Volume 2
Science Fiction, Horror & Fantasy

Science Fiction, Horror & Fantasy Film and Television Credits

Over 10,000 Actors, Actresses, Directors,
Producers, Screenwriters, Cinematographers, Art Directors,
and Make-Up, Special Effects, Costume and Other People;
Plus Full Cross-References from All Films and TV Shows

compiled by Harris M. Lentz, III

VOLUME 2

Section III: Film Index;
Section IV: Television Index

McFarland & Company, Inc., Publishers
Jefferson, North Carolina, and London

Library of Congress Cataloguing-in-Publication Data

Lentz, Harris M.
    Science fiction, horror & fantasy film and
television credits.

    Bibliography: p.
    Includes indexes.
    1. Science fiction films — Dictionaries. 2. Horror
films — Dictionaries.   3. Fantastic films — Dictionaries.
4. Science fiction television programs — Dictionaries.
5. Horror television programs — Dictionaries.
6. Fantastic television programs — Dictionaries.
I. Title.
PN1995.9.S26L46 1983   791.43′09′0915   82-23956

ISBN 0-89950-071-4 (set)
ISBN 0-89950-069-2 (v. 1)
ISBN 0-89950-070-6 (v. 2)

Manufactured in the United States of America.

McFarland & Company, Inc., Publishers
    Box 611, Jefferson, North Carolina 28640

ABBOTT AND COSTELLO GO TO MARS (1953)
Director: Charles Lamont
Bud Abbott (Lester), Lou Costello (Orville), Martha Hyer (Janie), Mari Blanchard (Allura), Robert Paige (Dr. Wilson), Hal Forrest (Dr. Nedring), Horace McMahon (Mugsy), Harold Goodwin (Dr. Coleman), Jack Kruschen (Harry), Joe Kirk (Dr. Orville), Jack Tesler (Dr. Holtz), Jean Willes (Captain), James Flaven, Russ Conway (policemen in bank), Syd Saylor (man at fountain), Anita Ekberg, Mackie Loughery, Jeri Miller, Judy Hatula, Patti McKay (Venusian guards), Ruth June Hampton, Jeanne Thompson, Valerie Jackson, Renate Huy, Elea Edsman (handmaidens), Paul Newlan (traffic cop), Tim Graham (cashier), Ken Christy (police officer), Douglas Henderson (announcer), Grace Lenard (French girl in restaurant), Billy Newell (drunk), Harry Lang (French waiter), Stanley Waxman (2nd announcer), Helen Noyes (Miss Pliny), Robert Forrest (observer), Dudley Dickerson (porter), Milton Bronson (announcer), Rex Lease (police sergeant), Sal Z. Martell (Rex Lease), Lester Dorr (customer), Scott Lee, Dale Van Sickel (policemen), Gloria Paul (tall girl), Frank Marlowe (bartender), Bary Curtis (boy), Helen Strohm (girl), Harold De Garro (tall cop), Jack Shutta (gurad), Jane Easton (javelin thrower), Rickey Van Dusen (girl), Betty Yeaton (contortionist), Harry Shearer (boy), Stanley Blystone, Carl Sklover, Bobby Barber, Sally Yarnell, Juanita Close, Cora Shannon.

ABBOTT AND COSTELLO MEET DR. JEKYLL AND MR. HYDE (1953)
Director: Charles Lamont
Bud Abbott (Slim), Lou Costello (Tubby), Boris Karloff (Dr. Jekyll), Helen Westcott (Vicky Edwards), Craig Stevens (Bruce Adams), Reginald Denny (Inspector), John Dierkes (Batley), Eddie Parker (Mr. Hyde), Patti McKaye, Betty Tyler, Lucille Lamarr (can-can dancers), Henry Corden (Javanese actor), Carmen De Lavallade (Javanese dancer), Marjorie Bennett (militant woman), Isabelle Dwan (Mrs. Penprase), Arthur Gould (bartender), Clyde Cook, John Rogers (drunks), Herbert Deans (victim), Gil Perkins, Judith Brian (couple on tandem bike), Hilda Plowright (nursemaid), Keith Hitchcock (jailer), Betty Fairfax (suffragette), James Aubrey (man), Susan Randall (girl), Harry Wilson (man with match), Duke Johnson (juggler), Wilson Benge (doorman), Al Ferguson (driver), Donald Kerr (chimneysweep), Michael Hadlow, Tony Marshe, Clive Morgan (bobbies).

ABBOTT AND COSTELLO MEET FRANKENSTEIN (1947)
Director: Charles T. Barton
Bud Abbott (Chick Young), Lou Costello (Wilbur Gray), Lon Chaney, Jr. (Lawrence Talbot), Bela Lugosi (Count Dracula), Glenn Strange (the Frankenstein Monster), Jane Randolph (Joan Raymond), Lenore Aubert (Sandra Mornay), Frank Ferguson (Mr. MacDougall), Charles Bradstreet (Dr. Stevens), Paul Strader (Sergeant), Harry Brown (photographer), Joe Kirk (man), Helen Spring (woman at baggage counter), Clarance Straight (man in armour), Vincent Price (voice of the Invisible Man), Bobby Barker.

ABBOTT AND COSTELLO MEET THE INVISIBLE MAN (1950)
Director: Charles Lamont
Bud Abbott (Bud Alexander), Lou Costello (Lou Francis), Nancy Guild (Helen Gray), Arthur Franz (Tommy Nelson), Adele Jergens (Boots Marsden), Sheldon Leonard (Morgan), Gavin Muir (Dr. Philip Gray), Paul Maxey (Dr. James C.

Turner), William Frawley (Detective
Roberts), John Day (Rocky Hanlon),
Sam Balter (radio announcer), Syd Say-
lor (waiter), Billy Wayne (Rooney),
George J. Lewis (Torpedo), Frankie
Van (referee), Bobby Barber (Sneaky),
Carl Sklover (Lou's handler), Charles
Petter (Rocky's handler), Ed Gargan
(Milt), Herb Vigran (Stillwell), Russ
Conway, Billy Snyder (newspapermen),
Franklin Parker, Ralph Montgomery
(photographers), Ralph Dunn (motor-
cycle cop), Harold Goodwin (bartender),
Richard Bartell (bald man), Walter F.
Appler (Dugan), Frank Dae (Col. Duf-
fle), Howard Banks (Officer), Perc
Launders (cop), Jack Shutta (attendant),
Milt Bronson (fight announcer), Donald
Kerr (ice cream vendor), Kit Guard
(fighter), Edith Sheets (nurse), Rory
Mallinson, Dick Gordon, Roy Darmour,
Ralph Brooks (men).

ABBOTT AND COSTELLO MEET THE
    KILLER, BORIS KARLOFF (1949)
    Director: Charles T. Barton
Bud Abbott (Casey Edwards), Lou Cos-
tello (Freddie Phillips), Boris Karloff
(Swami Talpur), Lenore Aubert (Ange-
la Gordon), Gar Wood (Jeff Wilson),
Alan Mowbray (Melton), Nicholas Joy
(Amos Strickland), James Flavin (Insp.
Wellman), Morgan Farley (Gregory
Milford), Donna Martell, Victoria Horne,
Mikel Conrad, Billy Gray, Percy Hel-
ton, Roland Winters, Marjorie Bennett,
Harry Hayden, Claire DuBrey, Vincent
Renno, Murray Alper, Frankie Van,
Patricia Hall, Gail Bonney.

ABBOTT AND COSTELLO MEET THE
    MUMMY (1955)
    Director: Charles Lamont
Bud Abbott (Pete Patterson), Lou Cos-
tello (Freddie Franklin), Marie Wind-
sor (Madame Rontru), Kurt Katch (Dr.
Zoomer), Michael Ansara (Charlie),
Dan Seymour (Josef), Richard Deacon
(Semu), Mel Welles (Iben), Richard
Karlen (Hetsut), George Khoury (Habid),
Eddie Parker (Klaris, the Mummy),
Vyola Vonn, Hank Mann, Mitchell Ko-
wal, Jan Arvan, Morris Ankrum, Do-
nald Kerr, Michael Vallon, Robin Morse,
Carole Costello, Ted Hecht, Kem Dibbs,
Paul Marion, Peggy King.

ABBY (1974)
    Director: William Girdler
William Marshall (Garnet Williams),
Carol Speed (Abby Williams), Juanita
Moore (Momma Potter), Terry Carter
(Emmett Williams), Austin Stoker (Cass

Potter), Charles Kissinger (Dr. Hen-
nings), Nathan Cook (Tafa Hassan), Elliott Moffitt (Russell Lang), Nancy Lee
Owens (Mrs. Wiggins), Bob Holt (voice
of the Demon).

ABOMINABLE DR. PHIBES, THE (1971)
    Director: Robert Fuest
Vincent Price (Dr. Anton Phibes), Jo-
seph Cotten (Dr. Vesalius), Hugh Grif-
fith (Rabbi), Terry-Thomas (Dr. Long-
street), Peter Jeffrey (Trout), Alex
Scott (Dr. Hargreaves), Peter Gilmore
(Dr. Kitaj), Maurice Kaufman (Dr.
Whitcombe), Virginia North (Vulnavia),
Edward Burnham (Dr. Dunwoody), David
Hutcheson (Dr. Hedgpath), Sean Bury
(Lem Vesalius), Susan Travers (Nurse
Allan), John Cater (Waverley), Aubrey
Woods (Goldsmith), Derek Godfrey (Crow),
Walter Horsbrugh (Ross), Barbara Keogh
(Mrs. Frawley), Norman Jones (Sgt.
Schenley), Dallas Adams (1st police of-
ficial), Alan Zipson (2nd police official),
Caroline Munro (Victoria Phibes).

ABOMINABLE SNOWMAN OF THE HIM-
    ALAYAS, THE (1957)
    Director: Val Guest
Peter Cushing (Dr. John Rollason), For-
rest Tucker (Tom Friend), Maureen
Connell (Helen Rollason), Richard Wat-
tis (Peter Fox), Robert Brown (Ed Shel-
ley), Wolfe Morris (Kusang), Arnold
Marle (Lhama), Michael Brill (McNee),
Anthony Chin (Major Domo).

ABSENT-MINDED PROFESSOR, THE
    (1961).
    Director: Robert Stevenson
Fred MacMurray (Prof. Ned Brainard),
Nancy Olson (Betsy Carlisle), Keenan
Wynn (Alonzo Hawk), Tommy Kirk (Bill
Hawk), Leon Ames (Pres. Rufus Dag-
gett), Edward Andrews (Defense Secre-
tary), Wally Brown (Coach Elkins), Ed
Wynn (Fire Chief), Jack Mullaney (Air
Force Captain), Forrest Lewis (Officer
Kelly), James Westerfield (Officer Han-
son), David Lewis (Gen. Singer), Wen-
dell Holmes (Gen. Poynter), Alan Hewitt
(Gen. Hotchkiss), Raymond Bailey (Ad-
miral Olmstead), Gage Clarke (Rev.
Bosworth), Elliott Reid (Shelby Ashton),
Belle Montrose (Mrs. Chatsworth), Alan
Carney (referee), Don Ross (Lenny),
Charlie Briggs (Sig), Wally Boag (TV
newsman), Leon Tyler (basketball player).

ACE DRUMMOND (1936) - serial in 13
    episodes
Chapters: 1. "Where East Meets West",
2. "Invisible Enemy", 3. "Doorway of

Doom", 4. "The Radio Riddle", 5. "Bullets of Sand", 6. "Evil Spirits", 7. "The Trackless Trail", 8. "The Sign in the Sky", 9. "Secret Service", 10. "Mountain of Jade", 11. "The Dragon Commands", 12. "Squadron of Death" & 13. "The World Akin".

Director: Ford Beebe & Cliff Smith John King (Ace Drummond), Jean Rogers (Peggy Trainor), Noah Beery, Jr. (Jerry), Selmer Jackson (Meredith, Sr.), Robert Warwick (Winston), Montague Shaw (Trainor), Lon Chaney, Jr. (Ivan), Guy Bates Post (Grand Lama), Jackie Morrow (Billy Meredith), James Eagle (Johnny Wong), Arthur Loft (Chang-Ho), Chester Gan (Kai-Chek), James B. Leong (Henry Kee), Al Bridge (Wyckoff), Ed Cobb (Nicolai), Richard Vessel (Boris), Sam Ash (Le Page), Hooper Atchley (Caldoni), Louis Vincinot (Lotan), Stanley Blystone (Sergei), Frederick Vogeding (Bauer).

ACE OF SCOTLAND YARD, THE (1929) - serial in 10 episodes
Director: Ray Taylor
Crauford Kent (Insp. Angus Blake), Monte Montague (Jarvis), Grace Cunard (Queen of Diamonds), Florence Allen (Lady Diana), Herbert Pior (Lord Planton), Albert Priscoe (Prince Darius).

ADDING MACHINE, THE (1969)
Director: Jerome Epstein
Milo O'Shea (Mr. Zero), Phyllis Diller (Mrs. Zero), Billie Whitelaw (Daisy), Sydney Chaplin (Lt. Charles), Julian Glover (Shrdlu), Raymond Huntley (Smithers), Phil Brown (Ben), Paddy O'Neill (Mabel), Libby Morris (Ethel), Hugh McDermott (Harry), Bill Nagy (lawyer), Carol Cleveland (Judy), Bruce Boa (detective), Kenny Damon (Joe), John Brandon (1st cell jailer), Hal Galili (2nd cell jailer), Tony Caunter (3rd cell jailer), Bill Hutchinson (Judy's lover), Helen Elliott (apartment girl), C. Denier Warren (jury foreman), Tommy Dugan (Judge), Gordon Sterne (yard guard), Lola Lloyd (coffee girl), Nicholas Stuart (District Attorney), Mike Reed (yard guard), George Margo (gateman), Janet Brown (Fat and Thin Woman), John Cook (husband), John Bloomfield, Alan Surtees, Helena Stevens, Christine Pryor, Shirley Cooklin, Cal McCord, Anthony Harwood (apartment tenants).

A. D. 3 OPERATION WHITE WHALE- FISH (1966-Ital.) (A. K. A. "A. D. 3 Operazione Squalo Bianco"; "Operation White Shark")

Director: Stanley Lewis
Janine Reynaud, Rodd Dana, Francesco Mule, Franca Polesello.

ADVENTURE AT THE CENTER OF THE EARTH (1964-Mex.) (A. K. A. "Aventura en el Centro de la Tierra)
Director: Alfredo B. Cravenna
Kitty de Hoyos, Javier Solis, Ramon Bagarini, Jose Elias Moreno, David Reynoso.

ADVENTURE IN THE NIGHT, AN (1947- Mex.) (A. K. A. "Una Aventura en la Noche)
Director: Rolando Aguilar
Luis Aguilar, Miroslava, Carlos Villarias, Susana Cora, Arturo Soto Rangel, Jorge Reyes.

ADVENTURES OF BARON MUNCHAUSEN, THE (1943-Ger.) (A. K. A. "Munchausen")
Director: Josef von Baky
Hans Albers (Baron Munchausen), Kathe Haack (Baroness Munchausen), Brigitte Horney (Catherine the Great), Michael Bohnen (Prince Karl of Brunswick), Wilhelm Bendow (Man in the Moon), Hans Brausewetter (Frederick von Hartenfeld), Marina von Ditmar (Sophie von Riedezel), Andrews Engelmann (Prince Potemkin), Herman Speelmanns (Christian Kuchenreutter), Ferdinand Marian (Count Cagliostro), Leo Slezak (Sultan Abd-ul-Hamid), Isle Werner (Princess Isabella d'Este), Gustav Waldau (Casanova), Walter Lieck (runner), Hubert von Heyerinck.

ADVENTURES OF CAPTAIN AFRICA, THE (1955) - serial in 15 episodes
Director: Spencer Gordon Bennet
John Hart (Captain Africa), Rick Vallin (Ted Arnold), June Howard (Princess Rhoda), Bud Osborne (Nat Coleman), Ben Welden (Omar), Paul Mario (Hamid), Michael Fox (Prime Minister), Lee Roberts (Boris), Terry Frost (Greg), Ed Coch (Balu).

ADVENTURES OF CAPTAIN MARVEL, THE (1941) - serial in 12 episodes
Chapters: 1. "Curse of the Scorpion", 2. "The Guillotine", 3. "Time Bomb", 4. "Death Takes the Wheel", 5. "The Scorpion Strikes", 6. "Lens of Death", 7. "Human Targets", 8. "Boomerang", 9. "Dead Man's Trap", 10. "Doom Ship", 11. "Valley of Death" & 12. "Captain Marvel's Secret".
Director: William Witney & John English
Tom Tyler (Captain Marvel), Frank Cogh-

lan (Billy Batson), Louis Currie (Betty
Wallace), Billy Benedict (Whitey Mur-
phy), Robert Strange (John Malcolm),
Bryant Washburn (Henry Carlyle), Har-
ry Worth (Prof. Bentley/the Scorpion),
George Pembroke (Dr. Stephen Lang),
Jack Mulhall (Howell), Nigel de Bru-
lier (Shazam), Leland Hodgson (Major
Rawley), Tetsu Komai (Chan Lai), Reed
Hadley (Rahman Bar), John Davidson
(Tal Chotali), Kenneth Duncan (Barnett),
Charleton Young (Martin), Stanley Price
(Owens), Peter George Lynn (Dwight
Fisher), Ernest Sarracino (Akbar),
John Bagni (Cowan), Wilson Benge (Ben-
son), Ken Terrell (Hawks), Edward
Cassidy (Dodge), Lynton Brent (Lefty),
Al Kikume (Native Chief), Paul Lopez
(Ali), Bud Geary (Pete), Jerry Jerome
(Brandon), Chuck Morrison (Carlson),
Eddie Dew (Cavalry Lieutenant), Fran-
cis Sayles (Carter), Frank Marlowe
(Gus), Major Sam Harris (Hudson), Ar-
mand Cortes (Hamid), Dick Crockett
(bridge heavy), Earl Bunn, George Su-
zanne (dam heavies), Loren Riebe (cu-
rio heavy), Ted Mapes (seaman), Loren Riebe, Duke Taylor (lab heavies),
Augie Gomez, Al Taylor, Curley Dresden, Henry Wills, Steve Clemente (natives), Marten Lamont (radio sergeant),
Frank Wayne (Steve), Carl Swolsman
(sentry), Ray Hanson (trucker), Victor
Cox, Joe Delacruz.

ADVENTURES OF REX AND RINTY
(1935) - serial of 12 episodes
    Director: Ford Beebe & B. Reeves
    Eason
Kane Richmond (Frank Bradley), Mischa Auer (Tanaga), Norma Taylor (Dorothy Bruce), Smiley Burnette (Jensen),
Harry Woods (Crawford).

ADVENTURES OF SHERLOCK HOLMES,
THE (1939)
    Director: Alfred Werker
Basil Rathbone (Sherlock Holmes), Ni-
gel Bruce (Dr. Watson), Ida Lupino (Ann
Brandon), George Zucco (Prof. Moriar-
ty), Alan Marshal (Jerrold Hunter), E. E.
Clive (Insp. Bristol), Henry Stephenson
(Sir. Ronald Ramsgate), Peter Willes
(Lloyd Brandon), Arthur Hohl (Bassick),
Mary Gordon (Mrs. Hudson), Holmes
Herbert (Justice), May Beatty (Mrs.
Jameson), Terry Kilburn (Billy), Wil-
liam Austin, George Regas, Anthony
Kemble Cooper, Mary Forbes, Frank
Dawson.

ADVENTURES OF SIR GALAHAD, THE
(1949) - serial in 15 episodes

    Director: Spencer Gordon Bennet
George Reeves (Sir Galahad), Nelson
Leigh (King Arthur), William Fawcett
(Merlin), Charles King (Bors), John
Merton (Ulric), Jim Diehl (Kay), Don
Harvey (Bartog), Marjorie Stapp (Queen
Guinevere), Hugh Prosser (Sir Lance-
lot), Pat Barton (Morgan le Fay), Lois
Hall (Lady of the Lake), Pierce Lyden
(Cawker), Rick Vallin, Ray 'Crash' Cor-
rigan.

ADVENTURES OF TARZAN, THE (1928) -
serial in 15 episodes
    Director: Robert F. Hill
Elmo Lincoln (Tarzan), Louise Lorraine
(Jane), Percy Pembroke (Clayton), Frank
Whitson (Rokoff), Lillian Worth (Queen
La of Opar), Joe Martin (the Ape), Tho-
mas Jefferson, James Inslee.

AELITA: THE REVOLT OF THE RO-
BOTS (1924-Sov.)
    Director: Yakov A. Protazanov
Nikolai M. Zeretelli (Los), Yulia Solnt-
seva (Queen Aelita), Igor Illinski (Busev),
Konstantin Eggert, Nikolai Batalov, Valentina Kuinzhi, V. Orlova, Yuri Savad-
sky.

AFRICA SCREAMS (1949)
    Director: Charles T. Barton
Bud Abbott (Buzz Johnson), Lou Costel-
lo (Stanley Livingston), Hilary Brooks
(Diana Emerson), Max Baer (Boots),
Buddy Baer (Grappler), Shemp Howard
(Gunner), Joe Besser (Harry), Clyde
Beatty (himself), Frank Buck (himself),
Charlie Gemora (the Ape).

AGAIN (1969-Ital./Span.) (A. K. A. "I
Caldi Amori di una Minorenne")
    Director: Julio Buchs
Brett Halsey, Marilu Tolo, Gerard Ti-
chy, Fabrizio Moroni, Romina Power.

AGENCY (1981)
    Director: George Kaczender
Robert Mitchum (Ted Quinn), Lee Ma-
jors (Philip Morgan), Valerie Perrine
(Brenda Wilcox), Saul Rubinek (Sam Gold-
stein), Alexandra Stewart (Mimi Oliveri),
Anthony Parr (Charlie), Michael Kirby
(Peters), Hayward Morse (Tony Flynn),
Gary Reineke (Jones), George Touliatos
(Sgt. Eckersley), Hugh Webster (inmate),
Jonathan Welsh (Detective Ross), Franz
Russell (George Miller).

AGENT 505 (1965-Ger./Ital./Fr.) (A. K. A.
"Agent 505 - Todesfalle Beirut")
    Director: Manfred R. Kohler
Frederick Stafford, Chris Howland, Ha-

rald Leiphitz, Genevieve Cluny, Gisella Arden.

AGENT FOR H. A. R. M. (1965)
    Director: Gerd Oswald
Mark Richman (Adam Chance), Carl Esmond (Prof. Janos Steffanic), Barbara Bouchet (Ava Vestok), Martin Kosleck (Malko), Wendell Corey (Jim Graff), Robert Quarry (Borg), Rafael Campos (Luis), Alizia Gur (Mid-Eastern Contact), Donna Michelle (Marian), Marc Snegoff (Conrad), Chris Anders (Schloss), Steve Stevens (Billy), Horst Ebersberg (Helgar), Ray Dannis (Manson), Robert Donner (morgue attendant), Ronald Von (Police Lieutenant), Robert Christopher (police officer).

AGENT JOE WALKER OPERATION
    FAR EAST (1966-Ital.) (A. K. A.
    "Agente Joe Walker Operazione Estremo Oriente")
        Director: Gianfranco Parolini/
        Frank Kramer
Tony Kendall, Brad Harris, Barbara Frey, Carlo Tamberlani, John F. Littlewords.

AGNET SIGMA 3 -- MISSION GOLDWA-
    THER (1968-Span./Ital.) (A. K. A.
    "Agente Sigma 3 -- Mision Goldwather")
        Director: Gian Paolo Callegari
Jack Taylor, Silvia Solar, Armando Calvo, Diana Martin, Frank Harris.

AGENT 353, MASSACRE IN THE SUN
    (1966-Ital./Fr./Span.) (A. K. A. "A-
    gente 353, Massacro al Sole")
        Director: Sergio Sollima/Simon
        Sterling
George Ardisson, Frank Wolff, Evi Marandi, Michel Lemoine, Luz Marquez, Leontine May, Fernando Sancho.

AGUIRRE, WRATH OF GOD (1972-Ger.)
    Director: Werner Herzog
Klaus Kinski (Don Lope de Aguirre), Ruy Guerra (Don Pedro de Ursua), Del Negro (Brother Gaspar de Carvajal), Helena Rojo (Inez), Peter Berling (Don Fernando de Guzman), Cecilia Rivera (Flores), Dany Ades (Perucho).

A-HAUNTING WE WILL GO (1942)
    Director: Alfred Werker
Oliver Hardy (Oliver), Stanley Laurel (Stanley), Sheila Ryan (Margo), Elisha Cook, Jr. (Frank Lucas), Addison Richards (Malcolm Kilgore), John Shelton (Tommy White), Edward Gargan (Foster), Willie Best (waiter), George

Lynn (Darby Mason), James Bush (Joe Morgan), Richard Lane (Parker), Lou Lubin (Dixie Beeler), Don Costello (Doc Lake), Robert Emmet Keane (Phillips), Dante the Magician, Frank Faylen, Walter Sande, Wade Boteler, Mantan Moreland, Terry More/Judy Ford.

AIR HAWKS (1935)
    Director: Albert Rogell
Ralph Bellamy (Barry), Tala Birell (Letty Lynn), Douglas Dumbrille (Arnold), Robert Allen (Lewis), Edward Van Sloan (Shulter), Victor Kilian (Tiny), Wiley Post (Wiley Post), Billie Seward (Mona), Robert Middlemass (Drewen), Geneva Mitchell (Gertie), Bill Irving (Leon), Wyrley Birch (Holden), C. Franklin Parker (Burbank), Al Hill (Pete), Peggy Terry (Blondie), Harry Strang (taxi driver).

ALADDIN AND HIS LAMP (1951)
    Director: Lew Landers
Patricia Medina (Jasmine), Noreen Nash (Passion Flower), John Sands (Aladdin), John Dehner (Bokra), Billy House (Kafan), Ned Young (Hassan), Richard Erdman (Mirza), Rick Vallin (Captain of the Guard), Charles Horvath (Genie), Arabella (maid-in-waiting), Sujata (dancing slave girl).

ALADDIN AND THE WONDERFUL LAMP
    (1917)
        Director: S. A. Franklin & C. H.
        Franklin
Elmo Lincoln (Genie), Buddy Messinger, Gertrude Messinger, Virginia Corbin, Francis Carpenter, Violet Radcliffe.

ALAKAZAM THE GREAT (1960-Jap.) -
    animated
        Director: Taiji Yabushita & Osamu Tezuka
Voices: Frankie Avalon, Jonathan Winters, Arnold Stang, Sterling Holloway, Dodie Stevens.

ALBINO (1980)
    Director: Jurgen Goslar
Christopher Lee, Sybil Danning, James Faulkner, Trevor Howard, Horst Frank.

ALERT IN THE SOUTH (1953-Fr./Ital.)
    (A. K. A. "Alerte au Sud"; "Allarme au Sud")
        Director: Jean Devejure
Jean-Claude Pascal, Erich von Stroheim, Gianna-Maria Canale, Peter Van Eyck, Jean Tissier, Jean Murat.

ALEX IN WONDERLAND (1970)

Director: Paul Mazursky
Donald Sutherland (Alex), Ellen Burstyn
(Beth), Meg Mazursky (Amy), Glenna
Sergent (Nancy), Joan Delaney (Jane),
Andre Philippe (Andre), Neil Burstyn
(Norman), Michael Lerner (Leo), Viola
Spolin (Mother), Carol O'Leary (Mar-
lene), Leon Frederick (Lewis), Moss
Mabry (Mr. Wayne), Paul Mazursky
(Hal Stern).

ALF'S BUTTON AFLOAT (1938)
Director: Marcel Varnel
Bud Flanagan (Alf Higgins), Chesney
Allen (Ches), Jimmy Nervo (Cecil), Ted-
dy Knox (Teddy), Charlie Naughton
(Charlie), Jimmy Gold (Jimmy), Ala-
stair Sim (Eustace), Wally Patch (Sgt.
Hawkins), Peter Gawthorne (Capt. Dris-
col), Glennis Lorimer (Frankie Dris-
col), James Carney (Lt. Hardy), Agnes
Laughlin (Lady Driscol), Bruce Winston
(Mustapha).

ALGOL (1920-Ger.)
Director: Hans Werkmeister
Emil Jannings (Mephisto), Kathe Haack,
John Gottowt, Ernst Hoffman, Hanna
Ralph, Erna Morena, Gertrud Welcker,
Hans Adalbert von Schlettow.

ALIAS JOHN PRESTON (1955)
Director: David MacDonald
Christopher Lee (John Preston), Alex-
ander Knox (Dr. Walton), Betta St. John
(Sally Sandford), Sandra Dorne (Maria),
John Longden (Mr. Sandford), John
Stuart (Dr. Underwood), Bill Fraser
(Joe Newton), Betty Anne Davies (Mrs.
Sandford), Patrick Holt (the Stranger),
Guido Lorraine, Dinah Ann Rogers,
Gabrielle Gay.

ALIAS NICK BEAL (1949)
Director: John Farrow
Ray Milland (Nick Beal), Thomas Mitch-
ell (Joseph Foster), Audrey Totter (Don-
na Allen), Geraldine Wall (Martha Fos-
ter), George Macready (Rev. Garfield),
Henry O'Neill (Judge Hobson), Darryl
Hickman (Larry Price), Fred Clark
(Frankie Faulkner), Nestor Paiva (Karl),
King Donovan.

ALI BABA AND THE FORTY THIEVES
(1944)
Director: Arthur Lubin
Jon Hall (Ali Baba), Maria Montez (A-
mara), Turhan Bey (Jamiel), Andy De-
vine (Abdullah), Kurt Katch (Hulagu
Khan), Frank Puglia (Cassim), Ramsay
Ames (Nalu), Moroni Olsen (Caliph
Hassan), Harry Cording (Mahmoud),

Scotty Beckett (Ali Baba as a child), Y-
vette Dugay (Amara as a child), Noel
Cravat (Mongol Captain), Robert Bar-
ron (Mongol Captain), Dick Alexander
(Mongol guard), Angelo Rossitto (Arab
dwarf), Charles Wagenheim (Barber),
Fortunio Bonanova (Old Baba), Jimmy
Conlin (Little Thief), Chris-Pin Martin
(Fat Thief), Ethan Laidlaw, Hans Her-
bert, John Calvert, Pedro Regas, Dick
Dickinson, Joey Ray, David Heywood
(thieves), Jerome Andrews, Ed Brown,
Dick D'Arcy, Eric Braunsteiner, Alex
Goudovitch, George Martin (dancers),
Belle Mitchell (nursemaid), Art Miles
(Mongol guard), Harry Woods (Mongol
guard), Rex Evans (Major Domo), Al-
phonse Berge (tailor), Wee Willie Davis
(Arab giant), James Khan (Persian
Prince), Theodore Patay (Arab priest),
Norman Willis, Don McGill, Pierce Ly-
den (guards).

ALICE IN WONDERLAND (1933)
Director: Norman Z. McLeod
Charlotte Henry (Alice), Richard Arlen
(Cheshire Cat), Roscoe Ates (the Fish),
William Austin (the Gryphon), Billy Bar-
ty (White Pawn), Billy Bevan (Two of
Spades), Colin Campbell (Garden Frog),
Gary Cooper (the White Knight), Leon
Errol (Uncle Gilbert), Louise Fazenda
(White Queen), W. C. Fields (Humpty
Dumpty), Cary Grant (the Mock Turtle),
Ethel Griffies (the Governess), Raymond
Hatton (the Mouse), Sterling Holloway
(the Frog), Polly Moran (Dodo Bird),
Roscoe Karns (Tweedledee), Jack Oakie
(Tweedledum), Edward Everett Horton
(the Mad Hatter), Charles Ruggles (the
March Hare), Harvey Clark (Father Wil-
liam), Alec B. Francis (King of Hearts),
Jack Duffy (Leg of Mutton), Skeets Gal-
lagher (the White Rabbit), Harry Ekezian
(First Executioner), Meyer Grace (Third
Executioner), Lillian Harmer (the Cook),
Colin Kenny (the Clock), Edna Mae Oli-
ver (the Red Queen), Mae Robson (Queen
of Hearts), Jackie Searl (the Door Mouse),
Patsy O'Byrne (the Aunt), Ned Sparks
(the Caterpillar).

ALICE IN WONDERLAND (1948)
Director: Dallas Bower
Carol Marsh (Alice), Pamela Brown
(Queen Victoria), Felix Aylmer (Dr. Lid-
del), Ernest Milton (Vice Chancellor),
David Read (Prince Consort), Stephen
Murray (Lewis Carrol), Raymond Bus-
sieres (the tailor), Elizabeth Hanson
(Lorene), Joan Dale (Edith).

ALICE IN WONDERLAND (1951) - anima-

ted
Producer: Walt Disney
Voices: Kathryn Beaumont (Alice), Ed Wynn (Mad Hatter), Richard Haydn (Caterpillar), Sterling Holloway (Cheshire Cat), Jerry Colonna (March Hare), Verna Felton (Queen of Hearts), Pat O'Malley (Walrus/Carpenter/Tweedledee/Tweedledum), Bill Thompson (White Rabbit/Dodo), Heather Angel (Alice's sister), Joseph Kearns (Doorknob), Larry Grey (Bill), Queenie Leonard (bird in the tree), Dink Trout (King of Hearts), Doris Lloyd (the Rose), James Macdonald (Dormouse), The Mello Men (Card Painters), Don Barclay.

ALICE'S ADVENTURES IN WONDERLAND (1910) - short
Director: Edwin S. Porter

ALICE'S ADVENTURES IN WONDERLAND (1972).
Director: William Sterling
Fiona Fullerton (Alice), Michael Crawford (the White Rabbit), Sir Ralph Richardson (the Caterpillar), Peter Sellers (the March Hare), Flora Robson (Queen of Hearts), Robert Helpmann (the Mad Hatter), Dudley Moore (the Dormouse), Spike Milligan (the Gryphon), Michael Jayston (Dodgson).

ALICE, SWEET ALICE (1976) (A. K. A. "Communion"; "Holy Terror")
Director: Alfred Sole
Paula Sheppard (Alice), Niles McMaster (Dominick), Linda Miller (Catherine), Alphonse de Noble (Mr. Alphonse), Brooke Shields (Karen), Rudolph Willrich (Father Tom), Mildred Clinton (Mrs. Tredoni), Jane Lowry (Aunt Annie), Lillian Roth (the Pathologist), Tom Signorelli (Detective Brenner), Kathy Rich (Angela), Louisa Horton (psychiatrist), Michael Hardstark (detective), Antonio Rocca (funeral attendant).

ALIEN (1979)
Director: Ridley Scott
Sigourney Weaver (Ripley), Ian Holm (Ash), Tom Skerritt (Dallas), Veronica Cartwright (Lambert), Yaphet Kotto (Parker), John Hurt (Kane), Harry Dean Stanton (Brett), Helen Horton (voice of Mother), Bolaji Badejo (the Alien), Eddie Powell (stuntman).

ALIEN DEAD, THE (1980) (A. K. A. "If Fell from the Sky")
Director: Fred Olen Ray
Mike Bonavia (Miller Haze), John Leirier (Paisley), Rich Vogan (Krelboin),

Buster Crabbe, Raymond Roberts, Linda Lewis.

ALIEN ENCOUNTERS (1979)
Director: James T. Flocker
Augie Tribach, Matt Boston, Phil Catalli, Patricia Hunt, Bonnie Henry, Eugene Davis.

ALIEN FACTOR, THE (1978)
Director: Donald M. Dohler
Don Leifert (Ben Zachary), Tom Griffith (Sheriff Cinder), Richard Dyszel (Mayor Wicker), Mary Mertens (Edie Martin), George Stover (Steven Price), Richard Geiwitz (Pete Evans), Anne Firth (Ruth Sherman), Johnny Walker (Rex), Eleanor Herman (Mary Jane), Christopher Gummer (Clay).

ALIEN LOVER (TVM-1975)
Director: Lela Swift
Kate Mulgrew (Susan), Pernell Roberts (Mike), Susan Brown (Marian), John Ventantonio (Marc), Steven Earl Tanner (Jude).

ALIENS ARE COMING, THE (TVM-1980) - 3-2-80
Director: Harvey Hart
Tom Mason (Scott Cryden), Max Gail (Russ Garner), Caroline McWilliams (Sue Garner), Melinda Fee (Irish O'Brien), Fawne Harriman (Joyce Cummings), Eric Braeden (Leonard Nero), Matthew Laborteaux (Timmy Garner), Ron Masak (Harve Nelson), John Milford (Eldon Gates), Curtis Credel (Frank Foley), Lorna Thayer (Waitress Sebastian), Hank Brandt (Lt. Col. John), Lawrence Haddon (Bert Fowler), Gerald McRaney (Patrolman Ashley), Richard Lockmiller (Patrolman Strong), Ed Harris (Chuck Polchek), Tom Lowell (intern), Nancy Priddy (teacher), John Gilgreen (Floyd), Peter Schuck (orderly), Sean Griffin (doctor), Tom Pittman (security guard), Chris O'Brien (technician), Dirk Olthof (waiter), Laurie Beach (student).

ALISON'S BIRTHDAY (1979-Austral.)
Director: Ian Coughlan
Joanne Samuel (Alison Findlay), Margie McCrae (Chrissie Willis), Martin Vaughan (Mr. Martin), Rosalind Speirs (Maggie Carlyle), Robyn Gibbes (Helen McGill), Lou Brown (Pete Healey), Ian Coughlan (Dave Ducker), Bunney Brooke (Aunt Jennifer), John Bluthal (Uncle Dean), Ralph Cotterill (Brian Healey), Marion Johns (Grandmother Thorne), George Carden (Druid Leader), Belinda Giblin (Isobel Thorne), Vincent Ball (Dr. Lyall), Lisa

Peers (Sally Brown), Eric Oldfield (priest), Sonia Peat (nurse).

ALL GUMMED UP (1947) - short
     Director: Jules White
Moe Howard, Larry Fine, Shemp Howard, Emil Sitka, Christine McIntyre.

ALL HALLOWE'EN (1952)
     Director: Michael Gordon
Sally Gilmour (Rowena), Oleg Briansky (Gervase), Jane Baxter (Lady Delville), Diane Cilento (Harriet), Clive Morton (Sir Arthur), Walter Hudd (Mr. Wilberforce), Hattie Jacques (Miss Quibble), Ferdy Mayne (soldier), Robert Mouney.

ALLIGATOR (1980)
     Director: Lewis Teague
Robert Forster (David Madison), Robin Riker (Marisa Kendall), Henry Silva (Col. Brock), Dean Jagger (Slade), Michael V. Gazzo (Chief Clark), Jack Carter (Mayor), Sidney Lassick (Guichei), Bart Braverman (Kemp, the reporter), James Ingersoll (Helms), Robert Doyle (Bill), Patti Jerome (Madeline), Perry Lang (Kelly), Sue Lyon (ABC newswoman), Angel Tompkins (newswoman), Leslie Brown (young Marisa), John Lisbon Wood (mad bomber), Buckley Norris (Bob), Royce D. Applegate (Callan), Jim Brockett (gator wrestler), Jim Boeke (Shamsky), James Arone (Sloan), Ed Brodow (Ross), Simmy Bow (Seedy), Stan Haze (Meyer), Peter Miller (Sparks), Pat Petersen (Joey), Micol (Joey's mother), Tom Kindle (announcer), Philip Luther (Purdy), Larry Margo (Stanley), John F. Goff (Ashe), Elizabeth Halsey (Policewoman), Barry Chase (1st Policeman), Richard Partlow (2nd Policeman), Kendall Carly Browne (Ann), Mike Mazurki (gatekeeper), Bella Bruck (Dot), Jeradio De Cordovier (Gator Vendor No. 1), Dick Richards (Gator Vendor No. 2), Vincent De Stefano (Gator Vendor No. 3), Jo Jo D'Amore (Gator Vendor No. 4), Corky Ford (Chi Chi), Charles R. Penland (Tyrone), Tink Williams (Hector), Danny Baseda (radioman), Anita Keith (old lady), Margaret Muse (society matron), Michael Misita (reporter No. 1), Harold Greene (reporter No. 2), Jim Alquist (reporter No. 3), Margie Platt (bride), Nike Zachmanoglou (maid at party), Gloria Morrison (woman at barbeque), Jack Tyree (stuntman).

ALLIGATOR PEOPLE, THE (1959)
     Director: Roy Del Ruth
Beverly Garland (Jane Marvin), Richard Crane (Paul Webster), George Macready

(Dr. Mark Sinclair), Lon Chaney, Jr. (Mannon), Bruce Bennett (Dr. Erik Lorimer), Frieda Inescort (Mrs. Henry Hawthorne), Douglas Kennedy (Dr. Wayne McGregor), Ruby Goodwin (Lou Ann), Dudley Dickerson (porter), Hal K. Dawson (conductor), Vince Townsend, Jr. (Toby), John Merrick (1st nurse), Lee Warren (2nd nurse), Bill Bradley (patient).

ALL SOUL'S EVE (1921)
     Director: Chester Franklin
Mary Miles Minter, Jack Holt, Clarence Geldert, Carmen Phillips, Mickey Moore, Lucien Littlefield, Lottie Williams, Alice Knowland, Fanny Midgely.

ALL THAT JAZZ (1979)
     Director: Bob Fosse
Roy Scheider (Joe Gideon), Jessica Lange (Angelique), Ann Reinking (Kate Jagger), Leland Palmer (Audrey Paris), Cliff Gorman (Davis Newman), Ben Vereen (O'Connor Flood), Erzsebet Foldi (Michelle), Michael Tolan (Dr. Ballinger), Max Wright (Joshua Penn), William LeMassena (Jonesy Hecht), Chris Chase (Leslie Perry), Deborah Geffner (Victoria), Kathryn Doby (Kathryn), Anthony Holland (Paul Dann), Robert Hitt (Ted Christopher), David Margulies (Larry Goldie), Sue Paul (Stacy), Keith Gordon (Young Joe), Frankie Man (Comic), Alan Heim (Eddie), John Lithgow (Lucas Sergeant), Robert Levine (Dr. Hyman), Phil Friedman (Murray Nathan), Stephen Strimpell (Alvin Rackmil), Sandahl Bergman, Eileen Casey, Bruce Davis, Gary Flannery, Jennifer Nairn-Smith, Denny Ruvolo, John Sowinski, Leland Schwantes, Candace Tovar, Rima Vetter (principal dancers), Trudy Carson, Mary Sue Finnerty, Lesley Kingley, P. J. Mann, Cathy Rice, Sonja Stuart, Terri Treas (fan dancers), Jan Flato, Ralph E. Berntsen, John Paul Fetta, Andy Schwartz (rock band), Leonard Drum (insurance man), Eugene Troobnick (insurance doctor), Jules Fisher (himself), Ben Masters (Dr. Garry), Leah Ayres (Nurse Capobianco), Joanna Merlin (Nurse Pierce), Catherine Shirriff (Nurse Briggs), Nancy Beth Fird (Nurse Bates), Harry Agress (Resident MD), C. C. H. Pounder (Nurse Gibbons), Tito Goya (attendant), Lotta Palfi-Andor (old woman), K. C. Townsend, Rita Bennett, Melanie Hunter (strippers), Gary Bayer (intern), Wayne Carson (assistant stage manager), Kerry Casserly (backstage dancer), Judi Passeltiner (backstage dancer), Nicole Fosse (dancer), Vicki Frederick, P. J. Mann (menage partners), Minnie Gaster (script super-

visor), Michael Green, Bruce MacCal-
lum (clapper boys), Steve Elmore, I. M.
Hobson, Mary McCarty, Theresa Mer-
ritt, Sammy Smith (cast of NY/LA),
Joyce Ellen Hill (Nurse Collins), Edith
Kramer (manager, rehearsal studio),
Barbara McKinley (Diane), Gavin Mo-
ses (apprentice editor), Mary Mon Toy
(dietician), Wallace Shawn (assistant
insurance man), Sloane Shelton (mother),
Jacqueline Solotar (autograph seeker),
Arnold Gross (pianist).

ALL THAT MONEY CAN BUY (1940)
    (A. K. A. "The Devil and Daniel Web-
    ster")
        Director: William Dieterle
Edward Arnold (Daniel Webster), Wal-
ter Huston (Mr. Scratch), James Craig
(Jabez Stone), Simone Simon (Bella Dee),
Gene Lockhart (Squire Slossum), Jane
Darwell (Ma Stone), John Qualen (Miser
Stevens), H. B. Warner (Justice Haw-
thorne), George Cleveland (Cy Bibber),
Jeff Corey (Tom Sharp), Frank Conlan
(Sheriff), Anne Shirley (Mary Stone),
Alec Craig (Eli Higgins), Carl Stock-
dale (Van Brooks), Rogert Strange (Clerk
of the Court), Sonny Bupp (Martin Van
Aldrich), Sarah Edward (Lucy Slossum),
Lindy Wade (Daniel Stone), Walter Baldwin (Hank), Robert Emmett Keane (husband), Fern Emmitt (wife), Eddie Dew
(farmer), Stewart Richards (doctor),
Virginia Williams (baby), Anita Lee
(infant), Harry Humphrey (minister),
Harry Hook (tailor), Patsy Doyle (servant), Ferris Taylor (President), Robert Dudley (Lem), Jim Toney (another
farmer), Bob Pittard (clerk), Frank
Austin (spectator), Charles Herzinger
(old farmhand), Sunny Boyne (man),
Sherman Sanders (caller), James Farley (studio gateman), William Alland
(guide).

ALONE IN THE DARK (1982)
        Director: Jack Sholder
Jack Palance (Frank Hawkes), Donald
Pleasence (Dr. Leo Bain), Martin Lan-
dao (Preacher Sutcliff), Dwight Schultz
(Dan Potter), Erland Van Lidth (Fatty
Elster), Deborah Hedwall (Nell Potter),
Lee Taylor-Allan (Toni Potter), Phil-
lip Clark (Tom Smith Skaggs).

ALONG THE MOON BEAM TRAIL (1920) -
    short
        Director: Willis O'Brien

ALONG WITH GHOSTS (1969-Jap.)
    (A. K. A. "Journey with Ghosts Along
    Tokaido Road")

        Director: Kimiyoshi Yasuda
Kojiro Hongo (Hyakutaro), Pepe Hozumi
(Shinta), Masami Rurukido (Miyo), Mut-
suhiro (Toura Saikichi), Yoshito Yamaji
(Higuruma), Bokuzen Hidari (Jinbei).

ALPHA INCIDENT, THE (1976)
        Director: Bill Rebane
Ralph Meeker, Stafford Morgan, Carol
Irene Newell, John Goff, John Alderman.

ALPHAVILLE (1965-Fr. /Ital.)
        Director: Jean-Luc Godard
Eddie Constantine (Lemmy Caution), An-
na Karina (Natacha von Braun), Akim
Tamiroff (Henri Dickson), Howard Ver-
non (Prof. Leonard Nosferatu), Jean-
Louis Comolli (Prof. Jeckell), Michel
Delahaye (Von Braun's assistant), Las-
zlo Szabo (Chief of Engineers).

ALRAUNE (1928-Ger.) (A. K. A. "Unholy
    Love")
        Director: Henrik Galeen
Brigitte Helm (Alraune), Paul Wegener,
Ivan Petrovitch, Alexander Sascha,
Georg John, Mia Pankau, Valeska Gert,
Louis Ralph, John Loder, Hans Traut-
ner, Wolfgang Lilzer, Heinrich Schroth.

ALRAUNE (1930-Ger.) (A. K. A. "Daugh-
    ter of Evil")
        Director: Richard Oswald
Brigitte Helm (Alraune), Albert Basser-
mann, Martin Kosleck, Kathe Haack,
Bernard Goetzke, E. A. Lichs, Paul
Westermeier, Harold Paulsen, Ivan Ko-
val-Samborski, Agnes Straub, Henry
Bender, Liselott Schaak.

ALRAUNE (1952-Ger.) (A. K. A. "Unna-
    tural")
        Director: Arthur Maria Rabenalt
Hildegard Neff (Alraune), Erich von
Stroheim (Ten Brinken), Karl Boehm
(Frank Braun), Harry Meyen (Count Ge-
roldingen), Harry Halm (Dr. Mohn), Ju-
lia Koschka (Prince Wolkonska), Denise
Vernac (Governess), Trude Hesterberg.

ALTERED STATES (1980)
        Director: Ken Russell
William Hurt (Dr. Edward Jessup), Blair
Brown (Emily Jessup), Bob Balaban (Ar-
thur Rosenberg), Charles Haid (Mason
Parrish), Thaao Penghlis (Eccheverria),
Miguel Godreau (Primal Man), Dori Bren-
ner (Sylvia Rosenberg), Peter Brandon
(Hobart), Charles White Eagle (the Bru-
jo), Drew Barrymore (Margaret Jessup),
Jack Murdock (Hector Ortego), Megan
Jeffers (Grace Jessup), Frank McCarthy
(Obispo), Evan Richards (Young Rosen-

berg), Hap Lawrence (Endocrinologist),
John Walter Davis (Medical Technician),
Deborah Baltzell (schizophrenic patient),
Susan Bredhoff (Eccheverria's girl),
Cynthia Burr (Parrish's girl), George
Gaynes (Dr. Wissenschaft), Paul Lar-
son (Charlie Thomas), John Larroquette
(X-Ray technician), Eric Forst (Mingus),
Adrianna Shaw (Dr. Antonini), Olivia
Michelle (Veronica), Martin Fiscoe
(graduate student), M. James Arnett
(stuntman).

ALUCARDA (1975-Mex.)
    Director: Juan Moctezuma
Claudio Brook (Dr. Oscheck), Tina Romero (Alucarda), Susana Kamini (Justine), David Silva (Father Lazaro).

AMAZING COLOSSAL MAN, THE (1957)
    Director: Bert I. Gordon
Glen Langan (Col. Glenn Manning), Ca-
thy Downs (Carol Forrest), William
Hudson (Dr. Paul Lindstrom), Russell
Bender (Richard Kingman), Larry Thor
(Dr. Eric Coulter), James Seay (Col.
Hallock), Lyn Osborn (Sgt. Taylor),
Scott Peters (Sgt. Lee Carter), Edmund
Cobb (Dr. McDermott), Judd Holdren
(Robert Allen), Hank Patterson (Henry),
Jack Kosslyn (lieutenant in briefing
room), Paul Hahn (attendant), Frank
Jenks (delivery man), June Jocelyn
(nurse), Diana Darrin (typist), William
Hughes (control officer), Harry Ray-
bould (army guard), Jimmy Cross (re-
ception desk sergeant), Jean Moorhead
(girl in bath), Myron Cook (Capt. Tho-
mas), Michael Harris (Police Lt. Keller), Richard Nelson (Sgt. Hanson), Bill
Cassady (Lt. Peterson), Stanley Lachman (Lt. Kline).

AMAZING DR. G., THE (1965-Ital./
    Span.) (A.K.A. "Due Mafiosi Contro
    Goldfinger", "Two Mafiosi Against
    Goldfinger")
    Director: G. Simonelli
Fernando Rey, Elisa Montes, Ciccio
Ingrassia, Franco Franchi, Gloria Paul.

AMAZING MR. BLUNDEN, THE (1972)
    Director: Leionel Jeffries
Laurence Naismith (Mr. Blunden), Lynne
Frederick (Lucy), Diana Dors (Mrs.
Wickens), James Villiers (Uncle Bertie),
David Lodge (Mr. Wickens), Rosalyn
Landor (Sarah), Marc Granger (George),
Gary Miller (James), Dorothy Alison
(Mrs. Allen), Madeline Smith (Bella),
Stuart Lock (Tom), Deddie Davis (Mea-
kin).

AMAZING MR. X, THE (1948)
    see "The Spiritualist" (1948)

AMAZING TRANSPARENT MAN, THE
    (1959)
    Director: Edgar G. Ulmer
Marguerite Chapman (Laura), Douglas
Kennedy (Joey Faust), Ivan Triesault
(Dr. Ulof), James Griffith (Krenner),
Red Morgan (Julian), Edward Erwin
(Drake), Carmel Daniel (Maria), Jona-
than Ledford (Smith), Norman Smith
(security guard), Patrick Cranshaw (se-
curity guard), Kevin Kelly (woman), Den-
nis Adams, Stacy Morgan (policemen).

AMBUSHERS, THE (1967)
    Director: Henry Levin
Dean Martin (Mat Helm), Senta Berger
(Francesca Medeiros), Janice Rule (Shei-
la Sommers), James Gregory (MacDo-
nald), Kurt Kasznar (Quintana), Albert
Salmi (Jose Ortega), Beverly Adams
(Lovey Kravezit), Roy Jenson (Karl),
John Brascia (Rocco), Linda Foster
(Linda), David Mauro (Nassim), Alexan-
dra Hay (secretary), John Indrisano (ra-
pist), Mauritz Hugo (man), Kyra Bes-
ter, Susanna Moore, Penny Brahms,
Ulla Lindstrom, Lena Cederham, Dee
Duffy, Yumiko Ishizuka, Marilyn Tin-
dall, Egidia Anabella Incontrera, Jann
Watson, Karin Fedderson, Terri Hughes,
Alena Johnston (Slaygirls).

AMERICAN WEREWOLF IN LONDON,
    AN (1981)
    Director: John Landis
Jenny Agutter (Alex Price), David Naugh-
ton (David Kessler), John Woodvine (Dr.
Hirsch), Griffin Dunne (Jack Goodman),
Lila Kaye (barmaid), Paul Kimber (Sgt.
McManus), David Schofield (dart player),
Brian Glover (chess player), Don Mc-
Killop (Insp. Villiers), Frank Oz (Mr.
Collins), Nina Carter (Naughty Nina),
Christopher Scoular (Sean), Mary Tem-
pest (Sean's wife), Joe Belcher (truck
driver), Anne-Marie Davies (Nurse Gal-
lagher).

AMERICATHON (1979)
    Director: Neil Israel
John Ritter (Chet Roosevelt), Harvey
Korman (Monty Rushmore), Fred Willard
(Vanderhoof), Richard Schaal (Jerry),
Chief Dan George (Sam Birdwater), Pe-
ter Riegert (Eric McMerkin), Nancy
Morgan (Lucy Beth), Zane Busby (Mou-
ling Jackson), Meat Loaf (Oklahoma Roy
Budnitz), Elvis Costello (Earl Manches-
ter), Terry McGovern (Danny Olsen),
Tommy Lasorda (announcer), Howard

Hesseman (Kip), Jay Leno (Larry), Peter Marshall (himself), Geno Andrews (Chris), Nellie Bellflower (VP Advertising), Jimmy Weldon (VP Research), Robert Beer (David Eisenhower), David Opatoshu, Allan Arbus (Hebrabs), Dorothy R. Stratten.

AMITYVILLE HORROR, THE (1979)
Director: Stuart Rosenberg
James Brolin (George Lutz), Margot Kidder (Kathleen Lutz), Rod Steiger (Father Delaney), Don Stroud (Father Bolen), Murray Hamilton (Father Ryan), John Larch (Father Nuncio), Val Avery (Sgt. Gionfriddo), Irene Dailey (Aunt Helen), Michael Sacks (Jeff), Natasha Ryan (Amy), K. C. Martel (Greg), Meeno Peluce (Matt), Amy Wright (Jackie), Helen Shaver (Carolyn), Marc Vahanian (Jimmy), Elsa Raven (Mrs. Townsend), Eddie Barth (Agucci), Ellen Saland (bride).

AMITYVILLE: THE POSSESSION (1982)
Director: Damiano Damiani
James Olson, Burt Young, Rutanaya Alda, Jack Magner, Ted Ross, George Lloyd, Diane Franklin.

AMONG THE LIVING (1941)
Director: Stuart Heisler
Albert Dekker (John Raden/Paul Raden), Susan Hayward (Millie Pickens), Frances Farmer (Elaine Raden), Harry Carey (Dr. Ben Saunders), Maude Eburne (Mrs. Pickens), Gordon Jones (Bill Oakley), Ernest Whitman (Pompey), Harlan Briggs (Judge), Jean Phillips (Peggy Nolan), Frank M. Thomas (Sheriff), Lee Shumway), Dorothy Sebastian.

AMPHIBIAN MAN, THE (1962-Sov.)
(A. K. A. "Cheloviek Amphibia")
Director: Gennadi Kazansky & Vladimir Chebotaryov
William Korenev (Pedro Zurita), Anastasia Virtinskaya (Alicia), Mikhail Kozakov, Anatoli Smiranin, Vladimir Davydov, Nikolai Simonov.

AMPHYTRION (1935-Ger./Fr.)
Director: Reinhold Schunzel & Albert Valentin
German cast: Willy Fritsch, Kathe Gold, Paul Kemp, Fitz Benkoff, Adele Sandrock, Hilda Hildebrand, Aribert Wascher.
French cast: Henri Garat (Amphytrion/Jupiter), Armand Bernard (Sosias/Mercury), Jeanne Boitel (Alcmene), Odette Florelle (Myrismis), Marguerite Moreno (Juno).

ANATOMIST, THE (1961)
Director: Leonard William
Alastair Sim, George Cole, Michael Ripper, Jill Bennett, Adrienne Corri, Margaret Gordon.

ANATOMY OF A PSYCHO (1961)
Director: Brooke L. Peters
Russell Bender (Frank), Darrell Howe (Chet), Ronnie Burns (Mickey), Pamela Lincoln (Pat), Pat McMahon (Arthur), Judy Howard (Sandy), Frank Kiliman (Bobbie), Mike Grainger (Lt. Mac), John B. Lee (District Attorney), Don Devlin (Moe), Robert Stabler (Prosecuting Attorney), Hon. Charles J. Simon (Judge).

AND MILLIONS WILL DIE! (1974)
Director: Leslie H. Martinson
Richard Basehart (Dr. Douglas Pruitt), Leslie Nielson (Jack Gallagher), Susan Strasberg (Heather Kessler), Joseph Furst (Franz Kessler), Alwyn Kurts (Dr. Mitchell), Peter Sumner (Dixie Hart), Tony Wager (Insp. Bigelow), George Assang (Chen), Jack Alleen (Tootoochey), Rowena Wallace (Maggie Christopher), Les Foxcroft (Henshaw), Willie Fennell (Sid Broomberg), Rich Scully (Officer), Nike Turner (Tootoochey's girl), Carmen Duncan (Jill Brennan), Russell Waters (Dr. Guttner), Sharriff Medon (postman), John Wallace (policeman), John Huggins (aide), Malik Selamat (Chi), Gary Mullay (Sgt. Wilson), Rici Effendi (Captain), Bill Jervis (Governor), James Ho (Ahn Nu), June Cheong (Gallagher's girl).

AND NOW THE SCREAMING STARTS (1973) (A. K. A. "Fengriffen")
Director: Roy Ward Baker
Peter Cushing (Dr. Pope), Herbert Lom (Henry Fengriffen), Ian Ogilvy (Charles Fengriffen), Stephanie Beacham (Catherine Fengriffen), Patrick Magee (Dr. Whittle), Guy Rolfe (Maitland), Geoffrey Whitehead (Silas, the woodsman), Rosalie Crutchley (Mrs. Luke), Janet Key (Bridget), Frank Forsyth (servant), Gillian Lind (Aunt Edith), Lloyd Lamble (Sir John Westcliffe), Sally Harrison (Sarah), Norman Mitchell (Constable).

ANDROMEDA STRAIN, THE (1971)
Director: Robert Wise
Arthur Hill (Dr. Jeremy Stone), James Olson (Dr. Mark Hall), David Wayne (Dr. Charles Dutton), Kate Reid (Dr. Ruth Leavitt), Paula Kelly (Karen Anson), George Mitchell (Jackson), Ramon Bieri (Major Manchek), Richard O'Brien (Grimes), Kermit Murdock (Dr. Robertson), Peter

Hobbs (Gen. Sparks), Richard Bull (Air Force Major), Walter Brooke (Secretary of Defense), Glenn Langan (Secretary of State), Ivor Barry (Murray), Emory Parnell (Old Doughboy), Eric Christmas (Senator from Vermont), Peter Helm (Sgt. Crane), Michael Pataki (Mic T), Ken Swofford (Toby), Mark Jenkins (Lt. Shawn), John Carter (Capt. Morton), Susan Stone (woman), Joe Di Reda (Burke), Susan Brown (Allison Stone), David McLean (Senator from New Mexico), Carl Reindel (Lt. Comroe), Bart LaRue (Medic Captain), Michael Bow (M.P. Sergeant), Judy Farrell (Pam), Garry Walberg (technician), Paul Ballantyne (hospital director), Johnny Lee (boy), William Dunbar (Air Force Sergeant), Joe Billings, Ray Harris, Ted Lehmann (scientists).

AND SOON THE DARKNESS (1970)
    Director: Robert Fuest
Pamela Franklin (Jane), Michele Dotrice (Cathy), Sandor Eles (Paul), John Nettleton (Gendarme), Claude Bertrand (Lassal), Hanna-Marie Pravda (Madame Lassal), Jean Carmet (Renier), John Franklyn (old man), Clare Kelly (schoolmistress).

AND THE BONES CAME TOGETHER
    (TVM-1973) - 2-15-73
    Director:
Laurence Luckinbill (Robert), Robin Strasser (Joyce), Herbert Berghoff (Maimonides Shim).

AND THEN THERE WERE NONE (1945)
    Director: Rene Clair
Louis Hayward (Philip Lombard), June Duprez (Vera Claythorne), Barry Fitzgerald (Judge Quincannon), Walter Huston (Dr. Armstrong), Roland Young (Blore), C. Aubrey Smith (Gen. Mandrake), Richard Haydn (Rogers), Queenie Leonard (Mrs. Rogers), Judith Anderson (Emily Brent), Mischa Auer (Prince Starloff), Harry Thurston (fisherman).

ANDY WARHOL'S FRANKENSTEIN (1974)
    (A.K.A. "Flesh for Frankenstein")
    Director: Paul Morrissey
Joe Dallesandro (Field Hand), Ulo Kier (Baron), Monique Van Vooren (Baron's wife), Arno Juerging (Otto), Dalila Di Lazzaro (girl zombie), Srdjan Zelenovic (farmer).

ANGEL, ANGEL, DOWN WE GO (1970)
    see "Cult of the Damned" (1970)

ANGEL FOR SATAN, AN (1966-Ital.)
    (A.K.A. "Un Angelo per Satana")
    Director: Camillo Mastrocinque
Barbara Steele, Claudio Gora, Ursula Davis, Antonio De Teffe, Marina Berti, Aldo Berti.

ANGEL LEVINE, THE (1970)
    Director: Jan Kadar
Zero Mostel (Moris Mishkin), Harry Belafonte (Alexander Levine), Ida Kaminska (Fanny Mishkin), Milo O'Shea (Dr. Arnold Berg), Gloria Foster (Sally), Barbara Ann Teer (welfare lady), Eli Wallace (store clerk), Anne Jackson (lady in store).

ANGEL OF H.E.A.T. (1982)
    Director: Helen Sanford
Marilyn Chambers (Angel), Mary Woronov (Samantha Vitesse), Gerald Okamura (Hans), Stephen Johnson, Milt Kogan, Remy O'Neil, Dan Jesse.

ANGEL ON EARTH (1961-Ger.) (A.K.A.
    "Ein Engel auf Erden")
    Director: Geza von Radvanyl
Romy Schneider, Henri Vidal, Jean-Paul Belmondo.

ANGEL ON MY SHOULDER (1946)
    Director: Archie Mayo
Paul Muni (Eddie Kagle/Judge Parker), Anne Baxter (Barbara Foster), Claude Rains (Nick), Hardie Albright (Smiley), Onslow Stevens (Dr. Higgins), James Flavin (Bellamy), Jonathan Hale (Chairman), Fritz Leiber (scientist), Sarah Padden (Agatha), Ben Welden (Shaggys), Kurt Katch (Warden), Addison Richards (Big Harry), George Meeker (Mr. Bentley), George Cleveland (Albert), Marion Martin (Mrs. Bentley), Maurice Cass (Lucius), Chester Clute (Kramer), Murray Alper (Jim), Erskine Sanford (minister), Joel Friedkin (Malvola), Lee Shumway.

ANGEL ON MY SHOULDER (TVM-1980) -
    5-11-80
    Director:
Peter Strauss (Eddie Kagel), Richard Kiley (Satan), Barbara Hershey (Julie), Seymour Cassel (Smiley Mitchell), Peter MacLean (Gregg Harlowe), Anne Seymour (Mrs. Martin), Janis Paige (Dolly Blaine), Frank Campanella (Giannelli), Terry Alexander (Luke), Scott Colomby (Tony), Janis Hansen (Cissy), Charles Cooper (Matt), Billy Jacoby (Joe Navotny).

ANGEL ON THE AMAZON (1948)
    Director: John H. Auer

George Brent (Jim Warburton), Brian Aherne (Anthony Ridgeway), Vera Hruba Ralston (Christine Ridgeway), Richard Crane (Johnny MacMahon), Constance Bennett (Dr. Karen Lawrence), Fortunio Bonanova (Sebastian Ortega), Ross Elliott (Frank Lane), Gus Schilling (Dean Hartley), Walter Reed (Jerry Adams), Alfonso Bedoya (Paulo).

ANGEL WHO PAWNED HER HARP, THE (1954)
    Director: Alan Bromly
Felix Aylmer (Joshua Webman), Diane Cilento (the Angel), Alfie Bass (Lennox), David Kossoff (Schwartz), Jerry Desmonde (Parker), Joe Linnane (Ned Sullivan), Philip Guard (Len Burrows), Robert Eddison (the Voice), Sheila Sweet (Jenny Lane), Genitha Halsey (Mrs. Burrows), Elaine Wodson (Mrs. Lane), Edward Evans (Sgt. Lane), Thomas Gallagher (Boyd), Phyllis Morris (Mrs. Trap), Raymond Rollett, Maurice Kaufman, June Ellis, Freddie Watts, Cyril Smith, Herbert C. Walton, Thomas Moore, Jean Aubrey.

ANGRY RED PLANET (1960)
    Director: Ib Melchior
Gerald Mohr (Col. Tom O'Banion), Nora Hayden (Dr. Irish Ryan), Les Tremayne (Prof. Gettell), Jack Kruschen (Sgt. Jacobs), J. Edward McKinley (Prof. Weiner), Paul Hahn (Gen. Treegar), Tom Daly (Dr. Gordon), Edward Innes (Gen. Prescott).

ANIMAL FARM (1954) - animated
    Director: John Halas & Joy Batchelor
Maurice Denham (voices).

ANIMAL WORLD, THE (1955)
    Director: Irwin Allen
John Storm, Theodore Von Eltz (Narrators).

ANNABELLE LEE (1972)
    Director: Harold Daniels
Margaret O'Brien.

ANNIE (1982)
    Director: John Huston
Albert Finney (Daddy Warbucks), Carol Burnett (Miss Hannigan), Aileen Quinn (Annie), Ann Reinking (Grace Farrell), Bernadette Peters (Lily St. Regis), Tim Curry (Rooster Hannigan), Geoffrey Holden (Punjab), Roger Minami (Asp), Edward Herrman (Franklin D. Roosevelt), Toni Ann Gisondi (Molly), Rosanne Sorrentino (Pepper), Lara Berk (Tessie), Lucie Stewart (Duffy), April Lerman (Kate), Robin Ignico (July), Lois De Banzie (Eleanor Roosevelt).

ANOTHER JOB FOR THE UNDERTAKER (1901) - short
    Director: Edwin S. Porter

ANTICHRISTO (1974-Ital.) (A.K.A. "The Tempter")
    Director: Alberto de Martino
Mel Ferrer (Massimo Oderisi), Arthur Kennedy (Bishop Oderisi), Alida Valli (Irene), Umberto Orsini (Psychiatrist), George Coulouris (Father Mittner), Carla Gravina (Ippolita), Anita Strindberg (Gretel), Mario Scaccia (Faith Healer).

ANTI-CLOCK (1980)
    Director: Jane Arden & Jack Bond
Sebastian Saville (Joseph Sapha/Prof. J.D. Zanof), Liz Saville (Sapha's sister), Susan Cameron (Alanda Clark), Louise Temple (Madame Luisa Aronowicz), Tom Gerrard (poker dealer), Yoshiro Matsuya, Katherine Newell (parapsychologists), Gia-Fu Feng (T'ai chi Master), Don Wilde (Alpha Therapist), Prof. Richard Feynman (the Physicist), Brian Jones, Robert Armstrong, Molly Tweedlie, Tony C.T. Tang, William K. Lam, Kenneth Pearson, Jasper Gough, Joe Chappell, Derek Osborne, Chan Fai, Pat Bond.

A-008 OPERATION EXTERMINATE (1965-Ital.)
    Director: Umberto Lenzi
Alberto Lupo, Ingrid Schoeller, Dina De Santis, Mark Trevor, John Heston, George Wang.

AOOM (1970-Span.)
    Director: Gonzale Suarez
Lex Barker (Ristel), Teresa Gimpera (Ana), Julian Ugarte (murderer), Luis Ciges (servant), Romy (woman), Craig Hill.

A*P*E (1976-Kor./U.S.)
    Director: Paul Leder
Rod Arrants, Joanne DeVerona, Alex Nicol.

APE, THE (1940)
    Director: William Nigh
Boris Karloff (Dr. Adrian), Maris Wrixon (Frances), Henry Hall (Sheriff), Gene O'Donnell (Danny), Jessie Arnold (Mrs. Brill), Jack Kennedy (Tomlin), Gertrude Hoffman (housekeeper), Selmer Jackson, George Cleveland.

APE MAN, THE (1943)

Director: William Beaudine
Bela Lugosi (Dr. James Brewster),
Louise Currie (Billie Mason), Wallace
Ford (Jeff Carter), Henry Hall (Dr.
George Randall), Minerva Urecal (Aga-
tha Brewster), Wheeler Oakman (Brady),
J. Farrell MacDonald (Captain), Ralph
Littlefield (Zippo), Jack Mulhall (re-
porter), Emil Van Horn (the Ape), Charles
Hall.

APE MAN OF THE JUNGLE (1964-Ital.)
   (A.K.A. "Tarzak Contro Gli Uomini
   Leopardo", "Tarzak Against the Leo-
   pard Men")
   Director: Carlo Veo
Ralph Hudson, Rita Klein, Nuccia Car-
dinali, John Chevron, Archie Savage.

APE WOMAN, THE (1964-Ital./Fr.)
   (A.K.A. "La Donna Scimmia", "The
   Monkey Woman")
   Director: Marco Ferreri
Ugo Tognazzi (Antonio Focaccia), Annie
Girardot (Maria), Achille Majeroni
(Majoroni), Elvira Pasoloni (Chamber-
maid), Filippo Pompa Marcelli (Bruno),
Ugo Rossi (Ponsioner), Ermelinda De
Felice (Sister Furgonicino).

APPEARANCE OF SUPER GIANT (1956-
   Jap.) (A.K.A. "Super Giant" No. 1
   & 2)
   Director: Teruo Ishii
Ken Utsui (Super Giant), Minoru Takada, Junko Ikeuchi, Ryo Iwashita, Minako Yamada, Utako Mitsuya.

APPLE, THE (1980-Ger./U.S.)
   Director: Menahem Golan
Vladek Sheybal (Mr. Buggallow), George
Gilmour (Alphie), Catherine Mary Ste-
wart (Bibi), Joss Ackland (Mr. Topps),
Grace Kennedy (Pandi), Allan Love
(Dandi), Ray Shell (Shake), Miriam
Margolyes (landlady), Derek Deadman
(Bulldog), Leslie Meadows (Ashley),
Gunter Notthoff (Farday), Clem Davies
(Clark James), Michael Logan (James
Clark), Coby Recht (Jean-Louis), George
S. Clinton (Joe Pittman), Iris Recht
(Dominique), Francesca Poston (Vam-
pire).

APRIL 1, 2000 (1953-Austr.)
   Director: Wolfgang Libeneiner
Curt Jurgens (Capitano Herakles), Pe-
ter Gerhard (Hieronymus Gallup), Eli-
zabeth Stemberger (Secretary), Paul
Horbiger (Augustin), Hilde Krahl (World
Security Council President), Josef
Meinrad (Prime Minister), Kald Er-
mann (Cabinet Chief), Guido Wieland

(Alessandro Vitalini), Heinz Moog (Hajji
Halef Omar), Robert Michal (Wei Yao
Chee), Ulrich Bettae (Moderato Robin-
son), Harry Fuss (Franz), Waltraut
Haas (Mitzi), Hans Moser (Composer).

AQUARIANS, THE (TVM-1970) - 10-24-
   70
   Director: Don McDougall
Jose Ferrer (Dr. Vreeland), Ricardo
Montalban (Dr. Luis Delgado), Kate
Woodville (Barbara Brand), Chris Ro-
binson (Ledring), Curt Lowens (Ehrlich),
Tom Simcox (Jerry Hollis), Elsa Ingram
(Jean Hollis), Lawrence Casey (Bob Exe-
ter), Leslie Nielsen (official), Joan
Murphy (Norma), Harlan Warde, Austin
Stoker, Napoleon Reed, Phil Philbin,
Ted Swanson, Ken Harris, Myron Nat-
wick, Henry Mortimer, Dan Chandler,
William Evenson, Roger Phillips.

ARABIAN ADVENTURE (1979)
   Director: Kevin Connor
Christopher Lee (Alquazar), Oliver To-
bias (Prince Hasan), Milo O'Shea (Kha-
sim), Emma Samms (Princess Zuleira),
Shane Rimmer (Abu), Hal Galili (Asaf),
Puneet Sira (Majeed), Peter Cushing
(Wazir Al Wuzara), Mickey Rooney (Daad
El Shur), Capucine (Vahishta), Milton
Reid (Genie), John Ryman (Bahloul),
John Ratzenberger (Achmed), Jacob Wit-
kin (Omar, the Goldsmith), Suzanne
Danielle (Eastern dancer), Athar Malik
(Mahmoud), Elizabeth Welch (beggarwo-
man).

ARABIAN NIGHTS, THE (1942)
   Director: John Rawlins
Maria Montez (Sherazade), John Hall
(Haroun-Al-Raschid), Sabu (Ali Ben Ali),
Billy Gilbert (Ahmad), Leif Erickson
(Kamar), Shemp Howard (Sinbad), Edgar
Barrier (Grand Vizier), Turhan Bey
(Captain of the Guard), Acquanetta (Ishya),
Thomas Gomez (Hakim), John Qualen
(Aladdin), Wee Willie Davis (Valda),
Emory Parnell (harem sentry), Robert
Greig (eunuch), Harry Cording (black-
smith), Richard Lane (Corporal), Adia
Kuznetzoff (auctioneer), Elyse Knox
(Duenna), Robin Raymond (slave girl),
Charles Coleman (eunuch), Jeni Le Gon
(dancer's maid), Carmen D'Antonio,
Virginia Engels, Mary Moore, Jean
Trent, Patsy Mace, Pat Starling, Nedra
Sanders, Veronika Pataky, Frances
Gladwin, Rosemarie Dempsey, June
Ealey (harem girls), Andre Charlot,
Art Miles, Anthony Blair, Frank Lack-
teen, Robert Barron, Murdock MacQuar-
rie (bidders), Crane Whitley, Duke York,

Charles Alvarado (Officers), Ken Christy (Provost Marshal), Kermit Maynard (soldier), Ernest Whitman (Nubian slave), Johnnie Berkes (blind beggar), Eva Puig (old woman), Mickey Simpson (hangman), Dave Sharpe (stuntman).

ARC, THE (1919-Ger.)
    Director: Richard Oswald
Eugen Klopfer.

ARGOMAN SUPERDIABOLICO (1966-Ital.) (A.K.A. "Come Rubare la Corona d'Inghilterra", "How to Steal the Crown of England")
    Director: Sergio Grieco/Terence Hathaway
Roger Browne, Dominique Boschero, N. Marlowa.

ARNOLD (1974)
    Director: Georg Fenady
Stella Stevens (Karen Llewelyn), Roddy McDowall (Robert), Elsa Lanchester (Hester), Shani Wallis (Jocelyn), Farley Granger (Evan Lyons), Patric Knowles (Douglas Whitehead), Bernard Fox (Constable Hooks), Victor Buono (Minister), John McGiver (Governor), Ben Wright (Jonesy), James Farr (Dybbi), Norman Stuart (Arnold), Wanda Bailey (Flo), Steven Marlo (1st dart player), Leslie Thompson (2nd dart player).

AROUND THE WORLD IN EIGHTEEN DAYS (1923) - serial in 12 episodes Chapters: 1. "The Wager", 2. "Wanted by the Police", 3. "The Apaches of Paris", 4. "The Man Who Broke the Bank at Monte Carlo", 5. "Sands of Doom", 6. "The Living Sacrifice", 7. "The Dragon's Claws", 8. "A Nation's Peril", 9. "Trapped in the Clouds", 10. "The Brink of Eternity", 11. "The Path of Peril" & 12. "The Last Race".
    Director: B. Reeves Eason & Robert F. Hill
William Desmond (Phileas Fogg, Jr.), Laura LaPlante (Martha Harlow), Wade Boteler (Wallace J. Brenton), William P. DeVaul (Jiggs), Percy Challenger (Rand), William Welsh (Matthew Harlow), Tom S. Guise (Davis), Hamilton Morse (Smith), Gordon Sackville (White), Alfred Hollingsworth (Phileas Fogg), L. J. O'Connor, Arthur Millett (detectives), Pat Calhoun (Harlow's butler), Spottiswoode Atkins (Piggott), Sidney DeGrey (Hippolyte Darcy), Harry De Vere (man who makes bet), Boyd Irwin (Munfare), Jean DeBrine (Desplayer).

AROUND THE WORLD UNDER THE SEA

(1966)
    Director: Andrew Marton
Lloyd Bridges (Dr. Doug Standish), Brian Kelly (Dr. Craig Mosby), David McCallum (Dr. Phil Wolker), Shirley Eaton (Dr. Maggie Hanford), Keenan Wynn (Hank Stahl), Gary Merrill (Dr. August Boren), Marshall Thompson (Dr. Orin Hillyard), Ron Hayes (Brinkman), Celeste Yarnall (secretary), George DeVries (Coast Guard Lieutenant), George Shibata (Prof. Hamuru), Don Wells (sonor man), Donald Linton (Vice President), Frank Logan (Captain of Diligence), Jack Ewalt (sup. mining barge), Joey Carter (technician), Paul Gray (pilot), Tony Gulliver (officer).

ARREST BULLDOG DRUMMOND (1938)
    Director: James Hogan
John Howard (Capt. Hugh C. Drummond), Heather Angel (Phyllis Clavering), H. B. Warner (Col. Nielson), E. E. Clive (Tenny), Reginald Denny (Algy Longworth), George Zucco (Rolf Alferson), Zeffie Tilbury (Aunt Meg), Leonard Mudie (Richard Gannett), Claude Allister (Sir Basil Leghorne), David Clyde (Constable McThane), Clyde Cook (Constable Sacker), Neil Fitzgerald (Sir Malcolm McLeonard), Ewan Thomas (Smith), George Regas (Soongh), Jean Fenwick (Lady Beryl Ledyard), John Sutton, John Davidson.

ARSENIC AND OLD LACE (1944)
    Director: Frank Capra
Cary Grant (Mortimer Brewster), Raymond Massey (Jonathan Brewster), Josephine Hull (Abby Brewster), Jean Adair (Martha Brewster), Peter Lorre (Dr. Einstein), John Alexander (Teddy Brewster), Priscilla Lane (Elaine Harper), Edward Everett Horton (Mr. Witherspoon), Jack Carson (O'Hara), James Gleason (Lt. Rooney), Grant Mitchell (Rev. Harper), Edward McNamara (Brophy), Chester Clute (Dr. Gilchrist), John Ridgely (Saunders), Charles Lane (reporter), Vaughan Glaser (Judge Cullman), Leo White (man in phone booth), Garry Owen (taxi driver), Edward McWade (Gibbs), Lee Phelps (umpire), Hank Mann (photographer), Spencer Charters (marriage license clerk).

ARTISTS AND MODELS (1955)
    Director: Frank Tashlin
Dean Martin (Rick Todd), Jerry Lewis (Eugene Fullslade), Shirley MacLaine (Bessie Sparrowbush), Dorothy Malone (Abigail Parker), Eva Gabor (Sonia), Anita Ekberg (Anita), Jack Elam (Ivan), George Winslow (Richard Stilton), Otto

Waldis (Kurt), Emory Parnell (Kelly),
Herbert Rudley (Secret Service Chief),
Kathleen Freeman (Mrs. Milldoon),
Carleton Young (Col. Drury), Eddie
Mayehoff (Mr. Murdock), Alan Lee
(Otto), Nick Castle (dancer), Art Ba-
ker (himself), Richard Webb, Richard
Shannon (secret service agents), Ste-
ven Geray, Frank Jenks, Martha Went-
worth, Ralph Dumke, Clancy Cooper,
Margaret Barstow, Sara Berner, Charles
Evans, Mike Ross, Patti Ross, Ann
McCrea, Mortimer Dutra, Glen Wal-
ters, Sharon Baird, Patricia Morrow,
Dale Hartleben, Sue Carlton, Mickey
Little, Larri Thomas.

ARTISTS'S DILEMMA, THE (1901) -
    short
    Director: Edwin S. Porter

ARTISTS' DREAM, THE (1898-Fr.)
    (A.K.A. "Reve d'Artists")
    Director: Georges Melies

ASPHYX, THE (1972)
    Director: Peter Newbrook
Robert Stephens (Hugo), Robert Powell
(Giles), Fiona Walker (Anna), Alex
Scott (President), John Lawrence (Ma-
son), Ralph Arliss (Clive), Terry Scul-
ly (Pauper), Jane Lapotaire (Christina),
David Gray (Vicar), Tony Caunter (War-
den), Paul Bacon (1st member).

ASSASSINATION BUREAU, THE (1969)
    Director: Basil Deardon
Oliver Reed (Ivan Dragomiloff), Diana
Rigg (Sonya Winter), Telly Savalas
(Lord Bostwick), Curt Jurgens (Gen.
Von Pinck), Philippe Noiret (Monsieur
Lucoville), Warren Mitchell (Herr Weiss),
Clive Revill (Cesare Spado), Kenneth
Griffith (Monsieur Popescu), Beryl
Reid (Madame Otero), Vernon Dobtcheff
(Mr. Muntzov), Anavella Incontrera
(Eleanora), Jeremy Lloyd, Olaf Pooley,
George Coulouris, Milton Reid, Roger
Delgado, Ralph Michael, Jess Conrad,
Peter Bowles, Eugene Deckers, Kath-
erine Kath, Gordon Sterne, George Mur-
cell, Maurice Browning, Clive Gazes,
Gerik Schielderup, Frank Thornton,
Michael Wolf, William Kendall.

ASSAULT ON PRECINCT 13 (1976)
    Director: John Carpenter
Austin Stoker (Bishop), Darwin Joston
(Wilson), Laurie Zimmer (Leigh), Tony
Burton (Wells), Nancy Loomis (Julie),
Charles Cyphers (Starker), Martin
West (Lawson), Peter Bruni (Ice Cream
Man), Marc Ross (Patrolman Tramer),

Alan Koss (Patrolman Baxter), Henry
Brandon (Chaney), John J. Fox (Warden),
Kim Richards (Kathy), Frank Doubleday
(White Warlord), Al Nakauchi (Oriental
Warlord), Gilbert De la Pena (Chicano
Warlord), Peter Frankland (Caudell),
James Johnson (Black Warlord), Gilman
Rankin (bus driver), Cliff Battuello (1st
guard), Horace Johnson (2nd guard), Va-
lentine Villareal (Chicano tough), Kenny
Miyamoto (Oriental tough), Len Whitaker
(Black hood), Jerry Viramontes (Chicano
hood), Maynard Smith (Police Commis-
sioner), Brent Keast (radio announcer),
Kris Young, Joe Woo, Jr., Warren Brad-
ley, III, Randy Moore, William Taylor
(gang members).

ASSIGNMENT OUTER SPACE (1960-Ital.)
    (A.K.A. "Space Men")
    Director: Anthony Dawson/Anton-
io Margheriti
Rik von Nutter (Ray Peterson), Gaby
Farinon (Ludy), Archie Savage (Al),
Dave Montressor (Gino), Alain Dijon
(Commander), Aldo Pini.

ASSIGNMENT TERROR (1970-Ital./Ger./
    Span.) (A.K.A. "El Hombre Que Vino
    de Ummo", "Dracula vs. Franken-
    stein", "Dracula Jagt Frankenstein",
    "The Man Who Came from Ummo",
    "Los Monstruous Del Terror")
    Director: Tulio De Michelli
Michael Rennie (Dr. Odo Warnoff), Ka-
rin Dor (Maleva), Paul Naschy (Walde-
mar), Craig Hill (Henry Kirian), Peter
Damon, Patty Sheppard, Angel Del Pozo,
Manuel de Blas.

ASTOUNDING SHE MONSTER, THE (1958)
    Director: Ron Ashcroft
Robert Clarke (Dick Cutler), Kenne Duncan (Nat Burdell), Shirley Kilpatrick
(the She-Monster), Marilyn Harvey (Margaret Chaffee), Jeanne Tatum (Esther
Malone), Ewing Brown (Brad Conley).

ASTRO-ZOMBIES (1968)
    Director: Ted V. Mikels
John Carradine (Dr. DeMarco), Wendell
Corey (Holman), Joan Patrick (Janine
Norwalk), Rafael Campos (Juan), William
Bagdad (Franchot), Tom Pace (Eric Por-
ter), Vince Barbi (Tiros), Victor Izay
(Dr. Petrovich), Tura Santanna (Santan-
na), Joe Hoover (Chuck Edwards), Wally
Moon (Mike Webber), Egon Sirany (Fo-
reign agent), John Hopkins (Thompson),
Lynnette Lantz (Ginger), Janis Saul
(Lynn), Vic Lance (chauffeur), Rod Wil-
moth (Astro Zombie).

ASTRONAUT, THE (TVM-1972) - 1-8-72
Director: Robert Michael Lewis
Monte Markham (Eddie Reese/Col.
Brice Randolph), Susan Clark (Gail
Randolph), Jackie Cooper (Kurt Ander-
son), Robert Lansing (John Phillips),
Richard Anderson (Dr. Wylie), Walter
Brooke (Tom Everett), John Lupton
(Don Masters), James Sikking (Higgins),
Paul Kent (Carl Samuels), Loretta Le-
versee (Toni Scott).

ASYLUM (1972)
Director: Roy Ward Baker
Patrick Magee (Dr. Rutherford), Her-
bert Lom (Byron), Charlotte Rampling
(Barbara), Peter Cushing (Mr. Smith),
Barry Morse (Bruno), Britt Ekland
(Lucy), Barbara Parkins (Bonnie), Ro-
bert Powell (Dr. Martin), Richard Todd
(Walter), Sylvia Sims (Ruth), Geoffrey
Bayldon (Max), James Villiers (George),
Megs Jenkins (Miss Higgins), Frank
Forsyth (gatekeeper).

ASYLUM OF SATAN (1975)
Director: William Girdler
Charles Kissinger, Carla Borelli, Nick
Jolly.

ATLANTIDE, L' (1921-Fr.) (A.K.A.
"Lost Atlantis")
Director: Jacques Feyder
Jean Angelo (Capt. Morhange), Stacia
Napierkovska (Antinea), Georges Mel-
choir (Lt. St. Avit), Marie-Louise
Iribe (Tanit Zerga), Abel-Kader-Beh-
Ali (Cegheir-ben-Cheikh), Mohammed-
Ben-Noni (Bon-Dejeina), M. Franceschi
(M. le Mesge), Andre Roanne.

ATLANTIDE, L' (1932-Ger.) (A.K.A.
"Die Herrin von Atlantis", "The Mis-
tress of Atlantis", "Lost Atlantis")
Director: G.W. Pabst
German cast: Brigitte Helm (Antinea),
Odette Florelle (Clementine), Vladimir
Sokoloff (Count Bielowsky/Jitomir Chief-
tain), Gustav Diesal (Capt. Morchange),
Heinz Klingenberg (Capt. St. Avit), Flo-
relle Tela-Tchai (Tanit-Zerga), Georges
Tourreil (Lt. Ferrieres), Mathias Wie-
mann (the Norwegian).
French cast: Brigitte Helm (Antinea),
Jean Angelo (Capt. Morchange), Pierre
Blanchar (Capt. St. Avit), Vladimir
Sokoloff (Count Bielowsky/Jitomir Chief-
tain), Odette Florelle (Clementine),
Florelle Tela-Tchai (Tanit Zerga),
Georges Toureil (Lt. Ferrieres), Jacques
Richet (Jean Chataignier), Mathias Wei-
mann (the Norwegian).

English cast: Brigitte Helm (Antinea),
Vladimir Sokoloff (Count Bielowsky/Jito-
mir Chieftain), Odette Florelle (Clementine), John Stuart, Gibb McLaughlin,
Gustav Diesal.

ATLANTIDE, L' (1961-Fr./Ital.) (A.K.A.
"Journey Beneath the Desert", "The
Lost Kingdom", "Antinea, l'Amante
della Citta Sepolta")
Director: Edgar G. Ulmer & Giu-
seppe Masini
Jean-Louis Trintignant (Pierre), Haya
Harareet (Antinea), Georges Riviere
(John), Amadeo Nazari (Tamal), Rad
Fulton (Robert), Giulia Rubini (Zinah),
Gabriele Tinti (Max), Giammaria Volonte
(Tarath).

ATLANTIS, THE LOST CONTINENT
(1961)
Director: George Pal
Anthony Hall (Demetrios), Joyce Taylor
(Antillia), John Dall (Zaren), Edward C.
Platt (Azor), Frank DeKova (Sonoy),
Berry Kroeger (Surgeon), Wolfe Bar-
zell (Petros), William Smith (Captain of
the Guard), Jay Novello (Xandros), Ed-
gar Stehli (King Kronas), Buck Maggei
(Andex), Paul Frees (Narrator), Gene
Roth.

ATLAS AGAINST THE CYCLOPS (1961-
Ital.) (A.K.A. "Maciste nella Terra
dei Ciclopi", "Maciste in the Land of
the Cyclops", "Monster from the Un-
known World")
Director: Antonio Leonviola
Mitchell Gordon, Chelo Alonso, Vira
Silenti.

ATOM AGE VAMPIRE (1963-Ital.) (A.K.A.
"Seddok, l'Erede di Satana")
Director: Anton Majano & Richard
McNamara
Sergio Fantoni (Pierre), Alberto Lupo
(Prof. Levin), Susanne Loret (Janette),
Franca Paridi Strahl (Monica), Robert
Berta (Sacha), Ivo Garrani, Andrea Scotti.

ATOMIC AGENT (1959-Fr.) (A.K.A.
"Nathalie, Secret Agent")
Director: Henri Decoin
Martine Carol (Nathalie), Howard Ver-
non (William Dantoren), Dany Saval (Pi-
voine), Noel Roquevert (Pierre Darbon),
Felix Marten (Jacques Fabre), Dario
Moreno (Dr. Alberto), Andre Versini
(Pellec), Jacques Berthier (Jean Darbon).

ATOMIC KID, THE (1954)
Director: Leslie H. Martinson
Mickey Rooney (Blix Waterberry), Robert

Strauss (Stan Cooper), Elaine Davis
(Audrey Nelson), Bill Goodwin (Dr.
Rodell), Whit Bissell (Dr. Edgar Pang-
born), Hal March (Ray), Joey Forman
(M. P.), Robert Emmett Keane (Mr.
Reynolds), Stanley Adams (Wildcat
Hooper), Peter Leeds (Bill), Fay Roope
(Gen. Lawlor), Bill Welsh (commenta-
tor), Charles J. Conrad (scientist),
Tommy Walker (enlisted man), Don
Haggerty Lieutenant), Milton Frome
(communications man), Sig Frohlich
(photographer), Dan Riss (Jim), Ray
Walker (newspaperman), Peter Brocco
(Mr. Mosley), Robert Nichols (techni-
cian), Paul Dubov (Mr. Anderson),
Billy Snyder (croupier), Frank Richards
(thug), Guy Way (Lieutenant), Allan
Ray, Joe Rocca (M. P. s), Slick Slaven
(Corporal), George Mather, Dick Win-
slow (sergeants).

ATOMIC MAN, THE (1956)
    Director: Ken Hughes
Gene Nelson (Mike Delaney), Faith Do-
mergue (Jill Friday), Peter Arne (Dr.
Rayner), Donald Gray (Maitland), Jo-
seph Tomelty (Insp. Cleary), Paul Hardt-
muth (Bressler), Martin Wyldeck (Dr.
Preston), Launce Maraschal (editor),
Vic Perry (Emanuel Vasquo), Charles
Hawtrey (Scruffy).

ATOMIC RULERS OF THE WORLD
    (1957-Jap.) (A. K. A. "Super Giant
    No. 3 & 4")
    Director: Teruo Ishii, Akira
        Mitsuwa & Koreyoshi Akasaka
Ken Utsui (Super Giant), Minako Yama-
da, Minoru Takada, Junko Ikeuchi, Kan
Hayashi, Chisako Tahara, Reiko Seto,
Akira Tamura.

ATOMIC SUBMARINE, THE (1959)
    Director: Spencer Gordon Bennet
Arthur Franz (Cmdr. Reef Holloway),
Dick Foran (Capt. Dan Wendover), Brett
Halsey (Carl Nelson), Tom Conway (Sir
Ian Hunt), Paul Dubov (Lt. David Mil-
burn), Victor Varconi (Dr. Clifford
Kent), Selmer Jackson (Admiral Ter-
hune), Jean Morehead (Helen), Bob
Steele (Griff), Joi Lansing (Julie), Jack
Mulhall (Murdock), Sid Melton (Chester),
Richard Tyler (Carney), Ken Becker
(Powell).

ATOM MAN VS. SUPERMAN (1950) -
serial in 15 episodes
Chapters: 1. "Superman Flies Again",
2. "Atom Man Appears!", 3. "Ablaze
in the Sky!", 4. "Superman Meets Atom
Man!", 5. "Atom Man Tricks Superman",

6. "Atom Man's Challenge", 7. "At the
Mercy of Atom Man!", 8. "Into the Emp-
ty Doom!", 9. "Superman Crashes
Through!", 10, "Atom Man's Heat Ray",
11. "Luthor's Strategy", 12. "Atom
Man Strikes!", 13. "Atom Man's Flying
Saucer", 14. "Rocket of Vengeance" &
15. "Superman Saves the Universe".
    Director: Spencer Gordon Bennet
Kirk Alyn (Clark Kent/Superman), Noel
Neill (Lois Lane), Lyle Talbot (Luthor),
Pierre Watkin (Perry White), Tommy
Bond (Jimmy Olsen), Jack Ingram (Fos-
ter), Don C. Harvey (Albert), William
Fawcett (the Mayor), Terry Frost (Bear),
Rusty Westcoatt (Carl), Wally West (Dorr),
George Robotham (Earl), Paul Stader
(Lawson), Fred Kelsey (Chief of Police),
Stanley Blystone (man in the street).

ATRAGON (1963-Jap.) (A. K. A. "Kaitei
    Gunkan", "Underwater Warship")
    Director: Inoshiro Honda
Tadao Takashima (the Photographer),
Yu Fujiki (the Sub Captain), Yoko Fuji-
yama (the Captain's daughter), Kenji
Sahara, Jun Tazaki, Akemi Kita, Hiroshi
Koizumi, Tetsuko Kobayashi, Ken Uehara.

ATTACK FROM SPACE (1958-Jap.)
    (A. K. A. "Super Giant No. 5 & 6",
    "Super Giant Against the Satellites")
    Director: Teruo Ishii
Ken Utsui (Super Giant), Utako Mitsuya,
Teruhishia Ikeda, Kan Hayashi, Hiroshi
Asami, Minoru Takada, Junko Ikeuchi.

ATTACK OF THE CRAB MONSTERS
    (1957)
    Director: Roger Corman
Richard Garland (Dale Drewer), Pamela
Duncan (Martha Hunter), Leslie Bradley
(Dr. Karl Weigand), Russell Johnson
(Hank Chapman), Mel Welles (Jules
Deveroux), Richard Cutting (Dr. James
Carson), Ed Nelson (Ensign Quinlan),
Tony Miller (Jack Sommers), Beech
Dickerson (Ron Fellows), Maitland Stuard,
Robin Riley, Charles B. Griffith, Doug
Roberts (seamen).

ATTACK OF THE FIFTY FOOT WOMAN
    (1958)
    Director: Nathan Hertz/Nathan
        Juran
Allison Hayes (Nancy Archer), William
Hudson (Harry Archer), Yvette Vickers
(Honey Parker), George Douglas (Sheriff
Dubbitt), Roy Gordon (Dr. Cushing), Otto
Waldis (Dr. Von Loeb), Frank Chase
(Charlie), Ken Terrell (Jessup Stout),
Thomas E. Jackson (prospector), Eileene
Stevens (nurse), Mike Ross (Tony), Dale

Tate (commentator).

ATTACK OF THE GIANT LEECHES
(1959) (A. K. A. "The Giant Leeches")
Director: Bernard Kowalski
Ken Clarke (Steve Benton), Yvette Vickers (Liz Walker), Jan Shepard (Nan Greyson), Tyler McVey (Doc Greyson), Bruno VeSota (Dave Walker), Michael Emmet (Cal Moulton), Gene Roth (Sheriff Kovis), George Cisar (Lem Sawyer), Dan White (Slim Reed).

ATTACK OF THE KILLER TOMATOES
(1978)
Director: John De Bello
David Miller (Mason Dixon), Sharon Taylor (Louise Fairchild), George Wilson (Jim Richardson), Rock Peace (Wilbur Finletter), Jack Riley (Agriculture Official), Eric Christmas (Sen. Polk).

ATTACK OF THE MAYAN MUMMY
(1963-Mex. /U. S.)
Director: Jerry Warren
Nina Knight, Richard Webb, Bruno VeSota, Steve Conte, John Burton.

ATTACK OF THE MONSTERS (1969-
Jap.) (A. K. A. "Gamera vs. Guiron")
Director: Noriaki Yuasa
Nobuhiro Kajima (Akio), Miyuki Akiyama (Tomoko), Yuko Hamada (Kuniko), Chrystopher Murphy (Tom), Eiji Funakoshi (Dr. Shiga), Kon Omura (Kondo).

ATTACK OF THE MUSHROOM PEOPLE
(1963-Jap.) (A. K. A. "Matango")
Director: Inoshiro Honda & Eiji Tsuburya
Akiro Kubo, Yoshio Tsuchiya, Kumi Mizuno, Hiroshi Koizumi, Miki Tashiro, Hiroshi Tachikawa.

ATTACK OF THE PUPPET PEOPLE
(1958)
Director: Bert I. Gordon
John Agar (Bob Westley), John Hoyt (Mr. Franz), June Kenney (Sally Reynolds), Michael Mark (Emil), Laurie Mitchell (Georgia), Jack Kosslyn (Sgt. Patterson), Scott Peters (Mac), Jean Moorhead (Janet), Ken Miller (Stan), Susan Gordon (Agnes), Marlene Willie (Laurie), June Jocelyn (Brownie leader), Hank Peterson (the Doorman), Hal Bogart (the mailman), Bill Giorgio (janitor), Jaime Forster (Ernie), Troy Patterson (elevator operator), George Diestel (switchboard operator), Mark Lowell (salesman).

ATTACK OF THE ROBOTS (1962-Fr. /
Span.) (A. K. A. "Cartes sur Table",
"Cards on the Table", "Cards Boca Arriba", "Cards Face Up")
Director: Jesus Franco
Eddie Constantine (Pereira), Sophie Hardy (Cynthia), Francois Brion (Lady Cecelia), Fernando Rey (Sir Percy), Alfredo Mayo, Marcello Arroita-Jaurequi.

AT THE EARTH'S CORE (1976)
Director: Kevin Connor
Doug McClure (David Innes), Peter Cushing (Dr. Abner Perry), Caroline Munro (Dia), Cy Grant (Ra), Sean Lynch (Hoojah), Keith Barron (Dowsett), Godfrey James (Ghak), Anthony Verner (Gadsby), Michael Crane (Jubal), Helen Gill (Maisie), Robert Gillespie (photographer), Bobby Parr (Sagoth Chief), Andee Cromarty (slave girl).

AT THE EDGE OF THE WORLD (1927-
Ger.) (A. K. A. "Am Rande der Welt")
Director: Karl Grune
Albert Steinrueck (the Miller), Brigitte Helm (Magda, the miller's daughter), Victor Janson (Captain), Wilhelm Dieterle (John), Camilla von Hollay (John's wife), Max Schreck (the pedler), Imre Raday (Michael), Erwin Faber (the Stranger), Jean Bradin (the Lieutenant).

AT THE SIGN OF THE JACK O'LANTERN
(1922)
Director: Lloyd Ingraham
Wade Boteler, Betsy Ross Clark, Victor Potel, Earl Schenck, Clara Clark Ward, Zella Ingraham.

AT THE VILLA ROSE (1920)
Director: Maurice Elvey
Manora Thew (Celia Harland), Teddy Arundell (Insp. Hanaud), Norman Page (Julius Ricardo), Langhorne Burton (Harry Weathermill), Joan Beverley (Adele Rossignol), Kate Gurney (Helene), J. L. Boston Besnard), Eva Westlake (Mme. Dauvray), Armand Lenders (Perichet).

ATTIC, THE (1980)
Director: George Edwards
Carrie Snodgress (Louise Elmore), Ray Milland (Wendell Elmore), Ruth Cox (Emily), Marjorie Eaton (Mrs. Fowler), Rosemary Murphy (Mrs. Perkins), Fern Barry (Mrs. Mooney), Francis Bay (the librarian), Angel (Dickey), Patrick Brennan (David Perkins), Phil Speary (travel agent), Michael Rhodes (the sailor), Mark Andrews (the gardener), Dick Welsbacher (Bureau of Missing Persons).

AUDREY ROSE (1977)
Director: Robert Wise

Anthony Hopkins (Elliot Hoover), Marsha Mason (Janice Templeton), John Beck (Bill Templeton), Susan Swift (Ivy Templeton), John Hillerman (Scott Velie), Norman Lloyd (Dr. Steven Lipscomb), Ivy Jones (Mary Lou Sides), Robert Walden (Brice Mack), Philip Sterling (Judge Langley), Stephen Pearlman (Russ Rothman), Mary Jackson (Mother Veronica), Aly Wassil (Maharishi Gupta Pradesh), Richard Lawson (1st policeman), David Wilson (2nd policeman), Tony Brande (Detective Fallon), Elizabeth Farley (Carol Rothman), Pat Corley (Dr. Webster), Eunice Christopher (Mrs. Carbone), Ruth Manning (customer in store), David Frescoe (Dominick), Karen Anders (waitress).

AU SECOURS! (1923-Fr.) (A. K. A. "Help!")
    Director: Abel Gance
Max Linder, Gina Palerme, Jean Toulout.

AUTOPSY (1978-Ital.)
    Director: Armando Crispini
Mimsy Farmer, Bary Primus, Ray Lovelock, Angela Goodwin.

AUTOPSY OF A GHOST (1967-Mex.)
    (A. K. A. "Autopsia de un Fantasma")
    Director: Ismael Rodriquez
Basil Rathbone (Canuto Perez), Cameron Mitchell (Moleculo), John Carradine (Satan), Amedde Chabot, Carlos Pinar, Vitola Susana Cabrera, Pompin Iglesias, Pancho Cordova.

AVENGER, THE (1960-Ger.) (A. K. A. "Der Raecher")
    Director: Karl Anton
Heinz Drache, Ingrid van Bergen, Benno Sterzenbach, Ina Duscha, Klaus Kinski, Maria Litto, Ludwig Linklin, Rainer Brandt.

AVENGING CONSCIENCE, THE (1914)
    Director: D. W. Griffith
Henry B. Walthall (the Nephew), Spottiswoode Aiken (the Uncle), Blanche Sweet (Nephew's sweetheart), Mae Marsh (the maid), Ralph Lewis (the detective), George Seigmann (an Italian), Donald Crisp, Dorothy Gish, Robert Harron.

AWAKENING, THE (1980)
    Director: Mike Newell
Charlton Heston (Matthew Corbeck), Susannah York (Jane Turner), Stephanie Zimbalist (Margaret Corbeck), Jill Townsend (Anne Corbeck), Patrick Drury (Paul Whittier), Bruce Myers

(Dr. Khalid), Ian McDiarmid (Dr. Richter), Nadim Sawalha (Dr. El Sadek), Ahmed Osman (Yussef), Miriam Margolyes (Dr. Kadira), Leonard Maguire (John Matthews), Michael Mellinger (Hamid), Ishia Bennison (nurse), Madhav Sharma, Michael Halphie, Roger Kemp (doctors), Chris Fairbanks (porter).

AWFUL DR. ORLOFF, THE (1961-Span. / Fr.) (A. K. A. "Gritos en la Noche", "Screams in the Night", "L'Horrible Dr. Orloff", "The Demon Doctor")
    Director: Jesus Franco
Howard Vernon (Dr. Orloff), Conrado San Martin (Insp. Tanner), Diano Lorys, Maria Silva, Perla Cristal, Ricardo Valle, Venacio Muro.

AXE (1977)
    Director: Frederick R. Friedel
Leslie Lee (Lisa), Jack Canon (Steele), Frederick Friedel (Billy), Ray Greene (Lomax), Douglas Powers (Grandfather), Frank Jones (Aubrey), Hart Smith (detective), George J. Managhan (Harold), Carol Miller (storewoman), Scott Smith (policeman).

AZTEC MUMMY, THE (1957-Mex.)
    (A. K. A. "La Momia")
    Director: Rafael Lopez Portillo
Ramon Gay, Rosita Arenas, Leslie Harryson, Crox Alvarado, Steve Grant, Luis Castaneda, Arturo Martinez.

BABES IN TOYLAND (1934) (A. K. A. "March of the Wooden Soldiers")
    Director: Gus Meins & Charles Rogers
Stan Laurel (Stanley Dum), Oliver Hardy (Oliver Dee), Charlotte Henry (Bo-Peep), Henry Kleinbach (Barnaby), Felix Knight (Tom-Tom), Florence Roberts (Widow Peep), William Burress (Toymaker), Virginia Karns (Mother Goose), Ferdinand Munier (Santa Claus), Johnny Downs, Marie Wilson.

BABES IN TOYLAND (1961)
    Director: Jack Donohue
Ray Bolger (Barnaby), Ed Wynn (Toymaker), Annette Funicello (Mary Contrary), Tommy Sands (Tom Piper), Henry Calvin (Gonsorgo), Gene Sheldon (Roderigo), Rommy Kirk (Grumio), Ann Jillian (Bo Peep), Mary McCarty (Mother Goose), Kevin Corcoran (Boy Blue), Brian Corcoran (Willie Winkle), Marilee and Melanie Arnold (twins).

BABY, THE (1973)
    Director: Ted Post

Anjanette Comer, Ruth Roman, Mariana Hill, Suzan Zenor, David Manzy.

BABYSITTER, THE (TVM-1980) - 11-28-80
Director: Peter Medak
Stephanie Zimbalist (Joanna Redwine), Patty Duke Astin (Liz), William Shatner (Jeff), Quinn Cummings (Tara), John Houseman (Doc), David Wallace (Scotty), Frank Birney (Farragut), Kenneth Tigar, Richard Ty Haller, Virginia Kiser, Hildy Brooks.

BACCHANTES, THE (1960-Ital./Fr.)
(A.K.A. "Le Baccanti")
Director: Giorgio Ferroni
Pierre Brice, Akim Tamiroff, Alberto Lupo, Tania Elg, Alessandra Panaro.

BACK FROM THE DEAD (1957)
Director: Charles Marquis Warren
Peggie Castle (Miranda Anthony), Arthur Franz (Dick Anthony), Marsha Hunt (Katy Hazelton), Don Haggerty (John), Marianne Stewart (Nancy Corodell), Evelyn Scott (Molly), James Bell (Mr. Bradley), Jeanne Bates (Agnes), Ned Glass (Doctor), Jean Wood (Miss Townsend), Helen Wallace (Mrs. Bradley), Otto Reichow (Father Renall), Frances Turner (babysitter), Joan Bradshaw.

BACK TO THE PLANET OF THE APES (1974)
see Television: Planet of the Apes (1974)

BADDESLEY MANOR (1926) - short
Director: Maurice Elvey

BAD SEED, THE (1956)
Director: Mervyn LeRoy
Nancy Kelly (Christine Penmark), Patty McCormack (Rhoda Penmark), Henry Jones (LeRoy), William Hopper (Kenneth Penmark), Eileen Heckart (Mrs. Daigle), Evelyn Varden (Monica Breedlove), Paul Fix (Richard Bravo), Jesse White (Emory), Gage Clarke (Reginald Tasker), Joan Croydon (Miss Fern), Frank Cady (Mr. Daigle).

BAD RONALD (TVM-1974) - 10-23-74
Director: Buzz Kulik
Scott Jacoby (Ronald Wilby), Kim Hunter (Elaine Wilby), Linda Watkins (Mrs. Schumacher), Cindy Fisher (Babs Wood), Cindy Eilbacher (Althea Wood), Lisa Eilbacher (Ellen Wood), Pippa Scott (Mrs. Wood), Dabney Coleman

(Mr. Wood), John Larch (Sgt. Lynch), Ted Eccles (Duane Mathews), Aneta Corsaut (Mrs. Mathews), Angela Hoffman (Carol Mathews), Linda Purl (Laurie Mathews), Lesley Woods (Aunt Margaret).

BAFFLED (TVM-1973) - 1-30-73
Director: Philip Leacock
Leonard Nimoy (Tom Kovack), Susan Hampshire (Michele Brent), Vera Miles (Andrea Glenn), Jewel Branch (Jennifer Glenn), Angharad Rees (Peggy Tracewell), Rachel Roberts (Mrs. Farraday), Christopher Benjamin (Verelli), Ewan Roberts (Hopkins), Mike Murray (Sanford), Valerie Taylor (Mrs. Sanford), Ray Brooks (Tracewell), Milton Johns (Dr. Reed), Al Mancini (TV interviewer), Shane Rimmer, John Rae, Roland Brand, Frank Mann, Dan Meaden, Bill Hutchinson, Patsy Smart, Michael Sloan.

BAIT (1954)
Director: Hugo Haas
Cleo Moore (Peggy), Hugo Hass (Marko), John Agar (Ray), Emmett Lynn (Foley), Bruno VeSota (Webb), George Keymas (Chuck), Jan Englund (waitress), Sir Cedric Hardwicke (Narrator).

BAMBOO SAUCER, THE (1968)
Director: Frank Telford
Dan Duryea (Hank Peters), John Ericson (Fred Norwood), Lois Nettleton (Anna Karachev), Bob Hastings (Garson), Vincent Beck (Zagorsky), Bernard Fox (Ephram), Nan Leslie (Dorothy Vetry), James Hong (Sam Archibald), William Mims (Joe Vetry), Robert Dane (Miller), Bartlett Robinson (Rhodes), Andy Romano (Blanchard), Rico Cattani (Dubovsky), Nick Katurich (Gadyakoff).

BANDITS OF CORSICA (1953)
Director: Ray Nazarro
Richard Greene (Mario/Carlos/Lucien), Paula Raymond (Christina), Raymond Burr (Jonatto), Raymond Greenleaf (Paoli), Dona Drake (Zelda), Lee Van Cleef (Nerva), Nestor Paiva (Lorenzo), Frank Puglia (Riggio), Peter Mamakos (Diegas), Peter Brocco (Angelo), Paul Cavanagh (Dianza), George Lewis (Arturo), Virginia Brissac, Michael Ansara, John Pickard, Clayton Moore, Francis J. McDonald, William Forrest.

BANG BANG (1968-Span./Ital.) (A.K.A. "The Bang Bang Kid")
Director: Luciano Lelly
Guy Madison (Bear Bullock), Tom Bosley (Merriweather Newberry), Sandra

Milo (Gwenda Skaggel), Jose Maria Caf-
farell (Mayor Skaggel), Diana Zurakowska (Betsy Skaggel), Guistino Durano
(Hotchkiss), Riccardo Garrone (Killer
Kissock).

BARBARELLA (1967-Ital. /Fr.)
     Director: Roger Vadim
Jane Fonda (Barbarella), John Phillip
Law (Pygar), Anita Pallenberg (the
Black Queen), Milo O'Shea (Durand-Du-
rand/Concierge), David Hemmings (Di-
ladano), Marcel Marceau (Prof. Ping),
Ugo Tognazzi (Mark Hand), Claude Dauphin (President of Earth), Antonio Sabato (Jean-Paul), Veronique Vendell
(Captain Moon), Serge Marquand (Captain Sun), Talitha Pol (pipe-smoking
girl), Nino Musco (the Generale), Sergio Ferrero (Black Queen's messenger),
Maria Theresa Orsini (suicide girls),
Catherine & Marie Therese Chevalier
(the twins), Chantal Cachin (female re-
volutionary), Romolo Valli, Franco
Gula, Carla Rousso, Barbara Winner.

BARON BLOOD (1972-Ital. /Ger.)
     Director: Mario Bava
Joseph Cotten (Alfred Becker/Baron von
Kleist), Elke Sommer (Eva Arnold),
Massimo Girotti (Karl Hummel), Rada
Rassimov (Christine Hoffman), Antonio
Cantafora (Peter Kleist), Humi Raho
(Police Inspector), Nicoletta Elmi (Gret-
chen), Dieter Tressler (Herr Dortmundt),
Alan Collins (Fritz).

BARON MUNCHAUSEN (1961-Czech.)
     (A. K. A. "Baron Prasil")
     Director: Karel Zeman
Milos Kopecky (Baron Munchausen),
Jana Brejchova (Bianca), Rudolph Jeli-
nek (Tonik), Karel Hoger (Cyrano), Rudolph Hrusinsky (Sultan).

BARRACUDA (1978)
     Director: Harry Kerwin
Wayne David Crawford (Mike Canfield),
Roberta Leighton (Liza Williams), Wil-
liam Kerwin (Sheriff Ben Williams),
Bert Freed (Papa Jack), Cliff Emmich
(Lester), Jason Evers (Dr. Elliot Snow),
Bobbie-Ellyne Kosstrin (Maggie Snow),
Bob J. Shields (Floyd), Jerry Rhodes
(Bubba), Scott Avery (Toby), Harry Ker-
win (agent arriving No. 1), Rick Rhodes
(agent arriving No. 2), Matt King (agent
leaving), Robert G. Noe (hotel clerk),
Leigh Walsh (girl student), William
Roundebush (boy student), Denise Tay-
lor (girl student), David Reiner (arguing man on street), Ray Michel (2nd
arguing man), Burt Richards (securi-

ity guard), Dick Sterling (security guard),
Bob Hiers (car fighting man), Elizabeth
Michel (car fighting woman), Scott Wohr-
man (lobster fishing boy), Ruth Miller
(Edna), Willis Knickerbocker (Bill),
Frank Logan (Sam), Julian Byrd (male
patient), Jill Shakorr (girl with dog),
Kim Nichols (girl on beach), Ed Lupin-
ski (boy on beach), Daniel L. Fitzgerald
(cook).

BARTON MYSTERY, THE (1920)
     Producer: Harry T. Roberts
Lyn Harding, Edward O'Neil, Vernon
Jones, Hilda Bayley, Eva Westlake, Ar-
thur Pussy, Ernest Cox.

BASILISK, THE (1914)
     Director: C. M. Hepworth
William Felton, Alma Taylor, Tom Powers.

BASKET CASE (1982)
     Director: Frank Henenlotter
Kevin Van Hentenryck (Duane Bradley),
Terri Susan Smith (Sharon), Beverly
Bonner (Casey), Lloyd Pace (Dr. Needle-
man), Diana Browne (Dr. Kutter), Ro-
bert Vogel (hotel manager), Joe Clarke
(O'Donovan), Bill Freeman (doctor).

BAT, THE (1926)
     Director: Roland West
Emily Fitzroy (Cornelia Van Gorder),
Louise Fazenda (Lizzie Allen), Jack Pick-
ford (Brooks), Tullio Carminati (Molet-
ti, the Bat), Eddie Gribbon (Detective
Anderson), Robert McKim (Dr. Wills),
Sojin (Billy), Lee Shumway (the Unknown),
Jewel Carmen (Dale Ogden), Andre de
Beranger (Gideon Bell), Arthur House-
man (Richard Fleming), Charles W. Her-
zinger (man in black mask).

BAT, THE (1958)
     Director: Crane Wilbur
Agnes Moorehead (Cornelia Van Gorder),
Vincent Price (Dr. Malcolm Wells), Ga-
vin Gordon (Lt. Anderson), John Sutton
(Warner), Lenita Lane (Lizzie Allen),
Elaine Edwards (Dale Bailey), Darla
Hood (Judy Hollender), John Bryant (Mark
Fleming), Harvey Stephens (Carter Fle-
ming), Riza Royce (Mrs. Patterson), Ro-
bert B. Williams (Detective), Mike Steele
(Jack Bailey).

BATMAN, THE (1943) - serial in 15 epi-
     sodes
Chapters: 1. "The Electric Brain", 2.
"The Bat's Cave", 3. "The Mark of the
Zombies", 4. "Slaves of the Rising Sun",
5. "The Living Corpse", 6. "Poison Pe-

ril", 7. "The Phoney Doctor", 8. "Lured by Radium", 9. "The Sign of the Sphinx", 10. "The Flying Spies", 11. "A Nipponese Trap", 12. "Embers of Evil", 13. "Eight Steps Down", 14. "The Executioner Strikes" & 15. "The Doom of the Rising Sun".

Director: Lambert Hillyer
Lewis Wilson (Bruce Wayne/Batman), Douglas Croft (Dick Grayson/Robin), J. Carrol Naish (Dr. Daka), William Austin (Alfred), Shirley Patterson (Linda), Charles C. Wilson (Captain Arnold), Gus Glassmire (Martin Warren), Charles Middleton (Ken Colton), Michael Vallon (Preston), Robert Fiske (Foster), Eddie Parker (stuntman).

BATMAN (1966)
Director: Leslie H. Martinson
Adam West (Bruce Wayne/Batman), Burt Ward (Dick Grayson/Robin), Cesar Romero (the Joker), Burgess Meredith (the Penguin), Frank Gorshin (the Riddler), Lee Meriwether (Kitka/the Catwoman), Alan Napier (Alfred), Neil Hamilton (Commissioner Gordon), Madge Blake (Aunt Harriet Cooper), Stafford Repp (Chief O'Hara), Reginald Denny (Commodore Schmidlapp), Sterling Holloway (Col. Terry), George Sawaya (Quetch), Dick Crockett (Morgan), Gil Perkins (Bluebeard), Milton Frome (Vice Admiral Fangschleister), Ivan Triesault.

BATMAN AND ROBIN (1949) - serial in 15 episodes (A. K. A. "The New Adventures of Batman and Robin") Chapters: 1. "Batman Takes Over", 2. "Tunnel of Terror", 3. "Robin's Wild Ride", 4. "Batman Trapped", 5. "Robin Rescues Batman", 6. "Target - Robin", 7. "The Fatal Blast", 8. "Robin Meets the Wizard", 9. "The Wizard Strikes Back", 10. "Batman's Last Chance", 11. "Robin's Ruse", 12. "Robin Rides the Wind", 13. "The Wizard's Challenge", 14. "Batman vs. Wizard" & 15. "Batman Victorious".

Director: Spencer Gordon Bennet
Robert Lowery (Bruce Wayne/Batman), John Duncan (Dick Grayson/Robin), Jane Adams (Vicki Vale), Lyle Talbot (Commissioner Gordon), Ralph Graves (Harrison), Don Harvey (Nolan), Leonard Penn (Carter), House Peters, Jr. (Earl), Michael Whalen (Dunne), William Fawcett (Hammil), Rick Vallin (Brown), Greg McClure (Evans), Rusty Wescoatt (Ives), Eric Wilton (Alfred), Marshall Bradford (Roger Morton), Jim Diehl (Jason), Eddie Parker (stuntman).

BAT PEOPLE, THE (1974)
Director: Jerry Jameson
Stewart Moss (Dr. John Beck), Marianne McAndrew (Cathy Beck), Michael Pataki (Detective Sgt. Ward), Paul Carr (Dr. Kipling), Arthur Space (derelict).

BATTLE BENEATH THE EARTH (1968)
Director: Montgomery Tully
Kerwin Mathews (Cmdr. Jonathan Shaw), Viviane Ventura (Tila Yung), Robert Ayres (Adm. Hillebrand), Martin Benson (Gen. Chan Lu), Peter Arne (Dr. Arnold Kramer), Earl Cameron (Sgt. Seth Hawkins), Al Mulock (Sgt. Mulberry), John Brandon (Maj. Frank Cannon), Peter Elliott (Kengh Lee), Michael McStay (Train Commander), Edward Bishop (Lt. Cmdr. Vance Cassidy), Bill Nagy, Bessie Love, Bee Duffell, Carl Jaffe, David Spencer, Paula Li Shiu, Larry Cross, Bill Hutchinson, Martin Terry, Norma West, Sarah Brackett, Chela Matthison, Frank Lieberman, Roy Pattison.

BATTLE BEYOND THE STARS (1980)
Director: Jimmy T. Murakami
Richard Thomas (Shad), John Saxon (Sador), George Peppard (Cowboy), Robert Vaughn (Gelt), Sybil Danning (St. Exmin), Darlanne Fluegel (Nanelia), Morgan Woodward (Cayman), Sam Jaffe (Dr. Hephaestus), Jeff Corey (Zed), Lynn Carlin (voice of Nell), Marta Kristen (Lux), Larry Meyers (Kelvin), Laura Cody (Kelvin), Earl Boen (Nestor No. 1), John McGowans (Nestor No. 2), Steve Davis (Quepeg), Eric Morris (Feh), Ron Ross (Dab), Don Thompson (Cush), Ansley Carlin (Wok), Doug Carleson (Pok), Julia Duffy (Mol), Daniel Carlin (Pez), Terrence McNally (Gar), Dallas Clarke, Rick Davidson, Brian Coventry, Whitney Rydbeck, Dan Vincent, Kerry Frank, Ron Henschel.

BATTLE BEYOND THE SUN (1962-U.S.S.R./U.S.) (A.K.A. "Nebo Zovyot")
Director: Thomas Colchart
Edd Perry/Ivan Pereverzev, Arla Powell/A. Popova, Andy Stewart, Bruce Hunter.

BATTLE FOR THE PLANET OF THE APES (1973)
Director: J. Lee Thompson
Roddy McDowall (Caesar), Claude Akins (Aldo), Natalie Trundy (Lisa), Severn Darden (Kolp), Paul Williams (Virgil), Lew Ayres (Mandemus), Austin Stoker (McDonald), Noah Keen (Teacher), Paul

Stevens (Mendez), John Huston (the
Lawgiver), France Nuyen (Alma), Bob-
by Porter (Cornelius), John Landis
(Jake's friend), Michael Stearns (Jake),
Richard Eastham (mutant captain), An-
dy Knight (mutant on motorcycle), Pat
Cardi (young chimp), Heather Loew
(doctor), Cal Wilson (soldier).

BATTLE IN OUTER SPACE (1960-Jap.)
(A. K. A. "Uchu dai Senso")
Director: Inoshiro Honda
Kyoko Anzai (Etsuko Shiroishi), Roy
Ikebe (Ichiro Katsuminya), Harold Con-
way (Dr. Immerman), Koreya Senda
(Prof. Adachi), Yoshio Tsuchiya (Koi-
chi Adachi), Hisaya Ito (Kogure), Fu-
yuki Murakami (Insp. Iriake), Leonard
Stanford (Dr. Richardson), Kozo Nomu-
ra (Rocket Commander), Minoru Takada
(Defense Commander), Elise Richter,
George Whyman.

BATTLE OF THE STARS (1979-Ital.)
Director: Alfonso Brescia/Al
Bradley
John Richardson, Jason Palance, Yanti
Somer.

BATTLE OF THE WORLDS (1960-Ital.)
(A. K. A. "Il Pianeta degli Uomini
Spenti", "The Planet of Extinguished
Men")
Director: Antonio Margheriti
Claude Rains (Prof. Benjamin Benson),
Maya Brent (Eva), Bill Carter (Fred
Steel), Umberto Orsini (Bob Cole), Ren-
zo Palmer (Gen. Verrick), Jacqueline
Derval (Cathy), Carol Danell (Mrs. Col-
lins).

BATTLESTAR GALACTICA (TVM-1978) -
9-17-78
Director: Richard A. Colla
Lorne Greene (Commander Adama), Ri-
chard Hatch (Apollo), Dirk Benedict
(Starbuck), Maren Jensen (Athena), Jane
Seymour (Serina), Laurette Spang (Cas-
siopea), Herb Jefferson, Jr. (Boomer),
Noah Hathaway (Boxey), John Colicos
(Baltar), Tony Swartz (Jolly), Ed Beg-
ley, Jr. (Greenbean), Rick Springfield
(Zac), George Murdock (Salik), Lew
Ayres (Adar), Ray Milland (Uri), John
Fink (Dr. Paye), Wilfrid Hyde-White
(Anton), Sarah Rush (Rigel), Bruce
Wright (deck hand), Chip Johnson (war-
rior), Geoffrey Binney (warrior), Ran-
di Oakes (young woman), Paul Coufos
(pilot), David Matthau (operative), Nor-
man Stuart (statesman), David Greenan
(bridge officer).

BATTLETRUCK (1982) (A. K. A. "War-
lords of the 25th Century")
Director: Harley Cokliss
Michael Beck (Hunter), Annie McEnroe
(Carlie), James Wainwright (Straker),
John Ratzenberger (Rusty), Randolph Pow-
ell (Judd), Diana Rowan (Charlene), John
Bach (Bone), Bruno Lawrence (Willie).

BAT WHISPERS, THE (1930)
Director: Roland West
Chester Morris (Detective Anderson),
Grayce Hampton (Cornelia Van Gorder),
Maude Eburne (Lizzy Allen), Una Mer-
kel (Dale Van Gorder), Gustav von Seyf-
fertitz (Dr. Venrees), DeWitt Jennings
(Police Captain), Richard Tucker (Mr.
Bell), William Bakewell (Brook), Spen-
cer Charters (the Caretaker), S. E. Jen-
nings (man in black mask), Charles Dow
Clark (Detective Jones), Sidney D'Al-
brook (Police Sergeant), Ben Bard (the
Unknown), Wilson Benge (the Butler),
Chance Ward (Police Lieutenant), Hugh
Huntley (Richard Fleming).

BAT WOMAN, THE (1967-Mex.) (A. K. A.
"La Mujer Murcielago")
Director: Rene Cardona
Mauro Monti, Armando Silvestre, Hec-
tor Godoy, Eric del Castillo, Robert
Canedo, David Silva.

BEAR, THE (1961-Fr.) (A. K. A. "L'Ours")
Director: Edmond Sechan
Renato Rascel, Francis Blanche, Daniel
Lecourtois, Yvette Etievant, Cora Ca-
moin, Jean Bellanger, Hubert De Lap-
parent, Gocha.

BEAST FROM HAUNTED CAVE, THE
(1959)
Director: Monte Hellman
Michael Forrest (Bill), Sheila Carol
(Gypsy), Frank Wolff (Alex), Wally Cam-
po (Byron), Richard Sinatra (Marty),
Chris Robinson (the Beast).

BEAST FROM 20,000 FATHOMS, THE
(1953)
Director: Eugene Lourie
Paul Christian (Tom Nesbitt), Paula Ray-
mond (Lee Hunter), Kenneth Tobey (Col.
Evans), Cecil Kellaway (Prof. Elson),
Donald Woods (Capt. Jackson), Lee Van
Cleef (Corporal Stone), Jack Pennick (Ja-
cob), Ross Elliott (George Ritchie), King
Donovan (Dr. Ingersoll), Steve Brodie
(Loomis), Frank Ferguson (Dr. Morton),
Ray Hyke (Sgt. Willistead), Mary Hill
(Nesbitt's secretary), Michael Fox (doc-
tor), Alvin Greenman (1st radar man),
Arthur Batanides, James Best.

BEAST IN SPACE (1978-Ital.)
    Director: Alfonso Brescia/Al
    Bradley
Sirpa Lane, Vassilli Caris, V. Venantini.

BEAST IN THE CELLAR, THE (1971)
    Director: Jeame Kelly
Beryl Reid (Ellie Ballantyne), Flora
Robson (Joyce Ballantyne), T. P. Mc-
Kenna (Superintendent Paddick), John
Hamill (Cpl. Alan Marlow), Vernon
Dobtcheff (Sir Bernard Newsmith), Pe-
ter Craze (Roy), David Dodimead (Dr.
Spencer), Tessa Wyatt (Joanna Suther-
land), Christopher Chittell (Baker),
Dafydd Harvard (Stephen Ballantyne),
John Kelland (Sgt. Young).

BEASTMASTER, THE (1982)
    Director: Don Coscarelli
Marc Singer (Dar), Tanya Roberts (Kirk),
Rip Torn (Maax), John Amos (Seth),
John Milrad (Tal), Rod Loomis (Zed),
Ben Hammer, Ralph Strait.

BEAST MUST DIE, THE (1974)
    Director: Paul Annett
Calvin Lockhart (Tom Newcliffe), Peter Cushing (Dr. Christopher Lundgren),
Charles Gray (Bennington), Anton Diffring (Pavel), Marlene Clark (Caroline
Newcliffe), Michael Gambon (Jan Jar-
mokowski), Ciaran Madden (Davina Gilmore), Sam Mansaray (Butler), Tom
Chadbon (Paul Foote), Andrew Lodge
(pilot), Carl Bohun, Eric Carte (hunters).

BEAST OF BABYLON AGAINST THE
SON OF HERCULES (1963-Ital.)
    (A. K. A. "L'Eroe di Babilonia", "The
    Hero of Babylon")
    Director:
Gordon Scott (Nippur), Moira Orfei,
Michael Lane, Genevieve Gard.

BEAST OF BLOOD (U. S. /Phil.) (A. K. A.
    "Blood Devils", "Beast of the Dead",
    "Return to the Horrors of Blood Is-
    land")
    Director: Eddie Romero
John Ashley (Dr. Bill Foster), Celeste
Yarnell (Myra Russell), Eddie Garcia
(Dr. Lorca), Liza Belmonte (Laida),
Bruno Punzalan (Razak), Alfonso Car-
vajal (Ramu), Beverly Miller (Captain),
Angel Buenaventura, Johnny Long.

BEAST OF HOLLOW MOUNTAIN, THE
    (1956-U. S. /Mex.) (A. K. A. "El Mon-
    struo de la Montana Hueca, "La Bes-
    tia de la Montana")

    Director: Edward Nassour & Is-
    mael Rodriguez
Guy Madison (Jimmy Ryan), Patricia
Medina (Sarita), Carlos Rivas (Felipe
Sanchez), Eduardo Noriega (Enrique
Rios), Mario Navarro (Panchito), Pas-
cual Garcia Pena (Pancho), Lupe Car-
riles (Margarita), Julius Villareal (Don
Pedro), Manuel Arvide (Martinez), Mar-
garito Luna (Jose), Lobo Negro (Jorge),
Roberto Contreras (Carlos), Jose Cha-
vez (Manuel), Armando Gutierrez, Jorge
Trevino.

BEAST OF MOROCCO, THE (1966)
    (A. K. A. "Hand of Night")
    Director: Frederic Goode
William Sylvester (Carver), Diane Clare
(Chantal), William Dexter (Leclerq),
Alicia Gur (Marisa), Terence De Mar-
ney (Omar), Edward Underdown (Gun-
ther).

BEAST OF THE YELLOW NIGHT (1971-
    Phil. /U. S.)
    Director: Eddie Romero
John Ashley (Joseph Langdon), Mary
Wilcox (Julia Rogers), Ken Metcalfe
(Earl Rogers), Vic Diaz (the Devil), Ed-
die Garcia (Detective Lt. Campos), An-
dres Centenera (the blind man).

BEAST OF YUCCA FLATS, THE (1961)
    Director: Coleman Francis
Tor Johnson (Dr. Joseph Jaworsky),
Douglas Mellor, Barbara Francis, Bing
Stafford, Larry Aten, John Morrison,
Linda Bielima, Tony Cardoza, Jim Oli-
phant, Alan Francis, Eric Tomlin, Bob
Labansat, George Prince, Conrad Brooks,
Ronald Francis.

BEAST WITH A MILLION EYES, THE
    (1955)
    Director: David Kramarsky
Paul Birch (Allan Kelly), Lorna Thayer
(Carol Kelly), Donna Cole (Sandy Kelly),
Richard Sargent (Larry), Leonard Tar-
ver (Him), Chester Conklin (Old Man
Webber).

BEAST WITH FIVE FINGERS, THE (1946)
    Director: Robert Florey
Peter Lorre (Hilary Cummins), Robert
Alda (Conrad Ryler), Andrea King (Julie
Holden), J. Carrol Naish (Ovidio Casta-
nio), Victor Francen (Francis Ingram),
Belle Mitchell (Savanna), Charles Dingle
(Raymond Arlington), Pedro de Cordoba.

BEAST WITHIN, THE (1981)
    Director: Phillippe Mora
Ronny Cox (Eli MacCleary), Bibi Beach

(Caroline MacCleary), Luke Askew
(Dexter Ward), Paul Clemens (Michael
MacCleary), Don Gordon (Judge Cur-
win), Logan Ramsay (Edwin Curwin),
L. Q. Jones (Sheriff Pool), Ron Soble
(Tom Laws), Meshach Taylor (Deputy),
R. G. Armstrong (Doc Schoonmaker),
John Dennis Johnson (Horace), Kitty
Ruth Moffat (Amanda Platt).

BEAUTIFUL DREAMER, THE (1953-
　　Mex.) (A. K. A. "El Bello Durmiente")
　　Director: Gilberto M. Solares
Tin Tan, Lilia Del Valle, Wolf Ruvinski,
Gloria Mestre.

BEAUTY AND THE BEAST (1946-Fr.)
　　(A. K. A. "La Belle et la Bete")
　　Director: Jean Cocteau
Jean Marais (Avenant/the Prince/the
Beast), Josette Day (the Beauty), Mar-
cel Andre (the Merchant), Mila Parely
(Adelaide), Nane Germon (Felicia), Mi-
chel Auclair (Ludovic).

BEAUTY AND THE BEAST (1963)
　　Director: Edward L. Cahn
Mark Damon (Duke Eduardo), Joyce
Taylor (Lady Althea), Eduard Franz
(Baron Orsini), Michael Pate (Prince
Bruno), Merry Anders (Princess Sy-
bel), Dayton Lummis (Count Roderick),
Walter Burke (Grimaldi).

BEAUTY AND THE BEAST (TVM-1976) -
　　12-3-76
　　Director: Fielder Cook
George C. Scott (the Beast), Trish Van
Devere (Belle Beaumont), Bernard Lee
(Edward Beaumont), Virginia McKenna
(Lucy), Patricia Quinn (Susan), Michael
Harbour (Anthony), William Relton
(Nicholas).

BEAUTY AND THE BEAST (1978-Czech)
　　Director: Juraj Herz
Zdena Studenkova (Beauty), Vlastimil
Harapes (the Beast), Vaclav Vosko (Beau-
ty's father), Jana Brejchova (Gavina),
Zuzana Kocurikova (Malinka).

BEAUTY AND THE ROBOT (1960) (A. K. A.
　　"Sex Kittens Go to College")
　　Director: Albert Zugsmith
Mamie Van Doren (Dr. Mathilda West),
Tuesday Weld (Jody), Louis Nye (Dr.
Zorch), Martin Milner (George Bar-
ton), Pamela Mason (Dr. Myrtle Car-
tle), John Carradine (Prof. Watts),
Mickey Shaughnessy (Boomie), Jackie
Coogan (Wildcat MacPherson), Maila
'Vampira' Nurmi (Etta Toodie), Mija-
nou Bardot (Zuzanne), Jody Fair (bar-

tender), Allan Drake (Legs Raffertino),
Arlene Hunter (nurse), Conway Twitty
(himself), Norman Grabowski (himself),
Irwin Berke (Prof. Towers), Babe London (Miss Cadwallader), Buni Bacon
(night club hostess).

BEAUTY OF THE DEVIL (1949-Fr.)
　　(A. K. A. "La Beaute du Diable")
　　Director: Rene Clair
Michel Simon (Mephisto), Gerard Phi-
lipe (Faust), Nicole Besnard (Margue-
rite), Simon Valere (Princess), Gino
Cervi (Prince), Raymond Cordy (ser-
vant), Paolo Stoppa, Tullio Carminati,
Carlo Ninchi, Gaston Modot.

BEDAZZLED (1967)
　　Director: Stanley Donen
Peter Cook (George Spiggott), Dudley
Moore (Stanley Moon), Raquel Welch
(Lilian Lust), Eleanor Bron (Margaret
Spencer), Michael Bates (Insp. Clarke),
Robin Hawdon (Randolph), Bernard Spear
(Irving Moses), Eric Chitty (Seed), Par-
nell McGarry (Gluttony), Howard Goor-
ney (Sloth), Barry Humphries (Envy),
Alba (Vanity), Daniele Noel (Avarice),
Robert Russell (Angel), Peter Hutchins
(P. C. Roberts), Michael Trubshawe
(Lord Dowdy), Martin Boddey (Cardinal),
Robin Tolhurst (Daphne), Lockwood West
(St. Peter), Max Faulkner (priest), Eve-
lyn Moore (Mrs. Wisby), John Steiner
(TV announcer), Anna Turner (shop as-
sistant).

BEDFORD INCIDENT, THE (1965)
　　Director: James B. Harris
Richard Widmark (Capt. Eric Finlander),
Sidney Poitier (Ben Munceford), James
MacArthur (Ensign Ralston), Wally Cox
(Sonar Man), Martin Balsam (Cmdr. Ches-
ter Potter), Eric Portman (Wolfgang
Schrepke), Michael Kane (Cmdr. Alli-
son), Donald Sutherland (Pharmacist's
Mate Nerney), Phil Brown (Chief Phar-
macist's Mate McKinley), Warren Stan-
hope (Pharmacist's Mate Strauss), Brian
Davies (Lt. Beekman), Gary Cockrell
(Lt. Bascombe).

BEDKNOBS AND BROOMSTICKS (1971)
　　Director: Robert Stevenson
Angela Lansbury (Eglantine Price), Roddy McDowall (Mr. Jelk), David Tomlinson (Emelius Browne), Sam Jaffe (Bookman), John Ericson (Col. Heller), Reginald Owen (Gen. Teagler), Tessie O'Shea
(Mrs. Hobday), Bruce Forsyth (Swinburne), Arthur Gould-Porter (Captain
Greer), Ben Wrigley (street sweeper),
Manfred Lating (German Sergeant), Rick

Traeger (German Sergeant), Roy Smart (Paul), Ian Weighall (Charlie), Cindy O'Callaghan (Carrie), John Orchard (vendor), Lennie Weinrib (voice of Secretary Bird and Lion), Ysabel MacCloskey.

BEDLAM (1946)
Director: Mark Robson
Boris Karloff (Master Sims), Anna Lee (Neil Bowen), Billy House (Lord Mortimer), Richard Fraser (Hannay), Ian Wolfe (Sidney Long), Leland Hodgson (John Wilkes), Robert Clarke (Dan the Dog), Jason Robards (Oliver Todd), Elizabeth Russell (Mistress Sims), Glenn Vernon (the Gilded Boy), Joan Newton (Dorothea the Dove).

BEDLAM IN PARADISE (1955) - short
Director: Jules White
Moe Howard, Shemp Howard, Larry Fine, Phil Van Zandt, Sylvia Lewis, Vernon Dent, Symone Boniface.

BED-SITTING ROOM, THE (1969)
Director: Richard Lester
Rita Tushingham (Penelope), Sir Ralph Richardson (Lord Fortnum), Michael Hordern (Capt. Bules Martin), Arthur Lowe (Dad), Mona Washbourne (Mum), Richard Warwick (Allan), Dudley Moore (Sergeant), Peter Cook (Inspector), Spike Milligan (Mate), Marty Feldman (Nurse Arthur), Ron Moody (Dwarf), Roy Kinnear (plastic fethishist), Harry Secombe (fallout shelter man), Gordon Rollings (patient), Ronald Fraser (Field Marshall Sergeant), Dandy Nichols (Ethyl Shroake), Frank Thornton (BBC man), Jack Shepherd (Underwater Vicar), Henry Wollf (electricity man), Bill Wallis (the P.M.), Ronald J. Brody (chauffeur), Cecil Cheng (Chinaman), Eddie Malin (club waiter), Jimmy Edwards (Nigel).

BEES, THE (1978-U.S./Mex.)
Director: Alfredo Zacharias
John Saxon (John Norman), Angel Tompkins (Sondra Miller), John Carradine (Dr. Sigmund Humel), Claudio Brook (Dr. Miller), Arnand Martin (Arthur), Alicia Encinias (Alicia), Julio Cesar (Julio), Jose Chavez Trowe (Father), Deloy White (Winkler), George Bellanger (Undersecretary Brennan), Roger Cudney (Blankeley), Chad Hastings (Gray), Elizabeth Wallace (secretary), Julia Yallop (model), Gray Johnson, Al Jones (muggers), Whitey Hughes (man in park), Eddie Alexander (announcer), Bill Bordy (newscaster), Brian Hanna, David Silverkleit, Alfred

Melhem (boys), Don Maxwell (U.S. General), Walter Hanna (President).

BEFORE DAWN (1933)
Director: Irving Pichel
Stuart Erwin (Dwight Wilson), Dorothy Wilson (Patricia Merrick), Warner Oland (Dr. Cornelius), Dudley Digges (Horace Merrick), Frank Reicher (Joe Valerie), Gertrude W. Hoffman (Mattie), Jane Darwell (Mrs. Marble), Oscar Apfel (Insp. O'Hara).

BEFORE I HANG (1940)
Director: Nick Grinde
Boris Karloff (Dr. John Garth), Evelyn Keyes (Martha Garth), Edward Van Sloan (Dr. Ralph Howard), Bruce Bennett (Dr. Paul Ames), Don Beddoe (Capt. McGraw), Ben Taggart (Warden Thompson), Pedro de Cordoba (Victor Sondini), Kenneth MacDonald (Anson), Robert Fiske (District Attorney), Wright Cramer (George Wharton), Bertram Marburgh (Stephen Barclay), Frank Richards (Otto Kron).

BEFORE MIDNIGHT (1933)
Director: Lambert Hillyer
Ralph Bellamy (Insp. Trent), June Collyer (Janet Holt), Claude Gillingwater (John Fry), Betty Blythe (Mavis Fry), Joseph Crehan (Capt. Flynn), Arthur Pierson (Dr. David Marsh), William Jeffrey (Edward Arnold), Bradley Page (Stubby), Otto Yanaoka (Kono).

BEGINNING OF THE END (1957)
Director: Bert I. Gordon
Peter Graves (Ed), Peggie Castle (Audrey), Morris Ankrum (Gen. Hanson), Richard Benedict (Corporal Mathias), James Seay (Capt. Barton), Thomas B. Henry (Col. Sturgeon), Than Wyenn (Frank), Pierre Watkin (Taggert), Frank Wilcox (Gen. Short), John Close (Major Everett), Don C. Harvey (1st patrolman), Larry J. Blake (2nd patrolman), Steve Warren (1st soldier), Frank Connor (2nd soldier), Don Eitner (3rd soldier), Frank Chase (4th soldier), Alan Reynolds, Alan Wells, Hylton Socher, Paul Grant, Eilene Janssen, Patricia Dean.

BEHIND THE MASK (1932)
Director: John Francis Dillon
Edward Van Sloan (Dr. Steiner), Boris Karloff (Henderson), Jack Holt (Jack Hart), Constance Cummings (Julie Arnold), Claude King (Arnold), Willard Robertson (Capt. Hawkes), Bertha Mann (Edwards).

BEING THERE (1979)

Director: Hal Ashby
Peter Sellers (Chance), Shirley Mac-
Laine (Eva Rand), Melvyn Douglas
(Benjamin Rand), Jack Warden (Pres.
Bobby), Richard Dysart (Dr.
Robert Allenby), Richard Basehart (Vladimir
Skrapinov), Ruth Attaway (Louise),
Dave Clennon (Thomas Franklin), Fran
Brill (Sally Hayes), Denise Dubarry
(Johanna Franklin), James Noble (Pre-
sidential Adviser), Oteil Burbridge
(Lolo), Ernest M. McClure (David),
Kenneth Patterson (Jeffrey), Ravenell
Keller, III (Abbaz), Alfredine Brown
(old woman), Brian Corrigan (police-
man by White House), Georgine Hall
(Rand's secretary), W. C. 'Mutt' Bur-
ton (Lewis), Richard Venture (Wilson),
Henry B. Dawkins (X-ray technician),
Arthur Grundy (Arthur), Neill P. Lea-
man (Nurse Constance), Villa Mae Bark-
ley (Nurse Teresa), Alice Hirson (First
Lady), Sandy Ward (Sen. Slipshod),
Katherine DeHetre (Kinney), Than Wyenn
(Ambassador Gaufridi).

BELA LUGOSI MEETS A BROOKLYN
  GORILLA (1952) (A. K. A. "The Boys
  from Brooklyn")
Director: William Beaudine
Bela Lugosi (Dr. Zabor), Duke Mitchell
(Duke), Sammy Petrillo (Sammy), Mu-
riel Landers (Salome), Mickey Simpson
(Chula), Al Kikume (Chief Rakos), Mil-
ton Newberger (Bongo), Martin Garra-
laga (Pepe Bordo), Charlita (Nona).

BELL, BOOK AND CANDLE (1958)
Director: Richard Quine
James Stewart (Sheperd Henderson),
Kim Novak (Gillian Holroyd), Jack Le-
mon (Nicky Holroyd), Ernie Kovacs
(Sidney Redlitch), Elsa Lanchester
(Queenie), Janice Rule (Merle Kittridge),
Hermione Gingold (Mrs. De Pass), Ho-
ward McNear (Andy White), Phillipe
Clay (French singer), Wolfe Barzell
(proprietor), Joe Barry (exterminator),
Bek Nelson (secretary), Gail Bonney
(Merle's maid), Monty Ash (herb store
owner), The Brothers Candoli (musicians).

BELL OF HELL, THE (1973-Span./Fr.)
  (A. K. A. "La Campana del Infierno")
Director: Claudio Guerin Hill
Renaud Verley, Maribel Martin, Viveca
Lindfors, Alfredo Mayo.

BELLS, THE (1926)
Director: James Young
Lionel Barrymore, Boris Karloff, Gus-
tav von Seyffertitz, Lola Todd, Fred
Warren, Edward Phillips, Otto Leder-
er, Lucille LaVerne, Caroline Frances
Cook, Lorimer Johnston.

BEN (1972)
Director: Phil Karlson
Lee Harcourt Montgomery (Danny Gar-
rison), Joseph Campanella (Cliff Kirt-
land), Meredith Baxter Birney (Eve Gar-
rison), Arthur O'Connell (Billy Hatfield),
Rosemary Murphy (Beth Garrison), Kaz
Garas (Joe Greer), Paul Carr (Kelly),
Kenneth Tobey (engineer), James Luisi
(Ed), Richard Van Vleet (Reade), Lee
Paul (Carey), Arlen Stuart (Mrs. Gray),
Scott Garrett (Henry Gray), Richard
Drasin (George), Norman Alden (police-
man).

BENEATH THE PLANET OF THE APES
  (1970)
Director: Ted Post
James Franciscus (Brent), Charlton
Heston (Taylor), Maurice Evans (Dr.
Zaius), Kim Hunter (Zira), Linda Har-
rison (Nova), David Watson (Cornelius),
Lou Wagner (Lucius), Jeff Corey (Cas-
par), Thomas Gomez (Minister), James
Gregory (Ursus), Victor Buono (Fat Mu-
tant), Don Pedro Colley (Negro Mutant),
Natalie Trundy (Albina), Gregory Sierra
(Verger), Paul Richards (Mendez), Tod
Andrews (Skipper), Eldon Burke (Goril-
la Sergeant).

BERKELEY SQUARE (1933)
Director: Frank Lloyd
Leslie Howard (Peter Standish), Heather
Angel (Helen Pettigrew), Irene Browne
(Lady Ann Pettigrew), Alan Mowbray
(Major Clinton), Beryl Mercer (Mrs.
Berwick), Betty Lawford (Marjorie
Frant), Olaf Hytten (Sir Joshua Rey-
nolds), David Torrence (Lord Stanley),
Samuel S. Hinds (American Ambassador),
Valerie Taylor (Kate Pettigrew), Juliette
Compton (Duchess of Devonshire), Colin
Keith-Johnston (Tom Pettigrew), Ferdi-
nand Gottschalk (Mr. Throstle).

BERMUDA DEPTHS, THE (1977)
Director: Tom Kotani
Burl Ives (Dr. Paulis), Leigh McCloskey (Magnus Dens), Connie Sellicca (Jennie Haniver), Carl Weathers (Eric), Julie Woodson (Doshan), Ruth Attaway (Delia).

BERSERK! (1967)
Director: Jim O'Connolly
Joan Crawford (Monica Rivers), Ty Har-
din (Frank Hawkins), Judy Geeson (Ange-
la Rivers), Diana Dors (Matlida), Robert
Hardy (Superintendent Brooks), Michael

Gough (Durando), George Claydon (Bruno), Geoffrey Keen (Commissioner Dalby), Sidney Tafler (Harrison Liston), Milton Reid (Strong Man), Howard Goorney (Emil), Ambrosine Phillpotts (Miss Burrows), Philip Madoc (Lazlo), Marianne Stone (Wanda), Thomas Cimarro (Gaspar), Ted Lune (Skeleton Man), Peter Burton (Gustavo), Miki Iveria (Gypsy fortune teller), Bryan Pringle (Constable Bradford), Golda Casimir (bearded lady), Reginald Marsh (Detective Sgt. Hutchins).

BESPOKE OVERCOAT, THE (1955)
Director: Jack Clayton
David Kossoff (Morry, the tailor), Alfie Bass (Fender), Alan Tilvern (Mr. Ranting), Alf Dean (grave digger).

BETWEEN THE NETS (1967-Span./Ital./Fr.) (A.K.A. "Entre las Redes")
Director: Riccardo Freda
Lang Jeffries, Sabine Suno, Frank Oliveras, Antonio Orengo, Silva Solar, Ida Galli.

BETWEEN TWO WORLDS (1944)
Director: Edward A. Blatt
John Garfield (Tom Prior), Paul Henried (Henry), Eleanor Parker (Ann), Edmund Gween (Scrubby), Sydney Greenstreet (Thompson), Faye Emerson (Maxine), George Tobias (Pete Musick), George Coulouris (Lingley), Sara Allgood (Mrs. Midget), Dennis King (Rev. William Duke), Gilbert Emery (Clivedon-Banks), Isobel Elsom (Mrs. Clivedon-Banks), Lester Matthews (dispatcher), Pat O'Moore (clerk).

BEWARE SPOOKS! (1939)
Director: Edward Sedgewick
Joe E. Brown (Roy Gifford), Mary Carlisle (Betty Lou Winters), Clarence Kolb (Commissioner Lewis), Don Beddoe (Nick Bruno), Marc Lawrence (Slick Eastman), George J. Lewis (Danny Emmett).

BEWARE! THE BLOB (1972) (A.K.A. "Son of the Blob")
Director: Larry Hagman
Robert Walker, Jr. (Bobby Hartford), Gwynne Gilford (Lisa Clark), Richard Webb (Sheriff Jones), Carol Lynley (Lesley), Gerrit Graham (Joe), Dick Stahl (Mr. Fascio), Godfrey Cambridge (Chester Hargis), Marlene Clark (Marian Hargis), Shelley Berman (Mr. Carmel, the barber), Dick Van Patton (Mr. Adelman), J.J. Johnson (Deputy Williams), Cindy Williams (Cindy), Randy Stonehill (Randy), Larry Hagman (drunk), Burgess Meredith (drunk), Rockne Tarkington, Tiger Joe Marsh, Danny Goldman, Del Close, Tim Baar, Preston Hagman, Fred Smoot, John Houser, William B. Foster, Byron Keith, Margie Adelman, Robert N. Goodman, Patrick McAllister, Larry Norman.

BEWARE THE BRETHREN (1972) (A.K.A. "Beware My Brethren", "The Fiend")
Director: Robert Hartford-Davies
Ann Todd (Birdie Wemys), Tony Beckley (Kenneth Wemys), Patrick Magee (Minister), Suzanna Leigh (Paddy Lynch), David Lodge (CID Inspector), Ronald Allen (Paul), Percy Herbert (Commissionaire), Madeline Hinde (Brigitte Lynch), Jeannette Wild (prostitute), Diana Chappell (poolside girl), Susanna East (teenage girl), Hani Borelle (riverside girl), Maxine Barrie (singer), Ian Kiddy (baptised boy), Katherine McDonald (child), Dee Shenderey, Brenda Kempner, Irving Lycett, James Watts (congregation members).

BEWITCHED (1945)
Director: Arch Oboler
Edmund Gwenn (Dr. Bergson), Phyllis Thaxter (Joan Alris Ellis), Addison Richards (John Ellis), Kathleen Lockhart (Mrs. Ellis), Will Wright (Mr. Herkheimer), Horace McNally (Eric Russell), Minor Watson (Governor), Virginia Bruce (Governor's wife), Henry H. Daniels, Jr. (Bob Arnold), Francis Pierlot (Dr. George Wilton), Gladys Blake (Glenda), Oscar O'Shea (Capt. O'Malley), Sharon McManus (small girl).

BEWITCHED DUNGEON (1900-Fr.) (A.K.A. "La Tour Maudite", "The Accursed Tower") - short
Director: Georges Melies

BEWITCHED INN, THE (1897-Fr.) (A.K.A. "L'Auberge Ensorcelee") - short
Director: Georges Melies

BEWITCHED TRUNK, THE (1904-Fr.) (A.K.A. "Le Coffre Enchante") - short
Director: Georges Melies

BEYOND, THE (1981-Ital.) (A.K.A. "E Tu Vivrai Nel Terrore! L'Aldila")
Director: Lucio Fulci
Katherine MacColl (Liza), David Warbeck (John), Sarah Keller (Emily).

BEYOND ATLANTIS (1973)
Director: Eddie Romero
John Ashley (Logan), Patrick Wayne
(Vic), Leigh Christian (Syrene), George
Nader (Nereus), Sid Haig (East Eddie),
Lenore Stevens (Kathy).

BEYOND EVIL (1980)
Director: Herb Freed
John Saxon (Larry), Lynda Day George
(Barbara), David Opatoshu (Dr. Solo-
mon), Michael Dante (Del), Mario Mi-
lano (Albanos), Anne Marisse (Leia),
Janica Lynde (Alma), Zitto Kazaan (Es-
teban).

BEYOND THE BERMUDA TRIANGLE
(TVM-1975) - 11-6-75
Director: William A. Graham
Fred MacMurray (Harry Ballinger),
Sam Groom (Jed Horn), Donna Mills
(Claudia), Suzanne Reed (Jill), Dana
Plato (Wendy), Dan White (Caldas),
John Disanti (Linder), Ric O'Feldman
(Doyle), Woody Woodbury (Borden),
Joan Murphy (Myra).

BEYOND THE DARKNESS (1976-Ger.)
Director: Michael Walter
Dagmar Hedrich, Werner Bruhns, Peter Martin Urtel, Rudolf Schundler, Michael Hinz, Eva Kinsky, Elizabeth Volk-
mann.

BEYOND THE DOOR (1974-Ital./U.S.)
(A.K.A. "Chi Sei?", "Who Are You?")
Director: Oliver Hellman
Richard Johnson (Dimitri), Juliet Mills
(Jessica), David Colin, Jr. (Robert),
Elizabeth Turner, Gabriele Lavia.

BEYOND THE DOOR II (1977-Ital.)
(A.K.A. "Shock")
Director: Mario Bava
Daria Nicoldi (Dora Baldini), John Stei-
ner (Bruno), David Colin, Jr. (Marco),
Ivan Rassimov (Psychiatrist).

BEYOND THE MOON (1954)
see Television: Rocky Jones, Space
Ranger (1954-55)

BEYOND THE REEF (1981)
Director: Frank C. Clark
Dayton Ka'ne (Tikoya), Maren Jensen
(Diana), Kathleen Swan (Milly), Keahi
Farden (Jeff), Oliveria Maciel Diaz
(Manidu).

BEYOND THE TIME BARRIER (1960)
Director: Edgar G. Ulmer
Robert Clarke (Maj. William Allison),
Darlene Tompkins (Princess Trirene),

Arianne Arden (Markova), John Van
Dreelan (Dr. Bourman), Ken Knox (Col.
Martin), Stephen Bekassy (Karl Kruse),
Red Morgan (the Captain), Jack Herman
(Dr. Richman), Neil Fletcher (Air Force
Chief of Staff), John Loughney (Gen.
LaMont), William Shapard (Gen. York),
James Altgerns (Secretary Patterson),
Russell Marker (Col. Curtis), Don Flour-
noy, Tom Ravick (mutants).

BEYOND TOMORROW (1940)
Director: A. Edward Sutherland
Harry Carey (Melton), C. Aubrey Smith
(Chadwick), Charles Winninger (O'Brien),
Maria Ouspenskaya (Tanya), Jean Par-
ker, Richard Carlson, Rod La Rocque,
Helen Vinson.

BIG BUS, THE (1976)
Director: James Frawley
Joseph Bologna (Dan Torrance), Stockard
Channing (Kitty Baxter), John Beck (Shoul-
ders O'Brien), Rene Auberjonois (Father
Kudos), Ned Beatty (Shorty Scotty), Bob
Dishy (Dr. Kurtz), Jose Ferrer (Iron-
man), Harold Gould (Prof. Baxter), Lar-
ry Hagman (parking lot doctor), Ruth
Gordon (old lady), Richard Mulligan
(Claude Crane), Richard B. Shull (Eme-
ry Bush), Sally Kellerman (Sybil Crane),
Lynn Redgrave (Camille Levy), Stuart
Margolin (Alex), Howard Hesseman (Jack),
Mary Wilcox (Mary Jane Beth Sue), Mur-
phy Dunne (Tommy Joyce), Vic Tayback
(Goldie), Walter Brooke (Mr. Ames),
James Jeter (bus bartender), Raymond
Guth, Miriam Byrd-Nethery, Dennis
Kort (farm family).

BIGFOOT (1969)
Director: Robert F. Slatzer
Chris Mitchum (Rick), Joi Lansing (Joi
Landis), Lindsay Crosby (Wheels), John
Carradine (Jasper B. Hawks), James
Craig (Sheriff Cyrus), Doodles Weaver
(Forest Ranger), John Mitchum (Elmer
Briggs), Judy Jordan (Chris), Ken May-
nard (Mr. Bennett), Joy Wilkerson (Peg-
gy), Noble Chissell (Hardrock), Dorothy
Keller (Nellie), Nick Raymond (Slim),
Sonny West (Mike), Lois Red Elk (Fall-
ing Star), Carolyn Gilbert (Mrs. Cum-
mings), Bill Bonner (Lucky), Suzy Mar-
lin Crosby (Suzy), Walt Swanner (Henry),
Kim Cardoza (Kim), Tony Cardoza (fish-
erman), James Stellar (Bigfoot), Nick
Raymond (evil creature), A'leshia Lea,
Nancy Hunter, Gloria Hill (female creatures), Jerry Maren (baby creature).

BIG GAME, THE (1972)
Director: Robert Day

Stephen Boyd (Leyton Von Dyke), Cameron Mitchell (Bruno Carstens), Ray Milland (Prof. Handley), France Nuyen (Atanga), Michael Kirner (Mark Handley), Brendon Boone (Jim Handley), John Van Dreelan (Lee), John Stacy (Gen. Stryker), Marie Du Toit (Lucie Handley), George Wang (Wong), Romano Puppo (Alberto), Larry McEvoy (Dr. Warden), Bill Brewer (Captain), Ian Yule (Officer in Command), Judy Washington, Anthony Pritchard.

BIG GRAY-BLUE BIRD, A (1970-Ger.)
(A. K. A. "Ein Grosser Grau-Blauer Vogel")
Director: Thomas Schamoni
Umberto Orsini, Klaus Lemke, Sylvia Winter, Olivera Vuco, Lukas Ammann.

BIG JACK (1949)
Director: Richard Thorpe
Wallace Beery (Big Jack Horner), Marjorie Main (Flapjack Kate), Richard Conte (Dr. Alexander Meade), Edward Arnold (Mayor Mahoney), Charles Dingle (Mathias Taylor), Vanessa Brown (Patricia Mahoney), Clinton Sundberg (C. Petronius Smith), Clem Bevans (Saltlick Joe), Will Wright (Will Farnsworth), Jack Lambert (Bud Valentine), Syd Saylor (Pokey), William Phillips (Toddy).

BIKINI BEACH (1964)
Director: William Asher
Frankie Avalon (Frankie), Annette Funicello (Dee Dee), Martha Hyer (Vivien Clements), Keenan Wynn (Harvey H. Honeywagon), Don Rickles (Big Drag), Harvey Lembeck (Eric von Zipper), John Ashley (Johnny), Jody McCrea (Deadhead), Meredith MacRae (Animal), Candy Johnson (Candy), Timothy Carey (Slim), Danielle Aubrey (Lady Bug), James Westerfield (Officer), Donna Loren (Donna), Paul Smith (Officer), Delores Wells (Sniffles), Janos Prohaska (Clyde), Val Warren (Teenage Werewolf), Boris Karloff (himself).

BILLION DOLLAR BRAIN, THE (1967)
Director: Ken Russell
Michael Caine (Harry Palmer), Karl Malden (Leo Newbegin), Ed Begley (Gen. Midwinter), Francoise Dorleac (Anya), Guy Doleman (Col. Ross), Oscar Homolka (Col. Stok), Milo Sperber (Basil), Vlademir Sheybal (Dr. Eiwort), Susan George (Russian girl in tavern), Donald Sutherland (scientist at computer), Gregg Palmer (1st Dutch businessman), John Herrington (2nd Dutch business-

man), Hans de Vries (3rd Dutch businessman), Janos Kurutz, Paul Tamarin, Alexei Jawdokimov, Iza Teller (Latvian gangsters), Mark Elwes (Birkenshaw), Fred Griffith (taxi driver), Stanley Caine (special delivery boy), John Brandon (Jim), George Roubicek (Edgar), Michael Stayner (scientist), Alex Marchevsky, Peter Forest (Russian radar operators), Brandon Brady (Chief of Security), Tony Harwood (Macey), Reed de Rouen (1st observer), James Woolf (caller), Jill Mai Meredith (Russian girl), Miki Iveria (Russian woman in tavern), Dolly Brennan (woman in gangster hut), Bill Mitchell (Midwinter's aide), Frederick Schrecker (old man on train), Steve Emerson (Russian plainclothesman), Max Moss (shoe shop assistant).

BILLION DOLLAR THREAT, THE (TVM-1979) - 4-15-79
Director: Barry Shear
Dale Robinette (Robert Sands), Ralph Bellamy (Miles Larson), Patrick MacNee (Horatio Black), William Bryant (Harry Grebe), Keenan Wynn (Eli), Robert Tessier (Benjamin), Karen Specht (Ivy), Beth Specht (Holly), Ronnie Carol (Marcia Buttercup), Stephen Keep (Harold Darling), Read Morgan (Charlie), Marianne Marks (Ming), Harold Sakata (Oriental man), Bob Hastings (desk clerk), Ned Wilson (Martian), Than Wyenn (assistant manager), Fil Formicola (bell boy), Jason Corbett (lab technician), Seth Foster, Cliff Carnell, Walt Davis, George Spicer, Robert Lone (technicians).

BILLY THE KID VS. DRACULA (1966)
Director: William Beaudine
John Carradine (Dracula), Chuck Courtenay (Billy the Kid), Melinda Plowman (Betty Bentley), Roy Barcroft (Marshal Griffin), Virginia Christine (Eva Oster), William Forrest (James Underhill), Hannie Landman (Lila Oster), Charlita (Nina), Bing Russell, Harry Carey, Jr., Richard Reeves, Olive Carey, Lennie Greer, Walter Janovitz, Marjorie Bennett.

BIRD IN THE HEAD, A (1946) - short
Director: Edward Bernds
Moe Howard, Larry Fine, Curly Howard, Vernon Dent, Frank Lackteen, Robert Williams.

BIRD OF PARADISE (1932)
Director: King Vidor
Dolores Del Rio (Luana), Joel McCrae (Johnny Baker), John Halliday (Mac), Lon Chaney, Jr. (Thornton), Bert Roach (Hector), Richard Gallagher (Chester),

Pukui (the Chief), Agostino Bergato (Medicine Man), Sophie Ortego (Old Native Woman).

BIRD OF PARADISE (1950)
Director: Delmer Daves
Louis Jourdan (Andre Laurence), Debra Paget (Kalua), Jeff Chandler (Tenga), Everett Sloane (the Beachcomber), Otto Waldis (Skipper), Jack Elam (the Trader), Maurice Schwartz (the Kahuna), Prince Lei Lani (Chief), Mary Ann Ventura (Noanoa), Alfred Zeisler (Van Hook), David K. Bray (Chanter), Violet Nathaniel (Chiefess), Sam Monsarrat (Tenga's friend), Solomon Pa (Chief's man).

BIRDS, THE (1963)
Director: Alfred Hitchcock
Rod Taylor (Mitch Brenner), Tippi Hedren (Melanie Daniels), Jessica Tandy (Mrs. Brenner), Suzanne Pleshette (Annie Hayworth), Veronica Cartwright (Cathy Brenner), Ethel Griffies (Mrs. Bundy), Malcolm Atterbury (Deputy Al Malone), Charles McGraw (Sebastian Sholes), Ruth McDevitt (Mrs. MacGruder), Lonny Chapman (Deke Carter), Elizabeth Wilson (Helen Carter), Karl Swenson (drunk), Doddles Weaver (fisherman), John McGovern (postal clerk), Joe Mantell (travelling salesman), Richard Deacon (man in elevator), Doreen Lang (woman), William Quinn (man), Suzanne Cupito.

BIRDS DO IT (1966)
Director: Andrew Marton
Soupy Sales (Melvin Byrd), Tab Hunter (Lt. Porter), Arthur O'Connell (Prof. Wald), Beverly Adams (Claudine Wald), Edward Andrews (Gen. Smithburn), Doris Dowling (Congresswoman Clanger), Louis Quinn (Sgt. Skam), Burt Taylor (Devlin), Courtney Brown (Arno), Julian Voloshin (Prof. Nep), Warren Day (Curtis), Russell Saunders (Clurg), Jay Laskay (Willie), Bob Bersell (doorman), Burt Leigh (radar operator).

BIRD WITH THE CRYSTAL PLUMAGE, THE (1969-Ital./Ger) (A.K.A. "L'-Uccello dalle Piume di Cristallo", "Phantom of Terror")
Director: Dario Argento
Tony Musante (Sam Delmas), Suzy Kendall (Julia), Eva Renzi (Monica), Mario Adorf (Berto), Umberto Raho (Ranieri), Renato Romano (Dover).

BISHOP MURDER CASE, THE (1929)
Director: Nick Grinde & David

Burton
Basil Rathbone (Philo Vance), Leila Hyams (Belle Dillard), Alec B. Francis (Prof. Bertrand Dillard), Roland Young (Sigurd Arnesson), George Mario (Adolph Drukker), Sydney Bracey (Pyne), Clarence Geoldert (John F. -X. Markham), Delmer Daves (Raymond Sperling), James Donlan (Ernest Heath), Carroll Nye (John E. Sprigg), Charles Quartermaine (John Pardee), Zelda Sears (Mrs. Otto Drukker).

BISHOP OF THE OZARKS, THE (1923)
Director: Finis Fox
Wilford W. Howard, Fred Kelsey, Cecil Holland, R.D. MacLean, Derelyn Perdue, William Kenton.

BISHOP'S WIFE, THE (1948)
Director: Henry Koster
Cary Grant (Dudley), Loretta Young (Julia Brougham), David Niven (Henry Brougham), Monty Woolley (Prof. Wutheridge), Elsa Lanchester (Matilda), James Gleason (Sylvester), Gladys Cooper (Mrs. Hamilton), Isabel Jewell (hysterical mother), Regis Toomey (Mr. Miller), Tito Vuolo (Maggenti), Sarah Edwards (Mrs. Duffy), Anne O'Neal (Mrs. Ward), Karolyn Grimes (Debby Brougham), Margaret McWade (Miss Trumbull), Ben Erway (Mr. Perry), Erville Alderson (Stevens), Bobby Anderson (Defense Captain), Eugene Borden (Michel), Almira Sessions (1st lady in Michel's), Claire Du Brey (2nd lady in Michel's), Florence Auer (3rd lady in Michel's), Margaret Wells (hat shop proprietress), Kitty O'Neill (hat shop customer), Dorothy Vaughan (Delia), David Leonard (blind man), Edgar Dearing (cop), Joseph J. Greene (Santa Clause), Edythe Elliott (saleslady).

BITE ME, DARLING (1970-Ger.) (A.K.A. "Beiss Mich, Liebling")
Director: Helmut Foernbacher
Eva Renzi, Patrick Jordan, Amadeus August, Brigitte Skay, Frederick Pressel.

BIZARRE (1970) (A.K.A. "Secrets of Sex")
Director: Antony Balch
Valentine Dyall (Narrator), Elliott Stein, Cathy Howard, Maria Frost, Anthony Rowlands, Dorothy Grumbar, Laurelle Stretter, Yvonne Quenet, Richard Schulman.

BLACK ABBOT, THE (1962-Ger.) ("Der Schwarze Abt")
Director: Franz J. Gottlieb

Joachim Fuchsberger, Klaus Kinski, Dieter Borsche, Eddie Arent, Charles Regnier.

BLACKBEARD'S GHOST (1968)
Director: Robert Stevenson
Peter Ustinov (Edward Teach), Dean Jones (Steve Walker), Suzanne Pleshette (Jo Anne Baker), Elsa Lanchester (Emily Stowecraft), Richard Deacon (Mr. Wheaton), Michael Conrad (Pinetop Purvis), Joby Baker (Silky Seymour), Norman Grabowski (Virgil), Hank Jones (Larken), Ted Markland (Charles), Lou Nova (Leon), Charlie Brill (Edward), Ned Glass (teller), Elliott Reid (TV commentator), Herbie Faye (croupier), Gil Lamb (waiter), Kelly Thordson (motorcycle cop), George Murdock (head official), Alan Carney (bartender), Herb Vigran, William Fawcett, Sara Taft, Betty Bronson, Elsie Baker, Kathryn Minner.

BLACK BELLY OF THE TARANTULA, THE (1972-Ital.) (A.K.A. "La Tarantola Dal Ventre Nero")
Director: Paolo Cavara
Giancarlo Giannini (Insp. Tellini), Claudine Auger (Laura), Barbara Bouchet (Maria Zani), Barbara Bach (Jenny), Stefania Sandrelli (Anna Tellini), Rossella Falk (woman with mole), Silvano Tranquilli (Paolo Zani), Annabella Incontrera (Mirta), Giancarlo Prete (Mario), Anna Saia (Amica Zani), Nini Vingelli (Commissario Di Giacomo), Ezio Marano (masseur), Eugene Walter (waiter), Daniele Dublini (entymologist), Giuseppe Fortis (psychiatrist), Giorgio Dolfin (policeman), Amata Garbini (police doctor), Carla Manchini (beauty parlor client), Fulvio Mingozzi (director of clinic), Guerrino Grovello (informer).

BLACKBIRD, THE (1926)
Director: Tod Browning
Lon Chaney, Sr. (Don Tate/the Blackbird/the Bishop of Limehouse), Renee Adoree (Fifi Lorraine), Doris Lloyd (Limehouse Polly), Owen Moore (Bertram P. Gladye/West End Bertie), William Weston (Red), Sidney Bracy (Eddy's No. 1 man), Ernie Adams (Eddy's No. 2 man), Polly Moran (flower woman), Frank Norcross (music hall announcer), Eric S. Mayne (sightseer), Andy McLennan (ghost), Lionel Belmore, James T. Mack, Peggy Best, Willie Fung.

BLACK BOX, THE (1915) - serial in 15 episodes
Chapters: 1. "An Apartment House Case", 2. "The Hidden Hands", 3. "The Pocket Wireless", 4. "An Old Grudge", 5. "On the Rack", 6. "The Unseen Terror", 7. "The House of Mystery", 8. "The Inherited Sin", 9. "Lost in London", 10. "The Ship of Horror", 11. "A Desert Vengence", 12. "Neath Iron Wheels", 13. "Tongues of Flame", 14. "A Bolt from the Blue" & 15. "The Black Box".
Director: Otis Turner
Herbert Rawlinson (Sanford Quest), Anna Little (Lenore MacDougal), Frank Lloyd (Ian MacDouglas), Laura Oakley (Laura), Mark Fenton (police officer), William Worthington (Prof. Ashleigh/Lord Ashleigh), Helen Wright (Mrs. Reinholdt), Frank MacQuarrie (Craig), Beatrie Van (Ashleigh's daughter).

BLACK CAMEL, THE (1931)
Director: Hamilton MacFadden
Warner Oland (Charlie Chan), Bela Lugosi (Tarneverro), Robert Young (Jimmy Bradshaw), Victor Varconi (Robert Fyfe), J.M. Kerrigan (Thomas MacMaster), Marjorie White (Rita Ballou), Mary Gordon (Mrs. MacMaster), C. Henry Gordon (Van Horn), Robert Homans (Chief of Police), Dwight Frye (Jessop), Sally Eilers (Julie O'Neil), Violet Dunn (Anna), Dorothy Reviere (Shelah Fane), Richard Tucker (Wilkie Ballou), Murray Kinnell (Smith), Otto Yamaoka (Kashimo), Rita Roselle (Luana), William Post (Alan Jaynes), Louise MacKintosh (housekeeper).

BLACK CASTLE, THE (1952)
Director: Nathan Juran
Boris Karloff (Dr. Meissen), Richard Greene (Richard Beckett), Stephen McNally (Count Von Bruno), Paula Corday (Elga), Lon Chaney, Jr. (Gargon), Michael Pate (Herr Von Melcher), Tudor Owen (Romley), Otto Waldis (Krantz), John Hoyt (Herr Stieken), Henry Corden (Fender).

BLACK CAT, THE (1934)
Director: Edgar G. Ulmer
Boris Karloff (Hjalmar Poelzig), Bela Lugosi (Vitus Verdegast), Jacqueline Wells (Joan Allison), David Manners (Peter Allison), Lucille Lund (Karen Poelzig), Egon Brecher (Andreas Sandomir), Henry Armetta (the Sergeant), John Carradine (man playing organ), Herman Bing (car steward), Harry Cording (Thamal), Luis Alberni (train steward), Anna Duncan (maid), Andre Cheron (train conductor), King Baggott, George Davis,

Michael Mark, Albert Conti, Paul Weigel, Alphonse Martell, Tony Parlow, Paul Panger.

BLACK CAT, THE (1941)
Director: Albert S. Rogell
Basil Rathbone (Montague Hartley), Broderick Crawford (Hubert 'Gill' Smith), Gale Sondergaard (Abigail Doone), Anne Gwynne (Elaine Winslow), Bela Lugosi (Eduardo), Hugh Herbert (Mr. Penny), Cecilia Loftus (Henrietta Winslow), Gladys Cooper (Myrna Hartley), Claire Dodd (Margaret Gordon), Alan Ladd (Richard Hartley), John Eldredge (Stanley Borden).

BLACK CAT, THE (1965)
Director: Harold Hoffman
Robert Frost (Lew), Robin Baker (Diana), Sadie French (Lilith), Scotty McKay, George R. Russell.

BLACK CAT, THE (1980-Ital.)
Director: Lucio Folco
Patrick Magee (Miles), Mimsy Farmer (Gil), David Warbeck (Gorley), Al Cliver (Brian).

BLACK CHRISTMAS (1975) (A. K. A. "Stranger in the House")
Director: Bob Clark
Olivia Hussey (Jess), Margot Kidder (Barb), Keir Dullea (Peter Smythe), John Saxon (Lt. Fuller), Andrea Martin (Phyl), Douglas McGrath (Sgt. Nash), Art Hindle (Chris), Marian Waldman (Mrs. Mac), James Edmond (Mr. Harrison), Lynne Griffin (Clare), Michael Rapport (Patrick).

BLACK CROWN, THE (1950-Fr./Span.)
(A. K. A. "La Corona Negra")
Director: Luis Saslavasky
Rossano Brazzi, Vittorio Gassman, Maria Felix, Antonia Plana, Jose M. Lado, Julia C. Alba.

BLACK DRAGONS (1942)
Director: William Nigh
Bela Lugosi (Dr. Melcher/Colomb), Joan Barclay (Alice), Clayton Moore (Don Martin), George Pembroke (Saunders), I. Stanford Jolley (the Dragon), Robert Frazer (Hanlin), Kenneth Harlan (Colton), Edward Piel, Sr. (Wallace), Bob Fiske (Ryder), Irving Mitchell (Van Dyke), Max Hoffman, Jr. (Kearney), Bernard Gorcey (cabby).

BLACKENSTEIN (1973) (A. K. A. "Black Frankenstein")
Director: William A. Levey

John Hart (Dr. Frankenstein), Joe DiSue (the Monster), Ivory Stone, James Cougar, Andrea King, Liz Renay, Nick Bolin, Cardella Di Milo, Roosevelt Jackson.

BLACK FOREST, THE (1954)
Director: Gene Martel
Akim Tamiroff, Peggy Ann Garner, Gordon Howard.

BLACK FRIDAY (1940)
Director: Arthur Lubin
Boris Karloff (Dr. Ernest Sovac), Bela Lugosi (Eric Marney), Stanley Ridges (Prof. George Kingsley), Anne Gwynne (Jean Sovac), Anne Nagel (Sunny Rogers), Virginia Brissac (Margaret Kingsley), Paul Fix (William Kane), Jack Mulhall (bartender), Raymond Bailey (Louis Devore), Edmund MacDonald (Frank Miller), Joe King (Chief of Police), Murray Alper (bellhop), John Kelly (taxi driver), James Craig, Eddie Dunn, Edward McWade, Emmett Vogan, Edwin Stanley, Harry Hayden, Frank Jaquet, Wallace Reid, Jr.

BLACK HARVEST OF COUNTESS DRACULA, THE (1972-Span.) (A. K. A.
"El Retorno de Walpurguis", "Curse of the Devil", "Le Messe Nere della Countessa Dracula")
Director: Leon Klimovsky
Paul Naschy (Waldemar Daninski), Paty Shepard (Countess Wandesa de Nadasdy).

BLACKHAWK (1952) - serial in 15 episodes
Director: Spencer Gordon Bennet & Fred F. Sears
Kirk Alyn (Blackhawk), Carol Forman (Laska), John Crawford (Chuck), Don Harvey (Olaf), Michael Fox (Mr. Case), Rick Vallin (Stan/Boris), Weaver Levy (Chop Chop), Larry Stewart (Andre), Marshall Reed (Aller), Zon Murray (Bork), Pierce Lyden (Dyke), Frank Ellis (Hendrickson), William Fawcett (Dr. Ralph), Nick Stuart (Cress), Rory Mallinson (Hodge).

BLACK HOLE, THE (1979)
Director: Gary Nelson
Maximilian Schell (Dr. Hans Reinhardt), Anthony Perkins (Dr. Alex Durant), Yvette Mimieux (Dr. Kate McCrae), Robert Forster (Capt. Dan Holland), Joseph Bottoms (Lt. Charles Pizer), Ernest Borgnine (Harry Both), Tommy McLoughlin (Capt. S. T. A. R.), Roddy McDowall (voice of Vincent), Slim Pickens (voice of Old Bob).

BLACK LIMELIGHT (1938)
Director: Paul Stein
Raymond Massey (Peter Charrington),
Joan Mario (Mary Charrington), Walter Hudd (Lawrence Crawford), Henry
Oscar (Insp. Tanner), Dan Tobin (reporter), Coral Browne (Lilly James),
Elliott Mason (Jemima), Diana Beaumont (Gwen), Leslie Brady (detective).

BLACK MAGIC (1944) (A. K. A. "Meeting at Midnight")
Director: Phil Rosen
Sidney Toler (Charlie Chan), Mantan
Moreland (Birmingham Brown), Joseph
Crehan, Jacqueline De Wit, Frances
Chan, Frank Jaquet, Claudia Dell, Ralph
Peters, Helen Beverly, Edward Earle,
Harry Depp, Charles Jordan, Richard
Gordon.

BLACK MAGIC (1949)
Director: Gregory Ratoff
Nancy Guild (Marie Antoinette/Lorenza),
Orson Welles (Cagliostro), Akim Tamiroff (Citano), Frank Latimore (Gilbert),
Margot Grahame (Madame Du Barry),
Stephen Bekassy (DeMontagne), Gregory
Gaye (Chambord), Charles Goldner (Dr.
Messmer), Valentina Cortese (Zoraida),
Berry Kroeger (Alexander Dumas, Sr.),
Raymond Burr (Alexander Dumas, Jr.),
Ronald Adam, Lee Kresel, Tamara
Shayne, Robert Atkins, Franco Corsaro,
Bruce Belfrage, Lee Lenoir, Peter
Trent, Alexander Danaroff, Aniello
Mele, Nicholas Bruce, Titiana Pavlowa,
Giovanna Van Hulzen, Giuseppe Varni.

BLACK MOON (1934)
Director: Roy William Neill
Jack Holt (Stephen Lane), Fay Wray
(Gail), Clarence Muse (Lunch), Mme.
Sul-te-wan (Ruva), Dorothy Burgess
(Juanita Lane), Lumsden Hare (Macklin),
Eleanor Wesselhoeft (Anna), Arnold
Korff (Dr. Perez), Lawrence Criner
(Kaia), Cora Sue Collins (Nancy Lane),
Edna Tichenor, Henry Kolker, Robert
Frazier.

BLACK MOON (1975-Fr.)
Director: Louis Malle
Cathryn Harrison (Lily), Theresa Giehse
(old woman), Alexandra Stewart (sister),
Joe Dalesandro (brother).

BLACK NOON (TVM-1971) - 11-5-71
Director: Bernard Kowalski
Roy Thinnes (Rev. Jonathan Keyes),
Ray Milland (Caleb), Yvette Mimieux
(Deliverance), Lyn Loring (Lorna
Keyes), Henry Silva (Moon), Gloria

Grahame (Bethia), Hank Worden (Joseph),
Buddy Foster (Ethan), William Bryant
(Jacob).

BLACK ORCHIDS (1916)
Director: Rex Ingram
Cleo Madison, Wedgewood Nowell, Francis McDonald, Howard Crampton.

BLACK ORPHEUS (1959-Braz./Fr.)
(A. K. A. "Orfeu Negro")
Director: Marcel Camus
Breno Mello (Orpheus), Marpessa Dawn
(Eurylice), Lourdes de Oliveira (Mira),
Lea Garcia (Serafina), Adhemar Da Silva (Death), Waldetar De Souza (Chico),
Alesandro Constantino (Hermes), Jorge
Dos Santos (Benedito), Aurion Cassanio
(Zeca).

BLACK OXEN (1923)
Director: Frank Lloyd
Corinne Griffith (Madame Zatianny/Mary
Ogden), Alan Hale, Sr. (Prince Hohenhauer), Clara Bow (Janet Oglethorpe),
Conway Tearle (Lee Clavering), Kate
Lester (Jane Oglethorpe), Thomas S.
Guise (Judge Gavin Trent), Thomas
Ricketts (Charles Dinwiddie), Fred Gambold (Oglethorpe's Butler), Otto Lederer
(Ausyrian advisor), Eric Mayne (Chancellor), Otto Nelson (Dr. Steinach), Carmelita Gerachty (Anna Goodrich), Claire
McDowell (Agnes Trevor), Harry Mestayer (James Oglethorpe), Lincoln Stedman (Donnie Ferris), Clarissa Selwyn
(Dora Dwight), Percy Williams (Ogden's
Butler), Mila Constantin, Hortense O'-
Brien, Ione Atkinson (flappers).

BLACK PANTHER OF RATANA, THE
(1963-Ger./Ital./Thai.) (A. K. A. "Der
Schwarze Panther von Ratana")
Director: Jurgen Roland
Marianne Koch, Horst Frank, Heinz
Drache, Brad Harris.

BLACK PEARL, THE (1928)
Director: Scott Pembroke
Lila Lee, Ray Hallor, Adele Watson,
Thomas Curran, Art Rowlands, Carlton
Stockdale.

BLACK PIT OF DR. M, THE (1959-Mex.)
(A. K. A. "Misterios de Ultratumbe",
"Mysteries from Beyond the Tomb")
Director: Ferdinand Mendez
Ralph Bertrand (Dr. Harrison Aldaman),
Mapi Cortes (Patricia Aldaman), Gaston
Santos (Dr. Masali), Carl Aucira (Edward Jameson), Caroline Barret, Beatrice Aguirre, Louis Aragon, Anthony
Raxel.

BLACK RAVEN, THE (1943)
Director: Sam Newfield
George Zucco, Wanda McKay, Noel
Madison, Bob Randall, Byron Foulger,
Glenn Strange, Charles Middleton, I.
Stanford Jolley.

BLACK ROOM, THE (1935)
Director: Roy William Neill
Boris Karloff (Anton Berkman/Gregor
Berkman), Katherine DeMille (Mashka),
Marian Marsh (Thea), Robert Allen (Lt.
Lussan), Thurston Hall (Col. Hassel),
Henry Kolker (De Berghman), John
Buckler (Beran), Edward Van Sloan
(Doctor), Egon Brecher, Frederick
Vogeding.

BLACK SABBATH (1964-Ital.) (A. K. A.
"I Tre Volti Della Paura", "The
Three Faces of Fear")
Director: Mario Bava
"The Drop of Water" segment: Jacque-
line Pierreux (Helen), Milly Monti (the
maid).
"The Telephone": Michele Mercier
(Rosy), Lidia Alfonsi (Mary).
"The Wurdalak": Boris Karloff (Gorca),
Susy Anderson (Sdenka), Mark Damon
(Vladimir D'Urfe), Glauco Onorato (Gi-
orgio), Rika Dialina (Giorgio's wife),
Massimo Right (Pietro).

BLACK SCORPION, THE (1957)
Director: Edward Ludwig
Richard Denning (Henry Scott), Mara
Corday (Theresa), Carlos Rivas (Artu-
ro Ramos), Mario Navarro (Juanito),
Carlos Muzquis (Dr. Velazco), Pas-
cual Pena (Jose de la Cruz), Pedro Gal-
van (Father Delgado), Fanny Schiller
(Florentina), Arturo Martinez (Major
Cosio).

BLACK SLEEP, THE (1956) (A. K. A.
"Dr. Cadman's Secret")
Director: Reginal LeBorg
Basil Rathbone (Sir Joel Cadman), Her-
bert Rudley (Dr. Gordon Ramsay), Pa-
tricia Blake (Laurie Munroe), Akim
Tamiroff (Odo), Bela Lugosi (Casimir),
Lon Chaney, Jr. (Mungo), Phyllis Stan-
ley (Daphne), Peter Gordon (Sgt. Steel),
John Carradine (Borg, the Crusader),
George Sawaya (K-6, the sailor), Sally
Yarnell (Nancy, the bald woman), Tor
Johnson (Curry), Claire Carleton (Miss
Carmona Daly), Louanna Gardner (Mrs.
Angelina Cadman), Johnny Sheffield
(Roundsman Blevins), Clive Morgan
(Constable Glenowen).

BLACKSNAKE (1973) (A. K. A. "Sweet

Suzy")
Director: Russ Meyer
Anouska Hempel (Susan), David War-
beck (Walker), Percy Herbert (Over-
seer), Thomas Baptiste (Isaiah), Milton
McCollin (Joshua), Dave Prowse (Jona-
than), Bernard Boston (Daladier), Vikki
Richards (slave).

BLACK SUNDAY (1961-Ital.) (A. K. A.
"The Mask of the Demon", "La Mas-
chera de Demonio", "Revenge of the
Vampire")
Director: Mario Bava
Barbara Steele (Princess Asa/Katia),
John Richardson (Dr. Gorobec), Ivo
Garrani (Prince Vaida), Andrea Checchi
(Dr. Choma), Arturo Dominici (Javuto),
Enrico Olivieri (Constantin), Antonio
Pierfederici (the Priest), Clara Bindi
(the innkeeper), Tino Bianchi (Ivan),
Germana Dominici (innkeeper's daugh-
ter), Mario Passante (Nikita).

BLACK TORMENT, THE (1964)
Director: Robert Hartford-Davis
John Turner (Sir Roger Fordyke), Hea-
ter Sears (Lady Elizabeth Fordyke), Ann
Lynn (Diane), Peter Arne (Seymour),
Raymond Huntley (Col. Wentworth), Jo-
seph Tomelty (Sir Giles Fordyke), Nor-
man Bird (Harris), Francis De Wolff
(Black John), Patrick Troughton (Ostler),
Annette Whiteley (Mary), Edina Ronay
(Lucy Judd), Charles Houston (Jenkins),
Kathy MacDonald (Kate), Roger Croucher
(apprentice), Derek Newark (coachman),
Jack Taylor, Frank Hayden, Bill Cum-
mings (soldiers).

BLACK WATERS (1929)
Director: Marshall Neilan
James Kirkwood (the Rev. Mr. Eph Kelly), John Loder (Charlie), Mary Brian
(Eunice), Frank Reicher (Randall), Noble Johnson (Jeelo), Hallam Cooley (Chester), Robert Ames (Jimmy Darcy), Ben
Hendricks (Olaf), Lloyd Hamilton (Temple).

BLACK WIDOW, THE (1947) - serial in
13 episodes (A. K. A. "Sombra, the
Spider Woman")
Director: Spencer Gordon Bennet
& Fred C. Brannon
Bruce Edwards (Steve Colt), Carol Vor-
man (Sombra), Virginia Lindley (Joyce
Winters), Anthony Warde (Nick Ward),
Virginia Carroll (Ruth Dayton), Ramsay
Ames (Dr. Curry), I. Stanford Jolley
(Jaffa), Ernie Adams (Blinkey), Theodore
Gottlieb (Hitomu), Sam Flint (Henry Wes-
ton), Forrest Taylor (Bradley), Dale

Van Sickel (Bass/Hodges/Bill/Smith), Robert Wilke (cab driver/jailer), Gene Stutenroth/Roth (John M. Walker), LeRoy Mason (Dr. Godfrey), Keith Richards (Burns), Tom Steele (Blair/Jack/Bard), George Chesebro (J. Carter), Maxine Doyle (fortune teller), Stanley Price (Fillmore Hagin), Frank Lackteen (A. Kabob), Ken Terrell (Mendoza), Robert Reeves (detective), Gil Perkins (Burke), Bud Wolfe (guard), George Douglas (Harris), Robert Barron (Link), Arvon Dale (1st triangulator), John Alban (2nd triangulator), Jack O'Shea (Finnegan), Frank O'Connor (Inspector), Peggy Wynne (Nurse MacIntyre), Duke Green (Ted Mills), Charles Sullivan (Officer), Hal Landon (Andy Baldwin), Larry Steers (Harcourt), Frank White (Lee), John Phillips (Mark), Bill Bailey (morgue attendant), Dave Anderson (porter), Jerry Jerome (reporter No. 1), Richard Gordon (reporter No. 2), Carey Loftin (Spike), Laura Stevens (Trixie), Ted Mapes (Slade).

BLACK ZOO (1963)
    Director: Robert Gordon
Michael Gough (Michael Conrad), Jeanne Cooper (Edna Conrad), Rod Lauren (Carl), Virginia Grey (Jenny), Jerome Cowan (Jeffrey Stengel), Elisha Cook (Joe), Edward C. Platt (Detective Rivers), Mirianna Hill (Audrey), George Barrows (the Ape), Oren Curtis (Radu), Warene Ott (Mary Hogan), Eilene Janssen (bride), Eric Stone (groom), Dani Lynn, Susan Slavin (art students), Douglas Henderson (Lt. Duggan), Claudia Brack (Carl's mother), Daniel Kurlick (Carl as a child), Byron Morrow (the coroner), Jerry Douglas (lab technician), Michael St. Angel (Officer Donovan).

BLACULA (1972)
    Director: William Crain
William Marshall (Mamuwalde), Vonetta McGee (Tina/Luva), Thalmus Rasulala (Dr. Gordon Thomas), Denise Nicholas (Michelle), Gordon Pinsent (Lt. Jack Peters), Charles Macaulay (Dracula), Elisha Cook, Jr. (Sam, the morgue attendant), Ji-Tu Cumbuka (Skillet), Emily Yance (Nancy), Ted Harris (Bobby), Rick Metzler (Billy), Ketty Lester (Juanita), Lance Taylor, Sr. (Swenson), Logan Field (Barnes), Eric Brotherson (real estate agent).

BLADE RUNNER (1982)
    Director: Ridley Scott
Harrison Ford (Rick Deckard), Rutger Hauer (Batty), Sean Young (Rachel), Edward James Olmos (Gaff), M. Emmett Walsh (Bryant), Daryl Hannah (Pris), Brion James (Leon), William Sanderson (Sebastian), Joe Turkel (Tyrell), Joanna Cassidy (Zhora), Morgan Paull (Holden), James Hong (Chew), Kevin Thompson (Bear), Hy Pyke (Taffey Lewis), John Edward Allen (Kaiser).

BLAKE OF SCOTLAND YARD (1927) -
    serial in 12 episodes
    Director: Robert F. Hill
Hayden Stevenson (Angus Blake), Grace Cunard (Queen of Diamonds), Gloria Gray (Lady Diane Blanton), Monty Montague (Jarvis).

BLAKE OF SCOTLAND YARD (1937) -
    serial in 15 episodes
    Director: Robert F. Hill
Ralph Byrd (Sir James Blake), Joan Barclay (Hope Mason), Dickie Jones (Bobby), Herbert Rawlinson, Lloyd Hughes, Bob Terry, Nick Stuart.

BLANCHEVILLE MONSTER, THE (1960-
    Span./Ital.) (A.K.A. "Horror")
    Director: Alberto de Martino/
    Martin Herbert
Gerard Tichy (Rodrique Blackford), Joan Hills (Emilie Blackford), Leon Archoriz (Dr. Atwell Larouche), Richard Davis (John), Helga Line (Eleonor, the governess), Frank Moran (Alaistair, the butler), Iran Eory (Alice), Emily Wolkawicz (Emily's wet-nurse), Harry Winter (gamekeeper).

BLAST OFF (1954)
    see Television: Rocky Jones, Space Ranger (1953-54)

BLIND BARGAIN, A (1922)
    Director: Wallace Worsley
Lon Chaney, Sr. (Dr. Lamb/Apeman), Jacqueline Logan (Angela), Raymond McKee (Robert), Fontaine LaRue (Mrs. Lamb), Virginia Madison (Angela's mother), Virginia True Boardman (Mrs. Sandell), Aggie Herring (Bessie).

BLIND MAN'S BLUFF (1936)
    Director: Albert Parker
Basil Sydney, James Mason, Enid Stamp Taylor, Iris Ashley, Barbara Greene.

BLITHE SPIRIT (1945)
    Director: David Lean
Rex Harrison (Charles Condomine), Constance Cummings (Ruth Condomine), Kay Hammond (Elvira Condomine), Margaret Rutherford (Madame Arcati), Joyce Carey (Mrs. Bradman), Hugh Wakefield

(Dr. Bradman), Jacqueline Clark (Edith, the maid).

BLOB, THE (1958)
　　Director: Irwin S. Yeaworth, Jr.
Steve McQueen (Steve Andrews), Aneta
Corseaut (Judy Martin), Earl Rose
(Dave), Steven Chase (Dr. Hallen), John
Benson (Burt), Olin Howlin (the old man),
Vince Barbi (George, the diner owner),
Audrey Metcalf (Mrs. Martin), Elinor
Hammer (Mrs. Porter), Keith Almoney
(Danny Martin), Julie Cousins (Sally
the waitress), Robert Fields (Tony
Gressette), James Bonnet (Mooch Miller), Anthony Granke (Al).

BLOOD! (1974)
　　Director: Andy Milligan
Allan Berendt (Dr. Lawrence Orlovski),
Hope Stansbury, Eve Crosby, Patti
Gaul, Pamela Adams.

BLOOD AND BLACK LACE (1964-Ital./
　　Fr./Mono.) (A.K.A. "Sei Donne per
　　l'Assassino", "Six Women for the
　　Murderer", "Fashion House of Death")
　　Director: Mario Bava
Eva Bartok (Contessa Cristiana), Cameron Mitchell (Massimo Morlacchi),
Thomas Reiner (Insp. Silvestri), Mary
Arden (Peggy), Arianna Gorini (Nicole),
Claude Dantes (Greta), Franco Ressel
(Riccardo), Dane Di Paolo (Antiquary
Franco Seala), Massimo Righi (Marco),
Luciano Pigozzi (Cesare Lazzarini),
Harriet While Medin (Clarice), Francesca Ungaro (Isabella), Giuliano Raffaelli (Asst. Insp. Zanchin), Enzo Cerusico, Nadia Anty, Lea Drugher.

BLOOD AND LACE (1971)
　　Director: Philip Gilbert
Gloria Grahame (Mrs. Deere), Melody
Patterson (Ellie Masters), Vic Tayback
(Calvin Carruthers), Len Lesser (Tom
Kredge), Milton Selzer (Mr. Mullins),
Terri Messina (Bunch), Ronald Taft
(Walter), Dennis Christopher (Pete),
Maggie Corey (Jennifer), Louise Sherrill (Edna Masters), Peter Armstrong
(Ernest), Mary Strawberry (nurse).

BLOOD AND ROSES (1960-Fr./Ital.)
　　(A.K.A. "Et Mourir de Plaisir",
　　"And Die of Pleasure")
　　Director: Roger Vadim
Mel Ferrer (Leopoldo de Karnstein),
Elsa Martinelli (Georgia Monteverdi),
Annette Vadim (Carmilla von Karnstein), Marc Allegret (Judge Monteverdi), Gabriella Farinon (Lisa),
Jacques-Rene Chauffard (Dr. Verari),

Alberto Bonucci (Carlo Ruggieri), Serge
Marquand (Giuseppe), Renato Speziali
(Guido Naldi), Gianni De Benedetto (Police Marshal), Carmilla Stroyberg (Martha), Edythe Peters (the cook), Nathalie
Le Foret (Marie).

BLOOD BATH (1966) (A.K.A. "Track
　　of the Vampire")
　　Director: Stephanie Rothman &
　　Jack Hill
William Campbell (Sordi), Lori Saunders,
Sandra Knight, Marissa Mathes.

BLOOD BEACH (1981)
　　Director: Jeffrey Bloom
Mariana Hill (Catherine), David Huffman (Harry Caulder), John Saxon (Pearson), Stefan Gierasch (Dimitrios), Burt
Young (Royko), Darrell Fetty (Hoagy),
Lynne Marta (Jo), Eleanor Zee (Mrs.
Selden), Pamela McMyler (Mrs. Hench),
Harriet Medin (Ruth), Lena Pausette
(Marie), Otis Young (Piantadosi), Mickey
Fox (Moose), Charles Rowe Rook (Todd
Bell), Laura Burkett (girl in sand), Marleta Giles (girlfriend), Jacqueline Randall (2nd girl), Read Morgan (newsman),
John Joseph Thomas (Mark), Julie Dolan
(Karen), Sandra Friebel (Sue), Christopher Franklin (David), Bobby Bass (rapist), Mary Jo Catlett (Harriett Crabbe),
James Ogg (Alan Hench), Robert Newirth
(Bleeker), Judy Walker (mother on beach).

BLOOD BEAST FROM OUTER SPACE
　　(1965) (A.K.A. "The Night Caller")
　　Director: John Gilling
John Saxon (Jack Costain), Alfred Burke
(Superintendent Hartley), Maurice Denham (Prof. Morley), Robert Crewdson
(Medra, the Alien), John Carson (Major),
Jack Watson (Sgt. Hawkins), Patricia
Denhan (Ann Barlow), Warren Mitchell
(Lilbum), Marianne Stone (Mrs. Lilbum),
Aubrey Morris (Thorburn), Barbara
French (Joyce Malone), Stanley Meadows
(Grant), Tom Gill (Police Commissioner's
secretary), Geoffrey Lumsden (Col. Davy), Ballard Berkeley (Cmdr. Savage),
David Gregory (Private Jones), Anthony
Wager (Private Higgins), John Sherlock
(TV newscaster), Vincent Harding (1st
R/T soldier), Douglas Livingstone (2nd
R/T soldier), Romo Gorrara (Lieutenant).

BLOOD DEMON (1967-Ger.) (A.K.A.
　　"Die Schlangengrube und das Pendel",
　　"The Snake Pit and the Pendulum",
　　"Torture Chamber of Dr. Sadism")
　　Director: Harald Reinl
Christopher Lee (Count Regula), Karin

Dor (Lillian von Drabante), Lex Barker
(Roger von Marienburg), Vladimir Me-
dar, Carl Lange.

BLOOD DRINKERS, THE (1966-Phil. /
U.S.) (A.K.A. "Vampire People")
    Director: Gerardo De Leon
Ronald Remy (Dr. Marco), Amelia Fu-
entes, Eva Montez, Eddie Fernandez,
Celia Rodriguez, Paquito Salcedo.

BLOODEATERS (1980)
    Director: Chuck McCrann
Charles Austin (Cole), Beverly Shapiro
(Polly), Paul Haskin (Briggs), John Am-
plas (Phillips), Dennis Helfend (hermit).

BLOOD FEAST (1963)
    Director: Herschell Gordon Lewis
Connie Mason, Thomas Wood, Lyn Bol-
ton, Mal Arnold, Toni Calvert, Scott
H. Hall, Gene Courtier, Ashlyn Mar-
tin, Jerome Eden, Craig Maudslay,
Jr., Sandra Sinclair, Al Golden.

BLOOD FIEND (1966) (A.K.A. "Theatre
of Death")
    Director: Samuel Gallu
Christopher Lee (Phillipe Darvas), Julian Glover (Charles Marquis), Lelia
Goldoni (Dani Gireaux), Jenny Till (Nicole Chapel), Ivor Dean (Insp. Mi-
cheaud), Evelyn Laye (Madame Angele).

BLOOD FOR DRACULA (1974-Ital./Fr.)
(A.K.A. "Andy Warhol's Dracula",
"Dracula Vuole Vivere: Cerca San-
gui di Vergine!")
    Director: Paul Morrissey
Joe Dallesandro (the Gardner), Udo
Kier (Count Dracula), Vittoria De Sica
(the Nobleman), Arno Juerging (Dracula's assistant), Maxime McKendry (Nobleman's wife), Roman Polanski (a villager), Stefanie Carsini, Dominique
Darrell, Silvia Dionisio, Milena Vuko-
tic (Nobleman's daughters).

BLOOD FROM THE MUMMY'S TOMB
(1971)
    Director: Seth Holt & Michael
    Carreras
Andrew Keir (Prof. Julian Fuchs), Va-
lerie Leon (Margaret Fuchs/Tera),
James Villiers (Prof. Corbeck), Hugh
Burden (Dandridge), George Coulouris
(Berigan), Rosalie Crutchley (Helen
Dickerson), Mark Edwards (Tod Brow-
ning), David Markham (Dr. Burgess),
Anbrey Morris (Dr. Putnam), Tama-
ra Ustinov (Veronica), Joan Young
(Mrs. Caporal), David Jackson (young
male nurse), James Cossins (older

male nurse), Graham James (youth in
museum), Jonathan Burn (saturnine
young man), Penelope Holt, Angela Gin-
ders (nurses), Tex Fuller (patient), Ma-
dina Luis, Abdul Kader, Oscar Charles,
Saad Ghazi, Omar Ammodi, Ahmed Osman, Soltan Lalani (priests).

BLOODLUST (1961)
    Director: Ralph Brooke
Wilton Graff (Albert Balleau), Lylyan
Chauvin (Sandra Balleau), Robert Reed
(Johnny Randall), June Kenny (Betty
Scott), Gene Persson (Pete Garwood),
Walter Brooke (Dean Gerrard), Joan
Lora (Jean Perry).

BLOOD OF A POET (1930-Fr.) (A.K.A.
"Le Sang d'un Poete")
    Director: Jean Cocteau
Enrique Rivero, Elizabeth Lee Miller,
Oddette Talazac, Pauline Carton.

BLOOD OF DRACULA (1957) (A.K.A.
"Blood of the Demon", "Blood Is My
Heritage")
    Director: Herbert L. Strock
Sandra Harrison (Nancy Perkins), Louise
Lewis (Miss Branding), Gail Ganley
(Myra), Jerry Blaine (Tab), Malcolm
Atterbury (Lt. Dunlap), Heather Ames
(Nola), Thomas B. Henry (Mr. Perkins),
Don Devlin (Eddie), Paul Maxwell (Mike),
Richard Devon (Sgt. Stewart), Jean Dean
(Mrs. Perkins), Carlyle Mitchell (Stan-
ley Mather), Shirley de Lancey (Terry),
Mary Adams (Mrs. Thorndyke), Michael
Hall (Glenn).

BLOOD OF DRACULA'S CASTLE (1967)
(A.K.A. "Dracula's Castle")
    Director: Al Adamson, Jr.
Alex D'Arcy (Count Townsend), Paula
Raymond (the Countess), John Carradine
(George, the butler), Robert Dix, John
Cardos, Ray Young, Ken Osborne, Bar-
bara Bishop, Gene O'Shane.

BLOOD OF GHASTLY HORROR (1970)
(A.K.A. "Man with the Synthetic
Brain")
    Director: Al Adamson, Jr.
John Carradine (Dr. Vanard), Tommy
Kirk (Detective Lt. Cross), Regina Car-
rol (Susan Vanard), Kent Taylor (Elton
Corey), Roy Morton (Joe Corey), Rich
Smedley (Al), Arne Warde (Sgt. Grimal-
di), Tacey Robbins (Linda Clarke), Kirk
Duncan (David Clarke), Tanya Maree
(Nicky), John Armond (Nick), Lyle Fe-
lice (Vito), Barney Gelfen (detective),
John Talbert (Curtis), Joey Benson (Lt.
Ward).

BLOOD OF NOSTRADAMUS, THE (1960-
Mex.) (A. K. A. "La Sangre de Nos-
tradamus")
Director: Frederick Curiel
German Robles (Nostradamus), Domin-
go Soler (Prof. Duran), Julio Aleman,
Aurora Alvarado.

BLOOD OF THE IRON MAIDEN (1969)
Director: Ben Benoit
John Carradine, Carol Kane, Marvin
Miller, Peter Duryea, Pat Heider, Bar-
bara Mallory.

BLOOD OF THE VAMPIRE (1958)
Director: Henry Cass
Sir Donald Wolfit (Dr. Callistratus),
Vincent Ball (Dr. John Pierre), Barba-
ra Shelley (Madeleine), Victor Maddern
(Carl), William Devlin (Kurt Urach),
John Le Mesurier (Chief Justice), John
Stuart (Madeleine's uncle), Bernard
Bresslaw (tall thief), Andrew Faulds
(Chief Guard Wetzler), Bryan Coleman
(Herr Auron), George Murcell (1st
guard), Henry Vidon (Meinster), Y-
vonne Buckingham (serving wench),
Cameron Hall (drunken doctor), Milton
Reid.

BLOOD ON SATAN'S CLAW (1970)
(A. K. A. "Satan's Skin")
Director: Piers Haggard
Patrick Wymark (the Judge), Linda
Hayden (Angel Blake), Barry Andrews
(Ralph Gower), Michele Dotrice (Mar-
garet), Wendy Padbury (Cathy Vespers),
Tamara Ustinov (Rosalind Barton), Si-
mon Williams (Peter Edmonton), An-
thony Ainley (Rev. Fallowfield), James
Hayter (Squire Middleton), Charlotte
Mitchell (Ellen), Avice Landon (Isobel
Banham), Robin Davies (Mark Vespers),
Howard Goorney (doctor).

BLOOD ORGY OF THE SHE DEVILS
(1972)
Director: Ted Mikels
Lila Zaborin (Mara), Tom Pace (Mark),
William Bagdad (Toruke), Leslie Mc-
Rae (Lorraine), Victor Izay (Dr. Hels-
ford), Ray Myles (Rodannus), Paul Wil-
moth (Barth), Kebrine Kincade (Sharon),
Curt Matson (Dr. Paxton), Linn Henson
(Roberta), John Nicolai (Dr. Everest),
John Ricco (Royce Littleton), Vincent
Barbi (Indian Chief), Annik Borell (witch
who is stoned), Sherri Vernon (witch
burned at stake), Erica Campbell (girl
at seance), Chris Capen (member at
seance).

BLOOD PIE (1971-Span.) (A. K. A.

"Pastel de Sangre")
Director: Jose Maria Valles --
"Tarota" segment, Emilio Marti-
nez Lazaro - "Victor Frankenstein"
segment, Francisco Bellmunt -
"Terror Entre Cristianos" seg-
ment, Jaime Chavarri - "The
Dance" segment
Marta May, Julian Ugarte, Charo Lopez,
Luis Ciges, Marisa Paredes, Carlos
Otero, Eusebio Poncela.

BLOOD-RELATIONS (1977-Dutch/Fr.)
(A. K. A. "Bloedverwanten", "Les
Vampires en Ont Ras de Bol")
Director: Wim Lindner
Maxim Hamel, Eddie Constantine, Gre-
goire Aslan, Sophie Deschamps, Robert
Dalban.

BLOOD ROSE, THE (1969-Fr.) (A. K. A.
"La Rose Ecorchee", "The Flayed
Rose", "Ravaged")
Director: Laude Mulot
Philippe Lemaire (Frederic Lansac),
Annie Duperey (Anne Lansac), Howard
Vernon (Prof. Rohmer), Elisabeth Tes-
sier (Barbara), Michelle Perello, Oli-
via Robin.

BLOOD-SPATTERED BRIDE, THE (1974-
Span.) (A. K. A. "La Novia Ensangren-
tada", "The Bloody Bride")
Director: Vincente Aranda
Alexandra Bastedo, Simon Andrieu, Ma-
ribel Martin, Dean Selmier, Monteser-
rat Julio, Rosa M. Rodriguez, Angel
Lombarte.

BLOODSUCKERS (1971) (A. K. A. "In-
cense for the Damned")
Director: Robert Hartford-Davis
Peter Cushing (Dr. Walter Goodrich),
Patrick Macnee (Maj. Derek Longbow),
Johnny Sekka (Robert Kirby), Alexander
Davion (Tony), Imogen Hassall (Chris-
seis), Patrick Mower (Richard), Made-
line Hinde (Penelope Goodrich), William
Mervyn, Edward Woodward.

BLOODSUCKING FREAKS (1976) (A. K. A.
"The Incredible Torture Show")
Director: Joel Reed
Seamus O'Brien (Sardu), Louie DeJesus
(Ralphus), Niles McMaster (Tom), Viji
Krim (Natasha), Alan Dellay (Crazy
Silo), Dan Fauci (Detective Sgt. Tucci),
Ernie Peysher, Lynette Sheldon, Karen
Fraser, Michelle Craig.

BLOOD THIRST (1971-Phil. /U. S.)
Director: Newt Arnold
Robert Winston, Vic Diaz, Yvonne Niel-

son, Katherine Henryk, Max Rojo, Mirda Moreno, Eddie Infante, Ching Tello.

BLOODTHIRSTY BUTCHERS, THE (1969)
Director: Andy Milligan
John Miranda (Sweeney Todd), Jan Helay (Maggie Lovett), Berwick Kaler, Annabella Wood.

BLOODTIDE (1982)
Director: Richard Jefferies
Lila Kedrova (Sister Anna), Deborah Shelton (Madeline), James Earl Jones, Jose Ferrer, Mary-Louise Weller, Martin Kove, Lydia Cornell.

BLOODY BIRTHDAY (1980)
Director: Ed Hunt
Susan Strasberg (Mrs. Davis), Jose Ferrer (the Doctor), Lori Lethin (Joyce Russel), Melinda Cordell (Mrs. Brody), Julie Brown (Beverly Brody), Joe Penny (Mr. Harding), Bert Kramer (Sheriff Brody), K. C. Martel (Timmy Russell), Elizabeth Hoy (Debbie Brody), Billy Jacoby (Curtis), Andy Freeman (Steven Seaton), Ben Marley (Duke), Erica Hope (Annie), Cyril O'Reilly (Paul), Shane Butterworth (Jimmy Phillips), Michael Dudikoff (Willard), Daniel Currie (Deputy Duncan), Norman Rice (Mr. Seaton), Georgie Paul (Miss Lawrence), Bill Boyett (Mr. Russell), Ellen Geer (Mrs. Seaton), Ward Costello (Curtis' grandfather), Ruth Silveira (nurse).

BLOODY PIT OF HORROR, THE (1965-Ital./U.S.) (A. K. A. "Il Boia Scarlatto", "The Scarlet Executioner", "The Crimson Executioner")
Director: Massimo Pupillo/Max Hunter
Mickey Hargitay (Anderson, the Crimson Executioner), Louise Barrett (Edith), Walter Brandi, Femi Martin, Rita Klein, Moa Thai, Alfred Rice, John Turner.

BLOODY VAMPIRE, THE (1961-Mex.) (A. K. A. "El Vampire Sangriento", "Count Frankenhausen")
Director: Miguel Morayta
Carlos Agosti (Count Frankenhausen), Begona Palacios, Erna Bauman, Bertha Moss, Raul Farrell, Antonio Raxel, Enrique Lucero.

BLOW OUT (1981)
Director: Brian DePalma
John Travolta (Jack Terri), Nancy Allen (Sally Bedina), John Lithgow (Burke),

Dennis Franz (Manny Karp), Curt May (Frank Donohue), Peter Boyden (Sam), Ernest McClure (Jim), Maurice Copeland (Jack Manners), Dave Roberts (1st anchor), Claire Carter (Joan), John Hoffmeister (McRyan), John Aquino (detective), Patrick McNamara (Officer Nelson), Terrence Currier (Lawrence Henry), Tom McCarthy (policeman), Dean Bennett (campus guard), Missy Cleveland.

BLUEBEARD (1944)
Director: Edgar G. Ulmer
John Carradine (Gaston), Nils Asther (Insp. Lefevre), Jean Parker (Lateille), Ludwig Stossel (Lamarte), Iris Adrian (Mimi), Henry Kolker (Deschamps), George Pembroke (Insp. Renard), Teala Loring (Francine), Emett Lynn (Le Soldat), Carrie Deven (Constance), Sonia Sorel (Renee), Patti McCarty (Bebette), Anne Sterling (Jeanette).

BLUEBEARD (1951-Fr.) (A. K. A. "Barbe Bleue")
Director: Christian-Jaque
Pierre Brasseur, Cecile Aubry, Hans Alberts, Jacques Sernas, Fritz Kortner, Robert Arnoux, Jean Debucourt, Ina Halley.

BLUEBEARD (1972-Ital./Fr./Ger.)
Director: Edward Dmytryk
Richard Burton (Bluebeard), Raquel Welch (Magdalena), Joey Heatherton (Anne), Virna Lisi (Elga), Nathalie Delon (Brigitte), Agostina Belli (Caroline), Karen Schubert (Greta), Sybil Danning (prostitute), Edward Meeks (Sergio), Jean Lefebvre (Greta's father), Mathieu Carriere (violinist).

BLUEBEARD'S TEN HONEYMOONS (1960)
Director: W. Lee Wilder
George Sanders (Henri Landru), Corinne Calvet (Odette Bois), Jean Kent (Madame Guillin), Patricia Roc (Madame Dureaux), Greta Gynt (Jeanette), Maxine Audley (Cynthia), George Coulouris (Lacoste), Peter Illing (Le Fevre), Paul Whitsun-Jones (Station Master), Ingrid Hafner (Giselle), Selma Vas Diaz (Madame Boyer), Sheldon Lawrence (Pepi), Keith Pyott (estate agent), Ian Fleming (attorney), John Gabriel (barber), Robert Rietty (bank clerk), Jack Melford (concierge), Milo Sperber (librarian), Harold Berens (jeweler), Mark Singleton (advertising clerk), C. Denier Warren (neighbor), Dino Galvani (hardware store owner).

BLUE BIRD, THE (1940)

Director: Walter Lang
Shirley Temple (Mytyl), Spring Byington (Mummy Tyl), Nigel Bruce (Mr. Luxury), Gale Sondergaard (Tylette), Eddie Collins (Tylo), Sterling Holloway (Wild Plum), Edwin Maxwell (Oak), Russell Hicks (Daddy Tyl), Johnny Russell (Tyltyl), Brandon Hurst (Footman), Helen Ericson (Light), Laura Hope Crews (Mrs. Luxury), Cecilia Loftus (Granny Tyl), Al Shean (Grandpa Tyl), Sybil Jason (Angela Berlingot), Ann Todd (little sister), Scotty Beckett (child), Jessie Ralph (Fairy Berylune), Leona Roberts (Mrs. Berlingot), Dorothy Dearing (Cypress), Stanley Andrews (Wilhelm), Frank Dawson (Caller of Roll), Gene Reynolds (studious boy), Thurston Hall (Father Time), Dewey Robinson (Royal Forester), Claire Du Brey (nurse), Herbert Evans (Footman), Keith Hitchcock (Major Domo), Tommy Baker (lover), Dorothy Joyce (lover), Payne Johnson (child), Juanita Quigley (child), Buster Phelps (boy inventor), Billy Cook (boy chemist), Diane Fisher (little girl).

BLUE BIRD, THE (1976-U. S. S. R. /U. S.)
Director: George Cukor
Elizabeth Taylor (Mother/Maternal Love/Witch/Light), Jane Fonda (Night), Ava Gardner (Luxury), Cicely Tyson (Cat), Robert Morley (Father Time), Harry Andrews (Oak), Todd Lookinland (Tvityl), Patsy Kensit (Myltyl), Will Geer (Grandfather), Mona Washbourne (Grandmother), George Cole (Dog), Richard Pearson (Bread), Nadia Pavlova (Blue Bird), George Vitzin (Sugar), Margareta Terechova (Milk), Oleg Popov (Fat Laughter), Leonid Nevedomsky (Father), Valentina Ganilae Ganibalova (Water), Yevgeny Scherbakov (Fire).

BLUE DEMON AND THE SEDUCTRESSES (1968-Mex.) (A. K. A. "Blue Demon y las Seductoras")
Director: Gilberto Martinez Solares
Blue Demon, Regina Torne, Augustin Martinez Solares, Enrique Aguilar, Sandra Boyd, Gina Morett, Oscar Moreli, Griselda Mejia.

BLUE DEMON VS. THE DIABOLICAL WOMEN (1967-Mex.) (A. K. A. "Blue Demon vs. las Diabolicas")
Director: Chano Urueta
Blue Demon, David Reynoso, Martha Cisneros, Ana Martin, Griselda Mejia, Barbara Angeli, Maria Salome.

BLUE DEMON VS. THE INFERNAL BRAINS (1967-Mex.) (A. K. A. "Blue Demon vs. Cerebros Infernales")
Director: Chano Urueta
Blue Demon, David Reynoso, Ana Martin, Noe Murayama, Barbara Angeli, Dagoberto Rodriguez.

BLUE DEMON VS. THE SATANICAL POWER (1964-Mex.) (A. K. A. "Blue Demon contra el Poder Satanico")
Director:
Blue Demon, Martha Elena Cervantes, Jaime Fernandez.

BLUE LIGHT, THE (1932-Ger. /Ital.)
(A. K. A. "Das Blaue Licht")
Director: Leni Riefenstahl
Leni Riefenstahl, Mathias Wieman.

BLUE SUNSHINE (1977)
Director: Jeff Lieberman
Zalman King (Jerry Zipkin), Mark Goddard (Edward Flemming), Robert Walden (David Blume), Deborah Winters (Alicia Sweeney), Charles Siebert (Detective Clay), Ann Cooper (Wendy Flemming), Richard Crystal (Frannie Scott), Ray Young (Wayne Mulligan), Bill Adler (Ralphie), Barbara Quinn (Stephanie), Alice Ghostley, Stephan Gierasch.

BOAT WITHOUT A FISHERMAN, THE (1964-Span.) (A. K. A. "La Barca sin Pescador")
Director: Jose Maria Forn
Julian Ugarte (Devil), Gerard Landry, Mabel Karr, Ampero Soler Leal.

BOCCACCIO '70 (1962-Ital. /Fr.)
Director: Federico Fellini
"The Temptation of Dr. Antonio" segment: Peppino De Filippo (Dr. Antonio), Anita Ekberg (Anita), Giacomo Furia, Dante Maggio, Alberto Sorrentino.

BODY BENEATH, THE (1970)
Director: Andy Milligan
Gavin Reed (Father Alexander Algernon Ford), Jackie Skarvelles (Susan Ford), Colin Gordon (Graham Ford), Berwick Kaler (Spool), Richmond Ross (Paul Donati), Susan Heart (Alicia Ford), Emma Jones (Candice Ford), Susan Clark, Judith Heard.

BODY DISAPPEARS, THE (1941)
Director: D. Ross Lederman
Jeffrey Lynn (Peter De Haven), Jane Wyman (Joan Shotesbury), Edward Everett Horton (Prof. Shotesbury), Willie Best (Willie), Craig Stevens (Robert Struck), Marguerite Chapman (Christine Lunce-

ford), David Bruce (Jimmie Barbour), Charles Halton (Prof. Moggs), Ivan Simpson (Dean Claxton), Sidney Bracy (Barrett), Wade Boteler (Insp. Deming), Herbert Anderson (George 'Doc' Appleby), DeWolf Hopper, Natalie Shaefer, Tod Andrews.

BODY SNATCHER, THE (1945)
Director: Robert Wise
Boris Karloff (John Gray), Henry Daniell (Dr. Wolfe MacFarlane), Bela Lugosi (Joseph), Russell Wade (Donald Fettes), Rita Corday (Mrs. Marsh), Edith Atwater (Meg Camden), Sharyn Moffett (Georgina Marsh), Robert Clarke (Richardson), Mary Gordon (Mrs. Mary McBride), Carl Kent (Gilchrist), Donna Lee (street singer), Jim Moran (horse trader), Larry Wheat (salesman), Ina Constant (maid), Jack Welch (boy), Bill Williams.

BODY SNATCHERS, THE (1956-Mex.)
(A. K. A. "Ladron de Cadaveres")
Director: Fernando Mendez
Wolf Ruvinski, Carlos Riquelme, Eduardo Alcaraz, Arturo Martinez, Guillermo Hernandez.

BOOGENS, THE (1981)
Director: James L. Conway
Rebecca Balding (Trish Michaels), Fred McCarren (Mark Kinner), Anne-Marie Martin (Jessica Ford), Jeff Harlan (Roger Lowrie), Med Flory (Dan Ostroff), John Crawford (Brian Deering), Jon Lormer (Blanchard), Peg Stewart (Victoria Tusker), Marcia Reider (Martha Chapman), Scott Wilkinson (Deputy Greenwalt).

BOOGEY MAN, THE (1980)
Director: Ulli Lommel
Suzanna Love (Lacy), Ron James (Jake), John Carradine (Dr. Warren), Nicholas Love (Willy), Raymond Boyden (Kevin), Felicite Morgan (Helen), Bill Rayburn (Uncle Ernest), Llewelyn Thomas (Father Reilly), Natasha Schiano (Young Lacey), Jay Wright (Young Willy), Gillian Gordon (mother), Howard Grant (the lover), Lucinda Ziesing (Susan), Jane Pratt (Jane), David Swim (Timmy), Catherine Tambini (Katy), Katie Casey, Ernest Meier, Stony Richards, Claudia Porcelli (teenagers).

BOOGIE MAN WILL GET YOU, THE (1942)
Director: Lew Landers
Boris Karloff (Prof. Nathaniel Billings), Peter Lorre (Dr. Lorentz), Maxie Rosenbloom (Maxie), Jeff Donnell (Winnie

Layden), Maude Eburne (Amelia Jones), Don Beddoe (J. Gilbert Brampton), Larry Parks (Bill Layden), Frank Puglia (Silvia Bacigalupi), George McKay (Ebenezer), Frank Sully (Officer Starrett), James Morton (Officer Quincy), Eddie Laughton (Johnson).

BOOM! (1968)
Director: Joseph Losey
Elizabeth Taylor (Flora Goforth), Richard Burton (Chris Flanders), Noel Coward (the Witch of Capri), Joanna Shimkus (Blackie), Michael Dunn (Rudy), Romolo Valli (Dr. Lullo), Veronica Wells (Simonetta), Fernando Piazza (Etti), Franco Pesci (Gens Block), Giovanni Paganelli (Sergio Carozzi), Howard Taylor (journalist), Claudye Ettori (manicurist).

BORDERLAND (1922)
Director: Paul Powell
Milton Sills, Fred Huntley, Bertram Grassby, Agnes Ayres, Frankie Lee, Sylvia Ashton.

BORMAN (1966-Ital./Fr.)
Director: Bruno Paolinelli/John Husley
Liana Orfei, Paul Muller, Sandro Meretti/Robert Kent, Dominique Boschero, Kitty Swan, Mao Thai.

BORROWERS, THE (TVM-1973) - 12-14-73
Director: Walter Miller
Eddie Albert (Pod Clock), Tammy Grimes (Homily Clock), Judith Anderson (Aunt Sophy), Barnard Hughes (Crampfurl), Beatrice Straight (Mrs. Crampfurl), Karen Pearson (Arrietty Clock), Dennis Larson (the Boy), Danny McIlvary (Tom), Murray Westgate (Ernie).

BOTTLE IMP, THE (1917)
Director: Marshall A. Neilan
Sessue Hayakawa, James Neill, Guy Oliver, Margaret Loomis.

BOWERY AT MIDNIGHT (1942)
Director: Wallace Fox
Bela Lugosi (Prof. Brenner/Karl Wagner), John Archer, Wanda McKay, Tom Neal, Dave O'Brien, Wheeler Oakman, Vince Barnett, J. Farrell MacDonald, George Eldredge, Lew Kelly, Anna Hope, John Berkes, Ray Miller, Lucille Vance.

BOWERY BOYS MEET THE MONSTERS, THE (1954)
Director: Edward Bernds
Huntz Hall (Sach Debussy Jones), Leo Gorcey (Slip Mahoney), Ellen Corby (Ame-

lia), John Dehner (Derek), Bernard Gorcey (Louie Dumbrowsky), Lloyd Corrigan (Anton), Paul Wexler (Grissom), Laura Mason (Francine), Bennie Bartlett (Butch), David Condon (Chuck).

BOWERY TO BAGDAD (1955)
    Director: Edward Bernds
Huntz Hall (Sach Debussy Jones), Leo Gorcey (Slip Mahoney), Joan Shawlee (Velma), Bernard Gorcey (Louie Dumbrowsky), Eric Blore (the Genie), Stanley Clements, Jean Willes, Robert Bice, Rick Vallin, Richard Wessel, Michael Ross, Rayford Barnes, Paul Marion, David Condon, Bennie Bartlett.

BOY AND HIS DOG, A (1975)
    Director: L. Q. Jones
Don Johnson (Vic), Susanne Benton (Quilla June), Jason Robards, Jr. (Lew), Alvy Moore (Dr. Moore), Helene Winston (Mez), Tim McIntire (voice of Blood), Hal Baylor (Michael), Charles McGraw (the Preacher), Ron Feinberg (Fellini), Mike Rupert (Gary), Don Carter (Ken), Michael Hershman (Richard).

BOY AND THE PIRATES, THE (1960)
    Director: Bert I. Gordon
Charles Herbert (Jimmy Warren), Susan Gordon (Katrina Van Keif), Murvyn Vye (Blackbear), Paul Guilfoyle (Snipe), Joseph Turkel (Abu the Genie), Than Wynn (Hunter), Morgan Jones (Mr. Warren), Timothy Carey (Morgan), Archie Duncan (Scoggins), Mickey Finn (Peake), Al Cavens (Dutch Captain).

BOY IN THE PLASTIC BUBBLE, THE (TVM-1976) - 11-12-76
    Director: Randal Kleiser
John Travolta (Tod Lubitch), Glynnis O'Connor (Gina Biggs), Diana Hyland (Mickey Lubitch), Robert Reed (Johnny Lubitch), Ralph Bellamy (Dr. Ernest Gunther), Karen Morrow (Martha Biggs), Vernee Watson (Gwen), Howard Platt (Pete Biggs), John Friedrich (Roy Slater), Buzz Aldrin (himself).

BOYS FROM BRAZIL, THE (1978)
    Director: Franklin J. Schaffner
Gregory Peck (Josef Mengele), Laurence Olivier (Ezra Lieberman), James Mason (Eduard Siebert), Lilli Palmer (Esther Lieberman), Uta Hagen (Frieda Maloney), Steven Guttenberg (Barry Kohler), Denholm Elliott (Sidney Beynon), Rosemary Harris (Mrs. Doring), Anne Meara (Mrs. Curry), John Dehner (Henry Wheelock), David Hurst (Strasser), John Rubinstein (David Ben-

nett), Michael Gough (Harrington), Bruno Ganz (Bruckner), Jeremy Black (Jack/Simon/Bobby), Wolfgang Preiss (Lofquist), Joachim Hansen (Fassler), Linda Hayden (Nancy), Carl Duering (Trausteiner), Guy Dumont (Hessen), Richard Marner (Doring), Gunter Meisner (Farnbach), George Marischka (Gunther), Prunella Scales (Mrs. Harrington), Jurgen Anderson (Kleist), Raul Faustino Saldenha (Ismael), Wolf Kahler (Schwimmer), David Brandon (Schmidt), Gerti Gordon (Berthe), Monica Gearson (Gertrud), Mervyn Nelson (Stroop).

BOY WHO CRIED WEREWOLF, THE (1973)
    Director: Nathan H. Juran
Kerwin Mathews (Robert Bridgeston), Elaine Devry (Sandy Bridgeston), Scott Sealey (Richie Bridgeston), Robert J. Wilke (Sheriff), George Gaynes (Dr. Marderosian), Susan Foster (Jenny), Bob Homel (Brother Christopher), Jack Lucas (Harry), Harold Goodwin (Duncan), Dave Cass (Deputy), Loretta Temple (Monica), Tim Haldeman (1st guard), John Logan (2nd guard), Eric Gordon (Jesus Freak), Paul Baxley (1st werewolf).

BOY WITH GREEN HAIR, THE (1948)
    Director: Joseph Losey
Pat O'Brien (Gramps), Robert Ryan (Dr. Evans), Dean Stockwell (Peter), Barbara Hale (Miss Brand), Richard Lyon (Michael), Regis Toomey (Mr. Davis), Samuel S. Hinds (Dr. Knudsen), Dwayne Hickman (Joey), Walter Catlett (the King), Charles Meredith (Mr. Piper), David Clarke (Barber), John Calkins (Danny), Billy Sheffield (Red), Teddy Infuhr (Timmy), Eilene Janssen (Peggy), Charles Arnt (Mr. Hammond), Curtis Jackson (classmate), Peter Brocco.

BRAIN, THE (1962-Brit. /Ger.) (A. K. A. "Ein Toter Sucht Seiner Morder", "A Dead Man Seeks His Murderer", "Vengeance")
    Director: Freddie Francis
Peter Van Eyck (Dr. Peter Corrie), Anne Heywood (Anna Holt), Bernard Lee (Frank Shears), Cecil Parker (Stevenson), Maxine Audley (Marion Fane), Jeremy Spenser (Martin Holt), Jack MacGowran (Furber), Miles Malleson (Dr. Milles), George A. Cooper (Gabler), Frank Forsyth (Francis), Ann Sears (secretary), Allan Cuthbertson (Dr. Silva), Ellen Schwiers (Ella), Irene Richmond (Mrs. Gabler), Alistair Williams (Insp. Pike), Siegfried Lowitz

(Martin), Hans Nielsen (Immerman), Victor Brooks (farmer), Kenneth Kendall (newscaster), Bandana Das Gupta (Miss Soong), John Junkin (Frederick), Richard McNeff (Parkin), John Watson (priest), Brian Pringle (Master of Ceremonies), Patsy Rowlands (dance hall girl).

BRAIN EATERS, THE (1958)
Director: Bruno VeSota
Ed Nelson (Dr. Kettering), Alan Frost (Glenn), Joanna Lee (Alice), Jody Fair (Elaine), Robert Ball (Dan Walker), David Hughes (Dr. Wyler), Jack Hill (Sen. Powers), Orville Sherman (Cameron), Leonard Nimoy (Protector), Greigh Phillips (Sheriff), Henry Randolph (telegraph operator), Doug Banks (doctor).

BRAIN FROM PLANET AROUS, THE (1958)
Director: Nathan Hertz/Nathan Juran
John Agar (Steve March), Joyce Meadows (Sally Fallon), Robert Fuller (Dan Murphy), Thomas B. Henry (John Fallon), Henry Travis (Col. Frogley), Tim Graham (Sheriff Paine), Ken Terrell (Colonel), E. Leslie Thomas (Gen. Brown), Bill Giorgio (Russian).

BRANIAC, THE (1961-Mex.) (A.K.A. "El Baron del Terror", "The Baron of Terror")
Director: Chano Urueta
Abel Salazar, German Robles, Ariadna Welter, Rosa Maria Gallardo, Ruben Rojo, Mauricio Garces, Carmen Montejo.

BRAIN OF BLOOD (1971) (A.K.A. "The Creature's Revenge")
Director: Al Adamson, Jr.
Grant Williams (Bob Nigserian), Kent Taylor (Dr. Trenton), Reed Hadley (Amir), Regina Carrol, John Bloom, Angelo Rossito, Vicki Volante.

BRAINSTORM (1965)
Director: William Conrad
Jeff Hunter (Jim Grayam), Anne Francis (Lorrie Benson), Dana Andrews (Cort Benson), Viveca Lindfors (Dr. E. Larstadt), Kathie Browne (Angie DeWitt), Stacy Harris (Josh Reynolds), Phillip Pine (Dr. Ames), Strother Martin (Mr. Clyde), Michael Pate (Dr. Mills), Pat Cardi (Bobby), Robert McQueeney (Sgt. Dawes), George Pelling (Butler), Joan Swift (Clara), Victoria Meyerink (Julie), Stephen Roberts (Judge).

BRAINSTORM (1982)
Director: Douglas Trumbull
Natalie Wood, Christopher Walken, Cliff Robertson, Louise Fletcher.

BRAIN THAT WOULDN'T DIE, THE (1959)
Director: Joseph Green
Jason Evers (Dr. Bill Cortner), Virginia Leith (Jan Compton), Adele Lamont (Doris Powell), Eddie Carmel (the Monster), Doris Brent (nurse), Bruce Brighton (Dr. Cortner), Leslie Daniel (Kurt), Lola Mason (Donna Williams), Audrey Devereau (Jeannie), Paula Maurice (B-girl), Bruce Kerr (announcer), Bonnie Shari (stripper).

BRANDED FOUR, THE (1920) - serial in 15 episodes
Chapters: 1. "A Strange Legacy", 2. "The Devil's Trap", 3. "Flames of Revenge", 4. "The Blade of Death", 5. "Fate's Pawn", 6. "The Hidden Cave", 7. "Shanghaied", 8. "Mutiny", 9. "The House of Doom", 10. "Ray of Destruction", 11. "Buried Alive", 12. "Lost to the World", 13. "Valley of Death", 14. "From the Sky & 15. "Sands of Torment".
Director: Duke Worne
Joseph Girard (Dr. Horatio Scraggs), Ben Wilson (A.B.C. Drake), Neva Gerber (Marion Leonard), Ashton Dearholt (Mr. Leonard), William Dyer (the lawyer), Pansy Porter (2nd daughter), William Carroll (Jason).

BRAND OF SATAN, THE (1917)
Director: George Archainbaud
Montague Love, Gerda Holmes, Evelyn Greeley.

BRASS BOTTLE, THE (1914)
Producer: Cecil Hepworth
Holman Clark, Alfred Bishop, Vane Featherstone, Lawrence Grossmith, Tom Mowbray, Denis Lytton, Mary Brough, Rudge Harding.

BRASS BOTTLE, THE (1923)
Director: Maurice Tourneur
Ernest Torrence, Tully Marshall, Barbara LaMarr, Ford Sterling, Harry Myers, Roy Collins.

BRASS BOTTLE, THE (1964)
Director: Harry Keller
Tony Randall (Harold Ventimore), Burl Ives (Fakrash), Barbara Eden (Sylvia Kenton), Kamala Devi (Tezra), Edward Andrews (Prof. Kenton), Ann Doran (Martha Kenton), Richard Erdman (Seymour Jenks), Kathie Browne (Hazel

Jenks), Parley Baer (Samuel Wacker-
bath), Philip Ober (William Beevor),
Herb Vigran (Eddie), Alan Dexter (Joe),
Howard Smith (Sen. Grindle), Aline
Towne (Miss Gidden), Jan Arvan (Se-
neschal), Alex Gerry (Dr. Travisley),
Nora Marlow (Mrs. McGruder), Robert
P. Lieb (Lawyer Jennings), Lulu Por-
ter (belly dancer).

BRAVE NEW WORLD (TVM-1980) - 3-
7-80
    Director: Burt Brinkerhoff
Kristoffer Tabori (John Savage), Mar-
cia Strassman (Lenina Disney), Keir
Dullea (Thomas Grahmbell), Bud Cort
(Bernard Marz), Julie Cobb (Linda Ly-
senko), Ron O'Neal (Mustapha Mond),
Dick Anthony Williams (Heimholtz Wat-
son), Beatrice Colen (Gamma Female),
Patrick Cronin (Gamma Male), Valerie
Curtin (Stalina Shell), Trish O'Neil
(Macina Krupps), Reb Brown (Henry),
John Doucette (cosmetization techni-
cian), Sam Chew, Jr. (Chief Dispen-
ser), Aron Kincaid (J. Edgar Mill-
house), June Barrett (June), Bruce
Wright (1st reporter), Lee Chamber-
lin (head nanny nurse), Sherry Brewer
(Hochina), Peter Elbling (Darwin Bona-
parte), Carole Mallory (Miss Trotsky),
Candy Mobley (Beta Secretary), Tara
Buckman (Alpha Seminarian), Delia
Salvi (High Priestess), Susan Krebs
(Anita Shapely), Perry Bullington (Ro-
ger), Sandra McCabe (Marta Edison),
Nicholas Savalas (Benito Hoover), Dee
Dee Rescher (neighbor), Caroline Smith
(Rona DeMille), Murray Salem (Chief
Engineer), Chesley Uxbridge (1st sa-
vage guide), Jonathan Segal (Chem-O-
Technician), Jonelle Adams, Victoria
Racimo.

BREAK, THE (TVM-1974) - 7-8-74
    Director:
Robert Shaw (Giles), Mary Ure (Jane),
Jack Hedley (Gerald), Gerald Sim (Julian), Suzan Farmer (Janet), Tony Selby (Crawford).

BRENDA STARR (TVM-1976) - 5-8-76
    Director: Mel Stuart
Jill St. John (Brenda Starr), Victor Buo-
no (Lance O'Toole), Sorrell Booke (A. J.
Livwright), Torin Thatcher (Willis Las-
siter), Marcia Strassman (Kentucky
Smith), Barbara Luna (Luisa Santama-
ria), Jed Allan (Roger Randall), Joel
Fabiana (Carlos Vegas), Art Roberts
(Dax Leander), Tabi Cooper (Hank O'-
Hare), Roy Applegate (Tommy).

BREWSTER McCLOUD (1970)
    Director: Robert Altman
Bud Cort (Brewster McCloud), Sally
Kellerman (Louise), Michael Murphy
(Frank Shaft), Shelley Duvall (Suzanne),
William Windom (Haskell Weeks), Stacy
Keach (Abraham Wright), Margaret Ham-
ilton (Daphne Heap), Rene Auberjonois
(the Lecturer), John Shuck (Alvin John-
son), Jennifer Salt (Hope McFarland),
G. Wood (Capt. Crandall), Angelin John-
son (Mrs. Breen), Bert Remsen (Doug-
las Breen), Corey Fischer (Lt. Hines),
William Baldwin (Bernard), William Hen-
ry Bennet (band conductor).

BRICK BRADFORD (1947) - serial in 15
episodes
Chapters: 1. "Atomic Defense", 2.
"Flight to the Moon", 3. "Prisoners of
the Moon", 4. "Into the Volcano", 5.
"Bradford at Bay", 6. "Back to Earth",
7. "Into Another Century", 8. "Buried
Treasure", 9. "Trapped in the Time
Top", 10. "The Unseen Hand", 11. "Poi-
son Gas", 12. "Door of Disaster", 13.
"Sinister Rendezvous", 14. "River of
Revenge" & 15. "For the Peace of the
World".
    Director: Spencer Gordon Bennet
        & Thomas Carr
Kane Richmond (Brick Bradford), Linda
Johnson (June Saunders), Rick Vallin
(Sandy Sanderson), Pierre Watkin (Prof.
Salisbury), Charles Quigley (Laydron),
Jack Ingram (Albers), Carol Forman
(Queen Khana), Leonard Penn (Byrus),
John Hart (Dent), Fred Graham (Black),
Wheeler Oakman (Walthar), Charles
King (Creed), Nelson Leigh (Prescott),
George de Normand (Meaker), Helene
Stanley (Carol Preston), Robert Barron
(Zuntar), John Merton (Dr. Tymak).

BRIDE AND THE BEAST, THE (1957)
    Director: Adrian Weiss
Charlotte Austin (Laura), Lance Fuller
(Dan), Johnny Roth (Taro), Steve Cal-
vert (the Beast), Jeanne Gerson (Marka),
William Justine (Dr. Reiner), Gil Frye
(Capt. Cameron), Slick Slavin (soldier),
Jean Anne Lewis (stewardess), Bhogwan
Singh (native).

BRIDE OF FRANKENSTEIN, THE (1935)
    Director: James Whale
Colin Clive (Dr. Henry Frankenstein),
Boris Karloff (the Monster), Elsa Lan-
chester (Mary Shelley/the Bride), Er-
nest Thesiger (Dr. Septimus Pretorius),
O. P. Heggie (the Blind Hermit), Dwight
Frye (Karl), Valerie Hobson (Elizabeth
Frankenstein), Una O'Connor (Minnie),

E. E. Clive (Burgomeister), Gavin Gordon (Lord Byron), Reginald Barlow (Hans), Mary Gordon (Hans' wife), Douglas Walton (Percy Shelley), Ted Billings (Ludwig), Gunnis Davis (Uncle Glutz), Lucien Prival (Albert, the butler), Sarah Schwartz (Marta), Tempe Pigott (Aunt Glutz), Neil Fitzgerald (Rudy), Anne Darling (shepherdess), Walter Brennan, Rollo Lloyd, Mary Steward (neighbors), Helen Parrish (communion girl), Edwin Mordant (priest), John Carradine, Robert Adair, John Curtis, Frank Terry (hunters), Grace Cunard, Anders Van Haden, Maurice Black, John George (villagers), George De-Normand (stuntman). Miniatures: Peter Shaw (the Devil), Norman Ainslee (the Archbishop), Arthur Byron (King Henry), Joan Woodbury (the Queen), Billy Barty (the Baby), Kansas DeForrest (the Dancer), Josephine McKim (the Mermaid).

BRIDE OF THE GORILLA (1951)
Director: Curt Siodmak
Barbara Payton (Dina Van Gelder), Paul Cavanagh (Klass Van Gelder), Lon Chaney, Jr. (Taro), Raymond Burr (Barney Chavez), Ton Conway (Dr. Viet), Ray 'Crash' Corrigan (the Ape), Giselle Werbisek (Al Long), Woody Strode (policeman), Martin Garralaga (native man), Carol Varga (Larina), Paul Maxey (Van Heussen), Moyna MacGill (Mrs. Van Heussen), Felippa Rock (Van Heussen's daughter).

BRIDE OF THE MONSTER (1955) (A.K.A. "Bride of the Atom")
Director: Edward D. Wood, Jr.
Bela Lugosi (Dr. Eric Varnoff), Tor Johnson (Lobo), Tony McCoy (Lt. Dick Cross), Loretta King (Janet Lawton), George Becwar (Prof. Vladimir Strowski), Harvey B. Dunn (Capt. Robbins), Bud Osborne (Officer Melton), Dolores Fuller (Marie), Don Nagel (Marty), Ann Wilner (Millie), William Benedict (newsboy), Eddie Parker (stuntman), John Warren, Ben Frommer, Paul Carco.

BRIDES OF BLOOD (1968-U.S./Phil.)
(A.K.A. "Island of Living Horror", "Blood Brides", "Brides of Death")
Director: Eddie Romero
Kent Taylor (Dr. Paul Henderson), Beverly Hills (Carla Henderson), John Ashley, Oscar Keesee, Eva Darren, Mario Montenegro.

BRIDES OF DRACULA, THE (1960)
Director: Terence Fisher

Peter Cushing (Dr. Van Helsing), David Peel (Baron Meinster), Martita Hunt (Baroness Meinster), Yvonne Monlaur (Marianne), Freda Jackson (Greta), Miles Malleson (Dr. Tobler), Mona Washbourne (Frau Lang), Henry Oscar (Herr Lang), Andre Melly (Gina), Fred Johnson (Cure), Harold Scott (Severin), Victor Brooks (Hans), Michael Ripper (coachman), Marie Devereux (village girl), Norman Pierce (landlord), Vera Cook (landlord's wife).

BRIDES OF FU MANCHU, THE (1966)
Director: Don Sharp
Christopher Lee (Fu Manchu), Douglas Wilmer (Nayland Smith), Howard Marion-Crawford (Dr. Petrie), Tsai Chin (Lin Tang), Heinz Drache (Franz), Marie Versini (Marie Lentz), Joseph Furst (Otto Lentz), Burt Kwouk (Fang), Rupert Davies (Merlin), Carole Gray (Michel), Kenneth Fortescue (Sgt. Spicer), Harald Leipnitz (Nikki Sheldon), Eric Young (assistant), Roger Nanin (Insp. Pierre Grimaldi), Poulet Tu (Lotus), Wendy Gifford (Louise), Rulmaan Peer (Abdul), Lucille Soong, Christine Rau, Dani Sheridan, Evelyne Dheliat, Daniele Defrere, Katarina Quest, Yvonne Ekman, Janette Napper, Grete-Lill Henden, Anje Langstraat, Gaby Schar.

BRIGADOON (1954)
Director: Vincente Minnelli
Gene Kelly (Tomy Albright), Van Johnson (Jeff Douglas), Cyd Charisse (Fiona Campbell), Elaine Stewart (Jane Ashton), Barry Jones (Mr. Lundie), Albert Sharpe (Andrew Campbell), Hugh Laing (Harry Beaton), Tudor Owen (Archie Beaton), Dody Heath (Meg Brockie), Dee Turnell (Ann), Owen McGiveney (Angus), Eddie Quillan (Sandy), Jimmy Thompson (Charlie Chisholm Dalrymple), Virginia Bosler (Jean Campbell).

BRIGHTON STRANGLER, THE (1945)
Director: Max Nosseck
John Loder (Reginald), June Duprez (April), Miles Mander (Allison), Rose Hobart (Dorothy), Ian Wolfe (Mayor), Matthew Boulton (Insp. Graham), Gilbert Emery (Dr. Manby), Olaf Hytten (Banks), Rex Evans (Shelton), Michael St. Angel (Bob), Lydia Bilbrook (Mrs. Manby).

BRILLIANT SHIP, THE (1920-Ger.)
(A.K.A. "Das Brillantenschiff", "The Spiders" Part II)
Director: Fritz Lang
Lil Dagover, Carl de Vogt, Paul Morgan, Ressel Orla, Friedrich Kuhne, Georg

John, Gilda Langer, Meinhardt Maur, Paul Biensfeldt.

BRING ME THE VAMPIRE (1964-Mex.)
(A. K. A. "Echemme al Vampire")
    Director: Alfredo E. Crevena
Maria Eugenia San Martin, Hector Godoy, Mantequilla, Carlos Riguelme, Pompin Iglias, Pascual Garcia Pena, Ramon Bugarini.

BRITANNIA HOSPITAL (1982)
    Director: Lindsay Anderson
Leonard Rossiter (Potter), Graham Crowden (Millar), Malcolm McDowell (Mike), Joan Plowright (Phyllis), Jill Bennett (Macmillan), Marsha Hunt (Amanda), Frank Grimes (Fred).

BROOD, THE (1979)
    Director: David Cronenberg
Oliver Reed (Dr. Raglan), Samantha Eggar (Nola Carveth), Art Hindle (Frank Carveth), Susan Hogan (Ruth), Cindy Hinds (Candice Carveth), Nicholas Campbell (Chris), Nuala Fitzgerald (Julianna), Henry Beckman (Barton Kelly), Michael McGhee (Insp. Mrazek), Bob Silverman (Jan Hartog), Gary McKeehan (Mike Trellan), Joseph Shaw (Dr. Desborough), Rainer Schwartz (Birkin), Larry Solway (Resnikoff), Felix Scilla (the Child).

BROTHERHOOD OF SATAN, THE (1971)
    Director: Bernard McEveety
Strother Martin (Doc Duncan), L. Q. Jones (Sheriff), Charles Bateman (Ben), Anna Capri (Nicky), Geri Reischi (Kiti), Charles Robinson (Priest), Alvy Moore (Tobey), Helene Winston (Dame Alice), Debi Storm (Billy Jo), Jeff Williams (Stuart), Judy McConnell (Phyllis), Joyce Easton (Mildred), Robert Ward (Mike), Ysabel MacCloskey, John Barclay, Phyllis Coughlan, Patrick Sullivan Burke, Cicely Walper.

BROTHERHOOD OF THE BELL (TVM-1970) - 9-17-70
    Director: Paul Wendkos
Glenn Ford (Andrew Patterson), Dean Jagger (Chad Harmon), Rosemary Forsythe (Vivien Patterson), Maurice Evans (Harry Masters), Will Geer (Mike Patterson), William Smithers (Jerry Fielder), Robert Pine (Philip Dunning), Eduard Franz (Konstantin Horvathy), William Conrad (Bart Harris), Logan Field (Thaddeus Burns), Lizabeth Hush (Betty Fielder), Dabney Coleman, Leon Lontoc, Joe Brooks, Robert Clarke, Virginia Gilmore, Marc Hannibal,

Scott Grahame.

BROTHER JOHN (1971)
    Director: James Goldstone
Sidney Poitier (Brother John Kane), Will Geer (Doc Thomas), Beverly Todd (Louisa Macgill), Bradford Dillman (Lloyd Thomas), Paul Winfield (Henry Birkhardt), Ramon Bieri (Orly Ball), Warren J. Kemmerling (George), Lincoln Kilpatrick (Charles Gray), Zara Culley (Miss Nettie), Gene Tyburn (Calvin), Richard Ward (Frank), Lynn Hamilton (Sarah), P. Jay Sidney (Rev. Macgill), Michael Bell (Deve), Howard Rice (Jimmy), Darlene Rice (Marsha), E. A. Nicholson (Perry), Harry Davis (turnkey), Bill Crane (Bill Jones), Richard Bay (lab deputy), Lynn Arden (nurse), John Hancock (Henry's friend), William Houze (motel owner), Lois Smith, Maye Henderson (neighbors).

BRUCE GENTRY (1948) - serial in 15 episodes
    Director: Spencer Gordon Bennet & Thomas Carr
Tom Neal (Bruce Gentry), Judy Clark (Juanita Farrell), Ralph Hodges (Frank Farrell), Tris Coffin (Krendon), Terry Frost (Chandler), Jack Ingram (Allen), Eddie Parker (Gregg), Charles King (Ivor), Stephen Carr (Hill), Forrest Taylor (Dr. Alexander Benson), Hugh Prosser (Radcliffe), Dale Van Sickel (Gregory).

BRUTE MAN, THE (1946)
    Director: Jean Yarborough
Rondo Hatton (Hal Moffat), Jane Adams (Helen), Jan Wiley (Virginia Scott), Tom Neal (Clifford Scott), Donald MacBride, Peter Whitney.

BUBBLE, THE (1966) (A. K. A. "The Fantastic Invasion of Planet Earth")
    Director: Arch Oboler
Michael Cole (Mark), Deborah Walley (Catherine), Johnny Desmond (Tony), Olan Soule, Vic Perrin, Virginia Gregg, Chester Jones, Barbara Eiler, Kassie McMahon.

BUCKET OF BLOOD, A (1959)
    Director: Roger Corman
Dick Miller (Walter Paisley), Anthony Carbone (Leonard), Ed Nelson (Art Lacroix), Barboura Morris (Carla), Julian Burton (Maxwell H. Brock), Bert Convy (Lou Raby), John Brinkley (Will), Judy Bamber (Alice), Jhean Burton (Naolia), John Shaner (Oscar), Myrtle Domerel (Mrs. Surchart), Bruno VeSota.

BUCK ROGERS (1939) - serial in 12
episodes (A. K. A. "Destination Sa-
turn", "Planet Outlaws")
Chapters: 1. "Tomorrow's World", 2.
"Tragedy on Saturn", 3. "The Enemy's
Stronghold", 4. "The Sky Patrol", 5.
"The Phantom Plane", 6. "The Unknown
Command", 7. "Primitive Urge", 8.
"Revolt of the Zuggs", 9. "Bodies with-
out Minds", 10. "Broken Barriers",
11. "A Prince in Bondage" & 12. "War
of the Planets".
    Director: Ford Beebe & Saul A.
Goodkind
Buster Crabbe (Buck Rogers), Constance
Moore (Wilma Deering), C. Montague
Shaw (Dr. Huer), Jackie Moran (Buddy
Wade), Anthony Warde (Killer Kane),
Jack Mulhall (Capt. Rankin), Guy Usher
(Aldar), Phillip Ahn (Prince Tallen),
Wheeler Oakman (Patten), Henry Bran-
don (Capt. Lasca), Kenneth Duncan (Lt.
Lacy), Carleton Young (Scott), William
Gould (Marshall Kragg), Reed Howes
(Roberts).

BUCK ROGERS IN THE 25th CENTURY
(1979)
    Director: Daniel Haller
Gil Gerard (Buck Rogers), Erin Gray
(Wilma Deering), Pamela Hensley (Princess Ardala), Tim O'Connor (Dr. Huer),
Henry Silva (Kane), Joseph Wiseman
(Draco), Felix Scilla (Twiki), Duke Butler (Tigerman), H. B. Haggerty (Tigerman No. 2), Caroline Smith (young woman), John Dewey-Carter (supervisor),
Kevin Coates (pilot), David Cadiente
(Comtel Officer), Gil Serna (technician),
Larry Duran (guard No. 1), Kenny En-
doso (guard No. 2), Colleen Kelly (Wra-
ther), Steve Jones (pilot No. 2), David
Buchanan (pilot No. 3), Eric Lawrence
(officer), Burt Marshall (wingman).

BUG (1975)
    Director: Jeannot Szwarc
Bradford Dillman (James Parmiter),
Joanna Miles (Carrie Parmiter), Richard
Gilliland (Gerald Metbaum), Alan Fudge
(Mark Ross), Jamie Smith Jackson (Nor-
ma Tacker), Jesse Vint (Tom Tacker),
Patty McCormack (Sylvia Ross), Bren-
don Dillon (Charlie), James Greene
(Rev. Kern), Fred Downs (Henry Ta-
cker), Jim Poyner (Kenny Tacker), Sam
Jarvis (taxi driver), Bard Stevens (se-
curity guard).

BULLDOG DRUMMOND AT BAY (1937)
    Director: Norman Lee
John Lodge (Hugh Drummond), Victor
Jory (Gregoroff), Claude Allister (Algy

Longworth), Richard Bird (Caldwell),
Dorothy Mackaill (Doris), Hugh Miller
(Kalinsky), Brian Buchel (Meredith),
Annie Esmond (Mrs. Caldwell), Leslie
Perrins (Greyson), William Dewhurst
(Reginald Portside), Frank Cochrane
(Dr. Belfrus), Jim Gerald (Veight), Ma-
rie O'Neill (Norah).

BULLDOG DRUMMOND COMES BACK
(1937)
    Director: Louis King
John Howard (Capt. Hugh Drummond),
John Barrymore (Col. Neilson), Louise
Campbell (Phyllis Clavering), E. E.
Clive (Tenny), Reginald Denny (Algy
Longworth), J. Carroll Naish (Mikhail
Valdin), Helen Freeman (Irena Soldanis),
Ivo Henderson (Morris), John Rogers
(Blanton), John Sutton, Zeffie Tilbury,
Rita Page.

BULLDOG DRUMMOND ESCAPES (1937)
    Director: James Hogan
Ray Milland (Capt. Hugh Drummond),
Sir Guy Standing (Insp. Nielson), Hea-
ther Angel (Phyllis Clavering), Reginald
Denny (Algy Longworth), E. E. Clive
(Dobbs), Porter Hall (Merridew), Wal-
ter Kinsford (Stanton), Fay Holden (Na-
talie), Clyde Cook (Alf), Frank Elliott
(Bailey), Patrick Kelly (Stiles), Charles
McNaughton (Constable Higgins).

BULLDOG DRUMMOND IN AFRICA (1938)
    Director: Louis King
John Howard (Capt. Hugh Drummond),
Heather Angel (Phyllis Clavering), J.
Carrol Naish (Richard Lane), H. B. War-
ner (Col. Nielson), E. E. Clive (Tenny),
Reginald Denny (Algy Longworth), An-
thony Quinn (Deane Fordine), Neil Fitz-
gerald (McTurk), Matthew Boulton (Ma-
jor Grey), Forrester Harvey (Constable
Jenkins), Leonard Carey (Phillips), Rol-
lo Dix (Acris), William von Brincken (Dr.
Stern), Michael Brooke (Baron Nevsky),
Paul Porcasi (hotel manager), Evan Tho-
mas (sergeant), Gerald Rogers (tailor),
Jean De Briac (waiter).

BULLDOG DRUMMOND'S PERIL (1938)
    Director: James Hogan
John Howard (Capt. Hugh Drummond),
John Barrymore (Col. Nielson), Louise
Campbell (Phyllis Clavering), Reginald
Denny (Algy Longworth), E. E. Clive
(Tenny), Elizabeth Patterson (Aunt Blanche),
Halliwell Hobbes (Prof. Bernard Good-
man), Porter Hall (Dr. Botulian), Zeffie
Tilbury (Mrs. Weevens), Michael Brooke
(Anthony Greer), Matthew Boulton (Sir
Raymond Blantyre), Nydia Westman

(Gwen Longworth), Clyde Cook.

BULLDOG DRUMMOND'S THIRD ROUND (1925)
Director: Sidney Morgan
Jack Buchanan, Allan Jeayes, Betty Faire, Austin Leigh, Frank Goldsmith.

BUNNY LAKE IS MISSING (1965)
Director: Otto Preminger
Carol Lynley (Ann), Keir Dullea (Steven), Laurence Olivier (Insp. Newhouse), Noel Coward (Wilson), Martita Hunt (Ada Ford), Anna Massey (Elvira), Clive Revill (Andrews), Finlay Currie (doll maker), Lucie Mannheim (cook).

BURKE AND HARE (1971)
Director: Vernon Sewell
Derren Nesbitt, Harry Andrews, Yootha Joyce, Robin Hawdon, Dee Shenderey, Alan Tucker, Glynn Edward Francoise Pascal.

BURNING, THE (1981)
Director: Tony Maylam
Brian Matthews (Todd), Leah Ayres (Michelle), Larry Joshua (Glazer), Brian Backer (Alfred), Jason Alexander (Dave), Ned Eisenberg (Eddy), Carolyn Houlihan (Karen), Carrick Glenn (Sally), Fisher Stevens (Woodstock), Lou David (Cropsy).

BURNING COURT, THE (1961-Fr. / Ital. /Ger.) (A. K. A. "La Chambre Ardent", "Das Brennende Gericht", "I Peccatori della Foresta Nera", "The Curse and the Coffin")
Director: Julien Duvivier
Nadja Tiller (Myra), Jean-Claude Brialy (Marc Desgrez), Edith Scob (Marie Boissard), Perrette Pradier (Lucie Desgrez), Duvalles (Mathias Desgrez), Claude Rich (Stephane Desgrez), Walter Giller (Michel Boissard), Antoine Balpetre (Dr. Hermann), Dany Jacquet (Freida), Rene Genin (Henderson), Helena Manson (Madame Henderson).

BURNING OF A THOUSAND SUNS, THE (1965-Fr.) (A. K. A. "La Brulere de Mille Soleils")
Director: Pierre Kast
Alexandra Stewart.

BURNT OFFERINGS (1976)
Director: Dan Curtis
Oliver Reed (Ben), Karen Black (Marian), Bette Davis (Aunt Elizabeth), Lee Harcourt Montgomery (David), Burgess Meredith (Arnold Allardyce), Eileen Heckart (Roz Allardyce), Dub Tay-

lor (Walker), Anthony James (the Chauffeur), Orin Cannon (Minister), Todd Turquand (Young Ben), Joseph Riley (Ben's father), James T. Myers (Dr. Ross).

BURN, WITCH, BURN (1961) (A. K. A. "Night of the Eagle")
Director: Sidney Hayer
Janet Blair (Tansy Taylor), Peter Wyngarde (Norman Taylor), Reginald Beckwith (Harold Bunnison), Margaret Johnston (Flora Carr), Anthony Nicholls (Harvey Sawtelle), Colin Gordon (Prof. Lindsay Carr), Kathleen Byron (Evelyn Sawtelle), Judith Stott (Margaret Abbott), Jessica Dunning (Hilda Gunnison), Bill Mitchell (Fred Jennings), Norman Bird (doctor), George Roubicek (cleaner's man), Frank Singuineau (truck driver), Gary Woolf (trucker's mate).

BUTCHER, BAKER, NIGHTMARE MAKER (1982) (A. K. A. "Night Warning")
Director: William Asher
Jimmy McNichol (Billy), Susan Tyrrell (Aunt Cheryl), Bo Svenson (Detective Carlson).

CABINET OF CALIGARI, THE (1962)
Director: Roger Kay
Glynis Johns (Jane Lindstrom), Dan O'-Herlihy (Paul Caligari), Richard Davalos (Mark), Constance Ford (Christine), Lawrence Dobkin (David), Estelle Winwood (Ruth), J. Pat O'Malley (Martin), Doreen Lang (Vivian), Vicki Trickett (Jeanie), Charles Fredericks (Bob), Phyllis Teagardin (little girl).

CABINET OF DR. CALIGARI, THE (1919-Ger.) (A. K. A. "Das Kabinett des Dr. Caligari")
Director: Robert Wiene
Werner Krauss (Dr. Caligari/Dr. Sonnow), Lil Dagover (Jane Olsen), Conrad Veidt (Cesare), Rudolf Klein-Rogge, Friedrich Feher, Rudolf Lettinger, Hans Heinz von Twardowski.

CABIN IN THE SKY (1943)
Director: Vincente Minnelli
Eddie Anderson (Little Joe Jackson), Rex Ingram (Lucius/Lucifer, Jr.), Ethel Waters (Petunia Jackson), Lena Horne (Georgea Brown), Bill Bailey (Bill), Butterfly McQueen (Lily), Ruby Dandridge (Bill), Mantan Moreland (1st idea man), Willie Best (2nd idea man), Moke/Fletcher Rivers (3rd idea man), Poke/Leon James (4th idea man), Bubbles/John W. Sublett (Domino Jackson), Kenneth Spencer (Rev. Green/General), Louis Armstrong (the Trumpeter), Ernest Whitman

(Jim Henry), Buck/Ford L. Washington (Messenger Boy), Oscar Polk (the Deacon/Fleetfoot), Nicodemus (Dude), Duke Ellington.

CABIRIA (1914-Ital.)
Director: Giovanni Pastrone
Italian Almirante Manzini, Lydia Quaranta, Bartolomeo Pagano, Umberto Mozzato, Ernesti Camelli.

CAGE, THE (1963-Fr.) (A. K. A. "La Cage")
Director: Robert Darene
Jean Servais (Michel), Marina Vlady (Isabelle), Philippe Maury (Philippe), Myriel David (Oyane), Colette Duval (Colette), Alain Bouvette (Contrematire).

CAGLIOSTRO (1920-Ger.) (A. K. A. "Der Grav von Cagliostro")
Director: Reinhold Schunzel
Conrad Veidt, Anita Berber, Reinhold Schunzel, Karl Gotz.

CAGLIOSTRO (1928-Fr.)
Director: Richard Oswald
Alfred Abel, Hans Stuwe, Rene Heribel, George Dullin.

CAGLIOSTRO (1974-Ital.)
Director: Daniele Pettinari
Bekim Fehmiu (Cagliostro), Curt Jurgens (Cardinal), Rossana Schiaffino (Lorenza), Robert Alda (Pope), Evelyn Stewart (Serafina), Massimo Girotti (Casanova), Luigi Pistilli.

CALLING DR. DEATH (1943)
Director: Reginald LeBorg
Lon Chaney, Jr. (Dr. Mark Steele), Patricia Morrison (Stella Madden), Ramsay Ames (Marcia Steele), David Bruce (Robert Duvall), Fay Helm (Mrs. Duvall), J. Carrol Naish (Insp. Gregg), Holmes Herbert (butler), Alec Craig (watchman), Isabel Jewell (night club singer), George Dolenz (man), Mary Hale (patient), Lisa Golm (mother), John Elliott (father), David Hoffman (Inner Sanctum).

CALLING PAUL TEMPLE (1948)
Director: Maclear Rogers
John Bentley (Paul Temple), Margaretta Scott (Mrs. Trevellyan), Alan Wheatley (Edward Lathom), Dinah Sheridan (Steve Temple), Abraham Sofaer (Dr. Kohima), Jack Raine (Sir Graham Forbes), Celia Lipton (Norma Rice), Wally Patch (Spider Williams), Hugh Pryse (Wilfred Davies), Merle Totten-

ham.

CALL ME BWANA (1963)
Director: Gordon Douglas
Bob Hope (Matt Merriwether), Anita Ekberg (Luba), Edie Adams (Frederica Larsen), Lionel Jeffries (Dr. Ezra Mungo), Percy Herbert, Al Mulock (henchmen), Paul Carpenter (Col. Spencer), Peter Dyneley (Williams), Bari Johnsonn (Uta), Mai Ling (Hyacinth), Mark Heath (Koba), Arnold Palmer (himself), Robert Nichols (American Major), Orlando Martins (Chief of Ekele Tribe), Kevin Scott, Robert Arden (CIA men), Neville Monroe, Richard Burrell, Michael Moyer (reporters).

CALL OF THE SAVAGE, THE (1935) - serial
Director: Lew Landers
Noah Beery, Jr. (Jan Trevor), Dorothy Short (Mona Andrews), Bryant Washburn (Dr. Harry Trevor), Walter Miller (Dr. Frank Bracken), John Davidson (Emperro), Fredric McKaye (Dr. Charles Phillips), Russ Powell (Andrews), H. L. Woods (Borno).

CALTIKI, THE IMMORTAL MONSTER (1961-Ital./U.S.) (A. K. A. "Caltiki, il Mostro Immortale")
Director: Robert Hampton/Ricardo Freda, Lee Kresel & Mario Bava
John Merivale (Prof. John Fielding), Didi Sullivan (Ellen Fielding), Gerald Haerter (Max), Daniela Rocca (Linda), Daniele Pitani (Bob), Gay Pearl (dancer), Giacomi Rossi-Stuart.

CAMELOT (1967)
Director: Joshua Logan
Richard Harris (King Arthur), Vanessa Redgrave (Guenevere), Franco Nero (Lancelot Du Lac), David Hemmings (Mordred), Laurence Naismith (Merlyn), Lionel Jeffries (King Pellinore), Estelle Winwood (Lady Clarinda), Sue Casey (Lady Sybil), Pierre Olaf (Dap), Peter Bromilow (Sir Sagramore), Anthony Rogers (Sir Dinaden), Gary Marshal (Sir Lionel), Gary Marsh (Tom of Warwick), Nicolas Beauvy (Arthur as a boy).

CAMILLE 2000 (1969)
Director: Radley Metzger
Daniele Gaubert (Marguerite Gautier), Nino Castelnuono (Armand Duval), Eleanora Rossi-Drago (Prudence), Philippe Forquet (DeVarville), Roberto Bisacco (Gaston), Silvana Venturelli (Olympe), Massimo Serato (Armand's father),

Zachary Adams (Gody).

CANADIAN MOUNTIES VS. ATOMIC
    INVADERS (1953) - serial (A.K.A.
    "Missile Base at Taniak")
    Director: Franklin Adreon
Bill Henry (Sgt. Don Roberts), Susan
Morrow (Kay Conway), Arthur Space
(Marlof/Smokey Joe), Pierre Watkin
(Cmdr. Morrison), Dale Van Sickel
(Beck), Stanley Andrews (Anderson),
Hank Patterson (Larson), Harry Lauter
(Clark), Edmund Cobb (Mr. Warner),
Mike Ragan (Reed), Jean Wright (Mrs.
Warner), Tom Steele (Mack), Gayle
Kellogg (Corporal Guy Sanders), Jeane
Wood (Mrs. Anderson), William Faw-
cett (Murphy), George DeNormand (Ed
Peters), Fred Graham (Mason), Robert
Reeves (bartender), Joe Yrigoyen (launch
heavy No. 1), Carey Loftin (launch hea-
vy No. 2), Kenner Kemp (officer), Paul
Palmer (Turner), Drew Cahill (Mills),
Gordon Armitage (Ed Olson), Jimmy
Fawcett, David Sharpe, Duke Taylor,
Earl Bunn, Bob Jamison.

CANDLE FOR THE DEVIL, A (1973-
    Span.) (A.K.A. "Una Vela Para el
    Diablo")
    Director: Eugenio Martin
Judy Geeson, Lone Fleming, Esperanza Roy, Aurora Bautista, Victor Alca-
zar, Carlos Pineiro, Blanca Estrada,
Loretta Tovar.

CANDY (1968-U.S./Fr./Ital.)
    Director: Christian Marquand
Ewa Qulin (Candy), Charles Aznavour
(the Hunchback), Marlon Brando (Grindl),
Richard Burton (McPhisto), Ringo Starr
(Emmanuel), James Coburn (Dr. Kran-
keit), John Huston (Dr. Dunlap), Walter
Matthau (Gen. Smight), John Astin (Dad-
dy/Uncle Jack), Sugar Ray Robinson
(Zero), Anita Pallenberg (Nurse Bul-
lock), Nicoletta Machiavelli (Marquita),
Elsa Martinelli (Aunt Livia), Florinda
Bolkan (Lolita), Marilu Tolo (Conchita),
Enrico Maria Salerno (Jonathan J. John),
Lea Padovani (Silvia), Joey Forman
(the cop), Neal Noorlac (Harold), Peggy
Nathan (Miss Quimby), Fabian Dean
(the Sergeant), Peter Dane (Luther),
Umberto Orsini (1st hood), Enzo Fiermonte (2nd hood), Tony Foutz (1st weirdo), Tom Keyes (2nd weirdo), Mark Salvage (Dr. Harris), Micaela Pignatelli
(girl).

CAN ELLEN BE SAVED? (TVM-1974) -
    2-5-74
    Director: Harvey Hart

John Saxon (James Hallbeck), Kathy
Cannon (Ellen Lindsey), Leslie Nielsen
(Arnold Lindsey), Louise Fletcher (Bea
Lindsey), Michael Parks (Joseph), Chris-
tina Hart (Hary), Kathleen Quinlan (Me-
lissa), Scott Colomby (Randy), William
Katt (Bob), Rutanya Alda (Rachael), Den-
nis Redfield (Daniel).

CAN HEIRONYMUS MERKIN EVER FOR-
    GET MERCY HUMPPE AND FIND
    TRUE HAPPINESS? (1969)
    Director: Anthony Newley
Anthony Newley (Heironymus Merkin),
Joan Collins (Polyester Poontang), Milton Berle (Good Time Eddie Filth), George
Jessel (the Presence), Stubby Kaye (Fat
Writer), Bruce Forsyth (Uncle Limelight), Victor Spinetti (Sharpnose), Con-
nie Kreski (Mercy Humppe), Berri Cor-
nish (Fran), Judy Cornwell (Filigree Fon-
dle), Rom Stern (Producer Ron), Patri-
cia Hayes (Grandma), Roy Desmond (the
Mask), Desmond Walter Ellis (Philip
Bluster), Isabel Huril (Marge), Sally
Douglas (Automation Bunny), Aleta Mor-
rison (Harriet), Tara Newley (Thumbelina), Alexander Newley (Thaxted), Ju-
lian Orchard (the Red Cardinal), Ronald
Radd (Bentley), Louis Negin (Producer
Peter), Gilly Frant (Miss Fern), Ronald
Rubin (Skinny Writer), Margaret Nolan
(Little Assistance).

CANNIBAL GIRLS (1973)
    Director: Ivan Reitman
Eugene Levy (Clifford Sturges), Ronald
Ulrich (Rev. Alex St. John), Andrea Martin (Gloria Wellaby), Randall Carpenter
(Anthea), Bonnie Neison (Clarissa), Mira Pawluk (Leona), Bob McHeady (Sheriff), May Jarvis (Mrs. Wainwright), Alan
Gordon (1st victim), Allan Price (2nd
victim), Earl Pomerantz (3rd victim).

CANTERVILLE GHOST, THE (1944)
    Director: Jules Dassin
Charles Laughton (Sir Simon de Canter-
ville), Robert Young (Cuffy Williams),
Margaret O'Brien (Lady Jessica de Can-
terville), William Gargan (Sgt. Benson),
Reginald Owen (Lord Canterville), Peter
Lawford (Anthony de Canterville), Marc
Cramer, Frank Reicher, Lumsden Hare,
Rags Ragland, Donald Stuart, Elisabeth
Risdon, Una O'Connor, Frank Faylen,
Mike Mazurki.

CANTERVILLE GHOST, THE (1954) -
    short
    Director:
Monty Woolley.

CAPE CANAVERAL MONSTERS, THE
(1960)
Director: Phil Tucker
Katherine Victor (Nadja), Jason Johnson, Linda Connell, Scott Peters, Frank Smith.

CAPRICORN ONE (1978)
Director: Peter Hyams
Elliott Gould (Robert Caulfield), Hal Holbrook (Dr. James Kelloway), James Brolin (Charles Brubaker), Brenda Vaccaro (Kay Brubaker), Sam Waterston (Peter Willis), O. J. Simpson (John Walker), Karen Black (Judy Drinkwater), David Doyle (Walter Loughlin), Telly Savalas (Albain), Robert Walden (Elliot Whitter), Denise Nicholas (Betty Walker), David Huddleston (Hollis Peaker), Alan Fudge (Capsule Communicator), Lee Bryant (Sharon Willis), Jon Cedar, James Karen, Paul Picerni, Lou Frizzell, Darrell Zwerling, Hank Stohl, Milton Selzer, Norman Bartold, Barbara Bosson.

CAPTAIN AMERICA (1944) - serial in 15 episodes (A. K. A. "Return of Captain America")
Chapters: 1. "The Purple Death", 2. "Mechanical Executioner", 3. "The Scarlet Shroud", 4. "Preview of Murder", 5. "Blade of Wrath", 6. "Vault of Vengeance", 7. "Wholesale Destruction", 8. "Cremation in the Clouds", 9. "Triple Tragedy", 10. "The Avenging Corpse", 11. "The Dead Man Returns", 12. "Horror on the Highway", 13. "Skyscraper Plunge", 14. "The Scarab Strikes" & 15. "The Toll of Doom".
Director: John English & Elmer Clifton
Dick Purcell (Grant Gardner/Captain America), Lorna Gray (Gail Richards), Lionel Atwill (Dr. Maldor/Scarab), Charles Trowbridge (Commissioner Dryden), George J. Lewis (Matson), John Davidson (Gruber), Russell Hicks (Mayor Randolph), Frank Reicher (Prof. Lyman), John Hamilton (Hillman), Robert Frazer (Dr. Clinton Lyman), Jay Novello (Simms), Tom Chatterton (Henley), John Bagni (Monk), Hugh Sothern (Prof. Dodge), Edward Keane (Dr. Baraca), Edward Van Sloan (Gregory), Norman Nesbitt (newscaster), Crane Whitley (Dirk), Dale Van Sickel (Rick/patrolman No. 1), Ken Terrell (Hunt/road heavy/lab heavy No. 1), Paul Marion (Agent 31/Booth), Tom Steele (Kent), Fred Graham (Blain/Burton/Mead), Lynton Brent (airport mechanic), Stanley Price (Carson), Howard Hickman

(Carter), Al Ferguson (detective No. 1), Post Parks (detective No. 2), Brooks Benedict (florist No. 1), Sam Ash (florist No. 2), Kenne Duncan (Ed Graham), Edward Cassidy (guard), Ben Taggart (Donovan), Robert Wilke (garage heavy), Robert Strange (Hines), Bud Geary (Kane), George DeNormand (Pete), Ralf Harolde (Tait), LeRoy Mason (Bates), Ben Erway (car lot manager), George Byron (Ewalt Davis), Wilson Benge (Jarvis), Harry Strang (mechanic), Terry Frost (police broadcaster), Duke Green (Barton/platinum heavy), George Sherwood (Clancy), Joe Yrigoyen (Burns/Lewis), Jerry Jerome (Eddie), Herb Lytton (Carl Evans), Frank O'Connor (estate guard), Jack Kirk (expressman No. 1), Jack O'Shea (expressman No. 2), Lorn Courdaye (gas station worker), Gil Perkins (Gordon/Joe/Norton), John Daheim (lab heavy No. 2), George Magrill (mechanic heavy), Tom London (Mac), Charles Hutchison (Merritt), Roy Brent (Nick), Jeffrey Sayre (Norden), Bert LeBaron (Perry/Stark), Allen Pomeroy (Walker/Walters), Glenn Knight (morgue truck driver), Hal Craig (patrolman No. 2), James Carlisle (J. V. Wilson), Helen Thurston.

CAPTAIN AMERICA (TVM-1979) - 1-19-79
Director: Rod Holcomb
Reb Brown (Steve Rogers/Captain America), Len Birman (Dr. Simon Mills), Steve Forrest (Lou Brackett), Heather Menzies (Dr. Wendy Day), Lance LeGault (Harley), Robin Mattson (Tina Hayden), Frank Marth (Charles Barber), Joseph Ruskin (Rudy Sandrini), Michael McManus (Ortho), Dan Barton (Jeff Hayden), James Ingersoll (Lester Wiant), Nocona Aranda (Throckmorton), Chip Johnson (Jerry), June Dayton, Jim Smith, Diane Webster, Jason Wingreen, Buster Jones, Ken Chandler.

CAPTAIN AMERICA II (TVM-1979) - 11-23-79 & 11-24-79
Director: Ivan Nagy
Reb Brown (Steve Rogers/Captain America), Christopher Lee (Miguel), Len Birman (Dr. Simon Mills), Connie Sellecca (Dr. Wendy Day), Christopher Cary (Prof. Ilson), William Lucking (Stader), Lana Wood (Yolanda), Katherine Justice (Helen), John Waldron (Peter Moore), Bill Mims (Dr. J. Brenner), Lachelle Chamberlain (young girl), Alex Hyde-White (young man), Arthur Rosenberg (doctor), Stanley Kamel, Ken Swofford.

CAPTAIN KRONOS - VAMPIRE HUNTER

(1972)
Director: Brian Clemens
Horst Janson (Kronos), Shane Briant (Paul Durward), Caroline Munro (Carla), Ian Hendry (Kerro), John Carson (Dr. Marcus), John Cater (Grost), Wanda Ventham (Lady Durward), Lois Daine (Sara Durward).

CAPTAIN MIDNIGHT (1942) - serial in 15 episodes
Chapters: 1. "Mysterious Pilot", 2. "Stolen Range Finder", 3. "The Captured Plane", 4. "Mistaken Identity", 5. "Ambushed Ambulance", 6. "Weird Waters", 7. "Menacing Fates", 8. "Shells of Evil", 9. "The Drop of Doom", 10. "The Hidden Bomb", 11. "Sky Terror", 12. "Burning Bomber", 13. "Death in the Cockpit", 14. "Scourge of Revenge" & 15. "The Fatal Hour".
Director: James W. Horne
Dave O'Brien (Capt. Albright/Capt. Midnight), Dorothy Short (Joyce Edwards), James Craven (Ivan Shark), Sam Edwards (Chuck), Bryant Washburn (Edwards), Luana Walters (Fury), Ray Teal (Borgman), Guy Wilkerson (Ichabod Mudd), Joe Girard (Maj. Steel), George Pembroke (Dr. Jordan), Charles Hamilton (Martel), Al Ferguson (Gardo).

CAPTAIN NEMO AND THE UNDERWATER CITY (1969)
Director: James Hill
Robert Ryan (Captain Nemo), Chuck Connors (Sen. Robert Fraser), Nanette Newman (Helena), Luciana Paluzzi (Mala), John Turner (Joab), Bill Fraser (Barnaby), Allan Cuthbertson (Lomax), Ralph Nosseck (engineer), Christopher Hartstone (Philip), Kenneth Connor (Swallow), Vincent Harding (mate/navigator), Michael McGovern, Anthony Bailey, Margot Ley, Alan Barry, Ann Patrice, Patsy Snell.

CAPTAIN SINBAD (1963)
Director: Byron Haskin
Guy Williams (Captain Sinbad), Heidi Bruhl (Princess Jana), Pedro Armendariz (El Kerim), Abraham Sofaer (Calgo), James Dobson (Effritch), Henry Brandon (Col. Kabar), Maurice Marsac (Ahmed), John Crawford (Aram), Bernie Hamilton (Quintus), Geoffrey Toone (Mohar), Helmut Schneider (Bendar), Rolf Wanka (the King), Walter Barnes (Rolf), Margaret Jahnen (lady-in-waiting).

CAPTAIN VIDEO (1951) - serial in 15 episodes

Chapters: 1. "Journey into Space", 2. "Menace to Atoma", 3. "Captain Video's Peril", 4. "Entombed in Ice", 5. "Flames of Atoma", 6. "Astray in the Atmosphere", 7. "Blasted by the Atomic Eye", 8. "Invisible Menace", 9. "Video Springs a Trap", 10. "Menace of the Mystery Metal", 11. "Weapon of Destruction", 12. "Robot Rocket", 13. "Mystery of Station X", 14. "Vengeance of Vultura" & 15. "Video vs. Vultura".
Director: Spencer Gordon Bennet & Wallace A. Grissell
Judd Holdren (Captain Video), Larry Stewart (Video Ranger), George Eldredge (Tobor), Gene Roth (Vultura), Don C. Harvey (Gallagher), Jack Ingram (Aker), William Fawcett (Alpha), I. Stanley Jolley (Zarol), William Bailey (Prof. Dean), Skelton Knaggs (Retner), Jimmy Stark (Rogers), Zon Murray (Elko), Oliver Cross (Prof. Markham), Rusty Westcoatt (Beal), George Robotham (Drock).

CAPTIVE WILD WOMAN (1943)
Director: Edward Dmytryk
Evelyn Ankers (Beth Colman), John Carradine (Dr. Sigmund Walters), Acquanetta (Paula Dupree), Martha Vickers (Dorothy Colman), Milburn Stone (Fred Mason), Lloyd Corrigan (John Whipple), Fay Helm (Miss Strand), Vince Barnett (Curley Barret), Paul Fix (Gruen, the feeder), Ray 'Crash' Corrigan (Chula, the ape).

CAPTIVE WOMEN (1953) (A. K. A. "1000 Years from Now")
Director: Stuart Gilmore
Robert Clarke (Rob), Margaret Field (Ruth), William Schallert (Carver), Ron Randell (Riddon), Gloria Saunders (Catherine), Robert Bice (Bram), Stuart Randall (Gordon), Douglas Evans (Jason), Eric Colmar (Sabron), Paul Dorety, Chili Williams (captives).

CAPTURE OF BIG FOOT, THE (1979)
Director: Bill Rebane
Stafford Morgan, Katherine Hopkins, Richard Kennedy, George 'Buck' Flower, John Goff, Otis Young, John Eimerman.

CAR, THE (1977)
Director: Elliot Silverstein
James Brolin (Wade Parent), Kathleen Lloyd (Lauren), Ronny Cox (Deputy Luke Johnson), John Marley (Sheriff Everett Peck), R. G. Armstrong (Amos Clements), John Rubenstein (John Morris), Roy Jenson (Ray Mott), Elizabeth Thompson (Margie Johnson), Kim Richards (Lynn Marie), Kyle Richards (Debbie),

Kate Murtagh (Miss McDonald), Doris Dowling (Bertha), Eddie Little Sky (Denson), Robert Phillips (Metcalf), Henry O'Brien (Chas), Read Morgan (Mac Gruder), Lee McLaughlin (Marvin Fats), Joshua Davis (Jimmy), Ernie Orsatti (Dalton), Margaret Willey (Navajo woman), Geraldine Keams (Donna), John Moio (Parker), James Rawley (Thompson), Hank Hamilton (Al), Melody Thomas (Suzie), Bob Woodlock (Pete), Bryan O'Byrne (Wally), Tony Brande (Joe), Don Keefer (Dr. Pullbrook), Steve Gravers (Mackey), Louis Welch (Berry).

CARDIAC ARREST (1980)
    Director: Murray Mintz
Garry Goodrow (Clancy Higgins), Mike Chan (Wylie Wong), Maxwell Gail (Leigh Gregory), Robert A. Behling (Harvey Nichols), John Allen Vick (Capt. Olderman), Mark Wheeler (Richie Walker), Susan O'Connell (Dianne Gregory), Ray Reinhardt (Dr. Norton Williams), Marjorie Morley Eaton (Mrs. Swan), Charlie Murphy (Duke Southwick), Ed Vasgersian (Mr. Singh), Matthew Locricchio (Fred Eaton), Bill Ackridge (Duke Miller), Janet McGrath (Antoinette Eaton), Cynthia Lee Brian (lady in red hat), Nancy Fish (Tiffany), Ann Macey (anthropologist), Dave McElhatton (reporter), Charlie Lehman (security guard), Dana Evans (police lab technician), Joe Bellan (luggage shop salesman), Christopher LeVan (child), Harry D. K. Wong (Sun Lim), Steve Eoff (junkie), Fred Ward (Jamie), Cary Bisagna (police garage mechanic), Joy Carlin (Dr. Burns), Douglas Johnson (banker), Drew Eshelman (jeweler), Buzz Borelli (Tom Moore), Terry McGovern (Brewer), Sheldon Feldner (pharmacist), Maurice Argent (deputy coroner), Allen Newman (Di Napoli).

CARNATION KILLER, THE (TVM-1973)
    Director: Robert Tronson
Norman Eshley (Page), Katharine Schofield (Julie), Derek Smith (Baverstock), Garrick Hagon (Peter), Geoffrey Chater (Graham), Eric Mason (Sgt. O'Farrell), Malcolm Terris (Detective Superintendent), Roy Stone (Detective Sergeant), Tim Wylton (Forbes), A.J. Brown (Judge), Michael Corcoran (flower seller), Herbert Ramskill (guard on train), Gigi Gurpinar (girl on train), Barry Ashton, Godfrey Jackman, Michael Stainton (policemen).

CARNIVAL OF BLOOD (1971)
    Director: Leonard Kirtman

Earle Edgerton (Tom), Judith Resnick (Laura), Martin Barolsky (Dan), John Harris (Gimpy), Kaly Mills (fortune teller), Gloria Spivak (fat blonde), Eve Packer (prostitute), Glenn Kimberley (sailor), William Grinnel (husband), Linda Kurtz (wife).

CARNIVAL OF SOULS (1962)
    Director: Herk Harvey
Candace Hilligoss (Mary Henry), Herk Harvey (the Man), Sidney Berger (John Linden), Frances Feist (landlady), Art Ellison (Minister), Stanley Leavitt (doctor), Tom McGinnis, Forbes Caldwell, Bill De Jarnette, T.C. Adams, Dan Palmquist, Steve Boozer, Pamela Ballard, Larry Sneegas, Cari Conboy, Sharon Scoville, Mary Ann Harris, Peter Schnitzler.

CAROLINA CANNONBALL (1954)
    Director: Charles Lamont
Judy Canova (Judy), Andy Clyde (Grandpa Canova), Ross Elliott (Don Mack), Sig Ruman (Stefan), Jack Kruschen (Hogar), Leon Askin (Otto), Frank Wilcox (Professor), Emil Sitka (technician).

CAROUSEL (1956)
    Director: Henry King
Gordon MacRae (Billy Bigelow), Shirley Jones (Julie), Cameron Mitchell (Jigger), Gene Lockhart (Starkeeper), John Dehner (Mr. Bascombe), Barbara Ruick (Carrie), Robert Rounseville (Mr. Snow), Susan Luckey (Louise), Claramae Turner (Cousin Nettie), Richard Deacon (policeman), Audrey Christie (Mrs. Mullin), Frank Tweddell (Capt. Watson), Dee Pollock (Enoch Snow, Jr.), William Le Massena (Heavenly Friend), Jacques D'Amboise (Louise's dancing partner), Angelo Rossitto, Sylvia Stanton, Marion Dempsey, Tor Johnson, Mary Orozco, Duke Johnson, Ed Mundy, Harry Johnson.

CARRIE (1976)
    Director: Brian De Palma
Sissy Spacek (Carrie White), Piper Laurie (Margaret White), Amy Irving (Sue Snell), Nancy Allen (Chris Hargenson), William Katt (Tommy Ross), John Travolta (Billy Nolan), Betty Buckley (Miss Collins), P.J. Soles (Norman Watson), Sydney Lassick (Mr. Fromm), Stefan Gierash (Mr. Morton), Michael Talbot (Freddy), Priscilla Pointer (Mrs. Snell), Doug Cox (the Beak), Noelle North (Frieda), Dierdre Berthron (Thonda), Harry Gold (George), Cindy Daly (Cora), Anson Downes (Ernest), Edie McClurg (Helen), Rory Stevens (Kenny), Cameron

DePalma (boy on bicycle).

CARRY ON SCREAMING (1966)
Director: Gerald Thomas
Harry H. Corbett (Detective Sgt. Bung),
Kenneth Williams (Dr. Watt), Joan
Sims (Emily Bung), Angela Douglas
(Doris Mann), Fenella Fielding (Vale-
ria), John Pertwee (Fettle), Tom Clegg
(Odbodd), Billy Cornelius (Odbodd, Jr.),
Bernard Bresslaw (Sockett), Jim Dale
(Albert Potter), Dennis Blake (Rubba-
titi), Charles Hawtrey (Dan Dann), Pe-
ter Butterworth (Detective Constable
Slobotham), Frank Thornton (Mr. Jones),
Norman Mitchell (Cabby), Michael Ward
(Vivian).

CARRY ON SPYING (1964)
Director: Gerald Thomas
Kenneth Williams (Desmond Simkins),
Bernard Cribbins (Harold Crump), Bar-
bara Windsor (Daphne Huneybutt), Charles
Hawtrey (Charlie Bind), Richard Wattis
(Cobley), Eric Pohlmann (the Fat Man),
Frank Forsyth (Prof. Stark), Victor
Maddern (Milchmann), Derek Sydney
(Algerian), Renee Houston (Madame),
Jim Dale (Carstairs), Norah Gordon
(elderly woman), Dilys Laye (Lila),
Norman Mitchell (native policeman),
Eric Barker (the Chief), Judith Furse
(Dr. Crow), Gerton Glauber (code clerk),
John Bluthal (headwaiter), Jill Mai
Meredith (cigarette girl), Hugh Futcher
(scrawny native), Angela Ellison (cloak-
room girl), Tom Clegg (doorman), An-
thony Baird, Jack Taylor, Patrick Dur-
kin, Bill Cummings.

CARRY ON UP THE JUNGLE (1970)
Director: Gerald Thomas
Sidney James (Bill Boosey), Charles
Hawtrey (Tonka), Kenneth Connor (Claude
Chumley), Joan Sims (Lady Evelyn Bag-
ley), Frankie Howerd (Tinkle), Ber-
nard Bresslaw (Upsidaisi), Edwina Car-
roll (Nevda), Valerie Leon (Leda), Jac-
ki Piper (June), Terry Scott (Jungle
Boy), Reuben Martin (Gorilla).

CARS THAT EAT PEOPLE, THE (1976-
Austral.) (A. K. A. "The Cars That
Ate Paris")
Director: Peter Weir
John Meillon (Mayor), Terry Camilleri
(Arthur), Kevin Miles (Dr. Midland),
Melissa Jaffa (Beth), Peter Armstrong
(Gorman), Max Gillies (Metcalf), Ed-
ward Howell (Tringham), Bruce Spence
(Charlie), Charlie Metcalfe (Clife),
Tim Robertson (Les), Frank Saba (Con),
Derek Barnes (Al), Chris Heywood (Da-

ryl), Max Phipps (Rev. Mowbray).

CARTER CASE, THE (1919) - serial in
15 episodes
Chapters: 1. "The Phosgene Bullet", 2.
"The Vacuum Room", 3. "The Air Terror", 4. "The Dungeon", 5. ?, 6. "The
Wireless Detective", 7. "The Nerva-
graph", 8. "The Silent Shot", 9. "The
Camera Trap", 10. "The Moonshiners",
11. "The White Damp", 12. "The X-Ray
Detective", 13. "The Ruse", 14. ? &
15. ?.
Director: Donald Mackenzie
Herbert Rawlinson (Craig Kennedy),
Ethel Grey Terry (Cleo Clark), Marguerite Marsh (Anita Carter), Colt Albertson (Lester Mason), William Pike (Walter Jameson), Donald Hall (Shelby Carter), John Reinhart (Count von der Witz),
Joseph Marba (Hugo Geist/Avion), Kemp-
ton Greene (Rance Dixon), Gene Baker
(Alma, the maid), Louis Wolheim (Eman-
on), Frank Wunderlee (Bull Rudkin), Leslie Stowe (Darky Joe).

CASE OF POISONS, THE (1955-Fr.)
(A. K. A. "L'Affaire des Poisons",
"The Poison Affair")
Director: Henri Decoin
Danielle Darrieux, Paul Meurisse, Viv-
iane Romance, Anne Vernon.

CASE OF THE FRIGHTENED LADY
(1933)
Director: George King
Marius Goring (Lord Lebanon), Felix
Aylmer (Dr. Amersham), Penelope Dud-
ley Ward (Isla Crane), Patrick Barr
(Dick Ferraby), George Merritt (Insp.
Tanner), Helen Haye (Lady Lebanon),
Roy Emerton (Gilder), Ronald Shiner
(Sgt. Totty), John Warwick (Studd), To-
rin Thatcher.

CASE OF THE FULL MOON MURDERS,
THE (1973) (A. K. A. "The Case of the
Smiling Stiffs")
Director: Sean S. Cunningham
Fred Lincoln, Ron Browne, Cathy Wal-
ker, Harry Reems, Jean Jennings.

CASE OF THE TWO BEAUTIES, THE
(1968-Span./Ger.) (A. K. A. "El Caso
de las Dos Bellezas")
Director: Jesus Franco
Janine Reynaud, Rossana Yanni, Adrien
Hoven, Michel Lemoine.

CASINO ROYALE (1967)
Director: John Huston, Val Guest,
Ken Hughes, Robert Parrish & Joe
McGrath

David Niven (Sir James Bond), Peter
Sellers (Evelyn Tremble), Ursula Andress (Vesper Lynd), Woody Allen (Jimmy Bond/Dr. Noah), Joanna Pettet (Mata Bond), Orson Welles (Le Chiffre),
Daliah Lavi (the Detainer), Deborah
Kerr (Agent Mimi/Lady Fiona), Charles
Boyer (Le Grand), Kurt Kasznar (Smer-
nov), William Holden (Ransome), John
Huston (McTarry/M), Tracey Crisp
(Heather), Barbara Bouchet (Moneypen-
ny), Jacqueline Bisset (Miss Goodthighs),
Gabriella Licudi (Eliza), Alexandra Bastedo (Meg), George Raft (himself), Anna Quayle (Frau Hoffner), Colin Gordon
(casino director), Tracy Reed (Fang leader), Richard Wattis (British army officer), Geoffrey Bayldon (Q), Bernard
Cribbins (taxi driver), Percy Herbert
(1st piper), Terence Cooper (Cooper),
Angela Scoular (Buttercup), Jean-Paul
Belmondo (French Legionnaire), Derek
Mimmo (Hadey), Elaine Taylor (Peg),
Ronnie Corbett (Polo), John Wells (Q's
assistant), John Bluthal (casino doorman), Duncan Macrae (Insp. Mathis),
Chic Murray (Chic), Graham Stark
(cashier), Jonathan Routh (John), Vladek Sheybal (Le Chiffre's representative), Penny Riley (control girl), Jeanne
Roland (Captain of the guard), Stirling
Moss (driver), Peter O'Toole (Scottish
piper).

CASK OF AMONTILLADO, THE (1954) -
  short
  Director:
Monty Woolley

CASTLE, THE (1968-Ger./U.S.) (A.K.A.
  "Das Schloss")
  Director: Rudolf Noelte
Maximillian Schell (K), Cordula Tran-
tow (Frieda), Franz Misar (Arthur),
Trudik Daniel (innkeeper's wife), Hel-
mut Qualtinger (Burgel), Johan Misar
(Jeremiah), Friedrich Maurer (Mayor),
Hans Ernst Jager (landlord), Else Eh-
ser (Mizzi), Iva Janzurova (Olga), Olse
Kunkele, Martha Wallner.

CASTLE IN THE AIR (1952)
  Director: Henry Cass
David Tomlinson (Earl of Locharne),
Margaret Rutherford (Miss Nicholson),
A.E. Matthews (Blair), Patricia Dain-
ton (Ermyntrude), Ewan Roberts (Men-
zies), Brian Oulton (Phillips), Clive
Morton (Macree), Gordon Jackson (Hi-
ker), John Harvey (Andrews), Helen
Cherry (Boss Trent), Russell Waters
(Moffat), Archie Duncan (Constable),
Barbara Kelly (Mrs. Clodfelter Dunne),

Pat Sandys (girl hiker), Stringer Davis
(hall porter), Esme Beringer (Mrs.
Thompson), Norman Macowan (Pettigrew), Helen Christie (Jessie), David
Hannaford (small boy), Winifred Willard
(Miss Miller), Paul Blake (hotel manager).

CASTLE IN THE DESERT (1941)
  Director: Harry Lachman
Sidney Toler (Charlie Chan), Victor Sen
Yung (Jimmy Chan), Douglass Dumbrille
(Manderley), Richard Derr (Carl Dethe-
ridge), Lenita Lane (Lucy Manderley),
Henry Daniell (Watson King), Steven
Geray (Dr. Retling), Milton Parsons
(Fletcher), Ethel Griffies (Madame Sa-
turnia), Edmund MacDonald (Walter
Hartford), Arlene Whelan (Brenda Hart-
ford), Lucien Littlefield.

CASTLE KEEP (1969)
  Director: Sydney Pollack
Burt Lancaster (Maj. Abraham Falco-
ner), Patrick O'Neal (Capt. Lionel Beck-
man), Peter Falk (Sgt. Orlando Rossi),
Jean Pierre Aumont (Comte de Maldo-
rais), Tony Bill (Lt. Adam B. Amber-
jack), Al Freeman, Jr. (Pfc. Alistair
Benjamin), Astrid Heeren (Therese),
Scott Wilson (Cpl. Ralph Clearboy),
Michael Conrad (Sgt. Juan De Vaca),
Bruce Dern (Lt. Billy Byron Bix).

CASTLE OF BLOOD (1964-Ital./Fr.)
  (A.K.A. "La Danza Macabra", "Cas-
  tle of Terror", "La Lunga Notte del
  Terrore", "The Long Night of Terror")
  Director: Antonio Margheriti/
  Anthony Dawson
George Riviere (Allan Foster), Barbara
Steele (Elizabeth Blackwood), Montgo-
mery Glenn, Phil Karson, Silvia Scren,
Johnny Waters, Margrete Robsahm,
Raul H. Newman, Ben Steffen, Merry
Powers.

CASTLE OF EVIL (1966)
  Director: Francis D. Lyon
Scott Brady (Matt Granger), Virginia
Mayo (Sable), Hugh Marlowe (Dr. Coro-
zal), Lisa Gaye (Carol Harris), David
Brian (Robert Hawley), Shelley Morri-
son (Lupe), Natividad Vacio (Machado),
Ernest Sarracino (Tunki), William Thourl-
by (Dr. Kovec/the Electronic Man).

CASTLE OF FU MANCHU, THE (1968-
  Ger./Span./Ital./Brit.) (A.K.A. "Die
  Folterkamer des Doktor Fu Manchu",
  "The Torture Chamber of Dr. Fu Man-
  chu")
  Director: Jesus Franco

Christopher Lee (Fu Manchu), Richard
Greene (Nayland Smith), Howard Ma-
rion-Crawford (Dr. Petrie), Tsai Chin
(Lin Tang), Maria Perschy, Rosalba
Neri, Gunther Stoll, Jose Manuel Mar-
tin, Werner Aprelat.

CASTLE OF LUST (1968-Ger.) (A. K. A.
"Im Schloss der Blutigen Begierde",
"In the Castle of Bloody Lust")
     Director: Percy G. Parker
Janine Reynaud, Howard Vernon, Michel
Lemoine, Jan Hendriks, Elvira Bern-
dorff, Pier A. Caminneci.

CASTLE OF THE DOOMED (1968-Span. /
Ger.) (A. K. A. "Besame, Monstruo",
"Kiss Me, Monster")
     Director: Jesus Franco
Janine Reynaud, Rossana Yanni, Adrian
Hoven, Chris Howland, Carlos Mendi,
Manuel Otero, Ana Cesares, Manolo
Velasco.

CASTLE OF THE LIVING DEAD, THE
(1964-Ital. /Fr.) (A. K. A. "Il Cas-
tello dei Morti Vivi", "Le Chateau
des Morts Vivants")
     Director: Luciana Ricci/Herbert
     Wise & Warren Kiefer
Christopher Lee (Count Drago), Gaia
Germani (Laura), Philippe LeRoy (Eric),
Jacques Stanislawski (Bruno), Antonio
De Martino (Neep), Mirko Valentin (San-
dro), Ennio Antonelli (Gianni), Donald
Sutherland (witch/sergeant).

CASTLE OF THE MONSTERS, THE
(1957-Mex.) (A. K. A. "El Castillo
de los Monstruos")
     Director: Julian Soler
German Robles (Count Dracula), Evangelina Elizondo, Carlos Orellana, Guillermo Orea, Clavillazo.

CATACLYSM (1980)
     Director: Tom McGowan, Greg
     Tallas & Philip Marshak
Cameron Mitchell (Lt. Stern), Marc
Lawrence (Deiter/Abraham Weis), Mau-
rice Grandmaison (Papini), Faith Clift
(Claire Hansen), Charles Moll (Prof.
James Hansen), Robert Bristol (Olivier),
Elizabeth Martin (Ann), Klint Stevenson
(Jim), Christie Wagner (Mrs. Roget),
Robyn Russell (Mrs. Zeigler), Georgia
Geerling (waitress), T. J. Savage (morgue
attendant), Phil Yordan, Jr. (Italian
waiter), Richard Bulik (Nazi).

CAT AND THE CANARY, THE (1927)
     Director: Paul Leni
Laura La Plante (Annabelle West),

Creighton Hale (Paul Jones), Tully Mar-
shall (Roger Crosby), Arthur Edmund
Carewe (Harry), Flora Finch (Aunt Su-
san), Gertrude Astor (Cecily), George
Siegmann (Hendricks), Forrest Stanley
(Charles Wilder), Lucien Littlefield (Dr.
Ira Lazar), Martha Mattox (Mammy Plea-
sant), Billie Engel (taxi driver), Joe
Murphy (milkman).

CAT AND THE CANARY, THE (1939)
     Director: Elliot Nugent
Bob Hope (Wally Hampton), Paulette
Goddard (Annabelle), Gale Sondergaard
(Miss Lu), John Beal (Fred Blythe),
Douglas Montgomery (Jack Wilder), E-
lizabeth Patterson (Aunt Susan), Nydia
Westman (Cicily), George Zucco (Law-
yer Crosby), Willard Robertson (Hen-
dricks), Charles Lane, John Wray,
George Regas.

CAT AND THE CANARY, THE (1978)
     Director: Radley Metzger
Carol Lynley (Annabelle West), Michael
Callan (Paul Jones), Honor Blackman
(Susan Sillsby), Wilfrid Hyde-White (Cy-
rus West), Peter McEnery (Charlie Wil-
der), Daniel Massey (Harry Blythe), Oli-
via Hussey (Cicily Young), Wendy Hiller
(Allison Crosby), Edward Fox (Hendricks),
Beatrix Lehmann (Mrs. Pleasant).

CAT CREATURE, THE (TVM-1973) -
12-11-73
     Director: Curtis Harrington
David Hedison (Roger Evans), Meredith
Baxter (Rena Carter), Stuart Whitman
(Lt. Marco), Gale Sondergaard (Hester
Black), Kent Smith (Frank Lucas), John
Abbott (Prof. Reinhart), Renne Jarrett
(Sherry Hastings), John Carradine (desk
clerk), Keye Luke (Joe Sung), Virgil
Frye (Donovan), Milton Parsons (coro-
ner), Peter Lorre, Jr. (pawnshop clerk),
William Sims (Bert).

CAT CREEPS, THE (1930)
     Director: Rupert Julian
Helen Twelvetress (Annabel West), Ray-
mond Hackett (Paul), Neal Hamilton
(Charlie Wilder), Jean Hersholt (Dr.
Patterson), Lilyan Tashman (Cicily),
Lawrence Grant (Crosby), Montague
Love (Hendricks), Elizabeth Patterson
(Susan), Theodore von Eltz (Harry
Bluthe), Blanche Frederici (Mammy
Pleasant), Lupita Tovar.

CAT CREEPS, THE (1930) - Spanish
language
     Director: George Melford
Lupita Tovar, Antonio Moreno, Manuel

Granado.

CAT CREEPS, THE (1946)
Director: Erle C. Kenton
Fred Brady (Terry Nichols), Lois Collier (Gay Elliot), Noah Beery, Jr. (Pidge Laurie), Douglas Dumbrille (Tom McGarvey), Paul Kelly (Ken Grady), Rose Hobart (Connie Palmer), Vera Lewis (Cora Williams), Jonathan Hale (Walter Elliot), Eris Clive (Kyra Gordon), William Davidson (editor).

CAT FROM OUTER SPACE, THE (1978)
Director: Norman Tokar
Ken Berry (Dr. Frank Wilson), Sandy Duncan (Dr. Elizabeth Bartlett), Roddy McDowall (Mr. Stallwood), McLean Stevenson (Dr. Carl Link), Jesse White (Earnest Ernie), Harry Morgan (Gen. Stilton), Alan Young (Dr. Wenger), John Alderson (Mr. Smith), Ronnie Schell (Sgt. Duffy), Hans Conreid (Dr. Heffel), William Prince (Mr. Olympus), James Hampton (Capt. Anderson), Ralph Manza (Weazel), Hank Jones (Officer), Tiger Joe Marsh (Omar), Rick Hurst (Dydee guard), Tom Pedi (Honest Harry), Howard T. Platt (Col. Woodruff), Arnold Soboloff (NASA executive), Alice Backes, Mel Carter, Jim Begg, Roger Price, Henry Slate, Rick Sorensen, Dallas McKennon, Gil Stratton, Roger Pancake, Jerry Fujikawa, Pete Renaday, Tom Jackman, Joe Medalis, Richard Warlock, Fred L. Whalen, Jana Milo.

CAT GIRL, THE (1957)
Director: Alfred Shaughnessy
Barbara Shelley (Lenora), Robert Ayres (Dr. Marlowe), Kay Callard (Dorothy Marlowe), Paddy Webster (Cathy), Ernest Milton (Edmund), Jack May (Richard), Lilly Kann (Anna), John Lee (Allan), John Watson (Roberts), Martin Body (Cafferty), Selma Vaz Dias (nurse), John Baker (male nurse), Geoffrey Tyrrell (caretaker), Frank Atkinson (guard).

CATHERINE AND I (1980-Fr./Ital.)
(A. K. A. "Io E Caterina")
Director: Alberto Sordi
Alberto Sordi (Enrico), Edwige Fenech (Elisabetta), Catherine Spaak (secretary), Rossano Brazzi (Arthur), Valeria Valeri (wife).

CATHOLICS (TVM-1973) - 11-29-73
Director: Jack Gold
Martin Sheen (Father James Kinsella), Trevor Howard (Abbot), Andrew Kier

(Father Matthew), Cyril Cusack (Father Manus), Tom Jordan (Father Terrence), Michael Gambon (Brother Kevin), Leon Vitale (Brother Donald), Godfrey Quigley (Father Walter), John Kelly (Brother Paul), Gilbert McIntyre (Brother John), Seamus Healy (Brother Pius), Cecil Sheridan (Brother Malachy), Patrick Long (Brother Sean), Richard Oliver (Brother Alphonsus), Conor Evans (Brother Michael), John Franklin (Brother Martin), Liam Burk (Brother Daniel), John Pine (Brother Benedict), Frank Howard (Father Colum), Derry Power (dirty monk), Geoffrey Golden (publican), Joe Pilkington (boatman).

CATHY'S CURSE (1977)
Director: Eddy Matalon
Alan Scarfe (George Gimble), Beverly Murray (Vivian Gimble), Randi Allen (Cathy Gimble), Hubert Noel (doctor), Roy Witham (Paul), Dorothy Davis (Mary), Mary Morter (medium), Renee Girard (Mrs. Burton), Sonny Forbes (policeman), Linda Koot (Laura), Bob Gerolami (vet), Peter McNeil (young George Gimble), Bryce Allen, Lisa Nickelt (Cathy's friends).

CATMAN OF PARIS, THE (1946)
Director: Lesley Selander
Carl Esmond (Charles Regnier), Lenore Aubert (Marie Audet), Douglas Dumbrille (Henry Borchard), Adele Mara (Marguerite Duval), Gerald Mohr (Insp. Severn), Francis Pierlot (Paul Audet), Fritz Feld (Prefect of Police), Robert J. Wilke (the Catman), Anthony Caruso, John Dehner, George Renavent.

CAT O'NINE TAILS, THE (1971-Ital./Ger./Fr.) (A. K. A. "Il Gatto a Nove Code", "Der Neunschwanzige Katze")
Director: Dario Argento
Karl Malden (Franco Arno), James Franciscus (Carlo Giordani), Rada Rassimov (Bianca Merusi), Catherine Spaak (Anna Terzi), Cinzia De Carolis (Lori), Horst Frank (Dr. Braun), Carlo Alighiero (Dr. Calabresi), Carrado Olmi (Morsella), Pier Paolo Capponi (Police Superintendent Spimi), Vittorio Congia (Cameraman Righetto), Aldo Reggiani (Dr. Casoni), Emilio Marchesini (Dr. Mombelli), Rino Carraro (Prof. Terzi), Tom Felleghy (Dr. Esson), Werner Pochet (Manuel).

CAT PEOPLE (1982)
Director: Paul Schrader
Nastassia Kinski (Irena Gallier), Malcolm McDowell (Paul Gallier), John Heard (Oliver Yates), Annette O'Toole

(Alice Perrin), Ruby Dee (Female), Ed Begley, Jr. (Joe Creigh), Frankie Faison (Detective Brandt), Ron Diamond (Detective Ron Diamond), Scott Paulin (Bill Searle), Lynn Lowry (Ruthie), Tessa Richarde (Billie), John Larroquette (Bronte Judson), Fausto Barajas (Otis), Patricia Perkins (taxi driver), Berry Berenson (Sandra), Emery Hollier (Yeatman Brewer), John H. Fields (massage parlor manager).

CAT PEOPLE, THE (1942)
Director: Jacques Tourneur
Simone Simon (Irena Dubrovna), Kent Smith (Oliver Reed), Jane Randolph (Alice Moore), Tom Conway (Dr. Judd), Alan Napier (Carver), Jack Holt (Commodore), Elizabeth Russell (Barbara Farren), Alec Craig (zookeeper), Bud Geary (mounted cop), Mary Halsey (Blondie), Murdock MacQuarrie (caretaker), Elizabeth Dunne (Miss Plunkett), Theresa Harris (Minnie), George Ford (whistling cop), Steve Soldi (organ grinder), Betty Roadman (Mrs. Hansen), Donald Kerr (taxi driver), Dot Farley (Mrs. Agnew), Charles Jordan (bus driver), Henrietta Burnside (woman), Connie Leon (woman), Eddie Dew (street cop), John Piffl (cafe proprietor), Leda Nicova (patient).

CAT-WOMEN OF THE MOON (1953)
Director: Arthur Hilton
Sonny Tufts (Laird Grainger), Victor Jory (Lt. Kip Reisler), Marie Windsor (Helen Salinger), Bill Phipps (Douglas Smith), Douglas Fowley (Walt Willis), Carol Brewster (Alpha), Susan Morrow (Lambda), Suzanne Alexander (Zeta), Judy Walsh, Betty Allen, Ellye Marshall, Roxann Delman (the Cat-Women).

CAULDRON OF BLOOD (1967-Span./U.S.) (A. K. A. "El Coleccionista de Cadaveres", "The Collector of Cadavers", "The Corpse Collector", "Blind Man's Bluff")
Director: Edward Mann/Santos Alcocer
Boris Karloff (Badulescu), Jean-Pierre Aumont (Marchand), Viveca Lindfors (Tania), Milo Quesada (Shanghai), Ruben Rojo (Pablo), Dianik Zurakowska (Elga), Rosenda Monteros (Valerie).

CAVEMAN (1981)
Director: Carl Gottlieb
Ringo Starr (Atouk), Barbara Bach (Lana), Jack Gilford (Gog), Shelly Long (Tala), Dennis Quaid (Lar), John Metuszak (Tonda), Cork Hubbert (Ta),

Mark King (Ruck), Paco Morayta (Flok), Evan Kim (Nook), Ed Greenberg (Kalta), Carl Lumbly (Bork), Jack Scalici (Folg), Erica Carlson (Folg's mate), Sara Lopez Sierra (Folg's daughter), Esteban Baldez (Folg's son), Anals de Melo (Meeks), Avery Schreiber, Richard Moll.

CAVEMAN, THE (1912)
Director: Ralph W. Ince
Edith Story (1st cavewoman), Rose Tapley (2nd cavewoman), Harry Northrup (1st caveman), Teft Johnson (caveman chief).

CAVE OF ALI BABA, THE (1954-Arg.) (A. K. A. "La Cueve de Ali Baba")
Director: Mario Lugones
Perla Cristal, Malisa Zini, Hector Calcano, Tono y Gogo Andreu, Jorge Ayala.

CAVE OF THE LIVING DEAD (1965-Ger./Yugo.) (A. K. A. "Der Fluch der Grunen Augen", "The Curse of the Green Eyes")
Director: Akos Von Ratony
Adrian Hoven (Insp. Doren), Karin Field (Karin), Wolfgang Preiss (Prof. Adelsberg), Erika Remberg (Maria), John Kitzmiller (John), Emmerich Schrenk (Thomas), Carl Mohner (the Doctor).

CHAIRMAN, THE (1969)
Director: J. Lee Thompson
Gregory Peck (Dr. John Hathaway), Arthur Hill (Shelby), Anne Haywood (Kay Hanna), Alan Dobie (Denson), Conrad Yama (the Chairman), Ori Levy (Alexander Shertov), Zienia Merton (Ting Ling), Bert Kwouk (Chang Shou), Keye Luke (Prof. Soong Li), Eric Young (Yin), Alan White (Col. Gardner), Francisca Tu, Janet Key, Robert Lee, Keith Bonnard, Mai Ling, Gordon Sterne, Helen Horton, Cecil Cheng, Simon Cain, Edward Cast, Lawrence Herder, Anthony Chinn.

CHALLENGE, THE (TVM-1970) - 2-10-70
Director: Allen Smithee
Darren McGavin (Jacob Gallery), Mako (Yuro), Broderick Crawford (Gen. Lewis Meyers), James Whitmore (Overman), Paul Lukas (Dr. Nagy), Skip Homeier (Lyman George), Sam Elliott (Bryant), Adolph Caesar (Opano), Arianne Ulmer (Sarah), Andre Philippe (Swiss Official), Bill Zuckert (Army Colonel), Gene LeBell (doctor), Davis Roberts (scientist), Byron Morrow (Defense Secretary), Lew Brown (sergeant), Garry Walberg (submarine captain), Mi-

chael Hinn (army captain), Bill Quinn
(Marine Colonel), Eddie Guardino (soldier).

CHALLENGE OF THE GIANT, THE
(1965-Ital.) (A. K. A. "La Sfida dei
Giganti")
Director: Maurizio Lucidi/Mau-
rice Bright
Reg Park, Gia Sandri, Luigi Barbini,
Adriana Ambesi.

CHAMBER OF HORRORS (1940) (A. K. A.
"The Door with Seven Locks")
Director: Norman Lee
Leslie Banks (Dr. Manetta), Lillie Pal-
mer (June Lansdowne), Gina Malo
(Glenda Blake), Richard Bird (Insp.
Sneed), Cathleen Nesbitt (Ann Cody),
David Horne (Edward Havelock), J. H.
Roberts (Luis Silva), Romilly Lunge
(Dick Martin), Aubrey Mallalieu (Lord
Selford), Ross Landon (John Selford),
Harry Hutchinson (Bevan Cody).

CHAMBER OF HORRORS (1966)
Director: Hy Averback
Cesare Danova (Anthony Draco), Patrick
O'Neal (Jason Cravette), Wilfrid Hyde-
White (Harold Cavernon Blount), Tun
Tun (Pepe de Reyes), Laura Devon (Ma-
rie Champlain), Marie Windsor (Mme.
Corona), Suzy Parker (Barbara Dixon),
Patrice Wymore (Vivian), Jeanette
Nolan (Mrs. Ewing Perryman), Barry
Kroeger (Chun Sing), Richard O'Brien
(Dr. Romulous Cobb), Vinton Hayworth
(Judge Randolph), Philip Bourneuf (Insp.
Matthew Strudwick), Wayne Rogers (Sgt.
Tim Alberson), Charles Seel (Dr. Hope-
well), Ayllene Gibbons (barmaid), Inger
Stratton (Gloria), Tony Curtis (card pla-
yer).

CHAMPIONS OF JUSTICE RETURN,
THE (1972-Mex.) (A. K. A. "Veulven
los Campeones Justicieros")
Director: Federico Curiel
Blue Demon, Mil Mascaras, El Fantas-
ma Blanco, El Rayo de Jalisco, El Avis-
pon Escarlata, Yolanda Lievana, Julio
Cesar, Martha Angelica.

CHANDU THE MAGICIAN (1932)
Director: William Cameron Men-
zies
Edmund Lowe (Chandu), Bela Lugosi
(Roxor), Irene Ware (Princess Najdi),
Herbert Mundin (Albert Miggies), Hen-
ry B. Walthal (Robert Regent), Weldon
Heyburn (Abdullah), Virginia Hammond
(Dorothy), June Vlasek (Betty Lou), Nes-
tor Aber (Bobby).

CHANGELING, THE (1980)
Director: Peter Medak
George C. Scott (John Russell), Trish
Van Devere (Claire Norman), Melvin
Douglas (Sen. Joe Carmichael), John
Colicos (De Witt), Barry Morse (Dr.
Pemberton), Jean Marsh (Joanna Rus-
sell), James Douglas (Eugene Carmi-
chael), Roberta Maxwell (Eva Lingstrom),
Bernard Behrens (Prof. Robert Ling-
strom), Helen Burns (Leah Harmon),
Ruth Springford (Minnie Huxley), Eric
Christmas (Albert Harmon), Madeleine
Thornton-Sherwood (Mrs. Norman),
Frances Hyland (Elizabeth Grey).

CHANGE OF MIND (1969)
Director: Robert Stevens
Raymond St. Jacques (David Rowe), Su-
san Oliver (Margaret Rowe), Janet Mac-
Lachlan (Elizabeth Dickson), Leslie Niel-
sen (Sheriff Webb), Jack Creley (Bill
Chambers), David Bailey (Tommy Ben-
son), Cosette Lee (Angela Rowe), Andre
Womble (Scupper), Clarisse Taylor (Rose
Landis), Donnelly Rhodes (Roger Mor-
row), Larry Reynolds (Judge Forrest),
Henry Ramer (Chief Enfield), Rudy
Challenger (Howard Culver), Joseph
Shaw (Gov. LaTourette), Hope Clarke
(Nancy), Franz Russell (Mayor Farrell),
Sydney Brown (Attorney Nash), Ron Hart-
mann (Dr. Kelman), Tony Kamreither
(Dr. Bornear), Murray Westgate (Judge
Stanton).

CHANO VS. THE TIGER AND THE VAM-
PIRE (1971-Mex.) (A. K. A. "Chanoc
contra el Tigre y el Vampiro")
Director: Gilberto Martinez Sola-
res
Tin Tan/German Valdes, Gregorio Ca-
sal, Aurora Cavel, Marisa, Lina Marin,
Carlos Nieto, Victor Alcocer.

CHARLEY AND THE ANGEL (1973)
Director: Vincent McEveety
Fred MacMurray (Charley Appleby),
Harry Morgan (the Angel), Cloris Leach-
man (Nettie Appleby), Kurt Russell (Ray
Ferris), Kathleen Cody (Leonora Apple-
by), Vincent Van Patten (Willie Appleby),
Scott Kolden (Rupert Appleby), George
Lindsey (Pete), Edward Andrews (ban-
ker), Richard Bakalyan (Buggs), Barba-
ra Nichols (Sadie), Liam Dunn (Dr.
Sprague), Larry D. Mann (Felix), Kelly
Thordsen (policeman), George O'Hanlon
(Police Chief), Susan Tolsky (Miss Par-
tridge), Mills Watson (Frankie Zuto),
Ed Begley, Jr. (Derwood Moseby), Christina Anderson (Susie), Pat Delany (girl
in Sadie's Palace), Roy Engel (driver),

Bob Hastings (news reporter), Jack
Griffin (2nd policeman).

CHARLIE CHAN AND THE CURSE OF
THE DRAGON QUEEN (1981)
    Director: Clive Donner
Peter Ustinov (Charlie Chan), Angie
Dickinson (Dragon Queen), Lee Grant
(Mrs. Lupowitz), Richard Hatch (Lee
Chan, Jr.), Roddy McDowall (Gillespie),
Brian Keith (Police Chief), Rachel Ro-
berts (Mrs. Dangers), Johnny Sekka
(Stefan), Michelle Pfeiffer (Cordelia
Ferrington, III), Paul Ryan (Masten).

CHARLIE CHAN AT THE OLYMPICS
(1937)
    Director: H. Bruce Humberstone
Warner Oland (Charlie Chan), Keye
Luke (Lee Chan), Katherine DeMille
(Yvonne Roland), Allan Lane (Richard
Masters), John Eldredge (Cartwright),
Jonathan Hale (Hopkins), C. Henry Gor-
don (Arthur Hughes), Andrew Tombes
(Police Chief Scott), Howard Hickman
(Dr. Burton), Pauline Moore (Betty
Adams), Layne Tom, Jr. (Charlie
Chan, Jr.), Morgan Wallace (Charles
Zaraka), Fredrik Vogeding (Capt. Stras-
ser), Minerva Urecal, George Chandler,
Lee Shumway, Philip Morris, Selmer
Jackson, Stanley Blystone, Emmett Vo-
gan, Paul W. Panzer.

CHARLIE CHAN AT THE OPERA (1936)
    Director: H. Bruce Humberstone
Warner Oland (Charlie Chan), Boris
Karloff (Grevelle), Keye Luke (Lee
Chan), Charlotte Henry (Mlle. Kitty),
Frank Conroy (Mr. Whitely), William
Demarest (Sgt. Kelly), Gregory Gaye
(Enrico Barelli), Neda Harrigan (Mme.
Anita Barelli), Thomas Beck (Phil Chil-
ders), Maurice Cass (Mr. Arnold), Guy
Usher (Insp. Regan), Tom McGuire
(Harris), Margaret Irving (Mme. Lilli
Rochelle), Joan Woodbury, Lee Shum-
way, Stanley Blystone, Fred Kelsey.

CHARLIE CHAN AT THE WAX MUSEUM
(1940)
    Director: Lynn Shores
Sidney Toler (Charlie Chan), Victor Sen
Yung (Jimmy Chan), C. Henry Gordon
(Dr. Cream), Marc Lawrence (Steve
McBirney), Marguerite Chapman (Mary
Bolton), Harold Goodwin (Edwards),
Michael Visaroff (Dr. Otto von Broom),
Charles Wangenheim (Willie Fern), Joan
Valerie (Lily Latimer), Eddie Marr
(Grenock), Ted Osborn (Tom Agnew),
Hilda Vaughn (Mrs. Rocke), Archie
Twitchell (Carter Lane), Joe King (Insp.

Matthews).

CHARLIE CHAN AT TREASURE ISLAND
(1939)
    Director: Norman Foster
Sidney Toler (Charlie Chan), Victor Sen
Yung (Jimmy Chan), Cesar Romero (Rhadini), Pauline Moore (Eve Cairo), Douglass Dumbrille (Thomas Gregory), Sally
Blane (Stella Essex), Wally Vernon (Elmer Kelner), Douglas Fowley (Pete Lewis), June Gale (Myra Rhadini), Louis
Jean Heydt (Paul Essex), Charles Halton
(Redley), Trevor Bardette (Abdul), Donald MacBride (Chief J. J. Kilvaine),
Billie Seward (Bessie Sibley).

CHARLIE CHAN IN EGYPT (1935)
    Director: Lewis King
Warner Oland (Charlie Chan), Rita Hay-
worth (Nayda), Stepin Fetchit (Snow-
shoes), Nigel de Brulier (Edfu Ahmed),
Frank Conroy (Prof. Thurston), Paul
Porcasi (Fouad Soueida), Jameson Tho-
mas (Dr. Anton Racine), Arthur Stone
(Dragoman), Thomas Beck (Tom Evans),
Pat Patterson (Carol Arnold), James
Eagles (Barry Arnold).

CHARLIE CHAN IN RENO (1939)
    Director: Norman Foster
Sidney Toler (Charlie Chan), Victor Sen
Yung (Jimmy Chan), Ricardo Cortez (Dr.
Ainsley), Phyllis Brooks (Vivian Wells),
Kane Richmond (Curtis Whitman), Slim
Summerville (Sheriff Fletcher), Robert
Lowery (Wally Burke), Pauline Moore
(Mary Whitman), Kay Linaker (Mrs.
Russell), Charles D. Brown (Chief of
Police King), Morgan Conway (George
Bently), Iris Wong (Choy Wong), Louise
Henry (Jeanne Bently), Eddie Collins
(cab driver), Hamilton MacFadden (night
clerk), Jim Aubrey, Fred Kelsey.

CHARLIE CHAN'S MURDER CRUISE
(1940)
    Director: Eugene Forde
Sidney Toler (Charlie Chan), Victor Sen
Yung (Jimmy Chan), Lionel Atwill (Dr.
Suderman), Leo G. Carroll (Prof. Gor-
don), Robert Lowery (Jack Kenyon), Mar-
jorie Weaver (Miss Drake), Leonard
Mudie (Gerald Pendleton), Don Beddoe
(James Ross), Charles Middleton (Mr.
Walters), Cora Witherspoon (Susie Wat-
son), James Burke (Wilkie), Claire Du
Brey (Mrs. Walters), Kay Linaker (Mrs.
Pendleton), Harlan Briggs (coroner),
Richard Keene (Buttons), Layne Tom
(Charlie Chan, Jr.), Montague Shaw.

CHARLIE CHAN'S SECRET (1936)

Director: Gordon Wiles
Warner Oland (Charlie Chan), Charles
Quigley (Dick Williams), Astrid Allwyn
(Janice Gage), Herbert Mundin (Baxter),
Egon Brecher (Ulrich), Jonathan Hale
(Warren T. Phelps), Arthur Edmund Ca-
rew (Prof. Bowan), Ivan Miller (Morton),
Edward Trevor (Fred Gage), Henrietta
Crosman (Henrietta Lowell), Rosina
Lawrence (Alice Lowell), Gloria Roy
(Carlotta), William Norton Bailey (Harris).

CHARLY (1968)
Director: Ralph Nelson
Cliff Robertson (Charly Gordon), Claire
Bloom (Alice Kinian), Lilia Skala (Dr.
Anna Straus), Dick Van Patton (Bert),
Leon Janney (Dr. Richard Nemur), Ruth
White (Mrs. Apple), William Dwyer
(Joey), Ed McNally (Gimpy), Barney
Martin (Hank), Dan Morgan (Paddy),
Frank Dolan (Eddie).

CHATTER-BOX (1977)
Director: Tom De Simone
Candice Rialson (Penelope Pittman),
Larry Gelman (Dr. Pearl), Jane Kean
(Eleanor Pittman), Perry Bullington
(Ted), Arlene Martel (Marlene), Mi-
chael Taylor (Dick), Rip Taylor (Mr.
Jo), Cynthia Hoppenfield (Linda Ann),
Robert Lipton (Jon David), Sandra Gould
(Mrs. Bugatowski), Trent Dolan (Frank
Rio), Professor Irwin Corey (himself).

CHESS PLAYER, THE (1927-Fr.) (A. K. A.
"Le Jouer d'Echecs")
Director: Raymond Bernard
Pierre Blanchar, Edithe Jehanne, Charles
Dullin.

CHESS PLAYER, THE (1937-Fr.) (A. K. A.
"Le Jouer d'Echecs")
Director: Jean Dreville
Conrad Veidt, Francoise Rosay.

CHILD, THE (1977) (A. K. A. "Kill and
Go Hide")
Director: Robert Voskanian
Laurel Barnet (Alicianne), Frank Jan-
son (Norden), Rosalie Cole (Rosalie),
Richard Hanners (Len), Ruth Ballen
(Mrs. Whitfield).

CHILDREN, THE (1980)
Director: Max Kalmanowicz
Martin Shaker (John Freemont), Gil
Rogers (Sheriff Billy Hart), Gale Gar-
nett (Cathy Freemont), Tracy Griswold
(Harry Timmons), Joy Glaccum (Suzie
MacKenzie), Shannon Bolin (Molly),
Michelle Le Mothe (Dr. Joyce Gould),
Suzanne Barnes (Leslie Button), Ed-

ward Terry (Hank), Peter Maloney (Frank),
Martin Brennan (Sanford Butler-Jones),
David Platt (chauffeur), John Codiglia
(Jackson Lane), Michael Carrier (Bob
Chandler), Diane Deckard (Rita Chand-
ler), Arthur Chase (Cyrus MacKenzie),
June Berry (waitress), Ray Delmolino
(bus driver), J. D. Clarke, James Kla-
win (hardhats), X. Ben Fakackt (news-
caster). The Children: Clara Evans
(Jenny), Jeptha Evans (Paul), Nathanael
Albright (Tommy), Sarah Albright (Ellen),
Julie Carrier (Janet).

CHILDREN OF THE DAMNED (1963)
Director: Anton Leader
Ian Hendry (Dr. Tom Lewellin), Alan
Badel (Dr. David Neville), Barbara Fer-
ris (Susan Eliot), Alfred Burke (Colin
Webster), Martin Miller (Prof. Gruber),
Harold Goldblatt (Harib), Sheila Allen
(Diana Looran), Bessie Love (Mrs. Rob-
bin), Ralph Michael (Minister of Defense),
Patrick White (Mr. Davidson), Andre
Mikhelson (Russian Official), The Child-
ren: Clive Powell (Paul), Frank Summer-
scale (Mark), Lee Yoke-Moon (Mi Ling),
Roberta Rex (Nina), Mahdu Mathen (Ra-
shid), Gerald Delsol (Ago).

CHILDREN SHOULDN'T PLAY WITH
DEAD THINGS (1972)
Director: Benjamin Clark
Alan Ormsby (Alan), Anya Ormsby (An-
ya), Valerie Mauches (Val), Jane Daly
(Terry), Paul Cronin (Paul), Jeffrey
Gillen (Jeff), Roy Engleman (Roy), Bob
Filep (Emerson), Bruce Solomon (Winns),
Alecs Baird (caretaker), Seth Sklarey
(Orville).

CHILD'S PLAY (1954)
Director: Margaret Thompson
Mona Washbourne, Carl Jaffe, Dorothy
Alison, Peter Martyn, Ingeborg Wells.

CHILD'S PLAY (1972)
Director: Sidney Lumet
James Mason (Jerome Malley), Beau
Bridges (Paul Reis), Robert Preston
(Joseph Dobbs), Kate Harrington (Mrs.
Carter), Ronald Weyand (Father Mozian),
Charles White (Father Griffin), David
Rounds (Father Penny).

CHINA SYNDROME, THE (1979)
Director: James Bridges
Jane Fonda (Kimberly Wade), Jack Lem-
mon (Jack Godell), Michael Douglas (Ri-
chard Adams), Daniel Valdez (Hector
Salas), Peter Donat (Don Jacovitch),
James Hampton (Bill Gibson), A. Wil-
ford Brimley (Ted Spindler), Richard

Herd (Evan McCormack), Stan Bohrman (Peter Martin), Michael Alaimo (Greg Minor), James Karen (Mac Churchill), Donald Hotton (Dr. Lowell), Paul Larson (D. B. Royce), Khalilah Ali (Marge), Ron Lombard (Barney), Nick Pellegrino (Borden), Tom Eure (Tommy), Daniel Lewk (Donny).

CHINATOWN CHARLIE (1928)
    Director: Charles Hines
Louise Lorraine, Harry Gribbon, Sojin, Fred Kohler, Anna May Wong, John Burdette, Scotter Lowry, Johnny Hines, George Kuwa.

CHINATOWN MYSTERY, THE (1928) - serial in 10 episodes
Chapters: 1. "The Chinatown Mystery", 2. "The Clutching Claw", 3. "The Devil's Dice", 4. "The Mysterious 13", 5. "Galloping Fury", 6. "The Depth of Danger", 7. "The Invisible Hand", 8. "The Wreck", 9. "Broken Jade" & 10. "The Thirteenth Hour".
    Director: J. P. McGowan
Francis Ford (the Sphinx), Joe Bonomo (Joe Masters), Ruth Hiatt (the chemist), Al Baffert (crook), Sheldon Lewis, Grace Cunard, Helen Gibson, Rosemary Theby, Peggy O'Day, Jack Richardson, Duke Worne, Ernest Shields.

CHINESE PARROT, THE (1927)
    Director: Paul Leni
Sojin (Charlie Chan), Hobart Bosworth, Slim Summerville, Edgar Kennedy, Marian Nixon, Edmund Burns, Etta Lee, Albert Conti, Florence Turner, George K. Kuwa, Dan Mason, Frederick Esmelton.

CHITTY CHITTY BANG BANG (1968)
    Director: Ken Hughes
Dick Van Dyke (Caractacus Potts), Sally Ann Howes (Truly Scrumptious), Lionel Jeffries (Grandpa Potts), Gert Frobe (Baron Bomburst), Adrian Hall (Jeremy Potts), Heather Ripley (Jemima Potts), Anna Quayle (Baroness Bomburst), James Robertson Justice (Lord Scrumptious), Robert Helpmann (Child Catcher), Benny Hill (Toymaker), Davy Kaye (Admiral), Barbara Windsor (Blonde), Desmond Llewelyn, Bernard Spear, Peter Arne, Victor Maddern, Max Bacon, Stanley Unwin, Alexander Dore.

C. H. O. M. P. S. (1979)
    Director: Don Chaffey
Wesley Eure (Brian Foster), Valerie Bertinelli (Casey Norton), Conrad Bain (Ralph Norton), Red Buttons (Bracken),

Jim Backus (Mr. Gibbs), Hermoine Baddeley (Mrs. Fowler), Chuck McCann (Brooks), Regis Toomey (Chief Patterson), Larry Bishop (Ken Sharp), Robert Q. Lewis (Merkle).

CHOSEN, THE (1977-Ital.) (A. K. A. "Holocaust 2000")
    Director: Alberto De Martino
Kirk Douglas (Robert Caine), Simon Ward (Angel Caine), Virginia McKenna (Eva Caine), Agostina Belli (Sara Golen), Anthony Quayle (Prof. Griffith), Adolfo Celli (Dr. Kerouac), Alexander Knox (Meyer), Romolo Valli (Monsignor Charrier), Spiros Focas (Prime Minister Harbin), Massimo Foschi (Arab assassin).

CHOSEN SURVIVORS (1974-U. S. /Mex.)
    Director: Sutton Roley
Jackie Cooper (Raymond Couzins), Alex Cord (Steven Mayes), Diana Muldaur (Alana Fitzgerald), Bradford Dillman (Peter Macomber), Richard Jaeckel (Gordon Ellis), Barbara Babcock (Lenore Chrisman), Pedro Armendarez, Jr. (Luis Cabral), Lincoln Kilpatrick (Woody Russo), Gwen Mitchell (Carrie Draper), Christina Moreno (Kristin Lerner), Kelly Lange (Mary Louise Borden), Nancy Rodman (Farraday).

CHRISTMAS CAROL, A (1938)
    Director: Edwin L. Marin
Reginald Owen (Ebenezer Scrooge), Gene Lockhart (Cratchit), Kathleen Lockhart (Mrs. Cratchit), Terry Kilburn (Tiny Tim), Leo G. Carrol (Marley's ghost), Ann Rutherford (Spirit of Christmas Present), D'Arcy Corrigan, Lionel Braham, Ronald Sinclair.

CHRISTMAS CAROL, A (1951)
    Director: Brian D. Hurst
Alastair Sim (Ebenezer Scrooge), Mervyn Johns (Bob Cratchit), Hermoine Baddeley (Mrs. Cratchit), Michael Hordern (Jacob Marley), Jack Warner (Mr. Jorkins), Kathleen Harrison (Mrs. Dilber), George Cole (Young Scrooge), Patrick MacNee (Young Marley), Miles Malleson (Old Joe), John Charlesworth (Peter Cratchit), Glyn Dearman (Tiny Tim), Rona Anderson (Alice), Clifford Malleson (Mrs. Wilkins), Peter Bull, Ernest Thesiger, Francis de Wolff, Hattie Jacques, Carol Marsh, Olga Edwards, Brian Worth.

CHRISTMAS THAT ALMOST WASN'T, THE (1966-Ital.) (A. K. A. "Il Natale Che Quasi No Fui")
    Director: Rossano Brazzi

Rossano Brazzi (Phineas T. Prune), Paul Tripp (Sam Whipple), Alberto Rabagliati (Santa Claus), Lidia Brazzi (Mrs. Santa Claus), Friedrich Ledebur (Vernet), Medeleine Damien (Marinette), Mario Feliciani (the doctor).

CHRONICLES OF THE GRAY HOUSE, THE (1925-Ger.) (A. K. A. "Zur Chronik von Grieshuus", "At the Grey House")
Director: Arthur von Gerlach
Paul Hartmann (Viscount Heinrich), Rudolf Rittner (Owe Helden), Lil Dagover (Barbara), Arthur Kraussneck (Old Grieshaus), Gertrud Welcker (Greine), Gertrude Arnold (Matte), Jahn Christen (Christof), Hans Peter Peterhaus (Enzio), Rudolf Forster (Viscount Detlef).

CINDERFELLA (1960)
Director: Frank Tashlin
Jerry Lewis (Fella), Ed Wynn (Fairy Godfather), Judith Anderson (Wicket Stepmother), Anna Maria Alberghetti (Princess Charmein), Henry Silva (Maximilian), Robert Hutton (Rupert), Count Basie (himself).

CIRCLE OF IRON (1978)
Director: Richard Moore
David Carradine (Chang-Sha/Monkey Man/Rhythm Man/Death), Jeff Cooper (Cord), Roddy McDowall (White Robe), Christopher Lee (Zetan), Eli Wallach (Man in Oil), Erica Creer (Tara), Earl Maynard (Black Giant), Anthony De Longis (Morthond), Heinz Bernard (Gerryman), Jeremy Kaplan (Monkeyboy), Ziplor Paled (Gerryman's wife), Kam Yuen (Red Band), Bobby Ne'eman (Thug leader), Elizabeth Motzkin (Japanese woman), Dov Friedman (young monk), Ronen Nabah (beautiful boy), Michal Nedivi (boy's mother), Nissim Zohar (boy's father).

CIRCUS OF HORRORS (1960)
Director: Sidney Hayer
Anton Diffring (Rossiter/Schuler), Yvonne Monlaur (Nicole), Erika Remberg (Elissa), Donald Pleasence (Insp. Vanet), Jane Hylton (Angela), Kenneth Griffith (Martin), Conrad Phillips (Insp. Arthur Ames), Yvonne Romain (Melina), William Mervyn (Dr. Morley), Walter Gotell (Von Gruber), Jack Gwillim (Superintendent Andrews), John Merivale (Edward Finsbury), Kenneth J. Warren (roustabout), Fred Haggerty (roustabout), Colette Wilde (Evelyn Morley), Peter Swanwick (Insp. Knopf), Vanda

Hudson (Magda), Carla Challoner (Nicole as a child), Chris Christian (Ringmaster), Sasha Coco (Luis the clown), Glyn Houston (barker), Jack Carson (Chief Eagle Eye), Malcolm Watson (elderly man).

CITY BENEATH THE SEA, THE (TVM-1971) - 1-27-71
Director: Irwin Allen
Stuart Whitman (Admiral Mathews), Rosemary Forsythe (Lia Holmes), Robert Wagner (Brett Mathews), Robert Colbert (Cmdr. Woody Patterson), Whit Bissell (Prof. Holmes), Burr DeBenning (Aguila), Susana Miranda (Elena), James Darren (Dr. Talty), Joseph Cotten (Dr. Ziegler), Richard Basehart (the President), Sugar Ray Robinson (Capt. Hunter), Paul Stewart (Barton), Tom Drake (Gen. Putnam), Larry Pennell (Bill Holmes), Bill Bryant (Capt. Lunderson), Charles Dierkop (Quinn), Edward G. Robinson, Jr. (Dr. Burkson), Bob Dowdell (young officer), Johnny Lee (Tony), Erik Nelson (Triton Controller), Glenna Sergent (Sally), Sheila Mathews (blonde woman), Ray Didsbury (security guard).

CITY DESTROYED, THE (1923-Fr.) (A. K. A. "La Cite Foudroyee")
Director: Luitz-Marat
Daniel Mendille, Jeanne Maguenat, Armand Morins.

CITY OF FEAR (1959)
Director: Irving Lerner
Vince Edwards (Vince Ryker), Lyle Talbot (Chief Jensen), John Archer (Lt. Mark Richards), Steven Ritch (Dr. Wallace), June Blair (June), Joe Mell (Crown), Sherwood Price (Hallon), Cathy Browne (Jeanne), Kelly Thordsen (Sgt. Johnson).

CITY OF THE LIVING DEAD (1980-Ital.)
Director: Lucio Fulci
Christopher George, Katherine MacColl.

CITY OF WOMEN (1980-Ital.)
Director: Federico Fellini
Marcello Mastroianni (Snaporaz), Ettore Manni (Dr. Xavier Zuberkock), Anna Prucnal (Elena), Bernice Stegers (woman on train), Donatella Damiani (feminist on roller skates/dancing girl), Sara Tafuri (other dancing girl), Joie Silvani (old woman on motorcycle), Carl Terlizzi (Dr. Zuberkock's 10,000th conquest), Katren Gebelein (Enderbreith Small), Dominique Labourier (feminist), Alessandra Panelli (housewife in feminist skit), Mara Clukleva (Dr. Zuberkock's elderly maid), Leordana Solfizi

(feminist in black who brings out night-
shirt), Aramando Paracino, Umberto
Zuanelli, Pietro Fumagalli (three trou-
badours on roller coaster), Gabriella
Giorgelli (fishwoman at San Leo), Tatiana & Brigitte Petronio (Lyonet & Ginette Lamour).

CLAIRVOYANT, THE (1935) (A. K. A.
"The Evil Mind")
    Director: Maurice Elvey
Claude Rains (Maximus), Fay Wray (Rene), Jane Baxter (Christine), David
Calthrop (derelict), Mary Clare (Madame), Ben Field (Simon), Denier Warren (Bimeter), Jack Raine (customs
officer), Margaret Davidge (lodging
housekeeper).

CLASH OF THE TITANS (1981)
    Director: Desmond Davis
Harry Hamlin (Perseus), Laurence Oli-
vier (Zeus), Judy Bowker (Andromeda),
Burgess Meredith (Ammon), Neil Mc-
Carthy (Calibos), Ursula Andress (Aph-
rodite), Maggie Smith (Thetis), Claire
Bloom (Hera), Sian Phillips (Cassiopeia),
Susan Fleetwood (Athene), Pat Roach
(Hephaestus), Jack Gwillam (Poseidon),
Donald Houston (Acrisius), Vida Taylor
(Danae), Tim Pigott-Smith (Thallo), Har-
ry Jones (huntsman), Flora Robson, An-
na Manahan, Freda Jackson (blind witches).

CLASS OF 1984
    Director: Mark Lester
Perry King (Andy Norris), Timothy
Van Patten (Peter Stegman), Merrie
Lynn Ross (Diane Norris), Roddy Mc-
Dowall (Terry Corrigan), Al Waxman
(Stawiski), Lisa Langlois (Patsy), Da-
vid Gardner (Morganthau), Stefan Arn-
grim (Drugstore), Neil Clifford (Fallon),
Keith Knight (Barnyard), Michael Fox
(Arthur), Erin Flannery (Deneen Bow-
den).

CLAWS (1977) (A. K. A. "Devil Bear")
    Director: Richard Bansbach &
    R. E. Pierson
Jason Evers, Leon Ames, Anthony Caruso, Myron Healey, Glenn Sipes, Carla Layton.

CLIMAX, THE (1944)
    Director: George Waggner
Boris Karloff (Dr. Hohner), Susanna
Foster (Angela), Turhan Bey (Franz),
Gale Sondergaard (Luise), Thomas Go-
mez (Count Seebruck), June Vincent
(Marcellina), Scotty Beckett (King),
Ludwig Stossel (Amato), Jane Farrar
(Jarmila Vadek), Lotte Stein (Mama

Hinzie), Dorothy Lawrence (Miss Metz-
ger), Erno Verebes (Brunn), Maxwell
Hayes (King's aide), William Edmunds
(Leon), Grace Cunard, George Dolenz,
William Desmond, Francis Ford, Stuart
Holmes, Maurice Costello, Jack Richard-
son, Eddie Polo.

CLOCKWORK ORANGE, A (1971)
    Director: Stanley Kubrick
Malcolm McDowall (Alex), Patrick Ma-
gee (Mr. Alexander), James Marcus
(Georgie), Warren Clarke (Dim), Mi-
chael Tarn (Pete), Adrienne Corri (Mrs.
Alexander), Sheila Raynor (Mum), Phi-
lip Stone (Dad), Michael Bates (Chief
Guard), Miriam Karlin (Catlady), Vir-
ginia Wetherell (stage actress), John
Clive (stage actor), Margaret Tyzack,
John Savident (conspirators), Aubrey
Morris (Deltoid), Clive Francis (lodger),
Pauline Taylor (psychiatrist), Anthony
Sharp (Minister), Carl Duering (Dr. Brod-
sky), Paul Farrell (tramp), Godfrey
Quigley (prison chaplain), Michael Go-
ver (prison governor), Madge Ryan (Dr.
Branom), Cheryl Grunwald (rape girl),
John J. Carney (C. I. D. man), Carol
Drinkwater (Nurse Feeley), George
Naught (Bootick clerk), Katya Wyeth
(girl in ascot fantasy), Jan Adair, Vivi-
enne Chandler, Prudence Drage (hand-
maidens), Neil Wilson, Gillian Hills,
David Prowse, Steven Berkoff, Barrie
Cookson, Gaye Brown, Peter Burton,
Lindsay Campbell, Lee Fox, Shirley
Jaffe, Craig Hunter, Barbara Scott.

CLONE MASTER (TVM-1978) - 9-14-78
    Director: Don Medford
Art Hindle (Simon Shane), Robyn Doug-
lass (Gussie Wujek), Ralph Bellamy (Ez-
ra Louthin), John Van Dreelen (Salt),
Ed Lauter (Bender), Mario Roccuzzo
(Harry Tiezer), Stacy Keach, Sr. (Adm.
Millus), Lew Brown, Ken Sansom, Bill
Sorrells.

CLONES, THE (1974)
    Director: Paul Hunt & Lamar Card
Michael Greene (Dr. Gerald Appleby),
Stanley Adams (Carl Swafford), Gregory
Sierra (Nemo), Otis Young (Sawyer), Su-
san Hunt (Penny), Barbara Burgdorf (Ja-
net), Ray Giddeon (Fred Kalif), Walter
Robles (Sheriff), Alex Nicol (Secretary
of HEW), John Drew Barrymore (hippie),
Angelo Rossitto (man in phone booth).

CLONING OF CLIFFORD SWIMMER,
    THE (TVM-1974) - 11-1-74
    Director: Lela Swift
Peter Haskell (Clifford Swimmer), Sher-

ree North (Janet), Keene Curtis, Lance Kerwin.

CLONUS HORROR, THE (1979) (A. K. A. "Parts: The Clonus Horror")
Director: Robert S. Fiveson
Tim Donnelly (Richard), Paulette Breen (Lena), Peter Graves (Jeff Knight), Dick Sargent (Dr. Jameson), Keenan Wynn (Jake Nobel), Frank Ashmore (George Walker), David Hooks (Richard Knight), Zale Kessler (Dr. Nelson), Lurene Tuttle (Anna Noble), James Mantell (Ricky), Boyd Holister (Senator).

CLOSE ENCOUNTERS OF THE THIRD KIND (1977)
Director: Steven Spielberg
Richard Dreyfuss (Roy Neary), Melinda Dillon (Jillian Guiler), Francois Truffaut (Claude Lacombe), Teri Garr (Ronnie Neary), Bob Balaban (David Laughlin), Lance Hendricksen (Robert), Cary Guffey (Barry Guiler), Warren Kemmerling (Wild Bill), Shawn Bishop (Brad Neary), Justin Dreyfuss (Toby Neary), Adrienne Campbell (Sylvia Neary), Phillip Dodds (Jean Claude), Roberts Blossom (farmer), George Dicenzo (Major Benchley), Merrill Connally (Team leader), Bruce Davison (World War II pilot), Jim Mills.

CLOUDS OVER EUROPE (1939) (A. K. A. "Q Planes")
Director: Tim Whelan & Arthur Woods
Sir Laurence Olivier (Tony McVane), Valerie Hobson (Kay Hammond), Ralph Richardson (Major Hammond), John Longden (Peters), Franklyn Fox (Karl), George Curzon (Jenkins), Gus McNaughton (Bleekinsop), Gordon McLeod (Baron), David Tree (Mackenzie), George Butler (Air Marshall Gosport), Sandra Storme (Daphne), George Merritt (Barrett), Hay Petrie (stage door keeper).

CLUTCHING HAND, THE (1936) - serial in 15 episodes
Chapters: 1. "Who Is the Clutching Hand?", 2. "Shadow", 3. "House of Mystery", 4. "The Phantom Car", 5. "The Double Trap", 6. "Steps of Doom", 7. "The Invisible Enemy", 8. "A Cry in the Night", 9. "Evil Eyes", 10. "A Desperate Chance", 11. "The Ship of Peril", 12. "Hidden Danger", 13. "The Mystic Menace", 14. "The Silent Spectre" & 15. "The Lone Hand".
Director: Albert Herman
Jack Mulhall (Craig Kennedy), William Farnum (George Gaunt), Marion Schil-

ling (Verna Gironda), Mae Busch (Mrs. Gironda), Robert Frazier (Dr. Gironda), Reed Howes (Sullivan), Bryant Washburn (Denton), Dick Alexander (Olaf), Yakima Canutt (Number Eight), William Desmond (bartender), Ruth Mix (Shirley McMillan), Gaston Glass (Louis Bouchard), Robert Walker (Mitchell), Frank Leigh (Wickham), Franklyn Farnum (Nicky), Henry Hall (Warden), Snub Pollard (Snub), Milburne Morante (Marty), Bull Montana (sailor), Rex Larse (Walter Jameson), Mahlon Hamilton (Montgomery), Joseph W. Girard (Cromwell), Charles Locher (Hobart), Knute Erickson (Capt. Hanson), John Elliot (Mrs. White), Olin Francis (guard), Artemus Nigolian (maid), Gordon S. Griffith (Hamick), George Morrell (Jenkins), Roger Williams (Ali), Ethel Grove (Margaret), Robert Russell (Trusty), Vera Steadman (secretary), Gail Patrick, Bert Howard, William Kent, Art Howard, Eugene Burr (Board of Directors), Bob Kortman, Roy Cardona (henchmen), Rom London, George Allen, Slim Whittaker, Art Felix (sailors), John Ince, John Cowell (policemen).

COBRA STRIKES, THE (1948)
Director: Charles F. Riesner
Sheila Ryan, Richard Fraser, Leslie Brooks, James Seay, Richard Loo, Philip Ahn, George Sorel, Pat Flaherty, Leslie Dennison, Fred Nurney, Lyle Latell, Herbert Heyes.

COBRA WOMAN (1944)
Director: Robert Siodmak
Maria Montez (Tollea/Nadja), Jon Hall (Ramu), Lon Chaney, Jr. (Hava), Sabu (Kado), Edgar Barrier (Martok), Lois Collier (Veeda), Samuel S. Hinds (Father Paul), Mary Nash (the Queen), Moroni Olsen (MacDonald), Fritz Leiber (Venreau), Eddie Parker, Dale Van Sickel, George Magrill (guards), Robert Barron (Chief Guard), Carmen D'Antonio (dancer), John Bagni (native), Belle Mitchell (native woman), Vivian Austin, Paulita Arvizu, Beth Dean (handmaidens).

COCKEYED MIRACLE, THE (1946)
Director: S. Sylvan Simon
Frank Morgan (Sam Griggs), Keenan Wynn (Ben Griggs), Richard Quine (Howard Bankson), Cecil Kellaway (Tom Carter), Audrey Totter (Jennifer Griggs), Marshall Thompson (Jim Griggs), Gladys Cooper (Amy Griggs), Leon Ames (Ralph Humphrey), Arthur Space (Amos Spellman), Morris Ankrum (Dr. Wilson), Jane Green (Mrs. Lynne).

CODE OF THE AIR (1928)
Director: James P. Hogan
Kenneth Harlan (Blair Thompson), Edna Mae Cooper (Mrs. Carson), William V. Mong (Prof. Ross), Paul Wiegel (Doc Carson), James Bradbury, Jr. (Stuttering Slim), Arthur Rankin (Alfred Clark), June Marlow (Helen Carson).

COLD BLOODED BEAST, THE (1972-Ital.) (A.K.A. "La Bestia Uccide a Sangue Freddo", "The Beast Kills in Cold Blood", "Slaughter Hotel", "Asylum Erotica")
Director: Fernando Di Leo
Klaus Kinski, Margaret Lee, John Karlsen, Rosalba Neri, Monica Sterbel, Jane Garret, John Ely, Sandro Rossi, Gloria Desideri, Fernando Cerulli.

COLD NIGHT'S DEATH, A (TVM-1973) - 1-30-73
Director: Jerrold Freedman
Robert Culp (Dr. Robert James), Eli Wallach (Dr. Frank Enari), Michael C. Gwynne (Val Adams), James McEachin (Ryan Horner).

COLD SUN, THE (1954)
see Television: Rocky Jones, Space Ranger (1953-54).

COLLECTOR, THE (1965)
Director: William Wyler
Terence Stamp (Freddie Clegg), Samantha Eggar (Miranda Grey), Mona Washbourne (Aunt Annie), Maurice Dallimore (neighbor).

COLONEL BOGEY (1947)
Director: Terence Fisher
Mary Jerrold (Aunt Mabel), June Barrett (Alice Graham), Jack Stone (Wilfred Barriteau), Ethel Coleridge (Emily), Hedli Anderson (Millicent), Jack Train (voice of Uncle James), Sam Kydd.

COLOR ME BLOOD RED (1964)
Director: Herschell Gordon Lewis
Don Joseph, Candi Conder, Elyn Warner, Scott H. Hall, Jerome Eden, Patricia Lee, Jim Jaekel.

COLOSSUS AND THE AMAZONS (1960-Ital.) (A.K.A. "La Regina delle Amazzoni", "The Queen of the Amazons")
Director: Vittorio Sala
Gianna Maria Canale, Ed Fury, Rod Taylor, Daniella Rocca, Dorian Gray.

COLOSSUS AND THE HEADHUNTERS (1962-Ital.) (A.K.A. "Maciste contro i Cacciatori di Teste")

Director: Guido Malatesta
Kirk Morris, Laura Brown, Frank Leroy, Alfredo Zammi, Demeter Bitenc.

COLOSSUS OF NEW YORK, THE (1958)
Director: Eugene Lourie
John Baragrey (Dr. Henry Spensser), Otto Kruger (Dr. William Spensser), Mala Powers (Anne Spensser), Ross Martin (Dr. Jeremy Spensser), Charles Herbert (Billy Spensser), Robert Hutton (Prof. John Carrington), Ed Wolff (Colossus).

COMA (1978)
Director: Michael Crichton
Genevieve Bujold (Dr. Susan Wheeler), Micahel Douglas (Dr. Mark Bellows), Richard Widmark (Dr. George Harris), Elizabeth Ashley (Mrs. Emerson), Rip Torn (Dr. George), Lois Chiles (Nancy Greenly), Hari Rhodes (Dr. Morelind), Tom Selleck (Sean Murphy), Lance Le-Gault (Vince), Richard Doyle (Jim), Charles Siebert (Dr. Goodman), Gary Barton (computer technician), Alan Haufrect (Dr. Marcus), Michael MacRae (Chief Resident), Betty McGuire (nurse), William Wintersole (lab technician).

COMEBACK, THE (1979)
Director: Pete Walker
Jack Jones (Nick), David Doyle (Webster), Pamela Stephenson (Linda), Bill Owen (Mr. B), Peter Turner (Harry), Holly Palance (Gail), Richard Johnson (Macauley), Patrick Brock, Penny Irving, Sheila Keith, June Chadwick, Jeff Silk.

COMEDY OF TERRORS, THE (1963)
Director: Jacques Tourneur
Vincent Price (Waldo Trumbull), Peter Lorre (Felix Gillie), Boris Karloff (Amos Hinchley), Basil Rathbone (John F. Black), Joyce Jameson (Amaryllis Trumbull), Joe E. Brown (Cemetary Keeper), Beverly Hills (Mrs. Phipps), Paul Barsolow (Riggs), Linda Rogers (Phipp's maid), Buddy Mason (Mr. Phipps), Luree Nicholson (Black's servant).

COMET'S COME BACK, THE (1916)
Director:
John Steppling (Prof. Peedeegue), John Sheehan (Fuller Speed), Carol Halloway (Claire), Dick Rosson (Hess E. Tate).

COMING, THE (1980)
Director: Bert I. Gordon
Susan Swift (Loreen Graham/Ann Putnam), Guy Stockwell (William Goode), Laureen Downing (Sarah Goode), John Peters (Reverend Parris), Jennine Babo (Dor-

cas Goode), Beverley Ross (Merlina).

COMIN' ROUND THE MOUNTAIN (1951)
Director: Charles Lamont
Bud Abbott (Al Stewart), Lou Costello
(Wilbert), Kirby Grant (Clark Winfield),
Joe Sawyer (Kalen McCoy), Dorothy
Shay (Dorothy McCoy), Glenn Strange
(Devil Dan Winfield), Margaret Hamilton (the Witch), Ida Moore (Granny Mc-
Coy), Shay Cogan (Clora McCoy), Guy
Wilkerson, Russell Simpson, Jack Kruschen, Norman Leavitt, Joe Kirk, Robert Easton, Hank Wordern, O. Z. Whitehead, Peter Mamakos, Slats Taylor,
Dean White, Harold Goodwin, Stanley
Waxman, William Fawcett, Jane Lee.

COMMANDO CODY (1953)
Director: Fred C. Brannon, Harry Keller & Franklin Adreon
Judd Holdren (Jeff King/Commando Cody), Aline Towne (Joan), Gregory Gaye
(Retik), Peter Brocco (Dr. Varney),
William Schallert (Ted Richards), Craig
Kelly (Henderson), Lyle Talbot, Coleman Francis.

COMPUTERCIDE (TVM-1982) (A. K. A.
"The Final Eye") - 8-1-82
Director: Robert Michael Lewis
Joseph Cortese (Michael Stringer), Susan George (Lisa Korter), Donald Pleasence (Dettler), David Huddleston (Sorenson), Tom Clancy (Hanrahan), Liam
Sullivan (Emery Korter), Roger Cudney
(Robbins), Peter Brandon (Kennison),
Carl Bellanger (security chief), Richard
Noriega (host), Elizabeth Wallace (hostess), William Benedict (elderly man),
Edgar Justice (store owner), Sue Palmer (lady artist), Linda Gillin (librarian), Rod Haase (1st cop), Brian Baker (2nd cop), Shelley Hoffman (intern),
Alan Conrad (gate guard), Raye Sheffield (1st reporter), Robert Power (2nd
reporter), J. D. Hall (3rd reporter),
Joseph Chapman (lab operator).

COMPUTER WORE TENNIS SHOES,
THE (1969)
Director: Robert Butler
Kurt Russell (Dexter Riley), Cesar Romero (A. J. Arno), Joe Flynn (Dean Higgins), William Schallert (Prof. Quigley),
Fritz Feld (Sigmund Van Dyke), Pat Harrington, Jr. (moderator), Bing Russell
(Angelo), Richard Bakalyan (Chillie
Walsh), Alan Hewitt (Dean Collingsgood),
Frank Webb (Pete), Jon Provost (Bradley), Alexander Clarke (Myles), Pete
Renoudet (Lt. Hannah), Michael Mc-
Greevey (Schuyler), Debbie Paine (An-

nie), Frank Welker (Henry), Fabian
Dean (Little Mac), Hillyard Anderson
(J. Reedy), Heather Menzies (girl).

CONAN THE BARBARIAN (1982)
Director: John Milius
Arnold Schwarzenegger (Conan), James
Earl Jones (Thulsa Doom), Sandahl Bergman (Valeria), Max von Sydow (King Osric), Gerry Lopez (Subotai), Ben Davidson (Rexor), Frank McRae (Yaro), Mako
(Wizard), Cassandra Gaviola (Witch),
Valerie Quennessen (Princess), William
Smith (Conan's father), Nadluska (Conan's
mother), Luis Barboo (Red Hair), Franco Columbo (Pictish scout), Leslie Foldvary (sacrificial snake girl), Gary Herman (Osric's guard), Erick Holmey
(Turanian War Officer), Akio Mitamura
(Mongol General), Jack Taylor (Priest),
Jorge Sanz (young Conan), Sven Ole
Thorsen (Thorgrim), Kiyoshi Yamasaki
(Swordmaster).

CONDEMNED MEN (1940)
Director: William Beaudine
Mantan Moreland, Dorothy Dandridge,
Niel Webster.

CONDEMNED TO DEATH (1932)
Director: Walter Forde
Edmund Gwenn (Banting), Gillian Lind
(Kate Banting), Arthur Wontner (Sir
Charles Wallington), Norah Howard
(Gwen), Gordon Harker (Sam Knudge),
Jane Welsh (Sonia Wallington), Cyril
Raymond (Jim Wrench), Griffith Humphreys (Prof. Michels), Gordon Blythe
(Nali), Gilbert Davies (Dr. Cornell),
Bernard Bruneel (Tobias O'Latern),
James Cunningham (Insp. Sweeting), H.
St. Barbe West (Sir R. Cantier, K. C.).

CONDEMNED TO LIVE (1935)
Director: Frank R. Strayer
Ralph Morgan (Paul Kristan), Maxine
Doyle (Marguerite Mane), Mischa Auer
(Zan), Russell Gleason (David), Pedro
de Cordoba (Dr. Anders Bizet), Carl
Stockdale (John Mane), Edward Cecil
(manservant), Robert Frazer (doctor),
Paul Weigel (old doctor), Hedi Shope (Anna), Lucy Beaumont (Mother Molly), Ted
Billings (bell ringer), Marilyn Knowlden
(Maria), Dick Curtis, Harold Goodwin,
Charles 'Slim' Whittaker, Frank Brownlee, Horace B. Carpenter (villagers),
Barbara Bedford (woman), Ferdinand
Schumann-Heinck (father).

CONDORMAN (1981)
Director: Charles Jarrott
Michael Crawford (Willy Wilkins), Oliver

Reed (Krokov), Barbara Carrera (Natalia), James Hampton (Harry), Dana Elcar (Russ), Vernon Dobtcheff (Russian Agent), Jean-Pierre Kalfon (Morovich), Robert Arden (CIA Chief).

CONFESSIONAL, THE (1975) (A. K. A. "House of Mortal Sin")
    Director: Pete Walker
Susan Penhaligon (Jenny), Anthony Sharp (Meldrum), Stephanie Beacham (Vanessa), Hilda Barry (Mrs. Meldrum), Norman Eshley (Bernard), Sheila Keith (Miss Brabazon), Stewart Beven (Terry), Julia McCarthy (Mrs. Davey), Mervyn Johns (Father Duggan), Jon Yule (Robert), Kim Butcher (Valerie), Victor Winding (Dr. Gaudio), Bill Kerr (Davey), Ivor Salter (gravedigger), Jack Allen, Andrew Sachs, Melinda Clancy, Jane Hayward, Austin King.

CONFESSIONS OF AN OPIUM EATER (1962) (A. K. A. "Evils of Chinatown")
    Director: Albert Zugsmith
Vincent Price (Gil De Quincey), Linda Ho (Ruby Low), Richard Loo (George Wah), June Kim (Lotus), Philip Ahn (Ching Foon), Victor Sen Yung (Wing Young), Caroline Kido (Lo Tsen), Miel Saan (Look Gow), Terence De Marney (scrawney man), Gerald Jann (fat Chinese), Joanne Miya (1st dancing girl), Keiko (2nd dancing girl), Geri Hoo (3rd dancing girl), Yvonne Moray (child), Arthur Wong (Kwai Tong), Ralph Ahn (Wah Chan), Alicia Li (Ping Toy), John Mamo (auctioneer).

CONGRESS OF LOVE, THE (1966-Ger./ U. S.) (A. K. A. "Der Kongress Amuesiert Sich")
    Director: Geza von Radvanyl
Lilli Palmer, Curt Jurgens, Walter Slezak, Paul Meurisse, Brett Halsey, Anita Hoefer, Hannes Messemer.

CONNECTICUT YANKEE, A (1931)
    Director: David Butler
Will Rogers (Hank/Sir Boss), Maureen O'Sullivan (Alisande), Myrna Loy (Queen Morgan Le Fay), William Farnum (King Arthur), Frank Albertson (Clarence), Brandon Hurst (Sagramor), Mitchell Harris (Merlin).

CONNECTICUT YANKEE AT KING ARTHUR'S COURT, THE (1920)
    Director: Emmett J. Flynn
Harry C. Myers (the Yankee), Pauline Starke (Sandy), Charles Clary (King Arthur), Rosemary Theby (Queen Morgan La Fay), Charles Gordon (Clarence),

Wilfred McDonald (Sir Launcelot), George Siegmann (Sir Sagamore), William V. Mong, Louise Lovely.

CONNECTICUT YANKEE IN KING ARTHUR'S COURT, A (1948)
    Director: Tay Garnett
Bing Crosby (Hank Martin), Rhonda Fleming (Alisande LaCarteloise), Sir Cedric Hardwicke (King Arthur), William Bendix (Sir Sagramore), Murvyn Vye (Merlin), Virginia Field (Morgan LeFay), Henry Wilcoxon (Sir Lancelot), Richard Webb (Sir Galahad), Joseph Vitale (Sir Logris), Julia Faye (Lady Penelope), Alan Napier (High Executioner).

CONQUEROR OF ATLANTIS, THE (1965-Ital./Egypt). (A. K. A. "Il Conquestadore dell'Atlantida", "Kingdom in the Sand")
    Director: Alfonso Brescia
Kirk Morris, Helen Chanel, Piero Lulli, Andrea Scotti, Luciana Gilli, Mahmud El Sabba.

CONQUEROR WORM, THE (1968) (A. K. A. "The Witchfinder General")
    Director: Michael Reeves
Vincent Price (Matthew Hopkins), Ian Ogilvy (Richard Marshall), Hilary Dwyer (Sara), Rupert Davies (John Lowes), Robert Russell (John Stearne), Patrick Wymark (Oliver Cromwell), Wilfred Brambell (Master Loach), Nicky Henson (Swallow), Michael Beint (Capt. Gordon), William Maxwell (Gifford), Maggie Kimberley (Elizabeth), John Trenaman (Harcourt), Tony Selby (Salter), Hira Talfrey (hanged woman), Bernard Kay (fisherman), Beaufoy Milton (priest), John Kidd (1st Magistrate), Peter Haigh (2nd Magistrate).

CONQUEST OF MYCENE (1963-Ital./ Fr.) (A. K. A. "Ercole Contro Molock", "Hercules Against Moloch")
    Director: Giorgio Ferroni
Gordon Scott, Rosalba Neri, Alessandra Panaro, Genevieve Grad.

CONQUEST OF SPACE, THE (1955)
    Director: Byron Haskin
Eric Felming (Barney Merritt), Walter Brooke (Samuel Merritt), Micky Shaughnessy (Mahoney), Ross Martin (Fodor), Phil Foster (Siegle), William Hopper (Fenton), William Redfield (Cooper), Benson Fong (Imoto), Vito Scotti (Sanella), Michael Fox (Elsbach), Iphigenie Castiglioni (Mrs. Fodor), John Dennis (Donkersgoed), Joan Shawlee (Rosie).

CONQUEST OF THE PLANET OF THE
APES (1972)
Director: J. Lee Thompson
Roddy McDowall (Milo/Caesar), Don
Murray (Governor Breck), Ricardo
Montalban (Armando), Hari Rhodes
(MacDonald), Natalie Trundy (Lisa),
Severn Darden (Kolp), H. M. Wynant
(Hoskyns), Lou Wagner (busboy), John
Randolph (Commission Chairman), Paul
Comi, John Dennis (policeman), Buck
Kartalian (Frank, the gorilla), Hector
Soucy (ape with chain), Gordon Jump
(auctioneer), Dick Spangler (announcer),
Asa Maynor (Mrs. Riley), Joyce Haber
(Zelda).

CONQUEST OF THE MOON (1960-Mex.)
(A. K. A. "Conquistador de la Luna")
Director: Rogelio A. Gonzalez
Andres Soler, Ana Luisa Peluffo, Os-
car Ortiz de la Pinedo, Clavillazo.

CONQUEST OF THE POLE, THE (1912-
Fr.) (A. K. A. "A la Conquete du
Pole")
Director: George Melies

CONSPIRACY OF TERROR (TVM-1975) -
4-10-75
Director: John Llewellyn Moxey
Michael Constantine (Jacob Horowitz),
Barbara Rhoades (Helen Horowitz), Da-
vid Opatoshu (Arthur Horowitz), Arlene
Martel (Leslie Horowitz), Jon Lormer
(Slate), Roger Perry (Fred Warnall),
Mariclare Costello (Mrs. Warnall), Lo-
gan Ramsey (Dale), Jed Allan (David
Horowitz), Stewart Moss (Rabbi), Eric
Olson (Roger Gordon), Norman Burton
(Lt. Rossos), Ken Sansom, Paul Smith,
Bruce Kirby, Paul Bryar, Beverly
Bremers, Murray McLeod, Judi Stein,
John Finnegan, Anthony Aiello, Charles
Cooper, Shelly Morrison, Bob Golden.

CONTAMINATION (1980-Ital.) (A. K. A.
"Alien Contamination", "Alien on
Earth")
Director: Luigi Cozzi
Ian McCulloch, Louise Marleau, Mari-
no Mase, Siegfried Rauch.

COPS AND ROBIN (TVM-1978) - 3-28-
78
Director: Allen Reisner
Ernest Borgnine (Joe Cleaver), John
Amos (Bill Bundy), Michael Shannon
(John Haven), Natasha Ryan (Robin Lo-
ren), Carol Lynley (Dr. Alice Alcott),
Terry Kiser (Wayne Dutton), Philip
Abbott (District Attorney Garfield),
Richard Bright (Richards), Jeff Davi-

dy (Jim Loren), Gene Rutherford (Carl
Tyler), James York (Richard), Walter
Costello (Dutton's lawyer), Ivan Bonnar
(Judge Wheeler), J. Kenneth Campbell
(Detective Furie).

CORPSE GRINDERS, THE (1971)
Director: Ted V. Mikels
Sean Kenney (Dr. Howard Glass), Moni-
ca Kelly (Angie Robinson), Sanford Mit-
chell (Landau), J. Byron Foster (Malt-
by), Vince Barbi (Monk), Warren Ball
(Caleb), Ann Noble (Cleo), Earl Burnam
(Mr. De Sisto), Ray Dannis (Mr. Bab-
cock), Zena Foster (Mrs. Babcock),
Harry Lovejoy (the Neighbor), Drucilla
Joy (Tessie), Charles Fox (Willie), Curt
Matson (Paul, the stranger), Stephen
Lester (the mortician), William Kirsch-
ner (B. K.), George Bowden (David, the
intern), Andy Collings (De Sisto's sec-
retary), Mike Garrison (assistant to De
Sisto), Don Ellis (factory workman),
Mary Ellen Burke (Annie).

CORPSE VANISHES, THE (1942) (A. K. A.
"The Case of the Missing Brides")
Director: Wallace Fox
Bela Lugosi (Prof. Lorenz), Tris Cof-
fin (Dr. Foster), Luana Walters (Patri-
cia Hunter), Vince Barnett (Sandy), Eli-
zabeth Russell (the Countess), Minerva
Urecal (Fagah), Angelo Rossitto, George
Eldredge, Kenneth Harlan, Joan Barclay,
Gwen Kenyon, Frank Moran, Gladys
Faye.

CORRIDOR OF MIRRORS (1948)
Director: Terence Young
Eric Portman (Paul Mangin), Edina Ro-
nay (Milfanway Conway), Joan Maude (Ca-
roline Hart), Barbara Mullen (Veronica),
Alan Wheatley (Edgar Orsen), Hugh Lati-
mer (Bing), Christopher Lee (Charles),
Lois Maxwell (Imogene), Valentine Dy-
all (Counsel for the Defense), Thora Hird
(old woman), Leslie Weston (Mortimer),
Bruce Belfrage (Sir David Conway), Hugh
Sinclair (Owen Rhys), John Penrose
(Brandy), Mavis Villiers (Babs), Gordon
MacLeod (Public Prosecutor), Noel How-
lett (psychiatrist).

CORRIDORS OF BLOOD (1958) (A. K. A.
"The Doctor from Seven Dials")
Director: Robert Day
Boris Karloff (Dr. Bolton), Betta St.
John (Susan), Francis Matthews (Jona-
than), Francis DeWolff (Black Ben), Ad-
rienne Corri (Rachel), Christopher Lee
(Resurrection Joe), Finlay Currie (Mathe-
son), Frank Pettingell (Blount), Nigel
Green (Insp. Donovan), Charles Lloyd-

Pack (Hardcastle), Marian Spencer (Mrs. Matheson), Basil Dignam (Chairman), Carl Bernard (Ned the Crow), Yvonne Warren (Rosa), Robert Raglan (Wilkes), Howard Lang (Chief Inspector), John Gabriel (dispenser), Julian D'Albie (bald man), Roddy Hughes (man with watch).

CORRUPTION (1967)
Director: Robert Hartford-Davis
Peter Cushing (Sir John Rowan), Sue Lloyd (Lynn Nolan), Kate O'Mara (Val Nolan), Noel Trevarthen (Dr. Stephen Harris), David Lodge (Groper), Vanessa Howard (Kate), Wendy Vernals (Terry), Anthony Booth (Mike Orme), Billy Murray (Rik), Jan Waters (girl in flat), Alexandra Dane (Sandy), Phillip Manikum (Georgie), Valerie Van Ost (girl on train), Diana Ashley (Claire), Shirley Stelfox (girl at party), Victor Baring (mortuary attendant).

CORRPUTION OF CHRIS MILLER, THE (1973-Span.) (A. K. A. "La Corruptions de Chris Miller", "Sisters of Corruption")
Director: Juan Antonio Bardem
Jean Seberg, Barry Stokes, Gerard Tichy, Marisol, Perla Cristal.

CORSICAN BROTHERS, THE (1941)
Director: Gregory Ratoff
Douglas Fairbanks, Jr. (Mario/Lucien), Ruth Warrick (Isabelle), Akim Tamiroff (Colonna), J. Carrol Naish (Lorenzo), H. B. Warner (Dr. Paoli), John Emery (Tomasso), Henry Wilcoxon (Count Franchi), Gloria Holden (Countess Franchi), Walter Kingsford (M. Dupre), Nana Bryant (Mme. Dupre), Pedro de Cordoba (Gravina), Veda Ann Borg (Maria), William Farnum (priest).

CORSICAN BROTHERS, THE (1961-Ital./Fr.) (A. K. A. "I Fratelli Corsi")
Director: Anton Giulio Magano
Geoffrey Horne, Jean Servais, Valerie Lagrange, Gerard Barray.

COSMIC MAN, THE (1959)
Director: Herbert Greene
Bruce Bennett (Dr. Karl Sorenson), John Carradine (the Cosmic Man), Angela Greene (Kathy Grant), Paul Langton (Col. Mathews), Lyn Osborn (Sgt. Gray), Scotty Morrow (Ken Grant), Walter Maslow (Dr. Richie), Herbert Lytton (Gen. Knowland).

COSMIC MONSTER, THE (1958) (A. K. A. "The Strange World of Planet X",

"The Crawling Terror", "Cosmic Monsters")
Director: Gilbert Gunn
Forrest Tucker (Gil Graham), Martin Benson (Smith), Gabe Andre (Michele Dupont), Alec Mango (Dr. Laird), Hugh Latimer (Jimmy Murray), Geoffrey Chater (Gerald Wilson), Wyndham Goldie (Brig. Cartwright), Patricia Sinclair (Helen Forsyth), Catherine Lancaster (Gillian Betts), Hilda Fenemore (Mrs. Hale), Richard Warner (Insp. Burns), Susan Redway (Jane Hale), Neil Wilson (P. C. Tidy).

COSMOS - WAR OF THE PLANETS (1977-Ital.) (A. K. A. "Cosmo 2000 - L'Invasion Degli Extracorpi")
Director: Alfonso Brescia/Al Bradley
John Richardson, Yanti Somer, Vasilli Kramensis, Gisella Hahn, W. Buchanan.

COUNTDOWN (1967)
Director: Robert Altman
James Caan (Lee Stegler), Joanna Moore (Mickey Stegler), James Duvall (Chiz), Charles Aidman (Gus), Steve Ihnat (Ross), Michael Murphy (Rick), Barbara Baxley (Jean), Ted Knight (Larson), John Rayner (Dunc), Stephen Coit (Ehrman), Charles Irving (Seidel), Bobby Riha, Jr. (Stevie).

COUNT DRACULA (1970-Span./Ital./Ger./Brit.) (A. K. A. "El Conde Dracula")
Director: Jesus Franco
Christopher Lee (Count Dracula), Herbert Lom (Dr. Van Helsing), Klaus Kinski (Renfield), Maria Rohm (Mina Harker), Soledad Miranda (Lucy Westenra), Frederick Williams (Jonathan Harker), Jack Taylor (Dr. Seward), Paul Muller, Teresa Gimpera, Quincey Morris.

COUNT DRACULA (TVM-1978)
Director: Philip Seville
Louis Jourdan (Count Dracula), Frank Finlay (Prof. Van Helsing), Susan Penhaligon (Lucy Westenra), Judi Bowker (Mina Westenra), Mark Burns (Dr. John Seward), Bosco Hogan (Jonathan Harker), Jack Shepherd (Renfield), Ann Queensbury (Mrs. Westenra), Sue Vanner, Belinda Meulddjk, Susie Hickford (vampires), Michael MacOwan (Mr. Hawkins), Richard Barnes (Quincy P. Holmwood).

COUNTERBLAST (1948)
Director: Paul L. Stein
Robert Beatty (Dr. Rankin), Mervyn Johns (Dr. Bruckner), Nova Pilbeam

(Tracy Shaw), Margaretta Scott (Sister Johnson), Karel Stepanek (Prof. Inman), Alan Wheatley (Kennedy), Karl Jaffe (Heinz), Gladys Henson (Mrs. Plum), Ronald Adam (Col. Ingram), Martin Miller (seaman), Marie Lohr (Mrs. Coles), Antony Eustral (Dr. Forrester), John Salew (Pedro), Syvilla Binder (Martha), Aubrey Mallalieu (Maj. Walsh), Horace Kennedy (taxi driver).

COUNTESS DRACULA (1970)
    Director: Peter Sasdy
Ingrid Pitt (Countess Elizabeth), Nigel Green (Captain Dobi), Maurice Denham (Master Fabio), Lesley Anne Down (Ilona), Sandor Eles (Imre Toth), Patience Collier (Julie), Peter Jeffrey (Captain Balogh), Marianne Stone (kitchen maid), Leon Lissek (bailiff sergeant), Nike Arrighi (gypsy), Jessie Evans (Rosa), Ian Trigger (clown), Joan Haythorne (cook), Charles Farrell (the seller), Anne Stallybrass (pregnant woman), Susan Brodrick (Teri), Peter May (Janco), Andrea Lawrence (Ziza), John Moore (priest), Sally Adcock (Bertha), Paddy Ryan (man), Michael Cadman (young man), Hulya Babus (belly dancer), Leslie Anderson, Diana Sawday, Bippy Hearne (gypsy dancers), Gary Rich, Andrew Burleigh (boys), Ismed Hassan, Albert Wilkinson (circus midgets).

COUNTRY WITHOUT STARS, THE (1945-Fr.) (A. K. A. "Le Pays san Etoiles")
    Director: Georges Lacombe
Pierre Brasseur, Jany Holt, Gerard Philippe.

COUNT YORGA, VAMPIRE (1970)
    Director: Bob Kelljan
Robert Quarry (Count Yorga), Roger Perry (Dr. Hayes), Michael Murphy (Paul), Donna Anders (Donna), Judith Lang (Erica), Edward Walsh (Brudah), Michael Macready (Michael), Paul Hansen (Peter), Julie Conners (Cleo), Sybil Scotford (Judy), Deborah Darnell (vampire), Marsha Jordan (mother), Erica Macready (nurse).

CRACK IN THE WORLD (1965)
    Director: Andrew Marton
Dana Andrews (Dr. Stephen Sorensen), Kieron Moore (Ted Rampion), Janette Scott (Maggie Sorensen), Alexander Knox (Sir Charles Eggerston), Peter Damon (Masefield), Gary Lasdun (Markov), Todd Martin (Simpson), Mike Steen (Steele), Jim Gillen (Rand).

CRASH! (1977)

Director: Charles Band
Jose Ferrer (Mark), Sue Lyon (Kim), John Ericson (Greg), Leslie Parrish (Kathy), John Carradine (Dr. Edwards), Jerome Guardino (Lt. Pegler).

CRASHING LAS VEGAS (1956)
    Director: Jean Yarbrough
Leo Gorcey (Slip Mahoney), Huntz Hall (Sach Debussy Jones), David Condon (Chuck), Don Haggerty, Terry Frost, Minerva Urecal, Mort Mills, Jimmy Murphy, Mary Castle, Nicky Blair, Jack Rice.

CRASH OF MOONS (1954)
    see Television: Rocky Jones, Space Ranger (1953-54).

CRATER LAKE MONSTER, THE (1977)
    Director: William R. Stromberg
Glenn Roberts (Arnie), Mark Siegel (Mitch), Kacey Cobb (Susan), Richard Cardella (Steve), Richard Harrison (Dan), Bob Hyman (Doc), Hal Scharm (birdwatcher).

CRAWLING EYE, THE (1958) (A. K. A. "The Trollenberg Terror")
    Director: Quentin Lawrence
Forrest Tucker (Alan Brooks), Janet Munro (Anne Pilgrim), Jennifer Jayne (Sarah Pilgrim), Laurence Payne (Philip Truscott), Warren Mitchell (Crevett), Andrew Faulds (Brett), Stuart Saunders (Dewhurst), Derek Sydney (Wilde), Colin Douglas (Hans), Frederick Schiller (Klein), Garard Green (pilot), Theodore Wilhelm (Fritz), Caroline Glazer (child), Leslie Heritage (Carl), George Herbert, Richard Golding, Anne Sharpe (villagers), Jeremy Longhurst, Anthony Parker (student climbers).

CRAWLING HAND, THE (1963)
    Director: Herbert L. Strock
Rod Lauren (Paul Lawrence), Sirry Steffen (Marta Farnstrom), Peter Breck (Steve Curan), Kent Taylor (Doc Weitzberg), Alan Hale, Jr. (Sheriff), Arline Judge (Mrs. Hotchkiss), Allison Hayes (Donna), Richard Arlen, Tris Coffin, Syd Sayler, Ross Elliott.

CRAZE (1974)
    Director: Freddie Francis
Jack Palance (Neal Mottram), Diana Dors (Dolly Newman), Julie Ege (Helena), Edith Evans (Aunt Louise), Trevor Howard (Superintendant Bellamy), Michael Jayston (Sgt. Wall), Martin Potter (Ronnie), Frank Forsyth (Frank Trainor), Suzy Kendall (Sally), Hugh Griffith (solicitor), Marianne Stone.

CRAZIES, THE (1972) (A. K. A. "Code
Name: Trixie")
Director: George Romero
Lane Carroll (Judy), Lynn Lowry (Kath-
ie), W. G. McMillan (David), Lloyd Hol-
lar (Col. Peckem), Richard Liberty
(Artie), Harold Wayne Jones (Clank),
Richard France (Dr. Watts), Harry
Spillman (Major Ryder), Will Disney
(Dr. Brookmyre), Leland Starnes (Shel-
by), Robert J. McCully (Hawks), A. C.
MacDonald (Gen. Bowden), W. L. Than-
hurst, Jr. (Brubaker), Edith Bell (wo-
man lab technician), Robert Karlowsky
(Sheriff).

CRAZY KNIGHTS (1944) (A. K. A. "Ghost
Crazy")
Director: William Beaudine
Billy Gilbert, Shemp Howard, Maxie
Rosenbloom, Minerva Urecal, John
Hamilton, Jayne Hazard, Art Miles,
Tim Ryan, Bernie Sell.

CRAZY RAY, THE (1923-Fr.) (A. K. A.
"Paris Qui Dort", "Paris Asleep",
"Le Rayon Invisible", "The Invisible
Ray")
Director: Rene Clair
Albert Prejean, Henri Rollan, Marcel
Vallee, Madeleine Rodrique, Charles
Martinelli.

CREATION OF THE HUMANOIDS, THE
(1962)
Director: Wesley E. Barry
Don Megowan (Cragis), Don Doolittle
(Dr. Raven), Erika Elliot (Maxine),
Frances McCann (Esme), David Cross
(Pax), Richard Vath (Mark), Malcolm
Smith (Court), George Milan (Acto),
Dudley Manlove (Logan), Reid Ham-
mond (Hart), Gil Frye (Orus), Pat Brad-
ley (Moffitt), William Hunter (Ward),
Paul Sheriff (cop), Alton Tabor (volun-
teer).

CREATURE FROM BLACK LAKE, THE
(1976)
Director: Joy Houck, Jr.
Jack Elam (Joe Canton), Dub Taylor
(Grandpa Bridges), John David Carson
(Rives), Dennis Fimple (Pahoo), Bill
Thurman (Sheriff Billy Carter), Becky
Smiser (Becky Carter), Roy Tatum
(Fred/the Creature), Michelle Willing-
ham (Michelle), Jim McCullough, Jr.
(Orville Bridges), Evelyn Hindricks
(Mrs. Bridges), Roger Pancake (H. B.),
Karen Brooks (Orville's mother), Chase
Tatum (little Orville), Bob Kyle (Ru-
fus), Catherine McClenny (waitress),
J. N. Houck, Jr. (Dr. Burch).

CREATURE FROM THE BLACK LAGOON,
THE (1954)
Director: Jack Arnold
Richard Carlson (David Reed), Julia Ad-
ams (Kay Lawrence), Richard Denning
(Mark Williams), Antonio Moreno (Carl
Maia), Whit Bissell (Edwin Thompson),
Nestor Paiva (Lucas), Rodd Redwing (Lou-
is), Ben Chapman (Creature on land),
Ricou Browning (Creature in water), Har-
ry Escalante (Chico), Bernie Gozier (Zee),
Julio Lopez (Tomas), Sidney Mason (Dr.
Matos).

CREATURE FROM THE HAUNTED SEA
(1961)
Director: Roger Corman
Anthony Carbone (Renzo Capeto), Betsy
Jones-Moreland (Mary-Belle), Edmundo
Rivera Alvarez (Col. Tostada), Edward
Wain (Sparks Moran), Robert Bean (Jack),
Sonya Noemi (Mango), Beech Dickerson
(Pete Peterson, Jr.).

CREATURE OF DESTRUCTION (1967)
Director: Larry Buchanan
Aron Kincaid (Capt. Theodore Dell), Les
Tremayne (Dr. John Basso), Pat Delaney
(Dorina), Neil Fletcher (Sam Crain), Ann
McAdams (Lynn Crain), Scotty McKay,
Suzanne Ray, Ron Scott, Byron Lord, Ro-
ger Ready, Barnett Shaw.

CREATURE OF THE WALKING DEAD
(1965-Mex. /U. S.)
Director: Frederic Corte
Rock Madison, Ann Wells, Katherine Vic-
tor, Bruno VeSota, George Todd, Willard
Gross, Fernando Casanova, Sonia Furio.

CREATURES, THE (1966-Fr. /Swed.)
(A. K. A. "Les Creatures")
Director: Agnes Varda
Catherine Deneuve (wife), Michel Piccoli
(writer), Eva Dahlbeck (hotel owner), Nino Castelnuovo (electrician), Ursula Kub-
ler (vamp), Jacques Charrier (young man).

CREATURES THE WORLD FORGOT, THE
(1970)
Director: Don Chaffey
Julie Ege (Nala), Robert John (Rool), To-
ny Bonner (Toomak), Brian O'Shaughnes-
sy (Mak), Rosalie Crutchley, Sue Wilson,
Gerard Bonthuys, Jusje Kiesouw, Marcia
Fox.

CREATURE WALKS AMONG US, THE
(1956)
Director: John Sherwood
Jeff Morrow (Dr. William Barton), Rex
Reason (Dr. Thomas Morgan), Leigh Snow-
den (Marcia Barton), Gregg Palmer (Jed

Grant), James Rawley (Dr. Johnson), Maurice Manson (Dr. Borg), Don Megoway (Creature on land), Ricou Browning (Creature in water), Frank Chase (steward), Larry Hudson (state trooper), Lillian Molieri (Mrs. Morteno), Paul Fierro (Morteno), David McMahon (Capt. Stanley).

CREATURE WASN'T NICE, THE (1981)
Director: Bruce Kimmel
Cindy Williams (McHugh), Patrick Mac-Nee (Stark), Leslie Nielsen (Jameson), Gerrit Graham (Rodzinski), Bruce Kimmel (John), Ron Kurowski (the Creature), Paul Brinegar (Dirty Harry), Jed Mills, Kenneth Tobey, Sheri Eichen, Alan Abalew, Ron Burke, Jeffrey Ward, Carol Ann Williams, Margaret Willock, Robert Dryer, Peter DuPre.

CREATURE WITH THE ATOM BRAIN (1955)
Director: Edward L. Cahn
Richard Denning (Dr. Chet Walker), Angela Stevens (Joyce Walker), Michael Granger (Frank Buchanan), Gregory Gaye (Prof. Steigg), Tristram Coffin (D. A. MacGraw), Pierre Watkin (Mayor Bremer), Nelson Leigh (Dr. Kenneth Norton), S. John Launer (Capt. Dave Harris), Linda Bennett (Penny Walker), Don Harvey (Lester Banning), Lane Chandler (Gen. Saunders), Charles Evans (Chief Camden), Edward Coch (Jason Franchot), Paul Hoffman (Dunn), Larry Blake, Harry Lauter (reporters), Karl Davis (1st creature), Charles Horvath (2nd creature).

CREATURE WITH THE BLUE HAND, THE (1971-Ger.) (A. K. A. "Die Blaue Hand")
Director: Alfred Vohner
Klaus Kinski (Dave Emerson/Richard Emerson), Ilse Steppat (Lady Emerson), Diana Kerner, Herman Lenschau, Ilse Page, Harald Leipnitz, Albert Bessler, Carl Lange, Siegfried Schurenberg, Gudrun Genest.

CREEPER, THE (1948)
Director: Jean Yarborough
Eduardo Ciannelli, Onslow Stevens, Ralph Morgan, June Vincent, John Baragrey, Janis Wilson, David Hoffman, Lotte Stein, Ralph Peters, Philip Ahn, Richard Lane.

CREEPING FLESH, THE (1972)
Director: Freddie Francis
Peter Cushing (Emmanuel Hildern), Christopher Lee (Dr. James Hildern),

Lorna Heilbron (Penelope Hildern), George Benson (Waterlow), Kenneth J. Warren (Lenny), Michael Ripper (Carter), Duncan Lamont (Inspector), Jenny Runacre (Mrs. Hildern), Hedger Wallace (Dr. Perry), Catherine Finn (Emily), Harry Locke (barman), Maurice Bush (Karl), Robert Swann (young aristocrat), David Bailie (young doctor), Marianne Stone (female assistant), Tony Wright (sailor), Alexandra Dane (whore), Larry Taylor (1st warder), Martin Carroll (2nd warder), Dan Meaden (lunatic).

CREEPING TERROR, THE (1964) (A. K. A. "The Crawling Monster")
Director: A. J. Nelson
Vic Savage, Shannon O'Neil, William Thourlby, Norman Boone, John Caresio, Buddy Mize, Robin James, Lewis Lawson, Ray Wickman, Connie Valdie, Rita Tubin, Kelly Adams, Karl Goldenberg, Jack King, Louise Lawson, Mary Price, Mark Field, Al Lewis, Ken Savage, Myra Lee, Jerre Kopp.

CREEPING UNKNOWN, THE (1955) (A. K. A. "The Quatermass Experiment")
Director: Val Guest
Brian Donlevy (Bernard Quatermass), Jack Warner (Insp. Lomax), Richard Wordsworth (Victor Carroon), Margia Dean (Judith Carroon), Thora Hird (Rosie), David King Wood (Gordon Briscoe), Harold Lang (Christie), Maurice Kauffman (Marsh), Gron Davies (Green), Gordon Jackson (TV producer), Lionel Jeffries (Blake), Stanley Van Beers (Reichenheim), Frank Phillips (BBC announcer), Jane Asher (little girl), Sam Kydd.

CREEPSHOW (1982)
Director: George Romero
"Father's Day": Carrie Nye (Sylvia Grantham), Viveca Lindfors (Aunt Bedelia), Jon Lormer (Nate Grantham), Elizabeth Regan (Cass Grantham).
"The Lonely Death of Jordy Verrill": Stephen King (Jordy Verrill).
"The Crate": Adrienne Barbeau (Wilma Northrop), Fritz Weaver (Dexter Stanley), Hal Holbrook (Henry Northrop).
"Something to Tide You Over": Leslie Nielsen (Richard Vickers), Ted Danson (Harry).
"They're Creeping Up on You": E. G. Marshall (Upson Pratt).
and with Ed Harris (Hank), Ted Atkins (Stan), Robert Harper (Charlie), Joe King (Billy).

CREMATORS, THE (1972)
Director: Harry Essex

Maria Di Aragon, Marvin C. Howard,
Eric Alison, Mason Caufield.

CRESCENDO (1969)
    Director: Alan Gibson
Stephanie Powers (Susan Roberts), James
Olson (Georges/Jacques), Margaretta
Scott (Danielle Ryman), Joss Ackland
(Carter), Kirsten Betts (Catherine),
Jane Lapotaire (Lillianne).

CRIES IN THE NIGHT (1980) (A. K. A.
    "Funeral Home")
    Director: William Fruet
Lesleh Donaldson (Heather), Barry
Morse (Mr. Davis), Kay Hawtrey (Maude
Chambers), Dean Garbett (Rick Yates),
Stephen Miller (Billy Hibbs), Harvey
Atkin (Harry Browning), Alf Humphries
(Joe Yates), Peggy Mahon (Florie), Do-
ris Petrie (Ruby), Les Rubie (Sam),
Bob Warners (Fred Ray).

CRIME DOCTOR'S COURAGE, THE
    (1945)
    Director: George Sherman
Warner Baxter (Dr. Robert Ordway),
Hillary Brooke (Kathleen Carson), Je-
rome Cowan (Jeffers Jerome), Lloyd
Corrigan (John Massey), Anthony Caru-
so (Miguel Bragga), Lupita Tovar (Do-
lores Bragga), Stephen Crane (Gordon
Carson), Charles Arnt (Butler), Emory
Parnell (Captain Birch), King Kong Ka-
shay (Lugar), Dennis Moore (David
Lee), Robert Scott (Bob Rencoret),
Jack Carrington (Detective Fanning).

CRIME DOCTOR'S MANHUNT (1946)
    Director: William Castle
Warner Baxter (Dr. Robert Ordway),
Ellen Drew, William Frawley, Claire
Carleton, Olin Howlin, Myron Healey,
Francis Pierlot.

CRIME DOCTOR'S WARNING (1945)
    Director: William Castle
Warner Baxter (Dr. Robert Ordway),
John Litel, Dusty Anderson, Miles
Mander, John Abbott, J. M. Kerrigan,
Eduardo Ciannelli, Coulter Irwin.

CRIME OF DR. CRESPI, THE (1935)
    Director: John Auer
Erich von Stroheim (Dr. Crespi), Dwight
Frye (Dr. Thomas), Paul Guilfoyle (Dr.
Arnold), Harriet Russell (Mrs. Ross),
John Bohn (the dead man), Geraldine
Kay (Miss Rexford), Jeanne Kelly (Miss
Gordon), Patsy Berlin (Jeanne), Joe
Verdi (Di Angelo), Dean Raymond (mi-
nister).

CRIMES AT THE DARK HOUSE (1940)
    Director: George King
Tod Slaughter (Sir Percival Glyde), Hay
Petrie (Dr. Fosco), Sylvia Marriott
(Laura Fairlie), Hilary Eaves (Marian
Fairlie), Geoffrey Wardwell (Paul Hart-
wright), David Horne (Mr. Fairlie), Mar-
garet Yarde (Mrs. Bullen).

CRIMES OF STEPHEN HAWKE, THE
    (1936) (A. K. A. "Strangler's Morgue")
    Director: George King
Tod Slaughter (Stephen Hawke), Marjorie
Taylor (Julia Hawke), Eric Portman
(Matthew Trimble), Gerald Barry (Miles
Archer), Ben Soutten (Nathaniel), D. J.
Williams (Joshua Trimble), Charles
Penrose (Sir Franklyn), Norman Pierce
(landlord).

CRIMES OF THE BLACK CAT (1972-
    Ital.) (A. K. A. "Sette Scialli di Seta
    Gialla")
    Director: Sergio Pastore
Antonio De Teffe, Sylva Koscina, Giacomo Rossi-Stuart, Umberto Raho, Shirley Corrigan.

CRIMES OF THE FUTURE (1970)
    Director: David Cronenberg
Ronald Mlodzik, Tania Zolty, Jack Mes-
singer, Jon Lidolt, Paul Mullholland,
William Haslam.

CRIMINAL AT LARGE (1932)
    Director: T. Hayes Hunter
Emlyn Williams (Lord Lebanon), Cath-
leen Nesbitt (Lady Lebanon), Gordon
Harker (Sgt. Totty), Cyril Raymond
(Sgt. Ferraby), D. A. Clarke-Smith (Dr.
Amersham), Finlay Currie (Brooks),
Belle Crystal (Aisla Crane), Julian Royce
(Kelver), Norman McKinnel (Chief Insp.
Tanner), Eric Roland (Studd), Percy
Parsons (Gilder).

CRIMINAL LIFE OF ARCHIBALDO DE
    LA CRUZ, THE (1955-Mex.) (A. K. A.
    "El Ensayo de un Crimen", "The Prac-
    tice of Crime")
    Director: Luis Bunuel
Ernest Alonso (Archibaldo de la Cruz),
Miroslava (Lavinia), Rita Macedo (Pa-
tricia), Andrea Palma (Cervantes), Ar-
iadna Welter (Carlota), Rodolfo Landa
(Alejandro), Leonor Llausas (Governess),
J. M. Linares Rivas (Willy), Carlos Ri-
quelme (Chief of Police).

CRIMSON CULT, THE (1968) (A. K. A.
    "Curse of the Crimson Altar", "The
    Crimson Altar")
    Director: Vernon Sewell

Boris Karloff (Dr. Marshe), Christopher Lee (J. D. Morley), Barbara Steele (Lavinia), Mark Eden (Robert Manning), Virginia Wetherell (Eve), Michael Gough (Elder), Rupert Davies (Dr. Radford), Rosemarie Reede.

CRIMSON GHOST, THE (1946) - serial in 12 episodes (A. K. A. "Cyclotrode X")
    Director: William Witney & Fred Brannon
Charles Quigley (Duncan Richards), Linda Stirling (Diana Farnsworth), Joe Forte (Prof. Parker/the Crimson Ghost), Clayton Moore (Ashe), Kenne Duncan (Prof. Chambers), I. Stanford Jolley (Blackton), Forrest Taylor (Van Wyck), Sam Flint (Maxwell), Emmett Vogan (Anderson), Stanley Price (Fator), Wheaton Chambers (Wilson), Dale Van Sickel (Harte/Carson), Tom Steele (Stricker/Karl/chauffeur), Fred Graham (Zane/Pete Snyder), Rex Lease (Bain), Bud Wolfe (Gross/Smith), Ken Terrell (Dikes), Eddie Parker (Sherman), Duke Taylor (Erickson), Robert Wilke (Scott), Bill Wilkus (Cole), George Magrill (Fiske), John Daheim (Kelly), Rose Plummer (Mrs. Malloy), Loren Riebe (Logan), Eddie Rocco (Kell), Bill Yrigoyen (Milt), Carey Loftin (Palmer), Rod Bacon (Rosso), Virginia Carroll (nurse), Dick Rush (police inspector), Joe Yrigoyen (Slim), Polly Burson.

CRIMSON PIRATE, THE (1952)
    Director: Robert Siodmak
Burt Lancaster (Vallo), Nick Cravat (Ojo), Torin Thatcher (Humble Bellows), Eva Bartok (Consuelo), James Hayter (Prudence), Leslie Bradley (Baron Gruda), Noel Purcell (Pablo Murphy), Margot Graham (Bianca), Frank Pettingill (Colonel), Frederick Leicester (El Libre), Dagmar Wynter (La Signorita), Christopher Lee (Atache), Eliot Makeham (Governor).

CRIMSON STAIN MYSTERY, THE (1916) - serial in 16 episodes
Chapters: 1. "The Brand of Satan", 2. "In the Demon's Spell", 3. "The Broken Spell", 4. "The Mysterious Disappearance", 5. "The Figure in Black", 6. "The Phantom Image", 7. "The Devil's Symphony", 8. "In the Shadow of Death", 9. "The Haunting Specter", 10. "The Infernal Fiend", 11. "The Tortured Soul", 12. "The Restless Spirit", 13. "Despoiling Brutes", 14. "The Bloodhound", 15. "The Human Tiger" & 16. "The Unmasking".

    Director: T. Hayes Hunter
Maurice Costello (Harold Stanley), Ethel Grandin (Florence Montrose), Thomas J. McGrane (Dr. Burton Montrose), Olga Olonova (Vanya Tosca), John Milton (Layton Parrish), Eugene Strong (Robert Clayton), N. J. Thompson (Jim Tanner), William H. Cavanaugh (doctor's assistant).

CROCODILE (1981-Thai.)
    Director: Sompote Sands
Nat Puvanai (Dr. Akom), Tany Tim (John), Kirk Warren (Tanaka), Angela Wells.

CROOKED CIRCLE, THE (1932)
    Director: H. Bruce Humberstone
Ben Lyon (Brand Osborne), Zasu Pitts (Nora), James Gleason (Crimmer), C. Henry Gordon (Yoganda), Roscoe Karns (Harry), Raymond Hatton (Harmon), Robert Frazer (the Stranger), Spencer Charters (Kinny), Christian Rub (Dan), Berton Churchill (Col. Wolters), Frank Reicher (Rankin), Irene Purcell (Thelma), Ethel Clayton (Yvonne), Paul Panzer.

CROSSTALK (1982-Austral.)
    Director: Mark Egerton
Gary Day (Ed Ballinger), Penny Downie (Cindy), Brian McDermott (Whitehead), Peter Collingwood (Hollister), Kim Deacon (Jane), Jill Forster (Mrs. Stollier), John Ewart (Stollier), Judith Woodroffe (Clair).

CROWHAVEN FARM (TVM-1970) - 11-24-70
    Director: Walter Grauman
Hope Lange (Maggie Porter), Paul Burke (Ben Porter), Lloyd Bochner (Kevin Pierce), John Carradine (Nate Cheever), Cyril Delevanti (Harold Dane), Virginia Gregg (Mercy Lewis), Milton Selzer (Dr. Terminer), Woodrow Parfrey (Sam Wardwell), Cindy Eilbacher (Jennifer), Patricia Barry (Felicia), June Dayton (Madeleine Wardwell), Ross Elliot (Fritz Allen), Louise Troy (Claire Allen), William Smith (Patrolman Hayes), Pitt Herbert (Pearson), Dennis Cross (Police Chief).

CRUCIBLE, THE (1957-Fr.) (A. K. A. "Les Sorcieres de Salem", "The Witches of Salem")
    Director: Raymond Rouleau
Simone Signoret (Elizabeth Proctor), Yves Montand (John Proctor), Mylene Demongeot (Abigail Williams), Raymond Rouleau (Danforth), Francoise Lugagne (Jane Putnam), Jean Debucourt (Parris), Alfred

Adam (Thomas Putnam), Jeanne Fu-
sier-Gir (Martha Corey), Yves Brain-
ville (Hale), Miss Darling (Tituba),
Chantal Gozzi (Francy Proctor), Jean
Gaven (Peter Corey), Pierre Larquey
(Francis Nurse), Alexandre Rignault
(Willard), Piscal Petit (Mary Warren).

CRUCIBLE OF HORROR (1971) (A. K. A.
   "Velvet House")
   Director: Viktor Ritelis
Michael Gough (Walter Eastwood), Y-
vonne Mitchell (Edith), Olaf Pooley
(Reid), Sharon Gurney (Jane), Simon
Gough (Rupert), David Butler (Gregson),
Nicholas Jones (Benjy), Howard Goor-
ney (gas station attendant), Mary Hig-
nett (servant).

CRUCIBLE OF TERROR (1971)
   Director: Ted Hooker
Mike Raven (Victor Clare), James Bo-
lam (John Davis), Mary Maude (Millie),
Ronald Lacey (Michael Clare), John Ar-
natt (Bill Cartwright), Beth Morris
(Jane), Melissa Stribling (Joanna Brent),
Betty Alberge (Dorothy Clare), Kenneth
Keeling (George Brent), Judy Matheson
(Marcia), Me Me Lay (Chi San).

CRUEL WOMEN, THE (1969-Span.)
   (A. K. A. "Las Crueles")
   Director: Vicente Aranda
Capucine, Teresa Gimpera, Judy Mathe-
son, Carlos Estrada, Alicia Tomas,
Jose Maria Blanco.

CRUISE INTO TERROR (TVM-1978) -
   2-3-78
   Director: Bruce Kessler
Dirk Benedict (Simon), Hugh O'Brian
(Andy), Ray Milland (Dr. Isaiah Bak-
kun), Frank Converse (Matt Lazarus),
Lee Meriwether (Lil Mather), Christo-
pher George (Neal Barry), John For-
sythe (Fev. Charles Mather), Jo Ann
Harris (Judy Haines), Stella Stevens
(Marilyn Magneson), Marshall Thomp-
son (Bennett), Hilary Thompson (Deb-
bie Porter), Roger E. Mosley (Nathan),
Ruben Moreno (Emanuel).

CRYING WOMAN, THE (1959-Mex.)
   (A. K. A. "La Llorona")
   Director: Rene Cardona
Maria Elena Marques, Carlos Lopez
Moctezuma, Eduardo Fajardo, Mauri-
cio Garces, Emma Roldan, Erna Mar-
tha Bauman.

CRY OF THE BANSHEE (1970)
   Director: Gordon Hessler
Vincent Price (Lord Edward Whitman),

Essy Persson (Lady Patricia Whitman),
Elisabeth Bergner (Oona), Hugh Griffith
(Mickey), Sally Geeson (Sarah), Patrick
Mower (Roderick), Hilary Dwyer (Maureen Whitman), Pamela Farbrother (Margaret), Carl Rigg (Harry Whitman), Marshall Jones (Father Tom), Quinn O'Hara
(tavern witchgirl), Michael Elphick (Burke),
Stephen Chase (Sean), Robert Hutton
(guest), Godfrey James (rider), Richard
Everett (Timothy), Terry Martin (brander), Andrew McCullough (bully boy),
Gertan Klauber (landlord), Jan Rossini
(tavern wench), Peter Forest (party
man), Joyce Mandre (party woman).

CRY OF THE BEWITCHED (1956-Mex.)
   (A. K. A. "Yambao")
   Director: Alfredo Crevenna
Nina Sevilla, Ramon Gay, Rose Elena
Durgel, Ricardo Roman.

CRY OF THE WEREWOLF (1944)
   Director: Henry Levin
Nina Foch (Celeste La Tour), Steve
Crane (Bob Morris), Osa Massen (Elsa
Chauvet), John Abbott (Peter Althius),
Barton MacLane (Lt. Barry Lane), Blanche
Yurka (Blanca), Ivan Triesault (Yan
Spavero), Fritz Leiber (Dr. Charles
Morris), Fred Graff (Pinkie), Milton
Parsons (Adamson), John Tyrrell (Mac),
Robert Williams (Max).

CUL-DE-SAC (1966)
   Director: Roman Polanski
Donald Pleasence (George), Lionel Stander (Richard), Francoise Dorleac (Teresa), Jack MacGowran (Albert), William
Franklyn (Cecil), Iain Quarrier (Christopher), Renee Houston (Christopher's
mother), Geoffrey Sumner (Christopher's
father), Jacqueline Bisset (Jacqueline),
Trevor Delaney (Nicholas), Robert Dorning (Mr. Fairweather), Marie Kean
(Mrs. Fairweather).

CULT OF THE COBRA (1955)
   Director: Francis D. Lyon
Faith Domergue (Lisa Moya), Richard
Long (Paul), Marshall Thompson (Tom),
Kathleen Hughes (Julia Thompson), Da-
vid Janssen (Rico), Jack Kelly (Carl Tur-
ner), William Reynolds (Pete Norton),
Edward C. Platt (High Priest), James
Dobson (Corporal Nick Nommell), Olan
Soule (Air Force doctor), Leonard Strong
(Darv), Walter Coy (Police Inspector),
Myrna Hansen (Marion Sheean).

CULT OF THE DAMNED (1970) (A. K. A.
   "Angel, Angel, Down We Go")
   Director: Robert Thom

Holly Near (Tara Nicole Steele), Jordan Christopher (Bogart Peter Stuyvesant), Jennifer Jones (Astrid Steele), Charles Aidman (Willy Steele), Roddy McDowall (Santoro), Lou Rawls (Joe), Davey Davison (Anna Livia).

CURIOUS FEMALE, THE (1969)
  Director: Paul Rapp
Angelique Pettyjohn, Charlene Jones, David Westberg, Michael Greer, Bunny Allister, Julie Conners.

CURLYTOP (1924)
  Director: Maurice Elvey
Wallace MacDonald, Warner Oland, Shirley Mason, George Kuwa, Diana Miller.

CURSED MEDALLION, THE (1975-Ital.) (A. K. A. "The Night Child")
  Director: Massimo Dallamano
Richard Johnson (Michael Williams), Joanna Cassidy (Countess Capella), Nicole Elmi (Emily), Evelyne Stewart, Edward Purdom, Lila Kedrova.

CURSE OF BIGFOOT (1972)
  Director: Don Fields
William Simonsen, Robert Clymire, Ken Kloepfer, Jan Swihart.

CURSE OF FRANKENSTEIN, THE (1957)
  Director: Terence Fisher
Peter Cushing (Baron Victor Frankenstein), Christopher Lee (the Creature), Hazel Court (Elizabeth), Robert Urquhart (Paul Kremple), Valerie Gaunt (Justine), Paul Hardtmuth (Prof. Bernstein), Noel Hood (Aunt Sophie), Patrick Troughton (Kurt), Fred Johnson (grandfather), Claude Kingston (little boy), Melvin Hayes (young Victor), Marjorie Hume (mother), Alex Gallier (priest), Raymond Ray (uncle), Andrew Leigh (Burgomeister), Ann Blake (Burgomeister's wife), Sally Walsh (young Elizabeth), Michael Mulcaster (warden), Middleton Woods (lecturer), Raymond Rollett (Father Felix), Ernest Jay (undertaker), Alex Gallier (priest), Henry Caine (schoolmaster), Bartlett Mullins (tramp), J. Trevor Davis (uncle), Eugene Leahy (priest), Joseph Behrman (Fritz).

CURSE OF KING TUT'S TOMB, THE (TVM-1980) - 5-8-80 & 5-9-80
  Director: Philip Leacock
Robin Ellis (Howard Carter), Raymond Burr (Sabastian), Eva Marie Saint (Sarah Morrissey), Harry Andrews (Lord Carnarvon), Wendy Hiller (Princess

Velma), Tom Baker (Daoud), Barbara Murray (Giovanna), John Palmer (Fishbait), Rupert Frazer (Collins), Darien Angadi (Nahas), Rex Holsworth (doctor), Alfred Hoffmann (Stallholder), Andy Pantelidou (Lieutenant), Paul Scofield (Narrator), Angaharad Rees, Faith Brook, Patricia Routledge.

CURSE OF MELISSA, THE (1971)
  Director: Don Henderson
Michael Berry, Emby Mellay, Yvonne Winslow, Lee Amber, Jeanne Gerson.

CURSE OF NOSTRADAMUS, THE (1960-Mex.) (A. K. A. "La Maldicion de Nostradamus")
  Director: Frederico Curiel
German Robles (Nostradamus), Domingo Soler (Prof. Duran), Julio Aleman.

CURSE OF THE AZTEC MUMMY, THE (1959-Mex.) (A. K. A. "La Maldicion de la Momia")
  Director: Rafael Portello
Ramon Gay, Rosita Arenas, Crox Alvarado, Lobo Negro, Mucielago Velazquez, Enrique Alberto.

CURSE OF THE BLACK WIDOW, THE (TVM-1977) - 9-16-77 (A. K. A. "Love Trap")
  Director: Dan Curtis
Anthony Franciosa (Mark Higbie), Donna Mills (Leigh Lockwood), Patty Duke Astin (Laura Lockwood), June Allyson (Olga), Vic Morrow (Lt. Gully Conti), Roz Kelly (Flaps), Robert Burton (Jeff Wallace), Jeff Corey (Aspa Soldado), Sid Caesar (Lazlo Cozart), Max Gail (Ragsdale), June Lockhart (Mrs. Lockwood), H. B. Hagerty (Popeye), Bryan O'Byrne (Oaks, the zoo watchman), Tracy Curtis (gymnast), Robert Nader (Hank, the morgue attendant), Michael DeLano (Carlo Lenzi), Rosanna Locke (Jennifer), Bruce French (Summers, the town clerk).

CURSE OF THE BLOOD GHOULS (1962-Ital.) (A. K. A. "La Strage dei Vampiri", "Slaughter of the Vampires")
  Director: Roberto Mauri
Walter Brandi (Wolfgang), Graziella Granata (Louise), Dieter Eppler (the Blood Ghoul), Paolo Solvay, Gena Gimmy, Edda Feronao, Alfredo Rizzo, Carla Foscari, Maretta Procaccini.

CURSE OF THE CAT PEOPLE, THE (1944)
  Director: Gunther Fritsch & Robert Wise
Kent Smith (Oliver Reed), Simone Simon

(Irena Dubrovna), Jane Randolph (Alice Reed), Elizabeth Russell (Barbara Farren), Julia Dean (Julia Farren), Ann Carter (Amy Reed), Eve March (Miss Callahan), Sir Lancelot (Edward), Joel Davis (Donald), Juanita Alvarez (Lois).

CURSE OF THE CRYING WOMAN, THE (1961-Mex.) (A. K. A. "La Maldicion de la Llorona", "La Casa Embrujada", "The Bewitched House")
Director: Raphael Baledon
Rosita Arenas, Abel Salazar, Domingo Soler, Rita Macedo, Carlos Moctezuma.

CURSE OF THE CYLONS (1979)
see Television: Battlestar Galactica (1978-79).

CURSE OF THE DEMON (1956) (A. K. A. "Night of the Demon")
Director: Jacques Tourneur
Dana Andrews (Dr. John Holden), Niall MacGinnis (Dr. Julian Karswell), Peggy Cummins (Joanna Harrington), Reginald Beckwith (Mr. Meek), Athene Seyler (Mrs. Karswell), Maurice Denham (Prof. Henry Harrington), Liam Redmond (Prof. Mark O'Brien), Ewan Roberts (Lloyd Williamson), Brian Wilde (Rand Hobart), Richard Leech (Insp. Mottram), Peter Elliott (Prof. K. T. Kumar), Rosamund Greenwood (Mrs. Meek), Lloyd Lamble (Detective Simmons), Peter Hobbs (Superintendent), Percy Herbert (farmer), Charles Lloyd-Pack (chemist), John Salew (librarian), Walter Horsbrugh (Bates, the butler), Shay Gorman (narrator), Leonard Sharp (ticket collector), Ballard Berkeley (1st reporter), Michael Peake (2nd reporter), Lynn Tracy (air hostess), Janet Barrow (Mrs. Hobart).

CURSE OF THE DOLL PEOPLE, THE (1960-Mex.) (A. K. A. "Munecos Infernales", "Devil Doll Man")
Director: Benito Alazarki
Ramon Gay, Elvira Quintana, Robert G. Rivera, Jorge Mondragon.

CURSE OF THE FACELESS MAN (1958)
Director: Edward L. Cahn
Richard Anderson (Dr. Paul Mallon), Adele Mara (Dr. Maria Fiorillo), Luis Van Rooten (Dr. Fiorillo), Elaine Edwards (Tina Enright), Felix Locher (Dr. Emanuel), Gar Moore (Dr. Enrico Ricci), Jan Arvan (Insp. Renaldi), Bob Bryant (Quintillus, the Faceless Man).

CURSE OF THE FLY, THE (1965)
Director: Don Sharp

Brian Donlevy (Henry Delambre), George Baker (Martin Delambre), Carole Gray (Patricia Stanley), Michael Graham (Albert Delambre), Jeremy Wilkins (Insp. Ronet), Charles Carson (Insp. Charas), Bert Kwouk (Tai), Yvette Rees (Wan), Mary Manson (Judith), Rachel Kempson (Madame Fournier), Warren Stanhope (hotel manager), Arnold Bell (porter), Stan Simmons (the Creature).

CURSE OF THE GHOST, THE (1970-Jap.) (A. K. A. "Yotsuya Kaidan - Oiwa no Borei")
Director: Issei Mori
Kei Sato (Iyemon Tamiya), Kazuko Inano (Oiwa), Yoshihiko Aoyama (Yemoshichi Sato), Kyoko Mikage (Osode), Shoji Kobayashi (Naokichi).

CURSE OF THE HEADLESS HORSEMAN (1971)
Director: John Kirkland
Ultra Violet (the Countessa), Claudia Ream (Brenda), Markland Proctor (Mark Callahan), B. G. Fisher (Solomon), Don Carrara (John), Lydia Rosenbloom (Lydia), Ray Saniger (Sandy), Randy Ornalez (Randy), Ritch Brinkley (Ritch), Timothy A. Gracy (Tim).

CURSE OF THE LIVING CORPSE, THE (1963)
Director: Del Tenney
Roy Scheider (Philip Sinclair), Helen Waren (Abigail Sinclair), Margot Hartman (Vivian Sinclair), Robert Milli (Bruce Sinclair), Hugh Franklin (James Benson), Candace Hilligoss (Deborah Benson), Dino Narizzano (Robert Harrington), Linda Donovan (Letty Crews), J. Frank Lucas (Seth Lucas), Paul Haney (Constable Barnes), George Cotton (Constable Winters), Jane Bruce (cook), William Blood (minister).

CURSE OF THE MUMMY'S TOMB, THE (1965)
Director: Michael Carreras
Terence Morgan (Adam Beauchamp), Fred Clark (Alexander King), Jeanne Roland (Annette Dubois), George Pastell (Hashmi Bey), Bernard Rebel (Prof. Dubois), Jack Gwillim (Sir Giles Dalrymple), Ronald Howard (John Bray), Dickie Owens (the Mummy), Harold Goodwin, Michael Ripper.

CURSE OF THE STONE HAND (1959-Mex.)
Director: Jerry Warren & Carl Schleipper
John Carradine, Katherine Victor, Ernest Walch, Lloyd Nelson, Sheila Bon.

CURSE OF THE SWAMP CREATURE
(1966)
Director: Larry Buchana
John Agar (Barry Rogers), Francine
York, Shirley McLine, Bill Thurman,
Jeff Alexander, Cal Duggan, Charles
McLine, Bill McGee, Rodger Ready,
Ted Mitchell, Tony Houston, Annabelle
Weenick, J. V. Lee, Gayle Johnson,
Michael Tolden, Pat Cranshaw, Naomi
Lee.

CURSE OF THE UNDEAD (1959)
Director: Edward Dein
Eric Fleming (Preacher Dan), Michael
Pate (Drake Robey), Kathleen Crowley
(Dolores Carter), John Hoyt (Dr. Car-
ter), Edward Binns (Sheriff), Bruce
Gordon (Buffer), Helen Kleeb (Dora),
Jimmy Murphy (Tim Carter), Jay Ad-
ler (bartender), Edwin Parker, Frankie
Van, John Taux, Rush Williams (hench-
men).

CURSE OF THE VAMPIRES (1970-U. S. /
Phil.) (A. K. A. "Creatures of Evil")
Director: Gerardo De Leon
Amalia Fuentes, Eddie Garcia, Johnny
Monteiro, Romeo Vasquez, Rosario Del
Pilar, Mary Walter, Paquito Salcedo,
Andrew Benitez, Francisco Cruz, Quiel
Mendoza, Luz Angeles, Linda Rivera,
Tessie Hernandez.

CURSE OF THE VOODOO (1964) (A. K. A.
"Curse of Simba")
Director: Lindsay Shonteff
Lisa Daniely (Janet), Dennis Price (Ma-
jor Lomas), Mary Kerridge (Janet's
mother), Bryant Haliday, Ronald Leigh
Hunt.

CURSE OF THE WEREWOLF, THE (1961)
Director: Terence Fisher
Oliver Reed (Leon, the Werewolf), Ewen
Solon (Don Fernando), Clifford Evans
(Don Alfredo Carido), Catherine Feller
(Christina), Warren Mitchell (Pepe Va-
liente), George Woodbridge (Dominique),
Richard Wordsworth (beggar), Yvonne
Romain (jailor's daughter), Michael
Ripper (old soaker), Peter Sallis (Don
Enrique), Anthony Dawson (Marquis),
Hira Talfrey (Teresa), Desmond Llewe-
lyn (servant).

CURSE OF THE WRAYDONS, THE (1946)
(A. K. A. "The Terror of London")
Director: Victor M. Glover
Tod Slaughter (Philip Wraydon), Bruce
Seton (Capt. Jack Clayton), Andrew
Lawrence (George Heeningham), Ga-
briel Toyne (Lt. Payne), Lorraine

Clewes (Helen Sedgefield), Pearl Came-
ron (Rose Wraydon), Barry O'Neill
(George Wraydon), Ben Williams (John
Rickers).

CURUCU, BEAST OF THE AMAZON
(1956)
Director: Curt Slodmak
Beverly Garland (the Doctor), John Brom-
field (the Plantation Owner), Tom Payne
(Tupanico), Harvey Chalk (Father Flavi-
ano), Larri Thomas, Sergio De Oliveira,
Wilson Viana.

CYBORG 2087 (1966)
Director: Franklin Adreon
Michael Rennie (Garth), Karen Steele
(Sharon Mason), Warren Stevens (Dr.
Carl Zeller), Eduard Franz (Prof. Marx),
Wendell Corey (Sheriff), Adam Roarke
(Deputy Dan), Sherry Alberroni (Laura),
Harry Carey, Jr. (Jay C.), John Beck
(Skinny), Dale Van Sickel (Tracer No. 1),
Troy Melton (Tracer No. 2), Tyler Mac-
Duff (Sam Gilmore), Betty Jane Royale
(Jill), Chubby Johnson (Uncle Pete), Jim-
my Hibbard (Rick), Jo Ann Pflugg (woman
in control booth), Larry Dean (man in
control booth), Byron Morrow (Mr. Sec-
retary), Richard Travis (General), Ruth
Foster (citizen), Ted Ryan (gate guard),
George C. Fisher (1st station attendant),
James Kline (2nd station attendant), Jo-
anne Gaylord (woman in station), Charles
Evans (man in station), Harry Hollins
(communications officer).

CYCLOPS, THE (1957)
Director: Bert I. Gordon
Gloria Talbot (Susan Winter), James
Craig (Russ Bradford), Lon Chaney, Jr.
(Martin Melville), Tom Drake (Lee Brandt),
Dean Parkin (the Cyclops).

DAGORA, THE SPACE MONSTER (1964-
Jap.) (A. K. A. "Uchu Daikaiju Dogora",
"Space Monster Dogora")
Director: Inoshiro Honda
Yosuke Natsuki, Yoko Fujiyama, Hiroshi
Koizumi, Akiki Wakabayshi.

DAIN CURSE, THE (TVM-1978) - 5-22-
78, 5-23-78 & 5-24-78
Director: E. W. Swackhamer
James Coburn (Hamilton Nash), Jason
Miller (Owen Fitzstephan), Nancy Addi-
son (Gabrielle Leggett), Hector Elizondo
(Ben Feeney), Jean Simmons (Aaronia
Haldorn), Paul Stewart (the old man),
Beatrice Straight (Alice Dain Leggett),
David Canary (Jack Santos), Ellis Rabb
(Joseph Haldorn), Roland Winters (Hu-
bert Collinson), Beeson Carroll (Marshall

Cotton), Tom Bower (Sgt. O'Gar), Martin Cassidy (Eric Collinson), Roni Dengel (Daisy Cotton), Karen Ludwig (Maria Grosso), Brent Spiner (Tom Fink), Hattie Winston (Minnie Hershey), Ron Weyand (Judge Cochran), Malachy McCourt (Mickey), Brian Davies (Tom Vernon), Paul Harding (Mr. Leggett).

DALEKS - INVASION EARTH 2150 A. D. (1966)
Director: Gordon Flemying
Peter Cushing (Dr. Who), Bernard Cribbins (Tom Campbell), Andrew Keir (Wyler), Roberta Tovey (Suand), Jill Curzon (Louise), Eddie Powell (Thompson), Roger Avon (Wells), Ray Brooks (David), Keith Marsh (Conway), Philip Madoc (Brockley), Geoffrey Cheshire (RoboMan), Steve Peters (RoboMan Leader), Godfrey Quigley (Dorfmun), Tony Reynolds (man on bicycle), Bernard Spear (man with carrier bag), Robert Jewell (leader of Dalek operation).

DAMIEN - OMEN II (1978)
Director: Don Taylor
William Holden (Richard Thorn), Lee Grant (Ann Thorn), Jonathan Scott-Taylor (Damien Thorn), Robert Foxworth (Paul Buher), Lew Ayres (Bill Atherton), Nicholas Pryor (Charles Warren), Sylvia Sidney (Aunt Marion), Lucas Donat (Mark Thorn), Elizabeth Shepherd (Joan Hart), Ian Hendry (Michael Morgan), Leo McKern (Bugenhagen), Lance Hendricksen (Sgt. Neff), Alan Arbus (Pasarian), Meshach Taylor (Dr. Kane), Fritz Ford (Murray), John J. Newcombe (Teddy), Paul Cook (Colonel), John Charles Burns (Butler), Diane Daniels (Jane), Robert E. Ingham (teacher), Russell P. Delia (truck driver), Judith Dowd (maid), William B. Fosser (minister), Corney Morgan (greenhouse technician), Thomas O. Erhart, Jr. (sergeant), Anthony Hawkins (Pasarian's assistant), Rusdi Lane (Jim), Robert J. Jones, Jr. (guide), Cornelia Sanders (girl), Felix Shuman (Dr. Fiedler), William J. Whelehan (guard), Charles Mountain (priest), James Spinks (technician), Owen Sullivan (Byron).

DAMNATION ALLEY (1977)
Director: Jack Smight
Jan-Michael Vincent (Tanner), George Peppard (Denton), Dominique Sanda (Janice), Paul Winfield (Keegan), Jackie Earle Haley (Billy), Murray Hamilton (Landers), Kip Niven (Perry), Robert Donner (man), Seamon Glass (mountain man), Mark L. Taylor (Haskins), Trent

Dolan (technician), Bob Hackman (Colonel), Terrence Locke (air policeman), Erik Cord (burning man), Marcia Holley (Gloria).

DAMN YANKEES (1958)
Director: Stanley Donen
Tab Hunter (Joe Hardy), Gwen Verdon (Lola), Ray Walston (Applegate), Shannon Bolin (Meg Boyd), Russ Brown (Van Buren), Jimmie Komack (Rocky), Rae Allen (Gloria), Nathaniel Frey (Smokey), Robert Shafer (Joe Boyd), Albert Linville (Vernon), Elizabeth Howell (Doris), Jean Stapleton (Sister), Bob Fosse (Mambo dancer).

DANGER DIABOLIK (1967-Ital./Fr.)
(A. K. A. "Diabolik!")
Director: Mario Bava
John Phillip Law (Diabolik), Marisa Mell (Eva), Michel Piccoli (Insp. Ginco), Adolfo Celi (Ralph Valmont), Terry-Thomas (Minister of Finance), Claudio Gora (Police Chief), Edward Febo Kelleng (Sir Harold Clark), Annie Gorassini (Rose), Giulio Donnini (Dr. Vernier), Caterina Boratto (Lady Clark), Renzo Palmer, Andrea Bosic, Mario Donen, Lucia Modugno, Giorgio Gennari, Carlo Croccolo, Giuseppe Fazio, Isarco Ravailoi, Tiberio Mitri, Lidia Biondi, Giorgio Sciolette, Federico Boito, Wolfgang Hillinger.

DANGEROUS AFFAIR, A (1931)
Director: Edward Sedgwick
Jack Holt (Lt. McHenry), Ralph Graves (Wally Cook), Sally Blane (Marjory Randolph), Edward Brophy (Nelson), William V. Mong (Lionel), Susan Fleming (Florence), Tyler Brooke (Harvey), Charles Middleton (Tupper), Sidney Bracy (Plunkett), Blanche Frederici (Letty), Frederick Stanley (Tom), Esther Muir (Peggy), DeWitt Jennings (city editor).

DANGERS OF THE CANADIAN MOUNTED (1948) - serial (A. K. A. "R. C. M. P. and the Treasure of Ghengis Khan")
Director: Fred Brannon & Yakima Canutt
Jim Bannon (Christopher Royal), Anthony Warde (Mort Fowler), I. Stanford Jolley (J. P. Belanco), John Crawford (Danton), Virginia Belmont (Bobbie Page), Bill Van Sickel (Dan Page), Frank O'Connor (U. S. Commissioner), Eddie Parker (Lowry), Dorothy Granger (Skagway Kate), Dale Van Sickel (Boyd/Bart/Pete/Scott/Steele), Tom Steele (Fagin/Carter/Lou/Sloane/Spike/driver), Ken Terrell (Art/Curry/Fenton/Grady/Masters/Tom/guard), Phil Warren (George Hale), James Dale (Andy

Film Index   813

Knight), Jack Clifford (Marshal), Lee
Morgan (Dale), Ted Adams (oldtimer),
Robert Wilke (Baxter), Al Taylor (track
heavy No. 1), Harry Cording (track
heavy No. 2), Bud Wolfe (Zeke/Vance),
Arvon Dale (Roy Watson), Marshall
Reed (Dave/Douglas/Jim Williams),
Carey Loftin (clerk/porter), Eddie Phil-
lips (Baker), Tom McDonough (Frank),
Paul Gustine (Ken), Charles Regan
(Ralph), House Peters, Jr. (Ford), Hol-
ly Bane (Garson), Ted Mapes (Mac),
Jack Kirk (A. L. Thomas), Roy Bucko,
David Sharpe.

DANGER WOMAN (1946)
   Director: Lewis D. Collins
Brenda Joyce (June), Don Porter (Claude
Ruppert), Patricia Morison (Eve Ruppert), Kathleen Howard (Eddie), Milburn Stone (Gerald King), Samuel S.
Hinds (Sears), Ted Hecht (Lane), Leonard East (Howard), Charles D. Brown
(Insp. Pepper), Griff Barnett (Dr. Carey), Keith Richards (1st reporter), Eddie Acuff (2nd reporter), Howard Negley (Maxwell), Ronnie Gilbert, Doug
Carter, Chuck Hamilton (reporters).

DANTE'S INFERNO (1935)
   Director: Harry Lachman
Spencer Tracy (Jim Carter), Claire
Trevor (Betty McWade), Henry B. Wal-
thall (Pop McWade), Alan Dinehart (Jone-
sy), Scotty Beckett (Alexander Carter),
Robert Gleckler (Dean), Willard Robert-
son (Insp. Harris), Morgan Wallace (Capt.
Morgan), Rita Cansino, Gary Leon (dan-
cers).

DARBY O'GILL AND THE LITTLE PEO-
PLE (1958)
   Director: Robert Stevenson
Albert Sharpe (Darby O'Gill), Janet
Munro (Katie), Sean Connery (Michael
McBride), Jimmy O'Dea (King Brian),
Kieron Moore (Pony Sugrue), Estelle
Winwood (Sheelah), Walter Fitzgerald
(Lord Fitzpatrick), J. G. Devlin (Tom
Kerrigan), Jack MacGowran (Phadrig
Oge), Nora O'Mahony (Molly Malloy),
Farrell Pelly (Paddy Scanlon).

DAREDEVIL IN THE CASTLE (1961-
Jap.) (A. K. A. "Osakajo Monogatari")
   Director: Hiroshi Inagaki
Toshiro Mifune, Kyoko Kagawa, Yurko
Hoshi, Akihiko Hirata, Isuzu Yamada,
Yoshiko Kuga.

DAREDEVILS OF THE RED CIRCLE
(1939) - serial in 12 episodes
Chapters: 1. "The Monstrous Plot",

2. "The Mysterious Friend", 3. "The
Executioner", 4. "Sabotage", 5. "The
Ray of Death", 6. "Thirty Seconds to
Live", 7. "The Flooded Mine", 8.
"S. O. S.", 9. "Ladder of Peril", 10.
"The Infernal Machine", 11. "The Red
Circle Speaks" & 12. "Flight to Doom".
   Director: William Witney & John
English
Charles Quigley (Gene Townley), Her-
man Brix/Bruce Bennett (Tiny Dawson),
David Sharpe (Burt Knowles), Miles Man-
der (Horace Granville), Carole Landis
(Blanche Granville), Charles Middleton
(Harry Crowell/No. 39013), George
Chesebro (Sheffield), C. Montague Shaw
(Dr. Malcolm), Raymond Bailey (Stan-
ley), Ben Taggart (Dixon), Corbet Mor-
ris (Klein), William Pagan (Chief Landon),
Fred Toones (Snowflake), Robert Winkler (Sammy Townley), John Merton (Davis), Ray Miller (Jeff), Al Taylor (Al
No. 1), Bud Robinson (Al No. 2), Regi-
nald Barlow (doctor No. 1), Lloyd Whit-
lock (doctor No. 2), Loren Riebe (der-
rick heavy No. 1), Reed Howes (derrick
heavy No. 2), Edmund Cobb (foreman),
Joe McGuinn (Ed), Yakima Canutt, Duke
Taylor, Mike Jeffers, George DeNormand, Robert Wilke (G-Men), Ken Terrell (gas heavy No. 1), Bill Wilkus (gas
heavy No. 2), Bud Wolfe (John), Harry
Strang (Peck), Earl Askam (Lutens), Bud
Geary (Rex), Stanley Price (Selden),
Monte Montague (Tom), Truda Marson
(Nurse Benson), Bernard Suss (Black),
Lee Frederick (Bob), Frank Wayne (Dan),
Earl Bunn (Frank), Howard Mitchell (dis-
patcher), Eddie Cherkose (Burton), Bert
LeBaron (Blake), Roy Brent (Bill), Roy
Barcroft (superintendent), Joe Yrigoyen
(power heavy No. 1), Cy Slocum (power
heavy No. 2), Wally West (power heavy
No. 3), Broderick O'Farrell (Graves),
Jack Chapin (Joe), Buel Bryant (lab hea-
vy), Earle Hodgins (Hinkle), Ray Largay
(police commissioner), Forrest Dillon
(Kid), Jerry Jerome (Marco), Dale Wen-
gren, Sailor Vincent, Jerry Frank (miners), Bill Wilkus (office heavy), Norman
Nesbitt (newscaster), George Turner,
Fred Schaefer, William Nestel (oil heavies), Charles Thomas (Sam), Jack Kenney (Steve), Arthur Fowler (Sloan), Dick
Scott, Bob Thom, Curley Dresden (sub-
station heavies), Max Marx, Oscar Hendrian (tank heavies), George Plues (Ted),
Harry Anderson (Ward), Edward Foster
(Zeke), Jerry Frank (truck heavy), Jimmy Fawcett, Ted Mapes, Millard McGowan.

DARK, THE (1979)

Director: John Cardos
William Devane (Roy Warner), Cathy
Lee Crosby (Zoe Owens), Richard Jae-
ckel (Detective Dave Mooney), Keenan
Wynn (Sherman Mossberg), Warren Zem-
merling (Captain Speer), Jacquelyn Hyde
(De Renzy), Vivian Blaine (Courtney
Floyd), Casey Kasem (Pathologist),
Biff Elliot (Bresler), William Derrin-
ger (Herman Burmeister), John Bloom
(the Dark), Jay Lawrence (Jim Hamp-
ton), Vernon Washington (Henry Lydell),
Russ Marin (Dr. Baronowski), Paula
Crist (stewardess), Joann Kirk (stewar-
dess), Roberto Contreras (Max), Ron
Iglesias (Rudy), Sandra McCulley (car
hop), Erik Howell (Mr. Antwine), Wil-
liam Lampley (young man), Valla Rae
McDade (Camille), Monica Peterson
(Mrs. Lydell), Kathy Richards (Shelly),
Philip Michael Thomas (Corn Rows),
Jeffrey Reese (Randy Morse), Penny
Ann Phillips (Zelza), Ken Minyard (TV
sportscaster), John Dresden, Mel An-
derson, Horton Willis, Mickey Alzola,
Mickey Guinn, Gene McLaughlin, Gary
Littlejohn, Everett Creach, Ernest Ro-
binson, Robert Sizer (policemen).

DARK AUGUST (1975) (A. K. A. "The
    Hant")
    Director: Martin Goldman
Kim Hunter, William Robertson.

DARK CRYSTAL (1982)
    Director: Jim Henson & Frank
    Oz
Jim Henson, Frank Oz, Dave Goelz,
Kathy Mullen, Steve Whitmire, Brian
Muehl, Amiel.

DARK DREAMS (1971)
    Director: Rober Guermontes
Tina Russell, Tim Long, Jane DuLu,
Patrice Deveur, Arlana Blue.

DARKENED ROOMS (1929)
    Director: Louis Gasnier
Evelyn Brent (Ellen), Neil Hamilton
(Emory Jago), Wallace MacDonald (Bert
Nelson), Doris Hill (Joyce Clayton),
Gale Henry (Mme. Silvara), David Ne-
well (Billy), E. H. Calvert (Mr. Clay-
ton), Blanche Craig (Mrs. Rogarty),
Sammy Bricker (sailor).

DARKER SIDE OF TERROR, THE (TVM-
    1979) - 4-3-79
    Director: Gus Trikonis
Robert Forster (Paul Corwin/the Clone),
Adrienne Barbeau (Margaret Corwin),
Ray Milland (Prof. Meredith), David
Sheiner (Prof. Hillstrom), John Lehne

(Lt. Merholz), Thomas Bellin (Ed Lin-
nick), Denise DuBarry (Ann Sweeney),
Jack DeMave (Roger), Heater Hobbs
(Jenny), Eddie Quillan (watchman).

DARKEST AFRICA (1936) (A. K. A. "King
    of the Jungleland", "Batmen of Afri-
    ca") - serial in 15 episodes
Chapters: 1. "Baru, Son of the Jungle",
2. "The Tiger-Men's God", 3. "Bat Men
of Joba", 4. "Hunter Lions of Joba", 5.
"Bonga's Courage", 6. "Prisoners of the
High Priest", 7. "Swing for Life", 8.
"Jaws of the Tiger", 9. "When Birdmen
Strike", 10. "Trial by Thunder Rods",
11. "Jars of Death", 12. "Revolt of Slaves",
13. "Gauntlet of Destruction", 14. "The
Divine Sacrifice" & 15. "Prophecy of
Gorn".
    Director: B. Reeves Eason & Jo-
    seph Kane
Clyde Beatty (Clyde Beatty), Elaine She-
pard (Valerie), Wheeler Oakman (Durkin),
Edmund Cobb (Craddock), Lucien Prival
(Dagna), Manuel King (Baru), Edward
McWade (Gorn), Ray Benard (Samabi),
Ray Turner (Hambone), Harrison Greene
(Driscoll), Joseph Boyd (Nagga), Donald
Reed (Negus), Henry Sylvester (Tomlin),
Prince Modupe (Tiger Chief), Ray 'Crash'
Corrigan (Bonga/Samabi), Edwin Parker
(Batman), Joseph Delacruz (slave).

DARK INTRUDER (1965) (A. K. A. "Black
    Cloak")
    Director: Harvey Hart
Leslie Nielsen (Brett Kingsford), Mark
Richman (Robert Vendenburg), Werner
Klemperer (Prof. Malaki), Judi Mere-
dith (Evelyn Lang), Gilbert Green (Har-
vey Misback), Vaughn Taylor (Dr. Bur-
dett), Peter Brocco (Chi Zang), Charles
Bolender (Nikola), Harriet Vine (Hannah).

DARK MIRROR, THE (1920)
    Director: Charles Giblyn
Dorothy Dalton, Huntley Gordon, Pedro
de Cordoba, Jessie Arnold, Walter Nee-
land, Lucille Carney.

DARK NIGHT OF THE SCARECROW
    (TVM-1981) - 10-24-81
    Director: Frank De Felitta
Charles Durning (Otis), Robert F. Lyons
(Skeeter), Claude Earl Jones (Philby),
Lane Smith (Harless), Tonya Crowe
(Marylee), Jocelyn Brando (Mrs. Ritter),
Larry Drake (Bubba Ritter), Tom Tay-
lor (Sam), Ivy Jones (Mrs. Williams),
Jim Tartan (Mr. Williams), Ed Call (de-
fense attorney), Richard McKenzie (judge),
Alice Nunn (Mrs. Bunch), John Steadman
(Mr. Loomis), David Adams (deputy),

Dennis Robertson (Ray), Ivy Bethune (lady), Modi Frank (waitress), Jetta Scelza (Mrs. Whimberley).

DARK PLACES (1972)
Director: Don Sharp
Christopher Lee (Dr. Mandeville), Robert Hardy (Edward Foster/Andrew Marr), Joan Collins (Sarah Mandeville), Jean Marsh (Victoria Marr), Michael McVey (Francis Marr), Jane Birkin (Alta), Charleton Hobbs (Old Marr), Jennifer Thanisch (Jessica Marr), Martin Boddey (Police Sgt. Riley), Roy Evans (Baxter), John Glyn Jones (bank manager), John Levene (doctor), Barry Linehan (gatekeeper), Earl Rhodes, Lysandre DeLahaye (children on hill), Linda Gray (woman on hill).

DARK SECRET (1949)
Director: MacLean Roberts
Emrys Jones, Dinah Sheridan, Percy Marmont, Irene Handl.

DARK SECRET OF HARVEST HOME, THE (TVM-1978) - 1-23-78 & 1-24-78
Director: Leo Penn
Bette Davis (Widow Fortune), David Ackroyd (Nick Constantine), Joanna Miles (Beth Constantine), Laurie Prange (Sophie Hook), Rene Auberjonois (Jack Stump), Norman Lloyd (Amys Penrose), John Calvin (Justin Hooke), Rosanna Arquette (Kate Constantine), Lina Raymond (Tamar Penrose), Michael O'Keefe (Worthy Pettinger), Stephen Joyce (Robert Dodd), Linda Marsh (Maggie Dodd), Tracy Gold (Missy Penrose), Dick Durock (Roy Soakes), Richard Venture (Richard), Michael Durrell (Ty Harth), Stephen Gustafson (Jimmy Minerva), Bill Balhatchet, Phoebe Alexander, John Daheim, Grace Grant, Kathleen Howland, Martin Shakar, Lori Street, Donald Pleasence (narrator).

DARK STAR (1972)
Director: John Carpenter
Brian Narelle (Doolittle), Dan O'Bannon (Pinback), Cal Kuniholm (Boiler), Andreijah Pahich (Talby), Joe Sanders (Powell).

DARK TOWER, THE (1943)
Director: John Harlow
Ben Lyon (Phil Danton), Anne Crawford (Mary), David Farrar (Tom Danton), Herbert Lom (Torg), William Hartnell (Towers), Frederick Burtwell (Willie), Elsie Wagstaffe (Eve), Josephine Wilson (Mme. Shogun), J. H. Roberts (Dr.

Wilson).

DARLING OF PARIS, THE (1916)
Director: J. Gordon Edwards
Theda Bara (Esmerelda), Glen White (Quasimodo), John Webb Dillon (Clopin), Walter Law (Claude Frollo), Louis Dean (Gringoire), Herbert Heyes (Capt. Phoebus), Carey Lee (Paquette), Alice Gale (Gypsy Queen).

DAUGHTER OF DARKNESS (1947)
Director: Lance Comfort
Siobhan McKenna (Emily Beaudine), Anne Crawford (Bess Stanforth), Barry Morse (Robert Stanforth), Maxwell Reed (Dan), Liam Redmond (Father Corcoran), Honor Blackman (Julie Tallent), Grant Tyler (Larry Tallent), Denis Gordon (Saul Trevethick), George Thorpe (Mr. Tallent), David Greene (David Price), Arthur Hambling (Jacob).

DAUGHTER OF DR. JEKYLL (1957)
Director: Edgar G. Ulmer
Gloria Talbott (Janet Smith), John Agar (George Hastings), Arthur Shields (Dr. Lomas), John Dierkes (Jacob), Martha Wentworth (Mrs. Merchant), Molly McCart (Maggie).

DAUGHTER OF THE DRAGON (1931)
Director: Lloyd Corrigan
Anna May Wong (Ling Moy), Warner Oland (Dr. Fu Manchu), Bramwell Fletcher (Ronald Petrie), Holmes Herbert (Sir John Petrie), Neila Walker (Lady Petrie), Frances Dade (Joan Marshall), Sessue Hayakawa (Ahi Kee), Lawrence Grant (Sir Basil), Olaf Hytten (the Butler), Nicholas Soussanin (Morloff), Harrington Reynolds (Hobbs), A. Alyn Lawrence (Lu Chow), Harold Minir (Rogers), Lie Chan (the Amah).

DAUGHTER OF THE GODS, A (1916)
Director: Herbert Brenon
Annette Kellermann, Stuart Holmes, Mark Price, William E. Shay, Violet Horner.

DAUGHTER OF THE MIND (TVM-1969) - 12-9-69
Director: Walter Grauman
Ray Milland (Prof. Constable), Don Murray (Dr. Alex Lauder), Gene Tierney (Lenore Constable), Pamelyn Ferdin (Mary Constable), Ivor Barry (Dr. Paul Cryder), Barbara Dana (Tina Cryder), Edward Asner (Saul Weiner), George Macready (Dr. Frank Ferguson), Frank Maxwell (Gen. Augstadt), Virginia Christine (Helga), William Beckley (Arnold Bessmer), Cecile Ozorio (Devi Bessmer),

John Carradine (Mr. Bosch), Hal Frederick (technician), Bill Hickman (cab driver).

DAUGHTERS OF DARKNESS (1971-Belg./Fr./Ital.) (A. K. A. "Le Rouge Aux Levres", "The Redness of the Lips", "The Promise of Red Lips")
Director: Harry Kumel
Delphine Seyrig (Countess Elisabeth Bathory), Daniele Ouimet (Valerie Tardieu), John Karlen (Stefan Chiltern), Andrea Rau (Ilona Harczy), Paul Esser (porter), George Jamin (the man), Fons Rademakers (mother), Joris Collet (the butler).

DAUGHTERS OF SATAN (1972-U. S. / Phil.)
Director: Hollingsworth Morse
Tom Selleck (James Robertson), Barra Grant (Chris Robertson), Vic Diaz (Carlos Ching), Tani Phelps Guthrie (Kitty Duarte), Vic Silayan (Dr. Dangal), Paraluman (Juana Rios), Gina Laforteza (Andrea), Ben Rubio (Tommy Tantuico), Bobby Greenwood (Mrs. Postelwaite), Chito Reyes (Guerille), Paquito Salcedo (Mortician).

DAWN OF THE DEAD (1979)
Director: George Romero
David Emge (Stephen), Ken Foree (Peter), Scott Reiniger (Roger), Gaylen Ross (Francine).

DAWN OF THE MUMMY (1981)
Director: Armand Weston
Joan Levy, Victoria Johnson, Eilen Falson, John Salvo, George Peck, Barry Sattles, Brenda King.

DAY AFTER HALLOWEEN, THE (1980-Austral.) (A. K. A. "Snapshot")
Director: Simon Wincer
Chantal Contouri (Madeline), Hugh Keays-Byrne (Linsey), Sigrid Thornton (Angela), Robert Bruning (Elmer), Vincent Gil (Daryl), Denise Drysdale (Lilly), Jacqui Gordon, Lulu Pinkus, Peter Stratford, Steward Faichney, Jon Sidney, Julia Blake, Christine Amor, Peter Flemingham, Chris Milne, Bob Brown.

DAY AFTER TOMORROW, THE (TVM-1975) - 12-9-75
Director: Charles Crichton
Nick Tate (Harry Masters), Brian Blessed (Tom Bowen), Joanna Dunham (Anna Bowen), Martin Lev (David Bowen), Katherine Levy (Jane Masters), Don Fellows (Jim Forbes), Edward Bishop

(Narrator).

DAY MARS INVADED EARTH, THE (1962)
Director: Maury Dexter
Kent Taylor (Dr. David Fielding), Marie Windsor (Claire Fielding), William Mims (Dr. Web Spencer), Betty Beall (Judi Fielding), Gregg Shank (Rocky Fielding), Lowell Brown (Frank).

DAY OF THE ANIMALS (1977)
Director: William Girdler
Christopher George (Steve Buckner), Lynda Day George (Terry Marsh), Michael Ansara (Daniel Santee), Leslie Nielsen (Mr. Jensen), Jon Cedar (Frank Young), Ruth Roman (Mrs. Shirley Goodwin), Richard Jaeckel (Prof. MacGregor), Paul Mantee (Roy Moore), Andrew Stevens (Bob Denning), Susan Backlinie (Mandy Young), Walter Barnes (Ranger Tucker), Michael Rougas (Military Officer), Kathleen Bracken (Beth Hughes), Michael Clifford (Sheriff), Bobby Porter (Jon Goodwyn), Garrison True (newscaster), Michelle Stacy (little girl).

DAY OF THE DOLPHIN, THE (1973)
Director: Mike Nichols
George C. Scott (Dr. Jake Terrell), Trish Van Devere (Maggie Terrell), Fritz Weaver (Harold DeMilo), Severn Darden (Schwinn), Leslie Charleson (Maryanne), Paul Sorvino (Mahoney), John Dehner (Wallingford), John David Carson (Larry), William Roerick (Dunhill), Elizabeth Wilson (Mrs. Rome), Julie Follansbee, Florence Stanley, Brooke Hayward, Pat Englund (women at the club), Victoria Racimo (Lana), Edward Herrmann (Mike), Willie Meyers (Stone), Jon Korkes (David), Phyllis Davis (secretary).

DAY OF THE NIGHTMARE (1965)
Director: John Bushelman
John Ireland, John Hart, Elena Verdugo, Liz Renay, James Cross.

DAY OF THE TRIFFIDS, THE (1963)
Director: Stephen Sekely
Howard Keel (Bill Masen), Nichole Maurey (Christine Durrant), Janette Scott (Karen Goodwin), Kieron Moore (Tom Goodwin), Mervyn Johns (Prof. Coker), Janina Faye (Susan), Alison Legatt (Miss Coker), Carole Ann Ford (Bettina), Ewan Roberts (Dr. Soames), Geoffrey Mathews (Luis), Gilgi Hauser (Teresa), Victor Brooks (Poiret), Colette Wilde (Nurse Jamieson), Katya Douglas (Mary), Sidney Vivian (ticket agent), Thomas Gallagher

(burley man), John Simpson (blind man), Gary Hope (pilot).

DAY OF WRATH (1943-Dan.) (A. K. A. "Vreden's Dag")
Director: Carl T. Dreyer
Thorkild Roose, Lisbeth Movin, Albert Hoeberg, Anna Svierkier, Sigrid Neilendam, Preben Lerdoff, Olaf Ussing.

DAY THE EARTH CAUGHT FIRE, THE (1962)
Director: Val Guest
Edward Judd (Peter Stenning), Janet Munro (Jeannie Craig), Leo McKern (Bill Maguire), Reginald Beckwith (Harry), Gene Anderson (May), Renee Asherson (Angela), Austin Trevor (Sir John Kelly), Edward Underdown (Sanderson), Arthur Christiansen (editor), Michael Goodliffe (night editor), Robin Hawdon (Ronnie), Geoffrey Chater (Holroyd), Jane Aird (Nanny), Ian Ellis (Michael), Charles Morgan (foreign editor), John Barron (1st sub editor), Peter Butterworth (2nd sub editor), Michael Caine.

DAY THE EARTH FROZE, THE (1959-Fin./Sov.) (A. K. A. "Sampa")
Director: Julius Standberg
Nina Anderson (Anniky), Jon Powers (Lemminkainen), Ingrid Elhardt (Loukhy the witch), Peter Sorenson (Ilmarinen), Marvin Miller (narrator).

DAY THE EARTH MOVED, THE (TVM-1974) - 9-18-74
Director: Robert Michael Lewis
Jackie Cooper (Steve Barker), Beverly Garland (Helen Backsler), Cleavon Little (Harley Copeland), Stella Stevens (Kate Barker), William Windom (Judge Backsler), Kelly Thordsen (Officer Pat Ferguson), E. J. Andre (Henry Butler), Lucille Benson (Miss Porter), Ellen Blake (Evelyn Ferguson), Sid Melton (Chief), Tammy Harrington (Angela).

DAY THE EARTH STOOD STILL, THE (1951)
Director: Robert Wise
Michael Rennie (Klaatu/Mr. Carpenter), Patricia Neal (Helen Benson), Hugh Marlowe (Tom Stevens), Billy Gray (Bobby Benson), Sam Jaffe (Dr. Bernhardt), Lock Martin (Gort), Frances Bavier (Mrs. Barley), Frank Conroy (Mr. Harley), Carleton Young (Colonel), Edith Evanson (Mrs. Crockett), Robert Osterloh (Major White), Tyler McVey (Brady), John Brown (Mr. Barley), Marjorie Crossland (Hilda), Olan

Soule (Mr. Kurll), Drew Pearson, Gabriel Heatter, H. V. Kaltenborn, Elmer Davis (themselves), Fay Roope (Major General), James Seay (Government agent), Glenn Hardy (interviewer), House Peters, Jr. (M. P. Captain), Herbert Lytton (Brigadier General), Gil Herman (Government agent), Rush Williams (M. P. Sergeant), Freeman Lusk (Gen. Cutler), George Lynn (Col. Ryder), John Burton (British radio announcer), Harry Harvey, Jr. (taxi driver), Harry Lauter (platoon leader), Charles Evans (Major General), Harlan Warde (Mr. Carlson), Dorothy Neumann (Barnhardt's secretary), Wheaton Chambers (jeweler), Elizabeth Flournoy (customer), Howard Negley (Colonel), Kim Spalding, Lawrence Dobkin (medical corps captains), James Doyle (medical corps major), Bill Gentry, Kip/Stuart Whitman, Michael Capanna, Michael Mahoney (sentries), Michael Regan (Army Captain), Jack Daly, Harmon Stevens (men), Marshall Bradford (government man), John M. Reed (tank driver), James Craven (businessman), Sammy Ogg, Ricky Regan (boys), Ted Pearson (Colonel), John Close (Captain), David McMahon (English sergeant), Gayle Pace (Captain), Grady Galloway (radar operator), John Costello (Cockney), Eric Corrie, Michael Merris (British soldiers), Hassan Khayyam (Indian radio announcer).

DAY THE FISH CAME OUT, THE (1967-Gr./Brit.)
Director: Michael Cacoyannis
Candice Bergen (Electra), Tom Courtenay (the Navigator), Colin Blakely (the Pilot), Sam Wanamaker (Elias), Ian Ogilvy (Peter), Nicox Alexiou (goatherd), Paris Alexander (Fred), Marthur Mitchell (Frank), Dimitris Nicolaidis (dentist), Patricia Burke (Mrs. Mavroyannis), Marlena Carrere (goatherd's wife), Tom Klunis (Mr. French), William Berger (man in bed), Alexander Lykourezos (Director of Tourism), Dora Stratou, Costa Papaconstantinou (travel agents), Tom Whitehead (Mike), Assaf Dayan (tourist).

DAY THE SKY EXPLODED, THE (1959-Ital./Fr.) (A. K. A. "La Morte Viene Dallo Spazio", "Death Comes from Outer Space")
Director: Paolo Heusch
Paul Christian (John Maclaren), Madeleine Fischer (Katy Dandridge), Fiorella Mari (Mary Maclaren), Ivo Garrani (Herbert Weisser), Dario Michaelis (Pierre Leducq), Peter Meersman (Gen.

Wandorf), Jean-Jacques Delbo (Sergei Boetnikov), Massimo Zeppieri (Dennis Maclaren), Sam Galter.

DAY THE WORLD ENDED, THE (1956)
Director: Roger Corman
Richard Denning (Rick), Lori Nelson (Louise Maddison), Paul Birch (Captain Jim Maddison), Mike 'Touch' Connors (Tony Lamont), Adele Jergens (Ruby), Raymond Hatton (Pete), Paul Dubov (Radek), Jonathan Haze (contaminated man), Paul Blaisdell (the Mutant).

DAY TIME ENDED, THE (1980)
Director: John Cardos
Chris Mitchum (Richard), Jim Davis (Grant Williams), Dorothy Malone (Anna Williams), Scot Kolden (Steven Williams), Natasha Ryan (Jenny), Marcy Lafferty (Beth), Roberto Contreras.

DAY WITH THE DEVIL, A (1945-Mex.)
(A.K.A. "Un Dia con el Diablo")
Director: Miguel M. Delgado
Cantinflas, Andres Soler, Rafael Icardo, Pedro Elviro, Miguel Arenas, Estanislao Schillinsky.

DEAD AND BURIED (1981)
Director: Gary Sherman
James Farentino (Dan), Melody Anderson (Janet), Jack Albertson (Dobbs), Bill Quinn (Ernie), Macon McCalman (Ben), Nancy Locke Hauser (Linda), Dennis Redfield (Ron), Robert Englund (Harry), Michael Currie (Herman), Lisa Marie (hitchhiker), Lisa Blount (girl on the beach), Joe Medalis (doctor), Estelle Omens (Betty), Christopher Allport (George Le Moyne/Freddie).

DEAD ARE ALIVE, THE (1972-Yugo./
Ger./Ital.) (A.K.A. "L'Etrusco Uccidi Encore", "The Etruscan Kills Again")
Director: Armando Crispino
Alex Cord (Jason), Samantha Eggar (Myra), John Marley (Nikos), Najda Tiller (Leni), Horst Frank (Stephan), Enzo Tarascio (Giuranna), Carlo De Mejo (Igor), Vladan Milasinovic (Otello), Daniela Surina (Irene), Mario Maranzana (Vitanza), Wendy D'Olive (Giselle), Pier Luigi D'Orazio (Minelli), Christiane Von Blank (Velia), Ivan Pavicevac (policeman).

DEAD DON'T DIE, THE (TVM-1975) -
1-14-75
Director: Curtis Harrington
George Hamilton (Don Drake), Linda

Cristal (Vera LaValle), Ray Milland (Jim Moss), Joan Blondell (Levenia), James McEachin (Frankie Specht), Ralph Meeker (Lt. Reardon), Reggie Nalder (Perdido), Jerry Douglas (Ralph Drake), Milton Parsons (undertaker), William O'Connell (priest), Yvette Vickers, Russ Grieves, Brendon Dillon, Bill Smiley.

DEAD EYES OF LONDON, THE (1961-
Ger.) (A.K.A. "Die Toten Augen von London")
Director: Alfred Vohrer
Joachim Fuchsberger (Holt), Karin Baal (Nora), Dieter Borsche (Paul), Klaus Kinski, Ady Berber, Eddie Arent, Wolfgang Lukschy, Bobby Todd, Hans Paetsch, Ann Savo, Rudolph Fenner, Ida Ehre, Harry Wustenhagen, Fritz Schroder-Jahn.

DEADLIER THAN THE MALE (1967)
Director: Ralph Thomas
Richard Johnson (Hugh Drummond), Elke Sommer (Eckman), Nigel Green (Weston), Sylvia Koscina (Penelope), Steve Carlson (Robert Drummond), Laurence Naismith (Sir John), Zia Mohyeddin (King Fedra), Suzanna Leigh (Grace), Leonard Rossiter (Bridgenorth), George Pastell (Carloggio), Milton Reid (Chang), Jill Banner (Pam), Justine Lord (Miss Ashendon), Lee Montague (boxer), Virginia North, Didi Sydow, Yasuko Nagazumi, Dervis Ward, John Stone.

DEADLY AUGUST (1966)
Director:
Macdonald Carey, Howard Duff, Mary Murphy.

DEADLY BEES, THE (1966)
Director: Freddie Francis
Suzanna Leigh (Vicki Robbins), Frank Finlay (Manfred), Guy Doleman (Ralph Hargrove), Catherine Finn (Mrs. Hargrove), Michael Ripper (Hawkins), John Harvey (Thompson), Katy Wild (Doris Hawkins), Michael Gwynne (Dr. Lang), Alistair Williamson (Inspector), Frank Forsyth (doctor), Anthony Bailey (Compere), Tim Barrett (Harcourt), Greta Farrer (sister), James Cossins (coroner), Gina Gianelli (secretary), Maurice Good (agent).

DEADLY BLESSING (1981)
Director: Wes Craven
Maren Jensen (Martha), Ernest Borgnine (Isaiah), Lois Nettleton (Louisa), Susan Buckner (Vicky), Lisa Hartman (Faith), Sharon Stone (Lana), Jeff East (John Schmidt), Coleen Riley (Melissa), Kevin

Cooney (Sheriff), Doug Barr (Jim), Michael Berryman (William Gluntz), Lawrence Montaigne (Matthew Gluntz), Jenna Worthen (Mrs. Gluntz), Jonathan Gulla (Tom Schmidt), Chester Kulas, Jr. (Leopold), Lucky Mosley (Sammy), Annabelle Weenick (Ruth Schmidt), Neil Fletcher (gravedigger), Kevin Farr (fat boy), Bobby Dark (theatre manager), Dan Shackelford (medic), Percy Rodrigues (narrator).

DEADLY DREAM, THE (TVM-1971) -
9-25-71
Director: Alf Kjellin
Richard Jaeckel (Delgreve), Don Stroud (Kagen), Philip Pine (Dr. Farrow), Janet Leigh (Laura Hanley), Lloyd Bridges (Jim Hanley), Carl Betz (Dr. Howard Geary), Leif Erickson (Dr. Malcolm), Herbert Nelson (Dr. Goodman).

DEADLY HARVEST (1972)
Director: Timothy Bond
Clint Walker (Grant Franklin), Nehemiah Persoff (Mort Logan), Kim Cattrall (Susan Franklin), David Brown (Charles Ennis), Gary Davies (Michael Franklin), Dawn Greenhaigh (Leah Franklin), Tami Tucker (Bobbie Franklin), Jim Henshaw (John McCrae), Dwayne Mclean (Frank Wilcox), Tim Whelan (James Ennis), John Stoneham (Sam), Nuala Fitzgerald (Joyce Ennis), Les Carlson (the Minister), Cec Linder (the Chairman), Sean Sullivan (Dr. Abbott), Leo Leyden (Minister of Agriculture), Michael Tait (the Politician), Peter Jobin (Pierce), Jan Rubes (Swenson), Wally Crouter (militiaman), Hoah Cowan, Richard Ayers, Marcer Berule, Terr Martin, Rebecca Lager, Brad Spurgeon, John Peter Linton, Tony Parr.

DEADLY MANTIS, THE (1957)
Director: Nathan Juran
Craig Stevens (Col. Joe Parkman), Alix Talton (Marge Blaine), William Hopper (Dr. Ned Jackson), Florenz Ames (Prof. Anton Gunther), Donald Randolph (Gen. Mark Ford), Pat Conway (Sgt. Pete Allen), Phil Harvey (Lou), Paul Smith (Corporal), Floyd Simmons (Army Sergeant), Paul Campbell (Lt. Fred Pizar), Harry Tyler (spectator), David McMahon (Capt. Frank Carver), Madelon Mitchell (mother), Ned Le Fevre (announcer), Jess Kirkpatrick (father), James R. Haskin (civilian announcer), Tom Greenway (reporter), Bing Russell (trooper), George Lynn (bus driver), Jack Mather (Officer), William A. Forester (announcer), Helen Jay (Mrs. Far-

ley), John Close (engineer), James Lanphier (Col. Hervey), Tom Cound (Group Captain Hawkins), Dick Paxton (Plotter), William Anders (Sergeant), Keith Aldrich (co-pilot), Sumner Williams (pilot), Marvin Bryan (machinegunner), Skipper McNally (policeman), Harold Lee (Eskimo Chief), Ernesto Morelli (Italian fisherman).

DEADLY VISITOR, THE (TVM-1973) -
7-3-73
Director:
Gwen Verdon, Perry King (Jamie), Stephen Macht (Mulvancy), James Keach (Virgil), Ann Miles (the Presence).

DEAD MAN'S EYES (1955)
Director: Reginald LeBorg
Lon Chaney, Jr. (Dave Stuart), Jean Parker (Heather Hayden), Paul Kelly (Alan Bittaker), Acquanetta (Tania Czoraki), Thomas Gomez (Capt. Drury), Jonathan Hale (Dr. Sam Welles), George Meeker (Nick Phillips), Edward Fielding (Stanley Hayden), Eddie Dunn (Policeman Moriarity), Pierre Watkin (attorney), Beatrice Roberts (nurse).

DEAD MEN TELL NO TALES (1938)
Director: David Macdonald
Emlyn Williams (Dr. Headlam), Marius Goring (Greening), Clive Morton (Frank Fielding), Lesley Brook (Elizabeth Orme), Hugh Williams (Detective Insp. Martin), Sara Seegar (Marjorie), Jack Vivian (Crump), Christine Silver (Miss Haslett), Anne Wilton (Bridget), Marjorie Dale (the singer).

DEAD MEN WALK (1942)
Director: Samuel Newfield
George Zucco (Dr. Harold Clayton/Elwyn Clayton), Dwight Frye (Zolarr), Robert Strange, Mary Carlisle, Fern Emmett, Ned Young, Sam Flint, Hal Price.

DEAD OF NIGHT (1945)
Director: Alberto Cavalcanti ("The Ventriloquist's Dummy" segment), Charles Crichton ("The Golfing Story" segment), Basil Deardon ("Hearse Driver" segment) & Robert Hamer ("The Haunted Mirror" segment)
Mervyn Johns (Walter Craig), Roland Culver (Eliot Foley), Frederick Valk (Dr. van Straaten), Googie Withers (Joan Cortland), Sally Ann Howes (Sally O'Hara), Michael Redgrave (Maxwell Frere), Judy Kelly (Joyce Grainger), Ralph Michael (Peter Cortland), Mary Merrall (Mrs. Foley), Hartley Power (Sylvester Kee), Miles Malleson (Hearse Driver), Eliza-

beth Welch (Beulah), Barbara Leake
(Mrs. O'Hara), Anthony Baird (Hugh
Grainger), Johnny Maguire (the Dum-
my), Basil Radford, Naughton Wayne,
Allan Jeayes, Garry Marsh, Renee
Gadd, Magda Kun, Esme Perry.

DEAD OF NIGHT (TVM-1977) - 3-29-
   77
   Director: Dan Curtis
"Second Chance": Ed Begley, Jr.
(Frank), Christina Hart (Helen), Ann
Doran (Mrs. McCauley), Orin Cannon
(old farmer), Jean Le Bouvier (Mrs.
Cantrell), Jeff Reese (young man), Mi-
chael Talbott (Vinnie McCauley), Dick
McGarvin (Mr. Dorset), Karen Hurley
(Mrs. Dorset).
"No Such Thing As a Vampire": Patrick
Macnee (Dr. Gheria), Horst Buchholz
(Michael), Anjanette Comer (Alexis),
Elisha Cook, Jr. (Karel), Gail Bowman
(Maria), Joan Lemmo (Eva).
"Bobby": Joan Hackett (Alma), Lee H.
Montgomery (Bobby), Larry Green (dwarf).

DEAD ONE, THE (1961)
   Director: Barry Mahon
John Jackay (John), Linda Ormond (Linda), Monica Davis (Monica), Clyde Kelley (Jonas), Darlene Myrick (Bella Bella).

DEAD RINGER (1964)
   Director: Paul Henreid
Bette Davis (Margaret de Lorca/Edith
Philips), Karl Malden (Sgt. Jim Hobb-
son), Peter Lawford (Tony Collins),
Philip Carey (Sgt. Hoag), Jean Hagen
(Dede Marshall), George Macready
(Paul Harrison), Estelle Winwood (Ma-
triarch), George Chandler (George),
Cyril Delevanti (Henry), Mario Alcaide
(Garcia), Monika Henreid (Janet), Ken
Lynch (Capt. Johnson), Bert Remsen
(Dan), Charles Watts (apartment mana-
ger).

DEAD SPEAK, THE (1935-Mex.) (A.K.A.
"Los Muertos Hablan")
   Director: Gabriel Soria
Julia Soler, Amalia de Ilisa, Manuel
Noriega.

DEALERS IN DEATH, THE (1966-Mex.)
(A.K.A. "Profanadores de Tumbas",
"Profaners of Tombs")
   Director: Jose Diaz Morales
Santo, Gina Romand, Mario Orea, Jorge
Peral, Lobo Negro, Jesus Camacho,
Jessica Munguia, Fernando Oses.

DEAR, DEAD DELILAH (1972)

Director: John Farris
Agnes Moorehead (Delilah), Will Geer
(Ray), Dennis Patrick (Alonzo), Michael
Ansara (Morgan), Patricia Carmichael
(Luddy), Robert Gentry (Richard), Anne
Meacham (Grace), Elizabeth Eis (Ellen),
Ruth Baker (Buffy), Ann Gibbs (Young
Luddy), John Mariott (Marshall).

DEATH AT LOVE HOUSE (TVM-1976) -
   9-3-76
   Director: E.W. Swackhamer
Robert Wagner (Joel Gregory), Kate
Jackson (Donna Gregory), Joan Blondell
(Marcella Gefenhardt), Sylvia Sydney
(Mrs. Clara Josephs), Dorothy Lamour
(Denise Christian), Bill Macy (Oscar
Payne), John Carradine (Conan Carroll),
Marianna Hill (Lorna Love), John A. Zee
(Eric Herman), Joseph Bernard (bus dri-
ver), Robert Gibbons (director), Al Han-
sen (policeman), Croften Hardester (ac-
tor in film).

DEATH BITE (1982)
   Director: William Fruet
Oliver Reed, Kerrie Keane, Peter Fon-
da, Al Waxman, Gerard Parkes, George
Bloomfield.

DEATH BY INVITATION (1971)
   Director: Ken Friedman
Shelby Leverington, Norman Paige, Aa-
ron Phillips, Denver John Collins.

DEATH CAR ON THE FREEWAY (TVM-
   1979) - 9-25-79
   Director: Hal Needham
Shelley Hack (Janette Clausen), George
Hamilton (Ray Jeffries), Peter Graves
(Lt. Haller), Frank Gorshin (Ralph Chan-
dler), Barbara Rush (Rosemary), Har-
riet Nelson (Mrs. Shell), Dinah Shore
(Lynn Bernhiemer), Alfie Wise (Ace
Durham), Abe Vigoda (Frisch), Hal
Needham (driving instructor), Morgan
Brittany (actress), Tara Buckman, Sid
Haig, Robert F. Lyons, Gloria Stroock,
Marguerite DeLain, Hank Brandt, Nancy
Stephens, Jack Collins, Jim Negele, Ro-
ger Aaron Brown, Craig Baxley, Buddy
H. Farmer.

DEATH CURSE OF TARTU (1966)
   Director: William Grefe
Sherman Hayes (Johnny), Fred Pinero
(Ed Tison), Babette Sherrill (Julie Ti-
son), Doug Hobart (Tartu), Gary Holtz
(Tommy), Mayra Cristine (Cindy), Mau-
rice Stewart (Joann), Frank Weed (Sam
Gunter), Bill Marcos (Billy/the Indian).

DEATH DIMENSION (1978)

Director: Al Adamson
Jim Kelly, George Lazenby, Harold
Sakata, Patch Mackenzie, Bob Minor,
Terry Moore, Myron Bruce Lee, April
Sommers.

DEATHDREAM (1972) (A. K. A. "Dead
of Night", "The Night Andy Came Home")
Director: Bob Clark
John Marley (Charles Brooks), Lynn
Carlin (Christine Brooks), Richard Bac-
kus (Andy Brooks), Henderson Forsythe
(Doc Allman), Anya Ormsby (Cathy
Brooks), Jane Daly (Joanne), Michael
Mazes (Bob), Arthur Anderson (post-
man), Bud Hoey (Ed), Virginia Cortez
(Rosalie), Arthur Bradley (Army Cap-
tain), David Gawlikowski (truck driver),
Raymond Michel (policeman), Robert
Cannon (drunk), Jeff Becker, Scott Bec-
ker, Kevin Schweizer, Greg Wells (boys),
Jeff Gillen (bartender), Mal Jones (She-
riff), Edward Anderson (Deputy), Alan
Ormsby (bystander), George Devries
(1st TV announcer), Robert Noble (2nd
TV announcer).

DEATH FROM A DISTANCE (1936)
Director: Frank R. Strayer
Lee Kohlmar (Prof. Ernst Einfeld),
Wheeler Oakman (Langsdale), Robert
Frazer (Morgan), John Davidson (Ah-
mad Haidru), Russell Hopton (Detective
Lt. Ted Mallory), Lola Lane (Kay Pal-
mer), Lew Kelly (Detective Regan),
Cornelius Keefe (Gorman), George Ma-
rion (Jim Gray), John St. Polis (Prof.
Trowbridge) E. H. Calvert (District At-
torney), John Dilson (Editor McConnell),
Henry Hall (Medical Examiner), Her-
bert Vigran (photographer), Jane Keck-
ley, Creighton Hale, Eric Mayne (wit-
nesses), Charles West (fingerprint expert), Hal Price (detective), Frank La-
Rue (desk sergeant), Joel Lyon, Lynton
Brent, Ralph Brooks (reporters).

DEATH IN SPACE (TVM-1974) - 6-17-
74
Director: Charles Dubin
George Maharis (Dan Summit), Came-
ron Mitchell (Arnold Chester), Robert
Walker, Jr. (Barry Wolf), Margaret
O'Brien (Pam Rhodes), Don Knight (Dr.
King), Susan Oliver (Carla Burke), Wil-
liam Bryant (Norman Burke), Lynnette
Mettey (Kim).

DEATH IN THE ARENA (1962-Ital.)
(A. K. A. "Maciste, il Gladiatore
Piu Forte del Monde", "Colossus
of the Arena")
Director: Michele Lupo

Mark Forest (Maciste), Scilla Gabel,
John Chevron, Jose Greci.

DEATHMASTER, THE (1971)
Director: Ray Danton
Robert Quarry (Khorda), Brenda Dick-
son (Rona), Bill Ewing (Pico), John
Fiedler (Pop), William Jordan (Monk
Reynolds), Betty Anne Rees (Esslin),
Le Sesne Hilton (Barbado), Tari Taba-
kin (Mavis), John Lasell (Detective),
Freda T. Vanterpool (dancer), Kitty
Vallacher, Michael Cronin, Olympia
Sylvers, Ted Lynn, Bob Wood, Charles
Hornsby.

DEATH MOON (TVM-1978) - 5-31-78
Director: Bruce Kessler
Robert Foxworth (Jason Palmer), France
Nuyen (Tapulua), Barbara Trentham
(Diane May), Dolph Sweet (Lt. Russ
Cort), Charles Haid (Earl Wheelie), De-
bralee Scott (Sherry Weston), John Free-
man (Mrs. Jennings), Joe Penny (Rick
Bladen), Branscombe Richmond (Vince
Tatupu), Albert Harris (Dr. Restin),
Don Pomes (Dr. Erlich), Carole Kai
(Tami Waimea), Mitch Mitchell (Jennings),
Lydia Lei Kayahara (Julie Chin), Jose
Bulatao (Wolf Man dancer), Terry Taka-
da, Bob Witthans, Carole Avery, Chris
Bailey, Donna White, Alan Vicencio,
Robert I. Preston.

DEATH OF THE APE-MAN (1962-Czech.)
(A. K. A. "Tarzanova Smrt")
Director: Jaroslav Balik
Rudolf Hrusinsky (Baron Wolfgang von
Hoppe/Tarzan), Jana Stepankova (Regi-
na), Margin Ruzek (Baron Heinrich von
Hoppe), Vlastimil Hasek (Dr. Foreyt),
Ilya Racek (Usher), Elena Halkova (Ba-
roness), Nina Popelikova (lady with buck-
teeth), Miroslav Homolka (S. A. man),
Slavka Budinova (ring director).

DEATH ON THE FOUR-POSTER (1963-
Ital./Fr.) (A. K. A. "Delitto ala Spec-
chio")
Director: Ambrogio Molteni & Jean
Josipovici
John Drew Barrymore, Gloria Milland,
Michel Lemoine, Antonella Lualdi, Ma-
rio Valdemarin, Luisa Rivelli.

DEATH RACE 2000 (1975)
Director: Paul Bartel
David Carradine (Frankenstein), Simone
Griffith (Annie), Sylvester Stallone (Ma-
chine Gun Joe Viterbo), Mary Woronov
(Calamity Jane), Roberta Collins (Mathil-
da the Hun), Martin Kove (Nero the Hero),
Louisa Moritz (Myra), Joyce Jameson

(Grace Pander), Don Steele (Junior Bruce), Sandy McCallum (Mr. President), Harriet Medin (Thomasina Paine), Carle Bensen (Harold), George Wagner (Lon), Vince Trankina (Lt. Fury), Fred Grandy (Herman the German), Leslie McRay (Cleopatra), William Shephard (Pete), Darla McDonell (Mrs. Rhonda Bainbridge), Jack Favorite (Henry), Wendy Bartel (Laurie), Paul Lawrence (special agent), John Landis (mechanic), Roger Rook (radio operator), Bill Morey (deacon), Sandy Ignon (FBI agent).

DEATH RAY 2000 (TVM-1981) - 3-5-81
      Director: Lee H. Katzin
Robert Logan (Thomas R. Sloane), Ann Turkel (Sabina Dorffman), Clive Revill (Erik Clawson), Ji-Tu Cumbuka (Torque), Dan O'Herlihy (the Director), Paul Mantee (James), Roger Til (Henri), Maggie Cooper (Chrissy Randall), Peter Nyberg (August Inmann), Diana Webster (Mother Superior), Michelle Carey (Voice of Effie), Yuliis Ruval (Ilse Lander), Fiona Gordon (Sister Trilby), Richard Lineback (enlister man), James Chandler (Gideon Peak guark), Ava Lazar (flight attendant), Paula Jones (ground hostess), Connie Garrison (model), Stephen Coit (coroner), Tonyo Melendez (Cuban officer), William Meigs (U.S. Army General), David Brandon (General's aide), Michael Yama (photographer), Penelope Windust, Fred Sadoff.

DEATH SHIP (1980)
      Director: Alvin Rakoff
George Kennedy (Ashland), Richard Crenna (Trevor Marshall), Sally Ann Howes (Margaret Marshall), Nick Mancuso (Nick), Kate Reid (Sylvia), Victoria Burgoyne (Lori), Jennifer McKinney (Robin), Danny Higham (Ben), Saul Rubinek (Jackie).

DEATHSPORT (1978)
      Director: Henry Suso & Allan
         Arkush
David Carradine (Kaz Oshay), Claudia Jennings (Deneer), Richard Lynch (Ankar), William Smithers (Dr. Karl), Jesse Vint (Polna), Will Walker (Marcus), David McLean (Lord Zirpola), H.B. Haggerty (jailer), Jim Galante (Tritan guard), John Himes (Tritan President), Peter Hooper (Bakkar), Brenda Venus (Adriann), Gene Hartline (sergeant), Chris Howell (officer), Valerie Rae Clark (dancer).

DEATH TAKES A HOLIDAY (1934)
      Director: Mitchell Leisen

Frederic March (Prince Sirki), Evelyn Venable (Princess Gratzia), Sir Guy Standing (Sir Lambert de Catolica), Gail Patrick (Rhoda Fenton), Kent Taylor (Corrado de Catolica), Kathleen Howard (Princess Maria), Catherine Alexander (Alda Countess di Parma), Helen Westley (Duchess Stephanie), Henry Travers (Baron Cesarea), G.P. Huntley, Jr. (Eric Bagleg), Edward Van Sloan (Dr. Valle), Otto Hoffmann (Fedele), Hector Sarno (Pietro), Anna de Linsky (maid), Frank Yaconelli (flower vendor).

DEATH TAKES A HOLIDAY (TVM-1971) - 10-21-71
      Director: Robert Butler
Monte Markham (David Smith), Yvette Mimieux (Peggy Chapman), Melvyn Douglas (Judge Earl Chapman), Myrna Loy (Selena Chapman), Bert Convy (John Cummings), Kerwin Matthews (Sen. Earl Chapman, Jr.), Maureen Reagan (Ellen Chapman), Austin Willis (Martin Herndon), Colby Chester (Tony Chapman), Priscilla Pointer (Marion Chapman), Mario Machado, Regis J. Cordic (TV announcers).

DEATH TO SISTER MARY (TVM-1974) - 5-21-74 (A.K.A. "Murder Is a One-Act Play")
      Director: Robert D. Cardona
Robert Powell (Rook), Jennie Linden (Sister Mary), George Maharis (Mark Fields), Anthony Newlands (Tony Barton), Derek Fowlds (Dicky), Joan Haythorne (Mother Superior), Leigh Lawson (Larry Turner), Windsor Davies (Detective Moore), Gerry Cowan (TV Director), Norman Mitchell (security man), Maggie Rennie (housekeeper), Jill Shakespeare (operator).

DEATHTRAP (1982)
      Director: Sidney Lumet
Michael Caine (Sidney Bruhl), Christopher Reeve (Clifford Anderson), Dyan Cannon (Myra Bruhl), Irene Worth (Helga Ten Dorp), Henry Jones (Porter Milgrim), Joe Silver (Seymour Starger), Tony di Benedetto (Burt, the bartender), Al LeBreton (handsome actor), The Rev. Francis B. Creamer, Jr. (Minister), Stewart Klein (Stewart Klein), Jeffrey Lyons (Jeffrey Lyons), Joel Siegel (Joel Siegel), Jenny Lumet (stage newsboy), Jayne Heller (stage actress), George Peck (stage actor), Perry Rosen (stage actor).

DEATH TRAVELS TOO MUCH (1965-Span./Fr./Ital.) (A.K.A. "La Muerte

Viaja Demasiado")
Director: Claude Autant-Lara,
Giancarlo Zagni & Jose M. Forque
Emma Penella, Pierre Brasseur, Folco Lulli, Alida Valli, Sylvie, Leo Anchoriz.

DEATH VALLEY (1982)
Director: Dick Richards
Paul Le Mat (Mike), Catherine Hicks (Sally), Stephen McHattie (Hal), A. Wilford Brimley (Sherriff), Edward Hermann (Paul Stanton), Jack O'Leary (Earl), Peter Billingsley (Billy), Mary Steelsmith (baby sitter), Gina Christian (R. V. girl), Kirk I. Kiskella, Frank J. Cimorelli (R. V. boys).

DEATHWATCH (1980-Fr. /Ger.)
Director: Bertrand Tavernier
Romy Schneider (Katherine Mortenhoe), Harvey Keitel (Roddy), Harry Dean Stanton (Vincent Ferriman), Max Von Sydow (Gerald Mortenhoe), Therese Liotard (Tracey).

DECOY, THE (1946)
Director: Jack Bernhard
Edward Norris (Jim Vincent), Robert Armstrong (Frank Olins), Sheldon Leonard (Joe Portugal), Jean Gillie (Margot Shelby), Herbert Rudley (Dr. Craig), Ray Teal, Philip Van Zandt, Donald Kerr, Bert Roach, William Ruhl, Carol Donne, Betty Lou Hear, John Shay, William Self, Judy Gilbert, Ferris Taylor, Walden Boyle, Rosemary Bertrand.

DEEP RED (1976-Ital.) (A. K. A. "The Hatchet Murders")
Director: Dario Argento
David Hemmings (Marc Daly), Daria Nicolodi (Gianna Brezzi), Macha Meril (Helga), Gabriele Lavia (Carlo), Eros Pagni (Calcabrini), Giuliana Calandra (Amanda), Clara Calamai (Marta), Glauco Mauri (Giordani), Nicoletta Elmi.

DELUGE (1933)
Director: Felix Feist
Peggy Shannon (Claire Arlington), Sidney Blackmer (Martin Webster), Lois Wilson (Helen Webster), Matt Moore (Tom), Ralf Harolde (Norwood), Fred Kohler (Jephson), Edward Van Sloan (Prof. Carlysle), Samuel S. Hinds (Chief Forecaster), Lane Chandler (survivor), Philo McCullough, Harry Semels (renegades).

DELUSION (1980)
Director: Alan Beattie
Joseph Cotten (Ivan Langrock), Patri-

cia Pearcy, John Dukakis, David Hayward, Leon Charles.

DEMENTED (1980)
Director: Arthur Jeffreys
Salle Elyse (Linda Rogers), Bruce Gilchrist (Matt Rogers), Deborah Alter (Annie), Kathryn Clayton (Carol), Bryan Charles (Dr. Dillman), Chip Mathews (Mark), Mark Justin, Robert Mendel, Douglas Price (Jokers), Stephen Blood (detective), Bosco Palazzolo (Manuel), John Green, J. Kelly (Police Officers), Bill Martin, Jay Belinkoff, Robert Mendel, Mark Del Castille (rapists).

DEMENTIA (1953)
Director: John Parker
Adrienne Barrett, Bruno VeSota, Richard Barron, Ben Roseman, Ed Hinkle, Lucille Howland, Debbie VeSota.

DEMENTIA 13 (1963)
Director: Francis Ford Coppola
William Campbell (Richard Haloran), Luana Anders (Louise Haloran), Patrick Magee (Justin Caleb), Mary Mitchell (Kane), Ethne Dunn (Lady Haloran), Bart Patton (Billy Haloran), Peter Reed (John Haloran), Karl Schanzer (Simon), Barbara Dowling (Kathleen), Derry O'Donovan (Lilian), Ron Perry.

DEMON, THE (1963-Ital. /Fr.) (A. K. A. "Il Demonio")
Director: Brunello Rondi
Daliah Lavi (Mira), Frank Wolff (Antonio), G. Cristofanelli (Padre Tommaso), N. Tagliacozzo (Zio Giuseppe).

DEMON (1976) (A. K. A. "God Told Me To")
Director: Larry Cohen
Tony LoBianco (Peter Nicholas), Deborah Raffin (Casey Forster), Sandy Dennis (Martha Nicholas), Richard Lynch (Bernard Phillips), Sylvia Sidney (Miss Mullen), Sam Levine (Everett Lukas), Mike Kellin (Deputy Commissioner), Robert Drivas (David Morten), Robert Nichols (Fletcher), Sammy Williams (Harold Gorman), Andy Kaufman (police assassin), William Roerick (Richards), Jo Flores Chase (Mrs. Gorman), Harry Bellaver (Cookie), George Patterson (Zero), Lester Rawlins (Board Chairman), John Heffernan (Bramwell), Walter Steele (junkie), Alan Cauldwell (Bramwell as a youth), Mason Adams (obstetrician).

DEMON, THE (1981)
Director: Percival Rubens

Jennifer Holmes (Mary), Cameron Mitchell (Col. Bill Carson), Zoli Markey (Jo), Craig Gardner, Peter S. Elliott, Moira Winslow, Mark Tanous, Diane Burmeister, George Korelin, Vera Blacker, John Parsonson, Ashleigh Sendin, Graham Kennard, April Galetti, Jannie Wienand, Amanda Wildman.

DEMON BARBER OF FLEET STREET, THE (1936) (A. K. A. "Sweeney Todd")
Director: George King
Tod Slaughter (Sweeney Todd), Bruce Seton (Mack), Eve Lister (Johanna), D. J. Williams (Stephen Oakley), Davina Craig (Nan), Stella Rho (Mrs. Lovat), Jerry Verno (Pearley), Johnny Singer (the Beadle).

DEMON! DEMON! (TVM-1975) - 11-11-75
Director: Richard Dunlap
Bradford Dillman (Samn), Juliet Mills (Isobel), Robert Symonds (Ruig), Robert Emhardt.

DEMONIACS (1977-Fr.)
Director: Jean Rollin
Lieva Lone, Joelle Coeur, Patricia Hermenier.

DEMON LOVER, THE (1977)
Director: Donald G. Jackson & Jerry Younkins
Gunnar Hansen (Prof. Peckinpah), Christmas Robbins (Laval Blessing), Val Meyerik (Damian Kaluta), Tom Hutton (Detective Tom Frazetta), Linda Conrad (Elaine Ormsby), Sonny Bell (Officer Lester Gould), Phil Foreman (Alex Redondo), Carol Lasowski (Sally Jones), Susan Bullen (Susan Ackerman), Ron Hiveley (Paul Foster), David Howard (Charles Wrightson), Jan Porter (Jane Corben), Kathy Stewart (Pamela Kirby), Michael McGivern (Garrett Adams), Priscilla Southwell (Mrs. Frazetta), Kevin Baetz (Pete), Steve Lincoln (Arnie).

DEMON POND (1980-Jap.) (A. K. A. "Yashaga Ike")
Director: Masahiro Shinoda
Tamasaburo Bando (Yuri/Princess Shirayuki), Go Kato (Akira Hagiwara), Koji Nanbara (Priest Shikami), Tsutomi Yamazaki (Gakuen Yamasawa), Yatsuko Tan-ami, Norihei Miki, Hisahi Igawa, Ryunosuke Kaneda, Juro Kara.

DEMON RAGE (1981) (A. K. A. "Satan's Mistress", "Dark Eyes")
Director: James Polakoff

Britt Ekland (Ann-Marie), Lana Wood (Lisa), Kabir Bedi (the Spirit), John Carradine (Father Stratten), Sherry Scott (Michelle), Don Galloway (Carl), Elise-Anne (Belline), Tom Hallick (Burt), Chris Polakof (Cissy), John Simon (Police Sergeant), Alan Harris (Dave), Howard Murphy (the Beast), Michael Blackburn (ambulance driver), Bennett Waxman (ambulance attendant), Rick Alan, La Donna, K. Starchuk, Rheya Ferroh, Michelle Waxman (Demons).

DEMONS, THE (1972-Port./Fr.) (A. K. A. "Les Demons")
Director: Jesus Franco
Anne Lipert, Howard Vernon, Alberto Dalbes, Britt Nichols.

DEMON SEED (1977)
Director: Donald Cammell
Julie Christie (Susan Harris), Fritz Weaver (Alex Harris), Gerrit Graham (Susan Harris), Berry Kroeger (Petrosian), John O'Leary (Royce), Alfred Dennis (Mokri), Larry Blake (Cameron), Lisa Lu (Soon Yen), David Roberts (Warner), Patricia Wilson (Mrs. Talbert), Michael Glass (technician), Monica MacLean (Joan Kemp), E. Hampton Beagle (night operator), Michelle Stacy (Marlene), Dana Laurita (Amy), Felix Scilla, Tiffany Potter (babies), Robert Vaughn (voice of Proteus).

DEMONS OF THE MIND (1971)
Director: Peter Sykes
Patrick Magee (Dr. Falkenberg), Robert Hardy (Frederich Zorn), Shane Briant (Emil Zorn), Gillian Hille (Elizabeth Zorn), Yvonne Mitchell (Hilda), Paul Jones (Carl Richter), Kenneth J. Warren (Klaus), Virginia Wetherell (Inge), Robert Brown (Fischinger), Michael Hordern (Priest).

DEMON WITCH CHILD (1976-Span.) (A. K. A. "El Poder de las Tinieblas")
Director: Armando Ossorio
Julian Mateos, Fernando Sancho, Marian Salgado, Lone Fleming, Angel Del Pozo.

DERANGED (1974)
Director: Jeff Gillen & Alan Ormsby
Roberts Blossom (Ezra Cobb), Cosette Lee (Amanda Cobb), Robert Warner (Harlan Kootz), Marcia Diamond (Jenny Kootz), Brian Sneagle (Brad Kootz), Robert McHeady (Sheriff), Arlene Gillen (Miss Johnson), Marion Waldman (Maureen Selby), Micki Moore (Mary Ransom), Pat Orr (Sally Peterson), Jack Mather (drunk),

Leslie Carlson (narrator).

DESPERATE LIVING (1977)
Director: John Waters
Liz Renay (Muffy St. Jacques), Mink
Stole (Peggy Gravel), Susan Lowe (Mole
McHenry), Edith Massey (Queen Carlotta), Jean Hill (Grizelda Brown), Mary
Vivian Pearce (Princess Coo-Coo),
Cookie Mueller (Flipper), Sharon Niesp
(Shotsie), Marina Melin (Shina), Ed
Peranio (Lt. Wilson), Channing Wilroy
(Lt. Williams), Steve Butow (Lt. Grogan), George Stover (Bosley Gravel),
Turkey Joe (motorcycle cop), Pirie
Woods (babysitter), Roland Hertz (Muffy's husband), H. C. Kliemisch (Big
Jimmy Dong), George Figgs (Herbert),
Dolores Deluxe (nurse), Pat Moran
(pervert), Peter Koper, Steve Parker,
Pete Denzer, David Klein, Chuck Yeaton, Ralph Crocker (goons).

DESTINATION INNER SPACE (1966)
Director: Francis D. Lyon
Scott Brady (Commander Wayne), Sheree North (Sandra), Gart Merrill (Dr.
LeSatier), Mike Road (Hugh), Ron Burke
(the Creature), Roy Barcroft, Wende
Wagner, John Howard, James Hong,
William Thourly, Glen Spies, Biff Elliot, Richard Niles, Ken Delo, Ed
Charles Sweeny.

DESTINATION MOON (1950)
Director: Irving Pichel
John Archer (Jim Barnes), Tom Powers
(Gen. Thayer), Warner Anderson (Dr.
Charles Cargraves), Dick Wesson (Joe
Sweeney), Erin O'Brien Moore (Mrs.
Cargraves).

DESTINATION NIGHTMARE (TVM-1958)
(A. K. A. "The Veil" pilot)
Director: Paul Landers
Boris Karloff (Host/Ira Perry/Pete
Wade, Sr./Prof. Charles Goncour/
Morgan Debs), Whit Bissell (Dr. Will
Madison), George Hamilton (Krishna
Vernois), Ron Hagerthy (Pete Wade,
Jr.), Myron Healey (Bill Tighe), Roy
Engel (Wally), Denise Alexander (Ruth
Cooper), Olive Blakeney, Frances O'-
Farrell, Eve Brent, Shirley Mitchell,
Iphigineie Castiglione, Julius Johnson,
Jean Del Val, Rusty Lane, Tod Andrews,
Lee Terrance, Pitt Herbert, Claudia
Bryar, Jack Lomas, Kelly Thordsen.

DESTINY (1921-Ger.) (A. K. A. "Der
Mude Tod")
Director: Fritz Lang
Bernard Goetzke (Death), Lil Dagover,

Rudolf Klein-Rogge, Walter Janssen,
Carl Kuckert, Hans Sternborg, Erich
Pabst, Karl Huszar-Puffy, Max Adalbert, Georg John, Paul Blensfeld, Edward von Winterstein, Karl Platen.

DESTINY (1944)
Director: Reginald LeBorg
Gloria Jean (Jane), Alan Curtis (Cliff),
Minna Gombell (Marie), Frank Craven
(Clem), Vivian Austin (Phyllis), Grace
McDonald (Betty), Frank Fenton (Sam).

DESTROY ALL MONSTERS (1968-Jap.)
(A. K. A. "Kaiju Soshingeki", "Attack
of the Marching Monsters")
Director: Inoshiro Honda
Jun Tazaki (Dr. Yoshido), Akira Kubo
(Capt. Katsuo Yamabe), Yoshio Tsuchiya
(Dr. Otani), Andrew Hughes (Dr. Stevenson), Yukiko Kobayshi (Kyoko), Kenji Sahara (Nishikawa), Kyoko Ai (Queen
of Kilaaks).

DESTROY ALL PLANETS (1968-Jap.)
(A. K. A. "Gamera tai Uchi Kaiju Bairusu", "Gamera vs. Outer Space Monster Viras", "Gamera tai Viras",
"Gamera vs. Viras")
Director: Kenji Yuasa
Kojiro Hongo (Nobuhiko Shimada), Toru
Takatsuka (Maseo Nakaya), Kurl Crane
(Jim Morgan), Michiko Yaegaki (Mairko
Nakaya), Mari Atsumi (Junko Aoyama).

DESTRUCTORS, THE (1967)
Director: Francis D. Lyon
Richard Egan (Dan Street), Patricia O-
wens (Charlie), John Ericson (Dutch
Holland), Joan Blackman (Stassa Gertmann),
Michael Ansara (Count Mario Romano),
David Brian (Hogan), Khigh Dhiegh (King
Chou Lai), Johnny Seven (Spaniard), Gregory Morton (Dr. Frazer), John Howard
(Bushnell), Jim Adams (Michael Dugan),
Eddie Firestone (Barnes), Jayne Massey
(Suzie).

DEVIL, THE (1920)
Director: James Young
George Arliss, Edmund Lowe, Sylvia
Breamer, Mrs. George Arliss, Lucy
Cotton, Roland Bottomley.

DEVIL AND MAX DEVLIN, THE (1981)
Director: Steven Hilliard Stern
Elliott Gould (Max Devlin), Bill Cosby
(Barney Satin), Susan Anspach (Penny
Hart), Adam Rich (Toby Hart), Julie
Budd (Stella Summera), David Knell (Nerve
Nordlinger), Sonny Shroyer (Big Billy
Hunniker), Ronnie Schell (Greg Weems),
Reggie Nalder (Chairman of the Devil's

Council), Lillian Muller (Veronica),
Vernon Weddle (Justice of the Peace),
Helene Winston (Agent Hargraves),
Charles Shamata (Jerry Nadler), Army
Archerd (himself), Deborah Baltzell
(Heidi), Stanley Brock (the counterman),
Vic Dunlop (Brian), Ted Zeigler (Mr.
Billings), Jeannie Wilson (Laverne Hun-
niker), Julie Parrish (Sheila), Made-
lyn Cates (Mrs. Trent), Denise DuBar-
ry (Stella's secretary), Gustaf Unger
(Gregory), Joseph Burke (Steven), Ber-
til Unger (Julian), Tak Kubota (Bruce),
Susan Tolsky (Nerve's mom), Sally K.
Marr (Mrs. Gormley), Stu Gilliam
(orderly No. 1), Dailey Pike (orderly
No. 2), Ruth Manning (Mrs. Davis),
Ernest Harada (motorcycle scout No.
1), Bill Saito (motorcycle scout No. 2),
Rahsaan Morris (Tremaine), Bartine
Zane (blind lady), Adam Starr (kid at
carnival), Chip Courtland, Rene Lamart,
Mark Andrews (jocks), Teri Landrum
(Susie), Tracie Savage (Pammy), Nan-
cy Bond (Mrs. Minushkin), Sheila Rogers (Mrs. Pepper), Robert Baron (Mr.
Pepper), Pete Renaday (studio engineer),
Albert Able (M. C. announcer), Roger
Price (old man), Robert S. Telford
(camper owner), Wally K. Berns (fan
at party), Mindy Sterling, Richard Las-
tings (fans at Grammy's), Richard Crystal (Grammy award presenter), Steve
Eastin (Larry Binder), James Almanzar (ticket taker), Jackie Russell (carnival kid's mom), Nick Angotti (TV reporter), Gary Morgan (record store
D. J.), Ted Noose (officer), Bari Roulette (maid of honor), Jan Jorden (woman in lounge).

DEVIL AND MISS SARAH, THE (TVM-
1971) - 12-4-71
    Director: Michael Caffrey
Gene Barry (Rankin), Janice Rule (Sa-
rah Turner), James Drury (Gil Turner),
Donald Moffat (Appleton), Logan Ramsey
(Holmes), Slim Pickens (Stoney), Charles
McGraw (Duncan).

DEVIL BAT, THE (1940)
    Director: Jean Yarborough
Bela Lugosi (Dr. Paul Carruthers),
Dave O'Brien (Johnny Layton), Suzanne
Kaaren (Mary Heath), Donald Kerr
('One Shot' McGuire), John Ellis (Roy
Heath), Edward Mortimer (Martin Heath),
Guy Usher (Henry Morton), John David-
son, Wally Rairdon, Alan Baldwin, Hal
Price, Arthur Bryan, Gene O'Donnell,
Yolande Mallott.

DEVIL BAT'S DAUGHTER (1946)

    Director: Frank Wisbar
Nolan Leary (Dr. Elliot), John James
(Ted), Molly Lamont (Ellen), Rosemary
LaPlanche, Edward Cassidy, Eddie Kane,
Frank Pharr, Michael Hale, Monica
Mars.

DEVIL COMMANDS, THE (1941)
    Director: Edward Dmytryk
Boris Karloff (Dr. Julian Blair), Richard
Fiske (Richard Sayles), Amanda Duff
(Anne Blair), Anne Revere (Mrs. Wal-
ters), Dorothy Adams (Mrs. Marcy),
Kenneth MacDonald (Sheriff Willis), Ralph
Penney (Karl), Walter Baldwin (Seth
Marcy), Shirley Warde (Helen Blair).

DEVIL DOG: THE HOUND OF HELL
(TVM-1978) - 10-31-78
    Director: Curtis Harrington
Richard Crenna (Mike Barry), Yvette
Mimieux (Betty Barry), Kim Richards
(Bonnie Barry), Ike Eisenmann (Char-
lie Barry), R. G. Armstrong (Dunworth),
Lou Frizzell (George Baskins), Victor
Jory (Shaman), Ken Kercheval (Miles
Amory), Martine Beswicke (red-haired
lady), Bob Navarro (newscaster), Lois
Ursoni (Mrs. Hadley), Jerry Fogel (doc-
tor), Warren Munson (superintendent),
Deborah Karpf, Kevin McKenzie, Shelley
Curtis, Jan Burrell, Jack Carol, James
Reynolds, E. E. Sirianni, Dana Laurita.

DEVIL DOLL, THE (1936)
    Director: Tod Browning
Lionel Barrymore (Paul Lavond/Madame
Mandelip), Maureen O'Sullivan (Lorraine
Lavond), Lucy Beaumont (Mme. Lavond),
Frank Lawton (Toto), Henry B. Walthall
(Marcel), Rafaela Ottiano (Malita), Grace
Ford (Lachna), Robert Greig (Coulvet),
Arthur Hohl (Radin), Pedro de Cordoba
(Matin), Rollo Lloyd, Sherry Hall, Chris-
tian J. Frank, Francis McDonald (detec-
tives), Eily Malyon (laundry proprietor),
Claire Du Brey (Mme. Coulvet), E. Al-
lyn Warren (Police Commissioner), Ja-
nita Quigley (Marguerite), Nick Thomp-
son (Police Sergeant), Robert Graves,
Edward Keane (gendarmes), Robert Du
Coeudic (policeman), Inez Palange (con-
cierge), Evelyn Selbie (flower woman).

DEVIL DOLL (1964)
    Director: Lindsay Shonteff
Bryant Halliday (the Great Vorelli), Wil-
liam Sylvester (Mark English), Sandra
Dorne (Magda), Yvonne Romain (Mari-
anne), Karel Stepanek (Dr. Haller), Fran-
cis de Wolff (Dr. Keisling), Philip Ray
(Uncle Walter), Nora Nicholson (Aunt
Eva), Alan Gifford (Bob Garrett), Heidi

Erich (His Grace), Trixie Dallas (Miss Penton), Margaret Durnell (the Countess), Guy Deghy (Hans), David Charlesworth (Hugo Novik), Lorenza Coalville (Mercedes), Ella Tracey (Louisa), Pamela Law (Garret's girl-friend), Anthony Baird (soldier), Jackie Ramsden (nurse), Ray Landor (twist dancer).

DEVIL GIRL FROM MARS (1955)
Director: David MacDonald
Hugh McDermott (Michael Carter), Hazel Court (Eileen Prestwick), Patricia Laffan (Nyah), Peter Reynolds (Albert), Adrienne Corri (Doris), Joseph Tomelty (Prof. Hennessey), John Laurie (Mr. Jamieson), Sophie Stewart (Mrs. Jamieson), Anthony Richmond (Tommy).

DEVIL IN LOVE, THE (1966-Ital.)
(A.K.A. "L'Arcidiavolo", "The Archdevil", "Il Diavolo Innarmorato")
Director: Ettore Scala
Vittorio Gassman (Belfagor), Mickey Rooney (Adramalek), Claudine Auger (Magdalena), Helene Chanel (Clarice), Ettore Manni (Captain of the Guard), Gabriele Ferzetti (Lorenzo de Medici), Luigi Vannucchi (the Prince), Paolo Di Credico (Cardinal Giovanni), Annabella Incontrera (Lucretia), Liana Orfei (innkeeper's wife), Giorgia Moll (aristocrat's wife).

DEVIL IN MISS JONES, THE (1973)
Director: Gerard Damiano
Georgina Spelvin (Justine), John Clemens (Abaca), Harry Reams (Teacher), Albert Gork (man in the cell), Marc Stevens, Sue Flaken, Rick Livermore.

DEVIL RIDES OUT, THE (1968) (A.K.A. "The Devil's Bride")
Director: Terence Fisher
Christopher Lee (Duc de Richleau), Charles Gray (Mocata), Nike Arrighi (Tanith), Leon Green (Rex von Ryn), Sarah Lawson (Marie Eaton), Patrick Mower (Simon Aron), Paul Eddington (Richard Eaton), Rosalyn Landor (Peggy Eaton), Gwen Frangcon-Davies (Countess d'Urfe), Russell Waters (Malin).

DEVILS, THE (1971)
Director: Ken Russell
Vanessa Redgrave (Sister Jeanne), Oliver Reed (Father Grandier), Dudley Sutton (Baron de Laubardemont), Max Adrian (Ibert), Gemma Jones (Madeleine), Murray Melvin (Mignon), Michael Gothard (Father Barre), Christopher Logue (Cardinal Richelieu), Andrew Faulds (Rangier), Georgina

Hale (Philippe), John Woodvine (Trincant), Kenneth Colley (Legrand), Graham Armitage (Louis XIII), Brian Murphey (Adam), Judith Paris (Sister Judith), Iza Teller (Sister Iza), Catherine Willmer (Sister Catherine).

DEVIL'S CLAIM, THE (1920)
Director: Charles Swickard
Colleen Moore, Sessue Hayakawa, Rhea Mitchell, Joe Wray.

DEVIL'S COMMANDMENT, THE (1956-Ital.) (A.K.A. "I Vampiri", "The Vampire", "Lust of the Vampire")
Director: Riccardo Freda
Gianna Maria Canale, Paul Muller, Antoine Balpetre, Wandissa Guida, Rentao Tontini, Carlo D'Angelo.

DEVIL'S DAFFODIL, THE (1961-Brit./Ger.) (A.K.A. "Das Geheimnis der Gelben Narzissen", "Daffodil Killer")
Director: Akos Rathony
William Lucas (Jack Tarling), Christopher Lee (Ling Chu), Marius Goring (Oliver Milburgh), Penelope Horner (Anne Rider), Walter Gotell (Superintendent Whiteside), Peter Illing (Jan Putek), Colin Jeavons (Peter Keene), Albert Lieven (Raymond Lyne), Dawn Beret (Katya), Jan Hendriks (Charles), Bettine Le Beau (Trudi), Ingrid Van Bergen (Gloria), Campbell Singer (Sir Archibald), Lance Percival (French Gendarme), Martin Lyder (Max), Gundel Sargent (hotel receptionist), Frederick Bartman (detective), Nancy Nevinson (sluttish woman), Irene Prador (Maisie).

DEVIL'S DAUGHTER, THE (TVM-1973) - 1-9-73
Director: Jeannot Szwarc
Shelley Winters (Lilith Malone), Belinda J. Montgomery (Diane Shaw), Robert Foxworth (Steve Stone), Jonathan Frid (Howard), Joseph Cotten (Judge Weatherby), Lucille Benson (Janet Poole), Thelma Carpenter (Margaret Poole), Martha Scott (Mrs. Stone), Diana Ladd (Alice Shaw), Abe Vigoda (Alikhine), Robert Cornthwaite (Peter Dixon), Nick Bolin (Turk), Ian Wolfe (Father MacHugh), Barbara Sammeth (Susan Sanford), Rozelle Gayle (Fedora), Lillian Bronson (landlady).

DEVIL'S ENVOYS, THE (1942-Fr.)
(A.K.A. "Les Visiteurs du Soir")
Director: Marcel Carne
Jules Berry (the Devil), Arletty, Alain Cuny, Maria Dea, Roger Blin, Marcel Herrand, Pierre Labry, Fernand Ledoux,

Gabriel Gabrio, Jean d'Yd.

DEVIL'S EYE, THE (1960-Swed.) (A. K. A.
"Djavulens Oga")
Director: Ingmar Bergman
Jarl Kulle (Don Juan), Bibi Anderson
(Britt-Marie), Stig Jarrel (Satan), Gun-
nar Bjornstrand (the Actor), Axel Du-
berg (Britt-Marie's fiancee), Nils Pop-
pe (the Pastor), Gertrude Fridh (Pas-
tor's wife), Sture Lagerwall (Pablo),
Gunnar Sioberg (the Marquis), George
Funkquist (the Count), Allan Edwall
(the Ear Devil).

DEVIL'S FOOT, THE (1921)
Director: Maurice Elvey
Eille Norwood (Sherlock Holmes), Hugh
Buckler, Hubert Willis, Harvey Braban.

DEVIL'S GARDEN, THE (1920)
Director: Kenneth Webb
Lionel Barrymore, May McAvoy, H.
Cooper Cliffe, Doris Rankin.

DEVIL'S GARDEN (1967-Fr. /Ital.)
(A. K. A. "Coplan Sauve Sa Peau",
"Coplan Saves His Skin", "L'Assas-
sino Ha le Ore Contate")
Director: Yves Boiset
Claudio Brook, Margaret Lee, Jean
Servais, Klaus Kinski, Bernard Blier,
Jean Topart, Nana Michael.

DEVIL'S HAND, THE (1942-Fr.) (A. K. A.
"La Main du Diable", "Carnival of
Sinners")
Director: Maurice Tourneur
Pierre Fresnay (Roland), Josselyne
Gael (Irene), Noel Roquevert (Melisse),
Palau (Small Man), Guillaume de Sax
(Gibelin), Rexiane (Mme. Denis), An-
dre Varennes (Colonel), Antoine Bal-
petre (Denis), Chamarat (Duval), Ro-
bert Vattier (Perrier), Jean Coquelin
(Le Moine).

DEVIL'S HAND, THE (1958) (A. K. A.
"Live to Love")
Director: William J. Hole, Jr.
Robert Alda (Rick), Linda Christian
(Bianca), Neil Hamilton (Frank), Bruno
VeSota, Ariadne Welter, Jeanne Car-
men, Diana Spears, Gene Craft, Julie
Scott.

DEVIL'S LOVERS, THE (1971-Span.)
(A. K. A. "Les Amantes del Diablo")
Director: Jose Maria Elorrieta/
John Lacy
Teresa Gimpera, Espartaco Santoni,
Krista Nell, Veronica Lujan.

DEVIL'S MASK, THE (1946)
Director: Henry Levin
Anita Louise, Jim Bannon, Barton Yarborough, Mona Barrie, Thomas Jackson, Ludwig Donath, Edward Earle, Michael Duane.

DEVIL'S MESSINGER, THE (1962-U. S. /
Swed.) (A. K. A. "No. 13 Demon Street")
Director: Curt Siodmak
Lon Chaney, Jr. (Lucifer), Karen Kadler (Satanya), John Crawford (the Photographer), Michael Hinn, Tammy Newma-
ra, Gunnel Brostrom.

DEVIL'S MISTRESS, THE (1966)
Director: Orville Wanzer
Joan Stapleton (Athaliah), Robert Grego-
ry (Frank), Arthur Resley (Jeroboam),
Forrest Westmoreland (Charlie), Doug-
las Warren (Joe), Oren Williams (Will).

DEVIL'S NIGHTMARE (1971-Belg. /Ital.)
(A. K. A. "La Plus Longue Nuit du
Diable", "The Longest Night of the
Devil")
Director: Jean Brismee
Erika Blanc, Daniel Emilfork, Jean Ser-
vais, Jacques Monseau, Ivana Novak,
Shirley Corrigan.

DEVILS OF DARKNESS (1965)
Director: Lance Comfort
William Sylvester (Paul Baxter), Hubert
Noel (Count Sinistre), Diana Decker (Ma-
deline Braun), Carole Gray (Tania), Pe-
ter Illing (Insp. Martin), Brian Oulton
(the Colonel), Marianne Stone (the Du-
chess), Victor Brooks (Insp. Hardwick),
Gerard Heinz (Bouvier), Rona Anderson
(Anne Forest), Avril Angers (Midge),
Rod McLennan (Dave), Burnell Tucker
(Derek), Frank Forsyth (Tarbuk), Geof-
frey Kenion (Keith Forest), Marie Burke
(old gypsy woman), Eddie Byrne, Tracy
Reed.

DEVIL'S OWN, THE (1966) (A. K. A. "The
Witches")
Director: Cyril Frankel
Joan Fontaine (Gwen Mayfield), Kay Walsh
(Stephanie Bax), Alec McCowen (Alan
Bax), Duncan Lamont (Bob Curd), Leo-
nard Rossiter (Dr. Wallis), Martin Ste-
phens (Ronnie Dowsett), Michele Dotrice
(Valerie), Ann Bell (Sally), Shelagh Fra-
ser (Mrs. Creek), Ingrid Brett (Linda
Rigg), Viola Keats (Mrs. Curd), Gwen
Frangcon-Davies (Granny Rigg), Bryan
Marshall (Tom), John Collin (Dowsett),
Carmel McSharry (Mrs. Dowsett).

DEVIL'S PARTNER, THE (1958)

Director: Charles Rondeau
Richard Crane (David), Ed Nelson (Nick),
Jean Allison (Nell), Edgar Buchanan
(Doc), Byron Foulger (Papers), Claire
Carleton (Ida), Spencer Carlisle (Tom).

DEVIL'S PRIZE, THE (1916)
Director: Marguerite Bartsch
Antonio Moreno, Naomi Childers, Tem-
pler Saxe, Albert S. Howson, Clio Ayres.

DEVIL'S RAIN, THE (1975)
Director: Robert Fuest
William Shatner (Mark Preston), Ernest
Borgnine (Corbis), Ida Lupino (Mrs.
Preston), Tom Skerritt (Tom Preston),
Eddie Albert (Dr. Richards), Joan Pra-
ther (Julie Preston), Keenan Wynn (She-
riff Owen), Woodrow Chambliss (John),
George Sawaya (Steve Preston), John
Travolta (Danny), Lisa Todd (Lilith),
Claudio Brook (Preacher), Anton La-
Vey (High Priest), Diane LaVey (Pri-
scilla Corbis), Robert Wallace (Matthew
Corbis), Erika Carlson (Aaronessa
Fyffe), Tony Cortez (1st captor).

DEVIL STONE, THE (1917)
Director: Cecil B. DeMille
Wallace Reid (Guy Sterling), Tully Mar-
shall (Silas Martin), Geraldine Farrar
(Marcia Manot), Hobart Bosworth, Gus-
tav von Seyffertitz, Mabel Van Buren,
Horace B. Carpenter, James Neill,
Ernest Joy, Lillian Leighton, Burwell
Mamrick.

DEVIL'S TOY, THE (1916)
Director: Harley Knoles
Edwin Stevens (the Devil), Montague
Love, Madge Evans, Arnold Lucy, A-
dele Blood, Jack Halliday.

DEVIL'S WEDDING NIGHT, THE (1973-
Ital.) (A.K.A. "Il Plenilunio Delle
Vergini", "The Full Moon of the
Virgins")
Director: Paul Solvay
Sara Bay (the Countess), Mark Damon
(Karl Schiller/Franz Schiller), Miriam
Barrios, Stan Papps, Frances Davis,
Alexander Getty.

DEVIL'S WIDOW, THE (1971) (A.K.A.
"Tam Lin")
Director: Roddy McDowall
Ava Gardner (Michaela Cazaret), Ian
McShane (Tom Lynn), Stephanie Bea-
cham (Janet Ainsley), Richard Wattis
(Elroy), Cyril Cusack (Vicar Julian
Ainsley), Fabia Drake (Miss Gibson),
Joanna Lumley (Georgia), Madeline
Smith (Sue), David Whitman (Oliver),

Jennie Hanley (Caroline), Sinead Cusack
(Rose), Bruce Robinson (Alan), Michael
Bills (Michael), Heyward Morse (Andy),
Virginia Tingwell (Lottie), Pamela Far-
brother (Vanna), Peter Henwood (Guy),
Oliver Norman (Peter), Julian Barnes
(Terry).

DEVIL TO PAY, THE (1920)
Director: Ernest C. Warde
Roy Stewart (Cullen Grant), Robert Mc-
Kim (Brent Warren), Fritzi Brunette
(Dare Keeling), George Fisher (Larry
Keeling), Evelyn Selbie (Mrs. Roan),
Joseph J. Dowling (George Roan), Ri-
chard Lapan (Dick Roan), Mark Fenton
(Dr. Jernigan), William Marion (Detec-
tive Potter).

DEVIL WAS COMING FROM AKASAWA,
THE (1971-Ger./Span.) (A.K.A. "Der
Teufel Kam aus Akasawa", "El Diab-
lo Venia de Adasawa")
Director: Jesus Franco
Fred Williams, Walter Rilla, Howard
Vernon, Paul Mueller, Ewa Stroemberg,
Susann Korda, Siegfried Schueremberg,
Horst Tappert, Balndine Ebinger.

DEVIL WITH HITLER, THE (1942)
Director: Gordon Douglas
Alan Mowbray (the Devil), Bobby Watson
(Hitler), Marjorie Woodworth (Linda),
Joe Devlin (Mussolini), George E. Stone
(Suki Yaki), Sig Arno (Julius), Herman
Bing (Louis), Douglas Fowley (Walter).

DEVIL WITHIN, THE (1921)
Director: Bernard J. Durning
Virginia Valli, Nigel DeBrulier, Ber-
nard Durning, Dustin Farnum, Evelyn
Selbie, Hazel Deane.

DEVIL WITHIN HER, THE (1973) (A.K.A.
"I Don't Want to Be Born")
Director: Peter Sasdy
Joan Collins (Lucy Carlesi), Donald
Pleasence (Dr. Finch), Ralph Bates
(Gino Carlesi), Eileen Atkins (Sister
Albana), Caroline Munro (Mandy), Hi-
lary Mason (Mrs. Hyde), Janet Key (Jill),
John Steiner (Tommy), George Claydon
(Hercules), Judy Buxton (Sheila), Stan-
ley Lebor (Police Sergeant), Derek Ben-
field (Police Inspector), John Moore
(priest), Phyllis McMahon (nun), Susan
Richards (old lady), Andrew Secombe
(delivery boy).

DEVIL WOLF OF SHADOW MOUNTAIN,
THE (1964)
Director: Gary Kent
Johnny Cardoz (Aven Hunter), Gene Pol-

lock (David Hunter).

DEVIL WOMAN (1970-Phil.)
    Director: Jose Flores Sibal
Eddie Garcia, Divina Valencia, Marissa Delgado, Carldad Sanchez, Roger Calvin, Perla Bautista, Gina Alajar, Eva Marie, Jose Morelos, Romy Nario, Eddie Mercado.

DIABOLIC WEDDING (1972)
    Director: Gene Nash
Margaret O'Brien.

DIABOLICAL DR. Z, THE (1965-Span./ Fr.) (A. K. A. "Miss Muerte", "Miss Death", "Dans les Griffes du Maniaque", "In the Grip of the Maniac")
    Director: Jesus Franco
Fernando Montes (Philip), Antonio J. Escribano (Dr. Von Zimmer), Mabel Karr (Irma), Estella Blain (Nadia), Howard Vernon, Marcello Arroita, Guy Mairesse, Lucia Prado.

DIABOLICAL HATCHET, THE (1964-Mex.) (A. K. A. "La Hacha Diabolica")
    Director: Jose Diaz Morales
Santo, Lorena Velazquez, Bety Gonzales, Fernando Oses, Mario Sevilla, Colocho.

DIABOLICAL SHUDDER (1971-Span.)
    (A. K. A. "Escalofrio Diabolico")
    Director: George Martin
Paty Shepard, George Martin, Cris Auerta, Marta Monterrey, Vidal Molina, Silvana Sandovel.

DIABOLIC DUCHESS, THE (1964-Mex.)
    (A. K. A. "La Duquesa Diabolica")
    Director: Arturo Martinez
Rodolfo De Anda, Afelia Montesco, Dagoberto Rodriguez, Carlos Lopez Moctezuma, Ariadne Welter, Roberto Canedo.

DIABOLIQUE (1955-Fr.) (A. K. A. "Les Diaboliques", "The Fiends")
    Director: Henri-Georges Clouzot
Simone Signoret (Nicole Horner), Vera Clouzot (Christina Delasalle), Paul Meurisse (Michel Delasalle), Charles Vanel (Insp. Fichet), Noel Roquevert (Monsieur Herboux), Therese Dorny (Madame Herboux), Michel Serrault (Monsieur Raymond), Pierre Larquey (Monsieur Drain), Jean Brochard (Plantiveau), Georges Charmarat (Dr. Loisy), Jean Pierre Bonnefous (De Gascuel), Roberto Rodrigo (Jose), Michel Dumur (Ritberger), Soudieu (Georges Poujouly), Henri Humbert (Patard), Moinet (Yves-Marie Maurin).

DIAMOND FROM THE SKY, THE (1915) - serial in 30 episodes
Chapters: 1. "The Heritage of Hate", 2. "An Eye for an Eye", 3. "The Silent Witness", 3. "The Prodigal's Progress", 5. "For the Sake of a False Friend", 6. "Shadows at Sunrise", 7. "The Fox and the Pig", 8. "A Mind in the Past", 9. "A Runaway Match", 10. "Old Foes with New Faces", 11. "The Web of Destiny or Plaything of the Papoose", 12. "To the Highest Bidder", 13. "The Man in the Mask", 14. "For Love and Money", 15. "Desperate Chances", 16. "The Path of Peril", 17. "King of Diamonds and Queen of Hearts", 18. "Charm Against Harm", 19. "Fire, Fury and Confusion", 20. "The Soul Stranglers", 21. "The Lion's Bride", 22. "The Rose in the Dust", 23. "The Double Cross", 24. "The Mad Millionaire", 25. "A House of Cards", 26. "The Garden of the Gods", 27. "Mine Own People", 28. "The Falling Aeroplane", 29. "A Deal with Destiny" & 30. "The American Earl".
    Director: William Desmond Taylor & Jacques Jaccard
Lottie Pickford (Esther Cummings), William Russell (Blair Stanley), Irving Cummings (Arthur Stanley), Charlotte Burton (Vivian Marston), Eugenie Ford (Hagar), George Periclat (Luke Lovell), Orral Humphrey (Dr. Lee), Lillian Buckingham (Mother Stanley), W. J. Tedmarsh (Chinaman), Charles Watt (Marmaduke Smythe).

DIAMOND MACHINE, THE (1956-Fr.)
    (A. K. A. "Vous Pigez?", "You Dig?")
    Director: Pierre Chevalier
Eddie Constantine, Maria Frau, Yves Royan.

DIAMOND MAKERS, THE (1913) (A. K. A. "Fortune and Misfortune")
    Director: Edwin S. Porter
Margarita Fischer (High Priestess), Robert Leonard (Felix Westerly).

DIAMOND MASTER, THE (1928) - serial in 10 episodes
Chapters: 1. "The Secret of the Night", 2. "The Diamond of Death", 3. "The Tunnel of Terror", 4. "Trapped", 5. "The Diamond Machine", 6. "The Wolf Pack", 7. "The Death Trap", 8. "Into the Flames", 9. "The Last Stand" & 10. "The Reckoning".
    Director: Jack Nelson
Louise Lorraine (Doris Harvey), Hayden Stevenson (Mark Allen), Monty Montague (Frank Wilson), Al Hart (Prof. Jason Ramsey), Louis Stern (Mr. Harvey),

Walter Maly (Drake).

DIAMOND QUEEN, THE (1921) - serial
in 18 episodes
Chapters: 1. "The Vow of Vengeance",
2. "The Plunge of Doom", 3. "Perils
of the Jungle", 4. "Fires of Hate", 5.
"The Tide of Destiny", 6. "The Colos-
sal Game", 7. "An Amazing Ultimatum",
8. "In Merciless Clutches", 9. "A Race
with Rogues", 10. "The Betrayal", 11.
"In Torture's Grip", 12. "The Kidnap-
ping", 13. "Weird Walls", 14. "The
Plunge", 15. "The Decoy", 16. "The
Dip of Death", 17. "The Hand of Hate"
& 18. "The Hour of Reckoning".
Director: Edward Kull
George Chesebro (Mark Allen), Eileen
Sedgwick (Doris Harvey), Al Smith
(Prof. Jason Ramsey), Lou Short (Mr.
Harvey), Frank Clarke (Frank Wilson),
Josephine Scott (Louise).

DIAMONDS ARE FOREVER (1971)
Director: Guy Hamilton
Sean Connery (James Bond), Jill St.
John (Tiffany Case), Charles Gray (Er-
nst Stavros Blofeld), Lana Wood (Plen-
ty O'Toole), Jimmy Dean (Willard Whyte),
Norman Burton (Felix Leiter), Lois
Maxwell (Miss Moneypenny), Bernard
Lee (M), Desmond Llewelyn (Q), Bruce
Glover (Wint), Putter Smith (Kidd),
Bruce Cabot (Saxby), Edward Bishop
(Klaus Hergersheimer), Laurence Nais-
mith (Sir Donald Munger), Joseph Furst
(Dr. Metz), David Bauer (Mr. Slumber),
Trina Parks (Thumper), Donna Garratt
(Bambi), Leonard Barr (Shady Tree),
Larry Blake (Barker), Tom Steele (guard),
Henry Rowland (dentist), Marc Lawrence
(attendant), Sid Haig (attendant), Shane
Rimmer (Tom), Karl Held (agent), Da-
vid Healy (Launt Director), George Coo-
per (SPECTRE agent), Clifford Earl
(immigration officer), Nicky Blair (Trop
the doorman), Constantin De Goguel
(Mertz's aide), Joe Robinson (Peter
Franks), David de Keyser (doctor), Margaret Lacey (Mrs. Whistler), Jay Sarno
(sideshow barker), Ed Call (Maxie),
Catherine Deeney (welfare worker), Denise Perrier (Marie), Gary Dubin (boy),
Raymond Baker (helicopter pilot), Brinsley Forde (houseboy), Frank Olegario
(man in fez), Mark Elwes (Sir Donald's
secretary), John Abineri (airline representative), Max Latimer (Blofeld's double), Gordon Ruttan (Vandenburg aide),
Michael Valente (attendant), Bill Hutchinson (Moon Crater Controller).

DIAMONDS FOR BREAKFAST (1968)

Director: Scott Wodehouse
Marcello Mastroianni (Nicky), Rita
Tushingham (Bridget), Charles Lloyd-
Pack (Butler), Leonard Rossiter (Inspec-
tor), Warren Mitchell (Popov), Nora
Nicholson (Anastasia), Maggie Blye (Ho-
ney), Bryan Pringle (Police Sergeant),
David Horn (Duke), Ian Trigger (Popov's
assistant), Ann Blake (Nashka), Fran-
cesca Tu (Jeanne), Elaine Taylor (Vic-
toria), Bill Fraser (Brookseller), The
Karlins (triplets).

DIAMOND WIZARD, THE (1954) (A. K. A.
"The Diamond")
Director: Dennis O'Keefe & Mont-
gomery Tully
Dennis O'Keefe (Joe Dennison), Marga-
ret Sheridan (Marlene Miller), Alan
Wheatley (Thompson Blake), Francis
De Wolff (Yeo), Philip Friend (Insp. Mc-
Laren), Paul Hardtmuth (Dr. Eric Mil-
ler), Donald Gray (Cmdr. Gillies), Cy-
ril Chamberlain (Castle), Colin Tapley
(Sir Stafford Beach), Eric Berry (Hun-
ziger), Michael Balfour (Hoxie).

DIARY OF A MADMAN (1962)
Director: Reginald LeBorg
Vincent Price (Simon Cordelier), Nancy
Kovack (Odette Duclasse), Elaine Devry
(Jeanne d'Arville), Ian Wolfe (Pierre),
Chris Warfield (Paul Duclasse), Lewis
Martin (priest), Nelson Olmstead (Dr.
Borman), Joseph Ruskin (the Horla), Ed-
ward Colmans (Andre D'Arville), Har-
vey Stephens (Girot), Mary Adams (Lou-
ise), Stephen Roberts (Rennedon).

DICK BARTON AT BAY (1950)
Director: Godfrey Grayson
Don Stannard (Dick Barton), Tamara Des-
ni (Anna), George Ford (Snowey White),
Meinhart Maur (Serge Volkoff), Percy
Walsh (Prof. Mitchell), Joyce Linden
(Mary Mitchell), Campbell Singer (Insp.
Cavendish).

DICK BARTON, SPECIAL AGENT (1948)
Director: Alfred Goulding
Don Stannard (Dick Barton), George Ford
(Snowey White), Jack Shaw (Jock), Geof-
frey Wincott (Dr. Caspar), Gillian Maude
(Jean Hunter), Beatrice Kane (Miss Hor-
rock), Ivor Danvers (Snub).

DICK BARTON STRIKES BACK (1949)
Director: Godfrey Grayson
Don Stannard (Dick Barton), Sebastian
Cabot (Fouracada), Jean Lodge (Tina),
Bruce Walker (Snowey White), James
Raglan (Lord Armadale), John Harvey
(Major Henderson), Humphrey Kent (Col.

Gardner).

DICK SMART 2/007 (1966-Ital.)
     Director: Franco Prosperi/Frank
     Shannon
Margaret Lee, Richard Wilen, Rozana
Tabajos.

DICK TRACY (1936) - serial in 15 epi-
     sodes
Chapters: 1. "The Spider Strikes", 2.
"The Bridge of Terror", 3. "The Fur
Pirates", 4. "Death Rides the Sky", 5.
"Brother Against Brother", 6. "Dan-
gerous Waters", 7. "The Ghost Town
Mystery", 8. "Battle in the Clouds", 9.
"The Stratosphere Adventure", 10. "The
Gold Ship", 11. "Harbor Pursuit", 12.
"The Trail of the Spider", 13. "The
Fire Trap", 14. "The Devil in White"
& 15. "Brothers United".
     Director: Ray Taylor & Alan
     James
Ralph Byrd (Dick Tracy), Kay Hughes
(Gwen), Smiley Burnette (Mike McGurk),
Lee Van Atta (Junior), Carleton Young
(Gordon Tracy), John Piccori (Moloch),
Francis X. Bushman (Anderson), Byron
K. Foulger (Korvitch), George de Nor-
mand (Flynn), Theodore Lorch (Pater-
no), John Dilson (Brewster), Wedge-
wood Nowell (Clayton), Fred Hamilton
(Steve), Richard Beach (Gordon Tracy),
Edwin Stanley (Odette), Herbert Weber
(Martino), Harrison Greene (Clogger-
stein), Buddy Roosevelt (Burke), Lou
Fulton (Elmer), Bruce Mitchell (Bran-
don), Ed Platt (Oscar), Milburn Mo-
rante (Death Valley Johnny), Sam Flint
(Brock), Monte Montague (Clancy), Kit
Guard (Farley), Edward LeSaint (Gover-
nor), John Holland (Carter), Forbes
Murray (Coulter), I. Stanford Jolley
(intern), Roy Barcroft (henchman), Al
Ferguson (Henderson), Burr Caruth
(Wickland), Loren Raker (Tony), Brooks
Benedict (pilot), Harry Strang (Moffett),
Walter Long (Whitney), Wilfred Lucas
(Vance), Jack Ingram, Charley Phillips,
Donald Kerr (reporters), Alice Fleming
(teacher), Andre Cheron (Renee), Bob
Reeves (Officer), Harry Hall (Pete),
Ann Ainslee (Betty Clayton), Louis Mor-
rell (Potter), Kernan Cripps (Announcer),
Roscoe Gerall (watchman), Mary Kelley
(Georgetta), Hal Price (Crane), Henry
Sylvester (Commander), Leander de Cor-
dova (Stevens), William Stahl (Fox),
Jane Keckley (Mrs. Henkin), Al Taylor
(Costain), Loren Riebe (Peters), John
Ward (Doctor), Wally West (Kraft),
John Bradford (Joe), Jack Cheatham
(Morris), John Butler (Noble), William

Humphrey (James), Jack Gardner (Mills),
Jack Stewart (cop), Eva Mackenzie (tea-
cher), John Mills, Edgar Allan, Philip
Mason, Harod De Garro, Buddy Williams,
Henry Guttman.

DICK TRACY, DETECTIVE (1945) (A. K. A.
     "Dick Tracy", "Splitface")
     Director: William Berke
Morgan Conway (Dick Tracy), Anne Jef-
freys (Tess), Mike Mazurki (Splitface),
Jane Greer (Judith Owens), Lyle Latell
(Pat Patton), Joseph Crehan (Chief Bran-
don), Mickey Kuhn (Tracy Jr.), Trevor
Bardette (Prof. Starling), Morgan Wal-
lace (Steve Owens), Milton Parsons (Death-
ridge), William Halligan (Mayor), Edythe
Elliott (Mrs. Caraway).

DICK TRACY MEETS GRUESOME (1947)
     (A. K. A. "Dick Tracy's Amazing Ad-
     venture")
     Director: John Rawlins
Ralph Byrd (Dick Tracy), Boris Karloff
(Gruesome), Anne Gwynne (Tess True-
heart), Howard Ashley (Dr. I. E. Thal),
Skelton Knaggs (X-Ray), June Clayworth
(Dr. I. M. Learned), Lyle Latell (Pat
Patton), Tony Barrett (Melody), Milton
Parsons, Sean McClory, Robert Clarke,
Jason Robards, Sr. , Joseph Crehan, Lex
Barker, Robert Bray, Ernie Adams,
Bert Roach.

DICK TRACY RETURNS (1938) - serial
     in 15 episodes
     Director: William Witney & John
     English
Ralph Byrd (Dick Tracy), Lynn Roberts
(Gwen), Charles Middleton (Pa Stark),
David Sharpe (Ron Merton), John Mer-
ton (Champ), Reed Howes (Rance), Jer-
ry Tucker (Junior), Ned Glass (the Kid),
Jack Ingram (Slasher), Lee Ford (Mike
McGurk), Raphael Bennett (Trigger),
Edward Foster (Joe Hanner), Robert
Terry (Reynolds), Jack Roberts (Dude),
Michael Kent (Steve), Alan Gregg (Snub),
Tom Seidel (Hunt), Eddie Parker (Bur-
ton), Tom Steele, Dick Bitgood, Bob
Thom, Pat O'Shea, Roy Darmour (agents),
Forrest Taylor (Cmdr. Grant), Bud
Wolfe (Jake No. 1), Harrison Greene
(Nicholi Kroner), Earl Askam (Tully),
Duke York (Jack), Al Taylor (Karl), Mon-
te Montague (Sam), Duke Green (agent/
garage heavy No. 1), Lynton Brent (at-
tendant), Archie Hall (Blackie), Bill Hun-
ter (Buck), Gordon Hart (Carston), Ralph
Bowman (Clark), Eddie Dew (Co-Pilot),
Maston Williams (Bill), James Blaine
(Clive Anderson), Eddie Cherkose (Brand),
Douglas Evans (Burke), William Stahl

(Casey), Ian Rayo (Clem), Frank Wayne, Jack Montgomery, Walter Jones (crusher heavies), Earl Bunn, Harry Tenbrook, George Magrill, Jerry Frank (fertilizer heavies), Frank Hall Crane (doctor), Charles McMurphy (driver), Larry Steers (Duke), Wedgewood Nowell (Draper), Jerry Frank, Millard McGowan (dock heavies), Sherry Hall (Dayton), Pat McKee (crusher heavy), William Kent (dam watchman), Malcolm Graham (Forbes), Henry Otho (foreman No. 1), Bruce Mitchell (foreman No. 2), Jack Mack (Gomez Junction operator), Henry Sylvester (Dr. Grant), Allen Pomeroy (garage heavy), Budd Buster (gas station attendant), Sam Lufkin (guard), Dan Wolheim (Hogan), Charles Sherlock (Jake No. 2), Charles Martin (Jones), J. P. McGowan (Kruger), Frank O'Connor (Mason), James Carlisle (Naval Commissioner), Sid Troy (Harmon), Gloria Rich (Irene), Oscar Hendrian (Joe), Richmond Lynch (Knox), Charles McAvoy (Malloy), Herbert Weber (Miller), Douglas Meins (newsboy), Jenifer Gray (nurse), Kernan Crips (Officer), Charles Sullivan (Pete), Allan Cavan (Plover), Ralph McCullough (Perlita operator), John Gustin (pilot), Loren Riebe, Ted Wells, Buddy Mason (power heavies), William Mitchell (proprietor), Jack Egan (radio announcer), Edward Coke (reporter), Pat Gleason (Richard), Walter Low (Rex), King Mojave (sailor), Frank Marlowe, Bill Hunter, Buel Bryant (siding heavies), Charley Phillips (Snakey), Virginia Carroll (stewardess), Frank Hagney (Slim), Richard Parker (Stanton), Frank LaRue (Strobach), Francis Sayles (Terhune), Warren Jackson (Sweeney), Hal Cooke (L. C. Trendall), Harry Anderson (Max Williams), John Wade (Worthing), Charles Emerson (tire shop owner), Brian Burke (Wilson), Walter Wills (Boris Zarkoff), Yakima Canutt, Wesley Hopper, Art Dillard, Charles Regan.

DICK TRACY'S DILEMMA (1947) (A. K. A. "Mark of the Claw")
    Director: John Rawlins
Ralph Byrd (Dick Tracy), Lyle Latell (Pat Patton), Kay Christopher (Tess), Jack Lambert (the Claw), Ian Keith (Vitamin Flintheart), Bernadene Hayes (Longshot Lillie), William B. Davidson (Peter Premium), Jimmy Conlin (Sightless), Tony Barrett (Sam), Richard Powers (Fred).

DICK TRACY'S G-MEN (1939) - serial in 15 episodes
    Director: William Witney & John English
Ralph Byrd (Dick Tracy), Phyllis Isley/ Jennifer Jones (Gwen), Irving Pichel (Zarnoff), Kenneth Harlan (Anderson), Kenneth Terrell (Ed), Walter Miller (Robal), Robert Carson (Scott), Ted Pearson (Steve Lockwood), Julian Madison (Foster), Ted Mapes, William Stahl, Robert Wayne (G-men), Joe McGuinn (Tommy), Harrison Greene (Baron), Harry Humphrey (Warden Stover), Earl Bunn (Al No. 1), Jack Ingram (Al No. 2), Bud Geary (Ben/mine heavy), Monte Montague (Bourke), George DeNormand (Jack/canyon heavy), Edward Cassidy (Captain), Reginald Barlow (Albert Guttenbach), Tom Steele (lighthouse heavy No. 1/house heavy No. 3), Lee Shumway (Burke), Bud Wolfe (Bill/cabin heavy), Al Taylor, Bert LeBaron, Bill Wilkus (cove heavies), Reed Howes (Slim), Stanley Price (Shang), Joe Forte (Stanton), George Cleveland (Williams), Ray Johnson (attendant), Eddie Parker, Allen Pomeroy, Fred Schaefer (dock heavies), Milton Frome (Officer), Forrest Taylor (Stevens), Edmund Cobb (Reynolds), Allan Cavan (Warden), Tris Coffin (Zobar), Merrill McCormick (assistant), Harry Lang (Barossa), Curley Dresden, Charley Phillips (boat heavies), Bob Terry (Benton), Charles Sullivan (Brody), Jim Cassidy (Ralph Collins), Charles Hutchison (Brandon), Budd Buster (Cappy), Joe Yrigoyen, George Allen (crewmen), Bigelow Sayre (Davis), Russell Coller (dispatcher), Charles Regan (dam heavy), Frank Meredith (Duffy), Jack Raymond (Gus Fleming), Peter Von Ziegler (Green), Robert Hartford (Gus No. 1), Ken Cooker (Gus No. 2), Bruce Mitchell (guard), Eddie Cherkose, Bill Lally (ghost town heavies), Cy Slocum, Jimmy Fawcett (house heavies), Bill Wilkus, Millard McGowan (hangar heavies), Bill Yrigoyen (Howard), Sailor Vincent (intern), Louis Caits (Jerry), Barry Hays (Johnson), Frank O'Connor (Huxley), Jerry Frank (Jake), Gilman Shelton (Joe), Ed Brady (Jonas), Robert Brister (Kranz), Bert Le Baron (lighthouse heavy No. 2), Allan Davis (Link), Bernard Suss (Lassen), Walter Merrill (junior officer), John Locke (newscaster), Ethan Laidlaw (Pete), Edward Hearn (Ranger), Herbert Weber (James Robinson), Lloyd Ingraham (Stoddard), Perry Ivins (Telef), Bob Jamison (track heavy), Ray Harper (A. B. Martin), Joseph Swickard (Huenemo Mendoza), Edward Peil, Sr. (Price), Ray Largay (Rifkin), Jack Roberts (Lenny Slade), Charles Murphy

(Stopes), John Moloney (Tim), Charles
Sherlock, Carey Loftin (troopers), A-
lan Gregg, William Nestel (truck hea-
vies), Sammy McKim (Sammy Williams),
Jack Kenney (Ward), Sid Troy, George
Burton.

DICK TRACY VS. CRIME, INC. (1941) -
serial in 15 episodes
	Director: William Witney & John
	English
Ralph Byrd (Dick Tracy), Ralph Morgan
(Morton/the Ghost), Jan Wiley (June
Chandler), Kenneth Harlan (Lt. Cos-
grave), Robert Fiske (Cabot), Jack
Mulhall (Wilson), Hopper Atchley (Trent),
Howard Hickman (Chandler), Chuck
Morrison (Trask), Anthony Warde (Do-
rey), John Davidson (Lucifer), Robert
Frazer (Brewster), John Dilson (Wel-
don), Michael Owen (Billy Carr), John
Merton (Brent), Terry Frost (Drake),
Bud Wolfe (grill room heavy), Forrest
Taylor (Butler), Robert Wilke (helms-
man), Wheaton Chambers (Henderson),
Fred Kholer, Jr. (house heavy), Ed-
mund Cobb (Kelly), Walter McGrail
(Marine Captain/junction heavy No. 1),
Eddie Parker (hideout heavy), Al Tay-
lor (launch heavy), Stanley Price (Jack-
son), Ralph Morgan (Metzikoff), C.
Montague Shaw (Jonathan Martin), John
Bagni, Buddy Roosevelt, George Allen,
David Sharpe (pier heavies), Selmer
Jackson (Vincent), Lynton Brent (ser-
viceman), Archie Twitchell (announcer),
Jack Kenney (Berke), Frank Meredith
(army officer), Ralphael Bennett, Jacques
Lory, Joseph Kirk (brownstone heavies),
Dick Lamarr (Canfield), Pat O'Shea
(car heavy), Barry Hays (Chester),
Bert Le Baron, Jimmy Fawcett, Bill
Wilkus, Ken Terrell, Bob Robinson,
Duke Taylor, Bud Geary, Al Seymour,
Evan Thomas, Charley Phillips (plant
heavies), Bill Wilkus (Chuck), Marjorie
Kane (cigarette girl), Bert Le Baron
(Pete Collins), Charles McAvoy (Clan-
cy), Richard Kipling (customs inspec-
tor), Fred Schaefer (Dawson), Frank
Alten (Arno Draga), Edward Hearn
(Cutter Captain), Nora Lane (Ella Gilbert), Charles Miller (Hawes), John
James (Davis), Duke Taylor (deck heavy), George Peabody (driver), Sam Bernard (Green), John Webb Dillon (Inspector), William Hamner (intern), Walter
Miller (Morgan), Carol Adams (nurse),
Benny Burt (Nick), Frances Morris
(operator), Warren Jackson (junction
heavy No. 3), Douglas Evans (police
broadcaster), Howard Mitchell (Riley), Julian Madison (Ranger), Wally

Rose (roof heavy), Sid Troy (Slade),
Max Waizman (telegrapher), Dick Rush
(Tom), Charles McMurphy (yard guard),
Alex Lockwood (Smith), Ray Hanson
(Tim), Griff Barnette (watchman).

DICK TRACY VS. CUEBALL (1946)
	Director: Gordon Douglas
Morgan Conway (Dick Tracy), Anne
Jeffreys (Tess), Lyle Latell (Pat Pat-
ton), Rita Corday (Mona Clyde), Dick
Wessel (Cueball), Ian Keith (Vitamin
Flintheart), Douglas Walton (Priceless),
Esther Howard (Flora), Joseph Crehan
(Brandon), Byron Foulger (Little), Jim-
my Crane (Junior), Milton Parsons (Hig-
by), Skelton Knaggs (Rudolph).

DIE! DIE! MY DARLING (1965) (A. K. A.
	"Fanatic")
	Director: Silvio Narizzano
Tallulah Bankhead (Mrs. Trefoile), Stefanie Powers (Patricia Carroll), Peter
Vaughan (Harry), Donald Sutherland (Joseph), Yootha Joyce (Anna), Maurice
Kaufmann (Alan), Robert Dorning (Ormsby), Gwendolyn Watts (Gloria), Philip
Gilbert (Oscar), Winifred Dennis (shopkeeper), Diane King (talkative woman).

DIE LAUGHING (1980)
	Director: Jeff Werner
Robby Benson (Pinsky), Charles Durning
(Arnold), Elsa Lanchester (Sophie), Bud
Cort (Mueller), Linda Grovenor (Amy),
Rita Taggart (Thelma), Larry Hanken
(Bock), Michael David Lee (Einstein),
Marty Zagan (Friend), Sammuel Krach-
malnik (Zhukov), Peter Coyote (Davis),
Charles Fleisher (Charlie), Melanie
Henderson, Chuck Dorsett, Joe Bellan,
Nick Outin, Maurice Argent, Charles
Harwood, Carel Struycken, James Cran-
na, John Tim Burrus, Rhoda Gemignani.

DIE, MONSTER, DIE (1965) (A. K. A.
	"Monster of Terror")
	Director: Daniel Haller
Boris Karloff (Nahum Witley), Nick A-
dams (Stephen Reinhart), Suzan Farmer
(Susan Witley), Terence de Marney (Mer-
wyn), Freda Jackson (Letitia Witley),
Patrick Magee (Dr. Henderson), Sheila
Raynor (Miss Bailey), Sydney Bromley
(Pierce), Paul Farrell (Jason), Billy
Milton (Henry), George Moon (cab-driver).

DIE SCREAMING, MARIANNE (1973)
	Director: Pete Walker
Susan George (Marianne Evans), Barry
Evans (Eli Frome), Christopher Sandford
(Sebastian Smith), Leo Genn (the Judge),
Judy Huxtable (Hildegarde), Kenneth Hen-

del, Paul Stassino, Martin Wyldeck, John Laurimore, Anthony Sharp, Alan Curtis.

DIGBY - THE BIGGEST DOG IN THE WORLD (1974)
Director: Joseph McGrath
Jim Dale (Jeff Eldon), Spike Milligan (Dr. Harz), Milo O'Shea (Dr. Jameson), Kenneth J. Warren (Gen. Frank), Angela Douglas (Janine White), Norman Rossington (Tom), Dinsdale Landon (Col. Masters), Victor Spinetti (Prof. Ribart), Bob Todd (the Great Manzini), Richard Beaumont (Billy White), John Bluthal (Jerry), Edward Underdown (grandfather), Clovissa Newcombe (bunny girl), Victor Maddern (dog home manager), Molly Urquart (Aunt Ina), Sandra Caron (General's aide), Sheila Steafel (control operator), Rob Stewart (train driver), Harry Towb (Ringmaster), Garfield Morgan (Rogerson), Margaret Stuart (assistant), Frank Thornton (estate agent), Ben Aris (army captain).

DIMENSION FIVE (1966)
Director: Franklin Adreon
Jeffrey Hunter (Justin Power), Donald Woods (Cane), France Nuyen (Kitty), Harold Sakata (Big Buddha), Robert Ito (Sato), David Chow (Stoneface), Linda Ho (Nancy Ho), Lee Kolima (Genghis), John Lormer, Bill Walker, Virginia Lee, Ken Spalding, Kam Tong, John McKie, Carol Byron, Tad Horino.

DINOSAUR AND THE MISSING LINK, THE (1917)
Director: Willis O'Brien

DINOSAURUS! (1960)
Director: Irvin S. Yeaworth, Jr.
Ward Ramsey (Bart Thompson), Kristina Hanson (Betty Piper), Fred Engelberg (Mike Hacker), Alan Roberts (Julio), Paul Lukather (Chuck), Gregg Martell (Neanderthal Man), Wayne C. Tredway (Dumpy), James Logan (O'-Leary), Jack Younger (Jasper), Luci Blain (Chica), Howard Dayton (Mousey).

DIRIGIBLE (1931)
Director: Frank Capra
Jack Holt (Bradon), Fay Wray (Helen), Ralph Graves (Frisky Pierce), Hobart Bosworth (Rondelle), Clarence Muse (Clarence), Roscoe Karns (Sock McGuire), Selmer Jackson (Lt. Rowland), Emmet Corrigan (Adm. Martin), Harold Goodwin (Hansen), Al Roscoe (Cmdr. of USS Lexington).

DIRTY KNIGHTS' WORK (1976) (A. K. A. "A Choice of Weapons")
Director: Kevin Connor
John Mills (Bertie), Donald Pleasence (Sir Giles), Barbara Hershey (Marion), David Birney (Sir John), Peter Cushing (Sir Edward), Margaret Leighton (Ma Gore), Neil McCarthy, John Savident, Roy Holder, Keith Buckley, Brian Glover, Thomas Heathcote, John Hallam, Alexander John, Una Brandon-Jones, Bernard Hill, Brian Hall, John Bindon, Kevin Lloyd, Bill Weston, Marc Harrison, Diane Langton, Peter Childs, Brian Coburn, Max Faulkner, Mike Horsburgh.

DIRTY WORK (1933)
Director: Lloyd French
Stan Laurel, Oliver Hardy, Lucien Littlefield, Sam Adams.

DISAPPEARANCE OF FLIGHT 412, THE (TVM-1974) - 10-1-74
Director: Jud Taylor
Glenn Ford (Col. Pete Moore), Bradford Dillman (Major Mike Dunning), Robert F. Lyons (Capt. Cliff Riggs), David Soul (Capt. Roy Bishop), Gregg Mullavey (Capt. Tony Podryski), Guy Stockwell (Col. Trottman), Stanley Clay (Ferguson), Kent Smith (Gen. Enright), Jack Ging (White), Jonathan Lippe (Smith), Edward Winter (McCheer), Simon Scott (Col. Freeman Barnes), Cynthia Hayward (Nina Moore), Jesse Vint, Morris Buchanan, Donald Scott, Kevin Kerchival, Brent Davis.

DISCIPLE OF DEATH (1972)
Director: Peter Newbrook
Mike Raven (the Stranger), Virginia Wetherall (Ruth), Ronald Lacey (Parson), Stephen Bradley (Ralph), Marguerite Hardiman, George Belbin, Nicholas Amer.

DISCREET CHARM OF THE BOURGEOISIE, THE (1972-Fr.) (A. K. A. "Le Charme Discret de la Bourgeoisie")
Director: Luis Bunuel
Fernando Rey (Ambassador), Delphine Seyrig (Mrs. Thevenot), Jean Pierre Cassel (Mr. Senechal), Stephane Audran (Mrs. Senechal), Michel Piccoli (Home Secretary), Bulle Ogier (Florence), Claude Pieplu (Colonel), Paul Frankeur (Mr. Trevenot), Julien Bertheau (Bishop), Muni (peasant girl).

DISEMBODIED, THE (1957)
Director: Walter Grauman
Allison Hayes (Tonda Metz), John Wengraf (Dr. Metz), Robert Christopher

(Joe Lawson), Paul Burke (Tom Maxwell), Eugenia Paul (Lara), Joel Marston, Paul Thompson, Norman Frederic.

DISTANT EARLY WARNING (TVM-1975) - 10-21-75
Director: H. W. Kenney
Herb Edelman (Doc Goldman), Michael Parks (Vic), Mary Frann (Jane), Tony Geary (Dennis), Ford Rainey (Pa).

DOC SAVAGE - THE MAN OF BRONZE (1975)
Director: Michael Anderson
Ron Ely (Doc Savage), Paul Gleason (Long Tom), Michael Miller (Monk), Bill Lucking (Renny), Eldon Quick (Johnny), Darrell Zwerling (Ham), Paul Wexler (Capt. Seas), Pamela Hensley (Monja), Janice Heiden (Andriana), Bob Corso (Don Rubio Gorro), Alberto Morin (Jose), Robyn Hilton (Karen), Carlos Rivas (Kulkan), Victor Millan (Chief Chaac), Frederico Roberto (El Presidente), Jorge Cervera, Jr. (Col. Ramirez), Chuy Granco (Cheelok), Robert Tessier (Dutchman), Scott Walker (Borden), Michael Berryman (coroner), Grace Stafford (little lady).

DR. BLACK, MR. HYDE (1975) (A. K. A. "The Watts Monster")
Director: William Crain
Bernie Casey (Dr. Henry Pride), Rosalind Cash (Dr. Billie Worth), Stu Gilliam (Silky), Milt Kogan (Lt. Harry O'Connor), Ji-Tu Cumbuka (Lt. Jackson), Delia Thomas (Bernice), Marie O'Henry (Linda Monty).

DOCTOR BLOOD'S COFFIN (1961)
Director: Sidney J. Furie
Kieron Moore (Peter Blood), Hazel Court (Linda Parker), Ian Hunter (Dr. Robert Blood), Fred Johnson (Mr. Morton), Kenneth J. Warren (Sgt. Cook), John Romane (Hanson), Andy Alston (Beale), Gerald C. Lawson (Sweeting), Paul Stockman (Steve Parker), Paul Hardtmuth (Professor).

DR. BUTCHER, M. D. (1980-Ital.)
(A. K. A. "Queen of the Cannibals")
Director: Frank Martin
Ian McCulloch (Peter), Alexandra Cole (Cori Ridgway), Sherry Buchanan (Kelly), Peter O'Neal (George), Donald O'Brian (Dr. Abrera).

DR. COOK'S GARDEN (TVM-1971) - 1-19-71
Director: Ted Post

Bing Crosby (Dr. Leonard Crook), Frank Converse (Jim Tennyson), Blythe Danner (Jane Rausch), Bethel Leslie (Essie Bullitt), Abby Lewis (Dora Ludlow), Barnard Hughes (Elias Hart), Carol Morley (Mary Booth), Staats Cotsworth (Ted Rausch), Fred Burrel (Harry Bullitt), Jordan Reed (Billy), Helen Stenborg (Ruth Hart), Tom Barbour (Reverend).

DR. COPPELIUS (1966-Span./U. S.)
(A. K. A. "El Fantastico Mundo del Dr. Coppelius")
Director: Ted Kneeland
Walter Slezak (Dr. Coppelius), Claudia Corday (Swanhilda/Coppelia), Caj Selling (Franz), Eileen Elliott (Brigitta), Carmen Rojas (Spanish doll), Veronica Kusmin (Roman doll), Milorad Miskovitch (Hungarian dancer), Luis Prendes (the Mayor).

DOCTOR CRIPPEN (1963)
Director: Robert Lynn
Donald Pleasence (Dr. Crippen), Coral Browne (Belle Crippen), Samantha Eggar (Ethel Le Neve), James Robertson Justice (Capt. Kendall), Geoffrey Toone (Mr. Tobin), Oliver Johnston (Lord Chief Justice), Edward Underdown (Prison Governor), Basil Henson (Paul), Elspeth March (Mrs. Jackson), Edward Ogden (Clerk of the Court), Douglas Bradley-Smith (Dr. Pepper), John Arnatt (Chief Insp. Dew), Paul Carpenter (Bruce Martin), Basil Beale (Sgt. Mitchell), Olga Lindo (Clara), Betty Baskcomb (Mrs. Stratton), Ted Cast, Ian Whittaker.

DR. CRIPPEN LIVES (1958-Ger.) (A. K. A. "Doktor Crippen Lebt")
Director: Erich Engels
Peter Van Eyck, Elizabeth Muller, Fritz Tillmann, Katarina Mayberg.

DOCTOR CYCLOPS (1939)
Director: Ernest B. Schoedsack
Albert Dekker (Dr. Alexander Thorkel), Thomas Coley (Bill Stockton), Janice Logan (Dr. Mary Robinson), Victor Killian (Steve Barker), Charles Halton (Dr. Bulfinch), Paul Fix (Dr. Mendoza), Frank Reicher (Prof. Kendall), Frank Yaconelli (Pedro), Bill Wilkerson (silent indian), Allen Fox (cab driver).

DOCTOR DEATH (1972)
Director: Eddie Saeta
John Considine (Dr. Death), Barry Coe (Fred Saunders), Cheryl Miller (Sandy), Stewart Moss (Greg Vaughn), Leon Askin (Thor), Florence Marly (Tana), Jo Mor-

row (Laura Saunders), Sivi Aberg (Venus), Larry Vincent (the Strangler), Moe Howard (volunteer), Robert Ball (Old Wizard), Jim Boles (Caretaker Franz), Lin Henson (TV watcher), Pierre Gonneau (Harry), Athena Lorde (spiritualist), Patrick Dennis-Leigh (old man in society), Anna Bernard (girl in phone booth), Barbara Boles (Alice), Larry Rogers (young man in park), Denise Denise (girl with flat tire), Jeffrey Herman (man wanting new body), Eric Boles (man at seance), Leon Williams (man to arrange seance).

DOCTOR DOLITTLE (1967)
    Director: Richard Fleischer
Rex Harrison (Dr. Dolittle), Anthony Newley (Matthew Mugg), Samantha Eggar (Emma Fairfax), Richard Attenborough (Albert Blossom), Peter Bull (Gen. Bellowes), Muriel Landers (Mrs. Blossom), Geoffrey Holder (Willie Shakespeare), William Dix (Tommy Stubbins), Portia Nelson (Sarah Dolittle), Norma Varden (Lady Petherington).

DOCTOR FAUSTUS (1967-Brit./Ital.)
    Director: Richard Burton & Nevill Coghill
Richard Burton (Doctor Faustus), Elizabeth Taylor (Helen of Troy), Andreas Teuber (Mestopheles), David McIntosh (Lucifer), Elizabeth O'Donovan (Empress), Richard Carwardine (Cornelius), Jeremy Eccles (Belzebub), Ram Chopra (Valdes), Adrian Benjamin (Pope), Richard Heffer (1st scholar), Hugh Williams (2nd scholar), Gwydion Thomas (3rd scholar/Lechery), Nicholas Loukes (Cardinal/Pride), Richard Durden-Smith (Evil Angel/Knight), Patrick Barwise (Wagner), Anges McIntosh (Jeremy Chandler), Nevill Coghill, Ambrose Coghill, John Sandbach, Anthony Kaufmann, Richard Harrison, Sebastian Walker, Julian Wontner, Valerie James, Michael Menaugh, Maria Aitkien, Petronella Pulsford, Jacqueline Harvey, Carolyn Bennitt, Bridget Coghill, Susan Watson, R. Peverello, Sheila Dawson, Jane Wilford.

DOCTOR FRANKEN (TVM-1980) - 1-13-80
    Director: Marvin J. Chomsky & Jeff Leiberman
Robert Vaughn (Dr. Arno Franken), Robert Perault (John Doe), Terri Garr (Kelli Fisher), Cynthia Harris (Anita Franken), David Selby (Dr. Mike Foster), Josef Sommer (Mr. Parker),

Stanja Lowe (Mrs. Parker), Addison Powell (Dr. Eric Kerwin), Rudolph Willrich (Arthur Guernsey), Theodore Sorel (Gerald Blake), Nicolas Surovy (Martin Elson), Tokayo Doran (Claire), Sam Schacht (Detective Pearson), Claiborne Cary (Jenny), Roger Hill (anesthesiologist), Debra Mooney (surgical nurse), Laurie Chock (floor nurse), William Houston (cop).

DR. FRANKENSTEIN ON CAMPUS (1970) (A.K.A. "Flick")
    Director: Gil Taylor
Robin Ward (Viktor Frankenstein), Sean Sullivan (Professor), Austin Willis, Kathleen Sawyer, Ty Haller, Tony Moffat-Lynch.

DR. GOLDFOOT AND THE BIKINI MACHINE (1965) (A.K.A. "Dr. G. and the Bikini Machine")
    Director: Norman Taurog
Vincent Price (Dr. Goldfoot), Frankie Avalon (Craig Gamble), Dwayne Hickman (Todd Armstrong), Susan Hart (Diane), Fred Clark (D.J. Pavney), Jack Mullaney (Igor), Vincent Barnett (janitor), Alberta Nelson (Reject No. 12), Hal Riddle (newsvendor), Milton Frome (motorcycle cop), Kay Elhardt (girl in nightclub), Joe Ploski (cook), William Baskin (guard), Deanna Lund, Sally Sachse, Marianna Gaba, Patti Chandler, Sue Hamilton, Issa Arnal, Sally Frei, Mary Hughes, Laura Nicholson, Pam Rodgers, Jan Watson, Luree Holmes, China Lee, Kay Michaels, Leslie Summers, Arlene Charles (robots), Harvey Lembeck, Aron Kincaid, Annette Funicello.

DR. GOLDFOOT AND THE GIRL BOMBS (1966-U.S./Ital.) (A.K.A. "Le Spie Vengono Dal Semifreddo", "The Spy Who Came in from the Semi-Cold")
    Director: Mario Bava
Vincent Price (Dr. Goldfoot), Fabian (Bill Dexter), Moana Tahi (Goldfoot's assistant), Laura Antonelli (Rosanna), Franco Franchi (Franco), Ciccio Ingrassia (Ciccio).

DR. HECKYL AND MR. HYPE (1980)
    Director: Charles B. Griffith
Oliver Reed (Dr. Heckyl/Mr. Hype), Mel Welles (Dr. Hinkle), Jackie Coogan (Sgt. Fleacollar), Corinne Calvet (Pizelle Puree), Sunny Johnson (Coral Careen), Virgil Frye (Lt. Mac Druck 'Il Topo'), Maia Danziger (Miss Finebaum), Kedrick Wolfe (Dr. Lew Hoo), Dick Miller (Irsil/Orson), Sharon Compton (Mrs.

Quivel), Charles Howerton (Clutch Cooger), Lucretia Love (Debra Kate), Jack Warford (Herringbone Flynn), Denise Hayes (Liza Rowne), Ben Frommer (Sgt. Gurnisht Hilfn), Jacque Lynn Colton (Mrs. Fran van Crisco), Lisa Zebro (Mrs. van Crisco), Stan Ross (Flash Flud), Mickey Fox (Mrs. Fritz L. Pitzle), Catalaine Knell (Mrs. Fritz L. Pitzle), Steve Ciccone (Dum-Dum), Duane Thomas (Bad William's Ideal), Joe Anthony Cox (Bad Williams), Michael Ciccone (Hollowpoint), Candi Brough (Teri Tailspin), Randi Brough (Toni Tailspin), Yehuda Efroni (Bull Quivel), Dan Sturkie (Naso Rubico, the wino), Herta Ware (old lady on bus), Dana Feller (Nurse Pertbottom), Carin Berger (Nurse Lushtush), Cindy Riegel (Nurse Rosenrump), Katherine Kirkpatrick (Nurse Nietkiester), Merle Ann Taylor (Nurse Talltale), Samuel Livner (Acuticklic Patient), Christina Ann Saul (Blinkin'), Ed Randolph (Midnight Eaglehead), Jessica Griffith (policeman's daughter).

DR. HEIDEGGER'S EXPERIMENT
(1954) - short
Director:
Monty Woolley.

DOCTOR JEKYLL, THE (1951-Ital.)
(A. K. A. "Il Dottor Jekyll")
Director: Mario Scoffi
Mario Scoffi, Anna Maria Campoy, Jose Cibrian.

DR. JEKYLL AND MISS OSBOURNE
(1981-Fr.)
Director: Wladimir Borowczyk
Udo Kier (Dr. Jekyll), Marino Pierro (Miss Osbourne), Patrick Magee, Howard Vernon, Clement Haragi.

DR. JEKYLL AND MR. HYDE (1912)
Director: Lucius Henderson
James Cruze (Dr. Jekyll), Henry Benham (Mr. Hyde), Marguerite Snow (Muriel Carew).

DR. JEKYLL AND MR. HYDE (1913)
Director: Herbert Brenon
King Baggott (Dr. Jekyll/Mr. Hyde), Jane Gail (Alice), Matt Snyder (Alice's father), Howard Crampton (Dr. Lanyon), William Sorrell (Utterson).

DR. JEKYLL AND MR. HYDE (1920)
Director: John S. Robertson
John Barrymore (Dr. Henry Jekyll/Mr. Oscar Hyde), Brandon Hurst (Sir George Carewe), Martha Mansfield

(Millicent Carewe), Nita Naldi (Miss Gina), George Stevens (Poole), Charles Lane (Dr. Lanyon), J. Malcolm Dunn (John Utterson), Cecil Clovelly (Edward Enfield), Louis Wolheim (music hall owner).

DR. JEKYLL AND MR. HYDE (1920)
Director:
Hank Mann (Dr. Jekyll/Mr. Hyde).

DR. JEKYLL AND MR. HYDE (1920)
Director:
Sheldon Lewis (Dr. Jekyll/Mr. Hyde), Dora Mills Adams (Mrs. Lanyon), Alexander Shannon (Dr. Lanyon), Gladys Field (Bernice Lanyon), Leslie Austin (Danvers Carew), Harold Forshay (Edward Utterson).

DR. JEKYLL AND MR. HYDE (1931)
Director: Rouben Mamoulian
Frederic March (Dr. Henry Jekyll/Mr. Edward Hyde), Miriam Hopkins (Ivy Parsons), Rose Hobart (Muriel Carewe), Halliwell Hobbes (Brig. Gen. Carewe), Holmes Herbert (Dr. Lanyon), Edgar Norton (Poole), Arnold Lucy (Utterson), Tempe Pigott (Mrs. Hawkins), Eric Wilton (Briggs), Colonel MacDonnell (Hobson), Murdock MacQuarrie (doctor), Douglas Walton (student), John Rogers (waiter).

DR. JEKYLL AND MR. HYDE (1941)
Director: Victor Fleming
Spencer Tracy (Dr. Henry Jekyll/Mr. Hyde), Ingrid Bergman (Ivy Peterson), Lana Turner (Beatrix Emery), Donald Crisp (Sir Charles Emery), Ian Hunter (Dr. John Lanyon), Peter Godfrey (Poole), C. Aubrey Smith (the Bishop), Barton MacLane (Sam Higgins), Sara Allgood (Mrs. Higgins), Frederic Worlock (Dr. Heath), Dennis Green (Freddie), Frances Robinson (Marcia), Billy Bevan (Mr. Weller), Forrester Harvey (Old Prouty), Lawrence Grant (Dr. Courtland), Lumsden Hare (Col. Weyworth), William Tannen (Interne Fenwick), John Barclay (Constable), Alec Craig.

DR. JEKYLL AND MR. HYDE (TVM-1973) - 3-7-73
Director: David Winter
Kirk Douglas (Dr. Jekyll/Mr. Hyde), Susan George (Annie), Susan Hampshire (Isabel), Michael Redgrave (Danvers), Donald Pleasence (Smudge), Stanley Holloway (Poole), Geoffrey Chater (Lanyon), Judy Bowker (Tupenny), Nicholas Smith (Hastings), John J. Moore (Utterson), Geoffrey Wright (Wainwright).

DR. JEKYLL AND SISTER HYDE (1971)
Director: Roy Ward Baker
Ralph Bates (Dr. Jekyll), Martine Beswicke (Sister Hyde), Gerald Sim (Prof. Robertson), Lewis Fiander (Howard), Susan Brodrick (Susan Spencer), Dorothy Alison (Mrs. Spencer), Paul Whitsun-Jones (Sgt. Danvers), Ivor Dean (Burke), Tony Calvin (Hare), Virginia Wetherall (Betsy), Philip Madoc (Byker), Dan Meaden (town crier), Irene Bradshaw (Yvonne), Anna Brett (Julie), Pat Brackenbury (Helen), Rosemary Lord (Marie), Julia Wright (street singer), Geoffrey Kenion (older policeman), Jackie Poole (Margie), Petula Portell (Petra), Liz Romanoff (Emma), Roy Evans (knife grinder), Derek Steen (sailor), Will Stampe (Mine Host), Jeannette Wild (Jill), John Lyons (sailor), Bobby Parr (young apprentice).

DR. JEKYLL AND THE WEREWOLF
(1971-Span.) (A. K. A. "Doctor Jekyll y el Hombre Lobo")
Director: Leon Klimovsky
Paul Naschy (Waldemar Daninsky), Shirley Corrigan, Jack Taylor.

DR. JEKYLL'S DUNGEON OF DEATH
(1982)
Director: James Wood
James Mathers (Dr. Jekyll), John Kearney, Tom Nicholson, Dawn Carver Kelly, Nadine Kalmes.

DR. MABUSE, THE (1971-Span./Ger.)
(A. K. A. "El Dr. Mabuse")
Director: Jesus Franco
Fred Williams, Ewa Stromberg, Roberto Camardiel, Ewa Garden, Gustavo Re, Moises A. Rocha.

DR. MABUSE THE GAMBLER (1922-
Ger.) (A. K. A. "Dr. Mabuse der Spieler")
Director: Fritz Lang
Rudolf Kelin-Rogge (Dr. Mabuse), Alfred Abel (Count Todd), Paul Richter (Edgar Hull), Aud Egede Nissen (Cara Carozza), Bernhardt Goetzke (Van Wenck), Gertrud Welcker (Countess Todd), Hans von Schlettow, Georg John, Julius Falkenstein, Forster Larrinaga, Greta Berger, Lydia Potechina.

DR. MABUSE VS. SCOTLAND YARD
(1963-Ger.) (A. K. A. "Die Scharlachrote Dschunke", "The Scarlet Jungle", "Scotland Yard Jagt Dr. Mabuse")
Director: Paul May
Peter Van Eyck, Werner Peters, Wal-

ter Rilla, Klaus Kinski, Dieter Borsche, Hans Nielsen, Sabine Bethman.

DR. NO (1962)
Director: Terence Young
Sean Connery (James Bond), Joseph Wiseman (Dr. No), Ursula Andress (Honey), Anthony Dawson (Prof. Dent), John Kitzmiller (Quarrel), Jack Lord (Felix Leiter), Bernard Lee (M), Lois Maxwell (Miss Moneypenny), Zena Marshall (Miss Taro), Eunice Gayson (Sylvia), Tim Moxom (Strangways), Reggie Carter (Jones), Louis Blaazer (Playdell-Smith), Peter Burton (Major Boothroyd), Lester Prendergast (Puss-Feller), Margaret LeWars (photographer), William Foster-Davis (Duff), Dolores Keaton (Mary), Michele Mok (Sister Rose), Yvonne Shima (Sister Lily).

DOCTOR OF DOOM (1962-Mex.) (A. K. A.
"Las Luchadoras contra el Medico Asesino", "The Wrestling Women vs. the Murdering Doctor")
Director: Rene Cardona
Armando Silvestre, Lorena Velazquez, Roberto Canedo, Irma Rodriguez, Martha 'Guera' Solis, Chucho Salinas, Sonia Infante, Elizabeth Campbell.

DR. ORLOFF'S MONSTER (1964-Span./
Austr.) (A. K. A. "El Secreto del Dr. Orloff", "The Secret of Dr. Orloff")
Director: Jess Franco
Hugo Blanco/Hugh White (Andros), Jose Rubio/Joseph Raven, Pastor Serrardor/Patrick Long, Agnes Spaak, Perla Cristal, Luisa Sala, Mercelo Arroita-Jaurequi.

DR. PHIBES RISES AGAIN (1972)
Director: Robert Fuest
Vincent Price (Dr. Phibes), Robert Quarry (Biederbeck), Fiona Lewis (Diana), Valli Kemp (Vulnavia), Peter Jeffrey (Insp. Trout), Terry-Thomas (Lombardo), Hugh Griffith (Ambrose), Beryl Reid (Mrs. Ambrose), Peter Cushing (the Captain), John Cater (Waverly), Gerald Sim (Hackett), Milton Reid (Cheng), Caroline Munro (Victoria Phibes), Louis Fiander.

DR. PYCKLE AND MR. PRIDE (1925)
Director:
Stan Laurel (Dr. Pyckle/Mr. Pride).

DR. RENAULT'S SECRET (1942)
Director: Harry Lachman
George Zucco (Dr. Renault), J. Carrol Naish (Noel), Lynne Roberts (Madeline), Sheppard Strudwick/John Shepperd (Forbes),

Jack Norton (Austin), Bert Roach (the proprietor), Ray 'Crash' Corrigan (the Ape), Charles Wagenheim, Mike Mazurki, Eugene Bordon, Arthur Shields, Jean Del Val.

DR. SATAN (1966-Mex.) ("El Dr. Satan")
Director: Miguel Morayta
Joaquin Cordero, Alma Delia Fuentes, Carlos Agosti, Jose Galvez, Judith Azcarraga, Antonio S. Raxel, Gina Romand, Quintin Bulnes.

DR. SATAN AND BLACK MAGIC (1967-Mex.) (A. K. A. "El Dr. Satan y la Magic Negra", "Vuelve el Doctor Satan", "Return of Dr. Satan")
Director: Rogelia Gonzalez
Joaquin Cordero, Noe Murayama, Luz Maria Aguilar, Sonia Furio, Aurora Clavel.

DR. SCORPION (TVM-1978) - 2-24-78
Director: Richard Lang
Nick Mancuso (Jonathan Shackelford), Roscoe Lee Browne (Dr. Cresus), Christine Lahti (Tania Reston), Granville Van Dusen (Terry Batliner), Denny Miller (the Dane), Lincoln Kilpatrick (Eddie), Bill Lucking (Whitey Ullman), Sandra Kerns (Sharon Shackelford), Zitto Kazann (Arubella), Philip Sterling (Adm. Gunwilder), Joseph Ruskin (Lt. Reed), Richard T. Herd (Bill Worthington).

DR. STRANGE (TVM-1978) - 9-6-78
Director: Philip DeGuere
Peter Hooten (Dr. Stephen Strange), Jessica Walter (Morgan le Fay), John Mills (Lindmer), Clyde Kusatsu (Wong), Eddie Benton (Clea), June Barrett (Sarah), David Hooks (Nameless One), Philip Sterling (Dr. Frank Taylor), Diana Webster (Head Nurse), Darah Rush (nurse), Blake Marion (department chief), Bob Delegall (intern), Inez Pedroza (Agnes Carson), Lady Rowlands (Mrs. Sullivan), Frank Catalano (orderly), Larry Anderson (magician), Michael Ansara (voice of the Ancient One).

DR. STRANGELOVE (1963) (A. K. A. "Dr. Strangelove: Or How I Learned to Stop Worrying and Love the Bomb")
Director: Stanley Kubrick
Peter Sellers (Capt. Lionel Mandrake/Pres. Muffley/Dr. Strangelove), George C. Scott (Gen. Buck Turgidson), Sterling Hayden (Gen. Jack D. Ripper), Slim Pickens (Maj. T. J. 'King' Kong), Keenan Wynn (Col. Bat Guano), Peter Bull (Amb. de Sadesky), James Earl

Jones (Lt. Lothar Zogg), Tracy Reed (Miss Foreign Affairs), Jack Creley (Mr. Staines), Frank Berry (Lt. H. R. Dietrich), Paul Tamarin (Lt. B. Goldberg), Glenn Beck (Lt. W. D. Kivel), Shane Rimmer (Capt. G. A. 'Ace' Owens), Gordon Tanner (Gen. Faceman), Robert O'Neil (Adm. Randolph), Roy Stephens (Frank), Laurence Herder, Hal Galili, John McCarthy (Defense Team Members).

DR. TERROR'S GALLERY OF HORRORS (1967) (A. K. A. "Return from the Past", "The Blood Suckers")
Director: David L. Hewitt
John Carradine (Narrator).
"The Witch's Mirror": John Carradine (Tristram Halbin), Roger Gentry (Bob Farrell), Karen Joy (Julie Farrell), Vic McGee (Dr. Finchley).
"King Vampire": Ron Doyle (Brenner), Ron Brogan (Marsh), Margaret Moore (Mrs. O'Shea), Roger Gentry (mob leader).
"Monster Raid": Rochelle Hudson (Helen Spalding), Ron Doyle (Dr. Spalding), Ron Gentry (Dr. Sewart), Vic McGee (Desmond).
"Spark of Life": Lon Chaney, Jr. (Dr. Mendell), Ron Doyle (Dr. Cushing), Vic McGee (Amos Duncan), Joey Benson (Dr. Sedgewick).
"Count Alucard": Mitch Evans (Count Alucard), Roger Gentry (Jonathan Harker), Vic McGee (Burgomeister), Karen Joy (Medina), Gray Daniels (coachman).

DR. TERROR'S HOUSE OF HORRORS (1964)
Director: Freddie Francis
Peter Cushing (Dr. Shreck).
"Werewolf": Neil McCallum (Jim Dawson), Ursula Howells (Deidre Biddulph), Katy Wild, Peter Madden.
"Creeping Vine": Alan Freeman (Bill Rogers), Jeremy Kemp (Jerry Drake), Bernard Lee (2nd botanist), Ann Bell, Sarah Nicholls.
"Voodoo": Roy Castle (Biff Bailey), Kenny Lynch, Christopher Carlos, Tubby Hayes Quartet.
"Disembodied Hand": Christopher Lee (Franklin Marsh), Michael Gough (Eric Landor).
"Vampire": Donald Sutherland (Dr. Bob Carroll), Max Adrian (Dr. Blake), Jennifer Jayne (Nicole Carroll).
and with: Edward Underdown, Harold Lang, Frank Forsyth, George Mossman, Thomas Baptiste, Ilsa Blair, Judy Cornwall, Brian Hankins, Kenneth Kove, Al Mulock, Irene Richmond, Russ Henderson, Hedger Wallace, Faith Kent, John

Martin, Walter Sparrow, Laurie Leigh, Frank Barry.

DR. WHO AND THE DALEKS (1965)
Director: Gordon Flemying
Peter Cushing (Dr. Who), Roy Castle (Ian), Jennie Linden (Barbara), Barrie Ingham (Alydon), Geoffrey Toone (Temmosus), Roberta Tovey (Susan), Michael Coles (Gamatus), Mark Peterson (Elyon), John Brown (Antodus), Yvonne Antrobus (Dyoni).

DOCTOR X (1932)
Director: Michael Curtiz
Lionel Atwill (Dr. Xavier), Fay Wray (Joan Xavier), Preston Foster (Dr. Wells), Lee Tracy (Lee Taylor), Arthur Edmund Carewe (Dr. Rowitz), Harry Beresford (Dr. Duke), John Wray (Dr. Haines), Robert Warwick (Commisioner Stevens), Willard Robertson (Insp. Halloran), Thomas E. Jackson (editor), George Rosener (Otto), Leila Bennett (Mamie), Tom Dugan (Sheriff), Harry Holman (policeman), Mae Busch, Selmer Jackson.

DOG, A MOUSE AND A SPUTNIK, A (1958-Fr.) (A. K. A. "A Pied, a Cheval et par Sputnik", "By Foot, by Horse and by Sputnik", "Sputnik")
Director: Jean Dreville
Mischa Auer (the Professor), Pauline Carton (Marie), Noel Roquevert (the Mayor), Denise Gray (Marguerite Martin), Noel-Noel (Leon Martin), Darry Dowl (the Deputy Attache), Natalie Nerval (Dina, the interpreter), Robert Lombard (Chief of Police), Francis Blanche (Chazot).

DOGS (1976)
Director: Burt Brinckerhoff
David McCallum, Eric Server, Sterling Swanson, Sandra McCabe, Fred Hice, Linda Gray, George Wyner, Holly Harris.

DOLL, THE (1962-Swed.) (A. K. A. "Vaxdockan")
Director: Arne Mattsson
Per Oscarsson, Gio Petre.

DOMINIQUE (1978)
Director: Michael Anderson
Jean Simmons (Dominique Ballard), Cliff Robertson (David Ballard), Ron Moody (Dr. Rogers), Jenny Agutter (Miss Ballard), Simon Ward (Tony Calvert), Flora Robson (Mrs. Davis), Michael Jayston (Arnold Cravan), Judy Geeson (Marjorie Cravan), Jack War-

ner (stonemason), David Tomlinson (lawyer), Michael Japher.

DONA FLOR AND HER TWO HUSBANDS (1977-Braz.)
Director: Bruno Barreto
Sonia Braga (Dona Flor), Jose Wilker (Vadinho), Mauro Mendonca (Teodoro), Dinorah Brillanti (Rozilda), Nelson Savier (Mirandao), Arthur Costa Filho (Carlinhos), Rui Rezende (Cazuzat), Mario Gusmao (Arigof).

DONKEY SKIN (1970-Fr.) (A. K. A. "Peau d'Ane", "The Magic Donkey")
Director: Jacques Demy
Catherine Deneuve (Peau d'Ane), Jean Marais (Blue King), Delphine Seyrig (Fairy Godmother), Micheline Presle (Red Queen), Fernand Ledoux (Red King), Jacques Perrin (Prince), Henri Cremieux.

DONOVAN'S BRAIN (1953)
Director: Felix Feist
Lew Ayres (Dr. Patrick J. Corey), Gene Evans (Dr. Frank Schratt), Nancy Davis (Janice Cory), Steve Brodie (Herbie Yocum), Lisa K. Howard (Chloe Donovan), Michael Colgan (Tom Donovan), Tom Powers (advisor), Kyle James (Ranger Chief Tuttle), Stapleton Kent (W. J. Higgins), Peter Adams (Mr. Webster), Victor Sutherland (Nathaniel Fuller), John Hamilton (Mr. MacNish), Harlan Warde (Mr. Brooke), Paul Hoffman (Mr. Smith), William Cottrell (Dr. Crane), Faith Langley (receptionist), Tony Merrill (hotel desk clerk), Mark Lowell (supply company clerk), Shimen Ruskin (tailor).

DON'T ANSWER THE PHONE (1980)
Director: Robert Hammer
James Westmoreland (Chris McCabe), Flo Gerrish (Dr. Lindsay Gale), Ben Frank (Hatcher), Nicholas Worth (Kirk Smith), Gary Allen (John Feldon), Stan Haze (Adkins), Pamela Bryant (Sue Ellen), Ted Chapman (bald man), Denise Galick (Lisa), Dale Kalberg, Tom Lasswell, Deborah Leah Land, Ellen Karston, Chuck Mitchell, Susanna Severeid, Chris Wallace, Mike Levine, Victor Mohica, Paula Warner.

DON'T BE AFRAID OF THE DARK (TVM-1973) - 10-10-73
Director: John Newland
Kim Darby (Sally Farnham), Jim Hutton (Alex Farnum), Pedro Armendariz, Jr. (Francisco Perez), Barbara Anderson (Joan), William Demarest (Harris), William Sylvester (Tom), Lesley Woods (Eth-

el), Don Mallon (Bob), J. H. Lawrence
(George), Robert Cleaves (doctor), Ster-
ling Swanson (policeman), Felix Silla,
Patty Mahoney, Tamarra De Treaux.

DON'T GO IN THE HOUSE (1980)
    Director: Joseph Ellison
Dan Grimaldi (Donny), Robert Osth
(Bobby), Ruth Dardick (Mrs. Kohler),
Bill Ricci (Vito), Charlie Bonet (Ben),
Dennis M. Hunter, Johanna Brushay,
John Hedberg, Darcy Shean, Jim Don-
negan, Denise Woods, Colin McInness,
Joey Peschi, Mary Ann Chin, Claudia
Folts, Pat Williams, Ralph D. Bow-
man, Connie Oaks, Jean Manning, Tom
Brumberger, Kim Roberts, Gloria
Szymkovicz, O'Mara Leary, Eileen
Dunn, David McComb, Ken Kelsch, Nik-
ki Kollins, Louise Grimaldi, David
Brody, Gail Turner, Christian Isodore.

DON'T GO INTO THE WOODS (1980)
    Director: Jim Bryan
Buck Carradine, Mary Gail Artz, James
P. Hayden, Ken Carter.

DON'T LOOK IN THE BASEMENT (1973)
    Director: S. F. Brownrigg
Rosie Holotik (Charlotte Beale), Anne
MacAdams (Dr. Masters), William Mc-
Ghee (Sam), Gene Ross (Judge Oliver
W. Cameron), Jessie Lee Fulton (Jane
St. Claire), Camilla Carr (Harriet),
Harriet Warren (Jennifer), Hugh Feagin
(Sgt. Jaffee), Rhea MacAdams (Mrs.
Callingham), Betty Chandler (Allyson),
Jessie Kirby (Danny), Robert Dracup
(Ray Daniels), Michael Harvey (Dr. Ste-
phens).

DON'T LOOK NOW (1974-Brit./Ital.)
    Director: Nicholas Roeg
Julie Christie (Laura Baxter), Donald
Sutherland (John Baxter), Hilary Mason (Heather), Clelia Matania (Wendy),
Massimo Serato (Bishop Barbarrigo),
Renato Scarpa (Insp. Longhi), David
Tree (Anthony Babbage), Ann Rye (Mandy Babbage), Sharon Williams (Christine Baxter), Nicholas Salter (Johnny
Baxter), Bruno Cattaneo (Detective Sab-
bione), Leopoldo Trieste (hotel manager), Georgio Trestini (workman), Ade-
lina Poerio (dwarf).

DON'T PLAY WITH THE MARTIANS
    (1967-Fr.) (A. K. A. "Ne Jouez Pas
    avec les Martians")
    Director: Henri Lanoe
Jean Rochefort, Macha Meril, Haydee
Politoff, Andre Vallardy, Pierre Dac.

DON'T TAKE IT TO HEART (1944)
    Director: Jeffrey Dell
Richard Greene (Peter Hayward), Patri-
cia Medina (Lady Mary), Richard Bird
(Arthur/Ghost), Alfred Drayton (Mr.
Pike), Joan Hickson (Mrs. Pike), George
Merritt (landlord), Esma Cannon (maid),
Edward Rigby (butler), Brefni O'Rorke
(Lady Chaunduyt), Patrick Curwen (Mr.
Smith), Margaret Withers (Mrs. Smith),
Wylie Watson (Harry Bucket), Claude
Dampler (Loopy), Ivor Barnard (bus dri-
ver), Harry Fowler (telegraph boy), Er-
nest Thesiger, David Horne, Ronald
Squire, Edie Martin.

DON WINSLOW OF THE NAVY (1942) -
    serial in 12 episodes
Chapters: 1. "The Human Torpedo", 2.
"Flaming Death", 3. "Weapon of Horror",
4. "Towering Doom", 5. "Trapped in the
Dungeon", 6. "Menaced by Man-Eaters",
7. "Bombed by the Enemy", 8. "The
Chamber of Doom", 9. "Wings of De-
struction", 10. "Fighting Fathoms Deep",
11. "Caught in the Caverns" & 12. "The
Scorpion Strangled".
    Director: Ford Beebe & Ray Tay-
    lor
Don Terry (Don Winslow), Walter Sande
(Lt. Red Pennington), Wade Boteler
(Mike Splendor), Paul Scott (Captain
Fairchild), Claire Dodd (Mercedes),
John Litel (Menlin), Peter Leeds (Chap-
man), Anne Nagel (Misty), Frank Lack-
teen (Koloki), Samuel S. Hinds, Ben Tag-
gert (men).

DOOMSDAY CHRONICLES (1979)
    Director: James Thornton
William Schallert (Narrator).

DOOMSDAY MACHINE (1972)
    Director: Lee Sholem
Ruta Lee, Grant Williams, Bobby Van,
Mala Powers, Denny Miller, Henry Wil-
coxon, Harry Hope, Casey Kasem, Mike
Farrell.

DOOMWATCH (1972)
    Director: Peter Sasdy
Ian Bannen (Dr. Dell Shaw), Judy Geeson
(Victoria Brown), Simon Oates (Dr. Ridge),
John Paul (Dr. Quist), George Sanders
(the Admiral), Percy Herbert (Hartwell),
Geoffrey Keen (Sir Henry Leyton), Joseph
O'Conor (Vicar), Jean Trend (Dr. Fay
Chantry), Shelagh Fraser (Mrs. Straker),
Norman Bird (Brewer), Joby Blanchard
(Bradley), George Woodbridge (ferry
skipper), Brian Anthony (Brian Murray),
James Cosmo (Bob Gillette), Rita Davies
(Mrs. Murray).

DOOR WITH SEVEN LOCKS, THE (1962-
Ger. /Fr.) (A. K. A. "Die Tur mit
den Sieben Schlossern")
Director: Alfred Vohrer
Heinz Drache, Werner Peters, Klaus
Kinski, Eddi Arent, Adi Berber, Sabi-
na Sesselman, Hans Nielsen, Pinkas
Braun.

DORELLIK (1967-Ital.) (A. K. A. "Arri-
va Dorellik")
Director: Stefano Steno
Margaret Lee, Terry-Thomas, Didi
Perego, Jimmy Dorelli, Alfred Adam,
Rosella Como, Jean Pierre Zola.

DORIAN GRAY (1970-Ital. /Ger.) (A. K. A.
"The Secret of Dorian Gray", "Das
Bildnis Des Dorian Gray", "Il Dio
Chiamato Dorian")
Director: Massimo Dallamano
Helmut Berger (Dorian Gray), Herbert
Lom (Henry Wotton), Richard Todd
(Basil), Marie Liljedahl (Sybil), Mar-
garet Lee (Gwendolyn), Isa Miranda
(Mrs. Ruxton), Maria Rohm (Alice),
Beryl Cunningham (Adrienne), Eleono-
ra Rossi Drago (Esther), Renato Roma-
no (Alan), Stewart Black (James Vane).

DOUBLE DECEPTION (1960-Fr.) (A. K. A.
"Les Magiciennes", "The Magicians",
"Frantic")
Director: Serge Friedman
Jacques Riberolles, Jean Mercure, Gi-
nette Le Clerc, Ellen Kessler, Alice
Kessler, Daniel Sorano.

DOUBLE DOOR, THE (1934)
Director: Charles Vidor
Mary Morris (Victoria Van Brett), Eve-
lyn Venable (Anne Darrow), Kent Taylor
(Rip Van Brett), Sir Guy Standing (Mor-
timer Neff), Anne Revere (Caroline Van
Brett), Halliwell Hobbes (Mr. Chase),
Colin Tapley (Dr. John Lucas), Virgi-
nia Howell (Avery), Frank Dawson (Tel-
son), Helen Shipmann (Louise), Ralph
Remley (Lambert), Leonard Carey (Wil-
liam), Burr Caruth (Rev. Dr. Loring).

DOWN TO EARTH (1947)
Director: Alexander Hall
Rita Hayworth (Terpsichore), Larry
Parks (Danny Miller), Edward Everett
Horton (Messenger 7013), James Glea-
son (Max Corkle), George Macready
(Joe Mannion), Roland Culver (Mr. Jor-
dan), Adele Jergens (Georgie Evans),
Marc Platt (Eddie), William Frawley
(Police Lieutenant), James Burke
(Kelly), Kathleen O'Malley (Dolly),
Jean Donahue (Betty), William Haade

(Spike), Fred Sears (orchestra leader).

DO YOU LIKE WOMEN? (1964-Ital. /
Fr.) (A. K. A. "Aimezvous les Fem-
mes? ")
Director: Jean Leon
Gregorie Aslan, Sophie Daumer, Ed-
wige Feuillere, Guy Bedos.

DRACULA (1930)
Director: Tod Browning
Bela Lugosi (Count Dracula), Helen
Chandler (Mina Seward), David Manners
(Jonathan Harker), Edward Van Sloan
(Dr. Van Helsing), Dwight Frye (Ren-
field), Herbert Bunston (Dr. Seward),
Frances Dade (Lucy Weston), Charles
Gerrard (Martin), Moon Carroll (Briggs),
Josephine Velez (English nurse), Mi-
chael Visaroff (innkeeper), Donald Mur-
phy (man in coach), Daisy Belmore (wo-
man in coach).

DRACULA (1930) - Spanish language
Director: George Melford
Carlos Villarias (Count Dracula), Lupita Tovar, Barry Norton, Carmen Guerrero.

DRACULA (TVM-1974) - 2-8-74
Director: Dan Curtis
Jack Palance (Count Dracula), Nigel
Davenport (Dr. Van Helsing), Murray
Brown (Jonathan Harker), Fiona Lewis
(Lucy Westerna), Penelope Horner (Mi-
na Murray), Simon Ward (Arthur Holm-
wood), Pamela Brown (Mrs. Westerna),
George Pravda (innkeeper), Roy Spen-
cer (Whitby Inn Clerk), Hanna-Maria
Pravda (innkeeper's wife), Virginia We-
therell, Sarah Douglas, Barbara Lindley
(Dracula's wives), John Challis (Stock-
ton-on-Tees clerk), Sandra Caron (Whit-
by Inn maid), Reg Lye (zookeeper), Ni-
gel Gregory (Midvale shipping clerk),
Gitta Denise (Mada Kirstoff), John Pennington (Richmond shipping clerk), Fred
Stone (priest), Martin Read (coast guard).

DRACULA (BBC-TVM-1970) (segment of
"Mystery and Imagination")
Director: Patrick Dromgoole
Denholm Elliott (Count Dracula), Susan
George (Lucy Weston), Bernard Archard
(Dr. Van Helsing), Corin Redgrave (Jo-
nathan Harker), Joan Hickson (Mrs. Wes-
ton), James Maxwell (Dr. Seward), Su-
zanne Neve (Mina Harker), Michael Da
Costa (Jenkins), James Pope (Bert),
Hedley Goodall (Swales), Helena McCar-
thy (Mrs. Hoskins), Phyllis Morris (Mrs.
Perkins), Tony Lane (coachman), Marie
Legrand, Semper Muller, Nina Baden,

Valerie Muller (vampire women).

DRACULA (1979)
    Director: John Badham
Frank Langella (Count Dracula), Lau-
rence Olivier (Dr. Van Helsing), Kate
Nelligan (Lucy Seward), Donald Plea-
sence (Dr. Seward), Trevor Eve (Jona-
than Harker), Jan Francis (Mina Van
Helsing), Tony Haygarth (Renfield),
Duvitski (Annie), Teddy Turner (Swales),
Ted Carroll (Scarborough sailor), Kris-
tine Howarth (Mrs. Galloway), Joe
Belcher (Tom Hindley), Frank Birch
(Harbourmaster), Peter Wallis (priest),
Gabor Vernon (Captain of Demeter),
Frank Henson (Demeter sailor).

DRACULA A. D. 1972 (1972) (A. K. A.
    "Dracula Today")
    Director: Alan Gibson
Christopher Lee (Count Dracula), Pe-
ter Cushing (Dr. Van Helsing), Chris-
topher Neame (Johnny Alucard), Ste-
phanie Beacham (Jessica Van Helsing),
Michael Coles (Insp. Murray), Caro-
line Munro (Laura Bellows), Janet Key
(Anna Bryant), Marsha Hunt (Gaynor),
Philip Miller (Bob Tarrant), William
Ellis (Joe Mitchum), David Andrews
(Detective Sergeant), Michael Kitchen
(Greg), Lally Bowers (matron).

DRACULA AGAINST DR. FRANKEN-
    STEIN (1971-Span. /Fr.) (A. K. A.
    "Dracula contra el Dr. Franken-
    stein", "Dracula Prisonnier du Doc-
    teur Frankenstein")
    Director: Jesus Franco
Howard Vernon (Dracula), Dennis Price
(Dr. Frankenstein), Fernando Bilbao
(Frankenstein's monster), Brit Nichols
(Lady Dracula), Alberto Dalbes (Dr.
Seward), Luis Barboo (Morpho), Mary
Francis.

DRACULA - FATHER AND SON (1976-
    Fr.) (A. K. A. "Dracula Pere et Fils")
    Director: Edouard Molinaro
Christopher Lee (Count Dracula), Ber-
nard Mendez (Ferdinand), Catherine
Breillat (Herminie), Marie-Helene
Breillat (Nicole), Jean-Claude Dauphin
(young man), Anna Gael (woman).

DRACULA HAS RISEN FROM THE GRAVE
    (1968)
    Director: Freddie Francis
Christopher Lee (Count Dracula), Ru-
pert Davies (Monsignor Ernst Muller),
Veronica Carlson (Maria Muller), Bar-
ry Andrews (Paul), Michael Ripper
(Max), Barbara Ewing (Zena), Ewan

Hooper (priest), George A. Cooper
(landlord), Marion Mathie (Anna), Carrie Baker (village girl), John D. Collins
(student), Chris Cunningham (farmer),
Norman Bacon (boy).

DRACULA IN ISTANBUL (1953-Turk.)
    (A. K. A. "Drakula Istanbulda")
    Director: Mehmet Muhtar
Atif Kaptan (Count Dracula), Annie Ball.

DRACULA, PRINCE OF DARKNESS
    (1965)
    Director: Terence Fisher
Christopher Lee (Count Dracula), An-
drew Keir (Father Shandor), Barbara
Shelley (Helen Kent), Francis Matthews
(Charles Kent), Suzan Farmer (Diana
Kent), Charles Tingwell (Alan Kent),
Philip Latham (Klove), Thorley Walters
(Ludwig), Jack Lambert (Brother Pe-
ter), Walter Brown (Brother Mark),
George Woodbridge (landlord), Philip
Ray (priest), John Maxim (coach driver),
Joyce Hemson (mother).

DRACULA'S DAUGHTER (1936)
    Director: Lambert Hillyer
Gloria Holden (Countess Marya Zaleska),
Otto Kruger (Dr. Jeffrey Garth), Edward Van Sloan (Dr. Van Helsing), Irving Pichel (Sandor), Marguerite Chur-
chill (Janet Blake), Hedda Hopper (Lady
Esme Hammond), Claud Allister (Sir
Aubrey Vail), Nan Grey (Lili, the model),
E. E. Clive (Sgt. Clive), Gilbert Emery
(Sir Basil Humphrey), Billy Bevan (Albert), Halliwell Hobbes (Constable Hawkins), Eily Malyon (Miss Peabody), Christian Rub (coachman), Guy Kingsford (radio announcer), David Dunbar (motor
bobby), Gordon Hart (host), Joseph E.
Tozer (Dr. Graham), Douglas Wood (Dr.
Townsend), Fred Walton (Dr. Beamish),
Paul Weigel (the innkeeper), George So-
rel (police officer), William von Brincken (policeman), Douglas Gordon (attendant), Eric Wilton (butler), Agnes
Anderson (bride), William Schramm
(groom), Owen Gorin (friend), Else
Janssen, Bert Sprotte (guests), John
Blood (bobby), Clive Morgan (desk sergeant), Hedwigg Reicher (wife), John
Power (police official).

DRACULA'S DOG (1977) (A. K. A. "Zol-
    tan. . . Hound of Dracula")
    Director: Albert Band
Michael Pataki (Michael Drake/Count
Dracula), Jose Ferrer (Insp. Branco),
Jan Shutan (Marla Drake), Libbie Chase
(Linda Drake), John Levin (Steve Drake),
Reggie Nalder (Veidt Smit), Arleen Mar-

tell (Major Hessle), Simmy Bow (fisherman), Jojo D'Amore (fisherman), Roger Schumacher (hiker), Cleo Harrington (Mrs. Parks), Katherine Fitzpatrick.

DRACULA'S GREAT LOVE (1972-Span.)
(A. K. A. "El Gran Amour del Conde Dracula", "The Great Love of Count Dracula")
Director: Javier Aguirre
Paul Naschy (Count Dracula/Wendell), Rossana Yanni, Haydee Politoff, Mirta Miller, Vic Winner, Ingrid Garbo.

DRACULA SUCKS (1979) (A. K. A. "Dracula's Bride")
Director: Philip Marshak
Jamie Gillis (Count Dracula), Reggie Nalder (Dr. Van Helsing), Serena (Lucy Webster), Annette Haven (Mina), John Leslie (Dr. Arthur Seward), John Holmes (Dr. John Stoker), Kay Parker (Dr. Sybil Seward), Richard Bulik (Richard Renfield), Paul Thomas (Jonathan Harker), Bill Margold (Henry), Mike Ranger (Dr. Peter Bradley), Pat Manning (Irene Renfield), Seka (Dr. Betty Lawson), David Lee Bynum (Jarvis, the butler), Irene Best (maid), George Lee (singing cowboy), Kurt Sjoberg (Adolph Hitler), Martin L. Dorf (Martin, the attendant), Renee Andre (1st hand-maiden), Slavica (2nd hand-maiden), Nancy Hoffman (Baby Jane), Ken Michaels, Mitch Morrill (patients).

DRACULA VS. FRANKENSTEIN (1971)
(A. K. A. "Blood of Frankenstein")
Director: Al Adamson, Jr.
J. Carrol Naish (Dr. Durea), Lon Chaney, Jr. (Groton), Anthony Eisley (Mike), Regina Carrol (Judith), Zandor Vorkov (Count Dracula), John Bloom (Frankenstein's monster), Angelo Rossito (Grazbo), Jim Davis (Sgt. Martin), Russ Tamblyn (Rico), Forrest J. Ackerman (Dr. Beaumont), Anne Morell (Samantha), Greydon Clark (Strange), William Bonner, Bruce Kimball (bikers), Maria Lease (Joan), Albert Cole, Irv Saunders (policemen), Gary Kent (beach boy), Connie Nelson (beach girl), Lu Dorn (hippie), Shelly Weiss (the Creature).

DRAGON MURDER CASE, THE (1934)
Director: H. Bruce Humberstone
Warren Williams (Philo Vance), Margaret Lindsay (Bernice), Lyle Talbot (Leland), Eugene Pallette (Sgt. Heath), Robert Barratt (Stamm), George E. Stone (Tatum), Robert Warwick (Dr. Halliday), George Meeker (Montague), Etienne Girardot (Dr. Doremus), Do-

rothy Tree (Ruby), William Davidson (Greeff), Robert McWade (Markham), Helen Lowell (Mrs. Stamm), Charles C. Wilson (Hennessey), Arthur Aylesworth (Trainor), Wilfred Lucas.

DRAGON OF PENDRAGON CASTLE, THE (1950)
Director: John Baxter
Robin Netscher (Peter Fielding), Hilary Rennie (Judy Fielding), Jane Welsh (Mrs. Fielding), Graham Moffatt (Paddy), J. Hubert Leslie (Sir William Magnus), David Hannaford (Bobby), Leslie Bradley (Mr. Ferber), C. Denier Warren (Mr. Morgan), Lily Lapidus (Mrs. Morgan).

DRAGONSLAYER (1981)
Director: Matthew Robbins
Sir Ralph Richardson (Ulrich), Peter MacNicol (Galen), Caitlan Clarke (Calerian), Peter Eyre (Cassiodorous), John Hallam (Tyrian), Albert Salmi (Greil), Chloe Salaman (Princess Elspeth), Roger Kemp (Horsrik), Emrys James (Simon), Sydney Bromley (Hodge).

DREAM CHEATER, THE (1920)
Director: Ernest C. Warde
J. Warren Kerrigan, Fritzi Brunette, Aggie Herring, Sam Southern.

DREAM OF A RAREBIT FIEND (1906) - short
Director: Edwin S. Porter

DREAMS OF DEATH (1950-Ger.) (A. K. A. "Die Todlichen Traume")
Director: Paul Martin
Rudolf Forster, Cornell Borchers, Will Quadflieg.

DRESSED TO KILL (1946)
Director: Roy William Neill
Basil Rathbone (Sherlock Holmes), Nigel Bruce (Dr. Watson), Edmond Breon (Julian Emery), Patricia Morison (Hilda Courtney), Frederic Worlock (Col. Cavanaugh), Carl Harbord (Insp. Hopkins), Patricia Cameron (Evelyn Clifford), Tom P. Dillon (Sgt. Thompson), Harry Cording (Hamid), Mary Gordon (Mrs. Hudson), Topsy Glynn (Kilgour child), Ian Wolfe (Scotland Yard Commissioner), Lillian Bronson (tourist).

DRESSED TO KILL (1980)
Director: Brian De Palma
Michael Caine (Dr. Robert Elliott), Angie Dickinson (Kate Miller), Nancy Allen (Liz Blake), Keith Gordon (Peter Miller), Ennis Franz (Detective Marino), David Marguiles (Dr. Levy), Brandon Maggart

(Cleveland Sam), Fred Weber (Mike Miller), Susanna Clemm (Bobbi), Ken Baker (Warren Lockman), Robert Lee Rush (1st hood), Bill Randolph (chase cabbie), Sean O'Rinn (museum cabbie), Mary Davenport (woman at coffee shop).

DRILLER KILLER (1979)
Director: Abel Ferrara
Caroly Marz, Jimmy Laine, Bob De Frank, Babyi Day, Peter Yellen, Harry Schultz.

DRIVE-IN MASSACRE (1976)
Director: Stuart Segall
Jake Barnes, Adam Lawrence, Newton Naushaus, Douglas Gudbye, Norman Sherlock, Valdesta.

DRUMS OF FU MANCHU (1940) - serial in 15 episodes
Director: William Witney & John English
Henry Brandon (Fu Manchu), Olaf Hytten (Dr. Petrie), William Royle (Sir Dennis Nayland Smith), Gloria Franklin (Fah Lo Suee), Luana Walters (Mary Randolph), Dwight Frye (Anderson), Wheaton Chambers (Dr. Humphrey), George Cleveland (Prof. Parker), Tom Chatterton (Prof. Randolph), John Dilson (Ezra Howard), Robert Kellard (Allen Parker), Lal Chend Mehra (Sirdar Prahin), John Merton (Loki), Guy D'Ennery (Ranah Sang), George Pembroke (C.W. Crawford), Philip Ahn (Chang), John Bagni (Dangra), Paul Marion (Native messinger), John Picorri (Krantz), Lee Shumway (Corrigan), Merrill McCormick (attendant No. 1), Walter Stirlitz (attendant No. 2), Michael Vallon, Tony Paton (temple guards), Lowden Adams (Blake), Evan Thomas (Carlton), James B. Leong (Chinese), Ann Baldwin (Miss Thomas (Carlton), James B. Leong (Chinese), Ann Baldwin (Miss Frisbie), Joe de Stefani (High Lhama), Charley Phillips (baggage clerk), Harry Strang (Wade), John Lester Johnson (Cardo), Jamiel Hasson (Chieftain), Bert LeBaron (fireman), John Meredith (gate sentry), Bill Yrigoyen (Hillman), Paul Renay (Khandar), Kam Tong (Oriental houseboy), Robert Blair (sergeant), Jenifer Gray (stewardess), Eric Lansdale (Richards), Francis Walker (Koomerow), Tofik Mickey (Hindu), Frank Ellis, Henry Wills, Victor Cox (Tartars), Robert Stevenson (Tartar Russian), George Bruggeman, Bill Nind (telegraphers), Akim Dobrynin (temple priest), Carl Sepulveda, Jack Montgomery, Bob Woodward (tribesmen), Nor-

man Nesbitt (Wally Winchester), John Ward (Wilson), Ernie Sarracino (Dowlah Rao), James Flatley (Pegai), Budd Buster, Eddie Kaye, Bob Jamison, Alan Gregg, Art Dillard, Al Taylor, Jack Roper, Vinegar Roan, Bill Wilkus, Tommy Coats, Frank Wayne, Ted Wells, Burt Dillard, Johnny Judd, Jimmy Fawcett, Duke Green, Augie Gomez, George Suzanne, Duke Taylor, Ken Terrell, Joe Yrigoyen (Dacroits), Hector Sarno, David Sharpe.

DRUMS OF JEOPARDY (1923)
Director: Edward Dillon
Wallace Beery, Jack Mulhall, Elaine Hammerstein, David Torrence, Maude George, Eric Mayne, Forrest Seabury.

DRUMS OF JEOPARDY (1931) (A. K. A. "Mark of Terror")
Director: George B. Seitz
Warner Oland (Boris Karlov), June Collyer (Kitty Conover), Lloyd Hughes (Prince Nicholas Petrov), Florence Lake (Anya Karlov), Mischa Auer (Piotr), Clara Blandick (Aunt Abbie), Hale Hamilton (Martin Kent), George Fawcett (General Petrov), Murdoch MacQuarrie (Stephens), Ernest Hilliard (Prince Ivan), Wallace MacDonald (Prince Gregor), Ann Brody (Tazia), Edward Homans (Detective Brett), Ruth Hall (girl), Harry Semels (henchman).

DRUMS OF THE CONGO (1942)
Director: Christy Cabanne
Stuart Erwin (Congo Jack), Peggy Moran (Enid), Turhan Bey (Juma), Don Terry (Kirk), Dorothy Dandridge (Malimi), Ona Munson (Dr. Ann Montgomery), Jules Bledsoe (Kalu), Richard Lane (Coutlass), Ernest Whitman (King Malaba), Ed Stanley (Col. Robinson), Jess Lee Brooks (Chief Madjeduka), Napolean Simpson (Taroka Leader).

DRUMS OF THE JUNGLE (1934) (A. K. A. "Ouanga", "Crime of Voodoo")
Director: George Terwilliger
Sheldon Leonard (Le Strange), Fredi Washington (Cleie Gordon), Philip Brandon (Adam Maynard), Marie Raxton (Eve Langley), Winifred Harris (Aunt Sarrah), Sid Easton (Jackson), George Spink (Johnson), Babe Joyce (Susie).

DRUMS O'VOODOO (1934) (A. K. A. "She Devil")
Director: Arthur Hoerl
Laura Bowman (Aunt Hagar), J. Augustus Smith (Elder Berry), Edna Barr (Myrtle Simpson), Lionel Monagas (Ebe-

nezer), A. B. Comathiere (Deacon Dunson), Morris McKinney (Thomas Catt), Alberta Perkins (Sister Knight), Fred Bonny (Brother Zero), Trixie Smith (Sister Marguerite), Paul Johnson (Deacon August), Carrie Hugg (Sister Zunan), James Davis (Brother Zumee), Harriet Daughtry (Sister Lauter), Ruth Morrison (Sister Gaghan), Bennie Small (Bou Bouche), Pedro Lopez (Marcon).

DUEL (TVM-1971) - 11-13-71
    Director: Steven Spielberg
Dennis Weaver (David Mann), Jacqueline Scott (Mrs. Mann), Lucille Benson (Snakearama owner), Lou Frizzell (bus driver), Eddie Firestone (cafe owner), Carey Loftin (truck driver), Shirley O'Hara (waitress), Alexander Lockwood (man in car), Amy Douglass (woman in car), Gene Dynarski (man in cafe), Charles Seel (old man), Tim Herbert (gas station attendant).

DUEL IN SPACE (1954)
    see Television: Rocky Jones, Space Ranger (1953-54).

DUEL OF THE TITANS (1961-Ital.)
    (A. K. A. "Romolo e Remo", "Romulus and Remus")
    Director: Sergio Corbucci
Steve Reeves (Romulus), Gordon Scott (Remus), Virna Lisi (Julia), Andrea Bosic (Faustolo), Jacques Sernas (Curzio), Ornella Vanoni (Tarpeja), Franco Volpi (Amulio), Giuliano Dell-Ovo (Publio), Laura Solari (Rea Siliva), Enzo Cerusico (Numa), Germano Longo (Servio), Piero Lulli (Sulpicio), Franco Balducci (Acilio), Jose Greci (Estria), Gianni Musy (Celere), Inge Nystrom (Sira), Enrico Glori (priest).

DUNGEON OF HORROR (1963)
    Director: Pat Boyett
Russ Harvey, Helen Hogan, Maurice Harris, Bill McNulty, Lee Morgan, Pat Boyett, Ron Russell.

DUNWICH HORROR, THE (1970)
    Director: Daniel Haller
Sandra Dee (Nancy Walker), Dean Stockwell (Wilbur Whateley), Ed Begley (Dr. Henry Armitage), Sam Jaffe (Old Whateley), Lloyd Bochner (Dr. Cory), Barboura Morris (Mrs. Cole), Talia Coppola Shire (Cora), Jason Wingreen (Police Chief), Michael Fox (Dr. Raskin), Joanna Moore Jordan (Lavinia), Beech Dickerson (Mr. Cole), Jack Pierce (Reege), Donna Baccala (Elizabeth Hamilton), Toby Russ (librarian), Michael

Haynes (guard).

DUSK TO DAWN (1922)
    Director: King Vidor
Florence Vidor, Jack Mulhall, Truman Van Dyke, James Neill, Lydia Knott, Herbert Fortier.

DYBBUK, THE (1967-Isr. /Ger.) (A. K. A.
    "Between Two Worlds")
    Director: Ilan Eldad
David Opatoshu (the Rabbi), Peter Frye, Tina Wodetzky, Moti Barkan, Raphael Catzkin, Baruch Klass, Tutte Lmeka, Devorah Kastellanetz.

DYING ROOM ONLY (TVM-1973) - 9-18-73
    Director: Phillip Leacock
Cloris Leachman (Jean Mitchell), Ross Martin (Jim Cutler), Ned Beatty (Tom King), Louise Latham (Vi), Dana Elcar (Sheriff), Dabney Coleman (Bob Mitchell), Ron Feinberg (Lou McDermott).

EARTHBOUND (1920)
    Director: T. Hayes Hunter
Mahlon Hamilton, Naomi Childers, Wyndham Standing, Alec B. Francis, Lawson Butt, Aileen Pringle, Flora Revalles, Kate Lester.

EARTHBOUND (1940)
    Director: Irving Pichel
Warner Baxter (Nick Desborough), Andrea Leeds (Ellen Desborough), Lynn Bari (Linda Reynolds), Henry Wilcoxon (Jeffrey Reynolds), Christian Rub (Almette), Russell Hicks (Prosecutor), Elizabeth Patterson (Beck Tilden), Ian Wolfe (Totten), Pedro de Cordoba (Minister), Charley Grapewin (Mr. Whimser), Reginald Sheffield (Defense Attorney), Lester Scharff (detective).

EARTH DIES SCREAMING, THE (1964)
    Director: Terence Fisher
Dennis Price (Quinn Taggett), Virginia Field (Peggy Taggett), Willard Parker (Jeff Nolan), Vanda Godsell (Violet Courtland), Thorley Walters (Edgar Otis), Anna Palk (Lorna), David Spenser (Mel).

EARTHQUAKE (1974)
    Director: Mark Robson
Charlton Heston (Stewart Graff), Ava Gardner (Remy Graff), Lorne Greene (Sam Royce), Genevieve Bujold (Denise Marshall), George Kennedy (Lew Slade), Richard Roundtree (Miles Quade), Marjoe Gortner (Jody), Lloyd Nolan (Dr. James Vance), Victoria Principal (Rosa Amici), Barry Sullivan (Dr. Willis Stoc-

kle), John Randolph (the Mayor), Walter Matthau (drunk), Pedro Armendariz, Jr. (Slade's partner), Gabriel Dell (Miles' manager), Donald Moffat (Dr. Harvey Johnson), Lloyd Gough (Cameron), Jesse Vint (Buck), Alan Vint (Ralph), Lionel Johnston (Hank), Scott Hylands (assistant dam caretaker), George Murdock (Colonel), John Dennis (brawny foreman), Monica Lewis (Royce's secretary), Tiger Williams (Corry Marshall), John Elerich (Carl Leeds), Donald Mantooth (Sid), John S. Ragin (Chief Inspector), Kip Niven (assistant seismologist), Michael Richardson (Sandy), Bob Cunningham (Dr. Frank Ames), Bob Gravage (Mr. Griggs), Gene Dynarski (dam caretaker), Alex A. Brown, H. B. Haggerty (pool players), Dave Morick (technician), Tim Herbert (man), Inez Pedroza (Laura), Debralee Scott (newlywed).

EARTH SPIRIT (1923-Ger.) (A. K. A. "Erdgeist")
Director: Leopold Jessner
Albert Bassermann, Alexander Granach, Asta Nielsen, Carl Ebert, Heinrich George, Rudolf Forster, Gustav Rickelt, Erwin Biswanger, Julius Falkenstein.

EARTH II (TVM-1971) - 11-28-71
Director: Tom Gries
Gary Lockwood (David Seville), Mariette Hartley (Lisa Karger), Tony Francoisa (Frank Karger), Gary Merrill (Walter Dietrich), Lew Ayres (Pres. Charles Carter), Hari Rhodes (Dr. Loren Huxley), Scott Hylands (Jim Capa), Inga Swenson (Ilyana Kovalefskii), Edward Bell (Anton Kovalefskii), Bart Burns (Steiner), Brian Dewey (Matt Karger), Diana Webster (Hannah Young), John Carter (Hazlitt), Herbert Nelson (Chairman), Bob Hoy (West), Vince Cannon (technician), Serge Tschernisch (Russian), David Sachs (surgeon).

EARTH VS. FLYING SAUCERS (1956)
Director: Fred F. Sears
Hugh Marlowe (Dr. Russell A. Marvin), Joan Taylor (Carol Marvin), Morris Ankrum (Gen. Hanley), Donald Curtis (Major Hughlin), John Zaremba (Prof. Kanter), Grandon Rhodes (Gen. Edmunds), Thomas B. Henry (Adm. Enright), Larry Blake (motorcycle officer), Paul Frees (voice of the Alien), Dale Van Sickel (stuntman), Frank Wilcox (Alfred Cassidy), Harry Lauter (Cutting), Charles Evans (Dr. Alberts), Clark Howat (Sgt. Nash), Alan Reynolds (Maj. Kimberly).

EATING RAOUL (1982)
Director: Paul Bartel
Paul Bartel (Paul Bland), Mary Woronov (Mary Bland), Robert Beltram (Raoul), Ed Begley, Jr. (hippy), Susan Saiger (Doris the Dominatrix), Dan Barrows (Robbie R.), Ralph Brannen (Paco), Dick Blackburn (James), Hamilton Camp (Mr. Peck), Buck Henry (Mr. Leech), Edie McClurg (Susan), John Parragon (sexshop salesman).

EEGAH! (1962)
Director: Nicholas Merriwether
Arch Hall, Jr. , Marilyn Manning, Richard Kiel, William Watters, Cash Flagg.

EFFECTS (1979)
Director: Dusty Nelson
John Harrison (Lacey), Susan Chapek (Celeste), Joseph Pilato (Dom), Bernard McKenna (Barney), Debra Gordon (Rita), Tom Savini (Nicky), Chuck Hoyes (Lobo), Blay Bahnsen (Scratch).

EGGHEAD'S ROBOT (1970)
Director: Milo Lewis
Roy Kinnear, Richard Wattis, Kathryn Dawe, Jeffrey Chegwin, Keith Chegwin.

8 1/2 (1963-Ital.)
Director: Federico Fellini
Marcello Mastroianni (Guido Anselmi), Anouk Aimee (Luisa Anselmi), Claudia Cardinale (Claudia), Sandra Milo (Carla), Barbara Steele (Gloria Morin), Rossella Falk (Rosella), Guido Alberti (the Producer), Jean Rougeul (the Writer), Annibale Ninchi (Anselmi's father), Giuditta Rissone (Anselmi's mother), Caterina Boratto (fashionable girl), Madeleine Lebeau (an actress), Edra Gale (La Saraghina), Tito Masini (the Cardinal), Yvonne Casadei (aging dancer), Jan Dallas (the Mind Reader), Eugene Walter (the journalist), Gilda Dahlberg (journalist's wife), Nadine Sanders (airline hostess), Georgia Simmons (Anselmi's grandmother), Annie Gorassini (producer's girl friend), Hazel Rogers (Negro dancer), Marco Gemini (Guido as a boy), Riccardo Guglielmi (Guido as a farm boy).

ELECTRONIC MONSTER, THE (1960) (A. K. A. "Escapement", "Zex, the Electronic Fiend")
Director: Montgomery Tully
Rod Cameron (Jeff Keenan), Mary Murphy (Ruth Vance), Peter Illing (Paul Zakon), Meredith Edwards (Dr. Maxwell), Carl Jaffe (Dr. Hoff), Carl Duering (Blore), Kay Callard (Laura Maxwell),

Roberta Huby (Verna Berteaux), Larry Cross (Brad Somers), John McCarthy (Claude Kenver), Felix Felton (Commissaire), Carlo Borelli (Signore Kallini), Jacques Cey (French doctor), Armande Guinle (French farmer), Pat Clavin (studio receptionist), Malou Pantera (clinic receptionist), Alan Gifford (Wayne).

ELEPHANT BOY (1937)
    Director: Robert Flaherty & Zoltan Korda
Sabu (Toomal), Allan Jeayes (Muchua Appa), Walter Hudd (Petersen), W. E. Holloway (Toomal's father), Wilfrid Hyde-White (Commissioner), Bruce Gordon (Rhan Lahl), D. J. Williams (hunter).

ELEPHANT MAN, THE (1980)
    Director: David Lynch
Anthony Hopkins (Dr. Frederick Treves), John Hurt (John Merrick), Anne Bancroft (Mrs. Kendall), John Gielgud (Carr Gamm), Wendy Hiller (Mothershead), Freddie Jones (Bytes), John Standing (Fox), Hannah Gordon (Mrs. Treves), Michael Elphick (night porter), Helen Ryan (Princess Alexandra), Lesley Dunlop (Nora), Dexter Fletcher (Bytes' boy), Phoebe Nicholls (Merrick's mother), Lydia Lisle (Merrick's mother), Pat Gorman (fairground bobby), Gerald Case (Lord Waddington), Kathleen Byron (Lady Waddington), Hugh Manning (Broadneck), Patsy Smart (distraught woman), Frederick Treves (Alderman), Kenny Baker (Plumed Dwarf), Claire Davenport (Fat Lady), Orla Pederson (Skeleton Man), Stromboli (the Fire Eater), Gilda Cohen, Marcus Powell (midgets), Chris Greener (giant), Lisa & Teri Scoble (Siamese twins), James Cormack (Pierce), Richard Hunter (Hodges), Robert Bush (messenger), Roy Evans (cabbie), Joan Rhodes (cook), Nula Conwell (Nurse Kathleen), Tony Landon (porter), Alfie Curtis (milkman), Carole Harrison (tart), Brenda Kempner, Bernadette Milnes (fighting women), Morgan Sheppard (man in pub), Deirdre Costello, Pauline Quirke (whores), David Ryall (man with whores), Fanny Carby (Mrs. Kendall's dresser), Dennis Burgess (1st Committeeman), Eiji Kusuhara (Japanese bleeder), Robert Day (Little John), Tommy Wright, Peter Davidson (bobbies), Patricia Hodge (screaming woman), John Rapley (King in Panto), Hugh Spight (Puss in Panto), Teresa Codling (Princess in Panto), Marion Betzold (principle boy), Beryl Hicks (Fairy), Victor Kravchenko (lion/

coachman), Florenzio Morgado, Caroline Haigh (trees), Janie Kells, Michele Amas, Penny Wright, Lucie Alford (horses).

ELEVENTH HOUR, THE (1923)
    Director: Bernard J. Durning
Alan Hale, Sr. (Prince Stefan de Bernie), Nigel De Brulier (Mordecai Newman), Richard Tucker (Herbert Glenville), Shirley Mason (Barbara Hackett), Walter McGrail (Dick Manley), June Elvidge (Estelle Hackett), Charles Jones (Brick McDonald), Fred Kelsey (Submarine Commander), Fred Kohler (foreman), Edward Martindel (Barbara's uncle).

EMBALMER, THE (1966-Ital.) (A. K. A "Il Mostro Di Venezia", "The Monster of Venice")
    Director: Dino Tavello
Maureen Brown, Gin Mart, Viki Castillo, Elmo Caruso, Alcide Gazzatto, Alba Brotto.

EMBRYO (1976)
    Director: Ralph Nelson
Rock Hudson (Dr. Paul Holliston), Diane Ladd (Martha), Barbara Carrera (Victoria), Roddy McDowall (Riley), Anne Schedeen (Helen), John Elerick (Gordon), Vincent Bagetta (Collier), Jack Colvin (Dr. Winston), Dick Winslowe (Forbes), Lina Raymond (Janet Novak), Joyce Spitz (trainer), Dr. Joyce Brothers (herself).

EMPEROR AND THE GOLEM, THE (1951-Czech.) (A. K. A. "Cisaruv Pekar, Pekaruv Cisar", "Emperor's Baker, Baker's Emperor", "Return of the Golem")
    Director: Martin Fric
Jan Werich, Marie Vaslova, Natasa Gollova, Frantisek Cerny, Jiri Plachy, Bohus Zahorssky, Frantisek Filiposky, Zdenek Stepanek.

EMPIRE OF DIAMONDS, THE (1920)
    Director: Leonce Perret
Robert Elliott (Matthew Versigny), Lucy Fox (Marguerite Versigny), Henry G. Sell (Paul Bernac), Leon Mathot (Arthur Graves), Jacques Volyns (Trazi d'Aricola), Ruth Hunter (Esther Taylor), L. Morlas (Andre Zarnoff), J. Mailly (Baron de Lambri).

EMPIRE OF THE ANTS (1977)
    Director: Bert I. Gordon
Joan Collins (Marilyn Fryser), Robert Lansing (Dan Stokely), John David Carson (Joe Morrison), Jacqueline Scott (Margaret Ellis), Pamela Susan Shoop

(Coreen Bradford), Albert Salmi (Sheriff Art Kincade), Robert Pine (Larry Graham), Brooke Palance (Christine Graham), Jack Kosslyn (Thomas Lawson), Ilse Earl (Mary Lawson), Irene Tedrow (Velma Thompson), Harry Holcombe (Harry Thompson), Edward Power (Charlie Pearson), Jami Gavin (Ginny), Norman Franklin (Anson Parker), Tom Fadden (Sam Russell), Florence McGee (Phoebe Russell), Mike Armstrong (Jim), Jim Wheelus (crewman), Tom Ford (Pete), Charles Red (taxi driver), Mark Hooker, Hugh Hooker (stuntmen).

EMPIRE STRIKES BACK, THE (1980)
(A. K. A. "Star Wars 5")
Director: Irvin Kershner
Mark Hamill (Luke Skywalker), Harrison Ford (Han Solo), Carrie Fisher (Princess Leia), Anthony Daniels (C-3PO), Kenny Baker (R2-D2), Billy Dee Williams (Lando Carlrissian), Peter Mayhew (Chewbacca), David Prowse (Darth Vader), Alec Guinness (Obi-Wan Kenobi), Frank Oz (Yoda), Jeremy Bulloch (Boba Fett), Clive Revill (voice of the Emperor), Jack Purvis (Chief Ugnaught), John Hollis (Lando's aide), Julian Glover (Gen. Veers), Des Webb (snow creature), Michael Culver (Capt. Needa), Kenneth Colley (Adm. Piett), Michael Sheard (Adm. Ozzel), Kathryn Mullen (assistant for Yoda), Milton Johns, Oliver Maguire, John Dicks, Mark Jones, Robin Scobey (Empire Officers), Bruce Boa (Gen. Rieekan), Dennis Lawson (Wedge), Christopher Malcom (Zev), Richard Oldfield (Hobbie), Ian Liston (Janson), John Morton (Dak), John Ratzenberger (Major Derlin), Jack McKenzie (Deck Lieutenant), Jerry Harte (Head Controller), Norman Chancer, Norwich Duff, Brigitte Kahn, Ray Hassett, Burnell Tucker (Rebel Officers).

ENCHANTED COTTAGE, THE (1924)
Director: John S. Robertson
May McAvoy (Laura Pennington), Holmes Herbert (Major Hillgrove), Richard Barthelmess (Oliver Bashforth), Ethel Wright (Mrs. Minnett), Florence Short, Alfred Hickman, Ida Waterman, Marion Coakley.

ENCHANTED COTTAGE, THE (1945)
Director: John Cromwell
Robert Young (Oliver), Dorothy McGuire (Laura), Herbert Marshall (Hillgrove), Mildred Natwick (Mrs. Minnett), Spring Byington (Violet Price), Hillary Brooke (Beatrice), Alec Englander (Danny),

Richard Gaines (Frederick), Mary Worth (Mrs. Stanton), Josephine Whittell (canteen manager), Robert Clarke, Eden Nicholas.

ENCHANTED FOREST, THE (1945)
Director: Lew Landers
Edmund Lowe (Steven Blaine), Brenda Joyce (Anne), John Litel (Henderson), Billy Severn (Jackie), Clancy Cooper (Bilson), Harry Davenport (Old John).

ENCOUNTERS WITH THE UNKNOWN (1975)
Director: Harry Thomason
Rod Serling (Narrator), Rosie Holotick, Gene Ross, Gary Brockette, Annabelle Weenick, Bob Ginnaven, Kevin Kieberly, August Sehven.

END OF AUGUST AT THE HOTEL OZONE (1965-Czech.) (A. K. A. "Konec Srpna v Hotelu Ozon", "The End of the World at the Ozone Hotel")
Director: Jan Schmidt
Ondrej Jariabek, Magda Siedlerova, Beta Ponicanova, Hana Vitkova, Jana Novakova.

END OF THE WORLD, THE (1930-Fr.)
(A. K. A. "La Fin du Monde")
Director: Abel Gance
Abel Gance, Victor Francen, Colete Darfeuil, Jeanne Brindeau, Sylvia Grenade, Samson Fainsilber, Jean d'Yd, George Colin.

END OF THE WORLD (1977)
Director: John Hayes
Christopher Lee (Father Pergado/Zandor), Kirk Scott (Prof. Andrew Boran), Sue Lyon (Sylvia Boran), Dean Jagger (Ray Collins), Lew Ayres (Cmdr. Joseph Beckerman), Macdonald Carey (John Davis), John Van Ness (Mr. Sanchez), Liz Ross (Sister Patrizia), Mary Daugherty, Jane Wilbur, Kathy Cunha, Evelyn Lipton, Pat Wylie (nuns), Roscoe Born (student), John Haues (driver on highway), Sammy Bow (diner owner), John Dennis, Frank Leo (Brinkerman's guards), Gene Walker, George Soviak (plant guards), Ron Carter, David Gold (Brinkerman's assistants).

ENEMY FROM SPACE (1957) (A. K. A. "Quatermass II")
Director: Val Guest
Brian Donleavy (Prof. Bernard Quatermass), John Longden (Lomax), Bryan Forbes (Marsh), Sidney James (Jimmy Hall), William Franklyn (Brand), Vera Day (Sheila), Percy Herbert (Gorman),

Michael Balfour (Harry), Michael Ripper (Ernie), Charles Lloyd-Pack (Dawson), John Van Eyssen (Public Relations Officer), John Stuart (Commissioner), George Merritt (Superintendent), John Rae (McLeod), Tom Chatto (Broadhead), Jan Holden (young girl), Ronald Wilson (young man), Betty Impey (Kelly), Marianne Stone (secretary), Jane Aird (Mrs. McLeod), Lloyd Lamble (Inspector), Joyce Adams (woman MP), Howard Williams (Michaels), Robert Raikes (lab assistant), Philip Baird (lab assistant), John Fabin (interne), Arthur Blake (constable), Gilbert Davies (banker), Edwin Richfield (Peterson).

ENTER THE DEVIL (1971) (A. K. A. "Disciples of Death")
Director: Frank Q. Dobbs
Josh Bryant (Glenn), Irene Kelly (Dr. Leslie Culver), Dave Cass (Jason Brooks), John Martin (Sheriff), Carla Bensen (Doc), Robert John Allen (Ellis), Linda Rascoe (Maria), Happy Shahan (Ozzie Perkins), Wanda Wilson (Juanita), Ed Geldart (Sam), Ray Demney (Jerry), Bryan Quesenberry (Dave), Willie Gonzales (Paco), Rex Reddneck (Deputy), Dave Ford (Gerald), George Kennedy, Harley David Lopp, Ray O'-Leary (hunters), Norris Dominique.

ENTER THE DRAGON (1973)
Director: Robert Clouse
Bruce Lee (Lee), John Saxon (Roper), Jim Kelly (Williams), Ahna Capri (Tania), Shih Kien (Han), Bob Wall (Oharra), Angela Mao (Su-Lin), Betty Chung (Mei-Ling), Yang Sze (Bolo), Geoffrey Weeks (Braithwaite), Peter Archer (Parsons).

ENTITY, THE (1982)
Director: Sidney J. Furie
Barbara Hershey, Ron Silver, Natasha Ryan, Alex Rocco, Melanie Gaffin, George Coe, David Lablosa, Michael Alldredge, Richard Bretoff, Jacqueline Brooks, Maggie Blye, Allen Rich, Ray Singer.

EQUINOX (1967)
Director: Mark McGee
Edward Connell (Dave), Barbara Hewitt (Susan), Jack Woods (Asmodeus), Frank Boers (Jim), Robin Christopher (Vicki), Fritz Leiber, Jr. (Dr. Waterman/old man), Jim Phillips (reporter), Patrick Burke (Branson), Jim Duron (orderly).

EQUINOX (1971-Ital.) (A. K. A. "Equinozio")
Director: Maurizio Ponzi
Claudine Auger, Paola Pitagora, Paolo Turco, Giancarlo Sbragia.

EQUUS (1977)
Director: Sidney Lumet
Richard Burton (Dr. Dysart), Peter Firth (Alan Strang), Colin Blakely (Frank Strang), Joan Plowright (Dora Strang), Jenny Agutter (Jill Mason), Harry Andrews (Harry Dalton), Eileen Atkins (Heather Saloman), Kate Reid (Margaret Dysart), John Wyman (the Horseman).

ERASERHEAD (1977)
Director: David Lynch
Jeanne Bates (Mrs. X), Jack Nance (Henry Spencer), Charlotte Stewart (Mary X), Allen Josephs (Mr. X), Judith Anna Roberts (girl across hall), Laurel Near (lady in radiator), Jean Lange (grandmother), Jack Fisk (man), V. Phipps-Wilson (landlady).

ESCAPE (TVM-1971) - 4-16-71
Director: John L. Moxey
Christopher George (Cameron Steele), Marilyn Mason (Susan Walding), John Vernon (Charles Walding), William Windom (Dr. Henry Walding), Gloria Grahame (Evelyn Harrison), Avery Schreiber (Nicholas Slye), Huntz Hall (Gilbert), William Schallert (Lewis Harrison), Mark Tapscott (Dan), Lucille Benson (Trudy), George Clifton (Roger), Lisa Moore, Ed Call, Merrana Henrig, Chuck Hicks, Lester Fletcher, Caroline Ross.

ESCAPE FROM NEW YORK (1981)
Director: John Carpenter
Kurt Russell (Snake Plissken), Adrienne Barbeau (Maggie), Isaac Hayes (the Duke), Ernest Borgnine (Cabbie), Donald Pleasence (the President), Lee Van Cleef (Commissioner Hauk), Harry Dean Stanton (Brain), Oz Baker (Slag), Tommy Atkins (Rehme), Frank Doubleday (Romero), Charles Cyphers (Secretary of State), Joe Unger (Taylor), Season Hubley (Girl in Chock Full O'Nuts).

ESCAPE FROM THE PLANET OF THE APES (1971)
Director: Don Taylor
Roddy McDowall (Cornelius), Kim Hunter (Zira), Bradford Dillman (Dr. Lewis Dixon), Eric Braeden (Dr. Otto Hasslein), William Windom (the President), Natalie Trundy (Dr. Stephanie Branton), Sal Mineo (Milo), John Randolph (Chairman), Albert Salmi (E-1), Jason Evers (E-2), Ricardo Montalban (Armando), Peter

Forster (Cardinal), Steve Roberts (Gen.
Brody), E. Emmet Walsh (Aide-Captain),
Roy E. Glenn, Sr. (lawyer), William
Woodson (Naval Officer), James Bacon
(Gen. Faulkner), Army Archerd (refe-
ree), John Alderman (Corporal), Harry
Lauter.

ESCAPE IN THE FOG (1945)
    Director: Oscar Boetticher, Jr.
Nina Foch (Ilene Carr), Otto Kruger
(Paul Devon), Konstantin Shayne (Fred
Schiller), Ivan Triesault (Hausmer),
Ernie Adams (George Smith), William
Wright (Aary Malcolm), Charles Jor-
dan (Simmons), Noel Cravet (Kolb),
John Tyrell (Brice), John H. Elliott
(Thomas), Mary Newton (Mrs. Devon),
Ralph Dunn (police sergeant).

ESCAPE TO WITCH MOUNTAIN (1975)
    Director: John Hough
Ike Eisenmann (Tony Malone), Kim Ri-
chards (Tia Malone), Eddie Albert (Ja-
son O'Day), Ray Milland (Aristotle
Bolt), Donald Pleasence (Lucas Dera-
nian), Denver Pyle (Uncle Bene), Al-
fred Ryder (Astrologer), Reta Shaw
(Mrs. Grindley), Harry Holcombe (Capt.
Malone), Lawrence Montaigne (Uber-
mann), Dan Seymour (psychic), George
Chandler (grocer), Rex Holman (hunter
No. 1), Tony Giorgio (hunter No. 2),
Walter Barnes (Sheriff Purdey), Terry
Wilson (Biff Jenkins), Dermott Downs
(Truck), Shepherd Sanders (Guru), Ti-
ger Joe Marsh (Lorko), Sam Edwards
(Mate), Don Brodie (gasoline attendant),
Paul Sorensen (Sgt. Foss), Alfred Rossi
(Police Officer No. 3), Al Dunlap (De-
puty), Eugene Daniels (Cort).

ESCARLATA (1969-Phil.)
    Director: Fely Crisostomo
Amelia Fuentes, Zaldy Zshornack, Bella Flores, Venchito Galves, Max Alvarado, Renato Robles, Alvaro Muhlach,
Alex Flores.

ESPIONAGE IN TANGIERS (1966-Span./
Ital.) (A.K.A. "S.007 Spionaggio a
Tangeri", "Marc Mato, Agente S.
007")
    Director: Greg Tallas
Perla Cristal, Luis Davila, Alberto
Dalbes, Jose Greci, Tomas Blanco.

ETERNAL RETURN, THE (1943-Fr.)
    (A.K.A. "L'Eternel Retour")
    Director: Jean Dellannoy
Jean Marais, Madeleine Sologne, Jean
Murat, Yvonne de Bray, Pieral, Alex-
ander Rignault, Jean d'Yd, Roland Tou-

tain, Junie Astor.

E.T. THE EXTRA-TERRESTRIAL (1982)
    Director: Steven Spielberg
Dee Wallace (Mary), Henry Thomas
(Elliott), Peter Coyote (Keys), Robert
MacNaughton (Michael), Drew Barry-
more (Gertie), K.C. Martel (Greg),
Sean Frye (Steve), Tom Howell (Tyler),
David O'Dell (schoolboy), Erika Eleniak
(pretty girl), Richard Swingler (science
teacher), Frank Toth (policeman), Ro-
bert Barton (ultra sound man), Michael
Darrell (van man).

EUGENIE... THE STORY OF HER
    JOURNEY INTO PERFERSION (1969-
    Brit./Span./Ger.)
    Director: Jesus Franco
Marie Liljedahl (Eugenie), Maria Rohm
(Madame Saint-Ange), Christopher Lee
(Dolmance), Paul Muller (Father), Jack
Taylor (Mirvel), Nino Korda (Roches),
Anney Kablan (Augustin), Herbert Fuchs
(Hardin), Marie Luise Ponte (mother),
Colette Giacobine (Colette), Kathy La-
garde (maid).

EVENING WITH EDGAR ALLAN POE,
    AN (1972)
    Director: Ken Johnson
Vincent Price (Narrator).

EVERYTHING'S DUCKY (1961)
    Director: Don Taylor
Mickey Rooney (Beetle McKay), Buddy
Hackett (Admiral John Paul Jones), Jack-
ie Cooper (Lt. Parnell), Roland Winters
(Capt. Lewis Bollinger), Richard Dea-
con (Dr. Deckham), Gordon Jones (Chief
Conroy), James Milhollin (George Im-
hoff), Alvy Moore (Jim Lipscott), Joanie
Sommers (Nina Lloyd), Elizabeth Mac-
Rae (Susie Penrose), Robert B. Williams
(duck hunter), Jimmy Cross (misanthro-
pist), Gene Blakely (Lt. Cmdr. Kemp),
King Calder (Frank), Ellie Kent (nurse),
Ann Morell (Wave), Harold Kennedy (Mr.
Johnson), Dick Winslow (Froehlich), Wil-
liam Hellinger (Corpsman).

EVERYTHING YOU ALWAYS WANTED
    TO KNOW ABOUT SEX (BUT WERE
    AFRAID TO ASK) (1972)
    Director: Woody Allen
Woody Allen (Victor/Fabrizio/Jester/
Sperm), John Carradine (Dr. Bernardo),
Burt Reynolds (Switchboard), Louise
Lasser (Gina), Lynn Redgrave (the Queen),
Anthony Quayle (the King), Lou Jacobi
(Sam), Tony Randall (the Operator), Gene
Wilder (Dr. Ross), Elaine Giftos (Mrs.
Ross), Heather MacRae (Helen), Titos

Vandis (Milos), Stanley Adams (Stomach Operator), Oscar Beregi, Jr. (Brain Control), Geoffrey Holder (Sorcerer), Alan Caillou (the Fool's father), Jay Robinson (the Priest), Jack Barry, Pamela Mason, Toni Hold, Robert Q. Lewis, Regis Philbin (themselves), Sidney Miller (George), Erin Fleming (the girl), Ref Chuy (Igor), Dort Clark (Sheriff), Baruch Lumet (Rabbi Baumel), Robert Walden (sperm), Inga Neilson (Royal Executioner), Tom Mack (football player), H. E. West (Bernard Jaffe).

EVE, THE SAVAGE VENUS (1968-Ital.) (A. K. A. "Eva, la Verene Selvaggio", "King of Kong Island")
Director: Robert Moris
Brad Harris, Esmeralda Barros, Mark Farran, Adriana Alben, Mario Donatone, Aldo Cecconi, Ursula Davis.

EVICTORS, THE (1979)
Director: Charles B. Pierce
Vic Morrow (Jake Rudd), Michael Parks (Ben Watkins), Jessica Harper (Ruth Watkins), Sue Anne Langdon (Olie Gibson), Bill Thurman (preacher), Dennis Fimple (Bumford), Harry Thomasson (Wheeler), Jimmy Clem (Buckner), Twyla Taylor (Mrs. Bumford), Glen Roberts (Dwayne).

EVIL, THE (1978)
Director: Gus Trikonis
Richard Crenna (C. J.), Joanna Pettet (Caroline), Andrew Prine (Raymond), Victor Buono (the Devil), Cassie Yates (Mary), Milton Selzer (realtor), Lynne Moody (Felicia), Mary Louise Weller (Laurie), George O'Hanlon, Jr. (Pete), Robert Viharo (Dwight), Ed Bakey (Sam), Galen Thompson (Vargas), Emory Souza (Demon).

EVIL BRAIN FROM OUTER SPACE, THE (1959-Jap.) (A. K. A. "Super Giant No. 7, 8 & 9")
Director: Chogi Akasaka & Akira Miwa
Ken Utsui (Super Giant), Chisako Tawara, Reiko Seto, Terumi Hoshi.

EVIL DEAD (1982)
Director: Sam Riami
Bruce Campbell, Betsy Baker, Sarah York, Hal Delrich, Ellen Sandweiss.

EVIL EYE, THE (1920)
Director: J. Gordon Cooper
Stuart Holmes, Benny Leonard, Marie Shotwell, Ruth Dwayer.

EVIL EYE, THE (1962-Ital.) (A. K. A. "La Ragazza Che Sapeva Troppo")
Director: Mario Bava
John Saxon (Dr. Marcello Bassi), Leticia Roman (Nora Dralston), Valentina Cortesa (Laura Terrani).

EVIL OF FRANKENSTEIN, THE (1964)
Director: Freddie Francis
Peter Cushing (Baron Frankenstein), Peter Woodthrope (Zoltan), Sandor Eles (Hans), Katy Wild (Rena, the beggar girl), Kiwi Kingston (the Creature), David Hutcheson (Burgomeister), James Maxwell (Priest), Alistair Williamson (landlord), Duncan Lamont (Chief of Police), Steve Geray (Dr. Sergado), William Phipps (Rena's father), Maria Palmer (Rena's mother), Tracy Stratford (Rena as a child), Howard Goorney (drunk), Frank Forsyth (man-servant), Anthony Blackshaw, David Conville (policemen), Caron Gardner (Burgomeister's wife), Patrick Horgan (David Carrell), Timothy Bateson (hypnotised man), Tony Arpino (body snatcher).

EVILSPEAK (1981)
Director: Eric Weston
Clint Howard (Coopersmith), R. G. Armstrong (Sarge), Charles Tyner (Col. Kincaid), Joe Cortese (Rev. Jameson), Lenny Montana (Jake), Claude Earl Jones (Coach), Lynn Hancock (Miss Freidermyer), Dawn Stark, Hamilton Camp, Hayward Nelson.

EXCALIBUR (1981)
Director: John Boorman
Nigel Terry (Arthur Pendragon), Nicol Williamson (Merlin), Cherie Lunghi (Guenevere), Helen Mirren (Morgana), Nicholas Clay (Lancelot), Katrina Boorman (Igrayne), Corin Redgrave (Cornwall), Robert Addie (Mordred), Keith Buckley (Uryens), Paul Geoffrey (Perceval), Liam Neeson (Gawain), Gabriel Byrne (Uther), Charlie Boorman (young Mordred).

EXO-MAN, THE (TVM-1977) - 6-18-77
Director: Richard Irving
David Ackroyd (Nick Conrad), Anne Schedeen (Emily Frost), Harry Morgan (Travis), Jose Ferrer (Kermit Haas), Kevin McCarthy (D. A. Kamenski), Donald Moffat (Rogers), Jack Colvin (Martin), Richard Narita (Jim Yamaguchi), Jonathan Segal (Eddie Rubinstein), A. Martinez (Raphael Torres), John Moio (Dominic Leandro).

EXORCISM'S DAUGHTER (1974-Span.)
Director: Rafael Morena Alba

Amelia Gade, Francisco Rabal, Espartaco Santoni.

EXORCISMO (1974-Span.)
    Director: Juan Bosch Palau
Paul Naschy, Maria Perschy, Grace Mills, Maria Kosti.

EXORCIST, THE (1973)
    Director: William Friedkin
Ellen Burstyn (Chris MacNeil), Max Von Sydow (Father Merrin), Linda Blair (Regan MacNeil), Jason Miller (Father Karras), Lee J. Cobb (Lt. Kinderman), Jack MacGowran (Burke Dennings), Barton Heyman (Dr. Klein), Kitty Winn (Sharon), Robert Symonds (Dr. Tanney), Rudolf Schundler (Karl), Peter Masterson (clinic director), Ron Faber (assistant director), Titos Vandis (Karras' uncle), Rev. William O'Malley (Father Dyer), Gina Petrushka (Willie), Rev. T. Bermingham (University President), Arthur Storch (psychiatrist), Vasiliki Maliaros (Karras' mother), Donna Mitchell (Mary Jo Perrin), Wallace Rooney (Bishop), Roy Cooper (Jesuit Dean), Robert Gerringer (Senator), Joanne Dusseau (Senator's wife), Richard Callinan (astronaut), John Mahon (language lab director), Yvonne M. Jones (nurse), Beatrice Hunter (woman), Rev. John Nicola (priest), Vincent Russell (derelict in subway), Mary Boylan (1st mental patient), Bob Dahdah (interne), Mercedes McCambridge, Kitty Malone, Liam Dunn, Victor Argo, Michael Cristofer, Maidie Norman, Mason Curry, Flaudia Lennear (voices).

EXORCIST II: THE HERETIC (1977)
    Director: John Boorman
Linda Blair (Regan MacNeil), Richard Burton (Father Philip Lamont), Louise Fletcher (Dr. Gene Tuskin), Max Von Sydow (Father Merrin), James Earl Jones (Kokumo), Kitty Winn (Sharon), Paul Henreid (the Cardinal), Ned Beatty (Edwards), Belindha Beatty (Liz), Barbara Cason (Mrs. Phalor), Joey Green (young Kokumo), Ken Renard (Abbot), Tiffany Kinney (deaf girl), Rose Portillo (Spanish girl), Fiseha Dimetros (young monk), Hank Garrett (conductor), Bill Grant (taxi driver), Lorry Goldman (accident victim).

EXPERIMENT IN TERRA (1979)
    see Television: Battlestar Galactica (1978-79).

EXPERIMENT PERILOUS (1944)
    Director: Jacques Tourneur

Hedy Lamarr (Allida Bedereaus), George Brent (Dr. Huntington Bailey), Paul Lukas (Nick Bederaus), Albert Dekker (Claghorne), Carl Esmond (Maitland), Olive Blakeney (Cissie Bederaux), George N. Neise (Alec), Margaret Wycherly (Maggie), Stephnie Bachelor (Elaine), Mary Servoss (Miss Wilson), Julia Dean (Deria), William Post, Jr. (District Attorney), Billy Ward (Alec as a child).

EXPLOITS OF ELAINE, THE (1914) -
    serial in 14 episodes
Chapters: 1. "The Clutching Hand", 2. "The Twilight Sleep", 3. "The Vanishing Jewels", 4. "The Frozen Safe", 5. "The Poisoned Room", 6. "The Vampire", 7. "The Double Trap", 8. "The Hidden Voice", 9. "The Death Ray", 10. "The Life Current", 11. "The Hour of Three", 12. "The Blood Crystals", 13. "The Devil Worshippers" & 14. "The Reckoning".
    Director: L. J. Gasnier & George B. Seitz
Pearl White (Elaine Dodge), Arnold Daly (Craig Kennedy), Sheldon Lewis (Clutching Hand), Creighton Hale (Jameson), William Riley Hatch (Pres. Taylor Dodge), Raymond Owens (Perry Bennett), Edwin Arden (Wu Fang), Robin Towney (Limpy Red), Floyd Buckley (Michael), M. W. Rale (Wong Long Sin), Paul Panzer.

EXTERMINATING ANGEL, THE (1963-Mex.) (A.K.A. "El Angel Exterminador").
    Director: Luis Bunuel
Claudio Brook (the Major-Dumo), Silvia Pinal (Letitia), Lucy Gallardo (Lucia Nobile), Enrique Rambal (Senor Nobile), Bertha Moss (Leonora), Xavier Masse (Eduardo), Ofelia Montesco (Betriz), Nadia Haro Oliva (Ana Maynar), Antonio Bravo (Russell), Xaviar Loya (Francisco), Jose Baviera, Luis Beristain, Rosa Elena Durgel, Jacqueline Andere, Angusuto Benedico, Cesar Del Campo, Enrique Garcia Alvarez, Tito Junco, Patricia Moran, Ofelia Guilmain, Angel Merino, Patricia De Morelos.

EXTERMINATORS, THE (1965-Fr./Ital.) (A.K.A. "Coplan FX 18 Casse Tout", "FX-18 Superspy")
    Director: Ricardo Freda
Richard Wyler (Coplan), Jany Clair, Valeria Ciangotini, Gil Delamare, Robert Manuel Jacques Dacqmine, Maria Rosa Rodriquez, Robert Favart.

EXTRAORDINARY SEAMAN, THE
(1968)
Director: John Frankenheimer
David Niven (Lt. Cmdr. Finchhaven),
Faye Dunaway (Jennifer Winslow), Alan
Alda (Lt. J/G Morton Krim), Mickey
Rooney (Cook W. J. Oglethorpe), Jack
Carter (Gunner's Mate Orville Toole),
Juano Hernandez (Ali Shar), Barry Kelly
(Adm. Barnwell), Jerry Fujikawa (Adm.
Shimagoshi) Manu Tupou (Seaman 1/C
Lightfoot Star), John Cochran, Leonard
O. Smith, Richard Guizquan (Dyaks).

EYEBALL (1978-Ital.) (A. D. A. "Gatti
Rossi in un Labirinto di Vetro")
Director: Umberto Lenzi
John Richardson, Martine Brochard,
Ines Pelegrin, George Rigaud, Silvia
Solar

EYE CREATURES, THE (1965)
Director: Larry Buchanan
John Ashley, Shirley McLine, Cynthia
Hull, Warren Hammack, Bill Peck,
Chet David.

EYE OF THE CAT (1969)
Director: David Lowell Rice
Michael Sarrazin (Wylie), Gayle Hun-
nicutt (Kassia), Eleanor Parker (Aunt
Danny), Tim Henry (Luke), Laurence
Naismith (Dr. Mills), Linden Chiles
(Rendetto), Mark Herron (Bellemondo),
Jennifer Leak (Poor Dear), Annabelle
Garth (socialite).

EYE OF THE DEVIL (1967)
Director: J. Lee Thompson
David Niven (Phillipe de Montfaucon),
Deborah Kerr (Catherine de Montfau-
con), David Hemmings (Christian de
Caray), Sharon Tate (Odile), Emlyn
Williams (Alain de Montfaucon , John
LeMesurier (Dr. Monnet), Flora Rob-
son (Countess Estelle), Donald Pleas-
ence (Pere Dominic), Edward Mulhare
(Jean-Claude Ibert), Michael Miller
(Grandec), Suky Appleby (Antoinette),
Robert Duncan (Jacques), Donald Bis-
set (Rennard), Frank Forsyth (party
guest).

EYES BEHIND THE STARS, THE (1978-
Ital.) (A. K. A. "Occhi Dalle Stello")
Director: Mario Garriazzo/Ray
Garrett
Nathalie Delon, Robert Hoffmann, Mar-
tin Balsam, Carlo Hinterman, Giorgio
Ardisson, Sherry Buchanan.

EYES OF ANNIE JONES, THE (1963)
Director: Reginald LeBorg

Francesca Annis (Annie Jones), Rich-
ard Conte (David Wheeler), Myrtle
Reed (Carol Wheeler), Joyce Carey
(Aunt Helen), Alan Haines (Constable
Marlowe), Shay Gorman (Lucas), Jean
Lodge (Geraldine Wheeler), Victor
Brooks (Police Sgt. Henry), Mark Dig-
nam (orphanage director), Mara Pur-
cell (orphanage matron), Max Bacon
(pub-keeper Hoskins), Barbara Leake
(Margaret), Patricia McCarron (sec-
retary).

EYES OF A STRANGER (1981)
Director: Ken Widerhorn
Lauren Tewes (Jane), John DiSanti
(Stanley Herbert), Jennifer Jason Leigh
(Tracy), Peter DuPre (David), Kitty
Lunn (Annette), Gwen Lewis (Debbie),
Timothy Hawkins (Jeff), Ted Richert
(Roger England), Bob Small (Dr. Bob),
Toni Crabtree (Mona), Stella Rivera
(dancer), Dan Fitzgerald (bartender),
Jose Behamande (Jimmy), Luke Halpin
(tape editor), Rhonda Flynn (woman in
car), Tony Federico (man in car), Amy
Krug (young Jane), Tabbetha Tracey
(young Tracy), Jillian Lindig (mother),
Sarah Hutcheson (friend), George De-
Vries (father), Melvin Pape (doctor),
Alan Lee (photographer), Robert Good-
man (crewman), Herb Holdstein (eld-
erly man), Sonia Zomina (elderly wo-
man), Joe Friedman (movie patron),
Kathy Suerglu (Karen), Pat Warren
(Susan), Richard Allen (news director),
Madeline Curtis (nurse), Michael de
Silva (technical director).

EYES OF CHARLES SAND, THE (TVM-
1972) - 2-29-72
Director: Reza Badiyi
Peter Haskell (Charles Sand), Sharon
Farrell (Emily Parkhurst), Bradford
Dillman (Jeffery Winslow), Barbara
Rush (Katharine Winslow), Joan Bennett
(Aunt Alexandria), Adam West (Dr. Paul
Scott), Ivor Francis (Dr. Ballard), Gary
Clarke (Raymond), Donald 'Red' Barry
(trainer), Larry Levine (groom).

EYES OF LAURA MARS (1978)
Director: Irvin Kershner
Faye Dunaway (Laura Mars, Tommy
Lee Jones (John Neville), Rene Auber-
jonois (Donald Phelps), Brad Dourif
(Tommy Ludlow), Raul Julia (Michael
Reisler), Frank Adonis (Sal Volpe),
Darlanne Fluegel (Lulu), Lisa Taylor
(Michele), Rose Gregorio (Elaine Cas-
sell), Meg Mundy (Doris Spenser), Mar-
ilyn Meyers (Sheila Weissman), Paula
Lawrence (Aunt Caroline), Steve Mara-

chuk (Robert), Michael Tucker (Bert),
Gary Bayer, Mitchell Edmonds (reporters), Jeff Niki (photo assistant),
Bill Boggs (himself), Toshi Matsuo
(photo assistant), Dallas Edward Hayes
(Douglas), John E. Allen (Billy T),
Joey R. Mills (make-up person), Hector Troy (cab driver), John Sahag (hairdresser).

EYES OF THE MUMMY, THE (1918-
Ger.) (A. K. A. "Die Augen der Mum-
ie Ma")
      Director: Ernst Lubitsch
Emil Jannings, Pola Negri, Max Laurence, Harry Liedtke, Margarethe Kupfer.

FABLE, A (1971)
      Director: Al Freeman, Jr.
Al Freeman, Jr. (Leader), Hildy
Brooks (Wife), James Patterson (Hus-
band).

FABULOUS JOE, THE (1946)
      Director: Harve Foster
Walter Abel, Margot Grahame, Donald
Meek, Clarence Kolby, Marie Wilson,
Sheldon Leonard, Lucien Littlefield,
John Eldredge, Nana Bryant, Ellen
Corby, Barbara Bates, Donald Mac-
Bride, Howard Petrie, Johnny Miles,
Dorothy Christy, Al Bridges, Charlotte
Wynters.

FABULOUS WORLD OF JULES VERNE,
THE (1958-Czech.) (A. K. A. "Vyna-
lez Zkazy", "An Invention of Destruction")
      Director: Karel Zeman
Lubor Tokos/Louis Tock (Simon Hall),
Arnost Navratil/Ernest Navara (Prof.
Roch), Milo Holl (Artigas), Van Kiss-
ling (Serke), Jane Salanta (Jana), Francis Sherr (Pirate Captain).

FACE AT THE WINDOW, THE (1920)
      Director: Wilfred Noy
C. Aubrey Smith (Bentick), Gladys
Jennings (Marie de Brisson), Charles
Quartermaine (Lucien Degradoff), Ben
Field (Peter Pottlebury), Kathleen
Vaughan (Babette), Jack Hobbs (Lucien
Cartwright), Sir Simeon Stuart (Henri
de Brisson), Kinsey Peile (Dr. le Blanc).

FACE AT THE WINDOW, THE (1932)
      Director: Leslie Hiscott
Raymond Massey, Claude Hulbert

FACE AT THE WINDOW, THE (1939)
      Director: George King
Tod Slaughter (Chevalier del Gardo),

Marjorie Taylor (Cecile de Brisson),
John Warwick (Lucien Cortier), Leonard Henry (Gaston), Aubrey Mallalieu
(de Brisson), Robert Adair (Insp. Guf-
fert), Wallace Evennett (Prof. le Blanc),
Kay Lewis (Babette), Margaret Yarde
(Le Pinan), Harry Terry (the Face).

FACE BEHIND THE MASK, THE (1941)
      Director: Robert Florey
Peter Lorre (Janos Szabo), Evelyn
Keyes (Helen Williams), Don Beddoe
(Jim O'Hara), George E. Stone (Dinky),
Stanley Brown (Harry), James Seay
(Jeff), John Tyrell (Watts), Charles
Wilson (Chief O'Brien), George McKay
(Terry Finnegan), Warren Ashe (John-
son), Al Seymour (Benson), Frank Rei-
cher, Ernie Adams, Lee Shumway.

FACE IN THE FOG, A (1936)
      Director: Robert Hill
June Collyer (Jean Monroe), Lloyd
Hughes (Frank Gordon), Forrest Taylor
(Cromwell), Jack Mulhall (Reardon),
Al St. John (Elmer), Sam Flint (Harri-
son), Lawrence Gray (Peter Fortune),
Jack Cowell (Wilson), John Elliott (Dav-
is), Robert Williams (policeman), Ed-
ward Cassidy (detective).

FACE OF EVE, THE (1968-Brit. /Span.)
(A. K. A. "Eva")
      Director: Jermy Summers
Celeste Yarnall (Eve), Robert Walker,
Jr. (Mike), Herbert Lom (Diego), Chris-
topher Lee (Col. Stuart), Fred Clark
(John Burke), Maria Rohm (Anna), Ro-
senda Monteros (Conchita), Jean Caffa-
rell (Pepe), Ricardo Diaz (Bruno).

FACE OF FIRE (1959)
      Director: Albert Band
Cameron Mitchell (Ned Trescott), James
Whitmore (Monk Johnson), Bettye Ack-
erman (Grace Trescott), Mike Oscard
(Jimmie Trescott), Royal Dano (Jake
Winter), Lois Maxwell (Ethel Winter),
Richard Erdman (Al Williams), Robert
Simon (the Judge), Howard Smith (Sher-
iff Nolan), Jill Donahue (Bella Kovac).

FACE OF FU MANCHU, THE (1965)
      Director: Don Sharp
Christopher Lee (Dr. Fu Manchu), Nigel Green (Nayland Smith), Howard
Marion-Crawford (Dr. Petrie), Tsai
Chin (Lin Tang), James Robertson Justice (Sir Charles), Joachim Fuchsberger (Jansen), Walter Rilla (Prof. Muller), Karin Dor (Maria).

FACE OF MARBLE (1946)

Director: William Beaudine
John Carradine (Dr. Charles Randolph),
Robert Shayne (Dr. David Cauklin),
Claudia Drake (Elaine Randolph), Maris
Wrixon (Linda Sinclair), Willie Best
(Shadrack), Thomas E. Jackson (Inspector), Rosa Rey, Neal Burns, Allan Ray,
Donald Kern.

FACE OF TERROR, THE (1962-Span.)
(A. K. A. "La Cara del Terror")
Director: Isidoro Martinez Perry
Lisa Gaye, Fernando Rey, Gerard Tichy,
Virgilio Teixeira, Conchita Cuetos, Carlos Casaravilla.

FACE OF THE SCREAMING WEREWOLF,
THE (1959-Mex.) (A. K. A. "La Casa
del Terror", "The House of Terror")
Director: Gilberto Martinez Solares
Lon Chaney, Jr. (the Werewolf), Tin
Tan (Casamiro), Yolanda Varela, Yerye
Beirute, Alfredo Barron, Oscar Ortiz
de Pinedo.

FADE TO BLACK (1980)
Director: Vernon Zimmerman
Dennis Christopher (Eric Binford), Linda
Kerridge (Marilyn), Tim Thomerson (Dr.
Moriarity), Gwynne Gilford (Anne), James
Luisi (Gallagher), Norman Burton (Morty
Berger), Morgan Paull (Gary Pialy), Marya Small (Doreen), Eve Brent Ashe (Aunt
Stella), Hennen Chambers (Bart), Melinda
Fee (talk show hostess), John Steadman
(Sam), Bob Drew (Rev. Shick), Mickey
Rourke (Richie), Peter Horton (Joey Madona), Anita Converse (Dee Dee), Marcie
Barkin (Stacy), Jane K. Wiley (go-fer),
Gilbert Lawrence Kahn (counterman).

FAHRENHEIT 451 (1966)
Director: Francois Truffaut
Oskar Werner (Montag), Julie Christie
(Linda/Clarisse), Cyril Cusack (the Captain), Anton Diffring (Fabian), Ann Bell
(Doris), Anna Palk (Jackie), Jeremy
Spenser (man with apple), Bee Duffell
(the book woman), Caroline Hunt (Helen),
Gilliam Lewis (TV announcer), Rona
Milne (neighbor), Arthur Cox (nurse),
Noel David (TV announcer), Donald Pickering (TV announcer), Eric Mason (nurse),
Gillian Aldam (Mrs. Gillian), Joan Francis (bar telephonist), Edward Kaye (Mr.
Gillian), Tom Watson (sergeant instructor), Alex Scott (The Life of Henri Brulard), Michael Balfour (Machiavelli's
Prince), Fred Cox (Pride), Frank Cox
(Prejudice), David Glover (Pickwick Papers), Yvonne Blake (The Jewish Question),
Dennis Gilmore (The Martian Chronicles).

FAIL-SAFE (1964)
Director: Sydney Lumet
Henry Fonda (the President), Dan O'-
Herlihy (Gen Black), Walter Matthau
(Groeteschele), Frank Overton (Gen.
Bogan), Edward Binns (Col. Grady),
Fritz Weaver (Col. Cascio), Larry
Hagman (Buck), Sorrell Booke (Congressman Raskob), Russell Hardie
(Gen. Stark), William Hansen (Secretary Swenson), Russell Collins (Knapp),
Dom DeLuise (Sgt. Collins), Nancy
Berg (Ilsa Wolfe), Stuart Germain (Mr.
Cascio), Louise Larabee (Mrs. Cascio),
Janet Ward (Mrs. Grady), Frank Simpson (Sullivan), Hildy Parks (Betty Black),
Dana Elcar (Foster), John Connell (Thomas), Frieda Altman (Jennie).

FALL OF THE HOUSE OF USHER, THE
(1928-Fr.) (A. K. A. "La Chute de la
Maison Usher")
Director: Jean Epstein
Margaret Gance, Jean Debucourt, Charles
Lamay, Pierre Hot, Abel Gance.

FALL OF THE HOUSE OF USHER, THE
(1948)
Director: G. Ivan Barnett
Kay Tendeter, Irving Steen, Gwendoline
Watford.

FALL OF THE HOUSE OF USHER, THE
(1979)
Director: James L. Conway
Martin Landau (Roderick Usher), Charlene Tilton (Jennifer), Ray Walston
(Thaddeus), Robert Hays (Jonathan),
Dimitra Arliss (Madeline),

FAME AND THE DEVIL (1950-Ital.)
(A. K. A. "Al Diavolo con Celebrita")
Director: Mario Monicelli
Mischa Auer, Leonardo Cortese, Marilyn Buferd, Aldo Silvani, Marcel Cerdan,
Ferruccio Tagliavini, Bill Tubbs, Carlo
Companini, Franca Marzi.

FAMILY PLOT (1976)
Director: Alfred Hitchcock
Karen Black (Fran), Bruce Dern (Lumley), William Devane (Adamson), Barbara Harris (Blanche), Ed Lauter (Maloney), Katherine Helmond (Mrs. Maloney), Cathleen Nesbitt (Julia Rainbird),
Edith Atwater (Mrs. Clay), Nicholas
Colasanto (Constantine), Marge Redmond
(Vera Hannagan), William Prince (Bishop), Warren J. Kemmerling (Grandson), John Lehne (Andy Bush), Alexander
Lockwood (Parson), Charles Tyner
(Wheeler), Martin West (Sanger).

FAN, THE (1981)
  Director: Edward Bianchi
Lauren Bacall (Sally Ross), James
Garner (Jake Berman), Maureen Sta-
pleton (Belle Goldman), Michael Biehn
(Douglas Breen), Hector Elizondo
(Ralph Andrews), Kurt Johnson (David
Branum), Anna Maria Horsford (Emily
Stolz), Felga Martinez (Elsa), Reed
Jones (choreographer), Charles Black-
well (John Vetta), Kalulani Lee (Doug-
las' sister), Dwight Schultz (director),
Dana Delaney (clerk).

FANGS OF THE LIVING DEAD (1968-
  Span./Ital.) (A.K.A. "Malenka")
  Director: Amando de Ossorio
Anita Ekberg, Julian Ugarte, Diana
Lorys, John Hamilton, Adriana Am-
besi.

FANTASIA (1940) - Animated
  Producer: Walt Disney
Deems Taylor (Narrator), Leopold
Stokowski (Conductor).

FANTASIES (TVM-1982) - 1-18-82
  Director: William Wiard
Suzanne Pleshette (Carla Sherman),
Barry Newman (Detective Flynn), Ro-
bert Vaughn (Girard), Patrick O'Neal
(John Sherman), Stuart Damon (Roy),
Robin Mattson (April Heffner), John
Gabriel (Quentin Mallory), Robert S.
Woods (Clint McDougall), Peter Berg-
man (Larry Malter), Allyn Ann McLerie
(Shirley Conforti), Ben Marley (Arthur),
Madlyn Rhue (Rebecca), Lenora May
(Sandy Sherman), Carole Smith (Madge
Grodowski), John Sanderford (Daniel
Delbert), Terry Alexander (Harold
Johnson), Barry Corbin (coroner),
Stacey Kuhne (Lilita), Hap Lawrence
(Glen), Bob Basso (locksmith), Laur-
ence Lau (delivery boy), Karen Austin
(young woman), John Gowans (moder-
ator), Ruth Cox (1st student), Larry
Flash Jenkins (2nd student), Susan
Brecht (hawk-face), Jack Garner (Tom-
my), Edith Fields (Mildred), Robert
Nadder (waiter), Selma Archerd (dress
clerk), J. Victor Lopez (Jerry), J.P.
Bumstead, Aarika Wells, Rick Gates.

FANTASTIC NIGHT (1942-Fr.) (A.K.A.
  "La Nuit Fantastique")
  Director: Marcel L'Herbier
Micheline Presle, Fernand Gravet,
Saturnin Fabre, Bernard Blier, Jean
Paredes.

FANTASTIC PLANET (1973-Fr.) (A.K.A.
  "La Planete Sauvage") - Animated

  Director: Rene Laloux
  Voices: Barry Bostwick, Marvin
Miller, Olan Soule, Cynthia Alder,
Nora Heflin, Hal Smith, Mark Gruner,
Monika Ramirez, Janet Waldo.

FANTASTIC VOYAGE (1966)
  Director: Richard Fleisher
Stephen Boyd (Grant), Raquel Welch
(Cora Peterson), Edmond O'Brien
(Gen. Carter), Donald Pleasence (Dr.
Michaels), William Redfield (Capt.
Bill Owens), Arthur O'Connell (Col.
Donald Reid), Arthur Kennedy (Dr.
Duval), Barry Coe (communications
aide), Jean Del Val (Jan Benes), James
Brolin (technician), Shelby Grant
(nurse), Ken Scott (secret service man),
Brendan Fitzgerald (wireless operator).

FANTASY ISLAND (TVM-1977) -
  1-14-77
  Director: Richard Lang
Ricardo Montalban (Mr. Roarke), Herve
Villechaize (Tattoo), Bill Bixby (Arnold
Greenwood), Hugh O'Brian (Paul Hen-
ley), Sandra Dee (Franchesca), Peter
Lawford (Grant Baines), Carol Lynley
(Liz Hollander), Eleanor Parker (Eu-
nice Hollander Baines), Victoria Prin-
cipal (Michelle), Dick Sargent (Charles
Hollander), Christina Sinatra (Connie
Raymond), John McKinney (hunter No. 1),
Cedric Scott (hunter No. 2), Peter Mac-
lean (hunter No. 3), Ian Abercrombie
(bartender), Elizabeth Dartmoor (bar-
maid), Jim Mills.

FANTOMAS (1914-Fr.) - serial in 5
  episodes
  Director: Louis Feuillade
Rene Navarre, James Breon, Jane Fa-
ber, Georges Louis Melchior, Yvette
Andreyov, Rennee Carll, Luitz Morat,
Francine Fabreges.

FANTOMAS (1920) - serial in 20 epi-
  sodes
  Chapters: 1. "On the Stroke of Nine",
2. "The Million Dollar Reward", 3.
"The Triple Peril", 4. "The Blades of
Terror", 5. "Heights of Horror", 6.
"Altar of Sacrifice", 7. "Flames of
Sacrifice", 8. "At Death's Door", 9.
"The Haunted Hotel", 10. "The Fatal
Card", 11. "The Phantom Sword", 12.
"The Danger Signal", 13. "On the Count
of Three", 14. "The Blazing Train",
15. "The Sacred Necklace", 16. "The
Phantom Shadow", 17. "The Price of
Fang Wu", 18. "Double-Crossed", 19.
"The Hawk's Prey" & 20. "The Hell
Ship".

Director: Edward Sedgwick
Edna Murphy, Edward Roseman, Eva
Balfour, Lionel Adams, John Walker,
John Willard, Irving Brooks.

FANTOMAS (1932-Fr.)
Director: Paul Frejos
Jean Galland, Tania Fedor, Thomy
Bourdelle.

FANTOMAS (1947-Fr.)
Director: Jean Sacha
Simone Signoret, Marcel Herrand,
Alexandre Regnault, Lucienne Lemarch-
and, Georges Gosset, Francoise Chris-
tophe, Andre Le Gall, Yves Deniaud.

FANTOMAS (1964-Fr.)
Director: Andre Hunebelle
Jean Marais (Fantomas/Fandor), Louis
De Funes (Insp. Juve), Mylene Demongeot (Helene), Marie-Helen Arnaud
(Lady Beltham), Jacques Dynam (Juve's
assistant), Christian Toma (Chief Inspector), Robert Dalban (newspaper
editor).

FANTOMAS STRIKES BACK (1965-Fr. /
Ital.) (A.K.A. "Fantomas se Cech-
aine")
Director: Andre Hunebelle
Jean Marais (Fantomas/Fandor), Louis
De Funes (Insp. Juve), Mylene Demongeot (Helene), Jacques Dynam (Juve's
assistant), Robert Dalban (newspaper
editor).

FANTOMAS VS. SCOTLAND YARD
(1967-Fr.) (A.K.A. "Fantomas
contre Scotland Yard")
Director: Andre Hunnebelle
Jean Marais (Fantojas/Fandor), Louis
De Funes (Insp. Juve), Mylene Demon-
geot (Helene), Francoise Christophe,
Henri Serre, Jean-Pierre Caussimon.

FAREWELL TO THE PLANET OF THE
APES (1974)
see Television: Planet of the Apes
(1974)

FATAL NIGHT, THE (1948)
Director: Mario Zampi
Patrick Macnee (Tony), Lester Fergu-
son (Puce), Jean Short (Geraldine),
Leslie Armstrong (Cyril), Brenda Ho-
gan (Julia), Aubrey Mallalieu (Yokel).

FATAL RING, THE (1917) - serial in
20 episodes
Chapters: 1. "The Violet Diamond", 2.
"The Cruching Wall", 3. "Borrowed
Identity", 4. "The Warning on the Ring",

5. "Danger Underground", 6. "Rays
of Death", 7. "The Signal Lantern",
8. "The Switch in the Safe", 9. "The
Dice of Death", 10. "The Perilous
Plunge", 11. "The Short Circuit", 12.
"A Desperate Chance", 13. "A Dash
for Arabia", 14. "The Painted Safe",
15. "The Dagger Duel", 16. "The
Double Disguise", 17. "The Death
Weight", 18. "The Subterfuge", 19.
"The Cryptic Maze" & 20. "The End
of the Trail".
Director: George B. Seitz
Pearl White, Warner Oland, Earle
Fox, Floyd Buckley, Ruby Hoffman,
Caesare Gravine, Mattie Ferguson.

FATAL WARNING, THE (1929) - ser-
ial in 10 episodes
Chapters: 1. "The Fatal Warning", 2.
"The Phantom Flyer", 3. "The Crash
of Doom", 4. "The Pit of Death", 5.
"Menacing Fingers", 6. "Into Thin
Air", 7. "The House of Horror", 8.
"Fatal Fumes", 9. "By Whose Hand?"
& 10. "Unmasked".
Director: Richard Thorpe
Ralph Graves, Boris Karloff, Phillips
Smalley, Helene Costello, Symona
Boniface, Lloyd Whitlock, George
Periolat, Syd Crossley.

FAT SPY, THE (1966)
Director: Joseph Cates
Phyllis Diller (Camille), Jack E. Leo-
nard (Irving/Herman), Jayne Mans-
field (Junior), Brian Donlevy (Welling-
ton), Jordan Christopher (Frankie),
Lou Nelson (the Sikh), Johnny Tilotson
(Dodo), Lauree Berger (Nanette), Toni
Lee Shelley (Mermaid), Penny Roman
(Secretary), Chuck Alden, Linda Har-
rison, Tommy Graves, Deborah White,
Tommy Trick, Tracy Vance, Eddie
Wright, Toni Turner, Jeanette Taylor,
Jill Bludner (treasure hunters), Adam
Keefe (voices).

FAUST (1909) - short
Director: Edwin S. Porter
William J. Sorelle (Mephistopheles).

FAUST (1926-Ger.)
Director: F.W. Murnau
Gosta Ekman (Faust), Emil Jannings
(Mephistopheles), William Dieterle,
Camilla Horn, Eric Barclay, Yvette
Guilbert, Hanna Ralph.

FAUST (1960-Ger.)
Director: Peter Gorski
Will Quadflieg (Faust), Gustof Grund-
gens (Mephisto), Ella Buchi (Gretchen),

Elisabeth Flickenschildt (Marthe), Max
Eckard (Valentine), Edward Marks
(Wagner), Hermann Schomberg (The-
atre Director), Heinz Reincke (Frosch),
Uwe Friedrichsen (pupil).

FAUST AND THE DEVIL (1948-Ital.)
(A. K. A. "La Leggenda di Faust")
    Director: Armine Gallone
Italo Tajo (the devil), Nelly Corradi,
Therese Dorny, Gino Matters, Gilles
Queant, Cesare Barbetti.

FAUSTINA (1956-Span.)
    Director: Jose Luis Saenz de
    Heredia
Conrado San Martin, Fernando Rey,
Elisa Montes, Jose Isbert, Maria
Felix, Fernando Fernan Gomez.

FEAR CHAMBER, THE (1968-Mex. /
U. S.)
    Director: Jack Hill
Boris Karloff, Carlos East, Julissa,
Isela Vega, Santannon.

FEAR IN THE NIGHT (1947)
    Director: Maxwell Shane
Paul Kelly (Cliff Harlan), DeForrest
Kelly (Vince Grayson), Ann Doran (Lil
Harlan), Robert Emmett Keane (Mr.
Beinap), Kay Scott (Betty Winters),
Charles Victor, Jeff Yorke.

FEAR IN THE NIGHT (1972)
    Director: Jimmy Sangster
Peter Cushing (Michael Carmichael),
Joan Collins (Molly Carmichael), Judy
Geeson (Peggy Heller), Ralph Bates
(Robert Heller), James Cossins (doc-
tor), Gillian Lind (Mrs. Beamish),
John Brown (1st policeman), Brian
Grellis (2nd policeman).

FEARLESS FRANK (1967) (A. K. A.
"Frank's Greatest Adventure")
    Director: Philip Kaufman
Jon Voight (Frank), Severn Darden
(Doctor/Brother/Claude), Monique
Van Vooren (Plethora), Joan Darling
(Lois), Anthony Holland (Alfred), Lou
Gilbert (Boss), David Steinberg (Rat),
Ben Carruthers (Cat), Nelson Algren
(Needles), David Fisher (Screwnose),
Ken Nordine (stranger).

FEARLESS VAMPIRE KILLERS, THE
(1967) (A. K. A. "Dance of the Vam-
pires")
    Director: Roman Polanski
Roman Polanski (Alfred), Jack Mac-
Gowran (Prof. Abronsius), Ferdy
Mayne (Count Kroloc), Sharon Tate

(Sarah), Alfie Bass (Yoine Chagal),
Terry Downes (Koukol), Ian Quarrier
(Herbert), Jessie Robbins (Rebecca),
Fiona Lewis (Magda), Ronald Lacey
(Village idiot), Sydney Bromley (sleigh
driver), Andre Malandrinos, Matthew
Walters, Otto Di Amant (woodcutters).

FEAR NO EVIL (TVM-1969) - 3-3-69
    Director: Paul Wendkos
Louis Jourdan (Dr. David Sorell),
Wilfrid Hyde-White (Harry Snowden),
Carroll O'Connor (Myles Donovan),
Bradford Dillman (Paul Varney), Mar-
sha Hunt (Mrs. Varney), Lynda Day
George (Barbara), Katharine Wood-
ville (Ingrid Dorne), Harry Davis
(Wyant), Katherine Victor (woman at
seance), Fosco Gianchetti, Robert
Sampson, Ivor Barry, Lyn Peters,
Susan Brown, Jeanne Buckler.

FEAR NO EVIL (1981)
    Director: Frank LaLoggia
Stefan Arngrim (Andrew), Elizabeth
Hoffman (Mikhail/Margaret Buchanan),
Frank Birney (Father Daly), Kathleen
Rowe McAllen (Gabrielle/Hulie), Jack
Holland (Rafael/Father Damon), Dan-
iel Eden (Tony), Barry Cooper (Mr.
Williams), Alice Sachs (Mrs. Williams),
Paul Haber (Mark), Roslyn Gugino
(Marie), Richard Jay Silverthorn (Lu-
cifer).

FEAST OF FLESH (1968-Span.)
    Director: Emilio Vieyra
Blanca Burgueno, Mauricio De Fer-
raris, Justin Martin, Alberto Candeau,
Edwardo Munoz, Ricardo Bauleo, Edwardo Kliche, Susana Beltram.

FEET OF CLAY (1924)
    Director: Cecil B. DeMille
Vera Reynolds (Amy Loring), Rod La-
Rocque (Kerry Harlan), Julia Fay
(Bertha Lansell), Ricardo Cortez (Tony
Channing), Robert Edeson (Dr. Fergus
Lansell), Theodore Kosloff (Bendick),
Victor Varconi (the Bookkeeper), Will-
iam Boyd (young society man), Lucian
Littlefield, Lillian Leighton.

FELLINI'S CASANOVA (1976-Ital.)
(A. K. A. "Casanova")
    Director: Federico Fellini
Donald Sutherland (Giacomo Casanova),
Daniel Emilfork (DuBois), John Karlsen (Lord Talou), Tina Aumont (Henriette), Dudley Sutton (Duke of Wurten-
berg), Reggie Nalder (Faulkircher),
Margareth Clementi (Maddalena), Clarissa Mary Roll (Anamaria) Cicely

Browne (Madame D'Urfe), Daniela Gatti
(Giselda), Clara Algranti (Marcolina),
Hans Van Den Hoek (Prince de Brando),
Sandra Elaine Allen (Giantess), Carmen
Scarpitta (Madame Charpillon) Silvana
Fusacchia (Silvana), Luigi Zerbinati
(the Pope), Adele Angela Lojodice (Doll
woman).

FELLINI SATYRICON (1969-Ital. /Fr.)
    (A. K. A. "Satyricon")
    Director: Federico Fellini
Capucine (Tyrphaena), Salvo Randone
(Eumolpus), Martin Potter (Encolpius),
Alain Cuny (Lichas), Hiram Keller
(Ascyltus), Max Born (Giton), Magali
Noel (Fortuanata), Tanya Lopert (Cae-
sar), Lucia Roşe (suicide wife), Joseph
Wheeler (suicide husband), Gordon
Mitchell (robber), Mario Romagnoli
(Trimalchio), Giuseppe Sanvitale (Hab-
innas), Fanfulla (Vernacchio), Donyale
Luna (Oenothea), Hylette Adolphe (ori-
ental slave girl), Genius (Cinedo),
Danica La Loggia (Scintilla), Sibil la
Sedat (nymphomaniac)) Lorenzo Piani
(nymphomaniac's husband), Luigi Zerbinati (her slave), Antonia Pietrosi
(widow of Ephesus), Carlo Giordana
(Captain of Ship), Wolfgang Hillinger
(soldier at tomb), Elio Gigante (owner
of Garden of Delights), Vittorio Vittori
(notary), Marcello Di Folco (Proconsul),
Elisa Mainardi (Ariadne), Luigi Monte-
fiori (Minotaur/Pasquale), Baldassare
(hermaphrodite).

FEMALE TROUBLE (1975)
    Director: John Waters
Divine (Dawn Davenport/Earl Peterson),
David Lochary (Donald Dasher), Mary
Vivian Pearce (Donna Dasher), Mink
Stole (Taffy Davenport), Edith Massey
(Ida Nelson), Michael Potter (Gater),
Susan Walsh (Chiclett), Cookie Mueller
(Concetta), Sandy McDonald (beauty shop
customer), Pat Moran (bitch prisoner),
George Stover (chaplain), Ed Peranio
(Wink), George Pigga (Dribbles), Paul
Swift (Butterfly), Susan Lowe (Vikki),
George Hulse (teacher), Roland Hertz
(Dawn's father), Betty Woods (Dawn's
mother), Hilary Taylor (Taffy as a child),
Channing Wilroy (prosecutor), Seymour
Avigdor (defense lawyer), Elizabeth
Coffey (Ernestine).

FER-DE-LANCE (TVM-1974) - 10-18-74
    Director: Russ Mayberry
David Janssen (Russ Bogan), Hope Lange
(Elaine Wedell), Ivan Dixon (Joe Voit),
Jason Evers (Cmdr. Kirk), Charles Knox
Robinson (Lt. Nicholson), Ben Piazza

(Lt. Whitehead), George Pan (Torquale),
Sherry Boucher (Liz McCord), Robert
Ito (Masai Ikeda), Bill Mims (Mayne
Bradley), Shizuko Hoshi (Suan Kuroda),
Richard LePore (Chief Hughes), Sandra
Ego (Terezita), Felipe Turich (Shaman),
Frank Bonner (Compton) Robert Burr
(Cmdr. Scott), Alain Patrick, Bill
Catching, Richard Guthrie, Elveen Har-
vard.

FERRYBOAT WOMAN MARIA (1935-
    Ger.) (A. K. A. "Fahrmann Maria")
    Director: Frank Wisbar
Sybille Schmitz (Maria), Peter Voss.

FIDDLERS THREE (1944)
    Director: Harry Watt
Francis L. Sullivan (Nero), Diana
Decker (Lydia), Ernest Milton (Titus),
Mary Clare (Columbia), Tommy Trinder
(Tommy), Frances Day (Poppaea),
Elisabeth Welch (Thora), Sonnie Hale
(Professor), Frederick Piper (auction-
eer), Russell Thorndike (High Priest),
Robert Wyndham (lion-keeper).

FIEND (1980)
    Director: Don Dohler
Don Leifert (Eric Longfellow), Richard
Nelson (Gary Kender), Elaine White
(Marsha Kender), George Stover (Dennis Frye), Del Winans (Jimmy Barnes),
Greg Dohler (Scotty), Kim Dohler (Kristy Michaels), Anne Fritch (Katie), Pam
Merenda (Jane Clayton), Steve Vertlieb
(announcer), Steve Frith (man in Cemetary), Denise Grzybowski (Kristy's
friend), Debbie Vogel (Helen Weiss),
Richard Geiwitz (Fred), Lydia Vuyno-
vich (girl in cemetary) Tom Griffith
(man with beard), Barbara Shuman
(woman with dog), Anna Dorbert (woman
with groceries), Phil DeFlavis (father
at academy), Dannielle DeFlavis (daughter at academy).

FIENDISH PLOT OF DR. FU MANCHU,
    THE (1980)
    Director: Piers Haggard
Peter Sellers (Dr. Fu Manchu/Nayland
Smith), Helen Mirren (Alice Rage),
David Tomlinson (Sir Robert Avery),
John Le Mesurier (Perkins), Simon
Williams (Robert Townsend), Steve
Franken (Pete Williams), Sid Caesar
(Joe Capone), Stratford Johns (Ismail),
Clement Harari (Dr. Wretch), John
Sharp (Sir Nules Thudd), Lee Kwan-
Young (Tong), Burt Kwouk (Fu's servant),
Clive Dunn (Keeper of the Keys), Philip
Tan, Johns Rajohnson, Pralith Ingam
Oeurn, John Tan, Serge Julien, Lim Bun

Song (Dacoits), David Powers (Bedser),
Grace Coyle (Queen Mary), Rene Aranda
(King George V), Iska Khan (Fu's sergeant), Jacqueline Fogt (woman dignitary),
Katia Chenko (tour guide), Marc Wilkinson (conductor), George Hilsden (newsvendor), John Taylor (Sellers' double).

FIEND WITHOUT A FACE (1958)
    Director: Arthur Crabtree
Marshall Thompson (Maj. Jeff Cummings),
Kim Parker (Barbara Griselle), Terence
Kilburn (Capt. Chester), Kynaston Reeves
(Prof. Walgate), Michael Balfour (Sgt.
Kasper), Gil Winfield (Dr. Warren), Stan-
ley Maxted (Col. Butler), James Dyren-
forth (Mayor Hawkins), Peter Madden
(Dr. Bradley), R. Meadows White (Ben
Adams), Launce Maraschal (Melville),
Lala Lloyd (Amelia Adams), Robert
Mackenzie (Gibbons), Shane Cordell
(nurse), Kerringan Prescott (atomic
engineer).

FIGHTING DEVIL DOGS (1938) (A. K. A.
"The Torpedo of Doom") - serial in 12
    episodes
    Director: William Witney, John
    English & Robert Beche
Lee Powell (Lt. Tom Grayson) Bruce
Bennett (Frank Corby), Eleanor Stewart
(Janet Warfield), Montague Love (Gen.
White), John Picorri (Gould) John Dav-
idson (Lin Wing), Hugh Sothern (Warfield/
the Lightning), Edmund Cobb (Ellis),
Carleton Young (Johnson), Reed Howes
(Parker), Sam Flint (Col. Grayson),
Perry Ivins (Crenshaw), Henry Otho
(Sam Hedges), Forrest Taylor (Benson),
Tom London (Wilson), Allan Mathews
(Todd), Thomas Carr (clerk), Jack
Ingram (derigible radioman), Alan Gregg
(Macro), Harry Strang (Bennett), Robert
Kortman, Bud Osborne (gun heavies),
Monte Montague (Jacobs), Ken Cooper,
Jerry Frank, Jack O'Shea, Millard Mc-
Gowan, Dirk Thane, Theodore Lorch,
Al Taylor, Robert Wilbur, Harry Ander-
son (heavies), F. Herrick (gun heavy), . .
Lloyd Whitlock (dirigible captain),
Sherry Hall (Brown), Duke York (Sam),
Buddy Roosevelt (Pawnee Lieutenant),
John Merton (Thompson), Edward Cas-
sidy (Pawnee Captain), George DeNor-
mand (room gaurd), Fred Schaefer
(ambulance driver), Howard Chase
(Cuttle), Lee Baker (derigible crewman),
George Magrill (Jamison), Jack Daley
(Inspector), Larry Steers (King), Robert
Wilke, Joe Delacruz (soldiers), Lee
Frederick, Buel Bryant, Tom Steele
(marine guards), William Stahl (Lake),
Bruce Lane (Marine Corporal), Joe

Delacruz (native), James Carlisle
(officer), Edward Foster (Pete),
Wesley Hopper (Pawnee radioman),
Earl Douglas, Eddie Dew, Jack Ro-
berts, Frederick Freeman (radiomen),
Victor Wong (Mikichan), John Hiestand
(newscaster), Francis Sayles (Renault),
Frank Baker (Snell), Ray Hanson
(Smith), Edward Argyle (watchman),
Eddie Parker, Ray Henderson, Duke
Green.

FIGHTING MARINES, THE (1935) -
    serial in 12 episodes
Chapters: 1. "Human Targets", 2.
"Isle of Missing Men", 3. "The Savage
Horde", 4. "The Mark of the Tiger
Shark", 5. "The Gauntlet of Grief", 6.
"Robber's Roost", 7. "Jungle Terrors",
8. "Siege of Halfway Island", 9. "Death
from the Sky", 10. "Wheels of Destruc-
tion", 11. "Behind the Mask" & 12.
"Two Against the Horde"
    Director: B. Reeves Eason &
    Joseph Kane
Grant Withers (Corporal Lawrence),
Adrian Morris (Sgt. McGowan), Ann
Rutherford (Frances Schiller), Robert
Warwick (Col. Bennett), George J.
Lewis (Schiller), Jason Robards, Sr.
(Kota), Warner Richmond (Metcalf),
Pat O'Malley (Capt. Grayson), Douglas
Frazer (Douglas), Frank Reicher
(Steinbeck), Frank Glendon (Buchanan),
Richard Alexander (Ivan), Milburn
Stone (Red), Donald Reed (Pedor), Tom
London (Miller), Stanley Blystone (Gib-
son), Billy Arnold (Capt. Henderson),
Grace Durkin (Miss Martin), Franklin
Adreon (Capt. Holmes), Lee Shumway
(Capt. Drake).

FINAL ASSIGNMENT (1980)
    Director: Paul Amond
Genevieve Bujold (Nicole Thomson),
Michael York (Lyosha Petrov), Burgess
Meredith (Zak), Colleen Dewhurst (Dr.
Valentine Ulanova), Alexandra Stewart
(Sam O'Donnell), Richard Gabourie
(Bowen).

FINAL CONFLICT, THE (1981)
    Director: Graham Birkin
Sam Neill (Damien Thorn), Lisa Harrow
(Kate Reynolds), Rossano Brazzi (Fa-
ther de Carlo), Don Gordon (Harvey
Dean), Mason Adams (President), Barn-
aby Holm (Peter Reynolds), Leueen
Willoughby (Barbara), Robert Arden
(Ambassador), Tommy Duggan (Brother
Matteus), Marc Boyle (Brother Benito),
Milos Kirek (Brother Martin), Louis
Mahoney (Brother Paulo), Richard

Oldfield (Brother Simeon), Tony Vogel (Brother Antonio), Norman Bird (Dr. Philmore), Arwen Holm (Carol), Hugh Moxey (manservant), Arnold Diamond (astronomer), William Fox, John Baskcomb (diplomats), Richard Williams (Vicar), Eric Richard (astronomer's technician), Marc Smith (press officer), Stephen Turner (Stigwell), Al Matthews (workman), Larry Martyn, Harry Littlewood, Frank Coda (orators), Hazel Court.

FINAL COUNTDOWN, THE (1980)
    Director: Don Taylor
Kirk Douglas (Capt. Matthew Yelland), Martin Sheen (Warren Lasky), Katharine Ross (Laurel Scott), James Farentino (Cmdr. Richard Owens), Charles Durning (Sen. Samuel Chapman), Victor Mohica (Black Cloud), Soon Teck Oh (Simura), Ron O'Neal (Cmdr. Dan Thurman), James C. Lawrence (Lt. Perry), Joe Lowry (Cmdr. Damon), Mark Thomas (Cpl. Kullman), Harold Bergman (Bellman), Alvin Ing (Kajima), Peter Douglas (Quatermaster), Phil Philbin (Admiral), Dan Fitzgerald (Navy doctor), Lloyd Kaufman (Lt. Cmdr. Kaufman), Ted Riehert, Gary Morgan, Richard Liberty, George Warren, Robert Goodman, Neil Ronco, Jack McDermott, Orwin Harvey, William Couch, Masuyuki Yamazuki, Colby Smith, George H. Strohsahl, Jr., Kenneth J. Jaskolski, Sergei M. Kowalchik, Ronald R. Stoops, Jake Dennis, Jim Toone.

FINAL EXAM (1981)
    Director: Jimmy Huston
Cecile Bagdadi (Courtney), Joel S. Rice, (Radish), Ralph Brown (Wildman), Deanna Robbins (Lisa), John Fallon (Mark), Sherry Willis-Burch (Janet), Jerry Rusing (coach), Terry W. Farren (pledge), Sam Kilman Sheriff), Don Hepner (Dr. Reynolds), Timothy L. Raynor (killer).

FINAL PROGRAMME, THE (1973) (A.K.A. "The Last Days of Man on Earth")
    Director: Robert Fuest
Jon Finch (Jerry Cornelius), Jenny Runacre (Miss Bruner), Sterling Hayden (Major Lindberg), Harry Andrews (John), Hugh Griffith (Prof. Hira), Patrick Magee (Dr. Baxter), Graham Crowden (Dr. Smiles), Basil Henson (Dr. Lucas), George Coulouris (Dr. Powys), Julie Ege (Miss Dazzle), Derrick O'Connor (Frank Cornelius).

FINAL WAR, THE (1960-Jap.) (A.K.A.

"Dai Sanji Sekai Taisen-Yonjuichi Jikan no Kyofu")
    Director: Shigeaki Hidaki
Tatsuo Umemiya, Yoshiko Mita, Noribumi Fujishima, Michiko Hoshi, Yayoi Furustao, Tukiko Nikaido.

FINGERS AT THE WINDOW (1942)
    Director: Charles Lederer
Lew Ayres (Oliver Duffy), Basil Rathbone Day (Edwina Brown), Basil Rathbone (Dr. Santelle), Walter Kingsford (Dr. Cromwell), Miles Mander (Dr. Kurt Immelman), Russell Gleason (Ogilvie), Russell Hicks (Dr. Chandley), Mark Daniels (Hagney), William Tannen (Devlan), Bert Roach (Krum), Charles D. Brown (Insp. Gallagher), Cliff Clark, James Flavin.

FINIAN'S RAINBOW (1968)
    Director: Francis Ford Coppola
Fred Astaire (Finian McLonergan), Petula Clark (Sharon McLonergan), Tommy Steele (Og), Keenan Wynn (Judge Rawkins), Dolph Sweet (Sheriff), Al Freeman, Jr. (Howard), Don Franks (Woody Mahoney), Barbara Hancock (Susan the Silent), Wright King (District Attorney), Louis Silas (Henry), Ronald Colby (Buzz Collins), Brenda Arnau (share-cropper), Roy Glenn, Jester Hairston, Avon Long (Passion Pilgrim Gospeleers).

FIRE AND ICE (1983) - animated
    Director: Ralph Bakshi

FIRE DETECTIVE, THE (1929) - serial in 10 episodes
Chapters: 1. "The Arson Trail", 2. "The Pit of Darkness", 3. "The Hidden Hand", 4. "The Convict Strikes", 5. "On Flaming Waters", 6. "The Man of Mystery", 7. "The Ape Man", 8. "Back from Death", 9. "Menace of the Past" & 10. "The Flame of Love".
    Director: Spencer Gordon Bennet & Thomas L. Storey
Gladys McConnell (Gladys Samuels), Hugh Allen (Capt. Jeff Tarrant), Leo Maloney (Chief Carson), Frank Lackteen (Mr. Tarrant), John Cossar (District Attorney Samuels), Lawrence W. Steers (Charles Lewis).

FIREFOX (1982)
    Director: Clint Eastwood
Clint Eastwood (Mitchell Gant), Freddie Jones (Kenneth Aubrey), David Huffman (Buckholz), Warren Clarke

(Pavel Upenskoy), Ronald Lacey (Semelovsky), Kenneth Colley (Col. Kontarsky), Klaus Lowitsch (Gen. Vladimirov), Nigel Hawthorne (Pyotr Baranovich), Stefan Schnabel (First Secretary), Thomas Hill (Gen. Brown), Clive Merrison (Major Lanyev), Kai Wulff (Lt. Col. Voskov), Dimitra Arliss (Natalia).

FIRE IN THE SKY, A (TVM-1978) - 11-26-78
Director: Jerry Jameson
Richard Crenna (Jason Voight), Elizabeth Ashley (Sharon Allan), David Dukes (David Allen), Joanna Miles (Jennifer Dreiser), Nicolas Coster (the Governor), Lloyd Bochner (Paul Gilliam), Cynthia Eilbacher (Paula Gilliam), Andrew Duggan (the President), Bill Williams (Dale Turner), William Bogert (Lustus), Jenny O'Hara (Ann Webster), Merlin Olsen (Stan Webster), Michael Biehn (Tom Reardon), Diana Douglas (Mrs. Reardon), George Petrie (Hank), Al White (Sgt. Lockett), Roy Gainter (Dr. Jesse), Cecelia Allen (Elizabeth Ritchie), Bud Conlon (Gen. Kloman), Elta Blake (co-ed), Bill Heywood (TV announcer), Patrick McMahon (news director), Burke Rhind (Chief Controller), Hank Kendrick (launch director), Dino Bachelor (Danny), Brad Zinn (Hutton), Maggie Wellman (Carol).

FIRE MAIDENS FROM OUTER SPACE (1955)
Director: Cy Roth
Anthony Dexter (Luther Blair), Susan Shaw (Hestia), Paul Carpenter (Larson), Sidney Tafler (Dr. Higgins), Harry Fowler (Sydney Stanhope), Rodney Diak (Anderson), Jacqueline Curtiss (Duessa), Owen Berry (Prasus).

FIRE MONSTERS AGAINST THE SON OF HERCULES (1962-Ital.) (A.K.A. "Maciste contro i Monstri", "Macister vs. the Monster", "Colossus of the Stone Age")
Director: Guido Malatesta
Reg Lewis (Maciste), Matgaret Lee, Luciano Marin, Andrea Akreli, Myra Kent

FIREWORKS (1947) - short
Director: Kenneth Anger
Kenneth Anger, Bill Seltzer, Gordon Gray.

FIRST MAN INTO SPACE (1959)
Director: Robert Day
Marshall Thompson (Cmdr. C.E. Prescott), Bill Edwards (Lt. Dan Prescott), Marla Landi (Tia Francesca), Bill Nagy

(Chief Wilson), Robert Ayres (Capt. Ben Richards), Carl Jaffe (Dr. Paul Van Essen), Roger Delgado (Mexican Consul), Richard Shaw (Witney), John McLaren (State Department officer), Bill Nick (Clancy), John Fabian, Spencer Teakle, Chuck Keyser (Control Room officers), Michael Bell (state trooper), Helen Forrest (Secretary), Mark Sheldon (doctor), Sheree Wilson (nurse), Rowland Brand (truck driver), Barry Shawzin (Mexican farmer), Franklin Fox (C.P.O.), Laurence Taylor (shore patrolman).

FIRST MEN IN THE MOON (1919)
Director: Bruce Gordon
Bruce Gordon (Hogben), Heather Thatcher (Susan), Hector Abbas (Samson Cavor), Lionel d'Aragon (Rupert Bedford), Cecil Morton York (Grand Lunar).

FIRST MEN IN THE MOON (1964)
Director: Nathan Juran
Edward Judd (Arnold Bedford), Lionel Jeffries (Joseph Cavor), Martha Hyer (Kate Callender), Erik Chitty (Gibbs), Marne Maitland (Dr. Tok), Miles Malleson (registrar), Hugh McDermott (Challis), Gladys Henson (matron), Gordon Robinson (Martin), Sean Kelly (Col. Rice), John Murray Scott (Nevsky), Betty McDowall (Maggie), Lawrence Herder (Glushkov), Paul Carpenter (announcer), Huw Thomas (announcer), Peter Finch (writ server).

FIRST SPACESHIP ON VENUS (1962-E. Ger./Pol.) (A.K.A. "Der Schweigende Stern", "The Silent Planet", "Spaceship Venus Does Not Reply")
Director: Kurt Matzig
Yoko Tani (Sumiko Ogimura), Oldrich Lukes (Harringway), Ignacy Machowski (Orloff), Julius Ongewe (Talua), Kurt Rockelmann (Sikarna), Michael Postmikov (Durand), Gunther Simon (Brinkman), Lucina Winnicka (Joan Moran), Tang-Hua-Ta (Tchen Yu).

FITZCARRALDO (1982-Ger.)
Director: Werner Herzog
Klaus Kinski (Brian Sweeney Fitzgerald/Fitzcarraldo), Claudia Cardinale (Molly), Jose Lewgoy (Don Quilino), Miguel Angel Fuentes (Cholo), Paul Hettscher (Captain), Huerequeque Enrique Bohorquez (Huerequeque, the cook), Grande Othelo (railway station chief), Peter Berling (opera director), David Perez Espinosa (Campa chief), Milton Nascimento (black attendant),

Salvador Godinez (old missionary), Dieter Milz (young missionary), Rui Polanah (rubber baron), Bill Rose (Notary), Leoncio Bueno (prison guard).

FIVE (1951)
Director: Arch Oboler
William Phipps (Michael Rogan), Susan Douglas (Roseanne), James Anderson (Eric), Charles Lampkin (Charles), Earl Lee (Oliver P. Barnstaple).

FIVE BLOODY GRAVES (1970)
Director: Al Adamson, Jr.
Robert Dix (Ben), Scott Brady (Jim), Jim Davis (Clay), John Carradine (Boone), John Cardos (Joe Satago), Gene Raymond (voice of Death), Paula Raymond (Kansas), Kent Osbourne (Dave), Tara Ashton (Althea), Vicki Volante (Nora), Ray Young (Horace), Denver Dixon (Rawhide), Julie Edwards (Lavinia), Maria Polo (Little Fawn), Fred Meyers (driver).

FIVE MILLION YEARS TO EARTH (1967)
A. K. A. "Quatermass and the Pit")
Director: Roy Ward Baker
Andrew Keir (Prof. Quatermass), James Donald (Dr. Mathew Roney), Julian Glover (Col. Breen), Barbara Shelley (Barbara Judd), Peter Copley (Howell), Bryan Marshall (Capt. Potter), Duncan Lamont (Sladden), Bee Duffell (Miss Dobson), Robert Morris (Watson), Thomas Heathcoate (Vicar), Edwin Richfield (Minister), Maurice Good (Sgt. Cheghorn), Grant Taylor (Police Sgt. Ellis), Hugh Manning (pub customer), Sheila Steafel (journalist), Hugh Morton (elderly journalist), Hugh Futcher (Sapper West), Noel Howlett (Abbey Librarian), Keith Mars (Johnson), Roger Avon (electrician), John Graham (Inspector), James Culliford (Corporal Gibson), June Ellis (blonde), Brian Peck (technical officer), Charles Lamb (newsvendor).

FIVE SINISTER STORIES (1919-Ger.)
(A. K. A. "Funf Unheimliche Geschichten", "Five Tales of Horror")
Director: Richard Oswald
Conrad Veidt, Reinhold Schunzel, Anita Berber, Georg John, Hugo Doblin, Paul Morgan.

5,000 FINGERS OF DR. T, THE (1953)
Director: Stanley Kramer
Hans Conried (Dr. Terwilliker), Peter Lind Hayes (Zabladowski), Tommy Rettig (Bart), Mary Healy (Mrs. Collins), Noel Cravet (Sgt. Lund), Henry Kulky (Stroogo), John Heasley (Uncle Whitney), Robert Heasley (Uncle Judson).

FLAME BARRIER, THE (1958)
Director: Paul Landres
Arthur Franz (Dave Hollister), Kathleen Crowley (Carol Dahlmann), Robert Brown (Matt Hollister), Vincent Padula (Julio), Rod Redwing (Waumi), Kaz Oran (Tispe), Grace Mathews (Mexican girl), Pilar Del Rey (Indian girl), Larry Duran (bearer), Bernie Gozier (wounded Indian), Roberto Contreras (village Indian).

FLAMING DISK, THE (1920) - serial in 18 episodes
Chapters: 1. "Rails of Death", 2. "Span of Life", 3."Perilous Leap", 4. "Fires of Hate", 5. "Vanishing Floor", 6. "Pool of Mystery", 7. "Circle of Fire", 8. "Through Walls of Steel", 9. "The Floating Mine", 10. "Spiked Death", 11. "The Dynamite Trail", 12. "The Tunnel of Flames", 13. "Caged In", 14. "The Purple Rays", 15. "Poisoned Waters", 16. "Running Wild", 17. "Rails of Destruction" & 18. "End of the Trail".
Director: Robert F. Hill
Elmo Lincoln (Elmo Gray/Jim Gray), Louise Lorraine (Helen), Monty Montague (Bat), Lee Kohlmar (Prof. Wade), George Williams (Stanley W. Barrows), Jenks Harris (Con), Roy Watson (Rodney Stanton), Fred Hamer (Briggs),

FLASH GORDON (1936) (A. K. A. "Rocket Ship". "Spaceship to the Unknown") - serial in 13 episodes
Chapters: 1. "The Planet of Peril", 2. "The Tunnel of Terror", 3. "Captured by Shark Men", 4. "Battling the Sea Beast", 5. "The Destroying Ray", 6. "Flaming Fortune", 7. "Shattering Doom", 8. "Tournament of Death", 9. "Fighting the Fire Dragon", 10. "The Unseen Peril", 11. "In the Claws of the Tigron", 12. "Trapped in the Turret" & 13. "Rocketing to Earth".
Director: Frederick Stephani
Buster Crabbe (Flash Gordon), Jean Rogers (Dale Arden), Charles Middleton (Ming), Priscilla Lawson (Aura), Frank Shannon (Dr. Zarkov), John Lipson (Vultan), Richard Alexander (Prince Barin), Duke York, Jr. (King Kala), Theodore Lorch (High Priest), George Cleveland (Professor Hensley), Earl Askam (Officer Torch), Richard Tucker (Flash Gordon, Sr.), James Pierce (King Thun), House Peters, Jr. (Shark Man), Muriel Goodspeed (Zona), Lane Chandler, Glenn Strange, Fred Kohler, Jr. , Al Ferguson (soldiers), Eddie Parker, Carol Borland.

FLASH GORDON (1980)
Director: Mike Hodges
Sam J. Jones (Flash Gordon), Melody Anderson (Dale Arden), Topol (Dr. Hans Zarkov), Max Von Sydow (Emperor Ming), Ornella Muti (Princess Aura), Timothy Dalton (Prince Barin), Brian Blessed (Prince Vultan), Peter Wyngarde (Klytus), Mariangela Melato (Kala), Richard O'Brian (Fico), John Osborne (Arborian priest), Philip Stone (Zogi, the High Priest), John Hallam (Lura), Suzanne Danielle (serving girl), William Hootkins (Munson), Oliver MacGreevey (Klytus' observer No. 1), John Hollis (Klytus' observer No. 2), Ted Carroll (Biro), Bobbie Brown (Hedonia), Stanley Lebor (Mongan doctor), Adrienne Kronenberg (Vultan's daughter), John Morton (airline pilot), Burnell Tucker (airline co-pilot), Robbie Coltrane (man at airfield), Peter Duncan (young Treeman), Ken Sicklen (Treeman), Tessa (Hawkwoman), Vanetia Spicer (Hawkwoman), Francis Mugham (wounded hawkman), Paul Bentall (Klytus' pilot), Tony Scannell (Ming's officer), Leon Greene (Colonel in battle control room), Graeme Crowther (battle room controller), David Neal (Captain of Ming's Air Force), Deep Roy (Princess Aura's pet), Sally Nicholson (Queen of Azuria), Doretta Dunkler (Queen of Frigia), Colin Taylor (King of Frigia), George Harris (Prince of Ardentia), Andrew Bradford, Bertram Adams, Terry Forrestal, Mike Potter, John Sullivan, John Lees, Eddie Stacy, Roy Scammell (Hawkmen), Kathy Marquis, Kathy September, Sophie, Glenna Forster Jones (Sandmoon girls), Rosanne Romine, Sneh, Shaka, Magda, Lindy, Viva, Camella, Frances Ward, Beverly Andrews, Kerry Lou Baylis (Cytherian girls), Lorraine Paul, Carolyn Evans, Ruthie Barnett, Celeste, Tina Thomas (Aquarian girls), Miranda Riley (Frigian girl), Trevor Ward, Alva Shelley, Joe Iles, Nik Abraham, Glen Whitter, Leonard Hay (Ardentian men), Jamalia, Sunanka, Jil Lamb, Karen Johnson (Ming's serving girls), Kenny Baker, Malcolm Dixon, Mike Edmonds, Tiny Ross, John Ghavan, Rusty Goffe, Mike Cottrell, Peter Burrows, Richard Jones, John Lummis (dwarfs), Robert Goody, Peter S. James, Steven Payne, Daniel Venn, Max Alford, Anthony Olivier, Stephen Calcutt, Stuart Blake, Nigel Jeffcoat, Jim Carter (Azurdian men), Racquel, Fai, Gina (Ming's exotic girls), Eddie Powell, Chris Webb, John Gallant, Les Crawford, Peter Brace, Terry Richards (Ming's brutes), Michelle Mildwater, Marie Green, Imogen Claire, Kay Zimmerman, Stephen Brigden, Ken Robertson, Fred Warder, Lionel Guyett

FLASH GORDON CONQUERS THE UNIVERSE (1940) (A. K. A. "Peril from the Planet Mongo", "Space Soldiers Conquer the Universe", "Purple Death from Outer Space") - serial in 12 episodes.
Chapters: 1. "The Purple Death", 2. "Freezing Torture", 3. "Walking Bombs", 4. "The Destroying Ray", 5. "The Palace of Terror", 6. "Flaming Death", 7. "The Land of the Dead", 8. "The Fiery Abyss", 9. "The Pools of Peril", 10. "The Death Mist", 11. "Stark Treachery" & 12. "Doom of the Dictator".
Director: Ford Beebe
Buster Crabbe (Flash Gordon), Carol Hughes (Dale Arden), Charles Middleton (Emperor Ming), Frank Shannon (Dr. Zarkof), Shirley Deane (Princess Aura), Anne Gwynne (Sonja), Roland Drew (Prince Barin), Michael Mark (Karm), Donald Curtis (Ronal), Herbert Rawlinson (Prof. Froman), Roy Barcroft, Lane Chandler (guards), John Hamilton (Prof. Gordon), Byron Foulger (Druk), Victor Zimmerman (Thong), Don Rowan (Torch), Lee Powell (Roka), Ben Taggart (Lupi), Edgar Edwards (Turan), Sigmund Nilssen (Korro), Harry C. Bradley (Keedish), Ray Mala (King's son), Luli Deste (Fria), Clarice Sherry (Grenda), Jeanne Kelly (Olga), Earl Dwire (Janda), Mimi Taylor (Verna), Allan Caven (Nobleman), Carmen D'Antonio (Dancer), Eddie Parker.

FLASH GORDON'S TRIP TO MARS (1938) (A. K. A. "Mars Attacks the World", "Deadly Ray from Mars") - serial in 15 episodes
Chapters: 1. "New Worlds to Conquer", 2. "The Living Dead", 3. "Queen of Magic", 4. "Ancient Enemies", 5. "The Boomerang", 6. "Tree-Men of Mars", 7. "The Prisoner of Mongo", 8. "The Black Sapphire of Kalu", 9. "Symbol of Death", 10. "Incense of Forgetfulness", 11. "Human Bait", 12. "Ming the Merciless", 13. "The Miracle of Magic", 14. "A Beast at Bay" & 15. "An Eye for an Eye".
Director: Ford Beebe & Robert F. Hill
Buster Crabbe (Flash Gordon), Jean Rogers (Dale Arden), Charles Middleton (Emperor Ming), Frank Shannon, (Dr. Zarkov), Richard Alexander, (Prince Barin), Beatrice Roberts (Azura),

Donald Kerr (Happy), Montague Shaw (King of the Clay People), Anthony Warde (King of the Tree People), Kane Richmond (Pilot Captain), Earl Askam (Officer Torch), George Cleveland (Prof. Hensley), Lane Chandler, Glenn Strange, Al Ferguson, Fred Kohler, Jr. (soldiers), Jack Mulhall, Eddie Parker, Ben Lewis.

FLASH GORDON - THE GREATEST ADVENTURE OF ALL (TVM-1982) - animated
    Producers: Lou Scheimer & Norm Prescott
Voices: Robert Ridgely (Flash Gordon), Diane Pershing (Dale Arden), Bob Holt (Dr. Zarkov), David Opatoshu (Thun), Vic Perrin (Ming), Melendy Britt (Aura), Ted Cassidy (Vultan), Robert Douglas (Prince Barin).

FLASHMAN (1967-Ital./Fr.) (A.K.A. "Flashman contra les Hommes Invisible"; "Flashman vs. the Invisible Men")
    Director: Mino Loy/J. Lee Donan
Paolo Goslino/Paul Stevens, Isarco Ravailoi/John Heston, Claudia Lange, Jacques Ary, Seyna Seyn, Michaela Candali.

FLESH AND BLOOD SHOW, THE (1972)
    Director: Pete Walker
Jenny Hanley, Ray Brooks, Luan Peters, Patrick Barr, Robin Askwith.

FLESH AND FANTASY (1943)
    Director: Julien Duvivier
Robert Benchley (Doakes), David Hoffman (Davis), Betty Field (Henrietta), Robert Cummings (Michael), Marjorie Lord (Justine), Edgar Barrier (bearded gentleman), Edward G. Robinson (Marshall Tyler), Thomas Mitchell (Septimus Podgers), Anna Lee (Rowena), Dame May Whitty (Lady Pamela Hardwick), C. Aubrey Smith (Dean of Norwalk), Edward Fielding, Heather Thatcher (guests), Charles Boyer (the Great Gasper), Barbara Stanwyck (Joan Stanley), Charles Winninger (King Lamarr), Clarence Muse (Jeff), June Lang (Angela), Mary Ann Hyde (Gaspar's partner), Grace McDonald (equestrienne), Ian Wolfe (librarian), Doris Lloyd (Mrs. Caxton), Joseph Crehan (acrobat), James Craven (radio announcer), Peter Lawford (Pierrot), Eddie Acuff (policeman), Lane Chandler (Satan), Jacqueline Dalya (Angel), Mary Forbes (Lady Thomas), Arthur Loft, Lee Phelps (Detectives), Charles Halton (old prospector), Gil Patrick (Death), George Lewis, Paul Bryar (Harlequins), Clinton Rosemond (old Negro).

FLESH AND THE FIENDS, THE (1960)
    (A.K.A. "Mania", "The Fiendish Ghouls")
    Director: John Gilling
Peter Cushing (Dr. Robert Knox), Donald Pleasence (William Hare), George Rose (William Burke), Dermot Walsh (Dr. Mitchell), June Laverick (Martha), Renee Houston (Helen Burke), Billie Whitelaw (Mary Patterson), George Woodbridge (Dr. Ferguson), Philip Leaver (Dr. Elliott), John Cairney (Chris Jackson), June Powell (Maggie O'Hara), Beckett Bould (Old Angus), John Rae (Rev. Lincoln), Esma Cannon (Aggie), Geoffrey Tyrrel (Old Davey), Andrew Foulds (McCulloch), Raf De La Torre (Baxter), Melvyn Hayes (Daft Jamie), Michael Balfour (drunker sailor), George Bishop (blind man), Michael Mulcaster (undertaker), George Street (barman), Jack McNaughton (stallholder).

FLESH EATERS, THE (1964)
    Director: Jack Curtis
Martin Kosleck (Prof. Bartell), Byron Sanders (Grant Murdoch), Barbara Wilkin (Jan Letterman), Rita Morley (Laura Winters), Ray Tudor (Omar).

FLESH FEAST (1970)
    Director: B.F. Grinter
Veronica Lake (Dr. Elaine Frederick), Phil Philbin, Heather Hughes, Chris Martel, Martha Mischon, Dian Wilhite, Yanka Mann.

FLESH GORDON (1972)
    Director: Mike Light
Jason Williams (Flesh Gordon), Suzanne Fields (Dale Ardor), William Hunt (Emperor Wang), Joseph Hudgins (Dr. Flexi Jerkoff), John Hoyt (Prof. Gordon), Mycle Brandy, Candy Samples, Lance Larson, Nora Witernik, Steven Grummette, Judy Ziehm, Linus Gator, Mark Fore, Donald Harris, Susan Moore, Maria Aranoff, Sally Alt, Leonard Goodman, Linda Shepard, Mary Gavin, Duane Paulsen, Rick Lutze, Dee Dee Dailes, Patricia Burns.

FLIGHT THAT DISAPPEARED, THE (1961)
    Director: Reginald LeBorg
Craig Hill (Tom Endicott), Paula Raymond (Marcia Paxton), Dayton Lummis (Dr. Morris), Addison Richards (the Sage), Roy Engel (Jamison), Meg Wyllie (Helen Cooper), Gregory Morton (the Examiner), Nancy Hale (Barbara Nielson), John Bryant (Hank Norton), Bernadette Hale (Joan Agnew), Brad Trumbull (Jack Peters), Harvey Stephens (Walter Cooper), Francis De Sales

(Manson), Eden Hartford (Miss Ford),
Jerry James (Ray Houser), Ed Stoddard
(O'Connor), Jack Mann (Garrett), Stephen Ellesworth Crowley (A. T. C. Official), Carl Princi (announcer), Joe Haworth (radio operator).

FLIGHT TO MARS (1951)
    Dierctor: Lesley Selander
Cameron Mitchell (Steve Abbott), Mar-
guerita Chapman (Alita), Arthur Franz
(Dr. Jim Barker), Virgina Huston (Carol
Stafford), John Litel (Dr. Lane), Morris
Ankrum (Ikron), Richard Gaines (Prof.
Jackson), Lucille Barkley (Terris), Ro-
bert Barratt (Tillamar), Edward Earle
(Justin), William Forrest (Gen. Archer),
Bob Peoples (soldier), Tony Marsh (at-
tendant), Tris Coffin (commentator), Bill
Neff (sergeant), Trevor Bardette (Alzar),
Russ Conway, Raymond Bond (astronom-
ers), Everett Glass (Montar), David Bond
(Ramay), Wibur Back, Stanley Blystone,
William Bailey, Frank O'Connor (Coun-
cilmen), Perc Launders (workman).

FLORENTINE DAGGER, THE (1935)
    Director: Robert Florey
Donald Woods (Cesare), Margaret Lindsay (Florence Ballau), C. Aubrey Smith
(Dr. Lytton), Robert Barrat (the Captain),
Henry O'Neill (Victor Ballau), Egon Brecher (Karl), Frank Reicher (Von Stein),
Rafaela Ottiani (Lili Salvatore), Eily
Malyon (Fredericka), Paul Porcasi (Antonio), Charles Judels (Salvatore), Florence Fair (Teresa), Henry Kolker
(auctioneer), Herman Bing (the baker).

FLY, THE (1958)
    Director: Kurt Neumann
David Hedison (Andre Delambre), Patri-
cia Owens (Helene Delambre), Vincent
Price (Francois Brandon), Herbert Mar-
shall (Insp. Charas), Charles Herbert
(Philip Delambre), Kathleen Freeman
(Emma), Eugene Borden (Dr. Ejoute),
Torben Meyer (Gaston), Betty Lou Ger-
son (Nurse Anderson), Harry Carter (or-
derly), Arthur Dulac (French waiter),
Franz Roehm (police doctor).

FLY-BY-NIGHT (1942)
    Director: Robert Siodmak
Richard Carlson, Nancy Kelly, Albert
Basserman, Miles Mander, Walter Kings-
ford, Marion Martin, Mary Gordon, Cy
Kendall, Oscar O'Shea, Martin Kosleck,
Ed Gargan, Arthur Loft, Clem Bevans.

FLYING CARPET, THE (1956-Sov.)
    (A. K. A. "Stari Khottabych")
    Director: G. Kanzansky

Nikolai Volkov (Khottabych), Alyosha
Litvinov (Volka), Genia Khudiakov (Jen-
ya), Lyova Kovalchuk (Goga), Edvard
Kapelyan (Mukhammedov), Vera Romanova (Goga's mother), Olga Cherkasova
(the teacher), Marya Blinova (the mother).

FLYING DISC, THE (1964-Ital.) (A. K. A.
    "Il Disco Volante")
    Director: Tinto Brass
Monica Vitti, Alberto Sordi, Silvana
Mangano, Guido Celano, Eleonora Rossi
Drago, Alberto Fogliani.

FLYING DISC MAN FROM MARS (1950)
    (A. K. A. "Missile Monsters") - ser-
    ial in 12 episodes.
Chapters: 1. "Menace from Mars", 2.
"The Volcan's Secret", 3. "Death Rides
the Stratosphere", 4. "Execution by
Fire", 5. "The Living Projectile", 6.
"Perilous Mission", 7. "Descending
Doom", 8. "Suicidal Sacrifice", 9. "The
Funeral Pyre", 10. "Weapons of Hate",
11. "Disaster on the Highway" & 12.
"Volcanic Vengeance".
    Director: Fred C. Brannon
Walter Reed (Kent Fowler), Lois Collier
(Helen), Gregory Gaye (Mota), James
Craven (Dr. Bryant), Harry Lauter
(Drake), Tom Steele (Taylor), Richard
Irving (Ryan), Michael Carr (Trent),
Jimmy O'Gatty (Grady), Lester Dorr
(Crane), Clayton Moore (Louis Ashe),
Dale Van Sickel (watchman), George
Sherwood (gateman), Sandy Sanders
(Steve), John DeSimone (Curtis, Dick
Cogan (Kirk), Ken Terrell (Graves),
Dick Crockett (Bill), Bill Wilkus (Cole),
Saul Gorss (Ed), Carey Loftin (Hagen),
John Daheim (Boyd), Barry Brooks
(Garrett), David Sharpe, Paul Gustine,
(technicians), Guy Teague (workman),
Chuck Hamilton (driver).

FLYING SAUCER, THE (1949)
    Director: Mikel Conrad
Mikel Conrad (Mike Trent), Pat Garrison (Vee Langley), Denver Pyle (Turner), Roy Engel (Dr. Carl Lawton),
Russell Hicks (Hank Thorn), Virginia
Hewitt (Nanette), Frank Darien (Matt
Mitchell), Lester Sharpe (Col. Mari-
koff), Earle Lyon (Alex Muller), Hanz
von Teuffen (Hans), Robert Boon (barge
captain), Garry Owen (bartender in
Ernie's), Phillip Morris (Dreamland
bartender), George Baxter.

FLYING SAUCERS, THE (1955-Mex.)
    (A. K. A. "Los Platillos Voladores")
    Director: Julian Soler
Andres Soler, Evangelina Elizondo,

Amalia Aguilar, Jose Venegas, Resortes, Pedro de Urdimalas.

FLYING SAUCER DAFFY (1958) - short
Director: Jules White
Moe Howard, Larry Fine, Joe Besser, Emil Sitka, Gail Bonney, Diana Darrin, Harriette Tarler, Bek Nelson.

FLYING SERPANT, THE (1945)
Director: Sherman Scott
George Zucco (Prof. Andres Forbes), Ralph Lewis (Richard Thorpe), Hope Kramer (Mary Forbes), Wheaton Chambers (Lewis Havener), Henry Hall (Billy Hayes), Milton Kibbee (Hastings), James Metcalf (Dr. Lambert), Eddie Acuff (Jerry Jones), Terry Frost (Bennett).

FLYING TORPEDO, THE (1916)
Director: John O'Brien
John Emerson (Winthrop Clavering), Bessie Love (Hulda), Spottiswoode Aitken (Bartholomew Thompson), Viola Barry (Adelaide E. Thompson), William E. Lawrence (William Haverman), Fred J. Butler (Chief of International Crooks), Ralph Lewis (Enemy Commander), Lucille Younge (Enemy Agent).

FOES (1979)
Director: John Coats
Macdonald Carey (McCarey), Alan Blanchard (Paul), Jan Wiley (Diane), John Coats (Larry), Jerry Hardin (Gen. Mason), Gregory Clemens (Vic).

FOG, THE (1980)
Director: John Carpenter
Adrienne Barbeau (Stevie Wayne), Jamie Lee Curtis (Elizabeth Solley), Hal Holbrook (Father Malone), Janet Leigh (Kathy Williams), Charles Cyphers (Dan O'Bannon), John Houseman (Machen), Nancy Loomis (Sandy Fadel), Tommy Atkins (Nick Castle), Ty Mitchell (Andy Wayne), John Goff (Al Williams), Jim Jacobus (Mayor), George Buck Flower (Tommy Wallace), John Vick (Sheriff Simms), Regina Waldon (Mrs. Kobritz), Jim Canning (Dick Baxter), Darrow Igus (Mel Sloan), Jim Haynie (Hank Jones), Darwin Joston (Dr. Phibes), Fred Franklyn (Ashcroft), Bill Taylor (bartender), Rob Bottin (Blake), Charley Nicklin (Blake's voice), Lee Sacks, Ric Moreno, Tommy Wallace (ghosts), John Strobel (grocery clerk), Laurie Arent, Lindsey Arent, Shari Jacoby, Christopher Cundey (children).

FOG FOR A KILLER (1962) (A.K.A. "Out of the Fog")
Director: Montgomery Tully
David Sumner (George Mallon), Susan Travers (June Lock), James Hayter (Daniels), Renee Houston (Ma), Jack Watson (Sgt. Tracey), George Woodbridge (Chopper), John Arnatt (Superintendent Chadwick), Anthony Oliver (Chaplain), Olga Lindo (Mrs. Mallon).

FOG MURDERER, THE (1964-Ger.)
(A.K.A. "Der Nebelmorder")
Director: Eugen York
Hansjorg Felmy, Ingmar Zeisberg, Elke Arendt, Ralph Persson.

FOLKS AT THE RED WOLF INN, THE (1972) (A.K.A. "Terror House")
Director: Bud Townsend
Janet Wood (Pamela), Margaret Avery (Edwina), Michael Macready (policeman), Earl Parker (pilot), Arthur Space, Linda Gillin, John Neilson.

FOOD OF THE GODS (1975)
Director: Bert I. Gordon
Marjoe Gortner (Morgan), Pamela Franklin (Lorna Scott), Ida Lupino (Mrs. Skinner), Ralph Meeker (Bensington), John McLiam (Mr. Skinner), John Cypher (Brian Oster), Belinda Balaski (Rita), Chuck Courtney (Robert Davis), Tom Stovall (Thomas).

FOOLS (1970)
Director: Tom Gries
Jason Robards (Matthew South), Katherine Ross (Anais), Scott Hylands (David Appleton), Robert C. Ferro, Jr. (private detective), Roy C Jenson, Mark Bramhall (men in park), Marc Hannibal (dog owner), Charles B. Dorsett (dentist), Laura Ash (patient), Robert Rothwell, Michael Davis (policemen), Vera Stough (girl in movie), Floy Dean (woman in restaurant), Roy Jelliffe (man in restaurant).

FOOLS IN THE DARK (1924)
Director: Al Santell
Matt Moore (Percy Schwartz), Patsy Ruth Miller (Ruth Rand), Bert Grassby (Kotah), Charles Belcher (Dr. Rand), Tom Wilson (Diplomat), John Steppling.

FORBIDDEN JUNGLE (1949)
Director: Robert Tansey
Don Harvey (Tom Burton), Forrest Taylor (Trader Kirk), Alyce Louis (Nita), Robert Cabal (Tawa).

FORBIDDEN MOON (1953)
see Television: Rocky Jones, Space

Ranger (1953-54)

FORBIDDEN PLANET (1956)
    Director: Fred M Wilcox
Leslie Nielsen (Cmdr. John J. Adams),
Walter Pidgeon (Dr. Edward Morbius),
Anne Francis (Altaira Morbius), Warren
Stevens (Lt. Doc Ostrow), Jack Kelly
(Lt. Farman), Earl Holliman (Cookie),
Richard Anderson (Chief Olonzo Quinn),
George Wallace (Bosun), Robert Dix
(Grey), Jimmy Thompson (Youngerford),
James Drury (Strong), Morgan Jones
(Nichols), Peter Miller (Moran), Harry
Harvey, Jr. (Randall), Roger McGee
(Lindstrom), Richard Grant (Silvers),
James Best, William Boyett (crewmen),
Frankie Darro, Frankie Carpenter (Rob-
by the Robot), Marvin Miller (Voice of
Robby), Les Tremayne (Narrator).

FORBIDDEN ROOM, THE (1914)
    Director: Allan Dwan
Lon Chaney, Sr., Murdock MacQuarrie,
Pauline Bush.

FORBIDDEN WORLD (1982) (A. K. A.
    "Mutant")
    Director: Allan Holzman
Jesse Vint (Mike Colby), June Chadwick
(Dr. Barbara Glaser), Dawn Dunlap
(Tracy Baxter), Linden Chiles (Dr. Gor-
don Hauser), Fox Harris (Dr. Cal Tin-
burgen), Raymond Oliver (Brian Beale),
Scott Paulin (Earl Richards), Michael
Bowen (Jimmy Swift).

FORBIDDEN ZONE (1980)
    Director: Richard Elfman
Herve Villechaize (King Fausto), Susan
Tyrrell (Queen), Viva (Ex-Queen), Marie-
Pascale Elfman (Frenchy).

FORBIN PROJECT, THE (1970) (A. K. A.
    "Colossus: The Forbin Project")
    Director: Joseph Sargent
Eric Braeden (Forbin), Susan Clark
(Cleo), Gordon Pinsent (the President),
William Schallert (Grauber), Leonid
Rostoff (First Chairman), Georg Stanford
Brown (Fisher), Alex Rodine (Kuprin),
Willard Sage (Blake), Martin Brooks,
(Johnson), Marion Ross (Angela), Byron
Morrow (Secretary of State), Dolph Sweet
(Missile Commander), Robert Cornth-
waite (1st scientist), James Hong (2nd
scientist), Lew Brown (Peterson), Rom
Basham (Harrison), Sergie Tschernisch
(translator), Paul Frees (voice of Col-
ossus).

FOREVER (1921)
    Director: George Fitzmaurice

Wallace Reid, Montague Love, Elliott
Dexter, Elsie Ferguson, Dolores Cassinelli, George Fawcett, Paul McAllister, Barbara Dean.

FOREVER, DARLING (1955)
    Director: Alexander Hall
Lucille Ball (Susan Vega), Desi Arnaz
(Lorenzo Xavier Vega), James Mason
(Guardian Angel), Louis Calhern
(Charles Y. Bewell), John Emery (Dr.
Edward R. Winter), John Hoyt (Bill
Finlay), Natalie Schafer (Millie Op-
dyke), Nancy Kulp (Amy), Ralph Dumke
(Henry Opdyke), Willis Bouchey (Mr.
Clinton), Ruth Brady (Laura), Mabel
Albertson (society reporter).

FORGOTTEN CITY OF THE PLANET
    OF THE APES, THE (1974)
    see Television: Planet of the Apes
    (1974)

FOR HEAVEN'S SAKE (1950)
    Director: George Seaton
Clifton Webb (Charles), Joan Bennett
(Lydia), Edmund Gwenn (Arthur),
Robert Cummings (Jeff Bolton), Joan
Blondell (Daphne), Gigi Perreau (Item),
Tommy Rettig (Joe), Jack La Rue
(Tony), Dick Ryan (Michael), Harry
Von Zell (Tex), Robert Kent (Joe's
father), Charles Lane (tax agent), Whit
Bissell, Sue Casey, Ashmead Scott,
Dorothy Neumann, Jack Daly, Gilbert
Fallman, Perc Launders, William
O'Leary, Bob Harlow, Esther Somers,
Betty Adams, Richard Thorne.

FOR LOVE... FOR MAGIC (1968-Ital.)
    (A. K. A. "Per Amore... per Mag-
    ica")
    Director: Duccio Tessari
Mischa Auer, Rossano Brazzi, Sandra
Milo, Harold Bradley, Rosemarie
Dexter, Paolo Poli, Lorella De Lucia,
Gianni Morandi.

FORMULA, THE (1980)
    Director: John G. Avildsen
George C. Scott (Barney Caine), Mar-
lon Brando (Adam Steiffel), Marthe
Keller (Lisa), John Van Dreelen (Hans
Lehman), John Gielgud (Dr. Esau),
Richard Lynch (Kladen/Tedesco), G. D.
Spradlin (Clements), Beatrice Straight
(Kay Neeley), Robin Clarke (Major
Neeley), Ferdy Mayne (Siebold), Ike
Eisenmann (Tony), Wolfgang Preiss
(Franz Tauber), Calvin Jung (Sgt.
Yosuta), David Byrd (Obermann), Alan
North (Nolan), Gerry Murphy (chauf-
feur), Francisco Prado (Mendose),

Werner Kreindl (Schellenberg), Jan Niklas (Gestapo Captain), Dieter Schidor (assassin), Marshall Thompson (Geologist).

FOR YOUR EYES ONLY (1981)
Director: John Glen
Roger Moore (James Bond), Carole Bouquet (Melina), Topol (Columbo), Julian Glover (Kristatos), Jill Bennett (Brink), Michael Gothard (Locque), Lynn-Holly Johnson (Bibi), Jack Hedley (Havelock), Cassandra Harris (Lisl), John Wyman (Kriegler), Desmond Llewelyn (Q), Lois Maxwell (Miss Moneypenny), Geoffrey Keen (Minister of Defense), James Villiers (Tanner), John Wells (Denis), Janet Brown (the Prime Minister), Aliks Kritikos, Toby Robins, Charles Dance.

FOUNTAIN OF LOVE, THE (1969-Austr.) (A.K.A. "Die Liebesquelle")
Director: Ernst Hofbauer
Eddi Arent (Alwin), Ann Smyrner (Stina), Hans-Jurgen Baumier (Leif), Sieghardt Rupp (Nils), Christa Linder (Britta), Hartmuth Minrichs (Carl), Christiane Rucker (Brit), Helga Marlo (Caroline), Werner Abrolat (John), Marianne Schonauer (Mrs. van Weyden), Emely Rauer (Frieda).

4-D MAN, THE (1959) (A.K.A. "The Evil Force", "Master of Terror")
Director: Irwin S. Yeaworth, Jr.
Robert Lansing (Scott Nelson), Lee Meriwether (Linda Davis), James Congdon (Tony Nelson), Guy Raymond (Fred), Edgar Stehli (Dr. Carson), Robert Strauss (Roy Parker), Patty Duke (Marjorie Sullivan), Jasper Deeter (Mr. Welles), George Kayara (Sgt. Todaman), Dean Newman (Dr. Schwartz), Elbert Smuiyh (Capt. Rogers), Chick James (B-girl).

FOUR FLIES ON GREY VELVET (1972-Ital./Fr.) (A.K.A. "Quattro Mosche di Velluto Grigio")
Director: Dario Argento
Michael Brandon (Robert Tobias), Mimsy Farmer (Nina Tobias), Jean Pierre Marielle (Arrosio), Francine Racette (Dalia), Bud Spenser (Godfrey), Calisto Calisti (Carlo Marosi), Marisa Fabbri (Hilda), Fabrizio Moroni (Mirko), Costanza Spada (Maria), Oreste Lionello (Professor), Stefano Sattaflores (Andrew).

FOUR NIGHTS OF THE FULL MOON, THE (1964-Span.) (A.K.A. "Los Cuatro Noches de la Luna Llena")
Director: Sobey Martin

Gene Tierney, Amalia Gade, Dan Dailey, Jaime de Moray Aragon, Perla Cristal, Nini Montian.

FOUR-SIDED TRIANGLE (1953)
Director: Terence Fisher
Barbara Payton (Lena/Helen), Stephen Murray (Bill), James Hayter (Dr. Harvey), John Van Eyssen (Robin), Kynaston Reeves (Lord Grant), Percy Marmont (Sir Walter), John Stuart (solicitor), Jennifer Dearman (Lena as a child), Sean Barrett (Robin as a child), Glyn Dearman (Bill as a child).

FOUR SKULLS OF JONATHAN DRAKE, THE (1959)
Director: Edward L. Cahn
Eduard Franz (Jonathan Drake), Henry Daniell (Dr. Zurick), Valerie French (Alison Drake), Grant Richards (Lt. Rowan), Paul Cavanagh (Kenneth Richards), Paul Wexler (Zutai), Frank Gerstle (Lee Coulter), Howard Wendell (Dr. Bradford), Lumsden Hare (Rogers).

48 HOURS TO LIVE (1959-Brit./Swed.) (A.K.A. "Man in the Middle")
Director: Peter Bourne
Anthony Steel (Mike Gibson), Lewis Charles (Marino), Marlies Behrens (Lena), Ina Anders (Annika), Haken Westergren (Prof. Christensen), Birger Maimsten (Paul), Ingemar Johansson (Himself), Rusty Rutledge (Anders), Peter Bourne (Carlson).

F.P. 1 DOES NOT RESPOND (1932-Ger.) (A.K.A. "F.P. 1 Antwortet Nicht")
Director: Karl Hartl
English version: Leslie Fenton (Capt. Droste), Conrad Veidt (Major Ellissen), Jill Esmond (Clare Lennartz), Donald Calthrop (photographer), George Merritt (Lubin), Nicholas Hannen (Matthias), William Freshman (Konrad), Philip Manning (doctor), Warwick Ward (first officer), Alexander Field, Francis J. Sullivan (sailors).
French Version: Charles Boyer, Jean Murat, Danielle Parola, Pierre Brasseur, Marcel Vallee, Ernest Ferny, Pierre Pierade.
German version: Hans Albers, Peter Lorre, Paul Hartmann, Sybille Schmitz, Rudolf Platte, Hermann Speelmans.

FRAGMENT OF FEAR (1971)
Director: Richard C. Sarafian
David Hemmings (Tom Brett), Gayle Hunnicutt (Juliet), Wilfrid Hyde-White (Mr. Copsey), Flora Robson (Lucy

Dawson), Daniel Massey (Major Rick-
etts), Roland Culver (Mr. Vellacot),
Adolfo Celi (Bardoni), Mona Wash-
bourne (Mr. Gray), Bernard Archard
(Priest), Derek Newark (Sgt. Matthews),
Arthur Lowe (Mr. Nugent), Yootha
Joyce (Mrs. Ward-Cadbury), Glyn Ed-
wards (CID Superintendent), Mary
Wimbush (Bunface), Patricia Hayes
(Mrs. Baird), John Rae (Uncle Stanley),
Angelo Infanti (Bruno), Hilda Barry
(Miss Dacey), Massimo Sarchielli
(Mario), Philip Stone (CID Sergeant),
Kenneth Cranham (Joe), Edward Kemp
(Kenny), Michael Rothwell (Rocky),
Kurt Christian (Nino), Richard Kerr
(pop singer).

FRANCIS (1949)
    Director: Arthur Lubin
Donald O'Connor (Peter Stirling), Chill
Wills (voice of Francis), Patricia Me-
dina (Maureen Gelder), Zasu Pitts
(Valerie Humpert), Eduard Franz (Col.
Plepper), John McIntire (Gen. Stevens),
Robert Warwick (Col. Carmichaels),
Mikel Conrad (Major Garber), Frank
Faylen (Sgt. Chillingacker), Tony Cur-
tis (Captain Jones), Charles Meredith
(Banker Monroe), Ray Collins (Col.
Hooker), James Todd (Col. Saunders),
Duke York (Sgt. Poor), Howland Cham-
berlin (Major Nadel), Loren Tindall
(Major Richards), Harry Harvey, How-
ard Negley, Peter Prouse (correspond-
ents), Robert Anderson (Capt. Grant),
Jack Shutter (Sgt. Miller), Tom Graham
(Lt. Gremm), Al Ferguson (Capt. Dunn),
Mickey McCardle (Capt. Addison), Jim
Hayward (Capt. Norman), Joseph Kim
(Japanese Lieutenant), Harold Fong
(Japanese soldier), Judd Holdren, Ro-
bert Blint (ambulance men), Marvin
Kaplan (1st M. C. Lt.).

FRANCIS COVERS THE BIG TOWN
    (1953)
    Director: Arthur Lubin
Donald O'Connor (Peter Stirling), Chill
Wills (voice of Francis), Gene Lockhart
(Tom Henderson), Nancy Guild (Alberta
Ames), Larry Gates (Dan Austin), Gale
Gordon (Evans), William Harrigan (Chief
Hansen), Forrest Lewis (Judge Stanley),
Yvette Dugay (Maria Scola), Silvio Min-
ciotti (Salvatore Scola), Hanley Stafford
(Dr. Goodrich), Lowell Gilmore (Gar-
net), Michael Ross (Parker), Charles
J. Flynn (Jones), Louis Mason (Mason).

FRANCIS GOES TO THE RACES (1951)
    Director: Arthur Lubin
Donald O'Connor (Peter Stirling), Chill

Wills (voice of Francis), Piper Laurie
(Frances Travers), Cecil Kellaway
(Col. Travers), Jesse White (Frank
Damer), Barry Kelley (Mallory),
Vaughn Taylor (Harrington), Hayden
Rorke (Rogers), Peter Brocco (Dr.
Marberry), Don Beddoe (Dr. Quimby),
Charles Meredith (Banker Monroe),
Dick Wessel (Chuck), Kenneth Mac-
Donald (steward), Larry Keating (head
steward), Ed Max (1st mug), Jack
Wilson (2nd mug), George Webster
(jockey), Bill Walder (Sam), Bernard
Szold (proprietor), Nolan Leary (dri-
ver), Peter Chong (Wong), Ewing
Mitchell (Smith), William Gould (Sher-
iff), Sam Flint (Jones), Mike Pat Don-
ovan (guard), Willard Waterman (exer-
ciser).

FRANCIS GOES TO WEST POINT (1952)
    Director: Arthur Lubin
Donald O'Connor (Peter Stirling), Chill
Wills (voice of Francis), Lori Nelson
(Barbara Atwood), William Reynolds
(Wilbur Van Allen), James Best (Cor-
poral Ransom), Les Tremayne (Col.
Daniels), David Janssen (Corporal
Thomas), Gregg Palmer (William Nor-
ton), Alice Kelly (Cynthia Daniels),
Otto Hulett (Chad Chadwick), Leonard
Nimoy (football player).

FRANCIS IN THE HAUNTED HOUSE
    (1956)
    Director: Charles Lamont
Mickey Rooney (David Prescott), Paul
Frees (voice of Francis), Virginia
Welles (Lorna), Paul Cavanagh (Neil
Frazer), David Janssen (Lt. Hopkins),
Richard Deacon (Jason), Ralph Dumke
(Mayor Hargrove), James Flavin (Chief
Martin), Charles Horvath (Malcolm),
Timothy Carey (Hugo), Mary Ellen
Kay (Lorna Ann), Richard Gaines
(District Attorney Reynolds), Helen
Wallace (Mrs. MacPherson), Edward
Earle (Howard Grisby), Dick Winslow
(Sgt. Arnold), John Maxwell (Edward
Ryan).

FRANCIS IN THE NAVY (1955)
    Director: Arthur Lubin
Donald O'Connor (Peter Stirling/Slicker
Donovan), Chill Wills (voice of Francis),
Martha Hyer (Betsy Donevan), Richard
Erdman (Murph), Jim Backus (Cmdr.
Hutch), Paul Burke (Tate), David Jans-
sen (Lt. Anders), Clint Eastwood
(Jonesy), Leigh Snowden (Appleby),
Martin Milner (Rick), Virginia O'Brien
(Nurse Kittridge), Myrna Hansen
(Helen), Betty Jane Howarth (Standish),

Phil Garris (Stover), Kenneth Mac-Donald (policeman).

FRANCIS JOINS THE WACS (1954)
Director: Arthur Lubin
Donald O'Connor (Peter Stirling), Chill Wills (voice of Francis/Gen Kaye), Julia Adams (Capt. Parker), Lynn Bari (Major Simpson), Allison Hayes (Lt. Dickson), Zasu Pitts (Lt. Humpert), Mamie Van Doren (Bunky), Mara Corday (Kate), Karen Kadler (Marge), Joan Shawlee (Sgt. Kipp), Elsa Homes (Bessie), Patti McKaye (Lt. Burke), Anthony Radecki (General's aide), Sam Woody (blue soldier), Richard Deems (jeep driver).

FRANKENSTEIN (1910)
Director: J. Searle Dawley
Charles Ogle (the monster), Augustus Phillips (Dr. Frankenstein), Mary Fuller (the sweetheart).

FRANKENSTEIN (1931)
Director: James Whale
Boris Karloff (the Monster), Colin Clive (Dr. Henry Frankenstein), Mae Clarke (Elizabeth), Frederick Kerr (Baron Frankenstein), Edward Van Sloan (Dr. Waldman), John Boles (Victor Morris), Dwight Frye (Fritz), Lionel Belmore (Vogel, the Burgomeister), Michael Mark (Ludwig, the peasant father), Forrester Harvey (Hans, the woodsman), Marilyn Harris (Maria), Francis Ford (wounded villager on hill), Arletta Duncan, Pauline Moore (bridesmaids), Mary Sherman.

FRANKENSTEIN (TVM-1973) - 1-16-73 & 1-17-73)
Director: Glenn Jordan
Robert Foxworth (Dr. Henry Frankenstein), Bo Svenson (the Monster), Susan Strasberg (Elizabeth Lavenza), Robert Gentry (Henry Clerval), Philip Bourneuf (Alphonse Frankenstein), John Karlen (Otto Roget), Heidi Vaughn (Agatha De-Lacey), William Hansen (Prof. Waldman), Willie Aames (William Frankenstein), George Morgan (Hugo), Brian Avery (Felix), Maliala Saint Duval (Safie), Rosella Olson (Bride of the Monster).

FRANKENSTEIN AND THE MONSTER FROM HELL (1974)
Director: Terence Fisher
Shane Briant (Dr. Simon Helder), Charles Lloyd-Pack (Prof. Durendel), Bernard Lee (Tarmud), Madeline Smith (Sarah), David Prowse (the Monster), Sydney Bromley (Muller), John Stratton (the asylum director), Patrick Troughton (body

snatcher).

FRANKENSTEIN CONQUERS THE WORLD (1964-Jap./U.S.) (A.K.A. "Furankenshutain tai Baragon", "Frankenstein vs. the Giant Devil Fish")
Director: Inoshiro Honda
Nick Adams (Dr. James Bowen), Kumi Mizuno (doctor), Tadao Takashima (scientist), Takashi Shimura, Toshio Tsuchiya.

FRANKENSTEIN CREATED WOMAN (1966)
Director: Terence Fisher
Peter Cushing (Baron Frankenstein), Susan Denberg (Christina), Thorley Walters (Dr. Hertz), Robert Morris (Hans), Barry Warren (Karl), Peter Blythe (Anton), Duncan Lamont (Han's father), Derek Fowlds (Johann), Peter Madden (Police Chief), Philip Ray (Mayor), Alan MacNaughtan (Kleve), Colin Jeavons (priest), Alec Mango (spokesman), Ivan Beavis (new landlord), Kevin Flood (jailer), Bartlett Mullins (bystander), John Maxim (police sergeant), Stuart Middleton (Hans as a boy).

FRANKENSTEIN - ITALIAN STYLE (1976-Ital.)
Director: Armando Crispino
Gianrico Tedeschi (Prof. Frankenstein), Aldo Maccione (the Monster), Ninetto Davoli (Igor), Jenny Tamburi.

FRANKENSTEIN MEETS THE SPACE-MONSTER (1965)
Director: Robert Gaffney
Robert Reilley (Col. Frank Saunders/Astrobot), James Karen (Dr. Adam Steele), Nancy Marshall (Karen Grant), Marilyn Hanold (Princess Marcuzan), Lou Cutell (Nadir), David Kerman (Gen. Bowers).

FRANKENSTEIN MEETS THE WOLF-MAN (1943)
Director: Roy William Neill
Lon Chaney, Jr. (Lawrence Talbot), Bela Lugosi (the Frankenstein Monster), Patric Knowles (Dr. Frank Mannering), Ilona Massey (Elsa Frankenstein), Dennis Hoey (Insp. Owen), Maria Ouspenskaya (Maleva), Lionel Atwill (Mayor of Vasaria), Dwight Frye (Rudi), Rex Evans (Vazec), Harry Stubbs (Bruno), Don Barclay (Francis), Adia Kuynetzoff, Beatrice Roberts (villagers), Doris Lloyd (hospital nurse), Martha Vickers (little girl), Eddie Parker

(stuntman), Jeff Corey, Torben
Meyer.

FRANKENSTEIN MUST BE DESTROY-
ED (1969)
    Director: Terence Fisher
Peter Cushing (Baron Frankenstein),
Simon Ward (Karl Holst), Veronica
Carlson (Anna), Thorley Walters (In-
pector Frisch), Freddie Jones (Dr.
Richter), Maxine Audley (Ella Brandt),
George Pravda (Dr. Brandt), Derek
Fowlds (Johann), Geoffrey Bayldon
(police doctor), Colette O'Neal (mad
woman), Harold Goodwin (burglar),
Frank Middlemass (third guest).

FRANKENSTEIN 1970 (1958)
    Director: Howard W. Koch
Boris Karloff (Victor von Frankenstein),
Tom Duggan (Mike Shaw), Jana Lund
(Carolyn Hayes), Donald Barry (Doug-
las Row), Irwin Berke (Insp. Raab),
Rudolph Anders (Wilhelm Gottfried),
Charlotte Austin (Judy Stevens), John
Dennis (Morgan Healey), Norbert Schil-
ler (Shuter), Mike Lane (Hans).

FRANKENSTEIN 1980 (1972-Ital.)
    (A.K.A. "Mosaic - Frankenstein
    1980")
    Director: Mario Mancini
John Richardson, Renato Romano, Ziro
Papas, Gordon Mitchell.

FRANKENSTEIN'S BLOODY TERROR
    (1968-Span.) (A.K.A. "La Marca
    del Hombre Lobo", "The Mark of
    the Wolf Man")
    Director: Enrique L. Equiluz
Paul Naschy (Count Waldemar Danin-
sky), Diana Zurakowska (Countess
Janice), Julian Ugarte (Dr. Mikelhov),
Michael Manza (Rudolph), Rossanna
Yanni (Wandessa), Joseph Morton/Jose
Nieto, Carl Casara/Carlos Casaravilla,
Anita Avery/Aurura De Alba, Gilbert
Granger/Gualberto Galban.

FRANKENSTEIN'S DAUGHTER (1958)
    Director: Richard Cunha
John Ashley (Johnny Bruder), Donald
Murphy (Oliver Frank), Sandra Knight
(Trudy Morton), Sally Tood (Suzie Law-
lor), Felix Locher (Carter Morton),
Harold Lloyd, Jr. (Don), Wolfe Bar-
zell (Elser), John Zaremba, George
Barrows, Robert Dix, Harry Wilson,
Charlotte Portney, Voltaire Perkins,
Bill Coontz.

FRANKENSTEIN'S ISLAND (1982)
    Director: Jerry Warren

John Carradine, Cameron Mitchell,
Robert Clarke.

FRANKENSTEIN: THE TRUE STORY
    (TVM-1973) - 11-30-73 & 12-1-73
    Director: Jack Smight
Leonard Whiting (Dr. Victor Franken-
stein), Michael Sarrazin (the Creature),
David McCallum (Dr. Henry Clervel),
James Mason (Dr. Polidori), Nicola
Pagett (Elizabeth Fanshawe), Jane
Seymour (Agatha/Prima), Michael
Wiling (Sir Richard Fanshawe), Agnes
Moorehead (Mrs. Blair), Margaret
Leighton (Francoise DuVal), Sir Ralph
Richardson (Mr. Lacey), Sir John
Gielgud (Chief Constable), Tom Baker
(Sea Captain), Clarissa Kaye (Lady
Fanshawe), Dallas Adams (Felix),
Arnold Diamond (passenger in coach),
Julian Barnes (young man), Yootha
Joyce, Peter Sallis.

FRANKENSTEIN, THE VAMPIRE AND
    CO. (1961) (Mex.) (A.K.A. "Frank-
    estein, el Vampiro y Cia")
    Director: Benito Alazraki
Manuel 'Loco' Valdes, Martha Elena
Cervantes, Robert G. Rivera, Joaquin
Garcia Vargas, Nora Veyran, Jose
Jasso, Quintin Bulnes, Arthur Castro.

FREAKS (1932)
    Director: Tod Browning
Olga Baclanova (Cleopatra), Harry
Earles (Hans), Henry Victor (Hercules),
Leila Hyams (Venus), Roscoe Ates
(Roscoe), Daisy Earles (Freida), Rose
Dione (Mme. Tetrallini), Wallace Ford
(Phroso, the clown), Daisy and Violet
Hilton (siamese twins), Edward Bro-
phy, Matt McHugh (Rollo brothers),
Angelo Rossito (Angelino), Ernie
Adams (sideshow patron), Elvire
Snow (Zip, the Pin-Head), Jennie Lee
Snow (Pip, the Pin-Head), Schlitze
(Pin-Head), Koo Koo (the Bird Girl),
Josephine Joseph (Half-man/Half-wo-
man), Frances O'Connor (the Living
Venus De Milo), Elizabeth Green (the
Human Stork), Prince Randian (the
Living Torso), Peter Robinson (the
Human Skeleton), Michael Visaroff
(Jean, the caretaker), Johnny Eck
(Half-boy), Martha Morris (Armless
woman), Olga Roderick (Bearded
Lady), Albert Conti (Monsieur Duval),
Louise Beavers (maid).

FREAKY FRIDAY (1977)
    Director: Gary Nelson
Barbara Harris (Ellen Andrews),
Jodie Foster (Annabel Andrews), John

Astin (Bill Andrews), Patsy Kelly (Mrs. Schmauss), Dick Van Patten (Harold Jennings), Sorrell Booke (Mr. Dilk), Kaye Ballard (Coach Betsy), Alan Oppenheimer (Mr. Joffert), Ruth Buzzi (opposing coach), Marc McClure (Boris Harris), Marie Windsor (Mrs. Murphy), Charlene Tilton (Bambi), Fritz Feld (Jackman), Laurie Main (Mills), Iris Adrian (Bus passenger), Ricki Schreck (Virginia), Ceil Cabot (Miss McGuirk), Karen Smith (Mary Kay Gilbert), Sparky Marcus (Ben Andrews), Brooke Mills (Mrs. Gibbons), Marvin Daplan (carpet cleaner), Al Molinaro (drapery man), Shelly Juttner (Hilary), Jack Sheldon (Lloyd), Lori Rutherford (Jo-Jo), Barbara Walden (Mrs. Benson), Don Carter (delivery boy), Dermott Downs (Harvey Manager), Fuddle Bagley (bus driver), Jimmy Van Patten (cashier).

FREE FOR ALL (1949)
Director: Charles T. Barton
Robert Cummings (Christopher Parker), Ann Blythe (Alva Abbott), Percy Kilbride (Mr. Abbott), Ray Kollins (Mr. Blair), Percy Helton (Mr. Hershey), Lester Matthews (Mr. Alberson), Frank Ferguson (Hap Ross), Mikhail Rasumny (Dr. Torgelson), Harry Antrim (Mr. Whiting), Donald Woods (Roger Abernathy), Wallis Clark (Mr. Van Alstyne), Dooley Wilson (Aristotle), Willard Waterman (Commander), Kenneth Tobey (pilot), Russell Simpson (farmer), Bill Walker (Herbert), Harris Brown (Colonel), Murray Alper (McGuiness).

FRENZY (1946)
Director: Vernon Sewell
Derrick DeMarney, Frederick Valk, Joan Greenwood.

FRENZY (1972)
Director: Alfred Hitchcock
Jon Finch (Richard Blaney), Barry Foster (Robert Rusk), Barbara Leigh-Hunt (Brenda Blaney), Anna Massey (Babs Milligan), Alec McCowen (Chief Insp. Oxford), Vivian Merchant (Mrs. Oxford), Bernard Cribbins (Felix Forsythe), Billie Whitelaw (Hetty Porter), Michael Bates (Sgt. Spearman), Jean Marsh (Monica Barling), Clive Swift (Johnny Porter), Rita Webb (Bob's mother), Jimmy Gardner (hall porter), Elsie Randolph (porter's wife), George Tovey (Mr. Salt), Madge Ryan (Mrs. Davison), John Boxer (Sir George), June Ellis (barmaid), Bunny May (barman), Gearld Sim, Noel Johnson, (pub customers), Robert Keegan (hospital patient).

FRIDAYS OF ETERNITY, THE (1981-Arg.) (A. K. A. "Los Viernes de la Eternidad")
Director: Hector Olivera
Thelma Biral (Delfina), Hector Alterio (Gervasio), Susan Campos (Paula), Silvia Kutika (Zulema), Nora Cullen (Gaspara), Estaban Orloff (Juan Ciricaco).

FRIDAY THE 13th (1944-Ger.) (A. K. A. "Freitag, der 13")
Director: Erich Engels
Fritz Kampers, Angelika Hauff, Rudolf Fernau, Fita Benkhoff.

FRIDAY THE 13th (1980)
Director: Sean S. Cunningham
Adrienne King (Alice), Betsy Palmer (Mrs. Voorhees), Kevin Bacon (Jack), Peter Brouwer (Steve Christy), Laurie Bartram (Brenda), Jeannie Taylor (Marcie), Harry Crosby (Bill), Mark Nelson (Ned), Ari Lehman (Jason), Robbie Morgan (Annie), Walt Gorney (Crazy Ralph), Ron Millkie (Officer Dorf), Ronn Carroll (Sgt. Tierney), Debra S. Hayes (Claudette), Sally Anne Golden (Sandy), Dorothy Kobs (Trudy), Willie Adams (Barry), Rex Everhart (truck driver), Ken L. Parker (doctor), Mary Rocco (operator).

FRIDAY THE 13th - PART TWO (1981)
Director: Steve Miner
Amy Steel (Ginny), John Furey (Paul), Lauren-Marie Taylor (Vickie), Tom McBride (Mark), Warrington Gillette (Jason), Adrienne King (Alice), Bill Randolph (Jeff), Walt Gorney (Crazy Ralph), Betsy Palmer (Mrs. Voorhees), Stu Charno (Ted), Marta Kober (Sandra), Kirsten Baker (Terry), Russell Todd (Scott), Lauren-Marie Taylor (Vickie).

FRIDAY THE 13th - PART THREE (1982)
Director: Steve Miner
Dana Kimmell (Chris), Richard Brooker (Jason), Catherine Parks (Vera), Paul Kratka (Rick), Jeff Rogers (Andy), Larry Zerner (Shelly), Tracie Savage (Debbie), Rachel Howard (Chili), David Katims (Chuck), Nick Savage (Ali), Gloria Charles (Fox), Kevin O'Brien (Loco).

FRIDAY THE 13th - THE ORPHAN (1979)
Director: John Ballard
Peggy Feury (Aunt Martha), Mark

Ownens (David), Joanna Miles (David's mother), Donn Whyte (David's father), Eleanor Stewart (Mary), Afolabi Ajayi (Akin), Stanley Church (Dr. Thompson), David Foreman (Percy Ford), Jane House (Jean Ford).

FRIGHT (1957)
    Director: W. Lee Wilder
Nancy Malone (Ann Summers), Eric Fleming (Dr. Hamilton), Frank Marth (Morley), Humphrey Davis (Prof. Gore), Dean L. Almquist (Cullen), Elizabeth Watts (Lady Olive), Amelia Conley (Miss Ames), Walter Klaven (warden), Ned Glass (taxi driver), Norman Burton (reporter), Tom Reynolds (city editor), Robert Gardett (managing editor), Norman MacKaye, Don Douglas (inspectors), Philip Kenneally (policeman), Sid Raymond (van driver), Chris Bohn (TV announcer), Alney Alba (lady in restaurant).

FRIGHT (1971)
    Director: Peter Collinson
Susan George (Amanda), Ian Bannen (Brian), Honor Blackman (Helen Lloyd), John Gregson (Dr. Cordell), George Cole (Jim), Denis Waterman (Chris), Tara Collinson (Tara Lloyd), Maurice Kaufman (Police Inspector), Michael Brennan (Police Sergeant), Roger Lloyd Pack (Constable).

FRIGHTMARE (1975)
    Director: Peter Walker
Rupert Davies (Edmund), Shelia Keith (Dorothy), Deborah Fairfax (Jackie), Paul Greenwood (Graham), Leo Genn (Dr. Lytell), Kim Butcher (Debbie), Fiona Curzon (Merle), Jon Yule (Robin), Pamela Farbrother (Delia), Tricia Mortimer (Lilian), Edward Kalinski (Alec), Victor Winding (Detective Inspector), Noel Johnson (Judge), Anthony Hennessy (Sergeant), Michael Sharvell-Martin (barman), Tommy Wright (nightclub manager), Nicholas John (Pete), Andrew Sachs (Barry), Gerald Flood (Matthew), John Dagmar (old man).

FROGS (1971)
    Director: George McCowan
Ray Milland (Jason Crockett), Sam Elliott (Pickett Smith), Joan Van Ark (Karen Crokett), Adam Roarke (Clint Crokett), Lyn Borden (Jenny Crokett), Jucy Pace (Bella Berenson), Nicholas Cortland (Kenneth Wooster), David Gilliam (Michael Wooster), George Skaff (Stuart Wooster), Holly Irving

(Iris Crockett Wooster), Mae Mercer (Maybelle), Lance Taylor, Sr. (Charles), Hal Hodges (Jay Crockett), Dale Willingham (Tina Crockett), Carolyn Fitzsimmons (lady in car), Robert Saunders (boy in car).

FROM BEYOND THE GRAVE (1973)
    (A. K. A. "Tales from Beyond the Grave", "Creatures from Beyond the Grave")
    Director: Kevin Connor
Ian Bannen (Lowe), Ian Carmichael (Reggie), Peter Cushing (the Proprietor), Donald Pleasence (Underwood), Diana Dors (Mable), Margaret Leighton (Madame Orloff), Nyree Dawn Porter (Susan), David Warner (Edward), Jack Watson (Sir Michael), Angelica Pleasence (Emily), Ian Ogilvy (William Seaton), Lesley Anne Down (Rosemary Seaton), Wendy Allnutt (Pamela), Tommy Godfrey (Mr. Jefferies), John O'Farrell (Stephen), Ben Howard (Paul Briggs), Rosalind Ayres (the prostitute), Marcel Steiner (the Face).

FROM HELL IT CAME (1957)
    Director: Dan Miller
Tod Andrews (Dr. William Arnold), Tina Carver (Dr. Terry Mason), Gregg Palmer (Kimo), John McNamara (Prof. Clark), Linda Watkins (Mrs. Kilgore), Suzanne Ridgway (Korey), Baynes Barron (Chief Maranka), Robert Swan (Tano, the Witch-Doctor), Mark Sheeler (Eddie), Lee Rhodes (Norgu), Grace Matthews (Orchid), Tani Marsh (Naomi), Chester Hayes (Maku), Lenmana Guerin (Dori).

FROM RUSSIA WITH LOVE (1964)
    Director: Terence Young
Sean Connery (James Bond), Daniela Bianchi (Tatiana Romanova), Pedro Armendariz (Kerim Bey), Lotte Lenya (Rosa Klebb), Robert Shaw (Red Grant), Euince Gayson (Sylvia), Bernard Lee (M), Lois Maxwell (Miss Moneypenny), Walter Gotell (Morzeny), Francis de Wolff (Vavra), Nadja Regin (Kerim's girl), Aliza Gur (Vida), Vladek Sheybal (Kronsteen), Peter Bayliss (Benz), Peter Madden (McAdams), Desmond Llewelyn (Boothroyd), Fred Haggarty (Krilencu), Martine Beswicke (Zora), George Pastell (train conductor), Neville Jason (Rolls chauffeur), Peter Brayham (Rhoda), Leila (belly dancer), Jan Williams (masseuse), Mushet Auzer (Mehmet), Hasan Ceylan (foreign agent).

FROM THE EARTH TO THE MOON (1958)
Director: Byron Haskin
Joseph Cotten (Joseph Barbicane), George Sanders (Stuyvesant Nicholl), Debra Paget (Virginia Nicholl), Don Dubbins (Ben Sharpe), Patric Knowles (Cartier), Ludwig Stossel (Von Metz), Melville Cooper (Bancroft), Henry Daniell (Morgana), Morris Ankrum (Gen. Ulysses S. Grant), Carl Esmond (Jules Verne).

FROM THE ORIENT WITH FURY (1965-Ital./Span./Fr.) (A.K.A. "Agente 077, dell Oriente con Furore")
Director: Sergio Grieco
Ken Clark, Margaret Lee, Fabienne Dali, Philippe Hersent, Vittorio Sanipoli.

FROZEN ALIVE (1964-Brit./Ger.) (A.K.A. "Der Fall X701")
Director: Bernard Knowles
Mark Stevens (Frank), Marianne Koch (Helen), Delphi Lawrence (Joan), Walter Rilla (Sir Keith), Joachim Hansen (Tony), Wolfgang Lukschy (Insp. Prentow), John Longden (Prof. Hubbard), Sigurd Lohde (Dr. Merkheirmer), Helmuth Weiss (Chairman), Albert Bessler (Martin), Wolfgang Gunter (Sgt. Grun).

FROZEN DEAD, THE (1966)
Director: Herbert J. Leder
Dana Andrews (Dr. Norberg), Anna Palk (Jean Norberg), Philip Gilbert (Dr. Ted Roberts), Kathleen Breck (Elsa Tenney), Karel Stepanek (Gen. Luback), Basil Benson (Capt. Tirpitz), Alan Tilvern (Karl Essen), Oliver MacGreevy (Joseph), Ann Tirard (Mrs. Schmidt), Tom Chatto (Insp. Witt), Edward Fox (Prisoner No. 3), John Moore (Station master), Charles Wade (porter).

FROZEN GHOST, THE (1945)
Director: Harold Young
Lon Chaney, Jr. (Alex Gregor), Evelyn Ankers (Maura Daniel), Tala Birell (Mme. Monet), Martin Kosleck (Rudi Poldan), Elena Verdugo (Nina Coudreau), Milburn Stone (George Keene), Douglas Dumbrille (Insp. Brant), Arthur Hohl (drunk contestant).

FROZEN SCREAM (1980)
Director: Frank Roach
Renee Harmon, Thomas Gowan, Lee James, Sunny Bartholomew.

FUGITIVE FROM THE EMPIRE (TVM-1981) (A.K.A. "The Archer") - 4-12-81
Director: Nicholas Corea
Lane Caudell (Toran), Kabir Bedi (Gar the Draikian), Belinda Bauer (Estra), George Kennedy (Brakus), Victor Campos (Slash), Marc Alaimo (Sandros), Richard Dix (Rak), Tony Schwartz (Riis), George Innes (Mak), Robert Feero (Captain Rio), Andrew Bloch (Rega), Ivan J. Rado (Bors), Sharon Barris (Madras, the Horse Chief), Fred Pinkard (merchant), Larry Douglas (Lazar-Sa), Richard Moll (the Bovum Ferryman), Dee Croxton (woman scholar), Chao-Li Chi (astrologer), Ivan Sarik, Skip Riley (Draikean troopers), Pricilla Pointer, John Hancock, Allan Rich.

FULL MOON HIGH (1981)
Director: Larry Cohen
Adam Arkin, Alan Arkin, Ed McMahon, Roz Kelly, Kenneth Mars, Demond Wilson, Louis Nye, Elizabeth Hartman, Bill Kirchenbauter.

FUNHOUSE (1981)
Director: Tobe Hooper
Elizabeth Berridge (Amy), Kevin Conway (the Barker), Sylvia Miles (Madame Zena), Cooper Huckabee (Buzz), William Finley (Marco the Great), Wayne Doba (the Creature), Largo Woodruff (Liz), Miles Chapin (Richie), Shawn Carson (Joey Harper), Jack McDermott (Mr. Harper), Jeane Austin (Mrs. Harper), Ralph Marino (truck driver), David Carson (Geek), Sonia Zomina (bag lady).

FURTHER MYSTERIES OF DR. FU MANCHU (1924) - series in 3 parts
Segments: 1. "The Coughing Horror", 2. "The Golden Pomegranates", & 3. "The Cragmire Tower".
Director: Fred Paul
Harry Agar Lyons (Dr. Fu Manchu), Fred Paul, Humbertson Wright, Dorinea Shirley, George Foley, Johnny Butt, Harry Rignold, Fred Morgan, Julie Suedo.

FURY, THE (1977)
Director: Brian de Palma
Kirk Douglas (Peter Sanza), John Cassavetes (Childress), Amy Irving (Gillian Bellaver), Carrie Snodgress (Hester), Andrew Stevens (Robin Sandza), Fiona Lewis (Susan Charles), Charles Durning (Dr. Jim McKeever), Melody Thomas (LaRue), Carol Rossen

(Dr. Ellen Lindstrom), William Finley
(Raymond), Hilary Thompson (Cheryl),
Rutanya Alda (Kristen), Joyce Easton
(Mrs. Bellaver), Sam Laws (Black-
fish), Alice Nunn (Mrs. Callahan),
Jane Lambert (Vivian Nuckells), Gor-
don Jump (Mr. Nuckells), Patrick
Billingsley (Lander), J. P. Bumstead
(Greene), J. Patrick McNamara (Ro-
bertson).

FURY OF HERCULES, THE (1961-
    Ital./Fr.) (A.K.A. "La Furia di
    Ercole")
    Director: Gianfranco Parolini
Brad Harris, Alan Steel, Brigitte
Corey.

FURY OF THE CONGO (1950)
    Director: William Berke
Johnny Weismuller (Jungle Jim),
Sherry Moreland (Leta), Lyle Talbot
(Grant), William Henry (Ronald Cam-
eron), Joel Friedkin (Prof. Dunham),
Paul Marion (Raadi), George Eldredge
(Barnes), Rusty Westcoatt (Magruder),
Blanca Vischer (Mahara).

FURY OF THE WOLFMAN, THE (1970-
    Span.) (A.K.A. "La Furia del Hom-
    bre Lobo")
    Director: Jose Maria Zabalza
Paul Nazchy (Waldemar Daninsky),
Perla Cristal, Veronica Lujan.

FUTURE COP (TVM-1976) - 5-1-76
    Director: Jud Taylor
Ernest Borgnine (Joe Cleaver), John
Amos (Bill Bundy), Michael Shannon
(John Haven), John Larch (Forman),
Shirley O'Hara (grandmother), Herbert
Nelson (Klausmeier), James Luisi (Pa-
terno), Ronnie Clair Edward (Avery),
Stephen Pearlman (Dorfman), James
Daughton (young rookie).

FUTURE WORLD (1976)
    Director: Richard T. Heffron
Peter Fonda (Chuck Browning), Blythe
Danner (Tracy Ballard), Arthur Hill
(Duffy), Yul Brynner (the Gunslinger),
John Ryan (Schneider), Stuart Margolin
(Harry), Jim Antonio (Ron), Robert
Cornthwaite (Mr. Reed), Angela Greene
(Mrs. Reed), Nancy Bell (Erica), John
Fujioka (Mr. Takaguchi), Dana Lee
(Mr. Takaguchi's aide), Darrell Larson
(Eric), Burt Conroy (Gen. Karnovski),
Dorothy Konrad (Mrs. Karnovski), Alex
Rodine (KGB man), Allen Ludden (game
show MC), Joanna Hall (maiden fair),
Judson Pratt (bartender).

GABRIEL OVER THE WHITE HOUSE
    (1933)
    Director: Gregory LaCava
Walter Huston (Judson Hammond),
Karen Morley (Pendola Molloy), Fran-
chot Tone (Hartley Beekman), Arthur
Byron (Jasper Brooks), C. Henry
Gordon (Nick Diamond), Dickie Moore
(Jimmy Vetter), Samuel Hinds (Dr.
Eastman), Jean Parker (Alice Bron-
son), David Landau (John Bronson),
William Pawley (Borell), Claire Du-
brey (nurse).

GALAXINA (1980)
    Director: William Sachs
Dorothy R. Stratten (Galaxina), Avery
Schreiber (Captain Butt), Stephen Macht
(Thor), James David Hinton (Buzz),
Ronald Knight (Odric), Tad Horino
(Sam Wo), Lionel Smith (Maurice),
Angelo Rossitto (Monster from Egg),
Fred D. Scott (Commander), Nancy
McCauley (Elexia), George E. Mather
(Horn Man), Heather O'Connell (little
girl), Bartine Zane (little old lady),
Mike Castle (red skin man), Susan
Kiger (blue girl), Marilyn Joe (winger
girl), Hugh Warden (Earthman), David
A. Cox (Mr. Spot bartender), Pete
Schrum (biker guard), Stephen Morrell
(Chopper), Dee Cooper (Gen. Custer),
Rhonda Shear (Mime), Herb Kaplowitz
(Rock Eater/Kitty/Ugly Alien woman),
John Sistrunk (stuntman biker).

GALAXY OF TERROR (1981) (A.K.A.
    "Mindwarp: An Infinity of Terror",
    "Planet of Horror")
    Director: B.D. Clark
Edward Albert (Cabren), Erin Moran
(Alluma), Ray Walston (Kore), Zalman
King (Baelon), Bernard Behrens (Ilvar),
Sid Haig (Quuhod), Grace Zabriskie
(Capt. Trantor), Robert Englund (Ran-
ger), Taaffee O'Connell (Damelia),
Jack Blessing (Cos), Mary Ellen O'Neill
(Mitre).

GAME OF DEATH, A (1945)
    Director: Robert Wise
John Loder (Rainsford), Audrey Long
(Ellen), Edgar Barrier (Kreiger), Russell Wade (Robert), Russell Hicks (Whitney), Jason Robards (Captain), Noble
Johnson (Carib), Robert Clarke (Helmsman), Gene Roth (Pleshke).

GAMERA VS. MONSTER X (1970) (A.K.A.
    "Gamera vs. Jiger", "Gamera tai
    Daimaju Jaiga")
    Director: Noriaki Yuasa
Tsutomu Takakuwa, Kelly Varis, Kon

Omura, Katherine Murphy, Junko Yashiro.

GAMERA VS. ZIGRA (1971-Jap.)
(A.K.A. "Gamera tai Shinkai Kaiju Jigura")
Director: Noriaki Yuasa
Ken Utsui, Yusuke Kawazu, Kayo Matsuo.

GAMES (1967)
Director: Curtis Harrington
Simone Signoret (Lisa Schindler), James Caan (Paul Montgomery), Katharine Ross (Jennifer Montgomery), Don Stroud (Norman Fields), Kent Smith (Harry), Estelle Winwood (Miss Beattie), Ian Wolfe (Dr. Edwards), Marjorie Bennett (Nora), Peter Brocco (Count), Anthony Eustrel (Winthrop), George Furth (Terry), Florence Marley (Baroness), Eloise Hardt (Celia), Carmen Phillips (Holly), Carl Guttenberger (Arthur), Richard Guizon (massuer), Stuart Nisbet (Detective), Pitt Herbert (pharmacist), Kendrick Huxham (bookseller).

GAMMA PEOPLE, THE (1955)
Director: John Gilling
Paul Douglas (Mike Wilson), Eva Bartok (Paula Wendt), Leslie Phillips (Howard Meade), Walter Rilla (Boronski), Martin Miller (Lochner), Philip Leaver (Koerner), Rosalie Crutchley (Frau Bikstein), Olaf Pooley (Bikstein), Jackie Lane (Anna), Paul Hardtmuth (Hans), Pauline Drewett (Hedda), Michael Caridia (Hugo), Cyril Chamberlain (Graf),, Leonard Sachs (telegraph clerk), St. John Stuart (1st goon).

GAMMERA THE INVINCIBLE (1966-Jap.) (A.K.A. "Daikaiji Gamera")
Director: Noriaki Yuasa
Brian Donlevy (Gen. Terry Arnold), Albert Dekker (Secretary of Defense), John Baragrey (Capt. Lovell), Dick O'Neill (Gen. O'Neill), Diane Findlay (Sgt. Susan Embers), Eiji Funakosji (Dr. Hidaka), Harumi Kititachi (Kyoko), Yoshire Uchida (Toshio), Michiko Sugata (Nobuyo), Junichiro Yamashita (Aoyagi), Yoshiro Kitahara (Sakurai), Jun Hamamura (Dr. Maurase).

GANG BUSTERS (1942) - serial in 13 episodes
Chapters: 1. "The League of Murdered Men", 2. "The Death Plunge", 3. "Murder Blockade", 4. "Hangman's Noose", 5. "Man Undercover", 6. "Under Crumbling Walls", 7. "The Water Trap",

8. "Murder by Proxy", 9. "Gang Bait", 10. "Mob Vengeance", 11. "Wanted at Headquarters", 12. "The Long Chance" & 13. "Law and Order".
Director: Ray Taylor & Noel Smith
Kent Taylor (Bill Bannister), Irene Hervey (Vicky Logan), Ralph Morgan (Prof. Morris), Robert Armstrong (Tim Nolan), Joseph Crehan (Chief O'Brien), Richard Davies (Happy Haskins), Ralf Harolde (Halliger), George Lewis (Mason), George Watts (Mayor Hansen), Victor Zimmerman (Barnard), John Gallaudet (Wilkinson), Grace Cunard.

GANJA AND HESS (1973) (A.K.A. "Blood Couple", "Double Possession")
Director: Bill Gunn
Duane Jones (Dr. Hess Green), Marlene Clark (Ganja), Bill Gunn (George), Sam Waymon (Rev. Williams), Leonard Jackson (Archie), John Hoffmeister (Jack), Mabel King (Queen of Myrthia), Candece Tarpley (girl in bar), Enrico Fales (Green's son), Tara Fields (woman with baby), Richard Harrow (dinner guest), Betty Barney (singer), Betsy Thurman (poetess), Tommy Lane (pimp).

GARDENER, THE (1974) (A.K.A. "Seeds of Evil")
Director: Jim Kay
Katherine Houghton (Ellen Bennett), Joe Dallesandro (Carl, the gardener), Rita Gam (Helene Boardman), James Congden (John Bennett), Anne Meacham, Theodorina Bello.

GARDEN MURDER CASE, THE (1936)
Director: Edwin L. Marin
Edmund Lowe (Philo Vance), Virginia Bruce (Zalia Graem), Gene Lockhart (Lowe Hammle), Benita Hume (Nurse Beeton), H.B. Warner (Major Fenwicke-Ralston), Nat Pendleton (Sgt. Heath), Kent Smith (Woode Swift), Frieda Inescort (Mrs. Fenwiche-Ralston), Henry B. Walthall (Dr. Garden), Grant Mitchell (Markham), Jessie Ralph (Mrs. Hammle), Charles Trowbridge (Insp. Colby), Douglas Walton (Floyd Garden), Etienne Girardot (Doremus).

GARDEN OF THE DEAD (1972)
Director: John Hayes
John Dennis, Duncan McCloud, Marland Proctor, Eric Stern.

GARGOYLES (TVM-1972) - 11-21-72
        Director: B. W. L. Norton
Cornel Wilde (Mercer Boley), Jennifer
Salt (Diane Boley), Bernie Casey (Head
Gargoyle), Woodrow Chambliss (Uncle
Willie), Grayson Hall (Mrs. Parks),
Scott Glenn (James Reeger), John Gru-
ber (Jesse), Tim Burns (Ray), William
Stevens (Police Chief), Jim Connell
(Buddy), Rock Walker, Greg Walker,
Mickey Alzola (Gargoyles).

GARU, THE MAD MONK (1970) (A. K. A.
        "Guru, the Mad Monk")
        Director: Andy Milligan
Neil Flanagan (Father Garu), Jacque-
line Webb (Olga), Judith Isral (Nadja),
Julia Willis, Ron Keith.

GAS-S-S-S! (1970) (A. K. A. "Gas, or
        It Became Necessary to Destroy the
        World in Order to Save It")
        Director: Roger Corman
Robert Corff (Coel), Elaine Giftos
(Cilla), Bud Cort (Hooper), Ben Ve-
reen (Carlos), Talia Coppola Shire
(Coralie), Cindy Williams (Marissa),
Alex Wilson (Jason), Pat Patterson
(Demeter), Alan Braunstein (Dr. Drake),
Jackie Farley (Ginny), George Armitage
(Billy the Kid), Lou Procopio (Marshall
McLuhan), Phil Borneo (Quant), County
Joe and the Fish (F. M. Radio).

GATES OF THE NIGHT, THE (1946-
        Fr.) (A. K. A. "Les Portes de la
        Nuit")
        Director: Marcel Carne
Yves Montand (Diego), Pierre Bras-
seur (Georges), Jean Vilar (Le Clo-
chard), Nathalie Naltier (Malou), Sat-
urnin Fabre (Monsieur Senechal),
Maddy Berry (Madame Quinquina),
Dany Robin (Etiennette), Serge Reg-
giani (Guy), Christian Simon (Cri-Cri),
Carette (Monsieur Quinquina), Sylvia
Bataille (Claire Lecuyer), Raymond
Bussieres (Raymond Lecuyer).

GAWAIN AND THE GREEN KNIGHT
        (1972) (A. K. A. "Sir Gawain and the
        Green Knight")
        Director: Stephen Weeks
Murray Head (Gawain), Nigel Green
(the Green Knight), Ciaran Madden
(Linet), Robert Hardy (Sir Bertilan),
Davil Leland (Humphrey), Anthony
Sharp (King), Ronald Lacey (Oswald),
Murray Melvin (Seneschal), Willoughby
Goddard (Knight), Tony Steedman
(Fortinbras), George Merritt (Old
Knight), Richard Hurndall (bearded
man), Peter Copley (pilgram), Pauline

Letts (Lady of Lyonesse), Geoffrey
Bayldon (Wiseman), Jerold Wells (ser-
geant), Jack Woolgar (porter), Michael
Crand (the Giant).

GEMINI MAN, THE (TVM-1976) (A. K. A.
        "Code Name: Minus One") - 5-10-76
        Director: Alan Levi
Ben Murphy (Sam Casey), Richard Dy-
sart (Dr. Leonard Driscoll), Katherine
Crawford (Dr. Abby Lawrence), Quinn
Redeker (Vince Rogers), Dana Elcar
(Dr. Harold Schyler), H. M. Wynant
(Capt. Ballard), Paul Shenar (Charles
Edward Royce), Len Wayland (Capt.
Whelan), Cheryl Miller (receptionist),
Michael Lane, Jim Raymond, Austin
Stoker, Gregory Walcott, Richard
Kennedy, Robert Forward.

GENESIS II (TVM-1973) - 3-23-73
        Director: John L. Moxey
Alex Cord (Dylan Hunt), Mariette
Hartley (Lyra-a), Ted Cassidy (Isiah),
Percy Rodriguez (Isacc Kimbridge),
Lynne Marta (Harper-Smythe), Harvey
Jason (Singh), Tito Vandis (Yuloff),
Leon Askin (Overseer), Harry Ray-
bould (Slan-u), Bill Striglos (Dr. Kel-
lum), Beulah Quo (Lu-Chan), Liam
Dunn (Janus), Linda Grant (Astrid),
Tom Pace (Brian), Ray Young (2nd
Tyranian teacher), Ed Ashley, Robert
Hathaway, David Westburg, Dennis
Young, Tammi Bula, Didi Conn, Dav-
id Westburg, Teryl Wills.

GENIE, THE (1953)
        Director: Lance Comford
Douglas Fairbanks, Jr., Yvonne Furneux,
Martin Miller.

GENII OF DARKNESS (1960-Mex.)
        (A. K. A. "Nostradamus, El Ginio
        de las Tinieblas")
        Director: Federico Curiel
German Robles (Nostradamus), Dom-
ingo Soler (Prof. Duran), Julio Aleman,
Aurora Alvarado, Rina Valdarno, Luis
Aragon, Fanny Schiller.

GENIUS AT WORK (1946)
        Director: Leslie Goodwins
Bela Lugosi (Stone), Wally Brown, Alan
Carney, Anne Jeffreys, Lionel Atwill,
Forbes Murray, Ralph Dunn, Robert
Clarke.

GHASTLY ONES, THE (1969)
        Director: Andy Milligan
Don Williams, Eileen Hayes, Carol
Vogel, Richard Ramos, Anne Linden,
Hal Borski, Fib LeBlanque, Neril

Flanders, Maggie Rogers, Hal Sherwood, Veronica Radburn.

GHIDRAH, THE THREE-HEADED
MONSTER (1965-Jap.) (A. K. A.
"Ghidorah, Sandai Kaiji Chikyu
Saidia No Kessen", "The Biggest
Fight on Earth", "The Greatest
Battle on Earth")
Director: Inoshiro Honda
Yosuke Natuski (Shindo), Yuriko
Hoshi (Naoko), Hiroshi Koizumi (Prof.
Morai), Kanji Sahara (Chief Editor
Kanamaki), Akihiko Hirata (Chief Detective (Okita), Takashi Shimura (Dr.
Tsukamotoa), Eiko Wakabayashi (Princess Salno), Hisaya Ito (Malness), Emi
& Yumi Ito (the Little Sisters).

GHOST, THE (1963-Ital.) (A. K. A.
"Lo Spettro de Dr. Hichcock", "The
Spectre")
Director: Riccardo Freda
Barbara Steele, Peter Baldwin, Harriet
White, Elio Jotta, Raoul H. Newman,
Reginald Price Anderson.

GHOST AND MR. CHICKEN, THE
(1966)
Director: Alan Rifkin
Don Knotts (Luther Heggs), Liam Redmond (Mr. Kelsey), Skip Homier (Ollie
Weaver), Dick Sargent (George Beckett),
Joan Staly (Alma Parker), Reta Shaw (Mrs. Maxwell), Lurene Tuttle (Mrs. Miller),
James Begg (Herkie), Charles Lane
(Whitlow), Harry Hickox (Art Fuller),
Jesslyn Fax (boarder), Sandra Gould
(spiritual woman), Herbie Faye (man
in cafe), J. Edward McKinley, James
Milhollin, George Chandler, Hope
Summers, Jim Boles, Robert Cornthwaite, Hal Smith, Nydia Westman,
Eddie Quillan, Ellen Corby, Cliff
Norton.

GHOST AND MRS. MUIR, THE (1947)
Director: Joseph Mankiewicz
Gene Tierney (Luck Muir), Rex Harrison (Capt. Daniel Gregg), George
Sanders (Miles Fairley), Edna Best
(Martha), Vanessa Brown (Anna), Natalie Wood (Anna as a child), Robert
Coote (Coembe), Anna Lee (Mrs. Miles
Fairley), Isobel Elsom (Angelica),
Victoria Horne (Eva), William Sterling
(Bill), Whitford Kane (Sproule), David
Thursby (Scrogglings).

GHOST AND THE GUEST, THE (1943)
Director: William Nigh
James Dunn, Florence Rice, Anthony

Caruso, Robert Bice, Mabel Todd,
Renee Carson.

GHOST BREAKER, THE (1922)
Director: Alfred Green
Wallace Reid, Lila Lee, J. Farrell
MacDonald, Arthur Carew, Snitz Edwards, Walter Hiers, Frances Raymond.

GHOST BREAKERS, THE (1940)
Director: George Marshall
Bob Hope (Larry Lawrence), Paulette
Goddard (Mary Carter), Richard Carlson (Geoff Montgomery), Willie Best
(Alex), Paul Lukas (Parada), Pedro de
Cordoba (Havez), Anthony Quinn (Ramon Mederos/Francisco Mederos), Tom
Dugan (Raspy Kelly), Paul Fix (Frenchy),
Lloyd Corrigan (Martin), Virginia Brissac (Mother Zombie), Noble Johnson
(Zombie), James Flavin (hotel porter),
Douglas Kennedy, Robert Ryan (interns),
Robert Elliott (Lt. Murray), Paul Newlan (baggage man), Emmett Vogan (announcer), Kay Stewart (telephone girl),
Jack Hatfield (elevator boy), Grace
Hayle (screaming woman), James Blaine
(police sergeant), David Durand (bellhop),
Jack Edwards (ship Bellboy), Francis
Maran (headwaiter), Max Wagner (ship
porter), Blanca Vischer (Dolores), Leonard Sues (newsboy), Jack Norton (drunk).

GHOST CATCHERS (1944)
Director: Edward F. Cline
Ole Olsen (Olsen), Chic Johnson (Johnson), Gloria Jean (Melinda), Martha
O'Driscoll (Susanna), Leo Carrillo
(Jerry), Andy Devine (Bear), Lon
Chaney, Jr. (Horsehead), Kirby Grant
(Clay), Ella Mae Morse (Virginia), Walter Catlett (Colonel), Henry Armetta
(Italian), Tor Johnson, Walter Kingsford, Tom Dugan, Wee Willie, Ralph
Peters, Bess Flowers, Edgar Dearing,
Jack Norton, Frank Mitchell, Edward
Earle.

GHOST CHASERS (1951)
Director: William Beaudine
Leo Gorcey (Slip Mahoney), Huntz Hall
(Sach Debussy Jones), Bernard Gorcey
(Louie Dumbrowski), Billy Benedict
(Whitey), Lloyd Corrigan, Philip Van
Zandt, Robert Coogan, Marshall Bradford, Argentina Brunetti, Jan Kayne,
Budd Gorman, Hal Gerard, Belle Mitchell, Doris Kemper, Lela Bliss, George
Gorcey.

GHOST CREEPS, THE (1940)
Director: Joseph H. Lewis
Bobby Jordan (Danny), Leo Gorcey (Muggs),

Dave O'Brien (Knuckles), Minerva Ur-
ecal (Agnes), Vince Barnett (Simp),
Dennis Moore (Giles), George Humbert
(Tony), Sunshine Sammy Morrison (Scru-
no), Donald Haines (Pee Wee), Hally
Chester (Boy), Forrest Taylor (Judge
Parker), Frankie Burke (Skinny), Jack
Edwards (Algy), Inna Gest (Louise),
David Gorcey (Ike), Alden Chase (Har-
rison), Jerry Mandy (cook).

GHOST FOR SALE, A (1952)
    Director: Victor M. Gover
Tod Slaughter (the Caretaker), Patrick
Barr (Husband), Tucker McGuire (wife).

GHOST GOES GEAR, THE (1966)
    Director: Hugh Gladwish
Spencer Davis, Stevie Winwood, Peter
York, Nicholas Parsons, Lorne Gibson,
Muff Winwood.

GHOST GOES WEST, THE (1936)
    Director: Rene Clare
Robert Donat (Murdoch Glourie/Donald
Glourie), Jean Parker (Peggy Martin),
Eugene Pallette (Mr. Martin), Elsa Lan-
chester (Lady Shepperton), Ralph Bun-
ker (Mr. Bigelow), Everly Gregg (Mrs.
Morton), Morton Selten (the Glourie),
Hay Petrie (the McLaggeren), Herbert
Lomas (Fergus), Patricia Hillary (Shep-
erdess), Quentin McPhearson (the cre-
ditor), Elliot Mason.

GHOST GOES WILD, THE (1947)
    Director: George Blair
James Ellison, Anne Gwynn, Grant
Withers, Edward Everett Horton, Jon-
athan Hale, Lloyd Corrigan, William
Austin, Edward Gargan, Charles Hal-
ton, Emil Rameau.

GHOST IN THE INVISIBLE BIKINI,
    THE (1966)
    Director: Don Weis
Tommy Kirk (Chuck Phillips), Deborah
Walley (Lilli Morton), Basil Rathbone
(Reginald Ripper), Boris Karloff (Hiram
Stokeley), Quinn O'Hara (Sinistra), Aron
Kincaid (Bobby), Jesse White (J. Sini-
ster Hulk), Harvey Lembeck (Eric Von
Zipper), Susan Hart (Cecily), Francis
X. Bushman (Malcolm), Nancy Sinatra
(Vicki), George Barrows (Monstro),
Patsy Kelly (Myrtle Forbush), Claudia
Martin (Lulu), Bobbi Shaw (Princess
Yolanda), Piccola Pupa (Piccola), Benny
Rubin (Chicken Feather), Andy Romano
(J. D.), Luree Holmes (Shirl), Alberta
Neison (Alberta), Ed Garner, Patti
Chandler, Sue Hamilton, Mary Hughes,
Frank Alexia, Salli Sachse, Jerry

Brutsche, John Macchia, Alan Fife,
Bob Harvey, Myrna Ross.

GHOST JESTERS, THE (1964-Mex.)
    (A. K. A. "Los Fantasmas Burlones")
    Director: Rafael Baledon
Tin Tan, Manuel 'Loco' Valdez, Sonia
Infante, M. Lopez, Maria Eugenia
San Martin, Clavillazo, Resortes.

GHOST OF DRAGSTRIP HOLLOW, THE
    (1959)
    Director: William Hole, Jr.
Jody Fair (Lois), Martin Braddock
(Stan), Russ Bender (Tom), Kirby
Smith (Wesley), Jack Ging (Tony), Nan-
cy Anderson (Nita), Leon Tyler (Bonzo),
Paul Blaisdell (the Ghost), Elaine
Dupont (Rhoda), Sanita Pelkey (Amelia),
Henry McCann (Dave), Dorothy Neumann
(Anastasia), Beverly Scott (Hazel),
Judy Howard (Sandra), Jean Tatum (Al-
ice), Bill St. John (Ed), Tommy Ivo
(Allen), Marvin Almars (Leon), George
Dockstader (motor cop).

GHOST OF FLIGHT 401, THE (TVM-
    1978) - 2-18-78
    Director: Steven Hilliard Stern
Ernest Borgnine (Dom Cimoli), Gary
Lockwood (Jordan Evanhower), Carol
Rossen (Maria Cimoli), Robert F. Lyons
(Bill Bowdish), Eugene Roche (Matt
Andrews), Alan Oppenheimer (Barton),
Tina Chen (Val), Kim Basinger (Prissy
Frazier), Beverly Todd (Dana), Allan
Miller (Les Garrick), Howard Hesse-
man (Bert Stockwell), Russell Johnson
(Loft), John Quade (Marshall), Mark
L. Taylor (Ron Smith), Tom Clancy
(Dutch), Angela Clarke (Mrs. Collura),
Byron Morrow (Bailey), Lynn Wood,
Anna Mathias, Luis Avalos, Meeno
Peluce, Tony Mattlanga, Deborah
Harmon.

GHOST OF FRANKENSTEIN, THE (1942)
    Director: Erle C. Kenton
Sir Cedric Hardwicke (Dr. Ludwig
Frankenstein), Lon Chaney, Jr. (the
Monster), Bela Lugosi (Ygor), Lionel
Atwill (Dr. Theodore Bohmer), Evelyn
Ankers (Elsa Frankenstein), Ralph
Bellamy (Erik Ernst), Janet Ann Gallow
(Cloestine), Barton Yarborough (Dr.
Kettering), Doris Lloyd (Martha), Olaf
Hytten (Russman), Leyland Hodgson
(Chief Constable), Holmes Herbert
(Magistrate), Michael Mark (Mayor's
assistant), Dwight Frye, Harry Cord-
ing (villagers), Eddie Parker (stuntman),
Lionel Belmore, Richard Alexander,
Lawrence Grant.

GHOST OF LOVE (1981-Ital. /Fr. /Ger.)
(A. K. A. "Fantasma D'Amore")
Director: Dino Risi
Marcello Mastroianni (Nino Conti),
Romy Schneider (Anna).

GHOST OF SLUMBER MOUNTAIN,
THE (1919)
Director: Herbert M. Dawley
Herbert M. Dawley (Uncle Jack),
Willis O'Brien (Mad Dick).

GHOST OF ST. MICHAEL'S, THE (1940)
Director: Marcel Varnel
Will Hay (William Lamb), Felix Ayl-
mer (Dr. Winter), Charles Hawtrey
(Percy Thorne), Hay Petrie (Procur-
ator Fiscal), Raymond Huntley (Mr.
Humphries), Claude Hulbert (Hilary
Teasdale), John Laurie (Jamie),
Elliot Mason (Mrs. Wigmore), Roddy
Hughes (Amberley), Manning Whiley
(Stock), Brefni O'Rorke (Sgt. MacFar-
lane), Derek Blomfield (Sunshine).

GHOST OF THE STRANGLER, THE
(1965-Mex.) (A. K. A. "El Espectro
del Estrangulador", "Santo contra el
Espectro")
Director: Rene Cardona
Santo, Roberto Canedo, Carlos Lopez
Moctezuma, Mariva Duval, Begonia
Palacios.

GHOST PATROL (1936)
Director: Sam Newfield
Tim McCoy (Tim), Claudia Dell (Nat-
alie Brent), Dick Curtis (Charlie),
Wheeler Oakman (Kincaid), Jim Bur-
tis (Henry), Walter Miller (Dawson),
Lloyd Ingraham (Prof. Brent), Jack
Casey (Mac), Artie Ortego (Ramon),
Fargo Bussey (Bill), Slim Whitaker
(Frank), Art Dillard (Shorty).

GHOST SHIP, THE (1943)
Director: Mark Robson
Richard Dix (Capt. Stone), Russell
Wade (Tom Merriam), Edith Barrett
(Ellen), Skelton Knaggs (Finn), Robert
Bice (Raphael), Ben Bard (Bowns),
Tom Burton (Benson), Laurence Tier-
ney (Louis), Edmund Glover (Sparks),
Steve Winston (Ausman), Dewey Rob-
inson (Boats).

GHOST SHIP (1952)
Director: Vernon Sewell
Hazel Court (Margaret), Dermot
Walsh (Guy), Hugh Burden (Dr. Faw-
cett), John Robinson (Mansel), Hugh
Latimer (Peter), Joan Carol (Mrs.
Martineau), Joss Ackland (Ron), Mig-

non O'Doherty (Mr. Manley), Joss
Ambler (yard manager), Meadows
White (yard surveyor), Pat McGrath
(Bert), Laidman Browne (coroner),
John King Kelly (Sid), Ian Carmichael.

GHOSTS IN ROME (1960-Ital.) (A. K. A.
"Fantasmi a Roma", "Phantom
Lovers")
Director: Antonio Pietrangeli
Vittorio Gassman (Caparra), Marcello
Mastroianni (Reginaldo), Sandra Milo
(Flora), Belinda Lee (Girl), Eduardo
de Filippo (Principe), Tino Buazzelli.

GHOSTS - ITALIAN STYLE (1967-Ital. /
Fr.) (A. K. A. "Questi Fantasmi")
Director: Renato Castellani
Sophia Loren (Maria), Vittorio Gass-
man (Pasquale), Mario Adorf (Alfredo),
Margaret Lee (Sayonara), Aldo Giuf-
fre (Raffaele), Francesco Tensi (Prof.
Santanna), Marcello Mastroianni (Head-
less Ghost).

GHOSTS OF BERKELEY SQUARE, THE
(1947)
Director: Vernon Sewell
Robert Morley (Gen. Burlap), Felix
Aylmer (Col. Kelsoe), Claude Hulbert
(Merryweather), A. E. Matthews (Gen.
Bristow), Martita Hunt (Lady Mary),
Abraham Sofaer (Disraeli), John Long-
den (Mortimer Digby), Ernest Thesiger
(Investigator), Wilfrid Hyde-White
(Captain), Martin Miller (Professor),
Wally Patch (Foreman), Mary Jerrold
(Lettie), Marie Lohr (Lottie), Yvonne
Arnaud (Millie), Esme Percy (Vizier),
Ronald Frankau (Tex Farnham), James
Hayter, Harry Fine.

GHOSTS ON THE LOOSE (1943)
Director: William Beaudine
Bela Lugosi (Emil), Ava Gardner
(Betty), Minerva Urecal, Leo Gorcey,
Billy Benedict, Wheeler Oakman, Bobby
Jordan, Stanley Clements, Jack Mul-
hall, Frank Moran, Huntz Hall, Rick
Vallin, Sunshine Sammy Morrison,
Peter Seal, Bill Bates, Bobby Stone,
Bob Hill, Tom Herbert.

GHOST STORY (1974)
Director: Stephen Weeks
Murray Melvin, Larry Dann, Vivian
Mackerall, Anthony Bate, Leigh Law-
son, Marianne Faithfull, Barbara
Shelley.

GHOST STORY (1981)
Director: John Irvin
Fred Astaire (Ricky Hawthorne), Melvyn

Douglas (Edward Wanderly), Douglas
Fairbanks, Jr. (Dr. John Jaffrey),
John Houseman (Sears James), Patricia
Neal (Stella Hawthorne), Craig Wasson
(Don Wanderly/David Wanderly), Alice
Krige (Alma Mobley/Eve Galli), Brad
Sullivan (Sheriff Hardesty), Miguel
Fernandez (Gregory Bate), Jacqueline
Brooks (Milly), Lance Holcomb (Fenny
Bate), Tim Choate (young Hawthorne),
Kurt Johnson (young Wanderley), Mark
Chamberlain (young Jaffrey), Ken Olin
(young James).

GHOSTS THAT STILL WALK (1977)
    Director: James T. Flocker
Ann Nelson (Alice Douglas), Matt Bos-
ton (Mark Douglas), Jerry Jenson
(Harold Douglas), Caroline Howe (Ruth
Douglas), Rita Crafts (Dr. Wills), Lee
James (Dr. Philip Stamely), David Kane
(X-ray technician), Janice Renney
(radiologist), Phil Catalli (tour guide).

GHOST TALKS, THE (1928)
    Director: Lewis Seiler
Helen Twelvetrees (Miriam Hall), Car-
mel Myers (Marie Haley), Arnold Lucy
(Julius Bowmar), Earle Foxe (Heimie
Heimrich), Stepin Fetchit (Christopher
C. Lee), Charles Eaton (Franklyn Green),
Joe Brown (Peter Accardi), Dorothy Mc-
Gowan (Miss Eva), Bess Flowers (Sylvia),
Henry Sedley (Joe Talles), Clifford Demp-
sey (John Keegan), Mickey Bennett
(bellboy), Baby Mack (Isobel Lee), Clar-
ence Geldert.

GHOST TALKS, THE (1949)
    Director: Jules White
Moe Howard, Shemp Howard, Larry
Fine, Kenneth MacDonald.

GHOST WALKS, THE (1934)
    Director: Frank R. Strayer
John Miljan (Prescott), June Collyer
(Gloria Shaw), Spencer Charters (the
Professor), Richard Carle (Herman
Wood), Johnny Arthur (Erskine), Henry
Kolker (Dr. Kent), Wilson Benge
(Jarvis), Donald Kirke (Terry), Doug-
las Gerrard (Carroway), Eve Southern
(Beatrice), Jack Shutta (head guard),
Harry Strang (guard).

GHOUL, THE (1933)
    Director: T. Hayes Hunter
Boris Karloff (Prof. Morlant), Sir
Cedric Hardwicke (Broughton), Ernest
Thesiger (Laing), Dorothy Hyson (Bet-
ty), Harold Huth (Aga Ben Bragore),
Anthony Bushell (Ralph Morlant), D. A.
Clarke-Smith (Mahmoud), Kathleen

Harrison (Kaney).

GHOUL, THE (1974)
    Director: Freddie Francis
Peter Cushing (Dr. Lawrence), John
Hurt (Tom), Alexandra Bastedo (An-
gela), Gwendoline Watford (Ayah), Ver-
onica Carlson (Daphne), Ian McCulloch
(Geoffrey), Stewart Bevan (Billy), Don
Henderson (the Ghoul).

GIANT BEHEMOTH, THE (1958)
    Director: Eugene Lourie & Doug-
    las Hickox
Gene Evans (Steven Karnes), Andre
Morell (Prof. Bickford), Leigh Madi-
son (Jean MacDougall), John Turner
(Ian Duncan), Henry Vidon (Thomas
MacDougall), Jack MacGowran (Dr.
Sampson), Maurice Kaufmann (Sub
Commander), Leonard Sachs (inter-
rupting scientist).

GIANT CLAW, THE (1957)
    Director: Fred F. Sears
Jeff Morrow (Mitch MacAfee), Mara
Corday (Sally Caldwell), Morris Ankrum
(Lt. Gen. Edward Lewis), Robert Shayne
(Gen. Ben Penner), Louis D. Merrill
(Pierre Broussard), Edgar Barrier
(Dr. Noyman), Clark Howat (Major
Sperling), Ruell Shayne (Pete), Morgan
Jones (Lieutenant).

GIANT FROM THE UNKNOWN, THE
    (1958)
    Director: Richard E. Cunha
Ed Kemmer (Wayne Brooks), Sally
Fraser (Janet Cleveland), Morris
Ankrum (Prof. Cleveland), Buddy Baer
(Vargas, the Giant), Bob Steele (Sher-
iff Parker), Jolene Brown (Ann Brown).

GIANT GILA MONSTER, THE (1959)
    Director: Ray Kellogg
Don Sullivan (Chance Winstead), Lisa
Simone (Lisa), Shug Fisher
(Mr. Harris), Fred Graham (Sheriff),
Ken Knox (Steamroller Smith), Jerry
Cortwright (Bob), Pat Reaves (Rick),
Beverly Thurman (Gay), Pat Simmons
(Sherry), Don Flourney (Gordy), Clarke
Browne (Chuck), Ann Sonka (Whila),
Cecil Hunt (Compton), Janice Stone
(Missy), Tommie Russel (Mrs. Blac-
well), Yolanda Salas (Liz Humphries),
Stormy Meadows (Agatha Humphries),
Howard Ware (Eb Humphries), Grady
Vaughn (Pat Wheeler), Desmond Dhooge
(hitchhiker).

GIANT OF METROPOLIS, THE (1962-
    Ital.) (A. K. A. "Il Gigante de

Metropolis")
Director: Umberto Scarpelli
Mitchell Gordon (Obro), Rolando Lupi
(Yotar), Liana Orfei (Queen Texen),
Bella Cortez (Mesede), Furio Meniconi
(Egor).

GIANTS OF THESALY, THE (1960-Ital. /
Fr.) (A.K.A. "I Giganti Della Tes-
saglia")
Director: Riccardo Freda
Roland Carey (Jason), Ziva Rodann
(Creusa), Massimo Girotti (Orpheus),
Moira Orfei, Nadine Duca, Luciano
Morin, Cathio Caro, Alberto Farnese.

GIANT SPIDER INVASION, THE (1975)
Director: Bill Rebane
Steve Brodie (J.R. Vance), Barbara
Hale (Dr. Jenny Langer), Robert Easton
(Dan Kester), Leslie Parrish (Ev Kes-
ter), Bill Williams (Dutch), Alan Hale,
Jr. (Sheriff), Dianne Lee Hart (Terri),
Christiane Schmidtmer (Helga).

GIFT OF TERROR, A (TVM-1973)
Director: Lela Swift
Denise Alexander (Laura), Michael
Callan (Steve), Christopher Connelly
(Danny), Will Geer (Ben), Jeff Donnell
(Mrs. Cummings), Edd Byrnes (Les Bar-
ker), Linda Kaye Henning (Marian), Car-
men Zapata (Aunt Caroline), Edmund
Cambridge (conductor), Laurie Brooks
Jefferson (Jeanie).

GIGANTIS, THE FIRE MONSTER (1955-
Jap.) (A.K.A. "Gojira no Gyakushyu",
Godzilla's Counterattack", "Godzilla
Raids Again", "The Volcano Monster")
Director: Motoyoshi Odo
Hiroshi Koizumi (Tsukioka), Minoru
Chiaki (Kobayahi), Stesuko Wakayama
(Hedemi), Takashi Shimura, Yujio
Kasama, Mayuri Mokusho, Masao
Chimizu, Minosuki Yamada, Sonosake
Sawamura, Takeo Oikawa.

GILDERSLEEVE'S GHOST (1943)
Director: Gordon Douglas
Harold Peary (Gildersleeve), Charles
Gemora (the Gorilla), Frank Reicher,
Amelita Ward, Marian Martin, Joseph
Vitale, Richard LeGrand, Emory Par-
nell, Freddie Mercer, Margie Stewart.

GIRL AND THE DEVIL, THE (1943-
Swed.) (A.K.A. "Flickan och Djav-
ulen")
Director: Hampe Faustman
Stih Jarrel (Satan), Gunn Wallgren, Lin-
nea Hillberg, Sven Miliander.

GIRL FROM SCOTLAND YARD, THE
(1937)
Director: Robert Vignola
Karen Morley (Viola Beech), Eduardo
Ciannelli (Franz Borg), Robert Baldwin
(Derrick Holt), Milli Monti (Milli Monti),
Lloyd Crane (Bertie), Katherine Alex-
ander (Lady Lavering), Bud Flanagan
(John), Lynn Anders (Mary Smith), Ma-
jor Farrell (porter), Don Brodie (Joe),
Phil Sleeman (1st valet), Alphonse Mar-
tel (2nd valet), Odette Myrtil (musician).

GIRL IN HIS POCKET (1957-Fr.) (A.K.A.
"Un Amour de Poche", "A Pocket
Love", "Nude in His Pocket")
Director: Pierre Kast
Jean Marais, Genevieve Page, Agnes
Laurent.

GIRL IN THE KREMLIN (1957)
Director: Russell Birdwell
Lex Barker (Steve Anderson), Zsa Zsa
Gabor (Lili Grisenko/Greta Grisenko),
Maurice Manson (Stalin), Jeffrey Stone
(Mischa Rimilkin), William Schallert
(Jacob Stalin), Michael Fox (Igor Smet-
ka), Kurt Katch (Commissar), Elena
Da Vinci (Olga Smetka), Aram Katcher
(Lavrenti Beria), Charles Horvath
(2nd Igor Smetka), Norbert Schiller
(man), Dale Van Sickel (cabby), Natalia
Daryll (Dosha), Phillipa Fallon (Nina),
Carl Sklover (Rashti), Alfred Linder
(Tata Brun), Gabor Curtis (Dr. Petrov),
Richard Richonne (Vedishky), Wanda
Ottoni (Girl at sidewalk cafe), Peter
Besbas (wine shop owner), Franz Roehn
(old man), Albert Szabo (truck driver),
Henry Rowland (policeman), Della Mal-
zahn (dancer), Vanda Dupre (girl).

GIRL MOST LIKELY TO..., THE
(TVM-1973) - 11-6-73
Director: Lee Philips
Stockard Channing (Miriam Knight),
Edward Asner (Detective Ralph Varone),
Jim Backus (Prof. David Tilson), Joe
Flynn (Dr. Green), Warren Berlinger
(Herman Anderson), Suzanne Zenor (Hei-
di Murphy), Cyril Delevanti (Minister),
Ruth McDevitt (house mistress), Larry
Wilcox (Moose Meyers), Carl Ballen-
tine (Dr. Hankim), Fred Grandy (Dr.
Ted Gates), Chuck McCann (Coach),
Daniel Spelling (Fred Ames), Victor
Izay, Reb Brown, Bill Zuckert, Angela
Clarke, Florence Lake, Dennis Dugan,
Bobby Griffin, Bob Hanley, Mary Linn,
John Kirby, Annette O'Toole, Warren
Burton, Charles Pinte, Lonny Stevens,
Jack Kutchell, Florence London.

GIRL, THE GOLD WATCH AND DYN-
AMITE, THE (TVM-1981) - 5-7-81
Director: Hy Averback
Philip MacHale (Kirby Winter), Lee
Purcell (Bonnie Lee Beaumont), Mor-
gan Fairchild (Stella Walker), Zohra
Lampert (Wilma Farnham), Burton
Gilliam (Hoover Hess), Jack Elam (Seth
Beaumont), Carol Lawrence (Sarah
Beaumont), Gene Barry (Andrew Sto-
vall), Gary Lockwood (Sheriff Earl
Baker), Jerry Mathers (Deputy Henry
Thomas), Larry Linville (Wesley
Raines), Mary Hanson (Lola), Michele
Butin (Michele), Jerry Hausner (bank
guard), Tom Poston (Omar Krepps),
Tony Matranga (hold-up man), Richie
Havens, Lyle Alzado.

GIRL, THE GOLD WATCH AND
EVERYTHING, THE (TVM-1980) -
5-27-80
Director: William Wiard
Robert Hays (Kirby Winter), Pam
Dawber (Bonnie Lee Beaumont), Ed
Nelson (Joseph Locordolos), Jill Ire-
land (Charla), Maurice Evans (Winter-
more), Zohra Lampert (Wilma), Bur-
ton Gilliam (Hoover Hess), Macdonald
Carey (Grumby), Peter Brown (Raoul),
Larry Hankin (Rene), Arthur Bernard
(Hank), John O'Leary (Hibber), Stef-
fan Zacharias (old man), Peter Kevoian
(man in heart).

GIRL WHO DARED, THE (1944)
Director: Howard Bretherton
Lorna Gray, Kirk Alyn, Grant Withers,
Veda Ann Borg, Roy Barcroft, John
Hamilton, Peter Cookson, Tom London,
Willie Best, Vivian Oakland.

GIRLY (1969) (A.K.A. "Mumsy, Nan-
ny, Sonny and Girly")
Director: Freddie Francis
Vanessa Howard (Girly), Ursula
Howells (Mumsy), Pat Heywood (Nanny),
Howard Trevor (Sonny), Michael Bryant
(new friend), Imogen Hassall (girlfriend),
Hugh Armstrong (friend in five), Michael
Ripper (zoo attendant), Robert Swan
(soldier).

GLADIATOR, THE (1938)
Director: Edward Sedgwick
Joe E. Brown (Hugo Kipp), June Travis
(Iris Bennett), Lucien Littlefield (Prof.
Danner), Dickie Moore (Bobby), Robert
Kent (Tom Dixon), Donald Douglas
(Coach Robbins), Eddie Kane (Speed
Burns), Ethel Wales (Mrs. Danner),
Man Mountain Dean (Himself), Lee
Phelps (Coach Stetson), Wright Kramer

(Dr. DeRay).

GLADIATORS, THE (1969-Swed.)
(A.K.A. "Gladiatorena", "The
Peace Game")
Director: Peter Watkins
Arthur Pentelow, Frederick Danner,
Kenneth Lo, Jeremy Child, Bjorn
Franzen, Erich Sterling.

GLASS SPHINX, THE (1967-Span. /
Ital.).(A.K.A. "La Esfinge de
Cristal")
Director: Luigi Scattine
Robert Taylor (Prof. Karl Nichols),
Anita Ekberg (Paulette), Giacomo
Rossi-Stuart (Ray), Gianna Serra
(Jenny), Jose Truchado (Theo), Angel
Del Pozo (Alex), Remo De Angelis
(Mirko), Emad Hamdy (Fouad).

GLEN AND RANDA (1971)
Director: Jim McBride
Steve Curry (Glen), Shelley Plimpton
(Randa), Woodrow Chambliss (Sidney
Miller), Garry Goodrow (Magician),
Roy Rox, Hubert Powers, Robert
Holmer, William Fratis, Ortega Sang-
ster, Alice Huffman, Richard Frazier,
Barbara Spiegel, Leonard Johnson,
Laura Hawbecker, Dwight Tate, Charles
Huffman, Martha Furey, Jack Tartar-
sky, Lucille Johnson, Mary Henry,
Bud Thompson, James Nankerius,
David Woeller, Matthew Levine, Tal-
made Holiday, Winona Tomanoczy.

GLEN OR GLENDA? (1952) (A.K.A.
"I Changed My Sex", "I Led Two
Lives")
Director: Edward D. Wood, Jr.
Bela Lugosi (Spirit/Mystic), Tommy
Haynes (Frank/Frankie), Daniel Davis/
Edward Wood, Jr. (Glen), Lyle Talbot
(Policeman), Dolores Fuller (Barbara),
Timothy Farrell (psychiatrist), George
Weiss, Conrad Brooks, Charles Crofts,
Henry Bederski.

G-MEN VS. THE BLACK DRAGON
(1943) (A.K.A. "Black Dragon of
Manzanar") - serial in 15 episodes
Chapters: 1. "The Yellow Peril", 2.
"Japanese Inquisition", 3. "Arsenal of
Doom", 4. "Deadly Sorcery", 5. "Cel-
estial Murder", 6. "Death and Destruc-
tion", 7. "The Iron Monster", 8. "Beast
of Tokyo", 9. "Watery Grave", 10. "The
Dragon Strikes", 11. "Suicide Mission",
12. "Dead on Arrival", 13. "Condemned
Cargo", 14. "Flaming Coffin", & 15.
"Democracy in Action".
Director: William Witney

Rod Cameron (Rex Bennett), Donald Kirke (Muller), Noel Cravat (Ranga), Maxine Doyle (Marie), George J. Lewis (Lugo), C. Montague Shaw (Prof. Nicholson), Lawrence Grant (Sir John Brookfield), Robert Homans (Captain Gorman), Forbes Murray (Kennedy), Edward Keane (Gordon), Pat O'Malley (Gibson), Kenneth Harlan (Lance), Crane Whitley (Burnell), John Hamilton (Martin), Stanley Price (Gibbs), William Forrest (Prof. Jackson), Edmund Cobb (Stewart), Constance Worth (Vivian Marsh), Roland Got (Chang), Harry Burns (Tony), Hooper Atchley (Caldwell), Nino Pipitone (Haruchi), Bud Geary (Morse), George Lynn (Garr), Virginia Carroll (nurse), Ivan Miller (Inspector), Allen Jung (Fugi), Walter Fenner (Williams), Mary Gayless (Matron), Elliott Sullivan (Turner), Tom Seidel (Spenser), Dick French (Norris), Paul Fung (Japanese Commander), Charles La Torre (Nick), Arvon Dale, Charles Flynn (pilots), Sam Bernard (Karl), Ray Parsons (Jones), John Wallace (Newman), Eddie Phillips (heavy), Norman Nesbitt (radio announcer), Johnny James (power company clerk), Edward Dew (Agent Z-24), Ken Terrell (Karl), Eddie Parder (Butler), Tom Steele (garage heavy/intern No. 1), Gil Perkins (intern No. 2), George De Normand, Charley Phillips (house heavies), Dale Van Sickel (pier heavy), Duke Taylor (truck heavy), Buddy Roosevelt (truck heavy's voice), Martin Faust (mill heavy), Harry Tauvera (seaman), Norman Willis (Tarner), Walter Theil (Tarner's voice), Walter Low (Graham), Bud Wolfe (warehouse heavy), Robert Strange (Kettler), John Daheim (balcony heavy), Otto Metzetti.

GNOME-MOBILE, THE (1967)
    Director: Robert Stevenson
Walter Brennan (D. J. Mulrooney/Knobby), Matthew Garber (Rodney Winthrop), Karen Dotrice (Elizabeth Winthrop), Ed Wynn (Rufus), Sean McClory (Horatio Quaxton), Richard Deacon (Ralph Yarby), Ellen Corby (Etta Pettibone), Jerome Cowan (Dr. Conrad Ramsey), Charles Lane (Dr. Scroggins), Cami Sebring (Violet), Tom Lowell (Jasper), Frank Cady (Charlie Pettibone), Maudie Prickett (Katie Barrett), Gil Lamb (gas attendant), Norman Grabowski (male nurse), Pamela Gail, Susan Gates, Jacki Ray, Joyce Menges, Susan Henning, Bunny Henning (Gnomes), Byron Foulger, Dale Van Sickle, Alvy Moore, Jesslyn Fax, Karl Held, Hal Baylor, William Fawcett, Parley Baer, Charles Smith,

Ernestine Barrier, Susan Flannery, Dee Carroll, Jack Davis, Mickey Martin, Jimmy Murphy, Robert S. Carson, John Cliff, Mark Allen.

GO AND GET IT (1920)
    Director: Henry R. Symonds & Marshall Neilan
Pat O'Malley, Wesley Barry, Noah Berry, Sr., Agnes Ayres, J. Barney Sherry, Charles Hill Mailes, Bull Montana (the Ape).

GODSEND, THE (1980-Australia)
    Director: Gabrielle Beaumont
Cyd Hayman (Kate Marlowe), Malcolm Stoddard (Alan Marlowe), Angela Pleasence (the Stranger), Patrick Barr (Dr. Collins), Wilhelmina Green, Lee Gregory, Joanne Boorman.

GODZILLA, KING OF THE MONSTERS (1954-Jap.) (A. K. A. "Gojira")
    Director: Inoshiro Honda
Raymond Burr (Steve Martin), Akihiko Hirata (Iwanaga), Akira Takarada (Dr. Serizawa), Takashi Shimura (Dr. Yamani), Momoko Kochi (Imiko Yamani), Sachio Sakai, Ren Yamamota, Tadashi Okabe, Fuijuki Murakami, Toyoaki Suzuki, Toranosuke Ogawa, Frank Iwanaga.

GODZILLA'S REVENGE (1969-Jap.) (A. K. A. "Ora Kaiji Daishingeki")
    Director: Inoshiro Honda
Kenji Sahara, Tomonori Yazaki, Sachio Sakai, Machiko Naka, Chotaro Togin, Yoshibumi Tumima.

GODZILLA VS. GIGAN (1971-Jap) (A. K. A. "Gojira tai Giagan")
    Director: Jun Fukuda
Hiroshi Ishikawa, Tomoko Umeda

GODZILLA VS. MEGALON (1973-Jap.) (A. K. A. "Gojira tai Megalon")
    Director: Jun Fukuda
Katsuhiko Sasaki, Hiroyuki Kawase, Robert Dunham, Yutaka Hayashi, Kotaro Tomita.

GODZILLA VS. THE COSMIC MONSTER (1974-Jap.) (A. K. A. "Gojira tai Mekagojira", "Godzilla vs. the Bionic Monster")
    Director: Jun Fukuda
Akihiko Hirata, Masaaki Daimon, Hiroshi Koisumi, Kazuya Aoyama.

GODZILLA VS. THE SEA MONSTER (1966-Jap.) (A. K. A. "Nankai no Dai Ketto", "Ebirah, Horror of the Deep")

Director: Jun Fukuda
Akira Takarada, Jun Tazaki, Kumi
Mizuno, Toru Watanabe, Hideo Suna-
zuka.

GODZILLA VS. THE SMOG MONSTER
(1971-Jap.) (A.K.A. "Gojira tai
Hedora")
Director: Yoshimitu Banno
Hiroyuki Kawase (Ken Yano), Akira
Yamaguchi (Dr. Yano), Toshie Ki-
mura (Mrs. Yano), Toshio Shibaki
(Yukio Keuchi), Keiko Mari (Miki
Fujiyama).

GODZILLA VS. THE THING (1964-
Jap.) (A.K.A. "Gojira tai Mo-
sura")
Director: Inoshiro Honda
Akira Takarada (the reporter), Yu-
riko Hoshi (the photographer), Hiroshi
Koizumi (the scientist), Emi & Yumi
Ito (the little sisters), Yu Fujiki.

GOG (1954)
Director: Herbert L. Strock
Richard Egan (David Sheppard), Con-
stance Dowling (Joanna Merritt), Her-
bert Marshall (Dr. Van Ness), John
Wengraf (Dr. Zeitman), Philip Van
Zandt (Dr. Elzevir), Michael Fox (Dr.
Hubertus), William Schallert (Engle),
Valerie Vernon (Mme. Elzevir), Steve
Roberts (Major Howard), David Alpert
(Peter Burden), Byron Kane (Dr. Car-
ter), Miriam Richman (Helen), Je-
anne Dean (Marna), Tom Daly (Sena-
tor), Alex Jackson (Vince), Aline
Towne (Dr. Kirby), Al Bayer (pilot),
Patti Taylor, Beverly Jocher (Acro-
bats), Andy Andrews, Julian Ludwig
(security guards).

GOKE, BODY SNATCHER FROM
HELL (1968-Jap.) (A.K.A. "Kyu-
ketsuki Gokemidoro")
Director: Jajime Sato
Hideo Ko (the Killer), Teruo Yoshida
(the pilot), Tomoni Sato (the steward-
ess), Eizo Kitamara (the Senator),
Masaya Takahashi (space biologist),
Cathy Holan (GI's wife).

GOLD (1934-Ger.)
Director: Karl Hartl
Hans Albers, Brigitte Helm, Michael
Bohnen, Lien Deyers, Ernst Karchow,
F. Kayssler.

GOLDEN ARROW, THE (1962-Ital.)
(A.K.A. "La Freccia d'Oro")
Director: Antonio Margheriti
Tab Hunter (Hassan), Rossana Podesta

(Jamila), Umberto Melnati (Thin
Genie), Giustino Durano (Absent-
Minded Genie), Mario Feliciani
(Baktlar), Gian Paola Rosmino (Mok-
bar), Jose Jaspe (Sabrath), Abdel
Moneim Ibrihim (Capt. Hamit), Re-
nato Baldini (Prince of Bassora),
Rosario Borelli (Prince of Aleppo),
Ceco Zamurovich (Prince of Samar-
kand), Calisto Calisti (Prince of
Bassora's General), Dominique Bos-
chero (Queen of Rocky Valley), Omar
Zoulfikar (Magician of Rocky Valley),
Claudio Scarchieli (Bandit).

GOLDEN BLADE, THE (1953)
Director: Nathan Juran
Rock Hudson (Harun), Piper Laurie
(Princess Khairuzan), Gene Evans
(Hadi), Kathleen Hughes (Bakhamra),
Steven Geray (Barcus), George
Macready (Jafar), Edgar Barrier (Ca-
liph), Vic Romito (Sherkan), Anita Ek-
berg, Erika Norden, Lori Nelson, Alice
Kelly, Valerie Jackson (handmaidens).

GOLDEN EARRINGS (1947)
Director: Mitchell Leisen
Ray Milland (Col. Ralph Denistoun),
Marlene Dietrich (Lydia), Murvyn
Vye (Zoltan), Reinhold Schunzel (Prof.
Krosigk), Bruce Lester (Byrd), Her-
mine Sterler (Greta Krosigk), Ivan
Triesault (Major Reimann), Dennis
Hoey (Hoff), Eric Feldary (Steig),
Quentin Reynolds (himself), Otto
Reichow, Fred Nurney (agents), Ver-
non Downing, Gordon Richards (club
members), Henry Rowland (Peiffer),
Larry Simms (page boy), Hans Schumm,
George Sorel (policemen), John Dehner
(S.S. man), Gisele Werbiseck (dowager),
Tony Ellis (dispatch rider), Haldor de
Becker (telegraph boy), Leslie Deni-
son (Miggs), Bob Stephenson (S.S.
guard).

GOLDEN GATE MURDERS, THE (TVM-
1979) (A.K.A. "Phantom of the
Golden Gate") 10-3-79
Director: Walter Grauman
David Janssen (Detective Sgt. Paul
Silver), Susannah York (Sister Vene-
cia), Kim Hunter (Sister Superior),
Tim O'Connor (Capt. Daniels), Sandy
Ward (George Walker), Alan Fudge
(Sgt. McNally), Lee Paul (Willie
Petersen), Eric Server (Stacy), Paul
Coufos (Butler), Jon Lormer (Arch-
bishop), Jason Wingreen (Larkin),
Wayne Hefley (bridge officer), Phil
Boyett (bridge operator), Dave Cass
(biker), Lloyd Bochner (doctor), Hank

Brandt (1st detective), Vince Howard (2nd detective), June Sanders (saleslady), Olive Behrend (Sister Teresa), Michael O'Dwyer (Father Connolly), Sam Hiona (tourist), Richard O'Brien, Kenneth Tigar, Richard Bull, Regis J. Cordic.

GOLDENGIRL (1979)
Director: Joseph Sargent
Susan Anton (Goldine Serafin), Curt Jurgens (Dr. Serafin), James Coburn (Dryden), Leslie Caron (Dr. Lee), Robert Culp (Esselton), Harry Guardino (Valenti), Sheila DeWindt (Debbie Jackson), Ward Costello (Cobb), Nicolas Coster (Dr. Dalton), James A. Watson, Jr. (Winters), John Newcombe (Armitage), Juliana Fjeld (Ingrid), Anette Tannander (Krull), Michael Lerner (Sternberg), Andrea Brown (teammate).

GOLDEN MISTRESS, THE (1954)
Director: Joel Judge
John Agar (Bill Buchanan), Abner Biberman (Carl Dexter), Rosemarie Bowe (Ann Dexter), Andre Marcisse (Iznard), Kiki (Cristofe), Jacques Molant (Ti Flute), Pierre Blain (the Houngan), Shibley Talamas (DuPuis), Andre Germain (untamed spearman), Andre Contant, Napolean Bernard (Domballa soloists).

GOLDEN NEEDLES (1974)
Director: Robert Clouse
Joe Don Baker (Dan Mason), Elizabeth Ashley (Felicity), Burgess Meredith (Sidney Winters), Jim Kelly (Jeff), Ann Sothern (Finzie), Roy Chiao (Lin Toa), Tony Lee (Kwan), Frances Fong (Su Lin), Alice Fong (Lotus), Clarence Barnes (Claude), Edgar Justice (Bobby), Pat Johnson (Winters' man).

GOLDEN RABBIT, THE (1962)
Director: David MacDonald
Timothy Bateson, John Sharp, Willoughby Goddard, Maureen Beck, Kenneth Fortecue.

GOLDEN SEA, THE (1919-Ger) (A. K. A. "Die Goldene See", "The Spiders" Part I)
Director: Fritz Lang
Lil Dagover, Carl de Vogt, Ressel Orla, Paul Morgan, Georg John, Bruno Lettinger, Thea Sander, Edgar Pauly, Paul Biensfeldt, Friedrich Kuhne.

GOLDEN VOYAGE OF SINBAD, THE (1973)
Director: Gordon Hessier
John Phillip Law (Sinbad), Caroline

Munro (Margiane), Tom Baker (Koura), Douglas Wilmer (Grand Vizier), Gregoire Aslan (Hakim), Kurt Christian (Haroun), Takis Emmanuel (Achmed), Martin Shaw (Rachid), Aldo Sambrell (Omar), John D. Garfield (Abdul).

GOLDFACE, THE FANTASTIC SUPERMAN (1967-Ital. /Span.) (A. K. A. "Goldface, il Fantastico Superman")
Director: Adalberto Albertini
Spartaco B. Santoni/Robert Anthony, Evi Marandi, Hugo Pimentel, Micaela Pignatelli, Big Mattews, Manuel Monroy, Leontine May.

GOLDFINGER
Director: Guy Hamilton
Sean Connery (James Bond), Gert Frobe (Goldfinger), Honor Blackman (Pussy Galore), Harold Sakata (Oddjob), Shirley Eaton (Jill Masterson), Tania Mallett (Tilly Masterson), Martin Benson (Solo), Bernard Lee (M), Lois Maxwell (Miss Moneypenny), Austin Willis (Simmons), Bill Nagy (Midnight), Bert Kwouk (Mr. Ling), Richard Vernon (Smithers), Cec Linder (Felix Leiter), Nadja Regin (Bonita), Raymond Young (Sierra), Hal Galili (Strap), Michael Mellinger (Kisch), Alf Joint (Capungo), Dennis Dowles (Brunskill), Varley Thomas (old lady), Lenny Rabon (henchman).

GOLD OF THE AMAZON WOMEN (TVM-1979) - 3-6-79
Director: Mark L. Lester
Bo Svenson (Tom Jensen), Anita Ekberg (Queen Na-Eela), Donald Pleasence (Clarence Blasko), Richard Romanus (Luis Rodriguez), Robert Minor (Noboro), Bond Gibson (Taimi), Susan E. Miller (Oriana), Sarita Butterfield (Barari), Maggie Jean Smith (Reina), Charles Reynolds (Jorn Abramson), Ian Edward (Heintz Gunther), Mary Peters (Polani), Yasmine (Lee-Leeo), Carl Low, John Anthony Sarno, Fred Berkoff, Joseph Gilbert, Robert Ross.

GOLDSTEIN (1963)
Director: Philip Kaufman & Benjamin Manaster
Lou Gilbert (Old Man), Eileen Madison (Sally), Severn Darden (doctor), Thomas Erhart (Sculptor), Charles Fischer (Mr. Nice), Benito Carruthers (Jay), Anthony Holland (Aid), Nelson Algren (himself), Jack Burns.

GOLEM, THE (1914-Ger.) (A. K. A.
"Der Golem", "The Monster of Fate")
    Director: Paul Wegener & Henrik Galeen
Paul Wegener (the Golem), Henrik
Galeen, Albert Steinruck, Lydia Salmonova, Ernst Deutsch.

GOLEM, THE (1920-Ger.) (A. K. A.
"Der Golem, Wie Er in die Welt
Kam")
    Director: Paul Wegener & Carl
    Boese
Paul Wegener (the Golem), Albert
Steinrueck (Rabbi Loew), Lydia Salmanova (Mirima Lowe), Ernest
Deutsch (Famulus), Hanns Sturm,
Henrik Galeen, Grete Schroder, Lother Muthel, Ferdinand von Alten,
Otto Gebuhr, Dora Paetzoid, Max
Kronert.

GOLEM, THE (1936-Fr.) (A. K. A.
"Le Golem", "The Legend of
Prague")
    Director: Julien Duvivier
Ferdinand Hart (the Golem), Charles
Dorat (Rabbi Jacob), Harry Baur
(Emperor Rudolph II), Germaine Aussey, Raymond Aimos, Roger Karl,
Jany Holt, Gaston Jacquet, George
Voskovec.

GOLEM, THE (1966-Fr.) (A. K. A.
"Le Golem", "Mask of the Golem")
    Director: Jean Kerchbron
Andre Reybaz (the Golem), Pierre
Tabard, Marika Green, Michel Etchevery, Francois Vibert, Douking, Magali Noel, Robert Etchevery.

GOLEM (1980-Pol.)
    Director: Piotr Szulkin
Marek Walezewski (Pernat), Krystyna
Janda (Rozyna), Joanna Zolkowska
(Miriam), Wieslaw Drzewica (Miriam's
father), Krzysztof Majchrzak (student),
Henryk Bak, Wojeiech Pszoniak, Jan
Nowicki, Ryszard Pietrucki, Marian
Opania, Andrezej Seweryn, Boguslaw
Sobczuk.

GOLIATH AGAINST THE GIANTS (1960-
Ital. /Span.) (A. K. A. "Goliath contro
i Giganti")
    Director: Guido Malatesta
Fernando Rey, Brad Harris, Gloria
Milland, Barbara Carrol, Lina Rosales,
Jose Rubio, Carmen Deliro.

GOLIATH AND THE BARBARIANS (1959-
Ital.) (A. K. A. "Il Terrore dei Barbari",
"The Terror of the Barbarians")
    Director: Carlo Campogalliani

Steve Reeves (Emiliano), Bruce Cabot
(Alboyna), Arturo Dominici (Delfo),
Andrea Checchi (Agnese), Giulia
Rubini (Sabina), Chelo Alonso (Londo),
Livio Lorenzon (Igor), Furio Meniconi
(Marco), Luciano Marin (Svevo), Febrizio Capucci (Bruno), Gino Scotti
(Count Danjele).

GOLIATH AND THE DRAGON (1960-
Ital. /Fr.) (A. K. A. "La Vendette
de Ercole", "The Vengeance of
Hercules")
    Director: Vittorio Cottafavi
Mark Forest (Goliath), Broderick
Crawford (Eurystheus), Eleonora
Ruffo (Dejanara), Gaby Andre (Alcinoe),
Sandro Maretti (Ismene), Phillipe
Hersent (Illus), Frederica Ranchi
(Thea).

GOLIATH AND THE SINS OF BABYLON
(1963-Ital.) (A. K. A. "Maciste
l'Roe Piu Grande del Mondo", " Maciste, the World's Greatest Hero")
    Director: Michele Lupo
Mark Forest (Goliath), Eleanora Bianchi (Resia), Giuliano Gemma (Alceo),
Jose Greci (Xandros), Erno Crisa
(Pergaso), Arnaldo Fabrizio (Morakeb),
John Chevron (Evandro), Piero Lulli
(Meneos), Scilla Gabel, Mimmo Palmara, Livio Lorenzon, Paul Muller.

GOLIATH AND THE VAMPIRES (1961-
Ital.) (A. K. A. "Maciste contro il
Vampiro", "Maciste vs. the Vampire",
"The Vampires")
    Director: Giacomo Gentilomo &
    Sergio Corbucci
Gordon Scott (Goliath), Gianna Maria
Canale (Astra), Jacques Sernas (Buona),
Leonora Ruffo (Julia), Annabella Incontrera (Magda), Van Aikens, Mario
Feliciani, Emma Baron, Rocco Vitolozzi, Guido Celano, Renato Terra
Caizzi.

GOLIATH AWAITS (TVM-1981) - 11-11-
81 & 11-12-81
    Director: Kevin Connor
Mark Harmon (Peter Cabot), Christopher
Lee (John McKenzie), Frank Gorshin
(Dan Wesker), Emma Samms (Lea
McKensie), Eddie Albert (Admiral),
Robert Forster (Cmdr. Jeff Selkirk),
Alex Cord (Dr. Marlow), John Carradine (Ronald Bentley), John McIntire
(Sen. Bartholomew), Jeannette Nolan
(Mrs. Bartholomew), Jean Marsh (Dr.
Goldman), Duncan Regehr (Paul Ryker),
Hedley Mattingley (Bailey), Kip Niven
(Gantman), Alan Caillou (Goliath's
Captain), Irene Hervey (Carrie), Lori

Lethin (Maria), Michael Evans (Eric Whittaker), Laurence Haddon (Capt. Volero), Jack Blessing (Koskoff), Julie Bennett (Sylvia King), Warwick Sims (Luke Crane), Peter von Zerneck (Hoffman), Tony Ballen (Edward R. Morrow), Belinda Mayne (Sally Crane), Lawrence Benedict (Young Bailey), Cristine Nigra (Beth), Peter Ashton (Communicator Enterprise), Sandy McCullum, Chris Winfield (guards), Teri Taylor (presslady), Alan Fudge (Sweeney), Clete Roberts (anchorman), John Brandon (chief engineer), Sandy Simpson (Moore), John Berwick (crewman), Bruce Heighley (technician), Michael White (PC 18 Officer), Colin Drake (old man), Tom Dunstan (Agra worker), Kirk Cameron (Liam), George Innes, John Ratzenberger, Peter Stader, Michael Vendrell, Larry Levine, Larry Weston, Karen Lustgarten.

GOOD AGAINST EVIL (TVM-1977) - 5-22-77
Director: Paul Wendkos
Dack Rambo (Andy Stuart), Elyssa Davalos (Jessica Gordon), Dan O'Herlihy (Father Kemschler), Leila Goldoni (Sister Monica), Richard Lynch (Mr. Rimmin), Kim Cattrall (Linday Isley), Peter Brandon (Dr. Price), Natasha Ryan (Cindy Isley), Sandy Ward (Lt. Taggert), Isaac Goz (Merlin), Richard Stahl (Brown), John Harkins (Father Wheatley), Peggy McCay (Irene), Lillian Adams (Beatrice), Jenny O'Hara (the woman), Richard Sanders (doctor), Erica Yohn (Agnes).

GOODBYE CHARLIE (1964)
Director: Vincente Minnelli
Tony Curtis (George), Debbie Reynolds (Charlie), Pat Boone (Bruce), Walter Matthau (Sartori), Martin Gabel (Morton Craft), Laura Devon (Rusty), Roger C. Carmel (the Inspector), Ellen McRae (Franny), Joanna Barnes (Janie), Harry Madden (Charlie Sorel), Michael Romanoff (Patron), Antony Eustrel (Butler), Michael Jackson (Michael Jackson), Myrna Hansen (starlet), Donna Michelle (guest on yacht).

GOODBYE GEMINI (1970)
Director: Alan Gibson
Judy Geeson (Jacki), Martin Potter (Julian), Michael Redgrave (James Harrington-Smith), Freddie Jones (David Curry), Peter Jeffrey (Detective Insp. Kingsley), Alexis Kanner (Clive Landseer), Terry Scully (Nigel Garfield), Mike Pratt (Rod Barstowe),

Marian Diamond (Denise Pryce-Fletcher), Daphne Heard (Mrs. McLaren), Joseph Furst (Georgiu), Ricky Renee (Myra), Laurence Hardy (minister), Brian Wilde (taxi driver), Barry Scott (Audrey), Jack Connell (barman), Hilda Barry (stallholder).

GORATH (1962-Jap.) (A. K. A. "Yosei Gorasu")
Director: Inoshire Honda
Ryo Ikebe, Jun Tazaki, Akihiko Hirata, Kumi Mizuno, Yumi Shirakawa, Takshi Shimura.

GORE GORE GIRLS, THE (1972)
Director: Herschell Gordon Lewis
Frank Kress (Abraham Gentry), Amy Farrell (Nancy Weston), Henny Youngman (Marzdone Mobilie), Ray Saber (bartender), Russ Badger (police lieutenant), Hedda Lubin (Marlene), Nora Alexis (Lola Prinze), Phil Laurensen, Frank Rice (policemen), Emily Mason (Mary McIlhenny), Corlee Bew, Lena Bousman, Marina Salli, Menda MacPhail, Luba Cherewchenko, Vicki Carr (Go-Go dancers), Frank Kawsh, John Sezonov, Alex Petrovic (mobsters), Jim Killen (doctor), Lauren Obeda (lady wrestler), Norman Dachman (Master of Ceremonies), Jeanne Molen (hysterical woman), Harry Dachman (cabdriver).

GORGO (1959)
Director: Eugene Lourie
Bill Travers (Joe), William Sylvester (Sam), Vincent Winter (Sean), Christopher Rhodes (McCartin), Joseph O'Conor (Prof. Hendricks), Martin Benson (Dorkin), Basil Dignam (Admiral), Bruce Seton (Prof. Flaherty), Maurice Kauffman (radio reporter), Howard Lang (1st Colonel), Thomas Duggan (1st Naval Officer), Dervis Ward (bosun), Barry Keegan (mate).

GORGON, THE (1964)
Director: Terence Fisher
Peter Cushing (Dr. Namaroff), Christopher Lee (Prof. Meister), Barbara Shelley (Carla), Richard Pasco (Paul), Michael Goodliffe (Heitz), Patrick Troughton (Kanof), Jack Watson (Ratoff), Michael Peake (policeman), Alistair Williamson (Cass), Joseph O'Conor (coroner), Toni Gilpin (Sacha), Joyce Hemson (Martha), Redmond Phillips (Hans), Jeremy Longhurst (Bruno), Prudence Hyman (Chatelaine), Sally Nesbitt (nurse).

GORILLA, THE (1927)
Director: Alfred Santell
Tully Marshall (Uriah Townsend),
Walter Pidgeon (Stevens), Claude
Gillingwater (Cyrus Townsend),
Charlie Murray (Garrity), Fred
Kelsey, Alice Day, Aggie Herring,
Gaston Glass, Brooks Benedict,
Sydney Crossley.

GORILLA, THE (1930)
Director: Bryan Foy
Lila Lee (Alice Denby), Walter
Pidgion (Arthur Marsden), Edwin
Maxwell (Cyrus Stevens), Purnell Pratt
(the Stranger), Roscoe Karns (Simmons),
Harry Gribbon (Mulligan), Joe Frisco
(Garrity), Landers Stevens (the Inspec-
tor), William Philbrick (Servant).

GORILLA, THE (1939)
Director: Allan Dwan
Jimmy Ritz (Garrity), Harry Ritz
(Harrigan), Al Ritz (Mulligan), Anita
Louise (Norma Denby), Lionel Atwill
(Walter Stevens), Patsy Kelly (Kitty),
Bela Lugosi (Peters), Paul Harvey
(Conway), Joseph Calleia (the Stran-
ger), Edward Norris (Jack Marsden),
Wally Vernon (Seaman), Art Miles
(the Gorilla).

GORILLA AT LARGE (1954)
Director: Harmon Jones
Cameron Mitchell (Joey Matthews),
Anne Bancroft (Laverne Miller),
Raymond Burr (Cyrus Miller), Lee
J. Cobb (Detective Sgt. Garrison),
Charlotte Austin (Audrey Baxter),
Peter Whitney (Kovacs), Warren
Stevens (Mack), Lee Marvin (Shaugh-
nessy), John G. Kellogg (Morse),
Charles Tannen (Owens), George Bar-
rows (the Gorilla).

GORILLA OF SOHO, THE (1968-Ger.)
(A. K. A. "Der Gorilla von Soho")
Director: Alfred Vohrer
Horst Tappart, Uschi Glas, Albert
Lieven, Uwe Friedrichsen, Inge Lang-
en, Hubert von Meyerinck, Herbert
Fux.

GOTO, THE ISLAND OF LOVE (1968-
Fr.) (A. K. A. "Goto I'lle d'Amour")
Director: Walerian Borowczyk
Pierre Brasseur, Ligia Brancice, Rene
Dary, Ginette Leclerc, Jean-Pierre
Andreani, Guy Saint-Jean, Fernand
Bercher.

GRADUATION DAY (1981)
Director: Herb Freed

Christopher George (Coach George
Michaels), Patch MacKenzie (Anne
Ramshead), Michael Pataki (Mr.
Guglione), E. Danny Murphy (Kevin),
E. J. Peaker (Blondie), Virgil Frye
(MacGregor), Carmen Argenziano
(Halliday), Denise Cheshire (Sally),
Linnea Quigley (Dolores), Hal Bokar
(Ronald Corliss), Beverly Dixon
(Elaine Ramshead), Richard
Balin (Roberts), Karen Abbott
(Joanne), Billy Hufsey (Tony), Carl
Rey (Ralph), Vanna White (Doris),
Erica Hope (Diane), Ruth Ann Llorens
(Laura Ramshead), Tom Hintnaus (Pete),
Aaron Butler (the photographer), Viola
Kates Stimpson (Mrs. Badger), Patrick
White (truck driver), Grant Loud
(singer).

GRAVE OF THE VAMPIRE (1972)
Director: John Hayes
William Smith (James Eastman),
Michael Pataki (Caleb Croft/Prof.
Lockwood), Lynn Peters (Anne
Arthur), Jay Scott (Paul), Kitty
Vallacher (Leslie), Jay Adler (Zack),
Lieux Dressler (Olga), Diane
Holden (Anita Jacoby), Carmen Ar-
genziano (Sam), William Guhl (Duf-
fy), Abbi Henderson (Carol), Eric
Mason (Panzer), Inga Neilsen (Tex),
Margaret Fairchild (Fenwick), Frank
Whiteman (Brian), Lindus Guiness
(cook).

GRAVEYARD OF HORROR (1971-
Span.) (A. K. A. "Necrophagus",
"El Descuartizador de Binbrook")
Director: Michael Skaife/Mi-
guel Madrid
Bill Curran, Jocasta Gray, Frank
Brana, J. R. Clark, Victor Israel,
Titania Clement, Marisha Shiero,
Sany Green, Antonio G. Escribano,
Catherine Ellison, Beatrice Lacy.

GREAT ALASKAN MYSTERY, THE
(1944) (A. K. A. "The Great North-
ern Mystery") - serial in 13
episodes
Chapters: 1. "Shipwrecked among
Icebergs", 2. "Thundering Doom",
3. "Battle in the Clouds", 4. "Masked
Murder", 5. "The Bridge of Disaster",
6. "Shattering Doom", 7. "Crashing
Timbers", 8. "In a Flaming Plane", 9.
"Hurtling Through Space", 10. "Tricked
by a Booby Trap", 11. "The Tunnel of
Terror", 12. "Electrocuted", & 13.
"The Boomerang".
Director: Ray Taylor & Lewis
D. Collins

Milburn Stone (Jim Hudson), Marjorie
Weaver (Ruth Miller), Samuel S. Hinds
(Herman Brock), Ralph Morgan (Dr.
Miller), Fuzzy Knight (Grit Hartman),
Anthony Warde (Brandon), Martin
Kosleck (Dr. Hauss), Joseph Crehan
(Bill Hudson), Harry Cording (Capt.
Greeder), Edgar Kennedy (Bosun),
Jay Novello (Eskimo Chief), Perc
Launders (Haegle), Edward Gargan
(Kurtz), Jack Clifford (Dunn), William
Ruhl (Grey), Richard Powers (Burger),
Jack Ingram, Gibson Gowland.

GREAT ALLIGATOR, THE (1979-Ital.)
   (A.K.A. "Big Alligator River")
   Director: Sergio Martin
Babara Bach, Mel Ferrer.

GREAT GABBO, THE (1929)
   Director: James Cruze
Erich Von Stroheim (Gabbo), Betty
Compson (Maria), Donald Douglas
(Frank), Margie Kane (eccentric
dancer), Helen Kane, Hugh Herbert.

GREAT GAMBINI, THE (1937)
   Director: Charles Vidor
Akim Tamiroff (Gambini), Marian
Marsh (Ann Randall), Genevieve Tobin
(Mrs. Randall), Edward S. Brophy
(Buckie), William Demarest (Kirby),
Lya Lys (Luba), John Trent (Grant
Naylor), Roland Drew (Stephen Danby),
Allen Birmingham (Lamb), Ralph
Peters (bartender).

GREAT HOUDINIS, THE (TVM-1976)
   - 10-8-76
   Director: Melville Shavelson
Paul Michael Glaser (Harry Houdini),
Sally Struthers (Bess Houdini), Ruth
Gordon (Mrs. Cecilia Weiss), Vivian
Vance (Minnie), Adrienne Barbeau
(Daisy White), Bill Bixby (Rev. Arthur
Ford), Peter Cushing (Arthur Conan Doyle),
Maurine O'Sullivan (Lady Doyle), Nina
Foch (Rev. Leveyne), Wilfrid Hyde-
White (Superintendent Melville), Jack
Carter (Theo Weiss), Geoffrey Lewis (Dr.
Crandon), Barbara Rhoades (Margery
Crandon), Clive Revill (Slater), Jerome
Thor (conductor).

GREAT IMPERSONATION, THE (1935)
   Director: Alan Crosland
Edmund Lowe (Everard Dominey/
Leopold von Ragenstein), Valerie
Hobson (Eleanor Dominey), Lumsden
Hare (Duke Henry), Spring Byington
(Duchess Caroline), Frank Reicher (Dr.
Schmidt), Dwight Frye (Roger Unthank),
Leonard Mudie (Mangan), Brandon

Hurst (Middleton), Clyde King (Sir
Gerald Hume), Ivan F. Simpson (Dr.
Harrison), Nan Grey (Middleton's
daughter), Henry Mollison (Eddie
Pelham), Priscilla Lawson (maid),
Vera Eangles (Princess Stephanie),
Charles Waldron (Sir Ivan Brun),
Esther Dale (Mrs. Unthank), Pat
O'Hara (chauffeur), Willy Castello
(Duval), Murray Kinnell (seaman),
Virgina Hammond (Lady Hume),
Thomas R. Mills (bartender), Frank
Terry, Tom Ricketts, Robert Bolder
(villagers), Violet Seaton (Nurse),
John Powers (policeman), Harry
Worth (Hugo), Lowden Adams (waiter),
Frank Benson, David Dunbar (farmers),
Adolph Milar (German), Leonid
Snegoff (Wolff), Larry Steers (Army
Officer), Douglas Wood (Nobleman),
Harry Allen (Parkins).

GREAT MUPPET CAPER, THE (1981)
   Director: Jim Henson
Charles Grodin (Nicky Holiday), Diana
Rigg (Lady Holiday), John Cleese,
Peter Ustinov, Robert Morley, Jack
Warden.
Muppet performers: Jim Henson,
Frank Oz, Jerry Nelson, Dave Hoelz,
Richard Hunt.

GREAT PHYSICIAN, THE (1913)
   Director: Richard Ridgely
Charles Ogle (Death), Mabel Trun-
nelle, Robert Brower, Helen Couglin.

GREAT WHITE (1982)
   Director: Enzo G. Castellari
James Franciscus (Peter Benton),
Vic Morrow (Ron Hammer), Micky
Pignatelli (Gloria Benton), Joshua
Sinclair (William Wells), Timothy
Brent, Chuck Kaufman, Thomas
Moore, Joyce Lee.

GREEN ARCHER, THE (1940) - serial
   in 15 episodes
   Director: James W. Horne
Victor Jory (Spike Holland), Iris
Meridith (Valerie Howett), James
Craven (Abel Bellamy), Robert
Fiske (Savini), Dorothy Fay (Elaine
Bellamy), Jack Ingram (Brad), For-
rest Taylor (Howett), Joseph W. Gi-
rard (Insp. Ross), Kit Guard (Dinky),
Fred Kelsey (Capt. Thompson).

GREEN ARCHER, THE (1961-Ger.)
   (A.K.A. "Der Grune Bogenschutze")
   Director: Jurgen Roland
Gert Frobe, Karin Dor, Charles
Pallent, Eddi Arent, Klausjurgen Wussow.

GREEN EYE OF THE YELLOW GOD,
THE (1913)
Director: Richard Ridgely
Charles Ogle.

GREEN HORNET, THE (1939) -
serial in 13 episodes
Chapters: 1. "The Tunnel of Terror",
2. "The Thundering Terror", 3. "Fly-
ing Coffins", 4. "Pillar of Flames",
5. "The Time Bomb", 6. "Highways
of Peril", 7. "Bridge of Disaster", 8.
"Dead or Alive", 9. "The Hornet
Trapped", 10. "Bullets and Ballots",
11. "Disaster Rides the Rails", 12.
"Panic in the Zoo" & 13. "Doom of
the Underworld".
Director: Ford Beebe & Ray
Taylor
Gordon Jones (Britt Reid/the Green
Hornet), Wade Boteler (Michael Ax-
ford), Keye Luke (Kato), Anne Nagel
(Lenore Case), Douglas Evans
(Mortison), Ralph Dunn (Andy),
Walter McGrail (Dean), Gene Rizzi
(Carney), Edward Earle (Felix Grant),
Philip Trent (Jasper Jenks), John
Kelly (Hawks), Arthur Loft (Joe Ogden),
Cy Kendall (Monroe), Alan Ladd (man),
Anne Gwynne (girl), Ann Doran (girl),
Selmer Jackson, Kenneth Harlan,
Lane Chandler.

GREEN HORNET STRIKES AGAIN, THE
(1940) - serial in 15 episodes
Chapters: 1. "Flaming Havoc", 2.
"The Plunge of Peril", 3. "The
Avenging Heavies", 4. "A Night of
Terror", 5. "Shattering Doom", 6.
"The Fatal Flash", 7. "Death in the
Clouds", 8. "Human Targets", 9.
"The Tragic Crash", 10. "Blazing
Fury", 11. "Thieves of the Night",
12. "Crashing Barriers", 13. "The
Flaming Inferno", 14. "Racketeer-
ing Vultures" & 15. "Smashing the
Crime Ring".
Director: Ford Beebe & John
Rawlins
Warren Hull (Britt Reid/the Green
Hornet), Wade Boteler (Michael
Axford), Keye Luke (Kato), Anne
Nagel (Lenore Case), Pierre Watkins
(Grogan), Eddie Acuff (Lowery), Joe Dev-
lin (Dolan), C. Montague Shaw (Weaver),
William Hall (Don DeLuca), Jay Mi-
chael (Foranti), Dorothy Lovett (Fran-
ces Grayson), Tris Coffin, Pat O'Malley,
Ray Teal, Roy Barcroft, James Seay,
Nestor Paiva, Eddie Parker, Lane
Chandler, Jason Robards, Sr., Walter
Sande.

GREEN MANSIONS (1959)

Director: Mel Ferrer
Audrey Hepburn (Rima), Anthony
Perkins (Abel), Lee J. Cobb (Nuflo),
Henry Silva (Kua-Ko), Nehemiah
Persoff (Don Panta), Sessue Hay-
akawa (Runi), Michael Pate (priest).

GREEN SLIME, THE (1969-U.S./
Jap.) (A.K.A. "Gammo Sango
ucho Daisakusen")
Director: Kinji Fukasaku
Robert Horton (Jack Rankin), Richard
Jaeckel (Cmdr. Vince Elliot),
Luciana Paluzzi (Lisa Benson), Bud
Widom (Gen. Jonathan Thompson),
Ted Gunther (Dr. Halvorsen), Robert
Dunham (Capt. Martin), William
Ross (Ferguson), Richard Hylland
(Michael), David Yorston (Lt. Curtis),
Gary Randolf (Cordier), Linda Miller.

GREEN TERROR, THE (1919)
Director: Will P. Kellino
Heather Thatcher, Aurele Sydney,
Cecil du Gue, W.T. Ellwanger, Maud
Yates, Arthur Poole.

GREETINGS FROM EARTH (1978)
see Television: Battlestar Galactica (1978-79)

GRENDEL GRENDEL GRENDEL (1981-
Australia) - animated
Director: Alexander Stitt
Voices: Peter Ustinov (Grendel), Keith
Mitchell, Arthur Dignam, Ed Rosser,
Ric Stone, Ernie Bourne, Bobby Bright,
Julie McKenna, Alison Bird, Barry
Hill.

GRIM REAPER, THE (1981-Ital.)
Director: Joe D'Amato
Tisa Farrow (Julie), Saverio Valione,
Vanessa Steiger, George Eastman,
Mark Bodin, Mark Logan, Zora
Kerova, Bob Larsen, Rubina Ray.

GRIZZLY (1976) (A.K.A. "Killer
Grizzly")
Director: William Girdler
Christopher George (Kelly), Andrew
Prine (Don), Richard Jaeckel (Scott),
Joan McCall (Allison), Joe Dorsey
(Kittridge), Charles Kissinger (Doc-
tor), Kermit Echols (Corwin), Mary-
ann Hearn (1st victim).

GROUNDSTAR CONSPIRACY, THE
(1972)
Director: Lamont Johnson
George Peppard (Tuxan), Michael
Sarrazin (John Welles), Christine
Belford (Nicole Devon), Cliff Potts
(Carl Mosely), Tim O'Connor

(Gossage), Alan Oppenheimer (Hack-itt), James Olson (Sen. Stanton), Ty Haller (Henshaw), James McEachin (Bender), Roger Dressler (Kitchen), Anna Hagen (Dr. Plover), John Destry Adams (Zabrinski), Hagen Beggs (Dr. Hagler), Milos Zatovic (Dr. Zahl), Robin Collier (secretary), Don Gran-berry (technician), Bob Meneray (M. P. sergeant), Martin Moore, Dick Sar-gent, John Mitchell (M. P. s), Ed Col-lier (Nicole's doctor), Peter Lavender, William Nunn, Barry Cahill, John Vance (reporters).

GRUESOME TWOSOME (1966)
Director: Herschell Gordon Lewis
Chris Martell, Elizabeth Davis, Gret-chen Welles, Rodney Bedell.

GUESS WHAT HAPPENED TO COUNT DRACULA (1970)
Director: Laurence Merrick
Des Roberts (Count Dracula), Claudia Barron (Angelica), Robert Branche (Dr. Harris), John Landon (Guy), Frank Donato (Imp), Damu King (Hunch), Jeff Cady (Larry), Sharon Beverly (Vamp), Jim Settler (Rubt), John King III (Gil), James Young-El (Ma-cumba initiate), Angela Carnon (nurse), Yvonne Guadry (gypsy).

GULLIVER'S TRAVELS (1977)
Director: Peter Hunt
Richard Harris (Gulliver), Catherine Schell (girl), Norman Shelley (father), Meredith Edwards (uncle). Voices: Michael Bates, Julian Glover, Stephen Jack, Murray Melvin, Robert Rietty, Denis Bryer, Bessie Love, Nancy Nevinson, Vladek Sheybal, Bernard Spear, Roger Snowden, Graham Stark.

GUNS ON ICE PLANET ZERO, THE (1978)
see Television: Battlestar Galac-tica (1978-79)

GUYANA: CULT OF THE DAMNED (1980-Mex. /Span. /Pan.)
Director: Rene Cardona, Jr.
Stuart Whitman (Rev. James Johnson), Gene Barry (Rep. Lee O'Brian), John Ireland (Dave Cole), Joseph Cotten (Richard Gable), Bradford Dillman (Dr. Gary Shaw), Yvonne de Carlo (Susan Ames), Jennifer Ashley (Anna Kazan), Nadluska (Leslie), Erika Carl-son (Marilyn), Hugo Stiglitz (Cliff), Tony Young (Ron), Robert Doqui (Oliver), Carlos East (Mike).

GUY NAMED JOE, A (1943)
Director: Victor Fleming
Spencer Tracy (Pete Sandidge), Irene Dunne (Dorinda Durston), Van John-son (Ted Randall), James Gleason (Nails Kilpatrick), Ward Bond (Al Yackey), Lionel Barrymore (the General), Don DeFore (James J. Rourke), Barry Nelson (Dick Rum-ney), Henry O'Neill (Col. Hendricks), Esther Williams (Ellen Bright), Ad-dison Richards (Major Corbett), Matt Willis (Lt. Hunter), Walter Sande (mess sergeant), Gibson Gowland (bartender), Frank Faylen (Major), Marshall Reed, Blake Edwards (fliers), Phil Van Zandt (Major), Kirk Alyn (officer in heaven), Charles Smith (Sanderson), Mary Elliott (dance hall girl), Gertrude Hoffmann (old woman), Maurice Murphy (Capt. Robertson), William Bishop (Ray), Earl Schenck (Col. Sykes), Mark Daniels (Lieu-tenant), Eve Whitney (powerhouse girl), John Whitney (officer in heaven), Kay Williams (girl at bar), James Millican (orderly), John Frederick (Lt. Ridley), Peter Cookson (Sgt. Hanson), Irving Bacon (Corporal), Jacqueline White (Helen), Ernest Severn (Davy), Raymond Severn (Cy-ril), Yvonne Severn (Elizabeth), Ed-ward Hardwicke (George), Christopher Severn (Peter).

GYPSY MOON (1954)
see Television: Rocky Jones, Space Ranger (1953-54)

HAGGARD'S SHE - THE PILLAR OF FIRE (1899-Fr.) (A. K. A. "La Danse du Feu", "La Colonne de Feu")
Director: Georges Melies

HAIL! (1972) (A. K. A. "Washington, B. C. ")
Director: Fred Levinson
Dan Resin (the President), Richard B. Shull (Secretary of Health), Dick O'Neill (Attorney General), Joseph Sirola (Rev. Williams), Gary Sandy (Tom), Lee Meredith (Mrs. Meredith), Phil Foster (Moloney), K Callan (Mr. Burd), William Waterman (the Vice President), Patricia Ripley (the First Lady), Constance Forslund (Sara).

HALF HUMAN (1955-Jap.) (A. K. A. "Jujin Yukiotoko", "Monster Snow-man")
Director: Inoshire Honda & Kenneth G. Crane (English

sequences)
Akira Takarada (Iijima), Kenji Kasa-
hara (Takeno), Nobuo Nakamura (Shi-
heki Koijumi), Momoko Kochi (Shinsuke
Takeno), Akemi Negishi (Chika), John
Carradine (Dr. John Raybourn), Morris
Ankrum (Dr. Carl Jordan), Russell
Thorson (Prof. Philip Osborne), Robert
Karnes (Prof. Alan Templeton).

HALFWAY HOUSE (1944)
    Director: Basil Deardon
Francoise Rosay (Alice Meadows),
Mervyn Johns (Innkeeper Rhys), Gly-
nis Johns (Gwenyth), Sally Ann Howes
(Joanne French), Tom Walls (Capt.
Meadows), Esmond Knight (David
Davis), Valerie White (Jill French),
Alfred Drayton (Oakley), Richard
Bird (Richard French), Pat McGrath
(Terence), Guy Middleton (Capt.
Fortescue), Phillipa Hiatt (Margaret).

HALLOWEEN (1978)
    Director: John Carpenter
Donald Pleasence (Dr. Sam Loomis),
Jamie Lee Curtis (Laurie Strode),
Nancy Loomis (Annie Brackett), P. J.
Soles (Lynda), Charles Cyphers
(Leigh Brackett), Brian Andrews
(Tommy), Kyle Richards (Lindsey),
Nancy Stephens (Marion), John Mich-
ael Graham (Bob), Mickey Yablans
(Richie), Adam Hollander (Keith),
Brent LePage (Lonnie), Robert Phalen
(Dr. Wynn), Arthur Malet (graveyard
keeper), Will Sanden (Michael at age
6), Tony Moran (Michael at age 23),
Sandy Johnson (Judith), David Kyle
(boy friend), Peter Griffith (Laurie's
father), Nick Castle (the Shape), Jim
Windburn (stuntman).

HALLOWEEN II (1981)
    Director: Rick Rosenthal
Donald Pleasence (Dr. Sam Loomis),
Jamie Lee Curtis (Laurie Strode),
Pamela Susan Shoop (Karen), Charles
Cyphers (Leigh Brackett), Ana Alicia
(Janet), Jeffrey Kramer (Graham),
Cliff Emmich (Mr. Garrett), Lance
Guest (Jimmy), Gloria Gifford (Mrs.
Alves), Nancy Stephens (Marion),
John Zenda (Marshall), Ford Rainey
(Dr. Mixter), Hunter Von Leer (Gary
Hunt), Leo Rossi (Budd), Tawny Moyer
(Jill), Lucille Bensen (Mrs. Elrod),
Dick Warlock (the Shape/policeman No.
3), Alan Haufrect (announcer), Cath-
erine Bergstrom (producer), Howard
Culver (man in pajamas), Bill Warlock
(Craig), Jonathan Prince (Randy),
Dana Carvey (assistant), Leigh French

(Gary's mother), Ty Mitchell (Gary),
Ken Smolka (1st policeman), Roger
Hampton (2nd policeman), Pamela
McMyler (Laurie's mother), Dennis
Holahan (Laurie's father), Nichole
Drucker (young laurie), Adam Gunn
(young Michael Meyers), Tony Moran
(Michael at age 23), Nancy Loomis
(Annie Brackett), Robin Coleman
(medic), Jack Verbois (Bennett Tram-
er), Kyle Richards (Lindsey), Brian
Andrews (Tommy), Anne Bruner
(Alice).

HALLOWEEN 3: SEASON OF THE
    WITCH (1982)
    Director: Tommy Lee Wallace
Tom Atkins, Dan O'Herlihy, Stacey
Nelkin.

HALLUCINATED ALCHEMIST, AN
    (1897-Fr.) (A. K. A. "L'Hallucina-
    tion de l'Alchimiste")
    Director: Georges Melies

HALLUCINATIONS OF BARON MUN-
    CHAUSEN, THE (1911-Fr.) (A. K. A.
    "Les Hallucinations du Baron de
    Munchausen")
    Director: Georges Melies

HAMMERSMITH IS OUT (1971)
    Director: Peter Ustinov
Richard Burton (Hammersmith), Eliz-
abeth Taylor (Jimmie Jean Jackson),
Beau Bridges (Billy Breedlove), Peter
Ustinov (Doctor), Leon Askin (Dr.
Krodt), John Schuck (Henry Joe), Leon
Ames (Gen. Sam Pembroke), George
Raft (Guido Scartucci), Marjorie Eaton
(Princess), Linda Gaye Scott (Miss
Quim), Anthony Holland (Oldham),
Carl Donn (Cleopatra), Lisa Jak (Kid-
do), Mel Berger (fat man), Brook
Williams (Pete Rutter), Jose Espinoza
(Dude).

HAND, THE (1960)
    Director: Henry Cass
Derek Bond (Capt. Roberts/Roger
Crawshaw), Ray Cooney (Detective
Sgt. Pollitt), Harold Scott (Charlie
Taplow), Ronald Leigh-Hunt (Insp.
Munyard), Reed de Rouen (Michael
Brodie), Tony Hilton (Foster),
Bryan Coleman (Adams), Walter
Randall (Japanese Commander),
John Norman (Peter Adams), Mich-
ael Moore (Dr. Metcalfe), Jean
Dallas (Nurse Geiber), Reginald
Hearne (Noel Brodie), Madeleine
Burgess (Mrs. Brodie), Gwenda

Ewen (Nurse Johns), Garard Green (Simon Crawshaw), David Blake Kelly (Marshall), Ronald Wilson (doctor), Pat Hicks (Mrs. Adams), Frances Bennett (Mother), Susan Reid (little girl).

HAND, THE (1969-Fr.) (A. K. A. "La Main")
    Director: Henri Glaeser
Nathalie Delon (Sylvie), Michel Dunchaussoy (Phillippe), Roger Hanin, Henri Serre, Pierre Dux.

HAND, THE (1981)
    Director: Oliver Stone
Michael Caine (Jon Lansdale), Andrea Marcovicci (Anne Lansdale), Charles Fleischer (David Maddow), Bruce McGill (Brian Ferguson), Viveca Lindfors (Doctor), Nicholas Hormann (Bill Richman), Annie McEnroe (Stella Roche), Rosemary Murphy (Karen Wagner), Mara Hobel (Lizzie Lansdale), Pat Corley (Sheriff), Ed Marshall (doctor), John Stinson (therapist), Sparky Watt (Sergeant), Richard Altman (Hammond), Tracey Walter (Cop), Oliver Stone (bum), Brian Kenneth Hume (boy in classroom), Lora Pearson (girl in classroom), Jack, Scott, Randy & Patrick Evans (country bumpkins).

HAND OF A DEAD MAN, THE (1963-Span.) (A. K. A. "La Mano de un Hombre Muerto")
    Director: Jesus Franco
Howard Vernon, Paula Matrel, Ana Castor, Fernando Delgado, Georges Rollin, Gogo Robins.

HAND OF DEATH (1961)
    Director: Gene Nelson
John Agar (Alex Marsh), Paula Raymond (Carol Wilson), Steve Dunne (Tom Holland), Roy Gordon (Dr. Ramsey), John Alonzo (Carlos).

HAND OF PERIL, THE (1916)
    Director: Maurice Tourneur
House Peters (James Kestner), June Elvidge (Maura Lambert), Ralph Delmore (Frank Lambert), Doris Sawyer (Bull's Eve Cherry), Ray Pilcer (Tony Morello).

HAND OF POWER (1970-Ger.) (A. K. A. "In Banne Des Umheimlichen")
    Director: Alfred Vohrer
Joachim Fuchsberger, Hubert V. Meyernick, Siw Mattson, Pinkas Braun.

HANDS OF A STRANGER (1960)
    Director: Newton Arnold
Paul Lukather (Dr. Gil Harding), John Harvey (Dina Paris), James Stapleton (Vernon Paris), Sally Kellerman (Sue), Ted Otis (Dr. Russ Compson), Irish McCalla (Holly), Michael DuPont (Dr. Ken Fry), Michael Rye (George Britton), Larry Haddon (Police Lt. Syms), Elaine Martone (Eileen Hunter), Barry Gordon (Skeet), George Sawaya (cab driver), David Kramer (carnival barker).

HANDS OF ORLAC, THE (1925-Australia) (A. K. A. "Orlac Hande", "Die Unheimlichen Hande des Dr. Orlak")
    Director: Robert Wiene
Conrad Veidt, Fritz Kortner, Carmen Cartellieri, Paul Adkonas, Alexandra Sorina, Fritz Strassny.

HANDS OF ORLAC, THE (1960-Brit./ Fr.) (A. K. A. "Les Mains d'Orlac", "Hands of a Strangler")
    Director: Edmond T. Greville
Mel Ferrer (Steven Orlac), Christopher Lee (Nero), Dany Carrell (Regina), Sir Donald Wofit (Prof. Volcheff), Felix Aylmer (Dr. Cochrane), Lucile Saint-Simon (Louise), Basil Sydney (Siedelman), David Peel, Donald Pleasence, Janine Faye.

HANDS OF THE RIPPER (1971)
    Director: Peter Sasdy
Eric Porter (Pritchard), Angharad Rees (Anna), Jane Merrow (Laura), Derek Godfrey (Dysart), Dora Bryan (Mrs. Golding), Marjorie Rhodes (Mrs. Bryant), Keith Bell (Michael), Norman Bird (Inspector), Lunda Baron (Long Liz), Marjorie Lawrence (Dolly), Margaret Rawlings (Mme. Bullard), Elizabeth MacLennan (Mrs. Wilson), A. J. Brown (Rev. Anderson), April Wilding (Catherine), Anne Clune, Vicki Woolf (cell whores), Katya Wyeth, Beulah Hughes, Tallalah Miller (pub whores), Peter Munt (Leasants), Molly Weir (maid), Philip Ryan (police), Charles Lamb (guard), David Frankham (Mr. Sanford), Severn Darden (Simon Baud).

HANGAR 18 (1980)
    Director: James L. Conway
Darren McGavin (Harry Forbes), Robert Vaughn (Gordon Cain), Gary Collins (Steve Bancroft), Philip Abbott (Frank Morrison), Joseph

Campanella (Frank Lafferty), Cliff Osmond (Sheriff Barlow), Tom Hallick (Phil Cameron), Steven Keats (Paul Bannister), William Schallert (Prof. Mills), Pamela Bellwood (Sarah Michaels), James Hampton (Lew Price), Andrew Bloch (Neal Kelso), H. M. Wynant (Flight Director), Bill Zuckert (Ace Landon), Stuart Pankin (Sam Tate), Betty Ann Carr (Flo Mattson), Debra Macfarlane (female speciman), Jesse Bennett, Ed E. Carroll, Craig Clyde, Anne Galvan, Michael Irving, Robert Bristol, J. R. Clark, John William Halt, Ken Hapner, Bruce Katzman, H. E. D. Redford, Ocie Robinson, Peter Liakakis, Chet Norris, Max Robinson, Michael Ruud.

HANGING WOMAN, THE (1971-Span:)
Director: John Davidson
Stanley Cooper, Vickie Nesbitt, Marcella Wright, Gerald Tichy, Carl Mansion, Charles Fay, Catherine Gilbert, Charles Quince, Janis Brown, Paul Nash, Harold Stancey, Joseph Carter.

HANGOVER SQUARE (1845)
Director: John Brahm
Laird Cregar (George Harvey Bone), Linda Darnell (Netta Longdon), George Sanders (Dr. Allen Middleton), Glenn Langan (Carstairs), Alan Napier (Sir Henry Chapman), Frederic Worlock (Superintendent Clay), Leyland Hodgson (Detective Sgt. Lewis), Francis Ford (Ogilby), J. W. Austin (Detective Insp. King), Faye Marlowe (Barbara Chapman), John Goldsworthy (Butler), Charles Irwin (manager), Connie Leon (maid), Michael Dyne (Mickey), Clifford Brooke (watchman), Frank Benson (newsman), Robert Hale (costermonger), Leslie Denison (policeman).

HANNAH, QUEEN OF THE VAMPIRES (1972) (A. K. A. "Crypt of the Living Dead", "Vampire Woman", "Young Hannah, Queen of the Vampires")
Director: Ray Danton
Mark Damon, Theresa Gimpera, Andrew Prine, Patty Shepard, Francisco Brana.

HAPPY BIRTHDAY TO ME (1981)
Director: J. Lee Thompson
Melissa Sue Anderson (Virginia), Glenn Ford (Dr. Faraday), Tracy Bregman (Ann), Matt Craven (Steve), Jack Blum (Alfred), Lawrence Dane (Hal), Lenore Zann (Maggie), David Eisner (Rudi), Lisa Langlois (Amelia), Sharon Acker

(Estelle), Frances Hyland (Mrs. Patterson), Michel Rene Labelle (Etienne), Richard Rebiere (Greg), Lesleh Donaldson (Bernadette), Earl Pennington (Lt. Tracy).

HAPPY BIRTHDAY, WANDA JUNE (1971)
Director: Mark Robson
Rod Steiger (Harold Ryan), Susannah York (Penelope Ryan), Pamela Ferdin (Wanda June), George Grizzard (Dr. Norbert Wodley), Don Murray (Herb Shuttle), William Hickey (Looseleaf Harper).

HAPPY LAND (1943)
Director: Irving Pichel
Don Ameche (Lew Marsh), Frances Dee (Agnes), Harry Carey (Gramp), Ann Rutherford (Leonore Prentiss), Cara Williams (Tony Cavrek), Dickie Moore (Peter Orcutt), Richard Crane (Rusty), Mary Wickes (Emmy), James West (Rusty as a teenager), Larry Olsen (Rusty at age 5), James J. Smith (Everett Moore), Bernard Thomas (Sam Kendall), Edwin Mills (Bud), Terry Masengale (Arch), Minor Watson, Paul Weigel, John Dilson, William Weber, Roseanne Murray, Oscar O'Shea, Ferris Taylor, Housley Stevens, Adeline De Walt Reynolds, Walter Baldwin, Lillian Bronson, Ned Dobson, Jr., Joe Bernard, Leigh Whipper, Robert Dudley, Richard Abbott, Larry Thompson, Jackie Averill, Milton Kibbee, Marjorie Cooley, Pall Le Noir.

HARLEQUIN (1980-Australia)
Director: Simon Wincer
Robert Powell (Gregory Wolfe), David Hemmings (Nick Rast), Broderick Crawford (Doc Wheelan), Carmen Duncan (Sandra Rast), Guy Mercurio (Mr. Bergier), Alan Cassell (Mr. Porter), Mark Spain (Alex Rast), Sean Myers (Benny Lucas), Neville Teede (Dr. Barthelemy), Bevan Lee (Robinson), John Frawley (Dr. Lovelock), Mary Mackay (Edith Twist), Alyson Best (Alice), Nita Pannell (Mabel Wheelan), Murray Ogden (prison officer), Peter West (Godfrey), Claus Schultz (Arthur), David Hough (Jepson).

HARPY (TVM-1971) - 3-13-71
Director: Jerald Seth Sindell
Elizabeth Ashley (Marian Clune), Hugh O'Brian (Peter Clune), Tom Nardini (John), Marilyn Mason (Alison Reed), Mark Miller (Don Haskins), Linda Watkins (Mrs. Reed).

HARVEY (1950)
Director: Henry Koster
James Stewart (Elwood P. Dowd), Charles
Drake (Dr. Sanderson), Josephine Hull
(Beta Louise Simmons), Victoria Horne
(Myrtle Mae Simmons), Cecil Kellaway
(Dr. Chumley), Peggy Dow (Miss Kelly),
Jesse White (Wilson), William Lynn
(Judge Gaffney), Clem Bevans (Herman),
Wallace Ford (Lofgren), Norman Lea-
vitt (cab driver), Almira Sessions (Mrs.
Halsey), Minerva Urecal (Nurse Dunphy),
Nana Bryant (Mrs. Chumley), Ida Moore
(Mrs. McGiff), Grace Mills (Mrs. Chau-
venel), Richard Wessel (Cracker), Mau-
die Prickett (Elvira), Ed Max (sales-
man), Pat Flaherty (policeman), Ruth
Elma Stevens (Miss LaFay), Grace
Hampton (Mrs. Strickleberger), Anne
O'Neal (nurse), Eula Guy (Mrs. John-
son), Sam Wolfe (Minninger), William
Val (chauffeur), Polly Bailey (Mrs.
Krausmayer), Harry Hines (Meegels),
Sally Corner (Mrs. Cummings), Aileen
Carlyle (Mrs. Tewksbury), Gino Cor-
rado (eccentric man), Don Brodie (mail-
man).

HATCHET FOR THE HONEYMOON
    (1970-Span./Ital.) (A.K.A. "Una
    Hacha Para la Luna de Miel", "Blood
    Brides")
    Director: Mario Bava
Stephen Forsyth, Dagmar Lassander,
Laura Betti, Gerard Tichy, Alan Collins,
Luciano Pigozzi, Jesus Puente, Antonia
Mas, Femi Benussi.

HAUNTED CASTLE, THE (1896-Fr.)
    (A.K.A. "Le Manoir du Diable",
    "The Manor of the Devil", "The De-
    vil's Manor")
    Director: Georges Melies

HAUNTED CASTLE, THE (1921-Ger.)
    (A.K.A. "Schloss Vogelod")
    Director: F.W. Murnau
Paul Hartmann, Arnold Korff, Paul
Bildt, Olga Tscechova, Lulu Keyser-
Korff, Lother Mehnert, Julius Falken-
stein, Hermann Vallentin.

HAUNTED CASTLE (1969) (A.K.A.
    "Hiroku Kaibyoden")
    Director: Tokuzo Tanaka
Kojiro Hongo, Naomo Kobayashi, Mit-
suyo Kamei, Koichi Uenoyama, Akane
Kawasaki.

HAUNTED GOLD (1933)
    Director: Mack V. Wright
John Wayne, Sheila Terry, Harry
Woods, Erville Anderson, Otto Hoff-
man, Martha Mattox, Blue Washington.

HAUNTED HARBOR (1944) - serial in
    15 episodes
    Director: Spencer G. Bennett &
    Wallace Grissell
Kane Richmond (Jim Marsden), Kay
Aldridge (Patricia Harding), Roy
Barcroft (Kane), Marshall J. Reed
(Tommy), Forrest Taylor (Dr. Oliver
Harding), Oscar O'Shea (Galbraith),
Hal Taliaferro (Lawson), George J.
Lewis (Dranga), Edward Keane (Fred-
erick Vorhees), Kenne Duncan (Gregg),
Bud Geary (Snell), Robert Homans,
(port captain), Robert Wilke (bartender
No. 1), Fred Graham (Stokes/bartender
No. 2), Dale Van Sickel (Duff/guard No.
1/sailor No. 1), Tom Steele (Ronson/
Clark/guard No. 2/store heavy), Kit
Guard (roustabout), Ken Terrell (Taola/
sailor No. 2), Duke Green (Neville/
Dunning/Gort/Grimes/guard No. 3/
Kassim/Bert Mead/rock heavy No. 1),
Jack O'Shea (rock heavy No. 2), Pietro
Sosso (priest), Rico de Montez (Teamil),
Bud Wolfe, Carey Loftin (cave heavies),
Dick Botiller, Fred Cordova (policemen),
Charles Hayes (citizen), Nick Thomp-
son (Native Chief), Clancy Cooper
(Yank), Harry Smith, Harry Wilson,
Eddie Parker, Herbert Evans.

HAUNTED HOUSE, THE (1928)
    Director: Benjamin Christensen
Chester Conklin (Mr. Rackham), Flora
Finch (Mrs. Rackham), Edmund Breese
(Uncle Herbert), Sidney Bracy (Tully),
Thelma Todd (Nurse), Montague Love
(Mad Doctor), Larry Kent (Billy), Bar-
bara Bedford (Nancy), Eve Southern
(somnambulist), William V. Mong
(caretaker).

HAUNTED PALACE, THE (1963)
    Director: Roger Corman
Vincent Price (Joseph Curwen/Charles
Dexter Ward), Debra Paget (Ann Ward),
Lon Chaney, Jr. (Simon Orne), Frank
Maxwell (Dr. Fillet), Leo Gordon (Wee-
den), John Dierkes (West), Elisha Cook,
Jr. (Smith), Milton Parsons (Jabez
Hutchinson), Cathy Merchant (Hester
Tillinghast), Barboura Morris (Mrs.
Weeden), Harry Ellerbe (minister),
Bruno Ve Sota (bartender), Guy Wilker-
son (Leach), Darlene Lucht (woman
victim), I. Stanford Jolley.

HAUNTED STRANGLER, THE (1958)
    (A.K.A. "The Grip of the Strangler")
    Director: Robert Day
Boris Karloff (James Rankin), Elizabeth
Allen (Mrs. Rankin), Anthony Dawson
(Superintendent Burk), Jean Kent (Cora),
Tim Turner (Dr. McColl), Vera Day

(Peral), Dorothy Gordon (Hannah),
Derek Birch (hospital superintendent),
Diane Aubrey (Lily), Leslie Perrins
(prison governor), Desmond Roberts
(Dr. Johnson), Max Brimmell (turn-
key), John Fabian (Young Blood),
Jessica Cairns (asylum maid).

HAUNTING, THE (1963)
    Director: Robert Wise
Julie Harris (Eleanor Vance), Claire
Bloom (Theodora), Richard Johnson
(Dr. John Markway), Russ Tamblyn
(Luke Sanderson), Rosalie Crutchley
(Mrs. Dudley), Valentine Dyall (Mr.
Dudley), Lois Maxwell (Grace Mark-
way), Ray Compton (Mrs. Sanderson),
Ronald Adam (Eldridge Harper), Paul
Maxwell (Bud), Howard Lang (Hugh
Crain), Pamela Buckley (1st Mrs.
Crain), Freda Knorr (2nd Mrs. Crain),
Janet Mansell (Abigail at age 6), Amy
Dalby (Abigail at age 80), Mavis Vil-
liers (landlady), Diane Clare (Carrie
Fredericks), Susan Richard (nurse),
Claude Jones (fat man), Verina Green-
law.

HAUNTING OF JULIA, THE (1977)
    (A.K.A. "Full Circle")
    Director: Richard Longcraine
Keir Dullea (Magnus), Mia Farrow
(Julia), Jill Bennett (Lily), Peter Sallis
(Mr. Branscombe), Cathleen Nesbitt
(Mrs. Rudge), Pauline Jameson (Mrs.
Branscombe), Tom Conti (Mark), Ro-
bin Gammell (Swift), Anna Wing (Mrs.
Flood), Samantha Gates (Olivia), Sophie
Ward (Kate).

HAUNTING OF M, THE (1979)
    Director: Anna Thomas
Sheelagh Gilbey (Marianna), Nini
Pitt (Halina), Alan Hay (Karol), Evie
Garratt (Daria), Jo Scott Matthews
(Aunt Teresa), William Bryan (Marion),
Peter Austin (Stefan), Ernest Bale
(Staho), Varvara Pepper (Irka), Peter
Stenson (doctor), Isolde Cazelet (Yola).

HAUNTING OF PENTHOUSE D, THE
    (TVM-1974) - 10-15-74
    Director: Henry Kaplan
David Birney (Perry), Farley Granger
(Ben), Barton Heyman (Boyle), Carole
Mallory (Dolcina), Merwin Goldsmith
(Sgt. Janowitz).

HAUNTING OF ROSALIND, THE (TVM-
    1973) - 4-10-73
    Director:
Frank Converse (Arthur), Susan Sarandon (Dita), Pamela Payton-Wright

(Rosalind), Addison Powell (Dr. Soames),
Dennis Higghin (Bernard).

HAUNTS (1977)
    Director: Herb Freed
May Britt (Ingrid), Aldo Ray (Sheriff),
Ben Hammer (Vicar), E. J. Andre
(Doc), Cameron Mitchell (Carl), Will-
iam Gray Espy (Frankie), Susan Nohr
(Nel), Kendall Jackson (Loretta).

HAUNTS OF THE VERY RICH, THE
    (TVM-1972) - 9-20-72
    Director: Paul Wendkos
Lloyd Bridges (Dave Woodbrough),
Cloris Leachman (Ellen Blunt), Ed
Asner (Al Hunsicker), Moses Gunn
(Seacrist), Anne Francis (Annette
Larrier), Robert Reed (Rev. Mr.
Fellows), Donna Mills (Laurie), Tony
Bill (Lyle), Phyllis Hill (Reta), Bev-
erly Gill (Miss Vick), Todd Martin
(Harris), Sammy Jackson (ham radio
operator).

HAUSER'S MEMORY (TVM-1970) - 10-
    24-70
    Director: Boris Sagal
David McCallum (Hillel Mondoro), Su-
san Strasberg (Karen Mondoro), Lilli
Palmer (Anna), Leslie Nielsen (Slaugh-
ter), Helmut Kautner (Kramer), Robert
Webber (Dorsey), Hans Elwenspoek
(van Kungen), Herbert Fleishmann
(Renner), Peter Capell (Shepilov), Bar-
bara Lass (Angelika), Peter Ehrlich
(Kucera), Gunther Meisner (Koroviev),
Otto Stern (Gessler), Art Brauss (Bak),
Jochen Busse (Dieter), Manfred Redde-
mann (Sorsen), Barbara Capell (young
Anna).

HAVE ROCKET, WILL TRAVEL (1959)
    Director: David Lowell Rich
Moe Howard, Joe DeRita, Larry Fine,
Jerome Cowan (J.P. Morse), Anna-
Lisa (Dr. Ingrid Naaveg), Robert Col-
bert (Dr. Ted Benson), Nadine Datas,
Marjorie Bennett.

HAWK OF THE WILDERNESS (1938)
    (A.K.A. "Lost Island of Kioga") -
    serial in 12 episodes
Chapters: 1. "Mysterious Island", 2.
"Flaming Death", 3. "The Tiger Trap",
4. "Queen's Ransom", 5. "Pendulum of
Doom", 6. "The Dead Fall", 7. "White
Man's Magic", 8. "Ambushed", 9. "Ma-
rooned", 10. "Caves of Horror", 11.
"Valley of the Skulls", & 12. "Trail's
End".
    Director: William Witney &
    John English

Bruce Bennett/Herman Brix (Kioga/Lincoln Rand, Jr.), Mala (Kias), Monte Blue (Yellow Weasel), Noble Johnson (Mokuyi), George Eldredge (Allan Kendle), Dick Wessel (Dirk), William Royle (Manuel Solerno), Tom Chatterton (Dr. Edward Munro), Jill Martin (Beth Munro), Lane Chandler (Lincoln Rand, Sr.), Patrick J. Kelly (William Williams), Iron Eyes Cody (Storm Cloud), Ann Evers (Helena Rand), Fred Miller (Jansen), Harry Tenbrook (Pete), Loren Riebe (Carl), Snowflake/Fred Toones (George), Earl Askam (Red), Alex Montoya (Shoshone), Jerry Sheldon (Joe), George Letz (Tom), William Stahl (Bart), Art Felix (Dark Feather), Jerry Frank (Running Water), Jerome DeNuccio (Snow Mountain), Frank Hill (Many Rivers), Henry Wills (Seven Feathers), John Roy (White Beaver), Jimmy Dime (Dark Cloud), Moe Malulu (Cherokee), Jack Minton (Chippewa), Tony Urchel (Geronimo), John Big Tree (Medicine Doctor), Art Miles (Okoboji), Joe Draper (Running Deer), L. Y. Maxwell (Thunder Rock), Clarence Chorre (Wahnee), Phillip Armenta (Indian Chief), Charley Randolph (Minnewaska), Jim I. Spencer (Ottawa), Gertrude Chorre (Squaw), Wally Rose (Willow Bush), Sonny Chorre (White Eagle).

HAWKS AND THE SPARROWS, THE (1965-Ital.) (A. K. A. "Ucellacci e Uccellini", "Bad Birds and Good Birds")
    Director: Pier Paolo Pasolini
Toto, Ninetto Davoli, Rossana Di Rocco, Ferni Benussi, Umberto Bevilacqua, Renato Capogna.

HAWK THE SLAYER (1980)
    Director: Terry Marcel
Jack Palance (Voltan), John Terry (Hawk), Bernard Bresslaw (Gort), Shane Briant (Drago), Ray Charleson (Crow), Morgan Sheppard (Ranulf), Warren Clarke (Scar), Delcan Mullholland (Sped), Peter O'Farrell (Baldwin), Cheryl Campbell (Sister Monica), Annette Crosbie (Abbess), Harry Andrews (High Abbott), Graham Stark (Sparrow), Ferdy Mayne (old man), Roy Kinnear (innkeeper), Patrick Magee (priest), Patricia Quinn (woman), Christopher Benjamin (Fitzwalter), Catriona MacCall (Elaine), Peter Benson (Black Wizard), Derrick O'Connor (Ralf), Maurice Coulbourne (axe man No. 1), Barry Stokes (axe man No. 2), John J. Carney (soldier), Anthony Milner (Ferret), Jo England, Frankie Cosgrave, Melissa Wiltsie

(nuns), Lindsey Brook (Little Sister), Eddie Stacey (Chak), Ken Parry (Thomas), Stephen Rayne (Brother Peter), Robert Putt, Mark Cooper (roughs in tavern).

HEAD, THE (1959-Ger.) (A. K. A. "Die Nackte und der Satan", "The Naked and Satan", "A Head for the Devil")
    Director: Victor Trivas
Horst Frank (Dr. Ood), Michel Simon (Prof. Abel), Karin Kernke (Irene), Paul Dahlke (Crime Commissioner), Christine Mayback (Lilly), Dieter Eppler (Paul), Kurt Muller-Graf (Dr. Burke), Helmut Schmid (Bert, the lab assistant), Maria Stadler (Mrs. Schneider), Otto Storr (bartender).

HEADLESS GHOST, THE (1959)
    Director: Peter Graham Scott
Richard Lyon (Bill), Lilliane Sottane (Ingrid), Clive Revill (Fourth Earl), Jack Ellen (Earl of Ambrose), Carl Bernard (Sgt. Grayson), Alexander Archdale (Randolph), Trevor Barnett (strong man), Josephine Blake (Dancer), Donald Bissett (guide), Patrick Connor (Constable), John Stacy (Parker), Mary Barclay (Lady Ambrose).

HEAD OF PANCHO VILLA, THE (1955-Mex.) (A. K. A. "La Cabeza de Pancho Villa")
    Director: Chano Urueta
Luis Aguilar, Flor Silvestre, Pascual Garcia Pena, Jaime Fernandez, Francisco Reiguera.

HEARSE, THE (1980)
    Director: George Bowers
Trish Van Devere (Jane Hardy), Joseph Cotton (Walter Pritchard), David Gautreaux (Tom Sullivan), Donald Petrie (Luke), Perry Lang (Paul Gordon), Donald Hotton (Rev. Winston), Med Flory (Sheriff Denton), Christopher McDonald (Pete), Olive Dunbar (Mrs. Gordon), Dominic Barto (Driver), Nicholas Shields (Dr. Greenwalt), Al Hansen (Bo Rehnquist), Fredric Franklyn (Gordon), Allison Balson (Alice), Victoria Eubank (Lois), Chuck Mitchell (counterman), Jimmy Gatherum (boy), Tanya Bowers (schoolgirl).

HEARTBEAT (1949)
    Director: William Cameron Menzies
Richard Hart.

HEARTBEEPS (1981)
    Director: Allan Arkush

Andy Kaufman (Val Com-17485), Bernadette Peters (Aquacom-89045), Kenneth McMillan (Max), Randy Quaid (Charlie), Jack Carter (voice of Catskill), Melanie Mayron (Susan Gort), Christopher Guest (Calvin Gort), Richard B. Shull (factory boss), Kathleen Freeman (helicopter pilot), Dick Miller (factory watchman), Mary Woronov (party house owner), Paul Bartel (party guest), Anne Wharton (party guest), Jeffrey Kramer (party butler robot), Stephanie Faulkner, Barry Diamond (firing range technicians), Karsen Lee Gould, Irene Forrest (party maid robots), David Gene Lebell (forkliff drive robot).

HEART TRUMP IN TOKYO FOR OSS 117 (1966-Fr. /Ital.) (A. K. A. "Terror in Tokyo", "Atout Coeur a Tokio Pour OSS 117")
　　Director: Michel Boisrond
Frederick Stafford (OSS 117), Marina Vlady (Eva), Inkijinoff (Chief), Henri Serre (Wilson), Colin Drake, Tetsuko Yoshimura.

HEAVEN CAN WAIT (1943)
　　Director: Ernst Lubitch
Gene Tierney (Martha), Don Ameche (Henry Van Cleve), Charles Coburn (Hugo Van Cleve), Laird Cregar (His Excellency), Spring Byington (Berta Van Cleve), Louis Calhern (Randolph Van Cleve), Signe Hasso (Mademoiselle), Aubrey Mather (James), Eugene Pallette (E. F. Strabel), Clarence Muse (Jasper), Michael Ames (Jack Van Cleve), Helene Reynolds (Peggy Nash), Dickie Moore (Henry at age 15), Dickie Jones (Albert at age 15), Scotty Beckett (Henry at age 9), Claire Du Brey (Miss Ralston), Charles Halton (clerk in Britano's), Edwin Maxwell (doctor), Doris Merrick (nurse), Grayce Hampton (Albert's mother), Alfred Hall (Albert's father), Gerald Oliver Smith (Smith), Marlene Mains (Mary), James Flaven (policeman), Anita Bolster (Mrs. Cooper-Cooper), Trudy Marshall (Jane), Clara Blandick (grandmother), Leonard Carey (Flogdell), Florence Bates (Mrs. Craig).

HEAVEN CAN WAIT (1978)
　　Director: Warren Beatty & Buck Henry
Warren Beatty (Joe Pendleton), Julie Christie (Betty Logan), Dyan Cannon (Julia Farnsworth), Charles Grodin (Tony Abbott), Jack Warden (Max Corkle), James Mason (Mr. Jordan),

Buck Henry (the Escort), Vincent Gardenia (Detective), Dolph Sweet (head coach), John Randolph (former owner), Keene Curtis (Oppenheim), R. G. Armstrong (General Manager), William Sylvester (nuclear reporter), Morgan Farley (Middleton), Frank Campanella (Conway), Hamilton Camp (Bentley), Stephanie Faracy (Corinne), Harry D. K. Wong (gardener), Joseph Maher (Sisk), Richard O'Brien (advisor), Arthur Malet (Everett), Jeannie Linero (Lavinia), George J. Manos (security guard), Dick Enberg (TV interviewer), William Larsen (Renfield), William Bogert (Lawson), Ed V. Peck (trainer), Larry Block (Peters), Joel Marston, Robert E. Leonard, Earl Montgomery, Robert C. Stevens, (board members), Bill Sorrells (Tomarken), Bernie Massa (guard), Will Hare (Doctor), Joseph F. Makel (Ambassador), Lee Weaver (attendant), Roger Bowen (newspaperman), Nick Outin (chauffeur), Peter Tomarken, Lisa Blake Richards (reporters), Jerry Scanlan (Hodges), Jim Boeke (Kowalsky), Deacon Jones (Gorman), Marvin Fleming (Gudnitz), Les Josephson (Owens), Jack T. Snow (Cassidy), Curt Gowdy (TV commentator), Charlie Charlies (highwire artist), Al DeRogatis (TV analyst).

HEAVENLY DAZE (1948) - short
　　Director: Jules White
Moe Howard, Shemp Howard, Larry Fine, Vernon Dent, Sam McDaniel.

HEAVEN ONLY KNOWS (1947)
　　Director: Albert S. Rogell
Robert Cummings (Archangel Michael), Brian Donlevy, Marjorie Reynolds, Stuart Erwin, Bill Goodwin, Gerald Mohr, Ray Bennett, John Litel, Edgar Kennedy, Lurene Tuttle, Jorja Cartright, Peter Miles.

HEAVY METAL (1981) - animated
　　Director: Gerald Potterton
Voices: Roger Bumpass, Jackie Burroughs, Joe Flaherty, Martin Lavut, Don Francks, John Candy, Eugene Levy, Alice Playton, August Schallenberg, Susan Roman, Al Yanovsky, John Vernon, Richard Romanos, Harold Ramis, Marilyn Lightstone.

HEIRESS OF DRACULA, THE (1971-Ger. /Span.) (A. K. A. "Vampyros Lesbos", "Die Erbin des Dracula", "El Signo del Vampire", "Las Vampiras", "The Sign of the Vampire",

"The Vampire Women")
Director: Jesus Franco
Dennis Priçe, Paul Muller, Soledad Miranda, Susann Korda, Geidrun Kussin, Ewa Stromberg, Victor Feldman.

HE KNOWS YOU'RE ALONE (1980)
Director: Armand Mastroianni
Don Scardino (Marvin), Caitlin O'Heaney (Amy), Elizabeth Kemp (Nancy), Patty Pease (Joyce), Tom Rolfing (the Killer), Lewis Arlt (Gamble), James Rebhorn (Professor), Dana Barron (Diana), Tom Hanks (Elliot), Joseph Leon (Ralph, the tailor), James Carroll (Phil), Paul Gleason (Daley), Brian Byers (Bernie), Robin Lamont (Ruthie), Peter Gumeny (Thompson), Curtis Hostetter (Tommy), Robin Tilghman (Marie), John Bottoms (Father McKenna), Debbie Novak, Laurie Faso, Ron Haskins, Jamie Haskins, Russell Todd, Dorian Lopinto, Steve W. James, Anthony Shaw, Barbara Quinn, Michael Fiorillo, Ron Englehardt.

HELICOPTER SPIES, THE (TVM-1967)
Director: Boris Sagal
see Television: Man from U.N.C.L.E.
- "The Prince of Darkness Affair"
(10-2-67 & 10-9-67)

HELLISH SPIDERS (1966-Mex.) (A.K.A.
"Aranas Infernales")
Director: Federico Curiel
Blue Demon, Blanquita Sanchez, Fernando Oses, Ramon Bugarini, Martha Elena Cervantes, Sergio Virell, Jessica Munguia, Frankenstein.

HELL NIGHT (1981)
Director: Tom De Simone
Linda Blair (Marti), Vince Van Patten (Seth), Kevin Brophy (Peter), Peter Burton (Jeff), Jenny Neumann (May), Suki Goodwin (Denise), Jimmy Sturtevant (Scott).

HELLO DOWN THERE (1969)
Director: Jack Arnold
Tony Randall (Fred Miller), Janet Leigh (Vivian Miller), Jim Backus (T.R. Hollister), Roddy McDowall (Nate Ashbury), Ken Berry (Mel Cheever), Richard Dreyfuss (Harold Webster), Harvey Lembeck (sonarman), Charlotte Rae (Myrtle Ruth), Lou Wagner (Marvin Webster), Bruce Gordon (Admiral), Arnold Stang (Jonah), Kay Cole (Lorrie Miller), Henny Backus (Mrs. Webster), Frank Schuller (Alan Briggs), Gary Tigerman (Tommie Miller), Bud Hoey (Mr. Webster), Lee Meredith (Dr. Cara

Wells), Jay Laskay (Philo), Merv Griffin (himself), Frank Logan (Captain), Charles Martin (Chief Petty Officer), Pat Henning (Reilly), Andy Jarrell (radio man), Lora Kaye (secretary).

HELLSTROM CHRONICLE, THE (1971)
Director: Walon Green
Lawrence Pressman (Dr. Neils Hellstrom).

HELLZAPOPPIN' (1941)
Director: H.C. Potter
Dale Van Sickel (Frankenstein's Monster).

HELP! (1965)
Director: Richard Lester
John Lennon (John), Paul McCartney (Paul), George Harrison (George), Ringo Starr (Ringo), Leo McKern (Clang), Eleanor Bron (Ahme), Roy Kinnear (Algernon), John Bluthal (Bhuta), Victor Spinetti (Foot), Patrick Cargill (Superintendent).

HENDERSON MONSTER, THE (TVM-1980) - 5-27-80
Director: Waris Hussein
Jason Miller (Dr. Thomas Debs Henderson), Christine Lahti (Louise Casmir), Stephen Collins (Pete Casmir), Nehemiah Persoff (Prof. Tedeschi), Larry Gates (President Doby), David Spielberg (Mayor Bellona), Josef Sommer (Dr. Martin Grossman), Peter Evans (Brother Harold).

HENRY ALDRICH HAUNTS A HOUSE (1943) (A.K.A. "Henry Haunts a House")
Director: Hugh Bennett
Jimmy Lydon (Henry Aldrich), John Litel, Lucien Littlefield, Mike Mazurki, Charles Smith, Olive Blakeney.

HERBIE GOES BANANAS (1980)
Director: Vincent McEveety
Cloris Leachman (Aunt Louise), John Vernon (Prindle), Elyssa Davalos (Melissa), Harvey Korman (Capt. Elythe), Richard Jaeckel (Shepard), Alex Rocco (Quinn), Fritz Feld (Chief Stewart), Stephan W. Burns (Pete), Joaquin Garay III (Paco), Charles Martin Smith (D.J.), Vito Scotti (Armando), Jose Gonzalez Gonzalez, Rubin Moreno, Allan Hunt, Tina Menard, Jorge Moreno, Tom Scott, Iris Adrian, Patricia Van Patten, Henry Slate, Ceil Cabot, Hector Morales, Jack Perkins.

HERBIE GOES TO MONTE CARLO
(1977)
Director: Vincent McEveety
Dean Jones (Jim Douglas), Julie Sommars (Diane Darcy), Don Knotts (Wheely Applegate), Roy Kinnear (Quincey), Eric Braeden (Bruno von Stickel), Laurie Main (Duval), Bernard Fox (Max), Alan Caillou (Emile), Jacques Marin (Insp. Bouchet), Zavier Saint Macary (Detective Fontenory), Francoise Lalande (Monsieur Ribeaux), Mike Kulcsar (Claude), Stanley Brock (taxi driver), Gerard Jugnot (waiter), Tom McCorrey, Jean-Jacques Moreau, Lloyd Nelson, Yveline Briere, Madeleine Damien, Raoul Delfosse, Sebastian Floche, Ed Marcus, Alain Janey.

HERBIE RIDES AGAIN (1972)
Director: Robert Stevenson
Helen Hayes (Mrs. Steinmetz), Ken Barry (Willoughby Whitfield), Stefanie Powers (Nicole), John McIntire (Mr. Judson), Keenan Wynn (Alonzo Hawk), Huntz Hall (Judge), Vito Scotti (taxi driver), Ivor Barry (chauffeur), Raymond Bailey (lawyer), Liam Dunn (doctor), Richard X. Slattery (Traffic Commissioner), Chuck McCann (Lostgarten), Dan Tobin (lawyer), Elaine Devry (secretary), Rob McCary (Red Knight), Hank Jones (Sir Lancelot).

HERCULES (1957-Ital.) (A.K.A. "Le Fatiche de Ercole", "The Labors of Hercules")
Director: Pietro Francisci
Steve Reeves (Hercules), Sylvia Koscina (Iole), Fabrizio Mioni (Jason), Ivo Garrani (Pelias), Gianna Maria Canale (Antea), Arturo Dominici (Eurysteus), Mimmo Palmara (Iphitus), Lidia Alfonsi (the Sybil), Andrea Fantasia (Laertes), Aldo Fiorelli (Argos), G. P. Gosmino (Esculapius), Afro Poli (Chiron), Gino Mattera (Orpheus), Gabriele Antonini (Ulysses), Gina Rovere (Amazon), Luciana Paluzzi.

HERCULES AGAINST ROME (1964-Ital./Fr.) (A.K.A. "Ercole contro Roma")
Director: Piero Pierotti
Sergio Ciani/Alan Steel (Hercules), Wandisa Guida, Livio Lorenzon, Domenico Palmara, Andrew Aureli, Daniele Vargas.

HERCULES AGAINST THE BARBARIANS (1964-Ital.) (A.K.A. "Maciste nell' Inferno di Gengis Khan", "Maciste in Ghengis Khan's Hell")
Director: Domenico Paolella
Mark Forest (Maciste), Gloria Milland, Ken Clark, Roldano Lupi, Jose Greci, Renato Rossini.

HERCULES AGAINST THE MOON MEN (1964-Ital./Fr.) (A.K.A. "Maciste contro gli Uomini Della Luna", "Maciste vs. the Moon Men", "Maciste e la Regina di Samar", "Maciste and the Queen of Samar", "Maciste contre les Hommes de Pierre", "Maciste vs. the Stone Men")
Director: Giacomo Gentilomo
Sergio Ciani/Alan Steel (Maciste), Jany Clair, Anna-Maria Polani, Nando Tamberlani, Jean-Pierre Honore.

HERCULES AGAINST THE SONS OF THE SUN (1964-Ital./Span.) (A.K.A. "Ercole contro i Figli del Sole")
Director: Osvaldo Civirani
Mark Forest (Hercules), Anna Maria Pace, Angela Rhu, Giuliano Gemma, Ricardo Valle, Giulio Donnini, Andrea Scotti.

HERCULES AND THE CAPTIVE WOMEN (1961-Ital./Fr.) (A.K.A. "Ercole alla Conquista di Atlantide", "Hercules and the Conquest of Atlantis", "Hercules Conquers Atlantis")
Director: Vittorio Cottafavi
Reg Park (Hercules), Fay Spain (Antinea), Ettore Manni (Androcles), Luciano Marin (Illus), Ivo Garrani, Laura Ailan, Mario Petri, Mimmo Palmara, Enrico-Maria Salerno, Salvatore Furnari, Gianmaria Volonte, Mario Valdermarin, Allesandro Sperli, Maurizio Caffarelli, Luciana Angiolillo.

HERCULES AND THE PRINCESS OF TROY (TVM-1965) - 9-12-65
Director: Albert Band
Gordon Scott (Hercules), Diana Hyland (Princess Diana), Giorgio Ardisson (Leander), Mart Hulswit (Ulysses), Paul Stevens (Diogenes), Roger Browne (Ortag), Steve Garrett (King Petra).

HERCULES AND THE TYRANTS OF BABYLON (1964-Ital.) (A.K.A. "Ercole contro i Tiranni di Babilonia")
Director: Domenico Paolella
Rock Stevens (Hercules), Helga Line, Mario Petri, Annamaria Polani, Tullio Altamura, Livio Lorenzon.

HERCULES IN NEW YORK (1970)
Director: Arthur A. Seidelman

Arnold Strong/Arnold Schwarzenegger (Hercules), Arnold Stang.

HERCULES IN THE HAUNTED WORLD (1961-Ital.) (A.K.A. "Ercole al Centro della Terra", "Hercules at the Center of the Earth")
Director: Mario Bava
Reg Park (Hercules), Christopher Lee (Lichas), Leonora Ruffo (Deianira), Giorgio Ardisson (Theseus), Ely Draco, Milton Reid, Ida Galli, Marisa Belli.

HERCULES IN THE VALE OF WOE (1963-Ital.) (A.K.A. "Maciste Against Gercules in the Vale of Woe")
Director:
Kirk Morris,(Hercules), Liana Orfei, Bice Valori, Franco Franchi, Frank Gordon.

HERCULES OF THE DESERT (1964-Ital.) (A.K.A. "La Valle dell' Eco Tonante", "The Valley of the Thundering Echo")
Director: Tanio Boccia/Amerigo Anton
Kirk Morris (Hercules), Spela Rozin, Helene Chanel, Furio Meniconi, Alberto Farnese, Rosalba Neri.

HERCULES, PRISONER OF EVIL (1964-Ital.) (A.K.A. "Terror of the Kirghiz")
Director: Antonio Margheriti
Reg Park, Ettore Manni, Mireille Granelli, Maria Teresa Orsini, Furio Meniconi.

HERCULES, SAMSON AND ULYSSES (1963-Ital.) (A.K.A. "Ercole Sfida Sansone", "Hercules Challenges Samson")
Director: Pietro Francisci
Kirk Morris (Hercules), Richard Lloyd (Samson), Enzo Cerusico (Ulysses), Liana Orfie (Delilah), Aldo Giuffre (Siren), Fulvia Franco.

HERCULES THE INVINCIBLE (1963-Ital.) (A.K.A. "Ercole l'Invincible")
Director: Alfredo Mancori/Al World
Don Vadis (Hercules), Spela Rozin, Ken Clark, Carla Calo, Hugo Arden, Jeanette Barton, Red Boss, Jon Simons.

HERCULES UNCHAINED (1959-Ital./Fr.) (A.K.A. "Ercole e la Regina di Lidia", "Hercules and the Queen of Lidia")
Director: Pietro Francisci

Steve Reeves (Hercules), Sylva Koscina (Iole), Primo Carnera (Antaeus), Sergio Fantoni (Eteocles), Carlo D'Angelo (Creon), Sylvia Lopez (Queen of Lydia), Patrizia Della Rovere (Penelope), Gabriele Antonini (Ulysses), Cesare Fantoni (Oedipus), Mimmo Palmara (Polinices), Andrea Fantasia (Laertes).

HERCULES VS. THE GIANT WARRIORS (1964-Ital.) (A.K.A. "Il Trionfo di Ercole", "The Triumph of Hercules", "Hercules and the Ten Avengers")
Director: Alberto De Martino
Don Vadis (Hercules), Moira Orfei, Piero Lulli, Marilu Tolo, Peirre Cressoy, Enzo Fiermonte, Renato Rossini.

HERE COMES MR. JORDAN (1941)
Director: Alexander Hall
Robert Montgomery (Joe Pendleton), Claude Rains (Mr. Jordan), Edward Everett Horton (Messenger 7013), James Gleason (Max Corkle), Rita Johnson (Julia), Evelyn Keyes (Bette), Donald MacBride (Williams), John Emery (Tony), Halliwell Hobbes (Sisk), Don Costello (Lefty), Benny Rubin (Bugs), Joseph Crehan (doctor), Ken Christy (plainclothesman), Billy Newell (handler), Joe Hickey (Gilbert), Billy Dawson (Johnny), Tom Hanlon (announcer), Warren Ashe (Charlie), Bobby Larson (Chips), Mary Currier (secretary), John Kerns (sparring partner), Chester Conklin (newsboy), Lloyd Bridges (co-pilot), Edmund Elton (elderly man).

HER JUNGLE LOVE (1938)
Director: George Archainbaud
Dorothy Lamour (Tura), Ray Milland (Bob Mitchell), Lynne Overman (Jimmy Wallace), J. Carrol Naish (Kuasa), Jonathan Hale (J.C. Martin), Archie Twitchell (Roy Atkins), Dorothy Howe (Eleanor Martin), Edward A. Earle (Capt. Avery), Sonny Choree (1st guard), Tony Urchell (2nd guard), Richard Denning, Philip Warren (Men).

HERO AT LARGE (1980)
Director: Martin Davidson
John Ritter (Steve Nichols), Anne Archer (J. Marsh), Bert Convy (Walter Reeves), Kevin McCarthy (Calvin Donnelly), Harry Bellaver (Eddie), Leonard Harris (Mayor), Rick Podell (Milo), Jane Hallaren (Gloria), Allan Rich (Marth Fields), Tony Cacciotti (Anthony Casselli), Anita Dangler

(Mrs. Havacheck), William Bogert
(TV moderator), A. J. Carothers (TV
commentator), Dr. Joyce Brothers
(Herself), Kenneth Tobey (Fire Chief),
Kurt Andon (fireman), Gerald Castillo,
Gerry Black (heros at fire), Robin
Sherwood, Bryan O'Byrne, Kevin
Bacon, Tony Crupi, Gary Goodrow,
Rod Haase, Natalie Cilona, Heidi
Gold, Michael Gorrin, Henrietta Ja-
cobson, Michael Leon, James O'Con-
nell, William Robertson, Joseph Stern,
Vanda Barra, David-James Carroll,
Gary Klar, Andrew Masset, Church
Ortiz, Marley Sims, Larry Atebery,
Gary Combs, Neill Barry, Rita Crafts,
Lionel Pina, Carol Martin, Chris Bor-
gen, Michael Prince, John Roland,
Jack Somack, Willy Stern, Marilyn
Salenger, Rolland Smith, Nancy Bleier,
Frank Casey, Kenneth Cory, Penny
Crone, Tyler Horn, Robert Carricart,
Tracey Cohn, Alberto Ferrara, Lenny
Geer, Peter Iacangelo.

HE WHO DIED OF LOVE (1945-Mex.)
    (A. K. A. "El Que Murio de Amor")
    Director: Miguel Morayta
Julian Soler, Hilda Kruger, Luis
Asdas, Ampara Morillo, Fernando
Cortes.

HE WHO GETS SLAPPED (1924)
    Director: Victor Seastrom
Lon Chaney, Sr. (He), John Gilbert
(Bezano), Norma Shearer (Consuelo),
Tully Marshall (Count Mancini), Ford
Sterling (Tricaud), Brandon Hurst
(Barkilphedro), George Davis, Clyde
Cook (clowns), Harvey Clark (Briquet),
Paulette Duval (Zinida), Ruth King
(He's wife), Marc MacDermott (Beau
Regnard).

HEX (1973)
    Director: Leo Garen
Keith Carradine (Whizzer), Scott
Glenn (Jimbang), Robert Walker,
Jr. (Chupo), John Carradine (Old
Gunfighter), Tina Herazo (Oriole),
Dan Haggerty (Brother Billy), Mike
Combs (Golly), Iggie Wolfington (Du-
zak), Patricia Ann Parker (Elma),
Hilarie Thompson (Acacia), Gary
Busey (Giblets), Doria Cook (China),
Tom Jones (Elston).

HIBERNATUS (1969-Fr./Ital.)
    Director: Edouardo Molinaro
Louis de Funes, Claude Gensac, Olivier
de Funes, Yves Vincent, Michel Lonsdale, Martine Kelly, Paul Preboist,
Bernard Allane, Elyette Gensac.

HIDDEN CODE, THE (1920)
    Director: Richard Lestrange
Grace Davison (Grace Lamont), Ralph
Osborne (Eben Lamont), Clayton
Davis (August Mason), Richard Le-
strange (Richard Leslie).

HIDDEN HAND, THE (1917) - serial
    in 15 episodes
Chapters: 1. "The Gauntlet of Death",
2. "Counterfeit Faces", 3. "The Is-
land of Dread", 4. "The False Locket",
5. "The Air-Lock", 6. "The Flower
of Death", 7. "The Fire Trap", 8.
"Slide for Life", 9. "Jets of Flame",
10. "Cogs of Death", 11. "Trapped
by Treachery", 12. "Eyes in the Wall",
13. "Jaws of the Tiger", 14. "The
Unmasking" & 15. "The Girl of the
Prophecy".
    Director:
Doris Kenyon (Doris Whitney), Sheldon
Lewis (Dr. Scarley), Arline Pretty
(Verda Crane), Mahlon Hamilton (Jack
Ramsay).

HIDDEN HAND, THE (1942)
    Director: Ben Stoloff
Craig Stevens (Peter Thorne), Elisa-
beth Fraser (Mary Winfield), Julie
Bishop/Jacqueline Wells (Rita), Willie
Best (Eustace), Frank Wilcox (Law-
rence), Milton Parsons (John Chan-
ning), Tom Stevenson (Horace Chan-
ning), Roland Drew (Walter Channing),
Cecil Cunningham (Lorinda), Ruth
Ford (Estelle), Inez Gary (Hattie),
Marian Hall (Eleanor Stevens), Kam
Tong (Mallo), Creighton Hale, Wade
Boteler, Monte Blue.

HIDDEN MENACE (1938) (A. K. A.
    "Star of the Circus")
    Director: Albert de Courville
John Clements (Paul), Gene Sheldon
(Peters), Otto Kruger (Garvin), Ger-
trude Michael (Yester), Patrick Barr
(Truxa), John Turnbull (Tenzler),
Barbara Blair (Hilda), Norah Howard.

HIDDEN POWER (1939)
    Director: Lewis D. Collins
Jack Holt (Dr. Garfield), Gertrude
Michael (Virginia Garfield), Dickie
Moore (Steve), Regis Toomey (May-
ton), Henry Kolker (Weston), Henry
Haydon (Downey), Holmes Herbert
(Dr. Morley), William R. Davidson
(Foster), Marilyn Knowlden (Imogene),
Helen Brown.

HIDEOUS SUN DEMON, THE (1959)
    (A. K. A. "Blood on His Lips")

Robert Clarke (Dr. Gilbert McKenna), Patricia Manning (Ann Russell), Nan Peterson (Trudy Osborne), Patrick Whyte (Dr. Frederick Buckell), Fred La Porta (Dr. Jacob Hoffman), Del Courtney (radio announcer), Bill Hampton (Police Lieutenant), Donna Conkling (mother), Xandra Conkling (little girl).

HIGH ANXIETY (1977)
    Director: Mel Brooks
Mel Brooks (Richard Thorndyke), Madeline Kahn (Victoria Brisbane), Cloris Leachman (Nurse Diesel), Harvey Korman (Dr. Charles Montague), Dick Van Patten (Dr. Wentworth), Howard Morris (Prof. Lilloman), Jack Riley (desk clerk), Ron Carey (Brophy), Charlie Callas (Cocker Spaniel), Ron Clark (Zachary Cartwright), Lee Delano (Norton), Rudy DeLuca (the Killer), Barry Levinson (bellboy), Richard Stahl (Dr. Baxter), Darrell Zwerling (Dr. Eckhardt), Murphy Dunne (piano player), Albert J. Whitlock (Arthur Brisbane), Al Hopson (man who is shot), Bob Ridgely (flasher).

HIGHLY DANGEROUS (1950)
    Director: Roy Ward Baker
Dane Clark (Bill Casey), Margaret Lockwood (Frances Gary), Marius Goring (Anton Razinski), Naughton Wayne (Hedgerley), Wilfred Hyde-White (Luke), Olaf Pooley (assistant), Michael Hordern (Rawlings), Eric Pohlman (Joe), Eugene Deckers (Alf), George Benson (customer), Paul Hardtmuth (priest), Anthony Newley (Operator), Gladys Henson (attendant), Patric Doonan (customs man), Joan Haythorne (Judy), Noel Johnson (voice of Frank Conway), John Gabriel, Ernest Butcher, Toni Frost, John Hosley, Jill Balcon, Michael Ritterman.

HIGH PLAINS DRIFTER (1973)
    Director: Clint Eastwood
Clint Eastwood (the Stranger), Verna Bloom (Sarah Belding), Mariana Hill (Callie Travers), Mitchell Ryan (Dave Drake), Billy Curtis (Mordecai), Jack Ging (Morgan Allen), Stefan Gierasch (Mayor Jason Hobart), Geoffrey Lewis (Stacey Bridges), Paul Brinegar (Lutie Naylor), Walter Barnes (Sheriff Sam Shaw), John Quade (Jake Ross), Robert Donner (Preacher), Belle Mitchell (Mrs. Lake), Anthony James (Cole Carlin), Richard Bull (Asa Goodwin), Jack Kosslyn (saddlemaker), Ted

Hartley (Lewis Belding), William O'Connell (barber), Don Vadis (Dan Carlin), James Gosa (Tommy Morrow), John Mitchum (Warden), Scott Walker (Bill Borders), Jane Aull (townswoman), Reid Cruickshanks (gunsmith), Russ McCubbin (Fred Short), Carl C. Piti (teamster), Chuck Waters (stableman), Buddy Van Horn (Marshall Jim Duncan).

HIGH TREASON (1929)
    Director: Maurice Elvey
Benita Hume (Evelyn Seymour), Jameson Thomas (Michael Deane), Basil Hill (President of Europe), Humberston Wright (Dr. Seymour), Raymond Massey, Milton Rosmer, Rene Ray, Henry Vibart.

HILDE WARREN AND DEATH (1916-Ger.) (A.K.A. "Hilde Warren und der Tod")
    Director: Joe May
Mia May, Bruno Kastner, Fritz Lang, Georg John, Hans Mierendorff, Ernst Matray.

HILLBILLYS IN THE HAUNTED HOUSE (1967)
    Director: Jean Yarborough
John Carradine (Dr. Himmil), Basil Rathbone (Gregor), Lon Chaney, Jr. (Maxmillian), Richard Webb (Jim Meadows), Joi Lansing (Boots Malone), Ferlin Husky (Woody Weatherby), Linda Ho (Madame Wong), Don Bowman (Jeepers), George Barrows (the Ape), Molly Bee, Jim Kent, Marcella Wright, Merle Haggard, Sonny James.

HILLS HAVE EYES, THE (1977)
    Director: Wes Craven
Robert Houston (Bobby Carter), Susan Lanier (Brenda Carter), Dee Wallace (Lynne Wood), Virginia Vincent (Ethel Carter), James Whitworth (Jupiter), Russ Grieve (Bob Carter), Martin Speer (Doug Wood), Brenda Marinoff (Katie Wood), Janus Blythe (Ruby), Arthur King (Mercury), Cordy Clark (Mama), Lance Gordon (Mars), John Steadman (Fred).

HIS HAND SLIPPED (1952-Mex.) (A.K.A. "Se le Paso la Mano")
    Director: Julian Soler
Abel Salazar, Andres Soler, Delia Magana, Martha Roth, Queta Lavat.

HIS LAST TWELVE HOURS (1953-Ital) (A.K.A. "Le Sue Ultime 12 Ore")
    Director: Luigi Zampa
Jean Gabin, Antonella Lualdi.

HIS PREHISTORIC PAST (1914)
Director: Charles Chaplin
Charles Chaplin, Mack Swain, Fritz
Schade, Gene Marsh, Al St. John,
Cecile Arnold, Hank Mann, Frank D.
Williams (Cavemen), Alice Howell
(Cavewoman).

H-MAN, THE (1958-Jap.) (A.K.A.
"Uomini H", "Bijyo to Ekitainin-
gen")
Director: Inoshiro Honda
Akihiko Hirata (the scientist), Yumi
Shirakawa (the girl), Kenji Sahara
(the detective), Eitaro Ozawa, Mit-
suru Sato, Koreya Senda.

HOBBIT, THE (TVM-1977) - animated
- 11-27-77
Director: Arthur Rankin, Jr. &
Jules Bass
Voices: Orson Bean (Bilbo), John
Huston (Gandalf), Richard Boone
(Smaug), Otto Preminger (Elf King),
Cyril Ritchard (Elrond), Hans Con-
reid (Thorin Oakenshield), Theodore
(Gollum), Paul Frees, Don Messick,
John Stephenson.

HOLD THAT GHOST (1941)
Director: Arthur Lubin
Bud Abbott (Chuck Murray), Lou
Costello (Ferdinand Jones), Richard
Carlson (Dr. Jackson), Evelyn Ankers
(Norma Lind), Marc Lawrence
(Charlie Smith), Joan Davis (Camille
Brewster), Mischa Auer (Gregory),
Nestor Paiva (Glum), Thurston Hall
(Alderman), Janet Shaw (Alderman's
girl), Russell Hicks (Lawyer Banni-
ster), Don Terry (Strangler), Edgar
Dearing (Irondome), Harry Hayden
(Jenkins), William Davidson (Moose
Matson), Milton Parsons (Harry Hos-
kins), Shemp Howard (soda jerk),
William Forrest (state trooper),
Frank Perry (Snake Eyes), Edward
Pawley (High Collar), William Ruhl
(customer), Joe LaCava (Little Fink),
Howard Hickman (Judge), Mrs. Gar-
dner Crane (Mrs. Gitledge), Frank
Richards (gunman), Jeanne Blanche
(pretty thing), Bobby Barker.

HOLD THAT HYPNOTIST (1957)
Director: Austen Jewell
Huntz Hall (Sach Debussy Jones),
Stanley Clements, Jane Nigh, David
Condon.

HOLD THAT LINE (1952)
Director: William Beaudine
Huntz Hall (Sach Debussy Jones),

Leo Gorcey (Slip Mahoney), Gil
Stratton, Jr. (Whitey), David Gorcey
(Chuck), Bennie Bartlett (Butch),
Bernard Gorcey (Louie Dumbrowsky),
Taylor Holmes (Dean), Frances
Pierlot (Billingsley), Pierre Wat-
kin (Stanhope), John Bromfield
(Biff), Bob Nichols (Harold), Mona
Knox (Katie), Gloria Winters (Penny),
Veda Ann Borg (Candy Calin), Al
Eben (Big Dave), Ted Stanhope (Prof.
Grog), Tom Kennedy (Murphy),
Bert Davidson (police sergeant),
Marjorie Eaton (Miss Whitsett),
Jeanne Dean, Steve Dayne (students),
Ted Jordan, George Sanders
(players), Marvelle Andre (girl),
Tom Hanlon (announcer), Bob
Peoples, Paul Bryar, George Lewis,
David Condon.

HOLE IN THE WALL, THE (1929)
Director: Robert Florey
Claudette Colbert (Jane Oliver),
Edward G. Robinson (the Fox),
Donald Meek (Goofy), David Newell
(Gordon Grant), Nellie Savage
(Madame Mystera), Alan Brooks
(Jim), Louise Closser Hale.

HOLLYWOOD BOULEVARD (1976)
Director: Joe Dante & Allan
Arkush
Mary Woronov (Mary McQueen),
Candice Rialson (Candy Wednesday),
Dick Miller (Walter Paisley), Jeff-
rey Kramer (Patrick Hobby), Rita
George (Bobbi Quackenbush), Tara
Strohmeier (Jill McBain), Paul
Bartel (Erich Von Leppe), Richard
Doran (P.G.), Jonathan Kaplan
(Scotty), George Wagner (camera-
man), John Kramer (Duke Mantee),
W.L. Luckey (Rico Bandello), Charles
B. Griffith (Mark Dentine), Glen Shi-
mada (ubiquitous Filipino), Barbara
Pieters (drive-in mother), Joe Mc-
Bride (drive-in rapist), Sue Veneer
(drive-in dyke), David Boyle (obnox-
ious kid), Todd McCarthy (author),
Roberta Dean (reporter), Milt Kahn
(reporter), Miller Drake (mutant),
Glen Shimada (Filipino), Forrest J.
Ackerman (party guest), Commander
Cody and the Lost Planet Airmen.

HOMEBODIES (1973)
Director: Larry Yust
Frances Fuller (Miss Emily), Peter
Brocco (Mr. Blakely), Ian Wolfe
(Mr. Loomis), Ruth McDevitt (Mrs.
Loomis), William Hansen (Mr. Sandy),
Paula Trueman (Mattie), Douglas

Fowley (Mr. Crawford), Linda Marsh (Miss Pollack), Wesley Lau (construction foreman), Kenneth Tobey (construction boss), William Benedict (night watchman), Norman Gottschalk (apartment superintendent), Jo De Meo (construction worker), Eldon Quick (insurance inspector), Irene Webster (woman in floppy hat), Nicholas Lewis, John Craig (construction workers), Alma Du Bus (superintendent's wife), Michael Johnson (policeman).

HOME FOR THE HOLIDAYS (TVM-1972) - 11-28-72
Director: John L. Moxey
Jessica Walter (Frederica Morgan), Sally Field (Christine Morgan), Julie Harris (Elizabeth Hall Morgan), Eleanor Parker (Alex Morgan), Jill Haworth (Joanna Morgan), Walter Brennan (Benjamin Morgan), John Fink (Dr. Ted Lindsay), Med Flory (Sherriff).

HOME SWEET HOME (1972-Fr.)
Director: Liliane De Kermadec
Julien Guiomar, Coline Deble, Denis Gunzbourg, Jacques Monory, Patrick Dumont.

HOMICIDAL (1961)
Director: William Castle
Glenn Corbett (Karl), Patricia Breslin (Miriam Webster), Jean Arless (Emily/ Warren), Eugenie Leontovich (Helga), Alan Bunce (Dr. Jonas), James Westerfield (Mr. Adrims), Hope Summers (Mrs. Adrims), Wolfe Barzell (Olie), Richard Rust (Jim Nesbitt), Gilbert Green (Lt. Miller), Teri Brooks (Mrs. Forest), Ralph Moody (1st clerk), Joe Forte (2nd clerk).

HOMUNCULUS (1916-Ger.)
Director: Otto Rippert
Olaf Fonss (Homunculus), Aud Egede Nissen, Theodore Loos, Maria Carmi, Friedrich Kuhne, Mechtilde Their, Lupu Pick.

HOP HARRIGAN (1946) - serial in 15 episodes
Director: Derwin Abrahams
William Bakewell (Hop Harrigan), Jennifer Holt (Gail Nolan), Emmett Vogan (Arnold), John Merton (Dr. Tobar), Ernie Adams (Retner), Wheeler Oakman (Ballard), Terry Frost (Barry), Jim Diehl (Carter), Anthony Warde (Edward), Jackie Moran (Fraser), Robert 'Buss' Henry (Jackie Nolan), Peter Michael (Craven), Bobby Stone (Gray), Claire James (Gwen Arnold), Jack Buchanan (Deputy Sheriff).

HORRIBLE DR. HITCHCOCK, THE (1962-Ital.) (A.K.A. "L'Orribile Segreto del Dottor Hichcock", "The Horrible Secret of Dr. Hichcock", "The Terror of Dr. Hichcock")
Director: Riccardo Freda
Barbara Steele, Robert Flemying, Teresa Fitzgerald, Montgomery Glenn, Harriet White.

HORRIBLE SEXY VAMPIRE, THE (1970-Span.) (A.K.A. "El Vampire de la Autopista", "The Vampire of the Turnpike", "Der Vampir von Schloss Frankenstein", "The Vampire of Castle Frankenstein")
Director: Jose Luis Madrid
Waldemar Wohlfahrt, Patricia Loran, Barta Barry, Adela Tauler, Luis Induni, Anastasio Campoy.

HORROR AT 37,000 FEET, THE (TVM-1973) - 2-13-73
Director: David Lowell Rice
Roy Thinnes (Aaron O'Neill), William Shatner (Paul Kovalik), Chuck Connors (Ernie Slade), Buddy Ebsen (Len Farlee), Tammy Grimes (Mrs. Pender), Lyn Loring (Manya), Jane Merrow (Sheila O'Neill), Paul Winfield (Dr. Enkalla), Will Hutchins (Holcomb), France Nuyen (Annalik), Darlene Carr (Margot), Brenda Benet (Sally), Russell Johnson, H.M. Wynant, Mia Bendixsen.

HORROR CASTLE (1963-Ital.) (A.K.A. "Le Vergine di Norimberga", "The Virgin of Nuremburg", "The Castle of Terror")
Director: Anthony Dawson/Antonio Margheriti
George Riviere (Max Hunter), Rossana Podesta (Mary Hunter), Christopher Lee (Erich), Jim Nolan (Selby), Anny Delli Uberti (Marta), Luigi Severini (Doctor), Luciana Miione (Trude).

HORROR CHAMBER OF DR; FAUSTUS, THE (1959-Fr.) (A.K.A. "Eyes Without a Face", "Yeux sans Visage")
Director: Georges Franju
Pierre Brasseur (Dr. Gennessier), Edith Scob (Christiane Gennessier), Alida Valli (Louise), Juliette Mayniel (Edna), Beatrice Altariba (Paulette).

HORROR EXPRESS (1972-Span. /
Brit.) (A.K.A. "Panico en el
Transiberiano", "Panic on the
Trans-Siberian")
Director: Gene Martin
Christopher Lee (Alexander Saxton),
Peter Cushing (Dr. Wells), Telly
Savalas (Kazan), Silvia Tortosa (Irina),
Jorge Riguad (Trovski), Julio Pena
(Mirov).

HORROR HIGH (1974) (A.K.A.
"Twisted Brain")
Director: Larry Stouffer
Pat Cardi (Vernon), Austin Stoker,
Rosie Holotik, John Niland, Joye
Hash.

HORROR HOSPITAL (1973) (A.K.A.
"Computer Killers")
Director: Antony Balch
Michael Gough (Dr. Storm), Dennis
Price, Robin Askwith, Vanessa Shaw,
Ellen Pollock, Kurt Christian, Skip
Martin, Barbara Wendy, Colin
Skeaping, Kenneth Benda, Martin
Grace, George Herbert.

HORROR HOTEL (1960) (A.K.A.
"The City of the Dead")
Director: John L. Moxey
Patricia Jessel (Mrs. Newless/Eli-
zabeth Selwyn), Christopher Lee
(Prof. Driscoll), Betta St. John (Pa-
tricia Russell), Dennis Lotis (Rich-
ard Barlow), Venetia Stevenson (Nan
Barlow), Norman MacOwan (Rev.
Russell), Tom Naylor (Tom Maitland),
Fred Johnson (Elder), Valentine
Dyall (Jethrow Keane), Ann Beach
(Lottie), Jimmy Dyrenforth (garage
attendant).

HORROR HOUSE (1969) (A.K.A.
"The Haunted House of Horror")
Director: Michael Armstrong
Frankie Avalon (Chris), Jill Haworth
(Sheila), Mark Wynter (Gary), Julian
Barnes (Richard), Dennis Price (Insp.
Wainwright), Gina Warwick (Sylvia),
George Sewell (Kellett), Richard
O'Sullivan (Peter), Carol Dilworth
(Dorothy), Jan Holden (Peggy), Ver-
onica Doran (Madge), Clifford Earl
(Police Sergeant), Robert Raglan
(Bradley), Robin Stewart (Henry).

HORROR ISLAND (1941)
Director: George Waggner
Dick Foran (Bill Martin), Leo Car-
rillo (Tobias Clumb), Peggy Moran
(Wendy), Fuzzy Knight (Stuff), Hobart
Cavanaugh (Jasper), John Eldredge

(George), Ralf Harolde (Rod Hogan),
Lewis Howard (Thurman), Foy Van
Dolson (the Phantom), Iris Adrian
(Arleen), Walter Catlett (McGoon),
Emmett Vogan (the Stranger).

HORROR OF FRANKENSTEIN, THE
(1970)
Director: Jimmy Sangster
Ralph Bates (Victor Frankenstein),
David Prowse (the Monster),
Veronica Carlson (Elizabeth), Gra-
ham James (Wilhelm), Dennis Price
(grave robber), Joan Rice (grave
robber's wife), Kate O'Mara (Alys),
Bernard Archard (father), John Finch.

HORROR OF IT ALL, THE (1964)
Director: Terence Fisher
Pat Boone (Jack Robinson), Erica
Rogers (Cynthia), Dennis Price
(Cornwallis), Andree Melly (Natalia),
Valentine Dyall (Reginal), Eric Chitty
(Grandpa), Jack Bligh (Percival),
Archie Duncan (Muldoon), Oswald
Laurence (young Doctor).

HORROR OF PARTY BEACH, THE
(1963)
Director: Del Tenney
Allen Lauren (Dr. Gavin), Alice
Lyon (Elaine Gavin), John Scott
(Hank Green), Marilyn Clark (Tina),
Agustin Mayer (Mike), Eulabelle
Moore (Eulabelle), Damon Klebroyd
(Lt. Wells), Carol Grubman, Emily
Laurel, Dina Harris (girls in car),
Diane Prizio, Sharon Murphy (girls).

HORROR OF THE BLOOD MONSTERS
(1970) (A.K.A. "Creatures of the
Prehistoric Planet", "Horror Crea-
tures of the Prehistoric Planet",
"Vampire Men of the Lost Planet")
Director: Al Adamson, Jr.
John Carradine (Dr. Rynning), Robert
Dix (Col. Manning), Vickie Volante
(Valerie), Joey Benson (Willy), Jen-
nifer Bishop (Lian Malian), Fred Mey-
ers (Bob Scott), Bruce Powers (Bryce),
Britt Semand (Linda), Theodore (nar-
rator).

HORROR OF THE ZOMBIES (1977-Span)
Director: Amando de Ossorio
Maria Perschy, Jack Taylor, Carlos
Lemos, Blanca Estrada, Manuel de
Blas, Barbara Rey.

HORROR ON SNAPE ISLAND (1971)
(A.K.A. "Tower of Evil", "Beyond
the Fog")
Director: Jim O'Connolly

Bryant Haliday (Brent), Jill Haworth
(Rose), Jack Watson (Hamp Gurney),
Anna Palk (Nora), Mark Edwards
(Adam), Derek Fowlds (Dan), Candace
Glendenning (Penny), George Coulouris
(John Gurney), William Lucas (Detec-
tive Superintendent Hawk), John Hamil
(Gary), Dennis Price (Bakewell), Robin
Askwith (Des), Anthony Valentine (Dr.
Simpson), Gary Hamilton (Brom), Fred-
ric Abbott (Saul), Mark McBride (Mi-
chael), Serretta Wilson (Mae), Mari-
anne Stone (nurse).

HORRORS OF SPIDER ISLAND, THE
(1959-Ger.) (A. K. A. "It's Hot in
Paradise", "Toter Hing im Netz",
"Dead Body in the Web", "The
Spider's Web", "Girls of Spider
Island")
    Director: Fritz Bottger/Jamie
Nolan
Alex D'Arcy, Barbara Valentine,
Helga Frank, Harald Maresch, Reiner
Brand, Helga Neuner.

HORRORS OF THE BLACK MUSEUM
(1959)
    Director: Arthur Crabtree
Michael Gough (Edmond Bancroft),
Graham Curnow (Rick), Geoffrey Keen
(Superintendent Graham), Shirley Ann
Field (Angela), June Cunningham (Joan
Berkley), Gerald Anderson (Dr.
Ballan), Beatrice Varley (Aggie), John
Warwick (Insp. Lodge), Austin Trevor
(Commissioner Wayne), Howard Greene
(Tom Rivers), Dorinda Stevens (Gail),
Malow Pantera (Peggy), Stuart Saun-
ders (fun fair barker), Vanda Godsell
(Miss Ashton), Geoffrey Denton (ser-
geant), Hilda Barry, Nora Gordon
(women in hall), Gerard Green (man),
Gerald Case (manager), Howard Pays
(constable), William Abner (constable),
Frank Hender (surgeon), Ingrid Car-
don (little girl).

HORROR STAR, THE (1982)
    Director: Norman Thaddius Vane
Ferdy Mayne (Conrad Ragzoff), Luca
Bercovici, Jennifer Starett, Nita Talbot,
Barbara Pilavin, Leon Askin.

HOUND OF BLACKWOOD CASTLE,
THE (1968-Ger.) (A. K. A. "Der
Hund von Blackwood Castle")
    Director: Alfred Vohrer
Heinz Drache, Karin Baal, Agnes
Windeck, Siegfried Schurenberg, Ilse
Page.

HOUND OF THE BASKERVILLES, THE

(1921)
    Director: Maurice Elvey
Ellie Norwood (Sherlock Holmes),
Hubert Willis (Dr. Watson), Rex
McDougall (Sir Henry Baskerville),
Lewis Gilbert (Stapleton), Mme.
d'Esterre (Mrs. Hudson), Robert
English (Dr. Mortimer), Catina
Campbell (Beryle Stapleton), Fred
Raynham (Barrymore), Robert Vallis
(Selden), Allen Jeayes.

HOUND OF THE BASKERVILLES,
THE (1914-Ger) (A. K. A. "Der
Hund von Baskerville")
    Director: Rudolf Meinert
Alwin Neuss (Sherlock Holmes), Er-
win Fichtner (Lord Henry Baskerville),
Friedrich Kuhne (Stapleton), Andreas
Van Horne (Barrymore), Hanni Weiss
(Laura Lyons).

HOUND OF THE BASKERVILLES,
THE (1917-Ger.) (A. K. A. "Der
Hund von Baskervilles")
    Director: Richard Oswald

HOUND OF THE BASKERVILLES,
THE (1929-Ger.) (A. K. A. "Der
Hund von Baskervilles")
    Director: Richard Oswald
Carlyle Blackwell (Sherlock Holmes),
Livio Pavanelli (Sir Henry Basker-
ville), Alexander Mursky (Sir Hugo
Baskerville), Georges Seroff (Dr.
Watson), Fritz Rasp (Stapleton), Betty
Bird (Beryl Stapleton), Alma Taylor
(Mrs. Barrymore).

HOUND OF THE BASKERVILLES,
THE (1931)
    Director: V. Gareth Gundrey
Robert Rendel (Sherlock Holmes),
John Stuart (Sir Henry Baskerville),
Frederick Lloyd (Dr. Watson), Hea-
ther Angel (Beryl), Reginald Bach
(Stapleton), Sam Livesey (Sir Hugo
Baskerville), Wilfred Shur (Dr. Mor-
timer), Elizabeth Vaughn (Mrs. Laura
Lyon), Leonard Hayes (Cartwright),
Sybil Jane (Mrs. Barrymore), Henry
Hallett (Barrymore).

HOUND OF THE BASKERVILLES,
THE (1936-Ger.) (A. K. A. "Der
Hund von Baskerville")
    Director: Karl Lamac
Bruno Guttner (Sherlock Holmes),
Fritz Odemar (Dr. Watson), Peter
Voss (Sir Henry Baskerville), Arthur
Malkowski (Sir Hugo Baskerville),
Fritz Rasp (Barrymore), Lilly Schon-
berg (Mrs. Barrymore), Ernest

Rotmund (Dr. Mortimer), Erich Ponto (Stapleton), Annelisse Brand, Friedrich Kayssler.

HOUND OF THE BASKERVILLES, THE (1939)
Director: Sidney Lanfield
Basil Rathbone (Sherlock Holmes), Nigel Bruce (Dr. Watson), Richard Greene (Sir Henry Baskerville), Lionel Atwill (Sir James Mortimer), Wendy Barrie (Beryle Stapleton), John Carradine (Barryman), Eily Malyon (Mrs. Barryman), Beryl Mercer (Mrs. Jennifer Mortimer), Ralph Forbes (Sir Hugo Baskerville), Morton Lowry (John Stapleton), Barlowe Borland (Mr. Frankland), Mary Gordon (Mrs. Hudson), E. E. Clive (cabby), Nigel DeBruglier (convict), Ian MacLaren, Ivan Simpson, John Burton.

HOUND OF THE BASKERVILLES, THE (1959)
Director: Terence Fisher
Peter Cushing (Sherlock Holmes), Christopher Lee (Sir Henry Baskerville), Andre Morell (Dr. Watson), Marla Landi (Cecile), Miles Malleson (Bishop Frankland), David Oxley (Sir Hugo Baskerville), Ewen Solon (Stapleton), Sam Kydd (Perkins), John Le Mesurier (Barrymore), Francis De-Wolff (Dr. Mortimer), Helen Goss (Mrs. Barrymore), Michael Hawkins (Lord Caphill), Elizabeth Dott (Mrs. Goodlippe), Ian Hewitson (Lord Kingsblood), Michael Mulcaster (Selden), Dave Birks (servant), Judi Moyens (servant girl).

HOUND OF THE BASKERVILLES, THE (TVM-1972) - 2-12-72
Director: Barry Crane
Stewart Granger (Sherlock Holmes), William Shatner (George Stapleton), Bernard Fox (Dr. Watson), Jane Merrow (Beryl Stapleton), John Williams (Arthur Frankland), Sally Ann Howes (Laura Frankland), Anthony Zerbe (Dr. John Mortimer), Ian Ireland (Sir Henry Baskerville), Brendan Dillon (John Barrymore), Arline Anderson (Eliza Barrymore), Alan Caillou (Insp. Lestrade), Billy Bowles (Billy Cartwright), Chuck Hicks (Seldon), Karen Kondan (Mrs. Mortimer).

HOUND OF THE BASKERVILLES, THE (1978)
Director: Paul Morrissey
Peter Cook (Sherlock Holmes),

Dudley Moore (Dr. Watson/Mr. Spiggot/Mrs. Holmes), Joan Greenwood (Beryl Stapleton), Kenneth Williams (Sir Henry Baskerville), Denholm Elliott (Stapleton), Terry-Thomas (Dr. Mortimer), Hugh Griffith (Frankland), Max Wall (Barrymore), Irene Handl (Mrs. Barrymore), Spike Milligan (Baskerville Police Force), Roy Kinnear (Seldon), Dana Gillespie (Mary), Prunella Scales (Glynes), Penelope Keith (massage parlor receptionist), Jessie Matthews.

HOUR OF THE WOLF (1967-Swed.)
(A. K. A. "Vargtimmen")
Director: Ingmar Bergman
Liv Ullmann (Alma Borg), Max von Sydow (Johan Borg), Ingrid Thulin (Veronica Bogler), Erland Josephson (Baron von Merken), Georg Rydeberg (Lindhorst), Gudrun Brost (Baron's mother), Bertil Anderberg (Ernst von Merkens), Gertrud Fridh (Corinne von Merkens), Ulf Johanson (Heerbrand), Agda Helin (maidservant), Naima Winstrand (old lady with hat), Mona Seilitz (woman in mortuary), Mikael Rundqvist (young boy), Lenn Hjortzberg (Kapellmeister Kreisler), Folke Sundquist (Timino).

HOUSE AND THE BRAIN, THE (TVM-1973) - 5-24-73
Director: Gloria Monty
Hurd Hatfield (Constantine), Gretchen Corbett (Kate), Carol Williard (Marianna), Keith Charles (David), Maryce Carter (Judith).

HOUSE BY THE LAKE, THE (1977)
(A. K. A. "Death Weekend")
Director: Gary Flanagan
Brenda Vaccaro (Diane), Don Stroud (Lep), Chuck Shamata (Harry), Kyle Edwards (Frankie), Richard Ayres (Runt), Don Gransberry (Stanley), Michael Kirby (Ralph), Denver Mattson (Smoker), Ed McNamara (Spragg), Al Bernardo (Mr. Doobie), Roselle Stone (Mrs. Doobie), Richard Donat (policeman), Elaine Yarish (campground girl).

HOUSE IN NIGHTMARE PARK, THE (1973) (A. K. A. "The Night of the Laughing Dead")
Director: Peter Sykes
Ray Milland (Stewart Henderson), Rosalie Crutchley (Jessica), Frankie Howerd (Foster Twelvetrees), Hugh Burden (Major Reginald Henderson), Elizabeth Maclennan (Verity Henderson),

John Bennett (Patel), Kenneth Griffith
(Ernest), Ruth Dunning (Agnes), Aimee
Delamain (Mother).

HOUSE IN THE WOODS, THE (1957)
Director: Maxwell Munden
Michael Gough (Geoff Carter), Patri-
cia Roc (Carol Carter), Ronald Howard
(Spencer Roland).

HOUSE OF DARKNESS (1948)
Director: Oswald Mitchell
Leslie Brooks (Lucy), Laurence
Harvey (Francis Merivale), Leslie
Osmond (Elaine Merivale), Alexan-
der Archdale (John), John Stuart
(lawyer), George Melachrino (him-
self), Henry Oscar (film director).

HOUSE OF DARK SHADOWS (1970)
Director: Dan Curtis
Jonathan Frid (Barnabas Collins),
Grayson Hall (Dr. Julia Hoffman),
Joan Bennett (Elizabeth Stoddard),
Kathryn Leigh Scott (Maggie Evans),
Roger Davis (Jeff Clark), John
Karlen (Willie Loomis), Nancy
Barrett (Carolyn Stoddard), Thayer
David (Prof. T. Elito Stokes), Den-
nis Patrick (Sheriff George Patter-
son), Louis Edmonds (Roger Collins),
David Hensey (David Collins), Donald
Briscoe (Todd Jennings), Lisa Rich-
ards (Daphne Budd), Barbara Cason
(Mrs. Johnson), Humbert Astredo
(Dr. Forbes), Jerry Lacy (Minister),
Paul Michael (old man), Terry Craw-
ford (Todd's nurse), Michael Stroka
(pallbearer).

HOUSE OF DRACULA (1945)
Director: Erle C. Kenton
Lon Chaney, Jr. (Lawrence Talbot),
John Carradine (Baron Latos), On-
slow Stevens (Dr. Edelmann), Mar-
tha O'Driscoll (Miliza Morell),
Lionel Atwill (Insp. Holst), Jane
Adams (Nina), Glenn Strange (Frank-
enstein's monster), Skelton Knaggs
(Steinmuhl), Joseph E. Bernard
(Brahms), Ludwig Stossel (Siegfried),
Gregory Muradian (Johannes), Fred
Cordova (Gendarme), Beatrice
Gray, Dick Dickinson, Harry Lamont
(villagers).

HOUSE OF EVIL (1968-Mex./U.S.)
Director: Jack Hill
Boris Karloff.

HOUSE OF EVIL (TVM-1974) -
5-31-74
Director: Bill Glenn

Salome Jens (Rachel), Jamie Smith
Jackson (Kitty), Andy Robinson
(Sheriff Moore), Lou Frizzel (Deputy),
Dabney Coleman (Howard Dale),
Sarah Cunningham (Dr. Cates), Gary
Pagett (Charlie Boys), Elayne
Heilveil (Rose), Mary Carver (Mary
Hogan).

HOUSE OF EXORCISM (1975-Ital.)
(A.K.A. "Lisa and the Devil",
"La Casa dell'Exorcismo")
Director: Mario Bava
Elke Sommer (Lisa), Telly Savalas
(Leandro), Robert Alda (Father
Michael), Sylva Koscina (Countess),
Alida Valli.

HOUSE OF FEAR, THE (1939)
Director: Joe May
William Gargan (Arthur McHugh),
Irene Hervey (Alice Tabor), Robert
Coote (Bobby Morton), Tom Dugan
(Mike), El Brendel (Jeff), Alan
Dinehart (Joseph Morton), Walter
Woolf King (Carleton), Donald Doug-
las (John Woodford), Dorothy Arnold
(Gloria DeVere), Harvey Stevens
(Dick Pierce), Jan Duggan (Sarah
Henderson), Emory Parnell (police-
man), Harry Hayden (coroner).

HOUSE OF FEAR, THE (1945)
Director: Roy William Neill
Basil Rathbone (Sherlock Holmes),
Nigel Bruce (Dr. Watson), Paul
Cavanaugh (Simon Merrivale), Holmes
Herbert (Alan Cosgrave), Harry Cord-
ing (John Simpson), Dennis Hoey
(Insp. Lestrade), Alec Craig (Angus),
Gavin Muir (Chalmers), Aubrey
Mather (Alastair), Florette Hillier
(Alison MacGregor), Dick Alexander
(King), Sally Shepherd (Mrs. Mon-
teith), David Clyde (Alex MacGregor),
Leslie Denison (Sgt. Bleeker).

HOUSE OF FRANKENSTEIN (1945)
Director: Erle C. Kenton
Boris Karloff (Dr. Niemann), Lon
Chaney, Jr. (Lawrence Talbot),
J. Carrol Naish (Daniel), John
Carradine (Count Dracula), Anne
Gwynne (Rita Hussman), Glenn
Strange (Frankenstein's Monster),
Elena Verdugo (Ilonka), Lionel Atwill
(Insp. Arnz), Peter Coe (Carl),
George Zucco (Prof. Bruno Lampini),
Sig Ruman (Hussman, the Burgo-
meister), Frank Reicher (Ullman),
Philip Van Zandt (Muller), Michael
Mark (Strauss), William Edmunds
(Fejos), George Lynn (man), Olaf

Hytten, Brandon Hurst (villagers),
Julius Tannen (Muller), Gino Cor-
rado (man at horror show), Joe
Kirk, Charles Miller.

HOUSE OF FREAKS (1973-Ital.)
  (A. K. A. "Dr. Frankenstein's
  Castle of Freaks")
  Director: Robert Oliver
Rossano Brazzi (Count Frankenstein),
Michael Dunn (Genz), Christiane
Royce (Krista), Edmund Purdom,
Alan Collins, Gordon Michael, Loren
Ewing, Boris Lugosi, Xiro Pappas.

HOUSE OF HATE (1918) - serial in
  20 episodes
Chapters: 1. "The Hooded Terror",
2. "The Tiger's Eye", 3. "A Woman's Perfidy", 4. "The Man from
Java", 5. "Spies Within", 6. "A
Living Target", 7. "Germ Menace",
8. "The Untold Secret", 9. "Poi-
soned Darts", 10. "Double Crossed",
11. "Haunts of Evil", 12. "Flashes
in the Dark", 13. "Enemy Aliens",
14. "Underworld Allies", 15. "The
False Signal", 16. "The Vial of
Death", 17. "The Death Switch",
18. "At the Pistol's Point", 19.
"The Hooded Terror Unmasked",
& 20. "Following Old Glory".
  Director: George B. Seitz
Pearl White (Pearl Waldon), Antonio
Moreno (Harvey Gresham), Paul
Clerget (the Hooded Terror), J. H.
Gilmour (Winthrop Waldon), John
Webb Dillon (Haynes Waldon), Peggy
Shanor (Zelda Waldon).

HOUSE OF HORROR, THE (1929)
  Director: Benjamin Christensen
Chester Conklin, Louise Fazenda,
Michael Visaroff, Thelma Todd, Dale
Fuller, William Orlamond, Emile
Chautard, William V. Mong, Tenen
Holtz.

HOUSE OF HORRORS (1946) (A. K. A.
  "Joan Medford is Missing")
  Director: Jean Yarbrough
Martin Kosleck (Marcel de Lange),
Virginia Grey (Joan Medford),
Rondo Hatton (the Creeper), Bill
Goodwin (Lt. Larry Brooks), Alan
Napier (F. Holmes Harmon), Robert
Lowrey (Steven Morrow), Howard
Freeman (Hal Ormiston), Byron
Foulger (Mr. Samuels), Joan Shawlee
(Stella McNally), Mary Field (Nora,
the switchboard operator), Virginia
Christine (lady of the streets), Janet
Shaw (cab driver), Kent Taylor.

HOUSE OF MYSTERY (1934)
  Director: William Nigh
Ed Lowry (Jack Armstrong), Verna
Hillie (Ella Browning), Mary Foy
(Mrs. Potter), Brandon Hurst (Hindu
Priest), George Cleveland (Clancy),
Harry C. Bradley (Prof. Potter),
Joyzelle (Chanda), John Sheehan
(Harry Smith), Fritzi Ridgeway
(Stella Walters), George Hayes
(David Fells), Clay Clement (John
Pren), Dale Fuller (Mrs. Carfax),
Dick Botiller (Hindu), Irving Bacon
(Ned Pickens), Samuel Godfrey
(Ellis), James Morton (Englishman),
Bruce Mitchell (bartender).

HOUSE OF MYSTERY (1939) (A. K. A.
  "At the Villa Rose")
  Director: Walter Summers
Walter Rilla (Ricardo), Clifford
Evans (Tace), Martita Hunt (Helen
Vaquier), Kenneth Kent (Insp. Han-
aud), Ronald Adam (Besnard),
Judy Kelly (Celia Harland), Antionette
Cellier (Adele Rossignol), Peter
Murray Hill (Harry Wethermill),
Ruth Maitland (Mme. Dauvray).

HOUSE OF MYSTERY (1961) (A. K. A.
  "The Unseen")
  Director: Vernon Sewell
Peter Dyneley (Mark Lemming),
Jane Hylton (Stella Lemming), Nan-
ette Newman (Joan Trevor), Maurice
Kaufmann (Henry Trevor), Colin
Gordon (Burdon), John Merivale
(Clive), Molly Urquhart (Mrs.
Bucknall), Colette Wilde (wife).

HOUSE OF PSYCHOTIC WOMEN,
  THE (1976-Span.) (A. K. A. "House
  of Doom")
  Director: Carlos Aured
Maria Perchy (Ivette), Paul Naschy,
Diana Lorys, Eduardo Calvo, Eva
Leon, Luis Ciges, Ines Morales,
Pilar Barden, Antonio Pica.

HOUSE OF SECRETS (1929)
  Director: Edmund Lawrence
Marcis Manning (Margery Gordon),
Joseph Striker (Barry Wilding), Her-
bert Warren (Joe Blake), Richard
Stevenson (Bill), Francis M. Verdi
(Sir Hubert Harcourt), Edward Rose-
man (Wu Chang), Walter Ringham
(Home Secretary Forbes).

HOUSE OF SECRETS (1936)
  Director: Roland Reed
Leslie Fenton (Barry Wiling), Sidney
Blackmer (Tom Starr), Holmes

Herbert (Sir Bertram Evans), Muriel
Evans (Julie Fenmore), Syd Saylor
(Ed), Noel Madison (Dan Wharton),
Morgan Wallace (Dr. Kenmore),
Jameson Thomas (Coventry), George
Rosener (Hector Munson), Ian Mc-
Laren (Commissioner Cross), Matty
Fain (Jumpy), Rita Carlyle (Mrs.
Shippam), Tom Ricketts (Peters),
David Thursby (Gregory), Ramsey
Hill (Police Inspector), R. Lancaster
(English policeman), Matty Kemp
(man on ship).

HOUSE OF SEVEN GABLES, THE
(1940)
Director: Joe May
George Sanders (Jaffray Pynchon),
Vincent Price (Clifford Pynchon),
Margaret Lindsay (Hepzibah Pynchon),
Nan Grey (Phoebe Pynchon), Dick
Foran (Matthew Maule), Cecil Kell-
away (Philip Barton), Alan Napier
(Fuller), Gilbert Emery (Gerald),
Edgar Norton (Pineas Weed), Miles
Mander (the Deacon), Charles Trow-
bridge (the Judge).

HOUSE OF THE BLACK DEATH
(1965) (A. K. A. "The Widderburn
Horror", "Night of the Beast",
"Blood of the Man Devil")
Director: Harold Daniels
John Carradine (Andre de Sade),
Lon Chaney, Jr. (Belial De Sade),
Jerome Thor (Paul De Sade), Do-
lores Faith, Tom Drake, Andrea
King, Margaret Shinn, Sherwood
Keith.

HOUSE OF THE DAMNED (1963)
Director: Maury Dexter
Ronald Foster (Scott Campbell), Merry
Anders (Nancy Campbell), Richard
Crane (Joseph Schiller), Erika Peters
(Loy Schiller), Georgia Schmidt (Pris-
cilla Rochester), Dal McKennon (Mr.
Quinby), Stacey Winters (nurse), Ri-
chard Kiel (the Giant), Ayllenne Gib-
bons (the Fat Woman), Frieda Pushnik
(the Legless Girl), John Wilmore
(the Legless Man).

HOUSE OF THE LIVING DEAD (1977)
Director: Ray Austin
Shirley Ann Field, Mark Burns.

HOUSE OF THE SEVEN CORPSES,
THE (1974)
Director: Paul Harrison
John Ireland (Eric Hartmann), Faith
Domergue (Gayle), John Carradine
(Mr. Price), Carole Wells (Anne),

Charles Macaulay (Christopher),
Jerry Strickler (Dave), Larry
Record (Tommy), Ron Foreman
(Ron), Marty Hornstein (Danny),
Charles Bail (Jonathan Anthony
Beal/Theodore Beal), Jeff Alexan-
der (Russell Beal), Jo Anne Mower
(Allison Beal), Lucy Doheny (Su-
zanne Beal), Ron Garcia (Charles
Beal), Wells Bond (the Ghoul).

HOUSE OF USHER (1960) (A. K. A.
"Fall of the House of Usher")
Director: Roger Corman
Vincent Price (Roderick Usher),
Myrna Fahey (Madeline Usher),
Mark Damon (Phillip Winthrop),
Harry Ellerbe (Bristol).

HOUSE OF WAX (1953)
Director: Andre De Toth
Vincent Price (Henry Jarrod), Phyl-
lis Kirk (Sue Allen), Frank Lovejoy
(Lt. Tom Brennan), Carolyn Jones
(Cathy Gray), Roy Roberts (Matthew
Burke), Paul Picerni (Scott Andrews),
Paul Cavanaugh (Sidney Wallace),
Dabbs Greer (Sgt. Jim Shane), Phi-
lip Tonge (Bruce Allison), Ned
Young (Leon Averill), Charles Buch-
insky/Bronson (Igor), Reggie Ryman
(Barker), Frank Ferguson (Medical
Examiner), Grandon Rhodes (sur-
geon), Leon Curley (portly man),
Oliver Blake (pompous man), Riza
Royce (Ma Flanagan), Mary Lou
Holloway (Millie), Merry Townsend
(ticket taker), Lyle Latell (waiter),
Richard Benjamin, Jack Mower
(detectives), Ruth Warren (scrub-
woman).

HOUSE OF WHIPCORD (1974)
Director: Pete Walker
Barbara Markham (Mrs. Wakehurst),
Patrick Barr (Justice Bailey), Penny
Irving (Ann-Marie Di Verney), Ray
Brooks (Tony), Anne Michelle (Julia),
Sheila Keith (Walker), Dorothy Gor-
don (Bates), Ivor Salter (Jack), Ro-
bert Tayman (Mark E. Dessart),
Judy Robinson (Claire), Karen Da-
vid (Karen), Jane Hayward (Estelle),
Celia Quicke (Denise), Celia Imrie
(Barbara), David McGillivray (Ca-
ven), Ron Smerczak (Ted), Barry
Martin (Al), Tony Sympson (Henry),
Rose Hill (Henry's wife), Dave
Butler (ticket collector), Denis
Tinsley (police sergeant), Pete
Walker (cyclist).

HOUSE ON HAUNTED HILL (1958)

Director: William Castle
Vincent Price (Frederick Loren), Carol Ohmart (Annabelle Loren), Richard Long (Lance Schroeder), Alan Marshall (Dr. David Trent), Julie Mitchum (Ruth Bridges), Elisha Cook, Jr. (Watson Pritchard), Carolyn Craig (Nora Manning), Leona Anderson (Mrs. Slykes), Howard Hoffman (Jonas).

HOUSE ON SKULL MOUNTAIN (1974)
Director: Ron Honthaner
Victor French (Andrew Cunningham), Lloyd Nelson (Sheriff), Mike Evans (Philippe), Janee Michelle (Lorena Christophe), Jean Durand (Thomas), Xernona Clayton (Harriet Johnson), Ella Woods (Louette), Mary J. Todd McKenzie (Pauline), Don Devendorf (priest), Leroy Johnson (Senator).

HOUSE THAT DRIPPED BLOOD, THE (1970)
Director: Peter Duffell
Framework Story: John Bennett (Holloway), John Bryans (Stoker). "Method for Murder": Denholm Elliott (Charles Hillyer), Joanna Dunham (Alice Hillyer), Tom Adams (Dominick), Robert Lang (Psychiatrist). "Waxworks": Peter Cushing (Philip Grayson), Joss Ackland (Rogers), Wolfe Morris (Waxworks owner). "Sweets to the Sweet": Christopher Lee (John Reid), Chloe Franks (Jane), Nyree Dawn Porter (Ann). "The Cloak": Jon Pertwee (Paul Henderson), Ingrid Pitt (Carla Lind), Geoffrey Bayldon (Von Hartmann).

HOUSE THAT SCREAMED, THE (1969) (A.K.A. "La Residencia", "The Boarding School")
Director: Narcisco Ibanez Serrador
Lilli Palmer (Mme. Fourneau), Cristina Galbo (Theresa), John Moulder Brown (Luis), Mary Maude (Irene), Tomas Blanco (M. Baldie), Candida Losada (Mille. Desprez), Pauline Challenor (Catherine), Maribel Martin (Isabelle), Victor Israel (Brechard), Conchita Paredes (Suzanne), Teresa Hurtado (Andree), Anne Marie Pol (Jacqueline), Gloria Blanco (Cecile), Maria Jose Valero (Helene), Maria del Carmen Duque (Julie), Clovis Dave (Henry), Juana Azorin (Susie), Elisa Mendez (Marie).

HOUSE THAT VANISHED, THE (1973) (A.K.A. "Scream...and Die!", "Don't Go into the Bedroom")
Director: Joseph Larrax

Andrea Allan (Valerie), Karl Lanchbury (Paul), Maggie Walker (Susanna), Peter Forbes-Robertson (Mr. Hornby), Judy Matheson (Lorna), Annabella Wood (Stella), Alex Leppard (Terry), Edmund Pegge (Kent), Lawrence Keane (Mike), Daphne Lea (Mrs. Dabney), Richard Aylen (Insp. Matheson), Barbara Meale (1st victim), Joshua Leppard (Peter), Raymond Young (car driver).

HOUSE THAT WOULDN'T DIE, THE (TVM-1970) (A.K.A. "Ammie, Come Home") - 10-27-70
Director: John Llewellyn Moxey
Barbara Stanwyck (Ruth Bennett), Katherine Winn (Sara Dunning), Richard Egan (Prof. Pat McDougall), Michael Anderson, Jr. (Stan Whitman), Mabel Albertson (Mrs. McDougall), Doreen Lang (Sylvia Wall).

HOUSE WHERE EVIL DWELLS, THE (1982)
Director: Kevin Connor
Edward Albert (Ted), Susan George (Laura), Doug McClure (Alex), Amy Barrett (Amy), Mako Hattori (Ofami), Toshiyuki Sasaki (Sugoro), Toshiya Maruyama (Masanori), Tsuyako Okajima (Majyo Witch), Henry Mitowa (Zen Monk), Mayumi Umeda (Noriko), Hiroko Takano (Wakako), Shuren Sakurai (Noh Mask Maker), Shoji Ohara (Assistant Mask Maker), Jiro Shirai (Tadashi), Kazuo Yoshida (editor), Kunihiko Shinjo (assistant editor), Gentaro Mori (Yoshio), Tomoko Shimizu (Aiko), Hideo Shimado (policeman).

HOUSTON, WE'VE GOT A PROBLEM (TVM-1974) - 3-2-74
Director: Lawrence Doheny
Robert Culp (Steve Bell), Gary Collins (Tim Cordell), Sandra Dee (Angie Cordell), Clu Gulager (Lou Mathews), Ed Nelson (Gene Kranz), Steve Franken (Shimon Levin), Robert Corff (Abraham Levin), Sheila Sullivan (Lisa Bell), Quinn Redeker (Lousma), Jack Hogan (Kerwin), Barbara Baldwin (Donna), Zoyla Tolma (Mrs. Levin), Eric Shea (Mike Matthews), Geoffrey Scott (Mel Anderson), James N. Harrell (newsman), Thomas P. Stafford (astronaut).

HOW AWFUL ABOUT ALLAN (TVM-1970) - 9-22-70
Director: Curtis Harrington
Anthony Perkins (Allan Colleigh), Julie Harris (Katherine Colleigh), Kent Smith

(Raymond Colleigh), Joan Hackett
(Olive), Robert H. Harris (Dr. El-
lins), William Erwin (Dr. Ames),
Billy Bowles (Harold Dennis), Trent
Dolan (Eric), Gene Lawrence (Allan
as a child), Jeannette Howe (Katherine as a child).

HOW DO YOU DOOO? (1945)
    Director: Ralph Murphy
Bert Gordon, Claire Windsor, Frank
Albertson, Keye Luke, Fred Kelsey,
Charles Middleton, Matt McHugh,
Thomas Jackson, Harry von Zell,
Cheryl Walker, James Burke, Fran-
cis Pierlot, Ella Mae Morse, Leslie
Denison, Sidney Marion.

HOWLING, THE (1981)
    Director: Joe Dante
Patrick Macnee (Dr. George Wagg-
ner), Dee Wallace (Karen White),
Christopher Stone (R. William Neill),
Dennis Dugan (Chris), Belinda Balaski
(Terry Fisher), Elisabeth Brooks
(Marsha), Robert Picardo (Eddie),
John Carradine (Earl Kenton), Kevin
McCarthy (Fred Francis), Slim Pick-
ens (Sam Newfield), Noble Willingham
(Charlie Barton), James Murtaugh
(Jerry Warren), Jim McKrell (Lew
Landers), Margie Impert (Donna),
Don McLeod (T.C.), Dick Miller
(Walter Paisley), Ivan Saric (Jack
Molina), Kenneth Tobey (older cop),
Steve Nevil (young cop), Forrest J.
Ackerman (bookstore customer), Joe
Bratcher (radio man), Herb Braha
(porno cashier), Mesach Taylor
(Shantz), Bill Sorells (Kline), Daniel
Nunez (liquor cashier), Chico Mar-
tinez (man on street), Roger Corman
(man by phone), Michael O'Dwyer
(drunk), Sabrina Grant (hooker),
Wendell Wright (man at bar).

HOWLING IN THE WOODS, A (TVM-
    1971) - 11-5-71
    Director: Daniel Petrie
Barbara Eden (Liza Crocker), Larry
Hagman (Eddie Crocker), Vera Miles
(Rose Saines), John Rubinstein (Jus-
tin Conway), Ruta Lee (Sharon), Ford
Rainey (Bud Henshaw), Tyne Daly
(Sally Bixton), George Murdock (Mel
Warren), Karl Swenson (Apperson),
Bill Vint (Lonnie Henshaw), Lisa
Gerritsen (Betsy Warren).

HOW TO MAKE A MONSTER (1958)
    Director: Herbert L. Strock
Robert H. Harris (Pete Drummond),
Paul Brinegar (Rivero), Gary Conway

(Tony Mantell), Gary Clarke (Larry
Drake), Malcolm Atterbury (Richards),
Dennis Cross (Monahan), Morris An-
krum (Capt. Hancock), Paul Maxwell
(Jeff Clayton), Robert Shayne (Gary
Droz), Walter Reed (Detective Thomp-
son), Heather Ames (Arlen Dow), Tho-
mas B. Henry (Martin Brice), Eddie
Marr (John Nixon), Jacqueline Ebeier
(Jane), John Phillips (Detective Jones),
Rod Dana (lab technician), Pauline
Myers (Mille, the maid), Joan Chand-
ler (Marilyn), John Ashley (guest star).

HOW TO STEAL THE WORLD (TVM-
    1967)
    Director: Sutton Roley
    see Television: Man From U.N.C.-
    L.E. - "The Seven Wonders of the
    World Affair" (1-8-68 & 1-15-68)

HOW WE STOLE THE ATOMIC BOMB
    (1967-Ital.) (A.K.A. "Come Ru-
    bammo la Bomba Atomica")
    Director: Lucio Fulci
Franco Franchi, Ciccio Ingrassia,
Eugenia Litrel, Julie Menard.

HU-MAN (1976-Fr.)
    Director: Jerome Laperrousax
Terence Stamp, Jeanne Moreau.

HUMAN DUPLICATORS, THE (1964)
    Director: Hugo Grimaldi
George Nader (Glenn Martin), George
Macready (Prof. Dornheimer), Bar-
bara Nichols (Gale Wilson), Dolores
Faith (Lisa), Hugh Beaumont (Austin),
Richard Kiel (Kolos), Richard Arlen
(Intelligence Agency Head), Lonnie
Sattin, Tommy Leonetti.

HUMAN EXPERIMENTS (1980)
    Director: J. Gregory Goodell
Linda Haynes (Rachel Foster), Geof-
frey Lewis (Dr. Kline), Ellen Travolta
(Mover), Mercedes Shirley (Warden
Weber), Lurene Tuttle (Granny), Jack-
ie Coogan (Sheriff Tibbs), Aldo Ray
(Mat Tibbs), Darlene Craviotto (Rita),
Marie O'Henry (Tanya), Wesley Marie
Tackitt (Jimmy), Caroline Davies
(Pam), Cherie Franklin (cell guard),
Bobby Porter (Derril Willis), James
O'Connell (father), Rebecca Bohanon
(mother), Theodora Tate (daughter),
Timothy Cole (son).

HUMAN FEELINGS (TVM- 1978) -
    10-16-78
    Director: Ernest Pintoff
Billy Crystal (Miles Gordon), Nancy
Miller (God), Pamela Sue Martin

(Verna Gold), Donna Pescow (Gloria Prentice), Jack Carter (Robin Dennis), John Fiedler (Lester), James Whitmore, Jr. (detective), Pat Morita (waiter), Armand Assanti (Johnny Turner), Anthony Charnota (Eddie), Tom Pedi (Frank), Squire Fridell (Phil Sawyer), Richard Dimitri (Garcia), Scott Walker (guard).

HUMAN MONSTER, THE (1939) (A.K.A. "Dark Eyes of London")
    Director: Walter Summers
Bela Lugosi (Dr. Orloff/John Dearborn), Hugh Williams (Insp. Holt), Greta Gynt (Diana Stuart), Edmon Ryon (Lt. O'Reilly), Alexander Field (Brogan), Wilfrid Walters (Jake), Arthur E. Owen (Dumb Lew), Gerald Pring (Henry Stuart), Julie Suedo (secretary), Charles Penrose (drunk), May Haliatt.

HUMANOID, THE (1979-Ital.)
    Director: George B. Lewis
Richard Kiel (Golob), Arthur Kennedy (Kraspin), Barbara Bach (Lady Agatha), Corinne Clery (Barbara Gibson), Leonard Mann (Nick), Ivan Rassimov (Grael), Marco Yeh (Tom Tom), Massimo Serata (Great Brother), Vito Fornal, Attillipo Dise, Vanantino Vanatini, Giuseppe Quaglip.

HUMANOIDS FROM THE DEEP (1980)
    Director: Barbara Peeters
Doug McClure (Jim Hill), Ann Turkel (Dr. Susan Drake), Vic Morrow (Hank Slattery), Cindy Weintraub (Carol Hill), Anthony Penya (Johnny Eagle), Denise Galik (Linda Beale), Meegan King (Jerry Potter), Lynn Theel (Peggy Larsen), Breck Costin (Tom Hill), Hoke Howell (Deke), David Strassman (Billy), Don Maxwell (Dick), Linda Shayne, Bruce Monette, Frank Arnold, Greg Trevis, Lisa Glaser, Shawn Erler, Amy Barrett, Henry T. Williams, Jonathan Lehan, Jo Williams, Lyle Isom.

HUMAN VAPOR, THE (1960-Jap.)
    (A.K.A. "Gasu-Ningen Dai Ichi-Go")
    Director: Inoshiro Honda
Yoshio Tsuchiya (Mizuno, the Vapor Man), Tatsuya Mihashi (Okamoto, the detective), Kaoru Yachigusa (Fujichiyo, the dancer), Keiko Sata (Kyoko, the reporter).

HUMONGOUS (1982)
    Director: Paul Lynch
Janet Julian (Sandy Ralston), David

Wallace (Eric Simmonds), Janit Baldwin (Donna Blake), John Wildman (Nick Simmonds), Joy Boushel (Carla Simmonds), Layne Coleman (Burt Defoe), Shay Garner (Eda Parsons), Ed McFadyen (Mr. Parsons).

HUNCHBACK AND THE DANCER, THE (1920-Ger.) (A.K.A. "Der Bucklige und die Tanzerin")
    Director: F.W. Murnau
Conrad Veidt, Lyda Salmanova, Sascha Gura.

HUNCHBACK OF NOTRE DAME, THE (1923)
    Director: Wallace Worsley
Lon Chaney, Sr. (Quasimodo), Patsy Ruth Miller (Esmerelda), Brandon Hurst (Jehan), Norman Kerry (Phoebus), Raymond Hatton (Gringoire), Tully Marshall (Louis XI), Ernest Torrence (Clopin), Nigel De Bruglier (Dom Claude), Gladys Brockwell (Sister Godule), John Cossar (Justice of the Court), Eulalie Jensen (Marie), Winifred Bryson (Fleur de Lys), William Parke, Sr. (Josephus), Harry von Meter (M. Neufchatel), Kate Lester (Mme. de Gondelavier), Nick F. de Ruiz (M. le Torteru), Ray Myers (Charmolu's assistant), Edwin N. Wallack (King's Chamberlain), Joe Bonomo (stuntman), Jay Hunt, Gladys Johnston, Edward Johnson, Jane Sherman, Roy Laidlaw, Pearl Tupper, Charles Haefeli, Albert MacQuarrie.

HUNCHBACK OF NOTRE DAME, THE (1939)
    Director: William Dieterle
Charles Laughton (Quasimodo), Maurene O'Hara (Esmeralda), Sir Cedric Hardwicke (Frollo), Alan Marshal (Phoebus), Edmond O'Brien (Gringoire), Thomas Mitchell (Clopin), Harry Davenport (King Louis XI), Rod LaRoque (Philippe), George Zucco (Procurator), Walter Hampden (Archdeacon), Fritz Leiber (Nobleman), Spencer Charters (Court Clerk), George Tobias (Beggar), Minna Gombell (Queen of Beggars), Arthur Hohl (Oliver), Helen Whitney (Fleur), Katherine Alexander (Fleur's mother), Etienne Girardot (doctor).

HUNCHBACK OF NOTRE DAME, THE (1956-Fr./Ital.) (A.K.A. "Notre Dame de Paris")

Director: Jean Dalonnoy
Anthony Quinn (Quasimodo), Gina
Lolobrigida (Esmeralda), Jean
Danet (Capt. Phoebus), Alain Cuny
(Claude Frollo), Philippe Clay
(Clopin Trouillefou), Robert Hirsch
(Gringoire), Jean Tissier (Louis XI),
Danielle Dumont (Fleur de Lys),
Marianne Oswald (La Falourdel),
Maurice Sarfati (Jehan Frollo), Pieral
(Le Nabot), Roger Blin (Mathis Hun-
gadi), Duphilo (Guillaume Rosseau),
Jacques Hilling (Charmolue).

HUNCHBACK OF NOTRE DAME; THE
(TVM-1978) - 7-18-78
Director: Alan Cooke
Warren Clarke (Quasimodo), Michelle
Newell (Esmeralda), Kenneth Haigh
(Archdeacon Claude Frollo), David
Rintoul (Jehan), Richard Morant
(Phoebus), Christopher Gable (Pi-
erre), Ruth Goring (Madame Gonde-
laurier), Henrietta Baynes (Fleur-
de-Lys), Liz Smith (La Falourdel),
John Ratcliff (Robin), Tony Caunter
(Clopin), Terence Bayler (Cardinal).

HUNCHBACK OF SOHO, THE (1966-
Ger.) (A. K. A. "Der Bucklige von
Soho")
Director: Siegfried Schurenberg
(Sir John), Pinkas Braun (Allan),
Eddie Arent (Chaplain), Monika Peitch
(Wanda), Richard Haller (the Hunch-
back).

HUNCHBACK OF THE MORGUE, THE
(1972-Span.) (A. K. A. "El Jorobado
de la Morgue")
Director: Javier Aguire
Paul Naschy (Wolfgang Gotho), Maria
Perchy, Rossana Yanni, Vic Winner,
Elena Arpon, Manuel De Blas, Alberto
Dalbes, Antonio Pica.

HUNDRED MONSTERS, THE (1968-
Jap.) (A. K. A. "Yokai Huaku
Monogatari")
Director: Kimiyoshi Yasuda
Jun Fujimaki (Yasutaro), Miwa
Takada (Okiku), Mikiko Tsubouchi
(Osen), Sei Hiraizumi (Takichi),
Takashi Kanda (Tajiya).

HUNGRY WIVES (1973) (A. K. A.
"Season of the Witch")
Director: George Romero
Jan White (Joan), Ray Laine (Gregg),
Anne Muffly (Shirley), Joedda McClain
(Nikki), Virginia Greenwald (Marion),
Neil Fisher (Dr. Miller), Bill Thun-
hurst (Jack), Esther Lapidus (Sylvia),

Jean Wechsler (Gloria), Shirley
Strasser (Grace).

HUNTER (TVM-1973) - 1-9-73
Director: Leonard Horn
John Vernon (David Hunter), Steve
Ihnat (Alain Praetorius), Sabina
Scharf (Anne Novak), Fritz Weaver
(Cirrak), Edward Binns (Owen Lark-
dale), Ramon Bieri (Mishani), John
Schuck (McDaniel), Woodrow Parfrey
(Tyson), Lonny Chapman (Albert
Treadway), Roger Bowen (Alfred
Blunt), Ed Flanders (Dr. Miles),
Lawrence Cook (Donnelly), Sheldon
Allman (Dr. Abrams), Tony Van
Bridge (Griggs), Davy Jones (Lub-
bock), Walter Stocker (Gunner),
Barbara Rhoades (girl).

HURRICANE ISLAND (1950)
Director: Lew Landers
Jon Hall (Capt. Carlos Montalvo),
Marie Windsor (Jane Belton), Edgar
Barrier (Ponce de Leon), Karen Ran-
dal (Maria), Marshall Reed (Rolfe),
Nelson Leigh (Padre), Don Harvey
(Valco), Rick Vallin (Padre), Marc
Lawrence (Angus Macready), Jo
Gilbert (Okahla), Lyle Talbot (Physi-
cian), Romo Vincent (Jose), Rus
Conklin (Owanca), Rusty Wescoatt
(Crandall), Alex Montoya (Alfredo),
Zon Murray (Lynch).

HUSH...HUSH SWEET CHARLOTTE
(1964)
Director: Robert Aldrich
Bette Davis (Charlotte Hollis), Olivia
DeHavilland (Mirian), Joseph Cotten
(Dr. Drew Bayliss), William Camp-
bell (Paul Marchand), Cecil Kellaway
(Harry Willis), Agnes Moorehead (Velma
Cruthers), Mary Astor (Mrs. Jewell
Mayhew), Victor Buono (Big Sam Hol-
lis), Bruce Dern (John Mayhew), Wes-
ley Addy (Sheriff), Percy Helton (Fun-
eral Director), George Kennedy (fore-
man), Frank Ferguson (editor), Dave
Willock (taxi driver), Michael Pettit
(gang leader), Idell James (Ginny Mae),
John Megna (newsboy), Alida Aldrich
(young girl), Kelly Flynn (2nd boy),
Kelly Aldrich (3rd boy), Helen Kleeb,
Ellen Corby, Marianne Stewart (town
gossips), William Aldrich (dancer),
Carol Delay (Geraldine), William Walker (chauffeur), Lillian Randolph,
Geraldine West, Mary Henderson
(cleaning women).

HYDE PARK CORNER (1935)
Director: Sinclair Hill

Gordon Harker (Cheatie), Eric Portman (Chester), Gibb McLaughlin (Sir Arthur Gannet), Robert Holmes (Concannon), Donald Wolfit (Howard), Eileen Peel (Barbara Ainsworth), Binnie Hale (Sophie), Harry Tate (taxi driver).

HYENA OF LONDON, THE (1964-Ital.) (A.K.A. "La Jena de Loudra")
    Director: Gino Mancini/Henry Wilson
Luciano Stella/Tony Kendall, Diana Martin, Anthony Wright, Bernard Price.

HYPNOS (1971-Ital./Span.) (A.K.A. "Massacre Mania")
    Director: Paola Bianchini/Paul Maxwell
Ken Wood/Giovanni Cianfriglia, Rada Rassimov, Fernando Sancho, Robert Woods.

HYPNOSIS (1962-Ital./Span./Ger.) (A.K.A. "Nur Tote Zeugen Schweigen", "Only the Dead Are Silent", "Dummy of Death")
    Director: Eugenio Marten
Heinz Drache, Massimo Serato, Hildegarde Kneff, Werner Peters, Eleanora Rossi-Drago, Gotz George, Mara Cruz, Jean Sorel.

HYPNOTIC EYE, THE (1959)
    Director: George Blair
Jacques Bergerac (the Great Desmond), Allison Hayes (Justine), Marcia Henderson (Marcia Blane), Merry Anders (Dodie Wilson), Guy Prescott (Dr. Philip Hect), Joe Patridge (Dave Kennedy), Carol Thurston (Doris Scott), Phyllis Colo (Mrs. McNear), Mary Foran (June Mayes), Holly Harris (Mrs. Stevens), James Lydon (medic), Fred Demara (hospital doctor), Eric Nord (bongo drummer), Lawrence Lipton (poet).

HYPNOTIST AT WORK, A (1897-Fr.) (A.K.A. "L'Magnetiseur")
    Director: Georges Melies

HYPNOTIST'S REVENGE, THE (1909)
    Director: Georges Melies

HYSTERIA (1964)
    Director: Freddie Francis
Robert Webber (Mr. Smith), Lelia Goldoni (Denise), Maurice Denham (Hemmings), Jennifer Jayne (Gina), Anthony Newlands (Dr. Keller),

Sandra Boize (English girl), Peter Woodthrope, Sue Lloyd, Kiwi Kingston.

HYSTERICAL (1982)
    Director: Chris Bearde
The Hudson Brothers, Robert Donner, Murray Hamilton, Cindy Pickett, Richard Kiel, Clint Walker, Julie Newmar, Keenan Wynn, Franklin Ajaye, Maureen Dean, Annie Gaybis, Helena Makela.

I BELIEVE (1916) (A.K.A. "The Man Without a Soul")
    Director: George Loane Tucker
Milton Rosmer, Barbara Everest, Edward O'Neill, Edna Flugrath, Charles Rock, Kitty Cavendish, Hubert Willis, Frank Stanmore, Kenelm Foss.

I BURY THE LIVING (1958)
    Director: Albert Band
Richard Boone (Robert Kraft), Theodore Bikel (Andy McKee), Howard Smith (George Kraft), Herb Anderson (Jess Jessup), Peggy Maurer (Ann Craig), Robert Osterloh (Lt. Clayborne), Glenn Vernon (Stu Drexel), Russ Bender (Henry Trowbridge), Matt Moore (Charles Bates, Sr.), Lynn Bernay (Beth Drexel), Cyril Delevanti (W. Isham), Ken Drake (Bill Honegger).

I DISMEMBER MAMA (1974) (A.K.A. "Poor Albert and Little Annie")
    Director: Paul Leder
Joanne Moore Jordan, Gred Mullavey, Zooey Hall, Geei Reischi, Marlene Tracy, Elaine Partnow, Frank Whiteman.

IDLE ROOMERS (1944) - short
    Director: Del Lord
Moe Howard, Curly Howard, Larry Fine, Vernon Dent, Christine McIntyre, Duke York.

I DRINK YOUR BLOOD (1971)
    Director: David Durston
Jadine Wong (Sue-Lin), Ronda Fultz (Molly), Bhaskar (Horace Bones), Riley Mills (Pete), Richard Bowler (Doc Bowler), Tyde Kierney (Andy), John Damon (Roger Davis), Elizabeth Marner-Brooks, George Patterson, Lynn Lowry, John Damon, Iris Brooks, Alex Mann, Mike Gentry.

I EAT YOUR SKIN (1964) (A.K.A. "Zombies", "Voodoo Blood Bath")

William Joyce (Tom Harris), Heather Hewitt (Jeanine Biladeau), Walter Coy (Charles Bentley), Betty Hyatt Linton (Carol Fairchild), Dan Stapleton (Duncan Fairchild), Robert Stanton (Dr. Biladeau), Vanore Aikens.

IF.... (1969)
   Director: Lindsay Anderson
Malcolm McDowell (Mick Travers), Anthony Nicholls (Gen. Denson), David Wood (Johnny), Richard Warwick (Wallace), Robert Swan (Rowntree), Guy Ross (Stephans), Sean Bury (Jute), Peter Jeffrey (Headmaster), Arthur Lowe (Housemaster), Graham Crowden (History Master), Mona Washbourne (Matron), Christine Noonan (the Girl), Hugh Thomas (Denson), Geoffrey Chater (Chaplain), Mary MacLeod (Housemaster's wife), Robin Askwith (Keating), Ben Aris (Undermaster), Rupert Webster (Bobby Philips), Charles Lloyd Pack (Classics Master), Nicholas Page (Cox), Peter Sproule (Barnes), Philip Bagenal (Peanuts), Michael Cadman (Fortinbras).

I KILLED EINSTEIN, GENTLEMEN (1971-Czech.) (A.K.A. "Zabil Jsem Einsteina, Panove")
   Director: Oldrich Lipsky
Jana Brejchova (Dr. Given), Jiri Sovak, Lobumir Lipsky, Iva Janzurova, Radoslav Brzobohaty, Petr Depek.

I KILLED RASPUTIN (1967-Fr./Ital.) (A.K.A. "J'ai Tue Raspoutine")
   Director: Robert Hossein
Gert Frobe (Rasputin), Geraldine Chaplin (Mounia), Peter McEnery (Youssopov), Ira Furstenbert (Princess), Robert Hossein (Serge), Ivan Desay (Grand Duke), Patrick Balkany.

I KILL, YOU KILL (1965-Ital./Fr.) (A.K.A. Lo Uccido, Tu Uccidi")
   Director: Gianni Puccini
"Giochi Acerbi"/"Unripe Games": Luciana Paluzzi, Marisa Pavan, Giuse Raspani Dandolo. "Il Pienilunio"/ "Full Moon": Eleanora Rossi Drago, Tomas Millan.

I'LL NEVER FORGET YOU (1951) (A.K.A. "The House in the Square")
   Director: Roy Ward Baker
Tyrone Power (Peter Standish), Ann Blyth (Helen), Irene Browne (Lady Ann Pettigrew), Dennis Price (Tom Pettigrew), Beatrice Campbell (Kate Pettigrew), Raymond Huntley (Mr. Throstle), Kathleen Byron (Duchess of Devonshire), Michael Rennie (Forsyth).

ILLUSTRATED MAN, THE (1968)
   Director: Jack Smight
Rod Steiger (Carl), Claire Bloom (Felicia), Robert Drivas (Willie), Don Dubbins (Pickard), Jason Evers (Simmons), Tim Weldon (John), Christie Matchett (Anna).

I LOVE A MYSTERY (1944)
   Director: Henry Levin
Jim Bannon (Jack Packard), Nina Foch (Ellen Monk), Barton Yarborough (Doc Long), George Macready (Jefferson Monk), Lester Matthews (Justin Reeves), Carole Mathews (Jean Anderson), Gregory Gaye (Dr. Hall), Frank O'Connor (Ralph Anderson), Joseph Crehan (Capt. Quinn), Isabel Withers (Miss Osgood), Leo Mostovoy (Vovaritch), Kay Dowd, Ernie Adams.

I LOVE A MYSTERY (TVM-1973) - 2-27-73
   Director: Leslie Stevens
Ida Lupino (Randy Cheyne), David Hartman (Doc Long), Les Crane (Jack Packard), Hagan Beggs (Reggie York), Don Knotts (Alexander Archer), Jack Weston (Job Cheyne), Terry-Thomas (Gordon Elliott), Karen Jensen (Faith), Deanna Lund (Hope), Melodie Johnson (Charity), Peter Mamakos, Francine York, Lewis Charles, Andre Philippe.

I LOVE YOU, I KILL YOU (1971-Ger.) (A.K.A. "Ich Liebe Dich, Ich Tote Dich")
   Director: Uwe Brandner
Rolf Becker (Hunter), Hannes Fuchs (Teacher), Helmut Basch (Mayor), Thomas Eckelmann, Nikolaus Dutsch (policeman), Marianne Blomquist, Monika Hansen (village girls), Wolfgang Ebert.

I LOVE YOU, I LOVE YOU (1968-Fr.) (A.K.A. "Je T'Aime, Je T'Aime")
   Director: Alain Resnais
Claude Rich (Claude), Olga Georges-Picot (Catrine), Amouk Ferjac (Wiana), Marie-Blanche Vergne (young woman), Dominique Rozan (Dr. Haesserts), Van Doude (Rouffers).

ILSA, HAREM KEEPER OF THE OIL

SHEIKS (1976)
Director: Don Edmonds
Dyanne Thorne (Ilsa), Michael Thayer
(Adam), Victor Alexander (El Sharif),
Tanya Boyd (Satin), Marilyn Joy (Vel-
vet), Wolfgang Roehm (Kaiser), Sharon
Kelly, Haji Cat, Uschi Digart, Joyce
Gibson, Su Ling.

ILSA, SHE WOLF OF THE SS (1974)
Director: Don Edmonds
Dyanne Thorne (Ilsa), Gregory Knoph,
Maria Marx, Uschi Digart, Jo Jo De-
ville.

IMAGES (1972)
Director: Robert Altman
Susannah York (Cathryn), Rene Auber-
jonois (Hugh), Hugh Millais (Marcel),
Marcel Bozzuffi (Rene), Cathryn
Harrison (Susannah).

I MARRIED A MONSTER FROM OUTER
SPACE (1958)
Director: Gene Fowler, Jr.
Tom Tryon (Bill Farrell), Gloria
Talbott (Marge Farrell), Ken Lynch
(Dr. Wayne), John Eldredge (Collins),
Valerie Allen (Francine), Alan Dexter
(Sam Benson), James Anderson (Wel-
don), Jean Carson (Helen), Ty Hardin
(Mac), Maxie Rosenbloom (Grady, the
bartender), Robert Ivers (Harry), Jack
Orrison (Schultz), Peter Baldwin
(Swanson), Chuck Wassil (Ted), Steve
London (Charles Mason).

I MARRIED A WITCH (1942)
Director: Rene Clair
Veronica Lake (Jennifer Wooley),
Frederic March (Wallace Wooley),
Susan Hayward (Estelle Masterson),
Robert Warwick (J. B. Masterson),
Cecil Kellaway (Daniel), Robert
Benchley (Dr. Dudley White), Eily
Malyon (Tabitha), Elizabeth Patter-
son (Margaret), Aldrich Bowker
(Justice of the Peace), Emma Dunn
(Justice's wife), Robert Greig (town
crier), Helen St. Rayner (vocalist),
Blossom Rock, Billy Bevan, Robert
E. Homans, Monte Blue, Emory Par-
nell, Lee Shumway, Ann Carter,
Chester Conklin, Wade Boteler, Reed
Hadley, Peter Leeds.

IMMORAL TALES (1974-Fr.) (A. K. A.
"Contes Immoraus")
Director: Walerian Borowczyk
"Erzsebet Bathory" segment: Paloma
Picasso (Countess Bathory), Pascale
Christophe.

IMMORTAL, THE (TVM-1969) -
9-30-69
Director: Joseph Sargent
Christopher George (Ben Richards),
Jessica Walter (Janet Braddock),
Carol Lynley (Sylvia Cartwright),
Barry Sullivan (Jordan Braddock),
Ralph Bellamy (Dr. Pearce), Vin-
cent Beck (Locke), Marvin Silbersher
(doctor), William Sargent (pilot),
Joseph Bernard (mechanic).

IMMORTAL WOMAN, THE (1962-Fr. /
Ital. /Turk.) (A. K. A. "L'Immor-
telle")
Director: Alain Robbe-Grillet
Francoise Brion (Woman), Jacques
Doniol-Valcroze (Man), Guido Celano,
Catherine Carayon, Ulvi Uraz.

I, MONSTER (1971)
Director: Stephen Weeks
Christopher Lee (Dr. Charles Mar-
lowe/Blake), Peter Cushing (Utterson),
Susan Jameson (Diane), Richard
Hurndall (Lanyon), Mike Raven (En-
field), Kenneth J. Warren (Deane),
Marjie Lawrence (Annie), George
Merritt (Poole), Aimee Delamain
(landlady), Michael Des Barres (boy
in Alley).

IMPOSSIBLE VOYAGE, AN (1904-Fr.)
(A. K. A. "Le Voyage a Travers
l'Impossible")
Director: Georges Melies

IMPULSE (1975)
Director: William Grefe
William Shatner, Ruth Roman, Harold
Sakata, Jennifer Bishop, Kim Nicho-
las, James Dobbs, Marcie Knight.

INAUGURATION OF THE PLEASURE
DOME (1954)
Director: Kenneth Anger
Samson De Brier, Cameron, Katy
Kadell, Anais Nin, Kenneth Anger,
Curtis Harrington, Peter Loome.

INCREDIBLE FACE OF DR. B, THE
(1961-Mex.) (A. K. A. "Rostro
Infernal"; "Hell Face")
Director:
Jaime Fernandez, Elsa Cardenas,
Erick Del Castillo, Rosa Carmina.

INCREDIBLE HULK, THE (TVM-
1977) - 11-4-77
Director: Kenneth Johnson
Bill Bixby (Dr. David Banner), Lou
Ferrigno (the Hulk), Jack Colvin (Jack
McGee), Susan Sullivan (Dr. Elaine

Marks), Susan Batson (Mrs. Jessie Maire), Lara Parker (Laura Banner), Mario Gallo (Martin Bram), Charles Siebert (Ben), Eric Devon (B. J. Maier), Jake Mitchell (Jerry), June Whitley Taylor (Mrs. Epstein), Eric Server (policeman), William Larsen (minister), Olivia Barash (girl at lake), George Brenlin (man at lake), Terrence Locke (young man).

INCREDIBLE MELTING MAN, THE (1977)
Director: William Sachs
Alex Rabar (Col. Steven West), Burr DeBenning (Dr. Ted Nelson), Myron Healey (Gen. Parry), Michael Alldredge (Sheriff Blake), Lisle Wilson (Dr. Loring), Ann Sweeny (Judy Nelson), Julie Drazen (Carol), Dorothy Love (Helen), Jonathan Demme (Matt), Edwin Max (Harold), Janus Blythe (Nell), Rainbeaux Smith (model).

INCREDIBLE MR. LIMPET, THE (1963)
Director: Arthur Lubin
Don Knotts (Henry Limpet), Jack Weston (Lt. George Stickle), Andrew Duggan (Adm. Harlock), Carole Cook (Bessie Limpet), Charles Meredith (Adm. Fourstar), Oscar Beregi (Adm. Doemitz), Paul Frees (voice of Crusty), Elizabeth MacRae (voice of Laydfish), Larry Keating.

INCREDIBLE PARIS INCIDENT (1968-Ital.)
Director:
Roger Browne (Argoman), Dominique Boschero (Jenabelle), Dick Palmer.

INCREDIBLE PETRIFIED WORLD, THE (1959)
Director: Jerry Warren
John Carradine (Dr. Wyman), Robert Clarke (Craig Randall), Phyllis Coates (Dale Marshall), Allen Windsor (Paul Whitmore), George Skaff (Matheny), Sheila Noonan (Lauri Talbot), Joe Maierhouser (Jim Wyman), Maurice Bernard (Ingol), Harry Raven (Captain), Lloyd Nelson (radioman), Jack Haffner (reporter).

INCREDIBLE SHRINKING MAN, THE (1957)
Director: Jack Arnold
Grant Williams (Scott Carey), Randy Stuart (Louise Carey), Paul Langton (Charlie Carey), April Kent (Clarice), Raymond Bailey (Dr. Thomas Silver),

William Schallert (Dr. Arthur Benson), Frank Scannell (Barker), John Hiestand (TV newscaster), Helene Marshall, Diana Darrin (nurses), Billy Curtis, Luce Potter (midgets).

INCREDIBLE SHRINKING WOMAN, THE (1981)
Director: Joel Schumacher
Lily Tomlin (Pat Kramer/Judith Beasley), Charles Grodin (Vance Kramer), Ned Beatty (Dan Beame), Henry Gibson (Dr. Eugene Nortz), Elizabeth Wilson (Dr. Ruth Ruth), Nicholas Hormann (Logan Carver), Pamela Bellwood (Sandra Dyson), John Glover (Tom Keller), Mark Blankfield (Rob), Maria Smith (Concepcion), Shelby Balik (Beth Kramer), Justin Dana (Jeff Kramer), James McMullan (Lyle Parks), Mike Douglas (himself), Jacki King (herself), Karen Knapp, Mary McCusker, Maria O'Brien, David Marsh, Betty McGuire, Julie Payne, David Rupprecht, Charles Woolf, Randolph Powell, Donovan Scott (neighbors), Macon McCalman (Dr. Atkins), Richard A. Baker (Sidney), Dick Wilson (store manager), Sally Kirkland (store cashier), Pat Ast, June Sanders, Dorothy Andrews (customers), Tommy McLoughlin (Toy).

INCREDIBLE TWO-HEADED TRANSPLANT, THE (1970)
Director: Anthony M. Lanza
Bruce Dern (Roger), Pat Priest (Linda), Albert Cole (Cass), John Bloom (Danny), Casey Kasem (Ken), Berry Kroeger (Max), Larry Vincent (Andrew), Jack Lester (Sheriff), Jerry Patterson (Deputy), Darlene Duralia (Miss Pierce), Ray Thorn, Donald Brody, Mary Ellen Clawson (motorcyclist), Janice P. Gelman, Andrew Schneider, Mike Espe, Eva Sorensen (teenagers), Bill Collins, Jack English (highway patrolmen), Robert Miller (station attendant), Laura Lanza, Carolyn Gilbert (nurses), Leslie Cole (Danny as young boy).

INCREDIBLY STRANGE CREATURES WHO STOPPED LIVING AND BECAME MIXED-UP ZOMBIES, THE (1963) (A. K. A. "Teenage Psycho Meets Bloody Mary")
Director: Ray Stecker/Cash Flagg
Cash Flagg (Jerry Wagner), Brett O'Hara (Madame Estrella), Carolyn Brandt (Marge), Atlas King (Harold),

Sharon Walsh (Angie), Gene Pollock, Madison Clarke, James Bowie, Jack Brady, Toni Carmel, Joan Howard, Neil Stillman, Bill Ward, Titus Moede, Whitey Robinson, Erina Enyo, Son Hooker.

INCUBUS (1965)
    Director: Leslie Stevens
William Shatner (Marc), Allyson Ames (Kia), Robert Fortier (Olin), Eloise Hart (Amael), Ann Atman (Arndis), Milos Milos (Incubus).

INCUBUS (1980)
    Director: John Hough
John Cassavetes (Sam Cordell), John Ireland (Hank Walden), Kerrie Keane (Laura Kincaid), Helen Hughes (Agatha Galen), Erin Flannery (Jenny Cordell), Duncan McIntosh (Tim Galen), Harvey Atkin (Joe Prescott).

INDESTRUCTIBLE MAN, THE (1956)
    Director: Jack Pollexfen
Lon Chaney, Jr. (Butcher Benson), Marian Carr (Eva Martin), Robert Shayne (Prof. Bradshaw), Casey Adams (Chasen), Ross Elliott (Paull Lowe), Kenneth Terrell (Joe Marcellia), Stuart Randell (Police Captain), Marvin Ellis (Spueamy Ellis).

INDIAN SCARF, THE (1963-Ger.)
    (A.K.A. "Das Indishe Tuch")
    Director: Alfred Vohrer
Heinz Drache, Klaus Kinski, Ady Berber, Siegfried Schurenberg, Hans Nielsen, Corny Collins.

INDIAN TOMB, THE (1920-Ger.)
    (A.K.A. "Das Indishe Grambal",
    "The Hindu Tomb")
    Director: Joe May
Conrad Veidt, Bernard Goetzke, Lya de Putti, Olaf Fønss, Erna Morena, Paul Richter, Mia May.

I NEVER PROMISED YOU A ROSE
    GARDEN (1978)
    Director: Anthony Page
Kathleen Quinlan (Deborah Blake), Bibi Andersson (Dr. Fried), Ben Piazza (Mr. Blake), Lorraine Gary (Mrs. Blake), Susan Tyrell (Lee), Darlene Craviotto (Carla), Signe Hasso (Helene), Norman Alden (McPherson), Martine Bartlett (Secret Wife of Henry VIII), Robert Viharo (Anterrabae), Jeff Conaway (Lactameaon), Barbara Steele (Idat), Dick Herd (Dr. Halle), June C. Ellis (the Spy), Patricia Singer (Kathryn), Sarah Cunningham

(Mrs. Forbes), Diane Varsi (Sylvia), Mary Carver (Eugenia), Donald Bishop (doctor in Ward D), Samantha Harper (teacher in Ward D), Dolores Quentin (receptionist), Pamela Seaman (student nurse), Cynthia Szigetti, Cherry Davis, Carol Androsky, Elizabeth Dartmoor (nurses), Lynn Stewart, Carol Worthington, Gertrude Granor, Margo Burdichevsky, Nancy Parsons, Leigh Curran, Irene Roseen, Helen Verbit, Jan Burrell (women in Ward D).

INFERNAL TRIO, THE (1974-Fr.)
    Director: Francis Girol
Romy Schneider (Philomene), Michel Piccoli (George Sarret), Mascha Gomska (Catherine), Andrea Ferreol (Neomie), Hubert Deschamps (Chambon), Monica Fiorentini (Magali).

INFERNO (1980-Ital.)
    Director: Dario Argento
Irene Miracle (Rose Elliot), Leigh McCloskey (Mark Elliot), Daria Nicoldi (Countess Elise), Eleonora Giorgi (Sara), Alida Valli.

INFERNO IN SPACE (1954)
    see Television: Rocky Jones,
    Space Ranger (1953-54)

INFRA-MAN (1977-Hong Kong)
    Director: Hua Shan
Li Hsiu-hsien, Wang Hsieh, Lin Wenwei, Terry Liu.

INGAGI (1930)
    Director: William Campbell
Charles Gemora (Ingagi), Sir Hubert Winstead, Daniel Swayne.

INHERITANCE, THE (1947) (A.K.A.
    "Uncle Silas")
    Director: Charles Frank
Jean Simmons (Carolin Ruthyn), Derrick De Marney (Uncle Silas), Katina Paxinou (Madame de la Rougierra), Sophie Stewart (Lady Monica Warning), Esmond Knight (Dr. Bryerly), Derek Bond (Lord Richard Ilbury), Reginald Tate (Austin Ruthyn), Manning Whiley (Dudley Ruthyn), Marjorie Rhodes (Mrs. Rusk), Guy Rolfe (Sepulchre Hawkes), Frederick Burtwell (Branston), John Laurie (Giles), George Curzon (Sleigh), O.B. Clarence (Vicar), Frederick Ranalow, Robin Netscher, Patricia Glyn, John Salew.

INHUMAN WOMAN, THE (1923-Fr.)
    (A.K.A. "L'Inhumaine")

Director: Marcel L'Herbier
Eve Francis, Georgette LeBlanc,
Philippe Heriat, Jacques Catelain.

INITIATION OF SARAH, THE (TVM-
1978) - 2-6-78
Director: Robert Day
Kay Lenz (Sarah), Shelley Winters
(Miss Erica), Morgan Brittany
(Patti), Morgan Fairchild (Jennifer),
Tisa Farrow (Mouse), Tony Bill
(Paul Yates), Kathryn Crosby (Mrs.
Goodwin), Robert Hays (Scott),
Nora Heflin (Barbara), Deborah
Ryan (Bobbie), Talia Balsam (Al-
lison), Elizabeth Stack (Laura),
Doug Davidson (Tommy), Karen
Purcil, Jennifer Gay, Michael Tal-
bot, Albert Owens, Madeline Kelly,
Susan Duvall, Debi Fries.

IN LIKE FLINT (1967)
Director: Gordon Douglas
James Coburn (Derek Flint), Lee J.
Cobb (Lloyd Cramden), Jean Hale
(Lisa), Andrew Duggan (Pres. Trent),
Steve Ihnat (Carter), Anna Lee (Elis-
abeth), Yvonne Craig (Natasha),
Herb Edelman (Russian Premier).
Hanna Landy (Helena), Thomas Has-
son (Avery), Diane Bond (Jan),
Totty Ames (Simone), Jacki Ray
(Denise), Mary Michael (Terry),
Buzz Henry (Austin), Mary Meade
French (Hilda), Henry Wills (Cooper),
W. P. Lear, Sr. (Bill Lear), Thordis
Brandt, Erin O'Brien, Marilyn
Hanold, Faye Farrington, Inge Jak-
lyn, Ginny Gan, Eve Bruce, Pat
Becker, Nancy Stone, Inga Neilsen,
Lyzanne La Due.

IN SEARCH OF DRACULA (1972-
Swed.)
Director: Calvin Floyd
Christopher Lee.

INNER SANCTUM (1948)
Director: Lew Landers
Fritz Leiber, Charles Russell, Mary
Beth Hughes, Billy House, Lee
Patrick, Roscoe Ates, Nana Bryant,
Eve Miller, Dale Belding, Eddie
Parks.

INNOCENTS, THE (1961)
Director: Jack Clayton
Deborah Kerr (Miss Giddens),
Pamela Franklin (Flora), Martin
Stephens (Miles), Michael Redgrave
(the Uncle), Peter Wyngarde (Peter
Quint), Megs Jenkins (Mrs. Grose),
Isla Cameron (Anna), Clyttie Jessop
(Miss Jessop).

INSEMINOID (1980)
Director: Norman J. Warren
Robin Clarke (Mark), Judy Geeson
(Sandy), Stephanie Beacham (Kate)
Steven Grives (Gary), Jennifer
Ashley (Cmdr. Holly Mackey),
Barry Houghton (Karl), Victoria
Tennant (Barbra), Rosalind Lloyd
(Gail), Trevor Thomas (Mitch),
David Baxt (Ricky), Heather Wright
(Sharon), Dominic Jephcott (Dean),
Robert Pugh (Roy), Kevin O'Shea
(Corin), John Segal (Jeff).

INSPECTOR CALLS, AN (1954)
Director: Guy Hamilton
Alistair Sim (Insp. Poole), Olga
Lindo (Mrs. Birling), Arthur Young
(Mr. Birling), Bryan Forbes (Eric
Birling), Eileen Moore (Sheila
Birling), Jane Wenham (Eva Smith),
Brian Worth (Gerald Croft), Olwen
Brooks (Miss Francis), Barbara
Everest (Committee Member),
George Woodbridge (Fish and Chips
Shop Owner), Charles Saynor (police
officer), John Welsh (shop walker),
Frances Gowens (small girl).

INSPIRATIONS OF HARRY LARRABEE,
THE (1917)
Director: Bertram Bracken
Clifford Gray (Harry Larrabee),
Margaret Landis (Carolyn Vaughn),
Winifred Greenwood (Madame Ba-
tonyi), Frank Brownlee (Mr. Batonyi/
the Wolf), William Ehfe (Dr. Stettina).

INTERNATIONAL HOUSE (1933)
Director: A. Edward Sutherland
W. C. Fields (Prof. Henry R. Quail),
Stuart Erwin (Tommy Naish), Bela
Lugosi (Gen. Nicholas Pertrosky
Pertronovitch), Edmund Breese
(Dr. Wong), Sari Maritza (Carol
Fortescue), Harrison Greene (Herr
Von Baden), Lumsden Hare (Sir
Mortimer Fortescue), Franklyn
Pangborn (hotel manager), George
Burns (Dr. Burns), Gracie Allen
(Nurse Allen), Peggy Hopkins Joyce
(herself), Sterling Golloway.

INTRIGUE, THE (1916)
Director: Frank Lloyd
Lenore Ulrich (Countess Sonia Varnli),
Cecil Van Auker (Guy Longstreet),
Howard Davies (Baron Rognait),
Herbert Standing (King), Paul Weigel
(Emperor), Florence Vidor (maid).

IN THE BOOGIE MANS CAVE (1908-
Fr.) (A. K. A. "La Cusine de l'O-
gre")
Director: Georges Melies

INTRUDER, THE (1932)
Director: Albert Ray
Monte Blue (John Brandt), Lila Lee
(Connie Wayne), Mischa Auer (Wild
Man), William B. Davidson (Samson),
Wilfred Lucas (Mr. Wayne), Arthur
Housman (Reggie Wayne), Harry Cord-
ing (Cramer), Gwen Lee (Daisy),
Jack Beek (Hanson), Sidney Bracy
(valet), Lynton Brent (purser), Allen
Caven (Captain).

INTRUDER WITHIN, THE (TVM-
1981) - 2-20-81
Director: Peter Carter
Chad Everett (Jake Nevins), Jennifer
Warren (Colette Boudreau), Joseph
Bottoms (Scott), James Hayden
(Harry), Lynda Mason Green (Robyn),
Rockne Tarkington (Mark), Mary
Ann McDonald (Wilma), Michael
Hogan (Chili), Paul Larson (Sam),
Matt Craven (Phil), Ed Laplante
(Ed), Joe Finnegan (Final Creature),
Mickey Gilbert.

INUGAMIS, THE (1977-Jap.)
Director: Kon Ichikawa
Koji Ishizaka (Detective Kindaichi),
Meiko Takamine (Matsuko Inugami),
Miki Sanjo (Takeko), Mitsuke Kus-
abue (Umeko), Takeo Chii (Suketake),
Hisashi Kawaguchi (Suketomo), Teru-
hiko Aoi (Sukekiyo), Akira Kawaguchi
(Sayoko), Ryunosude Kaneda (Torano-
suke), Shoji Kobayashi (Kokichi),
Yoko Shimada (Nonomiya).

INVADERS FROM MARS (1953)
Director: William Cameron
Menzies
Helena Carter (Dr. Pat Blake), Jimmy
Hunt (David MacLain), Arthur Franz
(Dr. Stuart Kellston), Leif Erickson
(George MacLain), Hillard Brooke
(Mary MacLain), Morris Ankrum
(Col. Fielding), Max Wagner (Sgt.
Rinaldi), Milburn Stone (Capt. Roth),
William Phipps (Maj. Cleary), Walter
Sande (Sgt. Finley), Douglas Kennedy
(Officer Jackson), Bert Freed (Chief
Barrows), Robert Shayne (Dr. William
Wislon), Janine Perreau (Kathy Wilson),
John Eldridge (Mr. Turner), Barbara
Billingsly (Dr. Kelston's secretary),
Frank Wilcox (Chief of Staff), William
Forrest (Gen. Mayberry), Richard
Deacon (Sentry Regan), Charles Kane

(Officer Blaine), Luce Potter (Martian Intelligence), Lock Martin, Max
Palmer, Billy Curtis (Martians).

INVADERS FROM OUTER SPACE,
THE (1967-Span.) (A. K. A. "Los
Invasores del Espacio")
Director: Guillermo Ziener
Angel Aranda, Jose Maria Prada,
Manuel Fernandez Aranda, Mairata
O'Wisiedo, Inma de Santi.

INVASION (1966)
Director: Alan Bridges
Edward Judd (Dr. Vernon), Yoko Tani
(Sita), Lyndon Brook (Brian Carter),
Tsai Chin (Lim), Barrie Ingham,
Eric Young, Glyn Houston, Valerie Gea-
ron.

INVASION FROM INNER EARTH (1977)
Director: Bill Rebane
Nick Holt, Debbie Pick, Paul Bentzen,
Karl Wallace.

INVASION OF CAROL ENDERS, THE
(TVM-1974) - 3-8-74
Director:
Meredith Baxter Birney (Carol En-
ders), Christopher Connelly (Adam),
Philip Pine (Detective Yuen), Charles
Aidman (Dr. Bernard), Kris Nelson
(Jason), George Di Cenzo (Dr. Pal-
mer).

INVASION OF THE ANIMAL PEOPLE
(1960-Swed. /U. S.) (A. K. A. "Ter-
ror in the Midnight Sun", "Space
Invasion of Lapland")
Director: Jerry Warren &
Virginia Vogel
John Carradine (Dr. Frederick Wil-
son), Robert Burton (Eric Engstrom),
Barbara Wislon (Diane Wilson), Stan
Gester, Jack Haffner.

INVASION OF THE BEE GIRLS (1973)
Director: Denis Sanders
William Smith (Neil Agar), Victoria
Vetri (Julie Zorn), Anitra Ford (Dr.
Susan Harris), Wright King (Dr.
Murger), Cliff Osmond (Capt. Peters),
Ben Hamner (Gerb Kline), Anna
Aries (Nora Kline), Katie Saylor
(Gretchen Grubowsky), Andre Phil-
lippe (Aldo Ferrara), Sid Kaiser
(Stan Williams), Beverly Powers
(Harriet Williams), Tom Pittman
(Harv), William Keller (Joe), Cliff
Emmich (coroner).

INVASION OF THE BLOOD FARMERS
(1971)

Director: Ed Adlum
Cynthia Fleming (Onhorrid), Norman
Kelly (Dr. Roy Anderson), Tanna
Hunter (Jenny Anderson).

INVASION OF THE BODY SNATCHERS
(1956)
Director: Don Siegel
Kevin McCarthy (Dr. Miles Bennell),
Dana Wynter (Becky Driscoll), King
Donovan (Jack Belicec), Carolyn Jones
(Theodora Belicec), Larry Gates (Dr.
Dan Kaufman), Ralph Dumke (Sheriff
Nick Grivett), Jean Willes (Sally Wi-
thers), Sam Peckinpah (Charlie Buck-
holtz), Virginia Christine (Wilma Lentz),
Tom Fadden (Ira Lentz), Bobby Clarke
(Jimmy Grimaldi), Beatrice Maude
(Grandma Grimaldi), Everett Glass (Dr.
Ed Pursey), Richard Deacon (Dr. Har-
vey Bassett), Whit Bissell (Dr. Hill),
Dabbs Greer (Mac), Kenneth Patterson
(Mr. Driscoll), Eileen Stevens (Mrs.
Grimaldi), Jean Andren (Aunt Eleda),
Guy Way (Sam), Marie Selland (Martha),
Guy Rennie (proprietor), Pat O'Malley
(baggage man).

INVASION OF THE BODY SNATCHERS
(1978)
Director: Philip Kaufman
Donald Sutherland (Matthew Bennell),
Brooke Adams (Elizabeth Driscoll), Leo-
nard Nimoy (Dr. David Kibner), Jeff
Goldblum (Jack Bellicec), Veronica
Cartwright (Nancy Bellicec), Art Hindle
(Geoffrey), Lelia Goldoni (Katherine),
Stan Ritchie (Stan), Tom Luddy (Ted
Hendley), David Fisher (Mr. Gianni),
Gary Goodrow (Boccardo), Don Siegel
(taxi driver), Kevin McCarthy (running
man), Tom Dahlgren (Detective), Jerry
Walter (restaurant owner), Maurice Ar-
gent (chef).

INVASION OF THE DEAD, THE
(1972-Mex.) (A.K.A. "Los
Invasion de los Muertos")
Director: Rene Cardona
Cesar Silva (Dracula), Tarzan Moreno
(Frankenstein's Monster), Blue
Demon, Crista Linder, Luis Maris-
cal, Zorek, Jorge Mistral.

INVASION OF THE NEPTUNE MEN
(1961-Jap.) (A.K.A. "Uchu
Daisoku-sen")
Director: Koji Ota
Sinichi Chiba, Kappei Matsumoto,
Mitsue Komiya, Shinjiro Ebara, Kyuko
Minakami.

INVASION OF THE SAUCER MEN

(1957)
Director: Edward L. Cahn
Steve Terrell (Johnny Carter),
Gloria Castillo (Jean Hayden), Frank
Gorshin (Joe Gruen), Lyn Osborn
(Art Burns), Raymond Hatton (Lar-
kin), Douglas Henderson (Lt. Wilk-
ins), Sam Buffington (Colonel), Rus-
sell Bender (doctor), Bob Einer
(soda jerk), Ed Nelson (boy), Scott
Peters (1st soldier), Calvin Booth
(Paul), Kelly Thorsden (Sgt. Bruce),
Ray Darmour (Sgt. Gordon), Don
Shelton (Mr. Hayden), Jan Englund
(waitress), Patti Lawler (Irene),
Jim Bridges (boy), Joan Dupuis,
Audrey Conti (girls), Jimmy Pickford,
Orv Mohler (boys in soda shop),
Buddy Mason (policeman), Angelo
Rossitto, Lloyd Dixon, Edward
Peter Gibbons, Dean Neville (Sau-
cer Men).

INVASION OF THE STAR CREATURES
(1962)
Director: Bruno Ve Sota
Dolores Reed (Prof. Puna), Frankie
Ray (Penn), Robert Ball (Philbrick),
Gloria Victor (Dr. Tanga), Mark
Ferris (Col. Rank), Jim Almanzer,
Slick Slavin, Anton von Stralen,
Allen Dailey, Joseph Martin, Mike
Del Piano, Sid Kane, Lenore Bond.

INVASION OF THE VAMPIRES
(1962-Mex.) (A.K.A. "La Invasion de los Vampiros")
Director: Miguel Moratya
Carlos Agosti (Count Frankenhausen), Erna Martha Bauman, Tito
Junco, Rafael del Rio, Bertha Moss.

INVASION OF THE ZOMBIES (1961-
Mex.) (A.K.A. "Santo vs. the
Zombies")
Director: Benito Alzraki
Santo, Carlos Agosti, Armando
Silvestre, Lorena Velazquez, Irma
Serrano, Ramon Bugarini, Jaime
Fernandez, Dagoberto Rodrequez.

INVASION SINITESTRA (1968-Mex. /
U.S.) (A.K.A. "The Incredible
Invasion")
Director: Juan Ibanez & Jack
Hill
Boris Karloff, Enrique Guzman,
Christa Linder, Yerye Beirute, Tene
Valez, Maura Monti, Sergio Kleiner.

INVASION U.S.A. (1952)
Director: Alfred E. Green
Dan O'Herlihy (Mr. Ohman), Peggie

Castle (Carla), Gerald Mohr (Vince),
Phyllis Coates (Mrs. Mulvory), Ro-
bert Bice (George Sylvester), Wade
Crosby (Congressman), Erik Blythe
(Ed Mulvory), Tom Kennedy (barten-
der), Aram Katcher (5th Columnist
Leader), Edward G. Robinson, Jr.,
Noel Neill.

INVENTOR CRAZYBRAINS AND HIS
    WONDERFUL AIRSHIP (1906-Fr.)
    (A. K. A. "Le Dirigeable Fantasti-
    que ou le Cauchemar d'un Inventeur")
    Director: Georges Melies

INVINCIBLE INVISIBLE MAN, THE
    (1969-Span./Ital./Ger.) (A. K. A.
    "Mr. Super Invisible", "Invencible
    Hombre Invisible", "Super Invisible
    Man")
    Director: Antonio Margheriti/
    Anthony M. Dawson
Dean Jones, Gastone Moschin, Ingeborg
Schoener, Roberto Camardiel, Rafael
Alonso, Peter Karstein.

INVINCIBLE MACISTE BROTHERS,
    THE (1964-Ital.) (A. K. A. "Gli
    Invincibili Fratelli Maciste")
    Director: Roberto Mauri
Richard Lloyd, Claudie Lange, Tony
Freeman, Antonio De Teffe/Anthony
Steffen, Pier Anna Quaglia/Ursula
Davis, Gia Sandri.

INVINCIBLE THREE, THE (1964-
    Ital.) (A. K. A. "Gle Invincibili
    Tre")
    Director: Gianfranco Parolini
Sergio Ciani/Alan Steel, Nimmo Pal-
mara, Carlo Tamberlani, Lisa Gastoni,
Rosalba Neri.

INVINCIBLE MASKED RIDER, THE
    (1965-Ital./Fr.)
    Director: Umberto Lenzi
Pierre Brice, Massimo Serato, Helene
Chanel, Daniele Vargas, Aldo Bufi-
landi, Romano Ghini.

INVISIBLE AGENT (1942)
    Director: Edwin L. Marin
Ilona Massey (Maria Goodrich), Jon
Hall (Frank Griffin), Peter Lorre
(Baron Ikito), Sir Cedric Hardwicke
(Conrad Stauffer), J. Edward Bromberg
(Karl Heiser), John Litel (John Gard-
iner), Holmes Herbert (Sir Alfred
Spenser), Keye Luke (surgeon), Matt
Willis (Nazi assassin), Lee Shumway
(Brigadier General), Duke York, Lane
Chandler, Donald Curtis (German
sentries), Milburn Stone (German

sergeant), James Craven (ship's
radioman), Mabel Colcord (maid),
Marty Faust (killer), Alberto Morin
(Free Frenchman), John Holland
(Spencer's secretary), Wolfgang
Zilzer (von Porten), Ferdinand
Munier (bartender), Henry Guttman
(Storm Trooper), Eddie Dunn, Hans
Schumm (SS men), John Burton
(RAF flier), Michael Visaroff (Veri-
chen), Lee Tung-Fo (Gen. Chin Lee),
Walter Tetley (newsboy), Pat West
(taxi driver), William Ruhl, Otto
Reichow (Gestapo agents), Leslie
Denison (British radio operator),
Wally Scott, Bobby Hale (English
Tommy), Pat McVey (German),
Phil Warren, John Merton, Charles
Flynn, Paul Bryar (German soldiers),
Henry Zynder (Col. Kelenski),
Ferdnand Schumann-Heink (German
telephone operator), Victor Zimmer-
man, Bill Pagan (Storm Troopers),
Charles Regan (ordinance car driver),
Sven Hugo-Borg (German Captain),
Eddie Parker (stuntman).

INVISIBLE ASSASSIN, THE (1964-Mex.)
    (A. K. A. "El Asesino Invisible")
    Director: Rene Cardona
Ana Bertha Lepe, Guilermo Murray,
El Enmascarado de Oro, Jorge Pous,
Miguel Arenas, Carlos Agosti, Adri-
ana Roel.

INVISIBLE AVENGER (1958)
    Director: James Wong Howe &
    John Sledge
Richard Derr (Lamont Cranston), Helen
Westcott (Tara), Mark Daniels (Jogen-
dra), Dan Mullin (Pablo Ramirez/Vic-
tor Ramirez), Jeanne Neher (Felicia
Ramirez), Lee Edwards (Colonel),
Steve Dano (Tony Alcalde), Sam Page
(Charlie), Jack Doner (Billy), Leo
Bruno (Rocco).

INVISIBLE BOY, THE (1957)
    Director: Herman Hoffman
Philip Abbott (Dr. Merrinoe), Diane
Brewster (Mary Merrinoe), Richard
Eyer (Timmie Merrinoe), Harold
J. Stone (Gen. Swayne), Than Wyenn
(Dr. Zeiller), Robert H. Harris (Prof.
Allerton), Alexander Lockwood (Arthur
Kelvaney), Gage Clark (Dr. Bannerman),
Dennis McCarthy (Col. Macklin), John
O'Malley (Dr. Baine), Jefferson Dud-
ley Searles (Dr. Foster), Alfred
Linder (Martin), Ralph Votrian (1st
gate sergeant), Michael Miller (2nd
gate sergeant.)

INVISIBLE CREATURE, THE (1960)
(A. K. A. "The House in Marsh
Road")
Director: Montgomery Tully
Sandra Dorne (Valerie Stockley),
Derek Aylward (Richard), Tony
Wright (David Linton), Patricia Dainton (Jean Linton), Anita Sharp Bolster (Mrs. O'Brien), Olive Sloane
(Mrs. Morris), Sam Kydd (Lumley),
Llewellyn Rees (Webster), Roddy
Hughes (Daniels), Geoffrey Denton.

INVISIBLE DR. MABUSE, THE
(1961-Ger.) (A. K. A. "Die Unsichtbaren Krallen des Dr. Mabuse", "The Invisible Claws of
Dr. Mabuse", "The Invisible
Horror")
Director: Harald Reinl
Wolfgang Preiss (Dr. Mabuse),
Siegfried Lowitz (Brahm), Lex
Barker, Karin Dor, Werner Peters,
Alan Dijon.

INVISIBLE GHOST, THE (1941)
Director: Joseph H. Lewis
Bela Lugosi (Charles Kessler), Betty
Compson (Mrs. Kessler), Clarance
Muse (Evans), Ernie Adams (Jules),
Jack Mulhall (Tim), Polly Ann Young
(Virginia), John McGuire (Ralph),
George Pembroke (Williams), Fred
Kesley (Ryan), Terry Walker (Cecile), Ottola Nesmith.

INVISIBLE INVADERS (1959)
Director: Edward L. Cahn
John Agar (Maj. Bruce Jay), John
Carradine (Dr. Karol Noymann),
Philip Tonge (Dr. Adam Penner),
Jean Byron (Phyllis Penner), Robert Hutton (Dr. John Lamont), Eden
Hartford (WAAF secretary), Paul
Langton (Gen. Stone), Chuck Niles
(hockey announcer), Hal Torey
(farmer), Jack Kenney (cab driver),
Don Kennedy (pilot).

INVISIBLE KILLER, THE (1940)
Director: Sherman Stout
William Newell, Ernie Adams, Grace
Bradley, Roland Drew, Jeanne Kelly.

INVISIBLE MAN, THE (1933)
Director: James Whale
Claude Rains (Jack Griffin), Gloria
Stuart (Flora Cranley), William
Harrigan (Dr. Kemp), Henry Travers (Dr. Cranley), Holmes Herbert
(Chief of Police), Una O'Connor
(Jenny Hall), Forrester Harvey
(Herbert Hall), E. E. Clive (Jaffers),

Dudley Digges (Chief of Detectives),
Dwight Frye (reporter), John Carradine (informer), Harry Stubbs (Insp.
Bird), Donald Stuart (Insp. Lane),
John Merivale (boy), Merle Tottenham (Milly), Walter Brennan (man
with bike), Jameson Thomas (doctor).

INVISIBLE MAN, THE (1959-Mex.)
A. K. A. "Los Invisibles")
Director: Jaime Salvador
Firuta, Capulina, Martha Elena,
Cervantes, Eduardo Fajardo, Jose
Jasso, Rosa Maria Gallardo, Chucho
Salinas.

INVISIBLE MAN, THE (TVM-1975) -
5-6-75
Director: Robert Michael Lewis
David McCallum (Daniel Weston),
Melinda Fee (Kate Weston), Jackie
Cooper (Carlson), Henry Darrow (Dr.
Nick Maggio), Arch Johnson (Gen.
Turner), Alex Henteloff (Steiner),
John McLiam (blind man), Ted Gehring (gate guard).

INVISIBLE MAN IN ISTANBUL (1956-
Turk.) (A. K. A. "Gorunmiyen
Adam Istanbulda")
Director: Lutfu Akad
Atif Kaptan, Nese Yulac, Turan Seyfioglu.

INVISIBLE MAN RETURNS, THE
(1939)
Director: Joe May
Vincent Price (Geoffrey Radcliffe),
Sir Cedric Hardwicke (Richard Cobb),
Nan Grey (Helen Manson), John Sutton
(Dr. Frank Griffin), Alan Napier
(Willie Spears), Cecil Kellaway (Insp.
Sampson), Forrester Harvey (Ben
Jenkins), Ivan Simpson (Cotton),
Edward Fielding (Governor), Frances Robinson (nurse), Harry Cording
(shopworker), Harry Stubbs (Constable
Dukesbury), Edmund MacDonald
(mineworker), Mary Field (woman),
Billy Bevan.

INVISIBLE MAN'S REVENGE, THE
(1944)
Director: Ford Beebe
Jon Hall (Robert Griffin), Alan Curtis (Mark Foster), Evelyn Ankers
(Julie), Lester Matthews (Sir Jasper
Herrick), Gale Sondergaard (Lady
Irene Herrick), John Carradine (Dr.
Peter Drury), Leon Errol (Herbert
Higgens), Halliwell Hobbes (Cleghorn),
Ian Wolfe (Jim Feeny), Skelton Knaggs
(Al Parry), Doris Lloyd (Maude),

Billy Bevan (Sgt. Frederic Travers).

INVISIBLE MONSTER, THE (1950)
(A. K. A. "Slaves of the Invisible
Monster") - serial in 12 episodes
Director: Fred C. Brannon
Richard Webb (Lane Carson), Aline
Towne (Carol Richards), Lane Brad-
ford (Burton), Stanley Price (the Phan-
tom Ruler), John Crawford (Harris),
Dale Van Sickel (Otto Wagner), Tom
Steele (Haines/Mac), George Meeker
(Harry Long), Ed Parker (Stoner),
Marshall Reed (Officer McDuff),
Keith Richards (doctor), Frank
O'Connor (Hogan), Charles Sullivan
(Grogarty), Charles Regan (Art),
Bud Wolfe (Harding), Forrest Burns
(guard), Harold Goodwin (Kirk),
Ken Terrell (Kern), Edward Keane
(Warren Madison), Tom Monroe
(Gates), Douglas Evans (James
Hunter), Duke Taylor (Officer),
Mark Strong (watchman No. 1), Bert
LeBaron (watchman No. 2), David
Sharpe (watchman No. 3/guard No. 1),
George Volk (guard No. 3), John
Hamilton (Henry Miller), Guy Teague
(Al), Roy Gordon (Moore), George
Magrill (Sam), Howard Mitchell
(night watchman).

INVISIBLE POWER, THE (1914)
Director:
William H. West, Paul C. Hurst,
Thomas Gillette, Jane Wolfe, Cloe
Ridgeley, James W. Horne, Frank
Jonasson.

INVISIBLE RAY, THE (1920) - serial
in 15 episodes
Director: Harry A. Pollard
Ruth Clifford (Mystery), Sidney
Bracey (Jean Deaux), Edward Davis
(John Haldene), Jack Sherrill (Jack
Stone), Corinne Uzzell (Crystal
Gazer), W. H. Tooker (gang member).

INVISIBLE RAY, THE (1935)
Director: Lambert Hillyer
Boris Karloff (Dr. Janos Rukh), Bela
Lugosi (Dr. Felix Benet), Frances
Drake (Diane Rukh), Frank Lawton
(Ronald Drake), Beulah Bondi (Lady
Arabella Stevens), Walter Kinsford
(Sir Francis Stevens), Violet Kemble
Cooper (Mrs. Rukh), Nydia Westman
(Briggs), Daniel Haines (Headman),
George Renavent (President of the
Senate), Frank Reicher (Prof.
Meiklejohn), Paul Weigel (Monsieur
Noyer), Ernie Adams, Lawrence
Stewart, Etta McDaniel, Adele St.

Maur, Inez Seabury, Winter Hall.

INVISIBLE TERROR, THE (1963-Ger.)
(A. K. A. "Der Unsichtbare")
Director: Raphael Nussbaum
Hanaes Hauser, Ilse Steppat, Ellen
Schwiers, Hans von Borsody, Herbert
Stass, Hannes Schmidhauser, Harry
Fuss, Ivan Desny, Christiane Nielson.

INVISIBLE WOMAN, THE (1941)
Director: A. Edward Sutherland
Virginia Bruce (Kitty Carroll), John
Barrymore (Prof. Gibbs), John Howard
(Dick Russell), Charles Ruggles (George),
Oscar Homolka (Blackie Cole), Charles
Lane (Growley), Thurston Hall (John
Hudson), Margaret Hamilton (Mrs.
Jackson), Mary Gordon (Mrs. Bates),
Anne Nagel (Jean), Edward S. Brophy
(Bill), Maria Montez (Marie), Shemp
Howard (Hammerhead/Frankie), Kathryn
Adams (Peggy), Donald MacBride (Fog-
horn), Kitty O'Neil (Mrs. Patton), Eddie
Conrad (Hernandez), Kay Leslie (model),
Kay Linaker, Sarah Edwards (fashion
show buyers), Harry C. Bradley (want-
ad man), Kernan Cripps (postman).

INVOCATION OF MY DEMON BROTHER
(1969) - short
Director: Kenneth Anger
Kenneth Anger, Bobby Beausoleil,
Anton Szandor La Vey, Speed Hacker,
Lenore Kandell, Van Leuvan.

IRON CLAW, THE (1916) - serial in
20 episodes
Chapters: 1. "The Vengeance of Legar",
2. "The House of Unhappiness", 3. "The
Cognac Mask", 4. "The Name and the
Game", 5. "The Incorrigible Captive",
6. "The Spotted Warning", 7. "The
Hooded Helper", 8. "The Stroke of 12",
9. "Arrows of Hate", 10. "The Living
Dead", 11. "The Saving of Dan O'Mara",
12. "The Haunted Canvas", 13. "The
Hidden Face", 14. "The Plunge for
Life", 15. "The Double Resurrection",
16. "The Unmasking of Davy", 17. "The
Vanishing Fakir", 18. "The Green-
Eyed God", 19. "The Dave of Despair"
& 20. "The Triumph of the Laughing
Mask".
Director: Edward Jose
Pearl White, Creighton Hale, Sheldon
Lewis, Harry Fraser, J. E. Dunn.

IRON CLAW, THE (1941) - serial in
15 episodes
Director: James V. Horne
Charles Quigley (Bob Lane), Joyce
Bryant (Patricia Benson), Walter

Sande (Jack Strong), Forrest Taylor (Anton Benson), Alex Callam (James Benson), James Metcalfe (Culver Benson), Norman Willis (Roy Benson), Allen Doone (Simon Leach), Charles King (Sild), John Beck (Gyves), Hal Price (O'Malley), Edythe Elliot (Milly Leach), James Morton (Casey).

I SAW WHAT YOU DID (1965)
Director: William Castle
Joan Crawford (Amy Nelson), Leif Erickson (Dave Mandering), John Ireland (Steve Marak), Sarah Lane (Kit Austin), Andi Garrett (Libby Mannering), Patricia Breslin (Ellie Mannering), John Archer (John Austin), Joyce Meadows (Judith Marak), Sharyl Locke (Tess Mannering), John Crawford (trooper).

ISLAND, THE (1980)
Director: Michael Ritchie
Michael Caine (Maynard), David Warner (Nau), Dudley Sutton (Dr. Brazil), Jeffrey Frank (Justin), Colin Jeavons (Hizzoner), Don Henderson (Rollo), Frank Middlemas (Windsoe), Angela Punch McGregor (Beth), Zakes Mosae (Wescott), Brad Sullivan (Stark), John O'Leary, Bruce McLaughlin, Jimmy Casino (doctors), Suzanne Astor (Mrs. Burgess), Susan Bredhoff (Kate), Cary Hoffman (Mr. Burgess), Reg Evans (Jack the Bat), William Schilling (Baxter), Stewart Steinbert (Hiller), Bob Westmoreland (Charter Boat Captain).

ISLAND AT THE TOP OF THE WORLD (1973)
Director: Robert Stevenson
David Hartman (Prof. Ivarson), Donald Sinden (Sir Anthony Ross), Jacques Marin (Capt. Brieux), David Gwillim (Donald Ross), Agneta Echemyr (Freyja), Gunnar Ohlund, Denny Miller, Ivor Barry, Lasse Kolstad, Rolf Soder, Sverre Osudal, Brendan Dillon, Lee Paul, Erik Silju, Torsten Wahlund, Niel Ninrichsen, James Almanzar.

ISLAND OF DR. MOREAU, THE (1977)
Director: Don Taylor
Burt Lancaster (Dr. Moreau), Michael York (Braddock), Barbara Carrera (Maria), Nigel Davenport (Montgomery), Richard Basehart (Sayer of the Law), Noel Cravat (M'Ling), John L. (Boarman), Bob Ozman (Bullman), Fumio Demura (Hyenaman), Gary Baxley (Lionman), David Cass (Bearman), John Gillespie (Tigerman).

ISLAND OF LOST SOULS, THE (1933)
Director: Erle C. Kenton
Charles Laughton (Dr. Moreau), Richard Arlen (Edward Parker), Leila Hyams (Ruth Walker), Arthur Hohl (Montgomery), Kathleen Burke (Lota, the Panther Woman), Bela Lugosi (Sayer of the Law), Stanley Fields (Capt. Davies), Tetsu Komai (M'Ling), Paul Hurst (Capt. Donahue), Hans Steinke (Ouran), George Irving (American Consul), Robert Kortman (Hogan), Rosemary Grimes (Samoan girl), Harry Ekezian (Gola), Charles Gemora (Gorilla), Alan Ladd, Joe Bonomo, Randolph Scott, Duke York, Jr., Constantine Romanoff, Robert Milasch, Jack Waltess, Bob Kerr, Jack Burdette, Buster Brody, John George, Evangelus Bergas (Beastmen).

ISLAND OF LOST WOMEN (1959)
Director: Frank W. Tuttle
Jeff Richards (Mark Bradley), Alan Napier (Dr. Lujan), Venetia Stevenson (Venus), Gavin Muir (McBain), Diane Jergens (Uarna), June Blair (Mercuria), John Smith (Joe Walker), George Brand (Garland).

ISLAND OF TERROR (1966)
Director: Terence Fisher
Peter Cushing (Dr. Brian Stanley), Edward Judd (Dr. David West), Carole Gray (Toni Merrill), Eddie Bryne (Dr. Landers), Sam Kydd (Constable Harris), Niall MacGinnis (Mr. Campbell), Joyce Hemson (Mrs. Bellows), Liam Caffney (Bellows), James Caffrey (Argyle), Roger Heath cote (Dumley), Shay Gorman (Morton), Keith Bell (Halsey), Peter Forbes Robertson (Dr. Phillips), Richard Bidlake (Carson), Edward Ogden (helicopter pilot).

ISLAND OF THE BURNING DAMNED (1967) (A.K.A. "Night of the Big Heat", "Island of the Burning Doomed")
Director: Terence Fisher
Christopher Lee (Hanson), Peter Cushing (Dr. Stone), Patrick Allen (Jeff Callum), Sarah Lawson (Frankie Callum), Jane Merrow (Angela), Kenneth Cope (Tinker Mason), William Lucas (Ken Stanley), Thomas Heathcote (Bob Hayward), Jack Bligh (Ben Siddle), Percy Herbert (Gerald Foster), Ann Turner (Stella Haywood), Sidney Bromley (old tramp), Barry Halliday (radar operator).

ISLAND OF THE DAMNED (1976-
Span.) (A.K.A. "Quien Puede
Matar a un Nino?", "Who Can Kill
a Child?", "Would You Kill A
Child?")
    Director: Narcisco Ibanez Ser-
rador
Lewis Fiander (Tom), Prunella Ran-
some (Evelyn), Antonio Iranzo, Mi-
guel Naros, Marisa Porcel, Maria
Luisa Arias.

ISLAND OF THE DINOSAURS (1966-
Mex.) (A.K.A. "La Isla de los
Dinosaurios")
    Director: Rafael Lopez Portillo
Armando Sivestre, Alma Delia Fuen-
tes, Jenaro Moreno, Elsa Cardenas,
Manolo Fabregas, Crox Alvarado,
Roberto Canedos, Regina Torne,
Tito Junco.

ISLE OF LOST SHIPS, THE (1923)
    Director: Maurice Tourner
Anna Q. Nilsson (Dorothy Fairfax),
Milton Sills (Frank Howard), Frank
Campeau (Detective Jackson), Her-
shall Mayall (Captain Clark), Walter
Long (Peter Forbes), Aggie Herring
(Mother Joyce), Bert Woodruff
(Patrick Joyce).

ISLE OF LOST SHIPS (1929)
    Director: Irvin Willat
Jason Robards, Sr. (Frank Howard),
Noah Berry, Sr. (Capt. Peter Forbes),
Virginia Valli (Dorothy Renwick),
Henry Cording (Gallagher), Clarissa
Selwynne (Aunt Emma), Robert E.
O'Connor (Detective Jackson), Mar-
garet Fielding (Mrs. Gallagher),
Katherine Ward (Mother Joyce Burke),
Robert Homans (Mr. Burke), Sam
Baker (Sam Baker), Jack Acroyd
(Harry).

ISLE OF THE DEAD (1945)
    Director: Mark Robson
Boris Karloff (Gen. Pherides), Ellen
Drew (Thea), Marc Cramer (Oliver),
Katherine Emery (Mrs. St. Aubyn),
Alan Napier (St. Aubyn), Ernst Dorian
(Dr. Drossor), Helene Thimig (Kyra),
Jason Robards, Sr. (Albrecht), Skel-
ton Knaggs.

ISN'T IT SHOCKING (TVM-1973) -
10-2-73
    Director: John Badham
Alan Alda (Sheriff Dan Barnes), Louise
Lasser (Blanche), Ruth Gordon (Marge
Savage), Lloyd Nolan (Jesse Chapin),
Edmond O'Brien (Justin Oates), Will

Geer (Lemuel Lovall), Dorothy Tris-
tan (Doc Lovall), Liam Dunn (Myron
Flagg), Michael Powell (Michael),
Pat Quinn (Ma Tate), Jacqueline Allen
McClure (Hattie).

I SPIT ON YOUR GRAVE (1978)
    (A.K.A. "Day of the Woman")
    Director: Meri Zarchi
Camille Keaton (Jennifer), Eron
Tabor (Johnny), Richard Pace
(Matthew), Anthony Nichols (Stanley),
Gunter Kleeman (Andy), Alexis Mag-
notti (attendant's wife), Tammy Zar-
chi, Terry Zarchi (children), Traci
Ferrante (waitress), Bill Tasgal
(porter), Isac Agami (butcher),
Ronit Haviv (supermarket girl).

IT (1966)
    Director: Herbert J. Leder
Roddy McDowall (Arthur Primm),
Jill Haworth (Ellen Grove), Paul
Maxwell (Jim Perkins), Aubrey
Richards (Prof. Weal), Oliver
Johnston (Trimingham), Ernest
Clark (Harold Grove), Noel Trevar-
then (Insp. White), Alan Sellers (It),
Richard Goolden (old man), Ian
McCulloch (Wayne), Dorothy Frere
(Miss Swanson), Steve Kirby (Ellis),
Tom Chatto (Captain), Russell
Napier (Boss), Brian Haines (Joe
Hill), Mark Burns (1st officer),
Raymond Adamson (2nd officer),
Lindsay Campbell (policeman), John
Baker (guard), Frank Sieman (work-
man).

IT CAME FROM BENEATH THE SEA
(1955)
    Director: Robert Gorrdon
Faith Domergue (Lesley Joyce), Ken-
neth Tobey (Pete Mathews), Donald
Curtis (John Carter), Ian Keith (Adm.
Burns), Harry Lauter (Bill Nash),
Dean Maddox, Jr. (Adm. Norman),
Richard W. Peterson (Capt. Stacy),
Del Courtney (Robert Chase), Ed
Fisher (McLeod), Rudy Puteska
(Hall), Jules Irving (King), Charles
Griffith (Griff), Tol Avery (Navy
Interne), Ray Storey (reporter).

IT CAME FROM OUTER SPACE (1953)
    Director: Jack Arnold
Richard Carlson (John Putnam),
Barbara Rush (Ellen Fields), Charles
Drake (Sheriff Warren), Russell
Johnson (George), Joseph Sawyer
(Frank Daylon), Alan Dexter (Dave
Loring), George Eldredge (Dr. Snell),
Brad Jackson (Snell's assistant),

Warren MacGregor (Toby), George
Selk (Tom), Edgar Dearing (Sam),
Kathleen Hughes (Jane), William Pul-
len (Deputy Reed), Virginia Mullen
(Mrs. Frank Daylon), Robert S. Car-
son (Dugan), Dick Pinner (Lober),
Ned Davenport (man), Whitey Haupt
(Perry).

IT CONQUERED THE WORLD (1956)
    Director: Roger Corman
Peter Graves (Paul Nelson), Beverly
Garland (Claire Anderson), Lee Van
Cleef (Tom Anderson), Sally Fraser
(Joan Nelson), Russ Bender (Gen.
Patrick), Charles B. Griffith (Pete
Sheldon), Dick Miller (Sgt. Neil),
Jonathan Haze (Private Manuel Ortiz),
Karen Kadler (Ellen Peters), Taggart
Casey (Police Chief N.J. Schallert),
Paul Harbor (Floyd Mason), Tom
Jackson (George Haskell), Marshall
Bradford (U.S. Secretary Platt),
David McMann (Gen. Carpenter), Jim
Knight (bazooka man), Paul Blaisdell
(the Monster).

IT GROWS ON TREES (1952)
    Director: Arthur Lubin
Irene Dunne (Polly Baxter), Dean
Jagger (Phil Baxter), Richard Crenna
(Ralph Bowen), Sandy Descher (Midge
Baxter), Les Tremayne (Finlay Murch-
ison), Forrest Lewis (Dr. Harold Bur-
rows), Thurston Hall (Sleamish),
Frank Ferguson (John Letherby),
Madge Blake (woman), Hal K. Dawson
(Tutt), Joan Evans (Diane Baxter),
Dee Pollack (Flip Baxter), Edith
Meiser (Mrs. Pryor), Malcolm Lee
Beggs (Henry Carrollman), Chuck
Courtney (paper man), Bob Sweeney
(McGuire), Clark Howat (mustache),
John Damler (cleanshave), Emile
Avery (TV man), Elmer Peterson (com-
mentator), Cliff Clark (Sergeant),
Dee J. Thompson (Miss Reid), Jimmy
Dood (Treeburger proprietor), Anthony
Radecki, Charles Gibb, Perc Launders,
Charles McAvoy (policemen), Mary
Benoit, Vera Burnett (assistants),
Bob Carney (bus driver), Burman Bodil
(badge vendor), Ralph Montgomery
(umbrella vendor), Jack Reynolds
(reporter), William O'Leary (Gonnigle),
Jeanne Blackford (lady), Bob Edgecomb
(interviewer), Walter Clinton (delivery
man), Frank Howard, Robert Strong
(cameramen).

IT HAPPENED AT LAKEWOOD MANOR
    (TVM-1977) (A.K.A. "Panic at Lake-
    wood Manor") - 12-2-77
    Director: Robert Sheerer
Robert Foxworth (Mike Carr), Lynda
Day George (Valerie Adams), Myrna
Loy (Ethel Adams), Gerald Gordon
(Tony Fleming), Suzanne Somers
(Gloria Henderson), Bernie Casey),
Steve Franken (White), Barry Van
Dyke (Richard Cyril), Anita Gillette
(Peggy Kenter), Karen Lamm (Linda
Howard), Barbara Brownell (Mar-
jorie West), Moosie Drier (Tommy
West), Brian Dennehy (Fire Chief),
Bruce French, Vincent Cobb, Stacy
Keach, Sr., Rene Enriquez.

IT HAPPENED HERE (1963)
    Director: Kevin Brownlow &
    Andrew Mollo
Pauline Murray, Sebastian Shaw,
Honor Fehrson, Fiona Leland, Percy
Binns, Frank Bennett.

IT HAPPENED ONE CHRISTMAS
    (TVM-1977) - 12-11-77
    Director: Donald Wrye
Marlo Thomas (Mary Hatch), Wayne
Rogers (George Hatch), Orson
Welles (Henry F. Potter), Cloris
Leachman (Clara), Dick O'Neill
(Mr. Gower), Richard Dysart (Peter
Bailey), Barney Martin (Uncle
Willie), Robert Emhardt (Judge),
Med Flory (Nick, the bartender),
Doris Roberts (Mrs. Bailey), Chris
Guest (Harry Bailey), Cliff Norton
(Martini), Karen Carlson (Violet),
Morgan Upton (Bert Andrews),
Ceil Cabot (Cousin Tillie), Jim
Lovelett (Sam Wainwright), Archie
Hahn (Ernie Baker), Gino Conforti
(Sassini), Bryan O'Byrne (doctor),
Lynn Moodlock (Mary at age 12).

IT HAPPENED TOMORROW (1944)
    Director: Rene Clair
Dick Powell (Larry Stevens), Linda
Darnell (Sylvia), Jack Okie (Cigolini),
Edgar Kennedy (Insp. Mulrooney),
George Cleveland (Mr. Gordon),
Edward Brophy (Jake Schomberg),
Sig Ruman (Mr. Bechstein), Paul
Guilfoyle (Shep), Eddie Acuff (Jim),
George Chandler (Bob), Robert E.
Homans (Mulcahey), Emma Dunn
(Mrs. Keever), Robert Dudley
(Justice of the Peace), Eddie Coke
(Sweeney), John Philliber (Pop
Benson), Jack Hardner (reporter),
Marion Martin (nurse).

IT HAPPENS EVERY SPRING (1949)
    Director: Lloyd Bacon
Ray Milland (Vernon Simpson), Jean

Peters (Deborah Greenleaf), Paul
Douglas (Monk Lanigan), Ray Collins
(Prof. Greenleaf), Ted de Corsia
(Dolan), Ed Begley (Stone), Jessie
Royce Landis (Mrs. Greenleaf), Alan
Hale, Jr. (Schmidt), William E.
Green (Prof. Forsythe), Bill Murphy (Isa-
bell), Gene Evans, Ray Teal, Mickey
Simpson, Edward Keane, Grandon
Rhodes, Harry Cheshire, Al Eben,
Robert B. Williams, Ruth Lee, Jane
Van Duser, Harry Seymour, John
Butler, Johnny Calkins, Charles
Flynn.

IT'S A BIRD! IT'S A PLANE! IT'S
    SUPERMAN!!! (TVM-1975) -
    2-21-75
    Director: Jack Regas
David Wilson (Clark Kent/Superman),
Lesley Ann Warren (Lois Lane),
Kenneth Mars (Max Mencken), Loretta
Swit (Sydney Carlton), Allen Ludden
(Perry White), David Wayne, Harvey
Lembeck, Malachi Throne.

IT'S ALIVE! (1968)
    Director: Larry Buchanan
Tommy Kirk (Wayne), Shirley Bonne
(Leslie), Bill Thurman (Greevie),
Carveth Austerhouse (Norman),
Annabelle Weenick (Belle).

IT'S ALIVE (1974)
    Director: Larry Cohen
John Ryan (Frank Davies), Sharon
Farrell (Lenore Davies), James Dixon
(Detective Lt. Perkins), Michael
Ansara (the Captain), Andrew Duggan
(Dr. Perry), Guy Stockwell (Clayton),
William Wellman, Jr. (Charlie),
Robert Emhardt (the Executive),
Shamus Locke (the Doctor), Mary
Nancy Burnett (nurse), Diana Hale
(secretary), Daniel Holzman (boy),
Patrick Macallister, Gerald York,
Gwill Richards, Jerry Taft, W. Allen
York (expectant fathers).

IT'S A WONDERFUL LIFE (1946)
    Director: Frank Capra
James Stewart (George Bailey), Donna
Reed (Mary Hatch Bailey), Lionel
Barrymore (Mr. Potter), Thomas
Mitchell (Uncle Billy), Henry Travers
(Clarence), Beulah Bondi (Mrs.
Bailey), Samuel S. Hinds (Pa Bailey),
Ward Bond (Bert), H. B. Warner (Mr.
Gower), Frank Faylen (Ernie),
Gloria Grahame (Violet Bick), Frank
Albertson (Sam Wainwright), Sarah
Edwards (Mrs. Hatch), Lillian
Randolph (Annie), Sheldon Leonard

(Nick), Frank Hagney (Potter's body-
guard), Charles Lane (real estate
salesman), Bill Edmunds (Martini),
Argentina Brunetti (Mrs. Martini),
Harry Holman (High School Principal),
Carl Switzer (Freddie), Stanley An-
drews (drinker), Mary Treen (Cousin
Tilly), Charles Williams (Cousin
Eustace), Tod Karns (Harry Bailey),
Virginia Patton (Ruth Dakin), Ronnie
Ralph (Little Sam), Jean Gale (Little
Mary), Bobby Anderson (Little George),
Danny Mummert (Little Marty Hatch),
Jeanine Anne Roose (Little Violet),
Georgie Nokes (Little Harry Bailey),
Ray Walker (Joe), Karolyn Grimes
(Zuzu Bailey), Carol Coomes (Janie
Bailey), Larry Sims (Pete Bailey),
Jimmy Hawkins (Tommy Bailey),
Bobby Scott (Mickey), Harry Cheshire
(Dr. Campbell), Ellen Corby.

IT'S GREAT TO BE ALIVE (1933)
    Director: Alfred Werker
Gloria Stuart (Dorothy Wilton),
Paul Roulien (Carlos Martin), Edna
May Oliver (Dr. Prodwell), Herbert
Mundin (Brooks), Robert Greig
(Perkins), Emma Dunn (Mrs. Wilton),
Edward Van Sloan (Dr. Wilton),
Dorothy Burgess (Al Moran), Joan
Marsh (Toots).

IT! THE TERROR FROM BEYOND
    SPACE (1958)
    Director: Edward L. Cahn
Marshall Thompson (Col. Edward Carr-
uthers), Shawn Smith (Ann Anderson),
Kim Spalding (Col. Van Heusen),
Dabbs Greer (Eric Royce), Ann Doran
(Mary Royce), Paul Langton (Calder),
Robert Bice (Purdue), Thom Carney
(Kienholz), Richard Benedict (Bob
Finelli), Richard Hervey (Gino Finelli),
Ray 'Crash' Corrigan (It).

I'VE LIVED BEFORE (1956)
    Director: Richard Bartlett
Jock Mahoney (John Bolan), Leigh
Snowden (Lois Gordon), Ann Harding,
(Jane Stone), John McIntire (Dr.
Thomas Bryant), Raymond Bailey
(Mr. Hackett), Phil Harvey (Dr.
Miller), James Seay (Fred Bolan),
Lorna Thayer (Mrs. Fred Bolan),
Jerry Paris (Russell Smith), Vernon
Rich (Mr. Anderson), Simon Scott
(Robert Allen), Teri Robin (stenoty-
pist), Jane Howard (secretary),
Madelon Mitchel (maid), April Kent
(stewardess), Brad Morrow (John
Bolan as a boy), Mike Dale (pilot),
Ray Quinn (intern), Bill Anders (air

control officer), Mike Portanova, Marjorie Stapp, Charles Conrad, Earl Hansen, Beatrice Gray (spectators), Jimmy Casino, Palmer Wray Sherrill, Blanche Taylor.

IVORY APE, THE (TVM-1980) - 4-18-80
    Director: Tom Kotani
Steven Keats (Baxter Mapes), Jack Palance (Marc Kazarian), Cindy Pickett (Lil Tyler), Celine Lomez (Valerie Lamont), Earle Hyman (Insp. St. George), Derek Partridge (Aubrey Range), William Horrigan (Captain), Lou David (Roomie Pope), Tricia Senbera (Vita Havermyer), David Mann (Dr. Cole), George Rushe (Wilkinson), John Lough (Trot Toomer), Leonard Daniels (Smith), John Truscott (Collins).

I WALKED WITH A ZOMBIE (1943)
    Director: Jacques Tourneur
James Ellison (Wesley Rand), Frances Dee (Betsy Connell), Tom Conway (Paul Holland), Edith Barrett (Mrs. Rand), Christine Hordon (Jessica Rand), James Bell (Dr. Maxwell), Darby Jones (Carre Four), Teresa Harris (Alma), Sir Lancelot (Calypso singer), Jeni Legon (dancer).

I WAS A TEENAGE FRANKENSTEIN (1957)
    Director: Herbert L. Strock
Whit Bissell (Prof. Frankenstein), Phyllis Coates (Margaret), Robert Burton (Dr. Karlton), Gary Conway (the Monster), Marshall Bradford (Dr. Randolph), George Lynn (Sgt. Burns), John Cliff (Sgt. McAffee), Joy Stoner (Arlene), Claudia Bryar (Arlene's mother), Russ Whiteman (Dr. Elwood), Angela Blake (girl), Charles Seel (the jeweler), Gretchen Thomas (woman in corridor), Paul Keast (Man at crash), Pat Miller (police officer), Larry Carr (young man).

I WAS A TEENAGE WEREWOLF (1957)
    Director: Gene Fowler, Jr.
Michael Landon (Tony Rivers), Whit Bissell (Dr. Alfred Brandon), Yvonne Lime (Arlene), Malcolm Atterbury (Charles), Vladimir Sokoloff (Pepi), Eddie Marr (Doyle), Louise Lewis (Miss Ferguson), S. John Launer (Bill), Tony Marshall (Jimmy), Ken Miller (Vic), Guy Williams (Chris Stanley), Dawn Richards (Theresa), Barney Phillips (Detective Donovan), Joseph Mell (Dr. Hugo Wagner), Cindy Robbins (Pearl), Dorothy Crehan (Mary), Michael Rougas (Frank), Robert Griffin

(Police Chief Baker).

I WAS A ZOMBIE FOR THE F. B. I. (1982)
    Director: Marius Penczner
Larry Raspberry (Ace Evans), James Raspberry (Rex Armstrong), Laurence Hall (Bert Brazzo), John Gillick (Bart Brazzo), Christina Wellford (Penny), Ken Zimmerman (Mr. Carson), Tony Isbell (Mins), Rick Crowe (Bush), Alan Zellner (Dr. Franz Kaufman), Jeff Bailey (Jensen), Nichols Wall (Charlie), D. M. Coger (Tom), David Mayo (Hank), Lisa Jones (Miss Grimes), Allen French (Marshall), Tom Mc-Crory (Marshall), Greg LeMay (Marshall), Rick Clodfelter (pilot), Chuck Cooper (photographer), Ira Pyland (worker), Max Cheney (news cameraman), Tom Disney (cop), Colonius Davis, Robert Page, Walter Hamby, Andy Diggs (diggers), Teresa Roberts, Olga Page (helpers), Bill Haines (fat man), Bill Haines (FAA Man), Sue Donelson (waiting lady), Ken Wilburn (secruity chief), Estelle Helm (grandmother), Chris Shadrack (McGraw), Rick Owings (guard), Glenda Mace (secretary), David Hyde, Evelyn Stanford, Olga Page, Deborah Hyatt (zombies), Valerie Miller, Jane Conway, Jolanda Penczner, Paul Penczner, Amy Smith, Michael Farrish, Robert Bruce, Virgil Holder, Nancy Ellis, Chuck Cooper, Walter Hamby, Karla Shanke, Max Cheney, Paul Malolensy, Jennifer Malolensy, Linda Lamb, Sharon Hancock, Teresa Roberts, Sue Donaldson.

JABBERWOCKY (1977)
    Director: Terry Gilliam
Michael Palin (Dennis Cooper), Deborah Fallender (Princess), John Le Mesuier (Chamberlain), Max Wall (King Bruno the Questionable), Bernard Bresslaw (Landlord), Derek Francis (Bishop), Graham Crowden (Fanatic's leader), Warren Mitchell (Mr. Fishfinger), Annette Badland (Griselda Fishfinger), Brenda Cowling (Mrs. Fishfinger), Gordon Rollings (Kins's taster), David Prowse (Black Knight), Brian Glover (Armourer), Harry H. Corbett (Squire), Rodney Bewes (Squire), Alexandra Dane (Betsy), Peter Cellier, Anthony Carrick, Frank Williams (merchants), Paul Curran (Mr. Cooper, Sr.), John Bird (herald), Neil Innes (herald and drummer), Glenn Williams, Bryan Pringle

(gate guards), Simon Williams (Prince), Gordon Kaye (Sister Jessica), Jerrold Wells (Wat Dabney), Harold Goodwin, Tony Sympson, Julian Hough, John Gorman (peasants).

JACK, THE MANGLER OF LONDON (1971-Span. /Ital.) (A. K. A. "Jack, el Destripador de Londres")
    Director: Jose Luis Madrid
Paul Naschy, Patricia Loran, Renzzo Marignaro, Andres Resino, Orquidea De Santis, Irene Mir.

J'ACCUSE (1938-Fr.) (A. K. A. "I Accuse", "That They May Live")
    Director: Abel Gance
Victor Francen (Jean Diaz), Marie Lou (Flo), Line Noro (Edith), Renee Devillers (Helene), Jean Max (Henri Chimay), Delaitre (Francios Laurin), Jean Louis Barrault.

JACK AND THE BEANSTALK (1952)
    Director: Jean Yarborough
Bud Abbott (Dinkelpuss), Lou Costello (Jack), Buddy Baer (Sgt. Riley/the Giant), William Farnum (the King), Dorothy Ford (Polly), Shaye Cogan (Eloise Larkin/the Princess), James Alexander (Arthur Royal/the Prince), David Stollery (Donald), Barbara Brown (Mother).

JACK ARMSTRONG (1947) - serial in 15 episodes
Chapters: 1. "Mystery of the Cosmic Ray", 2. "The Far World", 3. "Island of Deception", 4. "Into the Chasm", 5. "The Space Ship", 6. "Tunnels of Treachery", 7. "Cavern of Chance", 8. "The Secret Room", 9. "Human Targets", 10. "Battle of the Warriors", 11. "Cosmic Annihilator", 12. "The Grotto of Greed", 13. "Wheels of Fate", 14. "Journey into Space" & 15. "Retribution".
    Director: Wallace Fox
John Hart (Jack Armstrong), Rosemary La Planche (Betty), Wheeler Oakman (Prof. Zorn), Pierre Watkin (Uncle Jim Fairfield), Claire James (Alura), Jack Ingram (Blair), Charles Middleton (Jason Grood), Joe Brown, Jr. (Billy), Eddie Parker (Slade), John Merton (Gregory), Hugh Prosser (Vic Hardy), Russ Vincent (Umala), Frank Marlo (Naga), Gene Stutenroth/Roth (Dr. Albour).

JACK THE GIANT KILLER (1962)
    Director: Nathan Juran
Kerwin Mathews (Jack), Judi Meredith (Princess Elaine), Torin Thatcher (Pendragon), Walter Burke (Garna), Barry Kelley (Sigurd the Viking), Don Beddoe (the Imp), Roger Mobley (Peter), Dayton Lummis (King Mark), Anna Lee (Lady Constance), Tudor Owen (Chancellor), Helen Wallace (Jack's mother), Robert Gist (Capt.

McFadden), Ken Mayer (boatswain).

JACK THE RIPPER (1959)
    Director: Robert S. Baker & Monty Berman
Lee Patterson (Sam Lowry), Eddie Byrne (Insp. O'Neill), Betty Mc-Dowall (Anne Ford), Ewen Solon (Sir David Rogers), John LeMesurier (Dr. Tranter), George Rose (Clarke), George Woodbridge (Blake), Barbara Burke (Kitty Knowles), Anne Sharpe (Helen), Endre Muller (Louis Benz), Bill Shine (Lord Sopwith), Garard Green (Dr. Urquhart), Philip Leaver (music hall manager), Denis Shaw (Simes), Esma Cannon (Nelly), Marianne Stone (drunken woman), Jane Taylor (Hazel), Hal Osmonde (Snakey), Olwen Brooks (Mrs. Boulton), Jack Allen (Assistant Commissioner), Dorinda Stevens (Margaret), George Street (station sergeant), Helena Digby (1st victim).

JACK THE RIPPER (TVM-1958) (A. K. A. "The Veil")
    Director: Michael Plant
Boris Karloff (Host/Dr. Mason/Mr. Atterbury/Capt. Elwood), Nial MacGinnis, Nora Swinburne, Clifford Evans, Thomas B. Henry, Robert Griffin, Morris Andrum.

JACK THE RIPPER (1979-Ger. /Swiss)
    Director: Jesus Franco
Klaus Kinski, Josephine Chaplin, Herbert Fux, Lina Romay.

JADE BOX, THE (1930) - serial in 10 episodes
Chapters: 1. "The Jade of Jeopardy", 2. "Buried Alive", 3. "The Shadow Man", 4. "The Fatal Prophecy", 5. "The Unseen Death", 6. "The Haunting Shadow", 7. "The Guilty Man", 8. "The Grip of Death", 9. "Out of the Shadows" & 10. "The Atonement".
    Director: Ray Taylor
Louise Lorraine (Helen Morgan), Jack Perrin (Jack Lamar), Francis Ford (Martin Morgan), Wilbur S. Mack (Edward Haines), Leo White (Percy Winslow), Monroe Salisbury (John Lamar), Jay Novello.

JADE MASK, THE (1944) (A. K. A.
"Charlie Chan in the Jade Mask")
Director: Phil Rosen
Sidney Toler (Charlie Chan), Hardie
Albright (Meeker), James Warren
(Jean), Edith Evanson (Louise), Mantan
Moreland (Birmingham Brown), Edwin
Luke, Frank Reicher, Jack Ingram,
Dorothy Granger, Ralph Lewis, Henry
Hall, Lester Dorr.

JALOPY (1953)
Director: William Beaudine
Leo Gorcey (Slip Mahoney), Huntz Hall
(Sach Debussy Jones), Bernard Gorcey
(Louie Dumbrowsky), Robert Lowery
(Skid Wilson), Leon Belasco (Prof.
Elrod Bosgood), Richard Benedict
(Tony Lango), Jane Easton (Bonnie
Lane), Murray Alper (Red Baker),
David Condon (Chuck), Bennie Bartlett
(Butch), Tom Hanlon (announcer),
Mona Knox (girl), Barton MacLane,
Anthony Caruso, Lyle Talbot, Percy
Helton, Fritz Feld, John Harmon, Harry
Tyler, Michael Ross.

JAMES BOND, OPERATION D. U. E.
(1966-Ital. /Fr.)
Director: Bruno Corbucci
Landro Buzzanca, France Anglade,
Claudie Lange, Furio Meniconi, Loris
Gizzi, Mirko Valentin.

JAMES TONT, OPERATION U. N. O.
(1965-Ital.)
Director: Bruno Corbucci &
Gianni Grimaldi
Lando Buzzanca, Evi Marandi, George
J. Wang, Gina Rovere, Loris Gizzi,
Alighiero Noschese.

JANE EYRE (1944)
Director: Robert Stevenson
Orson Welles (Edward Rochester),
Joan Fontaine (Jane Eyre), John Sutton
(Dr. Rivers), Margaret O'Brien (Adele
Varena), Henry Daniell (Brocklehurst),
Aubrey Mather (Col. Dent), Sara Al-
good (Bessie), Agnes Moorehead (Mrs.
Reed), Edith Barrett (Mrs. Fairfax),
Hillary Brooke (Blanche Ingram), John
Abbott (Mason), Peggy Ann Garner
(Jane as a child), Yorke Sherwood
(Beadle), Mae Marsh (Leah), Ethel
Griffies (Grace Poole), Ronald Harris
(John), Barbara Everest (Lady Ingram),
Elizabeth Taylor.

JANUSKOPF, DER (1920-Ger.) (A. K. A.
"Janus-Faced", "Love's Mockery)
Director: F. W. Murnau
Conrad Veidt (Dr. Warren/Mr. O'Connor),

Bela Lugosi, Margarete Schlegel.

JASON AND THE ARGONAUTS (1963)
Director: Don Chaffey
Tod Armstrong (Jason), Nancy Kovack
(Medea), Gary Raymond (Acastus),
Laurence Naismith (Argus), Michael
Gwynn (Hermes), Niall MacGinnis
(Zeus), Douglas Wilmer (Pelias),
Jack Gwillim (King Aeetes), Nigel
Green (Hercules), Patrick Troughton
(Phineau), John Cairney (Hylas),
Honor Blackman (Hera), Andrew
Faulds (Phalerus), John Crawford
(Polydeuces), Gernando Poggi (Cas-
tor), Douglas Robinson (Euphemus).

JASPER (1942-1946) - shorts
Producer: George Pal

JASSY (1947)
Director: Bernard Knowles
Margaret Lockwood (Jassy Woodroffe),
Patricia Roc (Dilys Helmar),
Basil Sydney (Nick Helmar), Dermot
Walsh (Barney Hatton), Dennis Price
(Christopher Hatton), Esma Cannon
(Lindy), John Laurie (Woodroffe),
Linden Travers (Mrs. Helmar),
Nora Swinburne (Mrs. Hatton),
Grey Blake (Stephen Fennell), Clive
Morton (Sir William Pennell), Jean
Cadell (Meggie), Bryan Coleman
(Sedley), Cathleen Nesbit (Elizabeth
Twisdale), Grace Arnold (housemaid),
Torin Thatcher (Bob Wicks), Beatrice
Varley (Mrs. Wicks), Maurice Denham
(Jim Stoner).

JAWS (1975)
Director: Steven Spielberg
Roy Scheider (Martin Brody), Robert
Shaw (Quint), Richard Dreyfuss
(Matt Hooper), Lorraine Gary (Ellen
Brody), Murray Hamilton (Mayor
Larry Vaughn), Jeffrey Kramer
(Deputy Hendricks), Carl Gottlieb
(Harry Meadows), Susan Backlinie
(Chrissie), Jonathan Filley (Cassidy),
Chris Rebello, Jay Mello (Brody
children), Lee Fierro (Mrs. Kintner),
Craig Kingsbury (Ben Gardner),
Jeffrey Voorhees (Alex Kintner),
Tedd Grossman (estuary victim),
Robert Nevin (Medical Examiner),
Peter Benchley (TV newsman).

JAWS II (1978)
Director: Jeannot Szwarc
Roy Scheider (Martin Brody), Lorraine
Gary (Ellen Brody), Murray Hamilton
(Mayor Larry Vaughan), Ann Dusen-
berry (Tina Wilcox), Joseph Mascolo

(Len Peterson), Jeffrey Kramer (Deputy Hendricks), Barry Coe (Andrews), Mark Gruner (Mike Brody), Marc Gilpin (Sean Brody), Gary Springer (Andy), Donna Wilkes (Jackie), David Elliott (Larry Vaughan, Jr.), Collin Wilcox (Dr. Lureen Elkins), Susan French (old lady), G. Thomas Dunlop (Timmy), Gary Dubin (Ed), John Dukakis (Polo), Billy Van Zandt (Bob Burnside), Keith Gordon (Doug), Ben Marley (Patrick), Gigi Vorgan (Brooke), Cynthia Grover (Lucy), Martha Swatek (Marge), Jerry Baxter (Helicopter Pilot), Jean Coulter (ski boat driver).

J. D. 'S REVENGE (1976)
Director: Arthur Marks
Lou Gossett (Rev. Bliss), Joan Pringle (Christella), Glynn Turman (Ike), Carl Crudup (Tony), Alice Jubert (Roberta), James Louis Watkins (Carl), Stephanie Faulkner (Phyllis), Fred Pinkard (Theotis), Jo Anne Meredith (Sarah), Fuddle Bagley (Enoch), David McKnight (J. D. Walker).

JEKYLL AND HYDE... TOGETHER AGAIN (1982)
Director: Jerry Belson
Mark Blankfield (Dr. Jekyll/Mr. Hyde), Bess Armstrong (Mary Carew), Tim Thomerson (Dr. Knute Lanyon), Krista Errickson (Ivy), Michael McGuire (Dr. Carew).

JENNIFER (1978)
Director: Brice Mack
Lisa Pelikan (Jennifer Baylor), Bert Convey (Jeff Reed), Nina Foch (Mrs. Calley), John Gavin (Sen. Tremayne), Amy Johnston (Sandra Tremayne), Jeff Corey (Luke Baylor), Wesley Eure (Pit Lassiter), Louise Hoven (Jane Delano), Georganne La Piere (DeeDee Martin), Ray Underwood (Dayton Powell), Florida Friebus (Miss Tooker).

JESSE JAMES MEETS FRANKENSTEIN'S DAUGHTER (1965)
Director: William Beaudine
John Lupton (Jesse James), Narda Onyz (Maria Frankenstein), Steven Geray (Rudolph Frankenstein), Cal Bolder (Hank, the Monster), Jim Davis (Marshall McFee), Estelita (Juanita), Nester Paiva, Raymond Barnes, Rosa Turich, Felipe Turich, Dan White, Page Slattery.

JE T'AIME, JE T'AIME (1968-Fr.)
(A. K. A. "I Love You, I Love You")
Director: Alain Resnais

Olga Georges-Picot (Catrine), Claude Rich (Claude Ridder), Anouk Ferjac (Wiana Lust), Annie Fargue (Agnes de Smet), Yvette Etievant (Germane Coster), Bernard Fresson (Bernard Hannecart), Irene Tunc (Marcelle Hannecart), Dominique Rozan (Dr. Haesaerts), Van Doude (Jan Rouffer), Marie-Blance Vergne (young woman).

JETTY, THE (1962-Fr.) (A. K. A. "The Runway", "La Jetee")
Director: Chris Marker
Jean Negroni (Narrator), Helene Chatelain, Davos Hanich, Jacques Ledoux, Andre Heinrich, Jacques Branchu, Pierre Joffroy.

JOHNNY DOESN'T LIVE HERE ANY MORE (1944) (A. K. A. "And So They Were Married")
Director: Joe May
Simone Simon, James Ellison, Minna Gombell, Chick Chandler, Robert Mitchum, Janet Shaw, Alan Dinehart, William Terry, Gladys Blake, Jerry Maren, Grady Sutton.

JONATHAN (1970-Ger.)
Director: Hans W. Geissendorfer
Jurgen Jung (Jonathan), Paul Albert Krumm (the Count), Eleanore Schminke (Lena), Ilsa Kunkele (Lena's mother), Thomas Astan (Thomas), Ilone Grubel (Eleonore), Hans Dieter Jendreyko (Josef), Oskar Von Schab (Professor).

JOURNEY INTO DARKNESS (TVM-1969)
Patrick McGoohan (Host).
see Television: Journey to the Unknown - "The New People" (10-17-68) & "Paper Dolls" (11-21-68)

JOURNEY INTO MIDNIGHT (TVM-1969)
Sebastian Cabot (Host).
see Television: Journey to the Unknown - "The Indian Spirit Guide" (10-10-68) & "Poor Butterfly" (1-9-69)

JOURNEY TO THE BEGINNING OF TIME (1966-Czech. /U.S.) (A. K. A. "Cesta do Praveku", "Journey to a Primeval Age")
Director: Karel Zeman
James Lukas (Doc), Victor Betral (Jo-Jo), Charles Goldsmith (Ben), Peter Hermann (Tony).

JOURNEY TO THE CENTER OF THE
EARTH (1959)
Director: Henry Levin
James Mason (Prof. Oliver Linden-
brook), Pat Boone (Alec McEwen),
Arlene Dahl (Carla), Thayer David
(Count Saknussemm), Peter Ronson
(Hans), Diane Baker (Jenny), Alan
Caillou (Rector), Alan Napier (Dean),
Ben Wright (Paisley), Alex Finlayson
(Prof. Bayle), Frederick Hallidy
(Chancellor), Mary Brady (Kirsty),
Robert Adler (Groom).

JOURNEY TO THE CENTER OF
TIME (1968)
Director: David L. Hewitt
Scott Brady (Stanton, Jr.), Anthony
Eisley (Mark Manning), Gigi Perreau
(Karen White), Abraham Sofaer (Dr.
von Steiner), Austin Green (Mr. Den-
ning), Lyle Waggoner (Alien), Tracy
Olsen (Susan), Poupee Gamin (Vina),
Andy David (Dave), Larry Evans,
Jody Millhouse.

JOURNEY TO THE FAR SIDE OF
THE SUN (1969) (A.K.A. "Dop-
pelganger")
Director: Robert Parish
Roy Thinnes (Col. Glenn Ross), Ian
Hendry (John Kane), Herbert Lom
(Dr. Hassler), Patrick Wymark (Ja-
son Webb), Lynn Loring (Sharon Ross),
Loni von Fried (Lise), George Sewell
(Mark Neuman), Edward Bishop (David
Poulson), Franco Derosa (Paulo
Landi), Jacques Aubuchon.

JOURNEY TO THE LOST CITY (1959-
Ger.) (A.K.A. "Tiger of Bengal")
Director: Fritz Lang
Debra Paget (Seta), Paul Christian
(Allan Burton), Luciana Paluzzi
(Barani), Walther Reyer (Prince
Chandra), Claus Holm (Ramagani),
Ikijinoff (Modani), Rene Deltgen (Rho-
des), Sabine Bethmann (Irene).

JOURNEY TO THE UNKNOWN (TVM-
1969)
Joan Crawford (Host).
see Television: Journey to the Unknown - "Matakitas Is Coming"
(11-28-68) & "The Last Visitor"
(1-2-69)

JUDEX (1916-Fr.) - serial in 12
episodes
Director: Louis Feuillade
Rene Creste, Yvette Andreyor.

JUDEX (1933-Fr.)

Director: Maurice Champreux
Rene Ferte, Marcel Vallee, Jean
Lefebvre, Rene Navarre, Mihalesco.

JUDEX (1963-Fr. /Ital.) (A.K.A.
"L'Uomo in Nero")
Director: Georges Franju
Channing Pollock (Judex), Edith
Scob (Jacqueline Favraux), Sylvia
Koscina (Daisy), Francine Berge
(Marie), Theo Sarapo (Morales),
Michel Vitold (Banker Favraux),
Jacques Jouhanneau (Cocontin),
Rene Gennin (Kerjean), Phillippe
Mareuil (De la Rochefontaine).

JUDGE DEE AND THE MONASTERY
MURDERS (TVM-1974) - 12-29-74
Director: Jeremy Kagan
Khigh Dhiegh (Judge Dee), Mako
(Tao Gan), Soon-Taik Oh (Kang I-Te),
Miiko Taka (Jade Mirror), Irene
Tsu (Celestial Wife), Suesie Elene
(Miss Ting), James Hong (Prior),
Beverly Kushida (Bright Flower),
Ching Hocson (White Rose), Yuki
Shimoda (Pure Faith), Robert
Sadang (Tsung Lee), Keye Luke
(Lord Sun Ming), Frances Fong
(Mrs. Pao), Richard Lee-Sung
(Driver No. 1), Tommy Lee (True
Wisdom), Tadashi Yamashita (Motai).

JUGGERNAUT (1936)
Director: Henry Edwards
Boris Karloff (Dr. Sartorius), Morton
Selten (Sir Charles Clifford), Joan
Wyndham (Eva Rowe), Arthur Mar-
getson (Roger Clifford), Anthony
Ireland (Capt. Arthur Halliday), Gibb
McLaughlin (Jacques), Nina Bouci-
cault (Mary Clifford), J.H. Roberts
(Chalmers), V. Rietti (Dr. Bousquet).

JULIET OF THE SPIRITS (1964-
Ital.) (A.K.A. "Giulietta degli
Spiriti")
Director: Federico Fellini
Giulietta Masina (Giulietta), Sandra
Milo (Susy), Sylva Koscina (Sylva),
Lou Gilbert (Grandfather), Mario
Pisu (Husband), Caterina Boratto
(Mother), Valentina Cortese (Valen-
tina), Luisa Della Noce (Adele),
Waleska Gert (Bhisma), Silvanna
Jachino (Dolores), Jose de Villa-
longa (Spanish Gentleman), Elena
Fondra (Elena), Asoka Rubener,
Walter Harrison, Sujata Ruberner
(Bhisman's helpers), Edoardo Torri-
cella (Russian teacher), Anne Francine
(psychoanalyst), Alba Cancellieri
(Giulietta as a child), Mario Conocchi

(family lawyer), Fredrich Ledebur.

JUNGLE, THE (1952)
    Director: William Berke
Marie Windsor (Princess Mari),
Cesar Romero (Rama Singh), Rod
Cameron (Steve Bentley), David Ab-
raham (Prime Minister), Sulochana
(the Aunt), Ramakrishna (young boy),
M. N. Nambiar (Mahaji), Chitar Devi
(the dancer).

JUNGLE CAPTIVE (1945) (A. K. A.
    "Wild Jungle Captive")
    Director: Harold Young
Otto Kruger (Dr. Stendahl), Vicki
Lane (Paula Dupree), Amelita Ward
(Ann Forrester), Phil Brown (Don
Young), Rondo Hatton (Moloch),
Ernie Adams (Jim), Jerome Cowan
(Insp. Harrigan), Eddie Acuff (Bill),
Charles Wagenheim (Fred), Jack
Overman (detective), Eddy Chandler
(motor cop).

JUNGLE GIRL (1941) - serial in 15
    episodes
    Director: William Witney &
        John English
Frances Gifford (Nyoka), Tom Neal
(Jack Stanton), Gerald Mohr (Stick
Latimer), Trevor Bardette (Mere-
dith-Bradley), Eddie Acuff (Curley
Rogers), Frank Lackteen (Shamba),
Bud Geary (Brock), Tommy Cook
(Wakimbu), Al Taylor (Claggett), Al
Kikume (Lutembi), Robert Barron
(Bombo), Joe McGuinn (Bone), Ken
Terrell (Mananga), Jerry Frank
(Lion Chief), Yakima Canutt, Duke
Green, Duke Taylor, Tom Steele,
David Sharpe, Harry Smith, Helen
Thurston.

JUNGLE GODDESS, THE (1922) -
    serial in 15 episodes
Chapters: 1. "Sacrificed to the Lions",
2. "The City of Blind Waters", 3.
"Saved by the Great Ape", 4. "The
Hell Ship", 5. "Wild Beasts in Com-
mand", 6. "Sky High with a Leopard",
7. "The Rajah's Revenge", 8. "The
Alligator's Victim", 9. "At Grips
with Death", 10. "The Leopard Woman",
11. "The Soul of Buddha", 12. "The
Jaws of Death", 13. "The Cave of
Beasts", 14. "Jungle Terrors" & 15.
"The Mad Lion".
    Director: James Conway
Elinor Field (Betty Castleton/Jungle
Goddess), Truman Van Dyke (Ralph
Dean), Lafe McKee (Rajah), Marie
Pavis (Leopard Woman), Vonda Phelps

(Guardian of the Temple), Olin
Francis (High Priest), George
Reed (Native Guide), William Platt
(Constable), H. G. Wells (Lord
Castleton).

JUNGLE HELL (1956)
    Director: Norman A. Cerf
Sabu, K. T. Stevens, George E.
Stone, David Bruce.

JUNGLE JIM IN THE FORBIDDEN
    LAND (1951) (A. K. A. "The For-
    bidden Land")
    Director: Lew Landers
Johnny Weismuller (Jungle Jim),
Angela Greene (Linda Roberts),
Jean Willes (Denise), Lester Matt-
hews (Commissioner Kingston),
William Tannen (Doc Edwards),
George Eldredge (Fred Lewis),
Frederic Berest (Zulu), Clem
Erickson (giant man), Irmgard
H. H. Raschke (giant woman),
William Fawcett (Old One), Frank
Jacquet (Quigley).

JUNGLE LOVERS, THE (1915)
    Director: Lloyd E. Carleton
Bessie Eyton (Naida Rand), Edward
J. Peil (Van Cleeve), Richard
Morris (Starling), Tom Bates
(Jan Blass), Edwin Wallock (Her-
man Blass), Cash Darrell (Peter
Rand).

JUNGLE MANHUNT (1951)
    Director: Lew Landers
Johnny Weismuller (Jungle Jim),
Sheila Ryan (Anne Lawrence),
Bob Westerfield (Bob Miller),
Rick Vallin (Bono), Lyle Talbot
(Dr. Mitchell Heller), William P.
Wilkerson (Maklee Chief).

JUNGLE MOON MEN (1954)
    Director: Charles S. Gould
Johnny Weismuller (Himself), Jean
Byron, Helene Stanton, Bill Henry,
Billy Curtis, Myron Healy, Frank
Sully, Ed Hinton, Michael Granger,
Kenneth L. Smith, Benjamin F.
Chapman, Jr.

JUNGLE MYSTERY, THE (1932) -
    serial in 12 episodes
Chapters: 1. "Into the Dark Continent", 2. "The Ivory Trail", 3.
"The Death Streams", 4. "Poisoned
Fangs", 5. "The Mystery Cavern",
6. "Daylight Doom", 7. "The Jaws
of Death", 8. "Trapped by the Enemy",
9. "The Jungle Terror", 10. "Ambushed",

11. "The Lion's Fury" & 12. "Buried Treasure".
Director: Ray Taylor
Tom Tyler (Kirk Montgomery), William Desmond (Mr. Morgan), Noah Beery, Jr. (Fred Oakes), Cecilia Parker (Barbara Morgan), Philo McCullough (Shillow), Sam Baker (Sungu), Carmelita Geraghty (Belle Waldron).

JUNGLE PRINCESS (1936)
Director: William Thiel
Dorothy Lamour (Ulah), Akim Tamiroff (Karen Nag), Ray Milland (Christopher Powell), Lynne Overman (Frank), Mala (Nelon), Molly Lamont (Ava), Hugh Buckler (Col. Lane), Roberta Law (Lin), Sally Martin (Ulah as a child).

JUNGLE QUEEN (1945) - serial in 13 episodes
Chapters: 1. "Invitation to Danger", 2. "Jungle Sacrifice", 3. "The Flaming Mountain", 4. "Wildcat Stampede", 5. "The Burning Jungle", 6. "Danger Ship", 7. "Trip-Wire Murder", 8. "The Mortar Bomb", 9. "Death Watch", 10. "Execution Chamber", 11. "The Trail to Doom", 12. "Dragged Under" & 13. "The Great Secret of the Sword".
Director: Ray Taylor & Lewis D. Collins
Edward Norris (Bob Elliott), Lois Collier (Pamela Courtney), Eddie Quillan (Chuck Kelly), Douglas Dumbrille (Lang), Tala Birell (Dr. Elsie Bork), Ruth Roman (Lothel), Clarence Muse (Kyba), Cy Kendall (Tambosa Tim), Napoleon Simpson (Maati), Clinton Rosemand (Godac), Oliver Prickett (man).

JUNGLE RAIDERS (1945) - serial in 15 episodes
Director: Lesley Selander
Kane Richmond (Bob Moore), Eddie Quillan (Joe), Carol Hughes (Zara), Veda Ann Borg (Cora), Janet Shaw (Ann Reed), Jack Ingram (Tom), Ernie Adams (Charley), Charles King (Jake Rayne), John Elliott (Dr. Moore), I. Stanford Jolley (Brent), Bud Buster (Dr. Reed), Nick Thompson (the Chief), Kermit Murdock (Cragg), Jim Aubrey (Mark), George Turner (Carter).

JUNGLE WOMAN (1944)
Director: Reginald LeBorg
Acquanetta (Paula Dupree), J. Carroll Naish (Dr. Carl Fletcher), Evelyn Ankers, (Beth Colman), Milburn Stone (Fred Mason), Lois Collier (Joan Fletcher), Richard Davies (Bob Whitney), Eddie Hyams, Jr. (Willie), Christian Rub (George), Douglas

Dumbrille (District Attorney), Pierre Watkin (Dr. Meredith), Nana Bryant (Fletcher's nurse), Samuel S. Hinds (Coroner), Alec Craig (caretaker), Richard Powers (fingerprint man), Julie London (girl).

JUNIOR G-MEN (1940) - serial in 12 episodes
Chapters: 1. "Enemies Within", 2. "The Blast of Doom", 3. "Human Dynamite", 4. "Blazing Danger", 5. "Trapped by Traitors", 6. "Traitors' Treachery", 7. "Flaming Death", 8. "Hurled through Space", 9. "The Plunge of Peril", 10. "The Toll of Treason", 11. "Descending Doom" & 12. "The Power of Patriotism".
Director: Ford Beebe & John Rawlins
Billy Halop (Billy Barton), Huntz Hall (Gyp), Gabrial Dell (Terry), Philip Terry (Jim Bradford), Cy Kendall (Brand), Roger Daniels (Midge), Kenneth Howell (Harry Trent), Russell Hicks (Col; Barton), Bernard Punsley (Lug), Kenneth Lundy (Buck).

JUNIOR G-MEN OF THE AIR (1942) - serial in 12 episodes
Chapters: 1. "Wings Aflame", 2. "The Plunge of Peril", 3. "Hidden Danger", 4. "The Tunnel of Terror", 5. "The Black Dragon Strikes", 6. "Flaming Havoc", 7. "The Death Mist", 8. "Satan Fires the Fuse", 9. "Satanic Sabotage", 10. "Trapped in a Blazing Chute", 11. "Undeclared War" & 12. "Civilian Courage Conquers".
Directors: Ray Taylor & Lewis D. Collins
Billy Halop (Ace Holden), Gene Reynolds (Eddie Holden), Lionel Atwill (the Baron), Frank Albertson (Jerry Markham), Huntz Hall (Bolts Larson), Gabrial Dell (Stick Munsey), Richard Lane (Don Ames), Frankie Darro (Jack), Turhan Bey (Araka), Noel Cravat (Monk), John Bleifer (Beal), Edward Foster (Comora), Bernard Punsley (Greaseball Plunkett), David Gorcey (Double Face Barker), Jay Novello (Dogara), J. Pat O'Malley (conductor), John Bagni (Augar), Billy Benedict (Blackie), Hugh Prosser (Lt. in state guard), Win Wright, Guy Kinsford (soldiers), Guy Usher (Senator), Jack Arnold (Flyer), Paul Bryar (Oriental chemist), Ben Wright (Corporal), Jimmy O'Gatty (Alien Jap American), Eddy Waller (Jay), Paul Phillips (Dick Parsons), Fred Burton (Colonel), William Desmond, Rolland Morris (Customers), Mel

Ruick (official), George Sherwood (instructor), Bert Freeman (Scientist), Heenan Elliott (watchman), Angelo Cruz (Ito), Edward Colebrook (Uamatka), Lynton Brent (Sergeant), Ken Lundy (newsboy).

JUST BEFORE DAWN (1982)
    Director: Jeff Lieberman
George Kennedy, Deborah Benson, Chris Lemmon, Gregg Henry, Jamie Rose, Ralph Seymour, Mike Kellin.

JUST FOR FUN (1961)
    Director: Gordon Flemying
Mark Wynter (Mark), Richard Vernon (Prime Minister), Reginald Beckwith (Opposition Leader), Jeremy Lloyd (Prime Minister's son), Cherry Roland (Cherry), Edwin Richfield (man with badge), Harry Fowler, John Wood, Gordon Rollings, Irene Handl, Frank Williams, Douglas Ives.

JUST IMAGINE (1930)
    Director: David Butler
El Brendel (Single O), Maureen O'Sullivan (LN-18), John Garrick (J-21), Mischa Auer (B-36), Marjorie White (D-6), Frank Albertson (RT-42), Hobart Bosworth (Z-4), Ivan Linow (Boko/Loko), Joyzelle (Loo Loo/Boo Boo), Joseph Girard (Commander), Wilfred Lucas (X-10), Kenneth Thomson (MT-3), Sidney De Gray (AK-44), Bo-Peep Karlin, Leola Kenny.

KARATE KILLERS, THE (1967)
    Director: Barry Shear
    see Television: Man From U. N. C. -
    L. E. - "The Five Daughters Affair"
    (3-31-67 & 4-7-67)

KARZAN, THE FABULOUS JUNGLE
    MAN (1971-Ital.) (A. K. A. "Karzan, il Favoloso Ummo della Giunglia")
    Director: Miles Deem
Johnny Kismuller, Jr. , Ettore Manni, Simone Blondell.

KEEPER, THE (1976)
    Director: Tom Drake
Christopher Lee (the Keeper), Tell Schrieber, Sally Gray, Ross Vezarian.

KEEP MY GRAVE OPEN (1974)
    Director: S. F. Brownrigg
Camilla Carr (Lesley Fontaine), Gene Ross (Dr. Emerson), Stephen Tobolowsky (Robert), Ann Stafford (Suzie), Sharon Bunn (Twinkle), Chelsea Ross (Kevin), Annabelle Weenick (Vera),

Bill Thurman (hitchhiker), Jessie Lee Fulton (Miss Evie), Lucille Baldwin (Miss Ada), Desmond Dhooge (storekeeper), Skipper Richardson (prostitute), Cebe Reed (Ceasar).

KELLY OF THE SECRET SERVICE
    (1936)
    Director: Bob Hill
Lloyd Hughes (Ted Kelly), Fuzzy Knight (Lefty Hogan), Syd Saylor (Red), Sheila Manors (Sally Flint), Jack Mulhall (George Lesserman), Forrest Taylor (Dr. Marston), John Elliott (Dr. Walsh), Miki Moria (Ylon), Jack Cowell (Chief Wilson).

KEMEK (1970-Ger)
    Director: Theodore Gershuny
Alexandra Stewart, David Hedison, Mary Woronov, Helmut Schneider, Herbert Weissbach, Robert Wolders.

KID FOR TWO FARTHINGS, A (1956)
    Director: Carol Reed
Celia Johnson (Joanna), Diana Dors (Sonia), David Kosoff (Kandinsky), Joseph Tomelty (Vagrant), Brenda De Banzie (Lady Ruby), Joe Robinson (Sam), Irene Handl (Mrs. Abramowitz), Lou Jacobi (Blackie Issacs), Sidney James (Ice Berg), Jonathan Ashmore (Joe), Sydney Tafler (Madame Rita), Daphne Anderson (Dora), Primo Carnera (Python), Vera Day (Mimi), Danny Green (Baron).

KIDNAPPING OF THE PRESIDENT,
    THE (1980)
    Director: George Mendeluk
William Shatner (Jerry O'Connor), Hal Holbrook (Pres. Adam Scott), Miguel Fernandes (Roberto Assanti), Cindy Girling (Linda Steiner), Van Johnson (Vice President Ethan Richards), Ava Gardner (Beth Richards), Elisabeth Shepherd (Joan Scott), Michael J. Reynolds (MacKenzie), Gary Reineke (Dietrich), Murray Westgate (Archie), Maury Chaykin (Harvey Cannon), Michael Kane (Herb), Aubert Pallascio, Elias Zarov, Patrick Brymar, Jackie Burroughs, Virginia Podesser, Larry Duran, Gershon Resnik, Chappelle Jaffe, John Stocker, John Romaine.

KID WITH THE BROKEN HALO, THE
    (TVM-1982) - 4-5-82
    Director: Leslie Martinson
Gary Coleman (Andy), Robert Guillaume

(Blake), Ray Walston (Michael), June
Allyson (Dorothea), Georg Stanford
Brown (Rudy Desautel), Mason Adams
(Harry Tannenbaum), Lani O'Grady
(Julie McNulty), John Pleshette (Jeff
McNulty), Corey Feldman (Pete),
Don Diamond (Giuseppe), Billy Beck
(Fenton), David Ashrow (Dave), Traci
Lee Briggs (Haber), Barry Hope (Flan-
agan), Randy Kirby (Frank), Wesley
Ann Pfenning (Glynde), Rance Howard
(coach), Jim Begg (prospect), Doug
Toby (player), Claude Swonger (assistant
coach), Rachel Jacobs (Martha), Tal-
madge Scott (teamate), Gary Guttenberg
(1st kid), Ty Mitchell (2nd kid), Hugh
McPhillips (Pierce), Kim Fields,
Rick Fitts.

KIGANJO NO BOKEN (1965-Jap.)
  (A. K. A. "Adventure in the Strange
  Stone Castle")
    Director: Senkichi Taniguchi
Toshire Mifune, Mie Hama, Yumi
Shirakawa, Makoto Sato, Tadao Naka-
muru, Tatsuya Mihashi.

KILL AND KILL AGAIN (1981)
    Director: Ivan Hall
James Ryan (Steve Chase), Anneline
Kriel (Kandy Kane), Ken Gampu (Gorilla),
Stan Schmidt (the Fly), Michael Mayer
(Marduk), Norman Robinson (Gypsy
Billy), Bill Flynn (Hotdog), Marloe
Scott-Wilson (Minerva), John Rams-
bottom (Dr. Horatio Kane), Eddie Dorie
(Optimus).

KILL, BABY, KILL (1966-Ital.) (A. K. A.
  "Operazione Paura", "Operation
  Fear", "Curse of the Dead")
    Director: Mario Bava
Erika Blanc (Monica Schuftan), Giacomo
Rossi-Stuart (Dr. Paul Eswai), Fabi-
enne Dali (Ruth the Sorceress), Gianna
Vivaldi (Baroness Graps), Piero Lulli
(Police Commissioner Kroger), Max
Lawrence (Kerl), Franca Dominici,
Valerio Valeri, Micaela Esdra, Mariella
Panfili, Giuseppe Addobbati.

KILLDOZER (TVM-1974) - 2-2-74
    Director: Jerry London
Clint Walker (Lloyd Kelly), Carl Betz
(Dennis Holvig), James Wainwright
(Jules 'Dutch' Drasner), Neville Brand
(Chub Foster), Robert Urich (Mack
McCarthy), James Watson, Jr. (Al
Beltran).

KILLER APE (1953)
    Director: Spencer Gordon Bennet
Johnny Weismuller (Jungle Jim), Carol

Thurston (Shari), Ray 'Crash' Cor-
rigan (Norley), Nestor Paiva (An-
drews), Paul Marion (Mahara),
Burt Wenland (Ramada), Nick Stuart
(Maron), Eddie Foster (Achmed),
Rory Mallinson (Perry), Max Palmer
(Man-Ape).

KILLER BEES (TVM-1974) - 2-26-74
    Director: Curtis Harrington
Gloria Swanson (Mme. van Bohlen),
Edward Andrews (Edward van Bohlen),
Kate Jackson (Victoria Wells), Roger
Davis (Dr. Helmus van Bohlen),
Craig Stevens (Rudolph van Bohlen),
Liam Dunn (Zeb Tucker), John
Ragin (Jeffreys), Don McGovern
(Mathias), Heather Ann Bostain
(Roseanna), Jack Perkins (salesman),
Donald Gentry (lineman), John Getz,
Robert L. Balzar, Daniel Woodworth.

KILLER FISH (1979-Ital. /Braz.)
    Director: Anthony M. Dawson
Lee Majors (Robert Lasky), Karen
Black (Kate Neville), James Fran-
ciscus (Paul Diller), Marisa Berenson
(Ann), Margaux Hemingway (Gabrielle),
Gary Collins (Tom), Dan Pastorini
(Hans), Roy Brocksmith (Ollie),
Charlie Guardino (Lloyd), Frank
Pesce (Warren), Anthony Steffen
(Max), Fabio Sabag (Quintin), Chico
Arago (Ben), Sonia Citicica (nurse),
Celsa Faria (airline passenger),
Goerge Cherques (Inspector).

KILLER INSIDE ME, THE (1976)
    Director: Burt Kennedy
Stacy Keach (Lou), Tisha Sterling
(Amy), Keenan Wynn (Chester),
Charles McGraw (Howard), Royal
Dano (father), Julie Adams (Mother),
John Dehner (Bob), John Carradine
(Dr. Smith), Susan Tyrrell (Joyce),
Don Stroud (Elmer), Pepe Serna
(Johnny).

KILLER LACKS A NAME, THE (1966-
  Ital.) (A. K. A. "Two Boys for
  Murder")
    Director: Tullio Domichelli
Lang Jeffries, Barbara Nelli, Olga
Omar.

KILLERS ARE CHALLENGED, THE
  (1965-Ital. /Fr.) (A. K. A. "A 007,
  Sfida Ai Killers")
    Director: Anthony Dawson/
    Antonio Margheriti
Richard Harrison, Susy Andersen,
Mitsuoko, Wandisa Guida, Marcel
Charvey.

KILLERS FROM SPACE (1954)
Director: W. Lee Wilder
Peter Graves (Doug Martin), James
Seay (Col. Banks), Frank Gerstle
(Dr. Kruger), Barbara Bestar (Ellen
Martin), Steve Pendleton (Briggs),
John Merrick (Deneb Tala), Shep
Menken (Major Clift), Jack Daly (po-
wer house gaurd), Ron Kennedy
(sentry), Burt Wenland (sergeant),
Ben Welden (pilot), Lester Dorr (sta-
tion attendant), Robert Roark (guard),
Ruth Bennett (Secretary), Mark Scott
(narrator), Coleman Francis.

KILLER SHREWS, THE (1959)
Director: Ray Kellogg
James Best (Capt. Thorn Sherman),
Ken Curtis (Jerry Lacer), Ingrid
Goude (Ann Craigis), Baruch Lumet
(Dr. Craigis), Gordon McLendon
(Radford Baines), J.H. Dupree (Rook),
Alfredo DeSoto (Mario).

KILLER'S MOON (1978)
Director: Alan Birkinshaw
Anthony Forrest, Tom Marshall,
Georgina Kean, Nigel Gregory, David
Jackson.

KILLER WITH TWO FACES (TVM-
1974) - 12-3-74
Director: John Scholz-Conway
Ian Hendry (Bob/Terry), Donna Mills
(Patty Heron), David Lodge (Bradley),
Roddy McMillan (Insp. Fillory), Susan
Drury (Jenny), Robin Parkinson (Mr.
Holland), Sereta Wislon (Sara),
Susannah McMillan (Dorothy), James
Greene (policeman), Jonathan Dennis
(intern), Christine Shaw (woman).

KILLING BOTTLE, THE (1967-Jap.)
(A.K.A. "Zettai Zetsumei")
Director: Senkichi Taniguchi
Nick Adams, Jun Tazaki, Tatsuya
Mihashi, Kumi Mizuno, Makoto Sato,
Yoshio Tsuchiya.

KILLING GAME, THE (TVM-1975)
(A.K.A. "Where the Action Is")
- 2-17-75
Director: Don Leaver
Edd Byrnes (Eddie Vallance), James
Berwick (Daddy Burns), Ingrid Pitt
(Ilse), George Innes (Zac), Trevor
Baxter (Winters), Frank Coda (Pur-
sell), Larry Cross (Tommy Vaughan),
Oliver McGreevy (Henry), Ray Marion
(croupier), Suzannah Williams (maid).

KILLING IN EVERY CORNER, A
(TVM-1974) - 11-19-74

Director Malcolm Taylor
Patrick Magee (Dr. Carnaby), Jo-
anna Pettet (Sylvia), Eric Flynn
(Slattery/Adridge), Max Wall (Kes-
selheim), Petra Markham, Don
Henderson, Peter Settelen.

KILLING KIND, THE (1973)
Director: Curtis Harrison
Ann Sothern (Thelma Lambert),
John Savage (Terry Lambert), Ruth
Roman (Rhea Benson), Luana Anders
(Louise), Cindy Williams (Lori),
Sue Bernard (Tina), Helene Winston
(Flo), Marjorie Eaton (Mrs. Orland),
Peter Brocco (father).

KINDAR THE INVINCIBLE (1965-
Ital.) (A.K.A. "Kindar, L'Invul-
neralble")
Director: Osvaldo Civirani
Mark Forrest, Mimmo Palmara,
Dea Flowers, Rosalba Neri.

KING DINOSAUR (1955)
Director: Bert I. Gordon
Bill Bryant (Dr. Ralph Martin),
Wanda Curtis (Dr. Patricia Bennett),
Douglas Henderson (Richard Gordon),
Patricia Gallagher (Nora Pierce),
Marvin Miller (Narrator).

KINGDOM OF THE FAIRIES (1903-
Fr.) (A.K.A. "Le Royaume des
fees", "The Fairyland")
Director: Georges Melies

KINGDOM OF THE SPIDERS (1977)
Director: John Cardos
William Shatner (Rack Hanson),
Tiffany Bolling (Diane Ashley),
Woody Strode (Walter Colby), Roy
Engel (Mayor Connors), Lieux
Dressler (Emma Washburn),
David McLean (Sheriff Smith),
Marcy Rafferty (Terry Hanson),
Natasha Ryan (Linda Hanson),
Altovise Davis (Birch Colby), Joe
Ross (Vern Johnson), Adele Malis
(Betty Johnson).

KING KONG (1933)
Director: Merian C. Cooper
& Ernest B. Schoedsack
Fay Wray (Ann Darrow), Robert
Armstrong (Carl Denham), Bruce
Cabot (Jack Driscoll), Frank Reicher
(Capt. Englehorn), Sam Hardy
(Weston), Noble Johnston (Native
Chief), James Flavin (Briggs, the
second mate), Steve Clemento (Witch
King), Victor Wong (cook), Ethan
Laidlaw (mate), Charlie Sullivan

(sailor), Vera Lewis, Leroy Mason (theatre patrons), Dick Curtis (sailor), Lynton Brent, Frank Mills (reporter), Paul Porcase (apple vendor).

KING KONG (1976)
Director: John Guillerman
Jessica Lange (Dwan), Jeff Bridges (Prescott), Charles Grodin (Wilson), John Randolph (Captain Ross), Rene Auberjoins (Bagley), Ed Lauter (Carnahan), Mario Gallo (Timmons), Jack O'Halloran (Perko), Jorge Moreno (Garcia), John Agar (New York District Attorney), Julius Harris (Boan), John Lone (Chinese Cook), Sid Conrad (Petrox Chairman), Gary Walberg (Army General), George Whitman (Army helicopter pilot), Wayne Heffley (Air Force Colonel).

KING KONG ESCAPES (1967-Jap.) (A.K.A. "Kingu Kongu no Gyakushu", "King Kong's Counterattack", "King Kong's Revenge")
Director: Inoshire Honda
Mie Hama (Madame X), Rhodes Reason (Cmdr. Carl Nelson), Linda Miller (Susan), Akira Takarada (Jiro), Eisei Amamoto (Dr. Who).

KING KONG VS. GODZILLA (1962- Jap.) (A.K.A. "Kingu Kongu tai Gojira")
Director: Inoshiro Honda
Michael Keith (Eric Carter), James Yagi (Yakata Omura), Tadao Takashima (O. Sakurai), Mie Hama (Fumeko Sakurai), Kenji Sahara (Kazuo Fukita), Akihiko Hirata (Premier Shigezawa), Ichiro Arishima (Mr. Tako), Tatsuo Matsumura (Dr. Markino), Yu Fujiki (Insaburo Furue), Harry Holcombe (Dr. Arnold Johnson), Senkichi Omura (Konno), Eiko Wakabayshi (Tamiye).

KING OF THE CONGO (1952) - serial in 15 episodes
Director: Spencer Gordon Bennet & Wallace A. Grissell
Buster Crabbe (Thunda/Roger Crum), Leonard Penn (Boris), Gloria Dee (Pha), Jack Ingram (Clark), Rick Vallin (Andreov), Rusty Wescoatt (Kor), William Fawcett (High Priest), Alex Montoya (Lipah), Neyle Morrow (Nahee), Bernie Goizer (Zahlia), Frank Ellis (Ivan), Nick Stuart (Degar), Bart Davidson (Alexis), Lee Roberts (Blake).

KING OF THE JUNGLE (1927) - serial in 10 episodes
Director: Webster Cullison

Elmo Lincoln, True Boardman, Gordon Standing, Sally Long.

KING OF THE JUNGLE (1933)
Director: H. Bruce Humberstone & Max Marcin
Buster Crabbe (Kaspa, the Lion Man), Frances Dee (Anne Rogers), Sidney Toler (Mr. Forbes), Douglas Dumbrille (Ed Peters), Nydia Westman (Sue), Irving Pichel (Gorey), Robert Barrat (Joe Nolan), Warner Richman (Gus), Sam Baker (Gwana), William Farnum (Police Officer), Patricia Farley (Kitty), Robert Adair (John C. Knolls), Ronnie Crosby (Kaspa at age 3), Mabel Stark (woman mauled by tiger).

KING OF THE KONGO (1929) - serial in 10 episodes
Chapters: 1. "Into the Unknown", 2. "Terror of the Jungle", 3. "The Temple of the Beasts", 4. "Gorilla Warfare", 5. "Danger in the Dark", 6. "The Fight at the Lion's Pit", 7. "The Fatal Moment", 8. "Sentenced to Death", 9. "Desperate Chances" & 10. "Jungle Justice".
Director: Richard Thorpe
Jacqueline Logan (Diana Martin), Boris Karloff (Scarface Macklin), Robert Frazer (Native Chief), Walter Miller (Larry Trent), Richard Tucker (Secret Service Chief), Lafe McKee (Trader John), Larry Steers (Jack Drake), Joe Bonomo (Gorilla), Harry Todd (Commodore), J. P. Leckray (Priest), J. Gordon Russell (derelict), Richard Neill (prisoner), William Burt (Mooney), Ruth Davis (Poppy).

KING OF THE MOUNTIES (1942) - serial in 12 episodes
Chapters: 1. "Phantom Invaders", 2. "Road to Death", 3. "Human Target", 4. "Railroad Saboteurs", 5. "Suicide Dive", 6. "Blazing Barrier", 7. "Perilous Plunge", 8. "Electrocuted", 9. "Reign Of Terror", 10. "The Flying Coffin", 11. "Deliberate Murder" & 12. "On to Victory".
Director: William Witney
Allan Lane (Sergeant King), Gilbert Emery (Commissioner), Russell Hicks (Marshal Carleton), Peggy Drake (Carol Brent), George Irving (Prof. Brent), Nestor Paiva (Count Baroni), William Bakewell (Ross), Douglas Dumbrille (Harper), Abner Biberman (Adm. Yamata), Duncan Renaldo (Pierre), Jay Novello (Lewis),

Francis Ford (Collins), Anthony Warde (Stark), William Vaughn (Marshal Von Horst), John Hiestand (Lane), Bradley Page (Blake), Paul Fung (Jap Bobardier), Norman Nesbitt (radio announcer), Allen Jung (Sato), Arvon Dale (Craig), Harry Cording (Wade Garson), Ken Terrell (Al), Carleton Young (Gus), Hal Taliaferro (Ed Johnson), Duke Green (lookout), Tom Steele (Jack/spike No. 2), Stanley Price (McGee), Forrest Taylor (telegrapher), Frank Wayne (Brant), John Roy, Bud Weiser (barn Heavies), Duke Taylor (Becker/Mountie/smelter heavy No. 1), Pete Katchenaro (Falcon pilot), Kam Tong (Jap pilot), Tommy Coats (Mike), Bob Jamison (Pete), Earl Bunn (Joe), Jack Kenney (plant guard), Sam Serrano, King Kong (road Japs), Joe Chambers (shack heavy), Jimmy Fawcett (smelter heavy No. 2).

KING OF THE ROCKET MEN (1949) (A.K.A. "Lost Planet Airmen") - serial in 12 episodes
Chapters: 1- "Dr. Vulcan - Traitor", 2. "Plunging Death", 3. "Dangerous Evidence", 4. "High Peril", 5. "Fatal Dive", 6. "Mystery of the Rocket Man", 7. "Molten Menace", 8. "Suicide Flight", 9. "Ten Seconds to Live", 10. "The Deadly Fog", 11. "Secret of Dr. Vulcan", & 12. "Wave of Disaster".
      Director: Fred C. Brannon
Tris Coffin (Jeff King), Mae Clarke (Glenda Thomas), Don Haggerty (Tony Dirken), I. Stanford Jolley (Prof. Bryant/Dr. Vulcan), James Craven (Prof. Millard), House Peters, Jr. (Burt Winslow), Douglas Evans (Chairman), Dale Van Sickel (Martin/Drake/ Gates/Miller/Rand), Buddy Roosevelt (Phillips), Dave Sharpe (Blears/Cliff/ Stark), Tom Steele (Knox/Chase/cab driver), Eddie Parker (Rowan), Stanley Price (Gunther Von Strum), Frank O'Connor (guard), Marshall Bradford (Graffner), Arvon Dale (aide), Michael Ferro (Turk), Ted Adams (Martin Conway), Bud Wolfe (Clay), Bert LeBaron (Morgan), Carey Loftin (Sparks), Jack O'Shea (Walter), Art Gilmore (newscaster).

KING OF THE ROYAL MOUNTED (1940) - serial in 12 episodes
      Director: William Witney & John English
Allan Lane (Sergeant King), Robert Strange (Kettler), Lita Conway (Linda Merritt), Herbert Rawlinson (Insp. King), Harry Cording (Wade Garson),

Stanley Andrews (Merritt, Sr.), Bryant Wahsburn (Crandall), John Dilson (Dr. Wall), Lucien Prival (Admiral Johnson), Robert Kellard (Corporal Tom Merritt), Norman Willis (Capt. Tarner), Ken Terrell (Al), Budd Buster (Vinegar Smith), Tony Paton (Le Couteau), John Bagni (Higgins), Bud Geary (Klondike), Al Taylor (Red), Bill Wilkus (Bill), Sam Harris (Harold Bolton), George DeNormand (Kent), Charles Thomas (Bayliss), Ted Mapes (Blake), Dale Van Scikel (radioman), George Plues (brakeman), Richard Simmons (Carter), Wallace Reid, Jr. (Doyle), William Stahl (Bob Hastings), Frank Wayne (Brant), Loren Riebe (Dinwoodie), William Justice (Hallett), Earl Bunn (Joe), Curley Dresden (Kelly), Robert Wayne (Lieutenant), Tommy Coats (Mike), Dave Marks (knife heavy), William Kellogg (MacCloud), Alan Gregg (Mills), Bob Jamison (Pete), Douglas Evans (Sergeant), Cy Slocum (sanitarium heavy) Denny Sullivan, Walter Low, George Ford (paralytics), Duke Taylor, Jimmy Fawcett (smelter heavies), David Sharpe, Duke Green.

KING OF THE WILD (1931) - serial in 12 episodes
Chapters: 1. "Man Eaters", 2. "The Tiger of Destiny", 3. "The Avenging Horde", 4. "The Secret of the Volcano", 5. "The Pit of Peril", 6. "The Creeping Doom", 7. "Sealed Lips", 8. "Jaws of the Jungle", 9. "The Door of Dread", 10. "The Leopard's Lair", 11. "The Fire of the Gods" & 12. "Jungle Justice".
      Director: Richard Thorpe
Walter Miller (Robert Grant), Boris Karloff (Mustapha), Nora Lane (Muriel Armitage), Dorothy Christie (Mrs. LaSalle), Cyril MacLaglen (Bimi), Tom Santschi (Harris), Carroll Nye (Tom Armitage), Victor Potel (Peterson), Lafe McKee (Officer), Martha Lalande (Mrs. Colby), Mischa Auer (Dakka), Otto Hoffman, Albert De Warton, Earle Douglas, Fletcher Norton, Merrill McCormick, Larry Steers, Walter Ferdna, Dick La Reno, Eileen Schofield, Norman Feusier, Floyd Shackelford.

KING OF THE ZOMBIES (1941)
      Director: Jean Yarbrough
Dick Purcell (Mac McCarthy), Joan Woodbury (Barbara Windsor), Henry Victor (Dr. Miklos Sangre), John Archer (Bill Summers), Mantan

Moreland (Jefferson Davis), Patricia Stacey (Madame Alyce Sangre), Madame Sul-te-Wan (Tahama), Guy Usher (Adm. Wainwright), Jimmy Davis (Lazarus), Marguerite Whitten (Samantha), Lawrence Criner (Dr. Couille), John Carradine, Roy D'Arcy.

KING SOLOMON'S MINES (1937)
Director: Robert Stevenson
Sir Cedric Hardwicke (Allan Quartermaine), Paul Robeson (Umbopa), Roland Young (Cmdr. Good), John Loder (Henry Curtis), Anna Lee (Kathy O'Brien), Arthur Sinclair (O'Brien), Robert Adams (Twals), Sydney Fairbrother (Gagool), Frederick Lesiter (wholesaler), Arthur Goullett (Sylvestra), Majabalo Hlubi (Kapsie), Alf Goddard (Red).

KIRLIAN WITNESS, THE (1978)
Director: Jonathan Sarno
Nancy Snyder (Rilla), Nancy Boykin (Laurie), Joel Colodner (Robert), Ted Leplat (handyman), Lawrence Tierney.

KISS AND KILL (1968-Span./Ger./U.S./Brit.) (A.K.A. "Against All Odds", "Blood of Fu Manchu", "Fu Manchu y el Beso de la Muerte", Fu Manchu and the Kiss of Death")
Director: Jesus Franco
Christopher Lee (Fu Manchu), Richard Greene (Nayland Smith), Howard Marion-Crawford (Dr. Petrie), Shirley Eaton (the Black Widow), Tsai Chin (Lin Tang), Maria Rohm (Ursula Wagner), Goetz George (Carl Jansen), Ricardo Palacios (Sancho Lopez), Frances Kahn (Carmen).

KISSES FOR MY PRESIDENT (1964)
Director: Curtis Bernhardt
Fred MacMurray (Thad McCloud), Polly Bergen (Leslie McCloud), Eli Wallach (Valdez), Arlene Dahl (Doris Reid), Edward Andrews (Sen. Walsh), Donald May (John O'Connor), Anna Capri (Gloria McCloud), Ronnie Dapo (Peter McCloud), Harry Holcombe (Bill Richards), Bill Walker (Joseph), Adrienne Marden (Miss Higgins), Richard St. John (Jackson).

KISS FROM BEYOND THE GRAVE, THE (1962-Mex.) (A.K.A. "El Beso de Ultratumba")
Director: Carlos Toussaint
Ana Bertha Lepe, Sergio Jurado, Enrique Lucero, Maggo Donato.

KISS ME DEADLY (1955)
Director: Robert Aldrich
Ralph Meeker (Mike Hammer), Albert Dekker (Dr. Soberin), Paul Stewart (Carl Evello), Juano Hernandez (Eddie Yeager), Wesley Addy (Pat), Marian Carr (Friday), Jack Lambert (Sugar), Cloris Leachman (Christina), Jack Elam (Charlie Max), Percy Helton (morgue doctor), Mort Marshall (Diker), Fortunio Bonanova (Trivaco), Gaby Rodgers (Lily Carver), Jerry Zinneman (Sammy), Leigh Snowden (girl at pool), Robert Cornthwaite (FBI man), James Seay (FBI man), Nick Dennis (Nick), Maxine Cooper (Velda), Madi Comfort (night club singer), Silvio Minciotti (old man), Jesslyn Fax (Mrs. Super), James McCallion (Super), Mara McAfee (nurse).

KISS MEETS THE PHANTOM (TVM-1978) - 10-28-78
Director: Gordon Hessler
Gene Simmons, Peter Criss, Ace Frehley, Paul Stanley (Kiss), Anthony Zerbe (Abner Devereaux), Deborah Ryan (Melissa), Carmine Caridi (Calvin Richards), Terry Webster (Sam), John Lisbon Wood (Slime), John Dennis Johnston (Chopper), Lisa Jane Persky (Dirty Dee).

KISS OF THE TARANTULA (1972) (A.K.A. "Shudders")
Director: Chris Munger
Suzanne Ling (Susan Bradley), Eric Mason (Walter Bradley), Herman Wallner (John Bradley), Patricia Landon (Nancy Drury), Beverly Eddins (Martha Bradley).

KISS OF THE VAMPIRE (1963) (A.K.A. "Kiss of Evil")
Director: Don Sharp
Edward De Souza (Gerald Harcourt), Noel Willman (Dr. Ravna), Jennifer Daniel (Marianne Harcourt), Clifford Evans (Prof. Zimmer), Barry Warren (Karl Ravna), Jackie Wallis (Sabena Ravna), Peter Madden (Bruno), Isabel Black (Tania), Carl Esmond (Anton), Virginia Gregg (Rosa), Vera Cook (Anna), Noel Howlett (Father Xavier), Sheilah Wells (Teresa), Stan Simmons (Hans), John Harvey (Police Sergeant), Brian Oulton (1st disciple), Margaret Read (1st female disciple), Olga Dickie (woman at graveyard).

KISS THE GIRLS AND MAKE THEM DIE (1966-Ital.) (A.K.A. "Opera-

zione Paradise", "Operation Para-
dise")
    Director: Henry Levin & Dino
        Mairuri
Michael Connors (Kelly), Dorothy
Provine (Susan Fleming), Raf Vallone
(Mr. Ardonian), Margaret Lee (Grace),
Terry-Thomas (Lord Aldric/James),
Beverly Adams (Karin), Nicoletta
Machiavelli (Sylvia), Jack Gwillim
(British Ambassador), Oliver Mac-
Greevy (Ringo), Sandro Dori (Omar),
Senya Seyn (interpertor), Marilu
Tolo (Gioia), Andy Ho (King), Hans
Thorner (Kruger), Michael Audley
(Major Davis), Nerio Bernardi (Pa-
pal Envoy), Edith Peters (Maria),
Renato Terra, Roland Bartrop, George
Leech.

KNIFE FOR THE LADIES, A (1973)
    Director: Larry G. Spangler
Jack Elam, Ruth Roman, Jeff Cooper,
Gene Evans, John Kellogg, Joe Santos.

KNIGHT OF TERROR (1964-Span. /
    Ital. /Fr.) (A. K. A. "Los Jinetes
    del Terror")
    Director: Mario Costa
Tony Russell, Scilla Gabel, Pilar
Clemens, Yves Vincent.

KNIGHT OF THE NIGHT, THE (1953-
    Fr.) (A. K. A. "Le Chevalier de
    la Nuit")
    Director: Robert Darlene
Jean- Claude Pascal, Renee Saint-
Cyr, Louis de Funes, Gregoire
Aslan, Max Dalban.

KNIGHTRIDERS (1981)
    Director: George Romero
Ed Harris (Billy), Gary Lahti (Alan),
John Amplas (Whiteface), Amy Inger-
soll (Linet), Tom Savini (Morgan),
Patricia Tallman (Julie), Warner
Shook (Pippen), Christine Forrest
(Angie), Brother Blue (Merlin), Cyn-
thia Adler (Rocky), John Hostetter
(Tuck), Ken Hixon (Steve), Albert
Amerson (Indian), Steven King.

KNIGHTS OF THE ROUND TABLE
    (1953)
    Director: Richard Thorpe
Robert Taylor (Lancelot), Mel Ferrer
(King Arthur), Ava Gardner (Guinevere),
Anne Crawford (Morgan LeFay),
Felix Aylmer (Merlin), Stanley Baker
(Modred), Robert Urquhart (Gawaine),
Niall MacGinnis (the Green Knight),
Gabriel Woolf (Percival), Maureen
Swanson (Elaine), Anthony Forwood

(Gareth), Ann Hanslip (Nan), Stephen
Vercoe (Agravaine), Jill Clifford
(Bronwyn).

KNIVES OF THE AVENGER (1967-
    Ital.) (A. K. A. "Raffica di Coltelli",
    "Shower of Knives")
    Director: Mario Bava
Cameron Mitchell (Rurik), Fausto
Tozzi (Aghen), Giacome Rossi-
Stuart (Harald), Luciano Polliten
(Moki), Elisa Mitchell (Karen).

KONGA (1960)
    Director: John Lemont
Michael Gough (Dr. Charles Dexter),
Claire Gordon (Sandra Banks),
Jesse Conrad (Bob Kenton), George
Pastell (Prof. Tagore), Austin Tre-
vor (Dean Foster), Margo Johns
(Margaret), Jack Watson (Superin-
tendent Brown), Stanley Morgan (Insp.
Lawson), Vanda Godsell (Mrs.
Kenton), Leonard Sachs (Mr. Kenton),
Grace Arnold (Miss Barnesdell),
Frank Forsyth (Gen. Brennan),
Nicholas Bennett (Daniel), Waveney
Lee (Janet), Kim Tracy (Mary),
Rupert Osborne (Eric).

KONGO (1932)
    Director: William Cowen
Walter Huston (Flint), Lupe Valez
(Tula), Conrad Nagel (Dr. Kingsland),
Virginia Bruce (Ann), C. Henry
Gordon (Gregg), Forrester Harvey
(Cookie), Mitchell Lewis (Hogan).

KRAKATIT (1948-Czech.)
    Director: Otaker Vavra
Florence Marly (Princess Willy),
Karek Hoger.

KRIEMHILD'S REVENGE (1924-Ger.)
    (A. K. A. "Kriemhilds Rache",
    "Niebelungen Saga" Part II)
    Director: Fritz Lang
Paul Richter (Siegfried), Rudolf
Klein-Rogge (Attila), Margarete
Schon (Kriemhild), Theodore Loos,
Bernard Goetzke, Hans von Schlet-
tow, Hanna Ralph.

KRONOS (1957)
    Director: Kurt Neumann
Jeff Morrow (Les Gaskell), Barbara
Lawrence (Vena), Morris Ankrum
(Dr. Stern), John Emery (Elito),
George O'Hanlon (Culver), Jose
Gonzales (Manuel), John Parrish
(Gen. Parry), Kenneth Alton (Mc-
Crary), Richard Harrison (pilot),
Marjorie Stapp (nurse), Robert

Shayne (general), Don Eitner, John Halloran, Gordon Mills.

KRULL (1983)
Director: Peter Yates
Ken Marshall, Lysette Anthony, Freddie Jones, Bernard Bresslaw, David Battley, Michael Elphick, Francesca Annis.

KWAIDAN (1963-Jap.) (A.K.A. "Weird Tales")
Director: Masuki Kobayashi
Renato Mikuni (Sumarai), Michiyo Aratama (first wife), Misako Watanabe (second wife), Katsuo Nakamura (Hoichi), Takashi Shimura (Priest), Yoichi Hayashi (Yoshitsune), Tetsuo Tamba (Samurai), Kanyemon Kakamura (Kannai), Noboru Nakaya (Heinai).

LADIES IN RETIREMENT (1941)
Director: Charles Vidor
Ida Lupino (Ellen Creed), Elsa Lanchester (Emily Creed), Louis Hayward (Albert Feather), Evelyn Deyes (Lucy), Edith Barrett (Louisa Creed), Isobel Elsom (Miss Fiske), Queenie Leonard (Sister Agatha), Emma Dunn (Sister Theresa), Clyde Cook (Bates).

LADY AND THE MONSTER, THE (1944)
(A.K.A. "The Lady and the Doctor")
Director: George Sherman
Erich von Stroheim (Prof. Franz Mueller), Richard Arlen (Patrick Cory), Vera Hruba Ralston (Janice Farrell), Sidney Blackmer (Eugene Fulton), Helen Vinson (Chloe Donovan), Mary Nash (Mrs. Fame), Charles Cane (Grimes), Bill Henry (Roger Collins), Lane Chandler (White, the ranger), Sam Flint (G. Phipps, the bank manager), Harry Hayden (Dr. Martin), Edward Keane (Manning), Maxine Doyle (receptionist), William Benedict (bellhop), Juanita Quigley (Mary Lou), Wallis Chark (Warden), Josephine Dillon (Mary Lou's grandmother), Tom London (husky man in tails), Lola Montes, Antonio Triano (dancers), Herbert Clifton (Butler), Lee Phelps (head- waiter), Harry Depp (bank Teller), Janet Mertin (cafe singer), Frank Graham (narrator).

LADY FRANKENSTEIN (1971-Ital) (A.K.A. "La Figlia di Frankenstein", "The Daughter of Frankenstein", "Madame Frankenstein")
Director: Mel Welles
Sarah Bay (Lady Tanya Frankenstein), Joseph Cotten (Baron Frankenstein), Paul Mueller (Charles Marshall), Mickey Hargity (Insp. Harris), Paul Whiteman,

Herbert Fux.

LADY IN A CAGE (1964)
Director: Walter Grauman
Olivia De Havilland (Mrs. Hilyard), James Caan (Randall), Jennifer Billingley (Elaine), Rafael Campos (Essie), Ann Sothern (Sade), Jeff Corey (the Wino), Charles Seel (the Junkman), Scatman Crothers (Junkman's assistant), William Swan (Malcolm Hilyard).

LADY POSSESSED (1951)
Director: William Spier & Roy Kellino
James Mason (Del Palma), June Havoc (Jean Wilson), Fay Compton (Mme. Brune), Stephen Dunne (Tom Wilson), Pamela Mason (Sybil), Steven Geray (Dr. Stepanek), Diana Graves (Medium), Odette Myrtil (Mrs. Burrows), John P. Monoghan (Dave), Eileen Erskine (Violet), Enid Mosier (calypso singer), Hazel Franklyn (matron), Judy Osborn (secretary), Alma Lawton, Constance Cavendish, Tonyna Micky Dolly, Anna Grevler (nurses).

LADY, STAY DEAD (1982-Australia)
Director: Terry Bourke
Chard Hayward (Gordon Mason), Louise Howitt (Jenny Nolan), Deborah Coulls (Marie Coleby), Roger Ward (Officer Collings), James Elliott (Patrolman Dunbar), Lex Foxroft (Billy Shepherd).

LAKE OF DRACULA (1973-Jap.)
(A.K.A. "Chi O Suu Me"; "Bloodthirsty Eyes"; "Dracula's Lust for Blood")
Director: Michio Yamamoto
Midori Fujita (Akiko), Osahide Takahashi (Sacki), Sanae Emi (Natsuoke), Mori Kishida, Kaku Takashina.

LANCELOT OF THE LAKE (1975-Fr.) (A.K.A. "Lancelot du Lac")
Director: Robert Bresson
Luc Simon (Lancelot), Vladimir Antolek-Oresek (King Arthur), Laura Duke Condominas (Queen Guinevere), Humbert Balsan (Gawain), Arthur de Montalemberg (Lionel), Patrick Bernard (Mordred).

LAND OF THE MINOTAUR (1975)
(A.K.A. "The Devil's Men")
Director: Costa Carayiannis

Donald Pleasence (Father Roche),
Peter Cushing (Baron Corofax), Luan
Peters (Laurie), Nikos Verlekis
(Ian), Costas Skouras (Milo), Bob
Behling (Tom), Vanna Revilli (Beth),
Fernando Bislani (Police Sergeant),
Anna Mantzourani.

LAND THAT TIME FORGOT, THE (1975)
     Director: Kevin Connor
Doug McClure (Bowen Tyler), Susan
Penhaligon (Lisa Clayton), John
McEnery (Capt. Von Schoevorts),
Anthony Ainley (Lt. Diets), Keith
Barron (Bradley), Godfrey James
(Borg), Bobby Farr (Ahm), Declan
Mulholland (Olson), Ben Howard
(Benson), Colin Farrell (Whiteley),
Roy Holder (Plesser), Andrew McCul-
loch (Sinclair), Grahame Mallard
(Deusett), Brian Hall (Schwartz),
Peter Sproule (Hindle), Ron Pember
(Jones), Andrew Lodge (Reuther), Stan-
ley McGeagh (Hiller), Steve James
(1st Sto-Lu).

LAND UNKNOWN (1956)
     Director: Virgil Vogel
Jock Mahoney (Cmdr. Harold Roberts),
Henry Brandon (Dr. Carl Hunter),
Shawn Smith (Maggie Hathaway),
William Reynolds (Lt. Jack Carmen),
Phil Harvey (Steve Miller), Douglas
Kennedy (Capt. Burnaham), Andrew
Branham (Lieutenant).

LASERBLAST (1977)
     Director: Micheal Rae
Kim Milford (Billy Duncan), Cheryl
Smith (Kathy Farley), Gianni Russo
(Tony Craig), Keenan Wynn (Col.
Farley), Roddy McDowall (Dr. Mels-
ton), Ron Masak (Sheriff), Dennis
Burkley (Peter Ungar), Barry Cutler
(Jesse Jeep), Mike Bobenko (Chuck
Boran), Eddie Deezen (Froggy).

LAST BRIDE OF SALEM (TVM-1974) -
     5-8-74
     Director: Tom Donovan
Bradford Dillman (Matt Clifton),
Lois Nettleton (Jennifer Clifton),
Paul Harding (Sebastian Mayhew),
Joni Bick (Kelly Clifton), Murray
Westgate (Fletcher), Ed McNamura
(Seth), James Douglas (Dr. Glover),
Moya Fenwick (Elisbeth), Susan Rubis
(Grace), Patricia Hamilton (Rebecca),
Rex Hagon (Master), Robert Hawkins
(Thomas), Jim Barron (Abner), Rick
Bennett (1st son), John Candy (2nd
son).

LAST CHASE, THE (1980)
     Director: Martyn Burke
Lee Majors (Franklyn Hart), Chris
Makepeace (Ring McCarthy), Bur-
gess Meredith (Capt. J.C. Williams),
Alexandra Stewart (Eudora), George
Touliatos (Hawkins), Diane D'Aquila
(Santana), Harvey Atkin (Jud), Ben
Gordon (Morely), Doug Lennox
(Army Captain), George R. Robert-
son (announcer), Moses Znaimer
(reporter).

LAST CHILD, THE (TVM- 1971) -
     10-5-71
     Director: John L. Moxey
Michael Cole (Allen Miller), Janet
Margolin (Karen Miller), Van Heflin
(Sen. Quincy George), Ed Asner
(Barstow), Harry Guardino (Howard
Drumm), Kent Smith (Iverson),
Victor Izay (Silverman), Barbara
Babcock (Shelley), Philip Bournouf
(Dr. Tyler), Michael Larrain (Sandy).

LAST DINOSAUR, THE (TVM-1977) -
     2-11-77
     Director: Alex Grasshoff &
     Tom Kotani
Richard Boone (Masten Thrust),
Joan Van Ark (Frankie Bands),
Steven Keats (Chuck Wade), Luther
Rackley (Bunta), Tatsu Nakamura
(Dr. Kawamoto), Carl Hansen
(Barney), Mamiya Sekia (Prehistoric
Girl), William Ross (Expedition
Captain).

LAST HORROR FILM, THE (1982)
     Director: David Winters
Caroline Munro (Jana Bates), Joe
Spinell, Judd Hamilton.

LAST HOUR, THE (1930)
     Director: Walter Forde
Stewart Rome, Richard Cooper,
Alexander,Field, Kathleen Vaughan,
Wilfred Shine, James Raglan,
Frank Arlton, George Bealby, Billy
Shine.

LAST MAN ON EARTH, THE (1924)
     Director: Jack G. Blystone
Earle Foxe (Elmer Smith), Derelys
Perdue (Hattie), Gladys Tennyson
(Frisco Kate), Grace Cunard (Gertie),
Clarissa Selwynne (Dr. Pardwell),
Marie Astaire (Paula Prodwell),
Maryon Aye (Red Sal), Jean Johnson
(Hattie at age 6), Buck Black (Elmer
at age 8), William Steele (Hattie's
father), Jean Dumas (Hattie's mother),
Harry Dunkinson (Elmer's father),

Fay Holderness (Elmer's mother),
Pauline French (Furlong).

LAST MAN ON EARTH, THE (1963-
Ital./U.S.) (A.K.A. "L'Ultimo
Uomo Della Terra")
Director: Sydney Salkow
Vincent Price (Robert Morgan), Franca
Bettoia (Ruth), Emma Danielli (Vir-
ginia Morgan), Giacomo Rossi-Stuart
(Ben Cortman), Umberto Rau, Tony
Corevi, Hector Ribotta, Christi Court-
land.

LAST MOMENT, THE (1923)
Director: J. Parker Reed, Jr.
Henry Hull, Doris Kenyon, Louis
Wolheim, Louis Calhern, Jerry Peter-
son, Harry Allen, William Nelly,
Mickey Bennett.

LAST OF THE SECRET AGENTS?,
THE (1966)
Director: Norman Abbott
Marty Allen (Marty Johnson), Steve
Rossi (Dteve Donovan), John Williams
(J. Frederick Duval), Nancy Sinatra
(Micheline), Lou Jacobi (Papa Leo),
Harvey Korman (German Colonel),
Theo Marcuse (Zoltan Schubach),
Ben Lessy (Harry), Carmen (Baby
May Zoftig), Connie Sawyer (Florence),
Sig Ruman (Prof. Werner von Konig),
Remo Pisani (Them), Larry Duran
(Them), Emanuel Thomas (frogman),
Don Keefer (handsome spy), Aida
Fries (belly dancer), Whilhelm Von
Homburg (GGI man), Phyllis Davis
(young lady), Paul Daniels (milkman),
Edy Williams (1st beauty), Makee
Blaisdell (King), Thordis Brandt (Fred
Johnson), Madge Blake, Almira Ses-
sions (ladies), Joe Devlin (waiter),
Philip Sascombe (Englishman), Hoke
Howell (man in Adolph Hitler uniform),
Allen D. Jung (Kurawa from Japan).

LAST PERFORMANCE, THE (1927)
Director: Paul Frejos
Conrad Veidt (Erik the Great), Mary
Philbin (Julie), Fred Mackaye (Mark
Royce), Leslie Fenton (Buffo), Gustav
Partos (Theatre Manager), William
H. Turner (Booking Agent), Sam De
Grazee (District Attorney), Anders
Randolf (Judge), George Irving (De-
fense Attorney).

LAST RITES (1980) (A.K.A. "Dracula's
Last Rites")
Director: Domonic Paris
Patricia Lee Hammond (Marie), Gerald
Fielding, Victor Jorge, Mimi Weddell,

Michael Lally.

LAST WAR, THE (1961-Jap.) (A.K.A.
"Senkai Dai Senso", "The Final
War")
Director: Shue Matsubayashi
Akira Takarada, Frankie Sakai, Yuriko
Hoshi, Nobuko Otowa, Yumi Shirakawa.

LAST WARNING, THE (1928)
Director Paul Leni
Laura La Plante, Montagu Love, John
Boles, Roy D'Arcy, Margaret Living-
ston, Slim Summerville, Fred Kelsey,
Mack Swain, D'Arcy Corrigan, Burr
McIntosh, Bert Roach, Charles K.
French.

LAST WAVE, THE (1978-Australia),
Director: Peter Weir
Richard Chamberlain (David Burton),
Olivia Hamnett (Anne Burton), Freder-
ick Parslow (Rev. Burton), Gulpilil
(Chris Lee), Walter Amagula (Gerry
Lee), Vivean Gray (Dr. Whitbun),
Nanjiwarra Amagula (Charlie), Roy
Bara (Larry), Dedric Laira (Lindsey),
Morris Lalara (Jacko), Peter Carroll
(Michael Zeadler), Athol Compton
(Billy Corman), Hedley Cullen (Judge),
Michael Duffield (Andrew Potter),
Jennifer de Greenlaw (Zeadler's
secretary), Jo England (babysitter),
Wallas Eaton (morgue doctor), John
Muagher (morgue clerk), Merv Lilley
(publican), John Frawley (policeman),
Guido Rametta (Guido), Ingrid Wier
(Grace Burton), Katrina Sedgwick
(Sophie Burton), Malcolm Robertson
(Don Fishburn), Richard Henderson
(Prosecutor), Greg Rowe (Carl).

LAST WOMAN ON EARTH, THE (1960)
Director Roger Corman
Anthony Carbone (Harold), Betsy
Jones-Moreland (Evelyn), Edward Wain
(Martin).

LAST YEAR AT MARIENBAD (1961-
Fr./Ital.) (A.K.A. "L'Annee Der-
niere a Marienbad")
Director: Alan Resnais
Delphine Seyrig (Woman), Sacha
Pitoeff (Husband), Giorgio Albertazzi
(Stranger).

LATHE OF HEAVEN, THE (TVM-1980)
- 1-9-80
Director David Loxton & Fred
Barsyk
Bruce Davison (George Orr), Kevin
Conway (Dr. Walter Haber), Niki
Flacks (Miss Crough), Margaret

Avery (Heather Lelache), Peyton Park
(Mannie Ahrens), Jo Livingston (George's
father), Bernedette Whitehead (George's
mother), Vannon Clark (Aunt Ethel),
Tom Matts (Grandfather), Jane Roberts
(Grandmother), Frank Miller (parole
officer), Joye Nash, Gena Sleete (women
on subway), R. A. Mihaloff (orderly),
Ben McKinley, III (orderly).

LATIN QUARTER, THE (1945)
        Director: Gunther Krampf
Joan Greenwood, Derrick De Marney,
Martin Miller, Joan Seton, Frederick
Valk, Valentine Dyall, Lilly Kahn,
Beresford Egan.

LATITUDE ZERO (1969, Jap. /U. S.)
        (A. K. A. "Ido Zero Daisakusen")
        Director: Inoshiro Honda
Joseph Cotten (Capt. Craig McKenzie),
Cesar Romero (Malic), Richard Jaeckel
(Perry Lawton), Patricia Medina (Lu-
cretia), Linda Haynes (Dr. Anne Barton),
Akira Takarada (Ken Tashiro), Akihiko
Hirata (Dr. Sugata), Masumi Okada (Dr.
Jules Masson), Tetsu Nakamura (Dr.
Okada), Mari Nakayama (Tsurko Okada),
Hikaru Kuroki (Kroiga), Susamu Kurobe
(Chin).

LAUGH, CLOWN, LAUGH (1928)
        Director: Herbert Brenon
Lon Chaney, Sr. (Tito Beppi), Loretta
Young (Simonette), Nils Asther (Count
Luigi Ravelli), Gwen Lee (Diane), Bernard
Siegel (Simon), Cissy Fitzgerald (Giacinta),
Leo Feodoroff, Emmett King.

LAUGHING AT DANGER (1924)
        Director: James W. Horne
Richard Talmadge (Alan Remington),
Joe Girard (Cyrus Remington), Joe
Harrington (Prof. Leo Hollister), Eva
Novak (Corolyn Hollister), Stanhope
Wheatcroft (Darwin Kershaw).

LEECH WOMAN, THE (1960)
        Director: Edward Dein
Coleen Gray (June Talbott), Phillip Terry
(Dr. Paul Talbott), Grant Williams (Neil
Foster), Gloria Talbott (Sally), John Van
Dreelen (Garvey), Estelle Hemsley
(Old Malla), Kim Hamilton (Young Malla),
Chester Jones (Ladu), Arthur Batanides.

LEFT-HANDED FATE (1966-Span. /
        Ger.) (A. K. A. "Fata Morgana")
        Director: Vicente Aranda
Teresa Gimpera, Mirianne Bennet,
Marcos Marti, Alberto Dalbes, Antonio
Ferrandis.

LEGACY, THE (1979) (A. K. A. "The
        Legacy of Maggie Walsh")
        Director: Richard Marquand
Katherine Ross (Maggie Walsh),
Sam Elliott (Pete Danner), John
Standing (Jason Mountolive), Margaret
Tyzack (Nurse Adams), Charles Gray
(Karl), Lee Montague (Jacques),
Roger Daltrey (Clive), Ian Hogg
(Harry), Hildegard Neil (Barbara),
Marianne Broome (Maria), William
Abney (Butler), Patsy Smart (cook),
Reg Harding (gardner), Mathias
Kilroy (stable hand).

LEGACY OF BLOOD (1972)
        Director Carl Monson
Rudolfo Acosta (Sheriff Dan Garcia),
Merry Anders (Laura Dean), Norman
Bartold (Tom Drake), John Carradine
(Christopher Dean), Faith Domergue
(Victoria Dean), Jeff Morrow (Gregory
Dean), Ivy Bethune (Elga), Richard
Davalos (Johnny Dean), Buck Kartalian
(Igor), John Smith (Carl Isenburg),
John Russell (Frank Mantee), Brooke
Mills (Leslie Dean), Mr. Chin (Chin).

LEGACY OF HORROR (1976) (A. K. A.
        "Legacy of Blood")
        Director: Andy Milligan
Elaine Boies, Chris Broderick, Jeanne
Cusick, Marilee Troncone, Julia Curry,
Peter Barcia, Stanley Schwartz, Louise
Gallandra, Dale Hansen.

LEGACY OF SATAN (1973)
        Director: Gerard Damiano
Lisa Christian, John Francis, Paul
Barry.

LEGALLY DEAD (1923)
        Director: William Parke
Milton Sills (Will Campbell), Claire
Adams (Minnie O'Reilly), Brandon
Hurst (Dr. Gelzer), Margaret Camp-
bell (Mrs. Campbell), Edwin Sturgin
(Jack Dorr), Faye O Neill (Jack's
sweetheart), Joseph Girard (District
Attorney), Robert E. Homans (Detective
Powell), Albert Prisco (the Anarchis),
Herbert Fortier (the Judge), Charles
Wellesley (the Governor), Charles A.
Stevenson (Malcolm Steel).

LEGENDARY CURSE OF LEMORA, THE
        (1973) (A. K. A. "Lemora, the Lady
        Dracula", "Lady Dracula")
        Director: Richard Blackburn
Lesley Gilb (Lemora), Cheryl Smith
(Lila), Richard Blackburn (Reverend),
William Whitton (Alvin), Steve Johnson
(ticket man), Maxine Ballantyne (old

lady), Monte Pyke (bus driver), Parker West (young man), John Drury, Jack Fisher, Charla Hall, Alice Barid Johnson, Buck Buchanan.

LEGEND OF BLOOD CASTLE (1974-Span.) (A. K. A. "Female Butcher", "Blood Ceremony")
Director: Jorge Grau
Ewa Aulin, Lucia Bose.

LEGEND OF BOGGY CREEK, THE (1972)
Director: Charles B. Pierce
Willie E. Smith, John P. Hixon, Jeff Crabtree, John W. Oates, Herb Jones, Buddy Crabtree.

LEGEND OF HELL HOUSE, THE (1973)
Director: John Hough
Clive Revill (Dr. Curtis Barnett), Pamela Franklin (Florence Tanner), Roddy McDowall (Ben Fischer), Gayle Hunnicutt (Ann Barnett), Roland Culver (Rudolph Deutsch), Michael Gough (Balasco), Peter Bowles (Hanley).

LEGEND OF HILLBILLY JOHN, THE (1972)
Director: John Newland
Severn Darden (Mr. Marduke), Hedge Capers (John), Denver Pyle (Grand-pappy John), Susan Strasberg (Polly Witse), Alfred Ryder (O. J. Onselm), Percy Rodrigues (Captain Lojoie H. Desplain IV), R. G. Armstrong (Bristowe), Harris Yulin (Zebulon Yandro), Val Avery (Cobart), Chester Jones (Uncle Anansi), William Traylor (Rev. Millen), Sidney Clute (Charles), Sharon Henesy (Lily),

LEGEND OF HORROR (1972)
Director: Bill Davies
Karin Field.

LEGEND OF LIZZIE BORDEN, THE (TVM-1975) - 2-10-75
Director: Paul Wendkos
Elizabeth Montgomery (Lizzie Borden), Fritz Weaver (Andrew Borden), Katherine Helmond (Emma Borden), Helen Craig (Abby Borden), Fionnuala Flanagan (Bridget Sullivan), Don Porter (George Robinson), Ed Flanders (Hosea Knowlton), Alan Hewitt (Mayor Coughlin), Gail Kobe (Alice Russell), Bonnie Bartlett (Sylvia Knowlton), John Beal (Dr. Bowen).

LEGEND OF LYLAH CLARE, THE (1968)
Director: Robert Aldrich

Kim Novak (Lylah Clare/Elsa Brinkmann), Peter Finch (Lewis Zarkan), Ernest Borgnine (Barney Sheean), Milton Selser (Bart Langner), Rosella Falk (Rosella), Valentina Cortese (Countess Bozo Bedoni), Lee Meriwether (young girl), Robert Ellenstein (Mike), David Willock (cameraman), Michael Fox (announcer), Coral Browne (Molly Luther), Ellen Corby (script girl), Gabrielle Tinti (Paolo), Jean Carroll (Becky Langner), Michael Murphy (Mark Peter Sheean), Peter Bravos (Butler), Tom Patty (Bedoni's escort), Queenie Smith (hairdresser), Vernon Scott (himself), Sidney Skolsky (himself), James Lanphier (1st legman), Hal Maguire (2nd legman), Nick Dennis (Nick), Mel Warkmeister, Barbara Ann Warkmeister (aerialists).

LEGEND OF SLEEPY HOLLOW, THE (TVM-1980) - 10-31-80
Director: Henning Scherllerup
Jeff Goldblum (Ichabod Crane), Dick Butkus (Brom Bones), Meg Foster (Katrina Von Tassel), Paul Sand (Frederic), John Sylvester White (Vanderhoof), Laura Campbell (Thelma), Michael Ruud (Palmer).

LEGEND OF SPIDER FOREST, THE (1971) (A. K. A. "Venom")
Director: Peter Sykes
Simon Brent, Neda Arneric, Derek Newark, Sheila Allen.

LEGEND OF THE SEVEN GOLDEN VAMPIRES, THE (1973) (A. K. A. "The Seven Brothers Meet Dracula")
Director: Roy Ward Baker
Peter Cushing (Dr. Van Helsing), Julie Ege (Vannessa Buren), John Forbes-Robertson (Count Dracula), David Chiang (Hsi Ching), Robin Stewart (Leyland Van Helsing), Shin Szu (Mai Kwei), Chan Shen (Kah), Robert Hanna (British Consul).

LEGEND OF THE WEREWOLF (1974)
Director: Freddie Francis
Peter Cushing (Prof. Paul Cantaflanque), David Rintoul (Etoile, the Werewolf), Hugh Griffith (Maestro), Lynn Dalby (Christine), Ron Moody (the Zoo Keeper), Roy Castle (photographer), Renee Houston (Chou-Chou), Patrick Holt (Local Dignitary), Norman Mitchell (Tiny), Stefan Gryff (Insp. Gerard), John Harvey (Prefect of Police), Marjorie Yates (Madame), Mark Weavers (Etoile as a boy).

LEGEND OF THE WOLF WOMAN
(1977-Ital.) (A. K. A. "La Lupa
Mannara")
Director: Rino Di Silvestro
Annik Borel, Dagmar Lassander,
Fred Stafford, Howard Ross, Elio
Zamuto, Osvaldo Ruggieri, Tino
Carraro.

LEMON GROVE KIDS MEET THE
GREEN GRASSHOPPER AND THE
VAMPIRE LADY FROM OUTER
SPACE (1966) - short
Director: Ted Rotter
Ray Dennis Steckler/Cash Flagg,
Carolyn Brandt, Coleman Francis,
Mike Kannon.

LEMON GROVE KIDS MEET THE
MONSTERS, THE (1966) - short
Director: Ray Dennis Steckler
Ray Dennis Steckler/Cash Flagg,
Mike Kannon, Jim Harmon, Gary
Collins, Larry Byrd, Ron Haydock,
Bob Burns.

LEONOR (1975-Span. /Fr. /Ital.)
Director: Juan Bunuel
Liv Ullmann (Leonor), Michel Piccolo
(Richard), Ornella Muti (Catherine),
Antonio Ferrandis (Thomas), Jose
Maria Caffarel (Doctor), Angel Del
Pozo (Chapelain).

LEOPARD LADY, THE (1927)
Director: Rupert Julian
Jacqueline Logan (Paula), Robert
Armstrong (Chris), James Bradbury,
Sr. (Commissioner Berlitz), Alan
Hale, Sr. (Caesar), Dick Alexander,
Hedwig Reicher, Sylvia Ashton, William
Burt.

LEOPARD MAN, THE (1943)
Director: Jacques Tourneur
Dennis O'Keefe, Isabel Jewell (Maria),
Margo (Clo-Clo), Jean Brooks (Kiki),
James Bell (Galbraith), Abner Biber-
man (Charlie How-Come), Tula Parma,
Margaret Landry, Richard Martin.

LET'S KILL UNCLE (1966)
Director: William Castle
Nigel Green (Major Kevin Harrison),
Mary Badham (Chrissie Harrison),
Pat Cardi (Barnaby Harrison), Nestor
Paiva (steward), Linda Lawson (Jus-
tine), Robert Pickering (Sgt. Jack
Travis), Reff Sanches (Ketchman).

LET'S LIVE AGAIN (1947)
Director: Herbert Leeds
John Emery, Hillary Brooks, Taylor

Holmes, Diana Douglas, Jeff Corey,
James Millican, Percy Helton,
John Parrish, Dewey Robinson,
Charles D. Brown, Earle Hodgins,
Ralph D. Sanford.

LET'S SCARE JESSICA TO DEATH
(1971)
Director: John Hancock
Zohra Lampert (Jessica), Barton
Heyman (Duncan), Alan Manson
(Dorker), Kevin O'Connor (Woody),
Gretchen Corbett (vampire girl).

LIBERTY FOR US (1931-Fr.) (A. K. A.
"A Nous la Liberte")
Director: Rene Clair
Henri Marchand, Raymond Cordy,
Paul Olivier, Jacques Shelly, Rolla
France, Leon Lorin, Germaine
Aussey, Alex d'Arcy, Andre Michaud.

LICENSED TO LOVE AND KILL (1979)
(A. K. A. "An Orchid for No. 1")
Director: Lindsay Shonteff
Gareth Hunt, Nick Tate, Fiona
Curzon, Gary Hope, Geoffrey Keene,
John Arnatt.

LICENSE TO KILL (1964-Fr.) (A. K. A.
"Nick Carter Va Tout Casser")
Director: Henri Decoin & Philippe
Senne
Eddie Constantine (Nick Carter),
Daphne Dayle, Yvonne Monlaur,
Vladimir Inkijinoff, Paul Frankeur,
Charles Belmond.

LIFE, LIBERTY AND PURSUIT ON
THE PLANET OF THE APES (1974)
see Television: Planet of the Apes
(1974)

LIFE RETURNS (1935)
Director: Eugene Frenke
Onslow Stevens, George Breakston,
Valerie Hobson, Frank Reicher,
Lois Wilson, Stanley Fields, Richard
Carle, Lois January, Maidel Turner,
Otis Harlan, Dean Benton, Richard
Quine, George McQuarrie, Dr. Robert
E. Cornish.

LIFESPAN (1975-U. S. /Dutch)
Director: Alexander Whitelaw
Klaus Kinski, Tina Aumont, Hiram
Keller, Fons Rademakers, Eric
Schneider.

LIFE WITHOUT SOUL (1915)
Director: Joseph W. Smiley
Percy Darrell Standing (the Creation),
William W. Cohill (Dr. Frankenstein),

Lucy Cotton (Elizabeth), Jack Hopkins
(Victor), George DeCarlton (Franken-
stein's father), Pauline Curley (sister),
David McCauley (servant), Violet De
Biccari (maid).

LIGHT AT THE EDGE OF THE WORLD,
THE (1971-U.S./Span.)
Director: Kevin Billington
Kirk Douglas (Denton), Yul Brynner
(Kongre), Samantha Eggar (Arabella),
Fernando Rey (Capt. Moriz), Jean-
Claude Drouot (Virgilio), Renato
Salvatori (Montefiore), Aldo Sambrell
(Tarcante), Massimo Ranieri (Fe-
lipe), Tito Garcia (Emillo), Tony
Skios (Santos), Victor Israel (Das
Mortes), Luis Barbo (Celsa Larga),
Raul Castro (Malapinha), Alejandro
De Enciso (Morabbito), John Clark
(Matt), Juan Cazalilla (Capt. Lafay-
ette), Oscar Davis (Amando), Tony
Cyrus (Valgolyo), Martin Uvince
(Balduino), Maria Borge (Emily Jane).

LIGHTING BOLT (1966-Ital./Span.)
(A.K.A. "Operazione Goldman")
Director: Anthony Dawson/
Antonio Margheriti
Anthony Eisley (Harry Sennet), Wandisa
Leigh (Patricia), Folco Lulli (Rethe),
Diana Lorys, Ursula Parker, Maria
Caffarel, Oreste Palalla, Renato
Mantalbano, Paco Sanz.

LI'L ABNER (1959)
Director: Melvin Frank
Peter Palmer (Li'l Abner), Leslie
Parrish (Daisy Mae), Stela Stevens
(Appassionata von Climax), Howard
St. John (Gen. Bullnose), Stubby
Kaye (Marryin' Sam), Julie Newmar
(Stupfyin' Jones), Billie Hayes (Mammy
Yokum), Joe E. Marks (Pappy Yokum),
Robert Strauss (Romeo Scragg),
Bern Hoffman (Earthquake McGoon),
Alan Carney (Mayor Dawgmeat),
Carmen Alvarez (Moonbeam McSwine),
Williams Lanteau (Available Jones),
Al Nesor (Evil Eye Fleagle), Ted
Thurston (Sen. Jack S. Phogbound).

LILIOM (1930)
Director: Frank Borzage
Charles Farrell, Rose Hobart, Walter
Abel, Lee Tracy, H.B. Warner,
Guinn Williams, Estelle Taylor, James
Marcus, Dawn O'Day, Mildred Van
Dorn.

LILIOM (1934-Fr.)
Director: Fritz Lang
Charles Boyer (Liliom), Madeliene

Ozeray (Julie), Florelle (Mme.
Muscat), Robert Arnoux (Strong
Arm), Roland Toutain (Sailor),
Henri Richaud (Commissary), Alex-
andre Regnault (Hollinger), Leon
Arvel (clerk), Barency (Purgatory
Cop), Alcover (Alfred), Raoul
Marco (detective), Antouin Artaud
(knife grinder), Rene Stern (cashier),
Richard Darencet.

LION MAN, THE (1936)
Director: John P. McCarthy
Jon Hall, Kathleen Burke, Richard
Carlyle, Eric Snowden, Ted Adams,
Virginia Barton, Jimmy Aubrey,
Lal Chand Mehra, Bobby Fairy,
Henry Hale.

LION'S BREATH, THE (1916)
Director: Horace Davey
Neal Burns (Clarance), Billie Rhodes
(sweetheart), George French (Prof.
Giblets), Ray Gallagher (Spike),
Jean Hathaway (mother).

LIPS OF BLOOD (1972-Fr.) (A.K.A.
"Le Sang des Autres", "The Others'
Blood", "Les Chemins de la Violence",
"The Paths of Violence")
Director: Ken Rudder
Georges Rigaud, Michael Flynn, Manon
Treviere, Catherine Frank, Richard
Vitz, Jacques Bernard.

LISZTOMANIA (1975)
Director: Ken Russell
Roger Daltrey (Liszt), Sara Keselman
(Princess Carolyn), Fiona Lewis
(Countess Marie), Paul Nicholas (Wag-
ner), Veronica Quilligan (Cosima),
Andrew Reilly (Hans), Nell Campbell
(Olga), Ringo Starr (the Pope),
Imogen Claire (George Sand), John
Justin (Count D'Agoult), Anulka
Dziubinska (Lola Montez), Peter
Brayham (bodyguard), David English
(Captain).

LITTLE BIT OF MURDER, A (TVM-
1973) - 3-29-73
Director:
Elizabeth Hartman (Camilla), Roger
Davis (Jeff), Nina Foch (Nellie),
Sharon Farrell (Linda), Sharon Gless
(Mrs. Clay).

LITTLE GIRL WHO LIVES DOWN THE
LANE, THE (1977)
Director: Nicholas Gessner
Jodie Foster (Rynn Jacobs), Martin
Sheen (Frank Hallett), Scott Jocoby
(Mario Podesta), Alexis Smith (Mrs.

Hallet), Mort Shuman (Officer Miglioriti),
Hubert Noel (bank clerk), Jacques Fam-
ery (Bank Clerk), Dorothy Davis (town
hall clerk), Clesson Goodhue (bank
manager), Mary Morter, Judie Wildman (tellers).

LITTLE PRINCE, THE (1974)
    Director: Stanley Donen
Richard Kiley (the Pilot), Steven Warner
(the Little Prince), Gene Wilder (the
Fox), Joss Ackland (the King), Bob
Fosse (the Snake), Donna McKechnie
(the Rose), Clive Revill (the Business-
man), Graham Crowden (the General),
Victor Spinetti (the Historian).

LITTLE SHOP OF HORRORS, THE
    (1960)
    Director: Roger Corman
Jonathan Haze (Seymour Krelboined),
Jackie Joseph (Audrey), Mel Welles
(Mushnik), Dick Miller (Fouch), Myrtle
Vail (Winifred), Leola Wendorff (Mrs.
Shiva), Jack Nicholson (Wilbur Force).

LIVE AGAIN, DIE AGAIN (TVM-1974)
    - 2-16-74
    Director: Richard A. Colla
Donna Mills (Caroline Carmichael),
Walter Pidgeon (Thomas Carmichael),
Gearaldine Page (Sissie O'Neil), Cliff
Potts (Joe Dolan), Mike Farrell (James
Carmichael), Vera Miles (Marcia Car-
michael), Irene Tedrow (Miss Moritz),
Lurene Tuttle (Betty Simpson), Peter
Bromilow (Dr. Fellman), Walker Ed-
miston (Larry Brice), Stewart Moss
(Wilson), Tom Curtis, Florence Luke
(old friends).

LIVE AND LET DIE (1973)
    Director: Guy Hamilton
Roger Moore (James Bond), Yaphet
Kotto (Kananga/Mr. Big), Jane Seymour
(Solitaire), Clifton James (J.W. Pepper),
Julius W. Harris (Tee Hee), Geoffrey
Holder (Baron Samedi), David Hedison
(Felix Leiter), Bernard Lee (M), Lois
Maxwell (Miss Moneypenny), Gloria
Hendry (Rosie), Earl Jolly Brown
(Whisper), Roy Stewart (Quarrel),
Tommy Lane (Adam), Lon Staton (Strut-
ter), Ruth Kempf (Mrs. Bell), Michael
Ebbin (Dambala), B.K. Arnau (singer),
Arnold Williams (cab driver), Madeline
Smith (beautiful girl), Joie Chitwood
(Charlie), Kubi Chaza (sales girl).

LIVES OF JENNY DOLAN, THE (TVM-
    1975) - 10-27-75
    Director: Jerry Jameson
Shirley Jones (Jenny Dolan), Stephen Boyd

(Joe Rossiter), James Darren
(Orlando), Farley Granger (David
Ames), George Grizzard (Ralph
Stantlow), David Hedison (Dr. Wes
Dolan), Lyn Carlin (Nancy Royce),
Stephen McNally (Lt. Nesbitt),
Dana Wynter (Andrea Hardesty),
Paul Carr (Eddie Owens), Charles
Drake (Alan Hardesty), Collin
Wilcox (Mrs. Owens), Ian McShane
(Sanders), Jess Oppenheimer
(Springfield), Pernell Roberts
(camera shop proprietor), Virginia
Grey (landlady), Tony Young (interne).

LIVING DEAD, THE (1933-Ger.)
    (A.K.A. "Funf Unheimliche
    Gerschichten", "Five Sinister
    Stories", "Histoires Estraordin-
    aires")
    Director: Richard Oswald
Paul Wegener, Eugene Klopfer,
Roma Bohn, Harold Paulsen, Roger
Wisten.

LIVING DEAD, THE (1934) (A.K.A.
    "The Scotland Yard Mystery")
    Director: Thomas Bentley
Gerald Du Maurier, Henry Victor,
Grete Natzler, George Curzon, Belle
Crystal, Leslie Perrins, Frederick
Paisley.

LIVING DEAD AT THE MANCHESTER
    MORGUE, THE (1974-Span. /Ital.)
    (A.K.A. "Fin de Semana Para
    los Muertos", "Weekend with the
    Dead", "Don't Open the Window")
    Director: Jorge Grau
Ray Lovelock (George), Arthur Kennedy
(McCormick), Christine Galbo
(Edna), Jeanine Mestre (Katie),
Fernando Hilbeck (Guthrie), Jose
Ruis Lifante (Martin).

LIVING GHOST, THE (1942)
    Director: William Beaudine
James Dunn (Nick Trayne), Jan Wiley
(Tina Craig), Joan Woodbury (Billie
Hilton), Paul McVey (Ed Moline),
Minerva Urecal (Delia Phillips),
George Eldredge (Tony Weldon),
Lawrence Grant (Dr. Bruhling),
Vera Gordon (Sister Lapidus), J.
Farrell MacDonald (Lt. Peterson),
Gus Gassmire (Walter Craig), Norman
Willis (Cedric), Danny Beck (double
talker).

LIVING HEAD, THE (1959-Mex.) (A.K.A.
    "La Cabeza Viviente")
    Director: Chano Ureuta
Abel Salazar, German Robles, Maricio

Garces, Ana Luisa Peluffo, Antonio Raxel.

LIVING IDOL, THE (1957)
Director: Albert Lewis
Steve Forrest (Terry Matthews), Liliane Montevecchi (Juanita), Eduardo Noriega (Manuel), James Robertson Justice (Dr. Alfred Stoner), Sara Garcia (Elena).

LIVING LEGEND, THE (1979)
see Television: Battlestar Galactica (1978-79)

LIZZIE (1957)
Director: Hugo Hass
Eleanor Parker (Elizabeth Richmond), Richard Boone (Dr. Neal Wright), Joan Blondell (Aunt Morgan), Hugo Haas (Walter Brenner), Marion Ross (Ruth Seaton), John Reach (Robin), Ric Roman (Johnny Valenso), Dorothy Arnold (Elizabeth's mother), Jan England (Helen Jameson), Carole Wells (Elizabeth at age 13), Johnny Mathis (nightclub singer), Karen Green (Elizabeth at age 9), Michael Marks (bartender), Dick Paxton (waiter), Gene Walker (guard), Pat Golden (man in bar).

LOCH NESS HORROR, THE (1982)
Director: Larry Buchanan
Sandy Kenyon, Barry Buchanan, Cort Falkenberg, Preston Hansen, Stuart Lancaster, Mickie McKenzie

LODGER, THE (1927)
Director: Alfred Hitchcock
Ivor Novello, Malcolm Keen, Marie Ault, Arthur Chesney.

LODGER, THE (1944)
Director: John Brahm
Laird Cregar (the Lodger), George Sanders (John Warwick), Sir Cedrec Hardwicke (Robert Burton), Merle Oberon (Kitty), Aubrey Mathers (Superintendent Sutherland), Sara Allgood (Ellen), Doris Lloyd (Jennie), Queenie Leonard (Daisy), David Clyde (Sgt. Bates), Frederick Worlock (Sir Edward), Lumsden Hare (Dr. Sheridan), Olaf Hytten (Harris), Colin Campbell (Harold), Helena Pickard (Anne Rowley), Harold De Becker (Charlie), Anita Bolster (Wiggy), Billy Bevan (publican), Edmund Breon (manager), Harry Allen (conductor), Skelton Knaggs (costermonger), Forrester Harvey (cobbler), Charles Hall (comedian).

LOGAN'S RUN (1976)
Director: Michael Anderson
Michael York (Logan), Jenny Agutter (Jessica), Richard Jordan (Francis), Peter Ustinov (Old Man), Roscoe Lee Browne (Box), Michael Anderson, Jr. (Doc), Farrah Fawcett-Majors (Holly), Randolph Roberts (sanctuary man), Lara Lindsay (woman runner), Gary Morgan (Billy), Michelle Stacy (little girl), Denny Arnold (runner No. 1), Glen Wilder (runner No. 2), Bob Neill (sanctuary man), Camilla Carr (sanctuary woman), Greg Michaels, Roger Borden (ambush men), Ann Ford (woman on Lastday), Laura Hippe (New You Shop Customer).

LONDON AFTER MIDNIGHT (1927)
(A.K.A. "The Hypnotist")
Director: Tod Browning
Lon Chaney, Sr. (Insp. Edmund Berke/Col. Yates/"Man in the Beaver Hat"/Moody, the Vampire Man), Henry B. Walthall (Sir James Hamlin), Conrad Nagel (Arthur Hibbs), Marceline Day (Lucille Balfour), Polly Moran (Anne Smithson), Edna Tichenor (Lunette, the Bat Girl), Claude King (the Stranger), Jules Cowles (Gallagher), Percy Williams (the Butler), Andy McLennan (Scotland Yard detective).

LONG HAIR OF DEATH, THE (1964-Ital.) (A.K.A. "I Lunghi Capelli della Morte")
Director: Antonio Margheriti/Anthony Dawson
Barbara Steele, Giorgio Ardisson, Robert Rains, Halina Zalewska, Jean Rafferty.

LONG SWIFT SWORD OF SIEGRIED, THE (1971-Ger.) (A.K.A. "Siegfried und das Sagenhafte Liebesleben der Nibelungen", "The Erotic Adventures of Siegfried")
Director: Adrian Hoven & David Friedman
Raymond Harmstorf, Sybill Danning, Heidi Bohlen.

LOOKER (1981)
Director: Michael Crichton
Albert Finney (Dr. Larry Roberts), James Coburn (John Reston), Leigh Taylor-Young (Jennifer Long), Susan Dey (Cindy), Dorian Harewood (Lt. Masters), Darryl Hickman (Dr. Jim Belfield), Terri Welles (Lisa), Tim Rossovich (moustached man), Kathryn Witt (Tina), Ashley Cox (Candy), Donna Benz (Ellen), Catherine

Parks (Jan), Michael Gainsborough (Sen. Harrison), Terry Kiser (Commercial Director), Georgann Johnson (Cindy's mother), Richard Venture (Cindy's father), Terrence McNally, Anthony Charnota.

LOOK WHAT'S HAPPENED TO ROSE-
MARY'S BABY (TVM-1976) (A.K.A.
"Rosemary's Baby II") - 10-29-76
Director: Sam O'Steen
Stephen McHattie (Adrian/Andrew),
Ruth Gordon (Minnie Castavet),
Ray Milland (Roman Castavet),
Patty Duke Astin (Rosemary Wood-
house), Tina Louise (Marjean Dean),
George Maharis (Guy Woodhouse),
David Huffman (Peter Simon), Donna
Mills (Ellen), Broderick Crawford
(Sheriff Holtzman), Lloyd Haynes
(Laykin), Brian Richards (Dr. Lister),
Philip Boyer (Adrian/Andrew at age 8),

LORD OF THE FLIES (1963)
Director: Peter Brook
James Aubrey (Ralph), Hugh Edwards
(Piggy), Roger Elwin (Roger), Tom
Chapin (Jack), Tom Gaman (Simon),
Roger Allan, Peter Davey, Nicholas
Hammond, Alan Heaps, Burnes, Holly-
man, Richard Horne, David Brunjes,
Kent Fletcher, Christopher Harris,
Jonathan Haep, Andrew Horne, Timothy
Horne, Anthony McCall-Hudson, David
St. Clair, Jeremy Scuse, Peter Ksie-
zopolski, Malcolm Rodker, Rene
Sanfiorenzo, Jr., John Stableford,
Nicholas Valenburg, Edward Valencia,
Jeremy Willis, Patrick Walkenburg,
John Walsh, the Surtess twins.

LORD OF THE RINGS (1978) - Animated
Director: Ralph Bakshi
Voices: Christopher Guard (Frodo Baggins),
William Squire (Gandalf), Michael
Scholes (Samwise Gamges), John Hurt
(Aragorn), Simon Chandler (Meriadoc
Brandybuck), Dominic Guard (Peregrin
Took), Norman Bird (Bilbo Baggins),
Anthony Daniels (Legolas), David
Buck (Gimli), Michael Graham-Cox
(Boromir), Peter Woodthrope
(Gollum), Philip Stone (Treoden),
Andre Morell (Elrond), John Westbrook
(Treebeard), Fraser Kerr (Saruman),
Michael Deacon (Wormtongue), Alan
Tilvern (Innkeeper), Annette Crosbie
(Galadriel), Sharon Baird, Phil
Gale, John A. Neris, Michael Lee
Cogan, Patrick Sullivan Burke, Donn
Whyte, Paul Gale, Billy Barty,
Trey Wilson, Jeri Lea Ray, Patty Ma-
loney, Felix Silla, Larry Larsen,

David Dotson, Tommy Madden, Art
Hern, Mike Clifford, Angelo Ros-
sitto, Gary Jensen, Santy Josol,
John L., Sam Laws, Terry Lionard,
Peter Looney, Dennis Madalone,
Buck Maffei, Chuck Hayward, Eddy
Hice, Pete Risch, Jack Verbons,
Loren Janes, Gregg Walker, Stan
Barrett, Herb Braha, Hank Calia,
Frank Delfino, Russ Earnest, Louis
Elias, Aesop Aquarian, Jerry Maren,
Harry Monty, Frank Morson, Walt
Robles, Mic Rodgers, Lenny Gear,
Eddy Fax, Harriet Gibson, Bob
Haney.

LORD SHANGO (1974)
Director: Raymond Marsh
Lawrence Cook (Jabo), Marlene Clark
(Jenny), Wally Taylor (Memphis),
Avis McCarthur (Billie), John Russell
(Rev. Slater), Bill Overton (Femi),
B.A. Ward (Deacon Davis), Stanley
Greene (Deacon Tibbles), Sandi
Franklin (Bebe), Maurice Woods
(cult leader), Dwayne Oliver
(assistant leader), Ella Mitchell
(lead singer), Ethel Ayler (lady in
bar).

LOST CITY, THE (1935) - serial in
12 episodes
Chapters: 1. "Living Dead Men", 2.
"Tunnel of Death", 3. "Dagger Rock",
4. "Doomed", 5. "Tiger Prey", 6.
"Human Beasts", 7. "Spider Men",
8. "Human Targets", 9. "Jungle
Vengeance", 10. "The Lion Pit", 11.
"The Death Ray" & 12. "The Mad
Scientist".
Director: Harry Revier
Kane Richmond (Bruce Gordon),
William 'Stage' Boyd (Zolok), Claudia
Dell (Natacha), Gabby Hayes (Butter-
field), Eddie Fetherstone (Jerry),
Ralph Lewis (Reynolds), William
Bletcher (Gorzo), Josef Swickard
(Manyus), Milburn Moranti (Andrews),
Margot D'Use (Queen Rama), William
Millman (Colton), Sam Barker (Hugo),
Jerry Frank (Appolyn), Gino Corrado
(Ben Ali), Henry Hall (Officer),
Curly Dresden (Arab), Everett Brown
(Giant).

LOST CITY OF THE JUNGLE (1946) -
serial in 13 episodes
Chapters: 1. "Himalaya Horror", 2.
"The Death Flood", 3. "Wave Length
for Doom", 4. "The Pit of Pendrang",
5. "Fiery Danger", 6. "Death's
Shining Face", 7. "Speedboat Missing",
8. "Fire Jet Torture", 9. "Zalabar

Death Watch", 10. "Booby Trap Rendez-
vous", 11. "Pendrang Guillotine", 12.
"Jungle Smash-Up" & 12. "Atomic
Vengeance".
Director: Ray Taylor & Lewis
D. Collins
Russell Hayden (Rod Stanton), Jane
Adams (Marjorie Elmore), Lionel
Atwill (Sir Eric Hazarias), Keye Luke
(Tai Sahn), John Miljan (Caffron),
John Eldredge (Dr. Elmore), Ralph
Lewis (Kurtz), Helen Bennett (Indra),
John Gallaudet (Grebb), Ted Hecht
(Dr. Harris), George Sorel (Sir Eric
Hazarias - completed role when Atwill
died during production), Gene Roth,
Arthur Space, John Mylong, George
Lynn, Dick Curtis, Frank Lackteen.

LOST CONTINENT (1951)
Director: Sam Newfield
Eric Porter (Capt. Larsen), Hildegard
Neff (Eva Webster), Suzanna Leigh
(Unity), Tony Beckley (Harry Tyler),
Benito Carruthers (Rinaldi), Nigel Stock
(Dr. Webster), Dana Gillespie (Sarah),
Jimmy Hanley (Pat), Neil McCallum
(1st Officer Hemmings), James Cossins
(Chief), Victor Maddern (Mate), Michael
Ripper (sea lawyer), Reg Lye (helms-
man), Donald Sumpter (Sparks), Charles
Houston (Braemer), Norman Eshley
(Jonathan), Alf Joint (Jason), Shivendra
Sinha (Jurri Curri), Eddie Powell
(Inquisitor), Darryl Read (El Diablo),
Frank Hayden (Sergeant), Mark Heath,
Horace James (customs men).

LOST HORIZON (1937)
Director: Frank Capra
Ronald Colman (Robert Conway), Jane
Wyatt (Sondra), John Howard (George
Conway), H. B. Warner (Chang), Edward
Everett Horton (Lovett), Thomas Mitchell
(Barnard), Margo (Maria), Isabel Jewell
(Gloria), Sam Jaffe (High Lama), Hugh
Buckler (Lord Gainsford), John Miltern
(Carstairs), Val Duran (Talu), David
Torrence (Prime Minister), Noble John-
son (leader of porters), Willie Fung
(bandit leader), Max Rabinowitz (Sei-
veking), John Burton (Wynant), John
Tettener (Montaigne), John T. Murray
(Meeker), Wyrley Birch, Margaret
McWade, Carl Stockdale, Ruth Robinson
(missionaries), David Clyde (steward),
Neil Fitzgerald (radio operator), Leonard
Mudie (Foreign Secretary), Boyd Irwin,
Sr.,(Assistant Foreign Secretary),
Lawrence Grant (1st man), Dennis D'Au-
burn (aviator), Victor Wong (bandit
leader), Milton Owen (Fenner), Mary
Lou Dix, Beatrice Blinn, Beatrice

Curtis Arthur Rankin (passengers),
Eric Wilton (Englishman), George
Chan (Chinese priest), Richard Loo
(Shanghai airport official), Chief
Big Tree (porter), Darby Clark
(Radio Operator).

LOST HORIZON (1973)
Director: Charles Jarrott
Peter Finch (Richard Conway),
Liv Ullman (Catherine), Michael
York (George Conway), Sir John
Gielgud (Chang), George Kennedy
(Sam Cornelius), Sally Kellerman
(Sally Hughes), Olivia Hussey (Maria),
Bobby Van (Harry Lovett), James
Shigeta (Brother To-Linn), Charles
Boyer (High Lama), Kent Smith (Mr.
Ferguson), John Van Dreelan (Dr.
Virdon).

LOST JUNGLE, THE (1934) - serial
in 12 episodes
Chapters: 1. "Noah's Ark Island", 2.
"Nature in the Raw", 3. "The
Hypnotic Eye", 4. "The Pit of Croco-
diles", 5. "Gorilla Warfare", 6. "The
Battle of Beasts", 7. "The Tiger's
Prey", 8. "The Lion's Brood", 9.
"Eyes of the Jungle", 10. "Human
Hyenas", 11. "The Gorilla" & 12. "Take
Them Back Alive".
Director: Armand Schaefer &
David Howard
Clyde Beatty (Clyde Beatty), Syd
Saylor (Larry Henderson), Wheeler
Oakman (Kirby), Mickey Rooney
(Mickey), Cecilia Parker (Ruth
Robinson), Warner Richmond (Shar-
key), Maston Williams (Thompson),
Lloyd Whitlock (Howard), Edward J.
LeSaint (Capt. Robinson), J.
Crauford Kent (explorer), Lloyd
Ingraham (Bannister), Lew Meehan
(Flynn), Wes Warner (jackman),
Jim Corey (Steve), Ernie S. Adams
(Pete), Harry Holman (Maitland),
Wally Wales (Sandy), Jack Carlyle
(the cook), Max Wagner (Slade),
Charles Whittaker (Slim).

LOST MISSILE, THE (1958)
Director: Lester Berke
Robert Loggia (David Loring), Ellen
Parker (Joan Woods), Larry Kerr
(Gen. Barr), Philip Pine (Joe Freed),
Selmer Jackson (Secretary of State),
Marilee Earle (Ella Freed), Kitty
Kelly (Ella's mother), Bill Bradley
(Bradler), Joe Hyams (Young), Fred
Engleberg (TV personality).

LOST MOMENT, THE (1947)

Director: Martin Gabel
Robert Cummings (Lewis), Susan
Hayward (Tina), Agnes Moorehead
(Juliana), Eduardo Ciannelli (Father
Rinaldo), Frank Puglia (Pietro),
John Archer (Charles), Minerva
Urecal (Maria), Joan Lorring (Amelia),
William Edmunds (Vittorio), Eugene
Bordon, Chris Drake, Martin Garralaga,
Julian Rivero, Nicholas Khadarik,
Lillian Molieri.

LOST PLANET, THE (1953) - serial
  in 15 episodes
Chapters: 1. "The Mystery of the Guided
Missile", 2. "Trapped by the Axial
Propeller", 3. "Blasted by the Thermic
Disintergrator", 4. "The Mind Control
Machine", 5. "The Atomic Plane",
6. "Disaster in the Stratosphere", 7.
"Snared by the Pryamic Catapult", 8.
"Astray in Space", 9. "The Hypnotic
Ray Machine", 10. "To Free the Planet
People", 11. "Dr. Grood Defies Gra-
vity", 12. "Trapped in a Cosmic Jet",
13. "The Invisible Enemy", 14. "In
the Grip of the De-Thermo Ray" &
15. "Sentenced to Space".
    Director: Spencer Gordon Bennet
Judd Holdren (Rex Barrow), Vivian
Mason (Ella Dorn), Gene Roth (Rec-
kow), Michael Fox (Dr. Grood), Pierre
Watkin (Ned Hilton), Leonard Penn
(Ken Wolper), I. Stanford Jolley
(Robot No. 9), Ted Thorpe (Tim
Johnson), Karl Davis (Karlo), For-
rest Taylor (Prof. Dorn), John
Cason (Hopper), Joseph Mell (Lah),
Nick Stuart (Darl), Jack George (Jarva),
Frederic Berest (Alden).

LOST PLANET OF THE GODS (1979)
  see Television: Battlestar Galactica
  (1978-79)

LOST SHADOW, THE (1921-Ger.)
  (A.K.A. "Der Verlorene Schatten")
    Director: Paul Wegener
Paul Wegener, Lyda Salmanova,
Grete Schroder, Hannes Sterm,
Werner Schock.

LOST TRIBE, THE (1949)
    Director: William Berke
Johhny Weismuller (Jungle Jim), Myrna
Dell (Norina), Elena Verdugo (Li
Wanna), Joseph Vitale (Calhoun), Ralph
Dunn (Capt. Rawling), Paul Marion
(Chot), George J. Lewis (Whip Wilson),
Wally West (Eckle), Nelson Leigh
(Zoron), George De Normand (Cullen),
Rube Schaffer (Lerch).

LOST WORLD, THE (1925)
    Director: Harry O. Hoyt
Wallace Beery (Prof. Challenger),
Bessie Love (Paula White), Lloyd
Hughes (Ed Malone), Lewis Stone
(Sir John Roxton), Arthur Hoyt
(Prof. Summerlee), George Bunny
(Colin McArdle), Bull Montana
(Apeman), Margaret McWade (Mrs.
Challenger), Jules Cowles (Zambo),
Alma Bennett (Gladys Hungerford),
Charles Wellesley (Major Hibbard),
Finch Smiles (Austin, the Butler),
Virginia Brown Faire (Marquette).

LOST WORLD, THE (1960)
    Director: Irwin Allen
Claude Rains (Prof. Challenger),
Michael Rennie (Lord Roxton),
Jill St. John (Jennifer Holmes),
David Hedison (Ed Malone), Fernando
Lamas (Gomez), Richard Haydn (Prof.
Summerlee), Ray Stricklyn (David
Holmes), John Graham (Stuart
Holmes), Jay Novello (Costa), Ian
Wolfe (Burton White), Vitina Marcus
(Native Girl), Colin Campbell (Prof.
Waldron).

LOST WORLD OF SINBAD, THE (1963-
  Jap.) (A.K.A. "Daitozoku", "Sam-
  urai Pirate")
    Director: Senkichi Taniguchi
Toshiro Mifune (Sukezaemon/Luzon),
Jun Tazaki, Jun Funando, Makoto
Stach, Ichiro Arishima, Kumi
Mizuno, Mitsuko Kusabue, Takashi
Shimura, Tadao Nakamura, Miye
Hama, Eiko Wakabayashi.

LOST ZEPPELIN, THE (1929)
    Director: Edward Sloman
Conway Tearle (Commander Hall),
Virgina Valli (Miriam Hall),
Ricardo Cortez (Tom Armstrong),
Duke Martin (Lt. Wallace), Winter
Hall (Mr. Wilson), Kathryn McGuire
(Nancy).

LOVE AT FIRST BITE (1979)
    Director: Stan Dragoti
George Hamilton (Count Dracula),
Susan St. James (Cindy Sondheim),
Richard Benjamin (Dr. Jeff Rosenberg),
Arte Johnson (Renfield), Dick Shawn
(Lt. Ferguson), Isabel Sanford
(Judge), Sherman Hensley (Rev.
Mike), Eric Laneuville (Russell),
Barry Gordon (flashlight vendor),
Michael Pataki (mobster), Robert
Ellenstein (VW man), Rolfe Sedan
(Maitre'd), Bob Basso (TV repair-
man), Hazel Shermet (lady in

elevator), Ronny Schell (gay in elevator), Bryan O'Byrne (priest), Stanley Brock (cab driver), Lidia Kristen (woman commissar), Whitney Rydbeck (male commissar), Susan Tolsky (model agent), Laurie Beach (little girl), David Ketchum (customs inspector), Danny Dayton (Billy), Robin Dee Adler (woman in nightgown), John Anthony Bailey (New York thug), Charlie Dell (busboy), John Dennis (motorcycle cop), Paul Barselow (bloodbank guard), Shelly Garrett (New York thug), Jacque Lynn Colton (woman with cat), Rose Michton (elderly lady), Tiger Joe Marsh (citizen at castle), Dino Natali (man outside castle), Deborah Kim Moore (nurse), Ding Dingle (TWA agent), Joe Medalis (intern), Robert Nadder (Bellevue doctor), Judy Penrod (stewardess), Michael Heit (busboy No. 2), Ralph Manza (Limo driver), Hal Ralston (police sergeant), Merrie Lynn Ross (lady in apartment), Cicely Wolper (grandmother), Lavelle Roby (mourner), Ed Marshall (news reporter), David Lansberg (Marty), Alan Haufrect (photographer), Jerold Pearson (hippie in customs).

LOVE BUG, THE (1968)
    Director: Robert Stevenson
Dean Jones (Jim Douglas), Michele Lee (Carole Bennett), David Tomlinson (Peter Thorndyke), Buddy Hackett (Tennessee Steinmetz), Joe Flynn (Havershaw), Benson Fong (Mr. Wu), Joe E. Ross (detective), Barry Kelley (police sergeant), Iris Adrian (carhop), Ned Glass, Robert Foulk, Gary Owens, Pedro Gonzalez-Gonzalez, Alan Fordney, Gil Lamb, P. L. Renoudet, Andy Granatelli, Nicole Jaffe, Russ Caldwell, Wally Boag, Brian Fong, Stan Duke, Max Balchowsky, Chick Hearn.

LOVE CAPTIVE, THE (1934)
    Director: Max Marcin
Nils Asther (Dr. Alexis Collender), Gloria Stuart (Alice Trask), Paul Kelly (Dr. Norman Ware), Alan Dinehart (Roger Loft), John Wray (Jules Glass), Addison Richards (Doctor), Russ Brown (Larry Chapman), Franklyn Ardell (Pete Noland), Robert Greig (Butler), Renee Gadd (Valerie Loft),

LOVE, DEATH AND THE DEVIL
    (1934-Ger.) (A. K. A. "Liebe, Tod und Teufel")
    Director: Heinz Hilpert &

Reinhart Steinbicker
Brigette Horney, Kathe von Nagy, Albin Skoda, Rudolf Platte, Erich Ponto, Klaus Hellmer.

LOVE DOCTOR, THE (1917)
    Director: Paul Scardonl
Earle Williams, Patsy De Forest, Corinne Griffith, Adele De Garde, Evart Overton, Webster Campbell, Frank McDonald.

LOVE FROM A STRANGER (1936)
    Director: Rowland V. Lee
Basil Rathbone (Gerald Lovell), Ann Harding (Carol Howard), Bruce Seton (Ronald Bruce), Joan Hickson (Emmy), Binnie Hale (Kate Meadows), Bryan Powley (Dr. Gribble), Donald Calthrop (Bobson), Jean Cadell (Aunt Lou), Eugene Leahy (Mr. Tuttle).

LOVE OF SUNYA, THE (1927)
    Director: Albert S. Parker
Gloria Swanson (Sunya Ashling), John Boles (Paul Judson), Ian Keith (Louis Anthony), Ivan Lebedeff (Howard Morgan), Anders Randolf (Robert Goring), Flobelle Fairbanks (Rita Ashling), Raymond Hackett (Kenneth Ashling), Hugh Miller (the Outcast), Andre de Segurola (Paolo de Salvo), Pauline Garon (Anne Hagen), Robert Schable (Henri Picard), John Miltern (Asa Ashling), Basil Rathbone.

LOVE SLAVES OF THE AMAZON
    (1957)
    Director: Curt Siodmak
Don Taylor (Dr. Pete Masters), Eduardo Ciannelli (Crespi), Gianna Segale (Gina), Tom Payne (Mario), Harvey Chalk (Adhennar Silva), Wilson Viana (Fernando), Anne Marie Nabuco (Queen), John Herbert (hotel clerk), Eugenia Carlos (Fernando's brother), Gilda Nery (ugly girl), Louis Serrano (pilot).

LOVES OF EDGAR ALLAN POE, THE
    (1942)
    Director: Harry Lachman
Shepperd Strudwick (Edgar Allan Poe), Jane Darwell (Mrs. Clem), Frank Conroy (Joe), Henry Morgan (Burling), Mary Howard (Frances), Virginia Gilmore, Linda Darnell, Walter Kingsford, Morris Ankrum, Hardie Albright, William Bakewell, Gilbert Emery, Francis Ford, Freddie Mercer, Peggy McIntyre, Morton Lowry, Harry Denny, Skippy Wanders, Erville Alderson,

Frank Melton, Edwin Stanley.

LOVES OF HERCULES, THE (1960-
Ital. /Fr.) (A. K. A. "Gli Amore
di Ercole")
Director: Carlo Ludovico Bra-
gaglia
Jayne Mansfield, Mickey Hargitay,
Massimo Serato, Moira Orfei, Ros-
sella Como.

LOVE WAR, THE (TVM-1970) -
3-10-70
Director; George McCowan
Lloyd Bridges (Kyle), Angie Dickinson
(Sandy), Bill McClean (Reed), Harry
Basch (Bal), Dan Travanty (Tod),
Allen Jaffe (Hort), Byron Foulger,
Pepper Martin.

LUANA, VIRGIN OF THE JUNGLE
(1968-Ital.) (A. K. A. "Luana,
la Figlis della Foresta Vergine")
Director: Bob Raymond
Mei Chin (Luana), Evi Marandi (Isabelle), Glenn Saxon (George), Pietro
Tordi, Raf Baldassare.

LUCAN (TVM-1977) - 5-22-77
Director: David Greene
Kevin Brophy (Lucan), Stockard
Channing (Mickey), Ned Beatty (Larry
McElwaine), William Jordan (Gene
Boone), Lou Frizzell (Casey), John
Randolph (Dr. Hoagland), Ben David-
son (Coach Dalton), Hedley Mattingly
(Pres. Davies), George Wyner (Rant-
zen), John Finnegan (Jess), Richard C.
Adams (Coffin), Todd Olsen (Lucan
at age 10), George Reynolds (policeman),
Virginia Hawkins (woman).

LUCIFER COMPLEX, THE (1978)
Director: David L. Hewitt &
Kenneth Hartford
Robert Vaughn (Glenn Manning),
Keenan Wynn (the Chief), Merrie
Lynn Ross (April), Aldo Ray (Karl),
William Lanning, Victoria Carroll,
Glen Ranson, Lynn Cartwright, Ross
Durfee, Kieu Chinh, Colin Eliot Brown,
Gustof Unger, Carol Terry, Corinne
Cole, Bertil Unger, Chellio Campbell.

LUCK OF THE IRISH, THE (1948)
Director: Henry Koster
Tyrone Power (Stephen Fitzgerald),
Anne Baxter (Nora), Cecil Kellaway
(Horace, the Leprechaun), Lee J.
Cobb (David Augur), Jayne Meadows
(Francis Augur), James Todd (Bill),
J. M. Kerrigan, Phil Brown, Norman
Leavitt, Charles Irwin, Tim Ryan,

Margaret Wells, Louise Lorimer,
Harry Antrim, John Goldsworthy,
Bill Swingley, Tom Stevenson,
Douglas Gerrard, Hollis Jewell,
Frank Mitchell, Tito Vuolo, An-
drew Branham, Ruth Clifford,
Dorothy Neumann, Ann Frederick,
John Roy, Lee MacGregor, Eddie
Parks, Claribel Bressel, Jimmy
O'Brien.

LULU (1962-Australia)
Director; Rolf Thiele
Nadja Tiller (Lulu), Hildegard
Knef (Baroness), O. E. Hasse
(Schon), Georges Regnier (Jack
the Ripper), Mario Adorf (trainer),
Rudolph Forster (father), Leon
Askin (son).

LULU (1980-Fr. /Ger. /Ital.)
Director: Walerian Borowczyk
Ann Bennent (Lulu), Michele Placido
(Schwarz), Udo Kier (Jack the
Ripper), Jean-Jacques Delbo (Goll),
Hans Jurgen Schatz (Alwa), Heinz
Bennent (Schon), Beate Kopp (Gesch-
witz).

LURKING VAMPIRE, THE (1959-
Arg.) (A. K. A. "El Vampiro
Acecha")
Director:
German Robles, Nesor Zarrade,
Abel Salazar, Blanco del Pardo.

LUST FOR A VAMPIRE (1970) (A. K. A.
"To Love a Vampire")
Director: Jimmy Sangster
Ralph Bates (Giles Barton), Yutte
Stensgaard (Carmilla Karnstein/
Mircalla), Barbara Jefford (Countess
Herritzen), Michael Johnson (Richard
Lestrange), Susanna Leigh (Janet
Playfair), Mike Raven (Count Karn-
stein), David Healy (Pelley), Luan
Peters (Trudi), Eric Chitty (Prof.
Hertz), Pippa Steel (Susan), Chris-
topher Neame (Hans), Helen Christie
(Mrs. Simpson), Michael Brennan
(landlord), Jonathan Cecil (Arthur
Biggs), Carol Little (Isabel),
Harvey Hall (Heinrich), Christopher
Cunningham (coachman), Judy
Matheson (Amanda), Jack Melford
(the Bishop), Erica Beale, Melita
Clarke, Jackie Leapman, Patricia
Warner, Vivienne Chandler, Melinda
Churcher, Christine Smith, Sue
Longhurst (schoolgirls).

LUST OF THE AGES, THE (1917)
Director: Harry Revier

Lillian Walker (Lois Craig), Jack Mowers (Byron Master).

M (1931-Ger.)
Director: Fritz Lang
Peter Lorre (Franz Becker), Ellen Widmann (mother), Theodor Loos, Inge Landgut, Herta von Walter, Gustaf Grundgens, Otto Wernicke, Paul Kemp, Fritz Gnass, Fritz Odemar.

M (1951)
Director: Joseph Losey
David Wayne (M), Martin Gabel (Marshall), Howard da Silva (Carney), Luther Adler (Langley), Glenn Anders (Riggert), Walter Burke (McMahan), Steve Brodie (Lt. Becker), Raymond Burr (Pottsy), Norman Lloyd (Sutro), Karen Morley.

MACABRA (1980) (A. K. A. "Demonoid")
Director: Alfredo Zacharias
Samantha Eggar (Jennifer Baines), Stuart Whitman (Father Cunningham), Roy C. Jenson (Mark Baines), Erika Carlsson (Nurse Morgan), Lew Saunders (Sgt. Leo Matson), Narcisco Busquets (Dr. Julian Rivkin), Ted White (Frankie), Haji Catton (Angela), Jose Chavez Trowe (Pepe), George Soviak (Sgt. Needham), Al Jones (Patrolman Yates), Whitey Hughes (gambler).

MACABRE (1958)
Director: William Castle
William Prince (Dr. Rodney Barrett), Jim Backus (Sheriff Jim Tyloe), Jacqueline Scott (Polly Baron), Philip Tonge (Jode Wetherby), Susan Morrow (Sylvia Stevenson), Ellen Corby (Miss Kushins), Christine White (Nancy Wetherby), Howard Hoffman (Humelm), Jonathan Kidd (Ed Quigley), Linda Guderman (Marge), Dorothy Morris (Alice Barrett), Voltaire Perkins (Preacher).

MACABRE DR. SCIVANO, THE (1971-Braz.) (A. K. A. "O Macabro Dr. Scivano")
Director: Raul Calhado & Rosalvo Cacador
Raul Calhado, Luiz Leme, Henricao, Oswaldo De Souza, Lauro Sawaya, Genesio Aladim.

MACABRE TRUNK, THE (1936-Mex.) (A. K. A. "El Baul Macabro")
Director: Miguel Zacarias
Ramon Pereda, Rene Cardona, Manuel Noreiga, Esther Fernandez, Juanito

Castro, Carlos Lopez.

MACISTE AND THE KING OF SAMAR (1964-It°l. /Fr.) (A. K. A. "Maciste e la Regina di Samar")
Director: Giacomo Gentilomo
Sergio Ciani/Alan Steel (Maciste), Jany Clair, Jean-Pierre Honore, Anna Maria Polani, Mario Tamberlani, Delia D'Alberti.

MACISTE, SPARTAN GLADIATOR (1964-Ital. /Fr.) (A. K. A. "Maciste, Gladiatore di Sparta")
Director: Mario Caiano
Mark Forest, Marilu Tolo, Claudio Undari, Elisabeth Fanti, Ugo Attanasio, Ferruccio Amendola,

MACISTE IN HELL (1926-Ital.) (A. K. A. "Maciste all' Inferno")
Director: Guido Brignone
Umberto Guarracino, Mario Salo, Domenico Serra, Pauline Polaire, Bartolomeo Pagano.

MACUMBA LOVE (1960)
Director: Douglas Fowley
Walter Reed (Weils), Ziva Rodann (Venus de Viasa), William Wellman, Jr. (Sarah's husband), June Wilkinson (Sarah), Ruth de Souza (Mama Rataloy).

MAD ABOUT MEN (1954)
Director: Ralph Thomas
Glynis Johns (Miranda/Caroline), Anne Crawford (Barbara), Donald Sinden (Jeff), Margaret Rutherford (Nurse Cary), Noel Purcell (Old Salt), Irene Handl (Madame Blanche), David Hurst (Mantalini), Martin Miller (Dr. Fergus), Joan Hickson (Mrs. Forster), Dora Bevan (Berengaria), Nicholas Phipps (Barclay), Peter Martyn (Ronald), Deryck Guvler (editor), Judith Furst (Viola), Harry Welchman (Symes), Anthony Oliver (pawnbroker).

MADAME SIN (TVM-1972) - 1-15-72
Director: David Greene
Bette Davis (Madame Sin), Robert Wagner (Anthony Lawrence), Denholm Elliott (Malcolm DeVere), David Healey (Braden), Catherine Schell (Barbara), Charles Lloyd Pack (Willoughby), Gordon Jackson (Cmdr. Teddy Cavendish), Dudley Sutton (Monk), Paul Maxwell (Connors), Roy Kinnear (Holidaymaker), Arnold Diamond (Lengett), Alan Dobie (White), Pik-Sen Lim

(Nikko), Fred Middlemass (Dr. Henriques), Al Mancini (fisherman).

MAD BUTCHER, THE (1972) (A. K. A.
"Meat Is Meat")
	Director: Guido Zurli
Victor Buono (Otto Lehman), Brad
Harris (Mike Warren), Karin Field
(Mrs. Lehman), Franca Polcelli,
Sybil Martin, Arthur Mann, Carl
Stearns, Michael Turner.

MADCAP MODELS (1941-43) - shorts
	Producer: George Pal

MAD DOCTOR, THE (1940)
	Director: Tim Whelan
Basil Rathbone (Dr. George Sebastian),
Ellen Drew (Linda Boothe), John
Howard (Gil Sawyer), Martin Kosleck
(Maurice Gretz), Ralph Morgan (Dr.
Charles Downer), Barbara Jo Allen
(Louise Watkins), Kitty Kelly (Winnie), Hugh Sothern (Hatch), Hugh
O'Connell (Lawrence Watkin).

MAD DOCTOR OF BLOOD ISLAND,
	THE (1969-Phil. /U. S.)
	Director: Eddie Romero &
		Gerardo de Leon
John Ashley (Dr. Bill Foster), Angelique Pettyjohn (Sheila Willard),
Eddie Garcia (Dr. Lorca), Ronald
Remy, Alicia Alonzo.

MAD DOCTOR OF MARKET STREET,
	THE (1942)
	Director: Joseph H. Lewis
Lionel Atwill (Dr. Graham/Dr.
Benson), Una Merkel (Margaret
Wentworth), Nat Pendleton (Red
Hogan), Claire Dodd (Patricia
Wentworth), Hardie Albright (William
Saunders), Richard Davies (Jim),
Anne Nagel (Mrs. Saunders), John
Eldredge (Dwight), Al Kikume (Kalo),
Noble Johnson (Elon), Milton Kibbee
(Hadley), Rosina Galli (Tanao), Ray
Mala (Bareb), Byron Shores (Crandall), Tani Marsh, Billy Bunkley
(Tahitian dancers), Boyd Davis,
Bess Flowers, Alan Bridge.

MAD EXECUTIONERS, THE (1963-
	Ger.) (A. K. A. "Der Henker von
	London", "The Hangman of London")
	Director: Edwin Zbonek
Wolfgang Preiss (Morel Smith),
Chris Howland (Cabby Pennypacker),
Maria Perchy (Ann Barry), Dieter
Borsche (Dr. MacFergusson), Harry
Riebauer (Dr. Philip Trooper),
Hansjorg Felmy (John Hillier), Rudolf

Forster (Sir Frank Barry), Alexander Engel (Broker), Rudolf Fernau
(Jerome), Stanislav Ledinek (Jimmy
Brown), Albert Bessler (murderer),
Jan Hendricks (Joe the Knife).

MAD GENIUS, THE (1931)
	Director: Michael Curtiz
John Barrymore (Tsarakov),
Marian Marsh (Nana), Donald
Cook (Fedor), Boris Karloff
(Fedor's father), Charles Butterworth (Karimsky), Carmel Myers
(Preskoya), Luis Alberni (Bankiff),
Frankie Darro (Fedor as a child),
Mae Madison (Olga), Andre Luget
(Count Renaud).

MAD GHOUL, THE (1943)
	Director: James P. Hogan,
David Bruce (Ted Allison), George
Zucco (Dr. Alfred Morris), Evelyn
Ankers (Isabel Lewis), Turhan
Bey (Eric Iverson), Robert Armstrong
(Ken McClure), Charles McGraw
(Detective Garrity), Milburn Stone
(Sgt. Macklin), Addison Richards
(Gavigan), Rose Hobart (Della),
Andrew Tombes.

MADHOUSE (1974)
	Director: Jim Clark
Vincent Price (Paul Toombes), Peter
Cushing (Herbert Flay), Robert
Quarry (Oliver Quayle), Adrienne
Corri (Faye Flay), Natasha Pyne
(Julia), Julie Crosthwaite (Ellen),
Linda Harrison (Elizabeth Peters),
Catherine Wilmer (Louise Peters),
John Garrie (Insp. Harper),
Barry Dennen (Blount), Ian Thompaon (Bradshaw), Michael Parkinson
(TV interviewer), Ellis Dayle (Alfred Peters), Jenny Lee Wright
(Carol), Peter Halliday (psychiatrist).

MAD LOVE (1935) (A. O. A. "The
	Hands of Orlac")
	Director: Karl Freund
Peter Lorre (Dr. Gogol), Colin
Clive (Stephen Orlac), Frances
Drake (Yvonne Orlac), Ted Healy
(Reagan), Edward S. Brophy
(Rollo), Sarah Haden (Marie), Henry
Kolker (Prefect Rosset), May Beatty
(Francoise), Key Luke (Dr. Wong),
Isabel Jewell, Rollo Lloyd, Clarence
H. Wilson, Sam Ash, Ian Wolfe,
Sara Padden, Billy Gilbert, Charles
Trowbridge, Frank Darien, Carl
Stockdale, Robert Emmett Keane,
Harold Huber, Hooper Atchley,

Otto Hoffman.

MAD MAGICIAN, THE (1954)
Director: John Brahm
Vincent Price (Gallico), Mary Murphy
(Karen), John Emery (Rinaldi),
Lenita Lane (Alice Prentiss), Jay
Novello (Mr. Prentiss), Eva Gabor
(Claire), Donald Randolph (Ormond),
Patrick O'Neal (Bruce).

MADMAN (1982)
Director: Joe Giannone
Alexis Dubin (Betsy), Tony Fish
(T. P.), Seth Jones (Dave), Harriet
Bass (Stacey), Jan Claire (Ellie),
Jimmy Steele (Richie), Alex Murphy
(Bill), Paul Ehlers (Madman Marz),
Carl Fredericks (Max), Michael
Sullivan (Cook).

MADMAN OF LAB 4, THE (1967-Fr.)
(A. K. A. "Le Fou du Labo '4")
Director: Jacques Besnard
Pierre Brasseur (Father), Jean
Lefebvre (Fou), Maria Latour (Regina),
Bernard Blier (Chief), Margo Lion
(Mother), Michel Serrault (Boss).

MAD MAX (1979-Australia)
Director: George Miller
Mel Gibson (Max), Hugh Keays-Byrne
(the Toecutter), Joan Samuel (Jessie),
Steve Bisley (Jim Goose), Roger
Ward (Fifi Macaffe), Tim Burns
(Johnny the Boy), Geoff Parry (Bubba
Zanetti), Paul Johnstone (Cundalini),
John Ley (Charlie), Jonathon Hardy
(Labatoche), Sheila Florence (May
Swaisey), Vince Gil (Nightrider),
Reg Evans (station master), Stephen
Clark (Sarse), Howard Eynon (Dia-
bando), John Farndale (Grinner),
Max Fairchild (Benno), Jerry Day
(Ziggy), Peter Flemingham (senior
doctor), Phil Motherwell (junior
doctor), Mathew Constantine (toddler),
Nic Gazzana (Starbuck), Hunter Gibb
(Liar), David Cameron (underground
mechanic), Robina Chaffey (singer),
Bertrand Cadart (Clunk), David Bracks
(Mudguts), Brendan Heath (Sprog),
Steve Millicamp (Roop), Lulu Pinkus
(Nightrider's girl), George Novak
(Scuttle), Nick Lathouris (Grease Rat),
Lisa Aldenhoven (nurse), Andrew Gil-
more (Silvertongue), Nein Thompson
(TV newsreader), Gil Tucker (Peo-
ple's Overseer), Billy Tisdall (Midge),
Kim Sullivan (girl in chevy).

MADMEN OF MANDORAS (1963)
(A. K. A. "They Saved Hitler's Brain")

Director: David Bradley
Walter Stocker (Phil Daly), Audrey
Claire (Kathy Day), John Holland
(John Coleman), Carlos Rivas
(Camino), Dani Lynn (Suzanne
Coleman), Marshall Reed (Frank
Dvorak), Scott Peters (David
Garrick), Nestor Paiva (Police
Chief Alaniz), Keith Dahle (Tom
Sharon), Pedro Regas (Padua),
Bill Freed (Mr. H.).

MAD MONSTER, THE (1942)
Director: Samuel Newfield
George Zucco (Dr. Lorenzo Cameron),
Glenn Strange (Pedro), Mae Busch,
Johnny Downs, Anne Nagel, Sarah
Padden, Henry Hall, Robert Strange,
Reginald Barlow, Edward Cassidy.

MAD MONSTER PARTY? (1967) -
animated
Director: Jules Bass
Voices: Boris Karloff, Phyllis
Diller, Gale Garnett, Alan Swift.

MADNESS FROM TERROR (1960-
Mex.) (A. K. A. "Locura del
Terror")
Director: Julian Soler
Tin Tan, Andres Soler, Loco Valdes,
Sonia Fuiro, David Silva, Veronica
Loyo.

MAD ROOM, THE (1969)
Director: Bernard Girard
Stella Stevens (Ellen Hardy), Shelly
Winters (Mrs. Gladys Armstrong),
Michael Burns (George), Severn
Darden (Nate), Carol Cole (Chris),
Barbara Sammeth (Mandy), Skip
Ward (Sam Aller), Lloyd Haynes
(Dr. Marion Kincaid), Beverly
Garland (Mrs. Racine), Lou Kane
(Armand Racine), Jenifer Bishop
(Mrs. Ericson), Gloria Manon (Edna).

MADONNA OF THE SEVEN MOONS
(1944)
Director: Arthur Crabtree
Phyllis Calvert (Maddalena Lambardi/
Rosanna), Stewart Granger (Nino),
Patricia Roc (Angela Lambardi),
Reginald Tate (Ackroyd), John
Stuart (Guiseppe), Peter Murray
Hill (Logan), Peter Glenville
(Sandro), Dulcie Gray (Nesta),
Hilda Bayley (Mrs. Flake), Nancy
Price (Madame Barucci), Amy
Veness (Tessa), Alan Haines (Evelyn),
Evelyn Darvell (Millie), Jean Kent
(Vittoria).

MAFU CAGE, THE (1979) (A. K. A.
"My Sister, My Love")
Director: Karen Arthur
Carol Kane (Cissy), Lee Grant (Ellen),
James Olson (David), Will Geer (Zom).

MAGIC (1978)
Director: Richard Attenborough
Anthony Hopkins (Corky), Ann-Margret
(Peggy Ann Snow), Burgess Meredith
(Ben Greene), Ed Lauter (Duke), E. J.
Andre (Merlin), Jerry Houser (cab
driver), David Ogden Stiers (Todson),
Lillian Randolph (Sadie), Joe Lowry
(Club M. C.), Beverly Sanders (laughing
lady), Stephen Hart (Captain), Patrick
McCullough (doorman), I. W. Klein
(Maitre d'hotel), Brad Beesley (young
Corky), Mary Munday (mother), Scott
Garrett (brother), Bob Hackman (father),
Michael Harte (minister).

MAGIC CARPET, THE (1951)
Director: Lew Landers
Lucille Ball (Narah), John Agar
(Ramoth), George Tobias (Gazi),
Patricia Medina (Lida), Raymond Burr
(Boreg), Gregory Gaye (Ali), Rick
Vallin (Abdul), William Fawcett
(Akhmid), Joe Gilbert (Maras),
Doretta Johnson (Tanya), Eileen Howe
(Vernah), Linda Williams (Estar),
Winona Smith (Ziela), Perry Sheehan
(Copah), Minka Zorka (Nedda).

MAGIC CHRISTIAN, THE (1969)
Director: Joseph McGrath
Peter Sellers (Sir Guy Grand), Ringo
Starr (Youngman Grand), Wilfrid
Hyde-White (Klaus), Laurence Harvey
(Hamlet), Spike Milligan (Warden),
Christopher Lee (Vampire), Raquel
Welch (Slave Pirestress), Leonard
Frey (psychiatrist), Isabel Jeans (Aunt
Agnes), Richard Attenborough (Oxford
coach), Caroline Blakiston (Aunt
Esther), Dennis Price.

MAGIC FACE, THE (1951)
Director: Frank Tuttle
Luther Adler (Janus the Great), Patricia
Knight (Vera Janus), Ilka Windish (Carla
Harbach), Heinz Moog (Hans Harbach),
Manfred Inger (Heinrich Wagner),
Peter Preses (Warden), Jasper von
Oertzen (Maj. Weinrich), Toni Mitter-
wurzer (Hans), Sukman (Himmler),
Charles Koenig (Franz), Herman
Ehrhardt (Goering), Annie Maires
(Mariana), William L. Shirer (himself).

MAGIC FOUNTAIN, THE (1961)
Director: Alan David

Sir Cedric Hardwicke (Narrator),
Erik Jelde (King), Hans Conried
(voice of the Owl), Buddy Baer,
Peter Nestler, Catherine Hansen,
Helmo Kinderman, Joseph Marz,
Osman Ragher.

MAGICIAN, THE (1926)
Director: Rex Ingram
Paul Wegener (Dr. Haddo), Ivan
Petrovich (Dr. Burdon), Ruth Terry
(Margaret Dauncy), Michael Powell,
Gladys Hamer, Firmin Gemier.

MAGICIAN, THE (1958-Swed.) (A. K. A.
"Ansiktet", "The Face")
Director: Ingmar Bergman
Max von Sydow (Vogler), Ingrid
Thulin (Manda Aman), Bibi Andersson
(Sara), Gunnar Bjorstrand (Vergerus),
Bengt Ekerot (Spegel), Lars Ekborg
(Simson), Erland Josephson (Eger-
man), Naima Wifstrand (grandmother),
Gertrud Fridh (Ottilia), Toivo Pawlo
(Stardeck), Ake Fridell (Tubal), Ulla
Sjoblom (Henrietta), Birgita Pettersson
(Sonna), Oscar Ljung (Antonsson),
Axel Duberg (Rustan).

MAGIC SERPANT (1966-Jap.) (A. K. A.
"Kairyu Daikessen", "Froggo and
Droggo", "Grand Duel in Magic")
Director: Tetsuya Yamauchi
Hiroki Matsukata, Tomoko Ogawa,
Ryutaro Otomo, Bin Amatsu.

MAGIC SWORD, THE (1962)
Director: Bert I. Gordon
Basil Rathbone (Lodac), Estelle Win-
wood (Sybil), Gary Lockwood (St.
George), Anne Helm (Princess Helen),
Liam Sullivan (Sir Branton), John
Mauldin (Sir Patrick), Leroy Johnson
(Sir Ulrich), Angus Duncan (Sir James),
Jacques Gallo (Sir Dennis), David
Cross (Sir Pedro), Taldo Kenyon
(Sir Anthony), Jack Kosslyn (Ogre),
Maila Nurmi (Hag), Danielle De Metz
(French girl), Merritt Stone (King),
Angelo Rossito, Ted Finn (Dwarves),
Ann Graves (Princess Laura), Marlene
Callahan (Princess Grace), Lorrie
Richards (Anne), Richard Kiel (Pin-
head), Nick & Paul Bon Tempi (Siamese
twins).

MAGIC VOYAGE OF SINBAD, THE
(1953-Sov.) (A. K. A. "Sadko")
Director: Alexander Ptushko
Edward Stolar/Serge Stolayarov
(Sadko), Anna Larion/Alli Larionova
(Lyubava), Maurice Troyan/Mark
Troyankovskiy (Trifon), Y. Leonidov

(Kuzma), N. Malishevsky (Vyshata), L. Fenin (Maharajah), B. Surovtsev (Ivashka),S. Martinson (Monk), M. Astangov (Leader of the Varangians), S. Kayukov (Tsar of the Ocean), O. Viklandt (Tsarina), E. Myshkova (Princess Ilmen), L. Vertinskaya (the Pheonix).

MAGNETIC MONSTER, THE (1953)
Director: Curt Siodmak
Richard Carlson (Jeffrey Stewart), King Donovan (Dan Forbes), Jean Byron (Connie Stewart), Harry Ellerbe (Dr. Allard), Byron Foulger (Simon), Leonard Mudie (Denker), Michael Fox (Dr. Serny), John Vosper (Capt. Dyer), Leo Britt (Benton), John Zaremba (Chief Watson), Michael Granger (Smith), Bill Benedict (Albert), Lee Phelps (city engineer), Frank Gerstle (Col. Willis), Douglas Evans (pilot), Strother Martin (co-pilot), John Dodsworth (Cartwright), Kathleen Freeman (Nelly), Charlie Williams (cabby), Jarma Lewis (stewardess), Elizabeth Root (Joy), Watson Downs (Mayor).

MAGNETIC MOON (1954)
see Television: Rocky Jones, Space Ranger (1953-54)

MAGNIFICENT MAGNET OF SANTA MESA, THE (TVM-1977) (A. K. A. "Adventures of Freddie") - 6-19-77
Director: Hy Averback
Michael Burns (Freddie Griffith), Dick Blasucci (Cal Bixby), Keene Curtis (Mr. Undershaft), Jane Connell (Ida Griffith), Susan Blanchard (Marcie Hamilton), Tom Poston (Willard Bensinger), Susan Sullivan (C. B. Macauley), Harry Morgan (J. J. Strange), Conrad Janis (Mr. Kreel), Loni Anderson, Alex Sharp, Zachary A. Charles, Jack Frey, Lindy Davis, Martin Asarow, Gary Giem, Hal Floyd, Linda McClure, William Hubbard Knight

MAGUS, THE (1968)
Director: Guy Green
Anthony Quinn (Maurice Conchis), Michael Caine (Nicholas Urfe), Candice Bergen (Lily), Anna Karina (Anne), Julian Glover (Anton), George Pastel (Andreas-Priest), Corin Redgrave (Capt. Wimmel), Paul Stassino (Meli), Danielle Noel (Soula), Takis Emmanuel (Kapetan), Ethel Farrugia (Maria), Anthony Newlands (party host), Jerome Willis (German officer), Andreas Melandrinos (goatherd), Roger Lloyd Pack (young Conchis), George Kafkaris, Stack Constantino (partisans).

MAID OF SALEM (1937)
Director: Frank Lloyd
Claudette Colbert (Barbara Clark), Fred MacMurray (Roger Coverman), Gale Sondergaard (Martha Harding), Beulah Bondi (Abagail Goode), Aubrey Mather (Jeremiah), Madame Sul-te-wan (Tichiba), Virginia Weidler (Nabby Goode), William Farnum (Judge Sewell), Sterling Holloway (Miles Corbin), Lucy Beaumont (Rebecca Nurse), Bonita Granville (Ann Goode), E. E. Clive (Thomas Ezekiel Bilge), Henry Kelker (Chief Justice Laughton), Donald Meek (Mr. Cheeves), Pedro de Cordoba (Morse), Halliwell Hobbes (Jeremiah Adams), Louise Dresser (Ellen Clarke), Babs Nelson (Mercy Cheeves), Zeffie Tilbury (Goody Sarah Higgins), Benny Bartlett (Timothy Clarke), Ivan Simpson (Rev. Samuel Parris), Harvey Stephens (Judge Harding), Edward Ellis (Nathanial Goode), Tom Ricketts (Giles Cory), J. Farrell MacDonald, Lionel Belmore.

MAIN STREET KID, THE (1947)
Director: R. G. Springsteen
Al Pearce, Alan Mowbray, Adele Mara, Janet Martin, Roy Barcroft, Byron S. Barr, Emil Rameau, Douglas Evans, Arlene Marris, Phil Arnold, Earl Hodgins, Dick Elliott.

MAJIN (1966-Jap.) (A. K. A. "Daimajin", "Majin, the Monster of Terror", "Majin the Hideous Idol")
Director: Kimiyoshi Yasuda & Yoshiyuki Kuroda
Kiwa Takada (Kozasa Hanabusa), Yoshihiko Aoyama (Tadafumi Hanabusa), Tatsuo Endo (Gunjuro), Jun Fujimaki (Kogenta), Ryutaro Gomi (Samanosuke).

MAJIN STRIKES AGAIN (1966-Jap.) (A. K. A. "Daimajin Gyakushu")
Director: Issei Mori & Yoshiyuki Kuroda
Hideki Ninomiya, Masahide Kizuka, Shiel Iizuka, Shinj Hori, Menuyuki Nagatomo.

MAKO, JAWS OF DEATH (1976) (A. K. A. "The Jaws of Death")
Director: William Grefe
Richard Jaeckel, Jenifer Bishop, John Chandler, Harold Sakata, Buffy Dee, Ben Dronen, Milton Smith, Paul Preston, Robert Gordon, Luke Halpin, Jerry Albert, Marcie Knight.

MALATESTA'S CARNIVAL (1972)

Director: Christopher Speeth
Herve Villachaize, Janine Carazo,
Lenny Baker, Daniel Dietrich, Jerome
Dempsey, William Preston, Elizabeth
Henn, Paul Hostetler.

MALEVIL (1981-Fr./Ger.)
Director: Christian de Chalonge
Jean-Louis Trintignant (Rulbert),
Michel Serrault (Emmanuel), Robert
Dhery (Peyssou), Jacques Dutronc
(Colin), Penelope Palmer (Evelyne),
Jacques Villeret (Momo), Hanns Zisch-
ler (veterination), Jacqueline Parent
(Cathy).

MALPERTIUS (1972-Fr./Ger./Belg.)
Director: Harry Kumel
Orson Welles (Cassavius), Susan
Hampshire (Euryale/Nancy/Alice),
Mathieu Carriere (Yann), Walter Rilla,
Daniel Pilon, Jean-Pierre Cassel,
Michel Bouquet, Dora Van Der Groen,
Sylvie Vartan.

MALTESE BIPPY, THE (1968)
Director: Norman Panama
Dan Rowan (Sam Smith), Dick Martin
(Ernest Grey), Carol Lynley (Robin
Sherwood), Mildred Natwick (Molly
Fletcher), Fritz Weaver (Ravenswood),
Julie Newmar (Carlotta Ravenswood),
Robert Reed (Lt. Tim Crane), Leon
Askin (Axel Kronstadt), Dana Elcar
(Sgt. Kelvaney), Charles Strauss,
Mike Kellin.

MAMMA DRACULA (1980-Belg./Fr.)
Director: Boris Szulzinger
Louise Fletcher (Mamma Dracula),
Maria Schneider (Nancy Hawaii),
Marc-Henri Wajnberg (Vladimir), Alex-
ander Wajnberg (Ladislas), Jimmy
Shuman (Van Bloed), Michel Israel
(Rosa), Jesse Hahn (Superintendent).

MAN, THE (1972)
Director: Joseph Sargent
James Earl Jones (Douglass Dilman),
Martin Balsam (Jim Talley), Burgess
Meredith (Sen. Watson), Lew Ayres
(Noah Calvin), William Windom (Arthur
Eaton), Barbara Rush (Kay Eaton),
Georg Stanford Brown (Wheeler), Janet
MacLachlan (Wanda), Martin Brooks
(Wheeler's Lawyer), Simon Scott
(Hugh Gaynor), Patric Knowles (South
African Consul), Anne Seymour (Ma Blore),
Gilbert Green (Congressman Hand),
Lawrence Cook (Congressman Streller),
Vince Howard (Congressman Eckworth),
Leonard Stone (Congressman Parmel),
Philip Bourneuf (Chief Justice Williams),

Ted Hartley (Press Secretary),
Bob DoQui (Webson), Elizabeth Ross
(Mrs. Smelker), Reginald Fenderson
(Rev. Otis Waldren), Edward
Faulkner (secret service agent),
Barry Russo (Haley), Gary Walberg
(Pierce), Howard K. Smith, Jack
Benny, William Lawrence.

MAN AND THE BEAST, THE (1951-
Arg.) (A.K.A. "El Hombre y la
Bestia", "Dottor Yekyll")
Director: Mario Soffici
Mario Soffici, Ana Maria Campay,
Jose Cibrian, Olag Zubarry, Rafael
Frontura.

MAN AND THE MONSTER, THE (1958-
Mex.) (A.K.A. "El Hombre y el
Monstruo")
Director: Rafael Baledon
Enrique Rambal, Abel Salaza,
Martha Roth, Anita Blanch, Ofelia
Guilman, Jose Chavez, Carlos
Suarez, Mary Vela.

MAN AND THE SNAKE, THE (1972) -
short
Director: Stuare Rydman
John Fraser, Andre Morell, Clive
Morton, Madge Ryan, Damaris
Hayman, Stephen Waller, Brenda
Cowling.

MAN BEAST (1955)
Director: Jerry Warren
Rock Madison (Lon Raynon),
Virginia Maynor (Connie Hayward),
Lloyd Nelson (Trevor Hudson),
George Skaff (Varga), George Wells
Lewis (Dr. Erickson), Tom Maruzzi
(Steve Cameron), Jack Haffner
(Kheon), Won Sing (trader).

MAN CALLED DAGGER, A (1967)
Director: Richard Rush
Paul Mantee (Dick Dagger), Terry
Moore (Harper Davis), Jan Murray
(Rudolph Koffman), Sue Ann Langdon
(Ingrid), Leonard Stone (Karl
Rainer), Richard Kiel (Otto), Bruno
Ve Sota (Dr. Grulik), Maureen
Arthur (Joy), Eileen O'Neill (Erica),
Mimi Dillard (girl in auto).

MANCHURIAN CANDIDATE, THE (1962)
Director: John Frankenheimer
Frank Sinatra (Bennett Marco),
Laurence Harvey (Raymond Shaw),
Janet Leigh (Rosie), Angela Lansbury
(Raymond's mother), Henry Silva
(Chunjin), James Gregory (Sen.
John Iselin), Leslie Parrish (Jocie

Jordon), John McGiver (Sen. Thomas
Jordon), James Edwards (Corporal
Melvin), Lloyd Corrigan (Holborn
Gaines), Khigh Dhiegh (Yen Lo),
Douglas Henderson (Colonel), Barry
Kelley (Secretary of Defense), Nick
Bolin (Berezobo), Madame Spivy
(Berezovo's Lady), Whit Bissell
(Medical Officer), William Thourlby
(Little), Albert Paulsen (Zilkov),
Mimi Dillard (Melvin's wife), John
Laurence (Gossfeld), Richard La
Pore (Mavole), Anton Van Stralen
(officer), Tom Lowell (Lembeck),
Nick Blair (Silvers), Reggie Nalder
(Gomel), Bess Flowers (Gomel's
lady counterpart), Miyoshi Jingu (Miss
Gertrude), Irving Steinberg (Freeman),
John Francis (Haiken), Joe Adams
(psychiatrist), Anna Shin (Korean
girl).

MANDRAKE (TVM-1979) - 1-24-79
    Director: Harry Falk
Anthony Herrera (Mandrake), Ji-Tu
Cumbaka (Lothar), Simone Griffeth
(Stacy), Gretchen Corbett (Jennifer
Lindsay), Robert Reed (Arkadian),
Ron Randell (Cutter), David Hooks
(Dr. Malcolm Lindsay), Hank Brandt
(Alec Gordon), Peter Haskell (Wil-
liam Romero), James Hong (Theron),
Harry Blackstone, Jr. (Dr. Nolan),
Sab Shimondo (Ho), David Hollander
(young Mandrake), Allan Hunt (Walter
Kevan), Donna Benz (Cindy), Edmund
Balin (choreographer).

MANDRAKE THE MAGICIAN (1939) -
    serial in 12 episodes
    Director: Sam Nelson & Nor-
        man Deming
Warren Hull (Mandrake), Doris
Weston (Betty Houston), Al Kikume
(Lothar), Kenneth MacDonald (Web-
ster), Don Beddoe (Raymond), Dick
Curtis (Dorgan), Ernie Adams (Brown),
Rex Downing (Tommy), Forbes Mur-
ray (Houston), George Chesebro
(Baker), Edward Earle (Andre),
John Tyrrell (Dirk), George Turner
(Hall).

MANEATER (TVM-1973) - 12-8-73
    Director: Vince Edwards
Ben Gazzara (Nick Baron), Sheree
North (Gloria Baron), Laurette Spang
(Polly Brenner), Richard Basehart
(Carl Brenner), Claire Brennan
(Paula Brenner), Kip Niven (Shep
Sanders), Stewart Raffill (Louis),
Lou Ferragher (1st ranger), Jerry
Fitzpatrick (2nd ranger).

MAN-EATER OF HYDRA, THE (1967-
    Span. /Ger.) (A.K.A. "La Isla
    de la Muerte", "Island of the
    Doomed", "Island of the Dead",
    "The Blood Suckers")
Cameron Mitchell (Baron von Weser),
Elisa Montes (Beth Christiansen),
George Martin (David Moss), Kay
Fischer (Cora Robinson), Matilde
Sampedro (Myrtle Callahan), Ralph
Naukoff (James Robinson), Herman
Nelsen (Prof. Julius Demerist),
Mike Brendel (Baldi), Richard
Valle (Alfredo).

MANFISH (1956)
    Director: W. Lee Wilder
Lon Chaney, Jr., (Swede), John
Bromfield (Branigan), Victor Jory
(Professor), Barbara Nichols
(Mimi), Tessa Pendergast (Elita),
Eric Coverly (Chavez), Vincent
Chang (Domingo), Jack Lewis
(Warren), Theodore Purcell (Big
Boy), Vere Johns (Bianco), Arnold
Shanks (Lieppo), Clyde Hoyte
(Calypso).

MAN FROM ATLANTIS, THE (TVM-
    1977) - 3-4-77
    Director: Lee H. Katzin
Patrick Duffy (Mark Harris),
Victor Buono (Mr. Schubert), Be-
linda Montgomery (Dr. Elizabeth
Merrill), Dean Santoro (Ernie Smith),
Art Lund (Adm. Dewey Pierce),
Allen Case (Lt. Cmdr. Berkley),
Mark Jenkins (Lt. Ainsley), Law-
rence Pressman (Cmdr. Phil Roth),
Joshua Bryant (Dr. Doug Berkley),
Steve Franken, Virginia Gregg.

MAN FROM BEYOND, THE
    Director: Burton King
Harry Houdini, Nita Naldi, Erwin
Connelly, Jane Connelly, Luis
Alberni, Albert Tavernier, Arthur
Maude, Frank Montgomery.

MAN FROM NOWHERE, THE (1976)
    Director: James Hill
Sarah Hollis-Andrews, Ronald Adam,
Shane Franklin.

MAN FROM PLANET X, THE (1951)
    Director: Edgar G. Ulmer
Robert Clarke (Lawrence), Margaret
Field (Enid Ellitt), Raymond Bond
(Prof. Elliot), William Schallert
(Mears), Roy Engel (the Constable),
Gilbert Fallman (Dr. Blane), George
Davis (Geordie), David Ormont
(Inspector).

MAN FROM YESTERDAY (1949)
    Director: Oswald Mitchell
John Stuart (Gerlad Amersley),
Henry Oscar (Julius Rickman), Laur-
ence Harvey (John Matthews), Gwyneth
Vaughan (Doreen Amersley), Marie
Burke (Doris).

MANHUNT IN SPACE (1954)
    see Television: Rocky Jones,
    Space Ranger (1953-54)

MANHUNT OF MYSTERY ISLAND
    (1945) (A. K. A. "Captain Mephisto
    and the Transformation Machine") -
    serial in 15 episodes
    Director: Spencer Gordon
    Bennet, Wallace A. Grissell &
    Yakima Canutt
Richard Bailey (Lance Reardon), Linda
Sterling (Claire Forrest), Roy Bar-
croft (Mephisto/Higgins), Kenne
Duncan (Sidney Brand), Forbes Murray
(Henry Hargraves), Forrest Taylor
(Prof. Forrest), Jack Ingram (Ed-
ward Armstrong), Edward Cassidy
(Paul Melton), Harry Strang (Fred
Braley), Lane Chandler (Reed), Tom
Steele (Lyons), Russ Vincent (Ruga),
Dale Van Sickel (Barker), Frank
Alten (Raymond), Duke Green (Clark/
Harvey), Fred Graham (Blake),
Eddie Parker (Fallon/Captain), Si
Jenks (Joe Benson), Dale Van Sickel
(Frazier/Lewis/Ritter/Sardon),
Frederick Howard (C. D. Pembroke).

MANIAC (1934)
    Director: Dwain Esper
Bill Woods (Don Maxwell), Horace
Carpenter (Dr. Meirschultz), Ted
Edwards (Buckley), Phyllis Diller
(Mrs. Buckley), Jennie Dark (Maizie),
Thea Ramsey (Alice Maxwell), Marvel
Andre (Marvel), Celia McGann (Jo),
J. P. Wade (Mike, the morgue attend-
ant), Marion Blackton (neighbor).

MANIAC (1963)
    Director: Michael Carreras
Kerwin Mathews (Geoff Farell), Nadia
Gray (Eve Beynat), Liliane Brousse
(Annette Beynat), Donald Houston
(Georges Beynat), George Pastell
(Insp. Etienne), Norman Bird (Salon),
Justine Lord (Grace), Arnold Diamond
(Janiello), Jerold Wells (Giles), Leon
Peers (Blanchard).

MANIAC (1977) (A. K. A. "Assault on
    Paradise", "The Town That Cried
    Terror")
    Director: Richard Compton

Paul Koslo (Victor), Oliver Reed,
Stuart Whitman, John Ireland,
Deborah Raffin, Jim Mitchum.

MANIAC (1980)
    Director: William Lustig
Caroline Munro (Anna D'Antoni),
Joe Spinell (Frank Zito), Gail
Lawrence (Rita), Kelly Piper
(nurse), Rita Montone (Hooker),
Tom Savini (disco boy), Hyla Mar-
row (disco girl), James Brewster
(beach boy), Linda Lee Walter
(Beach girl), Tracie Evans (street
hooker), Sharon Mitchell (2nd
nurse), Carol Henry (deadbeat),
Louis Jawitz (art director), Nella
Bacmeister (Carmen Zito), Denise
Spagnuolo (Denise), Billy Spagnuolo
(Billy), Frank Pesce (TV reporter),
Kim Hudson (lobby hooker), Can-
dice Clements (1st park mother),
Diane Spagnuolo (2nd park mother),
Terry Gagnon (woman in alley),
Joan Baldwin, Jeni Paz (models),
Janelle Winsten (waitress), Randy
Jergensen, Jimmy Aurichio (cops).

MAN IN BLACK, THE (1940)
    Director: Frances Searle
Valentine Dyall (Storyteller), Betty
Ann Davies (Bertha Clavering),
Sidney James (Henry Clavering),
Anthony Forwood (Victor Clavering),
Sheila Burrell (Janice), Hazel
Penwarden (Joan), Lawrence Bask-
comb (Sandford), Courtney Hope
(Mrs. Carter).

MAN IN HALF MOON STREET, THE
    (1944)
    Director: Ralph Murphy
Nils Asther (Julian Karell), Helen
Walker (Eve Brandon), Reinhold
Schunzel (Dr. Kurt Van Bruecken),
Morton Lowry (Allen Gutherie),
Paul Cavanagh (Dr. Henry Latimer),
Matthew Boulton (Insp. Garth),
Reginald Sheffield (Mr. Taper),
Edmond Breon (Sir Humphrey Bran-
don), Forrester Harvey (Harris,
the cabby), Konstantin Shayne (Dr.
Vishanoff), Edward Fielding (Col.
Ashley), Brandon Hurst (Simpson,
the Butler), Arthur Mulliner (Sir
John Aldergate), Aminata Dyne
(Lady Minerva Aldergate), Eustace
Wyatt (Insp. Lawson).

MAN IN OUTER SPACE (1961-Czech.)
    (A. K. A. "Muzz Prvniho Stoleti",
    "Man from the First Century")
    Director: Oldrich Lipsky

Milos Kopecky, Radovan Lukavsky, Anita Kajlichova, Vit Olmer, Otomar Krejca.

MAN IN THE ATTIC (1953)
Director: Hugo Fregonese
Jack Palance (Slade), Constance Smith (Lily Bonner), Frances Bavier (Helen Harley), Rhys Williams (William Harley), Lillian Bond (Annie Rowley), Isabel Jewell (Katy), Lisa Daniels (Mary Lenihan), Byron Palmer (Paul Warwick), Tita Phillips (Daisy), Harry Cording, Leslie Bradley, Lester Mathews, Sean McClory.

MAN IN THE DARK (1953)
Director: Lew Landersl
Edmund O'Brien (Steve Rawley/James Blake), Audrey Totter (Peg Benedict), Ted de Corsia (Lefty), Horace McMahon (Arnie), Nick Dennis (Cookie), Dayton Lummis (Dr. Marston), John Harmon (Herman), Ruth Warren (Mayme), Dan Riss (Jawald), Shepard Menken (interne).

MAN IN THE MIRROR (1936)
Director: Maurice Elvey
Edward Everett Horton (Jeremy Dike), Genevieve Tobin (Helen), Ursula Jeans (Veronica), Felix Aylmer (Earl of Wigan), Aubrey Mather (Bogus of Bokhara), Renee Gadd (Miss Blake), Garry Marsh (Tarkington), Alastair Sim (Interpreter), Stafford Hilliard (Dr. Graves), Viola Compton (Mrs. Massiter).

MAN IN THE MOON (1960)
Director: Basil Dearden
Kenneth More (William Blood), Shirley Anne Field (Polly), Norman Bird (Herbert), Michael Hordern (Dr. Davidson), Bernard Hosrfall (Rex), Charles Gray (Leo), John Phillips (Prof. Stephens), John Glyn-Jones (Dr. Wilmot), Bruce Boa (Roy), Noel Purcell (Prosecutor), Newton Blick (Dr. Hollis), Ed Devereaux (storekeeper), Richard Pearson, Lionel Gamlin (doctors), Russell Waters (Woomera director), Danny Green (lorry drover), Jeremy Lloyd (Jaguar driver).

MAN IN THE TRUNK, THE (1942)
Director: Malcolm St. Clair
J. Carrol Naish Lynne Roberts, Raymond Walburn, Mat McHugh, Eily Malyon, Sid Saylor, Arthur Loft,

Douglas Fowley, Milton Parsons, Charles Cane, George Holmes, Joan Marsh, Tim Ryan, Dorothy Peterson, Theodore Von Eltz, Vivian Oakland.

MAN IN THE WHITE SUIT, THE (1951)
Director: Alexander Mackendrick
Alec Guiness (Sidney Stratton), Joan Greenwood (Daphne Birnley), Cecil Parker (Alan Birnley), Michael Gough (Michael Corland), Ernest Thesiger (Sir John Kierlaw), Howard Marion Crawford (Cranford), Duncan Lamont (Harry), Henry Mollison (Hoskins), Vida Hope (Bertha), Patric Doonan (Frank), Harold Goodwin (Wilkins), Olaf Olsen (Knudsen), Colin Gordon (Hill), Joan Herben (Miss Johnson), Miles Malleson (tailor), Arthur Howard (Roberts), Roddy Hughes (Green), Edie Martin (Mrs. Watson), George Benson (the lodger), Judith Furst (Nurse Gamage), Mandy Miller (little girl), Frank Atkinson (Baker), Billy Russell (nightwatchman), John Rudling (Wilson).

MANITOU, THE (1978)
Director: William Girdler
Tony Curtis (Harry Erskine), Michael Ansara (Singing Rock), Susan Strasberg (Karen Tandy), Stella Stevens (Amelia Crusoe), Jon Cedar (Dr. Jack Hughes), Ann Sothern (Mrs. Karmann), Jeanette Nolan (Mrs. Winconis), Burgess Meredith (Dr. Ernest Snow), Paul Mantee (Dr. Robert McEvoy), Joe Gieb (Misquamacas), Ann Mantee (floor nurse), Lurene Tuttle (Mrs. Hertz), Hugh Corcoran (MacArthur), Tenaya (Singing Rock's wife), Jan Heininger (Wolf), Carole Hemingway (prostitute), Beverly Kushida (second floor nurse), Michael Laren (Michael).

MAN-MADE MONSTER (1941) (A. K. A. "The Electric Man")
Director: George Waggner
Lon Chaney, Jr. (Dan McCormick), Lionel Atwill (Dr. Rigas), Anne Nagel (June Lawrence), Frank Albertson (Mark Adams), Samuel S. Hinds (Dr. Lawrence), William Davidson (District Attorney), John Dilson (medical examiner), Frank O'Connor (detective), Russell Hicks (Warden), Douglas Evans (man), Connie Bergen (nurse)

Douglas Evans (alien), Ben Taggart
(Detective Sergeant), George Meader
(Dr. Bruno), Ivan Miller (doctor),
Chester Gan (Chinese boy).

MAN OF A THOUSAND FACES (1957)
    Director: Joseph Pevney
James Cagney (Lon Chaney, Sr.),
Jane Greer (Hazel Bennet), Dorothy
Malone (Cleva Creighton Chaney),
Marjorie Rambeau (Gert), Jim Bac-
kus (Clarence Logan), Jack Albertson
(Dr. J. Winston Shields), Jeanne
Cagney (Carrie Chaney), Robert
Evans (Irving Thalberg), Celia Lov-
sky (Mrs. Chaney), Nolan Leary
(Pa Chany), Danny Beck (Max Dill),
Simon Scott (Carl Hastings), Clarence
Kolb (himself), Hank Mann, Snub
Pollard (comedy waiters), Phil Van
Zandt (George Loane Tucker), Dennis
Rush (Creighton Chaney at age 4),
Rickie Sorensen (Creighton at age 8),
Robert Lyden (Creighton at age 13),
Roger Smith (Creighton at age 21).

MAN ON A SWING (1974)
    Director: Frank Perry
Cliff Robertson (Lee Tucker), Joel
Grey (Franklin Wills), Dorothy
Tristan (Janet Tucker), George
Voskovec (Dr. Holnar), Elizabeth
Wilson (Dr. Wilson), Ron Weyand
(Dr. Fusco).

MAN'S GENESIS (1912)
    Director: D.W. Griffith
Robert Harron (Weakhands), Mae
Marsh (Lily White), Wilfred Lucas
(Brute Force), William Chrystie
Miller (old man), Charles Mailes
(boy), W. C. Robinson (girl).

MANSION OF THE DOOMED (1976)
    (A. K. A. "The Terror of Dr.
    Chaney")
    Director: Michael Patacki
Richard Basehart (Dr. Leonard Chaney),
Trish Stewart (Nancy Chaney), Gloria
Grahame (Nurse Katherine), Lance
Henriksen (Dan), Vic Tayback (de-
tective), Libbie Chase (girl).

MANSTER, THE (1962-U.S. /Jap.)
    (A. K. A. "The Split")
    Director: George Breakston
Peter Dyneley (Larry Stanford), Jane
Hylton (Linda Stanford), Satoshi
Nakamura (Dr. Suzuki), Norman Van
Hawley (Ian Matthews), Terri Zimmern
(Tara), Toyoko Takechi (Emiko),
Jerry Ito (Superintendent Aida), Alan
Tarlton (Jennsen).

MAN THEY COULD NOT HANG, THE
    (1939)
    Director: Nick Grinde
Boris Karloff (Dr. Henrik Savaard),
Robert Wilcox (Scoop Foley), Lorna
Gray (Janet Savaard), Roger Pryor
(District Attorney Drake), Don Beddoe
(Lt. Shane), Ann Doran (Betty Craw-
ford), James Craig (Watkins), Dick
Curtis (Keprnov), Charles Trowbridge
(Judge Bowman), Byron Foulger
(Lang), John Tyrrell (Sutton), Joseph
De Stephani (Dr. Stoddard).

MAN THEY COULDN'T ARREST, THE
    (1933)
    Director: T. Hayes Hunter
Gordon Harker (Tansey), Hugh Wakefield (John Dain), Garry Marsh (Del-
bury), Renee Clama (Marcia), Nicholas Hannen (Lyall), Robert Farqu-
harson (Count Lazard), Dennis
Wyndham (Shaughnessy).

MANTIS IN LACE (1968)
    Director: William Rotsler
Susan Stewart, M. K. Evans, Steve
Vincent, Vic Lance, Pat Barrington.

MAN WANTS TO LIVE (1961-Fr. /Ital.)
    (A. K. A. "Les Hommes Veulent
    Vivre!")
    Director: Leonide Moguy
Claudio Gora, John Justin, Yves
Massard, Jacqueline Huet.

MAN WHO COULD CHEAT DEATH,
    THE (1959)
    Director: Terence Fisher
Anton Diffring (Dr. Georges Bonner),
Christopher Lee (Dr. Pierre
Gerrard), Hazel Court (Janine),
Arnold Marle (Dr. Ludwig Weiss),
Francis de Wolff (Legris), Delphi
Lawrence (Margo), Charles Lloyd-
Pack.

MAN WHO COULD WORK MIRACLES,
    THE (1936)
    Director: Lothar Mendes
Roland Young (George McWhirter
Fotheringay), Joan Gardner (Ada
Price), Ralph Richardson (Col.) Win-
stanely), Edward Chapman (Major
Grigsby), Ernest Thesiger (Mr.
Maydig), Sophie Stewart (Maggie
Hooper), George Zucco (Moody),
Robert Cochran (Bill Stoker),
Wallace Lupino (P. C. Winch), Wally
Patch (Superintendent Smithells),
Bruce Winston (landlord), Gertrude
Musgrove (Effie Brickman), Law-
rence Hanray (Mr. Bampfylde), Lady

Tree (housekeeper), Bernard Nedell (reporter), Torin Thatcher (Observer, a god), George Sanders (Indifference, a god), Ivan Brandt (Player, a god).

MAN WHO FELL TO EARTH, THE (1976)
Director: Nicholas Roeg
David Bowie (Thomas Jerome Newton), Candy Clark (Mary Lou), Rip Torn (Nathan Bryce), Buck Henry (Oliver Farnsworth), Bernie Casey (Peters), Jackson D. Kane (Prof. Canutti), Tony Mascia (Arthur), Rick Riccardo (Trevor), Linda Hutton (Elaine), Adrienne Larussa (Helen), Hillary Holland (Jill), Peter Prouse (Peters' associate), Richard Breeding (receptionist), Lilybell Crawford (jewelry store owner), James Lovell (himself).

MAN WHO HAUNTED HIMSELF, THE (1970)
Director: Basil Deardon
Roger Moore (Pelham), Hildegard Neil (Eve), Thorley Walters (Bellamy), Anton Rodgers (Alexander), Olga Georges-Picot (Julie), John Welsh (Freeman), Freddie Jones (psychiatrist), Edward Chapman (Barton), Hugh Mackenzie (James), Laurence Hardy (Mason), Alastair Mackenzie (Michael), Kevork Malikyan (Luigi), John Carson, Charles Lloyd-Pack.

MAN WHO LAUGHS, THE (1927)
Director: Paul Leni
Conrad Veidt (Gwynplaine), Mary Philbin (Dea), Olga Baclanova (Duchess Josiana), Brandon Hurst (Barkilphedro), Stuart Holmes (Lord Dirry-Moir), Frank Puglia, Jack Goodrich (clowns), Torben Meyer (the Spy), Edgar Norton (High Chancellor), George Siegmann (Dr. Hardquanonne), Cesare Gravina (Ursus), Josephine Cromwell (Queen Anne), Sam de Grasse (King James II), Nick F. DeRuiz (Wapentake), Charles Puffy (inkeeper), Julius Molnar, Jr. (Gwynplaine as a boy), Lon Poff, Carmen Costello.

MAN WHO LAUGHS, THE (1965-Ital. / Fr.) (A.K.A. "L'Uomo Che Ride")
Director: Sergio Corbucci
Edmund Purdom (Cesare Borgia), Lisa Gastoni (Lucrezia Borgia), Jean Sorel (Angelo/Astorre), Ilaria Occhini (Dea), Linda Sini.

MAN WHO LIVED AGAIN, THE (1936)

(A.K.A. "The Man Who Changed His Mind", "The Brainsnatcher", "Dr. Maniac")
Director: Robert Stevenson
Boris Karloff (Dr. Laurience), Anna Lee (Clare Wyatt), John Loder (Dick Haslewood), Lyn Harding (Prof. Holloway), Frank Cellier (Lord Haslewood), Cecil Parker (Dr. Grattan), Donald Calthrop (Clayton),

MAN WHO LIVED TWICE, THE (1936)
Director: Harry Lachman
Ralph Bellamy (James Black/ Slick Rawley), Marian Marsh (Janet Haydon), Thurston Hall (Dr. Schuyler), Isabel Jewell (Peggy Russell), Ward Bond (Gloves), Henry Kolker (Judge Treacher), Nana Bryant (Mrs. Schuyler), Willard Robertson (Logan).

MAN WHO RECLAIMED HIS HEAD, THE (1934)
Director: Edward Ludwig
Claude Rains (Paul Verin), Joan Bennett (Adele Verin), Lionel Atwill (Henri Dumont), Henry O'Neill (Fernand De Marney), Wallace Ford (Culry), Lawrence Grant (Marchand), William Davidson (Charrus), Henry Armetta (Laurent), Rollo Lloyd (Jean, the butler), Gilbert Emery (His Excellency), Valerie Hobson (Mimi), Doris Lloyd (Lulu), Lloyd Hughes (Andre), Bryant Washburn (Antoine), Lionel Belmore (train conductor), Norman Ainsley (steward), Harry Cording (French mechanic), Grace Cunard (woman), Hugh O'Connell (Danglas), Baby Jane (Linette Verin), Bessie Barriscale (Louise), G. P. Huntley, Jr. (Pierre), Noel Francis (Chon-Chon), Phyllis Brooks (secretary), Carol Coombe (clerk), Montague Shaw, Walter Walker, Crawford Kent, Edward Martindel (dignitaries), Edward Van Sloan, Purnell Pratt, Jameson Thomas (Munition Board Directors), Judith Wood (Margot), Anderson Lawler (Jack), Will Stanton (drunk soldier), Boyd Irwin (lorry driver), Emerson Treacy (French student), John Rutherford, Lee Phelps, Hyram A. Hoover (soldiers), Rudy Cameron (Maitre D'hotel), Lilyan Irene (woman shopper), Russ Powell (station master), William Ruhl (shopkeeper's husband), Rolfe Sedan (waiter), Ben F. Hendricks (chauffeur), Maurice Murphy (Leon), Carl Stockade

(tradesman), William Gould (man),
Wilfred North (man), Nell Craig
(woman), Tom Ricketts, William
West, Jose Swickard, Colin Kenny
(citizens), Ted Billings (newsboy),
William Worthington (attendant),
John Ince (speaker), Margaret Mann
(Granny), Russ Clark (French
truck driver).

MAN WHO SAW TOMORROW, THE
    (1922)
    Director: Alfred E. Green
Thomas Meighan, Leatrice Joy,
Albert Roscoe, Alec Francis,
Theodore Roberts, Eva Novak, June
Elvidge.

MAN WHO SOLD HIS SOUL, THE
    (1943) (A.K.A. "L'Homme Qui
    Vendit Son Ame")
    Director: Jean-Paul Paulin
Pierre Larquey, Michele Alfa,
Dartique, Mona Goya, Renee Thorel,
Andre Luguet, Robert LeVigan,
Huguette Saint-Arnaud.

MAN WHO TURNED TO STONE,
    THE (1957)
    Director: Leslie Kardos
Victor Jory (Dr. Murdock), Charlotte
Austin (Carol Adams), William
Hudson (Dr. Jess Rogers), Frederick
Ledebur (Eric), Jean Willes (Tracy),
Ann Doran (Mrs. Ford), Paul Cava-
nagh (Cooper), Tina Carver (Big
Marge), Victor Varconi (Myer),
George Lynn (Freneau), Barbara
Wilson (Anna).

MAN WHO WAGGED HIS TALE,
    THE (1957-Span./Ital.) (A.K.A.
    "Un Angel Paso Sobre Brooklyn",
    "An Angel Passed Over Brooklyn")
    Director: Ladislao Vajda
Peter Ustinov (Mr. Bossi), Pablito
Calvo (Tonino), Aroldo Tieri (Bruno),
Silvia Marco (Giulia), Jose Isbert
(Pietrino), Maurizio Arena (Alfonso),
Isabel De Pomes (Tonino's mother).

MAN WHO WALKED THROUGH THE
    WALL, THE (1960-Ger.) (A.K.A.
    "Ein Mann Geht Durch die Wand",
    "A Man Goes Through the Wall")
    Director: Ladislao Vajda
Heinz Ruehmann, Nicole Courcel,
Rudolf Rhomberg, Anita von Ow,
Rudolf Vogel, Peter Vogel, Hans
Poessenbacher, Michael Burk,
Guenter Graewerl, Elfie Petramer,
Karl Lieffen, Hubert von Meyerinck,
Max Haufler, Richard Bonne, Hans

Leibell, Henry Vahl, K.M. Vogler,
George Lehn, Dietrich Eckhardt,
Friedrich Domin, Eduard Leibner,
Lina Carstens, Werner Hessenland,
E.F. Fuehringer.

MAN WHO WANTED TO LIVE FOR-
    EVER, THE (TVM-1970) - 12-15-
    70
    Director: John Trent
Burl Ives (T.M. Trask), Sandy
Dennis (Enid Bingham), Stuart
Whitman (McCarter Purvis), Jack
Creley (Dr. George Simmons),
Ron Hartman (Dr. John Emmett),
Tom Harvey (McBride), Allan
Doremus (Dr. Carl Bryant), Ro-
bert Goodier (Dr. Wilfred Morton),
Joseph Shaw (Dr. Franz Heine-
mann), Kenneth James (Clinton),
Clem Harbourg (pianist), Harvey
Fisher, James Forrest, John
Davies, Robert Warner, Robert
Mann.

MAN WHO WOULD BE KING,
    THE (1975)
    Director: John Huston
Sean Connery (Daniel Dravot),
Michael Caine (Peachy Carnehan),
Christopher Plummer (Rudyard
Kipling), Saeed Jaffrey (Billy
Fish), Shakira Caine (Roxanne),
Karroum Ben Bouih (Kafu-Selim),
Jack May (District Commissioner),
Doghmi Larbi (Ootah), Paul Antrim
(Mulvaney), Mohammed Shamsi (Babu),
Albert Moses (Ghulam).

MAN WHO WOULDN'T DIE, THE
    (1942)
    Director: Herbert I. Leeds
Lloyd Nolan (Michael Shayne),
Henry Wilcoxon, Richard Derr,
Jeff Corey, Marjorie Weaver,
Francis Ford, Helene Reynolds,
Billy Bevan, Olin Howland,
Robert Emmett Keane.

MAN WITH BOGART'S FACE, THE
    (1980) (A.K.A. "Sam Marlow,
    Private Eye")
    Director: Robert Day
Robert Sacchi (Sam Marlow),
Franco Nero (Hakim), Michelle
Phillips (Gena Anastas), Olivia
Hussey (Elsa Borsht), Misty Rowe
(Duchess), Victor Buono (Commo-
dore Anastas), Herbert Lom (Mr.
Zebra), Sybil Danning (Cynthia),
Dick Bakalyan (Lt. Bumbera), Gregg
Palmer (Sgt. Hacksaw), Jay Robin-
son (Wolf Zinderneuf), George Raft

(Petey Cane), Yvonne DeCarlo
(Theresa Anastas), Mike Mazurki
(himself), Victor Sen Yung (Wing),
Henry Wilcoxon (Chevalier), A'Le-
shia Brevard (Mother), Peter Mamakos
(Spoony Singh), Joe Theismann (Jock),
Buck Kartalian (Nicky̆), Martin Kos-
leck (Horst Borsht), Philip Baker
Hall (Dr. Inman), Mike Masters
(Ralph), Kathleen Bracken (Mona),
Larry Pennell (George), Ed McCready
(garbage man), Rozelle Gayle (Mas-
todon), Everett Creach (Buster),
Bill Catching (Nero's Uncle), Alan
Foster (Driver), Wally Rose, Ralph
Carpenter (gunmen), Jerry Somers
(Catalina driver), James Bacon,
Marilyn Beck, Frank Barron, Dick
Whittington, Robert Osborne, Will
Tusher (reporters).

MAN WITH NINE LIVES, THE (1940)
(A.K.A. "Behind the Door")
    Director: Nick Grinde
Boris Karloff (Dr. Karvaal), Roger
Pryor (Dr. Tim Mason), Byron
Foulger (Dr. Bassett), Stanley
Brown (Bob Adams), Hal Taliaferro
(Sheriff Stanton), Jo Ann Sayers
(Judith Blair), John Dilson (Haw-
thorne), Ernie Adams (Pete Daggett),
Ivan Miller (Sheriff Halley), Lee
Willard (Jasper Adams), Bruce
Bennett (state trooper), Charles
Trowbridge.

MAN WITHOUT A BODY, THE (1957)
    Director: W. Lee Wilder
Robert Hutton (Dr. Phil Merritt),
Julia Arnall (Jean Kramer), George
Coulouris (Karl Brussard), Nadja
Regin (Odette Vanet), Peter Copley
(Leslie), Michael Golden (Nostrada-
mus), Maurice Kauffman (Chauffeur),
Frank Forsyth (detective), Kim
Parker (maid), Sheldon Lawrence
(Lew), Tony Quinn (Dr. Brandon),
Norman Shelley (Dr. Alexander),
Stanley Van Beers (Madame Tuss-
aud's guide), Edwin Ellis (publican),
William Sherwood (Dr. Charot),
Donald Morley (stock broker),
Ernest Bale (customs officer).

MAN WITHOUT A FACE, THE
    (1950) (A.K.A. "El Hombre sin
    Rostro")
    Director: Juan Bustillo Oro
Arturo de Cordova, Fernando Gali-
ana, Carmen Molina, Miguel Arenas,
Matilde Palau, Miguel Angel Ferriz,
Quete Lavat.

MAN WITHOUT DESIRE, THE (1922)
    Director: Adrian Brunel
Ivor Novello (Count Vittorio
Donaldo), Nina Vanna, Christopher
Walker, Sergio Mari, Adrian
Brunel, Jane Dryden, Dorothy
Warren.

MAN WITH THE BRAIN GRAFT,
    THE (1972-Fr./Ital./Ger.)
    (A.K.A. "L'Homme au Cerveau
    Greffe")
    Director: Jacques Doniol
    Valcroze
Jean Pierre Aumont, Nicoletta
Machiavelli, Mathieu Carriere,
Michel Duchaussoy, Martine Sar-
cey, Christian Duroc, Marienne
Egerick, Benoit Allemande, Moni-
que Melinand, Andre Tainsy, Pierre
Santini, Max Vialle.

MAN WITH THE GOLDEN FIST,
    THE (1967-Ital./Span.) (A.K.A.
    "L'Uomo dal Pugno D'Oro")
    Director: Jaime Jesus Bal-
    cazar
German Cobos, Erika Blanc, An-
tonella Murgia, Tomas Torres,
Frank Rosell, Monica Randal.

MAN WITH THE GOLDEN GUN,
    THE (1974)
    Director: Guy Hamilton
Roger Moore (James Bond),
Christopher Lee (Scaramanga),
Britt Ekland (Mary Goodnight),
Maud Adams (Andrea), Herve
Villechaize (Nick Nack), Clifton
James (J.W. Pepper), Richard
Loo (Hai Fat), Marc Lawrence
(Rodney), Bernard Lee (M), Lois
Maxwell (Miss Moneypenny),
Desmond Llewellyn (Q), Marne
Maitland (Lazar), Soon Taik Oh
(Hip), Carmen Sautoy (Dancer
Saida).

MAN WITH THE POWER, THE (TVM-
    1977) - 5-24-77
    Director: Nicholas Sgarro
Bob Neill (Eric Smith), Persis
Khambatta (Princess Siri), Tim
O'Connor (Walter Bloom), Vic Mor-
row (Paul), Noel de Souza (Shanda),
Roger Perry (Farnsworth), Bill
Fletcher (Dilling), Rene Assa
(Major Sajid), James Ingersoll
(driver).

MAN WITH THE RUBBER HEAD,
    THE (1901-Fr.) (A.K.A. "L'Homme
    a la Tete en Caoutchouc")

Director: Georges Melies

MAN WITH TWO FACES, THE (1934)
Director: Archie Mayo
Edward G. Robinson (Damon Wells),
Mary Astor (Jessica Wells), Ricardo
Cortez (Ben Weston), Louis Calhern
(Stanley Vance), John Eldredge
(Barry), Mae Clarke (Daphne),
Arthur Byron (Dr. Kendall), Henry
O'Neill (Police Inspector), Virginia
Sale (Peabody), Margaret Dale
(Martha), Emily Fitzroy (Hattie),
Arthur Aylesworth (morgue keeper),
David Landau (Detective Curtis).

MAN WITH TWO HEADS, THE (1970)
Director: Andy Milligan
Denis De Marne (Dr. Jekyll/Mr.
Blood), Julia Stratton (April Conners),
Gay Feld (Mary Ann Marsden), Jac-
queline Lawrence (Carla), Bryan
Southcombe (Oliver Marsden),
Berwick Kaler (Smithers), Junniver
Summerfield (Vicky).

MAN WITH TWO LIVES, THE (1942)
Director: Phil Rosen
Edward Norris, Marlo Dwyer,
Addison Richards, Anthony Warde,
Hugh Sothern, Edward Keane, Ernie
Adams, Kenne Duncan, George
Kirby, Eleanor Lawson, Tom Seidel,
Jack Ingraham, Frederick Burton,
Jack Buckley, Lois Landon, Frances
Richards, George Dobbs.

MARA OF THE WILDERNESS (1965)
Director: Frank McDonald
Adam West (Ken Williams), Linda
Saunders (Mara Wade), Theo Marcuse
(Jarnagan), Denver Pyle (Kelly),
Sean McClory (Dr. Frank Wade),
Eve Brent (Mrs. Wade), Ed Kemmer
(1st pilot), Stuart Walsh (2nd pilot),
Roberto Contreras (Friday), Leila
Walsh (Mara as a child).

MARAT/SADE (1967) (A.K.A. "The
Persecution and Assassination of
Jean-Paul Marat as Performed
by the Inmates of the Asylum of
Charenton Under the Direction of
the Marquis de Sade")
Director: Peter Brook
Patrick Magee (Marquis de Sade),
Ian Richardson (Jean-Paul Marat),
Glenda Jackson (Charlotte Corday),
Freddie Jones (Cucurucu), Clifford
Rose (M. Coulmier), Brenda Kempner
(Mme. Coulmier), Ruth Baker (Mlle.
Coulmier), Michael Williams (Herald),
Jonathan Burn (Polpoch), Jeannette

Landis (Rossignol), Robert Lloyd
(Jacques Roux), Susan Williamson
(Simonne Evrard), John Steiner,
Mark Jones, John Harwood,
Henry Mellor, Michael Farns-
worth, Guy Gordon, Leon Lissek,
Morgan Sheppard, John Hussey,
Mary Allen, Tamara Fuerst,
Sheila Grant, Lyn Pinkney, Mar-
oussia Frank, Michael Callinan,
Nicholas Moes, Heather Canning,
Timothy Hardy, Michael Gould,
Patrick Gowers, Rainier Schuelein.

MARCH HARE, THE (1956)
Director: George More O'Fer-
rall
Peggy Cummins (Pat Maguire),
Terence Morgan (Sir Charles Hare),
Wilfrid Hyde-White (Col. Keene),
Martita Hunt (Lady Anne), Der-
rick De Marney (Capt. Marlow),
Cyril Cusack (Lazy Mangan),
Charles Hawtrey (Fisher), Ivan
Samson (Hardwicke), Macdonald
Parke (Maguire), Reginald Beckwith
(Broker), Maureen Delany (Bridget).

MARGUERITE OF THE NIGHT
(1955-Fr./Ital.) (A.K.A. "Mar-
guerite de la Nuit")
Director: Claude Autant-Lara
Yves Montand, Michele Morgan,
Massimo Girotti, Jean-Francoise
Calve, Jean Delaucourt, Louis
Seigner, Fernand Sardou, Palau.

MARIE CHANTAL AGAINST DR.
KHA (1965-Fr./Span./Ital./Mor.)
(A.K.A. "Marie Chantal contre
Dr. Kha", "The Blue Panther")
Director: Claude Chabrol
Marie Laforet (Marie Chantal),
Akim Tamiroff (Dr. Kha), Fran-
cisco Rabal (Paco), Serge Raggiani
(Ivanov), Roger Hanin (Bruno),
Charles Denner (Johnson), Stephane
Audran (Olga).

MARK DONEN AGENT 27 (1966-Ital./
Span./Ger.) (A.K.A. "Mark
Donen Agente Zet")
Director: Giancarlo Romitelli
Lang Jeffries (Mark Donen), Laura
Valanzuela, Carlo Hinterman, Mit-
suoko.

MARK OF DEATH, THE (1962-Mex.)
(A.K.A. "La Marca del Muerto")
Director: Fernando Cortes
Fernando Casanova, Sonia Furio,
Aurora Alvarado, Pedro de Aquillon,
Rosa Maria Gallard, E. Espino.

MARK OF THE DEVIL (1970-Ger. /
Brit.) (A.K.A. "Brenn: Gexe
Brenn", "Burn, Witch, Burn")
Director: Michael Armstrong
Herbert Lom (Lord Cumberland), Reggie
Nalder (Albino), Udo Kier (Baron Chris-
tian von Meru), Olivera Vuco (Vanessa),
Herbert Fux (Chief Executioner), Adrian
Hoven, Gaby Fuchs, Ingeborg Schoener,
Doris Van Danwitz, Dorothea Carrera,
Marlies Peterson, Michael Maien,
Gunther Clemens, Johannas Buzalski.

MARK OF THE DEVIL, PART II (1972-
Ger.) (A.K.A. "Hexen: Geschandet
und su Tode Gequalt", "Witches:
Violated and Tortured to Death")
Director: Adrian Hoven
Anton Diffring, Erika Blanc, Reggie
Nalder, Percy Hoven, Astrid Kilian,
Ellen Umlaud, Lukas Ammann, Jean-
Pierre Zole, Rosy-Rosy, Johannes
Buzulski, Harry Hardt.

MARK OF THE GORILLA (1950)
Director: William Berke
Johnny Weismuller (Jungle Jim), Trudy
Marshall, Onslow Stevens, Suzanne Dal-
bert, Robert Pursell, Selmer Jackson.

MARK OF THE VAMPIRE (1935)
Director: Tod Browning
Bela Lugosi (Count Mora), Lionel
Barrymore (Prof. Zelen), Lionel Atwill
(Insp. Neumann), Elizabeth Allan (Irena
Borotyn), Holmes Herbert (Sir Karell
Borotyn), Jean Hersholt (Baron Otto
von Zinden), Carol Borland (Luna Mora),
Donald Meek (Dr. Doskil), Ivan Simpson
(Jan), Egon Brecher (coroner), Henry
Wadsworth (Count Feodor Vincenty),
Eily Malyon (sick woman), Christian
Rub (deaf man), Torbin Meyer (card
player), Zeffie Tilbury (grandmother),
Rosemary Glosz (innkeeper's wife),
Claire Vedara (English woman), Guy
Bellis (English man), Baron Hesse (bus
driver), Mrs. Lesovosky (old woman in
inn), Robert Greig (fat man), James
Bradbury, Jr.

MARK OF THE WHISTLER (1944) (A.K.A.
"The Marked Man")
Director: William Castle
Richard Dix (Lee Nugent), Janis Carter
(Patricia Henley), Porter Hall (Joe
Sorsby), Paul Guilfoyle (Gimpy Smith),
John Calvert (Eddie Donnelly), Matt
Willis (Perry Connelly).

MARK OF THE WITCH (1972)
Director: Tom Moore
Robert Elston, Anitra Walsh, Darryl

Wells, Marie Santell, Barbara Brownell.

MARKET OF SOULS, THE (1919)
Director: Joseph De Grsse
Philo McCullough, Dorothy Dalton,
Dorcas Mathews, H. E. Herbert.

MAROONED (1969)
Director: John Sturges
Gregory Peck (Charles Keith),
Richard Crenna (Jim Pruett), David
Janssen (Red Dougherty), Gene Hack-
man (Buzz Lloyd), James Franciscus
(Clayton Stone), Lee Grant (Celia
Pruett), Nancy Kovack (Teresa
Stone), Mariette Hartley (Betty Lloyd),
Scott Brady (Public Affairs Officer),
George Gaynes (Mission Director),
Walter Brooke (Radin), Mauritz
Hugo (Hardy), Craig Huebing (Flight
Director), John Carter (Flight Sur-
geon), Frank Marth (Space Systems
Director), Tom Stewart (Houston
Cap Com), Dennis Robertson (Launch
Director), Duke Hobbie (Titan Sys-
tems Specialist), George Smith
(Cape Weather Officer), Vincent
Van Lynn (Cannon), Bill Couch
(Russian Cosmonaut), Mary Linda
Rapelye (Pricilla Keith).

MARS NEEDS WOMEN (1966)
Director: Larry Buchanan
Tommy Kirk (Dop), Yvonne Craig
(Dr. Marjorie Bolen), Byron Lord
(Col. Page), Anthony Houston, Larry
Tanner, Warren Hammack, Cal
Duggan (Martians), Bill Thurman,
Pat Delaney, Donna Lindberg,
Sherry Roberts, Bubbles Cash, Roger
Ready, Neil Fletcher, George
Edgley, Dick Simpson, Barnett Shaw,
Chet Davis, Ron Scott, Don Campbell,
Gordon Buloe, Claude Earls, Bob
Lorenz, David Englund, Ann Palmer,
Pat Cranshaw, Sally Casey, Syliva
Rundell, Terry Davis.

MARTA (1971-Span./Ital.)
Director: Jose Antonio Nieves
Conde
Stephen Boyd (Miguel), Marisa Mell
(Marta/Pilar), Isa Miranda (Elena),
Jesus Puente (Don Carlos), Jorge
Rigaud (Arutro), Howard Ross (Luis),
Melida Quiroga (Dona Clara).

MARTIAN CHRONICLES, THE (TVM-
1980) - 1-27-80, 1-28-80 & 1-29-80
Director: Michael Anderson
Rock Hudson (Col. John Wilder), Darren
McGavin (Capt. Sam Parkhill), Bernie

Casey (Capt. Jeff Spender), Gayle Hunnicutt (Ruth Wiler), Fritz Weaver (Father Peregrine), Roddy McDowall (Father Stone), Barry Morse (Peter Hathaway), Joyce Van Patten (Elma Parkhill), Bernadette Peters (Genevieve), Christopher Connelly (Ben Driscoll), Nicholas Hammond (Arthur Black), Maggie Wright (Ylla), James Faulkner (Mr. K), Maria Schell (Anna Lustig), Wolfgang Reichmann (David Lustig, Sr.), Michael Anderson, Jr. (David Lustig, Jr.), Robert Beatty (Gen. Malcolm Halstead), Nyree Dawn Porter (Alice Becker), Richard Heffer (Capt. Conover), John Cassady (Capt. Briggs), Peter Marinker (McClure), Alison Elliott (Lavinia), Jon Finch (Jesus Christ), Terence Longdon (Martian Edler), Vadim Glowna (Capt. Hinkson), Derek Lamden.

MARTIAN IN PARIS, A (1960-Fr.) (A.K.A. "Un Martien a Paris")
    Director: Jean-Daniel Daninos
Darry Cowl, Michele Verez, Nicole Mirel, Henri Vilbert, Rolande Segur, Giselle Grandre.

MARTIANS ARRIVED, THE (1964-Span./Ital.) (A.K.A. "Llegaron los Marcianos", "The Martians Have Twelve Hands")
    Director: Franco Castellano & Giuseppe Moccia/Pipolo
Umberto D'Oris, Margaret Lee, Paolo Panelli, Carlo Croccolo, Franco Franchi, Alfredo Landa, Raimondo Vianello, Enzo Garinei, Cristina Gajoni, Magali Noel, Jose Calvo.

MARTIN (1978)
    Director: George A. Romero
John Amplas (Martin), Lincoln Maazel (Cuda), Christine Forrest (Christina), Elayne Nadeau (Mrs. Santini), Tom Savini (Arthur), Al Levitsky (Lewis), Fran Middleton (train victim), Sarah Venable (housewife victim).

MARY, MARY, BLOODY MARY (1975-Mex.)
    Director: Juan Lopez Moctezuma
Christina Ferrari (Mary), John Carradine (the Man), David Young (Ben Ryder), Helena Rojo (Greta), Arthur Hansel (U.S. Agent), Enrique Lucero (Mexican Police Lieutenant), Susan Kamini (hitchhiker).

MARY POPPINS (1964)
    Director: Robert Stevenson
Julie Andrews (Mary Poppins), Dick Van Dyke (Bert), David Tomlinson

(Mr. Banks), Glynis Johns (Mrs. Banks), Karen Dotrice (Jane Banks), Matthew Garber (Michael Banks), Hermione Baddeley (Ellen), Ed Wynn (Uncle Albert), Arthur Treacher (Constable Jones), Elsa Lanchester (Karie Nanna), Jane Darwell (Bird Woman), Reginald Owen (Admiral Boom), Arthur Malet (Mr. Dawes, Jr.) Marjorie Eaton (Miss Persimmon), Lester Mathews (Mr. Tomes), Cyril Delevanti (Mr. Grubbs), Reta Shaw (Mrs. Brill), Marjorie Bennett (Miss Lark), Don Barclay (Mr. Binnacle), Alma Lawton (Mrs. Corry), Clive L. Halliday (Mr. Mousley), Doris Lloyd (depositor), James Logan.

MASK, THE (1961) (A.K.A. "Eyes of Hell")
    Director: Julian Roffman
Paul Stevens (Dr. Allan Barnes), Paul Nevins (Demon of the Mask), Claudette Nevins (Pamela Albright), Bill Walker (Lt. Martin), Martin Lavut (Michael Radin), Anne Collings (Miss Goodrich), Leo Leyden (Dr. Soames), Norman Ettlinger (Prof. Quincy), Eleanor Beecroft (Mrs. Kelly), Ray Lawlor (lab technician), William Bryden (Anderson), Stephen Appleby (museum guide), Jim Moran (himself), Nancy Island (girl who is killed), Rudi Linschoten (Dr. Barnes in dream sequence).

MASKED MARVEL, THE (1943) (A.K.A. "Sakima and the Masked Marvel") - Serial in 12 episodes
    Director: Spencer Gordon Bennet
William Forrest (Martin Crane), David Bacon (Bob Barton/Masked Marvel), Louise Currie (Alice Hamilton), Johnny Arthur (Mura Sakima), Rod Bacon (Jim Arnold), Anthony Warde (Killer Mace), Richard Clarke (Frank Jeffers), Tom Steele (Masked Marvel in mask/estate heavy), Gayne Whitman (Marvel's voice), Howard Hickman (Warren Hamilton), Bill Healy (Terry Morton), Thomas Louden (Mathews), Eddie Parker (Meggs), Wendell Niles (newscaster), Duke Green (Karl/Spike/Kaler), Dale Van Sickel (Kline/Bleek/Blunt), George Pembroke (Air Raid Warden), Lester Dorr (reporter No. 1), Stanley Price (Barnes), Ken Terrell (bridge heavy/dock heavy/foreman), Forbes Murray (Doctor), Crane Whitley (Curtiss), Robert J. Wilke (garage heavy), Nolan Leary (gas station attendant), Fred Graham (Hart/Janson/Pete),

Herbert Rawlinson (Kettering), George J. Lewis (Philip Morton), Roy Barcroft (Kern), Edward Van Sloane (A. M. MacRae), George Suzanne (pier heavy), Sam Flint (police sergeant), Bud Geary, Tom London (truckers), John Daheim (bartender), Kenneth Harlan (officer), Sam Ash (reporter No. 2), Ernie Adams (Wilson), Allen Pomeroy (Chef), Carey Loftin (Grail), Joe Yrigoyen (Gyp/Karnes), Harry Woods (Parsons), Lynton Brent, Lee Roberts (guards), Sam Bernard (Parker), Brooks Benedict (photographer), Jack O'Shea (Ross/station heavy No. 1), Pat O'Shea (station heavy No. 2), Nora Lane (secretary), Frank O'Connor (watchman), Charles Hutchinson, Preston Peterson, Thom Metzetti, Betty Miles.

MASK OF DIIJON, THE (1945)
Director: Lew Landers
Erich Von Stroheim (Diijon), Mauritz Hugo (Danton), Edward Van Sloan (Sheffield), Jeanne Bates, Will Wright, Hope Landin, Denise Vernac, Shimen Ruskin, Antonio Filauri, Roy Darmour, Robert Malcolm.

MASK OF FU MANCHU, THE (1932)
Director: Charles Brabin
Boris Karloff (Fu Manchu), Myrna Loy (Fah Lo See), Lewis Stone (Nayland Smith), Jean Hersholt (Von Berg), Lawrence Grant (Sir Lionel Barton), Karen Morley (Miss Barton), Charles Starret (Terrence Granville), David Torrence (McLeod), Herbert Bunston, Gertrude Michael.

MASQUE OF THE RED DEATH, THE (1964)
Director: Roger Corman
Vincent Price (Prince Prospero), Hazel Court (Juliana), Jane Asher (Francesca), David Weston (Gino), Nigel Green (Ludovico), Patrick Magee (Alfredo), Skip Martin (Hop Toad), John Westbrook (Man in Red), Paul Whitsun-Jones (Scarlatti), Jean Lodge (Scarlatti's wife), Julian Burton (Senor Veronese), Brian Hewlett (Lampredi), Gay Brown (Senroa Escobar), Vernia Greenlaw (Esmeralda), Robert Brown (guard), Harvey Hall (Clistor), Doreen Dawn (Anna-Marie).

MASSACRE AT CENTRAL HIGH (1976)
Director: Renee Daalder
Derel Maury (David), Andrew Stevens (Mark), Kimberly Beck (Teresa), Robert Carradine (Spoony), Lani

O'Grady (Jane), Cheryl 'Rainbeaux' Smith (Mary), Steve Bond (Craig), Roy Underwood (Bruce), Steve Sikes (Rodney), Damon Douglas (Paul), Dennis Court (Arthur), Thomas Logan (Harvey), Jeffrey Winner (Oscar).

MASSARATI AND THE BRAIN (TVM-1982) - 8-26-82
Director: Harvey Hart
Daniel Pilot (Massarati), Peter Billingsley (Christopher), Ann Turkel (Diana Meredith), Christopher Lee (Leopold).

MASTER AND MARGHERITE, THE (1972-Yugo./Ital.) (A.K.A. "Il Maestro e Margherita")
Director: Aleksandar Petrovic
Ugo Tognazzi (Master), Mimsy Farmer (Margarita), Alain Cuny (Satan/Prof. Woland), Bata Zivojinovic (Koroviev), Pavle Vojisic (Azazello), Ljuba Tadic.

MASTER KEY, THE (1945) - serial in 13 episodes
Chapters: 1. "Trapped by Flames", 2. "Death Turns the Wheel", 3. "Ticket to Disaster", 4. "Drawbridge Danger", 5. "Runaway Car', 6. "Shot Down", 7. "Death on the Dial", 8. "Bullet Serenade", 9. "On Stage for Murder", 10. "Fatal Masquerade", 11. "Crash Curve", 12. "Lightning Underground" & 13. "The Last Key".
Director: Ray Taylor & Lewis D. Collins
Milburn Stone (Tom Brant), Jan Wiley (Janet Lowe), Byron Foulger (Prof. Henderson), Addison Richards (Garret Donohue), Maris Wrixon (Dorothy Newton), Sarah Padden (Aggie), George Lynn (Herman), Lash LaRue (Migsy), Russell Hicks (Chief O'Brien), Dennis Moore (Jack Ryan), Ernie Adams, Gene Roth, Roland Varno, John Merton, Dick Alexander.

MASTER MIND, THE (1920)
Director: Kenneth Webb
Lionel Barrymore, Ralph Kellard, Gypsie O'Brien, Bradley Barker, Marie Shotwell, Charles Brandt.

MASTER MINDS (1949)
Director: Jean Yarbrough
Leo Gorcey (Slip Mahoney), Huntz Hall (Sach Debussy Jones), Glenn Strange (Atlas), Gabriel Dell (Gabe Moreno), Jane Adams (Nancy Marlowe),

Alan Napier (Dr. Drugili), Billy
Benedict (Whitey), Bernard Gorcey
(Louie Dumbrowsky), Minerva Urecal
(Mrs. Hoskins), Skelton Knaggs (Hugo),
Bennie Bartlett (Butch), William Yet-
ter (Otto), David Gorcey (Chuck),
Chester Clute (Mike Barton), Pat
Goldin (father), Robert Coogan (young
man).

MASTER MYSTERY, THE (1918) -
    serial in 15 episodes
    Director: Burton King
Harry Houdini (Quentin Locke), Mar-
guerite Marsh (Eve Brent), William
Pike (Peter Brent), Floyd Buckley
(Q the Automoton), Ruth Stonehouse
(Deluxe Dora), Edna Britton (maid),
Charles Graham (Madagascar Strang-
ler), Jack Burns (chemist).

MASTER OF HORROR (1960-Arg.)
    (A. K. A. "Obras Maestras del
    Terror", "Masterworks of Terror")
    Director: Enrique Carreras
Narcisco Ibanez Serrandor, Carlos
Estrade, Ines Moreno, Lillian Valmar,
Narcisco Ibanes Menta, Marcedes
Carreras.

MASTER OF THE WORLD, THE
    (1934-Ger.) (A. K. A. "Der
    Herrn der Welt")
    Director: Harry Piel
Sybille Schmitz, Walter Janssen,
Walter Franck, S. Schuerenberg.

MASTER OF THE WORLD (1961)
    Director: William Witney
Vincent Price (Robur), Charles
Bronson (Strock), Henry Hull (Pru-
dent), Mary Webster (Dorothy Pru-
dent), David Frankham (Philip),
Richard Harrison (Alistair), Vito
Scotti (Topahe), Ken Terrell (Shanks),
Wally Campo (Turner), Steve Masino
(Weaver), Peter Besbas (Wilson).

MASTERS OF VENUS (1962) - serial
    in 8 episodes
    Director: Ernest Morris
Norman Wooland (Dr. Ballantyne),
Robin Stewart (Jim Ballantyne),
Amanda Coxell (Pat Ballantyne),
Ferdy Mayne (Votan), George Pastell
(Kallas), Arnold Diamond (Imos),
Patrick Kavanagh (Mike), Robin
Hunter (Peter), Jackie Martin (Bor-
las).

MATCHLESS (1966-Ital.)
    Director: Alberto Lattuada
Patrick O'Neal (Perry Liston), Donald

Pleasence (Andreanu), Henry Silva
(Hank Norris), Ira Furstenberg
(Arabella), Howard St. John (Gen.
Shapiro), Sorrell Booke (Col. Cool-
pepper), Nicoletta Machiavelli
(Tipsy), Tiziano Cortini (Hogdon),
Valeri Inkijinov (hypnotizer),
Elizabeth Wu (O Lan), Andy Ho
(O'Chin), Jacques Herlin (O'Chin's
doctor), M. Mishiku (Li-Hunang),
Margaret Lee.

MAUSOLEUM (1982)
    Director: Robert Barich
Marjoe Gortner, Bobbie Bresee,
Norman Burton, LaWanda Page,
Maurice Sherbanee, Laura Hippe.

MAZE, THE (1953)
    Director: William Cameron
    Menzies
Richard Carlson (Gerald McTeam),
Veronica Hurst (Kitty Murray),
Michael Pate (William), Katherine
Emery (Mrs. Murray), Hillary
Brooke (Peggy Lord), Robin Hughes
(Richard Roblar), Lillian Bond
(Mrs. Dilling), John Dodsworth
(Dr. Bert Dilling), Owen McGiveney
(Simon), Stanley Fraser (Robert),
Clyde Cook (cab driver).

MEATCLEAVER MASSACRE (1977)
    (A. K. A. "The Hollywood Meat-
    cleaver Massacre")
    Director: Evan Lee
Christopher Lee (Narrator), Larry
Justin, Bob Clark, Bob Mead,
Sandra Crane, Jonathan Grant, Jim
Habif, Evelyn Ellis.

MEDUSA TOUCH, THE (1978)
    Director: Jack Gold
Richard Burton (John Morlar),
Lino Ventura (Brunel), Lee Remick
(Dr. Zonfeld), Harry Andrews
(Assistant Commissioner), Marie-
Christine Barrault (Patricia), Michael
Hordern (Atropos, the fortune teller),
Derek Jacobi (Townley, the publisher),
Robert Lang (Pennington), Jeremy
Brett (Parrish), Alan Badel (Bar-
ristor), Michael Byrne (Duff), Gordon
Jackson (Dr. Johnson), Robert
Flemying (Judge McKinley), Norman
Bird (father), Jennifer Jayne (mother),
Philip Stone (Dean), Maurice O'Con-
nell (Sgt. Robbins), Avril Elgar (Mrs.
Pennington), John Normington (School-
master), Malcolm Tierney (Deacon),
James Hazeldine (Lovelass), Mark
Jones (Sgt. Hughes), Wendy Gifford
(receptionist), Gordon Honeycombe

(TV newscaster), Frances Tomelty
(nanny), Brooks Williams (male nurse),
Victor Winding (senior police officer),
Anthony Blackett (mounted police
officer), John Flanagan (police constable), Denyse Alexander (hospital
doctor), Stanley Lebor (police doctor),
George Innes (Van Driver), Ian Marter
(detective in street), Cornelius Bowe
(young Morlar), Adam Bridges (Morlar
at age 10), Joseph Clark (Morlar at
age 14), Christopher Burgess (pilot),
Matthew Long (co-pilot), Earl Rhodes
(Parson), Colin Rix (engineer).

MEDUSA VS. THE SON OF HERCULES
   (1962-Ital. /Span.) (A. K. A. "Perseo
   l'Invinceble", "Perseus the Invincible",
   "El Valle de los Hombres de Piedra",
   "The Valley of the Stone Men", "Per-
   seus Against the Monsters")
   Director: Alberto de Martino
Richard Harrison (Perseus), Arturo
Dominici, Leo Anchoriz, Anna Ranalli,
Elisa Cegani.

MEET MR. LUCIFER
   Director: Anthony Pelissier
Stanley Holloway (Mr. Hollingsworth/
Mr. Lucifer), Peggy Cummins (Kitty),
Jack Watling (Jim), Joseph Tomelty
(Mr. Pedelty), Barbara Murray
(Patricia), Gordon Jackson (Hector),
Ernest Thesiger (Mr. MacDonald),
Kay Kendall (singer), Charles Victor
(Mr. Elder), Humphrey Lestocq
(Arthur), Joan Sims (Fairy Queen),
Jean Cadell (Mrs. MacDonald), Ray-
mond Huntley (Patterson), Ian Car-
michael (Man Friday), Olga Gwynne
(principal boy), Frank Pettingell (Mr.
Roberts), Irene Handl (lady with dog),
Gladys Henson (lady in the bus),
Roddy Hughes (Billings), Eliot Make-
ham (Edwards), Dandy Nichols (Mrs.
Clarke), Bill Fraser (band leader).

MEGAFORCE (1982)
   Director: Hal Needham
Barry Bostwick (Ace Hunter), Persis
Khambatta (Zara), Michael Beck
(Dallas), Edward Mulhare (Byrne-
White), George Furth (Prof. Eggstrum),
Henry Silva (Guerera), Michael Kulcsar
(Ivan), Evan Kim (Suki), Ralph Wilcox
(Zac), Anthony Penya (Sixkiller), J.
Victor Lopez (Lopez), Michael Carven
(Anton), Bobby Bass (motorcycle driver),
Samir Kamoun (aide), Youssef Merhi
(radio operator), Roger Lowe (chauffeur),
Robert Fuller (pilot), Ray Hill, Jr.
(tank commander).

MENACE (1934)
   Director: Ralph Murphy
John Lodge (Roland Cavendish),
Raymond Milland (Freddie Bastion),
Halliwell Hobbes (Skinner), Henri-
etta Crosman (Mrs. Thornton),
Robert Allen (Andrew Forsythe),
Doris Llewellyn (Cynthia Bastion),
Burton Churchill (Norman Bellamy),
Desmond Roberts (Underwood).

MENACE FROM OUTER SPACE (1954)
   See Television: Rocky Jones,
   Space Ranger (1953-54)

MEN MUST FIGHT (1933)
   Director: Edgar Selwyn
Diana Wynyard (Laura Seward),
Lewis Stone (Edward Seward),
May Robson (Mrs. Seward, Sr.),
Hedda Hopper (Mrs. Chase),
Mary Carlisle (Evelyn), Robert
Young (Geoffrey), Phillips Holmes
(Bob), Robert Greig (Albert), Ruth
Selwyn (Peggy Chase), Luis
Alberni (Soto), Donald Dillaway
(Steve).

MEPHISTO WALTZ, THE (1971)
   Director: Paul Wendkos
Alan Alda (Myles Clarkson), Jac-
queline Bisset (Paula Clarkson),
Barbara Parkins (Roxanne), Curt
Jergens (Duncan Ely), William
Windom (Dr. West), Bradford
Dillman (Bill Delancey), Kathleen
Widdoes (Maggie West), Pamelyn
Ferdin (Abby Clarkson), Khigh
Dheigh (Zanc Theun), Barry Kroe-
ger (Raymont), Lylyan Chauvin
(writer), Gregory Morton (conductor),
Curt Lowens (agency head), Alberto
Morin.

MERMAID, THE (1904-Fr.) (A. K. A.
   "La Sirene")
   Director: Georges Melies

MERMAIDS OF TIBURON (1962)
   (A. K. A. "The Aqua Sex")
   Director: John Lamb
Timothy Carey (Milo Sangster),
Diane Webber (Mermaid Queen),
John Mylong (Ernst Steinhauer),
George Rowe (Dr. Samuel Jami-
son), Jose Gonzales-Gonzales (Pepe
Gallardo), Gil Garetto (Senor
Barquero), Vicki Kantenwine, Nani
Morissey, Jean Carroll, Karen
Goodman, Judy Edwards, Diana
Cook, Nancy Burns (Mermaids).

MESA OF LOST WOMEN, THE (1952)

Director: Herbert Tevos
Jackie Coogan (Dr. Arana), Richard
Travis (Don Mulcahey), Allan Nixon
(Doc Tucker), Mary Hill (Doreen),
Robert Knapp (Grant Phillips),
Tandra Quinn (Tarantella), Harmon
Stevens (Masterson), Samuel Wu
(Wu), George Barrows (George),
Chris-Pin Martin, John Martin,
Angelo Rossitto, Fred Kelsey, Kath-
erine Victor, Lyle Talbot (Narrator),

MESSAGE FROM MARS (1913)
Director: J. Walett Waller
Charles Hawtrey, E. Holman Clark,
Frank Hector, Crissie Bell, Hubert
Willis, Evelyn Beaumont, Kate
Tyndale, Eileen Temple, B. Stan-
more, R. Crompton, Tonie Reith.

MESSAGE FROM MARS, A (1921)
Director: Maxwell Karger
Leonard Mudie, Bert Lytell, Gordon
Ash, Raye Dean, Alphons Ethier,
Maude Milton.

MESSAGE FROM SPACE (1978-Jap.)
Director: Kinji Fukasaku
Vic Morrow (Gen. Garuda), Sonny
Chiba (Hans), Peggy Lee Brannon
(Meia), Philip Casnoff (Aaron),
Tetsuro Tamba (Nogushi), Sue
Shiomi (Esmeralida), Miko Narita
(Rockseia XII), Makoto Sato (Uroc-
co), Masazumi Okabe (Jack), Hiro-
yuki Sanada (Shiro), Noburo Mitani
(Kamesasa), Junkichi Orimoto (Kido),
Isamu Shimuzo (Robot Beba 2), Hideyo
Amamoto (Dark), Harumi Sone (La-
zarl).

MESSALINA AGAINST THE SON OF
  HERCULES (1965-Ital.) (A.K.A.
  "Empress Messalina Meets the
  Son of Hercules")
Director:
Richard Harrison (Glaucus), Marilu
Tolo (Messalina), Lisa Gastoni.

MESSIAH OF EVIL (1975)
Director: Gloria Katz
Michael Greer (Thom), Marianna
Hill (Arletty), Joy Bang (Toni),
Anitra Ford (Laura), Elisha Cook,
Jr. (Charley), Royal Dano (Joseph
Lang).

METAL MESSIAH (1978)
Director: Tibor Takacs
John Paul Young (Max), Richard
Allen (Philip Chandler), David
Hensen (the Messiah).

METAMORFOSIS (1971-Span.)
Director: Jacinto Esteva
Julian Ugarte, Romy, Carlos Otero,
Luis Ciges, Matta May, Alberto
Puig.

METAMORPHOSIS (1975-Swed.)
  (A.K.A. "Forvandlingen")
Director: Ivo Dvorak
Peter Schildt (Gregor), Ernst
Gunther (Mr. Samsa), Gunn Wall-
gren (wife), Inga-Lill Carlsson
(Grete), Per Oscarsson (Gregor's
employer).

METEOR (1979)
Director: Ronald Neame
Sean Connery (Dr. Bradley),
Natalie Wood (Tatiana), Brian
Keith (Dr. Dubov), Karl Malden
(Sherwood), Martin Landau (Adlan),
Henry Fonda (the President),
Richard Dysart (Secretary of De-
fense), Bo Brundin (Manheim),
Katherine DeHetre (Jan), Trevor
Howard (Sir Michael Hughes),
Joseph Campanella (Easton),
James Richardson (Alan), Roger
Robinson (Hunter), Clyde Kusatsu
(Yamashiro), John Findlater (Tom
Easton), Gregory Gaye (Russian
Premier), Peter Bourne (UN Pres-
ident), Burke Byrnes (Coast Guard
Officer), Zitto Kazann (Party
Member), Paul Tulley (Bill Frager),
Michael Zaslow (Mason), Allen
Williams (Michael McKendrick),
John McKinney (Watson), Bibi
Besch (Mrs. Bradley), Sybil Danning
(girl skier), Larry Duran (stuntman).

METEOR MONSTER (1957) (A.K.A.
  "Teenage Monster")
Director: Jacques Marquette
Gloria Castillo (Kathy North), Stuart
Wade, Gilbert Perkins, Norman
Leavitt, Charles Courtney, Stephen
Parker, Jim McCullough, Gaybe
Mooradian, Frank Davis, Arthur
Berkeley.

METROPOLIS (1926-Ger.)
Director: Fritz Lang
Rudolf Klein-Rogge (Rotwang),
Alfred Abel (Jon Frederson),
Gustav Frohlich (Freder), Brigitte
Helm (Maria), Fritz Rasp (Slim),
Theodor Loos (Josaphat), Erwin
Biswanger (No. 11811), Hanns Leo
Reich (Marinus), Olaf Storm (Jan),
Heinrich George (Foreman), Georg
John, Margaretta Lanner, Heinrich
Gotho, Max Dietze, Walter Kohle,

Arthur Rheinhard, Grete Berger, Ellen Frey, Erwin Vater, Olly Boheim, Lisa Gray, Helene Weigel, Anny Hintze, Hilde Woitscheff, Rose Lichtenstein, Beatrice Garga, Fritz Alberti, Helen von Munchhofen.

MICROWAVE MASSACRE (1979)
Director: Wayne Burwick
Jackie Vernon, Loren Schein, Al Troupe, Claire Ginsberg, Sarah Alt.

MIDI—MINUIT (1970-Fr.) (A.K.A. "Noon to Midnight")
Director: Piere Philippe
Sylvie Fennec, Beatrice Arnac, Jacques Portet, Daniel Emilfork, Laurent Vergez, Patrick Jouanne.

MIDNIGHT MENACE (1937)
Director: Sinclair Hill
Charles Farrell (Brian Gaunt), Fritz Kortner (Peters), Danny Green (Socks), Margaret Vyner (Mary Stevens), Wallace Evennett (Smith), Dino Galvani (Tony), Monte de Lyle (Pierre), Dennis Val Norton (Vronsky), Arthur Finn (Mac), Raymond Lovell (Harris), Lawrence Hanray (Sir George), Billy Bray.

MIDNIGHT OFFERINGS (TVM-1981) - 2-27-81
Director: Rod Holcomb
Melissa Sue Anderson (Vivian Sotherland), Mary McDonough (Robin Prentiss), Patrick Cassidy (Dave), Cathryn Damon (Diane Sotherland), Gordon Jump (Sherm Sotherland), Peter MacLean (Mr. Prentiss), Marion Ross (Mrs. Moore), Ray Girardin (Clausen), Jeff MacKay (Nemenz), Jack Garner, Dana Kimmell.

MIDNIGHT WARNING, THE (1932)
Director: Spencer Gordon Bennet
William 'Stage' Boyd (William Cornish), Claudia Dell (Enid van Buren), Henry Hall (Dr. Barris), John Harron (Erich), Hooper Atchley (Dr. Stephen Walcott), Huntley Gordon (Mr. Gordon), Phillips Smalley (Dr. Brown), Lloyd Ingraham (Adolph Klein), Lloyd Whitlock (Rankin), Art Winkler, Lon Poff.

MIDSTREAM (1929)
Director: James Flood
Ricardo Cortez (James Satnwood), Claire Windsor (Helen Craig), Montague Love (Dr. Nelson), Larry Kent (Martin Baker), Helen Jerome Eddy (Mary Mason), Leslie Brigham (Mephistopheles), Genevieve Schrader (Marguerite), Louis Alvarez (Faust), Florence Foyer (Marthe).

MIDSUMMER NIGHT'S DREAM, A (1935)
Director: Max Reinhardt & William Dietelre
James Cagney (Bottom), Dick Powell (Lysander), Joe E. Brown (Flute), Jean Muir (Helena), Victor Jory (Oberon), Anita Louise (Titania), Frank McHugh (Quince), Mickey Rooney (Puck), Hugh Herbert (Snout), Olivia de Havilland (Hermia), Ian Hunter (Theseus), Grant Mitchell (Egeus), Ross Alexander (Demetrius), Verree Teasdale (Hippolyta, Queen of Amazons), Nini Theilade (first Fairy), Dewey Robinson (Snug), Otis Harlan (Starveling), Billy Barty (Mustardseed), Hobart Cavanaugh (Philostrate), Arthur Treacher (Ninny's Tomb).

MIGHTY GORGA, THE (1970)
Director: David L. Hewitt
Anthony Eisley, Scott Brady, Kent Taylor, Megan Timothy, Lee Parish, Bruce Kemp.

MIGHTY JOE YOUNG (1949)
Director: Ernest B. Schoedsack
Robert Armstrong (Max O'Hara), Terry Moore (Jill Young), Ben Johnson (Gregg), Regis Toomey (John Young), Frank McHugh (Windy), Dennis Green (Crawford), Douglas Fowley, Paul Guilfoyle, Nestor Paiva (drunks), Dale Van Sickel (stuntman), Primo Carnera, Wee Willie Davis, Henry 'Bomber Kulkavich' Kulky, Sammy Stein, Karl David, Ian 'Iron Man' Batchelor, Phil 'Swedish Angel' Olafsson, Frank 'Man Mountain Dean' Leavitt, Ivan Rasputin, Sammy Menacker (Strongmen), Selmer Jackson, Ellen Corby, Addison Richards, James Flavin, Iris Adrian, Lora Lee Michel.

MIGHTY PEKING MAN, THE (1977-Chin.) (A.K.A. "Goliathon")
Director: Ho Meng-hua/Homer Gaugh
Li Hsiu-hsien (Chen Cheng-feng), Evelyne Kraft (Ah Wei), Hsaiao Yao (Huang Tsui-hua), Ku Feng (Lu Tiern), Lin Wei-tu (Chen Shi-yu),

Hsu Shao-shing (Ah Lung), Chen Ping (Lucy), Wu Hang-sheng (Ah Pi).

$1,000,000 DUCK (1971)
    Director: Vincent McEvesty
Dean Jones (Prof. Albert Dooley), Sandy Duncan (Katie Dooley), Joe Flynn (Finley Hooper), Tony Roberts (Fred Hines), James Gregory (Rutledge), Jack Kruschen (Dr. Gottlieb), Virginia Vincent, Edward Andrews, Arthur Hunnicutt, Sammy Jackson.

MILLION EYES OF SU-MURU, THE (1967) (A.K.A. "Sumuru")
    Director: Lindsay Shonteff
Frankie Avalon (Tommy Carter), Shirley Eaton (Su-Muru), George Nader (Nick West), Klaus Kinski (Pres. Boong), Wilfrid Hyde-White (Col. Baisbrook), Marie Rohm (Helga), Salli Sachse (Mikki), Krista Nell (Zoe), Essie Huang (Kitty), Patti Chandler (Louise), Ursula Rank (Erna), Paul Chang (Insp. Koo), Jon Fong (Col. Medika), Jill Hamilton, Denise Davreux, Christine Lok, Mary Cheng, Lisa Gray, Margaret Cheung, Louise Lee (guards).

MILL OF THE STONE WOMEN (1960-Ital./Fr.) (A.K.A. "Il Mulino Delle Donne di Pietra", "Le Moulin des Supplices", "Drops of Blood")
    Director: Giorgio Ferroni
Pierre Brice (Hans), Scilla Gabel (Elfy Wahl), Herbert Boehme (Prof. Wahl), Wolfgang Preiss (Dr. Bolem), Marco Guglielmi (Raab), Danny Carrel (Lise), Olga Solbelli, Liana Orfei.

MIND BENDERS, THE (1963)
    Director: Basil Deardon
Dirk Bogarde (Dr. Henry Longman), Mary Ure (Oonagh Longman), Michael Bryant (Dr. Tate), Wendy Craig (Annabelle), Edward Fox (Stewart), Sir John Clements (Major Hall), Geoffrey Keen (Calder), Roger Delgado (Dr. Jean Bonvouloirs), Norman Bird (Aubrey), Harold Goldblatt (Prof. Sharpey), Terry Palmer (Norman), Terence Alexander (Coach), Georgina Moon (Persephone), Timothy Beaton (Paul), Teresa Van Hoorn (Penny), Christopher Ellis (Peers), Robin Hawdon (student at Oxford), Edward Palmer (porter), Philip Ray (father), Pauline Winter (mother).

MIND OF MR. SOAMES, THE (1970)
    Director: Alan Cooke
Terence Stamp (Joan Soames), Robert Vaughn (Dr. Bergen), Nigel Davenport (Dr. Maitland), Christian Roberts (Thomas Fleming), Judy Parfitt (Jenny Bannerman), Scott Forbes (Richard Bannerman), Norman Jones (David), Donal Donnelly (Joe Allen), Billy Cornelius (Sgt. Clifford), Dan Jackson (Nicholis), Joe McPartland (Insp. Moore), Jon Croft (guard), Bill Pilkington (Pub owner), Tony Caunter (schoolteacher), Pamela Moseiwitch (girl on train), Kate Bimchy (barmaid), Esmond Webb (ticket seller), Joe Gladwin (old man in car), Eric Brooks (TV floor manager).

MIND OVER MURDER (TVM-1979) - 10-23-79
    Director: Ivan Nagy
Deborah Raffin (Suzy), David Ackroyd (Ben), Bruce Davison (Jason), Andrew Prine (Bald Man), Penelope Willis (Pierce), Christopher Cary (John Povey), Paul Lukather (Capt. Moran), Jann Burrell (Mrs. Winterspoon), Michael Horsley (Rookie), Wayne Heffley (Lt. Wales), Rex Riley (Anderson), Clint Young (Mr. Glazier), Robert Englund (Ted), Paul Reid Roman (Arnold), Lanny Duncan (Cab Driver), Jack Griffin (cameraman), Carl Anderson (Baker), Craig Baxley (Bobby), Don Ray Hall (reporter), Linda Ryan (young woman), Amy Allen Darr (receptionist), Natalija Nogulich (girl), Lenny Geer (derelect), Richard Winterstein (bus driver).

MIND SNATCHERS, THE (1972) (A.K.A. "The Happiness Cage")
    Director: Bernard Gerard
Christopher Walken (Rese), Joss Ackland (Dr. Frederick), Ronny Cox (Miles), Ralph Meeker (the Major), Susan Travers (Nurse Schroeder), Marco St. John (Orderly), Tom Aldredge (medic), Bette Henritze (Anna Draus), Birthe Newmann (Lisa), Claus Nissen (psychiatrist).

MINOTAUR, THE (1960-Ital.) (A.K.A. "Teseo Contro il Minotauro", "Theseus Against the Minotaur", "Minotaur - The Wild Beast of Crete", "The Warlord of Crete")
    Director: Silvio Amadio
Bob Mathias (Theseus), Rosanna

Schiaffino (Phaedra/Ariane), Rick
Battaglia (Demetrius), Alberto Lupo
(Chrysone), Carlos Tammerlani (King
Minos), Nico Pepe (Gerione), Nerio
Bernardi (King Egea), Tina Lattanzi
(Queen Pasiphe), Paul Muller (Coctor),
Titiana Casetti (Elea), Alberto Plebani,
Susanne Loret.

MIRACLE IN MILAN (1951-Ital.)
(A. K. A. "Miracolo a Milano")
Director: Vittorio de Sica
Francesco Golisano/Toto (Toto), Paolo
Stoppa (the Bad Rappi), Emma Gramat-
ica (the Old Lolatta), Brunella Boyo
(the Little Edvige), Anna Carena (Sig-
nore Altezzosa), Guglielmo Barnabo
(the Rich Man), Alba Arnova (the
Statue), Virgilio Riento (the Sergeant),
Ermino Spalla (Gaetano), Flora Cambi
(the Unhappy Sweetheart), Arturo
Bragaglia (Alfredo), Riccardo Bertazzolo
(Wrestler), Angelo Prioli (1st Comman-
der), Francesco Rissone (2nd Commander), Granduani Gianni (Little Toto).

MIRACLE MAN, THE (1919)
Director: George Loane Tucker
Lon Chaney, Sr. (Frog), Joseph Dowling
(the Patriarch), Betty Compson (Rose),
Thomas Meighan (Tom Burke), W.
Lawson Butt (Richard King), J. M. Du-
mont (the Dope), Fred A. Turner (Mr.
Higgins), Lucille Hutton (Ruth Higgins),
Elinor Fair (Claire King), Frankie Lee.

MIRACLE ON 34th STREET (1947)
(A. K. A. "The Big Heart")
Director: George Seaton
Maurene O'Hara (Doris Walker), Edmund
Gwenn (Kris Kringle), John Payne
(Fred Gailey), Natalie Wood (Susan
Walker), William Frawley (Charles
Halloran), Jerome Cowan (D. A. Thomas
Mara), Gene Lockhart (Judge Henry
X. Harper), Porter Hall (Mr. Sawyer),
Philip Tonge (Mr. Shellhammer),
James Seay (Dr. Pierce), William
Forrest (Dr. Rogers), Percy Helton
(Santa Claus), Harry Antrim (Mr. Macy),
Jeff Corey (reporter), Anthony Sydes
(Peter), Thelma Ritter (Peter's mother),
Jack Albertson, Guy Thomajan (post
office employees), Sunb Pollard (mail-
bearing court official), Robert Karnes
(interne), Theresa Harris (Mrs. Mara),
Richard Irving (reporter), Lela Bliss
(Mrs. Shellhammer), Robert Hyatt (Tho-
mas Mara, Jr.), Albin Hammer (Mara's
assistant), Anne O'Neal (Sawyer's sec-
retary), Alvin Greenman (Alfred), Mary
Field (girl's mother), Jane Green (Mrs.
Harper), Joseph McInerney (bailiff),

Stephen Roberts (guard), Ida McGuire
(drum majorette), Marlene Lyden
(Dutch girl), Herbert H. Heyes
(Mr. Gimbell), Robert Lynn (Macy's
salesman), Teddy Driver (Terry),
Robert Gist (Window Dresser),
Patty Smith (Alice).

MIRACLE ON 34th STREET (TVM-
1973) - 12-14-73
Jane Alexander (Karen Walker),
David Hartman (Bill Schaffner),
Sebastian Cabot (Kris Kringle),
Roddy McDowall (Dr. Henry Sawyer),
Jim Backus (Horace Shellhammer),
David Doyle (R. H. Macy), James
Gregory (District Attorney), Tom
Bosley (Judge Harper), Roland
Winters (Mr. Gimbel), Conrad Janis
(Richardson), Ellen Weston (Celeste),
Suzanne Davidson (Susan Walker),
Liam Dunn (Reindeer Keeper).

MIRACLE RIDER, THE (1935) -
serial in 15 episodes
Director: B. Reeves Eason &
Armand Scheafer
Tom Mix (Tom Morgan), Charles
Middleton (Zaroff), Pat O'Malley
(Sam Morgan), Jason Robards, Sr.
(Carlton), Ernie Adams (Stetler),
Hal Taliaferro (Burnett), Bob Kortman
(Longboat), Robert Frazer (Chief
Black Wing), Edward Hearn (Janes),
Jean Gale (Ruth), George Chesebro,
Edward Earle.

MIRACLES FOR SALE (1939)
Director: Tod Browning
Robert Young (Michael Morgan),
Florence Rice (Judy Barclay), Henry
Hull (Dave Duvalio), Frank Craven
(Dad Morgan), Lee Bowman (La Clair),
Astrid Allwyn (Mrs. Zelma La Clair),
Cliff Clark (Insp. Gavigan), Walter
Kinsford (Col. Watrous), Gloria
Holden (Madame Rapport), Frederick
Worlock (Dr. Sabbat), William
Demerest (Quinn), Charles Lane
(hotel clerk), John Piccori (colonel),
Edward Earle (man), Richard Loo
(Chinese soldier), Frank Sully (bus
driver), Eddie Acuff (taxi driver),
Phillip Terry (Master of Ceremonies),
Chester Clute (waiter), Harold Minjir
(Tauro), Harry Tyler (taxi driver),
Truman Bradley (Master of Ceremonies),
E. Allyn Warren (Dr. Hendricks),
James C. Morton (electrician),
Paul Sutton (Capt. R. Z. Storm),
Armand Kaliz (Francois), Fred
Warren (Police Surgeon), Suzanne
Kaaren (girl), John Davidson (weird

voice), Claire McDowall (woman),
Alphonse Martell (headwaiter), Monte
Vandergrift (Bergin), Edward Kilroy
(attendant), Harry Vejar (citizen),
Manuel Paris (sinister man), Margaret
Bert (Mary), Frances McInerney (ma-
gician's assistant), William Norton
Bailey (man in box), Cyril Ring (num-
bers man), Amelia Stone.

MIRACLES OF THE JUNGLE (1921) -
serial in 15 episodes
    Director: E. A. Martin & James
    Conway
Al Ferguson, Ben Hagerty, Irene Wallace, Wilbur Higgins, Genevieve Burte,
John George.

MIRAGE (1965)
    Director: Edward Dmytryk
Gregory Peck (David), Diane Baker
(Sheila), Walter Matthau (Ted Casele),
Leif Erickson (Major Crawford), Wal-
ter Abel (Charles Calvin), Kevin Mc-
Carthy (Josephson), Jack Weston (Les-
ter), Anne Seymour (Mrs. Frances
Calvin), George Kennedy (Willard),
Robert H. Harris (Dr. Broden), House
B. Jameson (Bo), Hari Rhodes (Lt.
Franken), Neil Fitzgerald (Joe Turtle),
Syl Lamont (Benny), Eileen Baral
(Irene), Franklin B. Cover (group
leader).

MIRANDA (1948)
    Director: Ken Annakin
Glynis Johns (Miranda), Griffith Jones
(Paul Marten), Googie Withers (Clare
Martan), Margaret Rutherford (Nurse
Cary), Yvonne Owen (Betty), David
Tomlinson (Charles), John McCallum
(Nigel Hood), Maurice Denham (Cockle
Man), Brian Oulton (Manell), Zena
Marshall (secretary), Sonia Holm
(Isobel), Charles Penrose (stage mana-
ger).

MIRROR AND MARKHEIM, THE (1954)
- short
    Director: John Lamont
Maurice Goring (Narrator), Arthur
Lowe, Christopher Lee, Lloyd Lamble,
Ruth Sheil, Philip Saville.

MISADVENTURES OF MERLIN JONES,
THE (1963)
    Director: Robert Stevenson
Tommy Kirk (Merlin Jones), Annette
Funicello (Jennifer), Leon Ames (Judge
Holmby), Stuart Erwin (Capt. Loomis),
Michael Fox (Kohner), Alan Hewitt (Prof.
Shattuck), Connie Gilchrist (Mrs. Gos-
sett), Burt Mustin (Bailiff), Norman

Grabowski (Norman), Dal McKennon
(Detective Hutchins).

MISSILE TO THE MOON (1959)
    Director: Richard Cunha
Gary Clarke (Lon), Cathy Downs
(June Saxton), K. T. Stevens (Lido),
Laurie Mitchell (Lambda), Michael
Whalen (Kirk Green), Nina Bara
(Alpha), Richard Travis (Arnold
Dayton), Tommy Cook (Gary), Mar-
jorie Hellen (Zeema), Lee Roberts
(Henry Hunter), Lisa Simone, Henry
Hunter, Sandra Wirth, Tania Velia,
Pat Mowry, Sanita Pelkey, Renata
Hoy, Marianne Gaba, Mary Ford.

MISSING ARE DEADLY, THE (TVM-
1975) - 1-8-75
    Director: Don McDougall
Ed Nelson (Dr. Margolin), Leonard
Nimoy (Dr. Durov), Gary Morgan
(Jeff Margolin), George O'Hanlon,
Jr. (David Margolin), Marjorie
Lord (Mrs. Robertson), Jose Fer-
rer (Mr. Warren), Kathleen Quinlan
(Michelle), Irene Tedrow (Mrs.
Bates), John Milford (Capt. Frank-
lin), Armand Alzamora (Dr. Mart-
inez), Stuart Nisbet (grocer).

MISSING GUEST; THE (1938)
    Director: John Rawlins
Paul Kelly (Scoop Hanlon), Constance
Moore (Stephanie Kirkland), William
Lundigan (Larry Dearden), Selmer
Jackson (Frank Baldrich), John
Harmon (Baldrich's guard), George
Cooper (Jake), Edwin Stanley (Dr.
Carroll), Florence Wix (Linda
Baldrich), Billy Wayne (Vic), Pat-
rick J. Kelly (Edwards, the Butler),
Harlan Briggs (Frank Kendall),
Pat C. Flich (goofy inventor).

MISSING LINK, THE (1927)
    Director: Charles F. Reisner
Syd Chaplin (Arthur Wells), Ruth
Hiatt (Beatrice Braden), Tom
McGuire (Col. Braden), Crauford
Kent (Lord Dryden), Nick Cogley
(Captain), Sam Baker (Missing
Link).

MISSING REMBRANDT, THE (1932)
    Director: Leslie S. Hiscott
Arthur Wontner (Sherlock Holmes),
Ian Fleming (Dr. Watson), Minnie Raynor
(Mrs. Hudson), Dino Galvina (Carlo
Ravelli), Francis L. Sullivan (Baron
von Guntermann), Miles Mander
(Claude Holford), Philip Hewland
(Insp. Lestrade), Jane Welsh (Lady

Violet), Herbert Lomas (Manning),
Anthony Hollis (Marquis De Chaminade),
Takase (Chang Wu), Ben Welden (a-
gent).

MISSION GALACTICA: THE CYLON
   ATTACK (1979)
   see Television: Battlestar Galactica (1978-79)

MISSION MARS (1968)
   Director: Nick Webster
Darren McGavin (Mike Blaiswick),
Nick Adams (Nick Grant), Heather
Hewitt (Edith Blaiswick), George
DeVries (Duncan), Shirley Parker
(Alice Grant), Michael DeBeaussett
(Cliff Lawson), Ralph Miller (Simpson),
Chuck Zink (Chuck, the radio operator),
Bill Kelly (Russian astronaut), Mon-
roe Myers (Lawson's aide), Art Baker
(doctor),

MISSION STARDUST (1968-Span. /
   Ital. /Ger.) (A. K. A. "4... 3...
   2... 1... Morte"; "Perry Rhodan -
   SOS Aus dem Weltall"; Perry
   Rhodan - SOS from Space"; "Orbita
   Mortal"; Death Orbit")
   Director: Primo Zeglio
Lang Jeffries (Maj. Perry Rhodan),
Essy Persson (Thora), John Karel-
sen (Dress), Pinkas Braun (Rotkin),
Luis Davila (Capt. Bull).

MISTER FREEDOM (1968-Fr.)
   Director: William Klein
Donald Pleasence (Dr. Freedom),
Delphine Seyrig (Marie), Philippe
Noiret (Moukij-Man), John Abbey
(Mr. Freedom), Sam Frey (Christ-
man), Catherine Rouvel (Marie Rouge),
Jean Claude Drouot (Dick), Serge
Gainsbourg (Mr. Drugstore), Yves
Montand.

MISTER, YOU ARE A WIDOW (1971-
   Czech.) (A. K. A. "Pane, Vy Jste
   Vdova")
   Director: Vaclav Vorlicek
Olga Schoberova, Iva Janzurova.

MISTRESS OF THE APES (1979)
   Director: Larry Buchanan
Jenny Neumann, Garth Pillsbury,
Barbara Leigh, Paula Sills, Walt
Robin.

MODERN BLUEBEARD, A (1947-Mex.)
   (A. K. A. "El Moderno Barba-Azul")
   Director: Jaime Salvador
Buster Keaton, Angel Garasa, Virginia
Serret, Luis G. Burreriro, Fernando

Soto, Jorge Mondragon.

MODERN PROBLEMS (1981)
   Director: Ken Shapiro
Chevy Chase (Max), Patti D'Arban-
ville (Darcy), Mary Kay Place
(Lorraine), Nell Carter (Dorita),
Dabney Coleman (Mark), Brian
Doyle-Murray (Brian), Mitch Krein-
del (Barry), Arthur Sellers (Mobile
Supervisor), Neil Thompson, Carl
Irwin (Controllers), Ron House
(vendor), Henry Corden (Dubrovnik),
Buzzy Linhart (tile man), Christine
Nazareth (redhead), Jan Speck
(brunette), Luke Andreas (tough
guy), Vincenzo Gagliardi (singer),
Pat Proft (Maitre'd Hotel), Jim
Hudson (doctor), Francois Cartier
(pianist), Tom Sherohman (waiter),
Frank Birney (man in lobby), Reid
Olson (principal dancer).

MODESTY BLAISE (1966)
   Director: Joseph Losey
Monica Vitti (Modesty Blaise),
Terence Stamp (Willie Garvin),
Dirk Bogarde (Gabriel), Harry
Andrews (Sir Gerald Tarrant),
Alexander Knox (Minister), Michael
Craig (Paul), Rosella Falk (Mrs.
Fothergill), Scilla Gabel (Melina),
John Karlsen (Oleg), Oliver
MacGreevy (Tattoed Man), Michael
Chow (Weng), Saro Urzi (Basilio),
Joe Melia (Crevier), Tina Marquand
(Nicole), Marcello Turilli (Strauss),
Jon Bluming (Hans), Giuseppe Pagan-
elli (Friar), Wolfgang Hillinger
(Handsome), Roberto Bisacco (En-
rico), Lex Schoorel (Walter),
Sylvan (Pacco).

MOLE MEN VS. THE SON OF HER-
   CULES (1961-Ital.) (A. K. A. "Ma-
   ciste, l'Uomo Fiu Forte del Mondo",
   "Maciste, the Strongest Man in the
   World")
   Director: Antonio Leonviola
Mark Forest (Maciste), Moira
Orfie, Raffaella Carra, Paul Wynter,
Gianni Garko, Enrico Glori, Graziella
Granta.

MOLE PEOPLE, THE (1956)
   Director: Virgil Vogel
John Agar (Roger Bentley), Hugh
Beaumont (Dr. Bellamin), Cynthia
Patrick (Gizelle), Alan Napier (Elinu,
the High Priest), Nestor Paiva (Prof.
Etienne Lafarge), Phil Chambers
(Dr. Paul Stuart), Rodd Redwing
(Nazar), Robin Hughes (1st Officer),

Arthur D. Gilmour (Sharu), Yvonne De
Lavallade (Dancer), James Logan
(Officer), Kay Kuter, John Dodsworth,
Marc Hamilton (priests), Pat Whyte
(guard), Joseph Abdullah (Arab fore-
man), Billy Miller (Arab boy), Eddie
Parker (Moleman),

MONITORS, THE (1969)
    Director: Jack Shea
Guy Stockwell (Harry Jordan), Susan
Oliver (Barbara Cole), Avery Schrei-
ber (Max Jordan), Sherry Jackson
(Mona), Shepperd Strudwick (Tersh),
Larry Storch (Col. Stutz), Keenan
Wynn (Gen. Blackwish), Ed Begley
(the President), Alan Arkin, Adam
Arkin, Stubby Kaye, Barbara Dana,
Xavier Cugat, Sen. Everett Dirksen,
Fred Kaz, Lynn Lipton, Jackie Vernon
(cameos).

MONK, THE (1971-Fr. /Ital.) (A. K. A.
    "Le Moine")
    Director: Ado Kyrou
Franco Nero (Ambrosio), Nathalie
Delon (Mathilde), Nicol Williamson
(Duke), Nadja Tiller (mother), Eliana
De Santis (Antonia), Elisabeth Wiener
(nun).

MONKEY BUSINESS (1952)
    Director: Howard Hawks
Cary Grant (Barnaby Fulton), Ginger
Rogers (Edwina Fulton), Marilyn Mon-
roe (Lois Laurel), Charles Coburn
(Oliver Oxly), Hugh Marlowe (Harvey
Entwhistle), Henri Letondal (Dr. Sieg-
fried Kitzel), Robert Cornthwaite (Dr.
Zoldeck), Douglas Spencer (Dr. Brun-
ner), Larry Keating (G. J. Gulverly),
Esther Dale (Mrs. Rhinelander), George
Winslow (Little Indian), Emmett Lynn
(Jimmy), Joseph Mell (barber), George
Eldredge (auto salesman), Heinie
Conklin (painter), Kathleen Freeman
(nurse), Olan Soule (hotel clerk), Harry
Carey, Jr. (reporter), Don McKee
(photographer), Faire Binney (dowager),
Billy McLean (bellboy), Paul Maxey,
Mack Williams (dignitaries), Forbes
Murray (man), Marjorie Holliday
(receptionist), Harry Seymour (clothing
store salesman), Harry Carter, Harry
Bartell, Jerry Paris (scientists), Roger
Moore (man), Ruth Warren, Isobel
Withers, Olive Carey (laundresses),
Dabbs Greer (cabbie), Russ Clark, Rudy
Lee, Mickey Little, Brad Mora, Jimmie
Roebuck, Louis Littieri (boys), Robert
Nichols (garage man), Gil Stratton, Jr.
(Yale man).

MONKEY'S PAW, THE (1923)

Director: Manning Haynes
Moore Marriott, A. B. Imeson,
Marie Ault, Charles Ashton, Johnny
Butt, Tom Coventry, George Wynne.

MONKEY'S PAW, THE (1932)
    Director: Wesley Ruggles
C. Aubrey Smith, Ivan Simpson,
Herbert Bunston, Bramwell Flet-
cher, Louis Carter, Betty Lawford,
Winter Hall.

MONKEY'S PAW, THE (1948)
    Director: Norman Lee
Milton Rosmer (Mr. Trelawne),
Megs Jenkins (Mrs. Trelawne),
Joan Seton (Dorothy Lang), Norman
Shelley (Monoghan), Hay Petrie
(Grimshaw), Michael Martin Harvey
(Kelly), Alfie Bass (Manager),
Mackenie Ward (Noel Lang), Eric
Micklewood (Tom Trelawne), Brenda
Hogan (Beryl), Sidney Tafler.

MONKEY'S UNCLE (1965)
    Director: Robert Stevenson
Tommy Kirk (Merlin Jones), Annette
Funicello (Jennifer), Leon Ames
(Judge Holmsby), Frank Faylon (Mr.
Dearborne), Arthur O'Connell
(Darius Green, III), Connie Gilchrist
(housekeeper), Mark Goddard (Hay-
wood), Gage Clarke (College Presi-
dent), Cheryl Miller (Lisa), Norman
Grabowski (Norman), Leon Tyler
(Leon), Alan Hewitt (Prof. Shattuck),
Harry Holcombe (agent), Harry
Antrim, Alexander Lockwood (re-
gents).

MONK OF MONZA, THE (1963-Ital.)
    (A. K. A. "Il Monaco di Monza")
    Director: Sergio Corbucci
Lisa Gastoni, Toto, Moira Orfei,
Nino Taranto, Erminio Marcario.

MONK WITH THE WHIP, THE (1967-
    Ger.) (A. K. Al "Der Monch mit
    der Pfeitsche")
    Director: Alfred Vohrer
Joachim Fuchsberger, Siegfried
Schurenberg, Ilsa Page, Ursula
Glas, Grit Bottchen, Tilly Lauen-
stein.

MONOLITH MONSTERS, THE (1957)
    Director: John Sherwood
Grant Willliams (Dave Miller), Lola
Albright (Cathy Barrett), Les Tre-
mayne (Martin Cochrane), Trevor
Bardette (Prof. Arthur Flanders),
Linda Scheley (Ginny Simpson), Phil
Harvey (Ben Gilbert), William Flah-
erty (Police Chief Dan Corey), Harry

Jackson (Dr. Steve Hendricks), Steve
Darrell (Joe Higgins), Richard Cutting
(Dr. Reynolds), Dean Cromer (highway patrolman), William Schallert
(weatherman).

MONSIEUR VERDOUX (1947)
    Director: Charles Chaplin
Charles Chaplin (Verdoux), Martha
Raye, Isobel Elsom, Marjorie Bennett,
Arthur Hohl, Almira Sessions, William
Frawley, Virgina Brissac, Irving
Bacon, Mady Correll, Robert Lewis,
Ada-May, Audrey Betz, Allison Roddan,
Marilyn Nash, Helene Heigh, Edwin
Mills, Bernard J. Nedell, Fritz Leiber,
Barbara Slater, Christine Ell, Margaret
Hoffman, John Harmon, Eula Morgan,
Charles Evans, Vera Marshe, Lois
Conklin.

MONSTER (1978)
    Director: Kenneth Hartford
John Carradine, Diane McBain, Roger
Clark, Keenan Wynn, Stella Calle,
John Lamont, Kelly Sill, Fernando
Corredor, Jade Stuart, Glenn Ransom.

MONSTER, THE (1925)
    Director: Roland West
Lon Chaney, Sr. (Dr. Ziska), Johnny
Arthur (Johnny, the under clerk),
Gertrude Olmsted (Betty Watson), Ed-
ward McWade (Luke Watson), Charles
A. Sellon (Constable), Ethel Wales (Mrs.
Watson), George Austin (Rigo), Knute
Erickson (Daffy Dan), Hallam Cooley
(Hal, the head clerk), Walter James
(Caliban).

MONSTER A GO-GO (1965)
    Director: Herschell Gordon
        Lewis, & Bill Rebane
June Travis, Phil Morton, George
Perry, Lois Brooks, Henry Hite.

MONSTER AND A HALF, A (1964-
    Ital.) (A.K.A. "Un Mostro... e
    Mezzo")
    Director: Stefano Steno
Franco Franchi, Ciccio Ingrassia,
Margaret Lee, Alberto Bonucci, Lena
von Martens, Giuseppe Partile, Maruska
Rossetti.

MONSTER AND THE APE, THE (1945)
    - serial in 15 episodes
    Director: Howard Bretherton
Robert Lowery (Ken Morgan), Carole
Mathews (Babs Arnold), George Mac-
ready (Prof. Ernst), Ralph Morgan,
(Prof. Arnold), Willie Best (Flash),
Jack Ingram (Norkid), Eddie Parker

(Blake), Anthony Warde (Flint),
Stanley Price (Mead), Ray 'Crash'
Corrigan (the Ape), Ted Mapes.

MONSTER AND THE GIRL, THE
    (1941)
    Director: Stuart Heisler
Ellen Drew (Susan Webster), Paul
Lakas (W.S. Bruhl), George
Zucco (Dr. Parry), Rod Cameron
(Sam Daniels), Edward Van Sloan
(Warden), Onslow Stevens (Mc-
Masters), Gerlad Mohr (Munn),
Cliff Edwards (Teps), Robert
Paige (Larry Reed), Tom Dugan
(Capt. Alton), Joseph Calleia
(Deacon), Minor Watson (Judge
Pulver), Marc Lawrence (Sleeper),
Philip Terry (Scott Webster),
Willard Robertson (Lt. Strickland),
Frank M. Thomas (Janson), George
F. Meader (Dr. Knight), Charlie
Gemora (the Ape), Emma Dunn,
Abner Biberman.

MONSTER CLUB, THE (1971)
    Director: Roy Ward Baker
Vincent Price (Erasmus), John
Carradine (R. Chetwynd-Haynes),
Roger Sloman (Club Secretary),
Fran Fullenwider (Buxom Beauty),
Anthony Steel (Lintom Busotsky),
Suzanna Willis (the Stripper), The
Viewers, B.A. Robertson, Night,
Pretty Things (the Bands). "The
Shadmock Story": James Laurenson
(Raven), Barbara Kellerman (An-
gela), Simon Ward (George), Geof-
frey Bayldon (Psychiatrist); "The
Vampire Story": Donald Pleasence
(Pickering), Britt Ekland (Lintom's
mother), Richard Johnson (Lintom's
father), Warren Saire (Lintom),
Neil McCarthy (Watson), Anthony
Valentine (Mooney); "The Humgoo
Story": Stuart Whitman (Sam),
Lesley Dunlop (Luna), Patrick Ma-
gee (Innkeeper).

MONSTER DEMOLISTHER (1960-
    Mex.) (A.K.A. "Nostradamus y
    el Destructor de Monstruos")
    Director: Frederick Curiel
German Robles (Nostradamus),
Domingo Soler (Prof. Duran), Julio
Aleman, Aurora Alvarado, Regelio
Jimenez Pons.

MONSTER FROM A PREHISTORIC
    PLANET (1967-Jap.) (A.K.A.
    "Daikaju Gappa")
    Director: Harauyasu Nogushi
Tamio Kawaji, Yoko Yamamoto, Koji

Wada, Yuji Odaka, Tatsuya Fuji,

MONSTER FROM GREEN HELL (1957)
Director: Kenneth Crane
Jim Davis (Quent Brady), Robert E.
Griffin (Dan Morgan), Barbara Turner
(Lorna Lorentz), Vladimir Sokoloff
(Dr. Lorentz), Eduardo Ciannelli
(Mahri), Joel Fluellen (Arobi), LaVerne
Jones (Kuana), Tim Huntley (territorial
agent), Frederic Potler (radar opera-
ator).

MONSTER FROM THE OCEAN FLOOR
(1954)
Director: Wyatt Ordung
Stuart Wade (Steve Dunning), Anne
Kimball (Julie Blair), Dick Pinner
(Dr. Baldwin), Jack Hayes (Joe), Wyott
Ordung (Pablo), Inez Palange (Tula),
David Garcia.

MONSTER FROM THE SURF (1964)
(A. K. A. "The Beach Girls and the
Monster")
Director: Jon Hall
Jon Hall (Otto), Sue Casey (Vicki),
Walker Edmiston (Mark), Arnold Les-
sing (Richard), Read Morgan, Elaine
Dupont, Dale Davis.

MONSTER ISLAND (1980 U. S. /Span.)
Director: Juan Piquer
Terence Stamp (Taskinar), Peter
Cushing (Kolderup), Gerard Tichy
(Capt. Turkott), Paul Naschy (Flynt),
Ian Serra (Jeff Morgan), David Hutton
(Mr. Arttelet), Gasphar Ipua (Carefi-
natu), Blanca Estrada (Dominque),
Frank Brana (Birling), Ana Obregon
(Meg Hollaney).

MONSTER MAKER (1944)
Director: Samuel Newfield
J. Carroll Naish (Dr. Igor Markov),
Wanda McCay (Patricia), Ralph Morgan
(Lawrence), Tala Birell (Maxine), Sam
Flint (Dr. Adams), Terry Frost (Blake),
Alexander Pollard (the Butler), Glenn
Strange (the Giant).

MONSTER OF FRANKENSTEIN, THE
(1920) (A. K. A. "Il Monstro di Frank-
enstein"
Director: Eugenio Testa
Umberto Guarracino (the Monster),
Luciano Alberti.

MONSTER OF HIGHGATE PONDS, THE
(1961)
Director: Alberto Cavalcanti
Ronald Howard (Uncle Dick), Rachel
Clay (Sophie), Michael Balfour (Bert),

Terry Raven (Chris), Michael Wade
(David), Frederick Piper (Sam),
Beryl Cooke (Ms. Haggerty), Roy
Vincente (the Monster).

MONSTER OF LONDON CITY, THE
(1964-Ger.) (A. K. A. "Das
Ungeheur von London City")
Director: Edwin Zbonek
Marianne Koch (Ann Morlay), Hans-
joerg Felmy (Richard Sand),
Dietmar Schoenherr (Dr. Morely
Greely), Chariklia Baxevanos (Betty
Ball), Hans Nielsen (Dorne), Fritz
Tillmann (Sir George), Peer Schmidt
(Teddy Flynn), Walter Pfeil (Horr-
lick), Kurk Pieritz (Maylor),
Adelheid Hinz (maid), Manfred
Grothe (detective), Gudrun Schmidt
(Evelyn Nichols), Elsa Wagner
(housekeeper), Gerda Blisse (assis-
tant), Kai Fischer (Helen Capstick).

MONSTER OF PEIDRAS BLANCAS,
THE (1958)
Director: Irwin Berwick
Les Tremayne (Dr. Jorgenson),
Forrest Lewis (Sheriff Matson),
John Harmon (Sturges), Don Sullivan
(the biochemist), Jeanne Carmen
(the girl), Frank Arvidson (the store-
keeper), Joseph La Cava (Mike),
Peter Dunn (Eddie), Wayne Berwick
(Little Jimmy), Jack Kevan (the
Monster).

MONSTER OF THE SHADOW (1954-
Mex.) (A. K. A. "El Monstruo de
la Sombra")
Director: Zacarias Gomez
Urquizo
Eduardo Noriega, Martha Roth, Jaime
Fernandez, Carmen Montejo.

MONSTER OF THE VOLCANOS, THE
(1962-Mex.) (A. K. A. "El Monstruo
de los Volcanes")
Director: Jaime Salvador
Joaquin Cordero, Andres Soler, Anal
Berta Lepe, Antonio Raxel, Victor
Alcocor, Jose Chavez, David Hayat.

MONSTER ON THE CAMPUS (1958)
Director: Jack Arnold
Arthur Franz (Dr. Donald Blake),
Joannna Moore (Madeline Howard),
Troy Donahue (Jimmy Flanders),
Judson Pratt (Mike Stevens), Whit
Bissell (Dr. Oliver Cole), Helen
Westcott (Molly Riordan), Nancy
Walters (Sylvia Lockwood), Phil
Harvey (Sgt. Powell), Ross Elliott
(Eddie Daniels), Hank Patterson

(Mr. Townsend), Eddie Parker (the Monster).

MONSTER THAT CHALLENGED THE WORLD, THE (1957)
Director: Arnold Laven
Tim Holt (Lt. Col. John Twillenger), Audrey Dalton (Gail Mackenzie), Hans Conried (Dr. Jess Rogers), Harlan Warde (Lt. Bob Clemens), Casey Adams (Tad Johns), Mimi Gibson (Sandy MacKensie), Gordon Jones (Josh Peters), Marjorie Stapp (Connie Blake), Dennis McCarthy (George Blake), Barbara Darrow (Jody Sims), Bob Beneveds (Mort Beatty), Michael Dugan (Clarke), Mac Williams (Capt. Mastera), Milton Parsons (Lewis Clark Dobbs), Eileen Harley (Sally), Jody McCrea (Seaman Fred Johnson), William Swan (Seaman Howard Sanders), Hal Taggert (Mr. Davis), Byron Kane (Coroner), Charles Tannen (Wyatt), Dan Gachman (Deputy Brewer), Gil Frye (Deputy Scott), Ralph Moody (old gatekeeper).

MONSTER WALKS, THE (1932)
Director: Frank Strayer
Rex Lease (Ted Clayton), Vera Reynolds (Ruth Earlton), Mischa Auer (Hanns Krup), Sheldon Lewis (Robert Earlton), Martha Mattox (Mrs. Krug), Willie Best (Exodus), Sidney Bracy (Herbert Wilkes).

MONSTER ZERO (1965-Jap.) (A. K. A. "Kaiju Daisenso", "Invasion of the Astro-Monsters", "Battle of the Astros", "Invasion of the Astros")
Director; Inoshiro Honda
Nick Adams, Akira Takarada, Junl Tazaki, Kumi Mizuno, Akira Kubo.

MONSTROSITY (1963) (A. K. A. "The Atomic Brain")
Director: Joseph Mascelli
Frank Gerstle (Dr. Frank), Erika Peters (Nina), Marjorie Eaton (Mrs. Hetty Marsh), Judy Bamber (Bea), Lisa Lang (Anita), Frank Fowler (Victor), Margie Fisco (Zombie).

MONTY PYTHON AND THE HOLY GRAIL (1975)
Director: Terry Gilliam & Terry Jones
Graham Chapman, John Cleese, Terry Gilliam, Eric Idle, Michael Palin, Terry Jones, Carol Cleveland, John Young, Connie Booth.

MONTY PYTHON'S LIFE OF BRAIN (1979)
Director: Terry Jones
Graham Chapman (Brain/Wiseman), Terry Jones (Mandy, Mother of Brian), Ken Colley (Jesus), John Cleese (Wiseman/Reg), Michael Palin (Wiseman/Big Nose/Francis), Gwen Taylor (Mrs. Big Nose), Eric Idle (Cheeky/Stan/Harry the Hagler), Carol Cleveland (Mrs. Gregory), Terrence Bayler (Gregory), Sue Jones-Davis (Judith), John Young (Matthias), Bernard McKenna, Andrew MacLachlin (stoner's helpers), Neal Innes (Weedy Samaritan), John Case (Gladiator), George Harrison (Mr. Papadopoulis), Charles McKeowan (man in crowd), Terry Gilliam (man in crowd).

MOONCHILD (1972)
Director: Alan Gadney
Victor Buono (Maitre D'), John Carradine (the Walker), Mike Travis (the Student), Pat Renella (Manager of the Inn), Frank Corsentino (Homunculus), William Challee (Alchemist), Janet Landgard (girl), Marie Denn (maid).

MOON OF THE WOLF (TVM-1972) - 9-26-72
Director: Daniel Petrie
David Janssen (Sheriff Whitaker), Bradford Dillman (Andrew Rodanthe), Barbara Rush (Louise Rodanthe), John Beradino (Dr. Druten), Royal Dano (Gurmandy, Sr.), John Chandler (Gurmandy, Jr.), Geoffrey Lewis (Lawrence Burrifous), Paul R. DeVille (Hugh Burrifous), Claudia MacNeil (Sarah), Dan Priest (Sam Cairns), Robert Phillips (Deputy), Serena Sande (nurse).

MOON PILOT (1961)
Director: James Neilson
Tom Tryon (Capt. Richard Talbot), Dany Saval (Layrae), Tommy Kirk (Walter Talbot), Brian Keith (Gen. John Vannerman), Edmond O'Brien (McClosky), Kent Smith (Secretary of the Air Force), Nancy Kulp (nutritionist), Murial Landers (fat lady), Bob Sweeney (Sen. Henry McGuire), Simon Scott (Medical Officer), Sarah Selby (Celia Talbot), Bert Rensen (Agent Brown), Dick Whittinghill (Col. Briggs), Robert Brubaker, William Hudson.

MOONRAKER (1979)
Director: Lewis Gilbert
Roger Moore (James Bond), Michael Lonsdale (Drax), Lois Chiles (Holly Goodhead), Richard Kiel (Jaws), Geoffrey Keen (Frederick Gray), Corinne Clery (Corinne Dufour), Blanche Ravalec (Dolly), Bernard Lee (M), Lois Maxwell (Miss Moneypenny), Desmond Llewelyn (Q), Emily Bolton (Manuela), Alfie Bass (Consumptive Italian), Walter Gotell (Gen. Gogol), Toshiro Suga (Chang), Jean-Pierre Castaldi (Private Jet Pilot), Leila Shenna (Private Jet Hostess), Irka Bochenko (blonde), Arthur Howard (Cavendish), Douglas Lambert (Mission Control Director), Michael Marshall (Col. Scott), Anne Lonnberg (museum guide), Brian Keith (US Shuttle Captain), George Birt (Boeing 747 Captain), Georges Beller, Kim Fortune, Johnny Traver, Chichinou Kaeppler, Catherine Seere, Nicaise Jean-Louis, Chris Dillinger, Lizzie Warville, Francoise, Gayat, Christine Hui, Beatrice Libert.

MOONSHINE MOUNTAIN (1967)
Director: Herschell Gordon Lewis
Chuck Scott, Adam Sorg, Bonnie Hinson, Jeffrey Allen.

MOONSTONE, THE (1934)
Director: Reginald Barker
David Manners (Franklin Blake), Herbert Bunston (Sir John Verinder), Gustav von Seyffertitz (Septimus Lucker), John Davidson (Yandoo), Phyllis Barry (Anne Verinder), Evelyn Bostock (Roseanna Spearman), Claude King (Basil Wynard), Olaf Hytten (Dr. Ezra Jennings), Jameson Thomas (Godgrey Abelwhite), Elspeth Dudgeon (Betteredge), Fred Walton (Henry), Charles Irwin (Insp. Cuff).

MOON ZERO TWO (1969)
Director: Roy Ward Baker
James Olson (Bill Kemp), Catherine Schell (Clementine Taplin), Warren Mitchell (J. J. Hubbard), Adrienne Corri (Liz Murphy), Bernard Bresslaw (Harry), Neil McCallum (Space Captain), Sam Kydd (barman), Ori Levy (Karminski), Joby Blanshard (Smith), Carol Cleveland (hostess), Dudley Foster (Whitsun), Leo Britt (Senior Customs Officer), Keith Bonnard (Junior Customs Officer), Michael Ripper (1st card player), Robert Tayman (2nd card player), Roy Evans (workman), Tom Kempinski (Officer),

Chrissie Shrimpton (Boutique attendant), Simone Silvers, Amber Dean Smith (girls).

MORE THAN A MIRACLE (1966-Ital. /Fr.) (A. K. A. "C'ra una Volta")
Director: Francesco Rosi
Sophia Loren (Isabella), Omar Sharif (Prince Ramon), Dolores Del Rio (Princess Mother), Georges Wilson (Monzu), Leslie French (Brother Joseph), Carlo Pisacane (1st witch), Marina Malfatti (Devout Princess), Rita Forzano (Greedy Princess), Rosemary Martin (Vain Princess), Anna Nogara (Impatient Princess), Carlotta Barilli (Superstitious Princess), Fleur Mombelli (Haughty Princess), Anna Liotti (Infant Princess), Chris Huerta (Spanish groom), Pietro Carloni (Village Priest), Giovanni Tarallo (elderly monk), Renato Pinciroli (Princess' Chamberlain), Giacomo Furia (prior), Gladys Dawson, Kathleen St. John, Beatrice Greach (witches).

MORE WILD WILD WEST (TVM-1980) - 10-7-80 & 10-8-80
Director: Burt Kennedy
Robert Conrad (James T. West), Ross Martin (Artemus Gordon), Jonathan Winters (Albert Paradine II), Victor Buono (Dr. Henry Messenger), Harry Morgan (Robert T. Malone), Rene Auberjonois (Sir David Edney), Randi Brough (Yvonne), Candi Brough (Daphne), Liz Torres (Juanita), Dave Madden (German Ambassador), Avery Schrieber (Alexyi, the Russian Ambassador), Gino Conforti (Georges, the French Ambassador), Jack LaLanne (physical fitness instructor), Emma Sampson (Merriwell Meriweather), Sandy Halberg (Joseph), Dr. Joyce Brothers (bystander), James Bacon (Wheelman), Joe Alfasas (Italian Ambassador), Rick Pearson, Rick Drasnin (Abominable Brothers), Hector Elias (Spanish Ambassador), John Furlong (Bavarian Ambassador), Richard Hawk (Edward Jenson), Casey Tibbs, Tony Epper, Dave Cass (Juanita's brothers).

MORGAN! (1966) (A. K. A. "Morgan, a Suitable Case for Treatment")
Director: Karel Reisz
David Warner (Morgan Delt), Vanessa

Redgrave (Leonie Delt), Irene Handl (Mrs. Delt), Robert Stephens (Charles Napier), Bernard Bresslaw (Policeman), John Rae (Judge), Graham Crowden (Counsel), Nan Munro (Mrs. Henderson), Newton Blick (Mr. Henderson), Arthur Mullard (Wally), Peter Cellier (2nd Council), Angus MacKay (best man).

MORTUARY (1982)
Director: Howard Avedis
Mary McDonough, David Wallace, Lynda Day George, Christopher George, Bill Paxton, Beth Schaffel, Curt Ayres.

MOST DANGEROUS GAME, THE (1932) (A. K. A. "The Hounds of Zaroff")
Director: Irving Pichel & Ernest B. Schoedsack
Fay Wray (Eve Trowbridge), Joel McCrea (Robert Rainsford), Leslie Banks (Count Zaroff), Noble Johnson (Ivan), Robert Armstrong (Martin Trowbridge), Steve Clemento (servant), Hale Hamilton.

MOST DANGEROUS MAN ALIVE, THE (1958)
Director: Allan Dwan
Ron Randell (Eddie Candell), Debra Paget (Linda), Elaine Stewart (Carla Angelo), Morris Ankrum (Capt. Davis), Gregg Palmer (Lt. Fisher), Anthony Caruso (Damon), Steve Mitchell (Devola), Tudor Owens (Dr. Meeker), Joel Dante (Franscetti).

MOTEL HELL (1980)
Director: Kevin Connor
Rory Calhoun (Vincent Smith), Nancy Parsons (Ida Smith), Nina Axelrod (Terry), Paul Linke (Bruce Smith), Monique St. Pierre (Debbie), Rosanne Katon (Suzi), E. Hampton Beagle (Bob), Everett Creach (Bo), Wolfman Jack (Rev. Billy), Dick Curtis (Guy), Elaine Joyce (Edith), Michael Melvin (Ivan), Marc Silver, Gwil Richards, John Ratzenberger, Toni Gillman, Shaylin Hendrixson, Heather Hendrixson, Barbara Goodson, Margot Hope, Kim Fowler.

MOTHER'S DAY (1980)
Director: Charles Kaufman
Nancy Hendrickson (Abbey), Deborah Luce (Jackie), Tiana Pierce (Trina), Holden McGuire (Ike), Billy Ray McQuade (Addley), Rose Ross (Mother), Kevin Lowe (Ted), Karl Sandys (Brad), Stanley Knapp (Charlie), Robert Carnegie (Tex), Ed Battle (Doorman),

Marsella Davidson (Terry), Bobby Collins (Ernie), Scott Lucas (storekeeper).

MOTHRA (1961-Jap.) (A. K. A. "Mosura")
Director: Inoshiro Honda
Frankie Sakai (the reporter), Hiroshi Koizumi (the photographer), Emi & Yumi Itoh (the Little Sisters), Ken Uehara, Kyoko Kagawa.

MOUSE ON THE MOON, THE (1963)
Director: Richard Lester
Margaret Rutherford (Gloriana), Ron Moody (Mountjoy), Bernard Cribbins (Vincent), June Ritchie (Cynthia), David Kossoff (Kokintz), John Le Mesurier (British Delegate), Peter Sallis (Russian Delegate), John Phillips (Bracewell), Terry-Thomas (Spender), Archie Duncan (U. S. General), Edward Bishop, Bill Edwards (U. S. Astronauts), Tom Aldredge (Wendover), Roddy McMillan (Benter), John Bluthal (Von Neidel), Michael Trubshawe (British Aide), Richard Marner (Russian Air Force General), Jan Conrad (Russian Aide), Hugh Lloyd (plumber), Mario Fabrizi (valet), Coral Morphew (peasant girl), Stuart Saunders (sergeant), Clive Dunn (bandleader), Frank Lieberman (American civilian), Lucy Griffiths, Carol Dowell (Ladies in Waiting), Stringer Davis (1st Councillor), Carolyn Pertwee (June), Sandra Hampton (April), Kevin Scott (American Journalist), Guy Dighy (German Scientist), Laurence Herder, Harvey Hull (Russian Cosmonauts), Eric Barker (1st Member), Allan Cuthbertson (2nd Member), Gerald Anderson (4th Member), Robin Bailey (5th Member), Frankie Howerd (Fenwichian), Paul Cole, Larry Crosse, Beverly Bennett, Michael Caspi, Murray Kash, Robert Haynos.

MOUSE THAT ROARED, THE (1959)
Director: Jack Arnold
Peter Sellers (Gloriana/Mountjoy/ Tully Bascombe), Jean Seberg (Helen), David Kossoff (Prof. Kokintz), William Hartnell (Will), Leo McKern (Benter), Austin Willis (U. S. Secretary of Defense), Colin Gordon (BBC Announcer), Timothy Bateson (Roger), Monty Landis (Cobbley), Harold Krasket (Pedro), George Margo (O'Hara), MacDonald Parke (Snippet), Richard Gatehouse

(Mulligan), Jacques Cey (ticket Collector), Stuart Sanders (Cunard Captain), Ken Stanley (2nd Officer).

MR. DRAKE'S DUCK (1950)
Director: Val Guest
Douglas Fairbanks, Jr. (Don Drake), Howard Marion Crawford (Major Travers), Wilfred Hyde-White (Mr. May), Reginald Beckwith (Mr. Boothby), Tom Gill (Capt. White), John Pertwee (Reuben), Yolande Donlan (Penny Drake), Peter Butterworth (Higgins), A. E. Matthews (Brigadier), John Boxer.

MR. HEX (1946)
Director: William Beaudine
Leo Gorcey (Slip Mahoney), Huntz Hall (Sach Debussy Jones), David Gorcey (Chuck), Gabriel Dell (Gabe Moreno), Bernard Gorcey (Louie Dumbrowski), William Benedict (Whitey), Gale Robbins, Ian Keith, Bobby Jordan, Gene Roth, Ben Weldon, William Ruhl, Danny Beck, Joe Gray, Meyer Grace, Sammy Cohen, Rita Lynn, Eddie Gribbon, John Indrisano, Jimmy Aubrey, Dewey Robinson.

MR. PEABODY AND THE MERMAID (1948)
Director: Irving Pichel
William Powell (Mr. Peadody), Irene Hervey (Polly Peabody), Ann Blythe (the Mermaid), Andrea King (Cathy Livingston), Clinton Sundberg (Mike Fitzgerald), Lumsden Hare (Col. Mandrake), Fred Clark (Basil), Art Smith (Dr. Harvey), Beatrice Roberts (Mother), Hugh French (Major Hadley), James Logan (Lieutenant), Cynthia Corley (nurse), Mary Somerville (Lady Trebshaw), Mary Field (Wee Shop clerk), Tom Stevenson, Richard Ryan (waiters), Ivan H. Browning (Sidney), Bobby Hyatt (boy), Carol Savage (Daphne), Ola Lorraine (receptionist), Winifred Harris, Lydia Bilbrook (voices).

MR. PEEK-A-BOO (1950-Fr.) (A.K.A. "Le Passe-Muraille")
Director: Jean Boyer
Bourvil (Leon Dutilleul), Joan Greenwood (Susan), Marcelle Arnold (Germaine), Roger Treville (Burdin), Craddock C. Monroe (Elmer), Henri Cremieux (Lecuyer), Payne Williams (Jean-Paul), Charles Jarell (Maurice), Raymound Souplex, Gerard Oury, Jacques Erwin.

MR. SARDONICUS (1961)
Director: William Castle
Guy Rolfe (Sardonicus), Ronald Lewis

(Sir Robert Cargrave), Oscar Homolka (Krull), Audrey Dalton (Maude), Vladimir Sokoloff (Father), Lorna Hanson (Anna), Erika Peters (Elenka), James Forrest (Wainwright), Constance Cavendish (Mrs. Higgins), David Janti (Janku), Mavis Neal (Head Nurse), Tina Woodward (girl), Franz Roehn (gravedigger).

MR. SYCAMORE (1975)
Director: Pancho Kohner
Jason Robards, Jr. (John), Sandy Dennis (Jane), Jean Simmons (Estelle), Robert Easton (Fred), Brenda Smith (Daisy), Mark Miller (Fletcher), Richard Bull (Doctor), Ian Wolfe (Abner/Arnie), Lou Picetti (Humphrey), David Osterhout (Officer Kelly), Jerome Thor (Higgins), Curtis Taylor (Harry), Paul Berini, Eddie Lewis (milkmen), Darby Hinton (Frank), Sydna Scott (clubwoman), Ron D'Ippolito, Richard Redd (attendants), Hall Brock (Albert), Twana Nugent (Albert's sister), Don Spector, Wayne Smith (workmen), Walter Scott,(truck driver), Janine Johnson (piano student), Everet Smith (Officer), Lance Cremer (newsboy).

MR. WU (1927)
Director: William Nigh
Lon Chaney, Sr. (Mr. Wu), Louise Dresser (Mrs. Gregory), Renee Adoree (Nang Ping), Ralph Forbes (Basil Gregory), Holmes Herbert (Mr. Gregory), Gertrude Olmsted (Hilda Gregory), Claude King (Mr. Muir), Anna May Wong (Loo Song), Mrs. Wong Wing (Ah Wong), Sonny Loy (Little Wu).

MRS. DEATH (1968-Mex.) (A.K.A. "La Senora Muerte")
Director: Jaime Salvador
Regina Torne, John Carradine, Elsa Cardenas, Miguel Angel Alvarez, Victor Junco, Isela Vega, Frankenstein, Mario Orea, Patricia Ferrer, Carlos Ancira, Alicia Ravel, Carlos Ortigosa.

MUMMY, THE (1932)
Director: Karl Freund
Boris Karloff (Imhotep/Ardath Bey), Zita Johann (Helen Grosvenor), David Manners (Frank Whemple), Arthur Byron (Sir Joseph Whemple), Bramwell Fletcher (Ralph Norton), Edward Van Sloan (Dr. Muller), Leonard Mudie (Prof. Pearson), Eddie Kane

(Dr. Le Baron), Henry Victor (Marion), Kathryn Byron (Frau Muller), Noble Johnson (the Nubian), James Crane (the Pharoah), Arnold Grey (Knight), Tony Marlow (Police Inspector).

MUMMY, THE (1959)
    Director: Terence Fisher
Peter Cushing (John Banning), Christopher Lee (Kharis), Yvonne Furneaux (Isobel Banning/Ananka), Eddie Byrne (Insp. Mulrooney), George Pastell (Mehemet), Felix Aylmer (Stephen Banning), Raymond Huntley (Joseph Whemple), John Stuart (Coroner), Michael Ripper (poacher), Harold Goodwin (Pat), Dennis Shaw (Mike).

MUMMY'S BOYS (1936)
    Director: Fred Guiol
Bert Wheeler (Stanley), Robert Woolsey (Whittaker), Willie Best (Catfish), Moroni Olsen (Doc Sterling), Barbara Pepper (Mary), Frank M. Thomas (Browning), Francis McDonald (El Bey), Mitchell Lewis (Sheik), Charles Coleman (Butler), Frank Lackteen (2nd Oriental), Frederic Barton (Mr. Edwards).

MUMMY'S CURSE, THE (1944)
    Director: Leslie Goodwins
Lon Chaney, Jr. (Kharis), Peter Coe (Dr. Ilzor Zandaab), Virginia Christine (Ananka), Kay Harding (Betty Walsh), Martin Kosleck (Raghab), Dennis Moore (Dr. James Halsey), Kurt Katch (Cajun Joe), Addison Richards (Major Pat Walsh), Ann Codee (Tante Berthe), Holmes Herbert (Dr. Cooper), Charles Stevens (Skilles), William Farnum (Michael, the caretaker), Napoleon Simpson (Goobie), Claire Whitney.

MUMMY'S GHOST, THE (1943)
    Director: Reginald LeBorg
Lon Chaney, Jr. (Kharis), Ramsay Ames (Amina Mansori/Ananka), John Carradine (Youssef Bey), Robert Lowery (Tommy Harvey), Barton MacLane (Insp. Walgreen), Claire Whitney (Mrs. Ellen Norman), Frank Reicher (Prof. Norman), George Zucco (High Priest), Harry Shannon (Sheriff Elwood), Anthony Warde (Sheriff's associate), Ivan Triesault (Scripps Museum guide), Martha Vickers (Norman's girl student), Emmitt Vogan (the Coroner), Lester Sharpe (Dr. Ayab), Oscar O'Shea (nightwatchman), Dorothy Vaughan (Mrs. Ada Blake), Mira McKinney

(Mrs. Martha Evans), Eddy Waller (Ben Evans), Don Barclay (student), Bess Flowers (Mapleton woman).

MUMMY'S HAND, THE (1940)
    Director: Christy Cabanne
Dick Foran (Steve Banning), Peggy Moran (Marta Solvani), Tom Tyler (Kharis), Cecil Kellaway (Prof. Solvani), Wallace Ford (Babe Hanson), George Zucco (Prof. Andoheb), Eduardo Ciannelli (the High Priest), Charles Trowbridge (Prof. Petrie), Sig Arno (the beggar), Michael Mark (the bizarre owner), Mara Tarta (the girl), Leon Belasco (Ali), Harry Stubbs (bartender), Eddie Foster (Egyptian).

MUMMY'S SHROUD, THE (1966)
    Director: John Gilling
John Phillips (Stanley Preston), Andre Morell (Sir Basil Walden), David Buck (Paul Preston), Elizabeth Sellars (Barbara Preston), Maggie Kimberley (Claire), Michael Ripper (Longbarrow), Catherine Lacey (Haiti), Eddie Powell (Prem, the Mummy), Dickie Owen (Prem), Richard Warner (Insp. Barrani), Roger Delgado (Hasmid Ali), Tim Barrett (Harry Newton), Toni Gilpin (Pharoah's wife), Bruno Barnabe (the Pharoah), Andreas Malandrinos (curator), Toolsie Persaud (Kah-to-Bey).

MUMMY'S TOMB, THE (1942)
    Director: Harold Young
Lon Chaney, Jr. (Kharis), Turhan Bey (Mehemet Bey), Dick Foran (Stephen Banning), John Hubbard (John Banning), Elyse Knox (Isobel Evans), George Zucco (Andoheb), Virginia Brissac (Mrs. Evans), Wallace Ford (Babe Hanson), Mary Gordon (Jane Banning), Frank Reicher (Prof. Norman), Paul E. Burns (Jim), Emmett Vogan (coroner), Cliff Clark (Sheriff), Janet Shaw (girl in car), Eddie Parker (stuntman), Glenn Strange, Grace Cunard.

MUNSTER GO HOME (1966)
    Director: Earl Bellamy
Fred Gwyann (Herman Munster), Yvonne De Carlo (Lily Munster), Al Lewis (Grandpa), Butch Patrick (Eddie Munster), Debbie Watson (Marilyn Munster), Hermione Gingold (Lady Effigie Munster), Terry-Thomas (Freddie Munster), Robert

Pine (Roger Moresby), Bernard Fox
(Squire Moresby), John Carradine
(Cruickshank), Jeanne Arnold (Grace
Munster), Ben Wright (Hennesy),
Richard Dawson (Joey), Cliff Norton
(Herbert), Arthur Malet (Hennesy),
Maria Lennard (Millie), Diana Chesney
(Mrs. Moresby), Jack Dodson (ship-
mate).

MUNSTERS' REVENGE, THE (TVM-
    1981) - 2-27-81
    Director: Don Weis
Fred Gwynne (Herman Munster), Yvonne
De Carlo (Lily Munster), Al Lewis
(Grandpa), K. C. Martel (Eddie Mun-
ster), Jo McDonnell (Marilyn Munster),
Robert Hastings (the Phantom of the
Opera), Sid Ceasar (Dr. Diablo),
Colby Chester (Michael), Herbert
Voland (Chief Boyke), Peter Fox (Glen),
Michael McManus (Ralph).

MUPPET MOVIE, THE (1979)
    Director: James Frawley
Charles Durning (Doc Hopper), Mel
Brooks (Prof. Krassman), Austin
Pendleton, Edgar Bergen, Milton
Berle, James Coburn, Dom DeLuise,
Elliott Gould, Bob Hope, Madeline
Kahn, Carol Kane, Cloris Leachman,
Steve Martin, Richard Pryor, Telly
Savalas, Orson Welles, Paul Williams,
Jim Henson, Frank Oz, Jerry Nelson,
Richard Hunt, Dave Goelz, Carroll
Spinney, Steve Whitmire, Kathryn
Mullen, Bob Payne, Erne Ozker,
Carolyn Wilcox, Olga Felgemacher,
Bruce Schwartz, Michael Davis, Buz
Suraci, Tony Basilicato, Adam Hunt.

MURDER AT DAWN (1932) (A. K. A.
    "The Death Ray")
    Director: Richard Thorpe
Jack Mulhall (Danny), Josephine Dunn
(Doris), Mischa Auer (Henry), Eddie
Boland (Freddie), J. Crawford Kent
(Arnstein), Marjorie Beebe (Gertrude),
Phillips Smalley (Judge Folger), Frank
Ball (Dr. Farrington), Martha Mattox
(housekeeper), Al Cross (Goddard).

MURDER AT 45 R. P. M. (1960-Fr.)
    (A. K. A. "Meurtre en 45 Tours")
    Director: Etienne Perier
Danielle Darrieux, Jean Servais,
Michel Auclair.

MURDER BY DEATH (1976)
    Director: Robert Moore
Peter Falk (Sam Diamond), Peter
Sellers (Sidney Wang), David Niven
(Dick Charleston), Maggie Smith (Dora

Charleston), Elsa Lanchester
(Jessica Marbles), James Coco
(Milo Perier), Alec Guinness
(Bensonmum), Truman Capote
(Lionel Twain), Eileen Brennan
(Tess Skeffington), Estelle Win-
wood (Miss Winters), Nancy Walker
(Yetta), James Cromwell (Marcel),
Richard Narita (Willie Wang),
Keith McConnell (Sherlock Holmes),
Richard Peel (Dr. Watson).

MURDER BY DECREE (1979)
    Director: Bob Clark
Christopher Plummer (Sherlock
Holmes), James Mason (Dr. Watson),
David Hemmings (Insp. Foxborough),
Anthony Quayle (Sir Charles Warren),
Genevieve Bujold (Annie Crook), Frank
Finlay (Insp. Lestrade), Sir John
Gielgud (Prime Minister), Susan
Oliver (Mary Kelly), Donald
Sutherland (Robert Lees), Roy
Lansford (Sir Thomas Smiley),
Peter Fonfield (William Slade),
Teddi Moore (Mrs. Lees), Catherine
Kessler (Carrie), Ron Pember
(Makins), Ken Jones (dock guard).

MURDER BY INVITATION (1941)
    Director: Phil Rosen
Wallace Ford (Bob White), Sarah
Padden (Aunt Cassie), Marian
Marsh (Nora O'Brien), Gavin
Gordon (Garson Denham), Minerva
Urecal (Maxine Denham), Herb
Vigran (Eddie), Arthur Young
(Trowdridge), George Guhl (Sheriff
Boggs), Hazel Keener (Mary Denham),
Wallis Clark (Judge Moore), Lee
Shumway, Dave O'Brien, John James,
Philip Trent, Dav Deslys, Isabelle
La Mal.

MURDER BY TELEVISION (1935)
    Director: Clifford Sanforth
Bela Lugosi (Arthur Perry), June
Collyer (June Houghland), George
Meeker (Richard Grayson), Huntley
Gordon (Dr. Scofield), Henry
Mowbray (Chief of Police Nelson),
Hattie McDaniel, Charles Hill
Mailes, Henry Hall, Charles D.
French, Larry Francis, William
Sullivan, Allan Jung, Claire McDowell,
William Tooker.

MURDER BY THE CLOCK (1931)
    Director: Edward Sloman
William Boyd (Lt. Valcour), Irving
Pichel (Philip Endicott), Lilyan
Tashman (Laura Endicott), Regis
Toomey (Officer Cassidy), Blanche

Friderici (Julia Endicott), Walter McGrail (Herbert Endicott), Sally O'Neil (Jane), Martha Mattox (Miss Roberts), Lester Vail (Thomas Hollander), Frank Sheridan (Chief of Police), Lenita Lane (Nurse), Charles D. Brown (O'Brien), Frederick Sullivan (Medical Examiner), Harry Burgess (Coroner), John Rogers (Hollander's valet).

MURDER CLINIC, THE (1966-Ital. / Fr.) (A.K.A. "La Lama nel Corpo", "The Knife in the Body", "Les Nuits del Epouvante", "The Night of Terrors", "The Murder Society", "Revenge of the Living Dead")
    Director: Elio Scardamaglia/ Michael Hamilton
William Berger, Francoise Prevost, Barbara Wilson, Mary Young, Harriet White.

MURDERER'S COMMAND (1966-Span. / Port. /Ger.) (A.K.A. "Comando de Asesinos")
    Director: Julio Coll
Peter Van Eyck, Antonio Vilar, Letitia Roman, Klaus Juergen, Mikaela, Antonio Pica.

MURDERERS FROM OTHER WORLDS (1971-Mex.) (A.K.A. "Asesinos de Otros Mundos")
    Director: Ruben Galindo
Santo, Carlos Agosti, Carlos Suarez, Sasha Montenegro, Juan Gallardo.

MURDERER'S ROW (1966)
    Director: Henry Levin
Dean Martin (Matt Helm), Ann-Margret (Suzie Solaris), Karl Malden (Julian Wall), James Gregory (MacDonald), Robert Eastham (Dr. Solaris), Camilla Sparv (Coco Duquette), Beverly Adams (Lovey Kravezit), Marcel Hillaire (Devereaux), Duke Howard (Billy Orwitt), Tom Reese (Ironhead), Ted Hartley (guard), Robert Terry (Dr. Rogas), Corinne Cole (Miss January), Mary Jane Mangler, Mary Hughes, Dale Brown, Amedee Chabot, Lynn Hartoch, Jan Watson, Marilyn Tindall, Rena Horton, Barbara Burgess, Luci Ann Cook, Dee Dee Duffy, Rena Horton (Slaygirls).

MURDER, HE SAYS (1945)
    Director: George Marshall
Fred MacMurray, Helen Walker, Marjorie Main, Porter Hall, Peter Whitney, Jean Heather, Barbara Pepper, Mabel Paige.

MURDER IN SPACE (1979)
    see Television: Battlestar Galactica (1978-79)

MURDER IN THE BLUE ROOM (1944)
    Director: Leslie Goodwins
Anne Gwynne (Nan Kirkland), Donald Cook (Steve Randall), John Litel (Frank Baldrich), Regis Toomey (Insp. McDonald), Bill Williams (Larry Dearden), Ian Wolfe (Edwards, the butler), Grace McDonald (Peggy), Betty Kean (Betty), Victoria Horne (Maid), Nella Walker (Linda Baldrich), Emmett Vogan (Hannagan), June Preisser (Jerry), Andrew Tombes (Dr. Carroll), Frankie Marlow (Curtis).

MURDER IN THE RED BARN (1935) (A.K.A. "Maria Marten")
    Director: Milton Rosmer
Tod Slaughter (William Corder), Sophie Stewart (Maria Marten), Eric Portman (Carlos), Dennis Hoey (Gambler), Clare Greet (Mrs. Marten), D.J. Williams (Farmer Marten), Gerrard Tyrrell (Tim), Antonia Brough (Maud Sennett), Quentin McPhearson (Mr. Sennett), Ann Trevor (Nan), Herbert Leonard (Compere), Stella Rho (Gypsy Crone), Noel Dainton (Stell), J. Leslie Frith (lawyer).

MURDERS IN THE RUE MORGUE (1932)
    Director: Robert Florey
Bela Lugosi (Dr. Mirakle), Leon Waycoff/Leon Ames (Pierre Dupin), Sidney Fox (Camille L'Espanaye), Bert Roach (Paul), Noble Johnson (Janos), Brandon Hurst (Prefect of Police), Arlene Francis (Monette), Betsy Ross Clarke (the mother), D'Arcy Corrigan (the morgue keeper), Charlie Gemora (the Ape), Herman Bing.

MURDERS IN THE RUE MORGUE (1971)
    Director: Gordon Hessler
Jason Robards, Jr. (Cesar Charron), Herbert Lom (Marot), Christine Kaufmann (Madeline Charron), Lilli Palmer (Madeleine's mother), Michael Dunn (Pierre), Adolfo Celi (Vidocq), Maria Perschy (Genevre), Peter Arne (Aubert), Dean Selmeir (Jacques), Marshall Jones (Ornsini), Jose Calvo (Hunchback), Werner Umberg (theater

manager), Luis Rivera (actor), Rosalind Elliot (Gabrielle), Virginia Stach (Lucie), Ruth Platt (Orsini's assistant), Maria Martin (Mme, Adolphe), Xan Das Bolas (Orsini's assistant), Sally Longley, Pamela McInnes, Rafael Hernandez (Members of Repertory Company).

MURDERS IN THE ZOO (1933)
    Director: Edward Sutherland
Charles Ruggles (Peter Yates), Lionel Atwill (Eric Gorman), Gail Patrick (Jerry Evans), Randolph Scott (Dr. Woodford), Kathleen Burke (Evelyn Gorman), John Lodge (Roger Hewitt), Harry Beresford (Prof. Evans), Edward McWade (Dan).

MUSEUM OF HORROR (1964-Mex.)
    (A. K. A. "El Museo dol Horror")
    Director: Rafael Baledon
Julio Aleman, Patricia Conde, Carlos Lopez Moctezuma, Joaquin Cordero, David Reynoso, Sonia Infante.

MUTATIONS, THE (1972)
    Director: Jack Cardiff
Donald Pleasence (Prof. Nolter), Brad Harris (Brian), Julie Ege (Hedi), Jill Haworth (Lauren), Tom Baker (Lynch), Michael Dunn (Burns), Olga Anthony (Bridget), Scott Antony (Tony), Lisa Collings (prostitute).

MUTINY IN OUTER SPACE (1964)
    (A. K. A. "Space Station X14)
    Director: Hugo Grimaldi
William Leslie (Major Towers), Dolores Faith (Faith Montaine), Richard Garland (Col. Cromwell), Pamela Curran (Connie), James Dobson (Dr. Hoffman), Carl Crow (Webber), Glenn Langan, Harold Lloyd, Jr. , Gabriel Curtis, Ron Stokes, Robert Palmer.

MY BLOOD RUNS COLD (1965)
    Director: William Conrad
Troy Donahue (Ben Gunther), Joey Heatherton (Julie Merriday), Barry Sullivan (Julian Merriday), Jeanette Nolan (Aunt Sarah), Nicholas Coster (Harry Lindsay), Russell Thorson (Sheriff), Howard McNear (Henry), John Holland (Mr. Courtland), Bill Wright (Lansbury), Howard Wendell (the Mayor), Shirley Mitchell (Mrs. Courtland), John McCook (Owen).

MY BLOODY VALENTINE (1981)
    Director: George Mihalka
Paul Kelman (T. J.), Lori Hallier

(Sarah), Neil Affleck (Axel), Keith Knight (Hollis), Cynthia Dale (Patty), Alf Humphreys (Howard), Helene Udy (Sylvia), Rob Stein (John), Terry Waterland (Harriet), Gina Dick (Gretchen), Tom Kovacs (Mike), Carl Marotte (Dave), Jim Murchison (Tommy), Peter Cowper (Harry Warden), Patricia Hamilton (Mabel), Don Francks (Chief Newby).

MY BROTHER TALKS TO HORSES (1946)
    Director: Fred Zinnemann
Butch Jenkins (Louie), Peter Lawford, Charles Ruggles, Spring Byington, Beverly Tyler, Edward Arnold, O. Z. Whitehead.

MY FRIEND, DR. JEKYLL (1960-Ital.) (A. K. A. "Il Mio Amico, Jekyll")
    Director: Marino Girolami
Ugo Tognazzi, Raimondo Vianello, Carlo Croccolo, Helene Chanel, Abbe Lane.

MY SON, THE HERO (1961-Ital. /Fr.) (A. K. A. "Arrivano i Titani")
    Director: Duccio Tessari
Pedro Armendriz (Cadmus), Guiliano Gemma (Crios), Antonella Lauldi (Hermione), Jacqueline Sassard (Antiope), Gerard Sety (Hippolytos), Serge Nubret (Rator), Ingrid Schoeller (Emerate), Tanya Lopert (Licina).

MY SON, THE VAMPIRE (1952)
    (A. K. A. "Mother Riley Meets the Vampier", "Vampire Over London", "King Robot")
    Director: John Gilling
Arthur Lucan (Old Mother Riley), Bela Lugosi (Baron Van Housen), Kitty McShane (Kitty Riley), Charles Lloyd-Pack, Dora Bryan, Ian Wilson, Hattie Jacques, Dandy Nichols, Philip Leaver, Richard Wattis, Graham Moffatt, Arthur Brander, David Hurst, Judith Furse, Roderick Lovell, Maria Mercedes.

MYSTERIANS, THE (1957-Jap.)
    (A. K. A. "Chikyu Boeigun", "Earth Defense Forces")
    Director: Inoshiro Honda
Kenji Sahara (Joji Atsumi), Yumi Shirakawa (Etsuko Shiraishi), Momoko Koshi (Hiroko), Takashi Shimura (Dr. Adachi), Akihiko Hirata (Ryoichi Shiraishi), Susumu Fujita (Cmdr. Morita), Fuyuki Murakami (Dr. Kawanami), Yoshio

Kosugi (Cmdr. Sugimoto), Hisaya Ito (Capt. Seki), Minosuke Yamada (Gen. Hamamoto), Harold S. Conway.

MYSTERIES OF BLACK MAGIC (1957-Mex.) (A. K. A. "Misterios de la Magia Negra")
Director: Miguel M. Delgado
Aldo Monti, Carlos Riguelme, Lourdes Pargas, Nadia Haro Oliva, Angelines Fernandez.

MYSTERIOUS CONTRAGRAV, THE (1915)
Director: Henry McRae
Frank Stites (Prof. Coxheim).

MYSTERIOUS DOCTOR, THE (1943)
Director: Ben Stoloff
Jon Loder (Harry Leland), Eleanor Parker (Letty), Letser Mathews (Dr. Holmes), Matt Willis (Bart Redmond), Forrester Harvey (Hugh), Cylde Cook (Herbert), Stuart Holmes (Peter), Creighton Hale (Luke), Crawford Kent (Commandant), David Clyde (Tom Andrews), Art Foster (Saul Bevan), Bruce Lester (Lt. Christopher Hilton), Phyllis Barry (Ruby), Leo White (Headless Man).

MYSTERIOUS DR. FU MANCHU, THE (1929)
Director: Rowland V. Lee
Warner Oland (Dr. Fu Manchu), Jean Arthur (Lia Eltham). O. P. Heggie (Nayland Smith), Neil Hamilton (Dr. Jack Petrie), William Austin (Sylvester Wadsworth), Claude King (Gen. Petrie), Tully Marshall (Chinese Ambassador), Noble Johnson (Li Po), Evelyn Selbie (Fai Lu), Charles Giblyn, Lawford Davidson, Charles Stevens, Donald MacKenzie, Lask Winter, Chappel Dosset.

MYSTERIOUS DR. SATAN, THE (1940) (A. K. A. "Dr. Satan's Robot") - serial in 15 episodes
Director: William Witney & John English
Eduardo Ciannelli (Dr. Satan), Robert Wilcox (Bob Wayne/Copperhead), Ella Neal (Lois Scott), William Newell (Speed Martin), C. Montague Shaw (Prof. Scott), Charles Trowbridge (Gov. Bronson), Jack Mulhall (Chief of Police), Kenneth Terrell (Corwin), Bud Geary (Hallett), Tom Steele (Robot), Dorothy Herbert (Alice Brent), Walter McGrial (Stoner), Paul Marion (the Stranger), Edwin Stanley (Col. Bevans),

Joe McGuinn (Gort), Archie Twitchell (airport radio announcer), Lynton Brent (Scarlett), Alan Gregg (Red), Al Taylor (Joe), Edward Cassidy (Barton), Harry Strang (Davis), Kenneth Harlan (Lathrop), John Bagni (Gray), Wally West (Palmer), Yakima Canutt, Bud Wolfe (sailors), Tris Coffin (Wells), William Stahl (Brock), Jimmy Fawcett (Al), Frank Conklin (Burns), Eddie Parker (Chuck), Duke Green (Duke), Eddie Dew (gas station attendant), James Bush (co-pilot), Bert LeBaron (Fallon), Ted Stanhope (Glover), Jerry Jerome (Green), Al Seymour (Jake), Ernest Sarracino (Mike), Jack O'Shea (house heavy), Floyd Criswell (Officer), Robert Wayne (Perry), Virginia Carroll (Nurse), Frank Brownlee (Panamint Pete), Frank Ellis, Patrick Kelly (plant heavies), Charles Hutchison (proprietor), Bill Wilkus (truck heavy), George Allen (Spike), Davison Clark (Wagner), Lloyd Whitlock (Williams), Dave Sharpe, Sam Garrett, Cy Slocum, Helen Thurston, Bob Rogers, Fred Schaefer, Bill Yrigoyen.

MYSTERIOUS INTRUDER, THE (1946)
Director: William Castle
Richard Dix, Barton MacLane, Nina Vale, Mike Mazurki, Regis Toomey, Pamela Blake, Helen Mourey, Paul Burns, Charles Lane, Kathleen Howard, Harlan Briggs.

MYSTERIOUS ISLAND (1929)
Director: Lucian Hubbard, Maurice Tourneur & Benjamin Christensen
Lionel Barrymore (Count Dakkar), Lloyd Hughes (Nikolai), Montague Love (Falon), Harry Gribbon (Mikhail), Gibson Gowland (Dimitri), Dolores Brinkman (Teresa), Snitz Edwards (Anton), Jane Daly (Sonia), Pauline Starke, Karl Dane.

MYSTERIOUS ISLAND (1950) - serial in 15 episodes
Chapters: 1. "Lost in Space", 2. "Sinister Savages", 3. "Savage Justice", 4. "Wild Man at Large", 5. "Trail of the Mystery Man", 6. "The Pirates Attack", 7. "Menace of the Mercurians", 8. "Between Two Fires", 9. "Shrine of the Silver Bird", 10. "Fighting Fury", 11. "Desperate Chance", 12. "Mystery

of the Mine", 13. "Jungle Downfall",
14. "Men from Tomorrow" & 15. "The
Last of Mysterious Island".
Director: Spencer Gordon Bennet
Richard Crane (Capt. Harding), Leonard
Penn (Captain Nemo), Karen Randle
(Rulu), Marshall Reed (Jack Pencroft),
Ralph Hodges (Bert Brown), Terry
Frost (Ayrton), Gene Roth (Captain
Shard), Bernie Hamilton (Beb), Hugh
Prosser (Gideon Spilett), Rusty Wes-
coatt (Moley).

MYSTERIOUS ISLAND (1960)
Director: Cy Endfield
Michael Craig (Capt. Cyrus Harding),
Herbert Lom (Captain Nemo), Michael
Callan (Herbert Brown), Joan Green-
wood (Marquisa Maria Labrino), Gary
Merrill (Gideon Spilett), Percy Herbert
(Sgt. Pencroft), Beth Rogan (Elena),
Dan Jackson (Neb), Nigel Green (Tom).

MYSTERIOUS ISLAND OF BEAUTIFUL
WOMEN (TVM-1979) - 12-1-79
Director: Joseph Pevney
Steven Keats (Stapleton), Peter Lawford
(Gordon Duvall), Cllint Walker (Wendell),
Jaime Lyn Bauer (Lizabeth), Michael
McGreevey (Danny), Guich Koock (J.J.),
Deborah Shelton (Bambi), Rosalind
Chaio (Flower), Sandy McPeak (Stu),
Jayne Kennedy, Susie Coelho, Kathryn
Davis.

MYSTERIOUS ISLAND OF CAPTAIN
NEMO (1973-Fr./Ital.) (A.K.A.
"L'Ile Mysterieuse", "The Myster-
ious Island")
Director: Juan Colpi
Omar Sharif (Captian Nemo), Phillippe
Nicaud (Gideon Spilett), Gerard Tichy
(Cyrus Smith), Ambroise M'Bia (Nebu-
chadnezzar), Jesse Hann (Bonaventure
Pencroft), Gabriele Tinti (Ayrton),
Rafael Bardem (Harbert Brown), Vidal
Molina (Harvey), Rick Bataglea (Finch).

MYSTERIOUS MAGICIAN, THE (1965-
Ger.) (A.K.A. "Der Hexer"; "The
Wizard")
Director: Alfred Vohrer
Joachim Berger, Heinz Drache, Sophie
Hardy, Eddi Arent, Siegfried Lowitz.

MYSTERIOUS MR. M, THE (1946) -
serial in 13 episodes
Chapters: 1. "When Clocks Chime Death",
2. "Danger Downward", 3. "Flood of
Flames", 4. "The Double Trap", 5.
"Highway Execution", 6. "Heavier Than
Water", 7. "Strange Coliseum", 8. "When
Friend Kills Friend", 9. "Parachute

Peril", 10."The Human Time-Bomb",
11. "The Key to Murder", 12. "High-
Line Smash-Up" & 13. "The Real Mr.
M".
Director: Lewis D. Collins &
Vernon Keays
Richard Martin (Kriby Walsh), Pamela
Blake (Shirley Clinton), Dennis Moore
(Grant Farrell), Jane Randolph (Marina
Lamont), Virginia Brissac (Grandma
Waldron), Byron Foulger (Wehterby),
Joseph Crehan (Capt. Blair), Jack
Ingram (Shark), Danny Morton (Derek
Lamont), Edmund MacDonald (Anthony
Waldron).

MYSTERIOUS MR. WONG, THE (1935)
Director: William Nigh
Bela Lugosi (Mr. Wong), Wallace
Ford (Janson), Arline Judge (Peg),
Fred Warren (Tsung), Lee Shumway
(Brandon), Lotus Long (Moonflower),
Robert Emmett O'Connor (McGilli-
cuddy), Edward Peil (Jen Yu), Luke
Chan (Chan Fu), Etta Lee, Chester
Gan, Theodore Lorch, Ernest F.
Young, James B. Leong.

MYSTERIOUS STRANGER, THE (1980-
Ger.)
Director: Peter H. Hunt
Chris Makepeace (August Feldner),
Fred Gwynne (Balthazar Hoffman),
Lance Kerwin (No. 44), Herbert Fux
(Hans Katzenyammer), Christoph
Waltz (Ernest Wasseman), Bernhard
Wicki (Heinrich Stein), Paola Lowe
(Frau Stein), Astrid Lohel (Sara),
Bernd Stephan (Doangivadam), Karl
Friedrich (Father Julian), Erika
Domenik (Duffles), Erwin Stein-
hauer (Gustav Fischer), Vanessa
Knox-Mawer (Marget), Harry Hornisch
(Adam Binks), Erika Wackernagel
(Katrina).

MYSTERIOUS TWO, THE (TVM-1982) -
5-31-82
Director: Gary Sherman
John Forsythe (Ge), Priscilla Pointer
(She), James Stephens (Tim Arm-
strong), Robert Pine (Arnold Brown),
Vic Tayback (Ted Randall), Noah
Beery, Jr. (Virgil Molloy), Karen
Werner, E.J. Andre, Bruce French,
Lee Bryant, Lauren Frost, Bill Quinn,
Mo Malone, Robert Englund, Jerry
Hardin, Shannon Wilcox, Renny Baker,
Candy Mobley, Ed Call, George Paul,
Constance Pfeifer, Bill Smillie, James
Parker, Dale Reynolds.

MYSTERY AT THE VILLA ROSE (1930)

Director: Leslie Hiscott
Austin Trevor (Hanaud), Richard Cooper (Ricardo), Francis Lister, John Hamilton, Norah Baring, Amy Brandon-Thomas.

MYSTERY LINER (1934)
Director: William Nigh
Noah Beery (Captain Holling), Astrid Allyn (Lila), Gustav Von Seyffertitz (Von Kessling), Edwin Maxwell (Major Pope), Ralph Lewis (Grimson), Olaf Hytten (Grimson's assistant), George Hayes (watchman), George Cleveland (Simms), Howard Hickman (Dr. Howard), Zeffie Tilbury (Granny), Boothe Howard (Downey), Gordon De Main (Bryson), John Maurice Sullivan (Watson), Cornelius Keefe (Cliff), Ray Brown (His Excellency), Jerry Stewart (Edgar), George Nash (waiter).

MYSTERY MIND, THE (1920) - serial in 15 episodes
Chapters: 1. "The Hypnotic Clue", 2. "The Fires of Fury", 3. "The War of Wills", 4. "The Fumes of Fear", 5. "Thought Waves", 6. "A Halo of Help", 7. "The Nether World", 8. "The Mystery Mind", 9. "Dual Personality", 10. "Hounds of Hate", 11. "The Sleepwalker", 12. "Temple of the Occult", 13. "The Binding Ray", 14. "The Water Cure", & 15. "The Gold of the Gods".
Director: Fred W. Sittenham & William S. Davis
Violet MacMillan (Violet Bronson), Peggy Shanor (Vera Collins), Dr. J. Robert Pauline (Dr. Robert Dupont), Paul Panzer (Dr. Sutton), Ed Rogers (Carl Canfield), De Sacia Saville (the Pahntom Face).

MYSTERY MOUNTAIN (1934) - serial in 12 episodes
Chapters: 1. "The Rattler", 2. "The Man Nobody Knows", 3. "The Eye That Never Sleeps", 4. "The Human Target", 5. "Phantom Outlaws", 6. "The Perfect Crime", 7. "Tarzan the Cunning", 8. "The Enemy's Stronghold", 9. "The Fatal Warning", 10. "The Secret of the Mountain", 11. "Behind the Mask" & 12. "The Judgment of Tarzan".
Director: Otto Brower & B. Reves Eason
Ken Maynard (Ken Williams), Verna Hillie (Jane Corwin), Edward Earle (Blayden), Edmund Cobb (the Rattler), Syd Saylor (Breezy), Lynton Brent (Matthews), Carmencita Johnson (Little Jane), Al Bridge (Henderson), Bob Kortman (Hank), Lafe McKee (Corwin),

Gene Autry, George Chesebro, Tom London, Jack Kirk, Wally Wales, Hooper Atchley, Smiley Burnette, William Gould, Lew Meehan, Philo McCullough, Curly Dresden, Jack Rockwell, Art Mix, James Mason, Steve Clark, Cliff Lyons, Frank Ellis.

MYSTERY OF EDWIN DROOD, THE (1935)
Director: Stuart Walker
Claude Rains (John Jasper), David Manners (Edwin Drood), Heather Angel (Rosa Bud), Douglass Montgomery (Neville Landess), Valerie Hobson (Helen Landess), E. E. Clive (Thomas Sapsea), Forrester Harvey (Durdles), Walter Kingsford (Hiram Grewigious), Ethel Griffies (Miss Twinkleton), Vera Buckland (Tope), Francis L. Sullivan (Mr. Crisparkle), Louise Carter (Mrs. Crisparkle), George Ernest (Deputy), Zeffie Tilbury (Opium Den Hag), J. M. Kerrigan.

MYSTERY OF DR. FU MANCHU, THE (1923) - series in 15 parts
Chapters: 1. "The Silver Buddha", 2. "The Man with the Limp", 3. "The Fiery Hand", 4. "Clue of the Pigtail", 5. "The West Case", 6. "The Sacred Order", 7. "The Queen of Hearts", 8. "Aaron's Rod", 9. "The Miracle", 10. "The Shrine of the Seven Lamps", 11. "The Fungi Cellers", 12. "The Cry of the Nighthawk", 13. "The Scented Envelopes", 14. "The Knocking on the Door", & 15. "The Call of Siva".
Director: A. E. Coleby
Harry Agar Lyons (Dr. Fu Manchu), Joan Clarkson, H. Cundall, Frank Wilson, Humbertson Wright, Fred P. Paul.

MYSTERY OF MARIE ROGET, THE (1942) (A.K.A. "Phantom of Paris)
Director: Phil Rosen
Patric Knowles (Dr. Palu Dupin), Maria Montez (Marie Roget), Maria Ouspenskaya (Mme. Cecile Roget), John Litel (M. Henri Beauvais), Frank Reicher (Magistrate), Lloyd Corrigan (Insp. Gobelin), Paul E. Burns (Gardener), Charles Middleton (the zoo curator), Reed Hadley (Naval Officer), Paul Dubov (Pierre, the news vendor), Beatrice Roberts (wife on street), Raymond Bailey (gendarme), Nell O'Day (Camille Roget), Edward Norris (Marcel Vigneaux), Clyde Filmore (M. De Luc), Norma Drury

(Mme. De Luc), John Maxwell (detective), Joe Bernard, Frank O'Connor (men), Lester Dorr, Charles Wagenheim (Subordinates to Prefect), Francis Sayles (Parisian), Jimmie Lucas (Parisian), Alphonse Martel (vegetable cart driver), Caroline Cooke (woman).

MYSTERY OF THE MARIE CELESTE, THE (1936) (A. K. A. "The Phantom Ship")
　　Director: Denison Clift
Bela Lugosi (Anton Lorenzen), Shirley Grey (Sarah Briggs), Arthur Margaretson (Captain Briggs), Ben Welden (Boas Hoffman), Dennis Hoey (Tom Goodschard), Gibson Gowland (Andy Gillings), George Mozart (Tommy Duggan), Edmund Willard (Toby Bilson), Cliff McLaglen (Captain Morehead), Ben Soutten, Terence de Marney, Herbert Cameron.

MYSTERY OF THE PALLID FACE, THE (1935-Mex.) (A. K. A. "Misterio del Rostro Palido")
　　Director: Juan Bustillo Oro
Rene Cardona, Carlos Villarias, Manuel Noriega, Beatriz Ramoz, Natalia Ortiz, Joaquin Busquets, Miguel Arenas.

MYSTERY OF THE 13th GUEST (1943)
　　Director: William Beaudine
Dick Purcell, Helen Parris, Addison Richards, Tim Ryan, Frank Faylen, Paul McVey, John Duncan, Jacqueline Dalya, Jon Dawson, John Ingraham, Cyril Ring.

MYSTERY OF THE WAX MUSEUM, THE (1933)
　　Director: Michael Curtiz
Lionel Atwill (Ivan Igor), Fay Wray (Charlotte Duncan), Glenda Farrell (Florence Dempsey), Frank McHugh (Jim), Gavin Gordon (Harold Winton), Edwin Maxwell (Joe Eorth), Holmes Herbert (Dr. Rasmussen), Arthur Edmund Carewe (Sparrow), Allen Vincent (Ralph Burton), Monica Bannister (Joan Gale), Matthew Betz (Hugo), DeWitt Jennings (Captain of Police), Thomas E. Jackson (Detective), Bull Anderson (the janitor), Pat O'Malley.

MYSTERY OF THREE CONTINENTS, THE (1959-Ital. /Fr. /Ger.) (A. K. A. "Il Mistero dei Trie Continenti")
　　Director: William Dieterle
Martha Hyer, Micheline Presle, Sabu, Wolfgang Preiss, Lino Venturi, Carlos Thompson, Gino Servi, Carlo Giustini, George Riviere, Carl Lange, Charles Regnier, Jean Claude Michel, Hans

Nielson, Rolf von Nauckhoff.

MYSTERY OF 13, THE (1919) - serial in 15 episodes
Chapters: 1. "Bitter Bondage", 2. "Lights Out", 3. "The Submarine Gardens", 4. "the Lone Rider", 5. "Blown to Atoms", 6. "Single Handed", 7. "Fire and Water", 8. "Pirate Loot", 9. "The Phantom House", 10. "The Raid", 11. "Bare Handed", 12. "The Death Ride", 13. "Brother against Brother", 14. "The Man Hunt", & 15. "The 13th Card".
　　Director: Francis Ford
Francis Ford, Rosemar Theby, Pete Girard, Nigel De Brulier, Phil Ford, Mark Fenton, Jack Saville, Doris Dare, Jack Lawton, Ruth Maureice, V. Orilo.

MYSTERY SHIP, THE (1917) - serial in 18 episodes
Chapters: 1. "The Crescent Scar", 2. "The Grip of Hate", 3. "Adrift", 4. "The Secret of the Tomb", 5. "The Fire God", 6. "Treachery", 7. "One Minute to Live", 8. "Hidden Hands", 9. "The Black Masks", 10. "The Rescue", 11. "The Line of Death", 12. "The Rain of Fire", 13. "The Underground House", 14. "The Masked Riders", 15. "The House of Trickery", 16. "The Forced Marriage", 17. "The Deadly Torpedo", & 18. "The Fight in Mid-Air".
　　Director: Harry Harvey & Francis Ford
Ben Wilson (Miles Gaston, Jr.), Neva Gerber (Betty Lee), Nigel de Brulier (James Lee), Kingsley Benedict (Jack Fay), Duke Worne (Harry Russell), Elsie Van Name (Betty's aunt).

MYSTIC, THE (1925)
　　Director: Tod Browning
Aileen Pringle (Zara), David Torrence (James Bradshaw), Mitchell Lewis (Zazarack), Dewitt Jennings (Police Inspector), Conway Tearle (Michael Nash), Robert Ober (Anton), Gladys Hulette (Doris Merrick), Stanton Heck (Carlo).

MYSTIC HOUR, THE (1934)
　　Director: Melville DeLay
Montague Love (Captain James), Lucille Powers (Mary Marshall), Charles Middleton (Roger Thurston), Edith Thornton (Myra Marshall), Eddie Phillips (Bradley Thurston), Charles Hutchison (Robert Randall), James Aubrey (Blinkey).

MYSTIC MIRROR, THE (1928-Ger.)
Director: Karl Hoffmann &
Prof. Teschner
Fritz Rasp, Rina de Ligoure, Albach
Retty, Felicitas Malten.

MYSTIQUE (1981)
Director: Bobby Roth
Yvette Mimieux (Bianca Ray), Chris-
topher Allport (Jack Nilsson), Cindy
Pickett (Lyn Nilsson), John Considine
(Jordon Carelli), Scott Marlowe (Ted
Bartel), Walter Olkewitz (Buddy
Gordon), Carmen Argenziano (Tony
Annese), Mary McCusker (Jane
Annese), Hugh Gillin (Ben Davis),
Fran Ryan (Marie Davis), Leo Rossi
(Chris Morris), Hanna Hertelendy
(Sylvia Arnold), Danny Dayton (David
Arnold), Denny Miller (Uwe), Wally
Taylor (Charlie Carter), Francis
Grey (Bernice Carter), Tony Plana
(Reza Haddad), Susan Lynch (Clare
Bartel), Micol Mercurio (Mrs. Gordon),
Peggy Kaye (Mrs. Morris), Barbara
Thorpe (Mrs. Haddad).

MY WIFE IS A PANTHER (1961-Fr.)
(A.K.A. "Ma Femme Est une Pan-
there")
Director: Raymond Bailly
Jean Richard, Jean Poiret, Serault,
Silvana Blasi, Jean Max, Marcel
Lupovici.

NABONGA (1943) (A.K.A. "The Jungle
Woman", "Gorilla")
Director: Samuel Newfield
Buster Crabbe (Ray Gorman), Barton
MacLane (Carl Hurst), Fifi D'Orsay
(Marle), Herbert Rawlinson (Stock-k
well), Julie London (Doreen Stockwell),
Jackie Newfield (Doreen as a child),
Prince Modupe (Tobo), Bryant Wash-
burn (hunter).

NAIDRA, THE DREAM WOMAN (1914)
Director: George Kleine
Mignon Anderson (Naidra), Riley Cham-
berlain (the scientist), Carey L.
Hastings (father), Morris Foster (the
organist).

NAKED APE, THE (1973)
Director: Zev Bufman
Johnny Crawford (Lee), Victoria
Principal (Cathy), Dennis Olivieri
(Arnie), Diana Darrin, Robert Ito,
John Hellerman, Marvin Miller, Nor-
man Grabowski, Brett Parker, Helen
Horowitz.

NAKED EVIL (1966) (A.K.A. "Exorcism

at Midnight")
Director: Stanley Goulder
Anthony Ainley (Dick Alderson),
Basil Dignam (Benson), Suzanne
Neve (Janet), Richard Coleman
(Hollis), Ronald Bridges (Wilkins),
Pearl Prescod (landlady), George
A. Saunders (Danny), Carmen
Munroe (Beverly), Dan Jackson
(Lloyd), Brylo Ford (Amazon), Olaf
Pooley, Laurence Tierney, Bob
Allen, Nuba Stuart, Catharine
Erhardt, Oscar James, Addison
Greene, Brad Johnson.

NAKED EXORCISM (1975-Ital.) (A. K. A.
"Un Urlo Dalle Tenebre", "L'Es-
corcista No. 2")
Director: Angelo Pannaccio
Richard Conte, Francoise Prevost,
Jean-Claude Verne, Mimma
Monticelli.

NAKED JUNGLE, THE (1953)
Director: Byron Haskin
Charlton Heston (Christopher
Leiningen), Eleanor Parker (Joanna
Leiningen), William Conrad (the
Commissioner), John Dierkes
(Gruber), Abraham Sofaer (Incacha),
Douglas V. Fowley (Medicine Man),
Romo Vincent (boat captain),
Norma Calderon (Zala), Leonard
Strong (Kutina), John Mansfield
(Foreman), Rodd Redwing, Bernie
Gozier, Pilar Del Rey, Jerry
Groves, Carlos Rivero, Ronald
Alan Numekena, John Reitzen,
John E. Wood, Leon Lontoc.

NAKED WITCH, THE (1961) (A. K. A.
"The Naked Temptress")
Director: Andy Milligan
Beth Porter, Robert Burgos, Lee
Forbes.

NAME FOR EVIL, A (1970)
Director: Bernard Girard
Robert Culp, Samantha Eggar, Sheila
Sullivan, Mike Lane, Reed Sherman,
Clarence Miller, Sue Hathaway.

NAME OF THE GAME IS KILL, THE
(1968) (A. K. A. "The Female
Trap")
Director: Gunnar Hellstrom
Jack Lord (Symcha Lipa), Susan
Strasberg (Mickey Terry), Collin
Wilcox (Diz Tery), Tisha Sterling
(Nan Terry), T. C. Jones (Mr. Terry/
Mrs. Terry), Mort Mills (Sheriff
Fred Kendall), Marc Desmond
(Doctor).

NANNY, THE (1965)
    Director: Seth Holt
Bette Davis (Nanny), Pamela Franklin
(Bobby), Wendy Craig (Virgie), Jill
Bennett (Pen), William Dix (Joey),
Alfred Burke (Dr. Wills), Maurice
Denham (Dr. Beamaster), Jack
Watling (Dr. Medman), James Villiers
(Bill), Harold Lang.

NAN OF THE NORTH (1921) - serial
    in 15 episodes
Chapters: 1. "The Missile from Mars",
2. "Fountain of Fury", 3. "The Brink
of Despair", 4. "In Cruel Clutches",
5. "On Terror's Trail", 6. "The Cards
of Chance", 7. "Into the Depths", 8.
"Burning Sands", 9. "The Power of
Titano", 10. "A Bolt from the Sky", 11.
"The Ride for a Life", 12. "Adrift",
13. "Facing Death at Sea", 14. "The Volcano", & 15. "Consequences".
    Director: Duke Worne
Ann Little (Nan), Leonard Clapham
(Sgt. Colby), Joseph W. Girard (gang
leader), Edith Stoyart (gang leader's
mistress), J. Morris Foster (henchman), Hal Wilson (mounted policeman),
Howard Crampton (store owner).

NASTY RABBIT, THE (1964) (A. K. A.
    "Spies-a-Go-Go")
    Director: James Landis
Mischa Tery (Mischa Lowzoff), Arch
Hall, Jr. (Britt Hunter), Melissa Mor-
gan (Cecilia), William Matters (Malcolm
McKinley/Marshall Malouf), Little Jack
Little (Maxwell Stoppic), Ray Vegas
(Gonzales), John Akana (Col. Kobayaski),
Harold Brizzy (Heinrich Krueger),
Sharon Ryker (Jackie), Hal Bokar (Ga-
vin), George Morgan (Hubert Jackson),
Leslie Kovacs (the Idiot).

NAVY VS. THE NIGHT MONSTERS,
    THE (1966) (A. K. A. "Monsters of
    the Night")
    Director: Michael Hoey
Anthony Eisley (Lt. Charles Brown),
Mamie Van Doren (Lt. Nora Hall),
Billy Gray (Fred Twining), Bobby Van
(Ensign Rutherford Chandler), Walter
Sande (Dr. Arthur Beecham), Pamela
Mason, Philip Terry, Edward Faulkner,
Russell Bender.

NEANDERTHAL MAN, THE (1952)
    Director: E. A. Dupont
Robert Shayne (Dr. Cliff Groves),
Richard Crane (Dr. Ross Harkness),
Doris Merrick (Ruth Marshall), Joyce
Terry (Jan), Robert Long (Jim) Dick
Rich (Sheriff Andrews), Jean Quinn

(Celia), Robert Easton, Beverly
Garland.

NECROMANCY (1971) (A. K. A. "The
    Toy Factory")
    Director: Bert I. Gordon
Orson Welles (Mr. Cato), Pamela
Franklin (Lori Brandon), Michael
Ontkean (Frank Brandon), Lee Pur-
cell (Priscilla), Harvey Jason
(Jay), Sue Bernard (Nancy), Lisa
James (Georgette), Terry Quinn
(Cato's son).

NECROPOLIS (1970-Ital.)
    Director: Franco Brocani
Tina Aumant, Viva Audre, Pierre
Clementi, B. Corazzari, Paul
Jabara.

NEITHER THE SEA NOR THE SAND
    (1972)
    Director: Fred Burnley
Susan Hampshire (Anna Robinson),
Frank Finlay (George Dabernon),
Michael Petrovich (Hugh Dabernon),
Jack Lambert (Dr. Irving), Michael
Craze (Collie), David Garth (Mr.
MacKay), Anthony Booth (Delamare),
Betty Duncan (Mrs. MacKay).

NEPTUNE FACTOR, THE (1973)
    (A. K. A. "The Neptune Disaster")
    Director: Daniel Petrie
Ben Gazzara (Cmdr. Blake), Yvette
Mimieux (Leah Jansen), Walter
Pidgeon (Dr. Andrews), Ernest
Borgnine (Mack MacKay), Donnelly
Rhodes (Bob), Chris Wiggins (Captain),
Ed McGibbon (Norton), David Yor-
ston (Stephens), J. Reynolds (Hal),
Stuart Gillard (Bradley), Kenneth
Pogue (Thomas), Dan MacDonald
(Hobbs), Mark Walker (Mounton),
Frank Perry (Sub Captain), Leslie
Carlson (Briggs), Joan Gregson
(Dobson), Kay Fujiwara (Anita),
Dave Mann (Hawkes), David Renton
(Warrant Officer), Richard Whelan
(Radio Officer).

NEPTUNE'S DAUGHTER (1914)
    Director: Herbert Brenon
Annette Kellermann, Leah Baird,
Katherine Lee, William E. Shay, Wil-
liam Welsh, Herbert Brenon.

NESTING, THE (1981) (A. K. A.
    "Phobia")
    Director: Armand Weston
Robin Groves (Lauren Cochran),
Christopher Loomis (Mark Felton),
John Carradine (Col. LeBrun), Gloria

Grahame (Florinda Costello), John David Lally (Daniel Griffith), Bill Rowley (Frank Beasley), Patrick Farelley (Dr. Webb), David Tabor (Abner Welles), Bobo Lewis (Catherine Beasley), June Berry (Saphire), Cecile Lieman (Helga), Ann Varley (Gwen), Ron Levine (Leland LeBrun), Bruce Kronenberg (Young Abner), Jim Nixon (Young Frank), James Saxon (Earl), Cliff Cudney (Sheriff), Jeffrey McLaughlin (Butler), Lee Steele (doctor), James Hayden, Jerry Hewitt (GIs).

NEST OF SPIES (1967-Span. /Ital.)
(A. K. A. "Nido de Espias")
    Director: Gianfranco Baldanello/
    Frank G. Carroll
Gordon Scott, Alberto Dalbes, Delfy Maurenn, Ted Carter, Man Dean, Silvia Solar.

NETWORK (1976)
    Director: Sidney Lumet
William Holden (Max Schumacher), Peter Finch (Howard Beale), Faye Dunaway (Diana Christiansen), Robert Duvall (Frank Hackett), Ned Beatty (Arthur Jensen), Beatrice Straight (Mrs. Schumacher), Wesley Addy (Nelson Chaney), Arthur Burghardt (Great Ahmed Kahn), Kathy Cronkite (Mary Ann Gifford), John Carpenter (George Bosch), Bill Burrows (TV Director), Jordan Charney (Harry Hunter), Ed Crowley (Joe Donnelly), Conchata Ferrell (Barbara Schlesinger), Darryl Hickman (Bill Herron), Ken Kercheval (Merill Grant), Gene Gross (Milton K. Steinman), Jerome Dempsey (Walter C. Amundsen), Stanley Grover (Jack Snowedn), Cindy Grover (Caroline Schumacher), Mitchell Jason (Arthur Zangwill), Paul Jenkins (TV stage manager), Kenneth Kimmins (associate producer), Zane Lasky (audio man), Michael Lipton (Tommy Pellegrino), Roy Poole (Sam Haywood), Lane Smith (Robert McDonough), Bernard Pollack (Lou), Carolyn Krigbaum (Max's secretary), Lynn Klugman (TV production assistant), Russ Petranto (TV associate director), Pirie MacDonald (Herb Thackeray), Theodore Sorel (Giannini), Cameron Thomas (TV technical director), Sasha von Scherler (Helen Miggs), Fred Stuthman (Mosaic Figure), Lydia Wilson (Hunter's secretary), William Prince (Edward G. Ruddy), Marlene Warfield (Laureen Hobbs), Lee Richardson (Narrator).

NEUTRON AGAINST THE DEATH ROBOTS (1961-Mex.) (A. K. A. "Los Automatas de la Muerte", "The Robots of Death")
    Director: Federico Curiel
Wolf Ruvinskis (Neutorn), Rosita Arenas, Armando Silvestre, Claudio Brook, Julio Aleman, Beto El Boticario.

NEUTRON AND THE BLACK MASK (Mex. -1961) (A. K. A. "Neutron, el Enmascardo Negro")
    Director: Federico Curiel
Wolf Ruvinskis (Neutron), Rosita Arenas, Julio Aleman, Claudio Brook Armando Silvestre, Beto El Boticario.

NEUTRON BATTLES THE KARATE ASSASSINS (1962-Mex.)
    Director:
Wolf Ruvinskis (Neutron).

NEUTRON TRAPS THE INVISIBLE KILLER (1964-Mex.)
    Director:
Wolf Ruvinskis (Neutron).

NEUTRON VS. THE MANIAC (1961-Mex.) (A. K. A. "Neutron and the Cosmic Bomb")
    Director:
Wolf Ruvinski (Neutron).

NEUTRON VS. THE AMAZING DR. CARONTE (1963-Mex.) (A. K. A. "Neutron contra el Doctor Caronte")
    Director: Federico Curiel
Wolf Ruvinskis (Neutoro), Julio Aleman, Rosita Arensa, Armando Silvestre, Beto El Boticario.

NEW ADVENTURES OF TARZAN, THE (1935) (A. K. A. "Tarzan and the Green Goddess") - serial in 12 episodes
Chapters: 1. "The New Adventures of Tarzan", 2. "Crossed Trails", 3. "The Devil's Noose", 4. "River Perils", 5. "Unseen Hands", 6. "Fatal Fangs", 7. "Flaming Waters", 8. "Angry Gods", 9. "Doom's Brink", 10. "Secret Signals", 11. "Death's Fireworks" & 12. "Operator 17".
    Director: Edward Kull & W. F.
    McGaugh
Herman Brix/Bruce Bennett (Tarzan), Ula Holt (Ula Vale), Frank Baker (Maj. Martling), Dale Walsh (Alice Martling), Harry Ernest (Gordon Hamilton), Don Castello (Raglans), Lewis Sergent (George), Earl Dwire (renegade), Mrs. Gentry (Queen Maya), Merrill McCormick (Bouchart).

NEW EXPLOITS OF ELAINE, THE
(1915) - serial in 10 episodes
Chapters: 1. "The Serpent Sign", 2.
"The Cryptic Ring", 3. "The Watching
Eye", 4. "The Vengeance of Wu Fang",
5. "The Saving Circles", 6. "Spontan-
eous Combustion", 7. "The Ear in the
Wall", 8. "The Opium Smugglers",
9. "The Tell-Tale Heart", & 10.
"Shadows of War".
    Director: George B. Seitz
Pearl White (Elaine Dodge), Creighton
Hale (Jameson), Arnold Daly (Craig
Kennedy), Edwin Arden (Wu Fang),
M.W. Rale (Wong Long Sin).

NEW HOUSE ON THE LEFT (1978)
    Director: Evans Isle
Day Beal, Patty Edwards, Delbert
Moss, Norma Knight, Richard Davis.

NEW INVISIBLE MAN, THE (1957-
    Mex.) (A.K.A. "El Hombre Que
    Logro Ser Invisible", "Invisible Man
    in Mexico")
    Director: Alfredo Crevena
Arturo de Cordova, Ana Luisa Peluffo,
Augusto Benedico, Raul Meraz.

NEW, ORIGINAL WONDER WOMAN,
    THE (TVM-1975) - 11-7-75
    Director: Leonard Horn
Lynda Carter (Diana Prince/Wonder
Woman), Lyle Waggoner (Steve Trevor),
Cloris Leachman (Queen Mother), Red
Buttons (Ashley Norman), Stella Stevens
(Marcia), Kenneth Mars (Col. von
Blasko), Eric Breaden (Drangel), John
Randolph (Blankenship), Henry Gibson
(Nikolas), Fannie Flagg (the Doctor),
Severn Darden (Bad Guy), Ian Wolfe,
Fritzi Burr, Helen Verbit, Tom Rosqui.

NEW YEAR'S EVIL (1980)
    Director: Emmett Alston
Roz Kelly (Diane Sullivan), Kip Niven
(Ricard Sullivan), Louisa Moritz (Sally),
Chris Wallace (Lt. Clayton), Jed Mills
(Ernie), Grant Cramer (Derek Sullivan),
Taafe O'Connell (Jane), Jon Greene
(Sgt. Greene), Anita Crane (Lisa),
Alicia Dhanifu (Yvonne), John London
(floor manager), Barry Gibberman (hotel
guest), Teri Copley (teenage girl),
Jennie Anderson (Nurse Robbie), Wendy-
Sue Rosloff (make-up girl), John Alder-
man (Dr. Reed), Jerry Chambers (Clerk),
Mike Mihalich (policeman at hotel),
Jerry Zanitsch, Mark L. Rosen (drunks),
Bob Jarvis, Richard E. Kald (policeman),
Linda Terito (stunt woman), Mark de
Frani (teenage boy), Richard Brown
(Swamper), Lyle (space boy), Julie Kaye

Towery (space girl), Tim Cutt (ambulance attendant), Don Grenough
(punker), Ryan Collier, Mark Korn-
gute (bar hustlers), Celena Allen,
Edward Jackson, Bill Blair, Clarisse Kotkin, Roxanne Orbis, Michelle
Waxman, Ricky Israel, Cynthia
Macarthur, Justin Robin (punkers
in car), Randy Gould, Karen Mills,
Jodie Mann, Adrienne Upton (phone
girls), Doug Le Mille, Lyle Pearcy,
Jim Amormino, Larry Lindsey
(Clayton's men).

NEXT! (1971-Ital./Span.) (A.K.A.
    "Lo Strano Vizio Della Signora
    Wardh", "The Strange Weakness
    of Mrs. Wardh", "The Next Vic-
    tim!")
    Director: Luciano Martino
Alberto De Mendoze (Neil Ward),
Edwige Fenech (Julie Ward), Ivan
Rassimov (Jean), George Hilton
(George), Cristina Airoldi (Carol).

NEXT ONE, THE (1982)
    Director: Nico Mastorakis
Keir Dullea (Glenn), Adrienne Bar-
beau (Andrea Johnson), Jeremy
Licht (Tim Johnson), Peter Hobbs
(Dr. Barnaby Caldwell).

NEXT VOICE YOU HEAR, THE (1950)
    Director: William Wellman
James Whitomre (Joe Smith), Nancy
Davis (Mrs. Joe Smith), Gary Gray
(Johnny Smith), Jeff Corey (Freddie),
Lillian Bronson (Aunt Ethel), Art
Smith (Mr. Brannan), Tom D'Andrea
(Hap Magee).

NICK CARTER AND THE RED CLUB
    (1965-Fr.) (A.K.A. "Nick
    Carter et le Trefle Rouge")
    Director: Jean-Paul Savignac
Eddie Constantine (Nick Carter),
Nicole Courcel (Dora), Jeanne
Valerie (Cleo), Jo Dassin (Jolas),
Jacques Harden (Captain), Jean
Ozenne (Proffessor), Roger Rudel,
Michael Ruhl, Marcel Pagliero,
Pierre Rousseau, Santesso Felio,
Graziella Galvani, Gordon Felio.

NIGHT COMES TO SOON (1947)
    (A.K.A. "The Ghost of Rashmon
    Hall")
    Director: Denis Kavanagh
Valentine Dyall (Doctor), Anthony
Baird, Anne Howard, Alec Faversham,
Beatrice Marsen, David Keir, Howard
Douglas, Arthur Brander.

NIGHTCOMERS, THE (1972)
Director: Michael Winner
Marlon Brando (Peter Quint), Stephanie
Beacham (Miss Jessel), Thora Hird
(Mrs. Grose), Verna Harvey (Flora),
Christopher Ellis (Miles), Anna Palk
(new governess).

NIGHT CREATURE (1979) (A. K. A.
"Out of the Darkness", "Fear")
Director: Lee Madden
Donald Pleasence (Axel MacGregor),
Nancy Kwan (Leslie), Ross Hagen,
Jennifer Rhodes, Lesly Fine.

NIGHT CREATURES (1962) (A. K. A.
"Captain Clegg")
Director: Peter Graham Scott
Peter Cushing (Dr. Blyss/Capt.
Nathaniel Clegg), Michael Ripper
(Jeremiah Mipps), Patrick Allen
(Capt. Collier), Yvonne Romaine
(Imogene), Oliver Reed (Harry Crab-
tree), Martin Benson (Rash), Derek
Francis (Squire), Peter Halliday
(Jack Pott), Milton Reid (the Mulatto),
Sydney Bromley (Tom Ketch), David
Lodge (Bosun), Terry Scully (Dick
Tate), Gordon Rollings (Qurzel),
Daphne Anderson (Mrs. Rash), Rupert
Osborne (Gerry), Jack MacGowran
(frightened man), Bob Head (Peg-leg),
Colin Douglas (pirate bosun).

NIGHT CRIES (TVM-1978) - 1-29-78
Director: Richard Lang
Susan St. James (Jeannie Haskins),
Michael Parks (Mitch Haskins),
William Conrad (Dr. Whelan), Jamie
Smith Jackson (Peggy Barton), Cath-
leen Nesbitt (Mrs. Delesande), Do-
lores Dorn (Nurse Green), Ellen
Geer (Mrs. Whitney), Saundra Sharp
(Bea Pryor), Diana Douglas (Mrs.
Thueson), Britt Leach (Dr. Medlow),
Lee Kessler (Cynthia), Carl Byrd,
Jennifer Penny, James Keane.

NIGHT DIGGER, THE (1971) (A. K. A.
"The Road Builder")
Director: Alastair Reid
Patricia Neal (Maura), Pamela Brown
(Mrs. Prince), Nicholas Clay (Billy),
Jean Anderson (Mrs. McMurtrey),
Yootha Joyce (Mrs. Polafox), Graham
Crowden (Mr. Bolton), Peter Sallis
(Rev. Polafox), Brigit Forsyth (Dis-
trict Nurse), Diana Patrick (Mary
Wingate), Sebastian Breaks (Dr. Ro-
binson), Bruce Myles (bank clerk),
Jenny McCracken (farmwife).

NIGHT EVELYN CAME OUT OF THE

GRAVE, THE (1971-Ital.) (A. K. A.
"La Notte che Evelyn Usca'Della
Tomba")
Director: Emilio Miraglia
Anthony Steffen/Antonio De Teffe
(Lord Alan Cunningham), Marina
Malfatti (Gladys), Erika Blanc
(Susan), Rod Murdock (George),
Giacomo Rossi-Stuart, Umberto
Raho, Joan C. Davis, Roberto
Maldera.

NIGHT GALLERY (TVM-1969) -
11-8-69
Director: Boris Sagal,
Steven Spielberg & Barry
Shear
Joan Crawford (Miss Claudia Menlo),
Roddy McDowall (Jeremy), George
Macready (Hendricks), Richard
Kiley (Joseph Strobe), Sam Jaffe
(Bleum), Barry Sullivan (Dr. Hea-
therton), Ossie Davis (Osmond
Portifoy), Barry Atwater (Carson),
Tom Bosley (Sydney Resnick),
Norma Crane (Gretchen), Byron
Morrow (Packer), Tom Basham
(Gibbons), Garry Goodrow (Louis),
George Murdock (1st agent), Richard
Hale (doctor), Shannon Farnon (1st
nurse).

NIGHT GAMES (1970)
Director: Roger Vadim
Cindy Pickett (Valerie), Joanna
Cassidy (Julie), Barry Primus
(Jason), Paul Jenkins (Sion), Gene
Davis (Timothy), Clem Parsons
(Jun), Juliet Fabriga (Alicia),
Carla Reynolds (Valerie at age 13),
Pamela Mellish (Sandra), Rene
Knecht (Blake), Walter Fagerstrom
(rapist), Clarke Reynolds (Medavoy),
Hermin Aslanian (jewelry shop
salesgirl), Mario Munder (dress
shop salesman), Bob Mallett,
George Weber (policemen).

NIGHT GOD SCREAMED, THE (1975)
(A. K. A. "Scream")
Director: Lee Madden
Jeanne Crain, Alex Nicol, Daniel
Spelling, Michael Sugich, Dawn
Cleary, Barbara Hancock, Gary
Morgan.

NIGHT HAIR CHILD (1971) (A. K. A.
"Child of the Night")
Director: James Kelly
Mark Lester, Britt Ekland, Lilli
Palmer, Hardy Kruger, Harry An-
drews, Collette Jack, Conchita
Montez.

NIGHT HAS A THOUSAND EYES, THE
(1948)
Director: John Farrow
Edward G. Robinson (John Triton),
Gail Russell (Jean Courtland), John
Lund (Elliott Carson), Virginia Bruce
(Jenny), William Demarest (Lt.
Shawn), Richard Webb (Peter Vinson), Onslow
Stevens (Dr. Walters), Jerome Cowen
(Whitney Courtland), Luis Van Rooten
(Mr. Myers), Roman Bohnen (Special
Prosecutor), John Alexander (Mr.
Gilman), Henry Guttman (Butler).

NIGHT IN PARADISE, A (1946)
Director: Arthur Lubin
Merle Oberon (Delaria), Turhan Bey
(Jason), Gale Sondergaard (Attossa),
Thomas Gomez (King Croesus), John
Litel (Archon), Douglas Dumbrille,
Moroni Olsen (High Priests), Jane
Adams (Lotus), Paul Cavanagh (Cleo-
menes), Pedro De Cordoba (Magus),
Harry Cording (Captain), Colin Camp-
bell (Goatman), Ray Collins (Leonides),
Ernest Truex, Marvin Miller, Jerome
Cowan (Scribes), Wee Willie Davis
(Salabaar), George Dolenz (Frigid
Ambassador), Richard Bailey (Lieu-
tenant), Dick Alexander (Temple
Guard), Hans Herbert (priest), Rose-
anne Murray (Marigold), Francis
McDonald (High Priest), Jean Trent
(Iris), James Hutton (Delarai messenger),
Duan Kennedy, Julie London, Ruth
Valmy, Kathleen O'Malley, Barbara
Bates, Karen X. Gaylord, Karen
Randle, Audrey Young, Kerry Vaughn
(Palace Maidens), Eula Morgan,
Myrtle Ferguson, Art Miles, Frank
Hagney (villagers), Julie Lynne (song
specialty), John Merton (sailor),
Harlan Miller (slave), Don Stowell
(sentinel), Ann Everett, June Frazer,
Marguerite Campbell (flowery girls),
Nikki Kerkes, Mercedes Mockaitis
(water girls), Denny Burke (contor-
tionist), Neal Young (Nobleman), Joe
Bernard (old man), John Berkes,
Pietro Sosso, Al Ferguson (beggars),
Earle Oxman (temple guard), Jack
Overman (man), Kit Guard (man in
crowd), Rex Evans (chef), Wade
Crosby (rough man), Clyde Flynn,
Juan Estrada, Charles Bates, Joel
Goodkind, Jimmy Fresco, Robert
Espinosa, Louis Montoya, Mickey
Fresco (boys).

NIGHT KEY, THE (1937)
Director: Lloyd Corrigan
Boris Karloff (Dave Mallory), Jean
Rogers (Joan Mallory), Warren Hull

(Travers), Hobart Cavanaugh
(Petty Louis), Samuel S. Hinds
(Ranger), Alan Baxter (the Kid),
Ward Bond (Finger Man), Edwin
Maxwell (Druger), David Oliver
(Mike), George Cleveland, Frank
Reicher, Frank Hagney, Ethan
Laidlaw.

NIGHT LIFE OF THE GODS (1935)
Director: Lowell Sherman
Alan Mowbray (Hunter Hawky),
Florine McKinney (Meg), Peggy
Shannon (Daphne Lambert), Richard
Carle (Grandpa Lambert), Wesley
Barry (Alfred Lambert, Jr.),
Gilbert Emery (Betts), Douglas
Fowley (Cyril Sparks), William
'Stage' Boyd (Mulligan), Henry
Armetta (Roigi), Robert Warwick
(Neptune), Irene Ware (Diana), Ann
Doran (girl), Theresa Maxwell
Conover (Alice Lambert), Arlene
Carroll (Stella), Phillips Smalley
(Alfred Lambert), Paul Kaye
(Meray), Ferdinand Gottschalk
(Old Man Turner), Geneva Mitchell
(Hebe), Pat De Cicco (Perseus),
Marda Deering (Venus), Raymond
Benard (Apollo), George Hassell
(Bacchus).

NIGHTMARE (1956)
Director: Maxwell Shane
Edward G. Robinson, Kevin Mc-
Carthy, Virginia Christine, Rhys
Williams, Barry Atwater, Gage
Clarke, Connie Russell, Marian
Carr, Billy May.

NIGHTMARE (1963)
Director: Freddie Francis
David Knight (Henry Baxter),
Moria Redmond (Grace), Brenda
Bruce (Mary), Jennie Linden (Janet),
George A. Cooper (John), John
Welsh (Doctor), Irene Richmond
(Mrs. Gibbs), Hedger Wallace
(Sir Dudley), Timothy Bateson
(Barman), Clytie Jessop (woman
in white), Julie Samuel (maid), Isla
Cameron (mother), Frank Forsyth
(waiter), Elizabeth Dear (Janet as
a child).

NIGHTMARE (1981)
Director: Ramono Scavolini
Baird Stafford (George Tatum),
Sharon Mith (Susan Temper), C.J.
Cooke (C. J. Temper), Mik Cribben
(Bob Rosen), Kathleen Ferguson
(Barbara), Danny Ronan (Kathy),
John L. Watkins (man with cigar).

NIGHTMARE ALLEY (1947)
Director: Edmund Goulding
Tyrone Power (Stan Carlisle), Joan
Blondell (Zena), Coleen Gray (Molly),
Helen Walker (Lilith), Taylor Holmes
(Grindle), Mike Mazurki (Bruno),
Ian Keith (Pete), Julia Dean (Mrs.
Peabody), James Flavin (Hoatley),
Roy Roberts (McGraw), James Burke
(Town Marshal), Gene Roth, Henry
Hall.

NIGHTMARE CASTLE (1965-Ital.)
(A. K. A. "Amanti D'Oltretomba",
"Lovers from Beyond the Tomb",
"The Faceless Monster")
Director: Alan Grunewald/
Mario Caiano
Barbara Steele (Muriel Arrowsmith/
Jenny), Paul Miller (Dr. Stephen Ar-
rowsmith), Rik Battaglia (David),
Helga Line (Solange), Lawrence
Clift (Dr. Derek Joyce), John Mc-
Doulgas (Jonathan).

NIGHTMARE IN BLOOD (1978)
Director: John Stanley
Kerwin Mathews (Prince), Dan Caldwell
(Seabrook), Barrie Youngfellow
(Cindy), John J. Cochran (Scotty),
Ray K. Gorman (B. B.), Hy Pyke
(Harris), Drew Eshelman (Arlington),
Irving Isreal (Ben-Halik), Morgan
Upton (George), Justin Bishop (Un-
worth), Charles Murphy (Flannery),
Mike Hitchcock (Driscoll), Stan Rit-
chie Marsdon, Yvonne Young (Barbara),
Erika Stanley (girl).

NIGHTMARE IN WAX (1969) (A. K. A.
"Crimes in the Wax Museum")
Director: Bud Townsend
Scott Brady (Haskell), Cameron
Mitchell (Vincent), Anne Helm (Marie),
Berry Kroeger (Max Black), Victoria
Carrol (Teresa), James Forrest
(Arthur Herman), Philip Baird (Tony),
Hollis Morrison (Nick), Johnny Cardos
(assistant detective).

NIGHT MONSTER (1942) (A. K. A.
"House of Mystery")
Director: Ford Beebe
Bela Lugosi (Rolf), Irene Hervey
(Dr. Lynne Harper). Lionel Atwill
(Dr. King), Ralph Morgan (Kurg Ing-
ston), Nils Asther (Agor Singh), Don
Porter (Dick Baldwin), Leif Erickson
(Laurie, the chauffeur), Fay Helm
(Margaret Ingston), Doris Lloyd
(Miss Judd), Frank Reicher (Dr. Tim-
mons), Robert E. Homans Cap Beggs),
Cyril Delevanti (Torque), Janet Shaw

(Millie Carson), Eddy Waller (Jebb
Harmon), Francis Pierlot (Dr.
Phipps), Elyse Knox.

NIGHT MUST FALL (1937)
Director: Richard Thorpe
Robert Montgomery (Danny),
Rosalind Russell (Olivia), Dame
May Whitty (Mrs. Branson), Alan
Marshall (Justin), Kathleen
Harrison (Mrs. Terrence), Eily
Maylon (nurse), Merle Tottenham
(Dora), Matthew Boulton (Belsize),
Winifred Harris (Mrs. Laurie),
E. E. Clive (guide), Beryl Mercer
(saleslady).

NIGHT MUST FALL (1964)
Director: Karol Reisz
Albert Finney (Danny), Susan
Hampshire (Olivia), Mona Wash-
bourne (Mrs. Bramson), Shelia
Hancock (Dora), Joe Gladwin
(Dodge), John Gill (Foster),
Michael Medwin (Derek), Martin
Wyldeck (Insp. Willet).

NIGHT MY NUMBER CAME UP,
THE (1955)
Director: Leslie Norman
Michael Redgrave (Air Marshall
Hardie), Sheila Sim (Mary Camp-
bell), Alexander Knox (Owen Robert-
son), Denholm Elliott (Flight Lt.
McKenzie), Michael Hordern
(Lindsay), Ursula Jeans (Mrs.
Robertson), Nigel Stock (the pilot),
Geoffrey Tyrrell (Bennett's secre-
tary), George Rose (Bennett),
Ralph Truman (Wainwright), Alfie
Bass, Bill Kerr (soldiers), Victor
Maddern (engineer), David Orr
(co-pilot), David Yates (navigator),
Richard Davies (wireless operator),
Charles Perry (Kent), Doreen Aris
(Miss Robertson), Hugh Moxey
(Wing Commander).

NIGHT OF BLOODY HORROR (1969)
Director: Joy N. Houck, Jr.
Gerald McRaney (Welsey Stuart),
Gaye Yellen (Angelle Miliot), Herb
Nelson (Dr. Bennett Moss),
Evelyn Hendricks (Agatha Stuart),
Lisa Dameron (Susan Collins),
Charlotte Shite (Kay Jensen), Bert
Roberts (Mark Lewis), Nicholous
Krieger (Lt. James Cole), Michael
Anthony (Mario Spenelli), Gordon
Ogden (Tucker Fredricks).

NIGHT OF DARK SHADOWS (1971)
Director: Dan Curtis

David Selby (Quentin/Charles Collins),
Kate Jackson (Tracy Collins), Lara
Parker (Anfelique), Grayson Hall
(Carlotta Drake), John Karlen (Alex
Jenkins), Thayer David (Rev. Strack),
Nancy Barrett (Claire Jenkins), James
Storm (Gerard Styles), Monica Rich
(Sarah Castle), Diana Millay (Laura
Collins), Christopher Pennock (Gabriel
Collins), Clarisse Blackburn (Mrs.
Castle).

NIGHT OF HORROR, A (1916-Ger.)
(A.K.A. "Nacht des Grauens")
    Director: Arthur Robison
Werner Krauss, Emil Jannings, Lupu
Pick.

NIGHT OF TERROR (1933)
    Director: Benjamin Stoloff
Bela Lugosi (Degar), Sally Blane
(Betty Jane Young), George Meeker,
Tully Marshall, Edwin Maxwell,
Bryant Washburn, Wallace Ford
Dave O'Brien, Gertrude Michael.

NIGHT OF THE BLOOD BEAST (1958)
    Director: Bernard Kowalski
Michael Emmet (Maj. John Corcoran),
Angela Greene (Dr. Julie Benson),
Ed Nelson (Dave Randall), John Baer
(Steve Dunlap), Tyler McVey (Dr.
Alex Wyman), Georgianna Carter (Donna
Bixby, Ross Sturlin (the Monster).

NIGHT OF THE BLOOD MONSTER
(1970-Span./Ger./Ital.) (A.K.A.
"El Proceso de las Brujas", "The
Trial of the Witches", "The Bloody
Judge", "The Witch-Killer of Black-
moor", "Der Hexentoter von Black-
moor", "Il Trono di Fucco", "The
Throne of Fire")
    Director: Jesus Franco
Christopher Lee (Judge Jeffreys),
Leo Genn, Maia Schell, Maria Rohm,
Hans Hass, Margaret Lee, Jose Maria,
Prada.

NIGHT OF THE BLOODY APES (1968-
Mex) (A.K.A. "Horror y Sexo")
    Director: Rene Cardona
Armando Silvestre, Norma Lazar,
Gina Moret, Joe Elias, Carl Lopez,
August Martin, Noelia Noel, Gerard
Zepeda.

NIGHT OF THE COBRA WOMAN
(1972-Phil./U.S.) (A.K.A. "Mo-
vini's Venom")
    Director: Andrew Meyer
Joy Bang (Joanna), Marlene Clark
(Lena), Vic Diaz (Lope), Slash Marks

(Sgt. Merkle), Roger Garrett
(Duff).

NIGHT OF THE DAMNED (1971-
Ital.) (A.K.A. "La Notte del
Dannati")
    Director: Felippo Maria Ratti/
    Peter Rush
Pierre Brice, Patrizia Viotti,
Mario Carra, Angela De Leo, An-
tonio Pavan, Daniele D'Agostini.

NIGHT OF THE DEMON (1980)
    Director: Jim Wasson
Mike Cutt, Joy Allen, Richard
Fields.

NIGHT OF THE DEVILS, THE (1971-
Ital./Span.) (A.K.A. "La
Notte dei Diavoli")
    Director: Georgio Ferroni
Agostina Belli, Teresa Gimpera,
Gianni Garko, Mark Roberts,
Umberto Raho, Luis Saurez, Bill
Vanders, Cinzia De Carolis.

NIGHT OF THE FOLLOWING DAY,
THE (1968)
    Director: Herbert Cornfield
Richard Burton (Bud), Richard
Boone (Leer), Pamela Franklin
(the Girl), Rita Moreno (Vi), Jess
Hahn (Wally), Hughes Warner (the
father), Jacques Marin (bartender),
Gerard Buhr (gendarme/fisherman).

NIGHT OF THE GHOULS (1959)
    Director: Edward D. Wood, Jr.
Criswell (Himself), Tor Johnson
(Lobo), Maila 'Vampira' Nurmi
(Black Ghost), Keene Duncan (Dr.
Acula), Valda Hansen.

NIGHT OF THE HUNTER (1955)
    Director: Charles Laughton
Robert Mitchum (Harry Powell),
Shelly Winters (Willa Harper),
Lillian Gish (Rachel), Peter Graves
(Ben Haper), James Gleason
(Birdie), Billy Chapin (John),
Don Beddoe (Walt), Evelyn Varden
(Icey), Gloria Castillo (Ruby),
Sally Jane Bruce (Pearl), Mary
Ellen Clemons (Clary), Cheryl
Callaway (Mary).

NIGHT OF THE LEPUS (1972)
    Director: William F. Claxton
Stuart Whitman (Roy Bennett),
Janet Leigh (Gerry Bennett), De-
Forest Kelley (Elgin Clark), Rory
Calhoun (Cole Hillman), Paul Fix
(Sheriff Cody), Melanie Fullerton

(Amanda Bennett), Chris Morrell
(Jackie Hillman), Henry Wills (Frank),
William Elliott (Dr. Leopold), Chuck
Hayward (Jud), Francesca Jarvis
(Mildred), Robert Hardy (Prof. Dirk-
son), I. Stanford Jolley (dispatcher),
Inez Perez (housekeeper), Richard
Jacome (Deputy Jason), G. Leroy
Gaintner (Walker), Robert Gooden
(Leslie), Evans Thornton (Major
White), Walter Kelley (truck driver),
Don Starr (Cutler), Frank Kennedy
(Doctor), Peter O'Crotty (Arlen),
Russell Morrell (Priest), Phillip
Avenetti (Officer Lopez), Donna
Gelgur (wife in car), Stephen deFrance
(husband in car), Sherry Hummer,
Rick Hummer (children in car), Jerry
Dunphy (television newscaster).

NIGHT OF THE LIVING DEAD (1968)
     Director: George Romero
Judith O'Dea (Barbara), Russell
Streiner (Johnny), Karl Hardman
(Harry), Duane Jones (Ben), Keith
Wayne (Tom), Judith Ridley (Judy),
Kyra Schon (Karen), Marilyn Eastman
(Helen).

NIGHT OF THE SEAGULLS (1975-
     Span.) (A.K.A. "La Noche de las
     Gaviotas")
     Director: Armando De Ossorio
Victor Petit, Maria Kosti, Sandra
Mozarosky, Julie James.

NIGHT OF THE SORCERERS (1973-
     Span.) (A.K.A. "La Noche de los
     Brujos")
     Director: Armando De Ossorio
Jack Taylor, Simon Andreiu, Kali
Hansa, Maria Kosti, J. Thelman.

NIGHT OF THE THOUSAND CATS
     (1972-Mex.) (A.K.A. "La Noche
     de los Mil Gatos")
     Director: Rene Cardona
Anjanette Comer, Zulma Faiad,
Crista Linder, Hugo Stiglitz.

NIGHT OF THE WEREWOLF (1968-
     Span.) (A.K.A. "Las Noches del
     Hombre Lobo")
     Director: Rene Govar
Paul Naschy (Waldemar Daninsky).

NIGHT OF THE WITCHES (1970)
     Director: Deith Erik Burt/
     Keith Larsen
Keith Erik Burt (the Preacher), Randy
Stafford (Athena), Ron Taft (Frank
Evans), Kathryn Loder (Cassandra),
Leon Charles (Mr. Greenstreet), John

Jones (Timothy Gruper), Susie
Edgell (Rosita), Ernest L. Rossi.

NIGHT OF VIOLENCE (1965-Ital.)
     Director: Roberto Mauri
Alberto Lupo, Marilu Tolo, Lisa
Gastoni, Helene Chapel.

NIGHT SCHOOL (1931)
     Director: Ken Hughes
Leonard Mann (Lt. Judd Austin),
Rachel Ward (Eleanor Adjai),
Drew Snyder (Prof. Millett), Joseph
R. Sicari (Taj), Nicholas Cairis
(Gus).

NIGHT SLAVES (TVM-1970) -
     9-29-70
     Director: Ted Post
James Franciscus (Clay Howard),
Lee Grant (Marj Howard), Andrew
Prine (Fess Beany), Scott Marlowe
(Matthew Russell), Leslie Nielsen
(Sheriff Henshaw), Tisha Sterling
(Naillil), Russell Thorson (Dr.
Smithers), John Kellogg (Mr.
Fletcher), Virginia Vincent (Mrs.
Crawford), Morris Buchanan (Mr.
Hale), Victor Izay (Jeff Pardee),
Cliff Carnell (Spencer), Raymond
Mayo (Joe Landers), Nancy
Valentine (May).

NIGHT STALKER, THE (TVM-1972)
     - 1-11-72
     Director: John L. Moxey
Darren McGavin (Carl Kolchak),
Simon Oakland (Vincenzo), Barry
Atwater (Janos Skorzeny), Carolk
Lynley (Gail Foster), Claude
Akins (Sheriff Butcher), Kent Smith
(D. A. Paine), Ralph Meeker
(Bernie Jenks), Charles McGraw
(Chief Masterson), Stanley Adams
(Fred Hurley), Elisha Cook, Jr.
(Mickey Crawford), Larry Linville
(Mokurji), Jordan Rhodes (Dr.
O'Brien).

NIGHT STRANGLER, THE (TVM-
     1973) - 1-16-73
     Director: Dan Curtis
Darren McGavin (Carl Kolchak),
Simon Oakland (Tony Vincenzo),
Richard Anderson (Dr. Richard
Malcolm), Jo Ann Pflug (Louise
Harper), John Carradine (Llewellyn
Crossbinder), Margaret Hamilton
(Prof. Crabwell), Scott Brady (Capt.
Roscoe Schubert), Wally Cox
(Titus Berry), George Tobias
(Stacks), Nina Wayne (Charisma
Beauty), Ivor Francis (Dr. Chris-
topher Webb), Kate Murtaugh
(Janie), Virginia Peters (Wilma

Krankheimer), Regina Parton (Ethel Murray).

NIGHT THAT PANICKED AMERICA, THE (TVM-1975) - 10-31-75
Director: Joseph Sargent
Vic Morrow (Hank Muldoon), Cliff De Young (Stefan Grubowski), John Ritter (Walter Wingate), Will Geer (Reverend Davis), Walter McGinn (Paul Stewart), Michael Constantine (Jess Wingate), Eileen Brennan (Ann Muldoon), Tom Bosley (Norman Smith), Meredith Baxter (Linda Davis), Paul Shenar (Orson Welles), Josh Bryant (Howard Koch), Granville Van Dusen (Carl Philips), Liam Dunn (Charlie), Walker Edminston (Ron Rifkin, Casey Kasem, Marcus J. Grapes (radio actors), Burton Gilliam (Tex), Shelley Morrison (Toni), Art Hannes (announcer).

NIGHT THE WORLD EXPLODED, THE (1957)
Director: Fred F. Sears
Tris Coffin (Dr. Ellis Morton), Kathryn Grant (Laura Hutchison), William Leslie (Dr. David Conway), Charles Evans (Gen. Bates), Marshall Reed (General's aide), Raymond Greenleaf (Gov. Cheney), Frank Scannell (Sheriff Quinn), Fred Coby (Ranger Brown), Paul Savage (Ranger Kirk), Terry Frost (foreman).

NIGHT THEY KILLED RASPUTIN, THE (1960-Ital./Fr.) (A.K.A. "Les Nuits de Raspoutine", "Nights of Rasputin")
Director: Pierre Chenal
Edmund Purdom (Rasputin), Gianna Maria Canale (Czarina), John Drew Barrymore (Yousoupoff), Jany Clair (Irina Yousoupoff), Ugo Sasso (the Czar), Ivo Garrani, Livio Lorenzon, Miranda Compa, Giluia Rubina, Maria Crazia, Nerio Bernardi, Marco Guglielmi, Buccella.

NIGHT TIDE (1961)
Director: Curtis Harrinton
Dennis Hopper (Johnny Drake), Linda Lawson (Mora), Gavin Muir (Capt. Murdock), Luana Anders (Ellen Sands), Marjorie Eaton (Madame Romanovitch), H. E. West (Lt. Henderson), Tom Dillon (merry-go-round manager).

NIGHT UNTO NIGHT (1947)
Director: Don Siegel
Ronald Reagan (John), Viveca Lindfors (Ann), Broderick Crawford (Shawn), Rosemary De Camp (Thalia), Osa Massen (Lisa), Craig Stevens (Tony), John McGovern (Willie Shawn), Lillian Yarbo (Josephine), Art Baker (Dr. Poole), Erskine Sanford (Dr. Altheim), Lois Austin (Mrs. Rose), Almira Sessions (maid), Irving Bacon (real estate agent), Ross Ford (bellboy), Dick Elliott (auto court manager).

NIGHT VISITOR, THE (1971)
Director: Laslo Benedik
Max Von Sydow (Salem), Trevor Howard (Inspector), Per Oscarrson (Dr. Anton Jends), Liv Ullman (Esther Jenks), Andrew Kier (Dr. Kemp), Rupert Davies (Clemmens), Gretchen Franklin (Mrs. Hansen), Arthur Hewlett (Pop), Jim Kennedy (Carl), Hanne Bork (Emmie), Lottie Freddie (Britt), Bjorn Watt Boolsen (Tokens).

NIGHT WALKER, THE (1964)
Director: William Castle
Barbara Stanwyck (Irene Trent), Robert Taylor (Barry Morland), Hayden Rorke (Howard Trent), Lloyd Bochner (the Dream), Rochelle Hudson (Hilda), Jess Barker (Malone), Judi Meredith (Joyce), Pauelle Clark (Pat), Tetsu Komai (the gardener), Marjorie Bennett (manager).

NIGHT WATCH (1973)
Director: Brian G. Hutton
Elizabeth Taylor (Ellen Wheeler), Laurence Harvey (John Wheeler), Billie Whitelaw (Sarah Cooke), Robert Lang (Appleby), Tony Britton, (Tony), Linda Hayden (girl in car), Rosario Serrano (Dolores), Bill Dean (Insp. Walker), Michael Danvers-Walker (Sgt. Norris), Laon Maybanke (florist), Kevin Colson (Carl), Pauline Jameson (secretary).

NIGHT WE GOT THE BIRD, THE (1960)
Dora Bryan (Julie Skidmore), Reginald Beckwith (Chippendale Charlie), Kynaston Reeves (Mr. Warre-Monger), Robertson Hare (Dr. Vincent), Irene Handl (Ma), Liz Fraser (Fay), John Slater (Wolfie Green), Ronald Shiner (Cecil Gibson), Terry Scott (PC Lovejoy), Brian Rix (Bertie Skidmore), Leo Franklyn (Victor), John LeMesurier (Clerk), Vera Pearce (Aunt).

NIGHTWING (1979)
Director: Arthur Hiller
Nick Mancuso (Youngman Duran),
David Warner (Philip Payne), Stephan Macht (Walker Chee), Kathryn
Harrold (Anne Dillon), Strother Martin (Selwyn), Ben Piazza (Roger Piggott), George Clutesi (Abner Tasupi),
Donald Hotton (John Franklin), Judith
Novgrod (Judy), Charles Hallahan
(Henry), Pat Corley (Vet), Alice Hirson (Claire Franklins), Danny Dapien
(Joe Mamoa), Jose Toledo (Harold
Masito), Charlie Bird (Beejay), Peter
Prouse (Doctor), Richard Romacito
(Ben Mamoa), Flavio Martinez III
(Isla Lalama).

1984 (1956)
Director: Michael Anderson
Edmond O'Brien (Winston Smith),
Jan Sterling (Julia), Michael Redgrave (O'Connor), David Kossoff (Mr.
Charrington), Mervyn Johns (Jones),
Donald Pleasence (Parsons), Carol
Wolveridge (Selina Parsons), Ronan
O'Casey (Rutherford), Kenneth Griffith (prisoner), Ernest Clark (announcer), Micheal Ripper, Patrick Allen,
Ewen Solon.

99 & 44/100 PERCENT DEAD (1974)
Director: John Frankenheimer
Richard Harris (Harry Crown), Edmond
O'Brien (Uncle Frank), Ann Turkel
(Buffy), Chuck Connors (Marvin 'Claw'
Zuckerman), Bradford Dillman (Big
Eddie), David Hall (Tony), Constance
Ford (Dolly), Kathrine Baumann (Baby),
Janice Heiden (Clara).

NINTH GUEST, THE (1934)
Director: Roy William Neill
Donald Cook (Jim Daley), Genevieve
Tobin (Jean Trent), Hardie Albright
(Henry Abbott), Edward Ellis (Tim
Cronin), Edwin Maxwell (Jason Osgood), Vince Barnett (William Jones),
Samuel S. Hinds (Dr. Murray Reid),
Helen Flint (Sylvia Inglesby), Sidney
Bracey (Butler), Nella Walker (Margaret Chisholm).

NO BLADE OF GRASS (1970)
Director: Cornel Wilde
Nigel Davenport (John Custance), Jean
Wallace (Ann Custance), Lynne Frederick (Marry Custance), George Coulouris (Mr. Sturdevant), Anthony May
(Pirrie), M. J. Mathews (George),
Tex Fuller (Mr. Beaseley), Michael
Percival (Constable), Ruth Kettlewell
(fat woman), Simon Merrick (TV

interviewer), Wendy Richard (Clara),
Anthony Sharp (Sir Charles Brenner),
Max Hartnell (Lieutenant), Norman
Atkyns (Dr. Cassop), Derek Keller
(Scott), Nigel Rathbone (Davey),
John Avison (Yorkshire sergeant),
Malcolm Toes (Sergeant Major).

NOCTURNA (1978)
Director: Harry Tampa
Nai Bonnett (Nocturna), John Carradine (Dracula), Yvonne DeCarlo
(Jugulia), Tony Hamilton (Jimmy),
Brother Theodore (Theodore), Sy
Richardson (RH Factor), Ivery
Bell, Norris Harris, Michael
Harrison, William H. Jones, Jr.
(Moment of Truth), Adam Keefe
(B.S.A. President), Monica Tidwell
(Brenda), Thomas Ryan (policeman),
Pierre Epstein (John), Ron Toler
(taxi driver), Tony Sanchez (victim),
Albert M. Ottenheimer (Dr. Bernstein), Frank Irizarry (disc jockey),
John Blyth Barrymore, Toby Handman, Shelly Wyant, Angelo Vignari
(B.S.A. members), Marcus Anthony,
Irwin Keyes (Transylvanians), Al
Sapienza, Jerry Sroka, A.C. Weary
(musicians).

NO EXIT (1954-Fr.) (A.K.A. "Huis
Clos")
Director: Jacqueline Adury
Frank Villard, Arletty, Gaby
Sylvia, Nicole Courcel, Yves Deniaud,
Renuad-Mary, Danliele Delorme.

NO EXIT (1962-Arg./U.S.) (A.K.A.
"Huis Clos", "Stateless")
Director: Ted Danielewski
Viveca Lindfors (Inez), Rita Gam
(Estelle), Morgan Sterne (Garcin),
Ben Piazza (Camarero), Orlando
Sacha (Gomez), Mirtha Miller
(Carmencita), Susana Mayo (Florence), Manuel Roson (Captain),
Miguel A. Iriarte (Robert), Elsa
Dorian (Shirley), Carlos Brown
(Roger Delaney III), Mario Horna
(Albert).

NO HAUNT FOR A GENTLEMAN (1952),
Director: Leonard Reeve
Anthony Pendrell, Sally Newton,
Jack MacNaughton, Patience
Rentoul, Peter Swanwick, Dorothy
Summers.

NO HOLDS BARRED (1952)
Director: William Beaudine
Leo Gorcey (Slip Mahoney), Huntz
Hall (Sach Debussy Jones), Marjorie

Reynolds (Rhonda), Leonard Penn (Taylor), David Condon (Chuck), Sandra Gould (Mildred), Henry Kulky (the Mauler), Bennie Bartlett (Bûthc), Murray Alper (Barney), Lisa Wilson (Betty), Tim Ryan (Mr. Hunter), Barbara Gray (Gertie), Ray Walker (Max), Leo 'Ukie' Sherin (Sam), Mike Ruby (referee).

NO PLACE LIKE HOMICIDE (1961)
(A. K. A. "What a Carve-Up!")
Director: Pat Jackson
Kenneth Connor (Ernie), Sidney James (Syd), Shirley Eaton (Linda), Donald Pleasence (Mr. Sloane), Michael Gough (Fisk), Michael Gwynn (Malcolm), Dennis Price (Guy), George Woodbridge (Dr. Edward), Valerie Taylor (Janet), Esma Cannon (Aunt Emily), Philip O'Flynn (Gabriel/Arkwright), Timothy Bateson (the porter), Frederick Piper (hearse driver).

NO PLACE TO HIDE (1955)
Director: Josef Shaftel
David Brian, Marsha Hunt, Hugh Corcoran, Ike Jarlego, Jr. Eddie Infante, Celia Flor, Manuel Silos, Pianing Vidal, Vicenta Advincula, Alfronso Carvajal, Lou Salvador.

NORLISS TAPES, THE (TVM-1973) -
2-21-73
Director: Dan Curtis
Roy Thinnes (David Norliss), Angie Dickinson (Ellen Cort), Claude Akins (Sheriff Hartley), Don Porter (Sanford Evans), Hurd Hatfield (Charles Langdon), Michele Carey (Marsha Sterne), Vonetta McGee (Mme. Jechiel), Bob Schott (Sargoth), Nick Dimitri (James Cort), George DiCenzo, Stanley Adams, Brian O'Byrne, Edmund Gilbert, Robert Mandan.

NORMING OF JACK 243, THE (TVM-1975).
Director: Gloria Monty
David Selby (Jack 243), Leslie Charleson (Anne/Joan II).

NOSFERATU (1922-Ger.) (A. K. A.
"Nosferatu, eine Symphonie des Grauens", "Nosferatu, a Symphony of Terror", "Nosferatu, the Vampire")
Director: F. W. Murnau
Max Schreck (Count Orlok/Dracula), Alexander Granach (Knock/Renfield), Gustav von Wangenheim (Waldemar Hutter/Jonathan Harker), Greta Schroeder (Ellen/Nina Harker), G. H. Schnell

(Harding/Westenra), Ruth Landshoff (Annie/Lucy), John Gottow (Prof. Bulwer/Van Helsing), Max Nemetz (Ship Captain).

NOSFERATU, THE VAMPIRE (1978-
Ger.) (A. K. A. "Nosferatu - Phantom der Nacht")
Director: Werner Herzog
Klaus Kinski (Count Dracula), Isabelle Adjani (Lucy Harker), Bruno Hans (Jonathan Harker), Walter Ladengast (Dr. Van Gelsing), Roland Topor (Renfield), Jacques Dufilho (Captain), Dan Van Husen (Warden), Jan Groth (Harbormaster), Carsten Bodinus (Schrader), Martje Grohmann (Mina), Ryk De Gooyer (town official), Tim Beekman (coffinbearer).

NO SURVIVORS PLEASE (1963-Ger.)
(A. K. A. "Der Chef Wunscht Keine Seugen", "The Chief Wants No Survivors")
Director: Hans Albin & Peter Berneis
Maris Perschy, Robert Cunningham, Gustavo Rojo, Uwe Friedrichsen, Karen Blaguernon, Rolf von Naukhaff.

NOTHING BUT THE NIGHT (1972)
(A. K. A. "The Resurrection Syndicate")
Director: Peter Sasdy
Christopher Lee (Col. Bingham), Peter Cushing (Sir Mark Ashley), Georgia Brown (Joan Foster), Diana Dors (Anna Harb), Kathleen Byron (Dr. Rose), Duncan Lamont (Dr. Knight), Keith Barron (Dr. Haynes), Fulton MacKay (Cameron), Gwyneth Strong (Mary Valley), John Robinson (Lord Fawnlee), Michael Gambon (Insp. Grant), Morris Perry (Dr. Yeats), Shelagh Fraser (Mrs. Allison), Geoffrey Frederick (computer operator), Louise Nelson (nurse), Robin Wentworth (head porter), Michael Wynne (Donald), Andrew McCulloch (Malcolm), Michael Segal (1st reporter), John Kelland (2nd reporter), Ken Watson (Jamie), Paul Humpoletz (Angus), Stanley Lebor (policeman), Stuart Saunders (police sergeant), Michael Brennan (deck hand), Janet Bruce (Naureen Stokes), Beatrice Ward (Helen Van Trayler), Geoffrey Denton (Paul Anderson).

NOT OF THIS EARTH (1957)
Director: Roger Corman

Paul Birch (Mr. Johnson), Beverly Garland (Nadine Storey), Morgan Jones (Harry Sherbourne), William Roerick (Dr. Frederick W. Rochelle), Jonathan Haze (Jeremy Perrin), Dick Miller (Joe Piper), Anne Carrol (woman from Davanna), Tamar Cooper (Joanna Oxford), Roy Engel (Sgt. Walton), Pat Flynn (Officer Simmons), Gail Ganley, Ralph Reed (teenagers), Harold Fong (Oriental specimen).

NOW YOU SEE HIM, NOW YOU DON'T (1972)
Director: Robert Butler
Kurt Russell (Dexter Riley), Cesar Romero (A. J. Arno), Joe Flynn (Dean Higgens), Jim Backus (Timothy Forsythe), Alan Hewitt (Dean Collingsgood), William Windom (Lufkin), Kelly Thordsen (Sgt. Cassidy), John Myhers (golfer), Pat Delaney (secretary), Dave Willock (Mr. Bruns), Richard Bakalyan (Cookie), Frank Aletter (TV announcer) Edward Andrews (Mr. Sampson), Ed Begley, Jr. (Druffle), Joyce Menges (Debbie Dawson), Michael McGreevey (Richard Schuyler), Neil Russell (Alfred), Robert Rothwell (driver), Frank Welker (Myles), Jack Bender (Slither Roth), George O'Hanlon (Ted), Mike Evans (Henry Fathington), Billy Casper (golfer), Paul Smith (road block officer), Dave Hill (golfer).

NUDE BOMB, THE (1980) (A. K. A. "The Return of Maxwell Smart")
Director: Clive Donner
Don Adams (Maxwell Smart), Sylvia Kristel (Agent 34), Pamela Hensley (Agent 36), Andrea Howard (Agent 22), Rhonda Fleming (Edith Von Secondberg), Dana Elcar (Chief), Vittorio Gassman (Nino Salvatore Sebastiani), Norman Lloyd (Carruthers), Bill Dana (Jonathon Levinson Seigle), Walter Brooke (American Ambassador), Gary Imhoff (Jerry Krovney), Sarah Rush (Pam Krovney), Thomas Hill (President), Joey Forman (Agent 13), Ceil Cabot (landlady), Patrick Gorman (French delegate), Alex Rodine (Russian delegate), Vito Scotti (Italian Delegate), Horst Ehrhardt (Polish delegate), Earl Maynard (Jamacan delegate), Richard Sanders (German delegate), Byron Webster (English delegate), James Noble (Secretary of Defense), Anthony Herrera, James Gavin, Gary Young.

NUDE VAMPIRE, THE (1969-Fr.) (A. K. A. "La Vampire Nue")

Director: Jean Rollin
Oliver Martin, Maurice Lemaitre, Ly Lestrong, Caroline Cartier, Bernard Musson, Jean Aron, Christine Francios, Ursulle Pauly.

NURSE SHERRI (1977)
Director: Al Adamson
Jill Jackson, Geoffrey Land, Marilyn Joe, Mary Kay Pass, Prentiss Moulden, Clayton Foster.

NURSE WILL MAKE IT BETTER (TVM-1975) (A. K. A. "The Devil's Web") - 2-24-75
Director: Shaun O'Riordan
Diana Dors (Bessy Malone), Andrea Marcovicci (Ruth Harrow), Ed Bishop (Carson), Cec Linder (Edgar Harrow), Michael Culver (Simon), Patrick Troughton (Lyall), Linda Liles (Charley Harrow).

NUTTY PROFESSOR, THE (1962)
Director: Jerry Lewis
Jerry Lewis (Prof. Julius F. Kelp/ Buddy Love), Stella Stevens (Stella Purdy), Kathleen Freeman (Millie Lemmon), Del Moore (Dr. Hamius R. Warfield), Howard Morris (Mr. Kelp), Elvia Allman (Mrs. Kelp), Milton Frome (Dr. Leevee), Buddy Lester (bartender), Celeste Yarnell, Francine York, Julie Parrish, Henry Gibson, David Landfield (students), Norman Alden, Skip Ward, Ned Flory (football players), Marvin Kaplan (English student), Joe Forte (faculty member), Terry Higgins (cigarette girl), Murray Alper (judo member), Doodles Weaver (Rube), Dave Willock (bartender), Gavin Gordon (salesman clothier), Mushy Callahan (cab driver).

NYLON NOOSE, THE (1963-Ger.) (A. K. A. "Die Nylonschlinge")
Director: Rudolf Zehetgruber
Ady Berber, Richard Goodman, Dietmar Schonherr, Laya Raki, Gustav Knuth, Helga Sommerfeld.

OO-2 SECRET AGENTS (1964-Ital.) (A. K. A. "OO-2 Agenti Segretissimi")
Director: Lucio Fulci
Franco Franchi, Ciccio Ingrassia, Ingrid Schoeller, Aroldo Tieri, Anni Gorassini.

087 MISSION APOCALYPSE (1966- Span./Ital.) (A. K. A. "087 Missione Apocalisse)

Director: Guido Malatesta/James
Reed
Arthur Hansl, Moa Thai, Pamela
Tudor, Harold N. Bradley, Jorge
Riguad, Eduardo Fajardo.

OBLONG BOX, THE (1969)
Director: Gordon Hessler
Vincent Price (Julian Markham),
Christopher Lee (Dr. Neuhartt), Hilary
Dwyer (Elizabeth), Peter Arne (Samuel
Trench), Sally Geeson (Sally Baxter),
Ivor Dean (Hawthorne), Alastair Will-
iamson (Sir Edward Markham), Rupert
Davies (Joshua Kemp), Michael Balfour
(Ruddock), Harry Baird (N'Galo), Max-
well Shaw (Tom Hackett), Carl Rigg
(Mark Norton), Godfrey James (Weller),
Uta Levka, Hira Talfrey, James Mellor,
John Barrie, Betty Woolfe, Anne Clune,
Ann Barrass, Danny Daniels, John
Wentworth, Martin Terry, Jackie Noble,
Jan Rossini, Tara Fernando, Anthony
Bailey, Martin Wyldeck, Colin Jeavons,
Zeph Gladstone, Tony Thawnton, Richard
Cornish, Andreas Melandrinos, Edgar
Wallace.

OBSESSION (1976)
Director: Brain De Palma
Genevieve Bujold (Elizabeth Courtland/
Sandra Portinari), Cliff Robertson
(Michael Courtland), John Lithgow
(Robert LaSalle), Wanda Blackman
(Amy Courtland), Stanley J. Reyes
(Insp. Brie), Sylvia Kuuma Williams
(Maid), Nick Kreiger (Farber), Don
Hood (Ferguson), Stocker Fontellieu
(Dr. Ellman), Andrea Esterhazy (D'An-
nunzio), Patrick McNamara (3rd kid-
napper).

OCTAGON, THE (1980)
Director: Eric Karson
Chuck Norris (Scott James), Lee Van
Cleef (McCarn), Art Hindle (A. J.),
Karen Carlson (Justine), Carol Bagda-
sarian (Aura), John Fujioka (Isawa),
Tadashi Yamashita (Seikura), Larry
D. Mann (Tibor), Kim Lankford (Nancy),
Jack Carter (Sharkey), Yuki Shimoda
(Katsumato), Kurt Grayson (Doggo).

OCTAMAN, THE (1971) (A. K. A.
"Octa-Man")
Director: Harry Essex
Kerwin Mathews (Rick), Pier Angeli
(Susanne), Jeff Morrow (John), David
Essex, Jerome Guardino, Robert Warner,
Buck Kartalian, Norman Fields, Jax
Jason Carroll, Samuel Peloso, Wally
Rose, Richard Cohen.

OFFICER 444 (1926)
Director: Ben Wilson & Francis
Ford
Ben Wilson (Officer 444), Neva Gerber
(Gloria Grey), Al Ferguson (the Frog),
Phil Ford, August Vollmer (gang
members), Jack Mower (Officer
444's partner).

OF GODS AND THE DEAD (1970-
Braz.) (A. K. A. "Os Deuses e
os Mortos")
Director: Ruy Guerra
Norma Bengell (Soledad), Othon
Bastos (Man), Itala Nadl (Ereno),
Ruy Potanah (Urbano), Nelson Xavier
(Valu), Jorge Chaia (Santana),
Fredi Kleeman (man in white).

OH, BOY! (1938)
Director: Albert De Courville
Bernard Nedell (Angelo Tonelli),
Albert Burdon (Percy Flower),
Mary Lawson (June Messenger),
Robert Cochran (Albert Bolsover),
Jay Laurier (Horatio Flower), Ed-
mon Ryan (Butch), Marie O'Nell
(Mrs. Baggs), Syd Walker (sergeant),
Charles Carson (Governor), Billy
Milton (conductor), Jerry Verno
(shopwalker), John Wood (man).

OH DAD, POOR DAD, MAMMA'S
HUNG YOU IN THE CLOSET AND
I'M FEELING SO SAD (1965)
Director: Richard Quine
Rosalind Russell (Madame Rosepettie),
Robert Morse (Jonathan), Jonathan
Winters (Dad), Barbara Harris
(Rosalie), Hugh Griffith (Commodore),
Lionel Jeffries (Airport Commander),
Cyril Delevanti (Hawkins), George
Kirby (Moses), Hiram Sherman
(Breckenduff), Janis Hansen (the
other woman).

OH, GOD! (1977)
Director: Carl Reiner
George Burns (God), John Denver
(Jerry Landers), Teri Garr (Bobbie
Landers), Ralph Bellamy (Sam
Raven), William Daniels (George
Summers), Donald Pleasence (Dr.
Harmon), Barnard Hughes (Judge
Baker), Barry Sullivan (priest),
Jeff Corey (rabbi), Paul Sorvino
(Rev. Willie Williams), George
Furth (Briggs), Titos Vandis (Bishop),
Dinah Shore (herself), David Ogden
Stiers (market executive), Carl
Reiner (talk show guest).

OH, GOD! BOOK II (1980)

Director: Gilbert Cates
George Burns (God), Suzanne Pleshette
(Paula), David Birney (Don), John
Louie (Shingo), Hans Conried (Dr.
Barnes), Howard Duff (Dr. Whitley),
Conrad Janis (Mr. Benson), Wilfrid
Hyde-White (Judge Miller), Louanne
(Tracy), Anthony Holland (Dr. Jerome
Newell), Dr. Joyce Brothers, Bebe
Drake Massey, Hugh Downs, Marian
Mercer, Vernon Weddle, Mari Gorman,
Alma Beltran.

OH! HEAVENLY DOG (1980)
Director: Joe Camp
Chevy Chase (Benjamin Browning), Jane
Seymour (Jackie Howard), Omar Sharif
(Malcolm Bart), Robert Morley (Bernie),
Alan Sues (Freddie), Donnelly Rhodes
(Montanero), John Stride (Alistair Bec-
kett), Barbara Leigh-Hunt (Margaret),
Stuart Germain (Higgins), Margaret
Courtenay (Dady Chalmers), Frank
Williams (Mr. Easton), Albin Pahernik
(Pelican man), Lorenzo Music (Carlton),
Harry Hill (Jeffrey Edgeware), Susan
Kellerman (German clerk), Marguerite
Corriveau (Patricia Elliott), Joe Camp,
Neil Affleck, Gerald Iles, Dan Wit,
Norman Tavis, David Samain, Jennifer
Foote, Jerome Tiberghien, George E.
Zeeman, Jeannette Casenave, Doris
Malcolm, Steve Michaels, Wendy
Dawson, Gayle Garfinkle, Mary Rath-
bone, Henry Hardy.

OLD DARK HOUSE, THE (1932)
Director: James Whale
Boris Karloff (Morgan), Charles Laugh-
ton (Sir William Porterhouse), Melvyn
Douglas (Roger Penderal), Gloria
Stuart (Margaret Waverton), Ernest
Thesiger (Horace Femm), Raymond
Massey (Phillip Waverton), Lillian
Bond (Gladys DuCane), Eva Moore
(Rebecca Femm), Bramber Wells (Saul
Femm), John Dudgeon (Sir Roderick).

OLD DARK HOUSE, THE (1963)
Director: William Castle
Tom Posten (Tom Penerel), Robert
Morley (Roderick Femm), Fenella
Fielding (Morganna Femm), Peter Bull
(Casper Femm/Jasper Femm), Joyce
Grenfell (Agetha Femm), Janette Scott
(Cicely Femm), Mervyn Johns (Potiphar
Femm), Danny Green (Morgan Femm),
Amy Dalby (the Player).

OLD DRACULA (1976) (A.K.A. "Vam-
pira")
Director: Clive Donner
David Niven (Count Dracula), Teresa

Graves (Vampira), Peter Bayliss
(Maltravers), Nicky Henson (Marc),
Jennie Linden (Angela), Linda
Hayden (Helga), Veronica Carlson
(Ritva), Bernard Bresslaw (Pottin-
ger), Freddie Jones (Gilmore),
Patrick Newell, Aimi MacDonald
(couple in hotel room), Penny Irving,
Nicola Austine, Hoima McDonald
(Playboy Bunnies), Minah Bird (Rose),
Andrea Allan (Eve), Frank Thornton
(Mr. King), Christopher Sandford
(Milton), Cathy Shirriff (Nancy),

OLD MOTHER RILEY'S GHOSTS (1941)
Director: John Baxter
Arthur Lucan (Mother Riley), Kitty
McShane (Kitty Riley), John Stuart
(John Cartwright), John Laurie (Mc-
Adam), Dennis Wyndaham (Jem), A.
Bromley Davenport (Warrender),
Peter Gawthorne (Mr. Cartwright),
Henry Longhurst, Ben Williams,
Charles Paton.

OLDEST PROFESSION, THE (1967-
Fr./Ger./Ital.) (A.K.A. "Le
Plus Vieus Metier du Mond")
"Prehistoric Times".
Director: Franco Indovina.
Michele Mercier (Britt), Gabriele
Tinti (Man from the Sea), Enrico
Maria Salerno (Braque).
"Anticipation".
Director: Jean-Luc Godard.
Anna Karina (Miss Conversation),
Jean-Pierre Leaud (Bellboy), Marilu
Tolo (Miss Physical Love), Jacques
Charrier (Space Traveler).

O LUCKY MAN! (1973)
Director: Lindsay Anderson
Malcolm McDowall (Mick Travis),
Ralph Richardson (Monty/Sir James
Burgess), Rachel Roberts (Gloria/Mme.
Pallard/Mrs. Richards), Arthur Lowe
(Mr. Duff/Charlie Johnson/Dr. Munda),
Helen Mirren (Patricia), Dandy Nichols
(Tea Lady/neighbor), Mona Wash-
bourne (neighbor/usher/Sister Hallet),
Graham Crowden (Dr. Miller/Prof.
Stewart/Down & Out), Peter Jeffrey
(Factory Chairman/Prison Governor),
Philip Stone (Jenkins/Interrogator/
Salvation Army Major), Alan Price
(himself), Wallas Eaton (Stone/Steiger/
Executive/Warder), Warren Clarke
(M.C./Warner/male nurse), Bill
Owen (Barlow/Superintendent), Ed-
ward Judd (Oswald), Pearl Nunez
(Mrs. Naidu), Mary Macleod (Mary
Ball/Vicar's wife), Michael Bangerter
(William/interrogator/released

prisoner), Michael Medwin (Duke of
Belminster/Captain/Power Station
Technician).

OMEGA MAN, THE (1971)
    Director: Boris Sagal
Charlton Heston (Robert Neville),
Rosalind Cash (Lisa), Anthony Zerbe
(Matthias), Paul Koslo (Kutch), Eric
Laneuville (Richie), Lincoln Kilpatrick
(Zachary), Brian Tochi (Tommy), Anna
Aries (woman in cemetary), Jill Geraldi
(little girl), John Dierkes, Deveren
Bookwalter, Monika Henreid, Forrest
Wood, Linda Redfearn (family mem-
bers).

OMEGANS, THE (1968)
    Director: W. Lee Wilder
Keith Larsen (Chuck), Ingrid Pitt
(Linda), Lucien Pan (Valdemar),
Bruno Punzalan (Oki), John Yench
(McAvoy), Joaquin Fajardo (Tumba),
Jorge Santos (clerk), Joseph de Cor-
dova (Dr. Balani), Lina Inigo (singer).

OMEN, THE (1976)
    Director: Richard Donner
Gregory Peck (Robert Thorn), Lee
Remick (Katherine Thorn), David
Warner (Jennings), Billie Whitelaw
(Mrs. Baylock), Harvey Stephens
(Damien Thorn), Patrick Troughton
(Father Brennan), Martin Benson
(Father Spiletto), Anthony Nicholls
(Dr. Becker), Leo McKern (Bugenha-
gen), Holly Palance (Nanny), Sheila
Raynor (Mrs. Horton), Robert Mac-
Leod (Horton), Robert Rietty (Monk),
John Stride (psychiatrist), Tommy
Duggan (priest), Freda Dowie (nun),
Roy Boyd (reporter).

OMICRON (1963-Ital.)
    Director: Ugo Gregoretti
Renato Salvatore (Omicron/Angelo),
Rosemary Dexter (Lucia), Gaetano
Quartaro (Midollo), Mara Carisi (Mrs.
Midollo), Ida Serasini (Widow Piatt-
ino), Calisto Calisti (Torchio), Danti
di Pinto (Police Inspector).

OMOO OMOO, THE SHARK GOD (1949)
    Director: Leon Leonard
Trevor Bardette, Pedro De Cordoba,
Ron Randell, Michael Whalen, George
Meeker, Devera Burton, Lisa Kincaid,
Richard Benedict, Rudy Robles, Jack
Raymond.

ON A CLEAR DAY YOU CAN SEE
    FOREVER (1970)
    Director: Vincente Minelli

Barbra Streisand (Daisy Gamble),
Yves Montand (Dr. Marc Chabot),
Bob Newhart (Dr. Mason Hume),
Jack Nicholson (Tad Pringle), Larry
Blyden (Warren Pratt), Simon Oak-
land (Dr. Conrad Fuller), John
Richardson (Robert Tentrees), Irene
Handl (Winnie Wainwhistle), Roy
Kinnear (Prince Regent), Pamela
Brown (Mrs. Fitzherbert), Elaine
Giftos (Muriel), Kermit Murdock
(Hoyt III), Mabel Albertson (Mrs.
Hatch), Byron Webster (Prosecuting
Attorney), Leon Ames (Clews),
Paul Camen (Millard), Tony Colti
(Preston).

ON BORROWED TIME (1939)
    Director: Harold S. Bucquet
Lionel Barrymore (Gramps Julian
Northrup), Bobs Watson (Pud), Sir
Cedric Hardwicke (Mr. Brink), Una
Merkel (Marcia Glies), Eily Malyon
(Demetria Riffle), Beulah Bondi
(Granny Nellie Northrup), Nat
Pendleton (Grimes), Henry Travers
(Dr. Evans), Ian Wolfe (Charles
Wentworth), Grant Mitchell (Mr.
Pilbeam), Truman Bradley (James
Northrup), Charles Waldron (Rev.
Murdock), Philip Terry (Bill Lowry),
James Burke (Sheriff Burlingame).

ONCE (1973)
    Director: Morton Helig
Marta Kristen (Woman), Chris
Mitchum (Creation), Jim Malinda
(Destruction).

ONCE IN A NEW MOON (1935)
    Director: Anthony Kimmins
Morton Selten, Derrick de Marney,
John Clements, Rene Ray, Eliot
Makeham, Wally Patch, Gerald
Barry, H. Saxon-Snell, Mary Hinton,
Richard Goolden, John Turnbull.

ONCE UPON A SPY (TVM-1980) -
    9-19-80
    Director: Ivan Nagy
Ted Danson (Jack Chenault), Chris-
topher Lee (Marcus Valorium), Leon-
ard Stone (Dr. Webster), Terry
Lester (Rudy), Mary Louise Weller
(Paige Tannehill), Eleanor Parker
(the Lady), Jo McDonnell (Susan),
Irene Serris (Greta), Burke Byrnes
(Berkle), John Hostetter (Chief).

ONE DEADLY OWNER (TVM-1973) -
    11-6-73
    Director: Ian Fordyce
Donna Mills (Helen Cook), Jeremy

Brett (Peter Tower), Laurence Payne (John Jacey), Robert Morris (Freddy Green), Michael Beint (Hawkins), Eric Lander (Hans), Roy Marioni (Walter),

ONE-EYED SOLDIERS, THE (1965-Yugo./Brit./U.S.)
Director; Jean Cristophe Dale Robertson (Richard Owne), Luciana Paluzzi (Gava Berens), Andrew Faulds (Col. Ferrer), Guy Deghy (Harold Schmidt), Mila Avramovic (Caporelli, the dwarf), Dragi Nikol (the Mummer), Boza Drinic (Charles Berens).

ONE FRIGHTENED NIGHT (1935)
Director: Christy Cabanne Charles Grapewin (Jasper Whyte), Mary Carlisle (Doris Waverly), Regis Toomey (Tom Dean), Wallace Ford (Joe Luvalle), Arthur Hohl (Arthur Proctor), Evalyn Knapp (1st Doris), Hedda Hopper (Laura Proctor), Fred Kelsey (Jenks), Clarence H. Wilson (Felix), Lucien Littlefield (Dr. Denham), Rafaela Ottiano (Elvira), Adrian Morris (Deputy Sheriff).

ONE GLORIOUS DAY (1922)
Director: James Cruze Will Rogers, Lila Lee, Alan Hale, Sr., John Fox, George Nichols, Clarence Burton, Emily Rait.

ONE MILLION B.C; (1940) (A.K.A. "Cave Man", "Man and His Mate")
Director: Hal Roach & Hal Roach, Jr.
Victor Mature (Tumak), Carole Landis (Loana), Lon Chaney, Jr. (Akhoba), John Hubard (Ohtao), Jacqueline Dalya (Ataf), Nigel De Bruglier (Peytow), Mamo Clark (Nupondi), Edgar Edwards (Skakana), Mary Gale Fisher (Wandi), Inez Palange (Tohana), Conrad Nagel (Narrator), Creighton Hale, Jean Porter.

ONE MILLION YEARS B.C. (1966)
Director: Don Chaffey Raquel Welch (Loana), John Richardson (Tumak), Robert Brown (Okhoba), Martine Beswicke (Nupondi), Percy Herbert (Sakana), Jean Waldon (Ahot), Yvonne Horner (Ullah), Malya Nappil (Tohana), Lisa Thomas (Sura), William Lyon Brown (Payto), Richard James (young rock man), Frank Hayden (1st rock man), Terence Maidment (1st shell man), Mickey De Rauch (1st shell girl), Robert Beatty (Narrator).

ONE NIGHT---BY ACCIDENT (1964-Fr.) (A.K.A. "Un Soir --- Par Hasard")
Director: Ivan Govar Jean Servais, Pierre Brasseur, A. Stroyberg.

ONE OF OUR DINOSAURS IS MISSING (1975)
Director: Robert Stevenson Peter Ustinov (Hnup Wan), Helen Hayes (Hettie), Clive Revill (Quon), Derek Nimmo (Lord Southmere), Bernard Bresslaw (Fan Choy), Joan Sims (Emily), Joss Ackland (B.J. Spence), Natasha Pyne (Susan), Roy Kinnear (Superintendent Grubbs), Deryck Guyler (Harris), Andrew Dove (Lord Castleberry), Max Harris (Truscott).

ONE OF OUR SPIES IS MISSING (1966)
Director: E. Darrell Hallenbeck see Television: Man from U.N.C.-L.E. - "The Bridge of Lions Affair" (2-4-66 & 2-11-66)

ONE SPY TOO MANY (1966)
Director: Joseph Sargent see Television: Man from U.N.-C.L.E. - "The Alexander the Greater Affair" (9-17-65 & 9-24-65)

ONE TOUCH OF VENUS (1948)
Director: William A. Seiter Robert Walker (Eddie Hatch), Ava Gardner (Venus), Dick Haymes (Joe Grant), Eve Arden (Molly Stewart), Tom Conway (Whitfield Savory), James Flavin (Corrigan), Sara Allgood (landlady), Olga San Juan (Gloria).

ONE WAY STREET (1925)
Director: John Francis Dillon Ben Lyon (Bobby Austin), Anna Q. Nilsson (Lady Sylvia Hutton), Marjorie Daw (Elizabeth Stuart), Lumsden Hare (Sir Edward Hutton), Dorothy Cumming (Lady Frances), Mona Kingsley (Kathleen Lawrence), Thomas Holding (John Stuart), M. Gonzales (Don Jose), Jed Prouty (Fat Man).

ON HER MAJESTY'S SECRET SERVICE (1969)
Director: Peter Hunt George Lazenby (James Bond), Diana Rigg (Tracy), Telly Savalas (Blofeld), Ilse Steppat (Irma Bunt), George Baker (Sir Hilary Bray), Bernard Horsfall (Campbell), Bernard Lee

(M), Lois Maxwell (Miss Moneypenny),
Desmond Llewelyn (Q), Catherine von
Schell (Nancy), Virginia North (Olympe),
Geoffrey Cheshire (Toussaint), Gab-
riele Ferzetti (Draco), George Cooper
(Braun), Angela Scoular (Ruby), Yuri
Borienko (Grunther), Terry Mountain
(Raphael), Les Crawford (Felsen),
Brian Worth (Manuel), Irvin Allen
(Che Che), Bill Morgan (Klett), James
Bree (Gumpold), Bessie Love (casino
guest), Elliott Sullivan (casino guest),
Dudley Jones (hall porter), Dani
Sheridan (American girl), Julie Ege
(Scandanavian girl), Anoushka Hempel
(Australian girl), Mona Chong (Chi-
nese girl), Jenny Hanley (Italian girl),
Joanna Lumley (English girl), Ingrid
Black (German girl), John Crewdson
(helicopter pilot).

ONIBABA (1965-Jap.) (A.K.A.
  "The Demon", "Devil Woman",
  "The Hole")
  Director: Kaneto Shindo
Nobuko Otowa, Jitsuko Yoshimura,
Taiji Tonoyama, Kei Sato, Jukichi
Uno.

ONLY A COFFIN (1966-Span./Fr.)
  (A.K.A. "Solo un Ataud", "The
  Orgies of Dr. Orloff")
  Director: Santos Alcocer
Howard Vernon (Dr. Orloff), Danielle
Godet, Adolfo Aries, Maria Saavedra,
Jose Bastida.

ONLY A SCREAM AWAY (TVM-
  1974) - 2-18-74
  Director:
Hayley Mills (Samantha), Gary Collins
(Howard), David Warbeck (Robert),
Ronald Meyer (Dr. Lambert), Jeremy
Bullock (Tom), Joyce Carey (Liza),
Jonathan Elsom (John).

ON THE BEACH (1959)
  Director: Stanley Kramer
Gregory Peck (Dwight Towers), Ava
Gardner (Moira Davison), Fred As-
taire (Julian Osborn), Anthony Perkins
(Peter Holmes), Donna Anderson (Mary
Holmes), Guy Doleman (Farrel), John
Meillon (Swain), Loda Brooks (Lt.
Hosgood), John Tate (Adm. Bridle),
Harp McGuire (Sundstrom), Richard
Meikle (Davis), Ken Wayne (Benson),
Joe McCormick (Ackerman), Lou
Vernon (Davidson), Basil Buller-
Murphy (Froude), Paddy Moran (port
man), Kevin Brennan (Dr. Forster),
Grant Taylor (Morgan), Frank Gat-
cliff (radio officer), John Casson

(Salvation Army Captain), John Royle
(senior officer), Dale Van Sickel
(stuntman), C. Harding Brown,
Jerry Duggan, Harvey Adams,
Stuart Finch, Joe McCormick, Rita
Pauncefort, Elwyn Peers, Peter
Williams, Al Thomas, Norman
Cook, Collins Hilton, Peter O'Shaugh-
nessy, Audine Leith, Cyril Gardner,
Ronald Fortt, Richard Webb, Paul
Maloney, Peter Ashton, Joe Jenkins,
Jerry Ian Seals, Lucian Endicott,
Brian James, Paddy Fitzallen, John
Morgan, Colin Crane, Jack Boyer,
Mario Vecci, Hugh Wills.

ON TIME (1924)
  Director: Henry Lehraman
Richard Talmadge (Harry Willis),
Billie Dove (Helen Hendon), Stuart
Holmes (Richard Drake), George
Selgmann (Wang Wu), Charles Clary
(Horace Hendon), Tom Wilson (Cas-
anova), Douglas Gerard (Mr. Black),
Frankie Mann (Mrs. Spinks), Fred
Kirby (Dr. Spinks).

OPEN SEASON (1974-Span./Swiss)
  (A.K.A. "Los Cazadores")
  Director: Peter Collinson
Peter Fonda (Ken), John Philip Law
(Greg), Richard Lynch (Art), Corn-
elia Sharpe (Nancy), Albert Mendoza
(Martin), William Holden (Wolkowski).

OPERATION ATLANTIS (1965-Ital./
  Span.) (A.K.A. "Agente 503
  Operazione Atlantide", "Agent
  003, Operacion Atlantida")
  Director: Domenico Paolella/
  Paul Fleming
John Ericson, Berna Rock, Ericka
Blanc, Beni Deus, Carlo Hinterman,
Maria Granada, Jose Manuel Martin.

OPERATION COUNTERSPY (1965-
  Ital./Span./Fr.) (A.K.A. "Oper-
  azione Controspionaggio")
  Director: Nick Nostro
George A. Ardisson, Lena Von Mar-
tens, Helen Chanel, Joaquin Diaz,
Leontina Mariotti.

OPERATION GOLDSEVEN (1966-
  Ital./Span.) (A.K.A. "Opera-
  zione Goldseven")
  Director: Alberto Leonardi/
  Albert B. Leonard
Tony Rusell, Erika Blanc, Fernando
Cebrian, Conrado San Martin,
Dianik Zurakowska, Wilbert Braley,
Peter White.

OPERATION KID BROTHER (1967-
Ital.) (A. K. A. "O. K. Connery")
Director: Alberto De Martino
Neil Connery (Neil Connery), Daniela
Bianchi (Maya), Adolfo Celi (Thair
Beta), Bernard Lee (Cmdr. Cunningham),
Lois Maxwell (Max), Anthony Dawson
(Alpha), Aagta Flori (Mildred), Guido
Lollobrigida (Kurt), Yachuco Yama
(Yachuco), Franco Giacobini (Juan),
Mario Soria (Gamma), Nando Angelini
(Ward Jones), Anna Maria Noe (Lotte).

OPERATION POKER (1965-Ital. Span.)
(A. K. A. "Operazione Poker")
Director: Osvaldo Civirana
Roger Browne, Helga Line, Jose
Greci, Carla Calo/Carol Brown,
Sancho Gracia.

ORCA (1977)
Director: Michael Anderson
Richard Harris (Capt. Nolan), Char-
lotte Rampling (Rachel Bedford), Will
Sampson (Umilak), Bo Derek (Annie),
Keenan Wynn (Novak), Peter Hooten
(Paul), Robert Carradine (Ken), Don
'Red' Barry (dock worker), Scott
Walker (Swain), Wayne Heffley (priest),
Vincent Gentile (gas station attendant).

ORDER: FX 18 MUST DIE (1965-Span. /
Fr.) (A. K. A. "Orden: FX 18
Debe Morir")
Director: Maurice Cloche
Ken Clark, Jany Clair, Jacques Da-
comine, Guy Delorme.

ORGY OF THE DEAD, THE (1972-
Span. /Ital.) (A. K. A. "La Orgia
de los Muertos")
Director: Jose Luis Merino
Paul Naschy, Dianik Zurakowska, Car-
los Quieny.

ORGY OF THE DEAD (1966) (A. K. A.
"Revenge of the Dead")
Director: Edward D. Wood, Jr.
Criswell, Pat Barringer, William
Bates, Fawn Silver, John Andrews,
Louis Ojena.

ORLAK, THE HELL OF FRANKEN-
STEIN (1960-Mex.) (A. K. A. "Orlak,
el Infierno de Frankenstein")
Director: Rafael Baledon
Joaquin Cordero, Andres Soler,
Armando Calva, Rose de Castilla,
Irma Dorantes, Pedro D'Aquillon.

ORLOFF AND THE INVISIBLE MAN
(1970-Span. /Fr.) (A. K. A. "Orloff
y el Hombre Invisible")

Director: Pierre Chevalier
Howard Vernon (Dr. Orloff), Brigitte
Carva, Fernando Sancha, Evane
Hanska, Isabelle Del Rio, Francisco
Valladares.

ORPHEUS (1950-Fr.) (A. K. A.
"Orphee")
Director: Jean Cocteau
Jean Marais (Orpheus), Francois
Perier (Heurtebise), Marie Dea
(Eurydice), Maria Casares (the
Princess), Jacques Varennes (1st
Judge), Henri Cremieux (the Man),
Greco (Aglanoice), Pierre Bertin
(the Inspector), Roger Blin (the
Writer), Edouard Dermithe (Cegeste).

OSS 117 - MISSION FOR A KILLER
(1965-Fr.) (A. K. A. "Furia a
Bahia pour O. S. S. 117", "Trouble
in Bahia for O. S. S. 117")
Director: Andre Hunebelle
Frederick Stafford (OSS 117), Mylene
Demongeot (Ann Marion), Raymond
Pellegrin (Leardo), Perrette Pradier
(Consuelo), Francois Maistre (Carlo),
Annie Andersson (secretary), Jacques
Riberolles (Miguel).

OSS 117 TAKES A VACATION (1969-
Fr. /Braz.) (A. K. A. "OSS 117
Prend des Vacances")
Director: Pierre Dalfon
Luc Merenda (OSS 117), Norma
Bengell (Friend), Elsa Martinelli
(Elsa), Ewidge Feuillere (Aunt),
Genevieve Grad (Pauline), Joss
Morgane (Brother), Rosanna Ghezza
(Anna), Tarcizio Meira (Killer).

OTHER, THE (1912-Ger.) (A. K. A.
"Der Andere")
Director: Max Mack
Albert Bassermann (Dr. Hallers),
Emmerich Hanus, Hanni Weisse,
Relly Ridon, Leon Rosemann, Otto
Collot, Paul Pasarge, G. Lengling.

OTHER, THE (1930-Ger.) (A. K. A.
"Der Andere")
Director: Max Glass & Robert
Wiene
Fritz Kortner (Dr. Hallers), Kathe
von Nagy, Heinrich George, Hermine
Sterler, Eduard von Winterstein,
Ursula von Dieman.

OTHER, THE (1972)
Director: Robert Mulligan
Uta Hahen (Ada), Diana Muldaur
(Alexandra Perry), Chris Udvarnoky
(Niles Perry), Martin Udvarnoky

(Holland Perry), Norma Connolly
(Aunt Vee), Victor French (Angleini),
Lou Frizell (Uncle George), Jenny
Sullivan (Torrie), Loretta Lavarsee
(Winnie), Portia Nelson (Mrs. Rowe),
John Ritter (rider), Jack Collins (Mr.
P. C. Pretty), Clarence Crow (Russell),
Ed Bakey (Chan-yu).

OTHER FU MANCHU, THE (1945-
Span.) (A. K. A. "El Otro Fu
Manchu")
Director: Ramon Barreiro
Rosita Yarza, Adela Esteban, Dan-
dida Lopez, Alicia Torres, Mary
Gonzalez, Carlos Munos, Manuel
Requena.

OUR MAN FLINT (1965)
Director: Daniel Mann
James Coburn (Derek Flint), Lee J.
Cobb (Lloyd Cramden), Gila Golan
(Gila), Edward Mulhare (Malcolm
Rodney), Benson Fong (Dr. Schnei-
der), Rhys Williams (Dr. Krupov),
Peter Brocco (De. Wu), Russ Conway
(General), Stevan Geray (Israeli
Diplomat), Alberto Morin (Cuban
Diplomat), William Walker (American
Diplomat), Gianna Serra (Gina),
Sigrid Valdis (Anna), Shelby Grant
(Leslie), Helen Funai (Sakito), Michael
St. Clair (Gruber), Ena Hartman (WAX),
James Brolin (technician), Lewis
Charles.

OUR MOTHER'S HOUSE (1967)
Director: Jack Clayton
Dirk Bogarde (Charlie Hook), Pamela
Franklin (Diana Hook), Yootha Joyce
(Mrs. Quayle), Annette Carell (Mother),
Edina Ronay (Doreen), Anthony Nicholls
(Mr. Halbert), Gerald Sim (bank clerk),
Louis Sheldon Williams (Hubert Hook),
Mark Lester (Jiminee Hook), Gustav
Henry (Willy Hook), Margaret Brooks
(Elsa Hook), John Gugolka (Dunstan
Hook), Sarah Nicholls (Gerty Hook),
Farnhum Wallace (Louis), Claire
Davidson (Miss Bailey), Garfield
Morgan (Mr. Moley), Diana Ashley
(girl friend), Faith Kent, John Arnatt
(clients), Jack Silk (motorcyclist).

OUTER SPACE JITTERS (1957) -
short
Director: Jules White
Moe Howard, Larry Fine, Joe Besser,
Dan Blocker (the Goon), Gene Roth,
Phil Van Zandt, Diana Darrin, Emil
Sitka, Harriette Tarler, Joe Palma.

OUTLANDS (1981)

Director: Peter Hyams
Sean Connery (Federal District
Marshall William O'Neil), Peter
Boyle (Mark Sheppard), Frances
Sternhagen (Dr. Marian Lazarus),
James Sikking (Deputy Montone),
Clarke Peters (Deputy Ballard),
Kika Markham (Carol), Steven
Berkoff (Sagan), John Ratzenberger
(Tarlow), Manning Redwood (Lowell),
Hal Gallili (Nelson), Angus MacInnes
(Hughes), Nicholas Barnes (Paul O'Neil
O'Neil), Pat Starr (Mrs. Spector),
Stuart Milligan (Walters).

OUT OF THIS WORLD (1954)
see Television: Rocky Jones,
Space Ranger (1953-54)

OUTWARD BOUND (1930)
Director: Robert Milton
Leslie Howard (Tom Prior), Helen
Chandler (Ann), Douglas Fairbanks,
Jr. (Henry), Montague Love (Mr.
Lingley), Dudley Digges (the
Examiner), Alec B. Francis (Scrubby),
Beryl Mercer (Mrs. Midget), Alison
Skipworth (Mrs. Clivedon-Banks),
Walter Kingsford (policeman), Lyonel
Watts (Rev. William Duke).

PACK, THE (1977) (A. K. A. "The
Long Hard Night")
Director: Robert Clouse
Joe Don Baker (Jerry), Hope Alex-
ander-Willis (Millie), Ned Wertimer
(Walker), Richard B. Shull (Hardi-
man), R. G. Armstrong (Cobb),
Bibi Besh (Marge), Delos V. Smith,
Jr. (McMinnimee), Richard O'Brien
(Dodge), Sherry Miles (Lois), Paul
Wilson (Tommy), Eric Knight (Guy),
Steve Lytle (Paul), Rob Narke
(husband), Peggy Price (wife), Steve
Butts (Bobby).

PACT WITH THE DEVIL (1968-
Mex.) (A. K. A. "Pacto Diabolico")
Director: Jaime Salvador
John Carradine, Regina Torne, Isela
Vega, Miguel Angel Alvarez, Andres
Garcia, Guillermo Zetina, Gloria
Munguia, Laura Ferlo, Silvia
Villalobos, Angel Distenfani, Carlos
Suarez, Enriqueta Carrasco.

PAJAMA PARTY (1964)
Director: Don Weis
Tommy Kirk (Gogo/George), An-
nette Funicello (Connie), Elsa Lan-
chester (Aunt Wendy Carruthers),
Jesse White (J. Sinister Hulk),
Buster Keaton (Chief Rotten Eagle),

Harvey Lembeck (Eric von Zipper),
Don Rickles (Big Bang), Frankie
Avalon (Socum), Ben Lessy (Fleagle),
Jody McCrea (Big Lunk), Donna
Loren (Vicki), Dorothy Lamour
(fashion show hostess), Bobbi Shaw,
Chery Sweeten, Susan Hart, Luree
Holmes, Candy Johnson.

PALACE OF THE ARABIAN NIGHTS
(1905-Fr.) (A.K.A. "Le Palais
des Mille et Une Nuits")
Director: Georges Melies

PAN (1973-Ital.)
Director: George Moorse
Udo Kier (Pilgrim of Death), Louis
Waldon (Pan), Helga Anders, Gor-
don Mitchell, Herbert Fux, Evelyn
Opela, Dieter Schidor.

PANDEMONIUM (1982) (A.K.A.
"Thursday the 12th")
Director: Alfred Sole
Carol Kane, Tom Smothers, Marc
McClure, Debrales Scott, Tab Hunter,
Eve Arden, Donald O'Connor, Jim
Boeke, Candice Azzara, Judge Rein-
hold, Richard Romanus, Miles
Chapin, Teri Landrum.

PANDORA AND THE FLYING DUTCH-
MAN (1950)
Director: Albert Lewin
James Mason (Hendrick van der Zee),
Ava Gardner (Pandora Reynolds),
Nigel Patrick (Stephen Cameron),
Sheila Sim (Janet Fielding), Harold
Warrender (Geoffrey Fielding),
Marius Goring (Reggie), Pamela
Kellino Mason (Jenny Ford), John
Laurie (Angus), Abraham Sofaer
(Judge), Patricia Raine (Peggy Ford),
Margarita D'Alvarez (Senora Mon-
talvo), Mario Cabre (Juan Montalvo),
La Pillino (dancer), Francisco Igual,
Lila Molnar, Gabriel Carmona,
Phoebe Hodgson, Guillermo Beltran,
Antonio Martin.

PANDORA'S BOX (1928-Ger.) (A.K.A.
"Die Buchse der Pandora")
Director: G.W. Pabst
Louise Brooks, Fritz Kortner, Fran-
cis Lederer, Sig Arno, Daisy Dora,
Gustav Diessl, Carl Goetz.

PANIC AT MADAME TUSSAUD'S
(1949) (A.K.A. "Panic in a Wax
Museum")
Director: Peter Graham Scott
Harry Fine (Bugs Maloney), Harry
Locke (Gladstone Green), Patricia

Owens, Francis Clare, Sam Lee,
Ivan Craig.

PANIC IN THE CITY (1967)
Director: Eddie Davis
Howard Duff (Dave Pomeroy),
Linda Cristal (Dr. Paula Stevens),
Stephen McNally (James Kincade),
Nehemiah Persoff (August Best),
Anne Jeffreys (Myra Pryor), Oscar
Beregi, Jr. (Paul Cerbo), Dennis
Hopper (Goff), Gregory Morton
(Steadman), John Hoyt, Wesley
Lau, George Barrows, Steve
Franken, Stanley Clements, Hank
Brandt, Deanna Lund, George
Saways, Douglas Evans, Eddie
Firestone, Walter Reed, Mike
Farrell, James Seay, Jim Adams,
Cal Currens, Elaine Beckett,
Edith Loder, Robert Tery, Eilene
Jannsen, John Pickard, Jann Wat-
son, Leon Leontoci, Wendy Stuart,
Bee Thompkins, Jim Kline, Rush
Williams, Maurice Wells, Renee
Redman, Walter Scott, Al Shafran,
William Tannen, Dodie Warren,
Tex Armstrong.

PANIC IN THE YEAR ZERO (1962)
Director: Ray Milland
Ray Milland (Harry Baldwin),
Jean Hagen (Ann Baldwin), Frankie
Avalon (Rick Baldwin), Mary Mit-
chell (Karen Baldwin), Richard
Garland (Mr. Johnson), Shary
Marshall (Mrs. Johnson), Joan
Freeman (Marilyn Hayes), Rex
Holman (Mickey), Willis Bouchey
(Dr. Strong), Russ Bender (Hark-
ness), Byron Morrow (Haenel),
Neil Nephew (Andy), Richard
Bakalyan (Carl), O. Z. Whitehaed
(Hogan), Hugh Sanders (Becker).

PANIC ON THE AIR (1936)
Director: D. Ross Lederman
Lew Ayres (Jerry Franklin),
Florence Rice (Mary), Edwin
Maxwell (Gordon), Benny Baker
(Andy), Charles Wilson (Fitz-
gerald), Murray Alper (Danker),
Gene Morgan (Lefty Dugan), Eddie
Lee (McNulty), Robert Emmet
Keane.

PANTHER GIRL OF THE KONGO
(1955) (A. K. A. "The Claw
Monsters") - serial in 12
episodes
Director: Franklin Adreon
Phyllis Coates (Jean Evans),
Myron Healey (Larry Sanders),

Arthur Space (Dr. Morgan), Roy Glenn, Sr. (Chief Danka), Mike Ragan (Rand), John Day (Cass), Morris Buchanan (Tembo), Archie Savage (Ituri), Ramsay Hill (Commissioner Stanton), Naaman Brown (Orto), John Daheim (Cass), Dan Ferniel (Ebu), Fred Graham (Nick), James Logan (Harris), Steve Calvert (the Gorilla), Gene Stutenroth/Roth (bartender), Keith McConnell (Kent), Charles Sullivan (Davis), DeForest Covan (Koango), Walter Smith (Naganto), Daniel Elam, Wesley Gale (natives), Alan Reynolds (Stanley), Don Carlos (Semba), Martin Wilkins (Zemba), Tom Steele.

PANTHER WOMAN, THE (1966-Mex.) (A.K.A. "Las Mujeres Panteras")
Director: Rene Cardona
El Angel Ariadne Welter, Elisabeth Campbell, Erick del Castillo, Manuel 'Loco' Valdes, Eda Lorna.

PARACELSUS (1943-Ger.)
Director: G.W. Pabst
Werner Drauss, Fritz Rasp, Victor Janson, Bernhard Goetzke, Harald Kreutzbert, Mathias Wieman.

PARALLAX VIEW, THE (1974)
Director: Alan J. Pakula
Warren Beatty (Joseph Frady), Hume Cronyn (Rintels), William Daniels (Austin Tucker), Paula Prentiss (Lee Carter), Kenneth Mars (former FBI agent), Jim Davis (Senator Hammond), Walter McGinn (Parallax representative), Kelly Thordsen (Sheriff), Earl Hindman (Deputy), Bill Joyce (Senator Carroll), William Jordan (Tucker's aide), Bill McKinney (assassin), Ford Rainey (Commission Spokesman), Stacy Keach, Sr. (Commission Spokesman), Vernon Weddle, William Swan, Richard Bull, Ed Winter, John S. Ragin, JoAnne Harris, Robert Lieb, Doria Cook, Joe De Reda, Bettie Johnson, Al Beltram, Joan Lemmo, Penelope Gillette, Rhonda Copland, Lee Pulford, Chuck Waters, Patsy Garrett, Suzanne Cohane, Ted Gehring.

PARANOIA (1968-Ital./Fr.) (A.K.A. "Orgasmo", "Orgasm")
Director: Umberto Lenzi
Carrol Baker (Kathryn West), Lou Castel (Peter Donovan), Colette Descombes (Eva), Tino Carraro (Brian Sanders), Franco Pesce (Martino), Lilia Brignone (Teresa), Jacques Stany (Police Inspector), Sara Simoni (Kathryn's aunt), Gaetano Imbro, Calisto

Calisti, Mario Rosiello, Alberto Cocchi.

PARANOIAC (1963)
Director: Freddie Francis
Oliver Reed (Simon Ashby), Janette Scott (Eleanor Ashby), Alexander Davion (Tony), Lilliane Brousse (Franciose), Sheila Burrell (Aunt Harriet), Maurice Denham (John Kossett), John Stuart (Williams), John Bonney (Keith Kossett), Sydney Bromley (tramp), Harold Lang (RAF type), Colin Tapley (Vicar), Laurie Leigh (1st woman), Marianne Stone (2nd woman), Jack Taylor (sailor).

PARASITE (1982)
Director: Charles Band
Robert Giaudini (Dr. Paul Dean), Demi Moore (Patricia Welles), Luca Bercovici (Ricus), Al Fann (Collins), Vivian Blaine (Miss Daley), Cherie Currie (Dana), James Davidson (Merchant), Tom Villard (Zeke).

PARIS PLAYBOYS (1954)
Director: Willaim Beaudine
Huntz Hall (Sach Debussy Jones/Prof. Le Beau), Leo Gorcey (Slip Mahoney), Bernard Gorcey (Louie Dumbrowsky), Veola Vonn (Mimi), Steven Geray (Gaspard), John Wengraf (Vidal), Marianne Lynn (Celeste), Davis Condon (Chuck), Bennie Bartlett (Butch), Alphonse Martell (Pierre), Gordon Clark (Cambon).

PARIS WHEN IT SIZZLES (1964) (A.K.A. "The Girl Who Stole the Eiffel Tower")
Director: Richard Quine
William Holden (Richard Benson), Audrey Hepburn (Gabrielle Simpson), Gregory Aslan (Police Inspector), Raymond Bussieres (Gangster), Christian Duvallex (Maitre d'hotel), Mel Ferrer, Tony Curtis, Noel Coward, Marlene Dietrich.

PASSING OF THE THIRD FLOOR BACK, THE (1935)
Director: Berthold Viertel
Conrad Veidt (the Stranger), Anna Lee (Vivian), Frank Cellier (Wright), Jack Livesey (Larcombe), Mary Clare (Mrs. Sharpe), Sara Algood (Mrs. de Hooley), Beatrix Lehmann (Miss Kite), John Turnbull (Major Tomkins), Ronald Ward (Chris), Cathleen Nesbitt (Mrs. Tomkins), Barbara Everest (Cook), Alexander

Sarner (gramophone man), Rene Ray
(Stassia).

PASSPORT TO DESTINY (1943) (A. K. A.
"Passport to adventure")
Director: Ray McCarey
Elsa Lanchester, Lenore Aubert, Fritz
Feld, Gavin Muir, Lumsden Hare,
Philip Van Zandt, Lloyd Corrigan,
Olat Hytten, Gordon Oliver, Lionel
Royce.

PASSPORT TO PIMLICO (1948)
Director: Henry Cornelius
Stanley Holloway (Arthur Pemberton),
Margaret Rutherford (Prof. Hatton
Jones), Hermione Baddeley (Edie Ran-
dall), Raymond Huntley (Mr. Wix),
Jane Hylton (Molly), Basil Radford
(Gregg), Paul Dupuis (Duke of Burgundy),
Naughton Wayne (Straker), Betty Waren
(Connie Pemberton), Barbara Murray
(Shirley Pemberton), John Slater (Frank
Huggins), Philip Stainton (P. C. Spiller),
Michael Hordern (Bashford).

PATRIA (1916) - serial in 15 episodes.
Chapters: 1. "Last of the Fighting
Channings", 2. "The Treasure", 3.
"Winged Millions", 4. "Double Crossed",
5. "The Island God Forgot", 6. "Alias
Nemesis", 7. "Red Dawn", 8. "Red
Night", 9. "Cat's Paw and Scapegoat",
10. "War in the Dooryard", 11. "Sun-
set Falls", 12. "Peace on the Border",
13. "Wings of Death", 14. "Border
Peril", 15. "For the Flag".
Director: Leopold Wharton,
Theodore Wharton & Jacques
Jaccard
Irene Castle (Patria), Milton Sills
(Donald Parr), Floyd Buckley, Warner
Oland, Dorothy Green, Nigel Barrie,
Marie Walcamp, George Majeroni,
Allen Murnane.

PATRICK (1978-Australia)
Director: Richard Franklin
Susan Penhaligon (Kathy Jacquard),
Robert Helpmann (Dr. Roget), Robert
Thompson (Patrick), Rod Mullinar (Ed
Jacquard), Bruce Barry (Dr. Wright),
Julia Blake (Matron Cassidy), Helen
Hemingway (Sister Williams), Frank
Wilson (Detective Sgt. Grant), Peter
Culpan (Grant's assistant), Maria
Mercedes (Nurse Panicale), Marilyn
Rodgers (day desk nurse), Peggy
Nichols (night desk nurse), Carole-
Ann Aylett (Patrick's mother), Paul
Young (lover), Walter Pym (Capt.
Fraser).

PAWNS OF MARS (1915)
Director: Theodore Marston
Dorothy Kelly (Florence Lefone),
James Morrison (John Temple),
Charles Kent (Dr. Lefone), George
Cooper (Rizo Turbal).

PEARL OF DEATH, THE (1944)
(A. K. A. "Sherlock Holmes and
the Pearl of Death")
Director: Roy William Neill
Basil Rathbone (Sherlock Holmes),
Nigel Bruce (Dr. Watson), Evelyn
Ankers (Naomi Drake), Miles Mander
(Giles Conover), Rondo Hatton (the
Creeper), Dennis Hoey (Insp. Les-
trade), Mary Gordon (Mrs. Hudaon),
Ian Wolfe (Amos Hodder), Holmes
Herbert (James Goodram), Richard
Nugent (Bates), Charles Francis
(Digby), Harold DeBecker (Boss),
Leyland Hodgson (customs officer),
Audrey Manners (teacher).

PEEPING TOM (1960) (A. K. A.
"Face of Fear")
Director: Michael Powell
Carl Boehm (Mark Lewis), Moira
Shearer (Vivian), Anna Massey
(Helen Stephens), Maxine Audley (Mrs.
Stephens), Shirley Ann Field (Diane
Ashley), Esmond Knight (Arthur
Baden), Michael Goodliffe (Don
Jarvis), Brenda Bruce (Dora), Jack
Watson (Insp. Gregg), Martin Miller
(Dr. Rosan), Nigel Davenport (Sgt.
Miller), Veronica Hurst (Miss Simp-
son), Bartlett Mullins (Mr. Peters),
Brian Wallace (Tony), Pamela Green
(Milly), Susan Travers (Lorraine),
Miles Malleson (elderly gentleman),
Maurice Durant (publicity chief),
Brian Worth (assistant director),
Alan Rolfe (store detective).

PEER GYNT (1915)
Director:
Charles Ruggles, Cyril Maude, Myrtle
Stedman.

PEER GYNT (1934-Ger.)
Director: Fritz Wendhausen
Hans Albers, Marieluise Claudius,
Lucie Hoflich, Olga Ischechova.

PEER GYNT (1941)
Director: David Bradley
Charlton Heston (Peer Gynt), Francis
X. Bushaman (Voice of Boyg), Betty
Hanisse (Aase), Mrs. Herbert Hyde,
Sue Straub (old women), Kathryne
Elfstrom (Solveig), Lucielle Powell
(Kari), Charles Paetow, Morris

Wilson (Haegstad), Betty Barton (Ingrid), Alan Eckhart (Mads Moen), George B. Moll (Drunk), Sarah Merrill (hag in green), Audrey Wedlock (woman in green), Rose Andrews (Anitre), Warren McKenzie (Mr. MacPherson), Alan Heston (ugly urchin), Roy Eggert, Jr. (Monsieur Ballon/Dovre-King).

PENALTY, THE (1920)
     Director: Wallace Worsley
Lon Chaney, Sr. (Blizzard), Claire Adams (Barbara), Kenneth Harlan (Wilmot), Ethel Grey Terry (Rose), Milton Ross (Lichtenstein), Charles Clary (Doctor), Edouard Trebaol (Bubble), James Mason (Peter), Madalaine Travers.

PENITENTE MURDER CASE, THE (1936) (A. K. A. "The Lash of the Penitentes", "El Asasenato de los Penitentes")
     Director: Harry J. Revier
Jose Swickard (Dr. Robert Taylor), Marie de Forest (Raquel), Jose Rubio (Chico), William Marcos (Manuel).

PENTHOUSE, THE (1967)
     Director: Peter Collinson
Suzy Kendall (Barbara), Tony Beckley (Tom), Terence Morgan (Bruce), Martine Beswicke (Harry), Norman Rodway (Dick).

PEOPLE, THE (TVM-1972) - 1-22-72
     Director: Jon Korty
Kim Darby (Melodye Amerson), William Shatner (Dr. Curtis), Dan O'Herlihy (Sol Diemus), Diane Varsi (Valency), Chris Valentine (Francher), Laurie Walters (Karen Kingus), Johanna Baer (Bethie), Jack Dahlgren (Kiah), David Petch (Matt), Stephanie Valentine (Talitha), Andrew Crichton (Thann), Dorothy Drady (Dita), Anne Walters (Obla), Mary Rose McMaster (Maras), Tony Dario (Bram).

PEOPLE THAT TIME FORGOT, THE (1977)
     Director: Kevin Connor
Patrick Wayne (Ben McBride), Sarah Douglas (Lady Charlotte), Doug McClure (Bowen Tyler), Dana Gillespie (Ajor), Thorley Walters (Norfolk), Shane Rimmer (Hogan), Milton Reid (Sabbala), Kiran Shah (Bolam, the dwarf), John Hallam, Tony Britton, David Prowse, Richard Parmentier, Gaylor Reid, Jimmy Ray, Tony McHale.

PEOPLE WHO OWN THE DARK, THE (1975-Span.) (A. K. A. "Planeta Ciego")
     Director: Leon Klimovsky
Paul Naschy, Maria Perschy, Tony Kendall, Teresa Gimpera, A. de Mendoza.

PEOPLETOYS (1974) (A. K. A. "The Devil Times Five", "The Horrible House on the Hill")
     Director: Sean McGregor
Gene Evans, Sorell Booke, Dawn Lyn, Shirley Morrison, Leif Garrett, Taylor Lacher.

PERCEVAL (1978-Fr.)
     Director: Eric Rohmer
Fabrice Luchini (Perceval), Andre Dussolier (Gawain), Arielle Dombasle (Blanchefleur), Michel Etchverry (Fisher King), Marc Eyraud (King Arthur), Marie-Christine Barrault (Guenivere), Pascale de Boysson (Perceval's mother), Antoine Baud (Red Knight), Jacques le Carpentier (Proud Lord of the Heath), Clementine Amouroux (damsel in tent), Jocelyne Boisseau (damsel who laughs), Gerard Falconetti (Kay), Alaine Serve (the Fool), Daniel Tarrare (Yvonet), Rauol Billerey (Gornemant of Gohort), Guy Delomre Dacafos (Hideous Damsel), Jean Boissery (Guingambresil), Gilles Raab (Sagremor), Claude Jaeger (Thiegaut of Tintaguel), Frederique Cerbonnet (Thiebaut's elder daughter), Anne-Laure Meury (damsel with small sleves), Frederic Norbert (King of Escavalon), Christine Leitot (King's sister), Hubert Gignoux (hermit).

PERCY (1970)
     Director: Ralph Thomas
Hywel Bennett (Edwin Anthony), Elke Sommer (Helga), Denholm Elliott (Emmanuel Whitbread), Janet Key (Hazel), Britt Ekland (Dorothy Chiltern-Barlow), Tracey Crisp (Miss Elder), Patrick Mower (James Vaile), Tracy Reed (Mrs. Penney), Cyd Hayman (Moira Warrington), Sue Lloyd (Bernice), Antonia Ellis (Rita La Rousse), Pauline Delaney (Sister Flanagan), Julia Foster (Marilyn), Adrienne Posta (Maggie Hyde), Sheila Steafel (Mrs. Gold), Arthur English (MC), Rita Webb (Mrs. Hedges), Angus MacKay (TV producer), Charles Hodgson (TV interviewer), Denise Coffey (1st operator).

PERCY'S PROGRESS (1974) (A. K. A.
"It's Not the Size That Counts")
Director: Ralph Thomas
Leigh Lawson (Percy), Elke Sommer
(Clarissa), Denholm Elliott (Emmanuel
Whitebread), Vincent Price (Stavos),
Judy Geeson (Dr. Fairweather), Milo
O'Shea (Dr. Klein), Julie Ege (Miss
Hanson), George Coulouris (Professor).

PERFECT WOMAN, THE (1949)
Director: Bernard Knowles
Patricia Roc (Penelope), Stanley Hollo-
way (Ramshead), Nigel Patrick (Roger
Cavendish), Miles Malleson (Prof.
Belmon), David Hurst (Wolfgang Winkel),
Irene Handl (Mrs. Butter), Fred Berger
(Farini), Constance Smith (receptionist),
Anita Bolster (Lady Diana), Pamela
Davis (Olga the Robot), Philipa Gill,
Noel Howlett, Patti Morgan.

PERILS OF NYOKA (1942) (A. K. A.
"Nyoka and the Tiger Man", "Nyoka
and the Lost Secrets of Hippocrates")
- serial in 15 episodes
Director: William Witney
Kay Aldridge (Nyoka), Clayton Moore
(Dr. Larry Grayson), Tris Coffin
(Torrini), Charles Middleton (Cassib),
William Benedict (Red), George Rena-
vent (Maghreb), Kenneth Duncan (Abou),
George Pembroke (John Spencer),
Robert Strange (Prof. Gordon), Lorna
Gray (Vultura), John Davidson (Lhoba),
George Lewis (Batan), John Bagni
(Ben Ali), Arvon Dale (Bedouin), Ken
Terrell (Ahmed), Forbes Murray (Prof.
Campbell), John Daheim, Duke Taylor,
Tom Steele, Iron Eyes Cody (Arabs),
Joe Garcia, Ken Terrell, Loren Riebe,
Duke Taylor, Henry Willis (guards),
Robert Barron (Sidi), Herbert Rawlinson
(Reynolds), Art Dupuis (Hassan), Emil
Van Horn (Satan), Pedro Regas (Ibra-
him), Leonard Hampton (Yussuf), Bud
Wolfe (Taureg leader), Steve Clemente,
Yakima Canutt, David Sharpe, Art
Dillard, Duke Green, Jack O'Shea,
Cy Slocum, George Suzanne, Jerry
Frank, Carey Loftin, George Plues,
Harry Smith, Dirk Thane (Tauregs),
Helen Thurston, Babe Defreest.

PERILS OF PARIS, THE (1924) (A. K. A.
"Terror")
Director: Edward Jose
Pearl White (Helen Aldrich), Robert
Lee (Roger Durant), Arlette Marchal
(Mrs. Gauthier), Henry Bandin (Prof.
Aldrich), Martin Mitchell (Paul Peret),
George Vermoyal (Erdman).

PERILS OF PAULINE, THE (1914) -
serial in 20 episodes
Director: Donald McKenzie &
Louis J. Gasnier
Pearl White (Pauline), Crane Wilbur
(Harry Marvin), Donald MacKenzie
(Blinky Bill), Paul Panzer (Raymond
Owen), Walter McGrail, Milton
Berle, Francis Carlyle, Eleanor
Woodruff, Edward Jose, Clifford
Bruce, Sam Ryan, Dan Courtney.

PERILS OF PAULINE, THE (1934) -
serial in 12 episodes
Chapters: 1. "The Guns of Doom",
2. "The Typhoon of Terror", 3. "The
Leopard Leaps", 4. "Trapped by
the Enemy", 5. "The Flaming Tomb",
6. "Pursued by Savages", 7. "Tracked
by the Enemy", 8. "Danger Depths",
9. "The Mummy Walks", 10. "The
Night Attack", 11. "Into the Flames",
& 12. "Confu's Sacred Secret".
Director: Ray Taylor
Evalyn Knapp (Pauline Hargrave),
Robert Allen (Robert Ward), John
Davidson (Dr. Bashan), Frank Lack-
teen (Fang), William Desmond (Prof.
Thompson), James Durkin (Prof.
Hargrave), Josef Swickard (Foreign
Consul), William Worthington (Ameri-
can Consul), Sonny Ray (Willis
Dodge), Pat O'Malley (aviator),
Adolph Muller (Captain).

PERILS OF PAULINE, THE (1967)
Director: Herbert B. Leonard
Pamela Austin (Pauline), Pat Boone
(George), Terry-Thomas (Stan
Martin), Edward Everett Horton
(Casper Coleman), Vito Scotti
(Frandise), Kurt Kasznar (Consul
General), Leon Askin (Commissar),
Hamilton (Camp Thorpe), Aram
Katcher (Vizier), Doris Packer
(Mrs. Carruthers), Rick Natoli
(Prince Benji), Max Kevlin (the Gor-
illa).

PERRY GRANT, AGENT OF IRON
(1966-Ital.) (A. K. A. "Perry
Grant, Agente di Ferro")
Director: Luigi Capuano/
Lewis King
Giacomo Rossi-Stuart, Peter Holden,
Marilu Tolo, Seyna Seyn, Umberto
D'Orsi.

PERSECUTION (1974) (A. K. A. "The
Terror of Sheba")
Director: Don Chaffey
Lana Turner (Carrie Masters), Ralph
Bates (David Masters), Trevor Howard

(Paul Bellamy), Olga Georges-Picot
(Monique Kalfon), Suzan Farmer
(Janie Masters), Patrick Allen (Ro-
bert Masters), Mark Weavers (young
David).

PETER IBBETSON (1935)
    Director: Henry Hathaway
Gary Cooper (Peter Ibbetson), John
Halliday (Duke of Towers), Ida Lupino
(Agnes), Ann Harding (Mary, Duchess
of Towers), Douglas Dumbrille (Dol.
Forsythe), Virginia Weidler (Mimsey),
Doris Lloyd (Mrs. Dorian), Dickie
Moore (Gogo), Christian Rub (Major
Duquesnois), Donald Meek (Mr. Slade),
Elsa Buchanan (Mme. Pasquier),
Gilbert Emery (Wilkins), Namara
(Mme. Ginghi), Elsa Prescott (Kath-
erine), Adrienne d'Ambricourt (nun),
Marcella Corday (maid), Theresa
Maxwell Conover (Sister of Mercy),
Colin Tapley (1st clerk), Clive Morgan
(2nd clerk), Ambrose Barker (3rd clerk),
Thomas Monk (4th clerk), Blanche
Craig (the Countess).

PETE'S DRAGON (1977)
    Director: Don Chaffey
Helen Reddy (Nora), Jim Dale (Dr.
Terminus), Mickey Rooney (Lampie),
Red Buttons (Hoagy), Sean Marshall
(Pete), Shelley Winters (Lena Gogan),
Jane Kean (Miss Taylor), Jim Backus
(the Mayor), Robert Easton (store
proprietor), Charlie Callas (voice of
Elliott), Charles Tyner (Merle),
Robert Foulk (Old Sea Captain), Jeff
Conoway (Willis), Gary Morgan (Gro-
ver), Walter Barnes (Captain), Cal
Bartlett (Paul), Roger Price (man
with visor), Ben Wrigley (egg man),
Joe Ross (cement man), Al Checco,
Jack Collins, Henry Slate (fisherman).

PETEY WHEATSTRAW (1977)
    Director: Cliff Roquemore
Rudy Ray Moore, Jimmy Lynch,
Eboni Wryte, G. Tito Shaw, Wildman
Steve.

PHANTASM (1979)
    Director: Don Coscarelli
Michael Baldwin (Mike), Bill Thornbury
(Jody), Reggie Bannister (Reggie),
Angus Scrimm (the Tall Man), Kathy
Lester (the Lady In Lavender), Terrie
Kalbus (granddaughter), Ken Jones
(caretaker), Lynn Eastman (Sally),
Susan Harper (girl friend), David
Arntzen (Toby), Bill Cone (Tommy),
Ralph Richmond (bartender), Laura Mann
(double lavender), Myrtle Scotton (maid),

Mary Ellen Shaw (fortune teller).

PHANTOM, THE (1922-Ger.)
    Director: F.W. Murnau
Alfred Abel, Lil Dagover, Aud Egede
Nissen, Lya de Putti, Grete Berger,
Frieda Richard, Karl Ettlinger.

PHANTOM, THE (1943) - serial in
    15 episodes
    Director: B. Reeves Eason
Tom Tyler (the Phantom/Godfrey
Prescott), Jeanne Bates (Diana),
Frank Shannon (Prof. Davidson),
Joe Devlin (Singapore Smith), Kenneth
MacDonald (Dr. Bremmer), Ernie
Adams (Rusty), Guy Kingsford (Byron
Andrews), John S. Bagni (Moku).

PHANTOM BARON, THE (1943)
    (A.K.A. "Le Baron Fantome")
    Director: Serge de Poligny
Alain Cuny (Herve), Jany Holt (Anne),
Jena Cocteau (Baron), Odette Joyeux
(Eify), Claude Samval (Alberic),
Alerme, P. Dorian, Andre Lefaur.

PHANTOM CREEPS, THE (1939) -
    serial in 12 episodes
Chapters: 1. "The Menacing Power",
2. "Death Stalks", 3. "Crashing
Towers", 4. "The Invisible Terror",
5. "Thundering Rails", 6. "The Iron
Monster", 7. "The Menacing Mist",
8. "Trapped in the Flames", 9.
"Speeding Doom", 10. "Phantom
Footprints", 11. "The Blast", & 12.
"To Destroy the World".
    Director: Ford Beebe & Saul
    A. Goodkind
Bela Lugosi (Dr. Alex Zorka), Robert
Kent (Capt. Bob West), Regis Toomey
(Jim Daly), Dorothy Arnold (Jean Drew),
Edward Van Sloan (Chief Jarvis),
Roy Barcroft (Parker), Eddie Acuff
(Mac), Charles King (Buck), Jack
C. Smith (Monk), Robert Blair (Smith),
Jerry Frank (Jones), Anthony Averill
(Rankin), Forrest Taylor (Black),
Edwin Stanley (Dr. Mallory), Dora
Clement (Ann Zorka), Karl Hackett
(Brown), Hugh Huntley (Perkins),
Lee J. Cobb, Willard Parker, Lane
Chandler.

PHANTOM EMPIRE, THE (1935)
    (A.K.A. "Radio Ranch", "Men with
    Steel Faces") - serial in 12 episodes
    Director: Otto Brower & B.
    Reeves Eason
Gene Autry (Gene), Frankie Darro
(Frankie), Betsy King Ross (Betsy),
Wheeler Oakman (Argo), Dorothy

Christy (Queen Tika), Smiley Burnette
(Oscar), Charles R. French (Mal),
Frank Glendon (Prof. Beetson), War-
ner Richmond (Rab), William Moore
(Pete), Edward Piel, Sr. (Dr. Coo-
per), Jack Carlyle (Saunders), Fran-
kie Marvin (Frankie), Stanley G.
Blystone, Fred Burns, Jay Wilsey,
Henry Hall, Wally Wales, Jim Corey,
Frank Ellis, Richard Talmadge (Mu-
ranians).

PHANTOM FIEND, THE (1932) (A. K. A.
   "The Lodger")
   Director: Maurice Elvey
Elizabeth Allan (Daisy Bunting), Jack
Hawkins (Joe Martin), Ivor Novello
(Angeloff), Kynaston Reeves (Bob
Mitchell), Barbara Everest (Mrs.
Bunting), A. W. Bascomb (Mr. Bunting),
Peter Gawthorne (Lord Southcliff),
Shayle Gardner (Detective Snell).

PHANTOM FOE, THE (1920) - serial
   in 15 episodes
   Director: Bertram Millhauser
Juanita Hansen, Warner Oland, William
N. Bailey, Wallace McCutcheon, Harry
Semels.

PHANTOM FROM SPACE (1952)
   Director: W. Lee Wilder
Ted Cooper (Lt. Hazen), Noreen
Nash (Barbara Randall), James Seay
(Major Andrews), Harry Landers
(Lt. Bowers), Rudolph Anders (Dr.
Wyatt), Jack Daly (Wakeman), Dic
Sands (the Phantom), Michael Mark,
Jim Bannon.

PHANTOM FROM 10,000 LEAGUES,
   THE(1955)
   Director: Dan Milner
Kent Taylor (Ted Baxter), Cathy
Downs (Lois Kingg), Michael Whalen
(Prof. King), Helene Stanton (Wanda),
Vivi Janis (Ethel), Philip Pine (George
Thomas), Rodney Bell (Bill Grant),
Pierce Lyden (Andy), Michael Garth
(Sheriff).

PHANTOM IN SPACE (1978)
   see Television: Battlestar Galactica
   (1978-79)

PHANTOM KILLER (1942)
   Director: William Beaudine
Dick Purcell (Edward Clark), Joan
Woodbury (Barbara Mason), John
Hamilton (John G. Harrison), Mantan
Moreland (Nicodemus), J. Farrell
MacDonald (Police Captain), Kenneth
Harlan (Lt. Brady), Warren Hymer

(Sgt. Corrigan), George Lewis (Kramer),
Elliott Sullivan (Dave Rigby), Gayne
Whitman (District Attorney), Karl
Hackett, Harry Depp.

PHANTOM OF CRESTWOOD, THE
   (1932)
   Director: J. Walter Ruben
Karen Morley (Jenny Wren),
Ricardo Cortez (Gary Curtis), H. B.
Warner (Priani Andes), Gavin
Gordon (William Jones), Anita
Louise (Esther Wren), Ivan Simpson
(Henry T. Herrick), George E.
Stone (the Cat), Robert Elliott (Tall
Man), Robert McWade (Herbert
Walcott), Mary Duncan (Dorothy
Mears), Pauline Frederick (Faith
Andes), Aileen Pringle (Mrs.
Walcott), Richard Gallagher (Eddie
Mack), Sam Hardy (Pete Harris),
Hilda Vaughn (Carter), Matty Kemp
(Frank Andes), Tom Douglas.

PHANTOM OF HOLLYWOOD, THE
   (TVM-1974) - 2-12-74
   Director: Gene Levitt
Jack Cassidy (Otto Varner/Carl
Varner), Skye Aubrey (Randy Cross),
Jackie Coogan (Joanthan), Peter
Haskell (Ray Burns), John Ireland
(Lt. Gifford), Peter Lawford
(Roger Cross), Corinne Calvet
(Mrs. Wickes), Broderick Crawford
(Capt. O'Neal), Kent Taylor (Wickes),
Regis Toomey (Joe, the watchman),
Bill Williams (Fogel), Billy Halop
(studio engineer), Fredd Wayne
(Clyde), John Lupton (Al), Gary
Burton (Duke), Carl Byrd, Bill
Stout, George Nolan, Edward
Cross, Damon Douglas.

PHANTOM OF PARIS, THE (1931)
   Director: John S. Robertson
John Gilbert (Cheri-Bibi), Leila
Hyams (Cecile), Lewis Stone
(Costaud), C. Aubrey Smith
(Bourrelier), Ian Keith (Marquise
de Touchais), Jean Hersholt (Her-
man), Alfred Hickman (Dr. Gorin),
Natalie Moorhead (Vera).

PHANTOM OF SOHO, THE (1963-
   Ger.) (A. K. A. "Das Phantom
   von Soho")
   Director: Franz Josef
   Gottlieb
Dieter Borsche (Hugh Patton),
Werner Peters (Dr. Dalmar), Otto
Waldis (Liverspot), Barbara
Ruetting (Clarinda Smith), Hans
Sohnker (Sir Philip), Peter Vogel

(Hallam), Hans Lielsen (Lord Malhouse), Elisabeth Flickenschildt (Joanna), Helge Sommerfeld (Corinna Smith), Stanislav Ledinek (Gilard), Emil Feldmar (Daddy), Hans W. Hamacher (Captain), Harald Sawade (Charlis).

PHANTOM OF THE AIR, THE (1932) - serial in 12 episodes
Chapters: 1. "The Great Air Meet", 2. "Secret of the Desert", 3. "The Avenging Phantom", 4. "Battle of the Clouds", 5. "Terror of the Heights", 6. "The Wild Ride", 7. "Jaws of Death", 8. "Aflame in the Sky", 9. "The Attack", 10. "Runaway Plane", 11. "In the Enemy's Hands",' &12. "Safe Landing".
Director: Ray Taylor
Tom Tyler (Bob Raymond), LeRoy Mason (Mort Crome), Walter Brennan (Skid), William Desmond (Mr. Edmunds), Gloria Shea (Mary Edmunds), Hugh Enfield (Blade), Jennie Cramer (Marie), Sidney Bracey (Munsa), Cecil Kellogg (Joe).

PHANTOM OF THE CONVENT, THE (1934-Mex) (A.K.A. "El Fantasma del Convento")
Director: Fernando de Fuentes
Marta Roel, Carlos Villatoro, Enrique del Campo, Paco Martinez, Jose Rocha, Victorio Blanco.

PHANTOM OF THE MOULIN ROUGE, THE (1925-Fr.) (A.K.A. "Le Fantome du Moulin Rouge")
Director: Rene Clair
Albert Prejean, Jose Davert, George Vaultier.

PHANTOM OF THE OPERA, THE (1925)
Director: Rupert Julian
Lon Chaney, Sr. (Erik, the Phantom), Mary Philbin (Christine Daae), Norman Kerry (Raoul de Chagny), Snitz Edwards (Florine Papillon), Gibson Gowland (Simon), Arthur Edmund Carewe (the Persian), Edward Cecil (Faust), Virginia Pearson (Carlotta), Edith Yorke (Mamma Valerius), Bernard Siegel (Joseph Buquet), Alexander Bevani (Mephisto), John Miljan (Valentine), Edward Martindel (Phillippe de Chagny), Anton Vaverka (the Prompter), Olive Ann Alcorn (La Sorelli), Grace Marvin (Martha), Bruce Covington (M. Monacharimn), George B. Williams (M. Richard), Cesar

Gravina (retiring manager), Chester Conklin.

PHANTOM OF THE OPERA, THE (1943)
Director: Arthur Lubin
Claude Rains (Enrique Claudin), Nelson Eddy (Anatole Carron), Susanna Foster (Christine Dubois), Edgar Barrier (Raoul de Chagny), Steven Geray (Vercheres), Barbara Everest (the Aunt), Frank Puglia (Villeneuve), Fritz Feld (Lacours), Hume Cronyn (Gerard), Miles Mander (M. Pleyel), J. Edward Bromberg (Amoit), Fritz Leiber (Franz Liszt), Jane Farrar (Biancarolli), Gladys Blake (Jennie), Hans Herbert (Marcel), Leo Carillo, Kate Drain Lawson, Rosina Galli, Paul Marion.

PHANTOM OF THE OPERA, THE (1961)
Director: Terence Fisher
Herbert Lom (the Phantom), Edward De Souza (Harry Hunter), Heather Sears (Christine Charles), Michael Gough (Lord Ambrose D'Arcy), Marne Maitland (Xavier), John Harvey (Vickers), Ian Wilson (Dwarf), Michael Ripper (cabby), Patrick Troughton (rat catcher), Miles Malleson (cabby), Martin (Rossi), Harold Goodwin (Bill), Thorley Walters (Latimer), Liam Redmond, Renee Houston, Miriam Karlin.

PHANTOM OF THE OPERETTA, THE (1955-Arg.) (A.K.A. "El Fantasma de la Opereta")
Director: Enrique Carreras
Amelita Vargas, Alfredo Barbieri, Gogo Andreu, Tono Andreu, Inez Fernandez.

PHANTOM OF THE OPERETTA, THE (1960-Mex.) (A.K.A. "El Fantasma de la Opereta")
Director: Fernando Cortes
Tin Tan, Loco Valdez, Ana Luisa Peluffo, Vitola, Marcelo, Luis Aldaz.

PHANTOM OF THE PARADISE (1974)
Director: Brian De Palma
Paul Williams (Swan), William Finley (Winslow Leech), Jessica Harper (Phoenix), Gerrit Graham (Beef), George Memmoli (Philbin), Jeffrey Comanor (the Juicy Fruits),

Archie Hahn (the Beach Bums), Harold Oblong (the Undeads).

PHANTOM OF THE RUE MORGUE, THE (1953)
Director: Roy Del Ruth
Karl Malden (Dr. Marais), Steve Forrest (Paul Dupin), Patricia Medina (Jeanette Rovere), Claude Dauphin (Insp. Bonnard), Anthony Caruso (Jacques), Allyn McLerie (Yvonne), Merv Griffin (George Brevert), Paul Richards (Rene), Erin O'Brien Moore (wardrobe woman), Dolores Dorn (Camille), Veola Vonn (Arlette), Rolfe Sedan (Le Bon), Charlie Gemora (the Ape), Frank Lackteen, Henry Kulky.

PHANTOM PLANET (1961)
Director: William Marshall
Dean Fredericks (Capt. Frank Chapman), Coleen Gray (Liara), Dolores Faith (Zehta), Francis X. Bushman (Sesom), Anthony Dexter (Herron), Al Jarvis (Judge Eden), Richard Kiel (the Solarite), Richard Weber (Lt. Makonnen), Dick Haynes (Col. Lansfield), Michael Marshall (Lt. White), Mel Curtis (Lt. Cutler), Earl McDaniel (Pilot Leonard), John Herrin (Capt. Beecher), Jimmy Weldon (Navigator Webb), Lori Lyons (radar officer), Akemi Tani (communications officer).

PHANTOM RAIDERS (1940) (A. K. A. "Nick Carter In Panama")
Director: Jacques Tourneur
Walter Pidgeon (Nick Carter), Florence Rice (Cora Barnes), Joseph Schildkraut (Al Taurez), John Carroll (John Ramsell, Jr.), Nat Pendleton (Gunboat Jacklin), Donald Meek (Bartholomew), Cecil Kellaway (Franklin Morris), Alec Craig (Andy MacMillan), Steffi Duna (Dolores), Dwight Frye (Eddie Anders), Matthew Boulton (John Rmasell, Sr.), Thomas Ross (Dr. Grisson).

PHANTOM SPEAKS, THE (1944)
Director: John English
Richard Arlen (Matt Fraser), Lynne Roberts (Joan Renwick), Stanley Ridges (Dr. Paul Renwick), Tom Powers (Harvey Bogardus), Pierre Watkin (Charlie Davis), Jonathan Hale (Owen McAllister), Ralf Harolde (Frankie Teel), Marian Martin (Betty Hanzel), Garry Owen (Louis Fabian), Charlotte Wynters (Cornelia Willmont), Doreen McCann (Mary Fabian).

PHANTOM THIEF, THE (1946)
Director: D. Ross Lederman

Chester Morris (Boston Blackie), Jeff Donnell, Richard Lane, George E. Stone, Wilton Graff, Marvin Miller, Joseph Crehan, Forbes Murray, Frank Sully, Dusty Anderson, Murray Alper.

PHANTOM TOLLBOOTH, THE (1968) - animated
Director: Chuck Jones, Abe Levitow & David Monahan
Butch Patrick. Voices: Mel Blanc, Hans Conried, Les Tremayne, Daws Butler, Larry Thor, June Foray.

PHANTOM WAGON, THE (1939-Fr.)
(A. K. A. "La Charrette Fantome")
Director: Julian Duvivier
Pierre Fresnay, Marie Bell, Mita Parley, Louis Javet, Palau, Robert Le Vigan.

PHARMACEUTICAL HALLUCINATIONS OR THE TRICK OF POTARD (1908-Fr.) (A. K. A. "Hallucinations Pharmaceutiques ou Le Truc du Potard")
Director: Georges Melies

PHAROAH'S CURSE, THE (1957)
Director: Lee Sholem
Mark Dana (Captain Storm), Ziva Rodann (Simira), Diana Brewster (Sylvia Quinten), George Niese (Robert Quentin), Ben Wright (Walter Andrews), Kurt Katch (Hans Brecht), Terence de Marney (Sgt. Smollett), Guy Prescott (Dr. Michael Farady), Robert Fortin (Claude Beauchamp), Richard Peel (Sgt. Gromley), Alvaro Guillot (Numar), Ralph Clanton.

PHASE IV (1973)
Director: Saul Bass
Nigel Davenport (Hubbs), Michael Murphy (Lesko), Lynne Frederick (Kendra), Alan Gifford (Mr. Eldridge), Helen Horton (Mrs. Eldridge), Robert Henderson (Clete).

PHOBIA (1980)
Director: John Huston
Paul Michael Glaser (Dr. Ross), John Colicos (Barnes), Alexandra Stewart (Barbara), Susan Hogan (Jenny), Robert O'Ree (Bubba), David Eisner (Johnny), David Bolt (Henry), Lisa Langlois (Laura), Kenneth Welsh (Sgt. Wheeler), Patricia Collins (Dr. Toland), Gwen Thomas (Dr. Clemens), Neil Vipond (Dr. Clegg), Marian Waldman (Mrs. Casey), Paddy Campanero, Peter Hicks, John

Stoneham, Gerry Salsberg, Joan Fowler,
Terry Martin, Janine Cole, Wendy
Jewel, Diane Lasko, Ken Anderson,
Karen Pike, Coleen Embry.

PHOENIX, THE (1979)
    Director: Richard Caan
Richard Kiel, Betty Noonan.

PHOENIX, THE (TVM-1981) - 4-26-81
    Director: Douglas Hickox
Judson Scott (Bennu), Shelley Smith
(Noel Marshall), E.G. Marshall (Dr.
Ward Frazier), Fernando Allende
(Diego De Varga), Daryl Anderson
(Dr. Cliff Davis), Jimmy Mair (Tim),
Hersha Parady (Lynn), Wayne Storm
(patrolman), Jim Malinda (croupier),
Paul Marin (anesthesiologist), Bret
Williams (technician), Patricia Conklin
(surgical nurse), Terry Jastrow (hood),
Angus Duncan, Stanley Kamel, Lyman
Ward.

PICNIC AT HANGING ROCK (1979-
    Australia)
    Director: Peter Weir
Rachel Roberts (Mrs. Appleyard), Dom-
inic Guard (Michael Fitzhubert), Helen
Morse (Dianne De Poiters), Jacki
Weaver (Minnie), Kristy Child (Dora
Lumley), Vivean Gray (Miss McCraw),
Anne Lambert (Miranda), Karen Robson
(Irma), Christine Schuler (Edith), Jane
Vallis (Mairon), Margaret Nelson
(Sara), John Jarratt (Albert), Martin
Vaughan (Ben Hussey), Ingrid Mason
(Rosamund), Jack Fegan (Doc McKenzie),
Wyn Roberts (Sgt. Bumpher), Frank
Gunnell (Edward Whitehead), Garry
McDonald (Jim Jones).

PICNIC ON THE GRASS (1966-Fr.)
    (A.K.A. "Le Dejeuner sur l'herbe")
    Director: Jean Renoir
Paul Meurisse, Catherine Rouvel,
Jean Pierre Granval, Fernand Sardou,
Ingrid Nordine, Jean Claudio.

PICTURE MOMMY DEAD (1966)
    Director: Bert I. Gordon
Don Ameche (Edward Shelley), Martha Hyer
(Francene Shelly), Zsa Zsa Gabor (Jessica
Shelley), Susan Gordon (Susan Shelley),
Maxwell Reed (Anthony), Wendell Corey
(Clayborn), Signe Hasso (Sister Rene),
Anna Lee (Elsie Kornwald), Robert
Sherman, Paul Clark.

PICTURE OF DORIAN GRAY, THE
    (1916)
    Director: Fred W. Durrant
Henry Victor; Pat O'Malley, Sydney

Bland, Dorothy Fane, Jack Jordan,
Douglas Cox, Miriam Ferris, A.B.
Imeson.

PICTURE OF DORIAN GRAY, THE
    (1917-Ger.) (A.K.A. "Das
    Bildnis des Dorian Gary")
    Director: Richard Oswald

PICTURE OF DORIAN GRAY, THE
    (1945)
    Director: Albert Lewin
George Sanders (Lord Henry Wotton),
Hurd Hatfield (Dorian Gray), Angela
Lansbury (Sibyl Vane), Lowell Gil-
more (Basil Hallward), Donna Reed
(Gladys Hallward), Peter Lawford
(David Stone), Richard Fraaer
(James Vane), Robert Greig (Sir
Thomas), Miles Mander (Sir Robert
Bentley), Billy Bevan (Malvolio
Jones Chairman), Morton Lowry
(Adrian Singleton), Lydia Bilbrook
(Mrs. Vane), Lillian Bond (Kate),
Douglas Walton (Allen Campbell),
Mary Forbes (Lady Agatha), Moyna
MacGill (Duchess), Renie Carson
(young French woman), Bernard
Gorcey, Arthur Shields, Andrew
Branham, Lumsden Hare, Reginald
Owen.

PICTURE OF DORIAN GRAY, THE
    (TVM-1973) - 4-23-73 & 4-24-73
    Director: Dan Curtis
Shane Briant (Doria Gray), Nigel
Davenport (Harry Wotten), Fionuala
Flanagan (Felicia), Charles Aidman
(Basil Hallward), Linda Kelsey
(Beatrice), Vanessa Howard (Sibyl
Vane), Brendan Dillon (Victor),
John Karlen (Alan Cmpbell), Dixie
Marquis (Madame De Ferrol).

PIED PIPER, THE (1972-Brit./Ger.)
    Director: Jacques Demy
Donald Pleasence (Baron), Donovan
(the Piper), Jack Wild (Gavin), John
Hurt (Franz), Diana Dors (Frau
Poppendick), Roy Kinnear (Burgomei-
ster), Michael Hordern (Melius),
Cathryn Harrison (Lisa), Keith Buckley.

PIED PIPER OF HAMELIN, THE
    (1917-Ger.) (A.K.A. "Der Rat-
    tenfanger", "The Ratcatcher")
    Director: Paul Wegener
Paul Wegener, Lyda Salmonova,
Wilhelm Diegelmann, Jakob Tiedtke.

PIGSTY (1969-Ital./Fr.) (A.K.A.
    "Porcile", "Pigpen")
    Director: Pier Paolo Pasolini

Jean-Pierre Leaud (Julian), Pierre Clementi (Cannibal), Ugo Tognazzi (Herdhitze), Alberto Lionello (Klotz), Margarita Lozano (Mrs. Klotz), Anne Wiazemsky (Ida), Ninetto Davoli (Maracchione), Marco Ferreri (Hans), Franco Citty (2nd Cannibal).

PILLOW OF DEATH (1945)
    Director: Wallace Fox
Lon Chaney, Jr. (Wayne Fletcher), Brenda Joyce (Donna Kincaid), J. Edward Bromberg (Julian Julian), Clara Blandick (Belle Kincaid), George Cleveland (Sam Kincaid), Wilton Graff (Capt. McCracken), Victoria Horne (Vivian Fletcher), Rosalind Ivan (Amelia Kincaid), Bernard B. Thomas (Bruce Malone), Fern Emmet (Mrs. Williams), J. Farrell MacDonald (Sexton).

PINK FLAMINGOS (1974)
    Director: John Waters
Divine (Divine/Babs Johnson), David Lochary (Raymond Marble), Mink Stole (Connie Marble), Mary Vivian Pierce (Cotton), Edith Massey (Mama Edie), Danny Mills (Crackers), Cookie Mueller (Cookie), Channing Wilroy (Channing), Paul Swift (Eggman), Susan Walsh (1st kidnapped girl), Linda Olgeirson (2nd kidnapped girl).

PINK PANTHER STRIKES AGAIN, THE (1976)
    Director: Blake Edwards
Peter Sellers (Insp. Clouseau), Herbert Lom (Dreyfus), Colin Blakely (Alec Drummond), Leonard Rossiter (Quinlin), Burt Kwouk (Kate), Lesley-Anne Down (Olga), Marne Maitland (Deputy Commissioner), Richard Vernon (Dr. Fassbender), Andre Maranne (Farncois), Michael Robbins (Jarvis), Dick Crockett (President), Briony McRoberts (Margo Fassbender), Byron Kane (Secretary of State), Omar Shariff (Egyptian assassin).

PINOCCHIO IN OUTER SPACE (1965- U. S. /Belg.) (A. K. A. "Pinocchio dans l'Espace") - animated
    Director: Ray Goossens
Voices: Arnold Stang, Conard Jameson, Peter Lazar, Cliff Owens, Minerva Pious, Mavis Mims, Kever Kennedy.

PIRANHA (1978)
    Director: Joe Dante
Bradford Dillman (Grogan), Heather Menzies (Maggie McDeown), Barbara Steele (Dr. Mengers), Kevin McCarthy (Dr. Hoak), Dick Miller (Buck Gardner), Keenan Wynn (Jack), Bruce Gordon (Col. Waxman), Paul Bartel (Dumont), Richard Deacon (Earl Lyon), Barry Brown (trooper), Guich Koock (pitchman), Melody Thomas (Laura), Belinda Balaski (Betsy), Shannon Collins (Suzie), Janie Squire (Barbara), Shawn Nelson (Whitney), Roger Richman (David), Bill Smillie (Jailer), Eric Henshaw (father in canoe), Jack Pauleson (man in canoe), Robert Vinson (soldier), Virginia Dunnam (girl).

PIT, THE (1980) (A. K. A. "Teddy")
    Director: Lew Lehman
Jeannie Elias, Sammy Snyders.

PIT AND THE PENDULEM, THE (1961)
    Director: Roger Corman
Vincent Price (Nicholas Medina), Barbara Steele (Elizabeth Barnard Medina), John Kerr (Francis Barnard), Luana Anders (Catherine Medina), Anthony Carbone (Dr. Charles Leon), Patrick Westwood (Maximillian), Lynne Bernay (Maria), Mary Menzies (Isabella), Charles Victor (Barto-lome), Larry Turner (Nicholas as a child).

PLACE OF ONE'S OWN, A (1944)
    Director: Bernrad Knowles
James Mason (Mr. Smedhurst), Barbara Mullen (Mrs. Smedhurst), Dennis Price (Dr. Selbie), Margaret Lockwood (Annette), Helen Haye (Mrs. Manning-Puthorn), Dulcie Gray (Sarah), Michael Shepley (Mr. Manning-Puthorn), Gus McNaughten, Ernest Thesigner, Helen Goss, O. B. Clarence, Moore Marriott, Edie Martin.

A PLACE TO DIE (TVM-1975)
    Director: Peter Jeffries
Alexandra Hay (Tessa Nelson), Bryan Marshall (Dr. Bruce Nelson), John Turner (Bart), Glynn Edwards (Lob), Sydney Bromley (Seth), Sally Stephens (Jill), Jenny Laird (Nan), Juan Moreno (Ncik), Georgine Anderson (Jane), Graham Weston (Dan), John Gabriel (Dr. Sharp), Lila Kaye (Bess Tarling), Peggy Ann Wood (Belle), Bill Ward (Job), John Flint (Police Inspector), Arnold Ridley (1st old man), Harold Bennett (2nd old man), Elsie Wagstaff (old woman), Lewis Wilson (policeman).

PLAGUE (1978) (A.K.A. "M3: The
Gemini Strain")
Director: Ed Hunt
Daniel Pilon (Bill), Kate Reid (Jessica),
Celine Lomez (teacher), Michael J.
Reynolds.

PLAGUE OF THE ZOMBIES, THE (1965)
Director: John Gilling
Andre Morell (Sir James Forbes),
John Carson (Clive Hamilton), Diane
Clare (Sylvia Forbes), Alexander Davion
(Harry Denver), Jacqueline Pearce
(Alice Thompson), Brook Williams
(Dr. Peter Thompson), Marcus Ham-
mond (Martinus), Michael Ripper
(Sgt. Swift), Roy Royston (Vicar),
Dennis Chinnery (Constable Christian),
Jerry Verno (the landlord), Louis
Mahoney (servant), Ben Aris (John
Martinus, the zombie in the mine),
Jolyan Booth (coachman), Del Watson,
Peter Diamond (zombies), Timy Cond-
roy, Norman Mann, Bernard Egan,
Francis Wiley (Young Bloods).

PLANET EARTH (TVM-1974) - 4-23-74
Director: Marc Daniels
John Saxon (Dylan Hunt), Janet Mragolin
(Harper-Smythe), Ted Cassidy (Isiah),
Diana Muldaur (Marg), Majel Barrett
(Yuloff), Christopher Cary (Baylock),
Johana De Winter (Villar), James D.
Antonio, Jr. (Dr. O'Connor), Claire
Brennan (Delba), Sally Kemp (Treece),
Corrine Camacho (Bronta), John Quade
(Kreeg Commandant), Sarah Chattin
(Thetis), Raymond Sutton (Kreeg Cap-
tain), Rai Tasco (R. Kimbridge), Joan
Crosby (Kyla), Aron Kincaid (Gorda),
James Bacon (Bartha), Patricia Smith
(Skylar).

PLANET OF STORMS (1962-Sov.) (A.K.A.
"Planeta Burg", "Cosmonauts on
Venus")
Director: Pavel Klushantsev
Kyunna Ignatova, Gennadi Vernov,
Giorgi Zhonov, Vladimir Yemelianov,
Yurie Sarantsev.

PLANET OF THE APES (1968)
Director: Franklin J. Schaffner
Charlton Heston (George Taylor), Roddy
McDowall (Cornelius), Kim Hunter
(Dr. Zira), Maurice Evans (Dr. Zaius),
James Whitmore (Assembly President),
James Daly (Honorious), Lou Wagner
(Lucius), Linda Harrison (Nova),
Woodrow Parfrey (Maximus), Buck
Kartalian (Julius), Wright King (Dr.
Galen), Jeff Burton (Dodge), Norman
Burton (Hunt Leader), Paul Lambert

(Minister), Dianne Stanley (female
astronaut), Robert Gunner (Landon),
Priscilla Boyd (1st human), Jane
Ross (human), Robert Lombardo,
Chuck Fisher, Eldon Burke, Joseph
Anthony, Dave Rodgers, John
Quijada, Bill Graeff, Army Archerd
(gorillas), Felix Silla (child gorilla),
Billy Curtis, Jerry Maren, Buddy
Douglas, Frank Delfino, Harry
Monty, Cass Martin, Smokey Ro-
berds, Norma Jean Kron, George
Saski, David Chow (chimps).

PLANET OF THE DINOSAURS (1978)
Director: James Shea
James Whitworth (Jim), Louie Lawless
(Lee), Pamela Bottaro (Nyla),
Charlotte Speer (Charlotte).

PLANET OF THE VAMPIRES (1965-
Ital./Span.) (A.K.A. "Terrore
Nello Spazio", "Terror from Space",
"Planet of Terror", "The Demon
Planet", "Outlaw Planet", "Haunted
Planet")
Director: Mario Bava
Barry Sullivan (Capt. Mark Markary),
Norma Bengell (Sanya), Evi Marandi
(Tiona), Angel Aranda (Wess),
Fernadno Villena (Karan), Stelio
Candelli (Mud), Mario Morales (Eldon),
Massimo Righi (Nordeg), Franco
Andrei (Garr), Ivan Rassimov (Kell),
Alberto Cevenini (Wan), Rico Boido
(Keir),

PLANETS AGAINST US (1961-Ital./Fr.)
(A.K.A. "I Pianeti Contro di
Noi", "Le Monstre Aux Yeux Vert",
"The Monster with Green Eyes",
"Hands of a Killer", "Man with
the Yellow Eyes")
Director: Romano Ferrara
Michel Lemoine (Branco), Jany Clair
(Audrey), Maria Paluzzi (Marina),
Marco Guglielmi, Otello Toso, Piero
Palermini, Peter Dane, Jacopo
Tecchio.

PLAN 9 FROM OUTER SPACE (1956)
(A.K.A. "Grave Robbers from
Outer Space")
Director: Edward D. Wood, Jr.
Bela Lugosi (Ghoul Man), Lyle Talbot
(Gen. Roberts), Mona McKinnon
(Paula Trent), Gregory Walcott (Jeff
Trent), Tom Keene (Col. Edwards),
Tor Johnson (Insp. Clay), Maila
'Vampira' Nurmi (Ghoul Girl), Dudley
Manlove (Eros), Joanne Lee (Tanna),
Duke Moore (Lt. Harper), John
Breckinridge (the Ruler), Criswell

(Narrator), Dr. Tom Mason (Lugosi's double), Paul Marco, Conrad Brook.

PLAYGIRLS AND THE VAMPIRE (1960-Ital.) (A. K. A. "L'Ultima Preda del Vampiro", "The Last Prey of the Vampire", "Curse of the Vampire")
Director: Piero Regnoli
Walter Brandi (Count Gabor Kernassy), Lyla Rocco, Alfredo Rizzo, Mario Giovannini, Tilde Damiani.

PLAY MISTY FOR ME (1971)
Director: Clint Eastwood
Clint Eastwood (Dave), Jessica Walter (Evelyn Draper), Donna Mills (Tobie Williams), John Larch (Sgt. McCallum), Jack Ging (Dr. Dewan), James McEachin (Al Monte), Irene Hervey (Madge Brenner), Clarice Taylor (Birdie), Duke Everts (Jay Jay).

PLEASE DON'T EAT MY MOTHER (1972)
Director: Carl Monson
Buck Kartalian (Henry Fudd), Lyn Lundgren (Henry's mother), Rene Bond (the new widow), Alicia Friedland (the hooker), Dash Fremont (flower store owner), Flora Wiesel, Adam Blari, David Curtis.

PLEASE, DON'T FIRE THE CANNON (1965-Ital. /Span.) (A. K. A. "Per Piacere, Non Sparate Col Cannon")
Director: Mario Caiano
Frank Wolff, Rossella Como, Gerald Landry, Claudio Gora, Jesus Puente.

PLUCKED (1967-Ital. /Fr.) (A. K. A. "La Morte Ha Fatto L'Ouvo", "Death Has Laid an Egg", "A Curious Way to Love")
Director: Giulio Questi
Gina Lollobrigida, Jean-Louis Trintignant, Ewa Aulin, Renato Romano, Giulio Donnini, Jean Sobieski.

PLUMBER, THE (1980-Australia)
Director: Peter Weir
Judy Morris (Jill Cowper), Robert Coleby (Brain Cowper), Ivar Kants (Max, the plumber), Candy Raymond (Meg), Henri Szeps (department head).

PLUNDER (1922) - serial in 15 episodes
Chapters: 1. "The Bandaged Man", 2. "Held By the Enemy", 3. "The Hidden Thing", 4. "Ruin", 5. "To Beat a Knave", 6. "Heights of Hazard", 7. "Mocked from the Grave", 8. "The Human Target", 9. "Game Clear Through", 10. "Against Time", 11. "Spunk", 12. "Un-

der the Floor", 13. "The Swamp of Lost Souls", 14. "The Madman", & 15. "A King's Ransom"
Director· George B. Seitz
Pearl White, Harry Semels,, Warren Krech, Tom McIntyre, William Nally, Wally Oettel, Edward J. Pool.

POINT OF TERROR (1971)
Director: Alex Nicol
Peter Carpenter (Tony Trelos), Dyanne Thorne (Andrea), Lory Hansen (Helayne), Paula Micthell (Sally), Joel Marston (Martin), Leslie Simms (Fran), Roberta Robson (1st wife), Dana Diamond (barmaid), Al Dulnap (bartender), Ernest Charles (detective), Tony Kent (priest).

POISON PEN, THE (1919)
Director: Edwin August
June Elvidge (Allayne Filbert), Earl Metcalfe (David Alden), Joe Smiley (Bishop Filbert), Marion Barney (Mrs. Filbert), Jeanne Loew (Marion Stanley), George Bunny (Sims), Irving Brooks (Johnson), John M. Sainpolis (Dr. McKenna), J. Arthur Young (Granville Walters), Henry West (Dorgan), Marguerite Gale (Mrs. Wells), Charles Mackay (Morton Wells), Dan Comfort (boy).

POLTERGEIST (1982)
Director: Tobe Hooper
JoBeth Williams (Dianne Freeling), Craig T. Nelson (Steve Freeling), Beatrice Straight (Dr. Lesh), Dominique Dunne (Dana Freeling), Oliver Robins (Robbie Freeling), Heather O'Rourke (Carol Anne Freeling), Richard Lawson (Ryan), Zelda Rubinstein (Tangina), Martin Casella (Marty), James Daren (Teague), Michael McManus (Tuthill), Virginia Kiser (Mrs. Tuthill).

POOR DEVIL (TVM-1973) - 2-14-73
Director: Robert Scheerer
Sammy Davis, Jr. (Sammy), Jack Klugman (Burnett Emerson), Christopher Lee (Lucifer), Madlyn Rhue (Frances Emerson), Adam West (Crawford), Gino Conforti (Bligh), Emily Yancy (Chelsea), Ken Lynch, Alan Manson, Buddy Lester, Jo DeWinter, Owen Bush, Byron Webster, Stephen Coit.

POPEYE (1980)
Director: Robert Altman

Robin Williams (Popeye), Shelly Duvall (Olive Oyl), Ray Walston (Poopdeck Pappy), Paul L. Smith (Bluto), Richard Libertini (Geezil), MacIntyre Dixon (Cole Oyl), Roberta Maxwell (Nana Oyl), Donovan Scott (Castor Oyl), Allan Nicholls (Rough House), Paul Dooley (Wimpy), Donald Moffat (the Taxman), Bill Irwin (Ham Gravy), Wesley Ivan Hurt (Swee'pea), Peter Bray (Oxblood Oxheart), Linda Hunt (Mrs. Oxheart), David McCharen (Harry Hotcash), Paul Zegler (Mayor Stonefeller), Robert Fortier (Bill Barnacle), Sharon Kinney (Cherry), Susan Kingsley (LaVerne), Pamela Burrell (Mrs. Stonefeller), Ray Cooper (Preacher), Geoff Hoyle, Larry Pisoni, Michael Christensen, Karen McCormick, Wayne Robson, Carlo Pellegrini, Noel Parenti, John Bristol, Patty Katz, Nathalie Blossom, Carlos Brown, Hovey Burgess, Julie Janney, Dianne Shaffer, Dennis Franz, Ned Dowd, Roberto Messina.

POTRAIT OF JENNIE (1948) (A. K. A. "Tidal Wave", "Jennie")
    Director: William Dieterle
Jennifer Jones (Jennie Appleton), Joseph Cotten (Eben Adams), Ethel Barrymore (Spinney), Lillian Gish (Mother Mary of Mercy), Cecil Kellaway (Matthews), Albert Sharpe (Moore), Henry Hull (Eke), David Wayne (Gus), Clem Bevans (Capt. Calib Cobb), Felix Bressart (Pete), Florence Bates (Mrs. Jekes), Maude Simmons (Clara Morgan).

PORT SINISTER (1952)
    Director: Harold Daniels
James Warren (Tony Ferris), Lynn Roberts (Jean Hunter), Paul Cavanagh (John Kolvac), William Schallert (Collins), Helene Winston (Florence), Houes Peters, Jr. (Jim Gerry), Robert Bice (Burt), Ken Terrell (Hollis), Eric Colmar (Christie), E. Guy Hearn (Capt. Crawley), Merrit Stone (Nick), Dayton Loomis (Mr. Lennox), Norman Budd (Akers), Marjorie Stapp (technician), Anne Kimball (nurse), Charles Victor (Coast Guard Lieutenant).

POSSESSED (1947)
    Director: Curtis Bernhardt
Joan Crawford (Louise Howell), Van Heflin (David Sutton), Raymond Massey (Dean Graham), Geraldine Brooks (Carol Graham), Stanley Ridges (Dr. Harvey Williard), John Ridgley (Harder), Moroni

Olsen (Dr. Ames), Monte Blue (Norris), Douglas Kennedy (assistant District Attorney), Tris Coffin (man at concert), Creighton Hale (secretary), Wheaton Chambers (waiter), Erskine Sanford (Dr. Max Sherman), Gerald Perreau/Peter Miles (Wynn Graham), Griff Barnett (Coroner), Rory Mallinson (Coroner's assistant), Isabel Withers (Nurse Rosen), Don McGuire (Dr. Craig), Sarah Padden (caretaker's wife), Philo McCullough (butler), Lisa Golm (Elsie), Clifton Young (interne), Frank Marlowe (proprietor), Jacob Gimpel (Walter Sveldon), Ralph Dunn (motorman), James Conaty (foreman), Nell Craig (nurse), Bunty Cutler (nurse), Henry Sylvester (Dean's secretary), Eddie Hart (bartender).

POSSESSED, THE (TVM-1977) - 5-1-77
    Director: Jerry Thorpe
James Farentino (Devin Leahy), Joan Hackett (Louise Gelson), Ann Dusenberry (Weezie Sumner), Claudette Nevins (Ellen Sumner), Harrison Ford (Paul Winjam), P. J. Soles (Marty), Diana Scarwid (Lane), Eugene Roche (Sgt. Taplinger), Dinah Manoff (Celia), Carol Jones (Alex), Ethelinn Block (Barry), James R. Parkes, Lawrence Bame, Susan Walden, Catherine Cunneff.

POSSESSION (TVM-1973) - 4-12-73
    Director: John Cooper
Joanna Dunham (Penny Burns), John Carson (Ray Burns), James Cossins.

POSSESSION (1981-Fr. /Ger.)
    Director: Andrezej Zulawski
Isabelle Adjani (Anna/Helen), Sam Neill (Marc), Heinz Bennent (Heinrich), Margit Carstensen (Margie), Shaun Lawton (Zimmerman), Michael Hogben (Bob), Johanna Hofer (Mother).

POSSESSION OF JOEL DELANEY, THE (1971)
    Director: Philip Rosenberg
Perry King (Joel Delaney), Shirley MacLaine (Norah Benson), Lisa Kohane (Carrie Benson), Miriam Colon (Veronica), Michael Hordern (Dr. Reichman), Lovelady Powell (Erika), Teodorino Bello (Mrs. Perez), Jose Fernandez (Tonio Perez), David Ellicott (Peter Benson), Edmundo Rivera Alverez (Don Pedro), Peter Turgeon (Brady), Aukie Herger (Mr. Perez), Barbara Trentham (Sherry),

Marita Lindholm (Marta), Paulita Inglesias (Bruja), Ernesto Gonzalez (seance subject).

POWER, THE (1967)
Director: Byron Haskin
George Hamilton (Jim Tanner), Michael Rennie (Arthur Nordlund), Suzanne Pleshette (Margery Lansing), Nehemiah Persoff (Carl Melniker), Arthur O'Connell (Henry Hallson), Earl Holliman (Talbot Scott), Richard Carlson (N. E. Van Zandt), Yvonne DeCarlo (Sally Hallson), Gary Merrill (Mark Corlane), Aldo Ray (Bruce), Barbara Nichols (Flora), Miiko Taka (Mrs. Van Zandt), Ken Murray (Grover), Lawrence Montaigne (Briggs), Beverly Hills (Sylvia), Celia Lovsky (Mrs. Hallson), Vaughn Taylor (Mr. Hallson).

POWER GOD, THE (1925) - serial in 15 episodes
Chapters: 1. "The Ring of Fate", 2. "Trapped", 3. "The Living Dead", 4. "Black Shadows", 5. "The Death Chamber", 6. "House of Peril", 7. "Hands of the Dark", 8. "59th Second", 9. "Perilous Waters", 10. "The Bridge of Doom", 11. "Treachery", 12. "The Flaming Menace", 13. "The Purloined Papers", 14. "The Storms Lash", & 15. "The Wages of Sin".
Director: Ben Wilson
Ben Wilson (Jim Thorpe), Neva Gerber (Aileen Sturgess), Mary Brooklyn (Aileen's mother), John Bahaglia (John Sturgess), Mary Crane (maid).

POWER OF THE WHISTLER, THE (1945)
Director: Lew Landers
Richard Dix (William Everest), Jeff Donnell (Francie Lang), Tala Birell (Constantina Ivaneska), John Abbott (Kasper Andropolos), Janis Carter (Jean Lang), Murray Alper (Joe Blaney), Loren Tindall (Charlie Kent), Cy Kendall (druggist).

POWER WITHIN, THE (TVM-1979)
(A. K. A. "Power Man") - 5-11-79
Director: John L. Moxey
Art Hindle (Chris Darrow), Edward Binns (Gen. Tom Darrow), Dick Sargent (Capt. Ed Holman), Susan Howard (Dr. Joanne Mills), David Hedison (Danton), Eric Braeden (Stephens), Joe Rassulo (Bill Camelli), Isabell McCloskey (Grandma), Karen Lamm (Marvallee), K. C. Martel (small boy), Chris Wallace (1st guard), Bill Sorrells (2nd guard).

PREHISTORIC WOMEN (1950)
Director: Greg Tallas
Laurette Luez (Tigri), Allan Nixon (Engor), Mara Lynn (Arva), Joan Shawlee (Lotee), Judy Landon (Eras), Joe Carroll Dennison (Nika), Tony Devlin (Ruig), Kerry Vaughn (Tulle), James Summers (Adh), Jeanne Sorel (Tana), Dennis Dengate (Kama), Johann Peturrson (Guaddi), John Merrick (Tribe Leader), Janet Scott (wise old lady).

PREHISTORIC WOMEN (1966)
(A. K. A. "Slave Girls")
Director: Michael Carreras
Martine Beswicke (Kari), Edina Ronay (Saria), Michael Latimer (David), Stephanie Randall (Amyak), Carol White (Gido), Sydney Bromley (Ullo), Alexandra Stevenson (Luri), Yvonne Horner (1st Amazon), Robert Raglan (Col. Hammond), Mary Gignett (Mrs. Hammond), Frank Hayden (Arja), Steve Berkoff (John), Bari Jonson (High Priest), Danny Daniels (Jakara), Louis Mahoney (head boy).

PREMATURE BURIAL, THE (1962)
Director: Roger Corman
Ray Milland (Guy Carrell), Hazel Court (Emily Gualt), Heather Angel (Kate Carrell), Richard New (Miles Archer), Alan Napier (Dr. Gideon Gault), John Dierkes (Sweeney), Dick Miller (Mole), Brendan Dillon (Minister).

PREMONITION (1972)
Director: Alan Rudolph
Carl Crow (Neal), Tim Ray (Andy), Victor Izay (Kilkeny), Winfrey Hester Hill (Baker), Jon Huss (Jon), Judith Patterson (Janice), Cheryl Adams (Susan), Barry Brown (Michael), Eddie Patterson (Ralph), John Holman (Lotheridge), Michele Fitzsimmons (Denise), Doug Digioila (Norm), Diana Daves (Miss Thorsen), Lee Alpert (frat brother), Larry Loveridge (man in cabin), Andy Hare (drummer), Miles Tilton (promoter), Shelley Snell, Tom Akers, Paul Katz, Alex Del Zoppo, Joyce Rudolph.

PREMONITION, THE (1976)
Director: Robert Allen Schnitzer
Sharon Farrell (Sheri), Richard Lynch (Jude), Jeff Corey (Detective Denver), Ellen Barber (Andrea),

Edward Bell (Miles), Danielle Brise-
bois, Chiitra Neogy, Rosemary Mc-
Namara, Margaret Graham, Wilmuth
Cooper, Thomas Williams, Roy White,
Robert Harper.

PRESIDENT'S ANALYST, THE (1967)
     Director: Theodore J. Flicker
James Coburn (Dr. Sidney Schaefer),
Godfrey Cambridge (Don Masters),
Severn Darden (Kropotkin), Will Geer
(Evans), Pat Harrington, Jr. (Arling-
ton Hewes), William Daniels (Wynn
Quantrill), Joan Darling (Jeff Quantrill),
Walter Burke (Henry Lux), Edward
Franz (Ethan Allan Crocket), Jill
Banner (Snow White), Joan Delaney
(Nan Butler), Barry McGuire (Old
Wrangler), Sheldon Collins (Bing
Quantrill), Kathleen Hughes (White
House tourist), Arte Johnson (Sullivan),
Martin Horsey, William Beckley
(Puddlians).

PRESIDENT'S PLANE IS MISSING,
     THE (TVM-1971) - 10-23-71
     Director: Daryl Duke
Buddy Ebsen (Dermit Madigan), Rip
Torn (George Oldenberg), Peter Graves
(Mark Jones), Arthur Kennedy (Gunther
Damon), Louise Sorel (Joanna Spencer),
Raymond Massey (Freeman Sharkey),
Marcedes McCambridge (Hester Madigan),
James Wainright (Gen. Ben Dunbar),
Joseph Campanella (Col. Doug Henderson),
Dabney Coleman (Bert Haines), Tod
Andrews (President Jeremy Haines),
Richard Eastham (Gen Colton), Byron
Morrow (Adm. Phillips), Richard Bull
(1st Controller), Vernon Weddle (2nd
Controller), Hoke Howell (Control
Supervisor), Barry Cahill (Ground
Crew Chief), James Sikking (aide to
Dunbar), James B. Smith (Maj. Earl
Foster), George Barrows (Mr. Meyers),
Barbara Leigh (WAF), John Rayner (Aide
to Colton), John Amos (Marine Corporal),
Maida Severn (Judy Nance), Ivan Bonar
(Colonel to Dunbar), Bill Walker (Tho-
mas), Gary Haynes (Rod Pitcher), Ro-
bert Reiser (boy in desert), Patty
Bodeen (girl in desert), Richard Stahl
(dentist), Gil Peterson (tower contro-
ler), Dale Tarter (airman), Lillian
Lehman (Genesse), James W. Gavin
(helicopter pilot), Jerry Crews (news
cameraman), John Ward (Major D'Andrea), Jeff Burton (reporter).

PRETTY POISON (1968)
     Director: Noel Black
Tony Perkins (Dennis Pitt), Tuesday
Weld (Sue Ann Stepanek), Beverly

Garland (Mrs. Stepanek), John
Randolph (Mr. Azenauer), Dick
O'Neill (Bud Munsch), Clarice
Blackburn (Mrs. Bronson), Ken
Kercheval (Harry), Joseph Bova
(Pete), Parker Fennelly (night-
watchman), Paul Larson (Mrs.
Stepanek's boyfriend), William
Sorrells (cop at beanery), Tim Calla-
han (plainclothesman), George
Fisher (burly man).

PREVIEW MURDER MYSTERY,
     THE (1936)
     Director: Robert Florey
Reginald Denny (Johnny Morgan),
Frances Drake (Peggy Madison),
Gail Patrick (Claire Woodward),
Rod LaRoque (Neil Du Beck), Ian
Keith (E. Gordon Smith), Bryant
Washburn (Jennings), Thomas
Jackson (Lt. McKane), Lee Shum-
way (Chief of Police), Eddie Dunn
(Tub Wilson), Jack Mulhall (screen
heavy), Henry Kleinbach (screen
actor), Chester Conklin (himself),
George Barbier (Jerome Hewitt),
Conway Tearle (Edwin Strange),
Jack Raymond (Tyson).

PREY (1977)
     Director: Norman J. Warren
Glory Annen, Sally Faulkner, Barry
Stokes.

PRIMITIVE MAN, THE (1913)
     Director: D.W. Griffith
Robert Harron (Weakhands), Mae
Marsh (Lily White), Wilfred Lucas
(Brute Force), Edwin Curglot,
Alfred Paget, William J. Butler
(Cavemen), Jenny Lee (Cavewoman).

PRINCE OF TEMPTERS (1926)
     Director: Lothar Mendes
Ian Keith (the Devil), Lois Moran,
Lya De Putti, Mary Brian, Ben
Lyon, J. Barney Sherry, Sam Hardy,
Olive Tell.

PRINCESS AND THE MAGIC FROG,
     THE (1965)
     Director: Austin Green
David Bailey, Ernest Vaio, Nancy
De Carl, Clive Halliday, Frank
Delfino, Dick Reeves.

PRIVATE CLINIC OF PROFESSOR
     LUND, THE (1959-Ger.) (A. K. A.
     "Privat Klinik Professor Lund",
     "Doctor Without a Conscience")
     Director: Falk Harnack
Wolfgang Preiss, Ewald Balser,

Cornell Borchers, Karin Baal, Barbara
Ruetting, Erika Beer, Emmerich Schrend,
Wolfgang Kieling, Walter Jacob, Lena
Cartens.

PRIVATE EYES (1953)
    Director: Edward Bernds
Leo Gorcey (Slip Mahoney), Huntz
Hall (Sach Debussy Jones), Bernard
Gorcey (Louie Dumbrowski), David
Condon (Chuck), Bennie Bartlett (Butch),
Robert Osterloh, Joyce Holden, Wil-
liam Phillips, Rudy Lee, William
Forrest, Chick Chandler, Lou Lubin,
Tim Ryan, Peter Mamakos, Edith
Leslie, Myron Healey, Lee Van Cleef.

PRIVATE EYES, THE (1980)
    Director: Lang Elliott
Tim Conway (Dr. Tart), Don Knotts
(Insp. Winship), Trisha Noble (Mis-
tress Phyllis Morley), Bernard Fox
(Justin), Grace Zabriskle (Nanny),
John Fujioka (Mr. Uwatsum), Susie
Mandel (Hilda), Irwin Keyes (Jack),
Stan Ross (Tebit), Fred Stuthman (Lord
Morley), Mary Nell Santacroce (Lady
Morley), Patrick Carnshaw (Roy),
Robert V. Barron (gas station attendant).

PRIVATE LIFE OF ADAM AND EVE,
    THE (1959)
    Director: Albert Zugsmith &
    Mickey Rooney
Mickey Rooney (Nick Lewis/the Devil),
Mamie Van Doren (Evie Simms/Eve),
Fay Sapin (Lil Lewis/Lilith), Martin
Milner (Ad Simms/Adam), Mel Torme
(Hal Sanders), Tuesday Weld (Vangie
Harper), Cecil Kellaway (Doc Bayles),
Paul Anka (Pinkie Parker), Ziva Rodann
(Passiona), Theona Bryant, June
Wilkinson, Phillipa Fallon, Barbara
Walden, Toni Covington (Devil's Fam-
iliars), Nancy Root, Donna Lynne,
Sharon Wiley, Miki Kato, Andrea Smith,
Buni Bacon, Stella Garcia (Satan's
Sinners).

PRIVATE LIFE OF SHERLOCK HOLMES,
    THE (1970)
    Director: Billy Wilder
Robert Stephens (Sherlock Holmes),
Colin Blakely (Dr. John H. Watson),
Irene Handl (Mrs. Hudson), Genevieve
Page (Gabrielle Valladon), Christopher
Lee (Mycroft Holmes), Clive Revill
(Rogozhin), George Benson (Insp.
Lestrade), Tamara Toumanova (Pet-
rova), Mollie Maurenn (Queen Victoria),
Peter Madden (Von Tirpitz), Stanley
Holloway (1st gravedigger), Eric
Francis (2nd gravedigger), Michael

Balfour (cabby), Catherine Lacey
(old lady), Kynaston Reeves (old
man), Frank Thornton (porter),
Alex McCrindle (baggageman),
Graham Armitage (wiggins),
Godfrey James (Carter), Robert
Cawdron (hotel manager), Micael
Elwyn (Cassidy), James Copeland
(guide), Kenneth Benda (minister),
John Garrie (Carter), Ina De La
Haye (Petrova's maid), Anne Blake
(Madame), Marilyn Head, Wendy
Ligham, Sheena Hunter, Anna
Matisse, Penny Brahms (girls),
Daphne Riggs (Lady-in-Waiting),
Phillip Ross (McKeller), Annette
Kerr (Secretary), John Gatrell
(Equerry), Philip Anthony (Lt.
Commander), Tina & Judy Spooner
(twins).

PRIVATE PARTS (1972)
    Director: Paul Bartel
Ann Ruymen (Cheryl), Lucille
Benson (Aunt Martha), John Ven-
tantonio (George), Laurie Main
(Rev. Moon), John Lupton, Gene
Simms (policemen), Stanley Living-
ston (Jeff), Ann Gibbs (Judy), Len
Travis (Mike), Charles Woolf
(Jeff's dad), Dorothy Neumann
(Mrs. Quigley), Patrick Strong
(Artie).

PRIVILEGE (1967)
    Director: Peter Watkins
Paul Jones (Steve Shorter), Jean
Shrimpton (Vanessa Ritchie), Jean
Mark London (Alvin Kirsch), Max
Bacon (Julie Jordan), Jeremy
Child (Martin Crossley), William
Job (Andrew Butler), James Cossins
(Prof. Tatham), Frederick Danner
(Marcus Hopper), Arthur Pentelow
(Leo Stanley), Doreen Mantle (Miss
Crawford), Victor Henry (Freddie
K.), Steve Kirby (Squit), Michael
Barrington (Bishop of Essex), John
Gill (Bishop of Surrey), Edwin
Fink (Bishop of Cornwall), Norman
Pett (Bishop of Hersham), Alba
(Bishop of Rutland), Malcolm
Rogers (Rev. Jeremy Tate), Michael
Graham (TV director).

PROBE (TVM-1972) - 2-21-72
    Director: Russell Mayberry
Hugh O'Brian (Hugh Lockwood),
Burgess Meredith (B.C. Cameron),
Sir John Gielgud (Harold L. Stree-
ter), Angel Tompkins (Gloria
Harding), Elke Sommer (Ullie),

Kent Smith (Dr. Laurent), Alfred
Ryder (Cheyne), Lilia Skala (Frau
Ullman), Ben Wright (Van Niestat),
Jules Maitland (Brugge), Robert
Boon, Albert Popwell, Jacklyn Smith,
Ginny Golden, Jan Daley, Joanne
Frank, A. Martinez, Byron Chung,
Gun Sundberg.

PROFESSOR CREEPS (1942)
     Director: William Beaudine
Mantan Moreland, F. E. Miller,
Arthur Ray, Florence O'Brien.

PROJECTED MAN, THE (1966)
     Director: Ian Curteis
Bryant Halliday (Prof. Steiner), Mary
Peach (Dr. Pat Hill), Norman Wooland
(Dr. Blanchard), Ronald Allen (Chris-
topher Mitchell), Derek Farr (Insp.
Davis), Tracey Crisp (Sheila Anderson),
Gerard Heins (Prof. Lembach), Der-
rick de Marney (Dr. Latham), Sam
Kydd (Harry), Norma West (Gloria),
Terry Scully (Steve), Frank Gatliff
(Dr. Wilson).

PROJECT M7 (1953) (A. K. A. "The
     Net")
     Director: Anthony Asquith
Phyllis Calvert (Lydia), James Donald
(Neathley), Robert Beatty (Sam Sea-
gram), Herbert Lom (Alex Leon),
Patric Doonan (Brian Jackson), Noel
Willman (Dennis Boyd), Walter Fitz-
gerald (Sir Charles Cruddock), Maurice
Denham (Carrington), Muriel Pavlow
(Caroline Cartier), Marjorie Fielding
(Mama).

PROJECT MOONBASE (1953)
     Director: Richard Talmadge
Donna Martell (Col. Briteis), Hayden
Rorke (Gen. Greene), Barbara Morrison
(Polly Prattles), Ross Ford (Major
Moore), James Craven (Commodore
Carlson), Larry Johns (Dr. Wernher),
Robert Karnes (Sam), Herb Jacobs
(Mr. Roundtree), Ernestine Barrier
(Madame President), Peter Adams
(Captian Carmody), John Hedlow
(adjutant), John Straub (chaplain),
John Tomecko (blockhouse operator),
Charles Keane (spacom operator),
Robert Paltz (bellboy).

PROJECT X (1967)
     Director: William Castle
Christopher George (Hagen Arnold),
Monte Markham (Gregory Gallea),
Greta Baldwin (Karen Summers),
Henry Jones (Dr. Crowther), Harold
Gould (Col. Holt), Philip Pine (Lee

Craig), Ivan Bonar (Col. Cowen),
Keye Luke (Sen Shiu), Lee Delano
(Dr. Tony Verity), Robert Cleaves
(Dr. George Tarvin), Sheila
Bartold (Sybil Dennis), Ed Pren-
tiss (Hicks), Charles Irving
(Maj. Tolley), Patrick Wright
(Stover), Maresther Denver
(Overseer).

PROLIFIC MAGICAL EGG, THE
     (1901-Fr.) (A. K. A. "L'Oeuf
     du Sorcier", "L'Oeuf Magique
     Prolifique")
     Director: Georges Melies

PROM NIGHT (1980)
     Director: Paul Lynch
Jamie Lee Curtis (Kim), Leslie
Nielsen (Mr. Hammond), Antoinette
Bower (Mrs. Hammond), Eddie
Benton (Wendy), Casey Stevens
(Nick), Michael Tough (Alex),
Pita Oliver (Vicki), Joy Thompson
(Jude), Robert Silverman (Sykes),
Jeff Wincott (Drew), George
Touliatos (McBride), Marybeth
Rubins (Delly), David Mucci
(Lou), Melanie Morse MacQuarrie
(Henri-Ann), David Gardner (Dr.
Fairchild), Sheldon Rybowski
(Slick), David Bolt (Weller), Sonia
Zimmer (Melanie), Liz Stalker-
Mason (Adele), Rob Garrison
(Sayer), Beth Amos (Maude),
Sylvia Martin (Mrs. Cunningham),
Ardon Bess (teacher), Pam Henry
(car hop), Lee Wildgen (gang
member), Tammy Bourne, Brock
Simpson, Debbie Greenfield.

PROPHECY (1979)
     Director: John Frankenheimer
Robert Foxworth (Rob), Talia
Shire (Maggie), Richard Dysart
(Isley), Armand Assante (John
Hawks), Victoria Racimo (Ramona),
George Clutesi (M'Rai), Tom
McFadden (pilot), Burke Byrnes
(father), Johnny Timko (boy),
Mia Bendixsen (girl), Evans Evans
(cellist), Charles H. Gray (Sheriff),
Everett L. Creach (Kelso), Graham
Jarvis (Shusette), Lyvingston
Holmes (black woman), Renato
Moore, Roosevelt Smith, Mel
Waters, Eric Mansker, Jay
Durkus, Steve Shemayme, John
A. Shemayne, Bob Terhune, Lon
Katzman, James H. Burke.

PROPHETESS OF THEBES, THE
     (1908-Fr.) (A. K. A. "La

Prophetesse de Thebes")
Director: Georges Melies

PROVIDENCE (1977-Fr. /Swiss),
Director: Alain Resnais
Dirk Bogarde (Claude), Ellen Burstyn
(Sonia), John Gielgud (Clive), David
Warner (Kevin), Elaine Stritch (He-
len), Cyril Luckham (Mark), Dennis
Lawson (Dave), Kathryn Leigh Scott
(Boon), Peter Arne (Nils), Milo
Sperber (Jenner), Anna Wing (Karen).

PROVIDENCE OF THE WAVES, THE
(1904-Fr.) (A.K.A. "The Dream
of a Poor Fisherman", "La Providence de Notre-Dame des Flots")
Director: Georges Melies

PROWLER, THE (1981) (A.K.A.
"The Graduation")
Director: Joseph Zito
Farley Granger (Sheriff George
Fraser), Vicki Dawson (Pam Mc-
Donald), Cindy Weintraub (Lisa),
Christopher Goutman (Mark London),
John Seitz (Kingsley), Lawrence
Tierney.

PSYCHIC, THE (1979-Ital.) (A.K.A.
"Sette Note in Nero")
Director: Lucio Fulci
Jennifer O'Neill (Virginia), Gabriele
Ferzetti, Marc Porel, Gianni Garko,
Jenny Tamburi, Evelyn Stewart,
Fabrizio Jovine, Vito Passeri, Luigi
Diberti, Ricardo Parisio Perrotti.

PSYCHIC KILLER (1976)
Director: Ray Danton
Jim Hutton (Arnold), Nehemiah Per-
soff (Dr. Gubner), Paul Burke (Mor-
gan), Julia Adams (Dr. Laura Scott),
Whit Bissell (Dr. Taylor), Rod Cam-
eron (Dr. Commanger), Neville
Brand (Lemonowski), Aldo Ray (An-
derson), Harry Holcombe (Judge),
Joe Della Sorte (Sanders), Mary
Wilcox (Martha), Della Reese (Mrs.
Gibson), Robyn Raymond (jury foreman),
Diane Deininger (Arnold's mother),
Jerry James (dead doctor), John
Dennis (Frank), Bill Quinn (Coroner),
Walter Miles (Coroner), Judith Brown
(Anne), Marland Proctor (motorcycle
cop), Bill Bonner (ambulance driver),
Stack Pierce (Emilio), Mello Alex-
andria (cop), Greydon Clark (Sowash),
Ed Cross (old man), Sheldon Lee
(inmate).

PSYCHO (1960)
Director: Alfred Hitchcock

Anthony Perkins (Norman Bates),
Janet Leigh (Marion Crane), Vera
Miles (Lila Crane), John Gavin
(Sam Loomis), Martin Balsam
(Milton Arbogast), John McIntire
(Sheriff Chambers), Frank Albert-
son (Tom Cassidy), Simon Oak-
land (Dr. Richmond), Vaughn
Taylor (George Lowery), Lurene
Tuttle (Mrs. Chambers), Mort
Mills (policeman), John Anderson
(car salesman), Pat Hitchcock
(Caroline), George Eldredge,
Francis De Sales, Sam Flint (of-
ficials).

PSYCHO-CIRCUS (1967) (A.K.A.
"Circus of Fear")
Director: John L. Moxey
Christopher Lee (Gregor), Leo
Genn (Insp. Elliott), Heinz Drache
(Carl), Anthony Newlands (Bar-
berini), Margaret Lee (Gina),
Klaus Kinski (Manfred), Suzi Ken-
dall (Natasha), Skip Martin (Mr.
Big), Victor Maddern (Mason),
Cecil Parker (Sir John), Maurice
Kaufmann (Mario), Eddi Arent
(Eddie), Tom Bowman (Jackson),
Gordon Petrie (Negor), Fred Powell
(Red), Lawrence James (Manley),
Henry Longhurst (hotel porter),
Dennis Blakely (van guard), George
Fisher (4th man), Peter Brace
(man in speedboat), Roy Scammel
(man in speedboat), Geoff Silk,
Keith Peacock (secruity men).

PSYCHO LOVER, THE (1969)
(A.K.A. "The Psycho Killer")
Director: Robert Vincent
O'Neill
Lawrence Montaigne, Joanne Mere-
dith, Frank Cuva, Elizabeth Plumb,
John Vincent.

PSYCHOMANIA (1963) (A.K.A.
"Violent Midnight")
Director: Richard Hilliard
Lee Phillips (Elliot Freeman),
Jean Hale (Carol Bishop), Shepperd
Strudwick (Adrian Bennedict), James
Farentino (Charlie Perone), Sylvia
Miles (Silvia), Dick Van Patten
(Palmer), Lorraine Rogers (Alice
St. Clair), Margot Hartman (Lynn
Freeman), Day Tuttle (Mr. Mel-
bourne), Mike Keene (Insp. Grey),
Sheila Forbes (Janet Terhune),
Kaye Elhardt (Dolores Martello),
Mike O'Dowd (Max).

PSYCHOMANIA (1972) (A.K.A.

"The Frog", "The Living Dead", "The
Death Wheelers")
    Director: Don Sharp
George Sanders (Shadwill), Nicky
Henson (Tom Latham), Beryl Reid
(Mrs. Latham), Mary Larkin (Abby),
Ann Michelle (Jane Pettibone), Roy
Holder (Bertram), Robert Hardy (Chief
Insp. Hesseltine), Patrick Holt (Ser-
geant), Denis Gilmore (Hatchet), Miles
Greenwood (Chopped Meat), Rocky
Taylor (Hinley), Peter Whitting (Exesh),
Jacki Webb (mother), David Millett
(father), Linda Gray (grandmother),
Andrew Laurence (grandfather), Alan
Bennion, John Levene (constables),
Bill Pertwee (publican), Roy Evans
(motorits), Stanley Stewart (petrol
pump attendant), Serretta Wilson (Stella),
Lane Meddick (Mr. Pettibone), June
Brown (Mrs. Pettibone), Denis Carey
(Coroner's assistant), Martin Boddey
(Coroner), Ann Murray (motorist's
wife), Fiona Kendall (Monica), Ernest
C. Jennings (blind man), Heather Wright
(girl), Penny Leatherbarrow (woman
at police station).

PSYCHOPATH, THE (1965)
    Director: Freddie Francis
Patrick Wymark (Insp. Holloway),
Margaret Johnston (Mrs. Hedwig von
Sturm), John Standing (Mark von Sturm),
Alexander Knox (Frank Saville), Judy
Huxtable (Louise Saville), Colin Gordon
(Dr. Glyn), Thorley Walters (Martin
Roth), Robert Crewdson (Victor Ledoux),
Tim Barrett (Morgan), Frank Forsyth
(Tucker), John Harvey (Reinhardt
Klermer), Don Borisenko (Donald
Loftis), Harold Lang (Biggs), Olive
Gregg (Mary), Greta Farrer (cigarette
girl).

PSYCHOPATH (1974)
    Director: Larry Brown
Tom Basham (Tommy), Gene Carlson,
Gretchen Kanne.

PSYCHOTRONIC MAN, THE (1980)
    Director: Jack M.Sell
Peter Spelson (Rocky Foscoe), Curt
Colbert (Sgt. Chuck Jackson), Chris-
topher Carbie (Lt. Walter O'Brien),
Robin Newton (Kathy), Paul Marvel
(Dr. Steinberg), Jeff Caliendo (Officer
Maloney), Lindsey Novak (Mrs. Foscoe),
Irwin Lewin (Professor), Cornel Morgan
(SIA Agent Gorman), Bob McDonald
(old man).

PUFNSTUF (1970)
    Director: Hollingworth Morse

Jack Wild (Jimmy), Martha Raye
(Boss Witch), Billie Hayes (Witch-
iepoo), Mama Cass Elliott (Witch
Hazel), Angelo Rossito (Midget),
Billy Barty (Postman), Johnny
Silver (Dr. Blinky/Ludicrous Lion),
Joy Campbell (Orson Vulture/Fire-
man), Andy Ratoucheff (Fireman),
Sharon Baird (Shirley Pufnstuf),
Lou Wagner, Jane Dulo, Buddy
Douglas, Jan Davis, Ken Creel.

PUNISHMENT PARK (1970)
    Director: Peter Watkins
Jim Bohan (Captain), Van Daniels
(Sheriff), Frederick Franklyn
(Prof. Daly), Sanford Golden
(Senator), Harlan Green (Sheriff),
Rodger Greene (Marshall), Paul
Alelyanes, Carmen Argenziano,
Gary Johnson, Gladys Golden,
Stan Armsted, George Gregory,
Luke Johnson, Mike Hodel, Mitchell
Harding.

PUPPETOONS (1943-1947) - shorts
    Director: George Pal.

PURITAN PASSIONS (1923)
    Director: Frank Tuttle
Mary Astor, Glenn Hunter, Maude
Hill, Osgood Perkins, Frank
Tweed, Dwight Wiman, Thomas
Chalmers.

PURPLE MONSTER STRIKES,
    THE (1945) (A.K.A. "D-Day
on Mars") - serial in 15 episodes
Chapters: 1. "The Man in the Meteor",
2. "The Time Trap", 3. "Flaming
Avalanche", 4. "The Lethal Pit",
5. "Death on the Beam", 6. "The
Demon Killer", 7. "The Evil Eye",
8. "Descending Doom", 9. "The
Living Dead", 10. "House of Horror",
11. "Menace from Mars", 12.
"Perilous Plunge", 13. "Fiery
Shroud", 14. "The Fatal Trail", &
15. "Take-Off to Destruction".
    Director: Spencer Gordon
    Bennet & Fred C. Brannon
Dennis Moore (Craig Foster), Linda
Stirling (Sheila Layton), Roy
Barcroft (the Purple Monster),
James Craven (Dr. Cyrus Layton),
Bud Geary (Hodge Garrett), Keene
Duncan (Charles Mitchell), John
Davidson (Emperor of Mars),
Anthony Warde (Tony), Wheaton
Chambers (Benjamin), Joe Whitehead
(Carl Stewart), George Carleton
(Paul Meredith), Monte Hale (Harvey),

Emmett Vogan (Saunders), Mary Moore (Marica), Ken Terrell (Andy Martin), Rosemonde James (Helen), Frederick Howard (Crandall), Tom Steele (Fritz Benham/Joe/Mears), Fred Graham (Baker/Curry/Logan/ Ed Fletcher), Dale Van Sickel (policeman), George Chesebro (Shaw), Cliff Lyons (Clay), Carey Loftin (Mack), Robert Wilke (workman), John Daheim (Barnes), Henry Wills (Mason/Osborne), Robert Blair (Evans), Babe De Freest, Polly Burson.

PURSUING VENGEANCE, THE (1916)
    Director: Martin Sabine
Sheldon Lewis.

PURSUIT (TVM-1972) - 12-12-72
    Director: Michael Crichton
Ben Gazzara (Steve Graves), E. G. Marshall (James Wright), William Windom (Robert Phillips), Joseph Wiseman (Dr. Peter Nordmann), Martin Sheen (Timothy Drew), Wil Kuluva (Dr. Wolff), Jim McMullan (Lewis), Quinn Redeker (Capt. Morrison), Hank Brandt (agent), Joe Brooks, Conrad Beckman, Robert Cleaves.

PURSUIT TO ALGIERS (1945)
    Director: Roy William Neill
Basil Rathbone (Sherlock Holmes), Nigel Bruce (Dr. Watson), Marjorie Riordan (Sheila), Rosalind Ivan (Agatha Dunham), Morton Lowry (Sanford), Martin Kosleck (Mirko), Leslie Vincent (Nikolas), John Abbott (Jodri), Rex Evans (Gregor), Gerald Hamer (Kingston), Frederic Worlock (Prime Minister), Gregory Gaye (Ravez), Wee Willie Davis (Gubec), Wilson Benge (clergyman), Sven Hugo Borg (Johansson), Dorothy Kellogg (fuzzy looking woman), Tom Dillon (restaurant proprietor).

PYGMY ISLAND (1950) (A. K. A. "Pigmy Island")
    Director: William Berke
Johnny Weissmuller (Jungle Jim), Ann Savage, David Bruce, Steven Geray, William Tannen, Tris Coffin, Billy Curtis, Rusty Wescoatt, Billy Barty, Pierce Lyden, Tommy Farrell.

PYRO (1963-Span. /U.S.) (A. K. A. "Pyro--Man Without a Face", "Fuego", "Fire", "Wheel of Fire", "Phantom of the Ferris Wheel")
    Director: Julio Coll
Barry Sullivan (Vance Pierson), Martha Hyer (Larua Blanco), Sherry

Moreland (Verna Pierson), Soledad Miranda (Liz Frade), Luis Prendes (Police Inspector), Fernando Hilbeck (Julio), Carlos Casarivilla (Frade), Marisenka (Isabella).

PYX, THE (1973)
    Director: Harvey Hart
Karen Black (Elizabeth Lucy), Christopher Plummer (Jim Henderson), Donald Pilon (Pierre Paquette), Jean-Louis Roux (Keerson), Yvette Brind'Amour (Meg), Jacques Godin (Superintendent), Terry Haig (Jimmy), Lee Broker (Herbie Lefram), Robin Gammel (Worther), Louise Rinfret (Sandra).

QUATERMASS CONCLUSION, THE (1979)
    Director: Piers Haggard
John Mills (Prof. Bernard Quatermass), Simon MacCorkingdale (Dr. Joseph Kapp), Barbara Kellerman (Clare Kapp), Margaret Tyzack, Brewster Mason.

QUEEN KONG (1976-Brit. /Ital.)
    Director: Frank Agrama
Robin Askwith (Ray Fay), Rula Lenska (Luce Habit).

QUEEN OF BLOOD (1966) (A. K. A. "Planet of Blood")
    Director: Curtis Harrington
Basil Rathbone (Dr. Faraday), Florence Marly (Velena), John Saxon (Allan Brenner), Judi Meredith (Laura James), Robert Boon (Anders Brockman), Dennis Hopper (Paul Grant), Don Eitner (Tony Barrat), Forrest J. Ackerman (scientist), Robert Porter, Virgil Frye, Terry Lee.

QUEEN OF OUTER SPACE (1958)
    Director: Edward Bernds
Zsa Zsa Gabor (Talleah), Eric Fleming (Capt. Neil Patterson), Laurie Mitchell (Queen Yllano), Paul Birch (Prof. Konrad), Dave Willock (Lt. Michael Cruze), Patrick Waltz (Lt. Larry Turner), Barbara Darrow (Kaeel), Lisa Davis (Motiya), Marilyn Buferd (Odeena), Kathy Marlowe, Laura Mason, Tania Velia (Councilors), Lynn Cartwright (guard leader), Marjorie Durant, Marya Stevens, Colleen Drake, Mary Ford (guards), Gerry Gaylor (friendly guard).

QUEEN OF SPADES (1948)
Director: Thorold Dickinson
Anton Walbrook (Surovin), Edith
Evans (Countess R.) Yvonne Mitchell
(Lizavetta), Ronald Howard (Andrei),
Anthony Dawson (Fyodor), Mary Jer-
rold (Old Vararushka), Miles Malleson
(Tchybukin), Athene Seyler (Princess
Ivashin), Valentine Dyall, Gibb Mc-
Laughlin, Aubrey Woods, George
Woodbridge, John Howard, Michael
Medwin, Ivor Bernard, David Paltengi,
Violetta Elvin, Maroussia Dimitr-
vitch, Jacqueline Clarke, Gordon
Begg, Aubrey Mallalieu, Hay Petrie,
Ian Colin, Yussef Tamart, Yussef
Ramart, Drusilla Wills, Pauline
Jameson, Brown Derby, Clement
McCallin.

QUEEN OF SPADES (1960-Sov.) (A. K. A.
  "Pikovaya Dama")
Director: Roman Tikhomirov
Oleg Strizhenov (Hermann), Yelena
Polevitskaya (Countess), Olga Krasina
(Lisa), Vadim Medvedev (Tomski),
B. Kulik (Yeletski), I. Gubanova-Gurzo
(Polina).

QUEEN OF SPADES (1965-Fr.) (A. K. A.
  "La Dame du Pique")
Director: Leonard Keigel.
Dita Parlo, Jean Negroni, Katharina
Renn.

QUEEN OF THE JUNGLE (1935) -
  serial in 12 episodes
Chapters: 1. "Lost in the Clouds",
2. "Radium Rays", 3. "The Hand of
Death", 4. "The Native's Revenge",
5. "Black Magic", 6. "The Death
Vine", 7. "The Leopard Leaps", 8.
"The Doom Ship", 9. "Death Rides
the Waves", 10. "The Temple of Mu",
11. "Fangs in the Dark", & 12. "The
Pit of Lions".
Director: Robert Hill
Reed Howes (David Worth), Dickie
Moore (David as a child), Mary
Kornman (Joan Lawrence), Marilyn
Spinner (Joan as a child), William
Walsh (John Lawrence), George
Chesebro (Ken Roberts), Lafe McKee
(Kali), Eddie Foster (Rosco), Barney
Furey (Abdullah), Robert Borman
(Captain Blake).

QUEEN OF THE SEA (1918)
Director: John G. Adolphi
Annette Kellermann (Merilla), Hugh
Thompson, Mildred Keats, Beth
Irvins.

QUEST FOR FIRE (1981-Fr. /Can.)
  (A. K. A. "La Guerre du Feu")
Director: Jean-Jacques
  Annaud
Everett McGill (Naoh), Rae Dawn
Chong (Ika), Ron Perlman (Amoukar),
Nameer El Kadi (Gaw), Gary
Schwartz (Rouka), Naseer el Kadi
(Nam), Frank Olivier Bonnet
(Aghoo), Kurt Schiegl (Faum),
Brian Gill (Modoc), Terry Fitt
(Hourk), Bibi Caspari (Gammia),
Peter Elliott (Mikr), Michelle
Leduc (Matr), Robert Lavoie
(Tsor), Matt Birman (Morah),
Christian Benrad (Umbre).

QUEST FOR LOVE (1971)
Director: Ralph Thomas
Tom Bell (Colin), Joan Collins
(Ottilie), Denholm Elliott (Tom),
Larence Naismith (Sir Henry),
Neil McCallum (Jimmy), Simon
Ward (Jeremy), Lyn Ashley (Jen-
nifer), Juliet Harmer (Geraldine).

QUESTOR TAPES, THE (TVM-
  1974) - 1-23-74
Director: Richard A. Colla
Robert Foxworth (Questor), Mike
Farrell (Jerry Robinson), Dana
Wynter (Lady Helen Trimbal),
Lew Ayres (Dr. Vaslovik), John
Vernon (Darrow), James Shigeta
(Dr. Chen), Majel Barrett (Dr.
Bradley), Walter Koenig (Ad-
ministrative Assistant), Ellen
Weston (Allison Sample), Fred
Sadoff (Dr. Audret), Reuben Singer
(Dr. Gorlov), Robert Douglas
(Dr. Michaels), Alan Caillou
(Immigrations Officer), Patti
Cubbison (secretary), Eydse
Girard (stewardess).

QUIET PLACE IN THE COUNTRY,
  A (1968-Ital. /Fr.) (A. K. A.
  "Un Tranquillo Posto di
  Campagna")
Director: Elio Petri
Franco Nero (Leonardo), Vanessa
Redgrave (Flavia), Georges Geret
(Attilio), Gabriella Grimaldi
(Wanda), Madeleine Damien (Wan-
da's mother), Rita Calderoni
(Egle), Renato Menegotto (Egle's
friend), John Francis Lane (Asy-
lum attendant), David Maunsell
(medium), Mirta Simionato,
Camillo Besenson, Marino
Pagiola, Graziella Simionato,
Constantine De Luca, Piero De
Franceschi, Guilia Menin, Otello

Cazzola, Sara Momo (villagers).

QUINTET (1979)
    Director: Robert Altman
    Paul Newman (Essex), Vittorio
Gassman (St. Christopher), Fernando
Rey (Grigor), Bibi Andersson (Ambrosia), Brigette Fossey (Vivia),
Nina Van Pallandt (Deuca), Tom
Hill (Francha), David Langton (Goldstar), Craig Richard Nelson (Redstone), Maruska Stankova (Jaspera),
Monique Mercure (Redstone's mate),
Anne Gerety (Aeon), Francoise Berd
(charity house woman), Michael
Maillot (Obelus), Max Fleck (wood
supplier).

RABID (1977)
    Director: David Cronenberg
    Marilyn Chambers (Rose), Joe Silver
(Murray Cypher), Frank Moore
(Hart Read), Howard Ryspan (Dr. Dan
Keloid), Patricia Gage (Dr. Roxanne
Keloid), Susan Roman (Mindy Dent),
J. Roger Periard (Lloyd Walsh), Lynne
Deragon (Nurse Louise), Victor Deay
(Claude Lapointe), Gary McKeehan
(Smooth Eddie), Terry Schonblum
(Judy Glasberg), Julie Anna (Nurse
Rita), Terrence G. Ross (farmer),
Robert O'Ree (police sergeant), Greg
Von Riel (man in plaza), Miguel Fernandez (man in Cinema), Jerome
Tiberghien (Dr. Karl), Richard Farrell (camper man), Jeannette Casenave
(camper lady), Carl Wasserman
(camper child), Allan Moyle (young
man in lobby), John Boylan (young
cop in plaza), Malcolm Neithorpe
(older cop in palza), Vlasta Vrana
(cop at clinic), Kirk McColl (desk
sergeant), Yvon Lecompte (policeman),
Jack Messinger (policeman on highway),
Grant Lowe (trucker), John Gilbert
(Dr. Royce Gentry), Tony Angelo
(dispatcher), Una Kay (Jackie), Peter
McNeill (Leader), Madeline Pageau
(Beatrice Owen), Mark Walker (Steve),
Bob Silverman (man in hospital),
Ron Mlodzik (male patient), Monique
Belisle (Sheila), Terry Donald (cook),
Harry Hill (Stasiak), Isabelle Lajeunese (waitress), Louis Negin (Maxim),
Bob Girolani (newscaster), Kathy
Keefler (interviewer), Riva Spier
(Cicile), Marcel Fournier (cab driver),
Denis Lacroix (drunken Indian),
Sherman Maness (Indian), Valda
Dalton (car lady), Murray Smith
(interviewer), Basil Fitzgibbon (crazy
in plaza).

RACE WITH THE DEVIL (1975)
    Director: Jack Starrett
    Peter Fonda (Roger), Warren
Oates (Frank), Loretta Swit (Alice),
Lara Parker (Kelly), R. G. Armstrong (Sheriff), Wes Bishop
(Deputy Dave), Clay Tanner
(Delbert), Carol Blodgett (Ethel),
Ricci Ware (Ricci Ware), Paul A.
Partain (Cal Mathers), Arkey
Blue (Arkey Blue), James Harrell
(gun shop owner), Karen Miller
(Kay), Jack Starrett (gas station
man), Phil Hoover (mechanic).

RADAR MEN FROM THE MOON
    (1951) (A.K.A. "Retik, the Moon
    Menace") - serial in 12 episodes
Chapters: 1. "Moon Rocket", 2.
"Molten Terror", 3. "Bridge of
Death", 4. "Flight to Destruction",
5. "Murder Car", 6. "Hills of
Death", 7. "Human Targets", 8.
"The Enemy Planet", 9. "Battle
in the Stratosphere", 10. "Mass
Execution", 11. "Planned Pursuit",
& 12. "Take-off to Eternity".
    Director: Fred C. Brannon
    George Wallace (Jeff King/Commando
Cody), Roy Barcroft (Retik), Aline
Towne (Joan Gilbert), William Bakewell (Ted Richars), Peter Brocco
(Krog), Clayton Moore (Graber),
Tom Steele (Zerg), Dale Van Sickel
(Alon), Baynes Barron (Nasor),
Noel Cravat (Robal), Bob Stevenson
(Daly), Don Walters (Henderson),
Paul McGuire (Bream), Wilson
Wood (Hank), Dick Cogan (Jones),
Paul Palmer (Bill), Ted Thorpe
(bartender), Stephan Gregory
(Benson), Harry Hollins (Brad),
Jack Shea (Doyle), Carey Loftin
(citizen), Billy Dix (Duke), Claude
Dunkin (Kern), William Marke
(guard), Sam Sebby (Moon Scout 7),
Arthur Walsh (motorcycle officer),
Joe Bailey, Guy Teague, Dick Rich
(policeman), Tony Merrill (Sam),
John Marshall (Smith), Ken Terrell.

RADAR PATROL VS. SPY KING
    (1949) - serial in 12 episodes
    Director: Fred C. Brannon
    Kirk Alyn (Chris Calvert), Jean
Dean (Joan Hughes), Anthony Warde
(Ricco Morgan), George J. Lewis
(Manuel Agura), John Crawford
(Sands), Tris Coffin (Franklyn Lord),
Harold Goodwin (Miller), Dale Van
Sickel (Lentz/Thomas), Eddie Parker
(Dutch), John Merton (Baroda/Spy
King), Tom Steele (Gorman/Ames),

Forbes Murray (Chairman), Eve
Whitney (Nitra), Stephen Gregory
(Hugo), Frank O'Connor (Chairman),
Arvon Dale (trooper), David Sharpe
(Cliff), Frank Dae (Clark), Eddie
Parker (Bender/Malloy/Nash/White/
Herb), Bud Wolfe (Kraft), Ken Terrell
(Tami), Charles Flynn (Finney), Duke
Taylor (Link), John Daheim (Hanley/
Jackson), Bert LeBaron (Nick),
Carey Loftin (cave heavy), Art
Dillard, Louise Volding, Helen
Thurston, Joe Hooker.

RADAR SECRET SERVICE (1949)
    Director: Sam Newfield
John Howard (Bill), Adele Jergens
(Lila), Tom Neal (Moran), Ralph
Byrd (Static), Pierre Watkin (Hamil-
ton), Sid Melton (Pill Box), Tris
Coffin (Michael), Keene Duncan, Bill
Hammond (Michael's henchmen),
Myrna Dell (Marge), Robert Kent
(Benson), Bob Carson (Tom), Marshall
Reed, John McKee (bruisers), Riley
Hill (Blacky), Holly Bane (truck
operator), Bob Woodward, Boyd
Stockman (henchmen), Jan Kayne
(maid), Bill Crespinel (helicopter
operator).

RADIO DETECTIVE, THE (1926) -
    serial in 10 episodes
Chapters: 1. "The Kick-off", 2. "The
Radio Riddle", 3. "The Radio Wizard",
4. "Boy Scout Loyalty", 5. "The Radio
Secret", 6. "Fighting for Love", 7.
"The Tenderfoot Scout", 8. "The
Truth Teller", 9. "The Fire Fiend",
& 10. "Radio Romance".
    Director: William Craft &
        William A. Crinley
Jack Daugherty (Eastern Evans),
Margaret Quimby (Mrs. Evans),
Jack Mower (Craig Kennedy), Florence
Allen (Flo), John T. Prince
(syndicate boss), Sammy Gervon,
Wallace Balwin (Crooks), Howard
Enstedt (policeman).

RADIO KING, THE (1922) - serial
    in 10 episodes
Chapters: 1. "A Cry for Help", 2.
"The Secret of the Air", 3. "A Battle
of Wits", 4. "Warned by Radio", 5.
"Ship of Doom", 6. "S.O.S.", 7.
"Saved by Wireless", 8. "The Master
Wave", 9. "The Trail of Vengeance",
& 10. "Saved by Science".
    Director: Robert F. Hill
Louise Lorraine (Mary Harden), Roy
Stewart (Brad Lane), Sidney Bracy
(Marnee), Al Smith (John Leyden),

Clark Comstock (Commander
Nelson), Ernest Butterworth, Jr.
(Jake).

RADIO-MANIA (1923) (A.K.A.
    "Mars Calling", "The Man from
    Mars", "M.A.R.S.")
    Director: R. William Neill
Grant Mitchell (Arthur Wyman),
Margaret Irving (Mary Langdon),
Gertrude Hillman (Mrs. Langdon), W.H.
Burton (Mr. Sterling), J.D. Walsh
(Buz Buz), Betty Borders (Tuz Tuz),
J. Burke (Gin Gin), Peggy Smith
(Pux Pux), Isabelle Vernon (land-
lady), Alice Effinger, Peggy Wil-
liams (Martian flappers).

RADIO PATROL (1937) - serial in
    12 episodes
Chapters: 1. "A Million Dollar
Murder", 2. "The Hypnotic Eye",
3. "The Human Clue", 4. "Flaming
Death", 5. "The Flash of Doom",
6. "The House of Terror", 7. "Claws
of Steel", 8. "In Perfect Crime",
9. "Plaything of Disaster", 10.
"A Bargain with Death", 11. "The
Hidden Menace", & 12. "They Get
Their Man".
    Director: Ford Beebe & Cliff
        Smith
Grant Withers (Pat O'Hara), Frank
Lackteen (Thata), Catherine Hughes
(Molly Selkirk), Monte Montague
(Pollard), Mickey Rentschler (Pinky
Adams), Max Hoffman, Jr. (Selkirk),
Leonard Lord (Franklik), Adrian
Morris (Sam), Dick Botiller (Zutta),
C. Montague Shaw, Jack Mulhall,
Harry Davenport, Wheeler Oakman.

RAGE (1972)
    Director: George C. Scott
George C. Scott (Dan Logan), Richard
Basehart (Dr. Cardwell), Barnard
Hughes (Dr. Spencer), Martin
Sheen (Maj. Holliford), Ken Tobey
(Col. Nickerson), Paul Stevens
(Col. Franklin), Dabbs Greer (Dr.
Thompson), Lou Frizzell (Spike
Zoynton), John Dierkes (Bill Parker),
Nicholas Beauvy (Chris Logan),
Ed Lauter (Orderly Simpson),
Stephen Young (Major Reintz),
William Jordon (Major Cooper).

RAIDERS OF THE LOST ARK
    (1981)
    Director: Steven Spielberg
Harrison Ford (Indiana Jones),
Karen Allen (Marion Ravenwood),
Paul Freeman (Rene Belloq), Ronald

Lacey (Toht), Denholm Elliott (Brody),
John Rhys-Davies (Sallah), Wolf
Kahler (Dietrich), Anthony Higgins
(Gobler), Alfred Molina (Satipo),
William Hootkins (Major Eaton),
Vic Tablian (Barranca), Don Fellows
(Col. Musgrove), Fred Sorenson
(Jock), Bill Reimbold (bureaucrat),
Patrick Durkin (Australian climber),
Tuttte Lemkow (Imam), Malcolm
Weaver (ratty Napalese), Matthew
Scurfield (2nd Nazi), Sonny Caldinez
(mean Mongolian), Anthony Chinn
(Mohen), Pat Roach (giant Sherpa),
Christopher Frederick (Otto),
Ishaq Bux (Omar), Souad Messaoudi
(Feyah), Kiran Shah (Abu), Terry
Richards (Arab swordsman), Pat
Roach (1st mechanic), Steve Hanson
(German agent), Frank Marshall
(pilot), Martin Kreidt (young soldier),
George Harris (Katanga), Eddie
Tagoe (messenger pirate), John
Rees (Sergeant), Tony Vogel (Tall
Captain), Ted Grossman (Peruvian
porter).

RAISE THE TITANIC! (1980)
Director: Jerry Jameson
Jason Robards, Jr. (Adm. James
Sandecker), Richard Jordan (Dirk
Pitt), David Selby (Dr. Gene Seagram),
Anne Archer (Dana Archibald),
J. D. Cannon (Capt. Joe Burke),
Paul Carr (Nicholson), Alec Guinness
(John Bigalow), Michael C. Gwynne
(Bohannon), Dirk Blocker (Merker),
Norman Bartold (Kemper), Bo
Brundin (Capt. Andre Prevlov),
Charles Macaulay (Busby), Elya
Baskin (Marganin), Harvey Lewis
(Kiel), M. Emmet Walsh (MCPO
Vinnnie Giordino), Robert Broyles
(Willis), Stewart Moss, Michael
Pataki, Mark L. Taylor, Marvin
Silbersher, Nancy Nevinson, Trent
Dolan, Sander Vanocur, Ken Place,
Craig Shreeve, Jonathan Moore,
Michael Ensign, Brendan Burns,
Hilly Hicks, Mike Kulscar, George
Stover, Mark Hammer, George
Whitman, David Hammond, Ron
Evans.

RAMAR AND THE SEVEN CHAL-
LENGES (1953)
see Television: Ramar of the
Jungle (1952-53)

RAMAR AND THE UNKNOWN TERROR
(1953)
see Television: Ramar of the
Jungle (1952-53)

RAMAR OF THE JUNGLE (1952)
see Television: Ramar of the
Jungle (1952-53)

RANSOM (1928)
Director: George B. Seitz
Lois Wilson (Lois Brewster),
Edmund Burns (Burton Meredith),
William V. Mong (Wu Fang),
Blue Washington (Oliver), James
B. Leong (Scarface), Jackie
Coombs (Bobby).

RASHOMON (1950-Jap.)
Director: Akira Kruosawa
Toshiro Mifune (the Bandit),
Machiko Kyo (the woman), Masa-
yuki Mori (the man), Minoru
Chiaki (the priest), Takashi
Shimura (the firewood dealer),
Kichijiro Ueda (the commoner),
Fumiko Homma (the medium),
Daisuke Kato (the police).

RASPUTIN (1930-Ger.) (A. K. A.
"Rasputin Damon der Frauen",
"Rasputin, Demon with Women")
Director: Adolph Trotz
Conrad Veidt (Rasputin), Paul
Otto (Tsar), Kenny Rive (Tsarevich),
Carl Ludwig Diehl (Prince Felix),
Franziska King.

RASPUTIN (1938-Fr.) (A. K. A.
"Raspoutine")
Director: Marcel L'Herbier
Harry Baur (Rasputin), Marcelle
Chantal (the Czarian), Pierre-
Richard Willm (Count Igor Kourloff),
Jany Holt (Grousina), Corine
Nelson (Ania Kitina), Denis d'Ines
(Bishop Gregorina), Alexandre
Rignault (Capt. Block), Jean Worms
(the Czar), Jacques Baumer (Pro-
koff), Gabrielle Robinne (Czarina's
mother), Mady Berry.

RASPUTIN (1953-Fr.) (A. K. A.
"Raspoutine")
Director: Georges Combret
Pierre Brasseur (Rasputin), Isa
Miranda (Tsarine), Claude Laydu
(Moine Alexandre), Robert Bernier
(Tsar), Renee Faure (Vera),
Jacques Berthier (Officer), Miche-
line Francey, Milly Vitale, Jean
Wall, Etchevery, Robert Berri,
Raphael Patorin, Robert Lombard,
Denise Grey.

RASPUTIN AND THE EMPRESS
(1932)
Director: Richard Boleslavsky

Lionel Barrymore (Rasputin), John Barrymore (Prince Chegodieff), Ethel Barrymore (the Czarina), Ralph Morgan (the Czar), Edward Arnold (Dr. Remezov), C. Henry Gordon (Grand Duke Igor), Diana Wynward (Princess Natasha), Tad Alexander (the Czarevitch), Gustav von Seyffertitz (Dr. Wolfe), Mischa Auer (butler), Lucien Littlefield (reveler), Charlotte Henry (girl), Hooper Atchley (policeman), Frank Reicher (German Language teacher), Frank Shannon (Prof. Propotkin), Jean Parker (Maria), Dawn O'Day (Anastasia), Sarah Padden (landlady), Henry Kolker (Chief of Secret Police), Dave O'Brien, Maurice Black (soldier), Leo White (reveler).

RASPUTIN, THE BLACK MONK (1917)
    Director: Arthur Ashley
Montague Love (Rasputin), Henry Hull (Kerensky), Arthur Ashley (Raff), June Elvidge (Raff's wife), Lilian Cook (Raff's daughter), Julia Dean (Lady in Waiting), Bertram Granby (Alexis), Irving Cummings (Yusopof).

RASPUTIN, THE MAD MONK (1965)
    Director: Don Sharp
Christopher Lee (Rasputin), Barbara Shelley (Sonia), Renee Asherson (Tsarina), Richard Pasco (Dr. Zargo), Francis Mathews (Evan), Suzan Farmer (Vanessa), Joss Ackland (the Bishop), Alan Tilvern (Patron), Nicholas Pennell (Peter), Derek Francis (innkeeper), John Welsh (the Abbott), John Bailey (Court Physician), Robert Duncan (Tsarevitch).

RAT PFINK AND BOO BOO (1964)
    (A.K.A. "Rat Pfink a Boo Boo")
    Director: Ray Dennis Steckler
Dean Danger (Narrator), Carolyn Brandt, Vin Saxon, Titus Moede, George Caldwell, James Bowie, Mike Kannon, Keith Wester, Mary Joe Curts, Romeo Barrymore, Bob Burns.

RATS, THE (1982)
    Director: Robert Clouse
Sam Groom (Paul Harris), Sara Botsford (Kelly Leonard), Scatman Crothers (George Fosk), Lisa Langlois (Trudy White), Cec Linder (Dr. Louis Spenser), James B. Douglas (Mel Dederick), Lesleh Donaldson (Martha).

RATS ARE COMING! THE WERE-
    WOLVES ARE HERE!, THE (1972)
    Director: Andy Milligan
Hope Stansbury (Monica Mooney),

Berwick Kaler (Malcolm Mooney), Noel Collins (Mortimer Mooney), Jacqueline Skarvellis (Diana), Joan Ogden (Phoebe Mooney), Douglas Phair (Pa Mooney), Ian Innes (Gerald).

RATTLERS (1976)
    Director: John McCauley
Sam Chew (Dr. Parkinson), Elisabeth Chauvet (Ann), Dan Priest (Colonel), Ron Gold (Delaney), Richard Lockmiller (Deputy), Tony Ballen (Sheriff), Jo Jordan (Mother), Al Dunlap (General), Ancel Cook (janitor), Gary Van Ormand, Darwin Jostin (soldiers), Travis Gold, Alan Decker (boys).

RAVAGERS, THE (1979)
    Director: Richard Compton
Richard Harris (Falk), Ann Turkel (Faina), Ernest Borgnine (Rann), Art Carney (Sergeant), Anthony James (Leader), Woody Strode (Brown), Alana Hamilton (Miriam), Seymour Cassel (Blindman),

RAVEN, THE (1915)
    Director: Charles J. Brabin
Henry B. Walthall, Warda Howard, Ernest Maupin, Harry Dunkinson, Grant Foreman, Hugh E. Thompson, Frank Hmailton, Peggy Meredith.

RAVEN, THE (1935)
    Director: Lew Landers
Boris Karloff (Edmund Bateman), Bela Lugosi (Dr. Richard Vollin), Irene Ware (Jean Thatcher), Samuel S. Hinds (Judge Thatcher), Lester Matthews (Dr. Jerry Halden), Ian Wolfe (Pinky Geoffrey), Spencer Charters (Col. Bertram Grant), Arthur Hoyt (Chapman), Inez Courtney (Mary Burns), Maidel Turner (Harriet Grant), Walter Miller.

RAVEN, THE (1962)
    Director: Roger Corman
Vincent Price (Dr. Erasmus Craven), Peter Lorre (Dr. Bedlo), Boris Karloff (Dr. Scarabus), Jack Nicholson (Rexford Bedlo), Hazel Court (Lenore Craven), Olive Sturgess (Estele Craven), William Baskin (Grimes), Aaron Saxon (Gort), Connie Wallace (maid servant).

RAVEN, THE (1943-Ger.) (A.K.A. "Le Corbeau", "The Crow")
    Director: Henri-Georges Clouzot

Pierre Fresnay, Pierre Larquey,
Helena Manson, Ginette Leclerc,
Noel Roquevert, Micheline Francey.

RAW FORCE (1982)
    Director: Ed Murphy
Cameron Mitchell (Captain), Geoff
Binney (Mike), Jillian Kessner (Cookie),
John Dresden (John), Jennifer Holmes
(Ann), Hope Holiday (Hazel), Rey
King (Chin), Vic Diaz (Monk).

RAW MEAT (1972)
    Director: Gary Sherman
Donald Pleasence (Insp. Calhoun),
Norman Rossington (Detective Sgt.
Rogers), David Ladd (Alex Campbell),
Sharon Gurney (Patricia Wislon),
Christopher Lee (Stratton-Villers,
MI 5), Hugh Armstrong (the Man),
June Turner (the Woman), James
Cossins (James Manfred), Clive
Swift (Insp. Richardson), Heather
Stoney (D.C.W. Alice Marshall),
Hugh Dickson (Dr. Bacon), Jack
Woolgar (platform inspector), Colin
McCormack (1st constable), Gary
Winkler (2nd constable), Ron Pember
(lift operator), Suzanne Winkler (prostitute), James Culliford (publican),
Gerry Crampton, Gordon Petrie,
Terry Plummer (tunnel workers).

RED ALERT (TVM-1977) - 5-18-77
    Director: William Hale
William Devane (Frank Brolen), Ralph
Waite (Cmdr. Henry Stone), Michael
Brandon (Carl Wyche), Adrienne Barbeau (Judy Wyche), David Hayward
(Larry Cadwell), Jim Siedow (Howard
Ives), M. Emmet Walsh (Sheriff
Sweeney), Malcolm Wittman (Lou
Banducci), Lois Fleck (Marie), Dixie
Taylor (Mrs. Kerwin), Howard Finch
(Harry Holland), Charles Krohn
(Stover), Don Wiseman (Bill Yancy).

RED CIRCLE (1915) - serial in 14
    episodes
Chapters: 1. "Nevermore", 2. "Pity
the Poor", 3. "Twenty Years Ago",
4. "In Strange Attire", 5. "Weapons
of War", 6. "False Colors", 7. "Third
Degree", 8. "Peace at Any Price",
9. "Dodging the Law", 10. "Excess
Baggage", 11. "Seeds of Suspicion",
12. "Like a Rat in a Trap", 13.
"Branded as a Thief", & 14. "Judgement Day".
    Director: Sherwood MacDonald
Philo McCullough, Ruth Roland, Gordon
Sackville, Frank Mayo.

REDEEMER, THE (1977)
    Director: Constantine S. Gochis
T.G. Finkbinder (the Redeemer),
Jeannetta Arnette, Nick Carter,
Gyr Patterson, Damien Knight, Nikki
Barthen, Christopher Flint.

RED HOUSE, THE (1946)
    Director: Delmer Daves
Edward G. Robinson (Pete Morgan),
Judith Anderson (Ellen Morgan),
Rory Calhoun (Teller), Julie London
(Tibby Rinton), Lon McCallister
(Nath Storm), Harry Shannon (Dr.
Byrne), Walter Sands (Don Brent),
Ona Munson (Mrs. Storm), Arthur
Space (Officer), Allene Roberts (Meg).

RED INN, THE (1951-Fr.) (A.K.A.
    "L'Auberge Rouge")
    Director: Claude Autant-Lara
Fernandel (the Monk), Francoise
Rosay (Marie), Julian Carette
(Martin), Marie-Claire Olivia
(Mathilde), A. Vialla (Fetiche),
Andre Cheff (the Dandy), Nane
Germon (the Englishman), Didier
d'Yd (the Marchioness), Gaussimon,
Gregoire Aslan (passengers).

RED LIGHTS (1923)
    Director: Clarence G. Badger
Alice Lake (Norah O'Neill), Lionel
Belmore (Alden Murray), Jean
Hersholt (Ezra), Raymond Griffith
(Sheridan Scott), Marie Prevost
(Ruth Carson), John Walker (Blake),
Dagmar Godowsky (Roxy), William
Worthington (Luke Carson), Frank
Elliot (Kirk Allen), George Reed
(porter), Charles H. West (conductor),
Charles B. Murphy (henchman).

RED MILL, THE (1927)
    Director: Roscoe Arbuckle
Karl Dane (Capt. Jacob Edam), Louise
Fazenda (Gretchen), Snitz Edwards
(Timothy), Marion Davies (Tina),
Owen Moore (Dennis), George Siegmann
(William), J. Russell Powell (Burgomaster), Fred Gambold (innkeeper),
William Orlamond (Governor),
Sunshine Hart.

RED PLANET MARS (1952)
    Director: Harry Horner
Peter Graves (Chris Cronyn),
Andrea King (Linda Cronyn), Herbert
Berghof (Franz Calder), Marvin
Miller (Arjenian), Walter Sande
(Admiral Carey), Willis Bouchey
(President), Lewis Martin (Dr.
Mitchell), Morris Ankrum (Secretary

Sparks), House Peters, Jr. (Dr.
Boulting), Orley Lindgren (Stewart
Cronyn), Bayard Veiller (Roger
Cronyn), John Topa (Borodin), Claude
Dunkin (Peter Lewis), Tom Keene
(Gen. Burdette), Gene Roth (UMW
President), Bill Kennedy (commenta-
tor), Vince Barnett (man), Grace
Leonard (woman).

RED RIDING HOOD (1901-Fr.) (A. K. A.
"Le Petit Chaperon Rouge")
Director: Georges Melies

RED TENT, THE (1969-Ital. /Sov.)
(A. K. A. "La Tenda Rossa")
Director: Mikhail Kalatozov
Peter Finch (Umberto Nobile), Sean
Connery (Roald Amundsen), Claudia
Cardinale (Valeria), Hardy Kruger
(Lundborg), Mario Adorf (Biagi),
Massimo Girotti (Romagna), Donatas
Banionis (Mariano), Luigi Vannucchi
(Zappi), Boris Kmelnizki (Viglieri),
Jiri Vizbor (Behounek), Edward
Marzevuc (Malmgren), Jure Solomin
(Troiani), Otar Koberidze (Cecioni),
Nikita Mikhalkov (Chuknovsky),
Grigori Gaj (Samoilovich), Nicolai
Ivanov (Kolka).

REFLECTION OF FEAR, A (1971)
Director: William A. Fraker
Robert Shaw (Michael), Sally Keller-
man (Anne), Sondra Locke (Marguerite),
Mary Ure (Katherine), Signe Hasso
(Julia), Mitchell Ryan (McKenna),
Gordon DeVol (Hector), Liam Dunn
(the Coroner), Victoria Risk (Peggy),
Michael St. Clair (Kevin), Michele
Montau (Mme. Caraquet), Michelle
Marvin (nurse), Leonard John Crofoot
(Aaron), Gordon Anderson (voice of
Aaron).

REFLECTIONS OF MURDER (TVM-
1974) - 11-24-74
Director: John Badham
Tuesday Weld (Vicky), Joan Hackett
(Claire Elliott), Michael Lerner
(Jerry Steele), R. G. Armstrong
(Turner), Sam Waterston (Michael
Elliott), Lucille Benson (Mrs. Turner),
Lance Kerwin (Chip), John Levin
(Keith), William Turner (Mr. Grif-
fiths), James A. Newcombe (Peter),
Jesse Vint (cop on freeway), Ed
Bernard (coroner), Sam Henriot (David),
Don Sparks (photographer), Sandra
Coburn (woman), Rita Conde (maid).

REINCARNATE, THE (1971)
Director: Don Haldane

Jack Creley (Everet Julian), Jay
Reynolds (David Paine), Trudy
Young (Ruthie Montes), Hugh
Webster (Berryman), Gene Tyburn
(Stedley), Rex Hagon (Gene),
Colin Fox (Ormsby), Terry Tweed
(Ann Jameston).

REINCARNATION OF PETER PROUD,
THE (1975)
Director: J. Lee Thompson
Michael Sarrazin (Peter Proud),
Jennifer O'Neill (Ann Curtis),
Margot Kidder (Marcia Curtis),
Cornelia Sharpe (Nora Hayes),
Anne Ives (Ellen Curtis), Nor-
mann Burton (Dr. Frederick
Spear), Paul Hecht (Dr. Samuel
Goodman), Steve Franken (Dr.
Charles Crennis), Tony Stephano
(Jeff Curtis), Debralee Scott
(Suzy), Jon Richards (newspaper
custodian).

RELUCTANT ASTRONAUT, THE
(1967)
Director: Edward J. Montagne
Don Knotts (Roy Fleming), Arthur
O'Connell (Buck Fleming), Jeanette
Nolan (Mrs. Fleming), Leslie
Nielsen (Maj. Fred Gifford),
Joan Freman (Ellie Jackson),
Jesse White (Donelli), Paul
Hartman (Rush), Nydia Westman
(Aunt Zana), Guy Raymond (Bert),
Burt Mustin (Ned), Robert Pickerin
(Maran), Robert Simon (Cervantes),
Frank McGarth (Plank), Fabian
Dean (bus driver), Fay De Witt
(secretary), Joan Shawlee (blonde
in bar), Ceil Cabot (waitress).

REMARKABLE ANDREW, THE
(1941)
Director: Stuart Heisler
William Holden (Andrew Long),
Brain Donlevy (Gen. Andrew Jack-
son), Ellen Drew (Peggy Tobin),
Richard Webb (Randall Stevens),
Montague Love (George Washington),
Brandon Hurst (Chief Justice John
Marshall), Gilbert Emery (Thomas
Jefferson), Rod Cameron (Jesse
James), Jimmy Conlin (Private
Henry Bartholomew Smith), Minor
Watson (District Attorney Orville
Beamish), Spencer Charters (Dr.
Clarence Upjohn), George Watts
(Benjamin Franklin), Milton Parsons
(Purchase Agent Sam Savage),
Porter Hall (Chief Clerk Art
Slocumb), Clyde Fillmore (Mayor
Ollie Lancaster), Thomas W. Ross

(Judge Ormond Krebbs), Wallis Clark
(City Treasurer R. R. McCall), Nydia
Westman, Martha O'Driscoll, Frances
Gifford.

REMEMBER LAST NIGHT (1935)
Director: James Whale
Edward Arnold (Danny Harrison), Sally
Eilers (Bette Huling), Constance Cum-
mings (Carlotta Milburn), Robert Young
(Tony Milburn), Robert Armstrong
(Fred Flannagan), Reginald Denny (Jack
Whitridge), Edward S. Brophy (Maxie),
George Meeker (Vic Huling), Jack
LaRue (Baptiste), Gustav von Seyffer-
titz (Prof. Jones), Gregory Ratoff
(Faronea), Rafaela Ottiano (Mme.
Bouclier), Louise Henry (Penny Whit-
ridge), Arthur Treacher (Phelps),
Monroe Owsley (Billy Arnold).

RENEGADE SATELLITE, THE (1954)
see Television: Rocky Jones,
Space Ranger (1953-54)

RENTADICK (1972)
Director: Jim Clark
James Booth, Julie Ege, Richard
Briers, Ronald Fraser, Donald Sinden,
Kenneth Cope, Spike Milligan, Tsai
Chin.

REPEAT PERFORMANCE (1947)
Director: Alfred Werker
Louis Hayward (Barney Page), Joan
Leslie (Sheila Page), Richard Basehart
(William Williams), Virginia Field
(Paula Costello), Tom Conway (John
Friday), Natalie Schafer (Eloise Shaw),
Benay Venuta (Bess Nichols), Ilka
Gruning (Mattie).

REPTILE, THE (1966)
Director: John Gilling
Noel Willman (Dr. Franklyn), Jen-
nifer Daniel (Valerie Spalding),
Jacqueline Pearce (Anna Franklyn),
Ray Barrett (Harry Spaling), Michael
Ripper (Tim Bailey), Marne Maitland
(Malay), John Laurie (Mad Peter),
Charlse Lloyd-Pack (Vicar), George
Woodbridge (Old Garnsey), David
Baron (Charles Spalding), Harold Gold-
blatt (solicitor).

REPTILICUS (1962-U. S. /Dan.)
Director: Sidney Pink
Carl Ottosen (Mark Grayson), Ann
Smyrner (Lise Martens), Asbjorn
Anderson (Prof. Martens), Mimi
Heinrich (Karen Martens), Marla
Behrens (Connie Miler), Bent Majding
(Svend Viltofft), Ole Wisborg (Capt.

Brandt), Poul Wildaker (Dr. Dalby),
Dirk Passer (Dirk Mikkelsen).

REPULSION (1965)
Director: Roman Polanski
Catherine Deneuve (Carol), Ian
Hendry (Michael), Yvonne Furneaux
(Helen), John Fraser (Colin), Renee
Houston (Miss Balch), Patrick
Wymark (the Landlord), James
Villiers (John), Hugh Futcher (Reg-
gie), Helen Fraser (Bridget), Valerie
Taylor (Madame Denise), Monica
Merlin (Mrs. Rendlesham), Roman
Polanski (a spoons player), Mike
Pratt (a workman), Imogen Graham
(a manicurist).

RESCUED FROM AN EAGLE'S NEST
(1907) - short
Director: Edwin S. Porter

RESURRECTED MONSTER, THE
(1952-Mex.) (A. K. a. "El Monstruo
Resucitado")
Director: Chano Urueta
Carlos Navarro, Miroslava, Fernando
Wagner, Jose Maria Linares Rivas,
Alberto Mariscal.

RESURRECTION (1980)
Director: Daniel Petrie
Ellen Burstyn (Edna McCauley),
Sam Shepard (Cal Carpenter), Roberts
Blossom (John Harper), Eva Le
Galliene (Grandma Pearl), Richard
Farnsworth (Esco), Pamela Pay-
ton-Wright (Margaret), Jeffrey De
Munn (Joe MacCauley), Clifford
David (George), Madeline Thornton-
Sherwood (Ruth), Richard Hamilton
(Earl Carpenter), Lois Smith (Kathy),
Carlin Glynn (Suzy Kroll), Ebbe Roe
Smith (Hank Peterson), John Tillinger
(Dr. Herron), Ralph Roberts (Buck),
Bernard Behrens (Dr. Fisher),
Penelope Allen (Ellie), Lane Smith
(Don), Trazana Beverley (Dr.
Ellen Baxter), George Sperdakos
(Dr. Hankins), Vernon Weddle, James
Blendick, Harvey Christiansen, Lou
Fant, David Haney, James N.
Harrell, David Calkins, Therese
East, Jessie Lee Fulton, Claudette
Harrell, Jennifer McAllister, A. G.
Mills, Tom Taylor, Carol Williard,
Don Michaelson, Edith Mills,
Sylvia Walden, Tracy Wilson.

RESURRECTION OF ZACHARY
WHEELER, THE (1971)
Director: Robert Wynn
Bradford Dillman (Zachary Wheeler),

Angie Dickinson (Dr. Johnson), Leslie
Nielsen (Harry), James Daly (Dr.
Redding), Robert J. Wilke (Fielding),
Jack Carter (Dwight Chiles), Tris
Coffin (Dr. Keating), Tyler McVey
(George), Don Haggerty (Jake), Byron
Morrow (Gen. Townes), Harry Holcombe
(Wilson), Rodofo Hoyos (Medina), Lew
Brown (Collins), Richard Schuyler (Bates),
Richard Simmons (Adams), Ruben Mo-
reno (Gen. Manez), Peter Mamakos
(Premier Mabella), Steve Corey (Car-
son), Jim Healy (1st TV commentator),
Lee Giroux (2nd TV commentator),
Jill Jaress (Ensign Lee), Patrick O'Moore
(Matrin), Paul Sorenson (Thompson),
Del Murray (Williams), Tom Peters
(shipping clerk), Ray Fine (Jerry), John
Bill (medic), Steve Conte (radio operator),
Andy Davis (radio operator), Linda
Londan (nurse), Dean Stewart (orderly),
Thomas Dycus (Dr. Rand), Aly Yoder
(Mrs. Bleer).

RETURN, THE (1981) (A. K. A.   "Earth-
    right")
    Director: Greydon Clark
Cybill Shepherd (Jennifer Kramer),
Jan Michael Vincent (Wayne Thomp-
son), Raymond Burr (Dr. Joseph Kramer),
Martin Landau (Marshall Miles 'Buck'
Buchanan), Neville Brand (Walt), Vincent
Schiavelli (the Prospector), Brad Rear-
don (Eddie), Darby Hinton (Darren),
Ernest Anderson (Dr. Mostorff), Ken
Minyard, Candy Castillo (federal agents),
Steven Hirsch (Dr. Parkfield), Susan
Kiger Bunch (Young Jennifer), Zachary
Vincent (young Wayne), Robert M.
Magnus (town drunk), Michael R. Starita
(grandfather), Dorothy Constantine (motel
manager), Lynda Clark (girl), Buck Allen
(truck driver), Jacob Bresler (cafe
patron).

RETURN FROM WITCH MOUNTAIN
    (1978)
    Director: John Hough
Kim Richards (Tia Malone), Ike
Eisenmann (Tony Malone), Bette Davis
(Letha Wedge), Christopher Lee (Dr.
Victor Gannon), Denver Pyle (Uncle
Bene), Anthony James (Sickle), Ward
Costello (Clearcole), Jack Soo (Mr.
Yokomoto), Dick Bakalyan (Eddie),
Brad Savage (Muscles), Christian Jut-
tner (Dazzler), Jeffrey Jacquet (Rocky),

RETURN OF CAPTAIN INVINCIBLE,
    THE (1983)
    Director: Phillippe Mora
Alan Arkin, Christopher Lee, Bill
Hunter, Kate Fitzpatrick, Graham

Kennedy, Michael Pate, Max Phipps,
John Bluthal, Hayes Gordon, Noel
Ferrier, Arthur Dignam, Max Cullen,
Chris Haywood, Gus Mercurio,
Maggie Dences, Treach Lee, Norman
Erskine, Brian Adams.

RETURN OF CHANDU, THE (1934)
    (A. K. A. "Chandu on the Magic
    Island") - serial in 12 episodes
Chapters: 1. "The Chosen Victim",
2. "The House on the Hill", 3. "On
the High Seas", 4. "The Evil Eye",
5. "The Invisible Circle", 6. "Chan-
du's False Step", 7. "The Mysterious
Island", 8. "The Edge of the Pit",
9. "The Invisible Terror", 10. "The
Crushing Rock", 11. "The Uplifted
Knife", & 12. "The Knife Descends".
    Director: Ray Taylor
Bela Lugosi (Frank Chandler/Chandu),
Maria Alba (Princess Nadji),
Clara Kimball Young (Dorothy
Regent), Bryant Washburn (Prince
Andre), Phyllis Ludwig (Betty
Regent), Lucien Prival (Vindhyan),
Dean Benton (Bob Regent), April
Armbuster (Sertia), Elias Lazaroff
(Bara), Peggy Montgomery (Judy),
Dick Bottellier (Morta), Frazer
Acosta (Nito), Jack Clark (Vitras),
Harry Walker (Tagora), Isobel
LeMall (Mrs. James), Charles
Meecham (Mr. James), Josef
Swickard (Tyba), Murdock McQuaine
(voice of Ubasti), Henry Hall (curator),
Beatrice Roberts (lady), Don Brodie
(reporter), Edward Piel (airline
agent), Elias Schaffer (old man),
Iron Eyes Cody (Cat Man), Merrill
McCormick (sacrificial aide).

RETURN OF COUNT YORGA, THE
    (1971)
    Director: Bob Kelljan
Robert Quarry (Count Yorga), Mar-
iette Hartley (Cynthia Nelson),
Roger Perry (Dr. David Baldwin),
Yvonne Wilder (Jennifer), Tom
Toner (Rev. Thomas), Rudy Deluca
(Lt. Madden), Walter Brooke
(Bill Nelson), George Macready
(Prof. Rightstat), Edward Walsh
(Brudah), Mike Pataki (Joe),
Craig Nelson (Sgt. O'Connor),
Philip Frame (Tommy), Karen
Houston (Ellen), David Mapson
(Jason), Helen Baron (Mrs. Nelson),
Jesse Wells (Mitzi), Corrine Conley
(witch), Allen Joseph (Michael),
Peg Shirley (Claret), Liz Rogers
(Laurie Greggs), Paul Hansen
(Jonathan Greggs).

RETURN OF DRACULA, THE (1958)
(A. K. A. "The Curse of Dracula",
"The Fantastic Disappearing Man")
Director: Paul Landres
Francis Lederer ("Bellac Goudal"/
Count Dracula), Norma Eberhardt
(Rachel Mayberry), Greta Granstedt
(Cora Mayberry), Ray Stricklyn (Tim),
Jimmy Baird (Micky Mayberry),
John McNamara (Sheriff Bicknell),
Gage Clark (the Reverend), John
Wengraff (Mr. Meyerman), Norbert
Schiller (Bellac Goudal), Robert
Lynn (doctor), Hope Summers (Cor-
nelia), Virginia Vincent (Jenny),
Dan Gachman (county clerk), Mel
Allen (Porter), Harry Harvey, Sr.
(station master).

RETURN OF DR. FU MANCHU, THE
(1930)
Director: Rowland V. Lee
Warner Oland (Dr. Fu Manchu),
Jean Arthur (Lia Eltham), O. P.
Heggie (Nayland Smith), Neil Hamil-
ton (Dr. Jack Petrie), William Austin
(Sylvester Wadsworth), Shayle Gard-
ner (Insp. Harding), David Dunbar
(Lawrence), Tetsu Komai (Chang),
Evelyn Selby (Fai Lu), Margaret
Fealy (Lady Helen Bentley), Toyo
Fujita (Ah Ling), Ambrose Barker
(the reporter).

RETURN OF DR. MABUSE, THE
(1961-Ger.) (A. K. A. "Im Stahl-
netz des Dr. Mabuse", "In the
Steel Net of Dr. Mabuse")
Director: Harald Reinl
Wolfgang Preiss (Dr. Mabuse),
Gert Frobe, Lex Barker, Daliah
Lavi, Ady Berber, Fausto Tozzi,
Werner Peters.

RETURN OF DR. X, THE (1939)
Director: Vincent Sherman
Humphrey Bogart (Marshall Quesne),
Wayne Morris (Walter Barnett),
Rosemary Lane (Joan Vance), Dennis
Morgan (Michael Rhodes), John Litel
(Dr. Francis Flegg), Lia Lys (Angela
Merrova), William Hopper (Fenton),
Joe Crehan (editor), Charles Wilson
(Roy Kincaid), John Ridgely (Rodger),
Huntz Hall (Pinky), Creighton Hale
(hotel manager), Glenn Langan (in-
terne), Olin Howland (undertaker),
Cliff Saum (Detective Sgt. Moran),
Arthur Aylesworth (guide), DeWolfe
Hopper (interne), Ian Wolfe, Virginia
Brissac, George Reeves, John Har-
mon, Howard Hickman, Ed Chandler.

RETURN OF THE GIANT MAJIN,
THE (1966-Jap.) (A. K. A.
"Daimajin Ikaru")
Director: Kenji Misuni
Kojiro Hongo (Juro Chigusa),
Shiho Fujimura (Sayuri), Taro
Marui (Todohei), Takashi Kanda
(Danjo Mikoshiba).

RETURN OF MAURICE DONNELLY,
THE (1915)
Director: William Humphrey
Leo Delaney (young man), Leah
Baird (wife), Anders Randolph
(physician), Mary Maurice (mother),
Denton Vane (District Attorney),
Garry McGarry (warden), Josephe
Earle (nurse), William Dunn,
Daniel Hages (crooks).

RETURN OF PETER GRIMM, THE
(1926)
Director: Victor Schertzinger
Alec B. Francis (Peter Grimm),
Lionel Belmore (Rev. Bartholemy),
Elizabeth Patterson (Mrs. Bartho-
lomey), Janet Gaynor (Catherine),
John St. Pollis (Andrew McPherson),
Richard Walling (James Hartman),
John Roche (Frederick Grimm),
Florence Gilbert (Annemarie),
Bodil Rosing (Marta), Michey McBan
(William), Sammy Cohen (clown).

RETURN OF PETER GRIMM, THE
(1935)
Director: George Nicholls, Jr.
Lionel Barrymore (Peter Grimm),
Helen Mack (Catherine), Donald
Meek (Mr. Bartholomew), Ethel
Griffies (Mrs. Batholomew), George
Breakston (William), Lucien
Littlefield (Col. Lawton), Edward
Ellis (Dr. Andrew Macpherson),
Allen Vincent (Frederik), James
Bush (James), Greta Meyer (Marta).

RETURN OF SHERLOCK HOLMES,
THE (1929)
Director: Basil Dean
Clive Brook (Sherlock Holmse),
Harry T. Morey (Prof. Moriarty),
Donald Crisp (Col. Moran), H.
Reeves-Smith (Dr. Watson), Betty
Lawford (Mary Watson), Charles
Hay (Capt. Longmore), Hubert
Druce (Sgt. Gripper).

RETURN OF TARZAN, THE (1920)
Director: Harry Revier
Gene Pollar (Tarzan), Karla
Schramm (Jane), Armand Cortez
(Rokoff), George Romain (Count),

Franklin Coates (Paul D'Arnot),
Estelle Taylor (Countess de Coude),
Walter Miller.

RETURN OF THE APE MAN (1944)
    Director: Phil Rosen
Bela Lugosi (Prof. Dexter), John
Carradine (Prof. Gilmore), Tod
Andrews (Steve Rogers), Judy Gibson (Anne), George Zucco (the Ape
Man), Frank Moran (the Ape Man),
Ed Chandler (Sergeant), Mary Currier (Mrs. Gilmore), Ernie Adams
(bum), Horace Carpenter (watchman),
Mike Donovan, George Eldredge
(patrolmen), Frank Leigh.

RETURN OF THE EVIL DEAD, THE
    (1973-Span.) (A.K.A. "El Ataque),
    de los Muertos Sin Ojos")
Tony Kendall, Lone Fleming, Fernando
Sancho, E. Roy.

RETURN OF THE FLY, THE (1959)
    Director: Edward Bernds
Brett Halsey (Philippe Delambre),
Vincent Price (Francoise Delambre),
David Frankham (Dr. Alan Hines),
Dan Seymour (Max Berthold), John
Sutton (Insp. Charas), Danielle De-
Metz (Cecile Bonnard), Michael
Mark (Gaston), Janine Grandel (Mme.
Bonnard), Pat O'Hara (Detective
Evans), Jack Daly (Granville), Richard
Flato (Sgt. Dubois), Barry Bernard
(Lt. Maclish), Joan Cotton (nurse),
Florence Strom (Nun), Francisco
Villalobas (priest), Gregg Martell.

RETURN OF THE FROG, THE (1938)
    Director: Maurice Elvey
Gordon Harker (Insp. Elk), Una
O'Connor (Mum Oaks), Cyril Smith
(Maggs), Charles Carson (Commissioner), George Hayes (Lane), Rene Ray
(Lila), Charles Lefeaux (Golly Oaks),
Hartley Power (Sandford), Aubrey
Mallalieu (Banker), Meinhart Maur
(Aikman).

RETURN OF THE GIANT MONSTERS
    (1967-Jap.) (A.K.A. "Gamera
    vs Gyaos", "Gamera tai Gyaos")
    Director: Noriaki Yuasa
Kojiro Hongo (Shiro Tsitsmui), Kichi-
jiro Ueda (Tatsueman Kanamura),
Reiko Kasahara (Sumiko Kanamaru),
Naoyuki Abe (Eiichi), Taro Marui
(Kuma), Yukitaro Hataru (Hachiko).

RETURN OF THE KING, THE (TVM-
    1980) - animated - 5-11-80
    Director: Arthur Rankin, Jr. &

Jules Bass
Voices: Orson Bean (Frodo),
Roddy McDowall (Samwise), Theodore Bikel (Aragorn), John Huston
(Gandalf), William Conrad (Denethor), Theodore (Gollum), Glenn
Yarbrough (the Minstrel), Paul
Frees, Casey Kasem, Nellie
Bellflower, Don Messick, John
Stephenson, Sonny Melendrez.

RETURN OF THE TERROR, THE
    (1934)
    Director: Howard Bretherton
Mary Astor (Olga Morgan), Lyle
Talbot (Dr. Goodman), John Halliday (Dr. Redmayne), Frank Mc-
Hugh (Joe), Irving Pichel (Burke),
Frank Reicher (Reinhardt), J.
Carroll Naish (Steve Scola), Robert
Barrat (Pudge), Etienne Girardot
(Mr. Tuttle), George E. Stone
(Soapy), Renee Whitney (Virginia
Mayo), Robert E. O'Connor (Bradley), Maude Eburne, Frank Conroy,
Edmund Breese, Charles Grapewin,
Howard Hickman, Philip Morris.

RETURN OF THE VAMPIRE, THE
    (1943)
    Director: Lew Landers
Bela Lugosi (Armand Tesla), Nina
Foch (Nicki Saunders), Frieda
Inescort (Lady Jane Ainsley), Roland Varno (John Ainsley), Matt
Willis (Andreas Obry), Miles
Mander (Sir Frederick Freed),
Gilbert Emery (Prof. Saunders),
William C. P. Austin (Gannet),
Ottola Nesmith (Elsa), Leslie
Dennison (Lynch), George McKay,
Sherlee Collier, Billy Bevan,
Donald Dewar, Jeanne Bates.

RETURN OF THE WHISTLER (1948)
    Director: D. Ross Lederman
Michael Duane, Lenore Aubert,
Ann Doran, Anne Shoemaker,
Sarah Padden, Richard Lane,
Wilton Graff, Trevor Bardette,
James Cardwell, Olin Howlin,
Robert Emmett Keane, Edgar
Dearing.

RETURN OF WALPURGIS, THE
    (1973-Span.) (A.K.A. "El
    Retorno de Walpurguis", "Curse
    of the Devil")
    Director: Leon Klimovsky
Paul Naschy (Waldemar Daninsky/
Irineus Daninsky), Paty Sheppard
(Countess Wandesa de Nadasdy).

RETURN TO BOGGY CREEK (1977)
Director: Tom Moore
Dawn Wells (Mrs. Landry), Dana
Plato (Evie Joe Landry), John Hofeus.

RETURN TO FANTASY ISLAND (TVM-
1978) - 1-20-78
Director: George McGowan
Ricardo Montalban (Mr. Roarke), Herve
Villechaize (Tattoo), Horst Buchholz
(Charles Fleming), Adrienne Barbeau
(Margo Dean), Joseph Cotten (Mr. Grant),
Laraine Day (Mrs. Grant), George
Maharis (Benson), Joseph Campanella
(Brian Faber), George Chakiris (Pierre),
Pat Crowley (Lucy Faber), Cameron
Mitchell (Raoul), France Nuyen (Kito),
Karen Valentine (Janet Fleming), John
Zaremba, Kevi Kendall, Nancy McKeon,
Kristine Ritzke.

RETURN TO GLANNASCAUL (1951) -
short
Director: Hilton Edwards
Orson Welles, Michael Lawrence,
Sheila Richards, Helena Hughes.

RETURN TO YOUTH (1953-Mex.)
(A.K.A. "Retorno a la Juventud")
Director: Bustilo Oro
Andres Soler, Enrique Rambal, Carlos
Lopez Moctezuma, Rosario Grenados.

REVENGE! (TVM-1971) - 11-6-71
Director: Jud Taylor
Shelley Winters (Amanda Hilton), Stuart
Whitman (Mark Hembric), Bradford
Dillman (Frank Klaner), Carol Rossen
(Dianne Klaner), Roger Perry (Peter
Marsh), Gary Clarke (Ed Lucas),
Leslie Charleson (Nancy Grover),
Johnny Scott Lee (Jimmy Klaner).

REVENGE OF FRANKENSTEIN, THE
(1958)
Director: Terence Fisher
Peter Cushing (Dr. Victor Stein),
Francis Matthews (Dr. Hans Kleve),
Michael Gwynn (Karl), Eunice Gayson
(Margaret), John Welsh (Bergman),
Lionel Jeffries (Fritz), Oscar Quitak
(the Dwarf), Charles Lloyd-Pack
(President), John Stuart (Inspector),
Michael Ripper (Kurt), George Wood-
bridge (janitor), Arnold Diamond
(Molke), Margery Cresley (Countess
Barscynska), Anna Walmsley (Vera
Barscynask), Richard Wordsworth
(patient), Ian Whittaker (boy), Avril
Leslie (girl).

REVENGE OF THE BLOOD BEAST,
THE (1966-Ital.) (A.K.A. "La

Sorella de Santana", "The Sister
of Satan", "The She-Beast")
Director: Michael Reeves
John Karlson (Van Helsing), Barbara
Steele (Veronica), Ian Ogilvy (Philip),
Mel Welles, Jan Riley, Richard
Watson, Ed Randolph.

REVENGE OF THE CREATURE (1954)
Director: Jack Arnold
John Agar (Dr. Clete Ferguson), Lori
Nelson (Helen Dobson), John Brom-
field (Joe Hayes), Robert B. Williams
(George Johnson), Nestor Paiva (Lu-
cas), Grandon Rhodes (Jackson Fos-
ter), Dave Willock (Lou Gibson),
Charles Cane (Chief of Police),
Brett Halsey (Pete), Clint Eastwood
(Jennings), Ned Le Ferve (news-
caster), Diane De Laire (Miss Abbott),
Robert Nelson (Dr. McCuller), Robert
Wehling (Joe), Sydney Mason (announ-
cer), Don C. Harvey (Mac), Jack
Gargan (Skipper), Robert Hoy (Charlie),
Ricou Browning (the Creature), Mike
Doyle, Charles Gibb, Charles Victor,
(Cops), Don House.

REVENGE OF THE STEPFORD WIVES
(TVM-1980) - 10-12-80
Director: Robert Fuest
Sharon Gless (Kaye Foster), Arthur
Hill (Diz Coba), Julie Kavner (Megan
Brady), Don Johnson (Andy Brady),
Mason Adams (Wally), Audra Lindley
(Barbara Parkinson), Ellen Weston
(Kitten), Gay Rowan (Angelina),
Melissa Newman (Muffin), Tom Hill
(Dr. Edgar Trent), Joe Medalis
(real estate agent), Peter Malloney
(druggist), James McKrell (Bruce
Manson), Ed Bell (Gary Tarshis),
Lee Benard (Sally Tarshis), David
Boyle (Charlie Gray), Sheldon Feld-
ner (Norman Kahn), Dean Wein (am-
bulance driver), Stephanie Blackmore
(druggist's wife), Bonnie Sullivan
(Stepford wife), Gawanne Meyers
(Stepford wife attendant), Howard
Witt.

REVENGE OF THE ZOMBIES (1943)
(A.K.A. "The Corpse Vanished")
Director: Steve Sekely
John Carradine (Dr. Max Heinrich
Von Altermann), Robert Lowery
(Larry Adams), Gale Storm (Jennifer
Rand), Mantan Moreland (Jeff), Bob
Steele (Sheriff), Mauritz Hugo (Scott
Warrington), Veda Ann Borg (Lila
Von Altermann), Madame Sul-Te-Wan
(Beulah), James Baskett (Lazarus),
Barry McCollum (Dr. Keating),

Sybil Lewis (Rosella), Robert Cherry (Pete).

REVOLT OF THE GHOSTS (1946-
  Mex.) (A.K.A. "La Rebelion de
  los Fantasmas", "Rebellion of
  the Ghosts")
    Director: Alfredo Fernandez
    Bustamante
Gilbert Roland, Amanda Ledesma,
Angel Garasa, Luis G. Barreiro,
Nelly Montiel, Maria Conesa, Agus-
tin Lara.

REVOLT OF THE PRAETORIANS,
  THE (1964-Ital.) (A.K.A. "La
  Rivolta dei Pretoriani")
    Director: Alfonso Brescia
Richard Harrison, Moira Orfei,
Giuliano Gemma, Piero Lulli, Ivy
Holzer, Aldo Cecconi.

REVOLT OF THE ZOMBIES (1936)
    Director: Victor Halperin
Dean Jagger (Armand Louque), Roy
D'Arcy (Col. Mazovia), Dorothy
Stone (Claire Duval), George Cleve-
land (Gen. Duval), Teru Shimada
(Buna), Carl Stockdale (Ignacio Mc-
Donald), Robert Noland (Clifford
Grayson), William Crowell (Hsiang),
Selmer Jackson (Officer), Fred War-
ren (Dr. Trevissant), Hans Schumm
(German soldier).

RHINOCEROS (1973)
    Director: Tom O'Horgan
Zero Mostel (John), Gene Wilder
(Stanley), Karen Black (Daisy), Percy
Rodrigues (Mr. Nicholson), Robert
Weil (Carl), Joe Silver (Norman),
Marilyn Chris (Mrs. Bingham), Ro-
bert Fields (logician), Lou Cutell
(cashier), Lorna Thayer (restaurant
owner), Kathryn Harkin (lady with
cat), Howard Morton (doctor), Don
Calfa (waiter), Melody Santangelo
(young woman).

RIDERS TO THE STARS (1953)
    Director: Richard Carlson
Richard Carlson (Jerry Lockwood),
Herbert Marshall (Dr. Donald Stanton),
William Lundigan (Richard Stanton),
Martha Hyer (Jane Flynn), Lawrence
Dobkin (Dr. Delmar), Robert Karnes
(Walter Gordon), George Eldredge
(Dr. Drayden), Michael Fox (Dr.
Klinger), Ken Dibbs (Kenneth Wells),
Dawn Addams (Susan Manners), King
Donovan (Mr. O'Herli), James K.
Best (Sidney Fuller), Dan Riss (Dr.
Warner), John Hedlow (Archibald Guiness).

RING OF TERROR (1962)
    Director: Clark Paylow
George Mather (Lewis Moffitt),
Esther Furst (Betty Crawford),
Austin Green, Joseph Conway.

RIO '70 (1970-Span./Ger.) (A.K.A.
  "Sumuru", "River 70", "Die
  Sieben Mannder der Su-Muru",
  "The Seven Secrets of Su-Muru",
  "Future Women")
    Director: Jesus Franco
Shirley Eaton (Su Muru), George
Sanders, Maria Rohm, Elisa Mon-
tes, Marta Reeves, Richard Wyler,
Herbert Fleischman.

RISE AND RISE OF MICHAEL
  RIMMER, THE (1970)
    Director: Kevin Billington
Peter Cook (Michael Rimmer),
Denholm Elliott (Peter Niss),
Ronald Fraser (Tom Hutchinson),
Vanessa Howard (Patricia Cart-
wright), Arthur Lowe (Ferret),
Dennis Price (Fairburn), Harold
Pinter (Steven Hench), John Cleese
(Plumer), Roland Culver (Sir Eric
Bentley), Graham Chapman (Fromage),
George A. Cooper (Blackett), Nor-
man Bird (Alderman Poot), Elspeth
March (Mrs. Ferret), Dudley Fos-
ter (Federman), Norman Rossington
(guide), James Cossins (Crodder),
Ronnie Corbett (interviewer),
Nicholas Phipps (Snaggot), Diana
Coupland (Mrs. Spimm), Desmond
Walter-Ellis (Buffery), Percy
Edwards (bird impersonator), Julian
Glover.

RISK, THE (1960) (A.K.A. "Sus-
  pect")
    Director: Ray Boulting &
    John Boulting
Tony Britton (Bob Marriott), Vir-
ginia Maskell (Lucy Byrne), Peter
Cushing (Prof. Sewell), Ian Bannen
(Alan Andrews), Raymond Huntley
(Sir George Gatling), Donald
Pleasence (Brown), Spike Milligan
(Arthur), Thorley Walters (Mr.
Prince), Kenneth Griffith (Dr.
Shole), Basil Dignam (Dr. Childs),
Geoffrey Bayldon (Rosson), Sam
Kydd (Slater), Robert Bruce (Le-
vers), John Payne (Iverson), Andre
Charise (Heller), Brina Oulton
(Director), Murray Melvin (Teddy
Boy).

RITUAL OF EVIL (TVM-1970) -
  2-23-70

Director: Robert Day
Louis Jourdan (David Sorell), Diane
Hyland (Leila Barton), Wilfrid Hyde-
White (Harry Snowden), Anne Baxter
(Jolene Wiley), Belinda Montgomery
(Loey Wiley), John McMartin (Edward
Bolander), George Stanford Brown (Lar-
ry Richmond), Carla Borelli (Aline
Wiley), Johnny Williams (newscaster),
Regis Cordic (Sheriff), Dehl Berti
(Mora), Richard Alan Knox (hippie),
Jimmy Joyce (1st reporter), James
LaShane (2nd reporter).

RITUALS (1978)
Director: Peter Carter
Hal Holbrook (Harry), Jack Creley
(Jesse), Lawrence Dane (Mitzi), Robin
Gammell (Martni), Ken James (Able),
Gary Reineke (D. J.), Michael Zenon
(Matthew), Murray Westgate (Pilot).

ROAD GAMES (1981-Australia)
Director: Richard Franklin
Stacy Keach, Jr. (Pat Quid), Jamie
Lee Curtis (Hitch Pamela), Marion
Edwards (Fritz Frugal), Grant Page
(Smith or Jones), Bill Stacey (Captain
Careful), Thaddeus Smith (Abbott),
Stephen Millichamp (Costello), Alan
Hopgood (Lester), Robert Thompson
(Sneezy Rider), John Murphy (Benny),
Angie La Bozzetta (young hitchhiker),
Colin Vancao (Fred Frugal), Rochelle
Harris, Paul Harris (Frugal children),
Ed Turley (roadhouse proprietor).

ROAD TO BALI (1951)
Director: Hal Walker
Bob Hope (Harold Gridley), Bing Crosby
(George Cochran), Dorothy Lamour
(Lalah), Murvyn Vye (Den Arok), Peter
Coe (Gung), Ralph Moody (Bhoma Da),
Leon Adkin (Ramanyana), Dean Martin,
Jerry Lewis, Jane Russell (cameos),
Bernie Gozier (Bo Kassar), Harry
Cording (Verna's father), Herman Can-
tor (priest), Michael Ansara (guard),
Jack Claus (dancer), Allan Nixon (Eun-
ice's brother), Larry Chance (attendant),
Richard Keene (conductor), Bunny Lew-
bel (Lalah at age seven), Donald Layton
(employment agency clerk), Roy Gordon
(Eunice's father), Douglas Yorke (Ver-
na's brother), Jan Kayne (Verna),
Carolyn Jones (Eunice).

ROAD TO HONG KONG (1961)
Director: Norman Panama
Bing Crosby (Harry Turner), Bob Hope
(Chester Babcock), Joan Collins (Diane),
Dorothy Lamour (herself), Robert Morley
(the Leader), Walter Gotell (Dr. Zorbb),

Felix Aylmer (Grand Lama), Roger
Delgado (Jhinnah), Peter Madden
(Lama), Robert Ayres, Alan Gif-
fort, Robin Hughes (American of-
ficials), Bill Nagy (agent), Guy
Standeven (photographer), John
McCarthy (messenger), Julian
Sherrier (doctor), Katya Douglas
(receptionist), Simon Levy (servant),
Harry Baird, Irving Allen (Nubians),
Mei Ling (Chinese girl), Michael
Wynne, John Dearth, Jacqueline
Jones, David Randall, Roy Patrick,
Victor Brooks,

ROAD TO MANDALAY, THE (1926)
Director: Tod Browing
Lon Chaney, Sr. (Singapore Joe),
Lois Moran (Rosemary), Henry B.
Walthall (Father James Stevens),
Sojin (English Charlie Wing),
Owen Moore (Adm. Edward Her-
rington), John George (Yakmo),
Rose Langdon (Pansy), Lenore
Bushman, Eric S. Mayne, Virginia
Bushman, Robert Seiter.

ROAD TO MOROCCO (1942)
Director: David Butler
Bing Crosby (Jeff Peters), Bob
Hope (Turkey Jackson), Dorothy
Lamour (Princess Shalmar), An-
thony Quinn (Mullay Kasim), Vlad-
imir Sokoloff (Hyder Khan), Andrew
Tombes (Oso Bucco), Leon Belasco
(Yusef), Dan Seymour (Arabian
buyer), Mikhail Rasumny (Ahmed
Fey), George Givot (Neb Jolla),
Dona Drake (Mihirmah), Jamiel
Hasson (1st aide to Mullay Kasin),
Monte Blue (2nd aide to Mullay
Kasin), Brandon Hurst (English
announcer), Richard Loo (Chinese
announcer), Leo Mostovoy (Russian
announcer), Pete G. Katchenaro
(Philipine announcer), Nestor
Paiva (sausage vendor), Yvonne
DeCarlo, Louise LaPlanche, Theo
de Voe, Suzanne Ridgway, Patsy
Mace, Brooke Evans, Pappy Wilde
(Handmaidens), George Lloyd (1st
guard), Sammy Stein (Knife dancers),
Rita Christiani (dancer), Cy Kendall
(fruit stand proprietor), Michael
Mark (vendor), Stanley Price
(idiot), Kent Rogers, Sara Berner
(voice of camels), Robert Barron
(giant bearded Arab), Sylvia Opert,
Harry Cording, Dick Botiller (warriors), Edward Emerson (bystander).

ROAD TO RIO (1947)
Director: Norman Z. McLeod

Bing Crosby (Scat Sweeney), Bob Hope (Hot Lips Barton), Dorothy Lamour (Lucia Maria De Andrade), Frank Faylen (Harry), Gale Sondergaard (Catherine Vail), Joseph Vitale (Tony), Frank Puglia (Rodrigues), Nestor Paiva (Carodso), Robert Barrat (Johnson), Jerry Colonna, Raul Roulien (Cavalry Officers), Tad Van Brunt (pilot), Charles Middleton (farmer), Tor Johnson (Samson), George Meeker (Sherman Mallory), Stanley Andrews (Capt. Harmon), Harry Woods (ship's purser), Stanley Blystone (assistant purser), Laura Corbay, Albert Ruiz (dancers), Donald Kerr (steward), George Sorel (the Prefeito), Alan Bridge (ship's officer), Ray Teal (Buck), Gino Corrado (Barber), Ralph Dunn (foreman), George Chandler (valet), Arthur Bryan (Mr. Stanton).

ROAD TO UTOPIA (1945)
    Director: Hal Walker
Bing Crosby (Duke Johnson/Junior Hooton), Bob Hope (Chester Hooton), Dorothy Lamour (Sal Van Hoyden), Hillary Brooke (Kate), Douglass Dumbrille (Ace Larson), Jack La Rue (Le Bec), Robert Barrat (Sperry), Nestor Paiva (McGurk), Will Wright (Mr. Latimer), Robert Benchley (Narrator), Billy Benedict (newsboy), Alan Bridge (boat captain), Stanley Andrews (official at boat), Edgar Dearing (official), Arthur Loft (Purser), Charles Gemora (the Bear), Jimmy Dundee (ringleader of henchmen), Romaine Callender (Top Hat), Paul Newlan (ship's purser), Jack Rutherford (1st man), Al Hill (2nd man), Allen Pomeroy, Jack Stone (henchmen), Ronnie Rondell (hotel manager), Edward Emerson (M.C.), George McKay (waiter), Larry Daniels (ringleader), Ferdinand Munier (Santa Claus), Charles C. Wilson (official), Clair James, Maxine Fife (girls), Jim Thorpe (passenger).

ROAD TO ZANZIBAR (1941)
    Director: Victor Schertzinger
Bing Crosby (Chuck Reardon), Bob Hope (Fearless Frazier), Dorothy Lamour (Donna Latour), Una Merkel (Julia Quimby), Joan Marsh (Dimples), Eric Blore (Charles Kimble), George Renavent (Saunders), Nobel Johnson (Chief), Lionel Royce (Monsieur Lebec), Leigh Whipper (Scarface), Ernest Whitman (Whiteface), Norma Varden (Clara Kimble), Jules Strongbow (Solomon), Buck Woods (Thonga), Luis Alberni (proprietor of native booth), Iris Adrian (French Soubrette), Leo

Gorcey (boy), Robert Middlemass (Police Inspector), Paul Porcasi (Turk at slave market), Henry Roquemore (cafe proprietor), Pricsilla White, LaVerne Vess (Curzon sisters), Charlie Gemora (the Gorilla), Richard Keene (clerk), Ken Carpenter (commentator), Eddy Conrad (barber), James B. Carson (waiter), Alan Bridge (policeman).

ROAD WARRIOR, THE (1981-Australia) (A.K.A. "Mad Max II")
    Director: George Miller
Mel Gibson (Max), Bruce Spence (Gyro Captain), Vernon Wells (Wez), Emil Minty (Feral Kid), Kjell Nilsson (Humungus), Virginia Hey (Warrior Woman), Syd Heylen (Curmudgeon), Moria Claux (Big Rebecca), David Slingsby (Quiet Man), Steve J. Spears (Mechanic), Max Phipps (Toadie), Arkie Whiteley (Lusty Girl), William Zappa (Farmer), Jimmy Brown (Golden Youth).

ROBBING CLEOPATRA'S TOMB (1899-Fr.) (A.K.A. "Cleopatre")
    Director: Georges Melies

ROBERT MACAIRE AND BERTRAND (1906-Fr.)
    Director: Georges Melies

ROBINSON CRUSOE OF CLIPPER ISLAND (1936) (A.K.A. "Robinson Crusoe of Mystery Island", "S.O.S. Clipper Island") - serial in 14 episodes
    Director: Ray Taylor & Mack V. Wright
Mala (Mala), Mamo Clark (Princess Melani), Herbert Rawlinson (Jackson), Selmer Jackson (Canfield), William Newell (Hank), John Dilson (Ellsworth), George Chesebro (Draker), John Piccori (Porotu), Robert Kortman (Wilson), John Ward (Tupper), George Cleveland (Goebel), Lloyd Whitlock (Lamar), Tracy Layne (Larkin), Allen Connor (Taylor), Tiny Roebuck (Eppa), Herbert Weber (Stevens), Anthony Pawley (radio operator), Edmund Cobb (Crosby/Harris), Bud Osborne (Ellis), Edward Cassidy (Joe Davis), Lester Dorr (officer), Buddy Roosevelt (wireless operator), Val Duran (half caste), Evan Thomas (agent 1), Larry Thompson (agent 2), Allan Cavan (Captain), Ralph McCullough (chemist), Henry Sylvester (Fairchild),

David Horsley (Ed Varne/co-pilot),
Jack Mack (Fosdick), Oscar Hendrian (guard), Harry Strang (Grover), Loren Riebe (Johnson), Al
Taylor (Macro), Henry Hale (Mercer), Frank Ellis (Rontree), Jack
Mack (Manning), Allen Mathews
(M-2), Don Brodie (radioman),
Roscoe Gerall (Price), Eddie Phillips (operator), Charles McMurphy
(sergeant No. 1), Jack Stewart (sergeant No. 2), F. Herrick Herrick
(Tollar), Francis Walker (spy),
Frazer Acosta (Teekor), Jerry
Jerome (Wallace).

ROBINSON CRUSOE ON MARS (1964)
     Director: Byron Haskin
Paul Mantee (Cmdr. Christopher
Drake), Vic Lundin (Friday), Adam
West (Col. Dan McReady).

ROBOT MONSTER (1953) (A. K. A.
     "Monsters from the Moon")
     Director: Phil Tucker
George Barrows (Ro-Man), Gregory
Moffett (Johnny), George Nader
(Roy), Claudia Barrett (Alice),
John Mylong (the Professor), Selena
Royle (Martha), Pamela Paulson
(Carla), John Brown (voice of the
Great One and Ro-Man).

ROBOT OF REGALIO (1954)
     see Television: Rocky Jones,
     Space Ranger (1953-54)

ROBOT VS. THE AZTEC MUMMY,
     THE (1959-Mex) (A. K. A. "La
     Momia contra el Robot Humano",
     "El Robot Humano", "The Human
     Robot")
     Director: Rafael Portillo
Roman Gay, Rosita Arenas, Crox
Alvarado, Emma Roldan, Luis Aceves
Castenada.

ROCK 'N' ROLL HIGH SCHOOL (1979)
     Director: Allan Arkush
P. J. Soles (Riff), Vincent Van Patten
(Tom), Clint Howard (Eagelbauer),
Dey Young (Kate), Mary Woronov
(Miss Togar), Paul Bartel (McGree),
Dick Miller (Police Chief), Alix Elias
(Coach Steroid), Don Steele (Screamin'
Steve), Loren Lester (Hansel), Daniel
Davies (Gretel), Lynn Farrell (Angel
Dust), Grady Sutton (School Board
President), Herbie Braha (manager),
Barbara Ann Walters (cafeteria lady),
Maria Rosenfield (Cheryl), Terry Soda
(Norma), Chris Somma (Shawn), Joe
Van Sickle (cop), The Ramones (them-

selves), Ann Chatterton, Debbie
Evans, Jack Gill, Kay Kimler, John
Hately.

ROCKET ATTACK, U. S. A. (1960)
     Director: Barry Mahon
John McKay (John Manston), Monica
Davis (Tannah), Daniel Kern, Philip
St. George, Edward Czerniuk.

ROCKET MAN, THE (1953)
     Director: Oscar Rudolph
Charles Coburn (Mayor Ed Johnson),
Spring Byington (Justice Amelia
Brown), Anne Francis (June Brown),
John Agar (Tom Baxter), George
Winslow (Timmy), Emory Parnell
(Big Bill Watkins), Stanley Clements
(Bob), June Clayworth (Miss Snedley),
Beverly Garland (Ludine), Don Haggerty (Officer O'Brien), Lawrence
Ryle, Lillian Powell.

ROCKETSHIP X-M (1950)
     Director: Kurt Neumann
Lloyd Bridges (Floyd Oldham),
Osa Massen (Lisa Van Horn), John
Emery (Dr. Karl Eckstrom), Noah
Beery, Jr. (William Corrigan),
Morris Ankrum (Dr. Robert Fleming),
Hugh O'Brian (Harry Chamberlain),
Patrick Ahern, John Dutra, Katherine
Marlowe (reporters), Sherry Moreland (Martian girl), Judd Holdren.

ROCKING HORSE WINNER, THE (1949)
     Director: Anthony Pelissier
John Mills (Bassett), Valerie Hobson
(Hester Graham), Ronald Squire
(Oscar Cresswell), Hugh Sinclair
(Richard Grahame), John Howard
Davies (Paul Garhame), Charles
Goldner (Mr. Tsaldouris), Byril
Smith (the Bailiff), Susan Richards
(Nannie), Caroline Steer (Joan),
Melanie McKenzie (Matilda), Anthony
Hollies (Bowler Hat).

ROCKY HORROR PICTURE SHOW,
     THE (1975)
     Director: Jim Sharman
Tim Curry (Dr. Frank N. Furter),
Susan Sarandon (Janet Weiss),
Barry Bostwick (Brad Majors),
Richard O'Brien (Riff Raff), Patricia
Quinn (Magenta), Peter Hinwood
(Rocky Horror), Little Nell Campbell (Columbia), Jonathan Adams
(Dr. Everett V. Scott), Meatloaf
(Eddie), Charles Gray (the Criminiologist).

RODAN (1957-Jap.) (A. K. A. "Radon")

Director: Inoshiro Honda
Kenji Sahara (Shigeru), Yumi
Shirakawa (Kyo), Akihiko Hirata
(Dr. Kashiwagi), Akio Kobori
(Nishimura), Yusako Nakata (young
woman), Monosuke Yamada (Ohsaki),
Yoshimubi Tojima (Iseki), Kiyoharu
Ohnaka.

RoGoPaG (1962-Ital. /Fr.)
Director: Jean-Luc Godard
"Le Nouveau Monde"/"The New World":
Jean-Marc Bory, Alexandra Stewart.

ROGUES TAVERN, THE (1936)
Director: Bob Hill
Wallace Ford (Jimmy Flavin),
Barbara Pepper (Marjorie), Jack
Mulhall (Bill), Joan Woodbury
(Gloria Rohloff), Clara Kimball
Young (Mrs. Jamison), Earl Dwire
(Morgan), John Elliott (Mr. Jami-
son), John W. Cowell (Bert), Vin-
cent Dennis (Hughes), Arthur Loft
(Wentworth), Ivo Henderson (Har-
rison), Ed Cassidy (Mason).

ROLLERBALL (1975)
Director: Norman Jewison
James Caan (Jonathan E), John
Houseman (Bartholomew), Maud Adams
(Ella), John Beck (Moonpie), Moses
Gunn (Cletus), Pamela Hensley (Mackie),
Ralph Richardson (Librarian), Shane
Rimmer (Team Executive), Bert
Kwouk (Oriental doctor), Barbara
Trentham (Daphne), Alfred Thomas
(team trainer), Burnell Tucker
(Captain of Guard), Angus MacInnes
(guard No. 1), Nancy Blair (girl in
library), Rick Le Permentier (Bar-
tholomew's aide), Abi Gouhad, Loftus
Burton (black reporter), S. Newton
Anderson (teammate), Robert Ito
(Japanese player), Stephen Boyum,
Alan Haman, Bob Leon, Danny Wong,
(Bikers), Roy Brunaker, Bob Minor,
Craig Baxley, Gary Epper, Jim Nic-
kerson, Dar Robinson, Walter Scott,
Jerry Wills, Chuck Parkinson, Jr. ,
Roy Scammell, Dick Warlock (stunt-
men).

ROLLOVER (1981)
Director: Alan J. Pakula
Jane Fonda (Lee Winters), Kris
Kristofferson (Hub Smith), Hume
Cronyn (Maxwell Emery), Josef
Summer (Roy Lefcourt), Josef
(Sol Naftari), Macon McCalman (Mr.
Fewster), Jodi Long (Betsy Okomoto),
Ron Frazier (Gil Hovey), Marvin
Chantinover (Mr. Lipscomb), Crocker

Nevin (Warner Ackerman), Paul Hecht
(Khalid), Norman Snow (Hishan).

ROMANCE OF ELAINE, THE (1915) -
serial in 12 episodes
Chapters: 1. "The Lost Torpedo",
2. "The Gray Friar", 3. "The
Vanishing Man", 4. "The Submarine
Harbor", 5. "The Conspirators",
6. "The Wireless Detective", 7.
"The Death Cloud", 8. "The Search-
light Gun", 9. "The Life Chain", 10.
"The Flash", 11. "The Disappearing
Helmet", & 12. "The Triumph of
Elaine".
Director: George B. Seitz
Pearl White (Elaine Dodge), Creigh-
ton Hale (Jameson), Lionel Barry-
more (Marcus Del Mar/Mr. X),
Arnold Daly (Craig Kennedy), Warner
Oland.

ROMANCE OF TARZAN, THE (1918)
Director: Wilfred Lucan
Elmo Lincoln (Tarzan), Enid Markey
(Jane Porter), Thomas Jefferson
(Prof. Porter), Monte Blue, Cleo
Madison, True Boardman, Bessie
Toner, George French, Gordon
Griffith, Clyde Benson, Colin Kenny,
Kathleen Kirkham.

ROOM TO LET (1950)
Director: Godfrey Grayson
Jimmy Hanley (Curley Minter),
Valentine Dyall (Dr. Fell), Reginald
Dyson (Sgt. Cranbourne), Constance
Smith (Molly Musgrave), Charles
Hawtrey (Mike Atkinson), Merle
Tottenham (Alice), Christine Silver
(Mrs. Musgrave), J. Anthony la
Penna (J. J.).

ROSEMARY'S BABY (1968)
Director: Roman Polanski
Mia Farrow (Rosemary Woodhouse),
John Cassavetes (Guy Woodhouse),
Ruth Gordon (Minnie Castevet),
Sidney Blackmer (Roman Castevet),
Ralph Bellamy (Dr. Sapirstein),
Maurice Evans (Hutch), Angela
Dorian (Terry Fionoffrio), Patsy
Kelly (Laura-Louise), Charles
Grodin (Dr. Hill), Elisha Cook, Jr.
(Mr. Nicklas), Wende Wagner (Tiger),
Hope Summers (Mrs. Gilmore),
Almira Sessions (Mrs. Sabatini),
Robert Osterloh (Mr. Fountain),
William Castle (man in phone booth),
Roy Barcroft (sun-browned man),
Tony Curtis (voice of Donald Baum-
gart), Gail Bonney (voice of baby-
sitter), Phil Leeds (Dr. Shand),

Marianne Gordon (Joan Jellico),
Hanna Landy (Grace Cardiff), Gordon
Connell (Guy's agent), Janet Garland
(nurse), Joan T. Reilly (pregnant
woman), Walter Baldwin (Mr. Wees),
Patricia O'Neal (Mrs. Wees), Elmer
Modlin (young man), Charlotte Boer-
ner (Mrs. Fountain), Patricia Ann
Conway (Mrs. John Kennedy), Ernest
Kazuyoshi Harada (young Japanese
man), George Savalas (workman),
Sebastian Brooks (Argyron Stavro-
poulos), Natalie Park Masters (wo-
man), Burno Sidar (Mr. Gilmour),
Marily Harvey (Sapirstein's reception-
ist), Frank White (Hugo Dunstan),
Viki Vigen (Lisa), Paul A. Denton
(Skipper), Bill Baldwin (salesman),
Mary Louise Lawson (Portia Haynes),
Gale Peters (Rain Morgan), D'Urville
Martin (Diego), George Ross Robert-
son (Lou Comford), Carol Brewster
(Claudia Comford), Michael Shillo
(Pope), Lynn Brinker (Sister Veronica),
Jean Inness (Sister Agnes), Clay Tan-
ner (the Devil), Michael Gomez (Pedro),
Mona Knox (Mrs. Byron).

ROTWEILER (1982)
    Director: Worth Keeter
Earl Owensby, Herman Bloodsworth,
Jerry Rushing.

RUBEZAHL'S MARRIAGE (1916-
    Ger.) (A.K.A. "Rubezahls Hoch-
    zeit", "Old Nip's Wedding")
    Director: Paul Wegener
Paul Wegener, Lyda Salmanova,
Arthur Ehrens, Georg Jacoby, Mari-
anne Niemeyer, Emilie Kurz, Ernst
Waldow, Rochus Gliese.

RUBY (1977)
    Director: Curtis Harrington
Piper Laurie (Ruby Claire), Stuart
Whitman (Vince Kemper), Roger
Davis (Dr. Keller), Janit Baldwin
(Leslie Claire), Len Lesser (Barney),
Crystin Sinclaire (Lila June), Paul
Kent (Louie), Jack Perkins (Avery),
Sal Vecchio (Nicky), Edward Donno
(Jess), Fred Kohler (Jake).

RULING CLASS, THE (1972)
    Director: Peter Medak
Peter O'Toole (14th Earl of Gurney),
Alastair Sim (Bishop Lampton), Ar-
thur Lowe (Tucker), Coral Browne
(Lady Claire), Nigel Green (McKyle),
Harry Andrews (13th Earl of Gurney),
Michael Bryant (Dr. Herder), James
Villiers (Dinsdale), William Mervyn
(Sir Charles), Kay Walsh (Mrs. Piggot-

Jones), Hugh Burden (Matthew Peake),
Graham Crowden (Truscott), Carolyn
Weymour (Grace), James Grout
(Inspector), Patsy Byrne (Mrs.
Treadwell), Joan Cooper (Nurse
Brice).

RUN, STRANGER, RUN (1973)
    (A.K.A. "Happy Mother's Day...
    Love, George")
    Director: Darren McGavin
Patricia Neal (Cara), Cloris Leach-
man (Ronda), Ron Howard (John-
ny), Tessa Dahl (Celia), Kathie
Browne (Crystal), Bobby Darrin
(Eddie), Joe Mascolo (Piccolo),
Thayer David (Minister), Simon
Oakland (Roy), Gale Garnett (Yo-
landa).

SAADIA (1953)
    Director: Albert Lewin
Cornel Wilde (Si Lahssen), Rita
Gam (Saadia), Mel Ferrer (Henrik),
Michel Simon (Bou Rezza), Wanda
Rotha (Fatima), Cyril Cusack
(Khadir), Marcel Poncin (Moha),
Helene Vallier (Zoubida), Anthony
(Lt. Camuzac), Jacques Dufilho
(bandit leader), Richard Johnson
(Lt. Girard), Marne Maitland,
Edward Leslie, Peter Copley, Peter
Bull, Harold Hasket, Abdullah
Mennebhi.

SABAKA (1955) (A.K.A. "The Hindu")
    Director: Frank Ferrin
Boris Karloff, Reginald Denny,
Victor Jory, Jay Novello, Lisa
Howard, Peter Coe, Vito Scotti,
Larry Dobkin, Paul Marion, Jeanne
Bates, Nino Marcel, June Foray,
Lou Krugman, Lou Merrill.

SABU AND THE MAGIC RING (1957)
    Director: George Blair
Sabu (Sabu), William Marshall (the
Genie), Daria Massey, Vladimir
Sokoloff, George Khoury, Peter
Mamakos, Kenneth Terrell, Robert
Shafto, John Doucette, Bernie Rich,
Robin Morse, John Lomma.

SADIST, THE (1963) (A.K.A. "The
    Profile of Terror")
    Director: James Landis
Arch Hall, Jr. (Charley Tibbs),
Marilyn Manning (Judy Bradshaw),
Helen Hovey (Doris Page), Richard
Alden (Ed Stiles), Don Russell
(Carl Oliver).

SAFE PLACE, A (1971)

1062   Science Fiction, Horror, Fantasy

Director: Henry Jaglom
Orson Welles (the Magician), Tuesday
Weld (Susan/Noay), Jack Nicholson
(Mitch), Philip Proctor (Fred),
Dov Lawrence (Larry), Gwen Welles
(Bari), Fanny Birkenmaier (maid),
Sylvia Zapp (Susan at age 5), Rhonda
Alfaro (girl in rowboat), Jennifer
Walker, Julie Robinson, Roger
Garrett, Barbara Flood, Francesca
Hilton, Jordon Hahn, Richard Fin-
nochio.

SAGA OF THE DRACULAS, THE
(1972-Span.) (A. K. A. "La Saga
de los Dracula")
Director: Leon Klimovsky
Tina Sainz, Tony Isbert, Maria
Koski, Narciso Ibaniz Menta,
Helga Lime, Christina Suriani, J. J.
Paladino.

SAGA OF THE VIKING WOMEN AND
THEIR VOYAGE TO THE WATERS
OF THE GREAT SEA SERPANT,
THE (1957) (A. K. A. "The Viking
Women and the Sea Serpant")
Director: Roger Corman
Abby Dalton (Desir), Susan Cabot
(Enger), June Kenny (Asmild),
Richard Devon (Stark), Jonathan
Haze (Ottar), Betsy Jones-Moreland
(Thyra), Gary Conway (Jarl), Brad
Jackson (Vedric), Jay Sayer (Senja),
Signe Hack.

SALEM'S LOT (TVM-1979) - 11-17-79
& 11-24-79
Director: Tobe Hooper
David Soul (Ben Mears), James Mason
(Straker), Bonnie Bedelia (Susan
Norton), Lance Kerwin (Mark Petrie),
Ed Flanders (Dr. Norton), Lew Ayres
(Jason Burke), Reggie Nalder (Barlow),
Barbara Babcock (June Petrie), Geof-
frey Lewis (Mike Ryerson), Kenneth
McMillan (Constable), Bonnie Bartlett
(Ann Norton), Marie Windsor (Eva),
Elisha Cook, Jr. (Weasel), Robert
Lussier (Nolly Gardner), Julie Cobb
(Bonnie Sawyer), Fred Willard (Larry
Crockett), George Dzundza (Cully
Sawyer), Brad Savage (Danny Glick),
Ronnie Scribner (Ralphie Glick),
Josh Bryant (Ted Petrie), Clarissa
Kaye (Marjorie Glick), Ernie Phillips
(Royal Snow), James Gallery (Father
Callahan), Ned Wilson (Henry Glick),
Barney McFadden (Ned Tebbets),
Joe Brooks (guard).

SALVAGE (TVM-1979) - 1-20-79
Director: Lee Philips

Andy Griffith (Harry Broderick),
Trish Stewart (Melanie Slozar),
Joel Higgins (Skip Carmichael),
Richard Jaeckel (Jack Klinger),
J. Jay Saunders (Mack), Jacqueline
Scott (Lorene), Raleigh Bond (Fred),
Peter Brown (Bill Kelly), Lee DeBroux
(Hank Beddows), Richard Eastham
(commentator), Jim Mills.

SAMSON (1961-Ital.) (A. K. A.
"Sansone")
Director: Gianfranco Parloni
Brad Harris, Alan Steel, Walter
Reeves, Mara Berni, Carlo Tam-
berlani, Brigitte Corey, Irene Prosen.

SAMSON AND THE MIGHTY CHAL-
LENGE (1964-Ital.) (A. K. A.
"Ercole, Sansone, Maciste, Ursus:
gli Invincible", "Hercules, Samson,
Maciste, Ursus: the Invincibles",
"Samson and the Mighty Challenge")
Director: Giorgio Capitani
Alan Steel/Sergio Ciani, Moira Orfei,
Helene Chanel, Nadir Baltimor,
Renato Rossini, Livio Lorenzon,
Luciano Marin, Yann Larvor, Lia
Zoppelli.

SAMSON AND THE SEVEN MIRACLES
OF THE WORLD (1961-Ital.) (A. K. A.
"Maciste alla corte del Gran Khan",
"Maciste at the Court of the Great
Khan", "Goliath and the Golden
City")
Director: Riccardo Freda
Gordon Scott (Samson), Yoko Tani
(Princess Lei-Ling), Helen Chanel,
Dante Di Paolo, Leonardo Severini,
Gabrielle Antonini, Valery Inkijinoff.

SAMSON AND THE SLAVE QUEEN
(1963-Ital.) (A. K. A. "Zorro
contro Maciste", "Zorro Against
Maciste")
Director: Umberto Lenzi
Pierre Brice (Zorro), Alan Steel/
Sergio Ciani (Samson), Moira Orfei
(Malva), Massimo Serato (Garcia),
Andrea Aureli (Rabek), Maria
Grazia Spina (Isabella).

SAMSON IN KING SOLOMON'S MINES
(1964-Ital.) (A. K. A. "Maciste
nelle Miniere de Re Solomone")
Director: Piero Regnoli/Mar-
tin Andrews
Reg Park, Wandisa Guida, Dan Harrison, Lorris Loddi, Eleanora Bianchi, Elio Jotta, Carlo Tamberlani.

SAMSON VS. THE GIANT KING

(1963-Ital.) (A. K. A. "Maciste
alla Corte Dello Zar", "Maciste
at the Court of the Czar", "Giant
of the Lost Tomb", "Atlas Against
the Czar")
Director: Tanio Boccia/Anton
Amerigo
Kirk Morris, Massimo Serato, Ombretta Colli, Gloria Milland, Tom
Felleghi, Giulio Donini, Dada Gallotti.

SAMSON VS. THE PIRATES (1963-
Ital.) (A. K. A. "Sansone contro i
Parati")
Director: Tanio Boccia
Kirk Morris, Margaret Lee, Aldo
Bufilandi, Daniele Vargas.

SAMURAI (TVM-1979) - 4-30-79
Director: Lee H. Katzin
Dana Elcar (Frank Boyd), James
Shigeta (Takeo Chisato), Morgan
Brittany (Cathy Berman), Joe Penny
(Lew Cantrell), Geoffrey Lewis
(Harold Tigner), Michael Pataki
(Peter Lacey), James McEachin
(Richardson), Charles Cioffi (Amory
Bryson), Beulah Quo (Hana Mitsu-
bishi Cantrell), Norman Alden (Lt.
Al DeNisco), Ralph Manza (Irving
Berman), Philip Baker Hall (Prof.
Owens), Shane Sinutko (Tommy),
Bob Minor, Diana Webster, Randolph
Roberts, Don Keefer.

SANDCASTLES (TVM-1972) - 10-17-72
Director: Ted Post
Jan-Michael Vincent (Michael), Bonnie
Bedelia (Jenna Hampshire), Herschel
Bernardi (Alexis), Mariette Hartley
(Sarah), Gary Crosby (Frank Watson),
William Hansen (Sascha), Loretta
Laversee (Ruth Watson), Lloyd Gough
(Paul Fiedler), William Long, Jr.
(Bennington), Mimi Davis (Sister),
Jody Hauber (Sherry), Dick Valentine
(driver).

SANDOKAN THE GREAT (1965-Ital.)
(A. K. A. "I Pirati della Malesia",
"Sandokan, La Tigre di Mompracem",
"Sandokan, the Tiger of Mompracem",
"Sandolan")
Director: Umberto Lenzi
Steve Reeves (Sandokan), Rik Bat-
talgia (Sambighong), Andrea Bosic
(Yanez), Genevieve Grad (Mary Ann),
Mimmo Palmara, Maurice Poli, Jac-
queline Sassard.

SANTA CLAUS CONQUERS THE MAR-
TIANS (1964)
Director: Nicholas Webster

John Call (Santa Claus), Vincent
Beck (Yoldar), Leonard Hicks
(Kimar), Pia Zadora (Girmar),
James Cahill (Rigna), Carl Donn
(Cochem), Jim Bishop (Lomas),
Leila Martin (Momar), Christopher
Month (Bomar), Charles G. Renn
(Nargo), Victor Stiles, Bill Mc-
Cutcheon, Donna Conforti, Al
Nesor, Josip Elic, Lin Thurmond,
Ivor Bodin, Glen Schaffer, Tony
Ross, Doris Rich, Ned Wertimer,
Don Blair, Gene Lindsey, Ronald
Rotholz, Scott Aronesty.

SANTO AGAINST BLUE DEMON IN
ATLANTIS (1968-Mex.) (A. K. A.
"Santo contra Blue Demon en la
Atlantida")
Director: Julian Soler
Santo, Blue Demon, Jorge Rado,
Rafael Banquells, Magda Giner,
Silvia Pasquel, Rosa Maria Pineiro,
Marcello Villamil, Griselda Mejia,
Hector Guzman.

SANTO AGAINST THE BLACK MAGIC
(1972-Mex.) (A. K. A. "Santo
contra la Magia Negra")
Director: Alfredo B. Crevenna
Santo, Elsa Cardenas, Gerty Jones,
Sasha Montenegro, Guillermo Galvez,
Ismael Ramirez, Fernando Oses,
Carlos Saurez.

SANTO AND BLUE DEMON VS.
DRACULA AND THE WOLF MAN
(1972-Mex.) (A. K. A. "Santo y
Blue Demon Contra Dracula y el
Hombre Lobo")
Director: Miguel M. Delgado
Santo, Blue Demon, Aldo Monti
(Dracula), Eugenia San Martin, Maria
Eugenia San Martin, Don Gave, Nubia
Marti, Honore Mandragon, Wally
Baron, Lucy Fields, Lourdes Batista,
Antonio Raxel Garcia, Carlos Saurez,
Carlos Leon.

SANTO AND BLUE DEMON VS. THE
MONSTERS (1968-Mex.) (A. K. A.
"Santo y Blue Demon contra los
Monstruos")
Director: Gilberto Martinez
Solares
Santo, Blue Demon, Carlos Ancira
(Bruno Halder), Heidi Blue, Manuel
Leal, David Avizu.

SANTO AND DRACULA'S TREASURE
(1968-Mex.) (A. K. A. "El Vampiro
y el Sexo", "Aanto en el Tesore
de Dracula", "The Vampire and

Sex")
Director: Rene Cardona
Santo, Aldo Monti (Dracula), Noelia
Noel, Carlos Agosti, Robert Rivera,
Alberto Rojas, Gina Moret, Diana
Arriaga, Paulette.

SANTO ATTACKS THE WITCHES
(1964-Mex.) (A. K. A. "Santo
Ataca las Brujas")
Director: Jose Diaz Morales
Santo, Lorena Valazquez, Ramon
Bugarini, Maria Eugenia San Mar-
tin, Crox Alvarado, Eda Ena Ruiz,
Fernando Oses, Lobo Negro.

SANTO IN THE HOTEL OF THE DEAD
(1961-Mex.) (A. K. A. "Santo
en el Hotel de la Muerte")
Director:
Santo, Fernando Casanova, Ana
Bertha Lepe.

SANTO IN THE MUMMY'S REVENGE
(1971-Mex.) (A. K. A. "Santo en
la Venganza de la Momia")
Director: Rene Cardona
Santo, Eric del Castillo, Cesar
del Campo, Mary Montiel, Carlos
Ancira, Carlos Suarez, Alma Roko,
Nino Jorgito.

SANTO IN THE REVENGE OF THE
VAMPIRE WOMEN (1968-Mex.)
(A. K. A. "Santo en la Venganza
de las Mujeres Vampiro")
Director: Federico Curiel
Santo, Gina Romand, Aldo Monti,
Patricia Ferrer, Norma Lazareno,
Victor Junco, Federico Falcon.

SANTO IN THE WAX MUSEUM (1963-
Mex.) (A. K. A. "Santo en el Museo
de Cara")
Director: Alfonso Corona
Blake
Santo, Claudio Brook, Ruben Rojo,
Norma Mora, Jose Luis Jimenez,
Roxana Bellini, Victor Valazquez.

SANTO VS. BARON BRAKOLA (1965-
Mex.) (A. K. A. "Santo contra el
Baron Brakola", "Baron Brakola")
Director: Jose Diaz Morales
Santo, Fernando Oses, Meche Car-
reno, Ana Martin, Andrea Palma,
Mercedes Carreno, Susana Robles,
Antonio de Hud.

SANTO VS. CAPULINA (1971-Mex.)
Director:
Santo, Capulina, Crox Alvarado,
Liza Castro.

SANTO VS. THE DAUGHTER OF
FRANKENSTEIN (1971-Mex.)
(A. K. A. "Santo vs. la Hija de
Frankenstein")
Director: Miguel M. Delgado
Santo, Gina Romand, Roberto Canedo,
Anel, Carlos Agosti, Sonia Fuentes,
Jorge Casanova, Lucy Gallardo.

SANTO VS. THE KING OF CRIME
(1962-Mex.) (A. K. A. "Santo contra
el Rey de Crimen")
Director: Federico Curiel
Santo, Fernando Casanova, Ana
Berthe Lepe, Rene Cardona.

SANTO VS. THE MARTIAN INVASION
(1966-Mex.) (A. K. A. "Santo vs.
Invasion de los Marcianos")
Director:
Santo.

SANTO VS. THE STRANGLER (1965-
Mex.) (A. K. A. "Santo contra el
Estrangulador")
Director: Rene Cardona
Santo, Alberto Vazquez, Maria Duval,
Begona Palacios, Carlos Lopez
Moctezuma.

SANTO VS. THE VAMPIRE WOMEN
(1961-Mex.) (A. K. A. "Santo contra
las Mujeres Vampiros")
Director: Alfonso Corona Blake
Santo, Lorena Valazquez, Jaime
Fernandez, Orfelia Montesco, Lobo
Negro, Maria Duval, Augusto Bene-
dico.

SARAGOSSA MANUSCRIPT, THE
(1964-Pol.) (A. K. A. "Rekopis
Znaleziony w Saragossie", "Ad-
ventures of a Nobleman", "Manu-
script Found in Saragossa")
Director: Wojciech Jerzy Has
Zbigniew Cybulski (Alfons van Worden),
Kazimierz Opalinski (Hermit), Inga
Cembrzynska (Moorish Princess),
Joanna Jedryka (Moorish Princess),
Miroslawa Lombardo (Van Worden's
mother), Slowomir Linder (Van
Worden's father), Aleksander Fogiel
(Spanish Nobleman), Franciszek
Pieczka (Pascheco), Ludwig Benoit
(Pascheco's father), Barbara Kraff-
towna (Camilla).

SASQUATCH, THE LEGEND OF
BIGFOOT (1978)
Director: Ed Ragossini
George Lauris (Chuck), Steve
Goergadine (Hank), Ken Kenzle
(Josh), Jim Bradford (Barney),

William Emmons (Dr. Markham),
Joe Morello (Techka Blackhawk).

SATANAS (1919-Ger.)
Director: F.W. Murnau
Conrad Veidt (Satan).

SATAN BUG, THE (1965)
Director: John Sturges
George Maharis (Lee Barrett),
Richard Basehart (Dr. Hoffman),
Anne Francis (Ann), Dana Andrews
(the General), Edward Asner (Vere-
tti), Frank Sutton (Donald), Richard
Bull (Cavanagh), John Larkin
(Michaelson), John Anderson (Rea-
gan), Simon Oakland (Tasserly),
Harold Gould (Dr. Ostrer), Hari
Rhodes (Johnson), John Clarke
(Raskin), Russ Bender (Mason),
Martin Blaine (Martin), James
Hong (Dr. Yang), Henry Beckman
(Dr. Baxter), John Newton.

SATANIC RITES OF DRACULA
(1973) (A. K. A. "Count Dracula
and His Vampire Bride")
Director: Alan Gibson
Christopher Lee (Count Dracula),
Peter Cushing (Dr. Van Helsing),
Michael Coles (Insp. Murray),
Joanna Lumley (Jessica Van Helsing),
William Franklyn (Torrence), Fred-
die Jones (Prof. Julian Keeley),
Richard Vernon (Mathews), Patrick
Barr (Lord Carradine), Richard
Mathews (Porter), Barbara Yu Ling
(Chin Yang), Lockwood West (Free-
borne), Valerie Van Ost (Jane),
Peter Adair (doctor), Maurice
O'Connell (Hanson), Marc Zuber
(Mod C), Maggie Fitzgerald, Mia
Martin, Pauline Heart, Finnuala
O'Shannon (vampire girls).

SATANIK (1968-Span. /Ital.)
Director: Piero Vavirelli
Julio Pena, Magda Konopka, Ar-
mando Calvo, Luigi Montini, Umi
Raho, Nima Ippoliti, Antonio Pica.

SATAN IN PRISON (1907-Fr.)
(A. K. A. "Satan en Prison")
Director: Georges Melies

SATAN MURDERS, THE (TVM-1974)
- 1-11-74
Director: Lela Swift
Larry Blyden (Dr. Paul Adams),
Salome Jens (Ann), Susan Sarandon
(Kate), Chris Sarandon (George),
Barton Heyman (Lt. Mendoza),
Douglas Watson (Carter), Paul

Sparer (Sabdor), Mathew Anton,
Peter Brandon.

SATAN OF ALL HORRORS (1972-
Mex.) (A. K. A. "Satanas de Todos
los Horrores")
Director: Julian Soler
Enrique Lizalde, Enrique Rocha,
Carlos Lopez Moctezuma, Illya
Shannell, Jesus Gomez.

SATAN'S CHEERLEADERS (1976)
Director: Greydon Clark
John Ireland (Sheriff Bub), Yvonne
DeCarlo (Emm Bub), Kerry Sherman
(Patti), Alisa Powell (Debbie),
Sherry Marks (Sharon), Hillary
Horan (Chris), Jacqulin Cole (Ms.
Johnson), Jack Kruschen (Billy
Brooks), Sydney Chaplin (Mond),
John Carradine (bum), Lane Caudell
(Stevie), Joseph Carlo (Coach),
Michael Donavon O'Donnell (farmer),
Robin Greer (Baker girl).

SATAN'S FIVE WARNINGS (1945-
Mex.) (A. K. A. "Las Ginco
Advertencias de Satanas")
Director: Julian Soler
Abel Salazar, Fernando Soler,
Eduardo Arozomena, Olga Jimenez,
Maria Elena Marques, Beatriz
Ramos, Ana Bronte, Antonio Monsel.

SATAN'S SCHOOL FOR GIRLS (TVM-
1973) - 9-19-73
Director: David Lowell Rice
Pamela Franklin (Elizabeth Sayres),
Roy Thinnes (Dr. Clampett),
Kate Jackson (Roberta Lockhart),
Lloyd Bochner (Dr. Delacroix),
Jamie Smith Jackson (Debbie Jones),
Jo Van Fleet (Mrs. Williams),
Cheryl Stoppelmoor/Ladd (Jody
Keller), Bing Russell (Sheriff),
Frank Marth (Detective), Gwynne
Gilford (Lucy Dembrow), Terry
Lumley (Martha Sayres), Bill Quinn
(Gardener).

SATAN'S SLAVE (1977)
Director: Norman J. Warren
Michael Gough (Alexander Yorke),
Candace Glendenning (Catherine
Yorke), Martin Potter (Stephen Yorke),
Barbara Kellerman (Frances),
Michael Grace (John), James Bree
(Malcolm), Celia Hewitt (Alizabeth).

SATAN'S TRIANGLE (TVM-1975)
- 1-14-75
Kim Novak (Eva), Doug McClure
(Haig), Jim Davis (Hal), Alejandro

Rey (Martin), Ed Lauter (Strickland),
Titos Vandis (Salao), Michael Conrad
(Pagnolini), Zitto Kazann (Juano),
Buck Gee (DeSoma), Hank Stohl
(Coast Guard Captain), Peter Bourne
(Swedish Captain), Tom Dever (Miami
radio rescue officer), Trent Dolan
(Miami rescue lieutenant).

SATELLITE IN THE SKY (1956)
     Director: Paul Dickson
Kieron Moore (Michael), Lois
Maxwell (Kim), Sir Donald Wolfit
(Merrity), Bryan Forbes (Jimmy),
Allan Gifford (Col. Galloway),
Carl Jaffe (Bechstein), Jimmy
Hanley (Larry), Donald Gray (Capt.
Ross), Thea Gregory (Barbara),
Barry Keegan (Lefty), Walter Hudd
(Blandford), Shirley Laurence,
Peter Neill, Ronan O'Casey, Charles
Richardson, Rick Rydon, Robert
O'Neil, Trevor Reid, John Baker,
Alastair Hunter.

SATURDAY THE 14th (1981)
     Director: Howard R. Cohen
Richard Benjamin (John), Paula
Prentiss (Mary), Severn Darden
(Van Helsing), Jeffrey Tambor
(Waldemar), Kari Michaelsen (Deb-
bie), Roberta Collins (Cousin Rhonda),
Kevin Brando (Billy), Rosemary
De Camp (Aunt Lucille), Thomas
Newman (Cousin Phil), Craig Coulter
(Duane), Nancy Lee Andrews (Yo-
landa), Carol Androsky (Marge),
Annie O'Donnell (Annette), Michael
Miller (Ernie, the cop).

SATURN 3 (1980)
     Director: Stanley Donen
Kirk Douglas (Adam), Farrah Faw-
cett (Alex), Harvey Keitel (Benson/
James), Douglas Lambert (Captain
James), Ed Bishop (Harding),
Christopher Muncke (2nd crewman).

SAVAGE, THE (1926)
     Director: Fred Newmeyer
Ben Lyon (Danny Terry), May
McAvoy (Ysabel Atwater), Tom
Maguire (Prof. Atwater), Philo
McCullough (Howard Kipp), Sam
Hardy (managing editor), Charlotte
Walker (Mrs. Atwater).

SAVAGE BEES, THE (TVM-1976) -
     11-22-76
     Director: Bruce Heller
Ben Johnson (Sheriff McKew), Michael
Parks (Dr. Jeff DuRand), Gretchen
Corbett (Jeannie Devereaux), Horst

Buchholz (Dr. Jorge Mueller), James
Best (Pelligrino), Paul Hecht (Rufus),
Bruce French (Police Lieutenant),
Richard Boyle (Coast Guard Chief),
David Gray (Coast Guard Lieutenant),
Elliott Keener (Freighter Boatswain),

SAVAGE CURSE, THE (TVM-1974)
     (A.K.A. "Kiss Me and Die") -
     2-25-74
     Director: John Sichel
George Chakiris (Robert Stone),
Jenny Agutter (Dominie Landsford),
Anton Diffring (Jonathan Landsford),
Stephen Grief (Ben Droom), John
Sharpe (Jack Woodgridge), Russell
Hunter (Old Fred), Peggy Sinclair
(Miss Faversham), John Atkinson
(Ben Hawkes), Raymond Mason
(Bill Gurney), Peter Cassilas (Jim
Stone), Barry James (Tom Whidden),
Sue Robinson (Jenny), Peter Elliott
(the Emgy).

SAVAGE GIRL (1932)
     Director: Harry S. Fraser
Rochelle Hudson (the Goddess),
Walter Byron (the scientist), Harry
F. Myers (the millionaire), Theodore
Adams (the valet), Adolph Milar
(the German), Floyd Shackleford (the
chauffeur), Charles Gemora (the
gorilla).

SAVAGES (1972)
     Director: James Ivory
Louis J. Standlen (Julian), Anne
Francine (Carlotte), Thayer David
(Otto), Susan Blakely (Cecily), Salome
Jens (Emily), Kathleen Widdoes
(Leslie), Margaret Brewster (Lady
Cora), Russ Thacker (Andrew),
Neil Fitzgerald (Sir Harry), Ultra
Violet (Iliona), Paulita Sedgwick
(Penelope), Martin Kove (Archie),
Eva Saleh (Zia), Sam Waterston
(James), Asha Puthill (forest girl).

SCALPEL (1977) (A.K.A. "False
     Face")
     Director: John Grissmer
Robert Lansing (Philip), Judith
Chapman (Heather/Jane), Arlen
Dean Snyder (Uncle Bradley), David
Scarroll (Rboert), Sandy Martin
(Sandy), Bruce Atkins (plumber).

SCANNERS (1981)
     Director: David Cronenberg
Patrick McGoohan (Dr. Paul Ruth),
Stephen Lack (Cameron Vale), Jen-
nifer O'Neill (Kim), Michael Ironside
(Darryl Revok), Lawrence Dane

(Keller), Robert Silverman (Pierce), Charles Shamata (Gandi), Adam Ludwig (Crostic), Mavor Moore (Trevellyan), Victor Desy (Dr. Gatineau).

SCARECROW, THE (1981-N. Zeal.)
    Director: Sam Pillsbury
John Carradine (Salter), Jonathan Smith (Ned), Daniel McLaren (Les), Stephen Taylor (Herbert), Anne Flannery (Ma), Des Kelly (Pa), Paul Owen-Lowe (Jim Coleman), Bruce Allpress (Uncle Athol), Greer Robson (Lyentte), Tracy Mann (Prudence), Denise O'Connell (Angela Potroz), Greg Naughton (Victor Lynch), Jonathan Hardy (Charlie Dabney), Phillip Holder (Len Ramsbottom), Roy Billing (Mr. Potroz).

SCARECROW OF ROMNEY MARSH,
    THE (1964) (A.K.A. "Dr. Syn,
    Alias the Scarecrow")
    Director: James Neilson
Patrick McGoohan (Dr. Syn), George Cole (Mipps), Sean Scully (John Banks), Geoffrey Keen (Gen. Pugh), Patrick Wymark (Joe Ransley), Eric Flynn (Lt. Philip Brackenbury), Eric Pohlmann (King George III), Michael Hordern (Sir Thomas Banks), Tony Britton (Simon Banks), Jill Curzon (Kate Banks), David Buck (Harry Banks), Richard O'Sullivan (George Ramsley), Kay Walsh (Mrs. Waggett), Alan Dobie (Fragg), Robert Dodson (Kim Ransley), Robert Brown (Sam Farley), Percy Herbert (head jailer), Allan McClelland (2nd jailer).

SCARED STIFF (1952)
    Director: George Marshall
Dean Martin (Larry Todd), Jerry Lewis (Myron Mertz), Lizabeth Scott (Mary Carroll), Dorothy Malone (Rosie), Carmen Miranda (Carmelita Castina), Henry Brandon (Pierre), Jack Lambert (Zombie), Leonard Strong (Shorty), Tom Powers (Police Lieutenant), George Dolenz (Mr. Cortega), Tony Barr (Trigger), William Ching (Tony Warren), Hugh Sanders (policeman on pier), Paul Marion (the Carrison twins).

SCARED TO DEATH (1947)
    Director: Christy Cabanne
Bela Lugosi (Leonide), George Zucco (Dr. Van Ee), Molly Lamont (Laura), Douglas Fowley, Joyce

Compton, Roland Varno, Nat Pendleton, Angelo Rossito, Stanley Price, Gladys Blake, Stanley Andrews, Lee Bennett.

SCARED TO DEATH (1980)
    Director: Bill Malone
John Stinson (Ted Lonergan), David Moses (Lou Capell), Diana Davidson (Jennifer Stanton), Toni Jannotta (Sherry Carpenter), Walker Edminston (Police Chief Warren), Mike Muscat (Howard Tindall), Pam Bowman.

SCARLET CLAW, THE (1944)
    Director: Roy William Neill
Basil Rathbone (Sherlock Holmes), Nigel Bruce (Dr. Watson), Gerald Hamer (Alistair Ramson), Arthur Hohl (Emil Journet), Paul Cavanagh (Lord William Penrose), Kay Harding (Marie Journey), Miles Mander (Judge Brisson), Victoria Horne (Nora), Ian Wolfe (Drake), David Clyde (Sgt. Thompson), George Kirby (Father Pierre), Harry Allen (Taylor, the storekeeper), Frank O'Connor (cab driver), Gertrude Astor (woman).

SCARLET CLUE, THE (1945)
    Director: Phil Rosen
Sidney Toler (Charlie Chan), Benson Fong (Tommy Chan), Mantan Moreland (Birmingham Brown), Robert Homans (Captain Flynn), I. Stanford Jolley (Ralph Brett), Virginia Brissac (Mrs. Marsh), Jack Norton (Willie Rand), Janet Shaw (Gloria Bayne), Milton Kibbee (Herbert Sinclair), Leonard Mudie (Horace Carlos), Ben Carter (Ben), Reid Kilpatrick (Wilbur Chester), Victoria Faust (Hulda Swenson), Helen Devereaux (Diane Hall), Charles Jordan (Nelson), Charles Sherlock (Sgt. McGraw), Kernan Cripps (Detective).

SCARLET STREAK, THE (1926) -
    serial in 10 episodes
Chapters: 1. "The Face in the Crowd", 2. "Masks and Men", 3. "The Rope of Hazard", 4. "The Death Ray", 5. "The Lost Story", 6. "The Plunge of Peril", 7. "The Race of Terror", 8. "The Cable of Courage", 9. "The Dive of Death", & 10. "Universal Peace".
    Director: Henry McRae
Jack Daughtery (Bob Evans), Lola Todd (Mary Crawford), Albert J.

Smith (Richard Crawford), Albert
Prisco (Monk), Virginia Ainsworth
(Monk's accomplice).

SCARS OF DRACULA, THE (1970)
    Director: Roy Ward Baker
Christopher Lee (Count Dracula),
Jenny Hanley (Sarah Framsen),
Denis Waterman (Simon Carlson),
Patrick Troughton (Klove), Anoushka
Hempel (Tania), Christopher Mat-
thews (Paul Carlson), Michael
Gwynn (Priest), Wendy Hamilton
(Julie), Michael Ripper (Landlord),
Delia Lindsay (Alice), Bob Todd
(Burgomeister), David Lealand (1st
officer), Richard Durden (2nd officer),
Morris Bush (farmer), Toke Townley
(elderly wagonmaster), Olive Barrie
(fat young man), Margot Boht (land-
lord's wife).

SCHIZO (1978)
    Director: Peter Walker
Lynne Frederick (Samantha), John
Leyton (Alan), Stephanie Beacham
(Beth), John Fraser (Leonard),
Lindsay Campbell (Falconer), Colin
Jeavons (Commissioner), Queenie
Watts (Mrs. Wallace), Jack Watson
(Haskin), Trisha Mortimer (Joy),
Paul Alexander (Peter), Victoria
Allum (Samantha as a child), John
McEnery (Stephens), Raymond
Bowers (manager), Terry Duggan
(editor), Diane King (Mrs. Falconer),
Robert Mill (Maitre d'), Victor
Winding (Sergeant), Pearl Hackney
(lady at seance), Wendy Gilmore
(Samantha's mother), Prime
Townsend (secretary).

SCHIZOID (1971-Ital./Fr./Span.) (A.
    K.A. "A Lizard in a Woman's
    Skin", "Una Lucertola con la
    Pelle di Donna")
    Director: Lucio Folci
Florinda Bolkan (Carol Hammond),
Stanley Baker (Insp. Corvin),
Leo Genn (Edmund Brighton), George
Rigaud (Dr. Kerr), Jean Sorel
(Frank Hammond), Alberto De Men-
doza (Brandon), Mike Kennedy
(Hubert), Penny Brown (Jenny),
Silvia Monti (Deborah), Anita
Strindberg (Julia Durer), Edy Gall
(Joan), Franco Balducci (McKenna),
Ezio Marano (Lowell), Erzsi Paal
(Mr. Gordon), Jean Degrade (clenic
director), Gaetano Imbro, Luigi
Antonio Guerra (policemen).

SCHIZOID (1980)

Director: David Paulsen
Klaus Kinski (Dr. Peter Fales),
Mariana Hill (Julie), Craig Wasson
(Doug), Donna Wilkes (Alison Fales),
Joe Regalbuto (Jake), Richard
Herd (Donahue), Christopher Lloyd
(Gilbert), Kiva Lawrence (Rosemary),
Cindy Dolan (Sally), Claude Duver-
noy (Francoise), Flo Gerrish (Pat),
Danny Assael (Barney), Jon Greene
(Archie), Richard Balin (Freddy),
Kathy Garrick (Maxine), Tobar Mayo
(Francis), Fredric Cook (Willy),
Jonathan Millner (Francis' friend),
Gracia Lee (Bruce), Frances Nealy
(housekeeper), Jay May (Boy), Kim-
berly Jensen (girl), Cindy Riegel
(secretary), Tony Swartz (bartender).

SCHLOCK (1972)
    Director: John Landis
John Landis (Schlockthropus), Saul
Kahan, Eliza Garrett, Joseph
Piantadosi, Forrest J. Ackerman,
Eric Allison, Charles Villiers,
Enrica Blankey, John Chambers.

SCOTLAND YARD DRAGNET (1957)
    (A.K.A. "The Hypnotist")
    Director: Montgomery Tully
Roland Culver (Dr. Francis Pelham),
Patricia Roc (Mary Foster), Paul
Carpenter (Valentine Neal), Willam
Hartnell (Detective Insp. Ross),
Kay Callard (Susie), Ellen Pollock
(Barbara Barton), Gordon Needham
(Detective Sgt. Davis), Oliver John-
ston, Martin Wyldeck.

SCOUNDREL, THE (1935)
    Director: Ben Hecht
Noel Coward (Anthony Mallare),
Julie Haydon (Cora Moore), Stanley
Ridges (Paul Decker), Ernest Cossart
(Jimmy Clay), Lionel Stander
(Rothstein), Alexander Woolcott
(Vanderveer Veyden), Edward
Ciannelli (Maruice Stern), Harry
Davenport (Slevack), Martha
Sleeper (Julia Vivian), Frank
Conlan (Massey), Everly Gregg
(Mildred Langwiler), Rosita Moreno
(Carlotta), Helen Strickland (Mrs.
Rollinson), Hope Williams (Mathilde),
Richard Bond (Howard Gillette),
O. Z. Whitehead (Calhoun), Raymond
Bramley (Felix Abrams), William
Ricciardi (Luigi), Uhei Hasegawa
(Yoshiwara), Carl Schmidt (zither
player), Isabelle Foster (scrub wo-
man), Miss Shushinka (fortune teller).

SCOUNDRELS, THE (1969-Mex.)

(A. K. A. "Los Canallas", "Infernal Angels")
Director: Federico Curiel
Mil Mascaras, Regina Torne, Claudia
Martel, Manolo Munox, David Silva,
Federico de Castillo, Fernando Oses,
Atila Michel, Olga Marquez, Elvira
Mendoza, Cesar Gay.

SCRAMBLED BRAINS (1951) - short
Director: Jules White
Moe Howard, Shemp Howard, Larry
Fine, Babe London, Emil Sitka, Vernon Dent.

SCREAM AND SCREAM AGAIN (1969)
Director: Gordon Hessler
Vincent Price (Dr. Browning), Christopher Lee (Fremont), Peter Cushing
(Bendek), Judy Huxtable (Sylvia),
Michael Gothard (Keith), Alfred
Marks (Superintendent Bellaver),
Anthony Newlands (Ludwig), Marshall
Jones (Konratz), David Lodge (Detective Insp. Strickland), Peter Sallis
(Schweitz), Uta Levka (Jane), Judi
Bloom (Helen Bradford), Clifford
Earl (Detective Sgt. Jimmy Joyce),
Kenneth Benda (Prof. Kingsmill),
Yutte Stensgaard.

SCREAM, BABY, SCREAM (1969)
Director: Joseph Adler
Ross Harris, Chris Martell, Eugenie
Wingate, Suzanne Stuart, Jim Vance,
Larry Swanson, Naomi Fink.

SCREAM, BLACULA, SCREAM (1973)
Director: Bob Kelljan
William Marshall (Mamuwalde), Pam
Grier (Lisa), Don Mitchell (Justin),
Michael Conrad (Sheriff Dunlop),
Barbara Rhoades (Elaine), Richard
Lawson (Willis), Bernie Hamilton
(Ragman), Lynne Moody (Denny),
Janee Michelle (Gloria), Van Kirksey (Prof. Walston), Beverly Gill
(Maggie), Don Blackman (Doll Man),
Arnold Williams (Louis).

SCREAMER (TVM-1974) - 11-12-74
Director: Shaun O'Riordan
Pamela Franklin (Nicola Stevens),
Wolfe Morris (Balsam), Donal McCann
(Jeff Holt), Frances White (Virna
Holt), Derek Smith (Insp. Charles),
Jim Norton (the Man), Harry Walker
(Sergeant), Michael Hall (doctor),
Stephen Bateman (station master),
Corinthia West (policewoman), Peter
Howell (ward), Ambrosine Phillpotts
(lady on train).

SCREAMERS (1981-U. S. /Ital.) (A. K. A.
"The Fish Men", "L'Isola Degli
Uomini Pesce", "Something Waits
in the Dark")
Director: Sergio Martino
Barbara Bach (Amanda Rackham),
Richard Johnson (Edmund Rackham),
Joseph Cotten (Prof. Marvin), Mel
Ferrer (Radcliffe), Cameron Mitchell
(Decker), Claudio Cassinelli (Claude),
Beryl Cunningham (Shakira), Eunice
Bolt (Samantha), Tom J. Delaney
(Patterson).

SCREAMING MIMI (1958)
Director: Gerd Oswald
Anita Ekberg (Virginia Wilson), Phil
Carey (Bill Sweeney), Harry Townes
(Dr. Greenwood), Gypsy Rose Lee
(Joann Mapes), Romney Brent (Charlie Wilson), Oliver McGowan (Walter
Krieg), Vaughn Taylor (Raoul Raynarde),
Alan Gifford (Capt. Bline), Frank
Scannell (Paul), Linda Cherney
(Ketti), Stephen Ellsworth (Dr. Joseph Robinson).

SCREAMING SHADOW, THE (1920) -
serial in 15 episodes
Chapters: 1. "A Cry in the Dark", 2.
"The Virgin of Death", 3. "The Fang
of the Beast", 4. "The Black Seven",
5. "The Vapor of Death", 6. "The
Hidden Menace", 7. "Into the Depths",
8. "The White Terror", 9. "The Sleeping Death", 10. "The Prey of Mong",
11. "Liquid Fire", 12. "Cold Steel",
13. "The Fourth Symbol", 14. "Entombed Alive", & 15. "Unmasked".
Director: Duke Worne
Joseph Girard (Baron Valska), Ben
Wilson (John Rand), Neva Gerber
(Mary Landers), Howard Crampton
(J. W. Russell), William Dyer (Jake
Williams), William Carroll (Harry
Malone), Frances Terry (Nadia),
Claire Wille, Pansy Porter (young
maidens), Fred Gamble (Fred Wilson),
Joseph Manning (the butler).

SCREAMING SKULL, THE (1958)
Director: Alex Nicol
John Hudson (Eric), Peggy Webber
(Jenny), Russ Conway (Rev. Snow),
Toni Johnson (Mrs. Snow), Alex
Nicol (Mickey, the gardner).

SCREAMING SKULL, THE (TVM-1973)
- 2-14-73
Director: Gloria Monty
David MaCallum, Carrie Nye (Helen),
Vincent Gardenia (Ollie), Stuart Germaine, Witfied Connors, Sarah

Cunningham.

SCREAMING WOMAN, THE (TVM-
1972) - 1-29-72
Director: Jack Smithy
Olivia DeHavilland (Laura Wynant),
Joseph Cotten (George Tresvant),
Ed Nelson (Carl Nesbitt), Walter
Pidgeon (Dr. Amos Larkin), La-
raine Stephens (Caroline Wynant),
Alexandra Hay (Evie Carson),
Charles Knox Robinson (Howard
Wynant), Jackie Russell (Helen
Nesbitt), Jan Arvan (Martin), Lonny
Chapman (Sergeant), Russell G.
Wiggins (Harry Sands), Charles
Drake (Ken Bronson), John Alderman
(Slater), Joyce Cunningham (Bernice
Wilson), Ray Montgomery (Ted
Wilson), Gene Andrusco (Deputy
David).

SCREAM IN THE NIGHT, A (1919)
Director: Burton King
Ruth Budd (Darwa), Ralph Kellard
(Robert Hunter), John Webb Dillon
(Prof. Silvio), Edna Britton (Vaneva
Carter), Ed Roseman (Lotec),
Adelbert Hugo (Gloris), Stephen
Grattan (Sen. Newcastle).

SCREAM IN THE NIGHT (1935)
Director: Fred Newmeyer
Lon Chaney, Jr. (Jack Wilson/Butch
Curtain), Philip Ahn (Wu Ting),
John Ince (Bentley), Sheila Terry
(Edith Bentley), Merrill McCormick
(Arab), Richard Cramer (Insp.
Green), Zarah Tazil (Mora), Manuel
Lopez (Johnny Fly).

SCREAM OF FEAR (1961) (A.K.A.
"Taste of Fear")
Director: Seth Holt
Susan Strasberg (Penny Appleby),
Christopher Lee (Dr. Gerrard),
Ronald Lewis (Bob), Ann Todd (Jane
Appleby), John Serret (Insp. Legrand),
Leonard Sachs (Spratt), Anne Blake
(Marie), Fred Johnson (father),
Richard Klee (plainsclothesman),
Bernard Brown (gendarme), Mme.
Lobegue (Swiss air hostess).

SCREAM OF THE DEMON LOVER
(1970-Span. /Ital.) (A.K.A.
"Ivanna", "Killers of the Castle
of Blood")
Director: Jose Louis Merino
Charles Quiney/Jeffrey Chase (Baron
Janos Dalmar), Erna Schurer/Jen-
nifer Hartley (Jennifer), Agostino
Belli, Antonio Escribano, Christian

Pathe, Mariano Vidal Molina.

SCREAM OF THE WOLF (TVM-1974) -
1-16-74
Director: Dan Curtis
Peter Graves (John Wetherby), Clint
Walker (Byron Douglas), Jo Ann
Pflug (Sandy Miller), Don Megowan
(Grant), Philip Carey (Sheriff Vernon
Bell), Brian Richarsd (Deputy Chase),
Grant Owens (Deputy Bill), Dean
Smith (Lake), Orville Sherman
(coroner), Jim Storm (boy), Bonnie
Van Dyke (girl), Lee Paul (student),
Vernon Weddle, Douglas Bungert,
William Baldwin, Kenneth Stimson.

SCREAM, PRETTY PEGGY (TVM-
1973) - 11-24-73
Director: Gordon Hessler
Sian Barbara Allen (Peggy Johns),
Betty Davis (Mrs. Ellito), Ted
Bessell (Jeffrey Elliot), Tovah Feld-
shuh (Agnes Thornton), Charles
Drake (George Thornton), Allan
Arbus (Dr. Saks), Christiane Schmidt-
ner (Jennifer Elliott), Jessica Rains
(office girl), Johnnie Collins, III
(student).

SCREAMS OF A WINTER NIGHT (1979)
Director: James L. Wilson
Matt Borel (John), Gil Glascow (Sam),
Patrick Byers (Carl), Mary Agnes
Cox (Elaine), Robin Bradley (Sally),
Ray Gaspard (Harper), Beverly Allen
(Jookie), Brandy Barrett (Liz), Charles
Rucker (Alan), Jan Norton (Lauri).

SCROOGE (1935)
Director: Henry Edwards
Seymour Hicks (Ebenezer Scrooge),
Donald Calthrop (Bob Cratchit),
Barbara Everest (Mrs. Cratchit),
Robert Cochran (Fred), Maurice
Evans (poor man), Mary Glynne
(Belle), Philip Frost (Tiny Tim),
Marie Ney (Spirit of Christmas Past),
Oscar Asche (Spirit of Christmas
Present), C.V. France (Spirit of
Christmas Future), Garry Marsh
(Belle's husband), Charles Carson
(Middlemark), Mary Lawson (poor
man's wife), Athene Seyler (Scrooge's
charwoman), Eve Grey (Fred's wife),
Morris Harvey (poulterer), Hugh E.
Wright (Old Joe), Hubert Harben
(Worthington), D. J. Williams (un-
dertaker), Margaret Yarde (Scrooge's
laundress).

SCROOGE (1970)
Director: Ronald Neame

Albert Finney (Ebenezer Scrooge),
Alec Guinness (Marley's Ghost),
Edith Evans (Ghost of Christmas
Past), Kenneth More (Ghost of
Christmas Present), Paddy Stone
(Ghost of Christmas Yet to Come),
Laurence Naismith (Mr. Fesziwig),
Kay Walsh (Mrs. Fezziwig), David
Collings (Bob Cratchit), Anton Rod-
gers (Tom Jenkins), Michael Medwin
(nephew), Richard Beaumont (Tiny
Tim), Suzanne Neve (Isabel), Frances
Cuka (Mrs. Cratchit), Derek Francis,
Roy Kinnear (portly gentlemen),
Mary Peach (nephew's wife), Gordon
Jackson (nephew's friend), Geof-
frey Bayldon (toy shop owner), Molly
Weir, Helena Gloag (women debtors),
Marianne Stone (party guest), Keith
March (well wisher), Reg Lever
(Punch and Judy man).

SEA BAT, THE (1930)
    Director: Wesley Ruggles
Charles Bickford, Nils Asther, John
Miljan, Boris Karloff, Gibson Gow-
land, Raquel Torres, Edmund Breese,
George F. Marion, Mack Swain.

SEA HOUND, THE (1947) - serial in
    15 episodes
    Director: Walter B. Eason &
        Mack Wright
Buster Crabbe (Captain Silver), Ralph
Hodges (Jerry), Robert Barron
(Admiral), Stanley Blystone (Black
Mike), Milton Kibbee (John Whitney),
Rick Vallin (Manila), Jimmy Lloyd
(Tex), Jack Ingram (Murdock), Pamela
Blake (Ann Whitney), Hugh Prosser
(Rand), Al Baffert (Lon), Robert Dun-
can (Sloan), Spencer Chan (Kukai),
Pierce Lyden (Vardman), Rusty
Wescoatt (Singapore).

SEA RAIDERS (1941) - serial in 12
    episodes
Chapters: 1. "The Raider Strikes",
2. "Flaming Torture", 3. "The Tragic
Crash", 4. "The Raider Strikes Again",
5. "Flames of Fury", 6. "Blasted
from the Air", 7. "Victims of the
Storm", 8. "Dragged to Their Doom",
9. "Battling the Sea Beast", 10.
"Periled by a Panther", 11. "Entombed
in the Tunnel", & 12. "Paying the Pen-
alty".
    Director: Ford Beebe & John
        Rawlins
Billy Halop (Billy Adams), Huntz
Hall (Toby Nelson), Gabriel Dell
(Bilge), Bernard Punsley (Butch),
Hally Chester (Swab), Joe Recht

(Lug), William Hall (Brack Warren),
John McGuire (Tom Adams), Mary
Field (Aggie Nelson), Edward Keane
(Elliott Carlton), Marcia Ralston
(Leah Carlton), Reed Hadley (Carl
Tonjes), Stanley Blystone (Capt.
Olaf Nelson), Richard Alexander
(Jenkins), Ernie Adams (Zeke),
Jack Clifford (Anderson), Richard
Bone (Krans), Morgan Wallace (Capt.
Lester), Eddie Dunn (Capt. Meredith).

SEARCH FOR BRIDEY MURPHY,
    THE (1956)
    Director: Noel Langley
Teresa Wright (Ruth Simmons),
Louis Hayward (Morey Bernstein),
Kenneth Tobey (Rex Simmons),
Nancy Gates (Hazel Bernstein),
Richard Anderson (Dr. Deering),
Walter Kingsford (Professor), James
Bell (Hugh Lynn Cayce), Tom McKee
(Catlett), Janet Riley (Lois Morgan),
Charles Maxwell (Father Bernard),
Charles Boaz (Jerry Thomas),
Lawrence Fletcher (Cranmer),
Noel Leslie (Edgar Cayce), William
J. Barker (himself), James Kirk-
wood (Brian at age 68), Eilene
Janssen, Hallence Hill, Bradford
Jackson, Denise Freeborn, Ruth
Robinson, Marion Gray, Hugh
Corcoran, Dick Ryan, Flora Jean
Engstrom, Jeane Wood, Thomas P.
Dillon.

SEARCH FOR THE GODS (TVM-
    1975) - 3-9-75
    Director: Jud Taylor
Stephen McHattie (Willie Longfellow),
Kurt Russell (Shan Mullins), Vic-
toria Racimo (Genara Juantez),
Raymond St. Jacques (Raymond
Stryker), Ralph Bellamy (Dr. Hen-
derson), Albert Paulsen (Tarkanian),
John War Eagle (Lucio), Carmen
Argenziano (Wheeler), Joe David
Marcus (Elder), Joe Marcus, Jr.
(Council Indian), Larry Blake (jai-
ler), Jackson D. Kane (Glenn).

SEBASTIAN (1968)
    Director: David Greene
Dirk Bogarde (Segastian), Susannah
York (Becky Howard), Janet Munro
(Carol Fancy), John Gielgud (Head
of Intelligence), Lilli Palmer
(Elsa Shahn), Nigel Davenport (Gen.
Phillips), Ronald Fraser (Toby),
Ann Beach (Pamela), John Ronane
(Security Head Jameson), Susan
Whitman (Tilly), Ann Sidney (Naomi),
Jeane Roland (Randy), Louise

Pernell (Thelma), Veronica Clifford (Ginny), Lyn Pinkney (Joan), Margaret Johnston (Miss Elliott), Charles Lloyd Pack (chess player), Donald Sutherland (American), Portland Mason (the UG girl), Alan Freeman (TV disc jockey).

SECOND BEST SECRET AGENT IN THE WHOLE WIDE WORLD, THE (1965) (A. K. A. "Licensed to Kill")
Director: Lindsay Shonteff
Tom Adams (Charles Vine), Karel Stepanek (Henrik Jacobsen), Veronica Hurst (Julia Lindberg), Peter Bull (Masterman), Francis De Wolff (Walter Pickering), George Pastell, Oliver MacGreevy (Russian Commisars), John Arnatt (Rockwell), Felix Felton (Tetchnikov), Denis Holmes (Maltby), Tony Wall (Sadistikov), Paul Tann (Valdimir Sheehee), Billy Milton (Wilson), Judy Huxtable (Computer center girl), Harry Hope (army officer), Carole Blake (crossword puzzle girl), Stuart Saunders (police inspector), John Evitts (killer), Shelagh Booth (Governess), Robert Marsden (August Jacobsen), Claire Gordon, Mona Chong, Julian Strange, Sarah Maddern, Michael Godfrey, J. B. Dubin-Behrmann.

SECONDS (1966)
Director: John Frankenheimer
Rock Hudson (Antoichus Wilson), Salome Jens (Norma Marcus), John Randolph (Arthur Hamilton), Richard Anderson (Dr. Innes), Murray Hamilton (Charlie Evans), Jeff Corey (Mr. Ruby), Will Geer (Old Man), Karl Swenson (Dr. Morris), Khigh Dheigh (Davalo), Ned Young (Henry Bushman), Wesley Addy (John), Robert Brubaker (Mayberry), John Lawrence (Texan), Frances Reid (Emily Hamilton), Edgar Stehli (tailor shop presser), Dody Heath (Sue Bushman), Francoise Ruggieri (girl in bedroom), Elisabeth Fraser (plump blonde), Dorothy Morris (Mrs. Filter), Frank Campanella (man in station), Barbara Werle (secretary), Aaron Magidow (meat man), Thom Conroy (dayroom attendant), De De Young (nurse), Kirk Duncan (Mr. Filter), William R. Wintersole (doctor), Tina Scala (young girl).

SECRET AGENT FIREBALL (1965-Ital. /Fr.) (A. K. A. "Lie Spie Uccidone a Beirut", "The Spy Killers")
Director: Mario Donen
Richard Harrison (Robert Fleming), Wanda Guida (Elena), Dominique Boschero (Liz), Jim Clay (Russian agent), Alan Collins (Russian agent), Alcide Borik (taxi driver), Clement Harari, Audrey Fisher, Carrol Brown, Jean Ozenne, Franklin Fred, F. Unger.

SECRET AGENT SUPER DRAGON (1966-Ital. /Fr.) (A. K. A. "New York Chiama Superdrago", "New York Calling Superdragon")
Director: Giorgio Ferroni
Ray Danton (Bryan Cooper/Super Dragon), Margaret Lee (Cynthia Fulton), Marisa Mell (Charity Farrell), Gerhard Hearter (Coleman), Jess Hahn (Baby Face), Carlo D'Angelo (Fernand Lamas), Marco Guglielmi (Prof. Kurge), Adriana Ambesi (Verna), Solvi Stubing (Elizabeth), Jacques Herlin (Dumont).

SECRET AGENT 777 OPERATION MYSTERY (1965-Ital.) (A. K. A. "Agent Segreto 777 Operazione Mistero")
Director: Enrico Bomba/Henry Bay
Mark Damon, Louis Jourdan, Seyna Seyn, Mary Young, Stanley Kent.

SECRET BEYOND THE DOOR (1947)
Director: Fritz Lang
Joan Bennett (Celia Lamphere), Michael Redgrave (Mark Lamphere), Anne Revere (Caroline Lamphere), Barbara O'Neil (Miss Robey), Natalie Schafer (Edith Potter), James Seay (Bob Dwight), Paul Cavanagh (Rick Barrett), Virginia Brissac (Sarah), Rosa Rey (Paquita), Mark Dennis (David), Donald Kerr (ticket man), Annabel Shaw (intellectual sub-deb), Marie Harmon, Kay Morley (subdebs), Cran Whitley (Lavender Falls man), Virginia Farmer (Lavender Falls woman), Lucio Villegas (priest), Eddy C. Waller (Lem), Julian Rivero (proprietor), Danny Duncan (ferret-faced man), Paul Scardon (owl eyes), David Cota (knife fighter), Paul Fierro (fighter), Frank Dae (country squire), Pedro Regas (waiter), Donna Martell (Mexican girl), David Cota (Judge), Ralph Littlefield (station agent), Tom Chatterton (gothic man), Wayne Tredway (beefy man), Watson Downs (conductor), Jesse Graves (porter),

Robert Espinosa, Tony Rodriquez,
Robert Barber (altar boy), Peggy
Remington (Dean of Women), Harry
Denny (college president).

SECRET CODE, THE (1942) - serial
in 15 episodes
Director: Spencer Gordon
Bennet
Paul Kelly (Dan Barton), Anne
Nagel (Jean Ashely), Trevor Bardette
(Jensen), Gregory Gaye (Feldon),
Jacqueline Dalya (Linda), Lester
Dorr (Stahl), Clancy Cooper (Pat),
Robert O. Davis (Thyssen), Alex
Callam (Hogan), Louis Donath (Metz-
ger), Ed Parker (Berck), Beal
Wong (Quito), Eddie Woods (Kurt).

SECRET LIFE OF WALTER MITTY,
THE (1947)
Director: Norman Z. McLeod
Danny Kaye (Walter Mitty), Virginia
Mayo (Rosalind Van Hoorn), Boris
Karloff (Dr. Hugo Hollingshead),
Fay Bainter (Mrs. Mitty), Ann
Rutherford (Gertrude Griswold),
Thurston Hall (Bruce Pierce),
Florence Bates (Mrs. Griswold),
Gordon Jones (Tubby Wadsworth),
Konstantin Shayne (Peter Van Hoorn),
Henry Cordon (Hendrick), Fritz
Feld (Anatold), Milton Parsons
(Butler), Reginald Denny (R. A. F.
Colonel), Doris Lloyd (Mrs. Fol-
linsbee), Frank Riecher (Maasdam),
Sam Ash (art editor), Bess Flowers
(illustrator), John Hamilton (Dr.
Remington), Charles Trowbridge
(Dr. Renshaw), Lumsden Hare
(Dr. Pritchard-Mitford), Hank
Worden (western character), Henry
Kolker (Dr. Benbow), Pierre Watkin
(Minister), Mary Forbes (Mrs.
Pierce), Jack Overman (Vincent),
Mary Brewer, Betty Carlyle, Sue
Casey, Karen X. Gaylord, Jackie
Jordan, Mary Ellen Gleason, Lorraine
DeRome, Georgia Lange, Martha
Montgomery, Irene Vernon, Michael
Mauree, Pat Patrick, Lynn Walker
(Goldwyn Girls), George Magrill
(Wolf Man), Joel Friedkin (Mr.
Grimsby), Harry Harvey, Jr. (office
boy), Warren Jackson (business
manager).

SECRET OF DR; MABUSE (1964-
Ital, /Ger. /Fr.) (A. K. A. "Les
Rayons Mortels du Docteur Ma-
buse", "The Death Ray of Dr.
Mabuse")
Director: Hugo Fregonese

Wolfgang Priess (Dr. Mabuse), Peter
Van Eyck, Leo Genn, Werner Peters,
Yvonne Furneaux, Yoko Tani, O. E.
Hasse, Walter Rilla.

SECRET OF MY SUCCESS, THE (1965)
Director: A. L. Stone
James Booth (Arthur Tate), Stella
Stevens (Violet Lawson), Shirley
Jones (Marigold Murado), Honor
Blackman (Baroness von Lukenburg),
Lionel Jeffries (Insp. Hobart/Baron
von Lukenburg/Pres. Esteda/Earl
of Aldershot), Joan Hickman (Mrs.
Pringle), Amy Dalby (Mrs. Tate),
Nicolau Breyner.

SECRET OF NIMH, THE (1982) -
animated
Director: Don Bluth
Voices: Elizabeth Hartman (Mrs.
Frisby), Derek Jacobi (Nicodemus),
Dom DeLuise (Jeremy the crow),
Peter Strauss (Justin), Hermione
Baddeley (Auntie Shrew), Arthur
Malet (Mr. Ages), John Carradine
(the Great Owl), Paul Shenar (Jenner),
Tom Hattan (Farmer Fitzgibbons),
Shannen Doherty (Teresa), Will
Wheaton (Martin), Jodi Hicks (Cynthia),
Ian Fried (Timmy).

SECRET OF THE BLACK TRUNK,
THE (1962-Ger.) (A. K. A. "Das
Geheimnis der Schwarzen Koffer",
"Das Schloss des Schrekens",
"Castle of the Terrified")
Director: Werner Klinger
Senta Berger, Joachim Hansen,
Peter Carstens, Hans Reiser, Leonard
Steckel.

SECRET OF THE BLUE ROOM,
THE (1933)
Director: Kurt Neumann
Lionel Atwill (Robert von Heldorf),
Gloria Stuart (Irene von Heldorf),
Paul Lukas (Capt. Walter Brink),
Edward Arnold (Commissioner
Forster), William Janney (Thomas
Brandt), Onslow Stevens (Frank
Faber), Robert Barrat (Paul, the
Butler), Elziabeth Patterson (Mary),
James Durkin (Foster's assistant),
Muriel Kirkland (Betty), Anders
van Haden (the Stranger), Russell
Hopton (Max).

SECRET OF THE LOCH, THE (1932)
(A. K. A. "The Loch Ness Mystery")
Director: Milton Rosmer
Seymour Hicks (Prof. Heggie),
Gibson Gowland (Angus), Nancy O'Neil

(Angela Heggie), Rosamund Johns
(Maggie), Frederick Peisley (Jimmy
Andrews), Ben Field (Peirmaster),
Stafford Hilliard (Macdonald), Hu-
bert Harben (Prof. Fothergill),
Eric Hales (diver).

SECRET OF THE SUBMARINE,
    THE (1916) - serial in 15 episodes
    Director: George Sargent
Juanita Hansen (Cleo Burke), Tho-
mas Chatterton (Lt. Jarvis Hope),
Hylda Hollis (Olga Ivanoff), Lamar
Johnstone (Gerald Morton), George
Clancy (Hock Barnacle), William
Tedmarsh (Tatsuma), Joseph
Beaudry (Calvin Montgomery),
Harry Edmondson (Sextus), George
Webb (Mahlin), Hugh Bennett (Dr.
Ralph Burke).

SECRET OF THE TELEGIAN (1960-
    Jap.) (A.K.A. "Denso Ningen")
    Director: Jun Fukuda
Koji Tsuruta, Akihiko Hirata,
Yumi Shirakawa, Tadao Nakamura,
Seizaburo Kawaxu.

SECRET OF THE WHISTLER, THE
    (1946)
    Director: George Sherman
Richard Dix, Leslie Brooks, Mona
Barrie, Mary Currier, Michael
Duane, Ray Walker, Jack Davis,
Charles Trowbridge, Arthur Space,
Barbara Wooddell, Claire DuBrey.

SECRET OF TREASURE ISLAND,
    THE (1938) - serial in 15 episodes
    Director: Elmer Clifton
Don Terry (Larry Kent), Grant
Withers (Grindley), Hobart Bosworth
(Dr. X), Gwen Gaze (Toni Morrell),
William Farnum (Westmore), Dave
O'Brien (Jameson), Yakima Canutt
(Dreer), Colin Campbell (Hawkins),
Walter Miller (Collins), George
Rosener (Captain Custle), Warner
Richmond (Captain Facton), Bill
Boyle (Thorndyke), Joe Caits
(Jerry), Sandra Karina (Zanya),
Patrick J. Kelly (Professor).

SECRET ROOM, THE (1915)
    Director: Tom Moore
Tom Moore (Doctor), Marguerite
Courtot (daughter), Robert Ellis
(boyfriend), Ethel Clifton (mother),
Paton Gibbs (idiot), Betty Peterson
(nurse).

SECRET SERVICE IN DARKEST
    AFRICA (1943) (A.K.A. "Manhunt

in the African Jungle", "The
Baron's African War") - serial in
15 episodes
Chapters: 1. "North African In-
trigue", 2. "The Charred Witness",
3. "Double Death"; 4. "The Open
Grave", 5. "Cloaked in Flame",
6. "Dial of Doom", 7. "Murder
Dungeon", 8. "Funeral Arrangements",
9. "Invisible Menace", 10. "Racing
Peril", 11. "Lightning Terror",
12. "Ceremonial Execution", 13.
"Fatal Leap", 14. "Victim of Vil-
lainy", & 15. "Nazi Treachery Un-
masked".
    Director: Spencer Gordon Ben-
    net
Rod Cameron (Rex Bennett), Duncan
Renaldo (Pierre LaSalle), Joan
Marsh (Janet Blake), Kurt Katch
(Hauptmann), Lionel Royce (Sultan
Abou Ben Ali/Baron Von Rommler),
Ralf Harolde (Riverboat Captain),
Frederick Worlock (Sir James Lang-
ley), Frederic Brunn (Wolfe), Kurt
Kreuger (Ernst Muller), George
Renavent (Armand), Sigurd Tor (Luger),
William Vaughn (Capt. Beschert),
William Yetter (Commandant), Erwin
Goldi (Col. Van Raeder), Hans Von
Morhart (1st Officer), George Lewis
(Kaba), John Bleifer (Kasar), Jack
LaRue (Hassan), Anthony Warde
(Helzah), Paul Marion (Abdue),
Bud Geary (blacksmith), Tom Steele
(Cameron's double/cafe heavy No. 1),
George Magrill, Ken Terrell (machine
gunners), George DeNormand (Elmir),
Norman Nesbitt (broadcaster), Walter
Fenner (Sheik Feddallah), Eddie
Phillips (Bisra), George Sorel (French
doctor), Eddie Parker (Koshe), Jack
Chefe (French sentry), William Von
Brincken (Capt. Boschert), John
Davidson (Sheik), Ken Terrell (Ahmed),
Ali/fireman No. 1/guard No. 2/lobby
heavy No. 2/residence guard/Rokan),
Joe Yrigoyan (ambusher No. 2/Arab
No. 2/Wallah), Duke Green (ambusher
No. 2/Fezal/guard No. 1/Karl/sailor/
Rama/lobby heavy No. 2), Carey
Loftin (Arab No. 1/workman), Jacques
Lory (fireman No. 2), John Royce
(German soldier), Frank Alten (Schloss),
Jack O'Shea (Marga), Augie Gomez
(M-23), Emily LaRue (Zara), Nino
Bellini (supply officer), Ed Agresti
(French officer).

SECRETS OF A SOUL (1925-Ger.)
    (A.K.A. "Die Geheimnisse einer
    Seele")
    Director: G.W. Pabst

Werner Krauss, Jack Trevor, Ruth
Weyher, Ilka Gruning, Pavel Pavlov.

SECRET OF DR. CHALMERS, THE
(1970-Ital. /Span.) (A. K. A. "Il
Segreto del Dr. Chalmers", "L'Uomo
Che Visse due Volte", "The Man
Who Lived Twice", "Transplante
de un Cerebro", "Brain Transplant")
Director: Juan Logar/John
Somerset Logar
Frank Wolff, Simon Andreu, Silvia
Dionisio, Eduardo Fajardo, Nuria
Torray.

SECRETS OF THE FRENCH POLICE
(1932)
Director: Edward Sutherland
Frank Morgan (St. Cyr), Christian
Rub (Anton Dorain), John War-
burton (Leon Renault), Gwill Andre
(Eugenie Dorain), Murray Kinnell
(Bertillon), Gregory Ratoff (Gen.
Hans Moloff), Kendall Lee (Rena),
Lucien Prival (Baron Redor Lomzoi),
Julia Swayne Gordon (Madam Danton),
Arnold Korff (the Grand Duke).

SECRET WITNESS, THE (1931) (A. K. A.
"Terror by Night")
Director: Thornton Freeland
Una Merkel (Lois Martin), Zasu
Pitts (Bella), Nat Pendleton (Gunner),
Ralf Harolde (Lewis Leroy), Paul
Hurst (Brannigan), Greta Grandstedt
(Moll), William Collier, Jr. (Arthur
Jones), Clyde Cook (Larson), Rita
La Roy (Sylvia Folsom), Purnell
Pratt (Captain McGowan), June
Clyde (Tess), Hooper Atchley (Her-
bert Folsom), Clarence Muse (build-
ing engineer).

SEDUCTION, THE (1982)
Director: David Schmoeller
Morgan Fairchild (Jamie), Michael
Sarazin (Brandon), Andrew Stevens
(Derek), Colleen Camp (Robin),
Kevin Brophy (Bobby), Vince Ed-
wards (Maxwell), Joanne Linville
(Dr. Weston), Betty Kean (Mrs.
Caluso), Wendy Smith Howard (Julie),
Marri Mak (Liza), Woodrow Parfrey
(store salesman), Robert De Simone
(photographer), Richard Reed (floor
manager), Marilyn Staley (newscaster),
Marilyn Wolf (waitress), Jeffrey
Richman (technical director), Diana
Rose (Mrs. Wilson), Shailar Schmoel-
ler (Rickey Wilson), Deborah Kippel,
Kathryn Hart (teleprompter girls).

SEED OF MAN, THE (1969-Ital.)

(A. K. A. "Il Seme Dell'Uomo")
Director: Marco Ferreri
Annie Girardot, Rada Rassimov,
Marco Margine, Anna Wiazemski,
Maria Teresa Piaggio, Milva Fro-
sini, Angela Pagano.

SEIZURE (1974)
Director: Oliver Stone
Jonathan Frid (Edmund Blackstone),
Martine Beswicke (Queen of Evil),
Herve Villechaize (the Spider),
Henry Baker (Jackal, the Giant),
Christina Pickles (Nicole Black-
stone), Mary Woronov (Mikki), Joe
Sirola (Charlie), Troy Donahue
(Mark), Roger De Koven (Serge),
Anne Meacham (Eunice), Timothy
Ousey (Jason).

SENTINEL, THE (1977)
Director: Michael Winner
Cristina Raines (Allison Parker),
Chris Sarandon (Michael Lerman),
Burgess Meredith (Charles Chazen),
Ava Gardner (Miss Logan), Arthur
Kennedy (Franchino), John Carradine
(Father Halliran), Martin Balsam
(Prof. Ruzinsky), Jose Ferrer
(Robed Figure), Sylvia Miles (Gerde),
Deborah Raffin (Jennifer), Christopher
Walken (Rizzo), Eli Wallach (Gatz),
Jerry Orbach (director), Beverly
D'Angelo (Sandra), Hank Garrett
(Brenner), Robert Gerringer (Hart),
Tom Berenger (man at end), Nana
Tucker (girl at end), Gary Allen
(Malcolm Stinnett), William Hickey
(Perry), Tresa Hughes (Rebecca
Stinnett), Kate Harrington (Mrs.
Clark), Jane Hoffman (Lilian Clotkin),
Elaine Shore (Emma Clotkin), Sam
Gray (Dr. Aureton), Reid Shelton
(Priest), Fred Stuthman (Alison's
Father), Lucie Lancaster (Alison's
Mother), Zane Lasky (Raymond),
Jeff Goldblum (Jack), Anthony Hol-
land (party host), Mady Heflin
(Professor's student), Diane Stilwell
(Brenner's secretary), Ron McLarty
(real estate agent).

SEPARATION (1967)
Director: Jack Bond
Jane Arden (Jane), David De Keyser
(the husband), Iain Quarrier (the lover),
Terence De Marney (the old man),
Ann Lynn (the woman), Joy Bang,
Donald Sayer, Peter Thomas, Kath-
leen Saintsbury, Malou Pantera,
Theo Aygar, Ann Norman, Leslie
Linder, Fay Brook, Neil Holms.

SERGEANT DEADHEAD (1965)
(A. K. A. "Sergeant Deadhead the
Astronaut")
    Director: Norman Taurog
Frankie Avalon (Sgt. Deadhead/Sgt.
Donovan), Deborah Walley (Col.
Lucy Turner), Cesar Romero (Adm.
Stoneham), Fred Clark (Gen. Rufus
Fogg), Eve Arden (Lt. Kinsey),
Gale Gordon (Capt. Weiskopf),
Reginald Gardiner (Lt. Cmdr. Tal-
bott), John Ashley, Pat Buttram,
Buster Keaton.

SERPENT ISLAND (1954)
    Director: Bert I. Gordon
Sonny Tufts, Mary Munday.

SERPENT'S EGG, THE (1966-Ger. /
U. S.) (A. K. A. "Das Schlangenei")
    Director: Ingmar Bergman
Liv Ullmann (Manuela Rosenberg),
David Carradine (Abel Rosenberg),
James Whitmore (the Priest),
Gert Frobe (Insp. Bauer), Heinz
Bennent (Dr. Vergerus), Christian
Berkel (student), Paula Braend
(Mrs. Hemse), Toni Berger (Mr.
Rosenberg), Edna Bruenell (Mrs.
Rosenberg), Gaby Dohm (woman
with baby), Emil Feist (Cupid),
Paul Buerks (cabaret comedian),
Kai Fischer, Georg Hartmann,
Klaus Hoffmann, Edith Heerdegen,
Grisha Huber, Gunther Malzacher,
Volkert Kraeft.

SERPENTS, THE (1912)
    Director: Ralph Ince
Ralph Ince (Eric), Edith Storey
(Chloe), Taft Johnson (Haakon),
Helen Gardner (Linda), William
V. Raynous (idiot).

SEVEN DAYS IN MAY (1964)
    Director: John Frankenheimer
Burt Lancaster (Gen. James M.
Scott), Kirk Douglas (Col. Martin
'Jiggs' Casey), Fredric March (Pres.
Jordan Lyman), Edmond O'Brien
(Sen. Raymond Clark), Martin
Balsam (Paul Girard), Ava Gardner
(Eleanor Holbrook), George Mac-
ready (Christopher Todd), Whit
Bissell (Sen. Prentice), Hugh Mar-
lowe (Harold McPherson), Andrew
Duggan (Col. Mutt Henderson),
Richard Anderson (Col. Murdock),
Helen Kleeb (Esther Townsend),
John Houseman (Adm. Barnswell),
Jack Mullaney (Lt. Hough), Malcolm
Atterbury (White House Physician),
John Larkin (Col. Broderick),

Colette Jackson (bar girl).

SEVEN DAYS TO NOON (1950)
    Director: John Boulting &
    Roy Boulting
Barry Jones (Prof. Willingdon), Olive
Sloane (Goldie), Andre Morell (Super-
intendent Folland), Sheila Manahan
(Ann Willingdon), Hugh Cross (Ste-
phen Lane), Joan Hickson (Mrs.
Peckett), Ronald Adam (the Prime
Minister), Merill Mueller (American
commentator), Geoffrey Keen, Marie
Ney.

SEVEN DEAD IN THE CAT'S EYES
(1972-Ital. /Fr. /Ger.)
    Director: Antonio Margheriti
Anton Diffring, Jane Birkin, Francoise Christophe, Hiram Keller,
Dana Ghis, Venantini.

SEVEN FACES (1929)
    Director: Berthold Viertel
Paul Muni, Margaret Churchill,
Russell Gleason, Gustav von Seyf-
fertitz, Lester Lonergen, Euginie
Besserer.

SEVEN FACES OF DR. LAO (1964)
    Director: George Pal
Tony Randall (Dr. Lao/Merlin/the
Abominable Snowman/Appolonius/
Pan/the Medusa), Arthur O'Connell
(Clint Stark), John Ericson (Ed
Cunningham), Barbara Eden (Angela
Benedict), Noah Berry, Jr. (Tim
Mitchell), Argentina Brunetti
(Sarah Benedict), Lee Patrick (Mrs.
Howard Casin), Minerva Urecal
(Kate Rogers), Royal Dano (Carey),
John Qualen (Luther Rogers), Kevin
Tate (Mike Benedict), Edddie
Little Sky (George E. George), John
Douchette (Lucan), Peggy Rae
(Mrs. Peter Ramsey), Frank Cady
(James Sargent), Douglas Fowley
(toothless cowboy), Chubby Johnson
(fat cowboy), Dal McKennon (lean
cowboy).

SEVEN FOOTPRINTS TO SATAN
(1929)
    Director: Benjamin Christensen
Thelma Todd, Sheldon Lewis,
Creighton Hale, Sojin, Angelo
Rossito, Willaim V. Mong, DeWitt
Jennings, Ann Christy, Harry
Tenbrook, Nora Cecil, Charlie
Gemora (the Ape).

SEVEN PER-CENT SOLUTION, THE
(1976)

Director: Herbert Ross
Nicol Williamson (Sherlock Holmes),
Alan Arkin (Sigmund Freud),
Robert Duvall (Dr. Watson), Van-
essa Redgrave (Lola Deveraux),
Laurence Olivier (Prof.
Moriarty), Samantha Eggar (Mary Watson),
Joel Grey (Lowenstein), Jeremy
Kemp (Baron Von Leinsdorf), Charles
Gray (Mycroft Holmes), Georgia
Brown (Mrs. Freud), Anna Quayle
(Freda), Regina (Madam), Jill
Townsend (Mrs. Holmes), Leon
Greene (Squire Holmes), Alison
Leggatt (Mrs. Hudson), Gertan
Klauber (the Pasha), Michael
Blagdon (young Holmes).

SEVENTH SEAL, THE (1956-Swed.)
(A. K. A. "Det Sjunde Inseglet")
Director: Ingmar Bergman
Gunnar Bjornstrand (the Squire),
Max von Sydow (the Knight), Bibi
Andersson (Mia), Bengt Ekerot
(Death), Nils Poppe (Jof), Inga
Gill (Lisa), Maud Hansson (the Witch),
Inga Landgre (Knight's wife),
Bertil Anderberg (Raval), Gunnel
Lindblom (the Girl), Anders Ek
(the Monk), Ake Fridell (the Smith),
Erik Strandmark (Skat), Gunnar
Olsson (church painter), Benkt-
Ake Benktsson, Gudron Brost,
Lars Lind, Ulf Johansson.

SEVENTH VEIL, THE (1945)
Director: Compton Bennett
James Mason (Nicholas), Ann Todd
(Francesca Cunningham), Hugh
McDermott (Peter Gay), Herbert
Lom (Dr. Larsen), Albert Lieven
(Maxwell Leyden), Yvonne Owen
(Susan Brook), Muir Mathieson,
David Horne, Manning Whiley, John
Slater.

SEVENTH VICTIM, THE (1943)
Director: Mark Robson
Kim Hunter (Mary Gibson), Jean
Brooks (Jacqueline Ward), Hugh
Beaumont (Gregory Stone), Tom
Conway (Dr. Lewis Judd), Wally
Brown (Durk), Evelyn Brent (Natalie
Cortez), Erford Gage (Jason Hoag),
Chef Milani (Mr. Romari), Ben
Bard (Mrs. Brun), Margueritz
Sylva (Frances), Mary Newton (Mrs.
Redi), Elizabeth Russell, Barbara
Hale, Isabel Jewell, Feodor Chaliapin.

SEVENTH VOYAGE OF SINBAD,
THE (1958)
Director: Nathan Juran

Kerwin Mathews (Sinbad), Kathryn
Grant Crosby (Parisa), Richard
Eyer (the Genie), Torin Thatcher
(Sokurah), Alec Mango (Caliph),
Danny Green (Karim), Alfred
Brown (Harufa), Harold Kasket
(Sultan), Nana de Herrera (Sadi),
Virgilio Teixeira (Ali), Luis
Guedes (crewman), Nino Falanga
(gaunt sailor).

SEVERED ARM, A (1973)
Director: Thomas S. Alderman
Marvin Kaplan (Mad Man Herman),
Deborah Walley, Paul Carr, John
Crawford, David Cannon, Vincent
Martorano.

SEX OF THE WITCH, THE (1972-
Ital.) (A. K. A. "Il Sesso della
Strega")
Director: Elo Panaccio
Susan Levi, Jessica Dublin, Camille
Keaton, Marzie Damon, Sergio
Ferrero, Augusto Nobile, Lorenza
Guerrieri, Gianni Del, Donald O'Brien.

SHADOW, THE (1940) - serial in 15
episodes
Director: James W. Horne
Victor Jory (Lamont Cranston/Lin
Chang/the Shadow), Robert Fiske
(Stanford Marshall/the Black Tiger),
Veda Ann Borg (Margot Lane),
Jack Ingram (Flint), Charles King
(Russell), Charles Hamilton (Ro-
berts), Edward Piel, Sr. (Insp.
Joe Cardona), J. Paul Jones
(Turner), Roger Moore (Harry
Vincent), Gordon Hart (Hill), Frank
LaRue (Commissioner Ralph Weston),
Kit Guard, George DeNormand,
Lew Sergeant, Charles Sullivan,
Constantine Romanoff, Lloyd
Ingraham, Joe Caits.

SHADOW HOUSE (1972) - short
Director: Ken Dixon
John Carradine, Joanna Phillips,
John Friedman.

SHADOWMAN (1970-Fr.) (A. K. A.
"L'Homme Sans Visage")
Director: Georges Franju
Jacques Champreux (Shadowman),
Gayle Hunnicutt (the Girl), Gert
Frobe (Insp. Sorbier), Ugo Pagliai
(Paul), Josephine Chaplin (Martine),
Patrick Prejean (Seraphin), Clement
Harari (Dr. Dutreuil), Yvon Sarray
(Alvert), Henry Lincoln (Prof.
Petri).

SHADOW OF CHINATOWN (1936) -
serial in 15 parts
Chapters: 1. "The Arms of the God",
2. "The Crushing Walls", 3. "13
Ferguson Alley", 4. "Death on the
Wire", 5. "The Sinister Ray", 6.
"The Sword Thrower", 7. "The
Noose", 8. "Midnight", 9. "The
Last Warning", 10. "The Bomb",
11; "Thundering Doom", 12. "In-
visible Gas", 13. "The Brink of
Disaster", 14. "The Fatal Trap",
& 15. "The Avenging Powers".
    Director: Robert F. Hill
Bela Lugosi (Victor Poten), Joan
Barclay (Joan Whiting), Luana
Walters (Sonya Rokoff), Bruce
Bennett/Herman Brix (Martin An-
drews), Charles King (Grogan),
Maurice Liu (Willy Fu), Forrest
Taylor (Captain Walters), Henry
F. Tung (Dr. Wu), William Buchanan
(Healy), James B. Leong (Wong),
Paul Fung (Tom Chu), John Elliott
(Captain), Moy Ming (Wong's brother),
George Chan (Old Luee), Jack
Cowell (White Chink), Lester Dorr,
Roger Williams, Henry Hall.

SHADOW OF EVIL (1964-Fr. /Ital.)
    (A.K.A. "Banco a Bangkok pour
O.S.S. 117", "Jackpot in Bangkok
for O.S.S. 117")
    Director: Andre Hunebelle
Kerwin Mathews (Agent OSS-117),
Robert Hossein (Dr. Sinn), Pier
Angeli (Lila), Dominique Wilms
(Eva), Sing Milintrasai (Prasit),
Akom Mokranond (Sonsak), Jacques
Mauclair (Gamil Ratib), Henri
Virlogeux (Leasock).

SHADOW OF FEAR (TVM-1974) -
1-26-74
    Director:
Anjanette Comer (Dana Forester),
Claude Akins (Styron), Jason
Evers (Martin), Phil Carey (De-
tective Arnburg).

SHADOW OF TERROR (1945)
    Director: Lew Landers
Richard Fraser, Cy Kendall,
Kenneth MacDonald, Eddie Acuff,
Sam Flint, Emmett Lynn, Grace
Gillern.

SHADOW OF THE BAT (1966-Mex.)
    (A.K.A. "La Sombra del Mur-
cielago")
    Director: Federico Curiel
Blue Demon, Jaime Fernandez, Fernando Oses, Marta Romero, Jesus

Velazquez.

SHADOW OF THE CAT, THE (1961)
    Director: John Gilling
Barbara Shelley (Beth Venable), Andre
Morell (Walter Venable), Freda
Jackson (Clara), Alan Wheatley
(Insp. Rowles), Richard Warner
(Edgar), Vanda Godsell (Louise),
Conrad Phillips (Michael Latimer),
Catherine Lacey (Ella Venable),
William Lucan (Jacob), Charles
Stanley (Dobbins), Andrew Crawford
(Andrew), Kynaston Reeves (grand-
father), Vera Cook (mother), Kevin
Stoney (father), Howard Knight (boy),
Angela Crow (girl).

SHADOW OF THE EAGLE (1932) -
serial in 12 episodes
Chapters: 1. "The Carnival Mystery",
2. "Pinholes", 3. "The Eagle Strikes",
4. "The Man of a Million Voices",
5. "The Telephone Cipher", 6. "The
Code of the Carnival", 7. "Eagle
or Vulture?", 8. "On the Spot", 9.
"When Thieves Fall Out", 10. "The
Man Who Knew", 11. "The Eagle's
Wings", & 12. "The Shadow Unmasked".
    Director: Ford Beebe & B.
    Reeves Eason
John Wayne (Craig McCoy), Walter
Miller (Danby), Dorothy Gulliver
(Jean Gregory), Kenneth Harlan
(Ward), Yakima Canutt (Boyle), Roy
D'Arcy (Gardner), Pat O'Malley (Ames),
Richard Tucker (Evans), Edmund
Burns (Clark), Edward Hearn (Nathan
Gregory), Lloyd Whitlock (Green),
Billy West (clown), Ernie S. Adams,
Bud Osborne, Ivan Linow.

SHADOW OF THE HAWK (1976)
    Director: George McCowan
Jan Michael Vincent (Mike), Marilyn
Hassett (Maureen), Chief Dan George
(Old Man Hawk), Pia Shandel (Faye),
Marianne Jones (Dsonoqua), Jacques
Hubert (Andak), Cindy Griffith (secre-
tary), Anna Hagan (desk nurse), Mur-
ray Lowry (intern).

SHADOW OF THE PAST (1950)
    Director: Mario Zampi
Terence Morgan, Joyce Howard,
Michael Medwin, Marie Ney, Ronald
Adam, Andrew Osborn, Ian Fleming,
Louise Gainsborough, Wylie Watson,
Ella Retford.

SHADOW ON THE LAND (TVM-
1968) - 12-4-68
    Director: Richard C. Sarafian

John Forsythe (Gen. Bruce), Carol
Lynley (Abby Tyler), Jackie Cooper
(Lt. Col. Andy Davis), Janice Rule
(Capt. Everett), Gene Hackman
(Reverend), Marc Strange (Maj.
Shepherd McCloud), Myron Healey
(Gen. Hempstead), Bill Walker (Arnold), Scott Tomas (Felting), Jonathan Lippe (Lt. Allen), Mike Margotta (Timothy Willing), Frederick
Downs (Drucker), Ken Swofford,
Paul Sorenson, Paulene Myers,
Kay Stewart, Sandy Kevin, Mickey
Sholda, Ronnie Eckstein.

SHADOWS IN THE NIGHT (1944)
    Director: Eugene J. Forde
Warner Baxter (Dr. Robert Ordway), Nina Foch (Lois Garland),
George Zucco (Frank Swift), Minor
Watson (Frederick Gordan), Ben
Welden (Nick Kallus), Lester Matthews (Stanley Carter), Charles
Halton (Doc Stacey), Edward Norris
(Jess Hilton), Charles Wilson (Sheriff), Jeanne Bates (Adele Carter).

SHAGGY D.A., THE (1976)
    Director: Robert Stevenson
Dean Jones (Wilby Daniels), Suannne Pleshette (Betty Daniels),
Keenan Wynn (John Slade), Jo Anne
Worley (Katrinka Muggelberg),
Dick Van Patten (Raymond), Tim
Conway (Tim), Vic Tayback (Eddie
Roschak), Dick Bakalyan (Freddie),
Hans Conried (Prof. Whatley),
John Fiedler (Howie Clemmings),
Warren Berlinger (Dip), John Myhers (Admiral Brenner), Iris Adrian
(manageress), Ronnie Schell (TV
director), Jonathan Daly (TV interviewer), Shane Sinutko (Brian Daniels), Michael McGreevey (Sheldon),
Richard O'Brien (desk sergeant),
Dick Lane (roller rink announcer),
Benny Rubin (waiter), Ruth Gillette
(song chairman), Pat McCormick
(bartender), Hank Jones (policeman),
Milton Frome, Olan Soule, Walt
Davis, Mary Ann Gibson, Herb Vigran, Henry Slate, Albert Albe, Helene
Winston, Sarah Fankboner, Karl
Lukas, Christina Anderson, Joan
Crosby, Danny Wells, Vern Rowe,
John Hayes, George Kirby (canine
voices).

SHAGGY DOG, THE (1959)
    Director: Charles Barton
Fred MacMurray (Wilson Daniels),
Jean Hagen (Frieda Daniels), Tim
Considine (Buzz Miller), Kevin

Corcoran (Moochie Daniels), Annette Funicello (Allison D'Allessio),
Cecil Kellaway (Prof. Plumcutt),
Alexander Scourby (Dr. Mikhail
Andrassy), Strother Martin (Thurm),
Gordon Jones (Capt. Scanlon), Forrest Lewis (Officer Kelly), James
Westerfield (Officer Hanson), Roberta
Shore (Francesca Andrassy), Jacques
Aubuchon (Stefano), John Hart (police
broadcaster), Jack Albertson (reporter), Paul Frees (psychiatrist).

SHAME (1967-Swed.) (A.K.A. "Skamen")
    Director: Ingmar Bergman
Liv Ullmann (Eve Rosenberg), Max
Von Sydow (Jan Rosenberg), Sigge
Furst (Filip), Gunnar Bjornstrand
(Col. Jacobi), Birgitta Valberg
(Mrs. Jacobi), Hans Alfredson (Lobelius), Ingvar Kjellson (Oswald),
Raymond Lundberg (Jacobi's son).

SHAMROCK HILL (1948)
    Director: Arthur Dreifuss
Peggy Ryan, John Litel, Mary Gordon,
Rick Vallin, Ray McDonald, Trudy
Marshall, James Burke, Tim Ryan,
Lanny Simpson, Patsy Bolton, Tim
Graham, Douglas Wood, Barbara
Brier.

SHANKS (1973)
    Director: William Castle
Marcel Marceau (Malcolm Shanks/
Old Walter), Tsilla Chelton (Mrs.
Barton), Cindy Eilbacher (Celia),
Philippe Clay (Mr. Barton), Larry
Bishop (Napolien), Don Calva (Einstein), William Castle (the grocer),
Biff Manard, Helena Kallianiotes.

SHAPE OF THINGS TO COME, THE
    (1979)
    Director: George McCowan
Jack Palance (Omus), Carol Lynley
(Niki), Barry Morse (Dr. John
Caball), Eddie Benton (Kim Smedley),
Nicholas Campbell (Jason Caball),
John Ireland (Senator Smedley), Marc
Parr (Sparks), Greg Swanson (Sparks'
voice), William Hutt (voice of Lomax),
Ardos Bess (Merrick), Bill Lake
(astronaut), Lynn Green (lunar
technician), Albert Humphries (robot
technician), Michael Klinbell, Wili
Liberman, Rod McEwan, Jonathan
Hartman, Angelo Pedari (robots),
Danny Gage, Jo-Anne Lang, Terry
Martin, Lutz Brodie, Terry Spratt,
Linda Carter, Bill Jay (members
of Niki's Army).

SHARK'S CAVE, THE (1978-Ital. /
    Span.) (A.K.A. "Bermude: La
    Fossa Maledetta", "Cave of the
    Sharks")
    Director: Teodoro Ricci
Andres Garcia, Arthur Kennedy,
Janet Agren, Pino Colizzi.

SHE (1911)
    Director:
James Cruze, Marguerite Snow.

SHE (1916)
    Director: Will Barker
Alice Delysia, Henry Victor,
Sidney Bland, Blanche Forsythe,
J. Hastings Batson, Jack Denton.

SHE (1917)
    Director: Kenean Buel
Valeska Suratt.

SHE (1925)
    Director: Leander De Cordova
Betty Blythe, Carlyle Balckwell,
Marjorie Statler, Henry George,
Tom Reynolds, Jerrold Robertshaw,
Dorothy Barclay, Alexander Butler.

SHE (1935)
    Director: Irving Pichel &
    Lancing C. Holden
Helen Gahagan (She), Randolph
Scott (Leo Vincey), Nigel Bruce
(Holly), Helen Mack (Tanya Dugmore),
Gustav Von Seyffertitz (Billali),
Samuel S. Hinds (John Vincey),
Lumsden Hare (Dugmore), Noble
Johnson (Amahagger Chief), Jim
Thorpe, Anatol Winogardoff.

SHE (1965)
    Director: Robert Day
Ursula Andress (Ayesha), Peter
Cushing (Major Holly), Christopher
Lee (Billali), John Richardson
(Leo Vincey), Andre Morell (Haumeid),
Bernard Cribbins (Job), Rosenda
Monteros (Ustane).

S*H*E (TVM-1980) - 2-23-80
    Director: Robert Lewis
Cornelia Sharpe (Lavina Kean),
Omar Sharif (Cesare Magnasco),
Robert Lansing (Owen Hooper),
Anita Ekberg (Else), William
Traylor (Lacey), Tom Christopher
(Bronzi), Isabella Rye (Fanya),
Fabio Testi (Rudolph Caserta),
Mario Colli (Mucci), Claudio Ruf-
fini (LaRue), Fortunato Arena
(Paesano), Geoffrey Copplestone

(UN speaker), Gino Marturano
(Major Danilo), Emilio Messina
(Zee).

SHE CREATURE, THE (1956)
    Director: Edward L. Cahn
Marla English (Andrea), Tom
Conway (Timothy Chappel), Chester
Morris (Dr. Carlo Lombardi), Ron
Randell (Lt. Ed James), Freida
Inescort (Mrs. Chappel), Cathy
Downs (Dorothy Chappel), El
Brendel (Olaf, the Butler), Paul
Blaisdell (the Monster), Frank
Jenks (Police Sergeant), Lance Fuller
(Ted Erickson), Paul Dubov (Johnny),
Flo Bert (Martha), Kenneth MacDonald
(Prof. Anderson), William Hudson
(Bob), Jeanne Evans (Mrs. Brown).

SHE DEMONS (1958)
    Director: Richard Cunha
Irish McCalla (Jerri Turner), Tod
Griffin (Fred Maklin), Rudolph
Anders (Herr Osler), Victor Sen
Yung (Sammy Ching), Gene Roth
(Egore), Charlie Opuni (Kris Kamara),
Leni Tana (Mona), Billy Dix, Bill
Coontz.

SHE DEVIL (1956)
    Director: Kurt Neumann
Mari Blanchard (Kyra), Jack
Kelly (Dr. Scott), Albert Dekker
(Dr. Bach), John Archer (Kendall),
Blossom Rock (Hannah), Fay Baker
(Mrs. Kendall), Paul Cavanagh
(Sugar Daddy), Tod Griffin (interne),
Helen Jay (nurse), George Baxter
(floor manager), Joan Bradshaw
(red-head).

SHE-DEVILS ON WHEELS (1968)
    Director: Herschell Gordon
    Lewis
Betty Connell, Nancy Lee Noble,
Pat Poston, Christie Wganer, Ruby
Tuesday, John Weymer, Rodney
Bedell.

SHE FREAKS (1967)
    Director: Byron Mabe
Claire Brennan (Jade Cochran),
Bill McKinney (Steve St. John),
Lee Raymond (Blackie Fleming),
Lynn Courtney (Pat Mullins), Felix
Silla (Shorty), Van Teen (Mr.
Babcock), Claude Smith (Greasy),
Bill Bagdad (Pretty Boy), Marsha
Drake (Olga), Bobby Matthews
(Max), Ben Moore (advance man),
David Boudrot (customer in cage),
Madame Lee (Snake Charmer).

SHE GODS OF SHARK REEF (1958)
(A.K.A. "Shark Reef")
Director: Roger Corman
Don Durant (Lee), Bill Cord (Chris),
Lisa Montell (Mahia), Jeanne Gerson (Dua), Carol Lindsay (hula dancer).

SHE'LL FOLLOW YOU ANYWHERE (1971)
Director: David C. Rea
Keith Barron, Kenneth Cope, Richard
Vernon, Philippa Gail, Hillary
Pritchard, Penny Brahms, Sandra
Bryant.

SHERLOCK HOLMES (1922)
Director: Albert Parker
John Barrymore (Sherlock Holmes),
Roland Young (Dr. Watson), Gustav von Seyffertitz (Moriarty),
Louis Wolheim (Craigin), David
Torrence (Count von Stalberg),
Reginald Denny (Prince Alexis).
Hedda Hopper (Madge Larabee),
William Powell (Forman Wells),
Carol Dempster (Alice Faulkner),
Anders Randolf (James Larabee),
Peggy Bayfield (Rose Faulkner),
Percy Knight (Sid Jones), Robert
Schable (Alf Bassick), John
Willard (Insp. Gregson), Jerry
Devine (Billy).

SHERLOCK HOLMES (1932)
Director: William K. Howard
Clive Brook (Sherlock Holmes),
Miriam Jordan (Alice Faulkner),
Reginald Owen (Dr. Watson),
Ernest Torrence (Moriarty), Alan
Mowbray (Gore-King), Herbert
Mundin (pubkeeper), Montague
Shaw (Judge), Lucien Prival (Hans,
the Hun), Howard Leeds (Little
Billy), Arnold Lucy (Chaplain),
Stanley Fields (Tony Ardetti), Roy
d'Arcy (Manuel Lopez), Eddie Dillon (Ardetti's henchman), Brandon
Hurst (Erskine's secretary), Claude
King (Sir Albert Hastings), Robert
Graves, Jr. (Gaston Roux).

SHERLOCK HOLMES AND THE DEADLY
NECKLACE (1962-Ger.)
Director: Terence Fisher &
Frank Winterstein
Christopher Lee (Sherlock Holmes),
Thorley Walters (Dr. Watson),
Senta Berger (Ellen Blackburn),
Hans Sohnker (Prof. Moriarty),
Hans Nielson (Insp. Cooker),
Ivan Desny (Paul King), Leon
Askin (Chauffeur Charles), Wolfgang

Lukschy (Peter Blackburn), Bernard
Lajarrige (French Police Inspector),
Edith Schultze-Westrum (Mrs.
Hudson), Bruno W. Pantel (auctioneer), Linda Sini (light girl),
Roland Armontel (Doctor), Heinrich Gies (American), Max Strassberg (Johnny), Danielle Argence
(librarian).

SHERLOCK HOLMES AND THE
SECRET WEAPON (1943)
Director: Roy William Neill
Basil Rathbone (Sherlock Holmes),
Nigel Bruce (Dr. Watson), Lionel
Atwill (Prof. Moriarty), Kaaren
Verne (Charlotte Eberli), Dennis
Hoey (Insp. Lestrade), Phillip
Van Zandt (Kurt), Henry Victor
(Frederick Hoffner), Holmes
Herbert (Sir Reginald), Paul Fix
(Mueller), Harry Cording (Brady),
Mary Gordon (Mrs. Hudson),
Paul Bryar (waiter), Guy Kingsford
(London Bobby), George Eldredge
(policeman), Robert O'Davis (Braun),
Vicki Campbell (aviatrix), Gerard
Cavin (Scotland Yardman), James
Craven, Leslie Denison, Leyland
Hodgson, John Burton.

SHERLOCK HOLMES AND THE VOICE
OF TERROR (1942)
Director: John Rawlins
Basil Rathbone (Sherlock Holmes),
Nigel Bruce (Dr. Watson), Evelyn
Ankers (Kitty), Henry Daniell (Sir
Evan Basham), Montagu Love (Gen.
Jerome Lawford), Hilary Brooke
(Jill Grandis), Mary Gordon (Mrs.
Hudson), Olaf Hytten (Adm. Fabian
Prentice), Arthur Blake (Crosbie),
Leyland Hodgson (Capt. Roland
Shore), Harry Stubbs (taxi driver).

SHERLOCK HOLMES FACES DEATH
(1943)
Director: Roy William Neill
Basil Rathbone (Sherlock Holmes),
Nigel Bruce (Dr. Watson), Hillary
Brooke (Sally Musgrave), Milburn
Stone (Capt. Vickery), Halliwell
Hobbes (Brunton), Frederic Worlock (Geoffrey Musgrave), Dennis
Hoey (Insp. Lestrade), Olaf Hytten
(Capt. MacInstoh), Gavin Muir
(Philip Musgrave), Mary Gordon
(Mrs. Hudson), Gerald Phillips
(Mrs. Dowells), Vernon Downing
(Lt. Clavering), Ian Wolfe (antique
store clerk), Holmes Herbert (man),
Peter Lawford (2nd sailor), Harold
de Becker (pub proprietor), Heather

Wilde (Jenny), Norma Varden (Grace).

SHERLOCK HOLMES' FATAL HOUR (1931)
Director: Leslie S. Hiscott
Arthur Wontner (Sherlock Holmes), Ian Fleming (Dr. Watson), Minnie Rayner (Mrs. Hudson), Leslie Perrins (Ronald Adair), Jane Welsh (Kathleen Adair), William Frazer (Thomas Fisher), Phillip Hewland (Insp. Lestrade), Norman McKinnell (Col. Henslow), Sidney King (Tony Rutherford), Louis Goodrich (Col. Moran), Gordon Begg (Marston), Harry Terry (No. 16), Charles Paton (J. J. Godfrey).

SHERLOCK HOLMES IN NEW YORK (TVM-1976) - 10-18-76
Director: Boris Sagal
Roger Moore (Sherlock Holmes), Patrick Macnee (Dr. Watson), John Huston (Prof. Moriarty), Charlotte Rampling (Miss Irene Adler), David Huddleston (Insp. Lafferty), Signe Hasso (Fraulein Reichenbach), Gig Young (Mortimer McGraw), Leon Ames (Daniel Furman), Jackie Coogan (hotel proprietor), John Abbott (Heller), Geoffrey Moore (Scott Adler), Maria Grimm (Nicole), Marjorie Bennett (Mrs. Hudson).

SHERLOCK HOLMES IN WASHINGTON (1943)
Director: Roy William Neill
Basil Rathbone (Sherlock Holmes), Nigel Bruce (Dr. Watson), Henry Daniell (William Easter), Marjorie Lord (Nancy Partridge), George Zucco (Heinrich Hinkle), Holmes Herbert (Mr. Ahrens), Don Terry (Howe), Thurston Holmes (Sen. Henry Babcock), Bradley Page (Cady), Edmund MacDonald (Detective Grogan), Gavin Muir (Bart Lang), John Archer (Lt. Peter Merriam), Gilbert Emery (Sir Henry Marchmont).

SHERLOCK HOLMES' SMARTER BROTHER (1975)
Director: Gene Wilder
Gene Wilder (Sigi Holmes), Madeline Kahn (Jenny), Marty Feldman (Orville Sacker), Leo McKern (Moriarty), Roy Kinnear (Moriarty's assistant), Dom DeLuise (Gambetti), John Le Mesurier (Lord Redcliff), Douglas Wilmer (Sherlock Holmes), Thorley Walters (Dr. Watson), George Silmer (Bruner), Susan Field (Queen

Victoria).

SHE WAITS (TVM-1972) - 1-28-72
Director: Delbert Mann
Patty Duke Astin (Laura Wilson), David McCallum (Mark Wilson), Beulah Bondi (Mrs. Angela Medina), Lew Ayres (Dr. Sam Carpenter), Dorothy McGuire (Sarah Wilson), James Callahan (Dave Brody), Nelson Olmstead (Kurawicz),

SHE-WOLF, THE (1965-Mex.)
(A.K.A. "La Loba")
Director: Rafael Baledon
Kitty de Hoyos, Joaquin Cordero, Jose Elias Moreno, Noe Murayama, Adriana Roel.

SHE-WOLF OF DEVIL'S MOOR, THE (1978-Australia) (A.K.A. "Die Wolfin von Teufelsmoor", "The Devil's Bed")
Director: Helmut Pfandler
John Philip Law, Florinda Bolkan, Siegfried Wischnewski, Guido Wieland, Claudia Rieschel.

SHE-WOLF OF LONDON (1946)
(A.K.A. "Curse of the Allenbys")
Director: Jean Yarborough
June Lockhart (Phyllis Allenby), Don Porter (Barry Lanfield), Sara Haden (Martha Winthrop), Jan Wiley (Carol Winthrop), Dennis Hoey (Insp. Pierce), Lloyd Corrigan (Lathan), Martin Kosleck (Dwight Severn), Frederic Worlock (Constable), Eily Malyon (Hana), Clara Blandick.

SHIELDING SHADOW, THE (1916) - serial in 15 episodes
Chapters: "The Treasure Trove", 2. "Into the Depths", 3. "The Mystic Defender", 4. "The Earthquake", 5. "Through Bolted Doors", 6. "The Disappearing Shadow", 7. "The Awakening", 8. "The Haunting Hand", 9. "The Incorrigible Captive", 10. "The Vanishing Mantle", 11. "The Great Sacrifice", 12. "The Stolen Shadow", 13. "The Hidden Menace", 14. "Absolute Black", & 15. "The Final Chapter".
Director: Louis J. Gasnier & Donald Mackenzie
Grace Darmond, Ralph Kellard, Leon Bary, Madeline Travers.

SHINING, THE (1980)
Director: Stanley Kubrick
Jack Nicholson (Jack Torrance),

Shelley Duvall (Wendy Torrance), Danny Lloyd (Danny Torrance), Scatman Crothers (Halloran), Barry Nelson (Ullman), Joe Turkel (Lloyd), Philip Stone (Grady), Tony Burton (Durkin), Anne Jackson (Doctor), Barry Dennen (Watson), Lia Beldam (young woman in tub), Billie Gibson (old woman in tub), David Baxt, Manning Redwood (forest rangers), Lisa Burns, Louise Burns (Grady girls), Robin Pappas (nurse), Alison Coleridge (secretary), Burnell Tucker (policeman), Jana Sheldon (stewardess), Kate Phelps (receptionist), Norman Gay (injured guest).

SHIP OF THE MONSTERS, THE (1960-Mex.) (A.K.A. "La Nave de los Monstruos")
    Director: Rogelio A. Gonzales
Lalo Gonzalez, Ana Bertha Lepe, Lorena Velaquez, Manuel Alvarado, Consuelo Frank.

SHIRLEY THOMPSON VERSUS THE ALIENS (1972-Australia)
    Director: Jim Sharman
Jane Harders, John Ivkovitch, Tim Eliott, Helmut Bakaitis, June Collis, Ron Haddrick, John Llewellyn, Marion Johns.

SHIVERING SHERLOCKS (1948) - short
    Director: Del Lord
Moe Howard, Shemp Howard, Larry Fine.

SHOCK (1945)
    Director: Alfred Werker
Vincent Price (Dr. Cross), Lynn Bari (Elaine Jordan), Charles Trowbridge (Dr. Harvey), Reed Hadley (O'Neil), Frank Latimore (Lt. Paul Stewart), Anabel Shaw (Janet Stewart), Michael Dunne (Stevens), Pierre Watkins, Renee Carson, Selmer Jackson, Steve Dunne, Charles Tannen, Mary Young, Cecil Weston, John Davidson.

SHOCK CORRIDOR (1963)
    Director: Samuel Fuller
Peter Breck (Johnny), Constance Towers (Cathy), Gene Evans (Boden), James Best (Stuart), Philip Ahn (Dr. Fong), Hari Rhodes (Trent), Paul Dubov (Dr. Menkin), Frank Gerstle (Police Lieutenant), William Zuckert (Swanee), John Mathews (Dr. Cristo), Larry Tucker (Pag-

liacci), Chuck Roberson (Wilkes), Neyle Morrow (Psycho), John Craig (Lloyd), Linda Randolph (dance teacher), Rachel Romen (singer).

SHOCK TREATMENT (1973-Fr. / Ital.) (A.K.A. "Traitment de Choc")
    Director: Alain Jessua
Alain Delon, Annie Girardot, Michel Duchaussoy, Robert Hirsch, Jean-Francois Calve.

SHOCK TREATMENT (1981)
    Director: Jim Sharman
Cliff de Young (Brad Majors/Farley Flavors), Jessica Harper (Janet Majors), Richard O'Brien (Cosmo McKinley), Patricia Quinn (National McKinley), Charles Gray (Judge Oliver Wright), Nell Campbell (Nurse Ansalong), Ruby Wax (Betty Hapschatt), Jeremy Newson (Ralph Hapschatt), Barry Humphries (Bert Schnick), Manning Redwood (Harry Weiss), Rik Mayall (Rest Home Ricky), Darlene Johnson (Emily Weiss), Wendy Raebeck (Macy Struthers).

SHOCK WAVES (1975) (A.K.A. "Death Corps")
    Director: Ken Wiederhorn
Peter Cushing (Scar), Brooke Adams (Rose), John Carradine (Capt. Ben), Luke Halpin (Keith), Fred Buch (Chuck), Jack Davidson (Norman), D.J. Sidney (Beverly), Don Stout (Dobbs), Tony Moskal, Gary Levinson, Bob Miller, Bob White, Jay Meader, Talmadge Scott.

SHOES OF THE FISHERMAN, THE (1968)
    Director: Michael Anderson
Anthony Quinn (Kiril Lakota), Oskar Werner (Father David Telemond), Laurence Olivier (Piotr Ilyich Kamenev), David Janssen (George Faber), Vittorio De Sica (Cardinal Rinaldi), Leo McKern (Cardinal Leone), John Gielgud (the Elder Pope), Barbara Jefford (Dr. Ruth Faber), Frank Finlay (Igor Bounin), Rosemary Dexter (Chiara), Burt Kwouk (Peng), Clive Revill (Vucovich), George Pravda (Gorshenin), Niall MacGinnis (Capuchin Monk), Isa Miranda (the Marchesa), Marne Maitland (Cardinal Rahamani), Arnoldo Foa (Gelasio), Paul Rogers (Augustinian), Peter Copley, Arthur Howard (English Cardinals), George Harper (Brain), Leopoldo Trieste

(dying man's friend), Jean Rougeul
(Dominican).

SHOUT, THE (1978-Australia)
    Director: Jerzy Skolimowski
Alan Bates (Charles Crossley),
Susannah York (Rachel), John Hurt
(Anthony), Tim Curry (Robert),
Robert Stephens (Chief Medical
Officer), Julian Hough (Vicar),
Nick Stringer (cobbler), Carol
Drinkwater (cobbler's wife), John
Rees (Inspector), Susan Woolridge
(Harriet).

SHOW, THE (1927)
    Director: Tod Browning
John Gilbert (Cock Robin), Renee
Adoree (Salome), Lionel Barrymore
(the Greek), Edward Connelly (the
soldier), Gertrude Short (Lena),
Andy MacLennan (the Ferrett),
Edna Tichenor (Koko, the Human
Spider), Agostino Boragato (wise
old politician of Budapest), Zalia
Zarana (Living Half-Lady), Dorothy
Sebastian (Salvation Army girl),
Betty Boyd (Mermaid), Jacqueline
Gadsdon, Francis Powers, Cecil
Holland, Billy Seay, Jules Cowles,
Dorothy Seay, Ida May, Barbara
De Bozoky.

SHRIEK IN THE NIGHT, A (1933)
    Director: Albert Rey
Ginger Rogers (Patricia Morgan),
Lyle Talbot (Ted Rand), Arthur
Hoyt (Wilfred), Harvey Clark (Pete
Peterson), Purnell Pratt (Insp.
Russell), Lillian Harmer (Augusta),
Louise Beavers (maid), Maurice
Black (Martini), Clarence Wilson
(Editor Perkins).

SHRIEK OF THE MUTILATED (1974)
    Director: Michael Findlay
Alan Brock, Jennifer Stock, Cardy
Brown, Michael Harris, Tawm
Mellis.

SH! THE OCTOPUS (1937)
    Director: William McCann
Hugh Herbert (Kelly), Allen Jenkins
(Dempsey), John Eldredge (Paul
Morgan), Marcia Ralston (Vesta
Vernoff), George Rosener (Captain
Hook), Brandon Tynan (Mr. Cobb),
Margaret Irving (Polly Crane),
Eric Stanley (the Stranger), Elspeth
Dudgeon (Nanny).

SHUTTERED ROOM, THE (1966)
    Director: David Greene

Gig Young (Mike Kelton), Carol
Lynley (Susannah Kelton), Oliver
Reed (Ethan), Flora Robson (Aunt
Agatha), William Devlin (Zebulon),
Bernard Kay (Tait), Judith Artry
(Emma), Robert Cawdron (Luther),
Celia Hewitt (Aunt Sarah), Ingrid
Bower (village girl), Anita Ander-
son, Peter Porteous, Clifford Dig-
gins.

SIEGE OF SYRACUSE (1959-Ital./Fr.)
    (A.K.A. "L'Assedio di Siracusa")
    Director: Pietro Francisci
Rossano Brazzi (Archimedes), Tina
Louise (Diana), Sylva Koscina
(Clio), Enrico Maria Salerno (Gor-
gia), Gino Cervi (Gerone), Alberto
Farnese, Luciano Marin, Alfredo
Varelli.

SIEGFRIED (1923-Ger.) (A.K.A.
    "Niebelungen Saga" Part I)
    Director: Fritz Lang
Paul Richter (Siegfried), Margarete
Schoen (Kriemhilde), Rudolf Klein-
Rogge (Attila), Theodor Loos
(King Gunther), Hans Schlettow
(Hagen Tronge), Hanna Ralph
(Brunhilde), Gertrude Arnold,
Bernhard Goetzke, Hans Carl Muller,
Hardy von Francois, Erwin Biswan-
ger, Frieda Richard, George Jurow-
ski, Iris Roberts.

SIGN OF FOUR, THE (1932)
    Director: Graham Cutts
Arthur Wontner (Sherlock Holmes),
Ian Hunter (Dr. Watson), Isla
Bevan (Mary Morstan), Gilbert
Davis (Athelny Jones), Edgar
Norfolk (Capt. Morstan), Graham
Soutten (Jonathan Small), Miles
Malleson (Thaddeus Sholto), Claire
Greet (Mrs. Hudson), Togo (Tongo),
Roy Emerson (Bailey), Kynaston
Reeves (Bartholomew), Mr. Burnhett
(tattoo artist).

SILENCERS, THE (1965)
    Director: Phil Karlson
Dean Martin (Matt Helm), Stella
Stevens (Gail), Daliah Lavi (Tina),
Victor Buono (Tung-Tze), Arthur
O'Connell (Wigwam), Robert Webber
(Sam Gunther), James Gregory
(MacDonald), Beverly Adams (Lovey
Kravezit), Roger C. Carmel (An-
dreyev), Nancy Kovak (Barbara),
Cyd Charisse (Sarita), Richard Devon
(Domino), John Wills (M.C.), John
Reach (Traynor), Frank Gerstle
(Frazer), David Bond (Dr. Naldi),

Bill Couch, Robert Phillips, Chuck Hicks, Gary Lasdun (armed men), Grant Woods (radio man), Patrick Waltz (hotel clerk), Tom Steele, Todd Armstrong (guards), Guy Wilkerson (farmer), Ray Montgomery (Agent G), Harry Holcombe (Agent X), Vincent Van Lynn (Agent Z), Pat Renella (man).

SILENT NIGHT, BLOODY NIGHT (1972) (A.K.A. "Deathhouse")
Director: Theodore Gershuny
Patrick O'Neal (Carter), John Carradine (Towman), Mary Woronov (Diane), Walter Abel (Mayor), James Patterson, Astrid Hereen, Walter Klavun, Ondine, Philip Burns, Fran Stevens, Candy Darling, Tally Brown.

SILENT RAGE (1982)
Director: Michael Miller
Chuck Norris (Dan Stevens), Ron Silver (Dr. Tom Halman), Steven Keats (Dr. Philip Spires), Toni Kalem (Alison Halman), William Finley (Dr. Paul Vaughn), Brian Libby (John Kirby), Stephanie Dunnam (Nancy Halman), Stephen Furst (Charlie).

SILENT RUNNING (1971)
Director: Douglas Trumbull
Bruce Dern (Lowell), Cliff Potts (Wolf), Ron Rifkin (Barker), Jesse Vint (Keenan), Mark Persons, Steven Brown, Larry Whisenhunt, Cheryl Sparks (Drones), Roy Engel (Cmdr. Anderson).

SILENT SCREAM (1980)
Director: Denny Harris
Rebecca Balding (Scotty Parker), Cameron Mitchell (Lt. McGiver), Barbara Steele (Victoria Engles), Avery Schreiber (Sgt. Rusin), Yvonne DeCarlo (Mrs. Engels), Steve Doubet (Jack), Julie Andelman (Doris), Brad Reardon (Mason), John Widelock (Peter), Jack Stryker (Police Chief), Tina Taylor (Victoria at age 16), Jason Zahler (Mason at age 3), Thelma Pelish, Joan Lemmo, Ina Gould, Virginia Rose, Ernie Potvin, Rachel Bard.

SILENT STRANGER, THE (1916)
Director: King Baggot
King Baggot, Irene Hunt.

SILVER BLAZE (1937)
Director: Thomas Bentley

Arthur Wontner (Sherlock Holmes), Ian Fleming (Dr. Watson), Lyn Harding (Prof. Moriarty), John Turnbull (Insp. Lestrade), Robert Horton (Col. Ross), Arthur Macrae (Jack Trevor), Lawrence Grossmith (Sir Henry Baskerville), Judy Gunn (Diana Baskerville), Eve Gray (Mrs. Straker), Martin Walker (Straker), Arthur Goulet (Moran), Gilbert Davis (Miles Stamford), Minnie Rayner (Mrs. Hudson), D.J. Williams (Silas Brown), Ralph Truman (Bert Prince).

SILVER NEEDLE IN THE SKY (1954)
see Television: Rocky Jones, Space Ranger (1953-54)

SIMON (1980)
Director: Marshall Brickman
Alan Arkin (Simon Mendelssohn), Austin Pendleton (Becker), Madeline Kahn (Cynthia), Judy Graubart (Lisa), William Finley (Fichandler), Fred Gwynne (Korey), Wallace Shawn (Van Dongen), Max Wright (Hunderwasser), Jayant (Barundi), Adolph Green (commune leader), Ann Risley (Pam), Keith Szarabajka (Josh), Pierre Epstein (military aide), Roy Cooper (General's aide), Rex Robbins (army doctor), David Warrilow (Blades), Hetty Galen (voice of Mother), David Gideon (secruity guard), David Susskind (himself), Dick Cavett (himself), Remak Ramsay (TV newscaster), Hansford Rowe (TV priest), Jerry Mayer (TV scientist), William Griffis (TV senator), Yusef Bulos (TV philosopher), Slo Frieder (TV rabbi), Frank J. Lucan (TV psychologist).

SIMON, KING OF WITCHES (1971)
Director: Bruce Kessler
Andrew Prine (Simon), Brenda Scott (Linda Rackum), Normann Burton (Rackum), Ultra Violet (Sarah), Allyson Ames (Olivia Gebhart), George Paulsin (Turk), Michael C. Ford (Shay), Gerald York (Hercules), Lee Lambert (Troy), Angus Duncan (Colin), Richmond Shepard (Stanley), William Martel (Davies), Richard Ford Grayling (John Peter), Harry Rose (landlord), Mike Kopcha (lab technician), Ray Galvin (Chief Boyle), John Yates, Jerry Brooks (policemen), Buck Holland (detective), David Vaile (TV newscaster), Helen Jay (Mrs. Carter), Art Hern (Mayor), John Hart (Doctor), Sharon

Berryhill,(secretary), Frank Corsentino, John Copage, Earl Spainard, Bob Carlson, Bill McConnell (reporter), Luana Roberts, Elizabeth Saxon, Harri Sidonie, Jason Max, Stevi Freeman, Avanell Irwin, Jay Della, Eris Tillare (guests).

SINBAD AND THE EYE OF THE
   TIGER (1977)
   Director: Sam Wanamaker
Patrick Wayne (Sinbad), Taryn Power (Dione), Jane Seymour (Farah), Margaret Whiting (Zenobia), Patrick Troughton (Melanthius), Kurt Christian (Rafi), Nadim Sawaiha (Hassan) Bernard Kay (Zabid), Damien Thomas (Kassim), Salami Coker (Maroof), Bruno Barnabe (Balsora), David Sterne (Aboo-Seer).

SINBAD THE SAILOR (1946)
   Director: Richard Wallace
Douglas Fairbanks, Jr. (Sinbad), Maureen O'Hara (Shireen), Anthony Quinn (Emir), Walter Slezak (Melik), Jane Greer (Pirouze), Sheldon Leonard (auctioneer), Alan Napier (Aga), George Tobias (Abbu), John Miljan (Moga), Mike Mazurki (Yusuf), Cy Kendall (Kahn of Basra), Barry Mitchell (Muallin), Hugh Prosser (Captain of Guard), Billy Bletcher (Crier), Glenn Strange (Chief Overseer), Louis Jean Heydt (Corsair), Norbert Schiller (timekeeper), Wade Crosby (soldier), George Chandler (peddler), Max Wagner (assistant overseer), Ben Weldon (porter), Paul Guilfoyle (camel drover), Charles Soldani, Mikandor Dooraff, Joe Garcio, Chuck Hamilton (merchants), Harry Harvey (crier at execution), Nick Thompson (beggar on street), George Lloyd (lancer guard).

SINISTER HANDS (1932)
   Director: Armand Schaefer
Jack Mullhall (Detective Capt. Devlin), Phyllis Barrington (Ruth Frazer), Mischa Auer (Swami Yomurda), Crauford Kent (Judge McLeod), Jimmy Burtis (Watkins), Phillips Smalley (Richard Lang), Louis Natheaux (Nick Genna), Lloyd Ingraham (John Frazer), Helen Foster (Vivian Rogers), Gertrude Messenger (Betty Lang), Lillian West (Mrs. Lang), Bess Flowers (Mary Browne), Fletcher Norton (Lefty Lewis), Russell Collar (Tommy Lang).

SINISTER MONK, THE (1965-Ger.)
   (A.K.A. "Der Unheimliche
   Monch")
   Director: Harald Reinl
Ilse Steppat (Patricia), Siegfried Lowitz (Richard), Karin Dor (Gwendolin), Eddie Arendt (Smith), Harald Leipnitz (Insp. Bratt), Dieter Eppler, Uta Levka, Ursula Glas.

SINNERS IN SILK (1924)
   Director: Hobart Henley
Adolphe Menjou (Arthur Merrill), Conrad Nagel (Brock Farley), Jean Hersholt (Dr. Eustace), Eleanor Boardman (Penelope Stevens), Hedda Hopper (Mrs. Stevens), Edward Connelly (Bates), John Patrick (Powers), Virginia Lee Corbin (flapper), Frank Elliott (Sir Donald Ramsey), Bradley Ward (Ted), Dorothy Dawn (Rita), Peggy Elinor (Estelle), Mary Altkin (Peggy), Ann Luther (Mimi), Eugenie Gilbert (Cherie), Estelle Clark (Carmelita), Jerome Patrick (Jerry Hall), Miss Du Pont (Ynez).

SINS OF DORIAN GRAY, THE
   (1982)
   Director: Tony Maylam
Belinda Bauer (Dorian Gray), Joseph Bottoms (Stuart Vane), Anthony Perkins, Olga Karlatos.

SINTHIA THE DEVIL'S DOLL
   (1970)
   Director: Ray Steckler
Diane Webber, Maria Lease, Boris Balachoff, Shula Roan.

SIREN OF ATLANTIS (1947)
   Director: Gregg C. Tallas
Maria Montez (Antinea), Jean-Pierre Aumont (Andre St. Avit), Dennis O'Keefe (Jean Morhange), Henry Daniell (Blades), Morris Carnovsky (Le Mesge), Alexis Minotis (Cortot), Melada Mladova (Tanit Zerga), Russ Conklin (Eggali), Allan Nixon (Lindstrom), Herman Boden (Cegheir), Pierre Watkin (Colonel), Margaret Martin (handmaiden), Charles Wagenheim (doctor), Jim Nolan (Major), Joseph Granby (expert), John Shelton.

SIREN OF BAGHDAD (1952)
   Director: Richard Quine
Hans Conried (Ben Ali), Paul Henried, Patricia Medina, Laurette Luez, Charlie Lung, George Keymas, Anne Dore,

Vivian Mason.

SIRENS OF THE SEA (1917)
Director: Allen Holubar
Louise Lovely, Carmel Myers,
Jack Mulhall, William Quinn, Sydnea
Dean.

SIR HENRY AT RAWLINSON END
(1980)
Director: Steve Roberts
Trevor Howard (Sir Henry Rawlinson),
Patrick Magee (Rev. Slodden), Denise
Coffey (Mrs. E.), J.G. Devlin (Old
Scrotum), Harry Fowler (Buller
Bullethead), Sheila Reid (Florrie),
Daniel Gerroll (Rafe), Jeremy
Child (Peregrine), Vivian Stanshall
(Hubert), Suzanne Danielle (Candice),
Susan Porrett (Porcelain), Ben Aris
(Lord Tarquin of Staines), Liz Smith
(Lady Philippa of Staines).

SISTERS (1972) (A.K.A. "Blood
Sisters")
Director: Brian De Palma
Margot Kidder (Danielle Breton/
Dominique), Jennifer Salt (Grace
Collier), William Finley (Emil
Breton), Charles Durning (Private
Investigator), Dolph Sweet (Joseph
Larch), Barnard Hughes (Editor McLa-
ren), Lisle Wilson (Philip Woode), Mary
Davenport (Mrs. Collier).

SIX HOURS TO LIVE (1932)
Director: William Dieterle
Warner Baxter (Capt. Paul Onslow),
John Boles (Karl Kranz), Irene
Ware (the Woman), Beryl Mercer
(the Widow), Halliwell Hobbes (Baron
von Sturm), Edwin Maxwell (Police
Commissioner), Miriam Jordan
(Valerie von Sturm), John Davidson
(Kellner), Edward McWade (Ivan),
George Marion (Prof. Otto Bauer),
Dewey Robinson (Blucher).

SIX MILLION DOLLAR MAN, THE
(TVM-1973) - 3-7-73
Director: Richard Irving
Lee Majors (Steve Austin), Darren
McGavin (Oliver Spencer), Barbara
Anderson (Jean Manners), Martin
Balsam (Dr. Rudy Welles), Ivor
Barry (Geraldton), Robert Cornth-
waite (Dr. Ashburn), Olan Soule
(Saltillo), Charles Robinson (priso-
ner), George Wallace (General),
Dorothy Green (Mrs. McKay),
Maurice Sherbanee (Nudaylah),
Anne Whitfield (young woman),
Norma Storch (woman), Richard Webb.

SKELETON OF MRS. MORALES,
THE (1959-Mex.) (A.K.A. "El
Esqueleto de la Senora Morales")
Director: Rogelio A. Gonzeles,
Jr.
Arthuro de Cordova, Ampara Ri-
velles, Guillermo Orea, Elda Peralta,
Luis Aragon, Rosenda Monteros.

SKELETON ON HORSEBACK (1937-
Czech.) (A.K.A. "Bila Nemoc",
"The White Disease")
Director: Hugo Haas
Hugo Haas, Zdenek Stepanek, Bedrich
Karen, Karla Olicova, Vaclav Vydra.

SKULL, THE (1965)
Director: Freddie Francis
Peter Cushing (Christopher Mait-
land), Christopher Lee (Sir Matthew
Phillips), Patrick Wymark (An-
thony Marco), Jill Bennett (Jane
Maitland), Nigle Green (Insp. Wilson),
Patrick Magee (police surgeon),
Anna Palk (maid), Michael Gough
(auctioneer), Frank Forsyth (judge),
George Coulouris (Dr. Londe),
Peter Woodthorpe (Travers), Paul
Stockman (1st guard), Geoffrey
Cheshire (2nd guard), Maurice Good
(Phrenologist), April Olrich (French
girl), George Hilsdon (policeman),
Jack Silk (driver).

SKULLDUGGERY (1970)
Director: Gordon Douglas
Burt Reynolds (Douglas Temple),
Susan Clark (Dr. Sybil Greame),
Roger C. Carmel (Otto Kreps),
Paul Christian (Vancruysen), Alex-
ander Knox (Buffington), Chips
Rafferty (Pops Dillingham), Pat
Suzuki (Topazia), Wilfred Hyde-White
(Eaton), Edward Fox (Bruce Spofford),
William Marshall (Attorney Genral),
Mort Marshall (Dr. Figgins),
Booker Bradshaw (Smott), Michael
St. Claire (Tee Hee), Rhys Williams
(Judge Draper), John Kimberley
(Epstein), James Henry Eldridge
(Officer), James Bacon (commentator),
Totty Ames (motel manager), Gil-
bert Senior (Kauni), Clarence Harris
(Siria), John Woodcock (Spigget),
Wendell Baggett (Rev. Holzapple),
Burnal 'Custus' Smith (Chief),
Newton D. Arnold (Mimms), Mike
Preece (Naylor), Charles Washburn
(Papuan), Alex Gradussov (Russian
delegate), Eddie Fuchs (Israeli
delegate), Saul David (Berle Tanen),
Bernard Pike (associate judge), Cliff
Bell, Jr. (worker), Jim Alexander

(reporter).

SKY ABOVE HEAVEN (1964-Fr. /
Ital.) (A. K. A. "Le Ciel sur la
Tete")
Director: Yves Ciampi
Yvonne Monlaur, Andre Smagghe,
Jacques Monod, Marcel Bozzufi,
Yves Brainville, Guy Trejean, Jean
Daste.

SKY PIRATE (1939) (A. K. A. "Mys-
tery Plane")
Director: George Waggner
Jason Robards, Sr. , Milburn Stone,
Lucien Littlefield, Marjorie Rey-
nolds, Polly Ann Young.

SKY RANGER, THE (1921) (A. K. A.
"The Man Who Stole the Moon")
- serial in 15 episodes
Chapters: 1. "Out of the Clouds",
2. "The Sinister Signal", 3. "In
Hostile Hands", 4. "Desert Law",
5. "Mid-Air", 6. "The Crystal Prism",
7. "Danger's Doorway", 8. "Dropped
from the Clouds", 9. "The House
on the Roof", 10. "Trapped", 11.
"The Seething Pool", 12. "The Whirl-
ing Menace", 13. "At the Last Min-
ute", 14. "Liquid Fire", & 15. "The
Last Raid".
Director: George B. Seitz
June Caprice (June Elliot), George
B. Seitz (George Rockwell), Harry
Semels (Dr. Santro), Peggy Shanor
(Peggy Santro), Frank Redman (Prof.
Elliot), Joe Cuny (Joe Bentley).

SLAUGHTERHOUSE FIVE (1971)
Director: George Roy Hill
Michael Sachs (Billy Pilgrim), Ron
Leibman (Paul Lazzaro), Eugene
Roche (Edgar Derby), Valerie Perrine
(Montana Wildhack), Sharon Gans
(Valencia Marble Pilgrim), Perry
King (Robert Pilgrim), Sorrel
Booke (Lionel Merble), Roberts
Blossom (Wild Bob Cody), John
Dehner (Rumford), Friedrich Ledebur
(German leader), Holly Near (Barbara),
Lucille Benson (Billy's mother),
Kevin Conway (Weary), Nick Belle
(young German guard), Stan Gottlieb
(Hobo), Gary Waynesmith (Stanley),
Henry Bumstead (Eliot Rosewater),
Gilmer McCormick (Lily), Richard
Schaal (Campbell), Tom Wood (English-
man), Karl Otto Alberto (German
Guard Group 2).

SLAVE OF PARADISE, THE (1968-
Span. /Ital.) (A. K. A. "La Esclava

del Paraiso")
Director: Jose Maria Elorrieta
Jeff Cooper, Luciana Paluzzi, Perla
Cristal, Raf Vallone, Ruben Rojo,
Ricardo Palacios.

SLAVE OF THE CANNIBAL GOD
(1979-Ital.) (A. K. A. "La Mont-
agna del Dio Cannibale")
Director: Sergio Martino
Ursula Andress, Stacy Keach, Jr. ,
Claudio Cassinelli, Franco Fantasia.

SLEEPER (1973)
Director: Woody Allen
Woody Allen (Miles Monroe), Diane
Keaton (Luna Schlosser), John
Beck (Erno Windt), Peter Hobbs
(Dr. Dean), Mary Gregory (Dr.
Melik), Don McLiam (Dr. Agon),
Don Keefer (Dr. Tryon), Bartlett
Robinson (Dr. Orva), Marya Small
(Dr. Nero), Spencer Milligan (Jeb),
Chris Forbes (Rainer Krebs), Susan
Miller (Ellen Pogrebin), Brian
Avery (Herald Cohen), Lou Picetti
(M. C.), Spencer Ross (Sears Wig-
gles), Jessica Rains.

SLIME PEOPLE, THE (1963)
Director: Robert Hutton
Robert Hutton (Tom Gregory),
Susan Hart (Lisa Galbraith), Les
Tremayne (Norman Taliver), Ro-
bert Burton (Prof. Galbraith),
Judee Morton, John Close, William
Boyce.

SLITHIS (1978)
Director: Stephen Traxler
Alan Blanchard, Judy Motulsky,
Dennis Lee Falt, Win Condict, Hy
Pyke, Mello Alexandria, Don Cum-
mins.

SLUMBER PARTY MASSACRE,
THE (1982)
Director: Amy Jones
Michele Michaels, Robin Stille,
Michael Villela, Andre Honore.

SMILING GHOST, THE (1941)
Director: Lewis Seiler
Wayne Morris (Lucky Downing),
Brenda Marshall (Lil Forrester),
Alexis Smith (Eleanor Bently Far-
child), Willie Best (Clarence),
Alan Hale, Sr. (Norton), Helen
Westley (Grandma), Lee Patrick
(Rose), Roland Drew, David Bruce.

SNAKE PEOPLE, THE (1968-Mex. /
U. S.) (A. K. A. "La Muerte

Viviente", "The Living Death",
"Isla de los Muertos", "The Isle
of the Dead", "Isle of the Snake
People")
Director: Juan Ibanez
Boris Karloff (Carl Van Boulder/
Damballah), Rafael Bertrand (Capt.
Laresh), Julissa (Deidre), Charles
East (Lt. William), Tongolee
(Bondemo), Judy Carmichael (Mary
Ann Vanderberg), Quintin Miller
(Gomez).

SNAKE WOMAN, THE (1960)
Director: Sidney J. Furey
John McCarthy (Charles Prentice),
Susan Travers (Atheris), Geoffrey
Danton (Col. Wynborn), Arnold
Marle (Dr. Murton), Elsie Wagstaff
(Aggie), Hugh Moxey (Inspector),
John Cazabon (Dr. Adderson), Fran-
ces Bennett (Polly), Michael Logan
(Barkis), Jack Cunningham (Consta-
ble), Dorothy Feree (Martha), Ste-
venson Lang (Shepherd).

SNOWBEAST (TVM-1977) - 4-28-77
Director: Herb Wallerstein
Yvette Mimieux (Ellen Seberg), Bo
Svenson (Gar Seberg), Robert Logan
(Tony Rill), Sylvia Sidney (Carrie
Rill), Clint Walker (Sheriff Para-
day), Anne McEncroe (Heidi), Thomas
Babson (Buster), Kathy Christopher
(Jennifer), Michael J. London (the
Beast), Liz Jury, Jacquie Betts,
Ros McClung, Victor Raider-Wexler,
Ric Jury, Richard Jamison, Prentiss
Rowe.

SNOW CREATURE, THE (1954)
Director: W. Lee Wilder
Paul Langton (Dr. Frank Parrish),
Leslie Denison (Peter Welles),
Teru Shimada (Subra), William
Phipps (Lt. Dunbar), Robert Bice
(Fleet), Rudolph Anders (Dr. Dupont),
Darlene Fields (Joyce Parrish),
George Douglas (Corey, Jr.), Jack
Daly (Edwards), Robert Kino (Insp.
Karma), Rollin Moriyama (Leva),
Keith Richard (Harry Bennett),
Rusty Wescoatt (guard in warehouse),
Robert Hinton (airline manager).

SNOW DEVILS (1965-Ital.) (A.K.A.
"I Diavoli dello Spazio", "The
Devils from Space", "Space De-
vils", "The Devil Men from Space")
Director: Antonio Margheriti/
Anthony Dawson
Giacomo Rossi-Stuart, Amber Collins/
Ombretta Colli, Archie Savage,

Renato Baldini, Wilbert Bradley,
Halina Zalewska, Furio Meniconi,
Peter Martell, Iscaro Ravailoi,
Enzo Fiermonti, Freddy Hagar.

SNOW WHITE AND THE THREE
STOOGES (1961)
Director: Walter Lang
Carol Heiss (Snow White), Moe Howard,
Larry Fine, Joe DeRita, Edson Stroll
(Prince Charming), Patricia Medina
(Queen), Guy Rolfe (Oga), Buddy
Baer (Hordred), Edgar Barrier (King
Augustus), Peter Coe (Captain),
Michael David (Rolf), Chuck Lacy
(Frederick), Lisa Mitchell (Linda),
Blossom Rock (servant), Sam Flint
(Chamberlain), Owen McGiveney
(physician).

SOLARIS (1972-Sov.)
Director: Andrei Tarkovsky
Donatas Banionis (Chris Kelvin),
Natalya Bondarchuk (Hari), Yuri
Jarvet (Snauth), Anatoli Solonitsin
(Sartorius), Vladislav Dvorjetski
(Burton), Sos Sarkissian (Gibaryan),
Nikolia Grinko (father).

SOLDIER, THE (1982)
Director: James Glickenhaus
Ken Wahl (the Soldier), Klaus Kinski
(Dracha), William Prince (U.S.
President), Alberta Watson (Susan
Goodman).

SOLE SURVIVOR (TVM-1970) - 1-9-70
Director: Paul Stanley
Lou Antonio (Tony), Richard Basehart
(Gen. Russell Hamner), Vince
Edwards (Maj. Michael Devlin),
William Shatner (Lt. Col. Joe
Gronke), Alan Caillou (Corey), Pat-
rick Wayne (Mac), Dennis Cooney
(Brandy), Brad David (Elmo), Larry
Casey (Gant), Noah Keen (Gen. Shurm),
David Cannon (Capt. Patrick), Timur
Bashtu (Beddo), John Winston (Bri-
tish pilot), Ian Abercrombie (British
co-pilot), Julie Bennett (Amanda),
Bart Burns (older Senator).

SOLITARY GOES TO THE ATTACK,
THE (1968-Fr./Span.) (A.K.A.
"El Solitario Pasa al Ataque")
Director: Ralph Habib
Milo Quesada, Teresa Gimpera,
Roger Hanin, Sophie Agacinski, Jean
Lefebvre, Charles Millot, Gerard
Tichy.

SOME CALL IT LOVING (1973)
Director: James B. Harris

Zalman King (Robert Troy), Carol White (Scarlett), Richard Pryor (Jeff), Logan Ramsey (carnival doctor), Pat Priest (carnival nurse), Veronica Anderson (Angelica), Tisa Farrow (Jennifer), Brandy Herred (cheerleader), Ed Rue (mortician), Joseph DeMeo (bartender).

SOME GIRLS DO (1969)
    Director: Ralph Thomas
Richard Johnson (Hugh Drummond), Daliah Lavi (Helga), James Villiers (Carl), Maurice Denham (Mortimer), Robert Morley (Miss Mary), Beba Loncar (Pandora), Virginia North (No. 9), Vanessa Howard (No. 7), Ronnie Stevens (Carruthers), Sydney Rome (Flicky), Florence Desmond (Lady Manderley), Adrienne Posta (Angela).

SOMEONE AT THE TOP OF THE STAIRS (TVM-1973) - 2-12-73
    Director: John Sichel
Judy Carne (Jill), Donna Mills (Chrissie), Althea Charlton (Mrs. Oxley), David DeKeyser (Cartney), Francis Willis (Gary), Scott Forbes (Patrick), Peter Cellier, Brian McGrath, Clifford Parish.

SOMEONE BEHIND THE DOOR (1971) (A. K. A. "Quelqu'un Derriere la Porte")
    Director: Nicholas Gessner
Charles Bronson (the Stranger), Anthony Perkins (Laurence), Jill Ireland (Frances), Henri Garcin, Agathe Natanson, Adriano Magestretti.

SOMEONE IS WATCHING ME! (TVM-1978) - 11-29-78
    Director: John Carpenter
Lauren Hutton (Leigh Michaels), David Birney (Paul Winkless), Adrienne Barbeau (Sophie), Charles Cyphers (Gary Hunt), Len Lesser (burley man), George Skaff (Herbert Stiles), Grainger Hines (Steve), Jay Saunders (Police Inspector), James Murtaugh (Leone), John Mahon (Frimsin), Michael Laurence (TV announcer).

SOMETHING ALWAYS HAPPENS (1928)
    Director: Frank Tuttle
Esther Ralston (Diana), Neil Hamilton (Roderick), Sojin (Mr. Tsang), Lawrence Grant (Earl of Rochester), Mischa Auer, Noble Johnson, Roscoe Karns, Charles Sellon.

SOMETHING CREEPING IN THE DARK (1970-Ital.) (A. K. A. "Qualcosa Stricsia nel Buio")
    Director: Mario Colucci
Farley Granger, Giacomo Rossi-Stuart, Giulia Robal, Lucia Bose, Stan Cooper, Frank Beltramme, Francesco Lavagnino.

SOMETHING EVIL (TVM-1972) - 1-21-72
    Director: Steven Spielberg
Sandy Dennis (Marjorie Worden), Darren McGavin (Paul Worden), Jeff Corey (Gehrmann), Ralph Bellamy (Harry Lincoln), John Rubinstein (Ernest Lincoln), Johnny Whitaker (Stevie Worden), Margaret Avery (Irene), Sandy & Debbie Lempert (Laurie Worden), Laurie Hagan (Beth), David Knapp (John), Norman Barthold (Hackett), Lois Battle (Mrs. Farady), Herb Armstrong (Schiller), Sheila Barthold (Mrs. Hackett), Bella Bruck (Mrs. Gehrmann), Lynn Cartwright (secretary), Bruno VeSota, Alan Frost, John J. Fox, Carl Gottlieb, Crane Jackson, Paul Micale, John Nolan, Elizabeth Rogers, John Hudkins, Michael Macready, Margaret Muse, Connie Hunter Ragaway, Steven Spielberg.

SOMETHING WEIRD (1968)
    Director: Herschell Gordon Lewis
Tony McCabe, Elizabeth Lee, William Brooker.

SOMETHING WICKED THIS WAY COMES (1983)
    Director: Jack Clayton
Jason Robards, Jr.; Jonathan Pryce, Diane Ladd, Royal Dano, Vidal Peterson, Shawn Carson, Pam Greir, James Tacy, Dick Davalos, Ellen Geer, Mary Grace Canfield, Jack Dodson, Scott Wilson, Jake Dengal, Bruce M. Fischer.

SOMEWHERE IN TIME (1980)
    Director: Jeannot Szwarc
Christopher Reeve (Richard Collier), Jane Seymour (Elise McKenna), Christopher Plummer (W. F. Robinson), Teresa Wright (Laura Roberts), George Voskovec (Dr. Gerald Finney), Bill Erwin (Arthur), John Alvin (Arthur's father), Eddra Gale (Genevieve), Sean Hayden (young Arthur), Susan French (older Elise), Richard Matheson (astonished man), Audrey Bennett (Richard's date), W. H. Macy,

Laurence Coven (critics), Susan Bugg (Penelope), Christy Michaels (Beverly), Ali Matheson, George Wendt (students), Steve Boomer (hippie), Patrick Billingsley (professor), Ted Liss (agent), Taylor Williams (Matrie D'), Francis X. Keefe (desk clerk), Noreen Walker (librarian), David Hull (hotel manager), Evans Ghiselli (coin shop operator), Paul M. Cook (doctor), Don Franklin, Maud Strand, Barbara Giovannini, Victoria Michaels, William P. O'Hagen, Bo Clausen, Hal Frank, Val Bettin, James P. Dunnigan, Hayden Jones.

SONG OF THE SUCCUBUS (TVM-1975) - 3-7-75
    Director: Glenn Jordan
Brooke Adams (Olive Deems/Gloria Chambers), Scott Hylands (Alan Greene), George Gaynes (C. J. Meredith), Richard Schaal (Vic), Erica Yohn (Marybelle Rogers).

SON OF ALI BABA (1952)
    Director: Kurt Neumann
Tony Curtis (Kashma Baba), Piper Laurie (Kiki), Susan Cabot (Tala), William Reynolds (Mustafa), Victor Jory (Caliph), Hugh O'Brian (Hussein), Morris Ankrum (Ali Baba), Philip Van Zandt (Kareeb), Gregg Palmer (Farouk), Leon Belasco (Babu), Gerald Mohr (Capt. Youssef), Robert Barrat (Commandant), Alice Kelley (Calu), Milada Mladova (Zaza), Barbara Knudson (Theda), Katherine Warren (Princess Karma).

SON OF DRACULA (1943)
    Director: Robert Siodmak
Lon Chaney, Jr. (Count Alucard), Louise Allbritton (Katherine Caldwell), Evelyn Ankers (Claire Caldwell), Robert Paige (Frank Stanley), Frank Craven (Dr. Harry Brewster), J. Edward Bromberg (Prof. Lazlo), Samuel S. Hinds (Judge Simmons), Adeline Reynolds (Simba), George Irving (Col. Caldwell), Etta McDaniel (Sarah, the maid), Walter Sande (the jailor), Patrick Moriarity (the Sheriff), Cyril Delevanti (the coroner), Jack Rockwell (Deputy Sheriff), Jess Lee Brooks (Steven), Joan Blair (Mrs. Land), Sam McDaniel (Andy), Charles Moore (Mathew), Robert Dudley (Kirby), Charles Bates (Tommy Land), Emmett Smith (servant).

SON OF DRACULA (1974)

    Director: Freddie Francis
Harry Nilsson (Count Down), Ringo Starr (Merlin), Dennis Price (Van Helsing), Freddie Jones (Count Frankenstein), Rosanna Lee (Amber), Peter Frampton, Keith Moon, Skip Martin.

SON OF DR. JEKYLL (1951)
    Director: Seymour Friedman
Louis Hayward (Edward Jekyll), Alexander Knox (Dr. Kurt Lanyon), Jody Lawrence (Lynn), Lester Matthews (John Utterson), Gavin Muir (Richard Daniels), Paul Cavanagh (Insp. Stoddard), Rhys Williams (Michaels), Doris Lloyd (Lottie Sarelle), Claire Carleton (Hazel Sarelle), Patrick O'Moore (Joe Sarelle), James Logan, Leslie Dennison (Constables), Robin Camp (Willie Bennett), Bruce Lester (reporter), Holmes Herbert (local constable), Matthew Boulton (Insp. Grey), Pat Aherne (landlord), Wheaton Chambers (Magistrate), Vesey O'Davoren (Butler), Harry Martin (plainclothesman), Olaf Hytten (Prosecutor), Stapleton Kent (proprietor), Joyce Jameson (barmaid), Betty Fairfax (woman in window), Keith Hitchcock (Bobby), Ottola Nesmith (nurse), Ida McGill (woman), Carol Savage (young woman), Robin Hughes (Alec), Dave Dunbar, Frank Hagney (men in pub), Guy Kingsford (male nurse), Benita Booth (woman), Leonard Mudie (pharmacist), Phyllis Morris (tea woman), Alec Harford (clerk), David Cole (copy boy), Ola Lorraine (woman), Jimmie Long, Robert Reeves.

SON OF FLUBBER (1962)
    Director: Robert Stevenson
Fred MacMurray (Prof. Ned Brainard), Nancy Olson (Betsy Brainard), Keenan Wynn (Alonzo Hawk), Tommy Kirk (Biff Hawk), Joanna Moore (Desiree de la Roche), Ed Wynn (A. J. Allen), Ken Murray (Mr. Hurley), Leon Ames (Pres. Rufus Daggett), Charlie Ruggles (Judge Murdock), Stuart Erwin (Coach), Paul Lynde (sportscaster), Forrest Lewis (Officer Kelley), James Westerfield (Officer Hanson), Edward Andrews (Defense Secretary), Jack Albertson (Mr. Barley), Alan Carney (1st referee), William Demarest (Mr. Hummel), Burt Mustin (1st Bailiff), Byron Foulger (proprietor), J. Pat O'Malley (sign painter), Joe Flynn (commercial announcer), Robert Shayne (assistant

to defense attorney), Beverly Wills
(mother), Elliott Reid (Shelby Ashton),
Wed Miller (Baby Walter), Alan Hewitt
(prosecutor), Wally Boag (father),
Bob Sweeney (Mr. Harker), Leon
Tyler (Humphrey), Eddie Ryder (Mr.
Osborne), Lee Giroux (newscaster),
Alan Hewitt (prosecutor), Harriett
MacGibbon (Mrs. Daggett).

SON OF FRANKENSTEIN (1939)
    Director: Rowland V. Lee
Basil Rathbone (Baron Wolf von
Frankenstein), Boris Karloff (the
Monster), Bela Lugosi (Ygor), Jo-
sephine Hutchinson (Elsa von Frank-
enstein), Lionel Atwill (Insp. Krogh),
Edgar Norton (Thomas Benson, the
butler), Donnie Dunagan (Peter Von
Frankenstein), Emma Dunn (Amelia),
Lionel Belmore (Lang), Michael
Mark (Oswald Neumuller), Gustav
von Seyffertitz, Tom Ricketts, Lori-
mer Johnson (Burhers), Lawrence
Grant (Burgomeister), Perry Ivins
(Fritz), Caroline Cook (Mrs. Neu-
muller), Bud Wolfe, Eddie Parker
(stuntmen), Edward Cassiday, Dwight
Frye, Harry Cording, Ward Bond,
Jack Harris, Betty Chay.

SON OF GODZILLA (1968-Jap.)
    (A.K.A. "Gojira no Musuko")
    Director: Jun Fukuda
Tadao Takashima (Dr. Kuzumi),
Akira Kubo (Goro), Akihiko Hirata,
Kenji Sahara, Bibari Maeda, Yoshi
Tsuchiya.

SON OF HERCULES IN THE LAND
    OF DARKNESS, THE (1964-Ital.)
    Director:
Don Vadis, Spela Rozin, Carla Calo/
Carol Brown.

SON OF HERCULES IN THE LAND OF
    FIRE, THE (1963-Ital.) (A.K.A.
    "Ursus Nella Terra de Fuoco",
    "Ursus in the Land of Fire")
    Director: Giorgio Simonelli
Ed Fury (Ursus), Claudia Mori,
Luciana Gilli, Adriano Micantoni,
Nando Tamberlani, Pietro Ceccarelli,
Giuseppe Addobbati.

SON OF KONG (1933)
    Director: Ernest B. Schoedsack
Robert Armstrong (Carl Denham),
Helen Mack (Hilda Peterson), Frank
Reicher (Captain Englehorn), John
Marston (Helstrom), Victor Wong
(Charlie, the Cook), Lee Kohlmar
(Mickey), Ed Brady (Red), Noble

Johnson (Native Chief), Clarence
Wilson (Peterson), Katharine Ward
(Mrs. Hudson), Gertrude Sutton
(servant girl), Steve Clemento
(Witch King), Gertrude Short (girl
reporter), James L. Leong (Chinese
trader), Frank O'Connor (process
server).

SON OF SAMSON (1960-Fr. /Ital. /
    Yugo.) (A.K.A. "Maciste Neila
    Valle Dei Re", "Maciste in the Val-
    ley of the Kings")
    Director: Carlo Campogalliani
Mark Forest (Maciste), Chelo Alonso
(Queen Smedes), Angelo Sanolli
(Kenamun), Vera Silenti (Tekaet),
Carlo Tamberlani (Armittee),
Frederica Ranchi (Nofret), Peter
Dorric (Vizier).

SON OF SINBAD (1953)
    Director: Ted Tetzlaff
Dale Robertson (Sinbad), Sally For-
rest (Ameer), Vincent Price (Omar),
Lili St. Cyr (Nerissa), Mari Blan-
chard (Kristina), Leon Askin (Khalif),
Raymond Greenleaf (Simon), Jay
Novello (Jiddah), Ian MacDonald
(Murad), Larry Blake (Samit),
Donald Randolph (Councillor), Nejla
Ates (dancer in market), Kalantan
(dancer in desert).

SON OF TARZAN (1920) - serial in 15
    episodes
    Director: Harry J. Revier &
        Arthur Flaven
P. Dempsey Taylor (Tarzan), Karla
Schramm (Jane), Kamuela C. Searle
(Korak), Manilla Marta (Meriam),
Eugene Burr (Evan Paulovich), Mae
Giraci, Ray Thompson, Frank Morell,
Gordon Griffith.

SORCERERS, THE (1968)
    Director: Michael Reeves
Boris Karloff (Prof. Monserrat), Catherine Lacey (Estelle Monserrat), Ian O-
gilvy (Mike), Susan George (Audrey), I-
vor Dean (Insp. Matalon), Elizabeth Er-
cy (Nicole), Dani Sheridan (Laura), Victor Henry (Alan), Peter Fraser (Detective), Meier Tzelniker, Martin Terry,
Alf Joint, Bill Barnsley, Gerald Campion.

SORCERESS, THE (1955-Fr.) (A.K.A.
    "La Sorciere", "Blonde Witch")
    Director: Andre Michel
Maria Vlady (Aino), Maurice Ronet
(Laurent), Nicole Courcel (Kristina),
Michel Etcheverry (Camoin), Rume
Linstrom (the Pastor), Vela Lagnell

(Pastor's wife), Naina Wifstrand
(Maina), Ulf Palme (Matti), Erik
Hell (Pullinen), Eric Hellstrom (Erik).

SORROWS OF SATAN, THE (1926)
    Director: D.W. Griffith
Adolphe Menjou (Prince Lucio de
Rimarez), Ricardo Cortez (George
Tempest), Lya De Putti (Princess
Olga Godovsky), Ivan Lebedeff
(Amiel), Carol Dempster (Mavis
Claire), Dorothy Hughes (Mavis'
friend), Marcia Harris (landlady),
Lawrence D'Orsay (Earl of Elton),
Nellie Savage (dancer), Raymond
Griffith, Owen Nares.

SO SAD ABOUT GLORIA (1973)
    Director: Harry Thomason
Lori Saunders, Dean Jagger, Bob
Ginnaven, Lou Hoffman, Seymour
Treitman, Linda Wyse.

S.O.S. COAST GUARD (1937) -
    serial in 12 episodes
    Director: William Witney &
    Alan James
Ralph Byrd (Terry Kent), Bela
Lugosi (Boroff), Herbert Rawlinson
(Cmdr. Boyle), Maxine Doyle (Jean
Norman), Richard Alexander
(Thorg), John Picorri (Rickerby),
Carleton Young (Dodds), Thomas
Carr (Jim Kent), Lee Ford (Snapper
McGee), Lawrence Grant (Rabinisi),
Allen Connor (Dick Norman),
George Chesebro (Degado), Herbert
Rawlinson (Boyle), Joseph Girard
(Green), Edward Cassidy (Johnson),
Ranny Weeks (Wies), Roy Barcroft
(Goebel), Lester Dorr (intern),
Harry Strang (manager), Buddy
Roosevelt (Scott), Jack Ingram
(seaman), Herbert Weber (Belden),
Robert Walker (Black), Rex Lease
(orderly), Earl Bunn, Kit Guard
(kelp heavies), Frank Ellis (kelp
worker), Duke York, Forrest
Dillon (sea heavies), Joe Mack
(Adamic Captain), Dick Sheldon
(attendant), Gene Marvey (Blake),
Eddie Phillips, Reed Sheffield,
Frank Wayne, Warren Jackson,
Dick Scott (boat heavies), Jack
Clifford (Carver), Jack Daley (Cap-
tain), Tom Ung (Charlie), Lee
Frederick (citizen), King Mojave
(Driver), Curley Dresden, Henry
Morris, Vinegar Roan, James
Millican (dock heavies), Alexander
Leftwich (Froman), Jack Roberts
(Jones), Henry Hale (Krohn), Duke
Taylor (loader), Charles McMurphy

(Mate), Michael Morgan (Moore),
Edwin Mordant (Meade), Billie Van
Every (operator), Floyd Criswell
(motorcycle heavy), Alan Gregg
(Payne), Loren Riebe (Pete), Frank
Fanning, Frank Meredith, John
Gustin (policeman), Pat Mitchell
(radioman), Henry Otho (sailor),
Jerry Frank (Sam), Dan Wolheim
(Slarsen), Robert Williams (Sloan),
Frank Marvin (Sniper), Robert
Dudley (Stationmaster), Audrey Gaye
(supervisor), Yakima Canutt.

S.O.S. INVASION (1969-Span.)
    Director: Ailvio F. Balbeuna
Jack Taylor, Mara Cruz, Jose Maria
Tasso, Diana Sorel, Titania Climent,
Catherine Ellison, Vallerie Mulhol-
land.

S.O.S. TIDAL WAVE (1939)
    Director: John H. Auer
Ralph Byrd (Jeff Shannon), Frank
Jenks (Peaches Jackson), Marc
Lawrence (Sutter), Donald 'Red'
Barry (Curley), Raymond Bailey
(Roy Nixon), George Barbier (Un-
cle Dan), Dorothy Lee (Mabel),
Kay Sutton (Laurel Shannon), Oscar
O'Shea (Mike Holloran), Mickey
Kuhn (Buddy Shannon), Ferris Taylor
(Farrow).

SOUL OF A MONSTER (1944)
    Director: Will Jason
Rose Hobart (Lilyan Gregg), George
Macready (Dr. George Winson),
Jim Bannon (Dr. Roger Vance),
Jeanne Bates (Ann Winson), Erik
Rolf (Fred Stevens), Ernest Hil-
liard (Wayne).

SOUND OF HORROR (1964-Span.)
    (A.K.A. "El Sonido Prehistorico",
    "The Prehistoric Sound")
    Director: Antonio Nieves-Conde
James Philbrook (Pete), Arturo
Fernandez (Prof. Andre), Soledad
Miranda (Maria), Ingrid Pitt (Sofia),
Jose Bodalo, Francisco Piquer,
Antonio Casas, Lola Gaos.

SOYLENT GREEN (1973)
    Director: Richard Fleischer
Charlton Heston (Detective Thorn),
Edward G. Robinson (Sol Roth),
Leigh Taylor-Young (Shirl), Chuck
Connors (Tab Fielding), Joseph
Cotten (William Simonson), Brock
Peters (Hatcher), Paula Kelly
(Martha), Mike Henry (Kolozik),
Leonard Stone (Charles), Lincoln

Kilpatrick (Priest), Whit Bissell
(Governor Santini), Celia Lovsky
(Exchange Leader), Dick Van Patten
(Usher), Morgan Farley, Cyril
Delevanti, Belle Mitchell, John
Barclay (Books), John Dennis (Wag-
ner), Roy Jenson (Donovan), Forrest
Wood, Faith Quabius (attendants),
Jane Dulo (Mrs. Santini), Stephen
Young (Gilbert), Carlos Romero
(new tenant).

SPACE CASANOVA (1979)
see Television: Battlestar Galactica (1978-79)

SPACE CHILDREN, THE (1957)
Director: Jack Arnold
Adam Williams (Dave Brewster),
Peggy Webber (Anne Brewster),
Michael Ray (Bud Brewster), John
Crawford (Ken Brewster), Jackie
Coogan (Hank Johnson), Sandy
Descher (Eadie Johnson), Russell
Johnson (Joe Gamble), Johnny
Washbrook (Tim Gamble), Raymond
Bailey (Dr. Wahrman), Richard
Shannon (Lt. Col. Manley).

SPACED OUT (1981)
Director: Norman J. Warren
Barry Stokes (Oliver), Tony Maiden
(Willy), Gloria Annen (Cosia),
Michael Rowlatt (Cliff), Ava Cadell
(Partha), Lynne Ross (Prudence),
Kate Ferguson (Skipper).

SPACEFLIGHT IC-1 (1965)
Director: Bernard Knowles
Bill Williams (Capt. Mead Ralston),
Kathleen Breck (Kate Saunders), Do-
nald Churchill (Carl Walcott), Mark
Lester, Jeremy Longhurst, John Cair-
ney, Norma West, Linda Marlowe.

SPACE MASTER X-7 (1958)
Director: Edward Bernds
Bill Williams (John Hand), Lyn
Thomas (Laura Breeling), Paul
Frees (Dr. Charles Pommer),
Robert Ellis (Joe Rattigan), Thomas
B. Henry (Prof. West), Joan Barry
(Miss Meyers), Rhoda Williams
(Miss Archer), Moe Howard (cab
driver), Gregg Martell (engineer),
Fred Sherman (Morse), Thomas
Wilde (Collins), Carol Varga (Elaine
Frohman), Jesse Kirkpatrick (Cap-
tain), Court Shepard (Chief Hendry),
Al Baffert (passenger), Nesdon Booth.

SPACE MONSTER (1965)
Director: Leonard Katzman

Russ Bender (John Andros), James
B. Brown (Hank), Francine York
(Lisa), Baynes Barron (Paul).

SPACE PRISON (1979)
see Television: Battlestar Galactica (1978-79)

SPACE SHIP SAPPY (1957) -short
Director: Jules White
Moe Howard, Larry Fine, Joe
Besser, Doreen Woodbury, Benny
Rubin, Marilyn Hanold, Emil Sitka,
Lorraine Crawford, Harriette Tarler.

SPACE-WATCH MURDERS, THE
(TVM-1975)
Director:
Sam Groom, Tisha Sterling, Bar-
bara Steele, Joan Caulfield.

SPACEWAYS (1953)
Director: Terence Fisher
Howard Duff (Stephen Mitchell),
Eva Bartok (Lisa Frank), Alan
Wheatley (Smith), Philip Leaver
(Dr. Keppler), Andrew Osborn
(Philip Crenshaw), Michael Medwin
(Toby Andrews), Anthony Ireland
(Gen. Hayes), Hugh Moxey (Col.
Daniels), Cecile Chevreau (Vanessa
Mitchell), David Horne (Minister),
Jean Webster-Brough (Mrs. Daniels),
Leo Phillips (Sgt. Peterson), Mari-
anne Stone (Mrs. Rogers).

SPANIARD'S CURSE, THE (1958)
Director: Ralph Kemplen
Tony Wright (Charlie Manton), Lee
Patterson (Mark Brett), Michael
Hordern (Judge Manton), Henry
Oscar (Mr. Fredericks), Basil
Dignam (Guy Stevenson), Brian
Oulton (Frank Porter), Susan Beau-
mont (Margaret Manton), Ralph
Truman (Sir Robert Wyvern), Olga
Dickie (Hannah), Roddy Hughes
(Jody), John Watson.

SPASMO (1976-Ital.)
Director: Umberto Lenzi
Suzy Kendall (Barbara), Robert Hoffman (Christian), Monica Monet (Clor-
inda), Ivan Rassimov, Guido Alberti.

SPECKLED BAND, THE (1931)
Director: Jack Raymond
Raymond Massey (Sherlock Holmes),
Lyn Harding (Dr. Grimseby Rylott),
Athole Stewart (Dr. Watson), Angela
Baddeley (Helen Stoner), Nancy Price
(Mrs. Staunton), Marie Ault (Mrs. Hud-
son), Stanley Lathbury (Rodgers), Joyce

Moore (Violet), Charles Paton (builder).

SPECTRE (TVM-1977) - 5-21-77
Director: Clive Donner
Robert Culp (William Sebastian),
Gig Young (Dr. Ham Hamilton),
James Villiers (Sir Geoffrey Cyon),
John Hurt (Mitri Cyon), Ann Bell
(Anitra Cyon), Gordon Jackson (Insp.
Cabell), Jenny Runacre (Synda),
Majel Barrett (Lilith), Michael Lati-
mer, Linda Benson, Angela Grant.

SPECTRE OF EDGAR ALLAN POE,
THE (1972)
Director: Mohy Quandour
Robert Walker, Jr. (Edgar Allan
Poe), Cesar Romero (Dr. Grimaldi),
Carol Ohmart (Lisa Grimaldi),
Tom Drake (Dr. Forrest), Mary
Grover (Lenore), Karen Hartford
(night nurse), Mario Miland (Joseph),
Dennis Fimple (Farron), Frank
Packard (Jonah), Paul Bryar (Mr.
White), Marsha Mae Jones (Sarah).

SPELL, THE (TVM-1977) - 2-20-77
Director: Lee Phillips
Lee Grant (Marion Matchett), James
Olson (Glenn Matchett), Susan
Myers (Rita Matchett), Lelia Goldoni
(Jo Standish), Jack Colvin (Dale
Boyce), Barbara Bostock (Jill),
Wright King (Ryan Bellamy), Kathleen
Hughes (Fenitia), Doney Oatman
(Jackie Segal), James Greene (Stan
Restin), Helen Hunt (Kristina Matchett).

SPELL OF AMY NUGENT, THE
(1940) (A.K.A. "Spellbound",
"Passing Clouds")
Director: John Harlow
Derek Farr (Laurie Baxter), Gibb
McLaughlin (Gibb), Felix Aylmer
(Mr. Morton), Vera Lindsay (Diana
Hilton), Frederick Leister (Mr.
Vincent), Diana King (Amy Nugent),
Hay Petrie (Cathcart), W.G. Fay
(Johnnie), Marian Spencer (Mrs.
Stapleton), Hannen Swaffer (himself),
Irene Handl, Joyce Redman.

SPELL OF EVIL, THE (TVM-
1973) - 10-11-73
Director:
Diane Cilento (Clara), Edward de
Souza (Tony Mansell), William
Dexter (Mr. Pritchard), Jennifer
Daniels (Liz), Jeremy Longhurst
(George Mathews), Iris Russell
(Mrs. Roberts), Philip Anthony (Mr.
Todd), David Blecher (Dr. Peterson),
Martin Wyldeck (Mr. Laker), Linda

Cunningham (Suzy), Reg Lyle (Caretaker), Patricia Kneale (Mrs. Mansell).

SPHINX, THE (1933)
Director: Phil Rosen
Lionel Atwill (Jerome Breen), Sheila
Terry (Jerry Crane), Theodore Newton
(Jack Burton), Luis Alberni (Bacigalupi),
Robert Ellis (Insp. Riley), Paul Hurst
(Terrence Hogan), Lucien Prival, Paul
Fix, Hooper Atchley, Wilfred Lucas,
George Hayes, Lillian Leighton.

SPHINX, THE (1981)
Director: Franklin J. Schaffner
Lesley-Anne Down (Erica Baron),
Frank Langella (Ahmed Khazzan),
Sir John Gielgud (Abdu Hamdi),
Martin Benson (Muhammed), James
Cossins (Carter), John Rhys-Davies
(Stephanos Markoulis), Tutte Lem-
kow (Tewfik), Saeed Jaffrey (Selim),
Vic Tabian (Khalifa), Nadim Sawalha
(Gamal), William Hootkins (Don),
Eileen Way (Aida).

SPIDER, THE (1931)
Director: William C. Menzies &
Kenneth MacKenna
Edmund Lowe (Chatrand), Lois Moran
(Beverly Lane), George E. Stone
(Dr. Blackstone), El Brendel (Ole),
Earle Foxe (John Carrintgon),
Purnell Pratt (Insp. Riley), Howard
Phillips (Alexander), Warren Hymer
(Schmidt), William Pawley (Butch),
John Arledge (Tommy), Jesse De
Vorska (Goldberg), Ruth Donnelly
(Mrs. Wimbledon), Kendall McComas
(the Kid).

SPIDER, THE (1958) (A.K.A. "Earth
vs. the Spider")
Director: Bert I. Gordon
Ed Kemmer (Mr. Kingman), June
Kenny (Carol Flynn), Gene Persson
(Mike Simpson), Gene Roth (Sheriff),
Cagle), Hal Torey (Mr. Simpson),
June Jocelyn (Mrs. Flynn), Jack
Kosslyn (Mr. Fraser), Sally Fraser
(Helen Kingman), Mickey Finn (Mr.
Haskel), Hank Patterson (janitor),
Troy Patterson (Joe), Skip Young
(Sam), Bill Giorgio (Day Sheriff
Sanders), Howard Wright (Jake),
Bob Garnet (pest control man),
Shirley Falls (switchboard operator),
Bob Tetrick (Dave), George Stanley
(man in cavern), Merritt Stone (Mr.
Flynn), Nancy Kilgas (dancer),
David Tomack (line foreman).

SPIDER BABY (1965) (A.K.A.

"The Maddest Story Ever Told",
"The Liver Eaters", "Cannibal
Orgy")
Director: Jack Hill
Lon Chaney, Jr. , Carol Ohmart,
Mantan Moreland, Jill Banner, Quinn
Redeker, Beverly Washburn.

SPIDERMAN (TVM-1977) - 9-14-77
Director: E.W. Swackhamer
Nicholas Hammond (Peter Parker/
Spiderman), David White (J. Jonah
Jameson), Thayer David (Edward
Byron), Michael Pataki (Capt.
Barbera), Robert Hastings (Monahan),
Jeff Donnell (Aunt May), Lisa Eil-
bacher (Judy Tyler), Ivor Francis
(Prof. Noah Tyler), Holly Hicks
(Robbie Robinson), Barry Cutler
(purse snatcher), Dick Balduzzi
(delivery man), Len Lesser, Jim
Storm, Ivan Bonnar, Norman Rice,
Harry Caesar, George Cooper,
Roy West, James E. Brodhead,
Carmelita Pope, Kathryn Reynolds,
Robert Snively, Ron Gilbert, Larry
Anderson.

SPIDER RETURNS, THE (1941) -
serial in 15 episodes
Director: James W. Horne
Warren Hull (Richard Wentworth/
Blinky McQuade/the Spider), Mary
Ainslee (Nina Van Sloan), Dave O'Brien
Jackson), Corbet Harris (McLeod/
the Gargoyle), Kenne Duncan (Ram
Singh), Bryant Washburn (Westfall),
Joe Girard (Cmdr. Kirk), Anthony
Warck (Trigger), Charles Miller
(Van Sloan), Harry Harvey (Stephen),
Alden Chase.

SPIDER'S WEB, THE (1938) - serial
in 15 episodes
Director: Jamse W. Horne &
Ray Taylor
Warren Hull (Richard Wentworth/
Blinky McQuade/the Spider), Iris
Meredith (Nita Van Sloan), Charles
Wilson (Chase/the Octopus), Richard
Fiske (Jackson), Kenne Duncan (Ram
Singh), Forbes Murray (Commissioner
Kirk), Marc Lawrence (Steve),
Donald Douglas (Jenkins), Nestor
Paiva, Ernie Adams, Lane Chandler,
Edmund Cobb.

SPIDER WOMAN, THE (1943) (A.K.A.
"Sherlock Holmes and the Spider
Woman")
Director: Roy William Neill
Basil Rathbone (Sherlock Holmes),
Nigel Bruce (Dr. Watson), Gale
Sondergaard (Andrea Spedding),
Dennis Hoey (Insp. Lestrade), Alec
Craig (Radlik), Mary Gordon (Mrs.
Hudson), Harry Cording (Fred
Garvin), Arthur Hohl (Gilflower),
Vernon Downing (Norman Locke),
Teddy Infuhr (Larry), Stanley
Logan (Colonel), Lydia Bilbrook
(Colonel's wife), John Roche
(croupier), Donald Stuart (Artie),
John Burton (announcer), Belle
Mitchell (fortune teller).

SPIDER WOMAN STRIKES BACK,
THE (1946)
Director: Arthur Lubin
Gale Sondergaard (Zenobia Dollard),
Brenda Joyce (Jean Kingsley),
Kirby Grant (Hal Witley), Rondo
Hatton (Mario), Hobart Cavanaugh
(Mr. Stapleton), Milburn Stone
(Mr. Moore), Norman Leavitt (Tom),
Tom Daly (Sam Julian), Eula
Guy (Molly Corvin), Lois Austin
(Jinny Hawks), Adda Gleason (Mar-
tha), Ruth Robinson (Mrs. Wentley).

SPIES (1928-Ger.) (A.K.A. "Spi-
one", "The Spy")
Director: Fritz Lang
Rudolph Klein-Rogge (Haghi), Willy
Fritsch (Agent No. 326), Gerda
Maurus (Sonia), Fritz Rasp (Col.
Jellusic), Lien Deyers (Kitty),
Georg John (train conductor), Lupu
Pick (Dr. Matsumoto), Craighall
Sherry (Miles Jason), Paul Hor-
biger (Franz, the chaufferu), Louis
Ralph (Morrier), Hertha von Walther
(Lady Leslane), Paul Rehkopf
(Stroich), Julius Falkenstein (hotel
manager).

SPIES KILL SILENTLY (1966-Span. /
Ital.) (A.K.A. "Los Espias
Mantan en Silencio")
Director: Mario Caiano
Lang Jeffries (Michel), Emma
Danielli (Grace), Andrea Bosic
(Rachid), Jose Bodalo (Craig).

SPIES OF THE AIR (1939)
Director: David McDonald
Roger Livesey (Houghton), Basil
Radford (Madison), Felix Aylmer
(Col. Cairns), Joan Marion (Dorothy
Houghton), John Turnbull (Sir
Andrew Hamilton), Barry K. Barnes
(Jim Thurloe), Henry Oscar (Porter),
Edward Ashley (Stuart), Wallace
Douglas (Hooper), Everley Gregg
(Mrs. Madison).

SPIRAL STAIRCASE, THE (1945)
Director: Robert Siodmak
Dorothy McGuire (Helen Capel),
George Brent (Prof. Warren), Ethel
Barrymore (Mrs. Warren), Kent
Smith (Dr. Perry), Elsa Lanchester
(Mrs. Oates), Rhys Williams (Oates),
Sara Allgood (Nurse Barker),
Rhonda Fleming (Blanche), Gordon
Oliver (Steve Warren), James Bell
(Constable), Myrna Dell (murder
victim).

SPIRAL STAIRCASE, THE (1975)
Director: Peter Collinson
Jacqueline Bissett (Helen), Chris-
topher Plummer (Dr. Sherman),
John Philip Law (Steven), Mildred
Dunnock (Mrs. Sherman), Gayle
Hunnicutt (Blanche), Sam Wanamaker
(Lt. Fields), John Ronane (Dr.
Rawley), Ronald Radd (Oates),
Sheila Brennan (Mrs. Oates),
Elaine Strich (Nurse), Christopher
Malcolm (policeman), Heather Lowe
(blind girl).

SPIRIT IS WILLING, THE (1966)
Director: William Castle
Sid Ceasar (Ben Powell), Vera
Miles (Kate Powell), John McGiver
(Uncle George), John Astin (Dr.
Frieden), Cass Daley (Felicity
Twitchell), Mary Wickes (Gloria
Tritt), Jesse White (Fess Dorple),
Bob Donner (Ebenezer Twitchell),
Doodles Weaver (Booper Mellish),
Harvey Lembeck (Capt. Pederson),
Jill Townsend (Jenny/Priscilla
Weems/Carol Weems), J.C. Flippen
(mother), Nestor Paiva (father),
Barry Gordon (Steve Powell), Mickey
Deems (Rabbit Warren), Ricky
Cordell (Miles Thorpe).

SPIRIT OF THE BEEHIVE, THE
(1973-Span.) (A.K.A. "El
Espiritu de la Colmena")
Director: Victor Erice
Fernando Fernan Gomez, Teresa
Gimpera, Isabel Telleria, Ana
Torrent, Laly Soldevilla, Miguel
Picazo, Juan Margallo, Jose Villa-
sante (Frankenstein's monster).

SPIRITS OF THE DEAD (1967-Fr. /
Ital.) (A.K.A. "Histoires Ex-
traordinaires", "Tre Passi Nel
Delirio", Three Steps to Delirium",
"Tales of Mystery")
"Metzengerstein". Director: Roger
Vadim
Jane Fonda (Frederica), Peter Fonda

(Wilhelm), James Robertson Justice
(Countess' advisor), Philippe Lemaire
(Philippe), Annie Duperrey (1st
guest), Carla Marlier (Claude),
Serge Marquand (Hughes), Andrea
Voutsinas (2nd guest), Francoise
Prevost (friend of Countess),
Bouking (du Lissier), Audoin de
Bardot (Page).
"William Wilson". Director: Louis
Malle
Alain Delon (William Wilson),
Brigitte Bardot (Giuseppina), Katia
Critsina (young girl), Umberto
D'Orsi (Hans), Renzo Palmer (the
priest), Daniele Vargas (professor).
"Toby Dammit"/"Never Bet the
Devil Your Head". Director:
Federico Fellini.
Terence Stamp (Toby Dammit),
Salvo Randone (priest), Marina Yaru
(the Devil), Fabrizio Angeli (1st
director), Ernesto Colli (2nd director),
Anna Toniette (TV commentator),
Aleardo Ward (1st interviewer),
Paul Cooper (2nd interviewer).

SPIRITUALIST, THE (1948) (A.K.A.
"The Amaxing Mr. X")
Director: Bernard Vorhaus
Turhan Bey (Alexis), Lynn Bari
(Christine Faver), Richard Carlson
(Martin Abbott), Cathy O'Donnell
(Janet Burke), Donald Curtis (Paul),
Virginia Gregg, Harry Mendoza.

SPOOK BUSTERS (1946)
Director: William Beaudine
Leo Gorcey (Slip Mahoney), Huntz
Hall (Sach Debussy Jones), Bernard
Gorcey (Louie Dumbrowsky), Billy
Benedict (Whitey), David Gorcey
(Chuck), Gabriel Dell (Gabe Moreno),
Douglass Dumbrille, Bobby Jordan,
Richard Alexander, Charles Middle-
ton, Vera Lewis, Tanis Chandler,
Arthur Miles, Chester Clute, Maurice
Cass, Charles Millsfield.

SPOOK LOUDER (1943) - short
Director: Del Lord
Moe Howard, Curly Howard, Larry
Fine, Stanley Blystone, William
Kelly, Symona Boniface.

SPOOKS (1953) - short
Director: Jules White
Moe Howard, Shemp Howard, Larry
Fine, Philip Van Zandt, Tom Kennedy,
Norma Randall.

SPOOKS RUN WILD (1941)
Director: Phil Rosen

Bela Lugosi (Nardo), Dave O'Brien
(Jeff Dixon), Dennis Moore (Dr.
Von Grogh), Angelo Rossito (Luigi),
Dorothy Short (Linda Mason), Huntz
Hall (Glimpy), Leo Gorcey (Muggsy),
Bobby Jordan (Danny), David Gorcey
(Peewee), Sammy Morrison (Scruno),
Guy Wilkerson (Constable), George
Pembroke (Von Grosch), Rosemary
Portia (Margie), Donald Haines
(Skinny), Joe Kirk, Jack Carr.

SPOOK WHO SAT BY THE DOOR,
   THE (1973)
   Director: Ivan Dixon
Lawrence Cook (Dan), Paula Kelly
(Dahomey Queet), Byron Morrow
(General), Janet League (Joy), Paul
Butler (Do-Daddy), J. A. Preston
(Dawson), Don Blakely (Stud), David
Lemieux (Pretty Willie), Joseph
Mascolo (Senator), Jack Aaron
(Carstairs), Beverly Gill (Willa),
Bob Hill (Calhoun), Martin Golar
(Parkins), Jeff Hamilton (policeman),
Margaret Kromgols (old woman),
Tom Alderman (security officer),
Kathy Berk (Doris), Stephen Ferry
(Colonel), Stephen Ferry II (boy
guardsman), Anthony Ray (Shorty),
Harold Johnson (Jackson), Audrey
Stevenson (Mrs. Duncan), John Charles
(Stew), Frank Lesley (commentator),
Sidney Eden, Ponicano Olayta,
Jr., Colostine Boatwright, Cora
Williams, Johnny Williams, Bobbie
Gene Williams.

SPY IN THE GREEN HAT, THE (1966)
   Director: Joseph Sargent
   see Television: Man From U. N. C. -
   L. E. - "The Concrete Overcoat
   Affair" (11-25-66 & 12-2-66)

SPY IN THE SKY (1958)
   Director: W. Lee Wilder
Steve Brodie (Victor Cabot), George
Coulouris (Col. Benedict), Sandra
Francis Donat (Eva Brindisi), Bob
de Lange (Sidney Jardine), Andrea
Domburg (Alexandrine Duvivier),
Hans Tiemeyer (Dr. Keller), Dity
Oorthuis (Fritzi), Herbert Curiel
(Pepi), A. E. Collin, Alex Sweers,
Rob Milton, Leon Dorian, E. F.
Beavis, Harold Horsten.

SPY IN YOUR EYE (1965-Ital.)
   (A. K. A. "Berlino, Appunta-
   mento Per le Spie", "Berlin,
   Appointment for the Spies")
   Director: Vittorio Sala
Brett Halsey (Bert Morris), Pier

Angeli (Paula Krauss), Gastone
Moschin (Boris), Dana Andrews
(Col. Lancaster), Mario Valdemarin,
Tania Beryl, Aldo De Francisco,
Marco Guglielmi, Renato Baldini,
Luciana Angiolillo.

SPY LOVES FLOWERS, THE (1966-
   Ital.) (A. K. A. "Le Spie Amano
   i Fiori")
   Director: Umberto Lenzi
Daniele Vargas, Roger Browne,
Yoko Tani, Emma Danieli.

SPY SMASHER (1942) (A. K. A. "Spy
   Smasher Returns) - serial in
   12 episodes
Chapters: 1. "America Beware",
2. "Human Target", 3. "Iron
Coffin", 4. "Stratosphere Invaders",
5. "Decending Doom", 6. "The
Invisible Witness", 7. "Secret
Weapon", 8. "Sea Raiders", 9.
"Highway Racketeers", 10. "2700
Degrees Fahrenheit", 11. "Hero's
Death", & 12. "V...".
   Director: William Witney
Kane Richmond (Alan Armstrong/
Jack Armstrong/Spy Smasher), Sam
Flint (Admiral Corby), Marguerite
Chapman (Eve Corby), Hans Schumm
(the Mask), Tris Coffin (Drake),
Paul Bryar (Lawlor), George Rena-
vent (the Governor), Frank Corsaro
(Durand), Hans von Morhart (Capt.
Gerhardt), Henry Zynda (Lazar),
Robert O. Davis (Col. Von Kohr),
Tom London (Crane), Crane Whitley
(Dr. Hauser), Richard Bond (Hayes),
John James (Steve), George Lewis
(Stuart), Yakima Canutt (armored
car driver), Buddy Roosevelt (lieu-
tenant), Dudley Dickerson (Porter),
Ken Terrell (Jerry), John Buckley
(Walker), Bob Stevenson (Torpedo
Chief), Cy Clocum (French private),
Leonard St. Leo (French Lieutenant),
Marty Faust (Blacksmith), Martin
Garralaga (Commandant), Jack
Arnold (camera clerk), Hugh Prosser
(navigator), Jerry Jerome (Bunrs),
Lee Phelps (jail guard), George
Sherwood (jailor), Carleton Young
(Taylor), Pat Moran (waiter),
Arvon Dale (Thornton), William
Forrest (Douglas), John Peters
(Sub-Quatermaster), Gil Perkins
(Sub-Valve sailor), Charles Regan
(cafe manager), Frank Alten (Ger-
man officer), Lowden Adams (head-
waiter), Ray Parsons (Livingston),
Tom Steele, Eddie Jauregui, John
Daheim, Bob Jamison (brick heavies),

Bud Wolfe (Craig/policeman No. 2),
Robert Wilke (Chief Operative),
Howard Hughes, Charley Phillips
(barn heavies), Max Waizman (auto
clerk), Nick Vehr (dungeon guard),
Sid Troy (gold heavy), Louis Tomei
(Joe), Duke Taylor (Fritz), Lee
Phelps (guard), Carey Loftin (launch
heavy), Duke Green (lumber heavy),
Bert LeBaron (mechanic), Charles
Regan (manager), Jimmy Fawcett
(Lewis/policeman No. 3), Bill
Wilkus, Loren Riebe (pipe heavies),
Robert Stevenson (torpedo chief),
Jack O'Shea, James Dale.

SPY WHO LOVED ME, THE (1977)
    Director: Lewis Gilbert
Roger Moore (James Bond), Curt
Jurgens (Stromberg), Barbara
Bach (Major Anya Amasova), Richard
Kiel (Jaws), Caroline Munro (Naomi),
Walter Gotell (Gen. Gogol), George
Baker (Capt. Benson), Geoffrey Keen
(Minister of Defense), Bernard
Lee (M), Lois Maxwell (Miss Money-
penny), Desmond Llewelyn (Q),
Shane Rimmer (Capt. Carter),
Edward De Souza (Sheik Hosein),
Sidney Tafler (Liparus Captain),
Michael Billington (Sergie), Vernon
Dobtcheff (Max Kalba), Bryan Mar-
shall (Cmdr. Talbot), Olga Bisera
(Felicca), Nadim Sawalha (Fekkesh),
Valerie Leon (hotel receptionist),
Sue Vanner (log cabin girl), Milton
Reid (Sandor), Jeremy Bulloch
(Wayne crew member), Dawn Rod-
rigues, Jill Goodall, Anika Pavel,
Felicity York (Arab girls).

SPY WITH MY FACE, THE (1965)
    Director: John Newland
see Television: Man from
U. N. C. L. E. - "The Double
Affair" (11-17-64)

SQUIRM (1977)
    Director: Jeff Lieberman
John Scardino (Mick), Patricia Pearcy
(Geri Sanders), R. A. Dow (Roger
Grimes), Peter MacLean (Sheriff),
Jean Sullivan (Naomi), Frank Higgins
(Alma), William Newman (Quigley),
Barbara Quinn (Sheriff's girl),
Angel Sande (Millie), Carl Dagenhart
(Willie Grimes), Carol Jean Owens
(Bonnie), Walter Dimmick (Danny),
Kim Iocouvozzi (Hank), Julia Klopp
(Mrs. Klopp).

SSSSSSSSS! (1973)
    Director: Bernard Kowalski

Strother Martin (Dr. Carl Stoner),
Dirk Benedict (David Blake), Heather
Menzies (Kristine Stoner), Richard
B. Shull (Dr. Ken Daniels), Jack
Ging (Sheriff Hardisson), Tim O'Con-
nor (Kogen), Reb Brown (Steve
Randall), Kathleen King (Kitty),
Ted Grossman (deputy), Felix
Silla (Seal Boy), Charles Seel (old
man), Ray Ballard (tourist), Brendan
Burns, Rick Beckner (jocks), James
Drum, Ed McCready, Ralph Mont-
gomery, Frank Kowalski, Michael
Masters (hawkers), Bobbi Kiger
(kootch dancer), Noble Craig (Tim),
J. R. Clark (attendant), Chip Potter
(clerk).

STAIRWAY TO HEAVEN (1946)
    (A. K. A. "A Matter of Life and
    Death")
    Director: Michael Powell
David Niven (Peter Carter), Kim
Hunter (June), Roger Livesey (Dr.
Reeves), Marius Goring (Conductor
71), Robert Coote (Bob), Raymond
Massey (Abraham Farlan), Kathleen
Byron (Angel), Abraham Sofaer
(the Judge), Joan Maude (Chief
Recorder), Bob Roberts (Dr.
Gaertler), Betty Potter (Mrs. Ruc-
ker), Edwin Max (Mrs. McEwan),
Robert Atkins (the Vicar), Richard
Attenborough (English pilot), Bonar
Colleano (American pilot).

STALKER (1979-Sov./Ger.)
    Director: Andrei Tarkovsky
Alexander Kaidanovsky (Stalker),
Anatoly Solonitsyn (the writer),
Nikolia Grinko (the scientist), Alisa
Freindlich (Stalker's wife).

STANLEY (1972)
    Director: William Grefe
Chris Robinson (Tim Ochopee),
Alex Rocco (Richard Thomkins),
Susan Carrol (Susie Thomkins),
Steve Alaimo (Crail Denning), Rey
Baumel (Sidney Calvin), Marcie
Knight (Gloria Calvin), Mark Harris
(Bob Wilson), Paul Avery (Psycho),
Gary Crutcher (Dr. Everett), Mel
Pape (medical center guard), Butter-
ball Smith (stage manager), Pamela
Talus (Thomkin's girlfriend), Bill
Marquez (Wauchula).

STARCRASH (1979-Ital.)
    Director: Luigi Cozzi/Lewis
    Coates
Caroline Munro (Stella Star), Marjoe
Gortner (Akton), Christopher Plummer

(the Emperor), Joe Spinnell (Count Zarth Arn), Judd Hamilton (Elle), Robert Tessier (Thor), David Hasselhoff (Simon), Nadia Cassini (Queen of the Amazons), Hamilton Camp (voice of Elle).

STAR DUST (1978-E. Ger.) (A. K. A. "Im Staub der Sterne")
Director: Dr. Gottfried Kolditz
Jana Brejchova (Akala), Alfred Struwe (Suko), Ekkehard Schall (Chief), Milan Beli (Rink), Violeta Andrej (Rali), Sylvia Popovici (Illic), Leon Niemcyzk (Thob), Regeine Heintze (My), Mihai Merenta (Kte), Stefan Mihailescue Braila (Xik), Aurelia Dumitrescue (Chat).

STARK MAD (1929)
Director: Lloyd Bacon
Henry B. Walthall, Jacqueline Logan, Lionel Belmore, Irene Rich, John Miljan, J. B. Warner, Louise Fazenda, Audrey Ferris, Andre Beranger, Claude Gillingwater, William Collier, Jr.

STARLIGHT SLAUGHTER (1976)
(A. K. A. "Eaten Alive", "Slaughter Hotel", "Death Trap")
Director: Tobe Hooper
Neville Brand (Judd), Mel Ferrer (Harvey Wood), Carolyn Jones (Miss Hattie), Stuart Whitman (Sheriff Martin), William Finley (Roy), Marilyn Burns, Roberta Collins, Janis Lynn, Crystin Sinclaire, Robert Englund, Kyle Richards.

STARSHIP INVASION (1977)
Director: Ed Hunt
Robert Vaughn (Prof. Allan Duncan), Christopher Lee (Rameses), Tiiu Leek (Phi), Daniel Pilon (Anaxi), Victoria Johnson (Gezeth), Sherri Ross (Sagnac), Helen Shaver (Mrs. Duncan), Henry Ramer (Malcolm), Doreen Lipson (Dorothy).

STAR TREK - THE MOTION PICTURE (1979)
Director: Robert Wise
William Shatner (Adm. James T. Kirk), Leonard Nimoy (Mr. Spock), DeForest Kelley (Dr. Leonard 'Bones' McCoy), Persis Khambatta (Ilia), Stephen Collins (Capt. Decker), James Doohan (Scotty), George Takai (Sulu), Walter Koenig (Chekov), Nichelle Nichols (Uhura), Majel Barrett (Dr. Chapel), Grace Lee Whitney (Janice Rand), Mark Lenard (Klingon Captain), David

Gautreaux (Cmdr. Branch), Marcy Lafferty (Chief di Falco), Michael Rougas (Lt. Cleary), Howard Itzkowitz (Lt. Cmdr. Sonak), Terrence O'Connor (Chief Ross), Billy Van Zandt (Alien boy), Michele Ameen Billy (Lieutenant), Jeri McBride (technician), John D. Gowans (assistant to Rand), Gary Faga (airlock technician), Roger Aaron Brown (Epsilon technician).

STAR TREK II; THE WRATH OF KHAN (1982)
Director: Nicholas Meyer
William Shatner (Adm. James T. Kirk), Leonard Nimoy (Mr. Spock), DeForest Kelley (Dr. Leonard 'Bones' McCoy), Ricardo Montalban (Khan Noonian Singh), James Doohan (Chief Engineer Montgomery 'Scotty' Scott), Walter Koenig (Chekov), George Takei (Sulu), Paul Winfield (Capt. Clark Terrell), Nichelle Nichols (Communications Officer Uhura), Bibi Besch (Dr. Carol Marcus), Merritt Butrick (David Marcus), Kirstie Alley (Lt. Saavik), Ike Eisenmann (Midshipman First Class Peter Preston), Judson Scott (Joachim), John Vargas (Jedda), Nicholas Guest (Cadet), Kevin Sullivan (March), Russell Takaki (Madison), John Winston (Kyle), Paul Kent (Beach), Joel Marstan (Crew Chief), Bill Baker, Brian Davis, Ree Kai, Kim Ryusaki, Sergio Valentino (Starfleet Cadets).

STAR WARS (1977) (A. K. A. "Star Wars IV: A New Hope")
Director: George Lucas
Mark Hamill (Luke Skywalker), Harrison Ford (Han Solo), Carrie Fisher (Princess Leia Organa), Alec Guinness (Obi-Wan Kenobi), Peter Cushing (Grand Moff Tarkin), Anthony Daniels (See Threepio/C3PO), Kenny Baker (Artoo-Detoo/R2-D2), David Prowse (Lord Darth Vader), Peter Mayhew (Chewbacca), Phil Brown (Uncle Owen Lars), Shelagh Fraser (Aunt Beru Lars), Eddie Byrne (Gen. Willard), Alex McCrindle (Gen. Dodonna), Jack Purvis (Chief Jawa), Drewe Henley (Red Leader), Garrick Hagon (Red Three/Biggs), Dennis Lawson (Red Two/Wedge), Jack Klaff (Red Four/John D), William Hootkins (Red Six/Porkins), Angus McInnis (Gold Leader), Jeremy Sinden (Gold Two), Graham Ashley (Gold Five), Don Henderson (Gen. Taggi),

Richard Le Parmentier (Gen. Motti),
Leslie Schofield (Commander No. 1),
James Earl Jones (voice of Darth
Vader).

STEPFORD WIVES, THE (1975)
     Director: Bryan Forbes
Katharine Ross (Joanna), Paula Pren-
tiss (Bobby), Peter Masterson (Walter),
Patrick O'Neal (Dale Coba), Nanette
Newman (Carol), Tina Louise (Char-
maine), Carol Rossen (Dr. Francher),
William Prince (Ike Mazzard), Carole
Mallory (Kit Sunderson), Judith Bald-
win (Mrs. Cornell), Toni Reid (Marie
Axhelm), Barbara Rucker (Marie Ann
Stavros), George Coe (Claude Axhelm),
Michael Higgins (Mr. Cornell), Josef
Somer (Ted Van Sant), Simon Deckard
(Dave Markowe), Remak Ramsay (Mr.
Stkinson), Martha Greenhouse (Mrs.
Kirgassa), Paula Trueman (Welcome
Wagon lady), Joanna Cassidy.

STEPPENWOLF (1974-Brit./Fr./
     Ital./Ger.)
     Director: Fred Haines
Max von Sydow (Harry Haller), Do-
minique Sanda (Hermine), Pierre
Clementi (Pablo), Carla Romanelli
(Maria), Alfred Baillou (Goethe),
Roy Bosier (Aztec), Niels-Peter
Rudolph (Gustav).

STEREO (1969)
     Director: David Cronenberg
Ronald Mlodzik, Iain Ewing, Clara
Mayer, Jack Messinger, Paul Mull-
holland, Glenn McCauley, Arlene
Mlodzik.

STILL OF THE NIGHT (1982)
     (A.K.A. "Stab")
     Director: Robert Benton
Roy Scheider (Sam Rice), Meryl
Streep (Broke Reynolds), Jessica
Tandy (Grace Rice), Joe Grifasi (Jie
Vitucci), Sara Botsford (Gail Phil-
lips), Josef Sommer (George Bynum),
Irving Metzman (Murray), Rikke
Borge (Haether Wilson).

STING OF DEATH (1966)
     Director: William Grefe
Joe Morrison (John Hoyt), Deanna
Lund (Jessica), Valerie Hawkins
(Karen Richardson), Jack Nagle (Dr.
Richardson), John Vella (Egon),
Sandy Lee Kane (Louise), Lois
Etelman (Donna), Blanche Devreaux
(Susan), Judy Lee (Ruth), Robert
Stanton (Sheriff), Doug Hobart (the
Monster), Neil Sedaka (singer),

Barbara Paridon (1st girl), Tony
Gulliver (1st boy), Ron Pinchbeck
(2nd boy), John Castle (3rd boy).

STORY OF MANKIND, THE (1957)
     Director: Irwin Allen
Ronald Colman (Spirit of Man),
Vincent Price (the Devil), Hedy
Lamarr (Joan of Arc), Groucho
Marx (Peter Minuit), Harpo Marx
(Isaac Newton), Chico Marx (Monk),
Virginia Mayo (Cleopatra), Agnes
Moorehead (Queen Elizabeth),
Sir Cedric Hardwicke (High Judge),
Peter Lorre (Nero), Charles Coburn
(Hippocrates), Cesar Romero (Span-
ish Envoy), Dennis Hopper (Napoleon),
Helmut Dantine (Anthony), John Car-
radine (Khufu), Marie Wilson (Marie
Antoinette), Edward Everett Horton
(Sir Walter Raleigh), Marie Windsor
(Josephine), Reginald Gardiner (Shake-
speare), Melville Cooper (Major
Domo), Francis X. Bushman (Moses),
Bobs Watson (Hitler), Dani Crayne
(Helen of Troy), Austin Green
(Lincoln), Henry Daniell (Bishop of
Beauvais), Franklin Pangborn
(Marquis de Varennes), Anthony
Dexter (Columbus), Reginald Shef-
field (Caesar), Jim Ameche (Alex-
ander Graham Bell), Cathy O'Donnell
(early Christian woman), Nick Cravat,
Don Megowan, Tudor Owen, Abra-
ham Sofaer, Leonard Mudie, Toni
Gerry, George E. Stone, Richard
Cutting, Marvin Miller, William
Schallert, Ziva Rodann, David Bond,
Eden Hartford, Melinda Mars,
Nancy Miller, Harry Ruby, Alexander
Lockwood, Bart Mattson, Burt Nelson.

STORY OF THE BLOOD-RED ROSE,
     THE (1914)
     Director: Colin Campbell
Kathlyn Williams, Wheeler Oakman,
Charles Clary, Camille Astor,
Eugenie Besserer.

STORY WITHOUT A NAME, THE (1924)
     Director: Irvin Willet
Antonio Moreno (Alan Holt), Louis
Wolheim (Kurder), Agnes Ayres
(Mary Walsworth), Tyrone Power,
Sr. (Drakma), Dagmar Godowsky
(Claire), Jack Bohn (Don Powell),
Frank Currier (Admiral Wadsworth),
Maurice Costello (cripple), Ivan
Linow (laboratory assistant).

STOWAWAY TO THE MOON (TVM-
     1975) - 1-10-75
     Director: Andrew V. McLaglen

Lloyd Bridges (Charlie Englehardt), Michael Link (E. J. Mackernutt, Jr.), Jeremy Slate (Rick Lawrence), John Carradine (Jacob Avril), Kenne Curtis (Tom Estes), Walter Brooke (Whitehead), Jon Cedar (Jans Hartman), Jim McMullan (Ben Pelhan), Morgan Paull (Dave Anderson), Stephen Rogers (Joey), Jack Callahan (Dr. Jack Smathers), Edward Faulkner (Eli Mackernutt, Sr.), Barbara Faulkner (Mrs. Mackernutt), Charles Conrad (TV news commentator).

STRAIT-JACKET (1964)
    Director: William Castle
Joan Crawford (Lucy Harbin), Diane Baker (Carol), Leif Erickson (Bill Cutler), Howard St. John (Raymond Fields), John Anthony Hayes (Michael Fields), George Kennedy (Leo Krause), Rochelle Hudson (Emily Cutler), Edith Atwater (Mrs. Fields), Mitchell Cox (Dr. Anderson), Lee Yeary (Frank Harbin), Patricia Krest (Stella Fulton), Vickie Cos (Carol at age 3), Patty Lee, Laura Hess (little girls), Lyn Lundgren (beauty operator), Robert Ward (shoe clerk), Howard Hoffman.

STRAIGHT ON TILL MORNING (1972)
    Director: Peter Collinson
Rita Tushingham (Brenda Thompson), Shane Briant (Peter), Tom Bell (Jimmy Lindsay), Katya Wyeth (Caroline), John Bolam (Joey), Annie Ross (Liz), Claire Kelly (Margo), Harold Berens (Mr. Harris).

STRANGE ADVENTURE (1932)
    Director: Phil Whitman &
        Hampton Del Ruth
Regis Toomey (Lt. Mitchell), June Clyde (Toodles), William V. Mong (Silas Wayne), Lucille LaVerne (Mrs. Sheen), Eddie Phillips (Claude Wayne), Dwight Frye (Robert Wayne), Jason Robards, Sr. (Dr. Bailey), Alan Roscoe (Stephen Boulter), Snowflake/Fred Toomes (Jeff), Nadine Dore (Gloria), Isabelle Vecki (Sarah Boulter), Harry Myers (Officer Kelly), William J. Humphrey (coroner), Eddy Chandler (policeman).

STRANGE BEHAVIOR (1981-Australia/ N. Zeal.) (A. K. A. "Dead Kids")
    Director: Michael Laughlin
Michael Murphy (John Brady), Louise Fletcher (Barbara Moorhead), Fiona Lewis (Gwen Parkinson), Dan Shor (Pete Brady), Arthur Dignam (Dr.

LeSange), Marc McClure (Oliver), Scott Brady (Shea), Dey Young (Caroline), Charles Lane (Donovan), Jim Boelsen (Waldo), Beryl Te Wiata (Mrs. Haskell), B. Courtenay Leigh (Paula), William Hayward (Robinson), Elizabeth Cheshire (Lucy Brown), Billy Al Bengston (Felix Rowe), Jack Haines (Randy Morgan), William Condon (Bryan Morgan), Nicole Anderson (Flying Nun).

STRANGE AND DEADLY OCCURRANCE, THE (TVM-1974) - 9-24-74
    Director: John Llewellyn Moxey
Robert Stack (Michael Rhodes), Vera Miles (Christine Rhodes), L. Q. Jones (Sheriff Berlinger), Herb Edelman (Felix), Margaret Willock (Melissa Rhodes), Ted Gehring (Dr. Gilgreen), Aldin King (Rose), Dena Dietrich (Audrey), John McCallion (Ardie Detweiller), John Gruber (Deputy).

STRANGE CASE OF CAPTAIN RAMPER, THE (1927-Ger.) (A.K.A. "Ramper der Tiermensch"; "Ramper the Beastman")
    Director: Max Reichmann
Paul Wegener (Captain Ramper), Max Schreck, Kurt Gerron, Mary Johnson, George D. Gurtler, Hugo Doblin, Hermann Vallentin, Dillo Lombardi, Camilo Kossath, Raimondo van Riel.

STRANGE CASE OF DR. FAUST, THE (1969-Span.) (A.K.A. "Extrano Caso del Dr. Fausto")
    Director: Gonzale Suarez
Gonzale Suarez, Teresa Gimpera, Charo Lopez, Emma Cohen.

STRANGE CASE OF DR. JEKYLL AND MR. HYDE, THE (TVM-1968) - 1-7-68
    Director: Charles Jarrott
Jack Palance (Dr. Jekyll/Mr. Hyde), Billie Whitelaw (Gwyn), Denholm Elliott (Devlin), Oscar Homolka (Stryker), Leo Genn (Lanyon), Torin Thatcher (Sir John Turnbull), Duncan Lamont (Sgt. Grimes), Rex Sevenoaks (Dr. Wright), Tessie O'Shea (Tessie O'Toole), Gillie Fenwick (Poole), Jeannette Landis (Liz), Liz Cole (Hattie), Liza Creighton (Billie), Paul Harding (Constable Johnson), Donald Webster (Garvis), Geoffrey Alexander (Enfield), Patrick Crean

(Gerosi), William Nunn (Cassidy),

STRANGE CASE OF DR. RX, THE
(1941)
    Director: William Nigh
Patric Knowles (Jerry Church),
Anne Gwynne (Kit Cuhrch), Lionel
Atwill (Dr. Fish), Mona Barrie (Mrs.
Dudley Crispin), Paul Cavanagh
(John Crispin), Mantan Moreland
(Horatio), Shemp Howard (Sgt.
Sweeney), Samuel S. Hinds (Dudley
Crispin), Mary Gordon (Mrs. Scott),
Jan Wiley (Lily), Leyland Hodgson
(Butler), Edmund MacDonald (Capt.
Hurd), Boyd Davis (Police Commis-
sioner), Gary Breckner (announcer),
Ray 'Crash' Corrigan (the Gorilla),
Matty Fain (Zarini), Victor Zimmer-
man (Kirk), Eddy Chandler, Jack
Kennedy, Jack C. Smith (policeman),
Drew Demarest (club waiter), Harry
Harvey (night club manager), John
Gallaudet (man), Paul Bryar (bailiff),
Joe Recht (1st newsboy), Leonard
Sues (2nd newsboy), William Gould
(man).

STRANGE CONFESSION (1945)
    Director: John Hoffman
Lon Chaney, Jr. (Jeff Carter),
Brenda Joyce (Mary Carter), J.
Carrol Naish (Roger Graham),
Milburn Stone (Stevens), Addison
Richards (Dr. Williams), Lloyd Bridges
(David), Mary Gordon (Mrs O'Connor),
George Chandler (Harper), Christian
Rub (Mrs. Moore), Francis McDonald
(Hernandez), Gregory Muradian
(Tommy Carter), Wilton Graff
(Brandon), Jack Norton (drunk
boarder).

STRANGE DOOR, THE (1951)
    Director: Joseph Pevney
Charles Laughton (Alan de Maletroit),
Boris Karloff (Voltan), Sally Forrest
(Blanche de Maletroit), Richard
Stapley (Denis de Beaulieu), Paul
Cavanagh (Edmond de Maletroit),
Alan Napier (Count Gransin), Michael
Pate (Talcon), Morgan Farley (Ren-
ville), Charles Horvath (Turec),
Edwin Parker (Moret), William
Cottrell (Corbeau).

STRANGE EXORCISM OF LYNN HART,
THE (1974)
    Director: Marc Lawrence
Marc Lawrence (Zambrini), Toni
Lawrence (Lynn Hart), Jesse Vint,
Jim Antonio, Katherine Ross, Iris
Korn, Eric Holland, Walter Barnes,

William Michael, Larry Hussman,
Bone Adams, Don Skylar.

STRANGE HOLIDAY (1942) (A. K. A.
"The Day After Tomorrow")
    Director: Arch Oboler
Claude Rains (John Stephenson),
Gloria Holden (Mrs. Stephenson),
Milton Kibbee (Sam Morgan), Martin
Kosleck (the Examiner), Paul Hilton
(Woodrow), Barbara Bates (Peggy
Lee), Bobbie Stebbins (John Stephen-
son, Jr.), Walter White, Jr. (farmer),
Wally Maher (truck driver), Charles
McAvoy (guard), Helen Mack (secre-
tary), Tommy Cook, Ed Max, Pris-
cilla Lyons, Griff Barnett, Paul
Dubov, David Bradford.

STRANGE IMPERSONATION (1945)
    Director: Anthony Mann
Brenda Marshall, William Gargan,
Hillary Brooke, George Chandler,
H. B. Warner, Lyle Talbot, Ruth
Ford, Gay Forester, Mary Treen,
Richard Scott.

STRANGE MR. GREGORY, THE (1946)
    Director: Phil Rosen
Edmund Lowe (Mr. Gregory/Lane
Talbot), Jean Rogers (Ellen Randall),
Frank Reicher (Reicher), Jonathan
Hale, Don Douglas, Robert Emmett
Keane, Ferd A. Kelsey, Jack Norton,
Marjorie Hoshelle, Anita Turner,
Tom Leffingwell, Frank Mayo.

STRANGE NEW WORLD (TVM-1975) -
7-13-75
    Director: Robert Butler
John Saxon (Capt. Anthony Vico),
Kathleen Miller (Dr. Allison Crowley),
Kenne Curtis (Dr. William Scott),
James Olson (the Surgeon), Martine
Beswicke (Tania), Ford Rainey
(Sirius), Gerrit Graham (Daniel),
Catherine Bach (Lara), Reb Brown
(Sprang), Bill McKinney (Badger),
Cynthia Wood (Arana), Norland
Benson (Hide), Dick Farnsworth
(Elder).

STRANGE PEOPLE (1933)
    Director: Richard Thorpe
Hale Hamilton (J. E. Butron), Wilfred
Lucas (John Davis), Michael S.
Visaroff (Edwards), Stanley G.
Blystone (Burke), Gloria Shea
(Helen Mason), John Darrow (Jimmy
Allen), J. Frank Glendon (Crandall),
Jack Pennick (the plumber), Jerry
Mandy (the barber), Jane Keckley
(Mrs. Reed), Mary Foy (Mrs. Jones),

Frank H. LaRue (Kelly), Lew Kelly (insurance agent), Walter Brennan (radio repairman), Gordon DeMain (detective), Jay Wilsey (guest).

STRANGE POSSESSION OF MRS. OLIVER, THE (TVM-1977) - 2-28-77
    Director: Gordon Hessler
Karen Black (Mrs. Miriam Oliver), George Hamilton (Greg Oliver), Robert F. Lyons (Mark), Jean Allison (Mrs. Dempsey), Lucille Benson (housekeeper), Gloria LeRoy (saleslady), Burke Byrnes (bartender), Asher Brauner (dance partner in bar), Charles Cooper, Macon Mc-Calman, William Irwin, Delos V. Smith, Sunny Woods, Danna Hansen, Nancy Hahn Leonard, Bob Palmer.

STRANGER, THE (TVM-1973) - 2-26-73
    Director: Lee H. Katzin
Glenn Corbett (Neil Stryker), Cameron Mitchell (Benedict), Sharon Acker (Bettina Cooke), Lew Ayres (Prof. MacAuley), Steve Franken (Henry Maitland), Dean Jagger (Carl Webster), Tim O'Connor (Dr. Revere), George Coulouris (Max Greene), Arch Whiting (Mike Frome), Jerry Douglas (Steve Perry), H.M. Wynant (Eric Stoner), Buck Young (Nelson), Ben Wright (doctor), Virginia Gregg (ward administrator), William Bryant (truck driver), Steven Marlo (guard), Alan Foster, Philip Manson, Jon Blake, Jeanne Bates, Margaret Field, Gregg Shannon, William Harlow, James Chandler, Joie Magidow, Peggy Stewart, Heather McCoy, Kathleen M. Schultz.

STRANGER FROM VENUS, THE (1954) (A.K.A. "Immediate Disaster", "Stranger from the Stars")
    Director: Burt Balaban
Patricia Neal (Susan North), Helmut Dantine (the Stranger), Derek Bond (Arthur Walker), Cyril Luckham (Dr. Meinard), Stanley Van Beers (General), Graham Stuart (Police Chief), Marigold Russell (Gretchen), Kenneth Edwards (Charles Dixon), Willoughby Gray (Tom), David Garth (1st police officer), Nigel Green (2nd police officer), Arthur Young (scientist).

STRANGER IN OUR HOUSE (TVM-1978) - 10-31-78
    Director: Wes Craven
Linda Blair (Rachel Bryant), Lee

Purcell (Julia), Carol Lawrence (Leslie Bryant), Jeremy Slate (Tom Bryant), Jeff East (Peter Bryant), Macdonald Carey (Prof. Jarvis), Jeffrey McCracken (Mike Gallagher), Frank Drescher (Carolyn), Gwil Richards (Mr. Morgan), James T. Jarnagin (Bobby Bryant), Ed Wright (Mr. Wislon), Kerry Arquette (Anne), Patricia Wilson (Mrs. Gallagher), Beatrice Manley (Marge Trent), Billy Beck (Sheriff), Nicole Keller (Elizabeth).

STRANGER IS WATCHING, A (1982)
    Director: Sean S. Cunningham
Kate Mulgrew (Sharon Martin), Rip Torn (Artie Taggart), James Naughton (Steve Peterson), Barbara Baxley (Lally), Shawn Von Schreiber (Julie Peterson), James Russo (Ronald Thompson), Stephen Joyce (Detective).

STRANGER ON THE THIRD FLOOR (1940)
    Director: Boris Ingster
Peter Lorre (the Stranger), Elisha Cook, Jr. (Joe Briggs), Ethel Griffies (Mrs. Kane), Charles Halton (Meng), Cliff Clark (Martin), Oscar O'Shea (the Judge), Margaret Tallichet (Jane), Alec Craig (Defense Attorney), Charles Waldron (District Attorney), Otto Hoffman (Police Surgeon), John McGuire (Michael), Bud Osborne, Paul McVey, Emory Parnell.

STRANGER WITHIN, THE (TVM-1974) - 10-1-74
    Director: Lee Phillips
Barbara Eden (Ann Collins), George Grizzard (David Collins), Joyce Van Patten (Phyllis), David Doyle (Bob), Nehemiah Persoff (Dr. Klein).

STRANGE WORLD OF ZE DO CAIXAO, THE (1969-Braz.) (A.K.A. "O Estranho Mundo de Ze do Caixao")
    Director: Jose Mojica Marins
Jose Mojica Marins, Luiz Sergio Person, Rosavio Cacador, Iris Bruzzi, Jorge Michel.

STRANGLER, THE (1963)
    Director: Burt Topper
Victor Buono (Leo Kroll), Ellen Corby (Mrs. Kroll), David McLean (Lt. Benson), Baynes Barron (Sgt. Clyde), Jenane Bates (Clara), Russ Bender (Dr. Sanford), Byron Morrow (Dr. Morton), Diane Sayer (Barbara), Wally Campo (Eggerton), Davey Davison

(Tally), Mimi Dillard (Thelma),
Selette Cole (Helen), Michael M.
Ryan (Posner), Robert Cranford
(Jack Rosten), James Sikking (artist), Victor Masi (attendant), John
Yates (intern).

STRANGLER OF BLACKMOOR
CASTLE, THE (1963-Ger.) (A. K. A.
"Der Wurger von Schloss Blackmoor")
Director: Harald Reinl
Karin Dor, Ingmar Zeisberg, Harry
Fiebauer, Rudolf Furnau.

STRANGLER OF THE SWAMP (1945)
Director: Frank Wisbar
Rosemary LaPlanche (Maria),
Robert Barrat, Charles Middleton,
Blake Edwards, Frank Conlan,
Effie Parnell, Nolan Leary, Virginia
Farmer, Theresa Lyon.

STRANGLER OF THE TOWER (1966-
Ger.)
Director: Hans Mehringer
Charles Regnier, Kai Fisher, Hans
Reiser, Adi Berber, Christa Linder,
Ruth Jecklin, Ellen Schwiers, Gisela
Lorenz.

STRANGLERS OF BOMBAY, THE
(1959)
Director: Terence Fisher
Guy Rolfe (Capt. Lewis), George
Pastell (High Priest), Allan Cuthbertson (Connaught-Smith), Marne
Maitland (Patel Shari), Jan Holden
(Mary), Andrew Cruickshank (Col.
Henderson), Roger Delgado (Bundar),
Marie Devereux (Karim), John Harvey (Burns), Tutte Lemkow (Ram
Das), Michael Nightingale (Flood),
Steven Scott (Walters), Paul Stassino
(Silver), David Spenser (Gopali),
Margaret Gordon (Dorothy Flood),
Jack McNaughton (Corporal Roberts),
Ewen Solon (camel vendor).

STROKE OF A THOUSAND MILLIONS,
A (1966-Span./Ital./Fr.) (A. K. A.
"Un Golpe de Mil Millones")
Director: Paolo Heusch
Rik von Nutter, Marilu Tolo, Eduardo
Fajardo, Maximo Pietrobon.

STRONGER THAN DEATH (1915)
Director: Joseph de Grasse
Lon Chaney, Sr., Louise Lovely,
Millard D. Wilson, Arthur Shirley.

STRONGEST MAN IN THE WORLD,
THE (1975)

Director: Vincent McEveety
Kurt Russell (Dexter Riley), Cesar
Romero (A. J. Arno), Joe Flynn (Dean
Higgins), Eve Arden (Harriet), Dick
Van Patten (Harry), Phil Silvers (Krinkle), Michael McGreevey (Schuyler),
William Schallert (Quigley), Harold
Gould (Dietz), Dick Bakalyan (Cookie),
Benson Fong (Ah Fong), James
Gregory (Chief Blair).

STUDENT BODIES (1981)
Director: Mickey Rose
Kristen Riter (Toby), Matthew Goldsby
(Hardy), Richard Brando (the Breather), Joe Flood (Mr. Dumpkin),
Mimi Weddell (Miss Munsley), Joe
Talarowski (Principal Peters), Carl
Jacobs (Dr. Sigmund), Janice E.
O'Malley (Nurse Krud), Peggy Cooper
(Ms. Van Dyke).

STUDENT OF PRAGUE, THE (1913-
Ger.) (A. K. A. "A Bargain with
Satan", "Der Student von Prag",
"Asylum of Horror")
Director: Stellan Rye
Paul Wegener, Lyda Salmanova,
John Gottowt, Grete Berger, Fritz
Weldemann, Lother Korner.

STUDENT OF PARGUE, THE (1926-
Ger.) (A. K. A. "The Man Who
Cheated Life", "Der Student von
Prag")
Director: Henrik Galleen
Conrad Veidt (Baldwin), Werner
Krauss (Scapinelli), Agnes Esterhazy,
Eliza La Porta, Ferdinand von Alten.

STUDENT OF PRAGUE, THE (1935-
Ger.) (A. K. A. "Der Student von
Prag")
Director: Arthur Robinson
Anton Walbrook/Adolf Wohlbruk,
Dorothea Wieck, Erich Fielder,
Theodore Loos, Volker von Collande,
Franz Zimmermann.

STUDY IN SCARLET, A (1933)
Director: Edwin L. Marin
Reginald Owen (Sherlock Holmes),
Anna May Wong (Mrs. Pyke), June
Clyde (Eileen Forrester), John
Warburton (John Stanford), Allan
Dinehart (Thaddeus Merrydew),
Warburton Gamble (Dr. Watson),
Alan Mowbray (Insp. Lestrade), Billy
Bevan (Will Swallow), J. M. Kerrigan
(Jabez Wilson), Doris Lloyd (Mrs.
Murphy), Leila Bennett (Dolly),
Wyndham Standing (Capt. Pyke),
Halliwell Hobbes (Malcolm Dearing),

Temple Pigott (Mrs. Hudson), Tetsu
Komai (Ah Yet), Cecil Reynolds (Baker).

STUDY IN TERROR, A (1965)
     Director: James Hill
John Neville (Sherlock Holmes),
Donald Houston (Dr. Watson), An-
thony Quayle (Dr. Murray), John
Farser (Lord Carfax), Robert Morley
(Mycroft Holmes), Adrienne Corri
(Angela Osborne), Frank Finlay
(Insp. Lestrade), Barbara Windsor
(Annie Chapman), Judi Dench (Sally),
Cecil Parker (Prime Minister),
Peter Carsten (Max Steiner), Barbara
Leake (Mrs. Hudson), Barry Jones
(Duke of Shires), John Cairney (Mi-
chael), Dudley Foster (Home Secre-
tary), Georgia Brown (saloon singer),
Charles Regnier, Patrick Newell,
Edina Ronay, Kay Walsh.

SUCCUBUS (1968-Ger.) (A. K. A.
"Necronomicon - Gertraumte Sunden",
"Necronomicon - Dreamed Sins")
     Director: Jesus Franco
Janine Reynaud (Lorna), Howard
Vernon (Kapp), Michel Lemoine
(Pierce), Jack Taylor (Bill Mulligan),
Adrian Hoven, Nathalie Nord, Pier
A. Caminneci.

SUCKER MONEY (1933)
     Director: Dorothy Reid & Mel-
        ville Shyer
Mischa Auer (Swami Yomurda), Phyl-
lis Barrington (Claire Walton), Ralph
Lewis (John Walton), Mae Busch
(Mame), Fletcher Norton (Lukis),
Earl McCarthy (Jimmy Reeves),
Al Bridge, Mona Lisa, Anita Faye.

SUGAR HILL (1974)
     Director: Paul Maslansky
Marki Bey (Diana 'Sugar' Hill), Ro-
bert Quarry (Morgan), Don Pedro
Colley (Baron Samedi), Betty Anne
Rees (Celeste), Richard Lawson
(Valentine), Zara Culley (Mama
Maitresse), Larry D. Johnson (Lang-
ston), Charles Robinson (Fabulous),
Ed Geldhart (O'Brien), Rick Hagood
(Tank Watson), Thomas C. Carroll
(Baker), Albert J. Baker (George),
Raymond E. Simpson (King), Charles
Krohn (Capt. Merrill), Jack Bell
(Parkhurst), Judy Hanson (masseuse),
Tony Brubaker (head zombie), Peter
Harrell III (police photographer).

SUICIDE CLUB, THE (1914)
     Director: Maurice Elvey

Montagu Love, Fred Groves, Elizabeth Risdon, M. Gray Murray, A. V.
Bramble.

SUICIDE CLUB, THE (TVM-1973) -
     2-13-73
     Director: Bill Glenn
Peter Haskell (Tommy Kennicot),
Margot Kidder (Gerry Totten), Joseph
Wiseman (Silverado), Ivor Francis
(Jay Tileman), Maxine Stuart (Mrs.
Higbee), George Coulouris (Mullery),
Logan Ramsey (Pastorius), Jason
Wingreen (Cribbins), E. J. Andre
(Coleman Phipps), Ellen Weston (Les-
lie Woodruff), Ron Rifkin (Chanie
Summerhayes).

SUICIDE MISSION (1971-Mex.) (A. K. A.
     "Mision Suicida")
     Director: Federico Curiel
Santo, Lorena Velazquez, Elsa
Cardenas, Patricia Ferrer, Roxana
Bellini, Guillermo Galvez.

SUMMERFIELD (1977-Australia)
     Director: Ken Hannam
Nick Tate (Simon Robinson), Charles
Tingwell (Dr. Miller), John Walters
(David Abbott), Michelle Jarman (Sally
Abbott), Elizabeth Alexander (Jenny
Abbott), Max Cullen (Jim Tate),
Sheila Florance (Miss Gleeson),
Geraldine Turner (Betty Tate), Isabel
Harley (Miss Turner), Adrian Wright
(Peter Flynn), Joy Westmore (Mrs.
Shields), David Smeed (Mark), Max
Fairchild (Joe Baxter), Barry Donnelly
(Sgt. Potter).

SUNDAY OF LIVE, THE (1965-Fr. /
     Ger. /Ital.) (A. K. A. "Le Dimanche
     de la Vie")
     Director: Jean Herman
Danielle Darrieux, Jean-Pierre
Moulin, Olivier Hussenot, Francoise
Arnaul, Berthe Bovy.

SUNSET BOULEVARD (1950)
     Director: Billy Wilder
William Holden (Joe Gillis), Gloria
Swanson (Norma Desmond), Eric
Von Stroheim (Max von Mayerling),
Nancy Olson (Betty Schaefer), Fred
Clark (Sheldrake), Lloyd Gough (Mo-
rino), Jack Webb (Artie Green),
Franklyn Farnum (undertaker), Larry
J. Blake (1st finance man), Charles
Dayton (2nd finance man), H. B. War-
ner, Buster Keaton, Hedda Hopper,
Cecil B. DeMille, Jay Livingston,
Ray Evans, Anna Q. Nilsson, Bere-
nice Mosk (themselves), Tommy

Ivo (boy), Ken Christy (Captain of Homicide), Michael Brandon (salesman), Gertrude Astor, Virginia Randolph, Eva Novak, Frank O'Connor (courtiers), Eddie Dew (assistant coroner), E. Mason Hopper (doctor), Ottola Nesmith (woman), Len Hendry (police sergeant), Gerry Ganzer (Connie), Robert E. O'Connor (Jonesy), Ruth Clifford (Sheldrake's secretary), Stan Johnson (1st assistant director), William Sheehan (2nd assistant director), Howard Negley (Captain of Police), Gertie Messinger (hairdresser), John Skins Miller (electrician).

SUNS OF EASTER ISLAND, THE (1971-Fr./Braz.) (A.K.A. "Les Soleils de L'ile de Paques", "Os Sois da Ilha de Pascoa")
    Director: Pierre Kast
Norma Bengell (Norma), Francoise Brion (Francoise), Alexandre Stewart (Alexandra), Jacques Charrier (Alain), Maurice Garrel (scientist), Marcello Romo, Zozimo Bulbul, Ursula Kubler-Vian, Guy Guerra, Patricia Guzman, Caros Diegues.

SUPERARGO AND THE FACELESS GIANTS (1967-Ital./Span.) (A.K.A. "Superargo e i Giganti Senza Volto", "Superargo el Gigante", "Superargo the Giant", "Il Re dei Criminali", "The King of the Criminals")
    Director: Paolo Bianchini/ Paul Maxwell
Guy Madison, Lusia Baratto/Liz Baratt, Giovanni Cianfriglia/Ken Wood, Luciano Picozzi/Alan Collins, Diana Lorys, Tomas Blanco, Aldo Sambrell.

SUPERARGO VS. DIABOLICUS (1966-Ital./Span.) (A.K.A. "Superargo contra Diabolicus")
    Director: Nick Nostro
Giovanni Cianfriglia, Gerard Tichy, Lorendana Nusciak, Monica Randall, Francisco Castillo Escalona.

SUPERBEAST (1972)
    Director: George Schenck
Harry Lauter (Stewart Victor), Craig Littler (Dr. Bill Fleming), Antoinette Bower (Dr. Alix Pardee), Vic Diaz (Diaz), Jose Romulo (Vigo), Manny Oheda (Dr. Rojas), John Garwood (Cleaver).

SUPER FUZZ (1981-Ital./U.S.)
    Director: Sergio Corbucci

Terence Hill (Dave Speed), Joanne Dru (Rosy Labouche), Ernest Borgnine (Willy Dulop), Julie Gordon (Evelyn), Herb Goldstein (Silvius), Don Sebastian (Dingo), Marc Lawrence (Torpedo), Claudio Ruffini (Tragedy Row), Sal Borghese (Paradise Alley), Sergio Smacchi (Slot Machine), Lee Sandman (Chief McEnroy).

SUPERMAN (1948)
    Director: Spencer Gordon Bennet & Thomas Carr
Kirk Alyn (Clark Kent/Superman), Noel Neill (Lois Lane), Carol Forman (Spider Lady), Tommy Bond (Jimmy Olsen), Pierre Watkin (Perry White), George Meeker (Driller), Jack Ingram (Anton), Charles King (Conrad), Charles Quigley (Dr. Hackett), Luana Walters (Lara), Nelson Leigh (Jor-el), Herbert Rawlinson (Dr. Graham), Edward Cassidy (Eben Kent), Virginia Carroll (Martha Kent), Rusty Wescoatt (Elton), Forrest Taylor (Leeds), Terry Frost (Brock), Stephen Carr (Morgan), Alan Dinehard III (Clark Kent as a boy), Ralph Hodges (Clark Kent as a teen), Robert Barron (Rozan).

SUPERMAN AND SCOTLAND YARD (1954)
    see Television: Superman (1953-57)

SUPERMAN AND THE JUNGLE DEVIL (1954)
    see Television: Superman (1953-57)

SUPERMAN AND THE MOLE MEN (1951) (A.K.A. Television: Superman - "The Unknown People" (7-20-53 & 7-27-53)
    Director: Lee Sholem
George Reeves (Clark Kent/Superman), Phyllis Coates (Lois Lane), Jeff Corey (Luke Benson), Walter Reed (Bill Corrigan), Billy Curtis, Tony Baris, Jack Branbury, Jerry Marvin (Mole Men), Stanley Andrews (Sheriff), J. Farrell MacDonald (Pop Shannon), Ray Walker (John Craig), Paul Burns (Doc Saunders), Byron Foulger (Jeff Reagan), Irene Martin (Esther Pomfrey), Phil Warren (Deputy), Stephen Carr (Eddie), Hal K. Dawson (Weber), Margia Dean (Mrs. Benson), John Phillips (Matt), Beverly Washburn

(child), Frank Reicher (hospital super-
intendent), Adrienne Marden (nurse),
John Baer (interne), Florence Lake,
Ed Hinton.

SUPERMAN FLIES AGAIN (1954)
    see Television: Superman (1953-
54)

SUPERMAN IN EXILE (1954)
    see Television: Superman (1953-
54)

SUPERMAN'S PERIL (1954)
    see Television: Superman (1953-
54)

SUPERMAN - THE MOVIE (1978)
    Director: Richard Donner
Christopher Reeve (Clark Kent/
Superman), Marlon Brando (Jor-El),
Gene Hackman (Lex Luthor), Margot
Kidder (Lois Lane), Ned Beatty
(Otis), Jackie Cooper (Perry White),
Glenn Ford (Pa Kent), Valerie
Perrine (Eve Teschmacher), Marc
McClure (Jimmy Olsen), Susannah
York (Lara), Phyllis Baxter (Ma
Kent), Jeff East (young Clark Kent),
Terence Stamp (General Zod), Maria
Schell (Bond-Ah), Jack O'Halloran
(Non), Sarah Douglas (Ursa), Trevor
Howard (1st Elder), Harry Andrews
(2nd Elder), William Russell (8th
Elder), John Stuart (10th Elder),
Phil Brown (State Senator), Diane
Sherry (Lana Lang), Larry Hagman
(Colonel), Aaron Smolinski (Superman
as a baby), Jeff Atcheson (coach),
Rex Reed (himself), Jill Ingham (Per-
ry's secretary), Weston Gavin (mugger),
George Harris, II (Officer Mooney),
Rex Everhardt (desk sergeant), Jayne
Tottman (little girl), Paul Tuerpe
(Sgt. Hayley), Bill Bailey (State
Senator), Chief Tug Smith (Indian
Chief), Roy Stevens (Warden), Noel
Neill (woman on train), Kirk Alyn
(man on train), Alan Tilvern, Mark
Wynter, Vass Anderson, James
Garbutt, Daivd Neal, Penelope Lee,
Lee Quigley, John Hollis, Michael
Gover, Alan Cullen, David Petrou,
Robert Henderson, James Brocking-
ton, John F. Parker, Ray Evans,
Miquel Brown, Brad Flock, Billy J.
Mitchell, Larry Lamb, John Cassady,
Antony Scott, Su Shifrin, Vincent
Marzello, Lisa Hilboldt, Benjamin
Feitelson, Leueen Willoughby, Pieter
Stuyck, Stephen Kahan, Randy Jur-
genson, Colin Skeaping, Paul Avery,
Ray Hassett, Matt Russo, Bo Rucker,

David Maxt, Michael Harrigan,
Raymond Thompson, John Cording,
Oz Clarke, Frank Lazarus, Lawrence
Trimble, David Calder, Keith Alex-
ander, Brian Protheroe, Robert
Whelan, Norwick Duff, Michael
Ensign, Graham McPherson, Robert
O'Neill, John Ratzenberger, Burnell
Tucker, Norman Warwick, Colin
Etherington, Chuck Julian, David
Yorston, Robert MacLeod, Catherine
Reilly.

SUPERMAN II (1980)
    Director: Richard Lester
Christopher Reeve (Clark Kent/Super-
man), Margot Kidder (Lois Lane),
Terence Stamp (General Zod), Sarah
Douglas (Ursa), Jack O'Halloran (Non),
Gene Hackman (Lex Luthor), Jackie
Cooper (Perry White), Susannah
York (Lara), Valerie Perrine (Eve
Teschmacher), E.G. Marshall (the
President), Marc McClure (Jimmy
Olsen), Ned Beatty (Otis), Clifton
James (Sheriff), Shane Rimmer,
John Ratzenberger (controllers),
Hal Galili (man at bar), Michael
Shannon (President's aide), Leueen
Willoughby (Leueen), John Hollis
(Krypton elder), Robin Pappas (Alice),
Roger Kemp (spokesman), Anthony
Milner, Roger Brierley, Richard
Griffiths (terrorists), Alain Dehay
(gendarme), Alan Stuart (cab driver),
Melissa Wiltsie (nun), Marc Boyle
(C.R.S. man), John Morton (Nate),
Jim Dowdell (Boris), Angus McInnes
(prison warden), Elva May Hoover
(mother), Todd Woodcroft (father),
Antony Sher (bell boy), Hadley
Kay (Jason), Gordon Rollings (fish-
erman), Bill Bailey (J.J.), Peter
Whitman (Deputy), Dinny Powell
(Boog), Richard Parmentier (reporter),
Marcus D'Amico (Willie), Don Fel-
lows (General), Tony Sibbald (Presi-
dential imposter), Tommy Duggan
(diner owner), Pamela Mandell (wait-
ress), Eugene Lipinski (newsvendor),
Carl Parris, Cleon Spencer (kids),
Pepper Martin (Rocky).

SUPER MONSTER (1980-Jap.)
    Director: Noriaki Yuasa
Mach Fumiake (Kilara), Yaeko
Kojima (Marsha), Yoko Komatsu
(Mitan), Keiko Dudo (Gilge), Koichi
Maeda (Keiichi), Toshie Takada
(Keiichi's mother), Osamu Kobayashi
(voice of the Captain of the Zanon).

SUPERNATURAL (1933)

Director: Victor Halperin
Carole Lombard (Roma Courtney),
Randolph Scott (Grant Wilson),
Vivienne Osborne (Ruth Rogen),
H. B. Warner (Dr. Houston), William
Farnum (Robert 'Nicky' Hammond),
Alan Dinehard (Paul Bavian), Beryl
Mercer (Madame Gourjan), Willard
Robertson (Warden), Lyman Wil-
liams (John Courtney's ghost), George
Burr McAnnan (Max).

SUPERNATURAL (1981-Span.) (A. K. A.
"Sobrenatural")
Director: Eugenio Martin
Cristina Galbo, Maximo Valverde,
Candida Losada, Gerardo Maya,
Juan Jesus Valverde, Lola Lemos.

SUPER-SLEUTH (1937)
Director: Ben Stoloff
Jack Oakie (Willard Martin), Ann
Sothern (Mary Strand), Edgar
Kennedy (Lt. Garrison), Eduardo
Ciannelli (Prof. Herman), Joan
Woodbury (Doris Dunne), Willie
Best (Warts), Alan Bruce (Larry
Frank), Paul Guilfoyle (Gibbons),
Paul Hurst (motor cycle cop),
George Rosener (policeman), Philip
Morris (Sullivan), Fred A. Kelsey
(jailer), Bradley Page (Ralph War-
ing), Robert E. O'Connor (Casey),
Alec Craig (Eddie, the doorman),
Dick Rush (Grimes), William Corson
(Beckett), Richard Lane (Barker).

SUPER STOOGES VS. THE WONDER
WOMEN (1975-Span.)
Director: Alfonso Brescia
Yueh Hua, Karen Yeh, Nick Jordan,
Mark Hannibal, Genie Woods, Ricardo
Pizzuti, Malisa Longo, Kirsten Gilles.

SURVIVOR, THE (1981-Australia)
Director: David Hemmings
Robert Powell (Keller), Jenny
Agutter (Hobbs), Joseph Cotten
(the Priest), Angela Punch Mc-
Gregor (Beth Rogan), Peter Sumner
(Tewson), Ralph Cotterill (Slater),
Adrian Wright (Goodwin).

SUSPIRIA (1977-Ital. /U. S.)
Director: Dario Argento
Jessica Harper (Susy Banyon),
Joan Bennett (Madame Blank),
Alida Valli (Miss Tanner), Udo
Kier (Frank), Flavio Bucci (Daniel),
Stefania Casini (Sara), Miguel
Bose (Mark), Barbara Magnolfi (Olga),
Susanna Javicoli (Sonia), Margherita
Horowitz (a teacher), Jacopo Mariani

(Albert), Fulvio Mingozzi (taxi driver),
Renato Zamengo (Caroline), Rudolf
Schundler (Milius), Eva Axen (Pat),
Giuseppe Transocchi (Pavlo).

SVENGALI (1927-Ger.)
Director: Gennaro Righelli &
H. Grund
Paul Wegener (Svengali), Anita Dorris,
Alexander Granach, Andre Mattoni.

SVENGALI (1931)
Director: Archie Mayo
John Barrymore (Svengali), Marian
Marsh (Trilby), Bramwell Fletcher
(Billee), Donald Crisp (the Laird),
Luis Alberni (Gacko), Lumsden
Hare (Taffy), Carmel Myers (Honori),
Paul Porcasi (Manager).

SVENGALI (1954)
Director: Noel Langley
Donald Wolfit (Svengali), Hildegarde
Neff (Trilby), Terence Morgan
(Billy), Derek Bond (the Laird),
David Kossoff (Gecko), Alfie Bass
(Carrel), Noel Purcell (Patrick O'Fer-
ral), Harry Secombe (Barizel),
David Oxley (Dodor), Paul Rogers
(Taffy), Joan Haythorne (Mrs. Bagot),
Peter Illing (Police Inspector), Hubert
Gregg (Durien), Martin Boddey, Toots
Pound, Arnold Bell, Cyril Smith, Rica
Fox, Joan Heal, Neville Phillips.

SWAMP THING (1982)
Director: Wes Craven
Louis Jourdan (Arcane), Adrienna
Barbeau (Alice Cable), Ray Wise
(Dr. Alec Holland), Nanette Brown
(Linda Holland), Nicholas Worth
(Bruno), Don Knight (Ritter), David
Hess (1st henchman), Al Ruban
(Charlie), Dick Durock (Swamp Thing),
Ben Bates (Arcane monster), Tommy
Madden (Bruno monster).

SWARM, THE (1978)
Director: Irwin Allen
Michal Caine (Brad Crane), Katharine
Ross (Helena), Henry Fonda (Dr.
Walter Krim), Richard Widmark
(Gen. Slater), Olivia de Havilland
(Maureen Schuster), Fred Mac-
Murray (Clarence), Ben Johnson (Fe-
lix), Lee Grant (Anne MacGregor),
Jose Ferrer (Dr. Andrews), Richard
Chamberlain (Dr. Hubbard), Patty
Duke Astin (Rita Baird), Slim Pickens
(Jud Hawkins), Cameron Mitchell (Gen.
Thompson), Donald 'Red' Barry (Pete
Harris), Alejandro Rey (Dr. Mar-
tinez), Bradford Dillman (Major

Baker), Morgan Paull (Dr. Newman), Robert Varney (Mr. Durant), Patrick Culliton (Sheriff Morrison), Chris Petersen (Hal), Doria Cook (Mrs. Durant), Christian Juttner (Paul Durant), Arthur Space (engineer), John Williams (launching officer), Mara Cook (secretary), Stephen Powers (radarman), Steve Marlo (pilot No. 1), Ernie Orsatti (duty officer), John Furlong (cameraman), Jerry Toomey (Eddie), Joey Eisnach (bee boy), Chris Capen (Lieutenant), Tony Haig (Officer No. 2), Bill Snider (radarman No. 2), Arell Blanton (sergeant), George Simmons (nurse), Trent Dolan (radio sergeant), Phil Montgomery (mechanic), Marcia Nicholson (Captain), Art Balinger (radio announcer), Frank Blair (himself), Chuck Hayward (standby engineer), Michael Seehan (1st airman), Howard Culver (2nd airman), Glenn Charles Lewis (chemical warfare guard), Jim Mills.

SWEET KILL (1972) (A. K. A. "The Arousers")
Director: Curtis Hanson
Tab Hunter (Eddie Collins), Cheri Latimer (Lauren), Isabel Jewell (Mrs. Cole), Nadyne Turney (Barbara), John Aprea (Lauren's boyfriend), Kate McKeown (Sherry), Linda Leider (Bickie), Roberta Collins (call girl), Sandy Kenyon, Brandy Herred, Josh Green, Angel Fox, Rory Guy.

SWEET SOUND OF DEATH (1965-U.S./Span.)
Director: Javier Seto
Dianik Zurakowska, Emil Cape, Alba, Victor Israel, Sun Sanders, Daniel Blum.

SWEET SUGAR (1972)
Director: Michel Levesque
Phyllis E. Davis, Timothy Brown, Ella Edwards, Pamela Collins, Cliff Osomnd, Jackie Giroux, Albert Cole, Jim Houghton, Daryl Severns, James Whitworth.

SWEET, SWEET RACHEL (TVM-1971) - 10-2-71
Director: Sutton Roley
Alex Dreier (Dr. Lucas Darrow), Stefanie Powers (Rachel Stanton), Pat Hingle (Arthur Piper), Louise Latham (Lillian Piper), Steve Ihnat (Dr. Tyler), Brenda Scott (Nora Piper), Chris Robinson (Carey), John Alvin (surgeon), Mark Tapscott (Houseman), Len Wayland (minister), John Hiller-

man (medical examiner), Rod McCarey (Paul Stanton), William Bryant (doctor).

SWORD AND THE DRAGON, THE (1956-Sov.) (A. K. A. "Ilya Mourometz", "The Epic Hero and the Beast")
Director: Alexander Ptushko
Boris Andreyev (Ilya Muromets), Andrei Abrikosov (Prince Vladimir), Natalia Medvedeva (Princess Apraxia), Shukur Burkanov (Kalin-Tsar), Ninel Myshkova (Vasilisa).

SWORD AND THE SORCERER, THE (1982)
Director: Albert Pyun
Lee Horsley (Talon), Kathleen Beller (Alana), Richard Lynch (Cromwell), Simon MacCorkindale (Mikah), George Maharis (Machelli), Richard Moll (Xusia), Robert Tessier (Verdugo), Anthony DeLongis (Rodrigo), Nina Van Pallandt (Malia), Jeff Corey (Craccus), Anna Bjorn (Elizabeth), Joe Regalbuto (Darius), Christopher Cary (King Richard).

SWORD IN THE STONE, THE (1963) - animated
Director: Wolfgang Reitherman
Voices: Ricky Sorenson (Wart), Sebastian Cabot (Sir Ector), Karl Swenson (Merlin), Junius Matthews (Archimedes), Alan Napier (Sir Pelinore), Norman Alden (Kay), Martha Wentworth (Madame Mim/Granny Squirrel), Ginny Tyler (little girl squirrel), Barbara Jo Allen (scullery maid), Richard Reitherman, Robert Reitherman.

SWORD OF ALI BABA, THE (1964)
Director: Virgil Vogel
Peter Mann (Ali Baba), Jocelyn Lane (Amara), Gavin MacLeod (Hulagu Khan), Peter Whitney (Abou), Frank Puglia (Cassim), Frank De Kova (Baba), Morgan Woodward (Captain of the Guard), Greg Morris (Yusuf), Frank McGrath (Pindar).

SYLVIA AND THE PHANTOM (1945-Fr.) (A. K. A. "Sylvie et le Fantome")
Director: Claude Autant-Lara
Odette Joyeux, Jacques Tati, Francois Perier, Louis Salou, Jean Desailly, Pierre Larquey, Claud Marcy, Gabrielle Fontan, Marguerite Cassan.

SYSTEM OF DR. TARR AND PROF. FEATHER, THE (1972-Mex.) (A. K. A. "Dr. Tarr's Torture Dungeon")
Director: Juan Lopez Moctezuma
Claudio Brook, Ellen Sherman, Robert Dumont, Martin LaSalle, Arthur Hansel.

TAG (1982)
Director: Nick Castle
Robert Carradine (Alex), Linda Hamilton (Susan), Bruce Abbott (Gersh), Frazer Smith (Carpenter), Kristine DeBell (Nancy), Perry Lang (Frank), John Mengotti (Randy), Michael Winslow (Gowdy).

TALES FROM THE CRYPT (1971)
Director: Freddie Francis
Ralph Richardson (Crypt Keeper), Geoffrey Bayldon (the guide), "All Through the House": Joan Collins (Joanne Clayton), Chloe Franks (Carol Clayton), Oliver MacGreevy (Santa Claus), Martin Boddey (Richard Clayton). "Reflection of Death": Ian Hendry (Carl Maitland), Susan Denny (Mrs. Maitland), Frank Forsyth (Tramp), Angie Grant (Susan), Paul Clere (Maitland's son), Sharon Clere (Maitland's daughter). "Blind Alleys": Nigel Patrick (William Rogers), Patrick Magee (George Carter), Tony Wall (Attendant), Harry Locke (Cook), George Herbert (old blind man), John Barrard, Ernest C. Jennings, Hugo De Vernier, Carl Bernard, Chris Cannon, Louis Mansl (blind men). "Poetic Justice": Peter Cushing (Arthur Grimsdyke), Robin Phillips (James Elliot), David Markham (Edward Elliot), Ann Sears (Mrs. Carter), Robert Hutton (Mr. Baker), Edward Evans (Mr. Ramsay), Kay Adrian (Mrs. Davies), Irene Gawne (Mrs. Phelps), Clifford Earl (Police Sergeant), Manning Wilson (Vicar), Dan Caulfield (Postman), Melinda Clancy (Carter's daughter), Carlos Baker (Davies' son), Stafford Medhurse (Phelps son). "Wish You Were Here": Richard Greene (Ralph Jason), Roy Dotrice (Charles Gregory), Barbara Murray (Enid Jason), Hedger Wallace (Detective), Peter Thomas (pallbearer).

TALES OF TERROR (1962)
Director: Roger Corman
"Morella": Vincent Price (Locke), Leona Gage (Morella), Maggie Pierce (Lenora), Ed Cobb (driver). "The Black Cat": Vincent Price (Fortunato), Peter Lorre (Montresor), Joyce Jameson (Annabel), Wally Campo (bartender), Alan Dewit (Chairman), Lenny Weinrib, John Hackett (policemen). "The Case of M. Valdemar": Vincent

Price (Valdemar), Basil Rathbone (Carmichael), David Frankham (Dr. James), Debra Paget (Helene), Scotty Brown (servant).

TALES THAT WITNESS MADNESS (1973)
Director: Freddie Francis
Clinic Link Episode: Jack Hawkins (Nicholas), Donald Pleasence (Dr. Tremayne).
"Mr. Tiger": Georgia Brown (Fat Patterson), Donald Houston (Sam Patterson), Russell Lewis (Paul Patterson), David Wood (Tutor).
"Penny Farthing": Suzy Kendall (Ann/Beatrice), Peter McEnery (Timothy Patrick), Frank Forsyth (Uncle Albert), Beth Morris (Polly), Neil Kennedy, Richard Connaught (removal men).
"Mel": Joan Collins (Bella Thompson), Michael Jayston (Brian Thompson).
"Luau": Kim Novak (Auriol Pageant), Michael Petrovitch (Kimo), Mary Tamm (Ginny Pageant), Lesley Nunnerley (Vera), Leon Lissek (Keoki), Zohra Segal (Malia).

TALK OF THE DEVIL (1977) - short
Director: Francis Serle
Hugh Lattimer (Nick Beelzebub), Suzan Farmer (Wendy), Victor Maddern (Cinders), Tim Barrett (Stephen Wallace), Robert Gallico (Harvey).

TANYA'S ISLAND (1980)
Director: Alfred Sole
D. D. Winters (Tanya), Richard Sargent (Lobo), Don McCleod (Blue, the Beast), Mariette Levesque (Kelly).

TARANTULA (1955)
Director: Jack Arnold
John Agar (Dr. Matt Hastings), Mara Corday (Stephanie Clayton), Leo G. Carroll (Prof. Gerald Deemer), Nestor Paiva (Sheriff Jack Andrews), Eddie Parker (Paul Lund), Ross Elliott (Birch), Raymond Bailey (Townsend), Ed Rand (Lt. John Nolan), Bert Holland (Barney Russell), Steve Darrell (Andy Anderson), Hank Patterson (Josh), Clint Eastwood (1st pilot), Jane Howard (co-ed secretary), Billy Wayne (Murphy), Dee Carroll (telephone operator), Tom London, Edgar Dearing (miners), James J. Hyland (Trooper Grayson), Stuart Wade (Major), Vernon Rich (Ridley), Bob Nelson (Trooper), Bing Russell (Deputy), Ray Quinn (Trooper),

Robert R. Stephenson (warehouseman),
Don Dillaway (Jim Bagney), Bud
Wolfe (bus driver), Jack Stoney
(helper), Rusty Wescoatt (driver).

TARANTULAS: THE DEADLY
   CARGO (TVM-1977) - 12-28-77
   Director: Stuart Hagmann
Claude Akins (Bert Springer), Pat
Hingle (Doc Hodgins), Deborah
Winters (Cindy Beck), Charles
Frank (Joe Harmon), Bert Remsen
(Mayor Douglas), Sandy McPeak
(Chief Beasley), Tom Atkins (Buddy),
Charles Siebert (Rich Finley),
Noelle North (Honey Lamb), Howard
Hesseman (Fred), John Harkins
(Sylvan), Penelope Windust (Gloria
Bealsey), Edwin Owens (Frank),
Jerome Guardino (H. L. Williams),
Matthew Laborteaux (Chuck Beck),
Lanny Horn (Harry Weed).

TARGET EARTH! (1954)
   Director: Sherman Rose
Richard Denning (Frank), Virginia
Grey (Vicki), Kathleen Crowley
(Nora), Richard Reeves (Jim),
Whit Bissell (scientist), Arthur
Space (General), Steve Pendleton
(Colonel), House Peters, Jr.
(technician), Jim Drake (Lieuten-
ant), Mort Marshall (Otis), Robert
Roark (Davis).

TARGET FOR KILLING (1966-
   Australia/Ital.) (A.K.A. "Das
   Geheimnis der Gelben Monche",
   "Il Segreto dei Frati Gialli", "The
   Secret of the Yellow Monks")
   Director: Manfred R. Kohler
Stewart Granger, Karin Dor, Rupert
Davies, Curt Jurgens, Klaus Kinski,
Erika Remberg, Adolfo Celi, Scila
Gabel, Mollie Peters.

TARGETS (1967)
   Director: Peter Bogdanovich
Boris Karloff (Byron Orlock), Sandy
Baron (Kip Larkin), Tim O'Kelly
(Bobby Thompson), Nancy Hsueh
(Jenny), Peter Bogdanovich (Sammy
Michaels), James Brown (Robert
Thompson, Sr.), Arthur Peterson
(Ed Loughlin), Mary Jackson (Char-
lotte Thompson), Tanya Morgan
(Ilene Thompson), Monty Landis
(Marshall Smith), Mark Dennis
(salesman), Daniel Ades (chauffeur),
Paul Condylis (drive-in manager),
Stafford Morgan (salesman at gunshop).

TARZAN AND HIS MATE (1934)

   Director: Cedric Gibbons
Johnny Weismuller (Tarzan), Maureen
O'Sullivan (Jane Parker), Neil Hamil-
ton (Harry Holt), Paul Cavanagh
(Martin Arlington), Forrester Harvey
(Beamish), Desmond Roberts (Vanness),
Doris Lloyd (Mrs. Cutten), Nathan
Curry (Saidi), William Stack (Pierce).

TARZAN AND THE AMAZONS (1944)
   Director: Kurt Neumann
Johnny Weismuller (Tarzan), Brenda
Joyce (Jane), Johnny Sheffield (Boy),
Maria Ouspenskaya (Queen), Barton
MacLane (Ballister), J. M. Kerrigan
(Splivers), Don Douglas (Andres),
Steven Geray (Brenner), Henry
Stephenson (Henderson), Shirley O'Ha-
ra (Athena).

TARZAN AND THE GOLDEN LION
   (1926)
   Director: J. P. McGowan
James H. Pierce (Tarzan), Boris
Karloff (Waziri Chieftan), Dorothy
Dunbar (Jane), Edna Murphy (Flora
Hawks), Fred Peters (Esteban
Miranda), Harold Goodwin, Liu Yu-
Ghing, D'Arcy Corrigan, Robert
Bolder.

TARZAN AND THE GREAT RIVER
   (1966)
   Director: Robert Day
Mike Henry (Tarzan), Jan Murray
(Capt. Sam Bishop), Rafer Johnson
(Barcuna), Diana Millay (Dr. Ann
Phillips), Manuel Padilla, Jr. (Pepe),
Paulo Grazindo (Professor).

TARZAN AND THE HUNTRESS (1946)
   Director: Kurt Neumann
Johnny Weismuller (Tarzan), Brenda
Joyce (Jane), Johnny Sheffield
(Boy), Patricia Morrison (Tanya),
Barton MacLnae (Wier), Charles
Trowbridge (King Farrod), Wallace
Scott (Smithers), Ted Hecht (Prince
Ozira), John Warburton (Marley),
Maurice Tauzin (Prince Suli), Mickey
Simpson (Monak).

TARZAN AND THE JUNGLE BOY
   (1968)
   Director: Robert Day
Mike Henry (Tarzan), Alizia Gur
(Myrna Claudel), Rafer Johnson
(Nagambi), Steve Bond (Buhura),
Ronald Gans (Eric Brunik), Ed John-
son (Ken Matson).

TARZAN AND THE LEOPARD WOMAN
   (1945)

Director: Kurt Neumann
Johnny Weismuller (Tarzan), Brenda
Joyce (Jane), Johnny Sheffield (Boy),
Acquanetta (Lea), Edgar Barrier
(Lazar), Tommy Cook (Kimba),
Anthony Caruso (Mongo), Dennis
Hoey (Commissioner), George J.
Lewis (Corporal), King Kong Kashey,
Robert Barron, Doris Lloyd, George
Renavent, Marek Windheim, Iris
Flores, Lillian Molieri, Kay Solinas,
Helen Gerald, Louis Mercier.

TARZAN AND THE LOST SAFARI
(1956)
Director: Bruce Humberstone
Gordon Scott (Tarzan), Robert
Beatty (Tusker Hawkins), George
Coulouris (Carl Kraski), Wilfrid
Hyde-White (Doodles Fletcher),
Betta St. John (Diana Penrod),
Peter Arne (Dick Penrod), Yolande
Donlan (Gamage Dean), Orlando
Martins (Chief Ogonooro).

TARZAN AND THE MERMAIDS
(1947)
Director: Robert Florey
Johnny Weismuller (Tarzan), Brenda
Joyce (Jane), Linda Christian (Mara),
George Zucco (Palanth), Gustavo
Rojo (Tiko), Fernando Wagner
(Verga), Andrea Palma (Luana),
John Laurenz (Benji), Edward
Ashley (Commissioner), Matthew
Boulton (British Inspector General).

TARZAN AND THE SHE-DEVIL (1952)
Director: Kurt Neumann
Lex Barker (Tarzan), Joyce MacKen-
zie (Jane), Monique Van Vooren
(Lyra), Raymond Burr (Vargo),
Tom Conway (Fidel), Robert Bice
(Maka), Henry Brandon (M'Tara),
Michael Granger (Lavar), Mike
Ross (Selim).

TARZAN AND THE SLAVE GIRL
(1949) (A. K. A. "Tarzan and the
Jungle Queen")
Director: Lee Sholem
Lex Barker (Tarzan), Vanessa
Brown (Jane), Robert Alda (Neil),
Hurd Hatfield (the Prince), Denise
Darcel (Lola), Anthony Caruso
(Sengo), Arthur Shields (Randini
doctor), Robert Warwick (High
Priest), Mary Ellen Kay (Moana),
Tito Renaldo (Chief's son), Rose-
mary Bertrand, Shirley Ballard,
Gwen Caldwell, Josephine Parra,
Martha Clemmons, Mona Knox,
Jackee Waldron (slave girls).

TARZAN AND THE TRAPPERS (1958)
Director: H. Bruce Humber-
stone
Gordon Scott (Tarzan), Eve Brent,
Rickie Sorenson, Leslie Bradley,
Maurice Marsac.

TARZAN AND THE VALLEY OF GOLD
(1965)
Director: Robert Day
Mike Henry (Tarzan), Nancy Kovack
(Sophia Renault), Don Megowan (Mr.
Train), David Opatoshu (Vinaro),
Eduardo Noriega (Talmadge), Manuel
Padilla, Jr. (Ramel), John Kelly
(Voss), Enrique Lucero (Perez),
Francisco Riquerio (Manco), Carlos
Rivas (Romulo), Oswald Olvera
(Antonio), Frank Brandstetter (Ruiz),
Jorge Beirute (Rodriquez).

TARZAN ESCAPES (1936)
Director: James McKay, John
Farrow & Richard Thorpe
Johnny Weismuller (Tarzan), Maureen
O'Sullivan (Jane Parker), John
Buckler (Capt. Fry), Benita Hume
(Rita Parker), William Henry (Eric
Parker), Herbert Mundin (Herbert
Henry Rawlins), E. E. Clive (Masters),
Darby Jones (Bomba).

TARZAN FINDS A SON (1939)
Director: Richard Thorpe
Johnny Weismuller (Tarzan), Maureen
O'Sullivan (Jane), Johnny Sheffield
(Boy), Ian Hunter (Mr. Lancing),
Frieda Inescort (Mrs. Lancing),
Henry Wilcoxon (Mr. Sande), Laraine
Day (Mrs. Richard Lancing), Morton
Lowry (Richard Lancing), Henry
Stephenson (Sir Thomas Lancing).

TARZAN GOES TO INDIA (1962)
Director: John Guillermin
Jock Mahoney (Tarzan), Mark Dana
(O'Hara), Leo Gordon (Bryce), Simi
(Princess Kamara), Feroz Khan
(Rama/Raju Kumar), Murad (Ma-
harajah), Jai (Jai, the Elephant Boy),
Jagdish Raaj (Raaj), Aaron Joseph
(Drive), Pehelwan Ameer (Mooty),
C. Raghaven (Chakra), Abas Khan
(Pilot), K. S. Tripathi (Conservation
officer).

TARZAN OF THE APES (1971)
Director: Scott Sidney
Elmo Lincoln (Tarzan), Enid Markey
(Jane Porter), True Boardman (Lord
Greystoke), Kathleen Kirkham (Lady
Greystoke), Thomas Jefferson (Prof.
Porter), George French (Binns), Colin
Kenny.

TARZAN'S DEADLY SILENCE (1970)
see Television: Tarzan - "The
Deadly Silence" (10-28-66 & 11-
4-66)

TARZAN'S DESERT MYSTERY (1943)
Director: William Thiele
Johnny Weismuller (Tarzan), Johnny
Sheffield (Boy), Nancy Kelly (Connie
Bryce), Otto Kruger (Hendrix),
Robert Lowery (Prince Selim),
Joe Sawyer (Karl), Lloyd Corrigan
(the Sheik).

TARZAN'S FIGHT FOR LIFE (1958)
Director: H. Bruce Humberstone
Gordon Scott (Tarzan), Eve Brent (Jane),
Carl Benton Reid (Dr. Sturdy), Harry
Lauter (Dr. Ken Warwick), Woody
Strode (Ramo), James Edwards
(Futa), Rickie Sorensen (Tahut),
Jil Jarmyn (Anne Sturdy).

TARZAN'S GREATEST ADVENTURE
(1959)
Director: John Guillermin
Gordon Scott (Tarzan), Anthony
Quayle (Slade), Sean Connery
(O'Bannion), Niall MacGinnis
(Kruger), Sara Shane (Angie), Al
Mulock (Dino), Scilla Gabel.

TARZAN'S HIDDEN JUNGLE (1955)
Director: Harold Schuster
Gordon Scott (Tarzan), Vera Miles
(Jill Hardy), Peter Van Eyck (Dr.
Celliers), Jack Elam (Berger),
Don Beddoe (Johnson), Richard
Reeves (Reeves), Rex Ingram (Su-
kulu Makumwa), Charles Fredericks
(De Groot), Ike Jones (Malenki),
Maidie Norman (Suma), Jester
Hairston (Witch Doctor).

TARZAN'S JUNGLE REBELLION
(1967)
see Television: Tarzan - "The
Blue Stone of Heaven" (10-6-67
& 10-13-67)

TARZAN'S MAGIC FOUNTAIN (1948)
Director: Lee Sholem
Lex Barker (Tarzan), Brenda
Joyce (Jane), Albert Dekker (Trask),
Evelyn Ankers (Gloria James),
Alan Napier (Jessup), Charles
Drake (Dodd), Henry Kulky (Vredak).

TARZAN'S NEW YORK ADVENTURE
(1942)
Director: Richard Thorpe
Johnny Weismuller (Tarzan), Maureen O'Sullivan (Jane), Johnny

Sheffield (Boy), Charles Bickford
(Buck Rand), Virginia Grey (Connie
Beach), Russell Hicks (Judge Abbot-
son), Paul Kelly (Jimmy Shields),
Chill Wills (Manchester Mountford),
Miles Mander (Portmaster), Howard
Hickman (Blake Norton).

TARZAN'S PERIL (1950)
Director: Byron Haskins
Lex Barker (Tarzan), Virginia Hus-
ton (Jane), Glenn Anders (gun smug-
gler), George Macready, Douglas
Fowley (gun-runners), Dorothy Dan-
dridge (Jungle Queen), Frederick
O'Neal (Evil Chieftan), Edward
Ashley.

TARZAN'S REVENGE (1937)
Director: D. Ross Lederman
Glenn Morris (Tarzan), Eleanor
Holm (Eleanor), Hedda Hopper (Pen-
ny), C. Henry Gordon (Ben Alleu
Bey), George Meeker (Nevin), Joseph
Sawyer (Olaf), Corbet Morris (Jigger),
George Barbier (Roger), John Lester
Johnson (Koki).

TARZAN'S SAVAGE FURY (1951)
Director: Cyril Endfield
Lex Barker (Tarzan), Dorothy Hart
(Jane), Patric Knowles (Edwards),
Charles Korvin (Rokov), Tommy
Carlton (Joey).

TARZAN'S SECRET TREASURE (1941)
Director: Richard Thorpe
Johnny Weismuller (Tarzan), Maureen
O'Sullivan (Jane), Johnny Sheffield
(Boy), Barry Fitzgerald (O'Doul),
Reginald Owen (Prof. Elliott), Tom
Conway (Medford), Philip Dorn (Van-
dermeer).

TARZAN'S THREE CHALLENGES
(1963)
Director: Robert Day
Jock Mahoney (Tarzan), Woody Strode
(Tarim Khan), Ricky Der (Kashi),
Tsuruko Kobaysahi (Cho San), Salah
Jamal (Hani), Earl Cameron (Mang),
Anthony Chinn (Tor), Christopher
Carlos (Sechung), Robert Hu (Nari).

TARZAN THE APE MAN (1932)
Director: W.S. Van Dyke II
Johnny Weismuller (Tarzan), Maureen
O'Sullivan (Jane Parker), Neil Hamil-
ton (Harry Holt), C. Aubrey Smith
(James Parker), Forrester Harvey
(Beamish), Doris Lloyd (Mrs. Cut-
ten), Ivory Williams (Riano).

TARZAN THE APE MAN (1959)
Director: Joseph Newman
Denny Miller (Tarzan), Cesare
Danova (Holt), Joanna Barnes (Jane),
Parker), Robert Douglas (Col. Par-
ker), Thomas Yangha (Riano).

TARZAN THE APE MAN (1981)
Director: John Derek
Bo Derek (Jane Parker), Richard
Harris (Parker), Miles O'Keeffe
(Tarzan), John Phillip Law (Holt),
Steven Strong (Ivory King), Aku-
shula Selayah (Africa), Maxime Phi-
loe (Riano), Leonard Bailey (Fea-
thers), Harold Ayer, Wilfred Hyde-
White, Laurie Main (club members),
Helmut Dantine.

TARZAN THE FEARLESS (1933) -
serial in 12 episodes
Chapters: 1. "The Dive of Death",
2. "The Storm God Strikes", 3.
"Thundering Death", 4. "The Pit
of Peril", 5. "Blood Money", 6.
"Voodoo Vengeance", 7. "Caught by
Cannibals", 8. "The Creeping Ter-
ror", 9. "Eyes of Evil", 10. "The
Death Plunge", 11. "Harvest of
Hate", & 12. "Jungle Justice".
Director: Robert P. Hill
Buster Crabbe (Tarzan), Jacqueline
Wells (Mary Brooks), Frank Lack-
teen (Abdul), Mischa Auer (Eltar),
Edward Woods (Bob Hall), E. Alyn
Warren (Dr. Brooks), Philo McCul-
lough (Jeff), Carlotta Monti (Pries-
tess of Zar), Matthew Betz (Nick),
Symonia Boniface (Arab woman),
Darby Jones (head bearer), George
De Normand (guard), Al Kikume (war-
rior).

TARZAN THE MAGNIFICENT (1960)
Director: Robert Day
Gordon Scott (Tarzan), Jock Mahoney
(Coy Banton), Betta St. John (Fay
Ames), John Carradine (Abel Ban-
ton), Lionel Jeffries (Ames), Alex-
andra Stewart (Lori), Carl Cameron
(Tate), Charles Tingwell (Conway),
Al Mulock (Martin Banton), Ron
MacDonnell (Ethan Banton), Gray
Cockrell (Johnny Banton), Harry
Baird (Warrior Leader), John Sulli-
van (Winters), Christopher Carlos
(Native Chief), Thomas Duggan, Ewen
Solon, Peter Howell, George Taylor,
Jacqueline Evans, John Harrison.

TARZAN THE MIGHTY (1928) -
serial in 12 episodes
Director: Jack Nelson & Ray

Taylor
Frank Merrill (Tarzan), Natalie
Kingston (Mary Trevor), Al Fergu-
son (Black John), Bobbie Nelson
(Bobby Trevor), Lorimer Johnston
(Lord Greystoke).

TARZAN THE TIGER (1929) - serial
in 15 episodes
Director: Henry McRae
Frank Merrill (Tarzan), Natalie King-
ston (Mary Trevor), Al Ferguson
(Black John), Lillian Worth (Queen
La of Opar), Sheldon Lewis.

TARZAN TRIUMPHS (1942)
Director: William Thiele
Johnny Weismuller (Tarzan), Johnny
Sheffield (Boy), Frances Gifford
(Zandra), Stanley Ridges (Von
Reichart), Pedro de Cordoba (Pat-
riarch), Sig Ruman (Sergeant), Rex
Williams (Schmidt), Philip Van Zandt
(Bausch), Stanley Brown (Achmet).

TASTE OF BLOOD, A (1967)
Director: Herschell Gordon
Lewis
Bill Rodgers (John Stone), Elizabeth
Wilkinson (Helene Stone), Otto
Schlesinger (Dr. Howard Helsing),
Ted Schell (Lord Gold), Gail Janis
(Vivian), Eleanor Valli, Lawrence
Tobin, Thomas Wood.

TASTE OF EVIL, A (TVM-1972) -
5-13-72
Director: John Llewellyn
Moxey
Barbara Stanwyck (Miriam Jennings),
William Windom (Harold Jennings),
Barbara Parkins (Susan Jennings),
Roddy McDowall (Dr. Lomas), Bing
Russell (Sheriff), Arthur O'Connell
(John), Dawn Frame (young Susan).

TASTE THE BLOOD OF DRACULA
(1970)
Director: Peter Sasdy
Christopher Lee (Count Dracula),
Geoffrey Keen (William Hargood),
Gwen Watford (Martha Hargood),
Linda Hayden (Alice Hargood), Peter
Sallis (Samuel Paxton), Anthony
Corlan (Paul Paxton), Isla Blair
(Lucy Paxton), John Carson (Jon-
athan Secker), Martin Jarvis (Jer-
emy Secker), Ralph Bates (Lord
Courtley), Michael Ripper (Cobb),
Roy Kinnear (Weller), Russell Hun-
ter (Felix), Shirley Jaffe (Hargood's
maid), Keith Marsh (father), Peter
May (son), Maddy Smith (Dolly),

Reginald Barratt (Vicar), Malaika
Martin (snake girl), Lai Ling (Chinese girl).

TEENAGE CAVEMAN (1958) (A. K. A.
    "Out of the Darkness")
    Director: Roger Corman
Robert Vaughn (the Boy), Leslie
Bradley (the Symbol Maker), Darrah
Marshall (the Maiden), Frank De
Kova (the Villain), Robert Shayne,
Marshall Bradford, Beech Dickerson,
Jonathan Haze, Joseph H. Hamilton,
June Jocelyn, Charles P. Thompson
(Members of the Tribe).

TEENAGERS FROM OUTER SPACE
    (1959) (A. K. A. "The Gargon Terror")
    Director: Tom Graeff
David Love (Derek), Dawn Anderson
(Betty Morgan), Harvey B. Dunn
(Grandpa Morgan), Bryan Grant (Thor),
Tom Lockyear (Joe Rogers), Frederic
Welsh (Dr. Brandt), King Moody (Captain), Helen Sage (Miss Morse), Sonia
Torgeson (swimmer).

TEENAGE ZOMBIES (1958)
    Director: Jerry Warren
Don Sullivan (Regg), Katherine Victor (Dr. Myra), Nan Green (Dot),
Steve Conte (Whorf), Raul Pepper
(Skip), Bri Murphy (Pam), Jay Hawk
(Morrie), Mitzi Albertson (Julie),
S. L. D. Morrison (Brandt), Mike
Concannon (Sheriff), Don Neeley
(Major Coleman), Chuck Niles (Ivan).

TELEFON (1977)
    Director: Don Siegel
Charles Bronson (Grigori Borzov),
Lee Remick (Barbara), Donald Pleasence (Nicolai Dalchimsky), Tyne
Daly (Dorothy Putterman), Alan Badel
(Col. Malchenko), Patrick Magee (Gen.
Strelsky), Sheree North (Marie Wills),
Frank Marth (Harley Sandburg).

TELEPHONE BOOK, THE (1971)
    Director: Nelson Lyion
Sarah Kennedy (Alice), Norman Rose
(Smith), Jill Clayburgh (Eyemask),
Barry Morse (Har Poon), Roger C.
Carmel (analyst), James Harder (caller
No. 1), David Dozer (caller No. 2),
Ultra Violet (whip woman), Geri Miller
(dancer), Matthew Tobin (mugger),
William Hickey (man in bed), Ondine
(narrator).

TELEVISION SPY (1939)
    Director: Edward Dmytryk

William Henry, Anthony Quinn, Byron
Foulger, Richard Denning, Minor
Watson, Judith Barrett, Dorothy Tree,
John Eldredge, William Collier, Sr.,
Morgan Conway.

TELL-TALE HEART, THE (1927)
    Director: Charles F. Klein
Otto Matiesen, Herford de Fuerberg,
Darvas.

TELL-TALE HEART, THE (1934)
    (A. K. A. "A Bucket of Blood")
    Director: Brian Desmond Hurst
John Kelt (the old man), Norman Dryden (the boy), Yolanda Terrell (the
girl), Thomas Shenton (1st investigator),
James Fleck (2nd investigator), Colonel
Cameron (the doctor), H. Vasher (asylum superintendent).

TELL-TALE HEART, THE (1941) -
    short
    Director: Jules Dassin
Joseph Schildkraut, Roman Bohnen.

TELL-TALE HEART, THE (1953) -
    animated short
    Director: Ted Parmelee
James Mason (narrator).

TELL-TALE HEART, THE (1953)
    Director: J. B. Williams
Stanley Baker (Edgar Allan Poe).

TELL-TALE HEART, THE (1961)
    (A. K. A. "Hidden Room of 1000
    Horrors")
    Director: Ernest Morris
Laurence Payne (Edgar Marsh), Dermot Walsh (Carl Loomis), Adrienne
Corri (Betty Clare), Annette Carell
(Carl's landlady), John Scott (Inspector), Selma Vaz Dias (Mrs. Vine),
John Martin (Police Sergeant), David
Lander (jeweller), Susanne Fuller
(Dorothy), Rosemary Rotheray (Jackie), Yvonne Buckingham (Mina),
Richard Bennett (Mike), Elizabeth
Paget (Elsie), Frank Thornton (barman),
Joan Peart (street girl), Nada Beall
(old crone), Graham Ashley (Neston),
Pamela Plant (manageress), Patsy
Smart (Mrs. Marlow), Brian Cobby
(young man), Madeline Leon (young
woman).

TELL-TALE HEART, THE (1971) -
    short
    Director: Steve Carver
Alex Cord, Sam Jaffe.

TEMPEST (1982)

Director: Paul Mazursky
John Cassavetes (Phillip), Gena Rowlands (Antonia), Susan Sarandon (Aretha), Vittorio Gassman (Alonzo), Raul Julia (Kalibanos), Molly Ringwald (Miranda), Sam Robards (Freddy), Paul Stewart (Phillip's father), Jackie Gayle (Trin), Tony Holland (Sebastian), Jerry Hardin (Harry Gondorf), Lucianne Buchanan (Dolores).

TEMPLE OF THE WHITE ELEPHANTS (1964-Ital./Fr.) (A. K. A. "Il Tempio dell' Elefante Fianco", "Sandok, il Maciste dell Giugla", "Sandok, the Giant of the Jungle")
Director: Umberto Lenzi
Marie Versini, Sean Flynn, Mimmo Palmara, Giacomo Rossi-Stuart, Alessandra Panaro.

TEMPTATION OF ST. ANTHONY, THE (1898-Fr.) (A. K. A. "Tentation de Saint Antoine")
Director: Georges Melies

TENANT, THE (1975-Fr./U.S.) (A. K. A. "Le Locataire")
Director: Roman Polanski
Roman Polanski (Trelkovsky), Isabelle Adjani (Stella), Melvyn Douglas (Mr. Zy), Shelley Winters (the Concierge), Jo Van Fleet (Mme. Dioz), Lila Kedrova (Mme. Gaderian), Bernard Fresson (Scope), Rufus (Badar), Claude Pieplu (apartment neighbor), Jacques Monod (cafe proprietor), Patrice Alexandre (Robert), Josiane Balasko (Viviane), Jean Pierre Bagot (policeman), Michel Blanc (Scope's neighbor), Jacky Cohen (Stella's friend), Florence Blot (Mme. Zy), Claude Dauphin (man in accident), Bernard Donnadieu (bar waiter), Alain Frerot (beggar), Gerard Jugnot (office clerk), Raoul Guylad (priest), Helena Manson (head nurse), Arlette Reinerg (tramp), Eva Ionesco (Mme. Gaderian's daughter), Gerard Pereira (drunk), Maite Nahyr (Lucille), Andre Penvern (cafe waiter), Dominique Poulange (Simone Choule), Serge Spira (Philippe), Jacques Rosny (Jean-Claude), Vanessa Vaylord (Martine), Francois Viaur (police sergeant).

TENDER DRACULA (1974-Fr.) (A. K. A. "Tendre Dracula")
Director: Pierre Grunstein
Peter Cushing (MacGregor), Alida Valli (Heloise), Miou-Miou (Marie), Nathalie Courval (Madeleine), Stephane Shandor (Boris), Bernard Menez (Alfred), Julian Guiomar,

Percival Russel.

TEN LITTLE INDIANS (1965)
Director: George Pollock
Hugh O'Brian (Hugh Lombard), Shirley Eaton (Ann Clyde), Leo Genn (Gen. Mandrake), Fabian (Mike Raven), Stanley Holloway (William Blore), Dennis Price (Dr. Armstrong), Mario Adorf (Herr Grohmann), Wilfrid Hyde-White (Judge Cannon), Daliah Lavi (Ilona Bergen), Marianne Hoppe (Frau Grohmann).

TEN LITTLE INDIANS (1975) (A. K. A. "And Then There Were None")
Director: Peter Collinson
Oliver Reed (Hugh), Elke Sommer (Vera), Richard Attenborough (Judge), Stephane Audran (Ilona), Gert Frobe (Blore), Herbert Lom (Dr. Armstrong), Charles Aznavour (Raven), Alberto de Mondoza (Martino), Maria Rohm (Elsa), Adolfo Celi (General).

TENTACLES (1977)
Director: Oliver Hellman
John Huston (Ned Turner), Bo Hopkins (Will Gleason), Shelley Winters (Tillie Turner), Henry Fonda (Mr. Whitehead), Delia Boccardo (Vicki Gleason), Cesare Danova (John Corey), Alan Boyd (Mike), Claude Akins (Capt. Robards), Sherry Buchanan (Judy), Franco Diogene (Chuck), Marc Fiorini (Don), Helena Makela (Jaime's mother).

10,000 YEARS B.C. (1917)
Director: Willis O'Brien

TENTH VICTIM, THE (1965-Ital./Fr.) (A. K. A. "La Cecima Vittima")
Director: Elio Petri
Marcello Mastroianni (Marcello Poletti), Ursula Andress (Caroline Meredith), Elsa Martinelli (Olga), Salvo Randone (Professor), Massimo Serato (Lawyer), Milo Quesada (Rudi), Luce Bonifassy (Lidia), Mickey Knox (Chet), Evi Rigano (the victim), Anita Sanders (relaxatorium girl), Richard Armstrong (Cole), Walter Williams (Martin), George Wang (Chinese assistant).

TEOREMA (1968-Ital.) (A. K. A. "Theorem")
Director: Pier Paolo Pasolini
Terence Stamp (the Visitor), Silvana Mangano (the Wife), Massimo Girotti (the Husband), Anne Wiazemsky (the Daughter), Andres Jose Cruz (the Son), Laura Betti (the Maid), Ninetto Davoli (Angelino), Alfonso Gatto, Carlo

De Mejo, Adele Cambria, Soublette.

TERMINAL ISLAND (1973)
Director: Stephanie Rothman
Phyllis Davis (Joy Lang), Don Marshall (A. J. Thomas), Ena Hartman
(Carmen Sims), Marta Kristen (Lee
Phillips), Sean David Kennedy (Bobby
Farr), Barbara Leigh (Bunny Campbell),
Clyde Ventura (Julian 'Mother' Dylan).

THE TERMINAL MAN (1974)
Director: Mike Hodges
George Segal (Harry Benson), Joan
Hackett (Dr. Janet Rose), Jill Clayburgh (Angela Black), James Sikking
(Ralph Friedman), Michael C. Gwynne
(Dr. Robert Morris), Donald Moffatt
(Dr. Arthur McPherson), Richard
Dysart (Dr. John Ellis), Jason Wingreen
(instructor), Ian Wolfe (the priest),
Normann Burton (Detective Capt. Anders), William Hansen (Dr. Ezra
Manon), Robert Ito (anesthetist), Matt
Clark (Gerard), Burke Byrnes, Gene
Borkan (guards), Jim Antonio (Richards),
Dee Carroll (night nurse), Jordan Rhodes
(questioner No. 1), Steve Kanaly (Edmonds), Fred Sadoff (police doctor), Lee
De Broux (reporter), Victor Argo (orderly), Jack Colvin (coroner).

TERRIBLE SNOW GIANT, THE (1962-
Mex.) (A. K. A. "El Terrible Gigante de las Nieves")
Director: Jaime Salvador
Joaquin Cordero, Andres Soler, Ana
Bertha Lepe, David Hayat, Jose Chavez,
Elizabeth Dupeyron, Jose Eduardo
Perez.

TERRIBLE PEOPLE, THE (1928) -
serial in 10 episodes
Director: Spencer Gordon
Bennet
Allene Ray, Walter Miller, Wifred
North, Larry Steers, Tom Holding,
Allan Craven, Mary Foy, Fred Vroom.

TERRIBLE PEOPLE, THE (1960-Ger.)
(A. K. A. "Die Bande des Schreckens",
"Hand of the Gallows")
Director: Harald Reinl
Joachim Fuchsberger, Karin Dor, Chris
Howland, Fritz Rasp, Elizabeth Flickenschildt.

TERRIBLE TURKISH EXECUTIONER,
THE (1903-Fr.) (A. K. A. "Le
Bourreau Turo")
Director: Georges Melies

TERRIFIED (1962)

Director: Lew Landers
Rod Lauren (Ken), Tracy Olsen (Marge),
Denver Pyle (Sheriff), Barbara Luddy
(Mrs. Hawley), Sherwood Keith (Mr.
Hawley), Stephen Roberts (Wesley Blake),
Steve Drexel (Steve), Lee Bradley
(Mulligan), Ben Frank (Buell), Michael
Fellen (Buzzy), Danny Welton (drunk).

TERROR (1928)
Director: Louis King
Tom Tyler, Frankie Darro, Jane
Reid, Al Ferguson, Jules Cowles.

TERROR, THE (1928)
Director: Roy Del Ruth
May McAvoy (Olga Redmayne), Louis
Fazenda (Mrs. Elvery), Edward
Everett Horton (Ferdinand Fane),
Alec B. Francis (Dr. Redmayne),
Holmes Herbert (Henry Goodman),
John Miljan (Alfred Kalman), Otto
Hoffman (Soapy Marks), Joseph W.
Girard (Insp. Hallick), Matthew
Betz (Joe Connor), Frank Austin (Cotton), Conrad Nagel (Narrator), Carl
Stockdale, Reed Howes, Lester Cuneo.

TERROR, THE (1938)
Director: Richard Bird
Wilfred Lawson (Mr. Goodman),
Alastair Sim (Soapy Marks), Linden
Travers (Mary Redmayne), Arthur
Wontner (Col. Redmayne), Iris Hoey
(Mrs. Elvery), Bernard Lee (Ferdy
Fane), Henry Oscar (Connor), Lesley
Wareing (Veronica Elvery), Richard
Murdoch (PC Lewis), John Turnbull
(Insp. Hallick), Edward Lexy (Insp.
Dobie).

TERROR, THE (1963)
Director: Roger Corman
Boris Karloff (Baron von Leppe),
Jack Nicholson (Andre Duvalier),
Sandra Knight (Helene), Dick Miller
(Stefan), Jonathan Haze (Gustaf),
Dorothy Neumann (old woman).

TERROR (1979)
Director: Norman J. Warren
Michael Craze (Gary), John Nolan
(James), Carolyn Courage (Ann),
James Aubrey (Phillip), Tricia Walsh
(Viv), Rosie Collins (Diane), Sarah
Keller (Suzy), Glynis Barber (Carol),
L. E. Mack (Mad Dolly), Milton Reid,
Peter Mayhew, Peter Craze, William
Russell, Mike O'Malley, Colin Howells,
Mary Maude, Michael Cameron, Peter
Sproule, Peter Attard, Patti Love.

TERROR ABOARD (1933)

Director: Paul Sloane
Charles Ruggles, Neil Hamilton, Shirley Grey, John Halliday, Verree Teasdale, Morgan Wallace, Jack La-Rue, Leila Bennett, Paul Hurst, Charles Hancock, Stanley Fields, Frank Hagney, Leila Bennett, Thomas C. Jackson, William Janney, Bobby Dunn, Paul Porcasi, Clarence Wilson.

TERROR BENEATH THE SEA (1966-Jap.) (A.K.A. "Kaitei Daisenso", "Water Cyborgs")
Director: Hajime Sato
Sinichi Chiba, Peggy Neal, Gunther Braun, Franz Gruber, Andrew Hughes, Erick Nielson, Hideo Murota, Tsuneoi Miemachi, Mike Daneen, Beverly Kahlor.

TERROR BY NIGHT (1946) (A.K.A. "Sherlock Holmes in Terror by Night")
Director: Roy William Neill
Basil Rathbone (Sherlock Holmes), Nigel Bruce (Dr. Watson), Alan Mowbray (Major Duncan-Bleek), Renee Godfrey (Vivian Vedder), Mary Forbes (Lady Margaret), Dennis Hoey (Insp. Lestrade), Frederic Worlock (Prof. Kilbane), Billy Bevan (train attendant), Leland Hodgson (conductor), Geoffrey Steele (Ronald Carstairs), Janet Murdoch (Mrs. Shallcross), Gerald Hamer (Mr. Shallcross), Boyd Davis (McDonald), Skelton Knaggs (Sands), Harry Cording (Mock), Bobby Wissler (Mock, Jr.), Charles Knight (guard).

TERROR CIRCUS (1973)
Director: Alan Rudolph
Andrew Prine, Sherry Alberoni, Gyl Roland, Manuella Theiss, Al Cormier.

TERROR-CREATURES FROM THE GRAVE (1965-Ital.) (A.K.A. "Cinque Tombe per un Medium", "Five Graves for the Medium")
Director: Massimo Pupillo/ Ralph Zucker
Barbara Steele (Cleo Hauff), Walter Brandi (Kovaks), Richard Garret (Morgan), Alfred Rice (Dr. Nemek), Marilyn Mitchell (Corinne), Alan Collins (Kurt), Tilde Till (Louise, the maid).

TERROR FROM THE YEAR 5,000 (1958) (A.K.A. "Cage of Doom")
Director: Robert Gurney
Ward Costello (Robert Hedges), Joyce Holden (Claire Erling), Frederic Downs (Prof. Erling), John Stratton (Victor), Fred Herrick (Angelo),
Beatrice Furdeaux (Miss Blake), Jack Diamond, Fred Taylor (lab technicians), Salome Jens (5,000 A.D. woman).

TERROR FROM UNDER THE HOUSE (1971) (A.K.A. "Revenge", "Inn of the Frightened People")
Director: Sidney Hayers
Joan Collins (Carol), James Booth (Jim), Ray Barrett (Harry), Kenneth Griffith (Weely), Sinead Cusack (Rose), Zuleika Robson (Jill), Tom Marshall (Lee).

TERROR HOUSE (1942) (A.K.A. "The Night Has Eyes")
Director: Leslie Arliss
James Mason (Stephen Deremid), Wilfrid Lawson (Jim Sturrock), Joyce Howard (Marian Ives), Mary Clare (Mrs. Hanger), Tucker McGuire (Doris), John Fernald (Dr. Barry Randall).

TERROR IN THE CRYPT (1963-Span./ Ital.) (A.K.A. "La Maldicion de los Karnstein", "The Curse of the Karnsteins", "La Cripta e l'Incubo", "The Crypt and the Nightmare", "Crypt of Horror")
Director: Camillo Mastrocinque/ Thomas Miller
Christopher Lee (Count Ludwig von Karnstein), Adriana Ambesi/Audry Amber, Pier AnaQuaglia/Ursula Davis, Jose Campos, Nela Conjiu, Vera Valmont, Carla Calo, Jose Villasante, Angela Minervini.

TERROR IN THE HAUNTED HOUSE (1958) (A.K.A. "My World Dies Screaming")
Director: Harold Daniels
Gerald Mohr (Philip Tierney), Cathy O'Donnell (Sheila Wayne), John Qualen (Jonah Snell), William Ching (Mark Snell), Barry Bernard (Dr. Victor Forel).

TERROR IN THE WAX MUSEUM (1972)
Director: George J. Fenady
Ray Milland (Harry Flexner), Broderick Crawford (Amos Burns), Elsa Lanchester (Julia Hawthorn), Maurice Evans (Insp. Daniels), John Carradine (Claude Dupree), Shani Wallis (Laurie Mell), Mark Edwards (Sgt. Michael Hawks), Louis Hayward (Tim Fowley), Patrick Knowles (Mr. Southcott), Steven Marlo (Karkoff), Nicole Shelby (Meg), Leslie Thompson (Constable Parker), Lisa Lu (Madame Yang), Ben Wright

(1st constable), Matilda Calnan (1st charwoman), Peggy Stewart (2nd charwoman). Wax Figures: Don Herbert (Jack the Ripper), Judy Wetmore (Lizzie Borden), George Farina (Bluebeard), Jo Williamson (Mrs. Borden), Diane Wahrman (girl in bed), Rosa Huerta (Lucretia Borgia), Rickie Weir (Marie Antoinette), Ben Brown (Attila the Hun), Paul Wilson (Ivan the Terrible), Don Williamson (Constable Bolt), Ralph Cunningham (Willie Grossman), Evelyn Reynolds (flower woman).

TERROR IS A MAN (1959-U.S./Phil.)
(A.K.A. "Creature from Blood Island", "Blood Creature")
Director: Gary De Leon
Francis Lederer (Dr. Girard), Richard Derr (Fitzgerald), Greta Thyssen (Frances Girard), Flory Carlos (Man-Beast), Oscar Keesee (Walter), Lilia Duran (Selene), Peyton Keesee (Tiago).

TERROR ISLAND (1920)
Director: James Cruze
Harry Houdini (Harry Harper), Lila Lee (Beverly West), Eugene Pallette (Guy Mordaunt), Rosemary Theby (Stella Mordaunt), Jack Brammal (Starkey), Edward Brady (Captain Black), Wilton Taylor (Job Mordaunt), Frank Bonner (Chief Bakaida), Fred Turner (Mr. West), Ted E. Duncan (1st Officer Murphy).

TERRORNAUTS, THE (1966)
Director: Montgomery Tully
Simon Oates (Dr. Joe Burke), Zena Marshall (Sandy Lund), Max Adrian (Dr. Henry Shore), Charles Hawtrey (Joshua Yellowless), Patricia Hayes (Mrs. Jones), Stanley Meadows (Ben Keller), Leonard Cracknell (Nick), Richard Carpenter (Danny), Frank Barry (Burke as a child), Frank Forsyth (uncle), Robert Jewell (robot operator), Andre Maranne (gendarme).

TERROR OF MECHAGODZILLA (1975-Jap.) (A.K.A. "Mekagojira no Gyakushu")
Director: Inishiro Honda
Tomoko Ai, Akihiko Hirata, Kenji Sahara, K. Saski.

TERROR OF THE TONGS, THE (1961)
Director: Anthony Bushell
Christopher Lee (Chung King), Geoffrey Toone (Capt. Jackson), Bert Kwouk (Mr. Ming), Ewen Solon (Tongman Tang How), Milton Reid (Tong Guardian), Yvonne Monlaur (Lee), Marne Maitland

(beggar), Charles Lloyd-Pack (doctor), Barbara Brown (Helena), Bandana Das Dupta (Anna), Marie Burke (Maya), Brian Worth (Harcourt), Richard Leech (Dean), Michael Hawkins (priest).

TERROR OUT OF THE SKY (TVM-1978) - 12-26-78
Director: Lee H. Katzin
Efrem Zimbalist, Jr. (David Martin), Tovah Feldshuh (Jeannie), Dan Haggerty (Nick Willis), Lonny Chapman (Earl Logan), Ike Eisenmann (Eric), Steve Franken (Gladstone), Richard Herd (Col. Mangus), Joe E. Tata (Groves), Bruce French (Eli Nathanson), Bill Quinn (Old Dermott), Philip Baker (Starrett), Charles Hallan (Tibbles), Tony La Torre (Tibbles boy), Poindexter (Mike), Ellen Blake (Agent), Steve Tannen (sergeant), Melinda Peterson (computer operator).

TERROR TRAIN (1980)
Director: Roger Spottiswoode
Ben Johnson (Carne), Jamie Lee Curtis (Alana), Hart Bochner (Doc), David Copperfield (Magician), Sandee Currie (Mitchy), Derek MacKinnon (Kenny Hampson), Anthony Sherwood (Jackson), Timothy Webber (Mo), Howard Busgang (Ed), D.D. Winters (Merry), Joy Boushel (Pet), Steve Michaels (Brakeman), Greg Swanson (Class President), Victor Knight (engineer).

TESTAMENT OF DR. CORDELIER, THE (1959-Fr.) (A.K.A. "The Doctor's Horrible Experiment", "Le Testament du Dr. Cordelier", "Experiment in Evil")
Director: Jean Renoir
Jean-Louis Barrault (Dr. Cordelier/Opale), Micheline Gary, Michel Vitold, Teddy Bilis, Jean Topart, Gaston Modot.

TESTAMENT OF DR. MABUSE, THE (1932-Ger.) (A.K.A. "Das Testament des Dr. Mabuse", "Crimes of Dr. Mabuse")
Director: Fritz Lang
German language version: Rudolf Klein-Rogge (Dr. Mabuse), Oskar Beregi (Dr. Baum), Theodor Loos (Dr. Kramm), Gustav Diessl (Kent), Vera Liessen (Lily), Otto Warnicke (Insp. Lohmann), Camilla Spira (Anna), Karl Meixner (Hofmeister), E.A. Licho (monetary expert), Theo Lingen (jeweler), Oskar Hocker, Raymond Cordy.

French language version: Rudolf
Klein-Rogge (Dr. Mabuse), Oskar
Beregi (Dr. Baum), Jim Gerald,
Thomy Bourdelle, Raymond Cordy,
Maurice Maillot.

TESTAMENT OF DR. MABUSE, THE
(1962-Ger.) (A.K.A. "Das Testa-
ment des Dr. Mabuse", "Terror
of the Mad Doctor")
Director: Werner Klingler
Wolfgang Preiss (Dr. Mabuse), Gert
Frobe (Lohmann), Walter Rilla
(Polland), Claus Tinney (Jack), Hel-
mud Helmud Schmid (Johnny), Senta
Berger, Charles Regnier.

TESTAMENT OF ORPHEUS, THE
(1959-Fr.) (A.K.A. "Le Testa-
ment d'Orphee")
Director: Jean Cocteau
Jean Cocteau, Emouard Dermithe,
Jean Marais, Yul Brynner, Jean-
Pierre Leaud, Pablo Picasso, Henri
Cremieux, Francois Perier, Nicole
Courcel, Maria Casares, Daniel
Gelin, Claudine Oger, Charles Az-
navour, Luis-Miguel Dominguin,
Francoise Christophe.

TEST PILOT PIRX (1979-Pol.)
Director: Marek Piestrak
Sergei Desnitsky, Boleslaw Abart,
Vladimir Ivashov, Aleksander Kaj-
danowski, Zbigniew Lesien.

TEXAS CHAIN SAW MASSACRE, THE
(1974)
Director: Tobe Hooper
Marilyn Burns (Sally Hardesty), Paul
A. Partain (Franklin Hardesty),
Gunnar Hansen (Leatherface), Allen
Danziger (Jerry), Teri McMinn
(Pam), William Vail (Kirk), Edwin
Neal (hitchhiker), Jim Siedow (old
man), John Dugan (grandfather),
Joe Bill Hogan (drunk), Robert Cor-
ten (window washer), Jerry Lorenz
(pickup driver).

THARK (1932)
Director: Tom Walls
Robertson Hare (Hook), Tom Walls
(Sir Hector Benbow), Ralph Lynn
(Ronald Gamble), Mary Brough (Mrs.
Todd), Joan Brierley (Cherry Buck),
Claude Hulbert (Lionel Todd), Gor-
don James (Death), Evelyn Bostock
(Kitty Stratton), Marjorie Corbett
Warner), Beryl de Querton (Lady
Benbow).

THAT CURSED HOUSE CLOSE TO

THE MUSHROOM BED (1972-Ital.)
Director:
Irina Demick, Adolfo Celi, Patrizia
Adiutori, Pilar Velasquez, Robert
Hoffmann.

THAT HOUSE IN THE OUTSKIRTS
(1980-Span.) (A.K.A. "Aquella
Casa en las Afueras")
Director: Eugenio Martin
Javier Escriva (Joaquin), Silvia
Aguilar (Nieves), Alida Valli (Isabel),
Mara Goyanes, Carmen Maura.

THAT'S THE SPIRIT (1945)
Director: Charles Lamont
Peggy Ryan (Sheila), Jack Oakie (Steve),
Gene Lockhart (Jasper), June Vincent
(Libby), Andy Devine (Martin), Irene
Ryan (Bilson), Arthur Treacher (Mas-
ters), Buster Keaton (L.M.), Victoria
Horne (Patience), Edith Barrett (Abi-
gail), Johnny Coy (Martin, Jr.).

THEATRE OF BLOOD (1972)
Director: Douglas Hickox
Vincent Price (Edward Lionheart),
Diana Rigg (Edwina Lionheart), Ian
Hendry (Peregrine Devlin), Harry
Andrews (Trevor Dickman), Robert
Coote (Oliver Larding), Jack Hawkins
(Solomon Psaltery), Coral Browne
(Miss Chloe Moon), Michael Hordern
(George Maxwell), Robert Morley
(Meredith Merridew), Dennis Price
(Hector Snipe), Arthur Lowe (Horace
Sprout), Diana Dors (Mrs. Psaltery),
Joan Hickson (Mrs. Sprout), Milo
O'Shea (Insp. Boot), Renee Asherson
(Mrs. Maxwell), Madeline Smith
(Rosemary), Eric Sykes (Sgt. Dogge),
Bunny Reed, Peter Thornton (police-
men), Tony Calvin (police photographer),
Brigid Eric Bates (Agnes).

THEFT OF THE MUMMIES OF GUANA-
JUATO, THE (1972-Mex.) (A.K.A.
"Robo de las Momias de Guanajuato")
Director: Tito Novaro
Mil Mascaras, Tito Novaro, El Ray
de Jalisco, Blue Angel, Julio Cesar,
Rafael Rosales.

THEM! (1954)
Director: Gordon Douglas
James Whitmore (Sgt. Ben Peterson),
James Arness (Robert Medford),
Edmund Gwenn (Dr. Harold Medford),
Joan Welson (Dr. Patricia Medford),
Onslow Stevens (Brig. Gen. O'Brien),
Chris Drake (Officer Ed Blackburn),
Sean McClory (Major Kibbee), Sandy
Descher (little girl), Mary Ann Ho-

kanson (Mrs. Lodge), Fredrick J.
Foote (Dixon), Olin Howlin (Jenson),
Fess Parker (Crotty), Robert Scott
Correll (Jerry), Richard Bellis (Mike),
Joel Smith (Ben's driver), John Close
(pilot's voice), William Schallert
(intern), Leonard Nimoy (sergeant),
Don Shelton (Captain of Troopers),
Dub Taylor (watchman), Cliff Ferre
(lab man), Matthew McCue (Gramps),
Marshall Bradford (doctor), Ken
Smith, Kenner Kemp, Richard Boyer
(troopers), Joe Forte (Coroner Put-
nam), Wally Duffy (airman), Fred
Shellac (attendant), Ann Doran (psy-
chiatrist), Willis Bouchey (official),
Norman Field (General), Otis Garth
(Admiral), John Maxwell (Dr. Grant),
Janet Stewart (WAVE), Waldron
Boyle (doctor), Alexander Campbell
(2nd official), Dick Wessell (cop),
Russell Gage (coroner), Robert Ber-
ger (Sutton), John Berardino (Ryan),
Harry Tyler, Oscar Blanke (inmates),
Eddie Dew (officer), Dorothy Green
(matron), Dean Cromer (M. P. ser-
geant), Lawrence Dobkin (engineer),
James Cardwell (officer), Chad Mal-
lory (loader), Gayle Kellogg (gunner),
Booth Colman (newsman), Walter
Coy (2nd newsman), Victor Sutherland
(Senator), Charles Perry (soldier),
Warren Mace (radio operator), Jack
Perrin (Army officer), Hubert Kerns,
Royden Clark (jeep drivers).

THEMROC (1973-Fr.)
    Director: Claude Faraldo
Michel Piccoli (Themroc), Marilu
Tolo (Secretary), Beatrice Romand
(sister), Francesca R. Coluzzi
(woman across the street), Mme.
Merivale (mother), Romain Bouteille
(Chief Bureaucrat), Miou-Miou,
Patrick Dewaere.

THESE ARE THE DAMNED (1961)
    (A. K. A. "The Damned")
    Director: Joseph Losey
Macdonald Carey (Simon Wells),
Shirley Anne Field (Joan), Alexander
Knox (Bernard), Viveca Lindfors
(Freya), Oliver Reed (King), Walter
Gotell (Major Holland), James Vil-
liers (Capt. Gregory), Kenneth Cope
(Sid), James Maxwell (Mr. Talbot),
Barbara Everest (Miss Lamont),
Alan McClelland (Mr. Stewart),
Brian Oulton (Mr. Dingle), Nicholas
Clay (Richard), Caroline Sheldon
(Elizabeth), Rachel Clay (Victoria),
Siobhan Taylor (Mary), Kit Williams
(Henry), Christopher Witty (William),

Rebecca Dignam (Anne), John Thomp-
son (Charles), Thomas Kempinski
(Ted), Edward Harvey, Neil Wilson,
Fiona Duncan, Anthony Valentine,
Leon Garcia, David Gregory, Larry
Martyn, Geremy Phillips, David
Palmer.

THEY ALL DIED LAUGHING (1964)
    (A. K. A. "A Jolly Bad Fellow")
    Director: Don Chaffey
Leo McKern (Prof. Bowles-Ottery),
Janet Munro (Dalia), Maxine Audley
(Clarinda), Dennis Price (Hughes),
Duncan MacRae (Dr. Brass), Miles
Malleson (Dr. Wooley), Leonard
Rossiter (Dr. Fisher), Geoffrey
Bayldon (Epicine), George Benson
(Insp. Butts), Patricia Jessel (Mrs.
Pugh-Smith), Mark Dignam (the Mas-
ter), Jerome Willis (Armstrong),
Mervyn Johns.

THEY CAME FROM BEYOND SPACE
    (1967)
    Director: Freddie Francis
Robert Hutton (Dr. Curtis Temple),
Jennifer Jayne (Lee Mason), Bernard
Kay (Richard Arden), Zia Mohyeddin
(Farge), John Harvey (Bill Tretho-
wan), Michael Hawkins (Williams),
Frank Forsyth (Blake), Michael
Gough (Master of the Moon), Jack
Lambert (doctor in office), Geoffrey
Wallace (Alan Mullane), Maurice
Good (Stilwell), Tana King (Mrs.
Trethowan), Katy Wild (girl in street),
Luanshiya Greer (girl attendant),
Paul Bacon (Rogers), Dermot Cathie
(Peterson), Christopher Banks (doc-
tor in street), Norman Claridge (Dr.
Andrews), Leonard Grahame (McCabe),
Kenneth Kendall (commentator), James
Donnelly (Guard), Robin Parkinson
(Maitland), Edward Rees (bank mana-
ger).

THEY CAME FROM WITHIN (1975)
    (A. K. A. "The Parasite Murders",
    "Shivers")
    Director: David Cronenberg
Paul Hampton (Roger St. Luc),
Barbara Steele (Betts), Joe Silver
(Rollo Linsky), Lynn Lowry (Forsythe),
Ronald Mlodzick (Merrick), Alan
Migicovsky (Nicholas Tudor), Suan
Petrie (Janine Tudor).

THEY CAME TO A CITY (1944)
    Director: Basil Dearden
John Clements, Googie Withers,
Raymond Huntley, Renee Gadd,
Mabel Terry-Lewis, A. E. Matthews,

Ada Reeve, Norman Shelley, J. B. Priestley, Frances Rowe.

THEY MIGHT BE GIANTS (1971)
Director: Anthony Harvey
George C. Scott (Justin Playfair), Joanne Woodward (Dr. Mildred Watson), Jack Gilford (Wilbur Peabody), Kitty Winn (Grace), Lester Rawlins (Blevins Playfair), Ron Weyand (Dr. Strauss), Susie Bond (Maud), Theresa Merritt (Peggy), Staats Costworth (Winthrop), Rue McClanahan (Daisy), Peter Fredericks (Grace's boyfriend), Jenny Egan (Miss Finch), Oliver Clark (Mr. Small), M. Emmet Walsh, Louis Zorich (sanitation men), Al Lewis (messenger), Eugene Roche (policeman), Michael McGuire (telephone guard), Jane Hoffman, Dorothy Greener (telephone operators), Jacques Sandulescu (Brown's driver), James Tolkan (Mr. Brown), Worthington Miner (Mr. Bagg), Frances Fuller (Mrs. Bagg), Matthew Cowles (teenage boy), Candy Azzara (teenage girl), Tony Capodilupo (Chief), John McCurry (Police Lieutenant), F. Murray Abraham (usher), Paul Benedict (chestnut vendor), Ralph Clanton (store manager), Ted Beniades (cab driver).

THIEF OF BAGDAD, THE (1924)
Director: Raoul Walsh
Douglas Fairbanks, Sr. (the Thief), Julanne Johnston (the Princess), Sojin (Mongol Prince), Brandon Hurst (the Caliph), Anna May Wong (Mongol slave), Snitz Edwards (the Thief's evil associates), Noble Johnson (Indian Prince), Winter Blossom, Etta Lee, Tote Du Crow, Sadakichi Hartmann, K. Nambu.

THIEF OF BAGDAD, THE (1940)
Director: Ludwig Berger, Michael Powell & Tim Whelan
Sabu (Abu), Conrad Veidt (Jaffar), June Duprez (the Princess), Rex Ingram (Djinni), Miles Malleson (Sultan), John Justin (Ahmed), Mary Morris (Halima), Morton Selten (the Old King), Bruce Winston (merchant), Allan Jeayes (the Story Teller), Hay Petrie, David Sharpe.

THIEF OF BAGDAD, THE (1960-
Ital./Fr.) (A.K.A. "Il Ladro di Baggad")
Director: Arthur Lubin
Steve Reeves (Karim), Georgia Moll (Amina), Edy Vessel (Kadesjah),

Georges Charmarat (Magician), Arturo Dominici, Daniele Vargas.

THIEF OF BAGDAD, THE (TVM-
1978) - 11-23-78
Director: Clive Donner
Kabir Bedi (Prince Taj), Roddy McDowall (Hasan), Peter Ustinov (the Caliph), Terence Stamp (Wazir Jaudur), Pavla Ustinov (Princess Yasmine), Frank Finley (Abu Bakar), Marina Vlady (Perizadah), Ian Holm (gatekeeper), Daniel Emilfork (the Genie), Neil McCarthy, Arnold Diamond, Leon Greene, Geoffrey Cheshire, Kenji Tanaki, Bruce Montague, Gabor Vernon, Ahmed el-Shenawi, Vincent Wong, Raymond Llewellyn, Kevork Malikyan, Ahmed Khail, George Little, Michael Chesdon, Yasher Adem.

THIEF OF DAMASCUS, THE (1951)
Director: Will Jason
Paul Henreid (Abu Andar), John Sutton (Khalid), Jeff Donnell (Sheherazade), Lon Chaney, Jr. (Sinbad), Edward Colmans (Sultan Raudah), Philip Van Zandt (Ali Baba), Nelson Leigh (Ben Jammal), Elena Verdugo (Nella), Leonard Penn (Habayah), Larry Stewart (Hassan), Robert Clary (Aladdin), Helen Gilbert (Princess Zafir), Robert Conte (horse trader).

THIN AIR (1969) (A.K.A. "Invasion of the Body Stealers")
Director: Gerry Levy
George Sanders (Gen. Armstrong), Maurice Evans (Dr. Matthews), Patrick Allen (Bob Meagan), Neil Connery (Jim Radford), Robert Flemying (Wing Cmdr. Baldwin), Lorna Wilde (Lorna), Hilary Dwyer (Julie), Alan Cuthbertson (Hindsmith), Michael Culver (Bailes), Shelagh Fraser (Mrs. Thatcher), Carl Rigg (Pilot Officer Briggs), Sally Faulkner (Joanna), Jan Miller (Sally), Carol Ann Hawkins (Paula).

THING, THE (1951) (A.K.A. "The Thing from Another World")
Director: Christian Nyby & Howard Hawks
Kenneth Tobey (Capt. Patrick Hendry), Margaret Sheridan (Nikki Nicholson), James Young (Lt. Eddie Dykes), Dewey Martin (Sgt. Bob), Paul Frees (Dr. Voorhees), Robert Cornthwaite (Dr. Carrington), Douglas Spencer (Ned 'Scotty' Scott), Robert Nichols (Lt. Ken 'Mac' MacPherson), Eduard

Franz (Dr. Stern), John Dierkes (Dr. Chapman), James Arness (the Thing), Billy Curtis (the Thing while shrinking), William Self (Corporal Barnes), Everett Glass (Prof. Wilson), Sally Creighton (Mrs. Chapman), Tom Steele (stuntman), George Fenneman (Dr. Redding), Norbert Schiller (Dr. Laurenz), David McMahon (Gen Fogarty), Edmond Breon (Dr. Ambrose), William Neff (Olson), Lee Tung Foo, Walter Ng (cooks), Robert Stevenson (Capt. Smith), Robert Gutknecht (Cpl. Hauser), Robert Bray (Captain), Ted Cooper, Allan Ray (Lieutenants), Nicholas Byron (Ted Richards).

THING, THE (1982)
    Director: John Carpenter
Kurt Russell (MacReady), A. Wilford Brimley (Blair), T.K. Carter (Nauls), David Clennon (Palmer), Keith David (Childs), Richard Dysart (Dr. Cooper), Charles Hallahan (Norris), Peter Maloney (Bennings), Richard Masur (Clark), Donald Moffat (Garry), Joel Polis (Fuchs), Thomas Waites (Windows), Norbert Weisser (Norwegian), Larry Franco (Norwegian passenger with rifle), Nate Irwin (helicopter pilot), William Zeman (pilot).

THINGS HAPPEN AT NIGHT (1948)
    Director: Francis Searle
Gordon Harker (Joe Harris), Robertson Hare (Vincent Ebury), Beatrice Campbell (Joyce Prescott), Alfred Drayton (Wilfred Prescott), Gwyneth Vaughan (Audrey Prescott), Olga Lindo (Mrs. Ebury), Garry Marsh (Spender), Joan Young (Mrs. Venning), Wylie Watson (Watson).

THINGS TO COME (1936)
    Director: William Cameron Menzies
Raymond Massey (John Cabal/Oswald Cabal), Sir Ralph Richardson (Rudolph Black, the Boss), Margaretta Scott (Rowena Cabal/Roxanne Black), Edward Chapman (Pippa Pasworthy/Raymond Passworthy), Sir Cedric Hardwicke (Theotocopulos), Sophie Stewart (Mrs. John Cabal), Ann Todd (Mary Gordon), Derrick de Marney (Richard Gordon), Pearl Argyle (Katherine Cabal), Anthony Holles (Simon Burton), Allan Jeayes (Grandfather Cabal), John Clements (the Airman), Abraham Sofaer (Wadsky), Maurice Bardell (Dr. Harding), George Sanders (pilot), Charles Carson (great-grandfather), Ivan Brandt

(Mitani), Patricia Hilliard (Janet Gordon), Kenneth Villiers (Maurice Passworthy), Pickles Livingston (Horrie Passworthy).

THING THAT COULDN'T DIE, THE (1958)
    Director: Will Cowan
Andrea Martin (Linda Madison), William Reynolds (Gordon Hawthorn), Jeffrey Stone (Hank Huston), Carolyn Kearney (Jessica Burns), Robin Hughes (Gideon Drew), Charles Horvath (Mike), James Anderson (Boyd Abercrombie), Peggy Converse (Flavia McIntire), Forrest Lewis (Ash).

THING WITH TWO HEADS, THE (1972)
    Director: Lee Frost
Ray Milland (Dr. Maxwell Kirshner), Roosevelt Grier (Jack Moss), Don Marshall (Dr. Fred Williams), Chelsea Brown (Lila), Roger Perry (Dr. Philip Desmond), Roger Gentry (Police Sergeant), John Dullaghan (Thomas), Kathy Baumann (Patricia), John Bliss (Donald Smith), Jane Kellem (Miss Mullen), Wes Bishop (Dr. Smith), Britt Nilsson (nurse), Lee Frost (Sgt. Hacker), Bruce Kimball (Police Lieutenant), Phil Hoover (policeman), Michael Viner (prison guard), Tommy Cook (chaplain), Rick Baker (the Gorilla), Rod Steele (medical salesman), Dick Whittington (TV newscaster), William Smith (hysterical condemned man).

THIRD EYE, THE (1965-Ital.) (A.K.A. "Il Terzo Occhio")
    Director: Giacomo Guerrini/ James Warren
Franco Nero, Eleanora Bianchi, Olga Solbelli, G. Pascal, Diana Sullivan.

THIRST (1979-Australia)
    Director: Rod Hardy
Chantal Contouri (Kate Davis), David Hemmings (Dr. Fraser), Henry Silva (Dr. Gauss), Max Phipps (Hodge), Rod Mullinar (Derek), Shirley Cameron (Mrs. Barker), Robert Thompson (Sean), Walter Pym (Dichter), Rosie Sturgess (Lori), Amanda Muggleton (Martha), Lulu Pinkus (nurse).

THIRSTY DEAD, THE (1974)
    Director: Terry Becker
John Considine, Jennifer Billingsley, Judith McConnell, Fredricka Meyers,

Tani Guthrie.

13 GHOSTS (1960)
Director: William Castle
Donald Woods (Cyrus Zorba), Rosemary DeCamp (Hilda Zorba), Martin Milner (Ben Rush), Jo Morrow (Medea Zorba), Charles Herbert (Buck Zorba), Margaret Hamilton (Elaine Zacharides), John Van Dreelan (E. Van Allen).

THIRTEENTH CHAIR, THE (1929)
Director: Tod Browning
Conrad Nagel (Richard Crosby), Leila Hyams (Helen O'Neill), Bela Lugosi (Insp. Delzante), Margaret Wycherly (Madame Rosalie La Grange), Holmes Herbert (Sir Roscoe Crosby), Mary Forbes (Lady Crosby), Moon Carroll (Helen Trent), John Davidson (Edward Wales), Helen Millard (Mary Eastwood), Cyril Chadwick (Brandon Trent), Frank Leigh (Prof. Feringeea), Charles Quartermaine (Dr. Phillip Mason), Gretchen Holland (Grace Standish), Bertram Johns (Howard Standish), Clarence Geldert (Commissioner Grimshaw), Lal Chand Mehra (Chotee), Henry Daniell.

THIRTEENTH CHAIR, THE (1937)
Director: George B. Seitz
Dame May Whitty (Mme. Rosaile LaGrange), Madge Evans (Neil O'Neill), Lewis Stone (Insp. Marney), Henry Daniell (John Wales), Holmes Herbert (Sir Roscoe Crosby), Ralph Forbes (Lionel Trent), Heather Thatcher (Mary Eastwood), Charles Trowbridge (Dr. Mason), Janet Beecher (Lady Crosby), Elissa Landi (Helen Trent), Matthew Boulton (Commissioner Grimshaw), Thomas Beck (Dick Crosby).

THIRTEENTH GUEST, THE (1932)
Director: Albert Ray
Ginger Rogers (Marie Morgan/Lela), Lyle Talbot (Phil Winston), J. Farrell Macdonald (Captain Ryan), Paul Hurst (Detective Grump), John Ince (John Morgan), William B. Davidson (Captain Brown), Henry Hall (jail sergeant), James C. Eagles (Harold 'Bud' Morgan), Erville Anderson (John Adams), Eddie Phillips (Thor Jensen), Frances Rich (Marjorie Thornton), Phillips Smalley (Dick Thornton), Tom London (Detective Carter), Ethel Wales (Joan Thornton), Crawford

Kent (Dr. Sherwood), Al Bridge (policeman), Kit Guard (prisoner), Adrienne Dore (Winston's date), Isobel LeMall (Marie's mother), Harry Tenbrook (cab driver), Charles Meacham (Marie's father), Robert Klein (John Barksdale), Allan Cavan (Wayne Seymour), Lynton Brent (prisoner), Tiny Sandford (Mike, the jailer), Bobby Burns (photographer).

13th HOUR, THE (1927)
Director: Chester Franklin
Lionel Barrymore (Prof. Leroy), Jacqueline Gadsdon (Mary Lyle), Fred Kelsey, Polly Moran, Charles Delaney.

13th HOUR, THE (1947)
Director: William Clemens
Richard Dix, Karen Morley, Jim Bannon, Regis Toomey, John Kellogg, Anthony Warde, Selmer Jackson, Pat O'Malley, Ernie Adams, Ed Parker, Bernadene Hayes.

13 WOMEN (1932)
Director: George Archainbaud
Ricardo Cortez (Sgt. Clive), Irene Dunne (Laura), Myrna Loy (Ursula Georgi), Jill Esmond (Jo), Florence Eldredge (Grace), C. Henry Gordon (Swami Yogadachi), Julie Haydon (Mary), Harriet Hagman (May Raskob), Peg Entwistle (Hazel), Kay Johnson (Helen), Mary Duncan (Julie Raskob), Elsie Prescott (Nan), Edward Pawley (Burns), Wally Albright (Bobby), Blanche Frederici (teacher).

THIRTY FOOT BRIDE OF CANDY ROCK, THE (1958)
Director: Sidney Miller
Lou Costello (Artie Pinsetter), Dorothy Provine (Emmy Lou Raven), Gale Gordon (Raven Rossiter), Charles Lane (Stanford Bates), Will Wright (Pentagon General), Peter Leeds (Bill Burton), Robert Burton (1st General), Robert Nichols (bank manager), Jimmy Conlin (Magruder), Lenny Kent (Sergeant), Veola Vonn (Jackie Delaney), Ruth Perrott (Aunt May), Jack Straw (pilot), Doodles Weaver.

THIS HOUSE POSSESSED (TVM-1981) - 2-6-81
Director: William Wiard
Parker Stevenson (Gary), Lisa Eilbacher (Sheila), Shelley Smith (Tanya), Slim Pickens (Keene),

K. Callan (Lucille), David Paymer (Pasternak), Joan Bennett (Rag Lady), Bill Morey (Robbins), Jan Shutan (Helen), Mandy Wyss (Holly), John Dukakis (Donny), Ivy Bethune (Martha), Doug Johnson (orderly), Jack Garner (Feeny), Phillip Baker Hall (clerk).

THIS ISLAND EARTH (1954)
Director: Joseph M. Newman
Jeff Morrow (Exeter), Rex Reason (Cal Meacham), Faith Domergue (Dr. Ruth Adams), Russell Johnson (Steve Carlson), Douglas Spencer (Monitor), Robert Nichols (Joe Wilson), Karl Lindt (Dr. Adolph Engelborg), Lance Fuller (Brack), Reg Parton, Eddie Parker (Mutants), Olan Soule (1st reporter), Richard Deacon (pilot), Robert B. Williams (Webb), Mark Hamilton (Metalunan), Guy Edward Hearn, Les Spears (reporters), Edward Ingram, Jack Byron (photographers), Coleman Francis (expressman), Spencer Chan, Lizalotta Valesca (scientists).

THIS IS NOT A TEST (1962)
Director: Frederic Gadette
Seamon Glass, Mary Morlas, Thayer Roberts, Aubrey Martin.

THOMAS AND...THE BEWITCHED (1970-Ital.) (A.K.A. "Thomas e... gli Indemonati")
Director: Pupi Avati
Edmund Purdom, Bob Tonelli, Daniele Samovy, Anita Sanders, Gianni Cavina, Giulio Pizzirani.

THOR AND THE AMAZON WOMEN (1963-Ital.) (A.K.A. "Tarzan, Roi de la Force Brutale", "Tarzan, King of Brute Force"; "Thaur, King of Brute Force")
Director: Antonio Leonviola
Joe Robinson, Bella Cortez, Susy Anderson.

THOSE FANTASTIC FLYING FOOLS (1967) (A.K.A. "Jules Verne's Rocket to the Moon", "Blast Off!")
Director: Don Sharp
Burl Ives (Phineas T. Barnum), Troy Donahue (Gaylord Sullivan), Terry-Thomas (Capt. Sir Harry Washington Smythe), Gert Frobe (Prof. Von Bulow), Lionel Jeffries (Sir Charles Dillworthy), Hermione Gingold (Wayward Girl's Home Custodian), Dennis Price (Duke of Barset), Daliah Lavi (Madelaine), Edward De Souza

(Henri), Derek Francis (Puddleby), Jimmy Clitheroe (Gen. Tom Thumb), Klaus Kinski (Bulgeroff), Graham Stark (Grundle), Joachim Tege (Bulgeroff), Renata Holt (Ann), Judy Cornwall (Electra), Joan Sterndale Bennett (the Queen), Allan Cuthbertson (Scotland Yard man), Stratford Johns (warrant officer).

THOUSAND AND ONE NIGHTS, A (1945)
Director: Alfred E. Green
Cornel Wilde (Aladin), Evelyn Keyes (the Genie), Phil Silvers (Abdullah), Adele Jergens (Princess Armina), Philip Van Zandt (Grand Wazh Abn-Hassan), Dusty Anderson (Novira), Nestor Paiva (Kahna), Rex Ingram (Giant), Gus Schilling (Jafar), Dennis Hoey (Sultan Kameer Al-Kir/Prince Hadji), John Abbott (Ali, the tailor), Richard Hale (Kofie, the Sorcerer), Murray Leonard (camel driver), Shelley Winters, Pat Parcisn, Carole Matthews (handmaidens).

THOUSAND EYES OF DR. MABUSE, THE (1960-Ger./Ital./Fr.) (A.K.A. "Die Tausend Augen des Dr. Mabuse", "Le Diabolique Docteur Mabuse", "Eye of Evil")
Director: Fritz Lang
Wolfgang Preiss (Dr. Mabuse), Gert Forbe, Peter Van Eyck, Dawn Addams, Werner Peters, Andrea Checchi, Howard Vernon, Jean-Jacques Delbo.

THREE ARABIAN NUTS (1951) - short
Director: Edward Bernds
Moe Howard, Shemp Howard, Larry Fine, Philip Van Zandt, Dick Curtis, Wesley Bly, Vernon Dent.

THREE CASES OF MURDER (1955)
"Lord Mountdrago".
Director: George More O'Ferrall
Orson Welles (Lord Mountdrago), Alan Badel (Owen), Helen Cherry (Lady Mountdrago), Andre Morell (Dr. Audlin).
"In the Picture".
Director: Wendy Toye
Alan Badel (Mr. X), Eddie Byrne (Snyder), Hugh Pryse (Jarvis), Leueen MacGrath (the Woman).

THREE FANTASTIC SUPERMEN, THE (1967-Ital.) (A.K.A. "I

Tre Fantastic Superman")
  Director: Gianfranco Parolini/
  Frank Kramer
Luciana Stella/Tony Kendall, Brad
Harris, Nick Jordan, Sabine Sun,
Carlo Tamberlani, Jochen Brockmann,
Gloria Paul.

THREE LIVES OF THOMASINA, THE
(1963)
  Director: Don Chaffey
Patrick McGoohan (Andrew MacDhui),
Susan Hampshire (Lori MacGregor),
Karen Dotrice (Mary MacDhui), Vincent
Winter (Hughie Stirling), Finlay Currie
(Grandpa Stirling), Laurence Naismith
(Rev. Angus Peddie), Wilfrid Brambell
(Willie Bannock), Francis De Wolff (Tar-
gu), Joan Anderson (Mrs. MacKenzie),
Oliver Johnston (Mr. Debbie), Denis
Gilmore (Jamie McNab), Matthew Gar-
ber (Geordie), Jack Stewart (Birnie),
Ewan Roberts (Constable McQuarrie),
Elspeth March (Voice of Thomasina).

THREE MISSING LINKS (1938) - short
  Director: Jules White
Moe Howard, Jerry 'Curly' Howard,
Larry Fine, Monty Collins, Jane
Hamilton, James C. Morten.

THREE STOOGES IN ORBIT, THE
(1962)
  Director: Edward Bernds
Moe Howard, Larry Fine, Joe De-
Rita, Edison Stroll (Capt. Tom An-
drews), Norman Leavitt (Williams),
Carol Christensen (Carol), Nestor
Paiva (Chairman), Maurice Manson
(Mr. Lansing), Peter Brocco (Dr.
Appleby), Roy Engel (Welby), Emil
Sitka (Prof. Danforth), George N.
Neise (Ogg), Rayford Barnes (Zogg),
Don Lamond (Col. Smithers), Peter
Dawson (Gen. Bixby), Thomas Glynn
(George Galveston), Duane Ament
(personnel clerk), Jane Wald (bathing
girl), Bill Dyer (Col. Lane), Jean
Charney (WAF sergeant), Cheerio
Meredith (tooth paste old maid).

THREE STOOGES MEET HERCULES,
THE (1962)
  Director: Edward Bernds
Moe Howard, Larry Fine, Joe De-
Rita, Quinn Redeker (Schuyler David),
Samson Burke (Hercules), Gene Roth
(Captain), Vicki Trickett (Diane
Quigley), Gregg Martell (Simon),
George N. Neise (Odius), Marlon
McKeever (Argo), Hal Smith (Thesus),
Lewis Charles (Achilles), Mike
McKeever (Ajax), Emil Sitka (shepherd),

John Cliff (Ulysses), Diana Piper
(Helen), Barbara Hines (Anita),
Cecil Elliott (matron), Terry Hunt-
ington (Hecuba), Edward Foster
(Freddie), Rusty Wescoatt (Philo).

THREE SUPERMEN IN THE JUNGLE,
  THE (1971-Span./Ital.) (A.K. A.
  "Los Tres Supermen en la Selva")
  Director: Bitto Albertini
Brad Harris, Jorge Martin, Salvatore
Borghese, Pilar Zorrilla, Francisco
Brana, Femi Benussi, Tomas Torres.

THREE TALES DARK AND DANGER-
  OUS (1980)
"Silver Blaze".
  Director: John Davies
Christopher Plummer (Sherlock
Holmes), Thorley Walters (Dr. Wat-
son), Basil Henson (Col. Ross),
Gary Watson (Insp. Gregory).
"The Ugly Little Boy".
  Director: Barry Morse & Don
  Thompson
Kate Reid (Nurse Fellows), Barry
Morse (Dr. Hoskins), Guy Big (the
Boy).
"The Rocking Horse Winner".
  Director: Peter Medak
Kenneth More (Uncle Oscar), Nigel
Rhodes (Paul), Angela Thorne (Mo-
ther), Peter Cellier (Father), Chris
Harris (Bassett).

THREE WISE FOOLS (1946)
  Director: Edward Buzzell
Margaret O'Brien (Sheila O'Monohan),
Edward Arnold (Theodore Findley),
Lionel Barrymore (Dr. Richard
Gaunght), Lewis Stone (Judge Thomas
Trumbull), Thomas Mitchell (Terence
Aloysius O'Davern), Cyd Charisse
(Rena Fairchild), Henry O'Neill
(Horace Appleby), Jane Darwell
(Sister Mary Brigid), Charles Dingle
(Paul Badger), Harry Davenport
(the Ancient), Warner Anderson
(the O'Monahan), Billy Curtis (Dugan).

THREE WOMEN (1977)
  Director: Robert Altman
Sissy Spacek (Pinky Rose), Shelley
Duvall (Millie Lammoreux), Janice
Rule (Willie Hart), Robert Fortier
(Edgar), Ruth Nelson (Pinky's mo-
ther), John Cromwell (Pinky's father),
Craig Richard Nelson (Mr. Mass),
Sierra Pecheur (Bunweill), Maysie
Hoy (hospital attendant), Belita
Moreno (hospital attendant), Beverly
Ross (Deidre), John Davey (Dr.
Norton).

THREE WORLDS OF GULLIVER,
THE (1959)
Director: Jack Sher
Kerwin Mathews (Gullivar), Jo Morrow (Gwendolyn), June Thorburn
(Elizabeth), Sherri Alberoni (Glumdalclitch), Gregoire Aslan (King
Brobdingnag), Mary Ellis (Queen
Brobdingnag), Basil Sydney (Emperor
of Lilliput), Marian Spencer (Empress
of Lilliput), Charles Lloyd-Pack
(Makovan), Martin Benson (Flimnap),
Peter Bull (Lord Bermogg), Alec
Mango (Galbet), Lee Patterson (Reldresal).

THREE'S COMPANY (1953)
Director: Charles Saunders
"The Scream": Douglas Fairbanks,
Jr., Basil Sydney, Elizabeth Sellars,
George Benson, Constance Cummings.

THRESHOLD (1971) - short
Director: Jay Lovins
John Carradine (Death), William
Rothlein, Carol Young.

THRESHOLD OF THE VOID, THE
(1971-Fr.) (A.K.A. "Le Seuil
du Vide", "On the Edge of the
Void")
Director: Jean Francois Davy
Jean Servais, Catherine Rich, Michel
Lemoine, Dominique Erlanger, Pierre
Vaneck.

THRILL KILLERS, THE (1965)
Director: Ray Steckler/Cash
Flagg
Cash Flagg, Liz Renay, Brick Bardo,
Carolyn Brandt, Ron Burr, Garay
Kent, Keith O'Brien, Herb Robins,
Laura Benedict, Atlas King, George
J. Morgan, Erina Enyo, Titus Moede.

THROUGH THE MAGIC PYRAMID
(TVM-1981) - 12-6-81 & 12-13-81
Director: Ron Howard
Chris Barnes (Bobby Tuttle), Eric
Greene (Tutankhamen), Vic Tayback
(Horembeb), Kario Salem (Akhenaten),
Olivia Barash (Baket), Jo Anne Worley (Mutjnedjmet), James Hampton
(Sam Tuttle), Hans Conried (Ay),
Elaine Giftos, Woodrow Chambliss,
Betty Beaird, Robbie Rist, Mel Berger, Kurt Christian, David Darlow,
Len Lesser, Hoke Howell, Mary
Carver, Ralph Dougherty, Mike
Johnson, Richard Moll, Daniel Leon,
Linda Zernecke, Angela Lamonea,
Sydney Penney.

THUNDERBALL (1965)
Director: Terence Young
Sean Connery (James Bond), Claudine Auger (Domino Derval), Adolfo
Celi (Emilio Largo), Martine Beswicke (Paula), Luciana Paluzzi
(Fiona), Rik Von Nutter (Felix Leiter), Bernard Lee (M), Lois Maxwell (Miss Moneypenny), Desmond
Llewellyn (Q), Guy Doleman (Count
Lippe), Roland Culver (Foreign Secretary), Reginald Beckwith (Kennington), Earl Cameron (Pinder), Leonard Sachs (Air Secretary), George
Pravda (Kutze), Molly Peters (Patricia), Michael Brennan (Janni),
Philip Locke (Vargas), Bill Cummings (Quist), Bob Simmons (Jacques Boitier), Edward Underdown
(Air Vice Marshal), Rosa Alba
(Madame Boiter), Paul Stassino
(Palazzi), Maryse Guy Mitsouko
(Mlle. La Porte).

THUNDERBIRDS ARE GO (1966) -
marionettes
Director: David Lane
Voices: Ray Barrett, Sylvia Anderson, Peter Dyneley, Neil McCallum,
Shane Rimmer, Charles Tingwell,
Bob Monkhouse, David Graham.

THUNDERBIRDS 6 (1968) - marionettes
Director: David Lane
Voices: Peter Dyneley, Catherine
Finn, Sylvia Anderson, Keith Alexander, Jeremy Wilkin, John Carson,
David Graham, Shane Rimmer, Gary
Files.

THUNDERBIRDS TO THE RESCUE
(1968)
see Television: Thunderbirds
(1966-68)

THX 1138 (1969)
Director: George Lucas
Robert Duvall (THX 1138), Donald
Pleasence (SEN 5241), Don Pedro
Colley (SRT, the Hologram), Maggie
McOmie (LUH 3147), Ian Wolfe
(PTO), Sid Haig (NCH), John Pearce
(DWY), Marshall Efrom (TWA),
Irene Forrest (IMM), Claudette Bessing (ELC), John Seaton (OUE),
Eugene I. Sullivan (JOT), Gary Alan
Marsh (CAM), Raymond J. Walsh
(TRG), Johnny Weismuller, Jr.,
Robert Feero (Chrome Robots), Gary
Austin (man in yellow), Henry
Jacobs (Mark 8 student), Mello Alexander, Barbara J. Artis (dancers).

TIDAL WAVE (1975-Jap./U.S.) (A.K.A.
"Nippon Chinbotsu", "Japan Sinks",
"Submersion of Japan")
   Director: Shiro Moritani & An-
drew Meyer
Lorne Greene (Warren Richards),
Keiju Kobayashi (Dr. Tadokoro),
Hiroshi Fujioka (Toshio Onoda),
Tetsuro Tamba (Prime Minister
Yamoto), Rhonda Leigh Hopkins (Fran),
Shogo Shimada (Prince Watari), An-
drew Hughs (Australian Prime Minis-
ter), Nubuo Nakamura (Australian
Ambassador), Ayumi Ishida (Reiko),
John Jujioka (Narita), Marvin Miller.

TIGER WOMAN, THE (1944) (A.K.A.
"Jungle Gold", "Perils of the Dark-
est Jungle") - serial in 12 episodes
   Director: Spencer Gordon
Bennet & Wallace Grissell
Linda Stirling (Tiger Woman), Allan
Lane (Allen Saunders), Duncan Re-
naldo (Jose), George J. Lewis (Mor-
gan), Stanley Price (Slim), Robert
Frazer (High Priest), Kenne Duncan
(Gentry), LeRoy Mason (Walton),
Nolan Leary (Capt. Scott), Tom
Steele (Karl/Lance/Largo/temple
heavy), Eddie Parker (Travis/Blair/
Gherkin/guard/office heavy/trooper),
Cliff Lyons (Rand/Lafe/camp heavy
No. 1/temple heavy No. 2/trooper),
Ken Terrell (Dixon/driver/depot
heavy/Schlag), Duke Green (Flint/
camp heavy No. 2/Fritz Karnes/
Grat/boat heavy), Rico de Montez
(Tegula), Crane Whitley (Dagget),
Georges Renavent (Commandant),
Bud Geary (blacksmith heavy No. 1),
Bud Wolfe (Tony/blacksmith heavy No.
3), John Daheim (blacksmith heavy No.
2), Robert Wilke (hill heavy No. 1/
road heavy), Al Ferguson (hill heavy
No. 2/Lou), Marshall Reed (Foster),
Rex Lease (Mart), Fred Graham
(Goff/Joe/Steve), Frank Marlowe
(Burt), Charles Hayes (bartender),
Roy Darmour (officer), Paul Gustine
(pilot), Carey Loftin (Slim), Tom
London (Dumont), Bert LeBaron
(Pete), Walt LaRue (temple heavy No.
3), Herman Hack (Wilson), Babe De-
Freest, Harry Smith, Augie Gomez,
Joe Molina, Catherine McLeod.

TILL DEATH (1978)
   Director: Walter Stocker
Keith Atkinson, Marshall Reed, Be-
linda Balaski, Bert Freed, Keith
Walker, Jonathan Cole.

TIME AFTER TIME (1979)

   Director: Nicholas Meyer
Malcolm McDowell (Herbert G.
Wells), David Warner (Dr. John
Lesley Stevenson), Mary Steen-
burgen (Amy Robbins), Charles
Cioffi (Lt. Mitchell), Laurie Main
(Insp. Gregson), Andonia Katsaros
(Mrs. Turner), Patti D'Arbanville
(Shirley), Keith McConnell (Harding),
Geraldine Baron (Carol), James
Garrett (Edwards), Byron Webster
(McKay), Leo Lewis (Richardson),
Joseph Maher (Adams), Kent Wil-
liams (assistant), Bob Shaw (bank
officer), Karin Mary Shea (Jenny),
Ray Reinhardt (jeweler), Michael
Evans (sergeant), Stu Klitsner (cler-
gyman), Nicholas Shields (diner),
Larry J. Blake (guard), Read Morgan
(booking cop), Bill Bradley (pawn-
broker), Rita Conde (maid), Shelley
Hack (Docent), Clete Roberts (news-
caster), Gail Hyatt (woman cop),
Jim Haynie, Wayne Storm, John
Colton, Earl Nicols, Glenn Carlson
(cops), Gene Hartline (cab driver),
Shirley Marchant (Dolores), James
Cranna (man), Antonie Becker (nurse),
Clement St. George (Bobby), Hilda
Haynes (2nd nurse), Corey Feldman
(boy at museum), Mike Gainey (Lon-
don bobby), Daniel Leegant (man on
street), Liz Roberson, Regina Wal-
dron (women), Anthony Gordon, Lou
Felder, Doug Morrisson (men),
Everett Creach, Larry Duran, Gadie
David, Brad Eide (stuntmen).

TIME BANDITS (1981)
   Director: Terry Gilliam
Craig Warnock (Kevin), Jack Pur-
vis (Wally), Malcolm Dixon (Stutter),
David Rappaport (Randall), Kenny Ba-
ker (Fidget), Mike Edmonds (Og), Ti-
ny Ross (Vermin), Sean Connery (Agam-
memnon), David Warner (Evil Incar-
nate), Sir Ralph Richardson (Supreme
Being), Ian Holm (Napoleon), John
Cleese (Robin Hood), Peter Vaughan
(Ogre), Katherine Helmond (Ogre's
wife), Michael Palin (Vincent), Shelley
Duvall (Pansy), David Daker (Kevin's
father), Sheila Fearn (Kevin's mother),
Jim Broadbent (Compere), John Young
(Reginald), Leon Lissek (1st refugee),
Brian Bowes (stunt knight/Hussar),
Myrtle Devenish (Beryl), Terence
Bayler (Lucien), Preston Lockwood
(Neguy), David Leland (puppeteer),
Charles McKeown (theatre manager),
John Hushman (the Great Rumbozo),
Derrick O'Connor (robber leader),
Neil McCarthy (2nd robber), Declan

Mulholland (3rd robber), Peter Jonfield (arm wrestler), Jerrold Wells (Benson), Derek Deadman (Robert), Roger Frost (Cartwright), Marcus Powell (Horse Flesh), Martin Carroll (Baxi Brazilla III), Ian Muir (Giant), Winston Dennis (bull-headed warrior), Del Baker (Greek fighting warrior), Juliette James (Greek Queen), Mark Holmes (Troll father), Andrew MacLachlan (fireman), Chris Grant (voice of TV announcer), Tony Jay (voice of Supreme Being), Edwin Finn (Supreme Being's face).

TIME FLIES (1944)
Director: Walter Forde
Felix Aylmer (Professor), Leslie Bradley (Walter Raleigh), Evelyn Dall (Susie Barton), Tommy Handley (Tommy), George Moon (Bill Barton), Moore Marriott (Soothsayer), John Salew (William Shakespeare), Roy Emerton (Capt. John Smith), Olga Lindo (Queen Elizabeth), Iris Lang (Pocohontas), Graham Moffatt (nephew), Stephane Grappelly (troubadour).

TIME MACHINE, THE (1960)
Director: George Pal
Rod Taylor (George), Yvette Mimieux (Weena), Alan Young (David Filby), Doris Lloyd (Mrs. Watchett), Sebastian Cabot (Dr. Philip Hillyer), Whit Bissell (Walter Kemp), Tom Helmore (Anthony Bridewell), Paul Frees (voice of Talking Rings).

TIME MACHINE, THE (TVM-1978) - 11-5-78
Director: Henning Schellerup
John Beck (Neil Perry), Priscilla Barnes (Weena), Andrew Duggan (Bean Worthington), Whit Bissell (Ralph Branley), Rosemary DeCamp (Agnes), R.G. Armstrong (Gen. Harris), John Hansen (Ariel), Parley Baer (Henry Haverson), Jack Kruschen (John Bedford), John Doucette (Sheriff Finley), Bill Zuckert, Hyde Clayton, John Zaremba, Peg Stewart, Craig Clyde, Debbie Dutson, Paul Grace, Buck Flower, Scott D. Curran, Tom Kelly, Julie Parrish, H.E.O. Redford, Scott Wilkinson, Kerry Summers, Maurice Grandmaison, Walt Price, Michael Rudd, James Lyle Strong.

TIME MASTERS, THE (1982-Fr./ Swiss/Ger.) (A.K.A. "Les Maitres du Temps") - animated

Director: Rene Laloux
Voices: Saddy Rebot, Frederic Legros, Jean Valmont, Yves Marie, Monique Thierry, Michel Elias, Ludovic Baugin, Pierre Tourneur, Alain Cuny.

TIME OF THEIR LIVES, THE (1946)
Director: Charles Barton
Lou Costello (Horatio Prim), Bud Abbott (Cuthbert/Dr. Breenway), Marjorie Reynolds (Melody Allen), Binnie Barnes (Mrs. Prescott), Gale Sondergaard (Emily), John Shelton (Sheldon Gage), Jess Barker (Tom Danbury), Rex Lease (Sgt. Makepeace), Robert Barrat (Major Putnam), Ann Gillis (Nora), William Hall (Connors), Donald MacBride (Lt. Mason), Lynne Baggett (June Prescott), Harry Woolman (motorcycle rider), Marjorie Eaton, Myron Healey, Selmer Jackson, Kirk Alyn, John Crawford, Boyd Irwin, Walter Baldwin.

TIME SLIP (1980-Jap.) (A.K.A. "Sengoko Jieitai")
Director: Kosei Saito
Sonny Chiba (Lt. Iba), Isao Natsuki (Samurai leader), Miyuki Ono (village girl), Jana Okada (modern girl).

TIME TO DIE, THE (1969-Fr.) (A.K.A. "Le Temps de Mourir")
Director: Andre Farwagi
Anna Karina, Bruno Cemer, Catherine Rich, Jean Rochefort, Billy Kearns.

TIME TRAVELERS, THE (1964)
Director: Ib Melchior
Preston Foster (Dr. Erik von Steiner), Phil Carey (Steve Connors), John Hoyt (Varno), Merry Anders (Carol White), Steve Franken (Danny McKee), Dolores Wells (Reena), Joan Woodbury (Gadra), Dennis Patrick (Councilman Willard), Forrest J. Ackerman (technician), Gloria Leslie (Councilwoman), Margaret Seldeen (technician), Peter Strudwick (the deviant).

TIME TRAVELERS, THE (TVM-1976) - 3-19-76
Director: Alexander Singer
Sam Groom (Dr. Clinton Earnshaw), Tom Hallick (Jeff Adams), Richard Basehart (Dr. Henderson), Trish Stewart (Jane Henderson), Booth Colman (Dr. Cummings), Francine

York (Dr. Lene Sanders), Walter
Burke (Dr. Stafford), Baynes Barron
(Chief Williams), Victoria Meyerink
(Betty), Dabney Coleman (Dr. Stafford), Dort Clark (Sharkey), Kathleen Bracken (Irish girl), Richard
Webb (police sergeant), Albert Cole
(news vendor).

TIN DRUM, THE (1979-Ger./Fr.)
    Director: Volker Schlondorff
David Bennent (Oskar), Mario Adorf
(Alfred Matzerath), Angela Winkler
(Agnes Matzerath), Daniel Olbrychski
(Jan Bronski), Charles Aznavour
(Sigismund Markus), Katharine Tahlbach (Maria), Heinz Bennent (Greff),
Andrea Ferreol (Lina Greff), Fritz
Hakl (Bebra), Tina Engel (young
Anna Kollaiczek), Mariella Oliveri
(Raswithz Raguna), Berta Drews
(old Anna Kollaiczek), Roland Beubner
(Joseph Kollaiczek), Ernst Jacobs
(Gauleiter Lobsack), Werner Rehm
(Scheffler, the baker), Ilse Page
(Gretchen Scheffler), Wigand Witting
(Herbert Truczinski), Kate Jaenicke
(Mother Truczinski), Schugger-Leo
(Marek Walczewski), Wolchech
Pazoniak (Faingold), Karl-Heinz
Titelbach (Felix), Otto Sander (Meyn,
the musician), Bruno Thost (Corporal
Lankes), Zygmunt Huebner (Dr.
Michon), Gerda Blisse (Miss Spollenhauer), Joachim Hackethal (Father
Wiehnke), Mieczyslaw Czechowicz
(Kobyella), Emil Feist, Herbert
Behrent (circus performers).

TIN GIRL, THE (1970-Ital.) (A.K.A.
    "La Ragazza de Latta", "The Girl
    of Tin")
    Director: Marcello Aliprandi
Umberto D'Orsi, Sydne, Elena Persiani, Roberto Antonelli, Adriano
Amidei Migiano.

TINGLER, THE (1959)
    Director: William Castle
Vincent Price (Dr. William Chapin),
Judith Evelyn (Mrs. Higgins), Patricia Cutts (Isabel Chapin), Darryl
Hickman (David Morris), Philip
Coolidge (Ollie Higgins), Pamela
Lincoln (Lucy Stevens).

TIN MAN, THE (1935) - short
    Director: James Parrott
Thelma Todd, Patsy Kelly, Matthew
Betz, Clarence H. Wilson, Cy Slocum.

TOBOR THE GREAT (1954)
    Director: Lee Sholem

Charles Drake (Dr. Ralph Harrison),
Karin Booth (Janice Roberts), Taylor Holmes (Nordstrom), Billy
Chapin (Gadge Roberts), Lyle Talbot (Admiral), Peter Brocco (Dr.
Gustav), Hal Baylor (Max), Henry
Kulky (Paul), Steve Geray (man
with glasses), Robert Shayne (General), Franz Roehn (Karl), Alan
Reynolds (Gilligan), William Schallert (Johnston), Norman Field (Commissioner), Helene Winston (secretary), Emmett Vogan (1st Congressman), Jack Daly, Maury Hill
(scientists).

TODO MODO (1976-Ital.)
    Director: Elio Petri
Marcello Mastroianni (Don Gaetano),
Gian Maria Volonte (President),
Michel Piccoli (Excellency), Mariangela Melato (Giancinta), Franco
Citti (chauffeur), Renato Salvatori
(Judge), Ciccio Ingrasia (Voitrano), Cesare Gelli (Inspector),
Tino Scotti (Cook).

TO KILL A CLOWN (1972)
    Director: George Bloomfield
Alan Alda (Major Ritchie), Blythe
Danner (Lily Frischer), Heath
Lamberts (Timothy Frischer), Eric
Clavering (Stanley).

TOMB OF LIGEIA, THE (1964)
    (A.K.A. "Tomb of the Cat")
    Director: Roger Corman
Vincent Price (Verden Fell), Elizabeth Shepard (Rowena Trevanion/
Ligeia Fell), Derek Francis (Lord
Trevanion), John Westbrook (Christopher Gough), Oliver Johnston
(Kenrick), Richard Vernon (Dr.
Vivian), Ronald Adam (Parson).

TOMB OF THE BLIND DEAD
    (1972-Span./Port.) (A.K.A.
    "La Noche del Terror Ciego",
    "The Night of the Blind Terror")
    Director: Armando De Ossorio
Lone Fleming, Cesar Burner,
Joseph Thelman, Helen Harp, Maria
Silva.

TOMB OF TORTURE (1963-Ital./
    Ger.) (A.K.A. "Metempsycose")
    Director: Antonio Boccaci
Annie Albert (Anna), Thony Maky
(Dr. Darnell), Elizabeth Queen
(Elizabeth), Mark Marian/Marco
Mariani (George), William Gray,
Fred Pizzot, Terry Thompson, Emy
Eko, Bernard Blay.

TOMMY (1975)
Director: Ken Russell
Ann-Margret (Nora Walker), Roger
Daltry (Tommy), Oliver Reed (Frank
Hobbs), Elton John (Pinball Wizard),
Keith Moon (Uncle Ernie), Eric
Clapton (Preacher), Jack Nicholson
(Specialist), Tina Turner (Acid Queen),
Robert Powell (Captain Walker), Paul
Nicholas (Cousin Kevin).

TOMORROW AT SEVEN (1933)
Director: Ray Enright
Chester Morris (Neil Broderick),
Vivienne Osborne (Martha Winters),
Frank McHugh (Clancy), Allen Jen-
kins (Dugan), Grant Mitchell (Win-
ters), Henry Stephenson (Drake),
Oscar Apfel (Marsden), Charles
Middleton (Simons), Cornelis Keefe
(Henderson), Virginia Howell (Mrs.
Quincey), Gus Robinson (Pompey),
Edward Le Saint (coroner).

TOMORROW MAN, THE (1979)
Director: Tibor Takacs
Don Francks (the Warden), Stephen
Markle (Tom Weston), Michelle
Chicoine (Margaret Weston), Gail
Dahms (Maya).

TOMORROW'S CHILD (TVM-1982)
- 3-22-82
Director: Joseph Sargent
William Atherton (Dr. Jim Spence),
Stephanie Zimbalist (Kay Spence),
Ed Flanders (Anders Stenslund),
Arthur Hill (Gorham), Bruce Davi-
son (Cliff Bender), Salome Jens
(Dr. Pressburg), Susan Oliver (Mari-
lyn), James Shigeta (Dr. Shibura),
Teddi Sidall (Janice Bender), J. Vic-
tor Lopez (Roy), Jerry McNeely (Dr.
Sargent), Dave Turner (Lt. Wolders),
Virginia Bingham (Cheryl), Lana Ro-
sen (Chuck), Stephen Douglas Helm
(man at accident), Freddye Chapman
(Nurse), Jody Myler (Arlene), Shelly
O'Neil (secretary).

tom thumb (1958)
Director: George Pal
Russ Tamblyn (tom thumb), Alan Young
(Woody the Piper), Terry-Thomas
(Ivan), Peter Sellers (Tony), Jessie
Matthews (Anna), June Thorburn (the
Forest Queen), Bernard Miles (Jona-
than), Peter Bull (the Town Crier),
Ian Wallace (the Cobbler), Peter But-
terworth (Bandmaster), Barbara Fer-
ris (voice of Thumbelina), Stan Freberg
(voice of the yawning man), Dal Mc-
Kennon (voice of Con-fu-shon).

TONIGHT I WILL ENTER YOUR CORPSE
(1966-Braz.) (A.K.A. "Esta Noite
Encarnarei Seu Cadaver")
Director: Jose Mojica Marins
Mina Monte, Arlete Brasulin, Roque
Rodriquez, Oswaldo de Souza, Palito,
Tina Wholers, William Morgan.

TONIGHT'S THE NIGHT (1954) (A.K.A.
"Happy Ever After")
Director: Mario Zampi
David Niven (Jasper O'Leary), Yvonne
De Carlo (Serena McGlusky), Barry
Fitzgerald (Thady O'Haggerty), George
Cole (Terence), Robert Urquhart (Dr.
Flynn), Eddie Byrne (Lannigan), A. E.
Matthews (Gen. O'Leary), Joseph
Tomelty (Dooley), Noelle Middleton
(Kathy McGlusky), Liam Redmond
(Regan), Michael Shepley (Maj.
McGlusky), Anthony Nicholls (soli-
citor).

TOOLBOX MURDERS, THE (1978)
Director: Dennis Donnelly
Cameron Mitchell (Kingsley), Pamelyn
Ferdin (Laurie), Wesley Eure (Kent),
Nicholas Beauvy (Joey), Aneta Coraut
(Joanne), Tim Donnelly (Detective),
Evelyn Guerrero (Butch), Marciee
Drake, Faith McSwain, Mariane
Walter (victims).

TOOMORROW (1970)
Director: Val Guest
Olivia Newton-John (Olivia), Roy Do-
trice (John Williams), Tracey Crisp
(Suzanne Gilmore), Benny Thomas
(Benny), Karl Chambers (Karl), Vic
Cooper (Vic), Imogen Hassall (Amy),
Margaret Nolan (Johnson), Carl Rigg
(Matthew), Roy Marsden (Alpha),
Maria O'Brien (Francoise).

TOPO, EL (1971-Mex.) (A.K.A. "The
Mole", "The Gopher")
Director: Alexandro Jodorowsky
Alexandro Jodorowsky, Brontis Jo-
dorowsky, Mara Lorenzio, David
Silva, Hector Martinez, Paula Romo,
Jacqueline Luis.

TOPPER (1937)
Director: Norman McLeod
Ronald Young (Cosmo Topper), Cary
Grant (George Kirby), Constance Ben-
nett (Marion Kirby), Billie Burke (Mrs.
Topper), Alan Mowbray (Wilkins),
Eugene Pallette (Casey), Hedda
Hopper (Mrs. Stuyvesant), Arthur
Lake (elevator boy), J. Farrell Mac-
Donald (policeman), Virginia Sale
(Miss Johnson), Doodles Weaver, Si

Jends (rustics), Elaine Shepard (secretary), Theodore von Eltz (hotel
manager).

TOPPER (TVM-1979) - 11-9-79
Director:
Kate Jackson (Marion Kirby), Andrew
Stevens (George Kirby), Jack Warden
(Cosmo Topper), Rue McClanahan
(Clara Topper), Macon McCalman
(Wilkins), James Karen (Korbell),
Charles Siebert (Ogilvy), Larry
Gelman (mechanic).

TOPPER RETURNS (1941)
Director: Roy Del Ruth
Roland Young (Cosmo Topper), Joan
Blondell (Gail Richards), Billie Burke
(Mrs. Topper), Dennis O'Keefe (Bob),
Carol Landis (Ann Carrington), Eddie
'Rochester' Anderson (Eddie), H. W.
Warner (Carrington), George Zucco
(Dr. Jeris), Rafaela Ottiana (Lillian),
Trevor Bardette (Rama), Patsy Kelly
(Emily, the maid), Donald MacBride
(Sgt. Roberts).

TOPPER TAKES A TRIP (1938)
Director: Norman Z. MacLeod
Roland Young (Cosmo Topper), Con-
stance Bennett (Marion Kirby), Billie
Burke (Mrs. Topper), Alan Mowbray
(Wilkins), Verree Teasdale (Mrs.
Parkhurst), Alex D'Arcy (Baron),
Franklin Pangborn (hotel manager),
Paul Hurst (bartender), Leon Belasco
(bellboy), Irving Pichel (prosecutor),
Spencer Charters (judge), James C.
Morton (bailiff).

TORMENTED (1960)
Director: Bert I. Gordon
Richard Carlson (Tom Stewart),
Susan Gordon (Sandy), Juli Redings
(Vi Mason), Joseph Turkel (Nick),
Lugene Sanders (Meg), Vera Marshe
(the Mother), Gene Roth (lunch stand
operator), Lillian Adams (real estate
broker), Merritt Stone (clergyman),
Harry Fleer (the father).

TORTICOLA CONTRA FRANKENSBERG
(1952-Fr.) (A. K. A. "Twisted Neck
vs. Frankensberg")
Director: Paul Paviot
Roger Blin (Dr. Frankensberg), Vera
Norman (Lorelei), Michel Piccoli
(the Monster), Francois Patrice,
Helena Menson, Marc Boussac,
Daniel Gelin.

TORTURE DUNGEON (1969)
Director: Andy Milligan

Jeremy Brooks (Duke of Norwich),
Susan Cassidy (Heather), Neil Flana-
gan (Peter the Eye), Patricia Dillon
(Lady Jane), Donna Whitfield (Lady
Agatha), Maggie Rogen (Margaret),
Richard Mason (Ivan), Haal Boske
(Alfred), George Box, Don Lyra,
Robert Fricelle, Patricia Garvey,
Helen Adams.

TORTURE GARDEN (1967)
Director: Freddie Francis
Burgess Meredith (Dr. Diabolo),
Beverly Adams (Carla Hayes), Peter
Cushing (Lancelot Canning), Jack
Palance (Ronald Wyatt), Bernard
Kay (Dr. Heim), Robert Hutton (Bruce
Benton), John Phillips (Eddie Storm),
Michael Ripper (Gordon Roberts),
Maurice Denham (Colin's uncle),
Michael Bryant (Colin Williams),
Barbara Ewing (Dorothy Endicott),
Nicole Shelby (Millie), John Standing
(Leo Wilson), Catherine Finn (Nurse
Parker), Ursula Howells (Miss Cham-
bers), Michael Hawkins (Constable),
Niall MacGinnis (doctor), David Bauer
(Mike Charles), Clytie Jessop (Atro-
pos), Hedger Wallace (Edgar Allen
Poe), Timothy Bateson (fairground
barker), Frank Forsyth (tramp),
James Copeland, Roy Godfrey, Roy
Stevens, Barry Low, Norman Claridge,
Geoffrey Wallace.

TORTURE SHIP (1939)
Director: Victor Halperin
Irving Pichel, Lyle Talbot, Russell
Horton, Jacqueline Wells, Leander
de Cordova, Stanley Blystone, Sheila
Bromley, Wheeler Oakman, Eddie
Holden, Anthony Averill.

TO THE DEVIL - A DAUGHTER
(1976)
Director: Peter Sykes
Christopher Lee (Father Michael
Raynor), Richard Widmark (John
Verney), Nastassia Kinski (Catherine
Beddows), Michael Goodliffe (George
de Grass), Honor Blackman (Anna
Fountain), Anthony Valentine (David),
Denholm Elliott (Henry Beddoes),
Derek Francis (the Bishop), Anna
Bentinck (Isabel), Isabella Telezynska
(Margaert), Constantin De Gougel
(Kolide), Eva Maria Meineke (Eveline
de Grass), Irene Prador (German
matron), Petra Peters (Sister Helle),
William Ridoutt (airport porter),
Brian Wilde (Black Room attendant),
Howard Goorney (critic), Zoe Hendry
(1st girl), Lindy Benson (2nd girl),

Jo Peters (3rd girl), Bobby Sparrow (4th girl), Frances De La Tour (Salvation Army Major).

TOTO IN HELL (1955-Ital.) (A. K. A. "Toto all' Inferno")
Director: Camillo Mastrocinque
Toto, Maria Frau, Dante Maggio.

TOTO IN THE MOON (1958-Ital./Span.) (A. K. A. "Toto nella Luna")
Director: Stefano Steno
Toto, Sylva Koscina, Ugo Tognazzi, Sandra Milo.

TOTO THE SHEIK (1950-Ital.) (A. K. A. "Toto Sceicco")
Director: Mario Mattoli
Toto, Tamara Lees, Aroldo Tieri, Laura Gore, Ada Dondini.

TO TRAP A SPY (1965)
Director: Don Medford
see Television: Man from U. N. - C. L. E. - "The Vulcan Affair" (9-22-64)

TOURIST TRAP (1979)
Director: David Schmoeller
Chuck Connors (Mr. Slausen), Jon Van Ness (Jerry), Jocelyn Jones (Molly), Robin Sherwood (Eileen), Tanya Roberts (Becky), Keith McDermott (Woody), Dawn Jeffory (Tina), Shailar Coby (Davey).

TOWER OF LONDON (1908-Fr.) (A. K. A. "La Tour de Londres")
Director: Georges Melies

TOWER OF LONDON (1926)
Director: Maruice Elvey
Isobel Elsom, John Stuart.

TOWER OF LONDON (1939)
Director: Rowland V. Lee
Basil Rathbone (Richard III), Boris Karloff (Mord the Executioner), Barbara O'Neil (Queen Elizabeth), Ian Hunter (Edward IV), Vincent Price (Duke of Clarence), Nan Grey (Lady Alice Barton), Leo G. Carroll (Lord Hastings), John Sutton (John Wyatt), Rose Hobart (Anne Neville), Miles Mander (Henry VI), Ralph Forbes (Henry Tudor), Frances Robinson (Isobel), Lionel Belmore (Beacon), Donnie Dunagan (Richard as a child), John Herbert-Bond (Richard as an older child), John Rodion (Lord De Vere), Ronald Sinclair (Prince Edward), G. P. Huntley (Prince of

Wales), Ernest Cossart (Tom Clink), Ernie Adams, Nigel de Bruller, C. Montague Shaw, Russell Powell, Harry Cording, Ivan Simpson, Walter Tetley.

TOWER OF LONDON (1962)
Director: Roger Corman
Vincent Price (Richard of Gloucester), Michael Pate (Sir Ratcliffe), Joan Freeman (Margaret), Robert Brown (Sir Justin), Sandra Knight (Mistress Shore), Bruce Gordon (Earl of Buckingham), Justice Watson (Edward IV), Joan Camden (Anne), Sara Selby (Queen), Eugene Martin (Edward V), Richard McCauly (Clarence), Richard Hale (Tyrus), Donald Losby (Richard).

TOWER OF SCREAMING VIRGINS, THE (1971-Span./Ger.) (A. K. A. "Der Turm Der Verbotenen Liebe", "The Tower of Forbidden Love")
Director: Francois Le Grand
Terry Torday (Marguerite), Jean Piat (Capt. Bourdan), Veronique Vendell (Jeanne), Uschi Glas (Blanche), Frank Olivier/Armando Francioli (Orsini), Dada Gallotti (Fluerette), Marie-Agne Anies (Catherine), Rudolf Forster (Honore De La Tour), Franz Rudnik, Karlheim Fiege, Jorg Pleva, Jacques Herlin, George Markos, Rolf Becker, Werner Fliege.

TOWER OF TERROR (1941)
Director: Lawrence Huntington
Wilfrid Lawson (Wolfe Kristan), Michael Rennie (Anthony Hale), George Woodbridge (Jurgens), John Longden (Commander), Morland Graham (Kleber), Richard George (Capt. Borkman), Edward Sinclair (Fletcher), Charles Rolfe (Albers), Movita (Marie Durand), Victor Weske (Peters), Olive Sloane (florist), Eric Clavering.

TOWN THAT DREADED SUNDOWN, THE (1976)
Director: Charles B. Pierce
Ben Johnson (Capt. J. D. Morales), Dawn Wells (Helen Reed), Andrew Prine (Deputy Norman Ramsey), Jimmy Clem (Sgt. Mal Griffin), Charles B. Pierce (Patrolman A. C. Benson), Cindy Butler (Peggy Loomis), Mike Hackworth (Sammy Fuller), Earl E. Smith (Dr. Krees), Christine Ellsworth (Linda Mae Jendkins), Misty West (Emma Lou), Rick Hildreth (Buddy Turner), Robert Aquino (Sheriff Otis Barker), Jim Citty (Chief R. J. Sullivan), Steve Lyons (Roy Allen),

Bud Davis (the Phantom Killer).

TOY BOX, THE (1971)
Director: Ron Garcia
Evan Steele (the Benevolent Man),
Ann Myers (Donna), Neal Bishop
(Ralph), Deborah Osborne, Marie
Arnold, Lisa Goodman, Steve Moon,
T. E. Brown, Ralph Dale, Karen
Hutt, Marsha Jordan, Kathie Hilton,
Jack King, Patti Mendosa, Nancey
Freese, Casey Larrain.

TRACK OF THE MOON BEAST (1976)
Director: Richard Ashe
Chase Cordell (Paul Carson), Donna
Leigh Drake (Kathy Nolan), Gregorio
Sala (Johnny Longbow), Francine
Kessler (Janet Price), Joe Blasco
(the Monster), Patrick Wright, Craw-
ford MacCallum, Fred McCaffrey,
Timothy Wayne Brown, Alan Swain,
Tim Butler, Jeanne Swain.

TRANSATLANTIC TUNNEL (1935)
(A. K. A. "The Tunnel")
Director: Maurice Elvey
Richard Dix (McAllen), Madge Evans
(Ruth McAllen), Helen Vinson (Varlia
Lloyd), Leslie Banks (Robbie), George
Arliss (the Prime Minister), Basil
Sydney (Mostyn), C. Aubrey Smith
(Lloyd), Henry Oscar (Grellier), Wal-
ter Huston (U. S. President), Jimmy
Hanley (Geoffrey McAllen), Cyril
Raymond, Mary Jerrold.

TRAPPED (1982)
Director: William Fruet
Henry Silva (Henry Chatwill), Nicho-
las Campbell (Roger Michaels), Bar-
bara Gordon (Miriam Chatwill), Gina
Dick (Dana), Joy Thompson (Caroline),
Ralph Benmergui (Lee), Sam Malkin
(Jeb), Alan Royal (Leonard), Stuart
Culpepper (Myles), John Rutter (Sher-
iff), Jeff Toole (Dave), Canone Camden
(Amy), Ervin Melton (Professor),
Jere Beery (welfare agent), Wallace
Wilkinson, Lloyd Semlar, Randall
Deal, Leonard Flory (Elders).

TREACHERY AND GREED ON THE
PLANET OF THE APES (1974)
see Television: Planet of the Apes
(1974)

TREASURE OF SATAN (1902-Fr.)
(A. K. A. "Les Tresors de Satan")
Director: Georges Melies

TREASURE OF THE PETRIFIED FOR-
EST, THE (1965-Ital.) (A. K. A. "Il

Tesoro della Foresta Pietrifica-
ta")
Director: Enimmo Salvi
Gordon Mitchell, Eleanora Bianchi,
Ivo Payer, Pamela Tudor.

TRIAL, THE (1962-Fr. /Ital. /Ger.)
(A. K. A. "Le Proces")
Director: Orson Welles
Anthony Perkins (Joseph K.), Je-
anne Moreau (Burstner), Romy Schnei-
der (Leni), Elsa Martinelli (Hilda),
Akim Tamiroff (Bloch), Orson Welles
(Defense Attorney), Katina Paxinou,
Suzanne Flon, Arnoldo Foa, Michael
Lonsdale, Max Haufler, Madeleine
Robinson, Fernand Ledoux, Jess Hahn,
Thomas Holtzman, Wolfgang Reichman,
Max Bushman, Maurice Teynac.

TRIBE, THE (TVM-1974) - 12-11-74
Director: Richard A. Colla
Victor French (Mathis), Henry Wilcoxon
(Cana), Stewart Moss (Gato), Meg Wy-
lie (Herta), Adriana Shaw (Jen), War-
ren Vanders (Gorin), Sam Gilman
(Rouse), Tani Phelps Guthrie (Sarish),
Nancy Elliot (Ardis), Dominique Pi-
nassi (Kiska), Mark Gruner (Perron),
Jeannie Brown (Orda), Jack Scalici
(Neanderthal Leader).

TRILBY (1914)
Director: Harold Shaw
Herbert Beerbohm Tree, Vira Birkett,
Philip Merivale, Wyndham Guise,
Cicely Richards, Douglas Munro,
E. Ion Swinley, Charles Rook.

TRILBY (1915)
Director: Maurice Tourneur
Wilton Lackaye, Clara Kimball Young,
Paul McAllister, Chester Barnett.

TRILBY (1923)
Director: James Young
Arthur Edmund Carewe (Svengali),
Andree Lafayette (Trilby), Creighton
Hale (Little Billee), Philo McCullough
(Taffy), Wilfrid Lucas (the Laird),
Francis McDonald (Gecko), Maurice
Cannon, Gertrude Olmstead.

TRILOGY (1969)
Director: Frank Berry
"Miriam": Mildred Natwick (Mrs.
Miller), Susan Dunfee (Miriam), Carol
Gustafson (Miss Lake), Robin Ponteiro
(Emily), Beverly Ballard (Nina).

TRILOGY OF TERROR (TVM-1975) -
3-4-75
Director: Dan Curtis

"Julie": Karen Black (Julie), Robert Burton (Chad), Gregory Harrison (Arthur Moore), James Storm (Eddie Nells), Kathryn Reynolds (Anne Richards), Orin Cannon (motel manager). "Millicent and Therese": Karen Black (Millicent/Therese), George Gaynes (Dr. Ramsay), John Karlen (Thomas Anman), Tracy Curtis (little girl). "Amelia": Karen Black (Amelia).

TRIPLE CONJURER AND THE LIVING DEAD, THE (1900-Fr.) (A.K.A. "L'Illusionniste Double et la Tete Vivante")
    Director: Georges Melies

TRIPLE HEADED LADY, THE (1898-Fr.) (A.K.A. "Bouquet d'Illusions")
    Director: Georges Melies

TRIPLE LADY, THE (1898-Fr.) (A.K.A. "Dedoublement Cabalisteque")
    Director: Georges Melies

TRIP TO THE MOON, A (1902-Fr.) (A.K.A. "Le Voyage dans la Lune")
    Director: Georges Melies

TRIUMPH OF SHERLOCK HOLMES, THE (1935)
    Director: Leslie S. Hiscott
Arthur Wontner (Sherlock Holmes), Ian Fleming (Dr. Watson), Lyn Harding (Prof. Moriarty), Leslie Perrins (John Douglas), Jane Carr (Ettie Douglas), Minnie Rayner (Mrs. Hudson), Michael Shepley (Cecil Barker), Charles Mortimer (Insp. Lestrade), Ben Welden (Ted Balding), Conway Dixon (Ames), Wilfrid Caithness (Col. Sebastian Moran), Roy Emerson (Boss McGinty), Edmund D'Alby (Capt. Marvin).

TRIUMPH OF THE SON OF HERCULES (1962-Ital.) (A.K.A. "El Trionfo di Maciste", "The Triumph of Maciste")
    Director: Tanio Boccia/Amerigo Anton
Kirk Morris, Ljuba Bodine, Cathia Caro, Carlo Colo.

TROG (1970)
    Director: Freddie Francis
Joan Crawford (Dr. Brockton), Michael Gough (Sam Murdock), Robert Hutton (Dr. Richard Warren), Kim Braden (Ann Brockton), Robert Crewsdon (Dr. Pierre Duval), Bernard Kay (Insp. Greenham), David Griffin

(Malcolm Travers), John Hamill (Cliff), Thorley Walters (the Magistrate), John Cornelius (Trog), Jack May (Dr. Selbourne), Geoffrey Case (Bill), Chloe Franks (little girl), Maurice Good (1st reporter), Rona Newton-John (2nd reporter), Paul Hansard (Dr. Kurtlimer), David Warbeck (Alan Davis), Simon Lack (Col. Vickers), Golda Casimir (Prof. Manoskiensky), Brian Grellis (John Dennis), Cleo Sylvestre (nurse).

TROMBA, THE TIGER MAN (1949)
    Director: Helmut Weiss
Rene Deltgen (Tromba), Adrian Hoven, Angelika Hanuff, Gustav Knuth, Hilde Wissner, Grethe Weiser, Gardy Granass.

TRON (1982)
    Director: Steven Lisberger
Jeff Bridges (Kevin Flynn/Clu), Bruce Boxleitner (Allen Bradley/ Tron), David Warner (Ed Dillinger/ Sark), Cindy Morgan (Lora/Yori), Barnard Hughes (Dr. Walter Gibbs/ Dumont), Dan Shor (Ram), Peter Juraski (Crom), Tony Stephano (Peter/Sark's Lieutenant), Craig Chudy, Vince Deadrick (warriors), Sam Schatz (expert disk warrior), Jackson Bostwick (head guard), Dave Cass (factory guard).

TROUBLE FOR TWO (1936)
    Director: S. Walter Ruben
Robert Montgomery (Prince Florizel), Rosaline Russell (Miss Vandeleur/ Princess Brenda), Frank Morgan (Col. Geraldine), Reginald Owen (Dr. Noel), Walter Kingsford (Malthus), E. E. Clive (King), Louis Hayward (young man with cream tarts), Ivan Simpson (Collins), Pedro de Cordoba (Sergei), Robert Greig (fat man), Leland Hodgson (Captain Rich), Tom Moore (Major O'Rook), Guy Bates Post (Ambassador).

TRUNK CRIME (1939) (A.K.A. "Design for Murder")
    Director: Roy Boulting
Manning Whiley (Bentley), Barbara Everest (Ursula), Hay Petrie (Old Dan), Thorley Walters (Frazier), Michael Drake (Grierson), Eileen Bennett (Eve), Lewis Stringer (Hearty).

TUCK EVERLASTING (1981)
    Director: Frederick King Keller
Fred A. Keller (Angus Tuck), James

McGuire (man in the yellow suit), Margaret Chamberlain (Winnie), Paul Flessa (Jesse Tuck), Sonia Raimi (Mary Tuck), Bruce D'Aurio (Miles Tuck).

TUNNEL, THE (1933-Ger.) (A.K.A. "Der Tunnel")
Director: Kurt Bernhardt
German language version: Paul Hartmann, Otto Wernicke, Atila Horbiger, Oily von Flint, Elga Brink, Ferdinand Marian, Max Wedner.
French language version: Jean Gabin, Madeleine Renaud, Gustaf Grundgens.

TUNNEL UNDER THE WORLD, THE (1968-Ital.) (A.K.A. "Il Tunnel Sotto il Mondo")
Director: Luigi Cozzi.
Alberto Moro, Bruno Salviero, Anna Mantovani, Lello Maraniello, Gretel Fehr, Isabell Karilson, Pietro Rosati, Ivana Monti.

TUNNELING THE CHANNEL (1907-Fr.) (A.K.A. "La Tunnel sous le Manche", "Le Cauchemar Franco-Anglais")
Director: Georges Melies

TUNNELVISION (1976)
Director: Brad Swirnoff & Neil Israel
Phil Proctor (Christian Broder), Rick Hurst (Father Phaser Gun), Howard Hesseman (Sen. McMannus), Larraine Newman (Sonja), Roger Bowen (Kissinger), Chevy Chase, Ernie Anderson, James Bacon, Roberta Kent, Lynn Marie Stewart, Pamela Toll, Edwina Anderson, Ron Silver, Lorry Goldman, Gerrit Graham, Sam Riddle, Joe O'Flaherty, Roger Bowen, Nellie Bellflower, Betty Thomas, Bart Williams, Ron Prince, Tom Davis, Frank Von Zerneck, Wayne Stax, Al Franken, Doug Steckley, Michael Overly Band, William Schallert, Howard Storm, Michael Mislove, Bill Saluga, Neil Israel, Jimmy Martinez, Elizabeth Edwards, Frank Alesia, Julie Mannix, Ira Miller, Terri Seigel, Mary McCuster, Rod Gist, Jose Kent, Michael Popovich, Bo Kaprall, Larry Gelman, Barry Michlin, Danny Dark, Kurt Taylor, Joe Roth, C.D. Taylor, Bob McClurg, Cary Hoffman, Dody Dorn.

TURNABOUT (1940)
Director: Hal Roach
Adolphe Menjou (Phil Manning), Carole Landis (Sally Willows), John Hubbard (Tim Willows), William Gargan (Joel Clare), Joyce Compton (Irene Clare), Mary Astor (Marian Manning), Marjorie

Main (Nora), Franklin Pangborn (Mr. Pingboom), Donald Meek (Henry), Berton Churchill (Julian Marlowe), Inez Courtney (Miss Edwards), Veree Teasdale (Laura Bannister), George Renavent (Mr. Ram), Margaret Roach (Dixie Gale), Polly Ann Young (Miss Twill), Ray Turner (Mose), Eleanor Riley (Lorraine), Miki Morita (Ito), Norman Budd (Jimmy), Yolande Mollot (Marie), Murray Alper (masseur).

TURN OF THE SCREW (TVM-1974) - 4-15-74
Director: Dan Curtis
Lynne Redgrave (Miss Cubberly), Megs Jenkins (Mrs. Grose), Eva Griffith (Flora), Jasper Johns (Miles), John Baron (Fredericks), Kathryn Scott (Miss Jessel), James Laurenson (Quint), Anthony Langdon (Luke), Benedict Taylor (Timothy), Vivian Bennett (secretary).

12 TO THE MOON (1960)
Director: David Bradley
Anna-Lisa (Dr. Sigrid Bromark), Ken Clark (Capt. John Anderson), Tom Conway (Dr. Orloff), Michi Kobi (Dr. Murata), Tony Dexter (Dr. Luis Vargas), Roger Til (Dr. Martel), John Wengraf (Dr. Heinrich), Cory Devlin (Dr. Makonen), Richard Weber (Dr. Ruskin), Phillip Baird (Dr. Rochester), Tema Bey (Dr. Hamid), Bob Montgomery, Jr. (Roddy Murdock), Francis X. Bushman (Narrator).

TWENTIETH CENTURY SURGEON, A (1897-Fr.) (A.K.A. "Chirurgien Americain")
Director: Georges Melies

TWENTIETH CENTURY SURGERY (1900-Fr.) (A.K.A. "La Chirurgie de l'Avenier")
Director: Georges Melies

20 MILLION MILES TO EARTH (1957)
Director: Nathan Juran
William Hopper (Col. Calder), Joan Taylor (Marisa Leonardo), Frank Puglia (Dr. Leonardo), John Zaremba (Dr. Judson Uhl), Thomas B. Henry (Gen. A.D. McIntosh), Jan Arvan (Signore Contino), George Khoury (Verrico), Bart Bradley (Pepe), Tito Vuolo (Commissario of Police), George Pelling (Mr. Maples), Arthur Space (Sharman), Rollin Moriyama (Dr. Koroku), Don Orlando (Mon-

dello), Dale Van Sickel (stuntman).

27th DAY, THE (1956)
    Director: William Asher
Gene Barry (Jonathan Clark), Valerie
French (Eve Wingate), George Vos-
kovec (Prof. Klaus Bechner), Azemat
Janti (Ivan Godofsky), Marie Tsien
(Su Tan), Stefan Schnabel (the Dictator),
Arnold Moss (the Alien), Frederick
Ledebur (Dr. Karl Neuhaus), Ralph
Clanton (Mr. Ingram), Paul Birch
(Admiral), Grandon Rhodes (U. N.
Presiding Officer), Ed Hinton (Com-
mander), Doreen Woodbury (woman),
Jerry Janger (officer), Mark Warren
(Peter), Don Spark (Harry Bellows),
David Bond (Dr. Schmidt), Eric Fel-
dary (Russian sergeant), Weaver
Levy (Chinese sergeant), Monty Ash
(Russian doctor), Irvin Ashkenszy
(2nd man), Hank Clemin (Hans), Theo-
dore Marcuse (Col. Gregor), Peter
Norman (interrogator), John Bleifer
(spokesman), Mel Welles (Marshall),
Sigfrid Tor (Gen. Zamke), John Dods-
worth (British announcer), Jacques
Gallo (French announcer), Charles
Bennett (Gorki), Arthur Lovejoy (Bra-
covich), John Bryant (federal agent),
John Mooney (M. P. captain), Paul
Power (Army doctor), Michael Harris
(FBI man), Walda Winchell (nurse),
Tom Daly (Joe, the bartender), Ralph
Montgomery (man), Don Rhodes (TV
technician), Emil Sitka (newsboy),
Phil Van Zandt (taxi driver), Paul
Frees (newscaster).

20,000 LEAGUES UNDER THE SEA
    (1907-Fr.) (A. K. A. "Deux Cent
    Mille Lieues sous les mers")
    Director: Georges Melies

20,000 LEAGUES UNDER THE SEA
    (1916)
    Director: Stuart Paton
Matt Moore (Lt. Bond), Allen Hollu-
bar (Captain Nemo), June Gail (Prin-
cess Daaker), William Welsh (Charles
Denver), Curtis Benton (Ned Land),
Dan Hamlon (Prof. Aronnax), Edna
Pendleton (Miss Aronnax), Howard
Crampton (Cyrus Harding), Wallace
Clark (Pencroft), Martin Murphy
(Herbert Brown), Leviticus Jones
(Neb), Lois Alexander (Prince Das-
ker's daughter).

20,000 LEAGUES UNDER THE SEA
    (1954)
    Director: Richard Fleischer
Kirk Douglas (Ned Land), James

Mason (Captain Nemo), Paul Lukas
(Prof. Pierre Arronnax), Peter Lorre
(Conseil), Robert J. Wilke (First
Mate), Carleton Young (John Howard),
Ted de Corsia (Capt. Farragut), Fred
Graham (Casey Moore), J. M. Ker-
rigan (Billy), Percy Helton (diver),
Edward Marr (shipping agent), Harry
Harvey (shipping clerk), Herb Vigran
(reporter), Ted Cooper (mate on
Lincoln).

TWICE TOLD TALES (1963)
    Director: Sydney Salkow
"Doctor Heidegger's Experiment":
Vincent Price (Alex Medbourne), Se-
bastian Cabot (Dr. Carl Heidegger),
Mari Blanchard (Sylvia Ward).
"Rappaccini's Daughter": Vincent
Price (Dr. Rappaccini), Brett Halsey
(Giovanni Guasconti), Joyce Taylor
(Beatrice Rappaccini), Abraham
Sofaer (Prof. Pietro Baglioni").
"The House of the Seven Gables":
Vincent Price (Gerald), Richard
Denning (Jonathan Maulle), Beverly
Garland (Alice), Jacqueline DeWit
(Hannah), Flory Simmons (Matthew),
Gene Roth (cab driver).

TWILIGHT PEOPLE, THE (1971)
    Director: Eddie Romero
John Ashley (Matt Farrell), Pat
Woodell (Neva Gordon), Charles
Macaulay (Dr. Gordon), Eddie Garcia
(Pereira), Jan Merlin (Steinman),
Pam Grier (Ayesa, the Panther
Woman), Ken Metcalfe (the Antelope
Man), Tony Gosalves (the Bat Man),
Mona Morena (the Wolf Woman), Kim
Ramos (the Ape Man), Angelo Centenera,
Letty Mirasol, Cenon Gonzalez, Romeo
Mabutol, Max Rojo, Roger Ocomapo,
Vic Unson.

TWILIGHT'S LAST GLEAMING (1977)
    Director: Robert Aldrich
Burt Lancaster (Lawrence Dell), Ri-
chard Widmark (Gen. MacKenzie),
Charles Durning (Pres. Stevens),
Melvyn Douglas (Zachariah Guthrie),
Paul Winfield (Willis Powell), Jo-
seph Cotten (Arthur Renfrew), Ros-
coe Lee Browne (James Forrest),
Burt Young (Garvas), Vera Miles
(Victoria Stevens), Richard Jaeckel
(Capt. Stanford Towne), William
Marshall (William Klinger), Charles
Aidman (Col. Bernstein), Charles
McGraw (Peter Crane), Leif Erickson
(Ralph Whittaker), William Smith
(Hoxey), Gerald S. O'Loughlin (Michael
O'Rourke), Morgan Paull (1st Lt.

Louis Cannellis), Bill Walker (Willard).

TWINKLE, TWINKLE, KILLER
KANE (1980) (A.K.A. "The Ninth
Configuration")
    Director: William Peter Blatty
Stacy Keach (Col. Kane), Jason Miller
(Lt. Reno), Ed Flanders (Col. Fell),
Neville Brand (Groper), Moses Gunn
(Major Nammack), Robert Loggia (Lt.
Bennish), Alejandro Rey (Lt. Gomez),
Joe Spinnell (Spinnell), Scott Wilson
(Capt. Cutshaw), George Di Cenzo
(Capt. Fairbanks), Tom Atkins (Sgt.
Krebs), Steve Sandor (1st cyclist),
Richard Lynch (2nd cyclist), Mark
Gordon, Stephen Powers, Bruce Boa,
William Lucking, David Healy, Tom
Shaw, Gordon K. Kee, Bobby Bass,
Marilyn Raymon, Linda Blatty, William Paul, Bobby Gilman, Billy Blatty.

TWINS OF EVIL (1971)
    Director: John Hough
Peter Cushing (Gustav Weil), Madelaine Collinson (Frieda Gelhorn),
Mary Collinson (Maria Gelhorn),
Damien Thomas (Count Karnstein),
Kathleen Byron (Katy Weil), Dennis
Price (Dietrich), Alex Scott (Hermann),
Luan Peters (Gerta), Isobel Black
(Ingrid Hoffer), Harvey Hall (Franz),
Roy Stewart (Joachim), Katya Wyeth
(Countess), Maggie Wright (Aleta),
David Warbeck (Anton), Inigo Jackson
(woodman), Judy Matheson (woodman's daughter), Peter Thompson
(gaoler), Sheelah Wilcox (lady in
coach), Kirsten Lindholm (young
girl at stake).

TWISTED NERVE (1968)
    Director: Roy Boulting
Hywel Bennett (Martin Durnley/
Georgie Clifford), Hayley Mills
(Susan Harper), Billie Whitelaw
(Joan Harper), Frank Finlay (Henry
Durnley), Phyllis Calvert (Enid Durnley), Timothy West (Superintendent
Dakin), Thorley Walters (Sir John
Forrester), Christian Roberts (Philip), Barry Foster (Gerry Enderson),
Gretchen Franklin (Mrs. Clarke),
Clifford Cox (Insp. Goddard), Russell Napier (Prof. Fuller), Richard
Davies (Taffy Evans), Brian Peck
(Detective Sgt. Thompson), Mary
Ladd (Judy), Michael Cadman (Mac),
Russell Waters (hospital attendant),
Hazel Bainbridge (nursing sister).

TWITCH OF THE DEATH NERVE

(1971-Ital.) (A.K.A. "Antefatto",
"Carnage")
    Director: Mario Bava
Claudine Auger, Claudio Volonto,
Laura Betti, Luigi Pistilli, Brigitte Skay, Ana Maria Rosati.

TWO COSMONAUTS AGAINST THEIR
WILL (1965-Span./Ital.) (A.K.A.
"Dos Cosmonautas a la Fuerza")
    Director: Lucio Fulci
Franco Franchi, Ciccio Ingarssia,
Monica Randal, Emilio Rodriguez,
Maria Silva.

TWO DEATHS OF SEAN DOOLITTLE,
THE (TVM-1975) - 4-4-75
    Director: Lela Swift
George Grizzard (Sean Doolittle),
Jeremiah Sullivan (Fergus), Barnard Hughes (Warren), Grayson
Hall (Rhea), Diana Davila (Diana).

TWO FACES OF DR. JEKYLL, THE
(1960) (A.K.A. "House of Fright")
    Director: Terence Fisher
Paul Massie (Dr. Jekyll/Mr. Hyde),
Christopher Lee (Paul Allen), Dawn
Addams (Kitty Jekyll), David Kossoff
(Litauer), Janine Faye (Jane), Francis DeWolff (Inspector), Norma
Marla (Maria), Magda Miller (Sphinx
girl), Helen Goss (Nannie), Joe Robinson (Corinthia), William Kendall
(clubman), Pauline Shepherd (girl
in gin shop), Percy Cartwright (coroner), Arthur Lovegrove (cabby),
Oliver Reed (barman).

TWO GHOSTS AND A GIRL (1958-
Mex.) (A.K.A. "Dos Fantasmas
y una Muchacha")
    Director: Rogelio A. Gonzalez
Tin Tan, Ana Luisa Peluffo, Luis
Aldas, Loco Valdez, Migual Manzano.

TWO LOST WORLDS (1950)
    Director: Norman Dawn
James Arness (Kirk Hamilton), Gloria
Petroff (Janice Jeffries), Laura Elliott (Elaine Jeffries), Pierre Watkin
(Magistrate Jeffries), Bill Kennedy
(Martin Shannon), Tom Hubbard (John
Hartley), Jane Harlan (Nancy Holden),
James Guilfoyle (Dr. Wakeland),
Bob Carson (Cap'n Allison), Fred
Kohler, Jr. (Nat Mercer), Tom Monroe (Cap'n Tallman), Richard Bartell
(Mr. Davis), Guy Bellis (Governor),
Tim Grahame (Salty).

TWONKY, THE (1952)
    Director: Arch Oboler

Hans Conried (Kerry), William Lynn (Coach Trout), Gloria Blondell (Eloise), Janet Warren (Caroline), Norman Fields (Doctor), Ed Max (Ed), Trilby Conried (baby), Al Jarvis (mailman), Steve Roberts (government agent), William Phipps (student), Florence Ravenal (nurse).

TWO ON A GUILLOTINE (1964)
Director: William Conrad
Connie Stevens (Cassie Duquense/ Melinda Duquesne), Cesar Romero (John 'Duke' Duquense), Dean Jones (Val Henderson), Parley Baer (Buzz Sheridan), Connie Gilchrist (Ramona Ryerdon), John Hoyt (Carl Vickers), Virginia Gregg (Dolly Best), Russell Thorson (Carmichael).

2 + 5: MISSIONE HYDRA (1966-Ital.)
Director: Pietro Francisci
Leonora Ruffo/Leonor Curtis, Kirk Morris, Antony Freeman, Leontine Snell, Gordon Mitchell, Roland Lesaffre.

2000 MANIACS (1965)
Director: Herschell Gordon Lewis
Connie Mason, Thomas Wood, Shelby Livingston, Ben Moore, Vincent Santo, Gary Bakeman, Mark Douglas, Jeffrey Allen, Michael Korb.

2001: A SPACE ODYSSEY (1968)
Director: Stanley Kubrick
Keir Dullea (David Bowman), Gary Lockwood (Frank Poole), William Sylvester (Dr. Heywood Floyd), Douglas Rain (voice of Hal 9000), Leonard Rossiter (Smyslov), Daniel Richter (Moonwatcher), Robert Beatty (Halvorsen), Margaret Tyzack (Elena), Frank Miller (Mission Controller), Alan Gifford (Poole's father), Penny Brahms (stewardess), Edwina Carroll (stewardess), Sean Sullivan (Michaels), John Ashley (astronaut), Mike Lovely, Brian Hawley, S. Newton Anderson, Ann Gillis, Edward Bishop, Peter Delman, Danny Grover, Glenn Beck, Bill Weston, David Hines, Tony Jackson, John Hordan, Scott MacKee, Heather Downham, Jimmy Bell, David Charkham, Simon Davis, Jonathan Daw, Darry Paes, Joe Rafalo, Andy Wallace, Bob Willyman, Richard Wood, Laurence Marchant, Terry Dugan, David Fleetwood, Danny Grover, Brian Hawley.

2000 YEARS LATER (1968)
Director: Bert Tenzer
Terry-Thomas (Charles Goodwyn), Edward Everett Horton (Evermore), John Abbott (Gregorius), Pat Harrington, Jr. (Franchot), Lisa Seagram (Cindy), Monti Rock III (Tomorrow's leader), Rudi Gernreich (himself), John Myhers (the General), Myrna Ross (Miss Forever), Casey Kasem (disc jockey), Tom Melody (the Senator), Murray Roman (Superdude), Michael Christian (the Piston Kid), Milton Parsons.

TWO WEEKS TO LIVE (1942)
Director: Malcolm St. Clair
Chester 'Lum' Lauck, Norman 'Abner' Goff, Franklin Pangborn, Kay Linaker, Rosemary LaPlanche, Herbert Rawlinson, Charles Middleton, Irving Bacon, Danny Duncan, Luis Alberni, Tim Ryan, Edward Earle, Ivan Simpson, Evelyn Knapp, Jack Rice, Oscar O'Shea.

TWO WORLDS OF JENNIE LOGAN, THE (TVM-1979) (A. K. A. "The Passion of Jennie Logan") - 10-31-79
Director: Frank De Felitta
Lindsay Wagner (Jennie Logan), Marc Singer (David), Alan Feinstein (Michael), Linda Gray (Elizabeth), Henry Wilcoxon (Harrington), Irene Tedrow (Mrs. Bates), Joan Darling (Dr. Lauren), Gloria Stuart, Constance McCashin, Peter Hobbs, Charles Thomas Murphy, Pat Corley, Layla Galloway, Allen Williams, John Hawkins, Robert Nadder.

UFO INCIDENT, THE (TVM-1975) - 10-20-75
Director: Richard Colla
James Earl Jones (Barney Hill), Estelle Parsons (Betty Hill), Barnard Hughes (Dr. Benjamin Simon), Dick O'Neill (Gen. Davidson), Lou Wagner (Leader), Tony Swartz (Gill), Terrence O'Connor (Lisa MacRainey), Beeson Carroll (Lt. Col. John MacRainey), Joe Stefano (Henderson), Jeanne Joe (Examiner), Vic Perrin (Narrator), Eric Server, Eric Murphy.

UFOria (1982)
Director: John Binder
Cindy Williams (Arlene), Harry Dean Stanton (Brother Bud), Fred Ward (Sheldon).

UFO: TARGET EARTH (1974)

Director: Michael A. de
Gaetano
Nick Plakias, Cynthia Cline, Phil
Erickson, LaVerne Light, Martha
Corrigan, Kathleen Long, Tom Ar-
curagi, Billy Crane, Brooks Clift,
Emily Bell.

UGLY DUCKLING, THE (1959)
Director: Lance Comfort
Bernard Bresslaw (Henry Jekyll/
Teddy Hyde), Reginald Beckwith
(Reginald), Maudie Edwards (Hen-
rietta Jekyll), Jon Pertwee (Victor
Jekyll), Michael Ripper, Richard
Wattis.

ULTIMATE IMPOSTER, THE (TVM-
1979) - 5-12-79
Director: Paul Stanley
Joseph Hacker (Frank Monihan),
Keith Andes (Eugene Danzinger),
Erin Gray (Beatrice Tate), John
Van Dreelan (Ruben Parets), Tracy
Brooks Swope (Danielle Parets),
Macon McCalman (Dr. Jake McKee-
ver), Normann Burton (Papich),
Robert Phillips (Red Cottle), Greg
Barnett (Sgt. Williger), Thomas
Bellin (Joe Maslan), Rosalind Chao
(Lai-Ping), Bobby Riggs (himself),
Loren Berman (Dominic), Chip
Johnson (Martin), Mark Garcia
(Felipe), Bill Capizzi (Tony), Gray-
don Gould (Carl Lathrop), Candy
Castillo (Esteban), Mike Kulscar,
Harry Pugh, Joseph Hardin, Betty
Kwan, W.T. Zacha, Bob Thomas,
Roberto Ramirez, Tommy Reamon,
Chuck Tamburro.

ULTIMATE WARRIOR, THE (1975)
Director: Robert Clouse
Yul Brynner, Max von Sydow, Jo-
anna Miles, William Smith, Stephen
McHattie, Richard Kelton.

ULTRAMAN (1967)
Director: Eiji Tsuburaya &
Hajima Tsuburaya
Satoshi Furuya, Shoji Kobayashi,
Susumu Kurobe, Bin Furutani.

ULYSSES (1954-Ital.)
Director: Mario Camerini
Kirk Douglas (Ulysses), Silvano
Mangano (Penelope/Circe), Anthony
Quinn (Antinous), Rossana Podesta
(Nausicaa), Sylvie (Euriclea), Jac-
ques Dumesnil (Alcinous), Daniel
Ivernel (Euriloco), Franco Inter-
lenghi, Evi Maltagliati, Tania
Weber, Elena Zareschi, Piero

Lulli, Ludmila Dudarova, Allesandro
Fersen, Ferruccio Stagni, Oscar
Andriani, Gualtiero Tumiati, Mario
Feliciani, Teresa Pellati, Michele
Riccardini, Umberto Silvestri.

ULYSSES AGAINST THE SON OF
HERCULES (1961-Ital./Fr.)
(A.K.A. "Ulisse contro Erole",
"Ulysses vs. Hercules")
Director: Mario Caiano
Georges Marchal, Michael Lane,
Eleonora Bianchi, Alessandra
Panaro, Yvette Lebon, Raffaele
Baldassare, Gianni Santuccio.

ULYSSES AND GIANT POLYPHEMUS
(1905-Fr.) (A.K.A. "Lille de
Calpso", "Ulysse et le Geant
Polyphe")
Director: Georges Melies

UNCANNY, THE (1977)
Director: Denis Heroux
Link Story: Peter Cushing (Wilbur),
Ray Milland (Frank),
Malkin Story: Susan Penhaligon (Janet),
Joan Greenwood (Miss Malkin), Ro-
land Culver (Wallace), Simon Williams
(Michael).
Black Magic Story: Alexandra Stewart
(Mrs. Blake), Donald Pilon (Mr.
Blake), Chloe Franks (Angela), Renee
Giraud (Mrs. Maitland), Katrina
Holden (Lucy).
Film Studio Story: Donald Pleasence
(Valentine De'Ath), Samantha Eggar
(Edina), John Vernon (Pomeroy),
John LeClerc (Barrington), Sean
McCann (Inspector), Catharine
Begin (Madeline).

UNCLE JOSH IN A SPOOKY HOTEL
(1900)
Director: Edwin S. Porter

UNCLE WAS A VAMPIRE (1959-Ital.)
(A.K.A. "Tempi Duri per i Vam-
piri", "Hard Times for Vampires",
"My Uncle the Vampire")
Director: Stefano Steno
Christopher Lee (Baron Rodrigo),
Slyva Koscina, Susanne Loret, Kay
Fischer, Renato Rascel, Lia Zop-
pelli.

UNDEAD, THE (1956)
Director: Roger Corman
Richard Garland (Pendragon), Pamela
Duncan (Diana Love/Helene), Richard
Devon (Satan), Allison Hayes (Lydia),
Billy Barty (the Imp), Mel Welles
(Smoukin), Bruno VeSota (the Innkeeper),

Dorothy Newman (Meg Maud), Val
Dufour (Quintus), Dick Miller,
Aaron Saxon.

UNDERNEATH THE ARCHES (1937)
Director: Redd Davis
Bud Flanagan (Bud), Chesney Allen
(Ches), Stella Moya (Anna), Lyn
Harding (Pedro), Enid Stamp-Taylor
(Dolores), Edmund Willard (Chief
Steward), Edward Ashley (Carlos),
Aubrey Mather (Professor).

UNDERSEA KINGDOM (1936) (A. K. A.
"Sharad of Atlantis") - serial in
12 episodes
Chapters: 1. "Beneath the Ocean
Floor", 2. "Undersea City", 3.
"Arena of Death", 4. "Revenge of
the Volkites", 5. "Prisoners of
Atlantis", 6. "The Juggernaut Strikes",
7. "The Submarine Trap", 8. "Into
the Metal Tower", 9. "Death in the
Air", 10. "Atlantis Destroyed", 11.
"Flaming Death", & 12. "Ascent to
the Upperworld"
Director: B. Reeves Esaon &
Joseph Kane
Ray 'Crash' Corrigan (Crash Cor-
rigan), Lois Wilde (Diana), William
Farnum (Sharad), Monte Blue (Khan),
Boothe Howard (Ditmar), C. Mon-
tague Shaw (Prof. Norton), Smiley
Burnette (Briny), Lane Chandler
(Darius), Lee Van Atta (Billy Nor-
ton), Lon Chaney, Jr. (Hakur), Jack
Mulhall (Lt. Andrews), Tom Steele,
Eddie Parker, George de Normand,
Wes Warner, Alan Curtis, Don Rowan,
Al Seymour (guardsmen), John
Bradford (Joe), Raymond Hatton
(Gasspon), Frankie Marvin (Salty),
Ralph Holmes (Martos), Lloyd Whit-
lock (Capt. Clinton), Kenneth Lawton
(Naval Doctor), Everett Gibbons
(Antony), John Merton (Moloch),
Ernie Smith (Gourck), David Horsley
(naval sentry), Rube Schaeffer (Magna),
Bill Yrigoyen (charioteer), William
Stahl, Millard McGowan (chamber
guards), Jack Ingram, Tracy Layne.

UNDERTAKER AND HIS PALS, THE
(1967)
Director: David C. Graham
Robert Lowery, Ray Dannis, Warrene
Ott, Sally Frei, Charles Fox, Tif-
fany Shannon O'Hara.

UNDERWATER CITY, THE (1961)
Director: Frank McDonald
William Lundigan (Bob Gage), Julie
Adams (Dr. Monica Powers), Roy

Roberts (Tim Graham), Carl Benton
Reid (Dr. Halstead), Paul Dubov
(George Burnett), Karen Norris
(Phyllis Gatewood), Edward Mallory
(Lt. Wally Steele), Edmond Cobb
(Meade), George De Normand (Dr.
Carl Wendt), Kathie Browne (Dotty),
Chet Douglas (Chuck 'Cowboy' Mar-
low), Roy Damron (Winchell), Paul
Power (civilian).

UNDYING MONSTER, THE (1942)
(A. K. A. "The Hammond Mystery")
Director: John Brahm
John Howard (Oliver Hammond),
Bramwell Fletcher (Geoffrey Covert),
James Ellison (Robert Curtis),
Heather Angel (Helga Hammond),
Eily Malyon (Mrs. Walton), Alec
Craig (Will), Holmes Herbert,
Heather Thatcher, Matthew Boulton,
Halliwell Hobbes, Aubrey Mather,
Charles McGraw, Heather Wilde.

UNEARTHLY, THE (1957)
Director: Brooke L. Peters
John Carradine (Dr. Charles Conway),
Allison Hayes (Grace Thomas), Myron
Healey (Mark Houston), Sally Todd
(Natalie), Arthur Batanides (Danny
Green), Roy Gordon (Dr. Loren
Wright), Marilyn Buferd (Dr. Gil-
christ), Tor Johnson (Lobo), Guy
Prescott (Capt. Rogers), Harry
(Jedrow), Paul McWilliams (Police
Officer).

UNEARTHLY STRANGER (1963)
Director: John Krish
John Neville (Dr. Mark Davidson),
Gabriella Licudi (Julie Davidson),
Philip Stone (Prof. John Lancaster),
Warren Mitchell (Dr. Munro), Jean
Marsh (Ms. Ballard), Patrick Newell
(Major Clarke).

UNHOLY NIGHT, THE (1929)
Director: Lionel Barrymore
Ernest Torrence (Dr. Ballou),
Roland Young (Lord Montague),
John Miljan (Major Mallory), Lionel
Belmore (Major Endicott), Boris
Karloff (Abdoul), Sojin (the Mystic),
Natalie Moorhead (Lady Vi), Clarence
Geldert (Insp. Lewis), Claude Flem-
ing (Sir James Rumsey), Richard
Tucker (Col. Davidson), Sidney
Jarvis (Butler), Gerald Barry (Capt.
Bradley), John Roche (Lt. Savor),
Philip Strange (Lt. Williams),
Richard C. Travers (Major McDougal),
Polly Moran (maid), George Cooper
(orderly).

UNHOLY QUEST, THE (1934)
Director: R.W. Lotinga
Terence de Marney (Frank Davis),
Claude Bailey (Prof. Sorotoff), Cris-
tine Adrien (Vera), John Milton (Haw-
kins), Ian Wilson (Wilky), Harry
Terry (Soapy).

UNHOLY THREE, THE (1925)
Director: Tod Browning
Lon Chaney, Sr. (Prof. Echo/Granny
O'Grady), Harry Earles (Tweedledee),
Victor McLaglen (Hercules), Mae
Busch (Rosie O'Grady), Matt Moore
(Hector McDonald), Matthew Betz
(Regan), William Humphreys (Defense
Attorney), Walter Perry (dime museum
announcer), John Merkyl (jeweler),
Violet Cane (Arlington baby), Mar-
jorie Morton (Mrs. Arlington), Charles
Wellesley (John Arlington), Percy
Williams (Butler), Edward Connelly
(Judge), Lou Morrison (Police Com-
missioner), E. Allyn Warren (Prose-
cuting Attorney), Alice Julian (the
Fat Lady), Peter Kortos (Sword
Swallower), Walter P. Cole (the
Human Skeleton), John Millerta (Wild
Man from Borneo), Vera Vance
(dancer), Harvey Parry (stuntman),
Mickey McBan.

UNHOLY THREE, THE (1930)
Director: Jack Conway
Lon Chaney, Sr. (Prof. Echo/Granny
O'Grady), Harry Earles (Tweedle-
dee), Ivan Linow (Hercules), Lila
Lee (Rosie O'Grady), Elliott Nugent
(Hector), John Miljan, Crauford Kent,
Clarence Burton.

UNHOLY WISH, THE (1939-Ger.)
(A.K.A. "Die Unheimlichen
Wunsche")
Director: Heinz Hilpert
Olga Tschechowa, Kathe Gold, Hans
Holt, Paul Dahlke, Elizabeth Flicken-
schildt, Ewald Balser.

UNIDENTIFIED FLYING OBJECTS
(1955) (A.K.A. "U.F.O.") -
Documentary
Director: Winston Jones
Tom Towers (Albert M. Chop/Nar-
rator).

UNIDENTIFIED FLYING ODDBALL,
THE (1979) (A.K.A. "The Space-
man and King Arthur")
Director: Russ Mayberry
Dennis Dugan (Tom Trimble), Ken-
neth More (King Arthur), Ron Moody
(Merlin), Sheila White (Alisande),

Jim Dale (Sir Mordred), John Le
Mesurier (Sir Gawain), Robert Beatty
(Sen. Milburn), Rodney Bewes (Clar-
ence), Cyril Shaps (Dr. Zimmerman),
Pat Roach (Oaf), Kevin Brennan
(Winston), Reg Lye (prisoner), Ewen
Solon (Watkins).

UNINVITED, THE (1944)
Director: Lewis Allen
Ray Milland (Roderick Fitzgerlad),
Gail Russell (Stella Meredith),
Ruth Hussey (Pamela Fitzgerald),
Donald Crisp (Cmdr. Beech), Alan
Napier (Dr. Scott), Cornelia Otis
Skinner (Miss Holloway), Barbara
Everest (Lizzie Flynn), Dorothy
Stickney (Miss Birk), Jessica New-
combe (Miss Ellis), John Kieran
(forward narrator), Elizabeth Simpson,
Queenie Leonard, George Kirby, David
Clyde, Leyland Hodgson, Moyna
Macgill.

UNION CITY (1980)
Director: Mark Reichert
Deborah Harry (Lillian), Dennis
Lipscomb (Harlan), Irina Maleeva
(Contessa), Everett McGill (Larry
Longacre), Terina Lewis (Evelyn,
the secretary), Tony Azito (Alphonse),
Sam McMurray (young vagrant), Pat
Benatar (Jeannette), Paul Andor,
Cynthia Crisp, Taylor Mead, Charles
Rydell.

UNKNOWN, THE (1927)
Director: Tod Browning
Lon Chaney, Sr. (Alonzo, the Armless),
Norman Kerry (Malabar), Joan Craw-
ford (Estrellita), Nick de Ruiz (Zanzi),
John George (Cojo), Billy Seay (the
Little Wolf), Frank Lanning (Costra),
John St. Polis.

UNKNOWN, THE (1946)
Director: Henry Levin
Jim Bannon (Jack Packard), Barton
Yarborough (Doc Long), Karen Morley
(Rachel Martin), Robert Wilcox (Ri-
chard Arnold), Jeff Donnell (Nina
Arnold), James Bell (Edward Martin),
Wilton Graff (Ralph Martin), Robert
Scott (Reed Cawthorne), Boyd Davis
(Col. Selby Martin), Helen Freeman
(Phoebe Martin), J. Louis Johnson
(Joshua).

UNKNOWN HOUR, THE (1964-Span.)
(A.K.A. "La Hora Incognita")
Director: Mariano Ozores
Emma Penella, Jose Luis Ozores,
Fernando Rey, Mabel Karr, Carlos

1144 Science Fiction, Horror, Fantasy

Ballesteros, Antonio Ozores.

UNKNOWN ISLAND (1948)
Director: Jack Bernhard
Barton MacLane (Tarnowski), Richard
Denning (John Fairbanks), Virginia
Gray (Carol Lane), Philip Reed (Ted
Osborne), Dan White (Edwards), Dick
Wessell (Sanderson), Philip Nazir
(Golab).

UNKNOWN MAN OF SHANDIGOR,
THE (1967-Swiss) (A. K. A. "L'In-
connu de Shandigor")
Director: Jean-Louis Roy
Marie-France Boyer (Sylvaina), Ho-
ward Vernon (Yank), Daniel Emilfork
(Von Krantz), Ben Carruthers (Manual),
Jacques Dufilho (Russian).

UNKNOWN PURPLE, THE (1923)
Director: Roland West
Henry B. Walthall (Peter March-
mont), Alice Lake (Jewel Marchmont),
Stuart Holmes (James Dawson), John-
nie Arthur (Freddie Goodlittle),
Ethel Grey Terry (Mrs. Freddie
Goodlittle), Frankie Lee (Bobbie),
Helen Ferguson (Ruth Marsh), James
Morrison (Leslie Bradbury), Richard
Wayne (George Allison), Brinsley
Shaw (Hawkins), Mike Donlin (Burton).

UNKNOWN TERROR, THE (1957)
Director: Charles Marquis War-
ren
John Howard (Dan Mathews), Mala
Powers (Gina Mathews), Paul Ri-
chards (Pete Morgan), Gerald Milton
(Dr. Ramsey), May Wynn (Concha),
Sir Lancelot (himself), Duane Gray
(Lino), Charles Gray (Jim Wheatley),
Charles Postal (Butler), Patrick O'Moore
(Dr. Willoughby), William Hamel (trai-
ner), Richard Gilden (Raul Kom),
Martin Garralaga (old Indian).

UNKNOWN TOMORROW, THE (1923-
Austria) (A. K. A. "Der Unbekannte
Morgen")
Director: Alexander Korda
Marta Korda, Werner Krauss, Olaf
Fonss, Paul Lukas, Albert Kersten.

UNKNOWN TREASURES (1926)
Director: Archie Mayo
John Miljan, Gustav von Seyffertitz,
Robert Agnew, Jed Prouty, Gladys
Hulette, Bertram Marburgh.

UNKNOWN WORLD (1950)
Director: Terrell O. Morse
Jim Bannon (Andy Ostengaard),

Bruce Kellogg (Wright Thompson),
Marilyn Nash (Joan Lindsay), Vic-
tor Kilian (Prof. Jeremiah Morley),
Otto Waldis (Dr. Max A. Bauer),
Tom Handley (Dr. James Paxton),
Dick Cogan (George Coleman),
George Baxter (Presiding Officer).

UNMAN, WITTERING AND ZIGO
(1971)
Director: John MacKenzie
David Hemmings (John Ebony),
Carolyn Seymore (Silvia Ebony),
Douglas Wilmer (Headmaster), An-
thony Haygarth (Cary Farthingale),
Nicholas Hoye (Cloistermouth),
Michael Howe (Unman), Michael
Cashman (Terhew), Colin Barrie
(Wittering).

UNMASKED (1929)
Director: Edgar Lewis
Robert Warwick (Craig Kennedy),
Milton Krims (Prince Hamid), Susan
Conroy (Mary Wayne), Sam Ash
(Billy Mathews), Lyons Wickland
(Larry Jamieson), Charles Slattery
(Insp. Collins), William Corbett
(Franklin Ward), Roy Byron (Caf-
ferty), Kate Roemer (Madam Ramon),
Marie Burke (Mrs. Brookfield),
Helen Mitchell (Mrs. Ward), Clyde
Dillison (imposter), Waldo Edwards
(Gordon Hayes).

UNSEEN, THE (1945)
Director: Lewis Allen
Joel McCrae, Gail Russell, Herbert
Marshall, Phyllis Brooks, Isobel
Elsom, Elizabeth Risdon, Victoria
Horne, Norman Lloyd, Tom Tully,
Richard Lyon, Mikhail Rasumny,
Nona Griffith, Mary Field.

UNSEEN, THE (1981)
Director: Peter Foleg
Barbara Bach (Jennifer), Lelia
Goldoni (Virginia Keller), Stephen
Furst (Junior), Sydney Lassick
(Ernest Keller), Doug Barr (Tony),
Karen Lamm (Karen), Lois Young
(Vicki).

UNSEEN HANDS (1924)
Director: Jacques Jaccard
Wallace Beery, Joseph J. Dowling,
Cleo Madison, Fontaine La Rue,
Jamie Gray, Jack Rollins, Jim
Corey.

UNTAMED WOMEN (1952)
Director: Merle Connell
Mikel Conrad (Steve), Doris Merrick

(Sandra), Morgan Jones (Andy), Carol Brewster (Tennus), Lyle Talbot (Col. Loring), Richard Monohan (Benny), Midge Ware (Myra), Autumn Rice (Cleo), Mark Lowell (Ed), Judy Brubaker (Valdra), Montgomery Pittman (Prof. Warren), Miriam Kaylor (Nurse Edmunds).

UNUSUAL TALES (1949-Fr.) (A. K. A. "Histoires Extraorinaires")
Director: Jean Faurez
Jules Berry, Fernand Ledoux, Suzy Charrier, Olivier Hussenot, Jandeline.

UP FROM THE DEPTHS (1979)
Director: Charles B. Griffith
Sam Bottoms (Greg Oliver), Susanne Reed (Rachel McNamara), Virgil Frye (Earl Sheridan), Kedric Wolfe (Oscar Forbes), Denise Hayes (Iris Lee), Charles Howerton (David Whiting), Charles Doherty (Ed), Helen McNelly (Louellen).

UP IN SMOKE (1957)
Director: William Beaudine
Huntz Hall (Sach Debussy Jones), Byron Foulger (the Devil), Stanley Clements (Duke), Fritz Feld, David Gorcey, Eddie LeRoy.

URSUS IN THE VALLEY OF LIONS (1961-Ital.) (A. K. A. "Ursus nella Valle dei Leoni")
Director: Carlo Ludovico Bragglia
Ed Fury, Moira Orfei, Mary Marlon, Alberto Lupo, Gerard Haerter, Giacomo Furis, Andrea Scotti, Mariangela Giordano.

VALLEY OF GWANGI, THE (1968)
Director: Jim O'Connolly
James Franciscus (Tuck Kirby), Gila Golan (T. J. Breckenridge), Richard Carlson (Champ Connors), Laurence Naismith (Prof. Bromley), Freda Jackson (Tia Zorina), Gustavo Rojo (Carlos Dos Orsos), Curtis Arden (Lope), Dennis Kilbane (Rowdy), Mario de Barros (Bean), Jose Burgos (dwarf).

VALLEY OF THE DRAGONS (1961) (A. K. A. "Prehistoric Valley")
Director: Edward Bernds
Cesare Danova (Hector Servadac), Sean McClory (Denning), Joan Staley (Denna), Danielle de Metz (Nateeta), Gregg Martell (Ol-Loo), I. Stanford Jolley (Patoo), Michael Lane (Anoka), Roger Til (Vidal), Gil Perkins (Tarn/ Doctor), Jerry Sunshine (LeClerc), Dolly Gray (Mara), Mike Dempsey

(Andrews).

VALLEY OF THE EAGLES (1951)
Director: Terence Young
Jack Warner (the Inspector), John McCallum (Nils Ahlen), Nadia Gray (Kara), Anthony Dawson (Sven Nystrom), Mary Laura Wood (Helga Ahlen), Norman McOwen (McTavish), Alfred Maurstad (Trerik), Martin Boddey (Headman), Njama Wiwstrand (Baroness Erland), Christopher Lee, Ewen Solon (detectives), Peter Blitz (Anders), Sarah Crawford (Norma), Molly Warner (Frau Lund), Trillot Billquist (Col. Strand), Gosta Cederlund (Prof. Lind), Sten Lindgren (Director General), Kurt Sundstrom, Holger Kax.

VALLEY OF THE ZOMBIES (1946)
Director: Philip Ford
Robert Livingston (Dr. Terry Evans), Adrian Booth (Susan Drake), Ian Keith (Ormand Murks), Thomas Jackson (Blair), Charles Trowbridge (Dr. Rufus Maynard), William Haade (Tiny), Wilton Graff (Dr. Garland), LeRoy Mason (Hendricks), Earle Hodings (Fred Mays), Charles Cane (Insp. Ryan), Russ Clark (Lacy), Charles Hamilton (the driver).

VAMPIRE, THE (1957) (A. K. A. "Mark of the Vampire")
Director: Paul Landres
John Beal (Dr. Paul Beecher), Coleen Gray (Carol Butler), Kenneth Tobey (Buck Donnelly), Lydia Reed (Betsy Beecher), Dabbs Greer (Dr. Will Beaumont), Herb Vigran (George Ryan), Ann Staunton (Marion Wilkins), James Griffith (Henry Winston), Paul Brinegar (Willie), Natalie Masters, Raymond Greenleaf, Mauritz Hugo, Louise Lewis, Wood Romoff, Brad Morrow, Hallene Hill, Anne O'Neal, George Selk, Walter A. Merrill, Christine Rees, Arthur Gardner.

VAMPIRE, THE (1957-Mex) (A. K. A. "El Vampiro")
Director: Fernando Mendez
German Robles (Count Lavud), Abel Salazar (Dr. Enrique), Ariadne Welter (Marta), Carmen Montejo, July Danery, Jose Luis Jimenez, Joseph Chavez, Amando Zumaya.

VAMPIRE (TVM-1979) - 19-7-79
Director: E. W. Swackhammer
Jason Miller (John Rawlins), Richard Lynch (Anton Voytek), E. G. Marshall (Harry Kilcoyne), Jessica Walter

(Nicole), Barrie Youngfellow (Andrea),
Kathryn Harrold (Leslie Rawlins),
Adam Starr (Tommy), Michael Tuc-
ker (Christopher Bell), Wendy Cutler
(Iris), Jonelle Allen (Brandy), Joe
Spinell, David Hooks.

VAMPIRE AND THE BALLERINA,
THE (1962-Ital.) (A.K.A. "L'A-
mante del Vampiro", "The Vampire's Lover")
    Director: Renato Polselli
Helene Remy (Louisa), Walter Brandi
(Luca), Maria Luisa Rolando (Countessa Bathory), Tina Gloriani (Francesca), Iscaro Ravaioli (servant),
John Turner, Ugo Gragnani.

VAMPIRE BAT, THE (1933)
    Director: Frank R. Strayer
Lionel Atwill (Dr. Otto von Niemann),
Fay Wray (Ruth Bertin), Melvyn
Douglas (Karl Brettschneider), Dwight
Frye (Herman Gleib), Maude Eburne
(Gussie Schnappman), George E.
Stone (Kringen), Carl Stockdale
(Schmidt), Robert Frazer (Emil
Borst), Harrison Greene (Wein-
garten), Lionel Belmore (Gustav
Schoen), Rita Carlisle (Martha Muel-
ler), Stella Adams (Georgiana), Wil-
liam Humphrey (Dr. Haupt), Willaim
V. Mong (Sauer), Fern Emmett
(Gertrude), Paul Weigel (Holdstadt).

VAMPIRE-BEAST CRAVES BLOOD,
THE (1967) (A.K.A. "The Blood
Beast Terror")
    Director: Vernon Sewell
Peter Cushing (Insp. Quennell),
Robert Flemying (Prof. Mallinger),
Vanessa Howard (Meg Quennell),
Wanda Ventham (Clare), David
Griffin (William), John Paul (War-
render), Glynn Edwards (Sgt. Allan),
Roy Hudd (morgue attendant), Wil-
liam Wilde (Britewell), Kevin Stoney
(the butler), Russell Napier (the land-
lord), Leslie Anderson (the coachman),
Simon Cain (the gardener).

VAMPIRE CIRCUS (1971)
    Director: Robert Young
Adrienne Corri (Gypsy Woman),
Laurence Payne (Mueller), Thorley
Walters (Burgomeister), John Moul-
der Brown (Anton Kersh), David
Prowse (the strongman), Lynne
Frederick (Dora Mueller), Anthony
Corlan (Emil), Elizabeth Seal (Gerta
Hauser), Domini Blythe (Anna Muel-
ler), Richard Owens (Dr. Kersh),
Robin Sachs (Heinrich), Barnaby

Shaw (Gustav Hauser), Roderick Shaw
(Jon Hauser), Christina Paul (Rosa),
Skip Martin (Michael), Jane Darby
(Jenny), John Brown (Schilt), Dorothy
Frere (Grandma Schilt), Sibylla Kay
(Mrs. Schilt), Jason James (foreman),
Arnold Locke (old villager).

VAMPIRE DOLL, THE (1970-Jap.)
(A.K.A. "Chi o Suu Ningyo")
    Director: Michio Yamamoto
Kayo Matsuo, Akira Nakao, Yukiko
Kobayshi, Kaku Takashina, Artsuo
Nakamara, Yoko Minikaze.

VAMPIRE HAPPENING, THE (1971-
Ger.) (A.K.A. "Gebissen Wird nur
Nachts - Happening der Vampire")
    Director: Freddie Francis
Ferdy Mayne (Dracula), Pia Degemark,
Yvor Murillo, Thomas Hunter, Ingrid
van Bergen, Joachim Kemmer, Lyvia
Bauer.

VAMPIRE HOOKERS (1978)
    Director: Cirio H. Santiago
John Carradine, Bruce Fairbaird,
Karen Stride, Trey Wilson, Lex
Winter, Lenka Novak, Katie Dolan.

VAMPIRE LOVERS, THE (1970)
    Director: Roy Ward Baker
Ingrid Baker (Mircalla Karnstein/
Carmilla), Peter Cushing (Gen. von
Spielsdorf), Madeleine Smith (Emma
Morton), George Cole (Roger Morton),
Pippa Steel (Lara Von Spielsdorf),
Dawn Addams (the Countess), Kate
O'Mara (Madmoiselle Perrodon),
Douglas Wilmer (Baron Joachim Von
Hartog), Jon Finch (Carl Ebhardt),
Ferdy Mayne (the doctor), Harvey
Hall (Renton), Charles Farrell (Kurt),
Janey Key (Gretchen), John Forbes,
Robertson (Man-in-Black), Kirsten
Betts (vampire).

VAMPIRE MOTH, THE (1956-Jap.)
(A.K.A. "Kyuketsu Ga")
    Director:
Ryo Ikebe, Akio Kobori, Kinuko Ito,
Asami Kuji.

VAMPIRES, THE (1968-Mex.) (A.K.A.
"Las Vampiras", "The Vampire
Girls")
    Director: Frederico Curiel
John Carradine, Pedro Armendariz,
Jr., Mil Mascaras, Maria Duval,
Maura Monti, Martha Romero, Conselsa
Maria Dagoberto Rodriguez, Jessica
Munguia, Vianey Larraga, Manuel
Garay.

VAMPIRE'S COFFIN, THE (1957-
Mex.) (A. K. A. "El Ataud del
Vampiro")
Director: Fernando Mendez
German Robles (Count Lavud), Abel
Salazar (Dr. Enrique), Ariadne Wel-
ter (Marta), Yeire Beirute, Alicia
Montoya.

VAMPIRE'S GHOST, THE (1945)
Director: Lesley Selandor
John Abbott (Webb Fallon), Adele
Mara (Lisa), Grant Withers (Father
Gilchrist), Roy Barcroft (Jim Bar-
rat), Charles Gordon (Roy Hendrick),
Peggy Stewart (Julie Vance), Frank
Jacquet (the Doctor), Martin Wilkins
(Simon Peter), Emmett Vogan (Tho-
mas Vance), Jimmy Aubrey (the bum),
George Carlton, Floyd Shadelford,
Fred Howard, Zack Williams.

VAMPIRE: THRILLS (1970-Fr.)
(A. K. A. "Le Frisson des Vam-
pires", "Sex and the Vampire")
Director: Jean Rollin
Sandra Julien, Jean-Marie Durand,
Michel Delahaye, Jacques Robiolles,
Nicole Nancel, Marie-Pierre, Kue-
Lan, Dominique.

VAMPIRE WOMEN, THE (1967-Fr.)
(A. K. A. "Les Femmes Vampires")
Director: Jean Rollin
Solange Pradel, Ursulle Pauly, Ni-
cole Romain, Bernard Letrou, Catherine
Deville, Jacqueline Sieger.

VAMPYR (1932-Fr. /Ger.) (A. K. A.
"The Strange Adventure of David
Gray")
Director: Carl T. Dreyer
Julian West/Nicolas de Gunzberg
(David Gray), Henrietta Gerard (Mar-
guerite Chopin), Jan Hieronimko (the
Doctor), Sybille Schmitz (Leone),
Maurice Schutz (owner of the castle),
Rena Mandel (Gisele), Jane Mora
(the nurse), Albert Bras, A. Babanini
(servant).

VAMPYR (1970-Span.) (A. K. A.
"Vampire")
Director: Pedro Portabella
Christopher Lee, Soledad Miranda,
Fred Williams, Herbert Lom, Jack
Taylor.

VAMPYRES (1975) (A. K. A. "Vampyres,
Daughters of Darkness")
Director: Joseph Larraz
Marianne Morris (Fran), Anulka
(Miriam), Murray Brown (Ted), Brian

Deacon (John), Sally Faulkner (Harriet), Michael Byrne (playboy), Bessie Love.

VANISHED (TVM-1971) - 3-8-71 &
3-9-71
Director: Buzz Kulik
Richard Widmark (President Roude-
bush), James Farentino (Gene Cul-
ligan), E. G. Marshall (Arthur Ingram),
Skye Aubrey (Jill Nichols), Arthur
Hill (Arnold Greer), Robert Young
(Sen. Earl Gannon), Eleanor Parker
(Sue Greer), Robert Hooks (Larry
Storm), William Shatner (Dave Paulick),
Larry Hagman (Jerry Freytag),
Murray Hamilton (Nick McCann),
Stephen McNally (Gen. Palfrey),
Tom Bosley (Johnny Cavanaugh),
Sheree North (Beverly), Michael
Strong (Descourcy), Jim Davis (Capt.
Coolidge), Christine Belford (Gret-
chen Greer), Russell Johnson (Clyde
Morehouse), Robert Lipton (Loomis),
Don Pedro Colley (Mercurio), Neil
Miller (Toubo), Betty White, Chet
Huntley (Newscasters), Herb Vigran,
Ilka Windish, Stacy Harris, Richard
Dix, Russ Conway, Gil Stewart, James
Hong, Carlton Young, Stacy Keach,
Sr. , Helen Kleeb, Kevin Hagen,
Clark Howat, Lawrence Linville,
Barry Atwater, Susan Kussman, Earl
Ebi, Randolph Mantooth, Leo G.
Morrell, Vince Howard, Judy Jordan,
Nancy Lee Dix, Athena Lorde, Art
Balinger, Perry Ribiero, Stephen
Colt, Fred Holliday, Dick Kleiner,
Joseph Finnigan, Francis DeSales,
William Boyett, Vernon Scott, Her-
bert Kaplow, Martin Agronsky.

VANISHING LADY, THE (1896-Fr.)
(A. K. A. "Escamotage d'une Dame
chez Robert-Houdin", "Conjuring a
Lady at Robert-Houdin's")
Director: Georges Melies

VANSIHING SHADOW, THE (1934) -
serial in 12 episodes
Chapters: 1. "Accused of Murder",
2. "The Destroying Ray", 3. "Aval-
anche", 4. "Trapped", 5. "Hurled from
the Sky", 6. "Chain Lightning", 7.
"The Tragic Crash", 8. "Shadow of
Death", 9. "Blazing Bulkheads", 10.
"Iron Death", 11. "The Juggernaut",
& 12. "Retribution".
Director: Lew Landers
Onslow Stevens (Stanley Stanfield),
Ada Ince (Gloria), William Desmond
(MacDonald), Richard Cramer (Dor-
gan), Walter Miller (Ward Barnett),

Sidney Bracey (Denny), James Durkin (Carl Van Dorn), Eddie Cobb (Kent), Monty Montague.

VANITY'S PRICE (1924)
Director: R. William Neill
Anna Q. Nilsson (Vanna Du Maurier), Stuart Holmes (Henri De Greve), Wyndham Standing (Richard Dowling), Arthur Rankin (Teddy), Lucille Bickson (Sylvia), Robert Bolder (Bill Connors), Cissy Fitzgerald (Mrs. Connors), Dot Farley (Katherine, the maid), Charles Newton (Butler).

VARAN THE UNBELIEVABLE (1958) Jap./U.S.) (A.K.A. "Daikaiji Baran")
Director: Inoshiro Honda
Myron Healey (Cmdr. James Bradley), Tsuruko Kobayashi (Anna Bradley), Clifford Kawada (Capt. Kishi), Derick Shimatsu (Matsu), Akihiko Hirata, Kozo Nomura, Koreya Senda, Aymi Sonoda.

VAULT OF HORROR (1973)
Director: Roy Ward Baker
"Midnight Mess": Daniel Massey (Rogers), Anna Massey (Donna), Mike Pratt (Clive), Erik Chitty (old waiter), Frank Forsyth, Jerold Wells (waiters). "Bargain in Death": Michael Craig (Maitland), Edward Judd (Alex), Robin Nedwell (Tom), Geoffrey Davies (Jerry), Arthur Mullard (gravedigger). "This Trick'll Kill You": Curt Jurgens (Sebastian), Dawn Addams (Inez), Jasmina Hilton (Indian Girl), Ishaq Bux (Fakir). "The Neat Job": Terry-Thomas (Critchit), Glynis Johns (Eleanor), John Forbes-Robertson (Wilson), Marianne Stone (Jane). "Drawn and Quartered": Tom Baker (Moore), Denholm Elliott (Diltant), Terence Alexander (Breedley), John Witty (Gaskill).

VEIL, THE (TVM-1958)
Director: Herbert L. Strock
Boris Karloff, Patrick Macnee, Robert Griffin, Ray Montgomery, Terence De Marney, Jennifer Raine.

VELVET VAMPIRE, THE (1971)
Director: Stephanie Rothman
Michael Blodgett (Lee Ritter), Sherry Miles (Susan Ritter), Celeste Yarnall (Diane Le Fanu), Jerry Daniels (Juan), Paul Prokop (Cliff), Gene Shane (Carl), Chris Woodley (Cliff's girlfriend), Sandy Ward (Amos), Bob Tessier (biker).

VENETIAN AFFAIR, THE (1966)
Director: Jerry Thorpe
Robert Vaughn (Bill Fenner), Elke Sommer (Sandra Fane), Boris Karloff (Dr. Pierre Vaugirous), Felicia Farr (Claire Connor), Karl Boehm (Robert Wahl), Roger C. Carmel (Mike Ballard), Joe de Santis (Jan Aarvan), Luciana Paluzzi (Giulia Almeranti), Edward Asner (Frank Rosenfield), Fabrizio Mioni (Russo), Wesley Lau (Neill Carlson), Bill Weiss (Goldsmith).

VENGEANCE OF FU MANCHU, THE (1967)
Director: Jeremy Summers
Christopher Lee (Fu Manchu), Douglas Wilmer (Nayland Smith), Howard Marion-Crawford (Dr. Petrie), Tsai Chin (Lin Tang), Noel Trevarthen (Mark Weston), Maria Rohm (Ingrid), Horst Frank (Rudy), Tony Ferrer (Insp. Ramos), Peter Carsten (Kurt), Mona Chong (Jasmin), Susanne Roquette (Maria), Wolfgang Kieling (Dr. Lieberson).

VENGEANCE OF SHE, THE (1967)
Director: Cliff Owen
Olinka Berova (Carol), John Richardson (Killikrates), Edward Judd (Philip), Colin Blakely (George), Andre Morell (Kassim), George Sewell (Harry), Noel Willman (Za-Tor), Jill Melford (Sheila), Derek Godfrey (Men-Hari), Daniele Noel (Sharna), Gerald Lawson (the Seer), William Lyon Brown (Magus), Zohra Segal (Putri), Derrick Sherwin (No. 1), Charles O'Rourke (servant), Christine Pockett (dancer), Dervis Ward (lorry driver).

VENGEANCE OF THE MUMMY, THE (1973-Span.) (A.K.A. "La Venganza de la Momia")
Director: Carlos Aured
Paul Naschy, Jack Taylor, Maria Silva, Rina Otolina, Helga Line, Eduardo Calvo, Fernando S. Polack, Luis Davila.

VENGEANCE OF THE VAMPIRE WOMEN (1969-Mex.) (A.K.A. "La Venganza de las Mujeres Vampiro")
Director: Federico Curiel
Santo, Aldo Monti, Gina Romand, Norma Lazareno, Victor Junco, Patricia Ferrer, Federico Falcon, Alfonso Manquia, Yolanda Ponce, Ivone Clay, Lucy Linares.

VENGEANCE OF THE ZOMBIES
(1972-Span.) (A.K.A. "La Rebelion de las Muertas", "The Revolt of the Dead Ones")
Director: Leon Klimovsky
Paul Naschy, Mirta Miller, Luis
Ciges, Vic Miller, Romy.

VENOM (1982)
Director: Piers Haggard
Klaus Kinski (Jacmel), Oliver Reed
(Dave), Nicol Williamson (Cmdr.
William Bulloch), Sarah Miles (Dr.
Marion Stowe), Susan George (Louise),
Michael Gough (David Ball), Cornelia
Sharpe (Ruth Hopkins), Lance Hol-
comb (Philip Hopkins), Sterling Hay-
den (Howard Anderson), Mike Gwilym
(Detective Constable Dan Spencer),
Paul Williamson (Detective Sergeant
Glazer).

VENTURES OF MARGUERITE, THE
(1915) - serial in 16 episodes
Chapters: 1. "When Appearances
Deceive", 2. "The Rogue Syndicate",
3. "The Kidnapped Heiress", 4.
"The Veiled Priestess", 5. "A So-
ciety Schemer", 6. "The Key to a
Fortune", 7. "The Ancient Coin", 8.
"The Secret Message", 9. "The
Oriental's Plot", 10. "The Spy's
Ruse", 11. "The Crossed Clues", 12.
"The Tricksters", 13. "The Sealskin
Coat", 14. "The Lurking Peril", 15.
"The Fate of America", & 16. "The
Trail's End".
Director: Hamilton Smith,
John E. Mackin & Robert
Ellis
Marguerite Courtot (Marguerite),
Richard Pudon (Peter Enright), E.F.
Roseman (Ferris), Phil Hardy (Fen-
ton), R.A. Bennett (Kagler), Joseph
Sullivan (Wharton), Bradley Parker
(Bob Winters), Paula Sherman (maid),
Frank Holland (Leo), F.B. Venocy
(Hal Worth), Harry Edwards (Jones/
crook), Helen Lindroth (Helen),
Robert Vaughn (crook), Walter Mc-
Erven (Dunbar), Otto Neimeyer (Carlow),
William Sherwood (Rudolph), Julia
Hurley (Carrie), Eleanor Lewis
(Alota), Anna Raeder (Martha), Free-
man Barnes (Manforth), Stella Junno
(Irene), H.E. Barrows (Bolton),
Losis Howell (Bertha), A. Lever
(Gungha).

VENUS AGAINST THE SON OF HER-
CULES (1962-Ital.) (A.K.A.
"Marte, Dio della Guerra", "Mars,
God of War")

Director: Marcello Baldi
Massimo Serato, John Kitzmiller,
Roger Browne, Jackie Lane, Dante
Di Paolo, Linda Sini.

VENUS IN FURS (1970-Ger./Brit./
U.S./Ital.) (A.K.A. "Venus in
Peltz")
Director: Jesus Franco
James Darren (Jimmy), Barbara
McNair (Rita), Klaus Kinski (Ahmed),
Maria Rohm (Wanda), Dennis Price
(Kapp), Margaret Lee (Olga), Adolfo
Lastretti (Inspector).

VERTIGO (1957)
Director: Alfred Hitchcock
James Stewart (Scottie), Kim Novak
(Madeleine/Judy), Barbara Bel Geddes
(Midge), Tom Helmore (Gavin Elster),
Konstantin Shayne (Pop Leibel), Ray-
mond Bailey (doctor), Henry Jones
(coroner), Ellen Corby (manageress),
Lee Patrick (older mistaken identity).

VICTOR FRANKENSTEIN (1977-Swed./
Irish) (A.K.A. "Terror of Frank-
enstein")
Director: Calvin Floyd
Leon Vitali (Victor Frankenstein),
Per Oscarsson (the Monster), Nicho-
las Clay (Henry), Stacey Dorning
(Elisabeth), Jan Ohlsson (William),
Henricsson (Capt. Waldon), Archie
O'Sullivan (Prof. Waldhem), Olof
Bergstrom (father), Harry Brogan
(blind man).

VIDEODROME (1982)
Director: David Cronenberg
Deborah Harry (Nicki Brand), James
Woods (Max Renn), Jack Creley
(Prof. Brian O'Blivion), Sonja Smits
(Bianca O"Blivion).

VILLAGE OF THE DAMNED (1960)
Director: Wolf Rilla
George Sanders (Gordon Zellaby),
Barbara Shelley (Anthea Zellaby),
Laurence Naismith (Dr. Willers),
Michael Gwynne (Maj. Alan Bernard),
John Phillips (Gen. Leighton), Richard
Vernon (Sir Edgar Hargreaves),
Richard Warner (Mr. Harrington),
Martin Stephens (David Zellaby),
Thomas Heathcote (James Pawle),
Charlotte Mitchell (Janet Pawle),
Alexander Archdale (Coroner), Jenny
Laird (Mrs. Harrington), Rosamund
Greenwood (Miss Ogle), Susan Rich-
ards (Mrs. Plumpton), Sarah Long
(Evelyn Harrington), Robert Marks
(Paul Norman), John Stuart (Mr.

Smith), Bernard Archard (Vicar),
Pamela Buck (Milly), Billy Lawrence
(John Bush), Peter Vaughan (Constable
Gobbey).

VILLAGE OF THE GIANTS (1965)
     Director: Bert I. Gordon
Tommy Kirk (Mike), Tisha Sterling
(Jean), Beau Bridges (Fred), Johnny
Crawford (Horsey), Ronny Howard
(Genius), Charla Doherty (Nancy),
Joy Harmon (Merrie), Tim Rooney
(Pete), Kevin O'Neal (Harry), Bob
Random (Rick).

VIRGIN PRESIDENT, THE (1967)
     Director: Grame Ferguson
Severn Darden, Peter Boyle, Con-
rad Yama, Andrew Duncan, Richard
Schall.

VIRGINS AND THE VAMPIRES (1972-
     Fr.) (A.K.A. "Caged Virgins",
     "Vierges et Vampires", "The
     Crazed Vampire")
     Director: Jean Rollin
Marie Castel, Mireille D'Argent,
Phillippe Gaste, Dominique Toussaint, Dominique, Louise Dhour, Michel Delsalle, Oliver Francois, Antoine Mausin, Paul Bisciglia.

VIRGIN SPRING, THE (1960-Swed.)
     (A.K.A. "Jungfrukallan")
     Director: Ingmar Bergman
Max Von Sydow (Tore), Brigitta
Valberg (Frau Mareta), Gunnel Lind-
blom (Ingeri), Brigitta Pettersson
(Karin), Tor Isedal (the mute), Axel
Dunberg (thin man), Allan Edwall
(beggar), Axel Slangus (bridge keeper),
Oscar Ljung (Simon), Gundrun Brost
(Frida), Ove Porath (boy).

VIRGIN WITCH, THE (1970)
     Director: Ray Austin
Anne Michelle (Christine), Vicky
Michelle (Betty), Keith Buckley
(Johnny), Patricia Haines (Sybil),
Neil Hallett (Gerald), James Chase
(Peter), Paula Wright (Mrs. Wendell),
Christopher Strain.

VIRUS (1980-Jap.) (A.K.A. "Fukkatsu
     No Hi")
     Director: Kinji Fukasaku
Sonny Chiba (Dr. Yamauchi), Chuck
Connors (Captain MacCloud), Glenn
Ford (Pres. Richardson), Olivia
Hussey (Marit), George Kennedy
(Adm. Conway), Cec Linder (Dr.
Latour), Bo Svenson (Major Carter),
Henry Silva (Garland), Robert Vaughn

(Sen. Barkley), Stephanie Faulkner
(Sarah Baker), Masao Kusakari (Yoshi-
zumi), Stuart Gillard (Dr. Mayer),
Isao Natsuki (Dr. Nakanishi), Edward
J. Olmos (Capt. Lopez), Ken Ogata
(Prof. Tsuchiya), Yumi Takigawa
(Moriko), George Touliatos.

VISIONS... (TVM-1972) (A.K.A.
     "Visions of Death") - 10-10-72
     Director: Lee Katzin
Monte Markham (Prof. Mark Lowell),
Telly Savalas (Lt. Phil Keegan), Bar-
bara Anderson (Susan Schaeffer),
Lonny Chapman (Martin Binzech),
Tim O'Connor (Bert Hayes), Joe
Sirola (George Simpson), Jim Antonio
(Sgt. Ted Kroel), Elizabeth Moore (Mrs.
Metcalfe), Richard Erdman (Ellis),
Val de Vargas (Steve Curtis), Robert
Do Qui (Andrews).

VISIT FROM A DEAD MAN, A (TVM-
     1975) - 1-10-75
     Director: Lela Swift
Alfred Drake (Fred Carter), Heather
MacRae (Sally Carter), Stephen Col-
lins (Harry), Will Hare (Constable).

VISITING HOURS (1982)
     Director: Jean Claude Lord
Lee Grant (Deborah Ballin), Michael
Ironside (Colt Hawker), Linda Purl
(Sheila Munroe), William Shatner
(Gary Baylor), Helen Hughes (Louise
Shepherd), Harvey Atkin (Vince Brad-
shaw), Michael J. Reynolds (Porter
Halstrom), Maureen McRae (Elizabeth
Hawker), Kirsten Bishopric (Denise),
Debra Kirschenbaum (Connie Wexler),
Elizabeth Leigh Milne (Patricia Ellis).

VISITOR, THE (1980-Ital./U.S.)
     (A.K.A. "Il Visitatore")
     Director: Michael J. Paradise/
     Giulio Paradisei
John Huston (Jersey Colsowitz, the
Visitor), Paige Conner (Katie Collins),
Mel Ferrer (Dr. Walker), Shelley
Winters (Jane Phillips), Joanne Nail
(Barbara Collins), Lance Henriksen
(Raymond), Sam Peckinpah (Sam),
Ja Townsend, Jack Dorsey, Johnny
Popwell, Steve Somers, Wallace
Williamson, Low Walker, Walter
Gordon, Sr., Hsio Ho Chao, Calvin
Fenbry, Betty Turner, Steve Cunn-
ingham, Neal Bortz, Bill Ash, Char-
ley Hardnett, Jack H. Gordon, Steve
Belzer.

VISIT TO A SMALL PLANET, A (1959)
     Director: Norman Taurog

Jerry Lewis (Kreton), Joan Blackman (Ellen Spelding), Fred Clark (Roger Putnam Spelding), Earl Holliman (Conrad), Gale Gordon (Bud Mayberry), John Williams (Delton), Lee Patrick (Rheba Spelding), Jerome Cowan (George Abercrombie), Barbara Lawson (beatnik dancer), Ellen Corby.

VOICE FROM THE GRAVE (1933)
Director: Phil Goldstone
Zita Johann (Nora Moran), Paul Cavanagh (Dick, the Governor), Alan Dinehart (the District Attorney), Clare Dubrey (Governor's wife), John Miljan (Paulino), Henry B. Walthall (Father Ryan), Sarah Padden, Ann Brody, Aggie Herring, Syd Saylor, Harvey Clark, Otis Harlan.

VOICE FROM THE SKY, THE (1930)
- serial in 10 episodes
Chapters: 1. "Doomed", 2. "The Cave of Horror", 3. "The Man from Nowhere", 4. "Danger Ahead", 5. "Desperate Deeds", 6. "Trail of Vengeance", 7. "The Scarlet Scourge", 8. "Trapped by Fate", 9. "The Pit of Peril", & 10. "Hearts of Steel".
Director: Ben Wilson
Wally Wales, Jean Delores.

VOICE OF THE WHISTLER (1955)
Director: William Castle
Richard Dix, Rhys Williams, Donald Woods, Tom Kennedy, Egon Brecher, Gigi Perreau, Lynn Merrick.

VOICE ON THE WIRE, THE (1917) -
serial in 14 episodes
Chapters: 1. "The Oriental Death Punch", 2. "The Mysterious Man in Black", 3. "The Spider's Web", 4. "The Next Victim", 5. "The Spectral Hand", 6. "The Death Warrant", 7. "The Marked Room", 8. "High Finance", 9. "A Stern Case", 10. "The Guarded Heart", 11. "The Thought Machine", 12. "The Sign of the Thumb", 13. "'Twixt Death and Dawn", & 14. "The Light of Death".
Director: Stuart Paton
Neva Gerber, Ben Wilson, Francis MacDonald, Ernest Shields, Frank Tokonaga, Joseph Girard, Howard Crampton, Wadsworth Harris.

VOICES (1973)
Director: Kevin Billington
David Hemmings, Gayle Hunnicutt, Lynn Farleigh, Russell Lewis, Adam Bridge, Eva Griffiths, Peggy Ann

Clifford.

VOODOO BLACK EXORCIST (1974-Span.)
Director: Manuel Cano
Aldo Sombrel, Eva Leon.

VOODOO HEARTBEAT (1972)
Director: Charles Nizet
Ray Molina, Philip Ahn, Ern Dugo, Forrest Duke, Stan Mason, Mike Zapata, Mike Meyers, Ebby Rhodes, Mary Martinez, Ray Molina, Jr.

VOODOO ISLAND (1957)
Director: Reginald LeBorg
Boris Karloff (Dr. Phillip Knight), Beverly Tyler (Sara Adams), Elisha Cook, Jr. (Martin Schuyler), Jean Engstrom (Claire Winter), Rhodes Reason (Matthew Gunn), Mervyn Vye (Barney Finch), Owen Cunningham (Howard Carlton), Herbert Patterson (Dr. Wilding), Glenn Dixon (Mitchell), Jerome Frank (Vickers), Frederick Ledebur (native chief).

VOODOO MAN (1944)
Director: William Beaudine
Bela Lugosi (Dr. Richard Marlowe), Tod Andrews (Ralph Dawson), George Zucco (Nicholas), Louise Currie (Stella Saunders), John Carradine (Toby), Wanda McCay (Betty Benton), Ellen Hall (Mrs. Evelyn Marlowe), Henry Hall (Sheriff), Terry Walker (Alice), Pat McKee (Grego), Dan White (Deputy), Mici Gota (housekeeper), Mary Currier (Mrs. Benton), Claire James (zombie), Ralph Littlefield, Ethelreda Leopold.

VOODOO TIGER (1952)
Director: Spencer Gordon Bennet
Johnny Weismuller (Jungle Jim), Jean Byron (Phyllis Bruce), James Seay (Abel Peterson), Jeanne Dean (Shalimar), Robert Bray (Major Bill Green), Rick Vallin (Sgt. Bono), Paul Hoffman (Michael Kovacs), Michael Fox (Carl Werner), John Cason (Jerry Masters), Charles Horvath (Wombulu), Richard Kipling (Commissioner Kingston), Frederic Berest (Native Chief), Alex Montoya (Native Leader), William R. Klein (co-pilot), Tamba.

VOODOO WOMAN (1956)
Director: Edward L. Cahn
Marla English (Marilyn Blanchard),

Tom Conway (Dr. Roland Gerard),
Mike 'Touch' Connors (Ted Bronson),
Lance Fuller (Rick), Paul Dubov
(Marcel), Mary Ellen Kay (Susan
Gerard), Norman Willis (Harry West),
Martin Wilkins (Chaka), Otis Greene
(Bobo), Emmett E. Smith (Gandor),
Jean Davis (native girl), Giselle D'Arc
(singer), Paul Blaisdell (the Monster).

VOYAGE INTO SPACE (1965-Jap.)
    (A. K. A. "Johnny Sokko and His
    Giant Robot")
    Director;
Mitsunobu Kaneko, Akio Ito, Tomomi
Kuwabara, Shozaburo Date, Hirohiko
Sato.

VOYAGE TO THE BOTTOM OF THE
    SEA (1961)
    Director: Irwin Allen
Walter Pidgeon (Adm. Harriman
Nelson), Robert Sterling (Capt. Lee
Crane), Joan Fontaine (Dr. Susan
Hiller), Peter Lorre (Commodore
Lucius Emery), Barbara Eden
(Cathy Connors), Michael Ansara
(Miguel Alvarez), Frankie Avalon
(Chip Romano), Regis Toomey (Dr.
Jamieson), John Litel (Adm. B. J.
Crawford), Henry Daniell (Dr. Zucco),
Howard McNear (Rep. Llewellyn
Parker), Del Monroe (Kowski), Mark
Slade (Smith), Anthony Monaco (Coo-
kie), Larry Gray (Dr. Newmar), Jona-
than Gilmore (Young), Charles Tan-
nen (Gleason), Robert Easton (Sparks),
David McLean (Ned Thompson), George
Diestel (Lt. Hodges), Michael Ford,
Skip Ward (crew members).

VOYAGE TO THE END OF THE UNI-
    VERSE (1963-Czech.) (A. K. A.
    "Ikaria XB-1")
    Director: Jindrich Polak
Zdenek Stepenak/Dennis Stephens
(Cmdr. Vladimir), Dana Merdricka/
Dana Meredith (Nina), Frantisek
Smolik/Francis Smolen (Astronomer
Anthony Hopkins), Irene Kova (Brigit),
Miroslav Machacek (Marcel), Joseph
Adams, Martin Tapin, Rudolph Dial,
John Rose, Renza Nova, Jan Morris,
Joe Irwin, John Mares, Marcella
Martin.

VOYAGE TO THE PLANET OF PRE-
    HISTORIC WOMEN (1968)
    Director: Peter Bogdanovich
Mamie Van Doren (Moana), Paige Lee,
Mary Mark.

VOYAGE TO THE PREHISTORIC

PLANET (1965)
    Director: John Sebastian/
    Curtis Harrington
Basil Rathbone (Prof. Hartman), Faith
Domergue (Marcia), Marc Shannon,
John Bix, Christopher Brand, Lewis
Keane, Robert Chanta.

VULCAN, SON OF JUPITER (1962-
    Ital.) (A. K. A. "Vulcano Figlio
    di Giove")
    Director: Emimmo Salvi
Gordon Mitchell, Bella Cortez, Rod
Flash, Roger Browne, Furio Meniconi,
L. Zagra, Yonne Sura, O. Gargaro.

VULTURE, THE (1966)
    Director: Lawrence Huntington
Robert Hutton (Eric Luytens), Akim
Tamiroff (Prof. Koniglish), Brode-
rick Crawford (Brian Stroud), Diane
Clare (Trudy Luytens), Philip Friend
(the Vicar), Annette Carell (Ellen
West), Patrick Holt (Jarvis), Edward
Caddick (the Sexton), Gordon Sterne
(Edward Stroud), Keith McConnell
(Police Superintendent Wendell),
Margaret Robertson (nurse).

WAGER BETWEEN TWO MAGICIANS,
    A (1904-Fr.) (A. K. A. "Match de
    Prestidigitation")
    Director: Georges Melies

WALKING DEAD, THE (1936)
    Director: Michael Curtiz
Boris Karloff (John Ellman), Edmund
Gwenn (Dr. Beaumont), Ricardo
Cortez (Nolan), Marguerite Churchill
(Nancy), Barton MacLane (Loder),
Warren Hull (Jimmy), Henry O'Neill
(Werner), Robert Strange (Merritt),
Joe Sawyer (Trigger), Paul Harvey
(Blackstone), Addison Richards (Pri-
son Warden), Eddie Acuff (Betcha),
Kenneth Harlan (Stephen Martin),
Joseph King (Judge Shaw), Ruth Robin-
son (Mrs. Shaw), Miki Morita (Sako),
Adrian Rosley (florist), Wade Boteler,
Milton Kibbee.

WANDERING JEW, THE (1904-Fr.)
    (A. K. A. "Le Juif Errant")
    Director: Georges Melies

WANDERING JEW, THE (1923)
    Director: Maurice Elvey
Matheson Lang, Isobel Elsom, Hutin
Britton, Malvina Longfellow, Shayle
Gardner, Jerrold Rubertshaw, Florence
Sanders, Hubert Carter, Winifred Izard,
Lewis Gilbert, Lionel D'Aragon, Fred
Raynham, Hector Abbas, Gordon Hopkirk.

WANDERING JEW, THE (1933)
Director: Maurice Elvey
Conrad Veidt, Marie Ney, Dennis
Hoey, Felix Aylmer, Jack Livesey,
Arnold Lucy, Abraham Sofaer, Cecily
Oates, Anne Grey, Joan Maude, Basil
Gill, Bertram Wallis, John Stuart,
Francis L. Sullivan, Ivor Barnard,
Peggy Ashcroft.

WANDERING MINSTREL, THE (1899-
Fr.) (A.K.A. "Richesse et Misere",
"La Cigale et la Fourmi", "Riches
and Misery", "The Grasshopper and
the Ants")
Director: Georges Melies

WAR BETWEEN THE PLANETS
(1965-Ital.) (A.K.A. "Missione
Planeta Errante", "Mission Wan-
dering Planet", "Planet on the
Prowl")
Director: Anthony Dawson/
Antonio Margheriti
Giacomo Rossi-Stuart/Jack Stuart
(Cmdr. Rod Jackson), Ombretta Colli/
Amber Collins (Terry), Peter Martell,
John Bartha, Vera Dolen, Marco Bo-
gliani.

WAR GAME, THE (1965) - documentary
. Director: Peter Watkins
Michael Aspel, Dick Graham (Nar-
rators).

WAR-GODS OF THE DEEP (1965)
(A.K.A. "City Under the Sea")
Director: Jacques Tourneur
Vincent Price (the Captain), Tab
Hunter (Ben Harris), Susan Hart (Jill
Tregallis), John LeMesurier (Mr.
Ives), David Tomlinson (Harold Tiffin-
Jones), William Hurndell (Tom), Derek
Newark (Dan), Henry Oscar (Mumford),
Anthony Selby (George), Roy Patrick
(Simon), Michael Heyland (Bill), Jim
Spearman (Jack), Steven Brooke (Ted),
Dennis Blake (Harry), Arthur Hewlett,
Walter Sparrow, John Barrett (fisher-
men), Barbara Bruce, Hilda Campbell,
Bart Allison, George Ricarde (guests).

WAR IN SPACE (1977-Ital.) (A.K.A.
"Anna Zero Guerra Nello Spazio")
Director: Alfonso Brescia/Al
Bradley
John Richardson, Malisa Longo, West
Buchanan, Charles Borromel, Massimo
Bonetti, Y. Somer.

WARLOCK MOON (1975)
Director: William Herbert
Laurie Walters (Jenny Macallister), Joe

Spano (John Devers), Edna Macafee
(Agnes Abercrombi), Ray Goman
(Deputy), Charles Raino (Sheriff),
Harry Bauer (hunter), Steve Solinsky,
Richard Vieille (axemen), Michael
Herbert (lecturer), Joan Zerrien
(1st girl).

WAR LORD, THE (1965)
Director: Franklin Schaffner
Charlton Heston (Chrysagon), Richard
Boone (Bors), Rosemary Forsyth
(Bronwyn), Maurice Evans (Priest),
Guy Stockwell (Drado), Niall Mac-
Ginnis (Odins), James Farentino
(Marc), Henry Wilcoxon (Frisian
Prince), Woodrow Parfrey (Piet),
John Alderson (Golbracht), Michael
Conrad (Rainault), Sammy Ross
(Volc), Allen Jaffe (Tybald), Dal
Jenkins (Dirck), Forrest Wood
(Chrysagon man), Johnny Jensen
(Boy Prince), Belle Mitchell (old
woman).

WARLORDS OF ATLANTIS (1978)
(A.K.A. "7 Cities to Atlantis")
Director: Kevin Connor
Doug McClure (Greg Collinson), Lea
Brodie (Delphine), Peter Gilmore
(Charles), Shane Rimmer (Daniels),
Hal Galili (Grogan), Michael Gothard
(Atmir), Robert Brown (Briggs),
Daniel Massey (Atraxon), Cyd Cha-
risse (Atsil), John Ratzenberger
(Fenn), Donald Bisset (Aitken), Derry
Power (Jacko), Ashley Knight (Sandy).

WARNING FROM SPACE (1956-Jap.)
(A.K.A. "Uchujin Tokyo Arawaru",
"Spacemen Arrive in Tokyo",
"Mysterious Satellite")
Director: Koji Shima
Keizo Kawasaki (Toru), Toyomi
Karita (Hikari Aozora), Bin Yagasawa
(2nd Pairan), Shozo Nanbu (Dr. Isobe),
Bontaro Miake (Dr. Komura), Kiyoko
Hirai (Mrs. Matusuda), Mieko Nagai
(Taeko).

WAR O'DREAMS, THE (1915)
Director: E.A. Martin
Edwin N. Wallock (Prof. Arthur
Ensign), Lillian Hayward (Mrs.
Ensign), Bessie Eyton (Bessie En-
sign).

WAR OF THE COLOSSAL BEAST
(1958) (A.K.A. "The Terror Strikes")
Director: Bert I. Gordon
Sally Fraser (Joyce Manning), Dean
Parkin (Col. Glenn Manning), Roger
Pace (Major Baird), Russ Bender

(Dr. Carmichael), George Becwar
(Swanson), Roy Gordon (Mayor),
Robert Hernandez (Miquel), Charles
Stewart (Capt. Harris), Rico Alaniz
(Sgt. Luis Murillo), Jack Kosslyn
(newscaster), George Navarro (Mex-
ican doctor), Howard Wright (Medical
Corps Officer), George Millan (Gen.
Nelson), Bill Giorgio (bus driver),
Warren Frost (switchboard operator),
Stan Chambers (TV announcer),
Loretta Nicholson (Joan), June
Joselyn (mother), Bob Garnet.

WAR OF THE GARGANTUAS (1967-
Jap.) (A.K.A. "Sanda tai Gaila")
Director: Inoshiro Honda
Russ Tamblyn (Dr. Paul Stewart),
Kumi Mizuno, Jun Tazaki, Kenji
Sahara, Kipp Hamilton, Hisaya Ito,
Kiroshi Sekita, Ren Yamamoto,
Haruo Nakajima, Nadao Kirido,
Nobuo Makamura, Yoshibumi Tajima.

WAR OF THE GIANTS (1966-Span./
Ital.) (A.K.A. "Combate de Gi-
gantes")
Director: Giorgio Capitani
Sergio Ciani, Conrado San Martin,
Elisa Montes, Renato Rossini.

WAR OF THE GODS (1979)
see Television: Battlestar Galactica (1978-79)

WAR OF THE MONSTERS (1966-
Jap.) (A.K.A. "Gamera tai
Barugon", "Gamera vs. Barugon")
Director: Shigeo Tanaka
Kojiro Hongo (Keisuke Hirata),
Akira Natsuki (Ichiro Hirata), Kyoko
Enami (Karen), Koji Fujiyama (On-
odera), Yuzo Hayakawa (Kawajiri),
Ichiro Sugai (Dr. Matsushita).

WAR OF THE PLANETS (1965-Ital.)
(A.K.A. "I Diafanoidi Portano la
Mort", "The Diaphanoids Bring
Death", "The Deadly Diaphanoids")
Director: Antonio Margheriti/
Anthony Dawson
Tony Russell, Lisa Gastoni, Franco
Nero, Massimo Serato, Michel
Lemoine, Carlo Giustini.

WAR OF THE ROBOTS (1978-Ital.)
Director: Alfonso Brescia/
Al Bradley
Antonio Sabato, Yanti Somer, West
Buchana, Ines Pellegrini.

WAR OF THE SATELLITES (1957)
Director: Roger Corman

Richard Devon (Dr. Van Ponder),
Dick Miller (Dave Boyer), Susan
Cabot (Sybil Carrington), Robert
Shayne (Hodgkiss), Michael Fox
(Akad), Jerry Barclay (John), Mitzi
McCall (Mitzi), Eric Sinclair (Dr.
Lazar), Jay Sayer (Jay), Beech
Dickerson, John Brinkley (crew
members), Bruno VeSota.

WAR OF THE WORLDS, THE (1953)
Director: Byron Haskin
Gene Barry (Dr. Clayton Forrester),
Ann Robinson (Sylvia Van Buren),
Les Tremayne (Gen. Mann), Lewis
Martin (Pastor Matthew Collins),
Robert Cornthwaite (Dr. Pryor),
Sandro Giglio (Dr. Bilder beck),
William Phipps (Wash Perry), Paul
Birch (Alonzo Hogue), Jack Krus-
chen (Salvatore), Vernon Rich
(Col. Heffner), House Stevenson,
Jr. (General's aide), Paul Frees
(Radio Announcer), Henry Brandon
(cop), Carolyn Jones (blonde), Pierre
Cressoy (man), Nancy Hale (young
wife), Virginia Hall (girl), Walter
Sande (Sheriff Bogany), Charles
Gemora (Martian), Alex Frazer
(Dr. Hettinger), Ann Codee (Dr.
Duprey), Ivan Lebedeff (Dr. Gratz-
man), Robert Rockwell (Ranger),
Alvy Moore (Zippy), Frank Kreig
(Fiddler Hawkins), John Maxwell
(Doctor), Ned Glass (looter with
cash), Russell Conway (Rev. Bethany),
Cliff Clark (Australian policeman),
Edward Colmans (Spanish priest),
Jameson Shade (Deacon), David
McMahon (Minister), Gertrude Hoff-
man (newsvendor), John Mansfield
(man), Freeman Lusk (Secretary of
Defense), Don Kohler (Colonel),
Sydney Mason (Fire Chief), Peter
Adams (Lookout), Ted Hecht (KGEB
reporter), Teru Shimada (Japanese
diplomat), Herbert Lytton (Chief of
Staff), Ralph Dumke (Buck Monahan),
Edgar Barrier (Prof. McPherson),
Wally Richard (reporter), Morton
C. Thompson (cub reporter), Ralph
Montgomery (Red Cross Leader),
Russell Bender (Dr. Carmichael),
Douglas Henderson (staff sergeant),
Anthony Warde (M.P. driver), Jerry
James (2nd reporter), Bud Wolfe
(big man), Jimmie Dundee (Civil
Defense official), Joel Marston (M.P.),
Patricia Iannone (little girl), Bill
Meader (P.E. official), Al Ferguson
(police chief), Eric Alden (man),
Rudy Lee (boy), Gus Taillon (elderly
man), Ruth Barnell (mother), Dorothy

Vernon (elderly woman), George Pal, Frank Freeman, Jr. (bums), Hugh Allen (Brigadier general), Stanley W. Orr (Marine major), Charles J. Stewart (Marine captain), Freddie Zendar (Marine lieutenant), Jim Davies (Marine commanding officer), Dick Fortune (Marine captain), Edward Wahrman (cameraman), Martin Coulter (Marine sergeant), Waldon Williams (boy), Hazel Boyne (screaming woman), Cora Shannon (old woman), Mike Mahoney (young man), David Sharpe, Dale Van Sickel, Fred Graham (looters), Sir Cedric Hardwicke (Narrator).

WAR OF THE ZOMBIES, THE (1963) Ital.) (A.K.A. "Roma contro Roma", "Rome vs. Rome", "Night Star, Goddess of Electra")
Director: Giuseppe Vari
John Drew Barrymore (Aderbal), Susi Anderson (Tullia), Ettore Manni (Gaius), Ida Galli (Rhama), Mino Doro, Philippe Hersent, Ivano Staccioli, Guilio Naculani, Matilde Calman.

WARRIOR EMPRESS (1960-Ital.) (A.K.A. "Saffo, Venere di Lesbo")
Director: Pietro Francisci
Tina Louise (Sappho), Kerwin Mathews (Phaon), Susy Golgi (Actis), Riccardo Garrone (Hyperbius), Enrico Maria Salerno (Melanchrus), Alberto Farenese (Larious), Antonio Batistella (Paeone), Strelsa Brown (Priestess), Lilly Mantovani (Cleide), Annie Gorassini (Dyla).

WASP WOMAN, THE (1959)
Director: Roger Corman
Susan Cabot (Janice Starling), Barboura Morris (Mary Dennison), Fred Eisley/Anthony Eisley (Bill Lane), Michael Marks (Dr. Eric Zinthrop), Frank Gerstle (Hellman), William Roerick (Arthur Cooper), Bruno VeSota (night watchman), Frank Wolff.

WATCHER IN THE WOODS, THE (1980)
Director: John Hough
Bette Davis (Mrs. Aylwood), David McCallum (Paul Curtis), Carroll Baker (Helen Curtis), Ian Bannen (John Keller), Kyle Richards (Ellie Curtis), Lynn-Holly Johnson (Jan Curtis), Richard Pasco (Tom Colley), Frances Cuka (Mary Fleming), Benddict Taylor (Mike Fleming), Eleanor Summerfield (Mrs. Thayer), Katherine Levy (Karen Aylwood), Georgina Hale (young Mrs. Aylwood).

WATER BABIES, THE (1979)
Director: Lionel Jeffries
James Mason (Grimes), Billie Whitelaw (Mrs. Doasyouwouldbedoneby), Bernard Cribbins (Masterman), Joan Greenwood (Lady Harriet), David Tomlinson (Sir John), Paul Luty (Sladd), Tommy Pender (Tom), Samantha Gates (Ellie).

WATERMELON MAN (1970)
Director: Melvin Van Peebles
Godfrey Cambridge (Jeff Gerber), Estelle Parsons (Althea Gerber), Erin Moran (Janice Gerber), Scott Garrett (Burton Gerber), Howard Caine (Mr. Townsend), Kay Kimberly (Erica), Kay E. Kuter (Dr. Wainwright), Irving Selbat (Mr. Johnson), Mantan Moreland (Counterman), Emil Sitka (delivery man), D'Urville Martin (bus driver), Lawrence Park (1st passenger).

WATERSHIP DOWN (1978) - animated
Director: Martin Rosen
Voices: John Hurt (Hazel), Roy Kinnear (Pipkin), Sir Ralph Richardson (Chief Rabbit), Denholm Elliott (Cowslip), Harry Andrews (Gen. Woundwort), Zero Mostel (Kehaar), Clifton Jones (Blackavar), Joss Ackland (Black Rabbit), Michael Graham-Cox (Bigwig), John Bennett (Captain Holly), Richard Briers (River), Richard O'Callaghan (Dandelion), Hannah Gordon (Hyzenthlay), Simon Cadell (Blackberry), Nigel Hawthorne (Companion), Mary Maddox (Clover), Terence Rigby (Silver), Lyn Farleigh (Cat), Michael Hordern (Narrator).

WAXWORKS (1924-Ger.) (A.K.A. "Three Wax Men", "Das Wachsfigurenkabinett")
Director: Paul Leni
Conrad Veidt (Ivan the Terrible), Werner Krauss (Jack the Ripper), Emil Jannings (Haroun-alRaschid), Olga Belejieff, William Dieterle, John Gottowt, Ernst Legal, Georg John.

WAY...WAY OUT (1966)
Director: Gordon Douglas
Jerry Lewis (Peter Mattemore), Connie Stevens (Eileen Forbes), Dick Shawn (Igor), Anita Ekberg (Anna Sablova), Robert Morley (Harold Quonset), Dennis Weaver (Hoffman), Howard Morris (Schmidlap), Brian Keith (Gen. Hallenby),

Alex D'Arcy (Deuce), James Brolin
(Ted Robertson), Linda Harrison
(Peggy), Bobo Lewis (Esther Daven-
port), William O'Connell (Ponsonby),
Milton Prame (Russian delegate), Sig
Ruman.

WEAPONS OF VENGEANCE (1963-
Ital./Fr.) (A.K.A. "I Diavoli
di Spartivento", "The Devils of
Spartivento")
    Director: Leopoldo Savona
John Barrymore, Jr., Giacomo
Rossi-Stuart, Jany Clair, Scilla
Gabel, Romano Ghisi.

WEB OF THE SPIDER (1979-Ital./
Fr./Ger.) (A.K.A. "Nella
Stretta Morsa del Ragno", "In
the Grip of the Spider", "E Venne
l'Alba... Ma Tinta Dirosso",
"And Comes the Dawn... But
Colored Red")
    Director: Anthony Dawson/
    Antonio Margheriti
Anthony Francoisa (Alan Foster),
Michele Mercier (Elizabeth), Karen
Filed (Julia), Klaus Kinski (Edgar
Allan Poe), Irinia Maleva, Paolo
Goslino.

WEDNESDAY CHILDREN, THE (1973)
    Director: Robert D. West
Marji Dodril (Mrs. Miller), Donald
E. Murray (Miller), Tom Kelly
(Scott), Carol Cary (Mrs. Berlow),
Al Miskell (Fenton), Robert D.
West (Minister).

WEEKEND (1967-Fr./Ital.)
    Director: Jean-Lue Godard
Mireille Darc (Corinne), Jean Yanne
(Roland), Jean-Pierre Kalfon (F.L.-
S.O. Leader), Valerie Lagrange
(Moll), Jean-Pierre Leaud (Saint-
Just/man in phone booth), Yves
Alfonso (Gros Poucet), Yves Beney-
ton (F.L.S.O. member), Blandine
Jeanson (Emily/Bronte/girl in farm-
yard), Georges Staquet (tractor
driver), Virginie Vigon (Marie-
Madeleine), Anne Wiazemsky (F.L.-
S.O. member/girl in car crash),
Isabelle Pons (Monsieur Jojot), Jean
Eustache (hitchhiker).

WEEKEND MURDERS (1970-Ital.)
(A.K.A. "Concerto Per Pistola
Solista", "Concert for a Solo
Pistol")
    Director: Michele Lupo
Anna Moffo (Barbara), Lance Percival
(Insp. Grey), Gastone Moschin (Sgt.

Thorpe), Evelyn Stewart (Isabelle),
Giacomo Rossi-Stuart (Ted), Peter
Baldwin (Anthony), Christopher
Chittell (Georgio), Marisa Fabbri
(Aunt Gladys), Beryl Cunningham
(Pauline), Guinto Parmeggiana
(Lawrence), Orchidea De Santis
(maid), Robert Hundar (valet),
Franco Borelli (stranger).

WEIRD WOMAN (1944)
    Director: Reginald LeBorg
Lon Chaney, Jr. (Prof. Norman
Reed), Anne Gwynne (Paula Reed),
Evelyn Ankers (Ilona Carr), Elisa-
beth Risden (Grace Gunnison), Ralph
Morgan (Prof. Millard Sawtelle),
Lois Collier (Margaret Mercer),
Elizabeth Russell(Evelyn Sawtelle),
Phil Brown (David Jennings), Harry
Hayden (Prof. Septimus Carr), Hanna
Kaapa (Laraus), William Hudson,
Jackie Lou Harding (students), Kay
Harding.

WELCOME TO ARROW BEACH
(1973) (A.K.A. "Tender Flesh")
    Director: Laurence Harvey
Laurence Harvey (Jason Henry),
Joanna Pettet (Grace Henry), Stuart
Whitman (Deputy Rakes), Meg Foster
(Robbin Stanley), John Ireland (Sher-
iff H. Bingham), Dody Heath (Felice),
David Macklin (Alex Heath), Gloria
Leroy (Ginger), Florence Lake (land-
lady), June Hedin (the hostess), John
Hart (the doctor), Robert Lussier
(Deputy Lippincott), Andy Romano
(Bryant), Altovise Gore (Deputy
Molly), Peter Ireland (Dale), Winston
Pruet (Ape), Janear Hines (reporter),
Tony Ballen (Clifford), Elizabeth
St. Clair (head nurse), June Westherly
(hostess), Craig Baxley (hot rod
driver), Elizabeth Haskell (beach
girl), James Clarke (beach boy).

WELCOME TO BLOOD CITY (1977)
    Director: Peter Sasdy
Jack Palance (Frendlander), Keir
Dullea (Lewis), Samantha Eggar
(Katherine), Barry Morse (Super-
visor), Hollis McLaren (Martine),
Chris Wiggins (Gellor), Allan Royale
(Peter), Ken James (Flint), Henry
Ramer (Chumley), John Evans (Lyle).

WEREWOLF, THE (1956)
    Director: Fred F. Sears
Steven Ritch (Duncan March, The
werewolf), Don Megowan (Jack
Haines), Joyce Holden (Amy Standish),
Harry Lauter (Clovey), S. John Launer

(Dr. Emery Forrest), Larry J. Blake (Birgus), Ken Christy (Dr. James Gilchrist), George M. Lynn (Dr. Morgan Chambers), George Cisar (Oxie), Eleanore Tanin (Helen Marsh), Don C. Harvey (1st Deputy), Kim Charney (Chris Marsh), Jean Charney (Cora), Marjorie Stapp (Min), James Gavin (Fanning), Ford Stevens (1st reporter), Jean Harvey (old woman).

WEREWOLF AND THE YETI, THE (1976-Span.) (A.K.A. "La Maldicion de la Bestia", "Night of the Howling Beast")
Director: M.I. Bonns
Paul Naschy (Waldemar Daninsky), Gil Vidal, Silvia Solar, L. Induni, G. Mills.

WEREWOLF IN A GIRL'S DORMITORY (1963-Ital./Austria) (A.K.A. "Lycanthropus: Bei Vollmond Mord", "I Married a Werewolf")
Director: Richard Benson/ Paolo Heusch
Barbara Lass (Brunhilde), Carl Schell (Julian Olcott), Maurice Marsac (Sir Alfred Whiteman), Curt Lowens (Mr. Swift), Alan Collins (Walter), Maureen O'Connor (Leonor McDonald), Mary McNeeran (Mary Smith), Anni Steinert (Sheena Whiteman), Grace Neame (Sandy).

WEREWOLF OF LONDON, THE (1935)
Director: Stuart Walker
Henry Hull (Dr. Glendon), Valerie Hobson (Lisa Glendon), Warner Oland (Dr. Yogami), Lester Matthews (Paul Ames), Spring Byington (Ettie Coombes), Lawrence Grant (Sir Thomas Forsythe), J.M. Kerrigan (Hawkins), Clark Williams (Hugh Renwick), Ethel Griffies (Mrs. Whack), Reginald Barlow (Dr. Phillips), Charlotte Granville (Lady Forsythe), Jeanne Bartlett (Daisy), Zeffie Tilbury (Mrs. Mancaster), Louis Vincenot (head cooley), Eddie Parker, Tempe Pigott, Egon Brecher, Harry Stubbs, David Thursby.

WEREWOLF OF WASHINGTON, THE (1973)
Director: Milton Moses Ginsberg
Dean Stockwell (Jack), Biff McGuire (the President), Clifton James (Attorney General), Jane House (Marion), Beeson Carroll (Cmdr. Salmon),

Michael Dunn (Dr. Kiss), Barbara Siegel (Hippy), Stephen Cheng (Foreign Minister).

WEREWOLF OF WOODSTOCK, THE (TVM-1975) - 1-24-75
Director: John Moffitt
Tige Andrews (Bert/the Werewolf), Michael Parks (Moody), Meredith McRae (Kendy), Harold J. Stone (Lt. Martino), Richard Webb (Dr. Marlow), Ann Doran (Dora), Andrew Stevens (Dave).

WEREWOLF VS. THE VAMPIRE WOMAN, THE (1970-Span./Ger.) (A.K.A. "La Noche de Walpurgis", "Shadow of the Werewolf")
Director: Leon Klimovsky
Paul Naschy (Waldemar Daninsky), Gaby Fuchs (Elvire), Patty Sheppard (Wandesa Darvula de Nadasdy), Barbara Capell (Genevieve), Andrew Reese, Julio Pena, Yelena Samarine, Andres Resino.

WEREWOLVES ON WHEELS (1971)
Director: Michel Levesque
Severn Darden (One), Stephen Oliver (Adam), D.J. Anderson (Helen), Duece Berry (Tarot), Anna Lynn Brown (Shirley), William Gray (Bill), Barry McGuire (Scarf), Grey Johnson (Movie), Owen Orr (Mouse), Leonard Rogel (gas station operator), John Hull, N.A. Palmisano, Dan Kopp, Carl Lee, Keith Guthrie, Bart Smith, Tex Hall, Marilyn Munger.

WE SHALL SEE (1964)
Director: Quentin Lawrence
Maurice Kaufman, Alec Mango, Talitha Pol, Faith Brook, Hugh Paddick, William Abney, Bridget Armstrong, Alex McIntosh, Donald Morley.

WEST OF ZANZIBAR (1928)
Director: Tod Browning
Lon Chaney, Sr. (Prof. Phroso/ Dead Legs Flint), Lionel Barrymore (Crane), Mary Nolan (Maizie), Warner Baxter (Doc), Jane Daly/Jacqueline Gadsdon (Anna), Kalla Pasha (Babe), Roscoe Ward (Tiny), Edna Tichenor (girl in bar), Rose Dione (owner of Zanzibar dive), Curtis Nero (Bumba), Fred Gambold (vaudeville comedian), Mae Busch, Anita Page, Chaz Chase, Art Winkler, Richard Cummings, Ida May, Dan Wolheim.

WESTWORLD (1973)
    Director: Michael Crichton
Richard Benjamin (Peter Martin),
James Brolin (John Blane), Yul Bryn-
ner (Gunslinger), Alan Oppenheimer
(Chief Supervisor), Dick Van Patten
(Banker), Majel Barrett (Miss Carrie),
Steve Franken (technician), Nora
Marlowe (hostess), Victoria Shaw
(Medieval Queen), Linda Scott (Ar-
lette), Terry Wilson (Sheriff), Nor-
man Bartold (Medieval Knight), Mi-
chael Mikler (Black Knight), Wade
Crosby (bartender), Anna Randall
(servant girl), Sharyn Wynters (Apa-
che girl), Chris Holter (stewardess),
Lin Henson (ticket girl), Julie Mar-
cus (girl in dungeon), Charles Seel
(bellhop), Anne Bellamy (middle-
aged woman), Will J. White, Ben
Young, Tom Falk (workmen), Orville
Sherman, Lindsay Workman, Lauren
Gilbert, Howard Platt, David Roberts
(supervisors), Jared Martin, Richard
Roat, Kenneth Washington, Robert
Patten, David Frank, Kip King,
David Man, Larry Delaney (techni-
cians).

WHAT! (1963-Ital./Fr.) (A.K.A.
    "La Frusta e il Corpo", "The
    Whip and the Body", "Night Is
    the Phantom")
    Director: Mario Bava
Daliah Lavi (Nevenka), Christopher
Lee (Kurt), Tony Kendall (Christian),
Isli Oberon (Katia), Dean Ardow (Count
Vladimir), Harriet White (Giorgia),
Alan Collins (manservant), Jacques
Herlin (priest).

WHAT EVER HAPPENED TO AUNT
    ALICE? (1969)
    Director: Lee H. Katzin
Geraldine Page (Claire Marrable),
Ruth Gordon (Mrs. Dimmock), Rose-
mary Forsyth (Harriet Vaughn),
Robert Fuller (Mike Darrah), Mil-
dred Dunnock (Miss Tinsley), Valerie
Allen (Dottie), Peter Brandon (George
Lawson), Joan Huntington (Julia Law-
son), Michael Barbera (Jim Vaughn),
Peter Bonerz (Mr. Bentley), Claire
Kelly (Elva), Jack Bannon (Olin),
Richard Angarola (Sheriff Armijo),
Martin Garralaga (Juan), Seth Riggs
(Warren), Lou Kane (telephone man).

WHAT EVER HAPPENED TO BABY
    JANE? (1962)
    Director: Robert Aldrich
Bette Davis (Jane Hudson), Joan
Crawford (Blanche Hudson), Victor

Buono (Edwin Flagg), Marjorie Bennett
(Della Flagg), Anna Lee (Mrs. Bates),
Dave Willock (Ray Hudson), Maidie
Norman (Elvira Stitt), Wesley Addy
(the director), Bert Freed (the pro-
ducer), Gina Gillespie (Blanche as
a child), Julie Allred (Baby Jane),
Barbara Merrill (Liza Bates), Ann
Barton (Cora Hudson).

WHAT HAVE YOU DONE WITH SO-
    LANGE? (1971-Ital./Ger.) (A.K.A.
    "Cosa Avete Fatto a Solange?",
    "Das Geheimnis der Gruen Steck-
    nadeln", "The Secret of the Green
    Pins", "The School That Couldn't
    Scream")
    Director: Massimo Dallemano
Joachim Fuchsberger, Christina
Galbo, Gunther Stoll, Karin Baal,
Fabio Testi, Camille Keaton, Claudia
Buthenuth, Maria Monti, Daniele
Micheletti, Giancarlo Badessi, Pilar
Castel.

WHAT'S SO BAD ABOUT FEELING
    GOOD? (1968)
    Director: George Seaton
George Peppard (Pete), Mary Tyler
Moore (Liz), Don Stroud (Barney),
Nathaniel Frey (Conrad), Susan St.
James (Aida), Dom DeLuise (Mon-
roe), Charles Lane (Dr. Shapiro),
John McMartin (the Mayor), George
Furth (Murgetroyd), Jeanne Arnold
(Gerturde), Monty Gunty (Sgt. Funty),
Joe Ponazecki (Officer Ponazecki),
Emily Yancy (Sybil), John Ryan (Ro-
ger), Thelma Ritter (Mrs. Schwartz),
Gillian Spencer (the Sack), Joey Faye
(zoo keeper), Frank Campanella
(Capt. Wallace), Martin O'Hara
(TV newscaster), Donald Hutton
(Sam), Arny Freeman (first mate),
Moses Gunn, Lincoln Kilpatrick,
Cleavon Little, Victoria Racimo,
Peter Turgeon, Bob Kaliban, George
Petrie, Hy Anzell, Marc Seaton,
Mina Kolb, Kay Turner, Ira Lewis,
Hugh Franklin, Peter Gumeny, Jara
Kohout, Barbara Minkus, Franklin
Cover, George Sperdakos, Tom Ahearne,
James Noble, Nat Polan, Eda Reiss
Merin, Salem Ludwig, Louis Zorich,
Albert Henderson.

WHAT'S THE MATTER WITH HELEN?
    (1971)
    Director: Curtis Harrington
Debbie Reynolds (Adelle Bruckner),
Shelly Winters (Helen Hill), Dennis
Weaver (Lincoln Palmer), Agnes
Morrehead (Sister Alma), Michael

MacLiammoir (Hamilton Starr),
Helene Winston (Mrs. Greenbaum),
Yvette Vickers (Mrs. Barker), Pame-
lyn Ferdin (Kiddy M.C.), Logan
Ramsey (cab driver), Minta Durfee
(old lady), Peter Brocco (old man),
Timothy Carey (tramp), Sammee
Lee Jones (Winona Palmer), Ribbi
Morgan (Rosalie Greenbaum), Peggy
Rea (Mrs. Schultz), Tammy Lee
(Charlene Barker), Molly Dodd (Mrs.
Rigg), Paulle Clark (Mrs. Plumb),
Debbie Van Den Houten (Sue Anne
Schultz), Teresa De Rose (Donna
Plumb), Peggy Lloyd Patten (Ellie
Banner), Swen Swenson (Gigolo),
Harry Stanton (Malcolm Hays), Gary
Combs (Matt Hill), Annette Davis
(spinster), Peggy Walter (young girl),
Sadie Delfino (midget lady), Helene
Heigh (widow), Douglas Deane (fana-
tical man).

WHEN A STRANGER CALLS (1979)
    Director: Fred Walton
Carol Kane (Jill Johnson), Charles
Durning (John Clifford), Tony Beckley
(Curt Duncan), Rachel Roberts (Dr.
Monk), Colleen Dewhurst (Tracy),
Carmen Argenziano (Dr. Mandrakis),
Rutanya Alda (Mrs. Mandrakis),
Kirsten Larkin (Nancy), Ron O'Neal
(Lt. Charlie Garber), Bill Boyett
(Sgt. Sacker), Michael Champion
(Bill), Heetu (houseboy), Joe Beale
(bartender), Ed Wright (retired man),
Louise Wright (retired woman),
Carol O'Neal (Mrs. Garber), Dennis
McMullen (maintenance man), John
Tobyansen (bar customer), Wally
Taylor (cheater), Richard Ball (Ste-
vie Lockart), Sarah Dammann (Bianca
Lockart), Steven Anderson (Stephen
Lockart), Lenora May (Sharon),
Randy Holland (Maitre d'), Trent
Dolan, Frank DiElsi, DeForest
Covan, Arell Blanton, Charles Bos-
well (policemen).

WHEN DINOSAURS RULED THE
    EARTH (1970)
    Director: Val Guest
Victoria Vetri (Sanna), Robin Hawdon
(Tara), Patrick Holt (Ammon), Pat-
rick Allen (Kingsor), Drewe Henley
(Khaku), Magda Konopka (Ulido),
Sean Caffrey (Kane), Imogen Hassall
(Ayak), Maria O'Brien (Omah), Jan
Rossini (rock girl), Connie Tilton
(sand mother), Maggie Lynton (rock
mother), Carol-Anne Hawkins (Yanni),
Jimmy Lodge (fisherman), Ray Ford,
Billy Cornelius (hunters).

WHEN MICHAEL CALLS (TVM-1972) -
    2-5-72
    Director: Philip Leacock
Ben Gazzara (Doremus Connelly),
Elizabeth Ashley (Helen Connelly),
Michael Douglas (Craig), Marian
Waldman (Elsa Britton), Larry Rey-
nolds (Dr. Britton), Karen Pearson
(Peggy Connelly), Albert S. Waxman
(Sheriff Hap Washbrook), Alan McRae
(Harry Randall), Steve Weston (Enoch
Mills), John Bethune (Quinlan), Mi-
chele Chicoine (Amy), Chris Pellett
(Peter), William Osler (Prof. Swen),
Robert Warner (Sam).

WHEN THE SCREAMING STOPS (1974-
    Span.) (A.K.A. "Las Garras de
    Lorele", "The Lorelei's Grasp")
    Director: Amando de Ossorio
Tony Kendall, Helga Line, Silvia
Tortosa, Lolita Tovar.

WHEN WOMEN HAD TAILS (1970-
    Ital.) (A.K.A. "Quando le Donne
    Avevando la Coda")
    Director: Pasquale Festa Cam-
        panile
Senta Berger (Filli), Frank Wolff
(Grrr), Giuliano Gemma (Ulli), Lino
Toffolo (Put), Aldo Giuffre (Zug),
Lando Buzzanca (Kao), Renzo Montag-
nani (Malue), Francesco Mule (Uto).

WHEN WOMEN LOST THEIR TAILS
    (1971-Ital./Ger.) (A.K.A. "Quando
    le Donne Persero la Coda")
    Director: Pasquale Festa Cam-
        panile
Senta Berger, Frank Wolff, Mario
Adorf, Lando Buzzanca, Renzo Mon-
tagnani, Lino Toffolo, Aldo Puglisi.

WHEN WOMEN PLAYED DING DONG
    (1971-Ital.) (A.K.A. "Quando gli
    Uomini Amarano la Clava... e
    con le Donne Fecero Din-Don")
    Director: Bruno Corbucci
Antonio Sabato, Aldo Giuffre, Nadia
Cassini, Vittorio Caprioli, Valeria
Fabrizi, Ello Pandolfi, Renato Rossini,
Anabella Incontrera.

WHEN WORLDS COLLIDE (1951)
    Director: Rudolph Mate
Richard Derr (Dave Randall), Barbara
Rush (Joyce Hendron), Peter Hansen
(Tony Drake), John Hoyt (Sydney
Stanton), Stephen Chase (Dean George
Frey), Larry Keating (Dr. Cole Hen-
dron), Hayden Rorke (Dr. Emory
Bronson), Sandro Giglio (Dr. Ottinger),
Laura Elliot (stewardess), Frank Cady

(Harold Ferris), Judith Ames (Julie
Cummings), Jim Congdon (Eddie Gra-
son), Frances Sanford (Alice, the
secretary), Freeman Lusk (Rudolph
Marston), Joseph Nell (Glen Spiro),
Marcel de la Brosse (headwaiter),
Queenie Smith (matron), Art Gilmore
(Paul), Keith Richards (Stanley),
Gay Nelson (Leda), Rudy Lee (Mike),
John Ridgley (Chief Inspector), James
Seay (Donovan), Harry Stanton (Dr.
Zenta), Sam Finn, Gertrude Astor,
Estelle Etterre (travelers), Hassan
Khayyam (Indian chairman), Bill
Meader (clerk), Ramsay Hill (French-
man), Gene Collins (newsdealer),
Mary Murphy, Kirk Alyn, Stuart
Whitman, Robert Chapman, Charmienne
Harker, Walter Kelley, Chad Madison,
Dolores Mann, Robert Sully, Richard
Vath (students), Paul Frees (Narrator).

WHERE DO WE GO FROM HERE? (1945)
     Director: Gregory Ratoff
Fred MacMurray (Bill Morgan), Joan
Leslie (Sally), Gene Sheldon (Ali,
the Genie), Alan Mowbray (Gen.
George Washington), Anthony Quinn
(Indian Chief), June Haver (Lucilla),
Carlos Ramirez (Benito), Fortunio
Bonanova (Columbus), John Davidson
(Benedict Arnold), Herman Bing
(Hessian Colonel), Howard Freeman
(Kreiger), Rosina Galli (old lady),
Fred Essler.

WHERE EAST IS EAST (1929)
     Director: Tod Browning
Lon Chaney, Sr. (Tiger Haynes),
Lupe Valez (Toyo), Lloyd Hughes
(Bobby Bailey), Estelle Taylor (Ma-
dame), Louis Stern (Fra Angelo),
Mrs. Wong Wing (Ming), Duke Ka-
hanamoku (wild animal trapper),
Richard R. Neill.

WHERE HAVE ALL THE PEOPLE
GONE? (TVM-1974) - 10-8-74
     Director: John Llewellyn Moxey
Peter Graves (Steven Anders), Verna
Bloom (Jenny), Kathleen Quinlan
(Deborah Anders), George O'Hanlon,
Jr. (David Anders), Michael James
Wixted (Michael), Noble Willingham
(Guide), Doug Chapin (Tom Clancy),
Jay W. MacIntosh (mother), Dan
Barrows (man with gun), Ken Sansom
(man at store).

WHERE THE BULLETS FLY (1966)
     Director: John Gilling
Tom Adams (Charles Vine), Dawn
Adams (Felicity Moonlight), Tim

Barrett (Seraph), Michael Ripper
(Angel), Ronald Leigh-Hunt (Thursby),
Maggie Kimberley (Jacqueline),
Suzan Farmer (Caron), Gerard Heinz
(Venstram), Wilfred Brambell (train
conductor), Joe Baker (Minister),
Michael Balfour (bandleader), Marcus
Hammond (O'Neil), Sid James (mor-
tuary attendant), John Arnott (Rock-
well), Maurice Browning (Cherub),
Bryan Mosley (Connolly), Heidi
Erich (Carruthers), Sue Donovan
(Celia), Terence Sewards (Minister's
P. A.), Michael Ward (Michael),
Julie Martin (Verity), Tom Bowman
(Russian Colonel), Patrick Jordan
(Russian), James Ellio (Flight Lt.
Fotheringham), Tony Alpino (Butler),
Charles Houston (co-pilot), Michael
Cox (Lt. Gayfawkes), Garry Marsh
(Major), Peter Ducrow (Prof. Hard-
ing), Barbara French (Harding's
secretary), Michael Goldie (labourer),
John Horsley (Air Marshal), Joe
Ritchie (truck driver), John Watson
(controller), Roy Stephens (staff
officer), David Gregory (RAF ser-
geant).

WHERE TIME BEGAN (1977-Span.)
     (A. K. A. "Viaje al Centro de la
     Tierra", "Fabulous Journey to the
     Center of the Earth")
     Director: Juan Piquer
Kenneth More (Prof. Otto Lindens-
brock), Ivonne Sentis (Glauben),
Pep Munne (Axel), Frank Brana (Hans),
Lone Fleming (Molly), Jack Taylor
(Olsen), Jose Cafarel (Prof. Fridikson),
Emiliano Redondo (Cristoff).

WHILE LONDON SLEEPS (1926)
     Director: H. P. Betherton
Helene Costello, Walter Merrill,
Otto Matiesen, John Patrick, George
Kotsonaros, DeWitt Jennings.

WHILE LONDON SLEEPS (1934)
     (A. K. A. "Sabotage")
     Director: Adrian Brunel
Victor Varconi, Joan Maude, D. A.
Clarke-Smith, J. Hubert Leslie, J. A.
O'Rourke, Wilfred Noy, Joan Matheson,
Shayle Gardner.

WHILE PARIS SLEEPS (1920)
     Director: Maurice Tourneur
Lon Chaney, Sr. , J. Farrell Mac-
Donald, John Gilbert, Mildred Manning,
Hardee Kirkland, Jack McDonald.

WHIP HAND, THE (1951)
     Director: William Cameron Menzies

Elliott Reid (Matt Corbin), Edgar
Barrier (Dr. Edward Keller), Carla
Balenda (Janet Keller), Raymond
Burr (Steve Loomis), Otto Waldis
(Dr. Willem Bucholtz), Michael
Steele (Chick), Lurene Tuttle (Molly
Loomis), Olive Carey (Mrs. Turner),
Peter Brocco (Garr), Lewis Martin
(Peterson), Frank Darien (Luther
Adams), Jameson Shade (Sheriff),
Art Dupuis (speedboat pilot), Brick
Sullivan, Bob Thom (rangers), Robert
Foulk, William Challee (guards).

WHIRLPOOL (1949)
    Director: Otto Preminger
Gene Tierney (Ann Sutton), Richard
Conte (Dr. Bill Sutton), Jose Ferrer
(David Korvo), Charles Bickford (Lt.
Colton), Eduard Franz (Martin Avery),
Larry Keating (Mr. Simms), For-
tunio Bonanova (Peruccio), Barbara
O'Neil (Theresa Randolph), Constance
Collier (Tina Cosgrove), Ruth Lee
(Miss Hall), Bruce Hamilton (Lt.
Jeffreys), Ian MacDonald (store
detective), Alex Gerry (Dr. Peter
Duval), Larry Bodkin, Robert Faulk,
Helen Westcott, Eddie Dunn, Myrtle
Anderson, Jane Van Duser, Howard
Negley, Mauritz Hugo, Randy Stuart,
Mack Williams, John Trebash, Nancy
Valentine, Clancy Cooper, Charles
J. Flynn.

WHISPERING GHOSTS (1942)
    Director: Alfred Werker
John Carradine (Long Jack), Brenda
Joyce (Elizabeth Woods), John Shel-
ton (David Courtland), Grady Sutton
(Jonathan Flack), Willie Best (Euclid
White), Milton Berle (H.H. Van
Buren), Milton Parsons (Dr. Bas-
comb), Charles Halton (Gruber),
Edmund MacDonald (Gilpin), Arthur
Hohl (Insp. Norris), Abner Biberman
(Mack Wolf), Harry Hayden (Conroy),
Rene Riano (Meg).

WHISPERING SHADOW, THE (1933) -
    serial in 12 episodes
Chapters: 1. "The Master Magician",
2. "The Collapsing Room", 3. "The
All-Seeing Eye", 4. "The Shadow
Strikes", 5. "Wanted for Murder",
6. "The Man Who Was Czar", 7.
"The Double Room", 8. "The Red
Circle", 9. "The Fatal Secret", 10.
"The Death Warrant", 11. "The
Trap", & 12. "King of the World".
    Director: Albert Herman &
        Colbert Clark
Bela Lugosi (Prof. Strang), Henry

B. Walthall (Bradley), Vivian Tatter-
sall (Vera Strang), Robert Warwick
(Raymond), George Lewis (Bud
Foster), Roy D'Arcy (Steinbeck),
Karl Dane (Sparks), Ethel Clayton
(the Countess), Malcolm MacGregor
(Jack Foster), Lloyd Whitlock (Dr.
Young), Tom London (Dupont), Jack
Perrin (Williams), Bob Kortman
(Slade), Eddie Parker (driver), Lafe
McKee (Martin Jerome), Gordon
DeMain (detective), Kernan Cripps
(foreman), Lionel Backus (Jarvis).

WHISTLER, THE (1944)
    Director: William Castle
Richard Dix (Earl Conrad), J. Car-
roll Naish (the Killer), Gloria Stuart
(Alice Walker), Alan Dinehart (Gor-
man), Joan Woodbury (Toni Virgan),
Cy Kendall (bartender), Trevor
Bardette (the thief), Don Costello
(Lefty Vigran), Clancy Cooper (Briggs),
Byron Foulger (flophouse clerk),
Robert E. Keane (Charles McNear),
George Lloyd (Bill Tomley), Charles
Coleman (Jennings), Robert Homans
(dock watchman).

WHISTLING IN DIXIE (1942)
    Director: S. Sylvan Simon
Red Skelton (Wally Benton), Ann
Rutherford (Carol Lambert), George
Bancroft (Sheriff Claude Stagg), Guy
Kibbee (Judge George Lee), Rags
Ragland (Sylvester/Chester Conway),
Diana Lewis (Ellamae Downs), Peter
Whitney (Frank V. Bailie), Celia
Travers (Hattie Lee), Lucien Little-
field (Corporal Lucken), Louis Mason
(Lem), Mark Daniels (Martin Gordon),
Pierre Watkin (Doctor), Emmett
Vogan (radio producer), Hobart Cava-
naugh (Panky).

WHISTLING IN THE DARK (1941)
    Director: S. Sylvan Simon
Red Skelton (Wally Benton), Conrad
Veidt (Joseph Jones), Ann Rutherford
(Carol Lambert), Virginia Grey (Fran
Post), Rags Ragland (Sylvester), Henry
O'Neill (Philip Post), Eve Arden (Buzz
Baker), Paul Stanton (Jennings), Don
Douglas (Gordon Thomas), Don Costello
(Noose Green), William Tannen (Ro-
bert Graves), Reed Hadley (Beau
Smith), Mariska Aldrick (Hilda).

WHITE BUFFALO, THE (1977)
    Director: J. Lee Thompson
Charles Bronson (James Otis), Jack
Warden (Charlie Zane), Will Sampson
(Crazy Horse), Kim Novak (Poker

Jenny), Clint Walker (Kileen), Stuart Whitman (Coxy), John Carradine (Briggs), Slim Pickens (Pinkney), Cara Williams (Cassie), Ed Lauter (Capt. Tom Custer), Douglas V. Fowley (Bixby), Cliff Pellow (Holt), Martin Kove (Jack McCall), Shay Duffin (Brady), Scott Walker (Gyp Hook-Hand).

WHITE DOG (1982)
Director: Sam Fuller
Kristy McNichol (Julie Sawyer), Paul Winfield (Keys), Burl Ives (Carruthers), Jameson Parker (Roland Gray), Lynne Moody (Molly), Marshall Thompson (director), Bob Minor (Joe), Vernon Weddle (Vet), Christa Lang (nurse), Tony Brubaker (sweeper driver), Samuel Fuller (Charlie Felton), Paul Bartel (cameraman), Martine Dawson (Martine), Alex A. Brown (man in church), Parley Baer (Wilber Hull).

WHITE GORILLA, THE (1947)
Director: Harry L. Fraser
Ray 'Crash' Corrigan, Lorraine Miller.

WHITE PONGO (1945) (A. K. A. Adventure Unlimited")
Director: Sam Newfield
Richard Fraser, Maris Wrixon, Al Eben, Egon Brecher, Lionel Royce, Joel Fluellen, Larry Steers, Gordon Richards, Milton Kibbee, George Lloyd, Michael Dyne.

WHITE ZOMBIE (1932)
Director: Victor Halperin
Bela Lugosi (Murder Legendre), Madge Bellamy (Madeline Short), John Harron (Neil Parker), Joseph Cawthorn (Dr. Bruner), Robert Frazer (Charles Beaumont), Clarence Muse (coach driver), Brandon Hurst (Silver), Frederick Peters (Chauvin), George Burr McAnnan (Von Gelder), Dan Crimmins (Pierre), John Printz, John Fergusson, Claude Morgan (zombies), Annette Stone, Velma Gresham (maids).

WHO? (1974)
Director: Jack Gold
Joseph Bova (Dr. Lucas Martino), Elliot Gould (Sean Rogers), Trevor Howard (Col. Azarin), John Lehne (Haller), James Noble (Gen. Deptford), Lyndon Brook (Dr. Barrister), Michael Lombard (Dr. Besser), Ed Grover (Finchley), Kay Tornborg (Edith), John Stewart (Frank Heywood),

Joy Garrett (Barbara), Bruce Boa (Miller), Evan Desny (Gen. Sturmer), Fred Vincent (Douglas), Alexander Allerson (Dr. Korthu), Craig McConnell (Uncle Lucas), Craig McConnell (Tonino), Herb Andress, Frank Schuller, Dell Negro (FBI agents).

WHO DONE IT? (1956)
Director: Basil Dearden
Belinda Lee, David Kossoff, Ernest Thesiger, Denis Shaw, Thorley Walter, Gibb McLaughlin, Frederic Schiller, Irene Handl, Charles Hawtrey, Garry Marsh, Nicholas Phipps, Benny Hill, George Margo.

WHO IS HARRY KELLERMAN AND WHY IS HE SAYING THOSE TERRIBLE THINGS ABOUT ME? (1971)
Director: Ulu Grosbard
Dustin Hoffman (Georgie Solloway), Barbara Harris (Allison), Jack Warden (Dr. Moses), David Burns (Leon), Betty Walker (Margot), Dom DeLuise (Irwin), Rose Gregorio (Gloria), Gabriel Dell (Sid), Joe Sicari (Marty), Josip Elic (Chomsky), Amy Levitt (Susan), Ed Zimmerman (Holloran), Walter Hyman (flower vendor), Rudy Bond (newsdealer), Candice Azzara (Sally), James Hall (Lemuel), Robyn Millan (Samantha), Regina Baff (Ruthie).

WHO IS KILLING THE GREAT CHEFS OF EUROPE? (1978)
Director: Ted Kotcheff
George Segal (Robby), Jacqueline Bisset (Natasha), Robert Morley (Max), Jean-Pierre Cassel (Kohner), Peter Sallis (St. Claire), Phillippe Noiret (Moulineau), John LeMesurier (Dr. Deere), Joss Ackland (Cantrell), Madge Ryan (Beecham), Daniel Emilfork (Saint-Juste), Jean Rochefort (Grandvilliers), Luigi Proietti (Ravello), Frank Windsor (Blodgett), Stefano Satta Flores (Fausto Zoppi), Tim Barlow (Doyle), Jean Gavin (Salpetre), Jacques Balutin (Chappemain), Michael Chow (Soong), Jean Paredes (Brissac), Jacques Marin (Massenet), Anita Graham (blonde), Nicholas Ball (Skeffington), Nigel Havers (counterman), David Cook (Bussingbill), John Carlisle (actor), Sheila Ruskin (actress), Kenneth Fortescue (director), Strewan Rodger (assistant director), Derek Smith (man in corridor), Marjorie Smith (receptionist), Aimee Delamain (old woman), Sylvia Kay (reporter), Eddie

Tagoe (Mumbala), Caroline Langrishe (Loretta), Lyall Jones (driver).

WHO KILLED DOC ROBBIN? (1948)
(A. K. A. "Sinister House")
Director: Bernard Carr
Virginia Grey, George Zucco, Don
Castle, Grant Mitchell, Donald King,
Claire Dubrey, Whitford Kane.

WHO SLEW AUNTIE ROO? (1971)
(A. K. A. "Whoever Slew Auntie
Roo?")
Director: Curtis Harrington
Shelley Winters (Rosie Forrest),
Mark Lester (Christopher), Chloe
Franks (Katy), Ralph Richardson
(Mr. Benton), Lionel Jeffries (Insp.
Willoughby), Hugh Griffith (Mr.
Harrison, the Pigman), Pat Hey-
wood (Dr. Mason), Rosalie Crutch-
ley (Miss Henley), Judy Cornwell
(Clarine), Michael Gothard (Albie),
Richard Beaumont (Peter), Marianne
Stone (Miss Wilcox), Jacqueline
Cowper (Angela), Charlotte Sayce
(Katherine).

WHOM THE GODS WISH TO DESTROY
(1964-Ger./Yugo.) (A. K. A. "Nie-
belungen")
Director: Harald Reinl
Herbert Lom (Attila the Hun), Ewe
Byer (Siegfried), Karin Dor, Maria
Marlowe, Rolf Henninger, Massimo
Girotti, Siegfried Wischenewski.

WHY THOSE STRANGE DROPS OF
BLOOD ON THE BODY OF JENNI-
FER? (1972-Ital.) (A. K. A. "Per-
che Quelle Strane Gocce di Sangue
sul Corpe di Jennifer", "Erotic
Blue")
Director: Guiliano Carmineo/
Anthony Ascott
Edwige Fenech, George Hilton,
Carla Brait, Paola Quattrini, Anna-
bella Incontrera, Giampiero Alber-
tini.

WICKED, WICKED (1973)
Director: Richard Bare
David Bailey (Rick Stewart), Tiffany
Bolling (Lisa James), Scott Brady
(Sgt. Ramsey), Edd Byrnes (Hank
Lassiter), Diane McBain (Dolores
Hamilton), Madeleine Sherwood
(Lenore Kardyne), Randolph Roberts
(Jason Gant), Arthur O'Connell
(hotel engineer), Indira Danks (Genny),
Patsy Garrett (housekeeper), Kirk
Bates (Owen Williams), Roger

Bowen (manager), Jack Knight (Bill
Broderick), Robert Nichols (day
clerk), Maryesther Denver (organist).

WICKER MAN, THE (1972)
Director: Robin Hardy
Edward Woodward (Sgt. Howie),
Christopher Lee (Lord Summerisle),
Britt Ekland (Willow), Diane Cilento
(Miss Rose), Ingrid Pitt (Librarian),
Lindsey Kemp (Alder McGregor),
Ian Campbell (Oak), Aubrey Morris
(old gardener/gravedigger), Russell
Waters (harbor master), Walter
Carr (schoolmaster), Irene Sunters
(May Morrison), Geraldine Cowper
(Rowan Morrison), Jennifer Martin
(Myrtle Morrison), Roy Boyd (Broome),
S. Newton Anderson (Landers), Lesle
Blackater (hairdresser), Penny Cluer
(Gillie), Kevin Collins (old fisherman),
Myra Forsyth (Mrs. Grimmond),
Barbara Ann Brown (woman with
baby), Ross Campbell (communicant),
Donald Eccles (T. H. Lennox), John
Hallam (P. C. McTaggart), Alison
Hughes (Howie's fiancee), John Mac-
Gregor (baker), Charles Kearney
(butcher), Fiona Kennedy (Holly),
Jimmie MacKenzie (Brian), Peter
Brewis, Ian Cutler, Michael Cole,
Bernard Murray, Andrew Tomkins
(musicians), Tony Roper (postman),
Ian Wilson (communicant), Juliette
Cadsow, Helen Norman, Elizabeth
Sinclair (villagers), Leslie Mackie
(Daisy), Lorraine Peters (girl on
grave), John Sharp (Dr. Ewan),
John Young (fishmonger), Richard
Wren (Ash Buchanan).

WILD IN THE SKY (1972) (A. K. A.
"Black Jack")
Director: William T. Naud
Brandon De Wilde (Josh), Keenan
Wynn (Gen. Harry Gobohare), Tim
O'Connor (Sen. Bob Recker), James
Daly (the President), Robert Lansing
(Maj. Reason), Bernie Kopell (Pen-
rat), Georg Stanford Brown (Lynch),
Dub Taylor (Roddenberry), Phil Van-
dervort (Woody), Larry Hovis (Capt.
Breen), Joseph Turkel (Corazza),
Dick Gautier (diver).

WILD IN THE STREETS (1968)
Director: Barry Shear
Christopher Jones (Max Frost), Shel-
ley Winters (Mrs. Flatow), Hal Hol-
brook (Sen. Fergus), Diane Varsi
(Sally Leroy), Millie Perkins (Mrs.
Fergus), Bert Freed (Mr. Flatow),
Ed Begley (Sen. Allbright), Richard

Pryor (Stanley X), Larry Bishop
(Abraham), Kevin Coughlin (Billy
Cage), Michael Margotta (Jimmy
Fergus), Don Wyndham (Joseph
Fergus), Kellie Flanagan (Mary Fer-
gus), Salli Sachse (hippie mother),
May Ishinhara (Fuji Ellie), Paul
Frees (Narrator), Louis Lomax,
Walter Winchell, Dick Clark, Mel-
vin Belli, Kenneth Banghart, Pamela
Mason, Army Archard, Allan J.
Moll, Jack Latham (cameos).

WILD STRAWBERRIES (1958-Swed.)
    (A.K.A. "Smultronstallet")
    Director: Ingmar Bergman
Victor Sjostrom (Prof. Isak Borg),
Bibi Andersson (Sara), Ingrid Thulin
(Marianne), Max von Sydow (Akerman),
Gunnar Bjornstrand (Evald), Jullan
Kindahl (Agda), Bjorn Bjelvenstam
(Viktor), Folke Sundquist (Anders),
Naima Wifstrand (Isak's mother),
Gertrud Fridh (Isak's wife), Ake
Fridell (Isak's wife's lover), Gunnel
Brostrom (Mrs. Alman), Gunnar
Sjoberg (Alman), Per Sjostrand (Sig-
frid), Sif Ruud (Aunt), Yngve Nordwall
(Uncle Aron), Gio Petre (Sigbritt),
Gunnel Lindblom (Charlotta), Anne-
Mari Wiman (Mrs. Akerman), Per
Skogsberg (Hagbart), Eva Noree (Anna),
Maud Hansson (Angelica), Lena Berg-
man, Monica Ehrling (twins), Goran
Lundquist (Benjamin), Helge Wulff
(promoter).

WILD, WILD PLANET (1965-Ital.)
    (A.K.A. "I Criminali della Galas-
    sia", "The Criminals of the Galaxy")
    Director: Anthony Dawson/
        Antonio Margheritti
Tony Russell (Cmdr. Michael Halstead),
Lisa Gastoni (Connie Gomez), Mas-
simo Serato (Nels Nurmi), Franco
Nero (Jake), Charles Justin (Ken),
Umberto Raho (Maitland), Enzo
Fiermonte (General), Moha Tahi (A.G.
Chief), Freddy Unger (De Lauty),
Franco Ressel (Jeff), Rodolfo Lodi
(Claridge), Aldo D'Ambrosia (Fryd),
Sanda Mondini (Delfos), Isarco Ra-
vailoi (hotel agent), Lino Desmond
(Schneider), Giuliano Raffaelli (Fran-
cini), Renato Montalbano (detective),
Carlo Kechler (Werner), Margherita
Ovorvitz (Edith Halstead), Victoria
Ziny, Kitty Swan, Annelise Stern,
Rosemarie Martin (girls).

WILD WILD WEST REVISITED, THE
    (TVM-1979) - 5-9-79
    Director: Burt Kennedy

Robert Conrad (James T. West),
Ross Martin (Artemus Gordon),
Paul Williams (Michelito Loveless,
Jr.), Harry Morgan (Robert T.
Malone), Jo Ann Harris (Carmelita
Loveless), Rene Auberjonois (Capt.
Sir David Edney), Robert Shields
(Allan), Lorene Yarnell (Sonya),
Joyce Jameson (Lola), Skip Homeier
(Joseph), Trisha Noble (Penelope),
Susan Blu (Gabrielle), Paula Ustinov
(Nadia), Jeff MacKay (Hugo Kauf-
man), Jacqueline Hyde (Queen Vic-
toria), Wilford A. Brimley (Pres.
Cleveland), Ted Hartley (Russian
Tsar), Alberto Morin (Spanish King),
Mike Wagner, Jeff Redford, John
Wheeler.

WILD WOMEN OF WONGO (1958)
    Director: James L. Wolcott
Jean Hawkshaw (Omoo), Johnny
Walsh (Engor), Mary Ann Webb
(Mona), Cande Gerrard (Ahtee),
Ed Fury (Gahbo), Adrienne Bourbeau
(Wana), Roy Murray, Steve Klisanin,
Val Phillips, Pat Crowley, Rex
Richards.

WILD WORLD OF BATWOMAN,
    THE (1966)
    Director: Jerry Warren
Katherine Victor (Batwoman),
Steve Brodie, Lloyd Nelson, George
Andre, Richard Banks.

WILLARD (1971)
    Director: Daniel Mann
Bruce Davison (Willard Stiles),
Ernest Borgnine (Al Martin), Elsa
Lanchester (Henrietta Stiles), Sondra
Locke (Joan), Jody Gilbert (Char-
lotte Stassen), Michael Dante (Brandt),
Joan Shawlee (Alice), J. Pat O'Mal-
ley (Jonathan Farley), Almira Ses-
sions (Carrie Smith), William Hansen
(Mr. Barskin), Alan Baxter (Mr.
Spencer), Pauline Drake (Ida Stassen),
John Myhers (Mr. Carlson), Helen
Spring (Mrs. Becker), Paul Bradley
(chemist), Louise De Carlo, Arthur
Tovey, Shirley Lawrence (guests),
Lola Kendrick (Mrs. Martin), Sherri
Presnell (Spencer), Robert Golden
(motorcycle rider).

WILLY WONKA AND THE CHOCO-
    LATE FACTORY (1971)
    Director: Mel Stuart
Gene Wilder (Willy Wonka), Jack
Albertson (Grandpa Joe), Leonard
Stone (Mr. Beauregarde), Roy Kin-
near (Mr. Salt), Peter Ostrum

(Charlie), Michael Bollner (Augustus
Gloop), Julie Dawn Cole (Veruca Salt),
Ursula Reit (Mrs. Gloop), Denise
Nickerson (Violet Beauregarde),
Paris Themmen (Mike Teevee), Dodo
Denny (Mrs. Teevee).

WINDSOR CASTLE (1926)
    Director: Maurice Elvey
Isabel Jeans, Ian Wilson.

WINGED SERPENT, THE (1982)
    (A. K. A. "The Serpent", "Q")
    Director: Larry Cohen
Michael Moriarty (Jimmy Quinn),
David Carradine (Detective Shepard),
Candy Clark (Joan), Richard Round-
tree (Sgt. Powell), Malachi McCourt
(Police Commissioner).

WITCH, THE (1906-Fr.) (A. K. A.
    "La Fee Carabosse", "Le Poignard
    Fatal")
    Director: Georges Melies

WITCH, THE (1955-Mex.) (A. K. A.
    "La Bruja")
    Director: Chano Urueta
Lilia Del Valle, Ramon Gay, Julio
Villareal, Charles Rooner, Luis
Aceves Castaneda.

WITCHCRAFT (1954-Span. /Mex. /
    Arg.) (A. K. A. "Maleficio")
    Director: Leon Klimovsky,
    Fernando de Fuentes & Florian
    Rey
Narcisco Ibanez Menta, Olga Zubarry,
Jorge Mistral, Santiago Gomez Cou,
Antonio Vilar, Amparito Rivelles.

WITCHCRAFT (1964)
    Director: Don Sharp
Lon Chaney, Jr. (Morgan Whitlock),
Jack Hedley (Bill Lanier), Jill Dixon
(Tracy Lanier), Viola Keats (Helen
Lanier), Diane Clare (Amy Whitlock),
David Weston (Todd Lanier), Yvette
Ress (Vanessa Whitlock), Barry
Linehan (Myles Forrester), Marie
Ney (Malvina Lanier), Marianne
Stone (Forrester's secretary), Hilda
Fennemore (nurse), Victor Brooks,
John Dungar.

WITCHCRAFT 70 (1969-Ital.) (A. K. A.
    "Angeli Bianchi... Angeli Neri",
    "The Satanists")
    Director: Luigi Scattini
Edmond Purdom (Narrator).

WITCHES, THE (1965-Ital. /Fr.)
    (A. K. A. "Le Streghe")

"The Girl from Sicily"
    Director: Franco Rossi
Silvana Mangano, Pietro Tordi.
"The Earth as Seen from the Moon"
    Director: Pier Paolo Pasolini
Silvana Mangano, Toto, Laura Betti,
Ninetto Davoli, Luigi Leoni.
"A Night Like Any Other"
    Director: Vittorio De Sica
Silvana Mangano, Clint Eastwood,
Armando Bottin (Superman), Gianni
Gori (Diabolik), Angelo Santi (Flash
Gordon), Paolo Gozlino (Mandrake),
Piero Torrisi (Batman).

WITCHES' BREW (1979)
    Director: Richard Shore
Richard Benjamin, Terri Garr, Lana
Turner.

WITCHES MOUNTAIN (1972-Span.)
    (A. K. A. "El Monte de las Brujas")
    Director: Raul Artigot
Patty Shepard, John Caffari, Monica
Randall.

WITCHING EYES, THE (1934)
    Director: Henry Hathaway
Sir Guy Standing (Martin Prentice),
John Halliday (Jack Brookfield),
Richard Carle (Lew Ellinger), Judith
Allen (Nancy Brookfield), Ralf Harolde
(Frank Hardmuth), William Frawley
(Foreman of Jury), Tom Brown (Clay
Thorne), Purnell Pratt (District At-
torney), Gerturde Michael (Margaret
Price), Ferdinand Gottschalk (Dr.
Melklejohn), Olive Tell (Mrs. Thorne),
Frank Sheridan (Chief of Police).

WITCHING HOUR, THE (1921)
    Director: William D. Taylor
Elliot Dexter (Jack Brookfield), Winter
Hall (Judge Prentice), Ruth Renick
(Viola Campbell), Robert Cain (Frank
Hardmuth), Mary Alden (Helen Whip-
ple), Edward Sutherland (Clay Whip-
ple), Fred Turner (Lew Ellinger),
Charles West (Tom Denning), L. M.
Wells (Judge Henderson), Genevieve
Blirn (Mrs. Campbell), Clarence
Geldard (Col. Bailey), Jim Blackwell
(Harvey).

WITCH IN LOVE, A (1966-Ital.) (A. K. A.
    "La Strega in Amore", "The Strange
    Obsession")
    Director: Damiano Damiani
Richard Johnson (Segrio), Rosanna
Schiaffino (Aura), Gian Maria Volonte
(Fabrizio), Sarah Ferrati.

WITCH LOVE (1967-Span.) (A. K. A.

"El Amor Brujo")
    Director: Francisco Rovira-
    Beleta
Antonio Gades, Rafael de Cordova,
Nuria Torray, Morucha, Jose Manuel
Martin.

WITCHMAKER, THE (1969)
    Director: William O. Brown
Anthony Eisley (Victor Gordon),
Thordis Brandt (Tasha), Alvy
Moore (Ralph Haynes), John Lodge
(Luther the Berserk), Helene
Winston (old Jessie), Warene Ott
(young Jessie), Tony Benson,
Robyn Millan (students), Shelby
Grant (Maggie), Larry Vincent
(Amos Coffin), Diane Webber (Na-
utch of Tangier), Sue Bernard
(Felicity Johnson), Nancy Craw-
ford (Goody Hale), Carolyn Rhodi-
mer (Marta), Gwen Lipscomb
(Fong Quai), Kathy Lynn (Patty
Ann), Howard Viet (Sam Blas), Patty
Wymar (Hag of Devon), Del Kaye
(Le Singe), Valya Garanda (El
A Haish Ma), Burt Mustin (boat-
man).

WITCH'S CURSE, THE (1960- Ital.)
    (A. K. A. "Maciste all 'Inferno",
    "Maciste in Hell")
    Director: Ricardo Freda
Kirk Morris (Maciste), Andrea
Bosic (Mary Gaunt), Helene Chanel,
Angelo Zanolli, Charles Fawcett,
Vira Silenti.

WITCH'S MIRROR, THE (1961-
    Mex.) (A. K. A. "El Espejo de
    la Bruja")
    Director: Chano Urueta
Rosita Arenas, Armando Calvo,
Dina de Marco, Isabella Corona.

WITCH WHO CAME FROM THE SEA,
    THE (1976)
    Director: Matt Cimber
Millie Perkins (Molly), Lonny Chap-
man (Long John), Vanessa Brown
(Cathy), Rick Jason (Billy Batt),
Peggy Feury (Doris), Roberta
Collins (Clarissa), Jean-Pierre
Camps (Tadd), Mark Livingston
(Tripoli), Stan Ross (Jack Dracula),
S. Morgan (McPeak), Richard
Kennedy (Detective Beard), George
Buck Flowers (Detective Stone),
Lynne Guthrie (Carol), Gene Ruth-
erford (Sam Walters), Jim Sims
(Austin Slade), Sam Chu Linn
(newscaster), Anita Franklin (TV
commentator), John Goff (Molly's

father), Verkina (young Molly).

WITCH WITHOUT A BROOM, A
    (1966-Span. /U. S.) (A. K. A. "Una
    Bruja Sin Escoba")
    Director: Jose Elorietta/
    Joe Lacy
Jeffrey Hunter (Garver Logan),
Maria Perschy (Marianne), Perla
Cristal (Octavia), Gustavo Rojo
(Cayo), Reginald Gillam (Don
Ignacio), Al Mulock (Wurlitz the
Wizard), Katherine Ellison (Yolanda),

WITHOUT A SOUL (1916)
    Director: James Young
Clara Kimball Young (Lola), Alec
B. Francis (lover), Mary Moore
(sister), Irene Tams (mother),
Edward M. Kimball (father).

WITHOUT WARNING (1980) (A. K. A.
    "It Came... Without Warning")
    Director: Greydon Clark
Jack Palance (Taylor), Martin Lan-
dau (Fred), Cameron Mitchell
(hunter), Neville Brand (Leo), Sue
Anne Langdon (Aggie), Ralph Meeker
(Dave), Larry Storch (scoutmaster),
Tarah Nutter (Sandy), Christopher
S. Nelson (Greg), Lynn Theel (Beth),
Darby Hinton (Randy), David Caruso
(Tom).

WIZ, THE (1978)
    Director: Sidney Lumet
Diana Ross (Dorothy), Michael
Jackson (the Scarecrow), Nipsey
Russell (the Tinman), Ted Ross
(the Lion), Richard Pryor (the Wiz),
Lena Horne (Glinda the Good), Mabel
King (Evillene), Thelma Carpenter
(Miss One), Theresa Merritt (Aunt
Em), Stanley Greene (Uncle Henry),
Carlton Johnson (Head Winkie), Clyde
J. Barrett (subway peddler), Henry
Madsen (Cheetah), Vicki Baltimor
(Green Lady), Glory Van Scott (Rolls
Royce Lady).

WIZARD, THE (1927)
    Director: Richard Rossen
Edmund Lowe (Stanley Gordon),
Leila Hyams (Anne Webster), Gustav
von Seyffertitz (Prof. Paul Coriolos),
E. H. Calvert (Edwin Palmer),
Barry Norton (Reginald Van Lear),
Norman Trevor (Judge Webster),
Perlie Marshall (Detective Murphy),
Oscar Smith (Sam), Maude Turner
(Mrs. Van Lear), George Kotsonaros
(the Gorilla), Richard Frazier.

WIZARD OF BAGHDAD, THE (1960)
Director: George Sherman
Dick Shawn (Genie Ali Mahmud),
Diane Baker (Princess Yasemeen),
Barry Coe (Prince Husan), John
Van Dreelen (Jullnar), Robert F.
Simon (Shamadin), Vaughan Taylor
(Norodeen), Kim Hamilton (Teegra),
Stanley Adams (Kvetch), William
Edmonson (Asmodeus), Don Beddoe
(Raschid), Michael David (Meroki),
Michael Burns (young Prince Husan),
Leslie Wenner (Yasemeen as a child),
Hortense Peters (barmaid), Tiny
Tim Baskin (desert chieftan).

WIZARD OF GORE, THE (1970)
Director: Herschell Gordon
Lewis
Ray Sager (Montag the Magnificent),
Judy Cler (Sherry Carson), Wayne
Ratay (Jack Ward), Phil Laurenson,
Jim Rau, John Elliot, Don Alexander.

WIZARD OF MARS, THE (1964)
Director: David L. Hewitt
John Carradine, Roger Gentry, Vic
McGee, Jerry Rannow, Eve Bernhardt.

WIZARD OF OZ, THE (1939)
Director: Victor Fleming
Judy Garland (Dorothy), Jack Haley
(Tin Woodsman), Ray Bolger (the
Scarecrow), Bert Lahr (the Cowardly
Lion), Frank Morgan (Wizard),
Margaret Hamilton (Wicked Witch),
Billie Burke (Glenda, the Good
Witch), Clara Blandick (Aunt Em),
Charley Grapewin (Uncle Henry),
Pat Walsh (Nikki), Jerry Maren
(a Munchkin).

WIZARDS (1977) - animated
Director: Ralph Bakshi
Voices: Bob Holt (Avatar), Jesse
Wells (Elinore), Richard Romanus
(Weehawk), Steve Gravers (Black-
wolf), David Proval (Peace), James
Connell (President), Christopher
Tayback (Peewhittle), Barbara
Sloane (Fairy).

WOLF DOG, THE (1933) - serial in
12 episodes
Chapters: 1. "The Call of the Wilderness", 2. "The Shadow of a Crime",
3. "The Fugitive", 4. "A Dead Man's
Hand", 5. "Wolf Pack Law", 6. "The
Gates of Mercy", 7. "The Empty
Room", 8. "The Avenging Fangs", 9.
"Wizard of the Wireless", 10. "Accused!", 11. "The Broken Record",
12. "Danger Lights".

Director: Colbert Clark &
Harry Frazer
Frankie Darro (Frank), George J.
Lewis (Bob), Boots Mallory (Irene),
Fred Kohler (Stevens), Henry B.
Walthall (Jim Courtney), Hale Hamil-
ton (Bryan), Stanley Blystone, Sarah
Padden, Niles Welch, Carroll Nye,
Lane Chandler, Donald Reed, Tom
London, Max Wagner, Cornelius
Keefe, Dickie Moore, George Magrill,
Harry Northrup, Yakima Canutt,
Lionel Backus, Jack Kenney, Gordon
DeMain, Wes Wagner, Leon Holmes,
Lew Meehan.

WOLFEN (1981)
Director: Michael Wadleigh
Albert Finney (Dewey Wilson), Diane
Verona (Rebecca Neff), Gregory
Hines (Whittington), Dick O'Neill
(Warren), Edward James Olmos
(Eddie Holt), Tom Noonan (Ferguson),
Dehi Berti (Old Indian), Peter Michael
Goetz (Ross), Ralph Bell (Commis-
sioner), Sam Gray (Mayor), Max M.
Brown (Christopher Vandeveer), Anne
Marie Photamo (Pauline Vanderveer),
Sarah Felder (Cicely Rensselear),
Reginald Vel Johnson (morgue atten-
dant), Chris Manor (janitor), James
Tolkan (Baldy), John McCurry (Sayad
Alye), Frank Adonis (Scola), Jeffrey
Ware (interrogation operator), Richard
Minchenberg (policeman), E. Brian
Dean (Fouchek), Jeffrey Thompson
(Harrison), Victor Arnold (Rounden-
bush), Ray Serra, Thomas Ryan
(detectives), Ray Brocksmith (fat
jogger in park), Michael Wadleigh
(terrorist informer), Tony Latham,
David Connell, Jery Hewitt (victims),
Joaquin Rainbow, Pete Dyer, Paul
Skyhorse, Jane Lind, Gordon Eagle,
John Ferraro, Rino Thunder, Javier
First-Day-Of-Light, George Stonefish,
Julie Evening Lily, Glenn Benoit,
Ricky Hawkeye, Eddy Navas (Native
Americans), Annie Gagen, Max Goff,
Robert L. King, Caitlin O'Heaney,
William Sheridan, Cullen Johnson,
Robert Moberly, Tony Stratta (ESS
Operators), Linda Gary, Burr De-
Benning, Mel Welles, Pat Parris,
Dan Sturkie, Andre Stolka, Charles
Howerdton, Corey Burton (ESS voices).

WOLFMAN, THE (1941)
Director: George Waggner
Lon Chaney, Jr. (Lawrence Talbot),
Evelyn Ankers (Gwen Conliffe), Claude
Rains (Sir John Talbot), Warren
William (Dr. Lloyd), Ralph Bellamy

(Capt. Paul Montford), Maria Ous-
penskaya (Maleva), Bela Lugosi
(Bela, the Gypsy), Patric Knowles
(Frank Andrews), Fay Helm (Jenny
Williams), Forrester Harvey (Twid-
dle), J. M. Kerrigan (Charles Con-
liffe), Leyland Hodgson (Kendall),
Doris Lloyd (Mrs. Williams), Harry
Gording (Wykes), Harry Stubbs,
(Rev. Norman), Kurt Katch (Gypsy),
Martha Vickers, Margaret Fealy,
Caroline Cooke, La Riana, Jessie
Arnold, Connie Leon, Ottola Nesmith,
Eric Wilton, Olaf Hytten, Tom Ste-
venson, Ernie Statnon.

WOLFMAN (1979)
    Director: Worth Keeter
Earl Owensby (Colin Glasgow), Ed
L. Grady (Rev. Leonard), Victor
Smith (Luthor), Richard Dedmon
(Uncle Clement), Maggie Lauterer
(Aunt Elizabeth), Kristina Reynolds
(Lynn Randolph), Sid Rancer (Dr.
Tate), Helen Tryon (Grandmother).

WOMAN AND THE BEAST, THE
    (1958-Mex.) (A. K. A. "La Mujer
    y la Bestia")
    Director: Alfonso Corono
    Blake
Andres Soler, Ana Luisa Peluffo,
Ruben Rojo, Carlos Cores, Fanny
Schiller.

WOMAN EATER, THE (1957)
    Director: Charles Saunders
George Coulouris (Dr. James Moran),
Vera Day (Sally), Robert MacKen-
zie (Lewis Carling), Joy Webster
(Judy Ryan), Jimmy Vaughan (Tanga),
Peter Wayn (Jack Venner), Sara
Leighton (Susan Curtis), Joyce Gregg
(Mrs. Senator), Maxwell Foster
(Detective Insp. Brownlow), Edward
Higgins (Sgt. Bolton), Roger Avon
(Constable), Marpessa Dawn (native
girl), Norman Claridge (Dr. Pat-
terson), Peter Lewiston (Detective
Freeman), Stanley Platts (steward),
Susan Neil (coffee girl), Shief Ashanti
(Witch Doctor), John Tinn (the Las-
car), Alexander Field (rifle range
attendant), John Grant (rescue party
leader), Harry Ross (Bristow), David
Lawton (man in pub).

WOMAN IN GREEN, THE (1945)
    (A. K. A. "Sherlock Holmes and
    the Woman in Green")
    Director: Roy William Neill
Basil Rathbone (Sherlock Holmes),
Nigel Bruce (Dr. Watson), Hillary

Brooke (Lydia), Henry Daniell (Prof.
Moriarty), Frederic Worlock (Onslow),
Paul Cavangh (Fenwick), Mary Gordon
(Mrs. Hudaon), Tom Bryson (Williams),
Matthew Boulton (Insp. Gregson),
Olaf Hytten (Norris), Eve Amber
(Maude), Sally Shepherd (Crandon),
Percival Vivian (Dr. Simnell), Harold
De Becker (shabby man), Tommy
Hughes (newsman).

WOMAN IN THE MOON, THE (1929-
    Ger.) (A. K. A. "Die Frau im
    Mond")
    Director: Fritz Lang
Gerda Maurus (Friede Velten), Willy
Fritsch (Wolf Helius), Fritz Rasp
(Walt Turner), Klaus Pohl (Prof.
Georg Manfeldt), Gustav von Wangen-
heim (Hans Windegger), Josephine
(the Mouse), Margaret Kupfer (Mrs.
Hippolt), Gustl Stark-Gstettenbauer
(Gustav), Karl Platen (man at the
microphone), Max Maximilian (Grot-
jan), Alexa von Porembaka (flower
girl), Gerhard Dammann (Chief of
the Helius Hangers), Tilla Durieux,
Hermann Vellentin, Borwin Walt,
Max Zilzer, Mahmud Terja Bey (Brains
& Cheque Books), Heinrich Gotho.

WOMAN WHO CAME BACK, THE (1945)
    Director: Walter Colmes
Otto Kruger (Stevens), John Loder
(Dr. Adams), Ruth Ford (Ruth),
Nancy Kelly, J. Farrell MacDonald,
Emmett Vogan, Almira Sessions,
Jeanne Gail, Harry Tyler.

WOMAN WHO WOULDN'T DIE, THE
    (1964) (A. K. A. "Catacombs")
    Director: Gordon Hessler
Gary Merrill (Raymond Garth), Jane
Morrow (Alice Taylor), Georgina
Cookson (Ellen Garth), Neil McCallum
(Dick Corbett), Rachel Thomas (Chris-
tine), Jack Train (solicitor), Frederick
Piper (police inspector).

WOMANHUNT, THE (1972)
    Director: Eddie Romero
John Ashley, Eddie Garcia, Pat
Woodell, Sid Haig, Ken Metcalfe,
Lisa Todd, Charlene Jones, Laurie
Rose.

WOMEN OF THE PREHISTORIC PLANET
    (1966)
    Director: Arthur Pierce
Wendell Corey (Admiral King), Keith
Larsen (Cmdr. Scott), John Agar
(Dr. Farrell), Irene Tsu (Linda),
Merry Anders (Karen), Paul Gilbert

(Lt. Bradley), Stuart Margolin (Chief),
Robert Ito (Tang), Gavin McLeod
(radio operator), Suzie Kaye (crew
member), Stuart Laswell (Charles),
Adam Roarke (Centurian).

WONDERFUL WORLD OF THE BRO-
THERS GRIMM, THE (1962)
    Director: Henry Levin & George
    Pal
Laurence Harvey (Wilhelm Grimm),
Karl Boehm (Jacob Grimm), Claire
Bloom (Dorothea Grimm), Walter
Slezak (Stossel), Barbara Eden
(Greta Heinrich), Oscar Homolka (the
Duke), Ian Wolfe (Gruber), Betty
Garde (Miss Bettenhausen), Martita
Hunt (the Story Teller), Arnold Stang
(Rumpelstiltskin), Bryan Russell
(Friedrich Grimm), Walter Rilla
(Priest), Cherrio Meredith (Mrs.
von Dittersdorf).
"The Dancing Princess": Yvette Mim-
ieux (the Princess), Russ Tamblen
(the Woodsman), Jim Backus (the King),
Beulah Bondi (the Gypsy), Clinton
Sundberg (the Prime Minister).
"The Cobbler and the Elves": Walter
Brooke (the Mayor), Robert Foulk
(the Hunter), Sandra Gale Bettin (the
Ballerina).
"The Singing Bone"; Terry-Thomas
(Ludwig), Buddy Hackett (Hans), Otto
Kruger (the King), Robert Crawford,
Jr. (the Shepherd), Sydney Smith (the
Spokesman).

WONDER MAN (1944)
    Director: H. Bruce Humber-
    stone
Danny Kaye (Buzzy Bellew/Edwin
Dingle), Virginia Mayo (Ellen Shanley),
Vera-Ellen (Midge Mallon), Allen
Jenkins (Chimp), S. Z. Sakall (Schmidt),
Edward S. Brophy (Torso), Steve
Cochran (Ten Grand Jackson), Donald
Woods (Monte Rossen), Natalie Schae-
fer (Mrs. Hume), Otto Kruger (D. A.
O'Brien), Byron Foulger (customer),
Virginia Gilmore (girl on bench),
Huntz Hall (sailor), Luis Alberni
(prompter), Chester Clute (meek man
on bus), James Flavin (bus driver),
Ray Teal (ticket taker), Leon Belasco
(pianist), Mary Field (D. A.'s secre-
tary), Alice Mock (prima donna),
Richard Lane (acrobatic dancer),
Maurice Cass (stage manager),
Carol Haney (dancer), Ed Gargan
(cop at park), Gisela Werbiseck (Mrs.
Schmidt), Al Ruiz (dancer), Jack
Norton (drunk at table), Charles
Irwin (drunk at bar), Frank Orth

(bartender), Cecil Cunningham (bar-
ker), Willard Van Simons (specialty
dancer), Alma Carroll, Karen Gay-
lord, Ruth Valmy, Georgia Lange,
Mary Moore, Deannie Best, Mary
Meade, Ellen Hall, Gloria Delson,
Margie Stewart, Martha Montgomery,
Phyllis Forbes (Goldwyn Girls).

WONDERS OF ALADDIN, THE (1961-
Ital.) (A.K.A. "Le Meraviglie
di Aladino")
    Director: Henry Levin
Donald O'Connor (Aladdin), Vittorio
De Sica (Genie), Fausto Tozzi (Grank
Vizler), Michele Mercier (Zaina),
Noelle Adam (Djalma), Milton Reid
(Omar), Aldo Fabrizi (Sultan), Marco
Tulli (Fakir), Mario Girotti (Prince
Moluk), Raymond Bussieres (Magi-
cian), Vittorio Bonos (lamb mer-
chant), Alberto Franese (bandit
chieftain), Franco Ressel (Visier's
Lieutenant), Adriana Facchetti
(Mamma Benhai), Giovanna Galletti
(midwife).

WONDER WOMAN (TVM-1974) -
3-12-74
    Director: Vincent McEveety
Cathy Lee Crosby (Wonder Woman),
Ricardo Montalban (Abner Smith),
Anitra Ford (Ahnjayla), Andrew
Prine (George Calvin), Charlene
Holt (Hippolyte), Kaz Garas (Steve
Trevor), Richard X. Slattery (Col.
Henkins), Sandy Gaviola (Tina),
Beverly Gill (Dia), Donna Garrett
(Cass), Jordan Rhodes (Bob), Roberta
Brahm (Zoe), Robert Porter (Joe),
Ronald Long.

WONDER WOMEN (1973-U.S./Phil.)
    Director: Robert O'Neil
Nancy Kwan (Dr. Tsu), Ross Hagen
(Mike Harber), Sid Haig (Gregorious),
Vic Diaz (Lapu-Lapu), Maria De
Aragon (Linda), Roberta Collins
(Laura), Claire Hagen (Vera), Gail
Hansen (Gail), Tony Lorea (Paul-
son/Lorenzo), Shirley Washington
(Maggie), Eleanor Siron (Mei-Ling),
Joonee Gamboa (Won Ton Charlie),
Bruno Punzalan (Nono, the fisherman),
Rick Reveke (Paulson's attendant),
Rudy De Jesus (the boy), Wendy
Greene (the swimmer), Leila Benitez
(Lillian Taylor), Ross Rival (Ramon,
the Jai A'Lai player).

WON IN THE CLOUDS (1914)
    Director: Otis Turner
Herbert Rawlinson (Cecil James),

Frank Lloyd (Roy Knabenshue), Marie
Walcamp (Grace James), Rex De
Rosselli (Portugese Jack), Essie Fay
(Mary Bjornesn).

WON'T WRITE HOME, MOM - I'M
   DEAD (TVM-1975) (A.K.A. "Ter-
   ror from Within") - 3-3-75
   Director: James Omerod
Pamela Franklin (Abby), Ian Bannen
(Frank), Oliver Tobias (Alan Smerdon),
Suzanne Neve (Beryl), Christopher
Malcolm (Hank), Norman Scare
(cashier), Dallas Adams (Douglas
Sadler), Lesley North (Janet Sadler),
Diana Patrick (Jody), Anabel Little-
dale (Helen), Sarah Porter (Emma).

WORD, THE (TVM-1978) - 11-12-78,
   11-13-78, 11-14-78 & 11-15-78
   Director: Richard Lang
David Janssen (Steve Randall), James
Whitmore (George Wheeler), Florinda
Bolkan (Angela Monti), Geraldine
Chaplin (Naomi Dunn), Eddie Albert
(Ogden Towery), Hurd Hatfield (Ced-
ric Plummer), Ron Moody (LeBrun),
John Huston (Nathan Randall), John
McEnery (Florian Randall), Janice
Rule (Barbara Randall), David Ack-
royd (Tom Carey), Donald Moffatt
(Henri Aubert), Nicol Williamson
(Maertin de Vroome), Nehemiah
Persoff (Abbot Petropolous), Martha
Scott (Sarah Randall), Laura Betti
(Maria), Bo Brundin (Heldering),
Catherine Burns (Lori Cook), Roland
Culver (Dr. Jeffries), Tessie O'Shea
(herself), Nicholas Coster (Peter
Ajemian), John Korkes, Alan Miller,
Walter Gottell, John Van Dreelan,
Lynn Farleigh, Mario Scaccia, Alexa
Kenin, Chris Lloyd.

WORK IS A 4-LETTER WORD (1967)
   Director: Peter Hall
David Warner (Val Brose), Cilla
Black (Betty Dorrick), Zia Mohyed-
din (Dr. Narayana), Jan Holden (Mrs.
Price), Julie May (Mrs. Dorrick),
Alan Howard (Rev. Mort), Elizabeth
Spriggs (Mrs. Murray), Joe Gladwyn
(Pa Brose).

WORLD BEYOND THE MOON, THE
   (1952)
   see Television: Space Patrol
   (1950-55)

WORLD OF THE DEAD, THE (1968-
   Mex.) (A.K.A. "El Mundo de los
   Muertos")
   Director: Gilberto Martinez

Solares
Santo, Blue Demon, Mary Montiel,
Pilar Pellicer.

WORLD OF THE VAMPIRES, THE
   (1961-Mex.) (A.K.A. "El Mundo
   de los Vampiros")
   Director: Alfonso Corona Blake
Guillermo Murray (Subotel), Silvia
Fourneir (Martha), Martha Bauman
(Leonor), Mauricio Garces (Rudy),
Tito Suneo, Jose Baviera, Rafael
Del Rio.

WORLD, THE FLESH AND THE
   DEVIL, THE (1959)
   Director: Ranald MacDougall
Harry Belafonte (Ralph Burton),
Inger Stevens (Sarah Crandall), Mel
Ferrer (Benson Thacker).

WORLD WILL SHAKE, THE (1939-
   Fr.) (A.K.A. "Le Monde Tremblera")
   Director: Richard Pottier
Erich von Stroheim, Claude Dauphin,
Madeleine Solonge, Armand Bernard,
Roger Duchesne.

WORLD WITHOUT END (1955)
   Director: Edward Bernds
Hugh Marlowe (John Borden), Nelson
Leigh (Dr. Galbraithe), Nancy Gates
(Garnet), Rod Taylor (Herbert Ellis),
Shawn Smith (Elaine), Lisa Montell
(Deena), Everett Glass (Timek), Chris-
topher Dark (Henry Jaffe), Paul Brine-
gar (Vida), Stanley Fraser (Elda),
Rankin Mansfield (Beryl), William
Vedder (James), Mickey Simpson
(Naga), Booth Colman.

WORLD'S GREATEST ATHLETE,
   THE (1973)
   Director: Robert Scheerer
Jan-Michael Vincent (Nanu), John
Amos (Coach Archer), Roscoe Lee
Browne (Gazenga), Tim Conway (Milo),
Billy DeWolfe (Maxwell), Dayle
Haddon (Jane), Nancy Walker (land-
lady), Danny Goldman (Leopold),
Vito Scotti, Ivor Francis, Howard
Cosell, Liam Dunn, Don Pedro Colley,
Leon Askin, Bill Toomey, Jim McKay,
Bud Palmer, Frank Gifford.

WORLD WAR III (TVM-1982) - 1-31-82
   & 2-1-82
   Director: David Greene
Brian Keith (Secretary Gordy), Rock
Hudson (Pres. McKenna), David Soul
(Col. Jake Caffrey), Cathy Lee Crosby
(Kate), Jeroen Drabbe (Col. Vorashin),
Robert Prosky (Gen. Rudenski), Lee

Wallace (Farber), Katherine Helmond (Dorothy), James Hampton (Dick), Jerry Kardin (Gen. Olafson), Bruce Vikant (Leff), Bob Minor (Trimble), Thomas Kill (Budner), Michael Fairman (Tenant), Meeno Peluce (Andrei Gorky), Donegan Smith (Gen. Schiff), Liz Sheridan (Naomi Glass), Art Evans (Buford), Anne Gerety (Kortner), Lesley Woods (Martra Jones), Joe Medalis (David), Susan Kivan (Megan Hardy), Brad Blaisdell (Kimball), Joe Sagal (Fest), Robert O'Reilly (Veich), Harry Basch, Kai Wulff, Frank Dent, John Lehne, Steve Tannen, William Traylor, Richard Yniguez, Marcus Makai, Anthony Shaw, Lee Wallace.

WORM EATERS, THE (1977)
    Director: Herb Robins
Herb Robins (Hermann Umger), Lindsay Armstrong Black, Robert Garrison, Joseph Sackett, Mike Garrison, Muriel Cooper, Harry Hostetler.

WRECKING CREW, THE (1969)
    Director: Phil Karlson
Dean Martin (Matt Helm), Elke Sommer (Linka Karensky), Nancy Kwan (Yu-Rang), Sharon Tate (Freya Carlson), Nigel Green (Count Massimo Contini), Tina Louise (Lola Medina), Weaver Levy (Kim), John Larch (MacDonald), John Brascia (Karl), Fuji (Toki), Bill Saito (Ching), Pepper Martin (Frankie), Wilhelm von Homburg (Gregory), Lynn Borden, Joel Drayton, Dick Winslow, Rex Holman, Ted Jordan, Tony Giorgio, Josephine James, Harry Fleer, Harry Geldard, J. B. Beck, James Daris, Whitney Chase, Brick Huston, James Lloyd, Vincent Van Lynn, Allen Pinson.

WRESTLING WOMEN VS. THE AZ-
    TEC MUMMY, THE (1964-Mex.)
    (A. K. A. "Las Luchadoras contra
    la Momia")
    Director: Rene Cardons
Armando Silvestre, Lorena Velazquez, Elizabeth Campbell, Maria Eugenia San Martin.

WRESTLING WOMEN VS. THE MUR-
    DERING ROBOT, THE (1969-Mex.)
    (A. K. A. "Las Luchardos contra
    el Robot Asesion", "El Asesino
    Loco y el Sexo")
    Director: Rene Cardona
Joaquin Cordero, Regina Torne, Carlos Agosti, Hector Lechuga, Pascual Garcia Pena.

WRONG IS RIGHT (1982)
    Director: Richard Brooks
Sean Connery (Patrick Hale), George Grizzard (Pres. Lockwood), Robert Conrad (Gen. Wombat), Katharine Ross (Sally Blake), G. D. Spradlin (Philindros), John Saxon (Homer Hubbard), Leslie Nielsen (Mallory), Henry Silva (Rafeeq), Robert Webber (Harvey), Hardy Kruger (Helmut Unger), Rosalind Cash (Mrs. Ford), Dean Stockwell (Hacker), Cherie Michan (Erica), Ron Moody (King Awad), Tony March (Abu).

XANADU (1980)
    Director: Robert Greenwald
Olivia Newton-John (Kira), Gene Kelly (Danny McGuire), Michael Beck (Sonny Malone), James Slovan (Simpson), Katie Hanley (Sandra), Dimitra Arliss (Helen), Fred McCarren (Richie), Ren Woods (Jo), Sandahl Bergman, Lynn Latham, Cherlse Bate, Melinda Phelps, Juliette Marshall, Marilyn Tokuda, Teri Beckerman, Yvette Van Voorhees (Muses).

X-17 TOP SECRET (1965-Span./Ital.)
    Director: Amerigo Anton
Lang Jeffries, Eleanor Blanchi, Rafael Barden, Aurora De Alba, Moa Thai, Gloria Usuna, Vladimoro Tukovich, Joe Kamel, Angel Jordan.

X FROM OUTER SPACE, THE (1967-
    Jap.) (A. K. A. "Uchu Daikaiju
    Guilala", "Big Space Monster
    Guliala")
    Director: Kazui Nihonmatsu
Eiji Okada (Dr. Kato), Peggy Neal (Liza), Shinichi Yanagisawa (Miyamoto), Toshiya Wazaki (Sano), Itoke Harada (Michiko), Franz Gruber (Behrman), Mike Daneen (Stein).

X - THE MAN WITH X-RAY EYES
    (1963)
    Director: Roger Corman
Ray Milland (Dr. James Xavier), John Hoyt (Dr. Willard Benson), Diana Van Der Vlis (Dr. Diane Fairfax), Don Rickles (Crane), Harold J. Stone (Dr. Sam Brant), John Dierkes (Preacher), Kathryn Hart (Mrs. Mart), Lorie Summers (party dancer), Vicki Lee (young girl patient), Carol Irey (woman patient), Dick Miller, Barboura Morris.

X THE UNKNOWN (1956)
    Director: Leslie Norman
Dean Jagger (Dr. Adam Royston),

Leo McKern (Insp. McGill), William
Lucas (Peter Elliott), Edward Chapman
(Mr. Elliott), John Harvey (Major
Cartwright), Michael Ripper
(Sgt. Grimsdyke), Kenneth Cope
(Private Lancing), Anthony Newley
(Private Spider Webb), Peter Hammond
(Lt. Bannerman), Norman Macowan
(Old Tom), Marianne Brauns (Zena),
Fraser Hines (Ian Osborne), Ian
MacNaughton (Haggis), Archie Duncan
(Sgt. Yardye), Jameson Clark
(Jack Harding), Jane Aird (Vi Harding),
Michael Brook (Willie Harding), Edwin
Richfield (old soldier), Neil Hallet
(Unwin), Neil Wilson (Russell),
John Stone (Gerry), Edward Judd.

YEAR OF THE CANNIBALS, THE
  (1971-Ital.) (A. K. A. "I Cannibali",
  "The Cannibals")
  Director: Liliana Cavani
Britt Ekland (Antigone), Pierre
Clementi (Tiresias), Delia Boccardo
(Ismene), Tomas Milian (Emone),
Francesco Leonette (Emone's father),
Marino Mase (Ismene's fiancee), Alfredo
Bianchini, Cora Nazzoni,
Alessandro Cane, Francesco Arminio,
Sergio Serafini, Giampero Frondini,
Giancario Calo.

YEAR 2889 (1967) (A. K. A. "In the
  Year 2889)
  Director: Larry Buchanan
Paul Petersen (Steve), Quinn O'Hara
(Jada), Charla Doherty (Joanna),
Neil Fletcher (Captain John), Bill
Thurman (Tim), Hugh Feagin (Mickey
Brown), Max Anderson (Granger),
Byron Lord.

YETI (1977-Ital.)
  Director: Frank Kramer/Gianfranco
Parolini
Mimmo Caru (Yeti), Phoenix Grant
(Jane), John Stacey (Prof. Wassermann),
Jim Sillivan (Herbie), Eddie
Faye (Hunnicut), Tony Kendall (Cliff),

YOGI, THE (1916-Ger.) (A. K. A.
  "Der Yogi")
  Director: Paul Wegener
Paul Wegener.

YOG- MONSTER FROM SPACE
  (1970-Jap.) (A. K. A. "Nankai
  no Daikaiji", "Space Amoeba")
  Director: Inoshiro Honda
Akiro Kubo (Taro Dudo), Atsuko
Takahashi (Ayako Hoshino), Kenji
Sahara (Makoto Obata), Yoshio
Tsuchiya (Kyoichi Miya), Noritake

Saito (Rico), Yukiko Kobayshi (Saki),
Chotaro Togin (Yokoyama), Satashi
Nakamura (Ombo), Mataru Omae
(Sakura), Sachio Sakai (the Editor),
Yuko Sugihara (stewardess), Yu
Fujiki (promotion division manager).

YOU BETTER WATCH OUT (1980)
  Director: Lewis Jackson
Brandon Maggart (Harry Stadling),
Dianne Hull (Jackie Stadling), Scott
McKay (Fletcher), Joe Jamrog
(Frank Stoller), Peter Friedman
(Grosch), Ray Barry (Gleason),
Sam Gray (Grilla), Bobby Lesser
(Gottleib), Ellen McElduff (Harry's
mother), Patty Richardson (Moss'
mother).

YOU'LL FIND OUT (1940)
  Director: David Butler
Boris Karloff (Judge Mannering),
Bela Lugosi (Prince Saliano), Peter
Lorre (Prof. Fenninger), Kay Kyser
(himself), Dennis O'Keefe (Chuck
Deems), Helen Parrish (Janis
Bellacrest), Joseph Eggenton (Jurgen),
Alma Kruger (Aunt Margo),
Ginny Simms, Sully Mason, Ish
Kabibble, Harry Babbit.

YOU'LL LIKE MY MOTHER (1972)
  Director: Lamont Johnson
Patty Duke (Francesca), Rosemary
Murphy (Mrs. Kinsolving), Richard
Thomas (Kenny), Sian Barbara
Allen (Kathleen), Dennis Rucker
(Red Cooper), James Neumann
(Joey), Harold Congdon (man), James
Glazman (the Breadman).

YOU NEVER CAN TELL (1951)
  Director: Lou Breslow
Dick Powell (Rex Shepherd), Peggy
Dow (Ellen Hathaway), Charles
Drake (Perry Collins), Joyce Holden
(Goldie), Sara Taft (Mrs. Bowers),
Albert Sharpe (Grandpa Hathaway),
Lou Polan (Lt. Gilpin), Watson
Downs (Slott), Will Vedder (Nichols),
Henry Kulky (large prisoner), Frank
Nelson (policeman), Olan Soule
(salesman).

YOUNG FRANKENSTEIN (1974)
  Director: Mel Brooks
Gene Wilder (Dr. Frankenstein),
Peter Boyle (the Monster), Marty
Feldman (Igor), Madeline Kahn (Elizabeth),
Cloris Leachman (Frau
Blucher), Teri Garr (Inga), Kenneth
Mars (Insp. Kemp), Richard Haydn
(Herr Falkstein), Leon Askin (Herr

Waldman), Liam Dunn (Mr. Hilltop),
Oscar Beregi, Jr. (jailor), Gene
Hackman (blind hermit), Lou Cutell
(frightened villager), Danny Goldman
(medical student), Richard Roth (Insp.
Kemp's aide), Rusty Blitz, Monte
Landis (gravedigger), Arthur Malet
(village elder), Anne Beesley (little
girl), Terrence Pushman, Ian Abercrombie, Randolph Dobbs (villagers),
Anatol Winogradoff.

YOUNG JACOBITES, THE (1959)
Director: John Reeve
Francesca Annis, Frazer Hines,
Jeremy Bullock, John Pike, John
Woodnut, David Stuart, Michael
O'Brien, Michael Nightingale, Gareth
Tandy.

YOUNG, THE EVIL AND THE SAVAGE,
THE (1968-Ital.) (A.K.A. "Sette
Vergini per il Diavolo", "Seven
Virgins for the Devil")
Director: Anthony Dawson/
Antonio Margheriti
Michael Rennie (Insp. Duran), Mark
Damon (Richard), Eleanor Brown
(Lucille), Sally Smith (Jill), Ludmilla
Lvova (Miss Clay), Pat Valturri
(Denise), Frank De Rosa (Detective
Gabon), Alan Collins (DeBrazzi).

YOU ONLY LIVE TWICE (1967)
Director: Lewis Gilbert
Sean Connery (James Bond), Donald
Pleasence (Blofeld), Mie Hama (Sissy
Suzuki), Karin Dor (Helga Brandt),
Charles Gray (Henderson), Teru
Shimada (Osato), Bernard Lee (M),
Lois Maxwell (Miss Moneypenny),
Desmond Llewelyn (Q), Alexander
Knox (U.S. President), Akiko Waka-
bayashi (Aiki), Tsai Chin (Chinese
girl), Robert Hutton (President's
aide), Tetsuro Tamba (Tiger Tanaka),
Diane Cilento (Double), Bert Kwouk
(Spectre No. 3), Michael Chow (Spec-
tre No. 4).

XPOTRON - FINAL COUNTDOWN
(1966-Ital./Span.) (A.K.A. "A-
gente Logan Missione Ypotron",
"Agent Logan's Secret Mission",
"Operation 'Y'")
Director: Giorgio Stegani
Gaia Germani, Alberto Dalbes, Luis
Devill, Janine Reynaud, Jesus Pu-
ente, Alfredo Mayo.

Z7 OPERATION REMBRANDT (1967-
Span./Ital./Ger.) (A.K.A. "Z.7.
Operacion Rembrandt", "Karate

in Tangiers for Agent Z-7")
Director: Giancarlo Romitelli
Lang Jeffries, Laura Valenzuela,
Carlo Hinterman, Lorendana Nusciak,
Mitsuko.

ZAAT (1972) (A.K.A. "The Blood
Waters of Dr. Z")
Director: Don Barton
Marshall Grauer (Dr. Leopold), Paul
Galloway (Sheriff Lou), Dave Dicker-
son (Walker Stevenson), Sanna Ring-
haver (Martha Walsh), Wade Popwell
(Zaat), Gerald Cruse.

ZAMBA, THE GORILLA (1949)
Director: William Berke
Jon Hall (Steve), June Vincent (Jenny),
Beau Bridges (Tommy), George Cooper
(Doug), Jane Nigh (Carol), Darby
Jones (Keega), George O'Hanlon
(Marvin), Harry Lauter, Alphonse
Martel (Gaston), Pierre Watkin (Ben-
ton), Theron Jackson (Kayla), Ray
'Crash' Corrigan (Zamba).

ZAPPED! (1982)
Director: Robert J. Rosenthal
Scott Baio (Barney), Willie Aames
(Peyton), Felice Schachter (Berna-
dette), Robert Mandan (Johnson),
Scatman Crothers (Dexter), Heather
Thomas (Jane), Roger Bowen (Spring-
boro), Marya Small (Mrs. Springboro),
Greg Bradford (Robert), Hilary Beane
(Corrine), Sue Ane Langdon (Rose).

ZARDOZ (1973)
Director: John Boorman
Sean Connery (Zed), Charlotte Ramp-
ling (Consuella), Sara Kestleman
(May), John Alderton (Friend), Niall
Buggy (Arthur Frayn), Sally Anne
Newton (Avalow), Bosco Hogan (George
Saden), Reginald Jarman (Death),
Barbara Dowling (Star), Christopher
Casson (old scientist), Jessica Swift
(Apathetic).

ZETA ONE (1969)
Director: Michael Cort
Robin Hawdon (James Word), Yutte
Stensgaard (Ann Olsen), James Robert-
son Justice (Maj. Bourdon), Charles
Hawtrey (Swyne), Dawn Addams (Zeta),
Anna Gael (Clotho), Lionel Murton
(W), Brigette Skay (Lachesis), Carol-
Anne Hawkins (Zara), Valerie Leon
(Atropos), Wendy Lingham (Edwina
Strain), Yolande Del Mar (stripper).

ZOMBIE (1979-Ital.) (A.K.A. "Zombie 2")

1174   Science Fiction, Horror, Fantasy

Director: Lucio Fulci
Tisa Farrow (Ann Boles), Richard
Johnson (Dr. David Menard), Ian Mc-
Culloch (Peter West), Al Cliver (Brian),
Annetta Gay (Susan Barrett), Stefania
D'Amario (nurse), Olga Karlatos
(Mrs. Menard).

ZOMBIE OF MORA TAU (1957) (A. K. A.
  "The Dead That Walk")
Director: Edward L. Cahn
Gregg Palmer (Jeff Clark), Allison
Hayes (Mona Harrison), Morris An-
krum (Jonathan Eggert), Autumn
Russell (Jan Peters), Joel Ashley
(George Harrison), Marjorie Eaton
(Mrs. Peters), Gene Roth (Sam),
Leonard Geer (Johnny), Ray 'Crash'
Corrigan (sailor), Frank Hagny (Capt.
Jeremy Peters), Lewis Webb (Art),
Mel Curtis (Johnson), William Bas-
kin (zombie).

ZOMBIES OF THE STRATOSPHERE
  (1952) (A. K. A. "Satan's Satellites")
  - serial in 12 episodes
Chapters: 1. "The Zombies Vanguard",
2. "The Battle of the Rockets", 3.
"Undersea Agent", 4. "Contraband
Cargo", 5. "The Iron Executioner",
6. "Murder Mine", 7. "Death on the
Waterfront", 8. "Hostage for Murder",
9. "The Human Torpedo", 10. "Flying
Gas Chamber", 11. "Man vs. Monster",
& 12. "Tomb of the Traitors".
Director: Fred C. Brannon
Judd Holdren (Larry Martin), Aline
Towne (Sue Davis), Lane Bradford
(Marex), John Crawford (Roth), Leo-
nard Nimoy (Narab), Dale Van Sickel
(telegraph operator), Craig Kelly
(Mr. Steele), Jack Hardin (Kerr),
Gayle Kellogg (Dick), Roy Engle
(Lawson), Ray Boyle (Shane), Paul
Stader (fisherman), Jack Shea (police-
man), Tom Steele (truck driver/Walk-
er), Stanley Waxman (Harding),
Robert Garabedian (Elah), Wilson
Wood (Bob Wilson), Robert Strange
(Kettler), Jack Mack (Gomez Opera-
tor), Floyd Criswell, Davison Clark
(officers), Paul Gustine (pilot), Henry
Rowland (plane heavy), Borman
Willis (Tarner), Clifton Young (Ross),
George Magrill, Frank Alten (train
heavies), John Daheim, Ken Terrell.

ZOMBIES ON BROADWAY (1945)
  (A. K. A. "Loonies on Broadway")
Director: Gordon Douglas
Bela Lugosi (Prof. Richard Renault),
Wally Brown (Jerry Miles), Alan
Carney (Mike Strayer), Sheldon Leonard

(Ace Miller), Anne Jeffreys (Jean
La Danse), Frank Jenks (Gus), Ian
Wolfe (Prof. Hopkins), Joseph Vitale
(Joseph), Louis Jean Heydt (Douglas
Walker), Darby Jones (Kolaga),
Russell Hopton (Benny), Sir Lance-
lot.

ZONTAR, THE THING FROM VENUS
  (1966)
Director: Larry Buchanan
John Agar (Dr. Curt Taylor), Susan
Bjurman (Martha), Neil Fletcher
(Sheriff), Anthony Houston (Deith),
Bill Thurman, Patricia De Laney,
Warren Hammack.

ZOO IN BUDAPEST (1933)
Director: Rowland V. Lee
Loretta Young (Eve), Gene Raymond
(Zani), Paul Fix (Heinie), O. P.
Heggie (Dr. Grunbaum), Wally
Albright (Paul Vandor), Murray
Kinnell (Garbosh), Ruth Warren
(Katrina), Roy Stewart (Karl), Niles
Welch (Mr. Vandor), Russ Powell
(Toski), Frances Rich (Elsie), Lu-
cille Ward (Miss Murst), Dorothy
Libaire (Rosita).

ZOTZ! (1962)
Director: William Castle
Tom Poston (Prof. Jonathan Jones),
Julia Meade (Prof. Virginia Fenster),
Jim Backus (Horatio Kellgore),
Fred Clark (Gen. Bulliver), Cecil
Kellaway (Dean Updike), Margaret
Dumont (Persephone Updike), James
Milhollin (Dr. Kroner), Mike Ma-
zurki (Igor), Zeme North (Cynthia
North), Carl Donn (Josh Bates),
Jimmy Hawkins (Jimmy Kellgore),
Judee Morton (Miss Blakiston),
Russ Whiteman (Major Folger),
Bart Patton (Mr. Carne), Michael
Westfield (Capt. Byron), George
Moorman (Lt. Stefanski), Elaine
Martone (secretary), Susan Dorn
(nurse).

Z. P. G. (1971) (A. K. A. "Zero
  Population Growth")
Director: Michael Campus
Oliver Reed (Russ McNeil), Geraldine
Chaplin (Carole McNeil), Don Gor-
don (George Borden), Diane Cilento
(Edna Borden), Aubrey Woods (Dr.
Mallory), David Markham (Dr.
Herrick), Sheila Reid (Mary Herrick),
Bill Nagy (the President), Lotte
Tholander (telescreen nurse),
Ditte Maria (telescreen operator),
Wayne John Rhodda (Metromart

salesman), Lone Lindorff (mother),
Belinda Donkin (daughter), Birgitte
Federspiel (psychiatrist), Claus
Nissen, Jeff Slocombe (guards),
Dale Robinson (guide), Victor Lipari
(headwaiter), Paul Secon (tour guide),
Michael Hildesheim (thief), Carlotta
Magnoff (informer), Torben Hundahl
(Presidential Aide), Annelise Gabold
(baby shop mother), Sam Maisel
(baby shop father), Peter Ronild
(edict doctor), Theis Ib Husfelt
(Jessie), Birthe Tove, Birgitte
Frigast (nurses).

ZUDORA (1914) (A.K.A. "The
    Twenty Million Dollar Mystery")
    - serial in 20 episodes
Chapters: 1. "The Mystic Message
of the Spotted Collar", 2. "The Mys-
tery of the Sleeping House", 3. "The
Mystery of the Dutch Cheese Maker",
4. "The Mystery of the Frozen Laugh",
5. "The Secret of the Haunted Hills",
6. "The Mystery of the Perpetual
Glare", 7. "The Mystery of the
Lost Ships", 8. "The Foiled Elopement",
9. "Kidnapped or the Mystery of
the Missing Heiress", 10. "The
Gentleman Crooks and the Lady", 11.
"A Message from the Heart", 12.
"A Bag of Diamonds", 13. "The Se-
cret of Dr. Munn's Sanitarium", 14.
"The Missing Million", 15. "The
Ruby Coronet", 16. "The Battle on
the Bridge", 17. "The Island of Mys-
tery", 18. "The Cipher Code", 19.
"The Prisoner in the Pilot House",
& 20. "The Richest Woman in the
World".
        Director: Frederick R. Sul-
        livan & Howell Hansel
Marguerite Snow (Zudora), James
Cruze, Harry Benham, Elizabeth
Forbes, Sidney Bracey.

ABC STAGE '67.
"The Canterville Ghost" (11-2-66): Michael Redgrave (Sir Simon de Canterville), Douglas Fairbanks, Jr. (Ambassador Otis), Natalie Schaefer (Mrs. Otis), Tippy Walker (Virginia Otis), David Charkham (Mark Otis), Mark Colleano (Matthew Otis), Peter Noone.
"The People Trap" (11-9-66): Stuart Whitman (Steve), Vera Miles (Adele), Connie Stevens (Flame), Lew Ayres (Arthur), Estelle Winwood (Sarah), Lee Grant (Ruth), Pearl Bailey, Jackie Robinson, Michael Rennie, Cesar Romero, Mort Sahl, Mercedes McCambridge, Phil Harris, Betty Furness.

ABC THEATRE OF THE MONTH.
"The Elephant Man" (1-4-82): Philip Anglim (John Merrick), Kevin Conway (Frederick Treves), Penny Fuller (Mrs. Kendal), Richard Clarke (Gomm), Christopher Hewett (Ross), Veronica Castang, Glenn Close, Jarlath Conriy, William Duff-Griffin, Rex Everhart, Joe Grifasi, William Hutt, Myvanwy Jenn, John Neville-Andrews, Josephine Nichols, David Rounds, Jean-Pierre Stewart.

ADDAMS FAMILY, THE. 1964-66.
John Astin (Gomez Addams), Carolyn Jones (Morticia Addams), Jackie Coogan (Uncle Fester), Ted Cassidy (Lurch), Blossom Rock (Grandmama Addams), Lisa Loring (Wednesday Addams), Ken Weatherwax (Pugsley Addams), Felix Scilla (Cousin Itt).
"The Addams Family Goes to School" (9-18-64): Allyn Joslyn (Mr. Hilliard), Madge Blake (Miss Comstock), Nydia Westman (Miss Morrison), Rolfe Sedan (postman).
"Morticia and the Psychiatrist" (9-25-64): George Petrie (Dr. Black).
"Fester's Punctured Romance" (10-2-64): Merry Anders (Miss Car-

ver), Robert Nunn (newsboy).
"Gomez the Politician" (10-9-64): Eddie Quillan (George Bass), Allyn Joslyn (Sam Hilliard).
"The Addams Family Tree" (10-16-64): Frank Nelson (Cecil B. Pomeroy), Kim Tyler (Harold Pomeroy), Jonathan Hale (Prof. Simms).
"Morticia Joins the Ladies League" (10-23-64): George Barrows (Gorgo), Peter Leeds (Oscar), Dorothy Neumann (Mrs. Magruder).
"Halloween with the Addams Family" (10-30-64): Don Rickles (Claude), Skip Homeier (Marty).
"Green-Eyed Gomez" (11-6-64): Del Moore (Lionel Barker), Pattee Chapman (Mildred).
"The New Neighbors Meet the Addams Family" (11-13-64): Cynthia Pepper (Amanda Peterson), Peter Brooks (Hubert Peterson), Eddie Marr.
"Wednesday Leaves Home" (11-20-64): Jesse White (Sgt. Haley), Ray Kellogg (Off. Thompson).
"The Addams Family Meets the V.I.P.'s" (11-27-64): Frank Wilcox (Mr. Harris), Stanley Adams (Ila Karpe), Vito Scotti (Midi Haan).
"Morticia, the Matchmaker" (12-4-64): Lee Goodman (Clarence P. Harvey), Hazel Shermet (Melancholia), Barry Kelley.
"Lurch Learns to Dance" (12-11-64): Penny Parker (Sally O'Rourke), Jimmy Cross (Fred Walters).
"Art and the Addams Family" (12-18-64): Vito Scotti (Sam Picasso), Hugh Sanders (Bosley Swain).
"The Addams Family Meets a Beatnik" (1-1-65): Tom Lowell (Rockland Cartwright III), Barry Kelley (Rockland Cartwright II), Barry Brooks (Benson).
"The Addams Family Meets the Undercover Man" (1-8-65): Rolfe Sedan (Mr. Briggs), George N. Neise (Mr. Hollister), Norman Leavitt (Mr. Conkey).

(ADDAMS FAMILY cont.)
"Mother Lurch Visits the Addams
Family" (1-15-65): Ellen Corby (Mother
Lurch).
"Uncle Fester's Illness" (1-22-
65): Lauren Gilbert (Dr. Milford).
"The Addams Family Splurges"
(1-29-65): Olan Soule (Haywood Widdy),
Roland Winters (Ralph J. Hulen).
"Cousin Itt Visits the Addams
Family" (2-5-65): Alan Reed (Park Com-
missioner), Bill Baldwin (Announcer).
"The Addams Family in Court"
(2-12-65): Hal Smith (Judge Saunders),
James Flavin (Detective Lt. Poston).
"Amnesia in the Addams Family"
(2-19-65).
"Thing Is Missing" (3-5-65): Tom-
my Farrell (Sam Diamond), Ray Kellogg
(Detective), Charles Wangenheim (Bos-
well).
"Crisis in the Addams Family"
(3-12-65): Parley Baer (Arthur J. Hen-
son), Eddie Quillan (Horace Beesley),
Bebe Kelly (Secretary).
"Lurch and His Harpsichord" (3-
19-65): Byron Foulger (Mr. Belmont).
"Morticia, the Breadwinner" (3-
26-65): Milton Frome (Becker).
"The Addams Family and the Space-
men" (4-2-65): Tim Herbert (Hinckley),
Jimmy Cross (Gilbert), Vito Scotti (Prof.
Altschuler).
"My Son, the Chimp" (4-9-65).
"Morticia's Favorite Charity" (4-
16-65): Parley Baer (Arthur Henson),
Maida Severn (Mrs. Atherton), Donald
Foster (Mr. Clayton).
"Progress and the Addams Fami-
ly" (4-23-65): Parley Baer (Arthur Hen-
son), Natalie Masters (Phoebe Henson).
"Uncle Fester's Toupee" (4-30-
65): Elisabeth Fraser (Madelyn Smith),
Frederic Downs (Max).
"Cousin Itt and the Vocational Coun-
celor" (5-7-65): Richard Deacon (Mor-
timer Phelps).
"Lurch, the Teenage Idol" (5-14-
65): Herbie Styles (Bickle), Laurie Mitch-
ell (Gladys).
"The Winning of Morticia Addams"
(5-21-65): Lee Bergere (Dr. Francoise
Chalon), Jan Arvan (Drashi Dumo).
"My Fair Cousin Itt" (9-17-65):
Sig Ruman (Eric Von Bissel), Jimmy
Cross (Bennie), Douglas Evans (Sam
Derrick).
"Morticia's Romance" (9-24-65 &
10-1-65): Margaret Hamilton (Granny
Hester Frump), Edward Schaaf (Mini-
ster).
"Morticia Meets Royalty" (10-8-
65): Elvia Allman (Princess Millicent).

"Gomez - the People's Choice"
(10-15-65): Parley Baer (Arthur Henson),
Jack Barry (Newsman), Eddie Quillan
(Clyde Arbogast).
"Cousin Itt's Problem" (10-22-65):
Meg Wyllie (Myrtle Mae Dragwater),
Frankie Darro (delivery boy).
"Halloween - Addams Style" (10-
29-65): Yvonne Peattie (Penelope Sand-
hurst), Bob Jellison (Henry Sandhurst),
Don McArt (Cousin Cackle).
"Morticia, the Writer" (11-5-65):
Peter Bonerz (Boxwell).
"Feud in the Addams Family" (11-
12-65): Fred Clark (Henry Courtney),
Virginia Gregg (Mrs. Courtney), Kevin
Tate (Robspierre Courtney).
"Gomez, the Reluctant Lover" (11-
19-65): Jill Andre (Miss Dunbar), Tom
Brown Henry (Jennings).
"Morticia, the Sculptress" (11-26-
65): Hugh Sanders (Bosley Swain), Vito
Scotti (Sam Picasso).
"Gomez, the Cat Burgler" (12-3-
65).
"Portrait of Gomez" (12-10-65):
Ralph Montgomery (Photographer), Tom
D'Andrea (Examiner).
"Morticia's Dilemna" (12-17-65):
Anthony Caruso (Don Xavier Molines),
Yardena (Consuella Molines), Bella
Bruck (Maria), Carlos Rivas (Cardona).
"Christmas with the Addams Fami-
ly" (12-24-65): Gregg Martell (Mission
Santa).
"Uncle Fester, Tycoon" (12-31-65):
Roy Roberts (Thaddeus Logan), Harold
Peary (Dr. Brown).
"Morticia and Gomez vs. Fester
and Mama" (1-7-66): Irene Tedrow (Inez
Thudd), Loyal 'Doc' Lucas (Andre).
"Fester Goes on a Diet" (1-14-66):
Jack LaLanne (Jack LaGrann), William
Keene (Dr. Motley), Peggy Mondo (Yvette).
"The Great Treasure Hunt" (1-21-
66): Nestor Paiva (Capt. Grimby), Ri-
chard Reeves (Brack).
"Ophelia Finds Romance" (1-28-66):
Robert Nichols (Andre Bartholomew).
"Pugsley's Allowance" (2-4-66):
Parley Baer (Arthur Henson), Jack Col-
lins (Dr. Bird), Natalie Masters (Phoebe
Henson), Robert S. Carson (Glenville),
Tim Herbert (Bennie the Bookie).
"Happy Birthday, Grandma Frump"
(2-11-66): Margaret Hamilton (Grandma
Hester Frump), George Petrie (Dr. Jon-
ley).
"Morticia, the Decorator" (2-18-
66): Eddie Quillan (Joe Digby), Jeff Don-
nell (Eleanor Digby).
"Ophelia Visits Morticia" (2-25-66):
George Cisar (Montrose).

"Addams Cum Laude" (3-4-66): Allyn Joslyn (Sam Hilliard), Carol Byron (Secretary), Pat Brown (Mrs. Bennett).
"Cat Addams" (3-11-66): Marty Ingels (Dr. Marvin P. Gunderson), Loyal 'Doc' Lucas (Jungle Doctor).
"Lurch's Little Helper" (3-18-66).
"The Addams Policy" (3-25-66): Eddie Quillan (Joe Digby), Parley Baer (Arthur Henson).
"Lurch's Grand Romance" (4-1-65): Diane Jergens (Tiny Trivia).
"Ophelia's Career" (4-8-65): Ralph Rose (Signor Bellini), Ben Wright (Rudolpho).

ADVENTURES OF FU MANCHU, THE. 1956. Glenn Gordon (Dr. Fu Manchu), Laurette Luez (Lia Elthram), Clark Howat (Dr. Jack Petrie), Lester Stevens (Sir Dennis Nayland Smith), Lester Matthews (Malik), Carla Balenda (Karameneh), John George.
"The Prisoner of Dr. Fu Manchu" (9-3-56).
"The Secret of Dr. Fu Manchu" (9-10-56).
"The Slave of Dr. Fu Manchu" (9-17-56).
"Golden God of Fu Manchu" (10-1-56).
"The Vengeance of Fu Manchu" (10-8-56).
"Dr. Fu Manchu, Incorporated" (10-8-56).
"The Master Plan of Fu Manchu" (10-15-56).
"The Assassin of Dr. Fu Manchu" (10-22-56).
"Dr. Fu Manchu's Raid" (10-29-56).
"The Satellites of Dr. Fu Manchu" (11-5-56).
"The Plague of Dr. Fu Manchu" (11-12-56).

A FOR ANDROMEDA. British 1961. Julie Christie (Andromeda), Peter Halliday (Dr. John Fleming), Mary Morris, Frank Windsor, Esmond Knight, John Nettleton, John Barrett, Patricia Kneale.

ALCOA HOUR.
"The Stingiest Man in Town" (12-23-56): Basil Rathbone (Old Scrooge), Vic Damone (Young Scrooge), Johnny Desmond (Fred), Patrice Munsel (Belle), Martyn Green (Bob Cratchit), Robert Weede (Marley's Ghost), Betty Madigan (Martha Cratchit), Robert Wright (Spirit of Christmas Present), Denis Kohler (Tiny Tim).

ALCOA PREMIERE.
"The Jail" (2-6-62): John Gavin (William Fortnum), Betty Ackerman (Ellen), Nora Keen (Peters), James Barton (Hobbs), Barry Morse (guard), Robert Sampson (Dr. Bernard).
"Mr. Lucifer" (11-1-62): Fred Astaire (Mr. Lucifer), Elizabeth Montgomery (Iris Hecate), Frank Aletter (Tom Logan), Joyce Bullifant (Jenny Logan), Hal Smith (Belial), George Petrie (Beelzebub), Milton Frome (Mammon), Gaylord Cavallaro (Moloch).
"The Dark Labyrinth" (3-21-63): Patrick O'Neal (Frederic Warren), Salome Jens (Madelyn Warren), Carroll O'Connor (Charles Campion), Barbara Barrie (Virginia Stanley), Arthur Malet (Peter Fearmax).

ALCOA THEATRE.
"Strange Occurrence at Rokesay" (10-6-58): John Kerr (Flight Lt. Upton), Patrick MacNee (Sgt. Shaw), Tom Helmore (Commanding Officer).

ALFRED HITCHCOCK PRESENTS. 1955-62. Alfred Hitchcock (Host).
"Revenge" (10-2-55): Ralph Meeker (Carl Spann), Vera Miles (Elsa Spann), Ray Teal (Lieutenant), Frances Bavier (Mrs. Fergerson), John Gallaudet (Doctor), Ray Montgomery (man in grey suit), John Day (cop), Norman Willis (Sergeant).
"Premonition" (10-9-55): John Forsythe (Kim Stranger), Warren Stevens (Perry), George Macready (Doctor), Cloris Leachman (Susan).
"Triggers in Leash" (10-16-55): Gene Barry (Del Delaney), Darren McGavin (Red Hillman), Ellen Corby (Maggie Flynn).
"Don't Come Back Alive" (10-23-55): Sidney Blackmer (Frank Partridge), Edna Holland (Librarian), Virginia Gregg (Mildred Partridge), Irene Tedrow (Lucy), Robert Emhardt (Kettle).
"Into Thin Air" (10-30-55): Alan Napier (Sir Everett), Patricia Hitchcock (Diana Winthrop), Mary Forbes (Mrs. Winthrop), John Mylong (Doctor), Ann Codee (Doctor's wife), Maurice Marsac (clerk), Geoffrey Toone (Basil Farnham), Gerry Gaylor (maid).
"Salvage" (11-6-55): Gene Barry, Donald Cook, Nancy Gates.
"Breakdown" (11-13-55): Joseph Cotten (Callew), Raymond Bailey (Ed Johnson), Lane Chandler (Sheriff), Forrest Stanley (Hubka), Harry Shannon (Doc

(ALFRED HITCHCOCK PRESENTS cont.) Horner), Murray Alper (Lloyd), Marvin Press (Chessy).

"Our Cook's Treasure" (11-20-55): Beulah Bondi (Mrs. Sutton), Everett Sloane (Ralph Montgomery), Janet Ward (Mrs. Montgomery).

"The Long Shot" (11-27-55): John Williams (Walker D. Hendricks), Peter Lawford (Charlie), Charles Cantor (Tommy De Witt), Gertrude Hoffman (Marguerite Stoddard), Frank Gerstle (Mack), Robert Warwick (Matthew Kelson), Virginia Christine (Secretary), Tim Graham (bartender).

"The Case of Mr. Pelham" (12-4-55): Tom Ewell (Albert Pelham), Raymond Bailey (Dr. Harley), Jan Arvan (Harry), Kirby Smith (Tom Mason), Kay Stewart (Miss Clement), John Compton (Vincent).

"Guilty Witness" (12-11-55): Judith Evelyn (Amelia Verber), Joe Mantell (Stanley Krane), Robert F. Simon (Detective Halloran), Kathleen Maguire (Dorothy Krane).

"Santa Claus and the 10th Avenue Kid" (12-18-55): Barry Fitzgerald (Stretch Sears), Bobby Clark (10th Avenue Kid), Virginia Gregg (Miss Webster), Arthur Space (Mr. Chambers), Justice Watson (Mr. Shaw).

"The Cheney Vase" (12-25-55): Patricia Collinge (Martha Cheney), Darren McGavin (Lyle Endicott), Carolyn Jones (Pamela Waring), George Macready (Herbert Keather).

"A Bullet for Baldwin" (1-1-56): Sebastian Cabot (Baldwin), John Qualen (Stepp), Philip Reed (King), Cheryl Clark (Mrs. Baldwin), Don McArt (Albert), Kate Drain (Lawson's landlady), James Adamson (janitor), Bill Erwin (fireman).

"The Big Switch" (1-8-56): George Mathews (Sam), George E. Stone (Barney), Joseph Downing (Al), Beverly Michaels (Goldie), J. Edwards (Ed).

"You Got to Have Luck" (1-15-56): John Cassavetes (Sam), Marisa Pavan (Mary), Ray Teal (Warden), Bob Patten (Willis), Vivi Janiss (Maude), Hal K. Dawson (Secretary), Lamont Johnson (Davis), Steve Clark (Pilot).

"The Older Sister" (1-22-56): Joan Lorring (Emma), Pat Hitchcock (Margaret), Carmen Mathews (Lizzie), Polly Rowles (Nell), Kay Stewart (neighbor), Wendy Winkleman (little girl).

"Shopping for Death" (1-29-56): Robert H. Harris (Mr. Foxe), Jo Van Fleet (Mrs. Shrike), John Qualen (Mr. Shaw), Mike Ross (Mr. Shrike), Michael Ansara.

"The Derelicts" (2-5-56): Philip Reed (Ralph Cowell), Cyril Delevanti (Alfred Aloane), Robert Foulk (Monroney), Robert Newton (Goodfellow), Johnny Silver (Shanks), Peggy Knudsen (Herta).

"And So Died Riabouchinska" (2-12-56): Claude Rains (Fabian), Charles Bronson (Krovitch), Bill Haade (stagehand), Lowell Gilmore, Claire Carleton, Charles Cantor.

"Safe Conduct" (2-19-56): Jacques Bergerac (Jan), Claire Trevor (Mary), Werner Klemperer (Klopka), Peter Van Eyck (Officer), John Banner (Conductor), Ralph Manza (waiter), Konstantin Shayne (custom's officer).

"Place of Shadows" (2-26-56): Everett Sloane (Father Vincente), Mark Damon (Ray Clements), Sean McClory (Brother Gerard), Everett Glass (Brother Charles).

"Back for Christmas" (3-4-56): John Williams (Herbert), Isobel Elsom (Hermione), Gavin Muir (Mr. Wallingford), A. E. Gould-Porter (Major Sinclair), Lily Kemble-Cooper (Mrs. Sinclair), Katherine Warren (Mrs. Wallingford), Irene Tedrow (Mrs. Hewitt), Gerald Hamer (Mr. Hewitt).

"The Perfect Murder" (3-11-56): Hurd Hatfield (Paul Tallendier), Philip Coolidge (Henri Tallendier), Hope Summers (Marie), Mildred Natwick (Mme. Tallendier), Gladys Hurlbut (Ernestine).

"There Was an Old Woman" (3-18-56): Estelle Winwood (Miss Monica Laughton), Norma Crane (Lorna Bramwell), Charles Bronson (Frank Bramwell), Dan Greer (milkman), Emerson Tracy (druggist).

"Whodunit?" (3-25-56): John Williams (Alexander), Alan Napier (Wilfred), Amanda Blake (Carol), Philip Coolidge (Talbot), Jerry Paris (Wally), Ruta Lee (girl angel).

"Help Wanted" (4-1-56): Lorne Greene (Mr. X), John Qualen (Mr. Crabtree), Ruth Swanson (Miss Brown), Madge Kennedy (Laura Crabtree).

"Portrait of Jocelyn" (4-8-56): John Baragrey (Arthur Clymer), Philip Abbott (Mark Halliday), Nancy Gates (Debbie), Raymond Bailey (Jeff), Olan Soule (clerk).

"The Orderly World of Mr. Appleby" (4-15-56): Robert H. Harris (Mr. Appleby), Michael Ansara (Dizar), Louise Larabee (Lena), Gage Clark (Gainsboro), Helen Spring (Mrs. Grant), Mary Munday (Martha Sturgis), Edna Holland (Mrs. Murchie).

"Never Again" (4-22-56): Phyllis Thaxter (Karen Stewart), Warren Stevens (Jeff Simmons), Jack Mullaney (Marlow), Louise Allbritton (Renee Marlow), Mason Curry (Mr. Sterling), Joan Banks (Margaret).

"The Gentleman from America" (4-29-56): Biff McGuire (Howard Latimer), Ralph Clanton (Sir Stephen), Eric Snowden (Hanson), Geoffrey Steele (man), John Dodsworthy (Calender), John Irving (Derek), John Alderson (attendant).

"The Baby-Sitter" (5-6-56): Thelma Ritter (Lottie Slocum), Carmen Mathews (Clara Nash), Theodore Newton (Charlie Nash), Michael Ansara (Mr. Demario), Mary Wickes (Sophie Armstedder).

"The Belfry" (5-13-56): Patricia Hitchcock (Ella), Dabbs Greer (Sheriff), Jack Mullaney (Clint Ringle), Jim Hayward (Preacher), John Compton (Walt), Horst Ehrhardt.

"The Hidden Thing" (5-20-56): Robert H. Harris (Mr. Hurley), Biff McGuire (Dana Edwards), Judith Ames (Laura), Katherine Warren (Mrs. Edwards), Richard Collier (counterman), Theodore Newton (Detective).

"The Legacy" (5-27-56): Alan Hewitt (Howard Cole), Leora Dana (Irene Cole), Jacques Bergerac (Prince Burhan), Enid Markey (Cecelia Smithson), Walter Kingsford (Col. Blair), Ralph Clanton (Randolph Burnside), Rudolph Anders (Maitre D'), Roxanna Arlen (Donna Dew), Vikki Dougan (glamour girl).

"Mink" (6-3-56): Ruth Hussey (Paula Hudson), Vinton Hayworth (Sgt. Delaney), Mary Jackson (Mrs. Wilson), Veda Ann Borg (hairdresser), Anthony Eustral (furrier), Eugenia Paul (model), Vivi Janiss (police woman).

"The Decoy" (6-10-56): Robert Horton (Gill Larkin), Cara Williams (Mona Cameron), David Orrick (Ben), Jack Mullaney (disc jockey), Mary Jean Yamaji (dancer), Edo Mita (husband), Eileen Harley, Harry Lewis.

"The Creeper" (6-17-56): Constance Ford (Ellen Grant), Steve Brodie (Steve), Reta Shaw (Martha Stone), Percy Helton (George), Harry Townes (Ed Chase), Dick Foran.

"Momentum" (6-24-56): Joanne Woodward (Beth Paine), Skip Homeier (Dick Baine), William Newell (Charlie), Ken Christy (A. T. Burroughs), Mike Ragan (cab driver), Henry Hunter (man from finance company), Frank Kreig (janitor).

"Wet Saturday" (9-30-56): John

Williams (Capt. Smollett), Sir Cedric Hardwicke (Mr. Princey), Kathryn Givney (Mrs. Princey), Tita Purdom (Millicent), Harry Barclay (George), Irene Lang.

"Fog Closing In" (10-7-56): Phyllis Thaxter (Mary Summers), George Grizzard (Ted Lambert), Paul Langton (Arthur), Carol Veazie (Mrs. Connolly).

"De Mortuis" (10-14-56): Robert Emhardt (Clarence Rankin), Cara Williams (Irene Rankin), Henry Jones (Wally Long), Philip Coolidge (Bud Horton), William McLean (Benny), Haim Winant (truck driver).

"Kill with Kindness" (10-21-56): Hume Cronyn (Fitzhugh Oldham), Carmen Mathews (Katherine), James Gleason (Jorgy), Marjie Liszt (woman).

"None Are So Blind" (10-28-56): Mildred Dunnock (Muriel), Hurd Hatfield (Seymour), Dorothy Crehan (maid), K. T. Stevens (Liza), Rusty Lane (detective), Lillian Bronson (neighbor).

"Toby" (11-4-56): Jessica Tandy (Edwina), Robert H. Harris (Albert Birch), George Mathews (McGurk), Ellen Corby (Mrs. McGurk), Mary Wickes (Mrs. Foster), Penny Santon (Mrs. Schwartz).

"Alibi Me" (11-11-56): Lee Philips (Georgie), Chick Chandler (Lucky), Harvey Stephens (Insp. Larkin), Alan Reed (Uncle), Herb Vigran (newsman), Charlie Cantor (Barney), Shirley Smith (Goldie), Lee Erickson (messenger boy).

"Conversation over a Corpse" (11-18-56): Ray Collins (Mr. Brenner), Dorothy Stickney (Cissie Enright), Carmen Mathews (Johanna), Ted Stanhope (bank teller).

"Crack of Doom" (11-25-56): Robert Horton (Mason Bridges), Robert Middleton (Clinker), Gail Kobe (Jessie), Dayton Lummis.

"Jonathan" (12-2-56): Corey Allen (Gil Dalliford), Douglas Kennedy (Jonathan Dalliford), Walter Kingsford (Doctor), Nancy Kulp (Nurse Andrews), Georgann Johnson (Rosine), Hope Landin (housekeeper), Heidi Mullenger (nurse).

"A Better Bargain" (12-9-56): Robert Middleton (Louis Koster), Henry Silva (Harry Silver), Kathleen Hughes (Marian), Jack Lambert (Blady), Don Hanmer (Mr. Cutter).

"The Rose Garden" (12-16-56): John Williams (Alexander), Patricia Collinge (Julia), Evelyn Varden (Cordelia), Ralph Peters (cab driver).

"Mr. Blanchard's Secret" (12-23-56): Mary Scott (Babs Fenton), Dayton Lummis (Mr. Blanchard), Meg Mundy (Mrs. Blanchard), Robert Horn (John

(ALFRED HITCHCOCK PRESENTS cont.) Fenton).

"John Brown's Body" (12-30-56): Russell Collins (John Brown), Leora Dana (Vera Brown), Hugh Marlowe (Harold Skinner), Edmon Ryan (Dr. Croatman), Walter Kingsford (Dr. Helck), Jean Owens (Ellen).

"Crackpot" (1-6-57): Biff McGuire (Ray), Robert Emhardt (Mr. Moon), Michael Fox (Carpenter), Mary Scott (Meg), Raymond Guth (room clerk), Phil Garris (bellhop).

"Nightmare in 4-D" (1-13-57): Henry Jones (Harry Parker), Virginia Gregg (Norma), Barbara Baxley (Lainey Elliott), Percy Helton (janitor), Norman Lloyd (Lt. Orsatti), Norman Bartold (Sgt. Gold).

"My Brother Richard" (1-20-57): Royal Dano (Martin), Harry Townes (Richard), Inger Stevens (Laura), Ray Teal (Sheriff), Bobby Ellis (Tommy), Lisa Golm (Tommy's mother).

"Manacled" (1-27-57): Gary Merrill (Rockwell), William Redfield (Steve Fontaine), Rusty Lane (Conductor), Betty Harford (waitress), Edith Evanson (elderly woman).

"Bottle of Wine" (2-3-57): Herbert Marshall (Judge Harley Condon), Robert Horton (Wally Donaldson), Jarma Lewis (Grace).

"Malice Domestic" (2-10-57): Ralph Meeker (Carl Borden), Phyllis Thaxter (Annette Borden), Vinton Hayworth (Dr. Wingate), Ralph Clanton (Perry Harrison), Lili Kardell (Lorna Jenkins).

"Number 22" (2-17-57): Rip Torn (Steve Morgan), Russell Collins (Skinner), Ray Teal (Chief of Detectives), James Nolan (Kelly), Michael Ross (jailer), Peter Leeds (custodian), Hugh Sanders (booking officer), Paul Picerni (Assissi), Bob Ross (Bohlen), Charles Watts (Franklin), Martin Wilkins (man).

"The End of Indian Summer" (2-24-57): Gladys Cooper (Marguerite), Steve Forrest (Joe), James Gleason (Howard), Kathleen Maguire (Helen), Philip Coolidge (Henderson), Hal K. Dawson (Graham), Hope Summers (maid), Ned Wever (Saunders), Michael Kuhn (bellhop), Mason Curry (desk clerk).

"One for the Road" (3-3-57): John Baragrey (Charles), Georgann Johnson, Louise Platt.

"The Cream of the Jest" (3-10-57): Claude Rains (Charles Gresham), James Gregory (Wayne Campbell), Paul Picerni (Nick), Johnny Silver (Jerry), Joan Banks (Lee).

"I Killed the Count" (3-17-57, 3-24-57 & 3-31-57): Charles Davis (Raines), John Williams (Insp. Davidson), Alan Napier (Lord Sorrington), John Hoyt (Count Mattoni), Rosemary Harris (Louise), Melville Cooper (Mullet), Charles Cooper (Froy).

"One More Mile to Go" (4-7-57): David Wayne (Sam Jacoby), Louise Larabee (Martha Jacoby), Steve Brodie (Trooper), Norman Leavitt (attendant).

"Vicious Circle" (4-14-57): George Macready (Mr. Williams), Dick York (Manny Coe), Kathleen Maguire (Betty), Russell Johnson (Turk), Paul Lambert (Gallagher), George Brenlin (Georgie).

"The Three Dreams of Mr. Findlater" (4-21-57): Barbara Baxley (Lalaze), John Williams (Mr. Findlater), Isobel Elsom (Mrs. Findlater), Walter Kingsford (Manley), Arthur E. Gould-Porter (Rogers), Molly Glessing (Bridget).

"The Night the World Ended" (4-28-57): Russell Collins (Joe), Edith Barrett (Miss Green), Harold J. Stone (Halloran), Clark Howat (reporter), Robert Ellis (reporter), Bart Burns (Nick), Robert Ross (Ned Weaver).

"The Hands of Mr. Ottermole" (5-5-57): Theodore Bikel (Sergeant), Rhys Williams (Summers), Arthur E. Gould-Porter (Whybrow), Barry Harvey (Whybrow's nephew), Torin Thatcher (Constable), John Trayne (Policeman).

"A Man Greatly Beloved" (5-12-57): Sir Cedric Hardwicke (John Anderson), Evelyn Rudie (Hildegarde), Hugh Marlowe (Rev. Fell), Edith Barrett (Mrs. Whiteford), Rebecca Welles (Mrs. Fell).

"Marsha Mason, Movie Star" (5-19-57): Judith Evelyn (Mabel McKay), Robert Emhardt (Henry), Vinton Hayworth (Mr. Abernathy), Claire Carleton (Bernice), Rusty Lane (Police Detective), Karen Morris (Cora).

"The West Warlock Time Capsule" (5-26-57): Henry Jones (George Tiffany), Mildred Dunnock (Louise), Russell Thorson (Dr. Rhody), Charles Watts (Mayor), Sam Buffington (Waldron), James F. Stone (customer), Bobby Clark (Charles).

"Father and Son" (6-2-57): Edmund Gwenn (Joe Saunders), Frederick Worlock (Gus Harrison), Charles Davis (Sam), Pamela Light (Mae).

"The Indestructible Mr. Weems" (6-9-57): Russell Collins (Clarence Weems), Robert Middleton (Cato Stone), Joe Mantell (Harry Brown), Rebecca Welles (Laura Weems), Gladys Hurlbut (Sara Collins), Ted Newton (Doctor), Ferdi Hoffman (Minister).

"A Little Sleep" (6-16-57): Vic Morrow (Benny), Robert Karnes (Ed), Barbara Cook (Barby), John Carlyle (Chris Kymer).

"The Dangerous People" (6-23-57): Robert H. Harris (Mr. Bellefontaine), Albert Salmi (Mr. Jones), Harry Tyler (station agent), Ken Clarke (policeman), David Armstrong.

"The Glass Eye" (10-6-57): William Shatner (Jim), Ton Conway (Max Collodi), Rosemary Harris (Dorothy), Jessica Tandy (Julia), Billy Barty (George), Colin Campbell (old man), Patricia Hitchcock (saleslady), Arthur E. Gould-Porter (hotel man), Paul Playdon (Allan), Nelson Welch (emcee).

"The Mail Order Prophet" (10-13-57): Jack Klugman (George Benedict), E. G. Marshall (Roger Grimes), Judson Pratt (Postmaster), Ken Christy (office manager), Linda Watkins (barrom customer), Barbara Townsend (secretary), Victor Romito (waiter).

"The Perfect Crime" (10-20-57): Vincent Price (Charles Courtney), James Gregory (John Gregory), Mark Dana (Harrington), Gavin Gordon (Ernest West), Marianne Stewart (Alice West).

"Heart of Gold" (10-27-57): Mildred Dunnock (Martha), Nehemiah Persoff (Ralph Collins), Darryl Hickman (Jackie Blake), Edward Binns (Ned Brown), Cheryl Callaway (little girl).

"The Silent Witness" (11-3-57): Dolores Hart, Don Taylor.

"Reward to Finder" (11-10-57): Oscar Homolka (John Gaminsky), Jo Van Fleet (Anna Gaminsky), Claude Akins (policeman), Ann Hunter (saleslady), Robert Whitesides (boy).

"Enough Rope for Two" (11-17-57): Jean Hagen (Madge), Steve Brodie (Maxie), Steven Hill (ex-convict).

"The Last Request" (11-24-57): Harry Guardino (Gerald Daniels), Hugh Marlowe (Bernard Butler), Cara Williams (Mona), Karin Booth (Sheila), Mike Ross (Frank), Robert Carson (Harry), Fred Kruger (Warden).

"The Young One" (12-1-57): Carol Lynley (Janice), Vince Edwards (Tex), Stephen Joyce (boy friend).

"The Diplomatic Corpse" (12-8-57): Peter Lorre (Tomas Salgado), George Peppard (Evan Wallace), Mary Scott (Janet Wallace), Isobel Elsom (the aunt).

"The Deadly" (12-15-57): Craig Stevens (Lewis Brenner), Phyllis Thaxter (Margo Brenner), Frank Gerstle (police officer), Lee Phillips (Stanley), Anabel Shaw (Rhoda Forbes).

"Miss Paisley's Cat" (12-22-57): Dorothy Stickney (Miss Paisley), Raymond Bailey (Insp. Graun), Fred Graham (Rinditch), Harry Tyler (Jenkins), Mark Sheeler (shabby man).

"Night of the Execution" (12-29-57): Pat Hingle (Warren Selvey), Russell Collins (Ed Barnes), Georgann Johnson (Doreen Selvey), Harry Jackson (Vance).

"The Percentage" (1-5-58): Carmen Mathews (Fay), Alex Nicol (Eddie), Don Keefer (Pete).

"Together" (1-12-58): Joseph Cotten (Tony), Christine White (Shelley), Sam Buffington (Charles), Gordon Winn (Courtney), Sanford Gibbons (editorial writer).

"Sylvia" (1-19-58): John McIntire (father), Ann Todd (Sylvia), Philip Reed (husband).

"The Motive" (1-26-58): Carl Betz (Jerome), Skip Homeier (Tommy Greer), Carmen Phillips (Sandra), William Redfield (Richard).

"Miss Bracegirdle Does Her Duty" (2-2-58): Mildred Natwick (Millicent Bracegirdle), Gavin Muir, Tita Purdom.

"The Equalizer" (2-9-58): Leif Erickson (Phillips), Martin Balsam (Eldon), Norma Crane (Louise), Dudley Manlove (Harris), Robert Riordan (Mr. Sloan).

"On the Nose" (2-16-58): David Opatoshu (Bookie), Karl Swenson (Ed), Jan Sterling (Fran), Carl Betz (man).

"Ghost for Breakfast" (2-23-58): Scott McKay (Jordan Ross), Joan Tetzel (Eve Ross), Richard Sheppard (Chester Lacey).

"Return of the Hero" (3-2-58): Jacques Bergerac (Andre), Lilyan Chauvin (Sybil), Victor Varconi (Count d'Auberge), Iphigenie Castiglioni (Countess d'Auberge), Susan Kohner (Therese), Marcel Dalio (Marcel).

"The Right Kind of Life" (3-9-58): Jeanette Nolan (Sadie Grimes), Robert Emhardt (Waterbury), Harry Tyler (Aaron Hacker).

"Foghorn" (3-16-58): Michael Rennie (Allen), Barbara Bel Geddes (Lucia), Bartlett Robinson (John St. Rogers).

"Flight to the East" (3-23-58): Gary Merrill (Ted Franklin), Anthony George (Sashalsmail), Patricia Cutts (Barbara Denham), Konstantin Shayne, Mel Welles.

"Bull in a China Shop" (3-30-58): Dennis Morgan (Detective O'Finn), Estelle Winwood (Hildy Lou), Ellen Corby (Miss Aman), Ida Moore (Miss Birdie), Elizabeth Patterson (Miss Bessie).

"The Disappearing Trick" (4-6-58):

(ALFRED HITCHCOCK PRESENTS cont.) Robert Horton (Walter Richmond), Raymond Bailey (Herbert), Betsy Von Furstenberg (Laura Gild), Percy Helton (Mr. Brucie), Perry Lopez (Julius), Frank Albertson (Regis), Dorothea Lord (Nurse), Tom Wilde (Doctor).

"Lamb to the Slaughter" (4-13-58): Barbara Bel Geddes (Mary Maloney), Allan Lane (Patrick Maloney), Harold J. Stone (Lt. Noonan), Ken Clarke (Mike), Otto Waldis (Sam), Tom Waldis (Doctor), William Keene (print man).

"Fatal Figures" (4-20-58): John McGiver (Harold Goams), Vivian Nathan (Margaret), Ward Wood (McBane), Nesdon Booth (shopkeeper).

"Death Sentence" (4-27-58): James Best (Norman Frayne), Katherine Bard (Paula Frayne), Steve Brodie (Al Revenel).

"Festive Season" (5-4-58): Carmen Mathews (Celia), Richard Waring (Charlie Boerum), Edmon Ryan (John Benson).

"Listen, Listen...!" (5-11-58): Edgar Stehli (Mr. Morgan), Adam Williams (Lt. King), Daytom Lummis (Sgt. Oliver), Rusty Lane (Father Rafferty), Jackie Loughery (girl).

"Post Mortem" (5-18-58): Steve Forrest (Stephen Archer), Joanna Moore (Judy Archer), James Gregory (Westcott), David Fresco (reporter), Edgar Peterson (reporter).

"The Crocodile Case" (5-25-58): Denholm Elliott (Jack Lyons), Hazel Court (Phyllis), Arthur E. Gould-Porter (Arthur Chaundry).

"A Dip in the Pool" (6-1-58): Fay Wray (Mrs. Renshaw), Philip Bourneuf (Mr. Renshaw), Keenan Wynn (William Botibol), Louise Platt (Ethel Botibol), Doreen Lang (Emily), Doris Lloyd (Emily's friend), Ralph Clanton (ship's purser), Barry Harvey (steward), Owen Cunningham (auctioneer).

"The Safe Place" (6-8-58): Robert H. Harris (George Piper), Philip Pine (Victor Mapett), Wendell Holmes (Henry Farsworth), Jerry Paris (Fred Piper), Joanne Linville, Robert Karnes.

"The Canary Sedan" (6-15-58): Jessica Tandy (Mrs. Bowley), Gavin Muir (Thompson), Murray Matheson (Mr. Bowley), Patrick Westwood (Mason), Tetsu Komai (elderly Chinese), Owen Cunningham (Van Adams), Barry Bernard (bartender), Barry Harvey (steward).

"Impromptu Murder" (6-22-58):

Hume Cronyn (Henry Dow), Doris Lloyd (Miss Wilkinson), David Frankham (Holson), Robert Douglas (Insp. Tarrang), Arthur E. Gould-Porter (Betts), Valerie Cossart (Mary Dow), Molly Glessing (Lucy), Gwendolyn Watts (Mrs. Barrett), Frederic Worlock (farmer), George Pelling (ticket seller).

"Little White Frock" (6-29-58): Julie Adams (Carol Longworth), Tom Helmore (Adam Longworth), Herbert Marshall (Colin Branckner), Bartlett Robinson (Robinson), Jacqueline Mayo (Lila Gordon), Roy Dean (Terry Bane).

"Poison" (10-5-58): Wendell Corey (Timber Woods), Arnold Moss (Dr. Ganderbal), James Donald (Harry Pope), Weaver Levy (houseboy).

"Don't Interrupt" (10-12-58): Cloris Leachman (Mrs. Templeton), Cyril Wills (Kilmer), Biff McGuire (Mr. Templeton), Peter Lazer (Johnny), Jack Mulhall (conductor).

"The Jokester" (10-19-58): Albert Salmi (Bradley), Roscoe Ates (Pop Henderson), James Coburn (Andrews), Baynes Barron (bartender), Arthur Batanides (police sergeant), Jim Kirkwood, Jr. (Dave), Charles Watts (police captain), Jay Joslyn (Morgan).

"The Crocked Road" (10-26-58): Richard Kiley (Harry Adams), Patricia Breslin (Mary), Walter Mathau (Officer), Charles Watts (Judge Stanton), Richard Erdman (Charlie), Peter Dane (Police Officer).

"Two Million Dollar Defense" (11-2-58): Barry Sullivan (Mark Robison), Leslie Nielson (Lloyd Ashley), Lori March (Eve Ashley), Wendell Holmes (D. A. Herrick), Herbert Anderson (John Keller), Edwin Jerome (Justice Cobb), Herb Lytton (Doctor).

"Design for Loving" (11-9-58): Barbara Baxley (Ann), Norman Lloyd (Charlie Braling), Marian Seldes (Lydia Braling), Elliott Reid (Tom).

"Man with a Problem" (11-16-58): Gary Merrill (Carl Adams), Mark Richman (Policeman), Elizabeth Montgomery (Karen), Ken Lynch (Police Lieutenant), Bartlett Robinson (hotel manager), Alex Gerry (Dr. Landers).

"Safety for the Witness" (11-23-58): Art Carney (Cyril T. Jones), Robert Bray (Lt. Flannelly), James Westerfield (Commissioner Cummings), James Flavin (Desk Sergeant), Doris Lloyd (Mrs. Crawpit), Mary Scott (Nurse Copeland), Ken Patterson (Thomas Bergman), Karl 'Killer' Davis (Big Dan Foley), George Greico (Tarzan Joe Felix), Dorothea Lord (lady cashier), David Fresco (motel night clerk).

"Murder Me Twice" (12-1-58): Phyllis Thaxter (Lucy Prior), Tom Helmore (Miles Farham), Herbert Anderson (George), Alan Marshall (Will Prior), Ward Costello (Burke), Liz Carr (Adele), Robert Carson, King Calder.

"Tea Time" (12-14-58): Margaret Leighton (Iris), Marsha Hunt (Blanche), Murray Matheson (Oliver), George Navarro (waiter).

"And the Desert Shall Blossom" (12-21-58): Ben Johnson (Sheriff), Wesley Lau (Deputy), William Demarest (Tom), Roscoe Ates (Ben), Mike Kellin (Stranger).

"Mrs. Herman and Mrs. Fenimore" (12-28-58): Mary Astor (Mrs. Fenimore), Doro Merande (Mrs. Herman), Russell Collins (Uncle Bill), Wesley Lau (Detective).

"Six People, No Music" (1-4-59): John McGiver (Arthur Motherwell), Peggy Cass (Rhoda Motherwell), Wilton Graff (Agnew), Howard Smith (Stanton Baravale), Joby Baker (Thor).

"The Morning After" (1-11-59): Robert Alda (Ben Nelson), Jeanette Nolan (Mrs. Trotter), Fay Wray (Mrs. Nelson), Dorothy Provine (Sharon), Dorothea Lord (Maid), Lyn Statten (Secretary).

"A Personal Matter" (1-18-59): Wayne Morris (Bret Johnson), Joe Maross (Joe), Frank Silvera (Senor Rodriguez), Anna Navarro (Maria).

"Out There - Darkness" (1-25-59): Bette Davis (Miss Fox), James Congdon (Eddie), Frank Albertson (Kirby), Arthur Marshall (elevator man), James Cotton (job applicant).

"Total Loss" (2-1-59): Nancy Olson (Jan Manning), Ralph Meeker (Mel Reeves), Ruth Storey (Evy), Dave Willock (Frank Voss), Barbara Lord (Susan), Ray Teal (fire chief).

"The Last Dark Step" (2-8-59): Robert Horton (Brad Taylor), Fay Spain (Leslie Lenox), Joyce Meadows (Janice Wright), Herb Ellis (Breslin), David Carlile (Langley).

"The Morning of the Bride" (2-15-59): Barbara Bel Geddes (Helen), Don Dubbins (Philip), Patricia Hitchcock (Pat), Helen Conrad (Mrs. Beasley).

"The Diamond Necklace" (2-22-59): Claude Rains (Andrew Thurgood), Betsy Von Furstenberg (Mrs. Rudel), Selmer Jackson (clergyman).

"Relative Value" (3-1-59): Denholm Elliott (John Manbridge), Torin Thatcher (Felix), Tom Conway, Frede-

ric Worlock.

"The Right Price" (3-8-59): Eddie Foy, Jr. (burglar), Allyn Josslyn (Mort Bonner), Jane Dulo (Jocelyn).

"I'll Take Care of You" (3-15-59): Ralph Meeker (John Forbes), Elisabeth Fraser (Dorothy Forbes), Ida Moore (Kitty), Russell Collins (Dad).

"The Avon Emeralds" (3-22-59): Hazel Court (Lady Avon), Alan Napier (Sir Charles Harrington), Roger Moore (Insp. Benson), Gertrude Flynn (Mrs. Smedley).

"The Kind Waitress" (3-29-59): Olive Deering (Thelma), Celia Lovsky (Mrs. Mannerheim), Rick Jason (Arthur), Mary Alan Hokanson (Marion).

"Cheap Is Cheap" (4-5-59): Dennis Day (Alexander Gifford), Alice Backes (Jennifer Gifford), Fred Essler (Arthur).

"The Waxwork" (4-12-59): Barry Sullivan (Raymond Hewson), Everett Sloane (Marriner), Shari K. Ophir (Bourdette).

"The Impossible Dream" (4-19-59): Franchot Tone (Oliver Matthews), Mary Astor (Grace Dolan), Carmen Mathews (Miss Hall), Irene Windust (Myra).

"Banquo's Chair" (5-3-59): John Williams (Insp. Brent), Kenneth Haigh (John Bedford), Reginald Gardiner (Maj. Cooke-Finch).

"A Night with the Boys" (5-10-59): John Smith (Irv Randell), Joyce Meadows (Francie), Sam Buffington (Smalley).

"Your Witness" (5-17-59): Brian Keith (Arnold Shawn), William Hansen (Harry Babcock), Gordon Wynn (Kenneth Jerome, Sr.), Brian Hutton (Kenneth Jerome, Jr.).

"Human Interest Story" (5-24-59): Steve McQueen (Bill Everett), Arthur Hill (Yangan Dahl), Tyler McVey (Cargan), William Challee (Barney).

"The Dusty Drawer" (5-31-59): Dick York (Norman Logan), Philip Coolidge (Mr. Tritt), Wilton Graff (Mr. Pinkson).

"A True Account" (6-7-59): Kent Smith (Gilbert Hughes), Jane Greer (Maureen Cannon), Robert Webber (Paul Brett), Madge Kennedy (Mrs. Hughes).

"Touche" (6-14-59): Paul Douglas (Bill Fleming), Dody Heath (Lara Fleming), Hugh Marlowe (Phil Baxter), Robert Morse (Sandy).

"Invitation to an Accident" (6-21-59): Gary Merrill (Joseph Pond), Joanna Moore (Virgilia), Alan Hewitt (Albert Magnum), Peter Walker (Cam Bedsole).

"Arthur" (9-27-59): Laurence Harvey (Arthur Williams), Hazel Court (Helen), Patrick MacNee (Sgt. John Theron),

(ALFRED HITCHCOCK PRESENTS
cont.) Robert Douglas (Inspector),
Barry Harvey (Constable).
"The Crystal Trench" (10-4-59):
Patricia Owens (Stella Ballister), James
Donald (Mark Cavendish), Harald Dy-
renforth (Frederick Blaver), Patrick
MacNee (Prof. Kersley), Werner Klem-
perer (Herr Ranks).
"Appointment at Eleven" (10-11-
59): Clint Kimbrough (Davie), Amy
Douglass (Davie's Mother), Norma
Crane (blonde), Michael J. Pollard,
Clu Gulager, Sean McClory.
"Coyote Moon" (10-18-59): Mac-
Donald Carey (John Piltkin), Collin Wil-
cox (girl), Edgar Buchanan (Pops).
"No Pain" (10-25-59): Brian Keith
(Dave Ramey), Joanna Moore (Cindy),
Yale Wexler (Arnold Barrett).
"Anniversary Gift" (11-1-59):
Harry Morgan (Hermie Jensen), Bar-
bara Baxley (Myra Jensen), Jackie
Coogan (George Bates), Michael J.
Pollard (Hansel Eidelpfeiffer), James
Field (Doctor), Maurice Manson (post-
man).
"Dry Run" (11-8-59): Robert
Vaughn (Art), Walter Matthau (Moran),
David White (Barbossa), Valerie Allen
(Clare).
"The Blessington Method" (11-15-
59): Henry Jones (Mr. Treadwell),
Dick York (Bunce), Elizabeth Patter-
son (Grandma), Irene Windust (Mrs.
Treadwell).
"Dead Weight" (11-22-59): Jo-
seph Cotten (Court Masterson), Julie
Adams (Peg Valence), Claude Stroud
(Mr. Eldridge), Don Gordon (Rudy),
Angela Greene (Mrs. Masterson).
"Special Delivery" (11-29-59):
Steve Dunne (Hugh Fortnum), Beatrice
Straight (Cynthia Fortnum), Peter La-
zer (Tom), Ethel Shutta (Mrs. Good-
body), Michael Burns, Frank Maxwell,
Cece Whitney.
"Road Hog" (12-6-59): Richard
Chamberlain (Clay Pine), Raymond Mas-
sey (Sam Pine), Robert Emhardt (Ed
Fratus), Roscoe Ates.
"Specialty of the House" (12-13-
59): Robert Morley (Mr. Lafler), Ma-
dame Spivy (Spiro), Kenneth Haigh (Cos-
tain), George Keymas (Paul), Bettye
Ackerman (Henline).
"An Occurrence at Owl Creek
Bridge" (12-20-59): Ronald Howard
(Peyton Farquhar), Juano Hernandez
(Josh), Kenneth Tobey (Col. Venable),
James Coburn.
"Graduating Class" (12-27-59):
Wendy Hiller (Miss Siddons), Robert

H. Harris (Ben Proudy), Gigi Perreau
(Gloria Pope), Jocelyn Brando.
"The Ikon of Elijah" (1-10-60):
Oscar Homolka (Carpius), Sam Jaffe
(Archimandrite), Danielle de Metz (El-
phtheria), Arthur E. Gould-Porter (Maj.
Parslow), William Greene (Theodoras),
David Janti (Paul Carp), Robert Richards
(Brother Constantine), Fred Catania
(Brother Damianos), Richard Longman
(Callost Chiringirian).
"The Cure" (1-24-60): Nehemiah
Persoff (Jeff Jenson), Cara Williams
(Marie), Leonard Strong (Lutz), Mark
Richman (Mike).
"Backward, Turn Backward" (1-
21-60): Tom Tully (Phil Canby), Alan
Baxter (Sheriff Willett), Raymond Bai-
ley (Harris), Phyllis Love (Sue Thomp-
son), Paul Maxwell (Saul).
"Not the Running Type" (2-7-60):
Paul Hartman (Milton Potter), Robert
Bray (Capt. Fisher), Wendell Holmes
(John B. Halverson).
"The Day of the Bullet" (2-14-60):
John Graven (Clete Vine), Barry Gordon
(Iggy Kovacs), Glenn Walken (Clete Vine
as a boy).
"Hitchhike" (2-21-60): John McIn-
tire (Charles Underhill), Robert Morse
(boy), Suzanne Pleshette (Anne), Read
Morgan (police officer), Paul E. Burns
(proprietor).
"Across the Threshold" (2-28-60):
Barbara Baxley (Irma Collett), George
Grizzard (Hubert Wintor), Patricia Col-
linge (Mrs. Wintor).
"Craig's Will" (3-6-60): Dick Van
Dyke (Tom Craig), Stella Stevens (Judy),
Paul Stewart (Vincent Noonan), Harry
Tyler, Stephen Roberts.
"Man from the South" (3-13-60):
Peter Lorre (gambler), Steve McQueen
(young man), Neile Adams (young man's
wife).
"Mme. Mystery" (3-27-60): Aud-
rey Totter (Betsey Blake), Joby Baker
(Jimmy Dolan), Harp McGuire (Steven).
"The Little Man Who Was There"
(4-3-60): Norman Lloyd (little man),
Read Morgan (Ben), Arch Johnson (Ja-
mie), R.G. Armstrong (Okie), Clegg
Hoyt (Hutch).
"Mother, May I Go Out to Swim"
(4-10-60): Gia Scala (Lottie Rank), Wil-
liam Shatner (John Crane), Jessie Royce
Landis (Claire Crane), Robert Carson.
"The Cuckoo Clock" (4-17-60):
Beatrice Straight (Ida Blythe), Fay Spain
(Madeline), Patricia Hitchcock (Dorothy).
"Forty Detectives Later" (4-24-
60): James Franciscus (William Tyree),
Jack Weston (Otto), George Mitchell

(Munro Dean), Arlene McQuade (Gloria), Robert Kelljan (customer).

"The Hero" (5-1-60): Oscar Homolka (Jan Van der Klaue), Irene Tedrow (Lady Musgrave), Eric Portman (Sir Richard Musgrave), Sally Pearce (Elizabeth Musgrave), Ralph Clanton (purser), Jack Livesey (Captain), Irene Windust (Mrs. Boswell), Richard Lupino (photographer), Bartlett Robinson (American), Barry Harvey (steward), Barney Bernard (ship's bartender).

"Insomnia" (5-8-60): Dennis Weaver (Charlie Cavendar), Al Hodge (Mr. Turney), James Milhollin (Dr. Tedaldi), Jack Ragin (Jack Fletcher), Dorothea Lord (receptionist), Ken Clarke (fireman).

"I Can Take Care of Myself" (5-15-60): Linda Lawson (Georgia), Myron McCormick (Bert), Frankie Darro (Little Dandy), Will Kuluva (Joey Palermo), Leonard Weinrib (Amos), Pat Harrington, Jr. (insurance man), Edmon Ryan (Simpson), Bill Sharon (man).

"One Grave Too Many" (5-22-60): Jeremy Slate (Joe Helmer), Neile Adams (Mrs. Helmer), Biff Elliott (Lt. Bates), Tyler McVey (Sgt. Dugan), Howard McNear (Mr. Pickett), David Carlile (patrolman).

"Party Line" (5-29-60): Judy Canova (Helen Parch), Arch Johnson (Miller), Gertrude Flynn (Betty Nubbins), Royal Dano (Atkins), Ellen Corby (Emma).

"Cell 227" (6-5-60): Brian Keith (Herbert Morrison), Frank Maxwell (Maury Berg), Liam Sullivan (Father McCann), James Westerfield (Lt. Pops Lafferty), James Best (Hennessey), Sal Ponti (De Baca).

"The Schartz-Metterklume Method" (6-12-60): Elspeth March (Mrs. Wellington), Hermione Gingold (Miss Hope), Patricia Hitchcock (Rose), Doris Lloyd (Nannie), Noel Drayton (Huggins).

"Letter of Credit" (6-19-60): Bob Sweeney (William Spengler), Robert Bray (Henry Taylor), Cyril Delevanti (Josiah Wingate), Theodore Newton (Sam Kern), Ron Nichols (Arnold Mathias), Jacqueline Holt (Miss Fester), Joseph Hamilton (stationmaster).

"Escape to Sonoita" (6-26-60): Burt Reynolds (Bill), James Bell (Andy), Venetia Stevenson (Stephanie), Murray Hamilton (man), Dean Stanton (man), Robert Karnes (Ted), George Dockstader (trooper).

"Hooked" (9-25-60): Robert Horton (Ray Marchand), Anne Francis (Ni-

la Foster), John Hamilton (Floyd Foster), Vivienne Segal (Fladys Marchand), Joseph Hamilton (old man).

"Mrs. Bixby and the Colonel's Coat" (9-27-60): Audrey Meadows (Mrs. Bixby), Les Tremayne (Dr. Bixby), Stephen Chase (Colonel), Sally Hughes (Miss Pluteney), Maidie Norman (Eloise), Howard Crane (pawnbroker).

"The Doubtful Doctor" (10-4-60): Dick York (Ralph Jones), Gena Rowlands (Lucille Jones), Michael Burns (Sidney), John Zaremba (Talbert Collins), Ralph Smiley (waiter), Robert Sampson (Ted Parkinson).

"Very Moral Theft" (10-11-60): Betty Field (Helen), Walter Matthau (Harry Wade), Karl Swenson (John Thompson), David Fresco (Parker), Robert Sampson (Jimmy), Sam Gilman (Charlie), Claude Stroud (Orville), Keith Britton (guard), Charles Carlson (teller), Rusty Lane (Ivers), Sal Ponti (Carl), William Newell (Fescue).

"The Contest for Aaron Gold" (10-18-60): Barry Gordon (Aaron Gold), Sydney Pollack (Bernie Samuelson), Frank Maxwell (Lionel Stern), William Thourlby.

"The Five Forty-Eight" (10-25-60): Zachary Scott (James Blake), Phyllis Thaxter (Iris Dent), Irene Windust (Mrs. Compton), Raymond Bailey (Mr. Watkins).

"Pen Pal" (11-1-60): Clu Gulager (Rod Collins), Gloria Ellis (Margie), Katherine Squire (Aunt Margaret), Stanley Adams (Detective Berger), Roy Montgomery (intern).

"Outlaw in Town" (11-15-60): Ricardo Montalban (Tony Lorca), Constance Ford (Shasta Cooney), Arch Johnson (Bat McCormack), Patsy Kelly (Minnie), Bernard Kates (Billy Feeney).

"Oh, Youth and Beauty" (11-22-60): Gary Merrill (Cash Bentley), Patricia Breslin (Louise Bentley), David Lewis (Jim Blackwood), Theodore Newton (Doctor), Dick Winslow (Harry), Maurice Manson (Arthur), Dudley Manlove (George), Gloria Henninger (Cathy).

"The Money" (11-29-60): Robert Loggia (Larry Chetnik), Doris Dowling (Angie), Wolfe Barzell (Miklos), Will Kuluva (Stephen Bregornick), Monica May (receptionist).

"Sybilla" (12-6-60): Barbara Bel Geddes (Sybilla), Alexander Scourby (Horace).

"The Man with Two Faces" (12-13-60): Spring Byington (Mrs. Wagner), Steven Dunne (Lt. Meade), Harp McGuire (Leo), Bethel Leslie.

(ALFRED HITCHCOCK PRESENTS
cont.)
"The Baby Blue Expression" (12-
20-60): Sarah Marshall (Mrs. Bar-
rett), Peter Walker (Philip Weaver),
Richard Gaines, Liz Carr, Edith An-
gold, Leonard Weinrib, Chet Stratton.
"The Man Who Found the Money"
(12-27-60): Arthur Hill (William Ben-
son), Rod Cameron (Curtis Newsome),
R. G. Armstrong (Capt. Bone), Lucy
Prentis (Elaine Purdy), Baynes Barron
(Lent), Clancy Cooper (A. J. Meecham),
Charles Sherlock (croupier), Mark Al-
len (man), Mike Ragan (desk sergeant).
"The Changing Heart" (1-3-61):
Abraham Sofaer (Ulrich Klemm), Anne
Helm (Lisa), Robert Sampson (Jack),
David Fresco (clerk), Nicholas Pryor
(Dane Ross).
"Summer Shade" (1-10-61): Julie
Adams (Phyllis Kendall), James Fran-
ciscus (Ben Kendall), Susan Gordon
(Kate Kendall), John Hoyt (Rev. White),
Charity Grace (Amelia Gastell).
"A Crime for Mothers" (1-24-61):
Claire Trevor (Lottie Mead), Biff El-
liott (Phil Ames), Robert Sampson (Ralph
Birdwell), Patricia Smith (Jane Bird-
well), Howard McNear (Mr. Maxwell),
King Calder (Charlie Vance), Gail Bon-
ney (secretary), Sally Smith (young girl).
"The Last Escape" (1-31-61):
Keenan Wynn (Joe Ferlini), Jan Ster-
ling (Wanda Ferlini), John Craven (Tom-
my Baggett), Dennis Patrick (Phil Ros-
coe), Jack Livesey (Dr. Rushfield),
Sam Flint (business man), Robert Car-
son (police chief), Ronnie Rondell (Dave),
Claude Stroud (official), Charles Mere-
dith (clergyman), Ed Allen (musician).
"The Greatest Monster of Them
All" (2-14-61): Robert H. Harris (Mar-
ty Lenton), Richard Hale (Ernest von
Kroft), William Redfield (Fred Logan),
Sam Jaffe (Hal Ballew).
"The Landlady" (2-21-61): Dean
Stockwell (Billy Weaver), Patricia Col-
linge (landlady), Laurie Main (Wilkins),
George Pelling (Bert), Burt Mustin
(Garvis), Barry Harvey (Tom), Jill
Livesey (Rose).
"The Throwback" (2-28-61): Mur-
ray Matheson (Cyril Hardeen), Scott
Marlowe (Elliot Gray), Joyce Meadows
(Enid Patterson), John Indisano (Joseph).
"The Kiss-Off" (3-7-61): Rip
Torn (Ernie Walters), Mary Munday
(Florrie), Bert Freed (Detective Coo-
per), Ken Patterson (District Attor-
ney), Frank Sully (desk clerk), Flo-
rence MacMichael (woman witness),
Don Keefer (tax clerk), Harry Swoger

(taxi driver).
"The Horseplayer" (3-14-61):
Claude Rains (Father Amion), Ed Gard-
ner (Sheridan), Percy Helton (Sexton),
Kenneth MacKenna (Bishop Cannon),
Mike Ragan (Mr. Cheever), William
Newell (bank teller), David Carlile (bank
teller), Ada Murphy (elderly woman),
John Yount (altar boy), Jackie Carroll
(altar boy).
"Incident in a Small Jail" (3-23-
61): John Fiedler (Leon Gorwald), Ron
Nicholas (Sandy), Richard Jaeckel (me-
chanic).
"A Woman's Help" (3-28-61): Ge-
raldine Fitzgerald (Elizabeth Bourdon),
Scott McKay (Arnold Bourdon), Leon
Lontoc (Chester), Antoinette Bower
(Joan Grecco), Lillian O'Malley (woman).
"Museum Piece" (4-4-61): Myron
McCormick (Mr. Clovis), Larry Gates
(Clay Hollister), Edward C. Platt (Hen-
shaw), Bert Convy (Ben Hollister).
"Coming, Mama" (4-11-61): Ei-
leen Heckart (Lucy Baldwin), Don De-
Fore (Arthur Clark), Madge Kennedy
(Mrs. Baldwin), Jesslyn Fax (Mrs.
Evans).
"Deathmate" (4-18-61): Gia Scala
(Lisa Talbot), Lee Philips (Ben Conant),
Les Tremayne (Peter Talbot), Russell
Collins (Alvin Moss).
"Gratitude" (4-25-61): Peter Falk
(Meyer Fine), Paul Hartman (John Ingo),
Edmund Hashim (Frank Mazzotti), Karl
Lukas (Otto), Bert Remsen (Lt. Mc-
Dermott), John Dennis (Joe Dunphy),
Adam Stewart (Avery Combs, Jr.), Phil
Gordon (Frank), Clegg Hoyt (Hubert),
Forrest Lederer (croupier), Janos Czin-
gula (investigator).
"A Pearl Necklace" (5-2-61):
Ernest Truex (Howard Rutherford), Ha-
zel Court (Charlotte Jameson Ruther-
ford), Jack Cassidy (Mark Lansing),
Michael Burns (Billy Lansing), David
Faulkner (young man).
"You Can't Trust a Man" (5-9-61):
Polly Bergen (Crystal Coe), Frank Al-
bertson (George Wyncliff), Joe Maross
(Tony).
"The Gloating Place" (5-16-61):
Susan Harrison (Susan Harper), Henry
Brandt (Lt. Palmer), King Calder (Phil
Harper), Marta Kristen (Marjorie Stone).
"Self-Defense" (5-23-61): George
Nader (Gerald Clarke), Audrey Totter
(Mrs. Phillips), Jessalyn Fax (Mrs.
Gruber), Steve Gravers (Lt. Schwartz),
Selmer Jackson (clergyman), David Car-
lile (Sgt. Krebs).
"A Secret Life" (5-30-61): Ronald
Howard (James Howgill), Patricia Dona-

hue (Margery Howgill), Addison Richards (Crandall Johnson), Arte Johnson (Mr. Bates), Florence MacMichael (Mrs. Hackett), Meri Welles (Kathleen Perry), Mary Murphy (Estelle Newman).

"Servant Problem" (6-6-61): Jo Van Fleet (Molly Goff), John Emery (Kerwin Drake), Alice Frost (Mrs. Standish), Bartlett Robinson (Colton), Katherine Givney (Mrs. Colton), Grandon Rhodes (Standish), Joan Hackett (Sylvia).

"Coming Home" (6-13-61): Crahan Denton (Harry Beggs), Jeanette Nolan (Edith), Robert Carson (warden), Kreg Martin (bartender), Harry Swoger (prison cashier), Syl Lamont (man), Susan Silo (girl), Gil Perkins (bus driver), Josie Lloyd (bank teller).

"Final Arrangements" (6-20-61): Martin Balsam (Leonard Compson), Slim Pickens (Bradshaw), Bartlett Robinson (Dr. Maxwell), O. Z. Whitehead (Simms), Vivian Nathan (Elsie Compson).

"Make My Death Bed" (6-27-61): Diana Van Der Vlis.

"Ambition" (7-4-61): Leslie Nielsen (Rudolf Cox), Ann Robinson (Helen Cox), Harry Landers (Ernie Stillingwater), Harold J. Stone (Mac Davis), Charles Carlson (Cliff Woodman), Charles Arnt (Mayor), Bernard Kates (Lou Heinz), Syl Lamont (hood).

"The Hat Box" (10-10-61): Paul Ford (Prof. Jarvis), Billy Gray (Perry Hatch).

"Bang, You're Dead" (10-10-61): Billy Mumy (Jackie Chester), Biff Elliott (Fred Chester), Lucy Prentiss (Amy Chester), Steve Dunne (Rich Sheffield), Dean Moray (Gary), Kelly Flynn (Stephen).

"Maria" (10-24-61): Venus De Mars (Emila Maria Travatore), Norman Lloyd (Leo Torbey), Nita Talbot (Carole Torbey), Edmund Hashim (El Magnifico), Kreg Martin (Benny), Marjorie Bennett (elderly woman), Billy Curtis (midget), Doug Carlson (roustabout).

"Cop for a Day" (10-31-61): Walter Matthau (Phil), Glenn Cannon (Davey), Robert Reiner (policeman), George Kane (policeman), Tom Begley (bank messenger), Susan Brown (receptionist).

"Keep Me Company" (11-7-61): Anne Francis (Julia Reddy), Edmund Hashim (Marco Reddy), Anthony Hall (Sam Reddy), Jack Ging (Detective Parks), Billy Wells (Kenny Reddy), Hinton Pope (policeman), Howard McLeod (policeman).

"Beta Delta Gamma" (11-14-61): Burt Brinckerhoff (Alan), Duke Howard (Mark), Severn Darden (Franklin).

"You Can't Be a Little Girl All Your Life" (11-21-61): Dick York (Tom Barton), Caroline Kearney (Julie Barton), John Anderson (Nicholson), Ted de Corsia (Lt. Christensen).

"The Old Pro" (11-28-61): Richard Conte (Frank Burns), Sarah Shane (Loretta Burns), Stacy Harris (Cullen).

"I Spy" (12-5-61): Kay Walsh (Mrs. Morgan), William Kendall (Capt. Morgan), Cecil Parker (lawyer), Eric Barker.

"Services Rendered" (12-12-61): Hugh Marlowe (Dr. Mannix), Steve Dunne (young man).

"The Right Kind of Medicine" (12-9-61): Robert Redford (Charlie Pugh), Russell Collins (Mr. Fletcher), Joby Baker (Vernon), Gage Clark (Dr. Vogel).

"A Jury of Her Peers" (12-26-61): Ann Harding (Sarah Hale), Frances Reid (Mrs. Peters), June Walker (Millie Wright), Robert Bray (Henry Peters), Ray Teal (Jim Hale).

"The Silk Petticoat" (1-2-62): Michael Rennie (Humphrey Orford), Antoinette Bower (Elicia Minden), Jack Livesey (Dr. Minden), David Frankham.

"Bad Actor" (1-9-62): Robert Duvall (Bart Conway), Charles Robinson (Jerry Lane), Carole Eastman (Marjorie Rogers).

"The Door without a Key" (1-16-62): Claude Rains (amnesia victim), Billy Mumy (Mickey), John Larch (Sgt. Shaw), Robert Carson (Lieutenant).

"The Case of M. J. H. " (1-23-62): Richard Gaines (M. J. Harrison), Barbara Baxley (Maude Sheridan), Robert Loggia (Jimmy French), Ted Newton (Dr. Cooper).

"The Faith of Aaron Menefee" (1-30-62): Andrew Prine (Aaron Menefee), Robert Armstrong (Doc Buckles), Sidney Blackmer (Otis James), Maggie Pierce (Emily Jones), Olan Soule (Brother Fish), Gail Bonney (woman), Don Hammer (Vern Byers).

"The Woman Who Wanted to Live" (2-6-62): Lola Albright (Lisa), Charles Bronson (Ray Bardon), Ray Montgomery (attendant), Craig Curtis (Rook), Ben Bryant (fat boy), Robert Rudelson (Cuke).

"Strange Miracle" (2-13-62): David Opatoshu (Sequiras), Miriam Colon (Lolla), Eduardo Ciannelli (Priest), Frank de Kova (Vargas), Adeline Pedroza (Maria), Tina Menard (Nun).

"The Test" (2-20-62): Brian Keith (Vernon Wedge), Eduardo Ciannelli (Mr.

(ALFRED HITCHCOCK PRESENTS cont.) Bleeker), Rod Lauren (Benjy), William Bramley (Dr. Hagerty), Steven Gravers (Wickers), Tenen Holtz (Sol Dankers).

"Burglar Proof" (2-27-62): Robert Webber (Harrison Fell), Paul Hartman (Sammy Morrisey), Whit Bissell (Mr. Bliss), Philip Ober (Wilton Stark).

"The Big Score" (3-6-62): Evan Evans (Dora), Philip Reed (Mr. Fellows), Rafael Campos (Gino), John Zaremba (Larry), Tom Gilleran (Mike), Jesse Jacobs (Ozzie), Joe Trapaso (Murphy).

"Profit Sharing Plan" (3-13-62): Henry Jones (Miles Cheever), Ruth Storey (Mrs. Cheever), Rebecca Sand (Anita), Humphrey Davis (Mr. Dougherty), Jim Sweeney (elevator operator).

"Apex" (3-20-62): Patricia Breslin (Margo), Vivienne Segal (Clara), George Kane (Mr. Weeks), Mark Miller (Claude).

"The Last Remains" (3-27-62): Ed Gardner (Marvin Foley), John Fiedler (Amos Duff), Len Weinrib (Stanley), Walter Kinsella (Lt. Morgan).

"Ten O'Clock Tiger" (4-3-62): Frankie Darro (Boots), Robert Keith (Arthur Duffy), Karl Lukas (Soldier Fresno), Bruce Dushman (Buster), Chuck Hicks (Gypsy Joe), Charles E. Perry (handler), Andy Romano (cop).

"Act of Faith" (4-10-62): George Grizzard (Alan Chatterton), Dennis King (Mr. Temple), Florence MacMichael (Alice).

"The Kerry Blue" (4-17-62): Carmen Mathews (Thelma Malley), Gene Evans (Ned Malley), Rob Reiner (Doctor), John Zaremba (Dr. Chaff), David Carlyle (Detective), Warren Smith (intern).

"The Matched Pearl" (4-24-62): John Ireland (Capt. McCabe), Ernest Truex (Mr. Wilkens), Sharon Farrell (Lolly Wilkens), Emile Genest (Kirkwood), Michael King (Conroy).

"What Frightened You, Fred?" (5-1-62): Edward Asner (Warden Bragan), R. G. Armstrong (Fred Riordan), Adam Williams (Dr. Cullen), Eve McVeagh (Mae), Steven Peck (Tony Wando).

"Most Likely to Succeed" (5-8-62): Joanna Moore (Louise), Howard Morris (Dave Sumner), Jack Carter (Stanley Towers), Molly Glessing (maid).

"Victim Four" (5-15-62): John Lupton (Ralph Morrow), Peggy Ann Garner (Madeline Drake), Paul Comi (Joe Drake), Bryan O'Byrne (Mr. Tittle), Harry Hines (old man).

"The Opportunity" (5-22-62): Richard Long (Paul Devore), Rebecca Sand (Kate Devore), Coleen Gray (Lois Callen), Olive Dunbar (Mrs. Ranwiller).

"The Twelve Hour Caper" (5-29-62): Dick York (Herbert Wiggam), Sarah Marshall (Miss Pomfritt), Kreg Martin (Webster), Wendell Holmes (Sylvester Tupper), Gage Clarke (Frisbee), Tom Bellin (Brand), Lillian O'Malley (cleaning woman).

"The Children of Alda Nuova" (6-5-62): Jack Carson (Frankie Fane), Christopher Dark (Crowder), Stefan Schnabel (Siani), Thano Rama (Paolo), Lidia Vana (old woman), David Fresco (cripple), Carlo Tricoli (villager).

"First Class Honeymoon" (6-12-62): Robert Webber (Edward Gibson), Jeremy Slate (Carl Seabrook), John Abbott (Abner Munro), Kim Hamilton (maid), Marjorie Bennett (Mrs. Phalen), Elaine Martone (Marian), James Flavin (doorman).

"The Big Kick" (6-19-62): Anne Helm (Judy Baker), Wayne Rogers (Kenneth), Brian Hutton (Mitch).

"Where Beauty Lies" (6-26-62): George Nader (Collin Hardy), Cloris Leachman (Caroline Hardy), Charles Carlson (Paul Ross), Pamela Curran (Joan Blake), Norman Leavitt (painter), Marlyn Clark (Julie Ross), Raymond Bailey (Doctor).

ALFRED HITCHCOCK HOUR. 1962-64. Alfred Hitchcock (Host).

"A Piece of the Action" (9-20-62): Gig Young (Duke Marsden), Martha Hyer (Alice Marsden), Robert Redford (Chuck Marsden), Gene Evans (Ed Krutcher), Roger de Koven (Nate), Kreg Martin (Smiley).

"Don't Look Behind You" (9-27-62): Vera Miles (Daphne Grey), Jeffrey Hunter (Harold Lambert), Alf Kjellen (Edwin Volck), Abraham Sofaer (Dr. MacFarlane), Madge Kennedy (Mrs. MacFarlane), Dick Sargent (Dave Fulton), Ralph Roberts (Paul Hatfield).

"Night of the Owl" (10-4-62): Brian Keith (Jim Mallory), Patricia Breslin (Linda Mallory), Norman Leavitt (Ben Kaylor), Philip Coolidge (Locke), Robert Bray (Lt. Ames), Mike Kellin (Parker), Claudia Cravey (Anne Mallory), Terry Ann Ross (Barbara Mallory), Frank Ferguson (Capt. Parker).

"I Saw the Whole Thing" (10-11-62): John Forsythe (Mike Barnes), Kent Smith (Jerry O'Hara), Philip Ober (Col. Hoey), Evans Evans (Penny Sanford), John Zaremba, Rusty Lane.

"Captive Audience" (10-18-62):

James Mason (Warren Barrow), Angie Dickinson (Janet West), Arnold Moss (Victor Martmann), Roland Winters (Ivar West), Ed Nelson (Tom Keller), Geraldine Wall (Mrs. Hurley), Sara Shane (Mrs. Marrow).

"Final Vow" (10-25-62): Carol Lynley (Sister Pamela), Clu Gulager (Jimmy Bresson), Isobel Elsom (Reverend Mother).

"Annabel" (11-1-62): Susan Oliver (Annabel), Dean Stockwell (David Kelsey), Hank Brandt (Gerald Delaney), Charles Robinson (Wes), Lisabeth Hush (Linda), Kathleen Nolan.

"House Guest" (11-8-62): Macdonald Carey (John Mitchell), Peggy McCay (Sally Mitchell), Robert Sterling (Ray Roscoe), Billy Mumy (Tony Mitchell), Adele Mara (Eve Sherston), Robert Armstrong (Charles Faulkner).

"The Black Curtain" (11-15-62): Richard Basehart (Phil Townsend), Lee Philips (Frank Carlin), Lola Albright (Ruth), Harold J. Stone (taxi driver), Gail Kobe (Virginia), Neil Nephew (Chuck), James Farentino (Bernie), Celia Lovsky (Mrs. Fisher).

"Day of Reckoning" (11-22-62): Louis Hayward (Judge David Wilcox), Claude Akins (Sheriff Jordan), Barry Sullivan (Paul Sampson), Katherine Bard (Caroline Sampson), Dee Hartford (Felicity Sampson), Jeremy Slate (Tent Parker), Hugh Marlowe, K. T. Stevens.

"Ride the Nightmare" (11-29-62): Gena Rowlands (Helen Martin), Hugh O'Brian (Chris Martin), John Anderson (Adam), Gail Bonney (elderly woman), Olan Soule (Bill), Jay Lanin (Fred), Philippa Bevans (Mrs. Anthony), Richard Shannon (Steve).

"Hangover" (12-6-62): Jayne Mansfield (Marian), Tony Randall (Hadley Purvis), Dody Heath (Sandra Purvis), Robert P. Lieb (Bill Hunter), Tyler McVey (Driscoll), Robert Franchot (Albert), Myron Healey (Bob Blake), James Maloney (Cushman), Chris Roman (Cliff), June Levant (saleswoman), William Phipps (bartender).

"Bonfire" (12-13-62): Peter Falk (Robert Evans), Dina Merrill (Laura Freshwater), Patricia Collings (Naomi Freshwater), Sam Weston (taxi driver), Paul Von Schreiber (youth), Craig Curtis (young man), Craig Duncan (police officer).

"The Tender Poisoner" (12-20-62): Howard Duff (Peter Harding), Dan Dailey (Philip Bartel), Jan Sterling (Beatrice Bartel), Bettye Ackerman

(Lorna Dickson).

"The Thirty-First of February" (1-4-63): William Conrad (Sgt. Cresse), Elizabeth Allen (Molly O'Rourke), David Wayne (Andrew Anderson), William Sargent (Peter Granville), Bob Crane (Charlie Lessing), Staats Cotsworth (Mr. Vincent), King Calder (Riverton), Bernadette Hale (Miss Wright), Kathleen O'Malley (Valerie Anderson), Steven Gravers (psychiatrist).

"What Really Happened?" (1-11-63): Gladys Cooper (Mrs. Raydon), Anne Francis (Eve Raydon), Gene Lyons (Howard Raydon), Ruth Roman (Addie), Steve Dunne (Jack Wentworth).

"Forecast: Low Clouds and Coastal Fog" (1-18-63): Dan O'Herlihy (Simon Carter), Inger Stevens (Karen Wilson), Christopher Dark (Manuel Sanchez), Chris Robinson (Ricky), Richard Jaeckel (Tom).

"A Tangled Web" (1-25-63): Barry Morse (Karl Gault), Zohra Lampert (Marie), Robert Redford (David Chesterman), Gertrude Flynn (Ethel Chesterman), Cathleen Cordell (Mrs. Spaulding).

"To Catch a Butterfly" (2-1-63): Bradford Dillman (Bill Nelson), Diana Hyland (Janet Nelson), Ed Asner (Jack Stander), June Dayton (Barbara Stander), Mickey Sholder (Eddie Stander).

"The Paragon" (2-8-63): Joan Fontaine (Alice Pemberton), Gary Merrill (John Pemberton), Virginia Vincent (Madge Fletcher), William Sargent (Walter Fletcher), Richard Carlyle (Leo Wales), Linda Leighton (Evie Wales), June Walker (Mrs. Wales).

"I'll Be the Judge, I'll be the Jury" (2-15-63): Peter Graves (Mark Needham), Albert Salmi (Theodore Bond), Sarah Marshall (Louise Trevor), Ed Nelson (Alec Nelson), Rodolfo Hoyos (Insp. Ortiz), Eileen O'Neil (Laura Needham), Zolya Talma (Mrs. Bond), Eric Tovar (Perez).

"Diagnosis: Danger" (3-1-63): Charles McGraw (Dr. Simon Oliver), Michael Parks (Dr. Dan Dana), Stefan Gierasch (Sgt.. Boyle), Berkeley Harris (Deputy Sheriff Judd), Marc Cavell (Alf), Marc Rambeau (Doug).

"The Lonely Hours" (3-8-63): Nancy Kelly (Vera Brandon), Juanita Moore (Mrs. McFarland), Gena Rowlands (Louise Henderson), Joyce Van Patten (Grace Thrope), Jackie Russell (Sandra), Jennifer Gillespie (Celia), Jesslyn Fax (Miss McGuiness), Annette Ferra (Harriet), Sally Smith (Marjorie), Willa Pearl Curtis (Hassie).

"The Star Juror" (3-15-63): Dean

(ALFRED HITCHCOCK HOUR cont.)
Jagger (George Davies), Betty Field
(Jenny Davies), Will Hutchins (J. J.
Fenton), Crahan Denton (Sheriff Wat-
son), Katherine Squire (Mrs.
Fenton), Cathie Merchant (Lola), Harry Harvey,
Sr. (Dr. Vince), Josie Lloyd (Pauline
Davies).

"The Long Silence" (3-22-63):
Michael Rennie (Ralph Manson), Phyl-
lis Thaxter (Nora Cory Manson), Nat-
lie Trundy (Jean Dekker), James Mc-
Mullan (George Cory), Connie Gilchrist
(Emma), Vaughan Taylor (Dr. Babcock),
Claude Stroud (Edgar Ogden), Rees
Vaughan (Robbie Cory).

"An Out for Oscar" (4-5-63): Lin-
da Christian (Eva Ashley), Henry Silva
(Bill Grant), Larry Storch (Oscar Blin-
ny), Myron Healey (Pete Rogan), Alan
Napier (Mr. Hodges), Rayford Barnes
(Ronald), David White (Detective Burr),
John Marley (Mike Chambers), George
Petrie (Rogers).

"Death and the Joyful Woman" (4-
12-63): Laraine Day (Ruth Hamilton),
Gilbert Roland (Luis Aguilar), Don Gal-
loway (Les Aguilar), Thomas Lowell
(Dominic Felse), Laura Devon (Kitty),
Frank Overton (George Felse), Maggie
Pierce (Jean Aguilar).

"Last Seen Wearing Blue Jeans"
(4-19-63): Michael Wilding (David Saunders), Randy Boone (Pete Tanner), Katherine Crawford (Lauren Saunders),
Anna Lee (Roberta Saunders).

"The Dark Pool" (5-3-63): Madlyn
Rhue (Consuela Sandine), Lois Nettle-
ton (Dianne Castillejo), Anthony George
(Victor Castillejo), Doris Lloyd (Mrs.
Gibbs), David White (Lance Hawthorn),
John Zaremba (coroner).

"Dear Uncle George" (5-10-63):
Gene Barry (John Chambers), John Lar-
kin (Simon Aldrich), Patricia Donahue
(Louise Chambers), Lou Jacobi (Lt.
Wolfson), Dabney Coleman (Tom Este-
row), Robert Sampson (Sgt. Duncan),
Charity Grace (Mrs. Weatherby), Bren-
dan Dillon (Sam), Alicia Li (Bea).

"Run for Doom" (5-17-63): John
Gavin (Dr. Donald Reed), Diana Dors
(Niki Carroll), Scott Brady (Bill Floyd),
Carl Benton Reid (Horace Reed), Tom
Skeritt (Dr. Frank Farmer), Gail Bon-
ney (Sarah).

"Death of a Cop" (5-24-63): Victor
Jory (Reardon), Peter Brown (Philip
Reardon), Laurence Tierney (Herbie
Lane), Paul Hartman (Trenker), John
Marley (Singer), Richard Jaeckel (Box-
er), Wilton Graff (George Chaney),
Read Morgan (Freddie), Jean Willes

(Eva), Paul Genge (Lt. Tom Mills).

"A Home Away from Home" (9-
27-63): Ray Milland (Dr. Fenwick),
Claire Griswold (Natalie Rivers), Vir-
ginia Gregg (Miss Gibson), Peter Leeds
(Andrew), Mary La Roche (Ruth), Ben
Wright (Dr. Norton), Connie Gilchrist
(Martha), Beatrice Kay (Sara Sanders),
Jack Searle (Nicky Long), Ronald Long
(Major), Peter Brooks (Donald).

"A Nice Touch" (10-4-63): Anne
Baxter (Janice Brandt), George Segal
(Larry Duke), Harry Townes (Ed Brandt),
Charlene Holt (Darlene Vance), Mimi
Dillard (receptionist), Gil Stuart (actor),
Martha Stewart (secretary).

"Terror in Northfield" (10-11-63):
Dick York (Sheriff Will Pearce), Jacque-
line Scott (Susan Marsh), R. G. Armstrong
(John Cooley), Gertrude Flynn (Flora
Sloan).

"You'll Be the Death of Me" (10-
18-63): Robert Loggia (Driver Arthur),
Carmen Phillips (Betty Rose), Pilar
Seurat (Mieko), Kathleen Freeman (Mrs.
McCleod), Barry Atwater (Gar Newton),
Charles Seel (Doc Chalmont), Norman
Leavitt (Kyle Sawyer), Sondra Kerr (Ru-
by McCleod), Hal Smith (Tompy Dill).

"Blood Bargain" (10-25-63): Anne
Francis (Connie Breech), Richard Kiley
(Jim Derry), Richard Long (Eddie Breech),
Barney Martin (Rupert Harney).

"Nothing Ever Happens in Linville"
(11-8-63): Gary Merrill (Harry Jarvis),
Fess Parker (Sheriff Ben Wister), Phyl-
lis Thaxter (Mrs. Logan), George Furth
(Charlie), Cathie Merchant (receptionist),
Robert Lieb (Dr. Wyatt), Burt Mustin
(Mr. Bell), Jan Arvan (Al).

"Starring the Defense" (11-15-63):
Richard Basehart (Miles Crawford), Te-
no Pollick (Tod Crawford), Russell Collins (Sam Brody), Diane Mountford (Ruthie), S. John Launer.

"Body in the Barn" (11-22-63): Lillian Gish (Bessie Carnby), Maggie McNamara (Camilla), Peter Lind Hayes (Henry), Kent Smith (Dr. Adamson), Patricia
Cutts (Samantha), Kelly Thordsen (Sheriff Turnbull), Josie Lloyd (Norm), James
Maloney (storekeeper).

"The Dividing Wall" (12-6-63):
James Gregory (Fred Kruger), Chris Ro-
binson (Terry), Katherine Ross (Carol),
Norman Fell (Al Norman), Simon Scott
(Durrell), Robert Kelljan (Frank Ludden),
Rusty Lane (Otto Brandt), Judd Foster
(Polson), Erik Corey (boy), Renata Vanni
(customer).

"Goodbye, George" (12-13-63): Robert Culp (Harry), Stubby Kaye (George),
Patricia Barry (Lana Layne), Elliott Reid

(Dave Dennis).

"How to Get Rid of Your Wife" (12-20-63): Bob Newhart (Gerald Swinney), Jane Withers (Edith Swinney), Joyce Jameson (Rosie Feather), Mary Scott (Laura), George Petrie (Henry), Harold Gould (District Attorney), Bill Quinn (Mr. Penny), Helene Winston (Mrs. Penny), Gail Bonney (Mrs. Harris), Ann Morgan Guilbert (pet shop owner), Joseph Hamilton (stage doorman), Harry Hines (rat poison salesman), Robert Karnes (police sergeant).

"Two Wives Too Many" (1-3-64): Teresa Wright (Marion Brown), Dan Duryea (Mr. Brown), Jean Hale (Bernice Brown), Linda Lawson (Lucille Brown), Steve Gravers (Lt. Storber).

"The Magic Shop" (1-10-64): John Megna (Tony Grainger), Leslie Nielsen (Steven Grainger), David Opatoshu (Dulong), Peggy McCay (Hilda Grainger), Paul Hartman (Adams).

"The Cadaver" (1-17-64): Michael Parks (Skip Baxter), Ruth McDevitt (Mrs. Fister), Martin Blaine (Prof. Dawson), Joby Baker (Doc), Jennifer West (Ruby).

"Beyond the Sea of Death" (1-24-64): Mildred Dunnock (Minnie Briggs), Diana Hyland (Grace Renford), Jeremy Slate (Keith Holloway), Abraham Sofaer.

"Night Caller" (1-31-64): Felicia Farr (Marcia Fowler), Bruce Dern (Roy Bullock), David White (Jack Fowler), Angela Greene (Lucy Phillips), Diane Sayer (Nancy Willis), Leslie Barringer (Stevey Fowler).

"The Evil of Adelaide Winters" (2-7-64): Kim Hunter (Adelaide Winters), John Larkin (Edward Porter), Gene Lyons (Robert McBain), Bartlett Robinson (Mr. Thompson), Sheila Bromley (Mrs. Thompson).

"The Jar" (2-14-64): Pat Buttram (Charlie), James Best (Tom Carmody), Collin Wilcox (Thedy), William Marshall (Jahdoo), Slim Pickens (Clem), Carl Benton Reid (Gramps), Billy Barty (midget), George Lindsey (Juke Marmer), Jocelyn Brando (Emma Jane), Jane Darwell (Granny Carnation).

"Final Escape" (2-21-64): Ed Byrnes (Paul Perry), Stephen McNally (Capt. Tollman), Robert Keith (Doc).

"Murder Case" (3-6-64): John Cassavetes (Lee Griffin), Gena Rowlands (Diana Justin), Hedley Mattingley (Blackie), Ben Wright (Tony), Murray Matheson (Charles Justin).

"Anyone for Murder?" (3-13-64): Barry Nelson (James Parkerson), Edward Andrews (Bingham), Dick Dawson

(Robert Johnson), Patricia Breslin (Doris Parkerson), Richard X. Slattery.

"Beast in View" (3-20-64): Joan Hackett (Helen Clarvoe), Kathy Nolan (Dorothy Johnson), George Furth (Jack Terola), Kevin McCarthy (Paul), Brenda Forbes (Mrs. Clarvoe).

"Behind the Locked Door" (3-27-64): Gloria Swanson (Mrs. Daniels), James MacArthur (Dave Snowden), Lynn Loring (Bonnie), Whit Bissell (Adam).

"A Matter of Murder" (4-3-64): Telly Savalas (Philadelphia Harry), Darren McGavin (Sheridan Westcott), Patricia Crowley (Enid Bentley), Patrick McVey (Police Lieutenant), Howard Wendell (Flagstone), Than Wyenn (general delivery), Lewis Charles (Lopez), Jordan Grant (Al), Tyler McVey (Police Chief), Calvin Bartlett (Harv), Paul Potash (Winnie), Marc Rambeau (Weldon).

"The Gentleman Caller" (4-10-64): Roddy McDowall (Gerald Musgrove), Ruth McDevitt (Emmy Rice), Juanita Moore (Mrs. Jones), Diane Sayer (Milly), Naomi Stevens (Mrs. Goldy).

"The Ordeal of Mrs. Snow" (4-17-64): Patricia Collinge (Mrs. Snow), Jessica Walter (Lorna Richmond), George Macready (Hillary Prine), June Vincent (Ruth Prine), Bartlett Robinson (Harvey), Pamela Curran (Sally Wilson), Don Chastain (Bruce Richmond).

"Ten Minutes from Now" (5-1-64): Donnelly Rhodes (James Bellington), Lonny Chapman (Lt. Wymar), Lou Jacobi (Dr. Glover), Neile Adams (Sgt. Louise Marklen), Jess Kirkpatrick (Thomas Grindley), Sandra Gould (secretary), Betty Harford (woman in museum), Harold Ayer (salesman).

"The Sign of Satan" (5-8-64): Christopher Lee (Karl Jorla), Gia Scala (Kitty), Gilbert Green (Max Rubini), Adam Roarke (Ed Walsh), Myron Healey (Dave).

"Who Needs an Enemy?" (5-15-64): Steven Hill (Charlie Osgood), Richard Anderson (Eddie Turtin), Joanna Moore (Danielle), Barney Phillips (Detective).

"Bed of Roses" (5-22-64): Patrick O'Neal (George Maxwell), Kathie Browne (Mavis Maxwell), George Lindsey (Sam Kirby), Torin Thatcher (Hardwicke), Alice Backes (Mrs. Hinchley), Pauline Myers (Celeste), Alice Frost (Eda Faye Hardwicke).

"Second Verdict" (5-29-64): Martin Landau (Ned Murray), Frank Gorshin (Lew Rydell), Sharon Farrell (Melanie Rydell), John Marley (Tony), Harold J. Stone (Osterman), Nancy Kovack (Karen Osterman).

(ALFRED HITCHCOCK HOUR cont.)
"Isabel" (6-5-64): Bradford Dillman (Howard Clemens), Barbara Barrie (Isabel Smith), Edmon Ryan (Lt. Huntley), Les Tremayne (Selby), Dabney Coleman (Sgt. Snyder), Doris Lloyd (Martha), Ken Patterson (Warden).

"The Return of Verge Likens" (10-5-64): Peter Fonda (Verge Likens), Robert Emhardt (Riley McGrath), Sam Reese (Wilford Likens), Jim Boles (Sheriff).

"Change of Address" (10-12-64): Arthur Kennedy (Keith Hollins), Phyllis Thaxter (Elsa Hollins), Royal Dano (Miley), Tisha Sterling (Rachel), Victor Jory.

"Water's Edge" (10-19-64): John Cassavetes (Rusty Connors), Ann Sothern (Helen Krause), Rayford Barnes (Mike Krause).

"The Life and Work of Juan Diaz" (10-26-64): Alejandro Rey (Juan Diaz), Pina Pellicer (Maria Diaz), Frank Silvera (Alejandro), Larry Domasin (Jorge), Valentin de Vargas (Police Chief), Alex Montoya (coffin maker).

"See the Monkey Dance" (11-9-64): Efrem Zimbalist, Jr. (Stranger), Roddy McDowall (George), Patricia Medina (wife).

"The Lonely Place" (11-16-64): Teresa Wright (Stella), Bruce Dern (Jesse), Pat Buttram (Emery).

"The McGregor Affair" (11-23-64): Andrew Duggan (McGregor), Elsa Lanchester (Aggie McGregor), Michael Pate (Hare), Arthur Malet (Burke), John Hoyt (Dr. Knox), Bill Smith (Tommy Lad).

"Misadventure" (12-7-64): Lola Albright (Eva Martin), George Kennedy (George Martin), Barry Nelson (Colin), Michael Bragan (boyfriend).

"Triumph" (12-14-64): Ed Begley (Brother Thomas Fitzgibbon), Tom Simcox (Brother John Sprague), Maggie Pierce (Lucy Sprague), Jeanette Nolan (Mary Fitzgibbons).

"Memo from Purgatory" (12-21-64): James Caan (Jay Shaw), Lyn Loring (Filene), Walter Koenig (Tiger), Anthony Musante (Candle), Zalman King (Fish), Michael Lamont (Trooper).

"Consider Her Ways" (12-28-64): Barbara Barrie (Jane), Gladys Cooper (Laura), Leif Erickson (Dr. Hellyer), Robert H. Harris (Dr. Perrigan), Ellen Corby (Chief Nurse), Carmen Phillips (Mother Daisy), Diane Sayer (Mother Haze), Gene Lyons (Max Wilding), Eve Bruce (Amazon), Dee J. Thompson (1st doctor), Alice Backes (2nd doctor),

Virginia Gregg (3rd doctor).

"The Crimson Witness" (1-5-65): Peter Lawford (Ernest Mullett), Julie London (Barbara), Martha Hyer (Judith Mullett), Joanna Moore (Madeline), Roger C. Carmel (Farnum Mullett), Alan Baxter (Baldwin), Paul Comi (Modeer), Larry Thor (Haskel).

"Where the Woodbine Twineth" (1-11-65): Margaret Leighton (Nell Snyder), Juanita Moore (Suse), Carl Benton Reid (Capt. King Snyder), E. J. Andre (Preacher), Joel Fluellen (Jesse), Eileen Baral (Eva), Lila Perry (Numa).

"The Final Performance" (1-18-65): Franchot Tone (Rudolph), Sharon Farrell (Rosie), Roger Perry (Cliff Allen), Kelly Thordsen (Sheriff).

"Thanatos Palace Hotel" (2-1-65): Steven Hill (Robert Manners), Angie Dickinson (Ariane Shaw), Barry Atwater (Borchter), Bartlett Robinson (J. Smith), Rex Comeaux (Devereau).

"One of the Family" (2-8-65): Lilia Skala (Frieda), Kathryn Hays (Joyce Dailey), Jeremy Slate (Dexter Dailey), Olive Deering (Christine Callender).

"An Unlocked Window" (2-15-65): Dana Wynter (Sheila), Stephen Roberts (Boris Crispis), Louise Latham (Maude), John Kerr (Glendon Baker), Cathie Merchant (Frieda Little), E. J. Andre (Sam), John Willis (newscaster).

"The Trap" (2-22-65): Donnelly Rhodes (John Cochran), Anne Francis (Peg Beale), Robert Strauss (Ted Beale), Patricia Hanning (Jenifer Arnold), Walter Mathews (Glen Arnold).

"Wally the Beard" (3-1-65): Larry Blyden (Wally Mills), Kathie Browne (Noreen), Berkeley Harris (Curly), Katherine Squire (Mrs. Adams), George Mitchell (Keefer), Elizabeth Harrower (Mrs. Jones), Lee Bergere (Detective), Leslie Perkins (Lucy Jones), John Indrisano (bartender).

"Death Scene" (3-8-65): James Farentino (Leo Manfred), Vera Miles (Nicky Revere), John Carradine (Gavin Revere), Buck Taylor (Dancer), Leonard Yorr (Bill Wagner), Virginia Aldridge (Susan Revere), Horace Brown (Harry).

"The Photographer and the Undertaker" (3-15-65): Jack Cassidy (Arthur Mannix), Harry Townes (Hiram Price), Alfred Ryder (Rudolph), Philip Bourneuf (Silvester), Jocelyn Lane (Sylvia), Joan Swift (secretary), Richard Jury (Willis), Jack Bernardi (delicatessen man).

"Thou Still Unravished Bride" (3-22-65): Ron Randell (Tommy Bonn), Sally Kellerman (Sally Benner), David Carradine (Clarke), Kent Smith (Mr. Benner),

Michael Pate (Stephen Leslie), Ted Bessell (Elliot Setlin), Edith Atwater (Mrs. Benner), Alan Napier (Guerny), Virginia Gregg (Mrs. Setlin), Howard Caine (Mr. Setlin), Ben Wright (Sutherland).
"Completely Foolproof" (3-29-65): J. D. Cannon (Joe Brisson), Patricia Barry (Lisa Brisson), Geoffrey Horne (Bobby Davenport), Myron Healey (Foyle), Lester Mathews (Walter Dunham), Joyce Meadows (Anna).
"Power of Attorney" (4-5-65): Richard Johnson (James Jarvis), Geraldine Fitzgerald (Agatha), Fay Bainter (Mary Bawfield), Josie Lloyd (Eileen).
"The World's Oldest Motive" (4-12-65): Henry Jones (Alex Morrow), Kathleen Freeman (Angela Morrow), Linda Lawson (Fiona), Robert Loggia (man).
"The Monkey's Paw - A Retelling" (4-19-65): Leif Erickson (Paul White), Jane Wyatt (Anna White), Lee Majors (Howard White), Collin Wilcox (Celina), Zolya Talmer (Gypsy Woman), Janet MacLachlan (Gayle), Stuart Margolin (Robin), Dick Caruso (Gypsy Boy), Gil Stuart (British Man), Peter Howard (Curtis Welks), Marusia Toumanoff (Natasha), Carmen Phillips (Mary Smith).
"The Second Wife" (4-26-65): June Lockhart (Martha), John Anderson (Luke), Jim Boles (Rev. Mr. Gilfoyle), Eve McVeagh (Sylvia), Alice Backes (Helen).
"Night Fever" (5-3-65): Coleen Dewhurst (Ellen Hatch), Tom Simcox (Jerry Walsh), Joe DeSantis (Jake Martinez), Richard Bull (Dr. Michaels), Don Marshall (Joe Chandler), Laurie Mitchell (Pinky), Peggy Lipton (Mary Winters), Don Stewart (Gabe).
"Off Season" (5-10-65): John Gavin (Johnny Kendall), Indus Arthur (Sandy), Tom Drake (Sheriff Dade), Dody Heath (Irma Dade), Richard Jaeckel, William O'Connell.

ALMOST HEAVEN. Pilot (12-28-78): Eva Gabor (Lydia), Robert Hays (Dave), Laurie Heinemann (Annie), Larry Gelman (George), Richard Roat (Randall), Jay Leno, Anne Schedeen, Ellen Regan.

AMERICAN PLAYHOUSE.
"Any Friend of Nicholas Nickleby Is a Friend of Mine" (2-9-82): Fred Gwynne (Charles Dickens), Brian Svrusis (Ralph), George Womack (Mr. Wyneski), Les Podewell (Grandpa), Sadie Hawkins (Grandma), Deanna Dunagan (Emily Dickenson), Jim Pappas,

Frank Howard, Donna Gibbons.
"Come Along with Me" (2-16-82): Estelle Parsons (Mabel Lederer), Barbara Baxley (Mrs. Faun/her sister), Sylvia Sidney (Mrs. Flanner), Edward Meeking, Dennis J. Vero, Kimberly Carter, Mary Seibel, Martin Kern, Brina Rodin, Camilla Hawk, Anne Doyle, Adam Hirsh, Rosemary Dean, Frank Galati, Thomas Erhart, Ned Schmidtke, Dick Sallenberger, Sheilah Keenan, Ted Liss, R. G. Clayton, Everett F. Smith, Dana Reilly, Christy Michaels, Mary Beth Liss, James Paccarrella, Toni Fleming, Bob Jones, Jack Orend, P. L. Neuman.

AMERICAN SHORT STORY.
"Rappaccini's Daughter" (2-25-80): Kristoffer Tabori (Giovanni Guasconti), Kathleen Beller (Beatrice Rappaccini), Leonardo Cimino (Dr. Rappaccini), Michael Egan (Baglioni), Antonia Rey (Emma), Madeline Willemsen (Lisabetta).

AMERICA 2100. Pilot (7-24-79): Karen Valentine (Dr. Karen Harland), Jon Cutler (Chester Barnes), Mark King (Phil Keese), Sid Caesar (voice of Max the Computer).

ANDROMEDA BREAKTHROUGH. British 1962. Susan Hampshire (Andromeda), Peter Halliday (Dr. John Fleming), Mary Morris, David King, John Hollis, Noel Johnson, Barry Linehan, Mellan Mitchell.

ARK II. 1976. Terry Lester (Jonah), Jean Marie Hon (Ruth), Jose Flores (Samuel).

ARMSTRONG CIRCLE THEATRE.
"The House of Flying Objects" (10-29-58): William Le Massena (Mr. Herrmann), Joan Copeland (Mrs. Herrmann), Lynn Loring (Lucy Herrmann), David Kerman (Mr. Ligouri).

ARTEMIS 81. British 12-29-81. Hywel Bennett (Gideon Harlax), Dinah Stabb (Gwen Meredith), Dan O'Herlihy (Von Drachenfels), Ian Redford (Jed Thaxter), Margaret Whiting (Laura Guise), Sevilla Delofski (Magog), Roland Curram (Asrael), Sting (Helith), Anthony Steel (Tristram Guise), Mary Ellen Ray (Sonia), Cornelius Garrett (Pastor), Siv Borg (Pastor's wife), Sylvia Coleridge (Gorgon scholar), Daniel Day Lewis (exhibitioner), Ingrid Pitt (Hitchcock blonde).

ATOM SQUAD, THE. 1953. Bob Hastings (Steve Elliot), Bob Courtleigh, Bram Nossem.

AVENGERS, THE. British 1962-63. Patrick MacNee (John Steed), Honor Blackman (Catherine Gale).

"Mr. Teddy Bear": Bernard Goldman (Mr. Teddy Bear), Kenneth Kealing (Col. Wayne Gilley), Douglas Muir (One-Ten).

"The Death of a Great Dane": Frederick Jaeger (Getz), John Laurie (Sir James Arnall), Leslie French (Gregory), Frank Peters (Miller), Clare Kelly (Mrs. Miller), Billy Milton (Minister), Herbert Nelson (gravedigger), Michael Moyer (policeman).

"Concerto": Sandor Eles (Stefan Veliko), Geoffrey Colville (Burns), Bernard Brown (Peterson), Dorinda Stevens (Darleen), Nigel Stock (Zalenko), Valerie Bell (Polly White), Leslie Glazer (Robbins), Carole Ward (receptionist).

"Death A'La Carte": Henry Soskin (Emir Abdulla Akaba), Robert James (Mellor), Gordon Rollings (Lucien), Paul Dawkins (Dr. Spencer), David Nettheim (Umberto), Ken Parry (Arbuthrot).

"Propellant 23": Frederick Schiller (Jules Meyer).

"White Dwarf": George A. Cooper (Maxwell Barker), Philip Latham (Cartwright), Peter Copley (Henry Barker), Bill Nagy (Johnson), Keith Pyott (Prof. Richter), Paul Anil (Rahin), Daniel Thorndike (Minister).

"Don't Look Behind You": Janine Gray (Ola), Kenneth Colley (young man).

"The Grandeur That Was Rome": Hugh Burden (Bruno), John Flint (Marcus), Colette Wilde (Octavia).

"The Death of a Batman": David Burke (John Wrightson), Philip Madoc (Eric Van Doren), Katy Greenwood (Lady Cynthia).

"The Sellout": Jon Rollason (Dr. Martin King), Michael Mellinger (Fraser), Frank Gatliff (Harvey), Arthur Hewlett (One-Twelve), Carleton Hobbs (Monsieur Roland).

"Immortal Clay": Steve Greeb.

"The Undertakers": Patrick Holt (Madden).

"Build a Better Mousetrap": John Tate (Col. Wesker), Nora Nicholson (Ermyntrude), Athene Seyler (Cynthia).

"The Mauritius Penny": Richard Vernon (Lord Matterley), Philip Guard (Goodchild), David Langton (Gerald Shelley), Alfred Burke (Brown), Edwin Brown (lorry driver), Alan Rolfe (Burke), Edward Jewesbury (Maitland).

"Killer Whale": Kenneth Farrington (Joey Frazer), Patrick Magee (Pancho).

"November Five": Gary Hope (Michael Oyter).

"Second Sight": Steven Scott (Dr. Vilner).

"Conspiracy of Silence": Robert Rietty (Carlo), Sandra Dorne (Rickie), Artro Morris (James), John Church (Terry).

"The Nutshell".

"The Golden Fleece": Warren Mitchell (Captain Jason).

"The Man with Two Shadows": Daniel Moynihan (Gordon), Philip Anthony (Cummings), Paul Whitsun-Jones (Charles), Terence Lodge (Borowski), George Little (Sigi), Douglas Robinson (Rudi), Gwendolyn Watts (Julie), Geoffrey Palmer (Dr. Terrance), Anne Godfrey (Miss Quist).

"Intercrime": Kenneth J. Warren (Felder), Alan Browning (Moss), Julia Arnall (Hilda Stern), Patrick Holt (Manning), Donald Webster (Palmer).

"Death Dispatch": Richard Warner (Miquel Roas).

"Brief for Murder": Alec Rose (Wescott).

"Death on the Rocks": Gerald Cross (Fenton), Hamilton Dyce (Max Daniels), Toni Gilpin (Samuel Ross), Richard Clark (Van Berg), David Sumner (Nicky), Ellen Intosh (Liza Denham), Annette Kerr (Mrs. Ross), Naomi Chance (Mrs. Daniels), Douglas Robinson (Sid).

"Box of Tricks": Julie Stevens (Venus Smith).

"School for Traitors": Julie Stevens (Venus Smith), Richard Thorp (Robert).

"Bullseye".
"The Decapod".
"Dressed to Kill".
"Full Run".
"The Gilded Cage".
"The Little Wonders".
"Mandrake".
"Man in the Mirror".
"Six Hands Across a Table".
"Traitor in Zebra".
"Warlock".
"The Wringer".

AVENGERS, THE. 1966-69. Patrick Macnee (John Steed), Diana Rigg (Mrs. Emma Peel) 66-68, Linda Thorson (Tara King) 68-69, Patrick Newell (Mother) 68-69.

"The Cybernauts" (3-28-66): Michael Gough (Dr. Armstrong), Frederick Jaeger (Benson), Bernard Horsfall (Jeph-

cott), Bert Kwouk (Tusamo), Ronald
Leigh Hunt (Lambert), Gordon Whiting
(Hammond), John Hollis (Sensai).
"Small Game for Big Hunters" (4-
4-66): Bill Fraser (Col. Rawlings),
James Villiers (Simon Trent), Liam
Redmond (Prof. Swain), A. J. Brown
(Dr. Gimson), Peter Burton (Fleming),
Tom Gill (Tropical Outfitter), Esther
Anderson (Lala), Paul Danguah (Raza-
fi), Peter Thomas (Kendrick).
"Death at Bargain Prices" (4-11-
66): Andre Morell (Horatio Kane), T. P.
MacKenna (Wentworth), Allan Cuthbert-
son (Farthingale), John Cater (Jarvis),
Diane Clare (Julie), George Selway
(Massey), Peter Howell (Prof. Popple),
Harvey Ashby (Marco), Ronnie Stevens
(Glynn).
"The Hour That Never Was" (4-
25-66): Gerald Harper (Geoffrey Rids-
dale), Roy Kinnear (Hickey), Dudley
Foster (Philip Leas), Roger Booth (Por-
ky Purser), Daniel Moynihan (Corporal
Barman), Fred Haggerty (Wiggins), Da-
vid Morell (driver).
"Castle De'Ath" (5-2-66): Gordon
Jackson (Ian), Robert Urquhart (Angus),
James Copeland (Robertson), Jack Lam-
bert (McNab), Russell Waters (control-
ler).
"Two's a Crowd" (5-9-66): War-
ren Mitchell (Brodny), Wolfe Morris
(Pudeshkin), Julian Glover (Vogel),
John Bluthal (Ivenko), Alec Mango
(Shvedloff), Maria Machado (Alicia El-
ena).
"The House That Jack Built" (5-
16-66): Michael Godliffe (Prof. Keller),
Griffith Davies (Burton), Michael Wynne
(Withers), Keith Pyott (Pennington).
"The Murder Market" (5-30-66):
Patrick Cargill (Mr. Lovejoy), Peter
Bayliss (Dinsford), Suzanne Lloyd (Bar-
bara Wakefield), Naomi Chance (Mrs.
Stone), John Woodvine (Robert Stone),
Edward Underdown (Jonathan Stone),
John Forgham (Beale), Barbara Ros-
coe (receptionist).
"The Girl from A. U. N. T. I. E. "
(6-6-66): Liz Fraser (Georgie Price-
Jones), Alfred Burke (Gregorio Auntie),
Bernard Cribbins (Arkwright), Mary
Merrall (Old Lady), Sylvia Coleridge
(Aunt Hetty), David Bauer (Ivenov), Ray
Martine (taxi driver), John Rutland
(Fred Jacques), Yolande Turner (recep-
tionist), Maurice Browning (Russian).
"How to Succeed at Murder" (6-
13-66): Sarah Lawson (Mary Merry-
weather), Angela Browne (Sara Penny),
Anne Cunningham (Gladys Murkle), Zeph
Gladstone (Liz Purbright), Artro Mor-

ris (Henry Throgbottom), David Garth
(Barton), Christopher Benjamin (J. J.
Hooter), Sidonie Bond (Annie), Robert
Dean (Jack Finlay), Jerome Willis (Josh-
ua Rudge), Kevin Brennan (Sir George
Morton).
"A Sense of History" (6-20-66):
Nigel Stock (Richard Carlyon), John Bar-
ron (Dr. Henge), John Glyn-Jones (Grind-
ley), Patrick Mower (Duboys), John Ring-
ham (Prof. Acheson), Robin Phillips
(John Pettit), Jacqueline Pearce (Mari-
anne), Peter Blythe (Millerson), Peter
Bourne (Allen).
"Room with a View" (6-27-66):
Paul Whitsun-Jones (Chessman), Peter
Jeffrey (Varnals), Richard Debb (Dr.
Cullen), Philip Latham (Carter), Vernon
Dobtcheff (Pushkin), Peter Arne (Palold),
Peter Madden (Dr. Wadkin).
"The Danger Makers" (7-4-66):
Nigel Davenport (Major Robertson),
Douglas Wilmer (Dr. Harold Long), Mo-
ray Watson (Peters), Adrian Ropes (Lt.
Stanhope), Fabia Drake (Col. Adams),
John Gatrell (Gordon Lamble), Richard
Coleman (RAF Officer).
"The Master Minds" (7-11-66):
Laurence Hardy (Sir Clive Todd), Patri-
cia Haines (Holly Trent), Ian McNaugh-
ton (Dr. Fergus Campbell), Bernard
Archard (Desmond Leeming), John Went-
worth (Sir Jeremy), Georgina Ward (Da-
vinia Todd), Manning Wilson (Major
Plessy).
"Dial a Deadly Number" (7-21-66):
Clifford Evans (Henry Boardman), Jan
Holden (Ruth Boardman), Anthony New-
lands (Ben Jago), Gerald Sim (Frederick
Yuill), John Carson (Fitch), Peter Bowles
(John Harvey), John Bailey (Warner),
Michael Trubshawe (the General), Nor-
man Chappell (Macombie), Edward Cast
(waiter).
"What the Butler Saw" (7-28-66):
John LeMesurier (Benson), Thorley Wal-
ters (Hemming), Dennis Quilley (Group
Capt. Miles), Kynaston Reeves (Maj.
Gen. Goddard), Ewan Hooper (Sgt. Mo-
ran), Humphrey Lestocq (Vice Adm.
Willows), Leon Sinden (Squadron Leader
Hogg), Howard Marion Crawford (Brig.
Goddard), David Swift (Barber), Norman
Scace (Reeves), Peter Hughes (Walters).
"The Gravediggers" (8-4-66): Ro-
nald Fraser (Sir Horace Winslip), Paul
Massie (Johnson), Caroline Blakiston
(Miss Thirlwell), Victor Platt (Sexton),
Wanda Ventham (Nurse Spray), Charles
Lamb (Fred), Lloyd Lamble (Dr. Mar-
lowe), Ray Austin (Baron), Steven Ber-
koff (Sager), Bryan Mosley (Miller).
"Too Many Christmas Trees" (8-

(AVENGERS cont.) 11-66): Mervyn Johns (Brandon Storey), Barry Warren (Jeremy Wade), Edwin Richfield (Dr. Felix Teasel), Alex Scott (Martin Trasker), Jeannette Sterke (Janice Crane), Robert James (Jenkins).

"The Thirteenth Hole" (8-18-66): Patrick Allen (Reed), Hugh Manning (Col. Watson), Peter Jones (Dr. Adams), Francis Matthews (Collins), Victor Maddern (Jackson), Donald Hewlett (Waversham), Norman Wynne (Prof. Minley), Richard Marner (man on TV screen).

"The Man-Eater of Surrey Green" (8-25-66): Derek Farr (Sir Lyle Peterson), Athene Seyler (Dr. Sheldon), Gillian Lewis (Laura Burford), Alan Carter (William Job), Edwin Finn (Prof. Taylor), Harry Shacklock (Prof. Knight), Ross Hutchinson (Dr. Connelly), John G. Heller (Lennox).

"The Town of No Return" (9-1-66): Alan MacNaughton (Brandon), Patrick Newell (Smallwood), Terence Alexander (Piggy Warren), Jeremy Burnham (Vicar), Juliet Harmer (Jill Manson), Robert Brown (Saul), Walter Horsbrugh (school inspector).

"Honey for the Prince" (1966): Ron Moody (Ponsonby-Hopkirk), Zia Mohyeddin (Prince Ali), George Pastell (Arkadi), Roland Curram (Vincent), Ken Parry (B. Bumble), Bruno Barnabe (Grand Vizier), Jon Laurimore (Ronny Westcott), Reg Pritchard (postman), Richard Graydon (George Reed), Peter Diamond (Bernie), Carmen Dene (Eurasian girl).

"Silent Dust" (1966): William Franklyn (Omrod), Jack Watson (Juggins), Norman Bird (Croft), Conrad Phillips (Mellors), Charles Lloyd Pack (Sir Manfred Fellows), Aubrey Morris (Quince), Isobel Black (Clare Prendergast), Joanna Wake (Miss Snow).

"A Surfeit of H_2O" (1966): Noel Purcell (Jonah Barnard), Albert Lieven (Dr. Sturm), Sue Lloyd (Joyce Jason), Talfryn Thomas (Eli Barker), Geoffrey Palmer (Martin Smythe), John Kidd (Sir Arnold Kelly).

"A Touch of Brimstone" (1966): Peter Wyngarde (John Cartney), Colin Jeavons (Lord Darcy), Carol Cleveland (Sara), Robert Cawdron (Horace), Michael Latimer (Roger Winthrop), Jeremy Young (Willy Frant), Bill Wallis (Tubby Bunn), Steve Plytas (Kartovski), Art Thomas (Pierre), Alf Joing (big man), Bill Reed (huge man).

"Quick-Quick Slow Death" (1966): Eunice Gayson (Lucille Banks), Maurice Kaufmann (Ivor Bracewell), Carole

Gray (Nicki), Larry Cross (Chester Read), James Belchamber (Peever), John Woodnutt (Captain Noble), David Kernan (Peidi), Alan Gerrard (Fintry), Collin Ellis (Bernard), Graham Armitage (Huggins), Ronald Govey (bank manager), Charles Hodgson (Syder), Michael Peake (Wili Fehr).

"From Venus with Love" (1-20-67): Barbara Shelley (Venus Browne), Philip Locke (Dr. Henry Primble), Paul Gillard (Ernest Cosgrove), Jon Pertwee (Brigadier Whitehead), Derek Newark (Crawford), Jeremy Lloyd (Bertram Smith), Adrian Ropes (Jennings), Arthur Cox (Clarke), Kenneth Benda (Mansford), Michael Lynch (Hadley).

"The Fear Merchants" (1-27-67): Patrick Cargill (Pemberton), Brian Wilde (Raven), Annette Carell (Dr. Voss), Garfield Morgan (Gilbert), Andrew Keir (Crawley), Jeremy Burnham (Gordon White), Edward Burnham (Meadows), Bernard Horsfall (Fox), Declan Mulholland (Saunders), Ruth Trouncer (Dr. Hill), Philip Ross (hospital attendant).

"The See-Through Man" (2-3-67): Moira Lister (Elena), Warren Mitchell (Brodny), Roy Kinnear (Quilby), John Nettleton (Sir Andrew Ford), Jonathan Elsom (Ackroyd), Harvey Hall (Ulric), David Glover (Wilton).

"Escape in Time" (2-10-67): Peter Bowles (Thyssen), Geoffrey Bayldon (Clapham), Imogen Hassall (Anjali), Judy Parfitt (Vesta), Edward Caddick (Sweeney), Roger Booth (Tubby Vincent), Clifford Earl (Paxton), Nicholas Smith (Parker), Rocky Taylor (Mitchell), Richard Montez (Josino).

"The Winged Avenger" (2-17-67): Nigel Green (Sir Lexius Clay), Jack MacGowran (Prof. Poole), Neil Hallett (Arnie Packer), Colin Jeavons (Stanton), John Garrie (Tayling), Roy Patrick (Julian), Donald Pickering (Peter Roberts), A. J. Brown (Dawson), William Fox (Simon Roberts), Hilary Wontner (Dumayn), Ann Sydney (Gerda), John Crocker (Fothers).

"The Living Dead" (3-3-67): Julian Glover (Masgard), Howard Marion Crawford (Geoffrey), Pamela Ann Davy (Mandy), Jack Woolgar (hermit), Edward Underdown (Rupert), Jack Watson (Hopper), John Cater (Olliphant), Vernon Dobtcheff (Spencer), Alister Williamson (Tom).

"The Bird Who Knew Too Much" (3-10-67): Ron Moody (Jordan), Ilona Rodgers (Samantha Slade), Kenneth Cope (Tom Savage), Michael Coles (Verret), Anthony Valentine (Cunliffe), John Wood (Twitter), Clive Colin-Bowler (Robin),

John Lee (Mark Pearson).
"The Hidden Tiger" (3-17-67):
Ronnie Barker (Cheshire), Lyndon Brook
(Dr. Manx), Gabrielle Drake (Angora),
John Phillips (Nesbitt), Michael For-
rest (Peters), Stanley Meadows (Er-
skine), Jack Gwillim (Sir David Harper),
Frederick Treves (Dawson), Brian
Haines (Samuel Jones), John Moore
(Williams), Reg Pritchard (Bellamy).
"The Correct Way to Kill" (3-24-
67): Anna Quayle (Comrade Olga Savo-
novitch Negretiskina Volkowske), Mi-
chael Gough (Nutski), Philip Madoc (I-
van Peppitoperoff), Terence Alexander
(Ponsonby), Graham Armitage (Algy),
Timothy Bateson (Merryweather), Pe-
ter Barkworth (Percy), Edwin Apps
(Winters), Joanna Jones (Hilda), John
G. Heller (Groski).
"Never, Never Say Die" (3-31-
67): Christopher Lee (Professor Stone),
Jeremy Young (Dr. Penrose), Patricia
English (Dr. James), David Kernan
(Eccles), John Junkin (Sergeant), Chris-
topher Benjamin (Whittle), Geoffrey
Reed (Carter), Peter Dennis (Private),
Anan Chuntz (Selby), Karen Ford (nurse),
Arnold Ridley (elderly gent), David
Gregory (young man).
"Epic" (4-14-67): Peter Wyn-
garde (Stewart Kirby), Kenneth J. War-
ren (Z. Z. Von Schnerk), Isa Miranda
(Damita Syn), Anthony Dawes (actor),
David Lodge (policeman).
"The Superlative Seven" (4-21-67):
Charlotte Rampling (Hana), Brian Bles-
sed (Mark Dayton), James Maxwell
(Jason Wade), Hugh Manning (Max Har-
dy), Leon Greene (Freddy Richards),
Donald Sutherland (Jessel), John Hollis
(Kanwitch), Gary Hope (Joe Smith),
Margaret Neale (stewardess), Terry
Plummer (Toy Sung).
"A Funny Thing Happened on the
Way to the Station" (4-28-67): James
Hayter (ticket collector), John Laurie
(Crewe), Drewe Henley (Groom), Isla
Blair (Bride), Tim Barrett (Salt), Dy-
son Lovell (Warren), Michael Nightin-
gale (Lucas), Richard Caldicot (Admi-
ral), Peter J. Elliott (attendant), Noel
Davis (secretary).
"Something Nasty in the Nursery"
(5-5-67): Dudley Foster (Mr. Goat),
Yootha Joyce (Miss Lister), Paul Ed-
dington (Beaumont), Patrick Newell
(Sir George Collins), Paul Hardwick
(Webster), Geoffrey Sumner (Gen.
Wilmot), Trevor Bannister (Gordon),
Clive Dunn (Martin), George Merritt
(James), Louie Ramsay (Nanny Smith),
Enid Lorimer (Nanny Roberts), Pene-

lope Keith (Nanny Brown), Dennis Chin-
nery (Dobson).
"The Joker" (5-12-67): Peter
Jeffrey (Prendergast), Sally Nesbitt
(Ola), Ronald Lacey (young man).
"Who's Who???" (5-19-67): Pa-
tricia Haines (Lola), Freddie Jones (Ba-
sil), Campbell Singer (Major 'B'), Pe-
ter Reynolds (Tulip), Philip Levene
(Daffodil), Arnold Diamond (Krelmar),
Malcolm Taylor (Hooper).
"Mission... Highly Improbable"
(1-10-68): Ronald Radd (Shaffer), Jane
Merrow (Susan Rushton), Noel Howlett
(Prof. Rushton), Francis Matthews (Chi-
vers), Richard Leech (Col. Drew), Ste-
fan Gryff (Josef).
"The Positive-Negative Man" (1-
17-68): Ray McAnally (Cresswell), Ca-
roline Blakiston (Cynthia Wentworth-
Howe), Michael Latimer (Haworth),
Jeanne Dainton (Miss Clarke), Peter
Blythe (Mankin), Sandor Eles (Maurice
Jobert), Bill Wallis (Charles Grey), Ann
Hamilton (receptionist).
"You Have Just Been Murdered"
(1-24-68): Barrie Ingham (Unwin), Ro-
bert Flemying (Lord Maxted), George
Murcel (Needle), Leslie French (Rath-
bone), Simon Oates (Skelton), John Ba-
ker (Hallam), Geoffrey Chater (Jarvis),
Clifford Cox (Chalmers), Les Crawford
(Morgan), Frank Maher (Nicholls), Pe-
ter J. Elliott (Williams).
"Death's Door" (1-31-68): Clif-
ford Evans (Boyd), William Lucas (Stap-
ley), Allan Cuthbertson (Lord Melford),
Marne Maitland (Becker), Paul Dawkins
(Dr. Evans), Michael Faure (Pavret),
William Lyon Brown (Dalby), Terry
Maidment (Jepson), Peter Thomas (Saun-
ders), Terry Yorke (Haynes).
"Murdersville" (2-7-68): Colin
Blakely (Mickle), John Rohane (Hubert),
Ronald Hines (Dr. Haymes), John Sharp
(Prewitt), Sheila Fearn (Jenny), Eric
Flynn (Croft), Robert Cawdron (Banks),
Norman Chappell (Forbes), Marika Mann
(Miss Avril), Joseph Greig (Higgins),
Irene Bradshaw (Maggie), Langton Jones
(Chapman), Geoffrey Colville (Jeremy
Purser), Tony Caunted (Miller), John
Chandos (Morgan), Andrew Laurence
(Williams).
"Return of the Cybernauts" (2-21-
68): Peter Cushing (Paul Beresford),
Frederick Jaeger (Benson), Charles
Tingwell (Dr. Neville), Fulton Mackay
(Prof. Chadwick), Roger Hammond (Dr.
Russell), Anthony Dutton (Dr. Garnett),
Noel Coleman (Conroy), Aimi MacDonald
(Rosie), Redmond Phillips (Hunt), Terry
Richards (Cybernaut).

(AVENGERS cont.)

"The 50,000 Pound Breakfast" (2-28-68): Cecil Parker (Grover), Yolande Turner (Miss Pegram), David Langton (Sir James Arnall), Pauline Delaney (Mrs. Rhodes), Anneke Wills (Judy), Cardew Robinson (Minister), Eric Woofe (1st assistant), Philippe Monnet (2nd assistant), Richard Curnock (Rhodes).

"Dead Man's Treasure" (3-13-68): Norman Bowler (Mike), Valerie Van Ost (Penny), Neil McCarthy (Carl), Edwin Richfield (Alex), Arthur Lowe (Benstead), Ivor Dean (Bates), Penny Bird (Miss Peabody), Rio Fanning (Danvers), Gerry Crampton (1st guest), Peter J. Elliott (2nd guest).

"The Forget-Me-Knot" (3-20-68): Patrick Kavanagh (Sean), Jeremy Burnham (Simon Filson), Jeremy Young (George Burton), Alan Lake (Karl), John Lee (Dr. Soames), Douglas Sheldon (Brad), Beth Owen (Sally), Leon Lissek (taxi driver), Tony Thawnton (Jenkins), Edward Higgins (the gardener).

"Invasion of the Earthmen" (3-27-68): William Lucas (Gen. Brett), Christian Roberts (Huxton), Lucy Fleming (Emily), Christopher Chittell (Bassin), Wendy Allunutt (Sarah), Warren Clarke (Trump), George Roubicek (Grant).

"The Curious Case of the Countless Clues" (4-3-68): Anthony Bate (Earle), Kenneth Cope (Gardner), Peter Jones (Sir Arthur Doyle), Edward De Souza (Flanders), Tony Selby (Stanley), Tracy Reed (Janice), George A. Cooper (Burgess), Reginald Jessup (Dawson), Jean Inness (Mrs. Peterson), Eve McVeagh (Maude), Gregg Martell (blacksmith), John Rubinstein (boy).

"Split!" (4-10-68): Nigel Davenport (Lord Barnes), Julian Glover (Peter Rooke), Bernard Archard (Dr. Constantine), John G. Heller (Hinnell), Jayne Sofiano (Petra), Steven Scott (Kartovski), Christopher Benjamin (Swindin), Maurice Good (Harry Mercer), Iain Anders (Frank Compton), John Kidd (the butler).

"Get-A-Way" (4-24-68): Andrew Keir (Col. James), Peter Bowles (Ezdorf), Peter Bayliss (Dodge), Terence Longdon (George Neville), Neil Hallett (Paul Ryder), William Wilde (Baxter), Michael Culver (Price), Barry Linehan (Magnus), Michael Elwyn (Lt. Edwards), Robert Russell (Lubin), John Hussey (Peters), Vincent Harding (Rostov), James Belchamber (Bryant).

"Have Guns...Will Haggle" (5-

1-68): Johnny Sekka (Col. Nsonga), Nicola Pagett (Adriana), Jonathan Burn (Conrad), Timothy Bateson (Spencer), Michael Turner (Crayford), Robert Gillespie (life attendant), Roy Stewart (Giles), Peter J. Elliott (Brad).

"Look (Stop Me If You've Heard This One) But There Were These Two Fellers..." (5-8-68): Jimmy Jewel (Maxie Martin), Julian Chagrin (Jennings), Bernard Cribbins (Bradley Marler), John Cleese (Marcus Rugman), William Kendall (Lord Dessington), John Woodvine (Seagrave), Garry Marsh (Brigadier Wiltshire), Richard Young (Sir Jeremy Broadfoot), Talfryn Thomas (Fiery Frederick), Robert James (Merlin), Bill Shine (Cleghorn), Johnny Vyvyan (escapologist), Jay Denyer (tenor), Len Belmont (ventriloquist).

"Game" (9-23-68): Peter Jeffrey (Bristow), Garfield Morgan (Manservant), Aubrey Richards (Prof. Witney), Anthony Newlands (Brig. Wishforth-Brown), Alex Scott (Averman), Geoffrey Russell (Dexter), Achilles Georgiou (student), Desmond Walter-Ellis (manager).

"The Super Secret Cypher Snatch" (9-30-68): John Carlisle (Peters), Ivor Dean (Ferret), Simon Oates (Maskin), Alec Ross (1st guard), Lionel Wheeler (2nd guard), Clifford Earl (Jarret), Donald Gee (Vickers), Allan Cuthbertson (Webster), Nicholas Smith (Lather), Anne Rutter (Betty), Angela Scoular (Myra), Anthony Blackshaw (Davis).

"You'll Catch Your Death" (10-7-68): Roland Culver (Col. Timothy), Charles Lloyd Pack (Dr. Fawcett), Douglas Blackwell (Postman), Fulton Mackay (Glover), Andrew Laurence (Herrick), Fiona Hartford (Janice), Dudley Sutton (Dexter), Peter Bourne (Preece), Hamilton Dyce (Camrose), Bruno Barnabe (Farrar), Sylvia Kay (Matron), Henry McGee (Maidwell), Emma Cochrane (Melanie), Valentine Dyall (Butler), Jennifer Clulow (Georgina), Geoffrey Chater (Seaton), Willoughby Gray (Padley), Royston Tickner (little man).

"Noon-Doomsday" (10-28-68): Ray Brooks (Farrington), T. P. McKenna (Grant), Griffith Jones (Baines), Lyndon Brook (Lyall), Peter Bromilow (Kafka), Peter Halliday (Perrier), Anthony Ainley (Sunley), John Glyn-Jones (Hyde), David Glover (Carson), Lawrence James (Cornwall), Alfred Maron (taxi driver).

"Legacy of Death" (11-4-68): Stratford Johns (Sidney Street), Ferdy Mayne (Baron Von Orlak), Ronald Lacey (Humbert Green), Kynaston Reeves (Dickens), Richard Hurndall (Farrer), John Hollis

(Zoltan), Peter Swanwick (Oppenheimer), Tutte Lemkow (Gorky), Vic Wise (Slattery), Leon Thau (Ho Lung), Teddy Kiss (Winkler), Michael Bilton (Dr. Winter).

"They Keep Killing Steed" (11-11-68): Ian Ogilvy (Baron Von Curt), Ray McAnally (Arcos), Norman Jones (Zerson), Bernard Horsfall (Capt. Smythe), William Ellis, Hal Galili, Rosemary Donnelly, Nicole Shelby, Gloria Connell, Anthony Sheppard, George Ghent, Michael Corcoran, Reg Whitehead, Angharad Rees, Ross Hutchinson.

"Wish You Were Here" (11-18-68): Liam Redmond (Charles Merrydale), Robert Urquhart (Maxwell), Brook Williams (Basil), Dudley Foster (Parker), Richard Caldicot (Mellor), Gary Watson (Kendrick), Derek Newark (Vickers), David Garth (Brevitt), John Cazabon (Mr. Maple), Louise Pajo (Miss Craven), Sandra Fehr (attractive girl).

"False Witness" (11-25-68): Rio Fanning (Land), Barry Warren (Melville), John Atkinson (Brayshaw), William Job (Lord Edgefield), Peter Jesson (Penman), Rhonda Parker (Rhonda), Arthur Pentelow (Dr. Grant), Larry Burns (Gould), Jimmy Gardner (little man), Dan Meaden (Sloman), Michael Lees (Plummer), John Bennett (Sykes), Tony Steedman (Sir Joseph), Simon Lack (Nesbitt), Terry Eliot (Amanda).

"All Done with Mirrors" (12-2-68): Joanna Jones (Pandora), Bruno Elrington (Gozzo), Anthony Dutton (Seligman), Dinsdale Landen (Watney), Nora Nicholson (Miss Emily), Peter Copley (Sparshott), David Grey (Williams), Tenniel Evans (Carswell), Peter Thomas (Kettridge), Liane Aukin (Miss Tiddiman), Desmond Jordan (Guthrie), Edwin Richfield (Barlow), Michael Trubshawe (Col. Withers), Graham Askley (Markin), Michael Nightingale (Real Colonel), Robert Sidaway (Real Barlow).

"Whoever Shot Poor George Oblique Stroke XR40?" (12-9-68): Dennis Price (Jason), Clifford Evans (Sir Wilfred Pelley), Judy Parfitt (Loris), Anthony Nicholls (Ardmore), Frank Windsor (Tobin), Valerie Leon (Betty), Adrian Ropes (Baines), Arthur Cox (anaesthetist), Tony Wright (Keller), John Porter-Davison (Jacobs), Jacky Allouis (Jill).

"The Rotters" (12-16-68): Gerald Sim (Kenneth), Eric Barker (Pym), Jerome Willis (George), John Nettleton (Palmer), Frank Middlemass (Sawbow), Dervis Ward, Toni Gilpin, Harold Innocent, Amy Dalby, Noel Davis,

John Scott, John Stone, Charles Morgan, Harry Hutchinson.

"Killer" (12-30-68): Jennifer Croxton (Lady Diana Forbes-Blakeney), Grant Taylor (Merridon), William Franklyn (Brinstead), Charles Houston (Gillers), Richard Wattis (Clarke), Oliver MacGreevy, Anthony Valentine, Harry Towb, Michael Ward, Michael McStay, John Bailey, James Bree, Jonathan Elsom, Clive Graham.

"My Wildest Dream" (1-6-69): Peter Vaughan (Jaeger), Derek Godfrey (Tobias), Edward Fox (Chilcott), Philip Madoc (Slater), Susan Travers (Nurse Owen), Michael David (Reece), Murray Hayne (Gibbons), Hugh Moxley (Peregrine), Tom Kempinski (Dyson), John Savident (Winthrop).

"The Interrogators" (1-20-69): Christopher Lee (Col. Mannering), David Sumner (Minnow), Glynn Edwards (Blackie), Philip Bond (Caspar), Neil McCarthy (Rasker), Neil Stacy (Mullard), Neil Wilson (Norton), Cecil Cheng (Captain Soo), Cardew Robinson (Mr. Puffin), Mark Elwes (naval officer), David Richards (RAF Officer).

"The Morning After" (1-27-69): Peter Barkworth (Jimmy Merlin), Penelope Horner (Jenny Firston), Joss Ackland (Brigadier Hansing), Brian Blessed (Sgt. Hearn), Philip Dunbar (Yates), Donald Douglas (Major Parsons), Jonathan Scott (Harold Cartney).

"Love All" (2-3-69): Robert Harris (Sir Rodney Kellogg), Veronica Strong (Martha Roberts), Terence Alexander (Bromfield), Brian Oulton (Tait), Patsy Rowlands (Thelma), Frank Gatliff, Ann Rye, Zuelma Dene, Norman Pitt, Robin Tolhurst, David Baron, Peter Stephens, John Cobner, Larry Taylor.

"Take Me to Your Leader" (2-10-69): Henry Stamper (Major Glasgow), Patrick Barr (Stonehouse), Michael Hawkins (Shepherd), Michael Robbins (Cavel), John Ronane (Captain Tim), Penelope Keith, Hugh Cross, Elisabeth Robillard, Sheila Hammond, Raymond Adamson, Cliff Diggins, Bryan Kendrick, Matthew Long, Wilfred Boyle.

"Fog" (2-17-69): David Bird (Osgood), Nigel Green (Armstrong), Guy Rolfe (Travers), Paul Whitsun-Jones (Sanders), Terence Brady (Carstairs), David Lodge (Maskell), Norman Chappell (Fowler), Frank Sieman, Virginia Clay, John Garrie, Patsy Smart, Bernard Severn, John Barrard, Stan Jay, Arnold Diamond, Frederick Peisley, William Lyon Brown.

"Stay Tuned" (2-24-69): Gary Bond

(AVENGERS cont.) (Proctor), Kate
O'Mara (Lisa), Duncan Lamont (Wilke),
Howard Marion-Crawford (Collins), I-
ris Russell (Father), Denise Buckley
(Sally), Harold Kasket (Dr. Meitner),
Roger Delgado (Kreer), Ewan Roberts
(Travers), Patrick Westwood (taxi dri-
ver).

"Who Was That Man I Saw You
With" (3-3-69): William Marlowe (Fairfax), Ralph Michael (Gen. Hesketh),
Alan Browning (Zaroff), Alan MacNaughtan (Gilpin), Bryan Marshall (Phillip-
son), Alan Wheatley (Dangerfield), Aimee Delamain (Miss Culpepper), Richard Owens (Perowne), Nita Lorraine
(Kate), Ralph Ball (Hamilton), Neville
Marten (Pye), Ken Haward (Powell).

"Pandora" (3-10-69): Julian Glo-
ver (Rupert), James Cossins (Henry),
Kathleen Byron (Miss Faversham), John
Laurie (Juniper), Anthony Roye (Petti-
grew), Geoffrey Whitehead (Carter),
Peter Madden (Lasindall), Reginald
Barratt (Murray), Raymond Burke
(Young Gregory).

"Homicide and Old Lace" (3-17-
69): Joyce Carey (Harriet), Gerald
Harper (Col. Corf), Mary Merrall
(Georgina), Keith Baxter (Dunbar), Edward Brayshaw (Fuller), Donald Pickering (Cartwright), Bryan Mosley, Mark
London, Kristopher Kum, Gertan Klauber, Bari Jonson, Kevork Malikyan,
John Rapley, Stephen Hubay, Anne Rutter.

"Thingumajig" (3-24-69): Jeremy
Lloyd (Shelly), Iain Cuthbertson (Kruger), John Horsley (Dr. Grant), Russell Waters (Pike), Hugh Manning (Major Starr), Willoughby Goddard (Truman), Edward Burnham (Brett), Dora
Reisser (Inge), Vernon Dobtcheff (Stenson), Michael McKevitt (Philips), Neville Hughes (William), Harry Shacklock (Bill), John Moore (Greer).

"Requiem" (3-31-69): Angela
Douglas (Miranda), John Cairney (Firth),
John Paul (Wells), Katja Wyeth (Jil),
Mike Lewin (Barrett), Denis Shaw (Mur-
ray), Harvey Ashby (Bobby), Terence
Sewards (Rista), John Baker (Vicar).

"Take-Over" (4-14-69): Tom Adams (Grenville), Elisabeth Sellers (Laura Bassett), Hilary Pritchard (Circe),
Michael Gwynn (Bill), Garfield Morgan
(Sexton), Keith Buckley (Lomax), Anthony Sagar (Clifford), John Comer (Groom).

"Bizarre" (4-21-69): Roy Kinnear (Bagpipes Happychap), Sally Nesbitt (Helen), Fulton Mackay (Master),
James Kerry (Cordell), John Sharp
(Jupp), George Innes (Shaw), Michael

Balfour (Tom), Sheila Burrell (Mrs.
Jupp), Ron Pember (Charley), Patrick
Connor (Bob).

BATMAN. 1966-68. Adam West (Bruce
Wayne/Batman), Burt Ward (Dick
Grayson/Robin), Alan Napier (Alfred),
Neil Hamilton (Commissioner Gordon),
Madge Blake (Aunt Harriet Cooper),
Stafford Repp (Chief O'Hara), Yvonne
Craig (Barbara Gordon/Batgirl) 67-
68.

"Hey Diddle Riddle/Smack in the
Middle" (1-12-66 & 1-13-66): Frank
Gorshin (Riddler), Jill St. John (Molly),
Allen Jaffe, Michael Fox.

"Fine Feathered Finks/The Penguin's a Jinx" (1-19-66 & 1-20-66): Burgess Meredith (the Penguin), Leslie Parrish (Dawn), Dan Tobin (Mr. Jay), Walter Burke (Sparrow), Lewis Charles
(Hawkeye).

"The Joker Is Wild/Batman Gets
Riled" (1-26-66 & 1-27-66): Cesar Romero (the Joker), Nancy Kovack (Queenie), David Lewis (Warden Crichton),
Jerry Dunphy (Fred), Jonathan Hole.

"Instant Freeze/Rats Like Cheese"
(2-2-66 & 2-3-66): George Sanders (Mr.
Freeze), Selby Grant (Princess Sandra),
Robert Hogan, Troy Melton.

"Zelda the Great/A Death Worse
Than Fate" (2-9-66 & 2-10-66): Ann
Baxter (Zelda), Jack Kruschen (Eivol
Ekdol), Barbara Heller (Hillary Stone-
win).

"A Riddle a Day Keeps the Riddler
Away/When the Rat's Away, the Mice
Will Play" (2-16-66 & 2-17-66): Frank
Gorshin (the Riddler), Susan Silo (Mou-
sey), Reginald Denny, Tim Herbert.

"The Thirteenth Hat/Batman Stands
Pat" (2-23-66 & 2-24-66): David Wayne
(Jervis Tetch, the Mad Hatter), Diane
McBain (Lisa), Gil Perkins (Dicer), Ro-
land La Starza (Cappy), Monique Le-
maire, Sandra Wells.

"The Joker Goes to School/He
Meets His Match, the Grizzly Ghoul" (3-
2-66 & 3-3-66): Cesar Romero (the Jo-
ker), Donna Loren (Susie), Sydney Smith
(Vandergilt), Kip King (Nick), Bryan O'-
Byrne (Schoolfield).

"True or Falseface/Super Rat Race"
(3-9-66 & 3-10-66): Malachi Throne
(Falseface), Myrna Fahey (Blaze), S.
John Launer (George W. Ladd), Larry
Owens (Bevans), Joe Brooks (fat man),
Billy Curtis (midget), Patrick Whyte
(curator), Brenda Howard.

"The Purr-fect Crime/Better Luck
Next Time" (3-17-66 & 3-18-66): Julie
Newmar (Catwoman), Jock Mahoney (Leo),

Ralph Manza (Felix), Harry Holcomb (Mark Andrews).

"The Penguin Goes Straight/Not Yet, He Ain't" (3-23-66 & 3-24-66): Burgess Meredith (the Penguin), Kathleen Crowley (Sophia Starr), Al Checco (Dove), Harvey Lembeck (Eagle-Eye), William Beckley (Reggie), Bill Welsh (newsman), Jim Drum (policeman).

"Ring of Wax/Give 'Em the Axe" (3-30-66 & 3-31-66): Frank Gorshin (the Riddler), Elizabeth Harrower (Miss Prentice), Linda Scott (Moth), Michael Greene (Matches), Ann Ayers (Mme. Soleil).

"The Joker Trumps an Ace/Batman Sets the Pace" (4-6-66 & 4-7-66): Cesar Romero (the Joker), Dan Seymour (Maharajah), Jane Wald (Jill), Tol Avery (Prescott Belmont), Angela Greene (Mrs. Belmont), Norm Alden (Lookout), Jacques Roux (manager), Bebe Louie (clerk), Owen Buch (Caddy).

"The Curse of Tut/The Pharaoh's in a Rut" (4-13-66 & 4-14-66): Victor Buono (King Tut), Ziva Rodann (Queen Nefertiti), Don 'Red' Barry (Vizier), Olan Soule (newscaster), Frank Christi (Scrivener), Emanuel Thomas.

"The Bookworm Turns/While Gotham City Burns" (4-20-66 & 4-21-66): Roddy McDowall (Bookworm), Francine York (Lydia Limpet), John Crawford (Printer's Devil), Byron Keith, Jan Peters, Jerry Lewis.

"Death in Slow Motion/The Riddler's False Notion" (4-27-66 & 4-28-66): Frank Gorshin (the Riddler), Sherry Jackson (Pauline), Francis X. Bushman (Van Jones), Theo Marcuse (Von Bloheim), Richard Bakalyan (C.B.), Walter Woolf King (manager), Jim Begg (baker), Burt Brandon.

"Fine Finny Fiends/Batman Makes the Scene" (5-4-66 & 5-5-66): Burgess Meredith (the Penguin), Julie Gregg (Finella), Victor Lunden (Octopus), Dal Jenkins (Shark), Louie Elias (Swordfish), Howard Wendell (millionaire), Bill Williams (multi-millionaire), Lisa Mitchell (Miss Natural Resources).

"Shoot a Crooked Arrow/Walk the Straight and Narrow" (9-7-66 & 9-8-66): Art Carney (Archer), Sam Jaffe (Albert A. Aardvark), Barbara Nichols (Maid Marilyn), Robert Cornthwaite (Alan A. Dale), Loren Ewing (Big John), Doodles Weaver (Crier Tuck), Arch Moore (cameo), Dick Clark (cameo).

"Hot Off the Griddle/The Cat and the Fiddle" (9-14-66 & 9-15-66): Julie Newmar (Catwoman), Jack Kelly (Jack O'Shea), George Barrows (Charles),

Charles Horvath (Thomas), Buck Kartalian (John), David Fresco (Zubin Zucchini), Edy Williams (Hostess).

"The Minstrel's Shakedown/Barbecued Batman" (9-21-66 & 9-22-66): Van Johnson (the Minstrel), Leslie Perkins (Amanda), John Gallaudet (Courtland), Norm Grabowski (Treble), Remo Pisani (Bass), Army Archerd (Putnam), James O'Hara (man), Phyllis Diller (cameo), Del Moore (cameo).

"The Spell of Tut/Tut's Case Is Shut" (9-28-66 & 9-29-66): Victor Buono (King Tut), Michael Pataki (Amenophis Twefik), Mariana Hill (Cleo Patrick), Sid Haig (Royal Apothecary), Peter Mamakos (Royal Lapidary), Boyd Santell (Sethos), Bea Bradley (Susan Smith).

"The Greatest Mother of Them All/Ma Parker" (10-5-66 & 10-6-66): Shelley Winters (Ma Parker), Tisha Sterling (Legs), Mike Vandever (Mad Dog), James Griffith (Tiger), Robert Biheller (Pretty Boy), Peter Brooks (Machine Gun), David Lewis (Warden Crichton), Julie Newmar (Catwoman).

"The Clock King's Crazy Crimes/The Clock King Gets Crowned" (10-12-66 & 10-13-66): Walter Slezak (the Clock King), Eileen O'Neill (Millie Second), Herb Anderson (Harry Hummert), Ivan Triesault (Benson Parkhurst), Jerry Doggett (Forbes), Sammy Davis, Jr. (cameo), Linda Lorimer, Roger Bacon.

"An Egg Grows in Gotham/The Yegg Foes in Gotham" (10-19-66 & 10-20-66): Vincent Price (Egghead), Gail Hire (Miss Bacon), Edward Everett Horton (Chief Screaming Eagle), Steve Dunne (Tim Tyler), Ben Welden (Foo Long), Albert Carrier (Pete Savage), Gene Dynarski (Benedict), Bill Dana (cameo), Ben Alexander (cameo), Mae Clark (cameo), George Fenneman (cameo).

"The Devil's Fingers/The Dead Ringers" (10-26-66 & 10-27-66): Liberace (Chandell/Harry), Marilyn Hanold (Doe), Edy Williams (Rae), Sivi Aberg (Mimi), James Millhollin (Alfred Slye).

"Hizzoner the Penguin/Dizzoner the Penguin" (11-2-66 & 11-3-66): Burgess Meredith (the Penguin), Woodrow Parfrey (Rooper), Cindy Malone (Lulu), George Furth (Gallus), Fuzzy Knight (cameo), Dennis James (cameo), Don Wilson (cameo), Little Egypt (cameo), Allen Ludden (cameo), Chet Huntley (cameo), Jack Bailey (cameo), Paul Revere and the Raiders (cameo).

"Green Ice/Deep Freeze" (11-9-66 & 11-10-66): Otto Preminger (Mr. Freeze), Marie Windsor (Nellie), Dee Hartford (Miss Iceland), Byron Keith,

(BATMAN cont.) Nicky Blair.
"The Impractical Joker/The Joker's Provoker" (11-16-66 & 11-17-66):
Cesar Romero (the Joker), Kathy Kersh (Cornelia), Christopher Cary (Angus Ferguson), Louis Quinn (Latch), Larry Anthony (Bolt), Howard Duff (cameo).
"Marsha, Queen of Diamonds/Marsha's Scheme of Diamonds" (11-23-66 & 11-24-66): Carolyn Jones (Marsha), Estelle Winwood (Aunt Hilda), Woody Strode (Grand Mogul), James O'Hara (Sgt. O'Leary), H. Douglas (announcer).
"Come Back Shame/It's the Way You Play the Game" (11-30-66 & 12-1-66): Cliff Robertson (Shame), Joan Staley (Okie Annie), Jack Carter (Hot Rod Harry).
"The Penguin's Nest/The Bird's Last Jest" (12-7-66 & 12-8-66): Burgess Meredith (the Penguin), Grace Gaynor (Chickadee), Voltaire Perkins (Judge Moot), Vito Scotti (Matey Dee), Lane Bradford (Cordy Blue), James O'Hara (cop), Ted Cassidy (cameo).
"The Cat's Meow/The Bat's Kow Tow" (12-14-66 & 12-15-66): Julie Newmar (Catwoman), Joe Flynn (Benton Belgoody), Tom Castronova (Meanie), Chuck Henderson (Miney), Sharya Wynters (Eenie), Chad Stuart (himself), Jeremy Clyde (himself), Judy Stragis.
"The Puzzles Are Coming/The Duo Is Slumming" (12-21-66 & 12-22-66): Maurice Evans (the Puzzler), Barbara Stuart (Rocket O'Rourke), Paul Smith (Knab), Sonny Bono (cameo), Cher (cameo).
"The Sandman Cometh/The Catwoman Goeth" (12-28-66 & 12-29-66): Michael Rennie (the Sandman), Julie Newmar (Catwoman), Richard Peel (Snooze), Spring Byington (J. Pauline), Tony Ballen (Nap), Gypsy Rose Lee (cameo), Don Ho (cameo), Pat Becker, Jeanie Moore.
"The Contaminated Cowl/The Mad Hatter Runs Afoul" (1-4-67 & 1-5-67): David Wayne (Jervis Tetch, the Mad Hatter), Jean Hale (Polly), Barbara Morrison (Hattie Hatfield), Lennie Breman (Benny), Victor Ames (Skimmer).
"The Zodiac Crimes/The Joker's Hard Times/The Penguin Declines" (1-11-67, 1-12-67 & 1-18-67): Burgess Meredith (the Penguin), Cesar Romero (the Joker), Terry Moore (Venus), Joe Di Reda (Mars), Hal Baylor (Mercury), Dick Crockett, Charles Fredericks, Charles Picerni.
"That Darn Catwoman/Scat, Darn Catwoman" (1-19-67 & 1-25-67): Julie Newmar (Catwoman), Leslie Gore (Pus-

sycat), J. Pat O'Malley (Pat Pending), Jock Gaynor (Spade), George Sawaya (Templar), Allen Jenkins (Little Al).
"Penguin Is a Girl's Best Friend/Penguin Sets a Trend/Penguin's Disasterous End" (1-26-67, 2-1-67 & 2-2-67): Burgess Meredith (the Penguin), Carolyn Jones (Marsha), Estelle Winwood (Aunt Hilda), Alan Reed (Gen. MacGruder), Bob Hastings (Beasley).
"Batman's Anniversary/A Riddling Controversy" (2-8-67 & 2-9-67): John Astin (the Riddler), Deanna Lund (Anna Gram), Martin Kosleck (Prof. Charm), Ken Scott (Down), Jim Lefebvre (Across).
"The Joker's Last Laugh/The Joker's Epitaph" (2-15-67 & 2-16-67): Cesar Romero (the Joker), Phyllis Douglas (Josephin Miller), Lawrence Montaigne (Mr. Glee), J. Edward McKinley (Mr. Flamm).
"Catwoman Goes to College/Batman Displays His Knowledge" (2-22-67 & 2-23-67): Julie Newmar (Catwoman), Paul Mantee (Cornell), Sheldon Allman (Penn), Jacques Bergerac (Fat Freddy), Whitney Blake (Amber Forever), Paul Picerni (Brown), Art Linkletter (cameo).
"A Piece of the Action/Batman's Satisfaction" (3-1-67 & 3-2-67): Van Williams (the Green Hornet), Bruce Lee (Kato), Roger C. Carmel (Col. Gumm), Diane McBain (Pinky Pinkston), Edward G. Robinson (cameo), Alex Rocco.
"King Tut's Coup/Batman's Waterloo" (3-8-67 & 3-9-67): Victor Buono (King Tut), Grace Lee Whitney (Neila), Lee Meriwether (Lisa), Tim O'Kelly (Jester), Suzy Knickerbocker (cameo), Tol Avery, Lloyd Haynes, James O'Hara.
"Black Widow Strikes Again/Caught in the Spider's Den" (3-15-67 & 3-16-67): Tallulah Bankhead (Mrs. Max Black), Don 'Red' Barry (Tarantula), Grady Sutton (Irving Cash), Mike Lane (Daddy Long Legs), Al Ferrara (Trap Door), Meg Wylie (Grandma), George Raft (cameo).
"Pop Goes the Joker/Flop Goes the Joker" (3-22-67 & 3-23-67): Cesar Romero (the Joker), Diana Ivarson (Baby Jane Towser), Reginald Gardiner (Park), Jan Arvan.
"Ice Spy/The Duo Defy" (3-29-67 & 3-30-67): Eli Wallach (Mr. Freeze), Leslie Parrish (Glacia Glaze), Elisha Cook, Jr. (Prof. Isaacson), H.M. Wynant (Frosty), John Archer (Carlisle).
"Enter Batgirl, Exit Penguin" (9-14-67): Burgess Meredith (the Penguin), Elizabeth Harrower.
"Ring Around the Riddler" (9-21-67): Frank Gorshin (the Riddler), Joan

Collins (Siren), Peggy Ann Garner (Betsy Boldface), Jerry Quarry (cameo), Armando Ramos (cameo), Paul Rojas (cameo), James Brolin.
"The Wail of the Siren" (9-28-67): Joan Collins (Siren), Mike Mazurki.
"The Sport of Penguins/A Horse of Another Color" (10-5-67 & 10-12-67): Burgess Meredith (the Penguin), Ethel Merman (Lola Lasagne), Horace McMahon.
"The Unkindest Tut of All" (10-19-67): Victor Buono (King Tut), Patti Gilbert (Shirley), James Gammon (Osiris), Cathleen Cordell (Librarian).
"Louie the Lilac" (10-26-67): Milton Berle (Louie the Lilac), Lisa Seagram (Lila), Dick Bakalyan (Arbutus), Karl Lukas (Acacia), Schuyler Aubrey (Primrose).
"The Oog and I/How to Hatch a Dinosaur" (11-2-67 & 11-9-67): Vincent Price (Egghead), Anne Baxter (Olga), Alfred Dennis.
"Surf's Up! Joker's Under!" (11-16-67): Cesar Romero (the Joker), Sivi Aberg (Undine).
"The Londinium Larcenies/The Foggiest Notion/The Bloody Tower" (11-23-67, 11-30-67 & 12-7-67): Rudy Vallee (Lord Phogg), Glynis Johns (Lady Penelope Peasoup), Lyn Peters (Prudence), Lynley Lawrence (Kit), Stacey Maxwell (Rosamond), Aleta Rotell (Daisy), Larry Anthony (Digby), Maurice Dallimore (Watson), Monty Landis (Basil), Harvey Jason (Scudder).
"Catwoman's Dressed to Kill" (12-14-67): Eartha Kitt (Catwoman), Rudi Gernreich, James Griffith.
"The Ogg Couple" (12-21-67): Vincent Price (Egghead), Anne Baxter (Olga), Violet Carlson.
"The Funny Feline Felonies" (12-28-67): Eartha Kitt (the Catwoman), Cesar Romero (the Joker), Dick Kallman (Little Louie Kallman), Joe E. Ross (Fred Fandango), Ronald Long (Karnaby Katz), Sandy Kevin (Giggler), Bobby Hall (Laughter), David Lewis (Warden Crichton).
"The Joke's on Catwoman" (1-4-68): Eartha Kitt (Catwoman), Cesar Romero (the Joker), Pierre Salinger (Lucky Pierre).
"Louie's Lethal Lilac Time" (1-11-68): Milton Berle (Louie the Lilac), Nobu McCarthy (Lotus), Percy Helton, Ronald Knight, John Dennis.
"Nora Clavicle and Her Ladies' Crime Club" (1-18-68): Barbara Rush (Nora Clavicle), June Wilkinson (Evelina).

"Penguin's Clean Sweep" (1-25-68): Burgess Meredith (the Penguin), John Vivyan (bank director), John Beradino (doctor), Monique Van Vooren (Miss Clean), Charles Dierkop (Dustbag).
"The Great Escape/The Great Train Robbery" (2-1-68 & 2-8-68): Cliff Robertson (Shame), Dina Merrill (Calamity Jan), Hermione Baddeley (Frontier Fanny), Barry Dennen (Fred), Dorothy Kirsten (cameo), Brian Sullivan (cameo).
"I'll Be a Mummy's Uncle" (2-22-68): Victor Buono (King Tut), Angela Dorian (Florence of Arabia), Henry Youngman (cameo).
"The Joker's Flying Saucer" (2-29-68): Cesar Romero (the Joker), Corinne Calvet (Emerald), Richard Bakalyan (Verdigris), Jeff Burton (Shamrock), Byron Keith (Mayor Linseed), Tony Gardner (Chartreuse), Fritz Feld (Prof. Greenleaf).
"The Entrancing Dr. Cassandra" (3-7-68): Ida Lupino (Dr. Cassandra), Howard Duff (Cabala), David Lewis (Warden Crichton).
"Minerva, Mayhem and Millionaires" (3-14-68): Zsa Zsa Gabor (Minerva), Jacques Bergerac (Freddie the Fence), Bill Smith (Adonis), Mark Bailey (Apollo), All Ferrara (Atlas), Yvonne Arnett (Aphrodite), William Dozier (Monroe).

BATTLESTAR GALACTICA. 1978-79.
Richard Hatch (Captain Apollo), Dirk Benedict (Lt. Starbuck), Lorne Greene (Commander Adama), Herb Jefferson, Jr. (Lt. Boomer), Maren Jensen (Athena), Laurette Spang (Cassiopea), Tony Swartz (Flight Sgt. Jolly), Noah Hathaway (Boxey), Terry Carter (Col. Tigh), John Colicos (Count Baltar), Sarah Rush (Flight Corp. Rigel), David Greenan (Flight Officer Omega), Anne Lockhart (Sheba), George Murdock (Dr. Salik), John Dullaghan (Dr. Wilker), Janet Louise Johnson (Brie), Jack Stauffer (Bojay), Ed Begley, Jr. (Greenbean), Patrick Macnee (Voice of Imperious Leader), Dick Durock (Imperious Leader), Jonathan Harris (Voice of Lucifer).
"Lost Planet of the Gods" (9-24-78 & 10-1-78): Jane Seymour (Serina).
"The Lost Warrior" (10-8-78): Kathy Cannon (Bella), Lance LeGault (Bootees), Claude Earl Jones (LeCerta), Red West (Marco), Johnny Timko (Puppis), Rex Cutter (Red-Eye).
"The Long Patrol" (10-15-78): James Whitmore, Jr. (Robber), Ted Gehring (Croad), Sean McClory (Assault), Tasha Martell (Adultress), Cathy Paine

(BATTLESTAR GALACTICA cont.)
(Cora the Computer), John Holland (waiter).

"Gun on Ice Planet Zero" (10-22-78 & 10-29-78): Roy Thinnes (Croft), James Olson (Thane), Dan O'Herlihy (Dr. Ravashol), Denny Miller (Ser Five Nine), Christine Belford (Leda), Britt Ekland (Tenna), Larry Manetti (Giles), Curtis Credel (Haals), Richard Lynch (Wolfe).

"The Magnificent Warrior" (11-12-78): Brett Somers (Siress Belloby), Barry Nelson (Bogan), Eric Server (Dipper), Dennis Fimple (Duggy).

"The Young Lords" (11-19-78): Bruce Glover (Megan), Charles Bloom (Kyle), Audrey Landers (Miri), Adam Man (Nilz), Brigitte Muller (Ariadne).

"The Living Legend" (11-26-78 & 12-3-78): Lloyd Bridges (Cain), Rod Haase (Tolan), Junero Jennings (Pegasus launch officer).

"Fire in Space" (12-17-78): William Bryant (Fireleader), Jeff MacKay (crewman).

"War of the Gods" (1-14-79 & 1-21-79): Patrick Macnee (Count Iblis), Kirk Alyn (old man), Bruce Wright (guard), Paul Coufos (pilot), John Williams (statesman), Norman Stuart (2nd statesman), Paula Victor (old woman), Olan Soule (Carmichael).

"The Man with Nine Lives" (1-28-79): Fred Astaire (Chameleon), Anne Jeffreys (Siress Blassie), Lance LeGault (Maga), Robert Feero (Bora), Anthony DeLongis (Taba), Dan Barton (crewman), Patricia Stich (Zara).

"Murder on the Rising Star" (2-18-79): Frank Ashmore (Ortega), Luman Ward (Pallon), Brock Peters (Solon), Patricia Stitch (Zara), W. K. Stratton (Barton).

"Greetings from Earth" (2-25-79): Randy Mantooth (Michael), Bobby Van (Hector), Ray Bolger (Vector), Kelly Harmon (Sarah), Murray Matheson (Geller), Lloyd Bochner (Leiter).

"Baltar's Escape" (3-11-79): Ina Balin (Siress Tinia), Lloyd Bochner (Leiter), John Hoyt (Dombra), Lance LeGault (Maga), Robert Feero (Bora), Anthony De Longis (Taba).

"Experiment in Terra" (3-18-79): Edward Mulhare (John), Melody Anderson (Brenda), Nehemiah Persoff (Supreme Commander), Ken Swofford (Max), Logan Ramsay (Moore), Peter MacLean (President).

"Take the Celestra" (4-1-79): Ana Alicia (Aurora), Paul Fix (Kronus), Nick Holt (Charka), Randy Stumpf (Damon), Richard Styles (Hermes).

"The Hand of God" (4-29-79).

BELL, BOOK AND CANDLE. Pilot (9-8-76): Yvette Mimieux (Gillian Holroyd), Michael Murphy (Alex Brandt), Doris Roberts (Aunt Enid), John Pleshette (Nicky Holroyd), Bridget Hanley (Lois), Susan Sullivan (Rosemary), Edward Andrews (Bishop Fairbarn), Dori Whitaker (Melissa).

BEWITCHED. 1964-72. Elizabeth Montgomery (Samantha Stevens), Dick York (Darrin Stevens) 64-69, Dick Sargent (Darrin Stevens) 69-72, David White (Larry Tate), Agnes Moorehead (Endora), Alice Pearce (Gladys Kravitz) 64-66, Sandra Gould (Gladys Kravitz) 66-72, George Tobias (Abner Kravitz), Irene Vernon (Louise Tate), Marion Lorne (Aunt Clara) 64-68, Maurice Evans (Maurice) semi-regular, Paul Lynde (Uncle Arthur) semi-regular, Bernard Fox (Dr. Bombay) semi-regular, Robert F. Simon (Frank Stevens) 66-68 semi-regular, Roy Roberts (Frank Stevens) 68-72 semi, Mabel Albertson (Phyllis Stevens) semi-regular, Alice Ghostley (Esmeralda) 68-72 semi-regular.

BEYOND WESTWORLD. 1980. Jim McMullan (John Moore), James Wainwright (Simon Quaid), Connie Sellecca (Pamela Williams), William Jordan (Prof. Joseph Oppenheimer), Severn Darden (Foley), Ann McCurry (Roberta), S. Newton Anderson (Scotty).

"Westworld Destroyed" (3-5-80): Judith Chapman (Laura Garvey), Stewart Moss (Foley), Dennis Holahan (Capt. Farrell), Morgan Paull (Parker), John Kirby (Dudley), Alex Kubik (gunfighter), Mo Lauren (Jan), Nicholas Guest (sailor), Edward Coch, Jr. (chubby gunfighter), Paul Henry Itkin (Horton), Cassandra Peterson (dance hall girl), Larry Levine (technician).

"My Brother's Keeper" (3-12-80): Jeff Cooper (Dean Stoner), Christopher Connelly (Nick Stoner), John Shearin (Jason), Denny Miller (Earl), Bobby Van (Danny), Jack Carter (Charles Vincent), Anthony Davis (Mike Roth), Delvin Williams (End).

"Sound of Terror" (3-19-80): Ronee Blakley (Ruth Avery), Rene Auberjonois (Power), Dirk Blocker (Mace), Lawrence Casey (Ryder), Robert Ayres (Spooner), Louis Welch (Bobby Lee), Dewayne Jessie (Lingo), Sirri Murad (Hakim Fadar), Mary Carver (head nurse).

BIG TOWN.
"Comic Book Murder" (6-8-55):
Mark Stevens, Barry Kelley, Alan Reed,
Jeanette Nolan, Jack Klugman.

BIG FOOT AND WILD BOY. 1977-79.
Ray Young (Big Foot), Joseph Butcher
(Wild Boy), Yvonne Regalado (Cindy),
Monika Ramirez (Suzie).

BIONIC WOMAN, THE. 1976-78. Lind-
say Wagner (Jaime Sommers), Ri-
chard Anderson (Oscar Goldman),
Martin E. Brooks (Dr. Rudy Welles).
"Welcome Home, Jaime" Part
Two (1-21-76): Dennis Patrick (Carl-
ton Harris), Kip Niven (Donald Harris),
Gordon Jump (Charlet Butler), Martha
Scott (Helen Elgin), Ford Rainey (Jim
Elgin).
"Angel of Mercy" (1-28-76): Andy
Griffith (Jack Starkey), Claudio Marti-
nez (Julio), Jean Allison (Judith More-
house), James Karen (George More-
house), Bert Santos (guerrilla), Paul
Berrones (wounded soldier).
"A Thing of the Past" (2-18-76):
Donald O'Connor (Harry Anderson), Ro-
ger Perry (Stone), Don Gordon (Morgan),
W. T. Zacha (Raines), Lee Majors
(Steve Austin), Brian Cutler (Major
Mills), Robbie Walcott (Mark), Lori
Busk (Caroline), Christian Juttner (Ted-
dy), Alycia Gardner (Gwen).
"Claws" (2-25-76): Jack Kelly
(Charles Keys), William Schallert (Un-
cle Bill), Alicia Fleer (Katie), Tippi
Hedren (Susan Victor), Mills Watson
(Sheriff).
"The Deadly Missiles" (3-3-76):
Forrest Tucker (J. T. Connors), Lee
Majors (Steve Austin), Ben Piazza (War-
ren Rayker), Gary McLarty (guard),
Alicia Fleer (Katie), Christian Juttner
(Teddy).
"Bionic Beauty" (3-17-76): Bert
Parks (Ray Raymond), Martha Scott
(Helen Elgin), Helen Craig (Mrs. Bel-
ding), Gary Crosby (stage manager),
Cassie Yates (Miss Florida), Charlotte
Moore (reporter).
"Jaime's Mother" (3-24-76): Nor-
ma Connolly (Mrs. Noah), Barbara Rush
(Ann), Sam Chew, Jr. (security agent),
Joseph George (Vic Boylin), Dan Barton
(Henderson).
"Winning Is Everything" (4-7-76):
John Elerick (Rim Sanders), Alejandro
Rey (Carlo Scappini), Nancy Jeris (Rus-
sian woman), Frank Cala (bartender).
"Canyon of Death" (4-14-76):
Guillermo San Juan (Paco), Gary Col-
lins (Mallory), Paul Cavonis (Hender-

son), Don McGovern (Briggs), Nina Wein-
traub (Felicity).
"Fly Jaime" (5-5-76): Jerry Doug-
las (Connors), Vito Scotti (Romero),
Spencer Milligan (Reed), Arline Ander-
son (Mrs. Griffith), Christopher Stone
(Marlow), Dick Valentin (pilot), Jim
Raymond (co-pilot).
"The Jailing of Jaime" (5-12-76):
Barry Sullivan (Dr. Hatch), Philip Abbott
(John Naud), Skip Homeier (Investigator
Gregory), Ron Hayes (Carlson), Ross
Elliott (Gen. Partridge), Anne Schedeen
(Cindy Wilson), Sam Chew, Jr. (Mark
Russell), Tom Bower (Red Ryan).
"Mirror Image" (5-19-76): Don
Porter (Dr. James Courtney), Lindsay
Wagner (Lisa Galloway), Terry Kiser
(Mathews), John Fink (Perkins), Herb
Jefferson, Jr. (Bexley), Sam Chew, Jr.
(Mark Russell), Fuddle Bagley (barten-
der), Harry Wier (man in bar), Christo-
pher Barrett (intern).
"The Ghost Hunter" (5-26-76):
Paul Shenar (Dr. Alan Cory), Kristy
McNichol (Amanda Cory), Bo Brundin
(Emil Laslo), Merry Loomis (nurse),
Susan Fleming (Lisa).
"The Return of Bigfoot" Part Two
(9-22-76): Lee Majors (Steve Austin),
Sandy Duncan (Gillian), John Saxon (Ned-
lik), Stefanie Powers (Shalon), Ted Cas-
sidy (Bigfoot), Charles Cyphers (Faler),
Severn Darden (Apploy).
"In This Corner, Jaime Sommers"
(9-29-76): Norman Fell (Bigelow), Mar-
cia Lewis (April Armitage), Marcia Sha-
piro (Mary Maddox), Marj Dusay (Dr.
Brandes), Margaret Shocklee (Esther),
Lew Palter (announcer).
"Assault on the Princess" (10-6-
76): Ed Nelson (Lucky Harrison), Vito
Scotti (Romero), John Durren (Grover),
Steve Kanaly (Tanner), Dick Dinman
(bartender), Tony Giorgio (Creighton),
Ron Wilson (Joe).
"Road to Nashville" (10-20-76):
Hoyt Axton (Big Buck Buckley), Doc Se-
verinsen (Muffin Calhoun), Fionnuala
Flanagan (Tammy Dalton), Bert Kramer
(Penn Mathers), Scott Arthur Allen (Wo-
mullun), Robin Harlan (Pam), Dick Haynes
(announcer), Doy Daniels, Jr. (Harold).
"Kill Oscar" Part One & Part
Three (10-27-76 & 11-3-76): Lee Majors
(Steve Austin), John Houseman (Dr. Frank-
lin), Jack Colvin (Baron Constaine), Jen-
nifer Darling (Peggy Callahan), Corinne
Michaels (Lynda Wilson), Jack Ging (Han-
son), Janice Whitby (Katy), John Dewey-
Carter (Rawlins), Sam Jaffe (Admiral
Ricter), Byron Morrow (Adm. Wilkins),
Eugene Peterson (Gen. Williams), Jim

(BIONIC WOMAN cont.) McMullan (Cmdr. Gordon).

"Black Magic" (11-10-76): Vincent Price (Manfred/Cyrus), William Windom (Warfield), Abe Vigoda (Barlow), Hermione Baddeley (Tess), Julie Newmar (Claudette), George Margo (boatman), Alvan Stanley (agent).

"Sister Jaime" (11-24-76): Kathleen Nolan (Mother Superior), Ellen Geer (Sister Barbara), Catherine Burns (Sister Beverly), Dran Hamilton (Sister Margo), Ron Hayes (Father Thomas), Al Hansen (trucker), Cynthia Whitham (Marlene Stolen).

"The Vega Influence" (12-1-76): Rick Lenz (Michael Marchetti), Jamie Smith Jackson (Laure), Philip Carey (Major Andrews), Don Marshall (Capt. Colter), Roy Poole (Dr. Boylin), John Lawrence (Sgt. Roberts).

"Jaime's Shield" (12-15-76 & 12-22-76): George Maharis (Bob Welton), Rebecca Balding (Parker), Diane Civita (Arleen), Linden Chiles (Herb Partnow), William Bryant (Jetton), Arch Johnson (Commissioner Hart), James McEachin (Capt. Godfrey), Amy Joyce (Rosignano).

"Biofeed Back" (1-12-77): Granville Van Dusen (Darwin Jones), Peter Haskell (Payton Jones), Lloyd Bochner (Ivan Karp), Jan Aaris (Marek).

"Doomsday Is Tomorrow" (1-19-77 & 1-26-77): Lew Ayres (Dr. Elijah Cooper), Sam Chew (Mark Russell), Kenneth O'Brien (Victor Dimitri), David Opatoshu (Satari), James Hong (Kurosawa), Ed Vasgersian (technician), Stack Pierce (navigator), Guerin Barry (Alex), Ned Wilson (pilot).

"Deadly Ringer" (2-2-77 & 2-9-77): Lindsay Wagner (Lisa Galloway), Don Porter (Dr. James Courtney), Katherine Helmond (Dr. Harkens), Warren Kemmerling (Warden Cooper), John Zenda (Weber), Martha Scott (Helen Elgin), Ford Rainey (Jim Elgin), Don 'Red' Barry (Woody), Don Fenwick (Ohanian).

"Jaime and the King" (2-23-77): Robert Loggia (Ali Ben Gaziim), Joseph Ruskin (Hassan), Lance Kerwin (Ishmail), Tanya George (Marahna), Brioni Farrell (Ezelda), Annette Cardona (Emerald).

"Beyond the Cell" (3-9-77): Sam Groom (Maj. John Cross), Mariel Aragon (Kim), Sandy Ward (Col. Banning), Ford Rainey (Jim Elgin), Martha Scott (Helen Elgin), Ron McCabe (Private Luddick), Madison Arnold (Willet).

"The Dejon Caper" (3-16-77): Rene Auberjonois (Pierre Lambert), Sydney Chaplin (Moreau), Bernard

Behrens (Beaumont), Erik Holland (Alain), Ben Wright (Fournier), Roger Til (Rochette).

"The Deamon Creature" (3-23-77): Jeff Corey (Thomas Bearclaw), Gary Lockwood (Lyle Cannon), John Quade (Hawkins), Howard McGillin (Sgt. Woods), J. Jay Saunders (Capt. Anders).

"Iron Ships and Dead Men" (3-30-77): Ray Young (Bob Richards), Stephen Elliott (Duke), Edward Walsh (Zanetos).

"Once a Thief" (5-4-77): Elisha Cook, Jr. (Inky), Dick Bakalyan (Talvin), Ed Barth (Saul), Dick Balduzzi (Rogers), Fuddie Bagley (Reggie), Frank Cala (Steinhauer).

"The Bionic Dog" (9-10-77 & 9-17-77): Ford Rainey (Jim Elgin), Dale Robinette (Roger Grette), Taylor Lacher (Crosby), Lee Jones-de Broux (Bill Tyler), Will Hare (Harley).

"Fembots of Las Vegas" (9-24-77 & 10-1-77): James Olson (Rod Kyler), Michael Burns (Carl Franklin), Jennifer Darling (Peggy Callahan), Melinda Fee (Tami), Nancy Bieier (Gina).

"Rodeo" (10-15-77): Andrew Prine (Billy Cole), Donald Gentry (Teak), John Crawford (Crowley), Jason Evers (Radnick), Thomas Bellin (Janos).

"African Connection" (10-29-77): Dan O'Herlihy (Harry Walker), Raymond St. Jacques (Azzar), Don Pedro Colley (Duma), Joan Pringle (Leona Mombassa).

"Motorcycle Boogie" (11-5-77): Evel Knievel (himself), Bernard Behrens (Major Petrov), Spencer Milligan (Schmidt), Chris Anders (1st guard), Erik Holland (2nd guard).

"Brain Wash" (11-12-77): Jennifer Darling (Peggy Callahan), Michael Callahan (John Bernard), David Watson (Benny).

"Escape to Love" (11-26-77): Philip Abbott (Arlo Kelso), Mitchell Laurence (Sandor Kelso), Mark Richman (Dubnov), John Reilly (Hober).

"Max" (12-3-77): Neile Adams-McQueen (Valerie Breuer), Christopher Knight (Bobby), Bill Fletcher (Hobbs), Rudy Solari (Carson), Sandy Kenyon (Dr. Sanders).

"Over the Hill" (12-17-77): Richard Erdman (Terrence Quinn), Michael Thoma (Boris Slotsky), Whit Bissell (Wolfe), Jeff David (Vanovic), Felice Orlandi (Juan Robles).

"All for One" (1-7-78): Franklyn Ajaye (Benny), Roger Perry (Tom Tharp), Henry Kingi (Mango), Viola Kates Stimpson (Mrs. Simpson), Gary Barton (Stubbs), Garret Pearson (Raul).

"The Pyramid" (1-14-78): Eduard

Franz (Ky), Christopher Stone (Chris Williams), Gavan O'Herlihy (Jim Burns).

"The Antidote" (1-21-78): Jennifer Darling (Peggy Callahan), Christopher Stone (Chris Williams), Linda Wiser (Sarah), Suzanne Charny (nurse), James Blendick (Carson).

"The Martians Are Coming, the Martians Are Coming" (1-28-78): Jim McMullan (Casey), Jack Kelly (Ray Fisk), Lynn Carlin (Norma Fisk), Frank Marth (Bill Robbins).

"Sanctuary Earth" (2-11-78): Helen Hunt (Aura), Christopher Stone (Chris Williams).

"Deadly Music" (2-18-78): Henry Darrow (Dasovic), Frank Converse (Jed Kimball), Chip Lucia (Ritter), James Crittenden (Marsden), Roger Cruz (Frank Dade).

"Which One Is Jaime?" (2-25-78): Jennifer Darling (Peggy Callahan), Brock Peters (Stratton), Sam Chew, Jr. (Mark Russell), James Sikking (Burns).

"Out of Body" (3-4-78): Nehemiah Persoff (Philip Jennings), Charlie Hill (Tommy Littlehorse), Richard Lynch (Denton), Allan Magicovsky (Jacoby).

"Long Live the King" (3-25-78): John Reilly (Sam Sloan), Carmen Argenziano (King Kusari), Charles Cioffi (Mostafa), Rene Assa (Kia), Dov Gottesfeld (Sharokah).

"Rancho Outcast" (5-6-78): Keenan Wynn (Gustave), Don Civita (Petie 'The Weasel' Regan), Diane Civita (Madeline), Henry King (One-eyed One), Robert Easton (Colonel).

"On the Run" (5-13-78): Christopher Stone (Chris Williams), Andrew Duggan (Parr), Skip Homeier (Senator Renshaw).

BLAKE'S SEVEN. British 1978-81. Gareth Thomas (Roj Blake) 78-80, Paul Darrow (Kerr Avon), Jan Chappell (Cally), Michael Keating (Vila Restal), Sally Knyvette (Jenna Stannis) 78-80, David Jackson (Olag Gan) 78-79, Josette Simon (Dayna Mellanby) 80-81, Steven Pacey (Del Tarrant) 80-81, Peter Tuddenham (voice of Zen and Orac), Jacqueline Pearce (President Servalan), Steven Greif (Travis) 78-79, Brian Crouccher (Travis) 79-80, Glynis Barber (Soolin) 1981.

"The Way Back" (1-2-78): Robert Beatty (Bran Foster), Michael Halsey (Tel Varon), Pippa Steel (Maja), Jeremy Wilkin, Gillian Bailey.

"Space Fall" (1-9-78): Leslie Schofield (Sub-Commander Raiker),

Glyn Owen, Norman Tipton, David Hayward.

"Cygnus Alpha" (1-16-78): Brian Blessed (Vargas), Glyn Owen (Leylan), Peter Childs (Arco), Pamela Salem (Kara), Norman Tipton (Artiz), David Ryall (Selman), Robert Russell (Laran).

"Time Squad" (1-23-78): S. Newton Anderson (Luddy), Tony Smart, Mark McBride, Frank Henson.

"The Web" (1-30-78): Ania Marson (Geela), Miles Fothergill (Novara), Richard Beale.

"Seek - Locate - Destroy" (2-6-78): John Bryans, Peter Miles, Ian Oliver, Astley Jones, Ian Cullen.

"Mission to Destiny" (2-13-78): Barry Jackson, Beth Morris, Stephen Tate, John Leeson.

"Duel" (2-20-78): Isla Blair (Sinofar), Patsy Smart (Giroc), Carol Royle.

"Project Avalon" (2-27-78): Julia Vidler (Avalon), David Bailie (Chevner), Glynis Barber, John Baker.

"Breakdown" (3-6-78): Julian Glover (Kayn), Ian Thompson (Farren), Christian Roberts.

"Bounty" (3-13-78): T. P. McKenna (Sarkoff), Carinithia West (Tyce), Marc Zuber (Tarvin), Mark York, Derrick Branche.

"Deliverance" (3-20-78): Tony Caunter (Ensor), James Lister (Maryatt), Suzan Farmer.

"Orac" (3-27-78): Derek Farr (Ensor Sr.), James Muir, Paul Kidd.

"Redemption" (1-9-79): Sheila Ruskin, Harriet Philpin, Roy Evans.

"Shadow" (1-16-79): Derek Smith (Largo), Adrienne Burgess (Hanna), Karl Howman (Bek), Archie Tew, Vernon Dobtcheff.

"Weapon" (1-23-79).

"Horizon" (1-30-79): Darien Angadi (Ro), Souad Faress (Selma), William Squire (Federation Kommissar).

"Pressure Point" (2-6-79): Jane Sherwin (Kasabi), Yolande Palfrey (Veron), Alan Halley, Sue Bishop, Martin Connor.

"Trial" (2-13-79): John Bryans, Peter Miles, Kevin Lloyd, Victoria Fairbrother, Claire Lewis.

"Killer" (2-20-79): Ronald Lacey (Tynus), Paul Daneman (Bellfriar), Colin Higgins (Tak), Michael Gaunt (Bax).

"Hostage" (2-27-79): John Abineri (Ushton), Judy Buxton (Inga), James Coyle (Molok), Kevin Stoney.

"Countdown" (3-6-79): Paul Shelley (Major Provine), Tom Chadbon (Del Grant), Robert Arnold, Geoffrey Snell, Lindy Alexander.

(BLAKE'S SEVEN cont.)

"Voices from the Past" (3-13-79): Richard Bebb (Ven Glynd), Frieda Knorr (Governor LeGrand), Martin Read.

"Gambit" (3-20-79): Denis Carey (Docholli), Aubrey Woods (Krantor), John Leeson, Deep Roy, Nicolette Roeg.

"The Keeper" (3-27-79): Bruce Purchase (Gola), Freda Jackson (Tara), Shaun Curry (Rod), Arthur Hewlett (old man).

"Star One" (4-3-79): David Webb (Stot), Jenny Twigge, Gareth Armstrong, John Brown, Paul Toothill.

"Aftermath" (1-7-80): Cy Grant (Mellanby), Alan Lake (Chel), Sally Harrison (Lauren), Richard Franklin, Michael Melia (troopers).

"Powerplay" (1-14-80): Michael Sheard (Klegg), Doyne Byrd (Harmon), John Hollis (Lom), Michael Crane (Mall), Primi Townsend (Zee), Julia Vidler (Barr), Catherine Chase (nurse), Helen Blatch (receptionist).

"Volcano" (1-21-80): Michael Gough (Hower), Malcolm Bullivant (Bershar), Ben Howard (Mori), Judy Matheson, Alan Bowerman.

"Dawn of the Gods" (2-5-80): Marcus Powell (Thaarn), Sam Dastor, Terry Scully.

"The Harvest of Kairos" (2-4-80): Andrew Burt, Frank Gatliff, Anthony Gardner, Stuart Fell.

"City at the Edge of the World" (2-11-80): Valentine Dyall (Norl), Colin Baker (Bayban), Carol Hawkins (Kerril), John J. Carney (Sherm).

"Children of Auron" (2-19-80): Sarah Atkinson (Clinician Franton), Rio Fanning, Ric Young, Jack McKenzie.

"Rumours of Death" (2-25-80): Lorna Heilbron (Sula), John Bryans (Shrinker), Donald Douglas (Grenlee), Peter Clay (Chesku), David Haig (Forres), David Gillies (Hob), Philip Bloomfield (Balon).

"Sarcophagus" (3-3-80).

"Ultraworld" (3-10-80): Peter Richards, Stephen Jenn, Ian Barritt (Ultras), Ronald Govey (Relf).

"Moloch" (3-17-80): John Hartley (Grose), Mark Sheridan (Lector), Deep Roy (Moloch), Davyd Harries, Sabina Franklyn, Debbie Blythe.

"Death-Watch" (3-24-80): Mark Elliot (Vinni), David Sibley, Kathy Iddon, Stewart Bevan.

"Terminal" (3-31-80): Gillian McCutheon, Heather Wright, Richard Clifford, David Healy.

"Rescue" (9-28-81): Bob Middleton (Creature), Geoffrey Burridge (Do-

rian).

"Power" (10-5-81): Dicken Ashworth (Gunn Sar), Juliet Hammond-Hill (Pella), Alison Glennie (Kate), Jenny Oulton (Nina), Paul Ridley (Cato), Linda Barr (Luxia).

"Traitor" (10-12-81): Malcolm Stoddard (Leitz), Christopher Neame (Col. Quute), Robert Morris (Major Hunda), John Quentin (Practor), Edgar Wreford (Forbus), David Quiter (the Tracer), Neil Dickson (Avandir), Cyril Appleton (Sgt. Hask), George Lee (Igin).

"Stardrive" (10-19-81): Barbara Shelley (Dr. Plaxton), Damien Thomas (Atlan), Peter Sands (Bomber), Leonard Kavanagh (Napier).

"Animals" (10-26-81): Peter Byrne (Justin), William Lindsay (Captain), Max Harvey (Borr), Kevin Stoney (Ardus), David Boyce (Og).

"Headhunter" (11-2-81): John Westbrook (Muller), Lynda Bellingham (Vena), Douglas Fielding (technician), Nick Joseph (Android), Leslie Nunnerley (voice).

"Assassin" (11-9-81): Betty Marsden (Verlis), Richard Hurndall (Nebrox), Caroline Holdaway (Piri), John Wyman (Cancer), Peter Attard (Benos), Adam Blackwood (Tok), Mark Barratt (Servalan's Captain).

"Games" (11-16-81): Stratford Johns (Belkov), Rosalind Bailey (Gambit), David Neal (Gerran), James Harvey (guard), Michael Gaunt (computer).

"Sand" (11-23-81): Stephen Yardley (Reeve), Daniel Hill (Chasgo), Jonathan David (Keller), Peter Craze (Servalan's assistant), Michael Gaunt (computer).

"Gold" (11-30-81): Roy Kinnear (Keiller), Anthony Brown (doctor), Dinah May (woman passenger), Norman Hartley (pilot).

"Orbit" (12-7-81): John Savident (Egrorian), Larry Noble (Pinder).

"Warlord" (12-14-81): Roy Boyd (Zukan), Bobbie Brown (Zeeona), Dean Harris (Finn), Rick James (Chalsa), Simon Merrick (Bocrva), Brian Spink (Mida), Charles Augins (Lod).

"Blake" (12-21-81): Gareth Thomas (Blake), David Collings (Deva), Sasha Mitchell (Arlen), Janet Lees Price (Klyn).

BOB HOPE CHRYSLER THEATRE.

"Time of Flight" (9-21-66): Jack Kelly (Al Packer), Jack Klugman (Markos), Juliet Mills (Mary Lewis), Jeanette Nolan (Mrs. Gardner), Woodrow Parfrey (De Carlo), Michael Conrad (McWhorter),

Peter Brocco (L-Quar), Clarke Gordon (Dr. Gardner), Lloyd Haynes (Christensen), Bill Hart (Reed), Nancy Hsueh (Miss Chan), Dave Morick (man).

"The Blue-Eyed Horse" (11-23-66): Ernest Borgnine (Melvin Feebie), Joan Blondell (Mrs. Melvin Feebie), Paul Lynde (Judge), Barbara Heller (Jennie Haggerty), Joyce Jameson (Mrs. Rassendale), Ann Jillian (Sheila).

"Code Name: Heraclitus" (1-4-67 & 1-11-67): Stanley Baker (Gannon), Leslie Nielsen (Fryer), Jack Weston (Gerberson), Sheree North (Sally), Signe Hasso (Lydia), Kurt Kasznar (Constantine), Malachi Throne (Hoffman).

BROADWAY TELEVISION THEATRE. "Night Must Fall" (8-18-52): Bethel Leslie, Ruth Gates, Anthony Kemble-Cooper, Wright King.

"Mrs. Moonlight" (9-8-52): Beverly Whitney, Una O'Connor, Stephen Courtleigh.

"Outward Bound" (11-24-52): John Dall, Jean Adair, Ernest Truex, Estelle Winwood.

"The Enchanted Cottage" (12-22-52): Judith Evelyn.

"Death Takes a Holiday" (1-5-53): Nigel Green, Wendy Drew.

"Criminal at Large" (2-2-53): Basil Rathbone, Estelle Winwood, Anthony Kemble-Cooper.

"R. U. R." (2-9-53): Hugh Reilly, Dorothy Hart.

"The Bat" (11-23-53): Estelle Winwood, Jay Jostyn, Alice Pearce.

"The Gramercy Ghost" (1-4-54): Veronica Lake, Richard Hylton.

BUCK ROGERS. 1979-81. Gil Gerard (Buck Rogers), Erin Gray (Wilma Deering), Tim O'Connor (Dr. Huer) 79-80, Felix Scilla (Twiki), Mel Blanc (Voice of Twiki), Eric Server (Voice of Dr. Theopolis) 79-80, Thom Christopher (Hawk) 80-81, Wilfrid Hyde-White (Dr. Goodfellow) 80-81, Jay Garner (Adm. Asimov) 80-81.

"Planet of the Slave Girls" (9-27-79): David Groh (Duke), Jack Palance (Kaleel), Roddy McDowall (Saroyan), MacDonald Carey (Mallory), Brianne Leary (Ryma), Karen Carlson (Stella), Buster Crabbe (Brig. Gordon), Michael Mullins (Regis), Robert Dowdell (Galen), Sheila de Windt (Major Fields), Don Marshall (Julia), Diana Markoff (female pilot), June Whiteley Taylor (wife), Borah Silver (husband), Michael Masters (workman), Don Masters (guard).

"Vegas in Space" (10-4-79): Ri-

chard Lynch (Morgan Velosi), Juanin Clay (Maj. Marla Landers), Cesar Romero (Amos Armat), Joseph Wiseman (Carl Morphus), Pamela Shoop (Tangi), Ana Alicia (Falina Redding), James Luisi.

"The Plot to Kill a City" (10-11-79 & 10-18-79): Frank Gorshin (Kellogg), John Quade (Quince), Nancy DeCarl (Sherese), Anthony James (Varek), Markie Post (Joella Cameron), Robert Tessier (Maros), Victor Argo (Rafael Argus), James Sloyan (Barney Smith), Seamon Glass (pirate), John Furlong (1st cop), James McEachin (Richard Selvin), Mitch Reta (technician), Richard Reed (1st rowdy), Sena Black (woman), Gwen Mitchell (ticket clerk), Nonice Williams (Katrina), Whitney Rydbeck (Hardsteen).

"The Return of the Fighting 69th" (10-25-79): Peter Graves (Noah Cooper), Robert Quarry (Corliss), Elizabeth Allen (Roxanne Trent), K. T. Stevens (Harriet Twain), Woody Strode (Corporal Big Red McMurtrey), Katharine Wyberg (Alicia), Robert Hardy (Clayton), Dan Sturkie (Eli Twain), Eddie Firestone (Corporal M. K. Schultz), Clifford Turknett (war technician).

"Unchained Woman" (11-1-79): Jamie Lee Curtis (Jen Burton), Michael DeLano (Pantera), Robert Cornthwaite (Warwick), Walt Hunter (Hugo), Danny Ades (Gymon), Jim B. Smith (shuttle captain), Charles Walters (Lt. Zimmerman), Tara Buckman, Bert Rosario.

"Planet of the Amazon Women" (11-8-79): Anne Jeffreys (Prime Minister), Ann Dusenberry (Ariela), Jay Robinson (Thorne), Antoinette Stella (Jayel), Liberty Godshall (Nyree), Wendy Dates (Renna), Darrell Zwerling (Prof. Mason), Teddi Siddell (Linea), Wally K. Byrnes (pilot), James Fraracci (Karsh).

"Cosmic Wiz Kid" (11-22-79): Gary Coleman (Hieronymus Fox), Melody Rogers (Lt. Dia Zertan), Roy Walston (Roderick Zale), Albert Popwell (Koren), M. P. Toman (Lester Fletcher), Earl Boen (Selmar), Tobar Mayo (guard), Tonny Epper (drunk).

"Escape from Wedded Bliss" (11-29-79): Pamela Hensley (Ardala), Michael Ansara (Kane), H. B. Haggerty (Tigerman), Alfred Ryder (Garidon).

"Cruise Ship to the Stars" (12-27-79): Kimberly Beck (Alison Michaels), Trish Noble (Sabrina), Leigh McCloskey (Jay), Dorothy R. Stratten (Miss Cosmos), Brett Halsey (Captain), Patty Maloney (Tina), Timothy O'Hagan (young man).

"Space Vampire" (1-3-80): Christopher Stone (Royko), Nicholas Hormann

(BUCK ROGERS cont.) (the Vorvon), Lincoln Kilpatrick (Dr. Ekbar), Patty Maloney.

"Happy Birthday, Buck" (1-10-80): Morgan Brittany (Raylyn Merritt), Peter MacLean (Cornell Traeger), Tamara Dobson (Dr. Dolora Bayliss), Eric Mason (Lt. Garth), Clay Alexander (Marsden), Bruce Wright (Rorvik), Chip Johnson (Carew), Abe Alvarez (security agent), Harry Gold (Alien Squadron Leader), Tom Gagen (Niles), Victoria Woodbeck (technician), Gina Gallego (woman).

"A Blast for Buck" (1-17-80): Gary Coleman (Hieronymus Fox).

"Ardala Returns" (1-24-80): Pamela Hensley (Ardala), Michael Ansara (Kane), H. B. Haggerty (Tigerman), Bob Minor (guard), James Emery (pilot), Betty Bridges (technician).

"Twiki Is Missing" (1-31-80): John P. Ryan (Kurt Belzack), Eddie Benton (Stella), Eugenia Wright (Dawn), Janet Bebe Louie (Clare), David Darlow (Pinchas), Ken Letner (Oto Anad).

"Olympiad" (2-7-80): Barney McFadden (Jorez), Judith Chapman (Lara Tizian), Nicholas Coster (Alarik), Paul Mantee (Karl), Paul Coufos (Zogan), John Zee (Satrap), Elgin Baylor, Jerry Quarry, Bob Seagren, Thomas 'Hollywood' Henderson, Carlos Palomino, Anthony Davis.

"A Dream of Jennifer" (2-14-80): Anne Lockhart (Leila Markeson/Jennifer), Paul Koslo (Cmdr. Reeve), Mary Woronov (Nola), Gino Conforti (Magician), Shawn Michaels (supervisor), Jessie Lawrence Ferguson (Lt. Rekoff), Marsha Mercant (clerk), Denis Haysbert (guard), Cameron Young (Toby Kaplin), Mitchell Young-Evans (mime).

"Space Rockers" (2-21-80): Jerry Orbach (Lars Mangros), Nancy Frangoine (Karana), Judy Landers (Joanna), Leonard Lightfoot (Cirus), Jesse Goins (Rambeau), Jeff Harlan (Mark), Cynthia Leake (Elaine), Joseph Taggart (security man), Mitch Reta (technician), Richard Moll.

"Buck's Duel to the Death" (3-20-80): William Smith (the Trebor), Keith Andes (Darius), Elizabeth Stack (Dione), Robert Lussier (Dr. Albert), Stephanie Blackmore (Greta), Heidi Bohay (Maja), Francisco Lagueruela (Karen), Donald R. Bruce (young officer), Edward Powers, Fred Sadoff.

"Flight of the War Witch" (3-27-80 & 4-3-80): Pamela Hensley (Princess Ardala), Michael Ansara (Kane), Sam Jaffe (Keeper), Julie Newmar (Za-

rina), Donald Petrie (Kotus), Vera Miles (Tora), Kelley Miles (Shandar), Sid Haig (Spero), Tony Carroll (Pantherman), Larry Ward (Council Member), Brent Davis (General), Gary Adler (security guard), Don Maxwell (Draconian soldier).

"Time of the Hawk" (1-15-81): Barbara Luna (Koori), David Opatoshu (Llamajuna), Lavelle Roby (Thromis), Andre Harvey (Thordis), Susan McIver (Simmons), Michael Fox (High Judge), Tim O'Keefe (Bailiff), Ken Chandler (court clerk), J. Christopher O'Connor (young lieutenant), Dennis Haysbert (communications probe officer), Sid Haig, Lance LeGault, Kenneth O'Brien.

"Journey to Oasis" (1-22-81): Mark Lenard (Ambassador Duvoe), Paul Carr (Lt. Devlin), Felix Scilla (Odee-X), Len Birman (Admiral Zeit), Mike Stroda (Rolla), Alex Hyde-White (technician), Don Whyte.

"The Guardians" (1-29-81): Harry Townes (Janovus XXVI), Rosemary DeCamp (Mrs. Rogers), Barbara Luna (Koori), Paul Carr (Lt. Devlin), Vic Perrin (1st Guardian), Howard Culver (mailman), Dennis Haysbert (helmsman).

"Mark of the Saurian" (2-5-81): Linden Chiles (Ambassador Cabot), Kim Hamilton (Lt. Paulton), Paul Carr (Lt. Devlin), Vernon Weddle (Dr. Moray), Barry Cahill (Lt. Elif), Allan Hunt (wing man), Alex Hyde-White (technician), Stacy Keach, Sr. (senior officer), Frank Parker (captain), Andrea Pike (crew member).

"The Golden Man" (2-19-81): Anthony James (Graf), Russell Wiggins (Relcos), David Hollander (Velis), Roger Rose (Marcos), Paul Carr (Lt. Devlin), Michael Masters (jailer), Diana Chesney (hag), Bob Elyea (Alphie), Richard Wright (onlooker No. 1), Arthur Eisner (onlooker No. 2), Bruce M. Fisher.

"The Crystals" (3-5-81): Amanda Wyss (Laura), James Parkes (Kovick), Gary Bolen (Johnson), Alex Hyde-White (Lt. Martin), Sandy-Alexander Champion (CPO Hall), Leigh C. Kim (Petrie), Hubie Kerns, Jr. (Mummy Monster).

"The Satyr" (3-12-81): Anne E. Curry (Syra), Dave Cass (Pangor), Bobby Lane (Delph), Dennis Freeman (midshipman).

"The Derelict Equation" (3-19-81): Tommy Madden (Xces), Billy Curtis (Yoomak), Harry Monty (Sothoz), Charles Secor (Kuzan), Tony Cox (Zedht), John Edward Allen (Zoman), Spencer Russell (Towtuk), Alex Hyde-White (technician).

"The Hand of the Goral" (3-26-81):

William Bryant (Cowan), Dennis Haysbert (Lt. Parsons), John Fujioka (Old Man), Peter Kastner (Reardon), Michael Horsley (Yeoman James).

"The Dorian Secret" (4-16-81): Devon Ericson (Asteria), Walker Edmiston (Koldar), William Kirby Cullen (Demeter), Eldon Quick (Chronos), Stuart Nisbet (Rand), Dennis Haysbert (Ensign), Brady Rubin (Sylas), Michele Marsh (Cleis), Jackie Russell (Kally), Keith Atkinson (Johan), Lachelle Chamberlain (Darel), Denny Miller.

BUCK ROGERS IN THE 25th CENTURY. 1950-51. Kem Dibbs (Buck Rogers), Lou Prentis (Wilma Deering), Harry Kingston (Barney Wade), Harry Sothern, Sanford Bickart, Robert Pastene.

CAPTAIN MIDNIGHT. 1954-58. Richard Webb (Captain Midnight), Sid Melton (Ichabod Mudd), Olan Soule (Tut), Jan Shepard (Marcia Stanhope), Renee Beard (Chuck Ramsey).
"Murder By Radiation" (9-4-54): Jimmy Ivo, Wheaton Chambers.
"Electronic Killer" (9-11-54): Bob Bice.
"Deadly Diamonds" (9-18-54).
"The Lost Moon" (9-25-54).
"Death Below Zero" (10-2-54): David Colmans.
"Operation Failure" (10-9-54): John Mylong (Zabor).
"Trapped Behind Bars" (10-16-54): Mel Welles (Harga), Lennie Bremen (Pete Hardy), Don C. Harvey (Rocky Billings).
"The Walking Ghost" (10-30-54): William Fawcett, Belle Mitchell.
"Counterfeit Millions" (10-23-54): Ken Christy (Bradshaw), Byron Foulger (Doc), John Domler (Gourney).
"Secret of the Jungle" (11-6-54): John Banner (Goronov).
"Sabotage Under the Sea" (11-13-54): John Pickard, Philip Van Zandt.
"Isle of Mystery" (11-20-54): Nina Monsour, Zon Murray, David Garcia.
"The Curse of the Pharoahs" (11-27-54): George Eldredge, Sheila Ryan.
"The Deserters" (12-4-54): Stuffy Singer (Hi Foley).
"The Electrified Man" (12-11-54): Ian Keith (Prof. Bergland).
"The Young Criminal" (12-18-54): Jack Diamond, Dick Rich.
"The Deadly Project" (12-25-54): Franz Roehn (Vranki), Pierre Watkin (Dr. Morgan).

"The Secret Room" (10-29-55).
"Mission to Mexico" (11-5-55): Tyler McVey (Hobson).
"The Frozen Man" (11-12-55).
"Doctors of Doom" (11-19-55): Frances Karath (Gladys Murphy).
"Sunken Sapphires" (11-26-55): Donna Drew (Helen Orloff), Dickie Bellis (Billy Orloff).
"The Master Criminal" (12-3-55): Baynes Barron.
"The Secret of Superstition Mountain" (12-10-55).
"The Mountain of Fire" (12-17-55): Alex Montoya (Carlos Perez), Ralph Gamble (Frank White).
"The Jungle Pit" (12-24-55): John Banner.
"Flight into the Unknown" (12-31-55).
"The Runaway Suitcase" (1-7-56): Gregg Barton (Fred Connors), Jimmy Karath (Tom Blake), Tom McKee (Detective Swan).
"Million Dollar Diamond" (1-14-56): Butch Barnard (Jimmy Bigson), Linda Danson (Mrs. Drexel).
"The Human Bullet" (1-21-56).
"Touchdown Terror" (1-28-56): Terry Frost (Bates), Mark Andrews.
"Top Secret Weapon" (2-4-56).
"The Human Bomb" (2-11-56): Dick Rich (Volmer), Gayne Whitman (Judge Bell), Jarl Victor (Linden), John Force (Oratz), Robert Lyden (Billy Griffiths).
"The Mark of Death" (2-18-56): Ted Hecht (Bengra Tassi), David Colmans (Ram Das), Peter Brocco (Landru), Paul Marion (knife seller), Bobken Ben Ali (Kalyan Singh).
"Arctic Avalanche" (2-25-56): Philip Ahn (Sutoc), Tetsu Komai (Kindu), Lane Nakana (Groba), Marc Krah (Zarca).
"Mystery of the Forest" (3-3-56): Don C. Harvey (Gaynor), Terry Frost (Harris), Art Gilmore (Prof. Harlow).
"Invisible Terror" (3-10-56): George Eldredge (Dr. Hamilton), Jarl Victor (Gorley), Mel Welles (Mannlicher), Bert Le Baron (Raughlin), Greta Granstedt (Mrs. Radnor).
"Saboteurs of the Sky" (3-17-56): Frances Karath (Sally Jansen), Irene Rich (Mr. Jensen), George D. Barrows (Fleck), Dick Grant (salesman), Harold Dyrenforth (Lorenz), Dick Elliott.
"Peril from the Arctic" (3-24-56): Mel Welles.

CAPTAIN NICE. 1966-67. William Daniels (Carter Nash/Captain Nice),

(CAPTAIN NICE cont.) Alice Ghostley (Mrs. Nash), Ann Prentiss (Sgt. Candy Kane), Liam Dunn (Mayor Finney), William Zuckert (Police Chief Segal), Byron Foulger (Mr. Nash).

"The Man Who Flies Like a Pigeon" (1-9-67): Kelton Garwood (Gregory Omnus), Arthur Malet (Crook).
"How Sheik Can You Get?" (1-16-67): Larry D. Mann (Sheik Abdul Beimer), James Lanphier (Ibid).
"That Thing" (1-23-67): Johnny Haymer (Dr. Von Keppel), Frank Maxwell (Gen. Rock Ravage).
"That Was the Bridge That Was" (2-6-67): Edward Binns (Al Spencer), Phil Roth (Hal Porter), Sabrina Schraf.
"The Man with Three Blue Eyes" (2-20-67): John Dehner (The Great Medula), Florence Halop (Mrs. Kowalski), Ernest Sarracino (prisoner).
"Is Big Town Burning?" (2-27-67): Victor Tayback (Mr. Lipton), Marilyn Lowell (Miss Devine), Robert Munk, Hollis Morrison, Gene Reynolds, Tommy Farrell.
"Don't Take Any Wooden Indians" (3-6-67): Joe Flynn (Dr. John Edgars), Joseph Perry (Luna), Ben Wright (Dunbar).
"That's What Mothers Are For" (3-13-67): Felice Orlandi (Lucky), Dennis Cross (Larkin).
"Whatever Lola Wants" (3-20-67): Barbara Stuart (Lola), Jack Perkins.
"Who's Afraid of Amanda Woolf?" (3-27-67): Madlyn Rhue (Amanda Woolf), John Fiedler (Gunner).
"The Week They Stole Payday" (4-3-67): Pat Harrington (Arthur), Victor French (Anthony).
"It Tastes O.K., But Something's Missing" (4-10-67): Simon Oakland (Harry Houseman), Dick Curtis (Bostic), Johnny Silver (Small man).
"May I Have the Last Dance" (4-17-67): Celeste Yarnall (Rossalind), Marilyn Mason (receptionist).
"One Rotten Apple" (4-24-67): Bob Newhart (Lloyd Larchmont), John Milford (Lionel), Jo Anne Worley (Rusty), Shirley Bonne (Ellie), Charles Grodin (news vendor), Margaret Teale (Babsy).
"Beware of Hidden Prophets" (5-1-67): John Dehner (the Great Medula), Joseph Campanella (Kincade).

CAPTAIN SCARLET AND THE MYSTERONS. 1967. Marionette Voices: Francis Matthews (Captain Scarlet), Donald Gray (Colonel White/Mysteron voice), Paul Maxwell (Captain Gray/World President), Edward Bishop (Captain Blue), Jeremy Wilkins (Captain Ochre), Gary Files (Captain Magenta), Cy Grant (Lt. Green), Charles Tingwell (Dr. Fawn), Janna Hill (Symphony Angel), Sylvia Anderson (Melody Angel), Liz Morgan (Rhapsody Angel/Destiny Angel), Lian-Shin (Harmony Angel).

"The Mysterons".
"Winged Assassin".
"Big Ben Strikes Again".
"Manhunt".
"Point 783".
"Operation Time".
"Renegade Rocket".
"White As Snow".
"Seek and Destroy".
"Spectrum Strikes Back".
"Avalanche".
"The Shadow of Fear".
"The Trap".
"Special Assignment".
"Lunarville 7".
"Heart of New York".
"The Traitor".
"Model Spy".
"Fire at Rig 15".
"Flight to Atlantica".
"Crater 101".
"Dangerous Rendezvous".
"Noose of Ice".
"Treble Cross".
"Inferno".
"Flight 104".
"Place of the Angles".
"Expo 2068".
"The Launching".
"Code Name: Europa".
"Attack on Cloudbase".
"The Inquisition".

CAPTAIN VIDEO. 1949-56. Richard Coogan (Captain Video) 49-50, Al Hodge (Captain Video) 50-56, Don Hastings (the Video Ranger), Jack Orsen (Commissioner Carey) 49-50, Ben Lackland (Commissioner Carey) 50-56, Hal Conklin (Dr. Pauli), Nat Polen (Agent Carter), Dave Ballard (Dr. Tobor).

CAPTAIN Z-RO. 1955. Roy Steffins (Captain Z-Ro), Bobby Turnbull (Jet).
"Christopher Columbus" (12-18-55).
"Daniel Boone" (12-25-55).
"Marco Polo" (1-1-56).
"Benedict Arnold" (1-8-56).
"King John" (1-15-56).
"Magellan" (1-22-56).
"Pony Express" (1-29-56).

"William Tell" (2-5-56).
"Roger the Robot" (2-12-56).
"Blackbeard the Pirate" (2-19-56).
"Attila the Hun" (2-26-56).
"Robin Hood" (3-4-56).
"Washington and Howe" (3-11-56).
"Curse of Ra" (3-18-56).
"Hernando Cortez" (3-25-56).
"Molly Pitcher" (4-1-56).
"Discovery of Gold" (4-8-56).
"Meteor" (4-15-56).
"Captain Cook and the Hawaiian
Islands" (4-22-56).
"Aztec Papers" (4-29-56).
"Genghis Khan" (5-6-56).
"The Gread Pyramid" (5-13-56).
"Leonardo da Vinci" (5-20-56).
"William the Conqueror" (5-27-
56).
"Adventure in Space" (6-3-56).
"King Alfred" (6-10-56).

CBS DAYTIME 90.
"The Guest Room" (2-13-74): Gil-
mer McCormick (Susan Banks), Frank
Converse (John Banks).

CBS LIBRARY.
"Once Upon a Midnight Dreary"
(10-21-79): Vincent Price (Host).
"The Ghost Belonged to Me" seg-
ment: Christopher Berrigan, Jessica
Lynn Pennington (Blossom), Alexandria
Johnson (Ghost), Wayne Heffley (driver).
"The Legend of Sleepy Hollow"
segment: Rene Auberjonois (Ichabod
Crane), Pamela Brown (Katrina), Guy
Boyd (Brom Bones), Robert Foster
(Headless Horseman).
"The House with a Clock in It's
Walls" segment: Severn Darden (Uncle
Jonathan), Mary Betten (Selena), Mi-
chael Brick (Lewis), Pat Petersen (Tar-
by).
"Robbers, Rooftops and Witches"
(4-20-82):
"Invisible Boy" segment: Kate
Reid (Aunt), Christian Slater (Charlie).

CHALLENGE OF THE SUPERHEROES,
THE. 1-18-79. Adam West (Bat-
man), Burt Ward (Robin), Frank
Gorshin (the Riddler), Charlie Cal-
las (Sinestro), Jeff Altman (Weather
Wizard), Gabriel Dell (Mordru),
Mickey Morton (Solomon Grundy),
Howard Morris (Dr. Sivana), Wil-
liam Schallert (Retired Man), Ale-
shia Brevard (Giganta), Garrett
Craig (Captain Marvel), Howard
Murphy (Green Lantern), Danuta
(Black Canary).

CHAMPIONS, THE. 1968. Stuart Da-
mon (Craig Stirling), Alexandra Bas-
tedo (Sharon Macready), William
Gaunt (Richard Barrett), Anthony
Nicholls (W. L. Tremayne).
"To Trap a Rat" (6-10-68): Guy
Rolfe (Pelham), Edina Ronay (Sandra),
Kate O'Mara (Jane), Michael Standing
(Edwards), Toke Townley (Higgs).
"The Dark Island" (6-17-68): Vla-
dek Sheybal (Max Kellor), Alan Gifford
(Admiral).
"The Invisible Man" (6-24-68):
Peter Wyngarde (Hallam), James Culli-
ford (Sumner).
"Get Me Out of Here" (7-1-68):
Frances Cuka (Anna Maria Martes), Ro-
nald Radd (Commandante), Philip Madoc
(Angel Martes).
"The Gilded Cage" (7-8-68): John
Carson (Symons), Jennie Linden (Saman-
tha), Clinton Greyn (Lovegrove).
"The Mission" (7-15-68): Dermot
Kelly (Hogan), Anthony Bate (Pedersen).
"Operation Deep-Freeze" (7-29-
68): Patrick Wymark (Gen. Gomez),
Robert Urquhart (Hemmings).
"Happening" (8-12-68): Michael
Gough (Joss), Jack MacGowran (Banner),
Grant Taylor (Gen. Winters).
"The Night People" (8-19-68):
Adrienne Corri (Mrs. Trennick), Te-
rence Alexander (Douglas Trennick),
Anne Sharp (Jane Soames), David Lodge
(Porth).
"The Silent Enemy" (9-19-68):
Paul Maxwell (Capt. Baxter), James
Maxwell (Stanton), Warren Stanhope
(Adm. Parker), Marne Maitland.

CHEVY SHOW, THE.
"O'Halloran's Luck" (3-12-61):
Art Carney (Tim O'Halloran), Barbara
Cook (Kitty Malone), Warde Donovan
(Foreman), Barbara Robbins (Mrs.
Skiles), Al Henderson (Dennison), Gra-
nia O'Malley (Mrs. Malone), Dick O'-
Neill (Finnigan), John McGovern (Mc-
Cauky), George Turner (Butler), Pat
Harrington, Sr. (Mr. Malone).

CHILDREN'S STORY, THE. 2-18-82.
Mildred Dunnock (Miss Warden),
James McCall (Johnny), Michaela
Ross (the new teacher), Fitz Gitler,
Christin Fenton, Max Barabas, Vanes-
sa Biery, Kiernan Tate, Danielle
Duclos, Michael Bellaran, Christian
Moy, Leslie Weiner, Nicole Smith,
Toni Ann Gisandi, Michelle Francoeur,
Sal Sanchez, Romy Takagi, Jimmy
Stokes.

CHRISTMAS 2025. 1-1-78. James Cromwell (Spelvin), Frank Aletter (Dril), Elinor Donahue (Margaret Drill).

CIRCLE OF FEAR. 1973.
"Death's Head" (1-5-73): Janet Leigh (Carol), Rory Calhoun (Larry), Gene Nelson (Steve), Joshua Bryant (doctor), Doreen Lang (Mrs. Norman), Ayn Ruymen (gypsy).
"Dark Vengeance" (1-12-73): Martin Sheen (Frank), Kim Darby (Cindy), Shelly Novak (Art).
"Earth, Air, Fire and Water" (1-19-73): Frank Converse (Sam), Joan Blackman (Ellen), Scott Marlowe (Paul), Dabbs Greer (Bill), Brooke Bundy (Holly), Tim McIntire (Jake), Tyne Daly (Anna), Frances Spanier (customer).
"Doorway to Death" (1-26-73): Barry Nelson (Jim), Susan Dey (Peggy), Leif Garrett (Robert), Dawn Lyn (Jane), Henry Jones (Truthers), Scott Thomas (man upstairs).
"Legion of Daemons" (2-2-73): Shirley Knight (Beth), John Cyphers (Keith), Neva Patterson (Mary), Bridget Hanley (Dana), John Ventantonio (Al), James Luisi (Rick), Kathryn Hayes (Janet), Paul Carr.
"Graveyard Shift" (2-16-73): John Astin (Fred Colby), Patty Duke Astin (Linda Colby), Joe Renteria (Johnny Horne), Douglas Henderson (Jack Willis), Don 'Red' Barry (Charlie Durham), Paul Picerni (Dr. Richardson), I. Stanford Jolley (Wolfman), William Castle (studio head), Royce Wallace (nurse), Hal Bokar (Apeman), Mathias Reitz (the Claw).
"Spare Parts" (2-23-73): Susan Oliver (Ellen Pritchard), Rick Lenz (Dr. Stephen Crosley), Christopher Connelly (Chuck), Meg Foster (Penny Wiseman), Don Knight (Dr. Pritchard), Alex Rocco (Joseph Moretti), Lee Kroeger (Nurse Storman), Barbara Stuart (Nurse Georgia Grant).
"The Ghost of Potter's Field" (3-23-73): Tab Hunter (Bob Herrick), Louise Sorel (Nisa King), Gary Conway (John Walsh), Pat Harrington, Jr. (Mark Riceman), Myron Healey (Lt. Maloney), Philip Pine (Dolf Ellis), Paul Winchell (Carlson), Robert Mandan (Ted Murray).
"The Phantom of Herald Square" (3-30-73): Victor Jory (Old Man), David Soul (James Barlow), Sheila Larken (Holly Brown), Meg Wyllie (old woman), Murray Mathewson (Mathews), Dennis Lee Smith (art student).

CLIFFHANGERS. 1979.
"Stop Susan Williams" segment: Susan Anton (Susan Williams), Ray Walston (Richard), Michael Swan (Schoengarth), John Hancock (Gold Tooth), Albert Paulsen (Korf), Don Knight (Recruiter), Fred Sadoff (Samuelson), Ron Hasson (Miguel), Melora Marshall (Olga), Than Wyenn (Nikolai), Robert Lynn (Layton).
"The Silent Enemy" (2-27-79).
"Jungle Death Trap" (3-6-79).
"Thundering Doom" (3-13-79).
"Deadly Descent" (3-20-79).
"Watery Grave" (3-27-79).
"Cauldron of Fire" (4-3-79).
"River of Blood" (4-10-79).
"Wheels of Destruction" (4-17-79).
"Terror from the Sky" (4-24-79).
"The Villain Revealed" (4-31-79).
"The Secret Empire" segment: Geoffrey Scott (Marshal Jim Donner), Tiger Williams (Billy), Charlene Watkins (Millie), Diane Markoff (Tara), Jay Robinson (Demeter), Mark Lenard (Thorval), Peter Breck (Keller), S. Newton Anderson (Kalek), Pamela Brull (Maya), Sean Garrison (Yannuck), Peter Tomarken (Roe).
"Plunge into Mystery" (2-27-79).
"Prisoner of the Empire" (3-6-79).
"The Mind Twisters" (3-13-79).
"Seeds of Revolt" (3-20-79).
"Attack of the Phantom Riders" (3-27-79).
"Sizzling Threat" (4-3-79).
"Mandibles of Death" (4-10-79).
"The Last Gasp" (4-17-79).
"Return to Chimera" (4-24-79).
"Powerhouse" (4-31-79).
"The Curse of Dracula" segment: Michael Nouri (Dracula), Stephen Johnson (Kurt von Helsing), Carol Baxter (Mary), Antoinette Stella (Jill), Louise Sorel (Amanda Gibbings), Jo Anne Strauss (Sister Theresa), Bever-Leigh Banfield (Christina).
"Lifeblood" (2-27-79).
"Blood Stream" (3-6-79).
"Demons of the Dark" (3-13-79).
"Depository of Death" (3-20-79).
"Sepulchure of the Undead" (3-27-79).
"Threshold of Eternity" (4-3-79).
"Where Angels Fear to Tread" (4-10-79).
"Sealed in Blood" (4-17-79).
"Thirst for Death" (4-24-79).
"Pleas of the Undead" (4-31-79).

CLIMAX!
"Casino Royale" (10-21-54): Barry Nelson (James Bond), Peter Lorre

(Le Chiffre), Linda Christian (Valeria). "Dr. Jekyll and Mr. Hyde" (7-28-55): Michael Rennie (Dr. Henry Jekyll/Mr. Hyde), Sir Cedric Hardwicke (Utterson), Mary Sinclair (girl). "The Chinese Game" (11-22-56): Rita Moreno (Irene), Macdonald Carey (Harry Belgard), Constance Ford (Helen), Harry Townes (Arthur Cook), Anna May Wong (clerk). "Strange Deaths at Burnleigh" (5-2-57): Michael Rennie (James MacLennan), Sir Cedric Hardwicke (Dr. Martin Crandell), Joan Tetzel (Ann Laird). "Shooting for the Moon" (4-24-58): John Forsythe (Frank Colby), Dick York (Gordon Bates), Bethel Leslie (Jessica Colby), Alexander Scourby (Eric Betzdorff), Robert Armstrong (Barney Farrell).

CLOAK OF MYSTERY. "The 13th Gate" (7-20-65): David Opatoshu (Dr. Jason Banner), Alex Cord (Steve O'Hara), Karl Held (David Mathews), Joyce Taylor (Amy Hanson), Jeremy Slate (Maj. Andrew Clark).

COMEDY OF HORRORS. Pilot - (9-1-81): Patrick Macnee (Host), Walter Olkewicz (Danny Logan), Kip Niven (Michael), Jo de Winter (Eileen Mannings), Deborah Harmon (Molly), Ivana Moore, Patricia Conwell, Richard Roat, Vincent Schiavelli.

COMMANDO CODY. 1956. Judd Holdren (Commando Cody), Aline Towne (Joan Albright), William Schallert (Ted Richards), Richard Crane (Dick Preston), Gregory Gaye (Retik), Craig Kelly (Mr. Henderson), Peter Brocco (Dr. Varney), Lyle Talbot (Baylor), Gloria Pall (Ruler's Assistant), Denver Pyle (Groog), Mauritz Hugo (Narkos), Joanne Jordan (Queen of the Mercurians), John Crawford, Coleman Francis, Zan Murray. "Enemies of the Universe" (7-16-55). "Atomic Peril" (7-23-55). "Cosmic Vengeance" (7-30-55). "Nightmare Typhoon" (8-6-55). "War of the Space Giants" (8-13-55). "Destroyers of the Sun" (8-20-55). "Robot Monster from Mars" (8-27-55). "The Hydrogen Hurricane" (9-3-55). "Solar Sky Raiders" (9-10-55). "S.O.S. Ice Age" (9-17-55). "Lost in Outer Space" (9-24-55).

"Captives of the Zero Hour" (10-8-55).

CONFLICT. "The Man from 1997" (11-27-56): James Garner, Gloria Talbot, Jacques Sernas, Charles Ruggles.

CREATURE, THE. British (1-30-55): Peter Cushing (Dr. John Rollason), Stanley Baker, Wolfe Morris, Eric Pohlmann, Simon Lack, Arnold Marle.

DANNY AND THE MERMAID. Pilot (5-17-78): Patrick Collins (Danny Stevens), Harlee McBride (Aqua), Ray Walston (Prof. Stoneham), Rick Fazel (Turtle), Conrad Janis (psychiatrist), Ancel Cook (pilot).

DARKROOM. 1981-1982. James Coburn (Host). "Closed Circuit" (11-27-81): Robert Webber (Greg Conway), Richard Anderson (Bellamy), Mary Frann (Beckwith), Lavelle Roby (Dr. Wilkerson), John H. Fields (Frank Merriman), Lee Duncan (Steve), James Purcell (guard), Steve Whitmore (engineer), John M. Benson (1st intern), Cliff Frazier (strongarm No. 1), Kate Williamson (doctor), Rozelle Gayle (Arab), Michael O'Guinne (2nd engineer), Robin Coleman (2nd intern), John Randolph. "Stay Tuned, We'll Be Right Back" (11-27-81): Lawrence Pressman (Charlie Miller), Joanna Miles (Janet Miller), Bert Freed (Mr. Miller), Shane Butterworth, Robert Gray. "The Bogeyman Will Get You" (12-4-81): Helen Hunt (Nancy), Quinn Cummings (Dee Dee), Randolph Powell (Philip Ames), Gloria DeHaven (Louise), Arlen Dean Snyder, R.G. Armstrong, William E. Phipps, Rick Beckner. "Uncle George" (12-4-81): Claude Akins (Bert Haskell), June Lockhart (Margo Haskell), Dub Taylor (Dixie Weeks), Dick Whittington (Uncle George). "Needlepoint" (12-11-81): Esther Rolle, Lawrence Hilton Jacobs. "Siege of 31 August" (12-11-81): Ronny Cox (Neil), Gail Strickland (Helen), Patrick Brennan (Ben), Pat Corley (Colonel), Hank Brandt (Sheriff). "A Quiet Funeral" (12-18-81): Robert F. Lyon (Marty Vetch), Eugene Roche (Charlie), Misty Rowe (Leda), Carmen Argenziano, John Medici. "Make Up" (12-18-81): Billy Crystal (Paddy), Sian Barbara Allen (Brenda), Jack Kruschen (Sam), Signe Hasso (Mrs. Lamont Tremayne), Brian Dennehy (Ro-

(DARKROOM cont.) land), Robert O'-Reilly (Sebastian), Elvia Allman (manageress), Roland Spivey (Burt Leeds), William Long, Jr. (bartender), Jodie Mann (clerk).

"The Partnership" (12-25-81): Pat Buttram (Tad Miller), David Carradine (biker), Carole Cook (Sally Anne), John Tuell, Jonathan Stark.

"Daisies" (12-25-81): Lloyd Bochner (Dr. John Michaelson), Rue McClanahan (Louise Michaelson), Elizabeth Halliday (Miss Wilson).

"Catnip" (12-25-81): Cyril O'Reilly (Ronnie Shires), Jocelyn Brando (Mrs. Mingle), Lynn Carlin (Mrs. Shires), Michael V. Gazzo (Nino), Karin Argoud (Loretta).

"Lost in Translation" (1-8-82): Andrew Prine (Dr. Paul Hudson), Whit Bissell (Arthur), Cyndy Garvey (Jeanette Hudson), Michael Zand (translator).

"Guillotine" (1-8-82): Patti D'Arbanville (Babette), France Benard (Pierre), Michael Constantine (Monsieur de Paris), Lilyan Chauvin (Madame), Logan Ramsay (Monsieur Konthinor), Dick Balduzzi (Louie), Todd Martin (gendarme), David Daniels (doctor), Zale Kessler (barber), Peter Jan Van Niel (gate guard), Robert Feero (prisoner), Alfred Dennis (baker).

DARK SHADOWS. 1966-71. Jonathan Frid (Barnabas Collins), Joan Bennett (Elizabeth Collins Stoddard/Flora Collins), Alexandre Moltke (Victoria Winters), Nancy Barrett (Carolyn Stoddard/Charity/Letitia Faye), Louis Edmonds (Roger Collins/Edward Collins), Grayson Hall (Dr. Julia Hoffman/Magda/Julia Collins), Kathryn Leigh Scott (Maggie Evans/Josette), Joel Crothers (Joe Haskell/Nathan Forbes), Lara Parker (Angelique/Cassandra/Valerie Collins), David Selby (Quentin Collins), John Karlen (Willie Loomis/Desmond Collins), David Henesy (David Collins/Tad Collins), Roger Davis (Peter Bradford), Sharon Smyth (Sarah Collins), David Ford (Sam Evans/Andre), Clarice Blackburn (Mrs. Johnson/Abigail Collins), Chris Pennock (Cyrus Longworth/Jeb Hawks/Gabriel Collins), Mitchell Ryan (Burke Devlin), Dana Elcar (Sheriff Patterson), Dennis Patrick (Jason McGuire), Robert Gerringer (Dr. Woodward), Anthony George (Jeremiah Collins), Kate Jackson (Daphne Harridge), Michael Stroka (Bruno/Laszlo), De-

nise Nickerson (Amy), Lisa Richards (Sabrina Stuart), Diana Millay (Mrs. Collins), Terry Crawford (Beth/Edith Collins), Robert Rodan (Adam), Marie Wallace (Eve), Paul Richard (King Johnny), Kathy Cody (Hallie Stokes/Carrie Stokes), Thayer David (Prof. Elliot Stokes/Count Petofi/Mordecai Grimes), Jerry Lacy (Rev. Trask), Humbert A. Astredo (Balberith/Charles Dawson), David Jay (Alexander), Gene Lindsey (Rondell Drew), Donna McKechnie (Amanda Harris/Oliver Corey), Michael Maitland (Michael), Virginia Vestoff (Samantha Collins), Keith Prentice (Morgan Collins), Donna Wandrey (Roxanne Drew), Alex Stevens (the Werewolf), Alan Feinstein, Don Briscoe, Conrad Fowkes, Alan Yorke.

DAY OF THE TRIFFIDS, THE. British (9-10-81 - 10-15-81).* John Duttine (Bill Masen), Jonathan Newth (Dr. Soames), Emma Relph (Jo), Stephen Yardley (John), Maurice Colbourne (Jack Coker), David Swift (Geadley), Perlita Neilson (Miss Durrant), Ian Halliburton (Grant), Robert Robinson (Palanguez), Steven Jonas (Young Bill), Keith Alexander (newsreel voice), Edmund Pegge (Walter), Cleo Sylvestre (nurse), Chris Gannon (patient), Alan Helm (blind man), Bonita Beach (blind woman), Max Faulkner (Jo's attacker), Caroline Fabbri (Tina), Christina Schofield (Shirley), Albie Woodington (gang leader), Andrew Paul (gang member), Mario Renzullo (gang member), Susie Fenwick (blind girl), Lindsey Moore (singer), Elizabeth Chambers (car attacker), Morris Barry (car attacker), Bernie Searle (car attacker), Desmond Cullum-Jones (Tom), Beryl Nesbitt (Tom's wife), Donald Pelmear (University gateman), Denis De Marne (Major Anderson), Andrew Miller (Dr. Vorless), John Hollis (Alf), John Benfield (Ted), Eva Griffiths (teenage girl), Jean Perkins (hotel manageres), Jon Rumney (manager), Terry Andrews (Frank), Gary Olsen (red-haired man), Sally Lahee (woman in street), Gordon Case (dying man), Christopher Owen (Vicar), Emily Dean (Susan), Jenny Lipman (Mary Brent), Desmond Adam (Dennis Brent), Lorna Charles (Susan), Denis Gilmore (David), Claire Ballard (Alice), Jenny Lipman (Mary), Gary Olsen (Torrence), Desmond Adams (Dennis)

*Aired in multiple segments; dates show first and last segments.

DESILU PLAYHOUSE.
"The Time Element" (11-24-58):
William Bendix (Peter Jenson), Martin
Balsam (Dr. Gillespie), Jesslyn Fax
(maid), Jesse White (bartender), Daryl
Hickman (Ensign Janoski), Caroline
Kearney (Mrs. Janoski), Joe De Rita
(drunk), Paul Bryar (bartender).
"Man in Orbit" (5-11-59): Lee
Marvin (Capt. David Roberts), E. G.
Marshall (Prof. Eric Carson), Peggy
McCay (Marie), Martin Balsam (Gam-
betta), Robert F. Simon (Gen. Finch).

DOCTOR WHO. British 1963 . William
Hartnell (the Doctor) 63-66, Patrick
Troughton (the Doctor) 66-70, Jon
Pertwee (the Doctor) 70-74, Tom Ba-
ker (the Doctor) 74-81, Peter Davi-
son (the Doctor) 81+, William Rus-
sell (Ian Chesterton),63-65, Jacque-
line Hill (Barbara Wright) 63-65,
Carole Ann Ford (Susan Foreman)
63-64, Maureen O'Brien (Vicki) 1965,
Peter Purves (Steven Taylor) 65-66,
Adrienne Hill (Katarina) 65-66, Jean
Marsh (Sara Kingdom) 65-66, Jackie
Lane (Dorothea Chaplet) 1966, Mi-
chael Craze (Ben Jackson) 66-67,
Anneke Wills (Polly) 66-67, Frazer
Hines (Jamie McCrimmon) 66-69,
Deborah Watling (Victoria Water-
field) 67-68, Wendy Padbury (Zoe
Herriet) 68-69, Nicholas Courtney
(Brigadier Alastair Gordon Leth-
bridge-Stewart) 68-75, John Levene
(Sgt. Benton) 68-76, Caroline John
(Liz Shaw) 70-71, Katy Manning (Jo
Grant) 71-73, Roger Delgado (the
Master) 71-73, Richard Franklin
(Capt. Mike Yates) 71-74, Elisabeth
Sladen (Sarah Jane Smith) 73-76, Ian
Marter (Harry Sullivan) 74-75, Lou-
ise Jameson (Leela) 77-78, John
Leeson (voice of K-9) 77-78, Mary
Tamm (Romanadvoratrelundar) 78-
79, Lalla Ward (Romana) 79-80, Da-
vid Brierley (voice of K-9) 79-80,
Matthew Waterhouse (Adric) 80+, Sa-
rah Sutton (Nyssa) 81+, Janet Field-
ing (Tegan) 81+.
"An Unearthly Child" (11-23-63 -
12-14-63):* Jeremy Young (Kal), De-
rek Newark (Za), Alethea Charlton (Hur),
Eileen Way (old mother), Howard Lang
(Horg).
"The Dead Planet" (12-21-63 - 2-
1-64): Alan Wheatley (Temmosus), John
Lee (Alydon), Philip Bond (Ganatus),
Virginia Wetherell (Dyoni), Gerald Curtis (Elyon), Jonathan Crane (Kristas),

*Aired in multiple segments; dates show first and
last segments.

Marcus Hammond (Antodus), Chris
Browning (Thal), Katie Cashfield, Vez
Delahunt, Kevin Glenny, Ruth Harrison,
Lesley Hill, Steve Pokol, Jeanette Ros-
sini, Eric Smith (Thals), Robert Jewell,
Gerald Taylor, Kevin Manser, Peter
Murphy, Michael Summerton (Daleks),
David Graham, Peter Hawkins (Dalek
voices).
"Beyond the Sun" (2-8-64 - 2-15-
64):
"Marco Polo" (2-22-64 - 4-4-64).
Mark Eden (Marco Polo), Derren Nes-
bitt (Tegana), Zienia Merton (Ping-Cho),
Jimmy Gardner (Chenchu), Leslie Bates
(man at lop), Charles Wade (Malik),
Philip Voss (Acomat), Michael Guest
(Mongol bandit), Paul Carson (Ling-Tau),
Gabor Baraker (Wang-Lo), Peter Law-
rence (Vizier), Tutte Lemkow (Kuiju),
Martin Miller (Kublai Khan), Basil Tang
(Office Foreman), Claire Davenport
(Empress).
"The Keys of Marinus" (4-11-64 -
5-16-64): George Coulouris (Arbitan),
Robin Philips (Altos), Katherine Scho-
field (Sabetha), Edmund Warwick (Adr-
rius), Francis de Wolfe (Vasor), Mar-
tin Cort (Voord), Peter Stenson (Voord),
Gordon Wales (Voord), Heron Carvie
(voice of Morpho), Michael Allaby (Larn),
Alan James (Ice Soldier), Anthony Ver-
ner (Ice Soldier), Henry Thomas (Tar-
ron), Raf de la Torre (Senior Judge),
Alan James (Judge), Fiona Walker (Ka-
la), Martin Cort (Aydan), Donald Pickering (Eyesen), Sephen Dartnell (Yartek).
"The Aztecs" (5-23-64 - 6-13-64)::
Keith Pyot (Autloc), John Ringham (Tlo-
toxl), Ian Cullen (Ixta), Margot Van Der
Burgh (Cameca), Tom Booth (Victim),
David Anderson (Captain), Walter Ran-
dall (Tanila), Andre Boulay (Perfect
Victim).
"The Sensorites" (6-20-64 - 8-1-
64): Ilona Rogers (Carol), Stephen Dart-
nell (John), Lorre Cossette (Captain
Maitland), Eric Francis (1st Elder),
Bartlett Mullins (2nd Elder), Ken Tyll-
sen (Sensorite), Joe Greig (Sensorite),
Peter Glaze (Sensorite), Arthur Newall
(Sensorite), John Bailey (Commander),
Martyn Huntley (Survivor), Giles Phibbs
(Survivor).
"The French Revolution" (8-8-64 -
9-12-64): Laidlaw Dalling (Rouvray),
Neville Smith (D'Argenson), Peter Wal-
ker (small boy), Robert Hunter (Sergeant),
Ken Lawrence (Lieutenant), James Hall
(Soldier), Howard Charlton (Judge), Jack
Cunningham (Jailer), Jeffrey Wickham
(Webster), Dallas Cavell (Overseer), Den-
nis Cleary (Peasant), James Cairncross

(DOCTOR WHO cont.) (Lemaitre), Roy Herrick (Jean), Donald Morely (Renan), John Barrard (Shopkeeper), Caroline Hunt (Danielle), Edward Brayshaw (Colbert), Keith Anderson (Robespierre), Ronald Pickup (Physician), Terry Bale (Soldier), John Law (Barrass), Tony Wall (Bonaparte), Patrick Marley (Soldier).

"Planet of the Giants" (10-31-64 - 11-14-64): Alan Tilvern (Forester), Frank Crawshaw (Farrow), Reginald Barrat (Smithers), Rosemary Johnson (Hilda), Fred Ferris (Bert).

"The Dalek Invasion of Earth" (11-21-64 - 12-26-64): Benard Kay (Carl Tyler), Peter Fraser (David Campbell), Ann Davies (Jenny), Michael Goldie (Craddock), Graham Rigby (Larry Madison), Alan Judd (Dortmun), Martyn Bentley (Roboman), Peter Badger (Roboman), Robert Aldous (Rebel), Robert Jewell (Dalek), Gerald Taylor (Dalek), Nick Evans (Dalek), Peter Murphy (Dalek), Kevin Manser (Dalek), Peter Hawkins (Dalek voice), David Graham (Dalek voice), Michael Davis (Thomson), Richard McNeef (Baker), Nicholas Smith (Wells), Nick Evans (Slyther), Patrick O'Connell (Ashton), Jean Conroy (Woman), Meriel Horson (Woman).

"The Rescue" (1-2-65 - 1-9-65): Ray Barrett (Bennett/Koquilion), Tom Sheridan (Spaceship Captain), Sydney Wilson (Koquilion).

"The Romans" (1-16-65 - 2-6-65): Derek Francis (Emperor Nero), Kay Patrick (Poppea), Michael Peake (Tavius), Peter Diamond (Delos), Derek Sydney (Sevcheria), Nicholas Evans (Centurion), Margot Thomas (stall-holder), Edward Kelsey (slave-buyer), Bart Allison (Maximus Petulion), Barry Jackson (Ascaris), Dorothy-Rose Gribble (woman slave), Gerton Klauber (Galley Master), Earnest Jennings (man in market), John Caesar (man in market), Tony Cambden (messenger), Brian Proudfoot (Tigilinus), Ann Tirard (Locusta).

"The Web Planet" (2-13-65 - 3-20-65): Roslyn De Winter (Vrestin), Arthur Blake (Hrhoonda), Catherine Fleming (Voice of Aminus), Jocelyn Birdsall (Hylnia), Martin Jarvis (Captain Hilio), Joylyon Booth (Prapilius), Ian Thompson (Hetra), Barbara Joss (Nemini), Catherine Fleming (voice of the Animus), Robert Jewell (Zarbi), Jack Pitt (Zarbi), Gerald Taylor (Zarbi), Hugh Lund (Zarbi), John Scott Martin (Zarbi), Kevin Manser (Zarbi).

"The Lionheart" (3-27-65 - 4-

17-65): Julian Glover (King Richard), Jean Marsh (Joanna), Walter Randall (El Akir), Roger Avon (Saphadin), Bernard Kay (Saladin), John Flint (William des Preaux), David Anderson (Reynier de Marun), Bruce Wightman (William de Tornebu), Reg Pritchard (Ben Daheer), Tony Caunter (Thatcher), Derek Ware (Saracen Warrior), Valentino Musetti (Saracen Warrior), Anthony Colby (Saracen Warrior), Robert Lankesheer (Chamberlain), Zahra Segal (Sheyrah), Gabor Baraker (Luigi Ferrigo), Chris Konyils (Saracen guard), Raymond Novak (Saracen guard), John Bay (Earl of Leicester), Petra Markham (Safiya), George Little (Haroun), Sandra Hampton (Maimuna), Viviane Sorrel (Fatima), Diane McKenzie (Hafya), Tutte Lemkow (Ibrahim), Billy Cornelius (soldier).

"The Space Museum" (4-24-65 - 5-15-65): Richard Shaw (Lobos), Jeremy Bulloch (Tor), Peter Sanders (Sita), Peter Craze (Dako), Salvin Stewart (Messenger), Peter Diamond (technician), Ivor Salter (Commander), Billy Cornelius (guard), Murphy Grumbar (Dalek), Peter Hawkins (Dalek voice).

"The Chase" (5-22-65 - 6-26-65): Ian Thompson (Malsan), Peter Purves (Morton Dill), David Blake Kelly (Captain Briggs), Malcom Rogers (Count Dracula), John Maxim (Frankenstein's Monster), Edmund Warwick (Robot Doctor), Robert Marsden (Abraham Lincoln), Hugh Walters (William Shakespeare), Roger Hammond (Roger Bacon), Vivienne Bennett (Queen Elizabeth I), Richard Coe (TV Announcer), Jack Pitt (Mire Beast/steward), Gerald Taylor (Dalek), Kevin Manser (Dalek), Robert Jewell (Dalek), John Scott Martin (Dalek), Peter Hawkins (Dalek voice), David Graham (Dalek voice), Hywel Bennett (Rynian), Al Raymond (Prondyn), Arne Gordon (guide), Dennis Chinnery (Albert Richardson), Patrick Carter (Bosun), Douglas Ditta (Willoughby), Roslyn de Winter (Grey Lady), Murphy Grumbar (Mechanoid), Jack Pitt (Mechanoid), John Scott Martin (Mechanoid), Ken Tyllson (Mechanoid), David Graham (Mechanoid voices), Derek Ware (bus conductor).

"The Time Meddler" (7-3-65 - 7-24-65): Peter Butterworth (the Monk), Michael Miller (Wulnoth), Peter Russel (Eldred), Althea Charlton (Edith), Michael Guest (Hunter), Norman Hartley (Ulf), Geoffrey Cheshire (Viking Leader), David Anderson (Sven), Ronald Rich (Gunnar).

"Galaxy Four" (9-11-65 - 10-2-65): Stephanie Bidmead (Maaga), Marina Mar-

tin (Drahvin), Susanne Carroll (Drahvin), Lyn Ashley (Drahvin), Jimmy
Kaye (Chumblie), Angelo Muscat (Chumblie), William Shearer (Chumblie), Pepi Poupee (Chumblie), Tommy Reynolds
(Chumblie), Robert Cartland (voice of
the Rill), Barry Jackson (Garvey).
"Mission to the Unknown" (10-9-
65): Edward de Souza (Marc Cory),
Robert Cartland (Malpha), Jeremy
Young (Gordon Lowery), Robert Jewell
(Dalek), Kevin Manser (Dalek), Gerald
Taylor (Dalek), John Scott Martin (Da-
lek), Peter Hawkins (Dalek voice), Da-
vid Graham (Dalek voice).
"The Myth Makers" (10-16-65 -
11-6-65): Ivor Salter (Odysseus), Fran-
cis de Wolff (Agamamnon), Cavan Ken-
dall (Achilles), Alan Haywood (Hector),
Jack Melford (Menelaus), Tutte Lem-
kow (Cyclops), Max Adrian (Priam),
Barrie Ingham (Paris), James Lyam
(Troilus), Frances White (Cassandra),
Jan Luxton (Messenger).
"The Dalek Master Plan" (11-13-
65 - 1-29-66): Nicholas Courtney (Bret
Vyon), Brian Cant (Kert Gantry), Pam-
ela Greer (Lizan), Philip Anthony (Roald),
Kevin Stoney (Mavic Chen), Michael
Guest (Interviewer), Julian Sherrier
(Zephon), Roy Evans (Trantis), Doug-
las Sheldon (Kriksen), Dallas Cavell
(Bors), Geoffrey Cheshire (Garge),
Maurice Browning (Karlton), Roger A-
von (Daxtar), James Hall (Borkar), Bill
Meilen (Froyn), John Herrington (Rhyn-
mal), Terence Woodfield (Celation),
Peter Butterworth (Monk), Roger Brier-
ly (Trevor), Bruce Wightman (Scott),
Jeffrey Isaac (Khephren), Derek Ware
(Tuthmos), Walter Randall (Hyksos),
Brian Mosely (Malpha), Robert Jewell
(Dalek), Kevin Manser (Dalek), Gerald
Taylor (Dalek), John Scott Martin (Da-
lek), Peter Hawkins (Dalek voice), Da-
vid Graham (Dalek voice), Clifford Earl
(Sergeant), Norman Mitchell (Police-
man), Malcolm Rogers (Policeman),
Kenneth Thornett (Inspector), Reg Prit-
chard (man in mackintosh), Sheila Dunn
(Blossom Lefavre), Leonard Grahame
(Darcy Tranton), Royston Tickner (Stein-
berger P. Green), Mark Ross (Ingmar
Knopf), Conrad Monk (Assistant Direc-
tor), David James (Arab Sheik), Paula
Topham (Vamp), Robert Jewell (Clown),
Albert Barrington (Prof. Webster), Buddy Windrush (prop man), Steven Machin
(cameraman).
"The Massacre" (2-5-66 - 2-26-
66): Eric Thompson (Gaston), David
Weston (Nicholas), John Tillinger (Simon), Christopher Tranchell (Roger),

Erik Chitty (Charles Preslin), Annette
Robertson (Anne Chaplette), Andre Mo-
rell (Marshall Tavannes), Joan Young
(Catherine de Medici), Leonard Sachs
(Admiral de Coligny), Barry Justice
(King Charles IX), Edwin Fenn (landlord),
Clive Cazen (guard captain), Reginald
Jessup (servant), Cynthia Etherington
(old lady), Michael Bilton (Toligny),
Roy Danton (1st man), Ernest Smith
(2nd man), Jack Tarran (1st guard),
Leslie Bates (2nd guard), John Slavid
(Officer), William Hartnell (Abbot of
Amboise).
"The Ark" (3-5-66 - 3-26-66):
Eric Elliott (Commander), Inigo Jack-
son (Zeutos), Roy Spencer (Manyak),
Kate Newman (Mallium), Michael Sheard
(Rhos), Ian Frost (Baccu), Edmund Coul-
ter (Monoid), Frank George (Monoid),
Ralph Corrigan (Monoid), Roy Skelton
(Monoid voice), Stephanie Heesom (Guar-
dian), Paul Greenhalgh (Guardian), Te-
rence Woodfield (Maharis), Terence
Bayler (Yendon), Brian Wright (Dassuk),
Eileen Helsby (Venussa), Richard Beale
(Refusion voice), John Caesar (Monoid).
"The Celestial Toyroom" (4-2-
66 - 5-21-66): Michael Gough (Toyma-
ker), Campbell Singer (Joe the Clown),
Carmen Silvera (Clara, the Clown), Pe-
ter Stephens & Reg Levers (the Hearts
Family), Breyl Brabham (Dancing Doll),
Ann Harrison (Dancing Doll), Delia Lin-
den (Dancing Doll), Peter Stephens (Cy-
ril).
"The Gunfighters" (4-30-66 - 5-21-
66): John Alderson (Wyatt Earp). Antho-
ny Jacobs (Doc Holliday), David Cole
(Billy Canton), William Hurndell (Ike
Clanton), Maurice Good (Phineas Clanton),
Sheena Marshe (Kate), Shane Rimmer
(Seth Harper), David Graham (Charlie),
Richard Beale (Bat Masterson), Reed
de Rouen (Pa Clanton), Laurence Payne
(Johnny Ringo), Martyn Huntley (Warren
Earp), Victor Carin (Virgil Earp).
"The Savages" (5-28-66 - 6-18-66):
Ewen Solon (Chal), Patrick Godfrey (Tor),
Peter Thomas (Edal), Geoffrey Frede-
rick (Exorse), Frederick Jaeger (Jano),
Robert Sidaway (Avon), Kay Patrick
(Flower), Clare Jenkins (Nanina), Nor-
man Henry (Senta), Edward Caddick
(Wylda), Andrew Lodge (assistant), Chris-
topher Debham (assistant), Tony Holland
(assistant), John Dillon (savage), Tim
Goodman (guard).
"The War Machines" (6-25-66 -
7-16-66): Alan Curtis (Major Green),
John Karvey (Prof. Brett), Sandra Bry-
ant (Kitty), Ewan Proctor (Flash), William Mervyn (Sir Charles Summer), John

(DOCTOR WHO cont.) Cater (Prof. Krimpton), Ric Felgate (journalist), John Doye (interviewer), Desmond Cullum-Jones (tramp), Roy Godfrey (Taximan), Gerald Taylor (War Machine Operator), John Rolfe (Captain), John Boyd-Brent (Sergeant), Frank Jarvis (Corporal), Robin Dawson (soldier), Kenneth Kendall (himself), George Cross (Minister), Edward Colliver (mechanic), John Slavid (man in phone box), Dwight Whylie (announcer), Carl Conway (correspondent).

"The Smugglers" (9-10-66 - 10-1-66): Terence de Marney (Churchwarden), George Cooper (Cherub), David Blake Kelly (Jacob Kewper), Mike Lucas (Tom), Paul Whitsun-Jones (Squire), Derek Ware (Spaniard), Michael Godfrey (Pike), Elroy Josephs (Jamaica), John Ringham (Blake), Jack Bligh (Gaptooth).

"The Tenth Planet" (10-8-66 - 10-29-66): Robert Beatty (Gen. Cutler), Alan White (Schultz), Earl Cameron (Williams), Dudley Jones (Dyson), David Dodimead (Barclay), Shane Shelton (Tito), John Brandon (Sergeant), Steve Plytas (Wigner), Christopher Matthews (radar technician), Reg Whitehead (Krail/ Jarl), Harry Brooks (Jalon), Greg Palmer (Shav/Gern), Ellen Cullen (technician), Glen Beck (announcer), Callen Angelo (Cutler), Christopher Dunham (R/T Technician), Harry Brooks (Krang), Peter Hawkins (Cyberman voice), Roy Skelton (Cyberman voice).

"The Power of the Daleks" (11-5-66 - 12-10-66): Martin King (Examiner), Nicholas Hawtrey (Quinn), Bernard Archard (Bragen), Robert James (Lesterson), Pamela Ann Davy (Hensell), Edward Kelsey (Resur), Richard Kane (Valmar), Peter Phorbes-Robertson (guard), Steven Scott (Kebble), Robert Russell (guard), Robert Cuckham (guard), Gerald Taylor (Dalek), Kevin Manser (Dalek), Robert Jewell (Dalek), John Scott Martin (Dalek), Peter Hawkins (Dalek voice).

"The Highlanders" (12-17-66 - 1-7-67): William Dysart (Alexander), Donald Bisset (Laird), Hannah Gordon (Kirsty), Michael Elwyn (Ffinch), Peter Welch (Sergeant), David Garth (Grey), Sydney Arnold (Perkins), Tom Bowman (sentry), Dallas Cavell (Trask), Barbara Bruce (Mollie), Andrew Downie (Mackay), Peter Diamond (Sailor), Guy Middleton (Attwood).

"The Underwater Menace" (1-14-67 - 2-4-67): Joseph Furst (Prof. Zaroff), Catherine Howe (Ara), Tom Watson (Ramo), Peter Stephens (Lolem), Colin Jeavons (Damon), Gerald Taylor (Damon's assistant), Graham Ashley (Overseer), Tony Handy (guard), Paul Anil (Jacko), P. G. Stephens (Sean), Noel Johnson (Thous), Roma Woodnutt (Nola).

"The Moon Base" (2-11-67 - 3-4-67): Patrick Barr (Hobson), Andre Maranne (Benoit), Michael Wolf (Nils), John Rolde (Sam), Alan Rowe (Dr. Evans/ Space Control voice), Mark Heath (Ralph), Barry Ashton (crewman), Derek Calder (crewman), Arnold Chazen (crewman), Leon Maybank (crewman), Victor Pemberton (crewman), Edward Phillips (crewman), Ron Pinnell (crewman), Alan Wells (crewman), Robin Scott (crewman), Sonnie Willis (crewman), John Wills (Cyberman), Peter Greene (Cyberman), Reg Whitehead (Cyberman), Keith Goodman (Cyberman), Peter Hawkins (Cyberman voice), Dennis McCarthy (Controller Rinberg's voice).

"The Macra Terror" (3-11-67 - 4-1-67): Peter Jeffrey (Pilot), Graham Armitage (Barney), Ian Fairbairn (Questa), Jane Enshawe (Sunnaa), Sandra Bryant (Chicki), Maureen Lane (Majorette), Terence Lodge (Medok), Gerton Klauber (Ola), Graham Leaman (Controller), Anthony Gardner (Alvis), Denis Goacher (Control voice), Richard Beale (broadcast voice), Robert Jewell (Macra), John Harvey (Official), John Caesar (guard), Steve Emerson (guard), Danny Rae (guard), Roger Jerome (cheerleader), Terry Wright (cheerleader), Ralph Carrigan (cheerleader).

"The Faceless Ones" (4-8-67 - 5-13-67): James Appleby (Policeman), Colin Gordon (Commandant), George Selway (Meadows), Wanda Ventham (Jean Rock), Victor Winding (Spencer), Peter Whitaker (Gascoigne), Donald Pickering (Blade), Christopher Tranchell (Jenkins), Madalena Nicol (Pinto), Bernard Kay (Crossland), Pauline Collins (Samantha Briggs), Gilly Fraser (Ann Davidson), Brijit Paul (announcer), Barry Wilsher (Heslington), Michael Ladkin (pilot), Leonard Trolley (Reynolds).

"The Evil of the Daleks" (5-20-67 - 7-1-67): Alec Ross (Bob Hall), Griffith Davies (Kennedy), John Bailley (Edward Waterfield), Geoffrey Colvile (Perry), Robert Jewell (Dalek), Gerald Taylor (Dalek), Murphy Grumbar (Dalek), John Scott Martin (Dalek), Roy Skelton (Dalek voice), Peter Hawkins (Dalek voice), Jo Rowbottom (Mollie Dawson), Marius Goring (Theodore Maxtible), Brijit Forsyth (Ruth Maxtible), Windsor Davies

(Toby), Gary Watson (Terrall), Sonny Caldinez (Kemel).

"The Tomb of the Cybermen" (9-2-67 - 9-23-67): Roy Stewart (Toberman), Aubrey Richards (Prof. Parry), Cyril Shaps (Viner), Clive Merrison (Callum), Shirley Cooklin (Kaftan), George Roubicek (Hopper), George Pastell (Kleig), Alan Johns (Rogers), Bernard Holley (Haydon), Ray Grover (crewman), Michael Kilgarrif (Cyberman), Hans Le Vries (Cyberman), Tony Harwood (Cyberman), John Hogan (Cyberman), Richard Kerley (Cyberman), Ronald Lee (Cyberman), Charles Pemberton (Cyberman), Kenneth Seeger (Cyberman), Reg Whitehead (Cyberman), Peter Hawkins (Cyberman voice).

"The Abominable Snowmen" (9-30-67 - 11-4-67): Jack Watling (Prof. Travers), Norman Jones (Khrisong), David Spenser (Thonmi), David Grey (Rinchen), Raymond Llewellyn (Sapan), Charles Morgan (Songsten), Wolfe Morris (Padmasambhava), David Baron (Ralpachan), Reg Whitehead (Yeti), Tony Harwood (Yeti), John Hogan (Yeti), Richard Kerley (Yeti).

"The Ice Warriors" (11-11-67 - 12-16-67): Wendy Gifford (Miss Garrett), Peter Barkworth (Clent), George Waring (Arden), Malcolm Taylor (Walters), Peter Diamond (Davis), Angus Lennie (Storr), Peter Sallis (Penley), Bernard Bresslaw (Varga), Roy Skelton (Computer voice), Roger Jones (Zondal), Sonny Caldinez (Turoc), Tony Harwood (Rintan), Michael Attwell (Isbur).

"The Enemy of the World" (12-23-67 - 1-27-68): Henry Stamper (Anton), Rhys McConnochie (Rod), Simon Caine (Curly), Mary Peach (Astrid), Bill Kerr (Kent), Colin Douglas (Bruce), Milton Johns (Benik), George Pravda (Denes), David Nettheim (Fedorin), Carmen Munroe (Fariah), Gordon Faith (guard captain), Bill Lyons (Captain), Reg Lye (Griffin), Andrew Staines (Sergeant), Christopher Burgess (Swann), Adam Verney (Colin), Margaret Mickey (Mary), Dibbs Mather (guard), Elliott Cairnes (guard), Bob Anderson (guard), William McGuirk (guard), Patrick Troughton (Salamander).

"The Web of Fear" (2-3-68 - 3-9-68): Jack Watling (Prof. Travers), Tina Packer (Anne Travers), Frederick Schrecker (Julius Silverstein), Rod Beacham (Lane), Ralph Watson (Knight), Morgan Richardson (Blake), Jon Rollason (Chorley), Jack Woolgar (Arnold), Stephen Whittaker (Wems), Bernard G.

High (soldier), Joseph O'Connell (soldier), John Levene (Yeti), John Lord (Yeti), Gordon Stothard (Yeti), Colin Warman (Yeti), Jeremy King (Yeti), Roger Jacombs (Yeti), Derek Pollitt (Evans).

"Fury from the Deep" (3-16-68 - 4-20-68): Victor Maddern (Robson), Roy Spencer (Harris), Graham Leaman (Price), Peter Ducrow (guard), Jane Murphy (Maggie Harris), John Garvin (Curney), Hubert Rees (Chief Engineer), John Abineri (Van Lutyens), Richard Mayes (Baxter), Bill Burridge (Quill), John Gill (Oak), Margaret John (Megan Jones), Brian Cullingford (Perkins).

"The Wheel in Space" (4-27-68 - 6-1-68): Freddie Foote (Servo-Robot), Eric Flynn (Ryan), Anne Ridler (Dr. Corwyn), Clare Jenkins (Tanya Lernov), Michael Turner (Bennett), Donald Sumpter (Enrico Casali), Kenneth Watson (Duggan), Michael Goldie (Laleham), Derrik Gilbert (Vallance), Kevork Malikyan (Rudkin), Peter Laird (Chang), James Mellor (Flannigan), Jerry Holmes (Cyberman), Gordon Stothard (Cyberman), Peter Hawkins (Cyberman voice), Roy Skelton (Cyberman voice).

"The Dominators" (8-10-68 - 9-7-68): Ronald Allen (Rago), Kenneth Ives (Toba), Arthur Cox (Cully), Philip Voss (Wahed), Malcolm Terris (Etnin), Nicolette Pendrell (Tolata), Felicity Gibson (Kando), Giles Block (Teel), Johnson Bayly (Balan), Walter Fitzgerald (Senex), Ronald Mansell (Council Member), John Cross (Council Member), Alan Gerrard (Bovem), Brian Cant (Tensa), John Hicks (Quark), Gary Smith (Quark), Freddie Wilson (Quark), Sheila Grant (Quark voice).

"The Mind Robber" (9-14-68 - 10-12-68): Emrys Jones (Master of the Land), John Atterbury (White Robot), Ralph Carrigan (White Robot), Bill Weisner (White Robot), Terry Wright (White Robot), Hamish Wilson (Jamie), Philip Ryan (Redcoat), Bernard Horsfall (Gulliver), Barbara Loft (Child), Sylvestra Tozel (Child), Timothy Horton (Child), Martin Langley (Child), David Reynolds (Child), Christopher Reynolds (Child), Paul Alexander (Clockwork Soldier), Ian Hines (Clockwork Soldier), Richard Ireson (Clockwork Soldier), Christine Pirie (Rapunzel), Sue Pulford (Medusa), Christopher Robbie (Karkus), David Cannon (Cyrano), John Greenwood (D'Artagnan/Lancelot), Gerry Wain (Blackbeard).

"The Invasion" (11-2-68 - 12-21-68): Murray Evans (lorry driver), Walter Randall (Patrolman), Sally Faulkner

(DOCTOR WHO cont.) (Isobel Watkins), Geoffrey Cheshire (Tracy), Kevin Stoney (Tobias Vaughn), Peter Halliday (Packer), Edward Burnham (Prof. Watkins), Ian Fairbairn (Gregory), James Thornhill (Sgt. Walters), Robert Sidaway (Capt. Turner), Sheila Dunn (Operator), Edward Dentith (Rutlidge), Peter Thompson (workman), Dominic Allan (policeman), Stacy Davies (Perkins), Clifford Earl (Branwell), Norman Hatley (Peters), Reg Whitehead (Cyberman), Greg Palmer (Cyberman), Pat Gorman (Cyberman), Harry Brooks (Cyberman), John Wills (Cyberman), Tony Harwood (Cyberman).

"The Krotons" (12-28-68 - 1-18-69): James Copeland (Selris), Gilbert Wynne (Thara), Terence Brown (Abu), Madeleine Mills (Vana), Philip Madoc (Eelek), Richard Ireson (Axus), James Cairncross (Beta), Maurice Selwyn (Custodian), Bronson Shaw (student), Robert La Bassiere (Kroton), Miles Northover (Kroton), Rok Skelton (Kroton voice), Patrick Tull (Kroton voice).

"The Seeds of Death" (1-25-69 - 3-1-69): Alan Bennion (Slaar), Steve Peters (Ice Warrior), Philip Ray (Eldred), Louise Pajo (Gia Kelly), John Witty (computer voice), Ric Felgate (Brent), Harry Towb (Osgood), Ronald Leigh-Hunt (Radnor), Terry Scully (Fewsham), Christopher Coll (Phipps), Martin Cort (Locke), Tony Harwood (Ice Warrior), Sonny Caldinez (Ice Warrior), Derrick Slater (guard), Graham Leaman (Marshal), Hugh Morton (Sir James Gregson).

"The Space Pirates" (3-8-69 - 4-12-69): Brian Peck (Dervise), Dudley Foster (Caven), Jack May (Hermack), Donald Gee (Warne), George Layton (Penn), Nick Zaran (Sorba), Lisa Daniely (Madeleine), Anthony Donovan (guard), Gordon Gostelow (Clancey), Steve Peters (guard), Edmond Knight (Dom Issigri).

"The War Game" (4-19-69 - 6-21-69): Jane Sherwin((Lady Buckingham), David Savile (Carstairs), John Livesby (German soldier), Bernard Davies (German soldier), Brian Forster (Willis), Terence Buyler (Barrington), Noel Coleman (Gen. Smythe), Hubert Rees (Capt. Ransome), Esmond Webb (Burns), Richard Steele (Gorton), Peter Stanton (Chauffeur), Pat Gorman (policeman), Tony McEwan (Redcoat), David Valla (Crane), Gregg Palmer (Lucke), David Garfield (Von Weich), Edward Brayshaw (War Chief), Philip Madoc (War Lord), James Bree (Security

Chief), Bill Hutchinson (Thompson), Terry Adams (Riley), Leslie Schofield (Leroy), Vernon Dobtcheff (Scientist), Rudolph Walker (Harper), John Atterbury (Alien), Charles Pemberton (Alien), Michael Lynch (Spencer), Graham Weston (Russell), David Troughton (Moor), Peter Craze (Du Pont), Michael Napier (Villar), Stephen Hubay (Petrov), Bernard Horsfall (Time Lord), Trevor Martin (Time Lord), Clyde Pollitt (Time Lord), Clare Jenkins (Tanya), Freddie Wilson (Quark), John Levene (Yeti), Tony Harwood (Ice Warrior), Roy Pearce (Cyberman), Robert Jewell (Dalek).

"Spearhead from Space" (1-3-70 - 1-24-70): Hugh Burden (Channing), Neil Wilson (Seeley), John Breslin (Capt. Munro), Anthony Webb (Dr. Henderson), Helen Dorward (Nurse), Talfryn Thomas (Mullins), George Lee (Captain Forbes), Iain Smith (UNIT man), Tessa Shaw (UNIT man), Ellis Jones (UNIT man), Allan Mitchell (Wagstaff), Prentis Hancock (reporter), Derek Smee (Ransome), John Woodnutt (Hibbert), Betty Bowden (Meg Seeley), Hamilton Dyce (Scobie), Henry McCarthy (Dr. Beavis), Clifford Cox (soldier), Edmund Bailey (waxworks attendant).

"The Silurians" (1-31-70 - 3-14-70): John Newman (Spencer), Bill Matthews (Davis), Peter Miles (Dr. Lawrence), Norman Jones (Baker), Thomasine Heiner (Miss Dawson), Fulton Mackay (Dr. Quinn), Roy Braningan (Roberts), Ian Cunningham (Dr. Meredith), Paul Barrow (Hawkins), Pat Gorman (Silurian Scientist), Dave Carter (Old Silurian), Nigel John (Young Silurian), Paul Barton (Silurian), Simon Cain (Silurian), John Churchill (Silurian), Dave Carter (Silurian), Peter Halliday (Silurian voice), Nancie Jackson (Doris Squire), Gordon Richardson (Squire), Richard Steel (Hart), Ian Talbot (Travis), Geoffrey Palmer (Masters), Harry Swift (Robins), Brendan Barry (Doctor), Darek Pallitt (Wright), Alan Mason (Corporal Nutting).

"The Ambassadors of Death" (3-21-70 - 5-2-70): Robert Cawdron (Taltalian), Ric Felgate (Van Lynden), Ronald Allen (Ralph Cornish), Michael Wisher (John Wakefield), Cheryl Molineaux (Miss Rutherford), John Abineri (Carrington), Ray Armstrong (Grey), Robert Robertson (Collinson), Ivan Moreno (Dobson), James Haswell (Champion), Bernard Martin (Control Room Assistant), Dallas Cavell (Quinian), Steve Peters (Astronaut), Neville Simons (Astronaut), Gordon Sterne (Heldorf), William Dysart (Reegan), Cyril Shaps

(Lennox), John Lord (Masters), Max Faulkner (soldier), Joanna Ross (1st assistant), Carl Conway (2nd assistant), Ric Felgate (Astronaut), James Clayton (Parker), Peter Noel Cook (Alien), Peter Halliday (Alien voice), Neville Simons (Michaels), Steve Peters (Lefee), Geoffrey Reeves (Johnson).

"Inferno" (5-9-70 - 6-2-70): Olaf Pooley (Stahlman), Christopher Benjamin (Sir Gold), Ian Fairbairn (Bromley), Walter Randall (Slocum), Sheila Dunn (Petra Williams), Derek Newark (Greg Sutton), David Simeon (Latimer), Derek Ware (Wyatt), Roy Scannell (sentry), Keith James (Patterson), Dave Carter (Primord), Pat Gormon (Primord), Philip Ryan (Primord), Peter Thompson (Primord), Walter Henry (Primord).

"The Terror of the Autons" (1-2-71 - 1-23-71): John Baskomb (Rossini), Dave Carter (museum attendant), Christopher Burgess (Prof. Philips), Andrew Staines (Goodge), Frank Mills (radio-telescope director), David Garth (Time Lord), Michael Wisher (Rex Farrel), Barbara Leake (Mrs. Farrel), Harry Towb (McDermott), Stephen Jack (Farrel, Sr.), Roy Stewart (strong man), Terry Walsh (Auton), Pat Gorman (Auton), Haydn Jones (Auton voice), Dermot Tuohy (Brownrose), Norman Stanley (telephone man).

"The Mind of Evil" (1-30-71 - 3-6-71): Eric Mason (Green), Roy Purcell (Powes), Raymond Westwell (Governor), Simon Lack (Prof. Kettering), Michael Sheard (Dr. Summers), Bill Matthews (Officer), Barry Wade (Officer), Dave Carter (Officer), Martin Gordon (Officer), Neil McCarthy (Barnham), Olive Scott (Linwood), Fernanda Marlowe (Bell), Pik-Sen Lim (Chin-Lee), Kristopher Kum (Fu Peng), Haydn Jones (Vosper), William Marlowe (Mailer), Tommy Duggan (Alcott), David Calderisi (Charlie), Patrick Godfrey (Cosworth), Johnny Barrs (Fuller), Matthew Walters (prisoner).

"The Claws of Axos" (3-13-71 - 4-3-71): Peter Bathurst (Chinn), Paul Grist (Bill Filer), Fernanda Marlowe (Corporal Bell), Derek Ware (Pigbin Josh), Donald Hewlett (Sir George Hardiman), David Savile (Winser), Bernard Holley (Axos Man), Kenneth Benda (Minister), Tim Piggott (Harker), Michael Walker (radar operator), David G. March (radar operator), Nick Hobbs (driver), Royston Farrell (technician).

"Colony in Space" (4-10-71 - 5-15-71): Peter Forbes-Robertson (Time Lord), John Baker (Time Lord), Graham Leaman (Tim Lord), John Scott Martin (Robot), David Webb (Leeson), Sheila Grant (Jane), John Line (Martin), John Ringham (Ashe), Mitzi Webster (Mrs. Martin), Nicholas Pennell (Winton), Helen Worth (Mary Ashe), Roy Skelton (Norton), Pat Gorman (Primitive), Bernard Kay (Caldwell), Morris Perry (Dent), Tony Caunter (Morgan), John Herrington (Holden), Stanley McGeach (Allen), Pat Gorman (Long), Roy Heyman (Alien Priest), John Tardaff (Leeson), Norman Atkyns (Guardian).

"The Daemons" (5-22-71 - 6-19-71): Damaris Hayman (Miss Hawthorne), Eric Millyard (Fr. Reeves), David Simeon (Alistair Fergus), James Snell (Harry), Robin Wentworth (Prof. Horner), Rollo Gamble (Winstanley), Don McKillop (Bert), John Croft (Tom Girton), Christopher Wray (Groom), John Joyce (Garvin), Gerald Taylor (Baker's man), Stanley Mason (Bok), Alec Linstead (Osgood), John Owens (Thorne), Stephen Thorne (Azal), Matthew Corbett (Jones).

"The Day of the Daleks" (1-1-72 - 1-22-72): Jean McFarlane (Miss Paget), Wilfrid Carter (Sir Reginald Styles), Tim Condreen (guerilla), Rick Lester (Ogron), John Scott Martin (Chief Dalek), Oliver Gilbert (Dalek voice), Peter Messaline (Dalek voice), Aubrey Woods (Controller), Deborah Brayshaw (technician), Gypsie Kemp (radio operator), Anna Barry (Anat), Jimmy Winston (Shura), Scott Fredericks (Boaz), Valentine Palmer (Monia), Andrew Carr (guard), Peter Hill (manager), George Raistrick (guard), Alex Mackintosh (TV reporter).

"The Curse of Peladon" (1-29-72 - 2-19-72): Henry Gilbert (Torbis), David Troughton (Peladon), Geoffrey Toone (Hepesh), Gordon St. Clair (Grun), Nick Hobbs (Aggedor), Stuart Fell (Alpha Centauri), Ysanne Churchman (voice of Alpha Centauri), Murphy Grumbar (Arcturus), Terry Bale (voice of Arcturus), Sonny Caldinez (Sorg), Alan Bennion (Izlyr), George Giles (Captain), Wendy Danvers (Amazonia).

"The Sea Devils" (2-26-72 - 4-1-72): Clive Morton (Trenchard), Royston Tickner (Robbins), Edwin Richfield (Hart), Alec Wallis (Bowman), Neil Seiler (radio operator), Terry Walsh (Barclay), Brian Justice (Wilson), Jane Murphy (Jane Blythe), Hugh Futcher (Hickman), Declan Mulholland (Clark), Pat Gorman (Sea Devil), Peter Forbes-Robertson (Sea Devil), Eric Mason (Smedley), Donald Sumpter (Ridgeway), Stanley Mc-

(DOCTOR WHO cont.) Geagh (Drew),
David Griffin (Mitchell), Christopher
Wray (Lovell), Colin Bell (Summers),
Brian Vaughn (Watts), Martin Boddey
(Walker), Norman Atkyns (Admiral),
Rex Rowland (Girton), John Caesar
(Myers).

"The Mutants" (4-8-72 - 5-13-72):
Paul Whitsun-Jones (Marshal), Geof-
frey Palmer (administrator), Christo-
pher Coll (Stubbs), Rick James (Cotton),
James Mellor (Varan), Jonathan Sher-
wood (Varan's son), Garrick Magon
(Ky), George Pravda (Jaeger), John
Hollis (Sondergaard), Sidney Johnson
(old man), Roy Pearce (Solos guard),
David Arlen (guard warrior), John
Scott Martin (Mutt), Damon Sanders
(guard), Martin Taylor (guard), Peter
Howell (investigator).

"The Time Monster" (5-20-72 -
6-24-72): Wanda Moore (Dr. Ingram),
Ian Collier (Stuart Hyde), John Wyse
(Dr. Percival), Neville Barber (Dr.
Cook), Barry Ashton (Proctor), Donald
Eccles (Krasis), Keith Dalton (Neophite),
Terry Walsh (windowcleaner), George
Cormack (Dalios), Aidan Murphy (Hip-
pias), Marc Boyle (Kronos), Gregory
Powell (Knight), Simon Legree (Sergeant),
Dave Carter (Officer), George Lee
(farmworker), Ingrid Pitt (Galleia),
Susan Penhaligon (Lakis), Michael Wal-
ker (Miseus), Derek Murcott (Crito),
Dave Prowse (Minotaur), Melville
Jones (guard), Ingrid Bower (Face of
Kronos).

"The Three Doctors" (12-30-72 -
1-20-73): William Hartnell (1st Doctor),
Patrick Troughton (2nd Doctor), Stephen
Thorne (Omega), Graham Leaman (Time
Lord), Clyde Pollitt (Chancellor), Roy
Purcell (President), Laurie Webb (Mr.
Ollis), Patricia Prior (Mrs. Ollis),
Rex Robinson (Dr. Tyler), Denys Pal-
mer (Palmer).

"Carnival of Monsters" (1-27-73 -
2-17-73): Stuart Fell (Functionary),
Michael Wisher (Kalik), Terence Lodge
(Orum), Cheryl Hall (Shirna), Leslie
Dwyer (Vorg), Tenniel Evans (Major
Daly), Andrew Staines (Captain), Ian
Marter (Andrews), Jenny McCracken
(Claire), Peter Halliday (Pletrac).

"Frontier in Space" (2-24-73 - 3-
31-73): John Rees (Hardy), James Culliford (Stewart), Roy Pattison (Draconian Pirate), Peter Birrel (Draconian
Prince), Vera Fusek (President), Michael Hawkins (Williams), Louis Mahoney (newscaster), Karol Hagar (Secretary), Ray Lonnen (Gardiner), Barry
Ashton (Kemp), Lawrence Davidson

(Draconian First Secretary), Timothy
Craven (guard), Luan Peters (Sheila),
Caroline Hunt (technician), Madhav
Sharma (Patel), Richard Shaw (Cross),
Dennis Bowen (Governor), Harold Gold-
blatt (Prof. Dale), Laurence Harrington
(guard), Bill Wilde (Draconian Captain),
Stephen Thorne (Ogron), Michael Kil-
garriff (Ogron), Rick Lester (Ogron),
John Woodnutt (Emperor), Ian Frost
(Draconian Messenger), Clifford Elkin
(Earth Cruiser Captain), Ramsay Wil-
liams (Brook), Stanley Price (Pilot),
Bill Mitchell (Newscaster), John Scott
Martin (Dalek), Michael Wisher (Dalek
voice).

"Planet of the Daleks" (4-7-73 -
5-12-73): Bernard Horsfall (Taron),
Prentis Hancock (Vaber), Tim Preece
(Codal), Roy Skelton (Wester), Jane
How (Rebec), Hilary Minster (Marat),
Alan Tucker (Latep), Tony Starr (Da-
lek Supreme), John Scott Martin (Dalek),
Murphy Grumbar (Dalek), Cy Town (Da-
lek), Michael Wisher (Dalek voice), Roy
Skelton (Dalek voice).

"The Green Death" (5-19-73 - 6-
23-73): Stewart Bevan (Prof. Clifford
Jones), Jerome Willis (Stevens), John
Scott Martin (Hughes), Ben Howard
(Hinks), Tony Adams (Elgin), Mostyn
Evans (Dai Evans), Ray Handy (milkman),
Talfryn Thomas (Dave), Roy Evans
(Bert), John Dearth (voice of BOSS),
John Rolfe (Fell), Richard Beale (Mini-
ster), Mitzi McKenzie (Nancy), Jean
Burgess (Cleaner), Roy Skelton (James),
Terry Walsh (guard), Billie Horrigan
(guard), Brian Justice (guard), Alan
Chuntz (guard).

"The Time Warrior" (12-15-73 -
1-5-74): Kevin Lindsay (Linx), David
Daker (Irongron), John J. Carney (Blood-
axe), Sheila Fay (Meg), Donald Pelmear
(Prof. Rubeish), June Brown (Lady Elea-
nor), Alan Rowe (Edward of Wessex),
Gordon Pitt (Eric), Jeremy Bulloch (Hal),
Steve Brunswick (sentry).

"Invasion of the Dinosaurs" (1-12-
74 - 2-16-74): Noel Johnson (Charles
Grover), Peter Miles (Prof. Whitaker),
Pat Gorman (UNIT Corporal), Martin
Jarvis (Butler), James Marcus (peasant),
Ben Aris (Shears), John Caesar (soldier),
Gordon Reid (Phillips), George Bryson
(Ogden), Terry Walsh (Looter), John
Bennett (Gen. Finch), Martin Taylor
(Corporal Norton), Dave Carter (Duffy),
Terence Wilton (Mark), Brian Badcoe
(Adam), Carmen Silvera (Ruth), Colin
Bell (Bryson), Timothy Craven (Robin-
son).

"Death to the Daleks" (2-23-74 -

3-16-74): Arnold Yarrow (Bellal), Roy Heymann (Gotal), John Abineri (Railton), Duncan Lamont (Galloway), Julian Fox (Hamilton), Joy Harrison (Jill Tarrant), Neil Seiler (Stewart), Mostyn Evans (High Priest), Terry Walsh (Spaceman), Steven Ismay (Zombie), John Scott Martin (Dalek), Murphy Grumbar (Dalek), Cy Town (Dalek), Michael Wisher (Dalek voice).

"The Monster of Peladon" (3-23-74 - 4-27-74): Ralph Watson (Ettis), Donald Gee (Eckersley), Gerald Taylor (Vega Nexos), Nina Thomas (Queen Thalira), Frank Gatliff (Ortron), Stuart Fell (Alpha Centauri), Ysanne Churchman (Voice of Alpha Centaur), Michael Crane (Blor), Terry Walsh (Captain), Rex Robinson (Gebek), Graeme Eton (Preba), Nick Hobbs (Aggedor), Roy Evans (Rima), Sonny Caldinez (Sskel), Alan Bennion (Azaxyr), Max Faulkner (Miner).

"Planet of the Spiders" (5-4-74 - 6-8-74): John Dearth (Lupton), Terence Lodge (Moss), Andrew Staines (Keaver), Christopher Burgess (Barnes), Carl Forgione (Land), Cyril Shaps (Prof. Clegg), Kevin Lindsay (Cho-Je), John Kane (Tommy), Pat Gorman (soldier), Chubby Oates (policeman), Terry Walsh (man with hat), Michael Pinder (Hopkins), Stuart Fell (tramp), Ysanne Churchman (Spider voice), Kismet Delgado (Spider voice), Maureen Morris (Spider voice), Geoffrey Morris (Sabor), Joanna Monro (Rega), Gareth Hunt (Arak), Jenny Laird (Neska), Walter Randall (Captain), Max Faulkner (2nd Captain), Maureen Morris (Great One), George Cormack (K'Anpo).

"Robot" (12-28-74 - 1-18-75): Edward Burnham (Prof. Kettlewell), Michael Kilgariff (the Robot), Alec Linstead (Jellicoe), Patricia Maynard (Miss Winters), John Scott Martin (guard), Timothy Craven (Short).

"The Ark in Space" (1-25-75 - 2-15-75): Wendy Williams (Vira), Kenton Moore (Noah), Christopher Masters (Libri), John Gregg (Lycett), Richardson Morgan (Rogin), Stuart Fell (Wirrn), Nick Hobbs (Wirrn), Gladys Spencer (voice), Peter Tuddenham (voice).

"The Sontaran Experiment" (2-22-75 - 3-1-75): Kevin Lindsay (Field Major Styre), Peter Futherford (Roth), Peter Walsh (Efrak), Terry Walsh (Zake), Glyn Jones (Krans), Donald Douglas (Vural), Brian Ellis (prisoner).

"Genesis of the Daleks" (3-8-75 - 4-12-75): Michael Wisher (Davros), Peter Miles (Nyder), James Garbutt

(Ronson), Dennis Chinnery (Gharman), John Scott Martin (Dalek), Max Faulkner (Falek), Keith Ashley (Dalek), Cy Town (Dalek), Roy Skelton (Dalek voice), Guy Siner (Ravon), Richard Reeves (Kaled Leader), John Franklyn-Robbins (Time Lord), Stephen Yardley (Sevrin), Drew Wood (Tane), Jeremy Chandler (Gerrill), Pat Gorman (Thal soldier), Hilary Minster (Thal Soldier), John Gleeson (Thal Soldier), Andrew Johns (Kravos), Peter Mantle (Kaled guard), Harriet Philpin (Bettan), Max Faulkner (Thal guard), Michael Lynch (Thal politician), Ivor Roberts (Mogren), Tom Georgeson (Kavell).

"Revenge of the Cybermen" (4-19-75 - 5-10-75): Ronald Leigh-Hunt (Stevenson), Alec Wallis (Warner), Jeremy Wilkin (Kellman), William Marlowe (Lester), David Collins (Vorus), Michael Wisher (Magrik), Christopher Robbie (Cyberleader), Melville Jones (Cyberman), Kevin Stoney (Tyrum), Brian Grellis (Sheprah).

"Terror of the Zygons" (8-30-75 - 9-20-75): John Woodnutt (Duke of Forgill/Broton), Hugh Martin (Munro), Tony Sibbald (Huckle), Angus Lennie (Angus McRannald), Robert Russell (Cabler), Bruce Wightman (radio operator), Lillias Walker (Sister Lamont), Bernard G. High (Corporal), Peter Symonds (soldier), Keith Ashley (Zygon), Ronald Gough (Zygon).

"Planet of Evil" (9-27-75 - 10-18-75): Terence Brook (Braun), Tony McEwan (Baldwin), Frederick Jaeger (Sorenson), Ewen Solon (Vishinsky), Prentis Hancock (Salamar), Michael Wisher (Morelli), Graham Weston (De Haan), Louis Mahoney (Ponti), Haydn Wood (O'Hara), Melvyn Bedford (Reig).

"Pyramids of Mars" (10-25-75 - 11-15-75): Bernard Archard (Prof. Marcus Scarman), Gabriel Woolf (Sutekh), Vik Tablian (Ahmed), Peter Copley (Dr. Warlock), Peter Mayock (Namin), Michael Bilton (Collins), Michael Sheard (Laurence Scarman), George Tovey (Ernie Clements), Nick Burnell (Mummy), Melvyn Bedford (Mummy), Kevin Selway (Mummy).

"The Android Invasion" (11-22-75 - 12-13-75): Martin Friend (Styggron), Roy Skelton (Chedaki), Max Faulkner (Adams), Peter Welch (Morgan), Milton Johns (Guy Crayford), Stuart Fell (Kraal), Patrick Newell (Faraday), Dave Carter (Grierson), Heather Emmanuel (Tessa), Hugh Lund (Matthews).

"The Brain of Morbius" (1-3-76 - 1-24-76): Philip Madoc (Solon), Colin

(DOCTOR WHO cont.) Fay (Condo), Gilly Brown (Ohica), Cynthia Grenville (Maren), Michael Spice (voice of Morbius), Stuart Fell (Morbius Monster), John Scott Martin (Kriz), Sue Bishop (Sister), Janie Kells (Sister), Gabrielle Mowbray (Sister), Veronica Ridge (Sister).

"The Seeds of Doom" (1-31-76 - 3-6-76): Tony Beckley (Harrison Chase), John Challis (Scorby), John Gleeson (Charles Winlett), Michael McStay (Derek Moberley), Hubert Rees (John Stevenson), Kenneth Gilbert (Dunbar), Seymour Green (Hargreaves), Michael Barrington (Sir Colin Thackeray), Mark Jones (Arnold Keeler), Ian Fairbairn (Dr. Chester), Alan Chuntz (chauffeur), Sylvia Coleridge (Amelia Ducat), David Masterman (guard), Harry Fielder (guard), John Acheson (Major Beresford), Ray Barron (Sgt. Henderson), Mark Jones (Krynoid's voice).

"The Masque of Mandragora" (9-4-76 - 9-25-76): Jon Laurimore (Count Federico), Gareth Armstrong (Guilliano), Tim Pigott-Smith (Marco), Norman Jones (Hieronymus), Anthony Carrick (Capt. Rossini), Robert James (High Priest), Pat Gorman (soldier), James Appleby (soldier), John Clamp (soldier), Peter Walshe (pikeman), Jay Niel (pikeman), Brian Ellis (Brother), Peter Tuddenham (Mandragora's voice), Peggy Dixon (dancer), Jack Edwards (dancer), Alistair Fullarton (dancer), Michael Reid (dancer), Kathy Wolff (dancer), Stuart Fell (entertainer).

"The Hand of Fear" (10-2-76 - 10-23-76): Roy Pattison (Zazzka), Roy Skelton (Rokon), David Purcell (Abbott), Renu Setna (Intern), Rex Robinson (Dr. Carter), Robin Hargrave (guard), Glyn Houston (Prof. Watson), Frances Pidgeon (Miss Jackson), Roy Boyd (Driscoll), John Cannon (Elgin), Judith Paris (Eldrad), Stephen Thorne (Eldrad).

"The Deadly Assassin" (10-30-76 - 11-20-76): Peter Pratt (the Master), Llewellyn Rees (President), Angus Mackay (Cardinal Borusa), Bernard Horsfall (Chancellor Goth), George Pravda (Castellan Spandrell), Derek Seaton (Commander Hildred), Erik Chitty (Co-ordinator Engin), Hugh Walters (Commentator Runcible), John Dawson (Time Lord), Michael Bilton (Time Lord), Maurice Quick (Gold Usher), Peter Mayock (Solis), Helen Blatch (voice of the Network).

"The Face of Evil" (11-27-76 - 1-22-77): Leslie Schofield (Calib), Victor Lucas (Andor), Brendan Price (To-

mas), Lloyd McGuire (Lugo), Tom Kelly (guard), Brett Forrest (guard), Leon Eagles (Jabel), Mike Elles (Gented), Peter Baldock (Acolyte), Rob Edwards (voice of Xoanon), Pamela Salem (voice of Xoanon), Anthony Frieze (voice of Xoanon), Roy Herrick (voice of Xoanon).

"The Robots of Death" (1-29-77 - 2-19-77): Russell Hunter (Commander Ulanov), Pamela Salem (Toos), David Bailie (Dask), Rob Edwards (Chub), Brian Croucher (Borg), Tariq Yanus (Cass), David Collins (Poul), Tania Rogers (Zilda), Miles Fothergill (SV7), Gregory de Polnay (D84), Mark Blackwell Baker (Robot of Death), John Bleasdale (Robot of Death), Mark Cooper (Robot of Death), Peter Langtry (Robot of Death), Jeremy Ranchev (Robot of Death), Richard Seager (Robot of Death).

"The Talons of Weng-Chiang" (2-26-77 - 4-2-77): John Bennett (Li Hsen Chang), Deep Roy (Mr. Sin), Michael Spice (Weng-Chiang/Greel), Trevor Baxter (Prof. Litefoot), Christopher Benjamin (Henry Gordon Jago), Tony Then (Lee), Alan Butler (Buller), Chris Cannon (Casey), John Wu (Coolie), Conrad Asquith (PC Quick), David McKail (Sgt. Kyle), Patsy Smart (Ghoul), Judith Lloyd (Teresa), Vaune Craig-Raymond (cleaning woman), Penny Lister (singer), Vincent Wong (Ho).

"Horror of Fang Rock" (9-3-77 - 9-24-77): Colin Douglas (Reuben), John Abbott (Vince), Ralph Watson (Ben), Alan Rowe (Col. Skinsale), Annette Woollett (Adelaide), Sean Caffrey (Palmerdale), Rio Fanning (Harker).

"The Invisible Enemy" (10-1-77 - 10-22-77): Frederick Jaeger (Prof. Marius), Michael Sheard (Lowe), Brian Grellis (Safran), Jay Neill (Silvey), Edmund Pegge (Meeker), John Leeson (Nucleus voice), Anthony Rowlands (crewman), John Scott Martin (Nucleus Operator), Nell Curran (nurse), Jim McManus (Opthalmologist), Roderick Smith (Cruickshank), Kenneth Waller (Hedges), Elizabeth Norman (Marius' nurse), Roy Herrick (Parsons), Pat Gorman (medic).

"Image of the Fendahl" (10-29-77 - 11-19-77): Wanda Ventham (Thea Ransome/Fendahl Core), Denis Lill (Dr. Fendelman), Edward Arthur (Colby), Scott Fredericks (Steal), Edward Evans (Moss), Derek Martin (Mitchell), Daphne Heard (Martha Tyler), Graham Simpson (Hiker), Geoffrey Hinsliff (Jack Tyler).

"The Sun Makers" (11-26-77 - 12-17-77): Henry Woolf (Collector), Roy Macready (Cordo), Richard Leach (Gatherer Hade), Jonina Scott (Marn), Mi-

chael Keating (Goudry), William Simon
(Mandrel), Adrienne Burgess (Veet),
David Rowlands (Bisham), Colin Mc-
Cormack (Commander), Derek Crewe
(Synge), Carole Hopkin (nurse), Tom
Kelly (guard).

"Underworld" (1-7-78 - 1-28-78):
James Maxwell (Jackson), Alan Lake
(Herrick), Imogen Bickford-Smith (Ta-
la), Jonathan Newth (Orfe), Jimmy
Gardner (Idmon), Norman Tipton (Idas),
Godfrey James (Tarn), James Marcus
(Rask), Jay Neill (Klimt), Frank Jar-
vis (Ankh), Richard Shaw (Lakh), Sta-
cey Tendeter (Naia), Christine Pollon
(voice of the Oracle).

"The Invasion of Time" (2-4-78 -
3-11-78): Milton Johns (Kelner), John
Arnatt (Borusa), Stan McGowan (Var-
dan Leader), Chris Tranchell (Andred),
Dennis Edward (Gomer), Tom Kelly
(Vardan), Reginald Jessup (Savar),
Charles Morgan (Gold Usher), Hilary
Ryan (Rodan), Max Faulkner (Nesbin),
Christopher Christou (Chancery Guard),
Michael Harley (bodyguard), Ray Calla-
ghan (Ablif), Gai Smith (Presta), Mi-
chael Mundell (Jasko), Eric Danot (guard),
Derek Deadman (Stor), Stuart Fell (Son-
taran).

"The Ribos Operation" (9-2-78 -
9-23-78): Cyril Luckham (the White
Guardian), Iain Cuthbertson (Garron),
Nigel Plaskitt (Unstoffe), Paul Seed
(the Graff Vynda-K), Robert Keegan
(Sholakh), Timothy Bateson (Binro),
Prentis Hancock (Captain), John Hamill
(Shrieve), Oliver Macguire (Shrieve),
Ann Tirard (the Seeker).

"The Pirate Planet" (9-30-78 -
10-21-78): Bruce Purchase (Captain),
Andrew Robinson (Mr. Fibuli), Rosalin
Lloyd (the Captain's nurse), Bernard
Finch (the Mentiad), David Sibley (Pra-
lix), Ralph Michael (Balaton), Prime
Townsend (Mula), David Warwick (Ki-
mus), Clive Bennett (citizen), Adam
Kurakin (guard).

"The Stones of Blood" (10-28-78 -
11-18-78): Beatrix Lehmann (Prof. Emi-
lia Rumsford), Susan Engel (Vivien Fay),
Nicholas McArdle (DeVries), Gerald
Cross (voice of Guardian), Elaine Ives-
Cameron (Martha), David McAlister
(voice of Megara), James Murray (camper), Shirin Taylor (camper).

"The Androids of Tara" (11-25-
78 - 12-16-78): Neville Jason (Prince
Reynart), Peter Jeffrey (Count Grendel),
Simon Lack (Swordmaster), Paul Lavers
(Farrah), Declan Mulholland (Till), Lois
Baxter (Lamia), Martin Matthews (Kur-
ster), Cyril Shaps (Archimandrite).

"The Power of Kroll" (12-23-78 -
1-13-79): Neil McCarthy (Thawn), Phi-
lip Madoc (Fenner), Grahame Mallard
(Harg), John Leeson (Dugeen), Terry
Walsh (Mensch), Carl Rigg (Varlik),
John Abineri (Ranquin), Glyn Owen
(Rohm-Dutt), Frank Jarvis (Skart).

"The Armageddon Factor" (1-20-
79 - 2-24-79): Susan Skipper (Heroine),
Ian Liston (Hero), Ian Saynor (Merak),
Lalia Ward (Princess Astra), John Wood-
vine (the Marshal), William Squire (the
Shadow), Barry Jackson (Drax), John
Cannon (guard), Harry Fielder (guard),
Pat Gorman (pilot), Iain Armstrong
(technician), Valentine Dyall (Guardian),
Stephen Calcutt (the Mute).

"Destiny of the Daleks" (3-3-79 -
3-24-79): Tim Barlow (Tyssan), Peter
Straker (Cmdr. Sharrel), Suzanne Dan-
ielle (Agella), Tony Osoba (Lan), Cy
Town (Dalek Operator), Mike Mungarvan
(Dalek Operator), Roy Skelton (Dalek
Voice), Penny Casdagli (Jall), David
Yip (Veldan), David Gooderson (Davros),
Cassandra (Movellan Guard).

"City of Death" (3-31-79 - 4-28-
79): Julian Glover (Count), David Gra-
ham (Kerensky), Kevin Flood (Hermann),
Catherine Schell (Countess), Tom Chad-
bon (Duggan), Peter Halliday (soldier),
Pamela Stirling (Louvre guide), John
Cleese (art gallery visitor), Eleanor
Bron (art gallery visitor).

"Creature from the Pit" (5-5-79 -
5-26-79): Myra Frances (Adrasta), Eileen Way (Karela), David Teifer (Huntsman), John Bryans (Torvin), Edward
Kelsey (Edu), Tim Munro (Ainu), Terry
Walsh (Doran), Morris Barry (Tollund),
Geoffrey Bayldon (Organon), Tommy
Wright (guardmaster), Dave Redgrave
(guard), Philip Denver (guard).

"Nightmare in Eden" (6-2-79 - 6-
23-79): David Daker (Rigg), Stephen
Jenn (Secker), Geoffrey Bateman (Dy-
mond), Richard Barnes (crewman), Lewis Fiander (Tryst), Jennifer Lonsdale
(Della), Barry Andrews (Stott), Geoffrey
Hinsliff (Fisk), Peter Craze (Costa),
Maggie Peterson (passenger), Annette
Peters (passenger), Lionel Sansby (passenger), Peter Roberts (passenger), Sebastian Stride (crewman), Eden Phillips
(crewman).

"The Horns of Nimon" (6-20-79 -
7-21-79): Bob Hornery (Pilot), Malcolm
Terris (Co-Pilot), Michael Osborne (So-
rak), Janet Ellis (Teka), Simon Gipps-
Kent (Seth), Graham Crowden (Soldeed),
Robin Sherringham (Nimon), Trevor St.
John Hacker (Nimon), Bob Appleby (Ni-
mon), Clifford Norgate (voice of Nimon),

(DOCTOR WHO cont.) John Bailey (Sezom).

"The Leisure Hive" (8-30-80 - 9-20-80): Adrienne Corri (Mena), David Haigh (Pangol), Laurence Payne (Morix), John Collin (Brock), Nigel Lambert (Hardin), Martin Fisk (Vargos), David Allister (Stimson), Ian Talbot (Klout), Andrew Lane (Chief Foamasi), Roy Montague (Argolin Guide), Harriett Reynolds (Tannoy voice).

"Meglos" (9-27-80 - 10-18-80): Edward Underdown (Zastor), Jacqueline Hill (Lexa), Crawford Logan (Deedrix), Colette Gleeson (Caris), Bill Fraser (Grugger), Frederick Treves (Brotadac), Simon Shaw (Tigellan Guard), Christopher Owen (Earthling), Tony Allef (Gaztak), Ranjit Nakara (Gaztak), Hi Ching (Gaztak), Bruce Callender (Gaztak), John Holland (Gaztak), James Muir (Gaztak), Terence Creasey (Deons), Eddie Sommer (Deons), Ray Knight (Deons), Chris Marks (Deons), Stephen Nagy (Deons), Sylvia Marriott (Deons), Lewis Hooper (Deons), Michael Brydon (guard), David Cleeve (guard), Stephen Kane (savant), John Laing (savant), David Cole (savant), Howard Barnes (savant), Michael Gordon Browne (Tigellan), Harry Fielder (Tigellan), Laurie Good (Tigellan), Peter Gates Fleming (Tigellan), Geoff Whitestone (Tigellan).

"Full Circle" (10-25-80 - 11-15-80): Richard Willis (Varsh), Bernard Padden (Tylos), June Page (Keara), James Bree (Nefred), Alan Rowe (Garif), Leonard Maguire (Draith), George Baker (Login), Tony Calvin (Dexeter), Norman Bacon (Marsh Child), Andrew Forbes (Omril), Adrian Gibbs (Rysik), Barney Lawrence (Marshman).

"State of Decay" (11-22-80 - 12-13-80): William Lindsay (King Zargo), Rachel Davies (Queen Camilla), Emrys James (Aukon), Iain Rattrary (Habris), Thane Bettany (Tarak), Arthur Hewlett (Kalmar), Stacy Davies (Veros), Clinton Greyn (Ivo), Rhoda Lewis (Marta), Dean Allen (Karl), Stuart Blake (Zoldaz), Stuart Fell (Roga), Alan Chuntz (guard).

"Warrior's Gate" (12-20-80 - 1-10-81): Clifford Rose (Rorvik), Kenneth Cope (Packard), David Weston (Biroc), Jeremy Gittins (Lazlo), Freddie Earlie (Aldo), Harry Waters (Royce), David Kincaid (Lane), Vincent Pickering (Sagan), Robert Vowles (Gundan).

"The Keeper of Traken" (1-17-81 - 2-7-81): Anthony Ainley (Tremas), Sheila Ruskin (Kassia), Denis Carey

(the Keeper), John Woodnutt (Seron), Margot Van de Burgh (Katura), Robin Soans (Luvic), Roland Oliver (Naman), Geoffrey Beevers (Melkur), Liam Prendergast (Foster), Philip Bloomfield (Foster).

"Logopolis" (2-14-81 - 3-7-81): Anthony Ainley (the Master), John Fraser (Monitor), Adrian Gibbs (Watcher), Dolores Whiteman (Aunt Vanessa), Tom Georgeson (police detective), Christopher Hurse (security guard).

"Castrovalva" (1-4-82 - 1-12-82): Anthony Ainley (the Master), Frank Wylie (Ruther), Dallas Cavell (Head of Security), Michael Sheard (Mergrave), Derek Waring (Shardovan), Neil Toynay (Portreeve), Souska John (child).

"Four to Doomsday" (1-18-82 - 1-26-82): Stratford Johns (Monarch), Annie Lambert (Enlightenment), Paul Shelley (Persuasion), Philip Locke (Bigon), Illarrio Bisi Pedro (Kurkutji), Burt Kwouk (Lin Fitu), Nadia Hamman (Villagra).

"Kinda" (2-1-82 - 2-9-82): Richard Todd (Sanders), Simon Rouse (Hindle), Nerys Hughes (Todd), Roger Milner (Anicca), Anna Wing (Anatta), Jeffrey Stewart (Dukkha), Adrian Mills (Aris), Mary Morris (Panna), Sarah Prince (Karuna), Lee Cornes (Trickster).

"The Visitation" (2-15-82 - 2-23-82): John Savident (Squire John), Anthony Calf (Charles), John Baker (Ralph), Valerie Fyfer (Elizabeth), Peter Van Dissel (Android), Richard Hampton (villager), Michael Robbins (Richard Mace), James Charlton (Miller), Michael Melis (Terileptil Leader), Neil West (poacher), Eric Dodson (headman).

"Black Orchid" (3-1-83 & 3-2-82): Gareth Milne (the Unknown), Ahmed Khalil (Latoni), Timothy Block (Tanner), Michael Cochrane (Lord Cranleigh), Barbara Murray (Lady Cranleigh), Moray Watson (Sir Robert Muir), Brian Hawksley (Brewster), Ivor Salter (Sgt. Markham), Andrew Tourell (Constable Cummings).

"Earthshock" (3-8-82 - 3-16-82): Clare Clifford (Kyle), James Warwick (Scott), Steve Morley (Walters), Suzi Arden (Snyder), Ann Holloway (Mitchell), Anne Clements (1st trooper), Mark Straker (2nd trooper), David Banks (Cyber Leader), Mark Hardy (Cyber Lieutenant), Alec Sabin (Ringway), June Bland (Berger), Beryl Reid (Briggs), Mark Fletcher (1st crew member), Christopher Whittingham (2nd crew member).

"Time Flight" (3-22-82 - 3-30-82): Anthony Ainley (the Master), John Flint

(Capt. Urquhart), Peter Dahlsen (Horton), Judith Byfield (Angela Clifford), Brian McDermott (Sheard), Peter Cellier (Andrews), Richard Easton (Capt. Stapley), Michael Cashman (1st Officer Billings), Keith Drinkel (Flight Engineer Scobie), Nigel Stock (Hayter), Leon Ny Taiy (Kalid), Hugh Hayes (Anithon).

DOOMWATCH. British 1970-72. John Paul (Dr. Quist), Simon Oates (Dr. Ridge), Joby Blanchard (Bradley), Wendy Hall, Robert Powell 1970.

DOW HOUR OF GREAT MYSTERIES. 1960. Joseph Welch (Host).
  "The Bat" (3-31-60): Helen Hayes (Cornelia Van Gorder), Jason Robards, Jr. (Anderson), Margaret Hamilton (Lizzie), Martin Brooks (Brooks), Bethel Leslie (Dale Ogden), Karl Light (Richard Fleming), Shepperd Strudwick (Dr. Wells), Mark Satow (Billy).
  "The Burning Court" (4-24-60): Barbara Bel Geddes (Marie Stevens), George C. Scott (Gordon Cross), Anne Seymour (Mrs. Henderson), Robert Lansing (Edward Stevens), Raymond Bramley (Mr. Morley), Paul Stevens (Mark Devereaux).
  "The Woman in White" (5-23-60): Lois Nettleton (Anna Catherick/Laura Fairlie), Siobhan McKenna (Marion Halcombe), Walter Slezak (Count Fosco), Robert Flemying (Sir Percival Glyde), Arthur Hill (Walter Hartright), Rita Vale (Countess Fosco), Catherine Proctor (Mrs. Vesey).
  "The Dachet Diamonds" (9-20-60): Rex Harrison (Cyril Paxton), Tammy Grimes (Daisy Strong), Robert Flemying (Lawrence), David Hurst (Baron), Alice Ghostley (Charlotte), Reginald Denny (Insp. Ireland), Melville Cooper (Franklyn), George Turner (hotel manager), Laurie Main (Connors), Hedlie Rainie (Skittles).
  "The Cat and the Canary" (9-27-60): Collin Wilcox (Annabelle West), Sarah Marshall (Cicily Sellsby), Andrew Duggan (Paul Jones), Hortense Alden (Mrs. Pleasant), George Macready, Telly Savalas, Louis Edmonds, Jack Betts.
  "The Inn of the Flying Dragon" (10-18-60): Farley Granger (Richard Beckett), Barry Morse (Count St. Alyre), Hugh Griffith (Capt. Harmonville), Michael Shillo (Innkeeper), Macha Meril.
  "The Great Impersonation" (11-15-60): Keith Michell (Baron von Ragastein/Sir Edward Dominey), Eva

Gabor (Stephanie), Jeanette Starke (Rosamund), Theodore Marcuse (Brandt), Martin Kosleck (Schmidt), Otto Simanek (Kaiser Wilhelm), Alistair Cooke (Narrator).

DRAMA SPECIAL.
  "The Crucible" (5-4-67): George C. Scott (John Proctor), Colleen Dewhurst (Elizabeth Proctor), Fritz Weaver (Rev. Hale), Henry Jones (Rev. Parris), Cathleen Nesbitt (Rebecca), Will Geer (Giles), Tuesday Weld (Abigail), Melvyn Douglas (Deputy Governor).
  "Arsenic and Old Lace" (4-2-69): Helen Hayes (Abby Brewster), Lillian Gish (Martha Brewster), Bob Crane (Mortimer Brewster), Fred Gwynne (Jonathan Brewster), David Wayne (Teddy Brewster), Sue Lyons (Elaine Harper), Jack Gilford (Dr. Einstein), Victor Kilian (Gibbs), Frank Campanella (Officer Klein), Billy De Wolfe (Witherspoon), Bernard West (Benner), Bob Dishy (Officer Sampson).

DUPONT SHOW OF THE MONTH.
  "Harvey" (9-22-58): Art Carney (Elwood P. Dowd), Marion Lorne (Vera Louise Simmons), Larry Blyden (Dr. Sanderson), Loring Smith (Dr. Chumley), Charlotte Rae (Myrtle Mae Simmons), Ruth White (Mrs. Chumley), Jack Weston (Wilson), Elizabeth Montgomery (Miss Kelly), Fred Gwynne (cab driver), Ray Bramley (Judge Gaffney), Katherine Raht (Mrs. Chauvenet).
  "Aladdin" (2-21-59): Cyril Ritchard (Magician), Sal Mineo (Aladdin), Anna Maria Alberghetti (Princess Ming Chou), Dennis King (Astrologer), Basil Rathbone (Emperor), Una Merkel (Mother), Howard Morris (Wu Fang), George Hall (Chamberlain), Alec Clarke (Prime Minister).
  "Heaven Can Wait" (11-16-60): Anthony Francoisa (Joe Pendleton), Robert Morley (Mr. Jordan), Joey Bishop (Max Levene), Wally Cox (Messenger 7013), Frank McHugh (Lefty), Paul Stevens (Tony Abbott), Diana van der Vlis (Julia Farnsworth), Elizabeth Ashley (Bette), Paul Reed (Insp. Williams).
  "The Richest Man in Bogota" (8-5-62): Lee Marvin (Juan de Nunez), Miriam Colon (Marina), Richard Eastham (Elder), Eugene Iglesias (Pedro), Dan Frazer (Francesco), John W. Morley (Felipe).
  "The Legend of Lylah Clare" (5-19-63): Tuesday Weld (Elsie Brinkmann), Alfred Drake (Louis Zakin), Michael Tolan (Welles Resnick), Sorrell Booke (Jake Resnick), Johnny Haymer (Mickey Man-

(DUPONT SHOW OF THE MONTH cont.) dell), Janice Mars (Olga), Paul Sparer (Ben).

ELGIN HOUR.
"A Sting of Death" (2-22-55): Boris Karloff (Mr. Mycroft), Robert Flemying (Mr. Silchester), Hermione Gingold (Alice), Martyn Green (Mr. Hargrave).

ENCHANTED CASTLE, THE. British 1981. Candida Beveridge (Cathy), Diane Mercer (Mademoiselle), Simon Sheard (Gerald), Marcus Scott-Barrett (Jimmy), Cavan Kendall (Bailiff/Lord Yalding), Stephen Meredith (Alf), Georgia Slowe (Princess/Mabel), Gill Abineri (Eliza), Bartlett Mullins (Respectable/Mr. Ugli), Molly Weir (flowered hat), Susan Field (poke bonnet), Douglas Barlow (cricket cap), Brownie Maisey (office boy), Louis Hammond (Mr. James), Eliza Buckingham (Psyche), Alastair Hunter (Zeus), Brian Hawksley (Jefferson Conway), Sheila Beckett (Aunt).
"A Magic Day" (5-6-81).
"Moon Magic" (5-13-81).
"Magic Light" (5-20-81).
"Magic Journey" (5-27-81).
"Feast of Magic" (6-3-81).
"Magic End" (6-10-81).

ENIGMA. Pilot (5-27-77): Scott Hylands (Andrew Icarus), Guy Doleman (Baron Maurice Mockcastle), Barbara O. Jones (Miranda Larawa), Soon-Teck Oh (Mei San Gow), Melinda Dillon (Dora Herren), Peter Coffield (Peter McCauley), Percy Rodrigues (Idi Ben Youref), Sherry Jackson (Kate Valentine), Jim Davis (Col. Valentine), Bill Fletcher (Wolf), Morgan Farley (Benjamin Herren), Judith Brown (Marsha), Melodie Johnson (Dr. Beverly Golden).

EVIL TOUCH, THE. 1973-74. Anthony Quayle (Host).
"The Lake" (9-16-73): Robert Lansing (Arthur Randall), Anne Hardy (Ellen Randall), Ann Bowden (Sylvia).
"Heart to Heart" (9-23-73): Mildred Natwick.
"Dr. McDermit's New Patients" (9-30-73): Richard Lupino (Dr. Tom McDermit), Kim Hunter (Jill McDermitt), Pandora Bronsen (Nona).
"The Obituary" (10-7-73): Leslie Nielsen (Willie Tremaine), John Morris (Pettitt), June Thody (Susan).

"Happy New Year, Aunt Carrie" (10-14-73): Julie Harris.
"A Game of Hearts" (10-21-73): Darren McGavin (Doctor), Colin Croft (Marshall), Judi Farr (Anne Sullivan).
"Seeing Is Believing" (10-28-73): Robert Lansing (Archie MacGauffin), Alfred Sandor (Williams), John Derum (Charlie), Arna-Maria Winchester (Evie).
"The Upper Hand" (11-4-73): Peter Gwynne (Roger Carlyle), Julie Harris (Jenny), Max Cullen (Policeman), June Salter (Louise Carlyle).
"Murder's for the Birds" (11-11-73): Vic Morrow.
"Marci" (11-18-73): Susan Strasberg (Elizabeth), Elizabeth Crosby (Marci), Peter Gwynne (John).
"George" (11-25-73): Darren McGavin (George Manners), Jack Thompson (Hammer), Shirley Cameron (Blanche), Reg Gillam (Dr. Taylor).
"Scared to Death" (12-2-73): Mildred Natwick.
"The Homecoming" (12-9-73): Harry Guardino (Mark Harper), John Meillon (Sam Field), Elaine Lee (Marion Field), Mike Dorsey (Wallace).
"Dear Beloved Monster" (12-16-73): Ray Walston, Alastair Duncan (Watson), Jan Kingsbury (Anya), Mark Hashfield (Roke).
"Campaign 2" (1-13-74): James Daly.
"Faulkner's Choice" (1-20-74): Noel Harrison.
"The Trial" (2-3-74): Ray Walston.
"The Fans" (2-10-74): Vic Morrow.
"Kadaitcha Country" (2-24-74): Leif Erickson (Rev. Mr. Vincent), Tony Wagner (Dr. Dennis), Rowena Wallace (Jean), Jack Thompson (the Stockman).
"Gornak's Prison" (3-3-74): Darren McGavin (Alvin), Kathie Browne (Selma), Joseph Furst (Dr. Gornak).
"The Voyage" (3-10-74): Leslie Nielsen, Terence Cooper (Craig Larsen), Jill Forster (Pamela Larsen).
"Dear Cora, I'm Going to Kill You" (3-24-74): Carol Lynley (Cora Blake), Charles McCallum (Harry Winston), Dennis Clinton (Lt. Brennan).

FAERIES. (2-25-81): Voices: Hans Conried (Fairy King/Shadow), Morgan Brittany (Princess), Craig Schaeffer (Olsin), Bob Arbogast (Kobold), Frank Welker (Puck).

FAMILY THEATRE.
"The Canterville Ghost" (3-10-75):

David Niven (Sir Simon de Canterville), James Whitmore (Hiram), Audra Lindley (Lucretia), Flora Robson (Mrs. Umney), Lynne Frederick (Virginia), Bobby Doran (Jefferson), Christopher Morris (Lincoln), Maurice Evans (Lord Canterville), Nicholas Jones (Charles, Duke of Cheshire).

FANTASTIC JOURNEY, THE. 1977. Jared Martin (Varian), Roddy Mc-Dowell (Jonathan Willoway), Carl Franklin (Dr. Fred Walters), Ike Eisenmann (Scott Jordan), Katie Saylor (Liana).

"Vortex" (2-3-77): Scott Thomas (Paul Jordan), Susan Howard (Eve Costigan), Leif Erickson (Ben Wallace), Ian McShane (Camden), Don Knight (Paget), Gary Collins (Dar-L), Mary Ann Mobley (Rhea), Jason Evers (Atar), Karen Somerville (Jill Sands), Scott Brady (Carl), Jack Stauffer (Andy), Byron Chung (George), Tom McCorry (Scar), Lynn Borden (Enid Jordan).

"Atlantium" (2-10-77): Gary Collins (Dar-L), Mary Ann Mobley (Rhea), Jason Evers (Atar), Albert Stratton (Iltar).

"Beyond the Mountain" (2-17-77): John David Carson (Cyrus), Marj Dusay (Rachel), Lester Fletcher (Chef), Frank Corsentino (Toren), Joseph Dellasorte (Aren), Ron Burke (Robert), Brian Patrick Clarke (Daniel), Bud Kenneally (Veteran), Crofton Hardester (Michael).

"Children of the Gods" (2-24-77): Cosie Costa (Delta), Mark Lambert (Alpha), Mark Eilbacher (Sigma), Stanley Clay (Beta), Richard Natoli (Gamma), Al Eisenmann (Omega), Michael Baldwin (Rho).

"Dream of Conquest" (3-10-77): John Saxon (Consul Tarant), Morgan Paull (Lt. Argon), Lenore Stevens (Lara), Robert Patten (Major Consul Luther), John Doran (Nikki), Bobby Porter (the Neffring).

"An Act of Love" (3-24-77): Christina Hart (Gwenith), Ellen Weston (Maera), Jonathan Goldsmith (Zaros), Vic Mohica (Baras), Jeffrey Byron (Heras), Belinda Balaski (Arla), Jerry Daniels (Guard).

"Funhouse" (3-31-77): Mel Ferrer (Apollonius), Mary Frann (Roxanne), Richard Lawson (Barker).

"Turnabout" (4-7-77): Joan Collins (Queen Halyana), Paul Mantee (King Morgan), Julie Cobb (Adrea), Beverly Todd (Connell), Charles Walker II (Obril).

"Riddles" (4-21-77): Dale Robinette (Kedryn), Carole Demas (Kryata), William O'Connell (Simkin), Dax Xenos (the Rider), Lynn Borden (Enid Jordan).

"The Innocent Prey" (6-17-77): Lew Ayres (Rayat), Richard Jaeckel (York), Cheryl Ladd (Natica), Nicholas Hammond (Tye).

FANTASY ISLAND. 1978 . Ricardo Montalban (Mr. Roarke), Herve Villechaize (Tattoo), Wendy Schaal (Julie) 81-83.

"Escape"/"Cinderella Girls" (1-28-78): Bert Convy (Udall), Robert Clary (Ipsy Dauphin), Reggie Nalder (Commandant), Diana Canova (Ann Dowd), Georgia Engel (Maxine Bender), John Saxon (Dr. Sullivan), Bernard Fox (Count).

"Bet a Million"/"Mr. Irresistable" (2-4-78): Henry Gibson (Mr. Wade), Gilbert Green (Mr. Hayden), Jane Powell (Joan Wade), John Schuck (Chuck Hoffman), Sondra Kaye Theodore (Gloria), Mabel King (Lelani), Alana Collins (Nikki).

"The Prince"/"The Sheriff" (2-11-78): Dack Rambo (Prince Peter), Lisa Hartman (Chris), Ed Begley, Jr. (Jamie), Harry Guardino (John Burke), John Chandler (Ed Larson), Sheree North (Julie), Ron Soble (Tom Larson), Guy Stockwell (Logan), William Mims (Tim Beard), Tiger Williams (the Kid).

"Family Reunion"/"Voodoo" (2-18-78): John Gavin (Harry Kellino), Juliet Mills (Evelyn Kellino), David Hedison (Carlyle Cranston), Mary Frann (Grace), Lauren Tewes (Jane Howell), Howard Duff (Douglas Shane), Marjorie Lord (Beth Shane), Gary Collins (Bill Jordan).

"Lady of the Evening"/"The Racer" (2-25-78): Carol Lynley (Renee Lansing), Mark Richman (Roy Burke), Alan Hale (Corky), Jerry Van Dyke (Brennan), Paul Burke (Bill Fredericks), Christopher George (Jack Kincaid), Carol Lawrence (Rachek Kincaid), Clark Brandon (Patrick Kincaid).

"Treasure Hunt"/"Beauty Contest" (3-11-78): Gene Barry (Neville Quinn), Jo Ann Harris (Andrea), Peter Haskell (Jim), Michael Callan (Stuart), Maureen McCormick.

"Funny Girl"/"Butch and Sundance" (3-18-78): Marcia Strassman (Katherine Patrino), Dennis Cole (Lloyd Hopper), Edward Andrews (Oscar), Dennis Cort (soda jerk), Lurene Tuttle (Mrs. Emery), Olan Soule (proprietor), James MacArthur (Alex Fairly/Sundance), Christopher Connelly (Bill Cummings/Butch), Wil-

(FANTASY ISLAND cont.) liam Smith (Wyatt Earp), Henry Jones (bank teller), Bob Hoy (Slim).

"Superstar"/"Salem" (3-25-78): Gary Burghoff, Stuart Whitman, Vera Miles, Leslie Nielsen (Whitfield), Darleen Carr (Dora), Brendan Dillon (Goodfriend), Henry Beckman (Weaver), Ellis Valentine, George Brett, Ken Brett, Fred Lynn, Steve Garvey, Tom Lasorda.

"Trouble, My Lovely"/"The Common Man" (4-1-78): Don Knotts (Stanley Shecter), Lynda Day George (Iris Chandler), Rick Jason (Arthur Hemmings), Dennis Patrick (Theodore Chandler), John Fiedler (Mortimer Fox), Frank Aletter (Lt. Draper), Pamela Bryant (Peggy Chandler), Jack Ging (Sgt. Gus Fallon), Dave Cass (Fitz), Bernie Kopell (Fred Staunton), Julie Cobb (Florence Staunton), Nancy Walker (Mumsy), Kevin King Cooper (Arnold Staunton), Cordy Clark (piano player), Joseph Abdullah (Captain).

"The Over the Hill Caper"/"Poof! You're a Movie Star!" (4-15-78): Ray Bolger (Spencer McLean (Randolph), Harriet Nelson (Winnie McLean), Foster Brooks (Spider), Tom Ewell (Fingers), Jordan Clarke (Prentiss), Barbi Benton (Shirley Russell), Herb Edelman (Gantman), Michael Anderson, Jr. , Joanna Barnes, Phil Foster.

"Reunion"/"Anniversary" (4-29-78): Lucie Arnaz, Ronnie Cox, Pamela Franklin (Agnes), Sue Lyon (Jill), Michele Lee (Carol), Jim Backus (Cap), Hilary Thompson.

"King for a Day"/"Instant Family" (5-6-78): David Doyle (Ernie Miller/ King Albert), Diane Baker (Queen Aurora), Theodore Bikel (Eric Soro), William Glover (Cecil), George D. Wallace (Harry Sand), Don Pedro Colley (Emperor Bakota), Melinda Naud (Gail Grayson), Jane Wyatt (Mildred Grayson), Adam Rich (Herbie Bloch), Don Dubbins (Dr. Bloch), Kristi Jean Wood (Laurie), Christian Zika (Conrad), Fred Lerner (manager).

"Fool for a Client"/"Double Your Pleasure" (5-15-78): Rich Little (Herbert Costigan), Stephen McNally (Judge), Lana Wood (Cecile), Ken Berry (Larry Barber), Caren Kaye (Deena/Nina McKay), Mary Ann Mobley (Pamela Deering), Donald May (Marlowe), Sal Viscuso.

"Call Me Lucky"/"Torch Singer" (5-20-78): Richard Dawson, Kathryn Holcomb, Edd Byrnes (Neil), Joey Forman (Bugsy), Louis Quinn (Joe), Brad

Savage (Joey), Milton Selzer (Willie).

"The Sheikh"/"The Homecoming" (9-16-78): Arte Johnson (Ed Breen), Georgia Engel (Jasmine/Brenda), Sid Haig (Hakeem), Arnold Moss (Sheikh), David Birney (Paul/Alan), Lynda Day George (Nancy), Ronnie Scribner (Danny), Michael Gregory, Cassandra Peterson.

"Big Dipper"/"The Pirate" (9-23-78): Dan Rowan (Petee), Jill Whelan (Harmony), Sonny Bono (Kavanau), Diana Canova (Mary), Vivian Blaine (Mrs. Devere), Rory Calhoun (Wasson), Cameron Mitchell (Boylin), Richard Roat.

"Beach Comber"/"The Last Whodunit" (9-30-78): John Astin, Celeste Holm, Maurice Evans (Hemsley), Judith Chapman (Evelyn), Janis Paige (Charlotte), Howard Morton (Terence), Lyon Borden.

"War Games"/"Queen of the Boston Bruisons" (10-7-78): Greg Morris, Christopher George, Anne Francis, Joanna Barnes (Betty), Don DeFore (Mitch), Mary Jo Catlett (Hooligan).

"I Want to Get Married"/"The Jewel Thief" (10-21-78): Meredith MacRae, Steve Forrest, Ken Berry (Eddie), Leigh Taylor-Young (Leslie), Yale Summers (Phillip), Peter Palmer, Mark Richman.

"Best Seller"/"The Tomb" (10-28-78): Desi Arnaz, Jr. , Barry Sullivan, David Opatoshu (Abdul), Mark Savage (Aki), Janice Heiden (Audrey), Shelley Fabares (Jill), Gloria De Haven (Louise), Maureen McCormick (Angela), Jeannie Wilson.

"Let the Good Times Roll"/"Nightmare"/"Tigers" (11-4-78): Paul Sand, Pamela Franklin, Darren McGavin, Peter Isacksen (Smooch), Ray Milland (Weston), Mary Ann Mobley (Sheilah), Brett Halsey (Arthur).

"Return"/"The Toughest Man Alive" (11-11-78): Red Buttons, Samantha Eggar (Helena March), France Nuyen (Anna), Paul John Balson (Jamie), Chao-Li Chi (Elder).

"The Appointment"/"Mister Tattoo" (11-18-78): Bert Convy, Connie Stevens, Barbi Benton, Troy Donahue (Jack), Fred Grandy (Bernie), Trisha Noble (Denise), Nancy Kwan (Adela), Brian Avery.

"The Plight of the Great Yellow Bird"/"The Island of Lost Women" (11-25-78): Peter Graves, Robert Morse, Cyd Charisse (Queen Delphia), Barbara Rush (Andrea), Dan Reed (Micah).

"Carnival"/"The Vaudevillians" (12-2-78): Phil Silver, Phil Harris, Carol Lynley, Stuart Whitman (Tom), Ellen

Geer (Doris), Luke Askew (Sunglasses), Paul Cavonis, Patrick J. Cronin.

"Charlie's Cherubs"/"Stalag 3" (12-9-78): Brenda Benet (Ginny), Bond Gideon (Claudia), Melinda Naud (Amber), Yvonne DeCarlo (Fifi), Cornel Wilde (Danny Ryan), Bobby Troup (Johnny Fox), Joe Mantell (Eddie Hodges), Ivor Barry (David Garner), Nehemiah Persoff (Horst von Stern).

"Vampire"/"Widow" (12-16-78): Robert Reed, Eva Gabor, Jack Elam (Hollis), Lloyd Bochner (Benson), Julie Sommars (Carmen), Noah Keen (Paul), Tammy Lauren (Tracy), Erica Yohn (Erika).

"Seance"/"Treasure" (1-13-79): Eve Plumb, George Maharis, Leslie Nielsen (Victor), Marie Windsor (Mme. Voric), Shelley Fabares (Eva), Ross Bickell (Eddie), Joseph Hacker (Claude), Michael Fox.

"Cowboy"/"Substitute Wife" (1-22-79): Hugh O'Brian, Jayne Meadows, Sherry Jackson, Hans Conried (Dr. Van Helsing), Johnny Timko (Tommy), Peter Breck (Casey), Peter Lawford (Harvey).

"Photographs"/"Royal Flush" (1-27-79): Michele Lee, John Rubinstein, John McIntire (Victor Holly), Diana Muldaur (Elizabeth Castle), Mabel King (Bertha), Ronne Troup (Emily), Hank Brandt (Castle), Paul Picerni (Nick Lago).

"Stripper"/"Boxer" (2-10-79): Laraine Stephens, Ben Murphy, Forrest Tucker (Jake), Stacy Keach, Sr. (Banning), Maureen McCormick (Jennie Collins), Michael Callan (McCoy), Mamie Van Doren (Sheila), Chuck McCann (Whoopee Hoover), William Beckley (Barnaby).

"Pentegram"/"A Little Ball"/"Casting Director" (2-17-79): Florence Henderson, Don Knotts, Lisa Hartman, Abe Vigoda (Sid), John Saxon (Colin), Cesar Romero (Habeeb), Phyllis Davis (Jean), Ben Davidson (Hammerhead Harris), Edward Grover (Marsh).

"Spending Spree"/"The Hunted" (2-24-79): Diana Canova (Sally), Lola Falana (Esther), Stuart Whitman (Charles Wesley), James Shigeta (Gen. Lin Sun), Khigh Dhiegh (Chang), Byron Morrow (Doc), Doodles Weaver, Mel Berger.

"Birthday Party"/"Ghost Breaker" (3-3-79): Janet Leigh, Ken Berry, Annette Funicello (Edna), Larry Storch (Le Blanc), Christopher Stone (Tom Deerborn), Skye Aubrey (Tracy), Ray Malavasi (himself), Douglas V. Fowley (Jacoby).

"Yesterday's Love"/"Fountain of Youth" (/-17-79): Eleanor Parker (Peggy Atwood), Craig Stevens (Charles Atwood), Guy Madison (Brick Howard), Lou Frizzell (Willie Tucker), Lew Ayres (J. D. Pettigrew), Dennis Cole (Capt. Jeff Bailey), Mary Louise Weller (Tina Mason), Eddie Little Sky (Chief), Rick Flores (Sato), Bert Santos (the Priest).

"The Comic"/"The Golden Hour" (5-5-79): Fred Grandy, Toni Tennille, Jack Carter (Danny Baker), Michael Parks (Mike Banning), Pat Klous (Mary Doyle), Morgan Woodward (Victor), Freddy Weller (himself), Joan Roberts.

"Cornelius and Alfonse"/"The Choice" (5-6-79): Red Buttons (Cornelius), Billy Barty (Alphonse), Juliet Mills (Ruth Ewell), Regis Philbin (Craig), Mary Ann Mobley (Evie), Beth Brickell (Ella), Michael Anderson, Jr. (Joe).

"Bowling"/"Command Performance" (5-12-79): Al Molinaro, Joan Blondell, Roddy McDowall (Simmons), Rue McClanahan (Margaret), Kathie Browne (Elena), George Garro, Lynda Farrell.

"Amusement Park"/"Rock Stars" (5-13-79): Scott Baio (Rob), Jimmy Baio (Willie), Jill Whelan (Jody), Keith Mitchell (Scooter), Jarrod Johnson (Derrus), Vernee Watson (Aunt Andrea), Rip Taylor, Ted Lange.

"Hit Man"/"Swimmer" (9-7-79): David Doyle (Fred Forbush), Eve Plumb (Terri Summers), Peter Graves (Jack Summers), Kaye Ballard (Elvira), Eddie Mekka (Johnny Detroit), Gail Fisher.

"Goose for the Gander"/"The Stuntman" (9-14-79): Doris Roberts, Dale Robertson, Grant Goodeve (Bill), Hans Conried (Bouffetout), Abe Vigoda (Joe), Dana Wynter, Vito Scotti.

"Tattoo, the Love God"/"Magnolia Blossoms" (9-21-79): Pamela Franklin, Lisa Hartman, Dack Rambo (Rawlins), Christopher Connelly (Hampstead), Gene Evans (O'Grady), Marianne Marks, Esmond Chung, Luke Askew.

"The Baby"/"Marathon" (10-5-79): Barbi Benton, Peter Isacksen, Arlene Golonka, Bob Seagren (sportscaster), Dick Martin (Dr. Funk), Paul Petersen (Eugene Bodeen), Barbara Luna (Mary), Marilyn Michaels (Mrs. Dunlop).

"Chain Gang"/"The Boss" (10-20-79): Dennis Cole, Donna Mills, Cameron Mitchell (Eddie Collins), Roddy McDowall (Pointer), Brett Halsey (Brent), Pat Klous (Stacy), John Myhers, Mr. Blackwell.

"Red Baron"/"Young at Heart" (10-27-79): Don Adams, Diana Canova, Ron Ely (Red Baron), Martine Beswicke (Mo-

(FANTASY ISLAND cont.) nique), David Ladd (David), Dave Madden (Crane), Al Ruscio, Tom Kindle.

"The Wedding" (11-3-79): Samantha Eggar (Helena March), Paul John Balson (Jamie), Joseph Cotten (John Cummings), Laraine Day (Katherine Cummings), Don Ho (Himself).

"Tattoo's Romance"/"Handy Man" (11-10-79): Audrey Landers, Sonny Bono, Joey Forman (Spider Sloate), Carolyn Jones (Aunt Ellie), Shelley Fabares (Emily), Beverly Powers, Richard Paul.

"Nobody's There"/"The Dancer" (11-17-79): Toni Tennille, Max Baer, Carol Lynley (Valeska), Michael Callan (Nicky), Dick Sargent (Pepperhill), Lilyan Chauvin (Selena), Frank Aletter, Leslie Deutsch.

"The Pug"/"The Class of '69" (11-24-79): Gary Collins, K. C. Martel, Adrienne Barbeau (Brenda Richards), Sugar Ray Robinson (Opie), Fred Grandy (Bernie), Fred Williamson (Jackson), Tim Thomerson (Lance Reynolds), Dane Clark (Charlie), Bill Baldwin, Ric Carrott.

"The Victim"/"The Mermaid" (12-1-79): Joan Prather, John Saxon, Michelle Phillips (Nyah), Mary Ann Mobley (Amanda), James Darren (Duvalle), Yvonne DeCarlo (Madame Jeannot).

"Cheerleaders"/"Marooned" (12-8-79): Georgia Engel, Patricia McCormack, Vic Tayback, Norman Alden (George), Dan Pastorini (Roger), Jayne Meadows (Liz), Tom Rossovich (Monk).

"The Inventor"/"On the Other Side" (12-15-79): Arte Johnson (Prof. Kleve), Jeanette Nolan (Mrs. Erma Gideon), Marcia Wallace (Martha Meeks), Ike Eisenmann (Keith), Macdonald Carey (Hobart), Stefan Gierasch (Zoltan), Lurene Tuttle, Lewis Arquette.

"Lookalikes"/"Winemaker" (12-22-79): Ken Berry, Celeste Holm (Sister Veronica), Ross Martin (Armand Fernandel), Nita Talbot (Blanche), Johnny Timko (Jimmy), Michael V. Gazzo (Lassiter).

"Unholy Wedlock"/"Elizabeth" (1-12-80): David Cassidy, Tina Louise (Marge Corday), Misty Rowe (Christi), Eddie Mekka (Ken Jason), Michael Ansara (Marco), Nancy De Carl (Sue Raines), Anthony Penya.

"Rogues to Riches"/"Stark Terror" (1-19-80): John Schuck, Melissa Sue Anderson, Robert Goulet (Pete), Alan Hale (Winston), Dolly Martin (Margaret), Michael Constantine (Joshua), Gunilla Hutton (Priscilla), David Drucker.

"Play Girl"/"Smith's Valhalla" (1-26-80): Barbi Benton, Hugh O'Brian, Leslie Nielsen (Emil), Janet Blair (Jackie Flynn), Fabian Forte (Walter), Charles Dierkop (Weasel Forbes), Sean Garrison, Heather McAdam, Denny Miller.

"Aphrodite"/"Dr. Jekyll and Miss Hyde" (2-2-80): George Maharis, Maureen McCormick (Jennifer), Belinda J. Montgomery (Minnie Hale), Nehemiah Persoff (Andreas), Britt Ekland (Aphrodite), Rosemary Forsythe (Dr. Melanie Griffin), Don Stroud (Ross Hayden).

"Swinger"/"Terrors of the Mind" (2-9-80): Howard Morris (Herman), Anne Francis (Maxine), Judy Landers (Peggy), Jack Carter (Stan), Lou Richards (Duke), Ed Ruffalo (Hot Dog), Suzanne Copeland (Jill), Lisa Hartman (Sharon Sanders), Frankie Avalon (Martin), Stephen McNally (Emmett Slate), Eric Mason (Pit Boss), Tony Giorgio (croupier), Heather Hewitt (woman), Dennis Doderer (man).

"Nona"/"One Million B. C. " (3-1-80): Phyllis Davis, Peter Graves, Jo Ann Pflug, Joanna Pettet (Nona), Neville Brand (Gog), Edd Byrnes (Lucas), Peter Lupus (Antar), Morgan Woodward (Targ).

"Mary Ann and Miss Sophisticate"/"Jungle Man" (3-8-80): Annette Funicello (Mary Ann), Maren Jensen (Valerie), Don Galloway (George Reardon), Dennis Cole (David Farley), France Nuyen (Mara), Barbara Luna (Princess Rima), Dick Butkus (Derek Haskell), Manu Tupuo (Prester John).

"My Fair Pharoah"/"The Power" (5-10-80): Joan Collins, Larry Linville, Ron Ely (Mark Antony), Michael Ansara (Ptolemy), Ruth Roman (Flatateeta), Chris Capen (Claudio), Carol Lynley (Stephanie), Julie Sommars (Laura).

"The Eagleman"/"The Children of Menta" (5-17-80): Bob Denver, Vernee Watson, Larry Storch (Hal), Keith Mitchell (Barney), Jim Backus (H. H.), Ralph Bellamy (Dr. Gates), Mickey Morton (Curly).

"The Devil and Mandy Breem"/"The Millionaire" (10-25-80): Carol Lynley (Mandy Breem), Roddy McDowall (Mephistopheles), Adam West (Philip Breem), Arte Johnson (Fred Catlett), Arlene Golonka (Ava).

"The Mermaid Returns"/"Flying Aces" (11-1-80): Michelle Phillips (Princess Nyah), Tom Wopat (David Chilton), Sam Melville (Tony Chilton), Robert Mandan (Rosacker), Dolly Martin (Betty), Tom Demenkoff (Eddie Allen), Hal England (Harvey).

"Skater's Edge"/"Concerto of Death"/"The Last Great Race" (11-8-80): Charlene Tilton, Dennis Cole, Dick Shawn, Juliet Mills, Erin Gray (Carla), Jack Carter (Morgan Townsend), Bradford Dillman (Stolmann), Peggy Fleming (Laura), Dack Rambo (Michael), Mary Ann Mobley (Linda), Allan Ludden (Judge).

"Sex Symbol"/"Don Quixote" (11-15-80): Phyllis Davis, Paul Williams, David Doyle (Wolf), Mary Louise Weller (Dulcie), Don Stroud (Orville), Robert F. Lyons (Carl), Michael Callan (Sterling), Edd Byrnes (Ron).

"Possessed" (11-22-80): Barbara Parkins, Missy Gold (Stephanie).

"The Pleasure Palace"/"The Love Doctor" (11-22-80): Gary Burghoff, Loni Anderson, Barbi Benton (Molly), Christopher George (Dr. Greg Miller), Roz Kelly (Olivia), Ruben Moreno (Native Chief), Henry Jones (Judge Mix), Dane Clark (Blainey), Yolanda Marzuez (native mother).

"With Affection, Jack the Ripper"/"Gigolo" (11-29-80): Lynda Day George (Lorraine Peters), Alex Cord (Robert West), Victor Buono (Dr. Albert Z. Fell), Angela Slater (Gracie), Ken Barry (Stanley Hocker), Meredith MacRae (Deena De Winter), Carolyn Jones (Jessie De Winter), Lyle Waggoner (Monty), Frank Birney (headwaiter).

"Snow Bird"/"The Invisible Woman" (12-6-80): Doug Barr (Ned Pringle), George Maharis (Mario), Don Ameche (Arturo), Pamela Sue Martin (Velda), Debra Jo Fondren (Rose), Neile McQueen (Trish), Dick Gautier (Denny), Sonny Bono (Morty), Elaine Joyce.

"Crescendo"/"Three Feathers" (12-20-80): Monte Markham (Edmund Dumont), Toni Tennille (Susan Lohman), James Hong (Lee Soong), Hugh O'Brian (Alan Colshaw), Diane Baker (Lena), Peter Lawford (Jesse Mason), James Wainwright (Jake), Skip Homeier (Durwood).

"Sanctuary"/"My Late Lover" (1-3-81): Bobby Sherman (Thomas Henshaw), Morgan Brittany (Tessa Brody), Michael Cole (Falco), Sid Haig (Harlan), Georganne LaPierre (Sandra), Eva Gabor (Anastasia Dexter), Gene Barry (Dexter), Craig Stevens (Walter Blair), John Ericson (Ellis Lathrop), Russell Nype (Donald McKenzie).

"Reprisal"/"High Off the Hog" (1-10-81): Maureen McCormick (Trudy Brown), Janis Paige (Mabel Martin), Holly Goodman (Janet Martin), Bob

Seagren (Chad), Richard Gilliland (Bud Simmons), Joan Benedict (Matron), Holly Gagnier (Janet), Stephen Shortridge (Hadley Boggs), Noah Beery, Jr. (Otis T. Boggs), Misty Rowe (Emily Boggs), Dody Goodman (Ma Boggs), Shecky Greene (Roger Foxx), Kathrine Baumann (Kathi Foxx), Ed Ruffalo (Frank), Lewis Arquette (Slocumb).

"Elizabeth's Baby"/"The Artist and the Lady" (1-17-81): Eve Plumb (Elizabeth Blake), Don Reid (Steven Blake), Alison Arngrim (Liza Blake), Susan Cotton (Helen Blake), Jeff Pomerantz (Victor), Jerome Guardino (Eddie), Heather O'Rourke (Liza at age 5), Kim Marie (Liza at age 12), Michael & David Shackleford (twins), Danny Most (Kermit Dobbs), Peter Brown (Patrick O'Herlihy), Michelle Pfeiffer (Debra Dare), Mike Henry (Mike Sandrini), Don Rutton (Hud), Jenny Sherma (Maybelle), John Myhers (Santa), Nancy Roberts (Beauty).

"The Heroine"/"The Warrior" (1-25-81): Mary Ann Mobley (Florence Richmond), Cesare Danova (Brent Hampton), Don Galloway (Peter Stiles), Robert Loggia (Porter C. Brockhill), Victoria Carroll (Nina), James MacArthur (Robert Graham), Shelley Fabares (Edna Graham), Mako (Master Qwong), Kieuh Chinh (1st Oriental Woman), Richard Lee-Sung (1st Mongolian Warrior).

"The Man from Yesterday"/"The World's Most Desirable Woman" (1-31-81): Dennis Cole (Maj. Kelvin Doyle), Martin Milner (William Keating), Elizabeth Baur (Lucille), Pummel Mor (Petie), William Jarquez (1st fisherman), Barbi Benton (Carla Baines), Bert Convy (Hal Garnett), Edie Adams (Liz Fuller), M. G. Kelly (Mark Strutton), Melanie Vinoz (Judy), Blane Savage (Grady), Camille Villechaize (Camille), Cindy Appleton (Trish), Dolores Cantu (Kathi), Stephanie Faulkner (Pauline), Mary Bower (Joyce), Teri Copley (Joanne).

"The Chateau"/"White Lightning" (2-7-81): Pamela Franklin (Vicki Lee), David Hedison (Claude Duncan), Carolyn Jones (Clora McAllister), George Lindsey (Norris Scoggins), Ed Begley, Jr. (Amos McAllister), Randolph F well (R. J. Scoggins), Wendy Schaal (Ruth Ann McAllister).

"Loving Strangers"/"Something Borrowed, Something Blue" (2-14-81): Peter Marshall (Tom Wilkerson), Jane Powell (Margaret Wilkerson), Cesar Romero (Roger Alexander), Shelley Smith (Pamela Archer), John Gavin (Jack Foster), Marjoe Gortner (Nick), J. Pat O'Malley.

(FANTASY ISLAND cont.)
"Chorus Girl"/"Surrogate Father"
(2-21-81): Stuart Whitman (Franklin
Adams), Lisa Hartman (Sheila Richards),
Joe Bennett (Maxim), John Saxon (Evan
Watkins), Nicole Eggert (Amy Watkins),
Rosemary Forsythe (Margot Glenn),
Jason Evers (Ben), Charles Picerni
(Donovan), Elven Havard (Policeman).
"Portrait of Solange"/"Also Rans"
(2-28-81): Elissa Leeds (Solange), Da-
vid Groh (Mark Ellison), Larry Lin-
ville (Jerome Pepper), Joan Prather
(Thalia Latham), Don Porter (Emmett
Latham), Arlene Dahl (Amelia Selby),
Macdonald Carey.
"The Searcher"/"The Way We
Weren't" (3-7-81): Laurette Spang
(Karen Saunders Holmes), Paul Burke
(Noah/John Saunders), James Darren
(Brian Holmes), Leo Gordon (Chief
Guard), Jerry Van Dyke (Fred Cooper),
Laraine Stephens (Dottie Cooper), Jack
Carter (Vic), Dawn Wells (Myra), Her-
moine Baddeley (Aunt Bella).
"The Experiment"/"Proxy Bil-
lionaire" (3-21-81): James Broderick
(Dr. Lucas Bergman), Woody Strode
(Makala), Laurie Walters (Lisa Berg-
man), Robert Goulet (Frank Miller/
Avery Williams), Phyllis David (Eliza-
beth), Britt Ekland (Bernice Williams),
Troy Donahue (Paul Yaeger).
"Delphine"/"The Unkillable" (4-11-
81): Ann Jillian (Delphine MacNab),
Don Galloway (Gregg Randolph), Carl
Ballantine (Zachariah), Doris Roberts
(Cluny), Vic Tayback (Chet), Elinor
Donahue (Madge), Randolph Mantooth
(Dr. Paul Todd), Alex Cord (Kyle), An-
nette Funicello (Elizabeth Drake).
"Basin Street"/"The Devil's Tri-
angle" (5-2-81): Cleavon Little, Joe
Namath, Christopher Connelly, Trish
Stewart, Berlinda Tolbert (Billie Joe),
Raymond St. Jacques (Camptown Dodds),
Mabel King (Mama Parker), Howard
George (Lt. Lavalle), John Shull (Sgt.
McAndrews).
"Hard Knocks"/"Lady Godiva" (5-
9-81): Philip Levien, Robert Sacchi,
Michelle Phillips, Patrick Wayne (Sir
John), Martha Smith (Monica), Ken Ber-
ry (His Lordship), Gunilla Hutton (Her
Ladyship), Nina Axelrod (Doreen Rich),
Michael Alldredge (Tom), John Chand-
ler (Eddie Gunn), Morgan Woodward
(Nick Hall).
"Man-Beast"/"Ole Island Oprey"
(5-16-81): David Hedison, Wendy Schall,
Jimmy Dean, Carol Lynley (Elizabeth),
Anne Francis (Lottie), Kevin Hagen
(Sam Hagen).

"Paquito's Birthday"/"Technical
Advisor" (5-23-81): Randi Oakes, Jill
St. John (Helen), Linda Cristal (Dona
Dolores), A. Martinez (Manuel), Victo-
ria Racimo (Consuelo), Anthony Trujil-
lo (Paco), Jim Stafford (Gene).
"Show Me a Hero"/"Slam Dunk"
(10-10-81): Sonny Bono, Jenilee Harri-
son, Connie Stevens, Martin Milner
(Ted), David Hedison (Johnny), Peter
Isacksen (Skyhook), Forrest Tucker
(Red Donovan).
"The Devil and Mr. Roarke"/
"Ziegfield Girls"/"Kid Corey Rides A-
gain" (10-17-81): Roddy McDowall
(Mephistopheles), Barbi Benton (Joan),
Audrey Landers (Ruby), Arte Johnson
(Ned), Jack Elam (Kid Corey), Came-
ron Mitchell (Sheriff), Dack Rambo
(Carl), Anne Jeffreys, Charles W.
Young, Richard Lineback, Betty Kenne-
dy.
"Cyrano"/"The Magician" (10-24-
81): Carol Lynley, Bart Braverman,
John Saxon (Cyrano de Bergerac), Lloyd
Bochner (Marquis de Sade), Simon Mac-
Corkindale (Gaston), Arnie Moore (Lo-
ban).
"The Lady and the Monster"/
"Crusher" (10-31-81): Lynda Day George,
Stuart Whitman, William Smith (the Mon-
ster), Diane Baker (Maggie), Alex Ku-
bik (Crusher), Jimmy Baio (Josh).
"La Liberatora"/"The World's
Strongest Man" (11-7-81): Charo (Dolo-
res), Sherman Hemsley (Charlie Atkins),
Alex Cord (Arguello), Vernee Watson
(Carrie), Cesare Danova (Verdugo), Kee-
nan Wynn (Willie), H. B. Haggerty (Samp-
son), Bill Dana (Father Vincente), Herb
Edelman (Lou), Alberto Morin.
"A Night on the Harem"/"Druids"
(11-14-81): Paul Williams, Joan Pra-
ther, Jayne Meadows (Contessa), Dennis
Cole (Paul), Elke Sommer (Etain), Ca-
mille Villechaize (Wanda), Tony Longo.
"Perfect Husband"/"The Volcano"
(11-21-81): Susan Sullivan, George Ma-
haris, Lyle Waggoner (Gilbert), Misty
Rowe (Teddy), Rossano Brazzi (Jagger),
Richard Romanus (Robert), Constance
Towers.
"Lillian Russell"/"The Lagoon"
(11-28-81): Phyllis Davis (Lillian Mar-
tin), Claude Akins (Calvin Pierson),
Craig Stevens (Peter Whiting), Gene
Barry (Diamond Jim Brady), Pamela
Susan Shoop (Moira), Broderick Craw-
ford (Jake), Steve Sandor (Palmer).
"Night of the Tormented Soul"/
"Romance Times Three" (12-5-81): Di-
anne Kay, Stephen Shortridge, Georgia
Engel, David Groh (Ben), Richard Ander-

son (Richmond), Frank Converse (Tony), Elinor Donahue, Frank Bonner, Stephanie Faulkner.

"A Very Strange Affair"/"The Sailor" (1-2-82): Florence Henderson (Laura Miles), Peter Graves (Capt. Henrik), Shelley Smith (Miss Harbinger), Dick Smothers (Ron Price), Arlene Golonka (Elaine Price), Hans Conried (J. D. Stoneman), Peter Brocco (Servant), Brett Halsey.

"House of Dolls"/"Wuthering Heights" (1-9-82): Britt Ekland (Clarissa), Hugh O'Brian (Heathcliffe), Bob Denver (Francis Elkins), Barbi Benton (Courtney), Richard Anderson (Edgar), Wilfrid Hyde-White (Lord Wyndham), Larry Storch (Harry), Joey Forman (George), Deborah Shelton (Sally), Cathryn Hart (Sybil), Karlene Crockett (Mindy), Rocke Ackermann (Bailiff), Martin Eric (Joseph), Frank Birney (Mr. Whitehead), Robert Beecher (servant).

"The Magic Camera"/"Mata Hara"/"Valerie" (1-16-82): Bob Denver (Don Winters), Susan Richardson (Ellen), Stephanie Faulkner (bartender), William Bogert (salesman), Tim O'Keefe (policeman), Phyllis Davis (Martha Harris), Monte Markham (Walter Lucas), Helen Boll (Matron), George Chakiris (Capt. Claude Dumarque), Ed E. Carroll (Sgt. Moliere), Alfred Dennis (M'sieu Andre), Christopher George (William Lowell), Michelle Phillips (Valerie Larabee), Ralph Bellamy (Adam Larrabee), John Myhers (Mr. Lacy), Rex Holman (Sheriff Jimmy).

"King Arthur in Mr. Roarke's Court"/"Shadow Games" (1-23-82): Tommy Smothers (Mr. Ralph Rogers), Robert Mandan (King Arthur), Carol Lynley (Gwen), Linda Blair (Miss Rawlins), Peter Mark Richman (Sam), Donny Most (Todd).

"Daddy's Little Girl"/"The Whistle" (1-30-82): Genie Francis (Krista Ackland), Carolyn Jones (Elli Ackland), William Windom (Bill Ackland), Alan Hale, Jr. (Al Bond), Gene Nelson (Bert Wilson), John Ericson (Gene), James Daughton (George Stickney), Paul Vaughn (Minister), Peg Shirley (Alice), Ed Winter (Adrian Bryles), Ann Turkel (Lela Proctor), John Carradine (Mayor), Alvy Moore (Mr. Stone), Kathryn Fuller (Mrs. Abbott), Hal Smith (Mr. Quarry).

"Save Sherlock Holmes"/"The Case Against Mr. Roarke" (2-6-82): Ron Ely, Donald O'Connor (Dr. Watson), Peter Lawford (Sherlock Holmes), Mel Ferrer (Moriarty), Rita Jenrette (Nurse Heavenly), Stuart Damon (Dr. Randolph),

Laraine Stephens, Ian Abercrombie, George Reynolds, Joe Alfasa.

"The Challenge"/"A Genie Named Joe" (2-13-82): Kim Darby, Larry Linville, Vic Morrow (Douglas Picard), Jane Powell (Eunice), Dick Sargent (Justin).

"Funny Man"/"Tattoo, the Matchmaker" (2-20-82): Jimmy Dean (Bo Gillette), Vicki Lawrence (Jenny Casey), Jeanette Nolan (Mama Gillette), Morgan Woodward (Uncle Jack), Linda Thompson Jenner (Lindy), Misty Rowe (Claudia Mills), Laurie Walters (Harriett Wilson), Skip Stephenson (Ambrose Tuttle), Russ Francis (Boardwalk Brian Sims).

"Sitting Duck"/"Sweet Suzi Swann" (3-6-82): Chuck Connors (Frank Barton), Helen Reddy (Suzi Swann), James Darren (Claude), George Maharis (Jack Hecker), Camilla Sparv (Irena Revel), Carol Lineback (Vera).

"A Face of Love"/"Image of Celeste" (3-20-82): Joanna Pettet, Monte Markham, Robert Goulet (Gaughin), Dane Clark (Chevelle), Christopher Stone (Andre), Erin Gray (Celeste), Larry Manetti, Nicholas Savalas.

"Forget-Me-Not"/"The Quiz Masters" (4-10-82): Jill St. John (Ellen Layton), Dick Gautier (Michael), Brett Halsey (Charles), Jim McKrell (Byron), Gene Rayburn (Bob Barkley), Jan Murray (Ron Ellison), Vicki Carr (Lois), Prof. Toru Tanaka (Magog), Catherine Campbell, Michael G. Kelley, David Byrd.

"Nancy and the Thunderbirds"/"The Big Bet" (5-1-82): Mary Ann Mobley (Nancy), John James (Corky), Patrick Wayne (Woody), Lydia Cornell (Judy), Tim Rossovich (Ben), Paul Cavonis (Charlie), Howard Keel (Col. Kinross), Iron Eyes Cody (Chief Daniel), Edd Byrnes (Al Henshaw).

"The Ghost's Story"/"The Spoilers" (5-8-82): Tanya Roberts (Amanda Parsons), Bo Hopkins (Harry Bodeen), Dack Rambo (Captain Timothy Black), Robert Fuller (Nick Tanner), Jo Ann Pflug (Juliet), John McCook (Ross), Bernard Behrens (Prof. Ballentine), Matthew Faison (Dr. Daniels).

FAR OUR SPACE NUTS, THE. 1975-76.
Bob Denver (Junior), Chuck McCann (Barney), Patty Maloney (Honk), Eve Bruce (Lantana), Stan Jenson (Crakor).

FAVORITE STORY.
"The Transferred Ghost" (3-31-54): Tom Brown, Ed Clark.

(FAVORITE STORY cont.)
"Strange Valley" (5-19-54): Ken Tobey, Carla Balenda.
"Live Forever" (6-2-54): Jack Deutel, Mary Anderson.
"It Couldn't Happen" (6-9-54): Peter Hansen, Nancy Gates.
"The Magic Egg" (7-15-54): Walter Kingsford (Morgan the Magnificent), Leslie Banning.
"The Time Barrier" (7-21-54): Robert Carson, Stuart Nedd, Joanne Jordan.

FIREBALL XL-5. 1963-65. Marionette voices: Paul Maxwell, Sylvia Anderson, David Graham, John Bluthal.

FLASH GORDON. 1953. Steve Holland (Flash Gordon), Irene Champlin (Dale Arden), Joseph Nash (Dr. Alexis Zarkov).
"Akim the Terrible".
"The Brain Machine".
"The Breath of Death".
"The Claim Jumpers".
"The Dancing Death".
"Deadline at Noon".
"The Deadly Deception".
"Death in the Negative".
"Duel Against Darkness".
"The Earth's Core".
"The Electromen".
"Encounter with Evil".
"Escape into Time".
"The Forbidden Experiment".
"The Frightened King".
"The Great Secret".
"Heat Wave".
"The Hunger Invasion".
"The Law of Velorum".
"The Lure of Light".
"The Matter Duplicator".
"The Micro-Men Menace".
"Mission to Masca".
"The Mystery of Phoros".
"The Planet of Death".
"The Race Against Time".
"The Rains of Death".
"The Return of the Androids".
"Saboteurs from Space".
"The Shadowy Death".
"The Skyjackers".
"The Sound Gun".
"The Space Smugglers".
"Struggle to the End".
"The Subworld Revenge".
"The Vengeance of Rabeed".
"The Water World Menace".
"The Weapon That Walked".
"The Witch of Neptune".

FORD STAR JUBILEE.

"Blithe Spirit" (1-14-56): Lauren Bacall (Elvira Condomine), Claudette Colbert (Ruth Condomine), Noel Coward (Charles Condomine), Mildred Natwick (Madame Arcate), Marion Ross (Edith), Philip Tonge (Dr. Bradman), Brenda Forbes (Mrs. Bradman).

FORD STARTIME.
"Turn of the Screw" (10-20-59): Ingrid Bergman (Governess), Hayward Morse (Miles), Alexandra Wagner (Flora), Isobel Elsom (Mrs. Grose), Paul Stevens (Peter Quint), Laurinda Barrett (Miss Jessell).

FORD THEATRE.
"The Unlocked Door" (6-3-54): Diana Lynn (Louise Allison), Fay Bainter (Mrs. Allison), Phil Carey (Roy Allison), Ellen Corby (Mabel), Hayden Rorke (Dr. George Malcolm), Frank Sully (Carpenter), John Maxwell (Dr. Spangler).
"Hanrahan" (3-31-55): Cecil Kellaway (Timothy Hanrahan), Elsa Lanchester (Rosie Bowker), Arthur Franz (Joe Newbury), Kathryn Grant (Kitty), Richard Deacon (Planter O'Toole).

FOUR STAR PLAYHOUSE.
"The Devil to Pay" (11-10-55): Charles Boyer (Warren Grisby), Mary Field (Nora Grisby), Joi Lansing (Miss Wilson), Don Beddoe (Mr. Thompson).

FRONT ROW CENTER.
"Outward Bound" (8-10-55): Patricia Hitchcock, John Irving, Alan Napier, John Abbott, Wilfred Knapp, Dorothy Bernard.

FUTURE COP. 1977. Ernest Borgnine (Officer Joe Cleaver), John Amos (Officer Bill Bundy), Michael Shannon (Officer John Haven), Herbert Nelson (Capt. Skaggs), Irene Tsu (Dr. Tingley).
"Fighting O'Haven" (3-5-77): Michael V. Gazzo (Charlie Willis), Rod McCary (Jack Casey), Mwako Cumbuka (gang leader), Angela May (Peggy).
"The Mad, Mad Bomber" (3-25-77): Gerrit Graham (Yancey), Albert Salmi (Wheeler), Harry Guardino (Bannock), Dennis Bowen (Red), Rick Sawaya (Zack), Bill Zuckert (Fisk).
"Girl on the Ledge" (4-7-77): Katherine Cannon (Helen Redmont), H. M. Wynant (Nick Redmont), Tracy Reed (Natalie Bundy), John O'Connell (Hadley).
"The Carlisle Girl" (4-22-77): Sheree North (Claire Hammond), Peter

Donat (Herb Conroy), Tracy Reed (Natalie Bundy), Edward Bach (Fitzgerald), Kim Hamilton (June Bundy).

"The Kansas City Kid" (4-30-77): Don Reid (Geary), Joan Collins (Eve Di Falco), Joshua Bryant (Andrew), Angela May (Peggy).

G. E. THEATRE.

"Mischief in Bandy Leg" (11-3-57): Gower Champion (Thomas Birch), Marge Champion (Kathleen Magee), Alan Napier (Sean O'Donnell), Rhys Williams (Matthew Magee), Emory Parnell (Ben Day), James McCallion (photographer).

"The Devil You Say" (1-22-61): Ronald Reagan (George Willoughby), Sid Caesar (Nick Lucifer), Patricia Barry (Geraldine Willoughby).

GALACTICA 1980. 1980. Kent McCord (Capt. Troy), Barry Van Dyke (Lt. Dillon), Robyn Douglass (Jamie Hamilton), Lorne Greene (Cmdr. Adama), Patrick Stuart (Dr. Zee), Herb Jefferson, Jr. (Boomer), Jerry Supirin, Eric Taslitz, Michael Brick, Nicholas Davis, Michelle Larson, Tracy Justrich, Lindsay Kennedy, Mark Everett, Ronnie Densford, Georgi Irene, David Larson, Eric Larson (the Super Scouts).

"Galactica Discovers Earth" (1-27-80, 2-3-80 & 2-10-80): Robert Reed (Prof. Mortinson), Richard Lynch (Cmdr. Xavier), Pamela Shoop (Ms. Carlyle), Christopher Stone (Maj. Stockwell), Robbie Rist (Dr. Zee), Curt Lowens (German Commander), Fred Holliday (Mr. Brooks), Ted Gehring (Sheriff), Bruce Wright (aide), Missy Francis (little girl), Adam Starr (boy), Eric Forst (1st German Officer), Eric Holland (2nd German Officer), Todd Martin (3rd German Officer), John Zenda (cop), Sharon Acker, Albert Paulsen, Michael Strong, Louis Turene.

"The Super Scouts" (3-16-80 & 3-23-80): Alan Miller (Col. Sydell), Mike Kellin (Mr. Stockton), John Quade (Sheriff), Carlene Watkins (nurse), Simon Scott (pilot), Fred Holliday (Mr. Brooks), Ken Scott (co-pilot), Helen Page Camp (saleslady), Jack Ging, George Deloy, Caroline Smith, Michael Swan.

"Spaceball" (3-30-80): Alan Miller (Col. Sydell), Jeremy Brett (Lt. Nash/Xavier), Fred Holliday (Mr. Brooks), Paul Koslo (Billy Ayres), Bert Rosario (Hal).

"The Night The Cylons Landed" (4-13-80 & 4-20-80): Roger Davis (Andromus), Peter Mark Richman (Col. Briggs), Wolfman Jack (himself), William Daniels (Norman), Lara Parker (Shirley), Jed Mills (cabbie), Arthur Batanides (2nd cabby), Ken Lynch (Grover), Herb Vigran (Pop), Timothy O'-Hagan (Kanan), Sheila de Windt (stewardess), Rex Cutter (Centauri), Robert Lunny (Britton), Rene Levant (1st Officer), Ed Griffith (2nd Officer), John Finnegan (officer in trauma room), John Widlock (Chuck), Paul Tuerpe (fireman), Alexander Petala (1st mugger), Cosie Costa (2nd mugger), T. Miratti (3rd mugger), Louis Sarada (4th mugger), Dan Ferrone (police sergeant), Chip Lucia (M. C.), Bernie Hamilton, Marj Dusay, Val Bisoglio, Heather Young.

"Space Croppers" (4-27-80): Dana Elcar (John Steadman), Ned Romero (Hector Alonzo), Ana Alicia (Gloria Alonzo), Kenneth Tobey (Sheriff), Booth Colman (Rogers), Andy Jarrell (Maze), Phil Livien (Dante), Joaquin Garay III (Chris Alonzo), Stefan Haves (Drannon), Gordon Haight (Deacon), John Dantona (Foley), Lance Maggleton (pilot), Dennis Haysbert (the Creature), Bill Cort, Anna Navarro, Bill McKinney.

"The Return of Starbuck" (5-4-80): Dirk Benedict (Starbuck), Judith Chapman (Angela), Rex Cutter (Cy), Ellen Gurkin (girl).

GEMINI MAN, THE. 1976. Ben Murphy (Sam Casey), Katherine Crawford (Dr. Abby Lawrence), William Sylvester (Leonard Driscoll).

"Smitherinnes" (9-23-76): Alan Oppenheimer (Arthur Hale), Jim Stafford (Buffalo), Andrew Prine (Stark), Gil Serna (Hank).

"Minotaur" (9-30-76): Ross Martin (Carl Victor), Deborah Winter (Nancy Victor), Loren Jones (Minotaur), Michael Jay London (guard).

"Sam Casey, Sam Casey" (10-7-76): Nancy Malone (Armistead), Tony Young (Tanner), Leonard Stone (Robbins), Pamela Shoop (Barby), Mickey Morton (Alf), Jo Ann Pflug (Suzi), Joan Crosby (Dora).

"Night Train to Dallas" (10-14-76): Lane Bradbury, Ryan MacDonald (first agent), Carl Reindel (second agent), Ann Shoemaker (Mrs. Price), Dawn Jeffory (Leslie).

"Run, Sam, Run" (10-28-76): Terry Kister (Ted Benton), Warren Berlinger (Harris), Laurette Spang (Maggie), Michael Richardson (Bruce), Ron Pinkard (Willie), Ted Hartley (Frank DeBlazio).

GENERAL HOSPITAL.
"The Voyage of the Ice Princess"
(1981): Anthony Geary (Luke Spencer),
Genie Francis (Laura Baldwin), Tristan
Rogers (Robert Scorpio), John Colicos
(Mikos Cassadine), Renee Anderson
(Alexandria Quartermaine), Andre Land-
zaat (Tony Cassadine), Thaao Penghlis
(Victor Cassadine), Sharon Wyatt (Tif-
fany Hill), Billie Hayes (O'Riley), John
Cypher (Maximillian Von Stadt), Rosina
Widdowson (Noel Von Stadt), William
Beckley (Albert), Bernard Fox (Nigel),
Rod Loomis (Konrad Kaluga), David
Lewis (Edward Quartermaine), Frank
Maxwell (Dan Rooney), Eddy Ryder
(Slick Jones), Melanie Vincz (Corinne),
Michael Yama (Kimo), Arthur Roberts
(James Duvall), Merrie Lynn Ross (Em-
ma Lutz), Rachel Ames (Audrey Hardy),
John Beradino (Dr. Steve Hardy), De-
nise Alexander (Dr. Lesley Webber),
Chris Robinson (Dr. Rick Webber),
Elizabeth Taylor (Helena Cassadine),
Bob Hastings (Capt. Bert Ramsay),
Jacklyn Zeman (Bobbie Spencer), Rick
Springfield (Dr. Noah Drake), Peter
Hansen (Lee Baldwin), Anna Lee (Lila
Quartermaine), Loanne Bishop (Rose
Kelly), Susan Brown (Dr. Gail Baldwin),
Gail Rae Carlson (Susan Moore), Stuart
Damon (Dr. Alan Quartermaine), Les-
lie Charleson (Dr. Monica Quartermaine),
Norma Connolly (Ruby Anderson), Todd
Davis (Bryan Phillips), Steve Doubet
(Dr. Zack Stewart), Lieux Dressler
(Alice Grant), Robin Eisenman (Stacy
Rawlins), Bianca Ferguson (Claudia
Johnson), Susan Pratt (Anne Logan),
Lisa Figus (Georgia), Shell Kepler
(Amy Vining), Robin Mattson (Heather
Webber), Emily McLaughlin (Jessie
Brewer), Lisa Lindgren (Kathy Summers),
Rick Moses (Hutch), David Mendenhall
(Mike), Philip Tanzini (Jeremy Logan).

GET SMART. 1965-70. Don Adams
   (Maxwell Smart), Barbara Feldon
   (Agent 99), Edward Platt (the Chief),
   Bernie Kopel (Conrad Siegfried) semi-
   regular, Robert Karvelas (Larrabee)
   semi, Victor French (CONTROL A-
   gent 44) semi, William Schallert
   (Adm. Harold Harmon Hargrade)
   semi, Ellen Weston (Dr. Steele)
   semi, Dick Gautier (Hymie) semi,
   Robert Cornthwaite (Prof. Windish)
   semi, Kasey Steach (Charlson) semi,
   George Ives (Dr. Bascomb) semi,
   King Moody (Starker) semi, Jane
   Dulo (Agent 99's mother) semi.

GHOST AND MRS. MUIR, THE. 1968-

70. Edward Mulhare (Capt. Daniel
   Gregg), Hope Lange (Carolyn Muir),
   Reta Shaw (Martha Grant), Charles
   Nelson Reilly (Claymore Gregg),
   Harlen Carraher (Jonathan Muir),
   Kellie Flanagan (Candy Muir), Guy
   Raymond (Ed Peevey), Dabbs Greer
   (Noorie Coolidge), Gil Lamb (Ed's
   friend).

GHOSTBREAKER. Pilot (9-8-67): Ker-
   win Mathews (Prof. Barnaby Cross),
   Diana van der Vlis (Cassandra), Nor-
   man Fell (Lt. P. J. Hartunian), Lar-
   ry Blyden (Waldo Kent), Michael
   Constantine (Oscar Jensen), Richard
   Anderson (Timothy Selfridge), Mar-
   garet Hamilton (Ivy Rumson), Orson
   Bean (Bryant Manning), Kevin Mc-
   Carthy (Cameron Witherspoon).

GHOST BUSTERS, THE. 1975-76. Forrest Tucker (Kong), Larry Storch
   (Eddie Spencer), Bob Burns (Tracy).

GHOST OF A CHANCE. Pilot (7-7-80):
   Shelley Long (Jenny Chance Clifford),
   Barry Van Dyke (Wayne Clifford),
   Steven Keats (Tom Chance), Gretchen
   Wyler (Frances), Archie Hahn (Mi-
   chael), Rosalyn Kind (Leslie), John
   O'Leary (Minister).

GHOST STORY. 1972. Sebastian Cabot
   (Winston Essex).
   "The New House" (3-17-72): Bar-
   bara Parkins (Eileen), David Birney
   (John), Jeanette Nolan (Mrs. Ramsay),
   Sam Jaffe (DeWitt), Ivor Francis, John
   Crawford.
   "The Dead We Leave Behind" (9-
   15-72): Jason Robards, Jr. (Elliot
   Brent), Stella Stevens (Joanna Brent),
   Jack Kelly (motorist), John McLiam
   (Titus Paul), Burr Smidt (Jud), Hayden
   Rorke, Skip Ward.
   "The Concrete Captain" (9-22-72):
   Stuart Whitman (Ed Lucas), Gena Row-
   lands (Kate Lucas), Walter Burke (Dan-
   iel), Eugenia Stewart (Katherine), Glenn
   Wilder (Captain).
   "At the Cradle Foot" (9-29-72):
   James Franciscus (Paul), Elizabeth Ash-
   ley (Karen), Meg Foster (Julie), Jeremy
   Slate (Norris), Karl Swenson (Ed Barnes),
   George McAllister, Jr. (Raphael, Jr.),
   Lori Busk (Emily as a girl), Lisa James
   (Emily as a woman).
   "Bad Connection" (10-6-72): Ka-
   ren Black (Barbara Shepherd), Michael
   Tolan (Keith Norton), Kaz Garas (Phil
   Briggs), Skip Homeier (Steve), Curt Con-
   way (Prescott), Med Flory (Ed Talbot),

Ellen Geer (Marian), Sandra Deel (Angie), James A. Watson, Jr. (Appleton).

"The Summer House" (10-13-72): Carolyn Jones (Martha Alcott), Steve Forrest (Andrew Alcott), William Windom (Charlie Pender), Robert Mandan (Walter Jerrold), Darlene Conley (Ruth Jerrold), Regis Toomey (Sam Streeter).

"Alter Ego" (10-27-72): Helen Hayes (Miss Gilden), Michael-James Wixted (Robert), Colin Wilcox (Molly Cameron), Charles Aidman (Jack Cameron), Geoffrey Horne (Harkness), Janet MacLachlan (Mrs. Dillon), Phyllis Love (Joan Howard), Gene Andrusco (Davey).

"Half a Death" (11-3-72): Pamela Franklin (Christina/Lisa), Signe Hasso (Mrs. Eliscu), Eleanor Parker (Paula), Andrew Duggan (Jeremy), Tod Andrews (Andrew), Stephen Brooks (Ethan), Taylor Lacher (Charlie).

"House of Evil" (11-10-72): Melvyn Douglas (Grandpa), Mildred Dunnock (Mrs. Rule), Joan Hotchkiss (Fran), Jodie Foster (Judy), Richard Mulligan (Tom), Brad Savage (Kevin), Alan Fudge (Dr. Parker).

"Cry of the Cat" (11-24-72): Doug McClure (Dan Hollis), Lauri Peters (Mariah Hollis), Mariette Hartley (Sheila Conway), Jackie Cooper (Dumpy Coyle), Don 'Red' Barry (1st cowboy).

"Elegy for a Vampire" (12-1-72): Hal Linden (David Wells), Mike Farrell (Frank Simmons), Arthur O'Connell (Owen Huston), Marlyn Mason (Laura Benton), John Milford (Detective Thorpe), Sheila Larken (Marne Simmons), Heather North (Dana).

"Touch of Madness" (12-8-72): Geraldine Page (Hattie), Rip Torn (Jonathon), Lynn Loring (Janet), Michael Bell (Harry Collins), Richard Angarola.

"Creatures of the Canyon" (12-15-72): Angie Dickinson (Carol Finney), John Ireland (Arthur Mundy), Madlyn Rhue (Georgia Strauss), Robert Donner (Ralph), Mary Murphy (Maggy Mundy).

"Time of Terror" (12-22-72): Patricia Neal (Ellen Alexander), Craig Stevens (Brett), Alice Ghostley (Betty Carter), Douglas Henderson (George Carter), Elliott Montgomery (Harry Alexander), Robert P. Lieb (drunk), Fred Holliday (desk clerk), Mark Tapscott (security guard).

GIRL FROM U. N. C. L. E. , THE. 1966-67. Stefanie Powers (April Dancer), Noel Harrison (Mark Slate), Leo G. Carroll (Mr. Waverly), Randy Kirby (Randy Kovacs).

"The Dog-Gone Affair" (9-13-66): Kurt Kasznar (Apollo Zakinthlos), Marcel Hillaire (Antoine Fromage), Luciana Paluzzi (Tuesday Hajadakis), Jan Arvan (Patras), Beth Brickell (hostess), Susan Brown (secretary).

"The Prisoner of Zalamar Affair" (9-20-66): Michael Ansara (Vizier), Brenda Benet (Gizelle), Abraham Sofaer (Omar), John Gabriel (Prince Ahmed), Rafael Campos (Abou), Jason Wingreen (Fahd), Henry Calvin (Sheik Ali Hassen).

"The Mother Muffin Affair" (9-27-66): Boris Karloff (Mother Muffin), Robert Vaughn (Napoleon Solo), Bernard Fox (Rodney Babcock), Bruce Gordon (Vito Pomade), Maryesther Denver (Maude), Arthur Malet (William Mickleston), Mitzie Evans (Lisa), William Tuttle (Tuttle).

"The Mata Hari Affair" (10-4-66): Edward Mulhare (Sir Terrance Keats), Jocelyn Lane (Mandy Dean Tanner), Christopher Cary (Toby Gordon-Jones), David Hurse (Matthew Brecker), David Watson (Greg Tovar), Leslie Dean (Marta Hurens).

"The Montori Device Affair" (10-11-66): Edward Andrews (Conrad Brassano), Dee Hartford (Chu-Chu), John Carradine (Prof. Boris Budge), Ted Cassidy (Tullio), Lisa Loring (Felicia), Linda Watkins (Mme. Freuchen-Nagy), William Edmonson (Police Captain), Randy Whipple (Darby).

"The Horns-of-the-Dilemma Affair" (10-18-66): Fernando Lamas (Alejandro DeSada), Alejandro Rey (Paco Herrera), Peter Mamakos (THRUSH man), Harold Dryenforth (Fisvold), Sandra Sullivan (Sarita Diaz), Tony Davis (Roy).

"The Danish Blue Affair" (10-25-66): Dom De Luise (Stanley Umlaut), Lloyd Bochner (Ole Bargman), William Bramley (Ingo), Virginia Gregg (Granny), Cindy Taylor (Gretel), Mark De Vries (Hansel), Ivan Triesault (Prof. Voltan), Fritz Feld (Chef), Ernest Sarracino (Sandor).

"The Garden of Evil Affair" (11-1-66): Arnold Moss (Iman Abbas), Anna-Lisa (Brunhilde), Lisa Seagram (Miss Karem), Sabrina Scharf (Greta Wolf), Oscar Beregi, Jr. (Hugo Von Gerb), Patrick Horgan (Duke Cornwallis), Khigh Dhiegh (THRUSH Director).

"The Atlantis Affair" (11-15-66): Sidney Blackmer (Prof. Henry Antrum), Denny Miller (Vic Ryan), Claude Woolman (Honore Le Gallows).

"The Paradise Lost Affair" (11-22-66): Monty Landis (Genghis Gomez III), Chips Rafferty (Liverpool 'Enry),

(GIRL FROM U. N. C. L. E. cont.) Raymond St. Jacques (Big Feets Charley), Mokihana (Mme. Chop Chop), Harry Swoger (Capt. Stone).

"The Lethal Eagle Affair" (11-29-66): Margaret Leighton (Gita Volander), Michael Wilding (Franz-Joseph), Brian Avery (Dieter).

"The Romany Lie Affair" (12-6-66): Lloyd Bochner (Sadvaricci), Gladys Cooper (Mamma Rosha), Cal Bolder (Goru), Audrey Dalton (Mrs. Wainwright), Anna Mizrahi (Ponthea).

"The Little John Doe Affair" (12-13-66): Wally Cox (Little John Doe), Pernell Roberts (Joey Celeste).

"The Jewels of Topango Affair" (12-20-66): John Qualen (Dr. Elmer Spritzer), Leslie Uggams (Natasha Brimstone), Brock Peters (King M'Bala), Booker Bradshaw (Prince Nicholas), Barry Kelley (Whiteside), Patrick Horgan (Byron Cavendish), Guy Way (Georgie Gounod), Carol Wayne (girl), Kelton Garwood (poet), Milton Parsons (waiter).

"The Faustus Affair" (12-27-66): Raymond Massey (B. Elzie Bub), Tom Bosley (Jonathan Quantum), Dick Crockett (Goethe).

"The U. F. O. Affair" (1-3-67): Fernando Lamas (Salim Ibn Hydari), Joan Blondell (Madame), Janet MacLachlan (Nur), Anthony Caruso (Amintore Possetti), James Millhollin (aide), Lee Kolima (giant guard), Janine Clements (handmaiden).

"The Moulin Ruse Affair" (1-17-67): Shelly Berman (Dr. Toulouse), Yvonne DeCarlo (Nadia Marcolescu), Ellen Corby (Mme. Bloor).

"The Catacombs and Dogma Affair" (1-24-67): Eduardo Ciannelli (Prince Boriarsi), Fabrizio Mioni (Cesari Boriarsi), Danielle DeMetz (Adriana Raffaelli), Gerald Mohr (Dossetti), Peter Marcus (Hugo Horsch), Thordis Brandt (Miss Ibsen), John Destare (Italian guard), Bob Duggan (Yugoslav guard).

"The Drublegratz Affair" (1-31-67): Patricia Barry (Princess Rapunzel), Vito Scotti (Dr. Igor Gork), Jill Townsend (Sherilee), Christopher Held (Prince Efrem), The Daily Flash (the band).

"The Fountain of Youth Affair" (2-7-67): Gena Rowlands (Baroness Ingrid Blangsted), Philip Ahn (Premier Dao), Donnelly Rhodes (Peter Starker), Miiko Taka (Mme. Dao), Gene Raymond (Charles Vechten).

"The Carpathian Caper Affair" (2-14-67): Ann Sothern (Mother Magda), Stan Freeberg (Herbert Fummer), Jack Cassidy (Rock Munnis), Joyce Jameson (Shirley Fummer), George Furth (Miklos), Violet Carlson (Mama), Bobby Gilbert.

"The Furnace Flats Affair" (2-21-67): Peggy Lee (Packer Jo), Susan Browning (Ladybug Byrd), Ruth Roman (Dolly X), Herb Edelman (Asterick), Percy Helton (Mesquite Swede).

"The Low Blue C Affair" (2-28-67): Hermione Gingold (Major Stella), Renzo Cesana (Diplomat), Broderick Crawford (Soyil Irosian), Stanley Clements (Dwayne), Leonid Kinskey (Enzo Cannaloni).

"The Petit Prix Affair" (3-7-67): Nanette Fabray (Desiree d'Oeuf), Steve Harmon (Jean), Michael Shillo (Octave d'Eouf), Marcel Hillaire (Prof. Pamplemousse).

"The Phi Beta Killer Affair" (3-14-67): Victor Buono (Sir Cecil Seabrook), Lynn Bari (Miss Twickum), Alan Caillou (Sgt. Grimes), Barbara Nichols (Ida Martz), Dick Bakalayan (Brutis), Jack LaRue (Cassie), Jason Wingreen (Dictator), Jerry Lester (Big Julie), Donald Curtis (billionaire).

"The Double-0-Nothing Affair" (3-21-67): Sorrell Booke (Sydney Morehouse), Edward Asner (George Kramer), Don Chastain (Montgomery), Jesslyn Fax (Mrs. Barnes), China Lee (Vivian), Harry Harvey, Sr. (old man).

"The U. N. C. L. E. -Samurai Affair" (3-28-67): Signe Hasso (Sumata), James McCallion (Sean McNee), Michael J. Pollard (Herbie), Richard Roat (Cmdr. Scott), Angelique Pettyjohn (Cora Sue), Tiki Santos (cook).

"The High and Deadly Affair" (4-4-67): Murray Matheson (Dr. Albert Merek), Julie Adams (Julia Douglas), Grayson Hall (Mrs. Fowler), David Brian (Logan), Eileen Baral (Eris).

"The Kooky Spook Affair" (4-11-67): Estelle Winwood (Lady Bramwich), Arthur Malet (Treacle), Edward Ashley (Beaumont), John Orchard (Heathcliff), Harvey Jason (Cecil Bramwich), Kendrick Huxham (steward), Barry Malcolm (the Face).

GIRL WITH SOMETHING EXTRA, THE. 1973-74. Sally Field (Sally Burton), John Davidson (John Burton), Zohra Lampert (Anne), Jack Sheldon (Jerry Burton).

GOLDEN SHOWCASE.
"The Devil and Daniel Webster" (2-14-60): Edward G. Robinson (Daniel Webster), David Wayne (Devil), Tim O'Connor (Jabez Stone), Howard Freeman (Pinkham), Betty Lou Hol-

land (Dorcas Stone), Royal Beal (Justice Hawthorne), Stuart Germain (Stevens).

"The Picture of Dorian Gray" (12-6-61): John Fraser (Dorian Gray), George C. Scott (Lord Henry Wotton), Louis Hayward (Basil Hallward), Robert Walker, Jr. (James Vane), Susan Oliver (Sybil Vane/Hetty Merton), Margaret Phillips (Pamela), Norman Boller (Alan Campbell).

GOOD HEAVENS. 1976. Carl Reiner (Mr. Angel).

GREAT GHOST TALES. 1961.
"William Wilson" (7-6-61): Robert Duvall (William Wilson), Peter Brandon (Whisperer), Laurie Main (Sir Robert Tyne), Joanne Linville.
"Lucy" (7-13-61): Lee Grant (Lucy), Kevin McCarthy (Jerry).
"The Monkey's Paw" (7-20-61): Mildred Dunnock, R. G. Armstrong.
"Bye Bye Baby" (7-27-61): Janet Ward, Collin Wilcox, David J. Stewart, Edmon Ryan.
"August Heat" (8-3-61): James Broderick, Vincent Gardenia, Virginia Leith, Herbert Voland.
"Summer Rental" (8-10-61): Harry Millard, Cynthia Baxter.
"Mr. Arcularis" (8-17-61): Lois Nettleton, John Abbott.
"Sredni Vashtar" (8-24-61): Richard Thomas (Conradin), Judith Evelyn (Mrs. de Ropp).
"Phantom of Delight" (8-31-61): Blanche Yurka, Eric Berry, Clifford David, Anne Williams.
"Room 13" (9-7-61): William Redfield, Diana Van Der Vlis.
"The Wendigo" (9-14-61).
"Who Is the Fairest One of All?" (9-21-61): Salome Jens (Emily Hunter), Arthur Hill (Horace Kipper), Ruth White (Mrs. Pigott), Alvin Epstein (Dr. Kaplan).

GREAT MYSTERIES. 1973-74. Orson Welles (Host).
"A Terribly Strange Bed" (9-12-73): Edward Albert, Rupert Davies (Lemerie), Colin Baker (Barclay), Hugo de Vernier (Cropier).
"The Ingenious Reporter" (9-19-73): David Birney, Geoffrey Bayldon (Magistrate), James Maxwell (Defense lawyer).
"Farewell to the Faulkners" (9-26-73): Keith Baxter (Philip Faulkner), Jane Baxter (Harriet Faulkner).
"The Inspiration of Mr. Budd"

(10-3-73): Donald Connelly (Mr. Budd), Hugh Griffith (man).
"Money to Burn" (10-10-73): Olga Georges-Picot (Louise), Victor Buono.
"Battle of Wits" (10-17-73): Ian Bannen (Gregory Dean), Brewster Mason (Lumsden).
"The Dinner Party" (10-24-73): Joan Collins, Anton Rodgers (Edmund Blake), Anthony Sharp (J. J. McGill).
"The Monkey's Paw" (10-31-73): Cyril Cusack (Mr. White), Megs Jenkins (Mrs. White), Patrick Magee (Sgt. Morris), Michael Kitchen (Herbert).
"For Sale - Silence" (11-7-73): Jack Cassidy.
"Unseen Alibi" (11-14-73): Dean Stockwell.
"La Grande Breteche" (11-21-73): Peter Cushing, Susannah York.
"Death of an Old-Fashioned Girl" (11-28-73): Carol Lynley, Stephen Chase (Paul), Francisca Annis (Nicole), John Le Mesurier (Sid), Anne Stallybrass (Janet).
"Captain Rogers" (12-12-73): Donald Pleasence (Rogers), Joseph O'Connor (Mullet), Janey Key (Joan).
"Compliments of the Season" (12-19-73).
"Come into My Parlor" (12-26-73): Anne Jackson.
"In the Confessional" (1-9-74): Jose Ferrer, Milo O'Shea (Father Crumlish), Philip Davis (Johnny Sheehan), Shane Rimmer (Sgt. Warren).
"Ice Storm" (1-30-74).
"Power of Fear" (2-6-74): Don Murray, Shirley Knight.
"The Furnished Room" (2-13-74): Clarence Williams III.
"Under Suspicion" (2-20-74): Janice Rule.
"Where There's a Will" (3-6-74): Richard Johnson (Sexton), Hannah Gordon.
"The Trial for Murder" (3-13-74): Ian Holmes (Charles Stubbs).
"An Affair of Horror" (3-27-74): Harry Andrews (Sanderson).
"Point of Law" (4-3-74): Alec McCowan (James Addishaw).
"The Leather Funnel" (4-17-74): Christopher Lee (Arnaud), Simon Ward (Stephen).

GREATEST AMERICAN HERO, THE. 1981. William Katt (Ralph Hinkley), Robert Culp (Bill Maxwell), Connie Sellecca (Pam), Michael Pare (Tony), Brandon Williams (Kevin), Faye Grant (Rhonda), Don Cervantes (Rodriguez),

(GREATEST AMERICAN HERO cont.)
Jesse D. Goins (Cyler).
　　Pilot (3-18-71): Richard Herd
(Adam Taft), G. D. Spradlin (Nelson
Corey), Bob Minor (John Macke), Ned
Wilson (Shackelford), Robby Weaver
(Buck), Edward Bell (David Knight).
　　"The Hit Car" (3-25-81): Gwen
Humble (Starlet Wild), Gianni Russo
(Johnny Damanti), Kene Holliday (Ar-
nold Turner), Ernie Orsatti (Bob Ba-
ron), Bob Goldstein (maitre d'), Mel-
vin Allen (man), Virginia Palmer (wo-
man), Quin Kessler (hat check girl),
W. T. Zacha, Anthony Charnota.
　　"Here's Looking At You, Kid"
(4-1-81): James Whitmore, Jr. (Gor-
don McCready), June Lockhart (Mrs.
Davidson), Bob Hastings (Harry David-
son), Red West (Cliff), Thomas W.
Babson (Colvin), Will Gill, Jr. (Afri-
can Representative), Gerald Jann (A-
sian Representative), Eric Forst (Euro-
pean Representative), Roger Etienne
(Captain), Daniel Chodos (aide), Al
Dunlop (mechanic), Nick Ginardo (con-
sul), Bert Hinchman (bus driver), Blake
Clark (policeman).
　　"Saturday on Sunset Boulevard"
(4-8-81): William Bogert (Agent Car-
lisle), Aleya Hamilton (Theresa), Kai
Wulff (Serge Valenkov), David Tress
(Mikhail), Mal Steward (Sherman).
　　"Reseda Rose" (4-15-81): E. J.
Peaker (Rose Blake), Simone Griffeth
(Alicia Hinkley), Peter White (Semenko/
Simpson), Kurt Grayson (Zorin).
　　"My Heroes Have Always Been
Cowboys" (4-29-81): Jack Ging (Tracy
Winslow), John Hart (himself), Ferdy
Mayne (Figuera), Frank McCarthy (Ed-
ward Mcastelli), William Woodson (An-
nouncer).
　　"Fire Man" (5-6-81): Sandy Ward
(Lt. Rafferty), Timothy Carey (Came-
ron), Woody Eney (Moody), Mark Wi-
thers (Shaeffer), Raymond Singer (Kauf-
man), Steven Hirsch (Lane), Paul Cavo-
nis.
　　"The Best Desk Scenario" (5-13-
81): Eugene Peterson (Clarence), Dun-
can Regehr (Palmer Bradshaw), Michael
Ensign (Principal Kane), Tom Pletts
(Agent Genesta), Eric Server.
　　"The Two-Hundred-Mile-an-Hour
Fastball" (11-4-81): Markie Post (Deb-
bie Dante), Carmen Argenziano (Nick
Castle), Michael J. London (Raymond
Sloat), Richard Gjonola (Russ Decker),
Bruce Kirby, Hector Elias, William
Marquez, Stanley Brock, Ralph Maura,
Charles McDaniels, Porfirio Guzman
Berrones, Hank Robinson.

　　"Operation Spoil Sport" (11-11-
81): John Anderson (Gen. Stocker),
Dudley Knight (Charles Ratner), James
Burr Johnson (Major Dyle), Robin Riker
(Nancy Ratner), John Di Fusco (Sgt.
Jenson), John Brandon (Adm. Bailey),
Al White (Capt. Reilly), Don Maxwell,
Russ Martin.
　　"Don't Mess Around with Him"
(10-18-81): Joseph Wiseman (James J.
Beck), Byron Morrow (Marshall Dunn),
Stan Lachow (Jordan Heath), Bernard
Behrens (Dr. Springfield), Barry Cutler
(cab driver), Michael Alldredge (Vern),
W. T. Zacha.
　　"Hog Wild" (11-25-81): Gregory
Sierra (Sheriff Vargas), Dennis Burkley
(Preacher), Paul Koslo (Bad B), Mari-
anne Muellerleile (Stella), Tony Burton
(Curley), Dennis Fimple (Cile Kane),
Marland Proctor, Hoke Howell, Ter-
rence Beasor.
　　"Classical Gas" (12-2-81): Edward
Winter (Charley Wilde), George Loros
(Hydra), Garnett Smith (Hanson), Blake
Clark (Sgt. Crane), William Bogert.
　　"The Beast in Black" (12-9-81):
Christine Belford (Sheila Redman), Jane
Merrow (Betty), Rae Allen (Edith), Jeff
MacKay (Dr. Weinstein).
　　"The Lost Diablo" (12-16-81):
Fred Downs (Pop Casco), John Miranda
(Fletcher), Gary Grubbs (Doyle), Bill
Quinn.
　　"Plague" (1-6-82): Ed Grover (Bun-
ker), Arthur Rosenberg (Kelly), Jeff
Cooper (Reo), Glenn Wilder (Harvey
Locke), Melvin F. Allen (Arnold Diggs),
Richard Brand (Dr. Keene), James Dy-
bas (medic), Hand Salas (cadre man),
Robert Curtis (truck driver), Blake Ma-
rion (radar operator), William Bogert,
J. P. Bumstead, Chip Johnson.
　　"A Train of Thought" (1-13-82):
Milt Kogan (Doctor), James Lydon (Mc-
Givers), Judd Omen (Mohammed), Nick
Cinardo (Sylvester), Sonia Petrovna
(Sonja), Nick Shields, Robert Alan Browne,
Warren Munson.
　　"Now You See It" (1-20-81): Chris-
topher Lofton (Sen. Henderson), Jon Cy-
pher (Beller), Charles Bateman (Col.
Cullen), Laurence Haddon (Burke), Ro-
bert Covarrubias (De Jesus), Richard
Beauchamp (Phillipe), Joe Mantegna (Juan).
　　"The Hand-Painted Thai" (1-27-82):
James Shigeta (Shawn Liang), John Fujio-
ka (Gen. Vin Chow), Kurt Grayson (Tim
Lider), Hilary Labow (Erika Van Damm),
J. P. Bumstead.
　　"Send in the Clowns" (2-3-82):
Catherine Campbell (Erica), David Winn
(John), Kai Wulff (Peter), Alex Rodine

(Klaus), Derek Thompson, Richard Doyle.

"The Shock Will Kill You" (2-10-82): Don Starr (Crocker), Rod Colbin (Gen. Enright), Ray Girardin (Col. Nelson), Leonard Lightfoot (Lieutenant), Bert Hinchman.

"A Chicken in Every Plot" (2-17-82): Thalmus Rasulala (Col. Felipe Augereau), Ron O'Neal (Victor Suchet/ Etienne), Lincoln Kilpatrick (Le Masters), John Hancock (Gen. Louie Devout), Todd Armstrong (Ted McSherry).

"The Devil's Triangle and the Deep Blue Sea" (2-24-82): Jeremy Kemp (Devereaux), Glynn Turman (Le Clerc), Michael Halsey (Collins), Anne Bloom (Linda).

"It's All Downhill from Here" (3-3-82): Red West (Blandin), Sandra Kearns (Samantha), Bill Lucking (Klein), Norbert Weisser (Yuri), Michael Billington (Talenikov), Stefan Gierasch (Karpov), Sara Torgov (Anna), Craig Schaeffer.

"Dreams" (3-17-82): Michael Baseleon (Johnny Sanova), Elizabeth Hoffman (Margaret Detwiller), Robby Weaver (Ray Buck), Fred Stuthman (Evan Thoman), Nicholas Worth (Norm), James Costy (Duffy Magellan), Johnny Crear (Matty), John Le Bouvier (Irma Keeler), Charles Hutchinson (Ted Keeler), Peter Trancher (seminar guest speaker), Edward Bell, Nick Pellegrino, Milt Kogan.

"There's Just No Accounting..." (3-24-82): James Whitmore, Jr. (Byron), Jerry Douglas (Jack Martel), Marc Alaimo (Donnie Armus), Emily Moultrie (Debbie Sherwin), Cloyce Morrow (Penny Sherwin), Carole Mallory, Eugene Peterson, Ted Gehring, Ryan MacDonald.

"The Good Samaritan" (3-31-82): Keenan Wynn (Ira Hagert), Dennis Lipscomb (Dave Tanner), Carmen Argenziano (Murph), Harry Grant (Nino), Sandra McCulley (Judy), Bill Quinn (Harlan).

"Captain Bellybuster and the Speed Factory" (4-7-82): Chuck McCann, Anthony Charnota, Colin Hamilton, Jim Greenleaf.

"Who's Woo in America" (4-14-82): Barbara Hale (Mrs. Hinkley), Tom Hallick (Phillip Kaballa), Michael Prince (Prentice Hall), Jon Cedar (Heller), Hugh Gillin (C. C. Smith), Dave Cass (Goodwin), Daniel Chodos.

"Lilacs - Mr. Maxwell" (4-28-82): Ted Flicker (David), Adam Gregor (Yuri), Arnold Turner (insurance man), Dixie Carter, Gay Rowan, Trisha Hilka,

Gary Pagett, Craig Shreeve.

GREEN HORNET, THE. 1966-67. Van Williams (Britt Reid/The Green Hornet), Bruce Lee (Kato), Wende Wagner (Lenore 'Casey' Case), Walter Brooke (District Attorney F. P. Scanlon), Lloyd Gough (Mike Axford).

"The Silent Gun" (9-9-66): Charles Francisco (Al Trump), Lloyd Bochner (Dan Carley), Henry Evans (Renner), Kelly Jean Peters (Jackie), Ed. McGrealy (Olson), Max Kelvin (Stacey), L. McGranary (Minister).

"Give 'Em Enough Rope" (9-16-66): Diana Hyland (Claudia Bromley), Mort Mills (Alex Colony), Jerry Ayers (Pete), Joe Sirola (Charley), David Renard (Joe Sweek), Ken Strange (Big Bruiser).

"Programmed for Death" (9-23-66): Signe Hasso (Yolanda de Lukens), Richard Cutting (Frank Miller), Norman Leavitt (Walter Melvin), Pat Tidy (Charwoman), Barbara Babcock (Cathy Desmond), Gary Owens (Commentator), Sheila Leighton (D. A.'s secretary), Don Eitner (Pat Allen).

"Crime Wave" (9-30-66): Peter Haskell (Abel Marcus), Sheila Wells (Laura Spinner), Ron Burke (Joe), Gary Owens (Commentator), Denny Costello (detective), Jennifer Stuart (stewardess), Wayne Sutherlin (clown), Breland Rice (policeman), Wilkie de Martel (jeweler).

"The Frog Is a Deadly Weapon" (10-7-66): Victor Jory (Charles Delaclaire), Thordis Brandt (Nedra Vallen).

"Eat, Drink and Be Dead" (10-14-66): Jason Evers (Henry Dirk), Harry Lauter (Brannigan), Harry Fleer (Evans), William McLeannan (Winfield), Eddie Ness (Crandall).

"Beautiful Dreamer" (10-21-66 & 10-28-66): Geoffrey Horne (Peter Eden), Pamela Curran (Vanessa), Henry Hunter (Wylie), Jean Marie (Dorothy), Maurice Manson (Cavanaugh), Barbara Gates (Mary), Victoria George (Harriet), Fred Carson (Joel), Chuck Hicks (Cork), Jerry Catron (Johnny), Gary Owens (TV Announcer), Sandy Kevin (Phil).

"The Ray Is for Killing" (11-11-66): Robert McQueeney (Richardson), Bill Baldwin (Dr. Karl Bendix), Mike Mahoney (policeman), Grant Woods (Steve), Bob Gunner (detective), Jim Raymond (driver).

"The Preying Mantis Kills" (11-18-66): Mako (Low Sing), Tom Drake (Duke Slate), Gary Owens (Announcer), Allen Jung (Wing Ho), Al Huang (Jimmy Kee).

"The Hunters and the Hunted" (11-

(GREEN HORNET cont.) 25-66): Robert Strauss (Bud Crocker), Charles Bateman (Quentin Crane), Douglas Evans (Leland Stone), Rand Brooks (Conway).

"Deadline for Death" (12-2-66): James Best (Yale Barton), Lynda Day George (Ardis Ralston).

"Secret of the Sally Bell" (12-9-66): Warren Kemmerling (Bert Selden), Beth Brickell (Dr. Thomas), Jacques Denbeaux (Gus Wander), Greg Benedict (Carlos), Dave Perna (Wolfe).

"Freeway to Death" (12-16-66): Jeffrey Hunter (Emmet Crown), John Hubbard (Giles), Reggie Parton (Spike), David Fresco (Wiggins).

"May the Best Man Lose" (12-23-66): Harold Gould (Calvin Ryland), Linden Chiles (Warren Ryland), Robert Hoy (Woody), Troy Melton (Pete).

"Seek, Stalk and Destroy" (1-6-67): Ralph Meeker (Earl Evans), Raymond St. Jacques (Hollis Silver), Paul Carr (Eddie Carter), John Baer (Bradford Devlin), E.J. Andre (Paul), Harvey Parry (Bill).

"Corpse of the Year" (1-13-67 & 1-20-67): Joanna Dru (Sabrina), Celia Kaye (Melissa Neal), J. Edward McKinley (Simon Neal), Cesare Danova (Felix Garth), Tom Simcox (Dan Scully).

"Bad Bet on a 459 Silent" (2-3-67): Richard Anderson (Phil Trager), Richard X. Slattery (Steve Grant), Percy Helton (Gus), Tony Epper (Nixie), Bill Couch (Carns), Bill Hampton (Jess).

"Ace in the Hole" (2-10-67): Bert Freed (Sgt. Bert Clark), Jason Wingreen (Doctor), Brian Avery (Jim Dixon).

"Trouble for Prince Charming" (2-17-67): Edmund Hashim (Prince Rafil), Susan Flannery (Janet Prescott), Alberto Morin (Abu Bakr), James Lanphier (Sarajek).

"Alias the Scarf" (2-24-67): John Carradine (James Rancourt), Patricia Barry (Hazel Schmidt), Ian Wolfe (Peter Willman), Paul Gleason (Paul Garret).

"Hornet, Save Thyself" (3-3-67): Michael Strong (Dale Hyde), Marvin Brody (Eddie Rich).

"Invasion from Outer Space" (3-10-67 & 3-17-67): Larry D. Mann (Dr. Eric Mabouse), Arthur Batanides (Shugo), Linda Gaye Scott (Vama), Christopher Dark (Martin), Denny Dobbins (Colonel).

"The Hornet and the Firefly" (3-24-67): Gerald S. O'Loughlin (Ben Wade), Russ Conway (Commissioner Dolan).

GULLIVER IN LILLIPUT. British 1-3-82 - 1-24-82.* Andrew Burt (Gulliver), Linda Polan (Queen), Jonathan Cecil (King Bolbasto), Elizabeth Sladen (Lady Flimnap), George Little (Flimnap), Tilly Vosburgh (Cloren), Barry Andrews (Reldresal), Arthur Hewlett (old man), Jenny McCracken (Lady Bolgolam), John Baker (Frelock), Godfrey James (Bolgolam), Neil Fitzwiliam (Lalcon), Paul Hegarty (Mafrin Bolgolam), Leon Eagles (Balmuff), Bartlett Mullins (Clustril), John Crocker (Archelder), Andrew McCulloch (Sergeant), James Berwick (Limtoc), Peter Grayer (Degal), Richard Clifford (Captain), Brian Coburn (soldier), Danny Schiller (Ribble), Annabel Lanyon (Princess Glintchac), Neil Nisbet (Prince Lerbar), Murray Ewan (Royal tutor), Maggie Flint (Berella).

HALLMARK HALL OF FAME.
"Alice in Wonderland" (10-23-55): Gillian Barber (Alice), Martyn Green (the White Rabbit), Noel Leslie (Caterpillar), Mort Marshall (the Mad Hatter), Alice Pearce (Dormouse), Tom Bosley (Knave of Hearts), J. Pat O'Malley (Gryphon), Elsa Lanchester (Red Queen), Ronald Long (King of Hearts), Karl Swenson (Humpty Dumpty), Reginald Gardiner (White Knight), Bobby Clark (Duchess), Gilbert Mack (Frog Footman), Eva LeGallienne (White Queen).

"On Borrowed Time" (11-17-57): Ed Wynn (Gramps), Claude Rains (Mr. Brink), Beulah Bondi (Granny), Dennis Kohler (Pud), Margaret Hamilton (Aunt Demetria), Larry Gates (Mr. Pilbean), William LeMessena (Dr. Evans), William A. Lee (Mr. Grimes), Mildred Trares (Marcia), G. Wood (Jim), Dorothy Eaton (Susan).

"Berkeley Square" (2-5-59): John Kerr (Peter Standish), Edna Best (Lady Anne Pettigrew), Janet Munro (Helen Pettigrew), John Colicos (Tom Pettigrew), Frances Reid (Duchess of Devonshire), Mildred Trares (Marjorie Frant), Jeannie Carson (Kate Pettigrew), Norah Howard (Mrs. Barwick), Winston Ross (Major Clinton), Jerome Kilty (Mr. Throstle), Sheila Coonan (maid).

"The Tempest" (2-3-60): Maurice Evans (Prospero), Richard Burton (Caliban), Lee Remick (Miranda), Roddy McDowall (Ariel), Tom Poston (Trinculo), Liam Redmond (Gonzalo), Ronald Radd (Stephano), William H. Bassett (Ferdi-

*Aired in multiple segments; dates show first and last segments.

nand), Geoffrey Lumb (Alonso), William
Le Massena (Antonio), Paul Ballantyne
(Sebastian).

"Shangri-La" (10-24-60): Claude
Rains (High Lama), Richard Basehart
(Conway), Gene Nelson (Robert), Mari-
sa Pavan (Lo-Tsen), Alice Ghostley
(Mrs. Brinklow), John Abbott (Chang),
Helen Gallagher (Lise), James Valen-
tine (Mallinson).

"Arsenic and Old Lace" (2-5-62):
Tony Randall (Mortimer Brewster), Boris Karloff (Jonathan Brewster), Dorothy Stickney (Abby Brewster), Mildred
Natwick (Martha Brewster), Tom Bosley (Teddy Brewster), George Voskovec
(Dr. Einstein), Farrel Pelly (Rev. Harper), Dody Heath (Elaine Harper), Nathaniel Frey (Officer Klein), Ralph Dunn
(Lt. Rooney), Dort Clark (Officer Brophy), Alan MacAteer (Mr. Gibbs).

"Blithe Spirit" (12-7-66): Dirk
Bogarde (Charles Condomine), Rose-
mary Harris (Elvira), Rachel Roberts
(Ruth), Ruth Gordon (Mme. Arcati).

"Harvey" (3-22-72): James Stewart (Elwood P. Dowd), Helen Hayes
(Veta Louise Simmons), Jesse White
(Wilson), John McGiver (Dr. Chumley),
Madeline Kahn (Miss Kelly), Arlene
Francis (Mrs. Chumley), Martin Gabel
(Judge Gaffney), Fred Gwynne (cab driver), Marian Hallsey (Myrtle Mae Simmons), Richard Mulligan (Dr. Sanderson), Dorothy Blackburn (Mrs. Chauvenet).

"The Hunchback of Notre Dame"
(2-4-82): Anthony Hopkins (Quasimodo),
Lesley Anne Down (Esmeralda), Derek
Jacobi (Dom Claude Frollo), Robert
Powell (Phoebus), John Gielgud (Char-
molue), Gerry Sundquist (Pierre), Da-
vid Suchet (Trouillefou), Nigel Hawthorne
(Magistrate), Rosalie Crutchley (Simone),
Roland Culver (Bishop of Paris), Tim
Piggott-Smith (Philippe), Alan Webb
(Judge).

HALLOWEEN THAT ALMOST WASN'T,
THE. (10-28-79): Judd Hirsch (Dra-
cula), Henry Gibson (Igor), Mariette
Hartley (the Witch), John Schuck
(Frankenstein), Jack Riley (Werewolf),
Robert Fitch (the Mummy), Joseph
Elic (Zabaar the Zombie), Andrew
Duncan (newscaster), Jaime Ross
(father), Maggie Peters Ross (mo-
ther), Charlie Fields (boy), Kristen
Williams (girl).

HALLOWEEN WITH THE NEW ADDAMS
FAMILY. (10-30-77): John Astin
(Gomez Addams), Carolyn Jones

(Morticia Addams/Ophelia Frump),
Jackie Coogan (Uncle Fester), Ted
Cassidy (Lurch), Henry Darrow (Pan-
cho), Jane Rose (Grandmama), Lisa
Loring (Wednesday Sr.), Ken Wea-
thermax (Pugsley Sr.), Patrick Camp-
bell (Little Bo Peep), Parley Baer
(Boss Crook), Vito Scotti (Mickey),
Dean Sothern (Fake Gomez), Suzanne
Krazna (Countess Dracula), Jennifer
Surprenant (Wednesday Jr.), Kenneth
Marquis (Pugsley Jr.), Elvia Allman
(Mother Frump), David Johns (Hercu-
les), Clinton Beyerle (Atlas), Terry
Miller (Fake Morticia).

HAMMER HOUSE OF HORROR. British
1980 .

"Witching Time" (9-13-80): Jon
Finch (David), Patricia Quinn (Lucinda),
Prunella Gee (Mary), Ian McCulloch
(Charles), Lennard Pearce (Rector),
Margaret Anderson (Sister).

"The Thirteenth Reunion" (9-20-
80): Julia Foster (Ruth Cairns), Dinah
Sheridan (Gwen), Richard Pearson (Sir
Humphrey Chesterton), Norman Bird
(Basil), Warren Clarke (Ben), George
Innes (Cedric), James Cosmo (Willis),
Gerrard Kelly (Andrew), Michael Lati-
mer (Dr. Bradley), Barbara Keogh (Joan),
Paula Jacobs (Joyce), Roger Ostime
(the Butler), Kevin Stoney (Rothwell),
Peter Dean (Charlie), Louis Mansi (Ros-
si).

"Rude Awakening" (9-27-80): Den-
holm Elliott (Norman Shenley), Pat Hey-
wood (Emily Shenley), James Laurenson
(Mr. Rayburn), Lucy Gutteridge (Lolly),
Eleanor Summerfield (Lady Strudwick),
Patricia Mort (maid).

"Growing Pains" (10-4-80): Barbara Kellerman, Gary Bond.

"The Silent Scream" (10-11-80):
Peter Cushing (Martin Blueck), Brian
Cox (Chuck), Anthony Carrick (Aldridge),
Elaine Donnelly (Annie), Terry Kinsella
(Lionel), Robin Browne (police officer).

"The House That Bled to Death"
(10-18-80): Nicholas Ball (William),
Rachel Davies (Emma), Brian Croucher
(George), Pat Maynard (Jean), Milton
Johns (A. J. Powers), Emma Ridley
(Sophia), Joann White (Older Sophia),
George Tovey (old man), Una Brandon-
Jones (old woman), Jo Warne (1st mo-
ther), Sarah Keller (2nd mother), Max
Mason (journalist), Anny Perry (journa-
list).

"Charlie Boy" (10-25-80): Leigh
Lawson (Graham), Marius Goring (Heinz),
Angela Bruce (Sarah), Frances Cuka
(Gwen), David Healey (Peter), Michael

(HAMMER HOUSE OF HORROR cont.) Culver (Mark), Michael Deeks (Phil), Jeff Rawle (Franks), Janet Clare Fielding (secretary), Michael Stock (armourer), Lee Richards (actress), Andrew Pariss (boy), Charles Pemberton (policeman).

"The Children of the Full Moon" (11-11-80): Christopher Cazenove (Tom), Celia Gregory (Sarah), Diana Dors (Mrs. Ardoy), Robert Urquhart (Harry), Jacob Witkin (Woodcutter), Adrian Mann (Tibor), Sophie Kind (Eloise), Victor Wood (Sophy), Matthew Dorman (young boy), Wilhelmina Green (young girl), Corinna Reardon (small girl), Daniel Payne (small boy), Natalie Payne (Irenya), Daniel Kipling (Andreas).

"The Carpathian Eagle" (11-8-80): Suzanne Danielle (Natalie), Sian Phillips (Mrs. Henska), Anthony Valentine (Cliff), Barry Stanton (Tony), Jonathan Kent (Tadek), Matthew Long (Andy), Gary Waldhorn (Bacharach), Ellis Dale (police doctor), Jeffrey Wickham (Edgar), Morgan Sheppard (hospital gardner), Barry Stokes (first victim), Pierce Brosnan (last victim), Diane Adderley (policewoman), Richard Wren (chauffeur).

"Guardian of the Abyss" (11-15-80): Rosalyn Landor (Alison), Ray Lonnen (Michael), John Carson (Charles Randolph), Barbara Ewing, Paul Darrow.

"A Visitor from the Grave" (11-22-80): Kathryn Leigh Scott (Penny), Simon MacCorkindale (Harry), Gareth Thomas (Richard/Gupta), Mia Nadasi (Margaret), Stanley Lebor (Charles), Gordon Reid (Max).

"The Two Faces of Evil" (11-29-80): Anna Calder-Marshall (Janet Lewis), Gary Raymond (Martin Lewis), Paul Hawkins (David Lewis), Philip Latham (Hargreaves), Pauline Delany (Sister), Jenny Laird (Mrs. Roberts), William Moore (Mr. Roberts), Jeremy Longhurst (Dr. Cummings), Brenda Dowling (Nurse Davies), Mike Savage (P.C. Jenkins), Malcolm Hayes (attendant).

"The Mark of Satan" (12-6-80): Peter McEnery (Edwyn), Georginia Hale.

HARDY BOYS/NANCY DREW MYSTERIES, THE (1977-1979). The Hardy Boys: Parker Stevenson (Frank Hardy), Shaun Cassidy (Joe Hardy), Edmund Gilbert (Fenton Hardy), Edith Atwater (Gertrude Hardy) 77-78, Lisa Eilbacher (Calley Shaw) 77-78, Jack Kelly (Harry Morton) 1979.

Nancy Drew: Pamela Sue Martin (Nancy Drew), Janet Louise Johnson (Nancy Drew) 1978, William Schallert (Carson Drew), Jean Rasey (George Fayne), Susan Buckner (George Fayne) 1978, George O'Hanlon, Jr. (Ned Nickerson), Rick Springfield (Ned Nickerson) 1978, Ruth Cox (Bess), Robert Karnes (Sheriff King).

"The Mystery of the Haunted House" (1-30-77): The Hardy Boys: Jim Antonio (Rigby), John Kerry (Stratton), Roger Davis (Sonny), Simon Scott (man), Reggie Nalder (receptionist), Richard Kiel.

"The Mystery of Pirates Cove" (2-6-77): Nancy Drew: Monte Markham (Prof. Wall), Joe Penny (Brandon), Arthur Peterson (Jensen).

"The Mystery of the Witches' Hollow" (2-13-77): The Hardy Boys: Gary Springer (Chet Morton), Marc Vahanian (Simon), Bert Kramer (Steve Donner), Brad Trumbull (Sheriff Houghton), Sandy Ward (Capt. Maguire), Dimitra Arliss (Hazel Thompson), Bill Quinn (Andy Hudson).

"The Mystery of the Diamond Triangle" (2-20-77): Nancy Drew: Brian Byers (Morgan), Ralph Garrett (Slate), Phillip R. Allen (Everett), Len Lesser (Mackey), Gordon Jump (Officer Hooper).

"The Disappearing Floor" (3-6-77): The Hardy Boys: David Opatoshu (Prof. Desmond), Robin Chester (Marsha), Marj Dusay (Dr. Janice Craddock), Howard Platt (Sidney Tabor), Sam Gilman (Luther Hodges).

"The Secret of the Whispering Walls" (3-10-77): Nancy Drew: Queenie Smith (Lela), Irene Tedrow (Ruby), Archie Lewis (Dinko), Mary Jo Catlett (Dora), John Carter (Walter), Barbara Collentine.

"The Flickering Torch Mystery" (3-27-77): The Hardy Boys: Rick Nelson (Tony Bird), Robert Sampson (Lou Haskell), John Pleshette (Carl Fry), Herb Voland (Chief Colig), Deirdre Berthrong (Leslie Johnston), Ned Van Zandt (Richard Johnston).

"A Haunting We Will Go" (4-3-77): Nancy Drew: Dina Merrill (Thelma), Carl Betz (Alex), Victor Buono (Seth), Bob Crane (Danny), Pippa Scott (Janet).

"The Mystery of the Flying Courier" (4-10-77): The Hardy Boys: Dick Gautier (Tail Gunner Joe), Penny Peyser (Suzie Wilkens), Josh Taylor (Miles), Paul Tulley (Nash), Ken Swofford (Capt. Phelps).

"The Mystery of the Fallen Angel" (4-17-77): Nancy Drew: A Martinez

(Henry Salazar), Susan Pratt O'Hanlon (Ann), Robert Englund (Gar), Craig Littler (Vince), Robert Alda (Robert Jordan), Marjorie Lord (Clara Jordan), Beverly Garland (Thelma), Jamie Lee Curtis (Mary), Migdia Varela (Tina).

"Wipe Out" (4-24-77): The Hardy Boys: Shelly Novack (Wally), Titus Napoleon (Lew), James Shigeta (Kapala), Bruce Gordon (McGuire), Lisa Reeves (Becky), Frank Michael Liu (Lt. Kirk), Debbie Clinger (Liz).

"The Mystery of the Ghostwriter's Cruise" (5-1-77): Nancy Drew: David Wayne (John Addams), Dane Clark (Capt. Powers), H. M. Wynant (Howard), Joan Prather (Adriane), Les Lannom (George Tomkins), Susan Woollen (Cathy), Reb Brown (Rosselli), Derek Murcott (First Mate).

"The Mystery of the Jade Kwan Yin" (5-15-77): The Hardy Boys: Rosalind Chao (Lily), Richard Loo (Chen), Richard Lee Sung (Chu), David Tai Wai Chow (Wang), Bill Saito (Chao).

"The Mystery of the Solid Gold Kicker" (5-22-77): Nancy Drew: Mark Harmon (Chip Garvey), Terry Kiser (Ben Halstead), Martin Kove (Pete Miller), Michael Pataki, Jillian Kesner.

"The Hardy Boys and Nancy Drew Meet Dracula" (9-11-77 & 9-18-77): The Hardy Boys/Nancy Drew: Lorne Greene (Stavlin), Paul Williams (Allison Troy), John Van Dreelan (Mayor Haufman), Bernie Taupin (Tim Carstairs), Leon Askin.

"The Mystery of King Tut's Tomb" (9-25-77): The Hardy Boys: Taryn Power (Helene), Cesare Danova (Moustapha), Elyssa Davalos (Wendy Bonner).

"The Mystery of the Hollywood Phantom" (10-2-77 & 10-9-77): The Hardy Boys/Nancy Drew: James Wainwright (Arlo Wetherly), J. D. Cannon (Jason Fox), Clive Revill (Bronson), Casey Kasem (Hamilton), Dennis Weaver, Robert Wagner, Jaclyn Smith, Michael J. Quinn.

"The Mystery of the African Safari" (10-16-77): The Hardy Boys: Stuart Whitman (Trevor Masters), Anne Lockhart (Sarah Masters), Harold Sylvester (Ngoto), Percy Rodriguez, Peter Bromilow (Saunders), Albert Popwell (Keino).

"The Creature Came on Sunday" (10-30-77): The Hardy Boys: Bonnie Ebsen (Sharon Anderson), John Quade (Sheriff Oren), Victor Holchak (Berardi), Britt Leach (Farina), Danny Goodman).

"The Strange Fate of Flight 608" (11-6-77): The Hardy Boys: Robin Mattson (Carla), Thayer David (Goldman), Kitty Ruth (Beverly), Herb Braha (Prager), Don Marshall (Flight Engineer).

"Acapulco Spies" (11-13-77): The Hardy Boys: Craig Stevens (Cartell), Deborah Ryan (Jackie), Kimberley Beck (Sue).

"Nancy Drew's Love Match" (11-20-77): Nancy Drew: Maureen McCormick (Karen Phillips), Christopher Connelly (Castelli), Roger C. Carmel (John Bender), Nico Minardos (Paco), Stephen McNally (Phillips).

"The Silent Scream" (11-27-77): The Hardy Boys: Larry Storch (Jesse Miller), Trini Lopez (Julio Ramirez), Martha Gewertz (Alicia Peterson), Elizabeth Stack (Sally Kline), Val Avery (Alvin Tracey).

"Will the Real Santa Claus...?" (12-18-77): Nancy Drew: Dan O'Herlihy (Griffin), John Ericson (Capt. Rogers), Walt Davis (Stewart).

"The Lady on Thursday at Ten" (1-1-78): Nancy Drew: Simon Oakland (Eghan), John Karlen (Rocky), Nicholas Hammond (Burke), Tony Burton (Gilmore Lee).

"Oh Say Can You Sing" (1-8-78): The Hardy Boys: Gene Evans (Sgt. Reinauer), Guy Stockwell (Lt. Collins), Debra Clinger (Harriet Alexander), Raynold Gideon (Jerry Morgan), Nancy Stephens (Sally Morgan), Joe Bennett (Alex Campbell), Chip Lucia.

"The House on Possessed Hill" (1-22-78): The Hardy Boys: Dorothy Malone (Mrs. Blain), Melanie Griffith (Stacy Blain), Lloyd Bochner (Dr. Mann), Ed Crich (Jefferson), Wayde Preston (Sheriff Hollister), Royal Dano (Grant), Richard LePore (Allyn).

"Sole Survivor" (1-29-78): The Hardy Boys: Diana Muldaur (Lida), Robert Horton (Alan Kline), Barry Primus (Peter Abrams), Jean Marie Hon (Kim), James Hong (Dr. Low), Chao-Li Chi (Prof. Chiang), Michael Jackson (newscaster).

"Voodoo Doll" (2-12-78 & 2-19-78): The Hardy Boys/Nancy Drew: Ray Milland (Orrin Thatcher), Julius Harris (Dr. Dove), Kim Cattrall (Marie-Claire), Howard Duff (Lt. Martinelle), James Callahan (O'Hagerty), Johnny Sekka (Ambassador), Linda Dano (Josette), Madeleine Taylor Holmes.

"Mystery on the Avalanche Express" (2-26-78): The Hardy Boys/Nancy Drew: Deborah Walley (Gina Bartelli), Edd Byrnes (Hans Monckton), Troy Donahue

1252   Science Fiction, Horror, Fantasy

(HARDY BOYS/NANCY DREW MYSTE-
RIES cont.) (Alan Summerville), Gary
Crosby (Yates), Tommy Sands (Jerry
Kanner), Fabian Forte (Paul Leyton),
Vic Damone.
   "Death Surf" (3-12-78): The Har-
dy Boys: Maren Jensen (Marianne Dal-
ton), Jack Jones (Hubba), Jack Hogan
(Turner), Ken Scott (Lt. Conrad), John
Mark Robinson, Gary Wood.
   "Arson and Old Lace" (4-1-78):
The Hardy Boys/Nancy Drew: Joseph
Cotten (Walter Rathbone), Jack Kelly
(Insp. Helms), Pernell Roberts (Chief
Madison), Robert Sampson (Paul Kel-
ler), Cathy Rigby (Alice), Brian Cutler.
   "The Campus Terror" (5-7-78):
The Hardy Boys: Jack Ging (Insp. Ri-
chards), Valerie Bertinelli (Wendy
Chase), Kim Lankford (Alice Smith),
Derek Murcott (Dr. Llewellyn).
   "The Last Kiss of Summer" (10-
1-78 & 10-8-78): The Hardy Boys: Ka-
ren Brophy (Jocco Halsey), Kristie
Welsch (Jamie), Anne Lockhart (Jess),
Mills Watson (Dobson).
   "Assault on the Tower" (10-15-
78): The Hardy Boys: Patrick MacNee
(S), Pernell Roberts (Lt. Morley), Dana
Andrews (Townley), James Booth (Lt.
Buckley).
   "Search for Atlantis" (10-22-78):
The Hardy Boys: Lloyd Nolan (Prof.
Hendricks), Darleen Carr (Helena),
John Colicos (Morbius).
   "The Pirates" (10-29-78): The
Hardy Boys: Robert Loggia (Jean De-
veau), Dane Clark (Hubbard), June Lock-
hart (Mrs. Migley), Rebecca York (Rhea
Thomas), Phillip R. Allen (Gibbon).
   Title unknown (11-5-78): The
Hardy Boys: Craig Stevens (Franz Hol-
vard), Macdonald Carey (Sen. John Mar-
tin), Nina Axelrod (Kathryn Martin).
   "Defection to Paradise" (11-19-
78 & 11-26-78): The Hardy Boys: Da-
vid Gates (himself), Nehemiah Persoff
(Christovan), Pamela Franklin (Maria
Vichenko), Edd Byrnes (Paul Owens),
Bobby Van (Tom Dresden).
   "Deadly Game" (12-3-78): The
Hardy Boys: Mary Louise Wagner (An-
nie Metzger), Nancy Morgan (Melanie
Wilson), Jim Raymond.

HEAVEN ON EARTH. Pilot (6-28-79):
Carol Wayne (Roxy), Donna Ponter-
otto (Karen), William Daniels (Sebastian Parnell).

HEAVEN ON EARTH. Pilot (4-21-81):
Jack Gilford, Doug Sheehan (Jerry),
Ilene Graff (Katie), Ray Contreras

(Luis), Nora Morgan (Amy), Christopher J. Brown (Lenny), Rod Mc-
Cary (Harvey).

HERBIE, THE LOVE BUG. 1982. Dean
Jones (Jim Douglas), Patricia Harty
(Susan MacLane), Larry Linville
(Randy), Claudia Wells (Julie Mac-
Lane), Douglas Emerson (Robbie
MacLane), Nicky Katt (Matthew Mac-
Lane), Robert Paul (Bo Phillips).

HIGHCLIFFE MANOR. 1979. Shelley
Fabares (Helen Blacke), Eugenie Ross-
Leming (Frances Cascan), Audrey
Landers (Wendy Sparks), Gerald Gor-
don (Dr. Felix Morger), Stephen Mc-
Hattie (the Rev. Mr. Ian Glenville),
Jenny O'Hara (Rebecca), Christian
Marlowe (Bram Shelley), Ernie Hud-
son (Smythe), Harold Sakata (Cheng),
Luis Avalos (Dr. Sanchez), Marty
Zagon (Dr. Koontz), David Byrd (Dr.
Lester).

HIGHER AND HIGHER, ATTORNEYS AT
LAW. Pilot (9-9-68): Sally Keller-
man (Liz Higher), John McMartin
(John Higher), Dustin Hoffman (Ar-
thur Greene), Robert Forster (Doug
Payson), Alan Alda (Frank St. John),
Barry Morse (Colin St. John), Ruth
White (Ellen St. John).

HITCH-HIKER'S GUIDE TO THE GAL-
AXY, THE. British (6-4-81 - 7-9-
81).* Peter Jones (Voice of the Book),
Simon Jones (Arthur Dent), David
Dixon (Ford Prefect), Sandra Dickinson (Trillian), Mark Wing-Davey (Za-
phod Beeblebrox), Richard Vernon
(Slartibartfast), Joe Melia (Mr. Pros-
ser), Steve Conway (Barman), Martin
Benson (Vogon Captain), Michael Cule
(Vogon guard), David Learner (Mar-
vin), Stephen Moore (Voice of Marvin),
Rayner Bourton (newscaster), Gil Mor-
ris (Gag Halfrunt), David Tate (Voice
of Eddie the Computer), Antony Car-
rick (Lunkwill), Timothy Davies (Fook),
David Leland (Majikthise), Charles
McKeown (Vroomfondel), Matt Zim-
merman (Shooty), Marc Smith (Bang
Bang), Jack May (Garkbit), David
Prowse (bodyguard), Colin Jeavons
(Max Quordlepleen), David Rowlands
(hairdresser), Colin Bennet (Zarquon),
Peter Davison (Dish of the Day), Ray-
ner Bourton (newscaster), Aubrey
Morris (Captain), Matthew Scurfield
(No. 1), David Neville (No. 2), Geof-

*Aired in multiple segments; dates show first and
last segments.

frey Beevers (No. 3), Beth Porter (marketing girl), Jon Glover (management consultant).

HOLMES AND YOYO. 1976. Richard B. Shull (Sgt. Alexander Holmes), John Schuck (Sgt. Gregory 'Yoyo' Yoyonovich), Bruce Kirby (Capt. Harry Sedford), Andrea Howard (Maxine Moon), Ben Hammer (Chief Dwight Buchanan), Larry Hovis (Dr. Babcock), Fritzi Burr (Mrs. Buchanan), G. Wood (Police Commissioner).

HOLLYWOOD TELEVISION THEATRE. "The Police" (10-14-71): Murray Hamilton (Chief of Police), Fred Gwynne (Sergeant), John McGiver (General), Neva Patterson (wife), Bob Dishy (prisoner/aide).

"The Scarecrow" (1-10-72): Gene Wilder (Lord Ravenbane), Will Geer (Justice Mertons), Nina Foch (Goody Rickby), Norman Lloyd (Dickon), Blythe Danner (Rachel), Joan Tompkins (Cynthia Merton), Peter Duel (Richard Talbot), Tom Helmore (Sir Charles), Sian Barbara Allen (Amelia), Robert Karns (Minister Dodge), Peter Kastner (Captain Bugby), Ann Doran (Mistress Dodge), Vaughan Taylor (the Rev. Mr. Rand), Elisha Cook, Jr. (Micah), John Myhers (the Rev. Mr. Todd), Lizabeth Dean (Mistress Reddington).

"Steambath" (11-16-73): Bill Bixby (Tandy), Valerie Perrine (Meredith), Herb Edelman (Bieberman), Peter Kastner (Gottlieb), Kenneth Mars (Broker), Stephen Elliott (old-timer).

HUNCHBACK OF NOTRE DAME. British 1965. Peter Woodthorpe (Quasimodo), James Maxwell, Gary Raymond, Gay Hamilton, Suzanne Neve, Alex Davion, Norman Mitchell, Beatrix Lehmann, Jeffrey Isaac.

I DREAM OF JEANNIE. 1965-70. Barbara Eden (Jeannie), Larry Hagman (Capt. Tony Nelson), Bill Daily (Capt. Roger Healey), Hayden Rorke (Dr. Bellows), Philip Ober (Gen. Wingard Stone) 65-66, Karen Sharpe (Melissa Stone) 65-66, Emmaline Henry (Amanda Bellows) 66-70, Barton Mac-Lane (Gen. Peterson) 65-69, Vinton Hayworth (Gen. Schaeffer) 69-70.

IMMORTAL, THE. 1970-71. Christopher George (Ben Richards), David Brian (Maitland), Don Knight (Fletcher).

"Sylvia" (9-25-70): Carol Lynley

(Sylvia Cartwright), Glenn Corbett (David Hiller), Sherry Jackson (Sherry Hiller), Paul Langton (Walter Hiller), Angela Greene (Mrs. Hiller), Joey Tata (Monitor).

"White Elephants Don't Grow on Trees" (10-1-70): Ross Martin (Eddie Yeoman), Mitchel Vogel (Jud Yeoman), William Wintersole (plant manager), Read Morgan (Tucker), Elizabeth Harrower (Aunt Marge), Ed Begley, Jr. (attendant), Karl Lukas (superintendent), Virginia Carroll (waitress).

"Reflections on a Lost Tomorrow" (10-8-70): Jack Albertson (Dr. Kosler), Rosemary Forsythe (Anne), Philip Bourneuf (Dr. Hubner), Will Geer.

"Legacy" (10-15-70): Mario Alcaide (Ramos), Susan Howard (Annie), Manuel Padilla (Luis).

"The Rainbow Butcher" (10-22-70): Vic Morrow (Sheriff Wheeler), Collin Wilcox (Clarice), Byron Mabe (Deputy Collins), Tani Phelps (Martha), Jimmy Bracken (Donny).

"Man on a Punched Card" (10-29-70): Lynda Day George (Terry Kerwin), Lee Patterson (Duane Hollenback), Lori Busk (Bonita), Jim Wagerman (attendant), Ford Lile (Deputy), Hal Riddle (Morton).

"White Horse, Steel Horse" (11-5-70): John Dehner (George Allison), Warner Anderson (Judge Atkins), Robbie Porter (Robert Allison), Stephen Oliver (Nat), Bill Burton (Ray), John Picard (Katcher), Fredric Gavlin (Sheriff).

"Queen's Gambit" (11-12-70): Lee Meriwether (Sigrid Bergen), Nico Minardos (Simon Brenner), Karl Swenson (Dr. Lorenzo), Dom Tattoli.

"By Gift of Chance" (11-19-70): Michael Conrad (Monte Loomis), Herb Jefferson, Jr. (Garland), Art Lewis (Portland Bill), Jacqueline Scott (Alpha Henderson), Dan Haggerty (Danson), Paul Nuckles (Peters).

"Dead Man, Dead Man" (12-3-70): Henry Beckman (Kinneson), Brian Keith (Sheriff Holley), Joan Hotchkiss (Helen Stoner), Kem Dibbs (Bryer), John Garwood (McWard), Lal Baum (Frye), Lee Stanley (Deputy Barry).

"Paradise Bay" (12-10-70): Scott Brady (Brady), Tisha Sterling (Nancy/Julie), Howard Duff (Cameron), Aron Kincaid (Pete), Don Diamond (Warren), Joe Hooker (Eddie).

"The Return" (12-17-70): Richard Ward (Joe Carver), Harry Townes (Roy Adkins), Martine Bartlett (Mrs. Adkins), Marlene Clark (Carol Carver).

"To the Gods Alone" (12-31-70): Barry Sullivan (Jordan Braddock), Bruce

(IMMORTAL cont.) Dern (Luther),
Lynn Loring (Grace Lee).
"Sanctuary" (1-7-71): Sal Mineo
(Tainnajinni), Paul Picerni (Klabo),
Donald 'Red' Barry, Iron Eyes Cody,
Fred Lerner, Allen Gibbs.
"Brother's Keeper" (1-14-71):
Michael Strong (Jason Richards), Marj
Dusay (Allison Richards).

INCREDIBLE HULK, THE. 1978-81.
Bill Bixby (Dr. David Banner), Lou
Ferrigno (the Hulk), Jack Colvin
(Jack McGee).
"Final Round" (3-10-78): Martin
Kove (Rocky), Al Ruscio (Sariego),
Johnny Witherspoon (Tom), Fran Myers
(Mary).
"The Beast Within" (3-17-78):
Caroline McWilliams (Claudia), Dabbs
Greer (Dr. Malone), Richard Kelton
(Carl), Charles Lampkin (Joe), Jean
Durand (Jagger), Billie Joan Beach
(Rita).
"Of Guilt, Models and Murder"
(3-24-78): Jeremy Brett (Joslin), Loni
Anderson (Sheila), Deanna Lund (Terri
Ann), Ben Gerard (Sanderson).
"Terror in Times Square" (3-31-
78): Jack Kruschen (Norman), Pamela
Shoop (Carol), Arny Freeman (Leo),
Robert Alda (Jason).
"747" (4-7-78): Brandon Cruz
(Kevin), Edward Power (Phil), Sondra
Currie (Stephanie), Shirley O'Hara
(Mrs. MacIntire), Denise Galik (Denise),
Don Keefer (MacIntire), Howard Honig
(Jack), Susan Cotton (Cynthia Davis).
"The Hulk Breaks Las Vegas" (4-
21-78): Julie Gregg (Wanda), Dean San-
toro (Campion), Don Marshall (Lee),
Simone Griffith (Kathy), John Crawford
(Tom Elder), Paul Picerni (Charlie).
"Never Give a Trucker an Even
Break" (4-28-78): Jennifer Darling,
Frank Christi (Ted), Grand Bush (Mike),
John Calvin (Irishman), Charles Alvin
Bell (gas station man).
"Life and Death" (5-12-78): Diane
Civita (Carrie), Andrew Robinson (Dr.
Rhodes), John Williams (Dan), Julie
Adams (Ellen Harding), Carl Franklin
(Crosby), Al Berry (trucker).
"Earthquake's Happen" (5-19-78):
Peter Brandon (Hammond), Sherry Jack-
son (Diane Joseph), Kenne Holliday (Paul),
Lynne Topping (Nancy), Pamela Nelson
(Marsha), John Alvin (Dr. Patterson).
"The Waterfront Story" (5-31-78):
Sheila Larken (Josie), Jack Kelly (Tony),
James Sikking (McConnell), Candice
Azzara (Sarah), Ted Markland (Marty),
William Benedict (Vic).

"Married" (9-22-78): Mariette
Hartley (Dr. Caroline Fields), Brian
Cutler (Brad), Duncan Gamble (Mark),
Meehe Peluce (young boy), Diane Mar-
koff (girl), Joseph Kim (Justice of the
Peace).
"The Antowuk Horror" (9-29-78):
William Lucking, Debbie Lytton (Saman-
tha), Lance LeGault (Brad), Dennis Pa-
trick (Buck), Myron D. Healey (Cotton),
Gwen Van Dam (Mayor Murphy).
"Ricky" (10-6-78): Mickey Jones
(Ricky), James Daughton (Buzz), Robin
Mattson (Irene), Eric Server (Ted Ro-
berts), Gerald McRaney (Sam Roberts).
"Rainbow's End" (10-13-78): Ned
Romero (Logan), Craig Stevens (Carroll),
Michele Nichols (Kim), Gene Evans (Kel-
ley), Larry Volk (Andy Cardone), War-
ren Smith (guard).
"A Child in Need" (10-20-78): Den-
nis Dmister (Mark Hollinger), Sandy Mc-
Peak (Jack Hollinger), Sally Kirkland
(Margaret Hollinger), Rebecca York
(Mary Walker), Marguerite De Lain (re-
porter).
"Another Path" (10-27-78): Mako
(Li Sung), Tom Lee Holland (Frank Silva),
Irene Yah-Ling Sun (May Chuan), Richard
Lee Sung (Simon King), Jane Chung (Stam-
ma Loo), Joseph Kim (Fong).
"Alice in Disco Land" (11-3-78):
Donna Wilkes (Alice), Jason Kincaid
(Louie), Freeman King (D.J.), Mo Ma-
lone (Rosalyn Morrow), Marc Alaimo
(Ernie), Julie Hill (Molly), Betty Ann
Rees.
"Killer Instinct" (11-10-78): Den-
ny Miller (Tobey), Barbara Leigh (June
Tobey), Rudy Solari (Dr. Stewart), Wyatt
Johnson (Bowers), Herman Poppe (J.P.
Tobey), Tiger Williams (Tobey as a child).
"Stop the Presses" (11-24-79):
Mary Frann (Karen), Julie Cobb (Jill),
Sam Chew, Jr. (Joe Arnold), Art Me-
trano (Charlie Watts), Pat Morita (Fred),
Richard O'Brien.
"Escape from Los Santos" (12-1-
78): Shelley Fabares (Holly), Lee de
Broux (Deputy Evans), Dana Elcar (She-
riff Harris), W.K. Stratton.
"Wildfire" (1-17-79): John Ander-
son (Mike Callahan), Christine Belford
(Linda Callahan), Billy Green Bush (Tho-
mas), Dean Brooks (Adler), Ernie Orsat-
ti (Haze), John Petlock (Wade).
"A Solitary Place" (1-24-79): Kath-
ryn Leigh Scott (Gail), Jerry Douglas
(Frank), Bruce Wright (Richard), Hector Elias (Raul).
"Like a Brother" (1-31-79): Stuart
K. Robinson (Mike), Tony Burton (Taylor George), Carl Anderson (Oscar),

Austin Stoker (Rev. Williams), Dale Pullum (Bobby), Ernie Hudson (Lee).

"Haunted" (2-23-79): Carol Baxter (Renee), John O'Connell (Bernard), Johnny Haymer (Fred Lewitt), Jon Lormer (Dr. Rawlins), Randi Kiger (Renee as a child), Iris Korn (woman).

"Mystery Man" (3-2-79 & 3-9-79): Victoria Carroll (Rose), Aline Towne (Nurse Phalen), Howard Witt (Bob Cory), Bonnie Johns (Helen).

"The Disciple" (3-16-79): Mako (Li Sung), Rick Springfield (Michael), Gerald McRaney (Colin), Stacy Keach, Sr. (Tim), George Loros (Lynch).

"No Escape" (3-30-79): James Wainwright (Tom Wallace), Mariclare Costello (Kay), Sherman Hemsley (Robert), Thalmus Rasulala (Simon), Skip Homeier.

"Kindred Spirits" (4-6-79): Whit Bissell (Prof. Williams), Kim Cattrall (Dr. Gabrielle White), Chief Dan George (Lone Wolf), Rick Youngblood (A. Martinez).

"The Confession" (5-4-79): Markie Post (Pamela), Barry Gordon (Harold), Richard Herd (Mark Roberts).

"The Quiet Room" (5-11-79): Joanna Mills (Dr. Joyce Hill), Philip Abbott (Dr. Murrow), Sian Barbara Allen (Kathy), Robert F. Lyons (Sam).

"Vendetta Road" (5-25-79): Ron Lombard (Ray Floyd), Christina Hart (Cassie Floyd), Morgan Woodward (Madrid), Chip Johnson (Greg Bantam).

"Metamorphosis" (9-21-79): Mackenzie Phillips (Lisa Swan), Katherine Cannon (Jackie Swan), Gary Graham (Greg).

"Blind Rage" (9-28-79): Tom Stechschulte (Lt. Jerry Banks), Lee Bryant (Carrie Banks), Nicolas Coster (Coloner), Don Dubbins (Sgt. Murkland), Jack Rader (Major Anderson).

"Brain Child" (10-5-79): Robin Dearden (Joleen), June Allyson (Dr. Kate Lowell), Lynn Carlin (Elizabeth Collins), Henry Rowland (Dr. Saltz), Madeleine Taylor Holmes (La Bruja), Fred Carney (Mr. Sweeney), Stack Pierce (cop).

"The Slam" (10-19-79): Charles Napier (Blake), Marc Alaimo (Holt), Julius Harris (Doc).

"My Favorite Magician" (10-26-79): Ray Walston (Jasper Dowd), Anne Schedeen (Kimberly), Robert Alda (Giancarlo), Scatman Crothers (Edgar McGee), Joan Leslie (Lily), Bill Capizzi (Bill), Archie Lang (Justice of the Peace), Fritzi Burr (Rose Brown), Franklin Brown (Maurie Brown), Bob

Hastings (Earl).

"Jake" (11-2-79): L. Q. Jones (Jake White), James Crittenden (Leon White), Sandra Kerns (Maggie), Jesse Vint (Terry), Richard Fullerton (Buford), Buck Young (Bob Long).

"Behind the Wheel" (11-9-79): Esther Rolle (Coleen), Jon Cedar (Sam Egan), Michael Baseleon (Michael Swift), John Chandler (Eric), Margaret Impert (Jean), Albert Popwell (Calvin), Richard O'Keefe (owner), Jim Staskel (dealer), Ed Reynolds (driver).

"Homecoming" (11-30-79): Diana Muldaur (Dr. Helen Banner), John Marley (D. W. Banner), Regis J. Cordic (Dean Eckart), Guy Boyd (Steve Howston), Richard Armstrong (entomologist), Claire Malis (Mrs. Banner), Barbara Lynn Block (newscaster), Reed Diamond (Young David), Drew Snyder (Cross), Steve Burns.

"The Snare" (12-7-79): Bradford Dillman (Michael Sutton), Bob Boyd (pilot).

"Babalao" (12-14-79): Louise Sorel (Dr. Renee Dubois), Jarrod Johnson (Louie), Bill Henderson (Antoine Moray/Babalao), Michael Swan (Luc), Paulene Myers (Celine), Christine Avila (Denise), Morgan Hart (girl), John D. Gowans (local).

"Captive Night" (12-21-79): Anne Lockhart (Karen), Parley Baer (Raymond), Paul Picerni (Jim), Stanley Kamel (Gary).

"Broken Image" (1-4-80): Karen Carlson (Lorraine), John Reilly (Steve), Jed Mills (Teddy), George Caldwell (Pete).

"Proof Positive" (1-11-80): Caroline Smith (Pat Steinhauer), Walter Brooke (Mark Roberts), Wayne Storm (Chuck Schlosser), Charles Thomas Murphy (Garland), Isabel Cooley (Muriel).

"Sideshow" (1-25-80): Marie Windsor (Belle Starr), Judith Chapman (Nancy), Robert Donner (Benedict), Bruce Wright (Jimmy), Louisa Moritz (Beth), Allan Rich (Luther Mason), Tam Elliot (Candy), Essex Smith (Cox), Terence Evans (Cecil).

"Long Run Home" (2-1-80): Paul Koslo (Carl Rivers), Robert Tessier (Johnny), Mickey Jones (Doc), Stephen Keep (Fitzgerald), Edward Edwards (Bob), Albert Popwell (Doctor), Pamela Bryant (Ann), Nina Weintraub (Abigail), Galen Thompson (foreman).

"Falling Angels" (2-8-80): Annette Charles (Rita Montoya), Timothy O'Hagan (Peter Grant), Anthony Herrera (Don Sipes), Deborah Morgan-Weldon (Jodie), Cindy Fisher.

"The Lottery" (2-15-80): Robert Hogan (Harry), Peter Breck (Hull), Da-

(INCREDIBLE HULK cont.) vid Mc-
Knight (Clark), Adam Thomas (Steve),
Jimmy Hayes (guard), Luis Avalos.
    "The Psychic" (2-22-80): Brenda
Benet (Annie Caplan), Stephen Fenning
(Johnny Wolff), Jason Ross (cop).
    "A Rock and a Hard Place" (2-
29-80): Jeanette Nolan (Lucy Cash),
John McIntire (Preston Dekalb), Eric
Server (Randolph), J. Jay Saunders
(Garnett Simms), Robert Gray.
    "Deathmask" (3-14-80): Gerald
McRaney (Frank Rhodes), Frank Marth
(Mayor), Lonny Chapman (J. J. Hendren),
Joan Singer (Melendy Britt), Miriam
Charles (Marla Pennington), Don Mar-
shall (man), Dennis Bowen (Dale Jenks),
Michael Bond (Sid Fox), Kieran Mulla-
ney (young man), Desiree Kerns (young
blonde woman), Robert Luney (newsman).
    "Equinox" (3-21-80): Christine
DeLisle (Diane), Paul Carr (Allan Gra-
ble), Louis Turenne (Pierce), Henry
Polic II (Donald), Joy Garrett (Tina),
Bob Yannetti (Carlo), Mark McGee (Sir
Francis Drake), Kathie Spencer-Neff
(Inquisitor), Alexis Adams (girlfriend),
Danny Dayton.
    "Nine Hours" (4-4-80): Marc
Alaimo (Joe Franco), Sheila Larken
(Rhonda), David Comfort (Timmy), Sam
Ingraffia (Slick), Phil Rubinstein (Fats),
Doris Dowling (Nurse Grasso), Frank
De Kova (Sam Monte), Dennis Haysbert
(guard), John Medici (Danny), Hal Bo-
kar (Capt. Deeter).
    "On the Line" (4-11-80): Kathleen
Lloyd (Randy), Don Reid (Wilson), Joe
Di Reda (Mackie), Peter Jason (Bennett),
Tony Duke (reporter).
    "Prometheus" (11-7-80 & 11-14-
80): Laurie Prange (Katie Maxwell),
Monte Markham (Colonel), Whit Bissell
(Dr. John Zeiterman), Carol Baxter
(Charlena McGowan), Arthur Rosenberg
(Dr. Jason Spath), Stack Pierce (Ser-
geant), Roger Robinson (Captain Welsh),
John O'Connell (Col. Appling), John
Papais (corporal), Chip Johnson (pilot),
Jill Choder (lieutenant), Steve Bond
(young man), John Vargas (soldier),
Charles Castillan (man), J. P. Bum-
stead (2nd man).
    "Free Fall" (11-21-80): Sam Groom
(Hank Lynch), Jared Martin (Jack Ste-
wart), Sandy Ward (Max Stewart), Kelly
Harmon (Jean), Michael Swan (Woody
Turner), Ted Markland (Ike), Erik Hol-
land (Mead), John Zenda (Fowler),
George Brenlin (Hughes).
    "Dark Side" (12-5-80): Bill Lu-
cking (Mike Schulte), Rosemary For-
syth (Ellen), Philece Sampler (Lori),

Jonathan Perpich (Jimmy), Taaffe O'-
Connell.
    "Deep Shock" (12-12-80): Sharon
Acker (Dr. Louise Olson), Edward Po-
wer (Frank), Tom Clancy (Edgar Tu-
cker), Bob Hackman (Walt), M. P. Mur-
phy (1st security officer), Charles
Hoyes (2nd security officer), Helen Boll
(nurse), Saundra Sharp (reporter), Har-
riet Matthew (receptionist), Robert Alan
Browne (foreman), Stefan Gierasch.
    "Bring Me the Head of the Hulk"
(1-9-81): Jed Mills (La Fronte), Jane
Merrow (Dr. Jane Cabot), Walter Brooke
(Mark Roberts), Sandy McPeak (Alex),
Laurence Haddon (Hines), Murray Mac-
Leod (Lubin), Barbara Lynn Block (Pau-
line).
    "Fast Lane" (1-16-81): Robert F.
Lyons (Joe), Dick O'Neill (Callahan),
Victoria Carroll (Nancy), Alex Rebar
(Clyde), Lee de Broux (Leo), Frank Dou-
bleday (Danny), Ben Jeffrey (Clint),
John Finn (merchant).
    "Goodbye Eddie Cain" (1-23-81):
Cameron Mitchell (Eddie Cain), Donna
Marshall (Norma Crespi Lang), Anthony
Caruso (Dante Romero), Jennifer Holmes
(Victoria Lang), Gordon Connell (Mac),
Thomas MacGreevy (Sheehan), Ray Las-
ka (Jack Lewis), Roscoe Born (Sheldon),
Virginia Hahn (Mrs. Stauros).
    "King of the Beach" (2-6-81): Lou
Ferrigno (Carl Molino), Leslie Acker-
man (Mandy), Charlie Brill (Sol Diamond),
George Caldwell (Rudy), Nora Boland
(lady), Angela Lee (little Girl), Ken Wal-
ler (King), Kimberley Johnson (King's
girlfriend), Leo de Lyon (trainer).
    "Wax Museum" (2-13-81): Chris-
tine Belford (Leigh Gamble), Max Show-
alter (Walter Gamble), Ben Hammer
(Kelleher), Natalie Masters (woman),
Kiki Castillo (Andy), Michael Horsley
(news vendor).
    "East Winds" (2-20-81): William
Windom (Sgt. Jack Keeler), Richard Loo
(Kam Chong), Richard Narita (William),
Tony Mumolo (Officer Bill Menning),
Irene Yah Ling Sun (Tam), Beulah Quo
(landlady), Del Monroe (the lieutenant).
    "The First" (3-6-81 & 3-13-81):
Harry Townes (Dell Frye), Lola Albright
(Elizabeth Collins), Billy Green Bush
(Sheriff Carl Decker), Jack Magee (Walt),
Bill Beyers (Case), Dick Durock (Frye's
creature), Kari Michaelsen (Linda), Hank
Rolike (janitor), Julie Marine (Cheryl).
    "The Harder They Fall" (3-27-81):
Denny Miller (Paul), Peter Hobbs (Dr.
Hart), Diane Shalet (Judy), Joe Dorsey
(Al), Hugh Smith (Bernie), Alan Toy
(Bobby), Ralph Strait (bartender), William

Bogert.
"Interview with the Hulk" (4-3-81): Michael Conrad (Emerson Fletcher), Jan Sterling (Stella Verdugo), Walter Brooke (Mark Roberts).
"Half Nelson" (4-17-81): Tommy Madden (Buster Caldwell), H. B. Haggerty (Gregor Potemkin), Elaine Joyce (Mitzi), Sandy Dryfoos (Marsha), Paul Henry Itkin (Channing), Joey Forman, David Himes.
"Danny" (5-15-81): Don Stroud (Nat), Bruce Wright (Ben), Robin Dearden (Rachel), Taylor Lacher.
"Patterns" (5-22-81): Eddie Barth (Sam), Laurie Heineman (Liz), Paul Marin (Malamud), Robert O'Reilly (Sonny), Joshua Shelley (Solly).
"The Phenom" (10-2-81): Anne Lockhart (Audrey), Robert Donner (Devlin), Dick O'Neill (Cyrus), Brett Cullen (Joe Dunning), Ken Swofford.
"Two Godmothers" (10-9-81): Suzanne Charny (Barbara), Penny Peyser (Lannie), Sandra Kerns (Sondra), Kathleen Nolan (Hackett), Gloria Gifford (Grubb), John Steadman (Phil Giles), Gay Hagen (matron).
"Veteran" (10-16-81): Paul Koslo (Doug Hewitt), Wendy Girard (Lisa Morgan), Richard Yniguez (Frank Rivera), William Boyett (R. Harnell), Bruce Gray (Harrison Cole).
"Sanctuary" (11-6-81): Diana Muldaur (Sister Anita), Henry Darrow (Patrero), Guillermo San Juan (Roberto), Fausto Barajas (Rudy), Edie McClurg (Sister Mary Catherine).
"Triangle" (11-13-81): Andrea Marcovicci (Gale Webber), Peter Mark Richman (Jordan), Mickey Jones (George), Charles Napier (Bert), Jerry Sloan (Lyle), Don Maxwell, Bill Cross.
"Slaves" (5-5-82): John Hancock (Isaac Ross), Charles Ryner (Roy), Faye Grant (Christy), Jeffrey Kramer (Marty).
"A Minor Problem" (5-12-82): Nancy Grahn (Patty), Linden Chiles (Cunningham), Lisa Jane Persky (Rita), Kander Berkeley (Tom), John Walter Davis (Mark), Gary Vinson.

INNER SANCTUM. 1954. Paul McGrath (Raymond).
"The Stranger" (1-9-54): Kevin McCarthy, Dan Morgan, Dorothy Jalliffe, Crahan Denton, Pat Jenkins.
"Port of Regrets" (1-16-54): Ian Keith, Stefan Schnabel, Jeanne Shepherd.
"The Hermit" (1-23-54): John Marley.
"Guilty Secret" (1-30-54): Mil-

dred Dunnock, James Lipton, Ralph Santley, Jill Kraft.
"The Perfect Kill" (2-6-54): Joe Maross, Martin Newman.
"Face of Fear" (2-13-54): Paul Stewart, John Alexander.
"Never Die Again" (2-20-54): Peg Hillias, Everett Sloane, Alan Hewitt.
"The Yellow Parakeet" (2-27-54): Ernest Truex.
"A Second Life" (3-6-54): Anthony Ross, Margaret Draper, Rita Lynn.
"Lost in the Dark" (3-13-54): Everett Sloane.
"The Sound of Birds" (3-20-54): E. G. Marshall, Louise Horton.
"Cat Calls" (3-27-54): John Beal.
"Men of Iron" (4-3-54): Paul Stewart, Audrey Christie, Norma Crane, John Raby.
"The Sisters" (4-10-54): Mildred Dunnock, John Newland, Louisa Horton.
"The Good Luck Charm" (4-17-54): Murray Hamilton, Barbara Baxley.
"The Hands" (4-24-54): William Prince.
"Killer's Choice" (5-1-54): Warren Stevens, Sally Gracie.
"Watchers by the Dead" (5-8-54): John Beal, John Baragrey, Harry Townes.
"Identity Unknown" (5-15-54): Margaret Phillips, William Prince, Robert Simon.
"Queen of Spades" (5-22-54): Harry Townes, Joe De Santis, Edward Binns.
"Handle with Care" (5-29-54): Leonard Bell, Martin Huston.
"The Silent Bride" (6-5-54): Barbara Baxley, Alfred Ryder, Jane Seymour.
"Ghost Male" (6-12-54): Joseph Wiseman.
"Tomorrow Never Comes" (6-19-54): Warren Stevens, Harry Bellaver, Roy Fant.
"Nobody Laughs at Lou" (6-24-54).
"Family Skeleton" (7-3-54): Murray Hamilton, Edward Binns, Steve Elliott.
"Dark of the Night" (7-10-54): Wallace Ford, Betsy Palmer, Perry Wilson.
"Burial at High Point" (7-17-54): John Baragrey, Barbara Baxley, Theodore Newton.
"Hour of Darkness" (7-24-54): Jo Van Fleet, James Gregory, Philip Kenneally.
"Reward for Janie" (7-31-54): June Dayton, Barry Kroeger, John Kellogg.
"Face of the Dead" (8-7-54): Everett Sloane.
"The Lonely One" (8-14-54): Vaughn Taylor, Edward Binns, John Kellogg.
"Dream of Murder" (8-21-54):

(INNER SANCTUM cont.) Harry Townes, Luis van Rooten, Carol Wheeler.
"Pattern of Fear" (8-28-54): Beatrice Straight, Robert H. Harris, Nita Talbot.
"The Third Fate" (9-5-54): Louisa Horton, Donald Woods.
"The Landslide" (9-11-54).
"The Skull Beneath" (9-18-54): Robert H. Harris, Jack Albertson, Phyllis Hull.
"The Fatal Hour" (9-25-54): Shepherd Strudwick.
"Blind Luck" (10-2-54): Warren Stevens, Rusty Lane, June Dayton.

INVADERS, THE. 1967-68. Roy Thinnes (David Vincent), Kent Smith (Edgar Scoville).
"Beachhead" (1-10-67): Diane Baker (Kathy Adams), J. D. Cannon (Ben Holman), James Daly (Alan Landers), John Milford (Carver), Vaughn Taylor (Mr. Kemper), Ellen Corby (old lady), Bonnie Beecher, James Ward.
"The Experiment" (1-17-67): Roddy McDowall (Lloyd Lindstrom), Laurence Naismith (Dr. Curtis Lindstrom), Harold Gould (Dr. Paul Meuller), Dabbs Greer (the Minister), Willard Sage (Lt. James), Stuart Lancaster, Jackie Kendall.
"The Mutation" (1-24-67): Suzanne Pleshette (Vikki), Edward Andrews (Mark Evans), Lin McCarthy (Fellows), Roy Jenson (Alien), Rodolfo Hoyos (Miguel), Argentine Brunetti, Val Avery.
"The Leeches" (1-31-67): Arthur Hill (Warren Doneghan), Mark Richman (Tom Wiley), Diana van der Vlis (Eve Doneghan), Robert H. Harris (Hastings), Theo Marcuse (Noel Markham), William Wintersole (Alien), Peter Brocco (Millington), Noah Keen (Psychiatrist).
"Genesis" (2-7-67): Carol Rossen (Selene Lowell), Louise Latham (Joan Corman), Tim McIntire (Steve Gibbs), Phillip Pine (Hal Corman), William Sargent (Dr. Ken Harrison), John Larch (Greg Lucather), Frank Overton (Dr. Grayson).
"Vikor" (2-14-67): Jack Lord (George Vikor), Alfred Ryder (Nexus), Diana Hyland (Sherri Vikor), Richard O'Brien (Police Sergeant), Sam Edwards (Hank), Hal Baylor, Joe Di Reda, Larry Duran.
"Nightmare" (2-21-67): Kathleen Widdoes (Ellen Woods), Robert Emhardt (Mr. Ames), Jeanette Nolan (Miss Havergill), James Callahan (Ed Gidney), Nellie Burt (Lena Lapham),

Irene Tedrow (Clare Lapham), Logan Field (Carl Bidney), William Bramley (Constable Gabbard).
"Doomsday Minus One" (2-28-67): William Windom (Major Rick Graves), Andrew Duggan (Gen. Beaumont), Wesley Addy (Tomkins), Robert Osterloh (Carl Wyeth), Tom Palmer, Lee Farr, Rick Murray, Lew Brown.
"Quantity: Unknown" (3-7-67): James Whitmore (Harry Swain), Milton Selzer (A. J. Richards), William Talman (Col. Griffith), Susan Strasberg (Diane Oberly), Douglas Henderson (Lt. Farley), Barney Phillips (Walt Anson).
"The Innocent" (3-14-67): William Smithers (Nat Greely), Michael Rennie (Magnus), Robert Doyle (Sgt. Ruddell), Patricia Smith (Edna Greely), Paul Carr (Billy Stears), Katharine Justice (Helen), Dabney Coleman (Capt. Ross).
"The Ivy Curtain" (3-21-67): Jack Warden (Cahill), Susan Oliver (Stacy), David Sheiner (Mr. Burns), Murray Matheson (Mr. Reynard), Clark Gordon (Mr. Nova), Barry Russo (Lt. Alvarado), Byron Morrow, Paul Pepper.
"The Betrayed" (3-28-67): Ed Begley (Simon Carver), Laura Devon (Susan Carver), Nancy Wickwire (Evelyn Bowers), Norman Fell (Neal Taft), Victor Brandt (Joey Taft), Joel Fluellen (Butler), Bill Fletcher (1st Alien), Ivan Bonar (Older Alien), Gil Stuart.
"Storm" (4-4-67): Joseph Campanella (Father Joe), Barbara Luna (Lisa), Simon Scott (Dr. Gantley), Carlos Romero (Luis Perez), Dean Harens (Dr. Macleuen), John McLiam (clerk), Paul Comi, John Mayo.
"Panic" (4-11-67): Robert Walker, Jr. (Nick Baxter), Lynn Loring (Madeline Flagg), R. G. Armstrong (Gus Flagg), Len Wayland (Deputy Wallace), Ford Rainey (George Grundy), Ross Hagen (Jordan), Rayford Barnes.
"Moonshot" (4-18-67): John Ericson (Hardy Smith), Joanne Linville (Angela Smith), Kent Smith (Stan Arthur), Anthony Eisley (Tony LaCava), Richard X. Slattery (Riley), Paul Lukather (Correll), John Lupton (Major Banks), Peter Graves (Gavin Lewis), Strother Martin (Charlie Coogan), Robert Knapp (Lt. Col. Howell).
"Wall of Crystal" (5-2-67): Linden Chiles (Dr. Bob Vincent), Julie Sommars (Grace Vincent), Edward Asner (Tangus), Lloyd Gough (Joe McMullen), Russ Conway (Detective Harding), Jerry Ayres (Groom), Peggy Lipton (Bride), Mary Lou Taylor (Mrs. Endicott), Karen

Norris (Miss Johnson), Burgess Meredith (Theodore Booth), Ray Kellogg (policeman).

"The Condemned" (5-9-67): Ralph Bellamy (Morgan Tate), Marlyn Mason (Carol Tate), Murray Hamilton (Lewis Dunhill), Larry Ward (Detective Carter), Wright King (Ed Tonkin), Harlan Warde (Ed Peterson), Paul Bryan (Brock), John Ragin (John Finney), Gary Wallberg (Detective Regan).

"Condition: Red" (9-5-67): Antoinette Bower (Laurie Keller), Jason Evers (Dan Keller), Roy Engel (Dr. Rogers), Mort Mills (Mr. Arius), Robert Brubaker (Gen. Winters), Forrest Compton (Capt. Albertson), Burt Douglas (Capt. Conners), Jim Raymond (technician), Simon Scott (Maj. Pete Stanhope).

"The Saucer" (9-12-67): Anne Francis (Annie Rhodes), Charles Drake (Robert Morrison), Dabney Coleman (John Carter), Robert Knapp (Joe Bonning), Kelly Thordsen (Sam Thorne), Sandy Kenyon (Alien Leader), John Ward (Alien Pilot), Glenn Sipes (Doctor).

"The Watchers" (9-19-67): Shirley Knight (Margaret Cook), Kevin McCarthy (Paul Cook), Leonard Stone (Ramsey), Walter Brooke (Danvers), James Seay (Grayson), Harry Hickox (Bowman), John Zaremba (General), Robert Yuro (Simms).

"Valley of the Shadow" (9-26-67): Ron Hayes (Sheriff Clements), Nan Martin (Maria McKinley), Joe Maross (Capt. Taft), Harry Townes (Will Hale), Ted Knight (Major), Hank Brandt (Joe Manners), Jon Lormer (Minister), Wayne Heffley.

"The Enemy" (10-3-67): Barbara Barrie (Gale Frazer), Richard Anderson (Blake), Russel Thorson (Sheriff), Paul Mantee (Vern Hammond), Gene Lyons (Sawyer), George Keymas (Lavin).

"The Trial" (10-10-67): Don Gordon (Charlie Gilman), Lynda Day George (Janet Wilk), John Rayner (Fred Wilk), Harold Gould (Allen Slater), William Zuckert (Bert Wisnofsky), Russell Johnson (Robert Bernard), Malcolm Atterbury (Judge Symondson), James McCallion (Brennan), Selette Cole (waitress).

"The Spores" (10-17-67): Gene Hackman (Tom Jessup), John Randolph (Ernie Goldhaver), James Gammon (Hall), Judee Morton (Mavis), Kevin Coughlin (Roy), Mark Miller (Jack Palay), Patricia Smith (Sally), Wayne Rogers (John Mattson), Brian Nash (Mike), Joel Davidson (Earl), Jack Knight (Fred Mazo),

Jason Gero (Teddy), Victor Arnold (Ralph). "Dark Outpost" (10-24-67): William Sargent (Dr. John Devin), Tim McIntire (Hall), Andrew Prine (Vern), Dawn Wells (Eileen), Kelly Jean Peters (Nicole), White Bissell (Col. Harris), Tom Lowell (Steve), Susan David (Mrs. James).

"The Summit Meeting" (10-31-67 & 11-7-67): William Windom (Michael Tressider), Diana Hyland (Ellie Markham), Michael Rennie (Per Alquist), Eduard Franz (Thor Halvorsen), Ford Rainey (Jonathan Blaine), Martin West (Lieutenant), Ian Wolfe (Rosmundson), Vic Perrin (hypnotist), Troy Melton, Peter Hobbs, Richard Eastham, Victoria Hale, Hank Simms.

"The Prophet" (11-14-67): Pat Hingle (Brother Avery), Zina Bethune (Sister Claire), Roger Perry (Bill Shay), Richard O'Brien (Brother John), Bryon Keith (Brother James), Ray Kellogg (guard), Dan Frazer (reporter).

"Labyrinth" (11-21-67): Ed Begley (Dr. Samuel Crowell), Sally Kellerman (Laura Crowell), John Zaremba (Prof. Edward Harrison), James Callahan (Dr. Harry Mills), Ed Peck (Darrow), E. J. Andre (Henry Thorne), Virginia Christine (Mrs. Thorne).

"The Captive" (11-28-67): Dana Wynter (Dr. Katharine Serret), Fritz Weaver (Peter Borke), Don Dubbins (Sanders), Lawrence Dane (Josef), Peter Coe (Leo), K. L. Smith (foreman), Douglas Henderson (Martin), Robert Patten (Murphy).

"The Believers" (12-5-67): Carol Lynley (Elyse Reynolds), Anthony Eisley (Bob Torin), Than Wyenn (Torberg), Rhys Williams (Prof. Hollman), Donald Davis (Harland), Kathleen Larkin (Lt. Sally Harper), Richard Karlan (Charles Russell).

"The Ransom" (12-12-67): Alfred Ryder (Alien Leader), Anthony Eisley (Bob Torin), Laurence Naismith (Cyrus Stone), Karen Black (Claudia Stone), Lawrence Montaigne (Garth), Christopher Held (Lieutenant), John Ragin (Kent).

"Task Force" (12-26-67): Linden Chiles (Jeremy Mace), Nancy Kovak (June Murray), Martin Wolfson (William Mace), John Lassell (Bob Ferrara).

"The Possessed" (1-2-68): Michael Tolan (Ted Willard), Michael Constantine (Martin Willard), Katherine Justice (Janet Garner), William Smithers (Adam Lane), Charles Bateman (Burt Newcomb), Booth Colman (coroner).

"Counterattack" (1-9-68): Anna Capri (Joan Surrat), Lin McCarthy (Ar-

(INVADERS cont.) chie Harmon), John
Milford (Jim Bryce), Ken Lynch (Lt.
Conners), Donald Davis (Lucian), Pa-
mela Curran (Louise), Warren Vanders
(Earl), Don Chastain (Blake), Ross
Elliott (Eliot Kramer), Charles J. Ste-
wart (Robertson).

"The Pit" (1-16-68): Charles
Aidman (Julian Reed), Joanne Linville
(Pat Reed), Donald Harron (Jeff Brower).

"The Organization" (1-30-68): J.
D. Cannon (Peter Kalter), Chris Robinson (Mike Calvin), Barry Atwater (Dorcas), Larry Gates (Weller), Roy Poole
(Court), John Kellogg (Dom).

"The Peacemaker" (2-6-68): James
Daly (Gen. Sam Concannon), Lin Mc-
Carthy (Col. Archie Harmon), Phyllis
Thaxter (Sarah Concannon), Alfred Ry-
der (Ryder).

"The Vise" (2-20-68): Raymond
St. Jacques (James Baxter), Roscoe
Lee Browne (Arnold Warren), Janet
MacLachlan (Celia Baxter), Austin Wil-
lis (William Gehrig), Lou Gossett (Ol-
lie), Joel Fluellen (Homer Warren).

"The Miracle" (2-27-68): Barba-
ra Hershey (Beth Ferguson), Edward
Asner (Harry Ferguson), Arch Johnson
(Father Paul), Robert Biheller (Rickey),
Chris Shea (John).

"The Life Seekers" (3-5-68): Barry Morse (Keith), Diane Muldaur (Claire),
R. G. Armstrong (Capt. Battersea), Arthur Franz (Capt. Trench), Paul Comi
(Sgt. Leeds), Morgan Jones (Lt. Rawlings), Stephen Brooks (Officer Joe
Nash).

"The Pursued" (3-19-68): Suzanne
Pleshette (Anne Gibbs), Will Geer (Henry Willis), Gene Lyons (Corwin).

"Inquisition" (3-26-68): Mark
Richman (Andrew Hatcher), Susan Oliver (Joan Seeley), John Milford (Bolin),
Stewart Moss (Jenkins), Robert H. Harris (Stan Fredrickson).

INVISIBLE MAN, THE. 1958-60. Tim
Turner (Dr. Peter Brady), Lisa Dan-
iely (Diane Brady), Deborah Walting
(Sally Brady), Ernest Clark (Sir
Charles).

"Secret Experiment" (11-4-58):
Lloyd Lamble (Dr. Hanning).

"Crisis in the Desert": Adrienne
Corri (Yoland), Martin Benson (Omar),
Peter Sallis (Nerib), Eric Pohlmann.

"Behind the Mask": Dennis Price
(Mr. Constantine), Arthur Gomez (Pres.
Domecq), Edwin Richfield (Max), Bar-
bara Chilcott (Maria).

"Strange Partners": Griffith
Jones (Lucian Currie), Patrick Trough-

ton (Vickers), Jack Medford (Collins),
Victor Platt (Insp. Quillan).

"Point of Destruction": Duncan
Lamont (Scott), John Rudling (Dr. Court).

"Play to Kill": Helen Cherry (Barbara Crane), Colin Gordon (Colonel),
Hugh Latimer (Tom), Gary Thorne (Simon), Vincent Holman (Arthurson).

"The Decoy": Betta St. John (Terry Trent/Toni Trent), Robert Gallico
(Rubens).

"The Rocket": Glyn Owen (Smith),
Russell Waters (Reitter), Robert Brown
(Prof. Howard).

"Shadow Bomb": Jennifer Jayne
(Betty), Ronald Phillips (Finch).

"Man in Disguise": Tim Turner
(Nick), Leigh Madison (Madeleine), Lee
Montague (Matt).

"Bank Raid": Willoughby Goddard
(Crowther), Patricia Marmont (Headmis-
tress), Brian Rawlinson (Williams).

"Picnic with Death": Margaret
McCourt (Linda Norton), Derek Bond
(John Norton).

"Odds Against Death": Walter
Fitzgerald (Prof. Owens), Colette Wilde
(Lucia), Julia Lockwood (Suzy Owens),
Alan Tilvern (Caletta), Olal Pooley
(manager), Peter Taylor (Bruno), Pe-
ter Elliott (cropuier).

"Man in Power": Andre Morell
(Shafari), Vivian Matolon (King), Gary
Raymond (Prince Jonetta), Nadia Regin
(Princess Talma).

"The Big Plot": William Squire
(Waring), Barbara Shelley (Helen).

"Jailbreak": Dermot Walsh (Green),
Michael Brennan (Brenner), Ralph Michael (Governor), Ronald Fraser (Sharp).

"The Prize": Mai Zetterling (Tania), Anton Diffring (Gunzi), Tony Church
(Prof. Kenig).

"Flight into Darkness": Geoffrey
Keen (Dr. Stephens), Joanna Dunham
(Pat Stephens), Esmond Knight (Wilson),
John Harvey (Wade).

"The Locked Room": Zena Marshall (Tania), Lloyd Lamble (Dr. Hanning), Rupert Davies (Dushkin).

"The White Rabbit": Maria Landi
(Suzanne Dumasse).

"The Mink Coat": Derek Godfrey
(Walker), Harold Berens (Bunny), Murray Kash (Marcel).

"Death Cell": Lana Morris (Ellen
Summers), William Lucas (George Wilson).

"The Vanishing Evidence": Charles
Gray (Peter Thal), James Raglan (Prof.
Harper), Sarah Lawson (Jenny Reyden),
Ernest Clark (Col. Ward).

"Shadow on a Screen": Greta Gynt

(Sonia Vasa), Edward Judd (Stephen Vasa), Redmond Phillips (Bratski). "Blind Justice": Philip Friend (Arthur Holt), Honor Blackman (Katherine), Jack Watling (Sandy Mason). "The Gun Runners": Louise Allbritton (Zena Fleming), Bruce Seton (Col. Graham), Paul Stassino (Sardi).

INVISIBLE MAN, THE. 1975-76. David McCallum (Daniel Westin), Melinda Fee (Kate Westin), Craig Stevens (Walter Carlson).
"The Klae Resource" (9-8-75): Barry Sullivan (Lionel Parks), Robert Alda (James Fiedler), Conrad Janis (Homer), Paul Kent (Brian Kelly).
"The Fine Art of Diplomacy" (9-15-75): Ross Martin (Diego DeVega), Michael Pataki (Tandy), Vincent Beck (Vittorio Gregario), Pepe Callahan (Manuel), Paul Steward (Wood), Gwil Richards (capitol guard).
"Man of Influence" (9-22-75): John Vernon (Ernest Gide), Jack Colvin (Williams), Shirley O'Hara (Mrs. Margaret Hanover), Gene Raymond (Sen. Hanover), Alan Mandell (Sen. Baldwyn), Robert Douglas (Dr. Theophilus).
"Eyes Only" (9-29-75): Barbara Anderson (Paula Simon), Bobby Van (Tony Bernard), William Prince (Dr. Maynard), Thayer David (Jack Pierson), John Kerr (Kirk), Vince Martorano (Joe Palanzi), Frank Christi (Nick Palanzi), William Bronder (Marty), Tony Swartz (guard with dog).
"Barnard Wants Out" (10-6-75): Nehemiah Persoff (Dr. Leon Barnard), Jane Actman (Anna Barnard), Paul Shenar (Zartov), Cliff Osmond (elevator guard), Peter Colt (Petra), Macon McCalman (consul), George Fisher (Yuri).
"Panic" (10-20-75): Jamie Smith Jackson (Laurie Kappas), David Opatoshu (Neroda Kappas), Harry David (Jimmy James), Richard X. Slattery (Griggs), Al Ruscio (Mannie Hallman).
"Go Directly to Jail" (11-3-75): James McEachin (Leland McCallister), Pat Harrington, Jr. (Warden Stone), John Crawford (Coner), Paulene Myers (Mrs. McCallister), Eric Mason (Robles), Gregory Walcott (cop).
"Stop When the Red Lights Flash" (11-24-75): Roger C. Carmel (Armistead Jones), Scott Brady (Deputy Bentley), Frank Aletter (Charles Hootens).
"Pin Money" (12-1-75): Helen Kleeb (Margaret Carlson), John Zee (John Arnold), Thom Carney (Sgt. Mersky).
"The Klae Dynasty" (12-8-75):

Nancy Kovack (Caroline Klae), Farley Granger (Julian Klae), Peter Donat (Morgan Klae).
"Power Play" (1-19-76): Monte Markham.

IRONSIDE.
"Bubble, Bubble, Toil and Murder" (2-3-72): Raymond Burr (Chief Robert Ironside), Don Mitchell (Mark Sanger), Don Galloway (Sgt. Ed Brown), Elizabeth Baur (Fran Belding), Jodie Foster (Pip Barker), Lee Paul (Billy Mahan), John Schuck (Archie Baldwin), Rod Serling (Thyros), Paul Carr (Gerald Barker).
"Raise the Devil" (9-12-74 & 9-19-74): Raymond Burr (Chief Robert Ironside), Don Mitchell (Mark Sanger), Don Galloway (Sgt. Ed Brown), Elizabeth Baur (Fran Belding), Sian Barbara Allen (Susan Todd), Bill Bixby (Dr. Theodore Gallin), Carolyn Jones (Justice Cross), Michael Anderson, Jr. (Jeff Hanley), Dane Clark (James Todd), Paul Richards (Earl Jansen), Dennis Redfield (Rudy Sands), Dale Ishimoto (Yamato), Eric Chase (Neil).

ISIS. 1975-76. Joanne Cameron (Andrea Thomas/Isis), Brian Cutler (Rick Mason), Ronalda Douglas (Rennie), Joanna Pang (Cindy Lee).

IT'S ABOUT TIME. 1966-67. Frank Aletter (Mac), Jack Mullaney (Hector), Joe E. Ross (Gronk), Imogene Coca (Shad), Mary Grace (Mlor), Pat Cardi (Breer), Cliff Norton (the Cave Boss), Mike Mazurki (Clon), Kathleen Freeman (Mrs. Boss), Jan Arvan (Dr. Hamilton), Alan De Witt (Gen. Tyler).

JASON OF STAR COMMAND. 1978-80. Craig Littler (Jason), Charlie Dell (Dr. Parsafoot), Susan O'Hanlon Pratt (Nicole) 78-79, James Doohan (Commander Canarvin) 78-79, John Russell (the Commander) 79-80, Tamara Dobson (Samantha) 79-80, Sid Haig (Dragos).

JOHNNY JUPITER. 1953-54. Wright King (Ernest P. Duckweather), Vaughn Taylor (Mr. Frisbee) 1953, Cliff Hall (Mr. Frisbee) 1954, Gilbert Mack.

JOHNNY QUEST. Animated 1964-65. Voices: Tim Matheson (Johnny Quest), Mike Road (Roger 'Race' Bannon), John Stephenson (Dr. Benton Quest), Danny Bravo (Hadji), Don Messick (Bandit).

(JOHNNY QUEST cont.)
"Mystery of the Lizard Men" (9-
18-64).
"Splashdown Antarctica" (9-25-
64): Voices: Doug Young (Officer).
"The Curse of the Anubis" (10-2-
64): Voices: Vic Perrin (Ahmed).
"Pursuit of the Poho" (10-9-64).
"Treasure of the Temple" (10-23-
64): Voices: Henry Corden (Montoya),
Nestor Paiva (guard), Everett Sloane
(Perkin).
"Calcutta Adventure" (10-30-64).
"The Robot Spy" (11-6-64): Voices:
Vic Perrin (Dr. Zin).
"Double Danger" (11-13-64): Voi-
ces: Vic Perrin (Dr. Zin), Cathy Lewis
(Jade).
"Shadow of the Condor" (11-20-
64): Voices: Everett Sloane (Baron).
"Skull and Double Crossbones"
(11-27-64): Voices: Doug Young.
"The Dreadful Doll" (12-4-64):
Voices: Henry Corden (Lor).
"A Small Matter of Pygmies" (12-
11-64): Voices: Danny Bravo.
"Dragons of Ashida" (12-18-64):
Voices: Henry Corden (Dr. Ashida).
"Turu the Terrible" (12-25-64):
Voices: Everett Sloane (Deen).
"The Fraudulant Volcano" (12-31-
64): Voices: Vic Perrin (Dr. Zin),
Henry Corden (Governor).
"Werewolf of the Timberland" (1-
7-65): Voices: Doug Young (Wolf).
"Pirates from Below" (1-14-65).
"Attack of the Tree People" (1-
21-65).
"The Invisible Monster" (1-28-
65): Voices: John Stephenson (Dr. Nor-
man).
"The Devil's Tower" (2-4-65):
Voices: Henry Corden.
"The Quetong Missile" (2-11-65).
"The House of Seven Gargoyles"
(2-18-65): Voices: Cathy Lewis (Jade).
"Monster in the Monastery" (3-4-
65): Voices: Sam Edwards, Henry Cor-
den.
"The Sea Haunt" (3-11-65): Voices:
Keye Luke (Charlie).
"Riddle of the Gold" (4-22-65).

JOURNEY TO THE UNKNOWN. 1968-
69.
"Eve" (9-26-68): Carol Lynley
(Eve), Dennis Waterman (Albert Baker),
Michael Gough (Royal), Errol John
(George), Hermione Baddeley (Mrs.
Kass).
"Jane Brown's Body" (10-17-68):
Stephanie Powers (Jane Brown).
"The Indian Spirit Guide" (10-10-

68): Julie Harris (Leona Gillings), Tra-
cy Reed (Joyce), Catherine Lacey (Sarah
Prinn), Tom Adams (Jerry Crown),
Marne Maitland (Chardur), Dennis Rams-
den (Mrs. Hubbard), Jurlian Sherrier
(Bright Arrow).
"The New People" (10-17-68): Ro-
bert Reed (Hank Prentiss), Patrick Al-
len (Luther Ames), Milo O'Shea (Matt
Dystal), Jennifer Hillary (Ann Prentiss),
Adrienne Corri (Terry Lawrence), Me-
lissa Stribling (Helen Ames), Damien
Thomas (David Redford), Suzanne Mok-
ler (Susan Redford).
"Miss Belle" (10-24-68): Barbara
Jefford (Belle Weston), George Maharis
(Drake), Kim Burfield (Roberta), Adri-
enne Posta.
"Do Me a Favor and Kill Me" (11-
7-68): Joseph Cotten (Jeff Wheeler),
Faith Parfitt (Faith Wheeler), Kenneth
Haigh (Dirk), Douglas Wilmer (Harry),
Joyce Blair (Betty), David Warbeck
(Chris), Carol Cleveland (Lisa), Hugh
Futcher (wardrobe dresser).
"Somewhere in a Crowd" (11-14-
68): David Hedison (William Searle),
Ann Bell (Ruth Searle), Jane Asher
(Marielle), Jeremy Longhurst (Max New-
by), Ewen Solon (Douglas Bishop), Ten-
niel Evans (Hugh Baillie).
"Paper Dolls" (11-21-68): Michael
Tolan (Craig Miller), Nanette Newman
(Jill Collins), John Welsh (Bart Brere-
ton), Kenneth J. Warren (Joe Blake),
Michael Ripper (Albert Cole), Catherine
Finn (Elsie Cole), George Benson (the
Vicar), June Jago (Emily Blake), Barn-
aby Shaw (Boy), Roderick Shaw (Boy),
Noel Davis (Charles Phillips), Jerold
Wells (Mayhew), Joan Allison (Mrs.
Latham), Hazel Hughes (Mrs. Biddle),
Edward Hardwicke (Dr. Yarrow).
"Matakitas Is Coming" (11-28-68):
Vera Miles (June), Leon Lissek (Mataki-
tas), Gay Hamilton (Sylvia Ann), Lynn
Pinkney (Tracy), Dermot Walsh (Ken).
"The Beckoning Fair One" (12-12-
68): Robert Lansing (Jon Holden), Ga-
brielle Drake (Kit Beaumont), Gretchen
Franklin (Mrs. Barrett), John Fraser
(Derek Wilson), Clive Francis (Crich-
ton), Larry Noble (Barrett).
"One on a Desert Island" (12-19-
68): Brandon de Wilde (Alec Worthing),
Suzanna Leigh (Vicki), Robert Sessions
(Joe).
"Girl of My Dreams" (12-26-68):
Michael Callan (Greg Richards), Zena
Walker (Carrie Clark).
"The Last Visitor" (1-2-69): Patty
Duke Astin (Barbara), Kay Walsh (Mrs.
Walker), Geoffrey Bayldon (Mr. Plim-

mer), Joan Newell (Mrs. Plimmer).
"Poor Butterfly" (1-9-69): Chad
Everett (Steven Miller), Susan Brode-
rick (Rose), Bernard Lee (Ben Loker),
Fay Compton (Queen Victoria), Edward
Fox (Robert Sawyer), Susan Richards
(Mrs. Loker).
"Stranger in the Family" (1-16-
69): Anthony Corlan (Boy), Janice Rule
(Paula), Maurice Kaufmann (Sonny),
Jane Hylton (Margaret), Phil Brown
(Charles), Gerald Sim (Evans), Glynn
Edwards (Brown).
"The Killing Bottle" (1-23-69):
Roddy McDowall (Rollo Verdew), Bar-
ry Evans (Jimmy Rintoul), Ingrid Brett
(Vera Verdew), William Marlowe (Ran-
dolph Verdew).
"The Madison Equation" (1-30-
69): Barbara Bel Geddes (Inga Madi-
son), Jack Hedley (Adam Frost), Alan
Cuthbertson (Ralph Madison), Sue Lloyd
(Barbara Rossiter), Paul Daneman
(Stuart Crosbie).

JUDGEMENT DAY. Pilot (12-6-81):
Carol Lynley (Gov. Harriet Egan),
Victor Buono (Heavener), Roddy
McDowall (Heller).

K9 AND COMPANY. British 12-28-81.
John Leeson (voice of K9), Elizabeth
Sladen (Sarah Jane Smith), Colin
Jeavons (George Tracey), John Quarm-
by (Henry Tobias), Sean Chapman
(Peter Tracey), Nigel Gregory (Sgt.
Wilson), Mary Wimbush (Aunt Lavi-
nia), Linda Polan (Juno Baker), Bill
Fraser (Commander Pollock), Ian
Sears (Brendan Richards), Neville
Barber (Howard Baker), Gillian
Martell (Lilly Gregson), Stephen
Oxley (PC Carter).

KOLCHAK: THE NIGHT STALKER.
1974-75. Darren McGavin (Carl
Kolchak), Simon Oakland (Tony Vin-
cenzo), Jack Grinnage (Ron Updyke),
Ruth McDevitt (Emily Cowels).
"The Ripper" (9-13-74): Beatrice
Colen (Jane Plumm), Ken Lynch (Capt.
Warren), Mickey Gilbert (the Ripper),
Roberta Collins (Detective Cortazza),
Marya Small (masseuse), Ruth McDe-
vitt (woman), Donald Mantooth (police-
man).
"The Zombie" (9-20-74): Joseph
Sirola (Sposato), Earl Falson (Fran-
cois Edmonds), Charles Aidman (Win-
wood), Antonio Fargas (Sweetstick),
Carol Ann Susi (Monique), Paulene
Myers (Mamalois), Val Bisoglio (Vic-
tor Friese), John Fiedler (Gordon

Spangler), Scatman Crothers (Uncle
Filemon), J. Pat O'Malley (caretaker).
"U. F. O. " (9-27-74): James Gre-
gory (Captain Quill), Mary Wickes (Dr.
Weinstock), Dick Van Patten (Alfred
Brindle), John Fielder (Gordon Spang-
ler), Tony Rizzo (Leon Van Heusen),
Carol Ann Susi (Monique), Rudy Chal-
lenger (Stanley Wedemyer), Maureen
Arthur (woman speaker).
"The Vampire" (10-4-74): William
Daniels (Lt. Matteo), Kathleen Nolan
(Faye), Suzanne Charny (Catherine),
John Doucette (Deputy Sample), Larry
Storch (Swede), Milt Kamen (Gingrich),
Jan Murray (Ichabod Grace), Anne Whit-
field (call girl), Army Archerd (man).
"The Werewolf" (11-1-74): Eric
Braeden (Bernhardt Stieglitz), Nita Tal-
bot (Paula), Lewis Charles (Levitt),
Henry Jones (Captain), Dick Gautier
(Mel Tarter), Barry Cahill (Dr. Rose),
Jackie Russell (Wendy), Bob Hastings
(Hallem).
"Fire-Fall" (11-8-74): Fred Beir
(Ryder Bond), Philip Carey (Sergeant
Mayer), Madlyn Rhue (Marie), David
Doyle (Cardinale), Virginia Vincent
(Mrs. Markoff), Joshua Shelley (George).
Shropell), Alice Backes (Mrs.
Shropell), Joshua Shelley (George).
"The Devil's Platform" (11-15-
74): Tom Skerritt (Robert Palmer),
Ellen Weston (Lorraine Palmer), Julie
Gregg (Susan Driscoll), John Myhers
(James Talbot), Jeanne Cooper (Dr.
Kline), William Mims (Officer Hale).
"Bad Medicine" (11-29-74): Ra-
mon Bieri (Capt. Joe Baker), Alice
Ghostley (Agnes Temple), Victor Jory
(Chief Rolling Thunder), Richard Kiel
(Indian), Marvin Kaplan (Albert Delgado),
James Griffith (Schwartz), David Lewis
(auctioneer).
"The Spanish Moss Murders" (12-
6-74): Keenan Wynn (Captain Sisak), Se-
vern Darden (Dr. Pollack), Virginia
Gregg (Dr. Hollenbeck), Johnny Silver
(Pepe La Rue), Maurice Marsac (Henri
Villon), Randy Boone (Fiddler), Ned
Glass (Superintendent), Richard Kiel
(Monster), Elizabeth Brooks (nurse's
aide), Rudy Diaz (Sgt. Villaverde), Brian
Avery (record producer).
"The Energy Eater" (12-13-74):
William Smith (Jim Elkhorn), Michael
Strong (Walter Green), Elaine Giftos
(Janice Eisen), Tom Drake (Don Kibbey),
Michael Fox (Frank Wesley), Robert
Yuro (Capt. Webster), John Alvin (Dr.
Ralph Carrie), Joyce Jillson (Diana).
"Horror in the Heights" (12-20-74):
Phil Silvers (Harry Starman), Abraham
Sofaer (Indian), Herb Vigran (Goldstein),

(KOLCHAK cont.) Ned Glass (Jo), Eric
Server (Officer Boxman), Benny Rubin
(Buck Fineman), Naomi Stevens (Mrs.
Goldstein), Shelly Novack (Officer York).
"Mr. R. I. N. G." (1-10-75): Julie
Adams (Mrs. Walker), Corinne Michaels
(Leslie Dwyer), Bert Freed (Capt. A-
kins), Craig Baxley (Mr. R. I. N. G.),
Harry Beckman (Sen. Stephens), Robert
Easton (Bernard Carmichael), Donald
'Red' Barry (guard), Maidie Norman
(librarian).
　　"The Primal Scream" (1-17-75):
Pat Harrington, Jr. (Kitzmiller), John
Marley (Capt. Molnar), Lindsay Work-
man (Dr. Fisk), Katharine Woodville
(Dr. Lynch), Jamie Farr (Jack Burton),
Byron Morrow (Dr. Cowan), Regis J.
Cordic (Dr. Peel), Al Checco (Nils),
Sandra Gould (landlady), Barbara
Rhoades (secretary), Vince Howard
(policeman), Jeanie Bell (Rosetta).
　　"The Trevi Collection" (1-24-75):
Nina Foch (Mme. Trevi), Lara Parker
(Madelaine), Marvin Miller (Lecturer),
Priscilla Morrill (Griselda), Douglas V.
Fowley (superintendent), Peter Leeds
(photographer), Dick Bakalyan (1st hood),
Henry Slate (2nd hood).
　　"Chopper" (1-31-75): Larry Lin-
ville (Capt. Jonas), Sharon Farrell (Li-
la Morton), Art Metrano (Studs Spake),
Jay Robinson (Dr. Strig), Jim Backus
(Herb Bresson), Frank Aletter (Norman
Kahill), Steve Franken (morgue atten-
dant), Jesse White (1st watchman),
Joey Aresco (Electric Larry).
　　"Demon in Lace" (2-7-75): An-
drew Prine (Prof. C. Evan Spat), Kee-
nan Wynn (Capt. Joe Siska), Kristina
Holland (Rosalind Winters), Milton Par-
sons (Dr. Mozard), Jackie Vernon
(Coach Toomey), Caroline Jones (regis-
trar), Benjamin Masters (Mike Thomp-
son), Steve Stafford (Craig Donnelly).
　　"Legacy of Terror" (2-14-75):
Ramon Bieri (Capt. Webster), Pippa
Scott (Tillie Jones), Erik Estrada (Pepe
Torres), Sondra Currie (Vicky), Sor-
rell Booke (Eddy), Carlos Romero
(George Andrews), Victor Campos (Prof.
Rodriquez).
　　"The Knightly Murders" (3-7-75):
John Dehner (Capt. Vernon Rausch),
Hans Conreid (Mendel Boggs), Lieux
Dressler (Minervo Musso), Shug Fisher
(Pop Stenvold), Robert Emhardt (Ralph),
Lucille Benson (Mavra), Don Carter
(Morgue Assistant), Bryan O'Byrne
(Butler).
　　"The Youth Killer" (3-14-75):
Cathy Lee Crosby (Helen), Dwayne
Hickman (Sgt. Orkin), Kathleen Free-

man (Della Sarkof), John Fiedler (Gor-
don Spangler), Eddie Firestone (conven-
tioneer), Michael Richardson (Lance
Mervin), Penny Santon (Lance's mother),
Demosthenes (cab driver).
　　"The Sentry" (3-28-75): Kathie
Browne (Lt. Irene Lamont), Albert
Paulsen (Dr. James Verhyden), Tom
Bosley (Jack Flaherty), John Hoyt (La-
mar Beckwith), Frank Campanella (Ted
Chapman), Frank Marth (Col. Brody),
Margaret Avery (Ruth Van Galen), Cliff
Norton (Arnie Wisemore).

KORG: 70,000 B.C. 1974-75. Jim
Malinda (Korg), Bill Ewing (Bok),
Naomi Pollack (Mara), Christopher
Man (Tane), Charle Morted (Tor),
Janelle Pransky (Ree).

KRAFT THEATRE.
　　"The Man in Half Moon Street" (4-
30-53): John Newland.
　　"Alice in Wonderland" (5-5-54):
James Barton (Mock Turtle), Art Car-
ney (the Mad Hatter), Arthur Treacher
(Cheshire Cat), Joey Walsh (White Rab-
bit), Ernest Truex (Dormouse), Cliff
Hall (Duchess), Una O'Connor (Cook),
Arnold Moss (the Red Knight), Blanche
Yurka (Queen of Hearts), Fredd Wayne
(March Hare).
　　"A Connecticut Yankee in King Ar-
thur's Court" (7-8-54): Edgar Bergen
(the Boss), Victor Jory (Merlin), Carl
Reiner (Sir Kay), Jack Livesey (King
Arthur), Joey Walsh (Clarence), Sally
Gracie (Sandy), Ernest Graves (Sir
Lancelot).
　　"Death Takes a Holiday" (12-30-
54): Joseph Wiseman (Death), Lydia St.
Clair (Princess), Peter Brandon (Corra-
do), Lelia Barry (Grazia).
　　"Flying Objects at Three O'Clock
High" (6-20-56): Everett Sloane (Col.
Enright), Biff McGuire (William Lee),
Robert Simon (Col. Ross), Grant Ri-
chards (Major Dowd).

KROFFT'S SUPERSHOW, THE. 1976.
　　"Dr. Shrinker" segment. Jay Robinson (Dr. Shrinker), Billy Barty (Hugo), Susan Lawrence, Jeff McCay, Ted
Eccles.
　　"Electrawoman" segment. Deirdre Hall (Lori/Electrawoman), Judy
Strangis (Mara/Dynagirl), Norman Alden (Frank Hefflin).

LAND OF THE GIANTS. 1968-70. Gary Conway (Steve Burton), Don Matheson (Mark Wilson), Don Marshall
(Dan Erickson), Kurt Kasznar (Alex-

ander Fitzhugh), Deanna Lund (Valerie Scott), Heather Young (Betty Hamilton), Stefan Arngrim (Barry Lockridge), Kevin Hagen (Inspector Kobick).

"The Crash" (9-22-68): Don Watters (giant entomologist), Anne Dore (giant female assistant), Pat Michenaud (giant boy).

"Ghost Town" (9-29-68): Percy Helton (Akman), Amber Flower (granddaughter), Raymond Guth (tramp).

"Framed" (10-6-68): Paul Carr (giant photographer), Doodles Weaver (giant hobo), Linda Peck (giant model), Dennis Cross (giant policeman), Baynes Barron (giant policeman).

"Underground" (10-20-68): John Abbott (Gorak), Lance Le Gault (giant policeman), Jerry Catron (giant sentry), Ivan Markota (giant fugitive), Paul Trinka (giant guard No. 1), Jim Gosa (giant guard No. 2).

"Terror-Go-Round" (11-3-68): Joseph Ruskin (Carlos), Arthur Batanides (Luigi), Gerald Michenaud (Pepi), Arch Whiting (policeman).

"The Flight Plan" (11-10-68): Linden Chiles (Joe), William Bromley (1st giant), Myron Healey (2nd giant), John Pickard (giant guard).

"Manhunt" (11-17-68): John Napier (convict).

"The Trap" (11-24-68): Stewart Bradley (senior scientist), Morgan Jones (assistant scientist).

"The Creed" (12-1-68): Paul Fix (Dr. Brulle), Henry Corden (janitor), Harry Lauter (1st cop), Grant Sullivan (2nd cop), Wesley Lau (1st policeman), Gary Tigerman (delivery boy).

"Double Cross" (12-8-68): Willard Sage (Hook), Lane Bradford (Lobo), Howard Culver (curator), Ted Jordan (policeman at museum), Joseph Ryan (cabin policeman).

"The Weird World" (12-22-68): Glenn Corbett (Kagan), Don Gazzaniga (giant watchman).

"The Golden Cage" (12-29-68): Celeste Yarnall (Marna), Douglas Bank (giant scientist), Dawson Palmer (1st giant), Page Slattery (2nd giant).

"The Lost Ones" (1-5-69): Tommy Webb (Dolf), Jack Chaplain (Joey), Lee Jay Lambert (Hopper), Zalman King (Nick), Dave Dunlap (giant trapper).

"Brainwash" (1-12-69): Warren Stevens (Ashim), Leonard Stone (Dr. Kraal), Len Lesser (prisoner), Robert Dowdell (policeman).

"The Bounty Hunter" (1-19-69): Kimberly Beck (giant girl), Paul Sorensen (giant camper).

"On a Clear Day You Can See Earth" (1-26-69): Michael Ansara (Murtrah).

"Deadly Lodestone" (2-2-69): Paul Fix (Dr. Brule), Bill Fletcher (Sgt. Karf, Robert Emhardt (Mr. Secretary), Sheila Mathews (Nurse Helg), Gene Dynarski (Warden).

"The Night of the Thrombeldinbar" (2-16-69): Teddy Quinn (Garna), Michael A. Freeman (Tobek), Jay Novello (Okun), Miriam Schiller (housewife), Alfred Ryder (Parteg).

"Seven Little Indians" (2-23-69): Cliff Osmond (Grotius), Chris Alcaid (Sgt. Arnak), Garry Walberg (1st S. I. D. man), Rico Cattani (2nd S. I. D. man), Erik Nelson (3rd S. I. D. man).

"Target: Earth" (3-2-69): Dee Hartford (Altha), Arthur Franz (Franzen), Peter Mamakos (Logar), Denver Matson (Sergeant No. 1), Ivan Markota (Sergeant No. 2).

"Genius at Work" (3-9-69): Ronny Howard (Jodar), Jacques Aubuchon (Zurpin), Paul Trinka (Officer), Patrick Culliton (cop), Rusty Jones (boy witness), Vic Perrin (small giant man).

"Return of Inidu" (3-16-69): Jack Albertson (Inidu), Tony Benson (Grot), Peter Haskell (Enog), Steven Marlo (cop), Jerry Davis (Torg).

"Rescue" (3-23-69): Lee Meriwether (Mother), Don Collier (Father), Buddy Foster (Tedor), Blair Ashley (Leeda), Michael J. Quinn (Lt. Emar), Roy Rowan (newscaster), Tom Reese (Sgt. Gedo).

"Sabotage" (3-30-69): Robert Colbert (Bolgar), John Marley (Zarkin), Parley Baer (Obek), Elizabeth Rogers (secretary), Keith Taylor (newsboy), Douglas Bank (policeman).

"Shell Game" (4-13-69): Gary Dubin (Dal), Larry Ward (Talf), Jan Shepard (Osla), Tol Avery (Mr. Derg).

"The Chase" (4-20-69): Erik Nelson (S. I. D. man), Timothy Scott, Robert F. Lyons (Naylor), Patrick Sullivan Burke (Golan), Norman Burton (Sergeant).

"The Mechanical Man" (9-21-69): Broderick Crawford (Prof. Gorn), Stuart Margolin (Zoral), James Daris (super giant robot), William Chapman (Secretary Mek), Steven Marlo (minor S. I. D. official), Erik Nelson (minor S. I. D. official), Richard Carlyle (special policeman).

"Six Hours to Live" (9-28-69): George Mitchell (Harry Cass), Anne Seymour (Martha Cass), Richard Anderson (Joe Simmons), Bill Quinn (Warden Sloan), Larry Pennell (guard), Michael J. Quinn (gateman), Stewart Bradley (police ser-

(LAND OF THE GIANTS cont.) geant),
Max Power (pharmacist), Sam Elliott
(Martin Reed).

"The Inside Rail" (10-5-69): Arch
Johnson (Chief Rivers), Ben Blue (Moley), Joe Turkel (Sergeant), Vic Tayback (hood), John Harmon (groom).

"Deadly Pawn" (10-12-69): Alex
Dreier (Kronig), John Zaremba (Dr.
Lalor), Charlie Briggs (guard), Steve
Marlo (technician).

"The Unsuspected" (10-19-69):
Leonard Stone (Sgt. Eson).

"Giants and All That Jazz" (10-
26-69): Sugar Ray Robinson (Biff),
William Bramley (Hanley), Mike Mazurki (Loach), Diana Chesney (Nell).

"Collector's Item" (11-2-69):
Guy Stockwell (Garak), Robert H. Harris (Tojar), Susan Howard (Mrs. Garak), George Sperdakos (Goldsmith),
Erik Nelson (S. I. D. man).

"Every Boy Needs a Dog" (11-9-
69): Michael Anderson, Jr. (Ben), Oliver McGowan (Dr. Howard), Tom Nardini (Carl), Robert Shayne (Mr. Clinton).

"Chamber of Fear" (11-16-69):
Cliff Osmond (Jolo), Christopher Cary
(Deenar), Joan Freeman (Mara), Robert Tiedemann (the Monk), Don Kennedy (policeman).

"Comeback" (11-23-69): John
Carradine (Egor), Janos Prohaska (Gorilla), Jesse White (Manfred), Fritz
Feld (Quigg), James Jeter (studio gateman), Olan Soule (cameraman).

"The Clones" (11-30-69): William Schallert (Dr. Arno), Sandra Giles
(Dr. Greta Gault).

"A Place Called Earth" (12-7-69):
Warren Stevens (Olds), Jerry Douglas
(Fielder), Rex Holman (Mezron), Jerry Quarry (Bron), Gene Le Bell (Mezron's brother), John Mooney (pharama-
cist).

"Land of the Lost" (12-14-69):
Nehemiah Persoff (Titus), Clint Ritchie
(Andros), Peter Canon (slave No. 1),
Brian Nash (boy in park), Bob Braun
(balloon vendor), Ron Husmann (flight
controller), Fred Villani (sentry).

"Home Sweet Home" (12-21-69):
William H. Bassett (Ranger Jack), William Benedict (Villager Peabody), Robert Adler (Villager Sloacum), Pete
Kellett (guard), Mort Mills (constable),
June Dayton (Mrs. Perkins), John Milford (Ranger Wilson).

"Our Man O'Reilley" (12-28-69):
Alan Hale, Jr. (O'Reilly), Alan Berg-
mann (Krenko), Billy Halop (Bartender
Harry), Michael J. Quinn (Watchman

Jake), Lindsay Workman (Cunningham),
Edward Marr (Peddler Brynie), Dusty
Cadis (Store Guard Warner, Jr.).

"Nightmare" (1-4-70): Torin
Thatcher (Berger), Yale Summers (Andre).

"Pay the Piper" (1-11-70): Jonathan Harris (the Piper), Peter Leeds
(Senator), Michael James Wixted (Timmy).

"The Secret City of Limbo" (1-18-
70): Malachi Throne (Taru), Joseph
Ruskin (General Aza), Peter Jason (My-
lo), Whit Bissell (Dr. Krane).

"Panic" (1-25-70): Mark Richman
(Marad), Jack Albertson (Kirmus), Di-
ane McBain (Mrs. Evers), Edward G.
Robinson, Jr. (Guard Rogers), Patrick
Culliton (Officer Willis), Steven Marlo
(Officer Burns).

"The Deadly Dart" (2-1-70): Chris-
topher Dark (Sergeant Barker), Kent
Taylor (Doc Jelko), Madlyn Rhue (Ber-
tha Fry), John Dehner (Lt. Grayson),
Donald 'Red' Barry (Zoral), Willard
Sage (Insp. Swan).

"Doomsday" (2-15-70): Francine
York (Dr. North), Ed Peck (Warkin),
Charles Dierkop (Kamber), Tom Drake
(S. I. D. Sergeant).

"A Small War" (2-22-70): Sean
Kelly (Alek), Charles Darke (Mr. Er-
dap), Miriam Schiller (Nurse).

"The Marionettes" (3-1-70): Frank
Ferguson (Goalby), Bob Hogan (Brady),
Victoria Vetri (Lisa), Sandra Giles (Ha-
rem Dancer), Carl Carlsson (Knife
Thrower), Al Lampkin (Fire Eater),
Diane Krabbe (Diane), Bob Baker (Pup-
pet Man), Win Liverman (Trainer).

"Wild Journey" (3-8-70): Bruce
Dern (Thorg), Yvonne Craig (Berna),
Martin Liverman (1st security guard),
Erik Nelson (S. I. D. man), Sheila Ma-
thews (Collier), Marshall Stewart (man
passerby), Louise Lorimer (Miss Smith).

"Graveyard of Fools" (3-22-70):
Albert Salmi (Melzac/Bryk), John Crawford (Tagor), Michael Stewart (janitor).

LAND OF THE LOST. 1974-77. Spencer Mulligan (Rick Marshall) 74-76,
Wesley Eure (Will Marshall), Kathy
Coleman (Holly Marshall), Ron Harper (Uncle Jack) 76-77, Walter Edminston (Enik the Sleestak), Marvin Miller (Voice of Zarn), Van Snowden
(Zarn), Sharon Baird (Sa the monkey
girl), Phillip Paley (Chake the monkey boy), Scott Fullerton (Ta).

LANDON, LANDON AND LANDON. Pilot (6-14-80): William Windom (Ben

Landon), Nancy Dolman (Holly Landon), Daren Kelly (Nick Landon), Millie Slavin (Judith Saperstein), Richard O'Brien (Insp. Ulysses Barnes), Norman Bartold (George Rumford), Sudie Bond (Billie), Jason Wingreen (Darryl P. Goren), Arthur Adams (Coroner), Wil Albert (Reggie Ozer), Pat Studstill (Captain Nestor), Paul Tuerpe (White Suit), Maurice Hill (Cy Vorpal).

LIGHTS OUT. 1949-52. Jack LaRue (Host) 49-50, Frank Gallup (Host) 50-52.
"Episode One" (7-19-49): Frances Reid, Phil Arthur, Gladys Clark, Anita Anton.
"Episode Two" (7-26-49): William Post, Jr., Mary Patton, Eva Marie Saint.
"Long Distance" (8-2-49): Jan Minor.
"Conqueror's Isle" (11-7-49): Richard Derr, Vinton Hayworth, Mercer McLeod, Sarah Benham.
"The Fall of the House of Usher" (11-21-49): Helmut Dantine, Pamela Conroy, Stephen Courtleigh.
"I Dreamt I Died" (11-28-49): Alfreda Wallace, Philip Truex, Karen Stevens, Ross Martin.
"Something in the Wind" (12-5-49): John Graham, Douglas Chandler, Inga Adams.
"Justice Lies Waiting" (12-12-49): Larry Fletcher, Ray Rand, Mercer McLeod, Pat Jones, John Boruff.
"The Elevator" (12-19-49): Jack Hartley, Helene Dumas, James Van Dyke, Dolores Badioni.
"The Man Who Couldn't Lose" (12-26-49): Dean Harens, Alfreda Wallace.
"The Riverman" (1-2-50): Athena Lorde, Elizabeth Moore, Henry Brandon.
"Judgment Reversed" (1-9-50): King Calder, Nancy Coleman, Ralph Riggs, Bernard Nedell.
"The Green Dress" (1-16-50): Lynn Salisbury, Robert Pastene, Mercedes Gilbert, Candy Montgomery.
"The Devil to Pay" (1-23-50): Alfreda Wallace, Arnold Moss.
"Reservations - for Four" (1-30-50): Mercer McLeod, Dean Harens.
"Dead Pigeon" (2-6-50): Phil Coolidge, Joel Ashley, John Boruff, Florida Friebus.
"The Invisible Staircase" (2-13-50): Clairence Derwent, Elfreda Derwent.

"Graven Image" (2-20-50): Pat Jenkins, Dean Harens, John Clendinning.
"Portrait of a Dead Man" (2-27-50): Horace Braham, Dick Fraser.
"The Strange Case of John Kingman" (3-6-50): John Newland, Richard Purdy.
"The Emerald Lavalier" (3-13-50): Felicia Montealegre, Theodore Newton.
"The Scarab" (3-20-50): Vinton Hayworth, Richard Derr, Melba Rae.
"Mary" (3-27-50): Carol Ohmart, George Englund, Gage Jordan, John McQuade.
"The Queen Is Dead" (4-3-50): Mildred Natwick, Una O'Connor.
"The Faithful Heart" (4-10-50): Anne Francis, Liam Sullivan, Dorothy Francis, James O'Neil.
"A Toast to Sergeant Farnsworth" (4-17-50): Ross Martin, Dan Morgan.
"The Man Who Couldn't Remember" (4-24-50): Jack Palance, Tom Walsh, Roger De Koven.
"The Gloves of Gino" (5-1-50): Ross Martin, Bernard Nedell, Sarah Anderson, Leslie Barrett.
"The Silent Voice" (5-8-50): Douglas Parkhirst.
"The House That Time Forgot" (5-15-50): Dulcey Jordan.
"Rendezvous" (5-22-50): Richard MacMurray, Inge Adams.
"How Love Came to Professor Guildea" (5-29-50): Arnold Moss.
"The Heart of Jonathan O'Rourke" (6-5-60): Alfreda Wallace, Peter Capell, William Windom.
"The Determined Lady" (6-12-50): Ethel Griffies.
"A Child Is Crying" (6-19-50): David Cole, Frank Thomas, Jr., Leslie Nielsen.
"Encore" (6-26-50): Don Hanmer.
"I Dreamt I Died" (7-3-50): Alfreda Wallace, Philip Truex, Karen Stevens, Ross Martin.
"The Devil to Pay" (7-17-50): Theodore Marcuse, Grace Kelly, Jonathan Harris.
"The Strange Case of John Kingman" (7-31-50): Philip Coolidge, Oliver Cliff, John Baragrey.
"The Queen Is Dead" (8-14-50): Mildred Natwick, Una O'Connor.
"The Ides of April" (8-28-50): Ella Raines, George Reeves, Horace MacMahon.
"Benuili Chant" (9-4-50): Tom Drake, Ed Begley, Jean Sheppard.
"The Dark Corner" (9-11-50): John Newland, Mary Sinclair, Alan Marshall.
"The Leopard Lady" (9-18-50):

(LIGHTS OUT cont.) Boris Karloff. "Sisters of Shadow" (9-25-50): William Eythe, Elinor Randel. "The Posthumous Dead" (10-2-50): Ed Begley. "Just What Happened" (10-9-50): John Howard, Richard Purdy, Rita Lynn. "The Thing Upstairs" (10-16-50): Florence Reed, Freddy Bartholomew, Peggy Nelson. "The Skeptics" (10-23-50): E. G. Marshall. "The Martian Eyes" (10-30-50): Burgess Meredith, David Lewis, J. Pat O'Malley, Gavin Gordon. "The Half-Pint Flask" (11-6-50): John Carradine, Kent Smith. "The Waxwork" (11-13-50): John Beal, Nelson Olmstead. "Dr. Heidegger's Experiment" (11-20-50): Billie Burke, Gene Lockhart, Halliwell Hobbes, Thomas Poston. "The Mule Man" (11-27-50): Charles Korvin, Melba Rae, James O'Neil. "Beware This Woman" (12-4-50): Veronica Lake, Glenn Denning. "Masque" (12-11-50): Estelle Winwood, Mary Stewart, Lynn Salisbury. "The Men on the Mountain" (12-18-50): Lee Tracy, William Free, Vern Collett. "Jaspar" (12-25-50): Janis Carter, Johnny Johnston, Meg Mundy. "Tha Haunted Skyscraper" (1-1-51): Felicia Montealegre, Don Dickinson, Virginia Gilmore. "Bird of Time" (1-8-51): Jessica Tandy, David Lewis, Julie Bennett, Irving Ulinter. "The Bottle Imp" (1-15-51): Donald Buka, Glenn Langan. "For Release Today" (1-22-51): K. T. Stevens, Herbert Rudley, Vinton Hayworth. "The Masque of the Red Death" (1-29-51): Hurd Hatfield. "The House of Dust" (2-5-51): Nina Foch, Anthony Quinn. "Curtain Call" (2-12-51): Otto Kruger, Alan Bunce, Elinor Randel. "Strange Legacy" (2-19-51): Robert Stack, Margaret Hayes, Henry Hart, Joseph Sweeney. "The Dispossessed" (2-26-51): Jeffrey Lynn, June Dayton, Stefan Schnabel. "The Man with the Astrakhan Hat" (3-5-51): Paul Stewart, Ross Martin, Jim Bender, Peter Capell. "Leda's Portrait" (3-12-51):

Felicia Montealegre, George Reeves, John Emery. "Western Night" (3-19-51): Richard Derr, Biff Elliott, William Free. "The Power of the Brute" (3-26-51): Tom Drake, Richard Carlyle, Reba Tassell. "The Mad Dullaghen" (4-2-51): Glenn Langan, Stella Andrew, Berry Kroeger. "The Crushed Rose" (4-9-51): John Beal, Barbara Britton, Richard Purdy. "The Witness" (4-16-51): Dane Clark, Howard Smith, Florence Standley. "The Fonceville Curse" (4-23-51): Patrick Knowles, Rosalind Ivan, Alma Lawton, Donald Morrison. "Grey Reminder" (4-30-51): Beatrice Straight, John Newland. "The Lost Will of Dr. Kant" (5-7-51): Leslie Nielsen, Pat Englund, Russell Collins. "Dead Man's Coat" (5-14-51): Basil Rathbone, Norman Ross, William Post. "The Cat's Cradle" (5-21-51): Martha Scott, Murvyn Vye, Larry Kerr. "The Pattern" (5-28-51): John Forsythe, June Dayton, David Lewis. "The Martian Eyes" (6-4-51): Burgess Meredith, J. Pat O'Malley, David Lewis, John Baragrey. "Pit of the Dead" (6-11-51): Joseph Buloff, John Dall, Beatrice Kraft, Bill Darriet. "Dead Freight" (6-18-51): Charles Dingle, Louisa Horton. "The Passage Beyond" (6-25-51): John Buckmaster, Stella Andrew. "And Adam Begot" (7-2-51): Kent Smith. "The Meddlers" (7-9-51): John Carradine, E. G. Marshall, Dan Morgan. "The Devil in Glencairn" (7-16-51): Richard Carlson. "Zero Hour" (7-23-51): Denise Alexander, John O'Hare, Richard Wigginton. "The Fingers" (7-30-51). "The Faceless Man" (8-6-51): Robert Sterling, Ted Hecht, Gregory Morton. "The Man with the Watch" (8-13-51): Francis L. Sullivan, Gordon Clarke, Peggy French, Peter Capell. "Follow Me" (8-20-51): Peter Cookson, Doris Rich. "Mrs. Manifold" (8-27-51): Leslie Nielsen, Adelaide Klein, J. Pat O'Malley. "Blackwood Halt" (9-3-51): Stella Andrew, Frederick Tozere.

"Prophet of Darkness" (9-10-51): Sidney Blackmer, Ronola Robb.

"To See Ourselves" (9-17-51): Cathy O'Donnell, Henry Barnard, Mercer McLeod.

"Rappaccini's Daughter" (9-24-51): Eli Wallach, Hope Miller.

"Will-o'-the-Wisp" (10-1-51): Robert Stack, Louanna Gardner, Pat Browning.

"Dark Image" (10-8-51): Donald Woods, Ann Shepherd, Leni Stengel, Beatrice Kraft.

"I Spy" (10-15-51): Henry Hull, Dorothy Stickney, Dale Engel, Alfreda Wallace.

"The Deal" (10-22-51): Tom Ewell, Joseph Wiseman, Anne Marno, Martin Gabel.

"The Veil" (10-29-51): Lee J. Cobb, Arlene Francis.

"The Chamber of Gloom" (11-5-51): Geraldine Brooks, Arnold Moss, Andrew Branham.

"The Beast in the Garden" (11-12-51): Margaret Phillips, Jack Marivale.

"Friday the Nineteenth" (11-19-51): Eddie Albert.

"Far-Off Island" (11-26-51): Richard Greene, Gregory Morton, Lenka Peterson.

"The Silent Supper" (12-3-51): Vanessa Brown.

"The Angry Birds" (12-10-51): John Forsythe, Constance Dowling.

"Perchance to Dream" (12-17-51): William Eythe, Louanna Gardner.

"This Way to Heaven" (12-24-51): Burgess Meredith.

"Of Time and Third Avenue" (12-31-51): Henry Daniell, Bethel Leslie, Edward Gargan.

"School for the Unspeakable" (1-7-52): Donald Buka, Don Hanmer, Andrew Branham.

"Blood Relation" (1-14-52): Nina Foch, Franchot Tone.

"The Intruder" (1-21-52): Chester Morris, Jane Wyatt.

"The Third Door" (1-28-52): Vincent Price.

"The Chain" (2-4-52): Raymond Massey.

"Cries the String" (2-11-52): Signe Hasso, Gregory Morton.

"The Eyes from San Francisco" (2-18-52): Thomas Mitchell, Mary Heath, Stephen Hill.

"The Perfect Servant" (2-25-52): Henry Daniell, Albert Dekker, Joe Allen, Jr.

"Private - Keep Out" (3-3-52): Melvyn Douglas.

"The Upstairs Floor" (3-10-52): John Forsythe, Josephine Hull.

"The Borgia Lamp" (3-17-52): Grace Kelly, Robert Sterling, Hugh Griffith.

"Another Country" (3-24-52): Yvonne De Carlo.

"The Pit" (4-7-52): Murvyn Vye.

"The Men on the Mountain" (4-14-52): Lee Tracy, William Free, Vern Collett.

"A Lucky Piece" (4-21-52): Adelaide Klein, Henry Jones.

"For Rent" (4-28-52).

"Journey into the Shadows" (5-5-52): Robert Pastene, Katherine Bard.

"The Green Thumb" (5-12-52): George Mitchell, Victor Thorley.

"Little Girl" (5-19-52): Patsy Bruder, Frieda Altman.

"The Death's Head" (5-26-52): Steven Hill, Edgar Stehli.

"Night Walk" (6-2-52): Dan Hanmer, Susan Douglas.

"Blind Man's Bluff" (6-9-52): Mercer McLeod, Mary Farrell.

"Nightmare" (6-16-52): Joe Mantell, Perry Wilson, Mary Alice Moore.

"Coins of Death" (6-23-52): Joseph Anthony, Berry Kroeger.

"The Lonely Albatross" (6-30-52): John Carradine, William Redfield, Hildy Parks, Charles Egglestom.

"The Corpse in Room Thirteen" (7-7-52): Everett Sloane, Eleanor Lynn, Harold Gary, Charles Jordan.

"The Bog-Oak Necklace" (7-14-52): Jane Seymour, Carol Wheeler.

"Death Trap" (7-28-52): Clare Luce, Leslie Nielsen, John McQuade, J. Pat O'Malley.

"Man in the Dark" (8-4-52): Joseph Wiseman, Margaret Draper, Romney Brent, Joe De Santis.

"The Killer's Moon" (8-11-52): June Lockhart, Alfred Ryder, Michael Garrett, Neil Fisher.

"Twist of Fate" (8-18-52): E. G. Marshall, Constance Ford, Howard Smith.

"Death Is a Small Monkey" (8-25-52): Kevin McCarthy, Francis L. Sullivan, Andrew Branham, Constance Dowling, Missy Russell.

"The Verdict" (9-1-52): Everett Sloane.

"The Red Rose" (9-8-52): John Newland, Mary Phillips.

"The Darker Night" (9-15-52): Louisa Horton, Richard Derr.

"Flight Thirteen" (9-22-52): Josephine Hull, Alan Bunce.

"The Hollow Man" (9-29-52): Wil-

(LIGHTS OUT cont.) liam Bendix, Doris Dowling, Art Smith, Harry Bellows.

LIGHTS OUT.
"When Widows Weep" (1-15-72): Joan Hackett (Sabrina), Laurence Luckinbill (Howard), Louisa Horton (Karen), Michael McGuire (state trooper), Kathryn Walker (Helen).

LOGAN'S RUN. 1977-78. Gregory Harrison (Logan), Heather Menzies (Jessica), Donald Moffat (Rem), Randy Powell (Francis).
"Logan's Run" (9-16-77): Keene Curtis (Draco), Lina Raymond (Siri), Ron Hajek (Riles), J. Gary Dontzig (Akers), Anthony de Longis (Ketchman).
"The Collectors" (9-23-77): Linden Chiles (John), Leslie Parrish (Joanna), Angela Cartwright (Karen), Lawrence Casey (Martin), Perry Bullington, Ben Van Vector, Stan Stratton (Sandmen).
"Capture" (9-30-77): Horst Bucholz (Borden), Mary Woronov (Irene), Stan Stratton (Benjamin).
"The Innocent" (10-10-77): Lisa Eilbacher (Lisa), Lou Richards (Strong), Barney McFadden (Jeremy), Brian Kerwin (Patrick), Gene Tyburn (Friend).
"Man Out of Time" (10-17-77): Paul Shenar (David Eakins), Mel Ferrer (Analog), Woodrow Chambliss (Lab Tech One), Gene Tyburn (Comp Tech Four), Hank Brandt (Gold), Betty Bridges (Fontaine).
"Half Life" (10-31-77): William Smith (Patron/Modok), Len Birman (Positive No. 14/Brawn), Kim Cattrall (Rama II), Jeanne Sorel (Rama I), Betty Jinette (Woman-Positive), John Gowans (Engineer-Scientist).
"Crypt" (11-7-77): Christopher Stone (David Pera), Ellen Weston (Rachel Greenhill), Soon-Teck Oh (Dexter Kim), Neva Patterson (Victoria Mackie), Liam Sullivan (Frederick Lyman), Adrienne LaRussa (Sylvia Reyna), Peggy McCay (Dr. Krim), Richard Roat (man on video).
"Fear Factor" (11-14-77): Jared Martin (Dr. Paulson), Ed Nelson (Dr. Rowan), William Wellman, Jr. (Psychiatrist), Peter Brandon (Psychiatrist), Carl Byrd (Psychiatrist).
"Judas Goat" (12-19-77): Nicholas Hammond (Hal 14), Lance Legault (Matthew), Wright King (Jonathon), Spencer Milligen (Garth), Morgan Woodward (Morgan).
"Futurepast" (1-2-78): Mariette Hartley (Ariana), Michael Sullivan (Clay), Janis Jamison (the Woman),

Joey Fontana (Sandman), Ed Couppee (Sandman).
"Carousel" (1-16-78): Wright King (Jonathan), Rosanne Katon (Diane), Ross Bickell (Michael), Morgan Woodward (Morgan), Melody Anderson (Sheila), Regis J. Cordic (Darrel), Gary Swanson (Peter), Burton Cooper, William Molloy.
"Night Visitors" (1-23-78): George Maharis (Gavin), Barbara Babcock (Marianne), Paul Mantee (Barton).
"Turnabout" (1-30-78): Nehemiah Persoff (Asa), Gerald McRaney (Gera), Harry Rhodes (Samuel), Victoria Racimo (Mia), John Furey (Phillip), Anina Minotto (Aretha), Arell Blanton (Cell Guard One), Sherill Lynn Katzman (2nd woman).
"Stargate" (2-6-78): Eddie Firestone (Timon), Paul Carr (Morah), Darrell Fetty (Pata), Ian Tanza (Arcana).

LOST IN SPACE. 1965-68. Guy Williams (John Robinson), June Lockhart (Maureen Robinson), Jonathan Harris (Dr. Zachary Smith), Billy Mumy (Will Robinson), Mark Goddard (Donald West), Marta Kristen (Judy Robinson), Angela Cartwright (Penny Robinson), Bob May (the Robot).
"The Reluctant Stowaway" (9-15-65): Don Forbes (TV Commentator), Hal Torey (General), Byron Morrow (Lt. Gen. Squires), Hoke Howell (Sgt. Rogers), Tom Allen (Security Guard), Fred Crane, Brett Parker.
"The Derelict" (9-22-65): Don Forbes (TV Commentator), Dawson Palmer (Giant).
"Island in the Sky" (9-29-65).
"There Were Giants in the Earth" (10-6-65): Lamar Lundy (Cyclops monster).
"The Hungry Sea" (10-13-65).
"Welcome Stranger" (10-20-65): Warren Oates (Jimmy Hapgood).
"My Friend, Mr. Nobody" (10-27-65): William Bramley (Mr. Nobody).
"Invaders from the Fifth Dimension" (11-3-65): Ted Lahmann (Alien), Joe Ryan (Alien).
"The Oasis" (11-10-65).
"The Sky Is Fallyin" (11-17-65): Don Matheson (Retho), Francoise Ruggieri (Moela), Eddie Rosson (Lunon).
"Wish Upon a Star" (11-24-65): Dawson Palmer (Rubberoid).
"The Raft" (12-1-65): Dawson Palmer (Bush Creature).
"One of Our Dogs Is Missing" (12-8-65): Dawson Palmer (Mutant).
"Attack of the Monster Plants" (12-

15-65).

"Return from Outer Space" (12-29-65): Reta Shaw (Aunt Clara), Walter Sande (Sheriff Baxendale), Sheila Mathews (Ruth Templeton), Donald Loxby (Davey Sims).

"The Keeper" (1-12-66 & 1-19-66): Michael Rennie (the Keeper), Wilbur Evans.

"The Sky Pirate" (1-26-66): Albert Salmi (Alonzo P. Tucker).

"Ghost in Space" (2-2-66): Dawson Palmer (Uncle Thaddeus).

"The War of the Robots" (2-9-66).

"The Magic Mirror" (2-16-66): Michael J. Pollard (the Boy).

"The Challenge" (3-2-66): Michael Ansara (Ruler), Kurt Russell (Quano).

"The Space Trader" (3-9-66): Torin Thatcher (the Trader).

"His Majesty Smith" (3-16-66): Liam Sullivan (Nexus), Kevin Hagen (the Master).

"The Space Croppers" (3-30-66): Mercedes McCambridge (Sybilla), Sherry Jackson (Effra), Dawson Palmer (Keel).

"All That Glitters" (4-6-66): Werner Klemperer (Bolix), Dawson Palmer (Monster), Larry Ward (Ohan), Ted Lehmann (Voice).

"The Lost Civilization" (4-13-66): Royal Dano (Major Domo), Kym Karath (Princess), Dawson Palmer (Soldier).

"A Change of Space" (4-20-66): Frank Graham (Alien).

"Follow the Leader" (4-27-66): Gregory Morton (Alien Voice).

"Blast Off into Space" (9-14-66): Strother Martin (Nerim).

"Wild Adventure" (9-21-66): Vitina Marcus (Athena).

"The Ghost Planet" (9-28-66): Michael Fox (Summit Voice), Sue England (Space Control/Automation Voice).

"The Forbidden World" (10-5-66): Wally Cox (Tiabo), Janos Prohaska (Monster).

"Space Circus" (10-12-66): James Westerfield (Dr. Marvello), Melinda Fee (Fenestra), Harry Varteresian (Vicho), Michael Greene (Nubu), Dawson Palmer (Monster).

"The Prisoners of Space" (10-19-66): Dawson Palmer (Monster).

"The Android Machine" (10-26-66): Dee Hartford (Verda), Fritz Feld (Mr. Zumdish).

"The Deadly Games of Gamma 6" (11-2-66): Mike Kellin (Myko), Harry Monty (Geco), Ronald Weber (Gromack), Peter Brocco (Alien Leader), Chuck

Roberson (Giant).

"The Thief from Outer Space" (11-9-66): Malachi Throne (Thief), Ted Cassidy (Slave), Maxine Gates (Princess).

"The Curse of Cousin Smith" (11-16-66): Henry Jones (Jeremiah Smith).

"West of Mars" (11-30-66): Allan Melvin (Enforcer Claudius), Charles Arthur (Photo DBL), Mickey Manners (Dee), Lane Bradford (Pleiades Pete), Eddie Quillan (bartender).

"A Visit to Hades" (12-7-66): Gerald Mohr (Morbus).

"The Wreck of the Robot" (12-14-66): Jim Mills (Alien No. 1).

"The Dream Monster" (12-21-66): John Abbott (Sesmar), Dawson Palmer (Raddion), Harry Monty (1st midget), Frank Delfino (2nd midget).

"The Golden Man" (12-28-66): Dennis Patrick (Keema), Ron Gans (Frog Alien), Bill Troy (Frog Alien).

"The Girl from the Green Dimension" (1-4-67): Vitina Marcus (Athena), Harry Raybould (Urso).

"The Questing Beast" (1-11-67): Hans Conried (Sir Sagramonte), Sue England (Que Track Voice), Jeff County (Gundemar).

"The Toymaker" (1-25-67): Fritz Feld (Zumdish), Walter Burke (O. M.), Tiger Joe Marsh (Security Guard), Dawson Palmer (Monster), Larry Dean (Wooden Soldier).

"Mutiny in Space" (2-1-67): Ronald Long (Zahrt).

"The Space Vikings" (2-8-67): Sheila Mathews (Brynhilde), Bern Hoffman (Thor).

"Rocket to Earth" (2-15-67): Al Lewis (Zalto).

"The Cave of the Wizards" (2-22-67): Jim Mills (Eye), Dawson Palmer (Rock Creature), Michael Fox (Brain), Larry Dean (Mummy).

"Treasure of the Lost Planet" (3-1-67): Albert Salmi (Alonzo P. Tucker), Craig Duncan (Deek), Jim Boles (Smeek).

"Revolt of the Androids" (3-8-67): Dee Hartford (Verda), Don Matheson (IDAK), Dawson Palmer (Omega 17).

"The Colonists" (3-15-67): Francine York (Miolani).

"Trip Through the Robot" (3-22-67).

"The Phantom Family" (3-29-67): Alan Hewitt (Lemnoc).

"The Mechanical Men" (4-5-67): Jim Mills (Leader).

"The Astral Traveler" (4-12-67): Sean McClory (Hamish), Dawson Palmer (Angus).

(LOST IN SPACE cont.)
"The Galaxy Gift" (4-26-67): John
Carradine (Arcon), Jim Mills (Saticon
No. 1).
"Condemned of Space" (9-6-67):
Marcel Hillaire (Phanzig).
"Visit to a Hostile Planet" (9-13-
67): Pitt Herbert (Grover), Robert
Foulk (Cragmire), Robert Pine (Craig),
Norman Leavitt (Charlie), Claire Wil-
cox (Stacy).
"Kidnapped in Space" (9-20-67):
Grant Sullivan (Alien No. 764): Carol
Williams (Alien No. 1220), Joey Russo
(Smith as a boy).
"Hunter's Moon" (9-27-67): Vin-
cent Beck (Magazor).
"The Space Primevals" (10-4-67):
Arthur Batanides (Rangah).
"The Space Destructors" (10-11-
67): Tommy Farrell (Cyborg).
"The Haunted Lighthouse" (10-18-
67): Woodrow Parfrey (Col. Fogey),
Lou Wanger (J-5), Kenya Coburn (Zay-
bo).
"Flight into the Future" (10-25-67):
Don Eitner (Sgt. Smith), Lew Gallo
(Cmdr. Fletcher).
"Collision of the Planets" (11-8-
67): Dan Traverty (Ilan), Linda Gaye
Scott (Alien Girl), Joey Tata (Alien),
Dawson Palmer.
"The Space Creature" (11-15-67):
Ronald Gans (Creature).
"Deadliest of the Species" (11-22-
67): Lyle Waggoner (Mechanical Man
No. 1), Sue England (Female Robot
Voice), Ronald Gans (Alien Leader),
Ralph Lee (Mechanical Man No. 2).
"A Day at the Zoo" (11-29-67):
Leonard Stone (Farnum B. Showman),
Gary Tigerman (Oggo), Ronald Weber
(Mort).
"Two Weeks in Space" (12-13-67):
Fritz Feld (Zumdish), Richard Krisher
(MXR), Eric Matthews (QZW), Edy Wil-
liams (Non), Carroll Roebke (Tat).
"Castles in Space" (12-20-67):
Alberto Monte (Chavo), Corinna Tsopei
(Princess Reyka).
"The Anti-Matter Man" (12-27-
67).
"Target: Earth" (1-3-68): James
Gosa (Gilt Proto), Brent Davis (Mike
Officer), Thant Brann (2nd Officer).
"Princess of Space" (1-10-68):
Robert Foulk (Kraspo), Arte Johnson
(Fedor), Sheila Mathews (Aunt Gamma).
"The Time Merchant" (1-17-68):
John Crawford (Dr. Chronos), Byron
Morros (General), Hoke Howell (Ser-
geant).
"The Promised Planet" (1-24-68):

Gil Rogers (Bartholomew), Keith Taylor
(Edgar).
"Fugitives in Space" (1-31-68):
Tol Avery (Warden), Mike Conrad (Creech),
Charles Horvath (Guard).
"Space Beauty" (2-14-68): Leonard
Stone (Farnum B. Showman), Dee Hart-
ford (Nancy Pi Squared), Miriam Schil-
ler (Miss Teutonium).
"The Flaming Planet" (2-21-68):
Abraham Sofaer (Sobram).
"The Great Vegetable Rebellion"
(2-28-68): Stanley Adams (Tybo), James
Millhollin (Willoughby).
"The Junkyard of Space" (3-6-68):
Marcel Hillaire (Junk Man).

LOST PLANET, THE. British 1954.
Peter Kerr, Jack Stewart, Mary Law.

LOST SAUCER, THE. 1975-76. Ruth
Buzzi (Fi), Jim Nabors (Fum), Jar-
rod Johnson (Jerry), Alice Playten
(Alice).

LUCAN. 1977-78. Kevin M. Brophy
(Lucan), John Randolph (Dr. Hoag-
land), Don Gordon (Lt. Prentis).
"Listen to the Heart Beat" (9-12-
77): Stephanie Zimbalist (Tashi), Paul
Hecht (Miklos), Helen Lockwood (Elena),
Michael Keenan (Gheorghi).
"The Search" (12-26-77): Edward
Binns (Marston), Leslie Nielsen (Sheriff
Ramsey), Katherine Cannon (Penny),
G.W. Bailey.
"The Lost Boy" (1-2-78): Came-
ron Mitchell (Tilford Ames), Ray Under-
wood (Carl Bauer), Fred Downs (Frank
Bauer), Sarah Cunningham (Ida Mae
Bauer), Tisch Raye.
"How Do You Run Forever?" (1-9-
78): Diana Muldaur (Carol Demaree),
Monte Markham (Steven Demaree), Per-
cy Rodrigues (Dreber), Gail Landry (Dr.
Flemming), Bill Fletcher.
"One Punch Wolfson" (1-16-78):
Stan Shaes (Caldwell), Woodrow Parfrey
(Drummond), David Sheiner (Lt. Lanson),
James Karen (Murdoch), Pat Grundy
(Mrs. Caldwell), Allen Joseph.
"You Can't Have My Baby" (3-13-
78): Celeste Holm (Eva Jarrett), Pame-
la Franklin (Jodi), Don Reid (Ben), John
Chandler (Deputy), George Murdock, Ed
Griffith.
"The Pariah" (3-27-78): Robert
Reed (Les Braddock), Ellen Weston (An-
nie Braddock), Robbie Rise (Davy Brad-
dock), Shelley Fabares (Marsha), Mi-
chael V. Gazzo (Nick), John Horn (Joey
Talin).
"Nightmare" (11-13-78): John

Larch (Dr. Mason Walker), James Carroll Jordan (Dr. Ty Walker), Claudia Jennings (Debbie Kern).
"Brother Wolf" (11-20-78): Elisha Cook, Jr., Henry Jones, John McLain.
"Creature from Beyond the Door" (11-27-78): Barry Sullivan, Jenny Sullivan, William Smithers.
"Thunder God Gold" (12-4-78): Paul Brinegar (Willie), Gretchen Corbett (Bonnie), Matt Clark (Jake Jones), Sterling Holloway.

MAN AND THE CHALLENGE. 1959-60. George Nader (Glenn Barton).
"Sphere of No Return" (9-12-59): Paul Burke (Corey), Joyce Meadows (Lynn Allan), Raymond Bailey (Kramer), Keith Vincent (Regan), Frank Kirby (Mason).
"Maximum Capacity" (9-19-59): James Best (David Mallory), Mike Masters (Jerry Ogden), Robert Conrad (Bill Howard), Paula Raymond (Anne), Robert Karnes (Henderson).
"Odds Against Survival" (9-26-59): Robert Clarke (Dr. Wayne Robinson), Bethel Leslie (Nina Robinson), Whit Bissell (Dr. Robert Widener).
"Sky Diving" (10-3-59): Daniele Aubrey (Suzanne Bolet), John Van Dreelan (Georges Bolet), Alberto Morin (Raymond).
"Experiments in Terror" (10-10-59): Otto Kruger (David Mumford), Julia Adams (Linda Webb), Logan Field (Delmar Jervis).
"Invisible Force" (10-17-59): Debra Paget (Liza Dantes), William Conrad (Jim Harrigan), Carol Thurston (Alice Barron), Patrick Waltz (Jenks).
"Escape to Nepal" (10-24-59): Myron Healey (Dr. Morton Walker), John Maxwell (Dr. Warren Szold), John Granville (Marilyn Sidney).
"Border to Border" (10-31-59): Edward Kemmer (Tom Larson), Don Kennedy (Danny Ryan).
"Trial by Fire" (11-7-59): H. M. Wynant (Fred Conway), Joyce Taylor (Dorrie Conway).
"White Out" (11-14-59): Jan Shepard (Dr. Anna West), Phil Terry (Dr. William Ryder), Don Eitner (Lt. Joe Hale).
"The Breaking Point" (11-28-59): Alfred Ryder (Robert Carson), John Marley (Sam Randolph), Joyce Meadows (Lynn Allan), Tony Monaco (Leon Ulmer).
"Jungle Survival" (12-5-59): Dean Harens (Jim Connor), Mike Mas-

ters (Bill Locke), Marcia Henderson (Anne Sanders).
"I've Killed Seven Men" (12-12-59): Lin McCarthy (Paul Cheever).
"Man Without Fear" (12-19-59): John Day (Mike Mapes), Tracey Roberts (Helen), Frank Gerstle (Ed Burke), Nick Nicholson (Jim Phillips).
"The Visitors" (12-26-59): Bert Remsen (Ken), Fuzzy Knight (Burro Charlie), Robert J. Wilke (Old Gene), Len Lesser (Les), Jack Ging.
"The Storm" (1-2-60): Fred Gabourie (Roger Blanchard), Roberta Haynes (Patricia Halakua), Lee Johnson (Bill Blake), Byron Morrow (Dean Curtiss).
"Killer River" (1-9-60): John Archer (Sawyer), Michael Keith (Stanhope).
"Rodeo" (1-23-60): Ann Robinson (Sally Somers), Myron Healey (Dr. John Quint), Neil Grant (Big Ed Casey), Larry Mann (Jim Fitzpatrick), Chuck Parkerson (Announcer).
"The Windowless Room" (1-30-60): Jack Ging (Dan Wright), Sue Randall (Phyllis), Raymond Bailey (Dr. Kramer), Doris Fesette (Edith), Michael Keith (Ranger).
"Nightmare Crossing" (2-6-60): Keith Larson (John Napier), Tony Monaco (Harley), Mike Keene (Colonel), Pat McCaffrie (radio officer), Jack Catron (Winter).
"The Lure of Danger" (2-13-60): Miguel Landa (Cartina), Felipe Turich (Grantina), Abel Franco (Valencia), Robert Mercy (Arejevo), Edward Colmans (Dr. Lopez).
"Recovery" (2-20-60): Eloise Hardt (Madge Costain), John Archer (Capt. Norris), Jack Catron (Ensign Fowler).
"Buried Alive" (2-27-60): Robert Gothie (Buzz Harmon), Robert Bice (Carlson), Don Eitner (Doug), Don Harvey (Donaldson), Joyce Meadows (Lynn Allan).
"Recondo" (3-5-60): Jack Harris (Warden Tanner), Marianne Hill (Ruth), Arvid Nelson (Charlie Burke), Jay Douglas (Graham Landry), Bern Bassey (Darcy).
"Flying Lab" (3-12-60): Keith Vincent (Winters), Jack Hilton (Scott), Robert Knapp (Ryder), Page Slattery (Davis).
"Hurricane Mesa" (3-19-60): Jack Ging (Jim Harper), Robert Bice (Dr. Carlson).
"Astro Female" (3-26-60): Maureen Leeds (Gina Reed), Adrienne Hayes (Amy Brown), Joan Granville (Joan Lee),

(MAN AND THE CHALLENGE cont.)
Ethel Jensen (Jean Gillespie).
"The Extra Sense" (4-2-60):
Frank Maxwell (Col. Bill Blake), Paul
Comi (Sgt. Lowery).
"Man in the Capsule" (4-9-60):
Darryl Hickman (Max Edwards), Fred
Beir (Steve Paley), Dick Jeffries (radio
operator), Donald Gamble (Maxey).
"The Dropper" (4-23-60): Jack
O'Brien (Morgan Jones), Arthur Hel-
ler (Alan Wells), Jerry Summers (Drop-
per), Tyler McVey (Capt. Whitlow),
Howard McLeod (radio officer), Mike
Masters (judo man).
"High Dive" (4-30-60): Olive
Sturgess (Sylvia Honig), Charles Alvin
Bell (Ed Honig), Michael Keith (Matt
Adams), Vernon Rich (Judge Banner),
Charles R. Keene (Bill Andrews).
"Daredevils" (5-7-60): Don Ken-
nedy (Pete Knowland), Christine White
(Betty Knowland), Ted Knight (Dr. Her-
ter), Doris Fosette (Miss Johnson).
"Shooter McLaine" (5-21-60):
John Milford (McLaine), Mala Powers
(Betty Fuller), Dick Rich (John Mickel-
son), Charles Tannen (George Harley).
"Early Warning" (5-28-60): Phi-
lip Ober (Clifford Beck), Bethel Leslie
(Eleanor Beck), Andy Thompson (Col.
Pierce), Marshall Kent (Pentagon Chief).
"Breakoff" (6-4-60): Karl Swen-
son (Dr. Lindstrom), Miranda Jones
(Helen Vincent).
"Highway to Danger" (6-11-60):
Karen Scott (Kitty), Hank Patterson
(Swede), Barney Biro (Tamarin).

MAN CALLED SLOANE, A. 1979. Ro-
bert Conrad (Thomas Remington
Sloane III), Ji-Tu Cumbuka (Torque),
Dan O'Herlihy (Director), Karen Pur-
cill (Kelly), Michelle Carey (Voice of
Effie).
"Night of the Wizard" (9-22-79):
Roddy McDowall (Manfred Baranoff),
Diane Stilwell (Sara), Christian Mar-
lowe (Alexander), Chris de Lisle (Kris-
ta).
"The Seduction Squad" (9-29-79):
Robert Culp (Edward Danton), Lee Pur-
cell (Michele Blake), Anthony Eisley
(Herbert Davis), Laura Johnson (Joan-
na Ross).
"Tuned for Destruction" (10-6-
79): Geoffrey Lewis (Wild Bill McEvoy),
Sandra Kerns (Alice Baker), Denise
Du Barry (Corporal Comfort), Patrick
Culliton (Capt. Schturm), Laurence
Haddon (Updike).
"Masquerade of Terror" (10-13-
79): Richard Lynch (Jeremy Mason),

Len Birman (Forbes), LaVelda (Linda),
John Devlin (Toland).
"Demon's Triangle" (10-20-79):
Clive Revill (Morgan Lancaster), John
Reilly (David Clarke), Maurice Hill
(Hertzog), Marianne Marks (Lana), Jon
St. Elwood (Manu).
"The Venus Microbe" (10-27-79):
Monte Markham (Jonathan Cambro), Mor-
gan Fairchild (Melissa Nelson), Alex
Henteloff (Dr. Charles Franklyn), Dar-
rell Zwerling (Dr. Eckhart), Zacki Mur-
phy (Charlene Hutton), Robert Ellen-
stein (Dr. Davis), James Galante (Felix),
Faughn Armstrong (Snyder), Susette
Carroll (Dr. Jessica Barnes), Rita Wil-
son (Kathy), Ava Lazar (hostess).
"Collision Course" (11-17-79):
Eric Braeden (Crane), Nancy DeCarl
(Denise), Pat Klous (Elsa), Eldon Quick
(Dr. Ellman), Ben Wright (Mr. Har-
bridge), Michael Alldredge (Church),
Martina Deignan (Barbara Wilson), Richard Lockmiller (Emmett), Glenn Sipes
(hunt club manager), Laurence Bame
(truck driver), Roberta Lee Carroll
(missile thief).
"Samurai" (11-24-79): Mako (Ta-
naka), Nancy Conrad (Carrie), Nate
Esformes (Carlos Casal), Maria Rich-
wine (Maria), Richard Narita (Sato),
Elizabeth Chauvet (Carlotta), Jenny
Neumann (young girl), Bill Ewing (Tana-
ka's man), Earl Boen.
"Sweethearts of Disaster" (12-1-
79): Andrea Howard (Anna), Ted Ham-
ilton (Bannister), Lisa Shure (Vicki),
Jennifer Starrett (Paula).
"Lady Bug" (12-8-79): Edie Adams
(Lady Bug), Martin Kove (Roger), Bar-
bara Rucker (Dr. Chris Bishop), Stefan
Gierasch (Dr. Rand), Robin G. Eisen-
man (Ingrid).
"Architect of Evil" (12-15-79):
Michael Pataki (Worthing Pendergast),
Vonetta McGee (Tina Baldwin), Adrienne
La Russa (Serena), Lori Lethin (Helen),
Robert Phalen (Weems), John Aprea
(Harry Helms), Eric Server (Twilliger),
Linda Fontana (Terry), Robert Herman
(Scott), Lew Brown (Marvin).
"The Shangrila Syndrome" (12-22-
79): Dennis Cole (Hans Kruger), Jo Ann
Harris (Joanna), Daphne Maxwell (Dr.
Karla Meredith), Tony Epper (Penfold).

MANDRAKE THE MAGICIAN. 1954.
Coe Norton (Mandrake), Woody
Strode (Lothar).

MAN FROM ATLANTIS. 1977-78. Patrick Duffy (Mark Harris), Belinda J.
Montgomery (Dr. Elizabeth Merrill),

Alan Fudge (C.W. Crawford).
"The Death Scouts" (5-7-77):
Kenneth Tigar (Dr. Miller Simon), Tiffany Bolling (Lioa), Burr DeBenning (Xos), Hank Stohl (Wes), Annette Cardona (Ginny Mendoza), Alan Mandell (Grant Stockwood), Russell Arms (medical examiner).
"The Killer Spores" (5-17-77):
Kenneth Tigar (Dr. Miller Simon), Ivan Bonar (Edwin Shirley).
"The Disappearances" (6-20-77):
Kenneth Tigar (Dr. Miller Simon), Dennis Redfield (Dick Redstone), Darlene Carr (Mary), Pamela Solow (Jane), Ivor Francis (Dr. Medlow), Fred Beir (sub captain), Ruth Manning (Clara).
"Melt Down" (9-22-77): Victor Buono (Mr. Schubert), Robert Lussier (Brent), Richard Laurence Williams (Jomo), James E. Brodhead (Trubshawe), J. Victor Lopez (Chuey).
"The Mud Worm" (10-13-77):
Victor Buono (Mr. Schubert), Robert Lussier (Brent).
"Hawk of Mu" (10-18-77): Victor Buono (Mr. Schubert), Robert Lussier (Brent), Vicky Huxtable (Juliette), Carole Mallory (Vicki), Sydney Lassick (Smith).
"Giant" (10-25-77): Kareem Abdul Jabbar (Alien), Ted Neeley (Muldoon), John Dennis (bartender), Gene LeBelle (Dichter).
"Man O'War" (11-1-77): Victor Buono (Mr. Schubert), Robert Lussier (Brene), Harvey Jason (Dashki), Gary Owens (announcer).
"Shoot-Out at Land's End" (11-8-77): Patrick Duffy (Billy Jones), Richard Laurence Williams (Jomo), Pernell Roberts (Clint Hollister), Jamie Smith Jackson (Bettina), Noble Willingham (Washburn).
"Crystal Water, Sudden Death" (11-22-77): Victor Buono (Mr. Schubert), Rene Auberjonois (Havergal), Tina Lenert (Click One), Flip Reade (Click Two).
"The Naked Montague" (12-6-77):
John Shea (Romeo), Lisa Eilbacher (Juliet), Norman Snow (Tybalt), Lewis Arquette (Friar Laurance).
"C.W. Hyde" (12-13-77): Michele Carey (Belle), Val Avery (Calender), Pamela Solow (Sarah), Frank Bonner (bartender).
"Scavenger Hunt" (2-18-78): Ted Neeley (Muldoon), Ted Cassidy (Kanja), Eugenia Wright (Tiwi).
"Imp" (4-25-78): Pat Morita (Moby), Dick Gautier (Duke).
"The Siren" (5-2-78): Lisa Blake Richards (Jenny), Neville Brand (Stringer), Laurette Spang (Amanda), Michael Strong (Trevanian).
"Deadly Carnival" (6-6-78): Billy Barty (Moxie), Anthony James (Summersday), Sharon Farrell (Charlene), Donna Garrett (student).

MAN FROM U.N.C.L.E. 1964-68. Robert Vaughn (Napoleon Solo), David McCallum (Ilya Kuryakin), Leo G. Carroll (Alexander Waverly), Mario Siletti (Del Floria), May Heatherly (Heather).
"The Vulcan Affair" (9-22-64):
Patricia Crowley (Elaine May Donaldson), Fritz Weaver (Andrew Vulcan), William Marshall (Ashumen), Ivan Dixon (Soumarun), Eric Beery (Alfred Ghist), Rupert Crosse (Nobuk), Victoria Chaw (Gracie Ladovan).
"The Iowa-Scuba Affair" (9-29-64):
Katherine Crawford (Jill Dennison), Slim Pickens (Clint Spinner), Shirley O'Hara (Aunt Martha), Dorothy Neumann (scrub woman), Margarita Cardova (Latin woman).
"The Quadripartite Affair" (10-6-64): Jill Ireland (Marion Raven), Anne Francis (Gervaise Ravel), Richard Anderson (Adam Pattner), Roger C. Carmel (Horth), John Van Dreelen (Harold Bufferton), Robert Carricart (Karadian).
"The Shark Affair" (10-13-64):
Robert Culp (Capt. Shark), Sue Anne Langdon (Elsa Barnam), Herb Anderson (Harry Barnman), Hedley Mattingly (Capt. Fowler).
"The Deadly Games Affair" (10-20-64): Alexander Scourby (Prof. Amadeus), Ben Wright (stamp expert), Burt Brickerhoff (Chuck Boskirk), Janine Gray (Angelique), Brooke Bundy (Terry Brent).
"The Green Opal Affair" (10-27-64): Carroll O'Connor (Walter G. Brach), Milton Selzer (Dr. Shtallmacher), Joan O'Brien (Chris Brinel), Dovima (Mrs. Karda).
"The Giuoco Piano Affair" (11-10-64): Jill Ireland (Marion Raven), Anne Francis (Gervaise Ravel), John Van Dreelan (Harold Bufferton), James Frawley (Lt. Manuera), Gordon Gilbert (Smith).
"The Double Affair" (11-17-64):
Senta Berger (Serena), Sharon Farrell (Sandy Wister), Fabrizio Mioni (Arsene), Jennifer Billingsley (Taffy), Paula Raymond (Director), Donald Harron (Kitt Kittridge), Harold Gould (Doctor), Michael Evans (Darius Two), Jan Arvan (waiter), Michele Carey (Maggie), Nancy Hsueh (Wanda), Paul Siemion (clerk).
"The Project Strigas Affair" (11-

(MAN FROM U. N. C. L. E. cont.) 24-
64): William Shatner (Mike Donfield),
Leonard Nimoy (Vladeck), Woodrow
Parfrey (Linkwood), Narda Onyx (Mme.
Kurasov), Susan Kramer (Mr. Smith).
"The Finny Foot Affair" (12-2-
64): Kurt Russell (Chris Larson), Leo-
nard Strong (Gen. Yokura), Noel Dray-
ton (Dr. Parker).
"The Neptune Affair" (12-8-64):
Jeremy Slate (Gabe Melcroft), Marta
Kristen (Felicia Lavimore), Henry
Jones (Vincent Lockridge), Alex Lock-
wood (Dr. Lavimore).
"The Dove Affair" (12-15-64):
Ricardo Montalban (Satine), June Lock-
hart (Sarah Taub), Henry Lascoe (Pre-
mier Earnest), Clark Howat (Ambas-
sador), Emile Genset (Arseny Linz),
Robert Beach (Russel), Hans Difflipp
(Colonel), Leslie Towner (Linda), Jim-
my Bates (Kirk).
"The King of Knaves Affair" (12-
22-64): Paul Stevens (King Fazik), Di-
ana Millay (Ernestine Pepper), Arlene
Martel (Gemma Lusso), Jan Merlin
(Angel Galley), Gregory Morton (Carlo
Venerdi), Erik Holland (Bobo Barrett),
Tania Lemani (Venetia), John Sebastian
(Ernie Cadera).
"The Terbuf Affair" (12-29-64):
Madlyn Rhue (Clara Valdar), Jacques
Aubuchon (Emil), Michael Forest (Lt.
Fest), Kurt Kreuger (Stefan Valdar),
Albert Paulsen (Major Vicek).
"The Deadly Decoy Affair" (1-11-
65): Ralph Taeger (Egon Stryker), Jo-
anna Moore (Fran Parsons), Irene Ted-
row (Mrs. Thyssen), Charles Seel (Mr.
Thyssen), Berry Kroeger (Frame),
Edward Mallory (Narum).
"The Fiddlesticks Affair" (1-18-
65): Dan O'Herlihy (Marcel Rudolph),
Marlyn Mason (Susan Callaway), Ken
Murray (Anton Korbel).
"The Yellow Scarf Affair" (1-25-
65): Kamali Devi (Dierdre Purbhani),
Neile Adams (Sita Chandi), Linden
Chiles (Tom Simpson), Murray Mathe-
son (Maharajah), David Sheiner (Inspec-
tor).
"The Mad, Mad Tea Party Affair"
(2-1-65): Richard Haydn (Mr. Heming-
way), Zohra Lampert (Kay Lorrison),
Peter Haskell (Riley), Lee Meriwether
(Dr. Byrd), Peter Hansen (Morgan),
Dean Harens (Walter), Irving Steinberg
(Del Floria).
"The Secret Scepter Affair" (2-
8-65): Gene Raymond (Col. Allan Mor-
gan), Ziva Rodann (Aiz), Lili Darvas
(Madam Karim), Paul Lukather (Capt.
Ahmed).

"The Bow-Wow Affair" (2-15-65):
Susan Oliver (Alice Baldwin), Paul Lam-
bert (Andre Delgrovia), Antoinette Bo-
wer (Delilah Dovro), Pat Harrington,
Jr. (Guido Panzini), Jesslyn Fax (Mrs.
Clothilde Willard).
"The Four Steps Affair" (2-22-65):
Lee Chapman (Sarah), Michael Petit
(Miki), Susan Seaforth (Kelly Brown),
Luciana Paluzzi (Angela), Don Harron
(Kitt Kittridge), Robert Brubaker (Rud-
nick), Malachi Throne (Kaza).
"The See-Paris-and-Die Affair"
(3-1-65): Lloyd Bochner (Max Van
Schreeten), Gerald Mohr (Josef Van
Schreeten), Kathryn Hays (Mary Pil-
grim), Alfred Ryder (Corio).
"The Brain-Killer Affair" (3-8-
65): Elsa Lanchester (Dr. Agnes Da-
bree), Abraham Sofaer (Gabhail Samov),
Yvonne Craig (Cecile Bergstrom), Roose-
velt Grier (Jason), Nancy Kovack (Miss
Flostone).
"The Hong Kong Schilling Affair"
(3-15-65): Glenn Corbett (Bernie Oren),
Karen Sharpe (Heavenly Cortelle), Gavin
MacLeod (Cleveland), Richard Kiel
(Merry), Miiko Taka (Jade).
"The Never-Never Affair" (3-22-
65): Barbara Feldon (Mandy Stevenson),
Cesar Romero (Victor Gervais), Kate
Murtagh (Miss Raven), John Stevenson
(Varner).
"The Love Affair" (3-29-65): Ed-
die Albert (Brother Love), Maggie Pierce
(Pearl Rolfe), Robert H. Harris (Dr.
Janos Hradny), Tracey Roberts (Magda).
"The Gazebo in the Maze Affair"
(4-5-65): George Sanders (B. Emory
Partridge), Jeanette Nolan (Edith Par-
tridge), John Alderson (Jenkins), John
Orchard (Forrest), Donnie Franklin
(Peggy), Richard Peel (Forenaugh).
"The Girls of Nazarone Affair"
(4-12-65): Ben Wright (Dr. Nicole Bau-
rel), Kipp Hamilton (Lavinia Brown),
Marian Moses (Mme. Alceste Streigau),
Danica d'Hondt (Ludy).
"The Odd Man Affair" (4-19-65):
Martin Balsam (Albert Scully), Barbara
Shelley (Bryn Watson), Hedley Mattingly
(Wye), Ronald Long (Zed), Christopher
Cary (Ecky), Oscar Beregi, Jr. (Hollan-
der), Eve McVeagh (Baroness).
"The Alexander the Greater Affair"
(9-17-65 & 9-24-65): Rip Torn (Alexan-
der), Dorothy Provine (Tracey Alexan-
der), David Opatoshu (Kavon), David
Sheiner (Parviz), Yvonne Craig (Maude
Waverly), Leon Lontoc (Gen. Bon-Phou-
ma), James Hong (Prince Phanogg), Te-
ru Shimada (Pres. Sing-Mok), Robert
Karnes (Col. Hawks), Cal Bolder (Ingo

Lindstrum), Donna Michelle (Princess Nicole), Clarke Gordon (Claxon), Arthur Wong (Gen. Man-Phang), Robert Gibbons (Farrell), Carole Williams (receptionist).

"The Ultimate Computer Affair" (10-1-65): Charlie Ruggles (Gov. Callahan), Roger C. Carmel (Capt. Cervantes), Judy Carne (Salty Oliver), Judith Loomis (Flora), Paul Fierro (Feodore), Maurine Dawson (Sarah), Susan Wendell (Dora).

"The Foxes and Hounds Affair" (10-8-65): Vincent Price (Victor Marton), Patricia Medina (Lucia Belmont), Julie Sommars (Mimi Doolittle), Adam Roarke (Cantrell), Don Henley (Belmont's aide), Andre Phillippe (Merlin).

"The Discotheque Affair" (10-15-65): Ray Danton (Vincent Carver), Judi West (Sandy Wyler), Eric Braeden (Oakes), Harvey Lembeck (Tiger Ed), Evelyn Ward (Farina), Gene Benton (Sherman).

"The Re-Collectors Affair" (10-22-65): George Macready (Demos), Jocelyn Lane (Lisa Donato), Jacqueline Baer (Genevieve), Theodore Marcuse (Gregori Valetti).

"The Arabian Affair" (10-29-65): Phyllis Newman (Sophie), Michael Ansara (Sulador), Quinn O'Hara (Mitzi), Robert Ellenstein (David Lewin), Irene Tedrow (Hazel), Jerome Thor (Norman), Glenn Kramer (George), Tom Hatten (THRUSH Captain).

"The Tigers Are Coming Affair" (11-5-65): Jill Ireland (Suzanne de Serre), Lee Bergere (Prince Panat), Alan Caillou (Col. Quillan).

"The Deadly Toys Affair" (11-12-65): Angela Lansbury (Elfie Van Donck), Jay North (Bartlett), Diane McBain (Joanna Lydecker), John Hoyt (Headmaster), Arnold Moss (Noubar Telemakian), Gil Perkins (Dr. Warshowsky), Gloria Neil (Sarah), Ernst Winters (Basil), Christopher Essay (Steward).

"The Cherry Blossom Affair" (11-19-65): France Nuyen (Cricket Okasada), Woodrow Parfrey (Kutuzov), Beulah Quo (woman), Kam Tong (Yukio), Jeri Fujikawa (Harada), Beau Van den Ecker (Victor).

"The Virtue Affair" (12-3-65): Ronald Long (Jacques Robespierre), Mala Powers (Albert Dubois), Marcel Hillaire (Raoul Dubois), Frank Martha (Carl Voegler), Laurence Montaigne (Jailer).

"The Children's Day Affair" (12-10-65): Jeanne Cooper (Mother Fear), Warren Stevens (Capt. Jenks), Susan

Silo (Anna Paola), Eduardo Ciannelli (Carlo Farenti), Horst Ebersberg (Huck), Chris Anders (Tom), Joey Russo (Ricardo), Franco Corsaro (Alberto).

"The Adriatic Express Affair" (12-17-65): Jessie Royce Landis (Mme. Nemirovitch), Juliet Mills (Eya), Norbert Schiller (Little Man), Jennifer Billingsley (model), Jane Dulo (American woman), Henry Rowland (Fritz), Sig Ruman (conductor), Charles Hicks (Hans), Saul Gorss (Konrad).

"The Yukon Affair" (12-24-65): George Sanders (B. Emory Partridge), Marion Thompson (Victoria), Tianne Gabrielle (Murphy), Bernie Gozier (Headman).

"The Very Important Zombie Affair" (12-31-65): Claude Akins (El Supremo), Lisa Gaye Scott (Suzy), Rodolfo Acosta (Capt. Ramirez), Ken Renard (Delgado), Isabelle Cooley (Conchita), Maide Norman (Mama Lou).

"The Dippy Blonde Affair" (1-7-66): Joyce Jameson (JoJo Tyler), Robert Strauss (Simon Belanado), Rex Holman (Eddie), Fabrizio Mioni (Harry Pendleton), Robert Turnbull (Al), James Frawley (Max).

"The Deadly Goddess Affair" (1-14-66): Victor Buono (Col. Hubris), Michael Strong (Narouz), Steven Geray (Count Carragio), Brioni Farrell (Mia), Joseph Sirola (Malik), Marya Stevens (Angela), Dan Travanty (Luca), David Renard (Hamid), Stassa Damascus (Aeyesha).

"The Birds and the Bees Affair" (1-21-66): John McGiver (Mozard), Anna Capri (Tavis), John Abbott (Dr. Swan), Vincent Beck (Maples), Lorri Scott (dance instructor), Judy Cannon (cigarette girl).

"The Waverly Ring Affair" (1-28-66): Larry Blyden (George Dennell), Elizabeth Allan (Carla Drosten), Jim Boles (Dr. Lazarus), Allen Jaffe (Victor), Erik Holland (Agent 18), Alfred Hopson (photo clerk), Lee Delano (Victor).

"The Bridge of Lions Affair" (2-4-66 & 2-11-66): Maurice Evans (Sir Norman Swickert), Vera Miles (Mme. Desala), Bernard Fox (Jordan), Ann Elder (Joanna), Monica Keating (Olga), Dolorex Faith (Lorelei Lancer), Yvonne Craig (Wanda), Anna Capri (Do Do), Cal Bolder (Fleeton), James Doohan (Phillip Bainbridge), Robert Easton (Texan), Harry David Alexander (Gritsky), Antony Eustrel (steward), Ollie O'Toole (Corvy), Richard Peel (cat man), Barry Bernard (pet shop owner).

(MAN FROM U. N. C. L. E. cont.)
"The Foreign Legion Affair" (2-18-66): Howard Da Silva (Capt. Basil Calhoun), Danielle DeMetz (Barbara), Elizabeth Fraser (Macushia O'Shea), Michael Pate (Bey), Larry Chance (Bakim), Rupert Crosse (Corporal Remy), Viviane Ventura (Aisha), Michael Corhan (Colonel), Rockne Tarkington (domestic), Edward Hashim (Sheik),

"The Moonglow Affair" (2-25-66): Mary Ann Mobley (April Dancer), Norman Fell (Mark Slate), Kevin McCarthy (Arthur Caresse), Mary Carver (Jean Caresse).

"The Nowhere Affair" (3-4-66): Diana Hyland (Mara), Lou Jacoby (Arum Tertunian), David Sheiner (Longulius), J. Pat O'Malley (prospector), Leigh Chapman (Wanda), Mike Douglas (THRUSH Cowboy).

"The King of Diamonds Affair" (3-11-66): Ricardo Montalban (Rafael Delgado), Nancy Kovack (Victoria), Larry D. Mann (Blodgett), Mike St. Clair (Knox), Lisa Mitchell (Dolly), Ashley Cowan (Freddie).

"The 'Project Deephole' Affair" (3-18-66): Jack Weston (Buzz Conway), Barbara Bouchet (Narcissus Darling), Leon Askin (Marvin Elom), Walter Sande (Manager), Tony Monaco (Leon), Ralph J. Rose (Dr. Remington).

"The Round Table Affair" (3-25-66): Valura Noland (Vicky), Reginald Gardiner (Prince Fred), Bruce Gordon (Lucho Nostra), Don Francks (Artie King), Stuart Nisbit (Doc), Tom Barto (Bullets), Eric Lord.

"The Bat Cave Affair" (4-1-66): Martin Landau (Count Zark), Joan Freeman (Clemency McGill), Whit Bissell (Prof. Harvey Glomm), Peter Barone (Transon), Charles Horvath (Manservant), Tita Marsell (Spanish Dancer).

"The Minus X Affair" (4-8-66): Eve Arden (Prof. Lillian Stemmler), Sharon Farrell (Leslie), Theo Marcuse (Rollo), King Moody (Whittaker), John Bryant (Officer), Robert Doyle (Louis), Jan Peters.

"The Indian Affairs Affair" (4-15-66): Victoria Vetri (Charisma), Joe Mantell (L. C. Carson), Ted De Corsia (Chief Highcloud), Nick Colasanto (Ralph), Richard Loo (Dr. Yahama), Sharyn Hillyer (Wanda).

"Their Master's Voice Affair" (9-16-66): Estelle Winwood (Hester Partridge), Marianne Osborne (Verity Burgoyne), Joseph Ruskin (Jason Sutro), Victoria Young (Miki Matsu), Dale Ishi-

moto (Dr. Marsu), Cathy Ferrar (Suzy), Judy Franklin (Dottie), Diane Sayer (Kish), Larry Chance (Gratz), Clegg Hoyt (Duane).

"The Sort of Do-It-Yourself Dreadful Affair" (9-23-66): Jeannie Riley (Andy), Pamela Curran (Margo), Woodrow Parfrey (Dr. Pertwee), Barry Atwater (Lash), Fritz Feld (Toeffler), William Lanteau (analyst).

"The Galatea Affair" (9-30-66): Joan Collins (Rosy Shlagenheimer/Baroness Bibi di Chasseur), Noel Harrison (Mark Slate), Carl Esmond (Baron De Chasseur), Michael St. Clair (Olaf), Michael Angarola (Thirty), Paul Smith (American), Chris Essay (wine steward).

"The Super-Colossal Affair" (10-7-66): Shelly Berman (Veblen), J. Carroll Naish (Uncle Giuliano), Carol Wayne (Ginger Laveer), Bernard Fein (Cariago).

"The Monks of St. Thomas Affair" (10-14-66): David Stewart (Abbott Simon), Celeste Yarnall (Andrea Fouchet), Henry Calvin (Brother Peter), John Wengraf (Abbott John), Horst Ebersberg (Dolby), Roy Sickner (Prior), Iggie Wolfington (Brother Paulus), Ray Kellogg (wood chopper), Eugene Mate (customs man).

"The Pop Art Affair" (10-21-66): Sherry Alberoni (Sylvia Harrison), Sabrina Scharf (Mari Brooks), Robert H. Harris (Mark Ole), Nellie Burt (Mrs. Harrison), Charles Lane (Harrison), Sharyn Hillyer (Wanda), Stanley Ralph Ross (beatnik).

"The Thor Affair" (10-28-66): Bernard Fox (Brutus Thor), Linda Foster (Nellie Cranford), Ken Bernard (Dr. Diljohn), Arthur Batanides (Mohan Kiru), Harry Davis (Dr. Frazir Nahdi), Charles Giorgi (clerk), Antony Eustrel (butler), Ralph Traeger (hotel clerk).

"The Candidate's Wife Affair" (11-4-66): Diana Hyland (Miranda Bryant/Irina), Richard Anderson (Sen. Bryant), Larry D. Mann (Arnold Fairbanks), Anna Lisa (Signe), Than Wyenn.

"The Come with Me to the Casbah Affair" (11-11-66): Danielle DeMetz (Janine), Abbe Lane (Ayesha), Pat Harrington, Jr. (Pierrot La Mouche), Jacques Aubuchon (Col. Hamid).

"The Off Broadway Affair" (11-18-66): Shari Lewis (Janet Jarrod), Joan Huntington (Linda), Leon Askin (Machina), Charles Dierkop (Adolph), Lennie Weinrib (Winky Blintz), Peggy Taylor (Miss Osborne).

"The Concrete Overcoat Affair" (11-25-66 & 12-2-66): Jack Palance (Louis Strago), Janet Leigh (Miss Diketon), Eduardo Ciannelli (Fingers Stilletto),

Allen Jenkins (Pretty Stilletto), Jack LaRue (Feet Stilletto), Joan Blondell (Mrs. Fingers Stilletto), Ludwig Donath (Dr. Heinrich Von Kronen), Letitia Roman (Pia Monteri), Penny Santon (Grandmama Monteri), Elisha Cook (Arnold), Will Kuluva (Thaler), Maxie Rosenbloom (Crunch Battaglia), Vince Barnett (Scissors), Vincent Beck (Benjamin Luger).

"The Abominable Snowman Affair" (12-9-66): David Sheiner (Prime Minister), Anne Jeffreys (Calamith Rogers), Pilar Seurat (Amra Palli), Philip Ahn (High Lama), Stewart Hsieh (Baku).

"The My Friend the Gorilla Affair" (12-16-66): Vitina Marcus (Jungle Girl), Alan Mowbray (Harry Blackburn), Percy Rodriguez (Khufu), Raymond St. Jacques (Arunda), Joyce Jillson (Marsha Woodhugh), Arthur Malet (Professor), George Barrows (Baby, the gorilla).

"The Jingle Bells Affair" (12-23-66): Akim Tamiroff (Emissary Georgi Koz), Ellen Willard (Priscilla Worth), Leon Belasco (Maxim Radish), Leonid Kinskey (Ferenc Pifnic), Kent Smith (Macy).

"The Take Me to Your Leader Affair" (12-30-66): Nancy Sinatra (Coco Cool), Whitney Blake (Corinne), Paul Lambert (Simon Sparrow), Woodrow Parfrey (Dr. Adrian Cool), James Griffith (Dr. Trebush), Harry Swoger (Kalmus), Kay Michaels (Wanda).

"The Suburbia Affair" (1-6-67): Victor Borge (Dr. Rutters/Willoughby), Beth Brickell (Betsy), Reta Shaw (Miss Witherspoon), Richard Erdman (P. T. Barkley), Herb Anderson (Fletcher), King Moody (Barrows).

"The Deadly Smorgasbord Affair" (1-13-67): Lynn Loring (Neilla), Pamela Curran (Inga Anderson), Peter Brocco (Dr. A.C. Nillson), Robert Emhardt (Heinrich Beckman), Horst Ebersberg (Swen), Martin Koslech (Pederson), Craig Chudy (THRUSH Agent), Bill Hickman (Erik).

"The Yo-Ho-Ho and a Bottle of Rum Affair" (1-20-67): Dan O'Herlihy (Capt. Morton), Kevin Hagen (passenger), Eddie Quillan (Scotty), Peggy Taylor (Jenny Janue).

"The Napoleon's Tomb Affair" (1-27-67): Kurt Kasznar (Pres. Tunick), Joseph Sirola (Malanez), Ted Cassidy (Edgar), Mercedes Moliner (Candyce), Fritz Feld.

"The It's All Greek to Me Affair" (2-3-67): Harold J. Stone (Stavros), Linda Marsh (Kyra), George Keymas

(Manolakas), Ted Roter (Nico), Jacques Roux (Sauvignon), Michael Davis (Kostas).

"The Hula Doll Affair" (2-17-67): Jan Murray (Simon Sweet), Pat Harrington, Jr. (Peter Sweet), Patsy Kelly (Mama Sweet), Rex Holman (Oregano), Grace Gaynor (Wendy Thyme), Bobby Jordan (Marge), Jack Bernardi (Del Floria), James Milhollin (Cardaman).

"The Pieces of Fate Affair" (2-24-67): Sharon Farrell (Jacqueline Midcault), Theo Marcuse (Ellipsis Zark), Charles Seel (Uncle Charlie), Grayson Hall (Judith Merle), Richard Collier (Buck).

"The Matterhorn Affair" (3-3-67): Bill Dana (Marvin Klump), Norma Chase (Heather Klump), Oscar Beregi, Jr. (Backstreet), Vito Scotti (Beirut).

"The Hot Number Affair" (3-10-67): Sonny Bono (Jerry), Cher (Ramona), George Tobias (Harry Parkington), Ned Glass (Harry Signh), Richard Angarola (John Hardy), Bella Bruck (apartment manager).

"The When in Roma Affair" (3-17-67): Julie Sommars (Darlene), Cesare Danova (Cesare Guardia), Kathleen Freeman (Mrs. Sparks), Than Wyenn (Bruno), Sid Haig (Vito), Stuart Nisbit (Sparks).

"The Apple-A-Day Affair" (3-24-67): Robert Emhardt (Col. Picks), Jeannie Riley (Nina Lillette), Gil Lamb (Daddy Jo), Harry Swoger (Sheriff Skully), D'Urville Martin (Gardner).

"The Five Daughters Affair" (3-31-67 & 4-7-67): Joan Crawford (Amanda), Curt Jergens (Carl Von Kesser), Terry-Thomas (Constable), Telly Savalas (Count Fanzini), Herbert Lom (Randolph), Diane McBain (Margo), Danielle DeMetz (Yvonne), Kim Darby (Sandy True), Jill Ireland (Imogene), Irene Tsu (Reikko), Philip Ahn (Sazami Kyushn).

"The Cap and Gown Affair" (4-14-67): Henry Jones (Timothy Dwight), Carol Shelyne (Minerva Dwight), Melanie Alexander (Patricia), Larry D. Mann (Jonathan Trumbull), Martin Koslech (Dr. Neary), Zalman King (Haymish), Tom Palmer (Agent 24).

"The Summit-Five Affair" (9-11-67): Lloyd Bochner (Gerald Strothers), Albert Dekker (Harry Deldon), Susanne Cramer (Helga Deniken), Don Chastain.

"The Test-Tube Killer Affair" (9-18-67): Christopher Jones (Greg Martin), Lynn Loring (Christine Hobson), Martin Koslech (Porter), Paul Lukas (Dr. Stroller), Milton Parsons (waiter), D'Urville Martin (No. 5), John Nealson (No. 7), Lyn Peters (Mrs. Lamb).

(MAN FROM U. N. C. L. E. cont.)
"The 'J' for Judas Affair" (9-25-
67): Broderick Crawford (Mark Tenza),
Chad Everett (Adam Tenza), Delphi
Laurence (Olivia), Kevin Hagen (Da-
rien), Claude Woolman ('J').
  "The Prince of Darkness Affair"
(10-2-67): Carol Lynley (Annie), Brad-
ford Dillman (Luther), Lola Albright
(Azalea), John Carradine (Third-Way
Priest), Julie London (Laura Sebastion),
John Dehner (Dr. Kharmusi), Roy Jen-
son (Carl), H. M. Wynant (Aksoy Bro-
thers), Arthur Malet (White Hunter),
Kathleen Freeman (Mom), Barbara
Moore (Lisa), Robert Karnes (Ship's
Captain), Sid Haig (Alex), Lyzanne
Ladau (white-haired girl), Thordis
Brandt (Miss Zalamar).
  "The Master's Touch Affair" (10-
16-67): Jack Lord (Pharos Mandor),
Nehemiah Persoff (Stephan Valandros),
Leslie Parrish (Leslie Welling).
  "The THRUSH Roulette Affair"
(10-23-67): Michael Rennie (Barnaby
Partridge), Charles Drake (Taggart
Coleman), Nobu McCarthy (Monica),
Robert Ellenstein (Dr. Ieato), Eric
Feldary (Kramer), Charles H. Radilac
(Ambassador Vanderloon), Jacqueline
Dalya (Countess), Jean Durand (crou-
pier).
  "The Deadly Quest Affair" (10-30-
67): Darren McGavin (Viktor Karmak),
Marlyn Mason (Sheila Van Tilson), Ti-
mothy Carey (Stephan), Peter Bourne,
Bob Braiver.
  "The Fiery Angel Affair" (11-6-
67): Madlyn Rhue (Angela Abaca), Per-
ry Lopez (Carlos Abaca), Joseph Siro-
la (Paco), Victor Lundin (Vinay), Rodol-
fo Hoyos (Martine).
  "The Survival School Affair" (11-
20-67): Richard Beymer (Harry Wil-
liams), Chris Robinson (John Saimes),
Charles McGraw (Jules Cutter), Susan
Odin (Melissa Hargrove), Ray Girardin
(Andrew Hague).
  "The Gurnius Affair" (11-27-67):
George Macready (Zorcan Gurnius),
Judy Carne (Terry Cook), Will Kuluva
(Dr. Hans Von Etske), Joseph Ruskin
(Brown), Rudolph Anders (Hartmann),
Peter Arno (technician).
  "The Man from THRUSH Affair"
(12-4-67): John Larch (Dr. Killman),
Barbara Luna (Marnya), Mario Alcaide
(Marius), Robert Wolders (Andreas
Petros).
  "The Maze Affair" (12-18-67):
William Marshall (Dr. James Febray),
Anna Capri (Abbe), Laurence Mon-
taigne (Barnes), Barry Cahill (Cle-

mons), Ralph Moody (old man), Charles
Mayer.
  "The Deep Six Affair" (12-25-67):
Alfred Ryder (Commander Kohler), Di-
ana Van Der Vlis (Laura Adams), Pe-
ter Bromilow (Brian Morton), Dale Ish-
imoto (Yu), Gil Stuart (sub captain),
Peter Forster (uniformed guard).
  "The Seven Wonders of the World
Affair" (1-8-68 & 1-15-68): Leslie
Nielson (Gen. Maximilian Harmon), Elea-
nor Parker (Margitta), Barry Sullivan
(Robert Kingsley), Tony Bill (Steven
Garrow), Mark Richman (Mr. Webb),
Daniel O'Herlihy (Prof. David Garrow),
Albert Paulsen (Dr. Kurt Erikson),
Ruth Warwick (Mrs. Garrow), Hugh
Marlowe (Grant), Inger Stratton (Anna
Erikson), Richard Bull (Capt. Geiser),
Amy Thomson (Miss Carla), Anella
Varsett (Dr. Naomi Fisher), Edgar
Stehli (Veeth), David Hurst (Jan Vano-
vech), Arthur Hanson (Paul Mackie),
Barbara Moore (Lisa Rogers).

MASTERPIECE THEATRE.
  "Cold Comford Farm" (1-8-72):
Fay Compton (Aunt Ada), Sarah Badel
(Flora Poste), Alastair Sim (Amos).

MATINEE THEATRE.
  "Mr. Krane" (1-3-56): Sir Cecil
Hardwicke (Mr. Krane), John Hoyt (Har-
ry), Mary LaRoche (Elaine), Peter Han-
sen (Ken), Chris Alcaide (Norris).
  "The House of Seven Gables" (4-
6-56): John Carradine (Clifford), Mar-
shall Thompson (Holgrave), Helen Wal-
lace (Hepzibah), Alan Hewitt (Judge Jaf-
fray), Carlyn Craig (Phoebe), William
Lechner (Matthew Maule), Ray Spiker
(Hangman), Steve Carruthers (Lt. Go-
vernor).
  "Greybeards and Witches" (5-1-
56): Agnes Moorhead (Mrs. Barnes),
Cathy O'Donnell (Velna), Judy Nugent
(Emma), Louis Letteiri (Billy).
  "The Bottle Imp" (5-22-56).
  "The Fall of the House of Usher"
(8-6-56): Marshall Thompson (David
Grant), Tom Tryon (Roderick Usher),
Eduardo Ciannelli (Doctor).
  "Gramercy's Ghost" (9-7-56): Sa-
rah Churchill.
  "The Tell-Tale Heart" (11-6-56):
John Abbott.
  "Dracula" (11-23-56): John Carra-
dine (Count Dracula).
  "The Man in Half Moon Street" (1-
57).
  "Frankenstein" (2-5-57): Primo
Carnera (Frankenstein's monster).
  "One" (2-7-57): Everett Sloane,

Paul Langton.
"The Others" (2-15-57): Sarah
Churchill (Nina Varden), Geoffrey Toone
(Lorrain Daubiny), Doris Lloyd (Mrs.
Grose), Tommy Kirk (Miles), Karen
Sue Trent (Flora).
"Dr. Jekyll and Mr. Hyde" (3-8-
57): Douglas Montgomery (Henry Jek-
yll/Mr. Hyde), Lisa Daniels (Polly
Bannon), Chet Stratton (Utterson), Lums-
den Hare (Poole), Patrick Macnee (Pe-
ter).
"The Cask of Amontillado" (7-16-
57): Eduardo Ciannelli.
"The Invisible Man" (8-8-57):
Geoffrey Toone (Dr. Howard Kemp),
Chet Stratton (Griffin), Angela Thorn-
ton (Addy), Molly Roden (Mrs. Bunting),
Terence de Marney (Teddy).
"Mysterious Disappearance" (9-
19-57).
"Daniel Webster and the Sea Ser-
pant" (11-29-57): John Carradine.
"The Broom and the Groom" (12-
6-57): Russell Arms, Peggy King.
"Dark of the Moon" (12-13-57).
"The Suicide Club" (2-25-58):
John Abbott.
"Mrs. Moonlight" (3-7-58): Mar-
garet O'Brien.
"Death Takes a Holiday" (4-6-58):
Gene Raymond, Janice Rule.
"The Canterville Ghost" (4-15-
58): Ernest Truex, Sylvia Field.
"It Came from Out of Town" (4-
30-58).
"Angel Street" (5-9-58): Vincent
Price (Jack), Judith Evelyn (Bella),
Leo G. Carroll (Insp. Rough).
"Button, Button" (5-29-58).

McMILLAN AND WIFE.
"The Devil, You Say" (10-21-73):
Rock Hudson (Commissioner Stuart
McMillan), Susan St. James (Sally Mc-
Millan), Nancy Walker (Mildred), John
Schuck (Sgt. Enright), Keenan Wynn
(Zagmeyer), Werner Klemperer (Dr.
Bleeker), Robert Hooks (Sam Burke),
Barbara Colby (Linda Cosmac), John
Fiedler (Sykes), Joshua Shelley (Erwin
Blake).

MEDIC.
"Flash of Darkness" (8-29-55):
Richard Boone (Dr. Konrad Styner).

MEN INTO SPACE. 1959-60. William
Lundigan (Col. Edward McCauley),
Joyce Taylor (Mary McCauley), Co-
rey Allen (Lt. Johnny Baker), Kem
Dibbs (Capt. Harvey Sparkman).
"Moon Probe" (9-30-59): Angie

Dickinson (Mary McCauley), Paul Burke
(Maj. Billy Williams), Charles Herbert
(Pete McCauley), Paul Richards (USAF
Relations Officer).
Title unknown (10-7-59): Joe Ma-
ross (Maj. Patrick Donon), Charles
Herbert (Pete McCauley), Don Oreck
(Maj. Mason Trett), Karl Swenson (Sen.
Jim Sloane).
"Building a Space Station" (10-21-
59): Don Dubbins (Lt. Smith), Christo-
pher Dark (Capt. Forsythe), Nancy Had-
ley (Paula Smith), Bartlett Robinson
(Gen. Hicks), Don Kennedy (Capt. Mi-
chaels), Jack Mann (Major Hall).
"Water Tank Rescue" (10-28-59):
John Shepodd (Lt. Rick Gordon), Joan
Taylor (Carol Gordon), Paul Langton
(Major Warnecke), Gar Moore (Capt.
Hal Roberts).
"Lost Missile" (11-4-59): Harry
Townes (Dr. William Thyssen), Marcia
Henderson.
"Moonquake" (11-11-59): Arthur
Franz (Capt. Tom Farrow), Denver
Pyle (Dr. Peter Riber).
"Space Trap" (11-18-59): Peter
Hansen (Dr. Charles Cooper), Robert
Gist (Capt. Dan Freer), Russ Conway
(Gen. Devon), Dallas Mitchell (Lt. Pat
Warren), Ronald Foster (Lt. Neil Tem-
pleton).
"Asteroid" (11-25-59): Bill Wil-
liams (Dr. Stacy Croydon), Herbert
Rudley (Dr. Waring), Joyce Meadows
(Lynn Croydon).
Title unknown (12-2-59).
Title unknown (12-9-59): John
Sutton (Lt. Gen. Malcolm Terry), Lance
Fuller (Capt. Bob Stark), Robert Clarke
(Maj. Gibbie Gibson), Donna Martell
(Molly Gibson).
"First Woman on the Moon" (12-
16-59): Nancy Gates (Renza Hale), H. M.
Wynant (Major Hale), Tyler McVey (Maj.
Gen. Norgath), Harry Jackson (Major
Markey).
Title unknown (12-23-59): Keith
Larsen (Jim Nichols), Whit Bissell
(Oliver Farrar).
Title unknown (12-30-59): Warren
Stevens (Dr. Randolph), Simon Oakland
(Dr. Horton), John Milford (Dr. Hamil-
ton), Guy Stockwell (Lt. Murphy).
Title unknown (1-6-60): James
Drury (Maj. Nick Alborg), Philip Terry
(Col. Stoner), Murray Hamilton (Lt.
Col. Bill Alborg).
Title unknown (1-13-60): Fred
Beir (Lt. Art Frey), Jack Ging (Lt.
Jerry Rutledge).
"A Handful of Hours" (1-20-60):
William Schallert (Dr. Orrin), Mark

(MEN INTO SPACE cont.) Dana (Dr. Prescott), Peter Baldwin (Lt. Bob Kelly).

Title unknown (1-27-60): Robert Reed (Russell Smith), Anne Benton (Julie Wills), Byron Morrow (Glen Stillwell), John Garrett (Capt. Williams), Don Edmonds (Lt. Eden).

Title unknown (2-3-60): John Howard (Dr. Rowland Kennedy), Paul Comi (Maj. John Arnold), Donald May (Capt. Doug Bowers), Lillian Hamilton (Mrs. Bennett).

Title unknown (2-10-60): Harry Lauter (Jimmy Manx), Lisa Gaye (Joyce Lynn), Ray Montgomery (Paul Carlson).

"Mooncloud" (2-17-60): Robert Vaughn (Perry Holcomb), Allison Hayes (Mandy Holcomb), Douglas Dick (Harold Carter).

"Contraband" (3-2-60): James Coburn (Dr. Narry), Robert Osterloh (Dr. Rice), Robert Christopher (Dr. Bromfield), Don Ross (Dr. Orr).

Title unknown (3-9-60): Carol Ohmart (Muriel Gallagher), Dennis McCarthy (Dr. Caleb Fiske), Manning Ross (Dr. Torrance Alexander), William Lechner (Maj. Paul Ellis).

Title unknown (3-16-60): Peter Adams (Dr. Arnold Rawdin), Tod Andrews (Lt. Col. Vern Driscoll).

Title unknown (3-23-60): John Bryant (Major Bowers), Paul Carr (Capt. Swanson), Tyler McVey (Gen. Norgrath), Joe Flynn (Carey Stoddart).

Title unknown (3-30-60): Gerald Mohr (Dr. Bernard Bush), Harry Carey, Jr. (Major Boythe), Mort Mills (Dr. George Coldwell).

Title unknown (4-6-60): John Lupton (Dr. Guthrie Durlock), Joan Marshall (Lorrie Sigmund).

Title unknown (4-13-60): John Hudson (Capt. Kyle Rennish), Mimi Gibson (Jenny), Sally Bliss (Dr. Alice Roe).

Title unknown (4-20-60): Myron Healey (Maj. Steven Hawkes), Charles Cooper (Dr. Thomas Ward), Ralph Taeger (Cpl. Fred Jones).

Title unknown (4-27-60): Russ Conway (Gen. Devon), Edward C. Platt (Dr. Luraski), Alan Dexter (Gen. Brereton).

Title unknown (5-4-60): Donald Woods (Col. Jim Benson), Anne Neyland (Anne Benson), John Baer (Major Hodges).

Title unknown (5-11-60): Gene Nelson (Maj. Charles Randolph), James Best (Lt. John Leonard), Sally Fraser (Donna Talbot).

Title unknown (5-25-60): John Van Dreelan (Col. Tolchek), Jeremy Slate (Capt. Jim Nicholls), Jack Hogan (Major Ingram), Don Eitner (Maj. Ralph Devers), Tyler McVey (Gen. Norgath).

Title unknown (6-1-60): Dan Barton (Major Jackson), Richard Emory (Dr. Parker), Don Burnett (Capt. Dick Jackson), Robin Lory (Harriet).

Title unknown (8-17-60): Werner Klemperer (Major Kralenko), Edgar Barrier (Russian General), Skip Ward (Capt. Webb), Eric Feldary (Col. Alexandrov), Preston Hanson (Capt. Rumbough), Larry Thor (Maj. Gen. Mallon), Jay Warren (Russian Captain).

Title unknown (8-24-60): Paul Picerni (Bob King), Harp McGuire (Maj. Tex Nolan), Nelson Leigh (Gen. Adams).

"The Sun Never Sets" (8-31-60): John Sutton (Vice Marshal Terry), David Frankham (Neil Bedford Jones), Robin Hughes (Capt. Tom Hetherford), Mavis Dean (Lady Alice).

"Mystery Satellite" (9-7-60): Brett King (Maj. Tim O'Leary), Charles Maxwell (Col. Frank Bartlett), Edward Mallory (Capt. Don Miller), Mike Steele (Maj. Vic Enright), Harry Ellerbe (Maj. Gen. Albright), Mel Marshall (Sgt. Tucker), George Diestel (Maj. Bob Williams).

"Flight to the Red Planet" (1960): Marshall Thompson (Major Devery).

MOMENT OF FEAR. 1960.

"The Golden Deed" (7-1-60): Macdonald Carey (Jim Mellanby), Robert Redford, Nina Foch.

"Conjure Wife" (7-8-60): Larry Blyden.

"Fire by Night" (7-22-60): Mark Richman (Harry Jordan), Fay Spain (Marie Jordan), Phyllis Hill (Ruth Minton), Frank Overton (psychiatrist).

"Total Recall" (7-29-60): Inger Stevens (Nancy Derringer), Leslie Nielsen (Norman Derringer), Neva Patterson (Olivia Fairchild), Robert F. Simon (Dr. Lenbruck).

"The Third Party" (8-12-60): E. G. Marshall (B. J. Benedict), James Gregory (Sam Phillips).

"If I Should Die" (8-19-60): Donald Harron (Paul Baxter), Tim O'Connor (MacKay), Olive Deering (Florence Knapp), Scott McKay.

"The Accomplice" (8-26-60): Nehemiah Persoff, Geoffrey Horne, Will Kuluva, Robert Dowdell, Lilia Skala.

"Cage of Air" (9-9-60): Laraine Day, Robert Lansing, Meg Mundy.

MONSTER SQUAD, THE. 1976-77. Fred Grandy (Walt), Henry Polic II (Dracula), Buck Kartalian (Bruce W. Wolf), Michael Lane (Frank N. Stein), Paul Smith (Pff. McMac Mac).

MOONBASE 3. British 1973. Donald Houston (David Caulder), Ralph Bates, Christine Bradwill.

MORK AND MINDY. 1978-83). Robin Williams (Mork), Pam Dawber (Mindy McConnell), Conrad Janis (Fred McConnell), Elizabeth Kerr (Cora Hudson), Tom Poston (Mr. Bickley), Robert Donner (Exidor), Jay Thomas (Remo DaVinci) 79-, Gina Hecht (Jeanie DaVinci) 79-, Jim Staahl (Nelson) 79-, Ralph James (Orson), Shelley Fabares (Cathy McConnell) 80-, Jonathan Winters (Mearth) 81-.

MOST DEADLY GAME. "Witches' Sabbath" (10-17-70): Yvette Mimieux (Vanessa Smith), Ralph Bellamy (Ethan Arcana), George Maharis (Jonathan Croft), Jill Haworth (Lydia Grey), Richard Mulligan (Jordan), Barry Atwater (Harold Byers), Michael Baseleon (Milosz Patecky), Herb Armstrong (Dr. Halder), Martin Braddock (Ben Waterson), Jennie Blackton (Angie), Barbara Leigh (Karen), Sue Taylor (Gloria), Melora Conway (Mrs. Bridges).

MR. & MRS. DRACULA. Pilot (9-5-80): Dick Shawn (Vladimir Dracula), Carol Lawrence (Sonia Dracula), Gail Mayron (Minna Dracula), Anthony Battaglia (Sonny Dracula), Barry Gordon (Anton), Johnny Haymer (voice of Gregor), Rick Aviles (Mario), Robert Ellerbee, Ken Olfson, Susan Garia, Vicki Belmonte, Dick Wieand, Robert Ackerman.

MR. ED. 1960-66. Alan Young (Wilbur Post), Donnie Hines (Carol Post), Larry Keating (Roger Addison) 60-63, Edna Skinner (Kay Addison), Leon Ames (Gordon Kirkwood), Florence MacMichael (Winnie Kirkwood), Barry Kelly (Mr. Carlisle).

MR. MERLIN. 1981-82. Barnard Hughes (Max Merlin), Clark Brandon (Zachary Rogers), Elaine Joyce (Alex), Jonathan Prince (Leo).

MR. TERRIFIC. 1967. Stephen Strimpell (Stanley Beemish/Mr. Terrific), Dick Gautier (Hal), John McGiver

(Barton J. Reed), Paul Smith (Hanley Trent).

MUNSTERS, THE. 1964-66. Fred Gwynne (Herman Munster), Yvonne DeCarlo (Lily Munster), Al Lewis (Grandpa), Butch Patrick (Eddie Munster), Beverly Owen (Marilyn Munster) 64-65, Pat Priest (Marilyn Munster) 65-66.

"Munster Masquerade" (9-24-64): Linden Chiles (Tom Daly), Mabel Albertson (Agnes Daly), Frank Wilcox (Albert Daly), Lurene Tuttle (Mrs. Morton).

"My Fair Munster" (10-1-64): John Fiedler (Warren Bloom), Claire Carleton (Yolanda Cribbens), Edward Mallory (Jack).

"A Walk on the Mild Side" (10-8-64): Cliff Norton (Police Chief Harris), Larry Blake (desk sergeant), Barry Kelley (Commissioner Ludlow), Paul Baxley (purse snatcher), Harrison Lewis (drunk).

"Rock-A-Bye Munster" (10-15-64): Paul Lynde (Dr. Edward Dudley), Marilyn Lovell (Mrs. Dudley), Sid Melton (Diamond Jim).

"Pike's Pique" (10-22-64): Richard Deacon (Bordan T. Pike), Jane Withers (Fanny Pike).

"Low-Cal Munster" (10-29-64): Dick Winslow (Seymour Farber), Monty Margetts (Anna Farber), Paul Lynde (Dr. Dudley), Caryl Rowe (Nurse Fairchild).

"Tin Can Man" (11-4-64): Arch Johnson (Taggert), James Griffith (Balding).

"Herman the Great" (11-12-64): John Hubbard (Duke Ramsey), Joseph Mell (Hansen), Johnny Silver (Jerry).

"Knock Wood, Here Comes Charly" (11-19-64): Mike Mazurki (Leo 'Knuckles' Kraus), Jean Willes (Mrs. Cartwright).

"Autumn Croakus" (11-26-64): Linda Watkins (Lydia Gardner).

"The Midnight Ride of Herman Munster" (12-3-64): Lee Krieger (Al), Maxie Rosenbloom (Big Louie), Val Avery (Marty), Lennie Weinrib (Freddie), Joe Devlin (Police Sergeant).

"Sleeping Cutie" (12-10-64): John Hoyt (George Spelvin), Gavin MacLeod (Paul Newmar), Grant Williams (Dick Prince).

"Family Portrait" (12-17-64): Harvey Korman (Lennie Bates), Fred Beir (Chip Johnson).

"Grandpa Leaves Home" (12-24 64): Robert Strauss (night club manager),

(MUNSTERS cont.) Bill Dugan (fellow), Iris Adrian (woman), Nicky Blair (friend), Bill Couch (man), Sarah Jane Ross (dancer).

"Herman's Rival" (12-31-64): Lee Bergere (Ramon), Karen Flynn (Louisa), Irwin Charone (Lester), Chet Stratton (Mr. Haggerty), Tommy Farrell (assistant).

"Grandpa's Call of the Wild" (1-7-65): Don Haggerty (Haskell), Ed Peck (Willard), Curt Barrett (fisherman), Mike Ragan (1st ranger), Bing Russell (2nd ranger).

"All Star Munster" (1-14-65): Frank Maxwell (Coach Denham), Robert Easton (Moose Mallory), Gene Blakely (Jerry), Pat Buttram (Pop Mallory).

"If a Martian Answers, Hang Up" (1-21-65): Ronnie Dapo (Roger), Pat Rosson (Walt), Dort Clark (Mr. Andrews).

"Eddie's Nickname" (1-28-65): Paul Lynde (Dr. Dudley), Alice Backes (Nurse Fairchild).

"Bats of a Feather" (2-4-65): Gilbert Green (Mr. Brubaker), Alvy Moore (Dr. Grant), Barbara Babcock (Miss Guthrie), Tom McBride (Mr. Hazlett).

"Don't Bank on Herman" (2-11-65): Maurice Manson (Mr. Grover), Mousie Garner (Fingers), Jack Bernardi (Scotty), Pitt Herbert (Williams), Audrey Swanson (teller).

"Dance with Me, Herman" (2-18-65): Don Rickles (Doc Havemeyer), Joyce Jameson (Miss Valentine).

"Follow That Munster" (2-25-65): Ken Lynch (Mr. Kempner), Doris Singleton (Mrs. Andrews).

"Love Locked Out" (3-4-65): Elliot Reid (Dr. Baxter), Norman Grabowski (Winthrop), Bryan O'Byrne (Calvin).

"Come Back, Little Googie" (3-11-65): Bill Mumy (Googie Miller), Russ Conway (Mr. Miller).

"Far Out Munster" (3-18-65): Alex Gerry (Pops Murdock), Kelton Garwood (hermit).

"Movie Star Munster" (4-1-65): Jesse White (J. R. Finlater), Walter Burke (Alfred Swanson).

"Munsters on the Move" (3-25-65): Bert Freed (Dennison), Joey Scott (Jerry), Lenore Shanewise (Elmire), Jan Arvan (Poppa), Bella Brook (Momma), Charles Seel (elderly man), Nydia Westman (elderly woman), Alma Murphy (Susan).

"Herman the Rookie" (4-8-65): Leo Durocher (himself), Elroy Hirsch

(himself), Gene Darfler (Charlie).

"Country Club Munster" (4-15-65): Woodrow Parfrey (Petrie), Dan Tobin (Stubbs), J. Edward McKinley (Murdock), Al Checco (bartender), Johnny Jacobs (TV Announcer).

"Love Comes to Mockingbird Heights" (4-22-65): Charles Robinson (Alan Benson), Richard Hale (Uncle Gilbert), Duncan McLeod (Ben).

"Mummy Munster" (4-29-65): Philip Ober (Dr. Wilkerson), Pat Harrington, Jr. (Thatcher).

"Lily Munster, Girl Model" (5-6-65): John Alvin (Mr. Franklin), Roger C. Carmel (Laszlo Brastoff), Lois Roberts (Irving), Sally Morris (Colette), Sondra Matesky (Millicent), Nina Shipman (girl), Kimberly Beck (little girl).

"Munster the Magnificent" (5-13-65).

"Herman's Happy Valley" (5-20-65): John Hoyt (Barney Walters), Bartlett Robinson (Curtis), Richard Reeves (Gil Craig).

"Hot Rod Herman" (5-27-65): Henry Beckman (Leadfoot Baylor), Brian Corcoran (Sandy Baylor), Eddie Donno (mechanic).

"Herman's Raise" (6-4-65): Benny Rubin (Tom Fong), John Carradine (Mr. Gateman).

"Yes, Galen, There Is a Herman" (6-10-65): Brian Nash (Galen Stewart), Walter Brooke (John Stewart), Marge Redmond (Mrs. Stewart), Harvey Korman (Dr. Leinbach).

"Dancing Bear" (9-25-65): Gene Blakely (Leo), Michael Petit (Charlie Pike), Bill Quinn (White).

"Herman, the Master Spy" (9-23-65): Val Avery (Commissar), Leonard Yorr (Valesy), John Lawrence (Gregor), Edward Mallory (young man), Henry Hunter (older man), Bella Bruck (Ninotchka), Howard Wendell (John), Robert Miller (Roger), John Zaremba (Charlie), Jon Silo (Russian teletypist).

"Bronco Bustin' Munster" (9-30-65): Donald 'Red' Barry (Ted), William Phipps (Hank), Dick Lane (announcer), Leonard P. Geer (cowpoke).

"Herman Munster, Shutterbug" (10-7-65): Joe De Santis (Lou), Herbie Faye (Rod), Robert Morgan (Officer), Jefferson County (Daniel Boone), Alma Murphy (little old lady).

"Herman, Coach of the Year" (10-14-65).

"Happy 100th Anniversary" (10-21-65).

"Operation Herman" (10-28-65): Dayton Allen (Dr. Willoughby), Don Kee-

fer (Dr. Elliott), Marge Redmond (Miss Hazlet), Justin Smith (Doctor), Bill Quinn (attendant).
"Lily's House Guest" (11-4-65): Charles Bateman (Chester Skinner).
"Herman's Amnesia" (11-11-65): Willis Bouchey (Judge), Frank Maxwell (desk sergeant).
"Prince Charming" (11-18-65): Roger Perry (Ted Bradley).
"Herman's Driving License" (11-25-65): Charlie Ruggles (Charlie Wiggens).
"Will Success Spoil Herman Munster?" (12-9-65): Gary Owens (Dick Willet).
"Spot Is Missing" (12-16-65): J. Edward McKinley (Mayor Handley), Warren Parker (Ted), Bob Harvey (photographer), Helen Kleeb (woman), Jimmy Joyce (reporter).
"Morgan's Treasure" (12-23-65).
"Eddie and the Bully" (12-30-65): Jackie Minty (Mack McGinty), Bryan O'Byrne (Uriah), Chet Stratton (Clyde Thornton).
"Gambling Fever" (1-6-66): Barton MacLane (Big Roy), Joyce Jameson (Lou), Sammy Shore (Vic), Charlie Callas (Lefty).
"Herman, Disfigured" (1-13-66): Dom Deluise (Dr. Dudley), Joan Swift (nurse).
"Indian Herman" (1-20-66): Ned Romero (Wonga), Len Lesser (Manikoo), Felix Lochner (Powatuma), Sally Frei (Indian girl).
"Lily's Beauty Shop" (1-28-66): Eliva Allman (Mrs. Harkness), Charles Lane (Holmer), Adele Claire (Secretary), Mary Mitchel (Dorothea Harkness).
"Grandpa's Missing Wife" (2-3-66): Jane Withers (Pamela Thornton), Douglas Evans (Clarence).
"Cursed Ring" (2-10-66): Paul Reed (Henry J. Fregosi), Louise Glenn (telephone operator), Joan Swift (secretary).
"Zombo" (2-17-66): Louis Nye (Zombo), Digby Wolfe (director).
"Herman Munster, Poet" (2-24-66): Chet Stratton (Clyde Thornton), Joan Staley (Clara Mason).
"Tone Deaf Eddie" (3-3-66): John Carradine (Mr. Gateman).
"Missing Link Munster" (3-10-66): Harvey Korman (Prof. Fagenspahen), George Petrie (Prof. Hansen), Richard Poston (Doctor).
"Johan" (3-17-66): John Abbott (Dr. Frankenstein IV), Helen Kleeb (manager's wife), Forrest Lewis (mo-

tel manager).
"Boris the Robot" (3-24-66): Rory Stevens (Boris), Wendy Cutler (Sally).
"Fair Deal Dan" (3-31-66): Frank Gorshin (Fair Deal Dan), Rian Garrick (Corbett), Pat McCaffrie (Spengler).
"The Dragula" (4-7-66).
"Fraternity House" (4-14-66): David Macklin (Phil), Bonnie Franklin (Janice), Ken Osmond (John), Michael Blodgett (Jim), Vicki Fee (girl).
"Herman's Car Crash" (4-21-66): Dorothy Green (Mrs. Kingsley), Jerome Cowan (Ted Thatcher), Monroe Arnold (director).
"An Average American Family" (5-12-66): Willis Bouchey (Bradley), Pat Woodell (Miss Thompson).

MY FAVORITE MARTIAN. 1963-66. Ray Walston (Martin O'Hara), Bill Bixby (Tim O'Hara), Pamela Britton (Lorelei Brown), Alan Hewitt (Detective Bill Brennan), J. Pat O'Mally (Mr. Burns), Roy Engle (Police Captain).

MY LIVING DOLL. 1964-65. Bob Cummings (Dr. Bob McDonald), Julie Newmar (Rhoda), Henry Beckman (Dr. Carl Miller), Jack Mullaney (Peter Robinson), Doris Dowling (Irene).

MY MOTHER THE CAR. 1965-66. Jerry Van Dyke (Dave Crabtree), Maggie Pierce (Barbara Crabtree), Avery Schreiber (Captain Bernard Mancini), Ann Sothern (Voice of Mother), Cindy Eilbacher (Cindy Crabtree), Randy Whipple (Randy Crabtree).

MY PARTNER, THE GHOST. 1973. Kenneth Cope (Marty Hopkirk), Mike Pratt (Jeff Randall), Annette Andre (Jean Hopkirk), Ivor Dean (Inspector Large).

MYSTERY!.
"Dr. Jekyll and Mr. Hyde" (1-6-81 & 1-13-81): David Hemmings (Dr. Henry Jekyll/Mr. Edward Hyde), Lisa Harrow (Ann), Ian Bannen (Oliver Utterson), Clive Swift (Hastie Lanyon), Diana Dors (Kate Winterton), Gretchen Franklin (Cook), Toyal Wilcox (Janet), Roland Curram (Poule), Terry Downes (prisoner), Roger Davidson (Bradshaw), Anna Faye (Mary), Anthony Carrick (prison governor), Kenteas Brine (argyll prostitute), Tim Calver (argyll pimp), Sheelah Willcocks (Mrs. Willoughby), Sevilla Delofski (Fifi), Jane Slaughter (Gwen),

(MYSTERY! cont.) Gaye Brown (Diane),
Ashlen Knight (boy prostitute), Angela
Catherall (Dollymop).

MYSTERY AND IMAGINATION. British 1966. David Buck (Richard
Beckett, Host).
    "The Lost Stradivarius" (1-29-
66): Jeremy Brett, David Brett, David
Buck, Joyce Heron, Angela Morant,
Patricia Garwood, Edward Brayshaw.
    "The Body Snatcher" (2-5-66):
Trevor Baxter, Michael Johnson, James
Cossing, Ian Holm, Ann Ogden, Dermot Tyohy, Michael Gwynn.
    "The Fall of the House of Usher"
(2-12-66): David Buck, Susannah York,
Mary Miller, Denholm Elliott, Oliver
McGreevy, Dudley Jones.
    "The Open Door" (2-19-66): Jack
Hawkins, Rachel Gurney, Jill Meredith,
Henry Beltran, Debbie Bowen, Geoffrey
Sumner.
    "The Tractate Middoth" (2-26-66):
David Buck, Norman Scace, Jerry Verno, Tim Preece, Giles Block, Edwin
Finn, Cyril Renison, Helen Ford.
    "Lost Hearts" (3-5-66): Richard
Pearson, Freddie Jones, Megs Jenkins,
David Dodimead, Francis Thompson,
Roy Young, Darryl Read.
    "The Canterville Ghost" (3-12-
66): Bruce Forsyth, Doris Rogers,
John Falconer, David Stoll, David
Bauer, Libby Morris, Angela Thorne,
Colin Pilditch.
    "Room Thirteen" (10-22-66):
David Buck, David Battley, George
Woodbridge, Joss Ackland, Tessa Wyatt,
Carl Bernard.
    "The Beckoning Shadow" (10-29-
66): David Buck, Toni Palmer, Edwin
Richfield, Maureen Pryor, John Ronane,
Larry Noble, Julia McCarthy, Renny
Lister, Geoffrey Palmer.
    "The Flying Dragon" (11-5-66):
David Buck, Ann Bell, John Bryans,
John Phillips, Derek Smith, John Moffatt, Aubrey Morris.
    "Carmilla" (11-12-66): Natasha
Payne, Joseph O'Connor, Roy Marsden,
Laurél Mather, Sonia Dresdel, Terence
Bayler.
    "The Phantom Lover" (11-19-66):
David Buck, Robert Hardy, Virginia
McKenna, John Sharp, Richard Arthure,
Anthony Lindford.

MYSTERY SHOW. 1960. Walter Slezak (Host), Vincent Price (Host).
    "The Machine Calls It Murder"
(5-29-60): Larry Blyden (Peter Meineke), Everett Sloane (Lt. Malotte,

Betsy Von Furstenberg (Susan Jerome),
Peter Walker (Jerome), Lee Patrick
(Mrs. Endicott), Peg La Centra (Mrs.
Denton).
    "Thunder of Silence" (6-5-60):
James Whitmore (Philip Selby), John
Hoyt (Arnold Bellson), Sandy Kenyon
(Eddie), Jean Carson (drunk woman).
    "Summer Hero" (6-12-60): Zachary Scott (Damian Shea), Patty McCormack (Dotty Halsey), Ruth Ford (Julie
McCormick), Bobby Driscoll (Fred
Forbes), Paul Langton (Dr. Walter
Halsey), Florida Friebus (Lois Halsey),
Fred Beir (Bob Field).
    "Dark Possession" (6-19-60):
Diana Lynn (Charlotte Bell Wheeler),
Anne Seymour (Emily Bell), Marion
Ross (Ann Bell), Berry Kroeger (Gen.
Bell), W. H. Bassett (Dr. Roger Waring).
    "Fear Is the Parent" (6-26-60):
Mona Freeman (Avery Dow), Arthur
Franz (Simon Dow), Tracey Roberts
(Buff), Barbara Stuart (Claire), Nancy
Rennick (Louise), Chet Stratton (Whitman), Ross Elliott (Dr. Reinecke), Fay
Roope (Mr. Dow), Britt Osmond (Paul).
    "Murder Me Nicely" (7-3-60):
Everett Sloane (Alfred Emerson), Mark
Goddard (Peter Montopolis), Doreen
Lang (Marge Montopolis), Sylvia Field
(Mrs. Emerson), Hugh Sanders (Lt.
Hallaran), Yvonne Craig (Carolyn),
Henry Bernard (Sanford), Jack Stratton
(boy), Jerry Mobley (boy).
    "Dead Man's Walk" (7-10-60):
Robert Culp (Abel), Abby Dalton (Karen
Prescott), Bruce Gordon (Lt. Spear),
Arthur Batanides (Manny), Ellen Corby
(Maria), Paul Mazursky (Danny).
    "The Last Six Blocks" (7-17-60):
Dane Clark (Dr. Joseph Teague), Margarita Cordova (Esperanza), Jerome
Cowan (Harry Holmes), Berry Kroeger
(Bermudez), Pepe Hern (Mercado), Helen LeBerthon (Carla), Howard Ledig
(Greyson), John Hackett (Andrew Glenn),
Tony Maxwell (Felipe).
    "I Know What I'd Have Done" (7-
24-60): George Brent (Fred Girard),
Maggie Hayes (Muriel Girard), Nancy
Rennick (Nadine Girard), Anne Seymour
(Hazel), Charles Meredith (Gentry), Peter Walker (Lt. Phillips), Susan Davis
(Jerry), Paul Mazursky (reporter).
    "Enough Rope" (7-31-60): Richard
Carlson (Dr. Roy Flemming), Joan O'-
Brien (Susan), Barbara Stuart (Claire
Flemming), Bert Freed (Lt. Columbo),
Duncan MacLeod (Dave), Frank Behrens
(Harry), Mimi Walters (Miss Petrie),
Thomas Nello (Tommy).
    "Trial By Fury" (8-7-60): Agnes

Moorhead (Elizabeth Marshall), Laurie
Carroll (Joanne Marshall), John Alder-
man (Randolph Marshall), Warren Ste-
vens (Jim Powell), Donald Foster (Judge
Trask), Vinton Hayworth (Madigan),
Wesley Law (Lt. Crane), Hugh Sanders
(Edward Bennet), Charles Meredith
(Judge Bascomb).
  "Run-Around" (8-14-60): Vincent
Price (Michael Semmes), Everett Sloane
(Francis Rushmore), Nelson Holmes
(Felix McMahon), Thomas Nello (Dan
Nelson), Dahi Berti (Jerry), John Mil-
ford.
  "The Inspector Vanishes" (8-21-
60): Walter Slezak (Insp. Pierre Du-
mourier), Berry Kroeger (Commission-
er of Police), Erin O'Brien-Moore
(Mme. Petit), Barbara Stuart (Alice
Chatillon), Doris Dowling (Genevieve
Benoit), June Blair (Colette Dufour),
Chet Stratton (Arnold Beschamps).
  "Femme Fatale" (8-20-60): Janet
Blair (Lisa Townsend), Tracey Roberts
(Claire Bradford), Jack Cassidy (David
Townsend), Joe De Santis (Paul Otis),
Doris Lloyd (Nora Fleming).
  "Murder By the Book" (9-4-60):
Jeff Morrow (John Clayton), Carol Oh-
mart (Diane), Vanessa Brown (Carol
Penn), Hugh Sanders (Lt. Burdick),
Betty Garde (Mrs. Andrews), Thomas
Nello (Manny), Robin Blake (reception-
ist).
  "Blind Man's Bluff" (9-11-60):
John Ericson (Ray), Joan Evans (Blanche),
Jerome Cowan (Mr. Vandiver).
  "The Suicide Club" (9-18-60):
Cesar Romero, Everett Sloane.
  "A Perfect Alibi" (9-25-60): Ja-
net Blair.

NAME OF THE GAME, THE.
  "Tarot" (2-13-70): Gene Barry
(Glenn Howard), Jose Ferrer (Adrian
Blake), William Shatner (Peter), David
Carradine (Jason), Bethel Leslie (Ce-
lia), Luther Adler (Marc Osborne),
Gail Bonney (landlady), Frank Campa-
nella (detective), Carol Booth (Stephanie
White).
  "LA 2017" (1-15-71): Gene Bar-
ry (Glenn Howard), Sharon Farrell (San-
drelle), Severn Darden (Cameron), Bar-
ry Sullivan (Dana Bigelow), Paul Stewart
(Dr. Rubas), Edmund O'Brien (Berg-
man), Regis Cordic (Chairman), Louise
Latham (Helen), Geoffrey Lewis (Bates),
Jason Wingreen (Hammond), Michael
C. Gwynne (Dr. Parker), Stuart Nis-
bet (Dr. Simmons), Gloria Nanon (Dr.
Arnold), Phil Montgomery (Keeger),
Walt Davis (technician), Alicia Bond

(Dr. Barton).

N. E. T. PLAYHOUSE.
  "The Star Wagon" (6-2-67): Dus-
tin Hoffman (Hanus), Orson Bean (Ste-
phen Minch), Joan Lorring (Martha
Minch), Eileen Brennan (Hallie), Jo
Hurt (Mrs. Rutledge), Ed Zimmerman
(Charles).
  "Home" (1-19-68): Jenn Ben-Ya-
kov (Marcia), Jacque Lynn Colton (Sha-
ro), Irene Dailey (Ruth), Joel Fabiani
(John), Roger Davis (Roy), Dixie Mar-
quis (Cynthia), Louise Latham (Shami),
Dennis Patrick (Bert), Edward Winter
(George), Clement Fowler (Intruder).
  "1984" (4-19-68): Jane Merrow
(Julia), David Buck (Winston Smith),
Vernon Dobtcheff (Goldstein), Joseph
O'Conor (O'Brien).
  "They" (4-17-70): Cornelia Otis
Skinner (Kate), Gary Merrill (Barne),
Carmen Mathews (Annie), Joseph Wise-
man (Lev), Jack Gilford (Joey).

NEW AVENGERS, THE. 1978-79. Pa-
trick Macnee (John Steed), Joanna
Lumley (Purdey), Gareth Hunt (Mike
Gambit).
  "The Eagle's Nest" (9-5-78): Pe-
ter Cushing (Von Claus), Derek Farr
(Father Trasker), Brian Anthony (Stan-
nard), Neil Phillips (Main), Charles
Bolton (Ralph), Sydney Bromley (Hara), Frank
Gatliff (Karl), Sammie Winmill (Molly),
Joyce Carey (lady with dog), Maggy Max-
well (dowager), Peter Porteous (Nazi
corporal), Jerold Wells (Barker), Tru-
di Van Doorne (Gerda), Ron Forfar (Jud),
Raymond Mason (man with suitcase).
  "Target!" (9-12-78): Keith Bar-
ron (Draker), Robert Beatty (Ilenko),
Roy Boyd (Bradshaw), Deep Roy (Klokoe),
John Paul (Kendrick), Suzanna MacMillan
(Nurse), Robert Tayman (Palmer), Fre-
derick Jaeger (Jones), Dennis Blanch
(Talmadge), John Saunders (Titherbridge),
Peter Brace (Potterton), Marc Boyle
(McKay), Bruce Purchase (Lopez), Mal-
colm Stoddard (George Myers).
  "Angels of Death" (9-29-78): Dins-
dale Landen (Coldstream), Terence Alex-
ander (Manderson), Caroline Munro (Tam-
my), Michael Latimer (Refresby), Ri-
chard Gale (Pelbright), Lindsay Duncan
(Jane), Moira Foot (Cindy), Anthony Bai-
ley (Simon Carter), Pamela Stephenson
(Wendy), Hedger Wallace (Col. Tomson),
Melissa Stribling (Sally Manderson).
  "Sleeper" (10-6-78): Keith Buckley
(Brady), Sara Kestelman (Tina), Prentis
Hancock (Bart), Mark Jones (Chuck), Leo

(NEW AVENGERS cont.) Dolan (Bill), Gavin Campbell (Fred), David Schofield (Ben), Joe Dunne (Hardy), Peter Godfrey (Carter), Arthur Dignam (Dr. Graham), Jason White (1st policeman), Tony McHale (2nd policeman).

"Faces" (10-13-78): David De Keyser (Prator), Edward Petherbridge (Mullins), Neil Hallett (Clifford), Annabel Leventon (Wendy), David Webb (Bilston), Jill Melford (Sheila), Donald Hewlett (Torrance), Richard Leech (Craig), Michael Sheard (Peters), J. G. Devlin (tramp), Robert Putt (attendant).

"House of Cards" (10-20-78): Peter Jeffrey (Perov), Gordon Sterne (Prof. Vasil), Lyndon Brook (Cartney), Dan Meaden (Boris), Terry Plummer (Cristo), Frank Thornton (Roland), Annette Andre (Suzy Miller), Ina Skriver (Olga), Murray Brown (David Miller), Mark Burns (Spence), Anthony Bailey (Frederick), Jeremy Wilkin (Tulliver), Derek Francis (the Bishop), Geraldine Moffatt (Jo).

"Forward Base" (11-3-78): Jack Creley (Hosking), August Schellenberg (Bailey), Marilyn Lightstone (Ranoff), Nick Nichols (Malachev), David Calderisi (Halfhide), Maurice Good (Milroy), Anthony Parr (Glover), John Bethune (Doctor), Anne Cullinan Taylor (Laney), Toivo Pyyko (Clive), Les Rubie (Harper), Ara Hovanessiaan (Czibor), Richard Moffatt (radio operator).

"Obsession" (11-10-78): Martin Shaw (Larry), Mark Kingston (Gen. Canvey), Lewis Collins (Kilner), Terence Longdon (Cmdr. East), Anthony Heaton (Morgan), Tommy Boyle (Wolach), Roy Purcell (controller).

"Cat Amongst the Pigeons" (11-17-78): Vladek Sheybal (Zarcardi), Matthew Long (Turner), Hugh Walters (Lewington), Peter Copley, Kevin Stoney (Tomkins), Basil Dignam (Rydercroft), Patrick Connor (Foster), Brian Jackson (Controller), Andrew Bradford (Merton), Gordon Rollings (Bridlington), Joe Black (Hudson).

"Dead Men Are Dangerous" (11-24-78): Clive Revill (Mark Crayford), Richard Murdoch (Perry), Gabrielle Drake (Penny), Terry Taplin (Hara), Michael Turner (Dr. Culver), Roger Avon (Headmaster), Trevor Adams (Sandy), Gabor Vernon (Russian doctor).

"The Midas Touch" (12-1-68): John Carson (Freddy), David Swift (Prof. Turner), Ed Devereaux (Vann), Gilles Millinaire (Midas), Ronald Lacey (Hong Kong Harry), Geoffrey Bateman (Simpson), Robert Mill (Curator),

Lionel Guyett (Tayman), Kenneth Gilbert (Rostock), Pik-Sen Lim (Sing), Peter Winter (Morgan), Tania Mallett (Sara), Tim Condren (Boz), Bruce Bould (Froggart), Jeremy Child (Henry), Ray Edwards (Garvin), Chris Tranchell (Doctor), Pola Churchill (Princess), Bruno Elrington (Choy).

"Hostage" (12-8-68): William Franklyn (McKay), Simon Oates (Spelman), Michael Culver (Walters), Anna Palk (Suzy), Richard Ireson (Vernon), Barry Stanton (Packer), George Lane-Cooper (Marvin).

"The Lion and the Unicorn" (12-15-78): Jean Claudio (Unicorn), Maurice Marsac (Leparge), Raymond Bussieres (Henri), Jacques Maury (Ritter), Raoul Delfosse (Marco), Gerald Sim (Minister), Henri Dzarniak (Grima), Jean-Pierre Bernard (1st bodyguard), Ludwig Gaum (2nd bodyguard).

"Dirtier By the Dozen" (12-22-78): John Castle (Col. 'Mad' Jack Miller), Colin Skeaping (Travis), Shaun Curry (Sgt. Bowden), Michael Barrington (Gen. Stevens), Michael Howarth (Capt. Tony Noble), Brian Croucher (Terry), John Labanowski (Keller), Stephen Moore (Major Prentice), Alun Armstrong (Harris), Francis Mughan (Freddy), David Purcell (orderly), John Forbes-Robertson (Doctor), Ballard Berkeley (Col. Elroyd Foster), John Challis (soldier), Richard Derrington (Turner).

"Gnaws" (12-29-78): Julian Holloway (Charles Thornton), Morgan Shepherd (Walters), Peter Cellier (Carter), John Watts (Harlow), Ronnie Laughlin (motor mechanic), Anulka Dubinska (pretty girl), Ivan Chislenko (Ronnie Laughlin), Jeremy Young (Ivan Chislenko), Patrick Halahide (George Ratcliffe), Keith Marsh (Joe the Tramp), Ken Wynne (Arthur the Tramp), Keith Alexander (Malloy), Denise Reynolds (girl in car), Peter Richardson (boy in car).

"Complex" (1-5-79): Cec Linder (Baker), Harvey Atkin (Talbot), Vlasta Vrana (Karavitch), Rudy Lipp (Koschev), Jan Rubes (Patlenko), Michael Ball (Cope), David Nichols (Greenwood), Suzette Couture (Miss Cunnings), Gerald Crack (Berisford Holt).

"Three Handed Game" (1-12-79): David Wood (Ranson), Stephen Greif (Juventor), Tony Vogel (Ivan), Michael Petrovich (Larry), Terry Wood (Prof. Meroff), Gary Raymond (Masgard), Noel Trevarthen (Tony Field).

"The Gladiators" (1-19-79): Louis Zorich (Karl), Neil Vipond (Chuck Peters), Bill Starr (O'Hara), Yanci Buko-

vec (Barnoff), Peter Boretski (Tarno-
koff), Jan Muzynski (Cresta), Michael
Donaghue (Hartley), George Chuvalo
(huge man), Dwayne McLean (Rogers),
Patrick Sinclair (Ivan), Doug Lennox
(Nada).
   "Medium Rare" (1-26-79): Jon
Finch (Wallace), Mervyn Johns (elder-
ly man), Jeremy Wilkin (Richards),
Neil Hallett (Roberts), Sue Holderness
(Victoria Stanton), Maurice O'Connell
(McBain), Steve Ubels (man at seance),
Allen Weston (Mason), Celia Foxe (mo-
del girl), Diana Churchill (dowager la-
dy).
   "The Tale of the Big Why" (2-2-
79): Gary Waldhorn (Roach), Derek
Waring (Harmer), George A. Cooper
(Burt Brandon), Rowland Davies (Poole),
Roy Marsden (Turner), Maeve Alexan-
der (Mrs. Turner), Jenny Runacre (I-
rene), Geoffrey Toone (Minister).
   "Emily" (2-9-79): Jane Mallett
(Miss Daly), Les Carlson (Douglas Col-
lings), Peter Torokvei (Kalenov), Brian
Petchey (Reddington), Richard Davidson (Phillips), Jack Duffy (radio operator), Ed McNamara (chicken farmer),
Don LeGros (mechanic), Sandy Craw-
ley (1st policeman), John Kerr (2nd
policeman), Pat Patterson (3rd police-
man), Bill Ballentine (4th policeman).
   "To Catch a Rat" (2-16-79): Ian
Hendry (Gunner), Edward Judd (Cromwell), Robert Flemying (Quaintance),
Barry Jackson (Cledge), Jeremy Hawk
(Finder), Jo Kendall (Nurse), Anthony
Sharp (Grant), Bernice Stegers (operator), Sally-Jane Spencer (mother), Dallas Cavell (farmer), Genevieve Allen-
bury (Bridgit), Anita Graham (Helga).
   "Trap" (3-2-79): Terry Wood
(Soo Choy), Ferdy Mayne (Arcarti),
Robert Rietty (Dom Carlos), Kristo-
pher Kum (Tansing), Stuart Damon (Mar-
ty Brine), Yasuko Nagazumi (Yasko),
Bruce Boa (Mahon), Barry Lowe (Mur-
ford), Larry Lamb (Williams), Anne-
gret Easterman (Miranda), Maj-Britt
(girlfriend).
   "The Last of the Cybernauts...??"
(3-9-79): Robert Lang (Felix Kane),
Oscar Quitak (Malov), Basil Hoskins
(Prof. Mason), Robert Gillespie (Goff),
S. Newton Anderson (Kurtz), David
Horovitch (Fitzroy), Eric Carte (Ter-
ry), Gwen Taylor (Dr. Marlow), F.
Scott Graves (Dr. Warner), Davina Tay-
lor (Tricia), Pearl Hackney (Mrs.
Weir), Sally Bazely (Laura), Rocky
Taylor (Cybernaut), Ray Armstrong
(1st guard), Martin Fisk (2nd guard).
   "K Is for Kill" (3-23-79): Pierre

Vernie (Col. Martin), Maurice Marsac
(Gen. Gaspard), Charles Millot (Stanislav), Christine Delaroche (Jeanine Leparge), Paul Emile Deiber (Toy), Sacha
Pitoeff (Kerov), Sylvain Clement (Vas-
sili), Eric Desmaretz (Ivan), Tony Then
(monk), Krishna Clough (soldier), Eric
Allan (Penrose), Kenneth Watson (salvation army major), Guy Mairesse
(guard), Maxence Mailfort (Turkov),
Jacques Monnet (waiter), Cyrille Besnard (secretary), Frank Olivier (Minski),
Alberto Simono (Minister), Diana Rigg
(Mrs. Emma Peel).

NEXT STEP BEYOND. 1978-79. John
   Newland (Host).
   "Tsuname" (1-5-78).
   "The Return of Carrie Dewitt" (9-
13-78): Lewis Van Bergen (Carrie De-
witt), Karin Mani (Tiare Auber), Paul
Hampton (Surgeon), Alan Frost (Sgt.
Renaud), Anakorita (Madame Auber).
   "Possessed" (9-20-78): Gene Bua
(Paul Adams), Toni Bull Bua (Caroline
Adams), Biff Elliot (patrol sergeant),
Sam Chew, Jr. (Dr. Green), Bobb Hop-
kins (Officer Gates), Marco Lopez (Ro-
mero Robles).
   "The Love Connection" (9-27-78):
Kelly Gallagher (Jill August), Luana An-
ders (Harriet Jessup), Miles Shearer
(Frank Jessup), Jean Gillespie (Alice).
   "Ondine's Curse" (10-4-78): Me-
redith MacRae (Sara), Nick Holt (Tom),
Robert Cleaves (Anderson), Christopher
Ellis (hitchhiker).
   "Dream of Disaster" (10-11-78):
Meridith Baer (Helen Chambers), Peter
Skinner (Harry Chambers), Leonard
Stone (Dr. Whitewood), Eric Howell
(Steve Colton).
   "Ghost Town" (10-18-78): Kath-
leen King (Leslie DeLong), Paul Peter-
son (Mitch Mitchell), Michael Stroka
(Donk/Logan).
   "Drums at Midnight" (10-25-78):
Majel Barret (Neva Gillespie), Yvonne
Regalado (Montine Gillespie), Crane
Jackson (Dr. Deutsch), Sheldon Allman
(John Cooperman), Josephine Premice
(Mambo).
   "Portrait of the Mind" (11-1-78):
William Campbell (Chad Campbell), Eloy
Casados (Frank Mendoza), Ana Alicia
(Angela Mendoza), Edmund Stoiber (Sam
Landis).
   "Other Voices" (11-8-78): Robert
Walker, Jr. (Walter Harrison), Susan
Keller (Carrie Jarris), H.M. Wynant
(Frank Jarris), Audrey Christie (Elsie
Manning), Peter Forster (Jason).
   "A Matter of Pride" (11-15-78):

(NEXT STEP BEYOND cont.) Enrique Novi (Manny Guzman), Eileen Dietz (Melissa Guzman), Robert Contreras (Carlos), Martin Rudy (Dr. Hartfield).
"The Ghost of Cellblock Two" (11-22-78): Lana Wood (Sgt. Peg Enright), Kathleen Brown (Mary Sutter), Lee Warrick (Mrs. Jordan), Pat Renella (Officer Doug Taylor).
"The Legacy" (11-29-78): Delos V. Smith, Jr. (Gus Durning), Stephen A. Clark (Alan), Tasha Lee Zemrus (Patty), Doug Druse (Lt. Jeff Burns), Whitney Rydbeck (Officer John Woodward).
"Cry Baby" (12-6-78): Simone Griffith (Susan Elston), Joe E. Bratcher (Larry Elston), George Skaff (Doctor), Julie Parrish (Dr. Elizabeth Turner), Michael Haei (man), Marcia Mohr (woman).
"Greed" (12-13-78): Ben Andrews (Philip Barlow), Elaine Princi (Jan Barlow), Virginia Leith (Mrs. Whitaker), Larry Watson (Robert Whitaker), Larry Barton (hotel manager), Gil Lamb (store proprietor).
"Out of Body" (12-20-78): Larry Casey (David Peters), Deborah Alexakos (Susan Lacy), Marland Proctor (Vincent Tanner), James Houghton (Randall Prieste), Sandra McCully (Dorothy Peters), Henry Brandon (prosecuting attorney).
"Key to Yesterday" (12-27-78): David Gilliam (Daniel Gardner), Henry Brandon (Timothy Welling), Carol Connors (Valerie McKay), Clint Young (policeman), Nathan Adler (stage doorman), Sally Swift (Jessie).
"Woman in the Mirror" (1-3-79): Martine Beswicke (Helen Wiley), Noah Keen (Harold Cascomb), Craig Littler (Paul Marlin), Olive Dunbar (Mrs. Wyckoff), Louie Quinn (Ferris), John Lawrence (bartender).
"The Haunted Inn" (1-10-79): James Keach (Chris Stabler), Patricia Anne Joyce (Luciana Court), Lorna Thayer (Miss Argus), Buck Young (Sheriff), Robert Barron (Peter Combs).
"The Pact" (1-17-79): Tom Gerard (Teddy Mullins), Frank Ashmore (Peter Holmby), Lynn Benesch (Valerie Boardman), Diane Hale (the Gypsy), Scott Edward Allen (Young Peter), Jennifer Germaine (Young Valerie), Jeffrey Pinto (Young Teddy), Miles Masters (Sheriff),
"Sin of Omission" (1-24-79): Mark Goddard (Larry Hollis), Zina Bethune (Diane Hollis), John Harding (Dr. Carl Ferris), Bill Zuckert (Bart

Hudson), Ray Stricklyn (Mr. Morrison), Rhonda Hopkins (Mrs. Morrison), Shannon White (child).
"Thunderbolt" (1-31-79): Debbie Lytton (Carolyn Peters), Thomas Bellin (Alex Peters), Ryan MacDonald (George Chambers), Anne Helm (Ellen Chambers), Gary Vinson (factory foreman), M. G. Kelly (paramedic), Sonny Carver (bank guard), Paul E. Richards (insurance broker).
"The Confession" (2-7-73): Grace Lee Whitney (Dr. Dorothy Alsworth), Paulette Breen (Maggie Graham), Michael Christian (Carl Graham), George Ball (Ben Morrison), Terrance O'Connor (Helen Morrison), Peter Griffin (guard).
"Trance of Death" (2-28-79): Alexandra Morgan (Sharon Weaver), James Camino (Hank), Nancy Stevens (Christiana Hartford), Santy Josel (Tadashi), Colby Chester (Mark), Sandra Clark (Debbie).
"To Fight a Ghost" (3-7-79): Brione Farrell (Cathy Le Masters), Chuck Howerton (George Le Masters), Lisa Pera (Mrs. Riva), Radames Pera (Elton Connors).

NIGHT GALLERY. 1970-73. Rod Serling (Host).
"The Dead Man" (12-16-70): Carl Betz (Max Redford), Jeff Corey (Dr. Miles Talmadge), Louise Sorel (Velia Redford), Michael Blodgett (Fearing).
"The Housekeeper" (12-16-70): Larry Hagman (Cedric Acton), Jeanette Nolan (Miss Wattle), Suzy Parker (Carlotta), Cathleen Cordell (Miss Beamish).
"Room with a View" (12-23-70): Joseph Wiseman, Angel Tompkins (Lila), Diane Keaton (Nurse).
"The Little Black Bag" (12-23-70): Burgess Meredith (Dr. Fall), Chill Wills (Hepplewhite), George Furth (Gilling), E. J. Andre (Charlie).
"The Nature of the Enemy" (12-23-70): Joseph Campanella (Simms), Richard Van Vleet (Spaceman).
"The House" (12-30-70): Joanna Pettet (Elaine Chambrun), Paul Richards (Peugot), Steve Franken (Doctor).
"Certain Shadows on the Walls" (12-30-70): Agnes Moorhead (Emma Bigham), Louis Hayward (Stephen), Rachel Roberts (Rebecca), Grayson Hall (Ann).
"Make Me Laugh" (1-6-71): Godfrey Cambridge (Jackie), Jackie Vernon (Chatterje), Al Lewis (Mishkin), Tom Bosley (Jules).
"Clean Kills and Other Trophies"

(1-6-71): Raymond Massey (Dittman), Barry Brown (Archie), Herb Jefferson, Jr. (Tom), Tom Troupe (Pierce).

"Pamela's Voice" (1-13-71): Phyllis Diller, John Astin.

"Lone Survivor" (1-13-71): Torin Thatcher (Captain), John Colicos (the Survivor).

"The Doll" (1-13-71): Shani Wallis (Miss Danton), John Williams (Colonel), Henry Silva (Pandit Chola).

"The Last Laurel" (1-20-71): Jack Cassidy (Marius Davis), Martine Beswicke (Susan).

"They're Tearing Down Tim Riley's Bar" (1-20-71): William Windom (Lane), Diane Baker (Miss Alcott), Bert Convy (Doane), John Randolph (Pritkin), Henry Beckman (Policeman).

"Whisper" (5-13-71): Sally Fields, Dean Stockwell (Charlie), Kent Smith (Doctor).

"The Boy Who Predicted Earthquakes" (9-15-71): Clint Howard, Michael Constantine (Wellman), William Hansen (Grandfather).

"Miss Lovecraft Sent Me" (9-15-71): Sue Lyon, Joseph Campanella.

"The Hand of Borgus Weems" (9-15-71): Ray Milland (Dr. Ravdon), George Maharis (Lacland), Patricia Donahue (Dr. Innokenti), Joan Huntington (Susan), Peter Mamakos (Kazanzakis).

"The Phantom of What Opera?" (9-15-71): Leslie Nielsen (the Phantom), Mary Ann Beck.

"A Death in the Family" (9-22-71): Imogene Coca, King Donovan.

"The Class of '99" (9-22-71): Vincent Price (the Professor), Brandon de Wilde (Johnson), Frank Hotchkiss (Clinton), Randolph Mantooth (Elkins), Holly Hicks (Barnes), Barbara Shannon (Miss Peterson), Suzanne Cohane (Miss Fields).

"Witches' Feast" (9-22-71): Agnes Moorhead, Ruth Buzzi, Fran Ryan, Allison McKay.

"Since Aunt Ada Came to Stay" (9-29-71): Jeanette Nolan (Aunt Ada), James Farentino (Craig), Michele Lee (Joanne), Jonathan Harris (Prof. Porteus).

"With Apologies to Mr. Hyde" (9-29-71): Adam West (Mr. Hyde), Jack Laird (Assistant).

"The Flip Side of Satan" (9-29-71): Arte Johnson.

"Room for One Less" (9-29-71).

"A Fear of Spiders" (10-6-71): Patrick O'Neal (Justus), Kim Stanley (Elizabeth).

"Junior" (10-6-71): Wally Cox, Barbara Flicker.

"Marmalade Wine" (10-6-71): Rudy Vallee (Dr. Deeking), Robert Morse.

"The Academy" (10-6-71): Pat Boone, Leif Erikson (Director), Lawrence Linville (Sloane), Robert Gibbons (gatekeeper), E. A. Sirianni (chauffeur).

"The Phantom Farmhouse" (10-20-71): David McCallum, Linda Marsh (Mildred), David Carradine (Gideon), Bill Quinn (Dr. Tom), Trina Parks (Betty), Ford Rainey (Sheriff), Ivor Francis (Pierre), Gail Bonney (Mrs. Squire), Martin Ashe (Squire).

"Silent Snow, Secret Snow" (10-20-71): Orson Welles (Narrator), Radames Pera (Paul), Lonny Chapman (Father), Lisabeth Hush (Mother), Frances Spanier (Miss Buell), Jason Wingreen (Doctor).

"A Question of Fear" (10-27-71): Leslie Nielsen (Denny), Fritz Weaver (Mazi), Jack Bannon.

"The Devil Is Not Mocked" (10-27-71): Helmut Dantine (General), Francis Lederer (Master), Hank Brandt (Kranz).

"Midnight Never Ends" (11-3-71): Susan Strasberg (Ruth), Robert F. Lyons (Marine), Robert Karnes (Sheriff), Joseph Perry (Bateman).

"Brenda" (11-3-71): Glenn Corbett (Richard Alden), Laurie Prange (Brenda), Fred Carson (Thing), Barbara Babcock (Flora).

"Die Now, Pay Later" (11-3-71): Slim Pickens, Will Geer.

"The Diary" (11-10-71): Patty Duke Astin (Holly Schaefer), Virginia Mayo (Carrie Crane), David Wayne (Dr. Mills).

"A Matter of Semantics" (11-10-71): Cesar Romero (Dracula), E. J. Peaker.

"The Big Surprise" (11-10-71): John Carradine, Vincent Van Patton (Chris), Marc Vahanian (Jason), Eric Chase (Dan).

"Professor Peabody's Last Lecture" (11-10-71): Carl Reiner (Peabody), Johnnie Collins III (Lovecraft).

"House - With Ghost" (11-17-71): Jo Anne Worley, Bob Crane.

"Dr. Stringfellow's Rejuvenator" (11-17-71): Forrest Tucker (Dr. Stringfellow), Don Pedro Colley (Rolpho), Murray Hamilton (Snyder).

"Hell's Bells" (11-17-71): John Astin, Theodore Flicker (the Devil), Jody Gilbert (fat lady), John J. Fox (Mr. Tourist), Ceil Cabot (Mrs. Tourist).

"A Midnight Visit to the Neighbor-

(NIGHT GALLERY cont.) hood Blood
Bank" (11-17-71): Victor Buono.
"The Dark Boy" (11-24-71): Eli-
zabeth Hartman (Mrs. Timm), Gale
Sondergaard (Miss Abigail), Michael
Laird (Joel), Michael Baseleon (Tom),
Hope Summers (Miss Lettie).

"Keep in Touch - We'll Think of
Something" (11-24-71): Alex Cord
(Erik Sutton), Joanna Pettet (Claire
Foster), Richard O'Brien (Sgt. Brice).

"Pickman's Model" (12-1-71):
Bradford Dillman (Pickman), Louise
Sorel (Mavis), Donald Moffat (Uncle
George).

"The Dear Departed" (12-1-71):
Steve Lawrence (Mark), Maureen Arthur, Harvey Lembeck, Patricia Donahue.

"An Act of Chivalry" (12-1-71):
Ron Stein, Deidre Hudson, Jimmy Cross.

"Cool Air" (12-8-71): Barbara
Rush (Agatha), Henry Darrow (Munox),
Beatrice Kay (Mrs. Gibbons).

"Camera Obscura" (12-8-71):
Rene Auberjonois (Sharsted, Jr.), Ross
Martin (Gingold).

"Quoth the Raven" (12-8-71):
Marty Allen.

"The Messiah of Mott Street" (12-
15-71): Edward G. Robinson (Mr.
Goldman), Ricky Powell (Mickey), Tony Roberts (Dr. Levine), Yaphet Kotto
(Buckner), Anne Taylor (Miss Moretti).

"The Painted Mirror" (12-15-71):
Zsa Zsa Gabor, Arthur O'Connell,
Rosemary De Camp.

"The Different Ones" (12-29-71):
Dana Andrews (Paul), Jon Korkes (Victor).

"Tell David. . . " (12-29-71): Sandra Dee (Ann), Jared Martin (Tony/Da-
vid), Jenny Sullivan (Pat).

"Logoda's Heads" (12-29-71):
Denise Nichols, Patrick Macnee (Major
Crosby), Tim Matheson (Henley), Brock
Peters (Logoda), Zara Culley (Emba).

"Green Fingers" (1-5-72): Elsa
Lanchester, Cameron Mitchell, George
Keymas (Crowley), Harry Hickox (She-
riff).

"The Funeral" (1-5-72): Werner
Klemperer (Asper), Joe Flynn (Silkline),
Charles Macaulay (Count).

"The Tune in Dan's Cafe" (1-5-
72): Pernell Roberts (Joe), Susan Oliver (Kelly), James Davidson (Roy),
Brooke Mills (Red), James Nusser (Dan).

"Lindemann's Catch" (1-12-72):
Stuart Whitman (Lindemann), Anabel
Garth (Mermaid), Harry Townes (Suggs),
Jack Aranson (Doctor).

"A Feast of Blood" (1-12-72):

Sondra Locke (Sheila), Norman Lloyd
(Henry), Hermione Baddeley (Mrs.
Gary).

"The Late Mr. Peddington" (1-12-
72): Kim Hunter (Mrs. Peddington),
Harry Morgan (mortician), Randy Quade
(John).

"The Miracle at Camafeo" (1-19-
72): Harry Guardino (Rogan), Julie A-
dams (Gay Melcor), Ray Danton (Joe
Melcor).

"The Ghost of Sorworth Place" (1-
19-72): Richard Kiley, Jill Ireland (Ann),
John Schofield (Ghost), Mavis Neal (Mrs.
Ducker).

"The Waiting Room" (1-26-72):
Steve Forrest (Dichter), Gilbert Roland
(Bartender), Albert Salmi (Bristol),
Jim Davis (Bennett), Buddy Ebsen
(Soames), Les Barker (McKinley).

"The Last Rites for a Dead Druid"
(1-26-72): Bill Bixby (Bruce), Carol
Lynley (Jenny), Donna Douglas (Mildred),
Ned Glass (Bernstein), Janya Brant (Marta).

"Deliveries in the Rear" (2-9-72):
Cornel Wilde, Walter Burke (Jameson),
Rosemary Forsythe (Barbara), Kent
Smith (Bennett), Peter Brocco (Dr.
Shockman), Larry D. Mann (Hannify).

"Stop Killing Me" (2-9-72): Geraldine Page, James Gregory (Sergeant).

"Dead Weight" (2-9-72): Jack Albertson, Bobby Darin.

"I'll Never Leave You - Ever" (2-
16-72): Royal Dano (Owen), John Saxon
(Ianto), Peggy Webber (Crone), Lois
Nettleton.

"There Aren't Any More MacBanes"
(2-16-72): Joel Grey, Howard Duff, Darrel Larson (Elie), Barry Higgins (Mickey),
Ellen Blake (Creature).

"You Can't Get Help Like That Any-
more" (2-23-72): Broderick Crawford
(Fulton), Cloris Leachman (Mrs. Ful-
ton), Lana Wood (Maid), Henry Jones
(Hample), Severn Darden (Dr. Kessler),
Christopher Law (Foster), Pamela Shoop.

"The Sins of the Fathers" (2-23-
72): Richard Thomas (Ian), Geraldine
Page (Mrs. Evans), Michael Dunn (servant), Barbara Steele (widow).

"The Caterpillar" (3-1-72): Lau-
rence Harvey, Joanna Pettet (Rhona),
Don Knight (Tommy), Tom Helmore
(Warwick), John Williams (Doctor).

"Little Girl Lost" (3-1-72): Wil-
liam Windom, Ed Nelson (Burke), Ivor
Francis (Psychiatrist), John Lasell (Col.
Hawes).

"Satisfaction Guaranteed" (3-22-
72): Victor Buono, Cathleen Cordell
(Mrs. Mount).

"The Return of the Sorceror" (9-24-72): Vincent Price (Carnby), Bill Bixby (Noel Evans), Patricia Sterling (Fern).

"The Girl with Hungry Eyes" (10-1-72): James Farentino (David Faulkner), John Astin (Munsch), Joanna Pettit (girl).

"Fright Night" (10-15-72): Stuart Whitman (Tom Ogilvy), Barbara Anderson (Leona Ogilvy), Ellen Corby (Miss Patience), Alan Napier (Cousin Zachariah), Larry Watson (Longhair).

"Rare Objects" (10-22-72): Mickey Rooney (Augie Kolodney), Raymond Massey (Dr. Glendon), Fay Spain (Molly Mitchell), David Frescox (Blockman), Regis J. Cordic (Doctor), Victor Sen Young (Butler), Ralph Adano (Tony).

"Spectre in Tap Shoes" (10-29-72): Sandra Dee (Millicent/Marion), Dane Clark (Jason), Christopher Connelly (Sam), Russell Thorson (Dr. Coolidge), Michael Laird (Michael), Michael Richardson (mailman), Stuart Nisbet (policeman).

"The Ring with the Red Velvet Ropes" (11-5-72): Chuck Connors (Roderick Blanco), Gary Lockwood (Jim Figg), Joan Van Ark (Sandra Blanco), Ji-Tu Cumbuku (Big Dan Anger), Ralph Manza (Max), Charles Davis (Hayes), Frankie Van (referee).

"You Can Come Up Now, Mrs. Milliken" (11-12-72): Ozzie Nelson (Henry Milliken), Harriet Nelson (Helena Milliken), Roger Davis (George Beaumont), Michael Lerner (Burgess), Don Keefer (Coolidge), Margaret Muse (Steinhem), Lew Brown (1st officer), Stuart Nisbet (2nd officer).

"The Other Way Out" (11-19-72): Ross Martin (Bradley Meredith), Burl Ives (old man), Peggy Feury (Estelle), Jack Collins (Potter), Elizabeth Thompson (Miss Flannagan), Paul Micale (waiter), Adam Weed (Sonny).

"Finnegan's Flight" (12-17-72): Burgess Meredith (Finnegan), Cameron Mitchell (Tuttle), Barry Sullivan (Dr. Simsich), Kenneth Tobey (warden), Dort Clark (prisoner).

"She'll Be Company for You" (12-24-72): Leonard Nimoy (Henry Auden), Lorraine Gary (Barbara), Jack Oakie (Willy), Kathryn Hays (June).

"Something in the Woodwork" (1-14-73): Leif Erickson (Charlie Wheatland), Geraldine Page, Barbara Rhoades (Julie), Paul Jenkins (Joe Wilson), John McMurtry.

"Death on a Barge" (3-4-73): Lesley Ann Warren (Hyacinth), Lou

Antonio (Jake), Robert Pratt (Ron), Brooke Bundy (Phyllis), Jim Bokes (father), Arthur Spain (coastguardsman).

"The Doll of Death" (5-20-73): Susan Strasberg (Sheila), Alejandro Rey (Raphael), Barry Atwater (Brandon), Murray Matheson (Dr. Strang), Henry Brandon (Vereker), Jean Durand (Andrew).

"Hatred Unto Death" (5-27-73): Steve Forrest (Grant Wilson), Dina Merrill (Ruth Wilson), George Barrows (N'gi), Fernando Lamas.

"How to Cure the Common Vampire" (5-27-73): Richard Deacon (man with mallet), Johnny Brown (man with stake).

NIGHTMARE MAN, THE. British (5-1-81 - 5-22-81)*. James Warwick (Michael Gaffikin), Celia Imbrie (Fiona Patterson), Maurice Roeves (Insp. Inskip), Tom Watson (Dr. Goudry), Jonathan Newth (Col. Howard), James Cosmo (Sgt. Carch), Fraser Wilson (P. C. Malcolmson), Tony Sibbald (Dr. Symonds), Elaine Wells (Mrs. Mackay), Jeffrey Stewart (Drummond), Ronald Forfar (Campbell), Jon Croft (McGrath), Robert Vowles (Lt. Carey), Pat Gorman (the killer).

1984. British (12-12-54). Peter Cushing (Winston Smith), Andre Morell (O'Brien), Donald Pleasence (Syme), Yvonne Mitchell, Wilfred Brambell, Harry Lane, Campbell Gray.

1990. British 1977-79. Edward Woodward (Jim Kyle), Barbara Kellermann (Delly Lomas) 77-79, Robert Lang (Herbert Skardon), Clifton Jones (Henry Tasker) 77-78, George Murcell (Greaves) 77-78, Tony Doyle (Dave Brett), Paul Hardwick (Faceless), Donald Gee (Dr. Vickers) 77-78, Ray Smith (Charles Wainwright) 77-78, Richard Hurndall (Avery) 77-78, Simon Chandler (Brian) 77-78, John Castle (Philip Carter) 77-78, Anna Cropper (Susie Carter) 77-78, John Phillips (Atty. Gen. Graham) 77-78, John Bennett (Prosecutor) 77-78, Yvonne Mitchell (Kate Smith) 78-79, Lisa Harrow (Lynn Plake) 78-79, Clive Swift (Tony Doran) 78-79.

"Creed of Slaves".

"When Did You Last See Your Father?".

"Health Farm".

"Decoy".

*Aired in multiple segments; dates show first and last segments.

(1990 cont.)
"Voice from the Past".
"Whatever Happened to Cardinal Wolsey?".
"Witness".
"Non-Citizen".
"Pentagons".
"Black Market".
"Trapline".
"Ordeal By Small Brown Envelope".
"Hire and Fire".
"You'll Never Walk Alone".
"Grass Roots".
"What Pleases the Prince...".

NUTS & BOLTS. Pilot (8-24-81): Rich Little, Eve Arden, Jo Ann Pflug (Karen Prescott), William Daniels (Berlinger), Michael Young Evans, Tommy McLoughlin, Tammy Lauren, Justin Dana.

OMNIBUS.
"The Turn of the Screw" (2-13-55): Geraldine Page.

ONE STEP BEYOND. 1958-61. John Newland (Host).
"The Bride Possessed" (1-20-59): Virginia Leith (Sally Conroy), Skip Homeier (Matt Conroy), Harry Townes (Dr. Slawson), Ann Morrison (Mrs. Wharton).
"The Night of April 14th" (1-27-59): Barbara Lord (Grace Montgomery), Patrick Macnee (Erick Farley), Isobel Elsom (Mrs. Montgomery), Gavin Gordon (Rev. Morgan), Marjorie Eaton (Miss Parsons).
"Emergency Only" (2-3-59): Jocelyn Brando (Ellen Larrabee), Lin McCarthy (Arthur Douglas), Clark Howat (Jim Hennessey), Nan Adams (Mrs. March), Ann Staunton (Betty Hennessey), Ross Elliott (Charlie Towne), Paula Raymond (lady passenger), John Maxwell (conductor).
"The Dark Room" (2-10-59): Cloris Leachman (Rita Morrison), Marcel Dalio (man), Ivan Triesault (Inspector), Paul Dubov (Detective Marsac), Ann Codee.
"Twelve Hours to Live" (2-17-59): Jean Allison (Carol Jansen), Paul Richards (Will Jansen), Lillian Powell (Mrs. Ford), Larraine Gillespie (Debbie), Douglas Kennedy (Sergeant).
"Epilogue" (2-24-59): Charles Aidman (Carl Archer), Julie Adams (Helen Archer), Charles Herbert (Steve Archer), William Schallert (Dr. Sanders).
"The Dream" (3-3-59): Reginald Owen (Herbert Blakely), Molly Roden (Ethel Blakely), Philip Tonge (Lieutenant), Jack Lynn, Peter Gordon.
"Premonition" (3-10-59): Pamela Lincoln (Debbie Garrick), Beverly Washburn (Young Debbie Garrick), Julie Payne (Louise), Clare Corelli, Thomas B. Henry.
"The Dead Part of the House" (3-17-59): Mimi Gibson (Ann Burton), Philip Abbott (Paul Burton), Joanne Linville (Aunt Minna), Philip Ahn (Frank).
"The Vision" (3-24-59): Bruce Gordon (Capt. Emil Tremaine), Pernell Roberts (Sergeant), H. M. Wynant (Private Lacoste), Jerry Oddo (Private Mollene), Peter Miles (youth).
"The Devil's Laughter" (3-31-59): Alfred Ryder (John Marriott), Patrick Westwood (attendant), Ben Wright (executioner), Leslie Denis (chaplain), Alma Lawton (Liz), John Ainsworth, Lester Mathews.
"The Return of Mitchell Campion" (4-7-59): Patrick O'Neal (Mitchell Campion), Lilyan Chauvin (Francesca), Anatol Winogradoff (Alexis Paxinian), Richard Angalora (hotel clerk), Allegra Varron (restaurant operator).
"The Navigator" (4-14-59): Don Dubbins (First Mate Blake), Robert Ellenstein (Capt. Peabody), Joel Fluellen (Cook), Olan Soule (stowaway), Stephen Roberts (Second Mate Swanson), Robert Osterloh, Don Womack.
"The Secret" (4-21-59): Maria Palmer (Sylvia Ackroyd), Robert Douglas (Harry Ackroyd), Albert Carrier (Jeremy), Molly Glessing (Essie), Arthur Gould-Porter.
"The Aerialist" (4-28-59): Mike Connors (Mario Patruzzio), Yvette Vickers (Carlotta Patruzzio), Robert Carricart (Gino Patruzzio), Ruggero Romor (Paul Patruzzio), Penny Santon (Mama Patruzzio), Charlie Watts, Vernon Rice.
"The Burning Girl" (5-5-59): Luana Anders (Alice Denning), Sandra Knight (Patty Leland), Olive Deering (Mildred Denning), Edward C. Platt (Mr. Denning).
"The Haunted U-Boat" (5-12-59): Werner Klemperer (Herr Bautmann), Eric Feldary (Capt. Eric Kreig), Kort Falkenberg (Lt. Fridel), Wesley Lau (Lt. Schneider), Siegfried Speck, Paul Busch, Andrew Branham, Norberto Kerner, Frank Obershall.
"Image of Death" (5-19-59): Max Adrian (Marquis de la Rogert), Doris Dowling (Charlotte Landri), John Wengraf (Ernest), Deidre Owen (Rose), Gregory Gaye.

"The Captain's Guests" (5-26-59): Nancy Hadley (Ellen Courtney), Robert Webber (Andrew Courtney), Thomas Coley (Bill Oker), John Lormer.

"Echo" (6-2-59): Ross Martin (Paul Marlin), Ed Kemmer (Roger Wiley), Leslie Barrett (Daniel Cascomb), Rusty Lane (bartender).

"Front Runner" (6-9-59): Ben Cooper (Ronnie Watson), Walter Burke (Sam Barry), Sandy Kenyon (Tim Berryman).

"The Riddle" (6-16-59): Warren Stevens (Leonard Barrett), Bethel Leslie (Betty Barrett), Patrick Westwood (Kumar), Barry Atwater (Doctor).

"Delusion" (9-15-59): Norman Lloyd (Harold Stein), Suzanne Pleshette (Marta), David White (Lt. Barry), George Mitchell.

"Ordeal on Locust Street" (9-22-59): Augusta Dabney (Margaret Parish), Suzanne Lloyd (Anna Parish), David Lewis (Dr. Edward Brown), Jack Kirkwood.

"Brainwave" (10-6-59): George Grizzard (Harris), Whit Bissell (Capt. Fielding), Tod Andrews (Stacey), Raymond Bailey.

"Doomsday" (10-13-59): Torin Thatcher (Earl of Donamoor), Donald Harron (Jamie/William), Edmund Atienza (Doctor), Patricia Michon (Katherine).

"Night of the Kill" (10-20-59): Dennis Holmes (Davey Morris), Fred Beir.

"The Inheritance" (10-27-59): Sean McClory (Mario), Jan Miner (Grace), Iphigenie Castiglioni (Countess Ferenzi), Estelita (Nina).

"The Open Window" (11-3-59): Michael Harris (Anthony March), Louise Fletcher (Jeannie), Lori March (woman), Charles Seel.

"Message from Clara" (11-10-59): Barbara Baxley (Lois Morrison), Robert Ellenstein (Mr. Tomach), Oscar Beregi, Jr. (Dutchman), Celia Lovsky (landlady), Renata Vanna.

"Forked Lightning" (11-17-59): Ralph Nelson (George Chambers), Roberta Haynes (Ellen Chambers), Frank Maxwell (Alex Peters), Candy Moore (Carolyn Peters).

"Reunion" (11-24-59): Betsy von Furstenberg (Helga), Paul Carr (Peter), Rory Harrity (Hanns), Page Slattery (Theo).

"Dead Ringer" (12-1-59): Norma Crane (Esther Quentin), Grant Williams (Bill Quentin), Ed Prentiss (Dr. Parks), Olive Blakeney.

"The Stonecutter" (12-8-59): Walter Burke (Menzies), Joe Mantel (Stanley Lockhart), Arthur Shields (Pop Lockhart), Don Beddoe (Doc Simmons).

"Father Image" (12-15-59): Jack Lord (Dan Gardner), Cece Whitney (Valerie), Ian Wolfe (Timothy Welton), Frank Scannell (Barker), George Selk (stage doorman).

"Make Me Not a Witch" (12-22-59): Patty McCormack (Emmy Horvath), Eileen Ryan (Ma Horvath), Leo Penn (Pa Horvath), Robert Emhardt.

"The Hand" (12-29-59): Robert Loggia (Tom Grant), Miriam Colon (Alma), Pete Candoli (Johnny), Joe Sullivan.

"The Justice Tree" (1-5-60): Frank Overton (Cal Gannis), Sallie Brophy (Sally Dolan), Charles Herbert (Joey Dolan).

"Earthquake" (1-12-60): David Opatoshu (Gerald Perkins), Olan Soule (waiter), Martin Garralaga (Italian man), Elvira Curci (Italian woman).

"Forests of the Night" (1-19-60): Alfred Ryder (Ted Doliver), Stacy Graham (Nancy Doliver), Mark Roberts (Pete Rankin), Douglas Dick (Alec Brown).

"Call from Tomorrow" (1-26-60): Margaret Phillips (Elena Stacy), Arthur Franz (Kevin Stacy), Emily Lawrence (Mrs. Marpole), Daryn Hinton (child).

"Who Are You?" (2-2-60): Reba Waters (Laurie), Phyllis Hill (Phyllis Warren), Ross Elliott (George Warren), Philip Bourneuf (Carl Mason), Anna Lee (Helen Mason).

"The Day the World Wept" (2-9-60): Barry Atwater (Abraham Lincoln), Jeanne Bates (Mary Lincoln), Eric Sinclair (Secretary Hay), Theodore Newton (Minister Stroom).

"The Lovers" (2-16-60): Vanessa Brown (Elsa Schuldorf), John Beal (Otto Becher), Irene Tedrow (Dr. Sesselschreiber), Rudolph Anders (Josef), Sig Ruman (Uncle Franz), Lili Valenti.

"Vanishing Point" (2-23-60): Edward Binns (Fred Graham), June Vincent (Ruth Graham), Fredd Wayne (Lt. Barnes), William Allyn (District Attorney), Arthur Hanson (Prosecutor).

"The Mask" (3-1-60): Wesley Lau (Leonard Wilenski), Luis Van Rooten (Brimley), Joan Elan (Nurse), Stephen Bekassy (Doctor).

"The Haunting" (3-8-60): Ronald Howard (Colin Chandler), Christine White (Nancy), Keith McConnell (Peter Duncan), Doris Lloyd.

"The Explorer" (3-15-60): Gregory Morton (Dr. Einar Hansen), Bert Convy (Gus), Eddie Firestone (Anderson), John Wengraf (Felix Borgner), Jeremy

1296 Science Fiction, Horror, Fantasy

(ONE STEP BEYOND cont.) Slate (Eric),
Rudolph Anders, Edith Evanson.
"The Clown" (3-22-60): Mickey
Shaughnessy (Pippo), Yvette Mimieux
(Nonnie), Christopher Dark (Tom).
"I Saw You Tomorrow" (4-5-60):
John Hudson (Donald Stewart), Rose-
mary Murphy (Ellie Pelston), Narda
Onyx (Clair Seymour), Francis Bethen-
court (Carter Seymour).
"Encounter" (4-12-60): Robert
Douglas (Paul McCord), Barbara Stuart
(Helen Rand), John Carlyle (Tim Cole).
"The Peter Hurkos Story" (4-19-
60 & 4-26-60): Albert Salmi (Peter
Hurkos), Betty Garde (Tante Elsa),
Norbert Schiller (August Breitner),
Alf Kjellin (Lars Lindstrom), Justice
Watson (Capt. Kibbee), Andrew Prine
(Walter Bird), John Banner (Dr. Mol-
haus), Maurice Marsac (Prof. Grotius).
"Delia" (5-3-60): Lee Phillips
(Philip Wilson), Barbara Lord (Delia),
Maureen Leeds (Mrs. Garan), Murray
Matheson (Bentley), Peter Camlin, Sal-
vador Vaquez.
"The Visitor" (5-10-60): Joan
Fontaine (Ellen Grayson), Warren Beat-
ty (Harry Grayson), Charles Webster.
"Gypsy" (5-17-60): John Seven
(Gypsy), Robert Blake (Tom), Murvyn
Vye (Ape), John Kellogg (Folger).
"Contact" (5-24-60): Ron Randell
(Bill Dermott), Catherine McLeod (Ma-
ry Dermott), Jason Johnson (pawnbro-
ker), Rodney Bell (policeman), Alexan-
der Lockwood (Dr. Otis).
"The Lonely Room" (5-31-60):
Fabrizio Mioni (Henri), Carl Esmond
(Emile), Letizie Noverese (Therese),
Maurice Marsac (bartender), Peter
Camlin.
"House of the Dead" (6-7-60):
Mario Alcaide (Lt. Harry Fraser), La-
ya Raki (Mei Ling), Stephen Cheng (Mr.
Lum), Hilda Plowright (Mother Superior).
"Goodbye, Grandpa" (6-14-60):
Edgar Stehli (Grandpa), Anna Karen
(Nan Wylie), Donald Losby (Doug Wy-
lie), Candy Moore.
"The Storm" (6-21-60): Lee Ber-
gere (Joe Bernheim), Rebecca Welles
(Adele Bernheim), Argentina Brunetti
(Senora Castera), Danny Zaldivar (Jua-
nita).
"Tidal Wave" (8-30-60): Jean
Allison (Mrs. Margaret North), Dennis
Patrick (Emmet North), Cliff Hall (Capt.
Thomas Powers).
"Anniversary of a Murder" (9-27-
60): Harry Townes (Gerard Simms),
Randy Stuart (Frances Hillier), Am-
zie Strickland, Alexander Lockwood.

"The Death Waltz" (10-4-60): Eli-
zabeth Montgomery (Lillie Clarke), Joe
Cronin (Lt. Henry Buchanan), Ed Pren-
tiss (Col. Clarke), K. T. Stevens (Ber-
nice Clarke), Robert Sampson.
"The Return" (10-11-60): Dick
Davalos (Cpl. Fred Cossage), Jack
Mullaney (Cpt. Young Blood), Charles
Gray (Sgt. Kirsch), Chris Winters (Lt.
Heinmetz), Rex Holman (Private Atley).
"If You See Sally" (10-18-60):
Anne Whitfield (Sally Willis), George
Mitchell (Mr. Ellis), Mary Lou Taylor
(Mrs. Ellis), Pat McCaffrie (truck dri-
ver), Harry Jackson (salesman).
"Moment of Hate" (10-25-60): Jo-
anne Linville (Karen Wadsworth), John
Kellogg (Dr. Martin Llewellyn), Joyce
Chapman (Linda Lawson).
"To Know the End" (11-1-60): El-
len Willard (Emily), Sally Fraser (Ann),
Noel Drayton (Officer), Alex Davion
(Harry), James Forrest, Anthony Eus-
trell, Jean Fenwick.
"The Trap" (11-15-60): Mike Kel-
lin (Donovio/Gibbs), Alex Gerry (Dr.
Barnes), Ruth Storey (Florence Dono-
vio), Jeanne Bates, Francis De Sales.
"The Voice" (11-22-60): Robert
Lansing (Jared Corning), Luana Anders
(Joan Goss), Paul Genge (Tom Goss),
Carl Benton Reid (Brian Christopher),
David Lewis, Harry Stang.
"The Promise" (11-29-60): Wil-
liam Shatner (Carl Bremmer), Deidre
Owen (Lois Bremmer), Ben Wright (Capt.
George Davis), Guy Kingsford (newsman),
Queenie Leonard (Nurse O'Brien), Peter
Gordon (Colonel), Kurt Falkenberg (Ger-
man prisoner).
"Tonight at 12:17!" (12-6-60):
Peggy Ann Garner (Laura Perkins), John
Lasell (John Perkins), Jack Lester (Doc-
tor), Gene Lyons (Sam Blake), David
DeHaven (Frank).
"Where Are They?" (12-13-60):
Philip Pine (Harry Call), Joan Tompkins
(Jenny Call), Alan Dexter (Towers),
John Alvin (Bradley), Robert Williams
(Joe Tomlinson), Herb Patterson (Gar-
ner), Richard Devon.
"Legacy of Love" (12-20-60): Nor-
ma Crane (Marianne Darelle), Charles
Aidman (Norman Bromley), Ollie O'Toole,
Barbara Eiler (Mrs. Bromley), Joe Mc-
Guinn (station master), Jon Lormer (re-
sident), Alfred Hopson (taxi driver),
Louise Lorimer (Mrs. Darelle), Olan
Soule.
"Rendezvous" (12-27-60): Georg-
ann Johnson (Kate Maxwell), Donald Mur-
phy (Fred Summers), H. M. Wynant (Wil-
liam Cooper), Warren Kemmerling (Lt.

Walton), K. L. Smith (plainclothesman), Fred Coby (policeman).

"The Executioner" (1-3-61): Buzz Martin (Jess Bradley), Crahan Denton (Col. Martin), Tom Middleton (Sgt. Evans), Will J. White (Corporal), Don Ross (Pickets), Jeremy Slate (Capt. Adams).

"The Last Round" (1-10-61): Charles Bronson (Yank Dawson), Felix Deebank (Chipper White), Ronald Long (Alfie Jones), Wally Cassell (Collins), Gordon Richards (Doctor), Stewart Taylor.

"Dead Man's Tale" (1-17-61): Lonny Chapman (Philip Werris), Jean Engstrom (Jan Weeris), Lucy Prentiss (Mrs. Barton), Walter Reed (Robert Barton), Charles Seel (proprietor), Charles Tannen (hotel manager).

"The Scared Mushroom" (1-24-61).

"The Gift" (1-31-61): Betty Garde (Lola), Scott Marlowe (Mario), Mary Sinclair (Maude Gillespie).

"Persons Unknown" (2-7-61): David J. Stewart (Dr. Atl), Jay Novello (Gonzalez), Robert Carricart (Capt. Alvarez), Rudolfo Acosta (Col. Ferrero).

"Night of Decision" (2-21-61): Robert Douglas (George Washington), Richard Hale (Otumcas), Donald Buka (Marquis de Lafayette), Richard Tyler.

"The Stranger" (2-28-61): Peter Dyneley (Hadley), Bill Nagy (Jerome S. Cole), Patrick MacAlliney (Warden), Graham Stark (Peter), Ken Wayne (guard), Larry Cross (guard), Robert Percival (Doctor), Mark Baker (Barber).

"Justice" (3-7-61): Meredith Edwards (Wyndham Roberts), Clifford Evans (Constable Jones), Edward Evans, Barbara Mullen.

"The Face" (3-14-61): Sean Kelly (Stephen Bolt), Penelope Horner (Rosemary Hogan), John Brown (Mark Bolt), Gareth Tandy, Robin Summer.

"That Room Upstairs" (3-21-61): Lois Maxwell (Esther Hollis), David Knight (Will Hollis), Anthony Oliver (Hudson), Gilda Emmanueli (child), Carl Bernard (Doctor).

"Signal Received" (4-4-61): Mark Eden (Watson), Terry Palmer (Breed), Richard Gale (Hughes), Jennifer Daniel (girl), Viola Keats (Mrs. Breed).

"The Convession" (4-11-61): Donald Pleasence (Herbert Laurence),

Adrienne Corri (Sarah), Robert Raglan (policeman), Raymond Rollett (K. C.), Eileen Way (Mrs. Evans).

"The Avengers" (4-25-61): Andre Morell (the General), Lisa Gastoni (Marianne), Stanley Van Beers (Priest), Carl Jaffe (Doctor), Richard Leech (orderly), Steve Plytas (gardener), Robert Crewdson (musician), Jan Conrad (musician), Carl Duering (musician), Charles Russell (musician).

"The Prisoner" (5-2-61): Anton Diffring (German Soldier), Catherine Feller (Ruth Goldman), Faith Brook (Nurse Lentz).

"Blood Flower" (5-16-61): Larry Gates (Gavin Carrol), Eugene Iglesias (Simon Alcazan), Marya Stevens (Senorita Cavallera), David Garcia (Alfredo).

"The Sorcerer" (5-23-61): Christopher Lee (Wilhelm Reitlinger), Martin Benson (Klaus), Gabrielli Licudi (Elsa).

"The Villa" (6-6-61): Elizabeth Sellers (Mary Low), Michael Crawford (Tony Hudson), Geoffrey Toone (Jim Low), Marla Landi (Stella).

"The Tiger" (6-20-61): Pamela Brown (Miss Plum), Pauline Challenor (Pamela), Elspeth March (Mrs. Murphy), Patsy Smart.

"Nightmare" (6-27-61): Peter Wyngarde (Paul Roland), Ambrosine Philipotts (Lady Diana), Mary Peach (Jill Barrington), Ferdy Mayne (Geoffrey Heathcote), Jean Cadell.

"Eye Witness" (7-4-61): John Meillon (Henry Soames), Robin Hughes (Jake), J. G. Devlin (Leo), Rose Alba, Anton Rodgers.

OPERATION NEPTUNE. 1953. Tod Griffin (Commander Hollister), Humphrey Davis (Dink), Margaret Stewart (Empress Thirza), Richard Holland (Dick Saunders), Harold Conklin (Mersenus).

OUTER LIMITS, THE. 1963-65. Vic Perrin (the Control Voice).

"The Galaxy Being" (9-16-63): Cliff Robertson (Allan Maxwell), Jacqueline Scott (Carol Maxwell), Lee Phillips (Gene 'Buddy' Maxwell), Allyson Ames (Loreen), William O'Douglas, Jr. (the Andromedan), Burt Metcalfe (Eddie Phillips), Don Harvey, Mavis Neal, Peter Madsen, William Stevens, Joseph Perry.

"The Hundred Days of the Dragon" (9-23-63): Sidney Blackmer (William Lyons Selby), Philip Pine (Ted Pearson), Nancy Rennick (Carol Selby Carter), Mark Roberts (Bob Carter), Richard

(OUTER LIMITS cont.) Loo (Li Chin Sung), James Hong (Wen Lee), Aki Akeong (Chinese Scientist), Bert Remsen, James Yagi, James Camden, Clarence Yung, Henry Scott.

"The Architects of Fear" (9-30-63): Robert Culp (Allen Leighton), Geraldine Brooks (Yvette Leighton), Leonard Stone (Dr. Phillip Gainer), Douglas Henderson (Dr. Fredericks), Martin Wolfson (Dr. Herschel), Lee Zimmer (Ford), Clay Tanner, Hal Bokar, William Bush.

"The Man with the Power" (10-7-63): Donald Pleasence (Harold Finley), Priscilla Morrill (Vera Finley), Fred Beir (Steve Crandon), John Marley (Dr. Sigmund Hindeman), Edward C. Platt (Dean Radcliffe), Frank Maxwell (Keenan), Paul Lambert (Henshell), James McCallion (Tremaine), Anne Loos (Emily Radcliffe), Diane Strom (secretary), Paul Kent (detective), Pat O'Hara (surgeon), Harry Ellerbe (Finley's family doctor), Jane Barclay (nurse).

"The Sixth Finger" (10-14-63): David McCallum (Gwyllm Griffiths), Edward Mulhare (Prof. Mathers), Jill Haworth (Cathy), Constance Cavendish (Gert the Bread), Nora Marlowe (Mrs. Ives), George Pelling (deputy), Chuck Hayward (deputy), Robert Doyle (Wilt Morgan), Janos Prohaska (Darwin).

"The Man Who Was Never Born" (10-28-63): Martin Landau (Andro), Shirley Knight (Noelle Anderson), John Considine (Bertram Cabot), Maxine Stuart (Mrs. McCluskey), Karl Held (Capt. Joseph Reardon), Jack Raine (minister), Marlowe Jensen (old man).

"O. B. I. T." (11-4-63): Peter Breck (Sen. Jeremiah Orville), Jeff Corey (Byron Lomax), Joanne Gilbert (Barbara Scott), Harry Townes (Dr. Clifford Scott), Alan Baxter (Col. Grover), Konstantin Shayne (Dr. Philip Fletcher), Sam Reese (Clyde Wyatt), Jason Wingreen (Fred Severn), Robert Beneveds (Capt. James Harrison), Lindsay Workman (Dr. Anderson), Chuck Hamilton (Armand Younger).

"The Human Factor" (11-11-63): Harry Guardino (Maj. Roger Brothers), Gary Merrill (Dr. James Hamilton), Sally Kellerman (Ingrid Larkin), Joe De Santis (Col. William Campbell), Ivan Dixon (Major Giles), Shirley O'-Hara (Dr. Soldini), John Newton (Peterson), Art Alisi (Sergeant), James Sikking (orderly), Jane Langley, Matty Jordan.

"Corpus Earthling" (11-18-63):

Robert Culp (Dr. Paul Cameron), Salome Jens (Laurie Cameron), Barry Atwater (Dr. Jonas Temple), David Garner (Ralph), Ken Renard (caretaker).

"Nightmare" (12-2-63): Ed Nelson (Col. Luke Stone), David Frankham (Capt. Terry Brookman), Martin Sheen (Private Arthur Dix), Bernard Kates (Lt. Ezra Kruge), James Shigeta (Major Jong), John Anderson (Ebonite Interrogator), Bill Gunn (Lt. James Willamore), Lillian Adams (Mrs. Dix), Lisa Mann (Kruge's nurse), Sasha Harda (Kruge's grandfather), Ben Wright (Gen. Benton), Whit Bissell (General), William Sage (General).

"It Crawled Out of the Woodwork" (12-9-63): Scott Marlowe (Jory Peters), Michael Forest (Dr. Stuart Peters), Joan Camden (Prof. Stephanie Linden), Kent Smith (Dr. Block), Ed Asner (Det. Sgt. Thomas Siroleo), Barbara Luna (Gaby Christian), Gene Darfler (Warren Edgar Morley), Lea Marmer (cleaning lady), Ted De Corsia (2nd sentry), Tom Palmer (coroner).

"The Borderland" (12-16-63): Mark Richman (Ian Frazer), Nina Foch (Eva Frazer), Phillip Abbott (Lincoln Russell), Barry Jones (Dwight Hartley), Gene Raymond (Benson Sawyer), Gladys Cooper (Mrs. Palmer), Noel De Souza (Dr. Sung), Alfred Ryder (Edgar Price).

"Tourist Attraction" (12-23-63): Ralph Meeker (John Dexter), Janet Blair (Lynn Archer), Henry Silva (Gen. Juan Mercurio), Jerry Douglas (Tom Evans), Jay Novello (Prof. Arivello), Noel De Souza (Capt. Fortunato), William Sage (reporter), Stuart Lancaster (Skipper), Jon Silo, Edward Colmans, Martin Garralga, Henry Delgado, Roger Stern.

"The Zanti Misfits" (12-30-63): Michael Tolan (Prof. Stephen Grave), Bruce Dern (Ben Garth), Olive Deering (Lisa Lawrence), Robert F. Simon (Gen. Maximillian Hart), Claude Woolman (Maj. Roger Hill), Lex Johnson (communications operator), George Sims (computer technician), Joey Tata (radar operator), Mike Mikkler (armed guard).

"The Mice" (1-6-64): Henry Silva (Chino Rivera), Diana Sands (Julia Harrison), Michael Higgins (Dr. Thomas Kellander), Ron Foster (Robert Richardson), Francis De Sales (Warden), Hugh Langtry (Chromoite), Gene Tyburn (Goldsmith), Don Ross (Heddon), Dabney Coleman.

"Controlled Experiment" (1-13-64): Carroll O'Connor (Diemos), Barry Morse (Phobos), Grace Lee Whitney (Carla Duveen), Robert Fortier (Bert Hamill),

Robert Kelljan (Frank Brant), Kay Harris (blonde), Linda Hutchins.
"Don't Open Till Doomsday" (1-20-64): Miriam Hopkins (Mrs. Kry), Melinda Plowman (Vivia), Buck Taylor (Gard Hayden), John Hoyt (Emmett Balfour), David Frankham (Harvey Kry), Anthony Jochim (Justman, the Butler), Russell Collins (Justice of the Peace), Nellie Burt (Justice's wife).
"Zzzzz" (1-27-63): Philip Abbott (Ben Fields), Marsha Hunt (Francesca Fields), Joanna Frank (Regina), Booth Colman (Dr. Howard Warren).
"The Invisibles" (2-3-64): Don Gordon (Luis Spain), Tony Mordente (Gennaro Planetta), George Macready (Gov. Lawrence K. Hillman), Neil Hamilton (Gen. Hillary J. Clarke), Dee Hartford (Mrs. Clarke), Walter Burke (Castle), Richard Dawson (Oliver Fair), Len Lesser (guard), John Graham, William O. Douglas, Jr., Chris Warfield.
"The Bellero Shield" (2-10-64): Martin Landau (Richard Bellero, Jr.), Sally Kellerman (Judith Bellero), Neil Hamilton (Richard Bellero, Sr.), Chita Rivera (Mrs. Dame), John Hoyt (Alien).
"The Children of Spider County" (2-17-64): Lee Kinsolving (Ethan Wechsler), Kent Smith (Aabel), Bennye Gatteys (Anna Bishop), John Milford (John Bartlett), Crahan Denton (Sheriff Statefield), Dabbs Greer (Mr. Bishop), Joey Tata, Robert Osterloh.
"Specimen: Unknown" (2-24-64): Stephen McNally (Col. J. T. MacWilliams), Gail Kobe (Janet Doweling), Richard Jaeckel (Capt. Mike Doweling), Russell Johnson (Maj. Clark Benedict), Peter Baldwin (Lt. Gordon Halper), John Kellogg (Maj. Jennings), Arthur Batanides (Lt. Kenneth Gavin).
"Second Chance" (3-2-64): Simon Oakland (Empyrian), Don Gordon (Dave Crowell), Janet De Gore (Mara Matthews), John McLiam (Arjay Beasley), Angela Clarke (Sue Ann), Mimsy Farmer (Denise), Yale Summers (Buddy Lyman), Arnold Merritt (Tommy).
"Moonstone" (3-9-64): Ruth Roman (Prof. Diana Brice), Alex Nicol (Gen. Lee Stocker), Tim O'Connor (Maj. Clint Anderson), Curt Conway (Dr. Tom Mendl), Hari Rhodes (Lt. Ernie Travis).
"The Mutant" (3-16-64): Warren Oates (Reese Fowler), Betsy Jones Moreland (Julie Griffith), Larry Pennell (Dr. Evan Marshall), Walter Burke (Dr. Riner), Robert Sampson (Lt. Peter Chandler), Herbert Rudin (Henry LaCosta), Richard Derr (Philip Griffith).
"The Guests" (3-23-64): Geoffrey Horne (Wade Norton), Luana Anders (Tess Ames), Gloria Grahame (Florida Patton), Vaughn Taylor (Mr. Latimer), Nellie Burt (Ethel Latimer), Burt Mustin (old man).
"Fun and Games" (3-30-64): Nick Adams (Mike Benson), Nancy Malone (Laura Hanley), Bill Hart (Opponent), Theo Marcuse (Senator), Ray Kellogg, Robert Johnson.
"The Special One" (4-6-64): Flip Mark (Kenny Benjamin), Richard Ney (Mr. Zeno), Macdonald Carey (Roy Benjamin), Marion Ross (Agnes Benjamin), Edward C. Platt (Terrance), Bert Freed (Joe Hayden), Jason Wingreen (Turner).
"A Feasibility Study" (4-13-64): Sam Wanamaker (Dr. Simon Holm), David Opatoshu (Ralph Cashman), Joyce Van Patten (Rhea Cashman), Phyllis Love (Andrea Holm), Frank Puglia, Ben Wright.
"Production and Decay of Strange Particles" (4-20-64): George Macready (Marshall), Signe Hasso (Laurel), Allyson Ames (Arndis), Robert Fortier (Pollart), Leonard Nimoy, Joseph Ruskin, John Duke.
"The Chameleon" (4-27-64): Robert Duvall (Louis Mace), Howard Caine (Chambers), Henry Brandon (Gen. Crawford), Douglas Henderson (Tillyard), William O'Connell (1st Creature).
"The Forms of Things Unknown" (5-4-64): Vera Miles (Kassia Paine), Barbara Rush (Leonarda Edmond), David McCallum (Tone Hobart), Sir Cedric Hardwicke (Colas), Scott Marlowe (Andre Pavan), Clive H. Halliday (Timothy R. Edmont).
"Soldier" (9-19-64): Michael Ansara (Qarlo), Lloyd Nolan (Kagan), Tim O'Connor (Tanner), Jill Hill (Toni), Catherine McLeod (Abby), Ralph Hart (Loren), Ted Stanhope (Doctor), Jaime Forster (old man).
"Cold Hands, Warm Heart" (9-26-64): William Shatner (Jeff Barton), Geraldine Brooks (Ann Barton), Lloyd Gough (Gen. Claiborne), Malachi Throne (Dr. Mike), James Sikking (Botan), Henry Scott (electronics), Laurence Montaigne (construction), Julian Burton (reporter), Peter Madsen (reporter).
"Behold, Eck!" (10-3-64): Peter Lind Hayes (Dr. James Stone), Parley Baer (Dr. Bernard Stone), Joan Freeman (Elizabeth Dunn), Douglas Henderson (Detective Lt. Runyan), George Wilkerson (Sammy), Marcel Hobart (Miss Wilson), Jack Wilson (Sgt. Jackson),

(OUTER LIMITS cont.)   Paul Sorenson
(Grayson).
"Expanding Human" (10-10-64):
Skip Homeier (Dr. Roy Clinton), Keith
Andes (Dr. Peter Wayne), James Doo-
han (Lt. Branch), Vaughn Taylor (Dean
Flint), Aki Aloong (Akada), Jason Win-
green (Coroner Leland), Troy Melton
(Detective Sgt. Alger), Robert Doyle
(Marc Lake), Barbara Wilkins (Susan
Wayne), Peter Duryea (Morrow), Mary
Gregory (apartment manager), Shirley
O'Hara (receptionist), Marc Falcon
(elevator operator), Owen McGivney
(nightwatchman).
    "Demon with a Glass Hand" (10-
17-64): Robert Culp (Trent), Arline
Martel (Consuelo), Abraham Sofaer
(Arch), Rex Holman (Battle), Steve
Harris (Breech), Robert Fortier (Budge).
    "Cry of Silence" (10-24-64): Ed-
die Albert (Andy Thorne), June Havoc
(Karen Thorne), Arthur Hunnicut (La-
mont).
    "The Invisible Enemy" (10-31-
64): Adam West (Maj. Charles Mer-
ritt), Rudi Solari (Capt. Jack Burkley),
Chris Alcaide (Col. Danvers), Joe Ma-
ross (Gen. Weston), Ted Knight (Mr.
Jerome), Bob DoQui (Johnson), Mike
Mikler (Capt. Thomas), Peter Marko
(Vazzari), Anthony Costello (Lt. Bow-
man).
    "Wolf 359" (11-7-64): Patrick
O'Neal (Prof. Jonathan Merideth), Sara
Shane (Ethel Merideth), Peter Haskell
(Peter Jellicoe), Dabney Coleman (James
Custer), Ben Wright (Philip Exeter
Dundee).
    "I, Robot" (11-14-64): Leonard
Nimoy (Judson Ellis), Howard Da Silva
(Cutler), Marianna Hill (Nina Link),
Red Morgan (Adam Link), Ford Rainey
(D. A. Thomas Coyle), Hugh Sanders
(Barclay), John Hoyt (Prof. Hebbel),
Peter Brocco (Dr. Link).
    "The Inheritors" (11-21-64 & 11-
28-64): Steve Ihnat (Lt. Phillip Minns),
Robert Duvall (Adam Bullard), Ivan
Dixon (Sgt. James Conover), Dee Pol-
lock (PFC Francis Hadley), James Fraw-
ley (Renaldo), Donald Harron (Art Har-
ris), James Shigeta (Capt. Ngo Newa),
Ted DeCorsica (Branch), Dabbs Greer
(Larkin), Suzanne Cupito (Minerva),
Leon Askin (shop superintendent), Jan
Shutan (Mrs. Subiron), Kim Hector
(Johnny Subiron), Robert Cinder (Jes-
sup), David Brady (Danny Masters),
William Winterside (Prof. Andrew
Whitsett), Joanne Stewart (Miss Steen),
Linda Hutchings (nurse), Robert J.
Nelson (surgeon), Sy Prescott (guard),

Paulle Clark (2nd nurse).
    "Keeper of the Purple Twilight"
(12-5-64): Robert Webber (Ikar), War-
ren Stevens (Eric Plummer), Gail Kobe
(Janet Lane), Curt Conway (Franklin
Karlin), Edward C. Platt (David Hunt).
    "The Duplicate Man" (12-19-64):
Ron Randell (Henderson James I & II),
Sean McClory (Karl Emmett), Constance
Towers (Laura James), Stevan Geray
(Basil Jerichau), Konstantine Shayne
(Gardner), Ivy Bethune (Miss Thorson),
Mike Lane (the Megasoid), Alan Gifford
(guide), Jonathan Hole (pedestrian),
Jeffrey Stone (cop).
    "Counterweight" (12-26-64): Mi-
chael Constantine (Joe Dix), Crahan
Denton (Dr. James), Jacqueline Scott
(Dr. Alicia Hendrix), Sharry Marshall
(Maggie O'Hara), Sandy Kenyon (Prof.
Henry Craig), Larry Ward (Keith Ellis),
Charles Hardilac (Michael Lint).
    "The Brain of Colonel Barham"
(1-2-65): Grant Williams (Maj. Douglas
McKinnon), Elizabeth Perry (Jennifer
Barham), Anthony Eisley (Col. Alex
Barham), Douglas Kennedy (Gen. Daniel
Pettit), Wesley Addy (Dr. Rahm), Paul
Lukather (Nichols), Martin Kosleck (Dr.
Leo Hauser), Peter Hansen (Maj. Locke),
Robert Chadwick (guard).
    "The Premonition" (1-9-65): De-
wey Martin (Jim Darcy), Mary Murphy
(Linda Darcy), Emma Tyson (Jane Dar-
cy), Bill Bramley (Baldy Baldwin), Kay
Kuter (limbo being), Dorothy Green (ma-
tron), Coby Denton (sentry).
    "The Probe" (1-16-65): Mark Rich-
man (Jefferson Rome), Peggy Ann Gar-
ner (Amanda Frank), William Stevens
(Dexter), Ron Hayes (Coberly), William
Boyett (Beeman), Richard Tretter (radio
engineer), Janos Prohoska (the Mikie).

OUT OF THE BLUE. 1979. James Bro-
gan (Angel Random), Eileen Heckart
(Boss Angel), Dixie Carter (Marion
MacNelmore), Hannah Dean (Gladys),
Clark Brandon (Chris Richards), Oli-
via Barash (Laura Richards), Tammy
Lauren (Stacey Richards), Jason Kel-
ler (Jason Richards), Shane Keller
(Shane Richards).

OUT OF THE UNKNOWN. British 1965-
67.
    "Sucker Bait": Bill Nagy (Captain),
Clive Endersby (Mark Annuncio), John
Meillon (Dr. Sheffield), David Knight
(Dr. Cimon), Burt Kwouk (Noves), Ro-
ger Croucher (Fawkes), Tenniel Evans
(Rodriguez), David Sumner (Vernadsky).
    "The Machine Stops": Yvonne

Mitchell (Vashti).
"Frankenstein Mark II": Rachel
Roberts, Basil Henson.
"Immortality, Inc. ".
"Liar!".
"The Last Lonely Man".
"Beachhead".
"Random Quest".
"The Little Black Bag".
"Thirteen to Arcturas".
"The Naked Sun".
"Target Generation".

OUT OF THIS WORLD. British (June-
Sept., 1962). Boris Karloff (Host).
"Little Lost Robot": Maxine Aud-
ley.
"The Yellow Pill": Nigel Stock,
Richard Pasco, Peter Dyneley.
"The Cold Equation": Peter Wyn-
garde.
"Imposter".
"Botany Bay".
"Medicine Show".
"Divided We Fall".
"Pictures Don't Lie".
"Target Generation".
"Immigrant".
"I, Robot".
"The Tycoons".

PEACOCK SHOWCASE.
"The Electric Grandmother" (1-
17-82): Edward Herrmann, Maureen
Stapleton (Grandmother), Tara Kennedy
(Agatha), Paul Benedict (Guido Fantoc-
cini), Robert Macnaughton (Tom), Charlie Fields (Timothy), Truman Gaige
(Old Tom), Richard Whiting (Old Timothy), Paula Trueman (Old Agatha), Madeleine Thornton-Sherwood (Aunt Clara).

PHOENIX, THE. 1982. Judson Scott
(Bennu), Richard Lynch (Preminger).
"In Search of Mira" (3-26-82):
John Vernon (Atkins), E. G. Marshall
(Dr. Frazier), Bert Remsen (Hal
Massey), Jenny Parsons (Darlene),
Sandy Ward (Unger), Britt Leach,
Terry Wills.
"One of Them" (4-2-82): Andrea
Marcovicci, Carmen Zapata, Sheila
Frazier, Lawrence Casey, Marc Alai-
mo, Peter Michael Goetz, Debbie Rich-
ter, Behrouz Vossi, John Zenda, Josh
Cadman, Marshall Teague.
"Presence of Evil" (4-9-82): Kaz
Garas (Jack Houghton), Lee Purcell
(Cindy Houghton), Jeremy Light (Roddy),
Robert Reilly (Dolfo), Joan Foley (Fre-
da), Nancy Grahn (Holly).
"The Fire Within" (4-16-82):
John Milford (Harry Cartwright), Ei-

leen Davidson (Ellie), Tracey Gold (Jan),
Peter Iancangelo (Fred Barford), Nocona Aranda (Curator Fast), Carmen Argenziano (Dave), Sam Laws, Karen
Anders, Fred Franklin, S. Newton Anderson, Rick Grassi, Bret Shryer, Nelson Mashita, Noel Colton, Ned Bellamy.

PLANET OF THE APES. 1974. Ron
Harper (Allen Virdon), James Naugh-
ton (Pete Burke), Roddy McDowall
(Galen), Booth Colman (Dr. Zaius),
Mark Lenard (Gen. Urko).
"Escape from Tomorrow" (9-13-
74): Royal Dano (Farrow), Bobby Por-
ter (Arno), Woodrow Parfrey (Veska),
William Beckley (Grundig), Biff Elliot
(Ullman), Jerome Thor (Proto).
"The Gladiators" (9-20-74): John
Hoyt (Barlow), William Smith (Tolar),
Marc Singer (Dalton), Pat Renella (Ja-
son), Eddie Fontaine (Gorilla Sergeant).
"The Trap" (9-27-74): Norman
Alden (Zako), John Milford (Miller),
Cindy Eilbacher (Lisa Miller), Mickey
Leclair (Jick Miller), Wallace Earl
(Mary Miller), Eldon Burke (Olam),
Ron Stein (Mema).
"The Good Seeds" (10-4-74): Geof-
frey Deuel (Anto), Lonny Chapman (Po-
lar), Bobby Porter (Remus), Jacqueline
Scott (Zantes), Eileen Dietz (Jillia),
Dennis Cross (Gorilla Officer).
"The Legacy" (10-11-74): Zina
Bethune, Jackie Earle Haley, Wayne
Foster, Jon Lormer, Robert Phillips.
"Tomorrow's Tide" (10-18-74):
Roscoe Lee Browne (Hurton), Jay Ro-
binson (Bandor), John McLiam (Gahto),
Kathleen Bracken (Soma), Jim Storm
(Romar), Frank Orsatti, Tom McDonough.
"The Surgeon" (10-25-74): Martin
Brooks (Laander), Jacqueline Scott (Kira),
Michael Strong (Travin), Jaime Smith
Jackson (girl), Ron Stein (Haman/Lafer),
Peter Ireland.
"The Deception" (11-1-74): Jane
Actman (Fauna), John Milford (Sestus),
Baynes Barron (Perdix), Pat Renella
(Zon), Eldon Burke (Chilot), Tom Mc-
Donough (Macor), Ron Stein (Krona),
Hal Baylor.
"The Horse Race" (11-8-74): Bever-
ly Garland (Wanda), Anne Seymour (Ann),
Normann Burton (Yalu), Harry Townes
(Dr. Malthus), Eldon Burke (peasant),
Lynn Denesch (Nora), Wayne Foster
(Gorilla Lieutenant).
"The Tyrant" (11-22-74): Percy
Rodriguez (Aboro), Joseph Ruskin (Dako),
Tom Troupe (Augustus), Michael Conrad
(Janor), James Daughton (Mikal), Arlen
Stewart (Gola), Gary Combs (gorilla

(PLANET OF THE APES cont.) driver).
"The Cure" (11-29-74): David
Sheiner (Zoran), Sondra Locke (Amy),
Ron Soble (Kava), George Wallace (Tal-
bert), Albert Cole (Mason), Eldon
Burke (Inta).
"The Liberator" (12-6-74): John
Ireland, Jennifer Ashley, Ben Andrews,
Peter Skinner.
"Up Above the World So High"
(12-20-74): Joanna Barnes (Carsia),
Frank Aletter (Leuric), Martin E.
Brooks (Konag), William Beckley (Coun-
cil Orang), Ron Stein.

PLAY FOR TOMORROW. British.
"Crimes" (4-13-82): Sylvestra
Le Touzel (Jane), Peter Whitbread
(Ron), T. P. McKenna (Melvyn), Julia
Foster (Veronica), Stephen Sweeney
(Bill), Rufus Collins (Elliot), Dave Hill
(Smith), Donald Gee (Larry).
"Bright Eyes" (4-20-82): Robin
Ellis (Sam Howard), Sarah Berger (Ca-
thy), Corinna Reardon (Cathy as a child),
Kate Harper (Rachel), Constantine De
Goguel (John), Julian Curry (Charvier),
Stephen Grief (Shapiro), Gavin Camp-
bell (Michael Gilbert), Della Finch (TV
interviewer), Charles Baillie (TV cam-
eraman), John Hug (1st policeman),
Ian Flintoff (2nd policeman), Julian
Wadham (Oliver), Julia Gale (girl at
party), Adam Blackwood (boy at party).
"Cricket" (4-27-82): Malcolm
Terris (John Ridley), Anne Raitt (Mor-
na Ridley), Paul Antony-Barber (Willie
Ridley), Jeremy Child (Lord Slaggys-
ford), Simon Rouse (Colin Bayliss),
Terence Halliday (Tommy Coulthard).
"The Nuclear Family" (5-4-82):
Jimmy Logan (Joe Brown), Ann Scott-
Jones (Agnes Brown), Gerard Kelly
(Gary Brown), Lizzy Radford (Ann
Brown), Russell Hunter (Sgt. Smellie),
Sarah Thurstan (Able-bodied Andrews),
Gavin Campbell (newscaster), Barbara
Coles (scientist).
"Shades" (5-11-82): Tracey Childs
(Sheena/Angie), Stuart MacKenzie (Joe/
Malcolm), Emily Moore (Kate/Mary),
Neil Pearson (Adam/Peter), Shelagh
McLeod (Diana/Paula), Francesca Gon-
shaw (Julie/Sue), Michael Feldman (To-
ny).
"Easter 2016" (5-18-82): Denys
Hawthorne (Cyril Brown), Derrik O'Con-
nor (Lennie North), Bill Nighy (Connor
Mullan), Eileen Pollock (Clare Williams),
Gerard McSorley (John Bingham), Lise-
Ann McLaughlin (June Crawford), Colm
Meaney (Kevin Murphy), Susie Kelly
(Colette Brogan), Kenneth Branagh (stu-

dent).

PLAYHOUSE. British.
"The Witching Hour" (1-4-82):
Tony Boncza (Rufus), Geoffrey Bayldon
(Old Father Time), David Wood (F 28),
Maureen Lipman (Witch), Roy Kinnear
(Mirror), Brian Carroll (F 29).
"The Unknown Enchantment" (1-
18-82): John Savident (Lord Chamber-
lain), Brian Hawksley (Margrave), Ro-
salind Ayres (Elfriedra), Phyllida Law
(Countess Julie), Nigel Havers (Count
Kathka), Donna Evans (Princess Arabel-
la), Robin Davies (Count Pogo), Alec
Bregonzi (Abracadabra).
"The Queen of Annagh" (4-16-82):
Diane Fletcher (Nancy), Eamon Boland
(Michael Edward Ross), Trevor T. Smith
(the Officer).

PLAYHOUSE.
"The House on Judas Street" (1-
23-55): Jean Byron, Peter Votrain.

PLAYHOUSE 90.
"Forbidden Area" (10-4-56): Charl-
ton Heston (Maj. Jesse Price), Vincent
Price (Clark Simmons), Diana Lynn
(Katharine Hume), Tab Hunter (Stanley
Smith), Victor Jory, Charles Bickford.
"The Star Wagon" (1-24-57): Dia-
na Lynn (Martha Minch), Eddie Bracken
(Stephen Minch), Jackie Coogan (Hanus
Wicks), Margaret Hayes (Halle Arling-
ton), William Bishop (Charles Duffy),
Billie Burke (Mrs. Rutledge).
"Project Immortality" (6-11-59):
Lee J. Cobb (Dr. Lawrence Doner), Pat-
ty McCormack (Ketti Doner), Kenneth
Haigh (Martin Schramm), Gusti Huber
(Mrs. Doner), Michael Landon (Arthur
Doner).
"Alas, Babylon" (4-3-60): Dana
Andrews (Mark Bragg), Don Murray
(Randy Bragg), Kim Hunter (Helen Bragg),
Barbara Rush (Liz), Everett Sloane (Dr.
Gunn), Rita Moreno (Rita), Judith Evelyn
(Lavinia), Don Gordon (Pete), Robert
Crawford, Jr. (Richard), Gina Gillespie
(Laura), Burt Reynolds (Ace).

PLAYHOUSE OF THE STARS.
"The Black Mate" (6-18-54): Paul
Kelly (Winston Bunter), Lee Van Cleef
(Larkin), Robert Cornthwaite (Capt.
Johns), Bill Phillips (Forrest), Tom
Landon (Evans), George Khoury (Weber),
John Close (Hutton), John Harmon (Car-
ter).
"Gift of the Devil" (8-18-54): Will
Rogers, Jr. (Eli Hancock), Joan Cam-
den (Mrs. Pardee), Sally Fraser (Lucy

Mayer), Oliver Blake (Barnhart), Jack George (Uncle Bob), Ralph Moody (Mr. Moyer).

PLAY OF THE MONTH. British.
"I Have Been Here Before" (5-24-82): Herbert Lom (Dr. Gortler), Anthony Valentine (Walter Ormond), Lorne Heilbron (Janet), Diana Rayworth (Sally Pratt), Leslie Sands (Sam Shipley), James Griffiths (Oliver Farrant).

PLAY OF THE WEEK.
"House of Death" (10-4-55): Boris Karloff.
"Don Juan in Hell" (2-15-60): Hurd Hatfield (Don Juan), George C. Scott (the Devil), Siobhan McKenna (Dona Ana), Dennis King (the Statue), Marc Connelly (the Stage Manager).
"Night of the Auk" (2-20-61): William Shatner (Lewis Rohnen), Shepperd Strudwick (Dr. Bruner).
"The Enchanted" (4-3-61): Tom Poston (Supervisor), Rosemary Harris (Isabel), Walter Abel (Inspector), Arthur Treacher (Mayor), Cyril Cusack (Doctor), Nydia Westman (Armande Mangebois), James Mitchell (Ghost), Mary Finney (Leonide Mangebois), Joan Terrace (Lucy), Frances Lorrain Myers (Gilberte), Joseph Buloff (Executioner), Frederick Rolf (Executioner).
"The Dybbuk" (5-1-61): Theodore Bikel (Sender), Carol Lawrence (Leah), Ludwig Donath (Rabbi Azrael), Michael Tolan (Channon), Milton Selzer (Messenger), Vincent Gardenia (Nissen), Stefan Gierasch (Hassidim), Gene Saks (Hassidim), Jerry Rockwood (Hassidim), Theo Goetz (Meyer), Eli Mintz (Nachmon), Sylvia Davis (Frade), Michael Shillo (Rabbi Samson).
"No Exit" (2-10-62): Dane Clark, Colleen Dewhurst.

PLAY OF THE WEEK. British.
"Night of the Big Heat" (6-14-60): Patrick Holt, Melissa Stribling, Lee Montague, Bernard Cribbins.

PLAYWRIGHTS '55.
"The Answer" (10-4-55): Paul Douglas, Nina Foch, Albert Dekker, Walter Abel, Conrad Nagel.

POWERS OF MATTHEW STAR, THE. 1982-83. Peter Barton (Matthew Star), Lou Gossett, Jr.

PRODUCER'S SHOWCASE.
"Jack and the Beanstalk" (11-12-56): Joel Grey (Jack), Celeste Holm

(Mad Maggie), Cyril Ritchard (Peddler), Peggy King (Tillie), Billy Gilbert (Poodledoop), Arnold Stang (Little Giant), Leora Dana (Mother).

PRISONER, THE. 1968. Patrick McGoohan (Number Six), Angelo Muscat (the Butler), Peter Swanwick (the Supervisor).
"Arrival" (6-1-68): Guy Doleman (Number Two), Virginia Maskell (the Woman), George Baker (New Number Two), Paul Eddington (Cobb), Stephanie Randall (Maid).
"The Chimes of Big Ben" (6-6-68): Leo McKern (Number Two), Nadia Gray (Nadia), Richard Wattis (Fotheringay), Finlay Currie (the General).
"A, B & C" (6-15-68): Colin Gordon (Number Two), Katherine Kath (Engadine), Sheila Allen (Number 14), Peter Bowles (A), Georgia Cookson (blonde).
"Free for All" (6-29-68): Eric Portman (Number Two), Rachel Herbert (Number 58), Dene Cooper (photographer), George Benson (Labour Exchange Manager), John Cazabon, Harold Berens.
"The Schizoid Man" (7-6-68): Jane Merrow (Alison), Anton Rodgers (Number Two), Gay Cameron (Number 36), Earl Cameron (Supervisor).
"The General" (7-13-68): Colin Gordon (Number Two), John Castle (Number 12), Peter Howell (the Professor), Al Mancini (the Announcer), Betty McDowall.
"Many Happy Returns" (7-20-68): Donald Sinden (the Colonel), Patrick Cargill (Thorpe), Georgina Cookson (Mrs. Butterworth), Brian Worth (Group Captain), Jon Laurimore (Ernst), Richard Caldicot (the Commander), Dennis Chinnery (Gunther).
"Dance of the Dead" (7-27-68): Mary Morris (Number Two), Duncan Macrae (the Doctor), Norma West (Little Bo-Peep), Bee Duffell (Psychiatrist), Camilla Hasse (day supervisor), Alan White (Dutton), Denise Huckley (maid).
"Do Not Forsake Me, Oh My Darling" (8-3-68): Clifford Evans (Number Two), Zena Walker (Janet), Hugo Schuster (Selztman), Nigel Stock (the Colonel), John Wentworth (Sir Charles).
"It's Your Funeral" (8-10-68): Derren Nesbitt (New Number Two), Andre Van Geyseghem (Retiring Number Two), Annette Andre (the Watchmaker's Daughter), Martin Miller (Watchmaker), Mark Eden (Number 100), Wanda Ventham (Computer Attendant), Charles Lloyd-Pack (artist), Mark Burns (Number Two's Assistant), Arthur White (stall

(PRISONER cont.) holder), Grace Arnold (Number 36), Gerry Crampton (Kosho Opponent), Michael Bilton (M. C. Councillor).

"Checkmate" (8-17-68): Ronald Radd (the Rook), Peter Wyngarde (Number Two), Rosalie Crutchley (the Queen), Patricia Jessell (1st psychiatrist), Bee Duffell (2nd psychiatrist), George Coulouris (man with stick), Denis Shaw (the shopkeeper), Danver Walker (painter), Basil Dignam (supervisor), Victor Platt (assistant supervisor), Terence Donovan (sailer), Geoffrey Reed (skipper), Joe Dunne (1st tower guard), Romo Garrara (2nd tower guard).

"Living in Harmony" (1968): Alexis Kanner (the Kid), David Bauer (the Judge), Valerie French (Cathy), Gordon Tanner (town elder), Michael Balfour (Will), Larry Taylor (Mexican Sam), Gordon Sterne (the bystander).

"A Change of Mind" (8-24-68): John Sharpe (Number Two), Angela Browne (Number 86), George Pravda (Doctor), Kathleen Breck (Number 42), Michael Miller (Number 93), Bartlett Mullens (Committee Chairman), June Ellis (Number 48), Thomas Heathcote (Lobo Man), John Hamblin (1st woodland man), Michael Billington (2nd woodland man), Joseph Cuby (1st social group member), Michael Chow (2nd social group member).

"Hammer into Anvil" (8-31-68): Patrick Cargill (Number Two), Victor Maddern (Band Master), Basil Hoskins (Number 14), Norman Scace (Psychiatric director), Derek Aylward (New Supervisor), Hillary Dwyer (Number 73), Victor Woolf (shop assistant), Michael Segal (lab technician), Arthur Gross (Control Room Operator), Jackie Cooper (1st Guardian), Fred Haggerty (2nd Guardian), Eddie Powell (3rd Guardian), George Leach (4th Guardian), Susan Sheers (female cook expert), Margo Andrews (shop kiosk girl).

"The Girl Who Was Death" (9-7-68): Kenneth Griffith (Schnipps), Justine Lord (Sonia), Christopher Benjamin (Potter), Harold Berens (Boxing M. C.), Michael Brennan (Killer Karminski), Sheena Marsha (barmaid).

"Once Upon a Time" (9-14-68): Leo McKern (Number Two), John Maxim (Number 86), John Cazabon (Umbrella Man).

"Fall Out" (9-21-68): Leo McKern (Number Two), Alexis Kanner (Young Man), Kenneth Griffith (President), Michael Miller (delegate).

PROJECT UFO. 1978-79. William Jordan (Maj. Jake Gatlin) 1978, Edward Winter (Capt. Ben Ryan) 78-79, Caskey Swaim (Sgt. Harry Fitz), Aldine King (Libby) 1978.

Sighting 4001: "The Washington D. C. Incident" (2-19-78): Anne Schedeen (Helen McNair), Len Sayland (Operations Director), Frances Reid (Martha Carlyle), Linwood McCarthy (Senior Controller), Hoke Howell (Burke), John Findlater (Lt. Gary McNair).

Sighting 4002: "Welcome to Saucer City" (2-26-78): Jim Davis (Earl Clay), Barbara Luna (Helen Ramirez), Mills Watson (Barney Tomlinson), David Yanez (Pauley Ramirez), Colby Chester (Jim Rober), Olan Soule (George La Tourette), Parley Baer (Tom Fairly).

Sighting 4003: "The Fremont Incident" (3-12-78): Rod Perry (Robert Lee Armstrong), Frank Aletter (Milton Short), Herbert Rudley (Marsden), Kim Hamilton (Diane Armstrong), Gary Crosby (Maynard Timmons), Rod Cameron (Chief Gaffey).

Sighting 4004: "The Howard Crossing Incident" (3-19-78): Leif Erickson (Frederick Carlson), Maggie King (Jeannie Carlson), Claude Johnson (Martin Carlson), Ezra Stone (Prof. Hollander), Virginia Gregg (Greta Marshall), Lou Frizzell (Alex Marshall), Malachi Throne (Dr. Forrest), Richard Derr (Carryl Cochran), Jack Ging (Capt. Roy Gordon).

Sighting 4005: "The Medicine Bow Incident" (3-26-78): Paul Picerni (Ed Mason), Edward Winter (Brad Everett), Kenneth Mars (Gus Shafter), Anthony Eisley (Charles Lundman), Darrel Larson (Danny Peterson), Joan Freeman (Peggy Williams).

Sighting 4006: "The Nevada Desert Incident" (4-2-78): Scott Hylands (Lt. Paul Staley), Andrew Duggan (Dr. O'-Neill), Adrienne La Russa (Cynthia Staley), Buck Young (Major Birnham), Hank Brandt (Colonel Fox), Donna Douglas (Wendy).

Sighting 4007: "The Forest City Incident" (4-9-78): Stephen Hudis (Jerry Daniels), Michael Francis Blake (Clay Munson), Tim Donnelly (Stu Hadley), Don Dubbins (Charles Hamlin), Skip Homeier (Lt. Ed Coogan), Stacy Keach, Sr. (Marthis).

Sighting 4008: "The Desert Springs Incident" (4-23-78): Buckley Norris (Dave Chapman), Jack Sheldon (Mike Kirby), Peggy Webber (Emma Smith), Joseph Ruskin (Gist).

Sighting 4009: "The French Incident" (4-30-78): Jacques Aubuchon

(Marchand), Eric Braeden (Paul Gerard), Maria Grimm (Michelle Tanner), Morgan Woodward (Carlton Tanner).

Sighting 4010: "The Academy Incident" (5-7-78): Craig Stevens (Col. Delany), Anthony Geary (Darryl Biggs), Shane Sinutko (Timmy Delany), S. Newton Anderson (Jim Croft), Dr. Joyce Brothers (Dr. Paulson), Howard Culver (Dr. Bensinger), Winter Horton (Paul Radcliffe).

Sighting 4011: "The Doll House Incident" (5-20-78): Alf Kjellin (Carl Youngstrom), David Hedison (Frederick Flanagan), Linda Foster (Kristie Shields).

Sighting 4012: "The Rock-and-Hard Place Incident" (5-27-78): Elaine Joyce (Theresa Ball), Jack Hogan (Max Stacey), Paul Brinegar (Arley McCoy), Ann Doran (Annie Butler), Robert Ginty (Jeff Peters), Robert Patten (Col. Davis).

Sighting 4013: Title unknown (6-4-78): Pamela Franklin (Sister Lucy), Amzie Strickland (Sister Anne), Virginia Gregg (Sister Superior), David Watson (Monsignor Killian), Val de Vargas (Sheriff Diaz).

Sighting 4015: "The Underwater Incident" (9-21-78): Scott Thomas (Paul Marshall), Caroline McWilliams (Eve Summers), Laurette Spang (Linda Collins), Allen Case (Cmdr. Bell).

Sighting 4017: "The Devilish Lights Incident" (9-28-78): Kim Hunter (Dr. Samantha Klein), Jared Martin (Dr. Jon Robinson), Jenny Sullivan (Dr. Linda Robinson), Bob Dellegall (Capt. Harlan).

Sighting 4018: "The Pipeline Incident" (10-5-78): Randolph Mantooth (Tim Jenkins), Camerone Mitchell (Donald Worth), Donald May (Richard McLane), Brad Dexter (Lew Perrino).

Sighting 4019: "The Incident on the Cliff" (10-12-78): Trish Stewart (Lisa Forman), William Reynolds (Roger Forman), Kim Richards (Amy Forman).

Sighting 4020: "The Believe It or Not Incident" (10-19-78): Mark Slade (Roy Layton), Marie Windsor (Cara Layton), Anne Lockhart (Ann Booth), Olan Soule (Prof. Diedler).

Sighting 4021: Title unknown (11-2-78): Michael Strong (Charles Robinson), Gary Crosby (Ed Norwood), Normann Burton (Dr. Phil Greiner), Elaine Devry (Lida Robinson), Henry Jones (Harold Moon), Bradley Greene (Terry Robinson), Barry Cahill, Don 'Red' Barry.

Sighting 4022: "The Island Incident" (11-30-78): James Olson (Dr. Ted Saunders), Marlyn Mason (Donna Saunders), Cal Bellini (Peter Ueki), Ken Renard (Manuku), Sam Tampoya (Timi).

Sighting 4023: "The Superstition Mountain Incident" (12-7-78): Josh Albee (Charlie), Anna Karen (Clara), Leslie Ackerman (Laurie Pawling), William Bogert (Timothy Hooper), Dr. Joyce Brothers (Dr. Saginaw).

Sighting 4024: Title unknown (12-28-78): Pamelyn Ferdin (Cindy Harper), Whit Bissell (Harper), Malachi Throne (Prof. Lazlo).

Sighting 4017: Title unknown (1-4-79): Russell Wiggins (Andy McMurtry), Jim B. Smith (Chief Morton), Lou Frizzel (Luke Primrose), Joyce Jameson (Ella Primrose), Scott Mulhern (Sgt. Eddie Larkin), Kenneth Tigar (Roy Denby).

Sighting 4025: "The Spaceship Incident" (7-5-79): Peter Brown (Steve Rollins), John Anderson (Capt. Bergstad), Morey Amsterdam (Ollie Hyers), Jayne Meadows (Marlene Baker), Raymond Mayo (Helmsman), Donna Douglas (Mrs. Ferrall), Ed Deemer (radar operator).

Sighting 4026: Title unknown (7-12-79): Frank Holliday (Chuck Ryerson), Linda Foster (Janet Ryerson), Vic Perrin (Rashoon), Olan Soule (Emerson Keyes), Robert Patten (Felix Webster), Eddie Firestone (Silas Cob), Parley Baer, Sam Edwards.

Sighting 4027: "The Wild Blue Yonder Incident" (7-19-79): Rebecca York (Kay Galloway), W. K. Stratton (Doug Deweiler), Thomas A. Stewart (Roland Higbie), Fred Holliday (Captain Moran).

QUARK. 1977-78. Richard Benjamin (Adam Quark), Richard Kelton (Ficus) 1978, Timothy Thomerson (Gene/Jean), Conrad Janis (Palindrome), Bobby Porter (Andy the Robot), Tricia Barnstable (Betty 1), Cyb Barnstable (Betty 2), Alan Caillou (the Head).

Pilot (5-7-77): Douglas V. Fowley (O. B. Mudd), Misty Rowe (Interface).

"May the Source Be with You" (2-24-78): Hans Conried (Voice of the Source), Henry Silva (High Gorgon), Cris Capen (Gorgon Guard 1).

"The Old and the Beautiful" (3-3-78): Barbara Rhoades (Princess Carna).

"The Good, the Bad and the Ficus" (3-10-78): Geoffrey Lewis (Admiral Flint).

(QUARK cont.)
"Goodbye, Polumbus" (3-17-78).
"All the Emperor's Quasi-Norms"
(3-24-78 & 3-31-78): Ross Martin
(Zargon the Malevolent), Joan Van Ark
(Libido), Bruce M. Fischer (Baron).
"Vanessa 38-24-36" (4-7-78):
Marianne Bunch (Dr. Evans/Vanessa).

QUATERMASS AND THE PIT. British
1958-59. Andre Morell (Prof. Ber-
nard Quatermass), Cec Linder (Dr.
Matthew Roney), Anthony Bushell
(Col. James Breen), John Stratton
(Capt. Potter), Catherine Finn (Bar-
bara Judd), Van Boolen (truck dri-
ver), Michael Raghan (grap opera-
tor), Lionel Ngakane (workman),
John Rae (foreman), Arthur Hewlett
(Baines), Michael Bird (Armitage),
Janet Burnell (news interviewer),
Robert Perceval (Minister for War),
Richard Dare (Private Secretary),
Michael Ripper (Sergeant), Nan
Braunton (Miss Dobson), Harold
Goodwin (Corporal Gibson), John
Walker (Sapper West), Brian Gil-
mar (Sapper), Victor Platt (P. C.
Ellis), Clifford Cox (Sapper), Ian
Ainsley (Police Inspector), Patrick
Connor (policeman), Kenneth War-
ren (policeman), Howell Davies (Mr.
Chilcott), Hilda Barry (Mrs. Chil-
cott), Madge Brindley (Miss Groome),
Keith Banks (Nuttall), Tony Quinn
(news editor), Frank Crane (George),
Brian Worth (James Fullalove), Alan
McClelland (journalist), Stanley Vine
(journalist), Patrick Maynard (jour-
nalist), Anne Blake (journalist), Noel
Howlett (Vicar), Richard Shaw (Slad-
den), Edward Burnham (Official),
Harold Siddons (electrician), Antho-
ny Pendrell (TV Interviewer), John
Scott Martin (TV cameraman), Ber-
nard Spear (pub customer), Louise
Gainsborough (blonde), Sydney Brom-
ley (tattered man), Arthur Brander
(man in blazer), Stuart Nichol (Amer-
ican newscaster), Budd Knapp (Ameri-
can pilot).
  "The Halfmen" (12-22-58).
  "The Ghosts" (12-29-58).
  "Imps and Demons" (1-5-59).
  "The Enchanted" (1-12-59).
  "The Wild Hunt" (1-19-59).
  "Hob" (1-26-59).

QUATERMASS EXPERIMENT, THE.
British 1953. Reginald Tate (Prof.
Bernard Quatermass), Isobel Dean
(Judith Carroon), Hugh Kelly (John
Patterson), Moray Watson (Marsh),

Van Boolen (Len Matthews), W.
Thorp Devereaux (Blaker), Iris Ballard (Mrs. Matthews), Katie Johnson (Miss Wilde), Paul Whitsun-Jones
(James Fullalove), Neil Wilson (policeman), Oliver Johnston (news editor), Colyn Davies (fireman), Dominic le Foe (reporter), Patrick Westwood (reporter), Eugene Leahy (Police Insp. Wimbledon), Nicholas
Bruce (BBC newsreader), Duncan
Lamont (Victor Carroon), John Glen
(Dr. Gordon Briscoe), Denis Wynd-
ham (tipsy man), Pat McGrath (BBC
interviewer), Ian Colin (Chief Insp.
Lomax), Christopher Rhodes (Dr.
Ludwig Reichenheim), Frank Hawkins
(Detective Sgt. Best), Peter Bathurst
(Charles Greene), Stella Richman
(hospital sister), Enid Lindsay (Louisa Greene), Phil Vickers (American
journalist), Edward David (Indian
journalist), Jack Rodney (Ramsay),
Lewis Wilson (Walters), Anthony
Green (boy), Janet Joye (cinemagoer),
Keith Herrington (Space Lieutenant),
Pauline Johnson (space girl), Lee
Fox (cinema manager), Bernadette
Milnes (usherette), Richard Cuthbert
(chemist), Christie Humphrey (Janet),
John Stone (Ted), Frank Atkinson
(park keeper), Wilfred Brambell
(drunk), Reginald Hearne (police su-
perintendent), Neil Arden (TV inter-
viewer), Tony van Bridge (TV produ-
cer), John Kidd (Sir Vernon Dodds),
Josephine Crombie (TV assistant),
Arnold Diamond (man in bowler hat),
Kenneth Midwood (policeman), Andrew
Laurence (Major), Keith Pyott (per-
manent official).
  "Contact Has Been Established"
(7-18-53).
  "Person Reported Missing" (7-25-
53).
  "Very Special Knowledge" (8-1-53).
  "Believed to Be Suffering" (8-8-
53).
  "An Unindentified Species" (8-15-
53).
  "State of Evergency" (8-22-53).

QUATERMASS II. British 1955. John
Robinson (Prof. Bernard Quatermass),
Hugh Griffith (Dr. Leo Pugh), Monica
Grey (Paula), John Stone (Capt. John
Dillon), Brian Hayes (Sgt. Grice),
Tony Lyons (Trainee), Hilda Barry
(Mrs. Large), Eric Lugg (Fred Large),
Herbert Lomax (Robert), Richard
Cuthbert (landlord), Michael Brennan
(Dawson), Wilfred Brambell (tramp),
Hilda Fenemore (child's mother), Pe-

ter Carver (Inspector), Derek Aylward (Rupert Ward), Austin Trevor (Fowler), Rupert Davies (Vincent Broadhead, M. P.), Malvyn Hayes (Frankie), Sydney Bromley (Frankie's father), Ilona Ference (Frankie's mother), Roger Delgado (Hugh Conrad), Michael Golden (Paddy), John Rae (McLeod), Elsie Arnold (Mrs. McLeod), Ian Wilson (Ernie), Denis McCarthy (Doctor), Cyril Shaps (ground controller).
"The Bolts" (10-22-55).
"The Mark" (10-29-55).
"The Food" (11-5-55).
"The Coming" (11-12-55).
"The Frenzy" (11-19-55).
"The Destroyers" (11-26-55).

Q. E. D. 1982. Sam Waterston (Quentin E. Deverill), Julian Glover (Dr. Kilkiss), George Innes (Phipps), A. C. Weary (Charlie), Caroline Langrishe (Jenny).
"Target: London" (3-23-82): Sarah Berger (Betsy), Richard Morant (Richard), Frederick Jaeger (Kaiser), Ronald Lacey (Medium), John Abineri (Staff Officer), Robert Harris (Judge), Billy J. Mitchell (Professor), Robert Henderson (Old Professor), Edward Wiley (Young Professor), Jean Burgess (lady at seance), David Baron, Michael Stroud (guests at seance), Paul Jerricho (German sergeant), Constantin de Goguel (German Commander), Kenneth Owen (German Corporal), Paul Hompoletz (flunky), Michael Harbour (fisherman), Wolf Kahler, Steve Ubels (technician).
"The Great Motor Race" (3-30-82): Manning Redwood (Henry Ford), Henry McGee (Bassey), Biji Kusuhara (Count Oyama), Tim Woodward.
"Infernal Device" (4-6-82): Ian Ogilvy (Sidney Sarandon), George A. Cooper (Lord Eastleigh), Barrie Houghton (Kalnikov), Eric Kent (Blake), Bibs Ekkel (Hungarian), Patsy Smart (old woman), Ron Pember (cabby), Francine Morgan (Dolly), Tony Caunter (foreman), Michael Burrell (Official).
"The 4:10 to Zurich" (4-13-82): Paul Freeman (Prof. Rep), Elizabeth Shepherd (Lady Potts), Paul Angelia (Kroll), Chris Jenkins (Van Else), David Auker (taxi driver), Ben Feitelson (French chauffeur), Amy Dagley (young Dutch girl), Thea Ranft (Dutch girl's mother), Brenda Cowling (nun on train), Ingo Mogendorf (swarthy man).
"To Catch a Ghost" (4-20-82): Jean Anderson (Aunt Effie), Shelagh

McLeod (Caroline Makepeace), Cyril Luckham (Crabtree), John Vine (Gareth Makepeace), Pauline Quirke (Jane), Ann Way (Minnie).
"The Limehouse Connection" (4-27-82): Burk Kwouk (Dr. Lin), Sarah Lam (Priscilla), Barry Dennen (Al Russo).

QUICK AND QUIET. Pilot (8-18-81): William Windom, Rich Lohman, Lynda Day George (Margo Hilliard), Henry Jones (Walter Hilliard), Millie Slavin (Camille), Warren Berlinger (Leonard Plumb), Lois Areno (Bambi Wilson), Joan Roberts, Dallas Alinder, Lee Crawford, Jerry Maren, David Pritchard.

RAMAR OF THE JUNGLE. 1952-53. Jon Hall (Dr. Thomas Reynolds), Ray Montgomery (Prof. Ogden).

RENTAGHOST. British (4-24-81 - 5-29-81)*. Michael Staniforth (Timothy Claypole), Sue Nicholls (Nadia Popov), Molly Weir (Hazel the McWitch), Ann Emery (Ethel Meaker), Edward Brayshaw (Harold Meaker), Hal Dyer (Rose Perkins), Jeffrey Segal (Arthur Perkins), Christopher Biggins (Adam Painting), Robert East (Dr. Newman), Colin McCormack (police sergeant), Finola Keough (woman at door), Jeremy Truelove (boxer), Nigel Greaves (policeman), Norma Dunbar (newscaster), Paddie O'Neil (Queen Matilda), John Pennington (guard), Crispin Gillband (guard), Tony Caunter (Mr. Jackson).

RETURN OF CAPTAIN NEMO, THE. 1978. Jose Ferrer (Captain Nemo), Burgess Meredith (Prof. Cunningham), Tom Hallick (Cmdr. Tom Franklin), Burr De Benning (Lt. Jim Porter), Lynda Day George (Dr. Kate Melton), Mel Ferrer (Dr. Cook), Warren Stevens (Miller), Horst Bucholz (King Tibor), Anthony Geary (Bork), Yale Summers (Sirak), Med Flory (Tor), Randolph Roberts (helmsman), David Westberg (crewman), Anthony McHugh (radioman), Stephen Powers (Lloyd), Art Ballinger (TV announcer), Harvey Fisher (2nd radioman), Peter Jason (2nd helmsman), Richard Angarola (Trog).
"Deadly Blackmail" (3-8-78).
"Duel in the Deep" (3-15-78).
"Atlantis Dead Ahead" (3-22-78).

*Aired in multiple segments; dates show first and last segments.

1308   Science Fiction, Horror, Fantasy

RETURN TO THE LOST PLANET. British 1955. Peter Kerr, Jack Stewart, Mary Law.

RICHARD BOONE SHOW, THE.
"The Stranger" (10-22-63): Richard Boone (Dan Falco), Harry Morgan (Dr. Lindstrom), Bethel Leslie (Nell Braley), Lloyd Bochner (Anderson Carr), Robert Blake (the Stranger).

ROAD, THE. British 1963.

ROALD DAHL'S TALES OF THE UNEXPECTED. 1979-81. Roald Dahl (Host) 79-80, John Houseman (Host) 80-81.
"Dip in the Pool" (9-15-79): Jack Weston, Gladys Spencer, Don Fellows, David Harries.
"Man from the South" (9-22-79): Jose Ferrer, Katy Jurado, Michael Ontkean, Pamela Stephenson, Cyril Luckham.
"Mrs. Bixby and the Colonel's Coat" (9-29-79): Julie Harris, Michael Hordern, Richard Greene, Vass Anderson, Richard Hampton, Will Leighton, Alan Chuntz, Frederick Farley, Sandra Poyne.
"The Landlady" (10-6-79): Siobhan McKenna (Landlady), Leonard Preston (William Weaver).
"William and Mary" (10-13-79): Elaine Stritch, Marius Goring, Richard Hampton, Jane Paton, Jimmy Mac.
"Lamb to the Slaughter" (10-20-79): Susan George, Brian Blessed, Hugh Cross, Michael Byrne, George Little, Mark Jones, Andrew Fell, David English.
"Neck" (10-27-79): Joan Collins (Lady Natalia), Sir John Gielgud (Jelks, the Butler), Michael Aldridge (Sir Basil), Peter Bowles.
"Way Up to Heaven" (11-3-79): Julie Harris, Roland Culver.
"Edward the Conqueror" (11-10-79): Joseph Cotten, Wendy Hiller.
"Depart in Peace" (11-17-79): Joseph Cotten, Gloria Grahame.
"My Lady Love, My Dove" (11-24-79): Elaine Stritch.
"Skin" (12-1-79): Derek Jacobi.
"Taste" (12-8-79): Ron Moody.
"Royal Jelly" (12-15-79): Timothy West, Susan George.
"Galloping Foxley" (12-22-79): John Mills, Anthony Steel.
"The Hitchhiker" (12-29-79): Rod Taylor, Cyril Cusack.
"Genesis and Catastrophe" (1-5-80): Helmut Griem.

"The Umbrella Man" (1-12-80): Sir John Mills.
"Poison" (1-19-80): Andrew Ray, Anthony Steel.
"The Open Window" (1-26-80): Dina Merrill, Valerie Mahaffey.
"Nothin' Short of Highway Robbery" (2-2-80): Warren Oates, Bud Cort, Bettye Ackerman.
"In the Cards" (2-9-80): Susan Strasberg, Max Gail.
"Mr. Botibol's First Love" (9-13-80): Jack Weston (William Botibol), Anna Massey (Irene Wrzaszcyzk), Paul Bacon (Mason), Alan Rowe (Mr. Clements), Paul Greenhalgh (Mr. Simpson), Allan Corduner (store assistant).
"Man at the Top" (9-20-80): Peter Firth (Hardy), Rachel Davies (Diane), Cassie McFarlane (Estelle), John Rees (barman), Johnny Shannon (gambler), Paul McDowell (Schaefer).
"The Orderly World of Mr. Appleby" (9-27-80): Robert Lang (Arthur Appleby), Elizabeth Spriggs (Martha Appleby), Christopher Bramwell (Dominic), Cyril Luckham (Mr. Gainsborough), Nigel Caliburn (signwriter).
"Back for Christmas" (10-4-80): Richard Johnson (James Carpenter), Sian Phillips (Hermione Carpenter), Lynne Ross (Samantha), Cyril Luckham (Gavin), Avril Elgar (Nancy), Artro Morris (Tom), Mark Kenyon (Sebastian).
"Shatterproof" (10-11-80): Eli Wallach (Gerry Williams), Anthony Pullen-Shaw (Smith), Caroline Langrishe (Ellen), Godfrey Talbot (Emerson).
"Flypaper" (10-18-80): Alfred Burke (the Man), Lorna Yabsley (Sylvia Wilkinson), Pat Keen (Mabel), Stephanie Cole (Miss Harrison), Peggy Thorpe-Bates (Mrs. Wilkinson), Bernadette Windsor (Louise), Anthony Smee (the Vicar), Giles Phibbs (bus conductor).
"The Stinker" (10-25-80): Denholm Elliott (Harold Tinker), Patricia Quinn (Phyl Tinker), Joss Ackland (Jack Cutler), Diane Holland (Blanche Cutler), Tim Bentinck (Meech).
"The Best of Everything" (11-1-80): Michael Kitchen (Arthur), Judi Bowker (Ann Horton), Jeremy Clyde (Charlie Prince), Rachel Kempson (Mrs. Marsh), Brewster Mason (Horton).
"Vengeance Is Mine, Inc." (11-8-80): Bosco Hogan (Tom), Julian Fellowes (George), Betsy Blair (Mrs. Wilbur), Morris Barry (Mr. Wilbur), Robert Mill (Brewster), Stephan Boswell (doorman).
"Fat Chance" (11-15-80): John Castle (John Burge), Miriam Margolyes

(Mary Burge), Geoffrey Bayldon (Dr. Applegate), Sheila Gish (Frances). "The Sound Machine" (11-22-80): Harry Andrews (Klausner), James Warwick (Dr. Scott), Margery Mason (Mrs. Saunders). "Parson's Pleasure" (11-29-80): John Gielgud (Cyril Boggis), Bernard Miles (Mr. Rubbins), Lee Montague (Mr. Storker), Godfrey James (Claud), Harry Jones (Bert Rummins), Roger Milner (Mr. Hawkins), Virginia Clay (housekeeper), Irlin Hall (Lady). "Vicious Circle" (1-6-80): Siobhan McKenna (Mrs. Grady), Patrick Field (Rex Tobin), Forbes Collins (1st police officer), Roger Evans (2nd police officer), Graham Weston (superintendent), Kenneth Hadley (plain clothes officer). "I'll Be Seeing You" (12-13-80): Anthony Valentine (Roland Trent), Hilary Tindall (Vivienne Trent), Amanda Redman (Anna Warrack), Murray Ewan (Prof. George Coburn). "Proof of Guilt" (12-20-80): Roy Marsden (Chief Insp. Walters), Dudley Sutton (Detective Sgt. Jack Sherrard), Jeremy Clyde (George Stamford), Elizabeth Richardson (Clarissa Tower). "Never Speak Ill of the Dead" (12-27-80): Colin Blakely (Dr. David Rankin), Warren Clarke (Bob Streeter), Keith Drinkel (Sim Hoskins), Cheryl Hall (Irene Rankin), Brian Osborne (Police Sergeant). "Bird of Prey" (1-3-81): Sondra Locke (Edna), Frank Converse (Jack), Charles Hallahan (Charlie), Walker Edmiston (bird vocalizations). "The Best Policy" (1-10-81): Gary Burghoff (Flock), Logan Ramsey (Filbert), Deborah Harmon (Daisy), Edward Grover (Bailout), William Boyett (Simpson), Tad Horino (coroner), Robert Casper (Wheatley), Damian London (Mr. Grunge), Penelope Gillette (Mrs. Runion). "A Glowing Future" (1-17-81): Joanna Pettet (Betsy), John Beck (Jack), Bill LaVoie (moving man). "Turn of the Tide" (1-24-81): Richard Basehart (Slade), Gretchen Corbett (Martha), Nicholas Hormann (Spalding), Harry Northup (Fred), Maggie Peach (Fred's wife), Angie McCright (daughter). "Scrimshaw" (1-31-81): Joan Hackett (Brenda), Charles Kimbrough (Eric), Buddy Owen (sailor), A. C. Daily (beggar), Adair Jameson (gallery lady), Claude Anagram (bartender). "A Woman's Help" (2-7-81):

Tony Francoisa (Arnold Bourdon), Shirley Knight (Elizabeth Bourdon), Deborah Geffner (Miss Grecco), Annie McGreevey (nurse), Ian Martin (Dr. Ivey), Raymond Thorne (gardener), Imogene Bliss (mother).

ROBERT HERRIDGE THEATRE. "The Tell-Tale Heart" (9-24-61): Michael Kane. "The Lottery" (11-5-61): Edward Andrews (Joe Summers), Michael Higgins (Bill Hutchinson), Peggy Furey (Tessie Hutchinson).

ROBERT MONTGOMERY PRESENTS. "The House of Seven Gables" (5-21-51): Gene Lockhart, June Lockhart. "The Hunchback of Notre Dame" (11-8-54 & 11-15-54): Robert Ellenstein (Quasimodo), Hurd Hatfield (Gringoire), Celia Lipton (Esmeralda), Bramwell Fletcher (Frollo), Frederic Worlock (Provost), Mary Sinclair (Colombe), Scott Forbes (Phoebus). "Day of Grace" (7-16-56): John Gibson (William Potter), Jan Miner (Rosalie), Charles Drake (Jed), Mark K. Welles (Teresa). "Sunset Boulevard" (12-3-56): Mary Astor (Norma Desmond), Darren McGavin (Joe Gillis), Walter Kohler (Max). "Faust '57" (6-24-57): Bruce Gordon (Faust), Louis Edmonds (Green), Alfred Ryder (Smith), House Jameson (the Devil), Pamela Curran (Helen of Troy).

ROCKY JONES, SPACE RANGER. 1954-55. Richard Crane (Rocky Jones), Scotty Beckett (Winky), Sally Mansfield (Vena Ray), Maurice Cass (Prof. Newton), Robert Lyden (Bobby), Dian Fauntelle (Yarra), Ian Keith, Paul Marion.
"Gypsy Moon".
"Robot of Regalio".
"Menace from Outer Space".
"Beyond the Moon".
"Blast Off".
"Silver Needle in the Sky".
"Duel in Space".
"Inferno in Space".
"The Cold Sun".
"Menace from Outer Space".
"Crash of Moons".
"The Magnetic Moon".
"Out of This World".
"Manhunt in Space".

ROD BROWN OF THE ROCKET RANGERS. 1953-54. Cliff Robertson

(ROD BROWN OF THE ROCKET RAN-
GERS cont.) (Rod Brown), Jack
Weston (Wilbur Wormser), Bruce
Hall (Ranger Frank Boyle), John
Boruff (Commander Swift), Arthur
Batanides, Shirley Standlee.
"Operation Decoy" (4-18-53).
"The Case of the Invisible Sabo-
teurs" (4-25-53).
"The Planet of Ice" (5-2-53).
"Whispers in the Mind" (5-9-53).
"The Crater of Peril" (5-16-53).
"The Globe Men of Oma" (5-23-
53).
"The Adventures of the Venusian
Sea" (5-30-53).
"The Little Men of Mercury" (6-
6-53).
"World of the Doomed" (6-13-53).
"The Strangler Trees of Triton"
(6-20-53).
"Stranger from Outer Space" (6-
27-53).
"The Phantom Birds of Beloro"
(7-4-53).
"The Black Cloud of Calistro" (7-
11-53).
"The Suits of Peril" (7-18-53).
"Apples of Eden" (7-25-53).
"Space Bugs" (8-1-53).
"The Martian Queen" (8-8-53).
"The Fire Deamons of Deimos"
(8-15-53).
"The Big Hammer" (8-22-53).
"The Volcanos of Venus" (8-29-
53).
"The Death Ball" (9-5-53).
"The Unseen Planet" (9-12-53).
"The Madness from Space" (9-19-
53).
"The Looters of Leeron" (9-26-
53).
"The Octopus of Venus" (10-3-53).
"Colossus of Centauri" (10-10-
53).
"The Lights from Luna" (10-17-
53).
"The Twin Planet" (10-24-53).
"The Treasure of Tesoro" (10-31-
53).
"The Robot Robber of Deimos"
(11-7-53).
"The Magic Man of Mars" (11-14-
53).
"The Stickmen of Neptune" (11-
21-53).
"Money-Makers of Juno" (11-28-
53).
"The Deep Sleep" (12-5-53).
"The Cyclops of Themis" (12-12-
53).
"The Electric Man" (12-19-53).
"The Copernicus Diamond" (12-

26-53).
"The Stone Men of Venus" (1-2-
54).
"Energy Eaters from Luna" (1-9-
54).
Title Unknown (1-16-54).
"Operation Dinosaur" (1-23-54).
"Escape by Magic" (1-30-54).
"The Invisible Force" (2-6-54).
"Return of the Stickmen" (2-13-
53).
"The Fishman of the Venusian
Sea" (2-20-54).
"The Strong Man of Mayron" (2-
27-54).
"The Eel of Iapetus" (3-6-54).
"The Strange Man of Leefri" (3-
13-54).
"The Monkey That Couldn't Stop
Growing" (3-20-54).
"The Plan of Planet H" (3-27-54).
"Invasion from Dimension X" (4-
3-54).
"The Matter Transfer Machine"
(4-10-54).
"Terror in the Space Lighthouse"
(4-17-54).
"Assignment Danger" (4-24-54).
"Bird Girl of Venus" (5-1-54).
"The Exploding Man" (5-8-54).
"The Metal Eaters" (5-15-54).
"The Man Who Was Radioactive"
(5-22-54).
"The Cobalt Bomb" (5-29-54).

SALVAGE-1. 1979. Andy Griffith (Har-
ry Broderick), Joel Higgins (Skip
Carmichael), Trish Stewart (Mela-
nie Slozar), Richard Jaeckel (Jack
Klinger), Jacqueline Scott (Lorene),
J. Jay Saunders (Mack).
"Dark Island" (1-28-79): Henry
Goodwin), Ray Young (the Creature).
"Shangrila Lil" (2-5-79): Mako
(Toshiro), Dane Clark (Gen. Morse),
James Hong (Lee Chow).
"Shelter Five" (2-19-79): Sam
Groom (Maj. Phil Burke), Michelle Sta-
cy (Susan Burke).
"Ghost Trap" (2-26-79): Bert
Freed (Sam Bishop), Howard Mann (Kra-
mer), Henry Sutton (autioneer).
"The Bugatti Map" (3-5-79): Se-
vern Darden (Casper Beckman), David
Opatoshu (Max Jacoby), Ron Soble (Wil-
bur).
"The Golden Orbit" (3-12-79 & 3-
24-79): Edward Winter (Buck Fulton),
Ellen Bry (Vanessa Ashley), Barry Nel-
son (Dr. Singleton), Gary Stephan Swan-
son (Jim Webster), Jon Van Ness (M. P.
Kopple).
"Operation Breakout" (4-2-79):

Moses Gunn (Yaffert Boratu), John Crawford (Sanders), Hari Rhodes (Pierre).

"Mermadon" (4-16-79): Philip Abbott (Dr. Maven), Cliff Emmich (John Bevins), Kate Woodville (Bess Bevins), Julie Anne Haddock (Amelia).

"Up, Up and Away" (5-14-79): Christopher Connelly (Milo), Adam Roarke (Spiro), George Furth (Basset).

"Energy Solution" (5-21-79): Peter Donat (Dawson), Ben Piazza (Sanborne), Richard Eastham (Brinks).

"Confederate Gold" (5-28-79): R. G. Armstrong (Sheriff Moss), Dub Taylor (Shorty), Fran Ryan (Melba), Med Flory (Buster), Dirk Blocker (Billie), Kenneth White (Phil).

"Hard Water" (11-4-79 & 11-11-79): Michelle Ryan (Heather McAdam), Philip Charles MacKenzie (Kress), Bert Freed (Sam Bishop), Warren Kemmerling (Cameron), Rosemary Prinz (Faye Delmont), Cal Bowman (Filbert), Richard Dix (Adm. Seagrave), Michael Horsley (seaman), Ralph Montgomery (Magruder), Hank Underwood (Gruber), Cameron Young (Quartermaster), Paul Sorenson (Capt. Feeney), Dolores Albin (Ms. Flanders), Frank Campanella (Capt. Barlow), Norman Alexander Gibbs (missileman), Ned Mohell (lookout), David Pritchard (Gentry), Robert Eastham (Brinks).

SAPPHIRE AND STEEL. British 1979-1981. Joanna Lumley (Sapphire), David McCallum (Steel), David Collings (Silver) 80-81.

Series One (1979): Steven O'Shea (Rob Jardine), Tamasin Bridge (Helen Jardine), John Golightly (Mr. Jardine), Felicity Harrison (Mrs. Jardine), Val Pringle (Lead), Charles Pemberton (constable), Lee Clark (Victorian man).

Series Two (1979): Gerald James (Tully), Tom Kelly (Pearce), David Woodcock (voice of 1st submariner), David Carr (voice of 2nd submariner/ pilot).

Series Three (1980): Catherine Hall (Rothwyn), David Gant (Eldred), Russell Wooton (Changeling).

Series Four (1980): Alyson Spiro (Liz), Philip Bird (the Shape), Bob Hornery (the Shape), Natalie Hedges (child with parasol).

Series Five (1980): Patience Collier (Emma Mullrine), Nan Munro (Felicity McDee), Davy Kaye (Lord Mullrine), Jeffrey Wickham (Felix Harborough), Jeremy Child (Howard McDee), Jennie Stoller (Annabelle Harborough),

Peter Laird (Greville), Stephen MacDonald (George McDee), Patricia Shakesby (Anne Shaw), Christopher Bramwell (Tony Purnell), Debbie Farrington (Veronica Blamey).

Series Six (1981): Edward De Souza (man), John Boswall (old man), Johanna Kirby (woman), Christopher Fairbank (Johnny Jack).

SCIENCE FICTION THEATRE. 1955-57. Truman Bradley (Host).

"Beyond" (4-5-55): William Lundigan (Fred Gunderman), Ellen Drew (Helen Gunderman), Bruce Bennett (Gen. Troy), Tom Drake (Dr. Everett), Douglas Kennedy (Col. Barton), Basil Ruisdael (Dr. Carson).

"Time Is Just a Place" (4-15-55): Don DeFore (Al Brown), Marie Windsor (Nell Brown), Warren Stevens (Ted Heller), Peggy O'Connor (Ann Heller).

"No Food for Thought" (4-22-55): John Howard (Dr. Paul Novak), Otto Kruger (Prof. Emanuel Hall), Clarence Lung (Dr. Lee Suyin), Vera Miles (Jan Corey), Stanley Andrews (Sheriff Simpson), John Newland.

"Out of Nowhere" (4-29-55): Richard Arlen (Dr. Osborne), Jess Barker (Dr. Jeffries), Jonathan Hale (Dr. Milton), Hal Forest (Fleming), Irving Mitchell (superintendent), Carlyle Mitchell (Gen. Kenyon), Craig Duncan (Robb).

"Y. O. R. D. " (5-6-55): Walter Kingsford (Dr. Lawton), Judith Ames (Edna Miller), Louis Jean Heydt (Col. Van Dyke), DeForest Kelly (Capt. Hall, MD), Kenneth Tobey (Lt. Dunne).

"Stranger in the Desert" (5-13-55): Gene Evans (Bud Porter), Marshall Thompson (Gil Collins), Lowell Gilmore (Ballard).

"The Sound of Murder" (5-20-55): Howard Duff (Dr. Tom Mathews), Wheaton Chambers (Dr. Van Kamp), Russell Collins.

"The Brain of John Emerson" (5-27-55): John Howard (John Emerson), Joyce Holden (Joan), Michael Fox (Dr. Franklin), Ellen Drew (Mrs. Turner), Robert Simon (Captain Damon), Jackie Blanchard (nurse).

"Spider, Incorporated" (6-3-55): Gene Barry (Joe Ferguson), Audrey Totter (Ellie Ferguson), Ludwig Stossel.

"Death at 2 A. M. " (6-10-55): John Qualen (Dr. Samuel Avery), Skip Homeier (Bill Reynolds).

"Conversation with an Ape" (6-17-55): Barbara Hale (Nancy Stanton), Hugh Beaumont (Dr. Guy Stanton).

"Marked 'Danger'" (6-24-55): Otto

(SCIENCE FICTION THEATRE cont.)
Kruger (Dr. Engstrom), Nancy Gates
(Lois Strand), Arthur Franz (Fred
Strand).
　"Hour of Nightmare" (7-1-55):
William Bishop (Mel Wingate), Lynn
Bari (Verda Wingate), Charles Evans
(Ed Tratnor), Christopher Dark (Ra-
mon Sanchez), Tony Barrett (Comman-
dante).
　"The Strange Dr. Lorenz" (7-15-
55): Edmund Gwenn (Dr. Lorenz),
Kristine Miller (Helen), Donald Curtis
(Dr. Fred Garner).
　"100 Years Young" (7-22-55):
Ruth Hussey (Bernice Knight), John
Abbott (John Bowers), John Archer
(Mike Redding).
　"The Frozen Sound" (7-29-55):
Marshall Thompson (Dr. David Mas-
ters), Marilyn Erskine (Linda Otis),
Ray Collins (Dr. Milton Otis), Michael
Fox (Dr. Gordon).
　"The Stones Began to Move" (8-
12-55): Basil Rathbone (Victor Beren-
son), Jean Willes (Virginia Kincaid),
Jonathan Hale (Morton Archer), Ri-
chard Flato (Ahmed Abdullah).
　"The Lost Heartbeat" (8-19-55):
Zachary Scott (Dr. Richard Marshall),
Jan Shepard (Joan Crane), Walter Kings-
ford (Dr. John Crane).
　"The World Below" (8-26-55):
Gene Barry (Capt. Forester), Tol Avery
(Prof. Weaver), Marguerite Chapman
(Jean Forester).
　"Barrier of Silence" (9-9-55):
Adolphe Menjou (Dr. Elliott Harcourt),
Warren Stevens (Prof. Sheldon), Phyl-
lis Coates (Karen Sheldon), Charles
Maxwell (Thornton), John Doucette
(Neilson).
　"The Negative Man" (9-16-55):
Dane Clark (Vic Murphy), Beverly Gar-
land (Sally Torens), Carl Switzer (Pete).
　"Dead Reckoning" (9-29-55):
James Craig (Capt. John Berry), Adam
Williams (Lt. Bookman), Steve Brodie
(Lt. David Kramer), Arlene Whelan
(Evelyn Raleigh), Everett Glass (Dr.
Millard (Townsend), Art Lewis (Sgt.
'Corny' Cooper).
　"A Visit from Dr. Pliny" (9-30-
55): Edmund Gwenn (Dr. Pliny), Mor-
ris Ankrum (George Halsey), John Ste-
phenson (Dr. Brewster), William Schal-
lert (Mr. Thomas).
　"Dead Storage" (10-7-55): Vir-
ginia Bruce (Dr. Myrna Griffin), Wal-
ter Coy (Warren Keith), Robert H. Har-
ris (Dr. Robinson), Doug Henderson
(Dr. Avery), Booth Coleman (Dr. Mc-
Leod).

"The Strange People at Pecos"
(10-14-55): Arthur Franz (Jeff Jami-
son), Doris Dowling (Celia Jamison),
Dabbs Greer (Arthur Kern), Judith
Ames (Amy Kern), Andrew Glick (Ter-
ry Jamison), Barry Froner (Junior
Jamison), Beverly Washburn (Laurie).
　"The Human Equation" (10-21-55):
Macdonald Carey (Dr. Lee Seward),
Jean Byron (Nan Guild), Peter Adams
(Dr. Clements), Herbert Heyes (Gover-
nor), Tom McKee (Dr. Upton).
　"Target Hurricane" (10-28-55):
Marshall Thompson (James Tyler),
Margaret Field (Julie Tyler), Gary
Marshall (Bobby Tyler), Ray Collins
(Hugh Fredericks), Robert Griffin (Wal-
ter Bronson).
　"The Walter Maker" (11-4-55):
Craig Stevens (David Brooks), Virginia
Gray (Sheila Dunlap), William Talman
(Norman Conway).
　"The Unexplored" (11-11-55):
Kent Smith (Prof. Alex Bondar), Osa
Massen (Julie Bondar), Harvey Stephens
(Henry Stark), Madge Kennedy (Mrs.
Canby).
　"The Hastings Secret" (11-18-55):
Bill Williams (Bill Twinning), Barbara
Hale (Pat Hastings), Morris Ankrum
(Dr. Clausen).
　"Postcard from Barcelona" (11-
25-55): Keefe Brasselle (Dr. Burton),
Walter Kingsford (Dr. Cole), Christine
Larsen (Nina Keller).
　"Friend of a Raven" (12-2-55):
Richard Eyer (Tim Daniels), Virginia
Bruce (Jean Gordon), William Ching
(Walter Daniels), Charles Cane (Frank
Jenkins), Bernard Philipps (Dr. Hoster).
　"Beyond Return" (12-9-55): Zacha-
ry Scott (Dr. Erwin Bach), Joan Vohs
(Kyra Zelas), Peter Hansen (Dr. Dan
Scott).
　"Before the Beginning" (12-16-55):
Dane Clark (Dr. Ken Donaldson), Judith
Ames (Kate Donaldson), Phillip Pine (Dr.
Norman Heller).
　"The Long Day" (12-23-55): George
Brent (Sam Gilmore), Jean Byron (Laura
Gilmore), Steve Brodie (Robert Barton).
　"Project 44" (1-6-56): Bill Wil-
liams (Dr. Arnold Bryan), Doris Dow-
ling (Janice Morgan), Biff Elliott (Ed
Garrett).
　"Are We Invaded?" (1-20-56):
Pat O'Brien (Dr. Walter Arnold), Leslie
Gaye (Barbara Arnold), Anthony Eustral
(Mr. Galleon), Richard Erdman (Seth
Turner).
　"Operation Flypaper" (2-3-56):
Vincent Price (Dr. Philip Redmond),
John Eldridge (John Vollard), Kristine

Miller (Alma Ford), George Eldridge (David Vollard), Dabbs Greer (Mac-Namara).

"The Other Side of the Moon" (2-17-56): Skip Homeier (Lawrence Kerston), Beverly Garland (Katey Kerston), Philip Ober (Prof. Carl Schneider).

"Signals from the Heart" (4-6-56): Walter Kingsford (Prof. Tubor), Peter Hansen (Dr. Warren Stark), Joyce Holden (Alma Stark), Gene Roth (Patrolman Tom Horton).

"The Long Sleep" (4-13-56): Dick Foran (Dr. Samuel Willard), Nancy Hale (Ruth Taney), John Doucette (John Barton).

"Who Is This Man?" (4-20-56): Bruce Bennett (Dr. Hugh Bentley), Harlow Wilcox (Dr. Karl Krause), Charles Smith (Tommy Cooper).

"The Green Bomb" (4-27-56): Whit Bissell (Maxwell Carnaven), Kenneth Tobey (Frank Davis), Robert Griffin (Ralph Scott).

"When a Camera Fails" (5-4-56): Gene Lockhart (Dr. Richard Hewitt), Mack Williams (Dr. Johnston), Than Wyenn (Dr. Herbert).

"Bullet Proof" (5-11-56): Marshall Thompson (Jim Connors), Christopher Dark (Ralph Parr), John Eldridge (Prof. Rudman), Jacqueline Hold (Jean Rudman).

"The Flicker" (5-18-56): Victor Jory (Lt. Kiel), Michael Fox (Dr. Kinkaid), Steve Morris (Brad Jackson).

"The Unguided Missile" (5-25-56): Ruth Hussey (Jan O'Hara), Peter Hansen (Henry Maxon), Francis McDonald (Prof. Bernini).

"End of Tomorrow" (6-1-56): Christopher Dark (Keith Brandon), Diana Douglas (Jane Brandon), Dabbs Greer (Prof. Reimers), Walter Kingsford (Rudyard Parker).

"The Mind Machine" (6-8-56): Cyril Delevanti (Dr. Lewis Milton), Bill Williams (Dr. Alan Cathcart), Brad Trumbull (Dr. Mark Cook).

"The Missing Waveband" (6-15-56): Dick Foran (Dr. Milhurst), Stafford Repp (Prof. Van Boorne), Gene Roth (Dr. Lawrence), Michael Fox (Dr. Maxwell).

"The Human Experiment" (6-22-56): Marshall Thompson (Dr. Tom MacDougal), Jean Richardson (Claudia Barrett), Virginia Christine (Dr. Ballard).

"The Man Who Didn't Know" (6-29-56): Arthur Franz (Mark Kendler), Susan Cummings (Peggy Kendler), Bruce Wendell (Al Mitchell).

"The Phantom Car" (7-20-56):

John Archer (Arthur Gross), Judith Ames (Peggie Gross), Tyler McVey (Barney Cole).

"Beam of Fire" (7-27-56): Wayne Morris (Steve Conway), Frank Gerstle (Dr. Davis), Harlan Warde (Dr. Lindstrom).

"Legend of Crater Mountain" (8-3-56): Marilyn Erskine (Marion Brown), Brad Jackson (Dr. Jim Harris), Jo Ann Lilliquist (Rosellen Avitor), Freddy Ridgeway (Bobby Avitor), Nadene Ashdown (Susan Avitor).

"Living Lights" (8-10-56): Skip Homeier (Bob Laurie), Joan Sinclair (Grace Laurie), Mike Garth (Charles Irwin).

"Jupitron" (8-17-56): Bill Williams (Dr. John Barlow), Toni Gerry (Nina Barlow), Lowell Gilmore (August Wyckoff), Michael Fox (Dr. Norstad).

"The Throwback" (8-24-56): Peter Hansen (Norman Hughes), Virginia Christine (Anna Adler), Ed Kemmer (Joe Castle).

"The Miracle of Dr. Dove" (8-31-56): Gene Lockhart (Dr. Edward Dove), Robin Short (Jeff Spencer), Kay Faylen (Alice Kinder), Charles Wangenheim (Ed Gorman), Rhodes Reason (Sean Daly).

"One Thousand Eyes" (9-7-56): Vincent Price (Gary Williams), Jean Byron (Ada March), Bruce Wendell (Lt. Moss).

"Brain Unlimited" (9-14-56): Arthur Franz (Dr. Jeff Conover), Diana Douglas (Elaine Conover), Doug Wilson (Ralph Marken).

"Death at My Fingertips" (9-21-56): Dick Foran (Dr. Donald Stewart), June Lockhart (Eve Patrick), John Stephenson (Mark Davis).

"Sound That Kills" (9-28-56): Ludwig Stossel (Dr. Wissman), Ray Collins (Dr. Sinclair), Charles Victor (Ed Martin).

"Survival in Box Canyon" (10-12-56): Bruce Bennett (Dr. Sorenson), Susan Cummings (Ellen Barton), DeForest Kelley (Dr. Milo Barton).

"The Voice" (10-26-56): Donald Curtis (Roger Brown), Kristine Miller (Anna Brown), Anthony Eustral (Dr. Mendoza).

"Three Minute Mile" (11-9-56): Marshall Thompson (Nat Kendall), Martin Milner (Brit), Gloria Marshall (Jill).

"The Last Barrier" (11-16-56): Bill Ching (Robert Porter), Bruce Wendell (Dan Blake), Tom McKee (Wayne Masters).

"Signals from the Moon" (11-23-56): Bruce Bennett (Gen. Frank Ter-

(SCIENCE FICTION THEATRE cont.) rance), Michael Fox (Dr. Edwards), Bob Schield (Dr. Werth).

"Dr. Robot" (11-30-56): Peter Hansen (Dr. Edgar Barnes), Whit Bissell (Fred Lopert), Doug Wilson (Douglas Hinkle).

"The Human Circuit" (12-7-56): Marshall Thompson (Dr. Albert Neville), Joyce Jameson (Nina LaSalle), Bill Ching (Dr. George Stoneham).

"Sun Gold" (12-14-56): Marilyn Erskine (Susan Calvin), Ross Elliot (Howard Evans), Paul Fierro (Tawa).

"Facsimile" (12-21-56): Arthur Franz (George Bascomb), Aline Towne (Barbara Davis), Donald Curtis (Hugh Warner).

"The Miracle Hour" (12-28-56): Dick Foran (Jim Wells), Jean Byron (Cathy Parker), Charles Herbert (Tommy).

"The Killer Tree" (1-4-57): Bill Williams (Paul Cameron), Bonita Granville (Barbara), Keith Richards (Clyde Bishop).

"Gravity Zero" (1-11-57): Percy Helton (Dr. John Hustead), Lisa Gaye (Elizabeth Wickes), Bill Hudson (Ken Waring).

"The Magic Suitcase" (1-25-57): Charles Winninger (Grandpa Scott), William Vaughan (John Scott), Judith Ames (Eileen Scott).

"Bolt of Lightning" (2-1-57): Bruce Bennett (Dr. Sheldon Thorpe), Kristine Miller (Cynthia Blake), Sidney Smith (President Franklin).

"The Strange Lodger" (2-8-57): Peter Hansen (Dr. Jim Wallaby), Jan Shepard (Maggie Dawes), Charles Maxwell (Bill North).

SCIENCE SERIES.
"Our Mr. Sun" (1-19-56): Frank Baxter (Dr. Research), Eddie Albert (the Fiction Writer).

"Hemo the Magnificent" (3-20-57): Frank Baxter (Dr. Research), Richard Carlson (the Fiction Writer).

"The Strange Case of the Cosmic Rays" (10-25-57): Frank Baxter (Dr. Research), Richard Carlson (the Fiction Writer).

"The Unchained Goddess" (2-12-58): Frank Baxter (Dr. Research), Richard Carlson (the Fiction Writer), Mel Blanc, Hans Conried, Franklin Pangborn, Jay Novello, Ken Peters, Lurene Tuttle (voices).

SCREEN DIRECTOR'S PLAYHOUSE.
"The Carroll Formula" (7-18-56): Michael Wilding (David Scott),

Mavis Davenport (Sylvia), Steven Geray (Dr. Lehndorff), Roy Roberts (Gen. Lafferty), Don 'Red' Barry (Private Holmes), Donald MacBride (Col. Hobson), Howard McNear (Dr. Curtis).

SEARCH. 1972-73. Hugh O'Brian (Hugh Lockwood), Tony Francoisa (Nick Bianco), Doug McClure (Christopher R. Grove), Burgess Meredith (B.C. Cameron), Ford Rainey (Dr. Barnett), Angel Tompkins (Gloria Harding), Tom Hallick (Harris), Albert Popwell (Griffith), Byron Chung (Kuroda), Pamela Jones (Miss James), Ron Castro (Carlos), Ginny Golden (Miss Keach).

"The Murrow Disappearance" (9-13-72): O'Brian, Capucine (Silvana Tristano), Maurice Evans (Roger White), David White (Miles Llewellyn), Lawrence Cook (Compton), Vernon Weddle (McEgan), Ted Hartley (Lee Cardiff), Jay MacIntosh (Adele Murrow).

"One of Our Probes Is Missing" (9-20-72): Francoisa, Stefanie Powers (Jill Davenport), Jacquelyn Hyde (Lena Kapos), Milton Selzer (Lucas Kapos), Allen Garfield (Martin Zacharian), Larry Linville (Emery), Henry Capps (bartender), David Gilliam (Burrell).

"Short Circuit" (9-27-72): McClure, Jeff Corey (Dr. Moen), Mary Ann Mobley (Lelia Moen), Nate Esformes (Landis), Barbara Rucker (student), Jean Norman (rental agent), Ed Connelly (pilot).

"Moonrock" (10-4-72): O'Brian, Jo Ann Pflug (Dr. Laura Trapnell), George Pan (Abbas Mirzah), William Wintersole (Dr. Van Owen), David Mauro (Dimas), Gordon Rigsby (Dr. Ewing), Ann Prentiss.

"Live Men Tell Tales" (10-11-72): Francoisa, Louise Sorel (Magna), Leslie Charleson (Nancy), Martin Koslek (Josip), Torin Thatcher (Stonestreet).

"Operation Iceman" (10-25-72): Francoisa, Edward Mulhare (Pelham), Edward Bell (Gerard), James Gregory (Essex), Mary Frann (Burnside), Abraham Sofaer (Lokarno), Poupee Bocar (Kalia Sulvan), Russ Marin (Ginelli).

"The Antidote" (11-1-72): O'Brian, Ina Balin (Alexia), Robert Boon (Balzak), Malachi Throne (Nobokov), Alan Bergmann (Rolf), Byron Mabe (Egan), Peter von Zerneck (Bremer).

"In Search of Midas" (11-8-72): McClure, David Brian (Devlin), Barbara Feldon (Kate), Logan Ramsay (Wade), George Gaynes (Major Mathews).

"The Adonis File" (11-15-72): O'Brian, Bill Bixby (Mark Elliot), Victoria George (Anne Delaware), G.D. Spradlin (Ackerman), Brenda Benet (Ca-

rol Lescoe), Roy Jenson (Spencer),
Peggy Walton (Sandra Elliot).
"Flight to Nowhere" (11-22-72):
O'Brian, Joanna Cameron (Laura),
Linda Cristal (Antonia), Warren Van-
ders (Anderson), Don Dubbins (Neil
Corbett), William Patterson (Harry
Corbett), Joseph Alfasa (aide), Bob
Terhune (big man).
"The Bullet" (12-20-72): O'Brian,
Hurd Hatfield (Chen Kuo), Kurt Kasznar
(Harant), Michael Bow (Sutter), Bill
Fletcher (Gen. Chu), David Gilliam
(Burrell), Thelma Parrish (Taffy).
"Let Us Prey" (1-3-73): Fran-
coisa, Diana Hyland (Anjanette), Albert
Paulsen (Danzig), Walter Friedel (Rich-
ter), Mike DeAnda (Fuentes), Victor
Milan (Rodrigo).
"A Honeymoon to Kill" (1-10-73):
McClure, Luciana Paluzzi (Carla Luc-
chese), Rudy Solari (Luigi), Antoinette
Bower (Penny), Gary Clarke (Julian),
Peter Bromilow (Upson), George Cou-
louris (Carmine), Maurice Marsac (bus
driver), Tony Cacciotti (nurse).
"The Twenty-Four Carat Hit" (1-
24-73): Francoisa, Dane Clark (Bain),
Michael Conrad (Dunner), William
Smith (Roman), Lenny Montana (Ellis),
Nehemiah Persoff (Brugman), Wally
Cox (Brother Sam), Annette O'Toole
(Terry), Anitra Ford (Miss Lewis),
George Murdock (Pierson), Lane Brad-
ford (bartender).
"Numbered for Death" (1-31-73):
McClure, Luther Adler (Vollmer), Pe-
ter Mark Richman (Sam Boyce), Bert
Convy (Roger Allan), Whit Bissell (St.
Clair), Ramon Bieri (Inspector), Joan-
na Miles (Olivia Allan), Lauri Peters
(Trudy Hauser), Paulette Breen (Miss
Lund), Gloria Manon (Mona), Walter
Alzman (Stucke).
"Countdown to Panic" (2-7-73):
O'Brian, Ed Nelson (Parker), Howard
Duff (Jamison), Anne Francis (Beth
Parker), Robert Webber (Linden), Jack
Ging (Hall), Fred Downs (Avery).
"The Clayton Lewis Document"
(2-14-73): Francoisa, Rhonda Fleming
(Arlene Morrison), Anna Capri (Pam),
Don Gordon (Alex Nevin), Anthony
James (Barnsworth), Craig Stevens
(Clayton Lewis), Julie Adams (Jeanette
Ellis).
"Goddess of Destruction" (2-21-
73): McClure, Anjanette Comer (Anna
Raman), John Vernon (Paul Holloway),
Alfred Ryder (Dr. Sutra), Reggie Nal-
der (Lal Panjim), Than Wyenn (1st
representative), Gary Walberg (Lieu-
tenant), Jose DeVega (Prasad), Ken

Renard (Krishna Raman), George Kra-
mer (Baker).
"The Mattson Papers" (2-28-73):
Francoisa, Cameron Mitchell (Garrett),
Tim O'Connor (Kleinschmid), Ella Ed-
wards (Lenore), Don Pedro Colley (For-
bus), Terry Carter (Mattson), Nancy
Wilson (Sugar), Ivor Francis (DeMarig-
ny), Tony Epper (Crawford), John Kerr
(Senator Gordon).
"Moment of Madness" (3-14-73):
McClure, Patrick O'Neal (Ralph Byron),
Brooke Bundy (Ginny), Keith Andes (Dr.
Barnett), James Sikking (Callas), Frank
Maxwell (Hack), Lenore Kasdorf (Addie).
"Ends of the Earth" (3-21-73):
Francoisa, Sebastian Cabot (Tobler),
Diana Muldaur (Sheila), Jay Robinson
(Claude), William H. Bassett (Donald),
Simon Scott (Slater), Milt Kamen (Rico),
Judy Lewis (Ellen), Tom Palmer (Aus-
tin), George Wilbur (Mull).
"Suffer My Child" (3-28-73): O'-
Brian, Mel Ferrer (John Richman),
Paul Mantee (Sam Field), Dabney Cole-
man (Elliott), Byron Morrow (Martin
Honer), Dianne Hull (Tracy), Gerry
Goodrow (Lenny), Donna Baccala (Lynn
Wheatley), Bob Minor (Ken Castle).
"The Packagers" (4-11-73): Mc-
Clure, Michael Pataki (Pierre Karim),
Titos Vandis (President Sinhar), John
Holland (Gen. Harbison), Xenia Gratsos
(Zahura), James Almanzar (Marouk),
Roger Etienne (morgue inspector), Lo-
ren Janes (Craik).

SECOND HUNDRED YEARS, THE. 1967-
68. Monte Markham (Luke Carpen-
ter/Ken Carpenter), Arthur O'Connell (Edwin Carpenter), Frank Maxwell (Col. Garroway), Kay Reynolds
(Erica), Dan Beddow (Mr. Tolliver).

SHAZAM!. 1974-76. Michael Gray
(Billy Batson), Jackson Bostwick
(Captain Marvel) 74-75, John Davey
(Captain Marvel) 75-76, Les Tremayne
(Mentor).

SHEENA. 1956-57. Irish McCalla (Shee-
na), Christian Drake (Bob).
"Forbidden Cargo" (9-16-56).
"The Renegades" (9-23-56): Ro-
bert Shayne, John Banner, John Alvin,
Bob Goodwins, Anthony Ghazlo.
"The Sacred River" (9-30-56).
"Forbidden Land" (10-7-56): Fer-
dinand Wagner.
"The Test" (10-21-56).
"Trade of a Killer" (10-28-56):
Charles Horvath, Carlos Musquiz, Vir-
gil Richardson.

"The Ganyika Kid" (11-4-56):
Joe Adams, Howard Bryant, Andrew
Tavida.
"Mark of the Giant" (11-11-56):
Charles Horvath, Romney Brent.
"Curse of the Voodoo" (11-18-
56): Palmer Fallgren.
"The Elephant God" (11-25-56):
Barbara Bestar.
"Jungle Manhunt" (12-2-56): Su-
zanne Alexander.
"The Leopard Man" (12-9-56).
"Perilous Journey" (12-16-56):
Milton Reddi.
"Eyes of the Idol" (12-23-56):
Virgil Richardson.
"Jungle Pursuit" (12-30-56).
"The Lash" (1-6-57): Buddy
Baer, John Langley.
"Land of the Rogue" (1-13-57).
"The Rival Queen" (1-20-57).
"Fair Stranger" (1-27-57).
"Cry Wolf" (2-3-57): Melody
Kory.
"Crash in the Jungle" (2-10-57).
"Hot Treasure" (2-17-57).
"The Magic Bag" (2-24-57).
"Devil's Mountain" (3-3-57).
"Secret of the Temple" (3-10-
57): Eddie Brooks.
"Touch of Death" (3-17-57).

SHIRLEY TEMPLE STORYBOOK.
"Beauty and the Beast" (1-12-58):
Claire Bloom (Beauty), Charlton Hes-
ton (the Beast), E. G. Marshall (the
Merchant), June Lockhart (Beauty's
sister), Barbara Baxley (Beauty's sis-
ter).
"The Legend of Sleepy Hollow"
(3-5-58): Shirley Temple (Katrina Van
Tassel), Boris Karloff (Narrator), John
Ericson (Brom Bones), Jules Munshin
(Ichabod Crane), Fred Esler (Balthus
Van Tassel), Russell Collins (Alpheus).
"The Land of Green Ginger" (3-
18-58): Kuldip Singh (Abu Ali), Sue
England (Silverbud), Jack Albertson
(Tintac Ping Foo), Joey Faye (Rubdub
Ben Thud), Antony Eustrel (Aladdin).
"Rip Van Winkle" (5-8-58): E. G.
Marshall (Rip Van Winkle), Leora Da-
na (Dame Van Winkle), Ralph Dumke
(Tooley), Beverly Washburn (Judith),
Charles Davis (Alderman Donkle), Bil-
ly Barty (Dwarf), Terence de Marney
(Sergeant), Fred Sherman (Brom Dut-
cher), Paul Brinegar (Van Kimmel),
Owen McGiveney (Peter Vanderdonk).
"The Magic Fishbone" (8-20-58):
Barry Jones (King Watkins), Leo G.
Carroll (Mr. Gingery), Estelle Win-
wood (Fair Grandmarina), Lisa Dan-

iels (Princess Alicia), J. M. Kerrigan
(Mr. Pickles), Richard Lupino (Fish-
monger's boy), Rex Evans (Mr. Muf-
fins), Terry Burnham (Prince), Gary
Euer (Prince), Philip Walters (Prince),
Jimmy Carter (Prince), Christine An-
derson (Princess).
"The Wild Swans" (9-12-58): Phyl-
lis Love (Elisa), Melville Cooper (Bin-
ky), Grant Williams (King Julio), Jo-
seph Wiseman (Sorceror), Olive Dee-
ring (Queen Flavia), Alfred Ryder (First
Minister), Buzz Martin (brother), Bob
Chapman (brother), Bob Banas (brother).
"The Sleeping Beauty" (1-12-59):
Judith Evelyn (Black Fairy), Alexander
Scourby (King), Olive Deering (Grim-
gerda), Nancy Marchand (Queen), Anne
Helm (Sleeping Beauty).

SHIRLEY TEMPLE THEATRE.
"The Land of Oz" (9-18-60): Shirley Temple (Princess Ozma/Toto), Ag-
nes Moorehead (Mombi the Witch), Jona-
than Winters (Lord Nikidik), Ben Blue
(Scarecrow), Arthur Treacher (Graves),
Gil Lamb (Tin Woodsman), Sterling
Holloway (Pumpkinhead), Frances Ber-
gen (Glinda the Good), Charles Boaz
(Colonel), Mari Lynn (Jellia Jamb),
Norman Leavitt (repairman), Lou Mer-
rill (Court Doctor), William Keene (Ro-
yal Army).
"The Reluctant Dragon" (11-13-
60): Shirley Temple (Gillian), John
Rait (St. George), Alice Pearce (Rebec-
ca), Jonathan Harris (Voice of Dragon),
Jack Weston (Amos Overmuch), J. Pat
O'Malley (Mayor Godfrey), Charles
Herbert (Jeremy).
"The House of Seven Gables" (12-
11-60): Shirley Temple (Phoebe Pyn-
cheon), Agnes Moorehead (Hepzibah
Pyncheon), Robert Culp (Holgrave),
Jonathan Harris (Judge Jeffrey Pyncheon),
Martin Landau (Clifford Pyncheon),
John Abbott (Uncle Venner).
"Babes in Toyland" (12-25-60):
Shirley Temple (Floretta the Witch),
Jonathan Winters (Uncle Barnaby), Joe
Besser (Rodrigo), Jerry Colonna (Gon-
zales), Angela Cartwright (Jane), Han-
ley Stafford (Toymaker), Ray Kellogg
(Officer), Michael Petit (Alan), Carl
Ballantine (Gonzorgo), Bob Jellison
(jailer).
"The Terrible Clockman" (1-29-
61): Sam Jaffe (Zacharias), Eric Port-
man (Van Der Graf), Shirley Temple
(Gerande), Jacques Aubuchon (Burgo-
master), John Wengraf (King), Garrett
Lewis (Clockman), David Frankman
(Aubert), George Ives (Apothecary),

Betty Garde (Flower Woman), Arthur Malet (Cook), Jan Peters (Ironmonger), Joe Higgins (Tavernkeeper).

"The Little Mermaid" (3-5-61): Shirley Temple (Mermaid), Nina Foch (Merwich), Cathleen Nesbitt (Granny Mermaid), Donald Harron (Prince), Ray Walston (Sting Ray), John Hoyt (Prince's Aide), Torin Thatcher (Human King), Francine York (Human Princess), J. Pat O'Malley (Merking).

"The Princess and the Goblins" (3-19-61): Shirley Temple (Princess Irene), Jack Ging (Curdie Peterson), Irene Hervey (Esperanza), Mary Wickes (Lootie), Alice Pearce (Goblin Queen), Jack Weston (Goblin King), Herb Vigran (King Charles), Arte Johnson (Prince Gripe).

SHOWER OF STARS.
"A Christmas Carol" (12-23-54): Fredric March (Ebenezeer Scrooge), Basil Rathbone (Marley's Ghost), Ray Middleton (Nephew Fred/Spirit of Christmas Present), Sally Fraser (Belle/Spirit of Christmas Past), Bob Sweeney (Bob Cratchit), Christopher Cook (Tiny Tim), Queenie Leonard (Mrs. Cratchit), Craig Hill (Young Scrooge), Janine Perreau (Belinda), Peter Miles (Peter).

SIGMUND AND THE SEA MONSTERS.
1973-75. Billy Barty (Sigmund Ooz), Johnny Whitaker (Johnny Stuart), Scott Kolden (Scott Stuart), Mary Wickes (Zelda Marshall), Joe Higgins (Sheriff Chuck Bevins), Rip Taylor (Sheldon, the Sea Genie), Margaret Hamilton (Miss Eddels), Sparky Marcus (Shelby), Fran Ryan (Gertrude Gouch) 74-75, Sharon Baird, Van Snowden, Paul Gale, Walter Edmonds, Larry Larson.

SIX MILLION DOLLAR MAN, THE.
1973-78. Lee Majors (Col. Steve Austin), Richard Anderson (Oscar Goldman), Alan Oppenheimer (Dr. Rudy Welles) 73-75, Martin E. Brooks (Dr. Rudy Welles) 75-78.

"Wine, Women and War" (10-20-73): Earl Holliman (Harry Donner), David McCallum (Alexi Kaslov), Britt Ekland (Katrina Volana), Eric Braeden (Arlen Findlater), Lee Bergere (Masaha), Michele Carey (Cynthia), Simon Scott (Dawson), Bobbie Mitchell (stewardess), Catherine Ferrar.

"The Solid Gold Kidnapping" (11-17-73): Elizabeth Ashley (Dr. Erica Bergner), John Vernon (Julian Peck), Luciana Paluzzi (Contessa), Maurice

Evans (Chairman), Terry Carter (Mel Bristol), Leif Erickson (Cameron), Craig Huebing (Roger Ventriss), David White (Ambassador Scott), Polly Middleton (Chairman's secretary).

"Population: Zero" (1-18-74): Penny Fuller (Dr. Chris Forbes), Don Porter (Dr. Bacon), Paul Carr (Paul Cord), Walter Brooke (Gen. Harland Tate), Paul Fix (Joe Taylor), Morgan Jones (Major Phillips), Virginia Gregg (Mrs. Nelson), John Elerick (Corporal Ed Presley), Chester Colby (Joe Hollister), Stuart Nisbet (Harry Johnson), Mike Santiago (Frank), David Valentine (teletype operator), Bob Delegall (1st technician).

"Survival of the Fittest" (1-25-74): William Smith (Maxwell), James McEachin (Cromwell), Christine Belford (Colby), Laurette Spang (Helen), Randall Carver (Barris), Jo Anne Worley (Mona), W. T. Zacha (Roberts), Dale Johnson (Captain).

"Operation Firefly" (2-1-74): Pamela Franklin (Susan Abbott), Vic Mohica (Eddie), Simon Scott (Dr. Abbott), Joseph Ruskin (LeDuc), Erik Holland (Rawlins), Joe Kapp (Frank), John Belson (Jack Hogan), Bill Conklin (Hobbs).

"Day of the Robot" (2-8-74): Henry Jones (Dr. Jeffrey Dolenz), John Saxon (Dr. Sloane), Charles Bateman (Parnell), Lloyd Bochner (Wilson), Noah Keen (Gen. Tanhill), Robert Rothwell (Al), Louie Elias (Roy), Michael Alaimo (truck driver).

"Little Orphan Airplane" (2-22-74): Marge Redmond (Sister Annette), Greg Morris (Josh), Lincoln Kirkpatrick (Capt. Braco), Susan Gay Powell (Sister Terese), Stack Pierce (Bajad), Pierre Turner (Jajamin), Dave Turner (Farmer), Paul Bryar (Gen. Magoffin), Scoey Mitchell (Major Chooka).

"Doomsday and Counting" (3-1-74): Gary Collins (Vasily), Jane Merrow (Irina Leonova), Bruce Glover (Voda), William Smithers (Koslenko), Walter Edmiston (operator), William Boyett (Air Force General), Rico Cattani (1st technician), Anne Newman (2nd technician).

"Eyewitness to Murder" (3-8-74): Gary Lockwood (Hooper), William Schallert (Sandusky), Richard Webb (Sebastian), Leonard Stone (Tanner), Ivor Barry (Henley), Sal Ponti (Windom), Nicky Blair (Guido), Allen Joseph (Dorsey).

"Athena One" (3-15-74): Farrah Fawcett (Kelly Wood), Quinn Redeker (Capcom), Jules Bergman (himself), Paul Kent (Dr. Wolf), John S. Ragin

(SIX MILLION DOLLAR MAN cont.)
(Flight Director), Dean Smith (Oster-
man), Doug Collins (Retro).
"Dr. Wells Is Missing" (3-29-
74): John Van Dreelan (Alfredo), Mi-
chael Dante (Julio), Norbert Schiller
(Porter), Than Wyenn (desk clerk),
Curt Lowens (Anton), Terry Leonard
(Vincent), Jim Shane (Yamo), Dave
Cass (Kurt).
"The Last of the Fourth of Julys"
(4-5-74): Steve Forrest (Quail), Ar-
lene Martell (Violette), Hank Stohl
(Balsam), Ben Wright (Ives), Tom
Reese (Joe Alabam), Kevin Tighe (Root).
"Burning Bright" (4-12-74): Wil-
liam Shatner (Josh Lang), Quinn Rede-
ker (Calvin Billings), Warren Kemmer-
ling (Dr. Haldane), Rodolfo Hoyos (Ar-
ruza), Anne Schedeen (Tina), Mary
Rings (counter girl), Ron Stokes (M.
P.).
"The Coward" (4-19-74): George
Montgomery (Garth), George Takei
(Chin-Ling), France Nuyen (Marnu),
Martha Scott (Helen), Ken Endosa (Jo-
hara), Ron Soble (Quang-Dri), Kim
Kahana (Prokar), Fuji (Kai-sing).
"Run, Steve, Run" (4-26-74):
Henry Jones (Dr. Dolenz), George Mur-
dock (Rossi), Noah Beery, Jr. (Tom
Molson), Mike Henry (Cliff Platt), Me-
lissa Greene (Suzie), Victor Millan
(Art Ramirez), Bill Conklin (Smitty).
"Nuclear Alert" (9-13-74): Ca-
rol Lawrence (Dr. Clea Broder), Fred
Beir (Ted Swenson), George Gaynes
(Gen. Wilen), Felice Orlandi (Cal),
Thomas Bellin (Carson).
"The Pioneers" (9-20-74): Mike
Farrell (David), Joan Darling (Nicole),
Robert F. Simon (Sheriff), Vince Ho-
ward (Walker).
"Pilot Error" (9-27-74): Pat
Hingle (Senator Hill), Alfred Ryder
(Lannon), Hank Brandt (Cole), Hank
Stohl (Phillips), Stephen Nathan (Greg),
Suzanne Zenor (Jill Denby), Dennis
McCarthy (Doctor), Chet Douglas (re-
porter).
"The Pal-Mir Escort" (10-4-74):
Anne Revere (Salka Pal-Mir), Denny
Miller (Stellen), Leo Fuchs (Vani),
Nate Esformes (Shavid), Jamie Don-
nelly (Linda).
"The Seven Million Dollar Man"
(11-1-74): Monte Markham (Barney
Miller), Maggie Sullivan (Carla), Mar-
shall Reed (gate guard), Fred Lerner
(OSI man), Joan Van Ark.
"Straight on 'Til Morning" (11-8-
74): Meg Foster (Minonee), Christo-
pher Mears (Eymon), Cliff Osmond

(Sheriff Kemp), Jimmy Lyden (Dr. Wa-
ters), Donald Billett (Lohrman), Kurt
Grayson (Cockerell), Lucas White
(Packer), Al Dunlap (Ed Hermon).
"The Midas Touch" (11-15-74):
Farley Granger (Bert Carrington),
Noam Pitlik (MacGregor), Kate Mc-
Keown (Julie Farrell), Richard D.
Hurst (Connors), Woodrow Chambliss
(Pop), Marcus Smith (Sentry).
"The Deadly Replay" (11-22-74):
Clifton James (Shadetree Burns), Lara
Parker (Andrew Collins), Robert Sy-
monds (Jay Rogers), Jack Ging (Ted
Collins), Jack Manning (Carl Amison),
William Scherer (Simeon).
"Act of Piracy" (11-29-74): Le-
nore Kasdorf (Sharon), Hagan Beggs
(Jed), Stephen McNally (Dr. Craig),
Carlos Romero (Ferrage), Jorge Cer-
vera, Jr. (Lieutenant), David Domin-
guez (dock guard).
"Stranger in Broken Fork" (12-
13-74): Sharon Farrell (Angie), Robert
Donner (Horace), Bill Henry (Thurmond),
Arthur Franz (Dr. Carlton), Troy Mel-
ton (Corley Weems), Kristine Ritzke
(Jody).
"The Peeping Blonde" (12-20-74):
Farrah Fawcett (Victoria Webster), Ro-
ger Perry (Colby), Hari Rhodes (Karl),
W. T. Zacha (Victor), Christopher Staf-
ford Nelson (Billy Jackson), Martin
Speer (Flightcom).
"Cross Country Kidnap" (1-10-75):
Donna Mills (Lisa), Frank Aletter (Bor-
den), Tab Hunter (Blake), John Gabriel
(Shuster), Ben Wright (Benno), Jerome
Guardino (Veneman).
"Lost Love" (1-17-75): Linda
Marsh (Barbara Thatcher), Joseph Rus-
kin (Markos), Jeff Corey (Orin Thatcher),
Than Wyenn (Kosoyin), Wesley Lau
(Emil), Harry Pugh (waiter).
"The Last Kamikaze" (1-19-75):
John Fujioka (Kuroda), Robert Ito (Tho-
mas Gabella), Edmund Gilbert (Hay-
worth), Jimmy Joyce (Dr. Richmond),
Paul Vaughn (radio operator), Jane
Goodnow Gillett (Lorraine).
"Return of the Robot Maker" (1-
26-75): Henry Jones (Dolenz), Troy
Melton (Barney), Ben Hammer (Gen.
Stacy), Iris Edwards (Amy), Jean Lee
Brooks (Denise), Sarah Simmons (sec-
retary).
"Taneha" (2-2-75): Jess Walton
(E. J. Haskell), Bill Fletcher (Bleeker),
James Griffith (Will Long), Paul Brine-
gar (Rafe Morris), Jim B. Smith (Bob
Elliott), Trent Dolan (station attendant).
"Look Alike" (2-23-75): Robert
DoQui (Breezy), George Foreman (Mar-

cus Garvy), Jack Colvin (Ed Jasper),
Arthur Space (Carruthers), Robert
Salvio (La Salle), Mary Rings (Molly),
Susan Keller (Secretary).
"The E. S. P. Spy" (3-2-75): Rob-
bie Lee (Audrey Moss), Dick Van Pat-
ten (Harry), Philip Burns (Randolph),
George Patton (Jarecki), Bert Kramer
(George Vant), Alan Bergmann (Lund),
Paul Cavonis (Pierce).
"The Bionic Woman" (3-16-75 &
3-23-75): Lindsay Wagner (Jaime Som-
mers), Malachi Throne (Joseph Wrona),
Martha Scott (Helen Elgin), Ford Rai-
ney (Jim Elgin), Paul Carr (Timber-
lake), Harry Hickox (Jon Ellerton),
Sidney Clute (Schwartz).
"Outrage in Balinderry" (4-19-
75): Martine Beswicke (Julia Flood),
Gavan O'Herlihy (Dan), Richard O'Brien
(Breen), Alan Caillou (Gen. Carmichael),
Richard Erdman (Slaton), David Frank-
ham (Capt. Abbott), William Sylvester
(Frederick Collins), Margaret Fair-
child (Elinor Collins).
"Steve Austin, Fugitive" (4-27-
75): Gary Lockwood (Hooper), Jenni-
fer Darling (Peggy Callahan), Bernie
Hamilton (Lt. Dobbs), Reb Brown (Of-
ficer Atkins), Andy Romano (Charlie
Taylor), Marco Lopez (Portez), Am-
zie Strickland (old lady).
"The Return of the Bionic Woman"
(9-14-75 & 9-21-75): Lindsay Wagner
(Jaime Sommers), Richard Lenz (Dr.
Michael Marchetti), Tony Giorgio (Abe
Collins), Al Ruscio (Chester), Dennis
Patrick (Carlton Harris), Ford Rainey
(Jim Elgin), George Keymas (Arkoff),
Virginia Gregg (Mrs. Raymond).
"Price of Liberty" (9-28-75):
Chuck Connors (Niels Lindstrom), Hen-
strom), Henry Beckman (Robert Me-
yer), Sandy Ward (Doug Witherspoon),
Bill Quinn (Tom), George Jordan (Bill).
"The Song and Dance Spy" (10-5-
75): Sonny Bono (John Perry), Bruce
Glover (Buckner), Fred Holliday (Craw-
ford), Susie Coelho (Linda), Victor
Mohica (Lee Michaels), Robin Clarke
(Damon).
"The Wolf Boy" (10-12-75): John
Fujioka (Kuroda), Buddy Foster (Wolf
Boy), Teru Shimada (Ishikawa), Quinn
Redeker (Bob Masters), Bill Saito (To-
shio).
"The Deadly Test" (10-19-75):
Leigh Christian (Lt. Jan Simmons),
Martin Speer (David Levy), Erik Es-
trada (Prince Sakari), Tim O'Connor
(Col. Joe Gordon), Frank Marth (Win-
slow), William Scherer (Jim Barrows),
Harry Pugh (Pratt).

"Target in the Sky" (10-26-75):
Barbara Rhoades (Kelly Wixted), Denny
Miller (Jeremy Burke), Ivor Francis
(Dr. Morton Craig), Hank Stohl (Ben
Cosgrove), Rafer Johnson (Thaddeus
Jones).
"One of Our Running Backs Is
Missing" (11-2-75): Larry Csonka (Lar-
ry Bronco), Dick Butkus (Bob LaPort),
Les Josephson (Rick LaPort), Mike
Henry (Tatashore), Pamela Csonka (Pam
Bronco), Carl Weathers (Stolar), Al
Checco (George Yokum), Earl Faison
(Ailes).
"The Bionic Criminal" (11-9-75):
Monte Markham (Barney Miller), Donald
Moffat (Lester Burstyn), John Milford
(Shatley), Maggie Sullivan (Carla Peter-
son).
"The Blue Flash" (11-16-75): Rod-
ney Allen Rippy (Ernest Cook), Janet
MacLachlan (Mrs. Cook), Michael Con-
rad (Jimbo), Eddie Fontaine (Tony An-
derson), Jason Wingreen (Mr. Logan),
Garrison True (Harold), Barry Cahill
(Olmstead).
"The White Lightning War" (11-
23-75): Ben Hammer (Beauregard Wil-
lis), Hugh Gillin (Sheriff Weems), Kath-
erine Helmond (Middy), Austin Stoker
(Charles Quinten), Robert Donner (Ker-
mit), Randy Kirby (Johnny).
"Divided Loyalty" (11-30-75): Michael McGuire (Leon Jackson), Radames
Pera (Alex Jackson), Ned Romero (Bo-
ris), Johana de Winter (Edna Jackson),
Curt Lowens (Captain), Ralph Taeger
(Sergeant).
"Clark Templeton O'Flaherty" (12-
14-75): Lou Gossett (Clark Templeton
O'Flaherty), Louise Latham (Ms. Hal-
laway), Ryan MacDonald (Van Rensse-
laer), H. M. Wynant (McAdams), Lillian
Randolph (landlady), Susan Quick (tech-
nician), Linda Nesbit (woman).
"The Winning Smile" (12-21-75):
Jennifer Darling (Peggy Callahan), Mil-
ton Selzer (Dr. Emil Losey), Stewart
Moss (Dr. Gene Finney), Ben Andrews
(Agee), Harry Lewis (Hector), Robert
Delegall (Tom Depster), Rick Podell
(agent).
"Welcome Home, Jaime" Part
One (1-11-76): Lindsay Wagner (Jaime
Sommers), Martha Scott (Helen Elgin),
Ford Rainey (Jim Elgin), Richard Lenz
(Dr. Michael Marchetti), Dennis Patrick
(Carlton Harris), Roger Davis (Tom Hol-
loway), Dee Timberlake (Karen Stone),
Kraig Metzinger (Joey).
"Hocus-Pocus" (1-18-76): Per-
nell Roberts (Mark Wharton), Robbie
Lee (Audrey Moss), Jack Colvin (Will

(SIX MILLION DOLLAR MAN cont.)
Collins), Richard Geard (Dinallo),
W.T. Zacha (George), Chris Nelson (Jack).
"The Secret of Big Foot" (2-1-76
& 2-4-76): Stefanie Powers (Shalon),
Severn Darden (Apploy), Andre the
Giant (Bigfoot), Hank Brandt (Evan
Beckey), Penelope Windust (Marlene
Beckey), Charles Cypher (Faler),
Don Whyte (Tom Raintree), Ford
Lile (Captain), Chuck Bowman (guard),
Alan Mandell (technician).
"The Golden Pharoah" (2-8-76):
Farrah Fawcett (Trish Hollander),
Joe Maross (Gustav Tokar), Gordon
Connell (Wheel Jackson), Michael
Lane (Skorvic), Gary Vinson (Joe),
Rudy Challenger (Dave Martino),
Lyndel Stuart (secretary), Joseph
LaCava (croupier), Peter Ashton
(chauffeur).
"Love Song for Tanya" (2-15-76):
Cathy Rigby (Tanya), Terry Kiser
(Alexis), Kurt Grayson (Uri Gargon),
Alan Mason (Andre), Walker Edmiston (Ivan), Lindsay Wagner (Jaime
Sommers), Curtis Credel (Director),
Sheila Wills (saleslady), Michael
Cartel (guard).
"The Bionic Badge" (2-22-76):
Noah Beery, Jr. (Greg Banner),
Alan Bergmann (Burman), Thomas
Bellin (Gerry Martin), Stack Pierce
(Randolph), Susan Gay Powell (Cindy
Walker), Mike Santiago (Clint).
"Big Brother" (3-7-76): Michael A. Salcido (Carlos), Maria-
Elena Cordero (Margarite), Carl
Crudup (Smiley), Ralph Wilcox
(Larry Hamiln), John Hesley (Phil),
David Yanez (Chico), Renie Radich
(secretary), Jorge D. Cervera,
Jr. (Boy).
"The Return of Big Foot" Part
One (9-19-76): Lindsay Wagner (Jaime
Sommers), Sandy Duncan (Gillian),
John Saxon (Redlik), Stefanie Powers
(Shalon), Ted Cassidy (Bigfoot),
Severn Darden (Apploy), Charles
Cyphers (Faler), Stephen Young
(Dallet).
"Nightmare in the Sky" (9-26-76):
Farrah Fawcett (Kelly Wood), Dana
Elcar (Larry Stover), Donald Moffat
(Dr. Martin Davis), Hank Stohl (Mike).
"Double Trouble" (10-3-76):
Flip Wilson, Simon Scott (Dr. Barto),
Rick Rodell (Niko), Mira L. Waters
(Susan), Jerome Guardino (cab driver),
Borah Silver (doorman).
"The Most Dangerous Enemy"
(10-17-76): Cheryl Osborne.

"H+2+O=Death" (10-24-76): Elke
Sommers (Dr. Elsa Martin), Linden
Chiles (Olmega), John Van Dreelan
(Mr. Matheson), Todd Martin (Kirov),
Robert J. Hogan (Walker), Frank
Parker (Ed).
"Kill Oscar" Part Two (10-31-76):
John Houseman (Dr. Franklin), Corinne
Michaels (Lynda), Jennifer Darling
(Callahan), Jack Ging (Hanson).
"The Bionic Boy" (11-7-76):
Vincent Van Patten (Andy Sheffield),
Joan Van Ark (Valerie Sheffield),
Frank Gifford (himself), Kerry Sherman (Coline), Greg Evigan (Joe
Hamilton), Woodrow Chambliss (Mr.
Savannah), Nick David (Charlie),
Richard Erdman (Vernon), Dick Van
Patten (Palmer), Jack Bannon (Dr.
Melville), George Martin (Dr. Penny).
"The Vulture of the Andes" (11-
21-76): Barbara Luna (Leslie), Henry
Darrow (Falco), Bernie Kopell (Pete),
Zitto Kazann (Paul), Dallas Mitchell
(Maj. Reynolds).
"The Thunderbird Connection"
(11-28-76): Barry Miller (Prince
Hassad), Robert Loggia (Mahmud
Majid), Martine Beswicke (Shali
Biba), Jim McMullan (Col. Paul
Miller), Susanne Reed (Jan Lawrence),
Ned Romero (Akhmed Khadduri),
Erik Holland (Sgt. Young), Joe LoPresti (Arafa), Trent Dolan (Sgt.
Jones).
"A Bionic Christmas Carol"
(12-12-76); Ray Walston (Horton Budge),
Dick Sargent (Bob Crandall), Antionette Bower (Nora Crandall), Quinn
Cummings (Elsie Crandall), Adam
Rich (Bob Crandall, Jr.), Natasha
Ryan (Cissy Crandall), Noah Keen
(Dr. Hendricks), Ann Dusenberry
(girl clerk), June Drayton (secretary).
"Task Force" (12-19-76): Jennifer Darling (Peggy Callahan), Alex
Cord (Harraway), Taylor Lacher
(Nicolini), Edmund Gilbert (Major
Pell), Robert Forward (Air Force
General), Gary Cashdollar (MP),
Scott B. Wells (Sheriff).
"The Ultimate Imposter" (1-2-77):
David Sheiner (Stenger), Stephen Macht
(Joe Patton), Pamela Hensley (Jenny),
Margaret Fairchild (Lily Stenger),
Kim Basinger (Loraine), George Ball
(Mal).
"Death Probe" (1-9-77 & 1-16-77):
Jane Merrow (Irena Leonova), Nehemiah
Persoff (Popov), Beverly Garland
(Sonia), Don Dubbins (Zach Meesham),
Bill Fletcher (mechanic), Ross Elliott
(Sheriff), Walter Brooke (Gen. Wiley),

Austin Stoker (Captain), Philip Pine (Russian General), Ryan MacDonald (photographer), Judd Lawrence (technician).
"Danny's Inferno" (1-23-77): Larry Horn (Danny), Frank Marth (Bill Bruner), David Opatoshu (Dr. Monica), E. J. Peaker (Glennis), Mills Watson (Lazarus), John Hoyt.
"The Fires of Hell" (1-30-77): Heather Menzies (Allison Harker), Ken Swofford (Roy Palmer), Charles Aidman (Bertram Lomaz), Bruce Glover (Sheriff Burgess), Don 'Red' Barry (Howie), Bob Neill (driver), Natt Christian (worker).
"The Infiltrators" (2-6-77): Yvonne Craig (Lena), Michael Conrad (Retsky), Harold Sylvester (Tollombe), Cliff Carnell (Duclaire), Pervis Atkins (Mason), Joe Kapp (Cooper).
"Carnival of Spies" (2-13-77): Lloyd Bochner (Prof. Ulrich Rau), Cheryl Miller (Kim), Gloria Manon (Shira), Peter Weiss (Schmidt), H. M. Wynant (General), Michael Strong.
"U-509" (2-20-77): Guy Doleman (Bulman), Ian Abercrombie (Shoemacher), Steve Sandor (Covell), Ted Hamilton (Jaffe), William Sylvester (Prescott), Morgan Jones (Captain).
"Privacy of the Mind" (2-27-77): Suzanne Charny (Tamara Batalova), Leslie Moonves (Bob Kemps), Roger Perry (Dr. George Berman), Paul Mantee (Campbell), Curt Lowens (Kulikov), Bob Neill (Carlson).
"To Catch the Eagle" (3-6-77): George Loros (Lone Bear), Peter Breck (Silver Cloud), Kathleen Beller (Little Deer), Gerald McRaney (Bob Marsh), Dehl Berti (Iron Fist).
"The Ghostly Teletype" (5-15-77): Christina Hart (Margaret Waggner), Les Lannom (Davey Waggner), Larry Anderson (Murdoch), Robert H. Harris (Dr. Brenner), Elizabeth Kerr (Mrs. Waggner), Jodean Russo (Madame Marka), Linda Dano (Angela).
"Sharks" (9-11-77 & 9-18-77): Pamela Hensley (Cynthia), Stephen Elliott (Grayland), Gregory Walcott (Parker), William Sylvester (Adm. Prescott).
"Deadly Countdown" (9-25-77 & 10-2-77): Jenny Agutter (Dr. Leah Russell), Philip Abbott (Dave McGrath), Lloyd Bochner (Gordon Shanks), Crofton Hardester (Richman), Mills Watson (Webster), Sherry Hursey (Melissa), Martin Caidin (G. H. Beck).

"Bigfoot V" (10-9-77): Ted Cassidy (Bigfoot), Katherine DeHetre (Hope Langston), Geoffrey Lewis (Charlie), Tony Young (Jason), S. Newton Anderson (Higbee).
"Killer Wind" (10-16-77): Sheila Wills (Rhonda), Adam Roarke (Nash), James McEachin (Garth), Fred J. Gordon (Falco).
"Rollback" (10-30-77): Robert Loggia (Hendricks), Suzanne Charny (Maureen), Paul D'Amato (Brady), Rick Springfield.
"Dark Side of the Moon" (11-6-77 & 11-13-77): Jack Colvin (Dr. Charles Leith), Simone Griffith (Bess Fowler), Skip Homeier (Ted), Quinn Redeker (Frank), Bob Neill (Eric), Walter Brooke (Dr. Jellman).
"Target: Steve Austin" (11-27-77): Lynnette Mettey (Joan), Curt Lowens (Hellerman), Tony Epper (Rabbit), Quinn Redeker (Frank), Ian Abercrombie (man in van).
"The Cheshire Project" (12-18-77): Suzanne Somers (Jenny), Barry Cahill (Gen. Meyers), Jem Begg (Arthur Vale), John Larch.
"Walk a Deadly Wing" (1-1-78): Eric Braeden (Viktor Cheraskin), John Devlin (Dimitri), Eddie Fontaine (Sullivan).
"Just a Matter of Time" (1-8-78): Leigh Christian (Donna Hoffman), Charles Cioffi (Barris), Paul Carr (Essex), John Milford).
"Return of Death Probe" (1-22-78 & 1-29-78): Than Wyenn (Mahmoud), Ken Swofford (Dan Kelly).
"The Lost Island" (1-30-78): Robin Mattson (Da-Nay), Jared Martin (Torg), Alf Kjellin (Gerro), Robert Symonds (Jensen), Terence Burke (Zandor).
"The Madonna Caper" (2-6-78): Bibi Besch (Lysandra), Len Berman (Kane), Rudy Challenger (Tynan).
"Deadly Ringer" (2-13-78): Linda Dano (Margaret Winslow).
"Date with Danger" (2-20-78 & 2-27-78): Robert Walker, Jr. (Cloch/ Harold Bell), Elaine Giftos (Emily), Luke Askew (Banner), Hank Brandt (Fowler).
"The Moving Mountain" (3-6-78): Lisa Barringer (Andrea Mestrova), John Colicos (Gen. Gorbukov), George Clifton (Santos), Susan Fleming (Lorie), Keith Langsdale (Mishkin).

SIXTH SENSE, THE. 1972. Gary Collins (Michael Rhodes), Catherine Farrar (Nancy Murphy).

(SIXTH SENSE cont.)

"I Do Not Belong to the Human World" (1-15-72): Belinda Montgomery (Tina Norris), Jim McMullan (Pete Martin), Christina Crawford (Betty Blake), Kip Niven (Randy Blake), Bert Freed (Prof. Calvin Blake), John Milford (Detective).

"The Heart That Wouldn't Stay Buried" (1-22-72): Leif Erickson (Dr. Philip Ford), Laraine Day (Marion Ford), Jessica Walter (Jordana Theland), Michael Murphy (David Ford), Gene Tyburn (Joseph Ford), Jo DeWinter (nurse).

"Lady, Lady, Take My Life" (1-29-72): Tisha Sterling (Annette Gordon), John Saxon (Dr. Harry Auden), Alf Kjellin (Dr. Karl Rintels), Than Wyenn (Dr. Abishi), Walter Brooke (Walter), James McEachin (Richard Blain).

"The House That Cried Murder" (2-5-72): Carol Lynley (Gail Sumner), Corinne Camacho (Anne Carver), Larry Linville (Roger Carver), Robert Yuro (Frank Orley), Jim Antonio (Tom Walker), Kathleen King (Frances Dahl), William Bryant (Lt. Jensen), Patricia L. Mickey (Janet Lewis).

"The Man Who Died at 3 and 9" (2-26-72): Joseph Campanella (Paul Crowley), Simon Scott (Stuart Forbes), Susan Howard (Nita Forbes), Aly Wassil (Hari Narada), Chandrika (woman).

"Can a Dead Man Strike from the Grave" (2-26-72): William Shatner (Edwin Danbury), Anne Archer (Elizabeth Danbury), Bettye Ackerman (Helene), Pam Peters (Stephanie), Alison McKay (Phyllis Regan), Robert B. Williams (old man).

"With This Ring, I Thee Kill" (3-4-72): Lucie Arnaz (Marguerite Webster), Lee Majors (Clayton Ross), Richard Loo (Matsou), Will Geer (Father Jordan), Florence Lake (Desiree), Stacy Harris (Henry Webster), Dick Dinman (Doctor).

"Witch, Witch, Burning Bright" (3-11-72): Cloris Leachman (Judith Eaton), Tiffany Bolling (Damaris Eaton), Mike Farrell (Dr. Gil Clarke), Harry Townes (Martin Fletcher), Dana Elcar (Edward Winslow), Kermit Murdock (Judge Fuller), S. John Launer (Judge Fletcher), William Wintersole (Howland).

"Eye of the Hunted" (3-18-72): Mariette Hartley (Terry/Diana), James Wainwright (Wayne Bennett),

Louise Latham (Mrs. Bennett), Rudy Solari (Detective Woods), Mora Gray (Ada), Michael C. Gwynne (Lee).

"Echo of a Distant Scream" (4-1-72): Steve Forrest (Glenn Tuttle), Stefanie Powers (Paula Norris), A. Martinez (Billy), Jim Davis.

"Whisper of Evil" (4-8-72): Frank Converse (Perry Singleton), Carole Wells (Monique), Percy Rodrigues (Sgt. Bruckner), Coleen Gray (Joyce), Pat Delaney (Alice), Philip Pine (Dr. Lewis), Paul Stewart (Dr. Adamson), Henry Beckman (Bennington), Louis Quinn (Bernie), Murray MacLeod (Danny), Lewis Charles (Lee), Gracia Lee (Duke), Chris Hutson (nurse).

"Shadow in the Well" (4-15-72): Mary Ann Mobley (Lisa Wolf), Jeanette Nolan (Mrs. Wolf), Will Geer (Rev. Mr. Jordan), Henry Silva (Linchou), Mark Tapscott (Arnold).

"Face of Ice" (4-22-72): Bradford Dillman (George), Christine Belford (Anna), George Murdock (Victor), Michael Patacki (Sheriff).

"Coffin, Coffin, In the Sky" (9-23-72): Stephen McNally (Bud Fielding), Marge Redmond (Nurse Kelly), Barbara Babcock (Arlene), Ed Nelson (Pilot), Colby Chester (Co-Pilot), Sharon Gless (stewardess), James Daughton (Hank), Jess Walton (Lili), Casey MacDonald (Janice).

"Dear Joan, We're Going to Scare You to Death" (9-30-72): Joan Crawford (Joan Fairchild), Scott Hylands (Jason), David Ladd (Paul), Kelly Jean Peters (Lori), Anne Lockhart (Diana), Martine Bartlett (Carrie Malcolm), Lenore Kasdorf (Karen).

"Witness Within" (10-7-72): June Allyson (Mrs. Desmond), Tippy Walker (Julie Desmond), Michael Strong (Frank Moore), Willard Sage (Ansel Garnett).

"With Affection, Jack the Ripper" (10-14-72): Patty Duke Astin (Elizabeth), Robert Foxworth (Adam), Percy Rodrigues (Lt. Woods), Mitch Carter (policeman), Marilyn Nix (secretary), Heather Lowe (1st girl), Jannis Durkin (2nd girl).

"Once Upon A Chilling" (10-28-72): Susan Strasberg (Laura Anders), Ruth Roman (Mrs. Cloister), Joel Fabiani (Edward Melling), David Huddleston (Dr. Peace), John Hillerman (Adrain Weems).

"Through a Flame, Darkly" (11-4-72): Sandra Dee (Alice Martin), Charles Knox Robinson (Mike Martin),

John Anderson (Sheriff), John Karlen
(Ed), Val Bisoglio (Police Officer),
Peggy Feury (Dr. Milborn), Lenny
Montana (Barney).

"I Did Not Mean to Slay Thee"
(11-11-72): Pamela Franklin (Bonnie),
Michael Whitney (Jack Charleroi),
Pernell Roberts (Pettigrew), Michael
Baseleon (Dr. Vaughn), Jason Win-
green (Dr. Wilbur), Lindsay Workman
(Felton), Lyvonne Walder (Miss Hines),
Christine Dixon (Lynn Newland), Con-
nie Milton (nurse).

"And Scream By the Light of
the Moon, the Moon" (11-25-72): Jo-
sephine Hutchinson (Maude Hacker),
Sallie Shockley (Carol Kibben), Michael
Glaser (David Hall), Scott Glenn (Mark
Hall), Margaret Markov (Mary Ruth),
Chris Holter (Jeanne).

"If I Should Die Before I Wake"
(12-2-72): Stefanie Powers (Jean
Ames), Jane Wyman (Ruth Ames),
Gene Evans (Aaron Coe), Michael
Lane (Sam Fenwick), Dennis Dugan
(Bill Miller), Daniel Kemp (Sheriff),
Rod McCary (Dan Barr).

"Five Widows Weeping" (12-9-
72): Barry Sullivan (Amos Sutherland),
Mary Ann Mobley (Nancy Sutherland),
Ellen Weston (Joanna Sutherland),
William Jordan (John Sutherland),
Hank Brandt (Steve Sutherland), Wel-
son Welch (Eames), Read Morgan
(1st man).

"Gallows in the Wind" (12-16-72):
Meg Foster (Carey Evers), Gary
Clarke (Ed Sandifur), R.G. Armstrong
(Jack Preston), Virginia Gregg (Thelma
Young), George Ives (Frank Young),
Richard Hatch (Owen Preston), Conlan
Carter (Mack Burton).

"The Eyes That Would Not Die"
(12-23-72): Kathleen Gackle (Kathy
Turner), Rudy Solari (Dr. Simmons),
Percy Rodrigues (Lt. Woods), Tom
Bosley (Albert), Stanley Kamel (Kil-
ler), Regis J. Cordic (Commentator),
Laura Campbell (night nurse), Lisa
Moore (Nurse Greer), Sandy Champion
(orderly).

SPACE ACADEMY. 1977-79. Jon-
athan Harris (Gampu), Pamelyn
Ferdin (Laura Gentry), Ric Carrott
(Chris Gentry), Brian Tochi (Tee
Garsoom), Ty Henderson (Paul
Jerome), Maggie Cooper (Adrienne
Pryce-Jones), Eric Greene (Loki).

SPACE FORCE. 1978.
"Pilot" (4-28-78): William Phipps
(Cmdr. Irving Hinkley), Fred Willard

(Capt. Thomas Woods), Larry
Block (Pvt. Arnold Fleck), Jimmy
Boyd (Capt. Leon Stoner), Hilly
Hicks (Capt. Robert Milford), Mau-
reen Mooney (Sgt. Eve Bailey), Joe
Medalis (Lt. Kabar).

SPACE: 1999. 1975-77. Martin
Landau (Commander Koenig),
Barbara Bain (Dr. Helena Russell),
Barry Morse (Prof. Victor Berg-
man) 75-76, Nick Tate (Alan Car-
ter), Catherine Schell (Maya) 76-77,
Tony Anholt (Tony Verdeschi) 76-
77, Zienia Merton (Sandra Benes),
Clifton Jones (David Kano) 75-76,
Anton Phillips (Robert Mathias),
Prentis Hancock (Paul Morrow) 75-
76, Suzanne Roauette (Tanya Alex-
ander) 75-77, John Hug (Bill Fra-
ser) 76-77, John Alkin (Andy
Johnson) 76-77, Yasuko Nagazumi
(Yasko Nugami) 76-77, Jeffrey
Kissoon (Dr. Ben Vincent) 76-77,
Sarah Bullen (Main Mission Oper-
ative) 75-76.

"Breakaway" (9-9-75): Roy
Dotrice (Commissioner Simmonds),
Phillip Madoc (Commander Gorski),
Eric Carte (Eddie Collins), Lon
Satton (Ben Ouma).

"Matter of Life and Death" (9-
16-75): Richard Johnson (Lee Russell), Stuart Damon (Parks).

"Another Time, Another Place"
(9-23-75): Judy Geeson (Regina
Kesslann).

"Collision Course" (9-30-75):
Margaret Leighton (Arra).

"Force of Life" (10-7-75):
Ian McShane (Anton Zoref), Gay
Hamilton (Eva Zoref), Eva Rueber-
Staire (Jane), John Hamill (Mark
Dominix).

"Alpha Child" (10-14-75):
Julian Glover (Jarak), Cyd Hayman
(Cynthia Crawford/Rena), Wayne
Brooks (Jackie).

"Guardian of Piri" (10-21-75):
Catherine Schell (Servant of the Guardian), Michael Culver (Pete Irving).

"War Games" (10-28-75): Anthony Valentine (Male Alien), Isla
Blair (Female Alien).

"Mission of the Darlans" (11-
4-75): Joan Collins (Dara), Dennis
Burgress (Neman), Aubrey Morris
(Petros High Priest), Paul Antrim
(Lowry), Robert Russell (Hadin),
Gerald Stadden (male mute), Jackie
Horton (female mute).

"The Black Sun" (11-11-75):
Paul Jones (Mike Ryan), Jon Lauimore

(SPACE: 1999 cont.) (Smitty).
"End of Eternity" (11-18-75):
Peter Bowles (Balor), Jim Smilie
(Mike Baxter).
"Voyager's Return" (11-25-75):
Jeremy Kemp (Dr. Ernst Linden),
Barry Stokes (Jim Haines), Alex
Scott (Aarchon), Lawrence Trimble
(Abrams).
"The Testament of Arkadia"
(12-2-75): Orso Maria Guerrini (Luke
Ferro), Lisa Harrow (Anna Davis),
Anne Cullinan Taylor (Dani).
"The Last Enemy" (12-9-75):
Caroline Mortimer (Dione), Maxine
Audley (Theia), Kevin Stoney (Talos),
Carolyn Courage (1st girl).
"Dragon's Domain" (12-16-75):
Gianni Garko (Tony Cellini), Douglas
Wilmer (Commissioner Dixon),
Michael Sheard (Prof. Darwin King),
Susan Jameson (Dr. Juliet Mackie),
Barbara Kellerman (Dr. Monique
Fauchere).
"The Full Circle" (12-23-75):
Oliver Cotton (Spearman).
"Death's Other Dominion" (12-
30-75): Brian Blessed (Dr. Cabot
Rowland), John Shrapnel (Capt. Jack
Tanner), Mary Miller (Freda).
"Ring Around the Moon" (11-6-
76): Max Faulkner (Ted Clifford).
"Earthbound" (1-19-76): Chris-
topher Lee (Captain Zandor), Roy
Dotrice (Commissioner Simmonds).
"The Infernal Machine" (1-26-
76): Leo McKern (Companion/Delmer
Powys Plebus Gwent).
"The Missing Link" (2-2-76):
Peter Cushing (Raan), Joanna Dun-
ham (Vana).
"The Last Sunset" (2-9-76).
"Space Brain" (2-16-76): Shane
Rimmer (Kelly), Carla Romanelli
(Melita), Derek Anders (Wayland).
"The Troubled Spirit" (2-23-
76): Giancarlo Prette (Dan Mateo),
Hilary Dwyer (Laura Adams), Anthony
Nicholls (Dr. James Warren), Val
Musetti (Spirit).
"Metamorph" (9-18-76): Brian
Blessed (Mendor), Anoushka Hempel
(Annette Fraser).
"All That Glisters" (9-25-76):
Patrick Mower (Dave Reilly).
"Journey to Where" (10-2-76):
Freddie Jones (Dr. Logan), Isla
Blair (Carla), Laurence Harrington
(Jackson), Roger Bizley (MacDonald).
"The Taybor" (10-9-76): Wil-
loughby Goddard (Taybor).
"New Adam, New Eve" (10-
16-76): Guy Rolfe (Magus).

"Mark of Archanon" (10-23-76):
John Standing (Pasc), Michael Gal-
lagher (Etrec).
"Brian the Brain" (10-30-76):
Bernard Cribbins (Voice of Brian/
Capt. Michael).
"The Rules of Luton" (11-6-76):
David Jackson (Alien Strong), God-
frey James (Alien Invisible), Roy
Marsden (Alien Transport).
"A B Chrysalis" (11-13-76):
Ina Skriver (A), Sarah Douglas (B).
"The Catacombs of the Moon"
(11-20-76): James Laurenson (Pat-
rick Osgood), Pamela Stephenson
(Michelle Osgood).
"Seed of Destruction" (11-27-76).
"The Exiles" (12-12-76): Peter
Duncan (Cantar), Stacy Dorning (Ziva),
Margret Inglis (Mirella).
"Space Warp" (1-2-77).
"A Matter of Balance" (1-9-77):
Lynne Frederick (Shermeen Williams),
Stuart Wilson (Vindrus).
"The Beta Cloud" (1-16-77):
David Prowse (Creature).
"The Lambda Factor" (1-23-77):
Deborah Fallander (Carolyn Powell),
Jess Conrad (Mark Sanders).
"One Moment of Humanity"
(1-30-77): Billie Whitelaw (Aamara),
Leigh Lawson (Zarl), Geoffrey Bayl-
don (Number Eight).
"The Seance Spectre" (2-13-77):
Ken Hutchinson (Sanderson), Carolyn
Seymour (Eva).
"The Bringers of Wonder" (2-
20-77 & 2-27-77): Stuart Damon
(Guido Verdeschi), Patrick Westwood
(Dr. Shaw).
"Dorzak" (3-6-77): Lee Montague
(Dorazk), Jill Townsend (Sahala).
"The Immunity Syndrome" (3-
13-77).
"Devil's Planet" (3-20-77):
Hildegard Neil (Elizia).
"The Dorcons" (3-27-77): Ann
Firbank (Consul Varda).

SPACE PATROL. 1950-56. Ed
Kemmer (Buzz Corey), Lyn Os-
born (Cadet Happy), Rudolph
Anders (Dr. Van Meter), Virginia
Anders (Carol Karlyle), Nina
Bara (Tonga), Ken Mayer (Major
Robertson).
"Treachery on Mars" (12-30-50).
"The Lethal Lady" (1-6-51).
"Intrigue in the Cabinet" (1-
13-51).
"The Agra Ray" (1-20-51).
"The Ivy of Death" (1-27-51).
"Trouble on Saturn's Third

Moon" (2-3-51).
"Solo Flight to Jupiter" (1-10-51).
"Cosmic Debris Warning" (2-17-51).
"The Planos Epidemic" (2-24-51).
"Tunnel of Escape: Tunnel of Death" (3-3-51).
"The Perilous Sleep" (3-10-51).
"A Vacation at Lake Azure" (3-17-51): Perry Evans (Brand), Peter Foster (Zurach).
"Theft of the Zeta Ray" (3-24-51).
"Blackmail on Saturn" (3-31-51).
"The Man in the Radurium Glove" (4-7-51).
"Under the Red Lake of Jupiter" (4-14-51).
"The Counterfeit Commander" (4-21-51).
"Mysterious Mission to Canali" (4-28-51).
"The Major's Dilemma" (5-5-51).
"Isolation in Space" (5-12-51).
"The Tourist Trap" (5-19-51).
"Dangerous Intrigue" (5-26-51).
"The Secret Injection" (6-2-51).
"The Trecherous Technicians" (6-9-51): Lisa Howard (Lisa), Pierce Lyden (Chaney).
"Beyond the Rim of Space" (6-16-51).
"Race Against Death" (6-23-51).
"The Lost City of the Carnacans" (6-30-51).
"The Deadly Weapon" (7-7-51).
"The Legend of Wild Man's Ridge" (7-14-51).
"Way Station to the Stars" (7-14-51).
"The Hidden Reflector" (7-28-51).
"The Dangerous Discovery" (8-4-51).
"Spaceship on the Edge of Forever" (8-11-51).
"The Underwater Hideout" (8-18-51).
"A Big Wheel Named Ferri" (8-25-51).
"The Vindictive Brother" (9-1-51).
"Photograph of a Traitor" (9-8-51).
"The Courageous Coward" (9-15-51).
"The Theft of the Scrambler" (9-22-51).
"Prometheus Bound for Destruction" (9-29-51).
"Immediate Disaster" (10-6-51).

"Lunatics from the Future" (10-13-51).
"The Space Patrol Code Belt" (10-20-51).
"The Floating Image in Space" (10-27-51).
"Secret Peril" (11-3-51).
"The Parasite Disc" (11-10-51).
"The Secret of Terra" (11-17-51).
"Jungle of No Return" (11-24-51).
"Prison of Deadly Gas" (12-1-51).
"The Sacrifice" (12-8-51).
"Test Flight of the Galaxy" (12-15-51).
"Fair Exchange" (12-22-51).
"The Counterfeit Puzzle" (12-29-51).
"Flowers of Death" (1-5-52).
"Cosmic Smoke Guns" (1-12-52).
"Lost in the Snow-Cap Region of Mars" (1-19-52).
"Explosion on Morehouse Five" (1-26-52).
"The Evil Guardian of Harpola" (2-2-52).
"Hit By A Meteorite" (2-9-52).
"Planetold Plot" (2-16-52).
"Victim of Amnesia" (2-23-52).
"The Lieutenant's Revenge" (3-1-52).
"The Mind Readers" (3-8-52).
"Slaves of the Exonium Mine" (3-15-52).
"Abandoned in Outer Space" (3-22-52).
"The Great Bank Robbery" (3-29-52).
"The Mysterious Moonquakes" (4-5-52).
"The Phantom Fleet" (4-12-52).
"Trouble on Titan" (4-19-52).
"Sacrifice to the Moon God" (4-26-52).
"Uncertain Death" (5-3-52).
"Invasion" (5-10-52).
"A Threat to the United Planets" (5-17-52).
"The Threat of the Thormanoids" (5-24-52).
"Jungle Jeopardy" (5-31-52).
"The Scheming Sibling" (6-7-52).
"Danger on Mars" (6-14-52).
"Mission to Mercury" (6-21-52).
"The Deadly Ray Gun" (6-28-52).
"The Force Barrier" (7-5-52).
"The Iron Fist" (7-12-52).
"The Derelict Space Station" (7-19-52).
"The Mystery of Ancient Egypt" (7-26-52).
"Mystery of the Flying Pirate Ship" (8-2-52).

(SPACE PATROL cont.)
"Blackmail at Lake Axure"
(8-16-52).
"The Hidden Map" (8-23-52).
"The Green Mold of Mars"
(8-30-52).
"The Galactic War" (9-9-52).
"The Energy Thief" (9-13-52).
"Sabotage of the Jupiter Run"
(9-20-52).
"The Star Raiders" (9-27-52).
"The Code Breakers" (10-4-
52).
"Errand of Mercy" (10-11-52).
"Underwater Treachery"
(10-18-52).
"The Electronic Man" (10-
25-52).
"Treachery on Terra Five"
(11-11-52).
"Frontier Epidemic" (11-8-52).
"Powerdive" (11-15-52).
"Three Exiles" (11-22-52).
"The Shakedown" (11-29-52).
"The Human Trap" (12-6-52).
"The Chase in Time" (12-
13-52).
"The Deadly Sunbeam" (12-
20-52).
"The Conspiracy" (12-27-52).
"The Human Targets" (1-3-53).
"The Rifle Arsenal" (1-10-53).
"The Stolen Prisoner" (1-17-
53).
"The Deadly Flower" (1-24-53).
"Runaway Planetoid" (1-31-53).
"Radioactive Cave (2-7-53).
"Trip to Deimos" (2-14-53).
"Operation Rescue" (2-21-53).
"Survival in the Ice Desert"
(2-28-53).
"Space Fatigue" (3-7-53).
"Threat to Terra" (3-14-53).
"Jail Break" (3-21-53).
"The Laughing Alien" (3-28-53).
"The Vital Factor" (4-4-53).
"Space Mail Robbery" (4-11-
53).
"The Space Wanderer" (4-18-
53).
"Big Impersonation" (4-25-53).
"Electronic Space Storm"
(5-2-53).
"The Deadly Glacier" (5-9-53).
"The Mutation Bomb" (5-16-53).
"Phantom Space Ship" (5-23-53).
"The Green Plague" (5-30-53).
"The Fraud of Titan" (6-6-53):
Marvin Miller (Stanton), I Stanford
Jolley (Jim Todd), Edith Evanson
(Aunt Sybil), Wayne Taylor (Truck
Todd).
"The Man Who Stole a City"

(6-13-53).
"Gigantic Space Knife" (6-20-53).
"Space Patrol Microscope (6-
27-53).
"The Theft of the Terra Five"
(7-4-53).
"Mysterious Ocean in Space"
(7-11-53).
"The Stolen Evidence" (7-18-53).
"Traitorous Triangle" (7-25-53).
"Crash Landing" (8-1-53).
"The Brain Machine" (8-8-53).
"A Dangerous Smoke Cloud"
(8-15-53).
"The Black Falcon's Return"
(8-22-53).
"The Mystery of Planet X"
(8-29-53).
"The Trap of Planet X" (9-5-53).
"The Primitive Men of Planet
X" (9-12-53).
"The Hate Machine of Planet
X" (9-19-53).
"Black Falcon's Escape from
Planet X" (9-26-53).
"Resonance Impeller" (10-3-53).
"The Ice Demon of Planet X"
(10-10-53).
"The Slaves of Planet X" (10-
17-53).
"The Giant of Planet X" (10-
24-53).
"The Iron Eaters of Planet X"
(10-31-53).
"The Falcon's Web of Planet X"
(11-7-53).
"Castle's Destruction on Planet
X" (11-14-53).
"Valley of Illusion" (11-21-53).
"Doom of Planet X" (11-28-53).
"Alien and the Robot" (12-5-53).
"The Robot's Escape" (12-12-
53).
"The City of Living Statues"
(12-19-53).
"Mystery of the Missing As-
teroids" (12-26-53).
"The Phantom Space Pirate"
(1-2-54).
"The Space Vault Robbery"
(1-9-54).
"The Pirate's Escape" (1-16-
54).
"The Amazons of Cydonia"
(1-23-54).
"The Monsoon Trap on Cydonia"
(1-30-54).
"The Men-Slaves of Cydonia"
(2-6-54).
"The Deadly Radiation Cham-
ber" (2-13-54).
"The Plot in the Atomic Plant"
(2-20-54): Marvin Miller (Mr. Proteus).

"The Blazing Sun of Mercury"
(2-27-54).
"The Big Proteus Swindle"
(3-6-54).
"The Escape of Mr. Proteus"
(3-13-54).
"Mr. Proteus and Poison
Gas" (3-20-54).
"The Revenge of Mr. Proteus"
(3-27-54).
"The Capture of Mr. Proteus"
(4-3-54).
"Baccarratti's 'Z' Ray" (4-
10-54): Bela Kovacs (Prince Bac-
carratti/Zarra).
"Marooned in the Past" (4-
17-54).
"Evil Spirits of Great Thun-
derbird" (4-24-54).
"The Fall of the Kingdom of
Zarra (4-30-54).
"The Prisoners of the Giant
Comet" (5-7-54).
"The Demon Planet" (5-14-54).
"Lost in Galactic Space" (5-
21-54).
"The Hidden Treasure of
Mars" (5-28-54): I Stanford Jolley
(Dr. Lambert), Nestor Paiva (Car-
nacan).
"The Martian Totem Head"
(6-4-54).
"Trapped in a Pyramid" (6-
11-54).
"The Underwater Space Ship
Graveyard" (6-18-54).
"The Giant Marine Clam"
(6-25-54).
"Marooned on the Ocean Floor"
(7-2-54).
"Mystery of the Disappearing
Space Patrolmen" (9-4-54).
"The Space Patrol Periscope"
(9-11-54).
"The Space War" (9-18-54).
"The Defeat of Manza" (9-
25-54).
"The Giants of Pluto III" (10-
2-54).
"The Fiery Pit of Pluto III"
(10-9-54).
"Manhunt on Pluto III" (10-
16-54).
"Mystery of the Stolen Rocket
Ship" (10-23-54).
"The Atom Bomb" (10-30-54).
"Danger: Radiation" (11-6-54).
"The Exploding Stars" (11-
13-54).
"The Dwellers of the Prime
Galaxy" (11-20-54).
"Terra, the Doomed Planet"
(11-27-54).

"Revenge of the Black Falcon"
(12-4-54).
"The Sorcerers of Outer Space"
(12-11-54).
"The Defeat of Baccarratti"
(12-18-54).
"A Christmas Party for Happy"
(12-25-54).
"Lair of the Space Spider"
(1-1-55).
"Web of Arachna" (1-8-55).
"Collapse of the Spider's
Web" (1-15-55).
"The Androids of Algol" (1-
22-55): Larry Dobkins (Raymo),
Valerie Bales (Ula), Paul Cavanaugh
(Secretary General).
"Double Trouble" (1-29-55).
"The Android Invasion" (2-5-
55).
"The Wild Men of Procyon"
(2-12-55).
"Marooned on Procyon IV"
(2-19-55): Bert Holland (Survivor),
Charles Horvath (Survivor).
"The Atomic Vault" (2-26-55).

SPACE SCHOOL. British 1956.
John Stuart, Matthew Lane,
Donald Drummond, Julie Webb,
David Drummond.

SPIDERMAN. 1978-79. Nicholas
Hammond (Peter Parker/Spider-
man), Michael Pataki (Capt.
Barbera), Robert F. Simon (J.
Jonah Jameson), Chip Fields
(Rita), Ellen Bry (Julie) 1979.
"The Deadly Dust" (4-5-78 &
4-12-78): JoAnna Cameron (Gale),
Robert Alda (White), Randy Powell
(Gregg), Simon Scott (Dr. Baylor),
Anne Bloom (Carla), Steven A.
Anderson (Ted), Herbert S. Braha
(LeBeau), Emil Farkas (Benson),
Richard Kyker (Angel), Sid Clute
(Di Carlo).
"The Curse of Rava" (4-19-78):
Theodore Bikel (Mandak), Adrienne
LaRussa (Trina), Byron Webster
(Rusten), David Ralphe (Dr. Keller).
"Night of the Clones" (4-26-78):
Morgan Fairchild (Lisa Benson),
Lloyd Bochner (Dr. Moon), Rick
Traeger (Dr. Reichman), Irene
Tedrow (Aunt May).
"Escort to Danger" (5-3-78):
Alejandro Rey (President Calderon),
Barbara Luna (Lisa Alvarez),
Madeline Stowe (Maria Calderon),
Harold Sakata (Matsu), Michael
Marsellos (Sauti), Lachelle Price (Kim
Barker), Bob Minor (Curt Klein),

(SPIDERMAN cont.) Donna Hansen
(Mrs. Hays).
    "The Captive Tower" (9-5-78):
David Sheiner (Forster), Todd Sus-
man (Farnum), Fred Lerner (Duke),
Barry Cutler (Barry), Warren Vanders
(Hammer), Ed Sancho-Bonet (Ramirez).
    "A Matter of State" (9-12-78):
Nicolas Coster (Andre), John Crawford
(Evans), Michael Santiago (Carl),
James Victor (Martin).
    "The Con Caper" (11-25-78):
William Smithers (Colbert), Ramon
Bieri (Cates), Andrew Robinson (Mc-
Teague), Fred Downs (Warden Rischer).
    "The Kirkwood Haunting" (12-30-
78): Marlyn Mason (Lisa Kirkwood),
Peter MacLean (Dr. Polarsky), Paul
Carr (Ganz), Peggy McCay (Dr. Davis),
Del Monroe (thug).
    "Photo Finish" (2-7-79).
    "Wolfpack" (2-21-79): Gavan
O'Herlihy (David), Wil Seltzer (Art),
Allan Arbus (George Hansen).
    "The Chinese Web" (7-6-79):
Benson Fong (Min Lo Chan), Rosalind
Chao (Emily Loo T'ao), Hagan Beggs
(Evans), Richard Erdman (Zeider),
Myron Healey (Lt. Olson), John Milford.

SPOTLIGHT PLAYHOUSE. 1956.
    "The Magic Glass" (7-31-56):
Ruth Hussey (Trudy), William Hopper
(Walter), Dickie Bellis (Tommy),
Beverly Washburn (Linda), Claire
Carleton (Joan), Michael Raffetta
(tramp), Allen Pinson (lifeguard).

STAGE 7. 1954.
    "The Secret Weapon of 117"
(7-13-54): Ricardo Montalban, Susan
Morrow, Sheila Bromley, John Litel.
    "Tiger at Noon" (2-27-55): Ste-
phen McNally.

STARLOST. 1973-74. Keir Dullea
(Devon), Gay Rowan (Rachel), Robin
Ward (Garth), William Osler (Compu-
ter Voice).
    "Voyage of Discovery" (9-22-73):
Sterling Hayden (Jeremiah), George
Sperdakos (Jubal), Gillie Fenwick
(Old Abraham), Sean Sullivan (Rachel's
father), Aileen Seaton (Rachel's mother),
Jim Barron (Garth's father), Kay Haw-
trey (Garth's mother), Scott Fisher
(boy).
    "Lazarus from the Mist" (9-29-
73): Frank Converse (Dr. Gerald
Aaron), Vivian Reis (Mrs. Aaron),
Doug McGrath (the Sergeant), Mel
Tuck (1st tube dweller), Alan Bleviss
(2nd tube dweller).

    "The Goddess Calabra" (10-6-73):
John Colicos (the Governor), Barry
Morse (Shalith), Dominic Hogan (the
Priest), Michael Kirby (the Captain),
George Naklowych (Governor's Deputy),
Paul Geary (guard).
    "The Pisces" (10-13-73): Lloyd
Bochner (Garroway), Carol Lazare
(Teale), Diana Barrington (Teale),
Diana Barrington (Janice), Ted Beatie
(old man), Lillian Graham (old woman),
June Stacey (younger woman), Donna
Stacey (young girl), Susan Fleming
(technician).
    "Children of Methuselah" (10-
20-73): David Tyrell (Captain), Scott
Fisher (Prosecutor), Susan Stacey
("5"), Gina Dick (Supervisor).
    "And Only Man is Vile (10-27-73):
Simon Oakland (Dr. Asgard), Trudy
Young (Lethe), Irena Mayeska (Dr.
Diana Tabot), Tim Whelan (village
elder), John Bethune (Villager A).
    "The Alien Oro" (11-3-73):
Walter Koenig (Oro), Alexandra
Bastedo (Ydana).
    "Circuit of Death" (11-10-73):
Percy Rodrigues (Sakharov).
    "Gallery of Fear" (11-17-72):
Angel Tompkins (Doris), Jim Barron
(Garth's father), William Clune (Cap-
tain).
    "Mr. Smith of Manchester" (11-
24-73): Ed Ames (Mr. Smith), Pat
Galloway (Trent), Doris Petrie (nurse),
Nina Weintraub (girl).
    "The Astro Medics" (12-1-73):
Stephen Young (Dr. Chris), Meg
Hogarth (Dr. Jean), Budd Knapp (Dr.
Martin), Michael Zenon (Commander),
Bill Kemp (Captain).
    "The Implant People" (12-8-73):
Donnelly Rhodes (Roloff), Pat Collins
(Serina), Leo Leyden (Brant), Dino
Narizzano (Dumal).
    "The Return of Oro" (12-15-73):
Walter Koenig (Oro).
    "Farthing's Comet" (12-22-73):
Edward Andrews (Dr. Farthing), Linda
Sorensen (McBride).
    "The Beehive" (12-29-73): Will-
iam Hutt (Pete), Antoinette Bower
(Heather), Alan McRae (Callisher),
John Friesen (Keebie).
    "Space Precinct" (1-4-74): Ivor
Barry (Rafe), Nuala Fitzgerald (Reena),
Richard Alden (Mike).

STAR MAIDENS. 1977. Pierre Brice
(Adam), Gareth Ghomas (Shem),
Judy Geeson (Fulvia), Lisa Harrow
(Dr. Liz Becker), Christiane
Kruger (Octavia), Derek Farr

(Prof. Evans), Christian Quad-
flieg (Rudi Schmitt), Penelope
Horner (the Medusian P. A. An-
nouncer), Jenny Morgan (Date
Moss), Ann Maj Britt (Octavia's
assistant), Uschi Mellin (Andrea),
Ronald Hines (Insp. Stanley), Dawn
Addams (Clara).

STARSTRUCK. 1979.
  Pilot (6-9-79): Beeson Carroll
(Ben McCallister), Tania Myren (Kate
McCallister), Meegan King (Mark
McCallister), Kevin Brando (Rupert
McCallister), Guy Raymond (Ezra
McCallister), Elvia Allman (Abigail
McCallister), Lynne Lipton (Amber
LaRue), Sarah Kennedy (Delight),
Robin Strand (Chance), Joe Silver
(Max), Roy Brocksmith (Orthwaite
Frodo), Herb Kaplowitz (Dart), Ro-
bert Short (Hudson), Buddy Douglas
(Mrs. Bridges), J.C. Wells (Tashko),
Chris Walas (Mary-John), Cynthia
Latham (Madame Dumont).

STAR TREK. 1966-69. William Shat-
ner (Capt. James T. Kirk), Leonard
Nimoy (Mr. Spock), De Forest Kel-
ley (Dr. Leonard 'Bones' McCoy),
James Doohan (Montgomery Scott),
Nichelle Nichols (Lt. Uhura),
George Takai (Lt. Sulu), Majel
Barrett (Nurse Christine Chapel),
Grace Lee Whitney (Yeoman Janice
Rand) 66-67; Walter Koenig (Ensign
Pavel Chekov), 67-69; Jim Goodwin
(Lt. John Farrell) semi-regular.
  "The Man Trap" (9-8-66): Jeanne
Bal (Nancy Crater), Alfred Ryder
(Bob Crater), Michael Zaslow (Par-
nell), Bruce Watson (Green), Vince
Howard (crewman), Francine Pyne
(monster).
  "Charlie X" (9-15-66): Robert
Walker, Jr. (Charlie Evans), Abra-
ham Sofaer (the Thalasian), Patricia
McNulty (Lina Lawton), Charles J.
Stewart (Capt. Remart), Dallas Mitchell
(Tom Nellis).
  "Where No Man Has Gone Be-
fore" (9-22-66): Gary Lockwood
(Gary Mitchell), Paul Carr (Lt. Lee
Kelso), Sally Kellerman (Elizabeth
Dehner), Paul Fix (Dr. Piper), Lloyd
Haynes (Alden), Andrea Dromm (Yeo-
man Smith).
  "The Naked Time" (9-29-66):
Stewart Moss (Joe Tormolean), John
Bellah (Dr. Harrison), Bruce Hyde
(Kevin Riley).
  "The Enemy Within" (10-6-66):
Edward Maden (Fisher), Garland

Thompson (Wilson).
  "Mudd's Women" (10-13-66):
Roger C. Carmel (Harry Mudd),
Karen Steele (Eve McHuron), Susan
Denberg (Magda Kovacs), Maggie
Thrett (Ruth Bonaventure), Gene
Dynarski (Ben Childress), Seamon
Glass (Benton), John Kowal (Herm
Gossett).
  "What Are Little Girls Made Of?"
(10-20-66): Michael Strong (Dr.
Roger Korby), Sherry Jackson
(Andrea), Ted Cassidy (Ruk), Harry
Basch (Brown), Vince Deadrick (Mat-
thews), Budd Albright (Rayburn).
  "Miri" (10-27-66): Kim Darby
(Miri), Michael J. Pollard (John),
John Megna (fat boy), Steven McEveety
(redheaded boy), Ed McCready (crea-
ture).
  "Dagger of the Mind" (11-3-66):
James Gregory (Dr. Tristan Adams),
Marianna Hill (Dr. Helen Noel),
Morgan Woodward (Dr. Simon Van
Gelder), Suzanne Wasson (Lethe).
  "The Carbomite Maneuver"
(11-10-66): Anthony Call (Dave
Bailey), Clint Howard (Balck), Ted
Cassidy (Voice of Balck).
  "The Menagerie" (11-17-66 &
11-24-66): Jeffrey Hunter (Capt.
Christopher Pike), Susan Oliver
(Vina), Malachi Throne (Cmdr. Jose
Mendez), Meg Wylie (the Keeper),
Julie Parrish (Miss Piper), Majel
Barrett (Number One), John Hoyt
(Dr. Philip Boyce), Peter Duryea
(Lt. Tyler), Hagan Beggs (Lt. Hanson).
  "Conscience of the King" (12-
8-66): Arnold Moss (Anton Karidian),
Barbara Anderson (Lenore), Bruce
Hyde (Devin Riley), Eddie Paskey
(Lt. Leslie).
  "Balance of Terror" (12-15-66):
Mark Lenard (Romulan Commander),
Paul Comi (Andrew Stiles), Law-
rence Montaigne (Decius), John
Warburton (Centurion), Gary Walberg
(Hanson), Barbara Baldavin (Angela
Martine), Stephen Mines (Robert
Tomlinson).
  "Shore Leave" (12-29-66):
Emily Banks (Tonia Barrows), Oliver
McGowan (caretaker), Bruce Mars
(Finnegan), Perry Lopez (Rodriguez),
Shirley Bonne (Ruth), James Gruzaf
(Don Jaun), Sebastian Tom (Samurai).
  "The Galileo Seven" (1-5-67):
Don Marshall (Boma), John Crawford
(Commissioner Ferris), Peter Marko
(Gaetano), Phyllis Douglas (Yeoman
Mears), Grant Woods (Kelowitz),
Rees Vaughan (Latimer).

(STAR TREK cont.)

"The Squire of Gothos" (1-12-67): William Campbell (Trelane), Richard Carlyle (Jaeger), Michael Barrier (De Salle), Venita Wolf (Yeoman Ross).

"Arena" (1-19-67): Carole Shelyne (the Metron), Jerry Ayers (O'Herlihy), Tom Troupe (Lt. Harold), Grant Woods (Kelowitz), Sean Kenney (DePaul), James Falrey (Lang), Ted Cassidy (Voice of Gorn).

"Tomorrow Is Yesterday" (1-26-67): Roger Perry (Capt. Christopher), Ed Peck (Col. Fellini), Hal Lynch (Air Police Sergeant), Richard Merrifield (Technician Webb), John Winston (Transporter Chief Kyle).

"Court-Martial" (2-2-67): Percy Rodriguez (Commodore Stone), Elisha Cook, Jr. (Samuel Cogley), Joan Marshall (Areel Shaw), Richard Webb (Finney), Alice Rawlings (Jamie Finney), Hagan Beggs (Hanson), Winston DeLugo (Timothy).

"The Return of the Archons" (2-9-67): Harry Townes (Reger), Torin Thatcher (Marplon), Charles Macaulay (Landru), Christopher Held (Lindstrom), Sid Haig (First Lawgiver), Brioni Farrell (Tula), Jon Lormer (Tamar), Ralph Maurer (Bilar), Morgan Farley (Hacom), Eddie Paskey (Lt. Leslie), David L. Ross (guard).

"Space Seed" (2-16-67): Ricardo Montalban (Khan Singh), Madlyn Rhue (Marla McGivers), Blaisdell Makee (Spinelli), Mark Tobin (Joaquin).

"A Taste of Armageddon" (2-23-67): Gene Lyons (Ambassador Fox), David Opatoshu (Anan 879), Barbara Babcock (Mea 249), Robert Sampson (Sar 627), Miko Mayama (Yeoman Tamura), David L. Ross (Galloway).

"This Side of Paradise" (3-2-67): Jill Ireland (Leila Kalomi), Frank Overton (Elias Sandoval), Dick Scotter (Painter), Grant Woods (Kelowitz).

"Devil in the Dark" (3-9-67): Ken Lynch (Vandenberg), Barry Russo (Lt. Cmdr. Giotta), Brad Weston (Ed Appel), Biff Elliott (Schmitter), Janos Prohaska (the Horta).

"Errand of Mercy" (3-23-67): John Abbott (Ayleborne), John Colicos (Kor), Peter Brocco (Claymare), Victor Lundin (Klingon), David Hillary Huge (Trefayne).

"The Alternative Factor" (3-30-67): Robert Brown (Lazarus), Janet MacLachlan (Charlene Masters), Richard Derr (Commodore Barstow),

Eddie Paskey (Lt. Leslie), Arch Whiting (assistant engineer).

"The City on the Edge of Forever" (4-6-67): Joan Collins (Edith Keeler), John Harmon (Rodent), Hal Baylor (policeman), David L. Ross (Galloway), Bartell LaRue (Voice of the Guardian).

"Operation Annihilate" (4-13-67): Dave Armstrong (Kartan), Maurishka Taliferro (Yeoman Zara Jamal), Craig Hundley (Peter Kirk), Joan Swift (Aurelan Kirk).

"Amok Time" (9-15-77): Celia Lovsky (T'Pau), Arlene Martel (T'Pring), Lawrence Montaigne (Stonn), Byron Morrow (Komak).

"Who Mourns for Adonis?" (9-22-67): Michael Forest (Apollo), Leslie Parrish (Lt. Carolyn Palamas), John Winston (Kyle).

"The Changeling" (9-29-67): Blaisdell Makee (Singh), Arnold Lessing (Lt. Carlisle), Meade Martin (crewman), Barbara Gates (crewman), Vic Perrin (Voice of Nomad).

"Mirror, Mirror" (10-6-67): Barbara Luna (Marlena), Vic Perrin (Tharn).

"The Apple" (10-13-67): Keith Andes (Akuta), Celeste Yarnall (Martha Landon), Jay Jones (Ensign Mallory), David Soul (Makora), Shari Nims (Sayana).

"The Doomsday Machine" (10-20-67): William Windom (Commodore Decker), Elizabeth Rogers (Lt. Palmer), John Copage (Elliott), Richard Compton (Washburn), John Winston (Sgt. Kyle), Tim Burns (Russ).

"Catspaw" (10-27-67): Antoinette Bowers (Sylvia), Theo Marcuse (Korob), Michael Barrier (DeSalle), Jimmy Jones (Jackson).

"I, Mudd" (11-3-67): Roger C. Carmel (Harry Mudd), Mike Howden (Lt. Rowe), Richard Tatro (Norman), Micheal Zaslow (Ensign Jordan), Kay Elliott (Stella Mudd), Rhae & Alyce Andrece (Alice series), Tom & Ted LaGarde (Herman Series), Maureen & Coleen Thorton, Tamara & Starr Wilson.

"Metamorphosis" (11-10-67): Glenn Corbett (Zephram Cochrane), Elinor Donahue (Nancy Hedford).

"Journey to Babel" (11-17-67): Jane Wyatt (Amanda), Mark Lenard (Sarek), William O'Connell (Thelev), Reggie Nalder (Sharas), John Wheeler (Gav), James X. Mitchell (Lt. Josephs).

"Friday's Child" (12-1-67): Julie Newmar (Ellen), Tige Andrews (Kras), Michael Dante (Maab), Cal

Bolder (Keel), Kirk Raymone (Duur), Ben Gage (Teer Akaar), Robert Bralver (Grant).

"The Deadly Years" (12-8-67): Charles Drake (Commodore Stocker), Sarah Marshall (Janet Wallace), Beverly Washburn (Arlene Galway), Felix Locher (Johnson), Laura Wood (Mrs. Johnson), Carolyn Nelson (Yeoman Atkins).

"Obsession" (12-16-67): Stephen Brooks (Ensign Garrovick), Jerry Ayres (Ensign Rizzo).

"Wolf in the Fold" (12-22-67): John Fiedler (Hengist), Charles Macauley (Jaris), Pilar Seurat (Sybo), Joseph Bernard (Tark), Charles Dierkop (Morla), Judy McConnell (Tankris), Virginia Landridge (Karen Tracy), Tania Lemani (Kara), Judy Sherven (Nurse).

"The Trouble with Tribbles" (12-29-67): William Schallert (Nilz Barris), William Campbell (Koloth), Stanley Adams (Cyrano Jones), Whit Bissell (Lurry), Michael Pataki (Korax), Charlie Brill (Arne Darvin), Guy Raymond (Trader), Ed Reimers (Adm. Fitzpatrick), Paul Bradley (Ensign Freeman), David Ross (guard).

"The Gamesters of Trikelion" (1-5-68): John Ruskin (Galt), Angelique Pettyjohn (Shana), Jane Ross (Tamoon), Steve Sandor (Lars), Victoria George (Ensign Jana Haines), Mickey Morton (Kloog), Dick Crockett (Andoria Throll).

"A Piece of the Action" (1-12-68): Anthony Caruso (Bela Oxmyx), Victor Tayback (Jojo Karko), Lee Delano (Kalo), John Harmon (Tepo), Steve Marlo (Zabo), Sheldon Collins (boy), Dyanne Thorne (girl), Sharyn Hillyer (girl), Buddy Garion (hood).

"The Immunity Syndrome" (1-19-68).

"A Private Little War" (2-2-68): Nancy Kovack (Nona), Michael Whitney (Tyree), Booker Marshall (Dr. Mbenag), Arthur Bernard (Apella), Joe Romeo (Krell), Gary Pillar (Yotan), Janos Prohaska (the Mugato).

"Return to Tommorrow" (2-9-68): Diana Muldaur (Dr. Ann Mulhall).

"Patterns of Force" (2-16-68): David Brian (John Gil), Skip Homier (Melakon), Richard Evans (Isax), Valora Norland (Daras), William Wintersole (Abrom), Patrick Horan (Eneg), Bart LaRue (newscaster), Ralph Maure (SS Lieutenant), Pater Canan (Gestapo Lieutenant), Gilbert Green (SS Major), Paul Baxley (1st trooper).

"By Any Other Name" (2-23-68): Warren Stevens (Rojan), Stewart Moss (Hanar), Barbara Bouchet (Kelinda), Robert Fortier (Tomar), Carol Byrd (Lt. Shea), Leslie Dalton (Drea), Julie Cobb (Yeoman Leslie Thompson).

"The Omega Glory" (3-1-68): Morgan Woodward (Capt. Ronald Tracey), Roy Jenson (Cloud William), Irene Kelly (Sirah), David L. Ross (Galloway), Eddie Paskey (Lt. Leslie), Ed McReady (Dr. Carter), Morgan Farley (Yang Scholar), Lloyd Kino (Wu).

"The Ultimate Computer" (3-8-68): William Marshall (Dr. Daystrom), Barry Russo (Commander Wesley), Sean Morgan (Harper).

"Bread and Circuses" (3-15-68): William Smithers (Merik), Logan Ramsey (Claudius Marcus), Ian Wolfe (Septimus), Rhodes Reason (Flavius Maximus), Lois Jewell (Drusilla), Bart LaRue (Announcer), Jack Perkins (Master of Games);

"Assignment Earth" (3-29-68): Robert Lansing (Gary Seven), Teri Garr (Roberta Lincoln), Lincoln Demyan (Sgt. Rawlings), Don Keefer (Cromwell), Morgan Jones (Col. Nesvig).

"Spock's Brain" (9-20-68): Marj Dusay (Kara), James Daris (Morg), Sheila Leighton (Luma).

"The Enterprise Incident" (9-27-68): Joanne Linville (Romulan Commander), Richard Compton (technical officer), Jac Donner (Tal), Robert Gentile (Romulan technician), Mike Howden (guard), Gordon Coffey (soldier).

"The Paradise Syndrome" (10-4-68): Sabrina Scharf (Miramanee), Rudy Solari (Salish), Richard Hale (Goro), John Lindesmith, Lamont Laird.

"And the Children Shall Lead" (10-11-68): Melvin Belli (Gorgon), Craig Hundley (Tommy Starnes), Mark Robert Brown (Don), Pamelyn Ferdin (Mary), James Wellman (Prof. Starnes), Caesar Belli (Steve), Brian Tochi (Ray), Louis Elias (technician).

"Is There in Truth No Beauty" (11-19-68): Diana Muldaur (Dr. Miranda Jones), David Frankham (Lawrence Marvick).

"Spectre of the Gun" (10-25-68): Ron Soble (Wyatt Earp), Rex Holman (Morgan Earp), Charles Maxwell (Virgil Earp), Sam Gilman (Doc Holiday), Bonnie Beecher (Sylvia),

(STAR TREK cont.) William Zuckert (Sheriff Behan), Charles Seel (Ed), Ed McReady (barber), Richard Anthony (rider), Gregg Palmer (rancher), Abraham Soafaer (Melkotian voice).

"Day of the Dove" (11-1-68): Michael Ansara (Kang), Susan Howard (Mara).

"For the World Is Hollow and I Have Touched the Sky" (11-8-68): Kate Woodville (Natira), Byron Morrow (Adm. Westervleit), Jon Lormer (old man).

"The Tholian Web" (11-15-68).

"Plato's Stepchildren" (11-22-68): Michael Dunn (Alexander), Barbara Babcock (Philana), Liam Sullivan (Parmen), Ted Scott (Eraclitus), Derek Partridge (Donyd).

"Wink of an Eye" (11-29-68): Kathie Browne (Deela), Jason Evers (Rael), Eric Holland (Ekor), Geoffrey Binney (Compton).

"The Empath" (12-6-68): Kathryn Hays (Gem), Alan Bergman (Lal), Willard Sage (Thann), Jason Wingreen (Dr. Linde), Davis Roberts (Dr. Ozaba).

"Elaan of Troyius" (12-20-68): France Nuyen (Elaan), Jay Robinson (Petri), Tony Young (Kryton), Lee Duncan (Evans), K. L. Smith (Klingon), Victor Brandt (Watson), Dick Durock (guard), Charles Beck (guard).

"Whom Gods Destroy" (1-3-69): Steve Ihnat (Garth), Yvonne Craig (Marta), Key Luke (Corey), Gary Downey (Tellarite), Richard Geary (Andorian).

"Let That Be Your Last Battlefield" (1-10-69): Frank Gorshin (Bele), Lou Antonio (Lokai).

"The Mark of Gideon" (1-17-69): Sharon Acker (Odona), David Hurst (Hodin), Gene Dynarski (Krodack), Richard Derr (Adm. Fitzgerald).

"That Which Survives" (1-24-69): Lee Meriwether (Losira), Arthur Batanides (D'Amato), Naomi Pollack (Lt. Rahada).

"The Lights of Zetar" (1-31-69): Jan Shutan (Lt. Mira Romaine), John Winston (Lt. Kyle), Libby Erwin (Rindonian), Bud da Vinci (crewman's voice).

"Requiem for Methuselah" (2-14-69): James Daly (Flint), Louise Sorel (Reena).

"The Way to Eden" (2-21-69): Skip Homeier (Dr. Sevrin), Charles Napier (Adam), Mary Linda Rappelye (Irina), Victor Brandt (Tongo Rad),

Elizabeth Rogers (Lt. Palmer), Deborah Downey (hippie No. 1), Phyllis Douglas (hippie No. 2).

"The Cloud Minders" (2-28-69): Jeff Corey (Plasus), Diana Ewing (Droxine), Charlene Polite (Vanna), Fred Williamson (Anda), Ed Long (Midro).

"The Savage Curtain" (3-7-69): Lee Bergere (Abraham Lincoln), Barry Atwater (Surak), Philip Pine (Col. Green), Nathan Jung (Genghis Kahn), Carol Daniels Dement (Zora), Robert Herron (Kahless), Janos Prohaska (Yarnek), Bart LaRue (Yarnek's voice), Arell Blanton (Dickerson).

"All Our Yesterdays" (3-14-69): Mariette Hartley (Zarabeth), Ian Wolfe (Atoz), Kermit Murdock (Prosecutor), Johnny Haumer (Constable), Stan Barrett (jailer), Ed Baker (fop), Al Cavens (fop), Anna Karen (woman).

"Turnabout Intruder" (6-3-69): Sandra Smith (Dr. Janice Lester), Harry Landers (Dr. Coleman).

STATELY GHOSTS OF ENGLAND. (1-25-65). Margaret Rutherford (Host).

STICK AROUND. (1977). Pilot (5-30-77): Nancy New (Elaine Keefer), Fred McCarren (Vance Keefer), Andy Kaufman (Andy the Robot), Cliff Norton (Burkus), Craig Richard Nelson (Earl), Jeffrey Kramer (Ed).

STONE TAPE, THE. British (12-25-72). Michael Bryant, Jane Asher, Iain Cuthbertson, Michael Bates, Reginald Marsh.

STRANGE PARADISE. 1969. Colin Fox (Jean-Paul Desmond/Jacques Eloide Monde), Sylvia Feigel (Holly Marshall), Tudi Wiggins (Erica Desmond), Dawn Greenhaigh (Alison Kerr), Cosette Lee (Raxil), Kurt Schiegl (Quito), Angela Roland (Vangie), Paisley Maxwell (Elizabeth Marshall), Dan McDonald (Rev. Matthew Dawson), Bruce Gray (Tim Stanton), John Granik (Dan Forrest), Patricia Collins, Trudy Young.

STRANGE WORLD OF PLANET X, THE. British (1-15-56 - 10-20-56)*

*Aired in multiple segments; dates show first and last segments.

Helen Cherry, William Lucas,
David Garth.

STRUCK BY LIGHTNING. 1979.
Jack Elam (Frank), Jeffrey Kramer
(Ted Stein), Millie Slavin (Nora),
Bill Erwin (Glenn Hillman), Jeff
Cotler (Brian), Richard Stahl (Walt).

STUDIO ONE.
"U. F.O." (9-6-54): Parker
Fennelly, Dorothy Sands.
"It Might Happen Tommorrow"
(1-24-55): Barry Sullivan, Tony
Francoisa, Bert Freed, Russell Hicks,
Dana Wynter, Ben Hammer.
"Donovan's Brain" (2-28-55):
Wendell Corey (Dr. Cory), E. G. Mar-
shall (Dr. Shratt), June Drayton (Jan-
ice Cory), Don Hanmer (Yocum),
Lawrence Fletcher (Fuller), John
Reese, Patsy Bruder, Charles Pen-
man, Stanja Lowe.
"The Incredible World of Horace
Ford" (6-13-55): Art Carney (Horace
Ford), Leora Dana (Laura), Kathleen
Comegys (Mrs. Ford), House Jameson
(Mr. Judson), Jason Robards, Jr.
(Leonard O'Brien), Bettye Ackerman
(Betty).
"Mr. Arcularis" (6-25-56): John
Drainie (Mr. Arcularis), Bramwell
Fletcher (Dr. Alderton), Nancy Wick-
wire (Miss Carter/Miss Dean/Mrs.
Arcularis), Jonathan Harris (Dr.
Wetheril), John Mackwood (steward),
Gubi Mann (Nurse Carter).
"The Night America Trembled"
(9-9-57): Alexander Scourby (Phillips),
Robert Blackburn (director), Ed Asner
(actor), Frank Marth (actor), Ray
Boyld (actor), Norman Rose (announ-
cer), Casey Allen (announcer), Tom
Clancy (Tom), Vincent Gardenia (Dick),
Fred Scollay (Harry), James Coburn
(Sam), Crahan Denton (Mack), Pris-
cilla Gillette (Elaine), Fritz Weber
(card player), Warren Oates (card player),
Warren Beatty (card player), Larry
Robinson (card player), Susan Hallaran
(Millie), Al Markim (Brownie), Freda
Holoway (Mary), Clint Kimbrough (Bob),
John Gibson (father), Frank Daly
(editor), Bob Kilgallen (student).
"The Brotherhood of the Bell"
(1-6-58): Cameron Mitchell (James
Waterson), Tom Drake (Clark Sherrell),
Pat O'Brian (Mike Waterson), John
Baragrey (Chad Hammond), Joanne
Dru (Suzie Sherrell), Frank Wilcox
(Chief Councilor), Douglas Kennedy
(Mr. Gordon), Sheila Bromley
(Marie).

"The Other Place" (1-13-58):
Sir Cedric Hardwicke (Sir Alaric),
Richard Carlson (Harvey Lindfield),
Phyllis Avery (Paula), Marilyn Er-
skine (Mavis), Glenda Farrell (Mrs.
Endsley).

STUDIO 57.
"Ring Once for Death" (6-21-55):
John Howard (Dr. Mark Williams),
Emlen Davies (Edith Williams), Keye
Luke (Sam Kee), Alan Dinehart (Hardy
Williams), Noel Toy (Mrs. Kee).
"Secret Darkness" (11-12-57):
Vincent Price (Morius Lindsey),
Bethel Leslie (Ann Lindsey).
"Mr. November" (2-19-49):
Leo G. Carroll (Sheffild), William
Hopper (Kip), Robert Burton (Douglas),
Kasey Rogers (Nancy).

SUMMER FUN. 1966.
"Thompson's Ghost" (8-5-66):
Bert Lahr (Henry), Robert Rockwell
(Sam Thompson), Phyllis Coates
(Milly Thompson), Pamela Dapo (Ana-
bel Thompson), Barry Kelley (Chief
Watson), Willard Waterman (Dr.
Wheeler), Tim Matthieson (Eddie
Thompson), Trudy Howard (nurse).

SUMMER THEATRE. 1954.
"Experiment Perilous" (8-23-54):
Constance Ford (Kyra Zelas), Philip
Bourneuf (Dr. Fred Bach), Gene
Lyons (Dan), Augusta Dabney (Ellen).

SUNDAY SHOWCASE. 1959.
"Murder and the Android" (11-
8-59): Kevin McCarthy (James Jason
Valentine), Rip Torn (Rex), Vladimir
Sokoloff (Rostov), Suzanne Pleshette
(Mari), Sono Osato (Dallas Burton).

SUPERMAN. 1953-57. George Reeves
(Clark Kent/Superman), Phyllis
Coates (Lois Lane) 1953, Noel
Neill (Lois Lane) 53-57, John
Hamilton (Perry White), Jack
Larson (Jimmy Olsen), Robert
Shayne (Insp. Bill Henderson).
"Superman on Earth" (2-9-53):
Robert Rockwell, Herbert Rawlinson,
Stuart Randell, Aline Towne, Tom
Fadden, Frances Morris, Dani Nolan,
Dabbs Greer, Ross Elliott.
"The Haunted Lighthouse" (2-
16-53): Jimmy Ogg, Allene Roberst,
Sarah Padden, Steve Carr, Maude
Prickett.
"The Case of the Talkative
Dummy" (2-23-53): Tris Coffin
(Harry Green), Sid Saylor (Marco),

(SUPERMAN cont.) Pierre Watkin (Mr. Davis), Phil Pine, Robert Keat.
"The Mystery of the Broken Statues" (3-2-53): Tris Coffin (Paul Martin), Michael Vallon, Maurice Cass, Phillip Pine, Joey Ray, Wayde Crosby, Steve Carr.
"The Monkey Mystery" (3-9-53): Allene Roberts, Michael Vallon, Harry Lewis, William Challee.
"A Night of Terror" (3-16-53): Frank Richards, John Kellog, Ann Doran, Almira Sessions, Joel Friedkin, Steve Carr, Richard Benedict.
"The Birthday Letter" (3-23-53): Isa Ashdown, John Doucette, Virginia Carroll, Paul Marion.
"The Mind Machine" (3-30-53): Dan Seymour, Ben Weldon, Griff Barnett, James Seay.
"Rescue" (4-6-53): Houseley Stevenson, Sr. , Fred E. Sherman, Ray Bennett, Edmund Coff.
"The Secret of Superman" (4-13-43): Peter Brocco, Larry J. Blake, Steve Carr, Joel Friedkin, Helen Wallace.
"No Holds Barred" (3-20-53): Malcolm Mealey, Richard Reeves, Richard Elliott, Herbert Vigran.
"The Deserted Village" (4-27-53): Maudie Prickett, Fred E. Sherman, Edmund Cobb, Malcolm Mealey.
"The Stolen Costume" (5-4-53): Norman Budd, Frank Jenks, Dan Seymour, Veda Ann Borg, Bob Williams.
"Mystery in Wax" (5-11-53): Myra McKinney, Lester Sharpe.
"Treasure of the Incas" (5-18-53): Leonard Penn, Martin Garralaga, Juan DuVal, Hal Gerard, Juan Rivero.
"Double Trouble" (5-25-53): Howard Chamberlin, Selmer Jackson, Rudolph Anders, Jimmy Dodd, Steve Carr.
"The Runaway Robot" (6-1-53): Dan Seymour, John Harmon, Lucien Littlefield (Horatio Hinkle), Russell Johnson, Robert Easton, Herman Cantor.
"Drums of Death" (6-8-53): Harry Corden, Leonard Mudie, Milton Wood, Mabel Albertson, George Hamilton, Smoki Whitfield.
"The Evil Three" (6-15-53): Rhys Williams, Jonathan Hale, Cecil Elliot.
"Riddle of the Chinese Jade" (6-22-53): Victor Sen Yung (Lu Sung), James Craven, Gloria Saunders, Paul Burns.
"The Human Bomb" (6-29-53):

Trevor Bardette, Dennis Moore, Marshall Reed, Lou Lubin.
"Czar of the Underworld" (7-6-53): Paul Fix, John Maxwell, Tony Caruso, Roy Gordon, Steve Carr.
"The Ghost Wolf" (7-13-53): Jane Adams, Stanley Andrews, Lou Krugman, Harold Goodwin.
"The Unknown People" (7-20-53 & 7-27-53): Jeff Corey (Luke Benson), Walter Reed (Bill Corrigan), Stanley Andrews (Sheriff), Billy Curtis (Mole Man), Jack Branbury (Mole Man), Jerry Marvin (Mole Man), Tony Baris (Mole Man), Florence Lake, Ed Hinton, J. Farrell MacDonald, Frank Reicher, Paul Burns, Hal K. Dawson, Ray Walker, Beverly Washburn, Steve Carr, Margia Dean, Byron Foulger, Irene Martin, John Phillips, John Baer, Adrienne Marden.
"Crime Wave" (8-3-53): John Eldredge, Phil Van Zandt, Al Eben, Joseph Mell, Barbara Fuller.
"Five Minutes to Doom" (9-14-53): Dabbs Greer, Sam Flint, Lois Hall, John Kellogg, Jean Willes, Lewis Russell, Dale Van Sickel, William E. Green.
"The Big Squeeze" (9-21-53): Hugh Beaumont (Dan Grayson), John Kellogg, Aline Towne, Harry Cheshire, Bradley Mora, Ted Ryan, Reed Howes.
"The Man Who Could Read Minds" (9-28-53): Larry Dobkin, Veola Vonn, Richard Karlan, Tom Bernard, Russell Custer.
"Jet Ace" (10-5-53): Lane Bradford, Selmer Jackson, Richard Reeves, Jim Hayward, Sam Balter, Larry J. Blake, Mauritz Hugo, Bud Wolfe, Ric Roman.
"Shot in the Dark" (10-12-53): Billy Gray, Vera Marshe, John Eldredge, Frank Richards, Alan Lee.
"The Defeat of Superman" (10-19-53): Maurice Cass, Peter Mamakos, Nestor Paiva.
"Superman in Exile" (10-26-53): Leon Askin, Joe Forte, Phil Van Zandt, John Harmon, Robert S. Carson, Sam Balter, Gregg Barton, Don Dillaway.
"A Ghost for Scotland Yard" (11-2-53): Leonard Mudie (Brookhurst), Colin Campbell, Norma Varden, Patrick Aherne, Clyde Cook, Evelyn Halpern.
"The Dog Who Knew Superman" (11-9-53): Billy Nelson, Ben Welden, Lester Dorr, Dona Drake, John Daly.

"The Face and the Voice" (11-16-53): Hayden Rorke, I. Stanford Jolley, George Chandler, Percy Helton, Carlton Young, Nolan Leary, Sam Balter, William Newell.

"The Man in the Lead Mask" (11-23-53): Frank Scannell, John Crawford, Louis Jean Heydt, Paul Bryar, John Merton, Joey Ray, Lynn Thomas, Sam Balter.

"Panic in the Sky" (11-30-53): Jonathan Hale, Jane Frazee, Clark Howat, Thomas Moore.

"The Machine That Could Plot Crimes" (12-7-53): Sterling Holloway (Prof. Oscar Quinn), Billy Nelson, Sherry Moreland, Stan Jarman, Ben Welden, Sam Balter, Russell Custer.

"Jungle Devil" (12-14-53): Doris Singleton, Damian O'Flynn, Al Kikume, James Seay, Leon Lontoc, Steve Calvert, Bernard Gozier, Henry A. Escalante, Nacho Galindo.

"My Friend Superman" (12-21-53): Tito Vivolo, Yvette Dugan, Paul Burke, Terry Frost, Ralph Sanford, Edward Reider, Ruta Kilmonis, Frederick Berest.

"The Clown Who Cried" (12-28-53): Mickey Simpson, Peter Brocco, Harry Mendoza, George Douglas, Charles Williams, Richard D. Crockett, Richard Lewis, Harvey Parry.

"The Boy Who Hated Superman" (1-4-54): Roy Barcroft, Leonard Penn, Tyler McDuff, Charles Meredith, Richard Reeves.

"Simi-Private Eye" (1-11-54): Elisha Cook, Jr., Paul Fix, Richard Benedict, Alfred Linder, Douglas Henderson.

"Perry White's Scoop" (1-18-53): Steve Pendleton, Jan Arvan, Robert J. Wilke, Bibs Borman, Tom Monroe.

"Beware the Wrecker" (1-25-54): William Forrest, Pierre Watkin, Tom Powers, Denver Pyle, Renny McEvoy.

"The Golden Vulture" (2-1-54): Peter Whitney, Vic Perrin, Robert Rice, Murray Alper, Wes Hudman, Saul M. Gross, Carl H. Saxe, Dan Turner, William Vincent.

"Jimmy Olsen, Boy Editor" (2-8-54): Herb Vigran, Keith Richards, Dick Rich, Anthony Hughes, Jack Pepper, Ronald Hargrove, Bob Crosson.

"Lady in Black" (2-15-54): Frank Ferguson, Virginia Christian, John Doucette, Rudolph Anders,

Mike Ragan, Frank Marlowe.

"Star of Fate" (2-22-54): Lawrence Ryle, Jeanne Dean, Arthur Space, Paul Burns, Tony DeMario, Ted Hecht.

"The Whistling Bird" (3-1-54): Sterling Holloway (Prof. Oscar Quinn), Joseph Vitale, Otto Waldis, Marshall Reed, Allene Roberts, Toni Carroll, Jerry Hausner.

"Around the Wrodl" (3-8-54): Kay Morley, Patrick Aherne, Raymond Greenleaf, Judy Ann Nugent, Max Wagner, James Brown.

"Through the Time Barrier" (9-13-54): Sterling Holloway (Prof. Oscar Quinn), Jim Hyland, Florence Lake, Ed Hinton.

"The Talking Clue" (9-20-54): Billy Nelson, Richard Shakleton, Brick Sullivan, Julian Upton.

"The Lucky Cat" (9-27-54): Harry Tyler, Carl Hubbard, Ted Stanhope, John Phillips, Charles Watts.

"Superman Week" (10-4-54): Herb Vigran, Tamar Cooper, Jack George, Paul Burke, Buddy Mason.

"Great Caesar's Ghost" (10-11-54): Trevor Bardette, Jim Hayward, Olaf Hytten.

"Test of a Warrior" (10-18-54): Ralph Moody, Maurice Jara, Francis McDonald, George Lewis, Lane Bradford.

"Olsen's Millions" (10-25-54): Elizabeth Patterson, George E. Stone, Richard Reeves, Leonard Carey, Tyler McDuff.

"Clark Kent, Outlaw" (11-1-54): John Doucette, Sid Tomack, Tris Coffin, George Eldredge, Patrick O'Moore, Lyn Thomas.

"The Magic Necklace" (11-8-54): Leonard Mudie, Frank Jenks, John Harmon, Paul Fierro, Lawrence Ryle, Ted Hecht, Cliff Ferre.

"The Bully of Dry Gulch" (11-15-54): Raymond Hatton, Myron Healey, Martin Garralaga, Eddie Baker.

"Flight to the North" (11-22-54): Chuck Connors (Sylvester J. Superman), Ben Welden, Richard Garland, Ralph Sanford, Marjorie Owens, George Chandler.

"The Seven Souvenirs" (11-29-54): Philip Tead (Prof. Pepperwinkle); Arthur Space, Rick Vallin, Steve Calvert, Louise Lewis, Lennie Breman, Jack O'Shea.

"King for a Day" (12-6-54): Peter Mamakos, Leon Askin, Phil

(SUPERMAN cont.) Van Zandt, Jan Arvan, Steven Bekassy, Carolyn Scott, Chet Marshall.

"Joey" (9-12-55): Janine Perreau, Mauritz Hugo, Tom London, Billy Nelson, Jay Lawrence, Willard Kennedy.

"The Unlucky Number" (9-19-55): Elizabeth Patterson, Henry Blair, John Beradino, Russell Conklin, Jack Littlefield, Alan Reynolds, Tony DeMario, Alfred Linder.

"The Big Freeze" (9-26-55): Richard Reeves, George E. Stone, John Phillips, Rolfe Sedan, Eddie Baker.

"Peril By Sea" (10-3-55): Claude Akins, Julian Upton, Ed Penny.

"Topsy Turvy" (10-10-55): Phil Tead (Prof. Pepperwinkle), Ben Welden, Mickey Knox, Charles Williams.

"Jimmy the Kid" (10-17-55): Damian O'Flynn, Diana Darrin, Florence Ravenel, Rick Vallin, Jack Larson, Steven Conte.

"The Girl Who Hired Superman" (10-24-55): Gloria Talbott, Maurice Marsac, George Khoury, Lyn Guild, John Eldredge.

"The Wedding of Superman" (10-31-55): Milton Frome, Julie Bennet, Doyle Brooks, John Cliff, Nolan Leary, Dolores Fuller.

"Dagger Island" (11-7-55): Myron Healey, Dean Cromer, Raymond Hatton, Ray Montgomery.

"Blackmail" (11-14-55): Herb Vigran, Sid Tomack, George Chandler, Selmer Jackson.

"The Deadly Rock" (11-21-55): Robert Lowery, Lyn Thomas, Steven Geray, Robert Foulk, Ric Roman, Vincent G. Perry, Sid Melton, Jim Hayward.

"The Phantom Ring" (11-28-55): Paul Burke, Peter Brocco, Lane Bradford, Ed Hinton, Henry Rowland.

"The Jolly Roger" (12-5-55): Leonard Mudie, Myron Healy, Patrick Aherne, Jean Lewis, Pierre Watkin, Eric Snowden, Ray Montgomery, Dean Cromer, Chet Marshall.

"Peril in Paris" (9-10-56): Lilyan Chauvin, Peter Mamakos, Albert Carrier, Charles LaTorre, Franz Roehn.

"Tin Hero" (9-17-56): Carl Ritchie, Sam Finn, Frank Richards, Paula Houston, Jack Lomas.

"Money to Burn" (9-24-56): Mauritz Hugo, Dale van Sickel,

Richard Emory.

"The Town That Wasn't" (10-1-56): Frank Connor, Charles Gray, Richard Elliot, Terry Frost, Jack V. Littlefield, Michael Garrett, Phillip Barnes.

"The Tomb of Zaharan" (10-8-56): George Khoury, Jack Kruschen, Ted Hecht, Gabriel Mooradian, Jack Reitzen.

"The Man Who Made Dreams Come True" (10-15-56): Cyril Delevanti, Keith Richards, John Banner, Sandy Harrison, Hal Hoover, Laurie Mitchell.

"Disappearing Lois (10-22-56): Milton Frome, Ben Welden, Andrew Branham, Yvonne White.

"Close Shave" (10-29-56): Rick Vallin, Richard Benedict, Jack V. Littlefield, Missy Russell, John Lerry, Donald Diamond, Harry Fleer.

"The Phony Alibi" (11-5-56): Phil Tead (Prof. Pepperwinkle), John Cliff, Frank Kreig, Harry Arnie, William Challee.

"The Prince Albert Coat" (11-19-56): Raymond Hatton, Stephen Wooton, Daniel White, Ken Christy, Frank Fenton, Claire DuBrey, Phil Arnold, Jack Finch.

"The Stolen Elephant" (11-19-56): Gregory Moffet, Thomas Jackson, Eve McVeigh, Gregg Martell, I. Stanford Jolley.

"Mr. Zero" (11-26-56): Billy Curtis (Mr. Zero), Herb Vigran, George Barrows, Leon Allin, George Spotts.

"Whatever Goes Up" (12-3-56): Tris Coffin, Milton Frome.

"The Last Knight" (9-16-57): Marshall Bradford, Paul Power, Andrew Branham, Pierre Watkin, Jason Johnson, Ollie O'Toole, Thomas P. Dillon, Ronald Foster.

"The Magic Secret" (9-23-57): Freeman Lusk, George Selk, Jack Reynolds, Buddy Lewis, Kenneth Alton.

"Divide and Conquer" (9-30-57): Everett Glass, Donald Lawton, Robert Tafur, Jack Reitsen, Jack V. Littlefield.

"The Mysterious Cube" (10-7-57): Everett Glass, Ben Welden, Keith Richards, Bruce Wendell, Joel Riordin, John Ayres.

"The Atomic Captive" (10-14-57): Elaine Riley, Jan Arvan, Walter Reed, Raskin Ben-Ari, George Khoury, Mark Sheeler.

"The Superman Silver Mine" (10-21-57): Dabbs Greer, Charles Maxwell.
"The Big Forget" (10-28-57): Phil Tead (Prof. Pepperwinkle), Herb Vigran, Billy Nelson.
"The Gentle Monster" (11-4-57): Phil Tead (Prof. Pepperwinkle), Ben Welden, John Vivyan, Orville Sherman, Wilkie DeMartel.
"Superman's Wife" (11-11-57): Joi Lansing, John Eldredge, John Bennes, Harry Arnie, Wayne Heffley.
"Three in One" (11-18-57): Sid Tomack, Rick Vallin, Buddy Baer, Craig Duncan.
"The Brainy Burro" (11-25-57): Mark Cavell, Ken Mayer, Marritz Hugo, Edward LeVegue, Natividad Vacio, Sid Cassell.
"The Perils of Superman" (12-2-57): Michael Fox, Steve Mitchell, Andrew Branham, Missy Russell, Yvonne White.
"All That Glitters" (12-9-57): Phil Tead (Prof. Pepperwinkle), Len Hendry, Jack Littlefield, Myrna Fahey, Richard Elliot, George Eldredge, Paul Cavanagh.

SURVIVORS, THE. British 1975-77. Denis Lill, John Abineri, Lucy Fleming.

SUSPENSE. 1951.
"Dr. Jekyll and Mr. Hyde" (3-5-51): Basil Rathbone (Dr. Jekyll/Mr. Hyde).
"All Hallow's Eve" (10-28-52): Franchot Tone.

SUSPICION. 1958.
"The Voice in the Night" (5-26-58): Barbara Rush (Eleanor Thomason), James Donald (James Thomason), Patrick Macnee (Capt. Biersdorf), James Coburn (Matt Carson).

TABITHA. 1977-78. Lisa Hartman (Tabitha Stevens), David Ankrum (Adam Stevens), Karen Morrow (Aunt Minerva), Robert Urich (Paul), Mel Stewart (Marvin).

TALES OF FRANKENSTEIN. British. 1964. Anton Diffring (Dr. Frankenstein), Don Megowan (the Monster).

TALES OF THE HAUNTED. 1981. Christopher Lee (Host).
"Evil Stalks This House" (7-20-81- 7-25-81)*: Jack Palance

*Aired in multiple segments; dates show first and last segments.

(Richard Stokes), Helen Hughes (Maggie), Reginald Love (Adams), Frances Hyland.

TALES OF THE UNEXPECTED. 1977. William Conrad (Host).
"The Final Chapter" (2-2-77): Roy Thinnes (Frank Harris), Ned Beatty (McClaskey), Tim O'Connor (Zimmerman), Ramon Bieri (Warden Greer).
"The Mask of Adonis" (2-9-77): Robert Foxworth (Alexander), Marlyn Mason (Viviana), Linda Kelsey (Gerry), Victor Jory (Davidian), Clyde Kusatsu (Kanji), Steve Sandor (Peter Bolander).
"Devil Pack" (2-16-77): Ronny Cox (Jerry Colby), Christine Belford (Ann Colby), Van Williams (Sheriff), Russell Thorson (Scottie), Larry Mahan (Deputy), David Hollander (Todd Colby).
"The Nomads" (2-23-77): David Birney (Paul Rogers), Eugene Roche (Langston), David Huddleston (Sheriff Henry), Lynne Marta (Anne), Katherine Justice (Barbara), Read Morgan (Brody).
"A Hand for Sonny Blue" (3-9-77): Rick Nelson (Sonny Blue), Janice Lynde (Brenda), Carl Weathers (Dalby), Aldine King (Helen Dalby), Paul Cavonis (Art Winters), Henry Brown (Eugene).
"The Force of Evil" (3-13-77): Lloyd Bridges (Dr. Carrington), William Watson (Teddy Jakes), John Anderson (Floyd Carrington), Pat Crowley (Margaret), Eve Plumb (Cindy), Kirby Cullen (John William).
"You're Not Alone" (8-17-77): Joanna Pettet (Julie Thomas), Gary Collins (John Harris), Nina Gail Weintraub (Jennifer), Herb Edelman (Don Lucas), Patricia Smith (Amelia Brownlee), Jenny O'Hara (Mary Ann), Patricia Mattick (Betty), John Dullaghan (Detective Peterson), Jan Merlin (Phillip Mitchell), Sarah Hardy (Ellen), Ken Dibbs (Doorman).
"No Way Out" (8-24-77): Bill Bixby (John Kelty), Dean Stockwell (Richard Ayres), Robert Pine (Lt. Stevens), Hal England (Dr. John Kelty), Davey Davison (Amanda Kelty), Robert Hogan (Cmdr. Lear), Sheila Larken (Tracey Ayres).

TALES OF TOMORROW. 1951-53.
"Verdict from Space" (8-3-51): Lon McCallister, Martin Brandt, Andrew Branham.
"A Child Is Crying" (8-17-51): Walter Abel, Robin Morgan.

(TALES OF TOMORROW cont.)
"The Last Man on Earth" (8-31-51): John McQuade, Cloris Leachman.
"Errand Boy" (9-7-51): Joey Walsh.
"The Monsters" (9-14-51): Paul Langton, Barbara Boulton, Bert Kalmar, Jr.
"The Dark Angel" (9-28-51): Sidney Blackmer, Meg Mundy.
"The Crystal Egg" (10-12-51): Thomas Mitchell.
"Test Flight" (10-26-51): Lee J. Cobb.
"The Search for the Flying Saucer" (11-9-51): Jack Carter, Vaughn Taylor, Olive Deering.
"Enemy Unknown" (11-23-51): Lon McCallister, Walter Abel, Edith Fellows, Vince Otis.
"Sneak Attack" (12-7-51): Zachary Scott.
"The Invaders" (12-12-51): Eva Gabor, William Eythe.
"The Dune Roller" (1-4-52): Bruce Cabot, Virginia Gilmore.
"Frankenstein" (1-18-52): Lon Chaney, Jr. (the Monster), John Newland (Dr. Frankenstein), Mary Alice Moore.
"20,000 Leagues Under the Sea" (1-25-52 & 2-1-52): Thomas Mitchell, Leslie Nielson, Bethel Leslie.
"What You Need" (2-8-52): Billy Redfield, Edgar Stehli.
"Age of Peril" (2-15-52): Phyllis Kirk, Dennis Harris.
"Momento" (2-22-52): Boris Karloff, Barbara Joyce.
"The Children's Room" (2-29-52): Clare Luce, Una O'Connor, Terry Greene.
"Bound Together" (3-7-52): Nina Foch.
"The Diamond Lens" (3-14-52): Franchot Tone.
"Fountain of Youth" (3-21-52): Tom Drake.
"Flight Overdue" (2-28-52): Veronica Lake.
"And a Little Child" (4-4-52), Frank McHugh, Parker Fennelly, Iris Mann.
"Sleep No More" (4-11-52): Jeffrey Lynn.
"Time to Go" (4-18-52): Sylvia Sidney, Ed Peck.
"Plague from Space" (4-25-52): Gene Raymond.
"Red Dust" (5-2-52): Lex Barker.
"The Golden Ingot" (5-9-52):

Gene Lockhart.
"Black Planet" (5-16-52): Leslie Nielsen, Frank Albertson.
"World of Water" (5-23-52): Victor Jory.
"Little Black Bag" (5-30-52): Joan Blondell.
"Exile" (6-6-52): Chester Morris.
"All the Time in thw World" (6-13-52): Esther Ralston.
"The Miraculous Serum" (6-20-52): Lola Albright, Richard Derr.
"Appointment to Mars" (6-27-52): Leslie Nielsen, William Redfield.
"The Duplicates" (7-4-52): Darren McGavin.
"Ahead of His Time" (7-18-52): Paul Tripp.
"Sudden Darkness" (8-1-52): Olive Deering.
"Ice from Space" (8-8-52): Edmon Ryan (Capt. Boszik).
"A Child Is Crying" (8-15-52): Bert Lytell, Robin Morgan.
"A Bird in Hand" (8-22-52): Gina Niemilla, Peter Munsen.
"Thanks" (8-26-52): Joseph Anthony, Gregory Morton.
"The Seeing-Eye Surgeon" (9-5-52): Bruce Cabot.
"The Cocoon" (9-12-52): Jackie Cooper, Edith Fellows.
"The Chase" (9-19-52): Walter Abel.
"Youth on Tap" (9-26-52): Robert Alda.
"Substance 'X'" (10-3-52): Vicki Cummings.
"The Horn" (10-10-52): Franchot Tone.
"Double Trouble" (10-17-52): Paul Tripp, Ruth Enders.
"Many Happy Returns" (10-24-52): Gene Raymond.
"The Tomb of King Tarus" (10-31-52): Walter Abel.
"The Window" (11-7-52).
"The Camera" (11-14-52): Olive Deering, Donald Buka.
"The Quiet Lady" (11-21-52): Una O'Connor, John Conte.
"Invigorating Air" (11-28-52): Joseph Buloff.
"The Glacier Giant" (12-5-52): Chester Morris, Edith Fellows, Murray Tannenbaum.
"The Fatal Flower" (12-12-52): Victor Jory, Don Hamner.
"The Machine" (12-19-52): Gene Lockhart, Georgianne Johnson.
"The Bitter Storm" (12-26-52): Arnold Moss.

"The Mask of Medusa" (1-2-53): Raymond Burr, Steven Geray.

"Conqueror's Isle" (1-9-53): Ray Montgomery.

"Discovered Heart" (1-16-53): Susan Hallaran.

"The Picture of Dorian Gray" (1-23-53): John Newland (Dorian Gray), Peter Fernandez.

"Two-Faced" (1-31-53): Richard Kiley.

"The Build-Box" (2-6-53): Glenda Farrell.

"Another Chance" (2-13-53): Leslie Nielsen, Harold Mason.

"The Great Silence" (2-20-53): Burgess Meredith.

"Lonesome Village" (2-27-53): Constance Clausen.

"The End of the Cocoon" (3-6-53): Nancy Coleman, Peter Capell.

"The Squeeze Play" (3-13-53): John McQuade, Joseph Wiseman, Elizabeth Yorke.

"Read to Me, Herr Doktor" (3-20-53): Everett Sloane (Prof. Kimworth), Mercedes McCambridge (Patricia Kimworth), William Kemp (Sidney), Ernest Graves (Voice of Herr Doktor).

"Ghost Writer" (3-27-53): Leslie Nielsen, Gaby Rodgers.

"Past Tense" (4-3-53): Boris Karloff, Robert F. Simon.

"Homecoming" (4-10-53): Edith Fellows, Robert Keith, Hani Evans.

"The Rival" (4-17-43): Mary Sinclair, Anthony Ross.

"Please Omit Flowers" (4-24-53): Frank Albertson, Ann Burr.

"The Evil Within" (5-1-53): Margaret Phillips.

"The Vault" (5-8-52): Cameron Prud'homme, Dorothy Peterson.

"Ink" (5-15-53): Mildred Natwich, Joseph Anthony.

"The Spider Web" (5-22-53): Nancy Coleman.

"Lazarus Walks" (5-29-53): William Prince, Olive Deering.

"What Dreams May Come" (6-12-53): Arnold Moss.

TARZAN. 1966-68. Ron Ely (Tarzan), Manuel Padilla, Jr (Jai), Alan Caillou (Jason Flood), Rockne Tarkington (Rao), Stewart Rafill (Tall Boy).

"Eyes of the Lion" (9-8-66): Ned Romero (Oringa), Laurie Sibbald (Mara).

"The Ultimate Weapon" (9-16-66): Jock Mahoney (Roby Wallington),

Laurence Haddon (Walker Sully), Dennis Cross (Jim Haines), Sheilah Wells (Kathy Haines), Jerry Ayers (Peter Haines), Andrew Prine.

"Leopard on the Loose" (9-23-66): Russ Tamblyn (Bell), Morgan Jones (Galloway), Ken Scott (Morrisey).

"A Life for a Life" (9-30-66): Jon Alvar (Obasi), Danica d"Hondt (Maggie Calloway), John Levingston (Capt. Whittaker).

"The Prisoner" (10-7-66): Robert J. Wilke (Spooner), Charles Maxwell (Mac), Mina Dillard (Nione), Arthur Adams (Brouna).

"The Three Faces of Death" (10-14-66): Woody Strode (Jamayo), Ena Hartman (Laneen), Virgil Richardson (Nahnto).

"The Prodigal Puma" (10-21-66): Rafer Johnson (Spandrell), Gigi Perreau (Sheri Kapinski), Jan Merlin (Hacker).

"The Deadly Silence" (10-28-66 & 11-4-66): Jock Mahoney (Colonel): Bob DoQui (Metusa), Nichelle Nichols (Ruana), Kenny Washinton (Akaba), Woody Strode (Marshak), Lupe Garnica (Borua), Virgil Richardson (Tabor), Jose Chavez (Okala), Gregorio Acosta (Chico).

"The Figurehead" (11-11-66): Anthony Caruso (Grundy), Ronald Long (Toussaint), Ricky Cordell (Sharif).

"Village of Fire" (11-18-66): Nobu McCarthy (Dr. Haru), Joel Fluellen (Bwanichi), Chuck Wood (Totoni).

"Day of the Golden Lion" (12-2-66): Suzy Parker (Laura), Curt Lowens (Wilhelm), Rockne Tarkington (Ahmad), George Murdock (Karl), Ricardo Adalid (Mustafa), Chuck Wood (Naftel).

"Pearls of Tanga" (12-9-66): Carlos Rivas (Adm. Gloco), Pearla Walter (Lita), John Kelly.

"The End of the River" (12-16-66): Michael Whitney (Tyler), Robert J. Wilke (Gillian), Jill Donohue (Suzanne), George Murdock (Damian), Eric Davies (Batoba), Adam Wade (Sergeant).

"The Ultimate Duel" (12-23-66): Henry Silva (Ivor Merrick), Gail Kobe (Jean Merrick), Don Megowan (Rafelson), Booker T. Bradshaw (Dr. B'Dula), Vantile Whitfield (Kimpu).

"The Fire People" (12-30-66): Morris Erby (Chief Hamaar), Francisco Reyguera (Exaam), Elsa Cardenas

(TARZAN cont.) (Dr. Gloria Hal-
verson), Mel Lettman (David Chaddo).
Title unknown (1-6-68): Lloyd
Bochner (Bergstrom), Pippa Scott
(Diana Grayson), Harry Lauter (Curt
Grayson), Joel Fluellen (Chief Quar-
anga).

"The Day the Earth Trembled"
(1-13-67): Susan Oliver (Peggy),
John Anderson (Dolan), Jacques
Aubuchon (Joppo), Eugene Evans
(Thorn), John Edwards (Chico), Vin-
cent Arias (Pepito).

"Cap'n Jai" (1-20-67): Chips
Rafferty (Dutch), Gregg Palmer (Cookie), Russ McCubbin (Zanto).

"A Pride of Assassins" (1-27-67):
Gene Evans (Albers), Michael Whitney
(Baeder), Jill Donohue (Diana Lawton),
Victor French (Cotonasos).

"The Golden Runaway" (2-3-
67): Gia Scala (Martha Tolbooth),
Sean McClory (Red McGeehan), Stacy
Harris (Henry Fitzroy), Khalil Dezaleel
(Chundra Lal).

"Basil of the Bulge" (2-10-67):
Maurice Evans (Sir Basil Bertram),
Warren Stevens (Roger Bradley),
Lewis Martin (Commissioner West),
Bernie Hamilton (Mwanza), Howard
Morton, Dilliard Hayeson.

"Mask of Rona" (2-17-67):
Nancy Malone (Rona Swann), Leslie
Parrish (Beryl), Jock Mahoney (Cham-
bers), Martin Gabel (Peter Maas),
Howard Morton (District Officer).

"To Steal the Rising Sun" (2-24-
67): Roy Glenn, Sr. (King Lukumba),
James Earl Jones (Chief Bella),
John Van Dreelan (Duprez), Strother
Martin (Boggs), Henry Beckman
(O'Brian), Victoria Shaw (Lisa),
Roberto Lehouse (medicine man).

"Jungle Dragnet" (2-2-67):
Victoria Meyerink (Mandy Mason),
Simon Oakland (Thompson), William
Marshall (Kasembi), Pedro Galvin
(Mason), Virgil Richardson (Chief
M'Botu).

"The Perils of Charity Jones"
(3-10-67 & 3-17-67): Julie Harris
(Charity Jones), Woody Strode (Chaka),
Bernie Hamilton (Shambu), Edward
Binns (Pedro), Abraham Sofaer
(Commissioner).

"The Circus" (2-24-67): Chips
Rafferty (Dutch Jensen), Jack Elam
(Bellak), Sally Kellerman (Ilona),
Leo Gordon (Bull Thomas).

"The Ultimatum" (3-31-67):
Ruth Roman (Madiline Riker), Ralph
Meeker (Karnak), Henry Corden
(Romo), William Gunn, Jeff Burton.

"Algie B for Brave" (4-7-67):
Maurice Evans (Sir Basil Bertram),
Arthur Franz (Morrissey), Todd
Garrett (Algie Jenkins), Lewis Martin
(Commissioner West), Robert Bru-
baker.

"Man Killer" (4-14-67): Tammy
Grimes, Jeremy Slate, James Gregory,
Lloyd Haynes.

"Tiger, Tiger" (9-15-67):
James Whitmore (Cliff Stockwell),
Anne Jeffreys (Melody Stockwell),
Oscar Beregi, Jr. (Devereaux),
Michael Pate (Findley), Howard Mor-
ton (Commissioner).

"Voice of the Elephant" (9-22-67):
Murray Matheson (Judge Lawrence),
Percy Rodriguez (Matsui), John
Doucette (Brady), Rockne Tarkington
(Ramahit).

"Thief Catcher" (9-29-67):
George Kennedy (Crandell), Yaphet
Kotto (Kesho), John Haymer (Dawkins),
Don Mitchell (N'Duma).

"The Blue Stone of Heaven"
(10-6-67 & 10-13-67): Sam Jaffe
(Dr. Singleton), Ulla Stromstedt (Mary
Singleton), William Marshall (Col.
Tatakombi), Jason Evers (Ramon),
Lloyd Haines (Matto), Harry Lauter
(Josh Miller).

"Maguma Curse" (10-20-67):
Barbara Luna (Frankie McVeight),
Simon Oakland (Judson Burnett),
Sydney Charles McCoy (Daniel Buto),
Michael St. Clair (Mike Purdy),
Ken Renard (N'Gota), Izaac Field
(N'Boul).

"The Fanatics" (10-27-67):
Diana Hyland (Diana Russell), William
Smithers (Brooks), Don Marshall
(Kimini), George Murdock (Eric),
Chuck Wood (Bombi),

"The Last of the Supermen"
(11-3-67): Alf Kjellen (Von Wolvner):
Antionette Bower (Helge), Michael
Burns (Helmut Stever), Brock Peters
(M'Kone), William Wintersole (Kurt).

"Hotel Hurricane" (11-10-67):
Michael Tolan (John Turner), Bert
Freed (Bonacci), Jean Hale (Lora
Dunfee), Donnelly Rhodes (Hand).

"The Pride of a Lioness" (11-
17-67): Helen Hayes (Mrs. Wilson),
James MacArthur (Dr. Wilson),
Geoffrey Holder (Zwengi).

"Mountains of the Moon" (11-24-
67 & 12-1-67): Ethel Merman (Rosanna
McCloud), Harry Lauter (Whitehead),
Perry Lopez (Chigger), Strother
Martin (O'Keefe), William Marshall
(Likui), Harry Townes (Capt. Bates),
Sabrina (Millie).

"Jai's Amnesia" (12-15-67):
John Dehner (Crosby), John Alderson
(Molsen), Hal Baylor (Lee), John
Crawford (Captain).
"Creeping Giants" (12-29-67):
Raymond St. Jacques (Walter Wilson),
Robert J. Wilke (Yaeger), Will Kuluva
(Miguel Jimenez Brown).
"The Professional" (1-4-68):
Pat Conway (Col. Stone), Karl Swenson (Governor General), Jack Colvin
(Military Governor), Clarence Williams (Sorda), Anthony Costello (sergeant).
"The Convert" (1-12-68): Diana
Ross (Sister Terese), Cindy Birdsong (Sister Ann), Mary Wilson
(Sister Martha), Malachi Throne
(Larson), James Earl Jones (Nerlan),
Leonard O'Smith (Batu), Claude
Casey (Bleeker).
"King of the Dwsari" (1-26-68):
Robert Loggia (Brown), Morgan
Woodward (Blaine), Ernie Terrell
(Kwaku), Judy Pace (Abena).
"A Gun for Jai" (2-2-68):
Peter Whitney (Mulvaney), Geoffrey
Holder (Mayko), Bob DoQui (Charlie),
Ed Baker (Prince).
"Trek to Terror" (2-9-68):
Michael Ansara (Regis), John Pickard
(Elson), Booker T. Bradshaw (Dr.
Kenneth Kiley), Gregg Palmer
(Haines), Albert Popwell (Luonga).
"End of a Challenge" (2-16-68):
Chill Wills (Montrose), Henry Jones
(Leech), Woody Strode (Chief Bangu),
Pepe Brown (Ubi), Pedro Gonzalez-Gonzalez (Pedro).
"Jungle Ransom" (2-23-68):
Fernando Lamas (Ramon Velasquez),
Ted Cassidy (Samson), Barbara
Bouchet (Phyllis Fraser), Jack Hogan
(Larry Fraser).
"Four O'Clock Army" (3-1-68
& 3-8-68): Maurice Evans (Sir Basil
Bertram), Julie Harris (Charity Jones),
Bruce Gordon (Moussa), Bernie Hamilton (Chaka).
"Rendezvous for Revenge" (3-15-68): John Vernon (Dan Burton),
Laraine Stephens (Doria), Booth
Colman (Commissioner Lacing), Don
Knight (Odgers), Carey Wilson (Claude).
"Alex the Great" (3-22-68):
Neville Brand (Alex Spense), Michael
Dunn (Kamal Amir), Read Morgan
(Hamud), Diane Williams (Stacey
Wells), Dick Crockett (Yuseff), Jim
Shayne (Shamir).
"Trina" (4-5-68): Stacy Maxwell
(Trina MacKenzie), Nehemiah Persoff
(Chembe Knuji), Barbara Hancock

(Minette), Susan Howard (Gloria),
Sharon Harvey (Noreen), Suzie Kaye
(Maxine), Marianne Gordon (Marguerite).
Susan Trustman (Maggie), Barbara
Moore (Edith), Robert Monk (Doggu).

TEN LITTLE INDIANS. (1-18-59).
Nina Foch (Vera Claythorne),
Barry Jones (Judge Wargrave),
Kenneth Haigh (Philip Lombard),
Romney Brent (Dr. Armstrong),
Peter Bathurst (Gen. MacKensie),
Valerie French (Emily Brent),
Chandler Cowles (Arthur Marston),
George Turner (Rogers), James
Kenny (Blore), Jeremiah Morris
(Fred Narracott).

THEATRE. 1955.
"Gramercy's Ghost" (4-20-55):
James Broderick, Pat Carroll, Conrad
Janis.

THRILLER. 1960-62. Boris Karloff
(Host).
"The Twisted Image" (9-13-60):
Leslie Nielsen (Alan Patterson), Natalie
Trundy (Lily Hanson), George Grizzard (Merle Jenkins), Virginia Christine (Marge), Constance Ford (Louise),
Dianne Foster (Judy Patterson).
"Child's Play" (9-20-60): Tommy
Nolan (Hank Hattering), Frank Overton
(Bart Hattering), Bethel Leslie (Gail
Hattering), Parley Baer (Fisherman),
George Werier (Fisherman).
"Worse Than Murder" (9-27-60):
Constance Ford (Connie Walworth),
Harriett McGibbon (Myra), Christine
White (Anne), John Baragrey.
"Mark of the Hand" (10-4-60):
Mona Freeman (Sylvia Walsh), Shepperd Strudwick (Doug Kilburn), Jessie
Royce Landis (Mr. Kilburn), Judson
Pratt (Lt. Bill Gordon), Berry Kroeger (Paul Mowry), Terry Burnham (Tessa), Rachel Ames (Betty Follett), Woody
Strode.
"Rose's Last Summer" (10-11-60): Mary Astor (Rose French), Lin
McCarthy (Frank Clyde), Jack Livesey
(Haley Dalloway), Dorothy Green (Ethel
Goodfield), Lois E. Gridge (Mrs.
Cushman).
"The Guilty Men" (10-18-60):
Everett Sloane (Lou Adams), Frank
Silvera (Charlie Roman), Dorothy
Greene (Ethel), Jay C. Flippen (Harry
Gans), Anne Barton (Martha Adams),
John Marley (Dr. Tony Romano), Frank
Dana.
"The Purple Room" (10-25-60):
Rip Torn (Duncan Corey), Patricia

(THRILLER cont.) Barry (Rachel
Judson), Richard Anderson (Oliver
Judson), Alan Napier (Ridgewater),
Joanna Heyes (Caroline Vale), Ray
Teal (Wiley).
    "The Watcher" (11-1-60):
Martin Gabel (Frietag), Dick Cham-
berlain (Larry), Olive Sturgess (Beth
Pettit), Stu Erwin (Uncle Florian),
James Westerfield (Matthews), Irene
Hervey (Mrs. Pettit), Alan Baxter
(Sheriff Archer).
    "Girl with a Secret" (11-15-60):
Rhodes Reason (Tony Page), Myra
Fahey (Alice Page), Cloris Leachman
(Beatrice Stafford), Fay Bainter (Ger-
aldine Redfern), Victor Buono (Carolik),
Harry Ellerbe (Walter Devon), Ellen
Corby (Mrs. Peele), Paul Hartman
(George Stafford), James Seay (Herb
Innes), Esther Dale (Ellen), Rex Hol-
man (Evil Face).
    "The Prediction" (11-22-60):
Boris Karloff (Clayton Mace), Audrey
Dalton (Norine Burton), Alan Caillou
(Roscoe Burton), Alex Davion (Grant
Dudley), Abraham Sofaer (Gus Kos-
topopulos).
    "The Fatal Impulse" (11-20-60):
Elisha Cook, Jr. (Elser), Conrad
Nagel (Walker Wylie), Whitney Blake
(Jane Kimball), Robert Lansing (Lt.
Brian Rome), Steve Brodie (Sgt.
Dumont), Elaine Edwards (Marjorie
Dallquis), Lance Fuller (Larrimore),
Harry Bartell (Mr. Dallquis), Mary
Tyler Moore.
    "The Big Blackout" (12-6-60):
Jack Carson (Burt Lewis), Nan Leslie
(Midge Lewis), Jeannie Coper (Ethel),
George Mitchell (Doc Mulloy), Charles
McGraw.
    "Knock Three-One-Two" (12-
13-60): Joe Maross (Ray Kenton),
Beverly Garland (Ruth Kenton), War-
ren Oates (Benny), Charles Aidman
(George Milkos), Murray Alper
(bartender), Norman Leavitt (Charlie),
David Alpert (hoodlum), Meade Mar-
tin (young man).
    "Man in the Middle" (12-20-60):
Mort Sahl (Sam Lynch), Sue Randall
(Kay Salisbury), Frank Albertson
(Charles Slaisbury), Grace Albertson
(Mrs. Salisbury), Werner Klemperer
(Clark).
    "The Cheaters" (12-27-60):
Paul Newlan (Joe Henshaw), Mildred
Dunnock (Miriam Olcott), Jack Weston
(Edward Dean), Henry Daniell (Dirk
Van Prinn), Harry Townes (Sebastian
Grimm), Linda Watkins (Maggie
Henshaw), Dayton Lummis (Clarence),

Alan Carney (Burgin), Ed Nelson
(Charlie), Grandon Rhodes (Judge
Pfluger), Ralph Clanton (Thorgenson),
John Mitchum (Policeman), Joan
Tompkins (Ellen Grimm), Barbara
Eller (Olive Dean), Molly Glessing
(Mrs. Ames), Audrey Swanson (sales-
girl).
    "The Hungry Glass" (1-3-61):
William Shatner (Gil Trasker), Joanna
Heyes (Marcia Trasker), Russell
Johnson (Adam Talmadge), Elizabeth
Allen (Liz Talmadge), Donna Douglas
(Laura Bellman), Ottola Nesmith
(Old Laura Bellman), Clem Bevans
(Obed), Pitt Herbert (storekeeper),
Duane Grey (bearded man).
    "The Poisoner" (1-10-61):
Murray Matheson (Thomas Edward
Griffith), Sarah Marshall (Frances),
David Frankham (Proctor), Brenda
Forbes (Mrs. Abercrombe), Jennifer
Raine (Helen Abercrombe), Richard
Peel (Justin), Maurice Dallimore
(George Griffith), Seymour Green
(Sir John Herbert), Sam Edwards
(Charles Larrimore).
    "Man in a Cage" (1-17-61):
Philip Carey (Darrell Upshaw), Theo
Marcuse (Arthur Upshaw), Diana
Millay (Ellen), Guy Stockwell (Noel
Huston), Eduardo Ciannelli, Barry
Gordon.
    "Choose a Victim" (1-24-61):
Larry Blyden (Ralph Teal), Susan
Oliver (Edith Landers), Vaughn
Taylor (Phil), Guy Mitchell (Hazlett),
Billy Barty (Sam), Tracy Roberts
(Fay), Henry Corden (Sid Banajain).
    "Hay-Fork and Bill-Hook"
(2-7-61); Kenneth Haigh (Harry Ro-
berts), Alan Caillou (Sir Wilfred),
Audrey Dalton (Nesta), Alan Napier,
J. Pat O'Malley.
    "The Merriweather File" (2-14-
61): Bethel Leslie (Ann Merriweather),
Ross Elliott (Charles Merriweather),
James Gregory (Howard Yates),
Edward Binns (Giddeon), K. T. Stevens.
    "Fingers of Fear" (2-21-61):
Nehemiah Persoff (Wagner), Robert
Middleton (Ohrbach), H. M. Wynant
(Sid), Kevin Hagen (Spivak), Robert
J. Stevenson (Dr. Lascoe), Dick
Wessel (Zimmer), Thayer Roberts
(Merriman), Sam Gilman (Officer
Dutton).
    "Well of Doom" (2-28-62):
Robert Howard (Robert Penrose),
Henry Daniell (Squire Muloch), Torin
Thatcher (Jeremy Teal), Richard
Kiel (Styx), Fintan Meyler (Laura).
    "The Ordeal of Dr. Cordell"

(3-7-61): Robert Vaughn (Dr. Frank Cordell), Marlo Thomas (Susan Baker), Russ Conway (Boutaric), Kathleen Crowley (Dr. Lois Walker), Robert Ellenstein (Brauner).

"Trio for Terror" (3-14-61): Act I: Richard Lupino (Simon), Terence DeMarney (Uncle Julian), Iris Bristol (Katie), Gil Stuart (train guard), Nelson Welch (doctor). Act II: Reginald Owen (Hussar), Robin Hughes (Collins), Peter Brocco (Major Domo), Jacqueline Squire (old woman), Reginald Plato (croupier). Act III: John Abbot (Kriss Milo), Michael Pate (Shanner), Noel Drayton (superintendent), Richard Peel (inspector).

"Papa Benjamin" (3-21-61): John Ireland (Eddie Wilson), Jester Hairston (Papa Benjamin), Jeanne Bal (Judy), Robert H. Harris (Jerry Roberts), Henry Scott (Tommy Statts), Peter Forster (Insp. Daniels).

"A Late Date" (4-4-61): Edward Platt (Jimm Weeks), Larry Pennell (Larry), Judy Fair (Helen), Chris Seitz (Gordon), Stuffy Singer (Art Brinkerhoff), Steve Mitchell (Sid), Stuart Randall (Deputy Crowell), Richard Reeves (truck driver).

"Yours Truly, Jack the Ripper" (4-11-61): John Williams (Sir Guy), Edmond Ryan (Capt. Jago), Donald Woods (Carmody), Adam Williams (Hymie), Nancy Valentine (Arlene), Ransom Sherman.

"The Devil's Ticket" (4-18-61): Macdonald Carey (Hector Vane), Joan Tetzel (Marie Vane), John Emery (pawnbroker), Patricia Medina (Nadja), Robert Cornthwaite (Spengler), Bartlett Robinson (art critic), Hayden Rorke (doctor), Audrey Swanson (nurse).

"Parasite Mansion" (4-25-61): Pippa Scott (Marcia Hunt), James Griffith (Victor), Jeanette Nolan (Granny), Tommy Nolan (Rennie), Beverly Washburn (Lollie).

"A Good Imagination" (5-2-61): Patricia Barry (Louise Logan), Edward Andrews (Frank Logan), Ed Nelson (George), Glenn Strange (Indian), William Allyn (Randy Hagen), Ken Lynch (Joe Thorp), Jim Bannon (Sheriff), Britt Lomond (Arnold Chase), Mary Grace Canfield (Celia Perry).

"Mr. George" (5-9-61): Gina Gillespie (Priscilla), Virginia Gregg (Edna), Howard Freeman (Jared), Lillian Bronson (Adelaide), Joan Tompkins (Laura).

"Terror in Teakwood" (5-16-61): Guy Rolfe (Vladimir Vicek), Hazel Court (Leonie), Charles Aidman (Jerry), Vladimir Sokoloff (Glocky), Reggie Nalder (Gakfe), Linda Watkins (Sylvia Slattery), Bernard Fein (stage manager), George Kane (photographer).

"The Prisoner in the Mirror" (5-23-61): Lloyd Bochner (Harry Langham), Marion Ross (Kay), Jack Mullaney (Fred Forrest), Peter Brocco (Prof. Thibaut), Pat Michon (Yvette Dulaine), Henry Daniell (Count Cagliostro), David Frankham (Marquis de Chantenay).

"Dark Legacy" (5-30-61): Harry Townes (Mario Asparos/Radan), Ilka Windish (Monika Asparos), Henry Silva (Toby Wolfe), Alan Napier (attorney), Richard Hale (Eisenhart), Doris Lloyd (Mrs. Pringle), Ned Glass (Vince Fennaday).

"Pigeons from Hell" (6-6-61): Brandon DeWilde (Tim Brandon), Crahan Denton (Sheriff Buckner), Ken Renard (Jacob Blount), Guy Wilkerson (Howard), David Whorf (John Branner).

"The Grim Reaper" (6-13-61): William Shatner (Paul Graves), Natalie Shafer (Bea Graves), Elizabeth Allen (Dorothy Linden), Fifi D'orsay (Toinette), Scott Merill (Gerald Keller), Paul Newlan (Sgt. Bernstein), Henry Daniell (Pierre Radin), Robert Cornthwaite (Phillips).

"What Beckoning Ghost?" (9-18-61): Judith Evelyn (Mildred Beaumont), Tom Helmore (Eric Beaumont), Adele Mara (Lydia), Frank Wilcox (Detective).

"Guillotine" (9-24-61): Alejandro Rey (Robert Lamont), Danielle DeMetz (Babette Lamont), Robert Middleton (DeParis), Gregory Morton (prison director).

"The Premature Burial" (10-2-61): Boris Karloff (Dr. Thorne), Scott Marlowe (Julian Boucher), Sidney Blackmer (Edward Stapleton), Patricia Medina.

"The Weird Tailor" (10-16-61): George Macready (Joe Smith), Henry Jones (Erik Conrad), Sandra Kerr (Anna Conrad), Abraham Sofaer (Nicolai), Iphigenie Castiglione (Mme. Roberts), Stanley Adams (Mr. Schwenk).

"God Grante That She Lye Stille" (10-23-61): Ronald Howard (Dr. Edward Stone), Sarah Marshall (Lady Margaret), Henry Daniell (Vicar Weatherford), Avis Scott (Nurse Emmons), Victor Buono (Van de Velde), Madeleine Holmes (Sarah).

"Masquerade" (10-30-61):

(THRILLER cont.) Tom Poston (Charlie Denham), Elizabeth Montgomery (Rosamond Denham), John Carradine (Jed Carta), Jack Lambert (Lem Carta).

"The Last of the Sommervilles" (11-6-61): Boris Karloff (Dr. Farnham), Martha Hunt (Celia), Phyllis Thaxter (Ursula Sommerville), Peter Walker (Rutherford Sommerville), Chet Stratton (Mr. Parchester).

"Letter to a Lover" (11-13-61): Murray Matheson (Andrew Lawrence), Ann Todd (Sylvia Lawrence), Felix Deebank (Donald Carver), Avis Scott (Estelle Weber).

"A Third for Pinochle" (11-20-61): Edward Andrews (Maynard Thispin), Ann Shoemaker (Mrs. Thispin), Doro Merande (Melba), June Walker.

"The Closed Cabinet" (11-27-61): Olive Sturgess (Evie Bishop), David Frankham (Alan Mervyn), Peter Forster (George Mervyn), Jennifer Raine (Lucy Mervyn).

"Dialogs with Death" (12-4-61): "Friend of the Dead": Boris Karloff (Pop Jenkins), Ed Neslon (Tom), Ben Hammer (Dan Gordon). "Welcome Home": Boris Karloff (Col. Jackson), Estelle Winwood (Emily Jackson), Ed Nelson (Dan Lejan).

"The Return of Andrew Bentley" (12-11-61): John Newland (Ellis Corbett), Antoinette Bower (Sheila Corbett), Terence DeMarney (Uncle Amos), Philip Bourneuf (Dr. Weatherbee), Reggie Nalder (Andrew Bentley), Ken Renard (Jacob), Tom Hennesy (Familiar), Oscar Beregi, Jr. (Father Burkhardt), Norma Crane.

"The Remarkable Mrs. Hawk" (12-19-61): John Carradine (Jason Longfellow), Jo Van Fleet (Mrs. Hawk), Paul Newlan (Sheriff Willetts), Hal Baylor (Pete Grogan).

"Portrait Without a Face" (12-25-61): Robert Webber (Arthur Henshaw), Jane Greer (Ann Moffat), John Newland (Robertson Moffat), George Mitchell (Sheriff Pete Browning), Brian Gaffikan (Nat Fairchild).

"An Attractive Family" (1-1-62): Richard Long (Dick Farrington), Otto Kruger (Uncle Burt), Leo G. Carroll (Major Downey), Joyce Bouliphant (Jinny Willis), Joan Tetzel (Marion), Will Wright (Constable Walker), William Mims (George Drake).

"Waxworks" (1-8-62): Oscar Homolka (Pierre Jacquelin), Antoinette Bower (Annette), Ron Ely (Detective Hudson), Alan Baxter (Sgt. Dane), Booth Coman (Lt. Bailey).

"La Strega" (1-15-62): Alejandro Rey (Tonio Bellini), Ursula Andress (Luana), Jeanette Nolan (La Strega), Frank de Kova (Lt. Vincoli), Ramon Navarro (Maestro Giuliano), Ernest Sarracino (Padre Lupari).

"The Storm" (1-22-62): Nancy Kelly (Janet Wilson), David McLean (Ben Wilson), James Griffith (Ed Brandies), David Janssen, Jean Carroll.

"A Wig for Miss Devore" (1-29-62): Patricia Barry (Sheila Devore), John Fiedler (Herbert Bleake), John Baragrey (George Machink), Herbert Rudley (Max Quinke), Linda Watkins (Arabelle Foote), Bernard Fein (Lester Clyne), Ina Victor (Betty).

"The Hollow Watcher" (2-12-62): Audrey Dalton (Meg O'Dangh Wheeler), Sean McClory (Ian the O'Danagh), Warren Oates (Hugo Wheeler), Denver Pyle (Ortho Wheeler), Sandy Kenyon (Mason), Walter Burke (Croxton).

"Cousin Tundifer" (2-19-62): Edward Andrews (Miles Tundifer), Vaughn Taylor (Pontifer Tundifer), Sue Ann Langdon (Queenie De Lyte), Howard McNear (Jack Passasstroy), Dayton Lummis (Millard Braystone), Chet Stratton (Alfred Marvin), Jim Bannon (Lieutenant), Cyril Delevanti (old man), Hallene Hill (old woman).

"The Incredible Dr. Markesan" (2-26-62): Boris Karloff (Dr. Konrad Markesan), Dick York (Fred Bancroft), Carolyn Kearney (Molly Bancroft), Richard Hale (Prof. Latimer), Basil Howes (Prof. Charing), Henry Hunter (Prof. Angus Holden).

"Flowers of Evil" (3-5-62): Luciana Paluzzi (Madalana), Kevin Hagen (Arno Lunt), Jack Weston (Maurice Reynard), Gregory Gaye (President), Vladimir Sokoloff (janitor).

"Till Death Do Us Part" (2-12-62): Henry Jones (Carl Somer), Reta Shaw (Celia Hopper), Philip Ober (Elmer Hooper), Edgar Buchanan (Dr. O'Connor), Jocelyn Brando (Myrtle Hooper), Eve McVeagh (Bonnie), Jim Davis (Marshal), Frances Morris (Abbie).

"The Bride Who Died Twice" (2-19-62): Mala Powers (Consuela De La Verra), Eduardo Cianelli (Gen. De La Verra), Joe de Santis (Col. Sangriento), Robert Colbert (Capt. Fernandez), Carl Donn (Sergeant).

"Kill My Love" (3-26-62):
Richard Carlson (Guy Guthrie), K.T.
Stevens (Olive Guthrie), David Kent
(Julian Guthrie), Patricia Breslin
(Dinah Duffay), Casey Rogers (Anthea
Jason).
 "Man of Mystery" (4-2-62):
Mary Tyler Moore (Sherry Smith),
William Windom (Lou Waters), John
Van Dreelan (Joel Stone), William
Phipps (Harry Laxer), Ken Lynch
(Rudy), Ralph Clanton (Dr. Grail),
Mercedes Shirley (Jill Naylor).
 "The Innocent Bystanders" (4-
9-62): Steven Terrell (Bruce Evans),
Janet Lake (Elsie), John Anderson
(Jacob Grant), George Kennedy (John
Patterson), Gale Robbins (Mary
Jerold), Thann Wyenn (Vane).
 "The Lethal Ladies" (4-16-62):
"Murder on the Rocks": Rosemary
Murphy (Lavinia Sills), Howard
Morris (Myron Sills), Pamela Curran
(Gloria), Marjorie Bennett (Mercedes).
"Goodbye, Dr. Bliss": Rosemary
Murphy (Alice Quimby), Jackie Rus-
sell (Martha Foster), Howard Morris
(Dr. Wilfred Bliss), Henry Brandt
(Mr. Sutter).
 "The Specialists" (4-30-62):
Lin McCarthy (Pete Duncan), Su-
zanne Lloyd (Helen Coleman), Ronald
Howard (Martin Gresham), Ronald
Frankham (Joe Carter), Sean McClory
(Galt), Lauren Gilbert (Tracy), Robert
Douglas (Swinburne).

THUNDERBIRDS. 1964-66. Voices:
Peter Dyneley (Jeff Tracy), Shane
Rimmer (Scott Tracy), David
Holliday (Virgil Tracy), Matt
Zimmerman (Alan Tracy), David
Graham (Gordon Tracy/Prof.
Brains/Kyrano/Parker), Ray
Barrett (John Tracy/the Hood),
Sylvia Anderson (Lady Penelope
Creighton-Ward), Christine Finn
(Tin Tin Kyrano).
 "Trapped in the Sky".
 "Pit of Peril".
 "City of Fire".
 "Sun Probe".
 "The Uninvited".
 "The Mighty Atom".
 "Vault of Death".
 "Operation Crash Dive".
 "Move and You're Dead".
 "Martian Invasion".
 "Brink of Disaster".
 "The Perils of Penelope".
 "Terror in New York City".
 "End of the Road".
 "Day of Disaster".

 "The Edge of Impact".
 "Desperate Intruder".
 "30 Minutes After Noon".
 "The Imposters".
 "The Man from M. I. 5. ".
 "Cry Wolf".
 "Danger at Ocean Deep".
 "The Duchess Assignment".
 "Attack of the Alligators".
 "The Cham Cham".
 "Security Hazard".
 "Atlantic Inferno".
 "Path of Destruction".
 "Alias Mr. Hackenbacker".
 "Lord Parker's 'oliday".
 "Ricochet".
 "Give or Take a Million".

TIME MACHINE, THE. British.
 (1-25-49) Russell Napier (the Time
 Traveler), Mary Donn (Weena).

TIME EXPRESS. 1979. Vincent Price
 (Jason Winters), Coral Browne
 (Margaret Winters), James Reynolds
 (Robert Jefferson 'R. J. ' Walker),
 William Edward Phipps (Callahan),
 Woodrow Parfrey (ticket taker).
 "Garbage Man"/"Doctor's Wife"
 (4-26-79): Jerry Stiller (Eddie Cher-
 noff), Anne Meara (Gloria Chernoff),
 Michael Conrad (bartender), James
 MacArthur (Dr. Mark Toland), Pamela
 Toll (Olivia).
 "The Copy-writer"/"The Figure
 Skater" (5-3-79): Richard Masur (Sam
 Loring), Morgan Fairchild (Michelle),
 Lee Meriwether (Vanessa), Lyle
 Waggoner (David Laine), Terri Nunn
 (Jill Martin), Francois-Marie Benard
 (Paul).
 "Rodeo"/"Cop" (5-10-79): John
 Beck (Roy Culper), Kyle Richards
 (Billy Jane), Marcia Strassman,
 Robert Hooks (John Slocum), Vic
 Tayback (Enright).
 "Death"/"The Boxer" (5-17-79):
 Steve Kanaly (Michael Bennett), John
 Van Dreelan (Dr. Vall), Linda Scruggs
 Bogart, George Murdock (Max), Jaime
 Lyn Bauer (Elizabeth), Paul Sylvan
 (Tony Marcello).

TIME TUNNEL. 1966-67. James
 Darren (Tony Newman), Robert
 Colbert (Doug Phillips), Lee Meri-
 wether (Dr. Ann MacGregor), Whit
 Bissell (Gen. Heywood Kirk), John
 Zaremba (Dr. Raymond Swain),
 Wesley Lau (Sgt. Jiggs).
 "Rendezvous with Yesterday"
 (9-9-66): Michael Rennie (Capt. Mal-
 colm Smith), Gary Merrill (Sen. Leroy

(TIME TUNNEL cont.) Clark), Susan
Hampshire (Althea Hall), Don Knight
(Grainger), Gerald Michenaud (Mar-
cel), Michael Haynes (soldier).
    "One Way to the Moon" (9-16-
66): Larry Ward (Kane), James
Callahan (Beard), Ben Cooper (Nazar-
ro), Warren Stevens (Harlow), Ross
Elliott (Dr. Brandon), Barry Kelley
(Adm. Killian).
    "The End of the World" (9-23-
66): Paul Fix (Henderson), James
Westerfield (Sheriff), Paul Carr
(Blaine), Gregory Morton (Prof.
Ainsley), Sam Groom (Jerry), Nel-
son Leigh.
    "The Day the Sky Fell In" (9-
30-66): Lindon Chiles (Cmdr. Tony
Newman), Susan Flannery (Louise),
Lew Gallo (Lt. Anderson), Bob
Riordan (Adm. Brandt), Sheldon
Golomb (Little Tony), Sam Groom
(Jerry), Bob Okazaki.
    "The Last Patrol" (10-7-66):
Carroll O'Connor (Gen. Southall/
Col. Southall), Michael Pate (Capt.
Hotchkiss), John Napier (Capt. Jen-
kins), David Watson (Lt. Rynerson),
Jean Winston (British Sentry).
    "Crack of Doom" (10-14-66):
Torin Thatcher (Dr. Holland), Ellen
McRae (Eve Holland), Vic Lundin
(Karnosu), George Matsui (young
native).
    "The Revenge of the Gods" (10-
21-66): John Doucette (Ulysses),
Paul Carr (Paris), Dee Hartford
(Helen of Troy), Joseph Ruskin (Sar-
dis), Abraham Sofaer (Epeios), An-
thony Brand (Captain), Pat Culliton
(sentry).
    "Massacre" (10-28-66): George
Mitchell (Sitting Bull), Christopher
Dark (Crazy Horse), Joe Moross
(Gen. Custer), Perry Lopez (Dr.
Whitebird), Lawrence Montaigne
(Yellow Elk), Paul Comi (Capt.
Benteen), Jim Halferty (Tim).
    "Devil's Island" (11-11-66):
Marcel Hillarie (Boudaire), Theo
Marcuse (Lescaux), Oscar Beregi,
Jr. (Commandant), Ted Roter (Capt.
Dreyfuss), Steven Geray.
    "Reign of Terror" (11-18-66):
Monique Lemaire (Marie Antoinette),
David Opatoshu (shopkeeper), Louis
Mercier (Simon), Joey Tata (Lt.
Napoleon Bonaparte), Patrick Miche-
naud (Dauphin).
    "Secret Weapon" (11-24-66):
Nehemiah Persoff (Prof. Biraki),
Michael Ansara (Hruda), Gregory
Gaye (Alexis), Russell Conway (Gen.

Parker), Kevin Hagen (McDonnell),
Sam Groom.
    "The Death Trap" (12-2-66):
Scott Marlowe (Jeremiah), R.G.
Armstrong (Pinkerton), Tom Sker-
ritt (Matthew), Ford Rainey (Abraham
Lincoln).
    "The Alamo" (12-9-66): Rhodes
Reason (Col. William Travis), John
Lupton (Capt. Teynerson), Jim Davis
(Col. Bowie), Elizabeth Rogers (Mrs.
Reynerson), Rodolfo Hoyos (Capt.
Rodriguez), Edward Colmans.
    "Night of the Long Knives" (12-
16-66): Malachi Throne (Hira Singh),
David Watson (Rudyard Kipling),
Brendan Dillon (Col. Pettretch),
Peter Brocco (Kashi), Perry Lopez
(Major Kabir), George Keymas (Ali),
Ben Wright, Dayton Lummis.
    "Invasion" (12-23-66): John
Wengraf (Dr. Kleinmann), Lyle
Bettger (Maj. Hoffman), Joey Tata
(Verlaine), Robert Carricart (Mira-
beau), Michael St. Clair (Duchamps),
Francis DeSales (Dr. Shumate).
    "The Revenge of Robin Hood"
(12-30-66): Donald Harron (Robin
Hood/Earl of Huntington), John Orchard
(Engelard), John Crawford (King John),
John Alderson (Little John), Ronald
Long (Friar Tuck), James Lanphier
(DuBois), Erin O'Brien-Moore (Baro-
ness).
    "Kill Two By Two" (1-6-67):
Mako (Lt. Nakamura), Kam Tong
(Sgt. Itsugi), Philip Ahn (Dr. Naga-
mura), Vince Howard (medic), Brent
Davis (American Sgt.)
    "Visitors from Beyond the Stars"
(1-13-67): Jan Merlin (Centauri),
Fred Beir (Taureg), Ross Elliott
(Sheriff), Byron Foulger (Williams),
Tris Coffin (Crawford), John Hoyt
(Alien Leader), Gary Haynes (Deputy).
    "The Ghost of Nero" (1-20-67):
Eduardo Ciannelli (Count Galba),
Gunner Hellstrom (Major Niestadt),
John Hoyt (Dr. Steinholtz).
    "The Walls of Jericho" (1-27-67):
Rhodes Reason (Joshua), Myrna
Fahey (Rahab), Anrold Moss (Malek),
Lisa Gaye (Ahza), Abraham Sofaer
(Father), Michael Pate.
    "Idol of Death" (2-3-67): Teno
Pollick (Young Chief), Lawrence
Montaigne (Alvarado), Anthony Caruso
(Cortez), Rodolfo Hoyos (Castillano),
Peter Brocco (Retainer), Abel Fer-
nandez (Bowman).
    "Billy the Kid" (2-10-67):
Robert Walker, Jr. (Billy the Kid),
Allen Case (Sheriff Pat Garrett),

Harry Lauter (Wilson), Pitt Herbert (McKinney), John Crawford (Deputy John Poe), Phil Chambers (Marshall). "Pirates of Deadman's Island" (2-17-67): Victor Jory (Capt. Beal), Regis Toomey (Dr. Berkhart), Pepito Galindo (Armando), James Anderson (Hampton), Charles Bateman (Capt. Decatur), Alex Montoya (Spanish Captain). "Chase Through Time" (2-24-67): Robert Duvall (Nimon), Lew Gallo (Vokar), Vetina Marcus, Joe Ryan. "The Death Merchant" (3-3-67): Malachi Throne (Machiavelli/Michaels), John Crawford (Major), Kevin Hagen (Sgt. Maddux), Kevin O'Neal (Corporal). "Attack of the Barbarians" (3-10-67): John Saxon (Marco Polo), Vitina Marcus (Sarit), Arthur Batanides (Batu), Paul Mantee (Ambahai). "Merlin the Magician" (3-17-67): Christopher Carey (Merlin), James McMullan (Arthur), Lisa Jak (Guinevere), Vincent Beck (Wogan). "The Kidnappers" (3-23-67): Michael Ansara (Curator), Del Monroe (Ott), Bob May (Hitler). "Raiders from Outer Space" (3-31-67): John Crawford (Capt. Henderson), Kevin Hagen (Planet Leader). "Town of Terror" (4-7-67): Heather Young (Joan), Gary Haynes (Pat), Vincent Beck (Alien Leader), Kelly Thordsen (Alien-Sarah).

TOM CORBETT, SPACE CADET. 1950-56. Frankie Thomas (Tom Corbett), Al Markim (Astro), Jan Merlin (Roger Manning), Edward Bryce (Capt. Steve Strong), Carter Blake (Cmdr. Arkwright), John Fiedler (Cadet Alfie Higgins), Frank Sutton (Cadet Eric Raddison), Jack Grimes (Cadet T.J. Thistle), Patricia Ferris (Dr. Joan Dale) 50-53; Margaret Garland (Dr. Joan Dale) 53-56; Michael Harvey (Capt. Larry Strong), Beryl Berney (Betty), Marian Brash (Gloria). "Space Week" (7-7-51). "The Martian Revolt" (7-14-51): Joe DeSantis (Cmdr. Elblas), Ralph Camargo (Capt. Bex). "Trial in Space" (7-21-51): John Weaver (Cadet Harvey). "Graveyard of the Rockets" (7-28-51): James Van Dyke (Prof. Chambers), Ralph Riggs (Norgerson).

"The Asteroid of Death" (8-4-51): Clifford Sales (Jodie Morton). "The Mystery of Alkar" (8-11-51): Ralph Riggs (Luxor), Joe DeSantis (Elblas). "The Lost Colony of Venus" (8-18-51): Chet Stratton ('Ace of Space' Bradley). "Summer Space Maneuvers" (8-25-51 & 9-1-51). "The Million Dollar Patrol" (8-29-53). "The Trojan Planets" (9-12-53). "The Outpost of Danger" (9-26-53). "Target Danger" (10-10-53). "The Mountains of Fire" (10-23-53). "The Ghost Ship" (11-7-53). "The Beacon of Dangers" (11-21-53). "Spaceship of Death" (12-5-53). "The Raiders of the Asteroids" (12-19-53). "The Planet of Doom" (1-2-54). "Cargo of Death" (1-16-54): Humphrey Davis (Captain Brad Farley), Harry Bellaver (Dickson). "The Iron Major" (1-30-54). "The Space Projectile" (2-13-54). "Rescue in Space" (2-27-54). "The Earthdigger" (3-13-54). "Space Station of Danger" (3-27-54). "Treachery in Space" (4-10-54). "Comet of Death" (4-24-54). "Death Trap" (5-8-54). "The Runaway Rocket" (5-22-54). "The Atomic Curtain" (12-11-54). "Astro's Trial" (12-18-54). "The Runaway Asteroid" (1-1-55). "Suit Up For Danger" (1-8-55). "Mystery of the Mothball Fleet" (1-15-55). "The Life Ray" (1-22-55). "A Mighty Mite" (1-29-55). "Ace of the Space Lanes" (2-5-55): Ralph Camargo (Capt. Roy Cowan). "The Asteroid Station" (2-12-55). "The Grapes of Ganymede" (2-19-55). "Assignment: Mercury" (2-26-55). "Smugglers of Death" (3-5-55). "The Mystery of the Missing Mail Ship" (3-12-55): Ralph Camargo (Roy Cowan). "The Gremlin of Space" (3-19-55). "Terror in Space" (3-26-55). "Spaceship of Danger" (4-2-55). "The Magnetic Asteroid" (4-9-55): Bob Hastings (Jim Myers). "Danger in the Asteroid Belt" (4-16-55).

(TOM CORBETT, SPACE CADET.
cont.)
"False Alert" (4-23-55).
"Pursuit of the Deep Space Pro-
jectile" (4-30-55): Bill Lipton (Alex
Monroe).
"Outpost of Terror" (5-7-55):
Robert Dryden (Barker).
"An Exercise for Death" (5-14-
55): William Jonstone (Secretary
Masters).
"Ambush in Space" (5-21-55):
Bill Zuckert (Brock), Ralph Camargo
(Roy Cowan), Geoffrey Bryant (Care-
taker).
"The Stowaway" (5-28-55).
"Assignment: Survival" (6-4-
55).
"Space Blindness" (6-11-55):
Leon Janney (Prof. Hinkel).
"Comet of Danger" (6-18-55).
"The Final Test" (6-25-55).

TOMORROW PEOPLE, THE. British. 1973-77. Nicholas Young,
Peter Vaughan Clarke, Sammie
Winmill, Stephen Salmon, Elizabeth Adara.

TOPPER. 1953-55. Leo G. Carroll
(Cosmo Topper), Anne Jeffrey
(Marian Kirby), Robert Sterling
(George Kirby), Lee Patrick (Mrs.
Henrietta Topper), Thurston Hall
(Mr. Schuyler), Kathleen Freeman
(Katy, the maid).

TOPPER RETURNS.
Pilot (3-19-73): Roddy McDowall
(Cosmo Topper, Jr.), Stephanie
Powers (Marian Kerby), John Fink
(George Kerby), Reginald Owen
(Jones, the Butler).

TROLLENBERG TERROR, THE.
British (12-15-56 - 1-19-57)*
Sarah Lawson, Laurence Payne,
Rosemary Miller.

TV HOUR.
"Atomic Attack" (5-18-54):
Robert Keith (Dr. Lee), Phyllis
Thaxter (Gladys), Walter Matthau
(Dr. Spinelli), Audrey Christie (Mrs.
Moore), William Kemp (Jim Turner).

TV PLAYHOUSE.
"Visit to a Small Planet" (5-
8-55): Cyril Ritchard (Kreton), Alan
Reed (Gen. Powers), Ed Andrews
(Roger Spelding), Theodore Bikel

*Aired in multiple segments; dates show first and
last segments.

(Paul Laurent), Dick York (John
Randolph), Jill Kraft (Janet Spelding),
Sylvia Davis (Ellen Spelding), Gerald
Milton (2nd visitor), Bruce Kirby
(aide).
"The Dark Side of the Moon"
(8-18-57): Biff McGuire (Harry
Baker), Kathleen Maguire (Ellen
Baker), Alexander Scourby (Jordan),
Addison Powell (Majestic), Douglas
Watson (Cole), John Alexander (Col-
lins), Douglas Rodgers (Jansen),
Norma Moore (Pearle).

20th CENTURY-FOX HOUR.
"In Times Like These" (2-22-56):
MacDonald Carey (Lew Marsh), Fay
Wray (Agnes Marsh), Johnny Wash-
brook (Rusty at 12), Mark Damon
(Rusty at 17), Rodd Farrell (Rusty
at 6), Susan Lucky (Gretchen), James
Drury (Anton Cavrek), George Eld-
redge (Bill Beecher), Pamela Baird
(Lenore at 12), Lily Gentle (Lenore
at 17).
"Stranger in the Night" (10-17-
56): Joan Fontaine (Lynne Abbott),
Michael Wilding (Capt. Robert Wilton),
Elsa Lanchester (Ida Perkins), Ton
Conway (Craig Eaton), Jack Raine
(Royce), Philip Tonge (Smythe),
Ashley Cowan (Enguireies).

TWILIGHT ZONE. 1959-65. Rod Ser-
ling (Host).
"Where Is Everybody?" (10-2-
59): Earl Holliman (Mike Ferris),
James Gregory (General), Paul Lang-
ton, Gary Walberg, Carter Mulavey,
Jim Johnson, James McCallion, Jay
Overholtz, John Conwell.
"One for the Angels" (10-9-59):
Ed Wynn (Lew Bookman), Murray
Hamilton (Mr. Death), Merrit F.
Bohn (truck driver), Dana Dillaway
(little girl), Mickey Maga (little boy),
Jay Overholt (doctor).
"Mr. Denton on Doomsday"
(10-16-59): Dan Duryea (Al Denton),
Malcolm Atterbury (Henry J. Pate),
Martin Landau (Dan Hotaling), Doug
McClure (Peter Grant), Jeanne Cooper
(dance hall girl), Arthur Batanides
(Leader), Ken Lynch (Charlie), Robert
Burton (doctor), Bill Erwin (man).
"The Sixteen-Millimeter Shrine"
(10-23-59): Ida Lupino (Barbara Jean
Trenton), Martin Balsam (Danny Weiss),
Jerome Cowan (Jerry Hearndon),
Alice Frost (Sally), Ted de Corsia
(Marty Sall), John Clark (Herndon
on screen).
"Walking Distance" (10-30-59):

Gig Young (Martin Sloane), Frank
Overton (Mr. Sloane), Irene Tedrow
(Mrs. Sloane), J. Pat O'Malley (Mr.
Wilson), Bill Erwin (Mr. Wilcox),
Byron Foulger (Charlie), Ron Howard
(Wilcox boy), Sheridan Comerate
(attendant), Buzz Martin (teenager),
Joseph Corey (soda jerk).
    "Escape Clause" (11-6-59):
David Wayne (Walter Bedecker), Vir-
ginia Christine (Esther Bedecker),
Thomas Gomez (Cadwallader), Wen-
dell Holmes (Cooper), Raymond Bailey
(Doctor), Nesdon Booth (guard), Dick
Wilson (adjuster No. 1), Joe Flynn
(adjustor No. 2), Allan Lurie (subway
guard), Paul E. Burns (janitor).
    "The Lonely" (11-13-59): Jack
Warden (Jim Corry), John Dehner
(Allenby), Jean Marsh (Alicia), Ted
Knight (Adams), Jim Turley (Car-
stairs).
    "Time Enough At Last" (11-20-
59): Burgess Meredith (Henry Bemis),
Jacqueline DeWitt (Helen Bemis),
Vaughan Taylor (Mr. Carsville), Lela
Bliss (woman).
    "Perchance to Dream" (11-27-
59): Richard Conte (Edward Hall),
Suzanne Lloyd (Maya), John Larch
(Dr. Rathmann), Ted Stanhope (Stran-
ger), Russell Trent (rifle-range bar-
ker), Eddie Marr (girl show barker).
    "Judgment Night" (12-4-59):
Nehemiah Persoff (Lanser), Ben
Wright (Capt. Willoughby), Patrick
Macnee (Mr. Danbury), Hugh Sanders
(Mr. Potter), Leslie Bradley (Maj.
Devereaux), Deirdre Owen (Barbara),
Kendrick Huxham (bartender), James
Franciscus (Lt. Mueller), Richard
Peel (1st steward), Donald Journeaux
(2nd steward).
    "And When the Sky Was Opened"
(12-11-59): Rod Taylor (Lt. Col.
Clegg Forbes), Jim Hutton (Maj.
William Gart), Charles Aidman (Col.
Edward Herrington), Maxine Cooper
(Amy), Sue Randall (nurse), Paul
Bryar (bartender), Gloria Hall (girl).
    "What You Need" (12-25-59):
Ernest Truex (Mr. Pedot), Steve
Cochran (Fred Renard), William
Edmonson (bartender), Reed Morgan
(Lefty), Doris Karnes (woman), Ar-
line Sax (girl), Norman Sturgis (hotel
clerk), Judy Ellis (woman in street).
    "The Four of Us Are Dying" (1-
1-60): Harry Townes (Arch Hammer),
Phillip Pine (Sterig), Don Gordon
(Andy Marshak), Ross Martin (Johnny
Foster), Beverly Garland (Maggie),
Milton Frome (Detective), Bernard

Fein (Penell), Peter Brocco (Pop
Marshak).
    "Third from the Sun" (1-8-60):
Fritz Weaver (William Sturka), Joe
Maross (Jerry Riden), Edward An-
drews (Carling), S. John Launer
(loudspeaker voice), Lori March
(Eve), Denise Alexander (Jody),
Jeanne Evans (Ann), Will J. White
(guard).
    "I Shot an Arrow into the Air"
(1-15-60): Dewey Martin (Flight Of-
ficer Corey), Edward Binns (Capt.
Donlin), Ted Otis (Flight Officer
Pierson), Harry Bartel (Langford),
Leslie Barrett (Brandt).
    "The Hitchhiker" (1-22-60):
Inger Stevens (Nan Adams), Leonard
Strong (Hitchhiker), Adam Williams
(sailor), Lew Gallo (mechanic),
Eleanor Audley (Mrs. Whitney),
Dwight Townsend (highway flag man),
Russ Bender (counterman), Mitzi
McCall (waitress), George Mitch
(gas station man).
    "The Fever" (1-29-60): Everett
Sloane (Franklin Gibbs), Vivi Janiss
(Flora Gibbs), Art Lewis (drunk),
William Kendis (PR man), Lee Sands
(floor manager), Lee Millar (photogra-
pher), Marc Towers (cashier), Carole
Kent (girl), Jeffrey Sayre (croupier),
Arthur Peterson (Sheriff).
    "The Last Flight" (2-5-60):
Alexander Scourby (Gen. Harper),
Simon Scott (Major Wilson), Kenneth
Haigh (Lt. William Smith Decker),
Robert Warwick (Air Marsahl Mac-
Kaye), Jerry Catron (guard), Harry
Raybould (Corporal), Paul Baxley
(jeep driver), Jack Perkins (truck
driver), Frank Tallman (stunt pilot).
    "The Purple Testament" (2-12-
60): William Reynolds (Lt. Fitzgerald),
Dick York (Capt. Riker), Barney
Phillips (Capt. Gunther), William
Phipps (Sergenat), Michael Vandever
(Smitty), Marc Cavell (Freeman),
S. John Launer (Colonel), Warren
Oates (ambulance driver), Paul
Mazursky (orderly), Ron Masak (man
with harmonica).
    "Elegy" (2-19-60): Cecil Kell-
away (Jeremy Wickwire), Jeff Morrow
(Prof. Kurt Meyer), Don Dubbins
(Peter Kirby), Kevin Hagen (Capt.
James Weber).
    "Mirror Image" (2-26-60):
Vera Miles (Millicent Barnes), Martin
Milner (Paul Grinstead), Joe Hamil-
ton (ticket agent), Farris Taylor
(husband), Terese Lyon (old woman),
Naomi Stevens (woman attendant),

(TWILIGHT ZONE cont.) Edwin Rand (bus driver).

"The Monsters Are Due on Maple Street" (3-4-60): Claude Akins (Steve Brand), Jack Weston (Charlie), Barry Atwater (Mr. Goodman), Jan Handlik (Tommy), Mary Gregory (Tommy's mother), Lea Waggner (Mrs. Goodman), Anne Barton (Mrs. Brand), Sheldon Allman (Alien), Burt Metcalfe, Lyn Guild, Joan Sudlow, Ben Erway, Amzie Strickland, Jason Johnson.

"A World of Difference" (3-11-60): Howard Duff (Arthur Curtiss), Eileen Ryan (Nora Raigan), Gail Kobe (Sally), Frank Maxwell (Marty), David White (Brinkley), Peter Walker (Endicott), Susan Dorn (Marian), William Idelson (Kelly).

"Long Live Walter Jameson" (3-18-60): Kevin McCarthy (Walter Jameson), Edgar Stehli (Prof. Samuel Kittridge), Dody Heath (Susanna Kittridge), Estelle Winwood (Laurette Bowan).

"People Are Alike All Over" (3-25-60): Roddy McDowall (Sam Conrad), Paul Comi (Warren Macusson), Susan Oliver (Teenya), Byron Morrow (man), Vic Perrin (man), Vernon Bray (man).

"Execution" (4-1-60): Russell Johnson (Prof. George Manion), Albert Salmi (Joe Caswell), Thann Wyenn (Johnson), Jon Lormer (Reverend), George Mitchell (elderly man), Fay Roope (judge), Joe Haworth (cowboy), Richard Karlan (bartender).

"The Big, Tall Wish" (4-8-60): Ivan Dixon (Bolie Jackson), Steve Perry (Henry Temple), Kim Hamilton (Frances Temple), Walter Burke (Mizell), Henry Scott (Thomas), Charles Horvath (other fighter), Frankie Vann (referee), Carl McIntire (announcer).

"A Nice Place to Visit" (4-15-60): Larry Blyden (Rocky Valentine), Sebastian Cabot (Mr. Pip), Sandra Warner (1st beautiful girl), Suzanne Sturtridge (dancing girl), Barbara English (dancing girl), Nels Nelson (midget policeman), John Close (policeman), Peter Hornsby (craps dealer), Bill Mulliken (parking attendant), Wayne Tucker (croupier).

"Nightmare as a Child" (4-29-60): Janice Rule (Helen Foley), Suzanne Cupito (little girl), Sheppard Strudwick (Peter Selden), Terry Burnham (Markie), Michael Fox (Doctor), William Quinn (Doctor),

Vic Perry (police officer).

"A Stop at Willoughby" (5-6-60): James Daly (Gart Williams), Patricia Donahue (Jane Williams), Howard Smith (Mr. Misrell), Mavis Neal (Helen), Jason Wingreen (1st conductor), James Maloney (2nd conductor), Max Slater (man on wagon), Ryan Hayes (trainman), Bill Booth (1st boy), Butch Hengen (2nd boy).

"The Chaser" (5-13-60): George Grizzard (Roger Shakleford), Patricia Barry (Leila), John McIntire (Mr. Daemon), J. Pat O' Malley (man in homburg), Marjorie Bennett (fat lady), Barbara Perry (blonde), Rusty Wescoatt (tall man), Duane Gray (bartender).

"A Passage for Trumpet" (5-20-60): Jack Klugman (Joey Crown), John Anderson (Gabe), Frank Wolff (Baron), Mary Webster (Nan), Ned Glass (pawnshop owner), James Flavin (truck driver), Diane Honodel (woman pedestrian).

"Mr. Bevis" (6-3-60): Orson Bean (James B.W. Bevis), Henry Jones (J. Hardy Hempstead), Charles Lane (Mr. Peckinpaugh), Florence MacMichael (Margaret), William Schallert (policeman), House Peters, Jr. (2nd policeman), Dorothy Neuman (landlady), Horace McMahon (bartender), Vito Scotti (peddler), Colleen O'Sullivan (young lady), Timmy Cletro (little boy).

"After Hours" (6-10-60): Anne Francis (Martha White), Elizabeth Allen (saleslady), Nancy Rennick (Miss Pettigrew), James Milhollin (Armbruster), Patrick Whyte (Sloan), John Conwell (elevator operator).

"The Mighty Casey" (6-17-60): Jack Warden (Mouth McGarry), Robert Sorrells (Casey), Abraham Sofaer (Dr. Stillman), Jonathan Hole (Doctor), Rusty Lane (Commissioner), Alan Dexter (Beasley), Don O'Kelly (monk).

"A World of His Own" (7-1-60): Keenan Wynn (Gregory West), Phyllis Kirk (Victoria West), Mary LaRoche (Mary).

"King Nine Will Not Return" (9-30-60): Bob Cummings (Capt. Robert Embry), Paul Lambert (Doctor), Jenna MacMahon (nurse), Gene Lyons (psychiatrist), Seymour Green (British Officer), Richard Lupino (British man).

"Man in the Bottle" (10-7-60): Luther Alder (Arthur Castle), Bibi Janiss (Edna Castle), Joseph Ruskin (Genie), Lisa Golm (Mrs. Gumley),

Olan Soule (revenue man), Peter Coe (German Officer), Albert Szabo (German Officer).

"Nervous Man in a Four Dollar Room" (10-14-60): Joe Mantell (Jackie Rhodes), William D. Gordon (George).

"A Thing About Machines" (10-28-60): Richard Haydn (Bartlett Finchley), Barbara Stuart (Edith), Henry Beckman (Policeman), Barney Phillips (TV repairman), Margarita Cordova (girl on TV), Jay Overholts (intern), Lew Brown (telephone repairman).

"The Howling Man" (11-4-60): John Carradine (Brother Jerome), H.M. Wynant (David Ellington), Robin Hughes (Prisoner), Frederick Ledebur (Brother Christopher), Ezelle Poule (housekeeper).

"The Eye of the Beholder" (11-11-60): Donna Douglas (Janet Tyler), William D. Gordon (Doctor), Maxine Stuart (bandaged Janet Tyler), Edson Stroll (Walter Smith), Joanna Heyes (receptionist), Jennifer Howard (nurse), Arthur Keymas (Leader).

"Nick of Time" (11-18-60): William Shatner (Don Carter), Patricia Breslin (Pat Carter), Guy Wilkerson (counter man), Stafford Repp (mechanic), Walter Reed (desperate man), Dee Carroll (desperate woman).

"The Lateness of the Hour" (12-2-60): Inger Stevens (Jana Loren), John Hoyt (Dr. Loren), Irene Tedrow (Mrs. Loren), Mary Gregory (Nelda), Doris Karnes (Gretchen), Valley Keane (Suzanne), Tomas Palmer (Robert, the butler), Jason Johnson (Jensen).

"The Trouble with Templeton" (12-9-60): Brian Aherne (Booth Templeton), Pippa Scott (Laura Templeton), Sydney Pollack (Willis), Dave Willock (Marcel), King Calder (Sid Sperry), David Thursby (Eddie), Charles Carlson (Barney Flueger), Larry J. Blake (Freddie), John Kroger (Ed Page).

"A Most Unusual Camera" (12-16-60): Fred Clark (Chester Diedrich), Jean Carson (Paula Diedrich), Adam Williams (Woodward), Marcel Hillaire (waiter), Artie Lewis (tout).

"Night of the Meek" (12-23-60): Art Carney (Henry Corwin), John Fiedler (Mr. Dundee), Burt Mustin (Burt), Meg Wyllie (Sister Florence), Robert Lieb (Policeman Flaherty), Val Avery (bartender), Larraine

Gillespie (Elf), Kay Cousins (woman in the store).

"Dust" (1-6-61): John Alonso (Louis Gallegos), Thomas Gomez (Sykes), Vladimir Sokoloff (Mr. Gallegos), Paul Genge (Mr. Canfield), John Larch (Sheriff Koch), Dorothy Adams (Mrs. Canfield), Andrew Margolls (Estelita Gallegos), Douglas Heyes, Jr. (farmer boy), Duane Grey (Rogers), John Lormer (1st man), Daniel White (2nd man).

"Back There" (1-12-61): Russell Johnson (Peter Corrigan), Raymond Greenleaf (Jackson), Paul Hartman (Police Sergeant), John Lasell (Wellington/Booth), Bartlett Robinson (William), James Lydon (Patrolman), John Gavin (Policeman), Raymond Bailey (Millard), John Eldredge, Carol Rosen, J. Pat O'Malley, Jean Inness, Nora Marlowe, Lew Brown, Fred Kruger.

"The Whole Truth" (1-20-61): Jack Carson (Harvey Hunnicutt), Loring Smith (Honest Luther Grimbley), George Chandler (old man), Jack Ging (young man), Arte Johnson (Irv), Patrick Westwood (translator), Nan Peterson (girl).

"The Invaders" (1-27-61): Agnes Moorehead (old woman), Douglas Heyes (voice of astronaut).

"A Penny for Your Thoughts" (2-3-61): Dick York (Hector B. Poole), June Dayton (Miss Turner), Dan Tobin (Mr. Bagby), Cyril Delevanti (Mr. Smithers), Hayden Rorke (Mr. Sykes), Patrick Waltz (Mr. Brank), Harry Jackson (Mr. Brand), James Nolan (bank guard), Frank London (driver), Anthony Ray (newsboy).

"Twenty-Two" (2-10-61): Barbara Nichols (Liz Powell), Fredd Wayne (Barney Kaminer), Jonathan Harris (Doctor), Wesley Lau (airline agent), Norma Connolly (night nurse), Mary Adams (day nurse), Arline Sax (morgue nurse/stewardess), Jay Overholts, Joe Sergent, Carole Conn.

"The Odyssey of Flight 33" (2-24-61): John Anderson (Capt. Farver), Paul Comi (1st Officer Craig), Sandy Kenyon (Navigator Hatch), Harop McGuire (Flight Engineer Purcell), Wayne Heffley (2nd Officer Wyatt), Nancy Renick (Paula), Beverly Brown (Jane), Jay Overholts (passenger), Lester Fletcher (RAF man), Betty Garde (lady on plane).

"Mr. Dingle, the Strong" (3-3-61): Burgess Meredith (Luther Dingle), Don Rickles (Bettor), James

(TWILIGHT ZONE cont.) Wester-
field (Bartender O'Toole), James
Milhollin (Abernathy), Edward
Ryder (Joe Callahan), Jay Hector
(Boy), Michael Fox (Martian),
Douglas Spencer (Martian), Douglas
Evans, Donald Losby, Frank Rich-
ards, Bob Duggan, Phil Arnold,
Greg Irwin, Jo Ann Dixon.

"Static" (3-10-61): Dean
Jagger (Ed Lindsay), Carmen Mathews
(Vinnie Broun), Robert Emhardt
(Prof. Ackerman), Arch Johnson
(Roscoe Bragg), Steve Talbot (boy),
Alice Pearce, Bob Crane, Eddie
Marr, Clegg Hoyt, J. Pat O'Malley,
Jay Overholtz, Jerry Fuller, Lillian
O'Malley, Bob Duggan, Diane Strom,
Rob Rowan.

"The Prime Mover" (3-24-61):
Dane Clark (Ace Larsen), Buddy
Ebsen (Jimbo Cobb), Christine
White (Kitty Cavanaugh), Jane Bur-
gess (Sheila), Nesdon Booth (Big
Phil Nolan), Clancy Cooper (trucker),
Robert Riordan (hotel manager),
William Keene (desk clerk), Joe
Scott (croupier).

"Long Distance Call" (3-31-
61): Billy Mumy (Billy Bayles),
Philip Abbott (Chris Byles), Patri-
cia Smith (Sylvia Bayles), Lili Dar-
vas (Grandma Bayles), Henry Hunter
(Dr. Unger), Jenny Maxwell (Shirley),
Reid Hammond (Mr. Peterson),
Lew Brown (attendant), Bob McCord,
Jim Turley, Jutta Parr.

"A Hundred Yards Over the
Rim" (4-7-61): Cliff Robertson
(Chris Horn), Miranda Jones (Mar-
tha Horn), John Crawford (Joe),
John Astin (Charlie), Edward C.
Platt (Doctor), Robert L. McCord,
III (stuntman), Dave Armstrong
(stuntman).

"The Silence" (4-28-61):
Franchot Tone (Col. Archie Taylor),
Liam Sullivan (Jamie Tennyson),
Jonathan Harris (George Arnold),
Cyril Delevanti (Franklin), Everett
Glass (1st man), Felix Lochner (2nd
man), John Holland (3rd man).

"Shadow Play" (5-5-61):
Dennis Weaver (Adam Grant), Harry
Townes (Henry Ritchie), Wright
King (Paul Carson), Bernie Hamil-
ton (Coley), William Edmondson
(Jiggs), Gene Roth (Judge), Howard
Culver (Jury Foreman), Anne Barton
(Carol Ritchie), Tommy Nello (Phil-
lips), Mack Williams (Priest), Jack
Hyde (attorney), John Close.

"The Mind and the Matter"

(5-21-61): Shelley Berman (Archi-
bald Beechoraft), Jack Grinnage
(Henry), Chet Stratton (Mr. Rogers),
Jeanne Wood (landlady).

"Will the Real Martian Please
Stand Up?" (5-26-61): John Hoyt
(Ross), Morgan Jones (Dan Perry),
Jean Willes (Ethel McConnel), Jack
Elam (Avery), John Archer (Bill
Padgett), Barney Phillips (Haley),
Jill Ellis (Connie Price), Gertrude
Flynn (Rose Kramer), Ron Kipling
(George Price), Bill Erwin (Peter
Kramer), William Kendis (Olmstead).

"The Obsolete Man" (6-2-61):
Burgess Meredith (Romney Words-
worth), Fritz Weaver (Chancellor),
Josip Elic (Subaltern), Harry Fleer
(guard), Barry Brooks (1st man),
Harold Innocent (2nd man), Jane
Romeyn (woman).

"Two" (9-15-61): Charles Bronson (man), Elizabeth Montgomery
(woman), Sharon Lucas (stuntwoman).

"The Arrival" (9-21-61):
Harold Stone (Grant Sheckley), Fredd
Wayne (Paul Mally), Noah Keen
(Al Bengston), Bing Russell (ramp
attendant), Robert Brubaker (tower
operator), Robert Karnes (airline
official), Jim Boles (dispatcher).

"The Shelter" (9-29-61): Larry
Gates (Dr. William Stockton), Peggy
Stewart (Grace Stockton), Jack Al-
bertson (Jerry Harlowe), Jo Helton
(Mrs. Harlowe), Sandy Kenyon (Mr.
Henderson), Mary Gregory (Mrs.
Henderson), Joseph Bernard (Marty
Weiss), Moira Turner (Mrs. Weiss),
Mike Burns (Paul Stockton), John
McLiam (man).

"The Passerby" (10-6-61):
James Gregory (Sgt. Baxter), Joanna
Linville (Lavinia Goodwin), Rex
Holman (Charlie), Warren Kemmer-
ling (Jud), Austin Grene (Abraham
Lincoln), David Garcia (Lieutenant).

"A Game of Pool" (10-13-61):
Jonathan Winters (Fats Brown),
Jack Klugman (Jesse Cardiff).

"The Mirror" (10-20-61):
Peter Falk (Ramos Clemente), Will
Kuluva (Gen. DeCrul), Anthony
Carbone (Cristo), Arthur Batanides
(Tabal), Richard Karlan (D'Alles-
dandro), Vladimir Sokoloff (Priest),
Rodolfo Hoyos (Garcia), Val Ruffino
(guard).

"The Grave" (10-27-61): Lee
Marvin (Conny Miller), Richard
Geary (Pinto Sykes), James Best
(Johnny Rob), Strothers Martin
(Mothershed), Ellen Willard (Ione

Sykes), Stafford Repp (Ira Broadly), Larry Johns (Corcoran), Lee Van Cleef (Steinhart), William Challee (Jasen).

"It's a Good Life" (11-3-61): Billy Mumy (Anthony Fremont), John Larch (Mr. Fremont), Cloris Leachman (Mrs. Fremont), Jeanne Bates (Ethel Hollis), Tom Hatcher (Bill Soames), Alice Frost (Aunt Amy), Don Keefer (Dan Hollis), Casey Adams (Pat Riley), Lenore Kingston (Thelma Dunn).

"Death's Head Revisited" (11-10-61): Oscar Beregi, Jr. (Gunter Lutze), Joseph Shildkraut (Becker), Ben Wright (Doctor), Karen Verne (innkeeper), Robert Boone (taxi driver), Chuck Fox (Dachau victim).

"The Midnight Sun" (11-17-61): Lois Nettleton (Norma Forest), Betty Garde (Mrs. Bronson), Ned Glass (repairman), Tom Reese (the Man), Jason Wingreen (neighbor), Juney Ellis (neighbor's wife), John McLiam (policeman), William Keene (doctor), Robert J. Stevenson (announcer).

"Still Valley" (11-24-61): Gary Merrill (Joe Paradine), Vaughn Taylor (old man), Ben Cooper (William Dauger), Jack Mann (Mallory), Mark Tapscott (Lieutenant), Addison Myers (sentry).

"The Jungle" (12-1-61): John Dehner (Alan Richards), Walter Brooke (Chad Cooper), Hugh Sanders (Brooke Templeton), Emily Mc-Laughlin (Doris Richards), Howard Wright (Hardy), Donald Foster (Sinclair), Jay Adler (direlict), Jay Overholts (taxi driver).

"Once Upon a Time" (12-15-61): Buster Keaton (Woodrow Mulligan), Stanley Adams (Prof. Rollo), Milton Parsons (Prof. Gilbert), George E. Stone (Fenwick), Jesse White (repairman), Gil Lamb (policeman in 1890), James Flavin (policeman in 1962), Henry Fleer (2nd policeman in 1962), Warren Parker (store manager), Michael Ross.

"Five Characters in Search of an Exit" (12-22-61): Susan Harrison (Ballerina), William Windom (Major), Murray Matheson (Clown), Kelton Garwood (Tramp), Clark Allen (Bagpiper), Mona Houghton (girl), Carol Hill (woman).

"A Quality of Mercy" (12-29-61): Dean Stockwell (Lt. Katell/Lt. Yamuri), Albert Salmi (Sgt. Causarno), Leonard Nimoy (Hansen),

Ralph Botrain (Hanachek), Rayford Barnes (Watkins), Kale Ishmoto (Japanese soldier), Jerry Fujikawa (Japanese Captain), Michael Pataki (jeep driver).

"Nothing in the Dark" (1-2-62): Gladys Cooper (Wanda Dunn), Robert Redford (Patrolman Harold Beldon), R. G. Armstrong (contractor).

"One More Pallbearer" (1-12-62): Joseph Ruisman (Paul Radin), Katherine Squire (Mrs. Langford), Gage Clark (Rev. Hughes), Trevor Bardette (Col. Hawthorne), Josip Elic (electrician), Robert Snyder (electrician), Ray Galvin (policeman).

"Dead Man's Shoes" (1-19-62): Warren Stevens (Nate Bledsoe), Joan Marshall (Wilma), Richard Devon (Dagget), Florence Marly (Dagget's woman), Ben Wright (Chips), Ron Hagerty (Ben), Joe Mell (Jimmy), Harry Swoger (Sam), Eugene Borden (maitre d').

"The Hunt" (1-26-62): Arthur Hunnicutt (Hyder Simpson), Jeanette Nolan (Rachel Simpson), Robert Foulk (Gatekeeper), Charles Seel (Rev. Wood), Titus Moede (Wesley Miller), Orville Sherman (Tillman Miller), Dexter Dupont (Messenger).

"Showdown with Rance McGrew" (2-2-62): Larry Blyden (Rance McGrew), Arch Johnson (Jesse James), Robert Kline (Actor Jesse James), Robert Cornthwaite (Director), Hal K. Dawson (old man), Jay Overholts (cowboy), Troy Melton (cowboy), William McLean (property man), Robert J. Stevenson (bartender), Jim Turley (double).

"Kick the Can" (2-9-62): Ernest Truex (Charles Whitley), Russell Collins (Ben Conroy), John Marley (Mr. Cox), Hank Patterson (Frietag), Earle Hodgins (Agee), Marjorie Bennett (Mrs. Summers), Lenore Shanewise (Mrs. Densley), Eve McVeagh (Nurse), Anne O'Neal (Mrs. Wister), Burt Mustin (Carlson), Barry Truex (David Whitley), Marc Stevens, Gregory McCabe.

"A Piano in the House" (2-16-62): Barry Morse (Fitzgerald Fortune), Joan Hackett (Esther Fortune), Don Durant (Gregory Walker), Cyril Delevanti (Marvin Bridges), Philip Coolidge (Throckmorton), Muriel Landers (Marge Moore).

"The Last Rites of Jeff Myrtlebank" (2-23-62): James Best (Jeff Myrtlebank), Ralph Moody (Pa Myrtlebank), Sherry Jackson

1354 Science Fiction, Horror, Fantasy

(TWILIGHT ZONE cont.) (Comfort Gatewood), Lance Fuller (Orgram Gatewood), Edgar Buchanan (Doc Bolton), William Fawcett (Rev. Siddons), Ezelle Poulle (Ma Myrtlebank), Vicki Barnes (Liz Myrtlebank), Dub Taylor, Jon Lormer, Helen Wallace, Pat Hector, Mabel Forrest.

"To Serve Man" (3-2-62): Lloyd Bochner (Chambers), Susan Cummings (Pat), Richard Kiel (Kanamit), Hardie Albright, Theo Marcuse, Carleton Young, Nelson Olmstead, Robert Tafur, Lomax Study.

"The Fugitive" (3-9-62): J. Pat O'Malley (Ben), Susan Gordon (Jenny Lewis), Nancy Kulp (Mrs. Gates), Russ Bender (Doctor), Stephen Talbot (Howie), Wesley Lau (man), Paul Tripp (man), Johnny Eiman (pitcher).

"Little Girl Lost" (3-16-62): Robert Sampson (Chris Miller), Sara Marshall (Ruth Miller), Tracy Stratford (Tina Miller), Charles Aidman (Bill).

"Person to Persons Unknown" (3-23-62): Richard Long (David Gurney), Shirley Ballard (1st Wilma Gurney), Julie Van Zandt (2nd Wilma Gurney), Frank Silvera (Dr. Koslenko), Ed Glover (Mr. Huburtise), John Newton (Mr. Cooper), Michael Kelp (policeman), Joe Higgins (guard), Betty Harford.

"The Little People" (3-30-62): Joe Maross (Peter Craig), Claude Akins (William Fletcher), Michael Ford (Spacemen), Don Rhodes (Spaceman).

"Four O'Clock" (4-6-62): Theodore Bikel (Oliver Crangie), Phyllis Love (Mrs. Lucas), Linden Chiles (Hall), Moyna MacGill (Mrs. Williams).

"Hocus, Pocus and Frisby" (3-13-62): Andy Devine (Frisby), Howard McNear (Mitchell), Dabbs Greer (Scanlon), Clem Bevans (Old man), Milton Selzer (spaceman), Peter Brocco (spaceman), Larry Breitman (spaceman).

"The Trade-Ins" (4-20-62): Joseph Shildkraut (John Holt), Alma Platt (Martha Holt), Noah Keen (Mr. Vance), Theo Marcuse (Farraday), Edson Stroll (Young John Holt), Terence DeMarney (gambler), Billy Vincent (gambler), Mary McMahon (receptionist), David Armstrong.

"The Gift" (4-27-62): Geoffrey Horne (Williams), Cliff Osmond (Manuelo), Nico Minardos (doctor), Vito Scotti (Rudolfo), Henry Corden (Sanchez), Edmund Vargas (Pedro), Paul Mazursky (policeman), Vladimir Sokoloff (guitarist), Carmen D'Antonio.

"The Dummy" (5-4-62): Cliff Robertson (Jerry Etherson), Frank Sutton (Frank), John Harmon (Georgie), Sandra Warner (Noreen), Ralph Manza (doorkeeper), Rudy Dolan (emcee), George Murdock (Willie), Bethelynn Grey, Edy Williams (chorus girls).

"Young Man's Fancy" (5-11-62): Alex Nicol (Alex Walker), Phyllis Thaxter (Virginia Walker), Helen Brown (Mrs. Walker), Wallace Rooney (Mr. Wilkerson), Ricky Kelman (Alex at age 10).

"I Sing the Body Electric" (5-18-62): Josephine Hutchinson (Robot Grandmother), David White (George Rogers), Veronica Cartwright (Anne Rogers), Charles Herbert (Tom Rogers), Dana Dilaway (Karen), Doris Packer (Aunt Nedra), Vaughn Taylor (salesman), Judy Morton (Karen at age 18), Paul Nesbitt (Tom at age 20), Susan Crane (Anne at age 19), June Vincent.

"Cavender Is Coming" (5-25-62): Carol Burnett (Agnes Grep), Jesse White (Cavender), Howard Smith (Polk), Sandra Gould (woman), Frank Behrens (theatre manager), Jack Younger (truck Driver), John Fiedler (Field Representative), Donna Douglas (debutante), Albert Carrier (Frenchman), William O'Connell, Pitt Herbert, Stanley Jones (Field Representatives), Barbara Morrison, Roy Sickner, Norma Shattuc, Danny Kulick, Rory O'Brien, Maurice Dallimore, Adrienne Maredn.

"The Changing of the Guard" (6-1-62): Donald Pleasence (Prof. Ellis Fowler), Liam Sullivan (Headmaster), Phillippa Bevans (housekeeper), Bob Biheler (Graham), Kevin O'Neal (Butler), Jimmy Baird, Tom Lowell, Kevin Jones, Russ Horton, Buddy Hart, James Browning, Dennis Kerlee, Darryl Richard, Pat Close.

"In His Image" (1-3-63): George Grizzard (Alan Talbot), Gail Kobe (Jessica Connelly), Jamie Forster (hotel Clerk), Wallace Rooney (man), Katherine Squire (old woman), George Petrie (driver),

James Seay (Sheriff), Sherry Granato (girl), Joseph Sargent (double).

"The Thirty Fathom Grave" (1-10-63): Simon Oakland (Capt. Beecham), Mike Kellin (Bell), Bill Bixby (Officer of the Day), John Considine (McClure), Conlan Carter (Ensign Marmer), David Sheiner (Doctor), Forrest Compton (Officer), Tony Call (Lee Helmsman), Charles Kuenstle (Sonar Operator), Derrick Lewis (Helmsman), Henry Scott (Dr. O.O.D.), Vince Bagetta (sailor No. 1), Louie Elias (sailor No. 2).

"Valley of the Shadow" (1-17-63): David Opatoshu (Mayor Dorn), Ed Nelson (Phil Redfield), Natalie Trundy (Ellen Marshall), Jacques Aubuchon (Connolly), Suzanne Cupito (girl), James Doohan (girl's father), Dabbs Greer (Evans), Sandy Kenyon (gas attendant), Henry Beckman, Bart Burns, King Calder, Pat O'Hara (men).

"He's Alive" (1-24-63): Dennis Hopper (Peter Vollmer), Ludwig Donath (Ernest Ganz), Paul Mazursky (Frank), Curt Conway (Stranger), Wolfe Barzell (bartender), Howard Caine (Nick), Barnaby Hale (Stanley), Jay Adler (Gibbons), Bernard Fein (Heckler).

"The Mute" (1-31-63): Frank Overton (Harry Wheeler), Barbara Baxley (Cora Wheeler), Ann Jullian (Ilse Nielsen), Percy Helton (Tim Poulter), Robert Boon (Holger Nielson), Claudia Bryar (Frau Nielson), Oscar Beregi, Jr. (Karl Werner), Irene Dailey (Miss Frank), Eva Soreny (Frau Werner), Hal Riddle.

"Death Ship" (2-7-63): Jack Klugman (Capt. Ross), Ross Martin (Lt. Mason), Fred Beir (Lt. Carter), Ross Elliot (Kramer), Mary Webster (Ruth Mason), Tammy Marihugh (Jeannie Mason), Sara Taft.

"Jess-Belle" (2-14-63): Anne Francis (Jess-Belle), Jeannette Nolan (Granny Hart), James Best (Billy Ben Turner), Laura Devon (Eilwyn), Virginia Gregg (Ossie Stone), Jon Lormer (Minister), George Mitchell (Luther Glover), Helen Kleeb (Mattie Glover), Jim Boles (Obed Miller).

"Miniature" (2-21-63): Robert Duvall (Charlie Parkes), Pert Kelton (Mrs. Parkes), William Windom (Dr. Wallman), Barbara Barrie (Myra), John McLaim (museum guard), Claire Griswold (Doll), Chet Stratton (the guide), Joan Chambers (Harriet), Barney Phillips (Diemel), Len Weinrib (Buddy), Richard Angarola (suitor).

"Printer's Devil" (2-28-63): Burgess Meredith (Mr. Smith), Robert Sterling (Doug Winter), Pat Crowley (Jackie Benson), Ray Teal (Mr. Franklin), Charles Thompson (Andy Praskins), Doris Kemper (landlady), Camille Franklin (Molly), Ryan Hayes.

"No Time Like the Past" (3-7-63): Dana Andrews (Paul Driscoll), Patricia Breslin (Abby Sloan), Robert F. Simon (Harvey), Malcolm Atterbury (Prof. Elliot), Robert Cornthwaite (Hanford), John Zaremba (musician), Marjorie Bennett (Mrs. Chamberlain), Tudor Owen (Ship Captain), Lindsay Workman (bartender), James Yagi (policeman), Violet Rensing, Reta Shaw.

"The Parallel" (3-14-63): Steve Forrest (Bob Gaines), Jacqueline Scott (Helen Gaines), Philip Abbott (Gen. Easton), Paul Comi (psychiatrist), Frank Aletter (Col. Connacher), Shari Lee Bernath (Maggie Gaines), Morgan Jones (Captain), William Sargeant (Project Commander), Pete Masden, Robert Johnson.

"I Dream of Genie" (3-21-63): Howard Morris (George P. Hanley), Jack Albertson (Genie), Patricia Barry (Ann Lawson), Loring Smith (Watson), Joyce Jameson (starlet), Mark Miller (Roger), Bob Hastings (Sam), James Milhollin (Masters), Robert Ball (Clerk).

"The New Exhibit" (4-4-63): Martin Balsam (Martin L. Senescu), Maggie Mahoney (Emma Senescu), Will Kuluva (Mr. Ferguson), William Mims (Dave), Milton Parsons (Henri Desire Landru), Robert L. McCord (Burke), David Bond (Jack the Ripper), Bob Mitchell (Albert W. Hicks), Lennie Breman, Ed Barth, Craig Curtis, Marcel Hillaire, Phil Chambers.

"Of Late I Think of Cliffordville" (4-11-63): Albert Salmi (William J. Feathersmith), Julie Newmar (Miss Devlin), John Anderson (Diedrich), Wright King (Hecate), Gay Raymond (Gibbons), John Harmon (Clark), Hugh Sanders (Cronk), Christine Burke (Joanna Gibbons), Jamie Forster, Pat O'Hara, Mary

(TWILIGHT ZONE cont.) Jackson.

"The Incredible World of Horace Ford" (4-18-63): Pat Hingle (Horace Ford), Nan Martin (Laura Ford), Ruth White (Mrs. Ford), Vaughn Taylor (Mr. Judson), Phillip Pine (Leonard O'Brien), Mary Garver (Betty O'Brien), Jim E. Titus (Horace as a child), Jerry Davis (Hermy Brandt), Bella Bruck, George Spicer, Anthony Jochim, Bernadette Hale, Lester Maxwell, Harry Short, Billy Hughes.

"On Thursday We Leave for Home" (5-2-63): James Whitmore (Capt. William Benteen), Tim O'Connor (Col. Sloane), James Broderick (Al), Russ Bender (Hank), Paul Langton (George), Daniel Kulick (Jo Jo), Jo Helton (Julie), Lew Gallo (Lt. Engle), John Ward (man), Mercedes Shirley, Madge Kennedy, Shirley O'Hara (women), Anthony Benson (teenager).

"Passage on the Lady Anne" (5-9-63): Lee Philips (Alan Ransome), Joyce Van Patten (Eileen Ransome), Wilfrid Hyde-White (Mr. McKenzie), Gladys Cooper (Mrs. McKenzie), Cecil Kellaway (Burgess), Alan Napier (Capt. Protheroe), Cyril Delevanti (Officer), Don Keefer (Mr. Spieroto), Colin Campbell, Jack Raine.

"The Bard" (5-23-63): Jack Weston (Julius Moomer), John Williams (William Shakespeare), John McGiver (Mr. Shannon), Burt Reynolds (Rocky Rhodes), Doro Merande (Sadie), Henry Lascoe (Gerald Hugo), Howard McNear (Bramhoff), William Lanteau (Dolan), Judy Strangis (Dora), Clegg Hoyt (bus driver), Marge Redmond (secretary), Paul Dubov, Claude Stroud, George Ives, John Newton.

"In Praise of Pip" (9-27-63): Jack Klugman (Max Phillips), Billy Mumy (young Pip), Robert Diamonds (Lt. Pip), Connie Gilchrist (Mrs. Penny), S. John Launer (Moran), Russell Horton (George Reynold), Ross Elliot (doctor), Gerald Gordon (Lieutenant), Stuart Nisbit (surgeon), Kreg Martin (gunman).

"Steel" (10-4-63): Lee Marvin (Steel Kelly), Joe Mantell (Pole), Merritt Bohn (Nolan), Frank London (Maxwell), Chuck Nicks (Maynard Flash), Tipp McClure (Battling Maxo), Larry Barton (man's voice).

"Nightmare at 20,000 Feet"

(10-11-63): William Shatner (Bob Wilson), Christine White (Ruth Wilson), Ed Kemmer (co-pilot), Nick Cravat (Creature), Asa Maynor (stewardess).

"A Kind of Stop Watch" (10-18-63): Richard Erdman (Patrick McNulty), Leon Belasco (Potts), Roy Roberts (Cooper), Herbie Faye (Bartender), Doris Singleton (secretary), Ray Kellogg, Ken Drake, Richard Wessell, Sam Balter.

"The Last Night of a Jockey" (10-25-63): Mickey Rooney (Grady).

"The Living Doll" (11-1-63): Telly Savalas (Erich Streator), Tracy Stratford (Christine Streator), Mary LaRoche (Annabelle).

"The Old Man in the Cave" (11-8-63): James Coburn (French), John Anderson (Goldsmith), Josie Lloyd (Evelyn), Frank Watkins (Harber), Don Wilbanks (Furnam), John Marley (Jason), John Craven, Lenny Geer, Natalie Masters.

"Uncle Simon" (11-15-63): Sir Cedric Hardwicke (Simon Polk), Constance Ford (Barbara Polk), Ian Wolfe (Schwimmer), John McLiam.

"Probe 7 - Over and Out" (11-29-63): Richard Basehart (Col. Cook), Harold Gould (Gen. Larrabee), Antoinette Bower (Norda), Barton Heyman (Lt. Blane), Frank Cooper.

"The 7th Is Made Up of Phantoms" (12-6-63): Ron Foster (Sgt. Connors), Warren Oates (Corporal Langsford), Randy Boone (Private McCluskey), Robert Bray (Captain), Wayne Mallory (Scout), Greg Morris (Lieutenant), Jeffrey Morris (radio operator), Jacque Shelton, Lew Brown.

"A Short Drink from a Certain Fountain" (12-13-63): Patrick O'Neal (Harmon Gordon), Ruta Lee (Flora Gordon), Walter Brooke (Dr. Raymond Gordon).

"Ninety Years Without Slumbering" (12-20-63): Ed Wynn (Sam Forstmann), James Callahan (Doug Kirk), William Sargeant (Dr. Mel Avery), Carolyn Kearney (Marnie Kirk), Carol Byron (Carol Chase), John Pickard, Dick Wilson, Chuck Hicks.

"Ring-A-Ding Girl" (12-27-63): Maggie McNamara (Bunny Blake), Betty Lou Gerson (Cici), Mary Munday (Hildy), David Macklin

(Bud), George Mitchell, Vic Perrin, Hank Patterson, Bing Russell, Bill Hickman.

"You Drive" (1-3-64): Edward Andrews (Oliver Pope), Helena Westcott (Lillian Pope), Kevin Hagen (Pete Radcliff), John Hanek (policeman), Totty Ames (witness).

"The Long Morrow" (1-10-64): Robert Lansing (Doug Stanfield), George Macready (Dr. Bixler), Marlette Hartley (Sandy Horn), Edward Binns (Gen. Walters), William Swan (technician).

"The Self-Improvement of Salvatore Ross" (1-17-64): Don Gordon (Salvatore Ross), Gail Kobe (Leah Maitland), Vaughn Taylor (Mr. Maitland), Douglas Dumbrille (Mr. Holpert), J. Pat O'Malley, Seymour Cassel, Doug Lambert, Ted Jacques, Kathleen O'Malley.

"Number Twelve Looks Just Like You" (1-24-64): Collin Wilcox (Marilyn Cuberle), Pamela Austin (Val), Richard Long (Rock/Dr. Mann/Dr. Hortel/orderly/intern/Nickle), Suzy Parker (Lana/maid/patient/Simmons/Jane Doe).

"Black Leather Jackets" (1-31-64): Lee Kinsolving (Scott), Shelly Fabares (Ellen Tillman), Denver Pyle (Stu Tillman), Irene Hervey (Martha Tillman), Michael Forest (Steve), Michal Conrad (Sheriff Harper), Tom Gillerman (Fred), Wayne Heffley (furniture mover).

"Night Call" (2-7-64): Gladys Cooper (Elva Keen), Nora Marlowe (Margaret), Martine Bartlett (Miss Finch),

"From Agnes - With Love" (2-14-64): Wally Cox (James Elwood), Ralph Taeger (Walter Holmes), Sue Randall (Millie), Raymond Bailey (lab supervisor), Byron Kane, Nan Peterson, Don Keefer.

"Spur of the Moment" (2-12-64): Diana Hyland (Anne Henderson), Philip Ober (Mr. Henderson), Marsha Hunt (Mrs. Henderson), Roger Davis (David), Jack Raine, Robert Hogan.

"An Occurrence at Owl Creek Bridge" (2-28-64): Roger Jacquet (Peyton Farguhar), Anne Cornaly (Mrs. Farguhar).

"Queen of the Nile" (3-6-64): Ann Blythe (Pamela Norris), Lee Phillips (Jordon Herrick), Celia Lovsky (Mrs. Draper), Frank Ferguson, Ruth Phillips, James Tyler.

"What's in the Box?" (3-13-64):

William Demarest (Joe Britt), Joan Blondell (Phyllis Britt), Herbert C. Lytton (Doctor), Howard Wright (Judge), Sterling Holloway (TV repairman), Sandra Gould (girlfriend), Douglas Bank, Ron Stoker, Tony Miller, John L. Sullivan, Ted Christy.

"The Masks" (3-20-64): Robert Keith (Jason Foster), Milton Selzer (Wilfred Harper), Virginia Gregg (Emily Harper), Brooke Hayward (Paula Harper), Alan Sues (Wilfred Harper, Jr.), Willis Bouchey, Bill Walker.

"I Am the Night - Color Me Black" (3-27-64): Michael Constantine (Sheriff Koch), Paul Fix (Colbey), Terry Becker (Jagger), George Lindsay (Pierce), Ivan Dixon, Eve McVeagh, Elizabeth Harrower, Douglas Bank, Ward Wood.

"Sounds and Silences" (4-3-64): John McGiver (Roswell G. Flemington), Penny Singleton (Mrs. Flemington), Michael Fox (Psychiatrist), Francis de Sales (Doctor), William Benedict (Conklin), Renee Aubrey (secretary).

"Ceasar and Me" (4-10-64): Jackie Cooper (Jonathan West), Susanne Cupito (Susan), Sarah Selby (Mrs. Dudohy), Ken Konopka (Mr. Miller), Stafford Repp (pawnshop owner), Don Gazzinaga (detective), Sidney Marion (watchman), Olan Soule.

"The Jeopardy Room" (4-17-64): Martin Landau (Major Ivan Kuchenko), John Van Dreelan (Vassilov), Robert Kelljan (Boris).

"Stopover in a Quiet Town" (4-24-64): Barry Nelson (Bob Frazier), Nancy Malone (Millie Frazier), Denise Lynn, Karen Norris.

"The Encounter" (5-1-64): George Takei (Taro), Neville Brand (Fenton).

"Garrity and the Graves" (5-8-64): John Dehner (Jarred Garrity), J. Pat O'Malley (Gooberman), Stanley Adams (bartender), Norman Leavitt, Percy Helton, John Cliff.

"The Brain Center at Whipples" (5-15-64): Richard Deacon (Wallace Whipple), Paul Newlan (Hanley), Ted De Corsia (Dickerson), Jack Crowder (technician), S. Michaels (bartender), Burt Conroy.

"Come Wander with Me" (5-22-64): Gary Crosby (Floyd Burney), Bonnie Beecher (Mary Rachel), Hank Patterson (storekeeper), John Bolt (Billy Joe).

"The Fear" (5-29-64): Mark

(TWILIGHT ZONE cont.) Richman (Trooper), Hazel Court (Charlotte Scott).

"The Bewitchin' Pool" (6-19-64): Mary Badham (Sport), Tim Stafford (Jeb), Georgia Simmons (Aunt T.), Tod Andrews (Gil), Dee Hartford (Gloria), Kim Hector (Whitt), Harold Gould.

U.F.O. 1972-73. Ed Bishop (Cmdr. Edward Straker), George Sewell (Col. Alec Freeman), Gabrielle Drake (Lt. Gay Ellis), Michael Billington (Col. Paul Foster), Vladek Sheybal (Dr. Douglas Jackson), Wanda Ventham (Col. Virginia Lake), Grant Taylor (Gen. James Henderson), Harry Baird (Mark Bradley), Antoni Ellis (Lt. Joan Harrington), Dolores Mantez (Lt. Nina Barry), Anne Cullinan Taylor (Lt. Sharon Maltz), Peter Gordeno (Capt. Peter Karlin), Keith Alexander (Lt. Keith Ford), Patrick Allen (Tunner), Norma Roland (Miss Eland), Hugh Armstrong (Third Mobile Officer), Jeremy Wilkin (Skydiver navigator), Jon Kelly (Skydiver engineer), Georganna Moon (Skydiver operator), David Warbeck (Skydiver Captain), Andrea Allan (Moon Base operator), Ayshea (S.H.A.D.O. Operative), Penny Spencer (S.H.A.D.O. Operative), Louise Pajd (Miss Scott), Garry Myers (Lew Waterman), Mark Hawkins (intercepton pilot), Michael Ferrand (radar technician), Lois Maxwell (Miss Holland).

"Identified" (9-11-72): Basil Dignam, Shane Rimmer, Michael Mundell.

"A Question of Priorities" (9-18-72): Barnaby Shaw (John), Suzanne Neve (Mary), Mary Merall, Richard Aylen.

"The Dalotek Affair" (9-25-72): Tracy Reed (Jane Carson), David Weston, Philip Latham, Clinton Greyn, John Breslin.

"Confetti Check A-OK" (10-2-72): Suzanne Neve (Mary), Julian Grant, Michael Forest, Geoffrey Hinsliff, Frank Tregear.

"The Psychobombs" (10-9-72): Deborah Grant (Linda), David Collings (Clark), Mike Pratt (Mason), Tom Adams, Gavin Campbell.

"Court Martial" (10-16-72): Pippa Steel, Jack Hedley, Noel Davis, Neil McCallum (Mason).

"The Square Triangle" (10-23-72): Adrienne Corri (Liz Newton), Patrick Mowrer (Fowler), Allan Cuthbertson (Newton), Tutte Lemkow.

"Flight Path" (10-30-72): Keith Grenville (Dawson), George Cole (Paul Roper), Sonia Fox (Carol Roper), Maxwell Shaw.

"Mindbender" (11-6-72): Stuart Damon, Charles Tingwell, Craig Gunter, Al Mancini, Steven Berkoff.

"The Computer Affair" (11-13-72): Nigel Lambert, Maxwell Shaw, Hein Viljoen, Dennis Plenty.

"The Cat with Ten Lives" (11-20-72): Alexis Kanner (Regan), Geraldine Moffatt (Jean), Steven Berkoff, Al Manicni, Windsor Davies.

"The Sound of Silence" (11-27-72): Michael Jayston (Russell Stone), Susan Jameson (Anne), Nigel Gregory, Richard Vernon.

"Conflict" (12-4-72): Gerard Norman, David Courtland, Drewe Henley, Alan Tucker.

"Ordeal" (12-11-72): Quinn O'Hara (Sylvia Graham), David Healy, Mark Hawkins, Basil Moss, Joseph Morris.

"The Responsibility Seat" (12-18-72): Jane Merrow (Joe), Paul Gillard, Michael Kilgarriff.

"The Man Who Came Back" (12-25-72): Derren Nesbitt (Craig Collins), Gary Raymond (Col. Grey), Roland Culver, Mike Stevens.

"Kill Straker" (1-1-73): David Sumner, Annette Kerr, Peter Burton, Gary Files, Penny Jackson, Mark Hawkins.

"E.S.P." (1-8-73): John Stratton (Croxley), Douglas Wilmer, Deborah Stanford, Donald Tandy, Stanley McGeorgh.

"The Long Sleep" (1-15-73): Tessa Wyatt (Catherine), Christian Roberts (Tim), Christopher Roberts (Robbie), John Garrie, Anoushka Hempel.

"Reflections in the Water" (1-22-73): James Cosmo, Frank Mann.

"Destruction" (1-29-73): Philip Madoc, Stephanie Beacham, Edwin Richfield, Peter Blythe, Jimmy Winston.

"Close-Up" (2-5-73): Jean Marsh, Matt Zimmerman, Sue Gerrard, Robin Bailey, Paula Li Schiu.

"Sub-Smash" (2-19-73): Maxwell Shaw, Stanley McGeogh.

"Survival" (2-26-73): Gito Santana, Steven Berkoff.

"Timelash" (3-5-73): Fred
Santos, Philip Howard, Gerard Murray.

UNEXPECTED.
"The Witch of the Eight Islands"
(6-8-56): John Kellogg.

U.S. STEEL HOUR.
"The Bottle Imp" (3-13-57):
Farley Granger (Philip), Thayer
David (Andre Girard), Robert Fortin
(Rene), Geoffrey Holder (Calypso
Singer), Abe Simon (Pinaud), Paul
Andor (Uncle), Francis Compton (old
man).
    "The Two Worlds of Charlie
Gordon" (2-22-61): Cliff Robertson
(Charlie Gordon), Mona Freeman
(Jane Rawlins), Maxwell Shaw (Dr.
Strauss), Joanna Ross (Dr. Kinnian),
Gerald O'Loughlin (Joe).

VACATION PLAYHOUSE.
"The Big Brain" (8-19-63):
Frank Aletter (Lester Belstrup),
Ellen McRae (Ellen), Evelyn Ward
(Adele Weston), Mickey Sholdar
(Chuck Weston), George Niese (Sey-
mour), Bert Remsen (policeman).
    "The Good Old Days" (7-11-66):
Darryl Hickman (Rok), Kathleen
Freeman (Mommy), Ned Glass (Daddy),
Jacques Aubuchon (Soc), Dodo Denny
(Ugh), Chris Noel (Pantha), Dean
Moray (Kid).

VOYAGE TO THE BOTTOM OF THE
SEA. 1964-68. Richard Basehart
(Adm. Harriman Nelson), David
Hedison (Cmdr. Lee Crane), Robert
Dowdell (Lt. Cmdr. Chip Morton),
Del Monroe (Dowalski), Paul
Trinka (Patterson), Henry Kulky
(CPO Curley Jones) 64-65; Arch
Whiting (Sparks), Nigel McKeand
(Sonar) 64-65; Mark Slade (crew-
man) 64-65; Terry Becker (Chief
Sharkey) 65-68; Paul Carr (crew-
man), Allan Hunt (Stu Riley) 65-66;
Richard Bull (Doctor), semi-regular.
    "Eleven Days to Zero" (9-14-
64): Eddie Albert (Dr. Fred Wilson),
John Zaremba (Dr. Selby), Bill Hudson
Marcuse (Dr. Gamma), Bill Hudson
(Capt. Phillips), Booth Colman (chair-
man), Gordon Gilbert (O'Brien), Hal
Torey (Chairman), Barney Biro (Army
General).
    "The City Beneath the Sea" (9-
21-64): Hurd Hatfield (Zeraff), Linda
Cristal (Melina), John Anderson (Round-
Face), Peter Brocco (Xanthos), Peter
Mamakos (Nicolas), Al Ruscio (Dmitri).

"The Fear Makers" (9-28-64):
Edgar Bergen (Dr. Arthur Kenner),
Lloyd Bochner (Dr. Martin Davis),
Walter Brooke (Dan Case), William
Sargent (Anders), Martin Kosleck
(Cirector), Robert Payne (Murdock),
Ed Prentiss (James).
    "The Mist of Silence" (10-5-64):
Rita Gam (Detta Dasone), Mike Kellin
(Gen. Esteban D'Alvarez), Alejandro
Rey (Ricardo Galdez), Booth Colman
(Chairman), Edward Colmans (Presi-
dent Fuentes), Henry Del Gado (Capt.
Serra), Doug Lambert (Malone).
    "The Price of Doom" (10-12-64):
Jill Ireland (Julie Lyle), David Opatoshu
(Dr. Karl Reisner), John Milford (Philip
Wesley), Steve Ihnat (Pennell), Pat
Priest (Mrs. Pennell), Dan Seymour
(General), Ivan Triesault (crewcut man),
    "The Sky Is Falling" (10-26-64):
Charles McGraw (Rear Adm. Walter
Tobin), Adam Williams (Chief), Frank
Ferguson (Air Force General), Joseph
Di Reda (spaceman).
    "Turn Back the Clock" (10-26-
64): Nick Adams (Jason Kemp), Yvonne
Craig (Carol Denning), Les Tremayne
(Dr. Denning), Vitina Marcus (Native
Girl), Robert Cornthwaite (Zeigler).
    "The Village of Guilt" (11-22-
64): Richard Carlson (Mattson), Anna-
Lisa (Sigrid), Steven Geray (Dalgren),
G. Stanley Jones (Anderson), Torben
Meyer (Proprietor), Kort Falkenburg
(Father), Gordon Gilbert (O'Brien),
Erik Holland (Gartern), Frank Richards
(Hassler).
    "Hot Line" (11-9-64): Michael
Ansara (Gregory Malinoff), Everett
Sloan (Gronski), Ford Rainey (the
President), Robert Carson.
    "Submarine Sunk Here" (11-16-
64): Carl Reindel (Evans), Eddie Ry-
ker (Harker), Robert Doyle (Blake),
Wright King (Dr. Baines), Paul Comi
(Lt. Bishop), George Lindsey (Collins),
Derrik Lewis (O'Brien).
    "The Magnus Beam" (11-23-64):
Mario Alcaide (Major Amadi), Moni-
que Lemaire (Juana Rossi), Jacques
Aubuchon (Abdul Azziz), Malchi Throne
(Gen. Gamal).
    "No Way Out" (11-30-64): Than
Wyenn (Anton Koslow), Danielle De-
Metz (Anna Ravec), Jan Merlin (Victor
Vail), Oscar Beregi, Jr. (Col. Lascoe),
Richard Webb (Parker), Don Wilbanks
(Wilson).
    "The Blizzard Maker" (12-7-64):
Werner Klemperer (Frederick Cregar),
Milton Selzer (Dr. Charles Melton),
Kenneth McDonald (Surgeon).

(VOYAGE TO THE BOTTOM OF
THE SEA cont.)
"The Ghost of Moby Dick" (12-
14-64): Edward Binns (Dr. Walter
Bryce), June Lockhart (Ellen Bryce),
Bob Beekman (Jimmy Bryce).

"Long Live the King" (12-21-
64): Carroll O'Connor (Old John),
Michael Petit (Prince Ang), Michael
Pate (Col. Meger), Jan Arvan (Georges), Sara Shane (Countess).

"Hail to the Chief" (12-28-64):
Ford Rainey (the President), Viveca
Lindfors (Laura Rettig), David Lewis
(Dr. Kranz), Lorence Kerr (Ober-
hansly), John Hoyt (Gen. George
Beeker), James Doohan (Tobin), Nancy
Kovack (Monique), Tom Palmer (Dr.
Taylor).

"The Last Battle" (1-4-65): John
Van Dreelan (Col. Alfred Schroder),
Dayton Lummis (Dr. Gustav Reinhardt),
Joe De Santis (Anton Milkos), Ben
Wright (Benjamin Brewster), Rudy
Solari (Alejandro Tomas), Eric Fel-
dary (Col. Carl Deiner), Sandra
Williams (stewardess).

"Mutiny" (1-11-64): Harold J.
Stone (Adm. Jiggs Stark), Jay Lanin
(Captain), Steve Harris (Fowler),
Lew Brown (Jackson).

"Doomsday" (1-18-65): Ford
Rainey (the President), Donald Harron
(Cmdr. Corbett), Paul Genge (Gen.
Ashton), Sy Prescott (Corporal), Paul
Carr (Casey).

"The Invaders" (1-25-65): Robert
Duvall (Zar), Michael McDonald
(Foster).

"The Indestructible Man" (2-1-
65): Michael Constantine (Dr. Brand).

"The Buccaneer" (2-8-65):
Barry Atwater (Mr. Logan), George
Keymas (Igor), Emile Genest (French
Captain).

"The Human Computer" (2-15-
65): Walter Sande (2nd Admiral),
Herbert Lytton (1st Admiral), Ted
De Corsia (Foreign General), Simon
Scott (Reston), Harry Millard (agent).

"The Saboteur" (2-22-65): Warren Stevens (Forester), Bert Freed
(Dr. Ullman), James Brolin (Spencer), Russell Horton (Fred).

"Cradle of the Deep" (3-1-65):
John Anderson (Dr. Janus), Paul
Carr (Clark), Howard Wendell (Dr.
Andrew Benton), Derrick Lew (O'Brein),
Robert Pane (helmsman).

"The Amphibians" (3-8-65):
Skip Homeier (Dr. Jenkins), Curt
Conway (Dr. Winslow), Frank Graham
(Danny), Zale Perry (Andie).

"The Exile" (3-15-65): Edward
Asner (Alexsei Brynov), David Sheiner
(Josip), James Frawley (Semenov),
Jason Wingreen (Mikhail Brynov),
Harry Davis (Dr. Konstantin).

"The Creature" (2-22-65):
Leslie Nielsen (Capt. Wayne Adams),
Pat Culliton (crewman), William
Stevens (radar man), Robert Lipton.

"The Enemies" (3-29-65):
Henry Silva (Gen. Tau), Malchi
Throne (Dr. Shinera), Robert Sampson
(Capt. Williams), Tom Skerritt (Frank
Richardson).

"The Secret of the Lock" (4-5-
65): Hedley Mattingly (Insp. Lester),
Torin Thatcher (Prof. Alistari Mac-
Dougall), George Mitchell (Angus),
John McLiam (Andrews).

"The Condemned" (4-12-65):
J. D. Cannon (Adm. Falk), Arthur
Franz (Archer), Alvy Moore (Hoff),
John Goddard (Tracy).

"The Traitor" (4-19-65):
George Sanders (Maj. Gen. Fenton),
Michael Pate (Hamid), Susan Flannery
(Miss Nelson), Paul Kremin (waiter).

"Jonah and the Whale" (9-19-65):
Gia Scala (Dr. Katya Markhova),
Robert Pane (helmsman), Pat Culliton
(crewman).

"Time Bomb" (9-26-65): Ina
Balin (Litchka), John Zarmeba (Adm.
William Johnson), Susan Flannery
(Katie), Richard Loo (Li Tung), Dr.
Harald Dyrenforth (Doctor), Richard
Gilden (Tai), Jon Kowal (policeman),
Lee Millar (soldier), Frank Delfino
(boy).

"And Five of Us Are Left"
(10-3-65): Philip Pine (Lt. Ryan),
Robert Doyle (Frank Worden), James
Anderson (Lt. Wilson), Teru Shimada
(Nakamaru), Kent Taylor (Johnson),
Francoise Ruggieri (Brenda), Ed
McCready (Hill).

"The Cyborg" (10-10-65):
Victor Buono (Dr. Tabor Ulrich),
Nancy Hsueh (Tish Sweetly), Brooke
Bundy (Gundi), Fred Crane (Cyborg's
voice), Nick Colasanto (reporter),
Stanley Schneider (sailor), Tom Cur-
tis (1st technician).

"Escape from Venice" (10-17-
65): Renzo Cesana (Count Perdie
Straglione), Danica d'Hondt (Lola
Hale), Margot Stevenson (Betty
Harmon), Vincent Gardenia (Giuseppe
Bellini), Delphi Lawrence (Julietta),
Thomas Nello (Antonio), Ken Tilles
(gondolier), Rachel Romen (Alicia),
Freddie Roberto (croupier).

"The Left-Handed Man" (10-24-65):

Regis Toomey (George W. Penfield), Cyril Delevanti (Noah Grafton), Barbara Bouchet (Tippy Penfield), Charles Dierkop (Left-Handed Man), Judy Lang (Angie), Michael Barrier (Cabrillo), Fred Crane (Lasher).
"The Deadliest Game" (10-31-65): Lloyd Bochner (Gen. Hobson), Robert Cornthwaite (Gen. Reed Michaels), Audrey Dalton (Dr. Lydia Parrish), Robert F. Simon (the President).
"Leviathan" (11-7-65): Liam Sullivan (Dr. Anthony Sterling), Karen Steele (Cara Sloane).
"The Peacemaker" (11-14-65): John Cassavetes (Everett Lang), Whit Bissell (Connors), Irene Tsu (Su Yin), Walter Woolf King (Hansen), George Young (Lang's accomplice), Lloyd Kino (policeman), Lee Kolima (Junk Captain), George Zaima (scientist), Dale Ishimoto (Premier).
"The Silent Saboteurs" (11-21-65): Pilar Seurat (Moana Yutang), George Takei (Li Cheng), Bert Freed (Halden), Alex D'Arcy (Col. Lago), Phil Posner (Stevens), Robert Chadwick (1st astronaut), Ted Jordan (2nd astronaut).
"The X Factor" (12-5-65): John McGiver (Alexander Corby), Bill Hudson (Capt. Shire), Jan Merlin (Henderson), George Tyne (Liscomb), Anthony Brand (technician).
"The Machines Strike Back" (12-12-65): Roger C. Carmel (Adm. Halder), Bert Remsen (Sen. Kimberley), John Gallaudet (Adm. Johnson), Francoise Ruggeri (Verna Trober).
"Monster from Outer Space" (12-19-65): Wayne Heffley (Doctor), Hal Torey (Naval Commander), Preston Hanson (Flight Director), Lee Delano (technician).
"Terror on Dinosaur Island" (12-26-65): Paul Carr (Seaman Benson).
"The Killers of the Deep" (1-2-66): Michael Ansara (Capt. Tomas Ruiz), Patrick Wayne (Ensign Fraser), James Frawley (Manolo), John Newton (Cmdr. Richard Lawrence), Dallas Mitchell (Destroyer's sonar mate), Bruce Mars (bosun's mate), Gus Trikonis (sonar man).
"Deadly Creature Below" (1-9-66): Nehemiah Persoff (Francis J. Dobbs), Paul Comi (Joe Hawkins), Wayne Heffley (Doctor).
"The Phantom" (1-16-66): Alfred Ryder (Capt. Gerhard Krueger).
"The Sky's on Fire" (1-23-66): David J. Stewart (Dr. August Weber),

Robert H. Harris (Dr. Eric Carleton), Frank Marth (Cmdr. McHenry).
"Graveyard of Fear" (1-30-66): Robert Loggia (Dr. Crandall Ames), Marian Moses (Karyl Simmons).
"The Shape of Doom" (2-6-66): Kevin Hagen (Dr. Alex Holden).
"Dead Man's Doubloons" (2-13-66): Albert Salmi (Capt. Brent), Robert Brubaker (Adm. Howard), Allen Jaffe (Sebastian), Stan Kamber (sailor).
"The Death Ship" (2-20-66): Lew Gallo (Adm. Judson Stroller), June Vincent (Ava Winters), Ivan Triesault (Eric Klaus), Elizabeth Perry (Tracy Stewart), David Sheiner (Arthur Chandler), Herbert Voland (Glenn Carter), Harry David (Dr. Frank Templeton), Ed Connelly (Rourke), Alan Baxter (man), Bob Swimmer (pirate).
"The Monster's Web" (2-27-66): Mark Richman (Mark Gantt), Barry Coe (Cmdr. Bill Balter), Sean Morgan (sonar man).
"The Menfish" (3-6-66): Garry Merrill (Adm. Park), John Dehner (Dr. Borgman), Vic Lundin (Hansjurg), Wayne Heffley (Doctor), Roy Jenson (Johnson), George T. Sims (Bailey), Lawrence Mann (diver).
"The Mechanical Man" (3-13-66): James Darren (Omir), Arthur O'Connell (Paul), Seymour Cassel (Jensen), Cec Linder (Van Druten), Robert Riordan (Vendor).
"The Return of the Phantom" (3-20-66): Alfred Ryder (Capt. Gerhard Krueger), Vitina Marcus (Lani).
"The Monster from the Inferno" (9-18-66): Arthur Hill (Lindsey).
"Werewolf" (9-25-66): Charles Aidman (Dr. Hollis), Douglas Bank (Dr. Witt).
"The Day the World Ended" (10-2-66): Skip Homeier (Sen. William Dennis).
"Night of Terror" (10-9-66): Henry Jones (Elton Sprague), Jerry Catron (Buccaneer).
"The Terrible Toys" (10-16-66): Paul Fix (Sam Burke), Francis X. Bushman (Old Man), Jim Mills (voice).
"Day of Evil" (10-23-66)
"Deadly Waters" (10-30-66). Don Gordon (Stan Kowalski), Lew Gallo (Kruger), Harry Lauter (Cmdr. Finch).
"The Thing from Inner Space" (10-6-66): Hugh Marlowe (Bainbridge Wells), Dawson Palmer (Thing).
"The Death Watch" (11-13-66).

(VOYAGE TO THE BOTTOM OF
THE SEA cont.)
    "Deadly Invasion" (11-20-66):
Warren Stevens (Sam Garrity),
Michael Fox (Gen. Haines), Ashley
Gilbert (Kelly), Brent Davis (Peters).
    "The Haunted Submarine" (11-
27-66).
    "The Plant Man" (12-4-66):
William Smithers (Ben Wilson/John
Wilson).
    "The Lost Bomb" (12-11-66):
John Lupton (Dr. Bradley), Gerald
Mohr (Vadim), George Keymas
(Zane).
    "The Brand of the Beast"
(12-18-66).
    "The Creature" (1-1-67):
Lyle Bettger (Dr. King).
    "Death from the Past" (1-8-
67): John Van Dreelan (Adm.
Von Neuberg), Jan Merlin (Lt.
Froehlich).
    "The Heat Monster" (1-15-
67): Alfred Ryder (Dr. Olaf Berg-
strom), Don Knight (Sven Larson).
    "The Fossil Men" (1-22-67):
Brendan Dillon (Capt. Jacob Wren),
Jerry Catron (Richards).
    "The Mermaid" (1-29-67):
Diane Webber (Mermaid).
    "The Mummy" (2-5-67).
    "The Shadowman" (2-12-67):
Jerry Catron (Shadowman), Tyler
McVey.
    "No Escape from Death" (2-
19-67).
    "Doomsday Island" (2-26-67):
Jock Gaynor (Lars).
    "The Wax Men" (3-5-67):
Michael Dunn (Clown).
    "The Deadly Cloud" (3-12-67):
Robert Carson (Jurgenson), Bill
Baldwin.
    "Destroy Seaview!" (3-19-67):
Arthur Space (Dr. Land), Jerry
Catron (Leader).
    "Fires of Death" (9-17-67):
Victor Jory (Dr. Turner).
    "The Deadly Dolls" (9-24-67),
Vincent Price (Prof. Multiple),
Ronald P. Martin (Puppeteer).
    "Cave of the Dead" (10-8-67):
Warren Stevens (Lt. Cmdr. Peter
Van Wyck).
    "Journey with Fear" (10-15-
67): Gene Dynarski (Centaur I),
Jim Gosa (Centaur II), Eric Mat-
thews (Wilson).
    "Sealed Orders" (10-22-67).
    "Man of Many Faces" (10-29-
67): Jock Gaynor (Dr. Randolph Mason),
Brad Arnold (Page), Howard Culver

(reporter).
    "Fatal Cargo" (11-5-67): Wood-
row Parfrey (Leo Brock), Jon Lormer
(Dr. Pierre Blanchard).
    "Time Lock" (11-12-67): John
Crawford (Alpha).
    "Rescue" (11-19-67): Don
Dubbins (CPO Beach).
    "Terror" (11-26-67): Damian
O'Flynn (Dr. Thompson), Pat Cul-
liton (Dunlap), Thom Brann (crewman
No. 1), Brent Davis (crewman No. 2).
    "A Time to Die" (12-3-67):
Henry Jones (Mr. Pem).
    "Blow Up" (12-10-67).
    "Deadly Amphibians" (12-17-
67): Don Matheson (Proto), Joey
Tata (corpsman), Pat Culliton (guard).
    "The Return of Blackbeard"
(12-31-67): Malachi Throne (Black-
beard).
    "The Terrible Leprechaun"
(1-7-68): Walter Burke (Mickey/
Patrick), Ralph Garrett (Somers),
Pat Culliton (corpsman), John Bellah
(crewman).
    "The Lobster Man" (1-21- 68):
Vic Lundin (Lobster Man).
    "Nightmare" (1-28-68): Paul
Mantee (Jim Bentley).
    "The Abominable Snowman"
(2-4-68): Dusty Cadis (Rayburn),
Frank Babich (corpsman), Bruce
Mars (guard).
    "The Secret of the Deep" (2-11-
68): Mark Richman (John Hendrix).
    "Man-Beast" (2-18-68): Law-
rence Montaigne (Dr. Kermit Braddock).
    "Savage Jungle" (2-25-68):
Perry Lopez (Keeler), Patrick Cul-
liton (Alien).
    "Flaming Ice" (3-3-68): Michael
Pate (Gelid), Frank Babich (Frost
Man No. 1), George Robotham (Frost
Man No. 2).
    "Attack!" (3-10-68): Skip
Homeier (Robek), Kevin Hagen (Ko-
mal).
    "The Edge of Doom" (3-17-68):
Scott McFadden (helmsman).
    "The Death Clock" (3-24-68):
Chris Robinson (Corpsman Mallory).
    "No Way Back" (3-31-68):
Henry Jones (Mr. Pem), William
Beckley (Maj. John Andre), Barry
Atwater (Gen. Benedict Arnold).

WALT DISNEY.
    "Beyond Witch Mountain" (2-
20-82): Eddie Albert (Jason O'Day),
Efrem Zimbalist, Jr. (Aristotle Bolt),
Tracey Gold (Tia), Andy Freman
(Tony), J. D. Cannon (Deranian),

Noah Berry, Jr. (Uncle Bene), Stephanie Blackmore (Adrian Molina), Peter Hobbs (Dr. Morton), Gene Dynarski (Lawrence), William H. Bassett (Lowell Roberts), Eric Avid (Gregory), James Luisi (foreman), Lola Mason (lady driver), Hettie Lynn Hurtes (reporter), Kirk Cameron (boy).

WAY OUT. 1961. Roald Dahl (Host).
"William and Mary" (3-31-61).
"The Sisters" (4-14-61): Lois Smith, Carmen Mathews.
"Button, Button" (4-8-21): Warren Finnerty, Dick O'Neill.
"I Heard You Calling Me" (5-5-61): Constance Ford, Anthony Dawson.
"The Croaker" (5-12-61): John McGiver, Richard Thomas.
"False Face" (5-26-61): Alfred Ryder (Michael Drake), Martin Brooks (the Man), Gerry Jedd (Rita Singer), Lester Rawlins (Freddy Davis), Louise Larabee (waitress), Dana Elcar (hotel manager).
"Dissolve to Black" (6-2-61): Kathleen Widdoes (Bonnie Draco), Richard Morse (Daytime Harry), James Patterson (Nightime Harry), Mark Lenard (Daytime Paul), Leonardo Cimino (Daytime Murderer), Moultrie Patton (George Carver).
"Death Wish" (6-9-61): Charlotte Rae (Hazel), Don Keefer (George), Chuck Morgan (Charon), Heywood Hale Broun (Petard).
"The Overnight Case" (6-16-61): Kevin McCarthy (Dr. Paul Sandham), Barbara Baxley (Norma), Martin Balsam (Bill Clayton), Helen Stenborg (Miss Wickford), Leon B. Stevens (man).
"Hush-Hush" (6-33-61): Philip Coolidge (Prof. Ernest Lydecker), Rosemary Murphy (Bernice Lydecker), Woodrow Parfrey (William Rogers), Barry Newman (police officer), Mary Cushman (Maegaret Ainsley).
"Side Show" (6-30-61): Murray Hamilton (Harold Potter), Myron McCormick (Barker), Margeret Phillips (Cassandra), Doris Roberts (Edna Potter), Martin Huston (Ronnie).
"Soft Focus" (7-7-61): Barry Morse (Peter Pell), Joan Hotchkis (Louise Pell), Mitch Ryan (Bill Fontaine), Anne Meacham (Dolly Grainger), Dortha Duckworth (Mrs. Bickell).
"20/20" (7-14-61): Walter Slezak (Harvey Cartwright), Ruth

White (Stephanie Cartwright), Frederick Rolf (Jellifer), Sudie Bond (Mrs. Jellifer), Tom Shirley (Huddleston).

WEEKEND SPECIAL.
"The Girl with E.S.P." (10-20-79): Rachel Longaker (Laura), Lisa Alpert (Beth), Tracy Bergman (Jill).
"The Ghost of Thomas Kempe" (11-3-79 & 11-10-79): Robert Sampson (Harrison), Madelyn Cain (Mrs. Harrison), Portia Nelson (Mrs. Verity), Tara Talboy (Helen), Shane Sinutko, Garrett O'Connor.
"The Gold Bug" (2-2-80 & 2-9-80): Roberts Blossom (LeGrand), Geoffrey Holder (Jupiter), Sudie Bond (Agnes), Anthony Michael Hall.

WHEN WITCHES HOVERED. (10-31-73)
"The Devil's Hopyard": James Quinn (Abe Brown), Massie Owen (Obadiah Brown).
"The Machimoodus": John Colle (Narrator), Hal Dorsey (Parson Straightback), Randall Feldman (Acton), Robert Gustafson (Dr. Steele).

WHERE'S EVERETT?
Pilot (4-18-66): Alan Alda (Arnold Barker), Patricia Smith (Sylvia Barker), Nicholas Coster (Dr. Paul Jellicoe), Dorreen Miller (Lizzie), Frank DeVol (Murdock), Robert Cleaves (milkman).

WILD WILD WEST. 1965-69. Robert Conrad (James West), Ross Martin (Artemus Gordon), Charles Aidman (Jeremy Pike) 68-69.
"The Night of the Inferno" (9-17-65): Victor Buono (Wing Fat/Juan Manola), Suzanne Pleshette (Lydia Monteran), Nehemiah Persoff (Juan Manola/Gen. Andreas Cassinello), James Gregory (Pres. Ulysses S. Grant), Walter Woolf King (Col. Kelly Shear), Bebe Louie (Mei Mei), Alberto Morin (Major Domo), Chet Stratton (Bedford), Tom Reese (wagon driver), Phil Chambers (train captain), Warren Parker (train engineer), Clint Ritchie (lieutenant).
"Night of the Deadly Bed" (9-24-65): J.D. Cannon (Gen. Florey), Danica D'Hondt (Roxanne), Barbara Luna (Gatilla), Anna Shin (Margarita), Bob Heron (Capt. Jackson), Bill Catching (Angelo), Don Diamond (bartender), Jose Gallege (guitar player), Dale Van Sickel (guitar player).

(WILD WILD WEST cont.)

"The Night the Wizard Shook the Earth" (10-1-65): Michael Dunn (Dr. Miguelito Loveless), Leslie Parrish (Greta Lundquist), Richard Kiel (Voltaire), Phoebe Dorin (Antoinette), Sigrid Vladis (Miss Piecemeal), Harry Bartell (Prof. Neilsen), William Mims (Governor of California), Mike Masters (wrestler).

"The Night of the Sudden Death" (10-8-65): Robert Loggia (Warren Trevor), Julia Payne (Corinne Foxx), Antoinette Bower (Janet Coburn), Harlan Warde (Foxx), Elisa Ingram (Cossette), Sandy Kenyon (Hugo), Henry Hunter (Boone), Don Gazzaniga (hotel clerk), Bill Cassady (Sterling), Joel Fluellen (Chief Vonoma).

"The Night of the Casual Killer" (10-15-65): John Dehner (John Maxwell Avery), Ruta Lee (Laurie Morgan), Bill Williams (Marshal Kirby), Charles Davis (Tennyson), Len Lesser (Mason), Mort Mills (Harper), Curtis Taylor (Captain Davis), Ed Gilbert (Tom Hendrix), Dub Taylor (guard).

"The Night of a Thousand Eyes" (10-22-65): Jeff Corey (Captain Coffin), Diane McBain (Jennifer Wingate), Donald O'Kelly (Poavey), Barney Phillips (Captain Tenney), Linda Ho (Oriana), Janine Gray (Crystal), Jeanne Vaughn (Glory), Jack Searl (pilot), Victor French (Arnold), Celeste Yarnell (Miss Purviance).

"The Night of the Glowing Corpse" (10-29-65): Kipp Hamilton (Cluny Ormont), Philip Pine (Lt. Armand Renard), Charles Horvath (Ironfoot), Marion Thompson (Amelie Charlemont), Ron Whelan (Consul General Potez), Oscar Beregi, Jr. (Dr. Jean Paul Ormont), Ralph Roberts (Sen. Hastings), Frank Delfino (barker), Jayne Massey (Cecile), Louise Lawson (blonde).

"The Night of the Dancing Death" (11-5-65): Mark Richman (Prince Gio), Ilze Taurins (Marianna), Leslie Brander (Princess Gina Carlotta), Arthur Batanides (Marius Ascoli), Booth Colman (Amb. Xavier Perkins), Byron Morrow (Major Domo), Francoise Ruggieri (Baroness Nola Kolinski), Wolfe Barzell (Landgrave), Eva Soreny (Baroness), Lynn Carey (imposter).

"The Night of the Double-Edged Knife" (11-12-65): Leslie Nielsen (Maj. Gen. Ball), John Drew Barrymore (American Knife), Charles Davis (Tennyson), Katherine Ross (Sheila Parnell), Elisha Cook, Jr. (Mike McGreavy), Tyler McVey (Parnell),

Harry Townes (Penrose), Vaughn Taylor (Benjamin Adamson), Arthur Spree (Peter), Ed Peck (Merritt), Orrin Cobb (Simon), Harry Lauter.

"The Night That Terror Stalked the Town" (11-19-65): Michael Dunn (Dr. Miguelito Loveless), Richard Kiel (Voltaire), Phoebe Dorin (Antoinette), Jean Hale (Marie Pincher), Joe Hooker (Abernathy), Jordan Shelley (Baron Kolensky), Chuck O'Brien (Janus).

"The Night of the Red-Eyed Madmen" (11-26-65): Martin Landau (Gen. Grimm), Joan Huntington (Sgt. Musk), Shary Marshall (Jenny), Greg Martell (Otto), Tolan Matchings (Lola Bracer), Marianna Case (Cloris), Ted Markland (Jack Talbot), Nelson Olmsted (Sen. Rawls), Don Rizzan (Trooper), Ray Kellogg (Capt. Sandy O'Brien).

"The Night of the Human Trigger" (12-3-65): Burgess Meredith (Prof. Orkney Cadwallader), Kathie Browne (Faith Cadwallader), Greg Palmer (Thaddeus Cadwallader), Mike Masters (Hercules Cadwallader), Virginia Sale (Aunt Martha), Hank Patterson (Mr. Porter), James Jeter (Harry), Robert Phillips (Sam), Robert L. McCord (Sidney), William Henry (Sheriff), Lindsey Workman (bartender), Dick Winslow (piano player), Vernon Scott (clerk).

"The Night of the Torture Chamber" (12-10-65): Alfred Ryder (Horatio Bolt), Henry Beckman (Gov. Bradford/ Sam Jamison), Sigrid Valdis (Miss Piecemeal), Viviane Ventura (Angelique Lousea), H.M. Wynant (Durand), Nadie Sanders (Helva), Mike Abelar (guard).

"The Night of the Howling Light" (12-17-65): Sam Wanamaker (Dr. Arcularis), Scott Marlowe (Ahkeema), Ralph Moody (Ho-Tami), Linda Marsh (Indra), E.J. Andre (superintendant), Ottola Nesmith (Madame Lafarge), Clancy Cooper (Trowbridge), Roy Barcroft (Sikes), Don Kennedy (Junior Officer), Robert Bice (Captain), Dan Riss (Coast Guard Officer), Kay E. Kuter (caged man).

"The Night of the Fatal Trap" (12-24-65): Ron Randall (Col. Vasquez), Joanna Moore (Linda Medford), Joseph Ruskin (Viper), Don Briggs (Cantrell), Charles Davis (Tennyson), Walker Edmiston (Chalrie), Christian Anderson (Mark Dawson), Alan Sues (Matt Dawson), Dal Jenkins (Luke Dawson), Rodolfo Rayos (police chief).

"The Night of the Steel Assassin" (1-7-66): John Dehner (Iron Man Torres),

Sue Anne Langdon (Nina Gilbert),
Allen Jaffe (Guthrie), Sara Taft (Maria),
John Pickard (R. L. Gilbert), Arthur
Malet (Dr. Meyer), Roy Engel (Pres.
Grant), Bruno VeSota (bartender).

"The Night the Dragon Screamed"
(1-14-66): Pilar Seurat (Princess
Ching Ling), Ben Wright (Clive Allen-
by- Smythe), Beulah Quo (May Li),
Richard Loo (Wang Chung), Philip
Ahn (Quong Chu), Benson Fong (Mo
Ti), Gay Lee (Coolie No. 1), Michael
Sung (Coolie No. 2), Nancy Hsueh
(Tsu Hsi), Vince Eder (Lieutenant),
Paul King (oriental).

"The Night of the Grand Emir"
(1-28-66): Yvonne Craig (Ecstasy La
Joie), Robert Middleton (Emir El Emid),
Don Francks (T. Wiggett Jones), Ri-
chard Jaeckel (Christopher Cable),
James Lanphier (Dr. Mohammed Bey),
Tom Palmer (Willard Drapeau), Ar-
thur E. Gould-Porter (George), Ralph
Gary (Clay), Alene Charles (1st girl),
Phyllis Davis (2nd girl).

"The Night of the Flaming Ghost"
(2-4-66): John Doucette (John Obedian
Brown), Karen Sharpe (Barbara Bosley),
Lynn Loring (Carma Vasquez), Robert
Ellenstein (Luis Vasquez), Harry
Bartell (Will Glover), Charles Wagen-
heim (Shukie Summers).

"The Night of the Whirring Death"
(2-18-66): Michael Dunn (Dr. Miguelito
Loveless), Jesse White (Gov. Lewis),
Norman Fell (Jeremiah Ratch), Pamela
Austin (Priscilla Ames), Richard
Kiel (Voltaire), Phoebe Dorin (Antoi-
nette), Barbara Nichols (Bessie Bowen),
Val Avery (John Crane), Jason Wingreen
(policeman), Sam Flynn (clerk), Dick
Reeves.

"The Night of the Puppeteer"
(2-25-66): Lloyd Bochner (Zachariah
Skull), Imalda de Martin (Vivid), John
Hoyt (Justice Vincent Chayne), Nelson
Olmsted (Dr. Lake), Sara Taft (Mrs.
Chayne), Janis Hansen (waitress),
Len Rogel (sandwich-sign man), Jack
Tygett (butler), Wayne Albritton (har-
lequin), Walter Painter (caveman).

"The Night of the Bars of Hell"
(3-4-66): Arthur O'Connell (Warden
Ragan), Indus Arthur (Jenifer McCoy),
Elisha Cook (Gideon McCoy), Paul
Genge (Kross), Chet Stratton (Adams),
Milton Parsons (Executioner), Jenie
Jackson (Kitten), Bob Herron (Borg),
Roy Sickner (Driscoll), Shawn Michaels
(convict painter).

"The Night of the Two-Legged
Buffalo" (3-11-66): Nick Adams (Prince),
Dana Wynter (Lady Beatrice Marquand-

Gaynesford), Robert Emhardt (Claude
Duchamps), Paul Comi (Vittorie Pellegrini), Al Waytt (Coach Driver),
Clint Ritchie (bandit), Lindsay Workman (manager).

"The Night of the Druid's Blood"
(3-25-66): Don Rickles (Asmodeus),
Ann Elder (Lilith/Astarte Waterford),
Bartlett Robinson (Sen. Clay Water-
ford), Rhys Williams (Dr. Tristram),
Don Beddoe (Prof. Robey), Simon
Scott (Col. Fairchild), Sam Wade
(Robert Perry), Susan Browning
(Nurse), Emanuel Thomas (Butler).

"The Night of the Freebooters"
(4-1-66): Keenan Wynn (Thorwald
Wolfe), Maggie Thrett (Rita Leon),
William Campbell (Sgt. Bender),
Andre Phillippe (Enrique Leon),
James Gammon (Egan), Robert Matek
(Oldfield), James Connell (Richard
Henry), John Sterling (worker).

"The Night of the Burning Dia-
mond" (4-8-66): Robert Drivas (Midas
Morgan), Christine Schmidtmer (Lu-
cretia Ivronin), Dan Tobin (Thaddeus
Baines), Calvin Brown (Clive), Vito
Carbonara (Serbian Minister), Whitey
Hughes (Rudd), Chuck O'Brien (Ser-
bian guard).

"The Night of the Murderous
Spring" (4-15-66): Michael Dunn (Dr.
Miguelito Loveless), Jenie Jackson
(Kitten Twitty), Phoebe Dorin (Antoi-
nette), Bill McLean (hotel clerk),
Leonard Falk (attendant), Tod Garrett
(child), William Fawcett (man).

"The Night of the Sudden Plague"
(4-22-66): Theo Marcuse (Dr. Kirby),
Nobu McCarthy (Anna Kirby), Harvey
Levine (Clerk), H. M. Wynant (Coley
Rodman), Elliott Reid (Gov. Hawthorne),
Robert Phillips (Lafe), Eddie Durkin
(Frank Doyle).

"The Night of the Eccentrics"
(9-16-66): Victor Buono (Count Carlos
Manzeppi), Richard Pryor (Villar, the
ventriloquist), Anthony Eisley (Deadeye),
Paul Wallace (Tony Pie), Le Grand
Mellon (Miranda), Roy Jenson (Vance
Markham), Harry Ellerbe (Col. Arm-
strong), Frank Sorello (Benito Juarez),
Mike Masters (Titan).

"The Night of the Golden Cobra"
(9-23-66): Boris Karloff (Maharajah
Singh), Simon Scott (Col. Stanton
Mayo), James Westmoreland (Chandra),
Audrey Dalton (Veda), Jose de Vega
(John Mountaintop), Morgan Farley
(Muhjaj, the snake charmer), Michael
York (Goopta), John Alonzo (Sarcan),
John Mountanto (dancer), Sugata Osaka
(dancer).

"The Night of the Raven" (9-30-66): Michael Dunn (Dr. Miguelito Loveless), Phyllis Newman (Princess Wanakee), Phoebe Dorin (Antoinette), Howard Hoffman (War Eagle), Sandy Josel (Chawtaw), Bill Catching (man).

"The Night of the Big Blast" (10-7-66): Ida Lupino (Dr. Faustina), Mala Powers (Lily Fortune), Patsy Kelly (Prudence Fortune), Robert Miller Driscoll (Lyle Peters), Rita Damico (Carmen), Melville Ruick (Attorney General), Bruce Manning (Miklos).

"The Night of the Returning Dead" (10-14-66): Sammy Davis, Jr. (Jeremiah), Peter Lawford (Carl Jackson), Hazel Court (Elizabeth Carter), Ken Lynch (Tom Kellogg), Alan Baxter (Sheriff Ned Briggs), Frank Wilcox (Judge Bill Mott).

"The Night of the Flying Pie Plate" (10-21-66): William Windom (Ben Victor), Ford Rainey (Simon), Leslie Parrish (Morn), Woodrow Chambliss (Wingo), Pitt Herbert (Byron Pettigrew), Arlene Charles (Alena), Cindy Taylor (Pan).

"The Night of the Poisonous Posey" (10-28-66): Delphi Lawrence (Lucrece Posey), Percy Rodriguez (Brutus the Bonebreaker), Eugene Iglesias (Galleto), Shug Fisher (Sheriff Blayne Cord), George Keymas (Sergei Kaminsk), Michael Masters (Cyril the Firebug), H. M. Wynant (Little Pinto), Andre Phillippe (Ascot Sam), Christopher Cary (Snakes Tolliver), Hal Lynch (Sam Colbern).

"The Night of the Bottomless Pit" (11-4-66): Theo Marcuse (Gustave Maurais/Hubert Crandell), Joan Huntington (Camille Maurais), Tom Drake (Vincent Reed), Mabel Albertson (Mrs. Grimes), Steve Franken (Le Fou), Fred Carson (Le Cochon), Seymour Green (Lime), Chuck O'Brien (Andre Couteau), Greg Martell (guard), Ernie Misco (guard).

"The Night of the Watery Death" (11-11-66): John Van Dreelan (Philippe de La Mer), Jocelyn Lane (Demonique), John Ashley (Lt. Keighley), Forrest Lewis (Captain Pratt), James Galante (Naval Officer).

"The Night of the Green Terror" (11-18-66): Michael Dunn (Dr. Miguelito Loveless), Anthony Caruso (Bright Star), Paul Fix (Old Chief), Phoebe Dorin (Antoinette), Peggy Rea (Bright Star's wife).

"The Night of the Ready-Made Corpse" (11-25-66): Carroll O'Connor

(Fabian Lavendor), Alan Bergman (Claudio Antille/Murphy), Karen Sharpe (Rose Murphy), Patricia Huston (Leda Pellargo), Jack Perkins (Golo), Daniel Ades (Pellargo No. 1): Paul Comi (Pellargo No. 2), Gene Tyburn (Finley), Andi Garrett (barmaid).

"The Night of the Man-Eating House" (12-2-66): Hurd Hatfield (Liston Day), William Talman (Sheriff).

"The Night of the Skulls" (12-16-66): Donald Woods (Sen. Stephen Fenlow), Lisa Gaye (Lorelei), Douglas Henderson (Col. Richmond), Francis de Sales (Charleton), Sebastian Tom (the Samurai), Madame Spivy (the Axe Lady), Micheal Masters (Shanto the Beard), Calvin Browne (Ironhood Harper), Ann Dowd.

"The Night of the Infernal Machine" (12-23-66): Ed Begley (Judge M'Guigan), Bill Zuckert (Chief of Police Bulvon), Elaine Dunn (Vashti), Will Kuluva (Zeno Barota), Vito Scotti (Chef Oefali), John Lormer (Judge Vickerman), William Gwinn (Judge), John Harmon (Moody), Michael Pate (Bledsoe).

"The Night of the Lord of Limbo" (12-30-66): Ricardo Montalban (Vautrain), Dianne Foster (Amanda Vautrain), Felice Orlandi (Capt. Vincent Schofield), Gregory Morton (Levering), Ed Prentiss (Col. Fairchild).

"The Night of the Tottering Tontine" (1-6-67): Harry Townes (Prof. Raven), Robert Emhardt (Grevely), Lisa Pera (Amelia), Michael Road (Dexter), Henry Darrow (Maurice), Arthur Space (Applegate), William Wintersole (Baring).

"The Night of the Feathered Fury" (1-13-67): Victor Buono (Count Carlos Manzeppi), Michele Carey (Gerda), Perry Lopez (Dodo le Blanc), George Murdock (Luther Coyle), Hiedo Imamura (Benji), Oliver McGowan (Armstrong).

"The Night of the Gypsy Peril" (1-20-67): Arthur Batanides (Scullen), Ruta Lee (Zoe), Ronald Long (Sulton of Ramapur), Mark Slade (Hilliard), Johnny Seven (Mikolik), Charles Horvath (Gombol).

"The Night of the Tartar" (2-3-67): John Astin (Count Nikolai Sazanov), Malachi Throne (Kuprin), Susan Odin (Anastasia Rimsky), Andre Philippe (Feodor Rimsky), Martin Blaine (Millard Boyer), Walter Sande (Col. Crockett), Larry Anthony (detective), Michael Panaiv (Chekov), Chubby Johnson (old prospector), Lola Bell (lady bartender).

"The Night of the Vicious Valentine" (2-10-67): Agnes Moorehead (Emma Valentine), Diane McBain (Elaine Dodd), Henry Beckman (Paul J. Lambert), Sherry Jackson (Michelle LeMaster), J. Edward McKinley (Curtis Langley Dodd), Walter Sande (Col. Crockett), Sherman Menchen (E.N. Itnelav), Mitzi Evans (Gates), Quinn Cunningham (Minister), Don Delavay (Griffin, the Butler).

"The Night of the Braine" (2-17-67): Edward Andrews (Mr. Braine), Brioni Farrell (Voulee), Allen Jaffe (Leeto).

"The Night of the Deadly Bubble" (2-24-67): Alfred Ryder (Capt. Horatio Philo), Judy Lang (Prof. Abigail J. Pringle), Lou Krugman (Felix), Nelson Welch (Prof. McClendon), Nacho Galindo (Pepe), Kai Hernandez (maid).

"The Night of the Surreal McCoy" Michael Dunn (Dr. Miguelito Loveless), John Doucette (Axel Morgan), Ivan Treisault (Ambassador of Hertzburg), John Alonzo (Lightnin' McCoy), Quentin Sondegard (Gunman), Jose Moreno (bartender).

"The Night of the Colonel's Ghost" (3-10-67): Kathie Browne (Jennifer Caine), Lee Bergere (Col. Wayne Gibson), Alan Hewitt (Pernell), Walker Edmiston (Sheriff), Arthur Hunnicutt (Doc Gavin), Roy Engel (Pres. Grant).

"The Night of the Deadly Blossom" (3-17-67): Nehemiah Persoff (Adam Barclay), Miiko Taka (Haruko Ishuda), Pitt Herbert (Assistant Secretary of State Levering Davis), Reggie Valencia (Palea), George Keymas (Doctor), Lee Staley.

"The Night of the Cadre" (3-24-67): Donald Gordon (Gen. Titus Trask), Richard Jaeckel (Sgt. Stryker), Sheilah Wells (Josephine), Vince Howard (Ralph Kleed), Val Avery (Warden Primwick), Ken Drake (Dr. Frim).

"The Night of the Wolf" (3-31-67): Joseph Campanella (Talamantes), John Marley (King Stefan IX), Lori Scott (Leandra Novokolik), Jonathan Lippe (Capt. Adam Douchen), Eddie Fontaine (Sheriff Twilley), Michael Shillo (Dr. Hanska), Charlie Raddilack (Priest), Jimmy Booth (stagedriver).

"The Night of the Bogus Bandits" (4-7-67): Michael Dunn (Dr. Miguelito Loveless), Marianna Hill (Belladonna), Grace Gaynor (Pearling Hastings), Patsy Kelly (Mrs. Bancroft), Walter Sande (Col. Crockett), Donald 'Red' Barry (Rainey), Roland La Starza (Joe Kirby).

"Night of the Bubbling Death" (9-8-67): Harold Gould (Victor Freemantle), Madlyn Rhue (Carlotta Waters), William Schallert (Silas Grigsby), Timmy Brown (Clint Cartweel), Val Avery (Brad Logan), A.G. Ventana (Pima), John Mathews (driver).

"The Night of the Firebrand" (9-15-67): Pernell Roberts (Sean O'Reilly), Lana Wood (Sheila 'Vixen' O'Shaughnessy), Paul Lambert (Andre Durain), Paul Prokop (Clint Goxi), Russ McCubben (Briscoe), Zack Banks (Pierre), Len Wayland (Major Jason), Walter Sande (Col. Crockett), Whitey Hughes.

"The Night of the Assassin" (9-22-67): Robert Loggia (Col. Barbossa), Frank Sorrell (Pres. Benito Juarez), Conlan Carter (Halverson), Donald Woods (Griswold), Ramon Navarro (Don Tomas), Nina Roman (Col. Lupito Gonzalez), Phyllis Davis (Lt. Ramirez), Carlos Ramirez (Lieutenant), Nate Esformes (Perico Mendoza), Juan Talvera (soldier).

"The Night Dr. Loveless Died" (9-29-67): Michael Dunn (Werner Leibknicht/Miguelito Loveless), Susan Oliver (Triste), Robert Ellenstein (Arthur Tickle), Anthony Caruso (Deuce), Chubby Johnson (Sheriff Quayle), Jonathan Hole (Mr. Wells), Peter Hale (Layden), Lew Brown (guard), Debra Lee (girl), Marta Kopenhafer (girls).

"The Night of the Jack O'Diamonds" (10-6-67): Frank Silvera (El Sordo), Mario Alcaide (Fortuna), James Alexander (Gregorio), David Renard (Enrique).

"The Night of the Samurai" (10-13-67): Paul Stevens (Gideon Falconer), Irene Tsu (Reiko O'Hara), Thayer David (Hannibal Egloff), Khigh Dhiegh (Baron Saiga), John Hubbard (Clive Finsbury), Jane Betts (Madame Moustache), Jerry Fujikawa (Prince Shinosuke), Anders Andelius (Soapy), Candy Ward (handmaiden), Helen Funay (Japanese Maiden).

"The Night of the Hangman" (10-20-67): John Pickard (Amos Rawlins), Martin Brooks (Prof. Poore), Ahna Capri (Abigail), Sarah Marshal (Eugenia Rawlins), Dean Stanton (Lucius Brand), Paul Fix (Judge Blake).

"The Night of Montezuma's Hordes" (10-27-67): Ray Walston (Dr. Henry Johnson), Jack Elam (Zack Slade), Edmund Hashim (Col.

(WILD WILD WEST cont.) Pedro Sanchez), Roy Monsell (Dr. John Mallory), Roland La Starza (Jake), Hal Jon Norman (Juan), Carla Borelli (Sun Goddess).

"The Night of the Circus of Death" (11-3-67): Phil Bruns (Abner Lennox), Joan Huntington (Mary Lennox), Paul Comi (Bert Farnsworth), Arlene Martel (Erika), Florence Sundstrom (Mrs. Moore), Arthur Millay (Dr. Keyner), Dort Clark (Col. Housley), Sharon Kentran (Secretary), Ashley LaRue (Harry Holmes), Mary Ashley (Prescilla Goodbody), Red West.

"The Night of the Falcon" (11-10-67): Robert Duvall (Dr. Horace Humphries/the Falcon), Lisa Gaye (Lana Benson), Kurt Kreuger (Alex Heindorf), John Alderson (Clive Marchmont), George Keymas (Silvio Balya), Joseph Ruskin (Fediz Munez), Douglas Henderson (Col. Richamond), Edward Knight (Gen. Lassiter), Gene Tyburn (Felton), Warren Hammock (soldier), William Phipps (Marshal), Lynn Wood (mother), Michael Shea (boy), Michelle Tobin (Bonnie).

"The Night of the Cut Throats" (11-17-67): Bradford Dillman (Mike Trayne), Beverly Garland (Sally Yarnell), Walter Burke (John P. Cassidy), Shug Fisher (Jeremiah), Jackie Coogan (Sheriff Koster), Eddie Quillan (Hogan), Harry Swagger (Bartender), Lou Fraly (clerk), Quentin Sondergard (man), Red West.

"The Night of the Legion of Death" (11-24-67): Ken Smith (Gov. Winston E. Brubaker), Anthony Zerbe (Deke Montgomery), Donnelly Rhodes (Capt. Dansby), Karen Jensen (Catherine Kittridge), James Nusser (Reeves), Tolan Matchings (Henriette Faure), Alex Gerry (Judge), Walter Brooke (Prosecutor), Robert Terry (Daniel Dittridge), Eli Behar (Warden), Bill Erwin (jury foreman), Doug Rowe (attendant).

"The Night of the Turncoat" (12-1-67): John McGiver (Elisha Calamander), Marj Dusay (Crystal Fair), Bebe Louie (Song), Douglas Henderson (Col. Richmond), Warren Edmiston (Preacher), Brad Trumble (Doctor), Noel Swan (Collom), Andy Davis (Hansbury), Jim Driscoll (bartender), Rae Cousins (matron), John Armand (waiter), Fredrick Combs (elevator operator).

"The Night of the Iron Fist" (12-8-67): Mark Lenard (Count Draja), Ford Rainey (Pa Garrison), Bill Fletcher (Joe Stark), Ross Hagen (Gabe Kelso), Lisa Pera (Countess Zorana), William von Homburg (Abel Garrison), Bo Hopkins (Zack Garrison), James Gavin (Sheriff), Red West (Roy), Whitey Hughes (George), Fred Strombose (Cal), Troy Milton (Harry), Wayne Heffley (Deputy), Craig Shreeve (reporter).

"The Night of the Running Death" (12-15-67): Jason Evers (Christopher Kohner), Dub Taylor (Peter Carstairs), T.C. Jones (Enzo/Miss Tyler), Maggie Thrett (Deidra/Topaz), Ken Swofford (Sloane), Karen Arthur (Gerta), Oscar Beregi, Jr. (Col. Diebold), John Pickard (Gov. Ireland), Laurie Burton (Alice), Dante DePaulo (Jeff Smith), Tony Gage (waiter), Don Reisen, Whitey Hughes.

"The Night of the Arrow" (12-29-67): Robert J. Wilke (Gen. Titus Ord Baldwin), Jeannine Riley (Aimee Baldwin), Robert Phillips (Oconee), Frank Martin (Col. Theodore Rath), William Bassett (Lt. Carter), Roy Engle (Pres. Grant), Logan Field (Sergeant), Paul Sorenson (Major), William Massey (jailor).

"The Night of the Headless Woman" (1-5-68): Richard Anderson (Commissioner James Jeffers), Dawn Wells (Betsy Jeffers), Theo Marcuse (Abdul Hassan), John McLiam (Tucker), Pete Callahan (Jon), Sandra Wells (Mary), Don Rizzan (Groves), Harry Lauter (Marshal), Marlene Tracy (Joanne), Steve Mitchell (Ringo), Mary Ann Chin (Fatima), Quentin Sondergard (driver).

"The Night of the Vipers" (1-12-68): Donald Davis (Vance Beaumont), Nick Adams (Sheriff Dave Cord), Sandra Smith (Nadine Conover), Red West (Jack Claxton), Johnny Haymer (Aloyisius Moriarity), Richard O'Brien (Sheriff Tenney), Gwen Tolford (woman), Clay Hodges (boxer).

"The Night of the Underground Terror" (1-19-68): Jeff Corey (Col. Tacitus Mosely/Douglas Craig), Nehemiah Persoff (Major Hazzard), Sabrina Scharf (China Hazzard), Douglas Henderson (Col. Richmond), Kenya Colbern (Madam Pompadour), Red West (Lt. Maverly), Greg Martell (Cajun), Whitey Hughes (Priv. Steiner), Dick Ainge (Priv. Crowder), Terry Leonard (Corporal Quist), Louise Lawson (slave girl).

"The Night of the Death Masks" (1-26-68): Milton Selzer (Emmett

Stark), Patty McCormack (Betsy Cole/ Stark), Louis Quinn (Mr. Goff), Bill Quinn (Dr. Pryor), Douglas Henderson (Col. Richmond), Judy McConnell (Amanda Vale/Morrison), Bobbie Jordan (Fleur Fogerty), Sam Edwards (station master), Chuck Courtney (soldier), Dick Chauncey (soldier), Jerry Laverone (soldier).

"The Night of the Undead" (2-2-68): Hurd Hatfield (Dr. Articulus), John Zaremba (Dr. Paul Eddington), Priscilla Morrill (Pahlah), Joan Delaney (Maria Eddington), Roosevelt Grier (Tiny Joe), Kai Hernandez (Domino), David Fresco (Grizzly), Marvin Brodie (Harold), Rhys Williams (Gilly), Joseph Perry (bartender), Hal DeWitt.

"The Night of the Amnesiac" (2-9-68): Edward Asner (Furman Crotty), Sharon Farrell (Cloris Colter), Kevin Hagen (Silas Crotty), Gil Lamb (Claude Cooper), George Petrie (Col. Petrie), John Kellogg (Rusty), Jim Nolan (warden), Jack Rainey (bartender).

"The Night of the Simian Terror" (2-16-68): Dabbs Greer (Senator Buckler), Grace Gaynor (Naomi Buckley), John Abbott (Dr. Von Liebig), Felice Orlandi (Benjamin Buckley).

"The Night of the Death-Maker" (2-23-68): Wendell Corey (Cullen Dane), Angel Tompkins (Marcia), J. Pat O'Malley (Brother Angelo), Arthur Batanides (Sergeant), Roy Engel (Pres. Grant).

"The Night of the Big Blackmail" (9-27-68): Harvey Korman (Baron Hinterstoisser), William Von Homburg (Herr Hess), Roy Engel (Pres. Grant), Ron Rich (Dick January).

"The Night of the Doomsday Formula" (10-4-68): Kevin McCarthy (Maj. Gen. Walter Kroll), E.J. Andre (Prof. Crane), Melinda Plowman (Wilma Crane), Gail Billings (Verna Scott), Vince Howard (bartender), Fred Strombrose (gunslinger), Tom Huff (guard), Red West (guard), Dick Gainge (guard).

"The Night of the Juggernaut" (10-11-68): Simon Scott (Theodore Block), Floyd Patterson (Lyle Dixon), Peter Hale (Tom Harwell), Gloria Calamie (Lonnie Millard), Byron Foulger (County Clerk), Bart LaRue (Maddox), Wild Bill Reynolds (old geezer), Irving Mosley (farmer).

"The Night of the Sedgewick Curse" (10-18-68): Richard Hale

(Philip Sedgewick), Jay Robinson (Dr. Maitland), Arthur Space (A.T. Redmond), Sharon Acker (Lavinia Sedgewick), Lee Weaver (Hiram Gilter), Maria Leonard (Jessica), Frank Campanella (Fingers), Arthur Adams (2nd desk clerk), Robert McCord (prisoner), Anthony Jochim (prisoner), Red West (man).

"The Night of the Gruesome Games" (10-25-68): William Schallert (Rufus Draus), Robert Ellenstein (Dr. Theobald Raker), Sherry Jackson (Lola Cortez), Helen Page Camp (Charity Witherly), Astrid Werner (Ludmilla), Ken Drake (Gen. Crocker), Jacqueline Hyde (La Marchessa Bellini), Greg Palmer (Dr. Walter DeForrest), Lee Cleem (No Fon), Red West.

"The Night of the Kraken" (11-1-68): Jason Evers (Commander Beach), Ford Rainey (Adm. Charles Hammond), Ted Knight (Daniel), Marj Dusay (Dolores Hammond), Anthony Caruso (Jose Aguila), Brent Davis (Lt. Dave Bartlett).

"The Night of the Fugitives" (11-8-68): Simon Oakland (Diamond Dave Desmond), Susan Hart (Rhoda), Charles McGraw (Sheriff Baggs), J.S. Johnson (Plank), Mickey Hargitay (Monk).

"The Night of the Egyptian Queen" (11-15-68): Sorrell Booke (Heisel), Morgan Early (Logan), Tom Troup (Jason Starr), Walter Brooke (Finley), William Marshall (Amalek), Penny Gaston (Rosie Gaston), Cindy Hunter (Princess Miasemel), Gene Tyburn (gambler).

"The Night of Fire and Brimstone" (11-22-68): Charles Macaulay (Zack Morton), Robert Phillips (Frank Roach), Dabbs Greer (Capt. Lyman Butler), John Crawford (Prof. Philip Colchrist), Bill Quinn (Dr. Emmett Sloan), Leslie Charleson (Dooley Sloan), Ken Mayer (Hannon), Fred Stromose (Lefty), Red West (Chuck), Dick Gangey (Rusty).

"The Night of the Camera" (11-29-68): Charles Aidman (Jeremy Pike), Pat Paulsen (Bosley Cranston), Barry Atwater (Gidoen Stix), Fuji (Mandarin), Rico Cattani (Butler), Victor Sen Yung (Baron Kyosai), Julio Medina (Don Carlos), Ken Mendosa (Hatchetrain).

"The Night of the Avaricious Actuary" (12-6-68): Harold Gould (Tebory Kovacks/John Taney), Emily Banks (Arden Masters), Ross Elliott (Gen. Caswell), Jenny Maxwell (Billie),

(WILD WILD WEST cont.) Judy Sherwin (Miss Lester), Tom Avery (Asa), Fritz Feld (chef), Barbara Hemingway (fat lady), Frank Somenetti (fat man), Lou Krugman (maitre'd), Joseph Durkin (Steve Gravers), Bennett King (diner), Red West.

"The Night of Miguelito's Revenge" (12-13-68): Michael Dunn (Dr. Miguelito Loveless), Charles Aidman (Jeremy Pike), Susan Seaforth (Delilah), Byron Morrow (Judge Alonzo Farley), Douglas Henderson (Col. Richmond), Linda Chandler (Lynn Carstairs), Jim Shane (Ivan Petrovich Kalinka), Johnny Silver (Biff Trout), Percy Helton (newspaper salesman), Arthur Batanides (Philo), Don Pedro Colley (Abby Carter), Walter Corey (Cyrus Barlow), Wendy Douglas (Mrs. Carter), Paul Barslow, Dort Clark.

"The Night of the Pelican" (12-27-68): Khigh Dhiegh (Din Chang), Charles Aidman (Jeremy Pike), Francine York (Dr. Sara Gibson), Lou Cutell (Major Frederick Prey), Andre Phillippe (Jean Paul), Debbie Wong (Kuei), Ella Edwards (Amy Stafford), Buck Kartalian (Police Lt. Tom Bengston), James Shen (Quen Yung), John Cremer (Col. Kelton Moore), Jonathan Brooks (Sergeant), Vincent Beck (Corporal Simon), John Quey, Lorna Darnell, Linda Ho, Holly Mascot.

"The Night of the Spanish Curse" (1-3-69): Thayer David (Cortez), Tolan Matchings (Cosina), Richard Angarola (Allesandro), Edward Colman (Juan), Pepe Callahan (Officer Rojas), Gil Serna (Fernandez), Ted de Corsia (elder), Jon Lormer (elder).

"The Night of the Winged Terror" (1-17-68 & 1-24-68): William Schallert (Frank Harper), Christopher Cary (Tycho), Michele Carey (Laurette), Jackie Coogan (Mayor Pudney), Bernard Fox (Dr. Occularis-Jones), Robert Ellenstein (Dr. Occularis II), Roy Engel (Pres. Grant), Frank Sorrello (Amb. Ramirez), Valentine de Vargas (Col. Cheveros), John Harding (Thaddeus Toombs), Vic Perrin (Professor), Rico Alonzi, Peter Hale, Zack Wiggins, Annette Molen, Don Ross.

"The Night of the Sabatini Death" (2-2-69): Ted de Corsia (Johnny Sabatini/Capt. Alymer Nolan), Jill Townsend (Sylvia Nolan), Alan Hale, Jr. (Ned Brown), Douglas Henderson (Col. Richmond), Ben Wright (Clarence), Jim Backus (Fabian Swanson), Tom Geas (Sheriff Chayne), Bethel Leslie (Melanie Nolan/Laura Samples), Donald 'Red' Barry (Farnsworth/Harry Borman), Eddie Quillan (Snidley), Red West Heavy).

"The Night of the Janus" (2-15-69): Charles Aidman (Jeremy Pike), Jack Carter (Alan Thorpe), Anthony Eisley (Warren Blessing), Jackie DeShannon (Torry Elder), Gail Billings (Myra Bates), Arthur Malet (Prof. Montegue), Nicky Blair (Thompson), Benny Rubin (Janus), Anthony Eilow (messenger), Red West (villian), Tony Gangey (villain), Bob Dodson (villain).

"The Night of the Pistoleros" (2-21-69): Edward Binns (Col. Roper), Robert Pine (Lt. Murray), Henry Wilcoxon (Armando Gallando), Perry Lopez (Sanchez), Richard O'Brien (Sgt. Charlie Tobin), Eugene Iglesias (Bernal), William O'Connell (Dr. Winterich), John Pickard (duty sergeant), Jay Jostyn (Major).

"The Night of the Diva" (3-7-69): Patrice Munsel (Rosa Montebello), Patrick Horgan (Max Crenshaw), Beverly Todd (Angelique), Patricia Dunne (Ellen Collingwood), Martin Kosleck (Igor), Lester Fletcher (Karl Crenshaw), Douglas Henderson (Col. Richmond).

"The Night of Bleak Island" (3-14-69): John Williams (Sir Nigel Scott), Gene Tyburn (Mark Chambers), Robert H. Harris (Steven Rydell), Beverly Garland (Celia Rydell), Richard Erdman (Mordecai Krone), Jana Tyler (Alicia Crane), James Westerfield (Ronald McAvity), Yvonne Schubert (Nancy Conrad), Jon Lormer (Boatman), Lorna Lewis (Helen Merritt).

"The Night of the Cossacks" (3-21-69): Guy Stockwell (Prince Gregor), Nina Foch (Duchess Sophia), Donnelly Rhodes (Count Balkovitch), Jennifer Douglas (Princess Lina), Alicia Gur (Maria), Oscar Beregi, Jr. (Petrusky).

"The Night of the Tycoons" (3-28-69): Jo Van Fleet (Amelia Bronston), Steve Carlson (Lionel Bronston), Tol Avery (Mr. Gorhan), Joanie Sommers (Kyra Vanders), Richard O'Brien (Mr. Van Cleeve), Lee Duncan (bartender), E. A. Sirianni (O'Brien), Milton Parsons (Kessel), Virginia Peters (Matron), Nelson Wells (board manager), Maria Garcia (Honey), Mike Mahoney (Carl), Biff Brody, Jerry Mann.

"The Night of the Plague" (4-4-69): Lana Wood (Avri Trent), William Bryant (Duncan Lansing), James Lanphier (Malcolm Lansing), John Hoyt (Guild), Bill Zuckert (Sheriff Dan Cass), Douglas Henderson (Col. Richmond), Red West (Carl), Eddie Firestone (Stills), Cliff Norton (drummer), Pilar Del Rey (Mexican matron), Flora Plumb (saloon Girl), Jacqueline Saylis (saloon girl), Tyler McVey, Steve Rains, Wayne Cochran.

WINE OF INDIA. British (1-15-70). Annette Crosbie, Brian Blessed, John Standing, Rosemary Nicols, Ian Ogilvy, Catherine Lacey.

WONDERFUL WORLD OF PHILIP MALLEY, THE.
Pilot (5-18-81): Stephen Nathan (Prof. Philip Malley), William Daniels (Dean Carswell), Stubby Kaye (Ben), Lori Lethin (Meredith), John Calvin (Coach Bronson), David Knell (Hanson).

WONDER WOMAN. 1976-79. Lynda Carter (Wonder Woman/Diana Prince), Lyle Waggoner (Steve Trevor), Richard Eastham (Gen. Blankenship) 76-77, Beatrice Colen (Etta Candy) 76-77, Norman Burton (Atkinson) 1977.
"Wonder Woman Meets Baroness Von Gunther" (4-21-76): Christine Belford (Baroness Von Gunther), Bradford Dillman (Arthur Deal/Thor), Christian Juttner (Tommy), Ed Griffith (Hanson), Edmund Gilbert (Warden).
"Faustia, the Nazi Wonder Woman" (4-28-76): Lynda Day-George (Fausta), Christopher George (Rojack), Bo Brundin (Kesselmann).
"Beauty on Parade" (10-23-76): Anne Francis (Lola Flynn), Dick Van Patten (Jack Wood), Bobby Van (Monty Burns), Christa Helm (Rita), Jennifer Shaw (Suzan), William Lanteau (Col. Flint).
"The Feminum Mystique" (11-6-76 & 11-8-76): Debra Winger (Drusilla), John Saxon (Radl), Caroline Jones (Queen), Charles Frank (Peter Knight), Paul Shenar (Wertz), Pamela Shoop (Magda), Erica Hagen (Dalma), Kurt Kreuger (Hemmschler), Curt Lowens (Gen. Ulrich).
"Wonder Woman vs. Gargantua" (12-18-76): Robert Loggia (Hans Eichler), Gretchen Corbett (Erica Belgard), John Hillerman (Conrad Steigler), Mickey Morton (Gargantua),

Tom Reese (Carl Mueller).
"The Pluto File" (12-25-76): Robert Reed (Sean Fallon), Hayden Roarke (Prof. Warren), Kenneth Tigar (Dr. Barnes), Albert Stratton (Charles Benson), Michael Twain (Frank Willis), Jason Johnson (James Porter).
"The Last of the Two Dollar Bills" (1-8-77): James Olson (Wotan), Barbara Anderson (Maggie), Richard O'Brien (Frank Wilson), John Howard (Doctor), David Cryer (Hank), Dean Harens (Dan Fletcher), Victor Argo (Jason).
"Judgment from Outer Space" (1-15-77 & 1-17-77): Tim O'Connor (Andros), Scott Hylands (Paul Bjornsen), Kurt Kasznar (Von Dreiberg), Janet MacLachlan (Sakri), Vic Perrin (Gorel), Arch Johnson (Gen. Kane), George Cooper (Gen. Clewes), Hank Brandt (Graebner), Christopher Cary (Mallory), Fil Formicola (Sergeant), Patrick Skelton (Gormsby), Christiane Schmidtmer (Lisa Engel).
"Formula 407" (1-22-77): Nehemiah Persoff (Prof. Moreno), Marisa Pavan (Maria), John Devlin (Major Keller), Charles Macaulay (McCauley), Peter MacLean (Schmidt), Maria Grimm (Lydia Moreno), Armando Silvestre (Antonio Cruz).
"The Bushwackers" (1-29-77): Roy Rogers (Mr. Hadley), Henry Darrow (Walter Lampkin), Lance Kerwin (Jeff Hadley), Tony George (Emmett Dawson), David Clarke (Sheriff Bodie), David Yanez (Charlie), Christoff St. John (Linc), Justin Randi (Freddie), Carey Kevin Wong (Sen), Rita Gomez (Maria).
"Wonder Woman in Hollywood" (2-16-77): Debra Winger (Drusilla), Harris Yulin (Mark Bremer), Robert Hays (Jim Ames), Christopher Norris (Gloria Beverly), Charles Cyphers (Kurt), Carolyn Jones (Queen), Alan Bergmann (Director).
"The Return of Wonder Woman" (9-16-77): Fritz Weaver (Dr. Solano), Jessica Walter (Gloria), Beatrice Straight (Queen), Bettye Ackerman (Asclepia), Russ Marin (Kleist), David Knapp (Maj. Gaines), Frank Killmond (Logan), Dorrie Thompson (Evadne), Brooke Bundy (Beverly).
"Anschluss '77" (9-23-77): Mel Ferrer (Fritz Gerlich), Julio Medina (Gaitan), Leon Charles (Von Klemper), Kurt Kreuger (Koenig), Barry Dennen (Clones Hitler), Peter Nyberg (Strasser).

1372 Science Fiction, Horror, Fantasy

(WONDER WOMAN cont.)

"The Man Who Could Move the World" (9-30-77): Yuki Shimoda (Ishida), Lew Ayres (Dr. Wilson), James Long (Oshima), Peter Kwong (Massake).

"The Bermuda Triangle Crisis" (10-7-77): Charles Cioffi (Manta), Larry Golden (Lt. Mansfield), Herman Poppe (Sergeant).

"Knockout" (10-14-77): Ted Shackelford (Pete), Jayne Kennedy (Carolyn), Frank Marth (tall man), Arch Johnson (John Kelly), Burr DeBenning (Tom Baker), K. C. Martel (Ted), Abraham Alvarez (Officer Fernandez), Frank Parker (Lane Curran).

"The Pied Piper" (10-21-77): Martin Mull (Hamlin Rule), Eve Plumb (Elena Atkinson), Bob Hastings (gatekeeper), Denny Miller (Carl Schwartz), Sandy Charles (Louise).

"The Queen and the Thief" (10-28-77): Juliet Mills (Queen Kathryn), David Hedison (Evan Robley), John Colicos (Ambassador Orrick).

"I Do, I Do" (11-11-77): Celeste Holm (Dolly Tucker), John Getz (Christian Harrison), Simon Scott (Sam Tucker), Kent Smith (Justice Brown), Henry Darrow (David Allen), Steve Eastin (Johnny).

"The Man Who Made Volcanoes" (11-18-77): Roddy McDowall (Dr. John Chapman), Roger Davis (Jack Corbin), Irene Tsu (Mei Ling), Richard Narita (Lin Wan), Milt Kogan (Kalanin), Ray Young (Tobirov).

"Mind Stealers from Outer Space" (12-2-77 & 12-9-77): Norman Rambo (Andros), Vincent Van Patten (Johnny), Kristin Larkin (Debbie), Allan Migicovsky (Dr. Rand), Sol Weiner (Capt. Parelli), Earl Boen (Chaka), Pamela Mason (Carla Burgess), Curt Lowens (Nordling).

"The Deadly Toys" (12-30-77): Frank Gorshin (Dr. Hoffman), John Rubinstein (Major Dexter), Ross Elliott (Dr. Lazar), James A. Watson, Jr. (Dr. Prescott), Donald Bishop (Dr. Tobias), Randy Phillips (Doctor).

"Light-Fingered Lady" (1-6-78): Greg Morris (Anton Caribe), Joseph R. Sicari (Leech), Christopher Stone (Tony Ryan), Titos Vandis (Michael Sutton), Gray Crosby (Grease), Larry Ward (Adler), Bubba Smith (Rojak), Rick DiAngelo (Ross), Stack Pierce (desk sergeant), Saundra Sharp (Eve), Judyann Elder (Marge Douglass).

"Screaming Javelin" (1-20-78): Henry Gibson (Marion Mariposa), E. J. Peaker (Lois Taggart), Melanie Chartoff (Nadia Samara), Robert Sampson (Bo Taggart), Rick Springfield (Tom Hamilton), Vaughn Armstrong (Eric).

"Diana's Disappearing Act" (2-3-78): Dick Gautier (Count Cagliostro), Ed Begley, Jr. (Harold Famus), Brenda Benet (Morgana), Aharon Ipale (Emir), Saundra Sharp (Eve), J. A. Preston (Jazreel).

"Death in Disguise" (2-10-78): George Charkiris (Carlo Indrezzati), Charles Pierce (Starker), Joel Fabiani (Woodward Nightingale), Jennifer Darling (Violet), Lee Bergere (Marius), Arthur Batanides (Krug), Christopher Cary (Beamer).

"IRAC Is Missing" (2-17-78): Ross Martin (Bernard Havitol), Tina Lenert (Cori), Lee Paul (Dirk), W. T. Zacha (Dick), Jim Veres (Sgt. Dobson), Lloyd McLinn (guard), Cletus Young (official).

"Flight to Oblivion" (3-3-78): Corinne Michaels (Capt. Ann Colby), Alan Fudge (Maj. Alan Cornell), John Van Dreelan (Edmund Dante), Michael Shannon (Lt. Stonehouse), Mitch Vogel (Drummer), David Sak Cadiente (1st heavy).

"Seance of Terror" (3-10-78): Todd Lookinland (Matthew), Rick Jason (Koslo), Kres Mersky (Theodora), Hanna Hertelendy (Ms. Kell), John Fujioka (Yamura), Adam Ageli (Bakru).

"The Man Who Wouldn't Tell" (3-31-78): Gary Burghoff (Alan Akroy), Jane Actman (Meg), Philip Michael Thomas (Furst), Michael Cole (Ted).

"The Girl from Ilandia" (4-7-78): Julie Ann Haddock (Tina), Harry Guardino (Simon Penrose), Allen Arbus (Bleaker), Fred Lerner (Davis), Buck Young (Doctor).

"The Murderous Missile" (4-21-78): Warren Stevens (Sheriff Beal), James Luisi (George), Steve Inwood (Mac), Mark Withers (Luther), Lucille Benson (Flo), Hal England (Hal Shaver).

"One of Our Teen Idols is Missing" (9-22-78): Leif Garrett (Lana/Mike Dincaid), Dawn Lyn (Whitney Springfield), Michael Lerner (Ashton Ripley), Ablert Paulsen (Raleigh Crichton), Michael Baseleon (Morley).

"Hot Wheels" (9-29-78):

Peter Brown (Tim Bolt), Lance LeGault (Otis Fiskie), John Durren (Alfie), Marc Rose (Slim).

"The Deadly Sting" (10-6-78): Harvey Jason (Prof. Brubaker), Ron Ely (Bill Michaels), Scott Marlowe (Angie Cappucci), Danny Dayton (Louis the Lithuanian), Marvin Miller (Beamer), Roman Gabriel, Deacon Jones, Lawrence McCutcheon, Eddie Allen Bell, Gill Stratton.

"The Fine Art of Crime" (10-13-78): Roddy McDowall (Henry Roberts), Michael McGuire (Moreaux), Ed Begley, Jr. (Harold Farnum), Gavin MacLeod (Ellsworth), Patti MacLeod (Mrs. Ellsworth).

"Disco Devil" (10-29-78): Paul Sand (Del Franklin), Wolfman Jack (Infrared), Michael DeLano (Nick Moreno), Russell Johnson (Colonel), Ellen Weston (Angelique).

"Formicida" (11-3-78): Lorene Yarnell (Dr. Irene Janus/Formicida), Robert Shields (Doug), Robert Alda (Harcourt), Stan Haze (Cawley).

"Time Bomb" (11-10-78): Joan Van Ark (Cassandra Loren), Ted Shackelford (Adam Clement), Allan Miller (Dan Reynolds), Fredd Wayne (J. J. MacConnell).

"Skateboard Whiz" (11-24-78): Cynthia Eilbacher (Jaime O'Neill), Eric Braeden (Donelson), Ron Masak (Duane Morrisey), Art Metrano (Friedman), John Reilly (Skye Markham), James Ray (John Key).

"The Deadly Dolphin" (12-1-78): Penelope Windust (Dr. Sylvia Stubbs), Nicolas Coster (Silas Lockhart), Britt Leach (Billy), Albert Popwell (Gaffer), Brian Tochi (Darrel), Micheal Stroka (Henry).

"Stolen Faces" (12-15-78): Joseph Maher (Edgar Percy), Kenneth Tigar (John Austin), Bob Seagren (Roman), John O'Connell (Todd Daniels), Diana Lander (Nancy).

"Pot O'Gold" (12-22-78): Dick O'Neill (Pat O'Hanlon), Brian Davies (Thackery), Steve Allie Collura (Bonelli), Arthur Batanides (Maxwell), Ric De Angelo (Raucher), Sherrie Wills (Lisa).

"Gault's Brain" (12-29-78): John Carradine (voice of Gault), Floyd Levine (Stryker), Kathy Sherriff (Tara London), David Mason Daniels (Morton Danzig), Mark Richman (Dr. Crippin), Erik Stern (Turk).

"Going, Going, Gone" (1-12-79): Hari Rhodes (Como), Bo Brundin (Zukov), Kaz Garas (Lucas), Mako (Brown), Charlie Brill (Smith), Marc Lawrence (Jones), Milton Selzer (Captain Louie).

"Spaced Out" (1-26-79): Rene Auberjonois (Kimball), Stephen Anderson (Sylvester), Paul Lawrence Smith (Simon Rohan), George Chung (Mr. Munn), Bob Short (Robby the Robot).

"The Starships Are Coming" (2-2-79): Andrew Duggan (Mason Steele), Jeffrey Byron (Henry Wilson), Tim O'Connor (Col. Robert Elliott), David White (General), James Coleman (aide), Sheryl Lee Ralph (Bobbie), Frank Whiteman (newsman).

"Amazon Hot Wax" (2-16-79): Kate Woodville (Adelle Kobler), Bob Hoy (Marty), Sarah Purcell (Barbie), Curtis Credel (Eric Landau), Martin Speer (Billy Dero), Rick Springfield (Anton), Danil Torppe (Jerry), Michael Botts (Kim), Judge Reinhold (Jeff Gordon).

"The Richest Man in the World" (2-19-79): Jeremy Slate (Marshall Henshaw), Roger Perry (Lawrence Dunfield), Barry Miller (Barney), Marilyn Mason (Lucy DeWitt).

"A Date with Doomsday" (3-10-79): Hermione Baddeley (Mrs. Thrip), Donnelly Rhodes (Ward Selkirk), Carol Vogel (Dede), Taaffe O'Connell (Val), Arthur Malet (Prof. Zandor), Michael Holt (John Blake).

"The Girl with the Gift for Disaster" (3-17-79): Jane Actman (Bonnie Murphy), James Sloyan (Mark Reuben), Raymond St. Jacques (William Mayfield), Ina Balin (Elizabeth Koren), S. Newton Anderson (Pete Phillips), Charles Haid (Bob Baker), Dick Batkus (Neil), Dulcie Jordan (receptionist), Nina Weintraub (Abby).

"The Boy Who Knew Her Secret" (5-28-79 & 5-29-79): Clark Brandon (Skip Keller), Michael Shannon (Cameron Michaels), John Milford (Mr. Keller), Lenora May (Melanie Rose), Tegan West (Pete Pearson), Burt Remsen (Dr. Eli Jaffe), Joyce Greenwood (Mrs. Keller).

"The Man Who Could Not Die" (8-28-79): Bob Seagren (Bryce Kandel), Brian Davies (Joseph

(WONDER WOMAN cont.) Reichman), James Bond III (T. Burton Phipps III), John Durren (Dale Hawthorne), Robert Sampson (Dr. Martin Akers), John Aprea (Durpis).

"The Phantom of the Roller Coaster" (9-4-79 & 9-11-79): Joseph Sirola (Harrison Fynch), Jared Martin (Leon Hurney/David Gurney), Ike Eisenmann (Randy), Marc Alaimo (Pierce), S. Newton Anderson (Roberts), Jocelyn Summers (Ms. Patrick), Jessica Rains (secretary), Mike Kopsha (Sergeant), Judith Christopher (receptionist).

WORLD BEYOND, THE.
     Pilot (1-27-78). Granville Van Dusen (Paul Taylor), Jo-Beth Williams (Marian Faber), Richard Fitzpatrick (Frank Faber), Barnard Hughes (Andy Borchard), Jan Van Evera (Sam Barker).

WORLD OF DARKNESS, THE.
     Pilot (4-17-77): Granville Van Dusen (Paul Taylor), Tovah Feldshuh (Clara Sanford), Beatrice Straight (Joanna Sanford), Gary Merrill (Dr. Thomas Madsen), James Austin (John Sanford), Shawn McAnn (Matty Barker), Jane Eastwood (Helen), Al Bernardo (Max).

WORLD OF DISNEY.
     "Shadow of Fear" (1-28-79 & 2-4-79): Ike Eisenmann (Billy), John Anderson (Zook), Peter Haskell (Dave), Joyce Van Patten (Laura), Kip Niven (Jim), Lisa Whelchel (Robin).
     "The Ghosts of Buxley Hall" (12-21-80 & 1-3-81): Monte Markham (Col. Joe Buxley), Dick O'Neill (Gen. Eulace Buxley), Victor French (Sgt. Maj. Sweet), Louise Latham (Bettina Buxley), Vito Scotti (Count De Gonzini), Ruta Lee (Ernestine De Gonzini), Guy Raymond (Ben Grissom), Renne Jarrett (Emily Wakefield), Rad Daly (Jeremy Ross), Tricia Cast (Posie Taylor), Don Porter (Judge Oliver Haynes), Steve Franken (Virgil Quinby), Christian Juttner (Hubert Fletcher), Tony Becker (Todd), John Ericson (George Ross), Billy Jocoby (David Williams), John Myhers (E. L. Hart), Joe Tornatore (Vincent).

WORLD OF THE GIANTS. 1959.
     Marshall Thompson (Mel Hunter), Arthur Franz (Bill Winters).

"Look Up at a Monster".
"The Bomb".
"Teeth of the Watchdog".
"Death Trap".
"The Gambling Story".
"Ice Chamber".
"Feathered Foes".
"The Pool".
"Rainbow of Fire".
"The Smugglers".
"Unexpected Murder".
"Panic in 3-B": Marcia Henderson (Miss Brown).
"Off Beat": Johnny Silver.

WORZEL GUMMIDGE. British. 1979.
     Jon Pertwee (Worzel Gummidge), Jeremy Austin (John Peters), Charlotte Coleman (Sue Peters), Una Stubbs (Aunt Sally), Mike Berry (Mr. Peters), Geoffrey Bayldon (the Crowman), Barbara Windsor (Saucy Nancy), Norman Bird (Mr. Braithwaite), Megs Jenkins (Mrs. Braithwaite), Joan Sims (Mrs. Bloomsbury-Barton), Wayne Norman (Pickles Bramble), Lorraine Chase (Dolly Clothes-Peg) 80; Billy Connelly (Bogel McNeep) 80.

YEAR AT THE TOP, A. 1977. Greg Evigan (Greg), Paul Shaffer (Paul), Mickey Rooney (Mickey Durbin), Gabriel Dell (Frederick J. Hanover), Priscilla Lopez (Linda), Priscilla Morrill (Miss Worley), Nedra Volz (Grandma Bell Durbin), Julie Cobb (Trish).

YEAR OF THE SEX OLYMPICS, THE. British (7-29-68). Leonard Rossiter (Nat Mender), Suzanne Neve (Deanie).